THE FOLLETT
SPANISH DICTIONARY

SPANISH·ENGLISH
AND
ENGLISH·SPANISH

by

JOSEPH G. FUCILLA

Professor of Romance Languages
Northwestern University, Evanston, Illinois

FOURTH PRINTING

FOLLETT PUBLISHING COMPANY

CHICAGO · 1948 · ILLINOIS

PREFACE

This book has been compiled in response to the growing demand for a popularly priced, thoroughly modern dictionary of the Spanish and English languages. For several years there has been a steady increase in good-neighborly intercourse between the Spanish- and English-speaking peoples of North and South America. This has resulted in a tremendous growth of interest throughout the United States in the language of Spanish America. It has also stimulated among Spanish Americans a corresponding interest in the language of the United States.

This development greatly deserves to be encouraged, and one way of encouraging it is to implement the new interest in these two languages with suitable tools for their mastery. Among the tools of language mastery, few are more useful than a good bilingual dictionary. By a "good" dictionary we mean one that gives accurate translations of all the words and expressions in both languages that people must know to be able to read and speak these languages effectively.

That is the practical sort of tool this book is designed to be. A dictionary of this handy size naturally cannot include complete vocabularies of either language, and it is not offered to advanced students as equivalent in the length of its word list to the larger, more expensive works in this field, such as the Follett *Velázquez Spanish Dictionary*. But for all ordinary purposes we believe this dictionary will be found to contain virtually every word and expression needed for the effective mastery of both languages. It is designed to be as useful to the Spanish-speaking student learning English as to the English-speaking student learning Spanish.

Both sections of the book have been compiled with the utmost regard for the needs of the user. Among the needs that we have constantly kept in mind are:

1. All the words and expressions in popular use, including the vocabulary necessary for reading modern newspapers and for carrying on commercial correspondence.

2. For the more specialized user an adequate technical vocabulary in the fields of science, engineering, arts, trades, sports, etc.

3. Accurate translations into equivalent terms or (in cases where equivalent terms do not exist) clear definitions in the briefest possible form.

iii

4. Sufficient information about each word, such as its part of speech, gender, number, inflection, usage, etc., to insure its correct use.

5. A single all-inclusive word list for each half of the dictionary, avoiding the wasted time and annoyance of having to consult separate lists for proper nouns, abbreviations, idiomatic phrases, etc.

6. Large clear print that will make continued use of the dictionary a pleasure rather than a strain.

Special attention has been given to the inclusion of new words, many of which are of too recent origin to appear in dictionaries published prior to the outbreak of World War II. Among the hundreds of new entries that are to be found in the book are **radar, electronics, gremlin, air-raid warden, flak, strafe, blood plasma,** and many others of a technical scientific, and military nature.

Space for the inclusion of a great many additional words was gained by the decision to dispense with pronunciations. In the case of Spanish words, pronunciation is no problem to anyone who will take the trouble to consult—or, better yet, to learn—the few simple rules of pronunciation appearing at the start of the Spanish section. In the case of English words, language teachers are generally agreed that correct pronunciation cannot be conveyed without the use of a third language in the form of a complicated system of phonetic symbols. The experience of English-Spanish dictionaries employing such systems of pronunciation has shown that they do not have sufficient usefulness in a work of this scope to justify their inclusion. The space which they would have taken has been more profitably devoted to the use of larger type and to the translation of hundreds of additional words.

Other special features of this dictionary include: (1) an abundance of idiomatic phrases, each under its appropriate key word; (2) an indication of the gender of Spanish nouns in *both* sections, thus eliminating the necessity of turning from the English section to the Spanish section for this essential information.

Acknowledgment is due the following for expert assistance in the preparation of this work: GRACIANO SALVADOR, Professor of Languages at Loyola University (Chicago), and IDA NAVARRO DE HINOJOSA, formerly Instructor in the Normal School of Panama and Spanish-English Translator for *Rotary International*. Mrs. Hinojosa's painstaking care in thrice reading every entry in this dictionary has contributed largely to whatever scholarly excellence it may possess.

JOSEPH G. FUCILLA.

PART I

SPANISH - ENGLISH

~≈~

ESPAÑOL - INGLÉS

SPANISH PRONUNCIATION

VOWELS

a sounds as *a* in father. Example: *Ana*.

e has two sounds. At the end of a syllable and before *m*, *n*, or *s* it sounds like *e* in they but without the vanish into *ee* at the end. Examples: *seda, leve, pensar, mes*. Everywhere else it has the sound of *e* in ten. Examples: *puerta, rey, el*.

i sounds as *i* in machine. Ex.: *rico, mesita*.

o has two sounds. At the end of a syllable it has the sound of *o* in tone. Examples: *todo, sonar*. Everywhere else it sounds like *o* in gone. Examples: *soy, sol, contar*.

u sounds as *u* in rule, or as *oo* in soon. Ex.: *fruta, útil*.

y (sometimes used as a vowel) sounds as *i* in machine. Ex.: *y, ley, hay*.

CONSONANTS

b has a sound slightly softer than the English *b* when used at the beginning of a sentence or breath-group. Ex.: *bondad, bien*. Elsewhere it has the softer sound of the English *v*, but with the lips lightly touching. Examples: *sabe, habla*.

c if before *a*, *o*, or *u* has the sound of *k*. Ex.: *casa, cosa, Cuba*. If *c* appears before *e* or *i*, it sounds like *th* in think. Ex.: *cena, cinco*. However, in many parts of Spain and in all Spanish America the *c* before *e* or *i* has the sound of the regular Spanish *s*.

ch is a separate sound and is pronounced like *ch* in chin. Ex.: *chacho*.

d if between vowels sounds as the *th* in then. Ex.: *mudo*. Otherwise it is approximately as in English. Ex.: *débil*.

f is like *f* in English.

g before *a*, *o*, or *u* has the hard sound as in English *God*. Ex.: *gana*. Before *e* and *i* it has a soft sound like English *h*. Ex.: *gente, giro*.

h is *always* silent. Ex.: *hado*, pronounced *atho*.

j is like English *h* as in hot. Ex.: *jota*.

k which is like English *k*, is found only in a few borrowed words. Ex.: *kilo*.

l is like *l*.

ll is a separate sound and is pronounced *ly* like *lli* in million. Ex.: *llave*.

m is like *m*.

n is like *n*, except that it takes the sound of *m* before *b, v, f, p*, and *m*.

ñ is a separate sound and is pronounced *ny* like *ni* in onion. Ex.: *uña*.

p is like the English *p*, only softer.

q is found only in combination with *u*, which is a silent letter in the group; *que* is pronounced *ke* (pronouncing the *e* as in Spanish, that is, like in ten or pen), and *qui* is pronounced *key*.

r is pronounced approximately as it is in English. Ex.: *clero*.

rr is a separate sound and calls for the trilling of the tongue so as to produce several vibrations. Ex.: *sierra*.

s is like the English *s* in *see* or *list*. Ex.: *saco, resbalar, esmero*.

t is like the English *t*, but a little softer.

v has the same two sounds as the Spanish *b*. Examples: *vaca, grave*.

w is found in a few borrowed words and usually retains the sound of the language from which it is derived.

x is like the English *x*. Ex.: *existo*. In *México, mexicano* (written *Méjico, mejicano* in other Spanish-speaking countries outside of Mexico) and in a few other words of Mexican origin, the *x* is like the Spanish *j*. However, *x* before a consonant is pronounced *s*. Ex.: *extremo*.

y sounds as *y* in *yet*. Ex.: *yodo*. However, final *y* (ex.: *rey*) as well as *y* meaning *and* are pronounced like Spanish *i*.

z sounds as *th* in *thin* or *thought*. Ex.: *zapato*. However, in many parts of Spain and in all Spanish America it has the sound of the regular Spanish *s*.

ACCENTUATION

Words ending in a vowel or in *n* or *s* are accented on the next to the last syllable. Ex.: *seguro, hablan, comidas*.

Words ending in a consonant other than *n* or *s* are accented on the last syllable. Ex.: *papel, escribir, feroz*.

Stresses that do not conform to the above two rules call for a written accent. Ex.: *francés, lección, ánimo*.

SYLLABIFICATION

A. A single consonant between vowels begins a syllable. Ex.: *ca-sa*.

B. The single consonant sounds *ch, ll, rr*, as well as the consonant group followed by *l* or *r* (except *rl, sl, tl*), also begin a syllable. Ex.: *e-char, a-llanar, pe-rro, ha-blo, a-pli-co, ma-dre*.

C. *Rl, sl, tl*, and groups of two consonants, other than those mentioned in B, are divided so that one consonant goes with the preceding syllable and one with the following syllable. Ex.: *man-ta, que-rer-se, cir-cu-lo, cal-ce-tín*.

D. In groups of more than two consonants, the last consonant or the two consonants forming the indivisible group (*see* B) begin the syllable. Ex.: *ex-tre-mo, sor-pren-der, ins-tru-men-to*.

E. When two strong vowels—*a, e*, or *o*—come together, each one is a part of a different syllable. Ex.: *pa-se-o, lo-a*. If the strong vowels are preceded or followed by the weak vowels *i* and *u* (and sometimes *y*), the combination forms only one syllable. Ex.: *au-to, ai-re, pei-ne, ley*. However, where the weak vowels have a written accent in the last named combinations, they and the strong vowels form two syllables. Ex.: *dí-a, ma-íz, re-í, flú-ido*.

F. Prefixes form separate syllables except when followed by *s*. Examples: *ab-negar, des-engaño, cons-tante*.

ABBREVIATIONS

Abbreviations used in this dictionary.—Abreviaturas usadas en este diccionario.

adj.	adjective, adjetivo	Mex.	Mexico, Méjico
adv.	adverb, adverbio	mil.	military art, milicia
aer.	aeronautics, aeronáutica	min.	mining, minería
agr.	agriculture, agricultura	mus.	music, música
anat.	anatomy, anatomía	n.	noun, sustantivo
arch.	architecture, arquitectura	naut.	nautical, náutico or marino
Arg.	Argentina, Argentina		
art.	article, artículo	orn.	ornithology, ornitología
ast.	astronomy, astronomía	phot.	photography, fotografía
auto.	automobile, automóvil	phy.	physics, física
biol.	biology, biología	pl.	plural, plural
Bol.	Bolivia, Bolivia	poet.	poetry, poética
bot.	botany, botánica	pol.	politics, política
chem.	chemistry, química	p.p.	past participle, participio pasado
Col.	Colombia, Colombia		
coll.	colloquial, familiar	P. R.	Puerto Rico, Puerto Rico
com.	commerce, comercio	prep.	preposition, preposición
conj.	conjunction, conjunción	print.	printing, imprenta
def.	defective, defectivo	pron.	pronoun, pronombre
dent.	dentistry, dentistería	rad.	radio, radiocomunicación
eccl.	ecclesiastic, eclesiástico	rail.	railway, ferrocarril
Ecu.	Ecuador, Ecuador	rhet.	rhetoric, retórica
elec.	electricity, electricidad	sing.	singular, singular
ent.	entomology, entomología	Sp. Am.	Spanish America, Hispanoamérica
f.	feminine, femenino		
fig.	figurative(ly), figurado	theat.	theater, teatro
geog.	geography, geografía	v.	verb, verbo
geol.	geology, geología	va.	transitive verb, verbo activo
gram.	grammar, gramática		
imp.	impersonal, impersonal	Ven.	Venezuela, Venezuela
interj.	interjection, interjección	vet.	veterinary, veterinaria
interr.	interrogative, interrogativo	vi., vn.	intransitive verb, verbo neutro
m.	masculine, masculino	vr.	reflexive verb, verbo reflexivo
math.	mathematics, matemáticas		
mech.	mechanics, mecánica	vt.	transitive verb, verbo activo
med.	medicine, medicina	zool.	zoology, zoología

SPANISH — ENGLISH

A

a, *prep.* to, in, at, according to, on, by, for, of.
A.: Alteza, Highness; **Aprobado,** passed (in an examination); **autor,** author.
a. área, area; unit of measure equal to 100 square meters.
(a) alias, alias.
@ arroba, weight of about 25 pounds; measure of about 32 pints.
@ @ arrobas, *pl.* of @ arroba.
AA.: Altezas, Highnesses; **autores,** authors.
ab. abad, abbot.
ababa, *f.* red poppy.
abacá, *m.* (bot.) abaca; manila hemp.
abacería, *f.* retail grocery store.
abacero, *m.* retail grocer.
abacial, *adj.* pertaining to an abbot or an abbey.
ábaco, *m.* abacus (of a column); calculating frame.
abad, *m.* abbot.
abada, *f.* female rhinoceros.
abadejo, *m.* codfish; yellow wren; Spanish fly.
abadengo, ga, *adj.* belonging to an abbacy.
abadesa, *f.* abbess.
abadía, *f.* abbey; abbacy.
abajadero, *m.* slope.
abajo, *adv.* under, underneath, below; downstairs; **calle —,** down the street; **hacia —,** downward.
abalanzar, *va.* to balance, to counterpoise; to dart; to impel; **—,** *vn.* to rush on with impetuosity; to venture.
abaleador, *m.* grain cleaner or separator.
abalear, *va.* to separate grain from chaff after winnowing.
abalorio, *m.* glass bead.
aballestar, *va.* (naut.) to haul a cable.
abanar, *va.* to ventilate by means of fans.
abanderado, *m.* (mil.) ensign; standard bearer.
abanderar, *va.* to register a ship.
abanderizador, ra, *n.* ringleader.

abanderizar, *va.* to band together.
abandonamiento, *m.* abandonment; carelessness; debauchery.
abandonar, *va.* to abandon, to desert, to leave; **—se,** to despond, to despair.
abandono, *m.* abandonment, forlornness; debauchery; carelessness.
abanicar, *va.* to fan.
abanico, *m.* fan; small crane, derrick; **— de chimenea,** fire fan; **— neumático,** suction fan.
abaniquero, *m.* fanmaker.
abano, *m.* hanging fan, ventilator.
abanto, *m.* African vulture.
abaratar, *va.* to cheapen, to reduce in cost.
abarca, *f.* shoe of coarse leather; sandal.
abarcar, *va.* to clasp, to embrace; to contain; to comprise.
abarcón, *m.* iron ring, hoop.
abarloar, *va.* (naut.) to bring alongside a wharf.
abarquillar, *va.* to shape like a boat; to curl up, to form into a roll.
abarracarse, *vr.* to withdraw into barracks.
abarraganamiento, *m.* concubinage.
abarraganarse, *vr.* to live in concubinage.
abarrancadero, *m.* boggy place; precipice; difficult business.
abarrancamiento, *m.* fall into a pit or trap; embarrassment.
abarrancar, *va.* to dig holes; **—se,** to become embarrassed.
abarredera, *f.* broom, carpet sweeper.
abarrotar, *va.* to strengthen with bars; (naut.) to stow the cargo.
abarrote, *m.* (naut.) small stowage; (Mex.) retail grocery.
abastecedor, ra, *n.* purveyor, caterer.
abastecer, *va.* (EZCO, EZCA) to purvey, to supply.
abastecimiento, *m.* provision; supplying with provisions.
abastionar, *va.* to fortify with bastions.

1

abasto, m. supply of provisions.
abatanar, va. to full cloth.
abate, m. abbé.
abatido, da, adj. dejected, low-spirited; faint; abject, mean.
abatimiento, m. low spirits, depression; — de costado, (aer.) side drift.
abatir, va. to throw down; to humble; to depress; —, vn. to descend, to stoop; —se, to be dejected or crestfallen.
abdicación, f. abdication.
abdicar, va. to abdicate.
abdomen, m. abdomen.
abdominal, adj. abdominal.
abducción, f. abduction.
abecé, m. alphabet.
abecedario, m. alphabet; spelling book, primer.
abedul, m. birch tree.
abeja, f. bee; — maestra or madre, queen bee.
abejar, m. beehive.
abejarrón or abejorro, m. horsefly; bumblebee.
abejero, m. beekeeper.
abejón, m. drone; hornet.
abellacarse, vr. to degrade one's self.
aberración, f. aberration.
abertal, adj. easily cleft or cracked.
abertura, f. chink, cleft, opening; (fig.) plain dealing.
abestiado, da, adj. beastlike.
abeto, m. fir tree.
abetunado, da, adj. bituminous.
abey, m. jacaranda.
abierto, ta, adj. open; sincere; frank.
abigarrado, da, adj. flecked.
abigarrar, va. to variegate, to dapple; to diversify.
abigeato, m. cattle stealing.
abigeo, m. cattle thief.
abigotado, da, adj. wearing long whiskers.
abintestato, ta, adj. (law) intestate.
abiselar, va. to bevel.
Abisinia, f. Abyssinia.
abismal, adj. abysmal; —, m. clasp nail, shingle nail.
abismar, va. to depress, to humble; —se, (Sp. Am.) to be astonished.
abismo, m. chasm, abyss; gulf; hell.
abitaque, m. rafter.
abizcochado, da, adj. biscuitlike.
abjuración, f. abjuration.
abjurar, va. to abjure, to recant upon oath.
Abl. or ab.¹ abril, Ap. or Apr. April.
ablación, f. ablation, removal.
ablandamiento, m. mollification, softening.
ablandar, va. and vn. to mollify, to soften.
ablandativo, va, adj. mollifying, softening.
ablativo, m. (gram.) ablative.
ablución, f. ablution.
abnegación, f. abnegation.
abnegar, va. (IE) to renounce.
abobado, da, adj. stultified, silly.
abobamiento, m. stupefaction.

abobar, va. to stupefy.
abocado, adj. light (wine).
abocamiento, m. meeting, interview.
abocar, va. to seize with the mouth; —se, to meet by agreement.
abocardado, da, adj. wide-mouthed.
abocinado, da, adj. funnel-shaped, bell-mouthed.
abocinar, va. to shape like a trumpet; —, vn. (coll.) to fall upon one's face.
abochornar, va. to swelter; to provoke; to shame; —se, to be angry; to blush; to wilt.
abofetear, va. to slap or box someone's ears.
abogacía, f. profession of a lawyer.
abogado, m. lawyer; advocate; mediator.
abogar, vn. to advocate; to intercede.
abolengo, m. ancestry; inheritance from ancestors.
abolición, f. abolition, abrogation.
abolicionista, m. abolitionist.
abolir, va. def. to abolish.
abolladura, f. dent; relief.
abollar, va. to emboss; to confound; to tire, to bore.
abollonar, va. to emboss.
abombado, da, adj. bent; stunned, confused.
abombarse, vi. to begin to spoil or decompose (foods).
abominable, adj. abominable, cursed.
abominación, f. abomination, cursedness.
abominar, va. to detest.
abonado, da, n. subscriber; —, adj. reliable; fit for.
abonador, ra, n. a person who goes bail for another.
abonamiento, m. surety, bail.
abonanzar, va. to grow calm, to clear up.
abonar, va. to bail; to insure; to improve; to make good an assertion; to manure; (com.); to give one credit; to credit with, to pay on an account; —, vn. to clear up; —se, to subscribe to; — en cuenta, to credit to one's account.
abonaré, m. (com.) check, promissory note, due bill.
abono, m. approbation; subscription; bail; fertilizer; pledge; allowance, payment; (com.) entry of an amount collected; — de pasaje, season ticket.
abordador, m. (naut.) one who boards a ship; intruder.
abordaje, m. act of boarding a ship.
abordar, va. (naut.) to board a ship; to put into a port; to take up; to approach (a subject).
abordo, m. act of boarding a ship.
aborigen, adj. aboriginal, indigenous; —, m. aborigine.
aborrachado, da, adj. high-colored.
aborrascarse, vr. to grow stormy; to get tipsy.
aborrecer, va. (EZCO, EZCA) to hate, to abhor; to desert (used only of birds).
aborrecible, adj. hateful, detestable.

aborrecimiento, *m.* abhorrence, hatred.
abortamiento, *m.* abortion.
abortar, *vn.* to miscarry, to have an abortion.
abortivo, va, *adj.* abortive.
aborto, *m.* abortion; monstrosity.
abortón, *m.* abortion of a quadruped.
aborujarse, *vr.* to be muffled up.
abotagarse, *vr.* to be swollen.
abotinado, da, *adj.* shaped like a gaiter or boot.
abotonar, *va.* to button; —, *vn.* to bud.
abovedar, *va.* to arch, to vault.
aboyar, *va.* (naut.) to lay down buoys.
abr. abreviatura, abbr. abbreviation.
abra, *f.* bay; mountain gorge, mountain canyon.
abracijo, *m.* embrace, hug.
Abrahán, Abraham.
abrasador, ra, *adj.* burning, very hot.
abrasamiento, *m.* burning.
abrasar, *va.* to burn; to parch the ground; to squander; —se, to be agitated by a violent passion.
abrasilado, da, *adj.* of the color of brazil-wood.
abrasión, *f.* abrasion.
abrasivo, va, *adj.* abrasive.
abrazadera, *f.* clamp, clasp, loop, binding; curtain or shade hook.
abrazamiento, *m.* embracing.
abrazar, *va.* to embrace, to hug; to surround; to comprise, to contain.
abrazo, *m.* embrace, hug.
ábrego, *m.* southwest wind.
abrelatas, *m.* can opener.
¡abrenuncio! *interj.* far be it from me!
abrevadero, *m.* watering place for cattle.
abrevar, *va.* to water cattle.
abreviación, *f.* abbreviation, abridgment; shortening.
abreviador, ra, *n.* one who shortens.
abreviar, *va.* to abridge to cut short; to accelerate.
abreviatura, *f.* abbreviation.
abribonarse, *vr.* to act like a scoundrel.
abridero, *m.* nectarine, freestone peach.
abridor, *m.* nectarine tree; opener; — de latas,** can opener; — de láminas,** engraver; — en hueco,** diesinker
abrigaño, *m.* shelter for cattle.
abrigar, *va.* to shelter; to protect, to cherish; — la esperanza,** to hope; —se, to take shelter to protect one's self against the cold.
abrigo, *m.* shelter; protection; aid; wrap, overcoat; — de pieles,** fur coat.
abril, *m.* April.
abrillantador, *m.* diamond cutter; mercerizer.
abrillantar, *va.* to cut a diamond; to mercerize (cotton).
abrimiento, *m.* opening.
abrir, *va.* to open; to unlock; to disclose a secret; —se, to be opened; (Mex.) to turn coward.

abrochador, *m.* buttonhook.
abrochar, *va.* to button on, to clasp on.
abrogación, *f.* abrogation, repeal.
abrogar, *va.* to abrogate.
abrojo, *m.* (bot.) thistle, thorn; (mil.) caltrop; —s, *pl.* hidden rocks in the sea.
abromado, da, *adj.* (naut.) hazy, foggy.
abromarse, *vr.* (naut.) to be worm-eaten.
abroquelarse, *vr.* to shield one's self.
abrumador, ra, *adj.* troublesome, annoying; overwhelming.
abrumar, *va.* to overwhelm; to cause trouble.
abrupto, ta, *adj.* abrupt; craggy.
abrutado, da, *adj.* brutish.
absceso, *m.* abscess.
absentismo, *m.* absenteeism.
Abs. gen. Absolución general, general absolution.
absolución, *f.* forgiveness; absolution.
absolutamente, *adv.* absolutely.
absolutismo, *m.* absolutism, despotism.
absoluto, ta, *adj.* absolute, independent; sole; unconditional; imperious.
absolutorio, ria, *adj.* absolving.
absolver, *va.* (UE) to absolve; to pardon.
absorbencia, *f.* absorption.
absorbente, *m.* and *adj.* (med.) absorbent; — higiénico,** sanitary napkin.
absorber, *va.* to absorb.
absorción, *f.* absorption.
absorto, ta, *adj.* absorbed; amazed.
abstemio, mia, *adj.* abstemious.
abstención, *f.* abstention.
abstenerse, *vr.* (ABSTENGO, ABSTUVE) to abstain; to refrain from.
absterger, *va.* to cleanse, to sterilize.
abstinencia, *f.* abstinence.
abstinente, *adj.* abstinent, abstemious.
abstracción, *f.* abstraction; retirement.
abstracto, ta, *adj.* abstract.
abstraer, *va.* (ABSTRAIGO, ABSTRAJE) to abstract; —, *vn.* to leave aside; —se, to be lost in thought.
abstraído, da, *adj.* retired; absent-minded.
abstruso, sa, *adj.* abstruse, difficult.
absuelto, ta, *adj.* absolved, acquitted.
absurdidad, *f.* absurdity.
absurdo, da, *adj.* absurd; —, *m.* absurdity.
abuela, *f.* grandmother.
abuelo, *m.* grandfather; —s, *pl.* ancestors.
abultado, da, *adj.* bulky, large, massive; (print.) boldface type.
abultar, *va.* to increase, to enlarge; —, *vn.* to be bulky.
abundancia, *f.* abundance.
abundante, *adj.* abundant, copious.
abundar, *vn.* to abound.
abur, *interj.* good-by, see you later.
aburar, *va.* to burn, to scorch.
aburelado, da, *adj.* dark red.
aburrido, da, *adj.* bored, weary; boresome, tedious.
aburrimiento, *m.* tediousness.
aburrir, *va.* to vex, to weary, to bore; to hazard; to relinquish; —se, to be bored

aburujar, *va.* to press or heap together.
aburujarse, *vr.* to clot.
abusar, *va.* to abuse; to impose upon; —, *vn.* to take advantage.
abusión, *f.* abuse.
abusivo, va, *adj.* abusive.
abuso, *m.* abuse, misuse, ill-usage; — **de confianza,** breach of trust.
abyección, *f.* abjectness.
abyecto, ta, *adj.* abject, low, dejected.
a/c: a cuenta, (com.) on account, in part payment; **a cargo,** (com.) drawn on; in care of.
A.C. or **A. de C. Año de Cristo,** A.D. in the year of Our Lord.
acá, *adv.* here, hither.
acabado, da, *adj.* finished, perfect, accomplished.
acabalar, *va.* to complete.
acaballar, *va.* to cover a mare.
acaballerado, da, *adj.* gentlemanly.
acabar, *va.* and *vn.* to finish, to complete; to achieve; to die; to expire; **acaba de hacerlo,** he has just done it; —se, to grow feeble, to become run down.
acabildar, *va.* to put to a vote.
acacia, *f.* acacia tree or shrub.
academia, *f.* academy; literary society.
académico, *m.* academician; —, **ca,** *adj.* university; academic.
acaecedero, ra, *adj.* incidental.
acaecer, *vn.* and *imp.* (ACAEZCA) to happen.
acaecimiento, *m.* event, incident.
acal, *m.* Mexican canoe.
acalambrado, da, *adj.* cramped.
acalenturarse, *vr.* to be feverish.
acalia, *f.* (bot.) marsh mallow.
acalorar, *va.* to heat; —se, to get excited; to become warm.
acallar, *va.* to quiet, to hush; to soften, to assuage; to appease.
acamado, da, *adj.* laid flat.
acampamento, *m.* (mil.) encampment.
acampar, *va.* to camp; (mil.) to encamp.
acampo, *m.* common pasture.
acanalado, da, *adj.* striated, fluted, corrugated.
acanalador, *m.* grooving tool, grooving plane.
acanalar, *va.* to make a channel; to flute, to groove.
acandilado, da, *adj.* peaked, pointed (of hats).
acanelado, da, *adj.* of a cinnamon color.
acanillado, da, *adj.* ribbed (applied to cloth).
acanto, *m.* prickly thistle; acanthus leaf.
acantonamiento, *m.* cantonment.
acantonar, *va.* (mil.) to quarter troops.
acañonear, *va.* to cannonade.
acaparar, *va.* to monopolize, to corner.
acaparrosado, da, *adj.* copperas-colored.
acaponado, da, *adj.* caponlike; effeminate.
acaramelar, *va.* to ice, to candy.
acarar, *va.* to confront; to face.

acardenalar, *va.* to beat black and blue; —se, to be covered with livid spots.
acariciar, *va.* to fondle, to caress.
ácaro, *m.* (zool.) cheese mite.
acarreador, *m.* carrier.
acarrear, *va.* to convey in a cart, to transport; to occasion, to cause.
acarreo, *m.* carriage, portage; cartage.
acaso, *m.* chance, haphazard; —, *adv.* perhaps, by chance, **por si** —, if perchance.
acastorado, da, *adj.* beavered.
acatalepsia, *f.* (med.) acatalepsy, feeblemindedness.
acatar, *va.* to revere, to respect, to obey orders.
acatarrarse, *vr.* to catch cold.
acaudalado, da, *adj.* rich, wealthy.
acaudalar, *va.* to hoard up riches.
acaudillador, *m.* commander of troops.
acaudillar, *va.* to command troops.
acceder, *vn.* to accede, to agree.
accesibilidad, *f.* accessibility.
accesible, *adj.* attainable; of easy access.
acceso, *m.* access, approach; sexual intercourse.
accesorias, *f. pl.* outbuildings.
accesorio, ria, *adj.* accessory, additional; —, *m.* accessory.
accidental, *adj.* accidental, casual.
accidentarse, *vr.* to have a fit.
accidente, *m.* accident; haphazard; attack, fit.
acción, *f.* act, action, operation; battle; position, posture; (com.) share, stock; —**ones ordinarias,** common stock; —**ones preferentes,** preferred stock; — **de presencia,** (chem.) catalysis.
accionamiento, *m.* drive; — **del eje delantero,** front wheel drive; — **hidráulico,** hydraulic drive; — **por motor,** motor drive.
accionar, *vn.* to gesticulate.
accionista, *m.* and *f.* shareholder; stockholder.
accípitre, *m.* bird of prey.
acebo, *m.* holly tree.
acebuche, *m.* wild olive tree.
acebuchina, *f.* wild olive.
acecinar, *va.* to salt meat and smoke it; —se, to wither.
acechador, *m.* one who lies in ambush, prier.
acechar, *va.* to lie in ambush, to lurk; to waylay; to spy.
aceche, *m.* (chem.) copperas.
acecho, *m.* lying in ambush, waylaying.
acedar, *va.* to sour; to displease, to disquiet.
acedera, *f.* (bot.) sorrel.
acedía, *f.* acidity; heartburn; roughness; harshness of manner.
acedo, da, *adj.* acid; harsh.
aceitar, *va.* to oil.
aceite, *m.* oil; — **crudo,** crude oil; — **pesado,** heavy oil; — **secante,** drying oil; — **vegetal,** vegetable oil; — **de comer,** sweet oil; — **de hígado de bacalao,** cod-

liver oil; — **de palmacristi** or **de ricino** castor oil.

aceitera, *f.* oil cruet; oil can or jar; woman who sells oil.

aceitería, *f.* oilshop.

aceitero, *m.* oil seller; oil cruet; oiler.

aceitoso, sa, *adj.* oily, greasy.

aceituna, *f.* olive; **—s aliñadas** or **en salmuera,** pickled olives.

aceitunado, da, *adj.* olive green.

aceitunero, *m.* olive seller.

aceituno, *m.* olive tree.

aceleración, *f.* acceleration.

aceleradamente, *adv.* swiftly, hastily.

acelerador, *m.* accelerator.

acelerar, *va.* to accelerate; to hurry.

acelga, *f.* (bot.) beet.

acémila, *f.* beast of burden.

acemilar, *adj.* belonging to mules and muleteers.

acemilería, *f.* mule stable.

acemilero, *m.* muleteer.

acemita, *f.* graham bread.

acemite, *m.* fine bran.

acendrar, *va.* to refine metals; to free from blemish.

acensuar, *va.* to impose a tax (on property).

acento, *m.* accent.

acentuación, *f.* accentuation.

acentuar, *va.* to accentuate, to emphasize.

aceña, *f.* water mill.

aceñero, *m.* keeper of a water mill.

acepar, *vn.* to take root.

acepción, *f.* meaning of a word, import; approval.

acepilladora, *f.* planer, planing machine.

acepilladura, *f.* smoothing with a plane; **—s,** *pl.* chips, shavings.

acepillar, *va.* to plane; to brush.

aceptabilidad, *f.* acceptability.

aceptable, *adj.* acceptable; worthy of acceptance.

aceptación, *f.* acceptation; approbation; (com.) acceptance (of a bill); **presentar a la —,** to present for acceptance; **falta de —,** nonacceptance, nonpayment.

aceptador, ra, *n.* acceptor.

aceptante, *m.* acceptor.

aceptar, *va.* to accept, to admit; (com.) to honor; **— una letra de cambio,** to honor a bill of exchange or a draft.

acepto, ta, *adj.* agreeable.

acequia, *f.* canal, channel, drain; trench.

acequiar, *va.* to construct canals, drains or cisterns.

acequiero, *m.* inspector of canals.

acera, *f.* sidewalk; pavement.

acerado, da, *adj.* made of steel.

acerar, *va.* to steel.

acerbidad, *f.* acerbity, rigor.

acerbo, ba, *adj.* rigorous, harsh, rude; cruel; bitter.

acerca de, *prep.* about, relating to.

acercar, *va.* to bring near together; to approach; **—se,** to accost; to approach.

ácere, *m.* maple tree.

acería, *f.* steelwork.

acerico or **acerillo,** *m.* pin cushion; small bed pillow.

acerino, na, *adj.* made of steel.

acero, *m.* steel; edged small arms; (fig.) courage; **— aleación,** alloy steel; **— colado,** cast steel; **— fundido,** hard steel; **— níquel,** nickel steel; **— recocido,** tempered steel; **— al carbono,** carbon steel; **— al cromo,** chrome steel; **— al vanadio,** vanadium steel; **— en barras,** bar steel; **— en bruto,** raw steel.

acerolo, *m.* (bot.) hawthorn.

acérrimo, ma, *adj.* most strenuous, very vigorous.

acerrojar, *va.* to bolt, to lock.

acertadamente, *adv.* wisely, with knack.

acertado, da, *adj.* fit, proper; prudent; accurate.

acertador, ra, *n.* dead shot, true prophet.

acertar, *va.* (IE) to hit the mark; to conjecture right; to turn out true; **—,** *vn.* to happen unexpectedly; to take root.

acertijo, *m.* riddle, conundrum.

aceruelo, *m.* small packsaddle for riding.

acervo, *m.* heap, pile.

acetábulo, *m.* apothecary's measure.

acetato, *m.* (chem.) acetate.

acético, ca, *adj.* acetic.

acetilcelulosa, *f.* cellulose acetate.

acetileno, *m.* acetylene.

acetona, *f.* (chem.) acetone.

acetosa, *f.* (bot.) sorrel.

acetre, *m.* small bucket; holy-water fount.

aciago, ga, *adj.* unlucky, ominous; unhappy.

acial, *m.* barnacle.

aciano, *m.* corn flower.

acíbar, *m.* aloes; aloe tree; (fig.) bitterness, displeasure.

acibarar, *va.* to add juice of aloes; to gall; to embitter.

aciberar, *va.* to grind extremely fine.

acicalador, *m.* polisher; burnisher, burnishing tool.

acicaladura, *f.,* **acicalamiento,** *m.* burnishing.

acicalar, *vn.* to polish, to furbish; **—se,** to dress in style; to paint one's face.

acicate, *m.* pointed Moorish spur; goad.

acidez, *f.* acidity.

acidificar, *va.* to acidify.

acidismo, *m.* (med.) acidosis.

acidioso, sa, *adj.* lazy; weak.

ácido, *m.* (chem.) acid; **— bórico,** boric acid; **— carbónico,** carbonic acid; **— clorhídrico,** hydrochloric acid; **— fosfórico,** phosphoric acid; **— nítrico,** nitric acid; **— pícrico,** picric acid; **— sulfúrico,** sulphuric acid; **— sulfuroso,** sulphurous acid; **ensayo por —,** acid test; **exento de —,** acid-free; **—, da,** *adj.* acid, sour.

acidular, *va.* to acidify.

acídulo, la, *adj.* (chem.) acidulous, tart.

acierto, *m.* act and effect of hitting; dex-

terity, ability, knack; chance, casualty.
acijado, da, *adj.* copperas-colored.
acije, *m.* copperas.
acijoso, sa, *adj.* brownish.
acimboga, *f.* citron tree.
ación, *f.* stirrup leather.
acipado, da, *adj.* well-milled (of broadcloth).
acirate, *m.* landmark (to show boundaries).
acitara, *f.* rails of a bridge; partition wall.
acitrón, *m.* candied lemon.
aclamación, *f.* acclamation; **por —,** unanimously.
aclamar, *va.* to applaud, to huzza; to cry up.
aclaración, *f.* explanation.
aclarar, *va.* to clear; to brighten; to explain; to clarify; **—se,** to clear up.
aclimatación, *f.* acclimatization.
aclimatar, *va.* to acclimatize.
aclocarse, *vr.* (UE) to brood.
acne, *m.* (med.) acne.
acobardar, *va.* to intimidate.
acoceador, ra, *adj.* kicking (of horses).
acocear, *va.* to kick with hind legs (of horses).
acocharse, *vr.* to squat, to stoop down.
acochinar, *va.* to assassinate; to injure sorely.
acodar, *va.* to lean the elbow upon; to lay cuttings of vines, shrubs, etc., in the ground.
acodillar, *va.* to bend at an angle.
acodo, *m.* (bot.) layer, scion, shoot.
acogedizo, za, *adj.* gathered promiscuously.
acogedor, ra, *n.* harborer; protector.
acoger, *va.* to receive; to protect; to harbor; **—se,** to resort to.
acogeta, *f.* place of safety.
acogida, *f.* reception; asylum; confluence; **dar — a una letra,** to honor a draft; **tener excelente —,** to meet with favor, to have an excellent sale.
acogimiento, *m.* reception, asylum.
acogollar, *va.* to cover delicate plants with straw.
acogombrar, *va.* to dig up the ground about plants; to cover plants with earth.
acogotar, *va.* to kill by a blow on the back of the head or the neck.
acolada, *f.* accolade.
acolchar, *va.* to quilt.
acólito, *m.* acolyte; assistant.
acolladores, *m. pl.* (naut.) lanyards.
acollarar, *va.* to yoke horses, etc.; to couple hounds.
acometedor, ra, *n.* aggressor; enterpriser; **—,** *adj.* aggressive.
acometer, *va.* to attack; to undertake; to overtake; to steal over one (sleep).
acometida, *f.*, **acometimiento,** *m.* attack, assault.
acomodadizo, za, *adj.* accommodating.
acomodado, da, *adj.* commodious; suitable, convenient, fit; wealthy.
acomodador, *m.* usher.
acomodamiento, *m.* accommodation.
acomodar, *va.* to accommodate, to arrange;

—, *vn.* to fit, to suit; **—se,** to make one's self comfortable.
acomodaticio, cia, *adj.* accommodating.
acomodo, *m.* accommodation; employment.
acompañador, ra, *n.* companion, chaperon; (mus.) accompanist.
acompañamiento, *m.* attendance; following; (mus.) accompaniment.
acompañante, ta, *n.* attendant, companion, chaperon.
acompañar, *va.* to accompany; to join; (mus.) to accompany; (com.) to attach; **—se,** to consult with others.
acompasado, da, *adj.* measured; well-proportioned.
acomplexionado, da, *adj.* pertaining to the complexion; **bien —,** of a good complexion; **mal —,** of a bad complexion.
acomunarse, *vr.* to unite.
aconchar, *va.* to accommodate; (naut.) to embay.
acondicionado, da, *adj.* conditioned; **bien** or **mal —,** well- or ill-prepared, well- or ill-qualified.
acondicionar, *va.* to prepare, to arrange, to fit; **—se,** to acquire a certain quality.
acongojar, *va.* to oppress, to afflict; **—se,** to become sad, to grieve.
acónito, *m.* (bot.) aconite, monkshood.
aconsejable, *adj.* advisable.
aconsejador, ra, *n.* adviser, counsellor.
aconsejar, *va.* to advise; **—se,** to take advice.
aconsonantar, *va.* to make a word rhyme with another, to rhyme.
acontecedero, ra, *adj.* that which may happen; eventual; probable.
acontecer, *vn. def.* (ACONTEZCA) to happen.
acontecimiento, *m.* event, incident.
acopado, da, *adj.* cup-shaped, bell-shaped.
acopar, *vn.* to shape like a cup.
acopiamiento or **acopio,** *m.* gathering, storing.
acopiar, *va.* to gather, to store up.
acoplado, da, *adj.* coupled; **—,** *m.* trailer (vehicle).
acoplamiento, *m.* coupling, connection, clutch.
acoplar, *va.* to couple; to adjust or fit pieces of timber work.
acoquinar, *va.* to intimidate.
acorazado, da, *adj.* iron-clad; **—,** *m.* battleship; **— de bolsillo,** pocket battleship.
acorazonado, da, *adj.* heart-shaped.
acorcharse, *vr.* to dry up and shrivel (of fruits).
acordado, da, *adj.* deliberate; agreed upon.
acordar, *va.* (UE) to resolve; to tune musical instruments; **—,** *vn.* to agree; **—se,** to come to an agreement; to remember; **no — mal,** to remember rightly.
acorde, *adj.* conformable, in agreement; **—,** *m.* accord; (mus.) chord.
acordeón, *m.* accordion.
acordonar, *va.* (mil.) to form a cordon.

acornear, *va.* to gore with the horns.
ácoro, *m.* (bot.) sweet flag.
acorralar, *va.* to shut up cattle or sheep in pens, to corral; to intimidate.
acortar, *va.* to abridge, to shorten; — **el paso,** to slow down.
acorullar, *va.* to ship oars.
acosar, *va.* to pursue closely, to molest, to harass.
acostado, da, *adj.* reclining, stretched, laid down.
acostar, *va.* (UE) to put to bed; to lay down; —**se,** to incline to one side (of buildings); to lie down; to go to bed.
acostumbradamente, *adv.* customarily.
acostumbrado, da, *adj.* customary, accustomed.
acostumbrar, *va.* to accustom; —, *vn.* to be accustomed.
acotación, *f.* act of setting bounds; limitation; marginal note.
acotar, *va.* to set bounds; to make marginal notes; to watch for; to select.
acotillo, *m.* large sledge hammer.
acoyundar, *va.* to yoke oxen.
acre, *adj.* acid; sharp; bitter; —, *m.* acre.
acrecencia, *f.,* **acrecentamiento,** *m.* increase, augmentation, growth.
acrecentar (IE) or **acrecer** (EZCO), *va.* to increase, to augment.
acreditado, da, *adj.* accredited; authorized; having a good reputation.
acreditar, *va.* to assure, to authorize; to credit; to accredit; to give credit; —**se,** to gain credit.
acreedor, ra, *n.* creditor; —, *adj.* worthy; credit; **saldo** —, credit balance.
acremente, *adv.* bitterly.
acribadura, *f.* sifting.
acribar, *va.* to sift; to pierce like a sieve.
acribillar, *va.* to pierce like a sieve; to molest, to torment.
acriminación, *f.* accusation.
acriminador, ra, *n.* accuser.
acriminar, *va.* to accuse, to impeach.
acrimonia, *f.* acrimony; asperity.
acrisolar, *va.* to refine, to purify.
acritud, *f.* acrimony; asperity.
acrobacia, *f.* acrobatics.
acróbata, *m.* and *f.* acrobat.
acróstico, *m.* acrostic.
acta, *f.* act; minutes of proceeding; — **de venta,** bill of sale.
actitud, *f.* attitude, posture.
activar, *va.* to make active; to expedite, to hasten; to activate; — **la propaganda,** to give impulse to advertising.
actividad, *f.* activity; liveliness.
activo, va, *adj.* active, diligent; —, *m.* (com.) assets.
acto, *m.* act; action; function; thesis; sexual intercourse; — **continuo,** immediately; **en el** —, at once, immediately; — **del reconocimiento,** (com.) inspection.
actor, *m.* actor, player, comedian; plaintiff.

Actos, *m. pl.* Acts of the Apostles.
actriz, *f.* actress.
actuación, *f.* action, operation.
actuado, da, *adj.* actuated; experienced.
actual, *adj.* actual, present.
actualidad, *f.* actuality, current event; **en la** —, at present.
actualmente, *adv.* actually, at present.
actuar, *vn.* to act, to take action; to proceed; to support a thesis.
actuario, *m.* actuary, notary.
acuafortista, *m.* and *f.* etcher.
acuarela, *f.* water coloring; water color.
acuarelista, *m.* and *f.* painter in water colors.
acuario, *m.* aquarium, tank; Aquarius (sign of the zodiac).
acuartelamiento, *m.* quartering of troops.
acuartelar, *va.* (mil.) to quarter troops; (naut.) to furl sails.
acuático, ca, *adj.* aquatic, water.
acuátil, *adj.* aquatic.
acuatizar, *vn.* to light on water.
acubado, da, *adj.* resembling a pail or bucket.
acucia, *f.* zeal.
acuciar, *va.* to covet; to urge.
acucioso, sa, *adj.* zealous, eager.
acucharado, da, *adj.* spoonlike.
acuchillado, da, *adj.* experienced; slashed; stabbed.
acuchillador, ra, *n.* quarrelsome person, bully.
acuchillar, *va* to cut with a saber; —**se,** to fight with knives.
acudimiento, *m.* aid, assistance.
acudir, *vn.* to assist, to succor; to be present; — **a,** to resort to; to hasten to.
acueducto, *m.* aqueduct.
ácueo, ea, *adj.* watery.
acuerdo, *m.* agreement; resolution; tribunal; consent; **de** —, unanimously, by agreement; **de** — **con,** in accordance with; **ponerse de** —, to reach an agreement; **quedar de** —, to agree.
acuitar, *va.* to afflict, to oppress; —**se,** to grieve.
acullá, *adv.* on the other side, yonder.
acumen, *m.* acumen, quick understanding.
acumulación, *f.* accumulation.
acumulador, *m.* battery, electric storage battery.
acumular, *va.* to accumulate, to heap together; to impute.
acumulativamente, *adv.* (law) by way of prevention; jointly.
acuñación, *f.* coining.
acuñador, *m.* coiner, wedge.
acuñar, *va.* to coin, to mint; to wedge in, to fasten with wedges.
acuosidad, *f.* wateriness.
acuoso, sa, *adj.* watery.
acurrucado, da, *adj.* huddled, squatted.
acurrucarse, *vr.* to huddle up.
acusación, *f.* accusation.

acusado, da, *n.* defendant; accused.

acusador, ra, *n.* accuser.

acusar, *va.* to accuse; to reproach; **— recibo de,** acknowledge receipt of; **—se,** to acknowledge sins to a confessor.

acusativo, *m.* (gram.) accusative.

acusatorio, ria, *adj.* accusing.

acuse, *m.* declaring (in cards); **— de recibo,** acknowledgment of receipt.

acústica, *f.* acoustics.

acústico, ca, *adj.* acoustic.

acutángulo, *m.* acute angle.

achacar, *va.* to impute, to blame.

achacoso, sa, *adj.* sickly, unhealthy.

achaparrarse, *vr.* (agr.) not to grow.

achaque, *m.* habitual indisposition; (coll.) menstrual period; excuse; vice; subject matter.

acharolar, *va.* to lacquer.

achatar, *va.* to flatten.

achicado, da, *adj.* childish; diminished.

achicador, *m.* scoop for baling boats; ladle.

achicadura, *f.* diminution, reduction.

achicar, *va.* to diminish; to bail a boat; **—se,** to make oneself small; to humble oneself.

achicoria, *f.* (bot.) chicory.

achicharrar, *va.* to fry meat too much; to overheat; to burn to a crisp.

achisparse, *vr.* to get tipsy.

achocar, *va.* to knock asunder; to hoard money; **—se,** to become a dotard.

achuchar, *va.* (coll.) to crush with a blow.

achulado, da, *adj.* (coll.) rough, tough.

adagio, *m.* adage, proverb; (mus.) adagio.

adala, *f.* (naut.) pump dale.

adalid, *m.* chief, commander.

adamado, da, *adj.* effeminate, ladylike.

adamantino, na, *adj.* adamantine.

adamascado, da, *adj.* damasklike.

Adán, Adam.

adaptabilidad, *f.* adaptability.

adaptable, *adj.* adaptable.

adaptar, *va.* to adapt, to fit, to adjust.

adaraja, *f.* (arch.) projecting stones left to continue a wall.

adarga, *f.* oval shield.

adargar, *va.* to shield.

adarme, *m.* sixteenth part of an ounce; 179 centigrams.

adarvar, *va.* to bewilder; to stun.

adarve, *m.* flat top of a wall.

adatar, *va.* to open an account; to credit.

adecenar, *va.* to divide troops into companies of ten; to count by tens.

adecuación, *f.* fitness.

adecuado, da, *adj.* adequate, fit, able.

adecuar, *va.* to fit, to accommodate, to proportion.

adehala, *f.* tip, gratuity.

adehesar, *va.* to convert land into pasture.

Adela, Adeline, Adele.

Adelaida, Adelaide.

adelantadamente, *adv.* beforehand.

adelantado, da, *adj.* anticipated; onward, bold; advanced; **por —,** in advance.

adelantamiento, *m.* progress, improvement, advancement.

adelantar, *va.* and *vn.* to advance, to accelerate; to pay beforehand; to ameliorate, to improve; to further; **—se,** to take the lead; to outdo.

adelante, *adv.* onward, further off; henceforth; **en —,** from now on; **más —,** farther on, later; **salir —,** to go ahead, to advance.

adelanto, *m.* progress, advance.

adelfa, *f.* (bot.) rosebay.

adelgazar, *va.* to make thin or slender; (fig.) to discuss with subtlety; to refine; **—se,** to lose weight.

Adelina, Adeline.

ademán, *m.* gesture; attitude.

ademar, *va.* to line the sides of mines with planks.

además, *adv.* moreover, also, in addition; else; **— de,** besides, aside from.

adenoideo, *adj.* adenoid; **tumor —,** adenoids.

adenoso, sa, *adj.* glandular.

adentellar, *va.* to bite; to indent; **— una pared,** to leave bricks projecting from a wall so as to allow for later extension.

adentro, *adv.* within; inwardly; **tierra —,** inland.

adepto, ta, *adj.* adept, initiated; **—,** *m.* follower.

aderezar, *va.* to dress, to adorn; to prepare; to season; to clean, to trim, to repair.

aderezo, *m.* adorning; finery; arrangement; **— de caballo,** trappings.

adestrador, ra, *n.* trainer.

adestrar, *va.* (IE) to guide; to teach, to instruct; **—se,** to practice.

adeudado, da, *adj.* indebted.

adeudar, *va.* to be dutiable; to contract debts; to owe; **— en cuenta,** to charge to one's account; **—se,** to be indebted.

adeudo, *m.* indebtedness; customs duty; (com.) debit.

adherencia, *f.* adhesion, adherence, cohesion; alliance, kindred.

adherente, *adj.* adherent, cohesive.

adherir, *vn.* and *vr.* (IE) to stick; to adhere to a sect; to espouse a cause; to hold, to cling.

adhesión, *f.* adhesion; cohesion; adherence.

adiamantado, da, *adj.* adamantine.

adición, *f.* addition; **— de la herencia,** entry into an inheritance.

adicional, *adj.* additional, supplementary.

adicionar, *va.* to make additions.

adicto, ta, *adj.* addicted, devoted to.

adiestrar, *va.* = **adestrar.**

adietar, *va.* to put on a diet.

adifés, *adv.* on purpose.

adinamia, *f.* debility, prostration.

adinerado, da, *adj.* moneyed, rich; wealthy.

adinerar, *va.* to cash into money.

adiós, *interj.* good-by, adieu.

adiposo, sa, *adj.* adipose, fat.
adir, *va.* to accept (an inheritance).
aditamento, *m.* addition; attachment.
adiva, *f.,* **adive,** *m.* jackal.
adivinación, *f.* divination.
adivinador, ra, *n.* diviner, soothsayer.
adivinanza, *f.* enigma; divination, riddle.
adivinar, *va.* to foretell; to conjecture, to guess.
adivino, na, *n.* diviner, soothsayer; fortune-teller.
adj. adjetivo, adj. adjective.
adjetivar, *va.* to use as an adjective; (gram.) to make the adjective agree with the substantive.
adjetivo, *m.* adjective.
adjudicación, *f.* adjudication.
adjudicar, *va.* to adjudge; **—se,** to appropriate to oneself.
adjunta, *f.* (com.) letter enclosed in another.
adjuntar, *va.* to enclose, to attach.
adjunto, ta, *adj.* united, joined, attached, annexed; **—,** *m.* attaché; (gram.) adjective.
ad lib. a voluntad, ad lib. at pleasure, at will.
adminicular, *va.* to support with legal proof.
adminículo, *m.* legal proof or evidence.
administración, *f.* administration, management, direction; headquarters; **en —,** in trust.
administrador, ra, *n.* administrator, trustee, manager; **— de aduanas,** collector of customs; **— de correos,** postmaster.
administrar, *va.* to administer, to manage.
administrativo, va, *adj.* administrative.
admirable, *adj.* admirable, marvelous.
admiración, *f.* admiration; wonder; (gram.) exclamation point.
admirar, *va.* to admire; **—se,** to wonder at; to be surprised.
admisible, *adj.* admissible, acceptable.
admisión, *f.* admission, acceptancy; (aer.) intake; **múltiple de —,** intake manifold.
admitir, *va.* to admit, to accept; to acknowledge; to receive, to let in; to concede; to permit.
admón. administración, administration, management.
admonición, *f.* admonition, warning.
admor. administrador, adm. administrator, manager.
adobado, *m.* pickled pork.
adobar, *va.* to dress; to pickle; to stew; to tan hides.
adobe, *m.* adobe, sun-dried brick.
adobería, *f.* brickyard.
adobo, *m.* repairing, mending; preparation; pickle sauce; rouge; ingredients for dressing leather or cloth.
adocenado, da, *adj.* very common, ordinary; by the dozen.
adocenar, *va.* to count, sell, or make by dozens; to underrate (a person).

adolecente, *m.* and *f.* sufferer.
adolecer, *vn.* (EZCO) to be seized with illness; **— de,** to suffer or ail from; to be subject to.
adolescencia, *f.* adolescence, youth.
adolescente, *adj.* adolescent, young.
Adolfo, Adolph.
adonde, *adv.* whither, where.
adondequiera, *adv.* wherever.
adopción, *f.* adoption.
adoptar, *va.* to adopt.
adoptivo, va, *adj.* adoptive.
adoquín, *m.* paving stone.
adoquinar, *va.* to pave.
adorable, *adj.* adorable.
adoración, *f.* adoration, worship.
adorador, ra, *n.* adorer.
adorar, *va.* to adore; to love exceedingly.
adormecer, *va.* (EZCO) to lull to sleep; **—se,** to fall asleep.
adormecido, da, *adj.* drowsy, stilled, put to sleep.
adormecimiento, *m.* drowsiness, sleepiness.
adormidera, *f.* (bot.) poppy.
adormir, *va.* and *vr.* (UE) to make drowsy, to cause sleepiness.
adormitarse, *vr.* to become drowsy.
adornar, *va.* to embellish, to ornament, to trim.
adornista, *m.* painter of ornaments.
adorno, *m.* adornment; ornament, decoration.
adquirir, *va.* (IE) to acquire; to gain.
adquisición, *f.* acquisition; accomplishment; **poder de —,** purchasing power.
adrales, *m. pl.* sideboards (of wagons).
adrede, *adv.* purposely.
adrenalina, *f.* adrenalin.
adresógrafo, *m.* addressing machine.
Adriático, *m.* and *adj.* Adriatic, Adriatic Sea.
adscribir, *va.* to appoint a person to a post.
adsorción, *f.* adsorption.
aduana, *f.* customhouse; **derechos de —,** customhouse duties.
aduanar, *va.* to enter goods at the customhouse; to pay duty.
aduanero, *m.* customhouse officer; **—, ra,** *adj.* pertaining to customs or customhouse.
aduanilla, *f.* grocery store.
aduar, *m.* nomadic village of Arabs; horde of gypsies; camp.
aducción, *f.* adduction.
aducir, *va.* (ADUZCO, ADUJE) to adduce, to cite.
aduendado, da, *adj.* fairylike.
adueñarse, *vr.* to take possession of.
adufe, *m.* tambourine.
adufero, *m.* tambourine player.
aduja, *f.* (naut.) coiled cable.
adujar, *va.* (naut.) to coil a cable.
adulación, *f.* adulation, flattery.
adulador, ra, *n.* flatterer.
adular, *va.* to flatter; to fawn.

adulteración, *f.* adulteration.
adulterar, *va.* and *vn.* to adulterate.
adulterino, na, *adj.* begotten in adultery; misborn; falsified.
adulterio, *m.* adultery.
adúltero, ra, *n.* adulterer, adulteress.
adulto, ta, *adj.* adult, grown-up, mature.
adunar, *va.* to unite, to join.
adunco, ca, *adj.* curved, warped.
adustión, *f.* (med.) burning.
adusto, ta, *adj.* gloomy, intractable, austere.
adv. adverbio, adv. adverb.
ad val. ad valórem, en proporción al valor, ad val. ad valorem, in proportion to the value.
advenedizo, za, *adj.* parvenu; foreign; —, *m.* upstart.
advenimiento, *m.* arrival, long-awaited advent; Advent.
adventicio, cia, *adj.* adventiticus; accidental.
adverbial, *adj.* adverbial.
adverbio, *m.* adverb.
adversario, *m.* adversary; antagonist.
adversidad, *f.* adversity, calamity.
adverso, sa, *adj.* adverse, calamitous.
advertencia, *f.* admonition; warning; notice.
advertidamente, *adv.* deliberately.
advertido, da, *adj.* precautious; skillful, intelligent.
advertir, *va.* (IE) to advert, to take notice of, to give heed to, to warn; to mark.
adviento, *m.* Advent.
adyacencia, *f.* contiguity.
adyacente, *adj.* adjacent.
aechar, *va.* to winnow, to sift.
aecho, *m.* winnowing.
aeración, *f.* aeration.
aéreo, rea, *adj.* air, aerial.
aerodinámica, *f.* aerodynamics.
aerodinámico, ca, *adj.* streamlined.
aeródromo, *m.* airdrome.
aerograma, *m.* wireless message.
aeronauta, *m.* aeronaut, airman, aviator.
aeronáutica, *f.* aeronautics.
aeronáutico, ca, *adj.* aeronautical.
aeronave, *f.* airship, dirigible, aircraft.
aeroplano, *m.* airplane; **— de combate,** fighter plane.
aeropuerto, *m.* airport.
aerostática, *f.* aerostatics.
aeroterapia, *f.* aerotherapy.
afabilidad, *f.* affability, graciousness.
afable, *adj.* affable, complacent, courteous.
áfaca, *f.* (bot.) yellow vetch.
a/f. a favor, in favor.
afamado, da, *adj.* noted, famous.
afamar, *va.* to make famous.
afán, *m.* anxiety, solicitude, worry.
afanar, *va.* to press, to hurry; **—se,** to toil, to take pains, to work eagerly; to be oversolicitous.
afanoso, sa, *adj.* solicitous; painstaking.
afasia, *f.* aphasia.
afear, *va.* to deform, to mar, to misshape.

afección, *f.* affection; fondness, attachment; (med.) affection, disease.
afectación, *f.* affectation.
afectadamente, *adv.* affectedly; for appearance' sake.
afectar, *va.* to affect; to feign.
afectísimo, ma, *adj.* very affectionate, devoted; yours truly.
afectividad, *f.* affection.
afectivo, va, *adj.* fond, tender.
afecto, *m.* affection, fondness, love; —, **ta,** *adj.* fond of, inclined to.
afectuoso, sa, *adj.* affectionate; moving; tender.
afeitada, *f.* shave, shaving.
afeitar, *va.* to shave; to paint the face; **—se,** to shave oneself.
afeite, *m.* paint, rouge.
afelpado, va, *adj.* plushlike, velvetlike.
afeminación, *f.* effeminacy.
afeminado, da, *adj.* effeminate.
afeminar, *va.* to unman, to enervate.
aferrado, da, *adj.* stubborn, headstrong.
aferrar, *va.* to grapple, to grasp, to seize.
aferruzado, da, *adj.* angry.
afestonado, *adj.* worked in a wavy pattern, festooned.
Afganistán, *m.* Afghanistan.
afianzar, *va.* to bail, to guarantee; to become security for; to prop, to fix.
afición, *f.* affection; preference; fondness, fancy, liking, hobby.
aficionado, da, *n.* lover, devotee; amateur; sport fan.
aficionar, *va.* to inspire affection; **—se,** to give one's mind to; to be fond of, to have a taste for.
afidio, *m.* aphid.
afijo, ja, *adj.* suffixed; —, *m.* suffix.
afiladera, *f.* whetstone.
afilado, da, *adj.* sharp; clear cut; thin.
afilador, *m.* sharpener; grinder.
afilar, *va.* to whet, to sharpen, to grind.
afiliado, da, *adj.* affiliated; —, *m.* subsidiary.
afiligranado, da, *adj.* filigreelike.
afilón, *m.* whetstone.
afilosofado, da, *adj.* affecting the airs of a philosopher.
afín, *m.* and *f.* relation by affinity; —, *adj.* contiguous; related.
afinación, *f.* completion; refining; tuning of instruments.
afinado, da, *adj.* refined; well-finished.
afinador, *m.* tuner.
afinar, *va.* to complete; to tune musical instruments; to refine.
afinidad, *f.* affinity, attraction; relationship; analogy.
afino, *m.* refinement (metals).
afirmación, *f.* affirmation; statement.
afirmado, *m.* pavement, paving.
afirmar, *va.* to secure, to fasten; to affirm, to assure.
afirmativa, *f.* affirmation.

afirmativamente, *adv.* affirmatively.
afirmativo, va, *adj.* affirmative.
aflicción, *f.* affliction, grief, heartache, pain; misfortune.
aflictivo, va, *adj.* distressing.
afligido, da, *adj.* afflicted.
afligir, *va.* to afflict, to grieve, to torment; **—se,** to grieve; to lose heart.
aflogisticar, *va.* to render incombustible.
aflojar, *va.* to loosen, to slacken, to relax; to relent; **—,** *vn.* to grow weak; to abate; to grow cool in fervor.
afluencia, *f.* inflow; plenty; fluency.
afluente, *adj.* affluent, abundant; tributary; loquacious.
afluir, *vn.* flow into; to congregate, to assemble.
afmo. or **af.**ᵐᵒ **afectísimo,** very affectionate.
afollar, *va.* (UE) to blow with bellows.
afondar, *va.* to put under water; (naut.) to sink; **—,** *vn.* to go to the bottom.
aforado, *adj.* privileged.
aforar, *va.* to gauge; to measure; to calculate the duty on goods.
aforismo, *m.* aphorism.
aforístico, ca, *adj.* aphoristic.
aforo, *m.* gauging; customhouse examination of goods or luggage.
aforrar, *va.* to line (clothes); (naut.) to sheathe.
aforro, *m.* lining; sheathing.
afortunadamente, *adv.* fortunately, luckily.
afortunado, da, *adj.* fortunate, happy; successful.
afosarse, *vr.* (mil.) to entrench one's self.
afrancesar, *va.* to Frenchify; to give words a French termination; **—se,** to act like a Frenchman.
afrecho, *m.* bran.
afrenta, *f.* outrage; insult, offense; infamy; disgrace.
afrentar, *va.* to affront; to insult.
afrentoso, sa, *adj.* ignominious; insulting.
afretar, *va.* (naut.) to scour; to clean.
africano, na, *n.* and *adj.* African.
afrijolar, *va.* (Cuba) to kill by shooting.
afrodisíaco, ca, *adj.* aphrodisiac.
afrontar, *va.* to confront; to reproach one to one's face with a crime.
afto. or **af.**ᵗᵒ **afecto,** affectionate.
afuera, *adv.* out, outside, outward; abroad; ¡**—!** *interj.* stand out of the way!
afueras, *f. pl.* environs of a place; suburbs, outskirts.
afufar, *vn.* and *vr.* (coll.) to run away, to escape.
afuste, *m.* gun carriage.
agachadiza, *f.* (zool.) snipe; **hacer la —,** to hide one's self.
agachar, *va.* and *vn.* to lower, to crouch; **—se,** to stoop, to squat.
agalla, *f.* gallnut; **—s,** *pl.* glands of the throat; tonsils; gills of fishes.

agallado, da, *adj.* steeped in an infusion of gall.
agallón, *m.* large gallnut; **—llones,** *pl.* strings of large silver beads; wooden beads used for rosaries.
agamuzado, da, *adj.* chamois-colored.
agarbarse, *vr.* to cower, to squat.
agárico, *m.* (bot.) agaric (fungous excrescence on the trunks of trees).
agarradera, *f.* holder, handle.
agarradero, *m.* anchoring ground; hold, haft.
agarrado, da, *adj.* miserable, stingy.
agarrafar, *va.* to grapple hard in a scuffle.
agarrar, *va.* to grasp, to seize, to gripe; **—se,** to hold on.
agarro, *m.* grasp.
agarrotar, *va.* to compress bales with ropes; to apply the punishment of the garrote, to garrote.
agasajador, ra, *adj.* attentive, eager to please.
agasajar, *va.* to receive and treat kindly; to regale; to entertain.
agasajo, *m.* graceful reception; entertainment; kindness; friendly present.
Ágata or **Agueda,** Agatha.
ágata, *f.* agate.
agavillar, *va.* to tie up grain in sheaves; **—se,** to associate with a gang of sharpers.
agazapar, *va.* (coll.) to catch (a person); **—se,** to hide one's self; to crouch.
agencia, *f.* agency; **— de turismo,** touring agency; **— de vapores,** steamship agency.
agenciar, *va.* to solicit, to endeavor, to obtain a thing.
agencioso, sa, *adj.* diligent, active; officious.
agenda, *f.* notebook, memorandum; agenda.
agenesia, *f.* (med.) impotence.
agente, *m.* agent, representative, broker, attorney; **— comisionista,** commission agent; **— vendedor,** sales agent; **— viajero,** traveling salesman; **— de bolsa,** broker; **— de cobros,** collector; **— de privilegios,** patent agent; **— de seguros,** insurance agent.
agérato, *m.* (bot.) ageratum.
ágil, *adj.* nimble, fast, active.
agilidad, *f.* agility, nimbleness.
agilitar, *va.* to render nimble, to make active.
agio, *m.* stockjobbing; usury; profit derived from money exchange or payment of drafts.
agiotador or **agiotista,** *m.* (com.) money changer, bill broker, stockbroker; usurer.
agiotaje, *m.* stockjobbing.
agitación, *f.* agitation; excitement.
agitado, da, *adj.* excited, agitated.
agitanado, da, *adj.* gypsylike.
agitar, *va.* to agitate, to move; **—se,** to become excited.
aglomeración, *f.* conglomeration, heap.
aglomerar, *va.* and *vr.* to agglomerate, to conglomerate.

aglutición, *f.* (med.) aglutition.
Ag.ⁿ **Agustín,** Aug. Augustine.
agnación, *f.* (law) consanguinity.
agnado, da, or **agnaticio, cia,** *adj.* (law) consanguineous.
agnición, *f.* (poet.) recognition.
agnosticismo, *m.* agnosticism.
agobiar, *va.* and *vr.* to bend down to the ground; to oppress, to burden.
agolparse, *vr.* to assemble in crowds.
agonía, *f.* agony, anguish.
agonizante, *m.* and *f.* dying person; —, *adj.* dying, agonizing.
agonizar, *va.* to assist dying persons; —, *vn.* to be in the agony of death, to agonize.
agorar, *va.* (UE) to divine; to augur.
agorero, ra, *n.* diviner; fortuneteller.
agorgojarse, *vr.* to be destroyed by grubs (grain).
agostadero, *m.* summer pasture.
agostar, *va.* to parch with heat; to blight; —, *vn.* to pasture cattle on stubbles in summer.
agostero, *m.* harvester; religious méndicant (who begs grain in August).
agostizo, za, *adj.* born in August; weak.
agosto, *m.* August (month); harvest time.
agotado, da, *adj.* sold out, exhausted, spent.
agotamiento, *m.* exhaustion.
agotar, *va.* to misspend; to exhaust; to use up; —se, to run down; to run out of, to be sold out of.
agracejo, *m.* barberry.
agraciado, da, *adj.* graceful; refined; gifted.
agraciar, *va.* to embellish; to grace; to give employment to.
agradable, *adj.* agreeable, pleasant.
agradar, *va.* to please, to gratify.
agradecer, *va.* (EZCO) to appreciate a favor; to be thankful for.
agradecido, da, *adj.* thankful, grateful.
agradecimiento, *m.* gratitude, gratefulness, thankfulness.
agrado, *m.* agreeableness, courteousness; pleasure; liking; **ser de su —,** to be satisfactory to you.
agramadera, *f.* brake (for dressing flax or hemp).
agramar, *va.* to dress flax or hemp with a brake.
agramiza, *f.* stalk of hemp; refuse of hemp.
agrandamiento, *m.* enlargement.
agrandar, *va.* to enlarge, to extend; to aggrandize.
agranujado, da, *adj.* grained.
agrario, ria, *adj.* agrarian.
agravación, *f.* aggravation.
agravador, ra, *n.* aggravator, aggressor.
agravante, *adj.* trying.
agravar, *va.* to oppress; to cause grief; to aggravate; to make worse, to exaggerate.
agravatorio, ria, *adj.* (law) compulsory, aggravating.
agraviador, ra, *n.* injurer, offender.
agraviar, *va.* to wrong, to injure; to hurt, to

make worse; —se, to take offense.
agravio, *m.* offense, injury.
agraz, *m.* verjuice; unripe grape; **en —,** unseasonably.
agrazón, *m.* wild grape; gooseberry bush.
agregación, *f.* aggregation; collection.
agregado, *m.* aggregate; attaché.
agregar, *va.* to add, to aggregate, to heap together; to collect.
agremiar, *va.* to organize into a union; —se, to unionize.
agresión, *f.* aggression, attack.
agresivo, va, *adj.* aggressive.
agresor, *m.* aggressor, assaulter.
agreste, *adj.* wild, rude, rustic; produced by nature without cultivation.
agrete, *adj.* sour, acid.
agriar, *va.* to sour, to acidify; to exasperate.
agrícola, *adj.* agricultural.
agricultor, *m.* agriculturist, farmer.
agricultura, *f.* agriculture.
agridulce, *adj.* half sweet and half sour.
agrietado, da, *adj.* cracked.
agrietarse, *vr.* to crack.
agrifolio, *m.* holly tree.
agrillo, lla, *adj.* sourish, sharp to the taste.
agrimensor, *m.* land surveyor.
agrimensura, *f.* land surveying.
agrimonia, *f.* (bot.) agrimony.
agrio, ria, *adj.* sour, acrid; rough, craggy; sharp, rude, unpleasant; —, *m.* acidity.
agrisado, da, *adj.* grayish-colored.
agronomía, *f.* agronomy.
agronómico, ca, *adj.* agronomical.
agrónomo, *m.* agronomist, agricultural engineer.
agrumarse, *vr.* to clog.
agrupación, *f.* group, association, gathering, crowd.
agrupar, *va.* and *vr.* to group (in a picture); to cluster, to crowd.
agrura, *f.* acidity.
agte. agente, agt. agent.
Agte. Gral. Agente General, G. A. General Agent.
agto. or **ag.**ᵗᵒ **agosto,** Aug. August.
agua, *f.* water, liquid, rain; **— arriba,** upstream; **— carbónica,** seltzer water; **— corriente,** running water; **— cruda,** hard water; **— de cal,** lime water; **— de soda,** soda water; **— de tocador,** toilet water; **— destilada,** distilled water; **— dulce,** fresh or soft water; **— dura,** hard water; **— fresca,** cold water; **— gaseosa,** aerated water; **— jabonosa,** suds; **— llovediza** or **— lluvia,** rain water; **— salada,** salt water; **— tibia,** lukewarm water.
aguacate, *m.* avocadò, alligator pear.
aguacero, *m.* short, heavy shower of rain.
aguachirle, *f.* insipid wine.
aguada, *f.* flood in a mine; (naut.) fresh-water hold or supply on board ship; (art) water color; painting in water colors.
aguaderas, *f. pl.* wooden framework for the carriage of jars of water by mules.

aguadero, *m.* watering place for cattle, horsepond.

aguado, da, *adj.* watered; watery.

aguador, ra, *n.* water carrier.

aguafuerte, *f.* etching.

aguaje, *m.* rapid current of sea water; (naut.) spring tide.

aguamanil, *m.* earthen or metal basin for the washstand.

aguamanos, *m.* water for washing the hands; washstand.

aguamarina, *f.* aquamarine.

aguamiel, *f.* hydromel; honey and water.

aguanieve, *f.* sleet; (orn.) lapwing.

aguañón, *m.* artisan in charge of hydraulic works.

aguanoso, sa, *adj.* aqueous, watery.

aguantar, *va.* to sustain, to suffer; to endure, to bear.

aguante, *m.* firmness; patience.

aguapié, *m.* inferior wine.

aguar, *va.* to mix water with wine; **—se,** to be thinned out with water.

aguardar, *va.* to expect, to wait for; to grant time.

aguardentería, *f.* liquor shop.

aguardentero, *m.* keeper of a liquor shop.

aguardiente, *m.* inferior whiskey; **— de caña,** rum.

aguardo, *m.* place where a hunter waits to fire at the game, stand.

aguarrás, *m.* spirits of turpentine.

aguatero, *m.* (Sp. Am.) water carrier.

aguatocha, *f.* pump.

aguaza, *f.* juice extracted from trees by incision.

aguazarse, *vr.* to become boggy or marshy.

aguazo, *m.* painting in gouache.

agudeza, *f.* keenness, sharpness; acuteness; smartness.

agudo, da, *adj.* sharp-pointed; keen-edged; smart; fine; acute, witty; brisk; shrill.

aguerrido, da, *adj.* inured to war; strapping, buxom.

aguijada, *f.* spur, goad.

aguijar, *va.* to prick, to spur, to goad; to stimulate.

aguijón, *m.* sting of a bee, wasp, etc.; stimulation.

aguijonear, *va.* to prick, to spur; to stimulate.

águila, *f.* eagle; a gold coin.

aguileño, ña, *adj.* aquiline; hawk-nosed.

aguilucho, *m.* eaglet.

aguinaldo, *m.* Christmas or New Year's gift.

aguja, *f.* needle; hatpin; switch; **— de coser,** sewing needle; **— de hacer media** or **de tejer,** knitting needle; **— de marear,** marine compass, binnacle; **— de zurcir,** darning needle; **— fonográfica,** phonograph needle; **— hipodérmica,** hypodermic needle; **— náutica,** marine compass.

agujazo, *m.* prick with a needle.

agujerear, *va.* to pierce, to bore.

agujero, *m.* hole; needlemaker; needle seller.

agujeta, *f.* lace or tape tipped with ferrules; **—s,** *pl.* tip, gratuity; pains from fatigue.

aguosidad, *f.* lymph.

aguoso, sa, *adj.* aqueous, watery.

agusanarse, *vr.* to be worm-eaten.

Agustín, Augustine, Austin.

agustiniano or **agustino,** *m.* monk of the order of St. Augustine.

aguzadera, *f.* whetstone.

aguzanieve, *f.* (orn.) wagtail.

aguzar, *va.* to whet; to sharpen; to stimulate.

¡ah! *interj.* ah! oh!

aherrojar, *va.* to put in chains or irons.

ahí, *adv.* there; **de — (que),** for this reason; **por —,** that way, more or less.

ahidalgado, da, *adj.* gentlemanly, noble.

ahijada, *f.* goddaughter.

ahijado, *m.* godson.

ahijar, *va.* to adopt as one's child; **—,** *vn.* to bring forth young; to bud.

ahilarse, *vr.* to grow faint for lack of nourishment; to grow ropy (of wine).

ahilo, *m.* faintness for lack of food.

ahinco, *m.* zeal, earnestness, eagerness.

ahogar, *va.* and *vr.* to throttle, to smother; to drown, to suffocate; to oppress; to quench.

ahogo, *m.* suffocation; anguish.

ahondar, *va.* to sink, to deepen; **—,** *vn.* to penetrate far into a thing.

ahora, *adv.* now, at present; just now; **—,** *conj.* whether, or; **— mismo,** right now; **hasta —,** thus far; **por —,** for the present.

ahorcajarse, *vr.* to sit astride.

ahorcar, *va.* to kill by hanging, to hang; **—se,** to commit suicide by hanging.

ahorita, *adv.* (Sp. Am.) just now, in just a minute.

ahormar, *va.* to fit, to adjust; to break in shoes.

ahorquillado, da, *adj.* forked.

ahorquillar, *va.* to prop up with forks.

ahorrar, *va.* to save, to economize; to emancipate.

ahorrativo, va, *adj.* frugal, thrifty, saving; niggardly, stingy.

ahorro, *m.* parsimony, saving, thrift; **caja de —s,** savings bank; **— postal,** postal savings.

ahoyar, *vn.* to dig holes.

ahuchar, *va.* to hoard up.

ahuecar, *va.* to hollow, to scoop out; **—se,** to grow haughty.

ahumar, *va.* to smoke, to cure in smoke.

ahusar, *va.* to make a thing as slender as a spindle, **—se,** to taper.

ahuyentar, *va.* to put to flight.

aijada, *f.* goad; pungency.

ailanto, *m.* (bot.) ailanthus.

airar, *va.* to anger, to irritate; **—se,** to get angry.

aire, *m.* air, wind; gracefulness of manners; aspect, countenance; musical composition; choke of an auto; **— viciado,** foul air;

al — libre, outdoors; **a prueba de —,** airtight; **conductor de —,** airway; **chorro de —,** air blast; **darse —,** to fan oneself; **enfriamiento** or **refrigeración por —,** air-cooled; **purificación del —,** air-conditioning; **tirar** or **quitar el —,** to pull out the choke.

aireador, *m.* aerator; gas charger.

airear, *va.* to air, to ventilate, to charge with gas.

airón, *m.* violent gale.

airoso, sa, *adj.* airy; windy; graceful, refined; successful.

aislado, da, *adj.* insulated, isolated, cut off.

aislador, *m.* (elec.) insulator.

aislamiento, *m.* isolation; insulation; (fig.) solitude, loneliness; privacy.

aislante, *adj.* insulating.

aislar, *va.* to surround with water; to isolate; to insulate.

¡ajá! *interj.* aha!

¡ajajá! *interj.* aha; there!

ajar, *m.* garlic field; **—,** *va.* to rumple, to crumple.

aje, *m.* habitual complaint.

ajedrecista, *m.* chess player.

ajedrez, *m.* chess (game); (naut.) netting, grating.

ajedrezado, da, *adj.* checkered.

ajedrista, *m.* chess player.

ajenabe or **ajenabo,** *m.* (bot.) wild mustard.

ajenjo, *m.* wormwood; absinthe.

ajeno, na, *adj.* another's; foreign, strange; contrary to; ignorant; improper.

ajenuz, *m.* (bot.) fennel flower.

ajetrearse, *vr.* to exert one's self; to bustle; to toil; to fidget.

ají, *m.* chili pepper, chili.

ajiaco, *m.* kind of stew.

ajicola, *f.* glue made of scraps of leather boiled with garlic.

ajimez, *m.* arched window with a pillar in the center to support it.

ajipuerro, *m.* (bot.) leek.

ajo, *m.* garlic; garlic sauce; rouge; discreditable transaction taken part in by several persons; **¡—!** *interj.* darn!

ajobar, *va.* to carry heavy loads upon one's back.

ajolio, *m.* sauce made of oil and garlic.

ajonje, *m.* birdlime.

ajoqueso, *m.* dish made of garlic and cheese.

ajorca, *f.* gold and silver anklet worn by Moorish women.

ajornalar, *va.* to hire by the day.

ajuar, *m.* bridal apparel and furniture; trousseau; household furniture.

ajuiciado, da, *adj.* judicious, prudent, sensible.

ajustable, *adj.* adjustable.

ajustador, ra, *n.* fitter.

ajustamiento, *m.* agreement; (com.) settling of accounts.

ajustar, *va.* to regulate; to adjust; to tighten; **— cuentas,** to settle matters, to settle accounts; **—se,** to adjust or adapt one's self.

ajuste, *m.* agreement, pact; adjustment, settlement; accommodation.

ajusticiar, *va.* to execute a malefactor.

al, contraction for **a el,** to the (followed by the masculine gender); **— fin,** at last; **— instante,** at once.

ala, *f.* wing; aisle; row, file; brim of the hat; auricle; **—s,** *pl.* (naut.) upper studding sails; protection; **— de proa,** ship's head.

alabandina, *f.* manganese.

alabanza, *f.* praise, applause.

alabar, *va.* to praise, to applaud, to extol.

alabarda, *f.* halberd.

alabardero, *m.* halberdier; hired clapper in theaters.

alabastrado, da, *adj.* resembling alabaster.

alabastrino, na, *adj.* of alabaster.

alabastro, *m.* alabaster; gypsum.

álabe, *m.* drooping branch of an olive tree; flier of a water mill; fan wheel.

alabearse, *vr.* to warp.

alábega, *f.* (bot.) sweet basil.

alabeo, *m.* warp, warping.

alacena, *f.* cupboard, small cupboard in the wall closet.

alacrán, *m.* scorpion; ring of the mouthpiece of a bridle; stop, hook.

alacranado, da, *adj.* bitten by a scorpion; infected.

alacridad, *f.* alacrity.

alada, *f.* fluttering of the wings.

aladares, *m. pl.* forelock falling over the temples.

alado, da, *adj.* winged.

álaga, *f.* (bot.) spelt, a species of yellow wheat.

alambicado, da, *adj.* given sparingly, grudgingly; distilled; pedantic.

alambicar, *va.* to distil; to investigate closely.

alambique, *m.* still.

alambrado, *m.* wire fence, wire screen, wire netting.

alambrar, *va.* to fence around with wire.

alambre, *m.* wire, copper wire; sheep bells; **— conductor,** conducting wire; **— de púas,** barbed wire; **— envuelto a prensa,** sheathed wire.

alambrera, *f.* wire cage; wire netting or screen.

alameda, *f.* poplar grove; promenade.

álamo, *m.* poplar, poplar tree; cottonwood tree; **— temblón,** aspen tree.

alamud, *m.* door bolt; bar of a gate.

alancear, *va.* to dart, to spear; to wound with a lance.

alano, *m.* boar hound.

alaqueca, *f.* bloodstone.

alar, *m.* overhanging roof; snare of horse hair; (Col.) sidewalk.

alarde, *m.* military review; display, exhibition; **hacer —,** to boast.

alardear, *vn.* to brag, to boast.

alargamiento, *m.* elongation.

alargar, *va.* to lengthen; to extend; to hand.

alarida, *f.* hue and cry.

alarido, *m.* outcry, shout, howl; **dar —s,** to howl.

alarife, *m.* architect.

alarma, *f.* alarm; **— de incendios,** fire alarm; **— contra ladrones,** burglar alarm.

alarmado, da, *adj.* alarmed.

alarmante, *adj.* alarming.

alarmar, *va.* and *vr.* to alarm.

alarmista, *m.* and *f.* alarmist.

alaterno, *m.* (bot.) mock privet.

a la v/ a la vista, (com.) at sight.

alazán, ana, *adj.* sorrel-colored (of horses).

alazo, *m.* blow with the wings.

alba, *f.* dawn of day, daybreak; alb, surplice.

albacea, *m.* executor; **—,** *f.* executrix.

albaceazgo, *m.* office of an executor.

albada, *f.* morning serenade; dawn of day; (mil.) attack at daybreak.

albahaca, *f.* (bot.) sweet basil.

albanega, *f.* hair net.

albanés, esa, *n.* and *adj.* Albanian.

albañal or **albañar,** *m.* common sewer; gully-hole.

albañil, *m.* mason, bricklayer.

albañilería, *f.* masonry.

albar, *adj.* white, whitish.

albarán, *m.* placard for renting a house, "for rent" sign.

albarazado, da, *adj.* affected with the white leprosy; pale; (Mex.) of Chinese and half-breed parents.

albarazo, *m.* white leprosy.

albarda, *f.* packsaddle for beasts of burden.

albardar, *va.* to saddle with a packsaddle.

albardilla, *f.* small packsaddle; coping; ridge; wool tuft.

albaricoque, *m.* apricot.

albaricoquero, *m.* apricot tree.

albarillo, *m.* dance tune for the guitar; small kind of apricot.

albarrada, *f.* dry wall; trench.

albatros, *m.* albatross.

albayalde, *m.* white lead.

albazano, na, *adj.* of a dark chestnut color.

albear, *va.* to whiten.

albedrío, *m.* free will, freedom of will.

albéitar, *m.* veterinary surgeon.

albeitería, *f.* veterinary science.

albéntola, *f.* fine fishing net.

alberca, *f.* reservoir, cistern, pool, pond.

albérchiga, *f.* kind of peach.

albergar, *va.* to lodge, to house, to harbor; **—se,** to take shelter.

albergue, *m.* shelter; lodging house, charity school for orphans.

Alberto, Albert.

albillo, *m.* white grape; wine made from white grapes.

albina, *f.* marshy ground inundated with sea water.

albo, ba, *adj.* (poet.) white.

albogue, *m.* bagpipe; cymbal.

albohol, *m.* (bot.) poppy.

albóndiga, *f.* ball of forcemeat.

albor, *m.* (poet.) dawn; whiteness; (fig.) beginning.

alborada, *f.* first dawn of day; (mil.) action fought at the dawn of day; morning watch.

alborear, *vn.* to dawn.

alborga, *f.* matweed sandal.

albornía, *f.* large glazed jug.

albornoz, *m.* coarse woolen cloth; Moorish cloak.

alboroque, *m.* treat at the conclusion of a bargain.

alborotadizo, za, or **alborotado, da,** *adj.* restless, turbulent.

alborotapueblos, *m.* disturber, agitator; (coll.) promoter of festivities.

alborotar, *va.* to make a disturbance, to stir.

alboroto, *m.* noise, disturbance, tumult, riot.

alborozado, da, *adj.* excited.

alborozar, *va.* to exhilarate.

alborozo, *m.* joy, gaiety; excitement.

¡albricias! *interj.* good news!

albudeca, *f.* (bot.) poor quality melon.

albufera, *f.* lagoon by the sea.

albugíneo, nea, *adj.* albuminous.

álbum, *m.* album; **— de recortes,** scrap book.

albumen, *m.,* **albúmina,** *f.* albumen.

albuminuria, *f.* (med.) Bright's disease.

albur, *m.* dace, river fish.

albura, *f.* whiteness; sapwood.

alca, *f.* penguin.

alcabala, *f.* sales tax; duty.

alcacel or **alcacer,** *m.* green barley.

alcachofa, *f.* artichoke.

alcahaz, *m.* large bird cage.

alcahazar, *va.* to cage birds.

alcahuete, ta, *n.* pimp, bawd, procurer.

alcahuetear, *va.* to pander.

alcahuetería, *f.* bawdry, pandering.

alcaide, *m.* governor of a castle; jailer, warden.

alcaidesa, *f.* wife of a warden or jailer.

alcaidía, *f.* office of a warden or jailer.

alcalde, *m.* justice of the peace; mayor.

alcaldía, *f.* office and jurisdiction of an alcalde.

álcali, *m.* (chem.) alkali.

alcalino, na, *adj.* alkaline.

alcalizar, *va.* to alkalize.

alcaloide, *m.* alkaloid.

alcamonías, *f. pl.* various kinds of aromatic seeds.

alcance, *m.* reach, scope; balance of an account; arm's length; range of firearms; capacity, ability; fathom; hit; compass; **— del oído,** earshot.

alcancía, *f.* money box; (mil.) hand grenade.

alcanfor, *m.* camphor.

alcanforado, da, *adj.* camphorated.

alcantarilla, *f.* small bridge, culvert; drain, sewer; underground conduit.

alcantarillado, *m.* sewage.

alcanzado, da, *adj.* needy; wanting.

alcanzar, *va.* to overtake, to come up with, to reach; to get, to obtain; to be a creditor; —, *vn.* to suffice; to reach.

alcaparra, *f.*, **alcaparro,** *m.* caper bush; caper.

alcaraván, *m.* (orn.) bittern.

alcaravea, *f.* caraway seed.

alcarraza, *f.* unglazed and·porous jar.

alcartaz, *m.* paper cone.

alcatifa, *f.* fine carpet.

alcatraz, *m.* pelican.

alcayata, *f.* hook; clothes hook; spike.

alcázar, *m.* castle; fortress; (naut.) quarterdeck.

alcazuz, *m.* licorice.

alc.^{de} **alcalde,** mayor; justice of the peace.

alce, *m.* the cut (in cards); (zool.) elk or moose.

alcoba, *f.* alcove; bedroom.

alcohol, *m.* antimony; alcohol; — **desnaturalizado,** denatured alcohol; — **para fricciones,** rubbing alcohol.

alcoholar, *va.* to paint with antimony; to rectify spirits; to reduce to a powder.

alcohólicc, ca, *adj.* alcoholic.

Alcorán, *m.* Koran.

alcoranista, *m.* and *f.* expounder of the Koran.

alcornoque, *m.* cork tree; person of uncouth manners.

alcorza, *f.* sugar paste for frosting.

alcrebite, *m.* sulphur, brimstone.

alcurnia, *f.* lineage, race.

alcuza, *f.* oil can, vinegar and oil cruet.

aldaba, *f.* knocker, clapper of a door; crossbar; latch.

aldabada, *f.* rap with a knocker; sudden fear.

aldabazo, *m.* violent rap with the knocker.

aldabear, *vn.* to knock at the door with the knocker.

aldea, *f.* hamlet; large farm.

aldeano, na, *adj.* rustic, countrified, uncultured; —, *m.* peasant, countryman, rustic; —, *f.* countrywoman, peasant woman.

aleación, *f.* art of alloying metals.

alear, *vn.* to flutter; —, *va.* to alloy.

aledaño, ña, *adj.* bordering, pertaining to a boundary line; —, *m.* border, boundary.

alegación, *f.* allegation.

alegar, *va.* to allege, to maintain, to affirm; to quote.

alegato, *m.* allegation, statement of plaintiff's case.

alegoría, *f.* allegory.

alegórico, ca, *adj.* allegorical.

alegorizar, *va.* to allegorize.

alegrar, *va.* to gladden; to lighten; to exhilarate; to enliven; to beautify; —se, to rejoice; to grow merry with drinking.

alegre, *adj.* glad, merry, joyful, content; — **de cascos,** lightheaded; intoxicated.

alegría, *f.* mirth, gaiety, delight, cheer; (bot.) sesame; —s, *pl.* public festivals.

alegro, *m.* (mus.) allegro.

alegrón, *m.* (coll.) sudden joy; sudden flicker.

alejamiento, *m.* distance, remoteness; aloofness; removal.

Alejandría, *f.* Alexandria.

Alejandro, Alexander.

alejar, *va.* to remove to a greater distance; to separate, to take away; —se, to withdraw, to move away.

Alej.° **Alejandro,** Alex. Alexander.

alelado, da, *adj.* stupefied.

alelarse, *vr.* to become stupid.

alelí, *m.* (bot.) winter gilliflower; damewort (a European garden flower).

aleluya, *f.* hallelujah; Easter time.

alemán, ana, *adj.* and *n.* German, —, *m.* German language.

Alemania, *f.* Germany.

alentador, ra, *adj.* encouraging.

alentar, *vn.* (IE) to breathe; —, *va.* to animate; to cheer, to encourage.

alepín, *m.* a kind of bombazine.

alerce, *m.* larch tree.

alergia, *f.* (med.) allergy.

alero, *m.* gable end; eaves.

alerón, *m.* (aer.) aileron.

alerta, *adv.* vigilantly; **estar** —, to be on the alert; ¡—! *interj.* alert! on the watch!

alertamente, *adv.* alertly, vigilantly, on the alert.

alertar, *va.* to render vigilant.

alerto, ta, *adj.* alert, vigilant, open-eyed.

alesna, *f.* awl.

alesnado, da, *adj.* awl-shaped.

aleta, *f.* winglet, little wing; fin (of a fish); blade (of a propeller).

aletargarse, *vr.* to fall into a lethargic state; to sink to sleep.

aletazo, *m.* blow from a wing.

aletear, *vn.* to flutter, to flit, to flicker.

aleteo, *m.* flapping of wings; fluttering.

Aleutianas or **Aleutas,** *f. pl.* Aleutian Islands.

aleve, *adj.* treacherous, perfidious.

alevosía, *f.* treachery, perfidy.

alevoso, sa, *adj.* treacherous, perfidious.

alfa, *f.* alpha, first letter of the Greek alphabet; — **y omega,** beginning and end.

alfabéticamente, *adv.* alphabetically.

alfabético, ca, *adj.* alphabetical.

alfabeto, *m.* alphabet.

alfajor, *m.* gingerbread; kind of sweet paste made of corn and honey.

alfalfa, *f.* (bot.) alfalfa.

alfanjazo, *m.* cutlass wound.

alfanje, *m.* hanger, cutlass.

alfaque, *m.* sand bank.

alfaquí, *m.* fakir.

alfar, *m.* pottery; potter's clay.

alfarería, *f.* potter's art.

alfarero, *m.* potter.

alfeñicado, da, *adj.* sugared; delicate.

alfeñique, *m.* sugar paste; weakling.

alferecía, *f.* epilepsy.

alférez, *m.* ensign; second lieutenant.
alfil, *m.* bishop (in chess).
alfiler, *m.* pin; **—es,** *pl.* pin money; **— de corbata,** scarf pin; **— de pecho,** brooch; **— de seguridad** or **imperdible,** safety pin.
alfilerazo, *m.* prick of a pin; large pin.
alfiletero, *m.* pincushion.
Alf.º Alfonso, Alph. Alphonse.
alfolí, *m.* granary; salt warehouse.
alfoliero or **alfolinero,** *m.* keeper of a granary or storehouse.
alfombra, *f.* carpet; rug; **— de flores,** (poet.) field of flowers.
alfombrar, *va.* to carpet.
alfombrero, *m.* carpet maker.
alfombrilla, *f.* small carpet; small rug; (med.) measles.
alfóncigo, *m.* pistachio (tree or nut).
Alfonso, Alphonse, Alphonso.
alforfón, *m.* buckwheat.
alforja, *f.* saddlebag, knapsack.
alforjero, *m.* maker or seller of saddlebags.
alforza, *f.* tuck, pleat.
Alfredo, Alfred.
álg. álgebra, alg. algebra.
alga, *f.* (bot.) alga, seaweed.
algaida, *f.* sand dune.
algalia, *f.* civet; civet cat.
algarabía, *f.* Arabic tongue; gabble, jargon; clamor, din.
algarada, *f.* loud cry; noise of an attack or tumult; sudden attack.
algarroba, *f.* (bot.) carob bean.
algarrobera, *f.,* **algarrobo,** *m.* (bot.) carob tree.
algazara, *f.* Moorish war cry; din, hubbub, uproar.
álgebra, *f.* algebra.
algebraico, ca, *adj.* algebraic.
álgido, *adj.* icy, chilly.
algo, *pron.* some, something; anything; **—de,** a little; **— que comer,** something to eat; **en —,** somewhat, in some way, a bit; **por —,** for some reason; **—,** *adv.* a little, rather.
algodón, *m.* cotton, cotton plant, cotton wool; **— de pelo,** stapled cotton; **— en bruto** or **en rama,** raw cotton; **— en madeja,** skein cotton; **— flor,** select cotton; **— hilado,** spun cotton; **— pólvora,** guncotton or nitrocotton.
algodonado, da, *adj.* filled with cotton; wadded, padded.
algodonal, *m.* cotton plantation.
algodonero, *m.* cotton plant; dealer in cotton, cotton broker; **—, ra,** *adj.* pertaining to the cotton industry.
algoso, sa, *adj.* full of algae or seaweed.
alguacil, *m.* bailiff, constable.
alguien, *pron.* someone, somebody, anyone, anybody.
alguno (algún), na, *pron.* somebody, someone, some person, anybody, anyone; **—,** *adj.* some, any; **en modo —,** in any way;

—na cosa, anything; **en —na parte,** anywhere; **—s,** *pl.* a few.
alhaja, *f.* jewel, gem; ornate furniture.
alhajar, *va.* to supply with furniture or with jewels.
alharaca, *f.* clamor, vociferation; ballyhoo.
alhelí, *m.* (bot.) gilliflower; damewort (a European garden flower).
alheña, *f.* (bot.) privet; henna; mildew in grain.
alhoja, *f.* lark.
alhóndiga, *f.* public granary.
alhondiguero, *m.* keeper of a public granary.
alhucema, *f.* (bot.) lavender.
aliacanado, da, *adj.* jaundiced.
aliado, da, *adj.* allied; **—,** *n.* ally.
alianza, *f.* alliance, league.
aliarse, *vr.* to ally oneself, to become allied.
alias, *adv.* alias; otherwise.
alicaído, da, *adj.* weak, drooping, extenuated.
alicates, *m. pl.* pincers, nippers; pliers.
Alicia, Alice.
aliciente, *m.* attraction, incitement, inducement.
alicuanta, *adj.* aliquant (number).
alícuota, *adj.* aliquot (number).
alienista, *m.* and *f.* alienist.
aliento, *m.* breath; courage, encouragement; **dar —,** to encourage; **sin —,** without breath, without vigor.
aligación, *f.* alligation.
aligar, *va.* to tie, to unite.
aligeramiento, *m.* alleviation; lightening a burden, levitation.
aligerar, *va.* to lighten; to alleviate; to hasten.
alijador, *m.* (naut.) lighter; smuggler.
alijar, *va.* (naut.) to lighten, to smuggle; **—,** *m.* uncultivated ground.
alijo, *m.* lightening of a ship; alleviation; smuggled goods.
alimaña, *f.* destructive animal.
alimentación, *f.* maintenance; food, nourishment, meals; **— de gravedad,** (aer.) gravity feed.
alimentador, *m.* feeder.
alimentar, *va.* to feed, to nourish.
alimenticio, cia, *adj.* nutritious, nutritive.
alimentista, *m.* and *f.* boarder, pensioner.
alimento, *m.* nourishment, food; **— combustible,** carbohydrate food; **— plástico,** protein food; **—s,** *pl.* alimony.
alindar, *va.* to fix limits.
alineación, *f.* alignment.
alinear, *va.* to measure by line, to arrange in line; **—se,** to fall in line.
aliñar, *va.* to adorn; to season.
aliño, *m.* dress, ornament, decoration; dressing, seasoning.
alípede, *adj.* (poet.) with winged feet; swift-footed.
aliquebrado, da, *adj.* broken-winged; dejected, low-spirited.

alisadura, *f.* planing, smoothing, polishing; **—s,** *pl.* shavings, cuttings.
alisar, *va.* to plane, to polish; to smoothe.
aliseda, *f.* plantation of alder trees.
alisios, *m. pl.* trade winds.
aliso, *m.* alder tree.
alistado, da, *adj.* striped; enlisted.
alistador, *m.* one who enlists or enrolls.
alistamiento, *m.* enrollment, conscription, levy.
alistar, *va.* and *vr.* to enlist, to enroll; to get ready, to make ready.
aliviadero, *m.* emergency outlet.
aliviador, ra, *n.* assistant, helper.
aliviar, *va.* to lighten; to ease, to relieve, to mollify.
alivio, *m.* alleviation, mitigation; comfort.
aljaba, *f.* quiver (for arrows).
aljez, *m.* crude gypsum.
aljibe, *m.* cistern.
aljofaina, *f.* earthen jug; washbasin.
aljófar, *m.* misshapen pearl; (poet.) drop of dew; tear.
aljofarar, *va.* to adorn with pearls.
aljor, *m.* crude gypsum.
alma, *f.* soul; heart; human being; principal part of a thing; conscience; energy.
almacén, *m.* department store; warehouse, magazine; **tener en —,** to have in stock.
almacenaje, *m.* warehouse rent; **— de gasolina,** gasoline storage.
almacenar, *va.* to store, to lay up.
almacenero, *m.* warehouse keeper.
almacenista, *m.* shop owner; salesman in a shop; warehouse owner; wholesaler.
almáciga, *f.* mastic; nursery of trees.
almadén, *m.* mine.
almadía, *f.* Indian canoe; raft.
almadraba, *f.* tunny fishery.
almadreña, *f.* wooden shoe.
almaganeta, *f.* sledge hammer.
almagrar, *va.* to tinge with red ochre.
almagre, *m.* red ochre.
almanaque, *m.* almanac.
almanaquero or **almanaquista,** *m.* maker or seller of almanacs.
almarjal, *m.* low marshy ground.
almártaga, *f.* litharge; a sort of halter.
almástiga, *f.* mastic.
almastigado, da, *adj.* containing mastic.
almazara, *f.* oil mill.
almazarero, *m.* oil miller.
almazarrón, *m.* red ochre.
almeja, *f.* clam.
almena, *f.* battlement.
almenado, da, *adj.* embattled.
almenaje, *m.* series of turrets around a rampart.
almenar, *va.* to crown a rampart with battlements.
almendra, *f.* almond; **— garapiñada,** sugared, honeyed almond.
almendrada, *f.* almond milk.
almendrado, da, *adj.* almondlike; **—,** *m.* macaroon.

almendrera, *f.,* **almendrero** or **almendro,** *m.* almond tree.
almez or **almezo,** *m.* lotus tree.
almeza, *f.* lotus berry.
almiar, *m.* haystack.
almíbar, *m.* sirup; **—es,** *pl.* preserved fruit.
almibarar, *va.* to preserve fruit in sugar; to conciliate with soft and endearing words.
almidón, *m.* starch, farina.
almidonado, da, *adj.* starched; affected; stiff in mannerisms; spruce.
almidonar, *va.* to starch.
almilla, *f.* undervest; short military jacket; breast of pork.
alminar, *m.* minaret.
almiranta, *f.* flagship; the admiral's wife.
almirantazgo, *m.* admiralty; admiral's dues.
almirante, *m.* admiral; swimming teacher.
almirez, *m.* brass mortar; **— y mano,** mortar and pestle.
almizclar, *va.* to perfume with musk.
almizcle, *m.* musk.
almizcleño, ña, *adj.* musky.
almizclera, *f.* muskrat.
almo, ma, *adj.* (poet.) vivifying; nourishing; venerable, holy.
almocafre, *m.* gardener's hoe.
almofía, *f.* washbasin.
almohada, *f.* pillow, bolster; coach box; cushion.
almohadilla, *f.* small pillow; working case; sewing cushion; **— higiénica,** sanitary napkin.
almohadillado, da, *adj.* padded, cushioned; **—,** *m.* upholstery.
almohadón, *m.* large cushion.
almohatre, *m.* sal ammoniac.
almohaza, *f.* currycomb.
almohazador, *m.* groom, stable boy, ostler.
almohazar, *va.* to curry.
almojábana, *f.* cheesecake.
almoneda, *f.* auction.
almonedear, *va.* to sell at auction.
almoraduj or **almoradux,** *m.* (bot.) sweet marjoram.
almorí, *m.* sweetmeat or cake.
almorranas, *f. pl.* hemorrhoids, piles.
almorta, *f.* (bot.) vetch.
almorzada, *f.* double handful of grain.
almorzado, da, *adj.* having breakfasted.
almorzar, *va.* (UE) to breakfast; to eat lunch, to have lunch.
almotacén, *m.* inspector of weights and measures.
almotacenazgo, *m.* office of an inspector of weights and measures.
almozárabe, *m.* Christian subject of the Moors.
Almte. almirante, Adm. Admiral.
almud, *m.* measure of grain (the twelfth part of a **fanega**).
almudada, *f.* piece of ground which it takes half a **fanega** of grain to sow.
almuerza, *f.* double handful (of grain, fruits, etc.).

almuerzo, m. breakfast; lunch, luncheon.
Al.º Alonso, Al. Alonzo.
alobadado, da, adj. bitten by a wolf; (vet.) suffering from painful swellings.
alobunado, da, adj. wolf-colored.
alocado, da, adj. crack-brained; foolish, inconsiderate.
alocución, f. address, speech.
áloe, m. (bot.) aloes.
aloja, f. mead.
alojamiento, m. lodging; accommodation; (naut.) steerage.
alojar, va. to lodge; —se, to reside in lodgings.
alojería, f. place where mead is prepared and sold.
alojero, m. seller of mead; box near the pit in some theaters of Spain.
alomado, da, adj. crook-backed (of horses).
alomar, va. to plow in furrows; to distribute equally (a load on a pack animal); —, vr. to grow strong and vigorous (of horses).
alón, m. wing of a bird stripped of its feathers.
alondra, f. lark.
Alonso, Alonzo.
alopiado, da, adj. composed of opium.
aloque, adj. light-red (wine).
alosa, f. shad (a salt-water fish).
alpaca, f. (zool.) alpaca; fabric from the wool of the alpaca.
alpañata, f. piece of leather for smoothing pottery.
alpargata, f. hempen shoe.
alpargatar, va. to make hempen shoes.
alpargatero, m. manufacturer of hempen shoes.
alpargatilla, f. small hempen sandal; —, m. and f. (coll.) crafty person, wheedler.
Alpes, m. pl. Alps.
alpinismo, m. mountain climbing.
alpinista, m. and f. mountain climber.
alpino, na, adj. Alpine.
alpiste, m. canary seed.
alpistela or alpistera, f. cake made of flour, eggs, sesamum and honey.
alpistero, m. sieve for sifting canary seed.
alquería, f. grange, farmhouse.
alquifol, m. (min.) potter's ore.
alquiladizo, za, adj. for hire.
alquilador, ra, n. hirer, tenant.
alquilar, va. to let, to hire, to rent.
alquiler, m. wages, hire; house rent; de —, for hire, for rent.
alquilona, f. woman hired for odd jobs, such as cleaning.
alquimia, f. alchemy
alquimista, m. alchemist.
alquitara, f. still.
alquitarar, va. to distil.
alquitrán, m. tar, liquid pitch; — de hulla, coal tar; — de madera, pine tar.
alquitranado, m. (naut.) tarpaulin.
alquitranar, va. to tar.
alrededor, adv. around; — de, about, around.

alrededores, m. pl. environs; neighborhood.
Alsacia Lorena, f. Alsace-Lorraine.
alt.: altitud, alt. altitude; altura, ht. height.
alta, f. ancient court dance; discharge of a cured patient from a hospital; (mil.) document qualifying entrance of a man into active service; new member in a club, organization, etc.
altanería, f. haughtiness.
altanero, ra, adj. haughty, arrogant, vain, proud.
altar, m. altar; — mayor, high altar.
altarero, m. decorator of altars for festivals.
altavoz, m. loudspeaker.
altea, f. (bot.) marsh mallow.
alterabilidad, f. changeability; mutability.
alterable, adj. alterable, mutable.
alteración, f. alteration, change; mutation; strong emotion; disturbance, tumult.
alterar, va. to alter, to change; to disturb; —se, to become angry.
altercación, f. altercation, controversy; quarrel, contest, strife.
altercado, m. disagreement, quarrel
altercador, ra, n. wrangler.
altercar, va. to dispute, to altercate, to quarrel.
álter ego, m. alter ego, a friend to whom the greatest confidences are entrusted.
alternación, f. alternation.
alternador, m. (elec.) alternator.
alternar, va. and vn. to alternate
alternativa, f. alternative.
alternativo, va, adj. alternate.
Alteza, f. Highness (title).
alteza, f. height, elevation.
altibajo, m. kind of brocaded velvet; downward blow in fencing; uneven ground; —s, pl. vicissitudes of human affairs, ups and downs; uneven ground.
altillo, m. hillock; (Sp. Am.) garret.
altímetro, m. altimeter.
altiplanicie, f. highland.
altiplano, m. high plateau.
altísimo, ma, adj. extremely high; el A—, m. the Most High, God.
altisonante or altísono, na, adj. highsounding, pompous.
altitonante, adj. (poet.) thundering from above.
altitud, f. altitude.
altivez, f. pride, haughtiness, huff.
altivo, va, adj. haughty, proud.
alto, ta, adj. high, elevated; loud; tall; arduous, difficult; eminent; enormous, atrocious; —, m height, story, floor; highland; (mil.) halt; (mus.) tenor, tenor notes; — relieve, high relief; ¡—! or ¡— ahí! interj. stop there! ¡— de aquí! interj. move off!
altoparlante, m. loudspeaker.
altramuz, m. (bot.) lupine.
altruísmo, m. altruism, unselfishness.
altruísta, adj. altruistic, unselfish; —, m. and f. altruist, unselfish person.

altura, *f.* height; highness; mountain summit; altitude; —s, *pl.* the heavens.

alubia, *f.* kidney bean.

alucinación, *f.*, **alucinamiento,** *m.* hallucination.

alucinar, *va.* to blind, to deceive; —se, to deceive oneself, to labor under a delusion.

alucón, *m.* barn owl.

alud, *m.* avalanche.

aludido, da, *adj.* referred to, above-mentioned.

aludir, *vn.* to allude, to refer to.

alumbrado, da, *adj.* aluminous; lighted, illuminated; (coll.) a little tipsy; —, *m.* lighting, illumination; (aer.) flare; — **sin sombras,** floodlighting.

alumbramiento, *m.* illumination; childbirth.

alumbrar, *va.* to light, to illuminate; to enlighten, to instruct; to soak in alum water; —se, to become intoxicated.

alumbre, *m.* alum.

alumbrera, *f.* alum mine.

aluminado, da, *adj.* impregnated with alum.

aluminio, *m.* aluminum.

aluminoso, sa, *adj.* aluminous.

alumno, na, *m.* foster child; disciple, pupil.

alunado, da, *adj.* lunatic; spasmodic; long-tusked.

alusión, *f.* allusion, hint.

alusivo, va, *adj.* allusive.

alustrar, *va.* to give luster, to polish.

alutación, *f.* grains of gold brought to light by washing.

aluvión, *m.* alluvium; washout.

álveo, *m.* bed of a river.

alvéolo, *m.* socket of a tooth; honeycomb cell.

alverjas, *f. pl.* peas.

alvidriar, *va.* to glaze earthenware.

Alv.° **Álvaro,** (proper name, no English equivalent).

alza, *f.* advance in price; lift.

alzadamente, *adv.* wholesale; for a lump sum.

alzado, *m.* (arch.) plan of a building showing front elevation; lump sum; —, **da,** *adj.* fraudulent (of a bankruptcy).

alzadura, *f.* elevation.

alzamiento, *m.* raise; elevation; higher bid; uprising.

alzapaño, *m.* curtain holder.

alzaprima, *f.* lever.

alzaprimar, *va.* to raise with a lever; to excite; to spur on.

alzapuertas, *m.* role of a mute servant; dummy in a game.

alzar, *va.* to raise, to lift up, to heave; to construct, to build; to hide, to lock up; to cut cards; — **cabeza,** to recover from a calamity; —se, to rise in rebellion.

allá, *adv.* there; thither; in other times; **más —,** further on, beyond; **más — de,** beyond.

allanar, *va.* to level, to flatten; to overcome

difficulties; to pacify; to subdue; —se, to submit, to abide by.

allegadizo, za, *adj.* swept or scraped together.

allegado, da, *adj.* near; related; —, *n.* follower, ally.

allegador, *m.* reaper, gatherer; poker, fire rake.

allegar, *va.* to collect, to gather; —se, to approach.

allende, *adv.* on the other side, beyond.

allí, *adv.* there, in that place; **por —,** yonder.

alloza, *f.* green almond.

allozo, *m.* wild almond tree.

A.M. **antemeridiano,** A.M. or a.m., before noon.

ama, *f.* mistress, housewife; — **de llaves,** housekeeper; — **de leche,** wet nurse.

amabilidad, *f.* amiability, kindness, affability.

amable, *adj.* amiable, kind; lovely.

amado, da, *n.* beloved, darling.

amador, ra, *n.* one who loves.

amaestrado, da, *adj.* taught, trained; cunningly contrived.

amaestrar, *va.* to teach, to instruct, to train.

amagar, *va.* and *vn.* to threaten; to shake one's fist.

amago, *m.* threat; indication; symptom.

amainar, *va.* (naut.) to lower a sail; —se, to give up, to withdraw from.

amajadar, *va.* to pen (sheep).

amalgama, *f.* amalgam.

amalgamación, *f.* amalgamation.

amalgamar, *va.* to amalgamate.

Amalia, Amelia.

amamantar, *va.* to suckle, to nurse.

amancebamiento, *m.* concubinage.

amancebarse, *vr.* to live in concubinage.

amancillar, *va.* to stain, to defile; to injure; to tarnish one's reputation.

amanecer, *m.* dawn, daybreak; **al —,** at daybreak; —, *vn.* (EZCO) to dawn; to appear at daybreak.

amanerado, da, *adj.* affected, overrefined.

amanerarse, *vr.* to become affected, to acquire undesirable mannerisms.

amanojar, *va.* to gather by handfuls.

amansador, ra, *n.* tamer, subduer; soother.

amansamiento, *m.* taming.

amansar, *va.* to tame, to domesticate; to soften, to pacify.

amantar, *va.* to cover with a blanket.

amante, *m.* and *f.* lover.

amanuense, *m.* and *f.* amanuensis, clerk, copyist.

amañar, *va.* to do a thing cleverly; —se, to accustom one's self to do things expertly; to adapt oneself.

amaño, *m.* skill, dexterity; —s, *pl.* tools; implements; intrigue.

amapola, *f.* (bot.) poppy.

amar, *va.* to love.

amáraco, *m.* (bot.) marjoram.

amaranto, *m.* (bot.) amaranth.
amarar, *vn.* to land a plane on water.
amargamente, *adv.* bitterly.
amargar, *va.* to make bitter; to exasperate; —, *vn.* to be bitter; —se, to become bitter.
amargo, ga, *adj.* bitter, acrid; painful —, *m.* bitterness; candy made of bitter almonds; —os, *m. pl.* bitters.
amargón, *m.* (bot.) dandelion.
amargor, *m.* bitterness; sorrow, vexation, distress.
amargoso, sa, *adj.* bitter.
amargura, *f.* bitterness; sorrow.
amarillazo, za, *adj.* pale yellow.
amarillear, *vn.* to turn yellow.
amarillejo, ja, or amarillento, ta, *adj.* yellowish.
amarillez, *f.* yellowness.
amarillo, lla, *adj.* yellow; —, *m.* jaundice.
amarinar, *va.* (naut.) to man, to equip.
amarra, *f.* cable; martingale.
amarradero, *m.* a post to make fast to; (naut.) mooring berth.
amarrar, *va.* to tie, to fasten.
amarrazones, *m. pl.* (naut.) ground tackle.
amarre, *m.* mooring; mooring line or cable.
amartelar, *va.* to court, to make love; —se, to fall in love.
amartillar, *va.* to hammer; to cock a gun or pistol.
amasadera, *f.* kneading bowl, breadboard.
amasadería, *f.* bakery.
amasadura, *f.* kneading.
amasar, *va.* to knead; (fig.) to arrange, to prepare, to settle.
amasiato, *m.* (Sp. Am.) concubinage.
amasijo, *m.* mixed mortar; bread dough; medley.
Amata, Amy.
amatista, *f.* amethyst.
amatorio, ria, *adj.* amatory.
amazona, *f.* an amazon, masculine woman; Río A—s, *m.* Amazon River.
ambages, *m. pl.* circumlocution; sin —, in plain language.
ámbar, *m.* amber; — gris, ambergris.
ambarino, na, *adj.* amber, amberlike.
Amberes, *f.* Antwerp.
ambición, *f.* ambition; covetousness.
ambicionar, *va.* to crave, to covet; to aspire to.
ambicioso, sa, *adj.* ambitious.
ambidextro, tra, *adj.* ambidextrous.
ambiente, *m.* surrounding atmosphere; environment.
ambigú, *m.* light meal, buffet lunch.
ambigüedad, *f.* ambiguity.
ambiguo, gua, *adj.* ambiguous, doubtful, equivocal.
ámbito, *m.* circuit, circumference; border, limit; corner.
ambo, *m.* double lottery prize.
ambos, bas, *adj. pl.* both.
ambrosía, *f.* ambrosia; any delicious liquor; (bot.) buckthorn.

Ambrosio, Ambrose.
ambulancia, *f.* ambulance.
ambulante, *adj.* ambulatory; roving; músico —, street musician; vendedor —, peddler.
ambulativo, va, *adj.* of a roving disposition.
amechar, *va.* to put a wick in lamps, etc.
amedrentar, *va.* to frighten, to terrify, to intimidate.
amelga, *f.* ridge between two furrows.
amelgar, *va.* to open furrows with a plow.
ameliorar, *va.* to better, to improve.
amelonado, da, *adj.* melon-shaped.
amén, *m.* amen, so be it; acquiescence; en un decir —, in an instant; — de, besides; except.
amenaza, *f.* threat, menace.
amenazador, ra, *adj.* menacing, threatening.
amenazar, *va.* to threaten, to menace.
amenidad, *f.* amenity, agreeableness.
amenizar, *va.* to render pleasant; to adorn a speech.
ameno, na, *adj.* pleasant, amusing, entertaining; flowery (of language).
amerengado, da, *adj.* like meringue; (coll.) prudish.
América Central, *f.* Central America.
América del Norte, *f.* North America.
América del Sur, *f.* South America.
América Española, *f.* Spanish America.
americana, *f.* sackcoat, coat.
americano, na, *n.* and *adj.* American.
ametralladora, *f.* machine gun; — de mano, sub-machine gun; — pequeña, tommy gun, sub-machine gun; pistola —, sub-machine gun.
ametrallar, *va.* to machine-gun.
amianto, *m.* asbestos.
amiba, *f.* amoeba.
amiboideo, dea, *adj.* amoebic.
amicísimo, ma, *adj.* most friendly.
amiento, *m.* stay of a helmet; shoelace.
amiga, *f.* female friend; concubine; schoolmistress; — preferida, best girl.
amigable, *adj.* amicable, friendly; suitable.
amígdala, *f.* tonsil.
amigdalitis, *f.* tonsilitis.
amigo, *m.* friend; comrade; lover; —, ga, *adj.* friendly.
amilanar, *va.* to frighten, to terrify; —se, to become terrified.
amillaramiento, *m.* tax assessment.
amillarar, *va.* to assess a tax.
amillonado, da, *adj.* very rich; —, *n.* millionaire.
aminorar, *va.* to reduce, to lessen.
amistad, *f.* friendship; concubinage; hacer —, to become acquainted.
amistar, *va.* and *vr.* to make acquainted; to reconcile.
amistoso, sa, *adj.* friendly, cordial, amicable.
amito, *m.* amice; (part of a priest's vestments).
amnesia, *f.* amnesia.

amnistía, *f.* amnesty.

am.º amigo, friend.

amo, *m.* master of a house; proprietor, owner; foster father; overseer; boss.

amoblar, *va.* (UE) to furnish.

amodorramiento, *m.* stupor, sleepiness.

amodorrarse, *vr.* to grow sleepy.

amohecerse, *vr.* (EZCO) to grow moldy or rusty.

amohinar, *va.* to put out of humor.

amojonar, *va.* to set landmarks.

amoladera, *f.* whetstone, grindstone.

amolador, *m.* grinder.

amoladura, *f.* whetting, grinding, sharpening.

amolar, *va.* (UE) to whet, to grind, to sharpen.

amoldar, *va.* to mold; to adjust; **—se,** to adapt one's self to.

amolletado, da, *adj.* loaf-shaped, oval.

amonedar, *va.* to coin.

amonestación, *f.* advice, admonition; warning; publication of marriage bans.

amonestar, *va.* to advise, to admonish, to monitor; to publish bans of marriage.

amoníaco, *m.* ammoniac.

amonio, *m.* (chem.) ammonium.

amontarse, *vr.* to take to the woods.

amontonar, *va.* to heap together; to accumulate.

amor, *m.* love; fancy; flame; the object of love; **por — de,** for the sake of; **por — de Dios,** for God's sake; **— propio,** self-love; pride; **—es,** *pl.* love affairs.

amoral, *adj.* amoral.

amoratado, da, *adj.* livid, black and blue; purplish.

amorcillo, *m.* flirtation.

amordazado, da, *adj.* gagged, muzzled.

amordazar, *va.* to gag, to muzzle.

amorfo, fa, *adj.* amorphous.

amorío, *m.* love-making, love.

amoroso, sa, *adj.* affectionate, loving.

amorrar, *vn.* (coll.) to hang one's head; **—se,** to sulk, to be sullen.

amortajar, *va.* to shroud a corpse.

amortiguador, *m.* bumper (of an automobile); shock absorber.

amortiguar, *va.* to lessen, to mitigate, to soften; to deaden; to temper.

amortizable, *adj.* redeemable.

amortización, *f.* amortization.

amortizar, *va.* to entail an estate; to amortize; to pay, to liquidate, to discharge a debt.

amoscar, *va.* to whisk flies; **—se,** to drive off flies with the tail (of animals); to fly into a passion at nothing.

amostachado, *adj.* wearing a mustache.

amostazado, da, *adj.* (coll.) annoyed, angry, vexed.

amostazar, *va.* (coll.) to exasperate, to provoke; **—se,** to become irritated, to go into a rage.

amotinador, ra, *n.* mutineer.

amotinamiento, *m.* mutiny.

amotinar, *va.* to excite rebellion; **—se,** to mutiny.

amovible, *adj.* removable.

ampara, *f.* (law) distraint.

amparar, *va.* to shelter, to favor, to protect; **—se,** to claim protection.

amparo, *m.* protection, help, support; refuge, asylum.

ampelita, *f.* soft slate.

ampelografía, *f.* science of grape growing.

amperaje, *m.* (elec.) amperage.

amperímetro, *m.* (elec.) amperemeter, ammeter.

amperio, *m.* (elec.) ampere.

ampliación, *f.* amplification, enlargement.

ampliar, *va.* to amplify, to enlarge, to extend, to expand, to increase.

ampliativo, va, *adj.* amplifying.

amplificación, *f.* enlargement (of a photograph).

amplificador, *m.* amplifier.

amplificar, *va.* to amplify, to enlarge.

amplio, plia, *adj.* ample, extensive, vast, spacious.

amplitud, *f.* amplitude, extension, largeness; **— de miras,** broad-mindedness.

ampo (de la nieve), *m.* dazzling whiteness; snowflake.

ampolla, *f.* blister; snowflake; bulb; vial, flask; ampoule; decanter.

ampollar, *va.* to raise blisters; **—se,** to rise in bubbles; **—,** *adj.* bubble-shaped.

ampolleta, *f.* small vial; ampoule; hourglass.

ampuloso, sa, *adj.* affected, pompous, bombastic.

amputación, *f.* amputation.

amputar, *va.* to amputate.

amuchachado, da, *adj.* boyish, childish.

amueblar, *va.* to furnish.

amugronar, *va.* to propagate a plant by layering.

amujerado, da, *adj.* effeminate.

amuleto, *m.* amulet.

amunicionar, *va.* to supply with ammunition.

amuñecado, da, *adj.* doll-like, like a puppet.

amurallar, *va.* to surround with walls.

amurcar, *va.* to gore with the horns.

amurco, *m.* blow with the horns.

amusco, ca, *adj.* dark brown.

amusgar, *va.* to lay back the ears; to half close one's eyes to see better.

Ana, Ann, Anne, Anna, Hannah.

ana, *f.* ell (measure).

anacardo, *m.* cashew tree or fruit.

anaconda, *f.* anaconda, South American boa.

anacoreta, *m.* anchorite, hermit.

anacorético, ca, *adj.* relating to a hermit.

anacronismo, *m.* anachronism.

ánade, *m.* and *f.* duck.

anadear, *vn.* to waddle.

anadeja, *f.* duckling.
anadino, na, *n.* young duck.
anadón, *m.* mallard.
anafalla, *f.* thick corded silk.
anafe, *m.* portable stove.
anagrama, *m.* anagram.
anahora, *adv.* immediately.
anal, *adj.* (anat.) anal.
analéptico, ca, *adj.* (med.) restorative.
anales, *m. pl.* annals.
analfabetismo, *m.* illiteracy.
analfabeto, ta, *n.* illiterate person.
analgésico, ca, *adj.* (med.) analgesic, anodyne.
análisis, *m.* or *f.* analysis.
analista, *m.* writer of annals.
analítico, ca, *adj.* analytical.
analizar, *va.* to analyze.
analogía, *f.* analogy.
analógico, ca, *adj.* analogous, similar.
análogo, ga, *adj.* analogous, similar.
ananá, *m.* pineapple.
anaplastia, *f.* plastic surgery.
anaquel, *m.* shelf in a bookcase.
anaranjado, da, *adj.* orange colored.
anarquía, *f.* anarchy.
anárquico, ca, *adj.* anarchical; confused.
anarquismo, *m.* anarchism.
anarquista, *m.* and *f.* anarchist.
anascote, *m.* serge.
anat. anatomía, anat. anatomy.
anata, *f.* yearly income.
anatema, *m.* or *f.* anathema.
anatematizar, *va.* to anathematize.
anatomía, *f.* anatomy.
anatómico, ca, *adj.* anatomical.
anatomista, *m.* anatomist.
anatomizar, *va.* to anatomize, to dissect.
anca, *f.* buttock; hindquarters (of a horse).
ancianidad, *f.* old age; antiquity.
anciano, na, *n.* and *adj.* aged (man or woman); old, ancient.
ancla, *f.* anchor; **— de la esperanza,** sheet anchor; **echar —s,** to anchor.
anclaje, *m.* act of anchoring; anchoring place; anchorage.
anclar, *vn.* to anchor.
anclote, *m.* stream anchor, grapnel.
ancón, *m,* **anconada,** *f.* bay.
áncora, *f.* anchor.
ancorage, *m.* anchoring place.
ancorar, *vn.* to cast anchor.
ancorero, *m.* anchor smith.
ancheta, *f.* small merchandise taken somewhere for sale; amount made on a deal.
ancho, cha, *adj.* broad, wide, large; **—,** *m.* breadth, width.
anchoa, *f.* anchovy.
anchura, *f.* width, breadth.
anchuroso, sa, *adj.* spacious, vast, ample.
andaderas, *f. pl.* gocart.
andadero, ra, *adj.* accessible, easy to walk on.
andado, da, *n.* stepchild; **—,** *adj.* beaten, much frequented; threadbare.

andador, *m.* stroller; leading string; alley or small walk in a garden; **—, ra,** *adj.* fast-going.
andadura, *f.* walk; pace; amble.
Andalucía, *f.* Andalusia.
andaluz, za, *n.* and *adj.* Andalusian.
andamiaje, *m.* scaffolding.
andamio, *m.* scaffold, scaffolding; (naut.) gangplank, gangway.
andana, *f.* row, rank, line; **llamarse —,** (coll.) to unsay, to retract a promise.
andanada, *f.* grandstand; (naut.) broadside.
andaniño, *m.* gocart in which children learn to walk.
andante, *adj.* walking, errant; (mus.) andante.
andar, *vn.* (ANDO, ANDUVE) to go, to walk; to fare; to proceed, to behave; to function, to move (as a machine); to grope; **¡anda!** or **¡ándale!** *interj.* hurry up! move on! you don't say!
andaraje, *m.* wheel of a well.
andarín, *m.* fast walker; professional runner.
andarivel, *m.* ferry cable, safety rope.
andas, *f. pl.* handbarrow; bier with shafts; stretcher.
andén, *m.* shelf; pavement; sidewalk; (rail.) platform; horse path.
ándito, *m.* gallery around a building.
andorrear, *vn.* to gallivant, to wander about.
andrajo, *m.* rag (of worn clothes).
andrajoso, sa, *adj.* ragged.
Andrés, Andrew.
andrógino, na, *n.* hermaphrodite; **—,** *adj.* hermaphroditic.
andrómina, *f.* (coll.) trick, fraud, artifice.
andullo, *m.* (naut.) canvas shield on harpings; roll of tobacco.
andurriales, *m. pl.* byways.
aneaje, *m.* ell (measure).
anear, *va.* to measure by the ell.
aneblar, *va.* (IE) to cloud, to darken; **—se,** to become cloudy.
anécdota, *f.* anecdote.
anegación, *f.* overflowing, inundation.
anegadizo, za, *adj.* easily inundated.
anegar, *va.* (IE) to inundate, to submerge; **—se,** to drown or to be flooded.
anejo, ja, *adj.*=**anexo, xa.**
anemia, *f.* (med.) anemia.
anémico, ca, *adj.* anemic.
anemómetro, *m.* anemometer.
anestesia, *f.* (med.) anesthesia.
anestésico, ca, *m.* and *adj.* anesthetic.
anexar, *va.* to annex, to join; to enclose.
anexidades, *f. pl.* annexes; appurtenances.
anexión, *f.* annexation.
anexionar, *va.* to annex.
anexo, xa, *adj.* annexed, joined; **—,** *m.* attachment on a letter or document; **—s,** *m. pl.* belongings.
anfibio, bia, *adj.* amphibious; **—,** *m.* amphibian.
anfibología, *f.* words of double meaning.

anfión, *m.* opium.

anfiteatro, *m.* amphitheater; auditorium; balcony (in a theater); (med.) dissecting room for medical students.

anfitrión, *m.* host.

ánfora, *f.* voting box.

angarillas, *f. pl.* handbarrow; stretcher.

ángaro, *m.* signal smoke; beacon.

ángel, *m.* angel; **tener —,** to have a pleasing personality.

Ángela, Angela.

angelical, *adj.* angelic, heaven-born.

angelote, *m.* large figure of an angel (on altars); fat, good-natured child.

angina, *f.* (med.) angina; **— de pecho,** angina pectoris.

anglicismo, *m.* Anglicism.

anglosajón, ona, *n.* and *adj.* Anglo-Saxon.

angostar, *va.* to narrow, to contract.

angosto, ta, *adj.* narrow, close.

angostura, *f.* narrowness; narrow passage.

angra, *f.* small bay.

anguarina, *f.* long, loose coat.

anguila, *f.* (zool.) eel.

angular, *adj.* angular; **piedra —,** cornerstone.

angulema, *f.* hemp cloth; **—s,** *pl.* (coll.) silly flattery.

ángulo, *m.* angle, corner.

anguloso, sa, *adj.* angular, cornered.

angustia, *f.* anguish; heartache.

angustiado, da, *adj.* worried, miserable.

angustiar, *va.* to cause anguish.

angustioso, sa, *adj.* distressing, alarming.

anhelante, *adj.* eager.

anhelar, *vn.* to long for, to desire; to breathe with difficulty.

anhelo, *m.* vehement desire, longing.

anheloso, sa, *adj.* very desirous.

anidar, *vn.* to nestle, to make a nest; to dwell, to inhabit.

anilina, *f.* aniline.

anillo, *m.* ring, small circle; **— de empaquetadura del émbolo,** piston ring; **— de boda,** wedding ring; **— colector,** (elec.) collector ring.

ánima, *f.* soul; bore of a gun; **—s,** *pl.* bell ringing at sunset.

animación, *f.* animation, liveliness.

animado, da, *adj.* lively; animated.

animal, *m.* and *adj.* animal; brute.

animalazo, *m.* big animal.

animalejo, *m.* small animal, animalcule.

animalucho, *m.* ugly, hideous animal.

animar, *va.* to animate, to enliven; to abet; to comfort; to encourage; to revive; **—se,** to cheer up, to be encouraged.

ánimo, *m.* soul, spirit; courage; mind; intention, meaning; will; thought; **en su —,** to himself; **¡—!** *interj.* cheer up!

animosidad, *f.* animosity; valor, courage.

animoso, sa, *adj.* courageous, spirited.

aniñarse, *vr.* to act in a childish manner.

aniquilar, *va.* to annihilate, to destroy; **—se,** to decay; to humble; to consume.

anís, *m.* (bot.) anise.

anisado, da, *adj.* anisated, pertaining to aniseed spirits; **—,** *m.* aniseed spirits, anisette; **aguardiente —,** anisette.

anisar, *va.* to tincture with anise.

Anita, Annette, Little Anne.

aniversario, *m.* anniversary; **—, ria,** *adj.* annual.

ano, *m.* anus.

anoche, *adv.* last night.

anochecer, *vn.* (EZCO) to grow dark; to be or reach (somewhere) by nightfall.

anochecida, *f.* nightfall.

anodinar, *va.* to apply an anodyne.

anodino, na, *adj.* (med.) anodyne.

ánodo, *m.* (elec.) anode.

anomalía, *f.* anomaly.

anómalo, la, *adj.* anomalous.

anón, *m.* (bot.) custard apple tree; fruit of same tree.

anonadar, *va.* to annihilate; to crush; to lessen; **—se,** to humble one's self.

anónimo, ma, *adj.* anonymous.

anormal, *adj.* abnormal.

anotación, *f.* annotation, note.

anotar, *va.* to comment, to note.

ánsar, *m.* goose; **— macho,** gander.

ansarería, *f.* place where geese are raised.

ansarero, *m.* gooseherd.

ansia, *f.* anxiety, eagerness, yearning; worry.

ansiadamente, *adv.* longingly, anxiously.

ansiar, *va.* to desire exceedingly; to long for.

ansiedad, *f.* anxiety, worry.

ansioso, sa, *adj.* anxious, eager.

ant. anticuado, *obs.* obsolete.

anta, *f.* (zool.) moose; elk.

antagónico, ca, *adj.* antagonistic.

antagonista, *m.* and *f.* antagonist.

antaño, *adv.* long ago; yore.

antártico, ca, *adj.* Antarctic.

ante, *m.* dressed buffalo skin; first course of dishes; **—,** *prep.* before; in the presence of; **— todo,** above all else.

anteado, da, *adj.* buff-colored.

anteayer, *adv.* day before yesterday.

antebélico, ca, *adj.* prewar.

antebrazo, *m.* forearm.

antecama, *f.* carpet in front of a bed.

antecámara, *f.* antechamber; lobby, hall.

antecedente, *m.* and *adj.* antecedent.

anteceder, *va.* to precede, to forego.

antecesor, ra, *n.* predecessor; forefather.

antecoger, *va.* to bring any person or thing before one; to gather in fruit before the due time.

Antecristo, *m.* Antichrist.

antedata, *f.* antedate.

antedatar, *va.* to antedate.

antedicho, cha, *adj.* aforesaid.

antediluviano, na, *adj.* antediluvian.

antelación, *f.* precedence.

antemano, *adv.* **de —,** beforehand, in advance.

antemeridiano, na, *adj.* in the forenoon, a. m.

antemural, *m.* (mil.) outworks, fortress wall.

antemuralla, *f.*, **antemuro,** *m.* (mil.) rampart, parapet.

antena, *f.* feeler; antenna, aerial.

antenallas, *f. pl.* pincers.

antenatal, *adj.* prenatal.

antenoche, *adv.* the night before last.

antenombre, *m.* title prefixed to a proper name (as **Don, San,** etc.).

anteojera, *f.* spectacle case.

anteojo, *m.* spyglass, eyeglass; — **de larga vista,** telescope; —**s,** *pl.* spectacles, eyeglasses.

antepagar, *va.* to pay in advance.

antepasado, da, *adj.* passed, elapsed; **semana** —, week before last; —**s,** *m. pl.* ancestors.

antepecho, *m.* (mil.) breastwork, parapet; sill; footstep of a coach, harness.

antepenúltimo, ma, *adj.* antepenultimate.

anteponer, *va.* (ANTEPONGO, ANTEPUSE) to prefer; to place before.

antepuerta, *f.* door hangings.

antera, *f.* (bot.) anther.

anterior, *adj.* anterior, fore; former, previous; **año** —, preceding year.

anterioridad, *f.* priority; preference; **pagar con** —, to pay in advance.

anteriormente, *adv.* formerly, previously; — **mencionada,** above-mentioned.

antes, *adv.* first; formerly; before; beforehand; rather; — **bien,** on the contrary; — **de,** before (time); — **de que,** before; — **que,** before (position); **cuanto** —, as soon as possible.

antesala, *f.* antechamber; lounging room; **hacer** —, to wait in an antechamber.

antestatura, *f.* (mil.) light, hasty entrenchment of stakes and sandbags.

antevíspera, *f.* two days before a given date, the day before the eve of a certain date.

antiaéreo, rea, *adj.* pertaining to anti-aircraft; —**s,** *m. pl.* anti-aircraft.

anticipación, *f.* anticipation; **pagar con** —, to pay in advance.

anticipadamente, *adv.* in advance.

anticipado, da, *adj.* anticipated, in advance; **gracias** —**das,** thanks in advance.

anticipar, *va.* to anticipate; to forestall.

anticipativo, va, *adj.* anticipative.

anticipo, *m.* advance; — **de pago,** payment in advance, retainer.

anticlerical, *adj.* anticlerical; —**ismo,** *m.* anticlericalism.

anticlimax, *m.* anticlimax.

anticuado, da, *adj.* antiquated; obsolete.

anticuar, *va.* to antiquate, to outdate.

anticuario, *m.* antiquary, antiquarian.

anticuerpo, *m.* antibody.

antídoto, *m.* antidote.

antier, *adv.* (contraction) day before yesterday.

antiesclavismo, *m.* antislavery.

antífona, *f.* antiphony; anthem.

antifricción, *f.* antifriction.

antigualla, *f.* monument of antiquity; antique.

antiguamente, *adv.* anciently; formerly.

antigüedad, *f.* antiquity, oldness; ancient times; —**es,** *f. pl.* antiques.

antiguo, gua, *adj.* antique, old, ancient; former; —, *m.* senior.

antihigiénico, ca, *adj.* unsanitary.

antílope, *m.* antelope.

Antillas, *f. pl.* Antilles or West Indies.

antimonárquico, ca, *adj.* antimonarchic.

antimonio, *m.* antimony.

antipapa, *m.* antipope.

antipara, *f.* screen; gaiter.

antiparras, *f. pl.* (coll.) spectacles.

antipatía, *f.* antipathy; dislike.

antipático, ca, *adj.* antipathetic; disagreeable, displeasing.

antípodas, *m. pl.* antipodes.

antipútrido, da, *adj.* antiseptic.

antirraquítico, ca, *adj.* antirachitic.

antisemítico, ca, *adj.* anti-Semitic.

antisepsia, *f.* antisepsis.

antiséptico, ca, *adj.* antiseptic.

antisocial, *adj.* antisocial.

antitanque, *adj.* antitank.

antítesis, *f.* (gram.) antithesis.

antitóxico, ca, *adj.* antitoxic.

antitoxina, *f.* antitoxin.

Ant.º Antonio, Anth. Anthony.

antojadizo, za, *adj.* capricious, fanciful.

antojarse, *vr.* to long, to desire earnestly; to take a fancy for.

antojera, *f.* spectacle case; blinker (of horses).

antojo, *m.* whim; longing, fancy.

antología, *f.* anthology.

antónimo, ma, *adj.* (gram.) antonymous; —, *m.* antonym.

Antonio, Anthony.

antor, *m.* seller of stolen goods.

antorcha, *f.* torch, taper; — **de oxciacetileno,** oxyacetylene torch.

antr. anterior, former, preceding, previous.

antracita, *f.* anthracite, hard coal.

antro, *m.* (poet.) cavern, den, grotto.

antropófago, *m.* man-eater, cannibal.

antropoide, *m.* and *adj.* anthropoid.

antropología, *f.* anthropology.

antropomorfo, fa, *adj.* anthropomorphous.

antruejo, *m.* the three days of the carnival before Ash Wednesday.

antuvión, *m.* sudden stroke or attack.

anual, *adj.* annual.

anualidad, *f.* yearly recurrence; annuity.

anualmente, *adv.* annually, yearly.

anuario, *m.* annual; yearbook; trade directory.

anubarrado, da, *adj.* clouded; painted with clouds (of linens and silks).

anublar, *va.* to cloud, to obscure; —**se,** to become clouded; to fall through.

anudar, *va.* to knot, to tie, to join; —**se,** to waste away.

anuencia, *f.* assent, compliance.
anuente, *adj.* agreeing, yielding.
anulable, *adj.* annullable.
anulación, *f.* abrogation; cancellation; annulment.
anular, *va.* to annul; to make insignificant; —, *adj.* annular; **dedo** —, ring finger, fourth finger.
anulativo, va, *adj.* derogatory.
anunciador, *m.* announcer.
anunciante, *m.* advertiser.
anunciar, *va.* to announce; to advertise.
anuncio, *m.* advertisement; notice.
anverso, *m.* obverse (in coins).
anzuelo, *m.* fishhook; allurement; kind of fritter.
aña, *f.* (zool.) hyena.
añadidura, *f.* addition; **por** —, in addition to.
añadir, *va.* to add; to join.
añafea, *f.* brown paper.
añafil, *m.* Moorish trumpet.
añagaza, *f.* birdcall, decoy; enticement.
añal, *adj.* annual; yearling (lamb).
añalejo, *m.* ecclesiastical almanac.
añascar, *va.* (coll.) to collect (little objects).
añejar, *va.* to make old; —se, to grow old; to become stale.
añejo, ja, *adj.* old, stale, musty.
añicos, *m. pl.* bits, small pieces; **hacer** —, to break into small pieces; **hacerse** —, to overexert oneself.
añil, *m.* indigo plant; indigo; bluing.
añinos, *m. pl.* fleecy skins of yearling lambs.
año, *m.* year; — **bisiesto,** leap year; — **intercalar,** leap year; **al** or **por** —, per annum; **cumplir** —s, to reach one's birthday; **día de A— Nuevo,** New Year's; **el — pasado,** last year; **el — que viene,** next year; **entrado en** —s, middle-aged; **hace un** —, a year ago; **tener . . . —s,** to be . . . . years old.
añojal, *m.* fallow land.
añojo, *m.* a yearling calf.
añoranza, *f.* melancholy, nostalgia.
añublo, *m.* mildew.
añudar, *va.* to fasten with knots, to join.
aojador, ra, *n.* hoodoo, person who practices magic.
aojar, *va.* to charm, to bewitch, to fascinate.
aojo, *m.* witchery, fascination.
aorta, *f.* (anat.) aorta.
aovar, *va.* to lay eggs.
ap.: aparte, new paragraph; (theat.) aside; apart, separately; **apóstol,** apostle.
ap.ª, ap.º, or **aplica., aplico. apostólica, apostólico,** apostolic.
apabilar, *va.* to prepare the wick of a wax candle; —se, to expire.
apacentadero, *m.* pasture, grazing ground.
apacentar, *va.* (IE) to tend grazing cattle.
apacibilidad, *f.* placidity.
apacible, *adj.* affable, gentle, placid, peaceful, quiet.
apaciguador, *m.* pacifier, appeaser.

apaciguar, *va.* to appease, to pacify, to calm; —se, to calm down.
apacheta, *f.* heap of stones placed by Peruvian Indians on tops of hills for religious purposes.
apachurrar, *va.* to crush, to flatten.
apadrinar, *va.* to act as second or as a godfather; to support, to favor, to patronize.
apagado, da, *adj.* low, dull, muffled; submissive; pusillanimous.
apagador, *m.* extinguisher; damper; **— de incendios,** fire extinguisher.
apagaincendios, *m.* fire engine; fire extinguisher.
apagar, *va.* to quench, to extinguish, to put out; to damp; to destroy; to soften.
apagón, *m.* blackout.
apalabrar, *va.* to arrange for a meeting with someone to discuss something; to speak for.
apalancar, *va.* to lift with a lever.
apalear, *va.* to whip, to beat with a stick.
apancora, *f.* common crab.
apandillar, *va.* to form a faction.
apantanar, *va.* to make a pool of stagnant water.
apantuflado, da, *adj.* slipperlike.
apañado, da, *adj.* clothlike; skillful; (coll.) suitable.
apañar, *va.* to grasp; to seize; to pilfer; to patch; —se, (coll.) to be skillful.
apaño, *m.* grasp, seizure; patch.
apañuscar, *va.* to rumple, to crush.
apapagayado, da, *adj.* parrotlike.
aparador, *m.* buffet, sideboard; dresser (furniture); workbench; workshop; counter; showcase; **estar de** —, to be dressed for receiving visitors.
aparar, *va.* to stretch out the hands or skirts of clothes for catching anything; to dig and heap the earth around plants.
aparato, *m.* apparatus, appliance; preparation; ostentation; show; system; **— de aguas gaseosas,** soda fountain; **— de gobierno,** steering gear; **— destilatorio,** distillery; (aer.) **— de flotación,** flotation gear; **— de radio,** radio set; **— de salvamento,** fire escape; **— de seguridad,** safety apparatus.
aparatoso, sa, *adj.* pompous, showy.
aparcería, *f.* (law, com.) partnership.
aparcero, *m.* partner; associate.
aparear, *va.* to match, to pair; —se, to be paired off by twos.
aparecer, *vn.* (EZCO) to appear.
aparecido, *m.* apparition, ghost.
aparejar, *va.* to prepare; to harness horses; to rig a ship.
aparejo, *m.* preparation; harness; gear; tackle; sizing of linen or canvas; (naut.) tackle, rigging; —s, *pl.* tools, implements.
aparentar, *va.* to make a false show; to pretend, to deceive.
aparente, *adj.* apparent; fit, suitable; evident.

aparición, *f.* apparition, emergence.

apariencia, *f.* appearance, looks; —**s,** *pl.* scenic effects.

aparrado, da, *adj.* crooked (applied to trees and plants); vinelike.

aparroquiar, *va.* to bring customers to a shop.

apartadero, *m.* parting place; siding, side track; crossroads.

apartadijo, *m.* small part; adjoining closet.

apartado, *m.* detached or private apartment; post-office box; — **de correos,** post-office box; — **de habitaciones,** suite of rooms; —, **da,** *adj.* secluded.

apartamiento, *m.* secluded place; apartment, flat; — **amueblado,** furnished apartment; — **sin muebles,** unfurnished apartment.

apartar, *va.* to separate, to divide, to dissuade; to remove; to sort; —**se,** to withdraw; to be divorced; to desist.

aparte, *m.* break in a line; new paragraph; —, *adv.* apart, separately; aside on the stage.

aparvar, *va.* to arrange the grain for being threshed.

apasionado, da, *adj.* passionate; suffering; impulsive; devoted to, fond of.

apasionar, *va.* to excite a passion; —**se,** to become very fond (of); to be prejudiced (about).

apatía, *f.* apathy.

apático, ca, *adj.* apathetic, indifferent.

apda. apreciada, esteemed (letter).

apea, *f.* tether.

apeadero, *m.* horse block; landing place; flag stop, small railroad station; alighting place.

apeador, *m.* land surveyor.

apear, *va.* to dismount, to alight; to measure lands; to take a thing; to dissuade; —**se,** to get off a train, horse, etc., to alight.

apechugar, *va.* to push with the breast; to undertake a thing with spirit and boldness.

apedreado, da, *adj.* stoned, pelted; **cara** —, face pitted with the smallpox.

apedrear, *va.* to throw stones; to kill with stones; to lapidate; —, *vn.* to hail; to talk in a rude, uncouth manner; —**se,** to be injured by hail.

apegarse, *vr.* to become attached.

apego, *m.* attachment, fondness.

apelable, *adj.* appealable.

apelación, *f.* appeal; court appeal.

apelado, da, *adj.* of the same color (horses).

apelambrar, *va.* to soak hides in pits of limewater.

apelante, *m.* (law) appellant.

apelar, *vn.* to appeal; to have recourse to; to be of the same color (horses).

apelativo, *adj.* (gram.) **nombre** —, generic name.

apelmazar, *va.* to compress.

apelotonado, da, *adj.* huddled.

apelotonar, *va.* and *vr.* to form into balls; to huddle.

apellar, *va.* to dress leather.

apellidar, *va.* to call by the last name; to call to arms; to proclaim.

apellido, *m.* surname, family name; call to arms.

apenar, *va.* to cause pain; —**se,** to grieve.

apenas, *adv.* scarcely, hardly.

apéndice, *m.* appendix; supplement.

apendicectomía, *f.* appendectomy.

apendicitis, *f.* appendicitis.

Apeninos, *m. pl.* Apennines.

apeñuscar, *va.* to press together, to crowd.

apeo, *m.* survey, mensuration of land; props and stays for underpinning a building.

apeonar, *vn.* to run swiftly (usually birds or fowl).

aperador, *m.* wheelwright; foreman; farmer.

aperar, *va.* to repair or equip farming vehicles.

apercibir, *va.* to prepare; to provide; to warn, to advise.

apercollar, *va.* (UE) to seize by the collar; to snatch away secretly; to assassinate.

aperdigar, *va.* to broil (partridges); to brown (meat); to prepare something for a purpose.

aperitivo, *m.* appetizer, liqueur taken before a meal.

apernar, *va.* (IE) to seize by the thigh.

apero, *m.* farm implements; outfit, equipment; riding outfit; saddle.

aperreado, da, *adj.* harassed.

aperrear, *va.* to throw to the dogs; to molest; —**se,** to worry one's self to death.

apertura, *f.* aperture, opening, chink, cleft.

apesadumbrar, *va.* to cause trouble; —**se,** to be grieved, to lose heart.

apestar, *va.* and *vn.* to infect with the pestilence; to produce an offensive smell.

apetecer, *va.* (EZCO) to long for; to crave.

apetecible, *adj.* desirable.

apetitivo, va, *adj.* appetizing.

apetito, *m.* appetite; that which excites desire; **entrar en** —, to get hungry, to work up an appetite.

apetitoso, sa, *adj.* pleasing to the taste, appetizing.

apezuñar, *vn.* to tread heavily (of horses).

apiadarse, *vr.* to commiserate (with); to take pity (on).

apicarado, da, *adj.* roguish, knavish.

ápice, *m.* summit, point; smallest part of a thing.

apicultura, *f.* apiculture.

apilar, *va.* to pile up.

apimpollarse, *vr.* to germinate.

apiñado, da, *adj.* pyramidal; pine-shaped; crowded.

apiñar, *va.* to press things close together; —**se,** to clog, to crowd.

apio, *m.* (bot.) celery.

apiolar, *va.* to gyve (a hawk); to tie by the leg; to seize; to kill.

apisonador, *m.* tamper.
apisonar, *va.* to ram down earth.
apitonar, *vn.* to put forth shoots; to bud; —, *va.* to peck (as hens do their eggs); —se, to rail at each other.
aplacable, *adj.* placable.
aplacar, *va.* to appease, to pacify.
aplanadera, *f.* roller for leveling the ground.
aplanadora, *f.* steamroller.
aplanar, *va.* to level, to flatten; to astonish, —se, to fall to the ground.
aplanchado, da, *adj.* ironed, smoothed; —, *m.* bundle of clothes, or clothes to be ironed.
aplanchadora, *f.* ironer.
aplanchar, *va.* to iron or press (clothes).
aplantillar, *va.* to adjust or fit a stone, a piece of timber or a board, according to model.
aplastado, da, *adj.* crushed; dispirited.
aplastar, *va.* to flatten, to crush; to squelch or crush (an opponent); —se, to collapse.
aplaudir, *va.* to applaud; to extol.
aplauso, *m.* applause, approbation, praise.
aplazamiento, *m.* postponement; summons.
aplazar, *va.* to call together; to defer; to adjourn; to postpone.
aplicable, *adj.* applicable.
aplicación, *f.* application; attention; industriousness.
aplicado, da, *adj.* studious, industrious.
aplicar, *va.* to apply; to clasp; to stick; to attribute; —se, to devote oneself to anything; to earn a living.
aplomado, da, *adj.* lead-colored; leaden; heavy, dull.
aplomar, *vn.* to plumb; —se, to tumble, to fall to the ground.
aplomo, *m.* calmness, self-possession, tact, poise.
apocado, da, *adj.* pusillanimous, cowardly; humble.
Apocalipsis, *m.* Apocalypse.
apocar, *va.* to lessen, to diminish; to contract; —se, to humble oneself.
apócope, *m.* shortening, cutting off.
apócrifo, fa, *adj.* apocryphal; fabulous.
apodar, *va.* to give nicknames.
apoderado, da, *adj.* authorized, empowered; —, *m.* (law) legal representative, proxy, attorney in fact.
apoderar, *va.* to empower; to grant power of attorney; —se, to take possession.
apodíctico, ca, *adj.* (law) apodictic; indisputable.
apodo, *m.* nickname.
apogeo, *m.* apogee, highest degree.
apolillar, *va.* to gnaw or eat (of moths); —se, to be moth-eaten.
apología, *f.* defense; eulogy.
apoltronarse, *vr.* to grow lazy, to loiter.
apomazar, *va.* to glaze with pumice stone.
apoplejía, *f.* apoplexy.
apoplético, ca, *adj.* apoplectic.
aporcar, *va.* (UE) to cover plants with earth.

aporrar, *vn.* to stand mute, to remain silent. —se, to become importunate.
aporreado, da, *adj.* cudgeled; dragged along; —, *m.* (Cuba) kind of chopped beef stew.
aporrear, *va.* to cudgel, to knock; —se, to drudge, to work too diligently.
aportadera, *f.* provision chest for portage by mules.
aportadero, *m.* landing place.
aportar, *vn.* to arrive at a port; —, *va.* to bring, to contribute.
aportillar, *va.* to make a breach in a wall, to break down, to break open; —se, to tumble down.
aposentador, *m.* usher in a theater.
aposentar, *va.* to harbor; to house.
aposento, *m.* room, chamber; inn; a temporary habitation; opera box.
aposesionar, *va.* to give possession; —se, to take possession.
aposición, *f.* (gram.) apposition.
apósito, *m.* external medicinal application.
apóst. apóstol, apostle.
aposta or **apostadamente,** *adv.* on purpose.
apostadero, *m.* stand, station; (naut.) station, dockyard.
apostar, *va.* (UE) to bet, to lay a wager; to post soldiers; —se, to station oneself.
apostasía, *f.* apostasy.
apóstata, *m.* apostate.
apostatar, *vn.* to apostatize.
apostema, *f.* abscess, tumor.
apostilla, *f.* marginal note; postscript.
apostillar, *va.* to make marginal notes; —se, to become pock-marked.
apóstol, *m.* apostle.
apostolado, *m.* apostleship.
apostólico, ca, *adj.* apostolic.
apostrofar, *va.* to apostrophize.
apóstrofe, *m.* or *f.* (rhet.) apostrophe.
apóstrofo, *m.* (gram.) apostrophe.
apostura, *f.* neatness.
apotegma, *m.* apothegm.
apoteosis, *f.* apotheosis.
apoyar, *va.* to favor; to assist; to support; to found; —, *vn.* to rest on, to lie; —se, to lean upon.
apoyo, *m.* prop, rest, stay, support; protection.
apreciable, *adj.* appreciable, valuable, respectable; (com.) **su** —, your favor (letter).
apreciación, *f.* estimation; estimate, valuation; appreciation.
apreciar, *va.* to appreciate, to estimate, to value.
aprecio, *m.* appreciation; esteem, regard.
aprehender, *va.* to apprehend, to seize; to fancy; to conceive.
aprehensión, *f.* apprehension, seizure; perception.
aprehensivo, va, *adj.* apprehensive, quick to understand; fearful.
apremiar, *va.* to press, to compel; to hurry.

apremio, *m.* pressure, constriction; judicial compulsion.

aprender, *va.* to learn; **— de memoria,** to learn by heart.

aprendiz, za, *n.* apprentice.

aprendizaje, *m.* apprenticeship.

aprensar, *va.* to press, to calender.

aprensión, *f.* apprehension, fear, misgiving.

apresar, *va.* to seize, to grasp; to capture.

aprestar, *va.* to prepare, to make ready.

apresto, *m.* preparation.

apresurado, da, *adj.* hasty.

apresuramiento, *m.* haste.

apresurar, *va.* to accelerate, to hasten, to expedite; **—se,** to hurry, to hasten.

apretadillo, lla, *adj.* somewhat constrained, rather hard put to it.

apretado, da, *adj.* tight; mean, miserable, closehanded; hard, difficult.

apretador, *m.* one who presses, presser; **— de corredera,** zipper.

apretadura, *f.* compression.

apretar, *va.* (IE) to compress, to tighten, to squeeze; to constrain, to distress; to pinch (of shoes); to urge earnestly.

apretón, *m.* pressure; **— de manos,** handshake.

apretura, *f.* crowd.

apriesa, *adv.* in a hurry.

aprieto, *m.* crowd; conflict; difficulty; predicament; **estar en un —,** to be in need of cash.

aprisa, *adv.* swiftly, promptly.

aprisco, *m.* sheepfold.

aprisionar, *va.* to imprison.

aproar, *vn.* (naut.) to turn the prow.

aprobación, *f.* approbation, approval.

aprobado, *m.* passing grade; **—,** *adj.* passed (in an examination); approved, O.K.

aprobar, *va.* (UE) to approve, to approve of.

aproches, *m. pl.* (mil.) approaches.

aprontar, *va.* to prepare hastily, to get ready.

apronto, *m.* speedy preparation.

apropiación, *f.* appropriation, assumption.

apropiado, da, *adj.* appropriate, adequate, fit.

apropiar, *va.* to appropriate; **—se,** take possession of.

aprovechable, *adj.* available, usable.

aprovechamiento, *m.* profit, utility; progress; reclamation.

aprovechar, *va.* to avail, to make use of; **—,** *vn.* to progress in studies, art, etc.; **—se de,** to take advantage of; to avail oneself.

aproximación, *f.* approximation, nearness, approach.

aproximar, *va.* and *vr.* to approach; to move near, to approximate.

ápside, *m.* (ast.) apsis, apse.

áptero, ra, *adj.* without wings; **insecto —ro,** insect without wings.

aptitud, *f.* aptitude, fitness, ability; talent.

apto, ta, *adj.* apt, fit, able, clever.

apuesta, *f.* bet, wager.

apuesto, ta, *adj.* smart, elegant.

apulgarar, *va.* to press with the thumb; **—se,** to become spotted by moisture.

apuntación, *f.* annotation; musical notation; aim.

apuntado, da, *adj.* pointed.

apuntador, *m.* observer; prompter; (naut.) gunner.

apuntalamiento, *m.* propping, pinning; **— por la base,** underpinning.

apuntalar, *va.* to prop; (naut.) to shore a vessel.

apuntar, *va.* to aim; to level, to point out; to note; to write down; to mark, to begin to appear or show itself; (theat.) to prompt; **—se,** to begin to turn (of wine).

apunte, *m.* annotation; note, sketch; stage prompting.

apuñetear, *va.* to strike with the fist.

apurado, da, *adj.* poor, destitute; to be in need of cash; exhausted; to be in a hurry; **verse —,** to be in difficulties.

apurar, *va.* to rush, to hurry; to annoy; to exhaust (as patience); to purify (as gold); to drink up; to clear up; to verify; **—se,** to hurry oneself; to worry, to grieve, to fret.

apuro, *m.* want, indigence; affliction, pain; embarrassment; **salir de un —,** to get out of a difficulty.

aquejar, *va.* to fatigue, to afflict.

aquel, aquella, aquellos, llas, *pron.* and *adj.* that, that one; those.

aquello, *pron.* that, the former, the first mentioned, that matter.

aquerenciarse, *vr.* to be fond of a place.

aquese, sa, so, *pron.* (poet.) that.

aqueste, ta, to, *pron.* (poet.) this.

aquí, *adv.* here, in this place; **de —,** hence; **por —,** this way.

aquiescencia, *f.* consent.

aquietar, *va.* to quiet, to appease, to lull; **—se,** to become calm.

aquilatación, *f.* assay.

aquilatar, *va.* to assay gold and silver.

aquilón, *m.* north wind.

A. R. Alteza Real, R. H. Royal Highness.

ara, *f.* altar.

árabe, *n.* and *adj.* Arabic, the Arabic language; native of Arabia, an Arab.

arabesco, *m.* arabesque; **—, ca,** *adj.* Arabic.

arábico, ca, or **go, ga,** *adj.* Arabian, Arabic.

arácnido, *m.* (zool.) arachnid.

arado, *m.* plow; **— de azada,** hoe plow; **— desterrador,** stubble plow; **— de discos,** disc plow; **— de gancho,** hook plow; **— giratorio,** rotary plow; **— múltiple,** gang plow.

arador, *m.* plowman.

Aragón, *m.* Aragon.

aragonés, esa, *n.* and *adj.* Aragonese

arancel, *m.* fixed price of provisions; customs; tariff; **— de aduanas,** customhouse; tariff book.

arancelario, ria, *adj.* pertaining to tariff rates; **derechos —rios,** custom duties.

arándano, *m.* cranberry.

arandela, *f.* pan of the socket of a candlestick; ruffles of shirts or waists; washer.

aranzada, *f.* a measure of land.

araña, *f.* spider; chandelier.

arañar, *va.* to scratch; to scrape; to corrode.

arañazo, *m.* deep scratch.

araño, *m.* scratch, slight wound.

arar, *va.* to plow the land.

arbellón, *m.* gutter.

arbitraje, *m.* arbitration.

arbitrar, *va.* to arbitrate.

arbitrariedad, *f.* arbitrariness.

arbitrario, ria, or **arbitrativo, va,** *adj.* arbitrary.

arbitrio, *m.* free will, means, expedient, way; arbitration; compromise; **—s,** *pl.* excise taxes.

arbitrista, *m.* schemer, projector, contriver.

árbitro, *m.* arbiter, arbitrator; umpire.

árbol, *m.* tree; shaft; (naut.) mast; **— de eje,** or **de manivela,** crankshaft; **— de transmisión,** belt shaft.

arbolado, da, *adj.* forested, wooded; **—,** *m.* woodland.

arboladura, *f.* (naut.) masting, masts.

arbolar, *va.* to hoist, to set upright; **—se,** to rear on hind feet.

arboleda, *f.* grove.

arbolete, *m.* branch of a tree for fastening lime twigs.

arbolista, *m.* arborist.

arbollón, *m.* floodgate, sluice.

arbóreo, rea, *adj.* pertaining to trees.

arbotante, *m.* flying buttress.

arbusto, *m.* shrub.

arca, *f.* chest, wooden box; sepulchral urn; **— del Testamento,** Ark of the Covenant; **— de hierro,** strongbox, safe.

arcabucería, *f.* troop of harquebusiers; harquebus factory.

arcabucero, *m* harquebusier, harquebus maker.

arcabuz, *m.* harquebus.

arcada, *f.* retching; arcade.

arcaduz, *m.* conduit or pipe for conveying water; bucket.

arcaico, ca, *adj.* archaic, ancient.

arcaísmo, *m.* archaism.

arcángel, *m.* archangel.

arcano, na, *adj.* secret, very reserved (thing); **—,** *m.* very important secret, mystery.

arce, *m.* maple tree.

arcedo, *m.* maple grove.

arcilla, *f.* argil, clay.

arcilloso, sa, *adj.* clayey.

arco, *m.* arc; arch; fiddle bow; hoop; **— iris,** rainbow; **soldadura con —,** arc welding; **lámpara de —,** arc light or lamp.

arcón, *m.* large chest; bin.

Archibaldo, Archibald.

archiducado, *m.* archduchy.

archiducal, *adj.* archducal.

archiduque, *m.* archduke.

archiduquesa, *f.* archduchess.

archipiélago, *m.* archipelago.

archivar, *va.* to file; to place in archives.

archivero, ra or **archivista,** *m.* keeper of the archives; file clerk.

archivo, *m.* archives; files, letter file.

arder, *vn.* to burn, to blaze.

ardid, *m.* stratagem, artifice, cunning.

ardido, da, *adj.* heated (of grain, tobacco, etc.); in a state of fermentation.

ardiente, *adj.* ardent, fiery, intense.

ardilla, *f.* squirrel; **— voladora,** flying squirrel.

ardor, *m.* great heat; valor; vivacity, fieriness, fervor, zeal.

ardoroso, sa, *adj.* fiery, restless.

arduo, dua, *adj.* arduous, difficult.

área, *f.* area (of a building).

arena, *f.* sand; grit; arena.

arenal, *m.* sandy ground.

arenga, *f.* harangue, speech.

arengar, *vn.* to harangue.

arenilla, *f.* molding sand.

arenisco, ca, or **arenoso, sa,** *adj.* sandy.

arenque, *m.* herring; **— ahumado,** red herring; **— en escabeche,** pickled herring.

areómetro, *m.* hydrometer.

arepa, *f.* kind of corn griddle cake.

aretes, *m. pl.* earrings.

arfada, *f.* (naut.) plunging movement of a ship in a heavy sea.

argadijo or **argadillo,** *m.* reel; restless person; wicker basket.

argado, *m.* prank, trick, artifice.

argamandijo, *m.* set of small implements.

argamasa, *f.* mortar.

argamasar, *va.* to make mortar.

árgana, *f.* crane (machine); **—s,** *pl.* horse baskets, panniers.

arganeo, *m.* (naut.) anchor ring.

Argel, *m.* Algiers.

argentado, da, *adj.* silverlike.

argentar, *va.* to silverplate; to color.

argentería, *f.* gold or silver embroidery.

argentino, na, *adj.* silvery; Argentine; **voz —a,** silvery voice; **—,** *m.* Argentine gold coin.

argirol, *m.* argyrol.

argolla, *f.* large iron ring; pillory; collar.

argón, *m.* (chem.) argon.

argucia, *f.* subtlety; trick.

argüe, *m.* windlass.

argüir, *vn.* (uyo) to argue, to dispute, to oppose; **—,** *va.* to infer.

argumentación, *f.* argumentation.

argumentar, *vn.* to argue, to dispute, to conclude.

argumento, *m.* argument; plot of a play; (radio) script.

aria, *f.* (mus.) aria, air.

aridez, *f.* drought; barrenness.

árido, da, *adj.* arid, dry; barren.

Aries, *m.* Aries, the Ram (sign of the Zodiac).

ariete, *m.* battering ram; — **hidráulico,** hydraulic ram.

arijo, ja, *adj.* easily tilled (applied to soil).

arillo, *m.* a small hoop; earring.

arimez, *m.* projecting part of a building.

ario, ria, *n.* and *adj.* Aryan.

arisco, ca, *adj.* fierce, rude; surly.

aristarco, *m.* severe critic.

aristocracia, *f.* aristocracy.

aristócrata, *m.* and *f.* aristocrat.

aristocrático, ca, *adj.* aristocratic.

aristotélico, ca, *adj.* Aristotelian.

arit. aritmética, arith. arithmetic.

aritmética, *f.* arithmetic.

aritmético, ca, *adj.* arithmetical.

aritmómetro, *m.* calculating machine.

arlequín, *m.* harlequin, buffoon.

arma, *f.* weapon, arm; —**s, blancas,** side arms; **alzarse en** —**s,** to revolt; **clavar las** —**s,** to ground arms; **maestro de** —**s,** fencing master; **sobre las** —**s,** under arms.

armada, *f.* fleet, armada.

armadía, *f.* raft.

armadillo, *m.* armadillo.

armado, da, *adj.* armed, assembled.

armador, *m.* shipowner; ship outfitter; an assembler; privateer; jacket, jerkin.

armadura, *f.* armor; roof frame, framework; trestle work; truss armor; armature.

armamento, *m.* warlike preparation, armament.

armar, *va.* to furnish with arms; to man; to arm, to fit up; to assemble; — **un lío,** (coll.) to start a "row."

armario, *m.* clothespress; clothes closet; cupboard; bookcase.

armatoste, *m.* hulk; frame.

armazón, *f.* framework, skeleton; hulk of a ship; —, *m.* skeleton of the body.

armelina, *f.* ermine skin.

armella, *f.* staple, screweye.

armería, *f.* arsenal; heraldry; art of armormaking.

armero, *m.* armorer, keeper of arms.

armiño, *m.* ermine.

armipotente, *adj.* (poet.) mighty in war.

armisticio, *m.* armistice.

armonía, *f.* harmony.

armónico, ca, *adj.* harmonious, harmonic; —, *f.* harmonica, mouth organ.

armonio, *m.* harmonium, reed organ.

armonioso, sa, *adj.* harmonious; sonorous.

armonizar, *va.* to harmonize.

arna, *f.* beehive.

Arnaldo, Arnold.

arnés, *m.* harness, gear, trapping.

árnica, *f.* arnica, medicinal plant.

arnilla, *f.* small beehive.

aro, *m.* hoop of wood; iron staple.

aroma, *f.* flower of the aromatic myrrh tree; —, *m.* aroma, fragrance.

aromático, ca, *adj.* aromatic.

aromatizar, *va.* to perfume.

arpa, *f.* (mus.) harp.

arpado, da, *adj.* serrated, toothed.

arpar, *va.* to tear to pieces, to rend.

arpegio, *m.* (mus.) arpeggio.

arpeo, *m.* (naut.) grappling iron.

arpía, *f.* (poet.) harpy.

arpillera, *f.* sackcloth; burlap.

arpista, *m.* harpist.

arpón, *m.* harpoon.

arponado, da, *adj.* like a harpoon.

arponar, *va.* to harpoon.

arponero, *m.* harpooner.

arqueada, *f.* (mus.) stroke or movement of the violin bow.

arqueado, da, *adj.* arched, vaulted; bent.

arquear, *va.* to arch; to gauge the dimensions of ships.

arqueo, *m.* act of arching, system of arches; (naut.) tonnage; (com.) checking of money and papers in a safe.

arqueología, *f.* archaeology.

arqueológico, ca, *adj.* archaeological.

arquería, *f.* series of arches.

arquero, *m.* hoopmaker; cashier.

arqueta, *f.* small trunk.

arquilla, *f.* little chest.

arquitecto, *m.* architect.

arquitectónico, ca, *adj.* architectural.

arquitectura, *f.* architecture.

arquitrabe, *m.* (arch.) architrave.

arrabal, *m.* suburb; —**es,** *pl.* environs, outskirts.

arrabalero, *m.* suburban; very common person, churl.

arrabio, *m.* cast iron.

arracada, *f.* earring.

arracimarse, *vr.* to cluster.

arráez, *m.* captain of a ship.

arraigar, *vn.* to take root; to establish; to become deep-seated or fixed; **costumbre arraigada,** settled habit, second nature.

arraigo, *m.* landed property; settling in a place.

arramblar, *va.* to cover with sand (of torrents); to sweep away.

arrancadera, *f.* bell for leading cattle.

arrancador, *m.* starter (of a vehicle or motor); — **de inercia,** (aer.) inertia starter.

arrancar, *va.* to pull up by the roots; to force out; to wrest; —, *vn.* to start; (naut.) to set sail.

arrancasiega, *f.* mowing of stunted grain; altercation, dispute.

arranque, *m.* extirpation; sudden burst of rage or emotion, tantrum; (auto.) ignition, starter; — **automático** or **eléctrico,** electric or automatic starter, self-starter; **motor de** —, self-starting motor, engine with an automatic starter.

arrapiezo or **arrapo,** *m.* tatter, rag; worthless urchin.

arras, *f. pl.* dowry; earnest money; (naut.) wings of the hold.

arrasar, *va.* to demolish, to destroy; —, *vn.* to clear up (of the sky).

arrastrado, da, *adj.* dragged along; miserable, destitute.

arrastrar, *va.* and *vn.* to creep, to crawl; to drag along the ground; to lead a trump in cards.

arrastre, *m.* lead of a trump in cards; mining mill.

arrayán, *m.* myrtle; bayberry.

¡arre! *interj.* gee! get up!

arrear, *va.* to drive horses, mules, etc.; to urge on.

arrebañar, *va.* to scrape together, to pick up.

arrebatado, da, *adj.* rapid, violent, impetuous, rash, inconsiderate.

arrebatar, *va.* to carry off, to snatch with hurry and precipitation; to enrapture.

arrebatiña, *f.* carrying off a thing precipitately out of a crowd; scrimmage.

arrebato, *m.* surprise; sudden attack; fit; rapture.

arrebol, *m.* redness in the sky; rouge.

arrebolar, *va.* to paint red; to rouge.

arrebozarse, *vr.* to swarm (of bees, etc.); to wrap up oneself.

arrebujar, *va.* to crumple; to wrap up.

arreciar, *vn.* to increase in intensity.

arrecife, *m.* causeway; reef.

arrecirse, *vr.* and *def.* to grow stiff with cold.

arredrar, *va.* to remove to a greater distance; to terrify; **—se,** to lose courage, to become frightened.

arregazado, da, *adj.* turned up; cocked.

arregazar, *va.* to truss, to tuck up (clothes).

arreglado, *adj.* regular; moderate; neat.

arreglador, *m.* fitter, arranger.

arreglar, *va.* to regulate; to adjust; to arrange; **— una cuenta,** to settle an account; **—se,** to dress; to fix oneself up; to manage.

arreglo, *m.* rule, order; arrangement, settlement; **con — a,** according to.

arregostarse, *vr.* to relish.

arrejacar, *va.* to weed out.

arrejaco, *m.* (orn.) swift; martin.

arrejaque, *m.* three-pronged fork, trident.

arrellanarse, *vr.* to sit at ease; to make oneself comfortable.

arremangar, *va.* to tuck up (sleeves, skirts, etc.); **—se,** to be determined.

arremango, *m.* tucking up (clothes).

arremeter, *va.* to assail, to attack; to seize suddenly.

arremetida, *f.* attack, assault.

arrendadero, *m.* stable ring for tying horses.

arrendado, da, *adj.* rented; manageable, tractable (of horses).

arrendador, *m.* tenant, lessee; lessor, hirer.

arrendajo, *m.* mockingbird; mimic, buffoon.

arrendamiento, *m.* lease, leasing; rental; **contrato de —,** lease.

arrendar, *va.* (IE) to rent, to let out, to lease; to tie a horse by the reins; to mimic.

arrendatario, ria, *n.* tenant; lessee.

arreo, *m.* dress, ornament; **—s,** *pl.* appurtenances, accessories; **—,** *adv.* successively, uninterruptedly.

arrepápalo, *m.* sort of fritter or bun.

arrepentido, da, *adj.* repentant.

arrepentimiento, *m.* remorse, repentance, penitence.

arrepentirse, *vr.* (IE) to repent.

arrepistar, *va.* to grind or pound into a fine pulp.

arrequives, *m. pl.* dress ornaments; circumstances of a case; requisites.

arrestado, da, *adj.* intrepid, bold; arrested.

arrestar, *va.* to arrest, to imprison; **—se,** to be bold and enterprising.

arresto, *m.* boldness in undertaking an enterprise; prison, arrest.

arrezafe, *m.* place full of thistles, brushwood, and brambles.

arriada, *f.* flood, overflowing.

arriar, *va.* (naut.) to lower, to strike; **—se,** to be flooded.

arriata, *f.,* **arriate,** *m.* hotbed; border of a garden; causeway.

arriba, *adv.* above, over, up, high, overhead, upstairs; (naut.) aloft; **de — abajo,** from head to foot, top to bottom; **para —,** up, upwards.

arribada, *f.* arrival of a vessel in port.

arribar, *vn.* to arrive; (naut.) to put into a harbor; to fall off to leeward.

arribo, *m.* arrival.

arricete, *m.* shoal, sandbank.

arriendo, *m.* lease, farm rent.

arriería, *f.* muledriver's trade.

arriero, *m.* muleteer.

arriesgado, *adj.* risky, dangerous.

arriesgar, *va.* and *vr.* to risk, to hazard, to expose to danger.

arrimadero, *m.* scaffold; stick or support to lean upon.

arrimadillo, *m.* wainscoting, paneling.

arrimadizo, za, *adj.* sustaining, sustainable; **—,** *m.* parasite, sponger.

arrimador, *m.* backlog in a fireplace.

arrimar, *va.* to approach, to draw near; (naut.) to stow the cargo; to lay aside; to give up a command; to displace, to dismiss; **—se a,** to lean against, to seek shelter under; to join.

arrinconar, *va.* to put a thing in a corner; to lay aside; to drive from office; **—se,** to retire, to withdraw.

arriscado, da, *adj.* forward, bold, audacious, impudent; brisk.

arriscador, *m.* olive gleaner.

arrivista, *m.* and *f.* parvenu.

arrizar, *va.* (naut.) to reef; to tie or lash.

arroba, *f.* weight of twenty-five pounds; measure (thirty-two pints).

arrobadizo, za, *adj.* (coll.) feigning ecstasy.

arrobador, ra, *adj.* enchanting, entrancing.

arrobamiento, *m.* rapture; amazement; rapturous admiration.

arrobarse, *vr.* to be enraptured, entranced.

arrocero, *m.* rice grower; rice merchant.

arrocinado, da, *adj.* stupid, asinine; worn-out (applied to horses).

arrocinarse, *vr.* to become dull and stupid.

arrodillar, *va.* to make (someone) kneel down; **—se,** to kneel.

arrodrigar or **arrodrigonar,** *va.* to prop vines.

arrogación, *f.* arrogation; adoption.

arrogancia, *f.* arrogance, haughtiness.

arrogante, *adj.* haughty, proud, assuming; bold, valiant, stout; **caballo —,** mettlesome, spirited horse.

arrogar, *va.* to arrogate; **—se,** to appropriate to oneself.

arrojadamente, *adv.* daringly.

arrojadizo, za, *adj.* easily cast or thrown.

arrojado, da, *adj.* rash, inconsiderate; bold, fearless.

arrojallamas, *m.* flame-thrower.

arrojar, *va.* to dart, to fling, to jet; to dash; to shed (a fragrance); to emit (light); to shoot, to sprout; to throw out; **— un saldo,** (com.) to show a balance.

arrojo, *m.* boldness, intrepidity, fearlessness.

arrollamiento, *m.* winding, wrapping.

arrollar, *va.* to wind, to roll up, to coil, to revolve; to wrap; to sweep away; to overwhelm, to defeat; to confound an opponent.

arromar, *va.* to blunt.

arrompido, *m.* broken ground for cultivation.

arropar, *va.* to clothe, to dress; to cover (with blankets, etc.).

arrope, *m.* must (new wine boiled until it is as thick as sirup).

arropea, *f.* irons, fetters.

arropía, *f.* taffy.

arrostrar, *va.* to undertake bravely or cheerfully; to encounter (dangers); **—se,** to fight face to face.

arroyada, *f.* torrent.

arroyar, *va.* to run in arroyos or gullies.

arroyo, *m.* arroyo, gully, creek; dry creek bed.

arroz, *m.* rice.

arrozal, *m.* rice field.

arruar, *vn.* to grunt like a wild boar.

arrufar, *va.* (naut.) to incurvate.

arrufianado, da, *adj.* impudent; like a ruffian.

arruga, *f.* wrinkle; rumple.

arrugar, *va.* to wrinkle; to rumple, to fold; **— la frente,** to knit the brow; **—se,** to shrivel.

arruinado, da, *adj.* fallen.

arruinar, *va.* to demolish; to ruin; **—se,** to lose one's fortune.

arrullador, ra, *adj.* flattering, cajoling; **—,** *m.* rocker.

arrullar, *va.* to lull to rest; to court, to bill and coo.

arrullo, *m.* cooing of pigeons; lullaby.

arrumaco, *m.* caress.

arrumaje, *m.* stowage of a ship's cargo.

arrumar, *va.* to stow cargo.

arrumazón, *m.* (naut.) stowing; cloudy horizon.

arrumbar, *va.* to set aside; to refute or silence in conversation; to decant wine; **—se,** (naut.) to steer the proper course, to resume the proper course.

arrunflarse, *vr.* to have a flush in cards.

arrurruz, *m.* arrowroot.

arsenal, *m.* arsenal; dockyard.

arsénico, *m.* arsenic.

art. or **art.º artículo,** art. article.

arte, *m.* and *f.* art; skill; artfulness; **bellas —s,** fine arts.

artefacto, *m.* object manufactured; handiwork; appliance, device.

artejo, *m.* finger joint.

arteria, *f.* artery.

arterial, *adj.* arterial; **tensión —,** blood pressure.

artero, ra, *adj.* dexterous, cunning.

artesa, *f.* kneading trough; wooden bowl.

artesano, *m.* artisan, workman.

artesón, *m.* wooden tub for kitchen use; panel ornament on ceilings and domes.

artética, *f.* (med.) arthritis.

artético, ca, *adj.* arthritical; gouty.

ártico, ca, *adj.* Arctic.

articulación, *f.* articulation, enunciation, way of speaking; joining, joint; **— universal,** (mech.) universal joint.

articular, *va.* to articulate, to pronounce distinctly.

articulista, *m.* newspaper columnist.

artículo, *m.* article; clause; point; (gram.) article; **— de fondo,** editorial; **—s de fantasía,** novelties; **—s de tocador,** toilet articles; **—s para escritorio,** office supplies; **—s vendibles,** stock in trade.

artífice, *m.* artisan, artist.

artificial, *adj.* artificial.

artificio, *m.* workmanship, craft; artifice, cunning trick.

artificioso, sa, *adj.* skillful, ingenious; artful, cunning.

artillar, *va.* to mount (cannon).

artillería, *f.* gunnery; artillery; ordnance.

artillero, *m.* artilleryman.

artimaña, *f.* stratagem, deception.

artimón, *m.* (naut.) mizzenmast.

artista, *m.* and *f.* artist.

artístico, ca, *adj.* artistic.

artritis, *f.* (med.) arthritis.

artrópodo, *m.* arthropod.

Arturo, Arthur.

arúspice, *m.* augur, soothsayer.

arveja, *f.* (bot.) vetch; (Sp. Am.) green pea.

arz. or **arzbpo. arzobispo,** Abp. archbishop.

arzobispado, *m.* archbishopric, archdiocese.

arzobispal, *adj.* archiepiscopal.

arzobispo, *m.* archbishop.

arzón, *m.* bow of a saddle.

as, *m.* ace; as (Roman coin).

asa, *f.* handle, haft, hold.

asado, da, *adj.* roasted; **—,** *m.* roast.

asador, *m.* turnspit.

asadura, *f.* entrails, chitterlings; toll paid for cattle.

asaetinado, da, *adj.* silky, satiny.
asalariar, *va.* to give a fixed salary.
asaltador, *m.* assailant; highwayman.
asaltar, *va.* to attack; to storm a position; to assail, to fall upon; — **a mano armada,** to commit assault with a deadly weapon.
asalto, *m.* assault, storm against a place.
asamblea, *f.* assembly, meeting.
asar, *va.* to roast.
asargado, da, *adj.* sergelike.
asativo, va, *adj.* boiled in its own juice.
asaz, *adv.* (poet.) enough, quite.
asbestino, na, *adj.* pertaining to asbestos.
asbesto, *m.* asbestos.
ascalonia, *f.* (bot.) shallot.
ascendencia, *f.* ascending line; line of ancestors.
ascendente, *adj.* ascending.
ascender, *va.* and *vn.* (IE) to ascend, to climb; to be promoted to a higher dignity; to amount to.
ascendiente, *m.* ascendant, forefather; influence.
ascensión, *f.* feast of Ascension; ascent.
ascenso, *m.* promotion to a higher dignity or station; **indicador de** —, climb indicator; **velocidad de** —, rate of climb.
ascensor, *m.* elevator.
asceta, *m.* and *f.* ascetic.
ascético, ca, *adj.* ascetic, hermitic.
ascetismo, *m.* asceticism.
asco, *m.* nausea; loathing; disgust.
ascua, *f.* red-hot coal; **estar en** —**s,** (coll.) to be restless or excited; ¡—**s!** *interj.* ouch!
aseado, da, *adj.* clean, elegant, neat.
asear, *va.* to clean, to make neat.
asechanza, *f.* snare.
asedado, da, *adj.* silky.
asediar, *va.* to besiege.
asedio, *m.* siege.
aseglararse, *vr.* to secularize oneself.
asegundar, *va.* to repeat.
asegurable, *adj.* insurable.
aseguración, *f.* insurance.
asegurado, da, *adj.* assured, secured, insured; —, *n.* policyholder.
asegurador, *m.* fastener; insurer, underwriter.
asegurar, *va.* to secure, to insure; to assure; to affirm.
asemejar, *va.* to make similar; —**se,** to resemble.
asenderear, *va.* to persecute, to force one's way.
asenso, *m.* assent, consent.
asentaderas, *f. pl.* buttocks.
asentador, *m.* razor strop.
asentar, *va.* (IE) to place on a chair or other seat; to affirm, to assure; to adjust; to note; — **al crédito de,** to place to credit of; —, *vn.* to be becoming; —**se,** to settle (of liquids).
asentimiento, *m.* assent.
asentir, *vn.* (IE) to acquiesce, to concede.
asentista, *m.* purveyor, contractor.

aseo, *m.* cleanliness, neatness.
asepsia, *f.* asepsis.
aséptico, *adj.* aseptic.
asequible, *adj.* attainable, obtainable.
aserción, *f.* assertion, affirmation.
aserradero, *m.* sawmill.
aserraduras, *f. pl.* sawdust.
aserrar, *va.* (IE) to saw.
asertivo, va, *adj.* affirmative.
asesar, *vn.* to become prudent.
asesinar, *va.* to assassinate.
asesinato, *m.* assassination.
asesino, *m.* assassin; impostor, cheat.
asesor, *m.* counselor, assessor.
asesorar, *va.* to give legal advice to; —**se,** to employ counsel; to take advice.
asestar, *va.* to aim, to point; to strike.
aseverar, *va.* to asseverate, to affirm solemnly.
asexual, *adj.* asexual.
asfalto, *m.* asphalt.
asfixia, *f.* (med.) asphyxia, asphyxiation.
asfixiante, *adj.* asphyxiating, suffocating.
asfixiar, *va.* and *vr.* to asphyxiate, to suffocate.
asfódelo, *m.* asphodel, day lily.
así, *adv.* so, thus, in this manner; therefore, so that; also; — **bien,** as well; — **que,** as soon as, after; **así, así,** so, so; middling; — **y todo,** nevertheless.
Asia Menor, *f.* Asia Minor.
asiático, ca, *n.* and *adj.* Asiatic.
asidero, *m.* handle, hold; occasion, pretext.
asido, da, *adj.* fastened, tied, attached.
asiduidad, *f.* assiduity, diligence.
asiduo, dua, *adj.* assiduous; devoted; close.
asiento, *m.* chair, bench, stool; seat; contract; entry; residence; — **común,** privy; — **de zaga,** rumble seat; — **trasero,** back seat.
asignación, *f.* assignation; distribution; destination; allocation.
asignar, *va.* to assign; to attribute.
asignatura, *f.* each subject of a school course.
asilo, *m.* asylum, refuge.
asilla, *f.* small handle; slight pretext; clavicle, collar bone.
asimetría, *f.* asymmetry.
asimilar, *vn.* to resemble; —, *va.* to assimilate.
asimilativo, va, *adj.* assimilative.
asimismo, *adv.* similarly, in the same manner; likewise.
asinino, na, *adj.* asinine.
asir, *va.* and *vn.* (ASGO, ASÍ) to grasp, to seize; to hold, to grip; to take root.
asistencia, *f.* actual presence; attendance; assistance; help; **falta de** —, absence (from class, etc.); — **social,** social work.
asistenta, *f.* handmaid; servant maid.
asistente, *m.* assistant, helper; chief officer of justice; officer's servant, orderly; **los** —**s,** those present.
asistir, *vn.* to be present; to attend; —, *va.*

to help, to minister, to further; to attend a sick person; — **oyente,** to be an auditor in a school course.

asma, *f.* asthma.

asmático, ca, *adj.* asthmatic.

asn. asociación, assn. association.

asna, *f.* she-ass, jenny.

asnada, *f.* foolish action.

asnal, *adj.* asinine.

asnería, *f.* stud of asses; great blunder.

asnico, ca, *n.* little ass; —, *m.* andiron.

asnillo, lla, *n.* little ass; —, *m.* field cricket.

asno, *m.* ass; stupid fellow.

asobarcar, *va.* to pick up and put under one's arm.

asocarronado, da, *adj.* waggish; crafty.

asociación, *f.* association; partnership.

asociado, da, *n.* associate.

asociar, *va.* to associate; —**se,** to form a partnership.

asolanar, *va.* to parch, to dry up.

asolar, *va.* (UE) to destroy, to devastate; —**se,** to settle, to clear (of liquids).

asoleado, da, *adj.* sunny.

asolear, *va.* and *vr.* to expose to the sun.

asolvarse, *vr.* to be stopped (of pipes, canals).

asomada, *f.* sudden appearance, apparition.

asomar, *vn.* to begin to appear; to peep; to show; —**se,** (coll.) to look out; to lean out; to be befuddled with wine.

asombradizo, za, *adj.* fearful, timid, easily frightened.

asombrar, *va.* to frighten, to amaze; to astonish; (poet.) to obscure, to overshadow.

asombro, *m.* dread, terror; astonishment.

asombroso, sa, *adj.* astonishing, marvelous.

asomo, *m.* mark, token, indication; conjecture; **ni por —,** nothing of the kind, far from it.

asonancia, *f.* assonance; harmony.

asordar, *va.* to make deaf with noises.

asosegar, *va.* and *vr.* (IE) to pacify, to appease, to lull.

asotanar, *va.* to build arched cellars.

aspa, *f.* reel; — **de hélice,** propeller blade; wing of a windmill.

aspálato, *m.* (bot.) variety of rosewood.

aspar, *va.* to reel; to crucify; to vex, to mortify; —**se a gritos,** to cry out loudly, to yell.

aspaviento, *m.* exaggerated astonishment or fear, undue fuss.

aspecto, *m.* appearance; aspect.

aspereza, *f.* asperity; harshness; acerbity.

asperges, *m.* sprinkling with holy water; aspersion; **quedarse —,** to be disappointed.

asperillo, *m.* sour taste of unripe fruit.

áspero, ra, *adj.* rough, rugged; craggy, hirsute, knotty; horrid; harsh, hard; crabbed, severe, austere, gruff.

asperón, *m.* grindstone.

aspersión, *f.* aspersion; sprinkling.

aspersorio, *m.* water sprinkler.

áspid or **áspide,** *m.* asp, aspic.

aspiración, *f.* aspiration; ambition; (mus.) short pause for breath.

aspirado, da, *adj.* indrawn.

aspirador, *m.* aspirator; — **de polvo,** vacuum cleaner.

aspirante, *m.* and *f.* aspirant.

aspirar, *va.* to inhale; to aspire; (gram.) to aspirate.

aspirina, *f.* aspirin.

asqueroso, sa, *adj.* loathsome; dirty, filthy.

asta, *f.* lance; horn; handle of a brush; staff, pole.

ástaco, *m.* crawfish.

asterisco, *m.* asterisk.

asterismo, *m.* constellation.

asteroide, *m.* asteroid.

astigmatismo, *m.* astigmatism.

astil, *m.* handle, shaft.

astilla, *f.* chip; splinter; fragment.

astillar, *va.* to chip.

astillazo, *m.* blow from a chip or splinter.

astillero, *m.* dockyard, shipyard; rack for weapons.

astracán, *m.* astrakhan.

astral, *adj.* astral.

astricción, *f.* astriction; constriction.

astrictivo, va, *adj.* astrictive, styptic.

astricto, ta, *adj.* contracted, compressed.

astringente, *adj.* and *m.* astringent.

astringir, *adj.* to astringe, to contract.

astro, *m.* star.

astrofísica, *f.* astrophysics.

astrología, *f.* astrology.

astrológico, ca, *adj.* astrological.

astrólogo, *m.* astrologer.

astronomía, *f.* astronomy.

astronómico, ca, *adj.* astronomical.

astrónomo, *m.* astronomer.

astroso, sa, *adj.* indecent, sordid.

astucia, *f.* cunning, slyness; finesse.

astuto, ta, *adj.* cunning, sly, astute, foxy.

asueto, *m.* holiday, vacation.

asumir, *va.* to assume.

Asunción, *f.* ascent of the Virgin Mary to Heaven.

asunto, *m.* subject; matter; affair, business.

asurarse, *vr.* to be burned in cooking.

asurcar, *va.* to furrow or to plow land.

asustadizo, za, *adj.* easily frightened, shy.

asustar, *va.* to frighten; —**se,** to be frightened.

atabacado, da, *adj.* tobacco-colored.

atabal, *m.* kettledrum.

atabalear, *vn.* to make a noise like kettledrums.

atabalero, *m.* kettledrummer.

atabe, *m.* small vent left in waterpipes.

atabernado, da, *adj.* retailed in taverns.

atabladera, *f.* roller to level land sown with grain.

atablar, *va.* to level land sown with grain.

atacado, da, *adj.* irresolute; stingy; stricken; attacked.

atacador, *m.* aggressor; ramrod; poniard.

atacar, *va.* to attack, to ram; to ram the load into firearms; to button; to fit.

ataderas, *f. pl.* (coll.) garters.

atado, *m.* bundle, parcel; —, **da,** *adj.* pusillanimous, easily embarrassed; attached, tied.

atador, *m.* binder, tier.

atadura, *f.* knot, fastening.

atafagar, *va.* to stupefy, to take away one's breath; to tease.

atafetanado, da, *adj.* resembling taffeta.

ataharre, *m.* broad crupper of a packsaddle.

atahorma, *f.* (orn.) osprey.

ataire, *m.* molding in the panels and frames of doors and windows.

atajadizo, *m.* partition wall.

atajar, *va.* to cut off part of the road; to intercept, to stop, to obstruct; —se, to be bewildered with terror.

atajea or **atajía,** *f.* sewer, drain pipe.

atajo, *m.* by-path; short cut, crosscut.

atalaya, *f.* watchtower; —, *m.* guard in a watchtower.

atalayar, *va.* to watch from a watchtower; to spy into the action of others.

atanquía, *f.* depilatory; refuse of silk.

ataque, *m.* attack; (mil.) trenches; (med.) fit of illness; verbal dispute.

ataquizar, *va.* propagate a plant by layering.

atar, *va.* to tie, to bind, to fasten; to stop; —se, to be embarrassed or perplexed.

ataracea, *f.* marquetry, inlaid work.

ataracear, *va.* to checker, to inlay.

atarantado, da, *adj.* bitten by a tarantula; surprised, amazed.

atarazana, *f.* arsenal, dry dock.

atarazar, *va.* to bite.

atareado, da, *adj.* busy.

atarear, *va.* to impose a task; —se, to overdo one's self.

atarjea, *f.* protecting vault over the pipes of an aqueduct; small drain.

atarquinar, *va.* to bemire.

atarugar, *va.* to wedge, to plug; to stuff, to fill; (coll.) to silence.

atasajar, *va.* to jerk meat (cut it into strips and dry in the sun).

atascar, *va.* to stop a leak; to throw an obstacle in the way; —se, to become bogged.

ataúd, *m.* coffin.

ataujía, *f.* damaskeen.

ataujiado, da, *adj.* worked in a damaskeen fashion.

ataviar, *va.* to dress out, to trim, to adorn.

atavío, *m.* dress, ornament, finery.

atavismo, *m.* atavism.

ataxia, *f.* (med.) ataxia; — **locomotriz,** locomotor ataxia.

atediar, *va.* to disgust; —se, to be bored.

ateísmo, *m.* atheism.

ateísta, *m.* and *f.* atheist.

atemorizar, *va.* to strike with terror, to daunt, to frighten.

atemperación, *f.* moderation.

atemperar, *va.* to temper, to soften, to assuage; to accommodate; to cool.

atenacear or **atenazar,** *va.* to tear off the flesh with pincers.

Atenas, *f.* Athens.

atención, *f.* attention, heedfulness; civility, complaisance; observance, consideration; **en** —, attending; in consideration of; as regards; **llamar la** —, to attract attention; **prestar** —, to give attention.

atender, *vn.* (IE) to be attentive; to heed, to hearken; —, *va.* to expect, to wait for; to look after.

atenerse, *vr.* (ATENGO, ATUVE), to depend or rely (on).

ateniense, *n.* and *adj.* Athenian.

atentado, da, *adj.* discreet, prudent, moderate; noiseless; —, *m.* attempt, transgression, offense; attack; crime.

atentamente, *adv.* attentively; sincerely.

atentatorio, ria, *adj.* having a criminal intent.

atentar, *va.* (IE), to try; to attempt crime; to go about a thing deliberately.

atento, ta, *adj.* attentive; heedful; observing; mindful; polite, courteous, mannerly; compliant; notable.

atenuación, *f.* attenuation.

atenuar, *va.* to diminish, to lessen; to attenuate, to make up for.

ateo, ea, *n.* and *adj.* atheist, atheistic.

atercianado, da, *adj.* afflicted with the tertian fever.

aterciopelado, da, *adj.* velvetlike.

aterirse, *vr.* and *def.* (IE) to grow stiff with cold.

aternerado, da, *adj.* calflike.

aterrado, da, *adj.* terrified, appalled.

aterrador, ra, *adj.* terrifying, frightful.

aterrar, *va.* (IE) to prostrate; to terrify; —se, to be terrified.

aterrizador, *m.* (aer.) landing gear.

aterrizaje, *m.* (aer.) landing (of airplane); — **ciego,** blind landing; — **de tres puntos,** three-point landing; — **forzoso,** forced landing; — **seguro,** safe landing; — **sin motor,** dead-stick landing; **campo de** —, landing field; **pista de** —, landing strip; **tirantes de** —, landing wires; **tren de** —, landing gear.

aterrizar, *vn.* (aer.) to land.

aterronar, *va.* to clot, to coagulate.

aterrorizar, *va.* to frighten, to terrify.

atesorar, *va.* to treasure or hoard up riches.

atestación, *f.* testimony, evidence; affidavit.

atestado, da, *adj.* stubborn; crowded; —, *m.* certificate.

atestamiento, *m.* cramming, crowding.

atestar, *va.* (IE) to attest, to witness; to cram, to stuff, crowd; —se, to overeat.

atestiguar, *va.* to witness, to attest.

atetado, da, *adj.* mammiform.

atetar, *va.* to suckle.

atetillar, *va.* to lay bare the roots of trees.

atezado, da, *adj.* black; browned by the sun.
atezar, *va.* to blacken; —**se,** to become sunburnt.
atiborrar, *va.* to stuff with wool, etc.; —**se,** to eat one's fill.
aticismo, *m.* Atticism; joke, witticism.
ático, *m.* attic.
atiesar, *va.* and *vn.* to make stiff; to make taut.
atigrado, da, *adj.* tiger-colored.
atildado, da, *adj.* correct, neat.
atildar, *va.* to punctuate, to underline, to censure; to deck, to dress, to adorn.
atinar, *va.* and *vn.* to touch the mark, to reach the point; to hit; to guess.
atíncar, *m.* borax.
atiriciarse, *vr.* to grow jaundiced, to get the jaundice.
atisbadero, *m.* peephole, eyehole.
atisbadura, *f.* peek, peeking.
atisbar, *va.* to pry, to examine closely; to glance.
atisuado, da, *adj.* tissuelike.
atizar, *va.* to stir the fire with a poker; to stir up.
atizonar, *va.* to fill up the chinks in a wall; —**se,** to be smutted (applied to grain).
Atlántico, ca, *n.* and *adj.* Atlantic.
atlas, *m.* atlas (collection of maps); kind of rich silk.
atleta, *m.* and *f.* athlete.
atlético, ca, *adj.* athletic.
atmósfera, *f.* atmosphere.
atmosférico, ca, *adj.* atmospheric.
atoar, *va.* (naut.) to tow.
atocinar, *va.* to cut up (a pig); to make bacon; (coll.) to assassinate.
atocha, *f.* (bot.) tough feather grass; esparto grass.
atol or **atole,** *m.* corn-flour gruel; atoll.
atolón, *m.* atoll, coral island.
atolondramiento, *m.* stupefaction, consternation; perplexity.
atolondrar, *va.* to stun, to stupefy; —**se,** to be stupefied.
atolladero, *m.* miry place, bog; difficulty, obstacle.
atollar, *vn.* to fall in the mud.
atómico, ca, *adj.* atomic.
atomismo, *m.* atomism.
átomo, *m.* atom.
atondar, *va.* to spur a horse.
atonía, *f.* (med.) weakness, debility.
atónito, ta, *adj.* astonished, amazed.
átono, na, *adj.* atonic, unaccented.
atontar, *va.* to stun, to stupefy; —**se,** to grow stupid.
atorarse, *vr.* to choke; to stick in the mud.
atormentadamente, *adv.* anxiously; tormentingly.
atormentar, *va.* to torment, to give pain.
atornillar, *va.* to screw.
atorozonarse, *vr.* to suffer from gripes or colic.
atorrante, *m.* (Sp. Am.) vagabond.

atortolar, *va.* to intimidate.
atosigar, *va.* to poison; to harass, to oppress.
atóxico, ca, *adj.* non-poisonous.
atrabancar, *va.* to huddle; to do something in a hurry.
atrabilis, *f.* (med.) black bile; (fig.) melancholy.
atracadero, *m.* landing place.
atracar, *va.* to overhaul a ship; to glut, to pamper; —, *vn.* (naut.) to make shore.
atracción, *f.* attraction.
atractivo, va, *adj.* attractive; magnetic; —, *m.* charm, grace.
atraer, *va.* (ATRAIGO, ATRAJE) to attract, to allure.
atragantarse, *vr.* to choke; to get stuck in conversation.
atraíble, *adj.* attractable.
atraillar, *va.* to leash.
atramparse, *vr.* to be caught in a snare; to be stopped or blocked up; to be involved in difficulties.
atramuz, *m.* (bot.) lupine.
atrancar, *va.* to bar a door; —, *vn.* to take long steps; to read hurriedly, to skim through.
atranque, *m.* difficulty; tight place.
atrapamoscas, *f.* (bot.) Venus's-flytrap.
atrapar, *va.* to overtake, to nab; to deceive.
atrás, *adv.* backwards; behind; past; **hacerse** —, to fall back; **hacia** —, quite the contrary.
atrasado, da, *adj.* backward, behind the times; late, tardy; in arrears.
atrasar, *va.* to outstrip, to leave behind; to postpone; to delay; — **el reloj,** to set back a watch; —**se,** to be behindhand or behind time; to fall behind; (com.) to be in arrears.
atraso, *m.* backwardness; —**s,** *pl.* arrears of money.
atravesado, da, *adj.* squint-eyed; oblique; crosswise; cross-grained; mongrel, degenerate.
atravesaño, *m.* cross timber.
atravesar, *va.* (IE) to lay a beam of timber across a place; to run through with a sword; to cross; to pass over; to trump a trick; —**se,** to get in the way; to thwart one's purpose.
atreguado, da, *adj.* deranged.
atresnalar, *va.* to collect sheaves of grain into heaps.
atreverse, *vr.* to dare, to venture.
atrevido, da, *adj.* bold, audacious, daring; brazen, impudent.
atrevimiento, *m.* boldness, audacity.
atribución, *f.* attribution, imputation.
atribuir, *va.* (UYO) to attribute, to ascribe; to impute; —**se,** to assume.
atribular, *va.* to vex, to afflict.
atributivo, va, *adj.* attributive; characteristic.
atributo, *m.* attribute.
atrición, *f.* contrition.

atril, *m.* lectern; music stand; easel.
atrincheramiento, *m.* (mil.) entrenchment.
atrincherar, *va.* to entrench.
atrio, *m.* porch; portico.
atrito, ta, *adj.* contrite, penitent.
atrocidad, *f.* atrocity.
atrochar, *vn.* to take bypaths.
atrofia, *f.* atrophy.
atrófico, ca, *adj.* affected with atrophy.
atrompetado, da, *adj.* trumpetlike.
atronado, da, *adj.* ill-advised; thoughtless, rash.
atronar, *va.* (UE) to deafen, to stun, to din; **—se,** to be thunderstruck.
atronerar, *va.* to make embrasures in a wall.
atropado, da, *adj.* grouped, clumped.
atropar, *va.* to assemble in groups.
atropellado, da, *adj.* hasty, precipitate; **—,** *m.* person who has been run over.
atropellar, *va.* to trample; to run down, to run over; **—se,** to hurry, to flurry.
atropello, *m.* trampling; outrage, insult; **— de automóvil,** automobile collision.
atropina, *f.* (med.) atropine.
atroz, *adj.* atrocious; (coll.) enormous.
atrozar, *va.* (naut.) to truss a yard to the mast.
attmo. or **att.ᵐᵒ atentísimo,** very kind, very courteous.
atto. or **att.º atento,** kind, courteous.
atufar, *va.* to vex, to plague.
atún, *m.* tunny fish.
atunara, *f.* tunny fishery.
aturdido, da, *adj.* harebrained, rattled.
aturdimiento, *m.* stupefaction; astonishment; dullness.
aturdir, *va.* to bewilder, to confuse; to stupefy.
atusar, *va.* to cut the hair; to shear; **—se el bigote,** to twist the mustache.
auca, *f.* goose.
aud.ª audiencia, a kind of law court.
audacia, *f.* audacity, boldness.
audaz, *adj.* audacious, bold.
audibilidad, *f.* audibility.
audible, *adj.* audible.
audición, *f.* broadcasting; audition.
audiencia, *f.* audience; hearing; audience chamber; hearing in court; a kind of high court.
audífono, *m.* radio earphone.
audiofrecuencia, *f.* audiofrequency.
audiómetro, *m.* audiometer.
audión, *m.* audion.
auditivo, va, *adj.* auditory.
auditorio, *m.* assembly; audience.
auge, *m.* the pinnacle of power; apogee of a planet.
augur, *m.* augur.
augurar, *va.* to augur, to tell in advance, to predict.
Augusto, Augustus.
augusto, ta, *adj.* august, majestic; magnificent; stately.
aula, *f.* lecture room, classroom.

aullar, *vn.* to howl.
aullido or **aúllo,** *m.* howling; cry of horror.
aumentar, *va.* to augment, to increase; **—,** *vn.* to grow larger.
aumentativo, va, *adj.* increasing, enlarging, augmentative.
aumento, *m.* augmentation, increase, growth; promotion, advancement.
aun, *adv.* yet, as yet, nevertheless; still, farther, even, further; **— cuando,** even though; (written **aún** after a verb).
aunar, *va.* to unite, to assemble.
aunque, *conj.* though, notwithstanding.
¡aupa! *interj.* up! up!
aura, *f.* gentle breeze; **— popular,** popularity.
auranciáceo, cea, *adj.* (bot.) citrus.
áureo, rea, *adj.* golden, gilt; **—,** *m.* doubloon; druggist's weight.
aureola, *f.* glory; nimbus; halo.
aurícula, *f.* (anat.) auricle.
auricular, *adj.* within hearing; auricular; **—,** *m.* earphone.
aurífero, ra, *adj.* (poet.) containing gold.
aurora, *f.* first dawn of day; (poet.) origin or first appearance of a thing; **— boreal,** northern lights.
aurragado, da, *adj.* badly tilled.
auscultación, *f.* (med.) auscultation.
ausencia, *f.* absence.
ausentarse, *vr.* to absent one's self.
ausente, *adj.* absent.
auspicio, *m.* auspice; prediction; protection.
austeridad, *f.* rigor, austerity.
austero, ra, *adj.* austere, severe; crabbed.
austral or **austrino, na,** *adj.* austral, southern.
australiano, na, *n.* and *adj.* Australian.
austríaco, ca, *n.* and *adj.* Austrian.
austro, *m.* south wind.
autarquía, *f.* autarchy, economic self-sufficiency.
auténtica, *f.* certificate.
autenticar, *va.* to authenticate.
autenticidad, *f.* authenticity.
auténtico, ca, *adj.* authentic, true, genuine.
autillo, *m.* (orn.) horned owl; secret auto-da-fé.
auto, *m.* judicial sentence; warrant, edict, ordinance; auto, automobile; **— de auxilio,** wrecker (automobile); **— de fe,** auto-da-fé, sentence given by the Inquisition; **— sacramental,** religious, allegorical play; **dar un paseo en —,** to take an auto ride.
autobiografía, *f.* autobiography.
autobomba, *m.* fire truck.
autobús, *m.* motorbus, bus.
autocamino, *m.* motor road.
autocamión, *m.* auto truck, motor truck.
autocarril, *m.* rail car.
autoclave, *m.* autoclave, pressure cooker; (med.) sterilizing apparatus.
autocracia, *f.* autocracy.
autócrata, *m.* and *f.* autocrat.

autódromo, *m.* speedway, automobile race track.
autogiro, *m.* autogyro.
autógrafo, *m.* autograph.
autoinducción, *f.* (elec.) self-induction.
autoinflamación, *f.* spontaneous combustion.
autómata, *m.* automaton.
automático, ca, *adj.* automatic.
automatismo, *m.* automatism.
automotor, *adj.* self-propelling.
automotriz, *adj.* automotive.
automóvil, *m.* automobile; **— acorazado,** armored car; **— de plaza,** taxi, taxicab; **— de turismo,** touring car; **— de auxilio,** wrecker.
automovilista, *m.* motorist.
autonomía, *f.* autonomy.
autónomo, ma, *adj.* autonomous.
autopiano, *m.* player piano.
autopsia, *f.* autopsy.
autor, *m.* author; maker; writer.
autora, *f.* authoress.
autorcillo, *m.* (coll.) bad writer.
autoría, *f.* managership of a theater.
autoridad, *f.* authority.
autoritarista, *m.* authoritarian.
autoritativo, va, *adj.* authoritative.
autorización, *f.* authorization.
autorizado, da, *adj.* competent, reliable.
autorizar, *va.* to authorize.
autorretrato, *m.* self-portrait.
autorzuelo, *m.* scribbler.
autosugestión, *f.* autosuggestion.
autumnal, *adj.* autumnal.
auxiliar, *va.* to aid, to help, to assist; to attend a dying person; —, *adj.* auxiliary.
auxilio, *m.* aid, help, assistance; **acudir en — de,** to go to the assistance of; **primer —,** first aid.
Av. Avenida, Ave. Avenue.
a/v. a la vista, (com.) at sight.
avadarse, *vr.* to become fordable.
aval, *m.* (com.) endorsement.
avalentado, da, *adj.* bragging, vainly boasting.
avalo, *m.* slight shock; earthquake.
avalorar, *va.* to estimate, to value; to heighten the value of a thing; to inspirit, to animate.
avaluar, *va.* to estimate, to value, to evaluate, to appraise, to set a price.
avalúo, *m.* estimating, appraisal.
avambrazo, *m.* armor for the forearm.
avance, *m.* (mil.) advance, attack.
avantrén, *m.* (mil.) limbers of a gun carriage.
avanzada, *f.* (mil.) vanguard.
avanzar, *va.* and *vn.* to advance, to push forward.
avanzo, *m.* (com.) balance sheet.
avaricia, *f.* avarice.
avariento, ta, *adj.* avaricious, covetous.
avaro, ra, *adj.* avaricious, miserly; —, *m.* miser.

avasallar, *va.* to subdue, to enslave.
ave, *f.* bird; **— de corral,** fowl.
avecilla, *f.* fledgling.
avecindar, *va.* to admit someone as a town resident; **—se,** to settle in a town as a resident.
avechucho, *m.* sparrow hawk; ragamuffin.
avejentar, *va.* and *vr.* to make (or become) more than one's age.
avejigar, *va.* and *vn.* to blister.
avellana, *f.* filbert, hazelnut.
avellanar, *m.* plantation of hazels.
avellanarse, *vr.* to shrivel, to grow as dry as a nut.
avellano, *m.* hazelnut shrub or tree.
avemaría, *f.* Ave Maria, salutation of the Virgin Mary.
¡Ave María! *interj.* exclamation of surprise.
avena, *f.* oats.
avenamiento, *m.* drainage.
avenar, *va.* to drain or draw off water.
avenate, *m.* gruel; fit of madness.
avenencia, *f.* agreement, bargain; union, concord.
aveníceo, cea, *adj.* oaten.
avenida, *f.* flood, inundation; concurrence of several things; avenue, boulevard.
avenir, *va.* and *vr.* (AVENGO, AVINE) to reconcile; to accommodate; to be reconciled; to join, to consent.
aventador, *m.* winnower; fan.
aventadura, *f.* (vet.) windgall.
aventajado, da, *adj.* advantageous, excelling, superior.
aventajar, *va.* to surpass, to excel, to have the advantage.
aventar, *va.* (IE) to fan; to expel; to scatter; **—se,** to be puffed up.
aventura, *f.* adventure, event, incident, chance.
aventurar, *va.* to venture, to risk, to take chances.
aventurero, ra, *adj.* adventurous; —, *m.* adventurer, free lance.
avergonzado, da, *adj.* embarrassed, sheepish.
avergonzar, *va.* (UE) to shame, to abash; **—se,** to be ashamed.
avería, *f.* (naut.) average; damage; aviary; **— repentina,** breakdown.
averiado, da, *adj.* damaged by sea water.
averiarse, *vr.* to suffer damage at sea.
averiguación, *f.* investigation.
averiguar, *va.* to inquire, to investigate, to ascertain; to explore.
averío, *m.* flock of birds.
averno, *m.* (poet.) hell.
aversión, *f.* aversion, dislike; abhorrence.
avestruz, *m.* ostrich.
avezar, *va.* to accustom, to habituate.
aviación, *f.* aviation; **— comercial,** commercial aviation; **parque de —,** aviation ground.
aviador, ra, *n.* aviator.
aviar, *va.* to provision, to provide for a

journey; to equip; to hasten the execution of a thing; **—se,** to get ready.
avidez, *f.* covetousness.
ávido, da, *adj.* (poet.) greedy, covetous.
aviejarse, *vr.* to grow old.
aviento, *m.* pitchfork.
avieso, sa, *adj.* irregular, out of the way; mischievous, perverse.
avigorar, *va.* to inspire with vigor and spirit.
avilantez, *f.* forwardness, boldness.
avillanado, da, *adj.* boorish; mean, vile, base.
avillanar, *va.* to debase.
avinagrado, da, *adj.* soured, crabbed, peevish, bad-tempered.
avinagrar, *va.* to acidify.
avío, *m.* preparation, provision.
avión, *m.* (orn.) martin, swallow; airplane; **— de bombardeo,** bomber; **— de combate,** pursuit plane; **— de cubierta,** ship plane; **— postal,** mailplane; **por —,** by plane, by air mail.
avisado, da, *adj.* prudent, cautious; sagacious, skillful; **mal —,** ill-advised, injudicious.
avisador, *m.* adviser, announcer, informer.
avisar, *va.* to inform, to give notice; to admonish; to advertise.
aviso, *m.* information; intelligence; notice, advertisement; warning; hint; prudence; care; counsel, advice; **falta de —,** without advice; **sin otro —,** without further advice; **según —,** as per advice.
avispa, *f.* wasp.
avispado, da, *adj.* lively, brisk, vivacious.
avispar, *va.* to spur; to incite to alertness; **—se,** to be peevish.
avispero, *m.* wasps' nest.
avispón, *m.* hornet.
avistar, *va.* to descry at a distance; to have an interview, to transact business.
avituallar, *va.* (mil.) to supply with provisions.
avivar, *va.* to quicken, to enliven, to encourage.
avizorar, *va.* to spy, to search narrowly.
avocar, *va.* (law) to appeal.
avucasta or **avutarda,** *f.* (orn.) bustard.
axila, *f.* armpit.
axioma, *m.* axiom, maxim.
axiomático, ca, *adj.* axiomatic.
**¡ay! *interj.* alas! ¡— de mí! alas! poor me!
aya, *f.* governess, instructress.
ayer, *adv.* yesterday; lately; **— mismo,** only yesterday; **— por la mañana,** yesterday morning; **— por la tarde,** yesterday afternoon; **— por la noche,** yesterday evening.
ayes, *m. pl.* lamentations, sighs.
Ayte. ayudante, Adj. or Adjt. Adjutant.
Ayte. Gral. Ayudante General, A. G. Adjutant General.
ayuda, *f.* help, aid, assistance; support; syringe; **—, *m.* assistant; **— de cámara,** valet.

ayudante, *m.* assistant; caddie; (mil.) adjutant, aide-de-camp.
ayudar, *va.* to aid, to help, to assist, to further.
ayunar, *vn.* to fast, to abstain from food.
ayunas, en —, *adv.* fasting, without food; without knowledge, ignorant (of an affair).
ayuno, *m.* fast, abstinence from food; **—, na,** *adj.* fasting.
ayunque, *m.* anvil.
ayuntamiento, *m.* town council; city hall; municipal government.
ayustar, *va.* (naut.) to bend two ends of a cable.
azabachado, da, *adj.* jet-black.
azabache, *m.* jet.
azacán, *m.* water carrier.
azacaya, *f.* water pipe.
azada, *f.* spade, hoe.
azadón, *m.* pickax; hoe.
azadonar, *va.* to hoe.
azafata, *f.* queen's waiting woman.
azafrán, *m.* saffron.
azafranar, *va.* to dye with saffron.
azagador, *m.* cattle path.
azagaya, *f.* spear.
azahar, *m.* orange or lemon blossom.
azainadamente, *adv.* perfidiously; viciously.
azalea, *f.* (bot.) azalea.
azar, *m.* unforeseen disaster, unexpected accident; unfortunate card or throw in dice; disappointment; impediment; **al —,** at random.
azarbe, *m.* irrigation ditch.
azarja, *f.* silk reel.
azaroso, sa, *adj.* unlucky, ominous; hazardous.
aznacho or **aznallo,** *m.* Scotch fir.
ázoe, *m.* (chem.) nitrogen.
azófar, *m.* latten brass, a brass alloy.
azogadamente, *adv.* in a quick and restless manner.
azogar, *va.* to overlay with mercury; **— la cal,** to slake lime; **—se,** to suffer from mercury poisoning; to be in a state of agitation.
azogue, *m.* mercury; **—s,** *pl.* ships which carry mercury.
azoguería, *f.* amalgamation.
azolar, *va.* (UE) to cut timber with a hatchet.
azor, *m.* (orn.) goshawk.
azorar, *va.* and *vr.* to frighten, to terrify; to be agitated.
azorrarse, *vr.* to feel a heaviness in the head.
azotacalles, *m.* lounger, loafer.
azotaina, *f.* good beating or whipping.
azotar, *va.* to whip, to lash; to horsewhip.
azote, *m.* whip, lash given with a whip; scourge; calamity.
azotea, *f.* platform, flat roof of a house; roof garden.
azótico, ca, *adj.* (chem.) nitric.
azteca, *n.* and *adj.* Aztec (Indian tribe of Mexico).

azúcar, *m.* or *f.* sugar; **— blanco, ca,** refined sugar; **— cubicado, da,** cube sugar; **— de pilón,** loaf sugar; **— de plomo,** sugar of lead; **—de remolacha,** beet sugar; **— granulado, da,** granulated sugar; **— terciado, da,** or **moreno, na,** brown sugar.

azucarado, da, *adj.* sugared; sugary.

azucarar, *va.* to sugar, to sweeten.

azucarera, *f.* sugar bowl.

azucarero, *m.* sugar bowl; confectioner.

azucena, *f.* white lily.

azud, *m.* dam with a sluice or floodgate.

azuda, *f.* water works for irrigation.

azuela, *f.* adze.

azufaifa, *f.* jujube.

azufaifo, *m.* jujube tree.

azufrado, da, *adj.* whitened or fumigated with sulphur; sulphurous.

azufrar, *va.* to fumigate with sulphur.

azufre, *m.* sulphur, brimstone.

azufroso, sa, *adj.* sulphureous.

azul, *adj.* blue; **— celeste,** sky blue; **— subido,** bright blue; **— turquí,** deep blue.

azulado, da, *adj.* azure, bluish.

azular, *va.* to dye blue.

azulear, *vn.* to have a bluish tint.

azulejo, *m.* glazed tile; bluebird.

azulenco, ca, *adj.* bluish.

azumar, *va.* to dye (hair).

azumbre, *f.* liquid measure (half a gallon).

azur, *adj.* (poet.) blue (specially used in heraldry).

azutero, *m.* sluice master.

azuzador, ra, *n.* instigator.

azuzar, *va.* to set on dogs; to irritate, to stir up.

B

B.: Beato, blessed, holy; **Bueno,** Good (in an examination).

B/ or **b/ bala,** bale (of paper).

baba, *f.* drivel; drool, slobber.

bababuí, *m.* mockingbird.

babada, *f.* thighbone.

babadero or **babador,** *m.* bib.

babaza, *f.* slime; foam or froth from the mouth.

babear, *vn.* to drivel; to drool, to slobber.

babel, *m.* babel, confusion.

babera, *f.* chin piece of a helmet; bib.

babero, *m.* bib.

Babia, *f.* **estar en —,** to be absent-minded or dreaming.

babieca, *m.* and *f.* ignorant, stupid person.

Babilonia, *f.* Babylonia, Babel; babel, uproar, bedlam.

babor, *m.* (naut.) larboard, port; **de — a estribor,** athwart ship.

babosa, *f.* slug, limax; young onion.

babosear, *va.* and *vn.* to drool; to slobber.

baboso, sa, *adj.* driveling, slavering; silly; **—,** *n.* (Sp. Am.) fool, idiot.

babucha, *f.* Oriental slipper.

bacalao, *m.* codfish.

bacanales, *f. pl.* bacchanals.

bacante, *f.* bacchante.

bacía, *f.* basin, washbasin.

bacilo, *m.* bacillus.

bacinica, *f.* chamber pot for children.

bacteria, *f.* bacteria.

bactericida, *m.* germicide.

bacteriología, *f.* bacteriology.

bacteriológico, ca, *adj.* bacteriological.

bacteriólogo, *m.* bacteriologist.

báculo, *m.* walking stick; support; **— pastoral,** bishop's crosier.

bachiller, *m.* bachelor (degree), a college graduate, one who has received the bachelor's degree; babbler, prater.

bachillerato, *m.* bachelor's degree.

bachillerear, *vn.* to babble, to prattle.

badajo, *m.* clapper of a bell; (coll.) idle, foolish prattler.

badana, *f.* dressed sheepskin.

badea, *f.* insipid melon; stupid person.

badil, *m.*, **badila,** *f.* fire shovel.

badulaque, *m.* stupid fellow.

bagaje, *m.* pack animal; army baggage; luggage; **— de conocimientos,** wealth of knowledge.

bagajero, *m.* driver of pack animals; driver of military baggage.

bagatela, *f.* bagatelle, trifle.

bagazo, *m.* bagasse; sediment of grapes, olives, palms, etc.

bagre, *f.* an ugly woman; **—,** *m.* (Sp. Am.) kind of fresh-water fish; **—,** *adj.* pretentious, gaudy.

bahía, *f.* bay.

bailadero, *m.* public dance hall.

bailador, ra, *n.* dancer.

bailar, *vn.* to dance.

bailarín, ina, *n.* dancer, ballerina.

baile, *m.* dance, ball; bailiff; **— de etiqueta,** dress ball; **— de figuras,** square dance; **— de máscaras,** masked ball.

bajá, *m.* pasha.

baja, *f.* fall, diminution; fall in prices; loss in membership; (mil.) ticket of admission into a hospital.

Baja California, *f.* Lower California.

bajada, *f.* descent; downgrade; inclination.

bajamar, *f.* low water; low tide, ebb.

bajar, *va.* to lower, to let down; to decrease (the price); to lessen; to humble; to bend downward; **—,** *vn.* to descend; to grow less; **—se,** to crouch; to lessen.

bajel, *m.* vessel, ship.

bajelero, *m.* shipowner, shipmaster.

bajete, *m.* (mus.) baritone.

bajeza, *f.* meanness, abjectness; littleness; lowliness.

bajío, *m.* shoal, sandbank; decline; (Sp. Am.) lowland.

bajista, *m.* (com.) bear (in stocks); **tendencia —,** tendency to decline.

bajo, ja, *adj.* low; under; short; abject; despicable, low (vile); mean; faint; common; dull (of colors); bent; **tierra —,** lowland; **piso** or **planta —,** ground floor; **—jo,** *adv.* under; **—jo,** *prep.* under, underneath, below; **— par,** under or below par; **— techo,** indoors; **—cuerda,** underhandedly; **—,** *m.* (mus.) base.

bajón, *m.* bassoon.

bajonista, *m.* player on the bassoon.

bajorrelieve, *m.* bas-relief.

bakelita, *f.* bakelite.

bala, *f.* ball, bullet, shot; bale of paper containing ten reams; printer's inking ball.

balacear, *va.* (Mex.) to shoot at random.

balacera, *f.* (Mex.) shooting at random.

balada, *f.* ballad.

baladí, *adj.* mean, despicable, worthless.

baladre, *m.* (bot.) oleander.

baladrón, *m.* boaster, bully.

baladronada, *f.* boast, brag, bravado.

baladronear, *vn.* to boast, to brag.

bálago, *m.* straw; rick of straw; grain stalk; soapsuds.

balance, *m.* fluctuation; rolling of a ship; equipoise, balance; balance of accounts; balance sheet; **— de comprobación,** trial balance; **hacer un —,** to draw (or strike) a balance.

balancear, *va.* and *vn.* to balance; to roll; to waver; **—se,** to rock, to sway.

balanceo, *m.* rocking, swing, rolling (of a ship, plane, etc.).

balancín, *m.* swing bar; whiffletree; minting mill; rope dancer's pole; rocker arm.

balandra, *f.* (naut.) bilander.

balandrán, *m.* cassock.

balanza, *f.* scale; pair of scales; comparative estimate.

balanzario, *m.* balancer; weigher.

balar, *vn.* to bleat.

balasto, *m.* (rail.) ballast.

balaustrada, *f.* balustrade.

balaústre, *m.* baluster.

balazo, *m.* shot; bullet wound.

balboa, *m.* a coin of Panama normally worth $1.00.

balbucear, *va.* and *vn.* to speak indistinctly; to stammer.

balbuciente, *adj.* stammering, stuttering.

balbucir, *va., vn.* and *def.* (uzco) to stammer, to stutter.

balcón, *m.* balcony.

balconcillo, *m.* a small balcony.

balconaje, *m.* row or series of balconies.

baldar, *va.* to cripple.

balde, *m.* bucket, pail; **de —,** gratis, for nothing; **en —,** in vain.

baldear, *va.* (naut.) to wash the decks; to bail water from a ditch; to wash floors, sidewalks, etc., with pailfuls of water.

baldés, *m.* piece of dressed skin.

baldío, día, *adj.* untilled, uncultivated.

baldón, *m.* reproach; insult; disgrace.

baldosa, *f.* paving; flagstone; tile.

balduque, *m.* narrow red tape.

balería, *f.* pile of balls or bullets.

balido, *m.* bleating, bleat.

balín, *m.* buckshot.

balística, *f.* ballistics.

baliza, *f.* buoy.

balneario, *m.* bathing resort; **—, ria,** *adj.* relative to medicinal baths.

balompié, *m.* football.

balón, *m.* large ball; bale of goods; **juego de —,** basketball, ball game; **— de futbol,** football.

baloncesto, *m.* basketball.

balota, *f.* ballot.

balsa, *f.* pool; raft, float; ferry.

balsámico, ca, *adj.* balsamic; balmy.

bálsamo, *m.* balsam, balm.

balsear, *va.* to cross rivers on ferries or floats.

balsero, *m.* ferryman.

balsopeto, *m.* large pouch carried near the breast; bosom.

Báltico, *m.* Baltic Sea.

baluarte, *m.* bastion; bulwark; rampart.

balumba, *f.* bulk of things heaped together.

balumbo, *m.* bulky thing.

ballena, *f.* whale; whalebone.

ballenato, *m.* cub of a whale.

ballenero, *m.* (naut.) whaler.

ballesta, *f.* crossbow; **a tiro de —,** at a great distance.

ballestada, *f.* shot from a crossbow.

ballestear, *va.* to shoot with a crossbow.

ballestera, *f.* (mil.) loophole.

ballestería, *f.* archery; crossbows; crossbowmen.

ballestero, *m.* crossbowman; crossbow maker; king's armorer.

ballestilla, *f.* small crossbow.

bambalina, *f.* upper part of the scenery of a theater.

bambolear, *vn.* to reel, to sway.

bamboleo, *m.* reeling, staggering.

bambolla, *f.* (coll.) ostentation, vain show.

bambú or **bambuc,** *m.* bamboo.

bambuco, *m.* Colombian popular air and dance.

banal, *adj.* trite, commonplace.

banana, *f.* banana.

bananero, *m.* banana dealer; banana plant or fruit; **—, ra,** *adj.* pertaining to the banana.

banano, *m.* banana plant or fruit.

banasta, *f.* large basket.

banastero, *m.* basket maker.

banasto, *m.* large round basket.

banca, *f.* bench; washing box; (com.) banking; **casa de —,** banking house.

bancal, *m.* garden plot; bench cover.

bancario, ria, *adj.* banking.

bancarrota, *f.* bankruptcy; **tribunal de —,** bankruptcy court.

banco, *m.* bench; carpenter's bench; bench of rowers; bank; **— agrícola,** agricultural (or farmers') bank; **— de ahorros,** savings bank; **— de depósito,** trust bank; **— de descuento,** discount bank; **— de**

emisión, bank of issue; **— del estado,** state bank; **— de liquidación,** clearinghouse; **— de sangre,** blood bank; **— de taller,** workbench; **— hipotecario,** mortgage bank; **billete de —,** banknote; **empleado de —,** bank clerk; **libro de —,** passbook; **poner en el —,** to deposit in the bank.

banda, f. sash; ribbon; band; party; gang; crew; covey; bank, border.

bandada, f. covey, flock (of birds); drove.

bandearse, vr. to shift for oneself.

bandeja, f. tray.

bandera, f. banner, standard; flag; **— desplegada,** flying colors; **la — de parlamento,** flag of truce.

banderilla, f. small decorated dart used at a bullfight.

banderillear, va. to plant **banderillas** in a bull's neck or shoulder.

banderillero, m. thrower of **banderillas.**

banderizo, za, adj. factious; excitable.

banderola, f. streamer, pennant.

bandido, m. bandit, robber; knave.

bando, m. faction, party; team; proclamation.

bandolera, f. bandoleer; woman bandit.

bandolero, m. highwayman, robber.

bandolín, m., bandolina, f. mandolin.

banjo, m. banjo.

banquear, vn. (aer.) to bank.

banquero, ra, n. banker.

banqueta, f. sidewalk; three-legged stool; **— del piano,** piano stool.

banquete, m. banquet; feast.

baña, f., or **bañadero,** m. pool, puddle; bathing place.

bañar, va. to bathe; to tub; to water, to irrigate; to dip; to wash over a painting with a second coat of transparent colors; **—se,** to take a bath.

bañera, f. bathtub.

bañero, m. bathkeeper.

baño, m. bath; bathtub; bathroom; varnish; crust of sugar; coat of paint put over another; **— de ducha,** shower bath.

bao, m. (naut.) beam.

baqueta, f. ramrod; drumstick; (mil.) gantlet.

baquetazo, m. blow with a ramrod.

baqueteado, da, adj. inured, habituated.

báquico, ca, adj. bacchanal.

bar, m. bar (of a saloon).

baraja, f. playing card; complete pack of cards; game of cards.

barajadura, f. shuffling of cards.

barajar, va. to shuffle cards; to entangle.

¡barajo! interj. the deuce!

baranda, f. banister, railing; billiard-table cushion; **echar de —,** to exaggerate, to boast.

barandal, m. railing.

baratería, f. barratry; fraud.

baratero, m. cardsharper, card cheat; one who sells at a cheap price.

baratijas, f. pl. trifles, toys.

baratillero, m. peddler.

baratillo, m. secondhand shop; bargain counter.

barato, ta, adj. cheap, low-priced; **de —,** gratis; **—to,** adv. cheaply; **—,** m. cheapness, low price; money given by the winning gamblers to the bystanders.

baratura, f. cheapness.

baraúnda, f. noise, confusion.

barba, f. chin; beard, whiskers; **— a —,** face to face; **—,** m. actor who impersonates old men.

barbacana, f. (mil.) barbican.

barbacoa, f. barbecue.

barbada, f. jaw of a horse; dab (fish).

Barbadas, f. pl. Barbados.

barbado, da, adj. bearded.

barbar, vn. to grow a beard; to rear or keep bees; to take root.

Bárbara, Barbara.

barbaridad, f. barbarity, barbarism; rudeness; (coll.) ridiculous act; **una —,** a piece of nonsense; an "awful" lot; **¡qué —!** how terrible!

barbarie, f. barbarism, cruelty; rusticity.

barbarismo, m. barbarism, crowd of barbarians.

bárbaro, ra, adj. barbarous, savage; rash, bold, daring; rude, unpolished.

barbechar, va. to plow.

barbechera, f. series of successive plowings.

barbecho, m. first plowing, fallow.

barbería, f. barbershop.

barbero, m. barber.

barbeta, f. (naut.) rackline; (mil.) barbette.

barbiblanco, ca, adj. white-bearded.

barbicano, na, adj. gray-bearded.

barbihecho, cha, adj. fresh-shaved.

barbilampiño, ña, adj. thin-bearded, sparse-bearded.

barbilucio, adj. good looking and effeminate.

barbilla, f. point of the chin.

barbinegro, gra, adj. black-bearded.

barbirrubio, bia, adj. blond-bearded.

barbo, m. barbel (fish); catfish.

barbón, m. man with a thick, strong beard.

barbudo, da, adj. long-bearded.

barbulla, f. confused noise.

barbullar, vn. to talk confusedly and disorderly.

barbullón, ona, adj. talking loud, fast, and confusedly; **—,** n. one who talks fast and confusedly.

barca, f. boat, barge; **— de transbordo,** ferry.

barcada, f. passage in a ferryboat; boatload of persons or goods.

barcaje, m. fare; ferriage.

barcarola, f. barcarole.

barcaza, f. barge; privilege conceded in some ports of loading and unloading.

barco, m. boat, barge; ship; **— de guerra,** warship.

barda, f. bard. horse armor; thatch; reed.

bardal, *m.* mud wall, covered at the top with straw, brush or fence wood.

bardana, *f.* (bot.) common burdock.

bardar, *va.* to cover the top of walls with straw or brushwood; to thatch fences.

bardo, *m.* bard, poet.

bario, *m.* barium.

barítono, *m.* (mus.) baritone.

barjuleta, *f.* knapsack.

barloar, *vn.* (naut.) to grapple for the purpose of boarding.

barloventear, *vn.* (naut.) to tack, to tack about; to ply to windward.

barlovento, *m.* (naut.) windward; **ganar el —,** to get to windward.

Bar.^mé **Bartolomé,** Bart. Bartholomew.

barnacla, *f.* barnacle.

barniz, *m.* varnish.

barnizar, *va.* to varnish.

barógrafo, *m.* barograph.

barómetro, *m.* barometer; **indicación del —,** barometric reading.

barón, *m.* baron.

baronesa, *f.* baroness.

baronía, *f.* barony; baronage.

barquear, *vn.* to cross in a boat.

barquero, *m.* bargeman.

barquilla, *f.* (naut.) log; boat-shaped mold for making pastry; (aer.) nacelle.

barquillero, *m.* wafer baker; seller of rolled wafers.

barquillo, *m.* cone-shaped wafer.

barquín, *m.* large bellows for furnaces.

barquinazo, *m.* thud of a falling body.

barquino, *m.* wine bag.

barra, *f.* crowbar, lever; ingot of metal; rock, sandbank; **en —** or **en —s,** (metal) in bar or bars, as **oro en —,** bar gold, gold in bars, or bullion gold.

barrabasada, *f.* trick, plot, intrigue.

barraca, *f.* barrack; hut, cabin; shed; stall.

barraganete, *m.* (naut.) top timber.

barranca, *f.* cliff; gorge.

barranco, *m.* ravine; gorge; (fig.) great difficulty, embarrassment.

barrancoso, sa, *adj.* full of breaks and holes.

barrar, *va.* to barricade, to fortify; to daub; to smear.

barrear, *va.* to bar, to barricade; to cancel or cross off.

barredero, ra, *adj.* that drags along, sweeping; **—,** *m.* baker's mop; **—ra,** *f.* seine.

barredor, *m.* sweeper; **— al vacío,** vacuum cleaner; **— de alfombra,** carpet sweeper.

barreduras, *f. pl.* sweepings; remains, residue.

barrena, *f.* borer, gimlet, auger.

barrenar, *va.* to bore; (fig.) to frustrate one's designs.

barrendero, ra, *n.* sweeper, dustman or woman.

barreno, *m.* large borer; hole made with a borer or auger.

barreño, *m.*, **barreña,** *f.* earthen pan; tub; **—,** *m.* typical dance of Guatemala.

barrer, *va.* to sweep; to carry off the whole.

barrera, *f.* clay pit; bar, barrier; barricade; turnpike; **— antiaérea,** flak.

barrero, *m.* potter; clay pit.

barretear, *va.* to bar; to line the inside of shoes.

barretero, *m.* one who works with a crowbar, wedge or pick (in mines).

barriada, *f.* precinct, quarter, or ward of a city.

barrica, *f.* cask containing about 60 gallons; hogshead.

barricada, *f.* barricade.

barrido, *m.* sweep; **—, da,** *adj.* swept.

barriga, *f.* abdomen, belly; pregnancy; (naut.) middle part of a vessel.

barrigón, *m.* (Cuba) a small child; **—, ona,** *adj.* big-bellied.

barrigudo, da, *adj.* big-bellied.

barril, *m.* barrel; cask; jug.

barrilame, *m.*, **barrilería,** *f.* number of barrels collected in one place.

barrilero, *m.* barrelmaker.

barrilete, *m.* (naut.) mouse; keg; clamp.

barrilla, *f.* (bot.) saltwort, barilla, an impure soda.

barrillar, *m.* barilla pits.

barrio, *m.* district or section of a town; quarter; **—s bajos,** slums.

barrizal, *m.* clay pit.

barro, *m.* clay, mud; **vajilla de —,** earthenware; **— cocido,** terra cotta, baked clay.

barroco, *m.* baroque.

barroso, sa, *adj.* muddy; reddish, like clay; pimpled.

barrote, *m.* ironwork of doors, windows or tables; ledge of timber.

barrueco, *m.* pearl of irregular shape.

barruntador, ra, *n.* conjecturer.

barruntamiento, *m.* conjecturing, guessing.

barruntar, *va.* to foresee, to conjecture; to suspect.

barrunto, *m.* conjecture.

Bartolo, Bartolomé, Bartolomeo, Bartholomew.

bártulos, *m. pl.* household goods; tools; steps, means, ways (to get something done).

barzón, *m.* stroll.

barzonear, *vn.* to stroll; to loiter about.

basa, *f.* basis, base; pedestal.

basada, *f.* crane, derrick.

basado, da, *adj.* based.

basalto, *m.* basalt.

basamento, *m.* (arch.) pedestal and base of a column.

basar, *va.* to base; to found; to fix; to set; to support; to rest on.

basca, *f.* squeamishness; nausea.

bascosidad, *f.* nastiness, filth.

báscula, *f.* platform scale.

base, *f.* base, basis.

básico, ca, *adj.* basic, fundamental.

basílica, *f.* basilica (cathedral).

Basilio, Basil.

basilisco, *m.* basilisk.
basketbol, *m.* basketball.
basketbolista, *m.* and *f.* basketball player.
basketero, ra, *n.* basketball player.
basquear, *vn.* to be squeamish.
basquiña, *f.* kind of petticoat.
basta, *f.* basting; ¡—! *interj.* enough.
bastante, *adj.* sufficient, enough; quite; considerable; —, *adv.* enough; moderately; fairly; rather.
bastar, *vn.* to suffice, to be proportioned to something, to be enough.
bastarda, *f.* bastard file; piece of ordnance.
bastardear, *vn.* to degenerate.
bastardía, *f.* bastardy; meanness.
bastardilla, *f.* italic.
bastardo, da, *adj.* bastard, spurious; —, *m.* bastard.
bastear, *va.* to stitch loosely, to baste.
bastero, *m.* maker and seller of packsaddles.
bastidor, *m.* frame; embroidery frame; chassis; trestle; panel; —es, *pl.* stage scenery; wings; **detrás de —es,** backstage; **— de ventana** or **puerta,** sash; **— para camión,** truck frame; **— de pintor,** easel.
bastilla, *f.* hem, seam.
bastimentar, *va.* to supply with provisions.
bastimento, *m.* supply of provisions; (naut.) vessel.
bastión, *m.* (mil.) bastion.
basto, *m.* packsaddle for beasts of burden; —, **ta,** *adj.* coarse, rude, unpolished.
bastón, *m.* cane, stick; truncheon; staff of command.
bastoncillo, *m.* small cane; narrow lace.
bastonear, *va.* to beat with a cane or stick; to stir with a stick.
bastonero, *m.* cane maker or seller; marshal or manager of a ball, steward of a feast; assistant jailer.
bastos, *m. pl.* clubs (suit in cards).
basura, *f.* sweepings; refuse; garbage; dung.
basurero, *m.* dustpan; sweeper, duster (person); dunghill.
basurita, *f.* (Cuba) a tip; a little more.
bata, *f.* dressing gown; **— de casa,** negligee.
batacazo, *m.* noise of a fall.
batahola or **bataola,** *f.* hurly-burly, bustle.
batalla, *f.* battle, combat, fight; agitation of the mind; **— campal,** pitched battle; **orden de —,** battle array.
batallador, ra, *adj.* warlike; battling; —, *m.* combatant, warrior.
batallar, *vn.* to battle, to fight; to fence with foils; to dispute.
batallón, *m.* (mil.) battalion.
batán, *m.* fulling mill; —es, *pl.* kind of boys' game.
batanar, *va.* to full (cloth).
batanear, *va.* to beat, to handle roughly.
batanero, *m.* fuller.
batata, *f.* sweet potato.
batea, *f.* painted tray or hamper of lacquered wood; washing trough.
batear, *va.* and *vn.* (baseball) to bat.

batel, *m.* small boat.
batería, *f.* battery; **—cargada,** charged battery; **— de acumuladores,** storage battery; **— de cocina,** kitchen utensils; **— descargada,** discharged battery; **— de teatro,** stage lights; **— líquida,** wet battery; **— seca,** dry battery; **elemento de —,** battery cell.
batero, ra, *n.* maker of ladies' wrappers or negligees.
batey, *m.* (Cuba) premises of a sugar mill.
batida, *f.* hunting party.
batidera, *f.* beater (instrument for beating and mixing mortar).
batidero, *m.* continuous clashing of one thing against another; collision; uneven ground.
batido, da, *adj.* changeable (applied to silks); beaten, trodden (as roads); —, *m.* batter.
batidor, *m.* beater, chocolate beater; scout, ranger; outrider; one of the bodyguards who rides before a royal coach; **— de oro** or **plata,** gold or silver beater.
batiente, *m.* jamb or post of a door.
batihoja, *m.* gold beater; maker of sheet metal; warp of cloth.
batín, *m.* smoking jacket; doctor's gown.
batir, *va.* and *vn.* to beat; to dash; to clash; to demolish; to move in a violent manner; to strike (of the sun); **— banderas,** to salute with colors; **— palmas,** to clap, to applaud; **—se a muerte,** to fight to the death.
batista, *f.* batiste, cambric.
bato, *m.* simpleton, stupid man.
batón, *m.* large, loose gown, kimono.
baturrillo, *m.* hodgepodge; potpourri; medley.
batuta, *f.* baton; **llevar la —,** to lead, to preside.
baúl, *m.* trunk, chest; (coll.) belly; **— ropero,** wardrobe trunk.
bauprés, *m.* (naut.) bowsprit.
bausán, ana, *n.* fool; idiot.
bautismal, *adj.* baptismal.
bautismo, *m.* baptism.
bautisterio, *m.* baptistery.
bautizar, *va.* to baptize, to christen.
bautizo, *m.* baptism.
bauxita, *f.* bauxite.
baya, *f.* berry or other small round fruit.
bayeta, *f.* baize (kind of cloth); thick flannel.
bayetón, *m.* kind of cloth for making coats.
bayo, ya, *adj.* bay (of a horse).
bayoneta, *f.* bayonet.
bayonetazo, *m.* thrust with a bayonet.
baza, *f.* card trick.
bazar, *m.* bazaar; department store.
bazo, *m.* (anat.) spleen, milt.
bazofia, *f.* offal; refuse; swill.
bazucar, *va.* to stir liquids by shaking.
bazuqueo, *m.* stirring of liquids by shaking.
bca. barrica, bbl. barrel.
Bco. banco, bk. bank.

be, *m.* baa (cry of sheep); **la —,** *f.* the letter B.

beata, *f.* overly pious woman; hypocrite; woman engaged in charitable, religious work.

beatería, *f.* affected piety; bigotry.

beaterío, *m.* house or institution of pious women.

beatificación, *f.* beatification.

beatificar, *va.* to beatify; to hallow, to sanctify, to make blessed.

beatífico, ca, *adj.* beatific.

beatilla, *f.* a kind of fine linen.

beatísimo, ma, *adj.* most holy; **B— Padre,** Most Holy Father (the Pope).

beatitud, *f.* beatitude, blessedness.

beato, ta, *adj.* happy, blessed; devout; **—,** *n.* pious person.

Beatriz, Beatrice.

bebedero, *m.* drinking trough; drinking place for birds.

bebedizo, za, *adj.* drinkable.

bebedizo, *m.* love potion; poisonous drink.

bebedor, ra, *n.* tippler, drunkard, drinker.

beber, *va.* and *vn.* to drink; **—,** *m.* drinking.

bebible, *adj.* (coll.) drinkable, pleasant to the taste.

bebida, *f.* drink, beverage; **— alcohólica,** intoxicant.

bebido, da, *adj.* intoxicated.

bebistrajo, *m.* bad drink; mixture of drinks.

beborrotear, *va.* to sip often.

beca, *f.* part of a collegian's dress which is worn over the gown; fellowship; allowance, scholarship; **—s,** *pl.* strips of velvet, etc., with which the forepart of cloaks is lined by way of ornament.

becabunga, *f.* (bot.) brooklime.

becada, *f.* woodcock.

becafigo, *m.* (orn.) beccafico, figpecker.

becardón, *m.* snipe.

becerra, *f.* female calf; (bot.) snapdragon.

becerril, *adj.* pertaining to a calf.

becerrillo, *m.* calf; dressed calfskin.

becerro, *m.* yearling calf; calfskin; chartulary (of churches and monasteries); the Golden Book of the Castilian nobility at Simancas; **— marino,** sea calf; seal.

bedel, *m.* beadle; warden.

bedelía, *f.* beadleship; wardenship.

beduino, na, *adj.* Bedouin; uncivil.

befa, *f.* jeer, scoff, mock.

befar, *va.* to mock, to ridicule.

befo, fa, *adj.* blubber-lipped; knock-kneed.

begonia, *f.* (bot.) begonia.

behaviorismo, *m.* behaviorism.

bejucal, *m.* reed bank.

bejuco, *m.* tropical plant or vine; liana.

bejuquillo, *m.* small gold chain; thin **bejuco.**

beldad, *f.* beauty.

Belén, *m.* Bethlehem; scene representing the birth of Christ; **estar en —,** to be absent-minded.

beleño, *m.* (bot.) henbane.

belga, *adj.* and *n.* Belgian.

Bélgica, *f.* Belgium.

bélgico, ca, *adj.* Belgian.

Belice or **Beliza,** *f.* British Honduras.

bélico, ca, *adj.* warlike, martial.

belicoso, sa, *adj.* martial, pugnacious; aggressive.

beligerancia, *f.* belligerency.

beligerante, *n.* and *adj.* belligerent.

belitre, *adj.* vile, mean, worthless.

Beltrán, Bertram.

bellacada, *f.* action typical of knaves.

bellacamente, *adv.* knavishly, roguishly.

bellaco, ca, *adj.* sly, cunning, roguish; **—,** *m.* knave.

belladama or **belladona,** *f.* (bot.) deadly nightshade; (med.) belladonna.

bellaquear, *vn.* to cheat, to play roguish tricks.

bellaquería, *f.* knavery, roguery.

belleza, *f.* beauty.

bello, lla, *adj.* beautiful, handsome, fair, fine; perfect; **las —as artes,** the fine arts.

bellota, *f.* acorn; bottle of perfume or smelling salts.

bellote, *m.* large round-headed nail.

bellotear, *vn.* to feed on acorns.

bellotera, *f.* acorn season; acorn harvest.

bellotero, *m.* acorn picker or seller.

bemol, *m.* (mus.) flat.

bencina, *f.* (chem.) benzine.

bendecir, *va.* (BENDIGO, BENDIJE) to consecrate, to bless; to praise, to exalt.

bendición, *f.* benediction; blessing.

bendito, ta, *adj.* sainted, blessed; simple, silly; **—,** *m.* a saintlike person; **dormir como un —,** to sleep soundly; **¡—s sean!** bless their hearts!

benedícite, *m.* clergyman's leave of absence.

benedictino or **benito,** *m.* Benedictine.

benefactor, *m.* benefactor.

beneficencia, *f.* beneficence, charity.

beneficiado, da, *n.* incumbent of a benefice; beneficiary.

beneficiador, ra, *n.* benefactor; improver; careful administrator.

beneficiar, *va.* to profit; to benefit; to work and improve mines; **—se con** or **por,** to profit by.

beneficiario, *m.* beneficiary.

beneficio, *m.* benefit, favor, kindness; labor; culture; profit, gain; advantage; benefit night; (com.) premium; **a — de,** for the benefit of.

benéfico, ca, *adj.* beneficent, kind.

benemérito, ta, *adj.* meritorious, worthy.

beneplácito, *m.* good will, approbation.

benevolencia, *f.* benevolence, kindness, good will, charity.

benévolo, la, *adj.* benevolent, charitable; favorable; kindhearted.

benignidad, *f.* benignity, kindliness; mildness of the weather.

benigno, na, *adj.* benign; kind; mild.

Benito, Benedict, Bennet.

benzoico, ca, *adj.* (chem.) benzoic.
benzol, *m.* (chem.) benzol.
beodez, *f.* intoxication, drunkenness.
beodo, da, *adj.* drunk, drunken.
berberís, *m.* (bot.) barberry, berberry.
bérbero, *m.* barberry; a confection made of barberry.
bercería, *f.* vegetable market.
bercero, ra, *n.* green grocer.
berenjena, *f.* eggplant.
bergamota, *f.* (bot.) bergamot.
bergamote or **bergamoto,** *m.* bergamot tree.
bergante, *m.* brazen-faced villain, ruffian.
bergantín, *m.* (naut.) brigantine, brig.
beriberi, *m.* (med.) beriberi, a disease.
berilo, *m.* beryl, a precious stone.
berlina, *f.* berlin, kind of carriage.
berlinés, esa, *n.* and *adj.* Berliner, of or from Berlin, a native of Berlin.
bermejear, *vn.* to incline to red.
bermejizo, za, *adj.* reddish.
bermejo, ja, *adj.* reddish; crimson.
bermejura, *f.* reddishness.
bermellón, *m.* vermilion.
Bernardo, Bernard.
bernardo, da, *n.* Bernardine monk or nun.
Bern.º Bernardo, Bern. Bernard.
berra, *f.* coarse watercress plant.
berrear, *vn.* to low, to bellow.
berrenchín, *m.* foaming of a wild boar; crying of angry children.
berrendo, da, *adj.* tinged with two different colors.
berrido, *m.* bellowing of a calf.
berrín, *m.* child in a tantrum.
berrinche, *m.* anger, bad humor, sulkiness.
berrizal, *m.* place full of watercress.
berro, *m.* watercress.
berroqueño, ña, *adj.* granitelike; **piedra —ña,** very hard, stone-like granite.
Berta, Bertha.
berza, *f.* cabbage.
besa la mano or **— los pies,** (expression of courtesy and respect).
besamanos, *m.* kissing of hands; reception; court day.
besar, *va.* to kiss; to touch closely (inanimate things); **—se,** to kiss one another; to knock one's head against another's accidentally.
beso, *m.* kiss; collision of persons or things.
bestia, *f.* beast; animal; dunce, idiot.
bestiaje, *m.* herd of beasts.
bestial, *adj.* bestial, brutal.
bestialidad, *f.* bestiality.
besucar, *vn.* = **besuquear.**
besugo, *m.* sea bream.
besuquear, to spoon, to kiss repeatedly.
besuqueo, *m.* repeated kisses.
betabel, *m.* (Mex.) beet.
betarraga or **betarrata,** *f.* (bot.) beet.
betún, *m.* bitumen; shoe polish.
bey, *m.* bey, Turkish governor; honorary title.

bezo, *m.* blubber lip; proud flesh in a wound.
biazas, *f. pl.* leather saddlebags.
biberón, *m.* nursing bottle.
Biblia, *f.* Bible.
bíblico, ca, *adj.* Biblical.
bibliófilo, la, *n.* booklover, bibliophile.
bibliografía, *f.* bibliography.
bibliográfico, ca, *adj.* bibliographical.
bibliógrafo, *m.* bibliographer.
bibliomanía, *f.* bibliomania.
bibliómano, na, *adj.* bibliomaniac.
biblioteca, *f.* library; **— por subscripción,** circulating library.
bibliotecario, ria, *n.* librarian.
bicarbonato, *m.* bicarbonate; **— de sosa,** baking soda.
bíceps, *m.* (anat.) biceps.
bicicleta, *f.* bicycle; **montar en —,** to ride a bicycle.
biciclista, *m.* and *f.* bicyclist.
bicloruro, *m.* (chem.) bichloride.
bicoca, *f.* small fort; trifle, thing of little value.
bicúspide, *adj.* bicuspid.
bicho, *m.* vermin; insect; **mal —,** mischievous urchin.
biela, *f.* connecting rod.
bielda, *f.* pitchfork with six or seven prongs.
bieldar, *va.* to winnow grain.
bieldo or **bielgo,** *m.* winnowing fork.
bien, *m.* good; utility; benefit; welfare; **—es,** *pl.* property, riches; land; **—,** *adv.* well; right; all right; very; willingly; **¡—! interj.** fine! good! all right! **antes —,** rather, on the contrary; **— de salud,** well; **— or mal acondicionado,** in good or bad condition; **—es muebles,** goods and chattels; **—es raíces** or **inmuebles,** real estate; **— que,** although; **¡está —!** very well! good!
bienal, *adj.* biennial.
bienandante, *adj.* happy, fortunate, lucky.
bienandanza, *f.* prosperity, success.
bienaventurado, da, *adj.* blessed, happy, fortunate; simple, silly.
bienaventuranza, *f.* beatitude; prosperity; **—s,** *pl.* the beatitudes in the Bible.
bienestar, *m.* well-being; welfare; comfort.
bienhablado, da, *adj.* well and civilly spoken.
bienhadado, da, *adj.* lucky, happy.
bienhecho, cha, *adj.* well-shaped; well-done.
bienhechor, ra, *adj.* humane; **—,** *n.* benefactor.
bienio, *m.* space of two years.
bienquerencia, *f.* good will; affection, fondness.
bienquerer, *va.* (IE) to hold in esteem, to like.
bienquistar, *va.* and *vr.* to reconcile, to adjust differences.
bienquisto, ta, *adj.* generally esteemed and beloved.
bienvenida, *f.* welcome.

bienvenido, da, *adj.* welcome.

bienvivir, *vn.* to live in comfort; to live honestly.

bifocal, *adj.* bifocal.

biftec, *m.* = **bistec.**

bifurcación, *f.* junction; bifurcation, forking.

bigamia, *f.* bigamy.

bígamo, ma, *n.* bigamist.

bigardear, *vn.* to live licentiously.

bigardía, *f.* dissoluteness; trick, turn; jest.

bigardo, *m.* friar of loose morals; bum, tramp.

bigornia, *f.* anvil.

bigote, *m.* mustache; (print.) dash rule; **tener —s,** to be firm and undaunted.

bilateral, *adj.* bilateral.

bilingüe, *adj.* bilingual.

bilioso, sa, *adj.* bilious.

bilis, *f.* bile.

billar, *m.* billiards.

billarista, *m.* billiard player.

billete, *m.* ticket; billet, label; note, short letter; love letter; banknote bill; **— de andén,** platform ticket; **— de banco,** banknote; **— de banco falso,** counterfeit note; **— de deferencia,** accommodation bill; **— de entrada,** admission ticket; **— de estación,** season ticket; **— de ida y vuelta,** round-trip ticket; **— del tesoro,** treasury note; **— directo,** through ticket; **— sencillo,** one-way ticket.

billetera, *f.* billfold.

billetero, ra, *n.* (Sp. Am.) person selling lottery tickets.

billón, *m.* billion (one million millions— 1,000,000,000,000—in Spain, England, and Germany).

billonario, ria, *n.* billionaire.

bimbo, *m.* (Col.) a turkey.

bimembre, *adj.* having two parts.

bimestral, *adj.* bimonthly.

bimestre, *adj.* bimonthly; **—,** *m.* space of two months, bimonthly rent, salary, etc.

bimetalismo, *m.* bimetallism, use of two combined metals for coins.

bimotor, ra, *adj.* two-motored.

binar, *va.* to plow a piece of ground for the second time.

binario, *m.* binary.

binazón, *f.* plowing a second time.

binóculo, *m.* opera glass; binocular.

biofísica, *f.* biophysics.

binomio, mia, *adj.* binomial; **—,** *m.* binomial; **—mio de Newton,** (math.) binomial theorem.

biogénesis, *f.* biogenesis.

biografía, *f.* biography.

biógrafo, *m.* biographer.

biol. biología, biol. biology.

biología, *f.* biology.

biombo, *m.* screen.

bioquímica, *f.* biochemistry.

bióxido, *m.* (chem.) dioxide.

bipartido, da, *adj.* bipartite.

bípedo, *m.* biped.

biplano, *m.* biplane.

biricú, *m.* sword belt.

birimbao, *m.* jew's harp.

birla, *f.* bowling pin.

birlar, *va.* in bowling, to throw the ball a second time from the place it stopped the first time; (coll.) to kill with one shot; to dispossess.

birlocha, *f.* paper kite.

birlocho, *m.* light, two-seated wagon without a top.

Birmania, *f.* Burma.

birreta, *f.* cardinal's red cap.

birretina, *f.* grenadier's cap.

bisabuela, *f.* great-grandmother.

bisabuelo, *m.* great-grandfather.

bisagra, *f.* hinge; shoemaker's polisher.

bisecar, *va.* to bisect.

bisección, *f.* bisection.

bisectriz, *f.* bisector.

bisel, *m.* bevel.

biselar, *va.* to bevel.

bisemanal, *adj.* semiweekly.

bisiesto, *adj.* bissextile; **año —,** leap year.

bismuto, *m.* bismuth.

bisojo, ja, *adj.* squint-eyed, cross-eyed.

bisonte, *m.* bison.

bisoñada or **bisoñería,** *f.* action or speech by some inexperienced person.

bisoño, ña, *adj.* raw, undisciplined; inexperienced; **—,** *n.* novice.

bistec, *m.* beefsteak; **— de filete,** tenderloin steak; **— de solomillo y filete,** porterhouse steak.

bisulfato, *m.* bisulphate.

bisulfito, *m.* bisulphide.

bisutería, *f.* cheap or imitation jewelry.

bitor, *m.* (orn.) rail.

bituminoso, sa, *adj.* bituminous.

bivalvo, va, *adj.* bivalve, having two valves; **—vo,** *m.* bivalve.

bizarramente, *adv.* courageously, gallantly.

bizarrear, *vn.* to act in a spirited and gallant manner.

bizarría, *f.* gallantry, valor; liberality, generosity.

bizarro, rra, *adj.* brave, gallant; high-spirited; generous.

bizco, ca, *adj.* squint-eyed, cross-eyed.

bizcochero, *m.* biscuit cask; maker or seller of biscuits or cakes.

bizcocho, *m.* biscuit; cake, ladyfinger; sea biscuit; whitewash made of old plaster.

bizma, *f.* poultice.

biznieta, *f.* great-granddaughter.

biznieto, *m.* great-grandson.

bizquear, *vn.* to squint.

Blanca, Blanche.

blanca, *f.* half a maravedi, an old Spanish coin; (mus.) minim; magpie.

blanco, ca, *adj.* white, blank; **—,** *m.* blank; (print.) blank form; target; **— directo,** direct hit; **carta en —,** blank credit; **dar**

en el —, to hit the target; **en** —, in vain; **ropa** — **a,** linen.

blancura, *f.* whiteness; hoariness.

blancuzco, ca, *adj.* somewhat white, whitish.

blandear, *va.* to soften; to make one change his opinion; —, *vn.* to yield; **—se,** to sway, to waver.

blandir, *va.* and *def.* to brandish or flourish (a sword, lance, etc.) ; **—se,** to quiver.

blando, da, *adj.* soft, smooth; mellow; lithe; mild, gentle.

blandón, *m.* wax taper; church candlestick.

blanducho, cha, *adj.* flabby, loose, insecure.

blandura, *f.* softness; daintiness, delicacy; gentleness of temper; mild temperature.

blanqueador, ra, *n.* bleacher (person or thing that bleaches).

blanqueadura, *f.* bleaching; whitening.

blanquear, *va.* to bleach; to whitewash; to give coarse wax to bees in winter; —, *vn.* to show whiteness, to become white.

blanquecer, *va.* (EZCO) to blanch (silver coins) ; to whiten.

blanquecino, na, *adj.* whitish.

blanqueo, *m.* whitening; whitewash; bleaching.

blanquete, *m.* a whitening cosmetic.

blanquición, *f.* blanching (silver coins).

blanquimiento, *m.* bleaching liquid.

blanquizco, ca, *adj.* whitish.

blasfemador, ra, *n.* blasphemer.

blasfemamente, *adv.* blasphemously.

blasfemar, *vn.* to blaspheme.

blasfematorio, ria, *adj.* blasphemous.

blasfemia, *f.* blasphemy; oath; gross verbal insult.

blasfemo, ma, *adj.* blasphemous; —, *n.* blasphemer.

blasón, *m.* heraldry, blazonry; honor, glory.

blasonador, ra, *n.* boaster, braggart.

blasonar, *va.* to blazon; —, *vn.* to blow one's own horn, to boast.

bledo, *m.* (bot.) wild amaranth; **no me importa un** —, I don't give a rap, I don't care.

blindado, da, *adj.* ironclad, ironplated.

B.L.M. or **b.l.m.** besa la mano (expression of courtesy and respect).

bloc, *m.* bloc, political group; pad (of paper).

blonda, *f.* broad silk lace.

blondo, da, *adj.* light-haired; fair.

bloque, *m.* block.

bloquear, *va.* to blockade.

bloqueo, *m.* blockade.

B.L.P. or **b.l.p.** besa los pies (expression of courtesy and respect).

blusa, *f.* blouse.

B.ᵐᵒ P.ᵉ Beatísimo Padre, Most Holy Father (the Pope).

boa, *f.* (zool.) boa; boa (feather scarf).

boato, *m.* ostentation, pompous show.

bobada, *f.* folly, foolishness.

bobático, ca, *adj.* silly, stupid.

bobear, *vn.* to act or talk foolishly; to dally; to loiter about.

bobería, *f.* folly, foolishness.

bóbilis, de — —, *adv.* without more ado.

bobina, *f.* bobbin; coil; spool; (elec.) coil.

bobo, ba, *n.* dunce, fool; stage clown; —, *adj.* stupid; silly, foolish.

boca, *f.* mouth; entrance, opening; mouth of a river; **a pedir de** —, to one's heart's content; — **a** —, by word of mouth; — **abajo,** face down, on the stomach; **de manos a** —, suddenly; **hacerse agua la** —, to make the mouth water.

bocacalle, *f.* street intersection or opening.

bocací or **bocacín,** *m.* buckram.

bocadear, *va.* to divide (something) into various morsels.

bocadillo, *m.* lunch given to laborers in the field; kind of sandwich.

bocado, *m.* morsel, mouthful.

bocal, *m.* pitcher; mouthpiece of a trumpet.

bocamanga, *f.* part of a sleeve near the wrist; armhole.

bocamina, *f.* entrance to a mine.

bocanada, *f.* mouthful of liquid; puff (of smoke, etc.) ; — **de gente,** crowd of people.

bocarte, *m.* crushing mill.

bocatejas, *f. pl.* ridge tiles.

bocel, *m.* fluting plane.

boceto, *m.* sketch.

bocina, *f.* bugle horn; speaking trumpet; automobile horn; blowgun.

bocinar, *va.* to sound the horn.

bocinazo, *m.* honking.

bocinero, *m.* hornblower.

bocio, *m.* goiter.

bocón, ona, *n.* wide-mouthed person; braggart.

bocoy, *m.* large barrel.

bocudo, da, *adj.* large-mouthed.

boche, *m.* small hole in the ground for boys' games; blow with a wooden ball; (coll.) contempt, slight; **dar** — **a uno,** to slight or scorn some one.

bochinche, *m.* (Sp. Am.) mob, disorder, tumult, uproar.

bochorno, *m.* sultry weather, scorching heat; blush; humiliation; embarrassment.

bochornoso, sa, *adj.* shameful, reproachful.

boda, *f.* nuptials, wedding; **—s de plata** or **de oro,** silver or golden wedding.

bodega, *f.* wine cellar; growth of wine; warehouse; grocery store; (naut.) hold of a ship.

bodegón, *m.* cheap little restaurant or tavern; still-life painting.

bodegonear, *vn.* to frequent cheap little restaurants.

bodegonero, *m.* keeper of a **bodegón.**

bodigo, *m.* small loaf of finest flour presented as an offering in church.

bodijo, *m.* unequal or secret marriage.

bodoque, *m.* pellet; dunce, idiot.

bodoquera, *f.* mold for clay pellets; blowgun.

bodorrio, *m.* unequal or secret marriage.

bodrio, *m.* poor soup made of leavings; hodgepodge.

bóer, *n.* and *adj.* Boer.

bofes, *m. pl.* lungs.

bofetada, *f.* slap, box on the ear.

bofetón, *m.* box on the ear; folding doors on the stage.

boga, *f.* vogue, fad, popularity; kind of fish; rowing; —, *m.* rower; **estar en —,** to be fashionable, to be in vogue.

bogada, *f.* stroke in rowing.

bogador, ra, *n.* rower.

bogar, *vn.* to row, to paddle.

Bohemia, *f.* Bohemia.

bohemiano, na, *n.* and *adj.* Bohemian.

bohémico, ca, *adj.* Bohemian.

bohemio, mia, *n.* and *adj.* Bohemian; —, *m.* short cloak formerly worn by the guard of archers; gypsy.

bohemo, ma, *n.* and *adj.* Bohemian.

bohío, *m.* (Sp. Am.) Indian hut, hovel, cabin.

boicot, *m.* boycott.

boicotear, *va.* and *vn.* to boycott.

boina, *f.* beret, Basque cap, flat, round, woolen cap.

boj, *m.* boxwood, box tree.

boja, *f.* southernwood.

bojar or **bojear,** *va.* to sail round an island or cape, and measure the coast line thereof; to scrape off the rough integuments of leather; —, *vn.* to measure around.

bojedal, *f.* plantation of box trees.

bojeo, *m.* circumnavigation.

bola, *f.* ball; globe; bolus; bowling; marble; (coll.) lie, fib; disturbance; **escurrir la —,** to take French leave, to run away.

bolazo, *m.* blow of a bowling ball.

bolchevique, *m.* and *f.* and *adj.* Bolshevik.

bolchevismo, *m.* Bolshevism.

bolchevista, *n.* and *adj.* Bolshevik.

bolea, *f.* throw; (tennis) volley; **— alta,** (tennis) smash.

bolear, *vn.* to knock the balls about (billiards); to throw wooden balls; (Mex.) to shine shoes; to fail in a subject; to reject.

boleo, *m.* Spanish dance; bowling green.

bolero, *m.* Spanish dancer; Andalusian dance; runaway child; (Mex.) top hat; bootblack.

boleta, *f.* entrance ticket; soldier's billet; ballot.

boletero, *m.* ticket collector.

boletín, *m.* bulletin; warrant for payment of money; ticket for quartering of soldiers; **— de cotización,** list of quotations; **— meteorológico,** weather report.

boleto, *m.* ticket; **— de entrada,** admission ticket; **— de ida y vuelta,** round-trip ticket.

boliche, *m.* jack; small ball for bowling; small fish caught in a dragnet near the shore; dragnet.

bólido, *m.* shooting star.

bolillo, *m.* small bowling ball; bobbin; starching frame; (Mex.) kind of bread roll; **—s,** *pl.* starched cuffs.

bolina, *f.* noise, scuffle; (naut.) bowline; **ir a la —,** to sail on a wind.

bolívar, *m.* a coin of Venezuela.

boliviano, na, *adj.* and *n.* Bolivian; —, *m.* a Bolivian coin.

bolo, *m.* bowling pin, tenpin or ninepin; bolo (knife); notchboard of a winding staircase; **—s,** *pl.* bowling, game of tenpins or ninepins.

bolsa, *f.* purse, pouch; case; money exchange; stock exchange; richest vein of gold in a mine; **— de comercio** or **financiera,** stock exchange; **— para tabaco,** tobacco pouch; **corredor de —,** stock broker, exchange broker; **jugar a la —,** to speculate in stocks.

bolsería, *f.* purse factory.

bolsillo, *m.* pocket; money, funds.

bolsín, *m.* place where brokers meet out of exchange hours.

bolsista, *m.* speculator; stockbroker; jobber.

bolso, *m.* purse of money.

bollería, *f.* bakery shop.

bollero, ra, *n.* pastry cook.

bollo, *m.* small loaf or roll, penny roll, biscuit; cake, cooky.

bollón, *m.* brass-headed nail.

bollonado, da, *adj.* adorned with brass-headed nails.

bomba, *f.* pump; bomb; shell; **a prueba de —,** bombproof; **— de alimentación,** feed pump; **— de apagar incendio,** fire engine; **— de carena,** bilge pump; **— de circulación,** circulating pump; **— de compresión, — de impelente,** force pump; **— de fragmentación,** fragmentation bomb; **— de profundidad,** depth charge; **— de vacío,** vacuum pump; **— de vapor,** steam engine.

bombachos, *m. pl.* slacks.

bombardear, *va.* to bombard.

bombardeo, *m.* bombardment.

bombardero, *m.* bombardier; **— de pique,** dive bomber.

bombardino, *m.* (mus.) saxhorn.

bombasí, *m.* bombazine, dimity.

bombazo, *m.* report of a bursting bomb; throwing of a bomb.

bombeo, *m.* pumping.

bombero, *m.* fireman; pumper; (mil.) howitzer.

bombilla, *f.* light bulb; (Sp. Am.) a tube to sip maté.

bombo, *m.* large drum, bass drum.

bombón, *m.* bonbon, candy.

bonachón, ona, *n.* and *adj.* good-natured (person).

bonaerense, *m.* and *f.* and *adj.* native of or pertaining to Buenos Aires.

bonancible, *adj.* calm, fair, serene (of weather).

bonanza, *f.* fair weather; bonanza, abundance, wealth, prosperity, success.

bonazo, za, *adj.* good-natured, kind.

bondad, *f.* goodness; bounty; suavity; kindness, courtesy; excellence, healthfulness; **tenga la — de,** have the kindness to, please.

bondadoso, sa, *adj.* bountiful; kind; good-natured; **poco —,** unkind.

bonetada, *f.* salutation by raising the hat.

bonete, *m.* clerical hat; college cap; secular clergyman.

bonetería, *f.* hat-making; hat shop.

bonetero, *m.* cap or hat maker.

bongo, *m.* canoe used by Central American Indians; (Cuba) large river boat.

bonhomía, *f.* honesty; naiveté, simplicity.

boniato, *m.* sweet potato.

bonico, ca, *adj.* quite good, passable.

bonificación, *f.* allowance, bonus.

bonito, ta, *adj.* pretty; quite good, passable; affecting elegance and neatness; graceful; effeminate.

bonizal, *m.* cornfield.

bono, *m.* (com.) bond, certificate; **—s de gobierno,** government bonds.

boñiga, *f.* cow dung.

boqueada, *f.* act of opening the mouth; **la última —,** the last gasp.

boquear, *vn.* to gape, to gasp; to breathe one's last; **—,** *va.* to pronounce, to utter (a word).

boquera, *f.* sluice in an irrigating canal; eruption at the corners of the mouth.

boquerón, *m.* anchovy; large hole.

boquete, *m.* gap, narrow entrance.

boquiabierto, ta, *adj.* open-mouthed, gaping.

boquiancho, cha, *adj.* wide-mouthed.

boquiangosto, ta, *adj.* narrow-mouthed.

boquiduro, ra, *adj.* hard-mouthed (of horses).

boquifresco, ca, *adj.* fresh-mouthed (applied to horses).

boquifruncido, da, *adj.* having the mouth contracted.

boquihundido, da, *adj.* having the mouth sunk in from age or lack of teeth.

boquilla, *f.* little mouth; mouthpiece of a musical instrument or a pipe; cigar or cigarette holder; nozzle (of a hose).

boquirroto, ta, *adj.* loquacious, garrulous.

boquirrubio, bia, *adj.* (fig.) simple, easily imposed upon.

boquiseco, ca, *adj.* dry-mouthed.

boquituerto, ta, *adj.* wry-mouthed.

borato, *m.* borate.

bórax, *m.* borax.

borbollar, *vn.* to bubble out.

borbollón, *m.* bubbling; **a —ones,** hurriedly, impetuously.

borbotón, *m.* bubbling; gushing of water; **hablar a —es,** to speak in torrents.

borceguí, *m.* buskin, half boot.

borda, *f.* hut, cottage; (naut.) gun-wale.

bordado, *m.* embroidery.

bordador, ra, *n.* embroiderer.

bordadura, *f.* embroidery.

bordaje, *m.* side planks of a ship.

bordar, *va.* to embroider; to do anything artistically; **seda de —,** embroidery silk.

borde, *m.* border; edge, rim, fringe; margin; (naut.) board; **— de la acera,** curb.

bordear, *vn.* to border; (naut.) to ply to windward.

bordo, *m.* board; the side of a ship; (naut.) **a —,** on board; **franco a —,** free on board (f.o.b.).

bordón, *m.* pilgrim's staff; bass of a stringed musical instrument.

bordonero, ra, *n.* vagabond, roamer.

boreal, *adj.* boreal, northern.

Bóreas, *m.* Boreas, north wind.

Borgoña, *f.* Burgundy.

borgoña, *m.* Burgundy (wine.)

borgoñés, esa, or **borgoñón, ona,** *n.* and *adj.* Burgundian.

bórico, *adj.* boric; **ácido —,** boric acid.

borinqueño, ña, *n.* and *adj.* Puerto Rican

borla, *f.* tassel; tuft; doctor's hood; **— de empolvarse,** powder puff.

bornear, *va.* to bend, to turn or twist; (naut.) to swing the anchor around.

borní, *m.* (orn.) lanner (falcon).

borona, *f.* a grain similar to corn; bread made from the grain.

borra, *f.* yearling ewe; goat's hair; nap raised on cloth by shearers; hairy wool.

borrachear, *vn.* to be drunk, to get drunk habitually.

borrachera, *f.* drunkenness; hard drinking; revelry; madness.

borrachez, *f.* intoxication.

borracho, cha, *adj.* drunk, intoxicated; frenzied, infuriated.

borrachón, ona, *n.* great drinker, tippler.

borrachuela, *f.* (bot.) darnel.

borrador, *m.* eraser; rough draft.

borraja, *f.* (bot.) borage.

borrajear, *va.* and *vn.* to scribble.

borrar, *va.* to erase, blot, or efface a writing; to blur; to cloud, to obscure.

borrasca, *f.* storm, violent squall of wind; hazard, danger.

borrascoso, sa, *adj.* stormy.

borrasquero, ra, *n.* reveler.

borregada, *f.* large flock of sheep or lambs.

borrego, ga, *n.* yearling lamb; simpleton, blockhead.

borreguero, *m.* shepherd who tends lambs.

borrén, *m.* panel of a saddle.

borrica, *f.* she-ass, jenny.

borricada, *f.* drove of asses; cavalcade on asses; foolish action.

borrico, *m.* ass; blockhead.

borrilla, *f.* down or bloom on fruit.

borriqueño, ña, *adj.* asinine.

borriquero, *m.* one who drives asses.

borro, *m.* wether under two years of age; dolt.

borrón, *m.* ink blot, splotch, stain, tarnish;

blur; rough draft of a writing; first sketch of a painting; stigma.

borronear, *va.* to sketch, to scribble.

borroso, sa, *adj.* indistinct, blurred.

boruca, *f.* noise, clamor, excitement.

borujo, *m.* clot, lump; knot (in yarn).

boscaje, *m.* boscage; landscape (in painting).

Bosforo, *m.* Bosporus.

bosque, *m.* forest, grove, woods.

bosquejar, *va.* to make a sketch of a painting; to explain a thought rather obscurely; to make a rough model of a figure.

bosquejo, *m.* outline, sketch, summary; sketch of a drawing.

bosta, *f.* manure.

bostezar, *vn.* to yawn; to gape.

bostezo, *m.* yawn, yawning.

bot. botánica, bot. botany.

bota, *f.* wine bag; water cask; boot; — **de dos suelas,** double-soled boot; — **de montar,** riding boot.

botador, *m.* driver; punch (tool); kind of forceps.

botafuego, *m.* linstock (staff to hold a match for firing cannon).

botalón, *m.* (naut., mech.) boom.

botana, *f.* plug, stopper; scar.

botánica, *f.* botany.

botánico, ca, *adj.* botanical.

botánico, ca, or **botanista,** *n.* botanist.

botar, *va.* to cast, to fling, to throw; to launch.

botaratada, *f.* act or saying typical of a reckless person.

botarate, *m.* and *f.* madcap; spendthrift.

botarel, *m.* (arch.) abutment, support.

botarga, *f.* gaiters; harlequin's costume; harlequin; buffoon.

botavante, *m.* (naut.) grappling iron.

bote, *m.* boat, canoe; thrust with a pike or lance; rebound of a ball; (aer.) air gust "bump"; (Mex.) jail; — **automóvil** or **de gasolina,** motorboat, powerboat; — **salvavidas,** lifeboat; — **de sifón,** siphon bottle; **de — en —,** jammed.

botella, *f.* bottle, flask.

botequín, *m.* small boat.

botica, *f.* drugstore, pharmacy; saloon.

boticario, *m.* druggist, pharmacist.

botija, *f.* earthen jar with a short and narrow neck.

botijo or **botijón,** *m.* round earthen jar; plump little child.

botilla, *f.* small wine bag; woman's half boot.

botillería, *f.* ice-cream parlor; place where drinks are sold.

botillero, *m.* preparer or seller of iced liquids.

botín, *m.* buskin, half boot; legging, gaiter; booty, loot, spoils.

botina, *f.* kind of boot worn by women.

botinero, *m.* (mil.) booty guard; one who makes or sells gaiters.

botiquín, *m.* first-aid kit.

botivoleo, *m.* catching of a ball on the rebound.

boto, ta, *adj.* blunt; slow in understanding; —, *m.* leather bag for storing wine, lard, etc.

botón, *m.* button; bud; — **de contacto,** push button; — **de llamada,** call button; — **de manivela,** crankpin; **corchete de** —, buttonhook.

botonadura, *f.* set of buttons for a suit of clothes.

botonazo, *m.* thrust with a fencing foil.

botonero, ra, *n.* button maker; button seller.

bóveda, *f.* arch; vault; crypt; (arch.) apse.

bovino, na, *adj.* bovine.

boxeador, *m.* boxer, pugilist, prizefighter.

boxear, *vn.* to box.

boxeo, *m.* boxing, pugilism.

boya, *f.* (naut.) buoy; piece of cork fastened to a fishing net.

boyada, *f.* drove of oxen.

boyar, *vn.* to buoy, to be afloat.

boyera or **boyeriza,** *f.* ox stall, cow house.

boyero, *m.* ox herd; ox driver.

boyezuelo, *m.* young ox.

bozal, *m.* muzzle; —, *adj.* novice, inexperienced; pure, unmixed (of Negroes).

bozas, *f. pl.* (naut.) stoppers.

bozo, *m.* down which precedes the beard; headstall of a horse.

B.p. bendición papal, papal benediction.

brabante, *m.* Brabant or Flemish linen.

braceada, *f.* violent movement of the arms.

braceaje, *m.* coinage; coining of money; (naut.) depth of water.

bracear, *vn.* to swing the arms; —, *va.* (naut.) to brace.

bracero, *m.* day laborer; strong-armed man; **ir de** —, to walk arm in arm.

bracete, *m.* arm; **de** —, arm in arm.

Bracmán, *m.* Brahman.

braco, ca, *adj.* flat-nosed; —, *m.* pointer (dog).

braga, *f.* baby's diaper; —**s,** *pl.* breeches, trousers, pants, knickers.

bragadura, *f.* fork of the body; crotch of a pair of pants.

bragazas, *f. pl.* wide pants; —, *m.* (coll.) man who is easily dominated, particularly by women.

braguero, *m.* truss; bandage for a rupture.

bragueta, *f.* front opening of breeches or trousers.

braguillas, *f. pl.* little breeches; child wearing the first trousers; dwarfish person.

Brahmán, *m.* Brahman.

brama, *f.* rut, mating time (of animals).

bramadera, *f.* rattle.

bramadero, *m.* rutting place.

bramante, *m.* packthread, twine; Brabant linen; —, *adj.* roaring.

bramar, *vn.* to roar, to bellow; to storm, to bluster; to be in a fury.

bramido, *m.* cry uttered by wild beasts;

clamor of persons enraged; roaring of the elements.

brancada, *f.* dragnet, sweepnet.

branquias, *f. pl.* fish gills.

brasa, *f.* live coal; **estar hecho unas —s,** to be all in a blaze; to be flushed.

brasero, *m.* brazier, hearth.

Brasil, *m.* Brazil.

brasil, *m.* brazilwood; rouge.

brasilado, da, *adj.* ruddy.

brasileño, ña, *n.* and *adj.* Brazilian.

brasilero, ra, *adj.* (Sp. Am.) Brazilian.

brasmología, *f.* study of the rising and falling of the tides.

bravamente, *adv.* bravely, gallantly; cruelly; finely, extremely well.

bravata, *f.* bravado, boast, braggadocio.

braveador, ra, *n.* bully.

bravear, *vn.* to bully, to hector.

braveza, *f.* fury of the elements; bravery.

bravío, vía, *adj.* ferocious, savage, wild; coarse; **—,** *m.* fierceness, savageness.

bravo, va, *adj.* brave, valiant; bullying; savage, fierce; rude, unpolished; sumptuous; excellent, fine; **¡—!** *interj.* bravo!

bravura, *f.* ferocity; bravery; courage; bravado, boast.

braza, *f.* fathom.

brazada, *f.* extension of the arms; armful.

brazado, *m.* armful.

brazaje, *m.* (naut.) number of fathoms, depth of water.

brazal, *m.* bracer (piece of armor); biceps; arm pad of wood or leather.

brazalete, *m.* bracelet.

brazo, *m.* arm; branch of a tree; valor, strength, power; **— a —,** man to man; **a — partido,** with bare hands; **—s,** *pl.* hands, man power.

brazuelo, *m.* small arm; foreleg of animals; branch of the mouthbit of a bridle.

brea, *f.* pitch, tar; coarse cloth.

brear, *va.* to pitch, to tar; to vex, to plague; to play a joke on.

brebaje, *m.* beverage.

brecha, *f.* breach; gap; impression on the mind; **batir en —,** (mil.) to make a breach; to persecute.

brega, *f.* strife, struggle, contest; pun; joke, trick.

bregar, *vn.* to contend, to struggle; to struggle with difficulties; **—,** *va.* to work up dough on a board with a rolling pin.

breña, *f.* craggy, broken ground full of brakes and brambles.

breñal or **breñar,** *m.* briars, underbrush.

breñoso, sa, *adj.* craggy and brambled.

bresca, *f.* honeycomb.

brescar, *va.* to take honeycombs (from beehive).

Bretaña, *f.* Brittany; **Gran —,** Great Britain.

brete, *m.* fetters, shackles; (fig.) perplexity; difficulties.

bretón, ona, *n.* and *adj.* Breton; Briton.

bretones, *m. pl.* Brussels sprouts.

breva, *f.* early fig; early large acorn; a kind of cigar.

breval, *m.* (bot.) early fig tree.

breve, *m.* apostolic brief; (mus.) breve; **—,** *adj.* brief, short; **en —,** shortly.

brevedad, *f.* brevity, shortness, conciseness.

breviario, *m.* breviary; abridgement; brevier (small letter used in printing).

brezal, *m.* heath.

brezo, *m.* (bot.) heather.

briaga, *f.* rope made of bassweed.

briba, *f.* truancy, idleness.

bribón, ona, *adj.* vagrant; knavish, rascally; **—,** *n.* vagrant, tramp, bum; rogue, scoundrel.

bribonada, *f.* knavery, mischievous trick.

bribonear, *vn.* to rove; to lead a vagrant life.

bribonería, *f.* life of a vagrant; rascality.

bric a brac, *m.* bric-a-brac.

brida, *f.* bridle; horsemanship; (fig.) restraint, check, curb.

bridar, *va.* to bridle; to curb.

brigada, *f.* brigade.

brigadier, *m.* brigadier, brigadier general.

Brígida, Bridget.

brigola, *f.* battering ram.

brillador, ra, *adj.* brilliant, radiant.

brillante, *adj.* brilliant, bright, shining; **—,** *m.* brilliant, diamond.

brillantez, *f.* brilliancy, brightness.

brillantina, *f.* brilliantine.

brillar, *vn.* to shine, to sparkle, to glisten; to outshine in talents or merits.

brillo, *m.* brilliancy, brightness, splendor.

brincador, ra, *n.* jumper, leaper.

brincar, *vn.* to leap, to jump, to gambol; to omit something; to fly into a rage.

brinco, *m.* leap, jump, bounce; gambol; **dar —s,** to leap.

brindar, *vn.* to drink one's health, to toast; to salute (in a bullfight); **—,** *va.* to invite; to allure; to offer; **—se a,** to offer one's services.

brindis, *m.* health, toast.

brío, *m.* strength, vigor; spirit, courage.

briol, *m.* (naut.) bunt line.

briolín, *m.* (naut.) slab line.

briosamente, *adv.* spiritedly, courageously.

brioso, sa, *adj.* vigorous, fiery; full of spirit; courageous, lively.

briqueta, *f.* briquette.

brisa, *f.* breeze.

brisca, *f.* a card game.

briscar, *va.* to embroider with gold or silver twist mixed with silk.

bristol, *m.* Bristol board, Bristol paper.

británico, ca, *adj.* and *n.* British, Britisher.

brizar, *va.* to rock (the cradle).

brizna, *f.* fragment; blade.

brl. barril, bbl. barrel.

broca, *f.* spool for thread; drill; shoemaker's tack.

brocado, *m.* gold or silver brocade; **—, da,**

adj. embroidered, like brocade.

brocal, *m.* curbstone; metal rim of the scabbard of a sword.

brocatel, *m.* cloth made of hemp and silk.

bróculi, *m.* broccoli.

brocha, *f.* painter's brush; pencil.

brochada, *f.* stroke with a brush.

brochado, da, *adj.* figured (of cloth).

brochadura, *f.* set of hooks and eyes or fasteners.

broche, *m.* clasp; brooch.

brochón, *m.* large brush; plasterer's brush.

broma, *f.* clatter, noise; joke, jest; **dar —,** to tease; **tomar a —,** to take as a joke.

bromato, *m.* bromate.

bromear, *vn.* to jest, to joke.

bromhidrato, *m.* hydrobromide.

bromista, *m.* and *f.* joker, merry person, jolly companion.

bromuro, *m.* bromide.

bronca, *f.* quarrel.

bronce, *m.* bronze, brass, gun metal; (poet.) trumpet, bell.

bronceado, da, *adj.* bronzed; **—,** *m.* bronze color finish.

broncear, *va.* to bronze.

broncería, *f.* brassworks; brassware.

broncista, *m.* worker in bronze.

bronco, ca, *adj.* rough, coarse; crusty; crabbed; rude, hoarse; harsh (sounding).

bronconeumonía, *f.* bronchopneumonia.

bronquio, *m.* bronchial tube.

bronquitis, *f.* bronchitis.

broquel, *m.* shield, buckler; (fig.) support, protection; **rajar —es,** to bully, to swagger.

brotadura, *f.* budding.

brotar, *vn.* to bud, to germinate, to grow; to gush, to rush out; to break out, to appear (said of a disease).

brote, *m.* bud (of trees); shoot; crumb, bit.

broza, *f.* bark; vegetable rubbish; brushwood; printer's brush.

brozar, *va.* to brush (type).

brucero, *m.* one who makes or sells brushes or brooms.

bruces, a — or **de —,** face downward.

bruja, *f.* witch, hag; (Sp. Am.) a person temporarily out of money.

brujear, *vn.* to practice witchcraft.

brujería, *f.* witchcraft.

brujidor, *m.* glaziers' nippers.

brujir, *va.* to pare off the corners and edges (of glass).

brujo, *m.* sorcerer.

brújula, *f.* compass; magnetic needle; **— giroscópica,** gyrocompass.

brujulear, *va.* to turn up one card after another; to discover by deduction; to conjecture.

brujuleo, *m.* exposure of cards (in card games); close examination; conjecture.

brulote, *m.* fire ship.

bruma, *f.* mist, haze.

brumal, *adj.* wintry.

brumoso, sa, *adj.* misty, vague, hazy.

bruno, na, *adj.* dark brown.

bruñido, *m.* polish, burnish.

bruñidor, *m.* burnisher (person and instrument).

bruñir, *va.* to burnish; to polish; to put on rouge.

brusco, ca, *adj.* rude, gruff, peevish, forward.

Bruselas, *f.* Brussels.

brusquedad, *f.* rudeness.

brutal, *adj.* brutal, brutish; **—,** *m.* brute, rude person.

brutalidad, *f.* brutality; brutal action.

bruto, *m.* brute, beast, blockhead; **—, ta,** *adj.* brutal, stupid; crude (ore, oil, etc.); gross (profits, etc.); coarse, unpolished, in a rough state; **en —,** in a raw (unmanufactured) state, as **lino en —,** raw flax; in a coarse, unpolished, or rough state, as **diamante en —,** a rough diamond; **peso —,** gross weight.

bto.: bulto, pkg. package; **bruto,** gross (profits, etc.).

¡bu! *interj.* boo!

buba, *f.* pustule; bubo; **—s,** *pl.* (med.) buboes.

bubático, ca, *adj.* suffering from buboes.

bubilla, *f.* pimple, pustule.

bubón, *m.* large morbid tumor filled with matter.

bubónico, ca, *adj.* bubonic.

buboso, sa, *adj.* suffering from buboes.

bucanero, *m.* buccaneer.

bucarán, *m.* buckram.

Bucarest, *f.* Bucharest.

bucear, *vn.* to dive.

bucéfalo, *m.* Bucephalus; (coll.) rough, stupid person.

buceo, *m.* diving.

bucero, *adj.* black-nosed (applied to a hound).

bucle, *m.* curl.

bucólico, ca, *adj.* pastoral, rural, bucolic; **—,** *f.* pastoral poetry; (coll.) food.

buche, *m.* craw, crop, stomach of quadrupeds; mouthful; suckling ass; pucker or crease in clothes; (fig.) girl's bosom.

buchete, *m.* blown-out cheek.

Buda, Buddha.

buen, *adj.* good; **hacer — tiempo,** to be good weather; **tener — éxito,** to be successful.

buenamente, *adv.* easily, commodiously.

buenaventura, *f.* fortune, good luck.

bueno, na, *adj.* good, perfect; fair, plain; fit, proper; sociable, agreeable; strong; sound, healthy; useful; fine, liberal; well; **dar —na acogida,** to honor (a draft); **estar —,** to be well; **—no!** *interj.* all right! **¿de donde —no?** where do you come from? **de —na gana,** freely, willingly; **—no,** *adv.* enough, sufficiently; **—no esta,** enough, no more.

buey, *m.* ox, bullock.

¡buf! *interj.* pooh, pooh!

bufa, *f.* jeer, scoff, taunt, mock; (Cuba) drunkenness.

búfala, *f.* female buffalo.

bufalino, na, *adj.* pertaining to buffaloes.

búfalo, *m.* buffalo.

bufanda, *f.* scarf.

bufar, *vn.* to choke with anger; to huff; to snort.

bufete, *m.* desk, writing table; lawyer's office.

bufido, *m.* blowing of an animal; snorting of a horse; huff.

bufo, *m.* buffoon on the stage; —, **fa,** *adj.* comic; **ópera —fa,** comic opera.

bufón, *m.* buffoon; jester; —, **ona,** *adj.* funny, comical.

bufonada, *f.* buffoonery; raillery, sarcastic taunt.

bufonearse, *vr.* to jest, to make fun of.

bufonería, *f.* buffoonery.

buglosa, *f.* (bot.) bugloss, alkanet.

buhardilla, *f.* small garret, attic; dormer.

buhedera, *f.* embrasure, loophole.

buhero, *m.* owlkeeper.

buho, *m.* owl; an unsocial man.

buhonería, *f.* peddler's box.

buhonero, *m.* peddler, hawker.

buitre, *m.* vulture.

buitrero, *m.* vulture fowler; —, **ra,** *adj.* vulturine.

buje, *m.* bushing; axle box.

bujería, *f.* gewgaw, bauble, knickknack.

bujeta, *f.* box made of boxwood; perfume box.

bujía, *f.* spark plug; candle; candlestick; **— de cera,** wax candle; **— eléctrica,** electric lamp.

bula, *f.* papal bull.

bulbo, *m.* (bot.) bulb.

bulboso, sa, *adj.* bulbous.

buleto, *m.* apostolic letter.

bulevar, *m.* boulevard, parkway.

búlgaro, ra, *n.* and *adj.* Bulgarian.

bulto, *m.* bulk; mass; parcel; package; bundle; tumor, swelling; bust; luggage; baggage; **—s a la mano,** *pl.* (rail.) hand luggage; **a —,** indistinctly, confusedly; **en —,** by the lump; **comprar en —,** to purchase in a lump.

bulla, *f.* confused noise, clatter; crowd.

bullaje, *m.* noisy crowd; confusion caused by noisy crowd.

bullanguero, ra, *n.* noisy, turbulent person.

bullebulle, *m.* busybody.

bullicio, *m.* bustle; tumult, uproar; merry-making.

bullicioso, sa, *adj.* lively, restless, noisy, clamorous, busy; turbulent; boisterous.

bullidor, ra, *adj.* noisy; turbulent.

bullir, *vn.* (UYO) to boil; (fig.) to bustle, to hustle; —, *va.* to move, to stir.

bullón, *m.* boiling dye; metallic device to protect large book covers; type of knife used in olden times.

bumerang, *m.* boomerang.

buñolero, ra, *n.* maker or seller of buns.

buñuelo, *m.* bun; pancake, fritter, doughnut.

buque, *m.* boat, ship, vessel; bulk, capacity of a ship; hull of a ship; **— explorador,** scouting ship; **— fanal,** lightship; **— de guerra,** man-of-war; **— mercante,** merchant ship; **— petrolero,** tanker; **— taller,** repair ship; **— de torres,** turreted man-of-war; **— de vapor,** steamer; **— de vela,** sailboat.

buqueteatro, *m.* showboat.

burdel, *m.* brothel.

burdo, da, *adj.* coarse (of cloth); ordinary.

bureta, *f.* drop measurer.

burga, *f.* hot springs; spa.

burgomaestre, *m.* burgomaster.

burgués, esa, *adj.* bourgeois.

burguesía, *f.* bourgeoisie.

buril, *m.* burin, graver.

burilada, *f.* stroke of a burin.

buriladura, *f.* engraving.

burilar, *va.* to engrave with a graver.

burla, *f.* scoff, mockery, sneer; trick, slight deceit; hoax; **de —,** in jest; **hacer una —,** to play a joke.

burlar, *va.* to mock, to scoff; to hoax, to abuse, to play tricks, to deceive; to frustrate; **—se de,** to make fun of, to laugh at.

burlería, *f.* mockery, deceit; fabulous story; ridicule.

burlesco, ca, *adj.* burlesque, comical, funny.

burlón, ona, *n.* and *adj.* great wag; scoffer, insincere.

buró, *m.* bureau, chest of drawers.

burocracia, *f.* bureaucracy.

burocrático, ca, *adj.* bureaucratic.

burra, *f.* she-ass.

burrada, *f.* drove of asses; stupid action.

burrajo, *m.* dry stable dung for fuel.

burrero, *m.* asskeeper who sells asses' milk; (Mex.) owner or driver of donkeys.

burro, *m.* ass, donkey; stupid fellow; sawhorse.

bursátil, *adj.* relating to the bourse or exchange.

bus, *m.* bus (vehicle).

busca, *f.* search, examination; **en — de,** in search of.

buscada, *f.* research, inquiry.

buscador, ra, *n.* seeker, searcher, investigator.

buscapié, *m.* hint.

buscapiés, *m.* firecracker.

buscar, *va.* to seek, to search; to look for or after; to hunt after; to fetch; **ir a —,** to get (go after).

buscarruidos, *m.* quarrelsome fellow.

buscavidas, *m.* and *f.* prying person, spy, busybody.

buscón, *m.* searcher; cheat, pilferer, petty robber.

búsqueda, *f.* search.

busto, *m.* bust.

butaca, *f.* armchair; orchestra seat in a theater.

butadieno, *m.* butadiene.

butifarra, *f.* sausage made in Catalonia; **—as,** *pl.* gaiters; (Peru) kind of ham sandwich.

butílico, ca, *adj.* butylic.

butilo, *m.* butyl.

buzardas, *f. pl.* (naut.) breasthooks.

buzo, *m.* diver.

buzón, *m.* conduit, canal; mailbox; letter drop; cover of a cistern, pond, jar.

C

C. centígrado, C. Centigrade.

c.: capítulo, ch. or chap. chapter; **compañía,** co. company; **cuenta,** (com.) acc. or acct. account; **corriente,** c. or cur. current.

c/: cargo, (com.) cargo, charge; **contra,** against; **corriente,** current; **caja,** bx. box.

C.A. corriente alterna, A.C. alternating current.

c.ª compañía, co. company.

c/a. cuenta abierta, (com.) open account.

cabal, *adj.* just, exact; perfect, thorough, complete, accomplished.

cábala, *f.* cabala (mystical science); intrigue.

cabalgada, *f.* horseback excursion; cavalcade; (mil.) foray.

cabalgador, *m.* rider; horseman.

cabalgadura, *f.* sumpter mule, sumpter horse, beast of burden.

cabalgar, *vn.* ride on horseback; to take part in a cavalcade; to spring to horse.

cabalgata, *f.* cavalcade.

cabalístico, ca, *adj.* cabalistic.

cabalia, *f.* horse mackerel (fish).

caballaje, *m.* place where mares and she-asses are served by stallions; money paid for that service.

caballar, *adj.* equine.

caballear, *vn.* to go horseback riding often.

caballejo, *m.* nag; wooden frame for shoeing unruly horses.

caballerear, *vn.* to set up as a gentleman.

caballeresco, ca, *adj.* knightly; chivalrous; courteous.

caballerete, *m.* (coll.) fine young gentleman.

caballería, *f.* cavalry; cavalry horse; chivalry; knighthood; knight-errantry.

caballeriza, *f.* stable; number of horses, mules, etc., standing in a stable.

caballerizo, *m.* head groom of a stable.

caballero, *m.* knight; cavalier; gentleman; rider; horseman; **— andante** or **errante,** knight-errant.

caballerosidad, *f.* chivalry, nobleness, honorable behavior.

caballeroso, sa, *adj.* noble, gentlemanly.

caballerote, *m.* graceless, unpolished gentleman.

caballeta, *f.* field cricket.

caballete, *m.* ridge of a roof; trestle; sawhorse; horse (instrument of torture); painter's easel; hemp brake.

caballico, *m.* hobbyhorse, rocking horse.

caballista, *m.* horseman; good rider.

caballitos, *m. pl.* little horses; (coll.) merry-go-round.

caballo, *m.* horse; knight (in chess); **a —,** on horseback; **— de fuerza** or **potencia,** horsepower.

caballuno, na, *adj.* belonging to a horse.

cabaña, *f.* hut, cabin, shed, cottage; hovel; flock of ewes; drove of asses; line drawn on a billiard table, within which the players must play.

cabañal, *m.* mule or sheep track (of traveling or migratory herds).

cabañero, ra, *adj.* belonging to the droves of traveling mules and asses.

cabañil, *m.* keeper of a drove of mules or asses.

cabaret, *m.* cabaret, night club.

cabecear, *vn.* to nod with sleep; to shake one's head; (naut.) to pitch.

cabeceo, *m.* nod, shaking of the head; (aer.) pitching of a plane).

cabecera, *f.* beginning, chief part, upper end; head of a bed; pillow or bolster; headwaters; vignette; **médico de —,** attending physician.

cabecilla, *m.* ringleader.

cabellera, *f.* long hair spread over the shoulders; wig, head of hair; tail of a comet.

cabello, *m.* hair of the head.

cabelludo, da, *adj.* hairy, overgrown with hair; **cuero —,** scalp.

caber, *va.* and *vn.* (QUEPO, CUPE) to comprehend; to contain, to include; to fit; to be possible.

cabestraje, *m.* halter; money paid to a driver for conducting cattle to market.

cabestrar, *va.* to halter; to lead by a halter.

cabestrear, *vn.* to be led easily by the halter.

cabestrillo, *m.* sling, splint; necklace; gold chain.

cabestro, *m.* halter; leading ox.

cabeza, *f.* head; top; end; chief; leader; beginning of a thing; **— de partido,** county seat; **— de puente,** bridgehead; **por —,** per capita.

cabezada, *f.* headshake; headstall of a bridle; headband of a book; instep of a shoe.

cabezal, *m.* pillow; compress; post of a door.

cabezo, *m.* summit of a hill.

cabezón, ona, *adj.* big-headed; stubborn; **—,** *m.* collar of a shirt; opening in a garment for the passage of the head; noseband (for horses).

cabezorro, *m.* large, disproportionate head.

cabezudo, da, *adj.* big-headed; headstrong, obstinate.

cabezuela, *f.* small head; simpleton; coarse flour; rosebud for making rose water.

cabida, *f.* content, capacity; seating capacity; **tener — con una persona,** to be in high favor with one.

cabildear, *vn.* to lobby.

cabildeo, *m.* lobbying.

cabildo, *m.* chapter (of a cathedral or collegiate church); meeting of a chapter; town council.

cabina, *f.* cockpit (of an airplane); **— telefónica,** telephone booth.

cabizbajo, ja, or **cabizcaído, da,** *adj.* crestfallen; pensive; thoughtful.

cable, *m.* cable; rope; **— conductor,** electric cable; **— de mando,** (aer.) cable control; **— de remolque,** towline.

cablegrafiar, *va.* to cable.

cablegráfico, ca, *adj.* cable; **dirección —ca,** cable address.

cablegrama, *m.* cablegram.

cabo, *m.* extremity, cape, headland; end, tip; (mil.) corporal; **al —,** at last; **al — de,** at the end of; **llevar a —,** to finish, to carry out, to carry through, to accomplish.

Cabo de Buena Esperanza, Cape of Good Hope.

Cabo de Hornos, Cape Horn.

cabotaje, *m.* (naut.) coasting trade; pilotage.

cabra, *f.* goat.

cabrahigo, *m.* wild fig tree.

cabrería, *f.* place where goat's milk is sold.

cabrero, *m.* goat herd.

cabrestante, *m.* (naut.) capstan.

cabrilla, *f.* little goat; cabriolet; a kind of shellfish; **—s,** *pl.* Pleiades (constellation); blisters on legs caused by continuous proximity to fire.

cabrio, *m.* rafter, joist; chevron.

cabrío, *m.* flock of goats; **macho —,** buck.

cabriola, *f.* caper; gambol; pirouette.

cabriolar or **cabriolear,** *vn.* to cut capers; to curvet; to pirouette.

cabriolé, *m.* cabriolet, four-wheeled cart used in large factories to transport heavy loads; type of cloak used in olden times.

cabrita, *f.* small female kid; kidskin.

cabritero, *m.* dealer in kids; seller of kid-skins.

cabritilla, *f.* dressed kidskin.

cabrito, *m.* kid.

cabrón, *m.* buck, he-goat; one who consents to the adultery of his wife.

cabronada, *f.* infamous action which a man permits against his own honor.

cabruno, na, *adj.* goatish.

cacahual or **cacaotal,** *m.* plantation of chocolate trees.

cacahuate or **cacahuete,** *m.* peanut, goober.

cacao, *m.* (bot.) smooth-leaved chocolate nut tree; cacao.

cacareador, ra, *n.* crowing rooster, cackling hen; cackler; braggart, boastful person.

cacarear, *vn.* to crow, to cackle, to cluck; to brag, to boast.

cacareo, *m.* crowing of a rooster, cackling of a hen; boast, brag.

cacera, *f.* irrigating canal, channel, conduit.

cacería, *f.* hunting party.

cacerina, *f.* cartridge box.

cacerola, *f.* casserole, pan.

caceta, *f.* small pan.

cacique, *m.* cacique (prince or nobleman among the Indians); political leader, boss.

caco, *m.* pickpocket; coward.

cacofonía, *f.* cacophony, clashing sound.

cacto, *m.* cactus.

cacumen, *m.* height, top; acumen.

cacha, *f.* handle of a knife.

cachalote, *m.* cachalot, sperm whale.

cachamarín, *m.* (naut.) lugger.

cachar, *va.* to break in pieces.

cacharrero, ra, *n.* maker or seller of crockery.

cacharro, *m.* coarse earthen pot; potsherd; trash, rubbish.

cachaza, *f.* inactivity, tardiness.

cachemira, *f.* cashmere.

cachera, *f.* coarse, shaggy cloth.

cachete, *m.* cheek; blow with the fist.

cachetero, *m.* short, broad, sharp-pointed knife; bullfighter who kills the bulls with such a knife.

cachetudo, da, *adj.* chubby-cheeked.

cachicán, *m.* farm overseer.

cachidiablo, *m.* goblin.

cachigordete, *adj.* thick and short.

cachimba, *f.,* **cachimbo,** *m.* pipe (for smoking).

cachiporra, *f.* cudgel.

cachivache, *m.* broken pottery, potsherds; trumpery, trash; worthless person.

cacho, *m.* slice, piece (applied to lemons, oranges, etc.); horn; card game.

cachondo, da, *adj.* lustful; in heat, rutting (of animals).

cachorrillo, *m.* pocket pistol; little cub.

cachorro, rra, *n.* grown whelp or puppy; cub (of any animal).

cachucha, *f.* Spanish dance and its tune; cap.

cachuela, *f.* fricassee made of the livers and lungs of rabbits.

cachupín, *m.* Spanish settler in America.

cada, *pron.* each; everyone; everybody **—,** *adj.* each; every; **— cual,** everyone; each; **— uno,** everyone; each; **— vez,** every time; **— vez más,** more and more.

cadalso, *m.* scaffold; stage, platform.

cadarzo, *m.* floss silk.

cadáver, *m.* corpse, cadaver.

cadavérico, ca, *adj.* cadaverous; deathlike; deathly.

cadena, *f.* chain; series; network; **—antideslizante,** nonskid chain; **— de montañas,** range of mountains.

cadencia, *f.* cadence.

cadente, *adj.* declining; harmonious; well-modulated.

cadera, *f.* hip.

caderillas, *f. pl.* bustle.

cadete, *m.* (mil.) cadet.

cadillo, *m.* burr, burdock, bur-parsley.

caducar, *vn.* to dote; to lapse (of a legacy, etc.).

caduceo, *m.* caduceus, herald's staff.

caducidad, *f.* decrepitude.

caduco, ca, *adj.* worn out; enfeebled by age, decrepit; perishable; **mal —co,** epilepsy.

C.A.E. cóbrese al entregar, C.O.D. or c.o.d. cash or collect on delivery.

caedizo, za, *adj.* tottering, frail; deciduous.

caedura, *f.* loose threads dropping from the loom in weaving.

caer, *vn.* (CAIGO, CAÍ) to fall; to tumble down; to lapse; to befall, to happen, to come to pass; to die; (com.) to become due; **— bien,** to suit, to be pleasing; **— de bruces,** to fall headlong; **— en gracia,** to be liked; to win the favor of; **—se de suyo,** to be self-evident; **dejar —,** to drop.

C.A.F. or c.a.f. coste, seguro, y flete, c.i.f., cost, insurance, and freight.

café, *m.* coffee tree; coffee; café; **— cargado,** strong coffee; **— débil** or **claro,** weak coffee; **— molido,** ground coffee.

cafeína, *f.* caffeine.

cafetal, *m.* coffee plantation.

cafetera, *f.* coffee pot; (Arg.) a noisy motor-cycle; **— filtradora,** percolator.

cafetería, *f.* coffee store; coffeehouse.

cafetero, ra, *adj.* pertaining to coffee; **—,** *m.* café keeper; coffee planter or seller.

cafeto, *m.* coffee tree.

cafre, *adj.* savage, inhuman; rude.

cafúa, *f.* (Arg.) jail.

cagafierro, *m.* scoria, dross of iron.

cagajón, *m.* horse dung.

cagalar, *m.* rectum.

cagalera, *f.* looseness, diarrhea.

cagar, *vn.* and *vr.* to move the bowels.

cagarruta, *f.* dung of sheep or goats.

cagón, ona, *n.* person afflicted with diarrhea; cowardly person.

cahiz, *m.* a measure (about twelve bushels).

cahizada, *f.* tract of land which requires about one **cahiz** of grain to be properly sown.

caída, *f.* fall, falling; declivity, descent; **—de agua,** waterfall; **— de la tarde,** nightfall.

caído, da, *adj.* fallen.

caídos, *m. pl.* rents due but unpaid; arrears of taxes.

caimán, *m.* cayman, alligator; cunning man.

caimiento, *m.* low spirits; languidness; fall.

caja, *f.* box, case; coffin; money chest; body of a car; **— alta** or **baja,** upper or lower case in printing; **— de ahorros,** savings bank; **— de batería,** battery box; **— de cartón,** carton; **— de conexiones,** junction box; **— de engranajes,** gear case; **— de fusibles,** fuse box; **— de**

herramientas, tool chest; **— de hierro,** cashbox; **— de interrupción,** switch box; **— de reclutamiento,** recruiting branch; **— de ruptor,** breaker box; **— de seguridad,** safe-deposit box; **— de velocidades,** transmission-gear box; **— fuerte,** safe; **— registradora,** cash register; **libro de —,** cashbook.

cajero, *m.* cashier.

cajeta, *f.* snuff box, poor box; (Mex.) jelly made of goat's milk.

cajetilla, *f.* pack of cigarettes; (Arg.) dude.

cajetín, *m.* very small box.

cajista, *m.* compositor (in printing).

cajistería, *f.* typesetting.

cajón, *m.* drawer; locker; bookcase; caisson; wooden box; coffin; **ser de —,** (coll.) to be usual, to be customary.

cajonada, *f.* (naut.) lockers.

cajonería, *f.* chiffonier.

cal, *f.* lime; **— viva,** quicklime.

cala, *f.* cove, inlet, small bay; plug cut from a melon to test its ripeness; hole made in a wall to judge of its thickness.

calabacera, *f.* pumpkin; gourd; squash.

calabacero, *m.* retailer of pumpkins.

calabacín, *m.* small, young, tender pumpkin.

calabacino, *m.* wine gourd.

calabaza, *f.* pumpkin, gourd; **dar —s,** to jilt; to fail in a school subject, to flunk.

calabazada, *f.* butt (blow with the head).

calabozo, *m.* dungeon; jail.

calada, *f.* rapid flight of birds of prey.

calado, *m.* open work in metal, wood, or linen; (naut.) draft.

calador, *m.* probe (surgeon's instrument).

calafate, *m.* (naut.) calker.

calafatear, *va.* (naut.) to calk.

calafateo, *m.* (naut.) calking.

calafatería, *f.* (naut.) calking.

calamar, *m.* squid.

calambre, *m.* cramp.

calamidad, *f.* misfortune, calamity, misery.

calamina, *f.* calamine.

calamita, *f.* magnetic needle.

calamitoso, sa, *adj.* calamitous, unfortunate.

cálamo, *m.* (bot.) sweet flag; pen; shepherd's flute.

calamocano, *adj.* (coll.) fuddled, somewhat intoxicated, unsteady.

calandrajo, *m.* rag hanging down from a garment; ragamuffin.

calandria, *f.* (mech.) calender; (orn.) bunting.

calaña, *f.* character, quality.

cálao, *m.* (orn.) hornbill.

calar, *va.* to penetrate, to pierce; to discover a design; to make work in linen or metal, etc.; to put, to place; to sample, to gauge, to measure; **—se,** to introduce oneself; to insinuate oneself into; to stoop; to soak through.

calavera, *f.* skull; hotheaded fellow, daredevil, madcap.

calaverada, *f.* ridiculous, foolish action; escapade.

calaverear, *vn.* to act foolishly.

calcañal or **calcañar,** *m.* heel bone, heel.

calcar, *va.* to counterdraw; to trample on.

calcáreo, rea, *adj.* chalky.

calce, *m.* tire of a wagon wheel.

calcedonia, *f.* (min.) chalcedony.

calceta, *f.* stocking, hose.

calcetería, *f.* trade of a hosier; hosiery.

calcetero, ra, *n.* one who makes, mends or sells thread stockings; knitter.

calcetín, *m.* sock.

calcificación, *f.* calcification.

calcificar, *va.* to calcify.

calcina, *f.* mortar.

calcinar, *va.* to calcine; to scorch.

calcio, *m.* calcium.

calco, *m.* tracing.

calcografía, *f.* art of engraving.

calculable, *adj.* calculable.

calculador, *m.* calculator, computer, estimator.

calcular, *va.* to calculate, to reckon, to compute; to rate.

cálculo, *m.* calculation, computation; estimate; account; — **biliario,** (med.) gallstone.

Calcuta, *f.* Calcutta.

calda, *f.* warmth, heat; warming or heating; —**s,** *pl.* hot baths.

caldear, *va.* to weld iron; to warm, to heat.

caldera, *f.* caldron, kettle, boiler; **las —s de Pero Botero,** (coll.) hell.

calderada, *f.* a caldronful.

calderería, *f.* brazier's shop.

calderero, *m.* brazier, coppersmith; boilermaker.

caldereta, *f.* small caldron; — **de agua bendita,** holy-water font.

calderilla, *f.* holy-water font; copper coin.

caldero, *m.* bucket-shaped caldron.

calderón, *m.* copper, large caldron; paragraph; (mus.) sign denoting a hold.

calderuela, *f.* dark lantern (used by sportsmen to drive partridges into the net).

caldillo, *m.* gravy.

caldo, *m.* broth; bouillon; sauce; — **de carne,** consommé; —**s,** *pl.* spirituous liquors.

caldoso, sa, *adj.* having too much broth or gravy.

calefacción, *f.* heating; — **central,** central heating.

calendas, *f. pl.* calends, first day of every month.

calendario, *m.* almanac, calendar.

calentador, *m.* warming pan; heater; heating apparatus; — **de agua,** water heater.

calentar, *va.* (IE) to warm, to heat; —**se,** to grow hot; to dispute warmly; to be ruttish (of animals).

calentura, *f.* fever.

calenturiento, ta, *adj.* feverish.

calera, *f.* limekiln.

calería, *f.* place where lime is burned and sold.

calero, *m.* lime burner.

calesa, *f.* two- or four-wheeled carriage.

calesero, *m.* driver of a carriage.

calesín, *m.* one-horse chaise.

caletre, *m.* (coll.) understanding, judgment, discernment.

calibrador, *m.* gauge (instrument), caliper; — **para alambre,** wire gauge.

calibrar, *va.* to calibrate, to measure, to gauge.

calibre, *m.* caliber, gauge, inside diameter (of firearms, pipes, etc.); (fig.) sort, kind.

calicanto, *m.* allspice; stone masonry.

calidad, *f.* quality, condition, character; kind; — **media,** average quality.

cálido, da, *adj.* hot, warm.

calidoscópico, ca, *adj.* kaleidoscopic.

calidoscopio, *m.* kaleidoscope.

caliente, *adj.* hot, warm; fiery, vehement; **en —,** white-hot; immediately.

califa, *m.* caliph.

califato, *m.* caliphate.

calificación, *f.* qualification; mark (in school or an examination); judgment, censure.

calificar, *va.* to qualify; to rate; to describe, to characterize; to term; to authorize; to attest; to ennoble; —**se,** to prove one's noble birth.

caligrafía, *f.* calligraphy.

calígrafo, *m.* one who writes a beautiful hand.

calisténica, *f.* calisthenics.

cáliz, *m.* chalice; goblet; (bot.) calyx.

caliza, *f.* calcium carbonate, limestone.

calizo, za, *adj.* calcareous.

calma, *f.* calm; calmness, smooth sea; quiet; composure, tranquility.

calmante, *m.* (med.) anodyne; sedative.

calmar, *va.* to calm, to quiet, to pacify; —**se,** to be becalmed.

calmo, ma, *adj.* uncultivated, untilled.

calmoso, sa, *adj.* calm; tranquil.

caló, *m.* slang used by gypsies and ruffians.

calofriarse, *vr.* to shiver with cold; to have a chill.

calofrío, *m.* shivering with cold; chill.

calor, *m.* heat, hotness, ardor, fieriness; **hacer** or **tener —,** to be warm.

caloría, *f.* calorie.

calorífero, *m.* heater; radiator; — **de aire,** hot-air register; — **de vapor,** steam radiator.

calorífugo, ga, *adj.* nonconductor of heat; fireproof.

calorímetro, *m.* (chem.) calorimeter.

calumnia, *f.* calumny, slander.

calumniador, ra, *n.* calumniator, slanderer.

calumniar, *vn.* to calumniate, to slander.

calumnioso, sa, *adj.* calumnious, slanderous.

caluroso, sa, *adj.* warm, hot; lively.

calva, *f.* bald head; a children's game played with stones.

calvario, *m.* Calvary; series of troubles or adversities; (fig.) debts.

calvatrueno, *m.* baldness; wild person.

calvez or **calvicie,** *f.* baldness.

calvinismo, *m.* Calvinism.

calvinista, *m.* Calvinist.

calvo, va, *adj.* bald; barren.

calza, *f.* trousers; stockings.

calzada, *f.* causeway, highway; **— de acceso,** driveway.

calzado, *m.* any kind of shoe or footwear; **poner suela al —,** to sole.

calzador, *m.* shoe horn.

calzadura, *f.* putting on of shoes; felloe of a cartwheel.

calzar, *va.* to put on shoes; to block a wheel with a wedge, chock, etc.; to carry (bullets of a certain caliber); to fill (teeth).

calzón, *m.* ombre, a game of cards; (Mex.) a disease of sugar cane from lack of irrigation; **—es,** *pl.* trousers, breeches; **— de mujer,** bloomers.

calzonazo, *m.* big pair of breeches; **es un —,** he is a weak fellow.

calzoncillos, *m. pl.* drawers, men's underwear.

calzonudo, da, *adj.* (Arg.) stupid.

¡calla! *interj.* no! you don't mean it! hush!

callada, *f.* dish of tripe; **de —, a las —s,** without noise, privately.

callado, da, *adj.* silent, noiseless, quiet; discreet, close-mouthed; reserved.

callandico, *adv.* in a low voice; silently.

callar, *vn.* to keep silence, to be silent, to hold one's tongue; to conceal, to hush; **hacer —,** to silence.

calle, *f.* street; lane; alley; **¡—!** *interj.* strange! **arroyo de la —,** gutter; **— sin salida,** blind alley; **— transversal,** crossroad; **cruce de —,** street crossing; **doblar la —,** to turr the corner; **—s céntricas,** downtown.

callear, *va.* to clear (walks in a vineyard) of loose branches.

calleja, *f.* lane, narrow passage; alley.

callejear, *vn.* to loiter about the streets.

callejero, ra, *adj.* loitering, rambling.

callejón, *m.* alley, narrow pass; **— de entrada,** driveway; **— sin salida,** blind alley.

callejuela, *f.* lane, narrow passage; subterfuge, shift.

callista, *m.* or *f.* chiropodist.

callo, *m.* corn; wen; callus; **—s,** *pl.* tripe; **emplasto para los —s,** corn plaster.

callosidad, *f.* callosity, callousness.

calloso, sa, *adj.* callous; horny.

cama, *f.* bed, couch; litter; **— plegadiza,** folding bed; **guardar —,** to stay in bed; **hacer la —,** to make the bed.

camachuelo, *m.* (orn.) linnet.

camada, *f.* brood of young animals; layer (of cement, eggs, etc.); **— de ladrones,** nest of rogues.

camafeo, *m.* cameo.

camal, *m.* halter.

camaleón, *m.* chameleon.

camaleopardo, *m.* (ast.) the constellation Camelopard.

camamila, *f.* camomile.

camandulero, ra, *adj.* full of tricks, hypocritical; **—,** *n.* hypocrite.

cámara, *f.* hall; chamber; the two houses of a legislative body; camera; cockpit; chamber of a firearm; **— de aire,** inner tube; air chamber; **— de comercio,** chamber of commerce; **— de compensación,** clearing house; **— de escape,** exhaust; **— fotográfica para cine,** movie camera; **— frigorífica,** cold storage; **C— de Representantes,** House of Representatives.

camarada, *m.* comrade, companion.

camaradería, *f.* fellowship.

camaranchón, *m.* garret.

camarera, *f.* head waiting maid; waitress; chambermaid.

camarero, *m.* waiter; valet, steward; cabin steward.

camareta, *f.* (naut.) junior officers' mess room.

camariento, ta, *adj.* troubled with diarrhea.

camarilla, *f.* coterie of private advisers of the king; clique.

camarista, *m.* a member of the supreme council of **la Cámara;** (Mex.) valet; **—,** *f.* maid of honor of the queen.

camarlengo, *m.* lord of the bedchamber of the king.

cámaro or **camarón,** *m.* (zool.) shrimp.

camarote, *m.* berth, cabin, stateroom.

camasquince, *m.* busybody, meddler, kibitzer.

camastrón, *m.* cunning fellow.

cambalache, *m.* traffic by exchange, barter.

cambalachear, *va.* to barter.

cambalachero, ra, *n.* barterer.

cambiable, *adj.* fit to be exchanged.

cambial, *m.* bill of exchange.

cambiante, *adj.* changeable, changing; of varied hues; **—,** *m.* iridescence.

cambiar, *va.* to barter, to exchange; to change; to alter; to give or take money on bills, to make change (money).

cambiavía, *f.* (rail.) switch, switchman.

cambija, *f.* reservoir.

cambio, *m.* exchange, barter; change; bank; alteration; **— a la par,** exchange at par; **— con quebrado,** exchange under par; **— corriente,** current exchange; **— exterior** or **extranjero,** foreign exchange; **— de llantas,** change of tires; **— interior,** domestic exchange; **— de marchas** or **de velocidad,** gearshift; **— de moneda,** money exchange; **a — de,** in exchange for; **al — de,** at the rate of exchange; **¿a qué —?** at what rate of exchange; **en —,** on the other hand; **agente de —,** stockbroker; **casa de —,** exchange office; **corredor de —,** exchange broker; **letra**

de —, bill of exchange; **tipo de** —, rate of exchange.

cambista, m. banker, money broker.

cambray, m. cambric, fine linen.

Cambrige or **Cambrigia,** f. Cambridge.

cambrón, m. buckthorn; mock orange.

cambronal, m. thicket of brambles and thorns.

cambronera, f. (bot.) boxthorn.

camelia, f. camellia.

camellero, m. driver of camels.

camello, m. camel.

camellón, m. ridge turned up by a plow; flower bed; avenue, boulevard.

camilla, f. pallet, stretcher; bed for women after childbirth; clothes horse.

caminador, m. good walker.

caminante, m. traveler, walker.

caminar, vn. to travel, to walk, to march.

caminata, f. long walk.

camino, m. road, highroad, way; — **carretero** or **real,** highway; — **de hierro,** railroad; — **de hierro económico,** narrow-gauge railway; **gran** — **de hierro,** standard-gauge railway; **de** —, on the way; **ponerse en** —, to start out.

camión, m. truck, bus.

camioneta, f. small truck.

camisa, f. shirt; chemise; — **de fuerza,** strait jacket.

camisería, f. haberdashery.

camisero, m. haberdasher; shirt maker.

camiseta, f. undershirt.

camisola, f. ruffled shirt.

camisolín, m. shirt front.

camisón, m. nightgown; chemise.

camisote, m. coat of mail.

camomila, f. camomile.

camorra, f. quarrel, dispute.

camorrista, m. and f. quarrelsome person.

camote, m. sweet potato.

campal, adj. pertaining to camp or field; **batalla** —, pitched battle.

campamento, m. (mil.) encampment, camp.

campana, f. bell; — **de buzo,** diving bell; — **de chimenea,** funnel of a chimney; **juego de** —s, chimes.

campanada, f. sound of a bell; (fig.) scandal.

campanario, m. belfry, steeple.

campanear, vn. to ring the bell frequently; —, va. to divulge.

campanela, f. rapid rotation upon one foot in a Spanish dance.

campaneo, m. bell ringing, chime; affected manner of walking.

campanero, m. bell founder; bellman.

campanilla, f. hand bell; (anat.) uvula.

campanillazo, m. signal given with a bell.

campanillear, vn. to keep ringing a little bell.

campante, adj. excelling, surpassing; proud and unconcerned.

campanudo, da, adj. wide; puffed up; pompous, high-sounding.

campánula, f. (bot.) campanula.

campaña, f. campaign, level country; (mil.) campaign, expedition.

campar, vn. to encamp; to excel, to be ahead of.

campeador, m. warrior.

campear, vn. to be in the field; to frisk about in the fields; to excel.

campechano, na, adj. frank; hearty; cheerful.

campeche, m. campeachy wood, logwood.

campeón, m. champion.

campeonato, m. championship.

campesino, na, or **campestre,** adj. rural; —, n. peasant.

campiña, f. flat tract of arable land; country.

campiruso, sa, n. (Sp. Am.) a countryman or countrywoman.

campo, m. country; countryside; field; camp; ground; — **de deportes** or **de juegos,** playground; — **santo,** cemetery.

camueso, m. pippin tree; simpleton.

camuflaje, m. camouflage.

can, m. dog; (poet.) Dog Star.

cana, f. gray hair; **peinar** —s, to grow old.

canaco, adj. (Sp. Am.) pale, yellow.

Canadá, m. Canada.

canadiense, n. and adj. Canadian.

canal, m. channel, canal; gutter.

Canal de la Mancha, m. English Channel.

canalización, f. canalization; wiring.

canalizar, va. to dig canals in or for; (elec.) to wire.

canalizo, m. narrow channel, strait.

canalón, m. large gutter.

canalla, f. mob, rabble, populace; —, m. scoundrel.

canallada, f. despicable act.

canana, f. cartridge box.

canapé, m. canopy, sofa, lounge, settee.

canard, m. canard, false report.

canario, m. canary bird; (Sp. Am.) person who gives a large tip.

canasta, f. basket, hamper.

canastilla, f. small basket; layette.

canasto, m. large basket.

¡canastos! interj. confound it!

cáncamo, m. ringbolt; — **de ojo,** eye bolt.

cancel, m. screen (at church doors); royal box in the castle church.

cancela, f. grating of a door.

cancelación or **canceladura,** f. cancellation, erasure; settlement.

cancelar, va. to cancel, to erase; to efface from the memory.

cancelaría, f. papal chancery.

cancelario, m. chancellor.

cáncer, m. (med.) cancer.

Cáncer, m. Cancer, Crab (sign of the zodiac).

cancerarse, vr. to be afflicted with a cancer.

canceroso, sa, adj. cancerous.

canciller, m. chancellor; official assistant in a consulate or embassy.

canción, f. song.

cancionero, *m.* songbook; collection of poems.
canco, *m.* (Sp. Am.) buttock, hip.
canche, *adj.* (Sp. Am.) badly seasoned.
candado, *m.* padlock; earring.
candar, *va.* to lock, to shut.
candela, *f.* fire; light; candle; — **de cera,** wax candle.
candelabro, *m.* candlestick; candelabrum.
Candelaria, *f.* Candlemas.
candelejón, *m.* (Sp. Am.) a simple-minded, candid person.
candelero, *m.* candlestick; chandelier.
candelizas, *f. pl.* (naut.) brails.
candencia, *f.* incandescence.
candente, *adj.* red-hot.
candidato, ta, *n.* candidate; applicant.
candidatura, *f.* candidacy.
candidez, *f.* candor, frankness; whiteness.
cándido, da, *adj.* white, snowy; open, candid; simple.
candil, *m.* kitchen or stable lamp.
candilada, *f.* oil or grease spot.
candileja, *f.* (bot.) willow.
candiotera, *f.* wine cellar; storage place for casks, etc.
candonga, *f.* servile and hypocritical politeness; low cunning; old mule no longer fit for service.
candongo, ga, *adj.* cajoling, fawning.
candor, *m.* candor, ingenuousness, frankness.
caneca, *f.* a vitreous earthen bottle; liquid measure of 19 liters.
caneco, *adj.* (Sp. Am.) intoxicated.
canela, *f.* cinnamon.
canelo, *m.* cinnamon tree.
canelón, *m.* large gutter; icicle; cinnamon candy.
canesú, *m.* guimpe.
canfol, *m.* camphor.
canforato, *m.* camphorate.
cangallar, *va.* (Sp. Am.) to rob, to ransack.
cangilón, *m.* dipper.
cangrejo, *m.* crawfish, crab; (Sp. Am.) stupid person.
cangrena, *f.* gangrene.
cangrenarse, *vr.* to be afflicted with gangrene.
cangrenoso, sa, *adj.* gangrenous.
canguro, *m.* kangaroo.
caníbal, *m.* cannibal.
Canícula, *f.* Dog Star.
canícula, *f.* dog days.
canilla, *f.* shinbone; tap of a cask; spool.
caninez, *f.* canine appetite.
canino, na, *adj.* canine; **hambre —na,** canine appetite.
caniquí, *f.* fine muslin (from the East Indies).
canje, *m.* (mil.) exchange of prisoners of war; interchange of magazines, stamps, etc.
canjear, *va.* to exchange.
cano, na, *adj.* hoary, gray-headed.
canoa, *f.* canoe; conduit; trough.

canoero, *m.* person who paddles or rides in a canoe.
canon, *m.* canon; catalogue, list; (mus.) canon; (print.) canon type; **—es,** *pl.* canonical law.
canonesa, *f.* canoness.
canónico, ca, *adj.* canonical.
canónigo, *m.* canon, prebendary.
canonista, *m.* canonist.
canonización, *f.* canonization.
canonizar, *va.* to canonize.
canonjía, *f.* canonry; sinecure.
canoso, sa, *adj.* hoary, gray-headed.
cansado, da, *adj.* weary, wearied, tired; tedious, tiresome.
cansancio, *m.* lassitude, fatigue, weariness.
cansar, *va.* to weary, to fatigue; to harass, to molest; **—se,** to grow weary.
cantable, *adj.* tunable.
cantada, *f.* (mus.) cantata.
cantador, ra, *n.* singer of popular airs.
cantaleta, *f.* noisy, mocking serenade; tiresome singsong.
cantante, *m.* and *f.* singer.
cantar, *m.* song; **Cantar de los Cantares,** Song of Solomon; **—,** *va.* and *vn.* to sing; (in cards) to call out the trumps; **— de plano,** to make a full confession.
cántara, *f.* pitcher; a liquid meaure (containing about 32 pints).
cantárida, *f.* Spanish fly; kind of plaster made with this insect.
cántaro, *m.* pitcher; ballot box; **llover a —s,** to rain heavily, to pour.
cantata, *f.* cantata.
cantatriz, *f.* songstress.
cantera, *f.* quarry.
cantería, *f.* stonecutting trade; hewn stone.
cantero, *m.* stonecutter.
cántico, *m.* song, canticle.
cantidad, *f.* quantity, amount, number.
cantiga, *f.* poetical composition.
cantimplora, *f.* siphon; vessel for cooling liquors.
cantina, *f.* cellar; canteen; barroom.
cantinela, *f.* short song; tiresome repetition of a subject.
cantinero, *m.* butler; bartender.
cantizal, *m.* stony ground.
canto, *m.* song; singing; stone; edge; (poet.) canto.
cantón, *m.* corner; canton.
cantonearse, *vr.* to walk affectedly.
cantonera, *f.* corner plate; angle iron.
cantonero, ra, *n.* loafer.
cantor, ra, *n.* singer.
cantorral, *m.* place full of stones.
cantueso, *m.* (bot.) lavender, spike.
canturía, *f.* vocal music.
canturrear, *vn.* to hum, to sing in a low voice.
canutillo, *m.* stalk of a straw; small glass tube.
caña, *f.* cane, reed; stalk; (Sp. Am.) rum; **— del timón,** helm; **— dulce,** sugar cane.

cañada, *f.* dell, gulch, ravine; sheep walk.

cañal, *m.* fish garth; cane or reed plantation.

cañamar, *m.* hemp field.

cañamiel, *f.* sugar cane.

cáñamo, *m.* hemp; hempen cloth.

cañamón, *m.* hemp seed.

cañavera, *f.* reed grass.

cañaveral, *m.* sugar-cane plantation.

cañazo, *m.* blow with a cane.

cañería, *f.* conduit, pipe line; gas main; waterway.

cañero, *m.* conduit maker; director of water works; angler; sugar-cane dealer.

cañilavado, da, *adj.* small limbed (of horses).

cañiza, *f.* kind of coarse linen.

cañizo, *m.* hurdle.

caño, *m.* tube, pipe; gutter, sewer; **— de agua,** water faucet; **— de evacuación,** condenser pipe.

cañón, *m.* tube, pipe; gorge, canyon; cannon, gun; barrel of a gun; **— de campaña,** field piece; **— de órgano,** organ pipe.

cañonazo, *m.* cannon shot.

cañonear, *va.* to cannonade.

cañoneo, *m.* cannonade.

cañonera, *f.* embrasure for cannon; (naut.) gunboat.

cañonería, *f.* organ pipes; set of cannons.

cañonero, ra, *adj.* carrying guns.

cañonero, *m.* gunboat.

cañutillo, *m.* small tube or pipe.

cañuto, *m.* internode of a cane; phalange; pipe, tube.

caoba, *f.* mahogany.

caolín, *m.* kaolin.

caos, *m.* chaos; confusion.

caótico, ca, *adj.* chaotic.

cap.: capítulo, chap. chapter; **capitán,** capt. captain.

capa, *f.* cloak; mantle; layer, coating, stratum; cover; pretext; **de — y gorra,** in a plain manner.

capacidad, *f.* capacity; output; extent; talent.

capacitar, *va.* and *vr.* to enable, to qualify; to delegate.

capachero, *m.* basket maker; basket porter.

capacho, *m.* hamper; frail; bricklayer's hod; (orn.) barn owl.

capador, *m.* gelder; gelder's whistle.

capadura, *f.* castration, gelding.

capar, *va.* to geld; to castrate; (fig.) to curtail.

caparazón, *m.* caparison.

caparra, *f.* sheep louse; earnest money.

caparrós, *m.,* **caparrosa,** *f.* copperas.

capataz, *m.* overseer; warden; foreman.

capaz, *adj.* capacious, spacious, roomy; fit, apt; ingenious, clever, capable, able; liable.

capazo, *m.* rush basket, frail; blow with a cloak.

capcioso, sa, *adj.* captious.

capeador, *m.* bullfighter who challenges a bull with a cloak; cloak stealer.

capear, *va.* to rob a passenger of his cloak; to flourish one's cloak before a bull; **—,** *vn.* (naut.) to lay to.

capelo, *m.* dues received in olden times by bishops from their clergy; red hat (of a cardinal).

capellada, *f.* toe of a shoe.

capellán, *m.* chaplain, minister; almoner; **— castrense,** army chaplain; **— de navío,** navy chaplain.

capellanía, *f.* chaplainship.

capellina, *f.* (mil.) headpiece of a helmet; hood worn by country people.

capeo, *m.* challenging of a bull with a cloak.

capero, *m.* priest who carries the cope or pluvial in churches; cloak rack.

caperucita, *f.* small hood; **C— Roja,** Red Riding Hood.

caperuza, *f.* hood.

capeta, *f.* a short cape.

capialzado, *adj.* sloping on the outside and indented on the inside (in architecture).

capigorrista or **capigorrón, ona,** *n.* (coll.) vagabond; parasite.

capilar, *adj.* capillary.

capilla, *f.* hood; cowl; chapel.

capilleja, *f.* small chapel.

capillejo, *m.* small hood; skein of silk for sewing.

capiller or **capillero,** *m.* sexton, church warden.

capillo, *m.* child's cap; baptismal cap; hood used by countrywomen in olden times.

capilludo, da, *adj.* resembling a monk's cowl.

capirotada, *f.* batter made of herbs, eggs, garlic, and spice.

capirote, *m.* hood.

capisayo, *m.* garment which serves both as a cloak and riding coat.

capiscol, *m.* precentor.

capitación, *f.* poll tax.

capital, *m.* capital, stock, principal (money invested); estate (of a husband at time of marriage); **— circulante,** rolling capital; **— fluctuante,** floating capital; **colocar un —,** to invest capital; **—,** *f.* capital, metropolis; **—** *adj.* capital; principal.

capitalismo, *m.* capitalism.

capitalista, *n.* and *adj.* capitalist; **socio —,** partner who has capital in a firm.

capitalización, *f.* capitalization.

capitalizar, *va.* to capitalize.

capitán, *m.* captain; commander; **— de corbeta,** lieutenant commander; **— del puerto,** harbor master; **— general,** commander in chief; field marshal.

capitana, *f.* admiral's ship; flagship; (coll.) woman head of a troop; wife of a captain.

capitanazo, *m.* able general.

capitanear, *va.* to have the command of an army; to head a troop of people.

capitanía, *f.* captainship, captaincy.

capitel, *m.* spire over the dome of a church; capital (of a column).

capitolio, *m.* capitol.

capitón, *m.* striped mullet (fish).

capítula, *f.* part of the prayers read at divine service.

capitulación, *f.* capitulation; agreement; **—ones,** *pl.* matrimonial contract.

capitular, *vn.* to conclude an agreement; to yield; (mil.) to capitulate; to sing prayers at divine service; **—,** *va.* to accuse, to impeach; **—,** *m.* capitular; **—,** *adj.* capitulary.

capitulario, *m.* prayer book.

capítulo, *m.* chapter of a cathedral; assembly of the prelates of religious orders; chapter (of a book).

capn. or **cap.ⁿ capitán,** capt. captain.

capolar, *va.* to mince; to behead.

capón, *m.* eunuch; capon; (naut.) anchor stopper.

caponar, *va.* to geld; to curtail; to tie up vine branches.

caponera, *f.* coop (for capons).

caporal, *m.* chief, ringleader.

capota, *f.* cape; woman's bonnet; top (of certain vehicles, etc.).

capote, *m.* kind of cape, cloak, or coat; raincoat; (coll.) stern look; **decir para su —,** to say to oneself.

capotillo, *m.* short cloak.

capotón, *m.* large wide coat.

capotudo, da, *adj.* frowning.

capp.ⁿ capellán, chap. chaplain.

Capricornio, *m.* Capricorn (sign of the zodiac).

capricho, *m.* caprice, whim, fancy; (mus.) irregular but pleasing composition.

caprichoso, sa, *adj.* capricious, whimsical; fickle; obstinate; cranky.

caprichudo, da, *adj.* stubborn, capricious.

caprino, na, *adj.* goatish.

cápsula, *f.* capsule; bottle cap; cartridge shell; **— fulminante,** detonator; percussion cap.

capsular, *adj.* capsular.

captar, *va.* to captivate.

captura, *f.* capture, seizure.

capturar, *va.* to capture.

capucha, *f.* circumflex; cap, cowl, hood of a woman's cloak; monk's hood.

capuchina, *f.* Capuchin nun; (bot.) nasturtium.

capuchino, *m.* Capuchin monk; **—, na,** *adj.* appertaining to Capuchin monks or nuns.

capucho, *m.* cowl, hood.

capullo, *m.* pod of silkworm; bud; coarse cloth made of spun silk.

caqui, *adj.* khaki.

cara, *f.* face, visage, front; surface; **— a —,** face to face; **— de acelga,** sallow face; **— o cruz** or **— o sello,** heads or tails; **de —,** opposite, facing; **buena —,** cheerful mien; **mala —,** frown; **tener mala —,** to look bad.

carabina, *f.* carbine; **ser como la — de**

Ambrosio, to be good for nothing, to be worthless.

carabinero, *m.* carabineer.

cárabo, *m.* (orn.) horned owl.

caracol, *m.* snail; winding staircase.

caracolear, *vn.* to caracole, to wind.

¡caracoles! *interj.* Blazes! Confound it!

carácter, *m.* character, nature, disposition; quality; condition; character or letter used in writing or printing.

característica, *f.* and *adj.* characteristic.

característicamente, *adv.* characteristically.

característico, ca, *adj.* characteristic.

caracterizado, da, *adj.* characterized, distinguished; competent.

caracterizar, *va.* to characterize.

caracul, *m.* caracul, karakul.

caracumbé, *m.* (Chile) Negro dance.

caramanchón, *m.* garret.

¡caramba! *interj.* Good Lord! Heavens! Confound it!

carámbano, *m.* icicle; flake of ice.

carambola, *f.* carom (in billiards); trick; **por —,** indirectly, by chance.

carambolear, *vn.* to carom (in billiards).

caramelizar, *va.* to caramelize.

caramelo, *m.* caramel.

caramente, *adv.* dearly.

caramillo, *m.* small flute; gossip, tale carrying.

carángano, *m.* (coll.) louse.

carantoñero, ra, *n.* wheedler, cajoler.

carapacho, *m.* shell; (Cuba) a stew of shellfish.

carapato, *m.* castor oil.

carasol, *m.* sun parlor.

carátula, *f.* mask; histrionic art; title page.

caratulero, *m.* dealer in masks.

caravana, *f.* caravan; (Arg.) long earring; (Mex.) bow, curtsy.

caray, *m.* tortoise shell; **¡—!** *interj.* caramba! confound it!

carbohidrato, *m.* carbohydrate.

carbón, *m.* charcoal; coal; carbon; **copia al —,** carbon copy; **— bituminoso,** bituminous coal; **— animal,** bone black; **— de leña,** charcoal; **— de piedra,** mineral coal; **— fino,** culm; **papel —,** carbon paper; **— vegetal,** charcoal.

carbonada, *f.* large amount of coal for the furnace; broiled meat; kind of pancake.

carbonatado, da, *adj.* carbonated.

carbonatar, *va.* (chem.) to carbonate.

carbonato, *m.* carbonate.

carboncillo, *m.* charcoal pencil.

carbonear, *va.* to make coal out of wood.

carboneo, *m.* carbonization.

carbonera, *f.* coalpit, coalmine; (naut.) bunker.

carbonería, *f.* coalyard; coalshed; coalmine.

carbonero, *m.* charcoal burner; collier; man who mines or sells coal; **—, ra,** *adj.* pertaining to coal.

carbónico, ca, *adj.* carbonic.

carbonizar, *va.* to carbonize; to char.
carbono, *m.* (chem.) carbon; **dióxido de —,** carbon dioxide.
carborundo, *m.* carborundum.
carbunclo or **carbunco,** *m.* carbuncle; pustule.
carburador, *m.* carburetor.
carburo, *m.* (chem.) carbide.
carcaj, *m.* quiver (for a bow); rifle case or scabbard.
carcajada, *f.* hearty laughter; **soltar una —,** to burst out laughing.
carcajear, *va.* and *vr.* to laugh heartily.
carcañal or **carcañar** or **carcaño,** *m.* heel bone.
cárcava, *f.* gully; mound; hedge.
cárcel, *f.* prison; jail.
carcelaje, *m.* prison fees.
carcelería, *f.* imprisonment.
carcelero, *m.* jailer.
carcinoma, *m.* carcinoma, cancerous tumor.
cárcola, *f.* treadle.
carcoma, *f.* wood louse; dust made by the wood louse; grief; anxious concern.
carcomer, *va.* to gnaw, to corrode; **—se,** to grow worm-eaten.
carcomido, da, *adj.* worm-eaten.
carda, *f.* teasel; card (for carding wool); severe reprimand.
cardador, ra, *n.* carder, comber.
cardadura, *f.* carding.
cardar, *va.* to card wool; to raise the wool on cloth with a teasel.
cardelina, *f.* (orn.) goldfinch, redcap.
cardenal, *m.* cardinal; cardinal (bird); wale.
cardenalato, *m.* cardinalate, cardinalship.
cardenalicio, cia, *adj.* belonging to a cardinal.
cardencha, *f.* teasel; card, comb.
cardenillo, *m.* corrosion of copper, verdigris; Paris green.
cárdeno, na, *adj.* livid, purple.
cardero, *m.* maker of comb for carding wool.
cardíaco, ca, *adj.* cardiac.
cardico, *m.* small thistle.
cardillo, *m.* golden thistle.
cardinal, *adj.* cardinal (point); principal, fundamental.
cardiógrafo, *m.* (med.) cardiograph.
carditis, *f.* (med.) carditis.
Card.¹ Cardenal, cardinal.
cardo, *m.* thistle.
cardón, *m.* act of carding; (bot.) teasel.
carducha, *f.* large iron comb for wool.
carduzador, *m.* carder.
carduzar, *va.* to card or comb wool.
carear, *va.* to confront (criminals); to compare; to tend (a drove of cattle); **—se,** to assemble for business; to meet face to face; to settle something unpleasant.
carecer, *vn.* (EZCO) to want, to lack.
carena, *f.* careening or repairing of a ship.
carenar, *va.* to careen a ship.
carencia, *f.* lack; scarcity.
careo, *m.* (law) confrontation.

carero, ra, *adj.* in the habit of selling things high.
carestía, *f.* scarcity, want; famine; high price.
careta, *f.* mask.
careto, ta, *adj.* blazed (applied to horses).
carey, *m.* tortoise, shell turtle; tortoise shell.
carga, *f.* load, burden, pack; freight; cargo; load (of a firearm); impost, tax; (fig.) burden of the mind, heaviness; **— de vuelta,** return cargo; **la — de un carro,** carload.
cargadas, *f. pl.* a card game.
cargadero, *m.* loading place.
cargadilla, *f.* (coll.) increase of a debt due to accumulated interest.
cargado, da, *adj.* loaded, full; **— de espaldas,** round-shouldered.
cargador, *m.* freighter; loader; stoker; expressman; rammer.
cargamento, *m.* (naut.) load, cargo.
cargar, *va.* to load, to burden, to carry, to freight; to attack the enemy; to load a gun; to clog; to impose taxes; to impeach; **— en cuenta,** to charge on account, to debit; **— la mano,** to pursue with eagerness, to overcharge; **—,** *vn.* to incline, to tip.
cargazón, *f.* cargo (of a ship).
cargo, *m.* debit; burden; loading; employment; dignity; office; charge; care; obligation; accusation; **a — de,** in charge of or on account of; **a mi —,** for or on my account; **— de conciencia,** remorse, sense of guilt; **— y data,** creditor and debtor; **girar a nuestro (mi) —,** to draw on us (me); **hacerse — de,** to take into consideration, to realize; **librar a — de una persona,** to draw on a person.
cargoso, sa, *adj.* grievous, onerous; bothersome; **—,** *m.* (Sp. Am.) a bore, an annoying person.
carguera, *f.* nursemaid.
carguío, *m.* cargo of merchandise.
cariado, da, *adj.* carious.
cariaguileño, ña, *adj.* long-faced and crooknosed.
carialegre, *adj.* pleased-looking.
cariampollado, da, *adj.* round-faced.
cariancho, cha, *adj.* broad-faced, chubby.
cariarse, *vr.* to grow carious, to become decayed.
caribe, *adj.* Caribbean; cannibal.
caricatura, *f.* caricature.
caricia, *f.* caress.
caricioso, sa, *adj.* fondling, caressing.
caricuerdo, da, *adj.* having a composed look.
caridad, *f.* charity; benevolence; alms.
caridoliente, *adj.* sad-faced.
caries, *f.* (med.) caries, decay.
carifruncido, da, *adj.* having a wrinkled face.
carigordo, da, *adj.* full-faced.
cariharto, ta, *adj.* round-faced.
carilargo, ga, *adj.* long-faced.

carilucio, cia, *adj.* smooth-faced.

carilla, *f.* little face; mask used by bee-keepers.

carilleno, na, *adj.* full-faced.

carillón, *m.* carillon.

carinegro, gra, *adj.* swarthy-complexioned.

cariño, *m.* fondness, tenderness; endearing expression; love.

cariñoso, sa, *adj.* affectionate, endearing; loving.

carirraído, da, *adj.* brazen, impudent.

carirredondo, da, *adj.* round-faced.

carita, *f.* small face.

caritativo, va, *adj.* charitable, eleemosynary.

Carlos, Charles.

Carlota, Charlotte.

carmelita, *f.* and *adj.* Carmelite.

carmen, *m.* country house; Carmelite order.

carmenador, *m.* teaseler.

carmenar, *va.* to card wool; to pull out the hair of the head; to cheat at play.

carmes, *m.* kermes (cochineal insect).

carmesí, *m.* cochineal powder; crimson; purple.

carmín, *m.* and *adj.* carmine.

carnada, *f.* bait, lure.

carnadura, *f.* muscularity; flesh.

carnaje, *m.* salt beef.

carnal, *adj.* carnal, fleshy; sensual; related by blood; **primo —,** first cousin; **—,** *m.* time of the year in which meat may be eaten.

carnalidad, *f.* lustfulness; fleshliness.

carnaval, *m.* carnival.

carnaza, *f.* fleshy part of a hide; abundance of meat; bait.

carne, *f.* flesh, meat; pulp of fruit; **— asada en horno,** baked meat; **— asada en parrilla,** broiled meat; **— concentrada,** meat extract; **— cediza,** tainted meat; **— de gallina,** (fig.) gooseflesh; **— de membrillo,** preserved quinces; **— de pluma,** flesh of fowl; **— de vaca,** beef.

carnecilla, *f.* small excrescence on the body.

carnerada, *f.* flock of sheep.

carneraje, *m.* tax on sheep.

carnerear, *va.* to fine the proprietor of sheep which have done damage.

carnerero, *m.* shepherd.

carneril, *m.* sheepwalk.

carnero, *m.* sheep, mutton; family vault or burying place of olden times.

carneruno, na, *adj.* belonging to sheep.

carnestolendas, *f. pl.* Shrovetide.

carnet, *m.* notebook, memorandum book.

carnicería, *f.* butcher shop, meat market; shambles, slaughterhouse; carnage, slaughter.

carnicero, *m.* butcher; **—, ra,** *adj.* carnivorous.

carnicol, *m.* hoof of cloven-footed animals.

carnificarse, *vr.* to turn into, or become like, flesh.

carnívoro, *m.* carnivore; **—, ra,** *adj.* carnivorous.

carniza, *f.* refuse of meat.

carnosidad, *f.* proud flesh; fatness; fleshiness.

carnoso, sa, or **carnudo, da,** *adj.* fleshy; full of marrow.

caro, ra, *adj.* expensive; dear; **—ra mitad,** better half; beloved.

Carolina, Caroline, Carrie.

Carolina del Norte, *f.* North Carolina.

Carolina del Sur, *f.* South Carolina.

caromomia, *f.* dry flesh of a mummy.

carona, *f.* padding of a saddle; part of the animal's back on which the saddle lies.

caroquero, ra, *n.* wheedler, flatterer.

carótida, *f.* (anat.) carotid artery.

carozo, *m.* core of certain fruits.

carpa, *f.* carp (fish); part torn off a bunch of grapes; (Sp. Am.) a camping tent.

carpe, *m.* (bot.) witch hazel.

carpeta, *f.* table cover; portfolio.

carpintear, *vn.* to carpenter.

carpintería, *f.* carpentry; carpenter's shop.

carpintero, *m.* carpenter; **— de blanco,** joiner; **— de carretas,** cartwright; **— de obras de afuera,** carpenter who timbers or roofs houses; **— de ribera,** shipwright.

carpo, *m.* (anat.) wrist, carpus.

carraca, *f.* carack (ship); rattle.

carral, *m.* barrel, butt, vat.

carraleja, *f.* black beetle.

carralero, *m.* cooper, barrelmaker.

carrasca, *f.*, **carrasco,** *m.* evergreen oak.

carraspada, *f.* negus, mulled wine.

carraspera, *f.* hoarseness, sore throat.

carrasqueño, ña, *adj.* harsh, sharp; belonging to the evergreen oak.

carrera, *f.* career; education; course, race; race track; highroad; alley; row, line; course of life; **a la —,** very fast, running; **a — abierta,** at full speed.

carrerista, *m.* and *f.* race fan.

carreta, *f.* long narrow cart; wagon.

carretada, *f.* cartload; great quantity; **a —s,** in abundance.

carretaje, *m.* cartage.

carrete, *m.* spool, bobbin, reel; (elec.) coil.

carretear, *va.* to cart; to drive a cart.

carretel, *m.* spindle, fishing-rod reel; **— de carpintero,** carpenter's marking line.

carretela, *f.* light coach.

carretera, *f.* highway, main road; **— empedrada** or **pavimentada,** paved road.

carretería, *f.* number of carts; trade of a carman; cartwright's yard, wheelwright's shop.

carretero, *m.* cartwright; carman, carter, truckman.

carretilla, *f.* gocart; squib, cracker; wheelbarrow.

carretón, *m.* cart; truck.

carricera, *f.* (bot.) foxtail.

carril, *m.* cartway; cart rut; furrow; rail; railing.

carrilera, *f.* track (of a wheel); (Cuba) railroad track.
carrillada, *f.* hog's jowl; shiver which causes the jaws to quake.
carrillo, *m.* cheek; (naut.) hoisting tackle.
carrilludo, da, *adj.* round-cheeked.
carriola, *f.* trundlebed; small chariot, curricle.
carrizo, *m.* reed grass.
carro, *m.* cart, freight car, chariot, wagon, car; **la carga de un —,** carload; **— entero,** carload; **— lateral,** side car (of a motorcycle); **C— Mayor, C— Menor,** (ast.) Big Dipper, Little Dipper.
carrocería, *f.* car or truck body; carriage shop; carriage repair shop.
carrocín, *m.* chaise, curricle.
carromatero, *m.* charioteer, carman.
carromato, *m.* two-wheeled tilted cart.
carroña, *f.* carrion.
carroñar, *va.* to infect sheep with the scab.
carroño, ña, *adj.* putrid, rotten.
carroza, *f.* state coach; large coach; funeral car; (naut.) awning.
carruaje, *m.* carriage, vehicle.
carruajero, *m.* carrier, carter, wagoner.
carruco, *m.* small cart used in mountainous countries.
carta, *f.* letter; charter; map; (aer.) chart; **— aérea,** air letter; **— blanca,** carte blanche, **— certificada,** registered letter; **— circular,** circular letter; **— credencial** or **de crédito,** letter of credit; **— de amparo,** safe conduct; **— de ciudadanía,** citizenship papers; **— de fletamento,** charter party; **— de pedido,** letter ordering goods; **— de porte,** bill of lading; **— de presentación,** letter of introduction; **— en lista,** letter to be called for at post office, general delivery letter; **— general,** form letter.
cartabón, *m.* carpenter's square (tool).
cartapacio, *m.* memorandum book; portfolio.
cartear, *vn.* to play low cards; to see how the cards lie; **—se,** to keep up a correspondence by letter.
cartel, *m.* placard; handbill; poster, show bill; **no fijar —es,** post no bills.
cartela, *f.* slip of paper; cornice.
cartelera, *f.* billboard.
cartelón, *m.* show bill.
cárter, *m.* gear case (as in bicycle); **— del cigüeñal,** crankcase of an automobile.
cartera, *f.* portfolio, brief case, letter case; flap of a pocket; pocketbook; **— de bolsillo,** billfold.
carterista, *m.* and *f.* pickpocket.
cartero, *m.* letter carrier, postman, mailman.
cartilaginoso, sa, *adj.* cartilaginous.
cartílago, *m.* cartilage, gristle; parchment.
cartilla, *f.* short letter; primer.
cartografía, *f.* cartography, mapping.
cartógrafo, *m.* map maker, cartographer.
cartón, *m.* pasteboard; cardboard; drawing on strong paper; **— de paja,** strawboard; **— piedra,** pâpier-maché.
cartonero, *m.* pasteboard maker.
cartuchera, *f.* (mil.) cartridge box; cartridge pouch.
cartucho, *m.* cartridge; **— en blanco,** blank cartridge.
Cartuja, *f.* Carthusian order.
cartujo, *m.* Carthusian monk.
cartulina, *f.* Bristol board, fine cardboard.
carvi, *m.* (bot.) caraway seed.
casa, *f.* house; concern; home; **— al por mayor,** wholesale house; **— de banca,** banking house; **— de cambio,** exchange office; **— de campo,** country house; **— de correos,** post office; **— de comercio,** business house; **— de comisiones,** commission house; **— de compensación,** clearing house; **— de huéspedes,** boardinghouse; **— de locos,** madhouse; **— de máquinas,** engine house; **— de maternidad,** maternity hospital; **— de moneda,** mint; **— de préstamos** or **empeños,** pawnshop; **— editorial,** publishing house; **— matriz,** main office; **— mortuoria,** funeral parlor; **— solariega,** homestead; **en —,** at home; **poner —,** to set up housekeeping.
casabe, *m.* cassava.
casaca, *f.* frock coat.
casación, *f.* abrogation, repeal.
casadero, ra, *adj.* marriageable.
casamata, *f.* (mil.) casemate.
casamentero, ra, *n.* marriage maker.
casamiento, *m.* marriage, wedding.
casapuerta, *f.* vestibule.
casaquilla, *f.* short, loose jacket.
casar, *va.* to marry; to consort; to couple; to adjust; to abrogate; to annul; **—se,** to get married.
casatienda, *f.* house combining a store and living quarters.
casca, *f.* husks of grapes; bark for tanning leather.
cascabel, *m.* rattle, little round bell; sleigh bell; (zool.) rattlesnake.
cascabelada, *f.* jingling of small bells; inconsiderate speech or action.
cascabelear, *va.* to feed one with vain hopes; **—,** *vn.* to act with levity.
cascaciruelas, *m.* and *f.* (coll.) despicable person.
cascada, *f.* cascade, waterfall.
cascajal, *m.* place full of pebbles.
cascajo, *m.* gravel; fragments of broken vessels; rubbish; copper coin.
cascajoso, sa, *adj.* gravelly.
cascamajar, *va.* to pound a thing to bits.
cascanueces, *m.* nutcracker.
cascapiñones, *m.* pine-nut cracker; sheller of pine nuts.
cascar, *va.* to crack, to break into pieces; to lick, to beat; **—se,** to be broken open.
cáscara, *f.* rind, peel, husk; bark; **— sagrada,** cascara (sagrada).

¡cáscaras! *interj.* gosh!

cascarilla, *f.* Peruvian bark; (Arg.) person easily offended.

cascarón, *m.* eggshell.

cascarrón, ona, *adj.* rough, harsh, rude.

cascarudo, da, *adj.* thick-skinned, thick-peeled.

casco, *m.* skull, cranium; potsherd; helmet; hulk (of a ship); crown (of a hat); hoof (of a horse).

cascote, *m.* rubbish, fragments of material used in building.

cascudo, da, *adj.* large-hoofed.

cascundear, *va.* (Costa Rica) to beat, to flog.

caseína, *f.* casein.

caseoso, sa, *adj.* caseous, cheesy.

casera, *f.* housekeeper.

casería, *f.* (law) messuage; economical management of a house; (Sp. Am.) clientele.

caserío, *m.* series of houses; village.

caserna, *f.* (mil.) barracks.

casero, ra, *n.* landlord or landlady; agent; —, *adj.* domestic; familiar; homemade.

casi, *adv.* almost, nearly; — **que,** or — —, very nearly.

casia, *f.* (bot.) bastard cinnamon, cassia.

casilla, *f.* hut, booth, cabin; (naut.) cockpit; (aer.) nacelle; square (chess); point (of backgammon board); — **de correos,** mail box; —**s,** *pl.* pigeonholes; **sacar de sus** —, to infuriate, to drive crazy.

casillero, *m.* board with pigeon holes.

casimba, *f.* (Sp. Am.) well, spring.

casimir, *m.,* **casimira,** *f.* cashmere.

Casimiro, Casimir.

casino, *m.* casino, gambling house; clubhouse.

caso, *m.* case; occurrence, event; hap, casualty; occasion; (gram.) case; — **que,** in case; **en** — **de,** in the case of; **en** — **de fuerza,** in case of emergency; **en** — **de que,** in case; **en ese** —, in that case; **en todo** —, at all events; **no hacer** —, to pay no attention; **poner por** —, to state as an example.

casorio, *m.* hasty marriage; informal wedding.

caspa, *f.* dandruff, scurf.

Caspio, *m.* Caspian Sea.

¡cáspita! *interj.* Confound it! Gracious!

casquetazo, *m.* blow with the head.

casquete, *m.* helmet, cap; skull.

casquiblando, da, *adj.* soft-hoofed.

casquiderramado, da, *adj.* wide-hoofed.

casquijo, *m.* gravel.

casquilla, *f.* cell of the queen bee.

casquillo, *m.* iron socket; arrowhead; iron butt of a spear; (Sp. Am.) horseshoe.

casquimuleño, ña, *adj.* narrow-hoofed (like mules).

casquivano, na, *adj.* feather-brained.

casta, *f.* cast, race, lineage; breed; kind, quality.

castaña, *f.* chestnut; jug in the shape of a chestnut; knot of hair; — **pilonga,** dried chestnut; (Mex.) valise, suitcase.

castañal or **castañar,** *m.* chestnut grove.

castañazo, *m.* (Arg.) blow with the fist.

castañeta, *f.* castanet.

castañetear, *vn.* to rattle the castanets in dancing; to chatter (said of teeth).

castaño, *m.* chestnut tree; —, **ña,** *adj.* hazel; brown.

castañuela, *f.* castanet.

castañuelo, la, *adj.* chestnut-colored.

castellán, *m.* governor or warden of a castle.

castellanía, *f.* district belonging to a castle.

castellano, na, *n.* and *adj.* Castilian; Spanish language.

castidad, *f.* chastity.

castigador, ra, *n.* and *adj.* punisher.

castigar, *va.* to chastise, to punish; to afflict.

castigo, *m.* chastisement, punishment; correction; penalty (in games).

Castilla, *f.* Castile.

Castilla la Nueva, *f.* New Castile.

Castilla la Vieja, *f.* Old Castile.

castillejo, *m.* small castle; gocart (for little children).

castillo, *m.* castle; fortress; cell of the queen bee; (Arg.) a cart; — **de proa,** forecastle.

castizo, za, *adj.* of a noble descent; pure, uncorrupt.

casto, ta, *adj.* pure, chaste.

Cástor, *m.* (ast.) star in constellation Gemini.

castor, *m.* beaver.

castra, *f.* pruning of plants and trees.

castración, *f.* castration, emasculation.

castrar, *va.* to geld, to castrate; to prune; to cut the honeycombs out of beehives.

castrazón, *f.* cutting honeycombs out of hives.

castruera, *f.* (Col.) musical instrument.

casual, *adj.* casual, accidental, haphazard.

casualidad, *f.* casualty, accident; chance, coincidence.

casualmente, *adv.* accidentally, casually.

casucha, *f.* miserable hut.

casuista, *m.* and *f.* casuist.

casulla, *f.* chasuble.

cata, *f.* tasting; (Sp. Am.) a parrot.

catabolismo, *m.* catabolism.

cataclismo, *m.* cataclysm, violent catastrophe.

catacumbas, *f. pl.* catacombs.

catadura, *f.* act of tasting; (coll.) gesture, face, countenance.

catafalco, *m.* funeral canopy over a bier, catafalque.

catalán, ana, *n.* and *adj.* Catalan, Catalonian.

catalejo, *m.* telescope.

catalepsia, *f.* (med.) catalepsis.

Catalina, Catharine, Kate.

catálisis, *f.* (chem.) catalysis.

catalizador, *m.* (chem.) catalyzer.

catalogar, *va.* to catalogue, to list.

catálogo, *m.* catalogue; list.
catalpa, *f.* (bot.) catalpa.
Cataluña, *f.* Catalonia.
cataplasma, *f.* poultice.
catapulta, *f.* catapult.
catar, *va.* to taste; to inspect, to examine; to judge; to esteem.
catarata, *f.* cataract, waterfall, cascade; (med.) cataract.
catarata, *m.* (Arg.) policeman.
catarral, *adj.* catarrhal.
catarro, *m.* catarrh; **— epidémico,** influenza.
catarroso, sa, *adj.* catarrhal; subject to colds.
catártico, ca, *adj.* (med.) cathartic, purging.
catastro, *m.* general tax on land.
catástrofe, *f.* catastrophe, disaster.
catatán, *m.* (Chile) punishment.
catavino, *m.* small cup for tasting wine; **—s,** *m.* winetaster; tippler.
catecismo, *m.* catechism.
catecúmeno, *m.* novice, beginner; convert; newly ordained priest.
cátedra, *f.* professor's chair, professorship, subject taught by a professor.
catedral, *adj.* and *f.* cathedral.
catedrático, *m.* professor of a university.
categoría, *f.* category; rank; class.
categórico, ca, *adj.* categorical, decisive.
catequismo, *m.* instruction in religion.
catequista, *m.* catechist.
catequizar, *va.* to catechize; to instruct in Christianity.
caterva, *f.* mob, throng.
catimbao, *m.* (Chile) ridiculously dressed person.
catinga, *f.* (Arg.) body odor; (Chile) name given by the marines to the soldiers.
catire, *n.* and *adj.* (Sp. Am.) blond (usually applied to offspring of mulattoes and whites).
cativo, *m.* (C.R.) a kind of huge tree.
catódico, ca, *adj.* (elec.) cathodic.
cátodo, *m.* cathode.
catolicismo, *m.* Catholicism.
católico, ca, *adj.* and *n.* Catholic.
catorce, *m.* and *adj.* fourteen.
catorcena, *f.* group or set of fourteen units.
catorceno, na, *adj.* fourteenth.
catre, *m.* fieldbed; cot.
catricofre, *m.* folding bed.
caúca, *f.* wheat biscuit.
Cáucaso, *m.* Caucasus.
cauce, *m.* trench, ditch, drain; bed of a river.
caución, *f.* caution, security, guaranty.
caucionar, *va.* (law) to guarantee.
cauchal, *m.* rubber plantation or patch.
cauchera, *f.* rubber plant.
caucho, *m.* rubber, caoutchouc; **— artificial,** synthetic rubber; **— endurecido,** hard rubber; **— vulcanizado,** vulcanized rubber.
cauda, *f.* train of a bishop's robe.
caudal, *m.* property, fortune, wealth; fund,

stock; abundance, plenty; flow, discharge.
caudaloso, sa, *adj.* carrying much water (of rivers).
caudatario, *m.* trainbearer of a cardinal.
caudillo, *m.* chief, leader, dictator.
causa, *f.* cause; occasion; motive, reason; case, lawsuit; **a — de,** considering, because of, on account of, by reason of.
causal, *adj.* causal.
causante, *m.* and *f.* originator; constituent.
causar *va.* to cause, to produce; to occasion.
causídico, ca, *adj.* belonging to lawsuits; forensic.
causón, *m.* burning fever which lasts only a few hours.
cáustico, *m.* caustic; **—, ca,** *adj.* caustic.
cautamente, *adv.* cautiously.
cautela, *f.* caution, prudence; heedfulness.
cautelar, *va.* and *vn.* to take necessary precautions, to guard against.
cauteloso, sa, *adj.* cautious, heedful, prudent.
cauterio, *m.* (med.) cautery.
cauterizar, *va.* to cauterize; to reproach with severity.
cautivar, *va.* to take prisoner in war; to captivate, to charm, to attract.
cautiverio, *m.* captivity; confinement.
cautivo, va, *n.* captive, prisoner.
cauto, ta, *adj.* cautious, wary, prudent.
cava, *f.* digging and earthing of vines; wine cellar.
cavar, *va.* to dig, to excavate; **—,** *vn.* to penetrate far into a thing; to think profoundly; to paw (of horses).
caverna, *f.* cavern, cave.
cavernoso, sa, *adj.* cavernous.
cavial or **caviar,** *m.* caviar.
cavidad, *f.* cavity, hollow.
cavilar, *va.* to cavil, to criticize.
caviloso, sa, *adj.* captious; faultfinding.
cayada, *f.,* **cayado,** *m.* shepherd's crook.
Cayena, *f.* Cayenne.
cayo, *m.* rock, shoal.
Cayohueso or **Cayo Hueso,** *m.* Key West.
Cayos de la Florida, *m. pl.* Florida Keys.
caz, *m.* canal, trench; mill race.
caza, *f.* game; hunting, hunt; (aer.) pursuit plane.
cazasubmarinos, *m.* submarine chaser.
cazabe, *m.* (bot.) cassava, manioc.
cazadero, *m.* hunting ground.
cazador, *m.* hunter, huntsman; **— furtivo,** poacher.
cazar, *va.* to chase, to hunt.
cazatorpedero, *m.* torpedo-boat chaser or destroyer.
cazcarria, *f.* splashings of dirt.
cazo, *m.* copper saucepan with an iron handle; ladle.
cazudo, da, *adj.* thick-backed (of knives).
cazuela, *f.* stewing pan; crock.
cazumbrón, *m.* cooper.
cazurro, ra, *adj.* silent, taciturn.
cazuz, *m.* (bot.) ivy.

C.C. corriente continua, D.C. or d.c. direct current.

c/c: cuyo cargo, (com.) whose account; **cuenta corriente,** (com.) current account.

c/cta. cuya cuenta, (com.) whose account.

C.D. corriente directa, D.C. or d.c. direct current.

c/d cuenta de, (com.) account of.

C. de J. Compañía de Jesús, S. J. Society of Jesus.

¡ce! *interj.* hark! come hither!

cea, *f.* thighbone.

ceática, *f.* (med.) sciatica.

ceba, *f.* fattening of cattle.

cebada, *f.* barley; **— fermentada,** malt.

cebadera, *f.* nosebag (for horses).

cebadero, *m.* place where game or fowls are fed; bell mule.

cebador, *m.* primer (of a pump).

cebadura, *f.* act of feeding domestic animals.

cebar, *va.* and *vn.* to feed animals, to fatten. to stuff; to keep up a fire; to grapple; to prime (firearms); to start (machinery); to light (fireworks, etc.).

cebellina, *f.* (zool.) sable; sableskin.

cebo, *m.* food; bait, lure; priming.

cebolla, *f.* onion; bulb of the onion.

cebolleta, *f.* tender onion.

cebollino, *m.* onion seed.

cebolludo, da, *adj.* bulbous.

cebón, *m.* fat bullock or hog.

cebra, *f.* zebra.

cebruno, na, *adj.* reddish brown.

Cebú, *f.* Cebu.

cecear, *vn.* to pronounce the s in the same manner as the c (in Spanish); to lisp.

cecial, *m.* cod (fish).

Cecilia, Cecily, Cissy.

Cecilio, Cecil.

cecina, *f.* hung beef, salt beef, corned beef.

cedacero, *m.* sieve maker.

cedazo, *m.* sieve, strainer.

cedente, *m.* and *f.* indorser (of a draft).

ceder, *va.* to grant, to resign, to yield, to give up; **—,** *vn.* to submit, to comply, to give in; to abate, to diminish.

cedro, *m.* cedar.

cédula, *f.* slip of paper; bill; charter, patent; ticket; permit, license; **— de cambio,** bill of exchange; **— personal** or **de vecindad,** identification papers; **—s hipotecarias,** mortgage bank stock.

cedulón, *m.* proclamation; public notice.

cefalitis, *f.* cephalitis.

céfalo, *m.* mullet (a fish).

céfiro, *m.* zephyr, breeze.

cegar, *vn.* (IE) to grow blind; **—,** *va.* to deprive of sight; to darken; to shut.

cegarrita, *m.* and *f.* short-sighted person; **a —s,** with shut eyes.

ceguedad, *f.* blindness.

ceguera, *f.* blindness.

Ceilán, *f.* Ceylon.

ceja, *f.* eyebrow; edging of clothes; (mus.)

bridge of a stringed instrument; summit of a mountain.

cejar, *vn.* to go backward; to slacken, to give in.

cejo, *m.* thick mist or fog which usually arises from rivers.

cejudo, da, *adj.* having bushy eyebrows.

celada, *f.* sallet (type of helmet); ambush; clever trick.

celaje, *m.* color of the clouds; cloud scenery.

celandés, esa, *n.* and *adj.* New Zealander.

celar, *vn.* and *va.* to fulfil carefully the duties of an office; to watch over; to watch jealously over someone's actions; to conceal; to engrave.

celda, *f.* cell.

celdilla, *f.* cellule; cell in a beehive; capsule.

celebérrimo, ma, *adj.* most famous.

celebración, *f.* celebration; praise.

celebrante, *m.* and *f.* celebrant, person who celebrates.

celebrar, *va.* to celebrate; to praise; to be glad of; **— misa,** to say mass.

célebre, *adj.* famous, renowned; gay; agreeable in conversation.

celebridad, *f.* celebrity, fame.

celemín, *m.* dry measure (about a peck).

celeridad, *f.* celerity, velocity.

celerímetro, *m.* speedometer.

celeste, *adj.* heavenly, celestial, sky-blue.

celestial, *adj.* celestial; heavenly; perfect; excellent.

celibato, *m.* celibacy.

célibe, *m.* bachelor.

celo, *m.* zeal; rut (in animals); **—s,** *pl.* jealousy; **tener —s de,** to be jealous of.

celofán, *m.* cellophane.

celosía, *f.* lattice of a window; Venetian blind.

celoso, sa, *adj.* zealous, eager; jealous.

celta, *adj.* Celtic; **—,** *m.* or *f.* Celt.

céltico, ca, *adj.* Celtic.

célula, *f.* cell; **— fotoeléctrica,** electric eye.

celular, *adj.* cellular.

celuloide, *m.* celluloid.

celulosa, *f.* cellulose, woody fiber.

cementar, *va.* to cement.

cementerio, *m.* cemetery.

cemento, *m.* cement; putty, mastic; **— armado,** reinforced concrete; **— de caucho,** rubber cement.

cena, *f.* supper.

cenáculo, *m.* cenacle; hall in which Jesus administered the last supper.

cenacho, *m.* market basket.

cenadero, *m.* supper room; summerhouse.

cenador, *m.* one who sups; arbor.

cenagal, *m.* slough; quagmire.

cenagoso, sa, *adj.* miry, marshy.

cenar, *vn.* to have supper, to dine.

C. en C. Compañía en comandita, Ltd. limited partnership or company.

cenceño, ña, *adj.* thin, slender.

cencerrada, *f.* rough music; hubbub, clatter.

cencerrear, *vn.* to jingle continually; to

play badly or on an untuned guitar; to make a dreadful noise.

cencerro, *m.* bell worn by the leading mule; ill-tuned guitar; **a —s tapados,** privately, by stealth.

cencido, da, *adj.* untilled.

cendal, *m.* crepe; furbelow.

cendra, *f.* paste for cleaning silver.

cenefa, *f.* border; band or stripe on the edge of cloth; brim of a pond; **—s,** *pl.* fringes.

cenicero, *m.* ash heap, ash pit; engine pit; ash tray.

ceniciento, ta, *adj.* ash-colored.

cenit, *m.* zenith.

ceniza, *f.* ashes; **miércoles de —,** Ash Wednesday.

cenizo, za, *adj.* of the color of ashes.

cenobita, *m.* cenobite, monk.

cenojil, *m.* garter.

cenote, *m.* underground pool.

censatario, *m.* one who pays an annuity out of his estate.

censo, *m.* quit rent; census; **— de por vida,** life annuity.

censor, *m.* censor, reviewer, critic; censorious person.

censual, *adj.* pertaining to quit rent; rental.

censualista, *m.* life annuitant; lessor.

censura, *f.* critical review; censure, blame, reproach.

censurador, ra, *n.* faultfinder.

censurar, *va.* to review, to criticize; to censure, to blame.

cent. central, cen. or cent. central.

c/ent. color entero, solid color.

centauro, *m.* Centaur.

centavo, *m.* hundredth part; a cent, as the hundredth part of a **peso** (dollar).

centella, *f.* lightning, spark; thunderbolt.

centellar or **centellear,** *vn.* to sparkle.

centelleo, *m.* glittering, sparkle.

centena, *f.* hundred.

centenada, *f.* quantity of one hundred; **a —as,** by hundreds.

centenal, *m.* rye field.

centenar, *m.* hundred.

centenario, ria, *adj.* centenary, secular; **—,** *m.* centennial.

centeno, *m.* (bot.) rye; **—, na,** *adj.* hundredth.

centésimo, ma, *adj.* centesimal, hundredth.

centígrado, da, *adj.* centigrade.

centigramo, *m.* centigram.

centilitro, *m.* centiliter.

centímetro, *m.* centimeter.

céntimo, *m.* centime (French coin); cent.

centinela, *m.* and *f.* sentinel; **— avanzada,** advance guard; **— perdida,** (mil.) forlorn hope; **— a caballo,** vedette; **estar de** or **hacer —,** to be on guard.

centón, *m.* crazy quilt; cento (literary composition formed by joining scraps from other authors).

central, *adj.* central, centric; **—,** *f.* central or main station; powerhouse; (Sp. Am.)

sugar mill; **— telefónica,** telephone exchange.

centralista, *m.* (Sp. Am.) owner of a sugar mill.

centralización, *f.* centralization.

centralizar, *va.* to centralize.

centrar, *va.* to center.

céntrico, ca, *adj.* central.

centrifugar, *va.* to whirl in a centrifuge, to centrifuge.

centrífugo, ga, *adj.* centrifugal.

centrípeto, ta, *adj.* centripetal.

centro, *m.* center; principal object.

Centroamérica, *f.* Central America.

centroamericano, na, *adj.* and *n.* Central American.

cents. centavos, ¢ or c. cents.

cénts. céntimos, ¢ or c. cents.

centuplicar, *va.* to centuplicate.

céntuplo, pla, *adj.* centuple, hundredfold.

centuria, *f.* century.

cénzalo, *m.* mosquito.

ceñido, da, *adj.* moderate; encircled with rings; **—do al cuerpo,** close fitting.

ceñidor, *m.* belt, girdle.

ceñir, *vn.* (1) to gird, to surround, to circle; to environ; to reduce, to abbreviate, to abridge.

ceño, *m.* frown; ferrule.

ceñudo, da, *adj.* frowning, haughty, stern, gruff.

cepa, *f.* stock of a vine; origin of a family; hole.

cepejón, *m.* the larger end of a branch torn from a tree.

cepilladuras, *f. pl.* wood shavings.

cepillo, *m.* brush; plane, trowel; **— de dientes,** toothbrush; **— para el cabello** or **la cabeza,** hairbrush; **— para ropa,** clothesbrush.

cepo, *m.* block; trap; snare; poor box; (fig.) entanglement.

cequí, *m.* Venetian gold coin, sequin (obsolete coin).

cera, *f.* wax; wax taper, wax candle; **—s,** *pl.* honeycomb.

cerafolio, *m.* (bot.) chervil.

cerámica, *f.* ceramics.

ceramista, *m.* pottery maker, ceramist.

cerato, *m.* cerate.

cerbatana, *f.* peashooter; acoustic trumpet; blowpipe.

cerca, *f.* inclosure; fence; **—s,** *m. pl.* objects in the foreground of a painting; **—,** *adv.* near, at hand, close by; **— de,** close, near, about (approximately); by (location).

cercado, *m.* inclosure; fenced-in field or garden; lock.

cercanía, *f.* neighborhood, proximity.

cercano, na, *adj.* and *adv.* near, close by, neighbor, neighboring, adjoining.

cercar, *va.* to inclose, to environ, to surround, to circle; to fence.

cercenar, *va.* to pare; to retrench; to clip; to lop off; to reduce, to lessen; to curtail, to cut away; to abridge.

cerceta, *f.* (orn.) widgeon.

cercillo, *m.* tendril of the vine.

cerciorar, *va.* to assure, to ascertain, to affirm;—**se,** to make sure.

cerco, *m.* blockade of a place; circle; hoop; fence.

cerda, *f.* strong hair growing in a horse's tail or mane; bristle.

cerdear, *vn.* to be weak in the forequarter; to emit a harsh sound; to decline a request by subterfuges.

Cerdeña, *f.* Sardinia.

cerdo, *m.* hog, pig.

cerdoso, sa, or **cerdudo, da,** *adj.* bristly.

cereal, *m.* cereal; grain.

cerebelo, *m.* (anat.) cerebellum.

cerebral, *adj.* cerebral.

cerebro, *m.* brain.

ceremonia, *f.* ceremony.

ceremonial, *adj.* and *m.* ceremonial.

ceremonioso, sa, *adj.* ceremonious.

cerería, *f.* candle store.

cerero, *m.* candlemaker.

cereza, *f.* cherry.

cerezo, *m.* cherry tree.

cerilla, *f.* wax taper; wax tablet; earwax; wax match.

cerillo, *m.* wax match.

cermeña, *f.* muscadine pear.

cernada, *f.* leached ashes.

cernedero, *m.* apron worn for sifting flour; place for sifting flour.

cerneja, *f.* fetlock.

cerner, *va.* (IE) to sift, to strain; to bolt; —, *vn.* to bud and blossom; to drizzle; —**se,** to waddle; to hover.

cernido, *m.* sifting; sifted flour.

cernidura, *f.* sifting.

cero, *m.* zero; **ser un — a la izquierda,** to be insignificant, to be of no account.

cerollo, lla, *adj.* (applied to grain) reaped rather green and soft.

cerón, *m.* dregs of pressed wax formed into a cake.

cerote, *m.* shoemaker's wax; (coll.) panic, fear.

ceroto, *m.* soft cerate.

cerquillo, *m.* tonsure of a monk; small circle or hoop.

cerquita, *f.* small inclosure; —, *adv.* at small distance.

cerrada, *f.* hide covering the backbone of an animal.

cerradero, *m.* staple of a lock; —, **ra,** *adj.* locked; acting as a lock.

cerradizo, za, *adj.* capable of being locked.

cerrado, da, *adj.* close; reserved; concealed; stupid, dense.

cerradura, *f.* act of locking; lock; **— de golpe** or **de muelle,** spring lock.

cerrajear, *vn.* to do locksmith's work.

cerrajería, *f.* trade of a locksmith; lock-smith's shop.

cerrajero, *m.* locksmith.

cerramiento, *m.* stopping; inclosure; finishing of the roof of a building.

cerrar, *va.* and *vn.* (IE) to close, to shut; to obstruct a passage; to lock; to engage the enemy; **— una cuenta,** to close an account; **— una operación,** to close a transaction, to arrange a deal; —**se,** to be shut up; to be obstinate in an opinion; to grow dark.

cerrazón, *f.* dark and cloudy weather which precedes tempests.

cerrero, ra, *adj.* running wild; **caballo —,** unbroken horse, bronco.

cerril, *adj.* mountainous, rough; wild, untamed.

cerrión, *m.* icicle.

cerro, *m.* hill; neck of an animal; backbone; combed flax or hemp; **en —,** bareback (horseback riding).

cerrojo, *m.* bolt, latch (of a door).

certamen, *m.* literary contest; in olden times, oral examinations in schools to which the public was invited.

certero, ra, *adj.* certain, sure; well-aimed, accurate (of a shot); accurate (of a shooter).

certeza, *f.* certainty, assurance.

certidumbre, *f.* certainty, conviction.

certificación, *f.* certification, certificate; return of a writ.

certificado, *m.* certificate; —, **da,** *adj.* certified, registered (as a letter).

certificar, *va.* to certify, to affirm; to register (a letter).

certificatorio, ria, *adj.* authenticating.

cerúleo, lea, *adj.* cerulean, sky blue.

cerumen, *m.* earwax.

cerusa, *f.* white lead.

cerval or **cervario, ria,** *adj.* belonging to a deer or resembling it; **miedo —,** great timidity.

cervatillo, *m.* small deer.

cervato, *m.* fawn.

cervecería, *f.* brewhouse, brewery; beer saloon.

cervecero, *m.* brewer; —, **ra,** *adj.* fond of beer.

cerveza, *f.* beer, ale, lager; **— de jengibre,** ginger ale.

cervicabra, *f.* gazelle.

cerviguillo, *m.* thick nape of the neck.

cerviz, *f.* (anat.) cervix; nape of the neck; **doblar** or **bajar la —,** to humble oneself.

cervuno, na, *adj.* deer-colored.

cesación, *f.* cessation, ceasing, pause, discontinuation.

cesante, *m.* retired officer; dismissed public officer; —, *adj.* jobless.

cesar, *vn.* to cease, to desist, to stop.

César, Caesar; Roman emperor.

cesáreo, rea, *adj.* Caesarian; imperial; **operación —rea,** Caesarean operation.

cesión, *f.* cession, transfer; concession.

cesionario, ria, *n.* assignee, indorsee (of a negotiable instrument).

cesionista, *m.* and *f.* assignor.
césped, *m.* sod, turf covered with grass; grass plot, lawn.
cespedera, *f.* field where green sods are cut.
cesta, *f.* basket, pannier; scoop or racket (in pelota game).
cestada, *f.* basketful.
cestería, *f.* basket shop or factory.
cestero, ra, *n.* basketmaker or seller.
cesto, *m.* hand basket.
cetrino, na, *adj.* citrine, lemon-colored; jaundiced.
cetro, *m.* scepter.
cf: costo de flete, freight cost; **caballo de fuerza,** h.p. horsepower; **confesor,** confessor.
cg. centigramo, cg. centigram.
cgo. cargo, (com.) cargo, charge, care.
cía. or **C.ía Compañía,** Co. or co. Company; Soc. Society.
cía, *f.* hip bone.
cianuro, *m.* cyanide.
ciar, *vn.* to rein back; (naut.) to backwater; (fig.) to slacken in the pursuit of an affair.
ciática, *f.* (med.) sciatica.
ciático, ca, *adj.* sciatic.
cibera, *f.* mill hopper; grist put at once in the hopper; all seeds or grains fit for food; husks, grounds.
cicatero, ra, *adj.* niggardly; sordid.
cicatriz, *f.* cicatrice, scar.
cicatrizar, *va.* and *vn.* to cicatrize, to heal (as a wound).
cícero, *m.* (print.) pica type.
Cicerón, Cicero.
ciclismo, *m.* bicycling.
ciclista, *m.* and *f.* cyclist, bicyclist.
ciclo, *m.* cycle.
ciclómetro, *m.* cyclometer.
ciclón, *m.* cyclone.
cíclope or **ciclope,** *m.* Cyclops.
ciclorama, *m.* cyclorama.
cicuta, *f.* (bot.) hemlock.
cidra, *f.* citron.
cidro, *m.* citron tree.
ciegamente, *adv.* blindly.
ciego, ga, *adj.* blind; —, *n.* blind person; **a —gas,** blindly; **vuelo a —gas,** blind flying.
cielo, *m.* sky, heaven; atmosphere; climate; **— de la cama,** bed canopy; **— de la boca,** roof of the palate; **— máximo,** (aer.) ceiling.
ciempiés, *m.* centipede.
cien, *adj.* one hundred.
ciencia, *f.* science; **—s físicas,** physical science; **a — cierta,** with certainty; **hombre de —,** scientist.
cieno, *m.* mud, mire.
científico, ca, *adj.* scientific.
ciento, *adj.* one hundred; —, *m.* a hundred; **juego de los —s,** piquet (card game); **por —,** per cent; **tanto por —,** percentage.
cientopiés, *m.* centipede.

cierna, *f.* blossom of vines, plants, etc.
cierne, *m.* act of blossoming; **en —,** in blossom.
cierre, *m.* closing, fastening; close; **— de corredera,** zipper; **— de los libros,** (com.) closing the books.
cierro, *m.* inclosure.
cierto, ta, *adj.* certain, confident, true; **noticias —tas,** definite news; **por —to,** certainly.
cierva, *f.* doe; hind.
ciervo, *m.* deer, hart, stag; **— volante,** stag beetle.
cierzo, *m.* cold north wind.
c.i.f. costo, seguro y flete, c.i.f. (com.) cost, insurance, and freight.
cifra, *f.* cipher, number; abbreviation; sum total.
cifrado, da, *adj.* dependent; **— en,** dependent upon.
cifrar, *va.* to write in ciphers; to abridge; **— la esperanza en,** to place one's hope in.
cigarra, *f.* cicada, katydid.
cigarrera, *f.* cigar box; cigarette case; woman cigarette maker.
cigarrero, *m.* cigar seller.
cigarrillo, *m.* cigarette.
cigarrista, *m.* one who smokes many cigars.
cigarro, *m.* cigar; cigarette.
cigarrón, *m.* grasshopper.
cigoñal, *m.* well sweep.
ciguato, ta, *adj.* jaundiced.
cigüeña, *f.* (orn.) stork; (mech.) crank.
cigüeñal, *m.* crankshaft.
cigüeño, *m.* male stork.
cilicio, *m.* hair shirt.
cilindrar, *va.* to calender, to roll.
cilíndrico, ca, *adj.* cylindrical.
cilindro, *m.* cylinder; barrel.
cilla, *f.* granary.
cillazgo, *m.* storehouse fees paid for the tithes kept in a granary.
cillero, *m.* keeper of a granary; granary.
cima, *f.* summit, peak; top of trees.
cimbalillo, *m.* small bell.
cimbalo, *m.* cymbal.
cimbel, *m.* decoy pigeon.
cimborio or **cimborrio,** *m.* cupola.
cimbra, *f.* center of an arch.
cimbrado, *m.* quick movement in a Spanish dance.
cimbrar or **cimbrear,** *va.* to brandish a rod or wand; to sway, to bend; to vibrate; **— a alguno,** to give a beating; —, *vn.* to bend, to vibrate.
cimbreño, ña, *adj.* pliant, flexible.
cimbronazo, *m.* blow with the flat of a sword.
cimentado, *m.* refinement of gold.
cimentar, *va.* (ie) to lay the foundation of a building; to ground; to establish the fundamental principles (of religion, science, etc.); to refine metals.
cimento, *m.* = **cemento.**
cimera, *f.* crest (of a helmet or coat of arms).

cimero, ra, *adj.* uppermost; at the very top.
cimiento, *m.* groundwork of a building; basis, origin.
cimitarra, *f.* scimitar.
cimorra, *f.* glanders.
cinabrio, *m.* cinnabar; vermilion.
cinamomo, *m.* (bot.) bead tree.
cinc, *m.* zinc.
cinca, *f.* a fault in tenpins for which one loses five points.
cincel, *m.* chisel.
cincelador, *m.* engraver, sculptor.
cincelar, *va.* to chisel, to engrave.
cinco, *adj.* and *m.* five.
cincona, *f.* cinchona.
cincuenta, *m.* and *adj.* fifty.
cincuenteno, na, *adj.* fiftieth.
cincha, *f.* girth, cinch.
cinchar, *va.* to girth.
cinchera, *f.* girth place.
cincho, *m.* sash used to keep the body warm; belt, girdle.
cine, *m.* moving picture, cinema.
cinema, *m.* moving pictures, cinema.
cinemadrama, *m.* photoplay.
cinemática, *f.* kinematics.
cinematógrafo, *m.* moving-picture play or show; cinema.
cinestésico, ca, *adj.* kinesthetic.
cinética, *f.* kinetics.
cíngulo, *m.* girdle; ancient military insignia.
cínico, ca, *adj.* cynical.
cinismo, *m.* cynicism; impudence.
Cinosura, *f.* (ast.) Cynosure, the Little Dipper, or Little Bear.
cinqueño or **cinquillo,** *m.* game of cards played by five persons.
cinta, *f.* ribbon, tape, band, strip; — **de medir,** tape measure.
cintadero, *m.* notch in the crossbow to which the string is fastened.
cintagorda, *f.* coarse hempen net for the tunny fishery.
cinteado, da, *adj.* adorned with ribbons.
cintero, *m.* ribbon weaver or dealer.
cintillo, *m.* hatband.
cinto, *m.* belt, girdle.
cintura, *f.* girdle; waistline; belt.
cinturón, *m.* belt; — **salvavidas,** life belt.
cipo, *m.* signpost, milepost.
ciprés, *m.* cypress tree.
cipresal, *m.* grove of cypress trees.
cipresino, na, *adj.* resembling or belonging to cypress.
cir. cirugía, sur. surgery.
circo, *m.* circus.
circuir, *va.* (UYO), to surround, to encircle.
circuito, *m.* circuit; circumference; radio hookup.
circulación, *f.* circulation; currency; traffic.
circular, *adj.* circular, round, circulatory; **carta, —,** circular letter; —, *vn.* to circulate.
círculo, *m.* circle; circumference; district; orb; club.

circumcirca, *adv.* about; almost, more or less.
circumpolar, *adj.* circumpolar.
circuncidar, *va.* to circumcise.
circuncisión, *f.* circumcision.
circundar, *va.* to surround, to encircle, to make the circuit of.
circunferencia, *f.* circumference.
circunferencial, *adj.* circumferential, surrounding.
circunflejo, ja, or **acento —,** *m.* circumflex.
circunloquio, *m.* circumlocution.
circunnavegación, *f.* circumnavigation.
circunnavegar, *va.* to circumnavigate.
circunscribir, *va.* to circumscribe.
circunscripción, *f.* circumscription.
circunspección, *f.* circumspection.
circunspecto, ta, *adj.* circumspect, cautious.
circunstancia, *f.* circumstance, incident, event; state, condition, detail.
circunstanciado, da, *adj.* circumstantial, minute.
circunstancial, *adv.* circumstantial.
circunstante, *adj.* surrounding, attending; **—s,** *m. pl.* bystanders; audience.
circunvalar, *va.* to surround, to encircle.
circunvecino, na, *adj.* neighboring, adjacent.
circunvolución, *f.* convolution.
cirial, *m.* large candlestick.
cirio, *m.* wax candle.
cirro, *m.* indurated gland; tuft of horsehair.
cirrosis, *f.* cirrhosis.
ciruela, *f.* plum; — **seca** or **pasa,** prune.
ciruelo, *m.* plum tree.
cirugía, *f.* surgery.
cirujano, *m.* surgeon.
ciscar, *va.* to make dirty; **—se,** to have a bowel movement.
cisco, *m.* coal dust; (coll.) hubbub, noise.
cisión, *f.* incision.
cisma, *m.* and *f.* schism; disturbance.
cismático, ca, *adj.* schismatic; finicky.
cisne, *m.* swan; (fig.) outstanding poet or musician.
cisquero, *m.* coal-dust dealer; pounce bag.
cister, *m.* Cistercian order of St. Bernard.
cisterna, *f.* cistern; tank; reservoir.
cistitis, *f.* cystitis.
cisura, *f.* incision.
cita, *f.* citation, quotation; rendezvous; appointment.
citación, *f.* quotation; summons.
citado, da, *adj.* mentioned.
citar, *va.* to make an appointment to meet a person; to convoke; to cite; to quote; to summon; to give judicial notice.
cítara, *f.* (mus.) zither; cithara (ancient harplike musical instrument); partition wall of the thickness of a common brick.
citarista, *m.* and *f.* cithara or zither player.
citatorio, ria, *adj.* (law) citatory.
citerior, *adj.* nearer, toward this end; **España —,** northeastern part of Spain.

cítola, *f.* mill clapper.
citoplasma, *m.* cytoplasm.
citrato, *m.* citrate.
cítrico, ca, *adj.* (chem.) citric.
ciudad, *f.* city; civic body; — **natal,** city of birth; home town.
ciudadanía, *f.* citizenship; enfranchisement; citizens.
ciudadano, na, *n.* citizen; —, *adj.* civil; citylike, citified.
ciudadela, *f.* citadel.
civeta, *f.* civet cat.
civeto, *m.* civet perfume.
cívico, ca, *adj.* civic.
civil, *adj.* civil; polite, courteous; (law) not criminal.
civilidad, *f.* politeness, civility.
civilización, *f.* civilization; culture.
civilizador, ra, *adj.* civilizing.
civilizar, *va.* to civilize.
civismo, *m.* patriotism.
cizalla, *f.* fragments or filings of gold, silver, or other metal; shears.
cizaña, *f.* (bot.) darnel; pollution; vice; disagreement.
cl. centilitro, cl. centiliter.
c/l curso legal, legal tender.
claitonia, *f.* (bot.) spring beauty.
clamar, *vn.* to cry out in a mournful tone; to show a want of something.
clamor, *m.* clamor, outcry; exclamation; tolling of bells.
clamorear, *va.* and *vn.* to clamor; to toll the bell.
clamoreo, *m.* knell; prolonged clamor.
clamoroso, sa, *adj.* clamorous; **éxito —,** howling success.
clan, *m.* clan.
clandestino, na, *adj.* clandestine, secret, concealed.
clara, *f.* short interval of fair weather on a rainy day; white of an egg.
claraboya, *f.* skylight; bull's-eye.
claramente, *adv.* clearly; openly.
clarea, *f.* mulled wine.
clarear, *vn.* to dawn; —**se,** to be transparent; to clear up.
clarete or **vino —,** *m.* claret.
claridad, *f.* light, gleam, brightness, clearness.
clarificar, *va.* to brighten; to clarify.
clarificativo, va, *adj.* purifying, clarifying.
clarín, *m.* horn, bugle; organ stop; trumpet; trumpeter.
clarinero, *m.* trumpeter.
clarinete, *m.* clarinet; clarinet player.
clarividencia, *f.* clairvoyance.
claro, ra, *adj.* clear, bright; intelligible; light, evident, manifest; —, *m.* skylight; opening or space between the columns of a building; **¡—ro!** *interj.* of course!; **poner en —,** to set right.
claroscuro, *m.* (art) chiaroscuro.
clase, *f.* class, rank; order; kind; — **acomodada,** well-to-do gentry, wealthy class.

clásico, ca, *adj.* classical, classic.
clasificación, *f.* classification; filing.
clasificar, *va.* to classify, to class, to put in order.
Claudia, Claudina, Claudia.
claudicar, *vn.* to halt; to limp; to proceed bunglingly.
Claudio, Claude, Claudius.
claustral, *adj.* cloistral.
claustro, *m.* cloister; assembly of the faculty of a university; — **de universidad,** campus.
cláusula, *f.* period; clause.
clausular, *va.* to close a period; to conclude (a speech).
clausura, *f.* inner recess of a convent; confinement; conclusion, closing.
clausurar, *va.* to close; to adjourn.
clava, *f.* club, heavy stick; (naut.) scupper hole.
clavado, da, *adj.* exact, precise; nailed; furnished with nails.
clavar, *va.* to nail; to fasten in, to force in; to drive into; to drive a wedge; (fig.) to cheat, to deceive; — **la vista en,** to stare at.
clavazón, *f.* set of nails.
clave, *f.* key, code; (mus.) clef; **palabra —,** key word; —, *m.* harpsichord, clavichord.
clavel, *m.* (bot.) pink, carnation.
clavera, *f.* mould for nailheads; hole in a horseshoe.
clavero, *m.* aromatic clove tree; keeper of the keys.
clavetear, *va.* to ornament with nails.
clavicordio, *m.* clavichord, harpsichord.
clavícula, *f.* (anat.) clavicle, collarbone.
clavija, *f.* pin, peg; plug, key.
clavijado, da, *adj.* pegged, having pegs or pins.
clavo, *m.* nail; corn (on the feet); clove.
clemátide, *f.* (bot.) clematis.
clemencia, *f.* clemency, mercy.
clemente, *adj.* clement, merciful.
cleptomanía, *f.* kleptomania.
cleptomaníaco, ca, or **cleptómano, na,** *adj.* and *n.* kleptomaniac.
clerecía, *f.* clergy.
clerical, *adj.* clerical, pertaining to the clergy.
clericato, *m.* state and dignity of a clergyman.
clerigalla, *f.* priesthood (in contempt).
clérigo, *m.* clergyman.
clero, *m.* clergy.
cliente, *m.* and *f.* client; customer.
clientela, *f.* clientele, patronage.
clima, *m.* climate.
climax, *m.* climax.
clínica, *f.* clinic.
clínico, ca, *adj.* clinical.
clíper, *m.* clipper, flying boat.
clisar, *va.* to stereotype.
clisé, *m.* plate, mat, cut, type.

clister, *m.* (med.) clyster, an injection.
clivoso, sa, *adj.* (poet.) sloping.
clo-clo, *m.* clucking of a hen.
cloaca, *f.* sewer.
cloque, *m.* grapnel; harpoon.
cloquear, *vn.* to cluck.
cloqueo, *m.* cluck, clucking (of fowls).
cloquera, *f.* hatching of fowls; brooding time.
cloquero, *m.* harpooner in the tunny fishery.
clorhídrico, ca, *adj.* (chem.) hydrochloric.
cloro, *m.* (chem.) chlorine.
clorófila, *f.* chlorophyll (greenish coloring substance in plants).
cloroformizar, *va.* to administer chloroform.
cloroformo, *m.* chloroform.
clorosis, *f.* (med.) chlorosis.
cloruro, *m.* (chem.) chloride.
club, *m.* club, association.
clueca, *adj.* clucking and hatching (of a hen).
clueco, ca, *adj.* decrepit; (Sp. Am.) presumptuous, vain.
cllo. cuartillo, *pt.* pint; one fourth of a peck in dry measure.
cm. or **c/m centímetro,** cm. centimeter.
C.M.B. or **c.m.b. cuyas manos beso,** (expression of courtesy and respect).
Co. Compañía, Co. Company; Soc. Society.
c/o a cargo de, c/o or c.o. in care of.
coacción, *f.* coaction, compulsion.
coactivo, va, *adj.* coercive, compulsory.
coadyutor, *m.* coadjutor, assistant.
coadyuvador, *m.* fellow helper, assistant.
coadyuvar, *va.* to help, to assist.
coagular, *va.* and *vr.* to coagulate, to curd.
coágulo, *m.* coagulated blood.
coalición, *f.* coalition, confederacy.
coarrendador, *m.* joint partner in the rent of a property; colessor.
coartación, *f.* limitation, restriction; obligation of the holder of a benefice, or its recipient, to receive ordination.
coartada, *f.* (law) alibi.
coartar, *va.* to limit, to restrict, to restrain.
coate, coata, *n.* and *adj.* (Mex.) twin; pal.
coatí, *m.* coati (a raccoonlike animal).
cobalto, *m.* cobalt.
cobarde, *adj.* cowardly, timid; —, *m.* coward.
cobardía, *f.* cowardice.
cobertera, *f.* potlid; procuress.
cobertizo, *m.* small shed; hovel.
cobertura, *f.* coverlet; prerogative of the Spanish grandees to appear with covered head before the king.
cobija, *f.* gutter tile; head covering; (Mex.) bed cover, blanket.
cobijar, *va.* to cover; to shelter.
cobra, *f.* (zool.) cobra.
cobradero, ra, *adj.* recoverable.
cobrador, *m.* collector; streetcar or train conductor.
cobranza, *f.* recovery or collection of money.
cobrar, *va.* to collect; to recover; to receive; to charge (price, fee); **— ánimo,** to take

courage; **— fuerzas,** to gain strength; **— impuestos,** to tax; **letras** or **efectos a —,** bills receivable.
cobre, *m.* copper; copper or brass kitchen utensils; **— quemado,** copper sulphate; **moneda de —,** copper coin.
cóbrese al entregar, cash on delivery, C.O.D.
cobrizo, za, *adj.* coppery.
cobro, *m.* collection; payment; **presentar al —,** to present for payment.
coca, *f.* (bot.) coca, coca tea; (coll.) head.
cocaína, *f.* cocaine.
cocarar, *va.* to supply with coca leaves.
cocción, *f.* concoction.
coceador, ra, *adj.* kicking (of horses).
cocear, *va.* and *vn.* to kick; (fig.) to resist.
cocedero, ra, *adj.* easily cooked; —, *m.* cookery; bakery; kitchen.
cocedizo, za, *adj.* easily boiled.
cocer, *va.* (UE) to boil, to cook; —, *vn.* to boil; to ferment; **—se,** to suffer intense pain.
cocido, da, *adj.* cooked, boiled; (fig.) skilled, experienced; —, *m.* oglio, a dish made of boiled meat and vegetables.
cociente, *m.* quotient.
cocimiento, *m.* decoction; bath for dyeing.
cocina, *f.* kitchen, cuisine; **— económica,** cooking range.
cocinar, *va.* and *vn.* to cook; (coll.) to meddle.
cocinera, *f.* female cook.
cocinero, *m.* cook.
cocinilla, *f.* small kitchen, kitchenette; fireplace, cooking stove; **— sin fuego,** fireless cooker.
cocktail, *m.* cocktail.
coco, *m.* coconut, coconut tree; bogey, bugaboo; **agua de —,** coconut milk; **hacer —s,** to flirt.
cocodrilo, *m.* crocodile; (fig.) faithless person; **lágrimas de —,** crocodile tears.
cocoso, sa, *adj.* worm-eaten.
cocuyo or **cucuyo,** *m.* firefly.
cochambre, *m.* dirty, stinking object.
cochambrería, *f.* heap of nasty and filthy objects.
cochambroso, sa, *adj.* nasty, filthy, stinking.
cocharro, *m.* wooden cup.
cochastro, *m.* little sucking wild boar.
coche, *m.* coach; carriage; car; **— de alquiler,** cab; **— cama,** sleeping car; **— comedor,** diner; **— directo,** through coach; **— dormitorio,** sleeping car; **— fumador,** smoking car; **— restaurante,** dining car; **— salón,** parlor car.
cochear, *vn.* to drive a coach.
cochecillo, *m.* small carriage; **— de niño,** baby carriage.
cochera, *f.* coach house; garage.
cocheril, *adj.* pertaining to coachmen.
cochero, *m.* coachman, driver.
cochifrito, *m.* fricassee of lamb, mutton, etc.
cochina, *f.* sow.

cochinería, *f.* dirtiness, foulness.
cochinilla, *f.* wood louse; cochineal.
cochino, na, *adj.* dirty, nasty, filthy; —, *m.* pig.
cochiquera, *f.* pigsty.
coda, *f.* (mus.) finale.
codaste, *m.* (naut.) sternpost.
codazo, *m.* blow with the elbow.
codear, *vn.* to elbow.
codeína, *f.* codein.
códice, *m.* codex, old manuscript.
codicia, *f.* covetousness, lust, cupidity, greed.
codiciable, *adj.* covetable.
codiciar, *va.* to covet, to desire eagerly.
codicilar, *adj.* pertaining to a codicil.
codicilo, *m.* (law) codicil.
codicioso, sa, *adj.* greedy, covetous; diligent, laborious.
código, *m.* code of laws; — **de comercio,** code of commerce.
codillo, *m.* knee of quadrupeds; angle; crotch of a tree; codille, a term in ombre.
codo, *m.* elbow; bend, sharp turn; **dar de —,** to elbow; **charlar hasta por los —s,** to chatter like magpies.
codorniz, *f.* (orn.) quail.
coeducación, *f.* coeducation.
coeducar, *va.* to coeducate.
coeficiente, *m.* coefficient; — **de seguridad,** safety factor.
coerción, *f.* coercion, restraint.
coercitivo, va, *adj.* coercive.
coetáneo, nea, *adj.* contemporary.
coeterno, na, *adj.* coeternal.
coevo, va, *adj.* coeval.
coexistencia, *f.* coexistence.
coexistente, *adj.* coexistent.
coexistir, *vn.* to coexist.
cofa, *f.* (naut.) top of lower masts.
cofia, *f.* coif; silk hair net; headgear.
cofiador, *m.* (law) joint surety, fellow bondsman.
cofín, *m.* small basket for fruit.
cofradía, *f.* confraternity.
cofre, *m.* trunk; locker; box, chest; hood (of an automobile).
cofrero, *m.* trunk maker.
cogedera, *f.* hive used to gather an escaped swarm of bees; handle.
cogedizo, za, *adj.* gatherable.
cogedor, *m.* collector, gatherer; dustbin, dustpan.
coger, *va.* to catch, to lay hold of, to occupy, to take up; to surprise.
cogitabundo, da, *adj.* pensive, thoughtful.
cogitar, *va.* to reflect, to meditate.
cogollo, *m.* heart of a lettuce, cabbage, etc.; shoot of a plant.
cogote, *m.* occiput, back part of head or skull.
cogucho, *m.* (Cuba) inferior sugar.
cogujada, *f.* (orn.) crested lark.
cogujón, *m.* corner of a mattress or bolster.
cogulla, *f.* cowl, monk's hood.

cohabitar, *vn.* to cohabit, to live together.
cohechar, *va.* to bribe, to suborn; to plow just before sowing.
cohecho, *m.* bribery; season for plowing the ground.
coheredera, *f.* coheiress.
coheredero, *m.* coheir, joint heir.
coherencia, *f.* coherence.
coherente, *adj.* coherent, cohesive.
cohesión, *f.* cohesion.
cohete, *m.* skyrocket; firecracker; fuse; — **de señales,** (aer.) flare.
cohetero, *m.* rocket maker.
cohibir, *va.* to prohibit, to restrain.
cohombro, *m.* type of cucumber.
cohonestar, *va.* to give an honest appearance to an action.
cohorte, *f.* cohort.
coincidencia, *f.* coincidence.
coincidente, *adj.* coincident.
coincidir, *vn.* to coincide.
coito, *m.* cohabitation.
cojear, *vn.* to halt, to hobble; to deviate from virtue; to tilt.
cojera, *f.* lameness, halting.
cojijoso, sa, *adj.* peevish, irritable.
cojín, *m.* cushion; pillow, bolster.
cojinete, *m.* bearing (of an axle, etc.); — **de bolas,** ball bearing; — **de rodillos,** roller bearing.
cojo, ja, *adj.* lame, cripple, halt.
cojudo, da, *adj.* entire, not gelded, not castrated; —, *n.* (Sp. Am.) simple-minded, easily deceived person; a fool.
cok, *m.* coke.
col. or **col.ª: columna,** col. column; **colonia,** col. colony.
col, *f.* cabbage.
cola, *f.* tail; train (of a gown); line; glue; — **de pescado,** isinglass; **de la —,** behind, backwards; **hacer —,** to stand in line.
colaboración, *f.* collaboration, assistance.
colaborar, *vn.* to collaborate, to work together.
colación, *f.* lunch; (Col.) cake, biscuit; collation (bestowing an ecclesiastical benefice).
colacionador, *m.* collator.
colacionar, *va.* to collate, to compare.
coladera, *f.* strainer, colander.
coladero, *m.* colander; narrow passage.
colador, *m.* colander, strainer.
coladura, *f.* straining, filtering, seeping.
colanilla, *f.* small bolt.
colapez or **colapiscis,** *f.* isinglass.
colapso, *m.* (med.) prostration, collapse.
colar, *va.* and *vn.* (UE) to strain, to filter; to confer ecclesiastical benefices; to pass through a narrow place; to drink wine; —**se,** to be filtered.
colateral, *adj.* collateral.
colcha, *f.* coverlet, bedspread, quilt.
colchadura, *f.* quilting.
colchar, *va.* to quilt.
colchero, ra, *n.* quilt maker.

colchón, *m.* mattress; **— de muelles,** spring mattress; **— de pluma,** feather mattress; **— de viento,** air mattress.

colchonero, *m.* mattress maker.

coleada, *f.* wagging of an animal's tail.

colear, *vn.* to wag the tail.

colección, *f.* collection; line; set.

colecta, *f.* distribution of a tax levied on a town; collect (an oration of the mass); collection of offerings.

colectar, *va.* to collect (taxes, etc.).

colectividad, *f.* collectivity; community.

colectivismo, *m.* collectivism.

colectivo, va, *adj.* collective, aggregated; **contrato —,** closed shop; **sociedad —va,** general partnership.

colector, *m.* collector, gatherer; (elec.) commutator.

colega, *m.* and *f.* colleague.

colegial, *m.* collegian; **—,** *adj.* collegiate, pertaining to a college.

colegiala, *f.* college woman.

colegiata, *f.* collegiate church.

colegio, *m.* boarding school; college; society of men of the same profession.

colegir, *va.* (LIJO) to collect; to deduce.

cólera, *f.* anger, rage, fury; **montar en —,** to fly into a rage; **—,** *m.* (med.) cholera.

coléricamente, *adv.* in a rage.

colérico, ca, *adj.* choleric, irritable, angry, enraged.

colesterina, *f.* cholesterol, cholestrin.

coleta, *f.* queue of hair; short addition to a writing, postscript.

coletero, *m.* maker of buff jackets.

coleto, *m.* buff jacket; (coll.) interior of a person; **decir para su —,** to say to oneself.

colgadero, *m.* hook to hang things upon; **—, ra,** *adj.* fit to be hung up.

colgadizo, *m.* shed; **—, za,** *adj.* pendent, suspended.

colgador, *m.* hanger; **— de ropas,** clothes hanger.

colgadura, *f.* tapestry, drapery, bed hangings.

colgajo, *m.* tatter, rag.

colgante, *adj.* pendulous, hanging; **puente —,** suspension bridge.

colgar, *va.* (UE) to hang; to suspend; to adorn with tapestry; **—,** *vn.* to be suspended.

colibrí, *m.* hummingbird.

cólico, *m.* colic.

colicuar, *va.* to melt, to dissolve; **—se,** to become liquid.

coliflor, *f.* cauliflower.

coligación, *f.* connection, union, alliance.

colilla, *f.* cigar butt, cigarette butt.

colina, *f.* hill, hillock.

colinabo, *m.* turnip.

colindar, *vn.* to be contiguous; **— con,** adjacent (to).

colirrábano, *m.* kohlrabi.

coliseo, *m.* opera house, theater.

colisión, *f.* collision; friction.

colitigante, *m.* and *f.* litigant, party to a lawsuit.

colitis, *f.* (med.) colitis.

colmar, *va.* to heap up, to fill up; **—se,** to reach the limit.

colmena, *f.* hive, beehive.

colmenar, *m.* beehive stand, apiary.

colmenero, ra, *n.* beekeeper.

colmenilla, *f.* morel (mushroom).

colmillo, *m.* eyetooth; long tusk; premolar.

colmilludo, da, *adj.* having eyeteeth; (fig.) sagacious, quick-sighted.

colmo, *m.* heap; completion; crown; full; fill; height; highwater mark; **a —,** plentifully.

colocación, *f.* employment; arrangement; situation, place; allocation.

colocar, *va.* to arrange; to lay, to place; to give employment to; **— dinero,** to invest money.

colodra, *f.* milk pail; wooden can with which wine is measured.

colodrillo, *m.* back of the head.

coloide, *m.* colloid.

Colón, Columbus.

colon, *m.* (anat.) colon, large intestine.

colón, *m.* monetary unit of Costa Rica.

Colonia, *f.* Cologne.

colonia, *f.* colony; silk ribbon two inches wide; (Cuba) sugar-cane plantation; (Mex.) subdivision of land.

Colonia del Cabo, *f.* Cape Colony.

colonial, *adj.* colonial.

colonización, *f.* colonization.

colonizar, *va.* to colonize.

colono, *m.* colonist; farmer; sugar planter.

coloquio, *m.* colloquy, talk.

color, *m.* color, hue, dye; rouge; pretext; **so —,** on pretense, under pretext; **este — destiñe,** this color comes off.

coloración, *f.* coloring, coloration.

colorado, da, *adj.* ruddy, red.

colorante, *m.* coloring, dye.

colorar, *va.* to color; to tint, to dye.

colorativo, va, *adj.* coloring.

colorear, *va.* to color; to palliate, to excuse; **—,** *vn.* to grow red.

colorete, *m.* rouge.

colorido, *m.* coloring; pretext, pretense.

colorín, *m.* (orn.) linnet; vivid color; (Chile) a redheaded person.

colorinche, *m.* (Arg.) bright, vivid color.

colorir, *va.* to color.

colorista, *m.* and *f.* colorist.

colosal, *adj.* colossal, great.

coloso, *m.* colossus.

columbera, *f.* (Arg.) swing, seesaw.

Columbia Británica, *f.* British Columbia.

columbrar, *va.* to discern at a distance; to guess, to make out.

columna, *f.* column; **— de luz,** light beam; **quinta —,** fifth column.

Columnas de Hércules, *f. pl.* Pillars of Hercules.

columnata, f. colonnade.

columpiar, va. to swing to and fro.

columpio, m. swing, seesaw.

colusión, f. collusion.

colusorio, ria, adj. collusive.

colza, f. (bot.) rape, rapeseed.

collado, m. hillock.

collar, m. necklace, necklet.

collera, f. collar; clamp; chain gang; bush (in machinery); (Arg.) set of cuff links.

com.: comercial, com. or cml. commercial; **comercio,** com. commerce.

coma, f. comma (punctuation mark); (med.) coma.

comadre, f. midwife; title given godmother of one's child; also title given mother of child one has sponsored at christening; intimate friend, pal.

comadreja, f. weasel.

comadrería, f. gossiping.

comadrero, ra, adj. idle and gossiping.

comadrón, m. man midwife.

comadrona, f. midwife.

comandancia, f. command; commandant's office.

comandante, m. commander, chief; warden; major.

comandar, va. to command.

comandita, f. (com.) silent partnership.

comanditario, ria, adj. belonging or relating to a silent partnership; **socio —,** silent partner in a business.

comando, m. commando, expedition or raid by a military force.

comarca, f. territory, district; boundary, limit.

comarcano, na, adj. neighboring, bordering upon.

comarcar, va. to plant trees in a straight line; **—,** vn. to border, to abut.

comba, f. curvature; warp; bend; (Chile) hammer.

combar, va. to bend; **—se,** to warp.

combate, m. combat, conflict; fighting; **— singular,** duel; **fuera de —,** out of action; **aeroplano de —,** fighter plane.

combatidor, m. combatant.

combatiente, m. combatant; **no —,** noncombatant.

combatir, va. and vn. to combat, to fight; to attack; to contradict.

combinación, f. combination.

combinar, va. and vr. to combine.

combo, ba, adj. bent, crooked, warped; **—,** m. stand for cask.

combustible, adj. combustible; **—,** m. fuel; **aprovisionamiento de —,** fueling.

combustión, f. combustion.

comebolas, m. and f. (Col.) vagabond; (Cuba) fool, one who believes everything he hears.

comedero, ra, adj. edible.

comedia, f. comedy.

comediante, m. and f. actor, comedian.

comediar, va. to divide into equal shares.

comedido, da, adj. polite, gentle.

comedirse, vr. (I) to govern oneself.

comedor, ra, n. eater; feeder; **—,** m. dining room.

comején, m. white ant, wood borer, termite.

comendador, m. knight commander of a military order; head of a religious house.

comendadora, f. mother superior of a nunnery.

comendaticio, cia, or **comendatorio, ria,** adj. recommending, introductory (of letters).

comentador, ra, n. commentator.

comentar, va. to comment; to remark; to expound.

comentario, m. comment, commentary.

comento, m. comment; remark.

comenzar, va. and vn. (IE) to commence, to begin.

comer, va. to eat, to chew; to dine; to consume; to take a piece in chess; **dar de —,** to feed.

comerciable, adj. marketable; sociable.

comercial, adj. commercial.

comerciante, m. trader, merchant, tradesman, businessman.

comerciar, va. to trade, to have business intercourse with; **— en,** to deal in.

comercio, m. trade, commerce, business; communication, intercourse; company of merchants; **cámara de —,** chamber of commerce; **casa de —,** commercial house; **en el —,** in the shops; **junta de —,** board of trade.

comestible, adj. edible; **—s,** m. pl. provisions, food groceries; **tienda de —s,** grocery store.

cometa, m. comet; **—,** f. kite.

cometer, va. to commit, to charge; to intrust; to attempt.

cometido, m. task, trust, mission.

comezón, f. itch; ardent desire.

comicios, m. pl. elections; polls, voting places.

cómico, ca, adj. comic, comical, funny; **—,** n. actor, actress.

comida, f. eating, food; dinner; meal.

comidilla, f. favorite topic for gossip; hobby.

comienzo, m. beginning.

comilón, ona, n. great eater, glutton.

comillas, f. pl. quotation marks.

comino, m. cumin (plant or seed); **no valer un —,** to be worthless.

cominterno, m. comintern.

comisaría, f. comissaryship; commissariat; police department.

comisario, m. commissary; deputy.

comisión, f. trust, commission; mandate; committee; **a —,** on commission; **casa de —es,** commission house.

comisionado, m. commissioner.

comisionar, va. to commission, to depute.

comisionista, m. commissioner; commission agent, traveling salesman.

comis.° comisario, commissary.
comiso, *m.* confiscation; embargo.
comistrajo, *m.* (coll.) hodgepodge.
comité, *m.* committee.
comitiva, *f.* suite, retinue; cortege, followers.
cómitre, *m.* (naut.) boatswain on a galley.
como, *adv.* (*interrogative,* **cómo**) how, in what manner; as; in such a manner; like; — **quiera que,** whereas, inasmuch as; no matter how; **¿a cómo estamos?** what is the date?
cómoda, *f.* chest of drawers.
comodatario, ria, *n.* (law) borrower; pawnbroker.
comodidad, *f.* comfort, ease; convenience; profit, interest; **—es,** *pl.* wealth, estate.
cómodo, da, *adj.* convenient, commodious; comfortable.
comodoro, *m.* (naut.) commodore.
Comp. or **comp. Compañía,** Co. or co. Company; Soc. Society.
compactibilidad, *f.* compactness.
compacto, ta, *adj.* compact, close, dense.
compadecer, *va.* (EZCO) to pity, to sympathize with; **—se,** to agree with each other; — **de,** to pity.
compadrar, *vn.* to become a godfather.
compadrazgo, *m.* godfathership.
compadre, *m.* title given godfather of one's child; also title given father of child one has sponsored at christening; friend, old pal, compeer.
compadrería, *f.* friendly intercourse between friends or companions.
compaginar, *va.* to join, to couple.
compañero, ra, *n.* companion, comrade, friend, partner; — **de camarote,** cabin mate; — **de cuarto,** roommate; — **de viaje,** traveling companion.
compañía, *f.* company, society; partnership.
comparable, *adj.* comparable.
comparación, *f.* comparison.
comparar, *va.* to compare, to confront.
comparativo, va, *adj.* comparative.
comparecer, *vn.* (EZCO) to appear before a judge.
comparendo, *m.* summons.
comparición, *f.* (law) appearance.
comparsa, *m.* and *f.* (theat.) supernumerary actor; **—,** *f.* masqueraders in carnival.
comparte, *m.* joint party in a lawsuit.
compartir, *va.* to divide into equal parts; to share.
compás, *m.* pair of compasses; (mus.) measure, time; rule of life; pattern; — **de dos puntas,** dividers.
compasar, *va.* to measure with a compass.
compasión, *f.* compassion, commiseration, pity.
compasivo, va, *adj.* compassionate, merciful.
compatible, *adj.* compatible, consistent with.
compatriota, *m.* and *f.* countryman; countrywoman; fellow citizen.

compeler, *va.* to compel, to constrain.
compendiar, *va.* to epitomize, to abridge.
compendio, *m.* epitome, abridgment, summary.
compendioso, sa, *adj.* brief, abridged, compendious.
compensación, *f.* compensation; recompense; **casa de —,** clearing house.
compensar, *va.* and *vn.* to compensate; to make amends; to recompense.
competencia, *f.* competition, rivalry; competence.
competente, *adj.* competent, sufficient.
competer, *vn.* to be one's due, to be incumbent on.
competición, *f.* competition.
competidor, ra, *n.* competitor, rival.
competir, *vn.* (I) to vie; to contend, to compete, to compete with, to rival.
compilación, *f.* compilation.
compilador, *m.* compiler.
compilar, *va.* to compile.
compinche, *m.* comrade, confidant, crony.
complacencia, *f.* pleasure; compliance.
complacer, *va.* (AZCO) to please another; **—se,** to be pleased with.
complaciente, *adj.* pleasing; accommodating.
complejidad, *f.* complexity.
complejo, *m.* complex; **—, ja,** *adj.* complex, intricate.
complementario, ria, *adj.* complementary.
complemento, *m.* complement; completion; (gram.) object.
completamente, *adv.* completely.
completar, *va.* to complete.
completo, ta, *adj.* complete, perfect; absolute; **por —to,** completely.
complexión, *f.* constitution, physique.
complexionado, da, *adj.* complexioned; **bien** or **mal —,** of a good or bad complexion.
complexo, *m.* complex, integrated whole; **—, xa,** *adj.* complex, involved, intricate.
complicación, *f.* complication, entanglement.
complicar, *va.* to complicate.
cómplice, *m.* and *f.* accomplice.
complicidad, *f.* complicity.
complot, *m.* plot, conspiracy.
componedor, *m.* composer, author; compositor; referee; repairer.
componer, *va.* (COMPONGO, COMPUSE, COMPUESTO) to compose; to compound; to construct; to mend, to repair; to strengthen, to restore; to garnish; to adjust; to settle, to reconcile; to calm; **—se,** to arrange one's hair, clothes, etc.; **—se de,** to be composed of.
comportable, *adj.* supportable, tolerable, sufferable.
comportar, *va.* to suffer, to tolerate; **—se,** to comport oneself, to behave oneself.
composición, *f.* composition; composure; making; adjustment; agreement; musical

or literary composition; modest appearance; typesetting.

compositor, ra, *n.* composer; compositor.

compostura, *f.* composition, composure; mending, repairing; neatness of dress; accommodation, adjustment; modesty, demureness.

compota, *f.* preserves, sweetmeats.

compotera, *f.* vessel in which jams are served.

compra, *f.* purchase; necessaries bought for the daily use of the house; —s, purchases; **ir de —s,** to go shopping.

comprador, ra, *n.* buyer, customer, purchaser; caterer.

comprar, *va.* to buy, to purchase; — **al contado,** to buy for cash; — **al crédito** or **al fiado,** to buy on credit; — **al granel,** to buy in bulk; to buy wholesale; — **al por mayor (menor),** to buy at wholesale (retail); — **de ocasión,** to buy secondhand.

compraventa, *f.* bargain and sale.

comprender, *va.* to include, to contain, to comprise; to comprehend, to understand.

comprendido, da, *adj.* including, understood.

comprensibilidad, *f.* intelligibility.

comprensible, *adj.* comprehensible.

comprensión, *f.* comprehension, understanding.

comprensivo, va, *adj.* comprehensive.

compresible, *adj.* compressible.

compresión, *f.* compression, pressure.

compresivo, va, *adj.* compressive.

compresor, *m.* compressor.

comprimir, *va.* to compress; to condense; to repress, to restrain; —se, to restrain oneself, to control oneself.

comprobación, *f.* checking, verification.

comprobador, *m.* examiner.

comprobante, *adj.* proving; —, *m.* voucher.

comprobar, *va.* (UE) to verify, to check; to confirm; to prove.

comprometer, *va.* to compromise; to render one answerable for; to put in danger; —se, to commit oneself; to become engaged.

comprometido, da, *adj.* engaged, betrothed.

compromisario, *m.* arbitrator, umpire.

compromiso, *m.* compromise; commitment; engagement; pledge, obligation.

compuerta, *f.* half door; lock, floodgate, sluice.

compuesto, *m.* compound; —, **ta,** *adj.* composed, compounded, repaired; made up of; **interés —to,** compound interest.

compulsa, *f.* attested copy of an instrument.

compulsar, *va.* to make an authentic copy.

compulsión, *f.* duress.

compulsivo, va, *adj.* compulsive.

compulsorio, ria, *adj.* compulsory; —, *m.* (law) compulsory decree ordering an authentic copy to be made.

compunción, *f.* compunction, contrition.

compungirse, *vr.* to feel compunction.

computación, *f.* computation.

computar, *va.* to compute.

computista, *m.* and *f.* computer, computist.

cómputo, *m.* computation, calculation.

comulgar, *va.* and *vn.* to administer the sacrament; to take communion.

común, *adj.* common, usual, general; —, *m.* community, public; watercloset; **acciones en —,** common stock; **de — acuerdo,** by mutual consent; **en —,** jointly; **poco —,** unusual; **por lo, —** in general, generally.

comuna, *f.* town hall, municipality.

comunal, *m.* commonalty, common people; —, *adj.* community, communal.

comunero, ra, *adj.* popular; —, *m.* joint holder of a tenure of lands.

comunicación, *f.* communication, communiqué; — **radioeléctrica,** radio message.

comunicar, *va.* to communicate; —se, to have intercourse; to correspond; to be united.

comunicativo, va, *adj.* communicative.

comunidad, *f.* commonness; commonalty; community.

comunión, *f.* communion; fellowship; common possession.

comunismo, *m.* communism.

comunista, *m.* and *f.* communist.

comunizar, *va.* and *vn.* to communize.

comuña, *f.* mixed grains, mixed wheat and rye; —s, *pl.* seeds.

con, *prep.* with; by; — **que,** then, therefore; — **tal que,** on condition that; **dar —,** to find; **tratar —,** to do business with.

conato, *m.* endeavor, effort; crime attempted but not executed.

cóncava or **concavidad,** *f.* concavity.

cóncavo, va, *adj.* concave.

concebir, *va.* and *vn.* (I) to conceive (to imagine or comprehend); to conceive (to become pregnant).

conceder, *va.* to give; to grant; to concede, to allow.

concejal, *m.* councilman, councilor, alderman.

concejil, *adj.* relating to public boards.

concejo, *m.* civic body of a small town; town hall.

concentración, *f.* concentration; **campo de —,** concentration camp.

concentrado, da, *adj.* intensive.

concentrar, *va.* and *vr.* to concentrate.

concéntrico, ca, *adj.* concentric.

concepción, *f.* conception; idea.

conceptear, *vn.* to be clever in repartee, to make many jocular, smart remarks.

conceptible, *adj.* conceivable.

conceptista, *adj.* witty and subtle to excess; —, *m.* writer who overdoes witticism and subtlety.

concepto, *m.* conception, concept, idea, thought; judgment, opinion; (com.) account; item; **por todos —s,** by and large.

conceptuar, *va.* to conceive, to judge, to think.

conceptuoso, sa, *adj.* sharp, witty; sententious.

concernencia, *f.* respect, relation.

concerniente, *adj.* concerning, relating.

concernir, *v. imp.* (IE) to regard, to concern.

concertar, *va.* (IE) to concert, to settle; to adjust, to fix up; to conclude an agreement; to compose differences; —, *vn.* to agree, to accord.

concertina, *f.* concertina.

concertista, *m.* and *f.* concert performer or manager.

concesión, *f.* concession, grant, admission.

concesionario, ria, *n.* licensee, leaseholder.

conciencia, *f.* conscience.

concienzudo, da, *adj.* conscientious.

concierto, *m.* concert; agreement; accommodation; (mus.) concert; **de** —, according to agreement.

conciliación, *f.* conciliation, reconciliation.

conciliar, *va.* to conciliate, to reconcile; —, *adj.* conciliar, pertaining to councils.

conciliativo, va, *adj.* conciliatory.

conciliatorio, ria, *adj.* conciliatory.

concilio, *m.* council; assembly of bishops.

concinidad, *f.* harmony in language.

conciso, sa, *adj.* concise, brief.

concitar, *va.* to excite; to stir up commotions.

conciudadano, na, *n.* fellow citizen; countryman.

cónclave or **conclave,** *m.* conclave.

concluir, *va.* (UYO) to conclude, to complete; to convince; to infer, to deduce; to disarm an adversary by grasping the hilt of his sword.

conclusión, *f.* conclusion, end, finis; consequence.

concluso, sa, *adj.* ended, closed, concluded.

concluyente, *adj.* conclusive.

concolega, *m.* fellow collegian.

concomerse, *vr.* (coll.) to shrug the shoulders, to give a shrug.

concomitante, *adj.* concomitant, accompanying.

concomitar, *va.* to be concomitant, to accompany.

concordación, *f.* co-ordination.

concordancia, *f.* concordance, concord; harmony.

concordar, *va.* (UE) to accord; —, *vn.* to agree.

concordato, *m.* concordate.

concorde, *adj.* concordant, agreeing.

concordia, *f.* conformity, union, harmony; **de** —, by common consent.

concreción, *f.* concretion, solidifying, solidified mass.

concretar, *va.* to combine, to unite; to harmonize; to limit.

concreto, ta, *adj.* concrete, definite; **en** —**to,** in short.

concubina, *f.* concubine, mistress.

concubinato, *m.* concubinage.

concúbito, *m.* coitus, sexual intercourse.

conculcar, *va.* to trample under foot; to infringe.

concupiscencia, *f.* concupiscence, lust.

concurrencia, *f.* convention of persons; assembly, audience; concurrence; coincidence; confluence.

concurrentes, *m. pl.* those present at a gathering, guests.

concurrido, da, *adj.* crowded, well-attended.

concurrir, *vn.* to concur, to agree; to contribute; to coincide; to convene; to fall in.

concurso, *m.* concourse, crowd, assembly, meeting; aid; competition; — **de acreedores,** meeting of creditors; — **de belleza,** beauty contest.

concusión, *f.* concussion; shaking, shock.

concusionario, *m.* extortionist.

concha, *f.* shell; conch; oyster; tortoise shell.

conchabanza, *f.* act of making oneself comfortable; (coll.) plotting, conspiracy.

conchabar, *va.* to join, to unite; —**se,** to plot, to conspire.

conchado, da, *adj.* scaly; covered with shells.

conchil, *m.* rock shell.

conchudo, da, *adj.* scaly, crustaceous; cunning, crafty.

condado, *m.* earldom, county.

condal, *adj.* relating to an earl or count.

conde, *m.* earl, count; chief of gypsies.

condecente, *adj.* convenient, fit, proper.

condecorar, *va.* to adorn, to embellish, to confer a decoration on.

condenable, *adj.* damnable.

condenación or **condena,** *f.* condemnation.

condenar, *va.* to condemn, to sentence; to damn; to refute; to disapprove; —**se,** to condemn or blame oneself.

condenatorio, ria, *adj.* condemnatory.

condensación, *f.* condensation.

condensador, *m.* condenser.

condensar, *va.* and *vr.* to condense, to thicken.

condensativo, va, *adj.* condensative.

condesa, *f.* countess.

condescendencia, *f.* condescendence, condescension, compliance.

condescender, *vn.* (IE) to condescend, to yield, to comply; to reciprocate.

condestable, *m.* constable.

condestablía, *f.* constableship.

condición, *f.* condition, quality; state, footing; rank; clause, stipulation; **a** — **de que,** provided that; —**ones de pago,** terms of payment; **reunir las** —**ones necesarias,** to possess the necessary qualifications.

condicionado, da, *adj.* conditioned.

condicional, *adj.* conditional, not absolute.

condicionar, *vn.* to agree, to accord, to condition.

condigno, na, *adj.* condign; merited.

condimentar, *va.* to season (food).

condimento, *m.* condiment, seasoning; flavoring.

condiscípulo, la, n. fellow-disciple, fellow-student.

condolecerse or **condolerse,** *vr.* (UE) to condole.

condonación, *f.* pardoning, forgiving; condoning.

condonar, *va.* to pardon, to forgive; to condone.

cóndor, *m.* (orn.) condor.

conducción, *f.* conveyance; freight, express, conduct; payment for conducting; conduction; control.

conducente, *adj.* suitable, satisfactory; conducive.

conducir, *va.* and *vn.* (CONDUZCO, CONDUJE) to convey, to conduct, to lead; **— un automóvil,** to drive an automobile; **—se,** to conduct oneself.

conducta, *f.* conduct; behavior; conveyance.

conductivo, va, *adj.* conducive, conductory.

conducto, *m.* conduit, sewer, channel, drain; **por — de,** through (agent).

conductor, ra, *adj.* conductive; **—,** *m.* conductor, guide; (rail.) guard; driver (in golf); **hilo** or **alambre —,** electric wire.

condueño, ña, n. joint owner, partner.

conectar, *va.* to connect.

conectivo, va, *adj.* connecting.

conejal or **conejar,** *m.* rabbit warren.

conejera, *f.* warren, burrow; cavern inhabited by poor people.

conejero, ra, *adj.* trained to hunt rabbits.

conejo, ja, n. rabbit.

conejuna, *f.* rabbit fur.

conejuno, na, *adj.* pertaining to rabbits; rabbitlike.

conexidades, *f. pl.* (law) all matters pertinent to the principal subject.

conexión, *f.* connection, conjunction.

conexo, xa, *adj.* connected, united.

conf. or **confr. confesor,** confessor.

confabular, *va.* to confabulate; **—se,** to conspire.

confalón, *m.* gonfalon, banner, standard.

confección, *f.* (med.) compound; remedy; confection; **—es,** *pl.* ready-made dresses.

confeccionado, da, *adj.* ready-made.

confeccionador, *m.* confectioner.

confeccionar, *va.* to make, to put together; to compound; to prepare a prescription; to make preserves.

confederación, *f.* confederacy, confederation.

confederado, da, n. and *adj.* confederate.

confederar, *va.* and *vr.* to confederate; to federalize.

conferencia, *f.* conference; talk; lecture; **— de larga distancia,** long-distance call.

conferenciante, *m.* and *f.* public lecturer.

conferenciar, *vn.* to hold a conference; to consult together.

conferencista, *m.* and *f.* lecturer, speaker.

conferir, *va.* (IE) to confer, to grant.

confesar, *va.* (IE) to confess; to avow; to admit.

confesión, *f.* confession, avowal.

confesionario, *m.* treatise on hearing confessions; confessional.

confesionista, *m.* Lutheran.

confeso, sa, n. (law) one who confesses a crime.

confesonario, *m.* confessional.

confesor, *m.* confessor.

confetti, *m. pl.* confetti.

confiado, da, *adj.* confident; arrogant, forward.

confiador, *m.* (law) joint surety, fellow bondsman.

confianza, *f.* confidence, boldness; assurance; intimacy; trust; dependence; **de —,** informal; **digno de —,** reliable, trustworthy; **en —,** confidentially; **tener — en,** to trust.

confiar, *va.* and *vn.* to confide, to trust in; to hope, to count on; to give in charge.

confidencia, *f.* confidence.

confidencial, *adj.* confidential, off the record.

confidencialmente, *adv.* confidentially.

confidente, *m.* and *f.* confidant; **—,** *adj.* true, faithful, trusty.

configurar, *va.* to form, to shape.

confín, *m.* limit, boundary.

confinar, *va.* and *vn.* to exile; to confine, to limit; to border upon.

confirmación, *f.* confirmation.

confirmar, *va.* to confirm; to corroborate.

confiscación, *f.* confiscation, forfeiture.

confiscar, *va.* to confiscate.

confitar, *va.* to confect; to preserve, to candy.

confite, *m.* comfit, confection; candy, sugar-plum, bonbon.

confitera, *f.* candy box.

confitería, *f.* confectioner's shop.

confitero, ra, n. confectioner.

confitura, *f.* preserved or potted fruit; jam.

conflación, *f.* melting metals.

conflagración, *f.* conflagration.

conflicto, *m.* conflict, fight, struggle.

confluencia, *f.* confluence.

confluir, *vn.* (UYO) to join (said of rivers and sea currents); (fig.) to assemble or concur in one place.

conformar, *va.* to conform, to fit; **—,** *vn.* to suit, to fit; **—se,** to submit; to resign oneself.

conforme, *adj.* comfortable, suitable; **estar —,** to be in agreement; **—,** *adv.* according to.

conformidad, *f.* conformity; patience, resignation; **de —,** by common consent.

confort, *m.* comfort.

confortación, *f.* comfort, consolation.

confortante, *adj.* comforting; **—,** *m.* sedative.

confortar, *va.* to comfort; to strengthen; to console.

confortativo, va, *adj.* comfortable, comforting; cordial.

confracción, *f.* fracture, breaking.

confraternidad, *f.* confraternity, brotherhood.

confrontación, *f.* confrontation.

confrontar, *va.* to confront; to compare.

Confucio, Confucius.

confundir, *va.* and *vr.* to confound; to perplex; to huddle; to throw into confusion.

confusamente, *adv.* confusedly.

confusión, *f.* confusion, disorder; tumultous medley; perplexity, perturbation; obscurity; humiliation.

confuso, sa, *adj.* confused, confounded; obscure; perplexed.

confutación, *f.* confutation; disproof.

confutar, *va.* to confute; to refute.

conga, *f.* (Cuba) dance of African origin; (Col.) large poisonous ant.

congelación, *f.* congelation, solidification, freezing.

congelador, *m.* freezer.

congelar, *va.* and *vr.* to congeal, to freeze.

congeniar, *vn.* to be congenial.

congénito, ta, *adj.* congenital, connate.

congestión, *f.* (med.) congestion.

conglomeración, *f.* conglomeration.

conglomerado, *m.* hardpan.

conglutinar, *va.* to conglutinate, to cement.

congoja, *f.* anguish, grief; pang, heartbreaking.

congojoso, sa, *adj.* afflictive, painful.

congosto, *m.* canyon.

congraciar, *va.* to ingratiate, to flatter; **—se con,** to get into one's good graces.

congratulación, *f.* congratulation.

congratular, *va.* to congratulate.

congregación, *f.* congregation, assembly.

congregacional, *adj.* congregational.

congregar, *va.* to assemble, to meet, to collect.

congreso, *m.* congress.

congrua, *f.* an adequate sustenance for a priest.

congruamente, *adv.* congruously; suitably.

congruencia, *f.* convenience; opportunity; congruency.

congruente, *adj.* congruent; corresponding.

congruo, rua, *adj.* congruous; convenient, suitable.

cónico, ca, *adj.* conical.

conjetura, *f.* conjecture.

conjetural, *adj.* conjectural.

conjeturar, *va.* to conjecture.

conjugación, *f.* (gram.) conjugation.

conjugar, *va.* (gram.) to conjugate.

conjunción, *f.* conjunction, union.

conjuntamente, *adv.* together, jointly.

conjuntivitis, *f.* (med.) conjunctivitis, pink eye.

conjunto, ta, *adj.* united, conjunct; allied by kinship or friendship; **—,** *m.* the whole, the ensemble.

conjuración, *f.* conspiracy, plot.

conjurado, *m.* conspirator.

conjurador, *m.* conjurer; exorcist.

conjuramentar, *va.* to bind by an oath; to administer an oath.

conjurar, *va.* and *vn.* to conjure; to conspire.

conjuro, *m.* conjuration, exorcism.

conllevar, *va.* to aid or assist; to bear, to endure.

conmemoración, *f.* remembrance; commemoration; requiem.

conmemorar, *va.* to commemorate.

conmemorativo, va, *adj.* memorial, commemorative.

conmensuración, *f.* commensuration.

conmensurar, *va.* to commensurate.

conmigo, *pron.* with me, with myself.

conmilitón, *m.* comrade, fellow soldier.

conminación, *f.* commination, threat.

conminar, *va.* to threaten; to threaten a criminal with punishment.

conminatorio, ria, *adj.* comminatory, threatening.

conmiseración, *f.* commiseration, pity, compassion.

conmoción, *f.* commotion; concussion; fretting; tumult, disturbance.

conmovedor, ra, *adj.* affecting, moving, exciting, breath-taking.

conmover, *va.* and *vr.* (UE) to disturb, to excite.

conmutación, *f.* commutation, exchange, shift.

conmutador, *m.* electric switch; **— telefónico,** switchboard.

conmutar, *va.* to commute; to barter, to exchange.

connatural, *adj.* natural; according to nature.

connaturalizarse, *vr.* to accustom oneself to; to become accustomed or acclimated.

connivencia, *f.* connivance.

connotación, *f.* distant relationship; connotation.

connotado, *m.* remote relationship.

connotar, *va.* to connote, to imply.

connubio, *m.* (poet.) matrimony, wedlock.

cono, *m.* cone.

conocedor, ra, *n.* expert; connoisseur; **— de,** familiar with, expert in.

conocer, *va.* (OZCO) to know, to be acquainted; to understand; **—se,** to know one another.

conocido, da, *n.* acquaintance; **—,** *adj.* known.

conocimiento, *m.* knowledge, understanding; consciousness; connoisseurship; cognition; acquaintance; (com.) bill of lading; **poner en —,** to inform, to advise.

conocimto. conocimiento, (com.) B/L or b. l. bill of lading.

conque, *conj.* so then, well then.

conquista, *f.* conquest; acquisition.

conquistador, *m.* conqueror.
conquistar, *va.* to conquer.
conreinar, *vn.* to reign at the same time with another.
consabido, da, *adj.* already known; above-mentioned.
consagración, *f.* consecration.
consagrar, *va.* to consecrate, to dedicate, to hallow; **—se,** to devote oneself.
consanguíneo, nea, *adj.* consanguineous.
consanguinidad, *f.* consanguinity.
consciente, *adj.* conscious, of sound mind, aware.
consecución, *f.* attainment.
consecuencia, *f.* consequence; conclusion; result; **como —,** in consequence, consequently; **en —,** therefore.
consecuente, *m.* consequence, effect; (math.) consequent; **—,** *adj.* consequent, logical.
consecutivo, va, *adj.* consecutive.
conseguir, *va.* (I) to attain, to get (fetch).
conseja, *f.* fable, feigned story.
consejero, *m.* counselor; councilor; advisor.
consejo, *m.* counsel, advice; council; councilhouse; advisory board; **— de guerra,** court-martial; **— de ministros,** cabinet; **— directivo,** board of directors.
consenso, *m.* consensus, general agreement.
consentido, da, *adj.* spoiled (of children).
consentimiento, *m.* consent, assent.
consentir, *va.* (IE) to consent, to agree; to comply, to acquiesce; to overindulge, to coddle.
conserje, *m.* keeper or warden of a royal castle or public building; concierge, janitor.
conserva, *f.* conserve, preserve; **—s,** canned goods.
conservación, *f.* conservation, upkeep, maintenance.
conservador, *m.* conservator; curator; preserver; **—, ra,** *adj.* conservative.
conservar, *va.* to conserve; to candy fruit; to keep, to maintain.
conservativo, va, *adj.* conservative.
conservatorio, *m.* conservatory; **—, ria,** *adj.* conservatory, preservative.
considerable, *adj.* considerable; great, large.
consideración, *f.* consideration, regard; notice, sake, account; reflection.
consideradamente, *adv.* considerately.
considerado, da, *adj.* prudent, considerate, esteemed, respected.
considerando, *conj.* whereas.
considerar, *va.* to consider, to think over; to respect.
consign. consignación, (com.) consignment.
consigna, *f.* (mil.) watchword, countersign.
consignación, *f.* consignation; consignment; **a la — de,** consigned to.
consignador, *m.* one who consigns goods to a foreign correspondent, consignor, consigner.
consignar, *va.* to consign; to deposit; to

forward goods to a correspondent, to be sold for account of the consigners.
consignatario, *m.* trustee; consignee.
consigo, *pron.* with oneself.
consiguiente, *adj.* consequent, consecutive; consistent, logical; **—,** *m.* consequence, effect; **por —,** consequently.
consistencia, *f.* consistence, stability; solidity.
consistente, *adj.* consistent, firm, solid.
consistir, *vn.* to consist; to be contained.
consistorio, *m.* consistory; town house.
cons.º consejo, (law) counsel, advice, council.
consocio, *m.* partner, companion; fellow member.
consola, *f.* console, bracket, bracket shelf, cantilever.
consolación, *f.* consolation.
consolador, ra, *adj.* consòlatory, comfortable, cheering; **—,** *n.* consoler, soother.
consolar, *va.* (UE) to console, to comfort, to cheer.
consolidación, *f.* consolidation, merger.
consolidar, *va.* to consolidate, to strengthen; **—se,** (law) to tie up interest with principal; to become consolidated.
consolidativo, va, *adj.* consolidant, consolidative.
consonancia, *f.* consonance; congruence.
consonante, *m.* rhyme; **—,** *f.* (gram.) consonant; **—,** *adj.* consonant, conformable.
consorcio, *m.* partnership, society, trust.
consorte, *m.* and *f.* consort, companion; accomplice.
conspicuo, cua, *adj.* conspicuous; prominent.
conspiración, *f.* conspiracy, plot.
conspirador, ra, *n.* conspirator, plotter.
conspirar, *vn.* to conspire, to plot.
Const. Constitución, Const. Constitution.
Constancia, Constance.
constancia, *f.* constancy, steadiness, immutability.
constante, *adj.* constant, firm, unalterable; **—,** *f.* (math.) constant.
Constantino, Constantine.
Constantinopla, *f.* Constantinople.
constar, *v. imp.* to be evident or certain; to be composed of, to consist of; **hacer —,** to state; **me consta,** I know positively.
constelación, *f.* constellation.
consternación, *f.* consternation.
consternar, *va.* to strike with amazement, to confound; to dismay.
constipación, *f.* cold; constipation.
constipar, *va.* to cause a cold; to constipate; **—se,** to catch cold.
constitución, *f.* constitution (in all meanings).
constitucional, *adj.* constitutional.
constituir, *va.* and *vr.* (UYO) to constitute; to establish; to appoint.
constitutivo, va, *adj.* constitutive, essential.

constituyente, *n.* and *adj.* constituent.
const.¹ constitucional, constitutional.
constreñimiento, *m.* constraint.
constreñir, *va.* (I) to constrain, to force; (med.) to constipate.
constricción, *f.* constriction, contraction.
constrictivo, va, *adj.* astringent, binding.
construcción, *f.* construction, building, erection.
constructor, ra, *n.* builder.
construir, *va.* (UYO) to build, to construct; to construe.
consuegro, gra, *n.* parents of two children who marry each other.
consuelo, *m.* consolation, comfort; joy, merriment.
cónsul, *m.* consul.
consulado, *m.* consulate.
consular, *adj.* consular.
consulta, *f.* consultation; deliberation.
consultación, *f.* consultation.
consultar, *va.* to consult, to ask advice; to give advice.
consultivo, va, *adj.* consultative.
consultor, ra, *n.* adviser, counselor; —, *adj.* consulting; advisory, counseling.
consultorio, *m.* place of consultation; doctor's office; clinic; information bureau.
consumación, *f.* consummation, consumption, perfection, finishing.
consumado, da, *adj.* consummate, complete, perfect, accomplished, exquisite; —, *m.* jelly broth, consommé.
consumar, *va.* to consummate, to finish, to perfect.
consumidor, ra, *n.* consumer; —, *adj.* consuming.
consumir, *va.* to consume, to use up; to destroy; to waste, to exhaust; —se, to waste away, to languish.
consumo, *m.* consumption of provisions and merchandise; demand (for merchandise).
consunción, *f.* (med.) consumption; wasting; decline.
consustancial, *adj.* consubstantial.
contabilidad, *f.* accounting, bookkeeping; — por partida doble, double-entry bookkeeping; — por partida simple or sencilla, single-entry bookkeeping.
contacto, *m.* contact, touch; — del magneto, (aer.) ignition switch.
contadero, ra, *adj.* countable; —, *m.*, narrow passage where people or animals are counted.
contado, da, *adj.* scarce, rare; de —do, instantly; in hand; al —do, cash, ready money; $50 al —do, $50 down; tanto al —do, so much down.
contador, *m.* computer, accountant, reckoner; cash register; counter (table); counter (for games).
contaduría, *f.* accountant's office at the exchequer; auditorship.
contagiar, *va.* to infect.
contagio, *m.* contagion.

contagioso, sa, *adj.* contagious.
contaminación, *f.* contamination, pollution; defilement.
contaminar, *va.* to contaminate; to infect by contagion; to corrupt, to spoil.
contante, *adj.* fit to be counted; dinero — y sonante, ready cash.
contar, *va.* (UE) to count, to reckon, to compute, to calculate; to tell; — con, to rely upon.
contemplación, *f.* contemplation.
contemplar, *va.* to contemplate, to consider, to study, to observe; to meditate; to coddle.
contemplativo, va, *adj.* contemplative.
contemporáneo, nea, *n.* and *adj.* contemporary, coeval.
contemporizar, *vn.* to temporize; to comply.
contencioso, sa, *adj.* contentious; quarrelsome.
contender, *vn.* (IE) to contend, to strive; to contest, to debate.
contendiente, *m.* and *f.* competitor.
contener, *va.* (CONTENGO, CONTUVE) to contain, to comprise, to hold; —se, to refrain; to repress.
contenido, da, *adj.* moderate, temperate, modest; —, *m.* contents.
contentadizo, za, *adj.* bien —, easily contented; mal —, hard to please.
contentar, *va.* to content, to satisfy, to please; —se, to be pleased or satisfied.
contento, ta, *adj.* glad; pleased; content; —, *m.* contentment.
contestación, *f.* answer, reply; debate.
contestar, *va.* to prove, to attest; to answer, to reply; —, *vn.* to agree; to accord.
conteste, *adj.* confirming the evidence of another.
contexto, *m.* intertexture; context of a discourse.
contienda, *f.* contest, dispute, struggle, debate, fight.
contigo, *pron.* with thee.
contigüidad, *f.* contiguity.
contiguo, gua, *adj.* contiguous; close, near.
continencia, *f.* continence, abstinence, moderation.
continental, *adj.* continental.
continente, *m.* continent, mainland; countenance; —, *adj.* abstinent, moderate.
contingencia, *f.* possibility; contingency, contingence; risk.
contingente, *adj.* fortuitous, accidental; —, *m.* contingent; share.
continuación, *f.* continuation, continuance, lengthening; continuity; a —, below, herein.
continuamente, *adv.* continuously, continually.
continuar, *va.* and *vn.* to continue.
continuidad, *f.* continuity; sistema de —, follow-up system.
continuo, nua, *adj.* continuous, continual, ceaseless; de —nuo, continually.

conto. conocimiento, (com.) B/L or b.l. bill of lading.

contómetro, *m.* comptometer.

contonearse, *vr.* to walk in an affected manner.

contoneo, *m.* affected manner of walking.

contorcerse, *vr.* (UE) to distort; to twist one's body.

contorno, *m.* environs; contour, outline; **en —,** round about.

contorsión, f. contortion, wry motion.

contra, *prep.* against, contrary to, opposite to; **seguro — incendio,** fire insurance; **una letra —,** a draft on.

contraalmirante, *m.* rear admiral.

contraataque, *m.* counterattack.

contrabajo, *m.* counterbass; bass viol.

contrabalancear, *va.* to counterbalance.

contrabandista, *m.* smuggler, dealer in contraband goods.

contrabando, *m.* contraband trade, smuggling.

contrabatería, f. (mil.) counterbattery.

contracambio, *m.* re-exchange.

contracandela, f. (Sp. Am.) backfire.

contracarril, *m.* (rail.) counterrail.

contracción, f. contraction.

contracorriente, f. countercurrent, backwater.

contradanza, f. square dance; quadrille.

contradecir, *va.* (CONTRADIGO, CONTRADIJE) to contradict, to gainsay.

contradicción, f. contradiction; verbal opposition.

contradictorio, ria, *adj.* contradictory, opposite to.

contradique, *m.* counterdike.

contraer, *va.* and *vn.* (CONTRAIGO, CONTRAJE) to contract (an obligation or a disease); to reduce; **—se,** to shrink up.

contraescarpa, f. (mil.) counterscarp.

contraescritura, f. counterdeed.

contrafirmar, *va.* (law) to obtain a countermanding decree.

contrafoso, *m.* outer ditch of a fortress.

contrafuero, *m.* violation of a privilege.

contrafuerte, *m.* counterfort.

contragolpe, *m.* counterblow.

contraguardia, f. counterguard.

contrahacer, *va.* (CONTRAHAGO, CONTRAHICE) to counterfeit, to falsify; to pirate the works of an author.

contrahaz, *m.* wrong side (of cloth).

contrahecho, cha, *adj.* deformed, miscreated; counterfeited.

contralmirante, *m.* rear admiral.

contralor, *m.* controller, inspector.

contralto, *m.* and f. (mus.) contralto.

contramaestre, *m.* (naut.) boatswain; overseer of a factory.

contramalla, f. double net for catching fish.

contramallar, *va.* to make nets with double meshes.

contramandar, *va.* to countermand.

contramarca, f. countermark; customs

stamp duty, duty on goods.

contramarco, *m.* counterframe of a glass window.

contramarcha, f. countermarch.

contramarchar, *vn.* to countermarch.

contramarea, f. (naut.) countertide, springtide.

contramesana, f. (naut.) mizzenmast.

contramina, f. countermine.

contraminar, *va.* to countermine; to counterwork.

contramuralla, f. (mil.) low rampart, countermure.

contramuro, *m.* (mil.) countermure.

contraofensiva, f. counteroffensive.

contraorden, f. countermand.

contraordenar, *va.* to countermand.

contraparte, f. counterpart.

contrapartida, f. corrective entry in bookkeeping.

contrapasar, *vn.* to join the opposite party.

contrapaso, *m.* back step; (mus.) counternote.

contrapechar, *va.* to strike breast against breast (applied to horses in tournaments).

contrapelo, *adv.* **a —,** against the grain.

contrapesar, *va.* to counterpoise.

contrapeso, *m.* counterpoise, counterweight; ropedancer's pole; (Chile) uneasiness; **hacer — a,** to counterbalance.

contrapilastra, f. counterpilaster.

contraponer, *va.* (CONTRAPONGO, CONTRAPUSE) to compare, to oppose.

contraposición, f. counterview, contrast.

contraprueba, f. counterproof.

contrapuerta, f. inner hall door of a house.

contrapuntearse, *vr.* to quarrel with abusive language.

contrapunto, *m.* (mus.) counterpoint, harmony.

contrapunzón, *m.* counterpunch; gunsmith's countermark.

contraquilla, f. (naut.) false keel.

contrariamente, *adv.* contrarily, contrary to.

contrariar, *va.* to contradict, to oppose, to counteract, to vex.

contrariedad, f. contrariety, opposition; disappointment.

contrario, ria, *n.* opponent, antagonist; **llevar la —ria,** to take the opposite side; **— adj.** contrary, opposite, adverse, hostile; **al —rio,** on the contrary.

contrarreclamación, f. counterclaim.

contrarreforma, f. counterreformation.

contrarrestar, *va.* to strike back (a ball); to counteract, to offset, to oppose.

contrarresto, *m.* player who is to strike back the ball; opposition, contradiction.

contrarrevolución, f. counterrevolution.

contrarronda, f. (mil.) counterround.

contrasellar, *va.* to counterseal.

contraseña, f. countersign; (mil.) watchword, password.

contrastar, *va.* to contrast, to oppose; to

resist, to contradict; to assay metals; to examine measures and weights.

contraste, *m.* contrast; opposition; strife; assayer of the mint; assayer's office; assayer of weights and measures; (naut.) sudden change of the wind.

contrata, *f.* contract.

contratación, *f.* trade, commerce, business transaction.

contratante, *adj.* contracting; **partes —s,** contracting parties; **—,** *m.* contractor, trader.

contratar, *va.* to engage, to hire; to trade, to traffic; to contract, to stipulate.

contratiempo, *m.* disappointment, mishap.

contratista, *m.* contractor, lessee.

contrato, *m.* contract, pact; engagement; **celebrar un —,** to draw up a contract; **— de compraventa,** contract of bargain and sale.

contratreta, *f.* counterplot.

contratrinchera, *f.* countertrench.

contratuerca, *f.* lock nut.

contravalar, *va.* (mil.) to form a line of contravallation.

contravención, *f.* contravention, violation (of a law).

contraveneno, *m.* antidote.

contravenir, *va.* (CONTRAVENGO, CONTRAVINE), to contravene, to transgress; to oppose.

contraventana, *f.* window shutter.

contraventor, ra, *n.* offender, transgressor.

contravidriera, *f.* second glass window; storm window.

contribución, *f.* contribution; tax.

contribuir, *va.* (UYO) to contribute.

contributario, *m.* contributor, payer of taxes.

contribuyente, *adj.* contributing; contributory; **—,** *n.* contributor.

contrición, *f.* contrition, penitence.

contrincante, *m.* competitor, opponent.

contristar, *va.* to afflict, to sadden.

contrito, ta, *adj.* contrite, penitent.

control, *m.* control, check; **—es,** (aer.) controls.

controlabilidad, *f.* (aer.) controllability.

controversia, *f.* controversy, dispute.

controversista, *m. and f.* controversialist.

controvertir, *va.* (IE) to controvert, to dispute.

contumacia, *f.* obstinacy, stubbornness; (law) contumacy.

contumaz, *adj.* obstinate, stubborn; (law) contumacious.

contumelia, *f.* contumely, abuse.

contumelioso, sa, *adj.* contumelious, reproachful.

contundir, *va.* to beat together; to bruise; to cause a contusion.

conturbación, *f.* perturbation.

conturbar, *va.* to perturb, to disquiet.

contusión, *f.* contusion, bruise.

convalecencia, *f.* convalescence.

convalecer, *vn.* (EZCO) to recover from sickness; to recover lost prosperity or power.

convección, *f.* convection.

convecino, na, *adj.* neighboring.

convencer, *va.* to convince.

convencimiento, *m.* conviction.

convención, *f.* convention, pact.

convencional, *adj.* conventional, agreed upon by compact.

convenido, da, *adj.* agreed.

conveniencia, *f.* utility, profit; convenience; ease, commodity.

conveniente, *adj.* useful, advantageous; desirable, advisable, proper, convenient.

convenio, *m.* convention, contract; agreement, pact, compromise.

convenir, *vn.* (CONVENGO, CONVINE) to agree, to coincide; to compromise; to fit, to suit, to correspond; to assemble.

conventículo, *m.* conventicle.

convento, *m.* convent, monastery; **— de monjas,** nunnery.

conventual, *adj.* monastic.

convergencia, *f.* convergence.

conversación, *f.* conversation, easy talk; communication.

conversar, *vn.* to converse, to talk; to live together.

conversión, *f.* conversion, change.

converso, *m.* convert.

convertidor, *m.* converter.

convertir, *va.* (IE) to transform, to convert; to reform; **—se,** to convert oneself.

convexidad, *f.* convexity.

convexo, xa, *adj.* convex.

convicción, *f.* conviction.

convicto, ta, *adj.* convicted (found guilty).

convidada, *f.* a treat; an invitation.

convidado, da, *adj.* invited; **—,** *n.* invited guest.

convidar, *va.* to invite, to bid; to allure, to persuade; **—se,** to offer one's service spontaneously.

convincente, *adj.* convincing.

convite, *m.* invitation; feast to which persons are invited.

convocar, *va.* to convoke, to assemble.

convocatorio, ria, *adj.* that which convokes.

convólvulo, *m.* (bot.) convolvulus.

convoy, *m.* convoy, conduct, escort; (coll.) retinue; cruet.

convoyar, *va.* to convoy, to escort.

conv.te conveniente, advantageous, advisable, useful.

convulsión, *f.* convulsion.

convulsivo, va, *adj.* convulsive.

conyugal, *adj.* conjugal, connubial.

cónyuges, *m. pl.* married couple, husband and wife.

coñac, *m.* cognac, brandy.

cooperación, *f.* co-operation.

cooperador, ra, *n.* co-operator.

cooperador, ra, *adj.* co-operating

cooperar, *vn.* to co-operate.

cooperativo, va, *adj.* co-operative.

coopositor, *m.* competitor.
coordinación, *f.* co-ordination.
coordinar, *va.* to arrange, to classify; to co-ordinate.
copa, *f.* cup; goblet; top of a tree; crown of a hat; brazier; **—s,** *pl.* hearts (at cards); **tomar una —,** to have a drink (of liquor).
copado, da, *adj.* tufted, copped.
copal, *m.* copal.
Copenhague, *f.* Copenhagen.
copera, *f.* cupboard; china closet.
copero, *m.* sideboard.
copete, *m.* toupee; pompadour; crownwork of a looking-glass frame; top of a shoe; top, summit.
copetín, *m.* (Arg.) drink or aperitif before meals.
copetudo, da, *adj.* copped; supercilious on account of one's noble descent.
copia, *f.* plenty, abundance; copy, transcript; portrait taken from original design; imitation; (gram.) list of nouns and verbs.
copiador, *m.* copyist, copier.
copiar, *va.* to copy; to imitate, to draw from life; (poet.) to describe, to depict.
copilar, *va.* to compile.
copioso, sa, *adj.* copious, abundant, plentiful.
copista, *m.* and *f.* copyist.
copla, *f.* couplet; popular ballad, folksong; sarcastic remark.
coplear, *vn.* to make couplets.
coplero, *m.* poetaster; ballad seller.
copo, *m.* small bundle of cotton, flax, etc., put on the distaff to be spun; flake of snow.
copón, *m.* ciborium (cup used in Catholic churches); large cup.
copra, *f.* copra, dried coconut kernel.
copudo, *adj.* tufted, tufty, bushy.
cópula, *f.* joining of two things together; (arch.) cupola; (gram.) copula.
copulativo, va, *adj.* copulative.
coqueta, *f.* coquette, flirt.
coquetear, *vn.* to coquet, to flirt.
coquetería, *f.* coquetry, flirtation.
coquetón, ona, *adj.* flirtatious.
coquillo, *m.* coconut (of the Indian palm tree).
coquina, *f.* cockle.
coquito, *m.* grimace made to amuse children; small coconut.
coracero, *m.* cuirassier; (coll.) strong, bad cigar.
coracha, *f.* leather sack.
coraje, *m.* courage; anger.
corajudo, da, *adj.* angry, ill-tempered.
coral, *m.* coral; **—es,** *pl.* strings of corals; **—,** *adj.* choral.
coralero, *m.* worker or dealer in corals.
coralina, *f.* sea coralline.
corambre, *f.* hides and skins of animals, dressed or undressed.
corambrero, *m.* dealer in hides.

Corán, *m.* Koran.
coraza, *f.* cuirass; cuirassier, armor plate; shell of a turtle.
corazón, *m.* heart; core; benevolence; courage; center; pith of a tree; **de —,** heartily; **enfermedad del —,** heart trouble.
corazonada, *f.* inspiration; quick decision; presentiment.
corbachada, *f.* lash given with a whip.
corbacho, *m.* whip.
corbata, *f.* cravat, neckerchief, necktie.
corbatín, *m.* cravat with a clasp.
corbato, *m.* cooler (of a still).
corbeta, *f.* (naut.) corvette.
Córcega, *f.* Corsica.
corcel, *m.* steady horse, charger.
corcino, *m.* small deer.
corcova, *f.* hump; protuberance.
corcovado, da, *adj.* humpbacked, crooked.
corcovear, *vn.* to curvet, to cut capers.
corcovo, *m.* curvet; caper.
corchea, *f.* (mus.) an eighth note.
corchera, *f.* vessel made of pitched cork to cool liquor.
corcheta, *f.* eye of a hook or clasp.
corchete, *m.* clasp; locket; bench hook of a carpenter's bench; (coll.) constable.
corcho, *m.* cork; beehive; cork stopple.
cordaje, *m.* (naut.) cordage.
cordal, *m.* double tooth; string bar at the bottom of stringed instruments.
cordel, *m.* cord, rope; (naut.) line.
cordelazo, *m.* lash given with a rope.
cordelería, *f.* cordage; place where cord or twine is made or sold.
cordelero, *m.* ropemaker.
corderillo, *m.* dressed lambskin.
corderina, *f.* lambskin.
cordero, *m.* lamb; dressed lambskin; meek, gentle man.
cordial, *adj.* cordial, hearty, affectionate; **—,** *m.* cordial.
cordialidad, *f.* cordiality.
cordillera, *f.* range of mountains.
cordita, *f.* cordite.
Córdoba, *f.* Cordova.
cordobán, *m.* cordovan, cordwain.
cordón, *m.* cord, string; twisted lace; military cordon.
cordonería, *f.* lacemaking, twinemaking; shop where twine or round cord is sold.
cordonero, *m.* lacemaker; ropemaker.
cordura, *f.* prudence, practical wisdom; judgment.
coreo, *m.* harmonious blending of musical chords.
corezuelo, *m.* sucking pig; small leather hide.
corifeo, *m.* coryphaeus; leader.
corindón, *m.* corundum.
corista, *m.* chorister; **—,** *f.* chorus girl.
coriza, *f.* coryza, dry catarrh; peasant's sandal.
corladura, *f.* gold varnish.

cornada, *f.* thrust with a bull's horn.
cornadura, *f.* horns.
cornalina, *f.* cornelian, carnelian.
cornamenta, *f.* horns of an animal.
cornamusa, *f.* cornemuse, sort of rustic flute.
córnea, *f.* cornea.
cornear, *vn.* to butt with the horns.
corneja, *f.* crow.
cornejo, *m.* (bot.) dogwood.
Cornelio, Cornelius.
córneo, nea, *adj.* horny, callous.
cornerina, *f.* cornelian, carnelian.
corneta, *f.* cornet; hunting horn; cornet (ensign); **—,** *m.* bugler.
cornezuelo, *m.* instrument for bleeding horses; ergot of rye.
cornijal, *m.* corner of a building.
cornisa, *f.* cornice, molding.
corno, *m.* cornelian cherry tree.
cornucopia, *f.* cornucopia, horn of plenty; branched candlestick.
cornudo, da, *adj.* horned.
coro, *m.* choir, chorus; (poet.) summer solstitial wind.
corógrafo, ía, *n.* chorographer.
corola, *f.* corolla (petals of a flower).
corolario, *m.* corollary.
corona, *f.* crown; coronet; top of the head; clerical tonsure; crown (English silver coin); regal power; monarchy; honor, splendor, decoration; halo.
coronación, *f.* coronation.
coronar, *va.* to crown; to complete, to perfect; to ornament the top of a building.
coronario, ria, *adj.* relating to a crown; (bot.) coronary.
coronel, *m.* (mil.) colonel.
coronela, *f.* colonel's wife; **—,** *adj.* applied to the company, etc., belonging to a colonel.
coronilla, *f.* crown of the head.
coroto, *m.* (Col.) useless thing.
coroza, *f.* coronet of pasteboard worn as a mark of infamy.
corozo, *m.* bactris (a palm tree).
corpanchón, *m.* huge carcass.
corpiño, *m.* tight waist used as undergarment, corset cover.
corporación, *f.* corporation, guild.
corporal, *adj.* corporal, bodily; **—,** *m.* (eccl.) altar linen.
corporalidad, *f.* corporality, corporeity.
corpóreo, rea, *adj.* corporeal.
corpudo, da, *adj.* corpulent, bulky.
corpulencia, *f.* corpulence.
corpulento, ta, *adj.* corpulent, bulky.
Corpus, *m.* Corpus Christi, religious festival.
corpúsculo, *m.* corpuscle.
corral, *m.* yard; stockyards; corral; poultry yard; **aves de —,** poultry; **hacer —es,** (coll.) to play truant from school.
corralero, *m.* keeper of a dungyard.
correa, *f.* leather strap, thong; flexibility; belt; **tener —,** to bear teasing without annoyance.

correaje, *m.* heap of leather straps.
correar, *va.* to draw out (wool) and prepare it for use.
corrección, *f.* correction; reprehension; amendment; proper demeanor.
correctivo, va, *adj.* corrective.
correcto, ta, *adj.* exact, correct, right.
corrector, ra, *n.* corrector; proofreader.
corredera, *f.* race track; slide, runway, rail, roller.
corredizo, za, *adj.* easily untied; with a slipknot.
corredor, *m.* runner; racehorse; corridor, passage; broker; (mil.) scout; **—ra,** *f.* procuress.
corredura, *f.* liquor which flows over the brim of a vessel.
correduría, *f.* trade of a broker; brokerage.
correería, *f.* trade of a strap maker.
correero, *m.* strap maker or seller.
corregencia, *f.* coregency.
corregente, *m.* coregent.
corregidor, *m.* corrector; corregidor (Spanish magistrate).
corregidora, *f.* wife of a corregidor.
corregir, *va.* (CORRIJO, CORREGÍ), to correct, to amend; to reprehend; to mitigate.
correjel, *m.* sole leather.
correlación, *f.* correlation.
correlacionar, *va.* to correlate.
correlativo, va, *adj.* correlative.
correncia, *f.* (coll.) looseness of the bowels.
correo, *m.* mail; courier; mailman; post office; bag of letters; (law) accomplice; **a vuelta de —,** by return mail; **— aéreo,** air mail.
correoso, sa, *adj.* ductile, flexible; leathery.
correr, *vn.* to run; to race; to flow; to blow (applied to the wind); to pass away (applied to time); to take the proper course; to act heedlessly; **—,** *va.* to cause to move fast; to race (an animal); to make blush; to pursue; **a todo —,** at full speed; **—se,** to be ashamed; to become disconcerted; to fly into a rage; **— parejas,** to go together, to be on an equal footing.
correría, *f.* excursion, incursion; **—s,** youthful escapades.
correspondencia, *f.* correspondence; relation, intercourse, reciprocal intelligence; proportion; **— mercantil** or **comercial,** commercial correspondence; **estar en — con,** to correspond with; **llevar la —,** to be in charge of the correspondence.
corresponder, *va.* to make a suitable return; to correspond; to answer; to regard; to agree, to be congruent; **—se,** to correspond; to esteem one another.
correspondiente, *adj.* corresponding, conformable, suitable; **—,** *m.* correspondent.
corresponsal, *m.* correspondent.
corretaje, *m.* brokerage; money paid to a pimp; commission.
corretear, *vn.* to rove, to ramble; to run around (as children).

correvedile, *m.* talebearer; procurer, pimp.

corrida, *f.* course, race; **— de toros,** bull-fight; **de —,** at full speed.

corrido, da, *adj.* expert; artful; ashamed; **—,** *m.* (mus.) a special rhythm.

corriente, *f.* current (of water, electricity, etc.), stream, flow, course, progression; **— alterna** or **alternativa,** (elec.) alternating current; **— continua,** direct current; **— de aire,** air draft; **del —,** of the present (month); **poner al —,** to inform; **tener al —,** to keep advised; **—,** *adj.* current; fluent, easy, running; marketable; generally accepted.

corrillero, *m.* loafer.

corrillo, *m.* circle of persons generally gathered to loaf and gossip.

corro, *m.* circle formed by people who meet to talk or see a show; round (a dance).

corroborar, *va.* to corroborate, to strengthen.

corroer, *va.* to corrode.

corromper, *va.* to corrupt; to alter the form of a thing; to seduce a woman; to bribe, to suborn; **—,** *vn.* to stink; **—se,** to rot, to putrify; to become corrupt.

corronchoso, sa, *adj.* rude, rough.

corrosca, *f.* (Col.) straw hat.

corrosión, *f.* corrosion.

corrosivo, va, *adj.* corrosive.

corrte. or **cte.** or **corr.**te **corriente,** c. current, usual, common.

corrugación, *f.* corrugation.

corrupción, *f.* corruption, putrefaction; spurious alteration in a book or writing; depravity.

corruptela, *f.* corruption; (law) abuse.

corruptible, *adj.* susceptible of corruption.

corruptivo, va, *adj.* corruptive.

corrupto, ta, *adj.* corrupted, corrupt.

corruptor, ra, *n.* corrupter, misleader.

corsario, *m.* corsair, privateer.

corsé, *m.* corset.

corta, *f.* felling of wood.

cortabolsas, *m.* and *f.* (coll.) pickpocket.

cortacésped, *m.* lawnmower.

cortacircuitos, *m.* (elec.) circuit breaker.

cortadera, *f.* chisel for cutting hot iron; knife for extracting honeycombs.

cortadillo, *m.* small drinking glass; **echar —s,** to speak in an affected manner; to drink wine.

cortado, da, *adj.* sheepish, embarrassed; cut.

cortador, ra, *n.* cutter; **—,** *m.* butcher; **—es,** *pl.* incisors.

cortadora, *f.* cutter, mower, slicing machine.

cortadura, *f.* cut; cutting; incision; fissure; **—s,** *pl.* shreds, cuttings, parings.

cortafrío, *m.* chisel for cutting cold iron.

cortafuego, *m.* clear space to prevent fire from spreading.

cortapapel, *m.* paper cutter, paper knife.

cortapiés, *m.* thrust made at the legs in fencing.

cortaplumas, *m.* penknife, pocket knife.

cortar, *va.* to cut, to cut off, to curtail; to separate, to hew, to chop; (mil.) to cut off part of the enemy's army; to cut (in cards); to interrupt; to abridge; **—se,** to be ashamed or confounded; to coagulate.

corte, *m.* edge of knife, etc.; abscission, cutting; cut; felling of trees; expedient; cut goods to make a garment; **—,** *f.* (royal) court, the court of chancery; retinue; yard; courtship, flattery; **hacer la —,** to woo; **—s,** *f. pl.* Cortes, assembly of the states of the realm in Spain.

cortedad, *f.* smallness, littleness; stupidity; bashfulness; pusillanimity.

cortejante, *m.* courtier, gallant.

cortejar, *va.* to make love, to court; to accompany.

cortejo, *m.* homage; courtship; lover; gift, present; cortege, procession.

cortés, *adj.* courteous, genteel, polite.

cortesanazo, za, *adj.* awkwardly civil.

cortesanía, *f.* courtesy, politeness.

cortesano, na, *adj.* courtlike; courteous, gentle; **—,** *m.* courtier; **—,** *f.* courtesan.

cortesía, *f.* courtesy, good manners; polite form of speech in a letter.

corteza, *f.* cortex, bark; peel; crust; outward appearance; rusticity.

cortezudo, da, *adj.* barky; rustic, unmannerly.

cortijo, *m.* farmhouse, grange.

cortina, *f.* curtain; **— de humo,** smoke screen.

cortinaje, *m.* set of curtains.

corto, ta, *adj.* short; scanty, narrow, small, little; stupid; pusillanimous, fearful; concise; defective; **a la —ta o a la larga,** sooner or later.

cortocircuito, *m.* short circuit.

cortón, *m.* ringworm; fieldmouse.

corusco, ca, *adj.* (poet.) brilliant.

corva, *f.* bend of the knee; ham; curb (disease in horses' knees).

corvadura, *f.* curvature; bend of an arch.

corvaza, *f.* (vet.) curb.

corvejón, *m.* hock; spur of a cock.

corveta, *f.* curvet, bound of a horse.

corvetear, *vn.* to curvet, to leap.

corvo, va, *adj.* bent, crooked.

corzo, za, *n.* roe deer, fallow deer.

corzuelo, *m.* wheat which has been left in the husks by the thrashers.

cosa, *f.* thing; matter; **— de entidad,** important thing; **no hay tal —,** there is no such thing; **otra —,** something else; **ninguna —,** nothing.

cosaco, ca, *n.* and *adj.* Cossack.

coscoja, *f.* scarlet oak; dry leaves of the kermes oak; knob on the cross bit of a bridle.

coscojo, *m.* kermes grain.

cosecha, *f.* harvest; crop; harvest time; **de su —,** of one's own invention.

cosechar, *va.* to crop, to reap.

cosechero, *m.* harvester, husbandman; vintager.

coser, *va.* to sew; to join; **máquina de —,** sewing machine.

cosicosa, *f.* riddle.

cosido, *m.* stitching, sewing; **— de cama,** quilts and blankets stitched together.

cosmético, *m.* cosmetic.

cósmico, ca, *adj.* cosmic.

cosmografía, *f.* cosmography.

cosmología, *f.* cosmology.

cosmopolita, *n.* and *adj.* cosmopolite, cosmopolitan.

cosmos, *m.* cosmos.

cosquillas, *f. pl.* tickling; **hacer —,** to tickle.

cosquillear, *va.* and *vn.* to tickle.

cosquilloso, sa, *adj.* ticklish; easily offended.

costa, *f.* cost, price; charge, expense; fatigue, labor; coast, shore; **a toda —,** at any cost; **a lo largo de la —,** coastwise.

Costa del Marfil, *f.* Ivory Coast.

Costa del Oro, *f.* Gold Coast.

costado, *m.* side; (mil.) flank; side of a ship.

costal, *m.* sack, large bag; rammer beetle; **—,** *adj.* costal, pertaining to the ribs.

costalada, *f.* fall flat on the ground.

costalero, *m.* porter (who carries goods).

costanera, *f.* slope; **—as,** *pl.* rafters, timbers.

costanero, ra, *adj.* of the coast, coastwise; coastal; sloping.

costar, *vn.* (UE) to cost; to suffer detriment or loss.

coste, *m.* cost, expense; **a — y costas,** at cost; **precio de —,** cost price.

costear, *va.* to pay the cost; **—,** *vn.* to sail along the coast.

costera, *f.* side of a bale of goods; fisherman's basket; outside quire of a ream of paper.

costero, ra, *adj.* outward; belonging to a coast.

costilla, *f.* rib; (coll.) wife; stave; wealth; **—s,** *pl.* ribs of a ship.

costillaje or **costillar,** *m.* human ribs.

costo, *m.* cost, price, expense; **— de fabricación,** production cost; **precio de —,** cost price.

costoso, sa, *adj.* costly, dear, expensive.

costra, *f.* crust; broken biscuit given to the galley slaves.

costrada, *f.* kind of pastry.

costroso, sa, *adj.* crusty, with scabs.

costumbre, *f.* custom, habit; established manner; **de —,** usually; **tener por —,** to be in the habit of.

costura, *f.* seam; needlework; splicing of a rope; sewing.

costurera, *f.* seamstress; dressmaker.

cota, *f.* coat of mail.

cotarro, *m.* charity hut for the sheltering of beggars.

cotejar, *va.* to compare, to confront.

cotejo, *m.* comparison, collation.

cotí, *m.* ticking used for mattresses.

cotidiano, na, *adj.* daily.

cotilla, *f.* stays, corset.

cotillero, ra, *n.* staymaker.

cotillón, *m.* cotillion (dance).

cotización, *f.* (com.) quotation; **boletín de —,** list of quotations.

cotizar, *va.* to quote (a price).

coto, *m.* inclosure of pasture grounds; district; landmark; (med.) goiter.

cotón, *m.* printed cotton.

cotonada, *f.* calico, print, printed calico, prints.

cotonía, *f.* dimity; cotton goods.

cotorra, *f.* magpie; small parrot; (coll.) talkative woman.

cotorrera, *f.* hen parrot; (coll.) prattling woman.

cotorrería, *f.* loquacity.

coturno, *m.* cothurnus; buskin.

covacha, *f.* small cave, grotto.

covanilla, *f.*, **covanillo,** *m.* basket for gathering grapes.

coyote, *m.* coyote.

coyunda, *f.* strap with which oxen are tied to the yoke; (fig.) matrimonial union.

coyuntura, *f.* joint, articulation; conjuncture; occasion, opportunity.

coz, *f.* kick; recoil of a gun; flowing back of a flood; **a coces,** by dint of kicking.

C.P.B. or **c.p.b. cuyos pies beso,** (expression of courtesy and respect to a lady).

cps. compañeros, companions, partners; fellow members.

C.P.T. Contador Público Titulado, C.P.A. Certified Public Accountant.

c/r cuenta y riesgo, (com.) own account and risk.

crabrón, *m.* hornet.

cráneo, *m.* skull, cranium.

crápula, *f.* intoxication; licentiousness.

crasitud, *f.* grease, fat; corpulency.

craso, sa, *adj.* fat, greasy, thick.

cráter, *m.* crater of a volcano.

crátera, *f.* crater (large bowl for wine).

creación, *f.* creation.

Creador, *m.* the Creator, God.

creador, ra, *adj.* creative; **—,** *n.* one who creates, an originator.

crear, *va.* to create, to make; to establish.

crecer, *vn.* (EZCO) to bud forth; to increase; to swell.

creces, *f. pl.* augmentation, increase; additional quantity of corn paid by a farmer to a public granary besides what he borrowed from it; **pagar con —** to pay back generously, to pay more than is due.

crecida, *f.* swell of rivers.

crecido, da, *adj.* grown, increased; grave, important; **—s,** *m. pl.* widening stitches in knitting.

creciente, *f.* swell; leaven; crescent (of the moon); (naut.) flood tide; **—,** *adj.* growing, increasing; crescent (moon).

crecimiento, *m.* increase; growth; increment.
crec.te **creciente,** crescent (moon).
credencial, *f.* credential.
credibilidad, *f.* credibility.
crédito, *m.* credit; belief, faith; reputation; note, bill; — **mercantil,** good will; **a** —, on credit. —**s activos,** assets; —**s pasivos,** liabilities.
credo, *m.* creed; **en menos de un** —, in less than a jiffy.
credulidad, *f.* credulity.
crédulo, la, *adj.* credulous.
creencia, *f.* credence, belief; persuasion.
creer, *va.* (CREYÓ) to believe; to think; to credit; ¡**ya lo creo!** I should say so! of course!
creíble, *adj.* credible, believable.
crema, *f.* cream; custard; diaeresis; cosmetic; — **batida,** whipped cream; — **de afeitar,** shaving cream; — or **pasta dental,** tooth paste.
cremación, *f.* cremation.
cremallera, *f.* (mech.) ratch, rack.
cremar, *va.* to cremate.
crémor, — **tártaro,** *m.* cream of tartar.
crencha, *f.* parting of the hair; each of the two parts.
creosota, *f.* creosote.
crepuscular, *adj.* pertaining to twilight.
crepúsculo, *m.* crepuscule, twilight.
cresa, *f.* maggot.
crespo, pa, *adj.* crisp; curled, curly; obscure and bombastic; angry, displeased; —, *m.* (Sp. Am.) a curl.
crespón, *m.* crepe; — **de seda,** georgette, crepe de chine.
cresta, *f.* cockscomb; crest of some birds; top, summit of a mountain; (Col.) a thing one loves; love.
crestado, da, *adj.* crested.
crestomatía, *f.* anthology.
crestón, *m.* crest of a helmet.
Creta, *f.* Crete.
creta, *f.* chalk.
cría, *f.* breed or brood of animals; hatch; suckling; (coll.) child reared by a nurse.
criada, *f.* maid servant, handmaid.
criadero, *m.* nursery for trees; breeding place; —, **ra,** *adj.* fruitful, prolific.
criadilla, *f.* testicle; small loaf; truffle.
criado, *m.* servant; —, **da,** *adj.* educated, instructed, bred.
criador, *m.* creator; breeder; —, **ra,** *adj.* nourishing; creating, creative; fruitful.
crianza, *f.* breeding, education.
criar, *va.* to create, to produce; to breed, to procreate; to nurse; to suckle; to foster, to bring up.
criatura, *f.* child, baby, creature (in all its significations).
criba, *f.* sieve; sifting.
cribador, ra, *n.* sifter.
cribar, *va.* to sift, to screen.
cribo, *m.* sieve.

cric, *m.* jack, hoist.
crimen, *m.* crime.
criminal, *adj.* and *n.* criminal.
criminalidad, *f.* criminality.
criminalista, *m.* author who has written on criminal matters.
criminología, *f.* criminology.
crin, *f.* mane, horsehair.
crinolina, *f.* crinoline.
criollo, lla, *n.* Creole; —, *adj.* indigenous, native.
cripta, *f.* crypt.
crisálida, *f.* chrysalis, pupa.
crisantemo, *m.* chrysanthemum.
crisis, *f.* crisis; judgment passed after a mature deliberation.
crisma, *m.* and *f.* chrism; —, *f.* (coll.) head.
crismera, *f.* chrismatory.
crisol, *m.* crucible; melting pot.
crisolada, *f.* crucible full of metal.
crisolito, *m.* chrysolite; — **oriental,** yellow topaz.
cristal, *m.* crystal; crystal glass; — **tallado,** cut crystal.
cristalería, *f.* glassware.
cristalero, *m.* (Arg.) china closet.
cristalino, na, *adj.* crystalline, clear.
cristalización, *f.* crystallization.
cristalizar, *va.* to crystallize.
cristiandad, *f.* Christianity; observance of the law of Christ.
Cristianía, *f.* Christiana.
cristianismo, *m.* Christianism, Christendom.
cristianizar, *va.* to christianize.
cristiano, na, *n.* and *adj.* Christian.
Cristina, Christina, Christine.
Cristo, *m.* Christ.
Cristóbal, Christopher.
Cristóbal Colón, Christopher Columbus.
cristus, *m.* christcross (in olden times sign of the cross preceding the alphabet); **no saber el** —, to be very ignorant.
criterio, *m.* criterion, judgment.
crítica, *f.* criticism.
criticable, *adj.* subject to criticism.
criticador, ra, *n.* critic, censurer.
criticar, *va.* to criticize, to find fault.
crítico, *m.* critic, censurer; affected refiner of style and language; —, **ca,** *adj.* critical.
criticón, ona, *n.* faultfinder.
crocante, *m.* peanut or almond brittle.
cromático, ca, *adj.* chromatic.
cromato, *m.* chromate.
cromo, *m.* chromium, chrome.
crónica, *f.* chronicle, account, story.
crónico, ca, *adj.* chronic.
cronista, *m.* and *f.* chronicler; reporter; — **de salones,** society reporter.
cronógrafo, *m.* stop watch.
cronología, *f.* chronology.
cronológico, ca, *adj.* chronological.
cronómetro, *m.* chronometer.
croquet, *m.* croquet.
croqueta, *f.* croquette.

cruce, *m.* crossing; crossroads.

crucera, *f.* withers of a horse.

crucero, *m.* cross vault of a church under the dome; cross-bearer; piece of timber which lies across the rafters in a building; crick of a mill; (naut.) cruising station; cruiser; Cross (southern constellation).

crucetas, *f. pl.* bridging.

crucificar, *va.* to crucify; to molest; to torment.

crucifijo, *m.* crucifix.

crucigrama, *m.* crossword puzzle.

crudeza, *f.* unripeness; rudeness; cruelty; vain boasting; indigestion.

crudo, da, *adj.* raw, crude; green, unripe; rude, cruel; unfinished, immature; hard to digest; blustering, boasting; immature (of tumors).

cruel, *adj.* cruel; (fig.) insufferable; severe, hard; bloody, violent.

crueldad, *f.* cruelty, inhumanity, savageness.

cruento, ta, *adj.* bloody, cruel.

crujía, *f.* corridor, aisle of ward; — **de hospital,** hospital ward; — **de piezas,** suite of rooms.

crujido, *m.* crack, creak, clash, crackling.

crujir, *vn.* to crackle, to rustle; — **los dientes,** to grind the geeth.

crustáceo, cea, *adj.* crustaceous.

cruz, *f.* cross (as instrument, order, ensign of the Christian religion); (fig.) trial of patience, etc.

cruzada, *f.* crusade; expedition; indulgences granted to those who supported the crusade.

cruzado, da, *adj.* crossed; of crossed (breed, etc.); **paño** —, twilled cloth; —, *m.* old Spanish coin; crusader.

cruzamiento, *m.* crossing; — **de calle,** street crossing; — **de nivel,** (rail.) crossing road; — **de vía,** (rail.) junction.

cruzar, *va.* to cross; to cross a road; (naut.) to cruise; —**se,** to be knighted; to cross and trip, to stumble along (of horses).

cs.:cuartos, Spanish coin, ¼ real; **centavos, céntimos,** ¢ or c. cents.

c. s. f. costo, seguro y flete, c. i. f. cost, insurance, and freight,

ct. centavo, ¢ or c. cent.

cta. or **c.ta cuenta,** (com.) a/c or acc. account.

cta. cte. or **cta. corr.te cuenta corriente,** (com.) current account.

cta. de vta. or **cta. d/v cuenta de venta,** (com.) account sales.

cte. or **corr.te corriente,** current, usual, common.

c/u cada uno, each one, every one.

cuad. cuadrado, sq. square.

cuaderna, *f.* fourth part; (naut.) timberwork forming the ribs of a ship.

cuadernal, *m.* pulley, block, tackle.

cuadernillo, *m.* small parcel of paper; log (of a vessel).

cuaderno, *m.* parcel of paper stitched together; small memorandum book; four pages of printed matter; — **de bitácora,** logbook; — **de máquinas,** engine-room log.

cuadra, *f.* hall; drawing room; stable; block of houses.

cuadrado, da, *adj.* square, quadrate; perfect; —, *m.* square, quadrate; clock (in stockings); gusset of a shirt sleeve; (Cuba) rude and stupid in manners; **de** —**do,** in front, face to face; squared.

cuadragenario, ria, *adj.* forty years old.

cuadragesimal, *adj.* quadragesimal, lenten.

cuadragésimo, ma, *adj.* fortieth.

cuadrangular, *adj.* quadrangular, four-cornered.

cuadrángulo, *m.* quadrangle.

cuadrante, *m.* quadrant; dial plate of a sundial; square board put up in churches pointing out the order of masses to be celebrated.

cuadrar, *va.* and *vn.* to square; to square timbers; to multiply a number by itself; to fit, to suit, to correspond.

cuadratura, *f.* quadrature.

cuadricular, *va.* to copy by means of squares; —, *adj.* squared, in squares.

cuadriforme, *adj.* four-faced.

cuadrilátero, ra, *adj.* quadrilateral.

cuadrilongo, ga, *adj.* quadrangular, oblong.

cuadrilla, *f.* gang, crew, troop; meeting of four or more persons; band of armed men sent in pursuit of highwaymen; civil police; matador and his assistants; — **carrilana,** train gang.

cuadrillero, *m.* commander of an armed band; patrolman of the inquisition.

cuadriplicado, da, *adj.* quadrupled.

cuadrisílabo, ba, *adj.* quadrisyllabic.

cuadriyugo, *m.* cart with four horses.

cuadro, *m.* square; picture; picture frame; window frame; parterre in a garden; (mil.) square body of troops; (naut.) wardroom; — **de control,** (elec.) switchboard.

cuadrúpedo, da, *adj.* quadruped.

cuadruplicar, *va.* to quadruplicate.

cuádruplo, pla, *adj.* quadruple, fourfold.

cuajada, *f.* butter, curd, coagulated fat.

cuajaleche, *f.* (bot.) yellow bedstraw; cheese rennet.

cuajamiento, *m.* coagulation.

cuajar, *m.* rennet bag (of ruminants).

cuajar, *va.* to coagulate; to ornament too much; —, *vn.* to succeed; to please; —**se,** to coagulate, to curdle; (coll.) to fill up.

cuajarón, *m.* grume, clot, gore.

cuajo, *m.* rennet; coagulation.

cual, *pron.* and *adj.* which; such as; —, *adv.* as; how; like; **¿cuál?** *interr.* which (one)?

cualidad, *f.* quality.

cualquier, *adj.* any.

cualquiera, *adj.* and *pron.* any; anyone, someone, anybody, somebody.

cuan, *adv.* how, as (used only before adj.

or adv.); **cuán,** adv. how, what; **¡—
grande es Dios!** how great is God!
cuando (*interr.* **cuándo**), adv. when; in
case that; if; although; even; sometimes;
de — en —, from time to time; **— más,
— mucho,** at most, at best; **— menos,**
at least; **¿de cuándo acá?** since when?
cuantía, f. quantity; rank, distinction.
cuantioso, sa, adj. numerous, copious, rich.
cuantitativo, va, adj. quantitative.
cuanto, ta, adj. as many as, as much as, all,
whatever; **¿cuánto?** how much? **¿cuántos?** how many? **—,** adv. as; the more; **—
antes,** at once; **— más,** moreover, all the
more because; **en — a,** with regard to;
por —, inasmuch as.
cuarenta, adj. forty.
cuarentena, f. space of forty days; Lent;
quarantine.
cuarentón, ona, n. man or woman forty
years old.
cuaresma, f. Lent; collection of Lent
sermons.
cuaresmal, adj. lenten.
cuarta, f. quarter; sequence of four cards
in the game of piquet; quadrant (of a
circle); (naut.) quarter (point of the
compass).
cuartago, m. nag, hack; pony.
cuartal, m. quartern loaf; quarter (dry
measure).
cuartana, f. (med.) quartan.
cuartanal, adj. intermittent (of fever).
cuartanario, ria, adj. suffering from quartan (fever).
cuartear, va. to quarter, to divide into
four parts; to bid a fourth more at public
sales; to make a fourth person at a game;
—se, to split into pieces.
cuartel, m. quarter, fourth part; district of
a city; place where soldiers are lodged;
duty imposed on villages for the quartering
of soldiers; (coll.) dwelling, home; (naut.)
hatch; **— general,** headquarters.
cuartelero, m. soldier in each company who
keeps their apartment clean.
cuarterón, m. quartern, quarter; upper part
on windows, quadroon.
cuarteta, f. (poet.) quatrain.
cuarteto, m. quartet.
cuartilla, f. fourth part of an **arroba,** or
sixteenth part of a **quintal;** fourth part
of a sheet of paper; pastern of horses.
cuartillo, m. pint; fourth part of a peck in
grain; fourth part of a **real. ▪**
cuarto, m. fourth part, quarter; dwelling,
room, apartment; copper coin worth four
maravedís; pedigree; **—s,** pl. cash,
money; **—, ta,** adj. fourth.
cuartón, m. large joist.
cuarzo, m. quartz.
cuasi, adv. almost, nearly.
Cuasimodo, m. first Sunday after Easter.
cuate, m. and adj. (Mex.) twin.

cuatralbo, ba, adj. having four white feet
(horses).
cuatrero, m. horse thief.
cuatrinca, f. union of four persons or things;
four cards of the same suit.
cuatro, adj. four; **—,** m. figure four; (mus.)
quartet; **las —,** f. pl. four o'clock.
cuatrocientos, tas, n. and adj. four hundred.
cuatropea, f. horse tax.
cuatropeado, m. step in dancing.
cuatrotanto, m. quadruple.
cuba, f. cask; (fig.) toper, drunkard; tub.
cubano, na, adj. and n. Cuban.
cubero, m. cooper.
cubertura, f. cover, covering.
cubeta, f. small barrel; bucket.
cubeto, m. small pail or tub.
cubicado, adj. in cubes.
cubicar, va. to cube a number.
cúbico, ca, adj. cubic.
cubierta, f. cover; envelope; wrapping; pretext; deck of a ship; **— del motor,** (auto.)
hood.
cubierto, m. place for one at the table;
shelter; allowance of a soldier in a house;
course of dishes; regular dinner.
cubil, m. lair of wild beasts.
cubilete, m. copper pan for baking pies, etc.;
tumbler; dicebox; small pie stuffed with
mince meat; (coll.) high hat.
cubilla, f. blister beetle; flagpole socket.
cubismo, m. cubism.
cúbito, m. (anat.) ulna.
cubo, m. cube; pail; millpond; nave, hub
(of a wheel).
cubreasiento, m. seat cover.
cubrecama, f. bedspread.
cubrellanta, f. tire cover or casing.
cubrepán, m. fireshovel used by shepherds.
cubrir, va. to cover; to palliate; to disguise;
to spread over; to roof a building; to cover
a mare; **— una cuenta,** to balance an
account; **—se,** to put on one's hat.
cuca, f. edible cyperus; **mala —,** (coll.)
wicked person.
cucaña, f. greased pole to be climbed for a
prize; (coll.) anything acquired with little
trouble and at other people's expense.
cucañero, m. (coll.) parasite.
cucar, va. (Sp. Am.) to bother, to molest, to
provoke.
cucaracha, f. cockroach; (Ecu.) a ten-cent
coin.
cucarachero, ra, adj. (Cuba) very amorous; **—,** m. (Ven.) harmonious singing bird.
cucarda, f. cockade.
cuclillas, en —, adv. in a cowering manner; **sentarse en —,** to squat.
cuclillo, m. cuckoo; (fig.) cuckold.
cuco, ca, adj. (coll.) dainty, prim; sly,
crafty; **—,** m. cuckoo.
cucurucho, m. paper cone.
cuchara, f. spoon.
cucharada, f. spoonful, ladleful.

cucharita, *f.* teaspoon.

cucharón, *m.* ladle, dipper, large spoon; scoop; **— de almeja,** (mech.) clamshell bucket, grab bucket.

cuchichear, *vn.* to whisper.

cuchicheo, *m.* whispering, murmur.

cuchichero, ra, *n.* whisperer.

cuchilla, *f.* large kitchen knife; chopping knife; ancient poniard; (poet.) sword; bookbinder's knife.

cuchillada, *f.* cut with a knife; gash; **—s,** *pl.* wrangles, quarrels.

cuchillería, *f.* cutler's shop; cutlery.

cuchillero, *m.* cutler.

cuchillo, *m.* knife, edge; triangular gore or gusset of a garment; **— de postres,** fruit knife; **— mantequillero,** butter knife.

cuchufleta, *f.* joke, jest, fun.

cuelga, *f.* cluster of grapes hung up for use; birthday present.

cuello, *m.* neck; neck of a bottle; collar of a garment; small end of a wax candle shirt collar.

cuenca, *f.* wooden bowl; (geog.) valley, basin of a river; (anat.) eye socket.

cuenco, *m.* earthen bowl.

cuenta, *f.* computation, calculation; account; narrative; bead of a rosary; reason; satisfaction; **abonar en —,** to credit with; **adeudar en —,** to charge to one's account; **caer en la —,** to notice, to see; **cargar en —,** to charge to one's account, debit in account; **— abierta** or **corriente,** charge or checking account; **— atrasada,** overdue account; **— corriente,** account current or current account; **— de venta,** (com.) account sales; **— en participación,** joint account; **— pendiente,** unsettled account; **— simulada,** pro forma account; **dar — de,** to report on; **darse —,** to realize; **en — con,** in account with; **llevar —s,** to keep accounts; **por — y orden** (or **riesgo**) **de,** for account and order (risk) of; **tener en —,** to bear in mind; **tomar por su —,** to assume responsibility for.

cuentagotas, *m.* stactometer; medicine dropper, dropping tube.

cuentista, *m.* and *f.* talebearer.

cuento, *m.* story, tale, narrative; a million; prop, support; **— de hadas,** fairy tale.

cuerda, *f.* cord; string for musical instruments; match for firing a gun; spring of a watch or clock; Spanish measure of length; **bajo —,** underhandedly; **— de volatinero,** tightrope; **dar —,** to wind; **dar — al reloj,** to wind up the watch, or clock; **sin —,** unwound.

cuerdo, da, *adj.* prudent, judicious; in his senses.

cuerna, *f.* horn vessel into which cows, etc., are milked; stag's horn; huntinghorn.

cuerno, *m.* horn; corn, callosity; **— de abundancia,** horn of plenty.

cuero, *m.* hide, skin, leather; (fig.) great

drinker; **— cabelludo,** scalp; **imitación de —,** leatheroid, fabrikoid.

cuerpo, *m.* body; cadaver, corpse; staff, corps; **— de aviación,** air corps; **— volante,** flying column; **— a —,** hand to hand.

cuerva, *f.* (orn.) crow.

cuervo, *m.* (orn.) crow, raven.

cuesco, *m.* stone (of fruits); millstone of an oilmill.

cuesta, *f.* hill; rising ground with a slope; quest, charity; **ir — abajo,** to go down hill; **— arriba,** with great trouble and difficulty.

cuestión, *f.* question; dispute; quarrel; problem; matter.

cuestionable, *adj.* questionable, problematical.

cuestionar, *va.* to question, to dispute.

cuestionario, *m.* questionnaire.

cuestor, *m.* questor; alms gatherer.

cuestura, *f.* questorship.

cueva, *f.* cave, grotto, den.

cuévano, *m.* big basket for carrying grapes to the wine press.

cuezo, *m.* hod.

cuguar, *m.* (zool.) cougar, puma.

cugujada, *f.* sky lark.

cuguila, *f.* cowl, monk's hood.

cuidado, *m.* care, attention; solicitude, custody, trust; anxiety; accuracy; diligence; **estar con —,** to be worried; **estar de —,** to be dangerously ill; **tener —,** to be careful; **¡—!** *interj.* watch out!

cuidadoso, sa, *adj.* careful, heedful, vigilant.

cuidar, *va.* to heed, to care; to mind, to look after; **—se,** to be careful of one's health.

cuita, *f.* grief, affliction, trouble.

cuitado, da, *adj.* anxious, wretched, miserable; timid.

cuja, *f.* lance bucket; bedstead.

culada, *f.* fall on one's backside.

culantrillo, *m.* (bot.) maidenhair fern.

culantro, *m.* (bot.) coriander.

culata, *f.* breech of a gun; screwpin; back part of anything, butt; **— de cilindro,** cylinder head.

culatada, *f.* recoil or kick of a firearm.

culcusido, *m.* botched work, poorly sewed work.

culebra, *f.* snake; **— de cascabel,** rattlesnake.

culebrear, *vn.* to wriggle (as a snake).

culebrina, *f.* (mil.) culverin.

culera, *f.* stain of urine in the swaddling clothes of children; patch on the seat of pants.

culero, *m.* clout, diaper; disease in birds; **—, ra,** *adj.* slothful, lazy.

culminación, *f.* culmination; high-water mark.

culo, *m.* breech, backside; anus; bottom; socket.

culpa, *f.* misdemeanor, culpableness; sin;

guilt; **tener la —,** to be at fault.
culpable, *adj.* culpable, guilty.
culpado, da, *adj.* guilty.
culpar, *va.* to accuse, to blame.
culteranismo, *m.* high-flown style; affectation.
cultivación, *f.* cultivation, culture.
cultivador, *m.* cultivator.
cultivar, *va.* to cultivate, to till.
cultivo, *m.* cultivation; improvement; farming; culture of the mind and manners; culture (of bacteria).
culto, ta, *adj.* pure, elegant, correct; polished; enlightened, civilized; **—,** *m.* culture; worship, cult, religion, veneration; homage.
cultura, *f.* culture; elegance of style.
cumbre, *f.* top, summit; greatest height of favor, fortune, etc.
cumpleaños, *m.* birthday.
cumplido, da, *adj.* full, complete; plentiful; faultless; polished, polite, courteous; **—,** *m.* compliment.
cumplimentar, *va.* to compliment; to carry out.
cumplimentero, ra, *adj.* full of compliments; complaisant.
cumplimiento, *m.* compliment; accomplishment; fulfillment; expiration (of credit, etc.).
cumplir, *va.* to execute, to carry out; to provide; to fulfil; **— años,** to have a birthday; **—,** *vn.* to fall due, to expire; to perform one's duty.
cumquibus, *m.* (coll.) money.
cumulación, *f.* cumulation.
cumular, *va.* to accumulate.
cúmulo, *m.* heap, pile; (fig.) press of business; cumulus (clouds).
cuna, *f.* cradle; (fig.) native country; family, lineage; origin; **de humilde —,** of lowly birth.
cundir, *vn.* to spread (of oil, liquids, etc.); to extend (as news); to grow, to increase.
cunear, *va.* to rock (a baby's cradle); **—se,** to rock; to swing.
cuneta, *f.* gutter, ditch; drain.
cuña, *f.* wedge; die; (fig.) artifice, slyness.
cuñado, da, *n.* brother- or sister-in-law.
cuño, *m.* die for coining money; impression made by the die.
cuociente, *m.* quotient.
cuota, *f.* quota, fixed share; fee.
cupé, *m.* coupé; cab.
cupo, *m.* quota, share; tax rate.
cupón, *m.* (com.) coupon.
cúprico, ca, *adj.* (chem.) cupric.
cúpula, *f.* cupola, dome.
cupulino, *m.* sky lantern (small cupola raised upon another).
cuquillo, *m.* (orn.) cuckoo.
cura, *m.* parson; **—,** *f.* healing, cure, remedy.
curable, *adj.* curable, healable.
curación, *f.* cure, healing.
curado, da, *adj.* cured, seasoned.

curador, *m.* overseer; guardian; curator, administrator.
curadora, *f.* female guardian; woman who cures.
curaduría, *f.* guardianship.
cural, *adj.* pertaining to the parish or the priest; **casa —,** parsonage.
curandero, *m.* quack, medicaster.
curar, *va.* to cure, to heal; to prescribe the regimen of a patient.
curatela, *f.* tutorship.
curativo, va, *adj.* curative, healing.
curato, *m.* rectory, parsonage; parish, pastorate.
Curazao, *m.* Curaçao.
cureña, *f.* gun carriage; stay of a crossbow; **a — rasa,** (mil.) without a breastwork (applied to a barbet battery); without shelter.
curia, *f.* ecclesiastical court where church affairs are examined and decided in Rome; care and skill.
curial, *adj.* belonging to the Roman **curia; —,** *m.* member of the Roman **curia;** officer in courts of law.
curiosear, *vn.* to pry.
curiosidad, *f.* curiosity; neatness; object of curiosity, rarity.
curioso, sa, *adj.* curious, strange; neat, fine, beautiful; careful, attentive, diligent.
curruca, *f.* babbling warbler.
currutaco, *m.* beau, fop; **—, ca,** *adj.* foppish; affected.
cursado, da, *adj.* skilled; versed.
cursante, *adj.* frequenting; assiduous; **—,** *m.* student, scholar.
cursar, *va.* to frequent a place; to do a thing often; to study.
cursi, *adj.* pretentious, vulgar, shoddy.
cursillo, *m.* short course of lectures (in a university).
cursivo, va, *adj.* cursive; **letra —,** flowing handwriting; italics.
curso, *m.* course, direction; course (in schools); progress; current; **al — de la bolsa,** at the rate of exchange; **— legal,** legal tender; **perder el —,** to fail in a course.
curtidor, *m.* tanner, leather dresser.
curtidos, *m. pl.* tanned leather.
curtiduría, *f.* tannery.
curtir, *va.* to tan leather; to sunbrown; to inure to hardships.
curucusí, *m.* (Bol.) firefly.
curva, *f.* curve, bend, curved line; (naut.) knee; **— cerrada,** sharp bend; **— doble,** s-curve.
curvatura, *f.* curvature.
curvilíneo, nea, *adj.* curvilinear.
curvo, va, *adj.* curved, bent.
cuscurro, *m.* little crust of bread.
cúspide, *f.* cusp; apex, peak.
custodia, *f.* custody, keeping, hold; guard, escort; monstrance; reliquary in Catholic churches.

custodiar, va. to guard, to watch.
custodio, m. guard, keeper, watchman.
cutáneo, nea, adj. cutaneous.
cúter, m. (naut.) cutter.
cutí, m. ticking for mattresses.
cutícula, f. cuticle.
cutir, va. to knock one thing against another.
cutis, m. or f. skin, complexion.
cuto, m. (Bol.) one-handed person.
cuyo, ya, pron. of which, of whom, whose, whereof.
c/v or **c/vta cuenta de venta,** (com.) bill·of sale; account sales.
czar, m. czar.

Ch

ch/ cheque, check.
cha, f. tea (in the Philippines).
chabacanería, f. bungle; lack of art or taste; vulgar expression.
chabacano, na, adj. coarse, unpolished; awkward; **—,** m. (Mex.) a variety of apricot.
chacal, m. jackal.
chacó, m. military cap, shako.
chacolí, m. light red wine of a sourish taste.
chacota, f. noisy mirth; **hacer — de,** to make fun of.
chacotear, vn. to indulge in noisy mirth.
chacotero, ra, adj. waggish, acting the clown.
cháchara, f. (coll.) chitchat, chatter, idle talk.
chacharear, vn. to talk to no purpose.
chacharería, f. verbiage, garrulity.
chacharero, ra, n. prater.
chacho, m. stake at the game of ombre.
chafaldita, f. (coll.) teasing, merriment.
chafalditero, ra, n. teaser, chaffer.
chafallar, va. to botch, to mend poorly.
chafallo, m. coarse patch.
chafallón, ona, n. (coll.) botcher.
chafar, va. to mat down or flatten (the pile of velvet, blades of grass, etc.); to cut one short in his discourse.
chafarote, m. short, broad Turkish sword.
chafarrinada, f. blot or stain in clothes, etc.
chafarrinar, va. to blot, to stain.
chafarrinón, m. blot, stain.
chagrín, m. shagreen.
chal, m. shawl.
chalán, m. hawker, huckster; artful horse dealer; (Mex.) **— de río,** river ferry.
chalana, f. lighter, scow.
chalanear, va. to sell things artfully; **—,** vn. to deal in horses.
chalanería, f. artifice and cunning used by dealers in buying and selling.
chaleco, m. waistcoat, vest.
chalet, m. chalet, Swiss style cottage.
chalina, f. scarf.
chalote, m. (bot.) shallot.
chalupa, f. (Mex.) small canoe.

chamaco, ca, n. (Mex.) small boy or small girl.
chamarra, f. garment made of sheepskins or of very coarse cloth.
chamarreta, f. short, loose jacket.
chambergo, ga, adj. slouched, uncocked (applied to a hat).
chambón, ona, adj. awkward, bungling; **—,** n. unskillful person or gamester.
chambra, f. woman's dressing sack.
chamelote, m. camlet.
chamorra, f. (coll.) shorn head.
chamorro, rra, adj. with shorn hair; **—,** m. (bot.) beardless wheat.
champaña, m. champagne.
champú, m. shampoo.
champurrar, va. (coll.) to mix liquors; to speak gibberish.
chamucera, f. rowlock.
chamuscado, da, adj. tipsy, flustered with wine; addicted to some vice; scorched.
chamuscar, va. to singe, to scorch.
chamusquina, f. scorching; (coll.) scolding, wrangling.
chancear, vn. and vr. to joke, to jest.
chancero, ra, adj. jocose, sportive, merry; **—,** m. artful thief.
chanciller, m. chancellor.
chancillería, f. chancery.
chancla, f. old shoe.
chancleta, f. house slipper.
chanclo, m. patten, clog, galosh, rubber shoe.
chancro, m. (med.) chancre.
chandel, f. (aer.) chandelle.
chanfaina, f. ragout of livers and lungs.
chanflón, ona, adj. made in a bungling manner; **—,** m. kind of copper coin.
chantre, m. precentor.
chantría, f. office of a precentor.
chanza, f. joke, jest, fun.
chanzoneta, f. joke, jest; merry chansonnette, ballad.
chapa, f. thin metal plate which serves to strengthen or adorn the work it covers; flush on cheek; veneer.
chaparra, f. coach with a low roof.
chaparreras, f. pl. (Mex.) "chaps," leg covering of leather for riding through brush.
chaparro, m. evergreen oaktree; **—, rra,** adj. (Mex.) small or short (of a person).
chaparrón, m. violent shower of rain.
chapear, va. to garnish with metal plates, to veneer; **—,** vn. to splatter.
chapería, f. ornament consisting of a number of metal plates.
chapín, m. clog with a cork sole.
chapitel, m. capital of a column.
chaple, m. graver, tool used in engraving.
chapodar, va. to lop off the branches of trees.
chapotear, va. to wet with a cloth or sponge; **—,** vn. to paddle in the water; to dab.
chapucear, va. to botch, to bungle.

chapucería, *f.* clumsy performance, bungling work.

chapucero, *m.* blacksmith; nailer; bungler; **—, ra,** *adj.* clumsy, rude.

chapulín, *m.* grasshopper.

chapurrar or **chapurrear,** *va.* to speak a language brokenly; to mix liquors.

chapuz, *m.* act of ducking or sousing; clumsy performance.

chapuzar, *va.* and *vr.* to duck; to dive; to souse.

chaqueta, *f.* jacket, coat; **— de lana,** sweater.

chaquete, *m.* game resembling backgammon.

chaquetín, *m.* jerkin, jacket.

charada, *f.* charade.

charanga, *f.* brass band; flourish.

charca, *f.* pool of water, pond.

charco, *m.* pool of standing water.

charla, *f.* idle chitchat, prattle, talk.

charlador, ra, *n.* prater, garrulous person.

charladuría, *f.* garrulity, gossip

charlar, *vn.* to prattle, to chatter, to chat.

charlatán, ana, *n.* prater, idle talker; quack, mountebank.

charlatanería, *f.* garrulity; quackery.

charnela, *f.* hinge, joint.

charol, *m.* varnish; lacquer; enamel; patent leather.

charolar, *va.* to varnish, to enamel, to polish, to lacquer.

charolista, *m.* varnisher, lacquerer, enameler.

charpa, *f.* holster.

charrada, *f.* speech or action of a clown; a dance; any work made in a tasteless manner; tinsel, tawdriness.

charretera, *f.* epaulet.

charro, *m.* churl; Mexican in ornate riding habit; **—, rra,** *adj.* gaudy.

chasco, *m.* fun, joke, jest; disappointment; **llevarse —,** to be disappointed.

chasis, *m.* chassis (of automobile or camera).

chasquear, *va.* to crack a whip; to play tricks; to disappoint; to cheat; **—,** *vn.* to crack, to snap.

chasquí, *m.* foot messenger, runner (in Peru).

chasquido, *m.* crack of a whip; crack.

chata, *f.* flat-bottomed boat; bedpan.

chato, ta, *adj.* flat, flattish; flat-nosed.

chaveta, *f.* bolt, pin, key, pivot; **perder la —,** to become rattled, to lose one's bearings.

chaza, *f.* point where the ball is driven back or where it stops (in a kind of ball game).

chazador, *m.* person employed to stop the ball and mark the game.

chazar, *va.* to stop the ball before it reaches the winning point; to mark the point whence the ball was driven back.

checoeslovaco, ca, *n.* and *adj.* Czechoslovak, Czechoslovakian.

Checoeslovaquia, *f.* Czechoslovakia.

chelín, *m.* shilling.

cheque, *m.* (com.) check; **— al portador,** check to bearer; **— de viajeros,** traveler's check.

cheurón, *m.* chevron.

chibalete, *m.* (print.) composing frame or cabinet.

chicada, *f.* herd of sickly kids or goats; childish action.

chicle, *m.* (bot.) chicle; chewing gum.

chico, ca, *adj.* little, small; **—,** *n.* little boy or little girl.

chicolear, *vn.* to joke, to jest in gallantry.

chicoleo, *m.* jest in gallantry, joke.

chicoria, *f.* chicory.

chicorrotín, *adj.* (coll.) very small (applied to children).

chicote, ta, *n.* robust young person; (naut.) end of a cable; (coll.) cigar; (Sp. Am.) whip.

chicha, *f.* (Sp. Am.) fermented beverage made with corn.

chícharo, *m.* pea.

chicharra, *f.* harvest fly.

chicharrero, *m.* (coll.) hot place or climate.

chicharro, *m.* young tunnyfish; horse mackerel.

chicharrón, *m.* crackling, pork rind or fat cooked until crisp; any crisply cooked meat.

chichimeca, *m.* member of a Mexican Indian tribe.

chichisbear, *va.* to woo, to court.

chichisbeo, *m.* attendance paid to a lady; gallant, attendant on a lady.

chichón, *m.* lump on the head occasioned by a blow.

chifla, *f.* whistling, hissing; knife for paring leather (used by bookbinders).

chifladera, *f.* whistling.

chiflar, *vn.* to whistle; to mock, to jest: **—se,** (coll.) to become mentally unbalanced.

chiflido, *m.* sound of a whistle.

chile, *m.* (bot.) chili, red pepper.

chileno, na, *n.* and *adj.* Chilean.

chilindrón, *m.* game of cards.

chilla, *f.* call for foxes, etc.; **clavo de —,** tack; **tablas de —,** thin boards, clapboards.

chillar, *vn.* to scream, to shriek; to crackle, to creak; to hiss in frying.

chillido, *m.* squeak, shriek; **dar un —,** to utter a shriek, scream.

chillón, ona, *adj.* screachy, shrill; loud in color, showy; **—,** *n.* bawler, screamer; **—,** *m.* nail, tack.

chimenea, *f.* chimney, smokestack; (naut.) funnel.

chimpancé, *m.* chimpanzee.

china, *f.* pebble; porcelain; chinaware; China silk; (Cuba and P.R.) thin-skinned orange; Chinese woman.

chinarro, *m.* large pebble.

chinazo, *m.* blow with a pebble.

chincharrazo, *m.* thrust with a sword in a fight.

chincharrero, *m.* nasty place infested by vermin.

chinche, *m.* or *f.* bedbug; thumbtack; a bore.

chinchilla, *f.* chinchilla; its fur.

chinchona, *f.* quinine.

chinchorrería, *f.* (coll.) nuisance, impertinence; mischievous tale.

chinchorro, *m.* fishing boat; dragnet.

chinchoso, sa, *adj.* boring, troublesome; full of bedbugs.

chinela, *f.* house slipper.

chino, na, *n.* and *adj.* Chinese; —, *m.* Chinese language.

chiquero, *m.* hogsty.

chiquichaque, *m.* sawyer; noise made by things rubbing against each other.

chiquirritín, ina, *n.* (coll.) baby boy, baby girl.

chiquito, ta, *adj.* little, small; —, *n.* little boy; little girl.

chiribitil, *m.* crib; small room.

chirimía, *f.* flageolet; —, *m.* flageolete player.

chirinola, *f.* game played by boys; trifle.

chiripa, *f.* fluke (in billiards); (coll.) fortunate chance; **de —,** by mere chance.

chiripear, *vn.* to make flukes at billiards; to be fortunate in a game in spite of not understanding it well.

chiripero, ra, *n.* one who is lucky at games of chance; one who wins by flukes.

chirivía, *f.* (bot.) parsnip; (orn.) wagtail.

chirla, *f.* mussel.

chirlador, ra, *n.* (coll.) clamorous prattler.

chirlar, *vn.* to prattle.

chirlo, *m.* large wound in the face.

chirriar, *vn.* to hiss; to creak; to chirp.

chirrido, *m.* chirping of birds.

chirrío, *m.* creaking noise made by the wheels of a cart.

chirrión, *m.* tumbrel, creaking cart.

chirrionero, *m.* driver of a tumbrel.

chisgarabís, *m.* superficial meddler.

chisguete, *m.* small draft of wine.

chisme, *m.* misreport; gossip.

chismear, *va,* and *vn.* to tattle, to carry tales, to misreport.

chismero, ra, *n.* tattletale, talebearer.

chismoso, sa, *adj.* tattling, talebearing.

chispa, *f.* spark; very small diamond; short gun; small particle; slight intoxication; **¡—s!** *interj.* blazes! **echar —s,** to rave.

chispazo, *m.* the flying off of a spark from the fire, and the damage it does; tale mischievously circulated.

chispear, *vn.* to sparkle; to drizzle.

chispero, ra, *adj.* emitting a number of sparks, —, *m.* blacksmith.

chisporrotear, *vn.* to sparkle, to hiss (of liquids).

chisposo, sa, *adj.* sparkling.

chistar, *vn.* to mumble, to mutter.

chiste, *m.* witty saying; joke, jest.

chistera, *f.* hand basket for fishing; (coll.) silk hat, top hat.

chistoso, sa, *adj.* gay, cheerful; funny, comical.

¡chite! *interj.* silence! hush!

chiticalla, *m.* and *f.* (coll.) discreet and silent person; —, *m.* secret.

chiticallar, *va.* to keep silence; not to make a noise.

¡chito! or **¡chitón!** *interj.* hush! mum!

chivato, *m.* kid or young goat between six and twelve months old.

chivo, va, *n.* kid, goat.

¡cho! *interj.* whoa!

chocante, *adj.* repellent, repugnant.

chocar, *vn.* to strike, to knock; to encounter, to rush against each other; to fight, to combat; —, *va.* to provoke; to displease.

chocarrear, *vn.* to act a buffoon.

chocarrería, *f.* buffoonery.

chocarrero, *m.* buffoon; —, **ra,** *adj.* scurrilous, buffoonlike.

chocolate, *m.* chocolate.

chocolatera, *f.* chocolate pot.

chocolatero, *m.* chocolate manufacturer.

chocha, *f.* (orn.) woodcock.

chochear, *vn.* to dote.

chochera, *f.* second childhood.

chocho, cha, *adj.* doting.

chofer or **chófer,** *m.* chauffeur, driver; **carnet de —,** chauffeur's (driver's) license.

chofes, *m. pl.* livers and lungs.

chofeta, *f.* chafing dish.

chofista, *m.* a poor fellow who lives upon livers and lungs.

cholo, la, *n.* half-breed; pet name for some one with straight hair.

cholla, *f.* skull; (fig.) powers of the mind, judgment.

chopo, *m.* black poplar tree; (coll.) musket, gun.

choque, *m.* shock, collision, crash, clash; (mil.) skirmish; dispute, contest.

choquezuela, *f.* (anat.) kneepan.

choricero, ra, *n.* sausage maker or seller.

chorizo, *m.* pork sausage.

chorlito, *m.* (orn.) curlew, gray plover.

chorrear, *vn.* to drop from a spout, to gush, to drip; to come successively.

chorrera, *f.* spout or place from whence liquids drop; mark left by water or other liquids; frill of the breast of a shirt.

chorretada, *f.* water (or other liquid) rushing from a spout.

chorrillo, *m.* small spout; (coll.) the continual coming in and outgoing of money.

chorro, *m.* gush; **a —s,** abundantly.

chorrón, *m.* dressed hemp.

choto, *m.* sucking goat.

chotuno, na, *adj.* sucking (applied to young goats or kids).

chova, *f.* (orn.) jackdaw.

choza, *f.* hut, shepherd's cottage, cabin, hovel, shed.

chozuela, *f.* small hut.

chubasco, *m.* squall, shower.

chucero, *m.* (mil.) pikeman.

chuchear, *vn.* to whisper; —, *va.* to hunt fowl with calls, traps and nets.

chuchería, *f.* gewgaw, bauble, trinket, toy; curio.

chuchero, *m.* birdcatcher.

chucho, *m.* (coll.) dog; whip, scourge (in Cuba); word used to call a dog.

chuchumeco, *m.* a sorry, contemptible little fellow.

chuecazo, *m.* stroke (in playing ball).

chufeta, *f.* jest, joke; coal pan.

chufleta, *f.* taunt, jeer.

chufletear, *vn.* to sneer, to taunt.

chufletero, ra, *adj.* taunting, sneering.

chulada, *f.* droll speech or action.

chulear, *va.* to jest, to joke, to poke fun at; (Mex.) to woo.

chuleta, *f.* chop; — **de cordero,** lamb chop; — **empanada,** breaded chop; — **de puerco,** pork chop; — **de ternera,** veal chop.

chulo, la, *n.* punster, jester, clown; bull-fighter's assistant; —, *adj.* (Sp. Am.) pretty, attractive.

chumacera, *f.* (mech.) journal bearing; (naut.) rowlock.

chunga, *f.* jest, joke; **estar de** —, to be in good humor.

chunguearse, *vr.* to be in good humor, to jest.

chupa, *f.* waistcoat, jacket.

chupada, *f.* suction, sucking; —**do, da,** *adj.* lean, emaciated.

chupadero, ra, *adj.* sucking.

chupador, *m.* baby's teething ring.

chupar, *va.* to suck; (fig.) to sponge upon.

chupetear, *va.* to suck gently.

chupetín, *m.* doublet.

chupón, *m.* sucker (twig); (mech.) sucker, valve bucket, —, **ona,** *n.* swindler, sponger; —, *adj.* fond of sucking.

churdón, *m.* raspberry jam.

churre, *m.* thick, dirty grease.

churriburri, *m.* low fellow; rabble.

churriento, ta, *adj.* greasy.

churro, rra, *adj.* applied to sheep that have coarse wool.

churruscarse, *vr.* to be scorched.

churrusco, *m.* overtoasted bread.

churumbela, *f.* reed instrument resembling a flageolet; (Sp. Am.) small cup for maté.

chus ni mus, (coll.) **no decir** —, not to say a word.

chuscada, *f.* pleasantry, drollery.

chusco, ca, *adj.* pleasant, droll, merry.

chusma, *f.* rabble, mob.

chuzo, *m.* little spear or pike; **llover a** —**s,** to rain heavily.

D

D., Dn. or **D.ⁿ, Don,** Don, title equivalent to Mr., but used before given name.

d. or **da.: día,** d. day; **data,** date.

Da. or **D.ª, Doña,** Donna, title equivalent to Mrs. or Miss but used before given name.

dable, *adj.* easy, possible.

dactilografía, *f.* typewriting.

dactilografista, *m.* and *f.* typist, typewriter.

dactilógrafo, fa, *n.* typist; typewriter.

dactilología, *f.* dactylology, the art of talking by manual signs.

dactiloscopia, *f.* dactyloscopy, finger printing.

dadaísmo, *m.* dadaism.

dádiva, *f.* gift, present.

dadivoso, sa, *adj.* generous, open-handed.

dado, *m.* die (*pl.* dice) (*p.p.* of **dar**); — **que** or — **caso que,** in case that, provided that, since.

dador, ra, *n.* giver, bearer.

daga, *f.* dagger.

daguerrotipo, *m.* daguerreotype.

dala, *f.* (naut.) pump dale of a ship.

¡dale! *interj.* word used to express displeasure at another's obstinacy.

dalia, *f.* (bot.) dahlia.

dalmática, *f.* dalmatic, vestment worn by the deacons of the Roman Catholic church in the performance of divine service.

daltoniano, na, *adj.* color-blind.

daltonismo, *m.* color blindness.

dallador, *m.* lawn mower.

dallar, *va.* to mow grass.

dalle, *m.* scythe.

dama, *f.* lady, gentlewoman; mistress; king (in checkers); actress who performs the principal parts; —**s,** *pl.* checkers; **jugar a las** —**s,** to play checkers.

damascado, da, *adj.* damasklike.

damasco, *m.* damask (cloth); damson (plum).

damasina, *f.* light silk cloth resembling damask.

damasquino, na, *adj.* damaskeened.

damisela, *f.* young gentlewoman; girl about town.

damnificar, *va.* to hurt, to damage, to injure.

danés, esa, *n.* and *adj.* Danish.

Danubio, *m.* Danube.

danza, *f.* dance.

danzador, ra, *n.* dancer.

danzante, *m.* dancer; fickle, airy person.

danzar, *vn.* to dance; (coll.) to meddle.

danzarín, na, *n.* dancer; (coll.) meddling person.

dañar, *va.* to hurt, to damage; to injure, to spoil.

dañino, ina, *adj.* noxious; mischievous; harmful.

daño, *m.* damage, injury, loss; discount; —**s y perjuicios,** damages; **hacer** —, to hurt, to injure.

dañoso, sa, *adj.* hurtful, noxious.

dar, *va.* and *vn.* (DOY, DI) to give; to supply, to deliver; to confer, to grant; to represent; to hit; to strike; — **a conocer,** to make known; — **a la calle,** to face the street; — **a luz,** to give birth; — **de comer,** to feed; — **con,** to find, to meet; — **fe,** to certify, to attest; — **fianza,** to bail or give security; — **los buenos días,** to say good day; — **memorias,** to give regards; — **un paseo,** to take a walk; — **prestado,** to lend; — **que decir,** to give cause to criticize; — **que pensar,** to make suspicious, to cause to think; — **razón de,** to inform; —**se,** to give up; to conform to the will of another; —**se cuenta de,** to realize; —**se prisa,** to hurry.

dardo, *m.* dart, arrow.

data, *f.* date; article put down in an account.

datar, *va.* to date.

dátil, *m.* (bot.) date.

datilado, da, *adj.* resembling a date.

dativo, *m.* (gram.) dative.

dato, *m.* datum; —**s,** *pl.* data, information.

dauco, *m.* wild carrot.

DD. doctores, Drs. doctors.

de, *prep.* of; from; for; by; on; to; with.

dé, *imperative* of **dar,** give.

deán, *m.* dean.

deanato, *m.* deanship.

debajo, *adv.* under, underneath, below.

debate, *m.* debate, discussion, contest, altercation.

debatir, *va.* to debate, to argue, to discuss.

debe, *m.* (com.) debit; debtor side of an account; — **y haber,** debit and credit.

deber, *m.* obligation, duty; debt; —, *va.* to owe; to be obliged.

debidamente, *adv.* justly; duly, exactly, perfectly.

debido, da, *adj.* due; proper; **en forma —da,** in proper form.

débil, *adj.* feeble, weak; sickly; frail; pusillanimous.

debilidad, *f.* debility, weakness.

debilitación, *f.* emasculation.

debilitar, *va.* to debilitate, to weaken; —**se,** to become weak or feeble.

debitar, *va.* (com.) to debit.

débito, *m.* debt; duty.

debut, *m.* debut, first appearance.

debutante, *f.* debutante.

debutar, *vn.* to make one's debut, to make one's first appearance.

década, *f.* decade.

decadencia, *f.* decay, decline.

decadente, *adj.* decadent.

decaer, *vn.* (DECAIGO, DECAÍ) to decay, to decline, to fade.

decágono, *m.* decagon.

decagramo, *m.* decagram.

decaído, da, *adj.* crestfallen, prostrated, weak.

decaimiento, *m.* decay, decline.

decálogo, *m.* the Decalogue.

decampar, *vn.* to decamp.

decanato, *m.* seniority.

decano, *m.* senior, dean.

decantar, *va.* to cry up, to puff, to decant.

decapitación, *f.* decapitation, beheading.

decapitar, *va.* to behead.

decasílabo, *adj.* ten-syllable.

decena, *f.* denary, ten.

decenal, *adj.* decennial.

decenario, ria, *adj.* decennary.

decencia, *f.* decency.

decenio, *m.* decade.

deceno, na, *adj.* tenth.

decentar, *va.* (IE) to begin to make use of something (as cheese, bread, etc.); — **la salud,** to begin to lose one's health; —**se,** to get bedsores.

decente, *adj.* decent, honest; respectable.

decepción, *f.* disappointment.

decepcionar, *va.* to disappoint; —**se,** to be disappointed.

decible, *adj.* expressible.

decididamente, *adv.* decidedly.

decidir, *va.* to decide. to determine —**se,** to be determined, to decide.

decigramo, *m.* decigram.

decilitro, *m.* deciliter.

décima, *f.* (poet.) a stanza of ten lines.

decimal, *adj.* decimal; belonging to tithes.

décimo, ma, *adj.* tenth.

décimoctavo, va, or **deciocheno, na,** *adj.* eighteenth.

décimocuarto, ta, *adj.* fourteenth.

décimonono, na, *adj.* nineteenth.

décimoquinto, ta, *adj.* fifteenth.

décimoséptimo, ma, *adj.* seventeenth.

décimosexto, ta, *adj.* sixteenth.

décimotercio, cia, *adj.* thirteenth.

deciocheno, na, *adj.* eighteenth.

decir, *va.* (DIGO, DIJE) to say, to tell, to speak; to name; **querer —,** to mean; **por —lo así,** as it were; —, *m* familiar saying.

decisión, *f.* decision, determination.

decisivo, va, *adj.* decisive, final.

declamación, *f.* declamation. discourse, oration; oratorical invective; declamatory style of reading.

declamador, ra, *n.* declaimer, reciter

declamar, *vn.* to declaim, to harangue, to recite.

declamatorio, ria, *adj.* declamatory.

declaración, *f.* declaration, statement, explanation; interpretation; manifest; (law) deposition; railroad bill of lading.

declarar, *va.* to declare, to manifest, to state; to expound; to explain; (law) to decide; to depose upon oath; —**se,** to declare one's opinion; (coll.) to declare one's love.

declaratorio, ria, *adj.* declaratory, explanatory.

declinable, *adj.* (gram.) declinable.

declinación, *f.* declination, descent; decline; (gram.) declension.

declinar, *vn.* to decline; to bend, to slope· —, *va.* (gram.) to decline.

declinatoria, *f.* plea which attacks the competency of a judge.

declive, *m.* declivity, slope.
decocción, *f.* decoction.
decomisar, *va.* to confiscate, to forfeit, to seize.
decomiso, *m.* forfeiture, confiscation.
decoración, *f.* decoration, ornament; theatrical scenery, stage setting, stage scenery.
decorado, *m.* decoration, stage scenery.
decorador, ra, *n.* decorator; —, *adj.* decorating.
decorar, *va.* to decorate; to adorn; to illustrate.
decoro, *m.* honor, respect; circumspection; honesty; decency.
decoroso, sa, *adj.* decorous, decent.
decrecer, *vn.* (EZCO) to decrease, to diminish.
decreciente, *adj.* decreasing, diminishing.
decremento, *m.* decrease, diminution.
decrepitar, *va.* and *vn.* to decrepitate; to crackle in the fire.
decrépito, ta, *adj.* decrepit, crazy, worn out with age.
decrepitud, *f.* decrepitude.
decretal, *f.* letter of the pope which decides a question of ecclesiastical law; —, *adj.* decretal.
decretar, *va.* to decree, to decide, to resolve, to determine; to give a decree in a suit.
decreto, *m.* decree, decision; judicial decree.
décuplo, pla, *adj.* decuple, tenfold.
decuria, *f.* ten Roman soldiers under a decurion; class of ten students.
decurión, *m.* decurion; student who has the care of ten other students.
decursas, *f. pl.* arrears of rent.
decurso, *m.* course of time.
dechado, *m.* sample, pattern; sampler; model of virtue and perfection.
dedada, *f.* a pinch or portion (of anything).
dedal, *m.* thimble; very small drinking glass.
dedalera, *f.* (bot.) foxglove; digitalis.
dédalo, *m.* labyrinth; entanglement.
dedicación, *f.* dedication; consecration.
dedicado, da, *adj.* destined.
dedicar, *va.* to dedicate, to devote, to consecrate; —se, to apply oneself to.
dedicatoria, *f.* dedication.
dedillo, *m.* little finger; **saber una cosa al** —, to know a thing perfectly.
dedo, *m.* finger; toe; the forty-eighth part of a Spanish yard; finger's breadth, small bit; — **meñique,** little finger; — **pulgar,** thumb; — **del corazón,** middle finger; — **anular,** ring finger.
deducción, *f.* deduction, derivation, consequence.
deducir, *va.* (DEDUZCO, DEDUJE) to deduce, to infer; (law) to allege in pleading; (com.) to subtract.
defección, *f.* defection, apostasy.
defectible, *adj.* imperfect, deficient.
defectivo, va, *adj.* defective.
defecto, *m.* defect, fault, defectiveness; maimedness.

defectuoso, sa, *adj.* defective, imperfect, faulty.
defender, *va.* (IE) to defend, to uphold, to protect; to justify, to assert, to maintain; to prohibit, to forbid; to resist, to oppose.
defensa, *f.* defense, justification; apology; guard, shelter, protection, fence; (mil.) flanking defenses.
defensiva, *f.* defensive.
defensivo, *m.* defense, safeguard; —, **va,** *adj.* defensive.
defensor, ra, *n.* defender, supporter, protector; lawyer, counsel.
defensorio, *m.* plea, defense.
deferencia, *f.* deference.
deferente, *adj.* pliant, docile, yielding.
deferir, *vn.* (IE) to yield to another's opinion; —, *va.* to communicate.
deficiencia, *f.* deficiency.
deficiente, *adj.* deficient.
déficit, *m.* deficit.
definición, *f.* definition; decision.
definido, da, *adj.* definite.
definir, *va.* to define, to describe, to explain; to decide.
definitivo, va, *adj.* definitive, final; positive; **en** —, in short.
deformación, *f.* deformation.
deformado, da, *adj.* deformed.
deformar, *va.* to deform, to disfigure; —se, to become disfigured.
deforme, *adj.* deformed, ugly.
deformidad, *f.* deformity, ugliness; gross error.
defraudación, *f.* fraud, usurpation.
defraudador, ra, *n.* defrauder, usurper.
defraudar, *va.* to defraud, to cheat; to usurp; to disturb.
defuera, *adv.* externally, outwardly.
defunción, *f.* death; funeral.
degeneración, *f.* degeneracy.
degenerar, *vn.* to degenerate.
deglutir, *va.* to swallow.
degollación, *f.* decollation, beheading.
degolladero, *m.* throttle; slaughterhouse.
degollador, *m.* headsman, executioner.
degollar, *va.* (UE) to behead; to destroy, to ruin.
degradación, *f.* degradation.
degradar, *va.* to degrade; —se, to degrade or demean oneself.
degüello, *m.* decollation; act of beheading.
degustación, *f.* act of tasting.
dehesa, *f.* pasture ground.
dehesar, *va.* to turn arable land into pasture ground.
dehesero, *m.* keeper of a pasture ground.
deicidio, *m.* deicide, murder of Christ.
deidad, *f.* deity, divinity; goddess.
deificación, *f.* deification.
deificar, *va.* to deify.
deífico, ca, *adj.* divine.
deiforme, *adj.* godlike.
deísmo, *m.* deism.
deísta, *m.* deist.

dejadez, *f.* slovenliness, neglect, lassitude.

dejado, da, *adj.* slovenly, idle, indolent; dejected.

dejamiento, *m.* indolence, carelessness.

dejar, *va.* to leave, to let, to quit; to omit; to permit, to allow; to leave, to forsake; to bequeath; to pardon; **—se,** to abandon oneself (to).

dejativo, va, *adj.* slovenly, lazy.

dejo, *m.* end, termination; negligence, laziness; aftertaste, tang; effect; taste or flavor remaining after eating or drinking; particular accentuation on the last syllable of words.

del, *adj.* of the (contraction of **de el**).

delación, *f.* accusation, impeachment.

delantal, *m.* apron.

delante, *adv.* before (in the front; preceding in time; in preference to); **— de,** *prep.* in front of.

delantero, ra, *adj.* foremost, first; **—,** *m.* outrider; **—,** *f.* forepart; lead, advantage; front line seat; **tomar la —,** to get the start, to take the lead.

delatable, *adj.* accusable, blamáble.

delatante, *m.* and *f.* informer, accuser.

delatar, *va.* to accuse, to denounce.

delator, ra, *n.* accuser, informer, denouncer, delator.

delectación, *f.* pleasure, delight; **— morosa,** deliberate indulgence of some sensual pleasure that is contrary to good manners.

delegación, *f.* delegation; substitution.

delegado, da, *n.* delegate, deputy.

delegar, *va.* to delegate, to substitute.

deleitable, *adj.* delightful.

deleitar, *va.* to delight.

deleite, *m.* pleasure, delight; lust.

deleitoso, sa, *adj.* pleasing, delightful.

deletéreo, rea, *adj.* deleterious.

deletrear, *va.* and *vn.* to spell; to decipher, to interpret.

deletreo, *m.* spelling.

deleznable, *adj.* weak, fragile; slippery.

delfín, *m.* dolphin; dauphin.

delgado, da, *adj.* thin, delicate, light; slender, lean; acute, fine, ingenious; little, scanty.

deliberación, *f.* deliberation; resolution.

deliberadamente, *adv.* deliberately.

deliberar, *vn.* to consider, to deliberate; to consult.

deliberativo, va, *adj.* deliberative.

delicadeza, *f.* tenderness, softness; exquisiteness; delicacy, daintiness; subtlety; weakness of constitution.

delicado, da, *adj.* delicate, tender; faint; fastidious; exquisite; delicious, dainty; slender, subtle; weak in constitution, in poor health.

delicia, *f.* delight, pleasure.

delicioso, sa, *adj.* delicious, delightful.

delincuencia, *f.* delinquency; offense, guilt.

delincuente, *m.* and *f.* delinquent, culprit, offender.

delineación, *f.* delineation; sketch.

delineador, *m.* delineator.

delineamiento, *m.* delineament.

delinear, *va.* to delineate, to sketch; to describe.

delinquir, *vn.* to transgress the law.

deliquio, *m.* faint, languor.

delirante, *adj.* delirious.

delirar, *vn.* to be delirious, to rave; to talk nonsense.

delirio, *m.* delirium; dotage; nonsense.

delito, *m.* transgression of a law, crime.

delta, *f.* delta.

deltoide, *adj.* deltoid.

delusivo, va, *adj.* delusive.

delusorio, ria, *adj.* fallacious, deceiving.

della or **dello,** contractions of the words **de ella** or **de ello,** of her, of it (in old Spanish).

demacrado, da, *adj.* emaciated.

demacrarse, *vr.* to waste away, to become emaciated.

demagogia, *f.* demagogy.

demagogo, *m.* demagogue.

demanda, *f.* demand, claim; pretension; complaint; challenge; request; charity box; **oferta y —,** supply and demand.

demandadero, ra, *n.* servant of a convent or a jail.

demandado, da, *n.* defendant.

demandador, *m.* one who claims or demands; petitioner for charity for pious uses; plaintiff, demandant; claimant.

demandante, *m.* and *f.* (law) plaintiff.

demandar, *va.* to demand, to ask, to petition, to claim; to enter a claim; to start a suit.

demarcación, *f.* demarcation; boundary line.

demarcar, *va.* to mark out limits.

demás, *adj.* other; **los** or **las —,** the rest, the others; **—,** *adv.* besides; **y —,** and so on; **estar —,** to be over and above; to be useless or superfluous; **por —,** in vain, to no purpose.

demasía, *f.* excess in the price; overmuch; arduous enterprise; rudeness; want of respect; abundance, plenty; **en —,** excessively.

demasiado, da, *adj.* excessive, overmuch; bold, daring; useless; **—,** *adv.* enough, too much, excessively.

demencia, *f.* madness, insanity, dementia; **— precoz,** dementia praecox.

dementarse, *vr.* to become demented.

demente, *adj.* mad, insane.

demérito, *m.* demerit.

demeritorio, ria, *adj.* without merit.

demisión, *f.* submission, humility.

democracia, *f.* democracy.

demócrata, *m.* and *f.* democrat.

democrático, ca, *adj.* democratic.

democratizar, *va.* to democratize.

demografía, *f.* demography.

demoler, *va.* (UE) to demolish; to destroy.

demolición, *f.* demolition.
demonio, *m.* devil, demon; ¡—! *interj.* the deuce!
demonología, *f.* demonology.
demora, *f.* delay; demurrage.
demorar, *vn.* to delay, to tarry.
demostrable, *adj.* demonstrable.
demostración, *f.* demonstration; manifestation.
demostrar, *va.* (UE) to prove, to demonstrate, to show, to manifest.
demostrativo, va, *adj.* demonstrative.
demudar, *va.* to alter, to change; —se, to be changed.
demulcente, *adj.* (med.) emollient; —, *m.* emollient.
denegación, *f.* denial, refusal.
denegar, *va.* (IE) to deny, to refuse.
dengue, *m.* prudery; short veil.
denigración, *f.* defamation, disgrace.
denigrar, *va.* to blacken; to calumniate.
denodado, da, *adj.* bold, intrepid, audacious.
denominación, *f.* denomination, distinct appellation.
denominador, *m.* (math.) denominator.
denominar, *va.* to call, to give a name to.
denostar, *va.* to insult, to abuse.
denotación, *f.* denotation.
denotar, *va.* to denote, to express.
densidad, *f.* density; obscurity; — específica, specific gravity.
densimetría, *f.* densimetry.
densímetro, *m.* densimeter.
denso, sa, *adj.* dense, thick, compact.
dentado, da, *adj.* dentated, toothed; indented.
dentadura, *f.* set of teeth.
dental, *m.* bed to which plowshare is fixed; (agr.) wooden fork; —, *adj.* dental, pertaining to teeth or dentistry; clínica —, dental clinic.
dentar, *va.* and *vn.* (IE) to tooth; to indent; to teeth, to cut teeth.
dentellada, *f.* gnashing of the teeth; nip; pinch with the teeth; a —s, snappishly, peevishly.
dentellado, da, *adj.* denticulated.
dentellear, *va.* to bite.
dentera, *f.* setting on edge of teeth; (coll.) jealousy, envy.
dentición, *f.* dentition, teething.
denticular, *adj.* like teeth, toothed.
dentífrico, *m.* dentifrice; —, ca, *adj.* dentifrice; polvo —, toothpowder; pasta —, toothpaste.
dentista, *m.* dentist.
dentistería, *f.* dentistry.
dentro, *adv.* within, inside; — de, inside of; — de poco, shortly; hacia —, toward the inside; por —, on the inside.
dentudo, da, *adj.* uneven-toothed.
denudación, *f.* denudation.
denuedo, *m.* boldness, intrepidity.
denuesto, *m.* affront, insult.

denuncia, *f.* denunciation.
denunciable, *adj.* capable of being denounced.
denunciación, *f.* denunciation.
denunciador, ra, *n.* accuser, denunciator.
denunciar, *va.* to advise, to give notice; to denounce; to prognosticate.
denunciatorio, ria, *adj.* denunciatory.
deparar, *va.* to offer, to present, to bestow upon, to furnish.
departamental, *adj.* departmental.
departamento, *m.* department; section, bureau; (rail.) compartment.
depauperación, *f.* impoverishment.
depauperar, *va.* to impoverish.
dependencia, *f.* dependency; relation, affinity; business, affair.
depender, *vn.* to depend, to be dependent on; — de, to count on.
dependiente, *m.* dependent; hanger-on; subordinate; clerk.
depilatorio, *m.* depilatory.
deplorable, *adj.* deplorable, lamentable, wretched.
deplorar, *va.* to deplore, to regret.
deponer, *va.* (DEPONGO, DEPUSE) to depose, to declare; to displace; to deposit; —, *vn.* to evacuate the bowels.
deportación, *f.* deportation.
deportar, *va.* to transport; to deport, to banish.
deporte, *m.* sport, amusement.
deportivo, va, *adj.* sport, sporting.
deposición, *f.* deposition; assertion, affirmation; evacuation of the bowels; (law) deposition upon oath.
depositante, *m.* and *f.* depositor.
depositar, *va.* to deposit, to confide; to put in any place to be kept safe.
depositaría, *f.* depository.
depositario, *m.* depositary, trustee, receiver; —, ria, *adj.* relating to a depository.
depósito, *m.* deposit; warehouse.
depravación, *f.* depravity.
depravar, *va.* to deprave, to vitiate, to corrupt.
deprecación, *f.* petition; earnest entreaty.
deprecar, *va.* to beg, to implore.
depreciación, *f.* depreciation.
depreciar, *va.* to depreciate.
depredación, *f.* depredation.
depresión, *f.* depression, abasement, air pocket.
depresivo, va, *adj.* depressing.
deprimir, *va.* to depress, to humble, to deject.
depuración, *f.* purification.
depurador, *m.* purifier; converter (gas); dust chamber; cleansing tank.
depurar, *va.* to cleanse, to purify, to filter.
derecha, *f.* right hand, right side; right wing (in politics); a —s, right; well done; a la —, to the right-hand side.
derechamente, *adv.* directly, straight; rightly, prudently.

derechera, *f.* direct road.
derechista, *m.* and *f.* (pol.) rightist, reactionary.
derecho, cha, *adj.* right, straight; just, perfect, certain; —, *m.* right; justice, law; just claim; tax duty; fee; **dar —cho,** to entitle; **—os consulares,** consular fees; **—os de aduana** or **arancelarios,** customs duties; **—os de entrada,** import duties; **mercancías sujetas a —chos,** dutiable goods; **—os de autor,** royalty; **—os reservados,** all rights reserved.
derechura, *f.* rectitude, right way.
deriva, *f.* deviation, drift; ship's course; **indicador de —,** drift indicator.
derivación, *f.* derivation; source, origin.
derivado, *m.* by-product; (gram.) derivative; **—da,** *f.* (math.) derivative; **—, da,** *adj.* derived.
derivar, *va.* and *vn.* to derive; (naut.) to deflect from the course.
derivativo, va, *adj.* derivative.
dermatitis, *f.* dermatitis.
dermatología, *f.* dermatology.
dermatólogo, *m.* dermatologist.
derogación, *f.* derogation, abolition; deterioration; diminution.
derogar, *va.* to derogate, to abolish; to reform.
derogatorio, ria, *adj.* derogatory.
derrama, *f.* assessment of a tax or impost.
derramador, ra, *n.* and *adj.* prodigal, spendthrift.
derramamiento, *m.* effusion, waste; dispersion.
derramar, *va.* to drain off water; to spread; to spill, to scatter, to waste, to shed; **—se,** to be spread, to become scattered.
derrame, *m.* loss in measuring; leakage.
derrape, *m.* (aer.) yawing.
derredor, *m.* circumference, circuit; **al —** or **en —,** about, around.
derrelicto, ta, *adj.* derelict, abandoned; **—,** *m.* boat or thing abandoned in the sea.
derrelinquir, *va.* to abandon.
derrengado, da, *adj.* bent, crooked.
derrengar, *va.* (IE) to sprain the hip; to cripple; to bend.
derretimiento, *m.* fusion; melting.
derretir, *va.* (I) to melt; to consume, to expend; **—se,** to fall in love very easily; to be melted.
derribar, *va.* to demolish; to flatten, to throw down; to overthrow; **—se,** to throw oneself down on the ground.
derribo, *m.* demolition; debris.
derrocar, *va.* (UE) to pull down, to demolish.
derrochador, ra, *n.* prodigal, squanderer.
derrochar, *va.* to squander.
derrota, *f.* ship's course; road, path; defeat, rout (of an army, etc.).
derrotar, *va.* (naut.) to cause (a ship) to fall off her course; to destroy; to defeat.
derrotero, *m.* collection of sea charts; ship's course; (fig.) course, way.

derrotismo, *m.* defeatism.
derrotista, *m.* and *f.* defeatist.
derruir, *va.* (UYO) to demolish.
derrumbadero, *m.* precipice; thorny or arduous affair.
derrumbar, *va.* to throw down headlong; **—se,** to crumble away.
derrumbe, *m.* collapse, landslide.
derviche, *m.* dervish.
desabarrancar, *va.* to drag out of a ditch; to extricate from difficulties.
desabastecer, *va.* (EZCO) to cut off supplies from.
desabillé, *m.* dishabille, undress; morning gown.
desabollar, *va.* to take bulges out of pewter dishes, etc.
desabonarse, *vr.* to withdraw one's subscription.
desabor, *m.* displeasure; lack of taste.
desaborido, da, *adj.* tasteless.
desabotonar, *va.* to unbutton; **—,** *vn.* and *vr.* to blossom.
desabridamente, *adv.* insipidly.
desabrido, da, *adj.* tasteless, insipid; peevish.
desabrigado, da, *adj.* uncovered; shelterless.
desabrigar, *va.* to uncover; to deprive of clothes or shelter.
desabrigo, *m.* nakedness; destitution.
desabrimiento, *m.* insipidity; asperity of temper; dejection.
desabrir, *va.* to vex, to plague; to harass; **—se,** to be angry.
desabrochar, *va.* to unclasp, to unbutton, to unfasten; **—se** to unbosom, to reveal a secret in confidence.
desacalorarse, *vr.* to take the fresh air; to cool oneself.
desacatamiento, *m.* disrespect.
desacatar, *va.* to treat in a disrespectful manner.
desacato, *m.* disrespect, incivility.
desacertado, da, *adj.* mistaken, wrong; unwise.
desacertar, *vn.* (IE) to err, to commit a mistake.
desacierto, *m.* error, mistake, blunder.
desacobardar, *va.* to inspire courage, to remove fear from.
desacomodado, da, *adj.* destitute of the conveniences of life; out of service, out of employment.
desacomodamiento, *m.* incommodity, inconvenience.
desacomodar, *va.* to incommode, to molest; **—se,** to lose one's place.
desacomodo, *m.* discharge, loss of position; loss of comfort.
desacompañamiento, *m.* lack of company.
desacompañar, *va.* to leave the company of.
desaconsejado, da, *adj.* ill-advised.
desacordado, da, *adj.* discordant (applied to colors).

desacordar, *va.* (UE) to untune; —**se,** to be forgetful; to be at variance.

desacorde, *adj.* discordant; inharmonious.

desacorralar, *va.* to let the flock or cattle out of the fold.

desacostumbrado, da, *adj.* unaccustomed; unusual.

desacostumbrar, *va.* to break a habit; to become unaccustomed.

desacotar, *va.* to lay open a pasture ground; to withdraw a prohibition; to reject, to refuse.

desacreditar, *va.* to discredit.

desacuerdo, *m.* derangement of mental faculties; discordance, disagreement, disunion.

desaderezar, *va.* to disarrange, to disorder.

desadeudar, *va.* to pay one's debts, to get out of debt; —**se,** to be out of debt.

desadormecer, *va.* (EZCO) to wake, to rouse from sleep; to rouse from mental stupor.

desadornar, *va.* to divest of ornaments or decorations.

desadorno, *m.* lack of embellishments or charms.

desafección, *f.* disaffection.

desafecto, *m.* disaffection, discontent.

desaferrar, *va.* to weigh anchor; to loosen; to convince; to cause one to change an opinion.

desafiador, *m.* challenger.

desafiar, *va.* to challenge, to call out (to fight a duel); to defy.

desaficionar, *va.* to destroy one's affection for anything.

desafinar, *vn.* and *vr.* to be out of tune; to get out of tune.

desafío, *m.* challenge; struggle, contest, match, duel.

desaforado, da, *adj.* huge; disorderly, lawless, impudent.

desaforar, *va.* (UE) to encroach upon one's rights; (mil.) to cashier; —**se,** to be outrageous.

desaforrar, *va.* to take the lining from anything.

desafortunado, da, *adj.* unfortunate, unlucky.

desafuero, *m.* act of injustice; excess.

desagarrar, *va.* to release.

desagraciado, da, *adj.* ungraceful, inelegant.

desagraciar, *va.* to deform, to disfigure.

desagradable, *adj.* disagreeable, unpleasant.

desagradar, *va.* to displease, to offend.

desagradecer, *va.* (EZCO) to be ungrateful.

desagradecido, da, *adj.* ungrateful; —, *n.* ingrate.

desagradecimiento, *m.* ingratitude.

desagrado, *m.* asperity, harshness; displeasure.

desagraviar, *va.* to make amends for an injury.

desagravio, *m.* relief, satisfaction.

desagregar, *va.* to disjoin, to separate.

desaguadero, *m.* channel, drain; outlet, waste pipe.

desaguador, *m.* channel for carrying off water.

desaguar, *va.* to draw off water; —, *vn.* to empty or to flow into the sea.

desaguazar, *va.* to drain or draw off the water from a thing.

desagüe, *m.* channel, drain outlet, waste.

desahijar, *va.* to wean; —**se,** to swarm (of bees).

desahitarse, *vr.* to relieve indigestion.

desahogado, da, *adj.* petulant, impudent; in comfortable circumstances.

desahogar, *va.* to ease pain, to relieve; —**se,** to recover; to unbosom.

desahogo, *m.* ease, alleviation from pain, relief; unbosoming of one's troubles.

desahuciar, *va.* to despair; to give up; to dismiss a tenant; to declare (a patient) incurable.

desahucio, *m.* dismissing of a tenant or driving away cattle from a pasture ground (at the expiration of the stipulated time).

desahumar, *va.* to free from smoke.

desairado, da, *adj.* disregarded, slighted.

desairar, *va.* to disregard, to take no notice of; to rebuff.

desaire, *m.* disdain, disrespect; frown of fortune.

desajustar, *va.* to disproportion; to disadjust; —**se,** to withdraw from an agreement.

desajuste, *m.* lack of adjustment; disturbance of proper or regular conditions.

desalar, *va.* to cut off the wings; to take the salt out of fish, salt meat, etc., by steeping it in fresh water; —**se,** to run swiftly.

desalentar, *va.* (IE) to put out of breath; to discourage; —**se,** to lose hope, to be discouraged.

desalfombrar, *va.* to uncarpet.

desaliento, *m.* dismay, discouragement, dejection.

desaliñado, da, *adj.* slipshod.

desaliñar, *va.* to discompose, to disarrange.

desaliño, *m.* slovenliness; carelessness.

desalmado, da, *adj.* cruel, inhuman, impious.

desalmenado, da, *adj.* without turrets.

desalojar, *va.* to dislodge, to evict; to displace; —, *vn.* to move to other lodgings.

desalterar, *va.* to allay, to assuage, to settle.

desalumbrado, da, *adj.* dazzled; groping in the dark.

desamarrar, *va.* to unmoor a ship; to untie; to remove.

desamoldar, *va.* to unmold; to change the proportion or symmetry of anything.

desamorrar, *va.* to make a dull, silent person talk.

desamotinarse, *vr.* to withdraw from mutiny.

desamparar, *va.* to forsake, to abandon, to relinquish; to desist.

desamparo, *m.* abandonment; helplessness; dereliction.

desamueblar, *va.* to divest of furniture.

desancorar, *va.* (naut.) to weigh anchor.

desandar, *va.* (DESANDO, DESANDUVE) to retrograde, to go back the same road by which one came, to retrace.

desandrajado, da, *adj.* ragged, in tatters.

desangrar, *va.* to bleed one to excess; to drain a pond; (fig.) to exhaust one's means.

desanidar, *vn.* to forsake the nest; —, *va.* to dislodge from a post.

desanimado, da, *adj.* downhearted.

desanimar, *va.* and *vr.* to discourage.

desánimo, *m.* discouragement.

desanudar, *va.* to untie, to disentangle.

desapacibilidad, *f.* rudeness, churlishness, peevishness.

desapacible, *adj.* disagreeable, unpleasant, harsh.

desapadrinar, *va.* to disapprove, to disavow.

desaparear, *va.* to unmatch.

desaparecer, *va.* (EZCO) to remove out of sight; —, *vn.* to disappear.

desaparecimiento, *m.* disappearance.

desaparejar, *va.* to unharness beasts; (naut.) to unrig a ship.

desaparición, *f.* disappearance.

desapasionar, *va.* to root out a passion; to remove prejudice.

desapego, *m.* alienation of affection; coolness; disinterestedness.

desapercibido, da, *adj.* unprepared, unguarded.

desapercibimiento, *m.* unpreparedness.

desapestar, *va.* to cure persons infected with the plague.

desapiadado, da, *adj.* impious, merciless.

desaplicación, *f.* lack of application.

desaplicado, da, *adj.* indolent, careless, neglectful.

desapoderar, *va.* to dispossess; to repeal a power of attorney.

desapolillar, *va.* to free from moths; —se, (coll.) to go out after a long confinement when it is cold and sharp.

desaposentar, *va.* to turn someone out of his lodgings.

desaposesionar, *va.* to dispossess.

desapoyar, *va.* to withdraw support from.

desapreciar, *va.* to depreciate, to undervalue.

desaprender, *va.* to unlearn.

desapretar, *va.* (IE) to slacken, to loosen.

desaprisionar, *va.* to release from confinement; —se, to extricate oneself from difficulties.

desaprobación, *f.* disapprobation, disapproval.

desaprobar, *va.* (UE) to disapprove, to reprove.

desapropiamiento, *m.* alienation.

desapropiarse, *vr.* to alienate.

desaprovechado, da, *adj.* useless, unprofitable; backward.

desaprovechamiento, *m.* backwardness; waste of opportunities.

desaprovechar, *va.* to misspend, to turn to a bad use.

desapuntalar, *va.* to take away the props.

desapuntar, *va.* to unstitch; to lose one's aim, to aim firearms badly.

desarbolar, *va.* to unmast a ship; to clear of trees.

desarbolo, *m.* unmasting a ship.

desarenar, *va.* to clear a place of sand.

desarmable, *adj.* demountable.

desarmador, *m.* (Sp. Am.) screwdriver; hammer of a gun.

desarmadura, *f.* disarming.

desarmar, *va.* to disarm; to disband troops; to dismount (a crossbow, a cannon); to disassemble; (fig.) to pacify.

desarme, *m.* disarmament, disarming.

desarraigar, *va.* to root out; to extirpate.

desarraigo, *m.* eradication.

desarrapado, da, *adj.* ragged.

desarrebozar, *va.* and *vr.* to unmuffle; to manifest, to discover.

desarrebujar, *va.* to unfold, to spread out.

desarregladamente, *adv.* disorderly.

desarreglado, da, *adj.* immoderate in eating, drinking, etc.; disarranged; slovenly.

desarreglar, *va.* to disarrange, to derange.

desarreglo, *m.* disorder; licentiousness.

desarrimar, *va.* to remove; to dissuade.

desarrollar, *va.* and *vr.* to develop, to unroll, to unfold.

desarrollo, *m.* development; expansion; evolution; developing of a photo; evolvement.

desarropar, *va.* to undress; to take off covers or blankets.

desarrugar, *va.* to take out wrinkles.

desarrumar, *va.* to unload a ship.

desasear, *va.* to make dirty; to disorder.

desasentar, *va.* (IE) to remove; —, *vn.* to be disliked, to displease; —se, to stand up.

desaseo, *m.* uncleanliness, disorder.

desasimiento, *m.* letting loose; disinterestedness.

desasir, *va.* (DESASGO, DESASÍ) to loosen, to disentangle; —se, to extricate oneself. •

desasosegar, *va.* (IE) to disquiet, to disturb.

desasosiego, *m.* restlessness, uneasiness.

desastrado, da, *adj.* wretched, miserable; ragged.

desastre, *m.* disaster; misfortune.

desastroso, sa, *adj.* disastrous.

desatacar, *va.* to loosen, to untie; — una escopeta, to take the charge out of a gun.

desatar, *va.* to untie, to loose; to separate; to unriddle; —se, to give rein to one's tongue; to lose all reserve.

desatascar, *va.* to draw out of the mire; to extricate one from difficulties.

desataviar, *va.* to strip off decorations.

desatavío, *m.* lack of neatness in dress.

desatención, *f.* lack of attention, absence of mind; lack of politeness.

desatender, *va.* (IE) to pay no attention; to disregard, to neglect.

desatentado, da, *adj.* inconsiderate; thoughtless; excessive.

desatento, ta, *adj.* inattentive, careless; rude, uncivil.

desatesorar, *va.* to spend a treasure.

desatinado, da, *adj.* extravagant; tactless —, *m.* fool, madman.

desatinar, *va.* and *vn.* to derange one's mind; to throw into a violent rage; to talk nonsense; to become confused.

desatino, *m.* extravagance, folly; staggering; nonsense, blunder.

desatolondrar, *va.* to bring someone to himself; —se, to recover one's senses, to come to oneself.

desatollar, *va.* to pull out of the mire.

desatontarse, *vr.* to come to oneself (from a faint, stupefaction, etc.).

desatracar, *va.* (naut.) to sheer off.

desatrancar, *va.* to unbar; to clean out (a well, etc.).

desatufarse, *vr.* to grow calm.

desaturdir, *va.* to rouse from a state of dizziness or stupor.

desautorizar, *va.* to disauthorize.

desavahar, *va.* to ventilate, to air.

desavecindado, da, *adj.* deserted, unpeopled.

desavecindarse, *vr.* to change one's domicile.

desavenencia, *f.* discord, disagreement.

desavenido, da, *adj.* discordant, disagreeing.

desavenir, *va.* (DESAVENGO, DESAVINE) to discompose, to disconcert; —, *vn.* to quarrel; to disagree.

desaventajado, da, *adj.* disadvantageous, unprofitable.

desaviar, *va.* to deviate from the right road; to strip of necessaries.

desavío, *m.* going astray; lack of the necessary means.

desavisado, da, *adj.* ill-advised.

desavisar, *va.* to countermand.

desayunarse, *vr.* to breakfast; to learn about unexpected news for the first time, to be aware of something for the first time.

desayuno, *m.* breakfast.

desazogar, *va.* to take off the quicksilver (from a looking glass, etc.).

desazón, *f.* insipidity; disgust; uneasiness; unfitness of a soil for agricultural purposes.

desazonado, da, *adj.* ill-adapted; ill-humored; not in shape for cultivation.

desazonar, *va.* to render tasteless; to disgust; —se, to become indisposed.

desbancar, *va.* to clear a room of the benches; to break the bank (in gambling); (fig.) to supplant.

desbandarse, *vr.* to disband.

desbaratado, da, *adj.* wasted; broken up; (coll.) debauched, lewd.

desbaratar, *va.* to destroy; to defeat an army; to dissipate; — **la paz,** to break the peace; —, *vn.* to talk nonsense; —se, to be confounded; to break to pieces.

desbarato, *m.* destruction; defeat; dissipation.

desbarbado, da, *adj.* beardless.

desbarbillar, *va.* to prune the roots of young vines.

desbardar, *va.* to uncover a wall or fence.

desbarrar, *vn.* to slip, to steal away; to act or talk foolishly.

desbarretar, *va.* to unbar, to unbolt, to take off the bars and bolts.

desbarrigado, da, *adj.* little-bellied.

desbarrigar, *va.* to rip up, to open the belly.

desbarro, *m.* slipping; (fig.) nonsense, extravagance; frenzy.

desbastar, *va.* to smooth; to polish; to waste; to purify one's morals and manners.

desbaste, *m.* hewing, smoothing.

desbastecido, da, *adj.* without sufficient provisions.

desbecerrar, *va.* to wean (animals).

desblanquecido, da, *adj.* blanched.

desbocado, da, *adj.* open-mouthed (applied to a cannon); wild (applied to a horse); foul-mouthed, indecent.

desbocar, *va.* to break the brim of a jar or other vessel; —se, to be insensible of the bridle (as a runaway horse); to use abusive language.

desbordar, *vn.* and *vr.* to overflow; to give vent to one's temper or feelings.

desbordamiento, *m.* overflowing.

desborrar, *va.* to cut off the loose threads of cloth when it comes out of the loom; to lop off.

desboscar, *va.* to deforest.

desbragado, da, *adj.* without breeches; (coll.) shabby.

desbraguetado, da, *adj.* having the front of the breeches unbuttoned.

desbrevarse, *vr.* to evaporate, to lose body (in reference to wines).

desbrozar, *va.* to clear of rubbish.

desbrozo, *m.* clearing away rubbish.

desbuchar, *va.* to disclose one's secrets; to ease the stomach (applied to birds of prey).

descabalgar, *vn.* to alight from a horse; —, *va.* to dismount (a gun).

descabellado, da, *adj.* dishevelled; disorderly; wild, unrestrained; disproportional; violent.

descabellar, *va.* to disorder the hair.

descabezado, da, *adj.* beheaded; light-headed, giddy.

descabezar, *va.* to behead; to lop off; —se, to puzzle one's brains.

descabullirse, *vr.* (UYO) to steal away, to scamper; to elude difficulties cleverly.

descaderar, *va.* to sprain the hip.

descaecer, *vn.* (EZCO) to decline, to decay.

descaecimiento, *m.* weakness; languor.

descalabazarse, *vr.* to puzzle one's brains.

descalabrado, da, *adj.* wounded on the head.

descalabradura, *f.* contusion or wound in the head.

descalabrar, *va.* to break or wound the head; to attack one's character.

descalabro, *m.* calamity, considerable loss.

descalcez, *f.* nudity of the feet; barefootedness of monks.

descalificar, *va.* to disqualify.

descalzar, *va.* to pull off shoes and stockings.

descalzo, za, *adj.* barefooted.

descaminar, *va.* to misguide, to lead astray.

descamisado, da, *adj.* shirtless; very poor; shabby.

descampado, da, *adj.* disengaged, free, open.

descampar, *vn.* to leave off working; to cease raining; —, *va.* to clear off (a place).

descansado, da, *adj.* reposing; rested, refreshed; quiet.

descansar, *vn.* to rest; to pause in the execution of a thing; to repose, to sleep.

descanso, *m.* rest, repose.

descanterar, *va.* to take off corners or ends of (particularly crust of bread).

descantillar, *va.* to pare off; to lessen.

descañonar, *va.* to pluck out the feathers; (fig.) to cheat one out of his money.

descarado, da, *adj.* impudent, barefaced.

descararse, *vr.* to behave insolently.

descarbonizar, *va.* to decarbonize.

descarga, *f.* disburdening, unloading; volley, discharge; **hacer una —,** to open fire.

descargadero, *m.* wharf.

descargador, *m.* unloader.

descargar, *va.* to unload, to discharge, —**se,** to give a plea to an accusation.

descargo, *m.* discharge, acquittal; justification; unloading.

descargue, *m.* alleviation from any burden; license to unload a vessel.

descariño, *m.* coolness, loss of affection.

descarnar, *va.* to strip off the flesh; to clean away the flesh from; —**se,** to lose flesh; to dissipate, to squander one's wealth.

descaro, *m.* impudence.

descarriar, *va.* to lead astray; to separate cattle from one another; —**se,** to deviate from justice or reason.

descarrilamiento, *m.* (rail.) running off the rails.

descarrilar, *vn.* (rail.) to jump the track, to run off the rails; —, *va.* to derail.

descarrillar, *va.* to tear the jaws asunder.

descarrío, *m.* losing of one's way.

descartar, *va.* to discard; to dismiss; —**se,** to excuse oneself.

descarte, *m.* cards discarded; discarding; evasion, subterfuge.

descasar, *va.* to separate a husband and wife.

descascar, *va.* to shuck.

descascarador, ra, *n.* sheller, huller, husker.

descascarar, *va.* to peel, to husk; —**se,** to fall off.

descaspar, *va.* to remove dandruff from the head.

descasque, *m.* decortication.

descastado, da, *adj.* lacking in affection for one's relatives; ungrateful.

descastar, *va.* to exterminate (a breed of animals).

descendencia, *f.* descent, offspring.

descendente, *adj.* descending.

descender, *vn.* (IE) to descend, to walk downward; to flow; to be derived from.

descendiente, *adj.* and *m.* descending; descendant.

descendimiento, *m.* descent, lowering.

descensión, *f.* descent, descension.

descenso, *m.* descent; degradation.

descentralización, *f.* decentralization.

descentralizar, *va.* to decentralize.

desceñir, *va.* (I) to ungird.

descepar, *va.* to uproot, to root up; to clear a wood.

descerar, *va.* to take the empty combs (from a beehive).

descercado, da, *adj.* open, unfortified.

descercar, *va.* to destroy or pull down a wall.

descerrajar, *va.* to take off the lock of a door, etc.; to discharge firearms.

descifrable, *adj.* decipherable.

descifrar, *va.* to decipher; to decode; to make out.

descinchar, *va.* to ungirth a horse.

desclavador, *m.* nailclaw, clawhammer.

desclavar, *va.* to draw out nails.

descoagular, *va.* to liquefy, to dissolve a clot.

descobijar, *va.* to uncover, to take off blankets.

descocado, da, *adj.* bold, impudent.

descocar, *va.* to free trees from insects; —**se,** to be impudent.

descoco, *m.* impudence, sauciness.

descodar, *va.* to rip, to unstitch.

descogollar, *vn.* to prune plants.

descogotado, da, *adj.* barenecked.

descogotar, *va.* to knock off the horns of a stag at one blow.

descolchar, *va.* to untwist a cable.

descolgar, *va.* (UE) to unhang, to take down; —**se,** to come down gently; to glide.

descolmillar, *va.* to draw out the eyeteeth.

descolorar, *va.* to discolor.

descolorido, da, *adj.* pale, colorless, faded; off-color.

descolorimiento, *m.* discoloration.

descollar, *vn.* (UE) to overtop, to excel, to surpass.

descombrar, *va.* to disencumber.

descomedido, da, *adj.* impudent, insolent; huge.

descomedirse, *vr.* (I) to be rude or disrespectful.

descomodidad, *f.* inconvenience, discomfort.

descompasado, da, *adj.* excessive; disproportionate.

descompasarse, *vr.* to exceed all rule and measure.

descomponer, *va.* (DESCOMPONGO, DESCOMPUSE) to discompose, to spoil; to set at odds, to disconcert; (chem.) to decompose; —, *vn.* to be out of temper; to be indisposed; to change for the worse (of the weather); —se, to get out of order, to become spoiled.

descomposición, *f.* disagreement, discomposure; decomposition.

descompostura, *f.* disagreement; disorder, confusion; lack of modesty.

descompuesto, ta, *adj.* deranged; slovenly, disordered, out of order; distorted; spoiled (applied to food).

descomulgar, *va.* to excommunicate.

descomunal, *adj.* uncommon; beyond all measure.

desconceptuar, *va.* to discredit.

desconcertado, da, *adj.* disorderly, slovenly; baffled.

desconcertar, *va.* (IE) to disturb; to confound; to embarrass, to disconcert; —se, to disagree; to exceed the limits of prudence and judgment; to be out of joint.

desconcierto, *m.* discomposure; disorder, confusion; indolence, negligence.

desconchamiento, *m.* peeling; scaling (of a painted surface).

desconchar, *va.* to unscale; to strip off a surface (as varnish, plaster), etc.

desconectador, *m.* (elec.) switch; cutout.

desconectar, *va.* to disconnect; —se, to become disconnected.

desconfiado, da, *adj.* suspicious, mistrustful.

desconfianza, *f.* distrust, lack of confidence.

desconfiar, *vn.* to mistrust, to suspect.

desconformar, *vn.* to dissent, to differ.

desconforme, *adj.* discordant, contrary; unequal, unlike; unsatisfied.

desconformidad, *f.* disagreement, opposition; inequality, unlikeness, dissimilitude.

descongelar, *va.* to defrost.

desconocer, *va.* (OZCO) to disown, to disavow; to be totally ignorant of a thing; not to know a person; not to acknowledge (a favor received).

desconocido, da, *adj.* ungrateful; disguised; unknown, unrecognizable; —, *m.* stranger.

desconsiderado, da, *adj.* inconsiderate, imprudent.

desconsolado, da, *adj.* comfortless, dejected, downhearted, disconsolate.

desconsolador, ra, *adj.* lamentable; disconsolate; disconcerting.

desconsolar, *va.* (UE) to afflict; —se, to become afflicted; to lose one's spirit.

desconsuelo, *m.* affliction; dejection, grief.

descontable, *adj.* discountable.

descontagiar, *va.* to disinfect, to purify.

descontar, *va.* (UE) to discount; to abate, to diminish, to subtract.

descontentadizo, za, *adj.* squeamish, easily disgusted.

descontentar, *va.* to discontent, to displease.

descontento, *m.* discontent, dissatisfaction, disgust; —, **ta,** *adj.* unhappy, discontented.

descontinuar, *va.* to discontinue.

descopar, *va.* to lop off the branches of a tree.

descorazonado, da, *adj.* depressed (in spirit).

descorazonar, *va.* to pull out the heart; to dishearten, to discourage.

descorchar, *va.* to strip off the bark; to break a beehive to steal the honey; to break open (a chest or trunk).

descordar, *va.* (UE) to unstring an instrument.

descornar, *va.* (UE) to knock off the horns of an animal.

descorrear, *vn.* to loosen the skin that covers the tenderlings of a deer.

descorrer, *vn.* to run, to flow; —, *va.* to retrograde; — la cortina, to draw the curtain.

descortés, *adj.* impolite, uncivil.

descortesía, *f.* incivility, lack of politeness.

descortezar, *va.* to take off the crust of; (coll.) to polish or civilize.

descosedura, *f.* unseaming, ripping.

descoser, *va.* to unseam, to unstitch, to separate, —se, to give rein to one's tongue.

descosido, *m.* idle talker; ripped seam.

descostillar, *va.* to break the ribs; —se, to fall with great violence on one's back.

descostrar, *va.* to take off crust.

descotar, *va.* to remove the restrictions against the use of a path or road; —se, to expose the neck and shoulders.

descote, *m.* exposure of neck and shoulders.

descoyuntamiento, *m.* dislocation; pain from overexertion.

descoyuntar, *va.* and *vr.* to disjoint bones; to vex, to molest.

descrecer, *va.* and *vn.* (EZCO) to decrease, to diminish.

descrédito, *m.* discredit.

descreer, *va.* to disbelieve.

descreído, da, *n.* and *adj.* infidel, unbeliever.

descreimiento, *m.* lack of faith.

descriarse, *vr.* to decline, to deteriorate.

describir, *va.* to describe, to delineate.

descripción, *f.* delineation; description; inventory.

descriptible, *adj.* describable.

descriptivo, va, *adj.* descriptive.

descriptor, *m.* delineator.

descrito, ta, *adj.* described.

descruzar, *va.* to uncross.

descto., desct.º or **d.º descuento,** (com.) disc. discount.

descuadernar, *va.* and *vr.* to unbind (books); to disorder.

descuajar, *va.* to dissolve, to liquefy; to pluck up weeds; to dishearten.

descuajo, *m.* clearing ground of underbrush; eradication.

descuartizar, *va.* to quarter (to divide the body into four parts); to carve.

descubierta, *f.* (mil.) recognition; **a la —,** openly, clearly.

descubierto, ta, *adj.* uncovered, unveiled, bareheaded; **—,** *m.* deficit; solemn exposition of the sacrament; **al —,** sincere, aboveboard; **girar en —,** to overdraw.

descubridor, ra, *n.* discoverer, descrier; investigator; (mil.) scout; vessel on a voyage of discovery.

descubrimiento, *m.* discovery, disclosure.

descubrir, *va.* to discover, to disclose; to uncover; to reveal; (mil.) to overlook any place in a fortification; **—se,** to take off one's hat.

descuello, *m.* excessive stature; preeminence; haughtiness.

descuento, *m.* discount; diminution, decrease, rebate (on a debt, etc.).

descuerno, *m.* contempt; affront.

descuidado, da, *adj.* careless, negligent.

descuidar, *va.* and *vn.* to neglect, to relieve from care; to render careless; **—se,** to become negligent.

descuido, *m.* indolence, carelessness, negligence, forgetfulness; lack of attention, incivility; improper action; **al —,** affectedly careless.

descular, *va.* to break the bottom or end of a thing.

desde, *prep.* since, after, from; **— luego,** of course; **— entonces,** since then; **— que,** since.

desdecir, *va.* (DESDIGO, DESDIJE) to disavow; **—,** *vn.* to degenerate; to differ, to disagree; **—se,** to gainsay; to retract.

desdén, *m.* disdain, scorn, contempt; **al —,** affectedly careless.

desdentado, da, *adj.* toothless.

desdentar, *va.* (IE) to pull out teeth.

desdeñar, *va.* to disdain, to scorn; **—se,** to be disdainful.

desdeñoso, sa, *adj.* disdainful, contemptuous.

desdevanar, *va.* to unravel a clew or a ball (of yarn, etc.).

desdicha, *f.* misfortune, calamity; great poverty.

desdichado, da, *adj.* unfortunate, wretched, miserable.

desdoblar, *va.* to unfold, to spread open.

desdorar, *va.* to take off the gilding; to tarnish one's reputation.

desdoro, *m.* dishonor, blot on one's reputation.

deseable, *adj.* desirable.

desear, *va.* to desire, to wish; to require, to demand; **— saber,** to wonder.

desecación, *f.* desiccation.

desecar, *va.* to dry; to desiccate.

desecativo, *m.* healing plaster.

desechar, *va.* to depreciate; to reject, to refuse; to exclude; to reprove, to reprobate; to lay aside.

desecho, *m.* residue, remainder; refuse, offal; contempt.

desedificar, *va.* to set a bad example.

desellar, *va.* to unseal.

desembalar, *va.* to unpack, to open (merchandise).

desembarazar, *va.* to disembarrass; to clear; to disencumber; **—se,** to be extricated from difficulties.

desembarazo, *m.* disembarrassment; liberty to do a thing; ease; forwardness.

desembarcadero, *m.* landing place.

desembarcar, *va.* to disembark; **—,** *vn.* to disembark, to land.

desembarco, *m.* landing; disembarkment; landing of stairs.

desembargar, *va.* to raise an embargo.

desembargo, *m.* raising an embargo.

desembarque, *m.* landing.

desembaular, *va.* to empty a trunk; to disclose one's secret thoughts.

desembelesarse, *vr.* to recover from amazement.

desembocadero, *m.* mouth of a river or canal.

desembocar, *vn.* to put out of the mouth; to flow into; **— la calle,** to go from one street into another.

desembojar, *va.* to remove the silk pods from the southernwood.

desembolsar, *va.* to empty a purse; to disburse.

desembolso, *m.* disbursement, expenditure.

desemborrachar, *va.* to sober; **—,** *vn.* to become sober.

desemboscarse, *vr.* to get out of the woods; to get clear of an ambuscade.

desembozar, *va.* to unmuffle, to uncover.

desembozo, *m.* uncovering of the face.

desembragar, *va.* to disconnect; to disconnect the gears, to throw out of gear.

desembravecer, *va.* (EZCO) to tame, to domesticate.

desembriagar, *va.* and *vr.* to sober; to recover from drunkenness.

desembrollar, *va.* to disentangle, to disembroil.

desembuchar, *va.* to disgorge; (coll.) to unbosom.

desemejante, *adj.* dissimilar, different.

desemejanza, *f.* dissimilitude, unlikeness.

desemejar, *vn.* to be dissimilar.

desempacar, *va.* to unpack; **—se,** to cool off.

desempalagar, *va.* and *vr.* to remove nausea from; to restore the appetite; to clear a mill of stagnant water.

desempañar, *va.* to unswathe; to clean a tarnished glass.

desempapelar, va. to take paper off a wall.

desempaquetar, va. to unpack.

desemparejar, va. to unmatch, to make uneven.

desemparvar, va. to pile the threshed grain in heaps.

desempatar, va. to make unequal or uneven.

desempedrar, va. (IE) to unpave.

desempeñar, va. to redeem; to extricate from debt; to acquit; to perform (any duty); to discharge (any office).

desempeño, m. redeeming a pledge; performance or fulfillment of an obligation.

desemperezar, vn. to relinquish habits of laziness and indolence.

desempleado, da, adj. unemployed.

desempleo, m. unemployment.

desempolvar, va. to free from dust.

desemponzoñar, va. to expel poison; to cure a poisonous condition.

desempulgar, va. to unbend a bow.

desenalbardar, va. to take off a packsaddle.

desenamorar, va. and vr. to destroy love.

desencabalgar, va. (mil.) to dismount cannon.

desencabestrar, va. to disentangle a beast from the halter.

desencadenar, va. to unchain; to dissolve all connection or obligation.

desencajar, va. to take a thing out of its place.

desencajonar, va. to take out of a box.

desencalabrinar, va. to remove dizziness.

desencallar, va. and vn. to float a stranded vessel.

desencaminar, va. to lose one's way, to go astray.

desencantar, va. to disenchant, to disillusion.

desencanto, m. disenchantment, disillusion.

desencapotar, va. to strip of one's cloak; to uncover; to make manifest; to raise and keep up the head of a horse; —se, to put on a pleasing expression; to clear up (applied to cloudy skies).

desencaprichar, va. to dissuade from prejudice; —se, to get over a whim.

desencerrar, va. (IE) to free from confinement; to open, to unclose.

desenclavar, va. to draw out nails; to tear from its place.

desenclavijar, va. to take out the pegs of a musical instrument.

desencoger, va. to unfold, to spread out; —se, to grow bold.

desencolar, va. to unglue.

desencolerizarse, vr. to grow calm or appeased.

desenconar, va. to cure an inflammation; to appease one's anger; —se, to become milder; to be appeased.

desencono, m. cooling of anger.

desencordar, va. (UE) to unstring.

desencordelar, va. to untie, to take away ropes.

desencorvar, va. to straighten.

desencuadernar, va. to take off the binding of (a book).

desendemoniar or **desendiablar,** va. to exorcise.

desenfadado, da, adj. appeased in anger; free, unembarrassed; gay; wide, spacious.

desenfadar, va. to assuage or appease anger.

desenfado, m. ease; facility; calmness, relaxation.

desenfangar, va. to clear mud or filth from.

desenfardar or **desenfardelar,** va. to open bales of goods.

desenfrailar, vn. to leave the monastic life.

desenfrenado, da, adj. outrageous; ungovernable; licentious, wanton.

desenfrenar, va. to unbridle; —se, to give full play to one's desires; to fly into a rage.

desenfreno, m. licentiousness; unruliness; — de vientre, diarrhea.

desenfundar, va. to take out of a bag or pillowcase.

desenfurecerse, vr. (EZCO) to grow calm; to lay aside anger.

desenganchar, va. to unhook; to uncouple; to unhitch.

desengañado, da, adj. undeceived; disillusioned.

desengañar, va. and vr. to undeceive; to disillusion, to disappoint; to free from a mistake, to set right.

desengaño, m. undeception; disillusion, disappointment; naked truth; reproach, upbraiding.

desengarzar, va. to unravel; to take out of a setting.

desengastar, va. to take out of its setting (as a ring).

desengranar, va. to throw out of gear.

desengrasar, va. to take out the grease.

desengrosar, va. (UE) to extenuate, to make lean, to make thinner.

desengrudar, va. to scrape off the paste.

desenhebrar, va. to unthread; to unravel.

desenjaezar, va. to unharness horses.

desenjalmar, va. to take off a packsaddle from a beast of burden.

desenjaular, va. to let loose out of a cage.

desenlabonar, va. to unchain, to unlink.

desenlace, m. end of an affair; denouement, outcome, conclusion.

desenladrillar, va. to take up floor tiles or bricks.

desenlazar, va. to unlace, to untie; to unravel (a plot); —se, to come to a conclusion; to untangle oneself.

desenlosar, va. to unpave.

desenlutar, va. and vr. to cease mourning; to banish sorrow.

desenmarañar, va. to disentangle.

desenmudecer, va. (EZCO) to remove an impediment of speech; —, vn. to break a long silence.

desenojar, va. to appease; —se, to amuse oneself; to lose anger.

desenojo, m. abatement of anger.

desenredar, va. to disentangle; —se, to extricate oneself.

desenrizar, va. to uncurl.

desenrollar, va. to unroll.

desenroscar, va. to untwist, to unroll.

desensartar, va. to unthread; to unravel.

desensillar, va. to unsaddle.

desentablar, va. to rip off planks; to disturb; to embroil; to interrupt a friendly intercourse.

desentender, vn. and vr. (IE) to pretend not to understand; to pass by without noticing.

desenterramiento, m. disinterment.

desenterrar, va. (IE) to disinter, to unbury, to dig up; to recall to memory things forgotten.

desentoldar, va. to take away an awning; to strip a thing of its ornaments.

desentonación, f. dissonance.

desentonar, va. and vn. to humble; to be out of tune; —se, to raise the voice disrespectfully.

desentono, m. disharmony; rude tone of voice.

desentornillar, va. to unscrew.

desentorpecer, va. (EZCO) to free from torpor; —se, to lose numbness; to become lively, smart or pert.

desentramparse, vr. to free oneself from debts.

desentrañamiento, m. evisceration, disembowelment.

desentrañar, va. to gut, to eviscerate; to go into a matter very deeply; —se, to give away all one's fortune for love.

desentristecer, va. (EZCO) to banish sadness and grief.

desentronizar, va. to dethrone; to deprive of authority.

desentumecer, va. (EZCO) to restore motion to torpid limbs.

desenvainar, va. to unsheathe, to draw a sword; to bring to light; to stretch out the claws.

desenvenenar, va. to cure from poison.

desenvergar, va. to unbend a sail.

desenvoltura, f. sprightliness; cheerfulness; impudence, boldness; lewd posture or gesture; graceful, easy delivery of one's sentiments and thoughts.

desenvolver, va. (UE) to unfold; to unroll; to decipher, to unravel; to develop; —se, to be forward.

desenvuelto, ta, adj. forward; behaving with much assurance.

deseo, m. desire, wish.

deseoso, sa, adj. desirous.

desequilibrio, m. unsteadiness, lack of balance; disorder.

deserción, f. desertion.

desertar, va. (IE) to desert; to forsake one's colors or post; (law) to abandon a cause.

desertor, m. deserter, fugitive.

deservicio, m. disservice.

deservir, va. (I) to disserve; not to perform one's duty.

deseslabonar, va. to cut the links of a chain.

desesperación, f. despair, desperation; anger, fury.

desesperado, da, adj. desperate, hopeless.

desesperanzar, va. to deprive of hope; to make desperate.

desesperar, vn. to despair, to vex; —, va. to make desperate.

desesterar, va. to take away the mats from a room.

desestimación, f. disesteem, disregard.

desestimar, va. to disregard, to undervalue.

desfajar, va. to ungird.

desfalcar, va. to cut off, to lop off; to embezzle.

desfalco, m. diminution, deduction; embezzlement.

desfallecer, vn. (EZCO) to pine, to fall away; —, va. to cause to weaken.

desfallecido, da, adj. faint, languid.

desfallecimiento, m. languor, fainting, swoon; dejection.

desfavorable, adj. unfavorable.

desfavorecer, va. (EZCO) to disfavor; to contemn; to injure, to hurt; to contradict.

desfibradora, f. linter.

desfiguración, f. disfiguration; deformation.

desfigurar, va. to disfigure, to deform; to disguise; —se, to become disfigured or distorted.

desfigurado, da, adj. deformed.

desfijar, va. to take off, to remove.

desfiladero, m. defile, canyon; road at side of a precipice.

desfilar, vn. (mil.) to defile; to march in review.

desfile, m. parade.

desflemar, va. to clear of phlegm.

desfloración, f. defloration.

desflorar, va. to pull or pluck the flowers in a garden; to deflower; to tarnish.

desflorecer, vn. (EZCO) to wither.

desfogar, va. to make an opening for the fire; to express anger vehemently; —se, to give vent to one's anger.

desfogue, m. venting of one's anger.

desfondar, va. to break the bottom of any vessel; to penetrate the bottom of a ship.

desformar, va. to deform, to disfigure.

desfortalecer, va. (EZCO) to demolish the works of a fortress.

desgajar, va. to lop off the branches of trees; to break in pieces; —se, to be separated; to be torn in pieces.

desgalgadero, m. rugged or steep place.

desgalgar, va. and vr. to precipitate; to be thrown headlong.

desgana, f. lack of appetite; reluctance.

desganado, da, adj. having no appetite.

desganar, va. to deprive of the pleasure of doing something; —se, to lose all pleasure in doing a thing; to lose one's appetite.

desganchar, *va.* to lop off branches of trees.

desgano, *m.* lack of appetite; reluctance.

desgañifarse or **desgañitarse,** *vr.* to scream, to bawl.

desgarbado, da, *adj.* ungraceful, uncouth, gawky.

desgargantarse, *vr.* to become hoarse by bawling.

desgargolar, *va.* to ripple (flax or hemp); to take (a board) out of a groove.

desgaritar, *vn.* (naut.) to lose the course.

desgarrado, da, *adj.* licentious, dissolute; ripped, torn.

desgarrador, ra, *adj.* piercing; heart-rending.

desgarrar, *va.* to rend, to tear; —**se,** to get away from someone's company.

desgarro, *m.* rent, breach; impudence; idle boast; ogling.

desgarrón, *m.* large rent or hole; piece of cloth torn off.

desgastar, *va.* to consume, to wear out; to corrode; —**se,** to weaken, to lose strength.

desgaste, *m.* wastage.

desglosar, *va.* to scratch out marginal notes or remarks, to take out leaflets (from a book, etc.).

desglose, *m.* erasure of a note or comment.

desgobernar, *va.* (IE) to disturb the order of government; to misgovern; to dislocate; (naut.) to steer an unsteady course; to bar a vein on a horse's leg; —**se,** to affect ridiculous motions in dancing.

desgobierno, *m.* misgovernment, mismanagement.

desgonzar, *va.* to separate; to unhinge; to disjoint.

desgoznar, *va.* to unhinge; —**se,** to distort the body with violent motions.

desgracia, *f.* misfortune, mishap, grief; disgrace; unpleasantness; **por —,** unfortunately.

desgraciadamente, *adv.* unfortunately.

desgraciado, da, *adj.* unfortunate, unhappy, miserable; out of favor; disagreeable; ungrateful.

desgraciarse, *vr.* to fall out with; to be out of order; to degenerate.

desgramar, *va.* to pluck up grasses; to husk.

desgranar, *va.* to remove the kernels from the ears of corn; to scatter about; —**se,** to wear away (said of the touchhole of a firearm).

desgrasar, *va.* to remove the grease from.

desgregación, *f.* disintegration.

desgreñar, *va.* to dishevel the hair; to disorder.

desguarnecer, *va.* (EZCO) to strip clothes of trimmings and other ornaments; to deprive a thing of its strength; to disgarnish.

desguazar, *va.* to cut asunder timber.

desguindar, *va.* (naut.) to take and bring down; —**se,** to slide down by a rope.

desguinzar, *va.* to cut rags in paper mills.

deshabitado, da, *adj.* deserted, uninhabited, desolate.

deshabitar, *va.* to quit one's habitation; to unpeople.

deshabituar, *va.* to disaccustom.

deshacedor, *m.* undoer; — **de agravios,** avenger of injuries.

deshacer, *va.* (DESHAGO, DESHICE) to undo, to take apart, to destroy; to cancel, to efface; to rout an army; to melt; to cut up, to divide; to dissolve in a liquid; to violate (a treaty); to diminish; to disband troops; —**se,** to grieve, to mourn; to disappear; to do a thing with vehemence; to mollify; to grow feeble or meager; —**se de,** to get rid of.

desharrapado, da, *adj.* shabby, ragged, in tatters.

deshebillar, *va.* to unbuckle.

deshebrar, *va.* to unthread; to divide into filaments.

deshecha, *f.* simulation, fiction; polite farewell; a step in a Spanish dance; **hacer la —,** to feign, to pretend.

deshechizar, *va.* to disenchant.

deshechizo, *m.* disenchantment.

deshecho, cha, *adj.* undone, destroyed, wasted; melted; in pieces; **borrasca —cha,** violent tempest.

deshelar, *va.* (IE) to thaw; —**se,** to thaw, to melt.

desherbar, *va.* (IE) to weed.

desheredamiento, *m.* disinheriting.

desheredar, *va.* to disinherit; —**se,** to degenerate.

deshermanar, *va.* to remove the likeness or similarity of things; —**se,** to fall out or quarrel with one's brother.

desherrar, *va.* (IE) to unchain; to rip off the shoes of horses.

deshidratrar, *va.* (chem.) to dehydrate.

deshielo, *m.* thaw.

deshilachar, *va.* to ravel, to unweave.

deshilado, *m.* openwork; —, **da,** *adj.* marching in single file.

deshilar, *va.* to ravel; to convert into lint; to distract bees in order to get them into a new hive.

deshilo, *m.* obstructing the movement of bees to get them into a new hive.

deshincar, *va.* to draw out a nail; to tear up what is nailed fast.

deshinchar, *va.* to reduce a swelling; to appease one's anger; —**se,** to be removed (applied to a swelling); to abate presumption.

deshojar, *va.* to strip off the leaves.

deshollejar, *va.* to peel, to pare.

deshollinador, *m.* chimney sweeper, sweep; scraper for sweeping chimneys; (fig.) a careful examiner.

deshollinar, *va.* to sweep chimneys; to clean what is dirty; to view and examine with careful attention.

deshonestamente, *adv.* immodestly.

deshonestidad, *f.* immodesty, indecency; lewdness.

deshonesto, ta, *adj.* immodest; lewd; dishonest.

deshonor, *m.* dishonor; insult.

deshonorar, *va.* to deprive of an honor; to deprive of an office or employ.

deshonra, *f.* dishonor; seduction of a woman.

deshonrabuenos, *m.* calumniator, libeler; person who degenerates from his ancestors.

deshonrar, *va.* to affront, to insult, to defame; to dishonor; to seduce a woman.

deshonroso, sa, *adj.* dishonorable, indecent.

deshora, *f.* unseasonable time.

deshuesar, *va* to rid of bones.

deshumano, na, *adj.* inhuman.

deshumedecer, *va.* (EZCO) to deprive of humidity; —se, to grow dry.

desiderable, *adj.* desirable.

desidia, *f.* idleness, indolence.

desidioso, sa, *adj.* lazy, idle.

desierto, ta, *adj.* deserted, solitary; —, *m.* desert, wilderness.

designación, *f.* designation.

designar, *va.* to appoint; to express, to name; to designate.

designio, *m.* design purpose road, course.

desigual, *adj.* unequal, unlike; uneven, craggy, cliffy.

desigualar, *va.* to make unequal or dissimilar; —se, to excel, to surpass.

desigualdad, *f.* inequality, dissimilitude; inconstancy, knottiness, unevenness.

desilusión, *f.* disillusion.

desilusionar, *va.* to disillusion; —se, to become disillusioned.

desimpresionar, *va.* to undeceive.

desinclinar, *va.* to disincline.

desinfección, *f.* disinfection; deodorization.

desinfectante, *m.* disinfectant; deodorizer.

desinfectar, *va.* to disinfect, to sterilize.

desinficionar, *va.* to disinfect.

desinflación, *f.* deflation.

desinflamar, *va.* to cure an inflammation.

desinflar, *va.* to deflate.

desinterés, *m.* disinterestedness.

desinteresado, da, *adj.* disinterested, unselfish.

desintoxicar, *va.* to decontaminate.

desistir, *vn.* to desist, to cease, to stop.

desjarretadera, *f.* hooked knife for hocking or hamstringing cattle.

desjarretar, *va.* to hock, to hamstring; to deprive one of the means of making a fortune; to make one bleed to excess.

desjuntar, *va.* to disjoint; to divide, to separate.

deslamar, *va.* to clear of mud.

deslastrar, *va.* to unballast a ship.

deslavar, *va.* to wash superficially.

deslave, *m.* washout.

deslazar, *va.* to unlace.

desleal, *adj.* disloyal; perfidious.

deslealtad, *f.* disloyalty, breach of faith.

deslechugar, *va.* to prune the branches of vines.

desleír, *va.* (I) to dilute, to dissolve.

deslenguado, da, *adj.* foul-mouthed, loose-tongued.

deslenguar, *va.* to cut out the tongue; —se, to slander.

desliar, *va.* to untie.

desligar, *va.* to loosen, to unbind; to extricate.

deslindar, *va.* to mark the limits.

deslinde, *m.* demarcation.

desliz, *m.* slip, sliding; (fig.) slip, weakness; false step.

deslizadero, *m.* slippery place.

deslizadizo, za, *adj.* slippery, slippy, glib; lubricous.

deslizador, *m.* (aer.) glider.

deslizamiento, *m.* gliding.

deslizar, *vn.* and *vr.* to slip, to slide; to speak carelessly, to go too far in conversation.

deslomar, *va.* to break the back, to distort the loins, to chine.

deslucido, da, *adj.* unadorned; gawky; useless; **quedar** or **salir** —, to be a failure.

deslucimiento, *m.* disgrace, lack of success.

deslucir, *va.* and *vr.* (UZCO) to tarnish the luster; to obscure one's merit; to do poorly.

deslumbrador, ra, *adj.* dazzling.

deslumbramiento or **deslumbre**, *m.* overpowering luster; dazzle.

deslumbrar, *va.* to dazzle; to puzzle.

deslustrar, *va.* to tarnish; to obscure; to blast one's reputation.

deslustre, *m.* spot which obscures the luster; disgrace, ignominy.

deslustroso, sa, *adj.* unbecoming, ugly.

desmadejamiento, *m.* languishment.

desmadejar, *va.* to enervate, to produce languor.

desmagnetizar, *va.* to demagnetize.

desmalezar, *va.* to weed.

desmán, *m.* misbehavior; misfortune, disaster; misconduct.

desmandar, *va.* to countermand; to revoke a legacy; —se, to disband; to stray from the flock.

desmangar, *va.* to take off the handle of anything.

desmanotado, da, *adj.* unhandy, awkward.

desmantelado, da, *adj.* ruinous, dilapidated, dismantled, stripped.

desmantelamiento, *m.* dismantling.

desmantelar, *va* to dismantle; to abandon, to forsake; (naut.) to unmast.

desmañado, da, *adj.* clumsy, awkward, maladroit.

desmarañar, *va.* to disentangle.

desmarrido, da, *adj.* sad, dejected.

desmayado, da, *adj.* pale, wan; dismayed, appalled; fainted

desmayar, *vn.* to be dispirited or faint-hearted; —, *va.* to dismay, to dispirit; —se, to faint.

desmayo, *m.* swoon; dismay, discouragement.

desmazalado, da, *adj.* weak, dejected.

desmechado, da, *adj.* (Sp. Am.) with hair disheveled.

desmedido, da, *adj.* out of proportion; excessive.

desmedirse, *vr.* (I) to be beyond all measure.

desmedrado, da, *adj.* damaged, injured, thin.

desmedrar, *vn.* to decrease, to decay; —, *va.* to deteriorate.

desmejora, *f.* deterioration; loss.

desmejorar, *va.* to debase, to make worse.

desmelar, *va.* to take honey from a hive.

desmelenar, *va.* to dishevel.

desmembración, *f.* dismemberment.

desmembrar, *va.* (IE) to dismember; to curtail; to separate.

desmemoriado, da, *adj.* forgetful, devoid of memory.

desmenguar, *va.* to lessen, to decrease.

desmentida, *f.* act of contradicting.

desmentir, *va.* (IE) to contradict.

desmenuzable, *adj.* easily crumbled.

desmenuzar, *va.* to crumble, to chip, to fritter; to examine minutely.

desmerecer, *va.* and *vn.* (EZCO) to become undeserving of; to compare unfavorably.

desmerecimiento, *m.* demerit, unworthiness.

desmesura, *f.* excess, lack of measure.

desmesurado, da, *adj.* excessive; huge; immeasurable.

desmesurar, *va.* to perturb, to put out; to put out of order; —se, to talk impudently, to forget oneself.

desmigajar, *va.* to crumble, to break into bits.

desmigar, *va.* to crumble bread into small pieces.

desmilitarizar, *va.* to demilitarize.

desmochar, *va.* to lop; to mutilate.

desmoche, *m.* mutilation.

desmonetizar, *va.* to demonetize.

desmontable, *adj.* demountable.

desmontar, *va.* to cut down wood; to remove a heap of rubbish; to clear away (trees, dirt, rubbish, etc.); to uncock firearms; to take apart, to take to pieces; to dismount a troop of cavalry; to dismount cannon; —, *vn.* to dismount, to alight from a horse, etc.

desmonte, *m.* felling; clearing a wood.

desmoralización, *f.* demoralization.

desmoralizar, *va.* and *vr.* to demoralize.

desmoronadizo, za, *adj.* dilapidated, ruinous, rickety.

desmoronar, *va.* to destroy little by little; —se, to decay, to crumble.

desmotar, *va.* to burl; to gin.

desmovilizar, *va.* to demobilize.

desmullir, *va.* (UYO) to fluff what has been pressed and softened (as a pillow).

desnarigado, da, *adj.* noseless.

desnarigar, *va.* to cut off the nose.

desnatadora, *f.* cream separator.

desnatar, *va.* to skim milk; to take the choicest part.

desnaturalizado, da, *adj.* denatured; denaturalized.

desnaturalizar, *va.* to divest of naturalization rights; —se, to forsake one's country.

desnegar, *va.* (IE) to deny; —se, to retract.

desnervar, *va.* to enervate.

desnevar, *vn.* and *imp.* (IE) to thaw, to dissolve (as snow).

desnivel, *m.* unevenness of the ground.

desnucar, *va.* to break one's neck.

desnudar, *va.* to denude, to strip of clothes; to discover, to reveal; —se, to undress.

desnudez, *f.* nakedness.

desnudista, *m.* and *f.* nudist.

desnudo, da, *adj.* naked, bare, uncovered; ill-clothed; (fig.) plain, evident.

desnutrición, *f.* malnutrition, underfeeding.

desobedecer, *va.* (EZCO) to disobey.

desobediencia, *f.* disobedience; insubordination.

desobediente, *adj.* disobedient.

desobligar, *va.* to disoblige.

desobstruir, *va.* (UYO) to clear, to remove obstacles.

desocupación, *f.* leisure, lack of occupation.

desocupar, *va.* to quit, to empty; —se, to retire from a business; to disengage oneself from an occupation.

desodorante, *m.* deodorant.

desoír, *va.* (DESOIGO, DESOÍ) to pretend not to hear, to disregard.

desojar, *va.* and *vr.* to break the eye of a needle, etc.; to strain the sight by looking steadily at a thing.

desolación, *f.* destruction; affliction.

desolado, da, *adj.* desolate, disconsolate; lonely.

desolar, *va.* (UE) to lay waste; to harass.

desoldar, *va.* (UE) to unsolder.

desolladero, *m.* slaughterhouse.

desollado, da, *adj.* impudent, insolent, saucy.

desollar, *va.* (UE) to flay, to skin; (fig.) to extort an immoderate price.

desopinar, *va.* to defame.

desoprimir, *va.* to free from oppression.

desorden, *m.* disorder, confusion.

desordenado, da, *adj.* disorderly, unruly.

desordenar, *va.* to disorder, to disarrange; —se, to get out of order.

desorejar, *va.* to crop the ears.

desorganización, *f.* disorganization.

desorganizar, *va.* to disorganize.

desorientado, da, *adj.* confused, having lost one's bearings.

desorillar, *va.* to cut off the selvage of cloth.

desovar, *vn.* (UE) to spawn.

desove, *m.* spawning; spawn.

desovillar, *va.* to unwind; to unravel, to disentangle.

desoxidar, *va.* to deoxidize.

despabiladeras, *f. pl.* snuffers.

despabilado, da, *adj.* watchful, vigilant (at the time for sleeping).

despabilador, *m.* candle snuffer.

despabilar, *va.* to snuff a candle; (fig.) to dispatch briefly; —**se,** to rouse.

despacio, *adv.* slowly, leisurely; little by little; ¡—! *interj.* softly! gently!

despacito, *adv.* gently, leisurely; ¡—! *interj.* slowly!

despachar, *va.* to dispatch; to expedite; to dismiss; —**se,** to make haste.

despacho, *m.* dispatch, expedition; cabinet; office; countinghouse; commission; warrant, patent; shipment; official communication.

despachurrar, *va.* to squash, to crush; to mangle a speech.

despaldillar, *va.* to dislocate the shoulder of an animal.

despalmar, *va.* to clean and calk the bottoms of ships; to pare off a horse's hoof.

despampanar, *va.* to prune the shoots of vines; (fig.) to unbosom.

desparejar, *va.* to make unequal or uneven.

desparpajar, *va.* and *vr.* to undo in a disorderly manner; to prattle at random.

desparpajo, *m.* pertness of speech or action.

desparramar, *va.* to disseminate, to scatter, to overspread; to squander, to lavish; —**se,** to be dissipated.

desparvar, *va.* to take the sheaves of grain out of the stack to be threshed.

despatarrarse, *vr.* to fall on the ground with the legs widespread.

despavesar, *va.* to snuff (a candle).

despavorido, da, *adj.* frightened, terrified.

despavorir, *vn.* and *vr.* (*def.*) to be filled with terror.

despeado, da, *adj.* footsore (referring to animals).

despeadura, *f.* foundering.

despearse, *vr.* to bruise the feet or hoofs.

despechar, *va.* to enrage, to excite indignation; (coll.) to wean; —**se,** to despair.

despecho, *m.* indignation, displeasure; wrath; despite, spite; deceit; derision, scorn; **a — de,** in spite of.

despechugar, *va.* to cut off the breast of a fowl; —**se,** to uncover the breast; to walk with the breast open.

despedazar, *va.* to tear into pieces, to cut asunder; to mangle; —**se de risa,** to burst into fits of laughter.

despedida, *f.* farewell, dismissal, leave-taking; complimentary close (of letter).

despedir, *va.* (I) to discharge, to dart; to dismiss from office; —**se,** to take leave; to say good-by.

despegado, da, *adj.* unglued; separated; rough, sullen; indifferent, distant.

despegar, *va.* to unglue, to detach; (aer.) to take off; to get off the ground; —**se,** to withdraw one's affection.

despego, *m.* lack of love, coolness.

despegue, *m.* (aer.) take-off (of airplane).

despeinado, da, *adj.* uncombed, unkempt, tousled.

despeinar, *va.* to entangle the hair.

despejado, da, *adj.* sprightly, vivacious, quick, sagacious; clear, unobstructed; cloudless.

despejar, *va.* to clear away obstructions; —**se,** to cheer up; to amuse oneself; to become clear weather.

despejo, *m.* removal of obstacles; sprightliness; grace.

despeluzar, *va.* and *vr.* to make the hair stand on end.

despellejar, *va.* to skin.

despensa, *f.* pantry, larder; provisions.

despensero, ra, *n.* butler, caterer; steward on board ship; distributor.

despeñadero, *m.* precipice; (fig.) bold and dangerous undertaking.

despeñar, *va.* to precipitate, to fling down a precipice; —**se,** to throw oneself headlong.

despeño, *m.* precipitate fall; (med.) diarrhea.

despepitar, *va.* to remove the seeds from; —**se,** to give vent to one's tongue; to vociferate; to act imprudently.

desperdiciador, ra, *n.* spendthrift, squanderer.

desperdiciar, *va.* to squander; not to avail oneself of.

desperdicio, *m.* prodigality, profusion; residuum, remains; refuse.

desperdigar, *va.* to separate, to scatter.

desperezarse, *vr.* to stretch oneself on being roused from sleep.

despernado, da, *adj.* weary, tired of walking.

despernar, *va.* (IE) to break one's legs; to get one's legs tired.

despertador, *m.* alarm clock.

despertar, *va.* (IE) to awaken, to rouse from sleep; to excite; —**se,** to wake up; to grow lively or sprightly.

despiadado, da, *or* **desapiadado, da,** *adj.* pitiless, unmerciful, impious.

despido, *m.* discharge, dismissal.

despierto, ta, *adj.* awake; vigilant; brisk, sprightly.

despilfarrar, *va.* to waste through slovenliness, to squander.

despilfarro, *m.* slovenliness; waste; mismanagement.

despintar, *va.* to efface a painting; to obscure things; to mislead; —, *vn.* to degenerate; —**se,** to fade, to wash off.

despinte, *m.* (Chile) low-grade ore.

despinzar, *va.* to nap cloth.

despinzas, *f. pl.* tweezers, pincers.

despiojar, *va.* to delouse; (fig.) to relieve from misery.

despique, *m.* vengeance, revenge.

desplantar, *va.* to eradicate; to transplant;

—se, to lose one's erect posture (in fencing or dancing).

desplante, *m.* oblique posture in fencing; arrogant attitude.

desplazamiento, *m.* (naut.) displacement, shift.

desplegadura, *f.* explanation; unfolding, spreading out.

desplegar, *va.* (IE) to unfold, to display; to explain, to elucidate; (naut.) to unfurl; **—se,** to open, to unfold.

desplomar, *va.* to make a wall bulge out; **—se,** to bulge out; to fall flat to the ground.

desplome, *m.* downfall, collapse, tumbling down; (aer.) stall.

desplomo, *m.* jutting out of a wall.

desplumar, *va.* to deplume, to strip off feathers; (fig.) to despoil of one's property.

despoblación, *f.* depopulation.

despoblado, *m.* desert, uninhabited place; **—, da,** *adj.* depopulated.

despoblar, *va.* (UE) to depopulate; to desolate; **—se,** to become depopulated.

despojar, *va.* to despoil; to deprive of, to strip; **—se,** to undress.

despojo, *m.* spoliation; plunder; **—s,** *pl.* giblets (of fowls); remains; offal, debris, waste, junk.

desportillar, *va.* to break the neck of a bottle, pot, etc.

desposado, da, *adj.* newly married; handcuffed.

desposar, *va.* to marry, to betroth; **—se,** to be betrothed or married.

desposeer, *va.* to dispossess.

desposeimiento, *m.* dispossession.

desposorio, *m.* mutual promise to contract marriage, engagement.

déspota, *m.* despot, tyrant.

despótico, ca, *adj.* despotic.

despotismo, *m.* despotism.

despreciable, *adj.* contemptible, despicable, worthless.

despreciar, *va.* to scorn, to despise; to reject.

desprecio, *m.* scorn, contempt.

desprender, *va.* to unfasten, to loosen, to separate; **—se,** to give way, to fall down; to extricate oneself; to be inferred.

desprendimiento, *m.* alienation, disinterestedness.

despreocupado, *m.* nonconformist, freethinker; liberal; **—, da,** *adj.* unconcerned, unconventional.

despreocupar, *va.* and *vr.* to free from prejudice; to free from worry.

desprestigiar, *va.* to cause to lose one's reputation; to bring into disrepute.

deprestigio, *m.* loss of prestige.

desprevenido, da, *adj.* unprovided, unprepared.

desproporción, *f.* disproportion.

desproporcionar, *va.* to disproportion.

despropósito, *m.* absurdity, nonsense, irrelevant conversation.

desproveer, *va.* (DESPROVEÍDO, DESPROVISTO) to deprive of provisions; (mil.) to deprive of ammunition.

desprovisto, ta, *adj.* unprovided; devoid.

después, *adv.* after, afterward, later; then.

despumar, *va.* to skim, to remove foam (from).

despuntar, *va.* to blunt; (naut.) to double a cape; **—,** *vn.* to manifest wit and genius; **al — del día,** at break of day.

desquiciar, *va.* to unhinge; to discompose, to disorder.

desquijarar, *va.* to break the jaws.

desquitar, *va.* to retrieve a loss; **—se,** to recoup, to win one's money back again; to retaliate, to take revenge.

desquite, *m.* recovery of a loss; revenge, retaliation.

desreglado, da, *adj.* disorderly, irregular.

desreglarse, *vr.* to be irregular, to be ungovernable.

desrizar, *va.* to uncurl.

destacamento, *m.* (mil.) detachment.

destacar, *va.* (mil.) to detach (a body of troops); **—se,** to be ahead of, to stand out, to be conspicuous.

destajar, *va.* to hire or undertake work by the piece or job, to do piecework.

destajero, ra, *n.* pieceworker, one who undertakes work by the job.

destajo, *m.* job, undertaking work by the job.

destalonar, *va.* to wear out the heel of a shoe; to level horses' hoofs.

destapar, *va.* to uncover; **—se,** to be or become uncovered.

destapiar, *va.* to pull down mud walls.

destaponar, *va.* to uncork a bottle.

destartalado, da, *adj.* shabby; jumbled.

destazar, *va.* to cut to pieces.

deste, ta, to, *pron.* contraction for **de este, de esta, de esto** (in old Spanish).

destejar, *va.* to take away the tiles from; to leave a thing defenseless.

destejer, *va.* to unweave, to ravel.

destello, *m.* flowing out drop by drop; sparkle, gleam.

destemplado, da, *adj.* inharmonious, out of tune; incongruous (applied to paintings); intemperate.

destemplanza, *f.* intemperateness; unsteadiness of the weather; disorder; alteration in the pulse.

destemplar, *va.* to distemper, to alter, to disconcert; to untune; **—se,** to be ruffled; to be ill with a fever; to grow blunt; to act improperly.

destemple, *m.* discordance; disorder; intemperance; distemper; annealing.

desteñir, *va.* and *vr.* (DESTIÑO, DESTIÑENDO, DESTIÑO) to discolor, to fade.

desterrado, da, *n.* exile; **—,** *adj.* exiled, banished.

desterrar, *va.* (IE) to banish, to exile, to expel, to drive away.

desterradero, *m.* desert, wilderness.
desterronar, *vn.* to break the clods in the fields with a harrow or spade.
destetar, *va.* to wean.
destete, *m.* weaning.
destierro, *m.* exile, banishment.
destilación, *f.* distillation.
destiladera, *f.* still; alembic.
destilador, *m.* distiller; filtering stone; alembic.
destilar, *va.* and *vn.* to distil.
destilatorio, *m.* distillery; alembic.
destilería, *f.* distillery.
destinado, da, *adj.* destined.
destinar, *va.* to destine for, to intend for.
destinatario, ria, *n.* addressee, assignee.
destino, *m.* destiny; fate, doom; destination; office; job; **con — a,** bound for.
destitución, *f.* destitution, abandonment.
destituir, *va.* (UYO) to deprive; to dismiss from office.
destocar, *va.* to uncoif; to uncover the head.
destorcer, *va.* (UE) to untwist; to uncurl; (fig.) to arrange, to put in order; **—se,** (naut.) to deviate from one's course.
destornillador, *m.* screwdriver.
destornillar, *va.* to unscrew; (fig.) to act or speak rashly.
destrabar, *va.* to unfetter; (fig.) to separate.
destramar, *va.* to unweave; to break off an intrigue.
destrenzar, *va.* to undo a tress of hair.
destreza, *f.* dexterity, cleverness, cunning, expertness, skill.
destripar, *va.* to gut; to disembowel; to trample.
destripaterrones, *m.* day laborer; harrower.
destripular, *va.* to unrig a ship.
destriunfar, *va.* to extract all the trumps in cards.
destrocar, *va.* (UE) to return a thing bartered.
destronamiento, *m.* dethronement.
destronar, *va.* to dethrone, to depose.
destroncar, *va.* to lop, to cut short; to maim, to cut to pieces; (fig.) to ruin, to frustrate.
destróyer, *n.* (naut.) destroyer.
destrozado, da, *adj.* tattered, torn.
destrozar, *va.* to destroy, to break into pieces.
destrozo, *m.* breakage; destruction; (mil.) defeat, massacre.
destrucción, *f.* destruction, ruin.
destructible, *adj.* destructible.
destructivo, va, *adj.* destructive.
destructor, *m.* (naut.) destroyer.
destrueque, *m.* mutual restitution of things bartered or exchanged.
destruir, *va.* (UYO) to destroy, to ruin.
desuellacaras, *m.* bad barber; (coll.) shameless person.
desuello, *m.* (coll.) flaying; impudence; exorbitant price.
desuncir, *va.* to unyoke.

desunión, *f.* separation, disjunction; discord, dissension.
desunir, *va.* to separate, to disunite; to occasion discord.
desuñarse, *vr.* (coll.) to work one's fingers to the bone.
desurdir, *va.* to unweave cloth; to frustrate a plan.
desusar, *va.* and *vr.* to disuse, to become obsolete.
desuso, *m.* disuse; obsoleteness; desuetude.
desvahar, *va.* to trim off the withered part of a plant.
desvaído, da, *adj.* tall and ugly.
desvalido, da, *adj.* helpless, destitute.
desvaloración, *f.* devaluation.
desván, *m.* garret.
desvanecer, *va.* (EZCO) to divide into imperceptible parts; to cause to vanish; to undo, to remove; **—,** *vn.* and *vr.* to swell with pride; to faint; to grow vapid; to become insipid; to vanish; to be affected with giddiness.
desvanecimiento, *m.* pride, haughtiness; giddiness; swoon.
desvarío, *m.* delirium, raving; giddiness; inconstancy, caprice; extravagance.
desvedar, *va.* to revoke a prohibition against a thing.
desvelar, *va.* to keep awake; **—se,** to be watchful, to spend a sleepless night.
desvelo, *m.* lack of sleep; watchfulness; care.
desvenar, *va.* to take the veins from meat; to extract from the veins of mines.
desvencijado, da, *adj.* rickety, dilapidated.
desvencijar, *va.* and *vr.* to disunite, to weaken, to divide.
desvendar, *va.* to take off a bandage.
desventaja, *f.* disadvantage.
desventura, *f.* misfortune, calamity.
desventurado, da, *adj.* unfortunate, calamitous.
desvergonzado, da, *adj.* impudent, shameless.
desvergonzarse, *vr.* (UE) to speak or act in an impudent manner.
desvergüenza, *f.* shame; impudence; shameless word.
desviación, *f.* detour.
desviadero, *m.* sidetrack, railway switch.
desviar, *va.* and *vr.* to divert from the right way; to bypass; to dissuade; to parry (in fencing).
desvío, *m.* turning away, going astray; aversion; disdain; indifference; deviation; bypass.
desvirar, *va.* to pare off the superfluous part of a sole; to trim (a book).
desvirtuar, *va.* to rob of virtue or strength.
detalladamente, *adv.* in detail.
detallar, *va.* to detail, to relate minutely; to itemize.
detalle, *m.* detail; retail; **comprar** or **vender al —,** to buy or sell at retail.
detallista, *m.* retailer.

detective, *m.* detective.
detectivismo, *m.* detective service or force.
detector, *m.* detector.
detención, *f.* detention, delay.
detener, *va.* (DETENGO, DETUVE) to stop, to detain; to arrest; to keep back; to reserve; to withhold; **—se,** to tarry, to stay; to stop.
detenidamente, *adv.* carefully, thoroughly, painstakingly.
detenido, da, *adj.* sparing, niggardly; careful, painstaking; under arrest.
detentar, *va.* (law) to detain.
deterioración, *f.* deterioration, damage.
deteriorar, *va. and vr.* to deteriorate.
deterioro, *m.* deterioration.
determinación, *f.* determination, resolution; boldness; **tomar la —,** to make the decision.
determinado, da, *adj.* determinate; specific; resolute.
determinar, *va. and vr.* to determine, to fix; to resolve.
determinativo, va, *adj.* determinative.
determinismo, *m.* determinism.
detestable, *adj.* detestable, execrable.
detestación, *f.* detestation, abomination.
detestar, *va.* to detest, to abhor, to hate.
detonación, *f.* detonation.
detonador, *m.* detonator, fuse, blasting cap.
detractar, *va.* to detract, to defame, to slander.
detractor, *m.* slanderer, detracter.
detractora, *f.* detractress.
detrás, *adv.* behind; behind one's back, in the absence of; **por —,** from behind.
detrimento, *m.* detriment, damage, loss.
detrito, detritus, *m.* (geol.) detritus.
deuda, *f.* debt; fault; offense; **— consolidada,** funded debt; **— exterior,** external debt; **— flotante,** floating debt; **— pública,** public debt.
deudo, da, *adj.* relative, kindred.
deudor, ra, *n.* debtor.
Deuteronomio, *m.* Deuteronomy.
deutóxido, *m.* (chem.) dioxide.
devanadera, *f.* reel; movable decoration on the stage.
devanador, ra, *n.* winder; **—,** *m.* quill, piece of paper or other thing on which yarn is wound into a skein.
devanar, *va.* to reel; to wrap up.
devanear, *vn.* to rave, to talk nonsense; to dote.
devaneo, *m.* delirium; idle pursuit, frivolity.
devastación, *f.* devastation, desolation.
devastador, ra, *adj. and n.* desolator, devastator, harasser, spoiler.
devastar, *va.* to desolate, to lay waste.
devengar, *va.* to earn or draw (as salary, interest, etc.).
devoción, *f.* devotion, piety; strong affection, ardent love.
devocionario, *m.* prayer book.

devolución, *f.* (law) devolution; restitution, return.
devolutivo, *adj.* (law) transferable, devolutive; returnable.
devolver, *va.* (UE) to return; to restore; to refund, to pay back; to repay; (coll.) to vomit.
devorar, *va.* to devour, to swallow up.
devotería, *f.* exaggerated piety.
devoto, ta, *adj.* devout, pious; devoted, strongly attached.
dextrina, *f.* (chem.) dextrin.
dextrórsum, *adv.* toward the right.
dextrosa, *f.* (chem.) dextrose.
deyección, *f.* (geol.) debris, rock fragments; discharge of excrement; excrement.
dezmable, *adj.* tithable.
dezmar, *va.* to decimate; to tithe.
D. F. Distrito Federal, Federal District.
d/f or **d/fha. días fecha,** (com.) d.d. days after date.
Dg. decagramo, decagram.
dg.: decigramo, dg. decigram; **decagramo,** decagram.
dha. or **dho. dicha** or **dicho,** said, aforesaid, such.
día, *m.* day, daylight; **al otro —,** on the following day ; **a treinta —s vista,** at thirty days' sight; **— quebrado,** half holiday; **— festivo** or **de fiesta,** holiday; **dentro de ocho —s,** within a week (or eight days).
diabasa, *f.* diorite, kind of crystalline igneous rock.
diabetes, *f.* diabetes.
diabético, ca, *adj.* diabetic.
diabla, *f.* she-devil; **a la —,** carelessly; rudely.
diablazo, *m.* big devil.
diablear, *vn.* (coll.) to make mischief, to behave like devils.
diablejo, *m.* little devil, mischievous person.
diablillo, *m.* little devil; acute, clever man.
diablo, *m.* devil, Satan; person of a perverse temper; ugly, cunning or subtle person.
diablura, *f.* diabolical undertaking; devilishness.
diabólico, ca, *adj.* diabolical, devilish.
diacitrón, *m.* lemon peel preserved in sugar.
diaconato, *m.* deaconship.
diaconisa, *m.* deaconess.
diácono, *m.* deacon.
diacrítico, ca, *adj.* diacritical; (med.) diagnostic, distinguishing; **señal —ca,** diacritical mark.
diadema, *f.* diadem; halo.
diafanidad, *f.* transparency.
diáfano, na, *adj.* diaphanous, transparent.
diafragma, *m.* diaphragm, midriff.
diagnosticar, *va.* to diagnose.
diagnóstico, *m.* diagnosis; **—, ca,** *adj.* diagnostic.
diagonal, *adj.* diagonal; oblique.
diagrama, *m.* diagram, graph.
dialéctica, *f.* logic, dialectic.

dialéctico, *m.* logician; **—, ca,** *adj.* dialectical, logical.
dialecto, *m.* dialect.
dialogismo, *m.* dialogism.
diálogo, *m.* dialogue, conversation.
diamante, *m.* diamond; **— en bruto,** rough diamond; (coll.) diamond in the rough, something or someone rude in appearance but of sterling merit.
diamantino, na, *adj.* adamantine.
diamantista, *m.* diamond cutter; diamond dealer.
diametral, *adj.* diametrical, diametral.
diámetro, *m.* diameter.
diana, *f.* (mil.) reveille, the beating of the drum at daybreak.
diantre, *m.* deuce, devil.
diapasón, *m.* (mus.) diapason, octave; tuning fork.
diapositiva, *f.* lantern slide.
diaprea, *f.* small, round, tasty plum.
diariamente, *adv.* daily.
diario, *m.* journal, diary; daily newspaper; daily expense; **— de navegación,** log-book; **—, ria,** *adj.* daily.
diarismo, *m.* journalism.
diarista, *m.* journalist.
diarrea, *f.* diarrhea.
diástole, *f.* diastole.
diatermia, *f.* diathermy.
diatoma, *f.* diatom.
diatónico, ca, *adj.* (mus.) diatonic.
diatriba, *f.* diatribe.
dibujante, *m.* draftsman; one who draws.
dibujar, *va.* to draw, to design.
dibujo, *m.* drawing, sketch, draft, description.
Dicbre, diciembre, Dec. December.
dicción, *f.* diction, style, expression.
diccionario, *m.* dictionary.
dic.ᵉ, 10ᵉ, 10ᵇʳᵉ diciembre, Dec. December.
dicentra, *f.* (bot.) bleeding heart.
dicha, *f.* happiness, good fortune; **por —, a —,** by chance, luckily.
dicharacho, *m.* vulgar expression.
dichero, ra, *adj.* witty, cleverly facetious; **—,** *n.* witty and clever person.
dicho, *m.* saying, sentence, proverb; declaration; promise of marriage; **—, cha,** *adj.* said; **dejar — cho,** to leave word.
dichoso, sa, *adj.* happy, prosperous; lucky, fortunate.
diciembre, *m.* December.
dicotiledoneo, nea, *adj.* dicotyledonous.
dictado, *m.* a title of dignity or honor; dictate; dictation.
dictador, *m.* dictator.
dictadura, *f.* dictatorship.
dictáfono, *m.* dictaphone.
dictamen, *m.* opinion, notion; suggestion, insinuation.
dictar, *va.* to dictate.
dicterio, *m.* sarcasm, taunt, insult.
dictógrafo, *m.* dictograph.
diecinueve or **diez y nueve,** *m.* and *adj.* nineteen.

dieciocho or **diez y ocho,** *m.* and *adj.* eighteen.
dieciseis or **diez y seis,** *m.* and *adj.* sixteen.
diecisiete or **diez y siete,** *m.* and *adj.* seventeen.
Diego, *m.* James.
diente, *m.* tooth, fang, tusk, jag; **— de leche, — mamón,** milk tooth; **— molar,** molar tooth; **—s postizos,** false teeth; **hablar** or **decir entre —s,** to mumble, to mutter.
diéresis, *f.* diaeresis.
diestra, *f.* right hand; (fig.) favor, support, protection.
diestro, tra, *adj.* right; dexterous, skillful, clever; sagacious, prudent; sly, cunning; favorable, propitious; **—,** *m.* skillful fencer; halter, bridle.
dieta, *f.* diet, regimen; diet, assembly; daily salary of judges; **—s,** *pl.* cattle put on board a fleet to furnish fresh provisions for the sick.
dietario, *m.* book in which notable events were chronicled in olden times; family book of income and expense.
dietas, *f. pl.* traveling expenses or special fee allowed a public official.
dietética, *f.* dietetics.
diez, *adj.* and *m.* ten; **— de rosario,** each tenth bead of a rosary.
diezmar, *va.* to decimate; to tithe; to take the tenth; to destroy.
diezmero, *m.* tithepayer.
diezmesino, na, *adj.* ten months old.
diezmilésimo, ma, *adj.* ten-thousandth; **—,** *m.* one ten-thousandth.
diezmo, *m.* tithe; **—, ma,** *adj.* tenth.
difamación, *f.* defamation.
difamar, *va.* to defame, to libel.
difamatorio, ria, *adj.* defamatory, calumnious.
diferencia, *f.* difference; **a —,** with the difference; **—s,** *pl.* controversies, disputes.
diferencial, *adj.* differential, different; **—,** *m.* (auto.) differential.
diferenciar, *va.* to differ, to differentiate; **—se,** to differ, to distinguish oneself.
diferente, *adj.* different, unlike.
diferir, *va.* (ᵻᴇ) to defer, to put off; to differ.
difícil, *adj.* difficult.
dificultad, *f.* difficulty.
dificultar, *va.* to raise difficulties; to render difficult.
dificultoso, sa, *adj.* difficult; painful.
difidencia, *f.* diffidence.
difidente, *adj.* diffident, disloyal.
difractar, *va.* to diffract.
difteria, *f.* diphtheria.
difundir, *va.* to diffuse, to outspread; to divulge.
difunto, ta, *adj.* dead, deceased; late; **—,** *n.* deceased person.
difusamente, *adv.* diffusedly; verbosely.
difusión, *f.* diffusion, extension; expatiation.
difusivo, va, *adj.* diffusive.

difuso, sa, *adj.* diffusive, copious; large; prolix, circumstantial.

difusora, *f.* (rad.) broadcasting station.

digerible, *adj.* digestible.

digerir, *va.* (IE) to digest; to bear with patience; to meditate over something in order to understand it; to adjust, to arrange; (chem.) to digest.

digestible, *adj.* digestible.

digestión, *f.* digestion, concoction.

digestivo, va, *adj.* digestive.

digesto, *m.* (law) digest, compilation of statutes or legal decisions.

digital, *f.* (bot.) digitalis, foxglove; —, *adj.* pertaining to the fingers; **huellas —es,** fingerprints; —, *m. pl.* thumb notches.

dignación, *f.* condescension.

dignarse, *vr.* to condescend, to deign.

dignidad, *f.* dignity, rank; grandeur of mien; archbishop or bishop.

digno, na, *adj.* meritorious, worthy, deserving; suitable, appropriate.

digresión, *f.* digression; expatiation; **— de un astro,** departure of a planet from the equinoctial line.

dij or **dije,** *m.* charm, amulet; jewel.

dilacerar, *va.* to tear to pieces.

dilación, *f.* delay.

dilapidar, *va.* to dilapidate.

dilatable, *adj.* dilatable.

dilatación, *f.* dilatation, extension; calmness in sorrow; **bala de —,** dumdum, soft-nosed or hollow-pointed bullet.

dilatado, da, *adj.* large, extended; prolix; spacious, extensive; long delayed.

dilatar, *va.* to dilate, to expand; to spread out; to defer, to protract; **—se,** to expatiate; to speak largely and copiously; to delay.

dilatativo, va, *adj.* that which dilates.

dilatoria, *f.* waste of time; **traer a uno en —s, andar con —s,** to keep one waiting; to waste time with red tape.

dilatorio, ria, *adj.* dilatory.

dilección, *f.* love, affection, good will.

dilecto, ta, *adj.* loved, beloved.

dilema, *m.* dilemma.

diligencia, *f.* diligence; industriousness; affair, business; errand; stagecoach.

diligenciar, *va.* to exert oneself, to endeavor to obtain something.

diligente, *adj.* diligent, industrious, assiduous; prompt, swift.

dilogía, *f.* ambiguousness, double meaning.

dilucidación, *f.* explanation, illustration.

dilucidar, *va.* to elucidate, to explain.

dilucidario, *m.* explanatory writing.

diluir, *va.* and *vr.* (UYO) to dilute.

diluviano, na, *adj.* diluvian.

diluvio, *m.* deluge, inundation; vast abundance.

dimanación, *f.* emanation.

dimanar, *vn.* to spring from; to originate, to flow.

dimensión, *f.* dimension; extent, capacity, bulk.

dimes, *m. pl.* **andar en — y diretes,** (coll.) to contend, to argue back and forth.

diminución, *f.* diminution, decrease.

diminutamente, *adv.* diminutively; by retail.

diminutivo, va, *adj.* diminutive, little.

diminuto, ta, *adj.* defective, faulty; exceedingly small.

dimisión, *f.* resignation from an office.

dimisorias, *f. pl.* dimissory letters, papers granting leave to depart (to another diocese); (coll.) dismissal or discharge.

dimitir, *va.* to resign, to give up, to abdicate.

din, *m.* (coll.) money; **el — y el don,** money and quality (nobility); **el don sin el —,** nobility without riches.

dina, *f.* (phy.) dyne.

Dinamarca, *f.* Denmark.

dinámica, *f.* dynamics.

dinámico, ca, *adj.* dynamic.

dinamita, *f.* dynamite.

dínamo, *f.* (Sp. Am. **dínamo,** *m.*), dynamo.

dinastía, *f.* dynasty.

dineral, *m.* large sum of money.

dinerillo, *m.* small ancient coin; (coll.) small amount of money.

dinero, *m.* coin, money, coinage; currency; **— contante,** ready money, cash.

dinosauro, *m.* dinosaur.

dintel, *m.* doorframe.

diocesano, na, *adj.* diocesan.

diócesis, *f.* diocese.

dionisia, *f.* bloodstone.

diorama, *m.* diorama.

Dios, *m.* God; **— es grande,** let us trust in God, God will help us; **— mediante,** with the help of God, God willing.

dios, diosa, *m.* and *f.* god, goddess.

diploma, *m.* diploma; patent, license.

diplomacia or **diplomática,** *f.* diplomacy.

diplomarse, *vr.* to be graduated.

diplomático, ca, *adj.* diplomatic; —, *m.* diplomat.

dipsomanía, *f.* dipsomania, uncontrollable craving for alcohol.

dipsómano, *m.* dipsomaniac.

diptongo, *m.* diphthong.

diputación, *f.* deputation; object of a deputation.

diputado, *m.* delegate, representative.

diputar, *va.* to depute; to constitute.

dique, *m.* dike, dam, mole, breakwater, levee; **— de carena,** dry dock; **— flotante,** floating dock.

dirección, *f.* direction; guidance, administration; management; manager's office; address, addressing; **— telegráfica** or **cablegráfica,** cable address.

directamente, *adv.* directly.

directivo, va, *adj.* managing; —, *f.* governing body.

directo, ta, *adj.* direct, straight, nonstop; apparent, evident.

director, *m.* director; conductor; president; editor (of a publication); manager; **— de escena,** stage manager; **— espiritual,** father confessor, minister who gives spiritual advice; **— gerente,** managing director.

directora, *f.* directress, governess.

directorio, ria, *adj.* directive; directorial; **—,** *m.* directory; board of directors.

dirigente, *adj.* directing, ruling.

dirigible, *m.* airship, dirigible; **—,** *adj.* manageable.

dirigir, *va.* to direct; to conduct; to dedicate a work; to regulate, to govern; **— la palabra,** to address (someone); **—se,** to turn, to go, to address; **—se a,** to speak to, to turn to.

dirimente, *adj.* breaking off, dissolving.

dirimir, *va.* to dissolve, to separate; to declare void (as a matrimony); to adjust differences.

disanto, *m.* holy day.

discantar, *va.* to chant; to discourse on a subject, sometimes with impertinence; (mus.) to sing in counterpoint.

discante, *m.* tenor guitar; musical concert, especially of musical instruments.

discerniente, *adj.* discriminating.

discernimiento, *m.* discernment; appointment of a guardian by the proper magistrates.

discernir, *va.* (IE) to discern, to distinguish; to appoint a guardian.

disciplina, *f.* discipline; education; orderly training.

diciplinado, da, *adj.* disciplined, orderly.

disciplinar, *va.* to discipline.

disciplinario, ria, *adj.* disciplinary.

disciplinazo, *m.* blow with a lash.

discípulo, la, *n.* disciple, scholar, pupil.

disco, *m.* disk; face of the sun or moon; lens of a telescope; phonograph record; (rail.) disk, signal disk.

discóbolo, *m.* discus thrower.

díscolo, la, *adj.* ungovernable; peevish.

discordancia, *f.* disagreement, discord, disharmony.

discordante, *adj.* dissonant, discordant.

discordar, *vn.* (UE) to discord, to disagree.

discorde, *adj.* discordant; (mus.) dissonant.

discordia, *f.* discord, disagreement, clash.

discreción, *f.* discretion; acuteness of mind, sharpness of wit; **a —,** at one's good judgment; optional.

discrepancia, *f.* discrepancy.

discrepar, *vn.* to differ; to disagree.

discreto, ta, *adj.* discreet; ingenious, witty, eloquent.

disculpa, *f.* apology, excuse.

disculpar, *va.* and *vr.* to exculpate, to excuse, to acquit, to absolve.

discurrir, *vn.* to ramble about, to run to and fro; to discourse upon a subject; to discuss; **—,** *va.* to invent, to contrive.

discursivo, va, *adj.* discursive; contemplative.

discurso, *m.* discourse; reasoning; conversation; speech, dissertation; space of time.

discusión, *f.* discussion.

discutible, *adj.* debatable.

discutir, *va.* and *vn.* to discuss, to argue, to debate.

disecar, *va.* to dissect.

disección, *f.* dissection, anatomy.

disector, *m.* dissector, anatomist.

diseminación, *f.* dissemination; diffusion.

diseminar, *va.* to scatter as seed; to disseminate, to propagate.

disensión, *f.* dissension, misunderstanding, contest, strife.

disentería, *f.* dysentery.

disentimiento, *m.* dissent, disagreement.

disentir, *vn.* (IE) to dissent, to disagree.

diseñador, ra, *n.* designer.

diseñar, *va.* to draw, to design; to sketch.

diseño, *m.* design, draft; description; picture.

disertación, *f.* dissertation, discussion.

disertar, *vn.* to discourse, to debate (on a subject).

diserto, ta, *adj.* forceful, eloquent (in speech).

disfamación, *f.* defamation, injuring of a reputation by oral or written means.

disfavor, *m.* disregard, lack of favor.

disforme, *adj.* ugly, monstrous, formless; huge.

disfraz, *m.* mask, disguise; masquerade; dissimulation.

disfrazar, *va.* and *vr.* to disguise, to conceal; to cloak, to dissemble; to mask.

disfrutar, *va.* to enjoy.

disfrute, *m.* enjoyment.

disgregación, *f.* disintegration; disunion; act of disjoining.

disgregar, *va.* to disintegrate.

disgustar, *va.* to displease; to offend; **—se,** to be displeased, to fall out; to be worried.

disgusto, *m.* sorrow, grief; aversion; bad humor; **a —,** against one's will; **llevarse un —,** to be disappointed.

disidente, *adj.* and *n.* dissident, dissenter.

disimetría, *f.* lack of symmetry.

disimilitud, *f.* dissimilitude.

disimulación, *f.* dissimulation; hypocrisy.

disimulado, da, *adj.* reserved, dissembled; **a lo —do,** dissemblingly; reservedly.

disimulador, ra, *n.* pretender, dissembler.

disimular, *va.* to dissemble; to cloak; to hide; to pretend; to tolerate; to distort and misrepresent things.

disimulo, *m.* dissimulation; pretense; tolerance.

disipación, *f.* dissipation; (chem.) resolution into component parts; resolution into vapor.

disipado, da, *adj.* dissipated, prodigal.

disipador, ra, *n.* spendthrift.

disipar, *va.* and *vr.* to dissipate, to disperse, to scatter; to lavish, to squander.

dislate, *m.* nonsense, absurdity.
dislocación, *f.* dislocation.
dislocarse, *vr.* to be dislocated or put out of joint.
disminución, *f.* lessening, deterioration.
disminuir, *va.* to diminish.
disociación, *f.* dissociation.
disoluble, *adj.* dissoluble.
disolución, *f.* dissolution, breaking up; lewdness, licentiousness.
disolutivo, va, *adj.* dissolvent.
disoluto, ta, *adj.* dissolute, licentious, lewd.
disolvente, *m.* and *adj.* dissolvent.
disolver, *va.* (UE) to loosen, to untie; to dissolve, to disunite; to melt, to liquefy; **—se,** to dissolve, to break up.
disonancia, *f.* dissonance; disagreement.
disonante, *adj.* dissonant, inharmonious; (fig.) discordant.
disonar, *vn.* (UE) to disagree in sound; to disagree; to be repugnant.
dísono, na, *adj.* dissonant.
dispar, *adj.* unlike, unequal, different.
disparadero, *m.* trigger.
disparador, *m.* shooter; trigger of a gun.
disparar, *va.* and *vn.* to shoot, to discharge, to fire; to let off; to throw with violence; to talk nonsense; **—se,** to run headlong; to stoop, to dart down upon a prey.
disparatado, da, *adj.* inconsistent, absurd, extravagant.
disparatar, *vn.* to act foolishly; to talk nonsense.
disparate, *m.* nonsense, absurdity, extravagance; blunder.
disparejo, ja, *adj.* not uniform; unequal, uneven.
disparidad, *f.* disparity, inequality.
disparo, *m.* shot, discharge, explosion.
dispendio, *m.* extravagant expense; unnecessary waste of time or wealth.
dispendioso, sa, *adj.* costly, expensive.
dispensa, *f.* dispense; document granting a dispensation.
dispensable, *adj.* dispensable.
dispensación, *f.* dispensation, exemption.
dispensador, ra, *n.* one who excuses or grants a dispensation, dispenser.
dispensar, *va.* to dispense; to excuse, to absolve; to grant; to deal out.
dispensario, *m.* dispensary of drugs; clinic.
dispepsia, *f.* (med.) dyspepsia.
dispéptico, ca, *adj.* dyspeptic.
dispersar, *va.* and *vr.* to scatter.
dispersión, *f.* dispersion.
disperso, sa, *adj.* dispersed.
displicencia, *f.* displeasure, dislike.
displicente, *adj.* disagreeable, peevish.
disponer, *va.* and *vn.* (DISPONGO, DISPUSE) to arrange; to prepare; to dispose of; to resolve; **—se a,** to get ready to, to make arrangements.
disponible, *adj.* disposable, available.
disposición, *f.* disposition, arrangement; ordering; proportion; resolution; disposal;

command; power, authority.
dispositivo, va, *adj.* dispositive; **—,** *m.* device, mechanism, contrivance.
dispuesto, ta, *adj.* disposed, fit, ready; **bien —,** favorably inclined; **mal —,** unfavorably disposed.
disputa, *f.* dispute, controversy.
disputable, *adj.* disputable, controvertible.
disputador, ra, *n.* disputant, disputer.
disputar, *va.* and *vn.* to dispute, to controvert, to question; to debate, to argue.
distancia, *f.* distance, interval; difference.
distante, *adj.* distant, far off.
distar, *vn.* to be distant; to be different.
distender, *va.* and *vr.* (IE) (med.) to distend, to swell; to expand.
dístico, *m.* (poet.) distich, couplet.
distinción, *f.* distinction; difference; prerogative; **a —,** in contradistinction.
distinguido, da, *adj.* distinguished, prominent, conspicuous.
distinguir, *va.* to distinguish; to see clearly and at a distance; to discern; to show regard for; **—se,** to distinguish oneself, to excel.
distintivo, *m.* insignia, distinctive mark; particular attribute.
distinto, ta, *adj.* distinct, different; clear.
distracción, *f.* distraction, lack of attention; amusement, pastime.
distraer, *va.* (DISTRAIGO, DISTRAJE) to distract; to amuse, to entertain; **—se,** to be absent-minded, to be inattentive; to enjoy oneself.
distraído, da, *adj.* absent-minded; inattentive; dissolute, licentious.
distribución, *f.* distribution, division, separation; arrangement.
distribuidor, *m.* distributor; valve gear; slide valve; **— de alta presión,** high-pressure slide valve.
distribuir, *va.* (UYO) to distribute, to divide; to sort; to distribute type.
distributivo, va, *adj.* distributive.
distrito, *m.* district; territory.
disturbar, *va.* to disturb, to interrupt.
disturbio, *m.* disturbance, interruption.
disuadir, *va.* to dissuade.
disuasión, *f.* dissuasion.
disuasivo, va, *adj.* deterrent, dissuasive.
disyunción, *f.* disjunction; (gram.) disjunctive particle.
disyunta, *f.* (mus.) change of key.
disyuntivo, va, *adj.* disjunctive.
disyuntor, *m.* (elec.) circuit breaker.
dita, *f.* bond, security on a loan; bondsman.
diuresis, *f.* diuresis.
diurno, na, *adj.* diurnal; daily; **—,** *m.* prayer book.
diuturnidad, *f.* long duration.
diuturno, na, *adj.* lasting a long time.
diva, *f.* woman singer; prima donna.
divagación, *f.* wandering, digression.
diván, *m.* Divan (supreme council among the Turks); sofa.

divergencia, *f.* divergence
divergente, *adj.* divergent.
diversidad, *f.* diversity; variety of things.
diversificar, *va.* to diversify, to vary.
diversión, *f.* diversion, pastime, sport, amusement.
diverso, sa, *adj.* diverse, different; several, sundry.
divertido, da, *adj.* amused: amusing.
divertimiento, *m.* diversion, amusement, pastime, sport.
divertir, *va.* (IE) to divert (the attention); to amuse, to entertain; (mil.) to draw the enemy off from some design; **—se,** to have an enjoyable time.
dividendo, *m.* (math. and com.) dividend.
dividir, *va.* and *vr.* to divide, to disunite, to separate; to split, to break up.
divieso, *m.* (med.) boil.
divinamente, *adv.* splendidly, divinely.
divinidad, *f.* god, divinity; woman of exquisite beauty; **la D—,** the Deity.
divinizar, *va.* to deify; to sanctify.
divino, na, *adj* divine, heavenly; excellent.
divisa, *f.* motto, badge.
divisar, *vn.* to perceive indistinctly; to vary (in heraldry).
divisible, *adj* divisible.
división, *f.* division; partition; separation; difference; (gram.) hyphen.
divisor, *m.* (math.) divisor.
divisorio, ria, *adj.* divisive; **línea —,** dividing line.
divorciar, *va.* to pronounce a sentence of divorce; to divorce, to separate; **—se,** to be divorced.
divorcio, *m.* divorce; separation, disunion.
divulgación, *f.* disclosure, publication.
divulgar, *va.* to publish, to divulge.
diz, contraction of **dice,** says.
Dl. decalitro, Dl. or dkl. dekaliter or decaliter.
dl. decílitro, dl. deciliter.
dls. dólares, $ or dol. dollars.
Dm. decámetro, Dm. or dkm. dekameter or decameter.
dm. decímetro, dm. decimeter.
Dn., D.ⁿ or **d.ⁿ Don,** Don (title).
dna. or **doc. docena,** doz. dozen.
do, *m.* first note of the musical scale.
dobladillo, *m.* hem; strong knitting thread.
doblado, *m.* measure of the fold in cloth; **—, da,** *adj.* folded, robust, thickset; deceitful, dissembling.
dobladura, *f.* fold.
doblamiento, *m.* doubling, bending.
doblar, *va.* and *vn.* to double, to fold; to bend; to ring the passing bell; **—se,** to bend, to bow, to submit. **— la esquina,** to turn the corner.
doble, *adj.* double; thick and short, robust; artful, deceitful; **partida —,** double entry (bookkeeping); **al —,** doubly; **—,** *m.* fold, crease; toll of the passing bell.
doblegable, *adj.* flexible, pliant.

doblegar, *va.* to bend, to incurvate; to dissuade.
doblemente, *adv.* doubly; deceptively, maliciously.
doblete, *m.* false jewel, a stroke in billiards.
doblez, *m.* crease, fold; **—,** *m.* or *f.* duplicity in dealing.
doblón, *m.* doubloon.
doce, *adj.* and *m.* twelve.
docena, *f.* dozen; **por —s,** by the dozen.
docenal, *adj.* sold by the dozen.
doceno, na, *adj.* twelfth.
docente, *adj.* teaching; **personal —,** teaching staff.
dócil, *adj.* docile, tractable, obedient.
docilidad, *f.* docility, compliance, gentleness.
Doct., D.ʳ or **dr. Doctor,** Dr. Doctor.
docto, ta, *adj.* learned.
doctor, *m.* doctor; physician.
doctora, *f.* woman doctor; (coll.) wife of a physician or doctor.
doctorado, *m.* doctorate.
doctoral, *adj.* doctoral.
doctorando, *m.* one who is on the point of obtaining his doctor's degree.
doctorar, *va.* and *vr.* to graduate as a doctor.
doctrina, *f.* doctrine, instruction; science; discourse on the tenets of the Christan faith.
doctrinal, *m.* catechism; **—,** *adj.* doctrinal.
doctrinar, *va.* to teach, to instruct.
doctrinario, ria, *adj.* doctrinal; **—,** *n.* doctrinaire.
documentación, *f.* documentation; **— de a bordo,** ship's papers.
documento, *m.* document; deed of title, record.
docum.ᵗᵒ documento, doc. document.
dodecasílabo, *m.* dodecasyllable; **—, ba,** *adj.* having twelve syllables.
dogal, *m.* rope tied round the neck of asses, mules, etc.
dogma, *m.* dogma.
dogmático, ca, *adj.* dogmatic.
dogmatismo, *m.* dogmatism.
dogmatizador or **dogmatizante,** *m.* dogmatizer, dogmatist.
dogmatizar, *va.* to dogmatize.
dogo, *m.* terrier.
dolador, *m.* stonecutter; joiner.
doladura, *f.* chip, splinter.
dolamas, *f. pl.* or **dolames,** *m. pl.* ills, ailments; complaints.
dolar, *va.* to hew stone or wood.
dólar, *m.* dollar (U. S. monetary unit).
dolencia, *f.* disease, affliction.
doler, *vn.* and *vr.* (UE) to feel pain; to ache; to be sorry; to repent; to feel for the sufferings of others; to complain; **— la cabeza,** to have a headache.
doliente, *adj.* suffering; sorrowful; **—,** *m.* and *f.* mourner; patient (sick person).
dolo, *m.* fraud, deceit.

dolor, *m.* pain, aching, ache; affliction, grief; regret.

dolorido, da, *adj.* afflicted, painful, sore, tender; heartsick.

doloroso, sa, *adj.* sorrowful, afflicted, dolorous, dismal; painful.

doloso, sa, *adj.* deceitful, knavish.

domable, *adj.* tamable.

domador, ra, *n.* tamer, subduer; horsebreaker.

domadura, *f.* taming, subduing.

domar, *va.* to tame, to subdue, to master; **sin —,** untamed, unbroken.

domeñar, *va.* to make tractable, to tame.

domesticable, *adj.* tamable.

domesticar, *va.* to domesticate, to tame.

domesticidad, *f.* domesticity, domestication.

doméstico, ca, *adj.* domestic; **—,** *n.* domestic, menial.

domiciliado, da, *adj.* domiciliated; residing.

domiciliarse, *vr.* to establish oneself in a residence.

domicilio, *m.* habitation, domicile, home, abode; **— social,** firm's place of business.

dominación, *f.* dominion, domination, authority, power; **—ones,** *pl.* dominations (angelic beings).

dominador, ra, *adj.* dominating; overbearing; **—,** *n.* dominator.

dominante, *adj.* dominant, domineering.

dominar, *va.* to dominate; to control; to master (a language or a subject); **—se,** to control oneself.

dómine, *m.* grammarian; (coll.) pompous, empty-headed man.

Domingo, Dominic.

domingo, *m.* Sunday.

dominguero, ra, *adj.* done or worn on Sunday.

dominguillo, *m.* tumbler (a toy).

dominical, *adj.* manorial; dominical.

dominico, *m.* friar of the order of Saint Dominic.

dominio, *m.* dominion, domination, power, authority; domain.

dominó, *m.* domino (a masquerade garment); game of dominoes.

Dom.º Domingo, Dominic.

dom.º domingo, Sun. Sunday.

dompedro, *m.* (bot.) morning-glory.

don, *m.* Don, the Spanish title for a gentleman, (used only before Christian or given name).

don, *m.* gift, quality; **el — de la palabra,** the gift of speech; **— de gentes,** savoir-faire, courteous, pleasant manners.

donación, *f.* donation, gift.

donado, da, *n.* lay brother; lay sister.

donador, ra, *n.* donor, bestower, giver; **— de sangre,** blood donor.

donaire, *m.* grace, elegance; witty saying.

donante, *m.* and *f.* donor, giver.

donar, *va.* to make free gifts, to bestow.

donatario, ria, *n.* donee, recipient.

donativo, *m.* free contribution.

doncel, *m.* king's page; innocent young man.

doncella, *f.* virgin, maiden; lady's maid.

doncellez, *f.* virginity, maidenhood.

doncellona, *f.* old maid.

donde, *adv.* where; **¿de dónde?** whence? **¿hacia dónde?** in what direction? **¿por dónde?** by what way? for what reason?

dondequiera, *adv.* anywhere; wherever.

dondiego de noche, *m.* (bot.) jalap.

donillero, *m.* swindler, sharper; cheat.

donoso, *adj.* gay, witty; pleasant, comely.

doña, *f.* lady, mistress; title equivalent to Mrs. or Miss, but used only before Christian or given name.

doquier or **doquiera,** *adv.* anywhere.

Dor. deudor, Dr. or dr. debtor.

dorada or **doradilla,** *f.* gilthead (fish).

doradillo, *m.* fine brass wire; (orn.) wagtail.

dorado, da, *adj.* gilded; light (beer); **—,** *m.* gilding.

dorador, *m.* gilder.

doradura, *f.* gilding.

doral, *m.* (orn.) flycatcher.

dorar, *va.* to gild; (fig.) to palliate.

dórico, ca, *adj.* (arch.) Doric.

dormidero, ra, *adj.* sleepy, soporific; **—,** *m.* place where cattle repose; **—,** *f.* poppy.

dormido, da, *adj.* asleep.

dormilón, ona, *n.* (coll.) sleepyhead; **—,** *adj.* fond of sleeping.

dormir, *vn.* (UE) to sleep; **—se,** to fall asleep.

dormitar, *vn.* to doze, to be half asleep.

dormitorio, *m.* dormitory, bedroom.

Dorotea, Dorothy.

dorsal, *adj.* dorsal; **espina —,** spinal column.

dorso, *m.* back.

dos, *adj.* and *m.* two; **de — en —,** by two's, two abreast.

dosañal, *adj.* biennial.

doscientos, tas, *m.* and *adj.* two hundred.

dosel, *m.* canopy; platform.

doselera, *f.* valance.

dosis, *f.* dose.

dotación, *f.* dotation, endowment; equipment.

dotador, ra, *n.* one who endows; donor; institutor.

dotal, *adj.* pertaining to a dowry.

dotar, *va.* to endow with a fortune; to give a dowry to; to endue.

dote, *m.* and *f.* dower, dowry; **llevarse —,** to receive a dowry; **—s,** *pl.* gifts of nature; endowments.

dovela, *f.* stone of an arch.

dovelar, *va.* to hew a stone in curves.

doxología, *f.* doxology.

dozavo, va, *m* and *adj.* twelfth part.

d/p. días plazo, (com.) days' time.

Dr., Dʳ. or **dr. doctor,** Dr. or Doctor.

dra. dro. derecha, derecho, right-hand side.

dracma, *f.* drachm.
draga, *f.* dredger.
dragado, *m.* dredging.
dragaminas, *m.* minesweeper.
drago, *m.* (bot.) dragon tree.
dragón, *m.* dragon; (mil.) dragoon; (vet.) white spots in the pupils of horses' eyes.
dragona, *f.* (mil.) kind of epaulet; female dragon.
drama, *m.* drama.
dramática, *f.* dramatic art.
dramático, ca, *adj.* dramatic.
dramatizar, *va.* to dramatize.
dramaturgo, *m.* dramatist, playwright.
drástico, ca, *adj.* drastic, extreme in effect.
drenaje, *m.* drainage.
dríada or **dríade,** *f.* dryad.
dril, *m.* drill, coarse fabric of linen or cotton.
droga, *f.* drug; stratagem, artifice, deceit; (coll.) nuisance.
droguería, *f.* drugstore.
droguero, *m.* druggist.
droguista, *m.* druggist; cheat, impostor.
dromedario, *m.* dromedary.
druida, *m.* druid.
dúa, *f.* group of workmen for certain types of mining.
dualismo, *m.* dualism.
dubitativo, va, *adj.* doubtful, dubious, (often applied to conjunctions).
Dublín, *f.* Dublin.
ducado, *m.* duchy, dukedom; ducat.
ducal, *adj.* ducal.
ducho, cha, *adj.* dexterous; accustomed; —, *f.* shower bath; douche.
dúctil, *adj.* ductile, tractable.
duda, *f.* doubt, suspense, hesitation; **poner en —,** to question; **no cabe —,** there is no doubt.
dudable, *adj.* dubitable, dubious.
dudar, *va.* and *vn.* to doubt, to waver.
dudoso, sa, *adj.* doubtful, dubious.
duela, *f.* stave.
duelista, *m.* duelist, quarreler.
duelo, *m.* duel; grief; affliction; mourning; funeral.
duende, *m.* elf, goblin.
dueño, ña, *n.* owner, master, proprietor; **— de si mismo,** self controlled; **hacerse —,** to take possession; —, *f.* duenna, chaperon.
duermevela, *m.* (coll.) light sleep, doze; sleep frequently interrupted.
dúeto, *m.* duet.
dula, *f.* common pasture for cattle; all the horses from a community sent to pasture on a common ground.
dulcamara, *f.* (bot.) bittersweet; nightshade.
dulce, *adj.* sweet, pleasing to the taste; mild, soft, gentle, meek; —, *m.* candy, sweetmeat, confection.
dulcedumbre, *f.* softness, sweetness.
dulcémele, *m.* (mus.) dulcimer.
dulcería, *f.* confectionery store.

dulcificante, *adj.* sweetening.
dulcificar, *va.* to sweeten.
dulzaino, na, *adj.* excessively sweet.
dulzura, *f.* sweetness; gentleness, graciousness; pleasant manner in speaking or writing.
dulzurar, *va.* (chem.) to edulcorate.
dúo, *m.* (mus.) duo, duet.
duodecimal, *adj.* duodecimal.
duodécimo, ma, *adj.* and *m.* twelfth.
duodenal, *adj.* duodenal.
duodeno, *m.* duodenum.
dupdo. or **dup.**do **duplicado,** dup. duplicate, in duplicate.
dúplica, *f.* (law) reply.
duplicación, *f.* duplication.
duplicado, *m.* duplicate.
duplicar, *va.* to double, to duplicate; to repeat.
dúplice, *adj.* double.
duplicidad, *f.* duplicity; falseness.
duplo, *m.* double, duplex.
duque, *m.* duke.
duquesa, *f.* duchess.
dura, *f.* (coll.) duration, continuance.
durable, *adj.* durable, lasting.
duración, *f.* duration, term.
duradero, ra, *adj.* lasting, durable.
duraluminio, *m.* duralumin.
duramen, *m.* heartwood.
durante, *pres. p.* of **durar,** during; **— la guerra,** during the war.
durar, *vn.* to last, to endure; to wear well (as clothes).
duraznero, *m.* peach tree.
durazno, *m.* peach; peach tree.
dureza, *f.* hardness, solidity, firmness; acerbity; steadiness; lack of softness in paintings; tumor, callosity; **— de vientre,** constipation; **— de oído,** hardness of hearing.
durillo, *adj.* rather hard.
durmiente, *adj.* sleeping; —, *m.* dormer; dormant; (rail.) crosstie.
duro, ra, *adj.* hard, solid; unjust; oppressive, rigorous, cruel; stubborn; avaricious; rude, harsh, peevish, rough; stale (of bread); —, *m.* peso, dollar.
dux, *m.* doge (of Venice and Genoa).
d/v. días vista, (com.) days' sight.

E

e, *conj.* and (used only before words beginning with *i* or *hi*, when not followed by *e*).
E. este or **oriente,** E. east, orient.
ea, a kind of aspiration used to awaken attention; **¡— pues!** well then! let us see!
ebanista, *m.* cabinetmaker.
ébano, *m.* ebony.
ebonita, *f.* ebonite, vulcanite, hard rubber.
ebrio, ria, *adj.* inebriated, intoxicated, drunk.
ebullición, *f.* ebullition, boiling over.

ebúrneo, nea, *adj.* like ivory.

ec. ^{ca} or **ec.** ^{co} **eclesiástica, co,** ecclesiastic.

Eccehomo, *m.* Ecce Homo.

eclesiástico, *m.* clergyman, ecclesiastic; **—, ca,** *adj.* ecclesiastical.

eclipsable, *adj.* that may be eclipsed.

eclipsar, *va.* (ast.) to eclipse; to outshine; **—se,** to disappear.

eclipse, *m.* eclipse.

eclíptica, *f.* (ast.) ecliptic.

eco, *m.* echo.

economía, *f.* economy; **— política,** political economy, economics; **— dirigida,** planned economy.

económico, ca, *adj.* economic; economical, saving.

economista, *m.* economist; one who is a good manager of affairs.

economizar, *va.* to save up, to economize.

ecónomo, *m.* guardian, trustee; ecclesiastical administrator.

ecuación, *f.* equation.

ecuador, *m.* equator.

ecuánime, *adj.* equanimous, composed, fair, impartial.

ecuestre, *adj.* equestrian.

ecuménico, ca, *adj.* ecumenical, universal.

eczema, *f.* eczema.

echadero, *m.* place of rest or repose.

echadizo, za, *adj.* fit to be thrown away; suborned to pry into other people's actions; **—,** *m.* (coll.) foundling.

echar, *va.* to cast, to throw, to dart; to cast away: **— a correr,** to start running; **— a perder,** to spoil; **— carnes,** to grow fat; **— de menos,** to miss; **— de ver,** to notice; **— raíces,** to take root; **— un cigarro,** to smoke a cigar or cigarette; **—se,** to lie, to rest, to stretch oneself at full length; **— las cartas en el** (or **al**) **correo,** to mail the letters.

echazón, *f.* act of throwing; (law) jettison.

ed. edificio, bldg. building.

edad, *f.* age, epoch, era, time; **— media,** Middle Ages; **mayor de —,** of age; **ser menor de —,** to be a minor.

edecán, *m.* (mil.) aide-de-camp.

edema, *m.* edema.

Eden, *m.* Eden, paradise; delightful place.

edil, *m.* edile, a Roman magistrate.

edición, *f.* edition; published book, newspaper, magazine, etc.

edicto, *m.* edict.

edificación, *f.* construction; (fig.) good example.

edificar, *va.* to build; to fabricate; to construct a building; to set a good example.

edificativo, va, *adj.* edifying, exemplary, instructive.

edificio, *m.* building, structure.

Edimburgo, *m.* Edinburgh.

editor, ra, *n.* and *adj.* publisher; publishing; **casa —,** publishing house.

Edmundo, Edmund.

edredón, *m.* eiderdown; eiderdown quilt.

Eduardo, Edward.

educación, *f.* education; bringing up.

educado, da, *adj.* educated.

educador, ra, *n.* instructor, educator.

educando, da, *n.* pupil, scholar.

educar, *va.* to educate, to instruct, to train, to bring up (a child).

educativo, va, *adj.* educational.

educción, *f.* drawing forth, eduction, extraction.

educir, *va.* (EDUZCO, EDUJE) to educe, to extract, to bring out.

EE. UU. or **E.U. Estados Unidos,** U.S. United States.

efectista, *adj.* sensational, theatrical.

efectivamente, *adv.* effectually, powerfully; really.

efectividad, *f.* effectiveness; reality.

efectivo, va, *adj.* effective, true, certain; **—,** *m.* cash, specie; **— en caja,** cash on hand; **hacer —vo,** to cash; **valor —vo,** real value.

efecto, *m.* effect, consequence, purpose; **—s,** *pl* merchandise, wares, goods, belongings; **—s a cobrar** or **recibir,** bills receivable; **—s a pagar,** bills payable; **—s comerciales** or **de comercio,** commercial papers; **—s de escritorio,** stationery; **—s públicos,** public securities; **en —to,** in fact, in truth.

efectuación, *f.* accomplishment.

efectuar, *va.* to effect, to effectuate, to accomplish; **— un pago,** to make a payment.

efemérides, *f. pl.* notable events falling on a given day of any year.

efémero, *m.* (bot.) iris.

eferente, *adj.* efferent.

efervescencia, *f.* effervescence, ebullition; zeal, ardor, enthusiasm.

eficacia, *f.* efficacy.

eficaz, *adj.* efficacious, effective.

eficiente, *adj.* efficient, effective.

efigie, *f.* effigy, image.

efímero, ra, *adj.* ephemeral, passing.

eflorescente, *adj.* efflorescent.

efluvio, *m.* effluvium.

efugio, *m.* subterfuge.

efusión, *f.* effusion, gush.

Egeo, *m.* Aegean.

égida, *f.* protection, defense.

egipcio, cia, *n.* and *adj.* Egyptian.

Egipto, *m.* Egypt.

égloga, *f.* eclogue, pastoral poem.

egoísmo, *m.* selfishness, egoism.

egoísta, *adj.* egoistic, selfish, self-centered; **—,** *m.* and *f.* self-seeker.

egregio, gia, *adj.* egregious, eminent, remarkable.

egreso, *m.* debit, expense.

¡eh! *interj.* eh! here! ¿—? is that so? what?

Eje (el), *m.* the Axis (Germany, Italy, and Japan).

eje, *m.* axle tree, axle, axis, shaft; **— del timón,** (aer.) rudder post; **— de émbolo,**

(mech.) wrist pin; — **vertical,** (aer.) vertical axis.

ejecución, *f.* execution; carrying out, performance.

ejecutable, *adj.* performable.

ejecutante, *m.* and *f.* performer; (law) legal claimer of a debt.

ejecutar, *va.* to execute, to perform, to carry out; to put to death; (law) to distrain, to seize.

ejecutivo, va, *adj.* executive.

ejecutor, ra, *n.* executor; (law) distrainer.

ejecutoria, *f.* (law) writ of execution.

ejecutorial, *adj.* applied to the execution of the sentence of an ecclesiastical tribunal.

ejecutoriar, *va.* to obtain a verdict in one's favor; to make the truth of a thing evident.

ejecutorio, ria, *adj.* (law) executory.

ejemplar, *m.* exemplar; copy; sample; —, *adj.* exemplary.

ejemplificación, *f.* exemplification.

ejemplificar, *va.* to exemplify.

ejemplo, *m.* example; comparison; pattern, copy; **por —,** for instance.

ejercer, *va.* to exercise, to perform, to practice; **— la medicina,** to practice medicine.

ejercicio, *m.* exercise, practice; (mil.) drill; **— de tiro,** target practice.

ejercitación, *f.* exercise, practice.

ejercitar, *va.* to exercise, to put into practice; **—se,** to apply oneself to the functions of an office.

ejército, *m.* army.

ejido, *m.* common land; (Mex.) tract of land collectively owned by a legally organized group of peons.

el, *art. m.* the.

él, ella, ello, *pron.* he, she, it.

elaboración, *f.* elaboration, working out.

elaborado, da, *adj.* elaborate; manufactured.

elaborar, *va.* to elaborate; to manufacture.

elasticidad, *f.* elasticity; resilience.

elástico, ca, *adj.* elastic.

elche, *m.* renegade, apostate.

eléboro, *m.* (bot.) hellebore.

elección, *f.* election; discernment, choice.

electivo, va, *adj.* elective.

electo, ta, *adj.* elect; **presidente —,** president elect; **—,** *n.* person chosen or elected.

elector, *m.* elector.

electorado, *m.* electorate.

electoral, *adj.* electoral.

electricidad, *f.* electricity.

electricista, *m.* electrician.

eléctrico, ca, *adj.* electric, electrical.

electrificación, *f.* electrification.

electrización, *f.* electrification.

electrizar, *va.* to electrify.

electro, *m.* electrum.

electrocución, *f.* electrocution.

electrodinámica, *f.* electrodynamics.

electrodo, *m.* electrode.

electrofisiología, *f.* electrophysiology.

electrogalvanización, *f.* electroplating.

electroimán, *m.* electromagnet.

electrólisis, *f.* electrolysis.

electrolítico, *adj.* electrolytic.

electrólito, *m.* electrolyte.

electrolización, *f.* electrolyzation.

electrolizar, *va.* to electrolyze.

electromagnetismo, *m.* electromagnetism.

electrometalurgia, *f.* electrometallurgy.

electrometría, *f.* electrometry.

electrómetro, *m.* electrometer.

electromotor, *m.* electric motor.

electromotriz, *adj.* electromotive.

electrón, *m.* electron.

electronegativo, va, *m.* and *adj.* electronegative.

electrónica, *f.* electronics.

electroplatear, *va.* to electroplate.

electropositivo, va, *adj.* electropositive; **—,** *m.* electropositive.

electropuntura, *f.* electropuncture.

electroquímica, *f.* electrochemistry.

electroscopio, *m.* electroscope.

electrostática, *f.* electrostatics.

electrotecnia, *f.* electrotechnics, electrical engineering.

electroterapia, *f.* electrotherapy.

electrotipia, *f.* electrotyping.

electrotipo, *m.* electrotype.

elefante, *m.* elephant.

elefantino, na, *adj.* elephantine.

elegancia, *f.* elegance.

elegante, *adj.* elegant, fine.

elegía, *f.* elegy.

elegíaco, ca, *adj.* elegiac, mournful.

elegible, *adj.* eligible.

elegir, *va.* (LIJO) to choose, to elect.

elemental, *adj.* elemental, elementary.

elemento, *m.* element; ingredient; **—s,** *pl.* elements, rudiments, first principles.

Elena, Ellen, Helen.

elenco, *m.* catalogue, list, table, index; **— artístico,** cast (of a play).

elevación, *f.* elevation; highness; exaltation, dignity; ecstasy; rapture; haughtiness, pride, height; (aer.) altitude.

elevado, da, *adj.* elevated, lofty, high.

elevador, *m.* elevator, hoist.

elevar, *va.* to raise; to elevate; to heave; **—se,** to be enraptured; to be puffed up, to be conceited; to rise.

elidir, *va.* to weaken; (gram.) to elide.

eliminación, *f.* elimination.

eliminar, *va.* to eliminate.

elipse, *f.* (math.) ellipse.

elipsis, *f.* (gram.) ellipsis.

Elisa, Eliza.

Elíseos or **Elisios Campos,** *m. pl.* Elysian fields.

elisión, *f.* elision.

élitro, *m.* wing case (of insects).

elixir or **elíxir,** *m.* elixir.

elocución, *f.* elocution; effective diction.

elocuencia, *f.* eloquence.

elocuente, *adj.* eloquent.
elogiador, ra, *n.* eulogist, praiser.
elogiar, *va.* to praise, to eulogize.
elogio, *m.* eulogy, praise, compliment.
elucidación, *f.* elucidation, explanation.
eludir, *va.* to elude, to escape by stratagem.
ella, *pron.* she.
ello, *neut. pron.* it, that.
ellos, ellas, *pron. pl.* they (*masc.* and *fem.*)
E. M. Estado Mayor, (mil.) staff.
Em.ª Eminencia, Eminence.
Ema, Emma.
emaciación, *f.* emaciation.
emanación, *f.* emanation, waft.
emanar, *vn.* to emanate.
emancipación, *f.* emancipation; enfranchisement.
emancipar, *va.* to emancipate, to set free.
embadurnar, *va.* to smear, to bedaub.
embajada, *f.* embassy.
embajador, *m.* ambassador.
embalaje, *m.* packing, package.
embalar, *va.* to bale, to pack in bales.
embaldosado, *m.* tile floor.
embaldosar, *va.* to pave with tiles or flags.
embalsadero, *m.* pool of stagnant rain water.
embalsamador, *m.* embalmer.
embalsamar, *va.* to embalm; to perfume.
embalsar, *va.* to place on a raft; to impound (for irrigation purposes).
emballestarse, *vr.* to be on the point of discharging a crossbow.
embanastar, *va.* to put into a basket.
embanderar, *va.* to ornament with flags.
embarazado, da, *adj.* pregnant; **mujer —da,** pregnant woman.
embarazar, *va.* to embarrass; to make pregnant; **—se,** to become pregnant; to find oneself impeded by an obstacle.
embarazo, *m.* embarrassment; obstacle; pregnancy.
embarazoso, sa, *adj.* difficult, intricate, entangled.
embarbecer, *vn.* (EZCO) to appear, to begin to show (of one's beard); to be getting a beard.
embarcación, *f.* embarkation; navigation; any vessel or ship.
embarcadero, *m.* quay, wharf; port; harbor.
embarcar, *va.* to embark, to ship; **—se,** to go on shipboard, to embark; (fig.) to engage in any affair.
embargar, *va.* to lay on an embargo; to impede, to restrain.
embargo, *m.* embargo on shipping, sequestration; **sin —,** however, nevertheless.
embarnizador, *m.* varnisher.
embarnizadura, *f.* varnishing.
embarnizar, *va.* to varnish.
embarque, *m.* embarkation, shipment, shipping.
embarrador, *m.* plasterer; dauber.
embarradura, *f.* plastering (of walls, etc.), laying on of mortar.

embarrancar, *vn.* and *vr.* (naut.) to run aground; to get stuck in the mud.
embarrar, *va.* to coat with plaster; to bedaub; **—se,** to take to the trees (of frightened birds, etc.); to be smeared (with a viscous substance).
embarrilar, *va.* to pack in barrels.
embarullador, ra, *n.* bungler.
embarullar, *vt.* to bungle, to muddle.
embasamiento, *m.* (arch.) foundation (of a building).
embastar, *va.* to baste, to sew roughly.
embate, *m.* breakers, surf, surge; impetuous attack.
embaucador, *m.* sharper, impostor.
embaucamiento, *m.* deception, illusion.
embaucar, *va.* to deceive, to impose upon, to trick.
embaular, *va.* to pack up in a trunk; to cram, to fill with food beyond satiety.
embazar, *va.* to tinge, to shade; (fig.) to astonish; to impede, to stop, to check; **—,** *vn.* to be amazed; **—se,** to become tired; to be bored.
embebecer, *va.* (EZCO) to astonish, to stupefy, to amuse; **—se,** to be struck with amazement.
embebecimiento, *m.* amazement, astonishment.
embeber, *va.* to imbibe; to soak; to encase, to include; to squeeze, to press; **—,** *vn.* to shrink; **—se,** to be enraptured, to be absorbed; to retain firmly in the mind.
embelecar, *va.* to impose upon, to deceive.
embeleco, *m.* fraud, delusion, imposition.
embelesamiento, *m.* rapture.
embelesar, *va.* and *vr.* to amaze, to astonish; to charm.
embeleso, *m.* rapture, bliss, amazement, ravishment.
embellecer, *va.* (EZCO) to embellish, to beautify, to adorn.
embellecimiento, *m.* beautification, embellishment.
emberrincharse, *vr.* to fly into a tantrum (of children).
embestida, *f.* charge by the bull; assault, violent attack.
embestir, *va.* (I) to assail, to attack.
embetunar, *va.* to cover with pitch or tar; to blacken.
emblandecer, *va.* (EZCO) to soften, to appease; **—se,** to be moved to pity, to condescend through compassion.
emblanquecer, *va.* (EZCO) to whiten; **—se,** to grow white.
emblema, *m.* emblem, symbol.
embobamiento, *m.* astonishment; stupefaction.
embobar, *va.* to amuse, to divert from, to distract; **—se,** to be in suspense, to stand gaping.
embobecer, *va.* (EZCO) to stultify, stupefy; **—se,** to become stupefied or stultified.
embobecimiento, *m.* stupefaction.

embocadero, *m.* mouth of a channel or of a river.

embocadura, *f.* mouth piece; mouth of a river.

embocar, *va.* to put into one's mouth; to put one's mouth to; to swallow in haste; to enter by a pass; (fig.) to take hold of, to seize upon; to deceive.

embochinchar, *vn.* to provoke a riot, to instigate an uproar.

embodegar, *va.* to warehouse, to store.

embojo, *m.* shed for silkworms.

embolar, *va.* to put balls on the ends of bull's horns; to shine or polish shoes.

embolia, *f.* (med.) embolism.

embolismador, ra, *n.* detracter, reviler.

embolismar, *va.* and *vn.* (coll.) to propagate malicious rumors.

embolismo, *m.* embolism; imbroglio; confusion.

émbolo, *m.* (mech.) wrist pin; embolus, sucker or plunger of a pump; piston; **— vertical,** (aer.) vertical axis; **anillo de empaquetadura del —,** piston ring; **vástago del —,** piston rod.

embolsar, *va.* to put (money) into a purse.

embolso, *m.* putting (of money) into a purse.

embonar, *va.* to repair, to improve; (naut.) to sheathe.

emboque, *m.* passage of a ball through a ring, etc. (in games).

emborrachar, *va.* and *vr.* to intoxicate, to inebriate.

emborrar, *va.* to stuff, to wad; to comb the wool a second time; (coll.) to swallow food hastily, to cram (food).

emborrascar, *va.* to provoke, to enrage.

emborricarse, *vr.* to be stupefied; (coll.) to fall madly in love.

emborrizar, *va.* to give the first combing to wool.

emborronar, *va.* to blot, to get (a paper) spotted; to scribble, to write hastily.

emboscada, *f.* ambuscade; (mil.) ambush.

emboscar, *va.* (mil.) to post in ambush; **—se,** to retire into the thickest part of a forest; (mil.) to lie in ambush.

embotadura, *f.* bluntness (applied to weapons).

embotar, *va.* to blunt; (fig.) to enervate, to debilitate.

embotellamiento, *m.* bottling.

embotellar, *va.* to bottle.

embotijar, *va.* to lay a stratum of small earthen jars before the flooring is put down; to keep out the damp; to put into bottles; **—se,** to swell; to be in a rage.

embozado, da, *adj.* with face covered; involved.

embozar, *va.* to muffle the greater part of the face; (fig.) to cloak, to dissemble.

embozo, *m.* part of a cloak, veil or any other thing with which the face is muffled; muffling of one's face; upper fold in bed-

clothing; (fig.) artfulness in expression or action.

embragar, *va.* to throw in the clutch; (naut.) to sling.

embrague, *m.* clutch, coupling.

embravecer, *va.* and *vr.* (EZCO) to enrage, to irritate; **—,** *vn.* to grow strong and healthy (of plants).

embravecimiento, *m.* fury, rage.

embrazar, *va.* to clasp a shield.

embreadura, *f.* pitching or tarring of a ship.

embrear, *va.* to pitch a ship.

embriagante, *adj.* intoxicating.

embriagar, *va.* and *vr.* to intoxicate, to inebriate; to transport, to enrapture.

embriaguez, *f.* intoxication, drunkenness; rapture, transport of mind.

embridar, *va.* to bridle; to rule, to restrain.

embriología, *f.* embryology.

embrión, *m.* embryo.

embrionario, ria, *adj.* embryonic, embryonal.

embrocar, *va.* to pour out of one vessel into another, to decant.

embrollado, da, *adj.* tangled, confused.

embrollador, ra, *n.* entangler, confounder.

embrollar, *va.* to entangle, to embroil.

embrollo, *m.* tangle, trickery; embroiling.

embrollón, ona, *n.* talebearer, impostor; entangler.

embromado, da, *adj.* vexed, annoyed; (naut.) misty, hazy, foggy.

embromar, *va.* to cajole, to wheedle; to vex, to annoy; to banter.

embrujar, *va.* to bewitch.

embrutecer, *va.* (EZCO) to make stupid; to make irrational.

embuchado, *m.* large sausage made of pork, minced very small.

embuchar, *va.* to cram the maw of animals; to swallow food without chewing it.

embudar, *va.* to put through a funnel; to snare.

embudo, *m.* funnel; fraud, artifice.

embuste, *m.* lie; fraud, imposition; **—s,** *pl.* gewgaws, trinkets.

embustero, ra, *n.* impostor, cheat, liar.

embutido, da, *adj.* inlaid; stuffed; **—,** *m.* inlaid work; **fábrica de —s,** sausage factory.

embutir, *va.* to inlay; to incase one thing in another; to enchase; to mix confusedly; to cram, to eat too much.

emergencia, *f.* emergency; emergence; **campo de —,** (aer.) emergency landing field.

emérito, *adj.* emeritus.

emersión, *f.* emersion.

emético, ca, *adj.* emetic.

E. M. G. Estado Mayor General, (mil.) general staff.

emigración, *f.* emigration, migration.

emigrado, da, *adj.* and *n.* emigrated; emigrant.

emigrante, *m.* and *f.* emigrant.

emigrar, *vn.* to emigrate.

Emilia, Emily.

eminencia, *f.* eminence; height, hill.

eminente, *adj.* eminent, high; excellent, conspicuous.

emisario, *m.* emissary.

emisora, *f.* broadcasting station.

emitir, *va.* to emit, to send forth; to let go, to let fly.

Em.^{mo} or **Emmo. Eminentísimo,** most Eminent.

emoción, *f.* emotion.

emocionalismo, *m.* emotionalism.

emocionar, *va.* and *vr.* to touch, to move, to arouse emotion.

emoliente, *adj.* emollient, softening.

emolumento, *m.* emolument, fee, profit, advantage.

empachar, *va.* to impede, to embarrass; to cram, to surfeit; **—se,** to be ashamed, to be confounded.

empacho, *m.* indigestion; overloading; bashfulness, timidity; embarrassment; **sin —,** without ceremony; unconcernedly.

empachoso, sa, *adj.* embarrassing; bashful, timid.

empadronamiento, *m.* list of taxable persons.

empadronar, *va.* to enter on a list the names of those who are liable to pay certain taxes.

empajar, *va.* to thatch (a roof); to fill or cover with straw.

empalagamiento, *m.* surfeiting, surfeit, cloying.

empalagar, *va.* to mush; to loathe; to disgust; to trouble.

empalago, *m.* disgust, nausea.

empalagoso, sa, *adj.* mushy, cloying; wearisome.

empalar, *va.* to impale.

empalizada, *f.* (mil.) palisade.

empalizar, *va.* to enclose in a palisade.

empalmadura, *f.* joining of two pieces of wood; welding of metals.

empalmar, *va.* to join the ends of two pieces of timber.

empalme, *m.* (rail.) junction.

empanada, *f.* meat pie.

empanado, da, *adj.* breaded.

empanar, *va.* to cover with paste; to bread.

empandar, *va.* and *vr.* to bend in the middle, to sag.

empantanar, *va.* to submerge; to drag in the mud; to complicate a matter.

empañadura, *f.* swaddling of children; tarnishing.

empañar, *va.* to dim, to blemish; to swathe; to tarnish a glass with one's breath; to impeach one's reputation; **—se,** to grow dull; to become tarnished.

empañetar, *va.* (Sp. Am.) to plaster (walls, etc.).

empañicar, *va.* to hand or furl (a sail).

empanizado, da, *adj.* breaded.

empapar, *va.* to imbibe; to saturate, to soak, to drench; **—se,** to imbibe; to be soaked; to go deeply into a matter.

empapelador, ra, *n.* paperhanger.

empapelar, *va.* to wrap up in paper; to paper.

empaque, *m.* packing.

empaquetador, ra, *n.* packer.

empaquetadora, *f.* baling machine.

empaquetadura, *f.* packing.

empaquetar, *va.* to pack, to put in packages.

emparamentar, *va.* to bedeck (with hangings, etc.).

emparchar, *va.* to patch; to fill with plaster.

emparedado, *m.* sandwich; **—, da,** *adj.* shut up between walls.

emparedamiento, *m.* confinement; cloister.

emparedar, *va.* to confine, to immure.

emparejadura, *f.* equalization.

emparejar, *va.* to level; to match, to fit; to equalize.

emparentar, *vn.* (IE) to be related by marriage.

emparrado, *m.* vine arbor.

emparrar, *va.* to embower.

emparvar, *va.* to put grain in heaps for threshing.

empastadura, *f.* filling (of tooth).

empastar, *va.* to paste; to cover plentifully with colors; to fill (a tooth); to bind (books) with a stiff cover.

empatadera, *f.* (coll.) checking, suspension (as of a game, due to a tie, etc.).

empatar, *va.* to equal; to be a tie (in voting); to check, to obstruct.

empate, *m.* equality of votes, tie; stop, suspension.

empavesar, *va.* to deck out with flags; (naut.) to dress a ship.

empecatado, da, *adj.* turbulent; incorrigible, wicked; unlucky.

empecer, *va.* (EZCO) to harm, hurt; **—,** *vn.* to prevent.

empecimiento, *m.* injury, damage; obstacle.

empedernir, *va. def.* to harden; **—se,** to be petrified, to be inflexible.

empedrado, *m.* pavement.

empedrador, *m.* paver.

empedrar, *va.* (IE) to pave with stones.

empega, *f.* varnish of pitch; mark of pitch.

empegado, *m.* tarpaulin.

empegadura, *f.* varnish of pitch put on vessels.

empegar, *va.* to coat with pitch.

empeine, *m.* groin; instep; hoof of an animal.

empelar, *vn.* to grow hair.

empelotarse, *vr.* to get mixed up in a quarrel; to get lumpy (as cake batter).

empella, *f.* shoe vamp.

empellar, *va.* to jostle, to push.

empellejar, *va.* to cover with skins.

empellón, *m.* push, heavy blow; **a —ones,** rudely, by dint of blows.

empenachar, *va.* to adorn with plumes.

empeñar, *va.* to pawn, to pledge; to engage, to oblige; **—se,** to bind oneself to pay debts contracted; to persist in a resolution; to intercede.

empeño, *m.* obligation; engagement; courage; perseverance; protection; pawn.

empeoramiento, *m.* decline, deterioration.

empeorar, *va.* to make worse; **—,** *vn.* to grow worse.

empequeñecer, *va.* (EZCO) belittle, to minimize.

emperador, *m.* emperor.

emperatriz, *f.* empress.

emperejilar, *va.* to adorn profusely.

emperezar, *vn.* and *vr.* to be lazy or indolent.

empergaminar, *va.* to bind in parchment.

emperifollarse, *vr.* to overdress oneself.

empernar, *va.* to nail, to peg.

empero, *conj.* yet, however.

emperrarse, *vr.* (coll.) to be obstinate (about); to persist in.

empezar, *va.* (IE) to begin, to commence.

empicarse, *vr.* to be infatuated to excess, to become exceedingly fond (of).

empinado, da, *adj.* elevated, exalted, raised to a high dignity; steep.

empinadura, *f.* elevation, raising.

empinar, *va.* to raise, to lift; to exalt; to drink much; **—se,** to stand on tiptoe; to rise high.

empiolar, *va.* to tie the legs of hawks with jesses; to seize; to kill.

empíreo, *m.* empyrean (the highest heaven); **—, rea,** *adj.* celestial.

empírico, *m.* quack, empiric; **—, ca,** empirical.

empirismo, *m.* empiricism; quackery.

empizarrado, *m.* slate roofing.

empizarrar, *va.* to slate, to roof with slate.

emplastadura, *f.* plastering; application of cosmetics.

emplastar, *va* to apply plasters; to paint the face; to check the course of an affair; **—se,** to bedaub one's hands or feet.

emplastecer, *va.* (EZCO) (art) to smooth a rough area for painting.

emplasto, *m.* plaster.

emplástico, ca, *adj.* gluey, sticky like glue.

emplazador, *m.* (law) summoner.

emplazamiento, *m.* emplacement; site, location; (law) summons; citation.

emplazar, *va.* to summon.

empleado, da, *n.* employee, clerk.

emplear, *va.* to employ, to hire; to occupy; to use.

empleo, *m.* employ, employment, occupation.

emplomador, *m.* one who covers with lead.

emplomar, *va.* to lead; to line with sheet lead.

emplumar, *va.* to adorn with feathers; **—se,** to get feathers.

emplumecer, *vn.* (EZCO) to begin to get feathers.

empobrecer, *va.* (EZCO) to reduce to poverty; **—,** *vn.* to become poor.

empobrecimiento, *m.* impoverishing.

empolvado, da, *adj.* powdered; dusty.

empolvar, *va.* to powder, to sprinkle powder; **—se,** to become dusty.

empolladura, *f.* brood, hatch, covey (of birds); brood (of bees).

empollar, *va.* to brood, to hatch.

emponzoñador, ra, *n.* poisoner.

emponzoñamiento, *m.* poisoning.

emponzoñar, *va.* to poison; to taint; to corrupt.

emporcar, *va.* (UE) to soil, to dirty.

emporio, *m.* emporium.

empotrar, *va.* to embed in a wall or floor; to put (beehives) in a pit; to scarf, to splice.

empozar, *vn.* to form into puddles (water).

emprendedor, *m.* enterpriser; **—, ra,** *adj.* enterprising.

emprender, *va.* to enterprise, to undertake.

empreñar, *va.* to impregnate; **—se,** to beget.

empresa, *f.* enterprise, undertaking; symbol, motto; design, purpose.

empresario, *m.* impresario, contractor, manager.

empréstito, *m.* loan.

emprimar, *va.* to give (wool) a second combing; (coll.) to deceive, to take undue advantage of someone.

empringar, *va.* to grease.

empujar, *va.* to push, to shove, to press forward.

empuje, *m.* impulsion, impulse, pushing.

empujón, *m.* impulse, push; **a —ones,** pushingly, rudely.

empuñadura, *f.* hilt of a sword.

empuñar, *va.* to clinch, to clutch, to grip with the fist.

emulación, *f.* emulation, rivalry.

emular, *va.* to emulate, to rival.

émulo, la, *n.* competitor, rival.

emulsión, *f.* emulsion.

emulsionar, *va.* to emulsify.

emunción, *f.* (med.) excretion, exudation.

en, *prep.* in; for; on, upon; **— adelante,** in the future; **— cuanto,** as soon as; **— cuanto a,** as to; in regard to.

enaceitarse, *vr.* to become oily or rancid.

enagua, *f.*, **enaguas**, *pl.* underskirt, skirt, petticoat.

enaguachar, *va.* to overload with water; **—se,** to feel overstuffed with drink or fruit.

enajenable, *adj.* that can be alienated.

enajenación, *f.* alienation; absent-mindedness; inattention.

enajenamiento, *m.* change of affection; rapture, astonishment.

enajenar, *va.* to alienate; to rapture; **—se,** to fall out.

enalbardar, *va.* to lay a packsaddle on beasts of burden; to cover with a batter of eggs, flour, and sugar.

enaltecer, *va.* and *vr.* (EZCO) to praise, to exalt.

enamoradamente, *adv.* lovingly.

enamoradizo, za, *adj.* inclined to love.

enamorado, da, *adj.* in love, enamored, lovesick.

enamorador, *m.* lover, wooer.

enamoramiento, *m.* state of being in love; courtship.

enamorar, *va.* to inspire love; to woo; —se, to fall in love.

enamoricarse, *vr.* to be slightly in love.

enano, na, *adj.* dwarfish; —, *n.* dwarf, midget.

enantes, *adv.* (coll.) a little while ago.

enarbolar, *va.* to hoist, to raise high; —se, to become angry.

enarcar, *va.* to arch; to hoop (barrels); —se, to shrink, to become smaller.

enardecer, *va.* (EZCO) to fire with anger or excitement; to inflame.

enarenar, *va.* to fill with sand.

enastar, *va.* to put a handle to.

encabalgar, *va.* to provide horses; to rest or support one thing on another.

encabellecerse, *vr.* (EZCO) to grow hair.

encabestrar, *va.* to guide by a halter; —se, to be entangled in the halter.

encabezamiento, *m.* headline; heading; list of persons liable to pay a tax; tax, tribute; — de factura, billhead.

encabezar, *va.* to make up a tax list; to put a heading to; —se, to compound for taxes.

encabritarse, *vr.* to rear (of horses).

encachar, *va.* to line with concrete.

encadenamiento, *m.* linking together, chaining.

encadenar, *va.* to chain, to link together; to connect, to unite.

encajador, *m.* enchasing tool; one who enchases.

encajadura, *f.* enchasing.

encajar, *va.* to enchase; to fit in; to push or force in; —se, to thrust oneself into some narrow place; (coll.) to put on an article of clothing; to get into a place where one is not wanted.

encaje, *m.* chasing, inlaid work; lace; joining or fitting together; socket, groove; — de aguja, point lace; — de hilo, tatting.

encajera, *f.* lacewoman.

encajetillar, *va.* to put (cigarettes, tobacco) into packages.

encajonado, *m.* mudwall supported by pillars of bricks.

encajonamiento, *m.* packing into boxes, etc.

encajonar, *va.* to pack up in a box, to lay in a chest.

encalabrinar, *va.* to affect the head with some disturbing fume or vapor; to irritate or excite (one's nerves); —se, (coll.) to become obstinate.

encaladura, *f.* whitening, whitewash.

encalar, *va.* to whitewash.

encalvecer, *vn.* (EZCO) to lose one's hair.

encallar, *vn.* (naut.) to run aground; to be checked in the progress of some enterprise.

encallecer, *vn.* (EZCO) to get corns.

encamarar, *va.* to store (grain and fruit).

encamarse, *vr.* to lie in bed; to go to bed.

encaminar, *va.* to guide, to show the way; —se, to take a road, to be on the way.

encampanado, da, *adj.* bell-shaped; arrogant, exalted; (coll.) perched aloft; (coll.) left in the lurch.

encanalar or **encanalizar,** *va.* to convey through pipes or conduits.

encanallamiento, *m.* corruptness, degeneracy.

encanastar, *va.* to put in baskets.

encandecer, *va.* (EZCO) to heat to a white heat.

encandilar, *va.* to dazzle; to daze; to perplex; to become bloodshot (eyes).

encanecer, *vn.* (EZCO) to grow gray-haired; to grow old.

encanillar, *va.* to wind silk, wool or linen on a spool of cane.

encantador, ra, *adj.* charming, delightful, enchanting; —, *m.* enchanter, sorcerer, magician; —, *f.* sorceress, enchantress.

encantamiento, *m.* enchantment.

encantar, *va.* to enchant, to charm, to delight; to cast a spell.

encantarar, *va.* to put into a jar or a pitcher.

encante, *m.* public auction.

encanto, *m.* enchantment, spell, charm; delectation, delightfulness.

encanutar, *va.* to flute, to pleat.

encañado, *m.* conduit of water; hedge of canes or reeds.

encañar, *va.* to enclose with a hedge of cane; to convey water through conduits.

encañizada, *f.* fence made of cane and reeds for catching certain types of fish.

encañonar, *va.* and *vn.* to begin to fledge; to pleat, to fold; to put into pipes.

encapado, da, *adj.* cloaked.

encaperuzarse, *vr.* to cover one's head with a hood.

encapillar, *va.* (naut.) to rig (the yards); (min.) to start a new gallery; (coll.) to cover the head with a hood, etc.

encapotar, *va.* to cover with a cloak; —se, to be clouded; to look sullen.

encapricharse, *vr.* to become stubborn.

encapuchar, *va.* to cover anything with a hood.

encaramar, *va.* to raise; to extol; —se, climb.

encarar, *vn.* to face, to come face to face.

encarcelación, *f.* incarceration.

encarcelar, *va.* to imprison.

encarecer, *va.* and *vn.* (EZCO) to raise the price; (fig.) to enhance, to exaggerate; to recommend strongly.

encarecimiento, *m.* price raising; enhancement; earnest recommendation; exaggeration; **con —,** ardently.

encargar, *va.* to charge, to commission; **—se,** to take upon oneself; **—se de,** to take charge of, to see to it that.

encargo, *m.* charge, commission; order, request; responsibility; errand; office, employ.

encariñar, *va.* to inspire affection; **—se con,** to become fond of.

encarnación, *f.* incarnation; carnation, flesh color.

encarnado, da, *adj.* incarnate; red; dyed flesh color; **—,** *m.* flesh color.

encarnamiento, *m.* (med.) incarnation.

encarnar, *vn.* to incarnate, to embody; to form flesh; **—,** *va.* to give a flesh color to pieces of sculpture; to pierce the flesh; **—se,** to incorporate one thing with another.

encarnativo, *adj.* (med.) incarnative.

encarnizado, da, *adj.* fleshed; bloodshot, inflamed; irritated.

encarnizar, *va.* to satiate with flesh; to provoke, to irritate; **—se,** to be glutted with flesh; to be cruelly minded toward.

encarrilar or **encarrillar,** *va.* and *vr.* to place on the right track; to set right; to place a derailed vehicle on the rails.

encarrujarse, *va.* and *vr.* to twist, to coil; to kink.

encartamiento, *m.* outlawry, proscription.

encartar, *va.* to proscribe; to enter in the tax list; **—se,** to receive a card which spoils a game.

encarte, *m.* cards laid out (in a game).

encartonar, *va.* to bind in boards.

encascabelado, da, *adj.* decked with bells.

encasillado, *m.* set of pigeonholes.

encasillar, *va.* to put in pigeonholes; to assign, to distribute.

encasquetar, *va.* to cram a hat on one's head; (fig.) to induce one to adopt an opinion; **—se,** to be headstrong.

encastar, *va.* to improve a race of animals; to procreate, to generate.

encastillar, *va.* to fortify with castles; **—,** *vn.* to make the cell of the queen bee; **—se,** to shut oneself up for defense in a castle; to be headstrong.

encastrar, *va.* (mech.) to groove, to gear, to imbed.

encastre, *m.* groove; socket.

encauchado, da, *adj.* rubber-sheathed; **—,** *m.* raincoat.

encausar, *va.* to indict, to prosecute.

encavarse, *vr.* to hide in a cave or a burrow.

encebadar, *va.* and *vr.* (vet.) to surfeit.

encebollado, *m.* fricassee of beef or mutton and onions, seasoned with spice.

encefalitis, *f.* inflammation of the brain; **— letárgica,** sleeping sickness.

encelamiento, *m.* jealousy.

encellar, *va.* to mold curds or cheese in a basket.

encenagado, da, *adj.* mixed with mud.

encenagamiento, *m.* wallowing in dirt or in vice.

encenagarse, *vr.* to wallow in dirt or mire; (fig.) to wallow in vice.

encendedor, *m.* lighter; **— de cigarrillos,** cigarette lighter.

encender, *va.* (IE) to kindle, to light, to set on fire; to inflame, to incite; **—se,** to fire, to take fire; to fly into a rage.

encendido, da, *adj.* inflamed, high-colored; **—,** *m.* ignition; **—do prematuro,** backfiring.

encendimiento, *m.* inflammation; glow; firing, ignition.

encenizar, *va.* to cover with ashes.

encepador, *m.* stocker (of a gun).

encerado, da, *adj.* like wax, waxed; **—,** *m.* oilcloth; window blind; adhesive tape; blackboard; tarpaulin.

encerar, *va.* to wax; to fill or stiffen with wax.

encerotar, *va.* to wax thread.

encerradura, *f.,* **encerramiento,** *m.* act of locking up; isolation; imprisonment.

encerrar, *va.* (IE) to shut up, to confine; to contain; **—se,** to go into seclusion, to withdraw, to go behind closed doors.

encespedar, *va.* to turf.

encía, *f.* gum (of the teeth).

encíclica, *f.* encyclical epistle.

enciclopedia, *f.* encyclopedia.

enciclopédico, ca, *adj.* encyclopedic.

encierro, *m.* confinement, enclosure; cloister; prison; driving bulls into the pen.

encima, *adv.* above, over; at the top; over and above, besides.

encina, *f.* evergreen oak.

encinar, *m.* evergreen oak forest or grove.

encinta, *adj.* pregnant, in the family way.

enclaustrado, da, *adj.* shut up in cloisters.

enclavadura, *f.* groove; embedding.

enclavar, *va.* to nail.

enclavijar, *va.* to join closely; to put pegs in a musical instrument.

enclenque, *adj.* feeble, sickly; **—,** *m.* and *f.* weakling.

encobar, *vn.* and *vr.* to incubate.

encobrado, da, *adj.* mixed with copper; copper-colored.

encofrado, *m.* plank lining; **—os,** *pl.* sheeting, planking.

encoger, *va.* to contract, to shorten; to shrink; **—se,** to shrink; to be low spirited; to humble oneself.

encogidamente, *adv.* meanly, abjectly; bashfully.

encogido, da, *adj.* pusillanimous, timid, narrow-minded.

encogimiento, *m.* contraction; constriction; pusillanimity.

encojar, *va.* to cripple, to lame; **—se,** to grow lame; to feign sickness.

encoladura, *f.* gluing.

encolar, *va.* to glue.

encolerizar, *va.* and *vr.* to provoke, to irritate.

encomendar, *va.* (IE) to recommend; to instruct; —se, to commit oneself to another's protection.

encomiar, *va.* to praise.

encomiástico, ca, *adj.* complimentary, extolling.

encomienda, *m.* commission, charge; message; (mil.) commandery; patronage, protection; — **postal,** parcel post; —s, *pl.* compliments, regards.

encomio, *m.* encomium, praise, commendation.

enconar, *va.* to inflame, to irritate.

enconcharse, *vr.* (Sp. Am.) to isolate oneself from society; to get into one's shell, to keep aloof.

encono, *m.* malevolence, rancor, ill will.

enconoso, sa. *adj.* resentful; malevolent; irritating, inclined to bear ill-will toward others.

encontradizo, za, *adj.* that may be met on the way.

encontrado, da, *adj.* opposite, in front; opposed, contrary.

encontrar, *va.* and *vn.* (UE) to meet, to find, to encounter; to assemble, to come together; —se, to encounter in an hostile manner, to clash; to be of contrary opinions; —se con, to meet, to come upon, to find out.

encontrón, *m.* encounter, clash, collision.

encopetado, da, *adj.* presumptuous, boastful.

encorajar, *va.* to give courage, to inflame; —se, to be in a rage.

encorar, *va.* (UE) to cover with leather; —, *vn.* to heal, to grow new skin (over a wound).

encorchar, *va.* to hive bees; to provide with a cork.

encordar, *va.* (UE) to chord musical instruments.

encordelar, *va.* to tie with cords.

encorralar, *va.* to corral (cattle).

encorsetar, *va.* and *vr.* to put a corset on, especially a tight one.

encortinar, *va.* to provide (a room, etc.) with curtains.

encorvadura, *f.* act of bending; crookedness.

encorvar, *va.* to bend, to crook.

encostrar, *va.* to crust, to incrust; to rough cast; —se, to develop a scab.

encrespar, *va.* to curl, to frizzle; —se, to become rough (as the sea); to be enraged; to become complicated (as a discussion).

encrestado, da, *adj.* (fig.) haughty, lofty.

encrestarse, *vr.* to stiffen the crest (applied to a young cock).

encrucijada, *f.* crossroad; street intersection.

encrudecer, *va.* (EZCO) to make a wound worse; to exasperate, to irritate.

encrudecimiento, *m.* recrudescence.

encuadernación, *f.* binding books, bindery; — **de cartón,** cardboard binding; — **en tela,** cloth binding.

encuadernador, *m.* book binder.

encuadernar, *va.* to bind books.

encuadrar, *va.* to frame; to fit one thing into another.

encubar, *va.* to put liquids into casks.

encubiertamente, *adv.* secretly; deceitfully.

encubierto, ta, *adj.* hidden, concealed.

encubridor, ra, *n.* concealer, harborer; receiver of stolen goods.

encubrimiento, *m.* concealment, hiding.

encubrir, *va.* to hide, to conceal.

encuentro, *m.* shock, jostle; encounter, meeting, match.

encuitarse, *vr.* to grieve, to become despondent.

encumbrado, da, *adj.* high, elevated.

encumbramiento, *m.* elevation; height.

encumbrar, *va.* to raise, to elevate; to mount, to ascend a height; —se, to be raised.

encunar, *va.* to put in a cradle.

encurtido, *m.* pickle.

encurtir, *va.* to pickle.

enchapar, *va.* to veneer, to plate.

encharcarse, *vr.* to fall into the mire; (fig.) to fall into a difficult situation.

enchilada, *f.* (Mex.) kind of pancake stuffed with various foods and chili.

enchufar, *va.* to telescope.

enchufe, *m.* socket joint.

endeble, *adj.* feeble, weak.

endecasílabo, ba, *adj.* consisting of eleven syllables.

endecha, *f.* dirge, doleful ditty.

endechar, *va.* to sing funeral songs in honor and praise of the dead; —se, to grieve, to mourn.

endemoniado, da, *adj.* possessed with the devil; devilish.

endemoniar, *va.* to possess with the devil; to irritate, to provoke.

endentecer, *vn.* (EZCO) to cut teeth.

enderezadamente, *adv.* rightly; directly.

enderezamiento, *m.* straightening.

enderezar, *va.* to rectify; to straighten; —se, to stand upright.

endeudarse, *ve.* to contract debts; to feel indebted.

endiablada, *f.* mummery.

endiablado, da, *adj.* devilish, diabolical.

endibia, *f.* (bot.) endive.

endilgar, *va.* (coll.) to lead, to direct, to facilitate; to thrust something unpleasant (on someone).

endiosar, *va.* to deify; —se, to be puffed up with pride.

endocarditis, *f.* (med.) endocarditis.

endorso, *m.* endorsement.

endosante, *m.* indorser.

endosar, *va.* to indorse a bill of exchange.

endosatario, ria, *n.* indorsee.

endoso, *m.* indorsement of a bill of exchange.

endrina, *f.* (bot.) sloe.

endrino, *m.* sloe tree.

endrogarse, *vr.* to get into debt.

endulzar, *va.* to sweeten; to soften.

endurecer, *va.* (EZCO) to harden, to indurate; **—se,** to become cruel, to grow hard.

endurecidamente, *adv.* pertinaciously.

endurecido, da, *adj.* inured.

endurecimiento, *m.* hardening; obstinacy; hardness of heart.

ENE estenordeste, ENE or E.N.E. east-northeast.

enebro, *m.* (bot.) common juniper.

eneldo, *m.* (bot.) dill.

enema, *f.* enema.

enemigo, ga, *adj.* inimical, hostile, opposed; **—,** *n.* enemy.

enemistad, *f.* enmity, hatred.

enemistar, *va.* to make an enemy; **—,** *vn.* to become an enemy.

energía, *f.* energy, power, vigor; strength of will; **— vatimétrica,** (elec.) wattage.

enérgico, ca, *adj.* energetic; expressive.

energúmeno, na, *n.* demoniac, one possessed.

enero, *m.* January.

enervación, *f.* enervation.

enervar, *va.* to enervate.

enfadadizo, za, *adj.* irritable, irascible.

enfadado, da, *adj.* angry, irate; disgusted.

enfadar, *va.* and *vr.* to vex, to molest, to trouble; to become angry.

enfado, *m.* trouble, vexation, anger.

enfadoso, sa, *adj.* vexatious, troublesome.

enfaldar, *va.* to lop off the lower branches of trees; **—se,** to tuck up one's clothes.

enfardar, *va.* to pack, to bale goods.

enfardelar, *va.* to make up into bales.

énfasis, *m.* emphasis.

enfático, ca, *adj.* emphatic.

enfermar, *vn.* to fall ill; **—,** *va.* to make sick; to weaken.

enfermedad, *f.* indisposition, illness, disease.

enfermería, *f.* infirmary.

enfermero, ra, *n.* nurse; hospital attendant.

enfermizo, za, *adj.* infirm, sickly.

enfermo, ma, *adj.* sick, diseased, indisposed; **—,** *n.* sick person, patient; **ponerse —,** to get sick.

enfeudar, *va.* to invest with a fief, to accept as a vassal.

enfiestarse, *vr.* (Sp. Am.) to be on a lark, to enjoy oneself.

enfilar, *va.* to put in a row; (mil.) to put in closed ranks; to enfilade.

enflaquecer, *va.* (EZCO) to weaken, to make thin; **—se,** to lose weight.

enflaquecimiento, *m.* loss of weight; extenuation, maceration, enervation.

enfocar, *va.* to focus.

enfoque, *m.* focus.

enfoscado, da, *adj.* ill-humored; deeply engrossed in a business; cloudy.

enfoscarse, *vr.* to be perplexed or ill-humored; to be immersed in business; to be cloudy.

enfrailar, *va.* to make one a monk; **—se,** to become a monk.

enfranquecer, *va.* (EZCO) to exempt, to free.

enfrascar, *va.* to pour liquid into a flask; **—se,** to be entangled in brambles; to be involved in difficulties.

enfrenar, *va.* to bridle; to curb, to restrain.

enfrentar, *va.* to encounter, to confront, to face.

enfrente, *adv.* opposite, in front.

enfriadera, *f.* cooler, refrigerator.

enfriador, *m.* cooler, cold storage, refrigerator.

enfriamiento, *m.* refrigeration; cold, chill; **— por aire,** air-cooling.

enfriar, *va.* to cool, to refrigerate; **—se,** to cool down.

enfundar, *va.* to put into its case (as a pillow); to stuff, to fill.

enfurecer, *va.* (EZCO) to irritate, to enrage; **—se,** to grow boisterous or furious (of the wind and sea); to become furious or enraged.

enfurruñarse, *vr.* to grow angry, to frown.

engalanar, *va.* to adorn, to deck.

engallado, da, *adj.* erect, upright.

engalladura, *f.* tread, the germinating point in eggs of birds and reptiles.

engallarse, *vr.* to draw oneself up proudly.

enganchador, ra, *adj.* hitching, connecting; **—,** *m.* (mil.) recruiter.

enganchar, *va.* to hook, to snatch; to hitch, to connect; to ensnare; to decoy into the military service.

engañabobos, *m.* impostor; trickster.

engañadizo, za, *adj.* deceivable, easily deceived.

engañador, ra, *n.* cheat, impostor, deceiver; **—,** *adj.* deceiving; cheating.

engañar, *va.* to deceive, to cheat; **—se,** to be deceived; to make a mistake.

engaño, *m.* mistake, misunderstanding, deceit, fraud.

engañoso, sa, *adj.* deceitful, artful, false.

engarabatar, *va.* to hook; **—se,** to become shaped as a hook.

engarabitarse, *vr.* to climb, to mount; to cramp up (as the toes when they are cold).

engarce, *m.* linking, connection; hook.

engaritar, *va.* to place sentry boxes; to deceive cleverly.

engarrotar, *va.* to garrote; **—,** *va.* and *vr.* to stiffen (with cold).

engarzar, *va.* to chain, to link; to curl.

engastar, *va.* to enchase, to set a precious stone.

engaste, *m.* enchasing, setting.

engatar, va. (coll.) to cheat cleverly.
engatillar, va. to bind with a cramp iron.
engatusamiento, m. deception, cheating, coaxing.
engatusar, va. to wheedle, to coax.
engazar, va. to chain, to link; to splice an end of a rope in a circular form about a block; to dye cloth in the piece.
engendrar, va. to beget, to engender, to produce.
engendro, m. fetus, embryo; **mal —,** low breed; a perverse youth.
englobar, va. to consolidate, to consider various things as one.
engolfar, vn. to enter a gulf; **—se,** to be engaged in arduous undertakings or difficult affairs; to be deeply absorbed.
engolillado, da, adj. wearing the collar which is worn by lawyers in Spain; (coll.) fond of observing rigorously old styles.
engolosinar, va. to give a taste for; **—se,** to find delight in.
engolletarse, vr. (coll.) to become conceited or vain.
engomadura, f. gumming.
engomar, va. to gum, to glue; to rubberize.
engordar, va. to fatten; **—se,** to grow fat; to grow rich.
engorro, m. embarrassment, obstacle.
engorroso, sa, adj. troublesome, cumbrous.
engoznar, va. to hinge; to put hinges on.
Engracia, Grace.
engranaje, m. gear, gearing; **— de tornillo sin fin,** worm gear; **— recto,** spur gear; **— helicoidal,** helical gear; **caja de —,** gear case.
engranar, va. to throw into gear.
engrandecer, va. (EZCO) to augment, to aggrandize; to exaggerate; to exalt.
engrandecimiento, m. increase, aggrandizement; exaggeration; exaltation.
engranujarse, vr. to become covered with pimples; to acquire the ways of a rascal.
engrasador, m. lubricator, oiler; oil cup.
engrasar, va. to grease, to oil.
engreimiento, m. presumption, vanity; overindulgence.
engreír, va. (I) to make proud; to spoil, to overindulge; **—se,** to become vain; to become spoiled or overindulged.
engrescar, va. and vr. to goad into quarreling or fighting; to make others join in merrymaking.
engrifarse, vr. to stand up (as hair, from fright); to be displeased.
engringarse, vr. (coll.) to imitate the ways of foreigners or follow their customs.
engrosar, va. (UE) to make fat; **—,** vn. to increase in bulk.
engrudamiento, m. pasting, gluing.
engrudar, va. to paste.
engrudo, m. paste made of flour or starch.
engualdrapar, va. to caparison (a horse).
enguantarse, vr. to put gloves on.
enguijarrar, va. to pave with pebbles.

engullidor, ra, n. devourer; gobbler.
engullir, va. (UYO) to swallow, to gobble, to glut.
enhacinador, ra, n. one who gathers and binds into a sheaf (as wheat).
enharinar, va. to cover or sprinkle with flour.
enhastiar, va. to cause annoyance, to bore.
enhastillar, va. to put arrows in a quiver.
enhebrar, va. to thread a needle.
enhestar, va. and vr. (IE) to erect, to set upright.
enhilar, va. to thread.
enhorabuena, f. congratulation; felicitation; **—,** adv. well and good.
enhoramala, adv. in an evil hour.
enhornar, va. to place in an oven for baking.
enigma, m. enigma, riddle.
enigmático, ca, adj. enigmatical, of an obscure meaning.
enjabonadura, f. soaping.
enjabonar, va. to soap, to lather.
enjaezar, va. to caparison a horse.
enjalbegar, va. to whitewash the walls of a building; to paint (the face).
enjalma, f. packsaddle.
enjalmero, m. packsaddle maker.
enjambradero, m. place to which bees swarm to form their hives.
enjambrar, va. to gather a scattered swarm of bees; **—,** vn. to swarm; to multiply.
enjambrazón, f. swarming of bees.
enjambre, m. swarm of bees; crowd, multitude.
enjaretar, va. to run a string or a ribbon through lace or a hem; (coll.) to say something unthinkingly and hastily.
enjaular, va. to shut up in a cage; to imprison.
enjebar, va. to soak in lye.
enjebe, m. soaking in lye; bucking.
enjergar, va. (coll.) to start and direct a business.
enjertal, m. nursery of grafted trees.
enjoyar, va. to adorn with jewels; to set a ring with precious stones; to heighten the brilliancy of a thing.
enjuagadura, f. rinsing of the mouth.
enjuagar, va. to rinse the mouth and teeth; to rinse clothes.
enjuague, m. water used to rinse the mouth; intrigue.
enjugador, ra, n. one who dries; **—,** m. drum for drying clothes.
enjugar, va. to dry; to wipe off; **—se,** to dry up; to grow lean.
enjuiciar, va. to bring a lawsuit to trial; to pass judgment.
enjuncar, va. to tie with rush ropes.
enjundia, f. fat in the inside of fowls.
enjutar, va. to dry (plaster, etc.).
enjutez, f. dryness.
enjuto, ta, adj. dried; lean, slender; austere.
enlace, m. connection, coherence; link; kindred, affinity; wedding.

enladrillado, *m.* pavement of brick.
enladrillador, *m.* bricklayer.
enladrillar, *va.* to pave a floor with bricks.
enlardar, *va.* to rub with grease, to baste.
enlazable, *adj.* that can be fastened together.
enlazar, *va.* and *vr.* to join, to unite, to connect; to be joined in wedlock.
enlistonado, *m.* lath or batten work.
enlistonar, *va.* to lath, to batten.
enlodar, *va.* to bemire.
enloquecer, *va.* (EZCO) to madden, to make mad; —**se,** to become crazed or insane; to become infatuated.
enloquecido, da, *adj.* deranged.
enloquecimiento, *m.* enraging, maddening.
enlosar, *va.* to lay a floor with flags, tile or slabs.
enlozanarse, *vr.* to boast of one's dexterity or strength.
enlucido, *m.* plastering, plaster coating.
enlustrecer, *va.* to polish, to make something shiny.
enlutar, *va.* to put into mourning; —**se,** to go into mourning.
enllantar, *va.* to put a tire (on a vehicle).
enmaderar, *va.* to roof a house with timber.
enmantarse, *vr.* to be sad and melancholy (said of birds).
enmarañar, *va.* to entangle, to involve in difficulties; to puzzle.
enmarillecerse, *vr.* (EZCO) to become pale or yellow.
enmaromar, *va.* to tie with a rope (usually said of bulls and ferocious animals).
enmascarar, *va.* to mask; —**se,** to go in disguise, to masquerade.
enmasillar, *va.* to putty.
enmelar, *va.* (IE) to spread with honey; to sweeten, to mollify.
enmendación, *f.* emendation, correction.
enmendar, *va.* (IE) to correct, to reform; to repair; to compensate; to abrogate.
enmienda, *f.* correction, amendment; emendation; reward; compensation; parliamentary amendment.
enmohecer, *va.* (EZCO) to mold, to mildew; —**se,** to grow moldy or musty; to rust.
enmohecido, da, *adj.* rusty.
enmordazar, *va.* to put a muzzle on.
enmudecer, *vn.* (EZCO) to grow dumb; to be silent; —, *va.* to impose silence.
ennegrecer, *va.* (EZCO) to blacken; to darken, to obscure.
ennoblecer, *va.* (EZCO) to ennoble.
ennoblecimiento, *m.* ennoblement.
Eno. or **en.º enero,** Jan. January.
enodio, *m.* (zool.) fawn.
enojadizo, za, *adj.* fretful, peevish.
enojado, da, *adj.* angry, cross.
enojar, *va.* to irritate, to make angry; to tease; to molest; to offend; —**se,** to get cross, to become angry.
enojo, *m.* peevishness; anger, displeasure.
enojoso, sa, *adj.* offensive, vexatious.

enorgullecer, *va.* and *vr.* (EZCO) to fill with pride; to become proud.
enorme, *adj.* enormous, vast, huge; —**mente,** *adv.* hugely, enormously.
enormidad, *f.* enormity, monstrosity.
enrabiar, *va.* to enrage, to become furious.
enramada, *f.* hut covered with the branches of trees; shed; bower; arbor; ramification.
enramar, *va.* to cover with the branches of trees.
enranciarse, *vr.* to grow rancid.
enrarecer, *va.* (EZCO) to thin, to rarefy.
enredadera, *f.* climbing plant; vine.
enredador, ra, *n.* entangler; tattler; talebearer; busybody.
enredar, *va.* to entangle, to ensnare, to confound, to perplex; to puzzle; to sow discord; —**se,** to fall in love (unlawful love); to become entangled or involved.
enredo, *m.* entanglement; perplexity, embarrassment; mischievous lie; plot of a play.
enredoso, sa, *adj.* full of snares and difficulties.
enrejado, *m.* grating; railing; (as a fence); trelliswork; openwork embroidery.
enrejar, *va.* to fix a grating to a window; to grate, to lattice.
enrevesado, da, *adj.* difficult, stubborn, queer.
enriar, *va.* to soak hemp and flax in water.
enrielar, *va.* to put on the track; to lead, to guide.
Enrique, Henry.
enriquecer, *va.* (EZCO) to enrich; to adorn; —, *vn.* to grow rich.
Enriqueta, Harriet, Henrietta.
Enriquito, Harry, Hal.
enriscado, da, *adj.* mountainous, craggy.
enriscamiento, *m.* taking refuge among rocks.
enriscar, *va.* to place on the top of mountains or rocks; —**se,** to take refuge among rocks.
enristrar, *va.* to couch the lance; to range, to file; (fig.) to meet a difficulty.
enristre, *m.* couching a lance.
enrizar, *va.* and *vr.* to curl.
enrodrigonar, *va.* to prop vines with stakes.
enrojecer, *va.* and *vr.* (EZCO) to make red-hot; to blush.
enrollar, *va.* to wind, to roll, to coil.
enromar, *va.* and *vr.* to make something dull or blunt.
enronquecer, *va.* (EZCO) to make hoarse; —, *vn.* to grow hoarse.
enronquecimiento, *m.* hoarseness.
enroscadura, *f.* act of twisting; convolution.
enroscar, *va.* to twist; —**se,** to curl up.
enrubiar, *va.* to bleach or dye one's hair to blond.
ensabanar, *va.* to cover with sheets.
ensacar, *va.* to put (something) in a sack.
ensalada, *f.* salad; hodgepodge, medley.

ensaladera, *f.* salad bowl.

ensalmar, *va.* to set dislocated bones; to heal by spells.

ensalmo, *m.* enchantment, spell.

ensalobrarse, *vr.* to become bitter and salty (as water).

ensalzar, *va.* to exalt, to praise; to aggrandize; to exaggerate; **—se,** to boast.

ensamblador, *m.* joiner.

ensanchar, *va.* to widen, to extend, to enlarge; **—se,** to assume an air of importance; to expand.

ensanche, *m.* dilation, augmentation, widening; gore (in garments); increase.

ensangrentar, *va.* (IE) to stain with blood; **—se,** to be overzealous in the pursuit of a thing; to proceed in a cruel and barbarous manner; to cover oneself with blood.

ensañado, da, *adj.* vengeful, merciless; enraged.

ensañar, *va.* to revenge, to vent one's fury; to irritate, to enrage.

ensartar, *va.* to string (beads, etc.); (fig.) to go through a long story incoherently.

ensayar, *va.* to assay precious metals; to rehearse; to examine, to prove; to try; **—se,** to train, to practice.

ensaye, *m.* test (of materials).

ensayo, *m.* assay, trial, proof; rehearsal of a play; **pedido de —,** trial order.

ensebar, *va.* to grease.

ensenada, *f.* small bay.

enseña, *f.* colors; **—s,** *pl.* standard.

enseñanza, *f.* teaching, instruction; **primera —,** primary grades; **segunda —,** high-school grades.

enseñar, *va.* to teach, to instruct; to show; **—se,** to accustom oneself.

enseñorearse, *vr.* to domineer, to become lord and master (of something).

enserar, *va.* to cover with matting.

enseres, *m. pl.* chattels; implements, fixtures; household goods.

enseriarse, *vr.* (Sp. Am.) to become earnest or serious.

ensilaje, *m.* silage.

ensillado, da, *adj.* hollow-backed.

ensilladura, *f.* part of a horse or mule where the saddle is placed.

ensillar, *va.* to saddle.

ensimismarse, *vr.* to become engrossed in one's own importance.

ensoberbecer, *va.* (EZCO) to excite haughtiness or pride; **—se,** to become haughty; to become rough (as the sea).

ensopar, *va.* to dunk (food); **—,** *vn. and vr.* to drench.

ensordecer, *va.* (EZCO) to deafen; **—,** *vn.* to grow deaf; to become silent.

ensordecimiento, *m.* deafness.

ensortijamiento, *m.* curling the hair; hair ringlets.

ensortijar, *va.* to form into a ring; to curl.

ensuciar, *va.* to stain, to soil; to pollute with

vicious habits; **—se,** to dirty one's bed, clothes, etc.; to allow oneself to be bribed.

ensueño, *m.* dream, reverie, illusion.

entablado, da, *adj.* boarded, made of boards; **—,** *m.* floor made of boards.

entablar, *va.* to cover or floor with boards; to start or begin (a conversation, debate, etc.).

entablillar, *va.* to secure with small boards, to put in splints.

entallador, *m.* sculptor; engraver.

entalladura, *f.* sculpture; engraving.

entallar, *va.* to sculpture, to carve; to engrave; **—,** *vn.* to fit close to the body (of clothes, etc.).

entallecer, *vn.* (EZCO) to shoot, to sprout (of plants).

entapizar, *va.* to hang with tapestry, to upholster.

entarimado, *m.* bridging.

entarimar, *va.* to cover a floor with boards.

ente, *m.* entity, being; (coll.) ridiculous, worthless man.

entejar, *va.* to cover with tiles.

entenada, *f.* stepdaughter.

entenado, *m.* stepson.

entendederas, *f. pl.* (coll.) understanding, judgment.

entender, *va. and vn.* (IE) to understand, to comprehend; to remark, to take notice of; to reason, to think; **a mi —,** in my opinion; **—se,** to understand each other.

entendido, da, *adj.* wise, learned, prudent, knowing; **valor —do,** value stipulated or agreed on.

entendimiento, *m.* understanding, knowledge, judgment.

enteramente, *adv.* entirely, completely.

enterar, *va.* to inform thoroughly; to instruct; to let know; **—se (de),** to find out, to inform oneself, to be told.

entereza, *f.* entireness, integrity; fortitude; uprightness; perfection; firmness of mind.

entérico, ca, *adj.* (med.) enteric.

enteritis, *f.* (med.) enteritis.

enterizo, za, *adj.* entire, complete.

enternecer, *va.* (EZCO) to soften; to move to compassion; **—,** *vn.* to pity, to commiserate.

enternecimiento, *m.* compassion, pity.

entero, ra, *adj.* whole, entire; perfect, complete; sound; just, right; pure, uncorrupted; strong, robust; uncastrated; **por —ro,** entirely, completely; **color —ro,** solid color.

enterorragia, *f.* (med.) enterorrhagia, intestinal hemorrhage.

enterrador, *m.* gravedigger; sexton; undertaker, mortician.

enterrar, *va.* (IE) to inter, to bury.

entestado, da, *adj.* persistent, obstinate.

entibiar, *va.* to cool.

entidad, *f.* entity, real being; (fig.) consideration, importance.

entierro, *m.* burial; interment, funeral.

entintar, *va.* to dye or stain with ink.

entiznar, *va.* to stain with soot; to defame, to slander.

ento. entretanto, meanwhile.

entoldar, *va.* to cover with an awning; to adorn the walls with hangings; —**se,** to dress pompously; to become cloudy (said of the sky).

entomología, *f.* entomology.

entonación, *f.* modulation; intonation, tone, voice; blowing of the bellows of an organ; (fig.) presumption, pride.

entonador, *m.* organ blower; intoner of the first verse of a psalm.

entonar, *va.* to tune, to intonate, to chant; to blow the bellows of an organ; —**se,** to be puffed up with pride.

entonces, *adv.* then, at that time.

entonelar, *va.* to barrel.

entontecer, *va.* (EZCO) to make stupid, to fool; —**se,** to grow stupid.

entontecimiento, *m.* growing stupid.

entorchado, *m.* twisted cord which serves for embroideries.

entorchar, *va.* to twist a cord; to cover cords for musical instruments with wire.

entornar, *va.* to set ajar, to tilt.

entornillar, *va.* to make anything in the form of a screw or ring.

entorpecer, *va.* (EZCO) to benumb; to stupefy; to hinder.

entorpecimiento, *m.* torpor, numbness, stupefaction.

entortar, *va.* (UE) to bend; to make one cross-eyed.

entosigar, *va.* to poison.

entrada, *f.* entrance, entry, admission; —**s y gastos,** receipts and expenses; **pagar de** —, to pay as entrance or initiation fee.

entrambos, bas, *adj. pl.* both.

entrampar, *va.* to entrap, to ensnare; to involve in difficulties; to deceive; to encumber an estate with debts; —**se,** to become indebted.

entrante, *adj.* entering; coming, next (day, week, year); —, *m.* next month.

entrañable, *adj.* intimate, affectionate; profound.

entrañas, *f. pl.* entrails, intestines; (fig.) heart.

entrar, *va.* and *vn.* to enter, to go in; to commence.

entre, *prep.* between; in; among; — **manos,** in hand.

entreabrir, *va.* to half open a door, to leave it ajar.

entreacto, *m.* (theat.) intermission.

entreancho, cha, *adj.* of a medium width (neither wide nor narrow).

entrecano, na, *adj.* gray-black, grayish.

entrecavar, *va.* to dig lightly.

entrecejo, *m.* the space between the eyebrows; frowning, supercilious look.

entrecoger, *va.* to catch, to intercept.

entrecortado, da, *adj.* halting, hesitating, bewildered.

entrecruzar, *va.* to cross one another, to intertwine.

entrecubiertas, *f. pl.* (naut.) between decks.

entredicho, *m.* prohibition; ecclesiastical interdict.

entrefino, na, *adj.* between coarse and fine.

entrega, *f.* delivery; conveyance; surrender; **novela por** —**s,** serial or installment novel.

entregar, *va.* to deliver; to restore; —**se,** to deliver oneself up into the hands of another; to abandon oneself to vice; — **por extradición,** to extradite.

entrelazado, da, *adj.* interlaced, entwined, crisscross.

entrelazar, *va.* to interlace.

entrelistado, da, *adj.* striped, variegated.

entrelucir, *vn.* and *vr.* (UZCO) to show through.

entremedias, *adv.* in the meantime.

entremés, *m.* interlude; sidedish.

entremeter, *va.* to put one thing between others; —**se,** to intermeddle; to intrude.

entremetido, da, *n.* meddler, intruder; kibitzer; —, **da,** *adj.* meddling.

entremetimiento, *m.* interposition; meddling.

entremezclar, *va.* to intermix.

entrenador, *m.* trainer, coach.

entrenar, *va.* to train, to coach.

entreoír, *va.* (ENTREOIGO, ENTREOÍ) to overhear; to hear without perfectly understanding what is said.

entrepalmadura, *f.* disease in horses' hoofs.

entrepaño, *m.* panel.

entrepaso, *m.* rack (horse's gait).

entrepiernas, *f. pl.* opening between the legs; pieces put into the crotch of a pair of breeches.

entrepiso, *m.* space beteeen drifts or levels of a mine.

entrepuentes, *m. pl.* (naut.) between decks.

entresaca, *f.* cutting down of trees in order to thin a forest.

entresacar, *va.* to sift, to separate; to thin out (hair).

entresuelo, *m.* entresol, mezzanine; basement.

entretalladura, *f.* sculpture in bas-relief.

entretallar, *va.* to sculpture in bas-relief; to make elaborate work on goods.

entretanto, *adv.* meanwhile.

entretejer, *va.* to interweave.

entretela, *f.* buckram, stiff or strong linen; interlining.

entretelar, *va.* to put buckram or strong linen between the lining and cloth.

entretener, *va.* (ENTRETENGO, ENTRETUVE) to amuse; to entertain, to divert; to allay pain; —**se,** to amuse oneself.

entretenido, da, *adj.* pleasant, amusing; —, *m.* aspirant to an office, but meanwhile obtaining some remuneration.

entretenimiento, *m.* amusement, entertainment.

entretiempo, *m.* season between summer and winter (spring or autumn).

entrevenado, da, *adj.* intravenous.

entrevenarse, *vr.* to spread through the veins (liquid, etc.).

entrever, *va.* (ENTREVEO, ENTREVÍ) to have a glimpse of, to see imperfectly.

entreverado, da, *adj.* intermixed; interlined with fat and lean.

entreverar, *va.* to intermix, to mix together.

entrevista, *f.* interview.

entripado, da, *adj.* contained in the entrails.

entristecer, *va.* (EZCO) to sadden, to afflict; —se, to grieve, to be sad.

entrojar, *va.* to put up grain in barns.

entrometimiento, *m.* intrusion, interference, meddling.

entronar, *va.* = **entronizar.**

entroncar, *vn.* to belong to the same family; to make a junction.

entronización, *f.* elevation to a throne.

entronizar, *va.* to enthrone.

entronque, *m.* relationship with the chief of a family; crossroads, junction.

entruchada, *f.* clandestine operation, underhand business.

entruchar, *va.* to decoy, to lure into a trap.

entubar, *va.* to provide with pipes or tubes.

entuerto, *m.* affront, injury; —s, *pl.* afterpains.

entullecer, *va.* (EZCO) to obstruct, to check; —, *vn.* and *vr.* to be crippled.

entullecerse, *vr.* (EZCO) to become crippled or maimed.

entumecer, *va.* (EZCO) to benumb; —, *vn.* to become numb; to swell, to surge (as rivers).

entumecimiento, *m.* swelling; torpor.

enturbiar, *va.* to make turbid; to obscure, to confound; —se, to become muddy.

entusiasmar, *va.* to arouse enthusiasm, to elate, to transport, to enrapture; —se, to become enthusiastic.

entusiasmo, *m.* enthusiasm.

entusiasta, *m.* and *f.* enthusiast; —, *adj.* enthusiastic.

enumeración, *f.* enumeration.

enumerar, *va.* to enumerate.

enunciación, *f.* enunciation, declaration.

enunciar, *va.* to enunciate, to declare.

enunciativo, va, *adj.* enunciative.

envainar, *va.* to sheathe (as a sword).

envalentonar, *va.* to encourage, to inspirit, to make bold; —se, to become courageous.

envalijar, *va.* to put in a valise.

envanecer, *va.* (EZCO) to make vain; to swell with pride; —se, to become proud or vain.

envaramiento, *m.* stiffness, numbness.

envarar, *va.* and *vr.* to benumb.

envasador, *m.* funnel.

envasar, *va.* to barrel; to bottle; to can; to drink to excess.

envase, *m.* packing, bottling; container.

envejecer, *va.* (EZCO) to make old; —, *vn.* to grow old.

envejecido, da, *adj.* grown old; looking old.

envejecimiento, *m.* senescence, aging.

envenenador, ra, *n.* poisoner.

envenenamiento, *m.* poisoning.

envenenar, *va.* to envenom, to poison.

enverdecer, *vn.* and *vr.* (EZCA) to sprout, to become green (trees, fields, etc.).

envés, *m.* = **revés.**

envestidura, *f.* investiture.

envestir, *va.* (I) to confer or grant (as power).

enviado, *m.* envoy, messenger.

enviar, *va.* to send, to transmit, to convey, to dispatch.

enviciar, *va.* to vitiate, to corrupt; —se, to acquire bad habits.

envidar, *va.* to open the game by staking a certain sum.

envidia, *f.* envy; emulation.

envidiable, *adj.* enviable.

envidiar, *vn.* to envy, to grudge.

envidioso, sa, *adj.* envious, jealous.

envilecer, *va.* (EZCO) to vilify, to debase; —se, to degrade oneself.

envinagrar, *va.* to put vinegar into anything.

envío, *m.* sending, shipment, remittance.

envirar, *va.* to clasp together corkwood to form a beehive.

enviscar, *va.* to glue; to irritate, to anger; —se, to be glued with birdlime.

envite, *m.* opening the game by taking a certain sum; offer.

enviudar, *vn.* to become a widower or widow.

envoltorio, *m.* bundle of goods; defect in the weaving of cloth.

envoltura, *f.* wrapper, jacket; casing; —s, swaddling clothes.

envolver, *va.* (UE) to involve; to wrap up; —se, to be implicated in an affair.

envolvimiento, *m.* envelopment, involvement.

enyerbar, *va.* to sod; —se, to become covered with grass.

enyesadura, *f.* plastering.

enyesar, *va.* to plaster.

enyugar, *va.* to yoke cattle.

enzainarse, *vr.* to squint, to have a cast in one's eye; (coll.) to become treacherous or untrustworthy.

enzamarrado, da, *adj.* dressed in a shepherd's coat made of sheepskins, with the wool on.

enzarzado, da, *adj.* curled, matted.

enzarzar, *va.* to throw among brambles; to sow discord; —se, to be entangled among brambles; to be involved in difficulties.

eoceno, *m.* Eocene; —, **na,** *adj.* Eocene.

eón, *m.* eon.

epacta, *f.* (ast.) epact.
épico, ca, *adj.* epic.
epicúreo, rea, *adj.* epicurean.
epidemia, *f.* epidemic disease.
epidérmico, ca, *adj.* epidermic, epidermal.
epidermis, *f.* epidermis, cuticle.
Epifanía, *f.* Epiphany.
epiglotis, *f.* epiglottis.
epígrafe, *m.* epigraph, inscription; motto, device.
epigrama, *m.* epigram.
epilepsia. *f.* epilepsy.
epilogar, *va.* to conclude, to recapitulate, to sum up.
epílogo, *m.* epilogue.
epiqueya, *f.* mild and prudent interpretation of the law.
episcopado, *m.* episcopacy; bishopric.
episcopal, *adj.* episcopal.
episódico, ca, *adj.* episodic.
episodio, *m.* episode.
epistaxis, *f.* epistaxis, nosebleed.
epístola, *f.* epistle, letter; subdeaconship.
epistolar, *adj.* epistolary.
epistolario, *m.* collection of epistles which are read or sung at mass; guide for letter writing.
epitafio, *m.* epitaph.
epitalamio, *m.* nuptial song.
epitelio, *m.* epithelium.
epíteto, *m.* epithet.
epitomar, *va.* to epitomize.
epítome, *m.* epitome, compendium.
E.P.M. en propia mano, in one's own hands, personally.
época, *f.* epoch; age, era, period.
epopeya, *f.* epic; epic poetry.
epsomita, *f.* epsom salts.
epulón, *m.* great eater, indulger.
equidad, *f.* equity, honesty; impartiality, justice.
equidistante, *adj.* equidistant.
equidistar, *vn.* to be equidistant.
equilátero, ra, *adj.* equilateral, having all sides equal.
equilibrado, da, *adj.* balanced; **superficie —da,** (aer.) balanced surface.
equilibrar, *va.* to equilibrate; to counterpoise, to counterbalance.
equilibrio, *m.* equilibrium, balance; **— político,** balance of power.
equinoccial, *adj.* equinoctial.
equinoccio, *m.* equinox.
equipaje, *m.* baggage, luggage; equipment; (naut.) crew of a ship; (mil.) baggage train; **coche de —,** baggage car; **— de mano,** hand baggage; **exceso de —,** excess baggage; **jefe de —,** baggage master.
equipar, *va.* to fit out, to equip, to furnish.
equipo, *m.* equipment; (sports) team; **— corriente,** standard equipment.
equis, *f.* name of the letter *x*.
equitación, *f.* horsemanship.
equitativo, va, *adj.* equitable; just.

equivalencia, *f.* equivalence, compensation.
equivalente, *adj.* equivalent.
equivaler, *vn.* (EQUIVALGO, EQUIVALÍ) to be of equal value.
equivocación, *f.* mistake, error, misunderstanding.
equivocar, *va.* and *vr.* to mistake, to misconceive, to misunderstand.
equívoco, ca, *adj.* equivocal, ambiguous; **—,** *m.* equivocation, quibble.
equivoquista, *m.* equivocator.
era, *f.* era, age; threshing floor; plot in a garden.
eral, *m.* two-year-old ox.
erario, *m.* exchequer, public treasury, fisc.
erección, *f.* erection; elevation; foundation; establishment.
eremítico, ca, *adj.* hermitlike, solitary.
ergio, *m.* erg.
ergosterol, *m.* ergosterol.
erguir, *va.* (IRGO or YERGO, ERGUÍ) to erect, to raise up straight; **—se,** to be elated with pride.
erial, *adj.* untilled, uncultivated.
erigir, *va.* to erect, to raise, to build; to establish.
erisipela, *f.* (med.) erysipelas.
erisipelar, *va.* to cause erysipelas.
erizamiento, *m.* standing on end (of hair, etc.).
erizar, *va.* and *vr.* to bristle, to set on end (as hair).
erizo, *m.* hedgehog.
ermita, *f.* hermitage.
ermitaño, *m.* hermit; hermit crab.
Ernesto, Ernest.
erogar, *va.* to dispense or distribute funds.
erosión, *f.* erosion.
erosivo, va, *adj.* erosive.
erótico, ca, *adj.* erotic.
erradicable, *adj.* eradicable.
erradicación, *f.* extirpation.
erradicador, *m.* eradicator.
erradizo, za, *adj.* wandering to and fro.
errante, *adj.* errant, erring, roving; excursive.
errar, *va.* (YERRO, ERRÉ) to err, to commit errors; **—,** *vn.* to go astray; **— el blanco,** to miss one's mark.
errata, *f.* error in printing; **— de imprenta,** misprint.
erre, name of the double letter *rr*, also of the single letter *r* in some instances; **— que —,** (coll.) pertinaciously, obstinately.
erróneo, nea, *adj.* erroneous.
error, *m.* error, mistake, fault.
eructación, *f.* belching.
eructar, *vn.* to belch.
eructo, *m.* belch.
erudición, *f.* erudition, learning.
erudito, ta, *adj.* learned, lettered, erudite; **—,** *m.* sage, pundit, scholar.
erupción, *f.* eruption, outbreak, rash.
erutación, *f.* belching.
erutar, *vn.* to belch.

eruto, *m.* belch.
esbelto, ta, *adj.* tall and slender; well-shaped.
esbirro, *m.* bailiff, apparitor.
esbozar, *va.* to sketch, to outline.
esbozo, *m.* outline, sketch.
escabechar, *va.* to souse, to pickle.
escabeche, *m.* souse, pickle; pickled fish.
escabel, *m.* footstool.
escabrosidad, *f.* unevenness, roughness; asperity.
escabroso, sa, *adj.* rough, uneven; craggy, crabbed; rude, unpolished.
escabullirse, *vr.* (UYO) to escape, to evade; to slip through one's fingers.
escala, *f.* ladder; scale; (mus.) scale; (naut.) port; **hacer — en,** to stop at a port.
escalada, *f.* (mil.) escalade.
escalador, *m.* climber, he who scales walls.
escalafón, *m.* army register.
escaldado, da, *adj.* cautious, suspicious, wary; scalded.
escaldar, *va.* to scald.
escalera, *f.* staircase; ladder; **— de mano,** step ladder; **— móvil** or **movediza,** escalator, moving stairway.
escalfador, *m.* barber's pan for keeping water warm; chafing dish.
escalfar, *va.* to poach eggs; to scorch.
escalofrío, *m.* (med.) chill.
escalón, *m.* step of a stair; degree of dignity; (mil.) echelon.
escalonar, *va.* (mil.) to form in echelon; to step.
escalpelo, *m.* scalpel.
escama, *f.* fish scale; (fig.) resentment.
escamado, da, *adj.* taught by experience.
escamadura, *f.* scaling (of a fish); scalelike embroidery.
escamar, *va.* to take off the scales; **—,** *vn.* to embroider scale or shell fashion; **—se,** to cause mistrust or resentment.
escamoso, sa, *adj.* scaly.
escamotable, *adj.* retractable.
escamotar or **escamotear,** *va.* to make a thing disappear from one's hands (in conjuring).
escampar, *vn.* to stop raining; **—,** *va.* to clear a place.
escanciador, ra, *n.* one who pours the wine or liquor.
escanciar, *va.* to pour wine from one vessel into another to drink.
escanda, *f.* (bot.) speltwheat.
escandalizador, *m.* scandalmonger.
escandalizar, *va.* to scandalize, to shock; **—se,** to be scandalized.
escándalo, *m.* scandal.
escandaloso, sa, *adj.* scandalous, shameful; turbulent.
Escandinavia, *f.* Scandinavia.
escaño, *m.* bench with a back.
escapada, *f.* escape, flight.
escapar, *va.* to liberate from danger; to drive (a horse) very fast; **—,** *vn.* and *vr.* to escape, to flee.
escaparate, *m.* show window, showcase; cupboard, cabinet.
escapatoria, *f.* escape, flight; excuse.
escape, *m.* escape, flight; escapement (part of a watch); exhaust; **colector de —,** (aer.) exhaust collector ring; **múltiple de —,** (aer.) exhaust manifold; **a todo —,** with the utmost velocity, at full speed.
escapulario, *m.* scapulary.
escarabajear, *vn.* to crawl to and fro like insects; to scribble; to sting, to give pain.
escarabajo, *m.* scarab, tumblebug, beetle; short, ill-shaped person.
escaramuza, *f.* skirmish; dispute, quarrel.
escaramuzador, *m.* skirmisher; disputer.
escaramuzar, *vn.* to skirmish.
escarapela, *f.* cockade.
escarbadientes, *m.* toothpick.
escarbadura, *f.* act and effect of scratching.
escarbaorejas, *m.* earpick.
escarbar, *va.* to scratch the earth (as chickens do), to dig; to inquire minutely into.
escarcha, *f.* white frost.
escarchar, *vn.* to freeze, to frost.
escardadera, *f.* woman employed to clear fields of weeds.
escardador, *m.* weeder.
escardar, *va.* to weed.
escardillo, *m.* small weeding hook.
escariador, *m.* reamer.
escarlata, *f.* scarlet color; scarlet cloth.
escarlatina, *f.* scarlet fever, scarlatina.
escarmenar, *va.* to comb, to pick wool; to cheat gradually.
escarmentar, *vn.* (IE) to profit by experience; to take warning; **—,** *va.* to punish severely.
escarmiento, *m.* warning, caution; chastisement.
escarnecer, *va.* (EZCO) to mock, to ridicule.
escarnio, *m.* scoff, contemptuous ridicule.
escarola, *f.* (bot.) endive; pleated frill round the neck.
escarolado, da, *adj.* of the color of endive, pale yellowish; curled, frilled.
escarpa, *f.* declivity; (mil.) scarp.
escarpado, da, *adj.* sloped, craggy.
escarpar, *va.* to file works of sculpture with a rasp; (mil.) to escarp.
escarpia, *f.* meathook; spike.
escarpidor, *m.* wide, large-toothed comb.
escarpín, *m.* thin-soled shoe; woolen sock.
escasear, *va.* to give sparingly and with reluctance; to spare; **—,** *vn.* to grow less, to decrease.
escasez, *f.* scantiness, niggardliness; want.
escaso, sa, *adj.* small, short, little; sparing, niggardly; scanty, defective.
escatimar, *va.* to curtail, to lessen; to haggle; to corrupt the sense and meaning of words.
escayola, *f.* stucco.

escena, *f.* stage; scene; incident, episode.
escenario, *m.* scenario, stage.
escénico, ca, *adj.* scenic.
escepticismo, *m.* skepticism.
escéptico, ca, *adj.* skeptic, skeptical.
esclarecer, *va.* (EZCO) to lighten, to clear up, to illuminate; to illustrate; —, *vn.* to dawn.
esclarecido, da, *adj.* illustrious, noble.
esclarecimiento, *m.* dawn; illustriousness.
esclavina, *f.* pilgrim's pall; collar worn by priests; pelerine, fur cape.
esclavitud, *f.* slavery, servitude.
esclavizar, *va.* and *vr.* to enslave.
esclavo, va, *n.* slave, captive.
escleroma, *m.* (med.) scleroma, hardening of the tissues.
esclerosis, *f.* (med.) sclerosis.
esclusa, *f.* lock; sluice, floodgate; flume.
escoba, *f.* broom.
escobada, *f.* sweeping stroke; light sweeping.
escobajo, *m.* remains of an old broom; stalk of a bunch of grapes (without the fruit).
escobazo, *m.* blow given with a broom.
escobeta, *f.* floor brush.
escobilla, *f.* brush; small broom.
escobillón, *m.* artillery sponge.
escocer, *vn.* (UE) to feel a sharp lively pain; to be irritated; —se, to smart.
escocés, esa, *n.* and *adj.* Scotsman, Scotswoman; Scotch, Scottish.
Escocia, *f.* Scotland.
escofieta, *f.* women's headdress of gauze, etc.
escofina, *f.* rasp, file.
escofinar, *va.* to rasp.
escoger, *va.* to choose, to select.
escogidamente, *adv.* choicely, selectly.
escogido, da, *adj.* choice, selected.
escolar, *m.* scholar, student; —, *adj.* scholastic.
escolástico, ca, *adj.* scholastic; —, *m.* Scholastic (Christian philosopher of the Middle Ages).
escolio, *m.* scholion, comment, explanatory note.
escoliosis, *f.* (med.) scoliosis, lateral curvature of the spine.
escolta, *f.* (mil.) escort, convoy.
escoltar, *va.* to escort.
escollo, *m.* sunken rock, reef; difficulty, danger.
escombrar, *va.* to remove obstacles; to purify.
escombro, *m.* rubbish, debris; mackerel.
esconce, *m.* corner, angle.
escondedero, *m.* hiding place.
esconder, *va.* to hide, to conceal; to dissemble; to contain; —se, to lie hid.
escondidas or **escondidillas, (a —),** *adv.* in a secret manner.
escondido, da, *adj.* hidden.
escondite, *m.* concealment; hiding; hide-and-seek; **juego de —,** hide and seek.
escondrijo, *m.* hiding place.

esconzado, da, *adj.* oblique, angular.
escopeta, *f.* gun, shotgun; **a tiro de —,** within gunshot.
escopetazo, *m.* gunshot; gunshot wound.
escopetear, *va.* to discharge a gun repeatedly; —se, to discharge firearms at each other; to insult each other with foul language or to compliment each other back and forth.
escopeteo, *m.* discharge of firearms.
escopetero, *m.* musketeer; gunsmith.
escopladura or **escopleadura,** *f.* mortise hole made in timber.
escoplear, *va.* to chisel out.
escoplo, *m.* chisel.
escorar, *va.* (aer.) to bank (an airplane); (naut.) to prop, to shore up; —, *vn.* (naut.) to heel.
escorbútico, ca, *adj.* pertaining to or like scurvy.
escorbuto, *m.* scurvy.
escoria, *f.* dross, lee, clinker; worthless thing.
escoriación, *f.* excoriation, flaying.
escorial, *m.* dump pile.
escoriar, *va.* and *vr.* (med.) to excoriate, to flay.
Escorpio or **Escorpión,** *m.* Scorpio, Scorpion (sign of the zodiac).
escorpión, *m.* scorpion.
escorzo, *m.* foreshortening.
escorzonera, *f.* viper grass.
escotado, da, *adj.* low-necked, low-cut.
escotadura, *f.* low-cut in the neck of a dress.
escotar, *va.* to cut out a garment about the neck; to slope; to pay one's share of a joint expense.
escote, *m.* low-cut in a garment; tucker; one's share of a bill at a club.
escotero, ra, *adj.* free, disengaged.
escotilla, *f.* (naut.) hatchway.
escotillón, *m.* trapdoor; drop, stage trap (in theaters).
escozor, *m.* sharp pain; lively sensation or perception of the mind.
escriba, *m.* scribe (among the Hebrews).
escribanía, *f.* office of a notary; escritoire.
escribano, *m.* notary, scrivener; clerk.
escribidor, ra, *n.* poor writer.
escribiente, *m.* and *f.* amanuensis, clerk.
escribir, *va.* to write; to compose literary work; **— a máquina,** to typewrite.
escrit.ª escritura, deed.
escrito, *m.* literary composition; writing, manuscript; communication; (law) writ, brief; —, *p.p.* of **escribir,** written; **por —,** in writing.
escritor, ra, *n.* writer, author.
escritorio, *m.* writing desk; counting house; office, study.
escritura, *f.* writing; deed; **— de venta,** bill of sale; **— pública,** deed attested by a notary; **E—,** Scripture.
escriturar, *va.* to bind oneself legally.
escrofuloso, sa, *adj.* scrofulous.
escrupulizar, *vn.* to scruple, to doubt.

escrúpulo, *m.* doubt, scruple, scrupulousness; (ast.) minute on a graduated sphere.
escrupulosidad, *f.* scrupulosity.
escrupuloso, sa, *adj.* scrupulous; exact.
escrutinio, *m.* scrutiny, inquiry.
escrutiñador, *m.* scrutinizer, censor.
escuadra, *f.* square; squad; squadron; fleet; **— de reborde,** try square.
escuadrar, *va.* to square.
escuadrilla, *f.* escadrille.
escuadrón, *m.* squadron, troop of cavalry.
escuadronar, *va.* to form troops in squadrons.
escuadronista, *m.* (mil.) tactician.
escualidez, *f.* squalidness, misery.
escucha, *f.* sentinel, sentry; scout.
escuchar, *va.* to listen, to hearken.
escudar, *va.* to shield; to guard from danger; **—se,** to depend on some means of evading danger.
escudero, *m.* squire, escort.
escudilla, *f.* porringer.
escudillar, *va.* to pour out broth into bowls; to domineer.
escudo, *m.* shield, buckler; scutcheon of a lock; crown (gold coin); **— de armas,** coat of arms.
escudriñamiento, *m.* investigation, scrutiny.
escudriñar, *va.* to search, to pry into; to examine into.
escuela, *f.* school; **— de párvulos,** kindergarten; **— para externos,** day school; **— para internos,** boarding school; **escuela primaria,** elementary or grammar school; **— secundaria,** high school; **— superior,** college, university.
escueto, ta, *adj.* devoid of trimmings; strict; free, unencumbered.
esculcar, *va.* to spy; to search carefully; (Sp. Am.) to look for something hidden.
esculpir, *va.* to sculpture, to carve.
escultor, *m.* sculptor, carver.
escultura, *f.* sculpture; work of a sculptor.
escupidera, *f.* spittoon.
escupidero, *m.* spitting place.
escupidura, *f.* spittle; fever sore.
escupir, *va.* to spit.
escurreplatos, *m.* rack for draining dishes after washing.
escurrido, da, *adj.* having narrow hips; wearing skimpy clothing.
escurriduras, *f. pl.* dregs, lees.
escurrimiento, *m.* run-off, dripping, flow.
escurrir, *va.* to drain to the dregs; **—,** *vn.* to drop; to slip, to slide; to glide slowly; **—se,** to slip away.
esdrújulo, la, *adj.* (gram.) pertaining to a word whose accent falls on the antepenultimate syllable.
ESE estesudeste, ESE or E.S.E. east southeast.
ese, esa, *pron.* that.
esencia, *f.* essence.
esencial, *adj.* essential; principal.
esfera, *f.* sphere; globe; dial.

esférico, ca, *adj.* spherical.
esferoidal, *adj.* spheroid.
esferoide, *f.* spheroid.
esfinge, *m.* or *f.* sphinx.
esforzado, da, *adj.* strong, vigorous, valiant.
esforzar, *va.* (UE) to strengthen; **—se,** to exert oneself, to make an effort.
esfuerzo, *m.* effort, force; courage, spirit, vigor; **— de rotación,** (mech.) torque.
esfumarse, *vr.* to disappear.
esgarrar, *va.* and *vn.* to clear one's throat.
esgrima, *f.* fencing; **maestro de —,** fencing master.
esgrimador, *m.* fencer; fencing master.
esgrimir, *va.* to fence, to wield (a sword).
eslabón, *m.* link of a chain; steel for striking fire.
eslabonar, *va.* to link; to unite.
Eslavonia, *f.* Slavonia.
Eslovaquia, *f.* Slovakia.
esmaltador, *m.* enameler.
esmaltar, *va.* to enamel.
esmalte, *m.* enamel; fingernail polish.
esmerado, da, *adj.* painstaking, carefully done.
esmeralda, *f.* emerald.
esmerar, *va.* to polish; **—se** to do one's best, to take pains.
esmeril, *m.* emery.
esmerilar, *va.* to polish with an emery.
esmero, *m.* careful attention, elaborate effort; neatness.
eso, *dem. pron. neuter,* that (idea or statement); **— de,** that matter of; **a — de,** about; **por —,** for that reason, therefore.
esófago, *m.* gullet; throat, esophagus.
esotérico, ca, *adj.* esoteric, private, secret.
esotro, tra, *pron.* (contraction of **ese otro,** etc.) this or that other.
espabiladeras, *f. pl.* snuffers, candle snuffer.
espabilar, *va.* to snuff a candle.
espaciador, *m.* spacer.
espaciar, *va.* to extend, to dilate, to spread; (print.) to insert spaces; **—se,** to walk to and fro; to cheer up.
espacio, *m.* space, capacity; distance; slowness; (aer.) clearance.
espaciosidad, *f.* spaciousness, capacity.
espacioso, sa, *adj.* spacious, roomy; slow.
espada, *f.* sword; spade (in cards); **—,** *m.* swordsman; bullfighter who uses a sword.
espadachín, *m.* dexterous swordsman; bully.
espadaña, *f.* (bot.) cattail.
espadar, *va.* to break hemp or flax with a swingle.
espadería, *f.* sword cutler's shop.
espadero, *m.* sword cutler.
espadilla, *f.* swingle; ace of spades.
espadín, *m.* small short sword.
espalda, *f.* back; shoulders; shoulder of a bastion; **a —s,** behind one's back; **cargado de —s,** round-shouldered; **dar la —,** to turn one's back.
espaldar, *m.* backpiece of suit of armor; back of a seat; espalier in gardens.

espaldilla, *f.* shoulder blade.

espalmar, *va.* to pare a horse's hoof for shoeing.

espantadizo, za, *adj.* timid, easily frightened.

espantajo, *m.* scarecrow; bugaboo.

espantamoscas, *m.* fly swatter; anything to ward off flies.

espantapájaros, *m.* scarecrow.

espantar, *va.* to frighten, to daunt; to chase or drive away.

espanto, *m.* fright; menace, threat; wonder, surprise; apparition, spook.

espantosamente, *adv.* frightfully, horribly.

espantoso, sa, *adj.* frightful, dreadful; hideous.

España, *f.* Spain.

español, la, *n.* and *adj.* Spaniard; Spanish; —, *m.* Spanish language.

Española, *f.* Hispaniola.

españolismo, *m.* Hispanicism; fondness for things typical of Spain; idiomatic expression characteristic of Spain.

esparadrapo, *m.* court plaster, adhesive plaster.

esparaván, *m.* (vet.) spavin; sparrowhawk.

esparavel, *m.* casting net, dragnet.

esparcimiento, *m.* dispersal.

esparcir, *va.* to scatter; to divulge; —, *vn.* to effuse; —se, to amuse oneself.

espárrago, *m.* asparagus.

esparrancado, da, *adj.* with legs outstretched; spread asunder.

espartería, *f.* place where mats of esparto are made or sold.

espartero, *m.* maker and seller of esparto work.

esparto, *m.* (bot.) esparto, feather grass.

espasmo, *m.* spasm.

espasmódico, ca, *adj.* spasmodic.

espástico, ca, *adj.* (med.) spastic.

espato, *m.* spar; — flúor, fluor spar.

espátula, *f.* spatula.

especería, *f.* grocer's shop, grocery; spices.

especia, *f.* spice; —s, *pl.* medicinal drugs.

especial, *adj.* special, particular; en —, specially.

especialidad, *f.* specialty.

especialista, *m.* and *f.* specialist.

especializarse, *vr.* to specialize.

especie, *f.* species; matter; motive; class, sort, kind.

especiero, *m.* dealer in spices and aromatic drugs.

especificación, *f.* specification.

específicamente, *adv.* specifically.

especificar, *va.* to specify.

específico, ca, *adj.* specific; —, *m.* patented medicine.

espécimen, *m.* specimen, sample.

especioso, sa, *adj.* neat, beautiful, finished with care; specious, deceiving.

espectáculo, *m.* spectacle, sight; show.

espectador, *m.* spectator, onlooker.

espectral, *adj.* phantomlike.

espectro, *m.* specter, phantom, ghost, apparition; spectrum.

espectrómetro, *m.* spectrometer.

espectroscopio, *m.* (med.) spectroscope.

especulación, *f.* speculation, contemplation; commercial scheme.

especulador, ra, *n.* speculator.

especular, *va.* to speculate.

especulativo, va, *adj.* speculative; thoughtful.

espejismo, *m.* mirage.

espejo, *m.* looking glass, mirror; — de retrovisión, rear view mirror.

espelta, *f.* (bot.) spelt.

espeluznar, *va.* and *vr.* to set the hair on end (from shock).

espera, *f.* stay, waiting; (law) respite, adjournment, delay; sala de —, waiting room.

esperanto, *m.* Esperanto.

esperanza, *f.* hope, expectation; (naut.) áncora de —, sheet anchor.

esperanzar, *va.* to give hope.

esperar, *va.* to hope; to expect, to wait for.

esperezarse, *vn.* to stretch one's limbs.

esperma, *f.* sperm.

espermático, *adj.* spermatic.

espermatozoide, *m.* spermatozoon.

espernancado, da, *adj.* with widespread legs.

espesar, *va.* to thicken, to condense; —se, to grow thick, to solidify.

espeso, sa, *adj.* thick, dense.

espesor, *m.* thickness.

espesura, *f.* thickness, density, solidity.

espetar, *va.* to spit, to skewer; to pierce; (coll.) to spring (something) on one; —se, to be stiff and stately.

espetera, *f.* rack for kitchen utensils; kitchen equipment.

espetón, *m.* spit, poker, large pin; sea pike.

espía, *m.* and *f.* spy; — doble, spy who acts for contending parties.

espiar, *va.* to spy, to lurk.

espiga, *f.* ear (of grain); fuse of a bomb; sail of a galley; spike, peg.

espigadora, *f.* gleaner.

espigar, *vn.* to shoot into ears; to grow, to increase; —, *va.* to glean.

espigón, *m.* ear of corn; sting (as of a bee).

espina, *f.* thorn; thistle; spine, backbone; fishbone; — dorsal, spinal column; estar en —s, to be on needles and pins.

espinaca, *f.* (bot.) spinach.

espinar, *va.* to prick with thorns; —, *m.* place full of thornbushes, brambles, etc.; arduous undertaking.

espinazo, *m.* spine, backbone.

espinela, *f.* a ten-line octosyllabic meter.

espineta, *f.* (mus.) spinet.

espingarda, *f.* small piece of ordnance.

espinilla, *f.* shinbone; blackhead.

espino, *m.* thorn, prickly tree.

espinoso, sa, *adj.* thorny, spiny; arduous, dangerous.

espión, *m.* spy.

espiral, *adj.* spiral; —, *f.* spiral line.

espirar, *va.* to exhale; to instill, to move; —, *vn.* to breathe.

espirea, *f.* (bot.) spirea.

espiritar, *va.* (coll.) to possess with the devil; to wish someone to the devil; to irritate, to agitate; —se, to be possessed with an evil spirit.

espiritismo, *m.* spiritualism; spiritism.

espíritu, *m.* spirit, soul; genius; ardor; courage; (chem.) spirits; **el E— Santo,** the Holy Ghost; —s, *pl.* demons, goblins.

espiritual, *adj.* spiritual; ghostly.

espiritualidad, *f.* spirituality; principle and effect of what is spiritual.

espiritualizar, *va.* to spiritualize, to refine the intellect.

espirituoso, sa, *adj.* spirituous; vivid, lively.

espiroqueta, *f.* (biol.) spirochete.

espirómetro, *m.* spirometer, pulmotor.

espitar, *va.* to put a faucet in a tub.

esplendente, *adj.* (poet.) shining, resplendent.

esplendidez, *f.* splendor, magnificence.

espléndido, da, *adj.* splendid, magnificent; brilliant.

esplendor, *m.* splendor, radiance; magnificence.

espliego, *m.* (bot.) lavender.

esplín, *m.* melancholy.

espolazo, *m.* violent prick with a spur.

espolear, *va.* to spur, to instigate, to incite.

espoleta, *f.* fuse of a bomb; wishbone.

espolín, *m.* shuttle for brocading flowers on cloth.

espolique or **espolista,** *m.* running footman.

espolón, *m.* spur of a cock; icebreaker; (naut.) beak of a galley; (mil.) salient angle of a fortification.

espolvorear, *va.* and *vr.* to shake off the dust; to sprinkle with powder.

espondeo, *m.* (poet.) spondee.

esponja, *f.* sponge.

esponjadura, *f.* act of sponging.

esponjar, *va.* to sponge; —se, to be puffed up with pride.

esponjoso, sa, *adj.* spongy.

esponsales, *m. pl.* espousals, betrothal.

espontaneidad, *f.* spontaneity.

espontáneo, nea, *adj.* spontaneous; freewill.

espora, *f.* spore.

esposa, *f.* wife; —s, *pl.* manacles, handcuffs.

esposo, *m.* husband; —s, *pl.* married couple.

espuela, *f.* spur; stimulus; (bot.) larkspur; **— de caballero,** larkspur, delphinium.

espuerta, *f.* pannier, basket; **a —s,** in abundance.

espulgar, *va.* to delouse, to remove fleas from; to examine closely.

espulgo, *m.* cleaning from lice or fleas.

espuma, *f.* lather; froth, spume, foam.

espumadera, *f.* skimmer.

espumajear, *vn.* to froth at the mouth.

espumajoso, sa, *adj.* foamy, frothy, full of spume.

espumar, *va.* to skim, to take off the scum.

espumarajo, *m.* foam, froth (from the mouth).

espumosidad, *f.* foaminess.

espumoso, sa, *adj.* spumy, frothy, foamy.

espurio, ria, *adj.* spurious; adulterated, corrupted.

espurrir, *vn.* to stretch out the legs.

esputo, *m.* spit, sputum, saliva.

esq. esquina, *cor.* corner.

esquela, *f.* note, slip of paper.

esqueleto, *m.* skeleton.

esquema, *m.* scheme, diagram, sketch.

esquemático, ca, *adj.* schematic.

esquicio, *m.* sketch, drawn outline.

esquife, *m.* skiff, small boat.

esquilador, *m.* sheepshearer.

esquilar, *va.* to shear sheep.

esquileo, *m.* sheepshearing.

esquilmar, *va.* to gather and get in the harvest; to impoverish.

esquilmo, *m.* harvest; produce of vines, cattle.

esquilón, *m.* small bell, bell worn by cattle.

esquina, *f.* corner, angle; **doblar la —,** to turn the corner.

esquinado, da, *adj.* cornered, angled.

esquinar, *va.* to form into an angle.

esquinazo, *m.* corner; (Chile) serenade; **dar —,** (coll.) to jilt, to shake off.

esquisto, *m.* schist.

esquite, *m.* (Mex.) popped corn.

esquivar, *va.* to shun, to avoid, to evade; **— el cuerpo,** to dodge; —se, to disdain, to scorn.

esquivez, *f.* disdain, scorn.

esquivo, va, *adj.* scornful; shy, reserved.

estabilidad, *f.* stability; fixation.

estabilización, *f.* stabilization.

estabilizador, *m.* stabilizer; (aer.) fin.

estabilizar, *va.* to stabilize.

estable, *adj.* stable.

establecer, *va.* (EZCO) to establish, to found, to set; to decree.

establecimiento, *m.* establishment; founding; household.

establero, *m.* horsekeeper, groom, hostler.

establo, *m.* stable; cattlebarn.

estaca, *f.* stake; stick, cudgel.

estacada, *f.* (mil.) palisade; paling.

estacar, *va.* to enclose with stakes.

estacazo, *m.* blow given with a stake.

estación, *f.* station (railroad, radio, telegraph, etc.); position, condition, state, situation; season (of the year); **— de servicio,** (auto.) service station; **— de vehículos,** parking station; **red de — es,** network (radio).

estacional, *adj.* seasonal.

estacionamiento, *m.* stationing; (auto.) parking.

estacionar, *va.* (auto.) to park.

estacionario, ria, *adj.* stationary.

estadía, *f.* stay, sojourn; (naut.) demurrage.

estadio, *m.* racecourse, stadium; furlong.

estadista, *m.* statesman.

estadística, *f.* statistics; — **demográfica,** vital statistics.

estadístico, *m.* statistician; —, **ca,** *adj.* statistical.

estado, *m.* state, condition; — **de cuenta,** statement of an account; — **de guerra** or **de sitio,** martial law; — **mayor,** military staff; **hombre de —,** statesman.

Estados Unidos de América, *m. pl.* United States of America.

estadounidense or **estadunidense,** *adj.* of the United States of America; —, *m.* and *f.* person from the U. S. A.

estafa, *f.* trick, imposition; swindle.

estafador, *m.* impostor, swindler.

estafar, *va.* to deceive, to defraud; to swindle.

estafermo, *m.* wooden movable figure of an armed man; idle fellow who affects dignity and importance.

estafeta, *f.* courier, express; general post office for letters.

estafetero, *m.* postmaster.

estagnación, *f.* stagnation, paralyzation (of activities).

estalactita, *f.* stalactite.

estalagmita, *f.* stalagmite.

estallar, *vn.* to crack, to burst; to break out into fury.

estallido, *m.* crack, crackling, crash; blowout; outburst.

estambre, *m.* fine wool; stamen of flowers.

estamento, *m.* name given to each of the three estates of Spain composing the Cortes.

estameña, *f.* serge.

estampa, *f.* print, stamp; pattern, model.

estampador, *m.* stamper.

estampar, *va.* to print; to stamp; to imprint.

estampería, *f.* office for printing or selling prints.

estampero, *m.* maker or seller of stamps.

estampido, *m.* report of a gun, etc.; crack, crash.

estampilla, *f.* signet, rubber stamp; (Sp. Am.) postage stamp.

estancar, *va.* to check a current; to monopolize; to prohibit, to suspend.

estancia, *f.* stay, sojourn; mansion; (Sp. Am.) cattle ranch; living room; (poet.) stanza.

estanciero, ra, *n.* small farmer.

estanco, *m.* forestalling, monopoly; place where only monopoly goods are sold; —, **ca,** *adj.* (naut.) watertight.

estandarte, *m.* banner, standard.

estanque, *m.* pond, pool; basin.

estanquillero, *m.* tobacconist.

estanquillo, *m.* tobacconist's shop, cigar store.

estante, *m.* shelf; bookcase; **—s,** *pl.* (naut.) props of the cross beams.

estañador, *m.* tinman.

estañadura, *f.* tinning.

estañar, *va.* to tin; to solder.

estaño, *m.* (chem.) tin.

estaquilla, *f.* cleat, peg, spike.

estar, *vn.* (ESTOY, ESTUVE), to be; to be in a place; — **de prisa,** to be in a hurry; — **sobre sí,** to be cautious or wary; —**se parado** or **quieto,** to stand still; ¿**estamos?** do you understand? — **bien,** to be well; — **bueno,** to be well; — **de pie,** to be standing; — **malo,** to be ill.

estarcido or **estarcidor,** *m.* stencil.

estarcir, *va.* to stencil.

estática, *f.* statics, static.

estático, ca, *adj.* static; **techo —,** (aer.) static ceiling.

estatua, *f.* statue.

estatuario, *m.* statuary.

estatuir, *va.* (UYO) to establish, to determine; to enact.

estatura, *f.* stature.

estatuto, *m.* statute, law, bylaw.

estdo. estimado, esteemed.

este, *m.* east.

este, *m.,* **este,** *f. pron.* this, this one; **estos, tas,** *pl.* these.

esteapsina, *f.* steapsin.

estearina, *f.* stearine.

esteatita, *f.* soapstone.

Esteban, Stephen.

estenografía, *f.* stenography, shorthand writing.

estenógrafo, fa, *n.* stenographer, shorthand writer.

estenomecanografía, *f.* stenotyping.

estenomecanógrafo, fa, *n.* stenotypist.

estenotipia, *f.* stenotyping.

Ester, Esther.

éster, *m.* (chem.) ester.

estera, *f.* mat.

esterar, *va.* to cover with mats.

estercoladura, *f.* manuring.

estercolar, *va.* to dung, to manure; —, *vn.* to void the excrements.

estercolero, *m.* dunghill; dungpit.

estereóptico, *m.* stereopticon.

estereoscopio, *m.* stereoscope.

estereotipar, *va.* to stereotype.

estereotipia, *f.* stereotypography.

esterero, *m.* mat maker.

estéril, *adj.* sterile; barren.

esterilidad, *f.* sterility, barrenness.

esterilización, *f.* sterilization.

esterilizador, *m.* sterilizer.

esterilizar, *va.* to sterilize; to make barren or sterile; to free from germs.

esterilla, *f.* narrow braid of gold or silver; small mat.

esterlina, *adj.* sterling; **libra —,** pound sterling.

estero, *m.* estuary, firth; matting; matting season; (Arg.) swamp.

esteta, *m.* aesthete.
estética, *f.* aesthetics.
estetoscopio, *m.* stethoscope.
esteva, *f.* plow handle; long stick.
estevado, da, *adj.* bow-legged.
estiércol, *m.* dung; excrement, manure.
estigma, *m.* birthmark; stigma, affront.
estilar, *va.* and *vn.* to use, to be accustomed; **—se,** to be in style, to be customary.
estilete, *m.* stiletto.
estilo, *m.* stylus; style; use, custom; **por el —,** of the sort, kind.
estilográfico, ca, *adj.* stylographic; **pluma —,** fountain pen, stylographic pen.
estilógrafo, *m.* fountain pen, stylograph.
estima, *f.* esteem.
estimable, *adj.* estimable, worthy of esteem.
estimación, *f.* estimation, valuation, account.
estimar, *va.* to estimate, to value; to esteem; to judge.
estimular, *va.* to encourage, to stimulate; to sting, to excite, to goad.
estímulo, *m.* stimulus, encouragement, inducement.
estío, *m.* summer.
estipendiario, *m.* stipendiary.
estipendio, *m.* stipend, salary.
estíptico, ca, *adj.* styptic, astringent.
estipulación, *f.* stipulation.
estipular, *va.* to stipulate.
estirado, da, *adj.* forced.
estirador, *m.* drawing frame; stretcher (of curtains, etc.).
estirar, *va.* to dilate, to stretch out; to extend a discourse.
estirón, *m.* pulling; hauling; (coll.) **dar un —,** to grow rapidly.
estirpe, *f.* race, origin, stock.
estivador, *m.* stevedore, longshoreman.
esto, *pron. neuter,* this; **a —,** hereto, hereunto; **con —,** herewith; **en —,** at this juncture; **por —,** for this reason; **— es,** that is.
estocada, *f.* stab.
Estocolmo, *m.* Stockholm.
estofa, *f.* quilted material; quality.
estofado, da, *adj.* quilted; stewed.
estofar, *va.* to quilt; to stew meat.
estoicamente, *adv.* stoically.
estoico, *adj.* stoic, indifferent.
estola, *f.* priest's stole.
estolidez, *f.* coolness; stupidity; incapacity.
estólido, da, *adj.* stupid.
estomacal, *adj.* stomachic.
estomagar, *va.* to stomach, to resent; to enrage.
estómago, *m.* stomach.
estomatitis, *f.* (med.) stomatitis.
Estonia, *f.* Esthonia.
estopa, *f.* tow; burlap; oakum; waste for wiping machinery.
estopilla, *f.* fine spinning flax; lawn (cloth); **— de algodón,** cheesecloth.
estopín, *m.* quick match.

estopón, *m.* coarse tow.
estoposo, sa, *adj.* filamentous.
estoque, *m.* rapier.
estorbador, *m.* disturber.
estorbar, *va.* to hinder, to obstruct; to molest.
estorbo, *m.* hindrance, impediment.
estornudar, *vn.* to sneeze.
estornudo, *m.* sneeze.
estotro, tra, *pron.* (contraction for **este otro,** etc.) this other.
estrabismo, *m.* (med.) strabismus, cross-eye.
estrada, *f.* causeway.
estrado, *m.* drawing room; **—s,** *pl.* law courts.
estrafalario, ria, *adj.* slovenly, extravagant.
estragar, *va.* to deprave, to corrupt.
estrago, *m.* ravage; havoc.
estrambótico, ca, *adj.* extravagant, irregular; freakish.
estrangulador, ra, *n.* strangler; throttle of an engine.
estrangular, *va.* and *vr.* to choke, to strangle; (med.) to strangulate.
estratagema, *f.* stratagem; trick.
estrategia, *f.* strategy.
estratégico, ca, *adj.* strategic.
estrato, *m.* stratum, layer, stratus.
estratosfera, *f.* stratosphere.
estraza, *f.* rag; **papel de —,** brown paper.
estrechar, *va.* to tighten; to contract, to constrict; to clasp; to compress; **—se,** to bind oneself strictly; to reduce one's expenses; to communicate in confidence; to intensify one's friendship with someone.
estrechez, *f.* straitness, narrowness; intimate friendship; poverty.
estrecho, *m.* strait; narrow passage between two mountains; **—, cha,** *adj.* narrow, close; strait, tight; intimate; rigid, austere; exact; poor, indigent.
Estrecho de Magallanes, *m.* Strait of Magellan.
estregadura, *f.* friction, rubbing.
estregar, *va.* (IE) to rub one thing against another.
estrella, *f.* star.
estrellado, da, *adj.* starry; dashed to pieces; **huevos —s,** fried eggs.
estrellar, *va.* to dash to pieces; to crash, to hit against; to fry (eggs); **—se,** to be shattered (by).
estremecer, *va.* (EZCO) to shake, to make tremble; **—se,** to shake, to tremble; to thrill.
estremecimiento, *m.* trembling, shaking, shiver, thrill.
estrena, *f.* gift, handsel.
estrenar, *va.* to handsel; to regale; **—se,** to use for the first time; to begin.
estreno, *m.* début, first performance.
estrenuidad, *f.* energy, strength, vigor.
estreñimiento, *m.* obstruction; constipation.

estreñir, *va.* (1) to restrain; to constipate; —se, to restrain oneself; to become constipated.

estrépito, *m.* noise, clamor, bustle, noisiness, obstreperousness.

estrepitoso, sa, *adj.* noisy, rowdy.

estreptococo, *m.* streptococcus.

estría, *f.* groove.

estriadura, *f.* fluting.

estribar, *vn.* to prop; to found; to be supported; to depend upon; to rest on.

estribillo, *m.* refrain of a song.

estribo, *m.* buttress; stirrup; step on the side of a coach; running board; **perder los —s,** to talk nonsense; to lose one's head.

estricnina, *f.* strychnine.

estricto, ta, *adj.* strict, exact; severe.

estridente, *adj.* strident; obstreperous, clamorous.

estrofa, *f.* (poet.) stanza.

estropajear, *va.* to clean a wall with a dry brush.

estropajo, *m.* dishrag; worthless thing.

estropajoso, sa, *adj.* ragged; despicable; mean; stammering.

estropear, *va.* to spoil by rough usage; to maim, to cripple.

estropeo, *m.* weariness, fatigue; deterioration; rough treatment.

estructura, *f.* structure.

estruendo, *m.* clamor, noise; confusion, bustle; pomp, ostentation.

estrujadura, *f.* pressure, compressing.

estrujar, *va.* to press, to squeeze.

estrujón, *m.* last pressing of grapes; pressing, squeezing.

estuante, *adj.* exceedingly hot and glowing.

estuario, *m.* = **estero.**

estuco, *m.* stucco, plaster.

estuche, *m.* case for small articles; (fig.) a clever fellow.

estudiante, *m.* scholar, student.

estudiantil, *adj.* scholastic, pertaining to students.

estudiantina, *f.* roving band of students; **a la —,** in the manner of students.

estudiar, *va.* to study.

estudio, *m.* study; studio.

estudioso, sa, *adj.* studious.

estufa, *f.* stove; hothouse; heater.

estufador, *m.* stewpan.

estufero, *m.* stove maker.

estufilla, *f.* muff; small brazier.

estulto, ta, *adj.* silly, foolish.

estupefacción, *f.* stupefaction.

estupefacto, ta, *adj.* petrified with astonishment; stupefied.

estupendo, da, *adj.* stupendous, marvelous.

estupidez, *f.* stupidity.

estúpido, da, *adj.* stupid.

estupor, *m.* stupor; astonishment.

estuprador, *m.* ravisher, one who rapes.

estuprar, *va.* to ravish, to rape.

estupro, *m.* ravishment, rape.

estuque, *m.* = **estuco.**

etapa, *f.* (mil.) ration; stage, station, step.

etc. or &c. etcétera, etc. and so forth.

etcétera, *f.* et cetera, and so on.

éter, *m.* ether.

etéreo, rea, *adj.* ethereal.

eternidad, *f.* eternity.

eternizar, *va.* to eternalize, to perpetuate.

eterno, na, *adj.* eternal.

etesio, *adj.* etesian, annual; **viento —,** yearly wind.

ética, *f.* ethics.

ético, ca, *adj.* ethical, moral.

etileno, *m.* (chem.) ethylene.

etílico, ca, *adj.* ethylic; **alcohol —co,** ethylic alcohol.

etilo, *m.* ethyl.

etimología, *f.* etymology.

etimológico, ca, *adj.* etymological.

etiología, *f.* etiology.

Etiopía, *f.* Ethiopia.

etiqueta, *f.* etiquette, formality; label; **de —,** in formal dress.

étnico, ca, *adj.* ethnic.

etnografía, *f.* ethnography.

etnógrafo, *m.* ethnographer.

etnología, *f.* ethnology.

etnológico, ca, *adj.* ethnological.

etnólogo, *m.* ethnologist.

E. U. Estados Unidos, U. S. United States.

E. U. A. Estados Unidos de América, U. S. A. United States of America.

eucalipto, *m.* eucalyptus.

Eucaristía, *f.* Lord's Supper.

eucarístico, ca, *adj.* eucharistic.

eufonía, *f.* euphony.

eufónico, ca, *adj.* euphonious.

euforia, *f.* capacity to withstand the rigors of a disease; euphoria, well-being, buoyancy.

eugenesia, *f.* eugenics.

Eug.º Eugenio, Eug. Eugene.

Eugenio, Eugene.

eupepsia, *f.* (med.) normal digestion.

Euro, *m.* Eurus, the east wind.

Europa, *f.* Europe.

europeo, pea, *n.* and *adj.* European.

eutanasia, *f.* euthanasia.

Eva, Eve.

evacuación, *f.* evacuation; issue.

evacuar, *va.* to evacuate, to empty.

evadir, *va.* to evade, to escape.

Evang.º Evangelio, Gospel.

evangélico, ca, *adj.* evangelical.

evangelio, *m.* gospel.

evangelismo, *m.* evangelist.

evangelista, *m.* evangelist.

evangelizar, *va.* to evangelize.

evaporar, *va.* to evaporate; —, *vn.* to pass away; to grow vapid.

evasión, *f.* evasion, escape; subterfuge, poor excuse.

evasivo, va, *adj.* evasive, elusive, noncommittal.

eventual, *adj.* eventual, fortuitous.

eversión, *f.* destruction, devastation.
evicción, *f.* eviction, ejection.
evidencia, *f.* evidence, manifestation; **poner en —,** to make clear, to demonstrate.
evidente, *adj.* evident, clear, manifest.
evitable, *adj.* avoidable.
evitar, *va.* to avoid.
eviterno, na, *adj.* imperishable, indestructible (applied to the angels, the heavens, etc.).
evo, *m.* eon, eternity.
evocación, *f.* evocation; invocation.
evocar, *va.* to call out; to invoke.
evolución, *f.* evolution; evolvement.
evolucionario, ria, *adj.* evolutionary.
evolucionista, *m.* evolutionist.
ex abrupto, *adv.* abruptly, unceremoniously.
exacción, *f.* exaction; impost; contribution.
exacerbación, *f.* exacerbation.
exacerbar, *va.* to exasperate, to irritate.
exactitud, *f.* exactness, exactitude.
exacto, ta, *adj.* exact, punctual, assiduous.
exageración, *f.* exaggeration, overstatement.
exagerador, ra, *n.* amplifier, one that exaggerates.
exagerar, *va.* to exaggerate, to amplify.
exagonal, *adj.* hexagonal.
exaltación, *f.* exaltation, elevation.
exaltado, da, *adj.* hot-headed.
exaltar, *va.* to exalt, to elevate; to praise, to extol; **—se,** to become excited and
examen, *m.* examination, trial, inquiry; scrutiny; **sufrir un —,** to take an examination.
exámetro, *m.* hexameter (verse).
examinación, *f.* examination.
examinador, ra, *n.* examiner.
examinando, da, *n.* examinant.
examinar, *va.* to examine, to scrutinize.
exangüe, *adj.* exsanguine, bloodless.
exangular, *adj.* hexangular.
exánime, *adj.* spiritless, weak, dead.
exasperación, *f.* exasperation.
exasperar, *va.* to exasperate, to irritate.
Exc.ª Excelencia, Excellency.
excarcelar, *va.* to set a prisoner free.
excavación, *f.* excavation.
excavadora, *f.* excavator.
excavar, *va.* to excavate, to dig out.
excedente, *adj.* excessive, exceeding; **—,** *m.* surplus, excess.
exceder, *va.* to exceed, to surpass, to excel, to outdo.
Excelencia, *f.* Excellency (title).
excelencia, *f.* excellence.
excelente, *adj.* excellent.
excelso, sa, *adj.* elevated, sublime, lofty.
excentricidad, *f.* eccentricity.
excéntrico, ca, *adj.* eccentric.
excepción, *f.* exception.
excepto, *adv.* except that, excepting.
exceptuar, *va.* to except, to exempt.
excesivo, va, *adj.* excessive.

exceso, *m.* excess; **— de peso** or **de equipaje,** excess baggage.
excisión, *f.* excision.
excitable, *adj.* excitable, high-strung, nervous.
excitación, *f.* excitation.
excitante, *adj.* exciting, excitant.
excitar, *va.* to excite, to arouse, to urge; to enkindle.
exclamación, *f.* exclamation.
exclamar, *va.* to exclaim, to cry out.
excluir, *va.* (UYO) to exclude.
exclusión, *f.* exclusion; preclusion.
exclusivamente, *adv.* exclusively.
exclusive, *adv.* exclusively, exclusive, not included.
exclusividad, *f.* exclusiveness.
exclusivo, va, *adj.* exclusive, select.
excogitar, *va.* to cogitate, to contrive.
excomulgar, *va.* to excommunicate.
excomunión, *f.* excommunication.
excoriación, *f.* excoriation, flaying.
excoriar, *va.* and *vr.* to excoriate, to flay.
excremento, *m.* excrement.
excretar, *va.* to excrete.
excretorio, ria, *adj.* excretory.
exculpación, *f.* exculpation, clearing from an alleged fault.
excursión, *f.* excursion, outing; liquidation of the estate of a debtor for paying his debts; **ómnibus de —,** sight-seeing car.
excursionista, *m.* and *f.* excursionist; sight-seer.
excusa, *f.* excuse, apology, plea.
excusable, *adj.* excusable.
excusado, da, *adj.* excused; exempted, privileged; **—,** *m.* (in olden times) privilege of exemption from taxes; privy, water closet.
excusalí, *m.* apron, pinafore.
excusar, *va.* to excuse, to pardon; to exempt from taxes; to shun, to avoid; **—se,** to decline a request.
execrable, *adj.* execrable, accursed.
execración, *f.* execration, curse.
execrar, *va.* to execrate, to curse.
exégesis, *f.* exegesis.
exención, *f.* exemption, immunity, privilege.
exentar, *va.* to exempt, to privilege.
exento, ta, *adj.* exempt, free; **—,** *m.* officer in the Spanish lifeguards who held the rank of colonel.
exequias, *f. pl.* funeral rites, obsequies.
exhalación, *f.* exhalation; velocity; falling star.
exhalar, *va.* to exhale; **—se,** to evaporate.
exhausto, ta, *adj.* exhausted.
exhibición, *f.* exhibition, exposition.
exhibicionismo, *m.* exhibitionism.
exhibicionista, *m.* and *f.* exhibitionist.
exhibir, *va.* to exhibit, to display.
exhortación, *f.* exhortation.
exhortar, *va.* to exhort, to admonish.
exhorto, *m.* letters requisitorial sent by one judge to another.

exhumación, *f.* exhumation.
exhumar, *va.* to disinter, to unbury.
exigencia, *f.* exigency, demand.
exigente, *adj.* exigent.
exigible, *adj.* requirable.
exigir, *va.* to demand, to require.
exiguo, gua, *adj.* exiguous, small.
eximio, mia, *adj.* choice, excellent, famous, very eminent.
eximir, *va.* to exempt, to excuse.
existencia, *f.* existence, existency, being; **en —,** in stock.
existente, *adj.* existing, existent.
existir, *vn.* to exist, to be.
éxito, *m.* end, termination; issue; result, outcome; **buen —,** success.
ex-militar, *adj.* ex-service.
éxodo, *m.* exodus.
exoneración, *f.* exoneration.
exonerar, *va.* to exonerate, to unload.
exorbitancia, *f.* exorbitance.
exorbitante, *adj.* exorbitant, excessive, immoderate.
exorcismo, *m.* exorcism.
exorcista, *m.* exorciser, exorcist.
exorcizar, *va.* to exorcise.
exordio, *m.* exordium.
exotérico, ca, *adj.* exoteric.
exótico, ca, *adj.* exotic, foreign.
expansión, *f.* expansion, extension.
expansivo, va, *adj.* expansive; effusive.
expatriación, *f.* expatriation.
expatriarse, *vr.* to be exiled; to emigrate.
expectación, *f.* expectation.
expectativa, *f.* right or claim respecting some future thing; hope of obtaining a reward.
expectoración, *f.* expectoration.
expectorar, *va.* to expectorate.
expedición, *f.* expedition, speed, activity; shipment; **gastos de —,** shipping expenses.
expedicionario, *adj.* expeditionary.
expedidor, *m.* shipper.
expediente, *m.* affair of easy discussion and dispatch; expedient; pretext; provision; action, proceedings.
expedir, *va.* (I) to expedite, to dispatch, to ship, to forward; to issue; to make out (a check, etc.).
expeditivo, va, *adj.* expeditive, expeditious.
expedito, ta, *adj.* prompt, expeditious, speedy.
expeler, *va.* to expel, to eject.
expender, *va.* to expend, to lay out.
expendio, *m.* retail selling; (Mex.) cigar stand.
expensas, *f. pl.* expenses, charges; **a — de,** at the expense of.
experiencia, *f.* experience; trial.
experimentado, da, *adj.* experienced, expert.
experimental, *adj.* experimental.
experimentar, *va.* to experience; to experiment.
experimento, *m.* experiment, trial.

experto, ta, *adj.* expert, experienced; —, *n.* expert, old hand.
expiable, *adj.* expiable.
expiación, *f.* expiation, atonement; purification.
expiar, *va.* to atone for; to purify.
expiatorio, ria, *adj.* expiatory.
expirar, *vn.* to expire, to breathe the last.
explanada, *f.* esplanade.
explanar, *va.* to level, to grade; to explain.
explayar, *va.* to extend, to dilate; **—se,** to dwell upon, to enlarge upon.
expletivo, va, *n.* and *adj.* (gram.) expletive.
explicable, *adj.* explainable.
explicación, *f.* explanation.
explicaderas, *f. pl.* (coll.) manner in which anything is explained; facility of explaining.
explicar, *va.* to explain, to expound; **—se,** to speak plainly; to explain oneself.
explicativo, va, *adj.* explanatory; expository.
explícito, ta, *adj.* explicit, clear, distinct.
exploración, *f.* exploration.
explorador, ra, *n.* explorer; scout; pioneer; —, *adj.* exploring.
explorar, *va.* to explore; to inquire.
exploratorio, ria, *adj.* exploratory.
explosión, *f.* explosion.
explotación, *f.* working, exploiting.
explotar, *va.* to exploit, to profiteer; to operate.
expoliar, *va.* to despoil violently.
exponente, *m.* and *f.* exponent; —, *m.* (math.) exponent.
exponer, *va.* (EXPONGO, EXPUSE), to expose; to explain; to expose to danger, to jeopardize.
exportación, *f.* exportation, export.
exportador, ra, *adj.* exporting; **casa —ra,** export house; —, *m.* exporter.
exportar, *va.* to export.
exposición, *f.* exposition; exposure.
expósito, ta, *adj.* exposed; foundling; —, *n.* foundling.
expositor, ra, *n.* expounder, exhibitor; expositor.
expresar, *va.* to express.
expresión, *f.* expression, utterance.
expresivo, va, *adj.* expressive; affectionate.
expreso, sa, *adj.* expressed; express, clear, manifest, not dubious; —, *m.* express, courier; **—so aéreo,** air express.
express, *m.* (rail.) express train.
exprimidor, *m.* squeezer; wringer.
exprimir, *va.* to squeeze out, to wring; to express, to manifest.
ex profeso, *adv.* avowedly, on purpose.
expropiar, *va.* to expropriate, to commandeer.
expuesto, ta, *adj.* exposed; **lo —to,** what has been stated.
expulsar, *va.* to expel, to drive out.
expulsión, *f.* expulsion.
expulsivo, va, *adj.* expulsive; extrusive.

expulso, sa, *adj.* expelled; outcast.
expurgación, *f.* expurgation, purification.
expurgar, *va.* to purge, to purify.
exquisito, ta, *adj.* exquisite, consummate, excellent.
éxtasis, *m.* ecstacy, enthusiasm.
extático, ca, *adj.* ecstatic.
extender, *va.* (IE) to extend, to spread; to stretch out; **—se,** to be extended; to increase in bulk; to swell; to become generally known.
extensible, *adj.* tensile; extensible.
extensión, *f.* extension; extent; elongation.
extensivo, va, *adj.* extensive; extensible.
extenso, sa, *adj.* extensive, vast.
extenuación, *f.* extenuation, feebleness, debility.
extenuar, *va.* to extenuate, to debilitate.
exterior, *adj.* exterior, external; **—,** *m.* exterior, outward appearance.
exterioridad, *f.* exteriority; outward appearance; outside; pomp, ostentation.
exteriorizar, *va.* to make known, to express.
exteriormente, *adv.* externally.
exterminador, *m.* exterminator.
exterminar, *va.* to exterminate, to root out, to destroy.
exterminio, *m.* extermination, extirpation.
externo, na, *adj.* external, outward; foreign; **—,** *n.* day pupil of a school.
ex testamento, *adv.* by will or testament.
extinción, *f.* extinction.
extinguible, *adj.* extinguishable.
extinguir, *va.* to quench; to extinguish.
extintor, *m.* extinguisher, sprinkler.
extirpable, *adj.* eradicable.
extirpación, *f.* extirpation, extermination.
extirpador, *m.* extirpator; cultivator.
extirpar, *va.* to extirpate, to root out.
extorsión, *f.* extortion.
extra, *inseparable prep.* out of, beyond, extra (as a prefix); **—,** *adj.* unusually good.
extracción, *f.* exportation; extraction.
extractar, *vn.* to extract, to abridge.
extracto, *m.* extract.
extractor, ra, *n.* extractor.
extraer, *va.* (EXTRAIGO, EXTRAJE) to extract; to export.
extrajudicial, *adj.* extrajudicial.
extralegal, *adj.* extralegal.
extralimitarse, *vr.* to overstep one's authority; to take advantage of another's kindness.
extramuros, *adv.* outside (a town).
extranjero, ra, *adj.* foreign; **cambio —,** foreign exchange; **—,** *n.* foreigner, stranger, alien; **ir al —ro,** to go abroad.
extrañación, *f.* expatriation.
extrañar, *va.* to miss; to exile; to alienate; **—se,** to be surprised, to wonder at.
extrañeza, *f.* wonderment, surprise.
extraño, ña, *adj.* foreign; rare; singular, strange, odd.
extraoficial, *adj.* unofficial, off the record.

extraordinario, ria, *adj.* extraordinary, uncommon, odd.
extraterritorial, *adj.* extraterritorial.
extravagancia, *f.* folly, freak.
extravagante, *adj.* freakish; eccentric.
extraviar, *va.* to mislead; **—se,** to lose one's way.
extravío, *m.* deviation; misguidance; loss; madness; misplacement.
extremado, da, *adj.* extreme.
extremar, *va.* to exaggerate; **—se,** to exert oneself to the utmost.
extremaunción, *f.* extreme unction.
extremidad, *f.* extremity, brim of anything.
extremista, *n.* and *adj.* extremist.
extremo, ma, *adj.* extreme, last, **—,** *m.* extreme, highest degree; **de —mo a —mo,** from end to end; **en —mo, por —mo,** extremely.
extrínseco, ca, *adj.* extrinsic, external.
exuberancia, *f.* exuberance, luxuriance.
exudación, *f.* exudation.
exultación, *f.* exultation.
exvoto, *m.* votive offering.

F

f. franco, (com.) free.
f/ fardo, bl. bale; bdl. bundle.
fa, *m.* (mus.) fa.
fab. fabricante, mfr. manufacturer.
f.a.b. franco a bordo, (com.) f.o.b. free on board.
fábrica, *f.* fabrication; factory, factory works; building; **marca de —,** trade-mark.
fabricación, *f.* manufacture; **costo de —,** production cost; **— en serie** or **en gran escala,** mass production.
fabricado, da, *adj.* manufactured; synthetic.
fabricante, *m.* manufacturer, maker.
fabricar, *va.* to build, to construct; to fabricate, to manufacture, to process.
fabril, *adj.* manufacturing.
fabuco, *m.* beechnut.
fábula, *f.* fable; fiction; rumor, common talk.
fabulista, *m.* and *f.* writer of fables.
fabuloso, sa, *adj.* fabulous, fictitious, mythical.
facción, *f.* military exploit; faction; **—ones,** *pl.* features, physiognomy.
faccionario, ria, *adj.* factional.
faccioso, sa, *adj.* factious, turbulent; **—,** *n.* rebel.
facial, *adj.* facial; intuitive, perceiving.
fácil, *adj.* facile, easy.
facilidad, *f.* facility, easiness; ability; **—es,** *pl.* opportunities.
facilitar, *va.* to facilitate; to supply.
fácilmente, *adv.* easily.
facineroso, sa, *adj.* wicked, detestably bad; **—,** *n.* villain, scoundrel.
facistol, *m.* lectern.
facsímile, *m.* facsimile.
fact.ª factura, inv. invoice.
factible, *adj.* feasible, practicable.

facticio, cia, *adj.* factitious, sham.

factor, *m.* factor, element; (math.) factor; (com.) factor, agent; **— de seguridad,** safety factor.

factoría, *f.* factory; factorage, trading post.

factótum, *m.* factotum, jack-of-all-trades.

factura, *f.* invoice, bill; **— simulada,** pro forma invoice; **— de remesa** or **de expedición,** shipping invoice; **libro de —s,** invoice book.

facturar, *va.* to invoice, to bill; to check (baggage).

facultad, *f.* faculty, power, authority; ability.

facultado, da, *adj.* authorized.

facultativo, va, *adj.* optional; **—,** *m.* master of a science or art.

facundia, *f.* eloquence.

facha, *f.* appearance, aspect, mien, face.

fachada, *f.* façade, face, front.

fachenda, *adj.* vain, ostentatious; **—,** *m.* and *f.* one who boasts or brags.

fachendear, *vn.* to pretend to have important business on hand; to brag, to boast.

faena, *f.* work, labor; fatigue; work on shipboard.

faetón, *m.* phaeton.

faisán, *m.* pheasant.

faja, *f.* band, bandage, belt, sash; girdle; **— de terreno,** strip of land.

fajar, *va.* to swathe; to belt; to girdle.

fajero, *m.* knitted swaddling band for children.

fajina, *f.* toil, chore; kindling wood; **hacer —,** (coll.) to clean house thoroughly.

falacia, *f.* fallacy, fraud.

falange, *f.* phalanx.

falaz, *adj.* deceitful, fraudulent; fallacious.

falda, *f.* skirt; lap; flap; slope of a hill; **— pantalón,** culottes; **perrillo de —,** lap dog.

faldellín, *m.* short underskirt.

faldero, ra, *adj.* pertaining to the lap; fond of being constantly among women; **perrillo —,** lap dog.

faldillas, *f. pl.* small skirts.

faldón, *m.* long, flowing skirt; coattail.

falible, *adj.* fallible.

falsamente, *adv.* falsely.

falsario, ria, *adj.* falsifying, forging; **—,** *n.* forger, counterfeiter.

falsarregla, *f.* bevel square, bevel rule.

falsear, *va.* to falsify, to counterfeit; to forge; to distort; **—,** *vn.* to slacken; (mus.) not to agree in sound.

falsedad, *f.* falsehood, untruth.

falsete, *m.* spigot; falsetto voice.

falsificación, *f.* falsification, forgery.

falsificador, ra, *n.* falsifier.

falsificar, *va.* to falsify, to forge, to counterfeit.

falso, sa, *adj.* false, untrue; deceitful; feigned.

falta, *f.* fault, defect, mistake; want, lack;

absence; slight crime; failure; flaw; **— de aceptación,** nonacceptance; **— de pago,** nonpayment; **hacer —,** to be necessary; to be lacking; **poner —s,** to find fault; **sin —,** by all means; **no faltaba más,** (coll.) that's the last straw.

faltar, *vn.* to be wanting, to miss; to lack; to fail; not to fulfil one's promise; to need; to die.

falto, ta, *adj.* wanting, defective; devoid.

faltrero, *m.* pickpocket.

faltriquera, *f.* pocket (as in clothes).

falúa, *f.* (naut.) felucca.

fallar, *va.* to give sentence, to judge; to trump (in cards); **—,** *vn.* to fail, to miss; to be deficient.

fallecer, *vn.* (EZCO) to die.

fallecimiento, *m.* decease, death.

fallido, da, *adj.* disappointed, frustrated; bankrupt.

fallir, *vn.* to die; to fail (in a business, etc.); to comply with one's word.

fallo, *m.* judgment, sentence; being out of a certain suit (in cards); dictum.

fam. familiar, coll. colloquial.

fama, *f.* fame; reputation; **es —,** it is said.

famélico, ca, *adj.* ravenous, hungry.

familia, *f.* family; species.

familiar, *adj.* familiar; colloquial; informal; homelike; **—,** *m.* member of one's family; bosom friend; domestic servant.

familiaridad, *f.* familiarity, intimacy.

familiarizar, *va.* to familiarize; **—se,** to become familiar.

famoso, sa, *adj.* famous, renowned; noted.

fámulo, la, *n.* servant.

fanal, *m.* lantern; beacon, lighthouse; **buque —,** lightship.

fanático, ca, *adj.* fanatical; enthusiastic.

fanatismo, *m.* fanaticism.

fandango, *m.* fandango (lively Spanish dance).

fanega, *f.* a dry measure of approximately 1.6 bushel.

fanfarria, *f.* empty boast.

fanfarrón, ona, *adj.* boasting, bragging; **—,** *n.* bully; braggart.

fanfarronada, *f.* fanfaronade, boast, brag.

fanfarronear, *vn.* to boast, to brag.

fanfarronería, *f.* fanfaronade, vain boasting.

fango, *m.* mire, mud.

fangoso, sa, *adj.* muddy, miry.

fantaseador, ra, *n.* escapist, dreamer.

fantasía, *f.* fancy; fantasy; caprice; presumption; (mus.) fantasia.

fantasma, *m.* phantom, ghost.

fantasmagoría, *f.* phantasmagoria.

fantástico, ca, *adj.* fantastic, whimsical; presumptuous.

faquín, *m.* porter, carrier.

faquir, *m.* fakir.

faramalla, *f.* artful trick, cajolery; prattling; **—,** *m.* and *f.* (coll.) cajoling talebearer.

faramallón, ona, *n.* (coll.) tattling, deceitful person.

farándula, *f.* profession of a low comedian; artful trick.

farandulero, ra, *n.* actor, player; idle tattler, deceitful talker.

Faraón, *m.* Pharaoh; **f—,** faro (card game).

farda, *f.* ancient tax; bundle of clothing; **no pagar —,** (coll.) not to render homage.

fardel, *m.* fardel, bag, knapsack.

fardo, *m.* bale of goods, parcel, bundle.

farfantón, *m.* boasting babbler.

farfantonada, *f.* idle boast.

farfulla, *f.* (coll.) stammering; stammering person.

farfullar, *va.* and *vn.* to talk stammeringly; to do in a hurry and confusion.

faringe, *f.* (anat.) pharynx.

faringitis, *f.* (med.) pharyngitis.

farisaico, ca, *adj.* pharisaical.

farisaísmo, *m.* pharisaism.

fariseo, *m.* Pharisee; (coll.) very tall, austere person; hypocrite.

Farm. farmacia, phar. pharmacy.

farmacéutica, *f.* pharmaceutics.

farmacéutico, ca, *adj.* pharmaceutical.

farmacia, *f.* pharmacy.

farmacología, *f.* pharmacology.

farmacólogo, *m.* pharmacologist.

faro, *m.* (naut.) lighthouse; **— con luz amortiguada,** dimmed headlights.

farol, *m.* lantern, light; **— delantero,** headlight; **— de parada,** stop taillight; **— de tránsito,** traffic light; **— trasero** or **de cola,** taillight.

farola, *f.* street light lamp; beacon.

farolear, *vn.* (coll.) to boast, to brag.

farolero, *m.* lantern maker; lamplighter; (coll.) strutting coxcomb; **—, —ra,** *adj.* vain, ostentatious.

fárrago, *m.* farrago, medley.

farraguista, *m.* and *f.* person with head full of confused knowledge.

farsa, *f.* farce; company of players; sham, humbug.

farsante, *m.* actor, player (in olden times); (coll.) mountebank, charlatan; **—,** *adj.* boastful; deceitful.

fas (por) o por nefas, *adv.* justly or unjustly.

fasces, *f. pl.* fasces.

fascinación, *f.* fascination; deceit.

fascinador, ra, *adj.* fascinating.

fascinar, *va.* to fascinate; to charm; to enchant; to deceive.

fascismo, *m.* fascism.

fascista, *m.* and *f.* fascist.

fase, *f.* phase, aspect.

fastidiar, *va.* to sicken, to bore, to annoy.

fastidio, *m.* fastidiousness, squeamishness; disgust, annoyance, boredom, ennui.

fastidioso, sa, *adj.* squeamish, tiresome; annoying, vexing.

fastoso, sa, or **fastuoso, sa,** *adi.* proud, ostentatious.

fatal, *adj.* fatal; mortal; unfortunate; inevitable.

fatalidad, *f.* fatality, mischance, ill luck; fate.

fatalismo, *m.* fatalism.

fatalista, *n.* and *adj.* fatalist, fatalistic.

fatiga, *f.* toil; fatigue, weariness.

fatigado, da, *adj.* fatigued, weary, tired.

fatigar, *va.* and *vr.* to fatigue, to tire, to harass.

fatigoso, sa, *adj.* tiresome, boresome; tiring.

fatuidad, *f.* fatuity, foolishness, silliness.

fatuo, tua, *adj.* fatuous, stupid, foolish, silly, trifling; **fuego —,** ignis fatuus, will-o-the wisp.

fauces, *f. pl.* (anat.) fauces, gullet.

fauna, *f.* fauna.

fausto, ta, *adj.* happy, fortunate; **—,** *m.* splendor, pomp.

faustoso, sa, *adj.* haughty, ostentatious.

fautor, ra, *n.* abetter, accomplice.

fautoría, *f.* aid, help.

favonio, *m.* (poet.) westerly wind, zephyr.

favor, *m.* favor, good turn; protection, good graces; **a — de,** in favor of.

favorable, *adj.* favorable, advantageous, propitious.

favorcillo, *m.* slight favor.

favorecer, *va.* (EZCO) to favor, to protect.

favoritismo, *m.* favoritism.

favorito, ta, *adj.* favorite, beloved.

faz, *f.* face, front.

F.C. or **f.c. ferrocarril,** R.R. or r.r. railway.

F. ^{co} or **Franc.** ^{co} **Francisco,** Fran. Francis.

F. de T. Fulano de tal, John Doe, so-and-so.

fe, *f.* faith, belief; testimony; **a — mía,** on my honor; **dar —,** to certify, to attest; **en — de lo cual,** in testimony whereof.

fealdad, *f.* ugliness; turpitude, foulness.

feble, *adj.* weak, thin; deficient or weak in weight or quality (applied to metal coins, etc.).

Febo, *m.* (poet.) Phoebus (the sun).

Febo or **feb.° febrero,** Feb. February.

febrero, *m.* February.

febril, *adj.* febrile, feverish.

fecal, *adj.* (med.) fecal.

fecundar, *va.* to fertilize, to fecundate.

fecundidad, *f.* fecundity, fertility.

fecundo, da, *adj.* fruitful, fertile.

fecha, *f.* date (of letter, etc.); **a treinta días —,** at thirty days' sight; **hasta la —,** to date; **con —,** under date; **meses —,** (com.) months after date.

fechador, *m.* dater, dating machine.

fechar, *va.* to date (a letter, document, etc.).

fechoría, *f.* misdeed, villainy.

federación, *f.* federation, confederation.

federal, *adj.* federal.

federalismo, *m.* federalism.

Federica, Frederica.

Federico, Frederick, Fred.

fehaciente, *adj.* authentic.

feldespato, *m.* (min.) feldspar.

felicidad, *f.* felicity, happiness.
felicitación, *f.* congratulation.
felicitar, *va.* to congratulate, to felicitate.
feligrés, esa, *n.* parishioner.
feligresía, *f.* district of a parish.
Felipe, Philip.
Felisa, Felicia. Felicia.
feliz, *adj.* happy, fortunate; — **idea,** clever idea.
felonía, *f.* treachery; felony.
felpa, *f.* plush; a good drubbing.
felpilla, *f.* corded silk for embroidering; chenille.
felpudo, da, *adj.* plushy.
F. E. M. fuerza electromotriz, E. M. F. or e. m. f. electromotive force.
femenil, *adj.* feminine, womanly.
femenino, na, *adj.* feminine, female.
fementido, da, *adj.* false, unfaithful.
feminismo, *m.* feminism.
feminista, *m.* and *f.* feminist.
fémur, *m.* femur.
fenacetina, *f.* phenacetin.
fendiente, *m.* gash, deep cut.
fenecer, *va.* (EZCO) to finish, to conclude; —, *vn.* to come to an end; to die.
fenecimiento, *m.* termination, end.
Fenicia, *f.* Phoenicia.
fenicio, cia, *n.* and *adj.* Phoenician.
fénico, ca, *adj.* carbolic.
fénix, *m.* phoenix; king (in the sense of being the best or highest person or thing of its kind).
fenol, *m.* phenol, carbolic acid; — **rojo,** phenolphthalein.
fenolftaleína, *f.* phenolphthalein.
fenomenal, *adj.* phenomenal.
fenómeno, *m.* phenomenon.
feo, fea, *adj.* ugly; deformed.
feracidad, *f.* fertility, fruitfulness (of soil).
feraz, *adj.* fertile, fruitful (of vegetation).
féretro, *m.* bier, coffin; hearse.
feria, *f.* week day (not Saturday or Sunday); fair, market.
feriado, da, *adj.* suspended (applied to work); **día —do,** holiday.
ferial, *adj.* ferial.
feriar, *va.* to sell, to buy; to give fairings; —, *vn.* to suspend work for a few days.
ferina, *adj.* pertaining to a beast; **tos —,** whooping cough.
fermata, *f.* (mus.) pause, hold.
fermentación, *f.* fermentation.
fermentar, *vn.* to ferment.
fermento, *m.* ferment; leaven; (chem.) enzyme.
fernambuco, *m.* Pernambuco wood.
Fernando, Ferdinand.
Fern.do Fernando, Fer. or Ferd. Ferdinand.
ferocidad, *f.* ferocity, wildness; cruelty.
feróstico, ca, *adj.* (coll.) irritable, unruly; (coll.) exceedingly ugly.
feroz, *adj.* ferocious, cruel, savage, wild.
férreo, rrea, *adj.* iron, ferrous; **vía —rrea,** railroad.

ferrete, *m.* sulphate of copper used in dyeing; iron instrument for branding.
ferretería, *f.* hardware store.
férrico, ca, *adj.* ferric.
ferrocarril, *m.* railroad; — **aéreo,** elevated railroad; — **de cable,** cable railroad; — **de circunvalación,** girdle or belt railroad; — **de sangre,** animal-powered railroad; — **eléctrico,** electric railroad; — **funicular,** cable or funicular railroad; — **subterráneo,** subway; — **urbano** or **metropolitano,** street railroad; **por —,** by rail.
ferrocarrilero, ra, *adj.* (Sp. Am.) railroad; **acciones —as,** railroad stock.
ferrocromo, *m.* ferrochrome.
ferrotipia, *f.* (phot.) ferrotype, tintype.
ferroviario, ria, *adj.* railroad.
ferruginoso, sa, *adj.* like or containing iron.
fértil, *adj.* fertile, fruitful.
fertilidad, *f.* fertility, fecundity, fruitfulness.
fertilización, *f.* fertilization.
fertilizar, *va.* to fertilize.
férula, *f.* ferula, ferrule; yoke, authority rule, dominion; **estar bajo la — de otro,** to be under somebody else's rule or dominion.
feruláceo, cea, *adj.* like a ferrule.
férvido, da, *adj.* fervid, ardent.
ferviente, *adj.* fervent, ardent.
fervor, *m.* fervor, zeal, ardor; faith.
fervoroso, sa, *adj.* fervent, ardent, fervid, eager.
festejar, *va.* to feast, to celebrate; to court, to woo.
festejo, *m.* courtship; feast, entertainment.
festín, *m.* feast, banquet.
festividad, *f.* festivity; solemnization of some occurrence.
festivo, va, *adj.* festive; gay, merry; **día —vo,** holiday.
festón, *m.* garland; festoon.
festonear, *va.* to festoon.
fetal, *adj.* fetal.
fetiche, *m.* fetish.
fetichismo, *m.* fetishism.
fétido, da, *adj.* fetid, stinking.
feto, *m.* fetus.
feúcho, cha, *adj.* somewhat ugly.
feudal, *adj.* feudal.
feudalidad, *f.* feudality.
feudatario, ria, *n.* and *adj.* feudatory.
feudo, *m.* fief, tribute paid to a feudal lord.
fez, *m.* fez, former national headdress of the Turks.
fha. fecha, d. date.
fhdo. fechado, (com.) dated.
fiable, *adj.* responsible, worthy of trust.
fiado, da, *adj.* on trust; **al —do,** on trust, on credit; charged; **en —do,** on bail.
fiador, ra, *n.* bondsman, surety (person); —, *m.* loop of a cloak; fastener; catch of a lock; staple which supports a gutter.
fiambre, *adj.* cold (applied to meat); —, *m.* cold lunch.

fiambrera, *f.* pannier (for carrying cold lunch).

fianza, *f.* caution, security, guarantee, bail; **dar** or **prestar —,** to give security.

fiar, *va.* to bail; to sell on credit; to commit to another, to credit; **—,** *vn.* to confide, to trust.

fiasco, *m.* failure.

fiat, *m.* consent; (law) fiat.

fibra, *f.* fiber; **—s del corazón,** heartstrings.

fibroso, sa, *adj.* fibrous, fibroid.

ficción, *f.* fiction.

ficticio, cia, *adj.* fictitious.

ficha, *f.* counter (at games), chip; **catálogo de —s,** card catalogue; **— de referencia,** cross-reference card.

fichero, *m.* card index, file case.

fidedigno, na, *adj.* worthy of credit, deserving of belief.

fideicomisario, *m.* trustee.

fideicomiso, *m.* (law) trust.

fidelidad, *f.* fidelity; loyalty; punctuality; accuracy.

fideos, *m. pl.* vermicelli, spaghetti, noodles.

fiduciario, ria, *n.* and *adj.* fiduciary.

fiebre, *f.* fever; **— amarilla,** yellow fever; **— cerebral,** brain fever, meningitis; **— mediterránea,** undulant fever.

fiel, *adj.* faithful, loyal; **—,** *m.* inspector of weights and measures; needle of a balance; **—es,** *m. pl.* the faithful.

fielazgo, *m.* office of the town clerk.

fieltro, *m.* felt; felt rug, coat, or hat.

fiera, *f.* wild beast; fiendish person; (coll.) very able or shrewd person.

fierabrás, *m.* bully, braggart.

fiereza, *f.* fierceness, cruelty, ferocity; deformity.

fiero, ra, *adj.* fierce, cruel, ferocious; rough, rude.

fiesta, *f.* fiesta; feast; festivity, party; **—s,** *pl.* holidays, vacations.

fig. figura, fig. figure.

figón, *m.* small, unpretentious restaurant.

figonero, *m.* keeper of a small unpretentious restaurant.

figura, *f.* figure, shape; face card.

figurable, *adj.* imaginable; that which may be figured.

figurado, da, *adj.* figurative.

figurar, *va.* to shape, to fashion; **—,** *vn.* to figure, to be conspicuous; **—se,** to fancy, to imagine.

figurativo, va, *adj.* figurative.

figurero, *m.* mimic, ludicrous imitator; maker of images or figures.

figurilla, *f.* ridiculous little figure; statuette.

figurín, *m.* fashion plate.

figurón, *m.* low-bred person assuming an air of dignity and importance.

fijacarteles, *m.* man who pastes up bills or posters.

fijación, *f.* fixing; allocation; **— de carteles,** bill posting.

fijar, *va.* to fix, to fasten; to determine; to post; **—se,** to fix or settle itself in a place; to take notice (of), pay attention (to); **se prohibe — carteles,** post no bills.

fijeza, *f.* firmness, stability.

fijo, ja, *adj.* fixed, firm; settled, permanent; attentive; **precio —,** fixed price, one price for all.

fila, *f.* row, line of soldiers; **en —,** in a line, in a row.

Filadelfia, *f.* Philadelphia.

filamento, *m.* filament.

filantropía, *f.* philanthropy.

filantrópico, ca, *adj.* philanthropic.

filántropo, *m.* philanthropist.

filaria, *f.* (zool.) filaria.

filariosis, *f.* (med.) filariasis.

filarmonía, *f.* love of music or harmony.

filarmónico, ca, *adj.* philharmonic.

filatelia, *f.* philately, postage-stamp collecting.

filatélico, ca, *adj.* philatelic; pertaining to postage-stamp collecting.

filatelista, *m.* and *f.* philatelist.

filete, *m.* loin; (arch.) fillet; hem; small roasting spit; **— de vaca,** beef tenderloin.

filetear, *va.* to adorn with fillets.

filiación, *f.* affiliation; sonship; relation; regimental register of a soldier's height, age, etc.

filial, *adj.* filial.

filiar, *va,* to register one's descent; **—se,** to enroll.

filibustero, *m.* filibuster, freebooter.

filicida, *m.* and *f.* filicide, parent who kills his own child.

filigrana, *f.* filigree; delicate piece of work; **— de papel,** watermark (in paper).

fililí, *m.* (coll.) exquisite thing, delicacy.

filípica, *f.* philippic.

filipino, na, *n.* and *adj.* Philippine.

filis, *f.* grace and delicacy of action; bracelet, trinket.

filisteo, tea, *n.* and *adj.* Philistine; **—,** *m.* (coll.) tall, gigantic person.

filo, *m.* edge (of a sword, a knife, etc.).

filología, *f.* philology.

filológico, ca, *adj.* philological.

filólogo, *m.* philologist.

filosofar, *va.* to philosophize.

filosofía, *f.* philosophy.

filosófico, ca, *adj.* philosophical.

filosofismo, *m.* philosophism.

filósofo, *m.* philosopher.

filtración, *f.* filtration.

filtrar, *va.* to filter, to strain; **—se,** to leak out, to escape.

filtro, *m.* filter; love potion; **— de vacío,** vacuum filter.

fin, *m.* end, termination, conclusion; **al —,** at last; **en —, por —,** finally, lastly.

finado, da, *n.* and *adj.* dead, deceased.

final, *adj.* final; **—,** *m.* end, termination, conclusion, finale; **—es,** *pl.* finals (in sports events).

finalidad, *f.* finality.
finalista, *m.* and *f.* finalist.
finalización, *f.* finality.
finalizar, *va.* to finish, to conclude; —, *vn.* to be finished.
finalmente, *adv.* finally, at last.
finamente, *adv.* delicately, courteously.
financiamiento, *m.* financing.
financiar, *va.* to finance.
financiero, ra, *adj.* financial.
finca, *f.* land or house property; ranch.
Fineas, Phineas.
fineza, *f.* fineness, perfection; expression of courtesy; delicacy; friendly zeal; small, friendly gift.
fingido, da, *adj.* feigned, dissembled, sham.
fingimiento, *m.* simulation, pretense, false appearance.
fingir, *va.* and *vr.* to feign, to make believe, to dissemble; to imitate.
finiquitar, *va.* to settle or to close (an account).
finiquito, *m.* close of an account; final receipt or discharge.
finito, ta, *adj.* finite, limited, bounded.
Finlandia, *f.* Finland.
fino, na, *adj.* fine, perfect, pure; delicate, nice; acute, sagacious.
finura, *f.* fineness; courtesy.
fiordo, *m.* fiord.
firma, *f.* signature; company, firm.
firmamento, *m.* firmament, sky, heaven.
firmar, *va.* to sign, to subscribe.
firme, *adj.* firm, stable, strong, secure; constant, resolute.
firmeza, *f.* firmness, stability, constancy; fixation.
fiscal, *m.* attorney general, public prosecutor; —, *adj.* fiscal.
fiscalía, *f.* office and business of the fiscal.
fiscalizar, *va.* to accuse of a criminal offense.
fisco, *m.* fisc, exchequer.
fisga, *f.* three-pronged harpoon; grimace; raillery, jeering, banter.
fisgar, *vn.* to mock, to scoff, to jeer.
fisgón, *m.* punster, buffoon.
física, *f.* physics.
físico, ca, *adj.* physical; —, *m.* naturalist; physicist; physique; (coll.) face, physiognomy.
fisicoquímico, ca, *adj.* physiochemical.
fisiografía, *f.* physiography.
fisiógrafo, *m.* physiographer.
fisiología, *f.* physiology.
fisiólogo, *m.* physiologist.
fisionomía or **fisonomía,** *f.* physiognomy, countenance, features.
fisioterapia, *f.* physiotherapy.
fisonomista, *m.* and *f.* physiognomist.
fístula, *f.* (med.) fistula; water pipe; (mus.) reed, pipe.
flaco, ca, *adj.* thin, lean, meager; feeble, languid.
flacura, *f.* thinness, lack of flesh.
flagelación, *f.* flagellation.

flagelante, *m.* flagellant.
flagrante, *adj.* flagrant; **en —,** in the act, red-handed.
flagrar, *vn.* (poet.) to glow, to flame.
flamante, *adj.* flaming, bright; quite new.
flamear, *vn.* to flutter, to wave; to flame, to blaze.
flamenco, ca, *n.* and *adj.* Flemish; **baile —co,** Andalusian gypsy dance; —, *m.* flamingo.
flan, *m.* custard.
flanco, *m.* flank, side.
Flandes, *f.* Flanders.
flanquear, *va.* (mil.) to flank, to outflank.
flaquear, *vn.* to flag, to weaken; to grow spiritless; to slacken.
flaqueza, *f.* leanness, extenuation, meagerness, feebleness, weakness.
flato, *m.* flatulency; (Sp. Am.) melancholy.
flatulento, ta, *adj.* flatulent.
flauta, *f.* (mus.) flute.
flautado, da, *adj.* resembling a flute; —, *m.* flute stop of an organ.
flautero, *m.* flute maker.
flautín, *m.* piccolo, fife.
flautista, *m.* and *f.* flute player, flutist, piper.
flébil, *adj.* (poet.) lamentable, sad.
flebotomía, *f.* (med.) phlebotomy (bloodletting).
fleco, *m.* flounce, fringe; (Mex.) bangs (style of haircut).
flecha, *f.* arrow.
flechero, *m.* archer, bowman; arrow maker.
flema, *f.* phlegm.
flemático, ca, *adj.* phlegmatic.
flemón, *m.* boil; ulcer in the gums.
flemoso, sa, *adj.* phlegmy.
flemudo, da, *adj.* dull, sluggish; phlegmatic.
fletador, *m.* freighter; charterer.
fletamento, *m.* charter, chartering, **carta de —** or **póliza de —,** charter party.
fletante, *m.* shipowner.
fletar, *va.* to freight (a ship).
flete, *m.* (naut.) freight.
flexibilidad, *f.* flexibility, mobility.
flexible, *adj.* flexible, pliant; docile.
flexión, *f.* flexure; **resistencia a la —,** flexural strength.
flexural, *adj.* flexural; **resistencia —,** flexural strength.
flojedad, *f.* feebleness, laxity, laziness, negligence.
flojera, *f.* (coll.) laziness.
flojo, ja, *adj.* loose, flexible, lax, slack; insipid, feeble, weak; lazy; **pantalones —os,** slacks.
flor, *f.* flower; **echar —es,** to compliment, to flatter; **— de la edad,** prime of life.
flora, *f.* (bot.) flora.
florear, *va.* to adorn with flowers; —, *vn.* to flourish (of swords); (mus.) to flourish; to pay compliments (to).
florecer, *vn.* (EZCO) to blossom, to bloom.
floreciente, *adj.* in bloom.

Florencia, f. Florence (city).
florentino, na, n. and adj. Florentine.
florera, f. flower girl.
florero, m. flowerpot; flower vase.
floresta, f. forest, thicket, grove; collection of pleasing things.
florete, m. fencing foil.
floretista, m. fencer.
floricultor, ra, n. floriculturist.
floricultura, f. floriculture.
florido, da, adj. florid, flowery; choice, excellent.
florín, m. florin.
florista, m. florist.
florón, m. imprint; large flower; (arch.) fleuron, rosette.
flota, f. fleet; — aérea, air fleet.
flotación, f. flotation.
flotador, m. floater.
flotadura, f. flotation, floating.
flotante, adj. floating; deuda —, floating debt; póliza —, floating policy.
flotar, vn. to float; to wave.
flote, m. floating; a —, buoyant, afloat.
flotilla, f. small fleet, flotilla.
flox, m. (bot.) phlox.
fluctuación, f. fluctuation; uncertainty.
fluctuar, vn. to fluctuate; to be irresolute.
fluidez, f. fluidity, liquidness; fluency.
flúido, da, adj. fluid; (fig.) fluent; —, m. fluid.
fluir, vn. (UYO) to flow, to run (as a liquid).
flujo, m. (med.) flux; flowing; — de vientre, diarrhea.
flúor, m. (chem.) fluorine.
fluorescencia, f. fluorescence.
fluorita, f. (chem.) fluorite.
fluoroscopio, m. fluoroscope.
fluvial, adj. fluvial; vías —es, river waterways.
fluxión, f. (med.) flowing, fluction.
f.° or fol. folio, f. or fol. folio.
f. o. b. franco a bordo, (com.) f. o. b. free on board.
foca, f. (zool.) seal; piel de —, sealskin; piel de — de Alaska, Alaskan seal.
focal, adj. focal.
foco, m. focus; center; bulb (electric light).
fodolí, adj. meddlesome, officious.
fofo, fa, adj. spongy, soft, bland.
fogata, f. blaze; bonfire; heat caused by the fumes of wine.
fogón, m. hearth, fireplace, stove; caboose, vent of gun; — de un bajel, cookhouse.
fogonazo, m. flame of the priming of a gun; — del encendido, backfiring of an auto.
fogonero, m. fireman, stoker.
fogosidad, f. excessive vivacity, fieriness.
fogoso, sa, adj. fiery, ardent, fervent; impetuous, boisterous.
foguear, va. to accustom soldiers or horses to stand fire; to clean firearms by firing off a small quantity of gunpowder in them.

foliación, f. pagination (of books); (bot.) foliation.
foliar, va. to page.
foliatura, f. numbering the pages of a book; pagination.
folículo, m. follicle.
folio, m. folio, leaf of a book; de a —, (coll.) voluminous.
folklore, m. folklore.
folklórico, ca, adj. folkloric.
follaje, m. foliage.
follero, m. one who makes or sells bellows.
folletín, m. newspaper serial; small pamphlet.
folletista, m. pamphleteer.
folleto, m. pamphlet, booklet.
fomentación, f. fomentation.
fomentador, ra, n. booster, promoter.
fomentar, va. to foment; to promote, to encourage.
fomento, m. fomentation; promotion, fostering; improvement, development.
fonda, f. hotel, inn, lodging house.
fondeadero, m. anchoring place, anchorage.
fondear, va. (naut.) to sound; to search a ship; —, vn. to cast anchor.
fondillos, m. pl. seat of trousers.
fondista, m. innkeeper; caterer.
fondo, m. foundation; bottom; fund(s), capital, stock; essential nature; extent of a person's capacity; space occupied by ranks of soldiers; (art) background; intrinsic brilliance (of diamonds); — doble, false bottom; artículo de —, editorial article; —s públicos, public funds; dar —, to cast anchor; a —, perfectly, completely, fully.
fonética, f. phonetics.
fonético, ca, adj. phonetic.
fónico, ca, adj. phonic, pertaining to sound.
fonografía, f. phonography; shorthand, stenography.
fonógrafo, m. phonograph, gramophone.
fonolocalización, f. sound detecting; — de aviones, (aer.) sound detector.
fonología, f. phonology; phonics.
fontanería, f. art of making waterworks; conduit pipes, water duct.
fontanero, m. pipe maker, pipelayer, plumber.
forajido, da, n. outlaw, highwayman.
foral, adj. belonging to the statute law of a country.
foráneo, nea, adj. foreign, strange.
forastero, ra, adj. strange, exotic; —, n. stranger, foreigner.
forcejar or **forcejear,** vn. to struggle, to strive, to oppose.
forcejudo, da, adj. strong, robust.
forceps, m. forceps.
forense, adj. forensic.
forestal, adj. pertaining to the forest; explotación —, forest development.
forjador, m. framer, forger.
forjadura, f. forging.

forjar, *va.* to forge; to frame; to invent.

forma, *f.* form, shape, fashion; way; host to be consecrated by a priest; **de — que,** in such a manner that.

formación, *f.* formation; form, figure; twisted cord of silk, gold, silver, etc. used by embroiderers.

formado, da, *adj.* featured.

formal, *adj.* formal; proper, genuine; serious, grave.

formaldehído, *m.* formaldehyde.

formalidad, *f.* formality; punctuality; gravity; good behavior.

formalina, *f.* formalin.

formalismo, *m.* formalism.

formalizar, *va.* to put in final form; to comply with legal requisites; to put into legal form; **—se,** to grow formal, to become earnest.

formar, *va.* to form, to shape; **— causa,** to accuse, to bring suit.

formativo, va, *adj.* formative.

formato, *m.* (print.) format.

formero, *m.* centering of an arch.

fórmico, *m.* formic acid.

formidable, *adj.* formidable; dreadful, terrific.

formón, *m.* chisel; punch.

fórmula, *f.* formula.

formulación, *f.* formulation.

formular, *va.* to formulate, to draw up.

formulario, *m.* formulary; form (for filling in information).

fornicación, *f.* fornication.

fornicador, *m.* fornicator.

fornicar, *vn.* to commit fornication.

fornicario, ria, *adj.* relating to fornication.

fornitura, *f.* leather straps worn by soldiers; (print.) types cast to complete sorts.

foro, *m.* court of justice; bar; background of the stage; forum.

forraje, *m.* forage, fodder.

forrajeador, ra, *n.* forager.

forrajear, *va.* to gather forage.

forrar, *va.* to line (clothes, etc.); to cover (books, etc.).

forro, *m.* lining, facing; **— de papel,** jacket (of book).

fortalecer, *va.* (EZCO) to fortify, to strengthen, to encourage.

fortaleza, *f.* fortitude, valor, courage; strength, vigor; (mil.) fortress, stronghold; **— aérea,** flying fortress (big bomber).

fortificación, *f.* fortification.

fortificar, *va.* to strengthen, to comfort; to fortify a place.

fortín, *m.* small fort; bunker; **— con ametralladoras,** pillbox.

fortitud, *f.* strength, fortitude.

fortuito, ta, *adj.* fortuitous.

fortuna, *f.* fortune; **por —,** fortunately.

forzado, da, *adj.* forced, compelled; **—,** *m.* criminal sentenced to the galleys.

forzar, *va.* (UE) to force; to ravish.

forzosa, *f.* decisive move in a game; necessity.

forzosamente, *adv.* of necessity.

forzoso, sa, *adj.* indispensable, necessary.

forzudo, da, *adj.* strong, vigorous.

fosa, *f.* grave; (anat.) fossa.

fosfato, *m.* phosphate.

fosforescencia, *f.* phosphorescence.

fosforescente, *adj.* phosphorescent.

fosforescer, *vn.* to phosphoresce.

fosfórico, ca, *adj.* phosphoric.

fósforo, *m.* phosphorus; match; **— de seguridad,** safety match.

fósil, *adj.* and *m.* fossil.

foso, *m.* pit; moat, ditch, fosse; **— séptico,** septic tank.

fotocolografía, *f.* heliotype.

fotocromía, *f.* photochromy.

fotoeléctrico, ca, *adj.* photoelectric.

fotogénico, ca, *adj.* photogenic.

fotograbado, *m.* photoengraving, photogravure.

fotografía, *f.* photograph, picture, snapshot; **— instantánea de relámpago,** flashlight photography.

fotografiar, *va.* to photograph.

fotógrafo, *m.* photographer.

fotolitografía, *f.* photolithography.

fotometría, *f.* photometry.

fotómetro, *m.* photometer.

fotomicrografía, *f.* photomicrography.

fotoquímico, ca, *adj.* photochemical.

fotosíntesis, *f.* (chem.) photosynthesis.

fotostático, ca, *adj.* photostatic; **copia —,** photostatic copy.

fotóstato, *m.* photostat.

fototipia, *f.* collotype.

fotuto, *m.* (Cuba) automobile horn.

fr. franco, fr. franc.

fra. factura, inv. invoice.

F. R. A. Fuerza Real Aérea, R. A. F. Royal Air Force.

frac, *m.* evening coat, dress coat.

fracasar, *va.* to crumble, to break into pieces; **—,** *vn.* (naut.) to shatter to pieces; to fail.

fracaso, *m.* downfall, ruin, destruction; failure.

fracción, *f.* fraction.

fraccionario, ria, *adj.* fractional.

fractura, *f.* fracture.

fracturar, *va.* to fracture, to break.

fragancia, *f.* fragrance, perfume; (fig.) reputation for virtue.

fragante, *adj.* fragrant; flagrant; **en —,** in the act, red-handed.

fragata, *f.* (naut.) frigate.

frágil, *adj.* brittle, frail, weak.

fragilidad, *f.* fragility, brittleness; infirmity.

fragmentación, *f.* fragmentation.

fragmento, *m.* fragment.

fragor, *m.* noise, clamor.

fragosidad, *f.* roughness of the road; imperviousness of a forest.

fragoso, sa, *adj.* craggy, rough, uneven; noisy.

fragrancia, *f.* = **fragancia.**

fragrante, *adj.* = **fragante.**
fragua, *f.* forge; blacksmith's shop.
fraguar, *va.* to forge; to contrive; —, *vn.* to solidify, to harden (of mortar, clay, etc.)
fraile, *m.* friar, monk.
frambuesa, *f.* raspberry.
frambueso, *m.* raspberry bush.
francachela, *f.* elaborate repast, feasting to excess.
francamente, *adv.* frankly, openly.
francés, esa, *adj.* French; —, *m.* French language; Frenchman; —, *f.* French-woman.
francesilla, *f.* (bot.) crowfoot.
Francia, *f.* France.
Francisca, Frances.
Francisco, Francis, Frank.
franco, ca, *adj.* frank, liberal, open, sincere; **—co a bordo,** free on board; **—co de porte,** postpaid; prepaid; **—co sobre vagón,** free on rail; —, *m.* franc (French coin).
francolín, *m.* partridge.
francote, ta, *adj.* (coll.) frank, goodhearted, sincere.
franela, *f.* flannel.
franja, *f.* fringe; braid, border; stripe.
franquear, *va.* to exempt; to franchise; to disengage; to prepay postage; to stamp letters; **—se,** to give oneself up to the service of others; to unbosom oneself.
franqueo, *m.* postage.
franqueza, *f.* freedom, liberty; frankness, sincerity.
franquicia, *f.* immunity from taxes; franchise, grant.
frasco, *m.* flask, jar, vial, small bottle; powder flask; **— de perfume,** perfume bottle.
frase, *f.* phrase, sentence; **— en sentido figurado,** figure of speech.
fraseología, *f.* phraseology.
frasquera, *f.* bottle case, liquor case.
frasqueta, *f.* frisket of a printing press.
fraternal, *adj.* fraternal, brotherly.
fraternidad, *f.* fraternity, brotherhood.
fratricida, *m.* and *f.* fraticide (murderer of a brother).
fratricidio, *m.* fratricide (murder of a brother).
fraude, *m.* fraud, deceit, cheating.
fraudulento, ta, *adj.* fraudulent, deceitful.
fray, *m.* friar.
frazada, *f.* blanket.
frecuencia, *f.* frequency; **con —,** frequently.
frecuentación, *f.* frequentation.
frecuentar, *va.* to frequent.
frecuente, *adj.* frequent.
frecuentemente, *adv.* often, frequently.
fregadero, *m.* scullery, sink.
fregado, *m.* scouring of kitchen utensils; (fig.) intrigue; underhand work.
fregador, *m.* scrubbing brush, dishrag; —, **ra,** *n.* person who washes (dishes, etc.).
fregar, *va.* (IE) to rub, to cleanse, to scour; to wash (dishes); (coll.) to annoy.

fregona, *f.* kitchen maid (generally used in a depreciatory sense).
freidura, *f.* frying.
freír, *va.* (FRÍO, FREÍ) to fry.
fréjol, *m.* kidney bean.
frenar, *va.* to brake, to apply the brakes; to bridle.
frenesí, *m.* frenzy, madness; extravagant caprice.
frenético, ca, *adj.* mad, lunatic, insane, frantic, frenetic.
frenillo, *m.* impediment of the tongue.
freno, *m.* bridle; brake; **— de aire,** air brake.
frenología, *f.* phrenology.
frenópata, *m.* alienist.
frenopatía, *f.* study of mental diseases.
frente, *f.* face; forehead; **— a —,** face to face; —, *m.* (mil.) front rank of a body of troops; front line; **en —,** in front, opposite, across the way.
fresa, *f.* strawberry.
fresado, *m.* millwork.
fresal, *m.* strawberry plant.
frescachón, ona, *adj.* fresh looking and strong.
frescamente, *adv.* freshly; lately; bluntly.
fresco, ca, *adj.* fresh, cool; new; recent; plump, ruddy; brisk, bold; —, *m.* refreshing air; **tomar el —co,** to enjoy the cool air.
frescura, *f.* freshness, coolness; frankness; smart repartee; carelessness.
fresno, *m.* ash tree.
fresquería, *f.* (Sp. Am.) ice cream parlor.
friable, *adj.* friable.
frialdad, *f.* frigidity, coldness; indifference.
fricar, *va.* to rub together.
fricasé, *m.* fricassée.
fricción, *f.* friction.
friccionar, *va.* to rub.
friega, *f.* friction with flannel.
frígido, da, *adj.* cold, frigid.
frigorífero, *m.* refrigerator.
frigorífico, *m.* packing house; cold storage room; —, **ca,** *adj.* frigorific, refrigerating.
frijol, *m.* bean; **—es rojos** or **colorados,** kidney beans; **—es blancos,** navy beans.
frío, fría, *adj.* cold, frigid; indifferent; **sangre —ía,** presence of mind; —, *m.* cold; **hacer —** or **tener —,** to be cold.
friolento, ta, *adj.* very allergic to cold.
friolera, *f.* trifle.
frisadura, *f.* act of frizzling.
frisar, *va.* to frizzle; to rub against the grain; —, *vn.* to resemble; to approach.
friso, *m.* frieze; wainscot.
frisón, ona, *n.* and *adj.* Frisian; —, *m.* large draft horse.
fritada, *f.* dish of fried meat or fish.
frito, ta, *adj.* fried.
fritura, *f.* fry, fritter; **— de pescado,** fish fry.
frivolidad, *f.* frivolity.
frívolo, la, *adj.* frivolous, trifling, piddling.
fronda, *f.* (bot.) leaf; **—s,** *pl.* foliage.
frondosidad, *f.* foliage, tuft of leaves.

frondoso, sa, *adj.* leafy, abounding with leaves.
frontal, *m.* front ornament of an altar.
frontera, *f.* frontier, border.
fronterizo, za, *adj.* frontier; opposite.
frontis, *m.* face, façade.
frontispicio, *m.* frontispiece.
frontón, *m.* wall of a handball court; pelota court.
frotación or **frotadura,** *f.* friction, rubbing, rubdown.
frotar, *va.* to rub.
fructífero, ra, *adj.* fructiferous, fruitful.
fructificar, *vn.* to fructify; to yield profit.
fructosa, *f.* fructose, fruit sugar.
fructuoso, sa, *adj.* fruitful; useful.
frugal, *adj.* frugal, sparing.
frugalidad, *f.* frugality, parsimony.
fruición, *f.* fruition.
fruncidor, ra, *adj.* frowning; —, *n.* person who frowns; —, *m.* plaiter, gatherer (in sewing).
fruncimiento, *m.* wrinkling, corrugation; imposture.
fruncir, *va.* to pleat; to gather, to shirr; to reduce to a smaller size; to conceal the truth; **— las cejas,** to knit the eyebrows; **— los labios,** to curl the lips.
fruslería, *f.* trifle, futility; trinket.
frustrar, *va.* to frustrate, to thwart, to disappoint; **—se,** to miscarry; to fall through.
fruta, *f.* fruit; **— del tiempo,** fruit of the season; **— azucarada,** candied fruit.
frutal, *m.* fruit tree; —, *adj.* fruit-bearing.
frutera, *f.* fruit woman; fruit dish.
frutería, *f.* fruit store.
frutero, *m.* fruiterer; fruit basket.
frutilla, *f.* small fruit; strawberry (in Peru); round shell of which rosaries are made.
fruto, *m.* fruit; benefit, profit, reward, good results.
¡fu! *interj.* fie! shame! faugh!
fucsia, *f.* fuchsia.
fuego, *m.* fire; skin eruption; ardor; — **fatuo,** ignis fatuus, will-o-the-wisp; **¡—!** *interj.* fire! **—s artificiales,** fireworks.
fuelle, *m.* bellows, blower; (coll.) talebearer.
fuente, *f.* fountain; source; issue; spring (of water); platter, dish.
fuer, *m.* (contraction of **fuero, a — de**) as a, in the manner of.
fuera, *adv.* without; from outward; outside; over and above; **— de sí,** frantic, beside oneself; **¡—!** *interj.* out of the way!
fuero, *m.* statute law of a country; jurisdiction; privilege granted to a province; **— interno,** innermost conscience.
fuerte, *m.* fortification, fort; —, *adj.* vigorous, stout; strong; —, *adv.* strongly.
fuerza, *f.* force, strength, power, vigor; valor, courage; violence, coercion; **a — de,** by dint of; **— electromotriz,** electromotive force; **— mayor,** act of God; **—s,** *pl.* troops.

fuete, *m.* (Sp. Am.) horsewhip.
fuga, *f.* flight, escape; leak, leakage; (mus.) fugue.
fugarse, *vr.* to escape, to flee, to run away.
fugaz, *adj.* fugitive; volatile, passing; perishable.
fugitivo, va, *adj.* and *n.* fugitive.
fulano, na, *n.* such a one.
fulcro, *m.* fulcrum.
fulgente, *adj.* (poet.) brilliant.
fulgor, *m.* glow, brilliancy.
fulgurante, *adj.* resplendent.
fulgurar, *vn.* to emit flashes of light.
fulminación, *f.* flash; report; thundering.
fulminante, *m.* percussion cap, primer; —, *adj.* fulminating, explosive, thundering; overwhelming.
fulminar, *va.* to fulminate; to cause to explode.
fullería, *f.* cheating, cardsharping; fallacy.
fullero, *m.* cardsharper, cheat.
fumada, *f.* whiff (of smoke).
fumadero, *m.* smoking room.
fumador, *m.* smoker.
fumar, *va.* and *vn.* to smoke (cigars, etc.).
fumarada, *f.* blast of smoke; a pipeful of tobacco.
fumigación, *f.* fumigation.
fumigador, *m.* fumigator.
fumigatorio, ria, *adj.* fumigatory.
fumosidad, *f.* smokiness.
fumoso, sa, *adj.* full of smoke or fume, smoky.
funámbulo, la, *n.* ropedancer.
función, *f.* function, show, performance; solemnity, festival; (mil.) fight, battle.
funcional, *adj.* functional.
funcionamiento, *m.* working, functioning; performance; operation; action.
funcionar, *vn.* to function; to work, to run (as machines).
funcionario, *m.* official, functionary; **— público,** public official.
fund. fundador, founder.
funda, *f.* case, sheath; slip cover; **— de almohada,** pillowcase.
fundación, *f.* foundation; groundwork.
fundador, ra, *n.* founder (one who founds or establishes).
fundamental, *adj.* fundamental.
fundamentalismo, *m.* fundamentalism.
fundamento, *m.* foundation, base, groundwork; reason, cause; good behavior; orderliness.
fundar, *va.* to found; to establish, to ground.
fundible, *adj.* fusible.
fundición, *f.* fusion, melting; foundry; pig iron; (print.) font.
fundidor, *m.* founder, melter.
fundir, *va.* to melt metals.
fúnebre, *adj.* mournful, sad; funereal.
funeral, *adj.* funeral; **—es,** *m. pl.* funeral, obsequies.
funerario, ria, *adj.* funeral, funereal; —, *f.* undertaking establishment.

funesto, ta, *adj.* funereal, mournful, sad, dismal; disastrous.

fungo, *m.* fungus.

funicular, *adj.* funicular.

furgón, *m.* baggage car; freight car, express car.

furgonero, *m.* carter; carman; vanman.

furia, *f.* fury, rage; **a toda —,** with the utmost speed.

furibundo, da, *adj.* furious, furylike.

furioso, sa, *adj.* furious.

furor, *m.* fury.

furtivamente, *adv.* by stealth.

furtivo, va, *adj.* furtive, sly; **cazador —vo,** poacher.

furúnculo, *m.* (med.) boil.

fusa, *f.* (mus.) demisemiquaver.

fusco, ca, *adj.* fuscous, dusky, brownish-black.

fuselado, da, *adj.* streamlined.

fuselaje, *m.* fuselage.

fusible, *m.* (elec.) fuse; **caja de —s,** fuse box.

fusil, *m.* musket, rifle; **— que se carga por la recámara,** breechloader.

fusilar, *va.* to shoot.

fusilazo, *m.* musket shot.

fusilería, *f.* body of fusileers, rifle corps.

fusilero, *m.* fusileer, rifleman.

fusión, *f.* fusion, melting, union; **temperatura de —,** melting point.

fusique, *m.* kind of snuffbox.

fuste, *m.* tree and bows of a saddle; shaft of a lance; shaft of a column; nerve, character; **hombre de —,** man of character, man of initiative.

fustigar, *va.* to cudgel.

fútbol, *m.* football, soccer.

futilidad, *f.* futility.

futurismo, *m.* futurism.

futuro, ra, *adj.* and *m.* future.

fvda. favorecida, favored.

G

G. gracias, thanks.

g/ gramo, gr. gram.

g/ giro, draft.

gabacho, cha, *adj.* applied to the natives of some places at the foot of the Pyrenees; used also in derision to the French.

gabán, *m.* overcoat; **— de entretiempo,** lightweight coat.

gabardina, *f.* cassock; gabardine.

gabarra, *f.* (naut.) lighter (boat).

gabarrero, *m.* (naut.) lighterman.

gabela, *f.* tax, duty.

gabinete, *m.* cabinet, study, library, laboratory; **— de lectura,** reading room.

gacela, *f.* gazelle.

gaceta, *f.* newspaper.

gacetero, *m.* newswriter; newspaper seller.

gacetilla, *f.* news, tidings.

gacetillero, *m.* newswriter.

gacetista, *m.* newsmonger.

gachas, *f. pl.* porridge, mush, pap; caresses; **hacerse unas —,** to be soft or affectionate; **a —,** (coll.) on all fours.

gacho, cha, *adj.* curvated, bent downwards.

gaélico, ca, *adj.* Gaelic.

gafa, *f.* kind of hook; **—s,** *pl.* spectacles, goggles; **—s ahumadas,** smoked glasses.

gaguear, *vn.* (Sp. Am.) to stutter, to stammer.

gaita, *f.* bagpipe; flageolet.

gaitería, *f.* gay and gaudy dress.

gaitero, *m.* bagpiper, bagpipe player; **—, ra,** *adj.* gay, gaudy, showy.

gaje, *m.* salary, wages; **—s,** *pl.* fees; **—es del oficio,** annoyances caused by one's job or occupation.

gajo, *m.* branch of a tree broken off; part torn off a bunch of grapes; each section of an orange or other similar fruit.

gala, *f.* court dress; ceremony; gracefulness of expression; **día de —,** court day; **hacer —,** to glory in having done a thing, to boast.

galafate, *m.* artful thief; cunning rogue.

galán, *m.* gallant, gentleman in full dress; courtier; lover; actors who perform serious characters in plays, are distinguished in order as first, second, etc., **galán.**

galano, na, *adj.* elegant, neatly dressed; tasteful.

galante, *adj.* gallant, courtly; brave, generous, liberal; elegant.

galanteador, *m.* wooer, lover; flatterer.

galantear, *va.* to court, to woo; to philander.

galanteo, *m.* gallantry, courtship.

galantería, *f.* gallantry, elegance; liberality, generosity.

galápago, *m.* fresh-water turtle; (fig.) cunning man; English saddle; **—s,** *pl.* (naut.) cleats.

galardón, *m.* reward, recompense.

galardonar, *va.* to reward, to recompense.

galeón, *m.* (naut.) galleon; argosy.

galeota, *f.* (naut.) galliot.

galeote, *m.* galley slave.

galera, *f.* (naut.) galley; wagon; (print.) galley; reformatory for lewd women.

galerada, *f.* galley proof; carload.

galería, *f.* gallery; art museum; lobby.

Gales, *m.* Wales.

galés, galesa, *n.* and *adj.* Welsh, Gaelic, Welshman, Gael.

galga, *f.* greyhound bitch.

galgo, *m.* greyhound.

Galia, *f.* Gaul.

galicano, na, or **gálico, ca,** *n.* and *adj.* Gallican.

gálico, *m.* venereal disease, syphilis.

galicoso, sa, *adj.* syphilitic.

galillo, *m.* uvula.

galocha, *f.* clog, galosh.

galón, *m.* galloon; gallon.

galoneadura, *f.* ornamenting with galloons.

galonear, *va.* to lace, to trim with galloons.

galope, *m.* gallop; hasty execution of a thing.

galopear, *vn.* to gallop.

galopín, *m.* swabber; cabin boy; scullion; boy meanly dressed.

galvánico, ca, *adj.* galvanic.

galvanismo, *m.* galvanism.

galladura, *f.* tread (in an egg).

gallardear, *vn.* to do anything gracefully or elegantly.

gallardete, *m.* pennant, streamer.

gallardía, *f.* gallantry, elegance, gracefulness; activity, briskness; liberality.

gallardo, da, *adj.* gay, graceful, elegant, gallant; magnanimous; generous; brave, daring.

gallear, *va.* to tread (as cocks); —, *vn.* to assume an air of importance; to raise the voice menacingly.

gallego, ga, *n.* and *adj.* Galician.

galleta, *f.* hard tack; biscuit, cookie.

galletica, *f.* small cracker; — **salada,** oyster cracker.

gallina, *f.* hen; (fig.) coward; — **ciega,** blindman's bluff.

gallinaza, *f.* hen dung.

gallinazo, *m.* (zool.) turkey buzzard.

gallinero, ra, *adj.* preying or feeding upon fowls; —, *m.* poulterer; hen coop; hen roost; (coll.) the highest gallery in a theater.

gallineta, *f.* (orn.) sandpiper.

gallipavo, *m.* turkey; unexpected shriek of the voice in talking or singing.

gallito, *m.* small cock; (coll.) bully.

gallo, *m.* cock, rooster; chief of a village; **misa de** —, midnight mass.

gama, *f.* (mus.) gamut; (zool.) doe, she-deer.

gambeta, *f.* crosscaper in dancing.

gamella, *f.* yoke for oxen and mules; large wooden trough.

gamo, *m.* buck of the fallow deer.

gamuza, *f.* chamois; chamois skin.

gana, *f.* appetite; healthy disposition; desire, mind; **de buena** —, with pleasure, voluntarily; **de mala** —, unwillingly, with reluctance.

ganadería, *f.* breeding or feeding of cattle.

ganadero, *m.* cattle owner; dealer in cattle; sheepherder.

ganado, *m.* cattle; — **de cerda,** swine; — **en pie,** livestock; — **mayor,** horned cattle; mules; — **menor,** sheep; asses; — **merino,** merino sheep.

ganador, ra, *n.* winner, gainer; —, *adj.* winning, gaining.

ganancia, *f.* gain, profit, lucre; — **líquida,** net profit; —**s y pérdidas,** profit and loss.

ganancioso, sa, *adj.* gainful.

ganapán, *m.* porter, carrier; rude, coarse man.

ganar, *va.* to gain; to win; to beat (in a game); to earn.

gancho, *m.* hook; crook; peg; clip; — **de tendedero,** clothespin.

gandujado, *m.* fine or accordion pleating.

gandul, la, *n.* (coll.) idler, tramp, loafer.

ganga, *f.* European sand grouse; (min.) gangue, bed of minerals; (coll.) any valuable thing or profit acquired with little trouble or ado, bargain.

Ganges, *m.* Ganges.

ganglio, *m.* ganglion.

gangoso, sa, *adj.* snuffling.

gangrena, *f.* gangrene.

gangrenarse, *vr.* to become gangrenous.

gangrenoso, sa, *adj.* gangrenous.

ganguear, *vn.* to snuffle, to speak through the nose.

gangueo, *m.* snuffling, speaking through the nose.

ganoso, sa, *adj.* desirous, covetous.

gansarón, *m.* gosling; tall, thin man.

ganso, sa, *n.* gander; goose; tall slender person; foolish person; **hacer el** —, to try to be funny.

gañir, *vn.* to yelp or yowl.

gañote, *m.* windpipe; kind of fritter.

garabatear, *va.* to catch with a hook; to scrawl, to scribble.

garabato, *m.* pothook; attractive air of some women; —**s,** *pl.* scrawling letters or characters; awkward gestures or movements of the hands and fingers.

garage or **garaje,** *m.* garage.

garante, *m.* guarantor.

garantía, *f.* guarantee, pledge.

garantir, *va.* and *def.* to guarantee.

garantizar, *va.* to guarantee, to warrant.

garañón, *m.* jackass.

garapiña, *f.* sugar-coating; icing, frosting (of cake, candy, etc.); the congealed particles of any liquid; kind of black lace.

garapiñado, da, *adj.* candied, frosted, glacé; **almendras** —**das,** sugar-coated almonds.

garapiñar, *va.* to ice, to freeze (syrup, etc.); to candy.

garapiñera, *f.* ice-cream freezer.

garbanzal, *m.* piece of ground sown with chick-peas.

garbanzo, *m.* chick-pea.

garbanzuelo, *m.* spavin (foot disease in horses).

garbear, *vn.* to affect elegance or fineness.

garbillo, *m.* coarse sieve for grain; (min.) riddle; riddled ore.

garbo, *m.* gracefulness, elegance of manner; generosity; cleverness.

garboso, sa, *adj.* sprightly, graceful; liberal, generous.

gardenia, *f.* (bot.) gardenia.

garduña, *f.* (zool.) marten.

gargajear, *vn.* to spit, to expectorate phlegm.

gargajo, *m.* phlegm, spittle.

garganta, *f.* throat, gullet; instep; mountain flood, torrent; narrow pass between mountains or rivers; gorge.

gargantilla, *f.* woman's necklace.

gárgara, *f.* gargle; **hacer** —**s,** to gargle.

gárgola, *f.* gargoyle.
gargüero or **garguero,** *m.* gullet; windpipe.
garita, *f.* (mil.) sentry box; (rail.) line keeper's lodge.
garitero, *m.* operator or owner of a gambling house; gamester.
garla, *f.* (coll.) talk, prattle.
garlito, *m.* trap, snare; fish trap.
garnacha, *f.* counselor's robe; (Mex.) kind of meat tart.
garra, *f.* claw, talon, paw; clutch; hand (in contempt).
garrafa, *f.* decanter, carafe.
garrafal, *adj.* great, vast, huge.
garrafiñar, *va.* (coll.) to seize, to grapple.
garrapata, *f.* tick (insect).
garrapatear, *vn.* to scribble, to scrawl.
garrapato, *m.* clothes moth; pothook, scrawl.
garrocha, *f.* goad.
garrotazo, *m.* blow with a cudgel.
garrote, *m.* cudgel, club; garrote, capital punishment by strangling with an iron collar.
garrotillo, *m.* (med.) croup.
garrucha, *f.* pulley.
gárrulo, la, *adj.* chirping; chattering, prattling.
garulla, *f.* ripe grapes which remain in the basket; (coll.) rabble.
garza, *f.* heron (bird).
garzo, *m.* agaric; —, **za,** *adj.* blue-eyed.
garzota, *f.* night heron; plumage; crest of a helmet.
gas, *m.* gas; — **carbónico,** carbonic acid gas; — **cloro,** chlorine gas; — **de alumbrado,** illuminating gas; — **de nitrógeno,** nitrogen peroxide; — **sulfuroso,** sulphur dioxide; — **sulfhídrico,** hydrogen sulphide.
gasa, *f.* gauze, chiffon.
gaseoso, sa, *adj.* gaseous; —, *f.* soda water, pop.
gasista, *m.* gas fitter.
gasolina, *f.* gasoline; **tanque de —,** gasoline tank.
gasolinera, *f.* motor launch; filling station.
gasómetro, *m.* gasometer.
Gaspar, Jasper.
gastado, da, *adj.* worn-out, used, spent.
gastador, *m.* spendthrift, prodigal; corrupter; (mil.) army engineer; —, **ra,** *adj.* lavish, extravagant.
gastar, *va.* to expend; to waste; to spend; to wear out; to plunder; **—se,** to become old or useless.
gasto, *m.* expense, cost; — **adicional,** extra expense.
gastronomía, *f.* gastronomy.
gastrónomo, *m.* gourmet, epicure.
gastrópodo, *m.* gastropod.
gástrula, *f.* gastrula.
gata, *f.* she-cat; **a —s,** on all fours.
gatada, *f.* clawing; robbery effected in a cunning manner; cunning, shrewd action.

gatear, *vn.* to creep (as children); to climb up; —, *va.* (coll.) to scratch or claw; to steal.
gatera, *f.* cat's hole.
gatesco, ca, *adj.* feline, catlike.
gatillazo, *m.* click of the trigger in firing.
gatillo, *m.* tooth pincer; trigger of a gun.
gato, *m.* cat; jack; hooking tong; — **de algalia,** civet cat.
gatuno, na, *adj.* catlike, feline.
gaucho, *m.* cowboy, herdsman of the Argentine pampas.
gaveta, *f.* drawer of a desk, locker.
gavia, *f.* (naut.) main topsail; ditch; cell for insane persons; **—s,** *pl.* topsails of the mainmast and the foremast.
gavilán, *m.* (orn.) sparrow hawk.
gavilla, *f.* sheaf of grain; gang of suspicious persons.
gaviota, *f.* (orn.) gull, sea gull.
gavota, *f.* gavotte (French dance).
gayuba, *f.* red-berried arbutus.
gazapera, *f.* rabbit warren.
gazapo, *m.* young rabbit; artful knave; great lie.
gazmoñada or **gazmoñería,** *f.* prudery, hypocrisy.
gazmoñero, ra, or **gazmoño, ña,** *adj.* hypocritical.
gaznatada, *f.* blow on the throttle.
gaznate, *m.* throttle, windpipe.
gazpacho, *m.* cold soup made with bread, vinegar, and garlic; fried crumbs or bread.
gazuza, *f.* keenness of appetite.
géiser, *m.* geyser.
gelatina, *f.* gelatine, jelly.
gemelo, la, *n.* twin; **—os,** *pl.* opera glasses, binoculars; cuff links.
gemido, *m.* groan, moan, howl; **dar —s,** to groan.
Géminis, *m.* Gemini, Twins (sign of the zodiac); **g—,** kind of plaster.
gemir, *vn.* (I) to groan, to moan.
genciana, *f.* (bot.) gentian.
gendarme, *m.* gendarme, policeman.
gendarmería, *f.* gendarmery.
genealogía, *f.* genealogy.
genealógico, ca, *adj.* genealogical.
genealogista, *m.* genealogist.
generación, *f.* generation; progeny, lineage.
generador, *m.* generator.
general, *m.* general; —, *adj.* general, usual; **en —,** generally, in general; **por lo —,** as a rule.
generala, *f.* (mil.) general (a beat of the drum); a general's wife.
generalato, *m.* generalship.
generalidad, *f.* generality.
generalísimo, *m.* generalissimo.
generalizar, *va.* to generalize; to spread.
genérico, ca, *adj.* generic.
género, *m.* class, kind, species; sex, gender; — **humano,** mankind; **—s,** *pl.* goods, commodities.
generosidad, *f.* generosity.

generoso, sa, *adj.* noble, generous.
Génesis, *f.* Genesis, first book of the Pentateuch.
genética, *f.* genetics.
genial, *adj.* genial, pleasant, cheerful; outstanding, inspired, revealing creative genius.
genio, *m.* genius; temper; nature.
genital, *adj.* genital.
genitivo, *m.* (gram.) genitive case.
Gen.¹ General, Gen. General.
Génova, *f.* Genoa.
gente, *f.* people; nation; crowd; army troops; **— baja,** rabble, mob; **— común,** vulgar, common folk; **— menuda,** children.
gentecilla, *f.* mob, rabble.
gentil, *m.* pagan, heathen; **—,** *adj.* courteous; graceful, elegant, excellent.
gentileza, *f.* gentility, elegance of behavior; politeness; grace.
gentilhombre, *m.* gentleman.
gentilicio, cia, *adj.* pertaining to people or nations.
gentílico, ca, *adj.* pagan, heathenish.
gentilidad, *f.*, **gentilismo,** *m.* heathenism.
gentío, *m.* crowd, multitude.
gentuza, *f.* rabble, mob.
genuflexión, *f.* genuflection.
genuino, na, *adj.* genuine, pure.
geocéntrico, ca, *adj.* geocentric.
geodesia, *f.* geodesy.
geofísica, *f.* geophysics.
Geofredo, Geoffrey, Jeffrey.
geografía, *f.* geography.
geográfico, ca, *adj.* geographical.
geógrafo, *m.* geographer.
geología, *f.* geology.
geómetra, *m.* geometrician.
geometría, *f.* geometry; **— del espacio,** solid geometry; **— plana,** plane geometry.
geométrico, ca, *adj.* geometrical, geometric.
geopolítica, *f.* geopolitics.
geopónica, *f.* geoponics, the science of agriculture.
geotropismo, *m.* geotropism.
geranio, *m.* (bot.) geranium.
gerencia, *f.* management, administration (of a business or enterprise).
gerente, *m.* manager; **— director,** managing director.
geriatria, *f.* (med.) geriatrics.
Germania, *f.* Germany.
germanía, *f.* slang of gypsies and thieves.
germen, *m.* germ, bud; source, original cause.
germicida, *adj.* germicidal.
germinación, *f.* germination.
germinar, *vn.* to germinate, to bud.
Gertrudis, Gertrude, Gertie, Trudy.
gerundio, *m.* (gram.) gerund, present participle.
Gervasio, Gervas.
gestación, *f.* gestation.
gesticular, *vn.* to gesticulate.

gestión, *f.* management; effort, work, action, step; investigation.
gestionar, *va.* to manage, to negotiate; to take steps to obtain something desired.
gesto, *m.* face, visage; grimace, gesture; aspect, appearance; resemblance.
gestor, ra, *adj.* managing; **socio —,** active partner; **—,** *m.* manager.
géyser, *m.* geyser.
ghetto, *m.* ghetto.
giganta, *f.* giantess.
gigante, *m.* giant; **—,** *adj.* gigantic.
gigantesco, ca, *adj.* gigantic, giant, huge.
gigantilla, *f.* figure made of pasteboard with a very large head.
Gil, Giles.
gimnasia, *f.* gymnastics.
gimnasio, *m.* gymnasium; school, academy.
gimnástica, *f.* gymnastics.
gimnástico, ca, *adj.* gymnastic.
gimotear, *vn.* (coll.) to whine.
gimoteo, *m.* (coll.) whining.
Ginebra, *f.* Geneva.
ginebra, *f.* gin; confusion, bedlam.
ginecología, *f.* (med.) gynecology.
ginecólogo, *m.* gynecologist.
gineta, *f.* genet (kind of weasel).
girado, *m.* drawee of a draft.
girador, *m.* drawer of a draft.
girafa, *f.* giraffe.
giralda, *f.* weathercock in the form of a statue.
girándula, *f.* girandole.
girar, *vn.* to rotate; to revolve; to remit by bills of exchange; **— contra,** (com.) to draw on.
girasol, *m.* sunflower.
giratorio, ria, *adj.* gyratory, rotating, revolving; **silla —,** swivel chair.
giro, *m.* turn, bend; line of business, specialty; (com.) draft; **— a la vista,** sight draft; **— postal,** money order.
giroscopio, *m.* gyroscope.
gitanada, *f.* wheedling (like gypsies).
gitanear, *va.* and *vn.* to flatter, to wheedle.
gitanería, *f.* wheedling, flattery.
gitanesco, ca, *adj.* gypsylike.
gitano, na, *n.* gypsy; sly person; person of suave, pleasant manners.
glacial, *adj.* icy.
glaciar, *m.* glacier.
glacis, *m.* sloping bank, glacis.
gladiador or **gladiator,** *m.* gladiator, prizefighter.
gladíolo, *m.* (bot.) gladiolus.
glándula, *f.* gland.
glanduloso, sa, *adj.* glandulous.
glasé, *m.* glacé.
glaucoma, *m.* (med.) glaucoma.
glicerina, *f.* glycerine.
glicógeno, *m.* glycogen.
globo, *m.* globe; sphere; orb; **en —,** by the lump; **— aerostático,** air balloon; **— de barrera,** barrage balloon.
globoso, sa, *adj.* globular.

glóbulo, *m.* globule.
gloria, *f.* glory; sort of light, thin taffeta.
gloriarse, *vr.* to glory, to pride in; to take delight in.
glorieta, *f.* bower, arbor.
glorificación, *f.* glorification; praise.
glorificador, ra, *n.* glorifier; **—, ra,** *adj.* glorifying.
glorificar, *va.* to glorify; **—se,** to boast.
glorioso, sa, *adj.* glorious.
glosa, *f.* gloss, marginal footnote, commentary.
glosador, *m.* commentator, glosser.
glosar, *va.* to gloss, to comment.
glosario, *m,* glossary.
glotis, *f.* (anat.) glottis.
glotón, ona, *n.* and *adj.* glutton; gluttonous.
glotonería, *f.* gluttony.
glucosa, *f.* glucose.
glutinoso, sa, *adj.* glutinous, viscous.
gnomo, *m.* gnome.
gnosticismo, *m.* gnosticism.
G.º Gonzalo, Gonzalus.
gobernación, *f.* government; governor's office or mansion.
gobernador, *m.* governor.
gobernalle, *m.* rudder, helm.
gobernante, *m.* ruler, governor; **—,** *adj.* ruling, governing.
gobernar, *va.* (IE) to govern; to regulate; to direct.
gobierno, *m.* government; control; controls, helm.
gobio, *m.* bullhead (fish).
gob.º or **gob.ⁿᵒ gobierno,** govt. government.
gob.ʳ gobernador, gov. governor.
goce, *m.* enjoyment; possession; fruition.
Godofredo or **Gofredo,** Godfrey.
goleta, *f.* schooner.
golf, *m.* golf; **campo de —,** golf links.
golfo, *m.* gulf, bay; knave, rogue.
golilla, *f.* collar worn by magistrates of Spain; **—,** *m.* magistrate wearing a **golilla.**
golondrina, *f.* (orn.) swallow.
golosina, *f.* dainty, titbit.
goloso, sa, *adj.* gluttonous.
golpe, *m.* blow, stroke, hit; knock; unfortunate accident; **de —,** all at once; **— de estado,** 'coup d'état; **— de mar,** heavy sea, surge; **— de vista,** perception.
golpear, *va.* and *vn.* to beat, to knock; to give blows; to tap; to bruise.
goma, *f.* gum, rubber; **— elástica,** rubber; **— de mascar,** chewing gum; **— laca,** shellac; **— vulcanizada,** ebonite, hard rubber; **— para borrar,** eraser; **— para pegar,** mucilage.
gomosidad, *f.* gumminess, viscosity.
gomoso, sa, *adj.* gummy, viscous.
gónada, *f.* (anat.) gonad.
góndola, *f.* gondola.
gondolero, *m.* gondolier.
gonorrea, *f.* gonorrhea.
gordiflón, ona, *n.* (coll.) very corpulent person.

gordo, da, *adj.* fat, corpulent, plump.
gordura, *f.* grease; fatness, corpulence, obesity.
gorgojo, *m.* grub, weevil.
gorgojoso, sa, *adj.* full of grubs or weevils.
gorgorita, *f.* bubble formed on water by the fall of rain.
gorgoritear, *vn.* to warble, to quaver the voice.
gorgoritos, *m. pl.* quavers of the voice.
gorgoteo, *m.* gurgle.
gorigori, *m.* (coll.) song with which children mimic the clerk's chant at funerals.
gorila, *m.* (zool.) gorilla.
gorjear, *vn.* to warble; (mus.) to trill, to quaver.
gorjeo, *m.* trilling; quaver; chirping.
gorra, *f.* cap, bonnet; **de —,** (coll.) at others' expense, sponging.
gorrión, *m.* sparrow.
gorrista, *m.* and *f.* parasite, sponger.
gorro, *m.* cap or hood.
gota, *f.* drop; gout; **— coral** or **caduca,** (med.) epilepsy; **— serena,** (med.) amaurosis.
gotear, *vn.* to drip.
goteo, *m.* leak, leakage; **a prueba de —,** leakproof.
gotera, *f.* leak, leakage; gutter; fringe of bed hangings.
gótico, ca, *adj.* Gothic.
gotoso, sa, *adj.* gouty.
gozar, *va.* to enjoy, to have possession of; **— (de),** *vn.* to enjoy, to take pleasure (in).
gozne, *m.* hinge.
gozo, *m.* joy, pleasure, delight.
gozoso, sa, *adj.* joyful, cheerful, content, glad, merry, pleased.
gr. gramo, gr. gram.
grabado, *m.* engraving, illustration; **— al agua fuerte,** etching; **— al agua tinta,** aquatint.
grabador, *m.* engraver.
grabar, *va.* to engrave; to impress upon the mind; **— al agua fuerte,** to etch.
gracejo, *m.* graceful, pleasing manner.
gracia, *f.* grace; favor; benevolence; pardon; humor; **hacer —,** to amuse, to strike as funny; **tener —,** to be amusing; **—s,** *pl.* thanks; **dar —s,** to thank.
graciosidad, *f.* gracefulness, beauty, perfection.
gracioso, sa, *adj.* graceful, beautiful; funny, pleasing; benevolent; gratuitous; **—,** *m.* clown, buffoon.
grada, *f.* step of a staircase; harrow; **—s,** *pl.* seats of an amphitheater.
gradería, *f.* series of seats or steps.
gradilla, *f.* tile mold; small stepladder.
grado, *m.* step; degree; rank; will, pleasure; **de —,** willingly; **mal de su —,** against one's will.
graduación, *f.* graduation; (mil.) rank.
graduado, da, *n.* graduate, alumnus; **—,** *adj.* graduated.

graduador, *m.* graduator, gauge.
gradual, *adj.* gradual; **—,** *m.* a verse read between the epistle and the gospel at the celebration of mass.
graduando, *m.* graduate, candidate for academic degree.
graduar, *va.* to graduate; to classify, to grade; **—se,** to graduate, to obtain a degree.
gráfico, ca, *adj.* graphic; vivid; **—,** *m.* graph, diagram, sketch.
grafito, *m.* graphite.
grafología, *f.* graphology.
graja, *f.* (orn.) jay.
grajo, *m.* (orn.) jackdaw.
gral. general, gen. general.
grama, *f.* (bot.) dog's grass.
gramática, *f.* grammar.
gramatical, *adj.* grammatical.
gramático, *m.* grammarian.
gramo, *m.* gram, unit of measure.
gramófono, *m.* gramophone, phonograph.
gran, *adj.* contraction of **grande,** great, large, big.
grana, *f.* act of seeding; cochineal; scarlet grain; fine scarlet cloth.
granada, *f.* (mil.) grenade, shell; pomegranate; **— de metralla,** shrapnel.
granadero, *m.* (mil.) grenadier.
granadilla, *f.* passion flower; granadilla (fruit).
granadino, ra, *adj.* of Granada.
granado, da, *adj.* large, remarkable; select; illustrious; **—,** *m.* pomegranate tree.
granar, *vn.* to run to seed.
granate, *m.* garnet (precious stone).
granazón, *f.* seeding.
Gran Bretaña, *f.* Great Britain.
Gran Cañón, *m.* Grand Canyon.
grande, *adj.* great; large, big; **—,** *m.* grandee (Spanish nobleman).
grandeza, *f.* greatness; grandeur; grandeeship; body of grandees.
grandiosidad, *f.* greatness, grandeur; magnificence.
grandioso, sa, *adj.* grand, magnificent, grandiose.
grandor, *m.* size, bigness, extent, magnitude.
granear, *va.* to sow grain in the earth; to engrave; to grain leather.
granel, *m.* heap of grain; **a —,** in bulk.
granero, *m.* granary.
granito, *m.* granite.
granizada, *f.* copious fall of hail; multitude of things which fall in abundance.
granizar, *vn.* to hail.
granizo, *m.* hail; cloud in the eyes.
granja, *f.* grange, farm; summer resort; **— modelo,** model farm.
grano, *m.* grain, kernel; pimple; **ir al —,** to get to the point.
granoso, sa, *adj.* grainy; granular.
granuja, *f.* loose grape; **—,** *m.* (coll.) urchin, little rogue.
granulación, *f.* granulation.

granular, *adj.* granular.
gránulo, *m.* granule.
grasa, *f.* suet, fat, grease; shoe polish; **— de ballena,** whale oil, blubber.
grasiento, ta, *adj.* greasy, oily; filthy.
grasilla, *f.* pounce (fine powder).
gratificación, *f.* gratification, recompense; gratuity.
gratificar, *va.* to gratify, to reward, to recompense.
gratis, *adj.* gratis, free.
gratitud, *f.* gratitude, gratefulness.
grato, ta, *adj.* pleasant, pleasing; **su grata,** your favor (letter); **me es —o,** I have the pleasure.
gratuito, ta, *adj.* gratuitous, free.
gravamen, *m.* charge, tax; obligation; nuisance.
gravar, *va.* to burden, to oppress, to molest; to tax.
grave, *adj.* weighty, heavy; grave, serious, important; haughty; troublesome, grievous.
gravedad, *f.* gravity; seriousness.
gravemente, *adv.* gravely, seriously.
gravidez, *f.* pregnancy.
grávido, da, *adj.* pregnant; **estar en estado —do,** to be pregnant.
gravitación, *f.* gravitation.
gravitar, *vn.* to gravitate; to weigh down.
gravoso, sa, *adj.* onerous, unbearable.
graznar, *vn.* to croak; to cackle; to gaggle.
graznido, *m.* croak, cackle.
Grecia, *f.* Greece.
greco, ca, *adj.* Grecian; **—,** *n.* Greek.
greda, *f.* chalk, marl.
Greg.° Gregorio, Greg. Gregory.
Gregorio, Gregory.
greguería, *f.* outcry, confused clamor.
gremio, *m.* society; company, guild, corporation; trade union.
greña, *f.* tangled, matted hair.
greñudo, da, *adj.* disheveled, entangled.
gresca, *f.* clatter, tumult, outcry, confusion; wrangle, quarrel.
grey, *f.* flock (of sheep and goats); congregation of believers.
griego, ga, *adj.* Greek.
grieta, *f.* opening, crack, chink.
grifo, fa, *adj.* kinky, entangled (as hair); **—,** *m.* griffin; faucet.
grifón, *m.* water faucet, stopcock.
grilletes, *m. pl.* shackles, fetters.
grillo, *m.* cricket; **—s,** *pl.* fetters, irons.
grima, *f.* fright, horror.
gringo, ga, *n.* (Sp. Am.) (coll.) American or Englishman or Englishwoman.
gripe, *f.* grippe, influenza.
gris, *adj.* gray; **—,** *m.* miniver (Russian squirrel); (coll.) cold sharp air or weather.
gritador, ra, *n.* clamorer, bawler.
gritar, *vn.* to cry out, to clamor, to bawl.
gritería, *f.* outcry, clamor, confused cry of many voices.
grito, *m.* cry, call, scream; **a — herido,** with a clamorous cry.

gro, *m.* grosgrain (a silken fabric).
gro. género, sp. species.
Groenlandia, *f.* Greenland.
grosella, *f.* fruit of the red currant; gooseberry.
grosellero, *m.* currant bush.
grosería, *f.* coarseness, ill-breeding.
grosero, ra, *adj.* coarse, rude, unpolished.
grosura, *f.* suet, tallow; feet, liver, heart, etc., of an animal.
grotesco, ca, *adj.* grotesque.
grúa, *f.* crane (machine), hoist, derrick.
gruesa, *f.* gross (twelve dozen); chief part of a prebend.
grueso, sa, *adj.* bulky, gross, thick; large; coarse; —, *m.* corpulence.
grulla, *f.* (orn.) crane.
grumo, *m.* clod; curd; cluster, bunch; pith of trees.
grumoso, sa, *adj.* clotted.
gruñido, *m.* grunt, grunting; growl.
gruñidor, ra, *n.* grunter, mumbler.
gruñir, *vn.* (GRUÑO, GRUÑENDO) to grunt; to grumble; to creak (of hinges, etc.).
grupa, *f.* crupper, buttock.
grupera, *f.* crupper.
grupo, *m.* group.
gruta, *f.* grotto, grot.
gsa. gruesa, gro. gross.
gte. gerente, mgr. manager.
guacamayo, *m.,* **guacamaya,** *f.* macaw.
guaco, *m.* prairie chicken.
guadaña, *f.* scythe.
guadañadora, *f.* mower, mowing machine.
guadañero, *m.* mower.
gualderas, *f. pl.* sides; cheeks or brackets of a gun carriage.
gualdrapa, *f.* horse cloth; tatter, rag.
Gualterio, Walter.
guanábana, *f.* a yellowish tropic fruit.
guanaco, *m.* (zool.) guanaco.
guantada, *f.* slap given with the palm of the hand.
guante, *m.* glove; —s, *pl.* tip or extra fee.
guantería, *f.* glover's shop; glover's art.
guantero, *m.* glover, glovemaker.
guapear, *vn.* to boast of one's courage; to take a pride in fine dress.
guapeza, *f.* courage; ostentation in dress.
guapo, pa, *adj.* stout, courageous; valiant, bold; spruce, neat; ostentatious; gay, sprightly; elegant, handsome.
guaracha, *f.* variety of Spanish clog dance.
guarapo, *m.* sugar-cane juice.
guarda, *m.* and *f.* guard, keeper; —, *f.* custody, wardship, keeping.
guardaagujas, *m.* (rail.) switchman, pointsman.
guardaalmacén, *m.* storekeeper.
guardabarreras, *m.* (rail.) lineman.
guardabarro, *m.* mudguard, fender.
guardabosque, *m.* keeper of a forest, game warden.
guardabrisa, *m.* windshield.
guardacantón, *m.* spurstone, checkstone.

guardacostas, *m.* coast guard; coast-defense ship; revenue cutter.
guardafango, *m.* mudguard, fender; dashboard.
guardafrenos, *m.* brakeman.
guardafuego, *m.* fender, fire screen.
guardaludes, *m.* snowshed.
guardamonte, *m.* guard of a gunlock, sword, etc.
guardapelo, *m.* locket.
guardapolvo, *m.* any cloth or leather article worn on account of the dust; inner lid of a watch.
guardapuerta, *f.* storm door.
guardar, *va.* to keep, to preserve; to guard; —se, to be upon one's guard, to avoid, to abstain from.
guardarropa, *f.* wardrobe; —, *m.* and *f.* keeper of a wardrobe; —, *m.* coatroom.
guardarropía, *f.* wardrobe; theatrical wardrobe or costumes.
guardasellos, *m.* keeper of the seal; **G —
  del Rey,** Lord Privy Seal.
guardavía, *m.* (rail.) signalman; lineman.
guardavista, *m.* eyeshade.
guardia, *f.* guard; (naut.) watch; —, *m.*
  guardsman (soldier); — **civil,** national
  police of Spain.
guardián, ana, *n.* keeper; guardian.
guardianía, *f.* guardianship.
guardilla, *f.* garret; skylight.
guardín, *m.* tiller rope, wheel rope.
guarecer, *va.* (EZCO) to aid, to protect; to guard; to cure; —se, to take refuge or shelter.
guarida, *f.* den or lair of a wild beast; shelter; hiding place.
guarismo, *m.* cipher, number.
guarnecer, *va.* (EZCO) to garnish; to set (in gold, etc.); to adorn.
guarnición, *f.* flounce, facing; furbelow; gold setting; sword guard; garniture; (mil.) garrison.
guarnicionero, *m.* harness maker.
guasa, *f.* jewfish; (coll.) insipidity, dullness; (coll.) fun, jest.
guasón, ona, *adj.* (coll.) jocose; fond of teasing; witty; —, *n.* joker, jester; tease.
guatemalteco, ca, *n.* and *adj.* Guatemalan.
guayaba, *f.* guava (fruit); **guayabo,** *m.* guava (tree).
guayule, *m.* (bot.) guayule.
gubernamental, *adj.* governmental.
gubernativo, va, *adj.* administrative, governmental.
guedeja, *f.* forelock; long lock of hair; lion's mane.
guerra, *f.* war; hostility; — **rayo** or — **relámpago,** blitzkrieg; **hacer la —,** to wage war; **dar —,** to cause trouble or be a nuisance (usually a child).
guerreador, ra, *adj.* warlike.
guerrear, *vn.* to war, to wage war.
guerrero, *m.* warrior; —, **ra,** *adj.* martial, warlike.

guerrilla, *f.* band of guerrillas; war of guerrillas.

guerrillero, *m.* guerrilla, one engaged in guerrilla warfare.

guía, *m.* and *f.* guide, leader, director; —, *f.* guidebook; **— de bicicleta,** handle bar; **— sonora,** sound track (motion-picture film).

guiar, *va.* to guide, to lead; to drive.

Guido, Guy.

guija, *f.* pebble.

guijarral, *m.* place abounding in pebbles.

guijarrazo, *m.* blow with a pebble or a cobblestone.

guijarro, *m.* pebble; cobblestone; boulder.

guijarroso, sa, *adj.* pebbly.

Guillermina, Wilhelmina.

Guillermo, William.

Guill.º Guillermo, Wm. William.

guillotina, *f.* guillotine.

guillotinar, *va.* to guillotine.

guinda, *f.* kind of cherry.

guindar, *va.* to hang.

guindilla, *f.* (bot.) capsicum.

guindola, *f.* life buoy.

guinea, *f.* guinea (gold coin).

guinga, *f.* gingham.

guiñada, *f.* wink, hint.

guiñapo, *m.* tatter, rag.

guiñar, *va.* to wink, to hint.

guión, *m.* royal standard; banner; standard of the cross; (mil.) guidon; hyphen (in writing).

guirigay, *m.* (coll.) gibberish, confused language.

guirindola, *f.* frill of a shirt.

guirnalda, *f.* garland, wreath.

güiro, *m.* (bot.) bottle gourd.

guisa, *f.* manner, fashion; **a — de,** in the manner of.

guisado, *m.* ragout, fricassee, meat stew.

guisandero, ra, *n.* cook.

guisante, *m.* (bot.) pea.

guisar, *va.* to cook, to stew (meat), to dress foods.

guiso, *m.* seasoning of a dish; meat stew; condiment.

guisote, *m.* dish of meat cooked badly.

guitarra, *f.* guitar.

guitarrero, ra, *m.* guitar maker; guitar player.

guitarrista, *m.* and *f.* guitar player.

gula, *f.* gluttony.

guñir, *vn.* to grouch, to grunt, to sulk.

gusano, *m.* maggot, worm.

gusarapo, *m.* waterworm.

gustar, *va.* to taste, to try; —, *vn.* to like, to love; **— de,** to have a liking for, to take pleasure or delight in a thing.

Gustavo, Gustavus.

gusto, *m.* taste; gusto, pleasure, delight; liking, mind; election, choice; **a —,** at will; **tener — en,** to take pleasure in; **tanto —,** glad to meet you.

gustosamente, *adv.* tastefully; willingly.

gustoso, sa, *adj.* dainty; tasty; willing.

gutagamba, *f.* gamboge.

gutapercha, *f.* gutta-percha.

gutural, *adj.* guttural.

H

h. habitantes, pop. population.

¡ha! *interj.* ha! ah! alas!

haba, *f.* (bot.) bean.

Habana, *f.* Havana.

habanero, ra, *n.* and *adj.* native of Havana; of Havana; **—ra,** *f.* waltz tango, Cuban air and dance tune.

habano, *m.* Havana cigar; Havana tobacco.

hábeas corpus, *m.* habeas corpus.

haber, *va.* (HE, HUBE) to have (as an auxiliary verb); to exist; **—es,** *m. pl.* property, goods and chattels; (com.) credit; **ha de ser,** it must be.

habichuela, *f.* kidney bean; **— verde,** string bean.

hábil, *adj.* able, clever, skillful, dexterous, apt.

habilidad, *f.* ability, ableness, dexterity, aptitude.

habilitación, *f.* habilitation, qualification.

habilitado, da, *adj.* qualified; —, *m.* paymaster.

habilitar, *va.* to qualify, to enable; to equip, to supply with.

habitable, *adj.* habitable, lodgeable.

habitación, *f.* habitation, abode, lodging, dwelling, residence.

habitante, *m.* and *f.* inhabitant, dweller.

habitar, *va.* to inhabit, to reside.

hábito, *m.* dress, habit; habitude, customariness, custom.

habitual, *adj.* habitual, customary, usual.

habituar, *va.* to accustom; **—se,** to accustom oneself.

habitud, *f.* relation, connection.

habla, *f.* speech; language; discourse; talk, conversation; **sin —,** speechless.

hablador, ra, *n.* prattler; —, *adj.* talkative.

habladuría, *f.* impertinent speech; gossip.

hablar, *va.* and *vn.* to speak; to talk; to reason, to converse; to harangue.

hablilla, *f.* rumor, report; little tale.

hacedero, ra, *adj.* feasible, practicable.

hacedor, ra, *n.* maker, author; factor; able performer; creator; **el Supremo H—,** the Supreme Being.

hacendado, *m.* man of property; yeoman; landholder, planter, rancher, farmer; **—, da,** *adj.* landed.

hacendoso, sa, *adj.* industrious, diligent.

hacer, *va.* and *vn.* (HAGO, HICE) to make, to do; to manufacture; to perform; to matter; to fit, to suit; to cause; to compel; to earn; to accustom; **— agua** (naut.) to leak; **— alarde,** to boast; **— alto,** to halt; **— burla,** to poke fun at; **— calor,** to be warm; **— caso de,** to pay attention to; **— daño,** to hurt; **— de,** to act as;

— falta, to need, to be lacking; **— frío,** to be cold; **— fuego,** (mil.) to fire; **— la prueba,** to try an experiment; **— muecas,** to make faces; **— papel,** to play a role; **— presente,** to notify; **— saber,** to inform; **—se,** to become.

hacia, *prep.* toward; about; **— acá,** hitherward; **— atrás,** backward; **— abajo,** downward; **— arriba,** upwards.

hacienda, *f.* landed property; estate, fortune, wealth; domestic work; farmstead.

hacina, *f.* stack, rick.

hacinador, ra, *n.* stack maker.

hacinar, *va.* to stack or pile up sheaves of grain; to hoard.

hacha, *f.* large taper; axe, hatchet; **— de viento,** flambeau.

hachazo, *m.* blow with an axe.

hachero, *m.* torch stand; (mil.) pioneer; woodcutter, lumberjack.

hachón, *m.* large torch; cresset.

hada, *f.* fairy.

hado, *m.* fate, destiny.

halagar, *va.* to please; to cajole, to flatter.

halago, *m.* cajolery, caress; flattery.

halagüeño, ña, *adj.* pleasing; attractive, flattering.

halcón, *m.* falcon, hawk.

halconero, *m.* falconer.

hálito, *m.* breath; gentle breeze.

hallar, *va.* to find; to meet with; to discover; **—se,** to happen to find; to be pleased with a place; to find himself, to be (in a place).

hallazgo, *m.* finding, discovery; reward given for finding.

hamaca, *f.* hammock.

hambre, *f.* hunger; famine; eagerness, desire, greediness; **tener —,** to be hungry.

hambriento, ta, *adj.* hungry; starved; greedy, eager.

hangar, *m.* hangar.

haragán, ana, *n.* idler, loiterer, loafer, good-for-nothing; **—,** *adj.* lazy.

haraganear, *vn.* to loaf, to loiter.

haraganería, *f.* idleness, laziness.

harapo, *m.* rag, tatter.

haraposo, sa, *adj.* ragged.

harén, *m.* harem.

harina, *f.* flour; powder, dust; farina; **— de maíz,** corn meal.

harinero, *m.* flour dealer; **—, ra,** *adj.* made of flour, pertaining to flour.

harinoso, sa, *adj.* mealy.

harmonía, *f.* harmony.

harnero, *m.* sieve.

hartar, *va.* and *vr.* to cloy, to satiate; to gorge; to disgust.

harto, ta, *adj.* satiated; sufficient; **—,** *adv.* enough.

hartura, *f.* satiety; plenty, abundance.

hasta, *prep.* till, until; up to, as far as, down to; **— ahora** or **aquí,** till now; **— luego** or **después,** good-by; **— no más,** to the limit; **— la vista,** till we meet again; **—,** *conj.* also, even.

hastío, *m.* loathing; disgust; tedium.

hatajo, *m.* small herd of cattle; (coll.) assemblage, collection; **decir un — de disparates,** to utter many blunders.

hatillo, *m.* small bundle.

hato, *m.* clothes, wearing apparel; herd of cattle, flock of sheep; provisions for shepherds; heap, cluster; crowd, multitude.

Haya, (La) *f.* The Hague.

haya, *f.* beech tree.

haz, *m.* fagot, bundle of brushwood; (mil.) file of soldiers; **—,** *f.* face, visage; right side of cloth; surface of the ground.

hazaña, *f.* exploit, achievement, feat.

hazmerreír, *m.* ridiculous person, laughing-stock.

he, *adv.* behold, look here (generally followed by **aquí** or **allí**); **— allí,** there it is; **— aquí,** here it is; **—me aquí,** here I am.

Heberto, Herbert.

hebilla, *f.* buckle.

hebillaje, *m.* collection of buckles.

hebra, *f.* thread, filament; vein of minerals or metals.

hebraico, ca, *adj.* belonging to the Hebrews.

hebraísmo, *m.* Hebraism.

hebreo, ea, *n.* Hebrew; *m.*; **—,** Hebrew language; (coll.) usurer; **—, ea,** *adj.* Hebraic, Judaical.

hect, hectárea, hectare.

hectárea, *f.* hectare, unit of measure equal to 10,000 square meters, or 2.471 acres.

hectógrafo, *m.* hectograph.

hectogramo, *m.* hectogram.

hectolitro, *m.* hectoliter.

hectómetro, *m.* hectometer.

hechicería, *f.* witchcraft; charm.

hechicero, ra, *adj.* charming, bewitching; **—,** *n.* witch, hag; wizard.

hechizar, *va.* to bewitch; to enchant; to charm.

hechizo, *m.* bewitchment, enchantment, spell.

hecho, cha, *adj.* made, done; accustomed; **bien —cho,** well done; **mal —cho,** that's wrong; poorly made; **—,** *m.* fact; action, act, deed, feat.

hechura, *f.* form, shape, fashion; making; workmanship; creature; henchman, political follower.

heder, *vn.* (IE) to stink, to smell bad.

hediondez, *f.* strong stench.

hediondo, da, *adj.* fetid, stinking, malodorous.

hedonismo, *m.* hedonism.

hedor, *m.* stench, stink.

hegemonía, *f.* hegemony.

helada, *f.* frost; nip.

heladería, *f.* ice-cream parlor or store.

helado, da, *adj.* frozen; glacial, icy; astonished; astounded; **—,** *m.* ice cream.

helar, *va.* and *vn.* (IE) to congeal; to freeze, to ice; to astonish, to amaze; **—se,** to be frozen; to turn into ice; to congeal.

helecho, *m.* (bot.) fern.

Helena, Helen.
Hélice, —, f. (astron.) the Big Dipper, the Big Bear.
hélice, f. helix, helical line; screw propeller, spiral propeller.
helicóptero, m. helicopter.
helio, m. helium.
heliocromo, m. heliochromic process.
heliografía, f. heliograph, blueprint.
heliógrafo, m. heliograph.
helioscopio, m. helioscope.
helioterapia, f. heliotherapy.
heliotipo, m. heliotype.
heliotropismo, m. heliotropism.
hematites, f. hematite (iron ore).
hembra, f. female; eye of hook; nut of a screw.
hemicránea, f. (med.) hemicrania, migraine headache.
hemina, f. measure containing the third part of a **fanega.**
hemisferio, m. hemisphere.
hemofilia, f. (med.) hemophilia.
hemoglobina, f. (med.) hemoglobin.
hemopatía, f. (med.) disease of the blood.
hemoptisis, f. (med.) hemoptysis.
hemorragia, f. (med.) hemorrhage.
hemorroides, f. pl. piles, hemorrhoids.
hemóstasis, f. hemostasis.
henar, m. hay field.
henchir, va. (I) to fill up; **—se,** to fill or gorge oneself.
hendedura, f. fissure, chink, crevice.
hender, va. (IE) to chink, to split, to crack; to go through; to open a passage.
hendidura, f. rift.
heno, m. hay.
hepático, ca, adj. hepatic; **—ca,** f. (bot.) hepatica.
hepatisis, f. (med.) chronic consumption of the liver.
heraldo, m. herald.
herbaje, m. herbage, pasture.
herbolario, m. botanist; (coll.) ridiculous, extravagant man.
herborizar, vn. to study botany.
hercúleo, lea, adj. herculean, very strong.
heredable, adj. inheritable.
heredad, f. farm, country place; piece of cultivated land.
heredar, va. to inherit.
heredera, f. heiress.
heredero, m. heir.
hereditario, ria, adj. hereditary.
hereje, m. and f. heretic.
herejía, f. heresy.
herencia, f. inheritance, heritage; heirship.
herético, ca, adj. heretic.
herida, f. wound, hurt.
herido, da, adj. wounded, hurt.
herir, va. (IE) to wound, to hurt; to affect, to touch, to move; to offend.
hermafrodita, adj. hermaphrodite; **—,** m. androgyne.

hermanar, va. to match, to suit, to acknowledge as a brother; **—,** vn. to fraternize.
hermanastra, f. stepsister, halfsister.
hermanastro, m. stepbrother, half brother.
hermandad, f. fraternity; conformity; brotherhood, sodality.
hermano, na, n. brother, sister; mate (applied to objects); **primo** or **prima —,** first cousin; **—na de la caridad,** sister of charity.
hermético, ca, adj. hermetical, airtight.
hermosear, va. to beautify, to embellish, to adorn.
hermoso, sa, adj. beautiful, handsome.
hermosura, f. beauty.
hernia, f. hernia, rupture.
héroe, m. hero
heroicidad, f. heroism, heroic courage or virtue.
heroico, ca, adj. heroic.
heroína, f. heroine; (chem.) heroin.
heroísmo, m. heroism.
herpe, m. or f. skin eruption, such as eczema, etc.
herrada, f. pail, bucket; **agua —,** water in which red-hot iron has been cooled.
herrador, m. farrier.
herradura, f. horseshoe; **camino de —,** bridle path or road.
herraje, m. ironwork.
herramental, m tool bag.
herramienta, f. tool, implement; set of tools for workmen; **—tas,** pl. (coll.) teeth, grinders.
herrar, va. (IE) to shoe horses.
herrería, f. ironworks; blacksmith's shop; forge; clamor, confused noise.
herrero, m. smith.
herrumbre, f. iron rust.
hervidero, m. ebullition, boiling; small spring with gaseous bubbles; great quantity of people.
hervidor, m. boiler.
hervir, vn. (IE) to boil; to be fervent.
hervor, m. ebullition, boiling.
heterodina, f. heterodyne.
heterodoxia, f. heterodoxy.
heterodoxo, xa, adj. heterodox.
heterogeneidad, f. heterogeneousness.
heterogéneo, nea, adj. heterogenous.
hética, f. tuberculosis, consumption.
hético, ca, adj. hectic, consumptive.
hexágono, m. hexagon; **—, na,** adj. hexangular.
hexámetro, m. hexameter.
hez, f. lee, dregs; dross.
Hg. hectogramo, hg. hectogram.
hibisco, m. hibiscus.
hibridización, f. hybridization.
híbrido, da, adj. hybrid.
hidalgo, ga, n. hidalgo, hidalga (nobleman or noblewoman); **—,** adj. noble, illustrious.
hidalguía, f. nobility.
hidra, f. hydra.
hidrácido, m. (chem.) hydracid.

hidratación, f. hydration.
hidratar, va. (chem.) to hydrate.
hidrato, m. (chem.) hydrate; — **de carbono,** carbohydrate.
hidráulica, f. hydraulics.
hidráulico, ca, adj. hydraulic.
hidroavión, m. seaplane.
hidrocarburo, m. (chem.) hydrocarbon, carburated hydrogen.
hidroclorato, m. (chem.) hydrochlorate.
hidroclórico, ca, adj. (chem.) hydrochloric.
hidrodinámica, ca, adj. hydrodynamic.
hidroeléctrico, ca, adj. hydroelectric.
hidrófilo, la, adj. absorbent.
hidrofobia, f. hydrophobia.
hidrógeno, m. (chem.) hydrogen.
hidrografía, f. hydrography.
hidrólisis, f. hydrolysis.
hidropatía, f. hydropathy.
hidropesía, f. dropsy.
hidrópico, ca, adj. dropsical.
hidroplano, m. hydroplane.
hidroponía, f. hydroponics.
hidrósfera, f. hydrosphere.
hidrostática, f. hydrostatics.
hidrostático, ca, adj. hydrostatic.
hidrosulfúrico, ca, adj. hydrosulphuric.
hidrotecnia, f. hydraulic engineering.
hidroterapia, f. hydrotherapeutics.
hidróxido, m. (chem.) hydroxide.
hiedra, f. ivy.
hiel, f. gall, bile.
hielo, m. frost, ice.
hiena, f. hyena.
hierba, f. herb; grass, weed; — **becerra,** snapdragon.
hierbabuena, f. (bot.) mint.
hierbajo, m. weed; potion.
hierro, m. iron; brand; —**s,** pl. fetters; — **colado** or **de fundición** or **fundido,** cast iron; — **forjado** or **de fragua,** wrought iron; — **galvanizado,** galvanized iron; — **laminado,** sheet iron.
hígado, m. liver; (coll.) courage, valor.
higiene, f. hygiene.
higiénico, ca, adj. hygienic.
higo, m. fig; — **chumbo** or **de pala,** prickly pear; **no dársele a uno un —,** not to care a fig.
higuera, f. fig tree.
hijastro, tra, n. stepchild.
hijo, ja, n. son, daughter; child; young of animals; —**os,** m. pl. one's children, sons or daughters.
hijodalgo, m. nobleman.
hijuela, f. little daughter; patch (in sewing); a small drain; (law) inventory of the distributive shares of a succession; rural mail route.
hila, f. row, line; surgical gauze.
hilacha, f. filament or thread raveled out of cloth.
hiladillo, m. silk for ferreting; narrow ribbon or tape.
hilado, m. spun flax, wool, etc.

hilador, ra, n. spinner; —, f. spinning machine; —, adj. spinning.
hilandería, f. spinning mill.
hilandero, ra, n. spinner; —, m. spinning room.
hilar, va. to spin.
hilaridad, f. hilarity, mirth, gaiety.
Hilario, Hilary.
hilera, f. row, line, file.
hilo, m. thread; linen; wire.
hilván, m. basting.
hilvanar, va. to baste, to sew loosely; to perform in a hurry.
himeneo, m. (poet.) marriage.
himno, m. hymn; anthem.
hin, m. neighing.
hincapié, m. firm planting of one's foot; **hacer —,** to stress, to emphasize, to insist, to stand firm.
hincar, va. to thrust in, to drive into, to nail, to prick; — **la rodilla,** to kneel down.
hinchado, da, adj. swollen; vain, arrogant.
hinchador, m. pump; — **de neumáticos,** tire pump.
hinchar, va. to swell; —**se,** to swell, to grow larger; to be elated with arrogance.
hinchazón, f. swelling, tumid inflammation; ostentation, vanity.
hindú, m. and f. Hindu.
hinojo, m. knee; (bot.) fennel.
hipar, vn. to hiccough; to pant.
hipérbola, f. hyperbola, section of a cone.
hipérbole, f. hyperbole, exaggeration.
hiperbólico, ca, adj. hyperbolical.
hipercrítico, ca, adj. hypercritical.
hipertrofia, f. hypertrophy.
hipertrófico, ca, adj. hypertrophic.
hipnosis, f. hypnosis.
hipnótico, ca, adj. hypnotic.
hipnotismo, m. hypnotism.
hipnotizar, va. to hypnotize.
hipo, m. hiccough.
hipocondría, f. hypochondria.
hipocóndrico, ca, adj. hypochondriac.
hipocresía, f. hypocrisy.
hipócrita, adj. and n. hypocritical; hypocrite.
hipodérmico, ca, adj. hypodermic.
hipódromo, m. hippodrome, circus; race track.
hipofosfato, m. (chem.) hypophosphate.
hipogloso, m. halibut; —, sa, adj. hypoglossal.
hiponitrato, m. (chem.) subnitrate.
hipopótamo, m. hippopotamus.
hiposulfato, m. (chem.) hyposulphate.
hiposulfito, m. (chem.) hyposulphite.
hipoteca, f. mortgage.
hipotecar, va. to mortgage.
hipotecario, ria, adj. belonging to a mortgage.
hipotenusa, f. hypotenuse.
hipótesis, f. hypothesis, basis.
hipotético, ca, adj. hypothetical.

hirviente, *adj.* boiling.
hisopear, *va.* to sprinkle water about with a water sprinkler.
hisopo, *m.* (bot.) hyssop; water sprinkler.
hispano, na, *adj.* (poet.) Spanish.
Hispanoamérica, *f.* Spanish America.
hispanoamericano, na, *adj.* and *n.* Spanish-American.
histérico, ca, *adj.* hysterical.
histerismo, *m.* hysteria.
histología, *f.* histology.
historia, *f.* history; tale, story.
historiado, da, *adj.* ornate.
historiador, ra, *n.* historian, historiographer.
historiar, *va.* to record in history; to represent historical events in painting.
histórico, ca, *adj.* historical, historic.
historieta, *f.* short story, short novel.
histrión, *m.* player; clown.
hito, *m.* landmark; guidepost; mark to shoot at; **a —,** fixedly; **mirar de — en —,** to stare at, to look at from head to foot.
Hl. hectolitro, hectol. or hl. hectoliter.
Hm. hectómetro, hectom. or hm. hectometer.
Hno. Hermano, Bro. Brother.
Hnos. or **Hos. Hermanos,** Bros. Brothers.
hocicar, *va.* to break up the ground with the snout; **—,** *vn.* to fall headlong with the face to the ground.
hocico, *m.* snout, muzzle; flap-mouthed man; (coll.) face; **meter el — en todo,** to meddle in everything.
hocicudo, da, *adj.* long-snouted; blubber-lipped; flap-mouthed.
hogar, *m.* hearth, fireplace; house, residence, home.
hogaza, *f.* large loaf of household bread.
hoguera, *f.* bonfire; blaze.
hoja, *f.* leaf; blade (of knife, sword, etc.); sheet (of paper or metal); **— de afeitar,** razor blade; **— de apunte,** tally sheet; **— de estaño,** tinfoil; **— de lata,** tin; **— en blanco,** blank sheet form; **— de estaño,** tin foil.
hojalata, *f.* tin plate.
hojalatero, *m.* tinner, tinsmith.
hojaldre, *f.* light, flaky pastry.
hojaldrista, *m.* and *f.* pastry cook.
hojarasca, *f.* redundancy of leaves; foliage; useless trifles.
hojear, *va.* to turn the leaves of a book.
hojilla, *f.* leaflet.
hojuela, *f.* pastry; skins of olives after pressing.
hol. holandés, D. Dutch.
¡hola! *interj.* holla!
Holanda, *f.* Holland.
holandés, sa, *n.* and *adj.* Dutch.
holgachón, ona, *adj.* easy-going, lazy, indolent.
holgadamente, *adv.* loosely; leisurely.
holgado, da, *adj.* loose, wide, broad: at leisure; in easy circumstances.

holganza, *f.* comfort, ease, tranquility of mind; recreation, amusement.
holgar, *vn.* (UE) to rest; to be useless; **—se,** to sport, to be pleased with.
holgazán, na, *n.* idler, loiterer, vagabond.
holgazanear, *vn.* to idle, to loiter, to loaf, to lounge.
holgazanería, *f.* idleness, indolence.
holgura, *f.* frolic, merrymaking; width, breadth; ease, repose, comfort.
holocausto, *m.* holocaust.
hollar, *va.* (UE) to trample, to tread upon.
hollejo, *m.* pellicle, peel, chaff.
hollín, *m.* soot.
holliniento, ta, *adj.* sooty.
hombre, *m.* man, human being; ombre (card game); **— de bien,** honorable man; **¡— al agua!** man overboard!
hombrera, *f.* piece of armor for the shoulders.
hombría, *f.* manhood; **— de bien,** probity, honesty.
hombro, *m.* shoulder.
homenaje, *m.* homage, tribute.
homeópata, *m.* homeopath.
homicida, *m.* and *f.* murderer; **—,** *adj.* homicidal, murderous.
homicidio, *m.* murder.
homilía, *f.* homily, ecclesiastical sermon.
homogeneidad, *f.* homogeneity.
homogéneo, nea, *adj.* homogeneous.
homogenizar, va. to homogenize.
homógrafo, *m.* homograph.
homología, *f.* homology.
homólogo, ga, *adj.* homologous; synonymous.
homónimo, *m.* homonym.
honda, *f.* sling (instrument for throwing stones, etc.).
hondazo, *m.* throw with a sling.
hondear, *va.* (naut.) to sound.
hondero, *m.* slinger.
hondillo, *m.* any of the pieces of cloth which form the seats of pants.
hondo, da, *adj.* profound, deep; difficult.
hondonada, *f.* dale; ravine.
hondura, *f.* depth, profundity.
hondureño, ña, *n.* and *adj.* Honduran.
honestidad, *f.* honesty, modesty; urbanity.
honesto, ta, *adj.* honest; modest.
hongo, *m.* mushroom; fungus; Derby hat.
honguillo, *m.* fungus.
honor, *m.* honor.
honorable, *adj.* honorable.
honorario, ria, *adj.* honorary; **—rio,** *m.* salary, fee.
honorífico, ca, *adj.* creditable, honorable.
honra, *f.* honor, reverence; reputation; chastity (in women); **—s,** *pl.* funeral honors.
honradez, *f.* honesty, probity.
honrado, da, *adj.* honest, honorable, reputable.
honrar, *va.* to honor; **—se,** to deem it an honor.

honrilla, *f.* keen sense of honor.
honroso, sa, *adj.* honorable; honest.
hopalanda, *f.* gown worn by students.
hora, *f.* hour; time; **— de comer,** dinner-time; **—s,** *pl.* canonical hours; devotional book, prayer book.
Horacio, Horace.
horadar, *va.* to bore or perforate from one side to the other.
horario, ria, *adj.* horary, hourly; **—,** *m.* hour hand of a clock; time table; schedule of school hours.
horca, *f.* gallows; pitchfork; **carne de —,** gallows bird.
horcajadas or **horcajadillas** (**a —**), *adv.* astride.
horcajadura, *f.* fork formed by the two thighs.
horcate, *m.* yoke or collar of a horse; **— de yugo,** oxbow.
horchata, *f.* beverage made from crushed almonds or melon seeds.
horizontal, *adj.* horizontal.
horizonte, *m.* horizon.
horma, *f.* mold; **— de zapatos,** shoe tree.
hormero, *m.* maker of shoe lasts.
hormiga, *f.* ant.
hormigón, *m.* concrete; **— armado,** reinforced concrete.
hormigonera, *f.* concrete mixer.
hormigoso, sa, *adj.* formicine.
hormigueamiento, *m.* formication, itching (as if with ants).
hormiguear, *vn.* to itch; to run about like ants, to swarm.
hormiguero, *m.* anthill; place where there is a crowd of people moving.
hormiguillo, *m.* (vet.) scarf of the hoof; workers ranged in line, who pass the working materials from hand to hand; (Mex.) spicy sirup.
hormón, *m.* hormone.
hornacho, *m.* shaft of a mine.
hornachuela, *f.* hut, cave.
hornada, *f.* batch, bread baked at one time.
hornaza, *f.* goldsmith's furnace.
hornazo, *m.* Easter cake.
hornero, *m.* baker.
hornilla, *f.* grated compartment in a stove.
horno, *m.* oven, kiln, furnace; **— alto** or **de cuba,** blast furnace; **— de ladrillo,** brickkiln; **— Siemens-Martin,** open-hearth furnace.
horóscopo, *m.* horoscope.
horquilla, *f.* forked stick, pitchfork; hairpin; **— corrugada para el pelo,** bobby pin.
horrendo, da, *adj.* horrible, hideous; awful.
hórreo, *m.* granary.
horrible, *adj.* horrid, horrible.
horrísono, na, *adj.* (poet.) dreadful-sounding.
horror, *m.* horror, fright.
horrorizar, *va.* to cause horror, to frighten; **—se,** to be terrified.

horroroso, sa, *adj.* horrid, hideous, frightful.
hortaliza, *f.* vegetables.
hortelano, *m.* gardener, horticulturist; ortolan (bird).
Hortensia, Hortense.
hortensia, *f.* (bot.) hydrangea.
hortera, *f.* wooden bowl; **—,** *m.* nickname of shop boys in Madrid.
hortícola, *adj.* horticultural.
horticultura, *f.* horticulture.
hosco, ca, *adj.* dark; sullen, gloomy.
hospedador, ra, *n.* one who kindly receives and entertains guests and strangers; entertainer.
hospedaje, *m.* lodging.
hospedar, *va.* to lodge, to board; **—se (en),** to take lodging (at).
hospedería, *f.* hospitium, hospice.
hospedero, *m.* innkeeper.
hospicio, *m.* hospice, house of charity.
hospital, *m.* hospital; **— de sangre, de campaña,** field hospital.
hospitalario, ria, *adj.* hospitable; relative to a hospital.
hospitalero, ra, *n.* warden of a hospital.
hospitalidad, *f.* hospitality.
hospitalización, *f.* hospitalization.
hostería, *f.* inn, tavern.
hostia, *f.* host; wafer.
hostiario, *m.* wafer box.
hostigar, *va.* to trouble, to molest; to gall; to tire.
hostil, *adj.* hostile, adverse.
hostilidad, *f.* hostility, enmity.
hostilizar, *va.* to do harm to the enemy; to antagonize.
hotel, *m.* hotel.
hoy, *adv.* today, this day; **de — en adelante,** henceforth, henceforward; **— día,** nowadays.
hoya, *f.* hole, pit; sepulture.
hoyo, *m.* hole, pit, excavation.
hoyoso, sa, *adj.* full of holes.
hoyuelo, *m.* dimple.
hoz, *f.* sickle.
HP or **H.P. caballo de fuerza,** HP, H.P. or h.p. horsepower.
hta. hasta, until, up to.
hucha, *f.* large chest in which laboring people keep their clothes, money, and other valuable articles; money box.
huebra, *f.* day's work; extent of ground which a yoke of oxen can plow in a day; pair of mules with a plowman let out for a day's work.
hueca, *f.* notch at the small end of a spindle.
hueco, ca, *adj.* hollow, concave; empty, vain, ostentatious; **—,** *m.* interval; gap, hole; office vacancy.
huelga, *f.* rest, repose; recreation; fallow ground; strike of workmen.
huella, *f.* track, footstep, trace.
huérfago, *m.* heaves.
huérfano, na, *n.* and *adj.* orphan.

huero, ra, *adj.* empty, addle; (Mex.) blond, fair.

huerta, *f.* orchard, vegetable garden.

huerto, *m.* walled garden, fruit garden.

huesa, *f.* grave, sepulture.

hueso, *m.* bone; stone, core.

huesoso, sa, *adj.* bony.

huésped, da, *n.* guest; boarder, roomer, lodger; innkeeper; stranger; **casa de —des,** boardinghouse.

hueste, *f.* army in campaign.

huesudo, da, *adj.* bony.

huevar, *vn.* to lay eggs.

huevera, *f.* ovarium of birds; egg cup.

huevero, ra, *n.* dealer in eggs.

huevo, *m.* egg; ovum; spawn; **— cocido,** hard-boiled egg; **— condimentado con picantes,** deviled egg; **— de faltriquera,** candied egg; **— escalfado,** poached egg; **— frito** or **estrellado,** fried egg; **— pasado por agua,** soft-boiled egg; **— revuelto,** scrambled egg.

Hugo, Hugh.

hugonote, ta, *n.* and *adj.* Huguenot.

huída, *f.* flight, escape.

huir, *vn.* (HUYO) to flee, to escape.

hule, *m.* rubber; oilcloth.

hulla, *f.* soft coal, bituminous or pit coal.

humanarse, *vr.* to become man (applied to Jesus Christ); to become humane or meek.

humanidad, *f.* humanity, mankind; benevolence; (coll.) corpulence; **—es,** *pl.* humanities, human learning.

humanitario, ria, *n.* and *adj.* humanitarian.

humanitarismo, *m.* humanitarianism.

humano, na, *adj.* human; humane, kind.

humareda, *f.* great deal of smoke; confusion, perplexity.

Humberto, Humbert.

humeante, *adj.* smoking, steaming.

humear, *vn.* to smoke.

humedad, *f.* humidity, moisture, wetness.

humedecedor, *m.* humidifier.

humedecer, *va.* (EZCO) to moisten, to wet, to soak.

humedecido, da, *adj.* moistened, dampened.

húmedo, da, *adj.* humid, wet, moist, damp.

humero, *m.* tunnel; funnel; shaft of chimney; smoke pipe.

húmero, *m.* (anat.) humerus.

humildad, *f.* humility, humbleness; meanness; submission.

humilde, *adj.* humble, meek, lowly.

humillación, *f.* humiliation; submission.

humilladero, *m.* small chapel on the roads and near the villages.

humillar, *va.* to humble; to humiliate; **—se,** to humble oneself.

humo, *m.* smoke; fume.

humor, *m.* humor, disposition, temper, nature; **buen —,** good nature; **mal —,** ill temper; **estar de buen —,** to be gay.

humorada, *f.* graceful sprightliness; witty, humorous utterance or action.

humorado, da, *adj.* full of humors; **bien** or **mal —do,** in good or bad humor.

humorista, *m.* and *f.* humorist.

humoso, sa, *adj.* smoky.

humus, *m.* humus.

hundir, *vn.* to submerge; to sink, to overwhelm; to confound; **—se,** to sink, to go to the bottom; (coll.) to disappear; to lie hid.

Hunfredo, Humphrey.

húngaro, ra, *adj.* and *n.* Hungarian, **plato —ro,** goulash.

Hungría, *f.* Hungary.

huracán, *m.* hurricane, storm.

huraño, ña, *adj.* shy, unsociable, retiring.

hurgar, *va.* to stir; to excite quarrels.

hurgón, *m.* poker (for stirring a fire).

hurón, *m.* (zool.) ferret; ferreter; **—, ona,** *adj.* shy.

huronear, *vn.* to hunt with ferrets; (coll.) to pry into.

huronera, *f.* ferret hole; (coll.) hiding place.

¡hurra! *interj.* hurrah!

hurraca, *f.* magpie.

hurtadillas, (a), *adv.* by stealth.

hurtar, *va.* to steal, to rob.

hurto, *m.* theft, robbery.

húsar, *m.* (mil.) hussar.

husillo, *m.* clamp screw; **—s,** *pl.* drains.

husma, *f.* scenting; prying; **andar a la —,** (coll.) to pry into a thing, to spy out a secret.

husmear, *va.* to scent; to pry, to peep.

huso, *m.* spindle.

huta, *f.* hut.

I

ib. ibídem, ib. or ibid. in the same place.

ibérico, ca, *adj.* Iberian.

íbice, *m.* ibex.

ibídem, *adv.* in the same place.

ibis, *m.* ibis (wading bird).

iconoclasta, *m.* iconoclast, image breaker.

ictericia, *f.* jaundice.

ictiología, *f.* ichthyology.

íd. ídem, id. same, ditto.

ida, *f.* departure; sally; **—s,** *pl.* frequent visits; **—s y venidas,** coming and going; **billete de — y vuelta,** round trip.

idea, *f.* idea; scheme.

ideal, *m.* and *adj.* ideal.

idealismo, *m.* idealism.

idealista, *n.* and *adj.* idealist; idealistic.

idealización, *f.* idealization.

idealizar, *va.* and *vn.* to idealize.

idealmente, *adv.* ideally.

idear, *va.* to conceive: to think, to contrive, to plan.

ídem, item, the same, ditto.

idéntico, ca, *adj.* identical.

identidad, *f.* identity.

identificar, *va.* to identify; —**se,** to identify oneself.
ideograma, *m.* ideogram, ideograph.
ideología, *f.* ideology.
ideológico, ca, *adj.* ideological.
ideólogo, *m.* ideologist.
idilio, *m.* idyl.
idioma, *m.* language.
idiosincrasia, *f.* idiosyncrasy.
idiota, *m.* and *f.* idiot; —, *adj.* idiotic.
idiotismo, *m.* idiotism; ignorance.
idólatra, *m.* and *f.* idolater.
idolatrar, *va.* to idolize; to love with excessive fondness.
idolatría, *f.* idolatry.
ídolo, *m.* idol.
idoneidad, *f.* aptitude, fitness.
idóneo, nea, *adj.* fit, suitable.
i.e. esto es, i.e. that is.
igl.ª iglesia, ch. church.
iglesia, *f.* church.
Ignacio, Ignatius.
ignaro, ra, *adj.* ignorant, unlearned, uninstructed.
ígneo, nea, *adj.* igneous, fiery.
ignición, *f.* ignition.
Ign.º Ignacio, Ignatz; Ignatius.
ignominia, *f.* ignominy, infamy.
ignominioso, sa, *adj.* ignominious.
ignorancia, *f.* ignorance.
ignorante, *adj.* ignorant, stupid.
ignorar, *va.* to be ignorant of, not to know.
ignoto, ta, *adj.* unknown.
igual, *adj.* equal, similar; **al** —, equally.
igualación, *f.* equalization, matching, leveling.
igualar, *va.* to equalize, to equal; to match; —, *vn.* to be equal; —**se,** to place oneself on a level (with).
igualdad, *f.* equality.
igualmente, *adv.* equally.
iguana, *f.* iguana, large tropical lizard.
ijada, *f.* flank (of an animal); pain in the side.
ijadear, *vn.* to pant, to palpitate.
ijar, *m.* flank (of an animal).
ilación, *f.* inference, deduction; connectedness.
Il.º Ilustre, Illustrious.
ilegal, *adj.* illegal, unlawful.
ilegalidad, *f.* illegality.
ilegitimar, *va.* to render illegitimate.
ilegitimidad, *f.* illegitimacy.
ilegítimo, ma, *adj.* illegal; illegitimate.
ileso, sa, *adj.* unhurt.
ilícito, ta, *adj.* illicit, unlawful.
ilimitado, da, *adj.* unlimited, boundless.
iliterato, ta, *adj.* not learned, illiterate.
ilógico, ca, *adj.* illogical.
iluminación, *f.* illumination, lighting.
iluminar, *va.* to illumine, to illuminate, to enlighten.
ilusión, *f.* illusion.
ilusivo, va, *adj.* illusive.
iluso, sa, *adj.* deceived; fanatical; visionary.

ilusorio, ria, *adj.* illusory.
ilustración, *f.* illustration; explanation.
ilustrador, ra, *n.* illustrator.
ilustrar, *va.* to illustrate; to enlighten.
ilustre, *adj.* illustrious, celebrated.
imagen, *f.* image.
imaginable, *adj.* imaginable.
imaginación, *f.* imagination, fancy; conception.
imaginar, *va.* and *vn.* to imagine.
imaginaria, *f.* (mil.) reserves.
imaginario, ria, *adj.* imaginary, fancied.
imaginativo, va, *adj.* imaginative; —, *f.* imagination, fancy.
imaginero, *m.* painter of religious images.
imán, *m.* loadstone, magnet.
imantar, *va.* to magnetize.
imbécil, *m.* and *f.* imbecile, fool, idiot; —, *adj.* feeble-minded.
imbecilidad, *f.* imbecility.
imberbe, *adj.* beardless (applied to a young man).
imbuir, *va.* (UYO) to imbue; to infuse into the mind.
imitable, *adj.* imitable.
imitación, *f.* imitation, copy; **a** — **de,** in imitation of.
imitador, ra, *n.* imitator; (coll.) rubber stamp.
imitar, *va.* to imitate, to copy; to counterfeit.
imp. imprenta, print. printing, printing office.
impacción, *f.* impact.
impaciencia, *f.* impatience.
impacientar, *va.* to put one out of all patience; —**se,** to become impatient.
impaciente, *adj.* impatient, restless.
impalpable, *adj.* impalpable.
impar, *adj.* unequal, odd; uneven.
imparcial, *adj.* impartial.
imparcialidad, *f.* impartiality.
impartir, *va.* to impart.
impasibilidad, *f.* impassibility.
impasible, *adj.* impassible, unmoved.
impavidez, *f.* composure in the face of danger.
impávido, da, *adj.* calm in the face of danger.
impecabilidad, *f.* impeccability.
impecable, *adj.* impeccable.
impedimento, *f.* impediment, obstacle.
impedir, *va.* (I) to impede, to hinder, to prevent.
impeler, *va.* to impel; to incite, to stimulate.
impenetrable, *adj.* impenetrable, impervious; incomprehensible.
impenitencia, *f.* impenitence.
impenitente, *adj.* impenitent.
impensado, da, *adj.* unexpected, unforeseen.
imperar, *vn.* to rule, to command; to reign; to prevail.
imperativo, va, *adj.* imperative, pressing; —, *m.* (gram.) imperative (case).

imperatorio, ria, *adj.* imperial.
imperceptible, *adj.* imperceptible.
imperdonable, *adj.* unpardonable.
imperecedero, ra, *adj.* imperishable, undying.
imperfección, *f.* imperfection.
imperfecto, ta, *adj.* imperfect.
imperial, *f.* roof of a coach; —, *adj.* imperial.
imperialismo, *m.* imperialism.
imperialista, *adj.* imperialistic.
impericia, *f.* lack of experience or skill.
imperio, *m.* empire.
imperioso, sa, *adj.* imperious, pressing; arrogant, haughty.
imperito, ta, *adj.* unlearned, unskilled.
impermeable, *adj.* impermeable; waterproof; —, *m.* raincoat.
impermutable, *adj.* immutable.
impersonal, *adj.* impersonal.
impertérrito, ta, *adj.* intrepid, unterrified.
impertinencia, *f.* impertinence; troublesomeness.
impertinente, *adj.* impertinent; importunate.
impertinentes, *m. pl.* lorgnette.
imperturbable, *adj.* imperturbable.
impetración, *f.* plea; petition; thing obtained by petition.
impetrar, *va.* to beg, to beseech, to petition; to get by petition.
impetu, *m.* impetus; impetuosity.
impetuosidad, *f.* impetuosity.
impetuoso, sa, *adj.* impetuous.
impiedad, *f.* impiety; cruelty.
impío, pía, *adj.* impious.
implacable, *adj.* implacable, inexorable.
implicación, *f.* implication.
implicar, *va.* to implicate, to involve; to entangle; —, *vn.* to imply contradiction.
implícito, ta, *adj.* implicit.
implorar, *va.* to implore, to beg.
impolítica, *f.* incivility; impolicy.
impolítico, ca, *adj.* impolitic; impolite.
impoluto, ta, *adj.* not polluted, clear.
imponderable, *adj.* inexpressible, unutterable; imponderable.
imponente, *adj.* imposing, awe-inspiring.
imponer, *va.* (IMPONGO, IMPUSE) to impose a tax; to impute falsely; to advise; to impose upon; —se, to assert oneself.
impopular, *adj.* unpopular, out of favor.
importación, *f.* importation.
importador, ra, *n.* importer; —, *adj.* importing.
importancia, *f.* importance, import.
importante, *adj.* important, considerable.
importar, *vn.* to be important, to matter, to mind; to import; **no** —, not to mind.
importe, *m.* amount or gross amount; value, cost; — **bruto** or **total,** gross amount; — **líquido** or **neto,** net amount.
importunación, *f.* importunity.
importunar, *va.* to importune.
importunidad, *f.* importunity, annoyance.

importuno, na, *adj.* importunate, unreasonable; vexing, troublesome.
imposibilidad, *f.* impossibility.
imposibilitar, *va.* to render impossible; to disable.
imposible, *adj.* impossible.
imposición, *f.* imposition.
impostor, ra, *n.* impostor, cheater.
impostura, *f.* false imputation; imposture, deceit.
impotencia, *f.* impotence.
impotente, *adj.* impotent; helpless.
impracticable, *adj.* impracticable, unfeasible.
imprecación, *f.* imprecation, curse.
imprecar, *va.* to imprecate, to curse.
imprecatorio, ria, *adj.* containing curses, full of evil wishes.
impregnarse, *vr.* to become impregnated.
imprenta, *f.* printing; printing office.
imprescindible, *adj.* imperative; indispensable, essential.
impresión, *f.* impression; stamp; print; edition; influence; presswork.
impresionable, *adj.* impressionable; emotional.
impresionar, *va.* to impress, to imprint, to fix on the mind.
impresionismo, *m.* impressionism.
impreso, *m.* small book, short treatise; print; —s, *pl.* printed matter.
impresor, ra, *n.* printer.
imprevisión, *f.* lack of foresight; inadvertency.
imprevisto, ta, *adj.* unforeseen; unprovided against.
imprimación, *f.* priming coat (of paint, varnish, etc.); priming (of a gun).
imprimir, *va.* to print; to imprint; to stamp; to impress.
improbable, *adj.* improbable, unlikely.
improbo, ba, *adj.* corrupt, wicked; laborious; painful.
improductivo, *va. adj.* barren, unproductive.
impronunciable, *adj.* unpronounceable.
improperar, *va.* to upbraid, to taunt, to chide, to abuse.
improperio, *m.* contemptuous reproach, injurious censure.
impropiedad, *f.* impropriety.
impropio, pia, *adj.* improper, unfit; unbecoming.
improporción, *f.* disproportion.
improporcionado, da, *adj.* disproportionate.
improrrogable, *adj.* that which cannot be put off or deferred.
impróspero, ra, *adj.* unprosperous.
impróvido, da, *adj.* improvident, heedless.
improvisación, *f.* improvisation.
improvisar, *va.* to extemporize, to improvise.
improviso, sa, *adj.* improvised; unforeseen; not provided against; **de** —, unexpectedly.

imprudencia, *f.* imprudence; indiscretion.
imprudente, *adj.* imprudent, indiscreet.
impudencia, *f.* impudence.
impudente, *adj.* impudent, shameless.
impúdico, ca, *adj.* unchaste; shameless, brazen.
impuesto, *m.* tax, impost, duty; — **sobre rentas,** income tax.
impugnación, *f.* opposition, contradiction.
impugnar, *va.* to impugn, to oppose.
impulsar, *va.* to further, to impel; (mech.) to drive.
impulsivo, va, *adj.* impulsive.
impulso, *m.* impulse, impulsion, spur.
impune, *adj.* unpunished.
impunemente, *adv.* with impunity.
impunidad, *f.* impunity; guiltlessness.
impureza, *f.* impurity.
impuro, ra, *adj.* impure, foul.
imputable, *adj.* imputable, chargeable.
imputar, *va.* to impute, to attribute.
inaccesible, *adj.* inaccessible; (fig.) incomprehensible.
inacción, *f.* inaction, inactivity.
inaceptable, *adj.* unacceptable.
inactividad, *f.* inactivity.
inadecuado, da, *adj.* inadequate.
inadmisible, *adj.* inadmissible.
inadvertencia, *f.* oversight, inattention.
inadvertido, da, *adj.* inadvertent, unnoticed.
inafectado, da, *adj.* unaffected, genuine, natural.
inagotable, *adj.* inexhaustible.
inaguantable, *adj.* insupportable, insufferable, intolerable.
inajenable, *adj.* inalienable.
inalámbrico, ca, *adj.* wireless.
inalienable, *adj.* inalienable.
inalterable, *adj.* unalterable.
inane, *adj.* inane, useless, futile.
inanimado, da, *adj.* lifeless, inanimate.
inapelable, *adj.* unappealable.
inapreciable, *adj.* inappreciable; invaluable.
inastillable, *adj.* nonshattering; not chipping or splintering easily.
inaudito, ta, *adj.* unheard of, unusual.
inauguración, *f.* inauguration, consecration.
inaugurar, *va.* to inaugurate.
inca, *m.* Inca; Peruvian gold coin.
incandescencia, *f.* incandescence, white heat.
incansable, *adj.* indefatigable, untiring.
incapacidad, *f.* incapacity, inability; stupidity; incompetence.
incapacitar, *va.* to incapacitate, to disable.
incapaz, *adj.* incapable, unable.
incasto, ta, *adj.* unchaste, not pure.
incauto, ta, *adj.* incautious, unwary, heedless.
incendiar, *va.* to kindle, to set on fire.
incendiario, ria, *n.* and *adj.* incendiary.
incendiarismo, *m.* incendiarism.

incendio, *m.* fire, conflagration, combustion; **compañía de seguros contra —s,** fire insurance company; **boca de —,** fireplug.
incensar, *va.* (IE) to incense; (fig.) to flatter.
incensario, *m.* incensory, censer.
incentivo, *m.* incitement, inducement, incentive.
incertidumbre, *f.* incertitude, uncertainty.
incesante, *adj.* incessant, continual.
incesto, *m.* incest.
incestuoso, sa, *adj.* incestuous.
incidencia, *f.* incident; **por —,** accidently.
incidente, *m.* incident, event, accident.
incidir, *vn.* to fall upon, to meet with (as an error).
incienso, *m.* incense.
incierto, ta, *adj.* uncertain, doubtful.
incineración, *f.* incineration.
incinerador, *m.* incinerator.
incinerar, *va.* to incinerate.
incisión, *f.* incision, cut.
incisivo, va, *adj.* incisive.
inciso, *m.* (gram.) comma.
incitación, *f.* incitement.
incitar, *va.* to incite, to stir; to excite.
incitativo, va, *adj.* inciting.
incivil, *adj.* unpolished, uncivil.
inclemencia, *f.* inclemency, severity; **a la —,** openly, without shelter.
inclinación, *f.* inclination, slope; (aer.) airplane banking.
inclinar, *va.* to incline; to induce; —, *vn.* to resemble; —, *vr.* to incline, to slope; to be favorably disposed to.
inclinómetro, *m.* inclinometer; (aer.) banking indicator.
ínclito, ta, *adj.* famous, illustrious.
incluir, *va.* (UYO) to include, to comprise, to inclose.
inclusa, *f.* orphan asylum.
inclusión, *f.* inclusion.
inclusive, *adv.* inclusive, including.
incluso, sa, *adj.* inclosed.
incoado, da, *adj.* inchoate.
incoativo, va, *adj.* inchoative, inceptive.
incobrable, *adj.* irrecoverable; (com.) unable to be collected.
incógnito, ta, *adj.* unknown; **de —,** incognito.
incoherencia, *f.* incoherence.
incoherente, *adj.* incoherent.
incólume, *adj.* safe, unharmed.
incombustible, *adj.* incombustible.
incomodar, *va.* to inconvenience, to disturb; **—se,** to be angered.
incomodidad, *f.* uncomfortableness, inconvenience, annoyance.
incómodo, da, *adj.* uncomfortable, inconvenient.
incomparable, *adj.* incomparable, matchless.
incompatibilidad, *f.* incompatibility.
incompatible, *adj.* incompatible.
incompetencia, *f.* incompetency.

incompetente, adj. incompetent.
incompleto, ta, adj. incomplete.
incomplexo, xa, adj. simple, not complex.
incomprensible, adj. incomprehensible.
incompresible, adj. incompressible.
incomunicación, f. lack of communication.
incomunicado, da, adj. without communication.
inconcebible, adj. inconceivable.
inconciliable, adj. irreconcilable.
inconcuso, sa, adj. indisputable, incontrovertible.
inconexo, xa, adj. unconnected, incoherent; independent.
incongelable, adj. unfreezable; **solución —,** antifreeze.
incongruencia, adj. incongruity, incongruence.
incongruo, grua, adj. incongruous, disproportionate.
inconmensurable, adj. incommeasurable.
inconmovible, adj. unshakable, inexorable.
inconmutable, adj. incommutable.
inconquistable, adj. unconquerable.
inconsciencia, f. unconsciousness.
inconsciente, adj. unconscious.
inconsecuencia, f. inconsequence; inconsistency.
inconsecuente, adj. inconsequent; inconsistent.
inconsiderado, da, adj. inconsiderate, heedless.
inconsolable, adj. inconsolable.
inconstancia, f. inconstancy, unsteadiness; levity.
inconstante, adj. inconstant, variable, fickle.
inconstitucional, adj. unconstitutional.
incontestable, adj. indisputable, incontrovertible, incontestable.
incontinencia, f. incontinence, incontinency; unchastity.
incontinente, adj. incontinent.
incontrastable, adj. insurmountable; unconquerable; unanswerable.
inconveniencia, f. inconvenience; disadvantage.
inconveniente, adj. inconvenient; inadvisable; —, m. difficulty, obstacle; disadvantage.
incorporación, f. incorporation; annexation.
incorporar, va. to incorporate; to join; —se, to become incorporated; to sit up (in bed).
incorpóreo, rea, adj. incorporeal; immaterial.
incorrecto, ta, adj. incorrect.
incorregible, adj. incorrigible.
incorruptible, adj. incorruptible.
increado, da, adj. uncreated.
incredulidad, f. incredulity, incredulousness.
incrédulo, la, adj. incredulous.
increíble, adj. incredible.

incremento, m. increment, increase; growth.
increpación, f. reprehension, rebuke.
increpar, va. to chide, to reprehend, to scold.
incruento, ta, adj. unstained with blood (said specially of the sacrifice of the mass).
incrustación, f. incrustation.
incubación, f. incubation, hatching.
incubar, va. to hatch.
inculcar, va. to inculcate.
inculpable, adj. inculpable, unblamable.
inculpar, va. to accuse, to blame.
inculto, ta, adj. uncultivated, uneducated.
incumbencia, f. incumbency; duty.
incumbir, vn. to be incumbent upon one; to concern.
incurable, adj. incurable; irremediable.
incuria, f. negligence.
incurrir, vn. to incur.
incursión, f. incursion, incurring; (mil.) sortee; — **aérea,** air raid.
indagación, f. search, inquiry.
indagar, va. to search, to inquire, to investigate.
indebido, da, adj. undue; illegal, unlawful.
indecencia, f. indecency.
indecente, adj. indecent.
indecible, adj. inexpressible, unutterable.
indecisión, f. irresolution, indecision.
indeciso, sa, adj. irresolute; undecided, vague.
indeclinable, adj. firm, unshaken; (gram.) indeclinable.
indecoroso, sa, adj. indecent, unbecoming, indecorous.
indefectible, adj. unfailing.
indefendible, adj. indefensible.
indefenso, sa, adj. defenseless.
indefinible, adj. indefinable.
indefinido, da, adj. indefinite.
indeleble, adj. indelible.
indeliberado, da, adj. unpremeditated.
indemnización, f. indemnification, indemnity, compensation.
indemnizar, va. to indemnify.
independencia, f. independence.
independiente, adj. independent.
indescriptible, adj. indescribable.
indestructible, adj. indestructible.
indeterminado, da, adj. indeterminate; undetermined; irresolute.
indevoto, ta, adj. not devout, impious, irreligious.
indiana, f. chintz, printed cotton.
indiano, na, n. native or resident of West Indies; one who returns wealthy from America.
Indias, f. pl. Indies; — **Holandesas** (or **Neerlandesas**) **Orientales,** Dutch East Indies; — **Occidentales,** West Indies; **Mar de las —** or **Océano Indico,** Indian Ocean.
indicación, f. indication.
indicador, m. indicator, gauge; recorder;

— de deriva, shift or deviation gauge (of an aeroplane); **— de subida y bajada,** rate of climb indicator; **— de viraje,** bank indicator.

indicar, va. to indicate, to point out.

indicativo, va, adj. indicative, pointing; **—,** m. and adj. (gram.) indicative.

índice, m. mark, sign; hand of a watch or clock; index, table of contents; forefinger; **— de compresión,** compression rate.

indicio, m. indication, mark; sign, trace; token.

índico, ca, adj. pertaining to the East Indies; **Océano I—** (or **Mar de las Indias**), Indian Ocean; **Archipiélago I—,** Malay Archipelago.

indiferencia, f. indifference, unconcern.

indiferente, adj. indifferent.

indígena, adj. indigenous, native.

indigencia, f. indigence, poverty, need.

indigente, adj. indigent, poor, in want.

indigestión, f. indigestion.

indigesto, ta, adj. indigestible; (fig.) not properly thought or worked out.

indignación, f. indignation, anger.

indignado, da, adj. indignant, angry.

indignar, va. to irritate, to anger, to provoke, to tease.

indignidad, f. indignity; meanness.

indigno, na, adj. unworthy, undeserving; disgraceful.

índigo, m. indigo plant; indigo.

indio, dia, n. and adj. Indian.

indirecta, f. innuendo, hint, cue.

indirecto, ta, adj. indirect.

indisciplinado, da, adj. undisciplined.

indiscreción, f. indiscretion, imprudence.

indiscreto, ta, adj. indiscreet, inconsiderate.

indisculpable, adj. inexcusable.

indiscutible, adj. unquestionable.

indisoluble, adj. indissoluble.

indispensabilidad, f. indispensability.

indispensable, adj. indispensable.

indisponer, va. (INDISPONGO, INDISPUSE) to disable, to render unfit, to indispose; **—se,** to become ill; to fall out (with some one).

indisposición, f. indisposition, slight disorder.

indispuesto, ta, adj. indisposed.

indisputable, adj. indisputable, incontrovertible.

indistinto, ta, adj. indistinct.

individual, adj. individual.

individualidad, f. individuality.

individualizar, va. to specify individually.

individuo, m. individual.

indivisible, adj. indivisible.

indócil, adj. indocile; headstrong.

indocilidad, f. indocility.

índole, f. disposition, temper, peculiar genius; class, kind; nature.

indolencia, f. indolence, indifference.

indolente, adj. indolent, indifferent.

indomable, adj. untamable; unconquerable.

indomado, da, adj. untamed.

indómito, ta, adj. untamed, ungoverned, unruly.

indubitable, adj. unquestionable, indubitable.

inducción, f. induction, persuasion; **carrete de —,** or **bobina de —,** induction coil.

inducir, va. (INDUZCO, INDUJE) to induce, to persuade, to abet.

inductancia, f. inductance.

inductivo, va, adj. inductive.

inductor, m. inductor.

indudable, adj. undeniable; evident, certain, indubitable.

Indulg. plen. or **I.P. Indulgencia plenaria,** plenary indulgence.

indulgencia, f. indulgence, forgiveness.

indulgente, adj. indulgent.

indultar, va. to pardon; to exempt.

indulto, m. pardon, amnesty; privilege; exemption.

indumentaria, f. clothing, clothes outfit.

industria, f. industry.

industrial, adj. industrial.

industrialismo, m. industrialism.

industrialista, m. industrialist.

industriar, va. and vr. to instruct; to train, to coach.

industrioso, sa, adj. industrious; ingenious.

inédito, ta, adj. not published; unedited.

inefable, adj. ineffable, unspeakable, unutterable.

ineficacia, f. inefficacy.

ineficaz, adj. inefficacious.

ineludible, adj. inescapable.

ineptitud, f. inability, unfitness, ineptitude.

inepto, ta, adj. inept, unfit; useless.

inequívoco, ca, adj. unmistakable.

inercia, f. inertia; inactivity.

inerme, adj. disarmed, without arms.

inerte, adj. inert, dull, sluggish; unskillful, awkward.

Inés, Agnes, Inez.

inescrupuloso, sa, adj. unscrupulous.

inescrutable, adj. inscrutable.

inesperado, da, adj. unexpected, unforeseen.

inestimable, adj. inestimable.

inevitable, adj. unavoidable, inevitable.

inexactitud, f. inaccuracy, lack of exactness.

inexacto, ta, adj. not exact.

inexorable, adj. inexorable.

inexperto, ta, n. fledgling.

inexplicable, adj. inexplicable.

inexpuesto, ta, adj. (photo.) unexposed.

infalibilidad, f. infallibility.

infalible, adj. infallible.

infamador, ra, n. detractor.

infamante, adj. defamatory; opprobrious, disgraceful.

infamar, va. to defame, to disgrace.

infame, adj. infamous, bad; **—,** m. wretch, scoundrel.

infamia, *f.* infamy.
infancia, *f.* infancy, childhood.
infanta, *f.* infanta (royal princess of Spain or Portugal); wife of an **infante;** infant (female child under seven years old).
infante, *m.* infant; infantryman, foot soldier; any son of king of Spain, except the heir apparent.
infantería, *f.* infantry.
infanticida, *m.* infanticide (person).
infanticidio, *m.* infanticide (murder).
infantil, *adj.* infantile, childlike; **parálisis —,** infantile paralysis.
infanzón, *m.* nobleman.
infatigable, *adj.* indefatigable, untiring.
infatuación, *f.* infatuation.
infausto, ta, *adj.* unlucky, unfortunate, luckless; fatal.
infección, *f.* infection.
infectar, *va.* to infect.
infecto, ta, *adj.* infected.
infelicidad, *f.* misfortune, infelicity.
infeliz, *adj.* unhappy, unfortunate.
inferior, *adj.* inferior; lower.
inferioridad, *f.* inferiority; **complejo de —,** inferiority complex.
inferir, *va.* (IE) to infer; to inflict.
infernal, *adj.* infernal, hellish.
infestación, *f.* infestation.
infestar, *va.* to overrun, to harass, to annoy an enemy by incursions; to infect.
inficionar, *va.* and *vr.* to infect; to corrupt.
infidelidad, *f.* infidelity; treachery.
infiel, *adj.* infidel; faithless, false, disloyal; godless.
infierno, *m.* hell.
infiltración, *f.* (med.) infiltration.
infiltrar, *va.* and *vr.* to infiltrate; to filter; to imbue, to infuse.
ínfimo, ma, *adj.* lowest, lowermost.
infinidad, *f.* infinity, immensity.
infinitivo, *m.* (gram.) infinitive.
infinito, ta, *adj.* infinite, immense; **—,** *adv.* infinitely, immensely; **—,** *m.* infinity.
inflación, *f.* inflation.
inflamable, *adj.* inflammable.
inflamación, *f.* inflammation.
inflamar, *va.* to inflame; to kindle desires; to stir; **—se,** to catch on fire.
inflamatorio, ria, *adj.* inflammatory.
inflar, *va.* and *vr.* to inflate, to swell with wind.
inflexibilidad, *f.* inflexibility.
inflexible, *adj.* inflexible.
influencia, *f.* influence.
influenza, *f.* influenza, flu, grippe.
influir, *va.* (UYO) to influence, to prevail upon.
influjo, *m.* influx, influence.
influyente, *adj.* influential.
información, *f.* information; instruction; judicial inquiry.
informal, *adj.* not punctual; unreliable.
informalidad, *f.* unreliability.

informar, *va.* to inform, to let know, to report.
informe, *m.* information; report, account; **—,** *adj.* shapeless, formless.
infortunio, *m.* misfortune, ill luck.
infracción, *f.* infraction; breach, violation, trespass.
infractor, ra, *n.* violator.
infraestructura, *f.* substructure, underframe.
infrarrojo, ja, *adj.* infrared.
infrascripto, ta, or **infrascrito, ta,** *adj.* underwritten, undersigned; hereinafter mentioned.
infrecuente, *adj.* infrequent, unusual.
infringir, *va.* to infringe, to violate.
infructífero, ra, *adj.* unfruitful; useless.
infructuoso, sa, *adj.* fruitless, unproductive, unprofitable.
infundado, da, *adj.* groundless.
infundir, *va.* to infuse, to inspire with; to instill.
infusión, *f.* infusion.
infuso, sa, *adj.* infused (now used only with reference to the grace of God).
ingeniar, *va.* to conceive; to contrive; **—se,** to work in the mind, to endeavor to find out.
ingeniero, *m.* engineer.
ingenio, *m.* wit, ingenuity, talent, inventive mind, creative faculty, cleverness, skill; engine; **— de azúcar,** sugar mill.
ingenioso, sa, *adj.* ingenious, witty.
ingénito, ta, *adj.* inborn, natural.
ingenuidad, *f.* ingenuousness; candor, frankness, naiveté.
ingenuo, nua, *adj.* ingenuous, candid, open, naive.
ingerencia, *f.* interference.
ingerir, *va.* (IE) to insert; to introduce, to inclose; **—se,** to interfere officiously.
Inglaterra, *f.* England.
ingle, *f.* groin.
inglés, esa, *n.* and *adj.* Englishman, Englishwoman; English; **—,** *m.* English language.
ingratitud, *f.* ingratitude, thanklessness.
ingrato, ta, *adj.* ungrateful, thankless; disagreeable.
ingrediente, *m.* ingredient.
ingreso, *m.* (com.) receipts, revenue; entrance; ingress; earnings; surplice fees.
inhábil, *adj.* unable, incapable.
inhabilitar, *va.* to disqualify, to disable.
inhabitable, *adj.* uninhabitable.
inhalado, *adj.* indrawn.
inhalador, *m.* inhaler.
inherente, *adj.* inherent.
inhibición, *f.* inhibition, prohibition.
inhibir, *va.* to inhibit, to prohibit.
inhibitorio, ria, *adj.* prohibitory.
inhumación, *f.* inhumation, burial; **agencia de —,** funeral parlor.
inhumanidad, *f.* inhumanity.
inhumano, na, *adj.* inhuman, cruel.
inicial, *f.* and *adj.* initial.

iniciar, *va.* to initiate, to begin; —**se,** to be initiated; to receive the first orders.
iniciativo, va, *adj.* initiating, initiatory; —, *f.* initiative.
inicuo, cua, *adj.* iniquitous, unjust.
inimaginable, *adj.* unimaginable, inconceivable.
inimitable, *adj.* inimitable.
ininteligible, *adj.* unintelligible.
iniquidad, *f.* iniquity, injustice.
injertar, *va.* to graft (as a tree).
injerto, *m.* grafted tree; grafting.
injuria, *f.* offense, insult, harm.
injuriador, ra, *n.* injurer, wrongdoer.
injuriar, *va.* to insult, to harm.
injurioso, sa, *adj.* injurious; offensive.
injusticia, *f.* injustice.
injusto, ta, *adj.* unjust.
inmaculado, da, *adj.* immaculate.
inmanente, *adj.* immanent.
inmarcesible, *adj.* never-fading.
inmaturo, ra, *adj.* immature.
inmediación, *f.* neighborhood; vicinity; immediacy.
inmediatamente, *adv.* immediately, forthwith.
inmediato, ta, *adj.* immediate, next.
inmejorable, *adj.* unsurpassable.
inmemorial, *adj.* immemorial.
inmensidad, *f.* immensity.
inmenso, sa, *adj.* immense, infinite.
inmensurable, *adj.* immensurable.
inmersión, *f.* immersion, dip.
inmigración, *f.* immigration.
inmigrar, *vn.* to immigrate.
inminencia, *f.* imminence.
inminente, *adj.* imminent.
inmoble, *adj.* immovable; constant.
inmoderado, da, *adj.* immoderate.
inmodesto, ta, *adj.* immodest.
inmolar, *va.* to sacrifice.
inmoral, *adj.* immoral.
inmortal, *adj.* immortal.
inmortalidad, *f.* immortality.
inmortalizar, *va.* to immortalize.
inmóvil, *adj.* immovable, stable; deathlike.
inmovilidad, *f.* immobility.
inmueble, *adj.* (law) immovable (property); **bienes** —**s,** real estate.
inmundicia, *f.* nastiness, filth.
inmundo, da, *adj.* filthy, dirty; obscene.
inmune, *adj.* free, exempt.
inmunidad, *f.* immunity, privilege.
inmunizar, *va.* to immunize.
inmutabilidad, *f.* immutability.
inmutable, *adj.* immutable, unchangeable.
inmutar, *va.* to change, to alter; —**se,** to change expression due to sudden emotional disturbance.
innato, ta, *adj.* inborn, natural.
innegable, *adj.* incontestable, incontrovertible.
innoble, *adj.* ignoble; low-born.
innominado, da, *adj.* nameless, with no special name.

innovación, *f.* innovation.
innovador, ra, *n.* innovator.
innovar, *va.* to innovate.
innumerable, *adj.* innumerable, numberless.
inobediencia, *f.* disobedience.
inobediente, *adj.* disobedient.
inobservancia, *f.* inadvertency; inobservance.
inocencia, *f.* innocence.
inocente, *adj.* innocent.
inoculación, *f.* inoculation.
inocular, *va.* to inoculate.
inodoro, ra, *adj.* deodorized; —, *m.* water closet.
inofensivo, va, *adj.* harmless.
inoficioso, sa, *adj.* inofficious.
inolvidable, *adj.* unforgettable.
inopinado, da, *adj.* unexpected, unforeseen, sudden.
inq. inquisidor, inquisitor.
inquebrantable, *adj.* shatterproof, unbreakable; unswerving.
inquietar, *va.* to disquiet, to disturb, to worry.
inquieto, ta, *adj.* restless, anxious, uneasy.
inquietud, *f.* restlessness, worry, anxiety.
inquilino, na, *n.* tenant; boarder.
inquirir, *va.* (IE) to inquire, to investigate.
inquisición, *f.* inquisition; judicial inquiry.
inquisidor, *m.* inquirer; inquisitor.
insaciable, *adj.* insatiable, greedy.
insalubre, *adj.* insalubrious.
insalubridad, *f.* insalubrity, unhealthfulness.
insano, na, *adj.* insane, mad.
inscribir, *va.* to inscribe, to register.
inscripción, *f.* inscription.
insecticida, *m.* insecticide, insect poison, insect killer.
insecto, *m.* insect.
inseguro, ra, *adj.* uncertain, unsteady.
insensatez, *f.* insensateness, stupidity, folly.
insensato, ta, *adj.* insensate, stupid, insane.
insensibilidad, *f.* insensibility.
insensibilizar, *va.* to make insensible; to make insensitive.
insensible, *adj.* insensible; imperceptible.
insensiblemente, *adv.* by degrees; imperceptibly.
inseparable, *adj.* inseparable.
inserción, *f.* insertion.
insertar, *va.* to insert.
inservible, *adj.* unserviceable, useless.
insidioso, sa, *adj.* insidious.
insigne, *adj.* notable, famous.
insignia, *f.* badge; —**s,** *pl.* insignia.
insignificancia, *f.* insignificance.
insignificante, *adj.* insignificant.
insinuación, *f.* insinuation, hint.
insinuar, *va.* to insinuate, to hint; —**se,** to steal into imperceptibly; to ingratiate oneself.
insipidez, *f.* insipidity.
insípido, da, *adj.* insipid.

insipiencia, *f.* ignorance, lack of wisdom.
insistencia, *f.* persistence, steadiness.
insistir, *vn.* to insist; to emphasize.
insociable, *adj.* unsociable.
insolación, *f.* sunstroke, heatstroke.
insoldable, *adj.* that cannot be soldered; irreparable.
insolencia, *f.* insolence, impudence, effrontery.
insolente, *adj.* insolent, impudent.
in sólidum, *adv.* (law) jointly.
insólito, ta, *adj.* unusual.
insolvencia, *f.* insolvency.
insolvente, *adj.* insolvent.
insomnio, *m.* insomnia, sleeplessness.
insondable, *adj.* unfathomable; inscrutable.
insoportable, *adj.* insupportable.
inspección, *f.* inspection, survey, control.
inspeccionar, *va.* to inspect, to oversee, to examine.
inspector, *m.* inspector, superintendent.
inspiración, *f.* inspiration.
inspirar, *va.* to inspire.
instabilidad, *f.* instability, inconstancy, fickleness, mutability, fragility; giddiness.
instable, *adj.* unstable, inconstant, changing, mutable, fickle.
instalación, *f.* installation, fittings, fixtures; instalment; system; — **eléctrica,** electric plant, electric fixtures.
instalador, *m.* inductor.
instalar, *va.* to install; to induct (into office); —**se,** to settle, to be established.
instancia, *f.* instance; **elevar una —,** to make a petition.
instantáneo, nea, *adj.* instantaneous; —, *f.* snapshot.
instante, *m.* instant; **al —,** immediately, instantly.
instar, *va.* to press, to urge a request or petition; —, *vn.* to be pressing or urgent.
instaurar, *va.* to renew, to renovate.
instigación, *f.* incitement, impulse, instigation.
instigar, *va.* to instigate.
instilar, *va.* to instil, to impart gradually.
instintivo, va, *adj.* instinctive.
instinto, *m.* instinct; — **de conservación,** instinct of self-preservation.
institución, *f.* institution; —**ones,** *pl.* elements of a science.
institucional, *adj.* institutional.
instituir, *va.* (UYO) to institute, to establish.
instituto, *m.* institute.
institutriz, *f.* governess.
instrucción, *f.* instruction; education.
instructivo, va, *adj.* instructive, conveying knowledge.
instructor, *m.* instructor, teacher.
instruído, da, *adj.* educated.
instruir, *va.* (UYO) to instruct, to teach.
instrumentación, *f.* instrumentation.
instrumental, *adj.* instrumental.
instrumentista, *m.* and *f.* instrument maker; musical player.

instrumento, *m.* instrument; machine; means, expedient; — **de viento,** wind instrument; — **de cuerda,** string instrument; **tablero de —s,** instrument board; **vuelo con —s,** (aer.) blind flying.
insubordinación, *f.* insubordination.
insubordinado, da, *adj.* insubordinate, rebellious.
insubordinar, *va.* to stir to insubordination; —**se,** to rebel, to become insubordinated.
insubsistencia, *f.* instability.
insubsistente, *adj.* unable to subsist; unstable.
insubstancial, *adj.* not substantial; shallow.
insuficiencia, *f.* insufficiency, inadequacy.
insuficiente, *adj.* insufficient, inadequate.
insufrible, *adj.* insufferable, insupportable, intolerable.
insular, *m.* and *f.* islander; —, *adj.* insular.
insulina, *f.* insulin.
insulsez, *f.* insipidity, flatness.
insulso, sa, *adj.* insipid; dull, heavy; flat; cold.
insultar, *va.* to insult.
insulto, *m.* insult, offense; sudden and violent attack.
insuperable, *adj.* insuperable, insurmountable.
insurgencia, *f.* insurgence.
insurgente, *m.* and *adj.* insurgent.
insurrección, *f.* insurrection.
insurrecto, ta, *n.* and *adj.* insurgent, rebel.
intacto, ta, *adj.* untouched; entire; intact.
intachable, *adj.* blameless; irreproachable.
integración, *f.* integration.
integral, *adj.* integral, whole.
integridad, *f.* integrity, whole; uncorruptedness.
íntegro, gra, *adj.* integral, entire.
integumento, *m.* integument.
intelectual, *adj.* intellectual.
inteligencia, *f.* intelligence; understanding.
inteligente, *adj.* intelligent.
inteligible, *adj.* intelligible.
intemperancia, *f.* intemperance.
intemperie, *f.* rough or bad weather; **a la —,** outdoors.
intempestivo, va, *adj.* unseasonable, inopportune.
intención, *f.* intention, design, meaning, view.
intencionadamente, *adv.* intentionally.
intencionado, da, *adj.* inclined, disposed.
intendencia, *f.* administration; employment of an intendant.
intendente, *m.* intendant.
intensidad, *f.* intensity.
intensificar, *va.* to intensify.
intensión, *f.* intenseness; vehemence, zeal.
intenso, sa, *adj.* intense, ardent, vehement, zealous.
intentar, *va.* to try; to intend, to design.
intento, *m.* intent, purpose, design.

intentona, *f.* (coll.) extravagant design; rash attempt.

ínter, *prep.* between, in the midst (used as an inseparable prefix, except in phrase — **nos,** between us).

intercadencia, *f.* interruption; inconstancy; (med.) certain irregularity of the pulse.

intercalación, *f.* intercalation, insertion.

intercalar, *va.* to intercalate, to insert.

intercambiable, *adj.* interchangeable.

intercambio, *m.* interchange.

interceder, *vn.* to intercede.

interceptar, *va.* to intercept.

intercesión, *f.* intercession, mediation, entreaty.

intercesor, ra, *n.* intercessor, mediator.

intercostal, *adj.* intercostal.

interés, *m.* interest; concern; advantage; profit; — **compuesto,** compound interest; — **simple,** simple interest.

interesado, da, *adj.* interested; concerned; selfish; —, *n.* person interested, person concerned.

interesante, *adj.* interesting; useful, convenient.

interesar, *vn.* and *vr.* to be concerned or interested in; —, *va.* to interest; to concern, to give a share in.

interescolar, *adj.* interscholastic.

ínterin, *adv.* in the interim, in the meantime.

interinidad, *f.* temporary holding of office.

interino, na, *adj.* provisional (of an employ or office).

interior, *adj.* interior, internal; —, *m.* interior, inside; —**es,** *pl.* entrails, intestines.

interioridad, *f.* inside, interior.

interjección, *f.* (gram.) interjection.

interlineación, *f.* interlineation.

interlineal, *adj.* interlinear.

interlocución, *f.* interlocution, dialogue.

interlocutor, ra, *n.* interlocutor.

interlocutorio, ria, *adj.* interlocutory.

intermediar, *va.* to interpose.

intermediario, ria, *n.* and *adj.* intermediary.

intermedio, dia, *adj.* intermediate, intermedial; —, *m.* interval, interlude, recess; **por — de,** through, by means of.

interminable, *adj.* interminable, endless.

intermisión, *f.* intermission, interruption.

intermitente, *adj.* intermittent.

internacional, *adj.* international.

internacionalismo, *m.* internationalism.

internado, da, *adj.* interned; —, *m.* boarding-school system; group of boarding students.

internar, *va.* to intern; to place in a boarding school or asylum; —, *vn.* to pierce; —**se,** to insinuate, to wheedle.

interno, na, *adj.* interior, internal, inside; —, *n.* boarding-school student.

interpelación, *f.* interpellation, summons.

interpelar, *va.* to appeal to.

interpolación, *f.* interpolation; interruption.

interpolar, *va.* to interpolate; to interrupt.

interponer, *va.* (INTERPONGO, INTERPUSE) to interpose.

interposición, *f.* interposition; mediation.

interpretación, *f.* interpretation.

interpretar, *va.* to interpret, to explain; to translate.

intérprete, *m.* and *f.* interpreter.

interregno, *m.* interreign.

interrogación, *f.* interrogation, question.

interrogante, *adj.* interrogative; —, *m.* questioner.

interrogar, *va.* to interrogate, to question.

interrogativo, va, *adj.* interrogatory.

interrogatorio, *m.* interrogatory, cross-examination, questionnaire.

interrumpir, *va.* to interrupt.

interrupción, *f.* interruption, discontinuance.

interruptor, *m.* (elec.) switch.

intersección, *f.* intersection.

intersectario, ria, *adj.* interdenominational.

intersideral, *adj.* interstellar.

interuniversitario, ria, *adj.* intercollegiate.

intervalo, *m.* interval.

intervención, *f.* intervention, mediation.

intervenir, *vn.* (INTERVENGO, INTERVINE) to intervene, to mediate.

interventor, ra, *n.* intervener; controller.

intestado, da, *adj.* intestate.

intestino, na, *adj.* intestine, internal, interior; —, *m.* intestine.

intimación, *f.* intimation, hint.

intimar, *va.* to intimate, to hint.

intimidación, *f.* intimidation.

intimidad, *f.* intimacy.

intimidar, *va.* to intimidate; —**se,** to lose courage.

íntimo, ma, *adj.* internal, innermost; intimate, familiar.

intitular, *va.* to entitle; to confer a title on.

intolerable, *adj.* intolerable, insufferable.

intolerancia, *f.* intolerance.

intolerante, *adj.* intolerant.

intramuros, *adv.* within the walls.

intranquilo, la, *adj.* restless, uneasy.

intransitable, *adj.* impassable, impenetrable.

intransitivo, va, *adj.* (gram.) intransitive.

intratable, *adj.* intractable, ungovernable.

intrepidez, *f.* intrepidity; temerity.

intrépido, da, *adj.* intrepid, daring.

intriga, *f.* intrigue, plot.

intrigante, *m.* and *f.* intriguer; —, *adj.* intriguing, scheming.

intrigar, *vn.* to intrigue, to scheme.

intrincado, da, *adj.* intricate, involved.

intrincar, *va.* to entangle, to involve; to confound.

intrínseco, ca, *adj.* intrinsic, essential, inherent.

introducción, *f.* introduction.

introducir, *va.* (INTRODUZCO, INTRODUJE) to introduce; —**se,** to gain access (to).

introductor, ra, *n.* introducer.

introductorio, ria, *adj.* introductory.
introito, *m.* beginning of an oration; theatrical prologue.
introspección, *f.* introspection.
introverso, sa, *n.* introvert.
intrusión, *f.* intrusion, obtrusion.
intruso, sa, *adj.* intrusive, obtrusive; —, *n.* intruder.
intuición, *f.* intuition.
intuitivo, va, *adj.* intuitive.
inundación, *f.* inundation, deluge.
inundar, *va.* to inundate, to overflow.
inusitado, da, *adj.* unusual.
inútil, *adj.* useless, needless.
inutilidad, *f.* uselessness.
inutilizar, *va.* to render useless.
invadir, *va.* to invade, to attack a country.
invalidar, *va.* to invalidate, to render null and void.
inválido, da, *adj.* invalid, null; —, *n.* invalid.
invariable, *adj.* invariable.
invasión, *f.* invasion.
invasor, ra, *n.* invader.
invectiva, *f.* invective.
invencible, *adj.* invincible.
invención, *f.* invention.
inventar, *va.* to invent.
inventariar, *va.* to take inventory.
inventario, *m.* inventory.
inventiva, *f.* ingenuity, inventiveness, faculty of inventing.
invento, *m.* invention.
inventor, ra, *n.* inventor; fabricator.
inverisímil, *adj.* unlikely, improbable.
invernáculo, *m.* greenhouse.
invernada, *f.* hibernation.
invernadero, *m.* (mil.) winter quarters; greenhouse.
invernal, *adj.* wintry, winter.
invernar, *vn.* (IE) to pass the winter; to be the winter season.
invernizo, za, *adj.* pertaining to winter.
inverosímil, *adj.* unlikely, improbable.
inverosimilitud, *f.* unlikelihood, improbability.
inversión, *f.* inversion, investment; — de marcha, reverse.
inversionista, *m.* and *f.* investor.
inverso, sa, *adj.* inverted, reciprocal; —, *m.* wrong (side), opposite (side).
inversor, *m.* reversing switch.
invertebrado, da, *adj.* invertebrate; —, *m.* invertebrate.
invertir, *va.* (IE) to invert; (com.) to invest.
investidura, *f.* investiture.
investigación, *f.* investigation, research; inquest.
investigar, *va.* to investigate, to search out.
investir, *va.* (I) to invest, to confer upon, to endow.
inveterarse, *vr.* to become antiquated, to grow old.
invicto, ta, *adj.* unconquered.
invierno, *m.* winter.

inviolabilidad, *f.* inviolability.
inviolable, *adj.* inviolable.
invisible, *adj.* invisible.
invitación, *f.* invitation.
invitado, da, *n.* guest.
invitar, *va.* to invite.
invocación, *f.* invocation.
invocar, *va.* to invoke, to call upon.
involuntario, ria, *adj.* involuntary.
invulnerable, *adj.* invulnerable.
inyección, *f.* injection, hypodermic.
inyectar, *va.* to inject.
iodo = yodo, *m.* iodine.
ion, *m.* ion.
ionización, *f.* ionization.
ipso facto, *adv.* (law) immediately, without delay.
ir, *vn.* (VOY, FUÍ) to go, to walk; —se, to go away, to depart.
ira, *f.* anger, wrath.
iracundia, *f.* ire, irascibility.
iracundo, da, *adj.* wrathful; enraged.
iridiscencia, *f.* iridescence.
iris, *m.* rainbow; iris (of the eye).
Irlanda, *f.* Ireland.
irlandés, esa, *n.* and *adj.* Irishman, Irishwoman, Irish.
ironía, *f.* irony.
irónico, ca, *adj.* ironical.
irracional, *adj.* irrational.
irradiación, *f.* irradiation.
irradiado, da, *adj.* irradiated.
irrazonable, *adj.* unreasonable.
irreconciliable, *adj.* irreconcileable.
irrecusable, *adj.* unimpeachable.
irreflexión, *f.* rashness, inconsideration.
irrefragable, *adj.* undeniable, irrefutable.
irrefutable, *adj.* indisputable, irrefutable.
irregular, *adj.* irregular, abnormal, atypical.
irregularidad, *f.* irregularity, anomaly.
irreligioso, sa, *adj.* irreligious, impious.
irremediable, *adj.* irremediable, helpless.
irremisible, *adj.* irremissible, unpardonable.
irreparable, *adj.* irreparable, irretrievable.
irreprensible, *adj.* irreprehensible.
irresistible, *adj.* irresistible, resistless.
irresolución, *f.* irresolution.
irresoluto, ta, *adj.* irresolute.
irresponsabilidad, *f.* irresponsiblity.
irresponsable, *adj.* irresponsible.
irreverencia, *f.* irreverence, lack of reverence, respect or veneration.
irreverente, *adj.* irreverent.
irrevocable, *adj.* irrevocable.
irrisible, *adj.* laughable.
irrisión, *f.* mockery, mocking laughter.
irrisorio, ria, *adj.* ridiculous, laughable.
irritación, *f.* irritation; wrath.
irritar, *va.* to annul; to irritate, to exasperate.
irrupción, *f.* irruption, inroad.
Isabel, Isabel; Elizabeth.
Isidoro, Isidro, Isidor.
isla, *f.* isle, island.
Isla Española, *f.* Hispaniola.

Islandia, *f.* Iceland.
Islas Filipinas, *f. pl.* Philippine Islands.
isleño, ña, *n.* islander, from the Canary Islands.
isleta, *f.* islet.
islote, *m.* small, barren island.
isométrico, ca, *adj.* isometric.
isomorfo, fa, *adj.* isomorphic.
isósceles, *adj.* isosceles.
isotopos, *m.* isotope.
isotrópico, ca, *adj.* isotropic.
israelíta, *n.* and *adj.* Israelite, Jew, Jewish.
istmo, *m.* isthmus.
ít. ítem (artículo, suelto, capítulo, cláusula), article, chapter, clause, item.
Italia, *f.* Italy.
italiano, na, *n.* and *adj.* Italian; —, *m.* Italian language.
ítem, *m.* item, another article; —, *adv.* also.
itinerario, ria, *adj.* and *m.* itinerary.
izador, *m.* hoist.
izamiento, *m.* hoisting, raising, lifting.
izar, *va.* (naut.) to hoist.
izda., izq.ª or **izq.ᵈᵃ izquierda,** l. left, l.h. left hand.
izquierdo, da, *adj.* left; left-handed; —, *f.* left wing in politics; left, left hand.

J

jaba, *f.* crate; kind of basket.
jabalí, *m.* wild boar.
jabalina, *f.* wild sow; javelin.
jabón, *m.* soap; **pastilla de —,** cake of soap.
jabonado, *adj.* soaped; —, *m.* washing; laundry bundle.
jabonadura, *f.* soapsuds; lather.
jabonar, *va.* to soap.
jabonería, *m.* soap house.
jabonero, *m.* soapmaker or soap seller.
jaca, *f.* nag, pony.
jacal, *m.* (Mex.) wigwam, Indian hut.
jácara, *f.* song or dance tune; group of merrymakers at night singing **jácaras;** (coll.) annoyance; fabulous lie.
jacarear, *vn.* to sing **jácaras.**
jacinto, *m.* hyacinth.
jaco, *m.* nag, pony; short jacket.
Jacobo, Jacob.
jactancia, *f.* boasting.
jactancioso, sa, *adj.* boastful, vainglorious.
jactarse, *vr.* to boast.
jaculatoria, *f.* ejaculatory prayer, short and hurried prayer.
jadeante, *adj.* out of breath, panting.
jadear, *vn.* to pant.
jaez, *m.* harness; kind, quality.
jaguar, *m.* jaguar.
jagüey, *m.* (bot.) liana.
jai alai, *m.* Basque ball game.
jaiba, *f.* (Sp. Am.) crab.
Jaime, James.
jalapa, *f.* (bot.) jalap.
jalbegar, *va.* to whitewash, to make white;

—, *va.* and *vr.* (fig.) to put on makeup.
jalea, *f.* jelly.
jalear, *va.* to urge on hounds to the chase.
jaleo, *m.* halloo; Andalusian dance; scrimmage.
jaletina, *f.* jelly; gelatine.
jamás, *adv.* never; **para siempre —,** for ever and ever; **nunca —,** never, never more.
jamón, *m.* ham, gammon; **— planchado,** pressed ham.
jándalo, la, *adj.* having the gait and dialect of an Andalusian.
Japón, *m.* Japan.
japonés, esa, *adj.* and *n.* Japanese; —, *m.* Japanese language.
jaque, *m.* check (in chess); **— y mate,** checkmate.
jaquear, *va.* to check (in chess).
jaqueca, *f.* headache.
jarabe, *m.* sirup; **— tapatío,** kind of Mexican national dance.
jarana, *f.* merry clatter, outcry.
jarano, *m.* Mexican hat.
jarcia, *f.* bundle, packet; bundle or heap of odds and ends; (naut.) tackle.
jardín, *m.* garden; **— de la infancia,** kindergarten.
jardinería, *f.* gardening.
jardinero, ra, *n.* gardener.
jareta, *f.* fold or tuck for gathering.
jarra, *f.* jug, jar, pitcher; **en —** or **de —s,** with arms placed akimbo.
jarrete, *m.* hock.
jarretera, *f.* garter.
jarro, *m.* pitcher, jug.
jarrón, *m.* large jug, urn.
jaspe, *m.* (min.) jasper.
jaspear, *va.* to marble, to speckle.
jaula, *f.* cage; cell for insane persons; (rail.) cattle car.
jauría, *f.* pack of hounds.
Javier, Xavier.
jazmín, *m.* jessamine, jasmine.
jazz, *m.* jazz.
J.C. Jesucristo, J.C. Jesus Christ.
jedive, *m.* khedive.
jefatura, *f.* headquarters; leadership; **— de policía,** police headquarters.
jefe, *m.* chief, head, leader; **— de equipajes,** (rail.) baggage master; **— de tren,** guard, conductor.
jengibre, *m.* (bot.) ginger.
jenízaro, *adj.* cross-bred.
jerarquía, *f.* hierarchy.
jerárquico, ca, *adj.* hierarchical.
Jeremías, Jeremy, Jeremiah.
Jerez, *m.* **vino de —,** sherry wine.
jerga, *f.* coarse cloth; jargon, gibberish.
jergón, *m.* coarse mattress; (coll.) ill-fitting clothes; lazy, corpulent person.
jerigonza, *f.* jargon, gibberish.
jeringa, *f.* syringe; **— hipodérmica,** hypodermic syringe.
jeringar, *va.* to syringe, to squirt.

jeringazo, *m.* enema.
jeroglífico, ca, *adj.* and *m.* hieroglyphic.
Jerónimo, Jerome.
jersey, *m.* jersey.
Jerusalén, *m.* Jerusalem.
Jesucristo, *m.* Jesus Christ.
jesuíta, *m.* and *adj.* Jesuit.
jesuítico, ca, *adj.* jesuitical.
Jesús, Jesus.
jeta, *f.* thick lips; hog's snout.
Jhs. Jesús, J. Jesus.
jibia, *f.* cuttlefish.
jícara, *f.* chocolate cup; cup made from a gourd or similar substance.
jicotea, *f.* (Cuba) tortoise, turtle.
jigote, *m.* mincemeat.
jilguero, *m.* linnet.
jinete, *m.* cavalier, horseman, rider.
jingoísta, *m.* jingo, jingoist; —, *adj.* jingoist, jingoistic.
jipijapa, *f.* Panama hat straw; —, *m.* Panama hat.
jira, *f.* strip of cloth; picnic, excursion, outing, tour; — **campestre,** picnic; — **comercial,** business tour.
jirafa, *f.* giraffe.
jirón, *m.* shred, tear; facing of a skirt.
Joaquín, Joachim.
jobo, *m.* (bot.) Central American fruit similar to a plum, also the tree.
jocosidad, *f.* jocosity.
jocoso, sa, *adj.* waggish, good-humored.
jofaina, *f.* washbowl, washbasin.
Jonás, Jonah.
Jonatán, Jonatás, Jonathan.
Jorge, George.
jornada, *f.* one-day march; journey; military expedition; act (of a Spanish play).
jornal, *m.* daywork; day's pay; wages; **a —,** by the day.
jornalero, *m.* daylaborer.
joroba, *f.* hump.
jorobado, da, *adj.* hunchbacked.
jorobar, *va.* (coll.) to importune, to tease; **—se,** to bend over (as a hunchback).
José, Joseph.
Josefa, Josefina, Josephine.
Josefo, Josephus.
Josías, Josiah.
Josué, Joshua.
jota, *f.* the letter **j**; jot, tittle; Spanish dance; **no saber ni —,** not to know a thing, to be completely ignorant about something.
joven, *adj.* young; —, *m.* and *f.* young man, young woman.
jovial, *adj.* jovial, gay, merry.
jovialidad, *f.* joviality, gaiety.
Joviano, Jovian.
joya, *f.* jewel; present, gift.
joyel, *m.* small jewel.
joyería, *f.* jewelry store.
joyero, *m.* jeweler.
Juan, John.
Juana, Jane.
juanete, *m.* bunion, knucklebone of the big toe, especially when enlarged.

Juanita, Jenny; Jean; Jeanette.
Juanito, Johnny, Jack.
jubilación, *f.* festivity; pensioning off.
jubilar, *va.* to pension off; to superannuate; to lay aside as useless; —, *vn.* to become a pensioner on retiring or leaving office.
jubileo, *m.* jubilee.
júbilo, *m.* joy, merriment, festivity.
jubiloso, sa, *adj.* joyful, happy.
jubón, *m.* doublet, bodice, jacket.
judaico, ca, *adj.* Judaical, Jewish.
judaísmo, *m.* Judaism, Jewish religion.
judaizar, *va.* and *vn.* to judaize.
Judas, *m.* Judas; (fig.) traitor.
judía, *f.* French bean, kidney bean.
judicial, *adj.* judicial, juridical.
judío, día, *adj.* Jewish; —, *m.* Jew; (fig.) usurer.
Judit, Judith.
juego, *m.* play, amusement, game, sport, gambling; — **de balón,** basketball; — **de bolsa,** stock jobbing; — **de damas,** checkers; — **de muebles,** furniture set; **campo de —s,** playground.
juerga, *f.* (coll.) spree, carousal.
juev. jueves, Th. or Thur. Thursday.
jueves, *m.* Thursday.
juez, *m.* judge.
jugada, *f.* playing of a card; mean trick.
jugador, ra, *n.* player; gamester.
jugar, *va.* and *vn.* (UE) to play, to sport, to trifle, to toy; to gamble, to game; to intervene; to mock.
jugarreta, *f.* bad play, unskillful playing; trickery.
juglar, *m.* minstrel.
jugo, *m.* sap, juice.
jugoso, sa, *adj.* juicy, succulent.
juguete, *m.* toy, plaything, gewgaw, trinket.
juguetear, *vn.* to trifle, to fool.
juguetón, ona, *adj.* playful.
juicio, *m.* judgment, reason; trial; — **hipotecario,** foreclosure (of a mortgage).
juicioso, sa, *adj.* judicious, prudent.
Jul. julio, July.
julepe, *m.* julep; (coll.) reprimand.
Julián, Juliano, Julian.
Julio, Julius.
julio, *m.* July.
jumento, *m.* beast of burden; ass; stupid person.
Jun. junio, June.
junco, *m.* (bot.) rush; junk (Chinese ship).
juncoso, sa, *adj.* full of rushes.
junio, *m.* June.
junípero, *m.* (bot.) juniper.
junquillo, *m.* (bot.) jonquil; reed.
junta, *f.* congress, assembly, council; session, meeting; board; joint; coupling; — **directiva,** board of directors; — **de sanidad,** board of health; — **de comercio,** board of trade; — **universal,** universal joint; **llamar a —** or **convocar a una —,** to call a meeting.

juntamente, *adv.* jointly; at the same time.
juntar, *va.* to join, to unite; to collect, to gather; **—se,** to meet, to assemble; to be closely united.
junto, *adv.* near, close to; **de —,** or **por —,** by the bulk, in the lump; **—, ta,** *adj.* joined, united; **—os,** *pl.* together, side by side.
juntura, *f.* juncture; joint.
Júpiter, *m.* Jupiter (planet); (chem.) tin.
jura, *f.* oath, swearing; pledging allegiance; **— de la bandera,** pledging allegiance to the flag.
jurado, *m.* jury; juror, juryman; jurat.
jurador, ra, *n.* swearer.
juramentar, *va.* to swear; **—se,** to bind oneself by an oath.
juramento, *m.* oath.
jurar, *va.* and *vn.* to swear, to make oath; to curse.
jurídico, ca, *adj.* lawful, legal, juridical; done according to law.
jurisconsulto, *m.* lawyer, jurist.
jurisdicción, *f.* jurisdiction, legal authority; territory.
jurisperito, ta, *n.* professor of jurisprudence.
jurisprudencia, *f.* jurisprudence.
jurista, *m.* jurist, lawyer.
juro, *m.* right of perpetual property; **de —,** certainly.
justa, *f.* joust, tilt, tournament.
justamente, *adv.* justly, just.
justicia, *f.* justice; fairness, equity; **la —,** the police.
justiciero, ra, *adj.* fair, just.
justificación, *f.* justification; adjustment of lines of type.
justificado, da, *adj.* equal, justified; conformable to justice.
justificar, *va.* to justify; (print.) to adjust lines of type.
justificativo, va, *adj.* justificatory, justifying.
justillo, *m.* sleeveless jacket, jerkin.
Justiniano, Justinian.
Justino, Justin.
justipreciar, *va.* to estimate, to appraise.
justo, ta, *adj.* just; lawful; honorable; fair, upright; tight; **—,** *m.* just and pious man; **al —,** *adv.* fitly, duly; punctually.
juvenil, *adj.* juvenile, youthful.
juventud, *f.* youthfulness, youth.
juzgado, *m.* tribunal; judicature; court (of justice).
juzgar, *va.* and *vn.* to judge.

K

kaiser, *m.* kaiser.
kaki, *m.* and *adj.* khaki.
kaleidoscopio, *m.* kaleidoscope.
kan, *m.* khan, a Tartar chief; oriental prince.
kantiano, na, *n.* and *adj.* Kantian; a fol-

lower of Kant; pertaining to Kant's philosophy.
kantismo, *m.* Kantianism, philosophical doctrines of Immanuel Kant.
kantista, *n.* and *adj.* Kantian.
karakul, *m.* karakul; fur of a young karakul lamb.
Kc. Kilociclo, kc. kilocycle.
kepis, *m.* military cap.
kermes, *m.* kermes.
kerosina, *f.*, **kerosene** or **kerosén,** *m.* kerosene.
Kg. or **kg. kilogramo,** k. or kg. kilogram.
kilo, *m.* kilo, kilogram.
kilocaloría, *f.* kilocalorie.
kilociclo, *m.* kilocycle.
kilogramo, *m.* kilogram.
kilojulio, *m.* (elec.) kilojoule.
kilolitro, *m.* kiloliter.
kilometraje, *m.* mileage.
kilométrico, ca, *adj.* kilometric; (coll.) too long; **billete —,** mileage ticket; **discurso —,** a very long speech.
kilómetro, *m.* kilometer.
kilovatio, *m.* kilowatt.
kilovoltamperio, *m.* kilovolt-ampere.
kilovoltio, *m.* kilovolt.
kimono, *m.* kimono.
kiosco, *m.* kiosk, booth.
Kl. or **kl. kilolitro,** kl. kiloliter.
Km. or **km. kilómetro,** km. kilometer.
kodak, *m.* kodak.
kv. or **k.w. kilovatio,** kw. kilowatt.

L

L. Licenciado, licentiate, master; (Sp. Am.) lawyer.
l.: ley, law; **libro,** bk. book; **litro,** l. liter.
L/, l.ª, l. letra, bill, draft, letter.
£ libra esterlina, £ pound sterling.
la, *art.* the (feminine).
laberinto, *m.* labyrinth, maze.
labia, *f.* (coll.) winning eloquence.
labio, *m.* lip; edge of anything.
labor, *f.* labor, task; needlework; husbandry, tillage.
laborar, *va.* and *vn.* to work; to till.
laboratorio, *m.* laboratory.
laboreo, *m.* mine-working, mining.
laboriosidad, *f.* laboriousness, assiduity.
laborioso, sa, *adj.* laborious, industrious.
labrado, da, *adj.* worked (applied to figured cloth); **—,** *m.* cultivated land.
labrador, ra, *n.* laborer; cultivator, farmer; peasant.
labrantío, tía, *adj.* arable.
labranza, *f.* farming, tillage; husbandry; tilled land.
labrar, *va.* to work; to labor, to cultivate the ground; to build.
labriego, ga, *n.* peasant.
laca, *f.* lac, lacquer.
lacayo, *m.* lackey, footman.

laceración, *f.* laceration.
lacerar, *va.* to tear to pieces, to lacerate.
laceria, *f.* misery, poverty, wretchedness.
lacio, cia, *adj.* faded, withered; languid; straight (applied to hair).
lacónico, ca, *adj.* laconic, concise.
laconismo, *m.* laconism, brevity, conciseness.
lacra, *f.* mark left by a wound; fault, vice.
lacrar, *va.* to injure one's health; to damage financially; to seal with lacquer.
lacre, *m.* sealing wax; lacquer red.
lacrimal, *adj.* lachrymal.
lacrimoso, sa, *adj.* tearful, lachrymose.
lactancia, *f.* time of suckling.
lácteo, tea, *adj.* lactic, lacteous, milky; **ácido —teo,** (chem.) lactic acid; **vía —tea,** milky way.
lacticinio, *m.* any kind of milk food.
lactina, *f.* lactin.
lactosa, *f.* lactose.
ladear, *va.* to move to one side; to incline; **—,** *vn.* to incline to one side; **—se,** to incline to an opinion or party.
ladera, *f.* declivity; slope.
ladilla, *f.* crab louse.
ladino, na, *adj.* sagacious, cunning, crafty; adept as a linguist.
Ladislao, Ladislas.
lado, *m.* side; party; ¡**a un —!** clear the way!
ladrar, *vn.* to bark.
ladrido, *m.* barking; vociferation.
ladrillal or **ladrillar,** *m.* brickkiln.
ladrillo, *m.* brick; **— refractario,** firebrick.
ladrón, *m.* thief, robber, highwayman.
ladronera, *f.* den of robbers.
lagar, *m.* wine press.
lagarero, *m.* wine presser; one employed in olive pressing.
lagartija, *f.* (zool.) eft, newt.
lagarto, *m.* lizard; alligator; (coll.) sly person.
lago, *m.* lake; **— de leones,** den of lions.
lágrima, *f.* tear.
lagrimal, *m.* lachrymary bag; **—,** *adj.* lachrymal.
lagrimoso, sa, *adj.* weeping, shedding tears.
laguna, *f.* lagoon, pond; deficiency; blank space (as in a text), hiatus; gap.
lagunoso, sa, *adj.* marshy, fenny.
laico, ca, *adj.* lay, laic.
lama, *f.* mud, slime, ooze.
Lamberto, Lambert.
lamedor, ra, *n.* licker; **—,** *m.* (med.) cough sirup; (fig.) enticement, allurement.
lamedura, *f.* act of licking.
lamentable, *adj.* lamentable, deplorable, pitiable.
lamentación, *f.* lamentation, lament.
lamentar, *va.* to lament, to regret; **—,** *vn.* and *vr.* to lament, to complain, to cry.
lamento, *m.* lamentation.
lamer, *va.* to lick, to lap.
lámina, *f.* plate, sheet of metal; copper

plate; engraving, print, picture.
laminación, *f.* lamination.
laminar, *va.* to laminate.
lámpara, *f.* lamp; **— de arco,** arc light; **— de intermitencia,** flashlight; **— portátil,** emergency light; **— de radio,** radio tube; **— de soldar,** blowtorch; **— de tungsteno,** mazda lamp.
lamparero, ra, *n.* lamplighter; lamp maker or seller.
lamparilla, *f.* night light.
lamparón, *m.* large, unwieldy lamp; (med.) scrofula.
lampiño, ña, *adj.* beardless.
lampión, *m.* large lantern.
lamprea, *f.* lamprey (fish).
lamprear, *va.* to season with wine and sour gravy.
lana, *f.* wool; **— de acero,** steel wool; **— de vidrio,** spun glass.
lanar, *adj.* woolly.
lance, *m.* cast, throw; critical moment; chance, hazard; sudden quarrel.
lancear, *va.* to wound with a lance.
lancero, *m.* pikeman, lancer.
lanceta, *f.* lancet.
lancetada, *f.* lancing, cut of a lancet.
lancha, *f.* barge, lighter; launch; **— de carrera,** speedboat; **— de pescar,** fishing smack; **— de salvavidas,** lifeboat.
lanchaje, *m.* lighterage.
lanchón, *m.* (naut.) lighter, barge.
langosta, *f.* locust; lobster; sharper, swindler.
langostín, *m.* small locust.
languidecer, *vn.* (EZCO) to drop, to languish.
languidez, *f.* languidness.
lánguido, da, *adj.* languid, faint, weak; languorous, languishing.
lanilla, *f.* down, nap of cloth; fine flannel.
lanolina, *f.* lanolin.
lanoso, sa, *adj.* woolen.
lanudo, da, *adj.* woolly, fleecy.
lanza, *f.* lance, spear; pole of a coach; **—s,** *pl.* duty formerly paid by the nobility of the realm (in lieu of military services).
lanzabombas, *m.* bomb thrower, bomb release.
lanzada, *f.* stroke with a lance.
lanzadera, *f.* shuttle.
lanzaminas, *m.* mine layer.
lanzar, *va.* to throw, to dart, to launch, to fling; (law) to eject.
lanzatorpedos, *m.* torpedo tube; torpedo boat.
lapicero, *m.* pencil case; mechanical pencil.
lápida, *f.* flat stone, on which inscriptions are engraved; tombstone.
lapidario, ria, *n.* and *adj.* lapidary.
lápiz, *m.* lead pencil; black crayon used in drawing; black lead; **— para los labios** or **labial,** lipstick; **cortalápiz** or **tajalápiz,** *m.* pencil sharpener.
lapizar, *va.* to draw with a pencil; **—,** *m.* black-lead mine.

Laponia, *f.* Lapland.
lardar or **lardear,** *va.* to baste (meat); to scald with hot grease.
lardoso, sa, *adj.* greasy, fatty.
lares, *m. pl.* household gods of the ancient Romans; home.
larga, *f.* delay, adjournment; **a la —,** in the long run.
largamente, *adv.* for a long time; liberally.
largar, *va.* to loosen, to slacken; to let go; **—se,** (coll.) to get out, to leave; (naut.) to set sail.
largo, ga, *adj.* long; large, generous, liberal; copious; **—,** *m.* length; **todo lo — de,** the full length of.
largueza, *f.* length, largeness; liberality, generosity.
largura, *f.* length, longitude.
lárice, *m.* larch tree.
laringe, *f.* larynx.
laríngeo, gea, *adj.* laryngeal, pertaining to the larynx.
laringitis, *f.* (med.) laryngitis.
larva, (zool.) larva.
lasaña, *f.* fritter.
lascivia, *f.* lasciviousness; lewdness.
lascivo, va, *adj.* lascivious; lewd.
lasitud, *f.* lassitude, weariness.
lástima, *f.* compassion, pity; object of pity.
lastimar, *va.* to hurt; to wound; to move to compassion; **—se,** to be moved to compassion; to grieve.
lastimero, ra, *adj.* sad, mournful; lamentable.
lastimoso, sa, *adj.* grievous, mournful.
laso, sa, *adj.* tired, lax.
lastrar, *va.* to ballast a ship.
lastre, *m.* ballast; good judgment, sense.
lat.: latín, Lat. Latin; **latitud,** lat. latitude.
lata, *f.* tin can; (coll.) nuisance, annoyance; **dar —,** to waste time in idle chatter; **estar en la —,** to be penniless; **productos en —,** canned goods.
latebra, *f.* cave, hiding place.
latente, *adj.* dormant, concealed.
lateral, *adj.* lateral.
látex, *m.* (bot.) latex.
latido, *m.* pant, palpitation; barking of dogs.
latigazo, *m.* lash, crack of a whip.
látigo, *m.* whip.
latín, *m.* Latin language.
latinajo, *m.* (coll.) Latin jargon.
latinidad, *f.* Latinity, Latin language.
latinizar, *va.* to latinize.
latino, na, *adj.* Latin.
latinoamericano, na, *n.* and *adj.* Latin American.
latir, *vn.* to palpitate; to howl (as dogs).
latitud, *f.* breadth; width; latitude.
lato, ta, *adj.* ample, large, diffuse, extensive.
latón, *m.* brass; brassie.
latonero, *m.* brazier; worker in brass.
latoso, sa, *adj.* wearisome, annoying.

latría, *f.* worship, adoration due to God only.
latrocinio, *m.* larceny, theft, robbery.
laúd, *m.* lute (musical instrument).
laudable, *adj.* laudable, praiseworthy.
láudano, *m.* laudanum.
laude, *f.* tombstone with an epitaph engraved on it; **—s,** *pl.* (eccl.) Lauds.
laurear, *va.* to crown with laurel; to graduate; (fig.) to reward.
laurel, *m.* (bot.) laurel; laurel crown as a reward.
lauréola, *f.* crown of laurel.
lauro, *m.* (bot.) laurel; glory, honor.
lavabo, *m.* lavabo; washstand.
lavacaras, *m.* (fig. and coll.) flatterer.
lavadero, *m.* washing place; laundry.
lavado, *m.* washing, wash.
lavadura, *f.* wash, washing.
lavamanos, *m.* washing stand.
lavandera, *f.* laundress; **—ro,** *m.* laundryman.
lavandería, *f.* laundry.
lavar, *va.* to wash; to whitewash.
lavativa, *f.* enema.
lavatorio, *m.* act of washing; medicinal lotion; ceremony of washing the feet on Holy Thursday; lavatory.
lavazas, *f. pl.* dirty soap suds.
laxante, *m.* and *adj.* (med.) laxative.
laxar, *va.* to loosen, to soften.
laxativo, va, *m.* and *adj.* laxative.
laxitud, *f.* laxity; laxness; weariness.
laxo, xa, *adj.* lax, slack.
layar, *va.* to turn up the ground with a spade or hoe.
lazada, *f.* bowknot; loop.
lazareto, *m.* lazaretto.
lazarillo, *m.* boy who guides a blind man.
Lázaro, Lazarus.
lazo, *m.* lasso, lariat; slipknot; snare, trick; tie; bond; **— de zapato,** shoestring.
lb. libra, lb. pound.
l.c. loco citato, loc. cit. in the place cited.
Ldo., L.do or **l.do Licenciado,** licentiate, master; (Sp. Am.) lawyer.
le, *pron.* dative case of **él** or **ella.**
leal, *adj.* loyal, faithful.
lealtad, *f.* loyalty.
lebrel, *m.* greyhound.
lebrillo, *m.* glazed earthenware pan.
lección, *f.* reading; lesson; **dar una —,** to recite a lesson; **— práctica,** object lesson.
lecitol, *m.* substance found in egg yolk.
lector, ra, *adj.* reading; **—,** *n.* reader; **— de pruebas,** copyreader; **—,** *m.* instructor of the Gospel.
lectura, *f.* reading, lecture.
lechada, *f.* calcimine.
leche, *f.* milk.
lechera, *f.* milkmaid, dairymaid.
lechería, *f.* cow house, dairy.
lechero, *m.* milkman, dairyman; **—, ra,** *adj.* pertaining to milk.
lecho, *m.* bed; litter.

lechón, ona, *n.* sucking pig.
lechoso, sa, *adj.* milky.
lechuga, *f.* lettuce.
lechugado, da, *adj.* having leaves like lettuce.
lechuguilla, *f.* ruche.
lechuguino, *m.* bed of small lettuces; (coll.) dandy, dude.
lechuza, *f.* owl.
leer, *va.* (LEYÓ) to read; to lecture.
leg.: legal, legal; **legislatura,** legislature.
lega, *f.* (eccl.) lay sister.
legacía, *f.* legateship.
legación, *f.* legation, embassy.
legado, *m.* deputy, legate; legacy.
legajo, *m.* bundle of loose papers tied together; wrapper; file.
legal, *adj.* legal, lawful.
legalidad, *f.* legality, fidelity.
legalización, *f.* legalization.
legalizar, *va.* to legalize.
légamo, *m.* silt, mud.
legar, *va.* to depute; to bequeath.
legatario, ria, *n.* (law) legatee.
legendario, ria, *adj.* legendary.
legibilidad, *f.* legibility.
legible, *adj.* legible.
legión, *f.* legion.
legionario, ria, *adj.* legionary.
legislación, *f.* legislation.
legislador, ra, *n.* legislator, lawgiver.
legislar, *va.* to legislate.
legislativo, va, *adj.* legislative, lawgiving.
legislatura, *f.* legislature.
legista, *m.* legist, legal scholar, law professor.
legítima, *f.* (law) legitimate portion of the paternal or maternal estate.
legitimación, *f.* legitimation.
legitimar, *va.* to legitimate.
legitimidad, *f.* legitimacy.
legítimo, ma, *adj.* legitimate, lawful.
lego, *m.* (eccl.) layman.
legua, *f.* league (measure of length); **a —s,** very distant.
legumbre, *f.* legume; **—s,** *pl.* vegetables.
leguminoso, sa, *adj.* leguminous.
leído, da, *adj.* well-read.
lejanía, *f.* distance, remoteness.
lejano, na, *adj.* distant, remote, far.
lejía, *f.* lye, alkaline solution.
lejos, *adv.* at a great distance, far off; **—,** *m.* perspective, distant prospect.
lelo, la, *adj.* stupid, ignorant.
lema, *m.* theme of a literary composition explained in the title; motto; (math.) lemma.
lemur, *m.* (zool.) lemur.
lencería, *f.* linen goods; store selling linens.
lendroso, sa, *adj.* lousy.
lengua, *f.* tongue; language, tongue.
lenguaje, *m.* language, style of expression.
lenidad, *f.* lenity, mildness.
Leningrado, *m.* Leningrad.
lenitivo, va, *adj.* lenient, mitigant.
lente, *m.* or *f.* lens; monocle; **—s,** *pl.* glasses;

magnifying glasses; **—s contra resplandores,** sun or heat glasses; **— telefotográfica,** telephoto (or photographic) lens.
lenteja, *f.* (bot.) lentil.
lentejuela, *f.* spangle.
lentitud, *f.* slowness.
lento, ta, *adj.* slow, tardy, lazy.
leña, *f.* firewood, kindling wood.
leñador, ra, *n.* woodman (or woman), wood-cutter.
leñera, *f.* place for firewood.
leñero, *m.* timber merchant.
leño, *m.* block, log; trunk of a tree.
leñoso, sa, *adj.* woody.
León, Leo, Leon.
león, *m.* lion.
leona, *f.* lioness.
leonado, da, *adj.* lion-colored, tawny; fallow.
Leonardo, Leonard.
leonera, *f.* lion cage.
leonero, *m.* keeper of lions.
Leonor, Eleanor.
leopardo, *m.* leopard.
leopoldina, *f.* fob (as of watch).
Leopoldo, Leopold.
lepra, *f.* leprosy.
leproso, sa, *adj.* leprous.
lerdo, da, *adj.* slow, heavy; slow-witted, stupid.
lesión, *f.* hurt, damage, wound; injury.
lesna, *f.* awl.
leso, sa, *adj.* hurt, wounded.
letal, *adj.* mortal, deadly.
letanía, *f.* litany; **—s,** *pl.* supplicatory processions.
letárgico, ca, *adj.* lethargic.
letargo, *m.* lethargy; drowsiness; **— epidémico,** sleeping sickness.
letificar, *va.* to cheer; to invigorate.
letra, *f.* letter; handwriting; printing type; (com.) draft; inscription; words in a song; **— a la vista,** sight draft; **— a plazo,** time draft; **— de cambio,** bill of exchange, draft; **— gótica,** Old English type, black letter; **— mayúscula,** capital letter, upper-case type; **— minúscula,** small letter, lower-case type; **— redonda,** Roman type; **buena —,** good handwriting; **—s,** *pl.* learning; **Bellas L—s,** literary arts; **—s humanas or humanidades,** humanities.
letrado, da, *adj.* learned, lettered; **—,** *m.* lawyer; professor of law.
letrero, *m.* inscription, label, notice, poster, sign.
letrilla, *f.* short poem, generally written to be sung to music.
letrina, *f.* privy, toilet.
leucocito, *m.* leucocyte.
leucoma, *f.* (med.) leucoma.
leucorrea, *f.* (med.) leucorrhea, whites.
leudar, *va.* to leaven, to cause to ferment; **—se,** to ferment; to rise.
leva, *f.* act of weighing anchor; (mil.) levy;

(naut.) press, forcing into service; (mech.) cam.

levadizo, za, *adj.* that can be lifted or raised; **puente —,** drawbridge.

levadura, *f.* yeast, leaven, ferment; (med.) septic matter.

levantamiento, *m.* elevation; insurrection.

levantar, *va.* to raise, to lift up; to heave; to build up; to impute falsely; to elevate, to promote; **—se,** to rise; to get up from bed; to stand up.

levante, *m.* Levant; east; east wind.

leve, *adj.* light; trifling.

leviatán, *m.* leviathan.

levita, *m.* Levite; deacon; **—,** *f.* frock coat.

levitón, *m.* frock coat.

lexicografía, *f.* lexicography.

ley, *f.* law; loyalty; **—es,** *pl.* collection of laws; **fuera de —,** lawless.

leyenda, *f.* reading, inscription; legend.

lía, *f.* thin bass rope; pressed grapes; (coll.) **estar hecho una —,** to be intoxicated.

liar, *va.* to tie, to bind, to fagot.

libación, *f.* libation.

Líbano, *m.* Lebanon.

libelo, *m.* petition; written charge against a prisoner; lampoon, libel, roorback.

libélula, *f.* dragonfly.

liberación, *f.* liberation, deliverance.

liberal, *adj.* liberal, generous.

liberalidad, *f.* liberality, generosity.

liberalizar, *va.* to liberalize.

libertad, *f.* liberty, freedom; independence; freeness; **— de palabra,** freedom of speech; **— de imprenta,** freedom of press.

libertador, ra, *n.* deliverer, liberator.

libertar, *va.* to free, to set at liberty; to exempt, to clear from an obligation.

libertinaje, *m.* libertinism, licentiousness.

libertino, na, *adj.* and *n.* dissolute, licentious; lewd person.

liberto, ta, *n.* freedman or woman.

libídine, *f.* lewdness, lust.

libidinoso, sa, *adj.* libidinous, lewd, lustful.

libido, *m.* libido.

libra, *f.* pound (weight); **— esterlina,** pound sterling.

Libra, *f.* Libra, Balance (sign of the zodiac).

librado, da, *n.* drawee, accepter of a draft.

libramiento, *m.* order of payment; protection from danger.

libranza, *f.* draft, check, order of payment; **— postal,** money order.

librar, *va.* to free, to rid, to deliver; to give an order for paying a certain sum; to dispatch, to expedite; **— bien** or **mal,** to get over a thing well or ill; **—se,** to escape.

libre, *adj.* free; exempt; innocent; **— pensador, ra,** freethinker.

librea, *f.* livery.

librecambista, *m.* free trader.

librejo, *m.* little book, pamphlet.

libremente, *adv.* freely; boldly; audaciously, impudently.

librería, *f.* bookstore; library.

librero, *m.* book seller; (Mex.) bookcase.

libreta, *f.* memorandum book; loaf of bread weighing 16 ounces; **— de depósitos** or **de banco,** bank book; **— de la dotación,** enlistment record.

libreto, *m.* (mus.) libretto; (rad.) script.

librillo, *m.* small book; cigarette-paper book.

libro, *m.* book; **— copiador,** copybook; **— de actas,** minute book; **— de caballerías,** romance of chivalry; **— de caja,** cashbook; **— de cheques,** checkbook; **— de facturas,** invoice book; **— de memoria,** memo book; **— diario,** daybook or journal; **— mayor,** ledger; **— talonario,** check or stub book; **— culinario** or **— de cocina,** cookbook.

Lic. or **Licdo. licenciado,** licentiate, master; (Sp. Am.) lawyer.

licencia, *f.* permission, license; licentiousness; **— de conductor,** driver's license.

licenciado, *m.* licentiate; title given a lawyer.

licenciamiento, *m.* act of obtaining the degree of licentiate.

licenciar, *va.* to permit, to allow; to license; to discharge; **—se,** to become dissolute; to become a licentiate.

licencioso, sa, *adj.* licentious, dissolute.

liceo, *m.* lyceum.

licitación, *f.* bid, bidding (at an auction).

licitador, *m.* bidder.

lícitamente, *adv.* lawfully, licitly.

lícito, ta, *adj.* lawful, licit.

licor, *m.* liquor; anything liquid.

licorera, *f.* liquor case.

licorista, *m.* liquor maker, liquor dealer.

licuable, *adj.* that can be liquefied.

lid, *f.* contest, fight; dispute.

líder, *m.* and *f.* leader; (labor) instigator, agitator; chief.

lidiar, *vn.* to fight, to struggle, to contend.

lidiador, *m.* combatant.

liebre, *f.* hare.

liendre, *f.* louse egg.

liento, *adj.* moist, damp.

lienzo, *m.* linen, canvas, duck; painting; front of building.

liga, *f.* garter; bird lime; league, coalition; alloy.

ligadura, *f.* ligature, binding.

ligar, *va.* to tie, to bind, to fasten; to alloy; to confederate; **—se,** to league; to be allied; to bind oneself to the performance of a contract.

ligazón, *f.* union, connection; fastening.

ligereza, *f.* lightness; levity; swiftness.

ligero, ra, *adj.* light, swift, easy.

lignito, *m.* lignite.

ligustro, *m.* (bot.) privet.

lija, *f.* sandpaper; dogfish; dogfish skin.

lijar, *va.* to smooth, to polish.

lila, *f.* lilac color; lilac tree; lilac flower.

lima, *f.* file.

limadura, *f.* filing.

limar, *va.* to file; to polish.
limbo, *m.* limbo.
limeño, ña, *n.* native of Lima; —, *adj.* from Lima.
limitación, *f.* limitation, restriction.
limitado, da, *adj.* limited.
limitar, *va.* to limit; to restrain.
límite, *m.* limit, boundary; — **de velocidad,** speed limit.
limítrofe, *adj.* limiting, bordering.
limo, *m.* slime, mud, silt.
limón, *m.* lemon.
limonada, *f.* lemonade.
limonar, *m.* plantation of lemon trees.
limosna, *f.* alms, charity.
limosnero, ra, *adj.* charitable; —, *m.* almoner; (Sp. Am.) beggar.
limpiabotas, *m.* bootblack.
limpiadientes, *m.* toothpick.
limpiador, *m.* cleanser, scourer.
limpiadura, *f.* cleaning; —s, *pl.* dirt, waste, refuse, rubbish.
limpiar, *va.* to scour, to cleanse, to clear, to purify.
limpiauñas, *m.* nail cleaner.
limpiavidrio, *m.* windshield wiper.
limpido, da, *adj.* clear, limpid.
limpieza, *f.* cleanliness, neatness; chastity; integrity; purity of blood.
limpio, pia, *adj.* clean; limpid, neat; pure; **en —o,** clearly; **poner en —o,** to make a fair copy; **sacar en —o,** to infer, to understand.
lín. línea, l. line.
linaje, *m.* lineage, race, descent.
linar, *m.* flax field.
linaza, *f.* linseed.
lince, *m.* lynx; keen person; —, *adj.* lynx-eyed, keen-sighted.
lindar, *vn.* to be contiguous.
linde, *m.* or *f.* landmark, boundary.
lindero, *m.* landmark, boundary.
lindeza, *f.* neatness, elegance; —s, *pl.* (used ironically) insults.
lindo, da, *adj.* neat, handsome, pretty.
línea, *f.* line, boundary, limit; — **aérea,** airline; — **de fuego,** firing line; — **de vapores,** steamship line.
lineal, *adj.* lineal, linear.
lineamiento, *m.* outline, sketch.
linear, *va.* to draw lines.
linfa, *f.* lymph.
linfático, ca, *adj.* lymphatic.
lino, *m.* flax; linen.
linóleo, *m.* linoleum.
linotipo, *m.* linotype.
linterna, *f.* lantern; flashlight; — **delantera,** headlight; — **trasera** or **de cola,** taillight.
lío, *m.* bundle, parcel; scrape; conspiracy; **armar un —,** to start a "row"; **hacerse un —,** to become confused, to get into a mess.
liq.ⁿ liquidación, (com.) liquidation, settlement.

líq.º líquido, liq. liquid; net.
liquidación, *f.* liquidation, settlement; clearance sale.
liquidar, *va.* to liquefy, to melt; to clear accounts.
líquido, da, *adj.* liquid, net; **producto —,** net proceeds; **saldo —,** net balance.
lira, *f.* lyre; six, seven and eleven syllable verse lines with three rhymes.
lírico, ca, *adj.* lyrical, lyric.
lirio, *m.* iris (flower); lily.
lis, *f.* fleur-de-lis.
Lisandro, Lysander.
Lisboa, *f.* Lisbon.
lisiado, da, *adj.* crippled, lame.
lisiar, *va.* to lame, to cripple, to injure.
liso, sa, *adj.* plain, even, flat, smooth.
lisol, *m.* lysol.
lisonja, *f.* adulation, flattery.
lisonjear, *va.* to flatter.
lisonjero, ra, *n.* flatterer; —, *adj.* fawning; flattering; pleasing.
lista, *f.* slip of paper; shred of linen; list, catalogue; stripe; — **de correos,** general delivery; — **de pagos,** pay roll; — **de platos,** bill of fare, menu; — **de precios,** price list; — **nominal,** roll call; **pasar —,** to call the roll.
listerina, *f.* listerine.
listero, *m.* timekeeper.
listo, ta, *adj.* ready, prompt, active.
listón, *m.* large shred; ribbon.
lisura, *f.* smoothness; sincerity, candor.
lit. literalmente, lit. literally.
Lit. Literatura, lit. literature.
litera, *f.* litter; berth.
literal, *adj.* literal.
literario, ria, *adj.* literary.
literato, ta, *adj.* learned, lettered; —, *n.* literary person, writer.
literatura, *f.* literature.
litigante, *m.* and *f.* litigant.
litigar, *va.* to litigate, to carry on a cause.
litigio, *m.* lawsuit.
litigioso, sa, *adj.* litigious.
litio, *m.* (chem.) lithium.
litografía, *f.* lithography.
litografiar, *va.* to lithograph.
litográfico, ca, *adj.* lithographic.
litógrafo, *m.* lithographer.
litoral, *m.* littoral, coast; —, *adj.* littoral, pertaining to a coast.
litoscopio, *m.* lithoscope.
litosfera, *f.* lithosphere.
litro, *m.* liter.
Lituania, *f.* Lithuania.
lituánico, ca or **lituaniense,** *n.* and *adj.* Lithuanian.
liturgia, *f.* liturgy.
litúrgico, ca, *adj.* liturgical.
liviandad, *f.* lightness; levity, imprudence; incontinence.
liviano, na, *adj.* light; imprudent; unchaste; —os, *m. pl.* lungs.
lívido, da, *adj.* livid.

liza, f. prize ring.

lo, pron. it; **—,** art. the (used before an adjective).

loa, f. praise; prologue of a play; theatrical panegyric.

loable, adj. laudable.

loablemente, adv. commendably.

loar, va. to praise; to approve.

loba, f. she-wolf.

lobanillo, m. wen, cyst.

lobato, m. young wolf.

lobelia, f. (bot.) lobelia.

lobina, f. (fish) bass.

lobo, m. wolf.

lóbrego, ga, adj. murky, obscure; sad.

lobreguez, f. obscurity, darkness; dreariness.

lobuno, na, adj. wolfish.

local, adj. local; **—,** m. place.

localidad, f. locality; **—es,** pl. accommodations, tickets, seats.

localización, f. placing, location, fixing in a definite place.

localizar, va. to localize.

loción, f. lotion, wash.

loco, ca, adj. and n. mad, crackbrained; **casa de —s,** insane asylum; **— rematado,** stark-mad; **volverse —,** to go mad.

locomotora, f. locomotive.

locomóvil, adj. portable, movable; **—,** f. hauling or traction engine.

locuacidad, f. loquacity.

locuaz, adj. loquacious, garrulous.

locución, f. locution.

locuelo, la, n. giddy young person, madcap.

locura, f. madness, frenzy, folly; absurdity.

locutor, ora, n. announcer.

locutorio, m. receiving room in monasteries and prisons.

lodazal, m. muddy place.

lodo, m. mud, mire.

lodoso, sa, adj. muddy, miry.

log. logaritmo, log. logarithm.

logaritmo, m. logarithm.

lógica, f. logic.

lógico, ca, adj. logical, reasonable; **—,** m. logician.

lograr, va. to gain, to obtain; to succeed in an enterprise.

logrear, vn. to borrow or lend at interest.

logrero, ra, n. person who lends at interest, usurer.

logro, m. gain, benefit; attainment; interest; usury.

loma, f. hillock.

lombarda, f. red cabbage.

Lombardía, f. Lombardy.

lombriz, f. earthworm; **— solitaria,** tapeworm.

lomillo, m. small loin; cross-stitch (needlework).

lomo, m. loin; back of a book; crease of cloth; ridge between two furrows; **— plano,** flat back; **— hueco,** loose back; **llevar a** or **traer a —,** to carry on the back.

lona, f. canvas; sailcloth.

loncha, f. flagstone.

lóndiga, f. granary.

londinense, n. and adj. Londonese.

Londres, m. London.

long. longitud, long. longitude.

longanimidad, f. forbearance, patience.

longaniza, f. a long, slender pork-meat sausage (best kind).

longevidad, f. longevity.

longevo, va, adj. long-lived.

longitud, f. length; longitude.

lonja, f. (com.) exchange; grocery; warehouse; slice of ham or other meat.

lonjista, m. and f. grocer.

lontananza, f. distance; **en —,** far off, barely visible.

loor, m. (poet.) praise.

loquear, vn. to act a fool; to rejoice, to revel.

loquero, m. keeper of an insane asylum.

Lorena, f. Lorraine.

Lorenzo, Lawrence.

loro, m. parrot.

losa, f. flagstone; slab.

losange, m. lozenge.

Lotario, Lothaire.

lote, m. lot; share.

lotería, f. lottery; lotto.

loto, m. (bot.) lotus.

loza, f. delft, crockery, porcelain, chinaware.

lozanear, vn. to look fresh and healthy.

lozanía, f. verdure, exuberant growth of plants; vigor; vivacity.

lozano, na, adj. luxuriant; healthy, ruddy.

L. S. lugar del sello, L. S. place for stamp, stamp here.

Ltdo. Ltda. limitado, da, Ltd. limited.

lubricación, f. lubrication.

lubricador, ra, n. lubricator; **—,** adj. lubricating.

lubricante, adj. lubricant, lubricating.

lubricar, va. to lubricate.

lubrificar, va. to lubricate.

Lucas, Luke.

lucerna, f. light fixture, chandelier; (arch.) louver.

lucero, m. morning star, day star.

Lucía, Lucy.

Luciano, Lucian.

lúcido, da, adj. shining, magnificent, splendid; clear.

luciente, adj. bright, shining.

luciérnaga, f. glowworm, firefly, lightning bug.

Lucifer, m. Lucifer, Satan.

lucimiento, m. splendor, luster; success; brightness.

Lucio, Lucius.

lucio, cia, adj. lucid, bright.

lucir, vn. and vr. (UZCO) to shine, to be brilliant; to dress to advantage; to outshine; to show off.

lucrativo, va, adj. lucrative.

Lucrecia, Lucretia.

lucro, *m.* gain, profit, lucre; **—s y daños,** profit and loss.

lucha, *f.* struggle, strife, fight.

luchador, ra, *n.* wrestler, fighter; contender.

luchar, *vn.* to wrestle, to struggle, to fight.

ludibrio, *m.* mockery, derision.

luego, *adv.* presently, immediately; soon, afterwards; **desde —,** of course; **hasta —,** good-by; **— que,** as soon as.

luengo, ga, (poet.) *adj.* long, dilated; **—s años,** many years.

lug. lugar, pl. place.

lugar, *m.* place, spot; village; employment, office; room, space; cause, motive; (math.) locus; **en — de,** instead of; **— de diversión,** place of amusement; **—es comunes,** commonplaces; **— natal,** birthplace.

lugareño, ña, *adj.* and *n.* belonging to a village; inhabitant of a village.

lugarteniente, *m.* deputy, substitute; lieutenant.

lúgubre, *adj.* sad, gloomy; lugubrious.

Luis, Lewis, Louis.

Luisa, Louisa; Louise.

lujo, *m.* profuseness in pomp, dresses, fare; luxury; **de —,** de luxe, elegant.

lujoso, sa, *adj.* showy, profuse, lavish, sumptuous, luxurious.

lujuria, *f.* lewdness; luxury.

lujurioso, sa, *adj.* luxurious, voluptuous.

lumbago, *m.* lumbago.

lumbrada, *f.* large fire.

lumbre, *f.* fire; spark; light.

lumbrera, *f.* luminary; skylight; (arch.) louver.

luminaria, *f.* illumination; perpetual lamp in Catholic churches.

luminiscencia, *f.* luminescence.

luminoso, sa, *adj.* luminous, lucid, bright, brilliant.

lun. lunes, M. or Mon. Monday.

luna, *f.* moon; glass plate for mirrors; **— de miel,** honeymoon.

lunar, *m.* mole; blemish; **—,** *adj.* lunar.

lunático, ca, *adj.* lunatic, moon-struck.

lunes, *m.* Monday.

luneta, *f.* orchestra row seat (in theater); eyeglass.

lupanar, *m.* brothel.

lupia, *f.* encysted tumor.

lúpulo, *m.* (bot.) hops.

lustre, *m.* gloss, luster; splendor.

lustro, *m.* lustrum (space of five years).

lustroso, sa, *adj.* bright, brilliant.

luteranismo, *m.* Lutheranism.

luterano, na, *n.* and *adj.* Lutheran.

Lutero, Luther.

luto, *m.* mourning; bereavement; **de —,** in mourning.

Luxemburgo, *m.* Luxemburg.

luz, *f.* light; notice, information, hint; luster; **dar a —,** to give birth; **luces,** *pl.* culture, knowledge, enlightenment; **traje de —,** bullfighter's costume.

LL

llaga, *f.* wound, sore.

llagar, *va.* to wound, to hurt.

llama, *f.* flame; (zool.) llama.

llamada, *f.* call; (mil.) beat of the drum to summon troops; **— de incendios,** fire alarm; **— de larga distancia,** long-distance call.

llamado, da, *adj.* so-called, by the name of.

llamador, *m.* door knocker.

llamamiento, *m.* calling; convocation.

llamar, *va.* to call; to summon, to cite; to invoke; to knock at the door; **¿cómo se llama Ud.?** What is your name?

llamarada, *f.* sudden blaze of fire; sudden flush of the face.

llamativo, va, *adj.* showy, conspicuous, striking, provocative.

llamear, *vn.* to flame, to blaze.

llana, *f.* trowel; page (of a book, etc.).

llanada, *f.* wide tract of level ground; plain.

llanera, *f.* plainswoman.

llanero, *m.* plainsman.

llaneza, *f.* simplicity, sincerity, openness.

llano, na, *adj.* plain, even, level, smooth; meek, affable; clear, evident; **—,** *m.* level field; llano, plain.

llanta, *f.* rim, tire; **— balón,** balloon tire.

llanto, *m.* flood of tears, cry.

llanura, *f.* evenness, level; vast tract of level ground.

llares, *f. pl.* pot hanger.

llave, *f.* key; hammer (of a gun); **ama de —s,** housekeeper; **cerrar con —,** to lock; **— inglesa,** monkey wrench; **— maestra,** master key.

llavero, *m.* keeper of the keys; key ring; bunch of keys.

llegada, *f.* arrival, coming.

llegar, *vn.* to arrive; to reach; **— a ser,** to become; **—se,** to proceed to some neighboring place.

llena, *f.* flood, overflow.

llenar, *va.* to fill, to stuff, to gorge; to overwhelm (with compliments, kindness, etc.); **—se,** to feed gluttonously; to lose patience.

lleno, na, *adj.* full, replete; complete; **de —o,** entirely, fully.

llenura, *f.* abundance, plenty; fullness.

llevadero, ra, *adj.* tolerable.

llevar, *va.* to carry, to bear, to take away; to wear (clothes); to transport; to obtain; **— a cabo,** to complete, to accomplish; **— la correspondencia,** to carry on the correspondence; **— la voz por,** to speak for; **— los libros,** to keep books; **— puesto,** to be wearing, to have on; **—se,** to take away with; **—se bien,** to get along well together; **—se chasco,** to be disappointed.

lloraduelos, *m.* and *f.* (coll.) weeper.

llorar, *va.* and *vn.* to weep, to cry; to bewail.

lloriqueador, ra, crybaby.

lloriquear, *vn.* to whine.
lloro, *m.* weeping, crying.
llorón, ona, *n.* weeper.
lloroso, sa, *adj.* mournful, full of tears.
llovedizo, za, *adj.* pertaining to rain; **agua —za,** rain water.
llover, *v. imp.* (UE) to rain.
lloviznar, *v. imp.* to drizzle.
lluvia, *f.* rain.
lluvioso, sa, *adj.* rainy.

M

M.: Maestro, M. Master; **mediano,** med. medium; **Majestad,** M. Majesty; **Merced,** Grace or Worship.
m.: mañana, m. morning; **masculino,** m. masculine; **meridiano,** m. noon; **metro,** m. metro; **milla,** m. mile; **minuto,** m. minute.
m/: mi, my; **mes,** m. month.
M.ª María, Mary.
maca, *f.* blemish, flaw; deceit, trick; bruise (in fruit).
macabro, bra, *adj.* macabre, hideous.
macádam or **macadán,** *m.* macadam.
macadamizar or **macadanizar,** *va.* to macadamize.
macagua, *f.* macaw.
macanudo, da, *adj.* (Sp. Am.) (coll.) strong, robust, excellent, fine, magnificent, grand, first-rate.
macareno, na, *adj.* bragging, boasting.
macarrón, *m.* macaroon; **—es,** *pl.* macaroni.
macarse, *vr.* to rot (of fruit).
macear, *va.* to pound with a mallet; **—,** *vn.* to persist annoyingly, to harp upon.
macerar, *va.* to macerate, to soften.
macero, *m.* mace bearer.
maceta, *f.* flowerpot.
macilento, ta, *adj.* lean, extenuated; withered.
macillo, *m.* hammer (of a piano).
macizo, za, *adj.* massive, solid.
macrocosmo, *m.* macrocosm.
machaca, *m.* and *f.* ignorant, tiresome person; **—,** *f.* pounder, crusher.
machacar, *va.* to pound, to crush; **—,** *vn.* to importune, to molest; to harp upon.
machada, *f.* flock of he-goats; (coll.) stupidity.
machete, *m.* machete.
macho, *m.* male animal; he-mule; he-goat; pillar; hook to catch hold in an eye; **—,** *adj.* masculine, male; vigorous.
machón, *m.* buttress.
machorra, *f.* barren woman.
machucadura, *f.* pounding, bruising.
machucar, *va.* to pound, to bruise.
machucho, cha, *adj.* mature, ripe; judicious.
madama, *f.* madam.
madapolán, *m.* madapollam, percale.
madeja, *f.* skein of thread; lock of hair.

Madera, *f.* Madeira.
madera, *f.* timber, wood; wooden shutter; **— aserrada,** lumber; **de —,** wooden; **— contrachapada,** plywood; **— creosotada,** creosoted wood; **— de construcción,** building timber.
maderamen, *m.* timberwork.
maderería, *f.* lumberyard.
madero, *m.* beam of timber; lumberman, lumber dealer.
madrastra, *f.* stepmother.
madraza, *f.* (coll.) very fond mother.
madre, *f.* mother; womb, matrix; bed of a river.
madreperla, *f.* mother of pearl.
madreselva, *f.* honeysuckle.
madrigal, *m.* (poet.) madrigal.
madriguera, *f.* burrow; den, hiding place.
madrileño, ña, *n.* and *adj.* inhabitant of Madrid; from Madrid.
madrina, *f.* godmother.
madrona, *f.* mother who spoils her children by overindulgence; main irrigating ditch.
madroño, *m.* strawberry, strawberry plant; berry-shaped silk tassel.
madrugada, *f.* dawn; **de —,** at break of day.
madrugador, ra, *n.* early riser.
madrugar, *vn.* to get up early; to anticipate, to be beforehand.
madurar, *va.* to ripen; **—,** *vn.* to ripen, to grow ripe; to arrive at maturity.
madurez, *f.* maturity; prudence, wisdom.
maduro, ra, *adj.* ripe, mature; prudent, judicious.
maestra, *f.* school-mistress, woman teacher.
maestranza, *f.* equestrian club; dockyard; shipbuilding; machine shop, repair shop.
maestrazgo, *m.* grand mastership of a military order.
maestre, *m.* grand master of a military order; ship master; **— de raciones,** purser.
maestría, *f.* mastership, skill.
maestro, *m.* master; expert; teacher; **—, tra,** *adj.* masterly; **obra —,** master-piece.
Magdalena, Magdalena.
magdalena, *f.* oval-shaped biscuit made of flour and eggs.
magia, *f.* magic.
mágico, ca, *adj.* magical; **—,** *m.* magician.
magisterio, *m.* mastery; mastership; teachers as a class.
magistrado, *m.* magistrate; magistracy.
magistral, *adj.* magisterial; masterly; **—,** *m.* person who enjoys a prebend.
magistratura, *f.* magistracy.
magnanimidad, *f.* magnanimity.
magnánimo, ma, *adj.* magnanimous.
magnate, *m.* magnate, important personage.
magnesia, *f.* magnesia.
magnético, ca, *adj.* magnetic.
magnetismo, *m.* magnetism.
magnetita, *f.* magnetite.
magnetizar, *va.* to magnetize.
magneto, *m.* magneto.

magnificar, *va.* to exalt, to magnify.
magnificencia, *f.* magnificence, splendor.
magnífico, ca, *adj.* magnificent, splendid.
magnitud, *f.* magnitude; greatness, grandeur.
magno, na, *adj.* great.
magnolia, *f.* (bot.) magnolia.
mago, ga, *n.* magician, wizard.
magra, *f.* rasher, slice of pork.
magro, gra, *adj.* meager, thin.
maguey, *m.* (bot.) maguey, century plant.
magulladura, *f.* bruise, contusion.
magullar, *va.* to bruise, to contuse.
Mahoma, Mohammed.
mahometanismo, *m.* Mohammedanism.
mahometano, na, *n.* and *adj.* Mohammedan.
mahón, *m.* nankeen.
maillechort, *m.* white metal composed of nickel, copper, and zinc.
maitines, *m. pl.* (eccl.) matins.
maíz, *m.* corn, maize; **— machacado** or **molido,** hominy; **palomitas de —,** (Mex.) popcorn.
maizal, *m.* corn field.
maja, *f.* pestle of mortar.
majá, *m.* (Cuba) large, nonpoisonous snake.
majada, *f.* sheepfold.
majadería, *f.* absurd speech or act; insult; annoying and foolish action or saying; nonsense.
majadero, ra, *adj.* dull, silly, foolish; —, *n.* gawk, bore; —, *m.* pestle; **almirez y —ro,** mortar and pestle.
majadura, *f.* pounding, bruising.
majar, *va.* to pound.
majestad, *f.* majesty.
majestuoso, sa, *adj.* majestic, sublime.
majo, ja, *adj.* bold, gaudily attired; (coll.) good-looking, luxuriantly attired.
majuela, *f.* fruit of the white hawthorn.
majuelo, *m.* vine newly planted; hawthorn.
mal, *m.* evil, hurt, injury, ache; illness; **— de garganta,** sore throat; —, *adj.* (used only before masculine nouns) bad; **ir, caer** or **venir —,** to be unbecoming or displeasing.
mala, *f.* mail.
malacate, *m.* hoisting engine, windlass.
malaconsejado, da, *adj.* ill-advised.
malagradecido, da, *adj.* ungrateful.
malagueño, ña, *n.* and *adj.* of or pertaining to Malaga; **—ña,** *f.* popular song (of Malaga).
malamente, *adv.* badly, poorly; wrongly.
malandanza, *f.* misery, misfortune.
malandrín, *m.* highwayman; —, **na,** *adj.* malign, perverse.
malaria, *f.* malaria.
malavenido, da, *adj.* quarrelsome.
malaventura, *f.* calamity, misfortune.
malaventurado, da, *adj.* unfortunate.
malayo, ya, *n.* and *adj.* Malay, Malayan.
malbaratador, ra, *n.* spendthrift, lavisher.

malcaso, *m.* infamous act, treason.
malcomer, *va.* to eat poorly.
malcomido, da, *adj.* poorly fed.
malcontento, *m.* a card game; —, **ta,** *adj.* discontented, malcontent.
malcriado, da, *adj.* ill-bred, ill-behaved, unmannerly; naughty.
maldad, *f.* wickedness.
maldecir, *va.* (MALDIGO, MALDIJE) to curse.
maldición, *f.* malediction, curse, cursing.
maldito, ta, *adj.* perverse, wicked; damned, cursed; (coll.) little, not at all.
malear, *va.* to corrupt.
malecón, *m.* sea wall; levee, dike.
maledicencia, *f.* slander, calumny.
maleficiar, *va.* to adulterate, to corrupt; to bewitch.
maleficio, *m.* witchcraft, enchantment.
maléfico, ca, *adj.* mischievous, maleficent.
malestar, *m.* indisposition, uneasiness.
maleta, *f.* suitcase, satchel.
maletilla, *f.,* or **maletín,** *m.* handbag, satchel.
malevolencia, *f.* malevolence.
malévolo, la, *adj.* malevolent.
maleza, *f.* wickedness, malice; brambles, briars, underbrush.
malgastar, *va.* to waste, to lavish.
malhablado, da, *adj.* foul-mouthed.
malhadado, da, *adj.* unfortunate, wretched.
malhecho, *m.* evil act, wrong; —, **cha,** *adj.* malformed.
malhechor, ra, *n.* malefactor.
malherir, *va.* (IE) to wound grievously.
malhumorado, da, *adj.* ill-humored, peevish.
malicia, *f.* malice, perversity; suspicion; cunning, artifice; **tener —,** to suspect.
maliciar, *va.* to corrupt, to adulterate; —, *vn.* to suspect maliciously.
malicioso, sa, *adj.* malicious, wicked, malign.
malignidad, *f.* malignity, malice, evildoing.
maligno, na, *adj.* malignant, malicious.
malilla, *f.* manilla (card game).
malintencionado, da, *adj.* ill-disposed.
malmandado, da, *adj.* disobedient.
malmirado, da, *adj.* not considerate; disliked.
malo, la, *adj.* bad, ill, wicked; sickly.
malogramiento, *m.* failure, frustration.
malograr, *va.* to waste (as time or opportunity); **—se,** to fail of success.
malogro, *m.* disappointment, miscarriage.
malparado, da, *adj.* ill-conditioned, hurt.
malparida, *f.* woman who has had a miscarriage.
malparir, *va.* to miscarry.
malparto, *m.* abortion, miscarriage.
malquerer, *va.* (IE) to have a grudge against.
malquistar, *va.* to excite quarrels; to estrange friends.
malquisto, ta, *adj.* hated, detested.
malrotar, *va.* to misspend, to lavish.
malsano, na, *adj.* unhealthy, sickly; un-

healthful, unwholesome, unsanitary, insalubrious.

maltosa, *f.* maltose.

maltratamiento, *m.* ill treatment.

maltratar, *va.* to treat ill, to abuse, to maltreat.

malva, *f.* (bot.) mallow; **ser como una —,** to be docile and meek.

malvado, da, *adj.* wicked, very perverse; **—,** *n.* wrongdoer, villain.

malvasía, *f.* (bot.) malvasia; malmsey (wine made from the malvasia grape).

malvavisco, *m.* (bot.) althea.

malversación, *f.* malversation.

malversador, ra, *n.* person who misapplies property.

malversar, *va.* to misapply; to misappropriate.

malvís, *m.* (orn.) redwing.

malla, *f.* mesh; coat of mail.

mallo, *m.* mall; mallet.

Mallorca, *f.* Majorca.

mamá, *f.* mamma.

mamadera, *f.* nipple; nursing bottle.

mamar, *va.* and *vn.* to suck; (coll.) to cram and devour.

mamarracho, *m.* daub; grotesque ornament.

mameluco, *m.* mameluke; (coll.) simpleton; child's rompers.

mamífero, ra, *adj.* mammalian; **—s,** *m. pl.* mammals.

mamola, *f.* chuck under the chin.

mamón, ona, *n.* sucking animal; child who is suckled for a long time; **—,** *adj.* fond of suckling.

mamotreto, *m.* memorandum book.

mampara, *f.* screen.

mamparo, *m.* (naut.) bulkhead.

mampostería, *f.* rubblework, masonry.

mampuesto, *m.* parapet.

maná, *m.* manna.

manada, *f.* flock, drove of cattle; crowd, multitude; **— de lobos,** wolf pack.

manantial, *m.* source, spring; origin.

manar, *vn.* to spring from; to distil from; to issue; to abound.

mancar, *va.* to disable, to lame.

manceba, *f.* concubine.

mancebo, *m.* youth; companion; shop clerk.

mancilla, *f.* spot, blemish.

manco, ca, *adj.* handless; one-handed; maimed, faulty.

mancomún, de —, *adv.* jointly, by common consent.

mancomunar, *va.* to associate, to unite; to make two or more persons pay jointly the costs of a lawsuit; **—se,** to act together, to join in the execution of a thing.

mancomunidad, *f.* union, fellowship.

mancha, *f.* stain, spot, blot; **— de mosca,** flyspeck.

manchado, da, *adj.* spotted.

manchar, *va.* to stain, to soil, to spot.

manda, *f.* offer, proposal; legacy.

mandadero, *m.* errand boy.

mandado, *m.* mandate; command; errand, message.

mandamiento, *m.* mandate; commandment.

mandar, *va.* to command, to order; to offer; to bequeath; to send; **—,** *va.* and *vn.* to rule, to govern.

mandarín, *m.* mandarin.

mandatario, *m.* (law) attorney, agent; ruler of a nation, state, city, etc.

mandato, *m.* mandate, order; ecclesiastical ceremony of washing twelve persons' feet on Maundy Thursday; **por su —,** by your command.

mandíbula, *f.* jawbone, jaw.

mandil, *m.* coarse apron.

mando, *m.* command, authority, power; **—s,** *pl.* controls; **—s gemelos,** dual control.

mandolín, *m.,* or **mandolina,** *f.* mandolin.

mandón, ona, *adj.* imperious, domineering; **—,** *m.* imperious, haughty person.

mandril, *m.* (zool.) baboon; (mech.) spindle of a lathe.

maneable, *adj.* tractable.

manecilla, *f.* small hand; hand of a clock; book clasp.

manejable, *adj.* manageable.

manejar, *va.* to manage, to handle; to drive (a car, etc.); **—se,** to behave; to move about after having been deprived of motion.

manejo, *m.* managery, management, direction, administration; horsemanship.

manera, *f.* manner, mode; kind; **de ninguna —,** not at all.

manes, *m. pl.* manes (souls of the dead).

manga, *f.* sleeve; hurricane; cloak bag; straining bag; body of troops in a line.

manganato, *m.* (chem.) manganate.

manganeso, *m.* (chem.) manganese.

mangle, *m.* (bot.) mangrove.

mango, *m.* handle, haft; mango (a fruit).

mangoneo, *m.* pettifogging.

mangote, *m.* wide sleeve.

manguera, *f.* hose, hose pipe.

manguito, *m.* muff; (mech.) bushing sleeve.

maní, *m.* (Sp. Am.) peanut.

manía, *f.* frenzy, madness.

maniatar, *va.* to manacle, to handcuff.

maniático, ca, *adj.* maniac, mad, frantic.

manicero, *m.* peanut vendor.

manicomio, *m.* insane asylum.

manicura, *f.* manicure.

manicurista, *m.* and *f.* manicurist.

manicuro, ra, *n.* manicurist.

manifactura, manufactura, *f.* manufacture.

manifestación, *f.* manifestation, demonstration, declaration, statement.

manifestar, *va.* (IE) to manifest, to show.

manifiesto, ta, *adj.* manifest, open, clear; **—,** *m.* act of exposing the Holy Sacrament to the public adoration; manifesto; customhouse declaration.

manigua, *f.* (Cuba) thicket, jungle.

manigueta, *f.* handle haft; (naut.) kevel.

manija, *f.* handle, haft; crank; hopple; hand lever, stock; fetters; (mech.) ring, brace, clasp, clamp.

manilla, *f.* bracelet; handcuff, manacle.

maniobra, *f.* handiwork; handling; cleverness in handling; (mil.) maneuver.

maniobrar, *va.* to work with the hands; to work a ship; (mil.) to maneuver troops; to intrigue.

maniota, *f.* manacle, shackles.

manipulación, *f.* manipulation.

manipular, *va.* to manipulate, to manage.

manípulo, *m.* maniple; handful.

maniqueísmo, *m.* Manicheism.

maniqueo, ea, *n.* and *adj.* Manichean.

maniquí, *m.* mannikin.

manir, *va. def.* to keep meat until it grows tender.

manirroto, ta, *adj.* wasteful, too liberal.

manivacío, cía, *adj.* empty-handed.

manivela, *f.* (mech.) crank, crankshaft.

manjar, *m.* food, victuals; choice morsel of food.

Man.[1] **Manuel,** Manuel.

mano, *f.* hand; hand of clock or watch; coat of paint; **a —,** at hand; **a —s llenas,** liberally, abundantly; **tener buena —,** to be skillful; **— de obra,** labor, construction work; **de propia —,** with one's own hand; **venir a las —s,** to come to blows.

manojo, *m.* handful, bundle of herbs, etc.

manómetro, *m.* gauge, pressure gauge.

manopla, *f.* gauntlet; coachman's whip.

manosear, *va.* to handle; to muss.

manoseo, *m.* handling; mussing.

manotada, *f.* blow with the hand.

manotear, *vn.* to gesticulate with the hands.

manoteo, *m.* manual gesticulation.

mansedumbre, *f.* meekness, gentleness.

mansión, *f.* sojourn, residence; abode, home.

manso, sa, *adj.* tame; gentle, soft; **—,** *m.* leading male in a flock of goats, sheep or cattle.

manta, *f.* blanket; thrashing, drubbing; **— de viaje,** steamer rug.

manteamiento, *m.* tossing in a blanket.

mantear, *va.* to toss in a blanket.

manteca, *f.* butter, lard, fat; pomade.

mantecada, *f.* a type of cooky.

mantecado, *m.* butter cake; ice cream; **bloque de —,** brick ice cream.

mantecoso, sa, *adj.* greasy.

mantel, *m.* tablecloth.

mantelería, *f.* table linen.

manteleta, *f.* ladies' shawl.

mantenedor, *m.* president or chairman of a contest.

mantener, *va.* (MANTENGO, MANTUVE) to maintain, to support; to nourish; **—se,** to support oneself.

mantenimiento, *m.* maintenance; subsistence.

manteo, *m.* long cloak worn by priests and students.

mantequera, *f.* churn.

mantequero, *m.* butter seller, dairyman.

mantequilla, *f.* butter.

mantequillera, *f.* churn, butter churn, butter dish.

mantero, ra, *n.* blanket maker or vendor.

mantilla, *f.* mantilla, head-shawl; cloak; horsecloth; **—s,** *pl.* swaddling clothes.

mantillo, *m.* humus.

manto, *m.* mantle; cloak, robe.

mantón, *m.* large veil or shawl.

manual, *adj.* manual, handy; easily performed with the hand; **—,** *m.* manual.

manubrio, *m.* handle bar.

Manuel, Emanuel; Manuel.

manuf. manufactura, mfg. manufacturing.

manufactura, *f.* manufacture.

manufacturar, *va.* to manufacture.

manumitir, *va.* to release from slavery.

manuscrito, *m.* manuscript; **—, ta,** *adj.* written by hand.

manutención, *f.* maintaining; maintenance.

manzana, *f.* apple; block of houses.

manzanal or **manzanar,** *m.* apple orchard.

manzanilla, *f.* (bot.) common chamomile.

manzano, *m.* apple tree.

maña, *f.* handiness, dexterity, cleverness, cunning, artifice, skill, trick; evil habit or custom.

mañana, *f.* morning, morrow; **—,** *adv.* tomorrow; **pasado —,** day after tomorrow.

mañanear, *vn.* to rise early in the morning.

mañoso, sa, *adj.* skillful, handy; cunning.

mapa, *m.* map; **— turístico,** touring map.

mapache, *m.* raccoon; raccoon skin.

mapamundi, *m.* map of the world.

maquiavélico, ca, *adj.* Machiavelian.

maquilar, *va.* to take out the **maquila** (part of the flour given to the miller for grinding grain).

maquillaje, *m.* make-up.

máquina, *f.* machine, engine; **— de calcular,** calculating machine; **— de coser,** sewing machine; **— de escribir,** typewriter; **— de escribir portátil,** portable typewriter; **— de sumar,** adding machine; **— neumática,** air pump; **— para imprimir direcciones,** addressograph.

maquinación, *f.* machination.

maquinador, ra, *n.* schemer, machinator.

maquinalmente, *adv.* mechanically.

maquinar, *va.* to machinate; to conspire.

maquinaria, *f.* machinery; **— agrícola,** agricultural implements.

maquinista, *m.* machinist, mechanician; driver, engineer.

mar, *m.* or *f.* sea; **— alta,** rough sea; **— ancha,** high seas; **baja —,** low water; **— llena,** high water.

maraña, *f.* shrub, thicket; perplexity, puzzle; knot of a play.

marañón, *m.* fruit from which cashew nuts are obtained.

marasmo, *m.* (med.) marasmus.
maravedí, *m.* maravedi (smallest Spanish coin).
maravilla, *f.* wonder; **a las mil —s,** uncommonly well; exquisitely; **a —,** marvelously.
maravillar, *va.* to admire; **—se,** to wonder, to be astonished.
maravilloso, sa, *adj.* wonderful, marvelous.
marbete, *m.* tag, label.
marca, *f.* march (frontier province); due measure or weight of anything; mark, sign, brand; **— de fábrica,** trademark; **— del tipógrafo** or **— del editor,** printer's mark.
marcador, *m.* marker, assay master; **—, ra,** *adj.* marking.
marcar, *va.* to mark; to observe, to note, to designate.
marcasita, *f.* marcasite.
Marcelo, Marcellus.
marcial, *adj.* martial, warlike.
marcialidad, *f.* martial air or attitude.
marco, *m.* frame; frame of door, window, etc.; mark (weight of eight ounces); branding iron; measure of ground which may be sown with a **fanega** of grain.
márcola, *f.* pruning hook.
Marcos, Mark.
marcha, *f.* march; course; pace; **ponerse en —,** to proceed, to start off; **reducir** or **acortar la —,** to slow down.
marchamar, *va.* to put a mark on goods at the customhouse.
marchamo, *m.* mark put on goods at the customhouse.
marchar, *vn.* to go; to go off; to march; **— al encuentro,** to go to meet; **—se,** to go away.
marchitable, *adj.* perishable.
marchitar, *va.* and *vn.* to wither; to fade; to deprive of vigor.
marchito, ta, *adj.* faded, withered.
marea, *f.* tide; **— alta,** high tide; **— menguante,** ebb tide; **— muerta,** neap tide.
mareado, da, *adj.* dizzy, seasick.
mareaje, *m.* art of navigating a ship.
marear, *va.* to work a ship; to molest; **—se,** to become seasick.
marejada, *f.* sea swell, head sea.
mareo, *m.* seasickness.
marfil, *m.* ivory.
margarina, *f.* margarine.
Margarita, Margaret.
margarita, *f.* pearl; daisy; periwinkle.
margen, *m.* or *f.* margin; border; marginal note.
marginal, *adj.* marginal.
marginar, *va.* to make annotations on the margin.
margrave, *m.* margrave.
Marg.ᵗᵃ Margarita, Margaret.
María, Mary, Maria.
Mariana, Marian, Miriam.

marica, *f.* magpie; **—,** *m.* milksop, effeminate man.
maridillo, *m.* small brazier; pitiful husband.
marido, *m.* husband.
marihuana or **marijuana,** *f.* marihuana, marijuana.
marimacho, *m.* virago, mannish woman.
marimanta, *f.* bugbear.
marina, *f.* navy; shipping.
marinaje, *m.* seamanship; sailors.
marinar, *va.* to salt (fish).
marinería, *f.* seamanship; body of seamen.
marinero, *m.* mariner, sailor.
marinesco, ca, *adj.* nautical.
marino, na, *adj.* marine; **—,** *m.* mariner, seaman.
Mario, Marius.
mariposa, *f.* butterfly; rush light.
mariquita, *f.* (zool.) ladybird, ladybug.
mariscal, *m.* marshal; farrier; blacksmith; **— de campo,** major general, field marshal.
marisco, *m.* shellfish.
marital, *adj.* marital.
marítimo, ma, *adj.* maritime, marine.
maritornes, *f.* (coll.) ill-shaped, awkward woman.
marmita, *f.* kettle, pot.
marmitón, *m.* scullion.
mármol, *m.* marble.
marmolista, *m.* worker in marble.
marmóreo, rea, *adj.* marbled, marble.
marmota, *f.* marmot; prairie dog; woodchuck; groundhog.
maroma, *f.* rope; (Sp. Am.) feat, stunt (such as a somersault, etc.).
marqués, *m.* marquis.
marquesa, *f.* marchioness.
marquesado, *m.* marquisate.
marquesina, *f.* marquee, canopy.
marquesita, *f.* marcasite.
marrajo, *m.* white shark; **—, ja,** *adj.* sly, cunning.
marrana, *f.* sow.
marrano, *m.* pig, hog; a villainous person.
marrasquino, *m.* maraschino.
marro, *m.* quoits (game); disappointment, failure.
marrón, *m.* quoit, pitcher.
marroquí, *n.* and *adj.* Moroccan; **—,** *m.* morocco leather.
marrubio, *m.* horehound.
Marruecos, *m.* Morocco.
marrullería, *f.* knavery, cunning; prank, trick.
marrullero, ra, *adj.* crafty, cunning.
Marsella, *f.* Marseilles.
marsellés, *m.* shooting jacket; **—, sa,** *n.* and *adj.* native of Marseilles; of Marseilles.
marsopla, *f.* sperm whale.
marsupial, *m.* and *adj.* (zool.) marsupial.
mart. martes, Tu. Tuesday.
Marta, Martha.
marta, *f.* marten, marten fur.
martes, *m.* Tuesday.
martillada, *f.* blow with a hammer.

martillar, *va.* to hammer.
martillo, *m.* hammer.
Martín, Martin.
martinete, *m.* (orn.) martinette (a heron-like bird); drop hammer, pile driver; — **de fragua,** trip hammer.
martín pescador, *m.* (orn.) kingfisher.
mártir, *m.* or *f.* martyr.
martirio, *m.* martyrdom; torture.
martirizar, *va.* to martyr, to torture.
martirologio, *m.* martyrology.
marxista, *m.* Marxist.
marzo, *m.* March.
mas, *conj.* but, yet.
más, *adv.* more; besides; moreover; — **o menos,** more or less; **a — tardar,** at latest; **sin — ni —,** without more ado.
masa, *f.* dough, paste; mortar; mass; **las —s populares,** the lower classes.
masaje, *m.* massage.
mascada, *f.* (Mex.) fancy, large silk handkerchief.
mascadura, *f.* mastication.
mascar, *va.* to chew.
máscara, *m.* or *f.* mask, masquerader; —, *f.* mask, false face; **baile de —s,** masquerade dance.
mascarada, *f.* masquerade.
mascarilla, *f.* small mask.
mascarón, *m.* carved face on fountains and buildings.
mascota, *f.* mascot.
mascujar, *vn.* to masticate with difficulty; to pronounce with difficulty.
masculino, na, *adj.* masculine, male.
mascullar, *va.* to falter in speaking.
masera, *f.* kneading trough.
masilla, *f.* mastic, putty.
masonería, *f.* freemasonry.
masoquismo, *m.* masochism.
mastelero, *m.* mast, — **de gavia,** topmast.
masticación, *f.* mastication.
masticar, *va.* to masticate, to chew.
mástil, *m.* (naut.) topmast; pylon.
mastín, *m.* mastiff.
mastoides, *f.* and *adj.* mastoid.
mastuerzo, *m.* (bot.) common cress; simpleton.
Mat. matemática, math. mathematics.
mata, *f.* plant, shrub; sprig; blade; coppice; lock of matted hair.
matacandelas, *m.* extinguisher.
matachín, *m.* clown, buffoon; dance performed by grotesque figures.
matadero, *m.* slaughterhouse.
matador, *m.* murderer; bullfighter who kills bulls.
matadura, *f.* saddle gall.
matafuego, *m.* fire extinguisher.
matalotaje, *m.* (naut.) ship stores; (coll.) pile of things in disorder.
matanza, *f.* slaughtering; cattle to be slaughtered; massacre.
matar, *va.* to kill; to execute; to murder; to quench, to extinguish (fire); to slake

lime; to gall (a horse); **—se,** to kill oneself, to commit suicide.
matasanos, *m.* quack, charlatan, empiric.
matasiete, *m.* bully, braggadocio.
mate, *m.* checkmate; maté (Paraguayan tea); —, *adj.* unpolished.
matemática, *f.* mathematics.
matemático, ca, *adj.* mathematical; —, *m.* mathematician.
Mateo, Matthew.
materia, *f.* matter, material; subject; matter (pus); **primera —** or (Sp. Am.) — **prima,** raw material; **entrar en —,** to open or lead up to a subject.
material, *adj.* material, corporal; rude; uncouth; —, *m.* ingredient; cloth; materials.
materialidad, *f.* materiality; rudeness, coarseness.
materialismo, *m.* materialism.
materialista, *m.* or *f.* materialist; —, *adj.* materialistic.
maternal, *adj.* maternal, motherly.
maternidad, *f.* motherhood, motherliness.
materno, na, *adj.* maternal, motherly.
Matías, Mathias.
Matilde, Matilda.
matinal, *adj.* morning.
matiné, *f.* matinée.
matiz, *m.* shade of color; shading.
matizado, da, *adj.* variegated, many-hued.
matizar, *va.* to mix colors well; to beautify.
matón, *m.* bully.
matorral, *m.* shrub, thicket.
matraca, *f.* wooden rattle; jest, contemptuous joke; coxcomb.
matraquear, *vn.* to jest, to scoff, to mock, to ridicule.
matricida, *m.* or *f.* matricide (person).
matricidio, *m.* matricide (murder).
matrícula, *f.* register, list, license number; roster; — **para conducir vehículos,** driver's license.
matriculación, *f.* enrollment.
matricular, *va.* to matriculate; **—se,** to register; to enter a contest.
matrimonial, *adj.* matrimonial, connubial.
matrimonio, *m.* marriage; matrimony.
matriz, *f.* uterus, womb; mold, die; —, *adj.* main, parent; **casa —,** head or main office.
matrona, *f.* matron.
matutino, na, *adj.* morning.
maula, *f.* object found in the street; deceitful trick, imposition; —, *n.* (coll.) cheat, bad payer.
maulero, ra, *n.* impostor, cheat, swindler; dealer in remnants.
maullar, *vn.* to mew.
maullido, *m.* mew, cry of a cat.
Mauricio, Morris, Maurice.
mausoleo, *m.* mausoleum.
máxima, *f.* maxim, rule.
máxime, *adv.* principally.
Maximiliano, Maximilian.
máximo, ma, *adj.* maximum, chief, principal; very great.

may. letra mayúscula, cap. capital letter.
may.^{mo} **mayordomo,** majordomo, steward, butler.
mayo, *m.* May; Maypole.
mayólica, *f.* majolica ware.
mayonesa, *adj.* mayonnaise; **salsa —,** mayonnaise dressing.
mayor, *adj.* greater, larger; elder; **estado —,** military staff; **—,** *m.* superior; major; **—,** *f.* first proposition in a syllogism; **al por —,** wholesale.
mayoral, *m.* head shepherd; leader.
mayorazgo, *m.* first-born son with the right of primogeniture, son and heir; family estate entailed on the eldest son; (law) priority right to authority, inheritance, or succession.
mayordomía, *f.* administration, stewardship.
mayordomo, *m.* steward, superintendent; majordomo.
mayoría, *f.* majority, excellence, superiority; **— absoluta,** majority of votes in an election; **— relativa,** plurality.
mayormente, *adv.* principally, chiefly.
mayúscula, *f.* capital letter.
maza, *f.* club; mace; hub; (coll.) importunate, troublesome fellow.
mazada, *f.* blow with a mallet.
mazamorra, *f.* small bits, crumbs; corn pap or mush; (Col.) a sort of thick corn soup; (Arg. and Col.) whole corn, boiled; (naut.) mess made from broken biscuits.
mazapán, *m.* marzipan, marchpane.
mazmorra, *f.* Moorish dungeon.
mazo, *m.* mallet; bundle; (coll.) importunate, tiresome person.
mazorca, *f.* spindle full of thread; ear of corn.
mazurca, *f.* mazurka.
m/c mi cargo or **mi cuenta,** (com.) my account.
m/cta. mi cuenta, (com.) my account.
m/cte. m/c. moneda corriente, cur. currency.
Me **Madre,** Mother.
me, *pron.* me (dative case).
meada, *f.* urination.
meadero, *m.* urinal.
mear, *vn.* to urinate; to pump ship.
Meca, *f.* Mecca.
mecánica, *f.* mechanics; (coll.) mean, despicable thing; (mil.) management of soldiers, affairs.
mecánico, ca, *adj.* mechanical; **—,** *m.* mechanician, mechanic.
mecanismo, *m.* mechanism.
mecanizar, *va.* to mechanize.
mecanografía, *f.* typewriting.
mecanógrafo, fa, *n.* typist.
mecanotaquígrafo, fa, *n.* stenotypist.
mecedora, *f.* rocking chair, rocker.
Mecenas, *m.* Moecenas, patron who endows or otherwise fosters the arts.
mecer, *va.* to stir, to agitate; to rock; to

dandle a child to rest.
mecha, *f.* wick; bacon with which fowls and meat are larded; fuse, match.
mechar, *va.* to lard.
mechero, *m.* nozzle of a lamp; socket of a candlestick; **— de gas,** gas burner, gas jet.
mechinal, *m.* square stones left projecting in a wall to be continued; (coll.) very small room.
mechón, *m.* large lock of hair; large bundle of threads or fibers; large fuse.
Med. Medicina, Med. Medicine.
medalla, *f.* medal.
medallón, *m.* medallion; locket, lavalier.
media, *f.* stocking; **— vuelta,** right about.
mediación, *f.* mediation, intervention.
mediador, *m.* mediator; go-between.
mediados, a — de, *adv.* about the middle of.
medialuna, *f.* Crescent (emblem of the Turkish empire).
medianería, *f.* partition wall.
medianero, ra, *adj.* mediating, interceding.
medianía, *f.* moderation; mediocrity.
mediano, na, *adj.* moderate, middling; mediocre; medium.
medianoche, *f.* midnight.
mediante, *adv.* by means of, through; **Dios —,** God willing.
mediar, *vn.* to be in the middle; to intercede for another; to mediate.
mediator, *m.* ombre (game).
medicastro, *m.* charlatan, quack.
medicina, *f.* medicine.
medicinal, *adj.* medicinal.
medicinar, *va.* to give medicine, to treat a patient.
médico, *m.* physician; **—, ca,** *adj.* medical.
medida, *f.* measure; **— para líquidos,** liquid measure; **a la —,** made-to-measure, tailor-made; **a — que,** at the same time that, in proportion to; **— patrón,** standard measure.
medidor, *m.* meter; **— para neumáticos,** tire gauge; **—, ra,** *n.* measurer.
mediero, *m.* hosier, stocking dealer.
medieval, *adj.* medieval.
medio, dia, *adj.* half, halfway, mid, midway; mean; medium, average; **a — asta,** half mast; **a —as,** by halves; **de peso —,** middle weight; **—,** *m.* way, method; medium; middle; **—os,** *m. pl.* means.
mediocre, *adj.* middling, moderate, mediocre.
mediocridad, *f.* mediocrity.
mediodía, *m.* noon, midday; south.
medioeval, *adj.* medieval.
mediopaño, *m.* thin woolen cloth.
medir, *va.* (1) to measure; **—se,** to be moderate.
meditación, *f.* meditation.
meditar, *va.* and *vn.* to meditate; to brood.
Mediterráneo, *m.* Mediterranean.
mediterráneo, nea, *adj.* Mediterranean.
medra, *f.* progress, melioration, improvement.

medrar, *vn.* to thrive, to prosper; to improve.

medroso, sa, *adj.* fearful, timorous; terrible.

medula, or **médula,** *f.* marrow; principal substance, essence; (fig.) pith.

meduloso, sa, *adj.* full of marrow, marrowy.

megaciclo, *m.* megacycle.

megáfono, *m.* megaphone.

megalomanía, *f.* megalomania.

mego, ga, *adj.* meek, peaceful.

Mej. or **Mex. Méjico,** Mex. Mexico.

mejicano, na, or **mexicano, na,** *n.* and *adj.* Mexican.

Méjico, *m.* Mexico.

mejido, da, *adj.* beaten up with sugar and water (of eggs).

mejilla, *f.* cheek.

mejor, *adj.* and *adv.* better, best; — **dicho,** rather, more nearly proper; **a lo —,** when least expected.

mejora, *f.* improvement, melioration, growth.

mejoramiento, *m.* improvement, amelioration; enhancement.

mejorana, *f.* (bot.) sweet marjoram.

mejorar, *va.* to improve, to better, to meliorate, to heighten; to cultivate; to mend; —, *vn.* to recover, to grow well from a disease or calamity; —**se,** to improve, to grow better.

mejoría, *f.* improvement, melioration; mending; repairs; improvement in health; advantage; superiority.

melada, *f.* slice of toast dipped in honey.

melancolía, *f.* melancholy.

melancólico, ca, *adj.* melancholy, sad, gloomy.

melar, *va.* to boil clear (of sugar); to fill (combs) with honey.

melaza, *f.* molasses.

melcocha, *f.* taffy.

melena, *f.* dishevelled hair hanging loose over the eyes; foretop hair or mane; bobbed hair.

melenudo, da, *adj.* having bushy hair.

melífero, ra, *adj.* productive of honey.

melifluo, flua, *adj.* honey-mouthed; flowing with honey.

melindre, *m.* fritter made of honey and flour, ladyfinger; prudery, fastidiousness, affectation.

melindrear, *vn.* to act a prude.

melindroso, sa, *adj.* prudish, finical.

melocotón, *m.* (bot.) peach.

melodía, *f.* melody.

melodioso, sa, *adj.* melodious.

melodrama, *m.* melodrama.

melón, *m.* melon; — **de verano,** cantaloupe.

melonar, *m.* bed of melons.

melosidad, *f.* sweetness.

meloso, sa, *adj.* like honey, sweet; mellow.

melote, *m.* molasses.

mella, *f.* notch in edged tools; gap; **hacer —,** to affect.

mellado, da, *adj.* gap-toothed.

mellar, *va.* to notch; to deprive of luster and splendor.

mellizo, za, *n.* and *adj.* twin.

membrana, *f.* membrane.

membranoso, sa, *adj.* membranous, filmy.

membrete, *m.* memorandum, note; line of a letter containing the name of the addressee; invitation card.

membrillo, *m.* quince; quince tree.

membrudo, da, *adj.* strong, robust.

mementos, *m. pl.* two prayers at mass for the living and the dead.

memorable, *adj.* memorable.

memorándum, *m.* memorandum, notebook.

memoria, *f.* memory; souvenir; memoir; report (of a conference, etc.); —**s,** *pl.* compliments, regards.

memorial, *m.* memorandum book; memorial, brief.

memorialista, *m.* amanuensis; writer of petitions for others.

mención, *f.* mention.

mencionar, *va.* to mention.

mendaz, *adj.* lying, mendacious.

mendicante, *adj.* mendicant, begging; —, *m.* mendicant.

mendigar, *va.* to ask charity, to beg.

mendigo, *m.* beggar.

mendiguez, *f.* beggary.

mendrugo, *m.* broken bread given to beggars.

menear, *va.* to move from place to place; to manage; —**se,** to be brisk and active, to stir about; (coll.) to wriggle, to waddle.

meneo, *m.* waddling motion of the body.

menester, *m.* necessity, need, want; **ser —,** to be necessary; —**es,** *pl.* natural necessities.

menesteroso, sa, *adj.* needy, necessitous.

menestra, *f.* vegetable soup; dried legumes.

menestral, *m.* tradesman, handicraftsman.

meng. menguante, decreasing.

mengua, *f.* decay, decline; poverty; disgrace.

menguado, da, *adj.* cowardly; foolish; avaricious; **hora —,** fatal moment; —, *m.* stitch picked up in knitting.

menguante, *adj.* decreasing, diminishing; —, *f.* ebb tide, low water; decline.

menguar, *vn.* to decay, to fall off; to decrease, to diminish; to fail.

meningitis, *f.* (med.) meningitis.

menjurje, *m.* hodgepodge.

menopausia, *f.* (med.) menopause, change of life in women.

menor, *m.* and *f.* minor (one under age); —, *adj.* less, smaller, minor; **por —,** by retail, in small parts; minutely.

Menorca, *f.* Minorca.

menoría, *f.* inferiority; (law) minority, being under age.

menorragia, *f.* (med.) menorrhagia.

menos, *adv.* less; with exception of; **a lo—,**

or **por lo —**, at least, however; **lo — posible,** the least possible; **venir a —**, to get worse, to grow poor; **a — que,** unless.

menoscabar, *va.* to lessen; to make worse; to reduce.

menoscabo, *m.* diminution, deterioration, loss.

menospreciar, *va.* to undervalue, to underestimate; to despise, to contemn.

menosprecio, *m.* contempt, scorn.

mensaje, *m.* message, errand.

mensajero, ra, *n.* messenger.

menstruación, *f.* menstruation.

mensual, *adj.* monthly.

mensualidad, *f.* month's pay, month's allowance; monthly installment.

ménsula, *f.* (arch.) bracket, cantilever; rest for the elbows.

menta, *f.* (bot.) mint; **— verde,** spearmint.

mentado, da, *adj.* famous, renowned; mentioned, spoken of.

mental, *adj.* mental, intellectual.

mentalidad, *f.* mentality.

mentar, *va.* (IE) to mention.

mente, *f.* mind, understanding; sense, meaning.

mentecato, ta, *adj.* silly, crackbrained; **—,** *n.* fool, simpleton.

mentidero, *m.* (coll.) place where people gossip.

mentir, *vn.* (IE) to lie.

mentira, *f.* lie, falsehood; **parecer —,** to seem impossible.

mentirilla, *f.* fib, white lie.

mentiroso, sa, *adj.* lying, deceitful; **—,** *n.* liar.

mentís, *m.* giving the lie.

mentol, *m.* menthol.

mentolado, da, *adj.* mentholated.

mentón, *m.* chin.

menú, *m.* bill of fare.

menudear, *va.* to repeat, to detail minutely; **—,** *vn.* to occur frequently; to be plentiful; to go into detail.

menudencia, *f.* trifle; minuteness; **—s,** *pl.* small matters.

menudeo, *m.* retail; **al —,** at retail.

menudillos, *m. pl.* giblets of fowls.

menudo, da, *adj.* small; minute; of no moment; **a —do,** repeatedly, often; **—,** *m.* small change (money); tripe, entrails of an animal.

meñique, *m.* little finger.

meollo, *m.* marrow; judgment, understanding.

meón, ona, *adj.* continually urinating.

mequetrefe, *m.* insignificant, noisy fellow.

meramente, *adv.* merely, solely.

merca, *f.* (coll.) purchase.

mercachifle, *m.* huckster, merchant of small wares.

mercader, *m.* dealer, trader, merchant.

mercadería, *f.* commodity, merchandise; trade.

mercado, *m.* market; market place; **— de**

valores, stock market.

mercancía, *f.* trade, traffic; saleable goods, merchandise.

mercante, *adj.* merchant; **buque —,** merchant ship.

mercantil, *adj.* commercial, mercantile.

merced, *f.* favor, grace, mercy; will, pleasure; **estar a — de otro,** to be at another's command.

mercenario, *m.* day laborer; mercenary; member of **la Merced,** a religious order; **—, ria,** *adj.* mercenary.

mercería, *f.* dry-goods store.

mercerizar, *va.* to mercerize.

mercero, *m.* haberdasher.

mercurial, *m.* (bot.) dog's mercury (a European flowering weed); **—,** *adj.* mercurial.

mercurio, *m.* mercury, quicksilver.

mercurocromo, *m.* (med.) mercurochrome.

merecedor, ra, *adj.* deserving, worthy.

merecer, *va.* (EZCO) to deserve, to merit; **—,** *vn.* to be deserving, to be meritorious.

merecido, da, *adj.* deserved; **bien** or **mal —o,** well- or ill-deserved.

merecimiento, *m.* merit, desert.

merendar, *vn.* (IE) to lunch, to eat a light meal.

merengue, *m.* meringue.

mergo, *m.* diving bird, loon, cormorant.

meridiana, *f.* cot, couch.

meridiano, *m.* meridian; **pasado —,** afternoon; **—, na,** *adj.* meridional.

meridional, *adj.* southern, meridional.

merienda, *f.* luncheon, light repast.

merino, *m.* merino (sheep, wool, or cloth); royal judge and inspector of sheep pastures; shepherd of merino sheep; **—, na,** *adj.* moving from pasture to pasture.

mérito, *m.* merit, desert.

meritorio, ria, *adj.* meritorious, laudable.

merla, *f.* (orn.) blackbird.

merluza, *f.* hake (fish).

merma, *f.* waste, leakage; shortage.

mermar, *vn.* to waste, to diminish.

mermelada, *f.* marmalade.

mero, *m.* pollack (fish); **—, ra,** *adj.* mere, only; pure.

merodeador, ra, *n.* marauder; **—,** *adj.* marauding.

merodear, *vn.* to pillage, to go marauding.

mer.[s], merc.[s] mercancías, mercaderías, mdse. merchandise, goods.

mes, *m.* month.

mesa, *f.* table; landing (of a staircase); **— redonda,** round table; table for regular boarders; **poner la —,** to set the table; **quitar la —,** to clear the table.

mesada, *f.* monthly pay or wages or allowance.

mesana, *f.* (naut.) mizzenmast.

mesar, *va.* to tear one's hair out.

mescolanza, *f.* mess, jumble.

meseta, *f.* landing (of a staircase); tableland, plateau,

Mesías, m. Messiah.
mesmerismo, m. mesmerism.
mesodermo, m. mesoderm.
mesón, m. inn, hostelry.
mesonero, m. innkeeper.
mesozoico, adj. Mesozoic.
mesta, f. proprietors of cattle and sheep considered as a body; annual meeting of owners of flocks.
mestizo, za, adj. and n. mestizo (of mixed blood).
mesura, f. grave deportment, dignity; politeness; moderation.
mesurado, da, adj. moderate; modest; gentle; prudent.
mesurar, va. to instill moderation (in); —se, to refrain; to control oneself.
meta, f. boundary; goal, goal line.
metabolismo, m. metabolism.
metacarpo, m. (anat.) metacarpus.
metafísica, f. metaphysics.
metafísico, ca, adj. metaphysical; —, m. metaphysician.
metáfora, f. metaphor.
metafórico, ca, adj. metaphorical.
metal, m. metal; brass; tone or timbre of the voice.
metal. metalurgia, metal. metallurgy.
metálico, ca, adj. metallic, metal.
metalistería, f. metal work.
metalurgia, f. metallurgy.
metamorfismo, m. metamorphism.
metamorfosis, f. metamorphosis, transformation.
metatarsiano, na, adj. metatarsal.
metate, m. (Mex.) stone for grinding corn, etc.
metátesis, f. (gram.) metathesis, transposition.
meteoro, m. meteor.
meteorología, f. meteorology.
meteorologista, m. weatherman.
meter, va. to place, to put; to introduce, to insert; to smuggle goods into the country; —se, to meddle, to interfere.
meticuloso, sa, adj. meticulous, conscientious.
metilo, m. (chem.) methyl.
metódico, ca, adj. methodical, systematic.
método, m. method.
metralla, f. grapeshot.
métrico, ca, adj. metrical.
metro, m. meter; verse; (Spain, coll.) subway.
metrónomo, m. metronome.
metrópoli, f. metropolis; archiepiscopal church.
metropolitano, na, adj. metropolitan.
Mex. or **Mej. Méjico,** Mex. Mexico.
mezanina, f. mezzanine, half story.
mezcla, f. mixture, medley.
mezclador, ra, n. beater, mixer; —, adj. heating, mixing.
mezclar, va. to mix, to mingle; —se, to mix; to intermarry.

mezclilla, f. denim.
mezquindad, f. penury, poverty, avarice.
mezquino, na, adj. poor, indigent; avaricious, covetous, mean, petty.
mezquita, f. mosque.
m/f.: meses fecha, (com.) months after date; **mi favor,** my favor.
m/fha. meses fecha, (com.) months after date.
mg. miligramo, mg. milligram.
m/g mi giro, (com.) my draft.
mi, pron. my; —, m. mi, third note of the musical scale.
mí, pron. me (objective case of the pronoun yo).
miaja, f. crumb.
miar, vn. to mew.
miasma, m. (med.) miasma.
mica, f. mica, isinglass.
micado, m. Mikado.
micho, cha, n. (coll.) cat, pussy.
mico, m. monkey.
micra, f. micron.
microbio, m. microbe, germ.
microbiología, f. microbiology, bacteriology.
microbiólogo, m. microbiologist; bacteriologist.
microcefalia, f. microcephaly, microcephalism.
micrococo, m. micrococcus.
microcosmo, m. microcosm.
micrófono, m. microphone; receiver of a telephone.
microfotografía, f. microphotography.
micrométrico, ca, adj. micrometric.
micrómetro, m. micrometer.
microorganismo, m. micro-organism.
microscópico, ca, adj. microscopical.
microscopio, m. microscope.
miedo, m. fear, dread; **tener** —, to be afraid.
miel, f. honey; **luna de** —, honeymoon.
mielga, f. (bot.) lucern; small dogfish; rake.
miembro, m. member; limb.
mientras, adv. in the meantime; while; **— tanto,** meanwhile.
miérc. miércoles, Wed. Wednesday.
miércoles, m. Wednesday.
mierda, f. excrement, ordure.
mies, f. harvest.
miga, f. crumb.
migaja, f. scrap, crumb, small particle.
migajón, m. crumb without crust.
migar, va. to crumble.
Mig.[1] Miguel, Michael.
Miguel, Michael.
mijo, m. (bot.) millet.
mil, m. one thousand; **por** —, per thousand.
mil.: milicia, mil. militia; **militar,** mil. military.
milagro, m. miracle, wonder; offering hung up in churches in commemoration of a miracle.
milagroso, sa, adj. miraculous.

Milán, *f.* Milan.
milano, *m.* (orn.) kite, hawk.
milenario, ria, *adj.* millenary; —, *m.* millennium.
milés.³ **milésimos, mas,** thousandths.
milésimo, ma, *adj.* thousandth.
milicia, *f.* militia.
miliciano, *m.* militiaman; —, **na,** *adj.* military.
miligramo, *m.* milligram.
mililitro, *m.* milliliter.
milímetro, *m.* millimeter.
militar, *adj.* military; —, *vn.* to serve in the army.
militarismo, *m.* militarism.
milpa, *f.* (Sp. Am.) maize (corn) land.
milreis, *m.* milreis (Portuguese and Brazilian coin).
milla, *f.* mile.
millar, *m.* thousand.
millón, *m.* million.
millonario, ria, *n.* millionaire.
mimar, *va.* to coax, to wheedle, to flatter; to fondle, to caress.
mimbre, *m.* twig of a willow; wicker.
mimeógrafo, *m.* mimeograph.
mímico, ca, *adj.* mimic.
mimo, *m.* buffoon, clown; mime, mimic; prudery, delicacy; petting, indulgence.
mimosa, *f.* (bot.) mimosa.
mimoso, sa, *adj.* fastidious, finicky.
mina, *f.* mine; source of water, conduit, underground canal; (mil. or naut.) mine; **campo de** —**s,** mine field.
minador, *m.* miner.
minar, *va.* to undermine; to mine.
minarete, *m.* minaret, tower, belfry.
mineral, *m.* mineral; spring of water; —, *adj.* mineral.
mineralogía, *f.* mineralogy.
mineralógico, ca, *adj.* belonging to mineralogy.
minería, *f.* mining; — **de placer,** placer mining.
minero, *m.* miner; —, **ra,** *adj.* mining.
miniatura, *f.* miniature.
mínima, *f.* (mus.) minim.
mínimo, ma, *adj.* least, smallest.
minio, *m.* minium, red lead.
ministerio, *m.* ministry (office), cabinet; **M— de Fomento,** Department of Public Works; **M— de Gracia y Justicia,** Department of Justice; **M— de Hacienda,** Treasury Department; **M— de Relaciones Exteriores,** Department of Foreign Affairs.
ministril, *m.* petty officer of justice; player of wind instruments at churches.
ministro, *m.* minister of state; petty officer of justice.
min.º ministro, min. minister.
minorar, *va.* to lessen, to diminish.
minoría, *f.* minority.
minoridad, *f.* minority.

minucioso, sa, *adj.* minute, superfluously exact.
minué, *m.* minuet (music and dance).
minuendo, *m.* (math.) minuend.
minúscula, *adj.* small (applied to letters).
minuta, *f.* minute, first draft of an agreement in writing.
minutero, *m.* minute hand of a watch or clock.
minuto, *m.* minute.
mío, mía, *pron.* mine.
miocarditis, *f.* myocarditis.
miope, *n.* and *adj.* near-sighted; near-sighted person.
miopía, *f.* nearsightedness.
miosota, *f.* forget-me-not.
mira, *f.* sight of a gun; needle or point in mathematical instruments for directing the sight; purpose, intention; care; **estar a la** —, to be on the lookout.
mirada, *f.* glance; gaze; **clavar la** —, to peer, to stare.
mirador, ra, *n.* spectator, looker-on; —, *m.* bay window, observatory; veranda.
miramiento, *m.* consideration; circumspection, care.
mirar, *va.* to behold, to look; to observe, to spy; —, *v. imp.* to concern; —**se,** to look at oneself; to look at one another.
mirasol, *m.* (bot.) sunflower.
miriñaque, *m.* bauble, trinket; crinoline.
mirlo, *m.* blackbird.
mirón, ona, *n.* spectator, looker-on, bystander; prier, one who inquires with too much curiosity and officiousness; gazer; kibitzer.
mirra, *f.* myrrh.
mirto, *m.* myrtle.
misa, *f.* mass; — **del gallo,** midnight mass; **cantar** —, to say mass; — **de prima,** early mass.
misal, *m.* missal.
misántropo, *m.* misanthrope; misanthropist.
miscelánea, *f.* miscellany.
misceláneo, nea, *adj.* miscellaneous.
miserable, *adj.* miserable, wretched, unhappy; exhausted; avaricious.
miseria, *f.* misery; niggardliness; trifle.
misericordia, *f.* mercy; clemency, pity.
misericordioso, sa, *adj.* merciful, clement.
mísero, ra, *adj.* miserable, poor, wretched.
misia or **misiá,** *f.* (Sp. Am.) Mrs., Doña.
misión, *f.* mission.
misionero, *m.* missionary.
mismo, ma, *adj.* same, similar, equal; self.
misterio, *m.* mystery.
misterioso, sa, *adj.* mysterious, mystical.
mística, *f.* mysticism.
místico, ca, *adj.* mystic, mystical.
mitad, *f.* half; middle.
mítico, ca, *adj.* mythical.
mitigación, *f.* mitigation.
mitigar, *va.* to mitigate.
mitin, *m.* meeting.
mitología, *f.* mythology.

mitológico, ca, *adj.* mythological.
mitones, *m. pl.* mittens.
mitosis, *f.* mitosis.
mitra, *f.* (eccl.) miter.
mitrado, da, *adj.* (eccl.) mitered.
mixto, ta, *adj.* mixed, mingled.
mixtura, *f.* mixture.
m/l or **m/L mi letra,** my letter, my draft.
ml. mililitro, ml. milliliter.
mm milímetro, mm. millimeter.
m/n moneda nacional, national currency.
m/o mi orden, (com.) my order.
moaré, *m.* moire.
mobiliario, *m.* furniture; chattels.
mocasín, *m.* moccasin.
mocedad, *f.* youthfulness, youth.
moción, *f.* motion.
moco, *m.* mucus; snuff of a candle.
mocosidad, *f.* mucosity.
mocoso, sa, *adj.* sniveling, mucous.
mochar, *va.* to lop off, to cut.
mochila, *f.* knapsack.
mocho, cha, *adj.* dishorned, having the horns cut off; cropped, shorn; lopped, having the branches cut off; maimed, mutilated.
mochuelo, *m.* owl; **cargar con el —,** (coll.) to get the worst of an undertaking.
moda, *f.* fashion, mode; **de —,** fashionable; **última —,** latest fashion.
modales, *m. pl.* manners of a person, breeding.
modalidad, *f.* nature, character; (mus.) mode and tone.
modelado, *m.* modeling.
modelar, *va.* to model, to form.
modelo, *m.* model, pattern.
moderación, *f.* moderation, temperance.
moderado, da, *adj.* moderate, temperate.
moderador, *m.* moderator.
moderar, *va.* to moderate.
modernismo, *m.* modernistic movement in literature; modernism.
modernista, *adj.* modernistic.
modernización, *f.* modernization.
modernizar, *va.* to modernize.
moderno, na, *adj.* modern.
modestia, *f.* modesty, decency.
modesto, ta, *adj.* modest.
módico, ca, *adj.* moderate, reasonable (as price).
modificación, *f.* modification; limitation.
modificador, *m.* modifier.
modificante, *m.* modifier.
modificar, *va.* to modify.
modificativo, va, *m.* and *adj.* modificative.
modismo, *m.* idiom, idiomatic expression.
modista, *f.* dressmaker.
modo, *m.* mode, method, manner; moderation; mood; **de — que,** so that; **sobre —,** extremely.
modorra, *f.* drowsiness, doziness.
modorrar, *va.* to render heavy with sleep; **—se,** to become flabby, ready to rot (as fruit).

modorro, rra, *adj.* drowsy, sleepy.
modoso, sa, *adj.* well-behaved, temperate.
modrego, *m.* dunce, dolt.
modulación, *f.* modulation; **— de frecuencia,** frequency modulation; **— de amplitud,** amplitude modulation.
modulador, ra, *n.* modulator.
modulante, *adj.* modulating.
modular, *va.* to modulate, to transform.
módulo, *m.* (arch.) module, measure of columns; modulation of voice; unit of measure of running water; size of coins and medals; modulus.
mofa, *f.* mockery.
mofador, ra, *n.* scoffer, scorner.
mofar, *va.* and *vr.* to deride; to mock; to scoff.
moflete, *m.* fat cheek.
mogollón, *m.* hanger-on, parasite, sponger.
mohecer, *va.* (EZCO) to moss, to cover with moss.
mohín, *m.* grimace, wry face.
mohina, *f.* animosity, desire of revenge, resentment, grudge.
mohino, na, *adj.* fretful, peevish.
moho, *m.* (bot.) moss; rust.
mohoso, sa, *adj.* moldy, musty; mossy; rusty.
Moisés, Moses.
mojado, da, *adj.* wet.
mojadura, *f.* act of moistening or wetting.
mojar, *va.* to wet, to moisten; **—,** *vn.* to be immersed in an enterprise or business.
mojarse, *vr.* to become wet.
moje, *m.* gravy, sauce.
mojicón, *m.* kind of cooky; tea biscuit; (coll.) cuff, punch.
mojiganga, *f.* masquerade; mummery.
mojigato, ta, *adj.* hypocritical; **—,** *n.* hypocrite; fanatic.
mojón, *m.* landmark; heap; solid excrement.
mola, *f.* (med.) mole.
moldar, *va.* to mold.
molde, *m.* mold; pattern (for a dress, etc.); matrix, cast.
moldura, *f.* molding.
mole, *adj.* soft, mild; **—,** *f.* vast size or quantity; massiveness; **—,** *m.* (Mex.) kind of spicy sauce for fowl and meat stews.
molécula, *f.* molecule.
molecular, *adj.* molecular.
moledor, *m.* grinder; tiresome fellow, bore.
molendero, ra, miller; chocolate manufacturer.
moler, *va.* (UE) to grind, to pound; to vex, to molest; to waste, to consume by use.
molestar, *va.* to vex, to molest, to tease, to trouble.
molestia, *f.* injury, molestation.
molesto, ta, *adj.* vexatious, troublesome.
moletón, *m.* cotton flannel, flannelette.
molicie, *f.* tenderness, softness.
molienda, *f.* act of grinding or pounding; fatigue, lassitude.
molinero, *m.* miller.

molinete, *m.* windlass; turnstile.

molinillo, *m.* hand mill; grinder (for coffee, meat, etc.).

molino, *m.* mill.

mollar, *adj.* soft, pappy, pulpy; credulous.

molleja, *f.* gland; gizzard.

mollera, *f.* crown of head; **ser duro de —,** to be stupid, headstrong, hardheaded.

mollete, *m.* French roll; **—s,** *pl.* plump cheeks.

molletudo, da, *adj.* fat-cheeked.

molliznar or **molliznear,** *vn.* to sprinkle, to drizzle.

m/o, m/ or **m/m más o menos,** more or less.

momentáneo, nea, *adj.* momentary.

momento, *m.* moment, while.

momería, *f.* mummery.

momio, mia, *adj.* meager, lean.

momia, *f.* mummy.

momo, *m.* buffoonery, grimaces.

mona, *f.* female monkey; ludicrous imitator; drunkenness; drunkard.

monacal, *adj.* monkish.

monacillo, *m.* acolyte.

monada, *f.* grimace; (coll.) pretty child or thing.

monago or **monaguillo,** *m.* acolyte.

monarca, *m.* monarch.

monarquía, *f.* monarchy.

monárquico, ca, *adj.* monarchical.

monasterio, *m.* monastery, cloister.

monasticismo, *m.* monasticism.

monástico, ca, *adj.* monastic.

monast.º monasterio, mon. monastery.

monda, *f.* pruning of trees.

mondadientes, *m.* toothpick.

mondadura, *f.* cleaning; **—s,** *pl.* parings, peelings.

mondar, *va.* to clean, to cleanse; to trim, to husk, to peel; to deprive of money.

mondo, da, *adj.* neat, clean, pure; **—do, y lirondo,** without any admixture.

mondongo, *m.* paunch, tripe.

moneda, *f.* money, coinage, currency; **— corriente,** currency; **— falsa,** counterfeit; **— legal,** legal tender; **— nacional,** national currency; **casa de —,** mint; **papel —,** paper money.

monedar or **monedear,** *va.* to coin.

monedero, *m.* coiner.

monería, *f.* grimace, mimicry; trifle, gewgaw; cute action of a child.

monetario, *m.* coin collection ; **—, ria,** *adj.* monetary.

moniato, *m.* sweet potato.

monición, *f.* admonition; publication of the bans (of marriage).

monigote, *m.* lay brother; (coll.) bumpkin, dolt, lout; (coll.) poor painting or statue.

monismo, *m.* monism.

mónita, *f.* cunning, craft.

monitor, *m.* admonisher; (naut.) monitor; turret ship.

monje, *m.,* **monja,** *f.* monk; nun.

mono, na, *adj.* (coll.) neat, pretty; cute; **—,** *m.* monkey, ape.

monocromo, *m.* monochrome.

monóculo, *m.* monocle.

monogamia, *f.* monogamy.

monografía, *f.* monograph.

monograma, *m.* monogram.

monolito, *m.* monolith.

monólogo, *m.* monologue.

monomanía, *f.* monomania.

monomio, *m.* monomial.

monoplano, *m.* monoplane.

monopolio, *m.* monopoly.

monopolista, *m. and f.* monopolist, monopolizer.

monosílabo, ba, *adj.* monosyllabical; **—,** *m.* monosyllable.

monoteísmo, *m.* monotheism.

monoteísta, *n. and adj.* monotheist.

monotipia, *f.* monotyping.

monotipo, *m.* monotype.

monotonía, *f.* monotony.

monótono, na, *adj.* monotonous.

monóxido, *m.* (chem.) monoxide.

Mons. Monseñor, Msgr. Monsignor.

Monseñor, *m.* Monseigneur, Monsignor.

monstruo, *m.* monster.

monstruosidad, *f.* monstrosity.

monstruoso, sa, *adj.* monstrous.

monta, *f.* amount, sum total.

montacargas, *m.* elevator, hoist.

montaje, *m.* assembly, mounting; mounting of artillery; **—s,** *pl.* carriage or bed of a cannon.

montante, *m.* broadsword used in fencing; (com.) sum, amount.

montaña, *f.* mountain.

montañés, esa, *adj.* pertaining to the mountains; mountainous; **—,** *n.* mountaineer.

montañoso, sa, *adj.* mountainous.

montar, *vn.* to mount (on horseback); to amount to; **—,** *va.* to set (as diamonds).

montaraz, *adj.* mountainous; wild, untamed.

montazgo, *m.* toll to be paid for cattle passing from one province into another.

monte, *m.* mountain; wood, forest; difficulty; **— alto,** lofty grove; **— bajo,** copse, coppice, brush wood.

montera, *f.* peasant's cap.

montería, *f.* hunting, chase.

montero, *m.* huntsman, hunter.

montés, esa, or **montesino, na,** *adj.* bred or found in a forest or mountain.

monto, *m.* amount, sum.

montón, *m.* heap, pile; mass, cluster; **a —ones,** abundantly, by heaps.

montuoso, sa, *adj.* mountainous, hilly.

montura, *f.* horses and mules intended for the saddle; saddle and trappings; jewel setting.

monumental, *adj.* monumental.

monumento, *m.* monument.

monzón, *m.* monsoon.

moña, *f.* doll; ornament of ribbons for the head; (coll.) drunkenness.

moño, *m.* hair on the crown of the head tied together; tuft of feathers on the heads of some birds.

moquear, *vn.* to blow the nose.

moquete, *m.* blow on the face or nose.

moquillo, *m.* pip (disease in fowls).

moquita, *f.* sniffle, running from the nose.

mora, *f.* blackberry, mulberry.

morada, *f.* habitation, abode, residence.

morado, da, *adj.* violet, mulberry-colored, purple.

morador, ra, *n.* inhabitant, lodger, dweller.

moral, *m.* mulberry-tree; —, *f.* morals, ethics; —, *adj.* moral.

moralidad, *f.* morality, morals.

moralista, *m.* moralist.

moralizar, *vn.* to moralize.

moralmente, *adv.* morally.

morar, *vn.* to inhabit, to dwell.

moratoria, *f.* moratorium.

mórbido, da, *adj.* morbid, diseased, morbose; soft, mellow.

morbo, *m.* disease, distemper.

morboso, sa, *adj.* morbose, diseased, morbid.

morcilla, *f.* blood pudding, kind of sausage.

mordacidad, *f.* mordacity.

mordaz, *adj.* corrosive, biting; sarcastic; mordacious.

mordaza, *f.* gag.

mordedura, *f.* bite.

morder, *va.* (UE) to bite.

mordiente, *m.* mordant.

mordiscar, *va.* to gnaw, to nibble.

mordisco or **mordiscón,** *m.* bite.

morena, *f.* brown bread; sea eel; brunette girl; (geol.) moraine.

moreno, na, *adj.* brown, swarthy; brunette.

morfina, *f.* morphine.

morfológico, ca, *adj.* morphological.

morga, *f.* dregs of oil; coca leaves.

morganático, ca, *adj.* morganatic.

moribundo, da, *adj.* dying.

morigeración, *f.* temperance.

morigerar, *va.* to moderate.

morillo, *m.* andiron.

morir, *vn.* (UE) to die, to expire; —se, to go out, to be extinguished; to be benumbed.

morisco, ca, *adj.* Moorish; —, *m.* Morisco (name given to the Moors who remained in Spain after its restoration).

morisma, *f.* Mohammedan sect; multitude of Moors.

moro, ra, *adj.* and *n.* Moorish; Moor; Moslem; dark-skinned person.

morondanga, *f.* hodgepodge.

morondo, da, *adj.* bald; leafless.

morosidad, *f.* slowness, delay, tardiness, dilatoriness.

moroso, sa, *adj.* slow, tardy, heavy.

morrada, *f.* butting with the heads between two people.

morral, *m.* fodder bag, nose bag; sportsman's bag.

morralla, *f.* hodgepodge.

morrillo, *m.* pebble; fat of the nape of a sheep.

morriña, *f.* murrain; sadness, melancholy.

morrión, *m.* morion, helmet.

morro, *m.* any round skull-like object; overhanging lip.

morrongo, ga, morrono, na, *n.* cat.

morrudo, da, *adj.* blubber-lipped.

mortaja, *f.* shroud, winding sheet; mortise.

mortal, *adj.* mortal; fatal, deadly.

mortalidad, *f.* mortality.

mortandad, *f.* mortality, death rate; large number of deaths due to epidemics, etc.

mortecina, *f.* dead carcass, carrion.

morterete, *m.* small mortar for firing at festivities.

mortero, *m.* mortar.

mortífero, ra, *adj.* fatal.

mortificación, *f.* mortification; vexation, trouble.

mortificar, *va.* to mortify; to afflict, to vex.

mortuorio, *m.* burial, funeral; —, ria, *adj.* mortuary.

moruno, na, *adj.* Moorish.

Mosa, *m.* Meuse.

mosaico, ca, *adj.* Mosaic; —, *m.* tile.

mosca, *f.* fly.

moscardón, *m.* horsefly; importuning, sly fellow.

moscatel, *m.* muscadine or muscatel grape or wine.

moscón, *m.* large fly; crafty, deceitful fellow.

Moscú, *f.* Moscow.

mosquear, *va.* to shoo or drive away flies; to make an angry, clever retort; —se, to resent someone's remarks.

mosquero, *m.* flytrap.

mosquete, *m.* musket.

mosquetería, *f.* body of musketeers; musketry.

mosquetero, *m.* musketeer.

mosquitero, *m.* mosquito net.

mosquito, *m.* gnat, mosquito; tippler; toper, fuddler.

mostacho, *m.* mustache; —s del bauprés, (naut.) bowsprit shrouds.

mostachón, *m.* kind of candy or confection made from almond paste.

mostaza, *f.* mustard; mustard seed; hailshot.

mostillo, *m.* sauce made of must and mustard.

mosto, *m.* must, new wine.

mostrador, ra, *n.* demonstrator; —, *m.* counter; shop front.

mostrar, *va.* (UE) to show, to exhibit; —se, to appear, to show oneself.

mostrenco, ca, *adj.* strayed, ownerless; vagabond, vagrant; ignorant, stupid.

mota, *f.* bit of thread, etc., sticking to cloth; — de empolvarse, powder puff; slight defect or fault.

mote, *m.* nickname; device; (Chile) stewed corn.

moteado, da, *adj.* spotted.
motejar, *va.* to censure, to ridicule.
motilar, *va.* to cut off the hair, to crop.
motín, *m.* mutiny, riot.
motivar, *va.* to give a reason; to cause; to assign a motive.
motivo, *m.* motive, cause, reason; **con este —,** therefore; **con — de,** by reason of.
motocicleta, *f.* motorcycle.
motón, *m.* (naut.) block, pulley.
motonave, *f.* motorship.
motor, ra, *adj.* moving, movable; **—,** *m.* mover; motor, engine; **— de combustión interna** or **de explosión,** internal-combustion engine; **— Diesel,** Diesel engine; **poner en marcha el —,** to start or crank the engine.
motorización, *f.* motorization.
motorizar, *va.* to motorize.
motriz, *adj.* motor, motive, moving.
movedizo, za, *adj.* movable; variable, inconstant.
mover, *va.* (UE) to move; to touch pathetically; to stir up; to excite.
movible, *adj.* movable; motile.
móvil, *adj.* movable; **—,** *m.* motive, incentive.
movilidad, *f.* mobility; inconstancy.
movilización, *f.* mobilization.
movilizar, *va.* to mobilize.
movimiento, *m.* movement, motion; sedition.
moza, *f.* girl, lass; maidservant; last or deciding game.
mozalbete, *m.* lad.
mozo, za, *adj.* young; **—,** *m.* youth, lad; manservant; waiter; **— de caballos,** groom; **— de cuerda,** street porter.
m/p mi pagaré, (com.) my promissory note.
M. P. S. Muy Poderoso Señor, Almighty Lord.
mr. mártir, martyr.
m/r mi remesa, (com.) my remittance, my shipment.
mrd. merced, Grace, Honor (used as a title).
Mro. Maestro, Master, Lord, Teacher.
M.S. manuscrito, Ms. or MS. or ms. manuscript.
m.ˢ a.ˢ muchos años, many years.
M.SS. manuscritos, Mss. or MSS. or mss. manuscripts.
mtd. mitad, mid. middle; half.
muceta, *f.* mantelet worn by an officiating bishop.
mucilaginoso, sa, *adj,* mucilaginous.
mucílago, *m.* mucilage, viscous substance found in certain plants.
muchacha, *f.* girl, lass.
muchacho, *m.* boy, lad; **—, cha,** *adj.* boyish, girlish.
muchedumbre, *f.* crowd, multitude, plenty.
mucho, cha, *adj.* much, abundant; **—o,** *adv.* much.
muda, *f.* change, alteration; act of molting.

mudable, *adj.* changeable, variable, mutable.
mudanza, *f.* change; mutation; inconstancy; **estoy de —,** I am moving.
mudar, *va.* to change; to molt; **—se,** to change; to change one's clothes; to shift; to change house.
mudez, *f.* dumbness.
mudo, da, *adj.* dumb; silent, mute.
mueblaje, *m.* household furniture.
mueble, *m.* piece of furniture; **—s,** *pl.* furniture.
mueblista, *m.* furniture dealer.
mueca, *f.* grimace, wry face.
muela, *f.* upper millstone; grindstone; milldam; hillock; molar tooth; **— cordal** or **del juicio,** wisdom tooth.
muellaje, *m.* dockage.
muelle, *adj.* tender, delicate, soft; **—,** *m.* spring; regulator; quay, wharf; **— real,** mainspring.
muérdago, *m.* mistletoe.
muermo, *n.* (vet.) glanders.
muerte, *f.* death.
muerto, *m.* corpse; **—, ta,** *adj.* dead.
muesca, *f.* notch, groove.
muestra, *f.* pattern, sample; fag end of a piece of cloth; specimen, design, model; (mil.) muster roll; clock dial.
muestrario, *m.* samples, sample book.
mugido, *m.* lowing of an ox.
mugir, *vn.* to low, to bellow.
mugre, *f.* dirt.
mugriento, ta, *adj.* greasy, dirty, filthy.
muguete, *m.* lily-of-the-valley.
mujer, *f.* woman; wife.
mujeriego, *adj.* very fond of women (applied to men).
mujeril, *adj.* womanish, womanly.
mujerío, *m.* women's gathering.
mula, *f.* she-mule.
muladar, *m.* dung heap; anything very dirty.
mular, *adj.* belonging to mules.
mulatero, *m.* muleteer.
mulato, ta, *n.* and *adj.* mulatto.
muleta, *f.* crutch.
mulilla, *f.* small mule; type of ancient shoe.
mulo, *m.* mule.
multa, *f.* mulct, fine, penalty.
multar, *va.* to impose a pecuniary penalty.
multiforme, *adj.* multiform.
multígrafo, *m.* multigraph.
multimillonario, ria, *adj.* and *n.* multimillionaire.
múltiple, *adj.* multiple, manifold.
múltiplex, *adj.* (elec., rad.) multiplex.
multiplicación, *f.* multiplication.
multiplicador, ra, *n.* multiplier; **—,** *m.* (math.) multiplicator.
multiplicando, *m.* (math.) multiplicand.
multiplicar, *va.* to multiply.
multíplice, *adj.* multiple; multiplicious.
multiplicidad, *f.* multiplicity.
multitud, *f.* multitude, crowd.

mullir, *va.* to beat up, to shake up; to fluff.

mundano, na, *adj.* mundane, worldly.

mundial, *adj.* world-wide, of the whole world.

mundo, *m.* world; **todo el —,** everybody.

munición, *f.* ammunition.

municionar, *va.* to munition.

municipal, *adj.* municipal.

munificencia, *f.* munificence, liberality.

muñeca, *f.* wrist; child's doll.

muñeco, *m.* puppet; boy doll; effeminate fellow.

muñidor, *m.* beadle; messenger.

muñir, *va.* to summon; to decide; to direct.

muñón, *m.* brawn; stump of an amputated limb.

muralla, *f.* rampart, wall.

murciélago, *m.* (zool.) bat.

murmullo, *m.* murmur, mutter.

murmuración, *f.* backbiting, calumny; gossip.

murmurador, ra, *n.* detractor, backbiter, gossiper.

murmurar, *vn.* to murmur; to purl; to backbite; to gossip.

murmurio, *m.* murmur.

muro, *m.* wall.

murria, *f.* heaviness of the head.

musa, *f.* Muse.

musaraña, *f.* shrewmouse; goblin; vermin.

musco, ca, *adj.* dark brown; **—,** *m.* moss.

muscular, *adj.* muscular.

músculo, *m.* muscle; **— flexor,** (anat.) flexor.

muselina, *f.* muslin.

museo, *m.* museum.

muserola, *f.* noseband of a bridle.

musgo, *m.* moss.

música, *f.* music; **— de cámara,** chamber music; **— sagrada,** church music.

musical, *adj.* musical.

músico, ca, *n.* musician; **—,** *adj.* musical.

muslo, *m.* thigh.

mustiamente, *adv.* sadly, in a melancholy manner.

mustio, tia, *adj.* parched, withered; sad, sorrowful; musty.

musulmán, musulmano, na, *adj.* Mohammedan.

mutabilidad, *f.* mutability.

mutación, *f.* mutation, change.

mutilación, *f.* mutilation.

mutilador, ra, *n.* mutilator.

mutilar, *va.* to mutilate, to maim.

mutis, *m.* (theat.) exit.

mutismo, *m.* muteness, imposed or voluntary silence.

mutual or **mutuo, tua,** *adj.* mutual, reciprocal.

mutualidad, *f.* mutuality; mutual aid society.

muy, *adv.* very; greatly; **— ilustre,** most illustrious.

Mzo. or **mzo. marzo,** Mar. March.

N

N.: norte, N., No., or no. North; **Notablemente aprovechado,** notably proficient (in an examination).

n.: nacido, b. born; **noche,** night.

n/ nuestro, our.

N.A. Norte América, N.A. North America.

naba, *f.* rutabaga, Swedish turnip.

nabal or **nabar,** *m.* turnip field; **—,** *adj.* pertaining to turnips.

nabo, *m.* turnip.

Nac. nacional, nat. national.

nácar, *m.* mother of pearl.

nacarado, da, *adj.* set with mother-of-pearl; pearl-colored.

nacencia, *f.* tumor, growth.

nacer, *vn.* (NAZCO) to be born, to bud, to shoot (of plants); to rise; to grow; **—se,** to be propagated by nature (as grass).

nacido, da, *adj.* born; proper, apt, fit; **—,** *m.* tumor, abscess.

nacimiento, *m.* birth; Nativity.

nación, *f.* nation.

nacional, *adj.* national.

nacionalidad, *f.* national customs, nationality; citizenship.

nacionalismo, *m.* nationalism.

nacionalista, *m.* and *f.* nationalist.

nacionalización, *f.* nationalization.

nada, *f.* nothing; **—,** *adv.* in no way, by no means.

nadaderas, *f. pl.* swimming bladders (for learning to swim).

nadadero, *m.* swimming pool or beach.

nadador, ra, *n.* swimmer.

nadar, *vn.* to swim.

nadería, *f.* (coll.) a trifle, nothing.

nadie, *m.* nobody, no one.

nado, a —, *adv.* afloat.

nafta, *f.* naphtha.

naftalina, *f.* naphthalene.

naguas, *f. pl.* underskirt, petticoat.

naipe, *m.* playing card.

nalga, *f.* buttock, rump.

nansú, *m.* nainsook.

nao, *f.* ship, vessel.

Nápoles, *m.* Naples.

napolitano, na, *n.* and *adj.* Neapolitan.

naranja, *f.* orange; **jugo de —,** orange juice.

naranjada, *f.* orangeade.

naranjado, da, *adj.* orange-colored.

naranjal, *m.* orange grove.

naranjazo, *m.* blow with an orange.

naranjero, *m.* orange seller; orange tree.

naranjo, *m.* orange tree.

narciso, *m.* (bot.) daffodil; narcissus flower; precious stone of the color of daffodil; fop, coxcomb.

narcosis, *f.* narcosis; **— obstétrica parcial,** twilight sleep.

narcótico, ca, *adj.* and *m.* narcotic.

nardo, *m.* spikenard.

narigón, ona, *adj.* large-nosed; **—,** *m.* large nose; large-nosed person.

narigudo, da, *adj.* big-nosed.
nariz, *f.* nose; sense of smelling; nostril, nozzle.
narración, *f.* narration, account.
narrador, ra, *n.* narrator.
narrar, *va.* to narrate, to tell.
narrativa, *f.* narrative, relation; talent for narration.
N.ª S.ª Nuestra Señora, Our Lady.
nasa, *f.* fisherman's basket.
nasal, *adj.* nasal.
nasturcio, *m.* (bot.) nasturtium.
nata, *f.* cream, whipped cream; **la flor y —,** the cream, the elite.
natal, *adj.* natal, native.
natalidad, *f.* birthrate.
natalicio, cia, *adj.* pertaining to one's birthday; **—,** *m.* birthday.
natatorio, ria, *adj.* swimming; **—,** *m.* swimming place.
natillas, *f. pl.* custard.
natividad, *f.* nativity.
nativo, va, *adj.* native.
natural, *adj.* natural, native; common, usual; ingenuous, unaffected; **—,** *m.* temper, natural disposition; **al —,** unaffectedly; **del —,** from life.
naturaleza, *f.* nature.
naturalidad, *f.* birthright; naturalness; ingenuity; candor.
naturalista, *m.* naturalist.
naturalizar, *va.* to naturalize; **—se,** to become accustomed.
naturalmente, *adv.* naturally, of course.
naufragar, *vn.* to be shipwrecked, to suffer wreck; to suffer ruin in one's affairs.
naufragio, *m.* shipwreck.
náufrago, ga, *adj.* relating to shipwreck; **—,** *n.* shipwrecked person.
náusea, *f.* nauseousness, nausea.
náut. náutico, naut. nautical.
náutica, *f.* art of navigating.
nautilo, *m.* nautilus.
Nav. Navegación, nav. navigation.
náutico, ca, *adj.* nautical.
navaja, *f.* clasp knife; razor; **— de afeitar,** razor; **— de seguridad,** safety razor.
navajada, *f.* gash given with a knife.
navajero, *m.* razor case; shaving towel.
naval, *adj.* naval.
nave, *f.* ship; (arch.) nave.
navegable, *adj.* navigable.
navegación, *f.* navigation, shipping.
navegador or **navegante,** *m.* navigator.
navegante, *m.* navigator, seafarer.
navegar, *vn.* to navigate.
naveta, *f.* (eccl.) censer.
navidad, *f.* nativity; **N—,** Christmas.
naviero, ra, *adj.* shipping; **compañía —,** shipping company; **—,** *m.* shipowner.
navío, *m.* ship; **cocina de —,** cookhouse.
náyade, *f.* naiad, water nymph.
nazi, nazista, *n.* and *adj.* Nazi.
N.B. Nota Bene, (Latin) N.B. take notice.

n/c. or **n/cta. nuestra cuenta,** (com.) our account.
NE nordeste, NE or N.E. northeast.
neblina, *f.* mist, fine rain, drizzle.
nebulón, *m.* two-faced man, hypocrite.
nebuloso, sa, *adj.* misty, cloudy, nebulous, foggy, hazy, drizzling.
necear, *vn.* to talk nonsense.
necedad, *f.* gross ignorance, stupidity; nonsense; imprudence.
necesaria, *f.* privy, water closet, toilet.
necesario, ria, *adj.* necessary.
neceser, *m.* dressing case; vanity case, compact.
necesidad, *f.* necessity, need, want.
necesitado, da, *adj.* necessitous, needy.
necesitar, *va.* to necessitate; **—,** *vn.* to want, to need.
necio, cia, *adj.* ignorant, stupid; foolish; imprudent.
necrocomio, *m.* morgue.
necrología, *f.* necrology, an account of persons deceased.
necrópolis, *m.* burying ground.
necroscopia, *f.* autopsy.
néctar, *m.* nectar.
neerlandés, esa, *n.* and *adj.* Dutch; Dutchman, Dutchwoman; **—,** *m.* Dutch (the language).
nefalismo, *m.* total abstinence from alcohol.
nefando, da, *adj.* base, nefarious, abominable.
nefario, ria, *adj.* nefarious, heinous.
nefas, *adv.* **por fas o por —,** right or wrong.
nefasto, ta, *adj.* sad, unlucky.
negación, *f.* negation.
negar, *va.* (IE) to deny, to abnegate; to refuse; **—se,** to decline to do a thing.
negat. negativo, neg. negative.
negativa, *f.* negation; repulse, refusal; negative.
negativo, va, *adj.* negative.
negligencia, *f.* negligence.
negligente, *adj.* negligent, careless, heedless.
negociación, *f.* negotiation; commerce, business transaction.
negociado, *m.* bureau, division or section of business houses or government.
negociante, *m.* and *f.* trader, dealer, merchant.
negociar, *vn.* to negotiate (bills of exchange, political affairs); to trade.
negocio, *m.* business; affair; negotiation.
negrear, *vn.* to grow black, to appear black.
negrillo, *m.* black poplar.
negro, gra, *adj.* black; jetty; **—,** *n.* Negro; **— de humo,** lampblack.
negrura, *f.* blackness.
negruzco, ca, *adj.* blackish.
nemoroso, sa, *adj.* (poet.) woody, wooded.
nene, na, (coll.) baby.
neófito, *m.* neophyte, greenhorn.
neologismo, *m.* neologism.
neón, *m.* neon; **lámpara —,** neon light.

neoyorquino, na, *n.* and *adj.* New Yorker, from New York.

neozelandés, esa, *n.* and *adj.* New Zealander; of or from New Zealand.

nepotismo, *m.* nepotism.

nervio, *m.* nerve.

nervioso, sa, or **nervoso, sa,** *adj.* nervous; of or pertaining to nerves; excitable; sinewy, strong.

nervudo, da, *adj.* possessing strong and vigorous nerves.

nesga, *f.* gore (of a gown).

neto, ta, *adj.* neat, pure; net.

neumático, *m.* tire; **— balón,** balloon tire; **— desinflado,** deflated tire; **— de recambio** or **repuesto,** spare tire; **—, ca,** *adj.* pneumatic.

neumococo, *m.* pneumococcus.

neumonía, *f.* pneumonia.

neural, *adj.* neural.

neuralgia, *f.* neuralgia.

neurastenia, *f.* (med.) neurasthenia.

neuritis, *f.* (med.) neuritis.

neurología, *f.* neurology.

neurona, *f.* (anat.) neurone.

neuropatía, *f.* (med.) neuropathy.

neurosis, *f.* neurosis; **— de guerra,** shell shock, neurosis resulting from war.

neurótico, ca, *adj.* neurotic.

neutral, *adj.* neutral, neuter.

neutralidad, *f.* neutrality.

neutralización, *f.* neutralization.

neutralizar, *va.* (chem.) to neutralize.

neutro, tra, *adj.* neutral, neuter.

neutrón, *m.* neutron.

nevada, *f.* snowfall.

nevar, *vn. imp.* (IE) to snow.

nevera, *f.* icehouse; icebox.

nevería, *f.* place where ice cream or ices are sold.

nevisca, *f.* snowfall; light fall of snow.

nexo, *m.* nexus.

n/f. nuestro favor, our favor.

n/g. nuestro giro, (com.) our draft.

ni, *conj.* neither, nor.

nícalo, *m.* variety of mushroom.

nicaragüense, *n.* and *adj.* Nicaraguan.

Nicolás, Nicholas.

nicotina, *f.* nicotine.

nictalopia, *f.* night blindness.

nicho, *m.* niche.

nido, *m.* nest; habitation.

niebla, *f.* fog, mist.

nieta, *f.* granddaughter.

nieto, *m.* grandson.

nieve, *f.* snow.

nigromancia, *f.* necromancy, magic.

nigromante, *m.* necromancer, conjurer, magician.

nigromántico, ca, *adj.* necromantic.

nigua, *f.* chigoe, jigger flea.

Nilo, *m.* Nile.

nilón, *m.* nylon.

nimbo, *m.* nimbus, halo.

nimiamente, *adv.* excessively; minutely.

nimiedad, *f.* excess; extravagant nicety.

nimio, mia, *adj.* prolix; stingy; minute.

ninfa, *f.* nymph.

ningún, *adj.* (contraction of **ninguno**), no, not any (*used only before masculine nouns*); **de — modo,** in no way, by no means.

ninguno, na, *adj.* none, not one, neither.

niña, *f.* little girl; **— del ojo,** pupil of the eye; **— de los ojos,** pupil of the eye; (coll.) apple of one's eye.

niñada, *f.* puerility, childishness.

niñear, *vn.* to act like a child.

niñera, *f.* nursemaid.

niñería, *f.* puerility, childish action.

niñero, ra, *adj.* fond of children.

niñez, *f.* childhood.

niño, ña, *adj.* childish; **—,** *m.* child, infant; **desde —ño,** from infancy, from a child.

nipón, ona, *n.* and *adj.* Nipponese, Japanese.

níquel, *m.* nickel.

niquelado, da, *adj.* nickel-plated.

niquelar, *va.* to nickel-plate.

níspero, *m.* medlar tree; persimmon tree.

níspola, *f.* medlar (European fruit resembling a crabapple); (Sp. Am.) persimmon.

nítido, da, *adj.* neat, clean; pure; bright.

nitración, *f.* nitration.

nitrato, *m.* (chem.) nitrate, saltpeter.

nitrificación, *f.* nitrification.

nitrificar, *va.* to nitrify.

nitro, *m.* niter, saltpeter.

nitrobencina, *f.* nitrobenzine.

nitrocelulosa, *f.* nitrocellulose.

nitrógeno, *m.* nitrogen.

nitroglicerina, *f.* nitroglycerine.

nitroso, sa, *adj.* nitrous.

nivel, *m.* level, plane; **a —,** perfectly level.

nivelación, *f.* grading, leveling.

nivelador, *m.* leveler; **—, ra,** *adj.* leveling.

nivelar, *va.* to level.

n/l. or **n/L., nuestra letra,** (com.) our letter, our draft.

NNE nornordeste, NNE or N.N.E. northnortheast.

NNO nornoroeste, NNW or N.N.W. northnorthwest.

NO noroeste, NW or N.W. northwest.

no. or **n.º número,** no. number.

n/o. nuestra orden, (com.) our order.

no, *adv.* no; not.

noble, *adj.* noble, illustrious, generous.

nobleza, *f.* nobleness, nobility.

noción, *f.* notion, idea.

nocivo, va, *adj.* noxious, hurtful, injurious.

nocturno, na, *adj.* nocturnal, nightly; **—,** *m.* nocturn; (mus.) nocturne.

noche, *f.* night; **N— Buena,** Christmas Eve; **¡buenas —s!** good night!

nodriza, *f.* wet nurse.

nódulo, *m.* nodule.

nogal, *m.* walnut tree; walnut (wood).

nómade, *adj.* nomad, nomadic.

nombradía, *f.* and *n.* fame, reputation.

nombramiento, *m.* nomination; appointment.

nombrar, *va.* to name; to nominate; to appoint.

nombre, *m.* name; title; reputation.

nomenclatura, *f.* nomenclature; catalogue.

nomeolvides, *f.* (bot.) forget-me-not.

nómina, *f.* catalogue; pay roll; membership list.

nominador, ra, *n.* nominator, appointer; —, *adj.* nominating.

nominal, *adj.* nominal.

nominativo, *m.* (gram.) nominative.

non, *adj.* odd, uneven.

nona, *f.* (eccl.) nones.

nonada, *f.* trifle.

nonagenario, ria, *adj.* ninety years old; —, *n.* nonagenarian.

nonagésimo, ma, *adj.* ninetieth.

nonato, ta, *adj.* applied to one who has been born by Caesarian operation.

nono, na, *adj.* ninth.

non plus ultra, ne plus ultra, unexcelled, unsurpassed.

nordeste, *m.* northeast.

nórdico, ca, *adj.* and *n.* Nordic.

noria, *f.* chain pump; draw well.

norma, *f.* norm, standard, model, rule; square (tool).

normal, *adj.* normal.

normalidad, *f.* normality.

Normandía, *f.* Normandy.

nornordeste, *m.* north-northeast.

nornoroeste, *m.* north-northwest.

noroeste, *m.* northwest.

norte, *m.* north; rule, guide.

Norte América, *f.* North America.

norteamericano, na, *n.* and *adj.* North American.

Noruega, *f.* Norway.

noruego, ga, *n.* and *adj.* Norwegian.

nos, *pron.* dative of we.

nosotros, tras, *pron.* we, ourselves.

nostalgia, *f.* homesickness, nostalgia.

nota, *f.* note, notice, remark; order, bill; — **bene,** N. B. take notice. — **de entrega,** delivery order; — **musical,** musical note; — **de gastos,** bill of expenses.

notable, *adj.* notable, remarkable, distinguished.

notación, *f.* notation.

notar, *va.* to note, to observe, to mark; to remark.

notaría, *f.* profession of a notary; notary's office.

notario, *m.* notary.

noticia, *f.* notice, knowledge, information, note; news; **en espera de sus —s,** (com.) awaiting your reply.

noticiar, *va.* to inform.

niticiario (de radio), *m.* radio news.

noticioso, sa, *adj.* informed; learned; newsy.

notificación, *f.* notification.

notificador, ra, *n.* announcer.

notificar, *va.* to notify, to inform.

notoriedad, *f.* notoriety.

notorio, ria, *adj.* notorious, well-known.

novación, *f.* (law) novation, substitution of a new obligation for an old one.

noval, *adj.* grown on newly broken up ground; pertaining to newly broken up ground or to the fruits it produces.

novato, ta, *adj.* new; —, *n.* novice, greenhorn

novator, ra, *n.* innovator.

Novbre., nov.ᵉ,9ᵉ, or **9ᵇʳᵉ,noviembre,** Nov. November.

novecientos, tas, *adj.* and *m.* nine hundred.

novedad, *f.* novelty, modernness; admiration excited by novelties; fad; news; —**es,** *pl.* notions.

novela, *f.* novel; falsehood; fiction.

novelero, ra, *adj.* fond of novels; fond of hearing and telling news; new-fangled; inconstant; —, *m.* newsmonger.

novelista, *m.* and *f.* novelist, writer.

novena, *f.* Novena (term of nine days appropriated to some special worship.)

noveno, na, *adj.* ninth.

noventa, *m.* and *adj.* ninety.

novia, *f.* bride; fiancé, woman betrothed.

noviciado, *m.* novitiate.

novicio, cia, *n.* novice.

noviembre, *m.* November.

novilunio, *m.* new moon.

novilla, *f.* heifer.

novillada, *f.* drove of young bulls; fight of young bulls.

novillo, *m.* young bull or ox; **hacer —s,** (coll.) to play truant or hooky.

novio, *m.* bridegroom; fiancé, sweetheart (male).

novísimo, ma, *adj.* newest; —, *m.* each of the four last events of mankind (death, judgment, heaven and hell).

novocaína, *f.* novocaine.

n/p nuestro pagaré, (com.) our promissory note.

n/r nuestra remesa, (com.) our remittance or our shipment.

nra., nro., or **ntra., ntro. nuestra, nuestro,** our, ours.

N.S. Nuestro Señor, Our Lord.

N.S.J.C. Nuestro Señor Jesucristo, Our Lord Jesus Christ.

nto. neto, (com.) nt. net.

nubada, *f.* shower of rain; plenty.

nubado, da, *adj.* clouded (of cloth).

nubarrón, *m.* heavy shower of rain, large cloud.

nube, *f.* cloud; film.

nublado, da, *adj.* cloudy; —, *m.* clouds announcing a storm.

nublarse, *vr.* to be clouded, to become overcast.

nuca, *f.* nape, scruff of the neck.

núcleo, *m.* nucleus, core; kernel of a nut.

nudillo, *m.* knuckle; small knot made in stockings; nodule; small knot.

nudismo, *m.* nudism.

nudo, *m.* knot, gnarl; fastening; knuckle; — **corredizo,** slipknot.

nudoso, sa, *adj.* knotty.

nuera, *f.* daughter-in-law.

nuestramo, ma, *n.* (contraction of NUESTRO AMO) our lord, our lady; (Sp. Am.) the Holy Eucharist.

nuestro, tra, *adj.* and *pron.* our, ours.

nueva, *f.* news.

nuevamente, *adv.* recently, newly.

Nueva York, *f.* New York.

Nueva Zelandia, *f.* New Zealand.

nueve, *m.* and *adj.* nine.

nuevo, va, *adj.* new, modern, fresh; **de —vo,** once more, again; **¿qué hay de — vo?** is there any news? what news?

nuez, *f.* walnut; Adam's apple; **— moscada** or **de especia,** nutmeg.

nulidad, *f.* nullity, nonentity.

nulo, la, *adj.* null, void.

num. or **num.° número,** no. number.

numen, *m.* divinity; inspiration, poetical genius.

numeración, *f.* numeration, numbering.

numerador, *m.* numerator.

numeral, *adj.* numeral.

numerar, *va.* to number, to numerate, to count.

numerario, ria, *adj.* numerary; **—,** *m.* hard cash, coin.

numéricamente, *adv.* by numbers.

numérico, ca, *adj.* numerical.

número, *m.* number; cipher; **— atrasado,** back number; **— redondo,** round number.

numeroso, sa, *adj.* numerous.

numismática, *f.* numismatics.

numismático, *m.* numismatist.

nunca, *adv* never.

nunciatura, *f.* nunciature, office of nuncio.

nuncio, *m.* messenger; nuncio.

nuncupativo, va, *adj.* (law) nuncupative, oral (applied to wills).

nupcial, *adj.* nuptial.

nupcias, *f. pl.* nuptials, wedding.

nutra or **nutria,** *f.* otter.

nutrición, *f.* nutrition, feeding.

nutrimento, *m.* food, nourishment; nutrition.

nutrir, *va.* to nourish.

nutritivo, va, *adj.* nutritive, nourishing.

nutriz, *f.* wet nurse.

Ñ

ñagaza, *f.* birdcall.

ñame, *m.* (bot.) yam.

ñapa, *f.* (Sp. Am.) something over, lagniappe.

ñaque, *m.* hodgepodge.

ñiquiñaque, *m.* (coll.) trash, useless person or thing.

ñizca, *f.* (Sp. Am.) small piece, a little bit.

ñoclo, *m.* kind of macaroon.

ñoño, ña, *adj.* (coll.) decrepit, impaired by age.

ñoñería, *f.* dotage.

O

o, (**ó** when between numbers) *conj.* or.

¡o! *interj.* oh!

O. oeste, W. West.

o/ or **ord. orden,** (com.) ord. order.

oasis, *m.* oasis.

obcecación, *f.* obduracy, stubbornness.

obcecar, *va.* to blind, to darken.

obduración, *f.* obduracy.

obedecer, *va.* (EZCO) to obey.

obediencia, *f.* obedience.

obediente, *adj.* obedient.

obelisco, *m.* obelisk.

obenques, *m. pl.* (naut.) shrouds.

obertura, *f.* (mus.) overture.

obesidad, *f.* obesity.

obeso, sa, *adj.* obese, fat.

óbice, *m.* obstacle.

obispado, *m.* bishopric; episcopate.

obispo, *m.* bishop.

óbito, *m.* death, demise.

obituario, *m.* and *adj.* obituary.

objeción, *f.* objection, opposition; **poner —,** to raise an objection.

objetar, *va.* to object, to oppose.

objetivo, va, *adj.* objective; **—,** *m.* objective, purpose; eyepiece.

objeto, *m.* object, thing.

oblación, *f.* oblation, offering.

oblada, *f.* funeral offering.

oblea, *f.* wafer for sealing letters; (med.) pill, tablet.

oblicuidad, *f.* obliquity.

oblicuo, cua, *adj.* oblique.

obligación, *f.* obligation; bond, debt.

obligacionista, *m.* bondholder.

obligado, *m.* public contractor; (law) obligor; (mus.) obbligato.

obligar, *va.* to oblige, to force.

obligatorio, ria, *adj.* obligatory; required.

obliteración, *f.* obliteration.

oblongo, ga, *adj.* oblong.

ob.° or **obpo. obispo,** Bp. bishop.

oboe, *m.* (mus.) oboe; oboist.

óbolo, *m.* obolus (ancient Greek unit of weight); small contribution.

obra, *f.* work; means; virtue; power; toil, labor, employment; **poner por —,** to set to work; **— maestra,** masterpiece.

obrada, *f.* as much ground as two mules or oxen can plow in a day.

obrador, ra, *n.* workman, workwoman; **—,** *m.* workshop.

obrar, *va.* to work; to operate, to act; to put into practice; **—,** *vn.* to act; to ease nature.

obrepticio, cia, *adj.* (law) obreptitious.

obrero, ra, *n.* workman, workwoman; day-laborer.

obscenidad, *f.* obscenity.

obsceno, na, *adj.* obscene.

obscurantismo, *m.* obscurantism.

obscurecer, *va.* (EZCO) to obscure, to darken; **—,** *v. imp.* to grow dark; **—se,** to

disappear; to become dark.
obscurecimiento, *m.* blackout, darkening.
obscuridad, *f.* obscurity; darkness.
obscuro, ra, *adj.* obscure, dark; **a —as,** in the dark.
obsequiar, *va.* to court; to make a gift of; to entertain.
obsequio, *m.* obsequiousness, compliance; gift.
obsequioso, sa, *adj.* obsequious, compliant, officious.
observación, *f.* observation; remark; **—ones meteorológicas,** study about weather conditions.
observador, ra, *n.* observer; **—,** *adj.* observing.
observancia, *f.* observance, ceremonial reverence.
observar, *va.* to observe, to watch.
observatorio, *m.* observatory.
obsesión, *f.* obsession.
obsesionar, *va.* to obsess, to possess with an idea.
obstáculo, *m.* obstacle, bar, impediment, hindrance.
obstante, participle of **obstar; no —,** notwithstanding, nevertheless.
obstar, *vn.* to oppose, to obstruct, to hinder.
obstetricia, *f.* obstetrics.
obstinación, *f.* obstinacy, stubbornness.
obstinado, da, *adj.* obstinate.
obstinarse, *vr.* to be obstinate, to persist, to be stubborn.
obstrucción, *f.* obstruction.
obstruccionista, *m.* and *f.* obstructionist.
obstructivo, va, *adj.* obstructive.
obstruir, *va.* (UYO) to obstruct; to constipate; **—se,** to be blocked up, to be obstructed.
obtención, *f.* obtainment, attainment.
obtener, *va.* (OBTENGO, OBTUVE), to obtain, to get.
obturador, *m.* stopper; shutter of a camera; **—,** *adj.* able to stop or plug.
obtuso, sa, *adj.* obtuse, blunt.
obue, *m.* (mus.) oboe.
obús, *m.* (mil.) howitzer.
obvención, *f.* perquisite.
obviar, *va.* to obviate, to prevent.
obvio, via, *adj.* obvious, evident.
ocarina, *f.* ocarina (musical instrument).
ocasión, *f.* occasion, opportunity, chance; **de —,** used, secondhand.
ocasional, *adj.* occasional.
ocasionar, *va.* to cause, to occasion; to move, to excite.
ocaso, *m.* occident; decline; sunset.
occidental, *adj.* occidental, western.
occidente, *m.* occident, west.
occipucio, *m* occiput, back of the head.
Oceanía, *f.* Oceania.
océano, *m.* ocean.
oceanografía, *f.* oceanography.
ocelote, *m.* (zool.) ocelot.
ocio, *m.* leisure; pastime; idleness.

ociosidad, *f.* idleness, leisure.
ocioso, sa, *adj.* idle.
ocre, *m.* ochre.
octagonal, *adj.* octagonal.
octágono, *m.* octagon.
octano, *m.* (chem.) octane.
octava, *f.* octave.
octavario, *m.* eight days' festival.
Octavio, Octavius.
octavo, va, *adj.* eighth; **libro en —o,** octavo volume.
octeto, *m.* (mus.) octet.
Octbre, oct.ᵉ, 8 bre., 8ᵉ, or 8ᵇʳᵉ octubre, Oct. October.
octogenario, ria, *n.* octogenarian.
octogésimo, ma, *m.* and *adj.* eightieth.
octubre, *m.* October.
ocular, *adj.* ocular; **—,** *m.* eyeglass.
oculista, *m.* oculist.
ocultación, *f.* concealment.
ocultar, *va.* to hide, to conceal.
ocultismo, *m.* occultism.
oculto, ta, *adj.* hidden, concealed, secret.
ocupación, *f.* occupation; business, employment.
ocupado, da, *adj.* busy; occupied.
ocupar, *va.* to occupy, to hold an office; **—se,** to occupy, to follow a business; **— en** or **de,** to give attention to.
ocurrencia, *f.* occurrence, event, incident; accident; idea occurring to the mind; witty remark.
ocurrir, *vn.* to meet; to occur, to happen.
ochavado, da, *adj.* octagonal, eight-sided.
ochavar, *va.* to form an octagon.
ochavo, *m.* small Spanish brass coin valued at two maravedies.
ochenta, *m.* and *adj.* eighty.
ocho, *m.* and *adj.* eight.
ochocientos, *m.* and *adj.* eight hundred.
oda, *f.* ode.
odiar, *va.* to hate; **—se,** to hate one another.
odio, *m.* hatred.
odioso, sa, *adj.* odious, hateful.
odisea, *f.* odyssey.
odómetro, *m.* odometer, cyclometer.
odontología, *f.* odontology.
odontólogo, *m.* odontologist.
odontorrea, *f.* odontorrhagia (bleeding of gums).
odorífero, ra, *adj.* fragrant.
odre, *m.* wine bag; drunkard.
oesnorueste, *m.* west-northwest.
oessudueste, *m.* west-southwest.
oeste, *m.* west; west wind.
ofender, *va.* to offend, to injure; **—se,** to be vexed; to take offense.
ofensa, *f.* offense, injury.
ofensivo, va, *adj.* offensive, injurious.
ofensor, ra, *n.* offender; **—,** *adj.* offending.
oferta, *f.* offer; offering; **— y demanda,** supply and demand.
ofertorio, *m.* offertory.
oficial, *adj.* official; **—,** *m.* officer; official;

workman; clerk in a public office; — **de intercomunicación y coordinación,** liaison officer; — **de sanidad,** health officer; — **mayor,** chief clerk.

oficiala, *f.* trained working woman; forewoman.

oficiar, *va.* to officiate, to minister (of clergymen, etc.).

oficina, *f.* workshop; office, countinghouse; bureau.

oficio, *m.* office, employ, occupation, ministry; function; official letter; trade, business; notary's office; —s, *pl.* divine service.

oficiosidad, *f.* diligence; officiousness; importunity.

oficioso, sa, *adj.* officious, diligent; meddling.

ofrecer, *va.* (EZCO) to offer; to present; to exhibit; —se, to offer, to occur, to present itself.

ofrecimiento, *m.* offer, promise.

ofrenda, *f.* offering, oblation.

ofrendar, *va.* to present offerings to God.

oftalmía, *f.* ophthalmia.

oftalmología, *f.* ophthalmology.

oftalmólogo, *m.* occultist; ophthalmologist.

ofuscación, *f.* dimness of sight; obfuscation.

ofuscar, *va.* to darken, to render obscure; to confuse.

ogro, *m.* monster in fairy tales, ogre.

¡oh! *interj.* o! oh!

ohmio, *m.* (elec.) ohm.

oída, *f.* hearing; **de** or **por** —s, by hearsay.

oído, *m.* hearing; ear; touch hole; **hablar al** —, to whisper.

oidor, ra, *n.* hearer; —, *m.* special Spanish judge in olden times.

oír, *va.* (OIGO, oí), to hear; to listen; to understand.

ojal, *m.* buttonhole.

¡ojalá! *interj.* would to God! God grant!

ojaladura, *f.* the set of buttonholes in a suit of clothes.

ojalar, *va.* to make buttonholes.

ojeada, *f.* glance, look.

ojear, *va.* to eye, to view; to glance; to rouse or put up game by hallooing.

ojeo, *m.* putting up of game for the chase by hallooing.

ojera, *f.* dark circle under the eye (from illness or exhaustion); eyecup.

ojeriza, *f.* spite, grudge, illwill.

ojete, *m.* eyelet hole in clothes; (coll.) anus.

ojimel, *m.* oxymel.

ojiva, *f.* Gothic or painted window.

ojival, *adj.* ogival, having a pointed arch.

ojo, *m.* eye; sight; eye of a needle; **en un abrir y cerrar de** —s, in the twinkling of an eye, in a moment.

ola, *f.* wave, billow.

olaje, *m.* succession of waves, sea swell.

oleada, *f.* surge; violent emotion.

oleaginoso, sa, *adj.* oleaginous, oily.

oleaje, *m.* surf; **baño de** —, surf bathing.

olear, *va.* to administer extreme unction.

óleo, *m.* oil; extreme unction; holy oil.

oleoducto, *m.* oil pipe line.

oleomargarina, *f.* oleomargarine.

oler, *va.* (HUELO, OLÍ), to smell, to scent; —, *vn.* to smell; to smack of.

olfatear, *va.* and *vn.* to smell, to scent, to sniff.

olfato, *m.* sense of smell; scent.

oligarquía, *f.* oligarchy.

oligárquico, ca, *adj.* oligarchical.

olímpico, ca, *adj.* Olympic.

Olimpo, *m.* Olympus.

oliva, *f.* olive; olive tree; owl.

olivar, *m.* olive grove.

Oliverio, Oliver.

olivo, *m.* olive tree.

olmo, *m.* elm tree.

ológrafo, *adj.* holographic.

olor, *m.* odor, scent.

oloroso, sa, *adj.* fragrant, odorous, aromatic.

olvidadizo, za, *adj.* forgetful.

olvidar, *va.* and *vr.* to forget.

olvido, *m.* forgetfulness; oversight.

olla, *f.* round earthen pot, kettle; gulf, whirlpool; — **podrida,** dish composed of different boiled meats and vegetables.

ollería, *f.* pottery.

ollero, ra, *n.* potter.

ombligo, *m.* navel.

ombría, *f.* shady place.

ominar, *va.* to foretell.

ominoso, sa, *adj.* ominous.

omisión, *f.* omission.

omitir, *va.* to omit.

ómnibus, *m.* omnibus, bus.

omnipotencia, *f.* omnipotence.

omnipotente, *adj.* omnipotent, almighty.

omnipresencia, *f.* omnipresence.

omnisciente or **omniscio, cia,** *adj.* all knowing.

omnívoro, ra, *adj.* omnivorous.

omóplato, *m.* scapula, shoulder blade.

once, *m.* and *adj.* eleven.

onceno, na, *adj.* eleventh.

onda, *f.* wave (of water, etc.); (radio) wave; wave length; — **corta,** (radio) short wave; — **sonora,** sound wave.

ondear, *va.* and *vn.* to undulate, to wave; to fluctuate; —se, to seesaw.

ondómetro, *m.* radio-wave meter.

ondulación, *f.* corrugation, waving; — **permanente,** permanent wave.

ondulado, da, *adj.* corrugated, waved; —**o al agua,** water wave; —**o permanente,** permanent wave.

ondular, *vn.* to undulate, to ripple.

oneroso, sa, *adj.* burdensome, heavy.

ónice, ónique or **ónix,** *m.* (min.) onyx.

ONO oesnorueste, WNW or W.N.W. West-Northwest.

ontología, *f.* ontology.

onz. onza, oz. ounce.

onza, *f.* ounce (weight); ounce (snow leopard).

onzavo, va, *adj.* eleventh; —, *m.* eleventh part.

opacidad, *f.* opacity, gloom, darkness.
opaco, ca, *adj.* opaque, dark; melancholy, gloomy.
opalescencia, *f.* opalescence.
opalino, na, *adj.* opalescent.
ópalo, *m.* opal.
opción, *f.* option, choice.
ópera, *f.* opera.
operación, *f.* operation; business transaction; — **cesárea,** Caésarean operation.
operar, *va.* and *vn.* to operate, to act; —**se,** (med.) to have an operation.
operario, ria, *n.* operator, laborer.
opereta, *f.* operetta.
opiato, ta, *adj.* and *m.* opiate.
opilación, *f.* obstruction of the body; amenorrhea, stoppage of menstruation.
opilarse, *vr.* to contract amenorrhea.
ópimo, ma, *adj.* rich, fruitful.
opinable, *adj.* problematical.
opinar, *va.* and *vn.* to give an opinion.
opinión, *f.* opinion.
opio, *m.* opium.
opíparo, ra, *adj.* sumptuous.
oponer, *va.* (OPONGO, OPUSE), to oppose; —**se,** to oppose, to object, to be opposite.
oponible, *adj.* capable of being resisted.
oporto, *m.* port wine.
oportunamente, *adv.* opportunely, in due time.
oportunidad, *f.* opportunity, chance.
oportunismo, *m.* opportunism.
oportuno, na, *adj.* seasonable, opportune, timely.
oposición, *f.* opposition; competition of skill.
opositor, ra, *n.* opposer, opponent.
opresión, *f.* oppression.
opresivo, va, *adj.* oppressive.
opresor, ra, *n.* oppressor.
oprimir, *va.* to oppress; to crush, to press, to squeeze.
oprobio, *m.* opprobrium, ignominy, infamy.
optar, *va.* to choose, to elect.
optativo, *m.* (gram.) optative.
óptica, *f.* optics.
óptico, ca, *adj.* optic, optical; —, *m.* optician.
optimismo, *m.* optimism.
optimista, *m.* and *f.* optimist; —, *adj.* optimistic, hopeful.
óptimo, ma, *adj.* best.
optómetra, *m.* optometrist.
optometría, *f.* optometry.
opuesto, ta, *adj.* opposite, contrary.
opugnación, *f.* attack, opposition.
opulencia, *f.* wealth, riches.
opulento, ta, *adj.* opulent, wealthy.
opúsculo, *m.* opuscule.
oquedad, *f.* cavity, hollow; (fig.) emptiness or hollowness of what is written or said.
ora, *conj.* whether, either; — **esto,** — **aquello,** now this, now that.
oración, *f.* oration, speech; prayer; (gram.) sentence.
oráculo, *m.* oracle.

orador, ra, *n.* orator, speaker.
oral, *adj.* oral.
oralmente, *adv.* orally.
orangután, *m.* (zool.) orang-outang.
orar, *vn.* to harangue; to pray.
oratoria, *f.* oratory, rhetorical skill.
oratorio, *m.* oratory; oratorio; —, **ria,** *adj.* rhetorical.
orbe, *m.* orb, sphere, the earth; the globe; celestial body.
órbita, *f.* orbit, socket.
orbital, *adj.* orbital.
orden, *m.* order; — **de batalla,** battle array; — **del día,** order of the day; roster; —, *f.* order, command; **a sus órdenes,** at your service.
ordenación, *f.* arrangement; ordination; edict, ordinance.
ordenado, da, *adj.* neat, orderly.
ordenando, *m.* candidate for holy orders.
ordenanza, *f.* order; statute, rule; ordinance; ordination.
ordenar, *va.* to arrange; to order, to command; to ordain; —**se,** to take holy orders.
ordeñador, ra, *n.* and *adj.* milker; milking; **máquina** —, milking machine.
ordeñar, *va.* to milk.
ordinal, *adj.* ordinal.
ordinario, ria, *adj.* ordinary, usual, common; coarse; —, *m.* ordinary, established judge of ecclesiastical cases; carrier, carman; **acciones** —**rias,** common stock; **de** —**rio,** regularly, commonly, ordinarily.
orea, *f.* wood nymph.
orear, *va.* to cool, to refresh; to air; —**se,** to take the air.
orégano, *m.* wild marjoram (an aromatic mint plant).
oreja, *f.* auricle, ear; hearing; flap of shoe; —**s de mercader,** deaf ears; **con las** —**s caídas,** crestfallen.
orejera, *f.* ear muff, earflap.
orejón, *m.* pull by the ear; preserved peach; young nobleman of the ancient nobility of Peru.
oreo, *m.* breeze, fresh air.
orfandad, *f.* orphanage.
organdí, *m.* organdy.
organero, *m.* organ builder.
orgánico, ca, *adj.* organic; harmonious.
organillero, *m.* organ grinder.
organillo, *m.* hand organ.
organismo, *m.* organization; organism.
organista, *m.* and *f.* organist.
organización, *f.* organization; arrangement.
organizador, ra, *n.* and *adj.* organizer; organizing.
organizar, *va.* to organize.
órgano, *m.* organ; — **de cañones,** pipe organ.
orgía, *f.* orgy, drunken revel.
orgl. original, original; (print.) copy, manuscript.
orgullo, *m.* pride, haughtiness.

orgulloso, sa, *adj.* proud, haughty.
orientación, *f.* orientation, position, adjustment.
oriental, *adj.* oriental, eastern.
orientar, *va.* to orient, to adjust in or accommodate to a position; **—se,** to find one's bearings.
oriente, *m.* orient, east.
orificación, *f.* filling (of tooth).
orificio, *m.* orifice, mouth, opening.
origen, *m.* origin, source; natal country; family, extraction.
original, *adj.* original, primitive; novel, new; **—,** *m.* original, first copy.
originalidad, *f.* originality.
originar, *va.* and *vn.* to originate, to come from.
originario, ria, *adj.* originary, coming from.
orilla, *f.* limit, border, edge; margin; edge of cloth; sidewalk; shore.
orillar, *vn.* and *va.* to approach the shore; to arrange, to put in order.
orillo, *m.* list of cloth, selvage.
orín, *m.* rust; **—es,** *pl.* urine.
orina, *f.* urine.
orinal, *m.* chamber pot.
orinar, *vn.* to urinate.
oriol, *m.* (orn.) golden oriole or thrush.
oriundo, da, *adj.* derived from; native of.
orla, *f.* list, selvage, border.
orladura, *f.* border, edging, list.
orlar, *va.* to border, to edge.
orn. orden, ord. order.
ornamentación, *f.* ornamentation.
ornamento, *m.* ornament, embellishment.
ornar, *va.* to trim, to adorn.
ornato, *m.* ornament, decoration.
ornitología, *f.* ornithology.
ornitólogo, *m.* ornithologist.
oro, *m.* gold; money; **de —,** golden; **patrón —,** gold standard; **—s,** *pl.* diamonds (in cards).
oropel, *m.* tinsel.
orquesta, *f.* orchestra.
orquestación, *f.* orchestration.
orquídea, *f.* orchid.
ortiga, *f.* (bot.) nettle.
ortodoxia, *f.* orthodoxy.
ortodoxo, xa, *adj.* orthodox.
ortografía, *f.* orthography, spelling.
ortográfico, ca, *adj.* orthographical.
ortopédico, ca, *adj.* orthopedic.
ortopedista, *m.* and *f.* orthopedist.
oruga, *f.* (bot.) rocket; caterpillar.
orujo, *m.* peel of pressed grapes.
orza, *f.* jar, crock; (naut.) luff.
os, *pron.* dative of you, to you.
osa, *f.* she-bear; **O— Mayor,** (ast.) Great Bear, the Dipper.
osadamente, *adv.* boldly, daringly.
osadía, *f.* boldness, intrepidity; zeal, fervor.
osambre, *m.,* or **osamenta,** *f.* skeleton, bones.
osar, *vn.* to dare, to venture.
osar or **osario,** *m.* charnel house.

oscilación, *f.* oscillation.
oscilador, *m.* oscillator.
oscilar, *vn.* to oscillate.
ósculo, *m.* kiss.
oscurantismo, *m.* obscurantism.
oscurecer, *va.* (EZCA) to be cloudy; to become dark.
oscurecimiento, *m.* blackout, darkening.
oscuro, ra, *adj.* obscure, dark; **a —as,** in the dark.
óseo, sea, *adj.* osseous.
osificarse, *vr.* to ossify.
ósmosis, *f.* osmosis.
OSO oessudueste, WSW or W.S.W. westsouthwest.
oso, *m.* bear; **— blanco,** polar bear, **— pardo,** grizzly bear; **— hormiguero,** anteater.
ostensible, *adj.* ostensible, apparent.
ostensión, *f.* show, exhibition, manifestation.
ostensivo, va, *adj.* ostensive.
ostentación, *f.* ostentation, ambitious display, vain show.
ostentar, *va.* to show, to display; **—,** *vn.* to boast, to brag.
ostentoso, sa, *adj.* sumptuous, ostentatious.
osteología, *f.* osteology.
osteópata, *m.* and *f.* osteopath.
osteopatía, *f.* osteopathy.
ostiario, *m.* ostiary, doorkeeper.
ostra, *f.* oyster.
ostracismo, *m.* ostracism.
ostrera, *f.* oyster bed.
ostrogodo, da, *adj.* Ostrogothic.
osudo, da, *adj.* bony, full of bones.
otalagia, *f.* (med.) otalagia, earache.
otear, *va.* to observe, pry into.
otero, *m.* hill, knoll.
otología, *f.* (med.) otology.
otólogo, *m.* ear specialist.
otomano, na, *m.* and *adj.* Ottoman; **—,** *f.* couch, divan.
Otón, Otho.
otoñal, *adj.* autumnal.
otoñar, *vn.* to spend the autumn; to grow in autumn; **—se,** to be seasoned, to be tempered (applied to earth after rain).
otoño, *m.* autumn, fall.
otorgamiento, *m.* grant; license; contract.
otorgante, *m.* and *f.* maker (of a deed); grantor.
otorgar, *va.* to consent, to grant; to stipulate.
otoscopia, *f.* otoscopy.
otro, otra, *adj.* another, other.
otrosí, *adv.* besides, moreover; **—,** *m.* item; (law) any pleading subsequent to the original.
ovación, *f.* ovation.
ovalado, da, *adj.* oval-shaped.
óvalo, *m.* oval.
ovar, *vn.* to lay eggs.
ovario, *m.* ovary.
ovariotomía, *f.* (med.) ovariotomy.

ovaritis, *f.* (med.) ovaritis.
oveja, *f.* sheep.
ovejero, ra, *n.* shepherd, shepherdess; raiser of sheep.
ovejuno, na, *adj.* relating to sheep.
overal, *m.* flying suit.
Ovidio, Ovid.
ovillar, *vn.* to wind off from a reel, to reel off; to coil up; **—se,** to double oneself up.
ovillo, *m.* ball (of yarn, etc.); round, tangled thing; confusion of things.
ovíparo, ra, *adj.* oviparous, egg-bearing.
ovoso, sa, *adj.* full of seaweed.
óvulo, *m.* ovule.
oxiacetilénico, ca, *adj.* oxyacetylene.
oxidación, *f.* oxidation.
oxidar, *va.* and *vr.* to rust, to oxidize.
óxido, *m.* (chem.) oxide.
oxigenación, *f.* oxygenation.
oxigenado, da, *adj.* oxygenated; **rubia —da,** peroxide blonde.
oxígeno, *m.* (chem.) oxygen.
¡oxte! *interj.* keep off! begone! **sin decir — ni moxte,** without saying a word.
oyamel, *m.* (bot.) Mexican fir.
oyente, *adj.* and *n.* hearing; auditor, hearer; **—s,** *pl.* audience.
ozona, *f.,* **ozono,** *m.* ozone.

P

P.: Padre, Father; **Papa,** Pope; **pregunta,** Q. question.
p.: pagaré, (com.) promissory note; **pasivo,** pass. passive; **por,** per, for or by.
P.A.: por ausencia, in the absence; **por autorización,** by authority; **Prensa Asociada,** A.P. Associated Press.
pa. or p.ª para, for, to, in order to.
pabellón, *m.* pavilion; summer house; flag.
pábilo or **pabilo,** *m.* wick; snuff of a candle.
Pablo, Paul.
pábulo, *m.* food, nourishment; spiritual maintenance.
paca, *f.* paca, a South American rodent; bale, bundle.
pacana, *f.* pecan tree; pecan nut.
pacato, ta, *adj.* pacific, quiet, mild, gentle, tender, peaceable.
pacer, *vn.* (AZCO) to pasture, to graze.
paciencia, *f.* patience.
paciente, *adj.* and *n.* patient.
pacificación, *f.* pacification; peace of mind.
pacificador, ra, *n.* peacemaker.
pacificar, *va.* to pacify, to appease; **—,** *vn.* to deal for peace.
Pacífico, *m.* and *adj.* Pacific.
pacífico, ca, *adj.* pacific, peaceful.
pacifista, *m.* and *adj.* pacifist.
Paco, Frank.
paco, *m.* (zool.) alpaca.
pacotilla, *f.* goods shipped by sailors free of charge; business venture; **de —,** (coll.) of inferior quality.

pacotillero, ra, *n.* peddler, street vendor.
pactar, *va.* to contract, to stipulate.
pacto, *m.* contract, pact.
pachorra, *f.* sluggishness.
padecer, *va.* (EZCO) to suffer any bodily affliction; to sustain an injury; to be liable to.
padecimiento, *m.* suffering, sufferance.
padilla, *f.* little frying pan; small oven.
padrastro, *m.* stepfather; hangnail.
padrazo, *m.* overindulgent father.
padre, *m.* father; **—s,** *pl.* parents; ancestors; all the members of a religious congregation taken as a body.
padrenuestro, *m.* the Our Father, the Lord's Prayer.
padrinazgo, *m.* compaternity; sponsorship.
padrino, *m.* godfather; second, sponsor; protector; **— de boda,** groomsman.
padrón, *m.* poll, census; (coll.) indulgent parent; pattern, model.
paella, *f.* rice meat, rice chicken dish.
pág. página, p. page.
paga, *f.* payment, fee, wage.
pagadero, ra, *adj.* payable.
pagador, ra, *n.* payer; paying teller.
pagaduría, *f.* paymaster's office.
paganismo, *m.* paganism, heathenism.
pagano, *m.* heathen, pagan; one who pays or contributes his share; **—, na,** *adj.* heathenish; pagan.
pagar, *va.* to pay; to requite; to atone; **—se de,** to be pleased (with); to boast (about).
pagaré, *m.* bond, note of hand, promissory note, due bill, I. O. U.
pagd.º, pagd.ª pagado, pagada, (com.) pd. paid.
página, *f.* page of a book.
paginación, *f.* pagination.
pago, *m.* pay, payment; reward; **— al contado,** cash payment.
pagoda, *f.* pagoda.
paila, *f.* kettle; boiler; (Cuba) sugar pan.
país, *m.* country, region; **¡vaya un—!** some country! what a country!
paisaje, *m.* landscape.
paisanaje, *m.* peasantry, lay inhabitants of a country; relationship due to being of the same country.
paisano, na, *adj.* of the same country; **—,** *n.* countryman (or woman).
paja, *f.* straw; **echar —s,** to draw lots with straws.
pajar, *m.* straw loft.
pajarear, *va.* to go birdcatching; **—,** *vn.* to loiter about.
pajarera, *f.* aviary.
pajarero, ra, *adj.* gay, merry; **—,** *m,* bird-catcher.
pájaro, *m.* bird; sly, acute fellow; **a vista de —,** bird's-eye view; **— de cuenta,** person of importance.
pajarota or **pajarotada,** *f.* false, idle report.
pajarraco or **pajaruco,** *m.* large bird; cunning fellow.

paje, *m.* page.
pajera, *f.* stack of straw.
pajero, *m.* dealer in straw.
pajizo, za, *adj.* made of straw; thatched with straw; straw-colored.
pajuela, *f.* short straw; sulphur match.
pala, *f.* shovel; vamp of a shoe.
palabra, *f.* word; **a media —,** at the least hint; **de —,** by word of mouth. **dirigir la —,** to address; **libertad de —,** freedom of speech; **pedir la —,** to ask for the floor in public speaking; **tener la —,** to have the floor.
palabrada, *f.* low language, uncouth word.
palabrería, *f.* verbalism.
palabrero, ra, *adj.* talkative, loquacious.
palabrita, *f.* short word; word full of meaning.
palabrota, *f.* an uncouth word.
palaciego, ga, *adj.* pertaining or relating to the palace; **—,** *n.* courtier.
palacio, *m.* palace.
palada, *f.* a shovelful.
paladar, *m.* palate; taste, relish.
paladín, *m.* paladin, knight, champion.
paladino, na, *adj.* manifest, clear, public; **—,** *m.* paladin, champion.
palafrén, *m.* palfrey.
palafrenero, *m.* groom.
palanca, *f.* lever, bar, handle· **— de cambio de marcha,** reverse lever; **— de desenganche,** firing lever; **— de embrague,** clutch lever; **— de impulsión,** driving or operating lever; **— de hierro,** crowbar.
palancada, *f.* leverage
palancana or **palangana,** *f.* basin, washbowl.
palanquera, *f.* enclosure made with stakes.
palanqueta, *f.* bar shot; small lever.
palatinado, *m.* palatinate.
palatino, na, *adj.* belonging to the palace or courtiers.
palco, *m.* box in a theater.
palenque, *m.* passage from the pit to the stage in a theater; palisade; arena.
paleografía, *f.* paleography.
paleógrafo, *m.* paleographer.
paleolítico, *adj.* paleolithic.
paleontología, *f.* paleontology, study of fossils
paleontólogo, *m.* paleontologist.
paleozoico, *adj.* (geol.) Paleozoic.
palero, *m.* shoveler.
Palestina, *f.* Palestine.
palestra, *f.* inclosure, palisade: palaestra; art of wrestling; literary forum.
paleta, *f.* fire shovel; palette; trowel; **— de hélice,** propeller blade.
paletada, *f.* trowelful.
paleto, *m.* fallow deer; yokel, rustic.
paletó, *m.* man's frock coat.
palia, *f.* (eccl) altar cloth; pall.
paliar, *va.* to palliate, to excuse; to cloak.
paliativo, va, *adj.* palliative.
palidecer, *vn.* (EZCO) to turn pale.

palidez, *f.* paleness, wanness.
pálido, da, *adj.* pallid, pale, ghastly.
palillero, *m.* one who makes or sells toothpicks; toothpick case.
palillo, *m.* small stick; knitting needle case; rolling pin; toothpick; **—s,** *pl.* bobbins; drumsticks; castanets.
palinodia, *f.* palinody, recantation.
palio, *m.* cloak; pall.
palique, *m.* (coll.) trifling conversation.
palitroque, *m.* rough, ill-shaped stick.
paliza, *f.* cudgeling, drubbing with a stick.
palizada, *f.* palisade.
palma, *f.* date palm tree; palm of the hand; palm leaf; **ganar la —,** to carry the day; **batir —s,** to clap hands.
palmada, *f.* slap given with the palm of the hand, clap; **—s,** *pl.* clapping of hands.
palmatoria, *f.* low candlestick; (coll.) ferule.
palmear, *vn.* to clap hands.
palmera, *f.* palm tree.
palmeta, *f.* ferule.
palmito, *m.* palmetto.
palmo, *m.* palm; **— a —,** inch by inch.
palmotear, *vn.* to clap hands, to applaud.
palmoteo, *m.* clapping of hands.
palo, *m.* stick; cudgel; post; blow given with a stick; execution on the gallows; suit in cards; **—s,** *pl.* masting.
paloma, *f.* dove, pigeon; **— torcaz,** ring dove; **— viajera** or **mensajera,** homing pigeon, carrier pigeon; **— zorita,** wood pigeon.
palomar, *m.* pigeon house.
palomera, *f.* small dovecot; bleak place much exposed to the wind
palomilla, *f.* young pigeon; backbone of a horse; chrysalis; horse of a milk-white color; (Mex) boys' gang.
palomina, *f.* pigeon dung; (bot.) fumitory.
palomino, *m.* young pigeon; (coll.) stain of excrement upon the tail of a shirt.
palomita, *f.* squab; **—s de maíz,** popcorn.
palomo, *m.* cock pigeon.
palotada, *f.* stroke with a battledore.
palote, *m.* stick of a middling size; drumstick; stroke in penmanship.
paloteo, *m.* fight with sticks; clash.
palpabilidad, *f.* palpability.
palpable, *adj.* palpable, evident.
palpar, *va.* to feel, to touch, to grope.
pálpebra, *f.* eyelid.
palpitación, *f.* palpitation, panting.
palpitar, *vn.* to palpitate, to beat, to throb.
palpo, *m.* (zool.) feeler.
paludismo, *m.* malaria.
palurdo, da, *adj.* rustic, boorish, rude.
pampa, *f.* great plain, prairie; tree in Philippines; open field for military maneuvers.
pámpana, *f.* vine leaf.
pampanilla, *f.* loin cloth of leaves worn by the Indians.
pámpano, *m.* young vine-branch or tendril; pompano (a fish).

pampanoso, sa, *adj.* abounding in tendrils.
pampero, ra, *n.* Pampas man or woman; **—,** *adj.* relative to the Pampas; **—,** *m.* violent wind of South America.
pampirolada, *f.* kind of garlic sauce; (fig. and coll.) trivial nonsense.
pamplina, *f.* (bot.) chickweed; (coll.) nonsense; trifle.
pamplinada, *f.* nonsense; frivolity, trifle.
pamporcino, *m.* (bot.) cyclamen.
pampringada, *f.* slice of bread and gravy; (coll.) frivolous thing.
pan, *m.* bread; loaf; food in general; wheat; gold or silver leaf; **— tostado,** toasted bread.
pana, *f.* plush, corduroy, velveteen.
panacea, *f.* panacea, universal medicine.
panadería, *f.* trade of a baker; bakery.
panadero, ra, *n.* baker.
panal, *m.* honeycomb; sweet rusk.
panameño, ña, *n.* and *adj.* Panamanian, from Panama.
panarra, *m.* dolt, simpleton.
páncreas, *m.* pancreas.
pancromático, ca, *adj.* panchromatic.
panda, *f.* (zool.) panda; gallery in a cloister.
pandear, *vn.* to warp; to belly; to bulge.
pandemia, *f.* pandemia.
pandemónium, *m.* pandemonium.
panderada, *f.* group of tambourine players.
pandereta, *f.* tambourine.
pandero, *m.* timbrel, tambourine.
pandilla, *f.* plot, league; gang.
pando, da, *adj.* bulging, convex.
pandorga, *f.* (coll.) fat, bulky woman; kite.
panegírico, ca, *adj.* panegyrical; **—,** *m.* eulogy.
panegirista, *m.* panegyrist.
panera, *f.* granary; bread basket.
pánfilo, la, *n.* slow, sluggish, heavy person.
panfleto, *m.* roorback.
paniaguado, *m.* servant; protegé.
pánico, ca, *adj.* panic, frightful; **—,** *m.* panic, fright.
paniego, ga, *adj.* eating or yielding much bread; **—,** *m.* bag for carrying coal to be sold.
panilla, *f.* small measure of oil.
panizo, *m.* (bot.) panic grass.
panoja, *f.* (bot.) panicle.
panoplia, *f.* panoply.
panorama, *m.* panorama.
pantalones, *m. pl.* trousers, pants, pantaloons, panties; **— cortos** or **largos,** short or long pants or trousers; **— de mujer,** pantaloons, panties; **— bombachos,** slacks or loose-fitting pants; **— de media pierna para jugar al golf,** golf knickers; **— de equitación** or **de montar,** riding breeches.
pantalla, *f.* screen, fire screen; lamp shade; (fig.) person or object obstructing view.
pantano, *m.* pool of stagnant water, swamp, morass; tarn; (fig.) obstacle, difficulty, great hindrance.

pantanoso, sa, *adj.* marshy, fenny, boggy.
panteísta, *m.* and *f.* pantheist.
panteón, *m.* Pantheon; cemetery.
pantera, *f.* panther.
pantógrafo, *m.* pantograph.
pantomima, *f.* pantomime.
pantomímico, ca, *adj.* pantomimical.
pantomimo, *m.* pantomimist.
pantorrilla, *f.* calf (of the leg).
pantorrilludo, da, *adj.* having very large or thick calves.
pantufla, flo, *n.* slipper, shoe.
panza, *f.* belly, paunch.
panzada, *f.* bellyful of food.
panzudo, da, *adj.* big-bellied.
pañal, *m.* swaddling cloth; cloth in which anything is wrapped up; tail of a shirt; **estar en —es,** to be in an incipient stage.
pañero, *m.* wool merchant, clothier.
pañito, *m.* small cloth; **— de adorno,** doily.
paño, *m.* cloth, breadth of cloth; **— a cuadros,** checked cloth; **— rayado** or **listado,** striped cloth.
pañol, *m.* (naut.) storeroom; **— de granadas,** shell room.
pañuelo, *m.* handkerchief.
papa, *m.* Pope; **—,** *f.* potato; soft food for babies; (coll.) fib, exaggeration.
papá, *m.* papa, father.
papada, *f.* double chin; dewlap.
papadilla, *f.* the fleshy part under the chin.
papado, *m.* papacy.
papagayo, *m.* parrot.
papal, *adj.* papal, papistical.
papalina, *f.* cap with ear flaps; (coll.) drunkenness.
papamoscas, *m.* flycatcher (bird); (coll.) simpleton.
papanatas, *m.* (coll.) oaf, simpleton, ninny.
paparrucha, *f.* (coll.) fake news; nonsense.
papas, *f.* mush.
papaya, *f.* (bot.) papaw.
papel, *m.* paper; role, part; **— avitelado,** vellum paper; **— carbón,** carbon paper; **— celofán,** cellophane; **— encerado,** waxed paper; **— de entapizar,** wallpaper; **— de envolver,** wrapping paper; **— de escribir,** writing paper; **— de estraza,** brown paper; **— de excusado,** toilet paper; **— de lija,** sandpaper; **— de seda,** tissue paper; **— imitación chagrín,** granulated paper; **— jaspeado,** marbled paper; **— marquilla,** card or Bristol paper; **— moneda,** paper money; **— reactivo,** test or litmus paper; **— satinado,** glazed paper; **— secante,** blotter, blotting paper; **— sellado,** stamped paper.
papelear, *vn.* to look over papers.
papelera, *f.* writing desk; paper case.
papelería, *f.* stationery; stationery store; confused bundle of papers.
papelero, *m.* paper manufacturer; **—, ra,** *adj.* boastful.
papeleta, *f.* slip of paper on which something is written; ballot.

papelina, *f.* poplin; goblet.
papelón, ona, *adj.* boastful; —, *m.* large piece of paper; (Sp. Am.) raw sugar.
papera, *f.* goiter; —s, *pl.* (med.) mumps.
papilla, *f.* pap; guile, deceit.
papiro, *m.* papyrus.
papirolada, *f.* garlic sauce.
papirotada, *f.* tap on the neck or face; rap on the nose.
papirote, *m.* fillip.
papista, *n.* and *adj.* Papist, advocate of the Pope; **ser más — que el Papa,** to be more interested in something than the person directly concerned, to be over-enthusiastic about something which does not concern one.
papo, *m.* double chin, under chin; fowl's gizzard.
papudo, da, *adj.* double-chinned.
paq. paquete, pkg. package.
paquebot or **paquebote,** *m.* packet boat.
paquete, *m.* package, small packet, bundle; **— de planchas fotográficas,** film pack.
Paquita, Fanny.
par, *adj.* par, equal, alike, even; **sin —,** matchless; —, *m.* pair; par; equal, peer; peer (nobleman).
para, *prep.* for, to, in order to; toward, to the end that.
parabién, *m.* congratulation, felicitation.
parábola, *f.* parable; parabola.
parabólico, ca, *adj.* parabolical.
parabrisa, *m.* windshield.
paracaídas, *m.* parachute.
paracaidista, *m.* parachutist; —s, *pl.* para-troops.
Paracleto or **Paráclito,** *m.* Paraclete (name given to the Holy Ghost).
parachoques, *m.* (rail.) buffers; (auto.) bumper.
parada, *f.* halt; suspension; stop, pause; relay; dam, bank; stake, set, bet; (mil.) parade.
paradero, *m.* stopping place; whereabouts; station, depot; **— de aeroplanos,** airport.
paradigma, *m.* paradigm.
parado, da, *adj.* stopped (as a clock); spiritless; unoccupied; (Sp. Am.) standing up.
paradoja, *f.* paradox.
parador, *m.* one who stops or halts; inn.
parafina, *f.* paraffin.
parafrasear, *va.* to paraphrase.
paráfrasis, *f.* paraphrase.
paragoge, *f.* addition of a letter or syllable at the end of a word.
paragolpes, *m.* bumper.
paraguas, *m.* umbrella.
paraguayano, na, *n.* and *adj.* Paraguayan.
paraíso, *m.* paradise.
paraje, *m.* place, residence; condition; disposition.
paralaje, *m.* parallax.
paralelismo, *m.* parallelism.
paralelo, la, *adj.* and *n.* parallel.

paralelogramo, *m.* parallelogram, oblong.
parálisis, *f.* (med.) paralysis.
paralítico, ca, *adj.* paralytic, palsied.
paralizar, *va.* to paralyze, to stop, to impede; —se, to become paralyzed.
paralogismo, *m.* paralogism, false reasoning.
páramo, *m.* desert, wilderness; any place extremely cold.
parangón, *m.* paragon, model, comparison.
parangonar, *va.* to compare, to parallel.
paranoico, *m.* paranoiac.
parapeto, *m.* parapet, breastwork.
parar, *vn.* to stop, to halt; —, *va.* to stop, to detain; to treat ill; to bet at cards; **— en mal,** to have a bad end; **sin —,** instantly, without delay; —se, to stop, to halt; to stand up; —, *m.* lansquenet (card game).
pararrayo, *m.* lightning rod, conductor.
parasitario, ria, *adj.* parasitic.
parásito, *m.* parasite, sponger.
parasol, *m.* parasol.
paratifus, *m.* (med.) paratyphoid.
parca, *f.* fate; death.
parcamente, *adv.* sparingly.
parce, *m.* note given by grammar teachers as a reward to schoolboys, enabling them to escape punishment for later grammatical errors.
parcial, *adj.* partial; discriminating.
parcialidad, *f.* partiality, bias; party, faction.
parcialmente, *adv.* partially, in part.
parcidad, *f.* frugality.
parco, ca, *adj.* sparing, scanty; sober, moderate.
parchazo, *m.* large plaster; (fig.) deception, jest; (naut.) flapping of sails.
parche, *m.* patch; plaster; (mil.) drumhead.
pardal, *adj.* boorish, rustic; —, *m.* (orn.) linnet; (zool.) leopard; (coll.) astute, cunning man.
pardear, *vn.* to grow gray or brownish; to become dusky.
¡pardiez! *interj.* jocular affirmation or oath, by Jove!
pardillo, *m.* linnet.
pardo, da, *adj.* brown; cloudy; dark gray.
pardusco, ca, *adj.* grayish, grizzly.
pareado, *m.* a couplet of octosyllables or hendecasyllables.
parear, *va.* to match, to pair, to couple.
parecer, *m.* opinion, advice; mien; **al —,** apparently; —, *vn.* (EZCO) to appear, to seem; —se, to present oneself to view; to resemble.
parecido, da, *adj.* resembling, like; —, *m.* resemblance.
pared, *f.* wall; **— medianera,** party wall.
paredón, *m.* thick wall.
paregórico, *adj.* paregoric.
pareja, *f.* pair; couple, brace; team.
parentela, *f.* parentage, kindred, relatives.
parentesco, *m.* cognation, kindred, relationship.

paréntesis, *m.* parenthesis.
paresia, *f.* (med.) paresis.
pares o nones, *m. pl.* even or odd.
paria, *m.* pariah, the lowest caste in India.
parias, *f. pl.* tribute paid by one prince to another as an acknowledgment of superiority; placenta, afterbirth.
parida, *f.* woman lately delivered; —, *adj.* having lately given birth.
paridad, *f.* parity, equality.
pariente, ta, *n.* kinsman, kinswoman.
parihuela, *f.* barrow; stretcher.
parir, *va.* and *vn.* to bring forth; to produce; to give birth.
parisiense, *n.* and *adj.* Parisian.
parla, *f.* easy delivery, loquacity, gossip.
parlador, ra, *n.* prater.
parlamental, *adj.* parliamentary.
parlamentar, *vn.* to talk, to converse; to parley.
parlamentario, ria, *adj.* parliamentary; —, *m.* member of Parliament.
parlamento, *m.* harangue delivered in a public assembly; parliament.
parlanchín, ina, *adj.* and *n.* chatterer, jabberer; chattering.
parlar, *vn.* to chatter, to talk.
parlería, *f.* garrulity, gossip.
parlero, ra, *adj.* talkative.
parleta, *f.* conversation on trifling subjects.
parlotear, *vn.* to babble, to prattle.
parloteo, *m.* pitter-patter.
parmesano, na, *n.* and *adj.* Parmesan.
Parnaso, *m.* Parnassus.
paro, *m.* lockout, deadlock, suspension of work, unemployment; — **forzoso,** lockout.
parodia, *f.* parody.
parola, *f.* eloquence; chatter.
parótida, *f.* parotid gland; —s, *pl.* (med.) mumps.
paroxismo, *m.* paroxysm, fit.
parpadear, *vn.* to blink.
párpado, *m.* eyelid.
parque, *m.* park; (mil.) park of artillery.
parqueadero, *m.* parking place for cars.
parquedad, *f.* frugality.
parra, *f.* grapevine.
párrafo, *m.* paragraph; paragraph mark in printing.
parral, *m.* vine arbor; a large earthen jar.
parranda, *f.* carousal, revel; **andar de —,** to be on a spree, to be out having a good time.
parrandear, *vn.* to go on a lark or a spree.
parricida, *m.* and *f.* parricide (person).
parricidio, *m.* parricide (murder).
parrilla, *f.* gridiron, broiler.
parro, *m.* (orn.) duck.
párroco, *m.* parson.
parroquia, *f.* parish; customers collectively.
parroquial, *adj.* parochial.
parroquiano, *m.* parishioner; (com.) customer; —, **na,** *adj.* parochial.
parsimonia, *f.* parsimony.
Part. Partida, (com.) entry, consignment.

parte, *f.* part; side; party; **de ocho días a esta —,** within these last eight days; **de — a —,** from side to side, through; **por otra —,** on the other hand, besides; **— superior,** top.
partear, *va.* to deliver, to deliver a woman of a child.
partenogénesis, *f.* parthenogenesis.
partera, *f.* midwife.
partero, *m.* obstetrician.
partible, *adj.* divisible, partible.
partición, *f.* partition, division.
participación, *f.* participation, share.
participante, *m.* and *f.* participant.
participar, *va.* and *vn.* to participate, to partake; to communicate.
partícipe, *adj.* participant, sharing; —, *m.* and *f.* participator, participant.
participial, *adj.* participial.
participio, *m.* participle.
partícula, *f.* particle.
particular, *adj.* particular, special; —, *m.* private gentleman, civilian; topic.
particularidad, *f.* particularity; detail; characteristic.
particularizar, *va.* to particularize, to itemize; —se, to be distinguished (by).
particularmente, *adv.* particularly, especially.
partida, *f.* departure; party of soldiers; parcel; game at play; (com.) consignment; item in an account, entry; — **doble,** double entry.
partidario, ria, *adj.* partisan, adherent; —, *n.* partisan; advocate.
partidarismo, *m.* partisanship.
partido, *m.* party; district; match; **sacarle — a,** to take advantage of.
partidor, *m.* parter, divider.
partija, *f.* partition, division.
partir, *va.* to part, to divide; to cut, to break; —, *vn.* to depart; **a — de,** beginning with; —se, to differ in opinion.
partitivo, va, *adj.* (gram.) partitive.
partitura, *f.* (mus.) score.
parto, *m.* childbirth.
parva, *f.* unthreshed grain laid in heaps to be threshed; multitude.
parvedad or **parvidad,** *f.* littleness, minuteness.
parvo, va, *adj.* small, little.
párvulo, la, *adj.* very small; —, *m.* child; **escuela de —los,** kindergarten.
pasa, *f.* raisin; **ciruela —,** prune.
pasada, *f.* passage; pace, step; manner; (coll.) misbehavior; **de —,** on the way, in passing.
pasadera, *f.* steppingstone.
pasadero, ra, *adj.* supportable, sufferable; passable; —, *m.* steppingstone.
pasadizo, *m.* narrow passage; subway; alley, aisle.
pasado, *m.* past; (gram.) past tense; —s, *pl.* ancestors; —, *adj.* past; **— mañana,** day after tomorrow.

pasador, *m.* smuggler; door bolt; woman's brooch;—**de charnela** or **pivote,** kingpin.

pasadura, *f.* transit, passage; (fig.) convulsive weeping of children.

pasaje, *m.* passage; fare.

pasajero, ra, *adj.* transient, transitory, fugitive;—, *n.* traveler, passenger.

pasamanería, *f.* lacemaking; shop where lace, braid, cord, etc., are made.

pasamano, *m.* balustrade, hand rail, banister; lace, braid, cord, etc.

pasapasa, *m.* legerdemain.

pasaporte, *m.* passport; (mil.) furlough.

pasar, *va.* to pass; to surpass; to suffer; to strain; to dissemble; —, *vn.* to spend (time); —, *v. imp.* to happen; — **por alto,** to overlook; — **de largo,** to pass without stopping; —**se,** to go over to another party; to become corrupt or putrid.

pasatiempo, *m.* pastime, amusement.

pasavolante, *m.* sudden action.

Pascua, *f.* Passover; Christmas; Easter; **dar las** —**s,** to wish one a happy Christmas or Easter.

pascual, *adj.* (eccl.) paschal.

pase, *m.* permit.

paseador, ra, *adj.* and *n.* (person) fond of walking or fond of going out for amusement.

paseante, *m.* and *f.* stroller, promenader.

pasear, *va.* and *vn.* to take a walk; to walk about; —**se,** to walk for exercise or amusement; to loiter, to gape about.

paseo, *m.* walk, stroll, ride; sightseeing; — **en el campo,** hiking; **ir de** or **dar un** —, to go out walking or driving.

pasillo, *m.* small, narrow passage; corridor, aisle; short step.

pasión, *f.* passion.

pasionaria, *f.* passion flower.

pasito, *adv.* gently, softly; —, *m.* short step.

pasitrote, *m.* short trot.

pasividad, *f.* passivity.

pasivo, va, *adj.* passive, inactive; —, *m.* liabilities of a business house.

pasmar, *va.* to cause a spasm; to benumb; to chill; —, *vn.* to marvel, to wonder; —**se,** to suffer spasms; to be astonished.

pasmo, *m.* spasm, convulsion; astonishment, amazement.

pasmoso, sa, *adj.* marvelous, wonderful.

paso, *m.* pace, step; passage; manner of walking; flight of steps; accident; — **a nivel,** railroad crossing; **al** —, on the way, in passing; **abrirse el** —, to force one's way; **apretar el** —, to haste one's steps; **marcar el** —, to mark time.

paso doble, *n.* kind of musical rhythm, march.

pasquín, *m.* pasquinade, pasquil, lampoon, roorback.

pasta, *f.* paste; dough; binding for books; **buena** —, mild, gentle disposition.

pastar, *vn.* to pasture; —, *va.* to lead cattle to graze.

pastel, *m.* pie, cake, type of pastry; crayon.

pastelería, *f.* pastry cook's shop; pastry.

pastelero, ra, *n.* pastry cook.

pastelillo, *m.* tart; — **de manzanas,** apple tart.

pasteurización, *f.* pasteurization.

pasteurizar, *va.* to pasteurize.

pastilla, *f.* tablet, lozenge, drop; — **de limón,** lemon drop; — **de levadura,** yeast cake; — **de jabón,** cake of soap.

pastinaca, *f.* parsnip.

pasto, *m.* pasture.

pastor, *m.* shepherd; pastor, minister.

pastoril, *adj.* pastoral.

pastoso, sa, *adj.* mellow, doughy.

pastura, *f.* pasture; fodder.

pasturaje, *m.* pasturage.

pata, *f.* foot and leg of an animal; female duck; —**s arriba,** topsy-turvy.

patada, *f.* kick.

patagón, ona, *n.* and *adj.* Patagonian.

patalear, *vn.* to kick about violently.

pataleo, *m.* act of stamping one's foot.

patán, *m.* yokel, churl, countryman.

patarata, *f.* fiction, false story; trash.

patata, *f.* potato; — **frita,** fried potato; **puré de** —, mashed potatoes.

patear, *va.* and *vn.* to kick, to stamp the feet.

patena, *f.* paten (plate used for the Eucharist).

patente, *adj.* patent, manifest, evident; —, *f.* patent; warrant; letters of marque; — **de sanidad,** bill of health; — **real,** certificate of registry.

paternal, *adj.* paternal, fatherly.

paternalismo, *m.* paternalism.

paternalista, *adj.* paternalistic.

paternidad, *f.* paternity, fatherhood.

paterno, na, *adj.* paternal, fatherly.

patético, ca, *adj.* pathetic.

patíbulo, *m.* gibbet, gallows.

patilla, *f.* little foot; —**s,** *pl.* sidewhiskers.

patín, *m.* skate; ice spur; — **de hielo,** ice skate; — **de ruedas,** roller skate.

pátina, *f.* patina.

patinadero, *m.* skating rink.

patinador, ra, *n.* skater.

patinaje, *m.* skidding.

patinar, *vn.* to skate, to skid.

patio, *m.* court behind a house; pit in a theater; — **de universidad,** college campus.

patituerto, *m.* clubfoot; —, **ta,** *adj.* clubfooted.

pato, ta, *n.* duck.

patochada, *f.* blunder; silly, uncouth remark.

patogénico, ca, *adj.* pathogenic.

patología, *f.* pathology.

patológico, ca, *adj.* pathological.

patólogo, *m.* pathologist.

Patr. Patriarca, Patriarch.

patraña, *f.* fabulous story, fake, bunk.

patria, *f.* native country, fatherland; — **chica,** homeland (a regional home as opposed to a national home).

patriarca, *m.* patriarch.
patriarcado, *m.* patriarchate.
patriarcal, *adj.* patriarchal.
Patricio, Patrick.
patricio, *m.* patrician.
patrimonial, *adj.* patrimonial.
patrimonio, *m.* patrimony, inheritance.
patrio, tria, *adj.* native, paternal.
patriota, *m.* and *f.* patriot.
patriótico, ca, *adj.* patriotic.
patriotismo, *m.* patriotism.
patrocinar, *va.* to favor, to patronize, to protect.
patrocinio, *m.* protection, patronage.
patrón, *m.* patron, protector; ship captain; landlord of a house or inn; employer; guardian saint of a country, town, etc.; pattern, standard, model; stencil; — estarcidor, stencil; — oro, gold standard.
patrona, *f.* patroness; hostess; landlady.
patronímico, ca, *adj.* patronymic; —, *m.* patronymic, surname.
patrulla, *f.* (mil.) patrol; squad; gang.
patrullar, *vn.* to patrol (camp or garrison).
patuá, *m.* patois.
Paula, Paulina, Paula, Pauline.
paulatinamente, *adv.* slowly, by degrees.
pausa, *f.* pause; repose; **a —s,** by intervals.
pausado, da, *adj.* slow, deliberate; calm, quiet, paused.
pausar, *vn.* to pause.
pauta, *f.* ruler; standard, model; (mus.) ruled staff.
pava, *f.* turkey hen; peahen; **pelar la —,** (coll.) to flirt.
pavero, ra, *n.* one who feeds turkeys.
pavesa, *f.* embers, hot cinders.
pavía, *f.* clingstone peach.
pavimentar, *va.* to pave.
pavimento, *m.* pavement, floor.
paviota, *f.* sea gull.
pavipollo, *m.* young turkey.
pavo, *m.* turkey; — **real,** peacock.
pavón, *m.* peacock, peafowl.
pavonar, *va.* to blue steel.
pavonear, *vn.* to strut, to walk with affected dignity.
pavor, *m.* fear, terror.
pavoroso, sa, *adj.* awful, formidable.
pavura, *f.* fear, dread, terror.
payasada, *f.* clownish action.
payaso, *m.* clown.
payo, ya, *n.* yokel, churl.
payuelas, *f. pl.* chicken pox.
paz, *f.* peace; tranquillity, ease; **en —,** even, quits; **¡—!** *interj.* peace! hush!
pazguato, ta, *n.* stupid person, simpleton.
pbro. presbítero, priest.
p/cta. por cuenta, (com.) on account, for account.
P. D. posdata, P. S. postscript.
pdo. or **p.**do **pasado,** pt. past.
P.e **Padre,** Father.
peaje, *m.* bridge toll; ferriage.
peana or **peaña,** *f.* pedestal; foot stool.

peatón, *m.* pedestrian; rural postman.
pebete, *m.* incense stick; fuse, match.
pebetero, *m.* censer.
peca, *f.* freckle, spot.
pecado, *m.* sin.
pecador, ra, *n.* sinner, wrongdoer.
pecaminoso, sa, *adj.* sinful.
pecar, *vn.* to sin.
pécari, *m.* peccary.
pecblenda, *f.* pitchblende.
pecera, *f.* fish globe, aquarium.
pecina, *f.* slime; fish pond.
peciolo, *m.* leafstalk.
pecios, *m. pl.* flotsam and jetsam.
pécora, *f.* sheep; (coll.) cunning, designing person, particularly a woman.
pecoso, sa, *adj.* freckled.
pectina, *f.* (chem.) pectin.
pectoral, *adj.* pectoral; —, *m.* cross worn by bishops on the breast.
peculiar, *adj.* peculiar, special, strange.
pecuniario, ria, *adj.* pecuniary, financial.
pechar, *va.* to pay a land tax.
pechera, *f.* shirt bosom; (coll.) woman's bosom.
pechería, *f.* revenue, taxes.
pechero, ra, *adj.* liable to pay taxes; —, *m.* commoner, plebeian; bib.
pechicolorado, *m.* linnet.
pecho, *m.* breast; chest; teat; bosom; courage, valor; tax, contribution; **dar el —,** to suckle; **tener —,** to have patience; **tomar a —,** to take to heart.
pechuga, *f.* breast of a fowl; bosom.
pechuguera, *f.* cough, hoarseness.
pedagogía, *f.* pedagogy.
pedagógico, ca, *adj.* pedagogic.
pedagogo, *m.* pedagogue, teacher.
pedal, *m.* (mus.) pedal; (mech.) a treadle, as in a lathe.
pedante, *adj.* pedantic; —, *m.* coxcomb; private instructor at home.
pedantear, *vn.* to act like a pedant.
pedantería, *f.* pedantry.
pedantesco, ca, *adj.* pedantic.
pedantismo, *m.* pedantry.
pedazo, *m.* piece, bit; **hacer —s,** to break to pieces, to destroy.
pedernal, *m.* flint.
pedestal, *m.* pedestal, basis.
pediatría, *f.* pediatrics.
pedicular, *adj.* pedicular, pertaining to lice.
pedicuro, *m.* chiropodist.
pedido, *m.* request, order; — **de ensayo,** trial order; — **de precisión,** rush order.
pedigüeño, ña, *adj.* craving, demanding, beggary.
pedimento, *m.* petition.
pedir, *va.* (i) to ask, to solicit, to petition, to beg; to demand; to crave, to desire; — **cuenta,** to bring a person to account; — **prestado,** to borrow.
pedo, *m.* wind from the bowels, flatulence.
pedómetro, *m.* pedometer.

pedorrera, *f.* flatulency; **—s,** *pl.* tight pants.

pedorrero, ra, *adj.* flatulent.

pedrada, *f.* throw of a stone, blow.

pedregal, *m.* place full of stones.

pedregoso, sa, *adj.* stony.

pedrera, *f.* quarry, stone pit.

pedrería, *f.* collection of precious stones, jewelry.

pedrero, *m.* stonecutter; slinger; lapidary.

pedrisco, *m.* hailstone.

Pedro, Peter.

pedrusco, *m.* rough piece of stone.

pedúnculo, *m.* peduncle, flowerstalk.

peer, *vn.* and *vr.* to break wind.

pega, *f.* pitch; glue.

pegadizo, za, *adj.* clammy, sticky, viscous; contagious.

pegado, da, *adj.* mounted; glued, stuck; **—,** *m.* sticking plaster; poultice; patch.

pegadura, *f.* pitching; sticking.

pegajoso, sa, *adj.* sticky, viscous; contagious.

pegar, *va.* to cement, to stick, to paste; to join, to unite; to beat; **— fuego,** to set fire to; **—,** *vn.* to take root; **—se,** to intrude, to steal in; to adhere.

pegote, *m.* pitch plaster; impertinent intruder, hanger-on, sponger.

peinado, *m.* hairdressing; coiffure; **— al agua,** finger wave.

peinador, *m.* hairdresser; dressing gown.

peinadora, *f.* hairdresser.

peinar, *va.* to comb (the hair); **—se,** to comb one's hair.

peine, *m.* comb.

peinería, *f.* shop where combs are made and sold.

peinero, ra, *n.* combmaker.

peineta, *f.* convex comb for women.

p. ej. por ejemplo, e.g. for example.

peladilla, *f.* sugared almond, burnt almond; small pebble.

pelado, da, *n.* (Mex.) person of the lower classes; ignorant peasant; **—,** *adj.* coarse, vulgar.

peladura, *f.* plucking, peeling.

pelagallos, pelagatos, *m.* wretch, ragamuffin.

pelágico, ca, *adj.* pelagic, oceanic.

pelagra, *f.* (med.) pellagra.

pelaje, *m.* color or tint of animals' hair; hairiness, wooliness.

pelar, *va.* to pull out the hair; to strip off the feathers; to peel.

peldaño, *m.* step of a flight of stairs.

pelea, *f.* battle, fight; quarrel.

pelear, *vn.* to fight, to combat; **—se,** to scuffle, to fight one another.

pelele, *m.* man of straw; insignificant fellow.

peletería, *f.* trade or shop of a dealer in furs or hides.

peletero, *m.* furrier.

peliagudo, da, *adj.* downy, furry; (coll.) arduous, difficult; ingenious, dexterous.

pelícano, *m.* pelican; **—, na,** *adj.* grayhaired; hoary.

pelicorto, ta, *adj.* short-haired.

película, *f.* film; **rollo de —s,** film roll.

peliculero, ra, *n.* scenario writer.

peligrar, *vn.* to be in danger; to risk.

peligro, *m.* danger, risk, peril.

peligroso, sa, *adj.* dangerous, perilous.

pelillo, *m.* short hair; trifle.

pelo, *m.* hair; pile; flaw (in precious stones); **a —,** to the purpose, timely; **tomar el —,** to tease.

pelón, ona, *adj.* hairless, bald.

pelota, *f.* pelota, ball; **en —,** entirely naked.

pelotari, *m.* pelota or ball player.

pelotazo, *m.* blow with a ball.

pelote, *m.* goat's hair.

pelotear, *vn.* to play ball; to argue, to dispute; **—,** *va.* to audit (accounts).

pelotera, *f.* quarrel, brawl, riot, free-for-all.

pelotero, *m.* ball maker.

pelotón, *m.* large ball; crowd; (mil.) platoon.

peltre, *m.* pewter.

peltrero, *m.* pewterer.

peluca, *f.* wig; reproof.

peludo, da, *adj.* hairy; **—,** *m.* bast mat of an oval shape.

peluquería, *f.* shop where wigs are made and sold; barbershop, hairdresser's shop.

peluquero, *m.* barber, haircutter, hairdresser; wigmaker.

peluquín, *m.* small wig, wig for part of the head.

pélvico, ca, *adj.* pelvic.

pelvis, *f.* pelvis.

pelleja, *f.* skin stripped from an animal; (coll.) prostitute.

pellejo, *m.* skin, hide; pelt; peel; wineskin, leather bag for wine; oilskin; tippler, drunkard, fuddler.

pellejudo, da, *adj.* thick-skinned.

pellica, *f.* coverlet of fine furs.

pellico, *m.* shepherd's jacket made of skins.

pelliza, *f.* pelisse.

pellizcar, *va.* to pinch.

pellizco, *m.* pinch; nip; small bit.

pena, *f.* pain, punishment; embarrassment; trouble, grief, affliction; **a duras —s,** with difficulty; **merecer** or **valer la —,** to be worth while; **so — de,** under penalty of.

penacho, *m.* tuft on the heads of some birds; crest; pride, haughtiness.

penal, *adj.* penal; punitive.

penalidad, *f.* suffering, trouble; hardship; penalty; punishableness.

penar, *vn.* to suffer pain; to do penance; **—,** *va.* to chastise; to penalize; **—se,** to grieve, to mourn.

penates, *m. pl.* Penates, household gods.

pendencia, *f.* quarrel, dispute.

pendenciero, ra, *adj.* quarrelsome; (coll.) scrappy.

pender, *vn.* to impend, to hang over; to depend; to be irresolute; to be pending.

pendiente, *adj.* pendent, hanging; **— de**

pago, pending payment, unpaid; **—,** *m.* pendant; earring, eardrop; **—,** *f.* slope, grade, incline; **— arriba,** upgrade.

péndola, *f.* pendulum.

pendón, *m.* standard; banner, pennon.

péndulo, la, *adj.* pendent, hanging; **—,** *m.* pendulum.

pene, *m.* (anat.) penis.

penetrabilidad, *f.* penetrability.

penetrable, *adj.* penetrable; comprehensible.

penetración, *f.* penetration; complete intelligence.

penetrante, *adj.* penetrating, shrill, heartrending, pervasive.

penetrar, *va.* to penetrate; to enter; to permeate; to fathom, to comprehend.

penicilina, *f.* (med.) penicillin.

península, *f.* peninsula.

peninsular, *adj.* peninsular.

penique, *m.* penny.

penitencia, *f.* penitence, penance; penalty, fine.

penitencial, *adj.* penitential.

penitenciar, *va.* to impose a penance for a fault committed.

penitenciaría, *f.* office of a penitentiary.

penitenciario, *m.* penitentiary.

penitente, *adj.* penitent, repentant; **—,** *m.* penitent.

penología, *f.* penology.

penoso, sa, *adj.* painful; distressing, embarrassing.

pensado, da, *adj.* deliberate, thoughtful.

pensador, ra, *n.* thinker.

pensamiento, *m.* thought, thinking; (bot.) pansy.

pensar, *vn.* (IE) to think; to intend.

pensativo, va, *adj.* pensive, thoughtful.

penseque, *m.* (coll.) error due to carelessness or thoughtlessness.

pensilvano, na, *n.* and *adj.* Pennsylvanian.

pensión, *f.* pension; annuity; price of board and tuition.

pensionado, da, *n.* pensioner, pensionary; boarding school.

pensionar, *va.* to impose pensions.

pensionario, *m.* pensionary.

pensionista, *m.* and *f.* pensioner, pensionary; boarder.

pentágono, *m.* pentagon.

pentagrama, *m.* musical staff.

pentámetro, *m.* pentameter.

Pentateuco, *m.* the Pentateuch.

Pentecostés, *m.* Pentecost, Whitsuntide.

penúltimo, ma, *adj.* penultimate, last but one.

penumbra, *f.* penumbra, shade.

penuria, *f.* penury, poverty, indigence, neediness, extreme want.

peña, *f.* rock, large stone.

peñascal, *m.* rocky hill or mountain.

peñasco, *m.* large rock; strong, rough cloth.

peñascoso, sa, *adj.* rocky, mountainous.

peñón, *m.* rocky mountain; very large rock;

P— de Gibraltar, Rock of Gibraltar.

peón, *m.* pedestrian; laborer; foot soldier; top (toy); pawn (in chess); hive of bees; **— oriental,** coolie.

peonaje, *m.* peonage.

peonía, *f.* (bot.) peony; land granted to captured soldiers.

peonza, *f.* top; noisy little person.

peor, *adj.* and *adv.* worse; **tanto —,** so much the worse.

peoría, *f.* deterioration, detriment.

Pepe, Pepillo, Pepín, Joe.

pepinar, *m.* cucumber field.

pepino, *m.* cucumber.

pepita, *f.* kernel; pip, seed of some fruits, distemper in fowl; nugget.

pepitoria, *f.* fricassee made of giblets, livers and lungs; (Mex.) peanut brittle.

peplo, *m.* peplum.

pepsina, *f.* pepsin.

péptico, ca, *adj.* peptic.

peptona, *f.* peptone.

pequeñez, *f.* littleness, trifle; meanness.

pequeño, ña, *adj.* little, small, young.

pera, *f.* pear.

perada, *f.* pear preserves.

peral, *m.* pear tree; pear orchard.

percal, *m.* percale, muslin, calico.

percalina, *f.* percaline.

percance, *m.* perquisite; bad luck, misfortune.

percepción, *f.* perception, notion.

perceptible, *adj.* perceptible, perceivable.

percibir, *va.* to receive; to perceive, to comprehend.

percusión, *f.* percussion.

percha, *f.* perch; clothes hanger.

percherón, *m.* Percheron.

perder, *va.* (IE) to lose; **echar a —,** to ruin; **—se,** to go astray; to be lost; to be spoiled.

perdición, *f.* losing of a thing; perdition, ruin, loss.

pérdida, *f.* loss, damage.

perdido, da, *adj.* lost, strayed.

perdigón, *m.* partridge trained to decoy others; **—ones,** *pl.* bird shot.

perdiguero, ra, *adj.* setting, pointing (of dogs).

perdiz, *f.* partridge.

perdón, *m.* pardon, forgiveness.

perdonable, *adj.* pardonable.

perdonar, *va.* to pardon, to forgive.

perdurable, *adj.* perpetual, everlasting.

perecedero, ra, *adj.* perishable.

perecer, *vn.* (EZCO) to perish, to die; to perish for want of the necessaries of life; **—se,** to crave, to pine for.

pereda, *f.* pear orchard.

peregrinación, *f.* pilgrimage.

peregrinamente, *adv.* rarely, curiously.

peregrinar, *vn.* to go on a pilgrimage.

Peregrino, Peregrine.

peregrino, na, *adj.* foreign, traveling; going on a pilgrimage; strange; **—,** *n.* pilgrim.

perejil, *m.* parsley.

perendengues, *m. pl.* eardrops, earrings; cheap jewelry.

perenne, *adj.* perennial, permanent.

perentorio, ria, *adj.* peremptory, decisive.

pereza, *f.* laziness, idleness.

perezoso, sa, *adj.* lazy, idle.

perfección, *f.* perfection, fineness.

perfeccionado, da, *adj.* finished.

perfeccionamiento, *m.* perfecting, improvement, completion.

perfeccionar, *va.* to perfect, to improve; to complete, to finish.

perfecto, ta, *adj.* perfect, complete.

perfidia, *f.* perfidy.

pérfido, da, *adj.* perfidious, treacherous.

perfil, *m.* profile.

perfilado, da, *adj.* outlined; well-formed, delicate (of features).

perfiladura, *f.* art of profile drawing; sketching of outlines.

perfilar, *va.* to draw profiles; to sketch outlines; —se, to incline.

perforación, *f.* perforation, bore, drilling, puncture.

perforar, *va.* to perforate, to puncture.

perfumador, *m.* perfumer.

perfumar, *va.* to perfume.

perfume, *m.* perfume.

perfumería, *f.* perfumer's shop; perfumery.

perg. or **pno. pergamino,** parchment, diploma.

pergamino, *m.* skin dressed for writing; scroll, parchment.

pericardio, *m.* pericardium.

pericarditis, *f.* (med.) pericarditis.

pericia, *f.* skill, knowledge, connoisseurship, fineness.

periferia, *f.* periphery.

periférico, ca, *adj.* peripheral, external.

perifollo, *m.* (bot.) chervil, an aromatic herb; —s, *pl.* ribbons, finery.

perifonear, *va.* to broadcast (radio).

perifonía, *f.* radiobroadcasting.

perífono, *m.* radiobroadcaster.

perifrasear, *va.* to use circumlocution.

perífrasis, *f.* periphrasis, circumlocution.

perifrástico, ca, *adj.* periphrastic.

perigallo, *m.* loose skin hanging under the chin of lean persons; tall, lean, lank person; sling made of twine.

perihelio, *m.* (ast.) perihelion.

perilla, *f.* small pear; pear-shaped ornament; doorknob; goatee; **de —,** to the purpose, in time.

perillán, ana, *adj.* artful, knavish, vagrant; —, *n.* rascal, crafty person.

perímetro, *m.* circumference, perimeter.

perinola, *f.* die with four facets; neat little woman.

periódico, ca, *adj.* periodical; —, *m.* newspaper.

periodismo, *m.* journalism.

periodista, *m.* and *f.* editor of a periodical, journalist.

periodístico, ca, *adj.* journalistic.

período, *m.* period, term.

peripatético, ca, *adj.* peripatetic; (coll.) extravagant in opinion.

peripecia, *f.* change of situation (in a drama); unforeseen accident.

periquito, *m.* parakeet, lovebird.

periscopio, *m.* periscope.

perito, ta, *n.* and *adj.* expert; skillful, experienced.

peritoneo, *m.* peritoneum.

peritonitis, *f.* (med.) peritonitis.

perjudicar, *va.* to injure, to hurt, to damage.

perjudicial, *adj.* damaging, harmful, injurious.

perjuicio, *m.* injury, grievance, detriment; damage.

perjurar, *vn.* to forswear, to swear falsely; to swear; —se, to perjure oneself.

perjurio, *m.* perjury, false oath.

perjuro, ra, *adj.* perjured, forsworn; —, *n.* perjurer.

perla, *f.* pearl; **de —s,** much to the purpose; eminently fine.

perlesía, *f.* paralysis, palsy.

permanecer, *vn.* (EZCO) to remain, to stay.

permanencia, *f.* permanence, stay, sojourn.

permanente, *adj.* permanent.

permanganato, *m.* (chem.) permanganate.

permeable, *adj.* permeable.

permisión, *f.* permission, leave.

permiso, *m.* permission, leave, license.

permitir, *va.* to permit, to allow, to give leave; —se, to take the liberty.

permuta, *f.* permutation, exchange.

permutar, *va.* to exchange, to permute.

pernada, *f.* kick.

pernear, *vn.* to kick, to shake the legs; to fret.

pernera, *f.* leg of trousers.

pernicioso, sa, *adj.* pernicious, destructive.

pernil, *m.* ham.

pernio, *m.* hinge for doors and windows.

perniquebrar, *va.* (IE) to break the legs; —se, to break one's leg.

perno, *m.* spike, bolt; (mech.) joint pin.

pernoctar, *vn.* to pass the night.

pero, *conj.* but, yet, except; —, *m.* defect, fault; **poner —s,** to find fault.

perogrullada, *f.* platitude.

perol, *m.* boiler, kettle.

perón, *m.* (Mex.) variety of apple.

peroné, *m.* fibula.

peroración, *f.* peroration, the conclusion of an oration.

perorar, *vn.* to make an oration or a speech.

perorata, *f.* harangue, speech.

peróxido, *m.* peroxide; **— hidrogenado,** hydrogen peroxide.

perpendicular, *adj.* perpendicular.

perpendículo, *m.* plumb, plummet, pendulum.

perpetrar, *va.* to perpetrate, to commit (a crime).

perpetua, *f.* everlasting flower, xeranthemum, strawflower.

perpetuar, *va.* to perpetuate.
perpetuidad, *f.* perpetuity.
perpetuo, tua, *adj.* perpetual.
perplejidad, *f.* perplexity.
perplejo, ja, *adj.* perplexed.
perquirir, *va* (IE) to search diligently.
perra, *f.* bitch; drunkenness, intoxication;
— **chica**, coin worth five **céntimos**.
perramente, *adv.* miserably, wretchedly.
perrera, *f.* kennel; doghouse.
perrería, *f.* pack of dogs; drudgery.
perrero, *m.* beadle who drives dogs out of
the church; man fond of dogs.
perrillo, *m.* little dog; trigger; — **de falda**,
lap dog; — **de lanas**, poodle.
perro, *m.* dog; obstinate person; — **de
aguas**, water dog; — **de muestra**,
pointer; — **de presa**, bull dog; — **de
Terranova**, Newfoundland dog; — **galgo**,
greyhound; — **lebrero**, whippet.
persa, *adj.* and *n..* Persian.
persecución, *f.* persecution pursuit; harassing.
perseguidor, ra, *n.* persecutor, pursuer.
perseguir, *va.* (I) to pursue a fugitive; to
dun; to persecute.
perseverancia, *f.* perseverance, constancy.
perseverante, *adj.* perseverant.
perseverar, *vn.* to persevere, to persist.
persiana, *f.* window blind; Venetian blind.
pérsico, *m.* peach.
persignarse, *vr.* to make the sign of the cross.
persistencia, *f.* persistence, steadiness.
persistente, *adj.* persistent, tenacious;
—**mente**, *adv.* persistently.
persistir, *vn.* to persist.
persona, *f.* person; **por** —, per capita; **de
— a —**, from man to man.
personaje, *m.* personage; character (in a
play).
personal, *adj.* personal; —, *m.* personnel,
staff.
personalidad, *f.* personality.
personero, *m.* deputy, agent, attorney.
personificador, ra, *n.* impersonator.
personificar, *va.* to personify.
personilla, *f.* small, ridiculous person.
perspectiva, *f.* perspective, prospect; sight,
outlook.
perspicacia, *f.* perspicacity, clear-sightedness.
perspicaz, *adj.* perspicacious, quick-sighted;
sagacious, clear-sighted.
perspicuo, *adj.* perspicuous.
persuadir, *va.* to persuade, to convince;
—**se**, to be persuaded.
persuasión, *f.* persuasion.
persuasiva, *f.* persuasiveness.
persuasivo, va, *adj.* persuasive.
pertenecer, *vn.* (EZCO) to belong to, to
appertain; to concern.
perteneciente, *adj.* belonging.
pertenencia, *f.* right of property; appurtenance, dependence.
pértiga, *f.* long pole or rod.

pertiguero, *m.* verger.
pertinacia, *f.* pertinacity, obstinacy, stubbornness.
pertinaz, *adj.* pertinacious, obstinate.
pertinencia, *f.* relevance.
pertrechar, *va.* to supply a place with ammunition and other warlike stores; to
dispose, to arrange, to prepare; —**se**, to be
provided with the necessary defensive
stores and arms.
pertrechos, *m. pl.* ammunition, weapons
and other instruments of war; tools or
instruments; — **de guerra**, ordnance.
perturbación, *f.* disturbance, perturbation,
disquiet of mind.
perturbador, ra, *n.* perturber, disturber.
perturbar, *va.* to perturb, to disturb, to
trouble.
Perú, *m.* Peru.
peruano, na, *adj.* and *n.* Peruvian.
perversidad, *f.* perversity, malignity.
perversión, *f.* perversion; depravation, corruption.
perverso, sa, *adj.* perverse, extremely
wicked.
pervertir, *va.* (IE) to pervert, to corrupt.
pervigilio, *m.* sleeplessness, continuous
vigilance.
pesa, *f.* weight.
pesadez, *f.* heaviness, gravity, weight; slowness; peevishness, fretfulness; fatigue.
pesadilla, *f.* nightmare.
pesado, da, *adj.* peevish, troublesome; cumbersome; tedious; injurious; heavy, weighty.
pesadumbre, *f.* weightiness, gravity; quarrel, dispute; grief, trouble.
pesalicores, *m.* hydrometer.
pésame, *m.* message of condolence; condolence, sympathy.
pesantez, *f.* (phy.) gravity.
pesar, *m.* sorrow, grief; regret, repentance;
a — de, in spite of, notwithstanding;
—, *vn.* to weigh, to be of weight, to be
heavy; to repent; —, *va.* to weigh.
pesaroso, sa, *adj.* sorrowful, full of repentance.
pesca, *f.* fishing, fishery.
pescadería, *f.* fish market.
pescado, *m.* fish (when caught; in the water
it is **pez**).
pescador, ra, *n.* fisher, fisherman (or
woman).
pescante, *m.* crane; coach box.
pescar, *va.* to fish, to catch fish.
pescozón, *m.* slap on the neck with the open
hand.
pescuezo, *m.* neck.
pesebre, *m.* crib, manger.
pesebrera, *f.* row of mangers in a stable.
peseta, *f.* monetary unit of Spain worth
100 **céntimos**.
pesillo, *m.* small scales for weighing gold or
silver coin; diminutive of **peso**.
pesimista, *m.* and *f.* pessimist; —, *adj.*
pessimistic.

pésimo, ma, *adj.* very bad, abominable.
peso, *m.* monetary unit of Spain and several Sp. Am. countries; weight, heaviness; balance, scales; load; — **bruto,** gross weight; — **fuerte,** silver dollar; — **neto,** net weight; **en** —, bodily; — **mosca,** flyweight.
pespuntar, *va.* to backstitch.
pespunte, *m.* back stitch.
pesquera, *f.* fishery.
pesquisa, *f.* inquiry, examination; search.
pesquisar, *va.* to inquire; to search.
pesquisidor, *m.* examiner, inquirer; investigator.
pestaña, *f.* eyelash.
pestañear, *vn.* to move the eyelashes or eyelids, to wink.
pestañeo, *m.* moving of the eyelids or eyelashes.
peste, *f.* pest, plague, contagious disease.
pestífero, ra, *adj.* pestilential.
pestilencia, *f.* pestilence.
pestillo, *m.* bolt of a lock.
pesuño, *m.* foot of cloven-hoofed animals.
petaca, *f.* covered hamper; tobacco pouch, cigar case; leather trunk.
pétalo, *m.* petal.
petardear, *va.* to beat down a door with petards; —, *vn.* to cheat.
petardista, *m.* and *f.* deceiver, cheat.
petardo, *m.* petard, fire cracker; cheat, fraud, imposition.
petate, *m.* straw bed; (Sp. Am.) sleeping mat of the Indians; (naut.) sailor's bedding on board; passengers' luggage; (coll.) poor fellow.
petición, *f.* petition, demand, request, plea.
petimetre, *m.* fop, coxcomb, dude.
petirrojo, *m.* robin redbreast.
peto, *m.* breastplate; plastron.
pétreo, rea, *adj.* stony, of stone.
petrificación, *f.* petrification.
petrificar, *va.* and *vr.* to petrify.
petrografía, *f.* petrography.
petróleo, *m.* petroleum, oil, mineral oil.
petrología, *f.* petrology.
petulancia, *f.* petulance, insolence.
petulante, *adj.* petulant, insolent.
petunia, *f.* (bot.) petunia.
pez, *m.* fish (in the water); **peces de colores,** goldfish; —, *f.* pitch, tar; meconium; — **griega,** rosin.
pezón, *m.* leafstalk; nipple.
pezonera, *f.* linchpin; nipple shield.
pezuña, *f.* foot of cloven-hoofed animals.
Pf. peso fuerte, silver dollar.
piada, *f.* chirping of birds.
piadoso, sa, *adj.* pious, merciful.
Piamonte, *m.* Piedmont.
pian or **piano,** *adv.* gently, softly.
pianísimo, *m.* pianissimo.
pianista, *m.* and *f.* pianist.
piano, pianoforte, *m.* piano, pianoforte; — **de cola,** grand piano; — **mecánico,** player piano.

piar, *vn.* to squeak, to peep, to chirp.
piara, *f.* herd of swine; flock of ewes.
piastra, *f.* piaster, Turkish silver coin.
pica, *f.* pike, spear.
picacho, *m.* sharp point.
picada, *f.* puncture, pricking.
picadero, *m.* riding school; —**s,** *pl.* blocks of wood put under the keel of a ship while she is building.
picadillo, *m.* mincemeat, hash.
picado, da, *adj.* chopped; piqued, vexed.
picador, *m.* picador, horseman armed with goad in bullfights; riding master; pricker.
picadura, *f.* prick; puncture; bite (of an insect or snake); gusset in clothes; cut tobacco.
picaflor, *m.* hummingbird; fickle person, flirt.
picamaderos, *m.* (orn.) woodpecker.
picante, *adj.* sharp, pricking; hot, highly seasoned; piquant; —, *m.* piquancy, pungency; satire.
picaño, ña, *adj.* lazy; tattered and shameless.
picapedrero, *m.* stonecutter.
picaporte, *m.* picklock; catch bolt; door knocker; doorhandle; doorlatch.
picaposte, *m.* (orn.) woodpecker.
picar, *va.* to prick; to sting; to mince; to nibble; to pursue an enemy; to itch; —**se,** to be piqued; to be motheaten; to begin to rot (as fruit).
picardear, *vn.* to act like a knave.
picardía, *f.* knavery, roguery; deceit, malice; lewdness.
picaresco, ca, *adj.* roguish, knavish.
pícaro, ra, *adj.* knavish, roguish; mischievous, malicious; sly; merry, gay; —, *m.* rogue, knave.
picarote, *m.* notorious villain, great impostor.
picatoste, *m.* Spanish fried toast.
picazón, *f.* itching; prurience; displeasure.
pico, *m.* beak, bill; nib; peak; point; odd; loquacity; **perder por el** —, to lose by too much chattering; **cien dólares y** —, one hundred and odd dollars; **la una y** —, few minutes past one (o'clock).
picoso, sa, *adj.* pitted with the small pox; (Mex. coll.) hot, highly seasoned.
picotazo, *m.* peck of a bird.
picote, *m.* coarse cloth made of goat's hair; glossy silk cloth.
picotear, *va.* to peck (of birds); —, *vn.* to prattle, to chatter; —**se,** to wrangle (applied to women).
picotero, ra, *adj.* wrangling, chattering.
pícrico, ca, *adj.* (chem.) picric.
pictografía, *f.* pictography, picture writing; pictograph, picture character.
picudo, da, *adj.* beaked; sharp-pointed.
pichincha, *f.* a bargain.
pichón, *m.* young pigeon.
pie, *m.* foot; base, basis, foundation; trunk (of trees); occasion; (poet.) foot; —

cuadrado, square foot; **— de imprenta,** printer's mark; **al — de la letra,** literally; **a —,** on foot; **dar —,** to give occasion.

piedad, f. piety; mercy, pity.

piedra, f. stone; gem; gravel; hail; **— alum,** alum; **— angular,** cornerstone; **— de afilar,** whetstone; **— imán,** loadstone, magnet; **— lipis,** copper sulphate; **— miliaria,** milestone; **— de molino,** millstone.

piel, f. skin; fur; hide; peel.

piélago, m. high sea; great plenty, numberlessness.

pienso, m. common daily allowance given to horses or mules.

pierna, f. leg; branch or leg of a compass.

pietismo, m. pietism.

pieza, f. piece; piece of furniture; room.

pífano, m. fife; fife player; piper.

pifia, f. miscue in billiards; blunder.

pigmentación, f. pigmentation.

pigmeo, mea, n. and adj. dwarf; dwarfish.

pignoración, f. pledge.

pignorar, va. to pledge.

pigre, adj. negligent; slow; lazy.

pigricia, f. slothfulness, laziness; negligence.

pijamas, m. pl. pajamas.

pila, f. trough for water in which cattle drink; font; pile, battery; heap; holy-water basin; **nombre de —,** Christian name; **— seca,** dry battery.

pilada, f. quantity of mortar made at once; pile, heap.

pilar, m. large water basin of a fountain; pillar; **—,** va. to hull grain by pounding.

pilastra, f. pilaster.

píldora, f. pill.

pilón, m. pylon; large water basin, drinking trough; loaf of sugar.

pílora, m. pylorus.

pilotaje, m. pilotage.

piloto, m. (aer.) pilot; first mate; **— práctico,** coast pilot; **— de prueba,** test pilot.

piltrafa, f. piece of meat that is nearly all skin; **—s,** pl. scraps of food.

pillada, f. knavish trick.

pillaje, m. pillage, plunder.

pillar, va. to pillage, to plunder, to foray, to seize; to chop at.

pillería, f. gang of vagabonds or rogues; knavish trick or sham.

pillo, lla, adj. roguish; **—,** m. rogue, rascal, petty thief.

pilluelo, m. gamin.

pimental, m. pepper-bearing ground.

pimentero, m. pepper box; pepper plant.

pimentón, m. ground fruit of the pepper plant, paprika.

pimienta, f. pepper.

pimiento, m. (bot.) capsicum; pepper (the vegetable); pepper; red pepper (the spice).

pimpín, m. children's play.

pimpollo, m. sucker, sprout, bud.

pina, f. landmark in the form of a cone; felloe of a wheel.

pinacoteca, f. picture gallery.

pináculo, m. pinnacle.

pinar, m. grove of pines.

pincel, m. artist's brush.

pincelada, f. dash with a brush; touch.

pinchadura, f. puncture.

pinchar, va. to prick.

pinchazo, m. puncture; prick.

pinche, m. kitchen boy, scullion.

pincho, m. thorn.

pineal, adj. pineal.

pingajo, m. rag, tatter.

pingo, m. rag; **—s,** pl. (coll.) woman's clothes cheaply bought.

pingüe, adj. fat, greasy; fertile; prosperous.

pino, na, adj. steep; **—,** m. (bot.) pine.

pinocle, m. pinochle (card game).

pinocha, f. pine needle.

pinta, f. spot, blemish, scar; mark on playing cards; pint.

pintado, da, adj. painted, mottled; **venir —do,** to fit exactly.

pintamonas, m. and f. (coll.) bad painter, dauber.

pintar, va. to paint, to picture; to limn, to describe; to exaggerate; **—,** vn. to begin to ripen; to show, to give signs of; **—se,** to paint one's face.

pintarrajar, va. to variegate.

pintarrajo, m. daub.

pintiparado, da, adj. exactly like, closely resembling.

pintiparar, va. to compare.

pintor, ra, n. painter, artist.

pintoresco, ca, adj. picturesque.

pintorrear, va. to daub.

pintura, f. painting; picture.

pinzas, f. pl. pincers; nippers; forceps; **movimiento de —,** (mil.) pincers movement.

pinzón, m. (orn.) chaffinch.

piña, f. pineapple; fir cone; mass of silver in the shape of a pineapple.

piñata, f. potful of goodies broken by blindfolded children at games.

piñón, m. pineapple seed; pinion; spring nut of a gun.

piñonata, f. conserve of almonds.

piñonate, m. paste of almonds and sugar.

piñuela, f. cypress nut; agave; kind of figured silk material.

pío, pía, adj. pious, devout; piebald; merciful; **—,** m. cry of chickens.

piocha, f. ornament for women's headdresses; **—,** adj. (Mex. coll.) wonderful, highly pleasing.

piojería, f. abundance of lice; (coll.) misery.

piojo, m. louse; troublesome hanger-on.

piojoso, sa, adj. lousy; miserable, stingy.

piorrea, f. (med.) pyorrhea.

pipa, f. wine cask; pipe (liquid measure); tobacco pipe; pipe which children make of the stalks of corn; reed of a clarion; fuse of a bomb.

pipero, m. pipe or barrel maker.

pipiar, *vn.* to peep, to chirp.
pipote, *m.* keg.
pique, *m.* pique, offense taken; **echar a —,** to sink a ship; **a —,** in danger, on the point of; steep (shore).
piqué, *m.* piqué (a fabric).
piquera, *f.* bunghole of a barrel.
piquete, *m.* slight prick or sting; picket; (mil.) picket; **— de salvas,** firing party.
pira, *f.* funeral pyre.
piragua, *f.* piragua, dugout canoe.
piramidal, *adj.* pyramidal.
pirámide, *f.* pyramid.
pirata, *m.* pirate; cruel wretch.
piratear, *vn.* to pirate.
piratería, *f.* piracy.
Pirineos, *m. pl.* Pyrenees.
pirita, *f.* pyrite, marcasite.
piromanía, *f.* pyromania.
piropo, *m.* carbuncle; garnet; compliment, flattery.
pirotécnica, *f.* pyrotechny.
piroxilina, *f.* pyroxyline, guncotton.
pirueta, *f.* pirouette.
piruetar, *vn.* to pirouette.
pisada, *f.* footstep; footprint; footfall.
pisapapeles, *m.* paperweight.
pisar, *va.* to step, to tread, to trample; to stamp on the ground; to hammer down paving stones.
pisaverde, *m.* fop, coxcomb, jackanapes.
piscina, *f.* fishpond; swimming pool.
Piscis, *m.* Pisces, Fishes (sign of the zodiac).
piso, *m.* floor, story; pavement; apartment; **— bajo,** ground floor; **casa de tres —s,** three-story house.
pisón, *m.* rammer.
pisotear, *va.* to trample, to tread under foot.
pista, *f.* trace, footprint; track; racetrack.
pistilo, *m.* pistil.
pisto, *m.* thick broth.
pistola, *f.* pistol; **—pulverizadora,** spray gun.
pistolera, *f.* pistol holster.
pistoletazo, *m.* pistol shot.
pistolete, *m.* pocket pistol.
pistón, *m.* piston; percussion cap.
pita, *f.* (bot.) agave; maguey.
pitagórico, ca, *adj.* Pythagorean.
pitanza, *f.* pittance, daily allowance; price.
pitillo, *m.* cigarette.
pito, *m.* whistle; fife; **no me importa un —,** I don't care a straw.
pitón, *m.* tenderling; sprig, young shoot of a tree.
pitorra, *f.* woodcock.
pituitario, ria, *adj.* pituitary.
pizarra, *f.* slate; blackboard.
pizarral, *m.* slate quarry, slatepit.
pizarrón, *m.* blackboard.
pizca, *f.* mite; pinch; bit.
pl. plural, *pl.* plural.
placa, *f.* plaque; clasp of a sword belt; star, insignia of an order of knighthood; sheet of metal; **— de fábrica,** name plate.

pláceme, *m.* congratulation.
placentero, ra, *adj.* joyful, merry.
placer, *m.* pleasure, delight; (min.) placer; **—,** *v. def.* (AZCA) to please.
plaga, *f.* plague.
plagar, *va.* to plague, to torment.
plagiario, ria, *adj.* and *n.* plagiarizing; plagiarist.
plagio, *m.* plagiarism.
plan, *m.* plan; design, plot.
plana, *f.* trowel; page (of a book); level; **— mayor,** (mil.) staff office.
plancha, *f.* plate; flatiron; slab.
planchador, ra, *n.* ironer; presser.
planchar, *va.* to iron, to mangle.
planchear, *va.* to plate, to sheath.
planeador, *m.* (aer.) glider.
planeo, *m.* (aer.) gliding.
planeta, *m.* planet.
planetario, ria, *adj.* planetary; **—,** *m.* planetarium.
planilla, *f.* statement of expenses or charges.
plano, na, *adj.* plain, level, flat; **—,** *m.* plan, ground plan; (math.) plane; **de —no,** with full force, directly, flatly; **primer —no,** foreground.
planta, *f.* sole of the foot; plant; plantation; **— baja,** ground floor.
plantación, *f.* plantation; planting.
plantador, ra, *n.* planter.
plantaminas, *m.* mine layer.
plantar, *va.* to plant; to fix upright; to strike or hit a blow; to found, to establish; (coll.) to jilt; **—se,** to stand firm on a place.
plantear, *va.* to plan, to execute; to state (a problem).
plantel, *m.* nursery garden; training school.
plantilla, *f.* young plant; insole, inner sole of a shoe; vamp; plate of a gunlock.
plantillar, *va.* to vamp or sole shoes or stockings.
plantío, tía, *adj.* planted; ready to be planted; **—,** *m.* planting; nursery, garden bed.
plantón, *m.* scion, sprout; (mil.) sentry punished with extra duty.
plañidera, *f.* weeping woman.
plañir, *vn.* (PLAÑO, PLAÑENDO) to lament, to grieve, to bewail.
plasma, *m.* (biol. and min.), plasma, blood plasma.
plasta, *f.* paste, soft clay.
plastecer, *va.* (EZCO) to smear with sizing, to size.
plástico, ca, *adj.* plastic.
plata, *f.* silver; money; plate (wrought silver); **en —,** briefly, to the point; **— labrada,** silverware.
plataforma, *f.* platform; front and rear of a streetcar; **— giratoria,** (rail.) turnplate, turntable; **— de seguridad,** safety island.
platal, *m.* great wealth.
plátano, *m.* (bot.) plantain; banana (plant and fruit).

platea, _f._ (theat.) parquet, orchestra seats.
plateado, da, _adj._ silvery; silver-plated.
plateadura, _f._ silvering.
platear, _va._ to silver; to silverplate; to electroplate.
platería, _f._ silversmith's shop; trade of a silversmith.
platero, _m._ silversmith.
plática, _f._ discourse, conversation.
platicar, _vn._ to converse, to chat.
platilla, _f._ fine French linen.
platillo, _m._ saucer; side dish; (mus.) cymbal.
platina, _f._ platina, platinum; microscope slide; (print.) platen, bedplate.
platino, _m._ platinum.
plato, _m._ dish; plate; today's special; **lista de —s,** bill of fare, menu.
platónico, ca, _adj._ Platonic.
plausible, _adj._ plausible.
playa, _f._ shore, strand, beach.
plaza, _f._ square, place; fortified place; office, public employment; seat; enrolling of soldiers; **— de toros,** bull ring.
plazo, _m._ term, date of payment; **a —,** on credit, on time; **a — fijo,** for a fixed period.
pleamar, _f._ high water, high tide, flood tide.
plebe, _f._ common people, populace.
plebeyo, ya, _adj._ plebeian; **—,** _n._ commoner.
plebiscito, _m._ plebiscite, referendum.
plectro, _m._ plectrum.
plegable, _adj._ pliable.
plegadera, _f._ letter opener.
plegadizo, za, _adj._ folding, pliable.
plegador, _m._ folding instrument; pleater.
plegadura, _f._ fold; pleating.
plegar, _va._ (IE) to fold; to pleat.
plegaria, _f._ prayer.
pleita, _f._ pleated strand of fiber.
pleiteador, ra, _n._ pleader; wrangler.
pleitear, _va._ and _vn._ to plead, to litigate.
pleitesía, _f._ agreement, pact; **rendir —,** (coll.) to render tribute.
pleitista, _m._ and _f._ litigious person.
pleito, _m._ contract, bargain; dispute, controversy, debate; lawsuit.
plenamente, _adv._ fully, completely.
plenario, ria, _adj._ complete, full.
plenilunio, _m._ full moon.
plenipotenciario, ria, _n._ and _adj._ plenipotentiary.
plenitud, _f._ fullness, abundance, plenty.
pleno, na, _adj._ full; **sesión —na,** joint session.
pleonasmo, _m._ pleonasm.
plétora, _f._ (med.) plethora; overabundance.
pleura, _f._ (anat.) pleura.
pleuresía, _f._ pleurisy.
plexímetro, _m._ pleximeter.
plexo, _m._ plexus, network; **— solar,** (anat.) solar plexus.
plica, _f._ (law) escrow; (med.) matted hair.
pliego, _m._ sheet of paper; sealed envelope containing documents or papers; **— de condiciones,** specifications.
pliegue, _m._ fold, pleat.
plomar, _va._ to mark with a lead pencil.
plomero, _m._ plumber.
plomizo, za, _adj._ leaden.
plomo, _m._ lead; **— derretido,** melted lead.
pluma, _f._ feather, plume; pen.
plumada, _f._ dash with a pen.
plumado, da, _adj._ feathered.
plumaje, _m._ plumage; plume.
plumazo, _m._ stroke of the pen; large feather pillow or mattress.
plumero, _m._ bunch of feathers; feather duster.
plumista, _m._ petty writer, notary.
plúmula, _f._ plumule.
plural, _adj._ (gram.) plural.
pluralidad, _f._ plurality.
pluralizar, _va._ to pluralize.
plus, _m._ (mil.) bonus, extra pay.
pluscuamperfecto, _m._ (gram.) pluperfect tense.
plutocracia, _f._ plutocracy.
plutócrata, _m._ and _f._ plutocrat.
plutocrático, ca, _adj._ plutocratic.
plutónico, ca, _adj._ plutonic.
pluvial, _adj._ rainy.
P.M. or **p.m. pasado meridiano,** P.M. afternoon.
P.º Pedro, Peter.
p.º pero, but.
p/o or **P.O. por orden,** (com.) by order.
pobl. población, t. town.
población, _f._ population; town.
poblacho, _m._ populace, rabble.
poblado, _m._ town, village, inhabited place.
poblador, ra, _n._ populator, founder.
poblar, _va._ (UE) to populate, to people; to fill, to occupy; to bud, to get leaves.
pobre, _adj._ poor, indigent; deficient.
pobrete, ta, _n._ poor, unfortunate person; (coll.) useless but good-natured person.
pobreza, _f._ poverty, poorness.
pocero, _m._ well digger; sewerman.
pocilga, _f._ pigsty; any nasty, dirty place.
pocillo, _m._ chocolate cup.
pócima, _f._ potion, medicinal drink.
poción, _f._ potion.
poco, ca, _adj._ little, scanty; **—s,** _pl._ few; **—o,** _adv._ little; **— ha que,** lately, latterly; **— a —,** gently; little by little; **—,** _m._ a small part.
póculo, _m._ cup or glass for drinking.
poda, _f._ pruning of trees.
podadera, _f._ pruning knife.
podagra, _f._ gout in the joints of the feet.
podar, _va._ to prune.
podenco, _m._ hound.
poder, _m._ power, authority; command; force; **en — de,** in the hands of; **por —,** by proxy; **—,** _vn._ (PUEDO, PUDE) to be able; to possess the power of doing or performing; **—,** _v. imp._ to be possible.
poderhabiente, _m._ attorney in fact, agent.
poderío, _m._ power, authority; wealth, riches.

poderoso, sa, *adj.* powerful; eminent.
podio, *m.* (arch.) podium, large pedestal.
podre, *f.* pus, matter.
podredumbre, *f.* putrid matter; grief.
podrir, *vn.* (PUDRO, PUDRÍ) to rot, to putrefy, to spoil.
poema, *m.* poem.
poesía, *f.* poetry; poesy.
poeta, *m.* poet.
poética, *f.* art of writing poetry; essay on poetry writing.
poético, ca, *adj.* poetic.
poetisa, *f.* poetess.
poetizar, *va.* and *vn.* to poetize.
pogrom, *m.* pogrom.
póker, *m.* poker (card game).
polaco, ca, *adj.* and *n.* Polish; —, *m.* Polish language.
polaina, *f.* legging, gaiter.
polainas, *f. pl.* spats.
polar, *adj.* polar.
polaridad, *f.* polarity.
polariscopio, *m.* polariscope.
polarización, *f.* polarization.
polarizar, *va.* to polarize.
polca, *f.* polka.
polea, *f.* pulley; tackle block; — **con aparejo,** block and tackle.
polémica, *f.* polemics.
polémico, ca, *adj.* polemic.
polen, *m.* (bot.) pollen.
poleo, *m.* (bot.) pennyroyal.
poliandria, *f.* polyandry.
policía, *f.* police; politeness; neatness; **vigilante de** —, patrolman; —, *m.* policeman.
policíaco, ca, *adj.* pertaining to the police.
policopia, *f.* multigraphing.
policromo, ma, *adj.* polychrome, multicolored.
poliedro, *m.* polyhedron.
polifónico, ca, *adj.* polyphonic.
poligamia, *f.* polygamy.
polígamo, ma, *n.* and *adj.* polygamist.
polígono, *m.* polygon; —, **na,** *adj.* polygonal.
polilla, *f.* moth.
polimatía, *f.* great wisdom.
polimorfismo, *m.* polymorphism.
polinización, *f.* pollination.
polinizar, *va.* to pollinate.
polinomio, *m.* polynomial.
pólipo, *m.* polypus; octopus.
polisílabo, ba, *adj.* polysyllabic.
politécnico, ca, *adj.* polytechnic.
politeísmo, *m.* polytheism.
política, *f.* politics; policy.
político, ca, *adj.* political; polite; —, *m.* politician.
póliza, *f.* policy; check; passport; admission ticket; — **a prima fija,** fixed-premium policy; — **de seguro,** insurance policy.
polizón, *m.* bum, loafer; (naut.) stowaway.
polo, *m.* (geog. and elec.) pole; polo (game).
polonés, esa, *n.* and *adj.* Polish.

polonesa, *f.* (mus.) polonaise.
Polonia, *f.* Poland.
poltrón, ona, *adj.* idle, lazy; commodious, easy; **silla** —**ona,** armchair; —, *n.* poltroon.
poltronería, *f.* idleness, laziness, indolence.
polución, *f.* pollution.
polvareda, *f.* cloud of dust.
polvera, *f.* compact, vanity case, powder case.
polvo, *m.* powder, dust; — **dentífrico,** tooth powder; —**s de talco,** talcum powder; **en** —, powdered.
pólvora, *f.* gunpowder; fireworks.
polvorear, *va.* to powder.
polvoriento, ta, *adj.* dusty.
polvorín, *m.* gunpowder reduced to the finest dust; powder flask; powder magazine.
polvorista, *m.* manufacturer of gunpowder.
polvorizar, *va.* to pulverize; to powder.
polvoroso, sa, *adj.* dusty; **poner pies en** —**sa,** to scamper away.
polla, *f.* pullet; money bet at cards; pool; (coll.) young girl.
pollada, *f.* flock of young fowls; hatch, covey.
pollera, *f.* woman who deals with chickens; hen-coop; (Sp. Am.) wide skirt; national costume of Panama.
pollería, *f.* poultry market.
pollero, *m.* poulterer.
pollino, *m.* young, untamed ass; dull, stupid, heavy fellow.
pollo, *m.* young chicken; (coll.) young man.
poma, *f.* apple; smelling bottle.
pomada, *f.* pomatum, pomade, salve.
pomerano, na, *adj.* and *n.* Pomeranian; **perro** —, spitz.
pómez, *f.* pumice stone.
pomo, *m.* small bottle; apple; pommel.
pomología, *f.* pomology.
pompa, *f.* pomp; grandeur; **empresario de** —**s fúnebres,** undertaker, mortician.
pompón, *m.* pompon.
pomposo, sa, *adj.* pompous; magnificent.
pómulo, *m.* cheekbone.
poncil, *adj.* and *m.* bitter (orange or lemon).
ponche, *m.* punch (drink).
ponchera, *f.* punchbowl.
poncho, cha, *adj.* soft, mild; —, *m.* (Sp. Am.) poncho.
ponderable, *adj.* ponderable; measurable by scales; wonderful.
ponderación, *f.* ponderation, consideration; exaggeration.
ponderar, *va.* to ponder, to consider, to weigh; to exaggerate.
ponderativo, va, *adj.* exaggerating, hyperbolical.
ponedero, ra, *adj.* egg-laying; capable of being laid or placed; —, *m.* nest; nest egg.
poner, *va.* (PONGO, PUSE) to put, to place, to impose; to lay eggs; — **al corriente,** to acquaint (with), to inform; — **casa,**

to set up housekeeping; — **por escrito**, to put in writing; — **precio**, to set a price; — **la mesa**, to set the table; —**se**, to become, to set (of stars, etc.); —**se en marcha**, to start; —**se de pie**, to stand up.

poniente, *m.* west; west wind; —, *adj.* setting (as sun, etc.).

pontaje or **pontazgo**, *m.* bridge toll.

pontificado, *m.* pontificate.

pontifical, *adj.* and *m.* pontifical.

pontífice, *m.* Pope, pontiff.

pontificio, cia, *adj.* pontificial.

pontón, *m.* pontoon.

ponzoña, *f.* poison; harmful, immoral doctrine.

ponzoñoso, sa, *adj.* poisonous.

popa, *f.* (naut.) poop, stern.

popote, *m.* kind of Indian straw for brooms.

populacho, *m.* populace, mob.

popular, *adj.* popular.

popularidad, *f.* popularity.

populoso, sa, *adj.* populous.

poquedad, *f.* paucity, littleness; cowardice.

poquito, ta, *adj.* very little; —, *m.* a little; —**to a** —**to**, little by little.

por, *prep.* for, by, about, by means of; through; on account of; — **si acaso**, in case.

porcelana, *f.* porcelain, china.

porcentaje, *m.* percentage.

porcino, na, *adj.* porcine.

porción, *f.* part, portion, share; lot.

porcuno, na, *adj.* hoggish.

pordiosear, *vn.* to beg alms.

pordiosería, *f.* beggary.

pordiosero, ra, *n.* beggar.

porfía, *f.* obstinate quarrel; stubbornness; importunity; **a** —, emulously; with strife and contention.

porfiado, da, *adj.* obstinate, stubborn.

porfiador, ra, *n.* disputer, wrangler.

porfiar, *vn.* to dispute obstinately; to persist in a pursuit.

pórfido, *m.* porphyry.

pormenor, *m.* detail.

pornografía, *f.* pornography.

pornográfico, ca, *adj.* pornographic.

poro, *m.* pore.

porosidad, *f.* porosity.

poroso, sa, *adj.* porous.

porque, *conj.* because; so that, in order that.

porqué, *m.* cause, reason.

¿por qué? *interr.* why?

porquería, *f.* nastiness, foulness; brutishness, rudeness; trifle; dirty action.

porqueriza, *f.* pigsty.

porquero, *m.* swineherd.

porra, *f.* cudgel; (coll.) last player in boys' games.

porrazo, *m.* blow with a cudgel.

porrería, *f.* (coll.) stupidity, folly, silliness.

porrón, *m.* earthen pitcher for water.

portaaviones, *m.* (naut.) aircraft carrier.

portabandera, *f.* socket for a flagpole.

portacartas, *m.* mailbag.

portada, *f.* title page, front, frontispiece.

portadocumentos, *m.* brief case.

portador, ra, *n.* carrier, bearer, porter.

portaequipajes, *m.* luggage rack.

portaestandarte, *m.* (mil.) standard bearer; cornet.

portafusil, *m.* (mil.) sling of a musket or rifle.

portaguión, *m.* standard-bearer of cavalry.

portal, *m.* porch; portico, piazza.

portamanteo, *m.* portmanteau.

portamonedas, *m.* purse, pocketbook.

portaollas, *m.* pot holder.

portaparaguas, *m.* umbrella stand.

portapaz, *m.* or *f.* (eccl.) the image plate.

portaplumas, *m.* penholder.

portar, *va.* to carry, to bear (arms, etc.); —**se**, to behave, to comport oneself.

portátil, *adj.* portable.

portavoz, *m.* megaphone.

portazgo, *m.* toll, turnpike duty.

portazo, *m.* bang of a door; banging a door in one's face.

porte, *m.* portage, freight, postage; conduct; bearing, carriage; — **debido** or **a cobrar**, charge collect; — **pagado** or **cobrado**, charges prepaid; **carta de** —, railroad bill of lading.

porteador, ra, *adj.* carrying; **empresa** —, transport company.

portento, *m.* prodigy, portent, wonder.

portentoso, sa, *adj.* prodigious, marvelous, strange.

porteo, *m.* carrying, portage; **compañía de** —, express company.

portería, *f.* principal door of a convent; porter's office.

portero, ra, *n.* porter, gatekeeper, janitor or janitress, concierge; —, *m.* goal keeper (in Rugby, hockey).

portezuela, *f.* little door, carriage or car door.

pórtico, *m.* portico, porch, lobby.

portier, *m.* portiere.

portillo, *m.* aperture in a wall; gap, breach.

portón, *m.* inner door of a house.

portugués, esa, *n.* and *adj.* Portuguese.

porvenir, *m.* future.

¡porvida! *interj.* by the living God!

pos or **en** —, *adv.* after, behind; in pursuit of.

posada, *f.* boardinghouse, inn, hotel, dwelling; (Mex.) Christmas party.

posaderas, *f. pl.* buttocks.

posadero, *m.* innkeeper; backside, bottom.

posar, *vn.* to lodge; to sit down, to repose; —, *va.* to lay down a burden; —**se**, to perch.

posdata, *f.* postscript.

poseedor, ra, *n.* owner, possessor; —, *adj.* possessing.

poseer, *va.* to hold, to possess, to own.

poseído, da, *adj.* possessed.

posesión, *f.* possession.

posesivo, va, *adj.* (gram.) possessive.

posesor, ra, *n.* possessor.
posesorio, ria, *adj.* possessory.
posfecha, *f.* postdate.
posfechar, *va.* to postdate.
posibilidad, *f.* possibility.
posible, *adj.* possible; **hacer lo —,** to endeavor to do one's best; **lo más pronto —,** as soon as possible.
posición, *f.* position, place; posture; situation.
positivismo, *m.* positivism.
positivo, va, *adj.* positive.
pósito, *m.* public granary; **— pío,** granary for charity.
poso, *m.* sediment, dregs, lees.
posponer, *va.* (POSPONGO, POSPUSE) to postpone; to defer.
postal, *adj.* postal; **paquete —,** parcel post.
poste, *m.* post, pillar; **— de amarre,** mooring mast; **— de gasolina,** filling station.
postema, *f.* abscess, tumor; dull, troublesome person.
postergación, *f.* delaying, putting back, passing over.
postergar, *va.* to defer, to delay.
posteridad, *f.* posterity.
posterior, *adj.* posterior, back, rear.
posterioridad, *f.* posteriority.
posteriormente, *adv.* later, subsequently.
postigo, *m.* wicket; postern; pane or sash of a window.
postila, *f.* marginal note.
postillón, *m.* postilion.
postilloso, sa, *adj.* scabby, pustulous.
postizo, za, *adj.* artificial, false; **—,** *m.* false hair.
postludio, *m.* (mus.) postlude.
postmeridiano, na, *adj.* postmeridian.
postnatal, *adj.* postnatal.
postor, *m.* bidder at a public sale; bettor.
postración, *f.* prostration, breakdown.
postrar, *va.* to humble, to humiliate; **—se,** to prostrate oneself; to kneel down.
postre, *adj.* last in order; **a la —,** at last; **—,** *m.* dessert.
postrer or **postrero, ra,** *adj.* last in order, hindermost.
postulante, *m.* and *f.* postulant.
póstumo, ma, *adj.* posthumous.
postura, *f.* posture, position; tax on eatables; price asked or offered; bet, wager; agreement, covenant.
potable, *adj.* potable, drinkable.
potador, *m.* inspector of weights and measures.
potaje, *m.* pottage; drink made up of several ingredients; medley of various useless things.
potar, *va.* to equalize and mark weights and measures.
potasa, *f.* potash.
potasio, *m.* (chem.) potassium.
pote, *m.* pot, jar; flowerpot; standard measure or weight.
potencia, *f.* power; mightiness; strength;

las grandes —s, the great powers; **— luminosa,** candle power.
potencialidad, *f.* potentiality.
potentado, *m.* potentate, prince.
potente, *adj.* potent, powerful, mighty.
poterna, *f.* postern, sallyport.
potestad, *f.* power, dominion; jurisdiction.
pot-pourri, *m.* potpourri, hash.
potro, tra, *n.* colt; foal; rack; **— mesteño,** mustang.
potroso, sa, *adj.* afflicted with a rupture; (coll.) fortunate, lucky.
po. vo. próximo venidero, prox. in or of the coming month.
poyo, *m.* stone bench against a wall.
poza, *f.* puddle; hole.
pozal, *m.* bucket, pail.
pozo, *m.* well· (min.) shaft, pit.
P.P. porte pagado, p. p. postpaid.
p. p. por poder, (law) by power of attorney or by proxy.
ppdo., p. pdo or **p.º p.ᵈᵒ próximo pasado,** ult. in the past month.
p. pdo. participio pasado, p. p. past participle.
p. pr. participio presente, p. pr. present participle.
pr. or **p.ʳ por,** per, by, for.
práctica, *f.* practice.
practicable, *adj.* practicable, feasible.
practicante, *m.* and *f.* practicer; (med.) intern.
practicar, *va.* to practice; to exercise.
práctico, ca, *adj.* practical; skillful.
pradera or **pradería,** *f.* meadow, mead.
prado, *m.* lawn, meadow.
Praga, *f.* Prague.
pragmatism, *m.* pragmatism.
pral. principal, prin, principal.
prasio, *m.* prase, a semiprecious, green stone.
preámbulo, *m.* preamble, introduction, preface; circumlocution.
prebenda, *f.* prebend.
prebendado, *m.* prebendary.
prebendar, *va.* to give prebend.
preboste, *m.* provost.
precario, ria, *adj.* precarious.
precaución, *f.* precaution; prudence.
precaver, *va.* to prevent, to guard against.
precedencia, *f.* precedence; preference; superiority.
precedente, *adj.* precedent, foregoing.
preceder, *va.* to precede, to go before.
precepto, *m.* precept, order.
preceptor, *m.* master, teacher, preceptor.
preces, *f. pl.* prayers; devotions.
precesión, *f.* precession.
preciado, da, *adj.* priced, valued, esteemed; proud, presumptuous.
preciar, *va.* to value, to appraise; **—se de,** to take pride in, to boast.
precio, *m.* price, value; **— con rebaja** or **descuento,** trade price; **— de costo,** cost price; **— de venta,** sale price; **poner —,** to set a price; **último —,** best or

lowest price; — **tope** or **límite, máximo de** —**s**, price ceiling; **control de** —**s**, price control.
preciosidad, *f.* excellence, preciousness, beauty.
precioso, sa, *adj.* precious; beautiful; **piedra** —**sa,** gem.
precipicio, *m.* precipice, cliff; violent, sudden fall; ruin, destruction.
precipitación, *f.* precipitation, inconsiderate haste.
precipitado, da, *adj.* precipitate, headlong, hasty.
precipitante, *m.* (chem.) precipitant.
precipitar, *va.* to precipitate; —**se,** to run headlong to one's destruction.
precisar, *va.* to compel, to oblige, to necessitate; to state.
precisión, *f.* necessity, compulsion; preciseness; **con toda** —, on time, very promptly.
preciso, sa, *adj.* necessary, requisite; precise, exact; abstracted.
precocidad, *f.* precocity.
preconizar, *va.* to proclaim.
precoz, *adj.* precocious.
precursor, ra, *n.* precursor, forerunner; —, *adj.* preceding.
pred. predicado, pred. predicate.
predecesor, ra, *n.* predecessor, antecessor, forerunner.
predecir, *va.* (PREDIGO, PREDIJE) to foretell, to predict.
predefinir, *va.* to predetermine.
predestinación, *f.* predestination.
predestinar, *va.* to predestine.
predeterminación, *f.* predetermination.
predeterminar, *va.* to predetermine.
predicable, *adj.* fit to be preached; predicable.
predicación, *f.* preaching, sermon.
predicado, *m.* predicate.
predicador, *m.* preacher.
predicamento, *m.* predicament.
predicar, *va.* to publish; to preach.
predicativo, va, *adj.* predicative.
predicción, *f.* prediction.
predilección, *f.* predilection.
predilecto, ta, *adj.* darling, favorite; preferred.
predio, *m.* landed property; farm; — **rústico,** piece of cultivated ground; — **urbano,** town or country house.
predisponer, *va.* (PONGO, PUSE) to predispose, to prepare in advance.
predispuesto, ta, *adj.* biased, predisposed.
predominar, *va.* and *vn.* to predominate, to prevail.
predominio, *m.* predominant power, superiority.
preeminencia, *f.* pre-eminence, superiority of power.
preeminente, *adj.* pre-eminent, superior.
preexistencia, *f.* pre-existence.
preexistente, *adj.* pre-existent.

preexistir, *vn.* to pre-exist, to exist before.
pref. prefijo, pref. prefix.
prefacio, *m.* preface.
prefecto, *m.* prefect; county head.
prefectura, *f.* prefecture.
preferencia, *f.* preference; **de** —, preferably.
preferente, *adj.* preferred, preferable; **acciones** —**es,** preferred shares of stock.
preferible, *adj.* preferable.
preferir, *va.* (IE) to prefer.
prefijar, *va.* to prefix, to fix beforehand.
pregón, *m.* proclamation by the common crier, hue and cry.
pregonar, *va.* to proclaim in public places.
pregonero, *m.* common crier; —, **ra,** *adj.* announcing, proclaiming.
pregunta, *f.* question; inquiry; **hacer una** —, to ask a question.
preguntar, *va.* to question, to demand; to inquire; —**se,** to wonder.
preguntón, ona, *n.* inquisitive person; —, *adj.* inquisitive.
prehistórico, ca, *adj.* prehistoric.
prejuicio, *m.* prejudice.
prelación, *f.* priority, preference, preferment.
prelado, *m.* prelate.
preliminar, *adj.* and *m.* preliminary.
preludio, *m.* prelude.
prematuro, ra, *adj.* premature, precocious.
premeditación, *f.* premeditation, forethought.
premeditar, *va.* to premeditate; to think out.
premiar, *va.* to reward, to remunerate.
premio, *m.* reward, prize, recompense; (com.) premium; interest.
premisa, *f.* premise.
premura, *f.* narrowness; pressure; haste, hurry, urgency.
prenda, *f.* pledge, forfeit; pawn; piece of jewelry; trait, quality; person or thing dearly loved; —**s,** *pl.* accomplishments, talents, natural gifts; — **de vestir,** article of clothing.
prendar, *va.* to pledge; to ingratiate oneself; —**se,** to take a fancy to, to charm.
prendedero, *m.* broach, pin; hook.
prender, *va.* to seize, to catch; to imprison; —, *vn.* to catch or take fire; to take root; —, *vr.* to adorn oneself.
prendería, *f.* pawnbroker's shop; frippery.
prendero, *m.* pawnbroker; secondhand dealer.
prendido, *m.* attire of women; pattern for bone lace.
prendimiento, *m.* seizure; capture.
prensa, *f.* press, newspapers; **dar a la** —, to publish; **P— Asociada,** Associated Press.
prensado, *m.* luster, gloss.
prensadura, *f.* pressing, pressure.
prensapapeles, *m.* paperweight.
prensar, *va.* to press.
prensil, *adj.* prehensile.
prensista, *m.* pressman in a printing office.

preñado, da, *adj.* full; pregnant.
preñez, *f.* pregnancy.
preocupación, *f.* preoccupation; bias, prejudice; worry.
preocupar, *va.* to preoccupy; to prejudice; **—se,** to care about, to worry.
preordinación, *f.* preordination.
preordinar, *va.* to preordain, to predestine.
prep. preposición, prep. preposition.
preparación, *f.* preparation.
preparar, *va.* to prepare; **—se,** to be prepared.
preparativo, va, *adj.* preparative, qualifying; **—,** *m.* preparation.
preparatorio, ria, *adj.* preparatory.
preponderancia, *f.* preponderance.
preponderante, *adj.* preponderant.
preponderar, *vn.* to preponderate, to prevail.
preposición, *f.* (gram.) preposition.
prepositivo, va, *adj.* prepositional.
prepucio, *m.* prepuce, foreskin.
prerrogativa, *f.* prerogative, privilege.
presa, *f.* capture, seizure; prey; carcass of a fowl; dike, dam, mole; **—s,** *pl.* tusks, fangs, claws.
presagiar, *va.* to presage, to forebode.
presagio, *m.* presage, omen.
presbiterado or **presbiterato,** *m.* priesthood.
presbiterio, *m.* sanctuary.
presbítero, *m.* priest, clergyman; presbytery.
presciencia, *f.* prescience, foreknowledge.
prescindir, *vn.* to prescind, to do without; to cut off.
prescribir, *va.* to prescribe.
prescripción, *f.* prescription.
prescriptible, *adj.* prescriptible.
prescripto, ta, *adj.* prescribed.
presea, *f.* jewel, gem.
presencia, *f.* presence, coexistence.
presenciar, *va.* to witness, to see.
presentación, *f.* presentation, introduction; **a —,** at sight.
presentar, *va.* to present, to introduce; **— al cobro,** to present for payment; **—se,** to appear; to present (introduce oneself).
presente, *adj.* present; **—,** *m.* present, gift; instant; **al —,** at present, at the moment; **el 20 del —,** the 20th instant; **hacer —,** to call attention; **la —,** the present writing; **tener —,** to bear in mind.
presentemente, *adv.* presently, now.
presentimiento, *m.* presentiment, misgiving.
presentir, *va.* (IE) to have a presentiment.
presepio, *m.* manger; horse stable; barn for cattle.
preservación, *f.* preservation.
preservador, ra, *n.* and *adj.* preserver; preserving.
preservar, *va.* to preserve, to defend from evil.
preservativo, *m.* preservative, preventive; **—, va,** *adj.* preservative.

presidencia, *f.* presidentship; presidency, chairmanship.
presidencial, *adj.* presidential.
presidente, *m.* president; chairman.
presidiar, *va.* to garrison.
presidiario, *m.* convict.
presidio, *m.* penitentiary, prison; garrison of soldiers.
presidir, *va.* to preside.
presilla, *f.* small string; loop in clothes.
presión, *f.* pressure, pressing; **— de vapor,** steam pressure.
preso, sa, *n.* prisoner.
prestamista, *m.* and *f.* lender; pawnbroker.
préstamo, *m.* loan.
prestar, *va.* to lend, to loan; **pedir prestado,** to borrow.
presteza, *f.* quickness, haste, speed.
prestidigitador, ra, *n.* prestidigitator, juggler.
prestigiador, ra, *n.* cheat, impostor.
prestigio, *m.* prestige; spell, fascination.
presto, ta, *adj.* quick, prompt, ready; **—to,** *adv.* soon, quickly.
presumible, *adj.* presumable.
presumido, da, *adj.* presumptuous, arrogant.
presumir, *va.* to presume, to conjecture; **—,** *vn.* to boast, to have a high opinion of oneself.
presunción, *f.* presumption, conjecture; conceit.
presuntivo, va, *adj.* presumptive.
presunto, ta, *adj.* presumed, presumptive; **—to heredero,** heir apparent.
presuntuoso, sa, *adj.* presumptuous, vain.
presuponer, *va.* (PRESUPONGO, PRESUPUSE) to presuppose.
presupuesto, *m.* motive, pretext, pretense; presumed cost; estimate; budget.
presuroso, sa, *adj.* hasty, prompt, quick.
pretal, *m.* poitrel, breast leather of a horse.
pretender, *va.* to pretend, to claim; to try, to attempt.
pretendiente, *m.* pretender; suitor; candidate, office seeker.
pretensión, *f.* pretension, claim.
pretérito, ta, *adj.* preterit, past.
pretextar, *va.* to find a pretext or pretense.
pretexto, *m.* pretext, pretense.
pretil, *m.* battlement, breastwork; railing; parapet.
pretina, *f.* waistband; belt.
prevalecer, *vn.* (EZCO) to prevail; to outshine; to take root.
prevaricación, *f.* prevarication.
prevaricar, *va.* to prevaricate; to fail in one's duty.
prevención, *f.* prevention; disposition, preparation; supply of provisions; foresight.
prevenido, da, *adj.* prepared, provided; plentiful, abundant; provident, careful, cautious, foreseeing, forecasting.
prevenir, *va.* (PREVENGO, PREVINE) to pre-

pare; to foresee, to foreknow; to prevent; to advise; to warn; **—se,** to be prepared; to be predisposed.

preventivo, va, adj. preventive.

prever, va. (PREVEO, PREVÍ) to foresee, to forecast.

previo, via, adj. previous, former; **—vio el depósito de,** upon deposit of.

previsión, f. foresight, prevision, forecast.

previsor, ra, adj. foreseeing, farseeing; **—,** n. foreseer.

prez, m. or f. glory, honor.

priesa, f. haste, speed, hurry.

prieto, ta, adj. blackish, very dark; **—,** n. very dark brunette.

prima, f. the first three hours of the day; prime; (mus.) treble; (com.) premium; female cousin; **— donna,** prima donna.

primacía, f. priority; primateship, primacy.

primado, m. primeness; primate.

primario, ria, adj. first; **escuela —ria,** elementary school.

primavera, f. spring (the season).

primaveral, adj. springlike, pertaining to spring (the season).

primeramente, adv. in the first place, mainly.

primero, ra, adj. first, prior, former; **—ros auxilios,** first aid; **—ra enseñanza,** primary education; **—ro,** adv. rather, sooner.

primicia, f. first fruits.

primitivo, va, adj. primitive, original.

primo, ma, adj. first; **—,** n. cousin.

primogénito, ta, adj. and n. first-born; firstling.

primogenitura, f. primogeniture.

primor, m. beauty; dexterity, ability.

primoroso, sa, adj. neat, elegant, fine, excellent; handsome.

princesa, f. princess.

principado, m. princedom.

principal, adj. principal, chief, main; **—,** m. main floor.

principalmente, adv. mainly, principally, for the most part.

príncipe, m. prince.

principesco, ca, adj. princely.

principiante, m. and f. beginner, learner.

principiar, va. to commence, to begin.

principio, m. beginning, commencement; principle; **al —,** at the beginning.

pringada, f. slice of toast dipped in gravy.

pringar, va. to baste (in cooking); to grease; to take a share in; to stain one's reputation; **—se,** to embezzle, to misappropriate, to defraud.

pringón, ona, adj. dirty, greasy; **—,** m. grease stain.

pringoso, sa, adj. greasy, fat.

pringue, m. or f. grease, lard, gravy; grease stain.

prior, m. (eccl.) prior; **—,** adj. prior, preceding.

priora, f. prioress.

prioridad, f. priority.

prisa, f. celerity, promptness; haste; **a toda —,** at full speed; **darse —,** to hurry; **tener —,** to be in a hurry.

prisión, f. seizure, capture; prison; prey; duress.

prisionero, ra, n. prisoner; person captivated by love.

prisma, m. prism.

prismático, ca, adj. prismatic.

priv. privilegio, grant, patent, franchise, copyright.

privación, f. privation, want.

privada, f. filth or dirt thrown into the street.

privadamente, adv. privately.

privado, da, adj. private; secret; **—,** m. favorite (of a king, etc.).

privar, va. to deprive; to prohibit; **—se,** to deprive oneself.

privilegiado, da, adj. privileged, favorite.

privilegiar, va. to privilege, to favor.

privilegio, m. privilege; patent.

pro, m. or f. profit, benefit, advantage; **en — de,** in behalf of; **el — y el contra,** the pro and con.

proa, f. (naut.) prow, bow.

probabilidad, f. probability, likelihood.

probable, adj. probable, likely.

probablemente, adv. probably.

probado, da, adj. proved, tried.

probar, va. (UE) to try; to prove; to taste; **—,** vn. to suit, to agree; **—se,** to try on (clothes).

probatorio, ria, adj. probatory.

probeta, f. test tube.

probidad, f. probity, honesty.

problema, m. problem.

problemático, ca, adj. problematical.

probo, ba, adj. upright, honest.

procacidad, f. impudence, petulance.

procaz, adj. impudent, petulant, forward.

procedencia, f. derivation; origin, source.

procedente, adj. coming from, proceeding from; (law) according to rules, law, etc.

proceder, m. procedure; **—,** vn. to proceed, to go on; to issue; to prosecute any design.

procedimiento, m. proceeding; process; legal procedure.

proceloso, sa, adj. tempestuous, stormy.

prócer, adj. lofty; **—,** m. person in an exalted station; Father of the country (in American Republics).

procesado, da, adj. prolix and circumstantial (of legal papers); indicted.

procesar, va. to inform against, to prosecute; to indict.

procesión, f. procession.

procesional, adj. processional.

procesionario, m. processional.

proceso, m. process, lawsuit.

proclama, f. proclamation, publication.

proclamación, f. proclamation; acclamation.

proclamar, va. to proclaim.

procreación, f. procreation, generation.

procrear, va. to procreate, to generate.

procuración, *f.* power of attorney; procurement.

procurador, *m.* procurer; attorney; proctor; — **público,** attorney at law.

procuraduría, *f.* attorney's office; proctorship.

procurar, *va.* to solicit; to act as an attorney; to try, to attempt.

prodición, *f.* treachery, treason.

prodigalidad, *f.* prodigality; plenty, abundance.

prodigar, *va.* to waste, to lavish.

prodigio, *m.* prodigy, marvel, wonder.

prodigioso, sa, *adj.* prodigious, wonderful; excellent.

pródigo, ga, *adj.* prodigal, lavish.

producción, *f.* production.

producir, *va.* (PRODUZCO, PRODUJE) to produce, to yield; (law) to produce as evidence.

productivo, va, *adj.* productive, fertile; profitable.

producto, *m.* product; amount; — **bruto;** gross amount; — **neto** or **líquido,** net proceeds; —**s,** *pl.* produce; —**s alimenticios,** foodstuffs.

proejar, *vn.* to row (against the wind or tide).

proemio, *m.* preface, introduction.

proeza, *f.* prowess, exploit, valor, bravery.

prof.: profesor, prof. professor; **profeta,** prophet.

profanación, *f.* profanation.

profanar, *va.* to profane, to desecrate.

profano, na, *adj.* profane.

profecía, *f.* prophecy.

proferir, *va.* (IE), to utter, to say, to exclaim.

profesar, *va.* to profess, to exercise; to declare openly; to take the vows; to take the veil.

profesión, *f.* profession, following.

profesional, *adj.* professional, vocational.

profeso, sa, *adj.* professed.

profesor, ra, *n.* professor, teacher.

profesorado, *m.* body of teachers, faculty; professorship.

profeta, *m.* prophet.

profético, ca, *adj.* prophetic.

profetisa, *f.* prophetess.

profetizar, *va.* to prophesy.

proficiente, *adj.* proficient, advanced.

profiláctico, ca, *m.* and *adj.* prophylactic.

profilaxis, *f.* (med.) prophylaxis.

prófugo, ga, *adj.* fugitive.

profundamente, *adv.* profoundly, deeply.

profundidad, *f.* profundity, profoundness; depth; grandeur.

profundizar, *va.* to deepen; to penetrate.

profundo, da, *adj.* profound, deep.

profusamente, *adv.* profusely.

profusión, *f.* profusion, prodigality.

progenie, *f.* progeny, race, generation, offspring, issue.

progenitor, *m.* progenitor, ancestor, forefather.

progenitura, *f.* progeny; primogeniture.

programa, *m.* program; — **de estudios,** curriculum.

progresar, *vn.* to progress, to improve.

progresión, *f.* progression.

progresivo, va, *adj.* progressive.

progreso, *m.* progress, advancement.

prohibición, *f.* prohibition.

prohibicionista, *m.* and *f.* prohibitionist.

prohibido, da, *adj.* forbidden.

prohibir, *va.* to prohibit, to forbid, to hinder.

prohibitivo, va, *adj.* prohibitory, prohibitive.

prohijamiento, *m.* adoption.

prohijar, *va.* to adopt (a son).

prohombre, *m.* great man.

prójimo, *m.* fellow creature; neighbor.

pról. prólogo, prologue, introduction.

prole, *f.* issue, offspring, progeny, race.

proletariado, *m.* proletariat.

proletario, ria, *adj.* proletarian.

prolijidad, *f.* prolixity; minute attention to trifles.

prolijo, ja, *adj.* prolix, superfluous; tedious.

prólogo, *m.* prologue, introduction, preface.

prologuista, *m.* and *f.* writer of prologues; radio announcer.

prolongación, *f.* prolongation, continuance.

prolongado, da, *adj.* prolonged, extended, long.

prolongar, *va.* to prolong.

promediar, *va.* to share equally; to average; —, *vn.* to mediate.

promedio, *m.* average.

promesa, *f.* promise; pious offering.

prometedor, ra, *adj.* promising.

prometer, *va.* to promise, to assure; —, *vn.* to be promising; —**se,** to expect with confidence; to become betrothed.

prometido, da, *n.* and *adj.* betrothed; —, *m.* promise.

prominencia, *f.* protuberance, knob.

prominente, *adj.* prominent, jutting out.

promiscuo, cua, *adj.* promiscuous, confusedly mingled; ambiguous.

promisión, *f.* promise.

promoción, *f.* promotion.

promontorio, *m.* promontory.

promotor, ra, *n.* promoter, forwarder.

promover, *va.* (UE) to promote, to advance, to further.

promulgación, *f.* promulgation.

promulgador, ra, *n.* promulgator.

promulgar, *va.* to promulgate, to proclaim.

pron. pronombre, pron. pronoun.

prono, na, *adj.* inclined, prone.

pronombre, *m.* pronoun.

pronosticación, *f.* prognostication.

pronosticador, ra, *n.* foreteller, prognosticator.

pronosticar, *va.* to prognosticate, to predict, to foretell; to conjecture.

pronóstico, *m.* prognostic, prediction; omen, foreboding, foretoken; almanac published by astrologers.

prontitud, *f.* promptitude, promptness, speed.

pronto, ta, *adj.* prompt, ready; **—to,** *adv.* promptly; **—,** *m.* sudden impulse; **de —,** all of a sudden; **por lo —,** temporarily.

prontuario, *m.* memorandum book, handbook.

pronunciación, *f.* pronunciation.

pronunciamiento, *m.* (law) publication; insurrection, sedition.

pronunciar, *va.* to pronounce; **— un discurso,** to make a speech; **—se,** to rebel.

propagación, *f.* propagation; extension.

propagador, ra, *n.* propagator.

propaganda, *f.* propaganda; dissemination; advertising.

propagar, *va.* to propagate, to spread, to disseminate; **—se,** to multiply, to spread itself.

propalar, *va.* to publish, to divulge.

propasar, *va.* to go beyond, to exceed.

propender, *vn.* to incline.

propensión, *f.* propensity, inclination.

propenso, sa, *adj.* prone, inclined.

propiciación, *f.* propitiation, atonement.

propiciar, *va.* to propitiate.

propiciatorio, ria, *adj.* and *m.* propitiatory.

propicio, cia, *adj.* propitious, favorable.

propiedad, *f.* dominion, possession; property; right of property; propriety.

propietario, ria, *adj.* proprietary; **—,** *m.* proprietor; **—,** *f.* proprietress.

propina, *f.* tip, gratuity; **de —,** to boot, in addition.

propinar, *va.* to invite to drink; to prescribe (medicine).

propincuidad, *f.* propinquity.

propincuo, cua, *adj.* near, contiguous.

propio, pia, *adj.* proper; own; characteristic; same; **—s,** *m. pl.* lands, estates.

propronente, *m.* and *f.* proponent.

proponer, *va.* (PROPONGO, PROPUSE) to propose, to suggest; **—se,** to intend, to plan, to be determined.

proporción, *f.* proportion; symmetry.

proporcionado, da, *adj.* proportionate, fit.

proporcionar, *va.* to proportion; to adjust, to adapt; to provide, to afford, to supply.

proposición, *f.* proposition.

propósito, *m.* purpose; **a —,** adequate, fitting; **de —,** on purpose, purposely; **fuera de —,** untimely, not to the purpose; **a — de,** with regard to, speaking of, apropos of.

propuesta, *f.* proposal, offer, proposition; nomination.

propulsión, *f.* propulsion.

propulsor, ra, *n.* propeller; **—,** *adj.* propelling.

pror. procurador, atty. attorney.

prorrata, *f.* quota; **a —,** in proportion.

prorratear, *va.* to divide a quantity into certain shares; to apportion.

prorrateo, *m.* distribution.

prórroga, *f.* prolongation, extension, renewal.

prorrogable, *adj.* capable of being extended (in time).

prorrogar, *va.* to extend (in time), to prolong.

prorrumpir, *vn.* to break forth, to burst forth.

prosa, *f.* prose.

prosador, ra, *n.* prose writer; (coll.) impertinent speaker.

prosaico, ca, *adj.* prosaic.

prosapia, *f.* race, generation, ancestry.

proscenio, *m.* proscenium.

proscribir, *va.* to proscribe, to outlaw.

proscripción, *f.* proscription.

proscripto, *m.* outlaw; exile.

prosecución, *f.* prosecution; pursuit.

proseguir, *va.* (I) to pursue, to prosecute; to continue.

prosélito, *m.* proselyte.

prosodia, *f.* prosody.

prospecto, *m.* prospectus.

prosperar, *va.* to make happy; to favor; **—,** *vn.* to prosper, to thrive.

prosperidad, *f.* prosperity.

próspero, ra, *adj.* prosperous.

próstata, *f.* prostate gland.

prosternarse, *vr.* to prostrate oneself.

prostitución, *f.* prostitution.

prostituir, *va.* (UYO) to prostitute.

prostituta, *f.* prostitute.

protagonista, *m.* and *f.* protagonist.

protección, *f.* protection.

proteccionismo, *m.* protectionism.

protector, ra, *n.* protector, patron.

protectorado, *m.* protectorate.

proteger, *va.* to protect.

protegido, da, *n.* protegé.

proteiforme, *adj.* protean.

proteína, *f.* protein.

proterozoico, ca, *adj.* Proterozoic.

protervia, *f.* perversity.

protervo, va, *adj.* perverse, obstinate.

protesta, *f.* protest.

protestación, *f.* protestation.

protestante, *n.* and *adj.* Protestant.

protestar, *va.* to protest; to make public declaration of faith.

protesto, *m.* protest (of a draft); **gastos de —,** protest expenses.

protocloruro, *m.* (chem.) protochloride.

protocolo, *m.* protocol.

protomártir, *m.* the first martyr.

proton, *m.* (phy.) proton.

protoplasma, *m.* protoplasm.

prototipo, *m.* prototype.

protozoario, *m.* protozoan, one-celled organism.

protuberancia, *f.* protuberance.

prov.ª provincia, prov. province.

provecto, ta, *adj.* mature, advanced in knowledge, age or experience.

provecho, *m.* profit, benefit, advantage; **en su —,** in his favor.

provechoso, sa, adj. profitable, beneficial, favorable.
proveedor, ra, n. purveyor, provider.
proveer, va. (PROVEÍDO, PROVISTO) to provide; to provision, to supply; to confer; to decree; **—se (de),** to provide oneself (with).
provenir, vn. (PROVENGO, PROVINE) to issue, to arise or proceed from; to originate.
proverbial, adj. proverbial.
proverbio, m. proverb; **—s,** pl. Book of Proverbs.
providencia, f. providence; foresight; divine providence.
providencial, adj. providential.
providenciar, va. to take steps (to obtain something).
próvido, da, adj. provident.
provincia, f. province.
provincial, adj. and m. provincial.
provincialismo, m. localism.
provinciano, na, adj. provincial; **—,** n. provincial.
provisión, f. provision, supply, stock.
provisional, adj. provisional.
provisionalmente, adv. provisionally.
provisor, ra, n. provider; purveyor, contractor.
provocación, f. provocation.
provocador, ra, n. provoker.
provocar, va. to provoke, to excite.
provocativo, va, adj. provocative; quarrelsome.
prov.ᵒʳ **provisor,** purveyor, contractor, vicar-general.
prox. próximo, next, nearest.
proximidad, f. proximity; kindred by birth.
próximo, ma, adj. next, nearest, following.
proyección, f. projection.
proyectar, va. to project, to scheme, to plan.
proyectil, m. projectile.
proyecto, m. project, plan.
proyector, m. projector, spotlight.
Prudencia, Prudence.
prudencia, f. prudence, wisdom.
prudente, adj. prudent, cautious.
prueba, f. proof; trial, test; token; experiment; essay, attempt; taste; (phot. and print.) proof; (law) evidence; **a — de bala,** bullet-proof; **a — de bomba,** bombproof.
prurito, m. prurience; itching; persistent desire.
Prusia, f. Prussia.
prusiano, na, n. and adj. Prussian.
prusiato, m. (chem.) prussiate, cyanide.
prúsico, ca, adj. (chem.) prussic, hydrocyanic.
P. S. posdata, P. S. postscript.
ps. or $ pesos, $, dollars.
pseudónimo, ma, adj. pseudonymous; **—,** m. pseudonym.
psicoanálisis, m. or f. psychoanalysis.
psicoanalizar, va. to psychoanalyze.
psicología, f. psychology.
psicológico, ca, adj. psychological.

psicólogo, ga, n. psychologist.
psicópata, m. psychiatrist.
psicopático, ca, adj. psychopathic.
psicosis, f. psychosis.
psicoterapia, f. psychotherapy.
psiquiatra, m. psychiatrist.
psiquiatría, f. psychiatry.
psiquiátrico, ca, adj. psychiatric.
psíquico, ca, adj. psychic.
P. S. M. Por su mandato, By your, his, or her command.
pta.: pasta, bullion; (of books) bound in boards; (of paper) pulp; **peseta,** a Spanish coin.
pte. presente, pres. present.
p.ᵗᵉ **parte,** pt. part.
pto.: puerto, pt. port; **punto,** pt. pint.
púa, f. sharp point, prickle; shoot of a tree engrafted in another; weaver's reed; mental pain; (coll.) sly person.
pubertad, f. puberty.
publicación, f. publication.
publicano, m. publican.
publicar, va. to publish, to reveal; to publicize.
publicidad, f. publicity.
público, ca, adj. public; **—,** m. attendance, audience, crowd.
puchero, m. glazed earthen pot; meat boiled in earthen pot; **hacer —s,** to pout.
pudibundez, f. prudishness.
púdico, ca, adj. chaste, pure.
pudiente, adj. rich, opulent.
pudín, m. pudding.
pudor, m. bashfulness, modesty, decorum.
pudoroso, sa, adj. modest, shy.
pudrición, f. rottenness.
pudridero, m. rotting place.
pudrimiento, m. rottenness.
pudrir, va. (PODRIDO) to make putrid; **—,** vn. to rot, to be rotten.
pueblo, m. town, village; population; populace.
puente, m. bridge; (mus.) bridge; **— colgante,** suspension bridge; **— de barcas, — de pontones,** pontoon bridge; **— levadizo,** drawbridge.
puerca, f. sow.
puerco, ca, adj. nasty, filthy, dirty; rude; **—,** m. hog, pig; **carne de —co,** pork; **—co espín,** porcupine; **—co montés,** wild boar.
puericia, f. boyhood.
pueril, adj. boyish, childish.
puerilidad, f. puerility, boyishness.
puerro, m. (bot.) leek.
puerta, f. door, doorway, gateway; duty paid at the entrance of the gates in towns; **— de entrada,** front door; **— trasera,** back door; **—s vidrieras dobles,** French doors.
puertaventana, f. window shutter.
puerto, m. port, harbor, haven; narrow pass, defile; **— aéreo,** airport; **— franco,** free port.
pues, conj. as, since, because, for; **—,** adv.

then, therefore; ¡—! *interj.* well, then!

puesta, *f.* (ast.) set, setting; — **del sol,** sunset.

puesto, *m.* place; particular spot; retail shop; post; employment; barracks; booth; stand; blind for hunters; —, **ta,** *adj.* put, set, placed; — **que,** although.

¡**puf!** *interj.* poo! phew! (exclamation of disgust at a bad smell).

púgil or **pugilista,** *m.* prizefighter, boxer.

pugilato, *m.* pugilism, boxing; prizefight.

pugilístico, ca, *adj.* fistic.

pugna, *f.* combat, battle.

pugnar, *vn.* to fight, to combat; to solicit earnestly.

puja, *f.* outbidding at a public sale.

pujante, *adj.* powerful, strong, robust, stout, strapping.

pujanza, *f.* power, strength.

pujar, *va.* to outbid; to push ahead, to push through.

pujo, *m.* (med.) tenesmus; violent desire.

pulcritud, *f.* neatness, tidiness; pulchritude.

pulcro, cra, *adj.* neat, tidy.

pulga, *f.* flea; **tener malas —s,** to be easily piqued; to be ill-tempered.

pulgada, *f.* inch.

pulgar, *m.* thumb.

pulgarada, *f.* fillip; pinch (of salt, tobacco, etc.).

pulgón, *m.* plant louse.

pulguera, *f.* place abounding with fleas; (bot.) fleawort, fleabane.

pulicán, *m.* dentist's forceps.

pulidez, *f.* neatness.

pulido, da, *adj.* neat, nice; polished.

pulidor, *m.* polisher; instrument for polishing.

pulimento, *m.* polish, glossiness.

pulir, *va.* to polish, to burnish; to put the last touches to; **—se,** to adorn oneself; to become polished.

pulmón, *m.* lung.

pulmonía, *f.* pneumonia.

pulpería, *f.* (Sp. Am.) retail grocery.

púlpito, *m.* pulpit.

pulpo, *m.* cuttlefish; octopus; polypus.

pulposo, sa, *adj.* pulpous.

pulque, *m.* pulque (Mexican liquor).

pulsación, *f.* pulsation.

pulsar, *va.* to touch; to feel the pulse; to explore, to try; —, *vn.* to pulse.

pulsera, *f.* bracelet; wrist bandage.

pulso, *m.* pulse; firmness or steadiness of the hand; attention, care.

pulular, *vn.* to bud, to sprout.

pulverización, *f.* pulverization; atomizing, spraying.

pulverizador, *m.* atomizer, spray, sprayer, pulverizer.

pulverizar, *va.* to pulverize, to atomize, to spray; — **neumático,** airbrush.

pulla, *f.* smart repartee, taunt; obscene expression.

¡**pum!** *interj.* bang!

puma, *f.* puma, cougar, American panther.

puncha, *f.* sharp point, thorn.

pundonor, *m.* point of honor.

pundonoroso, sa, *adj.* having a nice sense of honor, punctilious.

punición, *f.* punishment, chastisement.

punitivo, va, *adj.* punitive.

punta, *f.* point, tip.

puntada, *f.* stitch made with a needle and thread.

puntal, *m.* prop, stay, buttress; stanchion.

puntapié, *m.* kick.

puntear, *va.* to play the guitar; to stitch; —, *vn.* (naut.) to tack.

puntel, *m.* iron tube for blowing glass.

puntería, *f.* aiming (of firearms); marksmanship.

puntero, *m.* pointer (stick); —, **ra,** *adj.* aiming well (with firearms).

puntiagudo, da, *adj.* sharp-pointed.

puntilla, *f.* small point; narrow lace edging; **de —s,** on tiptoe.

puntillo, *m.* small point, punctilio; (mus.) dot.

punto, *m.* point, end; dot; design; point of honor; object, aim; sight (of a gun); mesh (of a net); **al —,** instantly; **estar a — de,** to be about to; **hasta cierto —,** in some measure; — **de cadeneta,** lock stitch; — **de fuga,** vanishing point; — **de ojal,** herringbone; — **de partida,** or **de arranque,** starting point; — **de vista,** point of view; — **espigado,** tapered point; **son las dos en —,** it is exactly two o'clock, it is two o'clock sharp.

puntuación, *f.* punctuation.

puntual, *adj.* punctual, exact.

puntualidad, *f.* punctuality; certainty.

puntualizar, *va.* to fix in the mind or memory; to accomplish.

puntuar, *va.* to punctuate, to point.

punzada, *f.* prick, sting; pain; compunction.

punzador, ra, *n.* pricker.

punzadura, *f.* puncture, prick.

punzar, *va.* to punch, to prick, to sting.

punzón, *m.* punch, nail set.

puñado, *m.* handful.

puñal, *m.* poniard, dagger.

puñalada, *f.* stab with a dagger.

puñetazo, *m.* blow with the fist.

puño, *m.* fist; handful; wristband; hand ruffle; hilt; cuff.

pupa, *f.* pustule, pimple.

pupila, *f.* eyeball, pupil; orphan ward (girl).

pupilaje, *m.* pupilage; boardinghouse.

pupilo, *m.* pupil; scholar; boarder; orphan ward (boy).

pupitre, *m.* desk, writing desk.

puré, *m.* thick soup, purée.

pureza, *f.* purity, chastity.

purga, *f.* physic.

purgación, *f.* purgation; gonorrhea; catharsis.

purgante, *m.* purgative.

purgar, *va.* to purge, to purify; to atone, to expiate.

purgativo, va, *adj.* purgative, purging, cathartic.

purgatorio, *m.* purgatory.

purificación, *f.* purification.

purificador, ra, *n.* purifier; purificatory.

purificar, *va.* to purify; —**se,** to be purified, cleansed.

purismo, *m.* purism, affectation of purity in speech.

purista, *m.* and *f.* purist.

puritanismo, *m.* puritanism.

puritano, na, *adj.* puritanical; —, *n.* Puritan.

puro, ra, *adj.* pure, unmingled, mere; genuine, chaste, innocent, spotless; absolute; **a** —**ro,** by dint of; **de** —**ro,** extremely; —, *m.* cigar.

púrpura, *f.* purple, purple shell; emblem of ecclesiastical or royal dignity.

purpurado, *m.* cardinal.

purpurar, *va.* to color with purple.

purpurear, *vn.* to grow purple.

purpúreo, rea, *adj.* purple.

purulento, ta, *adj.* purulent.

pus, *m.* pus, matter.

pusilánime, *adj.* pusillanimous, faint-hearted.

pusilanimidad, *f.* pusillanimity.

pústula, *f.* pustule, pimple.

puta, *f.* prostitute, harlot.

putrefacción, *f.* putrefaction.

pútrido, da, *adj.* putrid, rotten.

puya, *f.* goad, stick.

pxmo. or **pxo. próximo,** next.

pza. pieza, pc. piece.

Q

q. or **q.º que,** which, that.

Q. B. S. M. or **q. b. s. m. que besa su mano,** (expression of courtesy and respect).

Q. B. S. P. or **q. b. s. p. que besa sus pies,** (expression of courtesy and respect).

qda. queda, curfew.

Q. D. G. or **q. D. g. que Dios guarde,** may God protect.

Q. E. G. E. or **q. e. g. e. que en gloria esté,** may (he, she) in glory be.

q. e. p. d. que en paz descanse, may (he she) rest in peace.

Q. E. S. M. or **q. e. s. m. que estrecha su mano,** yours truly.

ql. or **q.¹ quintal,** cwt. hundred-weight.

qq. quintales, cwts. hundred-weights.

que, *relative pron.* that, which, who, whom; **qué,** *interrogative* and *exclamatory pron.*, what; how; **sin** — **ni para** —, without reason; **no hay de** —, don't mention it; —, *conj.* that; than; whether; because; **a menos** —, unless; **con tal** —, provided.

quebracho, *m.* (bot.) quebracho.

quebrada, *f.* broken, uneven ground; (Sp. Am.) brook.

quebradero, *m.* breaker; — **de cabeza,** that which molests and importunes.

quebradizo, za, *adj.* brittle, flexible.

quebrado, *m.* (math.) fraction; —, **da,** *adj.* broken; bankrupt.

quebradura, *f.* fracture; rupture, hernia.

quebrantadura, *f.* fracture, rupture.

quebrantamiento, *m.* fracture, rupture, breaking out of prison; weariness, fatigue; violation of the law.

quebrantar, *va.* to break, to crack, to burst; to pound; to grind; to violate; —**se,** to fatigue; to weaken.

quebranto, *m.* weakness, lassitude; great loss, grief; severe damage.

quebrar, *va.* (IE) to break, to transgress a law, to violate; —, *vn.* to fail; —**se,** to break into pieces, to be ruptured.

quechemarín, *m.* (naut.) lugger.

queda, *f.* curfew.

quedamente, *adv.* in a low voice, softly.

quedar, *vn.* to stay, to remain; to be; to be left; — **suspenso,** to fail in a course, to be flunked; —**se con,** to keep.

quedito, *adv.* softly, gently.

quedo, da, *adj.* quiet, still; —**do,** *adv.* softly, gently.

quehacer, *m.* occupation, business, work; task, chore; daily routine, duty; —**es, de la casa,** chores or household duties.

queja, *f.* complaint.

quejarse, *vr.* to complain of; to moan.

quejido, *m.* complaint; groan.

quejoso, sa, *adj.* querulous; complaining.

quejumbroso, sa, *adj.* complaining, plaintive.

quema, *f.* burning, combustion, fire.

quemador, ra, *n.* incendiary; burner.

quemadura, *f.* mark made by fire, burn.

quemar, *va.* to burn; to kindle; —, *vn.* to be too hot; —**se,** to be parched with heat; to burn oneself.

quemazón, *f.* fire, conflagration; (coll.) smarting, burning sensation.

querella, *f.* complaint, lamentation; quarrel.

querellarse, *vr.* to lament, to complain; to file a complaint in a court of law.

querelloso, sa, *adj.* querulous.

querer, *va.* (QUIERO, QUISE) to wish, to desire; to will; to like, to love; to resolve; **sin** —, unwillingly; **como quiera,** anyhow, anyway; **cuando quiera,** at any time; **donde quiera,** anywhere.

querido, da, *adj.*. dear, beloved; —, *n.* darling, lover; —**do mío** or —**da mía,** my dear, my love, my darling.

querubín, *m.* cherub.

quesadilla, *f.* sweetmeat; cheesecake.

quesera, *f.* dairy; cheese dish.

quesero, *m.* cheese maker or cheese seller.

queso, *m.* cheese; — **helado,** brick ice cream; — **Gruyère,** Swiss cheese; — **de cerdo,** headcheese.

quetzal, *m.* (orn.) quetzal; quetzal, monetary unit of Guatemala.

quevedos, *m. pl.* pince-nez.

¡quiá! *interj.* come now!

quicial, *m.* side post; jamb.

quicio, *m.* hook, hinge (of a door); **estar fuera de —,** not to be in a regular or normal state.

quid, *m.* main point, reason, essence, gist.

quid pro quo, (Latin) an equivalent.

quiebra, *f.* crack, fracture; bankruptcy.

quiebro, *m.* (mus.) trill; inclination of the body.

quien, *pron.* who, which; **¿quién?** who?

quienquiera, *pron.* whosoever, whoever.

quieto, ta, *adj.* quiet, still, peaceable.

quietud, *f.* quietness, peace, tranquility, calmness.

quijada, *f.* jaw, jawbone.

quijarudo, da, *adj.* thick-jawed.

quijo, *m.* (min.) ore.

quijotada, *f.* quixotic action.

quijote, *m.* Quixote; quixotic person; cuisse.

quijotería, *f.* quixotism, quixotry.

quijotesco, ca, *adj.* quixotic.

quila, *f.* (Sp. Am.) a kind of strong bamboo.

quilatar, *va.* to assay.

quilate, *m.* carat.

quilo, *m.* (med.) chyle; kilogram.

quilla, *f.* keel.

quím. química, chem. chemistry.

quimbombó, *m.* (bot.) okra, gumbo.

quimera, *f.* chimera, foolish fancy; dispute, quarrel.

quimérico, ca, *adj.* chimerical, fantastic.

química, *f.* chemistry.

químico, *m.* chemist; **—, ca,** *adj.* chemical.

quimón, quimono or **kimono,** *m.* kimono; printed cotton, chintz.

quina, *f.* Peruvian bark.

quincalla, *f.* hardware, small metal wares.

quincallería, *f.* notion goods store; hardware, hardware store; ironmongery.

quince, *adj.* and *m.* fifteen; fifteenth; **— días,** two weeks.

quincena, *f.* fortnight; semimonthly pay.

quincenal, *adj.* semimonthly; fortnightly.

quinceno, na, *adj.* fifteenth.

Quincuagésima, *f.* Quinquagesima.

quincuagésimo, ma, *adj.* fiftieth.

quindenio, *m.* period of fifteen years.

quinientos, tas, *adj.* and *m.* five hundred.

quinina, *f.* quinine.

quinqué, *m.* lamp.

quinquenal, *adj.* quinquennial.

quinquenio, *m.* space of five years.

quinta, *f.* country seat, country house; levy, drafting of soldiers; quint (in piquet and fencing); (mus.) fifth.

quintacolumna, *f.* fifth column.

quintacolumnista, *m.* and *f.* fifth columnist.

quintaesencia, *f.* quintessence.

quintal, *m.* quintal, hundredweight.

quintana, *f.* country mansion.

quintar, *va.* to draw one out of five; to levy, to draft soldiers.

quintería, *f.* farm; grange.

quintero, *m.* farmer; servant who takes care of a farm.

quinteto, *m.* (mus.) quintette.

quintilla, *f.* metrical composition of five verses.

Quintín, Quintin, Quentin.

quinto, *m.* fifth; share of a pasture ground; drafted soldier; **—, ta,** *adj.* fifth.

quintúpleto, *m.* quintuplet.

quíntuplo, pla, *adj.* quintuple, fivefold.

quinzavo, va, *m.* and *adj.* fifteenth.

quiñón, *m.* share of profit or lands.

quiñonero, *m.* part owner.

quiosco, *m.* kiosk; summer house, pavilion, stand; **— de música,** bandstand; **— de periódicos,** newstand.

quiromancia, *f.* chiromancy, palmistry.

quiropráctico, *m.* chiropractor.

quirúrgico, ca, *adj.* surgical.

quisicosa, *f.* riddle; obscure question.

quisquilla, *f.* ridiculous nicety; trifling dispute.

quisquilloso, sa, *adj.* difficult, touchy, peevish, irritable.

quisto, ta, *adj.* only used with **bien** and **mal; bien —,** well received, generally beloved; **mal —,** ill received, hated.

¡quita! *interj.* God forbid! **¡— de ahí!** away with you!

quitación, *f.* pay, income.

quitaipón, *m.* headstall ornament for mules; **de —,** removable, off and on.

quitamanchas, *m.* cleaner of clothes.

quitanieve, *m.* snowplow.

quitapelillos, *m.* and *f.* (coll.) wheedler.

quitapesares, *m.* and *f.* (coll.) comfort, consolation.

quitapón, *m.* ornament for the headstall of mules; **de —,** off and on, removable.

quitar, *va.* to take away, to remove; to fetch away; to redeem a pledge; to abrogate, to annul; to free from an obligation; to parry (in fencing); **—se,** to get rid of.

quitasol, *m.* parasol.

quita y pon, (de), *adj.* that can be put on or off as one likes.

quite, *m.* obstacle, impediment.

quito, ta, *adj.* free from an obligation, exempt.

quizá, quizás, *adv.* perhaps.

quórum, *m.* quorum.

q. v. véase, q. v. which see.

R

R.: Reverendo, Rev. Reverend; **Respuesta,** reply; **Reprobado,** not passing (in an examination).

rabadán, *m.* head shepherd.

rabadilla, *f.* rump, croup.

rabanero, ra, *n.* seller of radishes.

rabaniza, *f.* radish seed.
rábano, *m.* radish; — **picante,** horse-radish.
rabia, *f.* rage, fury.
rabiar, *vn.* to be furious, to rage.
rabicorto, ta, *adj.* short-tailed.
rabieta, *f.* touchiness, petulance, bad temper.
rabilargo, ga, *adj.* long-tailed.
rabino, *m.* rabbi.
rabioso, sa, *adj.* rabid; furious.
rabo, *m.* tail.
rabón, ona, *adj.* docked, short-tailed.
rabosear, *va.* to spatter; to crumple, to rumple.
raboso, sa, *adj.* tattered.
rabotear, *va.* to cut or crop the tail.
rabudo, da, *adj.* long-tailed.
racimo, *m.* bunch, cluster (of grapes, etc.).
racimoso, sa, *adj.* having clusters.
raciocinar, *vn.* to reason, to argue.
raciocinio, *m.* reasoning; argument.
ración, *f.* ration, portion; prebend in Spanish cathedrals.
racional, *adj.* rational; reasonable.
racionalidad, *f.* rationality.
racionalismo, *m.* rationalism.
racionamiento, *m.* rationing.
racionar, *va.* to ration.
racismo, *m.* racism.
rada, *f.* anchorage for ships at some distance from shore, roadstead.
radiación, *f.* radiation.
radiador, *m.* radiator.
radiante, *adj.* radiant, beaming.
radiar, *vn.* (poet.) to radiate.
radicación, *f.* taking root; becoming rooted (of a habit).
radical, *adj.* radical, pertaining to the root; —, *m.* (math.) radical; extremist.
radicar, *vn.* to take root; —**se,** to take root; to settle, to establish oneself, to reside.
radio, *m.* or *f.* radio receiver; radio broadcasting station; (math., anat.) radius; (chem.) radium.
radioactividad, *f.* radioactivity.
radioactivo, va, *adj.* radioactive.
radioaficionado, *m.* radio amateur.
radioamplificador, *m.* radio amplifier.
radiocomunicación, *f.* wireless.
radiodifundir, *va.* to broadcast.
radiodifusión, *f.* radiobroadcasting; — **por fonógrafo,** electrical radio transcription.
radiodifusora, *f.* broadcasting station, radiobroadcaster.
radioemisión, *f.* wireless transmission.
radioemisor, ra, *adj.* broadcasting.
radioescucha, *m.* and *f.* radio listener.
radiofaro, *m.* radio beacon.
radiófono, *m.* radiophone.
radiofrecuencia, *f.* radiofrequency.
radiografía, *f.* radiography, X-ray picture.
radiógrafo, *m.* radiographer, X-ray specialist.
radiograma, *m.* radiogram.
radiómetro, *m.* radiometer.
radiorreceptor, *m.* radio receiving set.

radioso, sa, *adj.* radiant.
radiotelefonía, *f.* wireless.
radioteléfono, *m.* radiotelephone.
radiotelegrafista, *m.* and *f.* wireless operator.
radiotelégrafo, *m.* radiotelegraph.
radiotelegrama, *m.* radiotelegram.
radioterapia, *f.* radiotherapy.
radiotermia, *f.* (med.) radiothermy.
radiotransmisor, *m.* radio transmitter.
radioyente, *m.* and *f.* radio listener.
raedera, *f.* scraper, raker.
raedura, *f.* erasure; scrapings.
raer, *va.* to scrape, to grate; to erase.
Rafael, Raphael.
ráfaga, *f.* violent squall of wind.
Raf. Rafael, Raphael.
raglán, *m.* raglan.
raído, da, *adj.* scraped; worn out; impudent.
raigón, *m.* large strong root; root (of a tooth).
rail, *m.* (rail.) rail.
Raimundo, Ramón, Raymond.
raíz, *f.* root; base, basis; origin; **bienes raíces,** *pl.* landed property.
raja, *f.* splinter, chip of wood; slice (of fruit); chink, fissure, crack; coarse cloth.
rajá, *m.* rajah.
rajar, *va.* to split, to chop, to cleave; —, *vn.* (fig. and coll.) to boast.
ralea, *f.* race, breed; species.
ralear, *vn.* to become thin or sparse (as cloth or hair).
raleza, *f.* thinness; rarity.
ralo, la, *adj.* thin, sparse.
ralladura, *f.* mark left by the grater; small particles taken off by grating.
rallo, *m.* grater; ice scraper.
rama, *f.* branch (of a tree, of a family); printer's chase.
ramaje, *m.* foliage; flowering branches designed in cloth.
ramal, *m.* branch, ramification; halter.
rambla, *f.* sandy place; cavern in a rock.
ramera, *f.* whore, prostitute.
ramificación, *f.* ramification.
ramificarse, *vr.* to ramify, to branch out.
ramillete, *m.* nosegay, bouquet.
ramilletero, *m.* vase with artificial flowers for ornamenting altars.
ramo, *m.* branch (of a tree); branch (of trade, science, art, etc.); bunch, bouquet.
ramonear, *vn.* to cut off the branches of trees.
ramoso, sa, *adj.* branchy.
rampa, *f.* slope, ramp.
rampante, *adj.* rampant.
rampojo, *m.* rape of grapes (residue after pressing).
rampollo, *m.* shoot, sprig, sucker.
rana, *f.* frog.
rancidez, *f.* rancidness, rankness.
rancio, cia, *adj.* rank, rancid; old.
ranchear, *va.* and *vn.* to build huts; to lodge in huts.

ranchero, *m.* steward of a mess; small farmer, rancher.

rancho, *m.* mess; messroom; farm; cattle ranch.

randa, *f.* lace trimming.

randado, da, *adj.* trimmed with lace.

rangífero, *m.* reindeer.

rango, *m.* (mil.) rank.

ranúnculo, *m.* (bot.) buttercup.

ranura, *f.* groove.

rapa, *f.* olive tree blossom.

rapacería, *f.* puerility; childish action.

rapacidad, *f.* rapacity.

rapadura, *f.* shaving; baldness.

rapar, *va.* to shave; to plunder.

rapaz, za, *adj.* rapacious; —, *n.* young boy or girl.

rapazada, *f.* childish action or speech.

rape, *m.* hurried shaving; **pelar al** —, to cut hair very close.

rapé, *m.* snuff.

rápidamente, *adv.* rapidly.

rapidez, *f.* rapidity, speed.

rápido, da, *adj.* rapid, swift.

rapiña, *f.* rapine, robbery; **ave de** —, bird of prey.

rapiñar, *va.* to plunder.

raposa, *f.* female fox; cunning, deceitful person.

raposería, *f.* trick, wile, cunning.

raposo, *m.* male fox.

rapsodia, *f.* rhapsody.

rapto, *m.* rapine; ecstasy, rapture; ravishment, abduction.

raptor, *m.* ravisher.

Raquel, Rachel.

raqueta, *f.* racket, battledore.

raquítico, ca, *adj.* rickety.

raquitis, *f.*, **raquitismo,** *m.* rickets, rachitis.

rara avis, (Latin) rara avis, a rarity.

raramente, *adv.* rarely, seldom.

rarefacto, ta, *adj.* rarefied, thin.

rareza, *f.* rarity, rareness.

raridad, *f.* rarity.

raro, ra, *adj.* rare, scarce, extraordinary, strange.

ras, *m.* level, even surface.

rasadura, *f.* leveling with a strickle (in measuring grain).

rasar, *va.* to strike off with a strickle, or level a measure of grain.

rascacielo, *m.* skyscraper.

rascador, *m.* scraper; hatpin.

rascadura, *f.* act of scratching, scraping or rasping.

rascar, *va.* to scratch, to scrape, to scuff.

rascazón, *f.* itching.

rasero, *m.* strickle.

rasete, *m.* satinet, sateen.

rasgado, da, *adj.* torn, open; **boca** —**da,** wide mouth; **ojos** —**dos,** slanting eyes.

rasgar, *va.* to tear, to rend; to sliver.

rasgo, *m.* dash, stroke; grand or magnanimous action; feature, characteristic, trait.

rasgón, *m.* rent, rag, tatter.

rasguear, *vn.* to form bold strokes with the pen; (mus.) to play arpeggios.

rasgueo, *m.* arpeggio.

rasguñar, *va.* to scratch, to scrape.

rasguño, *m.* scratch.

raso, *m.* satin, sateen; glade; —, **sa,** *adj.* plain; flat; **al** —**so,** in the open air.

raspa, *f.* beard of a head of wheat or barley; backbone of fish; stalk of grapes; rasp.

raspadera, *f.* raker.

raspador, *m.* rasp; scraper.

raspadura, *f.* filing, scraping; filings; erasure.

raspar, *va.* to scrape, to rasp; to steal.

raspear, *vn.* to scratch (of pens).

rastra, *f.* sledge; **caminar a** —**s,** to crawl.

rastrallar, *vn.* to crack with a whip.

rastrear, *va.* to trace; to inquire into; —, *vn.* to skim along close to the ground (of birds).

rastrero, ra, *adj.* creeping; low, humble, cringing, reptile; —, *m.* inspector of a slaughterhouse.

rastrillador, ra, *n.* hackler, flax dresser; raker.

rastrillar, *va.* to hackle, to dress flax; to rake.

rastrillo, *m.* hackle; flax comb; portcullis; hammer of a gun; rake.

rastro, *m.* track; sledge; slaughterhouse; sign, token; trail.

rastrojera, *f.* stubble ground.

rastrojo, *m.* stubble.

rasurar, *va.* to shave.

rata, *f.* (zool.) rat.

ratear, *va.* to filch, to commit petty thefts; —, *vn.* to creep.

ratería, *f.* larceny, petty theft.

ratero, ra, *adj.* creeping, mean, vile; —, *n.* pickpocket; sneak thief.

ratificación, *f.* ratification.

ratificar, *va.* to ratify, to approve of.

ratina, *f.* ratteen.

rato, *m.* while; moment; **al poco** —, shortly, in a short while; **a** —**s,** occasionally; **a**—**s perdidos,** in leisure hours; **pasar el** —, to while away the time.

ratón, *m.* mouse.

ratonar, *va.* to gnaw (of animals).

ratonera, *f.* mousetrap; place where rats breed.

raudal, *m.* torrent; stream; abundance.

raya, *f.* stroke; stripe; streak; line; frontier; dash (in punctuation); **a** —, within bounds; —, *m.* ray (fish).

rayado, da, *adj.* striped.

rayano, na, *adj.* neighboring, contiguous, bordering on.

rayar, *va.* to draw lines, to rule; to stripe; to underline; — **en,** to border on.

rayo, *m.* ray, beam of light; flash of lightning; radius; — **equis,** X ray; — **visual,** field of vision.

rayón, *m.* rayon.

rayoso, sa, *adj.* radiating, striped.

raza, *f.* race, lineage; quality.

rázago, *m.* sackcloth.

razón, *f.* reason; cause, motive; ratio, rate; — **directa,** direct ratio; — **inversa,** inverse ratio; — **social,** firm name, name of a concern; **a — de,** at the rate of; **dar —,** to inform, to give account; **dar la —,** to agree with; **perder la —,** to go insane; **tener —,** to be right.

razonable, *adj.* reasonable.

razonado, da, *adj.* rational, prudent.

razonamiento, *m.* reasoning, discourse, argument.

razonar, *vn.* to reason, to discourse; to talk.

Rbí. or **R.**^bi **Recibí,** rec. receipt; recd. received.

R. D. Real Decreto, Royal Decree.

Rda. M. or **R. M. Reverenda Madre,** Reverend Mother.

Rdo. P. or **R. P. Reverendo Padre,** Reverend Father.

R.ᵉ**: Récipe,** (med.) ℞. take (Latin *recipe,* used in prescriptions); **registro,** record.

reacción, *f.* reaction.

reaccionar, *vn.* to react.

reaccionario, ria, *adj.* reactionary.

reacio, cia, *adj.* obstinate, refractory.

reactivo, *m.* (chem.) reagent.

reagravar, *va.* to aggravate anew.

real, *adj.* real, actual; royal; —, *m.* camp; real (a Spanish coin).

realce, *m.* embossment; flash; luster, splendor, enhancement.

realidad, *f.* reality, fact; sincerity.

realismo, *m.* realism.

realista, *m.* and *f.* royalist; realist.

realización, *f.* realization, fulfillment; (com.) bargain sale.

realizar, *va.* to realize, to fulfill; to perform; (com.) to sell, especially at a bargain.

realzar, *va.* to raise, to elevate; to emboss; to heighten.

reanimar, *va.* to cheer, to encourage; to reanimate.

reanudar, *va.* to renew, to resume.

reaparecer, *vn.* (EZCO) to reappear.

reasumir, *va.* to retake, to resume.

reasunción, *f.* resumption.

reata, *f.* collar, leash; rope tied to pack animals to keep them in line; pack train; (fig.) submission to the opinion of others.

reato, *m.* obligation of atonement for a sin which is unabsolved.

rebaja, *f.* abatement, deduction; reduction, rebate.

rebajar, *va.* to-abate, to lessen, to diminish, to curtail, to lower (as price); —se, to humble oneself.

rebalsa, *f.* pool, puddle.

rebalsar, *va.* to dam a stream.

rebanada, *f.* slice.

rebanador, *m.* slicer; —, ra, *adj,* slicing.

rebanar, *va.* to slice; to plane.

rebaño, *m.* flock of sheep, herd of cattle, drove.

rebasar, *va.* to go beyond, to exceed.

rebatir, *va.* to resist; to parry, to ward off; to refute; to repress.

rebato, *m.* unexpected attack, surprise; alarm, alarm bell.

Rebeca, Rebecca.

rebelarse, *vr.* to revolt; to rebel; to resist.

rebelde, *m.* rebel; —, *adj.* rebellious.

rebeldía, *f.* rebelliousness, contumaciousness, disobedience; (law) contumacy; **en —,** by default.

rebelión, *f.* rebellion, revolt.

rebenque, *m.* cat-o'-nine-tails.

reblandecer, *va.* (EZCO) to soften.

rebolledo, *m.* underbrush.

rebollo, *m.* trunk of a tree.

rebolludo, da, *adj.* thick-set.

rebombar, *vn.* to make a loud sound or report.

reborde, *m.* ledge, border.

rebosadura, *f.* overflow.

rebosar, *va.* to run over, to overflow; to abound.

rebotar, *va.* to clinch the point of a spike or nail; to repel; —, *vn.* to rebound.

rebote, *m.* rebound; **de —,** indirectly.

rebozo, *m.* muffling of oneself; woman's shawl; (fig.) pretext; **de —,** secretly; **sin —,** frankly, openly.

rebullir, *vn.* to stir, to begin to move.

reburujar, *va.* to wrap up, to pack up in bundles.

rebusca, *f.* research; refuge, remains.

rebuscador, ra, *n.* gleaner; researcher.

rebuscar, *va.* to glean the remains of grapes left by the vintagers; to search, to inquire.

rebuznar, *vn.* to bray.

rebuzno, *m.* braying of an ass.

recabar, *va.* to obtain by entreaty.

recadista, *m.* messenger boy.

recado, *m.* message; gift; compliments sent to an absent person.

recaer, *vn.* (RECAIGO, RECAÍ) to fall back again; to have a relapse; to behoove.

recaída, *f.* relapse.

recalcar, *va.* to emphasize; to squeeze; to stuff; —se, to utter repeatedly; to lean back in a chair.

recalcitrar, *vn.* to kick; to wince; to be recalcitrant.

recalentamiento, *m.* reheating.

recalentar, *va.* (IE) to heat again.

recalzar, *va.* to prick a design on paper; to hill (plants); to repair cement.

recamado, da, *adj.* decorated, embroidered.

recamar, *va.* to embroider with raised work.

recámara, *f.* boudoir, bedroom; chamber of a gun.

recantón, *m.* cornerstone.

recapacitar, *va.* to recall to mind.

recapitulación, *f.* recapitulation.

recapitular, *va.* to recapitulate.

recargar, *va.* to recharge; to charge again; to cram; to remand to prison on a new charge; to resurface (a road),

recargo, *m.* new charge or accusation; overload; additional tax; increase of a fever; resurfacing (of a road).

recatado, da, *adj.* prudent, circumspect, modest.

recatar, *va.* to conceal carefully; **—se,** to take care.

recato, *m.* prudence, care, circumspection; modesty; bashfulness.

recaudación, *f.* recovery of debts; collector's office.

recaudador, *m.* taxgatherer.

recaudar, *va.* to gather; to collect (rent or taxes); to obtain.

recaudo, *m.* rent or tax collection; bail; **a buen —,** under guard.

recavar, *va.* to dig the ground a second time.

recebar, *va.* to spread gravel.

recelar, *va.* to fear, to suspect, to misdoubt.

recelo, *m.* dread, suspicion, mistrust.

receloso, sa, *adj.* mistrustful, suspicious; shy.

recentadura, *f.* leaven kept for another batch of breadmaking.

recental, *adj.* sucking (of lambs).

recepción, *f.* reception; acceptance.

receptáculo, *m.* receptacle; refuge, asylum.

receptor, *m.* receiver, treasurer; investigating official; radio receiver.

receptoría, *f.* receiver's or treasurer's office.

receso, *m.* withdrawal, retirement; (Mex.) recess.

receta, *f.* recipe; prescription; account, list.

recetar, *va.* to prescribe medicines.

recetario, *m.* register of the prescriptions made by a physician; druggist's file.

recibí, *m.* (com.) receipt.

recibidor, *m.* receiver; receiving teller; entrance hall.

recibimiento, *m.* reception, receipt; antechamber.

recibir, *va.* to receive; to let in; to go to meet; **—se,** to be admitted.

recib.º recibido, recd. received.

recibo, *m.* receipt, voucher; **acusar —,** to acknowledge receipt; **estar de —,** to be at home for reception purposes; **día de —,** reception day.

recidiva, *f.* (med.) relapse.

recién, *adv.* recently, lately; **— casado, da,** newlywed.

reciente, *adj.* recent, new, fresh; modern.

recientemente, *adv.* recently, lately.

recinto, *m.* precinct, district; place.

recio, cia, *adj.* stout, strong, robust; coarse, thick; rude; arduous, rigid; **—,** *adv.* strongly, stoutly; **hablar —cio,** to talk loud.

récipe, *m.* prescription of a physician; (coll.) displeasure, disgust.

recipiente, *m.* recipient, container.

reciprocidad, *f.* reciprocity.

recíproco, ca, *adj.* reciprocal, mutual.

recisión, *f.* abrogation.

recitación, *f.* recitation.

recitar, *va.* to recite.

recitativo, va, *adj.* recitative.

reclamación, *f.* reclamation; remonstrance, claim, complaint.

reclamante, *m.* and *f.* claimant.

reclamar, *va.* to claim, to demand; to decoy birds with a call or whistle; (law) to reclaim.

reclamo, *m.* decoy bird; a bird trained to decoy others; call; an instrument for calling; allurement; reclamation; catchword (in printing); advertising; claim.

reclinación, *f.* reclining.

reclinar, *va.* and *vn.* to recline, to lean back.

reclinatorio, *m.* couch; object on which to recline.

recluir, *va.* and *vr.* (UYO) to shut up, to seclude.

reclusión, *f.* reclusion; recess.

recluta, *f.* recruiting; **—,** *m.* recruit.

reclutador, *m.* recruiting officer.

reclutamiento, *m.* recruiting; **caja de —,** recruiting branch for the army or navy.

reclutar, *va.* to recruit.

recobrar, *va.* to recover; **—se,** to recover from sickness; to recollect.

recobro, *m.* recovery.

recocer, *va.* (UE) to boil again; **—se,** to consume oneself with rage.

recocido, da, *adj.* overcooked; skillful, clever.

recodar, *vn.* to lean the elbow upon anything.

recodo, *m.* corner or angle jutting out; turn.

recogedero, *m.* meeting place, rendezvous; collecting instrument.

recogedor, ra, *n.* harborer, shelterer; gatherer; **—,** *m.* scraper (instrument).

recoger, *va.* to retake, to take back; to gather, to pick up; to shelter; to compile; to ask charity; **—se,** to take shelter or refuge; to retire to rest; to withdraw from the world.

recogido, da, *adj.* retired, secluded.

recogimiento, *m.* collection; retreat, shelter; abstraction from all worldly concerns.

recolchado, *m.* wadding.

recolección, *f.* summary; recollection.

recomendación, *f.* recommendation.

recomendar, *va.* (IE) to charge; to recommend.

recompensa, *f.* compensation; recompense, reward.

recompensar, *va.* to recompense, to reward.

recomponer, *va.* (RECOMPONGO, RECOMPUSE) to recompose.

reconcentrar, *va.* to concenter; to dissemble; to concentrate one's mind.

reconciliación, *f.* reconciliation.

reconciliar, *va.* to reconcile; **—se,** to become reconciled.

recondenado, *m.* sly fellow, old fox.

recóndito, ta, *adj.* recondite, secret, concealed.

reconocedor, ra, *n.* examiner, reviser.

reconocer, *va.* (RECONOZCO, RECONOCÍ) to examine closely; to acknowledge favors received; to admit; to recognize; to consider; (mil.) to reconnoiter; **—se,** to know oneself; to repent.

reconocido, da, *adj.* grateful.

reconocimiento, *m.* recognition; acknowledgment; gratitude; confession; submission; inquiry; reconnaissance; reconnoitering; **— médico,** medical examination; **aereoplano de —,** reconnaissance plane.

reconquista, *f.* reconquest.

reconquistar, *va.* to reconquer.

reconstituir, *va.* and *vr.* to reconstitute.

reconstituyente, *adj.* reconstituent; **—,** *m.* (med.) tonic.

reconstruir, *va.* (UYO) to reconstruct.

recontar, *va.* (UE) to recount, to count again; to relate.

recontento, ta, *adj.* much pleased; **—,** *m.* deep contentment.

reconvención, *f.* recrimination.

reconvenir, *va.* (RECONVENGO, RECONVINE) to retort, to recriminate.

recopilación, *f.* summary, abridgment.

recopilador, *m.* compiler.

recopilar, *va.* to compile; to abridge.

recordar, *va.* and *vr.* (UE) to remind; to remember; **—,** *vn.* to call to mind.

recordativo, va, *adj.* reminding, refresher.

recorredor, *m.* runner in a track meet.

recorrer, *va.* to run over, to peruse; to mend, to repair; to travel over.

recorrido, *m.* run, line; expedition; **final del —,** end of streetcar line, bus line, etc.

recortar, *va.* to cut away, to pare off, to trim.

recorte, *m.* outline; shred; **— de periódico,** newspaper clipping.

recoser, *va.* to sew again.

recostar, *va.* (UE) to lean against, to recline; **—se,** to recline, to rest.

recreación, *f.* recreation, amusement.

recrear, *va.* and *vr.* to amuse, to delight, to recreate.

recreativo, va, *adj.* recreative, diverting.

recrecimiento, *m.* increase, growth.

recreo, *m.* recreation, pastime, pleasure; recess, play; **campo** or **patio de —,** playground; **hora de —,** recess hour; **salón de —,** recreation hall.

recriminación, *f.* recrimination.

recriminar, *va.* to recriminate.

¡Recristo! *interj.* heavens!

recrudescencia, *f.* recrudescence.

recrudescente, *adj.* recrudescent.

rectamente, *adj.* justly, rightly.

rectángulo, la, *adj.* rectangular; **—,** *m.* rectangle.

rectificación, *f.* rectification.

rectificador, *m.* rectifier.

rectificar, *va.* to rectify, to correct.

rectilíneo, nea, *adj.* rectilinear.

rectitud, *f.* straightness; rectitude; justness, honesty; exactitude.

recto, ta, *adj.* straight, direct, right; just, honest.

rector, ra, *n.* superior of a community or establishment; rector, president or chancellor (of a university); curate, rector.

rectorado, *m.* rectorship.

rectoría, *f.* rectory, curacy; rectorship.

recua, *f.* drove of pack animals, pack train; (coll.) group of persons or things one after another.

recubrimiento, *m.* road surfacing.

recubrir, *va.* to cover again.

recudimiento, *m.* power vested in a person to collect rents or taxes.

recuento, *m.* inventory; recount.

recuerdo, *m.* remembrance, memory; souvenir; **—s,** *pl.* regards.

recuesto, *m.* declivity, gradual descent.

reculada, *f.* falling astern of a ship; recoil.

recular, *vn.* to recoil; to fall back, to back up.

recuperable, *adj.* recoverable.

recuperación, *f.* recovery.

recuperar, *va.* to recover; **—se,** to recover from sickness.

recurrir, *vn.* to recur; to turn to, to resort.

recurso, *m.* recourse; resource; **—s,** *pl.* means.

recusación, *f.* refusal; recusation.

recusar, *va.* to refuse; to refuse to admit.

rechazamiento, *m.* repulsion, rejection.

rechazar, *va.* to repel, to repulse, to reject; to contradict.

rechazo, *m.* rebound; rejection; recoil.

rechifla, *f.* mockery, derision.

rechiflar, *va.* to mock, to laugh.

rechinamiento, *m.* creaking of a machine; gnashing (of teeth).

rechinar, *vn.* to gnash the teeth; to creak.

rechino, *m.* creaking; gnashing.

rechoncho, cha, *adj.* (coll.) chubby.

red, *f.* net; web; grate through which fish or bread are sold; snare, wile, fraud; silk coif; **— barredera,** dragnet; **— de estaciones,** station network.

redacción, *f.* editing; editor's office; editorial staff.

redactar, *va.* to edit (a publication); to draw up, to draft.

redactor, *m.* editor.

redaño, *m.* (anat.) caul, omentum.

redecilla, *f.* hair net.

rededor, *m.* environs; **al — de,** around, more or less.

redención, *f.* redemption; ransom; assistance, support.

redentor, ra, *n.* and *adj.* redeemer; redeeming.

redil, *m.* sheepfold.

redimible, *adj.* redeemable.

redimir, *va.* to redeem, to ransom; to succor.

redingote, *m.* riding coat.

rédito, *m.* interest, yield of invested capital.

redoblado, da, *adj.* redoubled; stout and thick.

redoblar, *va.* to redouble; to rivet.
redoble, *m.* doubling, repetition; (mus.) octave; (mil.) roll of a drum.
redoma, *f.* vial.
redonda, *f.* (mus.) whole note.
redondear, *va.* to round off; to make round; —se, to extricate oneself from a difficulty.
redondel, *m.* round cloak; circle.
redondez, *f.* roundness, circular form.
redondilla, *f.* seven syllable verse in quatrains with alternate rimes.
redondo, da, *adj.* round; **a la —da,** round-about.
reducción, *f.* reduction; mutation; dissolution, liquefaction; exchange, change of money.
reducible, *adj.* reducible, convertible.
reducir, *va.* (REDUZCO, REDUJE) to reduce; to exchange; to convert; — **la marcha,** to slow down; —se, to cut down one's expenses; to economize.
reductor, ra, *adj.* reducing; **agente —or,** reducing agent.
redundancia, *f.* superfluity, redundance, excess.
redundante, *adj.* redundant, superfluous.
redundar, *va.* to overflow, to be redundant; to contribute; — **en,** to redound, to lead to, to result.
reedificación, *f.* rebuilding.
reedificar, *va.* to rebuild.
reeditar, *va.* to reprint.
reelección, *f.* re-election.
reelegir, *va.* (REELIJO, REELEGÍ) to re-elect, to substitute.
reembarque, *m.* reshipment.
reembolsar, *va.* to recover money advanced; to reimburse.
reembolso, *m.* reimbursement; **contra —,** by reimbursement.
reemplazar, *va.* to replace, to restore.
reemplazo, *m.* replacement; substitute in the militia.
reencarnación, *f.* reincarnation.
reencuentro, *m.* clash (of troops); collision.
reenganchar, *va.* (mech.) to recouple; (mil.) to re-enlist; —se, to enlist again.
reengendrar, *va.* to regenerate, to re-produce.
ref. referencia, ref. reference.
refacción, *f.* refection, refreshment; retribution, financing.
refajo, *m.* short petticoat.
refectorio, *m.* refectory.
referencia, *f.* reference.
referendario, *m.* officer appointed to countersign edicts or other documents.
referente, *adj.* referring, relating.
referir, *va.* (IE) to refer, to relate, to report; —se, to refer to, to relate to.
refigurar, *va.* to refigure.
refilón, de —, *adv.* obliquely, askance.
refinadera, *f.* refiner (a long cylindrical stone).
refinado, da, *adj.* refined; subtle, artful.

refinador, *m.* refiner.
refinadura, *f.* refining.
refinamiento, *m.* refinement, excellence.
refinar, *va.* to refine.
reflector, *m.* reflector, reverberator, searchlight.
reflejar, *va.* and *vr.* to reflect.
reflejo, *m.* reflex; reflection, light, glare.
reflexión, *f.* meditation, reflection.
reflexionar, *vn.* to reflect, to meditate, to consider.
reflexivo, va, *adj.* reflexive; reflective; pensive.
reflorecer, *vn.* (EZCO) to blossom again.
refluir, *vn.* (UYO) to flow back, to reflow.
reflujo, *m.* reflux, ebb tide; **flujo y —,** the tides.
refocilación, *f.* bracing recreation; reinvigoration.
refocilar, *va.* to brace up by healthful recreation; to reinvigorate.
reforma, *f.* reform; correction.
reformación, *f.* reformation, reform.
reformado, *m.* officer left without a command.
reformar, *va.* to reform, to correct, to restore; —se, to mend, to have one's manners reformed or corrected; to be prudent and moderate in speech and conduct.
reformatorio, *m.* reformatory.
reforzada, *f.* narrow tape.
reforzado, da, *adj.* reinforced; extra thick and strong at the breech (of firearms).
reforzar, *va.* (UE) to strengthen, to fortify; —se, to be strengthened and recovered.
refracción, *f.* refraction.
refractario, ria, *adj.* refractory; fireproof.
refrán, *m.* proverb, saying.
refregar, *va.* (IE) to rub one thing against another.
refregón, *m.* friction, rubbing of one thing against another.
refrenamiento, *m.* curb, refraining, restraint.
refrenar, *va.* to refrain, to restrain.
refrendación, *f.* countersigning.
refrendar, *va.* to countersign.
refrendario, *m.* officer appointed to countersign edicts, ordinances, or other public acts.
refrendata, *f.* countersignature.
refrescante, *adj.* refreshing, cooling.
refrescar, *va.* to refresh; —, *vn.* to cool; to take the air.
refresco, *m.* refreshment; lunch; cold drink.
refriega, *f.* affray, skirmish, encounter, fray.
refrigerador, *m.* refrigerator.
refrigerar, *va.* to cool, to refresh, to comfort, to refrigerate.
refrigerio, *m.* refrigeration, refreshment; consolation, comfort.
refringir, *va.* and *vr.* to refract.
refuerzo, *m.* reinforcement.
refugiado, da, *n.* refugee.

refugiar, *va.* to shelter; **—se,** to take refuge.
refugio, *m.* refuge, asylum; shelter; safety island.
refulgente, *adj.* refulgent.
refundición, *f.* remelting of metal, rearranging.
refundir, *va.* to melt metal again; to contain; to rearrange; to rehash.
refunfuñadura, *f.* growling, grumbling.
refunfuñar, *vn.* to snarl, to growl, to grumble.
refunfuño, *m.* growling, grumbling.
refutación, *f.* refutation.
refutar, *va.* to refute.
regadera, *f.* watering pot, sprinkler.
regadío, día, *adj.* irrigated, watered (of land).
regadizo, za, *adj.* that can be irrigated or watered.
regadura, *f.* irrigation, watering.
regalado, da, *adj.* convenient; pleasant; delicate, dainty; given as a present.
regalar, *va.* to regale; to make a present of; to caress; **—se,** to feast; to regale oneself.
regalía, *f.* regalia; privilege; royalty, share of profit.
regaliza, *f.* licorice.
regalo, *m.* present, gift, largess; regalement.
regañar, *vn.* to growl, to grumble; to quarrel; **—,** *va.* to scold, to reprimand.
regañón, ona, *adj.* snarling, growling, grumbling; scolding.
regar, *va.* (IE) to water, to irrigate; to spread.
regata, *f.* irrigating ditch; regatta.
regate, *m.* dribbling (in Rugby, basketball).
regatear, *vn.* to use evasions; **—,** *va.* to haggle, to higgle, to bargain.
regateo, *m.* act of haggling or bartering.
regatón, *m.* socket, ferrule; **—, ona,** *adj.* retailing.
regazo, *m.* lap of a woman.
regencia, *f.* regency; regentship.
regeneración, *f.* regeneration.
regenerar, *va.* to regenerate.
regenta, *f.* wife of a regent.
regente, *m.* regent; manager (in printing offices); registered pharmacist.
regiamente, *adv.* royally.
regidor, *m.* alderman; governor, prefect.
régimen, *m.* regimen, regime, management; (gram.) rules of verbs.
regimentar, *va.* (IE) to form regiments.
regimiento, *m.* administration, government; regimen; magistracy of a city; municipality; (mil.) regiment.
Reginaldo, Reginald.
regio, gia, *adj.* royal, kingly.
región, *f.* region, tract of country.
regionalismo, *m.* regionalism, sectionalism.
regir, *va.* (I) to rule, to govern, to direct.
—, *vn.* to be in force.
registrador, ra, *adj.* registering; **caja —,** cash register; **—,** *m.* registrar; inspector;
registrar, *va.* to survey, to inspect; to

examine; to search; to record, to enter in a register; **—se,** to register oneself.
registro, *m.* register, registration, examining or enrolling office; record; inspection; damper of a furnace; **— de efectos a cobrar,** bills-receivable book; **— de efectos a pagar,** bills-payable book.
regla, *f.* rule, law, statute, order, measure; rule, ruler; **— áurea,** golden rule; **— de cálculo,** slide rule; **— fija,** standard rule.
reglado, da, *adj.* regulated, temperate.
reglamento, *m.* by-law; set of rules and regulations.
reglar, *adj.* (eccl.) regular; **—,** *va.* to rule; to regulate; **—se,** to reform.
reglón, *m.* level (used by masons).
regocijado, da, *adj.* exultant.
regocijar, *va.* and *vr.* to rejoice; to gladden, to delight.
regocijo, *m.* joy, pleasure, merriment, rejoicing.
regoldar, *vn.* (ÜE) to belch.
regolfar, *vn.* to flow back.
regona, *f.* large irrigating canal.
regordete, *adj.* chubby, plump.
regresar, *vn.* to return to a place.
regreso, *m.* return, regression; **de — a,** on (my) way back to.
regüeldo, *m.* eructation, belch.
reguera, *f.* canal for watering lands or plants.
reguero, *m.* small rivulet; trickling line of spilt liquid; drain, gutter.
regulación, *f.* regulation; comparison, computation.
regulador, ra, *n.* regulator; timer; **—,** *m.* throttle valve.
regular, *va.* to regulate, to adjust; **—,** *adj.* regular; ordinary.
regularidad, *f.* regularity.
regurgitar, *va.* to regurgitate.
rehabilitación, *f.* rehabilitation.
rehabilitar, *va.* to rehabilitate.
rehacer, *va.* (REHAGO, REHICE) to repair, to make again; **—se,** to regain strength and vigor; (mil.) to rally.
rehecho, cha, *adj.* remade; squat, broadshouldered.
rehén, *m.* hostage.
rehilete, *m.* shuttlecock (in badminton).
rehogar, *va.* to roast.
rehuir, *va.* and *vr.* (UYO) to shun, to avoid; to back track.
rehumedecer, *va.* and *vr.* (EZCO) to dampen thoroughly.
rehundir, *va.* and *vr.* to sink; to remelt; to waste.
rehusar, *va.* to refuse, to decline.
reidor, ra, *adj.* jolly, laughing; **—,** *n.* person who laughs often.
reimpresión, *f.* reprint.
reimprimir, *va.* to reissue, to reprint.
reina, *f.* queen.
reinado, *m.* reign.

Reinaldo, Reynold.
reinar, *vn.* to reign, to govern.
reincidencia, *f.* reiteration, relapse.
reincidir, *vn.* to relapse, to fall back.
reino, *m.* kingdom, reign.
reintegración, *f.* reintegration, restoration.
reintegrar, *va.* to reintegrate, to restore; **—se,** to be reinstated or restored.
reintegro, *m.* reintegration; reimbursement.
reír, *vn.* (RÍo, REÍ) to laugh; **—se de,** to laugh at.
reiteración, *f.* repetition, reiteration.
reiterar, *va.* to reiterate, to repeat.
reja, *f.* plowshare; lattice; grating; railing; **—s,** bars.
rejalgar, *m.* (min.) realgar.
rejilla, *f.* small lattice or grating.
rejo, *m.* pointed iron bar or spike; sting of an insect.
rejón, *m.* dagger, poniard; spear used by bullfighters; short broad knife with a sharp point.
rejonazo, *m.* dagger thrust.
rejonear, *va.* to spear bulls.
rejuela, *f.* foot stove, warming pan.
rejuvenecer, *vn.* (EZCO) to grow young again, to be rejuvenated.
Rel. religión, rel. religion.
relación, *f.* relation; report; account; **—es,** *pl.* connections; **tener — con,** to be acquainted with.
relacionado, da, *adj.* related, connected, germane.
relacionar, *va.* to relate; to connect; to make acquainted.
relajación, *f.* relaxation; remission; laxity; commutation of a vow; remission of a criminal from an ecclesiastical to a secular court.
relajar, *va.* to relax, to slacken, to remit; **—se,** to be relaxed; to suffer from a hernia.
relamer, *va.* to lick again; **—se,** to lick one's lips; to relish; to paint oneself to excess.
relamido, da, *adj.* affected, overnice in dress.
relámpago, *m.* flash of lightning; **— sin trueno,** heat lightning.
relampaguear, *vn.* to lighten, to flash.
relapso, sa, *adj.* relapsed, fallen back into error or criminal ways.
relatar, *va.* to relate.
relatividad, *f.* relativity.
relativo, va, *adj.* relative, pertaining; **—vo a,** with regard to.
relato, *m.* statement; account, narrative.
relator, ra, *n.* relater, narrator.
relatoría, *f.* office of a reporter of judicial causes in a court of justice.
relegación, *f.* relegation, exile.
relegar, *va.* to relegate, to banish; to exile.
relente, *m.* evening dew; (coll.) boldness.
relentecer, *vn.* (EZCO) to grow soft or tender.
relevación, *f.* relevation; alleviation; relief; remission, pardon.

relevante, *adj.* great, eminent.
relevar, *va.* to emboss, to work in relief; to exonerate, to disburden; to relieve from a burden or charge; to assist; to succor; to forgive, to pardon; to exalt, to aggrandize; to paint an object to appear as if rising; to relieve, to substitute.
relevo, *m.* (mil.) relief.
relicario, *m.* reliquary.
relieve, *m.* relief (sculpture); **bajo —,** bas-relief.
religar, *va.* to bind more securely; to solder.
religión, *f.* religion.
religionario, ria, *n.* religionist; Reformist, Calvinist.
religiosidad, *f.* religiousness.
religioso, sa, *adj.* religious, pious.
relinchar, *vn.* to neigh.
relincho, *m.* neigh, neighing.
relindo, da, *adj.* extremely beautiful.
reliquia, *f.* residue, remains; saintly relic.
relocalización, *f.* relocation.
reloj, *m.* clock, watch; **— de pulsera,** wrist watch; **— marino,** chronometer; **movimiento de —,** works of a watch.
relojera, *f.* watchcase.
relojería, *f.* watchmaking; watch shop.
relojero, *m.* watchmaker.
reluciente, *adj.* resplendent, shining, glittering.
relucir, *vn.* (UZCO) to shine, to glitter; to excel, to be brilliant.
reluchar, *vn.* to struggle, to wrestle obstinately.
relumbrar, *vn.* to sparkle, to shine.
relumbrón, *m.* luster.
rellenar, *va.* to refill; to stuff.
relleno, *m.* fine-ground meat; refill; stuffing; **—, na,** *adj.* satiated.
remachado, da, *adj.* riveted.
remachador, *m.* riveter.
remachar, *va.* to rivet.
remache, *m.* rivet.
remaneciente, *adj.* reappearing.
remanente, *m.* residue, remains, remnant.
remangar, *va.* to tuck up (sleeves, dress, etc.).
remansarse, *vr.* to obstruct the course of a stream.
remanso, *m.* stagnant water; tardiness.
remar, *vn.* to row.
rematadamente, *adv.* entirely, totally.
rematado, da, *adj.* totally lost, utterly ruined; **loco —,** stark mad.
rematar, *va.* to terminate, to complete, to finish; to adjudge to the best bidder; **—,** *vn.* to be at an end; **—se,** to be utterly ruined.
remate, *m.* end, conclusion; auction sale.
remecer, *va.* (EZCO) to rock, to swing to and fro.
remedar, *va.* to copy, to imitate, to mimic.
remediable, *adj.* remediable.
remediador, ra, *n.* helper; curer.
remediar, *va.* to remedy; to assist, to help; to free from danger; to prevent.

remedio, *m.* remedy, reparation; help; amendment, correction; resource; refuge; **no tener —,** to be unavoidable; **sin —,** inevitable.

remedo, *m.* imitation, copy.

remellado, da, *adj.* jagged.

remendar, *va.* (IE) to patch, to mend; to correct.

remendón, *m.* patcher, cobbler.

remero, *m.* rower, oarsman.

remesa, *f.* sending of goods; remittance of money.

remiendo, *m.* patch, repair; correction; **a —s,** piecemeal.

remilgarse, *vr.* to be affectedly nice or grave.

remilgo, *m.* affected nicety or gravity.

reminiscencia, *f.* reminiscence, recollection.

remirado, da, *adj.* prudent, cautious.

remirar, *va.* to revise, to review; **—se,** to do very carefully; to consider.

remisible, *adj.* remissible.

remisión, *f.* act of sending back; remission, forgiveness; remittance.

remiso, sa, *adj.* remiss, careless, indolent.

remitente, *m.* and *f.* remitter, shipper, sender; **—,** *adj.* remittent.

remitir, *va.* to remit, to transmit; to pardon, to exempt from punishment; to suspend, to put off; **—,** *vn.* and *vr.* to slacken, to abate.

remo, *m.* oar; long and hard labor; **—s,** *pl.* limbs (of a person); legs (of an animal).

remoción, *f.* removal, remotion.

remojadero, *m.* soaking vat.

remojar, *va.* to soak; to steep.

remojo, *m.* steeping, soaking.

remolacha, *f.* beet.

remolcador, *m.* tug boat.

remolcar, *va.* (naut.) to tow.

remolinar, *vn.* to spin round; **—se,** to collect together tumultuously (of a crowd).

remolino, *m.* whirlwind; whirlpool; backwater.

remolón, ona, *adj.* soft, lazy; **—,** *m.* upper tusk of a wild boar.

remolonearse, *vr.* to refuse to move; to tarry, to delay.

remolque, *m.* towing a ship; trailer; **aeroplano de —,** towplane; **cable de —,** towline.

remono, na, *adj.* (coll.) very pretty, very cute.

remonta, *f.* (mil.) remount, supply of cavalry horses; resoling (of shoes).

remontar, *va.* to frighten away; to remount cavalry; to repair saddles; to resole (shoes); **—se,** to tower, to soar; **— a,** to go back to, to date from.

remontista, *m.* commissioner for the purchase of cavalry horses.

rémora, *f.* sucker (a fish); hindrance, cause of delay.

remordedor, ra, *adj.* causing regret, disquieting, discomposing.

remorder, *va.* (UE) to cause remorse; **—se,** to manifest or express concern; to bite again.

remordimiento, *m.* remorse.

remoto, ta, *adj.* remote, distant, far.

remover, *va.* (UE) to remove; to stir; to dismiss.

removimiento, *m.* removal; dismissal.

remozar, *va.* and *vr.* to rejuvenate.

rempujar, *va.* to push or shove a person out of his place.

rempujón, *m.* impulse, push, thrust, shove.

remudar, *va.* to replace, to substitute.

remuneración, *f.* remuneration, recompense.

remunerador, ra, *n.* remunerator.

remunerar, *va.* to reward, to remunerate.

remusgo, *m.* sharp, cold wind; presentiment.

renacer, *vn.* (AZCO) to be born again; to be new-born.

renaciente, *adj.* renascent.

Renacimiento, *m.* Renaissance.

renacimiento, *m.* regeneration; renascence; rebirth, new birth.

rencilla, *f.* quarrel or dispute which leaves a grudge.

rencilloso, sa, *adj.* peevish, quarrelsome.

rencor, *m.* rancor, grudge, spite; **guardar —,** to bear a grudge.

rencoroso, sa, *adj.* rancorous.

rendición, *f.* rendition; profit.

rendidamente, *adv.* humbly.

rendido, da, *adj.* worn-out, fatigued.

rendija, *f.* crevice, crack, cleft.

rendimiento, *m.* rendition; output, yielding; weariness, submission; humbling compliance; rent, income; (mech.) efficiency.

rendir, *va.* (I) to subject, to subdue, to produce, to yield; **—se,** to be tired, to be fatigued; to yield; to surrender; **— gracias,** to give thanks; **— un examen,** to take an examination.

renegado, *m.* apostate; wicked person.

renegar, *va.* (IE) to deny, to disown; to detest, to abhor; **—,** *vn.* to apostatize; to blaspheme, to curse.

renglón, *m.* written or printed line; (com.) part of one's income; item; **—ones,** *pl.* writings.

reniego, *m.* execration; curse; blasphemy.

reno, *m.* reindeer.

renombrado, da, *adj.* renowned.

renombre, *m.* surname; renown.

renovación, *f.* renovation, renewal; resuscitation.

renovador, *m.* renovator.

renovar, *va.* (UE) to renew, to renovate, to reform.

renquear, *vn.* to limp, to halt.

renta, *f.* rent, income.

rentero, *m.* renter, farmer.

rentista, *m.* and *f.* financier, independent person.

renuencia, *f.* unwillingness.

renuevo, *m.* sprout, shoot; renewal.

renuncia, *f.* renunciation, resignation; retraction.

renunciar, *va.* to renounce, to resign.

renuncio, *m.* renege or revoke (cards).

reñido, da, *adj.* at variance, at odds; hard-fought.

reñir, *va.* and *vn.* (RIÑÓ, RIÑENDO) to wrangle; to quarrel; to scold, to chide.

reo, *m.* offender, criminal.

reojo, *m.* **mirar de —,** to look at furtively, to look out of the corner of one's eye; to look contemptuously.

reorganización, *f.* reorganization.

reóstato, *m.* rheostat.

Rep. República, Rep. Republic.

repanchigarse, or **repantigarse,** *vr.* to stretch oneself out in a chair.

reparable, *adj.* reparable, remediable.

reparación, *f.* reparation, repair.

reparada, *f.* sudden bound of a horse.

reparar, *va.* to repair; to consider, to observe; to make amends; to give heed; to notice; **—,** *vn.* to parry.

reparativo, va, *adj.* reparative.

reparo, *m.* repair, reparation; notice; consideration; difficulty; cataplasm; **poner —,** to object.

repartición, *f.* distribution.

repartidor, ra, *n.* distributor; **—,** *m.* assessor of taxes.

repartimiento, *m.* distribution; assessment of taxes.

repartir, *va.* to distribute, to divide.

reparto, *m.* distribution; (theat.) cast of characters.

repasadora, *f.* wool comber.

repasar, *va.* and *vn.* to repass; to revise, to review, to look over; to clean (dyed wool); to mend (clothes).

repaso, *m.* revision, review; reprimand.

repatriación, *f.* repatriation.

repechar, *vn.* to ascend a slope.

repecho, *m.* declivity, slope.

repeladura, *f.* second shearing.

repelar, *va.* to tear out someone's hair; (Mex.) to grumble.

repeler, *va.* to repel; to refute, to reject.

repelón, *m.* tearing of hair; **a —ones,** by degrees, little by little; **de —,** by the way; in haste.

repello, *m.* plaster, plastering.

repensar, *va.* (IE) to think over, to reconsider.

repente, de —, *adv.* suddenly, on a sudden; offhand.

repentinamente, *adv.* suddenly.

repentino, na, *adj.* sudden, unforeseen.

repercusión, *f.* reverberation, repercussion.

repercutir, *vn.* to reverberate.

repertorio, *m.* repertory, index.

repetición, *f.* repetition; (mus.) repeat.

repetidor, ra, *n.* repeater.

repetir, *va.* (I) to repeat, to restate.

repicar, *va.* to chime, to ring a merry peal; **—se,** to pride oneself on.

repinarse, *vr.* to rise, to soar.

repique, *m.* chime, peal; dispute.

repiquetear, *va.* to ring merrily (bells); **—se,** to bicker, to wrangle with one another (two or more persons).

repiqueteo, *m.* pitter-patter.

repisa, *f.* pedestal or stand.

replegar, *va.* (IE) to redouble; (mil.) to wheel round the wing of an army; **—se,** (mil.) to fall back.

repleto, ta, *adj.* replete, very full.

réplica, *f.* reply, answer; repartee; replica.

replicar, *vn.* to reply, to answer; to argue.

repoblar, *va.* (UE) to repeople.

repollo, *m.* cabbage head.

repolludo, da, *adj.* cabbage-headed, round-headed.

reponer, *va.* (REPONGO, REPUSE) to replace; (law) to restore a case to a former or original state; **—se,** to recover lost health or property.

reportar, *va.* to refrain; to obtain, to reach; to attain; to carry, to bring.

reportorio, *m.* calendar, almanac.

reposado, da, *adj.* quiet, peaceful; settled (wine).

reposar, *vn.* to rest, to repose.

reposición, *f.* (law) restoring (of a case) to its primitive state.

reposo, *m.* rest, repose, quiescence.

repostería, *f.* pastry shop; butler's pantry.

repostero, *m.* pastry cook.

repreguntar, *va.* (law) to cross-examine.

reprender, *va.* to reprehend, to blame.

reprensible, *adj.* reprehensible.

reprensión, *f.* reprehension, blame, reproach.

represa, *f.* stoppage, retention; dam.

represalia, *f.* reprisal, reprise.

represar, *va.* to stop, to retain, to repress.

representable, *adj.* representable.

representación, *f.* representation; authority; performance.

representante, *m.* and *f.* representative; player; understudy (stage); **Cámara de R—s,** House of Representatives.

representar, *va.* to represent; to play on the stage.

representativo, va, *adj.* representative.

represión, *f.* repression.

reprimenda, *f.* reprimand.

reprimir, *va.* to repress, to refrain.

reprobable, *adj.* reprehensible.

reprobación, *f.* reprobation, reproof.

reprobar, *va.* (UE) to reject, to condemn, to upbraid; (coll.) to flunk.

réprobo, ba, *adj.* reprobate.

reprochar, *va.* to reproach.

reproche, *m.* reproach.

reproducción, *f.* reproduction.

reproducir, *va.* (REPRODUZCO, REPRODUJE) to reproduce.

reptil, *m.* reptile.

república, *f.* republic.

republicano, na, *adj.* and *n.* Republican.

repudiación, *f.* repudiation.

repudiar, *va.* to repudiate.

repudio, *m.* repudiation.

repuesto, *m.* stock, cupboard, dresser; **de —,** extra, spare; **— de neumático,** change of tire.

repugnancia, *f.* reluctance, repugnance, dislike.

repugnante, *adj.* repugnant, disgusting, forbidding.

repugnar, *va.* to oppose, to act with reluctance; to cause disgust.

repulgar, *va.* to hem; to overcast a seam; to put an edging on pastry.

repulgo, *m.* hem; border; fancy edging on pastry.

repulsa, *f.* refusal.

repulsión, *f.* repulsion.

reputación, *f.* reputation, renown.

reputado, da, *adj.* reputed.

reputar, *va.* to repute, to estimate.

requebrar, *va.* (IE) to break again something already broken; to woo, to court (a woman).

requerimiento, *m.* request, requisition; summons.

requerir, *va.* (IE) to notify; to request, to demand; to summon; to require, to need; to court, to woo.

requesón, *m.* cottage cheese, curds.

requiebro, *m.* flattery, compliment; endearing expression.

requilorios, *m. pl.* (coll.) useless ceremony; circumlocution.

requinto, *m.* small clarinet and its player; small guitar.

requisa, *f.* tour of inspection.

requisito, *m.* requisite, requirement; **—s de admisión,** admission requirements.

requisitorio, ria, *adj.* examinatory, requisitory; **—,** *m.* (law) request, petition.

res, *f.* head of cattle; beast; **carne de —,** beef.

resabiar, *va.* to contract evil habits; **—se,** to become vicious; to grumble.

resabio, *m.* unpleasant taste left on the palate; vicious habit, bad custom.

resaca, *f.* surge, surf; undertow.

resalado, da, *adj.* very salty; very graceful.

resaltante, *adj.* resilient, outstanding.

resaltar, *vn.* to rebound; to stand out; to be evident.

resarcimiento, *m.* compensation, reparation.

resarcir, *va.* to compensate, to make amends.

resbaladero, *m.* slippery place or road.

resbaladizo, za, *adj.* slippery, glib.

resbaladura, *f.* slippery track; backsliding.

resbalar, *vn.* and *vr.* to slip, to slide.

resbalón, *m.* slip, sliding.

resbaloso, sa, *adj.* slippery.

rescatar, *va.* to ransom, to redeem.

rescate, *m.* ransom.

rescindir, *va.* to rescind, to annul.

rescisión, *f.* rescission, revocation.

rescoldo, *m.* embers, cinders, scruple; misgiving.

rescripto, *m.* rescript.

resecar, *va.* and *vr.* to make too dry.

reseda, *f.* mignonette.

resentido, da, *adj.* resentful, angry.

resentimiento, *m.* resentment.

resentirse, *vr.* (IE) to begin to give way; to be impaired; to resent; to be hurt.

reseña, *f.* review; muster; signal; brief description.

reseñar, *va.* to make a rapid review, to summarize.

resequido, da, *adj.* parched.

reserva, *f.* reserve; reservation; **con** or **bajo la mayor —,** in strictest confidence.

reservado, da, *adj.* reserved, cautious, circumspect; **—,** *m.* booth.

reservar, *va.* to reserve; **—se,** to preserve oneself; to act with circumspection.

resfriado, *m.* cold (disease).

resfriar, *va.* to cool, to chill; **—se,** to catch cold.

resguardar, *va.* to preserve, to defend; **—se,** to be on one's guard.

resguardo, *m.* guard, security, safety; body of customhouse officers; voucher.

residencia, *f.* residence, dwelling.

residencial, *adj.* residential.

residenciar, *va.* to call a public officer to account for his administration, to impeach.

residente, *adj.* residing; **—,** *m.* and *f.* resident, inhabitant.

residir, *vn.* to reside, to dwell.

residual, *adj.* residual.

residuo, *m.* residue, remainder, by-product.

resignación, *f.* resignation, submission.

resignadamente, *adv.* resignedly.

resignado, da, *adj.* resigned.

resignarse, *vr.* to be resigned, to resign oneself.

resina, *f.* resin, rosin.

resinoso, sa, *adj.* resinous.

resistencia, *f.* resistance, opposition.

resistente, *adj.* resistant, strong, opposing.

resistibilidad, *f.* resistibility.

resistible, *adj.* resistible.

resistir, *vn.* and *va.* to resist, to bear; to oppose; to gainsay.

resma, *f.* ream (of paper).

resobrino, na, *m.* grandnephew, grandniece.

resol, *m.* glare of the sun.

resolución, *f.* resolution, boldness; decision; activity.

resoluto, ta, *adj.* daring, resolute.

resolver, *va.* (UE) to resolve, to decide; to analyze; **—se,** to resolve, to determine; to make up one's mind.

resollar, *vn.* (UE) to breathe; to take a breath; (coll.) to show up.

resonador, *m.* resonator, sounder.

resonar, *vn.* (UE) to resound, to ring.

resoplar, *vn.* to breathe audibly; to snort.

resoplido, *m.* continued audible breathing, snorting.

resorte, *m.* spring (elastic body); resort.

respaldar, *va.* to indorse; **—se,** to recline against a chair or bench; **—,** *m.* back (of seats).

respaldo, *m.* indorsement; back of a seat.

respble. respetable, honorable.

respectivo, va, *adj.* respective.

respecto, *m.* relation, respect; **al —,** relatively, respectively; in this regard; **—** **a** or **con — a,** in regard to.

respetable, *adj.* respectable, honorable.

respetar, *va.* to respect; to revere.

respeto, *m.* respect, regard, consideration; homage.

respetuoso, sa, *adj.* respectful.

respigar, *va.* to glean.

respigón, *m.* hangnail.

respingar, *vn.* to kick, to wince; (coll.) to mutter.

respingo, *m.* kick, jerk; (coll.) grumbling.

respiración, *f.* respiration, breathing; breath.

respiradero, *m.* vent, breathing hole; rest, repose.

respirar, *vn.* to respire, to breathe; **— el** **aire,** to take the air.

respiro, *m.* breathing; respite; (com.) extension for payment, time.

resplandecer, *vn.* (EZCO) to shine, to glitter.

resplandeciente, *adj.* resplendent, brilliant.

resplandor, *m.* splendor, brilliance; light.

responder, *va.* and *vr.* to answer; to re-echo; (com.) to correspond; to be responsible for.

responsabilidad, *f.* responsibility.

responsable, *adj.* responsible, accountable, answerable.

responso, *m.* response for the dead.

respta. respuesta, ans. answer.

respuesta, *f.* answer, reply.

resquebradura, *f.* cleft, crevice, split.

resquebrar, *va.* (IE) to crack, to start to break.

resquicio, *m.* aperture between the jamb and leaf of a door; crack, cleft; subterfuge, evasion.

resta, *f.* rest, residue, remainder.

restablecer, *va.* (EZCO) to re-establish; to restore; **—se,** to recover from a disease, etc.

restablecimiento, *m.* re-establishment.

restallar, *vn.* to smack, to click.

restante, *m.* rest, remainder; **—,** *adj.* remaining.

restañar, *va.* to stanch, to stop blood.

restar, *va.* to subtract; **—,** *vn.* to be left, to remain.

restauración, *f.* restoration.

restaurante, *m.* restaurant.

restaurar, *va.* to restore; to repair.

restinga, *f.* sand bar, shoal.

restitución, *f.* restitution.

restituir, *va.* (UYO) to restore; **—se,** to return.

resto, *m.* remainder, rest, balance.

restregar, *va.* (IE) to scrub, to rub.

restricción, *f.* restriction, limitation.

restringir, *va.* to restrain, to restrict, to limit.

restriñimiento, *m.* restriction.

restriñir, *va.* (RESTRIÑÓ, RESTRIÑENDO) to restrain.

resucitar, *va.* and *vn.* to resuscitate, to revive; to renew.

resudar, *vn.* to perspire, to transpire.

resuelto, ta, *adj.* resolute, determined, prompt.

resuello, *m.* breath, breathing; shortness of breath.

resulta, *f.* result, consequence; vacancy in an office; **de —s,** as a consequence.

resultado, *m.* result, consequence.

resultando, *m.* (law) finding.

resultar, *vn.* to result.

resumen, *m.* summary, recapitulation, précis.

resumir, *va.* to abridge; to resume; to summarize.

resurtir, *vn.* to rebound on impact.

resurrección, *f.* resurrection, revival, resuscitation.

resuscitar, *va.* to resurrect.

retablo, *m.* picture drawn on a board; altarpiece.

retacar, *va.* to hit a ball twice at billiards.

retaco, *m.* short, light shotgun.

retador, ra, *n.* challenger.

retaguardia, *f.* rear guard.

retahila, *f.* file, range, series.

retal, *m.* remnant.

retama, *f.* (bot.) broom, genista.

retar, *va.* to challenge, to call out.

retardar, *va.* to retard, to delay.

retardo, *m.* delay, procrastination.

retazo, *m.* remnant; cutting; **—s,** *pl.* odds and ends.

retejar, *va.* to repair the roof of a house.

retejo, *m.* repair of a roof.

retemblar, *vn.* (IE) to tremble repeatedly, to quiver.

retén, *m.* store, stock, reserve.

retención, *f.* retention.·

retener, *va.* (RETENGO, RETUVE) to retain, to keep back.

retentar, *va.* (IE) to threaten with a relapse (of a disease).

retentiva, *f.* circumspection, prudence; memory.

reticencia, *f.* reticence.

reticente, *adj.* reticent.

retina, *f.* retina.

retinitis, *f.* (med.) retinitis.

retintín, *m.* tinkling or jingling sound; affected tone of voice.

retiñir, *vn.* (RETIÑÓ, RETIÑENDO) to tinkle; to resound.

retirada, *f.* (mil.) retreat.

retirar, *va.* to withdraw, to retire; to print the back of a sheet; **—se,** to retire, to retreat.

retiro, *m.* retreat, retirement.
reto, *m.* challenge; threat, menace.
retocado, da, *adj.* refinished, retouched.
retocar, *va.* to retouch a painting or a photograph; to mend; to finish any work completely; to refurbish.
retoñar, *vn.* to sprout again.
retoño, *m.* aftermath, sprout, shoot.
retoque, *m.* finishing stroke; retouching.
retorcer, *va.* (UE) to twist; to retort.
retorcimiento, *m.* twisting, contortion.
retórica, *f.* rhetoric.
retórico, ca, *adj.* rhetorical; —, *m.* rhetorician.
retornar, *va.* to return, to give back; to turn, to twist; —, *vn.* to return.
retorno, *m.* return; barter, exchange.
retorta, *f.* retort.
retortero, *m.* twirl, rotation; **andar al** —, to hover about.
retortijón, *m.* twisting; — **de tripas,** cramp.
retozar, *vn.* to frisk, to skip; to frolic; to play the fool.
retozo, *m.* friskness, merrymaking; lascivious gaiety.
retozón, ona, *adj.* wanton, romping.
retracción, *f.* retraction.
retractación, *f.* retractation, recantation.
retractar, *va.* to retract, to unsay.
retracto, *m.* (law) retraction.
retraer, *va.* (RETRAIGO, RETRAJE) to draw back; to dissuade; —se, to take refuge; to flee.
retraimiento, *m.* retreat, asylum; seclusion; sanctum.
retrasar, *va.* to defer, to put off; —, *vn.* to retrograde; to be late; to be backward.
retraso, *m.* lateness; delay; **el tren ha tenido** —, the train is late.
retratar, *va.* to portray; to draw a portrait of; to photograph; to describe, to depict; —se, to be photographed, to sit for a portrait.
retratista, *m.* and *f.* maker of portraits.
retrato, *m.* portrait, photograph; effigy.
retreparse, *vr.* to lean back, to sit back in a chair.
retreta, *f.* (mil.) bugle sound for retreat; evening military parade; (Sp. Am.) open air concert by a military band.
retrete, *m.* closet; water closet, toilet.
retribución, *f.* retribution.
retribuir, *va.* (UYO) to repay.
retribuyente, *adj.* retributive.
retroacción, *f.* retroaction.
retroactivo, va, *adj.* retroactive.
retrocarga, *f.*, **de** —, breech-loading.
retroceder, *vn.* to go backward, to recede.
retrocesión, *f.* retrocession.
retroceso, *m.* backward motion.
retrogradar, *vn,* to retrograde.
retrógrado, da, *adj.* retrograde.
retronar, *vn.* (UE) to make a thunderous sound.

retrospectivo, va, *adj.* retrospective, backward.
retrucar, *vn.* to put backspin or draw on a ball (in billards).
retruécano, *m.* pun, play upon words.
retruque, *m.* backspin or draw in billiards; overbid in cards.
retumbar, *vn.* to resound, to jingle.
retumbo, *m.* resonance, echo.
reuma, *f.* (med.) rheum, rheumatism.
reumático, ca, *adj.* rheumatic.
reumatismo, *m.* rheumatism.
reunión, *f.* reunion, meeting.
reunir, *va.* to reunite, to gather; to unite; —se, to meet, to get together.
revalidación, *f.* confirmation, ratification.
revalidar, *va.* to ratify, to confirm; —se, to be admitted to a higher post or class.
revaluación, *f.* revaluation.
revancha, *f.* revenge.
revelación, *f.* revelation, disclosure, revealment.
revelador, *m.* tester; photograph developer.
revelamiento, *m.* revealment.
revelar, *va.* to reveal, to disclose; to develop (a photograph).
revenar, *vn.* to sprout.
revendedor, *m.* retailer, huckster, ticket scalper.
revender, *va.* to resell; to retail.
revenimiento, *m.* fermentation; shrinkage; (min.) cave-in.
revenirse, *vr. imp.* (VENGA) to shrink; to ferment, to turn sour.
reventa, *m.* resale.
reventadero, *m.* rough, uneven ground; laborious work.
reventar, *vn.* (IE) to burst, to crack; to toil, to drudge; —, *va.* to molest, to harass.
reventón, *m.* blowout.
reverberación, *f.* reverberation.
reverberante, *adj.* reverberant.
reverberar, *va.* to reverberate.
reverberatorio, ria, *adj.* reverberatory.
reverdecer, *vn.* (EZCO) to grow green again.
reverencia, *f.* reverence, respect, veneration; bow, curtsy.
reverencial, *adj.* reverential.
reverenciar, *va.* to venerate, to revere.
reverendo, da, *adj.* reverent.
reverente, *adj.* respectful, reverent.
reversibilidad, *f.* reversibility.
reversión, *f.* reversion, return.
reverso, *m.* reverse.
reverter, *vn.* (IE) to overflow.
revés, *m.* reverse, wrong side; misfortune; **al** —, backwards; inside out.
revesado, da, *adj.* obstinate; difficult, entangled, perplexed, obscure.
revestimiento, *m.* revetment.
revestir, *va.* (I) to dress; to coat or cover with; to revet; —se, to be invested with.
revisar, *va.* to revise, to review; to examine, to go over.
revisión, *f.* revision.

revisor, ra, *n.* reviser, corrector; —, *adj.* examining, revising.
revista, *f.* revision, review; magazine.
revistar, *va.* to review troops.
revivir, *vn.* to revive.
revocable, *adj.* revocable.
revocación, *f.* revocation, recall.
revocadura, *f.* plastering; (art) edge of the canvas turned over the stretcher.
revocar, *va.* to revoke.
revolar, *vn.* (ue) to hover (as birds).
revolcadero, *m.* wallow.
revolcarse, *vr.* (ue) to wallow; to be knocked down.
revolotear, *vn.* to flutter.
revoloteo, *m.* fluttering.
revoltillo, *m.* confusion, disorder.
revoltoso, sa, *adj.* turbulent, seditious; —, *n.* rioter.
revolución, *f.* revolution; disturbance, sedition.
revolucionar, *va.* to revolutionize.
revolucionario, ria, *adj.* revolutionary; —, *n.* revolutionist.
revolver, *va.* (ue) to turn over; to revolve; to stir; —**se,** to move to and fro; to change (of the weather).
revólver, *m.* revolver.
revoque, *m.* plastering.
revuelo, *m.* commotion, sensation.
revuelta, *f.* second turn; revolution, revolt.
revuelto, ta, *adj.* turned upside down, mixed up; mingled; restless, boisterous.
rey, *m.* king; king (in cards or chess).
reyerta, *f.* dispute.
rezagado, da, *adj.* left behind; **cartas —as,** unclaimed letters.
rezagar, *va.* and *vn.* to leave behind; to defer; to remain behind.
rezago, *m.* remainder, residue.
rezar, *va.* to pray, to say one's prayers.
rezo, *m.* prayer; divine office.
rezongar, *vn.* to growl, to mutter.
rezumarse, *vr.* to ooze, to run gently, to leak.
ría, *f.* estuary.
riada, *f.* inundation, overflow.
ribaldería, *f.* ribaldry, coarse abuse.
ribazo, *m.* hillock, ridge.
ribera, *f.* shore, strand, bank.
ribereño, ña, *adj.* belonging to the seashore or bank of a river.
ribete, *m.* trimming; seam, border.
ribetear, *va.* to hem, to border.
ricacho, cha, *adj.* (coll.) very rich.
Ricardo, Richard.
rico, ca, *adj.* noble, rich; delicious.
ridiculez, *f.* ridiculous action; absurdity; ridicule.
ridiculizar, *va.* to ridicule.
ridículo, la, *adj.* ridiculous.
riego, *m.* irrigation, watering.
riel, *m.* rail.
rienda, *f.* rein of a bridle; **a — suelta,** loose-reined, without restraint.

riente, *adj.* laughing, smiling.
riesgo, *m.* danger, risk, jeopardy.
rifa, *f.* scuffle, dispute; raffle, lottery.
rifar, *va.* to raffle.
rigidez, *f.* rigidity; stiffness.
rígido, da, *adj.* rigid, rigorous; severe.
rigor, *m.* rigor.
riguroso, sa, *adj.* rigorous, exact.
rija, *f.* lachrymal fistula; quarrel, scuffle, dispute.
rima, *f.* rhyme; pile, heap.
rimar, *va.* and *vn.* to rhyme.
rimero, *m.* collection of things placed regularly one over another.
Rin, *m.* Rhine.
rincón, *m.* corner, nook.
rinconada, *f.* corner formed by two houses, streets, etc.
rinconera, *f.* bracket, corner shelf or cupboard, whatnot.
ringlera, *f.* row, file.
rinoceronte, *m.* rhinoceros.
riña, *f.* quarrel, dispute.
riñón, *m.* kidney.
río, *m.* river, stream.
riolada, *f.* heap, large collection.
riostra, *f.* brace, bracket.
R. I. P. en paz descanse, may (he, she) rest in peace.
ripio, *m.* rubble, rubbish; word used only for purpose of completing a verse; verbiage.
riqueza, *f.* riches, wealth.
risa, *f.* laugh, laughter.
risada, *f.* horselaugh, guffaw.
risco, *m.* steep rock, cliff.
riscoso, sa, *adj.* steep and rocky.
risible, *adj.* risible, laughable.
risotada, *f.* outburst of laughter.
ristra, *f.* string of onions; row, file.
ristre, *m.* socket for a lance.
risueño, ña, *adj.* smiling, pleasant.
rítmico, ca, *adj.* rhythmical.
ritmo, *m.* rhythm.
rito, *m.* rite, ceremony.
ritual, *adj.* and *m.* ritual.
rival, *m.* and *f.* rival, competitor.
rivalidad, *f.* rivalry.
rivalizar, *vn.* to rival, to vie with.
rizar, *va.* to curl hair; to pleat.
rizo, *m.* curl, frizzle; crimping; cut velvet; **— marcel,** marcel (wave); —**s,** *pl.* short pieces of braided cordage.
rizoma, *m.* rhizome, rootstock.
R.¹ Real, R. Royal.
R. O. Real Orden, Royal Order.
robador, ra, *n.* robber.
róbalo, *m.* (zool.) bass.
robar, *va.* to steal; to rob, to plunder; to abduct; to kidnap.
Roberto, Robert.
roble, *m.* oaktree.
robledal, *m.* oak grove.
roblón, *m.* rivet, rivet plate; washer for screw bolt.
robo, *m.* robbery, theft.

robota, *f.* robot, mechanical man.

robustecer, *va.* and *vr.* (EZCO) to strengthen, to invigorate, to energize.

robustecimiento, *m.* invigoration; strengthening.

robustez, *f.* robustness.

robusto, ta, *adj.* robust, vigorous.

roca, *f.* rock, cliff; hard substance.

rocalla, *f.* pieces of rock crystal.

roce, *m.* friction; rub.

rociada, *f.* aspersion, sprinkling; dewdrops; malicious censure.

rociador, *m.* instrument for sprinkling cloth, sprinkler, sprayer.

rociar, *va.* to sprinkle; to scatter about; —, *vn.* to fall (of dew).

rocín, *m.* hack; stupid person.

rocinante, *m.* miserable hack, a low stature horse; an ignorant man.

rocío, *m.* dew.

rocoso, sa, *adj.* rocky.

rodada, *f.* rut, track of a wheel.

rodadura, *f.* act of rolling.

rodaja, *f.* small wheel; rowel of a spur; jagging iron used by pastry cooks; caster.

rodaje, *m.* wheelworks.

Ródano, *m.* Rhone.

rodapié, *m.* fringe round the foot of a bedstead; footrail on balconies.

rodaplancha, *f.* main ward of a key.

rodar, *vn.* (UE) to roll.

Rodas, *f. pl.* Rhodes.

rodear, *vn.* to encompass; to go a roundabout way; —, *va.* to wrap up, to circle, to compass.

rodela, *f.* shield, target.

rodeo, *m.* act of going round; detour; circuitous way; delay; subterfuge; rodeo.

Rodesia, *f.* Rhodesia.

rodete, *m.* roundlet of plaited hair; large wheel formed of many pieces; bolster; splinter bar; ward of a key; fifth wheel.

rodezno, *m.* water wheel; cogwheel.

rodilla, *f.* knee; clout; **de** —s, on one's knees.

rodillazo, *m.* push with the knee.

rodillo, *m.* roller, cylinder.

rodo, *m.* roller; **a** —, in abundance.

rododendro, *m.* (bot.) rhododendron.

Rodolfo, Rudolph.

rodrigar, *va.* to prop up (vines).

Rodrigo, Roderick.

rodrigón, *m.* prop for vines.

roedor, ra, *n.* gnawer; detractor.

roedura, *f.* gnawing.

roer, *va.* and *def.* (ROYENDO, ROYÓ) to gnaw, to corrode.

rogación, *f.* petition, supplication; —ones, *pl.* (eccl.) Rogation days.

rogar, *va.* (UE) to entreat, to beg; to pray.

rogativa, *f.* supplication, prayer.

Rogelio, Roger.

rojez, *f.* redness.

rojizo, za, *adj.* reddish.

rojo, ja, *adj.* red; ruddy.

rol, *m.* list, roll; catalogue; — **de la dotación,** muster roll.

Roldán, Rolando, Rowland, Roland.

roldana, *f.* pulley wheel, sheave.

rollizo, za, *adj.* plump, robust, sturdy.

rollo, *m.* roll; spiral.

Roma, *f.* Rome.

romadizo, *m.* catarrh; hay fever.

romana, *f.* steelyard.

romanar, *va.* to weigh with a steelyard.

romance, *adj.* Romance; —, *m.* Spanish language; ballad; novel of chivalry; romance; **hablar en** —, to speak plainly.

romancero, ra, *adj.* romancing; —, *m.* collection of romances or ballads; romancer.

romancista, *m.* romancist.

románico, ca, *adj.* Romanesque.

romano, na, *adj.* and *n.* Roman.

romanticismo, *m.* romanticism.

romántico, ca, *adj.* romantic; —, *m.* romanticist.

romaza, *f.* (bot.) sorrel.

rombo, *m.* rhomb.

romboide, *m.* rhomboid.

romería, *f.* pilgrimage, excursion, picnic.

romero, *m.* (bot.) rosemary.

romo, ma, *adj.* blunt, dull; flat-nosed.

rompecabezas, *m.* riddle, puzzle, jigsaw puzzle, rebus.

rompehielos, *m.* icebreaker.

rompenueces, *m.* nutcracker.

rompeolas, *m.* breakwater.

romper, *va.* and *vn.* to break, to dash, to fracture; to break up land; to pierce; to interrupt.

rompesquinas, *m.* (coll.) bully; street idler.

rompimiento, *m.* break; rupture; crack, cleft; first plowing of land.

ron, *m.* rum.

ronca, *f.* cry of a buck at rutting time; (coll.) menace, boast, brag.

roncar, *vn.* to snore; to make a harsh noise; to roar; to threaten, to boast, to brag.

roncear, *vn.* to be unwilling and poky; to kill time; (coll.) to flatter in order to gain an end; (naut.) to sail slowly.

ronco, ca, *adj.* hoarse; husky; coarse.

roncón, *m.* drone of a bagpipe.

roncha, *f.* wheal, pustule; —s, *pl.* (med.) hives.

ronda, *f.* night patrol; round (of drinks, cigars, etc.); last round in a game of cards; serenade; revelry; **hacer la** —, to pace one's beat.

rondador, *m.* watchman, night guard; patrolman; serenader; reveler.

rondar, *va.* and *vn.* to patrol; to take walks by night about the streets, to revel; to serenade; to go round.

rondel, *m.* roundelay.

rondín, *m.* round of an officer visiting sentinels.

rondó, *m.* (mus.) rondo.

ronquear, *vn.* to be hoarse.

ronquera, *f.* hoarseness.
ronquido, *m.* snore; rough, harsh sound.
ronronear, *vn.* to purr.
ronzal, *m.* halter.
ronzar, *va.* to chew hard things noisily.
roña, *f.* scab, mange; craft, fraud, cunning; nastiness, filth.
roñoso, sa, *adj.* scabby.
ropa, *f.* cloth, fabric; stuff; clothing; robe; costume; — **blanca,** (household) linen; — **de levantar** or **de cámara,** dressing gown; — **hecha,** ready-made apparel; — **interior,** underwear.
ropaje, *m.* clothing, wearing apparel; drapery.
ropavejería, *f.* frippery.
ropavejero, *m.* fripperer; old-clothes man.
ropería, *f.* trade in old clothes; clothes shop; wardrobe.
ropero, *m.* clothes merchant; wardrobe, clothes closet.
ropón, *m.* wide, loose gown; child's christening gown.
roque, *m.* rook (in chess).
roquete, *m.* roquet; barbed spearhead; (mil.) rammer, ramrod.
rorro, *m.* (coll.) baby.
rosa, *f.* rose; red spot appearing in any part of the body.
rosado, da, *adj.* crimsoned, flushed; rosy, pink.
rosal, *m.* rosebush, rosier.
Rosalía, Rosalie.
rosario, *m.* rosary; chain pump.
rosbif, *m.* roast beef.
rosca, *f.* screw and nut; anything round and spiral; ring-shaped biscuit.
roseta, *f.* rosette.
rosetón, *m.* carved rose (architecture).
rosicler, *m.* bright rose color; ruby silver.
rosoli, *m.* rossolis (a cordial).
rosquilla, *f.* sweet, spiral-shaped cake; doughnut; — **escarchada,** iced doughnut.
rostro, *m.* countenance, human face; rostrum.
rota, *f.* rout, defeat; ecclesiastical court in some Catholic countries.
rotación, *f.* rotation.
roto, ta, *adj.* broken, destroyed; leaky; debauched; —, *m.* (Chile) individual of the lowest class.
rotograbado, *m.* rotogravure.
rotondo, *f.* rotunda.
rotor, *m.* rotor.
rótula, *f.* patella, knee bone.
rotular, *va.* to inscribe, to label.
rótulo, *m.* inscription put on books and papers, label; sign; printed bill posted up in public places, show card.
rotundamente, *adv.* emphatically, peremptorily.
rotundo, da, *adj.* round, circular; peremptory.
rotura, *f.* fracture; rupture, crack, cleft; breakage.

roturación, *f.* breaking up of new ground.
roturar, *va.* to break up new ground.
roya, *f.* (bot.) rust, mildew.
rozadura, *f.* friction, graze, scratch.
rozagante, *adj.* trailing, sweeping (of gowns); (coll.) showy; splendid.
rozamiento, *m.* (mech.) friction; disagreement.
rozar, *va.* to stub up; to nibble the grass; to scrape; —, *vn.* to touch slightly; to rub against, to graze; to falter, to stammer.
roznar, *va.* to crack and grind hard things with the teeth; —, *vn.* to bray.
roznido, *m.* noise made by the teeth in eating, smacking of the lips; braying of an ass.
rozo, *m.* chip of wood; stubbing, weeding.
r. p. m. revoluciones por minuto, r. p. m. revolutions per minute.
rpte. representante, rep. representative.
Rubén, Reuben.
rubéola, *f.* (med.) measles.
rubí, *m.* ruby; **—es,** *pl.* jewels of a watch.
rubia, *f.* (bot.) madder; blonde girl.
rubicundo, da, *adj.* reddish, rubicund.
rubio, bia, *adj.* blonde, fair; reddish, ruddy; **—,** *m.* red gurnard.
rublo, *m.* ruble.
rubor, *m.* blush; bashfulness.
ruborizarse, *vr.* to blush, to flush.
rúbrica, *f.* bloodstone; red mark; flourish at the end of a signature; rubric.
rubricar, *va.* to mark with a red color; to sign with one's peculiar flourish; to subscribe, sign and seal a writing.
rucio, cia, *adj.* light gray; gray-haired (of horses); **—cio rodado,** dappled-gray (of horses); **—,** *m.* donkey.
ruda, *f.* (bot.) rue.
rudeza, *f.* roughness, rudeness; stupidity.
rudimento, *m.* beginning; **—s,** *pl.* rudiments.
rudo, da, *adj.* rude, rough, coarse; stupid.
rueca, *f.* distaff for spinning.
rueda, *f.* wheel, roller, circle, crown, sunfish; — **dentada,** gear wheel; cog wheel; — **catalina** or **de cabillas,** sprocket wheel; — **libre,** free wheeling; — **motriz,** driving wheel; — **de paletas,** paddle wheel; — **de la fortuna,** gambling wheel, roulette.
ruedo, *m.* rotation; circuit; border, selvage; round mat to sit upon; bottom of skirts.
ruego, *m.* request, prayer, petition, entreaty, plea, supplication.
rufián, *m.* ruffian; pimp, pander.
rufianesca, *f.* gang of ruffians; habits of ruffians.
Rufo, Rufus.
rufo, fa, *adj.* red-haired; frizzed, curled.
ruga, *f.* wrinkle.
rugar, *va.* to wrinkle.
rugido, *m.* roaring, roar.
rugiente, *adj.* bellowing, roaring.
ruginoso, sa, *adj.* rusty.

rugir, *vn.* to roar, to bellow; to crack.
rugoso, sa, *adj.* wrinkled.
ruibarbo, *m.* rhubarb.
ruido, *m.* noise.
ruidoso, sa, *adj.* noisy, clamorous, loud.
ruin, *adj.* mean, vile, despicable; wicked; avaricious.
ruina, *f.* ruin, downfall, destruction; —s, *pl.* ruins of an edifice.
ruindad, *f.* meanness, baseness, avarice.
ruinoso, sa, *adj.* worthless, ruinous, destructive.
ruiseñor, *m.* nightingale.
ruleta, *f.* roulette.
Rumania, *f.* Rumania.
rumba, *f.* rumba.
rumbo, *m.* point of the compass; course, direction; road, route, way; pomp, ostentation; **con — a,** bound for.
rumboso, sa, *adj.* magnificent, pompous; liberal.
rumiar, *va.* to ruminate; (coll.) to meditate.
rumión, ona, *adj.* ruminating much; (fig.) harping on a subject.
rumor, *m.* rumor, report.
Ruperto, Rupert.
ruptura, *f.* rupture, break.
rural, *adj.* rural.
Rusia, *f.* Russia.
ruso, sa, *n.* and *adj.* Russian.
rúst. rústica, (of books) unbound or in paper cover.
rusticidad, *f.* rusticity; coarseness.
rústico, ca, *adj.* rustic, rural; unbound or in a paper cover (of books); —, *m.* peasant.
ruta, *f.* route, road; itinerary.
rutilar, *vn.* (poet.) to radiate, to shine.
rutina, *f.* routine, habit formed from custom.
rutinario, ria, *adj.* routine; mechanical.
rutinero, ra, *adj.* of routine.

S

S.: San or **Santo,** St. Saint; **segundo,** second; **sur,** So. or so. south; **Sobresaliente,** S. Superior (in an examination).
s. substantivo, n. noun.
s: su, yr. your; **sobre,** over or about.
S.ª Señora, Mrs. Mistress.
S. A.: Sociedad Anónima, Corp. Corporation; **Su Alteza,** His or Her Highness.
sáb. sábado, Sat. Saturday.
sábado, *m.* Saturday; Sabbath.
sábana, *f.* bed sheet.
sabandija, *f.* grub, beetle, insect.
sabañón, *m.* chilblain.
sabedor, ra, *n.* well-informed person; —, *adj.* knowing, informed.
sábelotodo, *m.* jack-of-all-trades.
saber, *va.* (SÉ, SUPE) to know; to be able to; to experience; —, *vn.* to be very sagacious; — **a,** to taste of; —, *m.* learning, knowledge; **a —,** to wit; **es de —,** it is to be noted.

sabido, da, *adj.* learned, well-informed.
sabiduría, *f.* learning, knowledge, wisdom.
sabiendas, a —, *adv.* knowingly, consciously, with awareness.
sabina, *f.* (bot.) juniper.
sabio, bia, *adj.* sage, wise; —, *n.* sage, wise person, savant.
sablazo, *m.* saber cut.
sable, *m.* saber, cutlass.
sabor, *m.* relish, taste, savor, flavor.
saborear, *va.* to enjoy, to relish; to give a taste or zest; —se, to swallow slowly and with great enjoyment; to be pleased.
sabotaje, *m.* sabotage.
saboteador, *n.* saboteur.
saboyana, *f.* wide petticoat.
sabroso, sa, *adj.* savory; palatable, delicious; (coll.) saltish.
sabueso, *m.* bloodhound.
saca, *f.* exportation; sack.
sacabala, *f.* bullet drawer (used by surgeons).
sacabocado(s), *m.* puncheon, punch.
sacabotas, *m.* bootjack.
sacabuche, *m.* sackbut; small, contemptible man.
sacaclavos, *m.* nail puller.
sacacorchos, *m.* corkscrew.
sacadura, *f.* sloping cut by which tailors make clothes fit better.
sacamanchas, *m.* and *f.* scourer of clothes; — *m.* cleaner, spot remover.
sacamuelas, *m.* tooth drawer; (coll.) dentist.
sacar, *va.* to draw out; to except; to pull out; to draw lots; — **a luz,** to print; — **apodos,** to call names; — **en limpio,** to recopy neatly; to deduce.
sacarina, *f.* saccharine.
sacatrapos, *m.* worm of a ramrod.
sacerdocio, *m.* priesthood.
sacerdotal, *adj.* sacerdotal, priestly.
sacerdote, *m.* priest, clergyman.
sacerdotisa, *f.* priestess.
saciar, *va.* to satiate, to quench.
saciedad, *f.* satiety.
saco, *m.* sack, bag; man's coat; jacket; — **de yute,** gunny sack; **no echar en — roto,** not to forget, not to fail to take heed.
sacramental, *adj.* sacramental.
sacramento, *m.* sacrament.
sacrificar, *va.* to sacrifice; —se, to devote oneself to religion; to sacrifice oneself.
sacrificio, *m.* sacrifice.
sacrilegio, *m.* sacrilege.
sacrílego, ga, *adj.* sacrilegious.
sacristán, *m.* sacristan, sexton.
sacristía, *f.* sacristy, vestry.
sacro, *m.* (anat.) sacrum.
sacro, cra, *adj.* holy, sacred.
sacrosanto, ta, *adj.* very holy.
sacudida, *f.* shake, jerk, jolt.
sacudidura, *f.* dusting, cleaning.
sacudimiento, *m.* shaking off.
sacudir, *va.* to shake, to jerk; to dart; to

beat, to chastise with blows; **—se,** to reject with disdain.

sadismo, *m.* sadism.

saeta, *f.* arrow, dart.

saetar, *va.* to wound with an arrow.

saetazo, *m.* arrow wound.

saetín, *m.* mill trough, millrace, flume; peg, pin, tack; satin.

sáfico, ca, *adj.* (poet.) Sapphic.

saga, *f.* saga.

sagacidad, *f.* sagacity, shrewdness.

sagaz, *adj.* sagacious, sharp.

Sagitario, *m.* Archer (sign of the zodiac).

sagrado, da, *adj.* sacred, consecrated; **—,** *m.* asylum.

sagrario, *m.* place in a church wherein consecrated things are deposited; ciborium.

sahorno, *m.* chafing.

sahumar, *va.* to perfume; to smoke, to fume.

S. A. I. Su Alteza Imperial, His or Her Imperial Highness.

saín, *m.* grease or fat of an animal; grease on clothes.

sainete, *m.* farce, comedy; flavor, relish; delicate bit.

Sajonia, *f.* Saxony.

sal, *f.* salt; wit, grace, spice; **— de la Higuera,** Epsom salts.

sala, *f.* hall, parlor, courtroom; **— de clase,** classroom; **— de equipajes,** baggage room; **— de hospital,** hospital ward; **— de muestras,** showroom; **— de recreo,** amusement parlor.

saladero, *m.* salting place; salting tub.

salado, da, *adj.* salted, salty; witty, facetious.

saladura, *f.* salting.

salamandra, *f.* salamander.

salar, *va.* to salt.

salario, *m.* salary.

salazón, *f.* seasoning, salting.

salcochar, *va.* to boil with water and salt.

salchicha, *f.* small sausage; long fuse.

salchichería, *f.* shop in which sausages are sold.

salchichero, ra, *n.* maker or seller of sausages.

salchichón, *m.* large sausage.

saldar, *va.* to settle (an account), to pay.

saldo, *m.* balance; remnant sale at a dry-goods store; **— acreedor,** credit balance; **— deudor,** debit balance; **— líquido,** net balance.

saledizo, za, *adj.* salient.

salero, *m.* saltcellar; (coll.) gracefulness.

saleroso, *adj.* graceful.

salicilato, *m.* (chem.) salicylate.

salida, *f.* outgoing; outlet; issue, result; departure, exit; (mil.) sally; **— de sol,** sunrise.

saliente, *adj.* projecting, salient.

salina, *f.* salt pit, salt works, salt mine.

salinero, *m.* salter; saltmaker.

salino, na, *adj.* saline.

salir, *vn.* (SALGO, SALÍ) to go out, to depart to leave, to go away; to appear; to disappear; to be issued or published; to lose one's temper; **— bien en un examen,** to pass in an examination; **— fiador,** to procure or go surety, to bail, to be a guarantor; **— garante,** to be a responsible guarantor; **—se,** to drop, to leak; **—se de sus casillas,** to lose one's composure; **—se con la suya,** to accomplish one's end.

salitrado, da, *adj.* impregnated with saltpeter.

salitral, *m.* saltpeter works.

salitre, *m.* saltpeter, niter.

salitrería, *f.* saltpeter works.

salitrero, *m.* saltpeter refiner.

salitroso, sa, *adj.* nitrous.

saliva, *f.* saliva.

salivar, *vn.* to salivate, to spit.

salivoso, sa, *adj.* salivous.

salmista, *m.* psalmist.

salmo, *m.* psalm.

salmodia, *f.* psalmody.

salmón, *m.* salmon.

salmonado, da, *adj.* tasting or looking like salmon.

salmonete, *m.* red mullet.

salmuera, *f.* brine.

salobre, *adj.* brackish, salty.

Salomón, Solomon.

salón, *m.* parlor, hall, salon; **— de baile,** dance hall; **— de belleza,** beauty parlor; **— de refrescos,** ice-cream parlor; **— social,** lounging room; **— de ventas,** salesroom.

salpicadura, *f.* splash, spattering.

salpicar, *va.* to bespatter, to splash; to sprinkle.

salpicón, *m.* salmagundi; bespattering.

salpimentar, *va.* (IE) to season with pepper and salt.

salpimienta, *f.* mixture of salt and pepper.

salpresar, *va.* to salt; to preserve with salt.

salpullido, *m.* (med.) eruption, rash, prickly heat.

salpullir, *va.* and *vr.* (SALPULLÓ, SALPULLENDO) to break out in pustules or pimples on the skin.

salsa, *f.* sauce, dressing; **— francesa,** French dressing; **— de tomate,** tomato sauce, ketchup (or catsup); **— inglesa,** Worcestershire sauce.

salsera, *f.* gravy or sauce dish.

salserilla, *f.* small gravy dish; small saucer.

salsero, *m.* (bot.) Spanish thyme.

salsifí, *m.* salsify.

saltabancos, *m.* charlatan, mountebank.

saltadero, *m.* leaping place; artificial fountain, jet.

saltador, ra, *n.* jumper, leaper.

saltar, *vn.* to leap, to jump; to be irritated or agitated.

saltarín, ina, *n.* dancer; restless young rake.

salteador, *m.* highwayman.

saltear, *va.* to rob on the highway.
salterio, *m.* Psalter.
salto, *m.* leap, jump, omission; — **de agua,** waterfall; — **de viento,** sudden shifting of wind; **dar —s,** to jump; — **a la pértiga,** pole vault; — **de altura,** high jump.
saltón, *m.* grasshopper; —, **ona,** *adj.* hopping or leaping much.
salubre, *adj.* healthful.
salubridad, *f.* healthfulness.
salud, *f.* health; **estar bien** or **mal de —,** to be in good or poor health; ¡—! *interj.* hello! ¡**a su —!** to your health!
saludable, *adj.* salubrious, wholesome, healthful.
saludador, *m.* greeter; quack.
saludar, *va.* to greet, to salute, to bow.
saludo, *m.* (mil.) salute, greeting, salutation.
salutación, *f.* salutation, greeting; exordium.
salutífero, ra, *adj.* salubrious, healthful.
salva, *f.* (mil.) salvo; — **de aplausos,** thunderous applause.
salvación, *f.* salvation, deliverance.
salvado, *m.* bran.
Salvador, *m.* Savior; Salvador.
salvador, ra, *adj.* saving; —, *n.* savior, rescuer, redeemer.
salvadoreño, ña, *n.* and *adj.* Salvadorean, from El Salvador.
salvaguardia, *m.* safeguard.
salvaje, *adj.* savage, wild.
salvajería, *f.* rusticity, uncouth manners.
salvamento or **salvamiento,** *m.* safety, escape; **escalera de —,** fire escape.
salvar, *va.* to save, to rescue; to overcome (as a difficulty); —**se,** to escape from danger.
salvavidas, *m.* lifeboat, life preserver.
salvia, *f.* (bot.) sage, salvia.
salvilla, *f.* salver.
salvo, va, *adj.* saved, safe; **sano y —vo,** safe and sound; —**vo,** *adv.* excepting; —**vo error u omisión,** errors and omissions excepted.
salvoconducto, *m.* safe conduct.
sallar, *va.* to weed.
sámago, *m.* sapwood.
sambenito, *m.* garment, with a yellow cross at back and front, worn by penitents of the Inquisition; note of infamy.
san, *adj.* saint (before masculine proper names).
sanable, *adj.* curable, healable.
sánalotodo, *m.* panacea, general remedy.
sanamente, *adv.* naturally, agreeably.
sanar, *va.* and *vn.* to heal, to recover (health).
sanatorio, *m.* sanitarium, sanatorium.
sanción, *f.* sanction.
sancionar, *va.* to sanction.
sancochar, *va.* to boil with water and salt; to parboil.
sancocho, *m.* stew, chowder.
sandalia, *f.* sandal.

sándalo, *m.* sandalwood.
sandez, *f.* folly, stupidity.
sandía, *f.* watermelon.
sandio, dia, *adj.* foolish, nonsensical.
sandwich, *m.* sandwich.
saneamiento, *m.* surety, bail; sanitation, drainage.
sanear, *va.* to give bail; to indemnify; to drain; to improve lands.
sangradera, *f.* lancet; basin for blood; drain.
sangrador, *m.* bloodletter; outlet.
sangradura, *f.* bleeding.
sangrante, *adj.* bleeding.
sangrar, *va.* and *vn.* to bleed; —**se,** to be bled.
sangre, *f.* blood; **a — fría,** in cold blood; **a — y fuego,** without mercy; **banco de —,** blood bank; **donador** or **donante de —,** blood donor.
sangría, *f.* bleeding; wound, incision; tropical drink made with wine, sugar, and spices.
sangriento, ta, *adj.* bloody, stained with blood, gory; bloodthirsty.
sangüesa, *f.* raspberry.
sanguijuela, *f.* leech; sharper.
sanguinaria, *f.* knot grass; bloodstone.
sanguinario, ria, *adj.* sanguinary, cruel, bloody.
sanguíneo, nea, *adj.* sanguine; sanguineous.
sanidad, *f.* soundness, health; **patente de —,** bill of health.
sanitario, ria, *adj.* sanitary; —, *m.* health officer.
sano, na, *adj.* sound, sane; healthy.
santabárbara, *f.* powder magazine.
Santiago, James.
santiamén, *m.* moment, twinkling of an eye.
santidad, *f.* sanctity, holiness.
santificación, *f.* sanctification.
santificador, *m.* sanctifier.
santificar, *va.* to sanctify; to justify.
santiguador, ra, *n.* one who cures by making the sign of the cross.
santiguar, *va.* and *vr.* to make the sign of the cross; to bless; (coll.) to chastise, to punish.
santimonia, *f.* sanctity, sanctimony; chrysanthemum.
santísimo, ma, *adj.* most holy.
santo, ta, *adj.* and *m.* saint, holy; sacred; image of a saint; —**to y seña,** military watchword.
santón, *m.* hypocrite; Moslem monk or dervish.
santuario, *m.* sanctuary.
santurrón, ona, *n.* and *adj.* hypocrite pretending holiness.
santurronería, *f.* hypocrisy.
saña, *f.* anger, blind fury.
sañoso, sa, *adj.* furious, enraged, hotheaded.
sañudo, da, *adj.* furious, enraged.
sapo, *m.* large toad.
saponina, *f.* (chem.) saponin.

saporífero, ra, *adj.* imparting savor.
saque, *m.* striking the ball (tennis); kickoff (in football).
saqueador, ra, ransacker, freebooter, despoiler.
saquear, *va.* to ransack, to plunder, to foray.
saqueo, *m.* pillage, freebooting, foray.
S. A. R. Su Alteza Real, His or Her Royal Highness.
Sara, Sarah, Sally.
saragüete, *m.* (coll.) informal dance, party.
sarampión, *m.* measles.
sarape, *m.* serape, shawl, cloak.
sarcasmo, *m.* sarcasm.
sarcástico, ca, *adj.* sarcastic.
sarcófago, *m.* sarcophagus.
sardina, *f.* sardine.
sardinero, ra, *n.* dealer in sardines; —, *adj.* pertaining to sardines.
sardio or **sardo,** *m.* sard (semiprecious stone).
sardónice, *f.* sardonyx (semiprecious stone).
Sarg. Sargento, Sgt. Sergeant.
sarga, *f.* serge.
sargento, *m.* sergeant.
sarmiento, *m.* vine shoot.
sarna, *f.* itch; mange.
sarnoso, sa, *adj.* itchy, scabby, mangy.
sarpullido, *m.* rash, eruption.
sarracina, *f.* tumultuous contest between a number of persons.
sarria, *f.* wide net made of ropes, in which straw is carried.
sarro, *m.* incrustation of the mouth in protracted fevers; tartar on teeth; sediment which adheres to vessels.
sarroso, sa, *adj.* incrusted with sediment or tartar.
sarta, *f.* string of beads, pearls, etc.; string, row.
sartén, *f.* frying pan, saucepan.
S. A. S. Su Alteza Serenísima, His or Her Very Serene Highness.
sasafrás, *m.* (bot.) sassafras.
sastre, *m.* tailor.
sastrería, *f.* tailor's shop.
Satanás, *m.* Satan.
satánico, ca, *adj.* Satanic, devilish.
satélite, *m.* and *f.* satellite; (coll.) bailiff, constable; rubber stamp.
sátira, *f.* satire.
satírico, ca, *adj.* satirical.
satirizar, *va.* to satirize.
sátiro, *m.* satyr.
satisfacción, *f.* satisfaction; presumption; confidence; amends, apology.
satisfacer, *va.* (SATISFAGO, SATISFICE) to satisfy; to atone; —se, to satisfy oneself; to vindicate oneself.
satisfactorio, ria, *adj.* satisfactory.
satisfecho, cha, *adj.* satisfied, content.
sátrapa, *m.* satrap; (coll.) sly, crafty fellow.
saturación, *f.* (chem.) saturation.
saturnal, *adj.* saturnalian.

Saturno, *m.* Saturn; s—, (chem.) lead.
sauce, *m.* (bot.) willow.
saúco, *m.* (bot.) elder; second layer of a horse's hoof.
sauquillo, *m.* (bot.) dwarf elder.
savia, *f.* sap.
saxofón or **saxófono,** *m.* saxophone.
saya, *f.* skirt; ancient tunic or gown worn by men.
sayal, *m.* sackcloth.
sayalete, *m.* thin or light cloth.
sayo, *m.* smock; loose coat or similar garment.
sayón, *m.* corpulent, ill-looking fellow.
sayuelo, *m.* small jacket, little frock.
sazón, *f.* maturity; season, taste, flavor; opportunity; **en —,** seasonably, opportunely; **a la —,** then, at that time.
sazonadamente, *adv.* maturely, seasonably.
sazonado, da, *adj.* seasoned; witty.
sazonar, *va.* to season; to mature; —se, to ripen.
Sb.ⁿ Sebastián, Sebastian.
Sbre. or **7bre septiembre,** Sept. September.
S. C. su casa, (com.) your house, (expression of kind hospitality).
s. c. or **s/c.: su cargo** or **su cuenta,** (com.) your account; **su casa,** your house (expression of kind hospitality).
s/cta. or **s/c. su cuenta,** (com.) your account.
SE sudeste, SE or S. E. southeast.
sé, second person imperative singular of **ser,** to be; — **bueno,** be good; first person indicative singular of **saber,** to know; **yo — la lección,** I know the lesson.
se, the reflexive pronoun, possessive to the person or thing that governs the verb; used before the pronouns **me, te, le,** it reflects the action of the verb on the object which they represent. **Se** is used instead of other cases of the pronoun of the third person, as **¿Le entregó usted la carta? Sí, se la entregué.** Yes, I delivered it to him, to her. **Se** frequently introduces the passive form of a verb, as **Se dice,** It is said.
sebo, *m.* suet; fat; candle grease.
seboso, sa, *adj.* fat, greasy.
seca, *f.* drought, dry weather; inflammation and swelling in the glands.
secadero, *m.* place where fruit is dried.
secamente, *adv.* dryly, briefly.
secano, *m.* dry, arable land which is not irrigated.
secante, *m.* drying oil used for painting; blotter; —, *adj.* drying; **papel —,** blotting paper; —, *f.* (math.) secant.
secar, *va.* to dry; —se, to grow dry; to become meager; to decay.
sección, *f.* section.
secesión, *f.* secession.
seco, ca, *adj.* dry; not rainy; arid, sapless; meager; barren; lean, lanky.
secreta, *f.* privy, water closet; —s, *pl.*

private orisons said in a low voice by the priest at the beginning of the mass.

secretaría, *f.* secretaryship; secretariat; secretary's office.

secretario, ria, *n.* secretary; scribe; **— particular,** private secretary.

secreto, ta, *adj.* secret; hidden; **—,** *m.* secrecy; secret; **en—to,** in secret, in private.

secta, *f.* sect; doctrine.

sectario, ria, *adj.* and *n.* sectarian, sectary.

secuaz, *adj.* following a sect; **—,** *m.* sectary, follower, disciple of a sect.

secuela, *f.* sequel, continuation.

secuencia, *f.* sequence in prose or verse said in mass after the epistles.

secuestrar, *va.* to sequestrate; to kidnap.

secuestro, *m.* sequestration; kidnaping.

secular, *adj.* secular; lay; centenary; lasting for ages.

secularización, *f.* secularization.

secularizar, *va.* to secularize.

secundario, ria, *adj.* secondary; **escuela —ria,** high school.

secura, *f.* dryness.

sed, *f.* thirst; **tener —,** to be thirsty.

seda, *f.* silk (yarn, thread, or cloth).

sedal, *m.* fishing line; seton.

sedán, *m.* sedan.

sedar, *va.* to soothe, to appease.

sedativo, va, *adj.* sedative.

sede, *f.* see, seat of episcopal power; **— apostólica,** Apostolic See.

sedear, *va.* to clean jewels (gold or silver).

sedentario, ria, *adj.* sedentary.

sedería, *f.* silks; silk store.

sedero, *m.* silk seller.

sedición, *f.* sedition, mutiny.

sedicioso, sa, *adj.* seditious, mutinous.

sediento, ta, *adj.* thirsty; eagerly desirous.

sedimentación, *f.* sedimentation.

sedimento, *m.* sediment.

seducción, *f.* seduction.

seducir, *va.* (SEDUZCO, SEDUJE) to seduce; to attract, to charm.

seductivo, va, *adj.* seductive.

seductor, ra, *adj.* attractive, seductive, fascinating; **—,** *n.* seducer; charming person.

sefardí, *m.* Spanish Jew.

segadera, *f.* reaping hook, sickle.

segador, ra, *n.* mower, reaper, harvester; **— de césped,** lawn mower.

segar, *va.* (IE) to reap, to mow, to harvest.

Segismundo, Sigismund.

seglar, *adj.* worldly; secular; **—,** *m.* layman.

segmento, *m.* segment.

segregación, *f.* segregation, separation.

segregar, *va.* to separate, to set apart.

seguida, *f.* following; succession; **de —,** successively; **en —,** immediately, at once.

seguidilla, *f.* merry Spanish tune and dance; **—s,** *pl.* (coll.) diarrhea.

seguido, da, *adj.* continued, successive, followed.

seguidor. ra. n. follower: **—,** *m.* ruled paper

for teaching to write straight.

seguimiento, *m.* pursuit.

seguir, *va.* (SIGO, SEGUÍ) to follow, to pursue; **—se,** to ensue; to succeed.

según, *prep.* according to; **— aviso,** as per advice; **— y como,** it depends.

segundar, *va.* to second; **—,** *vn.* to be second.

segundario, ria, *adj.* secondary.

segundo, da, *adj.* second; **—,** *m.* second (of time).

segur, *f.* axe, large hatchet.

seguramente, *adv.* certainly, surely.

seguridad, *f.* security, surety, certainty, safety, assurance; **caja de —,** safety deposit vault; **fiador de —,** safety catch.

seguro, ra, *adj.* secure, safe, sure; firm, constant; **—,** *m.* insurance; leave, safe conduct; **a buen —ro,** certainly; **al —ro,** securely; **de —ro,** assuredly; **compañía de —ros,** life insurance company; **corredor de —ros,** insurance broker; **póliza de —ro,** insurance policy; **—ro sobre la vida,** insurance policy.

seis, *adj.* six, sixth (of the month); **—,** *m.* six.

seiscientos, tas, *adj.* six hundred.

selección, *f.* selection, choice.

selectividad, *f.* selectivity.

selectivo, va, *adj.* selective.

selecto, ta, *adj.* select, choice.

selva, *f.* forest.

sellador, ra, *n.* sealer, one who seals or stamps (documents, letters, etc.).

selladura, *f.* sealing (documents, letters, etc.).

sellar, *va.* to seal, to stamp; to finish.

sello, *m.* seal; stamp; stamp office; medicinal wafer; **— de correo,** postage stamp; **— de impuesto,** revenue stamp; **— de bicicleta or de entrega inmediata,** special delivery stamp.

semáforo, *m.* semaphore, signal mast.

semana, *f.* week.

semanal, *adj.* weekly.

semanario, ria, *adj.* weekly; **—,** *m.* weekly publication.

semántica, *f.* semantics.

semblante, *m.* face; countenance.

sembradío, día, *adj.* fit or prepared for sowing.

sembrado, *m.* sown field.

sembrador, ra, *n.* sower, planter, seeder.

sembradura, *f.* sowing.

sembrar, *va.* (IE) to sow, to plant.

semejante, *adj.* similar, like; **—,** *m.* fellow creature.

semejanza, *f.* resemblance, likeness.

semejar, *vn.* to resemble.

semen, *m.* semen; (bot.) seed.

sementar, *va.* (IE) to sow, to plant.

sementera, *f.* sowing; land sown with seed.

semestral, *adj.* semiyearly.

semestre, *m.* semester.

semi, prefix denoting half.

semianual, *adj.* semiannual.

semibreve, *f.* (mus.) semibreve, whole note.

semicircular, *adj.* semicircular.
semicírculo, *m.* semicircle.
semicopado, da, *adj.* (mus.) syncopated.
semicorchea, *f.* (mus.) semiquaver.
semidiós, *m.* demigod.
semiesfera, *f.* hemisphere.
semifusa, *f.* (mus.) double demi-semiquaver.
semilla, *f.* seed.
semillero, *m.* seed plot; hotbed.
seminario, *m.* seminary; origin, course; graduate school.
seminarista, *m.* scholar in a seminary.
semínima, *f.* (mus.) crotchet.
semiplena, *adj.* (law) imperfect; **prueba —,** imperfect proof, insufficient evidence.
semítico, ca, *adj.* Semitic.
semitono, *m.* (mus.) semitone.
semitropical, *adj.* semitropical.
semivocal, *f.* and *adj.* semivowel.
sémola, *f.* groats.
sempiterna, *f.* serge cloth.
sempiterno, na, *adj.* everlasting, eternal.
Sena, *m.* Seine.
senado, *m.* senate.
senadoconsulto, *m.* decree of (ancient Roman) senate.
senador, *m.* senator.
senatorio, ria, *adj.* senatorial.
S. en C. Sociedad en Comandita, silent partnership.
sencillez, *f.* slightness; simplicity; naturalness, candor.
sencillo, lla, *adj.* simple; plain, light in weight; artless, natural.
senda, *f.* path, footpath.
sendero, *m.* path, trail.
sendos, das, *adj. pl.* respective one for each of two or more persons or things; **tienen — caballos,** they have a horse for each one.
senescal, *m.* seneschal.
senil, *adj.* senile.
seno, *m.* breast, bosom; lap; womb; hole, cavity; sinus; asylum, refuge; interior (of a letter); **de cuyo — retiramos,** from which letter we have detached, in which we have found inclosed; (math.) sine.
sensación, *f.* sensation, feeling.
sensatez, *f.* reasonableness, good sense.
sensato, ta, *adj.* judicious, reasonable, wise.
sensibilidad, *f.* sensibility.
sensibilización, *f.* (photo.) sensitization.
sensibilizar, va, to sensitize.
sensible, *adj.* sensible; sensitive; regrettable; softhearted.
sensitiva, *f.* sensitive plant.
sensitivo, va, *adj.* sensitive; sensible.
sensorio, ria, *adj.* sensory.
sensual, *adj.* sensitive; sensual, lewd.
sensualidad, *f.* sensuality; carnal desire.
sentado, da, *adj.* seated; **dar por —do,** to take for granted.
sentar, *va.* (IE) to sit, to set up; to suit; to seat; **— en cuenta de,** to enter to the account of; **—se,** to sit down.

sentencia, *f.* sentence, opinion; verdict; **pronunciar la —,** to pass judgment.
sentenciar, *va.* to sentence, to pass judgment; to give one's opinion.
sentencioso, sa, *adj.* sententious.
sentido, *m.* sense; reason; signification; meaning; **— práctico,** common sense; **—, da,** *adj.* hurt, sorrowful.
sentimental, *adj.* sentimental.
sentimentalista, *m.* and *f.* sentimentalist.
sentimiento, *m.* sentiment; grief; feeling; sensation, resentment; opinion.
sentina, *f.* sink, drain; (naut.) scuppers.
sentir, *va.* (IE) to feel; to regret; to hear, to perceive; to suffer; to grieve, to mourn; to judge, to think; to foresee; **—se,** to find oneself; to be moved, to feel pain; to crack (of walls, etc.).
seña, *f.* sign, mark, token, signal, password; **—s,** *pl.* address; **—s dactiloscópicas,** fingerprints; **hacer —s,** to hail (someone).
señal, *f.* sign, signal; token; landmark; footstep; earnest money; **— de alto** or **de parada,** stop signal.
señaladamente, *adv.* especially; namely.
señalado, da, *adj.* famous, celebrated, noble.
señalamiento, *m.* assignation.
señalar, *va.* to stamp, to mark; to point out; to sign decrees; to signalize; **—se,** to distinguish oneself, to excel.
señor, *m.* lord; sir; sacrament of the Eucharist; **muy — mío** or **nuestro,** dear sir; **el S—,** the Lord.
señora, *f.* lady; mistress; gentlewoman; **Nuestra S—,** Our Lady.
señorear, *va.* to master, to domineer; **—se,** to govern one's temper or demeanor; to affect a peculiar gravity in one's deportment.
señoría, *f.* lordship; person to whom this title is given.
señoril, *adj.* lordly.
señorío, *m.* seigniory; self-control in action; dominion, command.
señorita, *f.* young lady, miss; (coll.) mistress of the house.
señorito, *m.* young gentleman; master (title); (coll.) master of the house.
señuelo, *m.* lure, enticement.
sépalo, *m.* (bot.) sepal.
separable, *adj.* separable.
separación, *f.* separation, division, dissociation.
separado, da, *adj.* separate, apart; **por —do,** under separate cover.
separar, *va.* to separate; **—se,** to separate, to be disunited; to withdraw.
sepelio, *m.* burial.
sepia, *f.* sepia; cuttlefish.
sepsis, *f.* (med.) sepsis.
Sept. sept.º 7bre or **7º septiembre,** Sept. September.
septentrión, *m.* north.
septentrional, *adj.* northern.
septicemia, *f.* (med.) blood poisoning.

séptico, ca, *adj.* septic.
septiembre, *m.* September.
séptimo, ma, *adj.* seventh.
septuagenario, ria, *n.* and *adj.* septuagenarian.
septuagésimo, ma, *adj.* seventieth.
septum, *m.* septum.
séptuplo, pla, *adj.* septuple, sevenfold.
sepulcral, *adj.* sepulchral.
sepulcro, *m.* sepulcher, grave, tomb; **Santo —,** Holy Sepulcher.
sepultar, *va.* to bury, to inter.
sepultura, *f.* sepulture, interment, grave.
sepulturero, *m.* gravedigger, sexton; mortician.
sequedad, *f.* aridity, dryness.
sequía, *f.* dryness; thirst; drought.
séquito, *m.* retinue, suite; public applause; following.
ser, *vn.* (SOY, FUÍ) to be; to exist; **llegar a —,** to become; **—,** *m.* being, life.
sera, *f.* large pannier.
seráfico, ca, *adj.* seraphic.
serafín, *m.* seraph.
serenar, *va.* and *vn.* to clear up; to settle, to grow clear; to pacify, to tranquilize; to be serene; **—se,** to calm down, to compose oneself.
serenata, *f.* serenade.
serení, *m.* (naut.) yawl, light boat.
serenidad, *f.* serenity, quiet.
sereno, *m.* evening dew; night watchman; **—, na,** *adj.* serene, calm, quiet, cloudless.
sergas, *f. pl.* exploits, achievements.
serie, *f.* series.
seriedad, *f.* seriousness; sternness of mien, gravity; sincerity.
serijo or **serillo,** *m.* small basket made of palm leaves.
serio, ria, *adj.* serious, grave; severe; earnest.
sermón, *m.* sermon.
sermonear, *va.* to lecture, to reprimand.
serón, *m.* large pannier used to carry figs, raisins, etc.
serosidad, *f.* (med.) serosity.
seroso, sa, *adj.* serous; thin.
serpentear, *vn.* to move like a serpent; to wriggle.
serpentina, *f.* coiled confetti; hammer of a gun; culverin.
serpiente, *f.* serpent, snake.
serpol, *m.* (bot.) wild thyme.
serrador, *m.* sawyer.
serraduras, *f. pl.* sawdust.
serrallo, *m.* seraglio, harem.
serranía, *f.* range of mountains, mountainous country.
serrano, na, *n.* mountaineer.
serrar, *va.* (IE) to saw.
serrín, *m.* sawdust.
serrucho, *m.* handsaw with a small handle.
servible, *adj.* fit for service.
servicial, *adj.* obsequious, serviceable, accommodating; **—,** *m.* (coll.) enema.

servicio, *m.* service; attendance; good turn; divine service; utility; chamber pot; service for the table; **— diurno,** day service; **— nocturno,** night service.
servidero, ra, *adj.* serviceable.
servidor, *m.* servant, waiter; **su —,** at your service; yours truly.
servidora, *f.* maidservant; **su —,** at your service; yours truly.
servidumbre, *f.* attendance, servitude; slavery; servility; privy, sewer.
servil, *adj.* servile.
servilleta, *f.* napkin.
servir, *va.* (I) to serve; to wait at table; **—se,** to deign, to please; **—se de,** to make use of.
serv.º servicio, service.
serv.ᵒʳ servidor, servant.
sesada, *f.* fried brains.
sesenta, *m.* sixty; **—,** *adj.* sixtieth.
sesentón, ona, *n.* person sixty years of age, sexagenarian.
sesera, *f.* brainpan; brain.
sesgadura, *f.* slope, sloping; bevel.
sesgar, *va.* to slope, to cut on the bias.
sesgo, *m.* slope; bias; **—, ga,** *adj.* sloping, oblique; grave; **al —go,** obliquely, on the bias.
sesión, *f.* session, meeting; conference.
seso, *m.* brain.
sestear, *vn.* to take a nap after dinner.
sesudo, da, *adj.* judicious, discreet, prudent.
seta, *f.* bristle; fungus (in general).
set.ᵉ or **set.ᵇʳᵉ setiembre,** Sept. September.
setecientos, tas, *adj.* seven hundred.
setena, *f.* heptad.
setenario, ria, *adj.* septenary.
setenta, *m.* and *adj.* seventy.
setentón, ona, *adj.* septuagenarian.
seto, *m.* fence, enclosure, hedge.
seudo, *adj.* pseudo, false.
seudónimo, *m.* nom de plume, pseudonym.
S. E. u O. or **s. e. u. o. salvo error u omisión,** E. & O. E. errors and omissions excepted.
severamente, *adv.* severely, sternly.
severidad, *f.* severity; austerity, strictness.
severo, ra, *adj.* severe, rigorous; grave, serious.
Sevilla, *f.* Seville.
sevillano, na, *n.* and *adj.* from Seville.
sexagenario, ria, *adj.* and *n.* sixty years old; person sixty years old, sexagenarian.
sexagésimo, ma, *adj.* sixtieth.
sexenio, *m.* space of six years.
sexo, *m.* sex.
sexta, *f.* sequence of six cards at piquet; sixth (minor canonical hour after tierce).
sexto, ta, *adj.* sixth; **—,** *m.* book containing canonical decrees.
s/f. su favor, your favor.
s/g: su giro, (com.) your draft; **sin gastos,** (com.) without expense or charge.
si, *conj.* if, whether, when, although; in case that; provided that; **— acaso,** or

por — acaso, by chance; — **no,** if not; —, *m.* (mus.) seventh note of the scale.

sí, *adv.* yes, without doubt; indeed; **de —,** spontaneously; —, *pron.* himself; herself; itself; themselves; **de por —** , by itself; **volver en —,** to come to, to recover one's senses.

sibarítico, ca, *adj.* sybaritical, luxurious.

sibila, *f.* prophetess; sibyl.

Sicilia, *f.* Sicily.

siciliano, na, *n.* and *adj.* Sicilian.

sicómoro, *m.* (bot.) sycamore.

siderurgia, *f.* siderurgy.

sidra, *f.* cider.

siega, *f.* harvest, mowing.

siembra, *f.* seedtime; sowing, seeding.

siempre, *adv.* always, ever; — **jamás,** for ever and ever.

siempreviva, *f.* (bot.) strawflower, everlasting flower.

sien, *f.* temple (of the head).

sierpe, *f.* serpent, snake.

sierra, *f.* saw; range of mountains; — **de armadura,** bucksaw; — **de cinta,** scroll saw; — **de vaivén,** jigsaw.

siervo, va, *n.* serf, slave; servant.

siesta, *f.* siesta, afternoon nap.

siete, *m.* and *adj.* seven.

sietemesino, na, *adj.* of seven months' time; —, *n.* child born seven months after conception.

sífilis, *f.* syphilis.

sifón, *m.* siphon, siphon bottle.

sig. or **sig.**te **siguiente,** fol. following.

sigilo, *m.* seal; secret; reserve.

sigiloso, sa, *adj.* reserved, silent.

siglo, *m.* century; **la consumación de los —s,** the end of the world.

signar, *va.* to sign, to seal; —**se,** to make the sign of the cross.

signatario, *m.* signatory.

signatura, *f.* sign, mark; signature (in printing).

significación, *f.* signification, significance, meaning.

significado, *m.* significance, meaning.

significar, *va.* to signify; to mean.

significativo, va, *adj.* significant, full of meaning.

signo, *m.* sign, mark.

siguiente, *adj.* following, successive, sequent.

sílaba, *f.* syllable; métrical composition.

silabario, *m.* primer.

silabear, *vn.* to spell out by syllables.

silabeo, *m.* syllabication.

sílabo, *m.* syllabus.

silbar, *va.* to hiss; —, *vn.* to whistle.

silbato, *m.* whistle.

silbido or **silbo,** *m.* hiss, whistling.

silenciador, *m.* silencer, muffler (of an automobile).

silencio, *m.* silence; ¡—! *interj.* silence! hush!

silencioso, sa, *adj.* silent.

sílex, *m.* (min.) silex.

silguero, *m.* (orn.) linnet.

sílice, *f.* silica, silicon dioxide.

silo, *m.* subterranean granary for wheat; silo.

silogismo, *m.* syllogism.

silogizar, *vn.* to reason, to argue.

silueta, *f.* silhouette, outline.

silva, *f.* an eleven- and seven-syllable meter with no fixed rhyme order.

Silvestre, Sylvester.

silvestre, *adj.* wild, uncultivated; savage.

silvicultura, *f.* forestry.

silla, *f.* chair; saddle; ecclesiastical see; — **de cubierta,** deck chair; — **de montar,** riding saddle; — **de ruedas,** wheel chair; — **giratoria,** swivel chair; — **para inválidos,** invalid's chair; — **plegadiza,** folding chair; — **poltrona,** armchair; easy chair; **de — a —,** face to face.

sillar, *m.* square-hewn stone.

sillería, *f.* set of chairs; saddler's shop; stalls about the choir of a church; building of hewn stone.

sillero, *m.* saddler; chairmaker.

silleta, *f.* small chair, stool; chamber stool.

sillico, *m.* basin of a chamber stool.

sillón, *m.* large armchair; sidesaddle.

sima, *f.* deep and dark cavern; abyss, gulf.

simbarra, *f.* furnace poker.

simbiosis, *f.* (biol.) symbiosis.

simbólico, ca, *adj.* symbolical.

simbolismo, *m.* symbolism.

simbolizar, *vn.* to symbolize.

símbolo, *m.* symbol; device.

simetría, *f.* symmetry.

simétrico, ca, *adj.* symmetrical.

simia, *f.* female ape or monkey.

simiente, *f.* seed.

símil, *m.* resemblance; (rhet.) simile; —, *adj* similar, like.

similar, *adj.* similar.

similitud, *f.* similitude.

simio, mia, *adj.* simian; —, *n.* ape or monkey.

simón, *m.* cab, hack.

simonía, *f.* simony.

simoníaco, ca, *adj.* guilty of simony; —, *n.* person guilty of simony.

simpatía, *f.* sympathy; charm; **tener — por,** to like someone, to find (someone) pleasant and congenial.

simpático, ca, *adj.* sympathetic; likable, winsome, charming.

simpatizar, *vn.* to sympathize; to be congenial.

simple, *adj.* single, simple, silly; insipid; —, *m.* simple (medicinal plant).

simpleza, *f.* simpleness, silliness; rusticity.

simplicidad, *f.* simplicity.

simplificar, *va.* to simplify, to make simple.

simulación, *f.* simulation.

simulacro, *m.* simulacrum, idol; sham battle.

simuladamente, *adv.* deceptively, hypocritically,

simulado, da, *adj.* feigned; **factura** or **cuenta** —, pro forma invoice or account.
simular, *va.* to simulate, to feign, to pretend.
simultaneidad, *f.* simultaneity.
simultáneo, nea, *adj.* simultaneous.
sin. sinónimo, syn. synonymous.
sin, *prep.* without, besides; — **embargo,** notwithstanding, nevertheless; — **duda,** doubtlessly.
sinagoga, *f.* synagogue.
sincerar, *va.* and *vr.* to exculpate, to justify.
sinceridad, *f.* sincerity.
sincero, ra, *adj.* sincere, ingenuous, honest.
síncopa, *f.* (gram., mus.) syncope; syncopation.
sincopar, *va.* to syncopate.
síncope, *m.* (med.) syncope, fainting fit.
sincrónico, ca, *adj.* synchronous, simultaneous.
sincronizar, *va.* to synchronize.
sindéresis, *f.* judgment, discretion.
sindicalismo, *m.* syndicalism.
sindicar, *va.* to inform, to accuse; to unionize.
sindicato, *m.* syndicate; — **(gremio) de obreros,** labor union.
sindicatura, *f.* trusteeship, receivership.
síndico, *m.* syndic; trustee or receiver in bankruptcy.
sinfonía, *f.* symphony.
singular, *adj.* singular; particular; unique.
singularidad, *f.* singularity.
singularizar, *va.* to distinguish; to singularize; —**se,** to distinguish oneself, to be singular.
singulto, *m.* hiccough, sob.
siniestra, *f.* left hand.
siniestro, tra, *adj.* left (side); sinister; unhappy; —, *m.* depravity; evil habit.
sinnúmero, *m.* no end; numberless quantity.
sino, *conj.* (after a negative), but; except; besides; only; —, *m.* destiny, fate.
sinodal, *adj.* synodic, synodal; —, *m.* examiner of curates and confessors.
sínodo, *m.* synod; conjunction of the heavenly bodies.
sinónimo, *m.* synonym.
sinónimo, ma, *adj.* synonymous.
sinopsis, *f.* synopsis, epitome, compendium.
sinóptico, ca, *adj.* synoptic.
sinrazón, *f.* injustice, wrong, injury.
sinsabor, *m.* displeasure, disgust.
sintaxis, *f.* syntax.
síntesis, *f.* synthesis.
sintético, ca, *adj.* synthetic, artificial.
síntoma, *m.* symptom.
sintonización, *f.* dialing.
sintonizar, *va.* (rad.) to syntonize, to tune.
sinuosidad, *f.* sinuosity.
sinuoso, sa, *adj.* sinuous, winding.
siquiera, *conj.* at least; though, although; **ni** —, not even.
sirena, *f.* foghorn, siren; mermaid.
sirga, *f.* towrope, towline.
sirgar, *va.* to tow a vessel.

sirte, *f.* moving sandbank; danger.
sirviente, ta, *n.* servant.
sisa, *f.* petty theft; clippings which tailors steal in cutting clothes; assize; excise.
sísmico, ca, *adj.* seismic.
sismógrafo, *m.* seismograph.
sismología, *f.* seismology.
sisón, *m.* filcher, pilferer; a Spanish wading bird.
sistema, *m.* system, plan.
sistemático, ca, *adj.* systematic.
sístole, *f.* systole.
sitiador, *m.* besieger.
sitiar, *va.* to besiege.
sitio, *m.* place; situation (of a town, etc.); (mil.) siege, blockade.
sito, ta, *adj.* situated.
situación, *f.* situation, state, condition.
situado, da, *adj.* situated, located.
situar, *va.* to place, to situate; to assign a fund; —**se,** to be established in a place or business; to station oneself.
ski, *m.* ski.
s/l or **s/L su letra** (com.) your letter or draft.
S. M. Su Majestad, His or Her Majesty.
S. M. A. Su Majestad Apostólica, His or Her Apostolic Majesty.
S. M. I. Su Majestad Imperial, His or Her Imperial Majesty.
smoking, *m.* Tuxedo coat.
S.ⁿ San, St. Saint.
S. N. Servicio Nacional, National Service.
SO sudoeste, SW or S. W. Southwest.
s/o su orden, (com.) your order.
so, *prep.* under; below (used in composition, it occasionally diminishes the import of the verb); — **pena de multa** or **muerte,** under penalty of fine or death; ¡—! *interj.* whoa!
soba, *f.* act of making something soft; beating; massage.
sobaco, *m.* armpit, armhole.
sobadura, *f.* kneading, rubbing.
sobajar, *va.* to rub hard.
sobar, *va.* to handle, to soften; to massage; to pummel, to beat, to whip; to scrub, to rub hard; to rumple clothes.
sobarba, *f.* noseband (of a bridle).
sobarbada, *f.* chuck under the chin; jerk; (fig.) reprimand, scolding.
soberanía, *f.* sovereignty.
soberano, na, *adj.* and *n.* sovereign.
soberbia, *f.* pride, haughtiness; presumption.
soberbio, bia, *adj.* proud, haughty.
sobina, *f.* wooden pin or peg.
sobornador, ra, *n.* suborner, briber.
sobornar, *va.* to suborn, to bribe.
soborno, *m.* subornation, bribe.
sobra, *f.* overplus, surplus, excess; rest, remainder; offense; **de** —, over and above; **hay de** —, there's more than enough.
sobradamente, *adv.* superabundantly.
sobradillo, *m.* small granary; shelter over a balcony.

sobrado, da, *adj.* excessive, abundant.

sobrante, *m.* residue, superfluity, surplus; **—s,** *pl.* odds and ends.

sobrar, *vn.* to have more than is necessary; to be more than enough; to remain, to be left.

sobrasar, *va.* to make a fire under (a pot or pan).

sobre, *prep.* above, over; moreover; a little more; on, upon, about; **cambio — Londres,** exchange on London; **— cero,** above zero; **— la mesa,** on the table; **— la par,** above par; **— todo,** above all; **—,** *m.* envelope.

sobreabundancia, *f.* superabundance.

sobreabundar, *vn.* to superabound.

sobreagudo, *m.* (mus.) highest treble.

sobrealimentar, *va.* to overfeed; to supercharge (a motor).

sobrealzar, *va.* to praise, to extol.

sobrebarato, ta, *adj.* extremely cheap.

sobrecama, *f.* coverlet, quilt, bedspread.

sobrecaña, *f.* tumor in a horse's leg.

sobrecarga, *f.* additional bundle thrown over a load; surcharge, overburden.

sobrecargador, *m.* (aer.) supercharger.

sobrecargar, *va.* to overload; to fell (in sewing).

sobrecargo, *m.* supercargo, purser.

sobreceja, *f.* part of the forehead over the eyebrows.

sobrecejo or **sobreceño,** *m.* frown.

sobrecoger, *va.* to surprise; **—se,** to become afraid or apprehensive.

sobrecomida, *f.* dessert.

sobrecubierta, *f.* double cover; (naut.) upper deck.

sobredicho, cha, *adj.* above-mentioned.

sobrediente, *m.* projecting tooth.

sobredorar, *va.* to overgild; to palliate, to exculpate.

sobreexcitación, *f.* overexcitement, dither.

sobreexcitarse, *vn.* to be in a dither, to be overexcited.

sobrehueso, *m.* morbid swelling on the bones or joints; trouble, encumbrance.

sobrehumano, na, *adj.* superhuman.

sobrellevar, *va.* to ease, to alleviate; to suffer, to tolerate.

sobremanera, *adv.* excessively, exceedingly.

sobremesa, *f.* table cover; dessert; **de —,** immediately after dinner.

sobrenadar, *vn.* to swim on the surface, to float.

sobrenatural, *adj.* supernatural.

sobrenombre, *m.* surname; nickname.

sobrentender, *va.* (IE) to understand; **—se,** to go without saying.

sobrepaga, *f.* increase or augmentation of pay.

sobreparto, *m.* confinement after childbirth.

sobrepasar, *va.* to surpass.

sobrepelliz, *f.* surplice.

sobrepeso, *m.* overweight.

sobrepié, *m.* osseous tumor at the top of horses' hoofs.

sobreplán, *m.* (naut.) rider.

sobreponer, *va.* (SOBREPONGO, SOBREPUSE) to put a thing over or on another; **—se,** to master; to put oneself out of reach of, to show oneself superior to.

sobreprecio, *m.* extra price.

sobreproducción, *f.* overproduction.

sobrepujanza, *f.* excessive strength.

sobrepujar, *va.* to exceed, to surpass, to excel.

sobrerropa, *f.* overcoat.

sobresaliente, *adj.* outstanding, conspicuous; excellent, excelling; **—,** *m.* and *f.* substitute, understudy.

sobresalir, *vn.* (SOBRESALGO, SOBRESALÍ) to exceed in height, to surpass; to be prominent; to extrude.

sobresaltado, da, *adj.* terrified, startled.

sobresaltar, *va.* to make an unexpected attack; to frighten.

sobresalto, *m.* sudden assault; sudden dread.

sobrescrito, *m.* address of a letter, superscription.

sobresdrújulo, la, *adj.* accented on any syllable preceding the antepenult.

sobresello, *m.* double seal.

sobrestadía, *f.* demurrage.

sobrestante, *m.* overseer; foreman.

sobresueldo, *m.* addition to one's pay or allowance.

sobretodo, *m.* topcoat, overcoat.

sobrevenir, *vn.* (SOBREVENGO, SOBREVINE) to happen, to come unexpectedly; to supervene.

sobreviviente, *m.* and *f.* survivor; **—,** *adj.* surviving.

sobrevivir, *vn.* to survive.

sobriedad, *f.* sobriety, moderation, temperance.

sobrina, *f.* niece.

sobrino, *m.* nephew.

sobrio, ria, *adj.* sober, frugal.

Soc. Sociedad, Soc. Society.

socaliña, *f.* extortion, cheating.

socaliñar, *va.* to extort by cunning.

socarrar, *va.* to singe, to scorch.

socarrón, ona, *adj.* cunning, sly, crafty.

socarronería, *f.* craft, cunning, artfulness.

socavar, *va.* to undermine; to excavate.

sociabilidad, *f.* sociability.

sociable, *adj.* sociable.

social, *adj.* social; **razón —,** firm name.

socialidad, *f.* sociality.

socialismo, *m.* socialism.

socialista, *m.* and *f.* socialist; **—,** *adj.* socialistic.

socialización, *f.* socialization.

socializar, *va.* to socialize.

sociedad, *f.* society, company, partnership; **— anónima,** corporation; **— benéfica,** benevolent, charity or welfare society; **— colectiva,** general partnership; **— en comandita** or **comanditaria,** limited

(silent) partnership; — **regular colectiva,** general partnership, copartnership.
Sociedad de las Naciones, League of Nations.
socio, *m.* associate, companion, partner, member; — **colectivo,** copartner; — **comanditario,** silent partner; — **gerente** or **gestor,** managing partner; — **industrial,** working partner.
sociología, *f.* sociology.
sociológico, ca, *adj.* sociological.
sociólogo, *m.* sociologist.
socolor, *m.* pretext, pretense.
socorredor, ra, *n.* succorer, helper.
socorrer, *va.* to succor, to help, to rescue.
socorrido, da, *adj.* furnished, supplied.
socorro, *m.* succor, help, aid.
sodio, *m.* sodium.
sodomía, *f.* sodomy.
sodomita, *m.* and *f.* sodomite.
soez, *adj.* mean, vile, lousy.
sofá, *m.* sofa, couch, lounge.
Sofía, Sophia.
sofisma, *m.* sophism.
sofista, *m.* sophist.
sofistería, *f.* sophistry.
sofisticar, *va.* to sophisticate.
sofístico, ca, *adj.* sophistical.
soflamar, *va.* to swindle; —**se,** to get scorched.
sofocación, *f.* suffocation, smothering.
sofocante, *adj.* suffocating, stifling.
sofocar, *va.* to suffocate, to smother; to harass.
sofrenada, *f.* sudden check given to a horse with the bridle; severe reprimand.
sofrenar, *va.* to check a horse by a violent pull of the bridle; to reprimand severely.
soga, *f.* rope.
soguería, *f.* ropewalk, rope yard.
soguero, *m.* ropemaker.
soja, *f.* (bot.) soybean.
sojuzgador, *m.* conqueror, subduer.
sojuzgar, *va.* to conquer, to subdue.
sol, *m.* sun; a silver coin of Peru; (mus.) sol; **hace —,** it is sunny; **puesta del —,** sunset; **rayo de —,** sunbeam; **salida del —,** sunrise.
solamente, *adv.* only, solely.
solana, *f.* sunny place; sunroom, sun porch; sun bath.
solanera, *f.* sunburn, sun bath.
solano, *m.* easterly wind.
solapa, *f.* lapel; pretense, pretext.
solapado, da, *adj.* cunning, crafty, artful.
solapar, *va.* to button one's coat across; to hide under a false pretense.
solar, *m.* building lot; real estate; ancestral mansion of a noble family; —, *adj.* solar; **luz —,** sunshine; —, *va.* (UE) to floor a room; to sole shoes or boots.
solariego, ga, *adj.* belonging to the ancestral mansion of a noble family, noble, old.
solaz, *m.* solace, consolation; **a —,** pleasantly, agreeably.

solazar, *va.* to solace, to comfort.
solazo, *m.* scorching sun.
soldada, *f.* wages.
soldadesca, *f.* soldiery.
soldadesco, ca, *adj.* soldierly, soldierlike.
soldado, *m.* soldier; — **de a caballo,** cavalryman; — **de infantería de marinos,** marine private; — **de marina,** marine; — **de reserva,** reservist; — **raso,** (coll.) buck private.
soldador, *m.* solderer; soldering iron.
soldadura, *f.* soldering; solder; correction; — **de arco,** arc welding.
soldar, *va.* (UE) to solder; to mend; —**se** to stick together.
solecismo, *m.* solecism.
soledad, *f.* solitude; lonely place; desert.
solejar, *m.* sunny place.
solemne, *adj.* solemn; celebrated; grand, high; gay, cheerful.
solemnidad, *f.* solemnity, pomp.
solemnizar, *va.* to solemnize, to praise.
soler, *vn. def.* (UE) to be accustomed, to be in the habit of.
soleta, *f.* linen sole put into stockings.
solfa, *f.* (mus.) gamut; solmization; accordance, harmony; sound flogging.
solfeador, *m.* songster; music master; dealer of blows.
solfear, *vn.* (mus.) to solfa, to solmizate.
solfeo, *m.* solfeggio.
solicitación, *f.* solicitation.
solicitante, *m.* and *f.* applicant.
solicitar, *va.* to solicit; to apply for.
solícito, ta, *adj.* solicitous, careful.
solicitud, *f.* solicitude, application, petition; **a —,** on request.
solidaridad, *f.* solidarity.
solidario, ria, *adj.* solidary, jointly liable.
solidez, *f.* solidity.
sólido, da, *adj.* solid.
soliloquio, *m.* soliloquy, monologue.
solimán, *m.* (chem.) bichloride of mercury.
solio, *m.* throne with a canopy.
solista, *m.* and *f.* soloist.
solitaria, *f.* post chaise for a single person; tapeworm.
solitario, ria, *adj.* solitary, lonely; —, *m.* hermit; solitaire (game).
solivantar, *va.* to induce, to incite.
soliviar, *va.* to raise up, to help raise up; —**se,** to lift oneself up half way.
solo, *m.* (mus.) solo; —, **la,** *adj.* alone, single; **a solas,** alone, unaided; **a sus solas,** quite alone.
sólo, *adv.* only.
solomillo or **solomo,** *m.* loin, chine; sirloin.
solsticio, *m.* solstice.
soltadizo, za, *adj.* easily untied.
soltar, *va.* (UE) to untie, to loosen; to set at liberty; —**se,** to get loose; to lose all decency and modesty.
soltera, *f.* unmarried woman, spinster, old maid.
soltería, *f.* celibacy.

soltero, ra, *adj.* unmarried; —, *m.* bachelor; —, *f.* bachelor girl, unmarried woman.

solterón, ona, *n.* old bachelor, old maid.

soltura, *f.* liberation; release; agility, activity; ease.

soluble, *adj.* soluble; solvable.

solución, *f.* solution; denouement of a drama.

solucionar, *va.* to solve.

solvencia, *f.* solvency.

solventar, *va.* to settle (debts).

solvente, *adj.* dissolvent; solvent.

sollo, *m.* sturgeon.

sollozar, *vn.* to sob.

sollozo, *m.* sob.

sombra, *f.* shade, shadow.

sombraje, *m.* covering of branches, mats, etc., to shelter from the sun.

sombrar, *va.* to astonish.

sombrear, *va.* to shade, to shadow.

sombrerazo, *m.* large hat; slap with a hat.

sombrerera, *f.* hatbox; woman who makes or sells hats.

sombrerería, *f.* hat factory; hat shop.

sombrerero, *m.* hatter, hatmaker.

sombrero, *m.* hat; — **de jipijapa,** Panama hat, — **de paja,** straw hat.

sombrilla, *f.* umbrella, parasol.

sombrío, bría, *adj.* shady; (poet.) darksome, gloomy, bleak.

someter, *va.* to submit; to subject; to subdue; —**se,** to humble oneself; to submit.

sometimiento, *m.* submission.

somnambulismo, *m.* = **sonambulismo.**

somnolencia, *f.* sleepiness, drowsiness.

somorgujar, *va.* and *vr.* to duck, to dive.

son, *m.* sound, report; Cuban musical rhythm; **a — de,** at the sound of; **en — de,** as, like, in the manner of; **en — de burla,** in a mocking manner.

sonado, da, *adj.* celebrated; famous; generally reported.

sonaja, *f.* jingle; timbrel (musical instrument).

sonajero, *m.* rattle.

sonambulismo, *m.* somnambulism.

sonámbulo, la, *n.* and *adj.* somnambulist.

sonar, *va.* (UE) to play upon a musical instrument; —, *vn.* to sound; to ring; —**se,** to blow one's nose.

sonata, *f.* (mus.) sonata.

sonda, *f.* sounding; catheter.

sondar or **sondear,** *va.* (naut.) to sound, to measure depth; to sound (another person's intentions); to probe.

sondeable, *adj.* fathomable.

soneto, *m.* sonnet.

sonido, *m.* sound.

sonómetro, *m.* sonometer.

sonoro, ra, *adj.* sonorous, ringing, tuneful.

sonreír, *vn.* and *vr.* (SONRÍO, SONREÍ) to smile.

sonrisa, *f.* smile.

sonrojar, *va.* and *vr.* to make one blush; to blush.

sonrojo, *m.* blush; offensive word which causes a blush.

sonrosado, da, *adj.* pink.

sonrosar or **sonrosear,** *va.* to dye a rose color; —**se,** to blush.

sonroseo, *m.* blush.

sonsacador, ra, *n.* wheedler.

sonsacamiento, *m.* wheedling, extortion.

sonsacar, *va.* to pump a secret out of a person.

sonsonete, *m.* tapping noise; scornful, derisive tone.

soñador, ra, *n.* dreamer, escapist.

soñar, *va.* and *vn.* (UE) to dream.

soñoliento, ta, *adj.* sleepy, drowsy; causing sleep; dull, lazy.

sopa, *f.* soup.

sopalanda, *f.* gown worn by students in olden times.

sopera, *f.* soup tureen.

sopero, *m.* soup plate; person fond of soups.

sopetón, *m.* hard box on the ears; **de —,** suddenly.

soplado, da, *adj.* blown; (coll.) overnice, fastidious.

soplar, *va.* and *vn.* to blow; to blow bellows; to steal in an artful manner; to suggest; to inspire; to tipple, to drink much; to accuse, to denounce anyone; —**se,** to swell up; to stuff oneself.

soplete, *m.* blowtorch, blowpipe; — **oxhídrico,** oxyhydrogen torch.

soplo, *m.* blowing; puff of wind; advice given secretly; instant, moment.

soplón, ona, *n.* talebearer.

soponcio, *m.* faint, swoon.

sopor, *m.* drowsiness, sleepiness.

soporífero, ra, *adj.* soporific, soporiferous.

soportable, *adj.* tolerable, supportable.

soportal, *m.* portico.

soportar, *va.* to suffer, to tolerate, to bear; to support.

Sor. Señor, Mr.

sor, *f.* sister (used only to nuns).

sorber, *va.* (UE) to sip, to suck; to absorb, to swallow; to imbibe.

sorbete, *m.* sherbet.

sorbo, *m.* sipping; a little; small quantity of anything; **tomar a —s,** to sip.

sordera, *f.* deafness.

sordidez, *f.* sordidness, nastiness, covetousness.

sórdido, da, *adj.* sordid; nasty, dirty; licentious.

sordina, *f.* damper; (mus.) sordine, mute.

sordo, da, *adj.* deaf; silent, quiet; secret.

sordomudo, da, *n.* and *adj.* deaf and dumb, person who is deaf and dumb.

sorgo, *m.* sorghum.

sorna, *f.* sluggishness, laziness, slowness.

sorprendente, *adj.* striking, surprising.

sorprender, *va.* to surprise, to fall upon unexpectedly.

sorpresa, *f.* surprise; **de —,** unawares.

sorteador, *m.* one who casts lots; dexterous bullfighter.

sortear, *vn.* to draw or cast lots; to fight bulls with skill and dexterity.

sorteo, *m.* act of casting or drawing lots, raffle.

sortija, *f.* ring; hoop; buckle.

sortilegio, *m.* sortilege, sorcery.

sosa, *f.* soda; (bot.) glasswort, kelp.

sosegado, da, *adj.* quiet, peaceful.

sosegar, *va.* (IE) to appease, to placate, to calm; **—,** *vn.* to rest, to repose; to be calm or composed.

sosería, *f.* insipidity.

sosiego, *m.* tranquillity, calmness, heart's ease.

soslayar, *va.* to do or place a thing obliquely.

soslayo, *adj.* oblique; **al** or **de —,** askew, sideways.

soso, sa, *adj.* insipid, tasteless.

sospecha, *f.* suspicion, mistrust.

sospechar, *va.* and *vn.* to suspect.

sospechoso, sa, *adj.* suspicious, mistrustful.

sostén, *m.* support; steadiness of a ship in pursuing her course.

sostener, *va.* (SOSTENGO, SOSTUVE) to sustain, to maintain; **—se,** to support or maintain oneself.

sostenido, da, *adj.* sustained; **—,** *m.* (mus.) sharp (tone and character ♯).

sostenimiento, *m.* sustenance.

sota, *f.* jack (in cards).

sotana, *f.* cassock; (coll.) flogging, drubbing.

sótano, *m.* cellar underground.

sotavento, *m.* (naut.) leeward, lee.

sotechado, *m.* roofed or covered place.

soterrar, *va.* (IE) to bury, to put underground.

soto, *m.* grove, thicket; undergrowth.

soviet, *m.* soviet.

soviético, ca, *adj.* soviet.

sovoz, a —, *adv.* sotto voce.

soya, *f.* soybean.

s/p su pagaré, (com.) your promissory note.

spre. siempre, always, ever.

Sr. or **S.ʳ Señor,** Mr. Mister.

s/r su remesa, (com.) your remittance or shipment.

Sra. or **S.ʳᵃ Señora,** Mrs. Mistress.

sre. sobre, over, on, above.

Sres. or **S.ʳᵉˢ Señores,** Messrs. Messieurs.

Sría. Secretaría, secretary's office.

srio. or **s.ʳⁱᵒ secretario,** sec. secretary.

S. R. M. Su Real Majestad, His or Her Royal Majesty.

Srta. or **S.ʳᵗᵃ Señorita,** Miss.

S. S. or **s. s. seguro servidor,** devoted servant.

S. S. Su Santidad, His Holiness.

S. S.ᵃ Su Señoría, His Lordship.

SS.AA. Sus Altezas, Their Highnesses.

SSE. sudsudeste, SSE or S.S.E South-Southeast.

SS. MM. Sus Majestades, Their Majesties.

SS.ᵐᵒ Santísimo, Most Holy.

SS.ᵐᵒ P. Santísimo Padre, Most Holy Father.

SS.ⁿᵒ escribano, scrivener, public writer.

SSO sudsudoeste, SSW or S.S.W. south-southwest.

S.S.S. or **s.s.s. su seguro servidor,** your devoted servant, yours truly.

SS. SS. SS. or **ss. ss. ss. sus seguros servidores,** your devoted servants, yours truly.

Sta. Santa, St. Saint (feminine).

Sto. Santo, St. Saint (masculine).

su, *pron.* his, her, its, one's; **sus,** their.

suave, *adj.* smooth, soft, delicate; gentle, mild, meek.

suavidad, *f.* softness, sweetness; suavity; gentleness.

suavizar, *va.* to soften; **—se,** to grow mild, to become soft; to temper.

subacetato, *m.* (chem.) subacetate.

subagencia, *f.* subagency.

subalterno, na, *adj.* subaltern, inferior, subordinate.

subarrendador, ra, *n.* undertenant.

subarrendar, *va.* (IE) to sublet, to sublease.

subarriendo, *m.* sublease.

subasta, *f.* auction, open sale; **sacar a pública —,** to sell at public auction.

subastar, *va.* to sell by auction.

subcarbonato, *m.* (chem.) subcarbonate.

subconsciente, *adj.* subconscious.

subcutáneo, nea, *adj.* subcutaneous.

subdelegación, *f.* subdelegation, substitution.

subdelegado, da, *n.* subdelegate.

subdelegar, *va.* to subdelegate.

subdiaconado or **subdiaconato,** *m.* subdeaconship.

subdiácono, *m.* subdeacon.

súbdito, ta, *adj.* subject (of a king, etc.).

subdividir, *va.* to subdivide.

subdivisión, *f.* subdivision.

subgerente, *m.* assistant manager.

subida, *f.* mounting; ascent, acclivity, rise; enhancement, augmentation of value or price.

subido, da, *adj.* deep-colored; very fine, very excellent; raised on high.

subintrar, *va.* to enter afterwards or in place of another.

subir, *vn.* to mount, to ascend, to climb; to increase, to swell; to enter leaves (of silk-worms, in making their cocoons); to rise in dignity, fortune, etc.; **—,** *va.* to ascend; to go up; to enhance.

súbito, ta, *adj.* sudden, hasty, unforeseen.

subjuntivo, *m.* (gram.) subjunctive.

sublevación, *f.* sedition, revolt.

sublevar, *va.* and *vn.* to excite a rebellion; to rise in rebellion.

sublimado, *m.* (chem.) sublimate.

sublime, *adj.* sublime, exalted.

sublimidad, *f.* sublime, sublimity.

submarino, *m.* submarine.

subnormal, *adj.* subnormal.
subordinación, *f.* subordination.
subordinado, da, *n.* and *adj.* subordinate.
subordinar, *va.* to subordinate.
subrayar, *va.* to underline, to underscore.
subrepción, *f.* hidden action, underhand business; subreption.
subrepticio, cia, *adj.* surreptitious.
subrogación, *f.* surrogation, subrogation, substitution.
subrogar, *va.* to surrogate, to subrogate.
subsanar, *va.* to excuse; to mend, to repair.
subscribir, *va.* and *vr.* to subscribe, to sign.
subscripción, *f.* subscription.
subscrito, ta, *adj.* subscribed, undersigned.
subsecretario, ria, *n.* undersecretary, assistant secretary.
subsecuente, *adj.* subsequent.
subseguir, *vn.* (I) to be subsequent, to follow.
subsidiario, ria, *adj.* subsidiary.
subsidio, *m.* subsidy, aid.
subsiguiente, *adj.* subsequent.
subsistencia, *f.* subsistence; permanence, stability.
subsistir, *vn.* to subsist, to last.
substancia, *f.* substance.
substancial, *adj.* substantial.
substancialmente, *adv.* substantially.
substanciar, *va.* to abridge; to aver; to verify, to substantiate.
substancioso, sa, *adj.* substantial, nutritive, nutritious.
substantivo, *m.* substantive, noun.
substitución, *f.* substitution, replacement.
substituir, *va.* (SUBSTITUYÓ, SUBSTITUYENDO) to substitute, to replace.
substituto, ta, *n.* and *adj.* substitute.
substracción, *f.* subtraction.
substraer, *va.* (SUBSTRAIGO, SUBSTRAJE) to subtract; —se, to retire, to withdraw.
subsuelo, *m.* subsoil.
subteniente, *m.* second lieutenant.
subterfugio, *m.* subterfuge.
subterráneo, nea, *adj.* subterraneous, underground; —, *m.* subterrane.
subtítulo, *m.* subtitle.
subtropical, *adj.* subtropical.
suburbano, na, *adj.* suburban; —, *n.* suburbanite.
suburbio, *m.* suburb.
subvención, *f.* subsidy; subvention.
subvenir, *va.* (SUBVENGO, SUBVINE) to aid, to succor; to defray.
subversión, *f.* subversion, overthrow.
subversivo, va, *adj.* subversive.
subvertir, *va.* (IE) to subvert, to destroy, to ruin.
subyugar, *va.* to subdue, to subjugate.
succión, *f.* suction.
suceder, *vn.* to succeed, to inherit; to happen.
sucesión, *f.* succession; issue, offspring; hereditary succession.
sucesivamente, *adv.* successively, consecu-

tively; **y así —,** and so on.
sucesivo, va, *adj.* successive; **en lo —vo,** from now on, in the future.
suceso, *m.* outcome, event; success.
sucesor, ra, *n.* successor, succeeder, heir.
suciedad, *f.* nastiness, filthiness, dirt, mire.
sucinto, ta, *adj.* succinct, concise.
sucio, cia, *adj.* dirty, nasty, filthy; obscene; dishonest.
sucre, *m.* sucre, coin of Ecuador.
Suc.res **Sucesores,** Successors.
suculento, ta, *adj.* succulent, juicy.
sucumbir, *vn.* to succumb, to perish, to sink.
sucursal, *adj.* subsidiary; —, *f.* branch, annex.
sud, *m.* south; south wind (used instead of **sur,** when joined to another word).
sudafricano, na, *n.* and *adj.* South African.
sudamericano, na, *adj.* and *n.* South American.
sudar, *va.* and *vn.* to sweat, to perspire; (coll.) to give with repugnance.
sudario, *m.* sweat cloth, shroud.
sudeste, *m.* southeast.
sudoeste, *m.* southwest.
sudor, *m.* sweat, perspiration.
sudoriento, ta, *adj.* moist with sweat.
sudorífico, ca, *adj.* sudorific, inducing sweat.
sudoso, sa, *adj.* sweaty.
sudsudeste, *m.* south-southeast.
sud-sudoeste, *m.* south-southwest.
Suecia, *f.* Sweden.
sueco, ca, *n.* and *adj.* Swedish.
suegra, *f.* mother-in-law.
suegro, *m.* father-in-law.
suela, *f.* sole of the shoe; sole leather.
sueldo, *m.* salary, pay; sou, sol, solidus (coins).
suelo, *m.* soil, surface; ground, pavement
suelta, *f.* loosening; tethers; hobbles; **dar —,** to liberate for a short time.
suelto, *adj.* loose; expeditious, swift; —, *m.* change (money); newspaper item.
sueño, *m.* sleep; vision, dream; **tener —,** to be sleepy.
suero, *m.* whey; serum (of blood); **— de manteca** or **mantequilla,** buttermilk.
suerte, *f.* chance, lot, fortune, fate, good luck; kind, sort; species; manner; **tener —,** to be lucky; **echar —es,** to draw lots.
suficiencia, *f.* sufficiency; **a —,** sufficiently, enough.
suficiente, *adj.* sufficient, fit, capable.
sufijo, *m.* suffix.
sufragáneo, *m.* suffragan, subordinate bishop; **—neo, nea,** *adj.* depending on another's authority or jurisdiction.
sufragar, *va.* to aid, to assist; to defray.
sufragio, *m.* vote, suffrage; aid, assistance.
sufrible, *adj.* sufferable.
sufrido, da, *adj.* long suffering, patient.
sufrimiento, *m.* sufferance, patience.
sufrir, *va.* to suffer, to bear with patience; to permit; to undergo.

sufusión, *f.* (med.) suffusion.
sugerir, *va.* (IE) to suggest.
sugestión, *f.* suggestion.
sugestionar, *va.* and *vr.* to influence by the power of suggestion.
suicida, *m.* and *f.* person committing suicide.
suicidarse, *vr.* to commit suicide.
suicidio, *m.* suicide.
Suiza, *f.* Switzerland.
suizo, za, *n.* and *adj.* Swiss.
sujeción, *f.* subjection; control; **con — a,** subject to.
sujetador, *m.* clasp, clamp, fastener.
sujetar, *va.* to subdue; to subject; to hold.
sujeto, ta, *adj.* subject, liable, exposed; **—,** *m.* subject; matter under discussion.
sulfanilamida, *f.* sulfanilamide.
sulfanilamidos, *m. pl.* sulfa drugs.
sulfapiridina, *f.* sulfapyridine.
sulfatiazol, *m.* sulfathiazole.
sulfato, *m.* (chem.) sulphate.
sulfhidrato, *m.* (chem.) hydrosulphide.
sulfhídrico, ca, *adj.* (chem.) hydrosulphuric.
sulfido, *m.* (chem.) sulphide.
sulfúreo, rea, *adj.* sulphureous.
sulfúrico, *adj.* sulphuric.
sultán, *m.* sultan.
sultana, *f.* sultana.
suma, *f.* sum; substance; amount; **en —,** in short.
sumamente, *adv.* extremely, highly.
sumar, *va.* to add, to sum up; to amount to.
sumario, ria, *adj.* summary; **—,** *m.* compendium, summary.
sumergible, *m.* submarine; **—,** *adj.* sinkable, submergible.
sumergir, *va.* and *vr.* to submerge, to sink.
sumersión, *f.* submersion, immersion.
sumidad, *f.* summit.
sumidero, *m.* sewer, drain.
suministración, *f.* supply, furnishing.
suministrador, ra, *m.* provider.
suministrar, *va.* to supply, to furnish.
sumir, *va.* to take, to receive the chalice at mass; **—se,** to sink under ground; to be sunken (of one's features).
sumisión, *f.* submission, acquiescence.
sumiso, sa, *adj.* submissive, humble.
sumo, ma, *adj.* highest, greatest; **a lo —mo,** at most; to the highest pitch.
sunción, *f.* (eccl.) receiving holy communion at mass.
suntuosidad, *f.* sumptuousness.
suntuoso, sa, *adj.* sumptuous.
sup. súplica, plea.
supeditación, *f.* subjection.
supeditar, *va.* to subject, to oppress.
superable, *adj.* superable, conquerable.
superabundancia, *f.* superabundance.
superabundar, *vn.* to superabound.
superar, *va.* to surpass, to excel.
superchería, *f.* deceit, fraud.
superentender, *va.* (IE) to oversee, superintend.

superficial, *adj.* superficial, shallow.
superficie, *f.* surface, area.
superfino, na, *adj.* superfine.
superfluidad, *f.* superfluity.
superfluo, lua, *adj.* superfluous, unnecessary.
superfosfato, *m.* superphosphate; **— de cal,** superphosphate of lime.
superheterodino, na, *adj.* superheterodyne.
superhombre, *m.* superman.
superintendencia, *f.* superintendence.
superintendente, *m.* superintendent, intendant, director.
superior, *adj.* superior; upper (in geography); **parte —,** topside; **—,** *m.* superior.
superioridad, *f.* superiority.
superlativo, va, *adj.* and *m.* (gram.) superlative.
supernumerario, ria, *adj.* supernumerary.
superstición, *f.* superstition.
supersticioso, sa, *adj.* superstitious.
super.^{te} superintendente, supt. superintendent.
supervivencia, *f.* survival; privilege to receive a dead person's pension; **— del más apto,** survival of the fittest.
supino, na, *adj.* supine, on one's back; indolent; **—,** *m.* (gram.) supine.
suplantación, *f.* supplanting.
suplantar, *va.* to falsify or tamper with a document; to supplant.
suplemento, *m.* supplement.
suplente, *adj.* substitute, alternate.
súplica, *f.* petition, plea, request, supplication.
suplicante, *adj.* and *m.* supplicant.
suplicar, *va.* to supplicate, to entreat; to pray, to plead; to appeal from a judgment;
suplicio, *m.* capital punishment; torture; grief, anguish.
suplir, *va.* to supply; to serve instead of, to perform another's functions; to disguise; to supplement.
supl.^{te} suplente, sub. substitute.
suponer, *va.* (SUPONGO, SUPUSE) to suppose, to surmise.
suposición, *f.* supposition, conjecture, basis.
supradicho, cha, *adj.* above-mentioned.
suprarrenal, *adj.* suprarenal, adrenal.
supremo, ma, *adj.* supreme.
supresión, *f.* suppression.
suprimir, *va.* to suppress; to abolish, to take out.
sup.^{te} suplicante, supplicant.
supuesto, *m.* supposition; **—, ta,** *adj.* supposed, false, assumed; **— que,** allowing that, granting that; **por —,** of course.
supuración, *f.* suppuration, coming to a head (of boils, etc.).
supurar, *vn.* to suppurate, to generate pus.
supurativo, va, *adj.* promoting suppuration.
Sur or **Sud América,** *f.* South America.
sur, *m.* south; south wind.
surcador, *m.* plowman.

surcar, *va.* to furrow; (fig.) to plow (as a ship through waves).

surco, *m.* furrow.

surgidero, *m.* anchoring place, anchorage.

surgir, *vn.* to anchor; to surge, to rise; to present itself, to emerge.

suroeste, *m.* southwest.

surtido, *m.* assortment, supply.

surtidor, ra, *n.* purveyor, caterer; —, *m.* waterspout; **—dor de gasolina,** filling station.

surtir, *va.* to supply, to furnish, to provide.

Susana, Susan.

susceptible, *adj.* susceptible.

suscitar, *va.* to excite, to stir up.

suscribir, *va.* and *vr.* to subscribe.

suscripción, *f.* subscription; signature.

suscriptor, ra, *n.* subscriber.

susidio, *m.* anxiety.

susodicho, cha, *adj.* above-mentioned, aforesaid.

suspender, *va.* to suspend, to stop, to cease, to raise up.

suspensión, *f.* suspension.

suspensivo, va, *adj.* suspensive.

suspenso, sa, *adj.* suspended, unfinished; —, *m.* failure (in an examination).

suspicacia, *f.* suspiciousness, distrust.

suspicaz, *adj.* suspicious, distrustful.

suspirar, *vn.* to sigh.

suspiro, *m.* sigh; kind of pastry.

sustancia, *f.* substance.

sustancioso, sa, *adj.* substantial, nutritious.

sustantivar, *va.* to use adjectives, etc., as substantives.

sustantivo, va, *adj.* and *m.* (gram.) substantive, noun.

sustentación, *f.* sustentation, support.

sustentar, *va.* to sustain; to support, to nourish.

sustento, *m.* food, sustenance, support.

sustitución, *f.* substitution.

sustituir, *va.* (SUSTITUYÓ, SUSTITUYENDO) to substitute.

sustituto, ta, *adj.* and *n.* substitute.

susto, *m.* fright, sudden terror; **llevarse un —,** to get a scare.

sustraendo, *m.* subtrahend.

sustraer, *va.* (SUSTRAIGO, SUSTRAJE), to subtract; **—se,** to retire, to withdraw.

susurrar, *vn.* to whisper, to divulge a secret; to murmur (of streams); to rustle.

susurro, *m.* whisper, murmur.

sutil, *adj.* subtle.

sutileza, *f.* subtlety, cunning; fineness, finesse; delicacy; perspicacity; slimness.

sutilizar, *va.* to subtilize; to polish; to discuss profoundly.

sutura, *f.* seam; (med.) suture.

suyo, ya, *adj.* his, hers, theirs, one's, his, her, its own, one's own or their own; **de —yo,** in itself, spontaneously; **los —s,** *m. pl.* their own, near friends, relations, acquaintances, servants.

svástica, *f.* swastika.

T

t. tarde, afternoon.

taba, *f.* jackstone.

tabacal, *m.* tobacco field.

tabaco, *m.* tobacco; **— en polvo,** snuff.

tábano, *m.* horsefly.

tabaquera, *f.* snuffbox.

tabaquería, *f.* cigar store; cigar factory.

tabaquero, *m.* tobacconist.

tabardillo, *m.* burning fever; **— pindado,** spotted fever.

tabasco, *m.* tabasco sauce.

taberna, *f.* tavern, saloon.

tabernáculo, *m.* tabernacle.

tabernero, *m.* tavern keeper, bartender.

tabes, *f.* (med.) consumption.

tabicar, *va.* to wall up.

tabique, *m.* thin wall; partition wall.

tabla, *f.* board; table; butcher's block; index of a book; bed of earth in a garden; **—s,** *pl.* tables containing the Decalogue; backgammon board; **— de materias,** table of contents; **— sinóptica,** synoptic table; **poner en —,** to tabulate.

tablado, *m.* scaffold, stage; frame of a bedstead; (naut.) platform.

tablajero, *m.* maker of scaffoldings.

tablazo, *m.* blow with a board; arm of the sea or of a river.

tablazón, *f.* boarding, planking decks and sheathing of a ship.

tablero, *m.* planed board; chessboard; checkerboard; stock of a crossbow; tailor's cutting board; blackboard; **— de dibujar,** drafting board.

tableta, *f.* tablet; cracknel.

tablilla, *f.* tablet, slab; bulletin board; **— de mesón,** sign of an inn.

tabuco, *m.* hut, small room.

taburete, *m.* chair without arms, stool.

tacañería, *f.* malicious cunning; niggardliness.

tacaño, ña, *adj.* artful, knavish; miserly, stingy; sordid.

tácito, ta, *adj.* tacit, silent; implied.

taciturno, na, *adj.* taciturn, silent; melancholy.

taco, *m.* stopper, stopple; wad; rammer; billiard cue; (Mex.) type of sandwich.

tacón, *m.* heel; **— de goma** or **de caucho,** rubber heel.

taconear, *vn.* to walk on one's heels.

taconeo, *m.* clatter of the heels in dancing.

táctico, ca, *adj.* tactical.

táctil, *adj.* tactile.

tacto, *m.* touch, feeling; tact.

tacha, *f.* fault, defect; small nail; stain, blemish.

tachar, *va.* to find fault with; to reprehend; to blot, to efface.

tachonar, *va.* to ornament with trimming; to stud with gilt-headed nails.

tachuela, *f.* tack, nail.

tafanario, *m.* (coll.) breech, seat, buttocks.

tafetán, *m.* taffeta; **— inglés,** court plaster; adhesive plaster; **—tanes,** *pl.* flags, colors.

tafilete, *m.* morocco leather.

tagornina, *f.* cheap cigar, stogy.

taha, *f.* region, district.

tahalí, *m.* shoulder belt.

tahona, *f.* horse mill; crushing mill; bakery.

tahonero, *m.* miller (of a horse mill); owner of a bakery.

tahur, *m.* gambler, gamester.

tahurería, *f.* gambling house; fraudulent gambling.

taimado, da, *adj.* sly, cunning, crafty.

taja, *f.* cut, incision; dissection; tally.

tajada, *f.* slice; (coll.) hoarseness.

tajadera, *f.* chopping knife.

tajador, ra, *n.* chopper, cutter; chopping block; trencher.

tajadura, *f.* cut, notch; section.

tajalápices, *m.* pencil sharpener.

tajaplumas, *m.* penknife.

tajar, *va.* to cut, to chop; to hew; to cut a quill.

tajo, *m.* cut, incision; cutting of a quill with a penknife; chopping block.

tajuela, *f.* low stool with three legs.

tal, *adj.* such; **con — que,** provided that; **no hay —,** no such thing; **¿qué —?** how goes it? how are you getting along? **— vez,** perhaps.

tala, *f.* felling of trees.

talabarte, *m.* sword belt.

talabartería, *f.* saddlery.

talador, ra, *n.* destroyer; drilling or boring machine.

taladradora, *f.* drilling machine; **— de fuerza,** power drill.

taladrar, *va.* to bore, to pierce, to punch.

taladro, *m.* borer, gimblet, auger, drill.

tálamo, *m.* bridal chamber; bridal bed.

talanquera, *f.* parapet, breastwork.

talante, *m.* manner of performance; appearance, aspect; pleasure; mien, countenance; humor; **de mal —,** unwillingly; ill disposed; **de buen —,** willingly, well disposed.

talar, *va.* to fell trees; to desolate, to make havoc; **—,** *adj.* trailing, down to the heels (of clothes); **—es,** *m. pl.* wings on the heels of Mercury.

talco, *m.* talc.

talega, *f.* bag; bagful.

talego, *m.* bag, sack; (coll.) clumsy, awkward fellow; **— de noche,** sleeping bag.

taleguilla, *f.* small bag.

talento, *m.* talent.

talión, *m.* retaliation, requital, talion.

talismán, *m.* talisman.

Talmud, *m.* Talmud, civil and canonical law book of the Jews.

talo, *m.* thallus.

talofitas, *f. pl.* (bot.) Thallophyte; Thallophyta.

talón, *m.* heel; heel of a shoe; baggage check; receipt; (Sp. Am.) duplicate check, coupon.

talonario, libro talonario, *m.* stub book; checkbook.

talonear, *vn.* to walk fast.

talla, *f.* raised work; sculpture; stature, size; measure of any thing; hand, draw, turn (in games); **de —,** of carved wood (frame); **media —,** half relief (in sculpture).

tallado, da, *adj.* cut, carved, engraved.

tallador, *m.* engraver.

tallar, *va.* to cut, to chop; to carve in wood; to engrave; **—,** *m.* forest of wood fit for cutting.

tallarín, *m.* noodle (for soup); **sopa de tallarines,** noodle soup.

talle, *m.* shape, size, proportion; waist.

taller, *m.* workshop, laboratory; **— de reparaciones,** repair shop.

tallista, *m.* woodcarver, engraver.

tallo, *m.* shoot, sprout, stem.

talludo, da, *adj.* thick-stalked.

tamal, *m.* tamale.

tamañito, ta, *adj.* very small.

tamaño, *m.* size, shape, bulk; **—, ña,** *adj.* showing the size, shape or bulk of anything.

tamarindo, *m.* tamarind tree and its fruit.

tamarisco or **tamariz,** *m.* tamarisk shrub.

tambalear, *vn.* and *vr.* to stagger, to waver.

tambaleo, *m.* staggering, reeling.

también, *adv.* also, too, likewise; as well.

tambor, *m.* drum; drummer; iron cylinder; small inclosure as a screen to the gates of of a fortress; **— mayor,** (mil.) drum major.

tambora, *f.* bass drum.

tamboril, *m.* tabor, timbrel.

tamborilear, *vn.* to tabor; (print.) to plane or level types.

tamborilero or **tamboritero,** *m.* tabor player or drummer.

tamborilete, *m.* planer (in printing).

Támesis, *m.* Thames.

tamiz, *m.* fine sieve.

tamo, *m.* fuzz or fluff from cloth; house dust; dust of grain.

tampoco, *adv.* neither, not either (used to enforce a foregoing negative).

tamujo, *m.* (bot.) boxthorn, buckthorn.

tan. tangente, tan. tangent.

tan, *m.* sound of the tabor; **—,** *adv.* so, so much, as well, as much.

tanda, *f.* turn; rotation; task; gang, number of persons employed in a work; each division of a performance, shift.

tangente, *f.* (math.) tangent.

tangerina, *f.* tangerine.

tangible, *adj.* tangible.

tango, *m.* tango, dance of Spanish-American origin.

tánico, ca, *adj.* tannic.

tanque, *m.* tank; reservoir, pool; dipper; bee glue.

tantear, *va.* to measure, to proportion; to mark the game with counters; to consider; to examine; **—se,** to redeem a barony or lordship.

tanteo, *m.* computation, calculation; playing counters; valuation, score.

tanto, *m.* certain sum or quantity; copy of a writing; —, **ta,** *adj.* so much, as much; very great; —, *adv.* so, in such a manner; a long time; **mientras** —, meanwhile; **por lo** —, therefore; —**s,** *pl.* score, points.

tanza, *f.* fishing line.

tañedor, ra, *n.* player on a musical instrument.

tañer, *va.* (TAÑÓ, TAÑENDO) to play a musical instrument.

tañido, *m.* tune; sound, clink.

tapa, *f.* lid, cover; — **de los sesos,** top of the skull.

tapacubo, *m.* hub cap or cover.

tapadera, *f.* lid of a pot, cover.

tapadero, *m.* large stopper.

tapadillo, *m.* concealment of a woman's face with a veil; stop on a pipe organ; **de** —, secretly, discreetly.

tapadura, *f.* act of covering, filling.

tapafunda, *f.* holster cover.

tapar, *va.* to stop up, to cover, to close; to conceal, to hide.

tapete, *m.* small carpet.

tapia, *f.* mud wall, wall fence.

tapial, *m.* mold for making mud walls.

tapiar, *va.* to wall up with a mud wall; to stop up a passage.

tapicería, *f.* tapestry, upholstery.

tapicero, *m.* tapestry maker, upholsterer.

tapioca, *f.* tapioca.

tapir, *m.* (zool.) tapir.

tapiz, *m.* tapestry.

tapizar, *va.* to hang with tapestry.

tapón, *m.* cork, plug, bung; (med.) tampon.

tapujarse, *vr.* to muffle oneself up.

taqueómetro or **taquímetro,** *m.* tachometer.

taquigrafía, *f.* shorthand writing, stenography.

taquígrafo, fa, *n.* shorthand writer, stenographer.

taquilla, *f.* box office, ticket office, ticket window; booking office.

taquillero, *m.* ticket seller.

tara, *f.* tare, deduction of weight.

taracea, *f.* checkerwork, inlaid work.

taracear, *va.* to make inlaid work.

tarambana, *m.* and *f.* giddy-headed person.

tarantela, *f.* tarantella, Neapolitan peasant dance; its tune.

tarántula, *f.* tarantula.

tararear, *va.* to hum a tune.

tarasca, *f.* figure of a serpent borne in processions, indicating the triumph of Christ over the devil; (coll.) ugly, ill-natured woman.

tarascada, *f.* bite; (coll.) pert, harsh answer.

tarazón, *m.* large slice, especially of fish.

tardanza, *f.* slowness, delay.

tardar, *vn.* and *vr.* to delay, to put off, to tarry; **a más** —, at the latest.

tarde, *f.* afternoon; evening; —, *adv.* late.

tardío, día, *adj.* late; slow, tardy.

tardo, da, *adj.* sluggish, tardy.

tarea, *f.* task.

tarifa, *f.* tariff, charge, rate, fare; price list.

tarima, *f.* platform; low bench; stand.

tarjeta, *f.* visiting card, card; — **postal,** post card.

tarlatana, *f.* tarlatan (cloth).

tarpón, *m.* tarpon.

tarro, *m.* glazed earthen pan; jar; pot.

tarso, *m.* tarsus.

tarta, *f.* tart; pan for baking tarts.

tartalear, *vn.* to reel, to stagger; to be perplexed.

tartamudear, *vn.* to stutter, to stammer.

tartamudo, da, *n.* and *adj.* stammerer, stammering.

tartana, *f.* tartan; two-wheeled carriage.

Tártaro, *m.* Tartar; Tartarus, hell.

tártaro, *m.* argol, cream of tartar; tartar of teeth.

tartera, *f.* baking pan (for tarts).

tarugo, *m.* wooden peg or pin.

tasa, *f.* rate, assize; measure, rule; valuation.

tasación, *f.* valuation, appraisement.

tasado, da, *adj.* limited, scanty; **con el dinero** —**do,** with a limited amount of money.

tasador, *m.* appraiser.

tasajo, *m.* jerked beef.

tasar, *va.* to appraise, to value.

tascar, *va.* to break flax or hemp; to nibble grass; to champ the bit.

tasco, *m.* refuse of flax or hemp; toppings of hemp.

tatarabuela, *f.* great-great-grandmother.

tatarabuelo, *m.* great-great-grandfather.

tataranieta, *f.* great-great-granddaughter.

tataranieto, *m.* great-great-grandson.

¡tate! *interj.* take care! beware! look out!

tatuaje, *m.* tattoo, tattooing.

taumaturgo, *m.* miracle worker.

Tauro, *m.* Taurus (sign of the zodiac).

taxi, *m.* taxicab.

taxidermista, *m.* and *f.* taxidermist.

taxímetro, *m.* taximeter; taxicab.

taza, *f.* cup; cupful; bowl; fountain basin.

tazmía, *f.* share of tithes.

te, *pron.* objective and dative cases of **tú** (thou).

té, *m.* tea.

tea, *f.* candlewood; torch.

teatral, *adj.* theatrical.

teatro, *m.* theater, playhouse, auditorium.

tecla, *f.* key of an organ or pianoforte; key of a typewriter.

teclado, *m.* keyboard.

teclear, *vn.* to finger a keyboard; to typewrite; —, *va.* (coll.) to resort to (an expedient).

tecleo, *m.* drumming on a keyboard; typing.

tecnicalidad, *f.* technicality.

tecnicismo, *m.* technicism, technical term.

técnico, ca, *adj.* technical; —, *f.* technique; —, *m.* technician.

tecnicolor, *m.* technicolor.

tecnológico, ca, *adj.* technological.

techo, *m.* roof, ceiling; shed; (coll.) dwelling house; **bajo —,** indoors.

techumbre, *f.* upper roof, ceiling.

Tedéum, *m.* Te Deum (song of thanksgiving).

tediar, *va.* to hate, detest; to be tired of.

tedio, *m.* disgust, dislike, abhorrence; boredom.

teja, *f.* roof tile.

tejado, *m.* roof covered with tiles.

tejamanil, *m.* shingle.

tejano, na, *n.* and *adj.* Texan, from Texas.

tejar, *m.* tileworks; **—,** *va.* to tile.

Tejas, *m.* Texas.

tejedor, ra, *n.* weaver.

tejedura, *f.* texture, weaving; woven stuff.

tejer, *va.* to weave, to knit.

tejera or **tejería,** *f.* tilekiln.

tejero, *m.* tilemaker.

tejido, *m.* texture, web; textile, fabric; (anat.) tissue.

tejo, *m.* quoit; yew tree.

tejón, *m.* badger.

tela, *f.* cloth; woven material; **— de hilo,** linen.

telar, *m.* loom.

telaraña, *f.* cobweb.

telef. teléfono, tel. telephone.

telefonear, *va.* and *vn.* to telephone.

telefonista, *m.* and *f.* telephone operator.

teléfono, *m.* telephone; **— automático,** dial telephone.

telefoto, *f.* wire photo.

teleg.: telegrama, tel. telegram; **telégrafo,** tel. telegraph.

telegrafiar, *va.* and *vn.* to telegraph.

telegráfico, ca, *adj.* telegraphic.

telégrafo, *m.* telegraph.

telegrama, *m.* telegram.

telémetro, *m.* range finder.

teleológico, ca, *adj.* teleological.

telepatía, *f.* telepathy.

telescopio, *m.* telescope.

teletipo, *m.* teletype.

telina, tellina, *f.* clam.

telón, *m.* backdrop in a theater; **— de boca,** theater curtain.

tema, *m.* theme; subject; **—,** *f.* obstinacy; contention; mania.

temático, ca, *adj.* thematic.

temblar, *vn.* (IE) to tremble, to quiver.

tembleque, *m.* jeweled hair ornament mounted on a wire; person or thing that trembles excessively.

temblón, ona, *adj.* tremulous.

temblor, *m.* trembling, tremor; **— de tierra,** earthquake.

tembloroso, sa, *adj.* trembling, shaky, tremulous.

temer, *va.* and *vn.* to fear, to doubt.

temerario, ria, *adj.* rash, temerarious; **—,** *n.* daredevil.

temeridad, *f.* temerity, imprudence; folly.

temeroso, sa, *adj.* timid, timorous.

temible, *adj.* dreadful, terrible; inspiring awe or fear.

temor, *m.* dread, fear.

temp. temperatura, t. temperature.

témpano, *m.* tympanum; block; iceberg.

temperamento, *m.* temperament, nature, temper.

temperar, *va.* to temper; **—,** *vn.* to go away for the summer.

temperatura, *f.* temperature.

tempestad, *f.* tempest, storm; violent commotion.

tempestivo, va, *adj.* seasonable, opportune.

tempestuoso, sa, *adj.* tempestuous, stormy.

templadamente, *adv.* temperately, moderately.

templado, da, *adj.* temperate, tempered, lukewarm.

templador, ra, *n.* tuner, temperer; **—,** *m.* tuning key.

templanza, *f.* temperance, moderation; temperature.

templar, *va.* to temper, to moderate, to cool; to tune; **—se,** to be moderate.

templario, *m.* templar.

temple, *m.* temperature; temper, temperament; harmonious accordance of musical instruments; **al —,** painted in distemper.

templo, *m.* temple, church.

Témpora, *f.* Ember days.

temporada, *f.* certain space of time, epoch, period, season.

temporal, *adj.* temporary, temporal; **—,** *m.* season; tempest, storm.

temporalidad, *f.* temporality.

tempóraneo, *adj.* deciduous.

temprano, na, *adj.* early, anticipated; **—no,** *adv.* very early, prematurely.

tenacidad, *f.* tenacity; obstinacy.

tenacillas, *f. pl.* small tongs, pinchers, pincers, pliers.

tenada, *f.* sheepfold, shed for cattle.

tenaz, *adj.* tenacious; stubborn.

tenaza, *f.* tongs, pincers.

tenazmente, *adv.* tenaciously; obstinately.

tenca, *f.* tench (fish).

tendedera, *f.* clothesline.

tendedor, ra, *n.* one who spreads clothes to dry.

tendencia, *f.* tendency; trend, leaning.

tender, *va.* (IE) to stretch out, to spread, to expand, to extend; to have a tendency; **—se,** to stretch oneself at full length.

ténder, *m.* (rail.) tender.

tendero, ra, *n.* haberdasher, shopkeeper.

tendido, *m.* row of seats (for the spectators at a bullfight); amount of clothes spread out to dry.

tendinoso, sa, *adj.* sinewy, gristly.

tendón, *m.* tendon, sinew; **— de Aquiles,** Achilles' tendon.

tenebrario, *m.* large candlestick with a triangular branch, holding 15 candles (in Roman Catholic churches).

tenebroso, sa, *adj.* dark, obscure; gloomy.

tenedor, *m.* holder, keeper, tenant; fork; payee (of bill of exchange); **— de libros,** bookkeeper, accountant.

tenedora, compañía —, *f.* holding company.

teneduría, *f.* position and office of the bookkeeper; **— de libros,** bookkeeping.

tenencia, *f.* possession; lieutenancy.

tener, *va.* (TENGO, TUVE) to take, to hold, to possess; to have; **— cuidado,** to be careful; **— derecho a,** to have the right to; **— empeño,** to be eager; **— en cuenta,** to take into consideration; **— inconveniente,** to have an objection; **— a menos,** to scorn; **—se,** to take care not to fall; to stop; to halt; to resist; to adhere.

tenería, *f.* tanyard, tannery.

teniente, *m.* lieutenant.

tenis, *m.* tennis.

tenista, *m.* and *f.* tennis player.

tenor, *m.* kind; condition, nature; literal meaning of a sentence or an article; (mus.) tenor.

tensión, *f.* tension, strain; **— arterial,** blood pressure.

tensor, *m.* turnbuckle.

tentación, *f.* temptation.

tentáculo, *m.* tentacle.

tentador, ra, *adj.* attractive, tempting; **—,** *n.* tempter.

tentar, *va.* (IE) to touch; to try; to grope; to tempt; to attempt.

tentativa, *f.* attempt, trial.

ten.ᵗᵉ **teniente,** Lt. or Lieut. Lieutenant.

tentempié, *m.* snack, bite.

tenue, *adj.* thin, tenuous, slender.

tenuidad, *f.* slenderness, weakness; trifle.

teñidura, *f.* dyeing.

teñir, *va.* (I) to tinge, to dye.

Teodora, Theodora.

Teodoro, Theodore.

Teófilo, Theophilus.

teologal, *adj.* theological.

teología, *f.* theology, divinity.

teológico, ca, *adj.* theological.

teólogo, *m.* theologian, divine.

teorema, *m.* theorem.

teoría, or teórica, *f.* theory.

teórico, ca, *adj.* theoretical.

teorista, *m.* doctrinaire.

teorizar, *va.* to theorize.

teosofía, *f.* theosophy.

tequila, *m.* tequila (kind of Mexican liquor).

terapéutico, ca, *adj* therapeutic, remedial, curative; **—,** *f.* therapeutics.

tercamente, *adv.* stubbornly.

tercenista, *m.* keeper of a wholesale tobacco warehouse.

tercería, *f.* mediation, arbitration; depositary.

tercero, ra, *adj.* third; **—,** *m.* third person; pimp; mediator.

tercerola, *f.* short carbine.

terceto, *m.* terza rima, tercet; (mus.) trio.

tercia, *f.* third; canonical hour falling at three o'clock; series of three cards.

terciado, da, *adj.* slanting, crosswise; **—,** *m.* cutlass.

terciana, *f.* tertian fever.

tercianario, ria, *n.* sufferer from tertian fever.

terciar, *va.* to put on sideways; to divide into three parts; to plow the third time; **—,** *vn.* to mediate.

tercio, cia, *adj.* third; **—,** *m.* third part; half a load; Spanish regiment (in the 16th century); **hacer buen —cio,** to do good to.

terciopelado, da, *adj.* velvety; **—,** *m.* velvetlike goods.

terciopelero, *m.* velvet weaver.

terciopelo, *m.* velvet.

terco, ca, *adj.* pertinacious, obstinate; stubborn; very hard.

Teresa, Theresa.

tergiversación, *f.* misrepresentation; evasion; tergiversation.

tergiversar, *va.* to misrepresent; to tergiversate.

terliz, *m.* tick, ticking (for beds, etc.).

termal, *adj.* thermal.

termas, *f. pl.* hot baths, hot springs.

terminación, *f.* termination; conclusion; last syllable of a word.

terminal, *adj.* terminal, final; **—,** *m.* terminal.

terminante, *adj.* decisive; absolute, strict; **orden —,** strict order.

terminar, *va.* to terminate, to end, to finish.

terminativo, va, *adj.* terminative.

terminantemente, *adv.* decidedly, absolutely.

término, *m.* term; end; boundary; limit.

terminología, *f.* terminology.

termita, *f.* termite; (chem.) thermite.

termodinámica, *f.* thermodynamics.

termómetro, *m.* thermometer.

termos, *m.* thermos bottle, vacuum bottle.

termoscopio, *m.* thermoscope.

termóstato, *m.* thermostat.

terna, *f.* ternary number.

ternero, ra, *n.* calf; veal; heifer.

terneza, *f.* softness, delicacy, tenderness; endearment.

ternilla, *f.* gristle, cartilage.

ternilloso, sa, *adj.* gristly, cartilaginous.

terno, *m.* ternary number; ornaments for celebrating high mass; three-piece suit.

ternura, *f.* tenderness.

terquedad, *f.* stubbornness, obstinacy.

terracota, *f.* terra cotta.

terrado, *m.* terrace.

terraja, *f.* screw plate.

Terranova, *f.* Newfoundland.

terraplén, *m.* horizontal surface of a rampart; terrace, platform.

terraplenar, *va.* to make a platform or terrace.

terraza, *f.* terrace, veranda, verandah; roof

garden; sidewalk tables (of a café); glazed jar with two handles.

terremoto, *m.* earthquake.

terrenal, *adj.* terrestrial, earthly.

terreno, na, *adj.* earthly, terrestrial; —, *m.* land, ground, field.

terrestre, *adj.* terrestrial, earthly.

terrible, *adj.* terrible, dreadful; ferocious.

territorial, *adj.* territorial.

territorio, *m.* territory.

terrón, *m.* clod of earth, mound; lump; —ones, *pl.* landed property.

terror, *m.* terror, dread, fear.

terrorismo, *m.* terrorism.

terrorista, *m.* and *f.* terrorist; scaremonger.

terruño, *m.* native land.

tersar, *va.* to smooth.

terso, sa, *adj.* smooth, glossy; terse.

tersura, *f.* smoothness, purity.

tertulia, *f.* informal gathering for conversation; conversation; party.

tesauro, *m.* thesaurus.

tesis, *f.* thesis.

tesón, *m.* tenacity, firmness.

tesorería, *f.* treasury.

tesorero, ra, *n.* treasurer.

tesoro, *m.* treasure; exchequer.

testa, *f.* head; top of head; front, face; (coll.) brains, cleverness.

testado, da, *adj.* leaving a will.

testador, *m.* testator.

testadora, *f.* testatrix.

testadura, *f.* erasure.

testamentaría, *f.* testamentary execution.

testamentario, *m.* executor of a will; —, **ria,** *adj.* testamentary.

testamento, *m.* will, testament.

testar, *va.* and *vn.* to make one's will; to bequeath; to scratch out.

testarudo, da, *adj.* obstinate, wrongheaded.

testera, *f.* front of anything; back seat of a carriage.

testerada, *f.* blow with the head; stubbornness.

testículo, *m.* testicle.

testificación, *f.* attestation.

testificar, *va.* to attest, to witness.

testificativo, va, *adj.* declaratory, testimonial.

testigo, *m.* witness, deponent.

testimonial, *adj.* testimonial; —es, *f. pl.* testimonials.

testimoniar, *va.* to attest, to bear witness.

testimonio, *m.* testimony; instrument legalized by a notary.

test.ᵐᵗᵒ **testamento,** testament, will.

test.º **testigo,** witness.

testuz, *m.* back of the head, nape (of animals).

tesura, *f.* stiffness, firmness; affected gravity.

teta, *f.* dug, teat.

tétano, *m.* (med.) tetanus, lockjaw.

tetar, *va.* to suckle, to give suck.

tetera, *f.* teapot, teakettle.

tetilla, *f.* small teat.

tetramotor, *m.* four-engined airplane.

tetrarca, *m.* tetrarch.

tétrico, ca, *adj.* gloomy, sullen, surly; dark.

tetróxido, *m.* (chem.) tetroxide.

tetuda, *adj.* having large teats or nipples; —, *f.* oblong olive.

textil, *adj.* and *m.* textile.

texto, *m.* text; a certain size of type.

textual, *adj.* textual.

tez, *f.* shining surface; complexion of the face; hue.

ti, *pron.* objective or dative case of **tú.**

tía, *f.* aunt; (coll.) good old woman.

tiara, *f.* tiara.

Tiberio, Tiberius.

tibia, *f.* shinbone.

tibieza, *f.* lukewarmness.

tibio, bia, *adj.* lukewarm; remiss.

tiburón, *m.* shark.

tictac, *m.* ticktock.

tiempo, *m.* time, term; season, weather; tempo; occasion; — **atrás,** some time ago; — **desocupado,** spare time; **a** —, in time; **a** —**s,** at times; **a su** — **debido,** in due time; **a un** —, at once, at the same time; **de** — **a** —, from time to time; **hacer buen** —, to be good weather; **más** —, longer; **tomarse** —, to take time, to defer; **en un** —, formerly.

tienda, *f.* tent; (naut.) awning; tilt; shop; — **oxígena,** (med.) oxygen tent.

tienta, *f.* probe (for surgeons); cleverness, sagacity; **andar a** —**s,** to grope in the dark.

tiento, *m.* touch; circumspection; **a** —, gropingly.

tierno, na, *adj.* tender; young; delicate, soft.

tierra, *f.* earth; land, ground; native country; — **de sombra,** umber.

tieso, sa, *adj.* stiff, hard, firm; taut; robust; valiant; stubborn.

tiesto, *m.* potsherd; flowerpot.

tifoideo, dea, *adj.* typhoid; —, *f.* typhoid fever.

tifus, *m.* (med.) typhus.

tigre, *m.* tiger.

tijeras, *f. pl.* scissors.

tijeretas, *f. pl.* tendrils; small scissors.

tijeretear, *va.* to cut with scissors; to dispose of other people's affairs at one's pleasure.

tila, *f.* lime tree, linden tree, flower of same; linden tea.

tildar, *va.* to blot; to brand, to stigmatize; to accuse; to put a tilde over, as letter **ñ.**

tilde, *f.* tilde, diacritical sign of the letter **ñ;** iota, tittle; very small thing.

tilo, *m.* linden tree.

tilla, *f.* (naut.) partial deck.

timbal, *m.* kettledrum.

timbalero, *m.* kettledrummer.

timbrazo, *m.* ringing of a doorbell.

timbre, *m.* stamp; call bell; crest of a coat of arms; timbre.

timidez, *f.* timidity.
tímido, da, *adj.* timid, shy.
timo, *m.* (anat.) thymus.
timón, *m.* helm, rudder; **— de dirección,** rudder.
timonera, *f.* (naut.) wheelhouse, pilothouse.
timonero, *m.* helmsman.
timorato, ta, *adj.* timorous; God-fearing.
Timoteo, Timothy.
timpanitis, *f.* (med.) tympanitis.
tímpano, *m.* kettledrum; (anat.) tympanum; tympan of a printing press.
tina, *f.* dyer's copper; large earthen jar; tub.
tinaja, *f.* large earthen jar for water.
tinajero, *m.* maker of water jars.
tinajón, *m.* large tub.
tinglado, *m.* shed, cart house.
tiniebla, *f.* darkness, obscurity; **—s,** *pl.* utter darkness.
tino, *m.* skill in discovering things by feeling; judgment, prudence.
tinta, *f.* tint, hue; ink; **— china,** India ink; **— de imprenta,** printer's ink; **— simpática,** invisible ink; **saber algo de buena —,** to know something on good authority.
tinte, *m.* tint, dye.
tintero, *m.* inkwell, inkstand.
tintinear, *vn.* to tinkle.
tintineo, *m.* tinkling of a bell.
tinto, ta, *adj.* deep-colored (of wine).
tintorería, *f.* dyer's shop.
tintorero, *m.* dyer.
tintura, *f.* tincture.
tinturar, *va.* to tinge, to dye, to tincture.
tiña, *f.* (med.) ringworm of the scalp; beehive spider; (coll.) poverty, want.
tiñoso, sa, *adj.* scabby, scurvy; niggardly.
tío, *m.* uncle; good old man.
tiovivo, *m.* merry-go-round.
típico, ca, *adj.* characteristic; typical.
tiple, *m.* (mus.) treble; one who sings treble; small guitar; **—,** *f.* soprano voice or singer.
tipo, *m.* type, model, pattern; rate, standard; **— cícero,** pica type; **— de cambio,** rate of exchange; **— de cartel,** large type; **— de descuento,** rate of discount; **— delgado,** light-faced type; **— de interés,** rate of interest; **— negro,** bold-faced type; **— usual,** body type.
tipografía, *f.* typography; typesetting.
tipográfico, ca, *adj.* typographical.
tipógrafo, *m.* printer.
típula, *f.* daddy longlegs.
tira, *f.* long and narrow strip; sliver; **—s,** *pl.* clerks' fees formerly paid in cases of appeal.
tirabraguero, *m.* truss.
tirabuzón, *m.* corkscrew; ringlet.
tirada, *f.* cast, throw; distance from one place to another; stroke (golf); edition, issue; presswork; **— aparte,** reprint.
tirador, ra, *n.* thrower; drawer; **—,** *m.* (print.) pressman; marksman; **— de oro,** maker of gold wire.

tiranía, *f.* tyranny.
tiránico, ca, *adj.* tyrannical, domineering.
tiranizar, *va.* to tyrannize.
tirano, na, *adj.* tyrannical; **—,** *n.* tyrant.
tirante, *m.* joist which runs across a beam; trace; gear; brace of a drum; **—s,** *pl.* suspenders; **—,** *adj.* taut, extended, drawn.
tirantez, *f.* tenseness, tightness, strain.
tirapié, *m.* stirrups, strap.
tirar, *va.* to throw, to toss, to cast; to pull; to draw; to fire off; to persuade; to draw metal into slender threads; **—,** *vn.* to tend, to incline; **— al blanco,** to shoot at a target.
tiritaña, *f.* thin silk cloth; thing of little value.
tiritar, *vn.* to shiver.
tiritona, *f.* (coll.) affected shiver.
tiro, *m.* cast, throw, shot; prank; imposition; set of coach horses; trace (of harness); **de — rápido,** rapid fire; **errar el —,** to miss (in shooting); **— al blanco,** target practice; **—s,** *pl.* sword belts.
tirocinio, *m.* apprenticeship.
tiroideo, dea, *adj.* (anat.) thyroid.
tiroides, *adj.* and *f.* (anat.) thyroid (gland).
tirón, *m.* pull, haul, tug; **de un —,** all at once, at one stroke.
tirona, *f.* seine, net.
tirotear, *vn.* to shoot at random.
tiroteo, *m.* random shooting, snapshooting; skirmish.
tirria, *f.* antipathy.
tirso, *m.* thyrsus, wand covered with ivy leaves, used in sacrifices to Bacchus.
tisana, *f.* ptisan (a drink).
tísico, ca, *adj.* tubercular, consumptive.
tisis, *f.* phthisis, consumption, tuberculosis.
tisú, *m.* tissue.
tít. or **tít.º título,** title.
titán, *m.* titan.
titánico, ca, *adj.* titanic, colossal.
títere, *m.* puppet; ridiculous little fellow.
titímalo, *m.* (bot.) spurge.
titiritero, *m.* puppet player.
Tito, Titus.
tito, *m.* chick-pea.
titubear, *vn.* to stammer; to vacillate, to hesitate; to totter, to waver.
titubeo, *m.* vacillation, hesitation, wavering.
titular, *va.* to title; **—,** *vn.* to obtain a title; **—,** *adj.* and *n.* titular.
título, *m.* title; name; headline; **a —,** on pretense, under pretext.
tiza, *f.* chalk.
tiznar, *va.* to smut; to tarnish.
tizne, *m.* soot, smut of coal.
tiznón, *m.* spot, stain.
tizo, *m.* half-burnt charcoal.
tizón, *m.* half-burnt wood.
t.º or **tom. tomo,** vol. volume.
toalla, *f.* towel; **— sin fin,** roller towel.
toalleta, *f.* small towel.
Tobías, Tobias.
tobillera, *f.* anklet.

tobillo, *m.* ankle.

toca, *f.* hood; a thin cloth for making hoods.

tocado, *m.* headdress, headgear.

tocador, *m.* one who touches; dressing table, toilet table, boudoir; (mus.) player.

tocante, *adj.* touching; **— a,** concerning, relating to.

tocar, *va.* to touch; to attain with the hand; (mus.) to play; to ring a bell, to try metals on a touchstone; **—,** *vn.* to belong; to concern; to be a duty or obligation; to behoove, to fall to one's share; **—se,** (coll.) to put on one's hat, to cover the head.

tocayo, ya, *n.* namesake.

tocinero, *m.* seller of pork and bacon.

tocino, *m.* bacon, salt pork.

tocón, *m.* stump (of a tree, arm, leg, etc.)

todavía, *adv.* nevertheless; yet, still.

todo, da, *adj.* all, every; entire; **todo el año,** all year around; **—s los días,** every day; **todo el mundo,** everybody; **de —s modos,** anyhow, anyway; **—,** *m.* whole, entirety; **ante —do,** first of all; **con —do,** notwithstanding; **sobre —do,** above all, especially.

todopoderoso, *adj.* almighty.

toesa, *f.* toise, fathom (French measure).

toga, *f.* toga; superior judgeship.

togado, da, *adj.* gowned.

tolano, *m.* tumor in horses' gums; **—s,** *pl.* short hair on the neck.

toldillo, *m.* small awning; covered sedan chair.

toldo, *m.* awning; tarpaulin; (Sp. Am.) Indian hut; tent.

tolerable, *adj.* tolerable, supportable.

tolerancia, *f.* tolerance, indulgence.

tolerante, *adj.* tolerant.

tolerar, *vn.* to tolerate, to suffer, to bear.

tolueno, *m.* toluene.

tolva, *f.* mill hopper.

tolvanera, *f.* dust storm, dust cloud.

toma, *f.* anything taken; capture, seizure; water faucet.

tomadero, *m.* handle; tap; outlet.

tomaína, ptomaine.

tomar, *va.* to take, to seize, to grasp; to understand, to interpret, to perceive; **— a cuestas,** to take upon oneself; **— el pelo,** to tease; **— la revancha,** to turn the tables; **—se,** to get rusty, to rust (metals).

Tomás, Thomas, Tom.

tomate, *m.* tomato.

tomatera, *f.* tomato plant.

tomillar, *m.* bed of thyme.

tomillo, *m.* (bot.) thyme.

tomo, *m.* bulk; tome; volume.

ton. tonelada, tn. ton.

ton, *m.* tone; **sin — ni son,** without rhyme or reason.

tonada, *f.* tune, melody, air.

tonadilla, *f.* interlude of music; short tune.

tonar, *vn.* (poet.) to thunder.

tonel, *m.* cask, barrel.

tonelada, *f.* ton; collection of casks in a ship; (naut.) tonnage duty.

tonelaje, *f.* tonnage.

tonelería, *f.* cooperage, barrelmaking; cooper's workshop.

tonelero, *m.* cooper, barrelmaker.

tonelete, *m.* little barrel.

tónico, ca, *adj.* tonic, strengthening: **—,** *m.* tonic; **—,** *f.* (mus.) tonic.

tono, *m.* tone.

tonsila, *f.* tonsil.

tonsilitis, *f.* tonsilitis.

tonsura, *f.* tonsure; haircutting; shearing.

tonsurar, *va.* to give the tonsure to; to cut the hair of; to shear, to fleece.

tontada, *f.* nonsense.

tontear, *vn.* to talk nonsense, to act foolishly.

tontería, *f.* foolery, nonsense.

tontillo, *m.* farthingale, hoop skirt.

tonto, ta, *adj.* stupid, foolish; **—,** *n.* dupe, fool, dunce.

topacio, *m.* topaz.

topar, *va.* to run or strike against.

tope, *m.* butt, rub; scuffle; **—s,** *pl.* (rail.) buffers.

topera, *f.* molehole.

topetada, *f.* butt (by a horned animal).

topetar, *va.* and *vn.* to butt.

topetón, *m.* collision, encounter, blow.

tópico, ca, *adj.* topical; **—,** *m.* topic, subject.

topinera, *f.* molehill.

topo, *m.* mole; stumbler; (coll.) dunce.

topografía, *f.* topography.

topográfico, ca, *adj.* topographical.

topógrafo, *m.* topographer, surveyor.

toque, *m.* touch; bell ringing; crisis; (mil.) call.

torada, *f.* drove of bulls.

toral, *adj.* principal, main.

tórax, *m.* thorax.

torbellino, *m.* whirlwind; lively, boisterous, restless person.

torcaz, *f.* ring dove, wild pigeon.

torcecuello, *m.* (orn.) wryneck.

torcedor, ra, *adj.* twisting; **—,** *m.* twister (spindle); anything causing displeasure.

torcedura, *f.* twisting; wrench; light, weak wine.

torcer, *va.* (UE) to twist, to double, to curve, to distort; to refute an argument; **—se,** to go crooked or astray.

torcida, *f.* wick.

torcidillo, *m.* twisted silk.

torcido, da, *adj.* oblique, tortuous, twisted.

torcimiento, *m.* bending, deflection; circumlocution; twisting.

tórculo, *m.* rolling press for prints.

tordo, *m.* thrush; **— mimo,** catbird.

toreador, *m.* bullfighter.

torear, *vn.* to fight bulls.

toreo, *m.* bullfighting.

torero, *m.* bullfighter.

toril, *m.* place where bulls are shut up prior to a fight.

torillo, _m._ little or young bull.
tormenta, _f._ storm, tempest, thunder-shower, thunderstorm.
tormento, _m._ torment, pain, anguish; torture; tedious affliction.
tornaboda, _f._ day after a wedding.
tornado, _m._ tornado.
tornaguía, _f._ debenture.
tornar, _va._ and _vn._ to return; to restore; to repeat.
tornasol, _m._ (bot.) sunflower; heliotrope.
tornasolado, _adj._ changing colors; watered (silk); iridescent.
torneador, _m._ turner.
tornear, _va._ and _vn._ to turn (on a lathe); to turn; to tilt at tournaments.
torneo, _m._ tournament.
tornera, _f._ doorkeeper of a nunnery.
tornero, _m._ turner.
tornillo, _m._ screw; vise; bolt; **— de presión** or **de retén,** setscrew.
torniquete, _m._ turnpike; (med.) tourniquet.
torno, _m._ wheel; lathe; winch, windlass; **en — de,** around.
toro, _m._ bull; **corrida de —s,** bullfight.
toronja, _f._ grapefruit.
toronjil, _m._ (bot.) balm.
torozón, _m._ gripes (among animals).
torpe, _adj._ dull, heavy; torpid; stupid; awkward; unchaste; obscene; infamous.
torpedero, _m._ torpedo boat.
torpedo, _m._ torpedo.
torpeza, _f._ heaviness, dullness; torpor; obscenity; stupidity.
torre, _f._ tower; turret; steeple of a church; **— de mando,** (naut.) conning tower.
torrecilla, _f._ turret.
torrefacción, _f._ roasting (of coffee, etc.).
torreja, _f._ (Sp. Am.) fritter.
torrejón, _m._ ill-shaped turret.
torrente, _m._ torrent.
torreón, _m._ fortified tower.
torrezno, _m._ rasher of bacon.
tórrido, da, _adj._ torrid, parched, hot.
torsión, _f._ twist, torsion.
torso, _m._ trunk, torso.
torta, _f._ tart, shortcake, cake.
tortada, _f._ meat pie.
tortera, _f._ pan for baking tarts.
tortícolis, _m._ stiff neck.
tortilla, _f._ tortilla, Mexican flat round corn-cake.
tórtola, _f._ turtledove; **— gemidora,** mourning dove.
tortuga, _f._ tortoise; turtle.
tortuoso, sa, _adj._ tortuous; crooked.
tortura, _f._ tortuosity; state of being twisted; rack, torture.
torvo, va, _adj._ stern, grim, severe, dour, fierce.
torzal, _m._ cord, twist.
tos, _f._ cough.
toscamente, _adv._ coarsely, grossly.
Toscana, _f._ Tuscany.
tosco, ca, _adj._ coarse, ill-bred, clumsy.

toser, _vn._ to cough.
tósigo, _m._ poison (from the yew tree); anguish, grief.
tostada, _f._ slice of toast; (Mex.) open-faced meat tart.
tostado, da, _adj._ parched; sunburned; light yellow, light brown; toasted.
tostador, ra, _n._ toaster (person); **—,** _m._ toasting fork, toaster.
tostar, _va._ to toast, to roast.
total, _m._ whole, totality; **—,** _adj._ total, entire.
totalidad, _f._ totality, whole.
totalitario, ria, _adj._ totalitarian.
totalizar, _va._ to add, to total.
tótem, _m._ totem.
toxemia, _f._ (med.) toxemia.
tóxico, ca, _adj._ toxic.
toxina, _f._ (med.) toxin.
tpo. tiempo, t. time.
tr. transitivo, tr. transitive.
traba, _f._ obstacle, impediment; trammel, fetter.
trabacuenta, _f._ error in accounts; dispute, controversy.
trabajador, ra, _n._ worker, laborer; painstaker; **—,** _adj._ hard-working, industrious.
trabajar, _va._ and _vn._ to work, to labor.
trabajo, _m._ work, labor, toil; workmanship; difficulty, trouble; **—s, forzados,** hard labor; **costar —,** to be difficult.
trabajosamente, _adv._ laboriously, with difficulty.
trabajoso, sa, _adj._ laborious; painful.
trabar, _va._ to join, to unite; to dispute, to quarrel; to take hold of; to fetter, to shackle; to set the teeth of a saw; **— amistad,** to make friends; **—se,** to become interlocked; to become confused or rattled.
trabazón, _f._ juncture, union.
trabilla, _f._ gaiter strap; small clasp; stitch dropped in knitting.
trabucar, _va._ to derange, to confound; **—se,** to become confused.
trabucazo, _m._ shot with a blunderbuss; sudden fright.
trabuco, _m._ catapult; blunderbuss.
Tracia, _f._ Thracia, Thrace.
tracoma, _f._ (med.) trachoma.
tractor, _m._ tractor; **— de orugas,** caterpillar tractor.
tradición, _f._ tradition.
tradicional, _adj._ traditional.
traducción, _f._ translation.
traducir, _va._ (TRADUZCO, TRADUJE) to translate.
traductor, ra, _n._ translator.
traer, _va._ (TRAIGO, TRAJE) to bring, to carry, to attract; to wear; to persuade; **—se,** to be dressed (well or poorly).
traficación, _f._ traffic, trade.
traficante, _m._ merchant, dealer.
traficar, _vn._ to traffic, to commerce, to do business, to deal (in).
tráfico, _m._ traffic, trade.

tragadero, *m.* esophagus, gullet; gulf, abyss;
tener buenos —s or **buenas tragaderas,**
to be very credulous.

tragador, ra, *n.* glutton, gobbler.

tragaldabas, *m.* (coll.) glutton.

tragaleguas, *m.* great walker.

tragaluz, *m.* skylight.

tragar, *va.* to swallow, to glut; to swallow up;
—se, to dissemble, to stand (an insult or
an affront).

tragedia, *f.* tragedy.

trágico, ca, *adj.* tragic.

trago, *m.* draft of liquor; adversity, misfortune; **a —s,** by degrees.

tragón, ona, *adj.* gluttonous.

traición, *f.* treason.

traicionar, *va.* to betray.

traidor, ra, *n.* traitor; **—,** *adj.* treacherous.

traílla, *f.* leash, lash; road scraper.

traillar, *va.* to level the ground.

traje, *m.* dress, suit, costume; **— académico,**
cap and gown; **— a la medida,** suit made
to order; **— de etiqueta,** evening clothes,
dress suit; **— hecho,** ready-made suit or
dress; **— sastre,** tailored suit.

trajín, *m.* bustling about one's work.

trajinar, *va.* to convey; (coll.) to bustle
about one's work.

trajinero, *m.* wagoner.

trama, *f.* plot, conspiracy, complot; weft
or woof (of cloth).

tramador, ra, *n.* plotter; artful contriver.

tramar, *va.* to weave; to plot, to machinate.

tramitación, *f.* transaction.

trámite, *m.* path; requirement; step, passage; (law) procedure.

tramo, *m.* piece, morsel; piece of ground
separated from another; flight of stairs;
section or span of a bridge.

tramontana, *f.* north wind; vanity, pride.

tramontar, *vn.* to cross the mountains;
to set (as the sun); **—,** *va.* to assist, to
relieve; **—se,** to flee, to escape.

tramoya, *f.* scene, theatrical decoration;
craft, wile, artful trick.

tramoyista, *m.* scene painter; sceneshifter;
swindler, humbug.

trampa, *f.* trap, snare; trap door; fraud;
bad debt; **hacer —,** to cheat.

trampantojo, *m.* (coll.) trick played before
one's eyes.

trampear, *vn.* and *va.* to swindle out of
one's money; to impose upon, to deceive.

trampista, *m.* and *f.* cheat, impostor.

trampolín, *m.* springboard.

tramposo, sa, *adj.* deceitful, swindling.

tranca, *f.* crossbar, crossbeam.

trancar, *va.* to barricade.

trancazo, *m.* blow with a bar; *m.* (coll.)
grippe, influenza.

trance, *m.* danger; state of insensibility;
hypnotic condition; last stage of life;
sale of a debtor's property; **a todo —,**
at all costs.

tranco, *m.* long step or stride.

tranchete, *m.* shoemaker's knife.

tranquilidad, *f.* tranquility; repose, heart's
content.

tranquilizar, *va.* and *vr.* to soothe, to quiet,
to calm.

tranquilo, la, *adj.* tranquil, calm, quiet.

transacción, *f.* transaction; accommodation, adjustment.

transatlántico, ca, *adj.* transatlantic; **—,**
m. transatlantic liner.

transbordar, *va.* to transfer, to change cars.

transcendencia, *f.* transcendency; importance.

transcender, *vn.* (ie) to go beyond, to rise
above; to transcend; to emit a strong and
pleasant odor.

transcontinental, *adj.* transcontinental.

transcribir, *va.* to transcribe, to copy.

transcurrir, *vn.* to pass, to elapse (as time).

transcurso, *m.* course (of time).

¡tránseat! *interj.* let it pass!

transeúnte, *adj.* transitory; **—,** *m.* passenger, passer-by.

transferencia, *f.* transfer.

transferir, *va.* (ie) to transfer; to defer.

transfigurable, *adj.* changeable.

transfiguración, *f.* transformation, transfiguration.

transfigurarse, *vr.* to be transfigured; to be
metamorphosed.

transfixión, *f.* transfixing.

transflorear, *va.* to enamel.

transformación, *f.* transformation.

transformador, *m.* transformer.

transformar, *va.* to transform; **—se,** to
become transformed; to change one's
sentiments or manners.

tránsfuga, *m.* and *f.* or **tránsfugo,** *m.* deserter, fugitive.

transfundir, *va.* to transfuse; to communicate.

transfusión, *f.* transfusion.

transgresión, *f.* transgression.

transgresor, ra, *n.* transgressor, lawbreaker.

transición, *f.* transition.

transido, da, *adj.* worn out with anguish;
avaricious.

transigir, *va.* to accommodate differences,
to compromise; **—,** *vn.* to give in.

transitar, *vn.* to travel, to pass by a place.

transitivo, va, *adj.* transitive.

tránsito, *m.* passage; transition; road, way;
change, removal; death of holy or virtuous persons; traffic; **señal de —,** traffic
sign.

transitorio, ria, *adj.* transitory.

transmigración, *f.* transmigration.

transmigrar, *vn.* to transmigrate.

transmisión, *f.* transmission; sending; **engranaje de —,** transmission gear.

transmisor, *m.* transmitter.

transmitir, *va.* to transmit, to send.

transmutable, *adj.* transmutable, changeable.

transmutación, *f.* transmutation.

transmutar, *va.* to transmute.

transparentarse, *vr.* to be transparent; to shine through.

transparente, *adj.* transparent, perspicuous.

transpiración, *f.* transpiration.

transpirar, *vn.* to transpire, to perspire.

transponer, *va.* (TRANSPONGO, TRANSPUSE) to transport, to transfer; —se, to get out of sight by turning a corner; to be drowsy.

transportación, *f.*, **transportamiento,** *m.* transportation.

transportar, *va.* to transport, to convey; (mus.) to transpose; —se, to be in a transport, to be carried away.

transporte, *m.* transportation; transport, conveyance; transport ship.

transposición, *f.* transposition, transposal.

transubstanciación, *f.* transubstantiation.

transversal, *adj.* transverse; collateral; **calle** —, crossroad.

tranvía, *m.* streetcar.

tranzadera, *f.* knot of pleated cords or ribbons; tape.

trapajo, *m.* rag, tatter.

trapajoso, sa, *adj.* ragged, tattered.

trápala, *f.* noise and confusion of people; galloping of horses; (coll.) lie, deceit; —, *m.* and *f.* babbler; cheat; —, *m.* garrulity.

trapería, *f.* frippery; rags; rag shop.

trapero, ra, *n.* dealer in rags.

trapiche, *m.* olive press; sugar mill.

trapisonda, *f.* bustle, noise, confusion; snare, deception.

trapo, *m.* rag, tatter; — **de limpiar,** cleaning rag.

tráquea, *f.* (med.) trachea, windpipe.

traquear, *vn.* to crack; —, *va.* to shake, to agitate.

traqueo, *m.* noise of fireworks; shaking; moving to and fro.

tras, *prep.* after, behind; — **de,** after, back of, besides; —, *m.* breach; blow attended with noise; —, —, bang, bang.

trasanteanoche, *adj.* three nights ago.

trasanteayer, trasantier, *adv.* three days ago.

trasatlántico, ca, *adj.* transatlantic.

trascendencia, *f.* transcendency; importance.

trascendental, *adj.* transcendental.

trascender, *vn.* (IE) to go beyond; to rise above, to transcend; to emit a strong and pleasant odor.

trascolar, *va.* (UE) to cross a mountain; to strain, to percolate.

trascordarse, *vr.* (UE) to forget.

trascorral, *m.* back yard.

trascurso, *m.* course (of time).

trasegar, *va.* (IE) to upset; to decant.

trasera, *f.* back part.

trasero, ra, *adj.* hind, hinder; **asiento** —, back seat; —, *m.* buttock.

trasferir, *va.* (IE) to transfer.

trasgo, *m.* goblin; lively, restless, noisy boy.

trashojar, *va.* to turn over the leaves, to skim through a book.

trashumar, *vn.* to roam to or from the pasture ground; to roam like sheep.

trasiego, *m.* removal; decanting of liquors.

trasladar, *va.* to transport, to transfer; to translate; to postpone; to transcribe, to copy.

traslado, *m.* copy; transcript, transfer.

traslapado, da, *adj.* overlapping.

traslucirse, *vr.* (UZCO) to be transparent; to be inferable.

traslumbrarse, *vr.* to be dazzled with excessive light; to vanish.

trasluz, *m.* light which passes through a transparent body; transverse light.

trasmallo, *m.* trammel net.

trasminar, *vn.*, to excavate; to pierce, to permeate; —se, to be diffused throughout.

trasmochar, *va.* to cut branches for use as fuel.

trasnochador, ra, *n.* night owl; night watcher.

trasnochar, *vn.* to watch, to sit up a whole night.

trasojado, da, *adj.* careworn, emaciated.

traspapelarse, *vr.* to be mislaid among other papers.

traspasar, *va.* to pass over; to remove, to transport; to transfix, to transpierce; to return, to repass; to exceed the proper bounds; to trespass; to transfer.

traspaso, *m.* conveyance; transfer; trespass.

traspié, *m.* slip, stumble; trip, wrestler's trick.

trasplantar, *va.* to transplant.

trasponer, *va.* (TRASPONGO, TRASPUSE) to transfer, to transport; —se, to take a circuitous road in order to get out of sight; to be drowsy.

traspuesta, *f.* transposition; hiding place in a wood; flight.

traspuesto, ta, *adj.* transported.

traspunte, *m.* (theat.) prompter.

traspuntín, *m.* bed mat; seat cushion.

trasquilador, *m.* shearer, clipper.

trasquiladura, *f.* shearing.

trasquilar, *va.* to shear sheep; to clip.

trasquilón, *m.* cut of the shears; hair badly cut.

traste, *m.* fret of a guitar; **dar al** — **con,** to ruin, to spoil.

trasteado, *m.* set of frets on a guitar.

trasteador, ra, *n.* one who frets a guitar.

trastear, *va.* to put frets on a guitar; —, *vn.* to move furniture.

trastejador, *m.* tiler.

trastejar, *va.* to cover with tiles.

trastería, *f.* heap of household goods; ridiculous or foolish action.

trastero, ra, *n.* garret, place reserved for household goods not in use.

trastienda, *f.* back room behind a store; prudence; forecast.

trasto, *m.* furniture or piece of household goods; kitchen utensil.

trastornado, da, *adj.* unbalanced, crazy.

trastornador, ra, *n.* disturber, turbulent person.

trastornar, *va.* and *vr.* to overthrow, to upset; to madden; to overturn; to perplex.

trastorno, *m.* confusion, upset, overthrow.

trastrocar, *va.* (UE) to invert the order of things.

trastumbar, *va.* to overturn, to let fall.

trasudar, *va.* to sweat, to perspire.

trasunto, *m.* likeness, copy; imitation.

trasverter, *vn.* (IE) to overflow.

trasvolar, *va.* (UE) to fly across.

trata, *f.* trade; slave trade; — **de blancas,** white slavery.

tratable, *adj.* tractable, compliant, pliant.

tratado, *m.* treaty, convention; treatise.

tratamiento, *m.* treatment; style of address.

tratante, *m.* dealer in provisions.

tratar, *va.* to treat on a subject; to traffic, to trade; to use, to treat; to be careful to attain an object; —**se,** to entertain a friendly intercourse; —**se de,** to be a question of.

trato, *m.* treatment; manner, address; trade, traffic; conversation; deal; dealing.

trauma, *m.* (med.) trauma.

traumático, ca, *adj.* traumatic.

traumatismo, *m.* traumatism.

través, *m.* bias; reverse; **a — de,** across.

travesaño, *m.* cross timber; crossbar, crossbeam; transom.

travesero, ra, *adj.* transverse, cross; —, *m.* bolster of a bed.

travesía, *f.* crossing, voyage; distance; (naut.) side wind.

travestido, da, *adj.* disguised.

travesura, *f.* mischief; prank.

travieso, sa, *adj.* mischievous; restless, uneasy, fidgety; turbulent; lively; debauched.

trayectoria, *f.* trajectory.

traza, *f.* first sketch; trace, outline; project; manner; means; appearance.

trazar, *va.* to plan out; to project; to trace.

trazo, *m.* sketch, plan, design.

trébol, *m.* (bot.) trefoil; clover.

trece, *m.* and *adj.* thirteen; thirteenth; **estarse en sus —es,** to persist in holding an opinion.

trecientos, tas, *adj.* three hundred.

trecho, *m.* space, distance of time or place; **a —s,** at intervals.

tregua, *f.* truce, cessation of hostilities; recess; **sin —,** unceasingly.

treinta, *m.* and *adj.* thirty.

treintavo, va, *m.* and *adj.* thirtieth.

treinteno, na, *adj.* thirtieth.

tremendo, da, *adj.* tremendous; terrible, formidable; awful, imposing.

trementina, *f.* turpentine.

tremés or **tremesino, na,** *adj.* three months old.

tremolar, *va.* and *vn.* to hoist the colors; to wave.

tremolina, *f.* rustling of the wind; bustle, confused noise.

trémulo, la, *adj.* tremulous, trembling.

tren, *m.* train, retinue; show; ostentation; (rail.) train; — **de ruedas,** running gear; — **elevado,** elevated train.

trencilla, *f.* braid, lace, plait or tape.

trencillo, *m.* gold or silver hatband.

trenza, *f.* braided hair, pleated silk.

trenzadera, *f.* tape; knot of pleated cords or ribbons.

trenzado, *m.* braided hair.

trenzar, *va.* to braid the hair.

trepador, ra, *adj.* climbing.

trepar, *vn.* to climb, to crawl.

trepidación, *f.* vibration; trepidation.

tres, *adj.* and *m.* three.

trescientos, tas, *adj.* three hundred; —, *m.* three hundred.

treta, *f.* feint (in fencing); trick, wile.

triaca, *f.* antidote.

triangulación, *f.* triangulation.

triangular, *adj.* triangular; —, *va.* to triangulate.

triángulo, *m.* triangle.

trib.¹ tribunal, tribunal, court of justice.

tribu, *f.* tribe.

tribulación, *f.* tribulation, affliction.

tribuna, *f.* tribune, platform, rostrum.

tribunal, *m.* tribunal, court of justice.

tribuno, *m.* tribune; orator.

tributar, *va.* to pay tribute; to contribute to; to pay homage and respect.

tributario, ria, *adj.* tributary.

tributo, *m.* tribute; tax.

tricentésimo, ma, *m.* and *adj.* three-hundredth.

triciclo, *m.* tricycle.

tricolor, *adj.* tricolored.

tricorne, *adj.* three-horned.

tricornio, *m.* three-horned hat.

tridente, *adj* three-pronged; —, *m.* trident.

triduano, na, *adj.* of three days' duration.

trienal, *adj.* triennial.

trienio, *m.* space of three years.

trifloro, ra, *adj.* three-flowered.

trifolio, *m.* trefoil, shamrock.

trigaza, *f.* short straw of wheat.

trigésimo, ma, *adj.* thirtieth.

trigo, *m.* wheat; — **mocho,** winter wheat.

trigon. trigonometría, trig. trigonometry.

trigonométrico, ca, *adj.* trigonometric.

trigueño, ña, *adj.* swarthy, brunette.

triguero, ra, *adj.* growing among wheat; —, *m.* winnowing sieve, screen; grain merchant.

trilogía, *f.* trilogy.

trillado, da, *adj.* beaten; trite, stale, hackneyed; **camino —,** common routine.

trillador, ra, *n.* thresher or thrasher; —, *f.* threshing machine; —, *adj.* threshing or thrashing; **máquina —,** threshing machine.

trilladura, *f.* act of threshing.
trillar, *va.* to thrash.
trillo, *m.* flail; threshing machine.
trimestre, *m.* space of three months.
trimotor, *m.* three-engined airplane.
trinado, *m.* trill, quaver.
trinar, *vn.* to trill, to quaver.
trincar, *va.* to break into small pieces; (naut.) to keep close to the wind; to fasten the rope ends.
trinchante, *m.* carver; carving knife.
trinchar, *va.* to carve, to divide meat; (coll.) to decide with an air of authority.
trinchera, *f.* trench, entrenchment.
trinchero, *m.* trencher; side table.
trinchete, *m.* knife used by shoemaker for cutting soles.
trineo, *m.* sleigh, sled.
Trinidad, *f.* Trinity.
trinitaria, *f.* (bot.) pansy, heartsease.
trino, na, *adj.* containing three distinct things; —, *m.* trill.
trinquete, *m.* foremast; kind of ball game.
trío, *m.* (mus.) trio.
trioxido, *m.* trioxide.
tripa, *f.* gut, entrails, tripe, intestine; belly of a vessel; core; **hacer de —s corazón,** to pluck up courage.
tripartir, *va.* to divide in three parts.
tripe, *m.* shag, plush.
tripería, *f.* tripe market, tripery.
tripero, *m.,* or **tripicallero, ra,** *n.* tripe-seller.
triplano, *m.* triplane.
triple, *adj.* triple, treble, three-ply.
triplicar, *va.* to treble, to triple.
tríplice, *adj.* triplex, treble, triple.
triplo, la, *adj.* treble, triplicate.
trípode, *m.* or *f.* tripod, trivet.
triptongo, *m.* triphthong.
tripudo, da, *adj.* big-bellied.
tripulación, *f.* crew of a ship.
tripular, *vn.* to man ships; to fit out.
triquina, *f.* trichina.
triquinosis, *f.* (med.) trichinosis.
triquitraque, *m.* clack, clatter, clashing; firecracker.
tris, *m.* noise made by the breaking of glass; trice, instant; **estar en un —,** to be on the point of.
triscar, *vn.* to make a noise with the feet; to frisk about.
trisecar, *va.* to trisect.
trisílabo, ba, *adj.* trisyllabic.
triste, *adj.* sad, mournful, melancholy.
tristeza, *f.* melancholy, sadness, dreariness.
trítono, *m.* tritone, musical interval of three tones.
trituración, *f.* pulverization; crushing.
triturador, ra, *adj.* crushing; —, *m.* crusher, crushing machine.
triturar, *va.* to reduce to powder, to grind, to pound.
triunfal, *adj.* triumphal.
triunfante, *adj.* triumphant, exultant.

triunfar, *vn.* to triumph; to trump at cards.
triunfo, *m.* triumph; trump (in cards).
triunvirato, *m.* triumvirate.
trivial, *adj.* frequented; vulgar; trivial.
trivialidad, *f.* vulgarity; trifle.
triza, *f.* mite; bit, shred; cord, rope.
trobador, *m.* troubadour.
trocar, *va.* (UE) to exchange, to barter; **—se,** to be changed or reformed.
trocha, *f.* trail, path; (rail.) gauge.
trochemoche, a —, *adv.* helter-skelter.
trofeo, *m.* trophy.
troj or **troje,** *f.* granary, fruit loft.
tromba, *f.* waterspout.
trombón, *m.* (mus.) trombone.
trombosis, *f.* (med.) thrombosis.
trompa, *f.* trumpet; proboscis, trunk (of elephants); humming top; **— de Eustaquio,** (anat.) Eustachian tube.
trompada, *f.* (coll.) fisticuff.
trompazo, *m.* heavy blow; adverse accident.
trompeta, *f.* trumpet, horn; —, *m.* trumpeter.
trompetear, *vn.* to sound the trumpet.
trompetero, *m.* trumpeter; trumpet maker.
trompetilla, *f.* small trumpet; speaking trumpet.
trompicar, *vn.* and *va.* to stumble frequently; to trip, to cause stumbling.
trompicón, *m.* stumbling.
trompo, *m.* spinning top.
tronada, *f.* thunderstorm.
tronar, *vn.* (UE) to thunder.
troncar, *va.* to truncate, to mutilate.
tronco, *m.* trunk; log of wood; stock; origin.
tronchar, *va.* to cut off at the stalk.
troncho, *m.* sprig, stem or stalk.
tronchudo, da, *adj.* having a long stem or stalk.
tronera, *f.* embrasure of a battery; loophole; dormer; hare-brained person; pocket of a pool table.
trono, *m.* throne; (eccl.) shrine; **—s,** *pl.* seventh choir of angels.
tronzar, *va.* to shatter, to break into pieces; to pleat, to fold.
tropa, *f.* troop; **—s de asalto,** storm troops; **—s ligeras,** skirmishers; **— de línea,** regular army.
tropel, *m.* confused noise; hurry, bustle, confusion, heap of things; crowd; **de —,** in a tumultous and confused manner.
tropelía, *f.* precipitation, hurry, confusion, vexation, oppression.
tropezadero, *m.* any stumbling or slippery place.
tropezar, *vn.* (IE) to stumble; to be detained or obstructed; to meet accidentally; to cut the feet in walking (horses).
tropezón, ona, *adj.* stumbling; —, *m.* tripping; **a —ones,** impeded and obstructed.
tropical, *adj.* tropical.
trópico, *m.* tropic; **—, ca,** *adj.* tropical.
tropiezo, *m.* stumble, trip; obstacle; slip; fault; quarrel; dispute.

tropo, *m.* figure of speech.
trotador, ra, *n.* trotter; —, *adj.* trotting.
trotar, *vn.* to trot.
trote, *m.* trot; **a** —, in haste.
trovador, ra, *n.* minstrel, troubadour.
trovar, *va.* to parody, to versify; —, *vn.* to versify, to write poetry.
Troya, *f.* Troy.
troyano, na, *n.* and *adj.* Trojan.
trozo, *m.* piece, bit, fragment; selection; (rail.) section of a line.
truculencia, *f.* truculence.
truculento, ta, *adj.* savage, truculent.
trucha, *f.* trout; crane.
trueno, *m.* thunderclap.
trueque, *m.* exchange, barter.
trufa, *f.* (bot.) truffle; hoax, fraud.
truhán, ana, *n.* buffoon; rascal; —, *adj.* knavish, rascally.
truhanear, *vn.* to play the buffoon.
truhanería, *f.* buffoonery.
truhanesco, ca, *adj.* rascally; clownish.
trujal, *m.* oil mill.
trulla, *f.* bustle, noise; crowd.
truncar, *va.* to truncate, to maim.
truquero, *m.* keeper of a pool table.
tu, *adj.* possessive sing. of pronoun **tú.**
tú, *pron.* thou.
tuba, *f.* tuba, bass horn.
tuberculosis, *f.* (med.) tuberculosis.
tubería, *f.* pipe line; tubing; piping.
tubiforme, *adj.* tubular, tubiform.
tubo, *m.* tube, pipe, duct; — **acústico,** speaking tube; — **de alimentación,** standpipe; — **de escape,** exhaust pipe; — **de radio,** radio tube; — **lanzatorpedos,** torpedo tube.
tubular, *adj.* tubular.
tuerca, *f.* screw.
tuerto, ta, *adj.* one-eyed; squint-eyed.
tuétano, *m.* marrow.
tufarada, *f.* strong scent or smell.
tufo, *m.* warm vapor arising from the earth; offensive smell; lock of hair over the temple.
tul, *m.* tulle (cloth).
tulipán, *m.* tulip.
tullido, da, *adj.* crippled, maimed.
tullimiento, *m.* maiming.
tullir, *va.* (TULLÓ, TULLENDO) to maim, to cripple; —, *vn.* to drop excrement (of birds); —se, to be crippled or maimed.
tumba, *f.* tomb, grave; roof of a coach; tumble.
tumbaga, *f.* pinchbeck, tombac (cheap alloy imitating gold).
tumbar, *va.* to tumble (to throw down); —, *vn.* to tumble (to fall down); —se, to lie down to sleep.
tumefacción, *f.* swelling, tumefaction.
tumescencia, *f.* tumescence.
tumescente, *adj.* tumescent.
tumor, *m.* tumor, morbid swelling.
túmulo, *m.* tomb, sepulchral monument.
tumulto, *m.* tumult, uproar.

tumultuoso, sa, *adj.* tumultuous.
tuna, *f.* prickly pear; idle life.
tunante, *adj.* cunning; leading a licentious life; —, *m.* rake, lazy loiterer; rascal.
tunar, *vn.* to lead a licentious life; to loiter.
tunda, *f.* act of shearing cloth; (coll.) severe chastisement.
tundidor, *m.* shearer of cloth.
tundidora, *f.* cloth-shearing machine.
tundir, *va.* to shear; to cudgel, to flog.
tundra, *f.* tundra.
tunecino, na, *n.* and *adj.* Tunisian.
túnel, *m.* tunnel.
Túnez, *f.* Tunis.
tungsteno, *m.* tungsten, wolfram.
túnica, *f.* tunic.
tuno, *m.* truant, rake; —, **na,** cunning; rascally.
tupé, *m.* toupee, foretop; (coll.) audacity, gall.
tupir, *va.* to press close; to make compact; —se, to stuff oneself with eating and drinking.
turba, *f.* crowd, rabble; turf, sod.
turbación, *f.* perturbation, confusion, trouble, disorder.
turbante, *m.* turban.
turbar, *va.* and *vr.* to disturb, to trouble; to embarrass.
turbina, *f.* turbine.
turbio, bia, *adj.* muddy, troubled.
turbión, *m.* heavy shower of rain; hurricane.
turbulencia, *f.* turbulence, disturbance.
turbulento, ta, *adj.* turbid, muddy; stormy, turbulent.
turco, ca, *n.* and *adj.* Turkish.
turismo, *m.* touring, tourism; **coche de** —, touring car.
turista, *m.* and *f.* tourist.
turnar, *vn.* to alternate.
turno, *m.* turn; vicissitude; — **diurno,** day shift.
turpial, *m.* (orn.) troupial, Central and South American oriole.
turquesa, *f.* turquoise.
turquí, *adj.* deep blue.
Turquía, *f.* Turkey.
turrar, *va.* to toast, to roast.
turrón, *m.* nougat.
turronero, *m.* nougat maker or seller.
turumbón, *m.* contusion on the head.
tute, *m.* a kind of card game.
tuteamiento, *m.* using **tú** instead of **usted,** i.e., familiar speech.
tutear, *va.* to use **tú** instead of **usted,** i.e., familiar form of speech.
tutela, *f.* guardianship, tutelage.
tutelar, *adj.* tutelar, tutelary.
tutor, *m.* guardian, tutor.
tutora, *f.* tutoress.
tutoría, *f.* tutelage.
tuya, *f.* (bot.) thuya, arborvitae.
tuyo, ya, *adj.* thine; **los** —s, *pl.* thy family, thy people, etc.

U

U. or **Ud. Usted,** you (*sing.*).
u, *conj.* or (used instead of **o,** when the following word begins with an *o*).
ubérrimo, ma, *adj.* fruitful, very plentiful.
ubicación, *f.* location, situation.
ubicar, *vn.* and *vr.* to be located.
ubre, *f.* dug, teat, udder.
uesnorueste, *m.* west-northwest.
uessudueste, *m.* west-southwest.
Uds. ustedes, you (*pl.*).
¡uf! interjection used to denote annoyance or weariness.
ufanamente, *adv.* ostentatiously, boastfully.
ufanarse, *vr.* to boast.
ufanía, *f.* haughtiness.
ufano, na, *adj.* haughty, arrogant; gay, cheerful.
ujier, *m.* usher, doorkeeper.
úlcera, *f.* ulcer.
ulceración, *f.* ulceration.
ulcerar, *vn.* to ulcerate.
ulceroso, sa, *adj.* ulcerous.
Ulpiano, Ulpian.
ulpo, *m.* (Sp. Am.) maize or corn gruel.
ulterior, *adj.* ulterior, farther, further.
últimamente, *adv.* lately.
ultimátum, *m.* ultimatum.
último, ma, *adj.* last, latest, hindmost; late, latter; remote, final; **a —mos del mes, de la semana, etc.,** at the latter part of the month, week, etc.; **por —mo,** lastly, finally.
últ.º último, ult. last.
ultra, *adv.* besides; used also as a prefix of some adjectives to indicate excess or exaggeration, as in **ultrafamoso,** ultrafamous; used with some nouns it has the meaning of *beyond,* as in **ultramar,** beyond the seas, overseas.
ultrajador, ra, *n.* one who outrages or insults.
ultrajar, *va.* to outrage; to despise, to scorn; to abuse.
ultraje, *m.* outrage.
ultramar, *adj.* and *m.* overseas.
ultramarino, na, pertaining to overseas merchandise; **—,** *m.* deep-blue dye; **azul —no,** ultramarine blue; **—nos,** *m. pl.* fancy groceries, usually from overseas.
ultramontano, na, *adj.* ultramontane.
ultranza, a —, *adv.* at all costs, at risk of death.
ultravioleta, *adj.* ultraviolet.
úlula, *f.* (orn.) owl.
umbilical, *adj.* umbilical.
umbral, *m.* threshold, doorstep; architrave; beginning, rudiment.
umbría, *f.* shade, grove.
umbroso, sa, *adj.* shady.
un, una, *adj.* a, an; one.
unánime, *adj.* unanimous.
unanimidad, *f.* unanimity.

unción, *f.* unction; extreme or last unction, **—ones,** *pl.* course of salvation.
uncir, *va.* to yoke.
undécimo, ma, *adj.* eleventh.
undísono, na, *adj.* (poet.) billowy.
undoso, sa, *adj.* wavy, rising in waves.
undular, *vn.* to undulate.
ungido, *adj.* and *m.* anointed of the Lord, king, sovereign.
ungir, *va.* to anoint.
ungüento, *m.* unguent, ointment; **— de soldado,** mercury ointment; **— de petróleo,** vaseline, petroleum jelly.
unicameral, *adj.* unicameral.
únicamente, *adv.* only, simply.
unicelular, *adj.* unicellular.
único, ca, *adj.* singular, unique, only.
unicornio, *m.* unicorn.
unidad, *f.* unity; unit; conformity, union.
unidamente, *adv.* jointly, unanimously.
unificación, *f.* unification.
uniformar, *va.* to make uniform.
uniforme, *adj.* uniform; **—,** *m.* (mil.) uniform, regimentals.
uniformidad, *f.* uniformity, evenness.
unigénito, *adj.* only-begotten.
unilateral, *adj.* unilateral.
unión, *f.* union.
unionismo, *m.* unionism.
unionizar, *va.* to unionize.
unir, *va.* to join, to unite; to mingle, to bind, to tie; **—se,** to associate, to get together.
unísono, na, *adj.* unison.
universal, *adj.* universal.
universalidad, *f.* universality.
universidad, *f.* universality; university.
universo, *m.* universe.
uno, *m.* one; **—, na,** *adj.* one; sole, only; **— a otro,** one another; **— a —,** one by one; **a una,** jointly, together.
untar, *va.* to anoint; to grease; to spread; **—se,** to be greased with unctuous matter; to bribe.
unto, *m.* grease; fat of animals.
untuoso, sa, *adj.* unctuous, greasy.
untura, *f.* unction; unguent.
uña, *f.* nail; hoof; claw, talon; pointed hook of instruments; **ser — y carne,** to be close friends.
uñada or **uñarada,** *f.* scratch with the nail.
uñero, *m.* whitlow; hangnail; ingrown nail.
uñeta, *f.* sculptor's gouge; nail claw; pitching pennies (boy's game).
¡upa! *interj.* up! up! (to make children get up from the ground).
uranio, *m.* uranium.
urbanidad, *f.* urbanity, good manners, politeness.
urbanización, *f.* urbanization.
urbanizar, *va.* to urbanize.
Urbano, Urban.
urbano, na, *adj.* polite, well-bred; urban.
urbe, *f.* metropolis.
urdidor, ra, *n.* warper; warping mill.
urdidura, *f.* warping.

urdimbre, f. chain, warp.
urdir, va. to warp; to contrive.
uremia, f. (med.) uremia.
urémico, ca, adj. uremic.
uretritis, f. urethritis.
urgencia, f. urgency, hurry, pressure of difficulty, need, necessity.
urgente, adj. pressing, urgent.
urgentemente, adv. urgently.
urgir, vn. to be urgent.
úrico, ca, adj. uric.
urinálisis, f. (med.) urinalysis.
urinario, ria, adj. urinary.
urna, f. urn; glass case in which small statues or images are kept.
urraca, f. magpie.
U.R.S.S. Unión de las Repúblicas Soviéticas Socialistas, USSR, U.S.S.R. Union of Soviet Socialist Republics.
urticaria, f. hives, rash.
uruguayo, ya, n. and adj. Uruguayan.
usado, da, adj. used; experienced.
usanza, f. usage, use, custom.
usar, va. to use, to make use of; to accustom; **—se,** to be in use, to be wont.
Usía, (= **Vuestra Señoría**), f. Your Lordship.
uso, m. use, service; custom; mode.
Usted or **usted,** pron. you (sing.) (contraction of **Vuestra Merced**); **Ustedes** or **ustedes,** you (plural)
usual, adj. usual, customary.
usufructo, m. usufruct, enjoyment, profit.
usufructuar, va. to enjoy the usufruct of anything; to render productive.
usufructuario, ria, adj. possessing the usufruct of anything.
usura, f. usury.
usurear or **usurar,** vn. to practice usury, to profiteer.
usurero, ra, n. usurer.
usurpación, f. usurpation.
usurpador, ra, n. usurper.
usurpar, va. to usurp.
utensilio, m. utensil.
uterino, na, adj. uterine.
útero, m. uterus, womb.
útil, adj. useful, profitable; helpful; **—es,** m. pl. utensils, tools.
utilidad, f. utility; usefulness; profit.
utilitario, ria, adj. utilitarian.
utilizable, adj. usable.
utilización, f. utilization.
utilizar, va. to make useful; to make use of; **—se,** to be made useful.
utopía, f. Utopia, utopia.
UU. ustedes, you (pl.).
uva, f. grape; barberry.
uxoricida, m. uxoricide, wife killer.

V

V.: usted, you (sing.); **valor,** val. value; **véase,** vid. see, refer to; **Venerable,** Venerable.

v.: vapor, ss. steamship; **véase,** vid. see, refer to; **verbo,** verb; **viuda,** widow.
v/valor, val. value; amt. amount.
V. A.: Vuestra Alteza, Your Highness, **Versión Autorizada,** A. V. Authorized Version.
vaca, f. cow.
vacaciones, f. pl. holidays, vacations.
vacada, f. drove of cows.
vacante, adj. vacant; **—,** f. vacancy.
vacar, vn. to be vacant.
vaciadero, m. drain, sink.
vaciador, m. molder; dumper.
vaciar, va. to empty, to clear; to mold; **—,** vn. to fall, to decrease (of waters); **—se,** to be spilt, to be emptied.
vacilación, f. vacillation, hesitation; irresolution.
vacilante, adj. irresolute, uncertain; feebleminded.
vacilar, vn. to vacillate; to hesitate, to waver.
vacío, cía, adj. void, empty; unoccupied; concave; vain; presumptuous; unemployed; **—,** m. vacuum; concavity.
vacuna, f. cowpox, vaccine virus.
vacunar, va. to vaccinate.
vacuno, na, adj. bovine, belonging to cattle.
vadeable, adj. fordable.
vadear, va. to wade, to ford.
vado, m. ford.
vagabundo, da, adj. vagabond, hobo, tramp.
vagamundear, vn. to rove or loiter about.
vagamundo, da, n. and adj. vagabond, tramp.
vagancia, f. vagrancy.
vagar, vn. to rove or loiter about; to wander; to be loose and irregular; **—,** m. leisure; slowness.
vagido, m. cry of a child; convulsive sob.
vagina, f. (anat.) vagina.
vago, ga, adj. vagrant; restless; vague; **—,** m. vagabond; **en —go,** unsteadily.
vagón, m. car, freight car, coach; **— cama,** sleeping car; **— de cola,** caboose; **— de ganado,** cattle car; **— de mercancías,** freight car.
vahido, m. vertigo, dizziness.
vaho, m. steam, vapor.
vaina, f. scabbard, sheath; knife case; pod, husk.
vainica, f. little sheath; hemstitch.
vainilla, f. (bot.) vanilla.
vaivén, m. fluctuation, vacillation, instability; dizziness; motion; risk, danger.
vajilla, f. table service, set of dishes; **— de plata,** silverware.
vale, m. farewell; promissory note, I.O.U.
valedero, ra, adj. valid, efficacious, binding.
valencia, f. (chem.) valence, valency.
valenciano, na, adj. and n. Valencian, from Valencia.
valentía, f. valor, courage; brag, boast.
Valentín, Valentine.

valentón, *m.* braggart, bully, swashbuckler.

valentonada, *f.* brag, boast.

valer, *vn.* (VALGO, VALÍ), to be valuable, to be worth, to be deserving; to be marketable; to prevail; to avail; to be valid; to have power; to yield; to produce; to amount to; to have influence; to be equivalent to; to be current; **—,** *va.* to protect, to favor; **— la pena,** to be worth while; **—se,** to employ, to make use of; to have recourse to.

Valeriano, Valerian.

valeroso, sa, *adj.* valiant, brave; strong, powerful.

valerosamente, *adv.* courageously.

valetudinario, ria, *adj.* valetudinarian, sickly.

valía, *f.* valuation; credit, favor; party; worth.

validación, *f.* validation.

validar, *va.* to give validity.

validez, *f.* validity, stability.

valido, da, *adj.* esteemed, respected; **—,** *m.* favorite of a prince or high dignitary.

válido, da, *adj.* valid; obligatory.

valiente, *adj.* valiant, brave, courageous; vigorous.

valija, *f.* valise; mail bag.

valijero, *m.* mailman.

valimiento, *m.* use, utility, advantage; contribution; favor, protection, support.

valor, *m.* value, price; validity; force, power; courage, valor; **por dicho —,** for the above amount; **— nominal** or **aparente,** face value; **sin —,** worthless.

valorar or **valorear,** *va.* to value.

vals, *m.* waltz.

valuación, *f.* valuation, appraisement, appraisal.

valuar, *va.* to value, to appraise.

válvula, *f.* valve, aperture; **— de seguridad,** safety valve; **— corrediza,** slide valve; **— de aire,** air valve.

valla, *f.* entrenchment; barricade; fence; obstacle, impediment.

vallado, *m.* enclosure with stakes or palisades.

valle, *m.* dale, valley.

¡vamos! *interj.* well! let's go! stop!

vampiro, *m.* vampire.

vanadio, *m.* vanadium.

vanagloria, *f.* vainglory, conceit.

vanagloriarse, *vr.* to be vainglorious, to boast of.

vandalismo, *m.* vandalism.

vándalo, la, *m.* and *adj.* vandal.

vanear, *vn.* to talk nonsensically.

vanguardia, *f.* vanguard, van.

vanidad, *f.* vanity; ostentation; futility; flirtation; illusion, phantom.

vanidoso, sa, *adj.* vain, showy; haughty, conceited.

vanilocuencia, *f.* wordiness, verbosity.

vano, na, *adj.* vain; useless; frivolous; arrogant; futile; **en —no,** in vain.

vapor, *m.* vapor, steam; breath; (naut.) steamer, steamship.

vaporizador, *m.* vaporizer, spray, sprayer.

vaporoso, sa, *adj.* vaporous, ethereal.

vapular, *va.* to whip, to flog.

vaquerizo, za, *adj.* relating to cows; **—,** *m.* cowherd.

vaquero, *m.* cowherd; herdsman, cowboy; **—, ra,** *adj.* belonging to cowherds or cowboys.

vaqueta, *f.* sole leather; ramrod.

V. A. R. Vuestra Alteza Real, Your Royal Highness.

vara, *f.* rod; pole, staff; wand; verge; yard (measure); **— alta,** sway, high hand; **—s,** *pl.* shafts of a coach.

varadero, *m.* shipyard; iron sheet protecting the side of ship where the anchor rests.

varadura, *f.* (naut.) grounding (of a ship).

varal, *m.* long pole; tall, slender person.

varapalo, *m.* long perch; blow with a pole; trouble, vexation.

varar, *va.* to launch (a ship); **—,** *vn.* and *vr.* to ground, to be stranded.

vardasca, *f.* a thin twig.

vardascazo, *m.* stroke with a twig.

vareaje, *m.* selling or measuring by the yard.

varear, *va.* to knock the fruit off trees with a pole; to goad a bull; to measure or sell by the yard; **—se,** to grow thin or lean.

vareta, *f.* lime twig for catching birds; stripe in any kind of cloth different in color from the ground; (coll.) **irse de —,** to suffer from diarrhea.

vareteado, da, *adj.* flecked.

varga, *f.* steepest part of a hill or incline.

variable, *adj.* variable, changeable.

variación, *f.* variation, change.

variado, da, *adj.* variegated, varied.

variante, *f.* difference, discrepancy; **—,** *adj.* varying.

variar, *va.* to vary, to change; **—,** *vn.* to vary.

varicela, *f.* chicken pox.

varicoso, sa, *adj.* varicose.

variedad, *f.* variety; diversity.

variedades, *f. pl.* vaudeville performance.

varilla, *f.* small rod; curtainrod; spindle, pivot; **—s,** *pl.* jawbones; rib of a fan.

vario, ria, *adj.* various, different; vague; variegated; **—s,** *pl.* some, several.

variómetro, *m.* variometer.

varón, *m.* man, male human being; man of respectability.

varona, *f.* mannish woman; woman.

varonesa, *f.* woman, female human being.

varonía, *f.* male issue; male descendants.

varonil, *adj.* male, masculine; manful.

Varsovia, *f.* Warsaw.

vasallaje, *m.* vassalage.

vasallo, *m.* vassal, liegeman.

vasar, *m.* buffet on which glasses or vessels are put.

vasco, ca, *n.* and *adj.* Basque.

vascuence, *m.* Basque language; (coll.) gibberish.

vaselina, *f.* vaseline, petroleum jelly.

vasija, *f.* pot; vessel (in which liquors are kept).

vaso, *m.* vessel; jar; vase; reservoir; — **de untar,** grease cup.

vástago, *m.* bud, shoot; descendant, offspring.

vastamente, *adv.* vastly.

vasto, ta, *adj.* vast, huge.

vate, *m.* poet, bard.

vatiaje, *m.* wattage.

vaticinador, *m.* prophet, diviner.

vaticinar, *va.* to divine, to foretell.

vaticinio, *m.* divination.

vatio, *m.* watt; — **hora,** watt hour.

¡vaya!, *interj.* well, now!

V. B.^d **Vuestra Beatitud,** Your Beatitude.

Vd. usted, you (*sing.*).

vda. viuda, widow.

Vds. or **VV. ustedes,** you (*pl.*).

V. E. Vuestra Excelencia, Your Excellency.

véase, see, refer to.

vecera, vecería, *f.* pack, herd.

vecindad, *f.* inhabitants of a place; neighborhood.

vecindario, *m.* number of inhabitants of a place, neighborhood, district.

vecino, na, *adj.* neighboring; near; —, *m.* neighbor, inhabitant.

vector, *m.* (math. and phy.) vector.

Veda, *m.* Hindu sacred writings, Veda.

veda, *f.* prohibition; closed season.

vedado, *m.* park, inclosure.

vedar, *va.* to prohibit, to forbid; to impede.

vedija, *f.* tangled lock of wool; flake; tuft of tangled hair, matted hair.

veedor, *m.* prier, busybody; overseer, inspector.

veeduría, *f.* inspector's office.

vega, *f.* meadow; plain; flat lowland well watered and very fertile.

vegetación, *f.* vegetation.

vegetal, *adj.* and *m.* vegetable.

vegetar, *vn.* to vegetate.

vegetariano, na, *adj.* and *m.* vegetarian.

vehemencia, *f.* vehemence, force.

vehemente, *adj.* vehement, violent.

vehículo, *m.* vehicle.

veintavo, *m.* and *adj.* twentieth.

veinte, *adj.* and *m.* twenty.

veintena, *f.* score, twenty.

veinteno, na, *adj.* twentieth.

veintitantos, tas, *adj. pl.* twenty-odd.

vejación, *f.* vexation, molestation; oppression.

vejamen, *m.* taunt; vexation.

vejar, *va.* to vex, to molest; to censure.

vejete, *m.* ridiculous old man.

vejez, *f.* old age.

vejiga, *f.* bladder; blister; — **de la bilis,** gall bladder.

vejigatorio, *m.* blistering plaster; —, **ria,** *adj.* raising blisters.

vela, *f.* watch; watchfulness; night watch; candle; a horse's ear; sail; ship; **hacerse**

a la —, to set sail.

velación, *f.* watching; —**ones,** *pl.* nuptial benedictions.

velada, *f.* evening entertainment, soiree.

velador, *m.* watchman; careful observer; large wooden candlestick; lamp stand or table.

velamen, *m.* set of sails.

velar, *vn.* to watch; to wake; to be attentive; to appear above the water (as rocks); —, *va.* to guard, to watch; to veil (a bride and groom) at a nuptial mass.

veleidad, *f.* whimsicalness, fickleness; feeble will; inconstancy.

veleidoso, sa, *adj.* inconstant, fickle.

velero, ra, *adj.* swift sailing; —, *m.* sailboat.

veleta, *f.* weathercock.

velo, *m.* veil; pretext.

velocidad, *f.* velocity, speed; **a toda —,** at full speed; **cambio de —,** gear shift; — **máxima,** speed limit; — **reducida,** slow motion.

velocímetro, *m.* speedometer.

velón, *m.* oil lamp.

velonero, *m.* lampmaker.

veloz, *adj.* swift; feathered.

velozmente, *adv.* swiftly.

vello, *m.* down; gossamer; short downy hair.

vellocino, *m.* fleece.

vellón, *m.* fleece; lock of wool; copper coin of the province of Castile.

velloso, sa, *adj.* downy, cottony, fluffy.

velludo, da, *adj.* shaggy, wooly, hairy.

vena, *f.* vein, blood vessel.

venablo, *m.* javelin.

venado, *m.* deer; venison.

venal, *adj.* belonging to the veins; salable; mercenary.

venalidad, *f.* venality.

vencedor, ra, *n.* conqueror, victor, foiler; —, *adj.* victorious.

vencejo, *m.* (orn.) swift, martin.

vencer, *va.* to conquer, to vanquish; —, *vn.* to fall due; —**se,** to govern one's desires, to control oneself.

vencible, *adj.* vincible, conquerable.

vencido, da, *adj.* conquered; due; **darse por —,** to give up, to yield; **letra —,** overdue draft.

vencim.^{to} **vencimiento,** (com.) expiration.

vencimiento, *m.* victory; bending down; expiration (term of a note).

venda, *f.* bandage; fillet; diadem.

vendaje, *m.* brokerage; bandage, dressing of wounds; — **enyesado,** plaster cast.

vendar, *va.* to bandage; to hoodwink.

vendaval, *m.* a strong south-by-west wind; — **de polvo,** dust storm.

vendedor, ra, *n.* seller; — **ambulante,** huckster; — **de periódicos,** newsboy.

vendeja, *f.* sale, auction.

vender, *va.* to sell.

vendible, *adj.* salable, vendible.

vendimia, *f.* vintage.

vendimiador, ra, *n.* vintager.

vendimiar, *va.* to gather the vintage.
venduta, *f.* (Sp. Am.) auction, sale.
Venecia, *f.* Venice.
veneno, *m.* poison, venom.
venenoso, sa, *adj.* venomous, poisonous.
venera, *f.* porcelain shell; badge worn by the knights of military orders.
venerable, *adj.* venerable.
veneración, *f.* veneration, worship.
venerar, *va.* to venerate, to worship.
venéreo, rea, *adj.* venereal.
venero, *m.* vein of metal in a mine; source of water.
venezolano, na, *adj.* and *n.* Venezuelan.
vengador, ra, *n.* avenger.
venganza, *f.* revenge, vengeance.
vengar, *va.* to revenge, to avenge; **—se,** to be revenged on.
vengativo, va, *adj.* revengeful.
venia, *f.* pardon; leave, permission; bow.
venial, *adj.* venial.
venida, *f.* arrival; return; overflow of a river.
venidero, ra, *adj.* future, coming, next; **próximo —ro,** the coming month; **—os,** *m. pl.* posterity.
venir, *vn.* (VENGO, VINE) to come, to arrive; to follow, to succeed; to spring from; to fit, to suit; **— a menos,** to decay, to decline; **¿ a qué viene eso?** to what purpose is that?; **el mes que viene,** next month; **—se,** to ferment.
venoso, sa, *adj.* veiny, veined.
venta, *f.* sale; roadside inn; **—s,** *pl.* turnover.
ventaja, *f.* advantage; **con — recíproca,** to mutual advantage; **llevar —,** to have an advantage over; (sports) handicap.
ventajoso, sa, *adj.* advantageous.
ventana, *f.* window; window shutter; **— de la nariz,** nostril; **repisa de —,** window sill; **vidrio de —,** windowpane.
ventanaje, *m.* number of windows in a building.
ventanilla, *f.* small window; peephole.
ventarrón, *m.* violent wind.
ventear, *v. imp.* to blow (as the wind); **—,** *va.* to smell, to scent; to investigate, to examine; to expose to the air; **—se,** to be filled with wind; (coll.) to break wind.
ventero, ra, *n.* keeper of a roadside inn.
ventilación, *f.* ventilation; discussion.
ventilador, *m.* ventilator; fan.
ventilar, *va.* and *vr.* to ventilate; to fan; to air; to discuss.
ventisca, *f.,* **ventisco,** *m.* snowstorm.
ventiscar, *v. imp.* to drift, to lie in drifts (snow).
ventisquero, *m.* snowdrift; **—s,** *pl.* glaciers.
ventolera, *f.* gust; pride, loftiness.
ventor, ra, *n.* pointer, setter (dog).
ventorrillo, *m.* roadside tavern.
ventosa, *f.* air hole; cupping glass.
ventosear, *vn.* and *vr.* to break wind.
ventosidad, *f.* flatulency.
ventoso, sa, *adj.* windy; flatulent.
ventrículo, *m.* ventricle.

ventril, *m.* counterpoise.
ventrílocuo, *m.* ventriloquist.
ventrudo, da, *adj.* big-bellied.
ventura, *f.* luck, favorable chance, fortune; **por —,** by chance.
venturina, *f.* aventurine, goldstone.
venturoso, sa, *adj.* lucky, fortunate, happy.
Venus, *f.* Venus (goddess or planet).
ver, *va.* (VISTO) to see, to look; to observe; to visit; to examine; **a —,** let's see; **hacer —,** to pretend; to show; **—se,** to find oneself; **—se en apuros,** to be in trouble; **—,** *m.* sense of sight, seeing, view; **a mi —,** in my opinion, as it looks to me.
vera, *f.* edge, border.
veracidad, *f.* veracity.
veranda, *f.* veranda, verandah.
veranear, *vn.* to pass the summer season.
veraneo, *m.* summering; **lugar de —,** *m.* summer resort.
verano, *m.* summer.
veras, *f. pl.* truth, sincerity; **de —,** in truth really.
veraz, *adj.* veracious, truthful.
verbal, *adj.* verbal, oral.
verbena, *f.* (bot.) verbena; festival on eve of a saint's day.
verbigracia, *adv.* for example.
verbo, *m.* word, term; (gram.) verb.
verbosidad, *f.* verbosity.
verboso, sa, *adj.* verbose.
verdacho, *m.* green chalk.
verdad, *f.* truth, veracity, reality; certain existence of things; **— de Perogrullo,** truism; **en —,** really, truly.
verdaderamente, *adv.* truly, in fact; indeed.
verdadero, ra, *adj.* true, real; sincere.
verde, *m.* and *adj.* green.
verdear or **verdecer,** *vn.* to grow green.
verdecillo, *m.* greenfinch.
verdegay, *m.* and *adj.* light yellowish green.
verdinegro, gra, *adj.* deep green.
verdolaga, *f.* (bot.) portulaca, purslane.
verdor, *m.* verdure; vigor; youth; green; **—es,** *pl.* age of vigor.
verdoso, sa, *adj.* greenish.
verdugado, *m.* farthingale.
verdugo, *m.* young shoot of a tree; hangman; very cruel person.
verduguillo, *m.* small, narrow razor; rapier.
verdulería, *f.* vegetable stand.
verdulero, *m.* grocer, vegetable man.
verdura, *f.* verdure; vegetables, garden stuff.
vereda, *f.* path, trail; circular order sent to several towns or places.
verga, *f.* (anat.) penis; cord of the crossbow; **— de garra,** topsail mast.
vergel, *m.* flower garden.
vergonzante, *adj.* bashful, shamefaced.
vergonzoso, sa, *adj.* bashful, shy; shameful.
vergüenza, *f.* shame; bashfulness; confusion; **tener —,** to be ashamed.
vericueto, *m.* rough road.
verídico, ca, *adj.* veridical, truthful, worthy of faith.

verificación, *f.* verification.
verificador, *m.* tester, checker.
verificar, *va.* to verify, to check; **—se,** to be verified, to turn out true; to take place.
verificativo, va, *adj.* tending to prove.
verisímil, *adj.* plausible, credible, probable.
verja, *f.* grate, lattice.
vermífugo, *adj.* and *m.* vermifuge.
verminoso, sa, *adj.* verminous, full of grubs.
veronal, *m.* (med.) veronal.
verónica, *f.* (bot.) speedwell; a feat in bullfighting.
verosímil, *adj.* plausible, credible, probable.
verosimilitud, *f.* verisimilitude.
verraco, *m.* boar.
verruga, *f.* wart, pimple; (col.) nuisance.
verrugoso, sa, *adj.* warty.
versado, da, *adj.* versed, skilled, experienced; conversant.
versal, *adj.* and *f.* (print.) capital (of letters).
Versalles, *m.* Versailles.
versar, *vn.* and *vr.* to be versed; to grow skillful; to treat of.
versátil, *adj.* versatile.
versículo, *m.* versicle; verse of a chapter.
versificación, *f.* versification.
versificador, *m.* versifier.
versificar, *va.* and *vn.* to versify.
versión, *f.* translation, version, interpretation.
verso, *m.* verse, stanza; **— blanco,** blank verse; **—s pareados,** doggerel; **— suelto** or **libre,** free verse.
vértebra, *f.* vertebra.
vertebrado, da, *m.* and *adj.* vertebrate.
vertedero, *m.* sewer, drain.
vertedor, ra, *n.* emptier; **—,** *m.* conduit, chute, sewer; (naut.) scoop for bailing boats.
verter, *va.* and *vr.* (IE) to spill, to shed; to empty; to pour; to translate; **—,** *vn.* to flow.
vertical, *adj.* vertical, upright.
vértice, *m.* vertex, zenith; crown of the head.
vertiente, *m.* waterfall, cascade; slope.
vertiginoso, sa, *adj.* giddy; dizzy; very fast.
vértigo, *m.* dizziness, vertigo; giddiness.
Véspero, *m.* Vesper (evening star).
vespertino, na, *adj.* evening.
vestíbulo, *m.* vestibule, lobby.
vestido, *m.* dress, suit of clothes.
vestidura, *f.* dress, wearing apparel; robe of distinction.
vestigio, *m.* vestige, trace; footprint.
vestiglo, *m.* horrid monster.
vestir, *va.* (I) to clothe, to dress; to accouter; to adorn; to cloak, to disguise.
vestuario, *m.* apparel, clothes; uniform; vestry.
Vesuvio, *m.* Vesuvius.
veta, *f.* vein (in mines, wood, etc.); stripe of a different color in cloth.
vet(e)ado, da, *adj.* striped, veined.
veter. veterinario, vet. veterinary.

veterano, na, *adj.* experienced, long practiced; **—,** *m.* veteran, old soldier.
veterinario, *m.* veterinary.
vetusto, ta, *adj.* very ancient.
vez, *f.* turn, time; **a la —,** at the same time; **a la — que,** while; **a veces,** sometimes; **en — de,** instead of; **otra —,** again; **repetidas veces,** again and again; **tal —,** perhaps; **una —,** once.
vg., v.g., or **v. gr. verbigracia,** e.g. for example.
vía, *f.* way, road, route, mode, manner, method; (rail.) railway, railway line; **— aérea,** air mail; **— crucis,** way of the cross; **— transversal,** crossroad.
viabilidad, *f.* viability.
viaducto, *m.* viaduct, underpass.
viajante, *adj.* excursive; traveling; **—,** *m.* traveling salesman.
viajar, *vn.* to travel.
viaje, *m.* journey, voyage, travel; **— sencillo,** one-way trip; **— redondo** or **de ida y vuelta,** round trip.
viajero, ra, *n.* traveler.
vial, *m.*, tree-lined street.
vialidad, *f.* system of public roads.
viandas, *f. pl.* food, victuals.
viático, *m.* viaticum; traveling expenses.
víbora, *f.* viper.
viborezno, *m.* young viper.
vibración, *f.* vibration.
vibrador, *m.* vibrator.
vibrante, *adj.* vibrating, vibrant.
vibrar, *va.* to vibrate, to brandish; to throw, to dart; **—,** *vn.* to vibrate.
vicaría, *f.* vicarship, vicarage.
vicariato, *m.* vicarage.
vicario, *m.* vicar; **—, ria,** *adj.* vicarial.
vicealmiranta, *f.* the galley next in order to that of the admiral.
vicealmirante, *m.* vice-admiral.
vicecanciller, *m.* vice chancellor.
vicecónsul, *m.* vice-consul.
viceconsulado, *m.* vice-consulate.
vicegobernador, *m.* lieutenant governor.
Vicente, Vincent.
vicepresidente, *m.* vice-president, vice-chairman.
viceversa, *adj.* vice versa; **—,** *m.* illogical statement, ambiguous statement.
viciar, *vn.* to vitiate, to corrupt; to annul; to deprave; **—se,** to become vitiated; to give oneself up to vice.
vicio, *m.* vice, folly.
vicioso, sa, *adj.* vicious, bad.
vicisitud, *f.* vicissitude.
Vict.ᵃ Victoria, Victoria.
Vic.ᵗᵉ Vicente, Vincent.
víctima, *f.* victim; sacrifice; **—s,** *pl.* casualties.
víctor, *m.* shout, acclamation; **¡—!** *interj.* long live!
victorear, *va.* to shout, to cheer.
victoria, *f.* victory.
victorioso, sa, *adj.* victorious.

victrola, *f.* victroia (trade name).
vid, *f.* (bot.) vine.
vida, *f.* life; **en su —,** never; **¡por —!** my word!
vidriado, da, *adj.* glazed; **—,** *m.* glazed earthenware, crockery.
vidriar, *va.* to glaze earthenware.
vidriera, *f.* glass case; shopwindow.
vidriería, *f.* glazier's shop; glass house.
vidriero, *m.* glazier.
vidrio, *m.* glass; **— cilindrado,** plate glass; **— inastillable,** nonshatter glass; **— soluble,** water glass.
vidrioso, sa, *adj.* glassy, brittle; slippery; very delicate.
viejo, ja, *adj.* old; ancient, antiquated.
Viena, *f.* Vienna.
vienés, esa, *adj.* and *n.* Viennese.
viento, *m.* wind; air; **hace —,** it is windy.
vientre, *m.* belly.
vier. viernes, Fri. Friday.
viernes, *m.* Friday; **V— Santo,** Good Friday.
viga, *f.* beam (large and long piece of timber); **— transversal,** crossbeam.
vigente, *adj.* in force.
vigésimo, ma, *adj.* twentieth.
vigía, *f.* watchtower; watch, watching; (naut.) shoal, rock; **—,** *m.* lookout, watch.
vigilancia, *f.* vigilance, watchfulness, care.
vigilante, *adj.* watchful, vigilant; **—,** *m.* guard.
vigilar, *va.* and *vn.* to watch over.
vigilia, *f.* nocturnal study; vigil; watch; fast; eve.
vigor, *m.* vigor, strength.
vigorización, *f.* invigoration; strengthening.
vigorizar, *va.* to energize.
vigoroso, sa, *adj.* vigorous, hardy.
vihuela, *f.* guitar.
vihuelista, *m.* and *f.* guitar player.
vil, *adj.* mean, sordid, low; worthless; infamous; ungrateful.
vileza, *f.* meanness, lowness; abjectness.
vilipendiar, *va.* to contemn, to revile.
vilipendio, *m.* contempt, disdain.
vilmente, *adv.* vilely; abjectly.
vilorta, *f.* ring made of twisted willow; cricket (in Old Castile).
villa, *f.* town.
Villadiego, *m.* **tomar las de —,** to run away, to sneak out.
villancico, *m.* Christmas carol.
villanesco, ca, *adj.* rustic.
villanía, *f.* lowness of birth; villainy; indecorous word or act.
villano, na, *adj.* rustic, boorish; villainous; **—,** *m.* villain; rustic.
villorrio, *m.* miserable little hamlet.
vinagre, *m.* vinegar.
vinagrera, *f.* bottle for vinegar.
vinagrero, *m.* vinegar merchant.
vinajera, *f.* wine vessel for the mass.
vinariego, *m.* vintager.
vinatería, *f.* wine trade.

vinatero, *m.* vintner, wine merchant.
vinculable, *adj.* that may be entailed.
vinculación, *f.* (law) entail.
vincular, *va.* to entail an estate; to perpetuate; to link.
vínculo, *m.* tie, link, bond, chain; entail.
vincha, *f.* (Sp. Am.) ribbon tied around the head.
vindicación, *f.* vindication, revenge.
vindicar, *va.* to vindicate; to avenge.
vindicativo, va, *adj.* vindictive.
vindicta, *f.* vengeance.
vino, *m.* wine; **— tinto,** red wine.
vinolento, ta, *adj.* excessively fond of wine.
vinoso, sa, *adj.* vinous, vinose.
v. intr. verbo intransitivo, v.i. intransitive verb.
viña, *f.* vineyard; grapevine.
viñador, *m.* keeper of a vineyard.
viñedo, *m.* vineyard.
viñero, *m.* keeper of a vineyard, viticulturist.
viñeta, *f.* (print.) headpiece; vignette.
viola, *f.* (mus.) viola; (bot.) violet.
violáceo, cea, *adj.* violet-colored.
violación, *f.* violation.
violado, da, *adj.* violet-colored; violated.
violador, ra, *n.* violator; profaner.
violar, *va.* to violate; to ravish; to profane a church.
violencia, *f.* violence.
violentar, *va.* to enforce by violent means.
violento, ta, *adj.* violent, forced; absurd.
violeta, *f.* (bot.) violet; **—,** *adj.* violet (color).
violín, *m.* violin, fiddle.
violinista, *m.* and *f.* violinist.
violón, *m.* bass viol.
violoncelo, *m.* violoncello.
viperino, na, *adj.* viperine.
vira, *f.* welt of a shoe.
virada, *f.* (naut.) tacking.
virago, *f.* virago, quarrelsome woman.
virar, *va.* to tack; **—,** *vn.* (coll.) to turn back.
virgen, *adj.* and *f.* virgin.
Virgilio, Virgil.
virginal, *adj.* virginal.
virginidad, *f.* virginity, maidenhood.
Virgo, *m.* Virgo (sign of the zodiac).
virgulilla, *f.* stroke or line, such as a comma or an accent mark.
viril, *m.* clear and transparent glass; monstrance; **—,** *adj.* virile, manly.
virilidad, *f.* virility, manhood; vigor.
virolento, ta, *adj.* diseased with smallpox; pitted from smallpox.
virote, *m.* dart, arrow; showy, vain loiterer; conceited person.
virreinato, *m.* viceroyship.
virrey, *m.* viceroy.
virtud, *f.* virtue; efficacy; vigor, courage; **—es,** *pl.* the fifth of the nine celestial choirs.
virtuosidad, *f.* virtuosity.
virtuoso, sa, *adj.* virtuous.
viruela, *f.* smallpox; **—as locas,** chicken pox.

virulencia, *f.* virulence.
virulento, ta, *adj.* virulent.
viruta, *f.* wood or metal cuttings; **—s,** *pl.* shavings.
visa, *f.* visa.
visaje, *m.* grimace; visage.
visar, *va.* to countersign; to visa a passport.
víscera, *f.* internal organ; **—s,** *f. pl.* viscera.
viscosidad, *f.* viscosity.
viscoso, sa, *adj.* viscous, glutinous, viscid.
visera, *f.* visor, eyeshade.
visible, *adj.* visible; apparent.
visillo, *m.* window shade.
visión, *f.* sight, vision; frightful, ugly or ridiculous person; phantom.
visionario, ria, *adj.* visionary.
visir, *m.* vizier.
visita, *f.* visit; visitor, guest; **hacer —s,** to pay visits; **— de cumplimento,** formal call.
visitación, *f.* visitation.
visitador, ra, *n.* visitor; surveyor.
visitante, *m.* and *f.* visitor.
visitar, *va.* to visit; **—se,** to be on visiting terms, to visit.
vislumbrar, *va.* to catch a glimpse; to perceive indistinctly; to know imperfectly, to conjecture.
vislumbre, *f.* glimmering light, conjecture; imperfect knowledge; slight resemblance.
viso, *m.* prospect; luster; pretext; apparent likeness.
víspera, *f.* evening before; day before; **—s,** *pl.* vespers.
vista, *f.* sight, view, vista; seeing; vision; eye; eyesight; glance; appearance; purpose; judgment; (law) trial; **— de pájaro,** bird's-eye view; **— de un pleito,** day of trial; **a la —,** on sight; **a primera —,** at first sight; **corto de —,** short-sighted; **echar una —,** to look after; **en — de,** in view of, considering; **hasta la —,** good-by; **—s,** *pl.* prenuptial gifts exchanged by bride and groom.
vistaria, *f.* (bot.) wisteria.
vistazo, *m.* glance.
vistillas, *f. pl.* height affording an extensive prospect.
visto, *adj.* obvious; **— que,** considering that; **por lo —,** apparently; **— bueno,** O.K., all right, correct.
vistoso, sa, *adj.* beautiful, showy.
visual, *adj.* visual, pertaining to the sight.
visualización, *f.* visualization.
vital, *adj.* vital, essential.
vitalicio, cia, *adj.* during life; **—,** *m.* life insurance policy.
vitalidad, *f.* vitality.
vitalismo, *m.* vitalism.
vitamina, *f.* vitamin.
vitela, *f.* calf; vellum, calfskin.
viticultura, *f.* viticulture, husbandry of vineyards.
¡vítor! *interj.* long life!
vitorear, *va.* to cheer, to applaud.

vitrina, *f.* showcase.
vitriolo, *m.* vitriol.
vitualla, *f.* victuals.
vituperable, *adj.* blamable.
vituperación, *f.* blame.
vituperador, ra, *n.* blamer.
vituperar, *va.* to blame.
vituperio, *m.* blame; infamy.
viuda, *f.* widow; dowager.
viudedad, *f.* widow's pension.
viudez, *f.* widowhood.
viudo, *m.* widower; **—, da,** *adj.* applied to the remaining bird when one of a pair dies.
¡viva! *interj.* hurrah! hail!
vivacidad, *f.* vivacity, liveliness.
vivamente, *adv.* vividly; deeply.
vivandero, *m.* (mil.) sutler.
vivaque or **vivac,** *m.* (mil.) bivouac.
vivaquear, *vn.* (mil.) to bivouac.
vivar, *m.* warren; vivary.
vivaracho, cha, *adj.* lively, smart, sprightly.
vivera, *f.,* **vivero,** *m.* warren; fishpond; vivary; (bot.) nursery.
víveres, *m. pl.* provisions.
viveza, *f.* liveliness, vehemence; perspicacity.
vividero, ra, *adj.* habitable.
vividor, ra, *adj.* thrifty; **—,** *n.* one who likes to impose on others, sponger.
vivienda, *f.* dwelling house.
viviente, *adj.* alive, living.
vivificación, *f.* vivification.
vivificador, ra, *n.* one who vivifies, animates or enlivens; **—,** *adj.* vivifying, animating.
vivificar, *va.* to vivify, to enliven.
vivificativo, va, *adj.* animating, comforting.
vivíparo, ra, *adj.* viviparous.
vivir, *vn.* to live; to last.
vivisección, *f.* vivisection.
vivo, va, *adj.* living; lively; ingenious, bright; **a lo —vo** or **al —vo,** vivid, naturalistic.
vizcaíno, na, *adj.* and *n.* Biscayan; **bacalao a la —na,** codfish Biscayan style.
vizcondado, *m.* viscountship.
vizconde, *m.* viscount.
vizcondesa, *f.* viscountess.
V. M. Vuestra Majestad, Your Majesty.
v.n. verbo neutro, vn. verb neuter.
V.º B.º visto bueno, O.K. all correct.
vocablo, *m.* word, term, diction.
vocabulario, *m.* vocabulary; dictionary.
vocación, *f.* vocation, calling.
vocal, *f.* vowel; **—,** *m.* member of a board of directors; **—,** *adj.* vocal, oral.
vocalización, *f.* (mus.) vocalization.
vocativo, *m.* (gram.) vocative.
voceador, *m.* vociferator; town crier.
vocear, *vn.* to cry, to scream, to bawl, to shriek.
vocería, *f.* clamor, outcry.
vociferación, *f.* vociferation; praise.
vociferador, ra, *n.* boaster, bragger.
vociferar, *vn.* to bawl, to proclaim in a loud voice.
vocinglería, *f.* clamor, outcry; loquacity.

vocinglero, ra, *adj.* brawling, prattling, noisy.

vodca, *f.* vodka.

vol.: volumen, vol. volume; **voluntad,** will; (com.) good will.

volador, ra, *adj.* flying; running fast; —, *m.* flying fish; rocket.

voladura, *f.* blast, explosion.

volandas, en —, *adv.* in the air; rapidly, as if flying.

volandera, *f.* runner (in oil mills); movable ledge on a type galley; (coll.) lie.

volandero, ra, *adj.* volatile; casual; unsettled.

volandillas, en —, *adv.* in the air; rapidly, as if flying.

volante, *adj.* flying; unsettled; —, *m.* screen; shuttlecock; servant, footman; steering wheel, flywheel; flier, note, memorandum; ruffle.

volantín, *m.* fishing apparatus.

volar, *vn.* (UE) to fly; to pass or to move swiftly; to execute with great promptitude and facility; —, *va.* to rouse game; to blow up, to discharge a mine; to irritate.

volatería, *f.* fowling; fowls; **de —,** incidentally; at random.

volátil, *adj.* volatile; flying.

volatilizar, *va.* to volatilize.

volatín, *m.* ropewalker, acrobat.

volatinero, ra, *n.* ropewalker, acrobat.

volcán, *m.* volcano.

volcánico, ca, *adj.* volcanic.

volcar, *va.* and *vr.* (UE) to upset; to turn up; to make giddy; to tire out one's patience.

volea, *f.* singletree, whippletree.

voleador, *m.* batter (in baseball).

volear, *vn.* to throw up in the air; —, *va.* to bat (in baseball).

voleo, *m.* volley; step in a Spanish dance.

volframio, *m.* wolfram, tungsten.

voltaico, ca, *adj.* voltaic.

voltaje, *m.* (elec.) voltage, tension.

voltámetro, *m.* voltameter.

voltamperio, *m.* volt-ampere.

volteador, ra, *n.* tumbler, acrobat.

voltear, *va.* to whirl, to overset; —, *vn.* to tumble.

volteo, *m.* whirl; overturning; **caja de —,** dump body of a truck.

voltereta or **volteta,** *f.* light tumble in the air, handspring; turning up of a trump (in cards).

voltímetro, *m.* voltmeter.

voltio, *m.* (elec.) volt.

volubilidad, *f.* volubility.

voluble, *adj.* inconstant, fickle.

volumen, *m.* volume; size.

voluminoso, sa, *adj.* voluminous.

voluntad, *f.* will; (com.) good will.

voluntariamente, *adv.* willingly, voluntarily.

voluntario, ria, *adj.* voluntary; —, *m.* volunteer.

voluntarioso, sa, *adj.* willful.

voluptuoso, sa, *adj.* voluptuous.

voluta, *f.* scroll, volute.

volver, *va.* and *vn.* (UE) to return; to restore, to repay; to turn; to send back a present; to change a thing from one place to another; **— en sí,** to recover one's senses; **— la cara,** to face about; **—se,** to turn sour; to turn towards; to retract an opinion.

vómica, *f.* (med.) vomica.

vomitar, *va.* to vomit.

vomitivo, va, *adj.* and *m.* emetic.

vómito, *m.* vomiting.

vomitón, ona, *adj.* often throwing up milk from the stomach (of a sucking child).

vomitona, *f.* violent vomiting after eating heartily.

voracidad, *f.* voracity.

vorágine, *f.* vortex, whirlpool.

voraz, *adj.* voracious, greedy.

vorazmente, *adv.* voraciously, greedily.

vórtice, *m.* vortex, whirlpool.

vos, *pron.* you, ye.

vosotros, tras, *pron. pl.* you, ye.

votación, *f.* voting.

votador, ra, *n.* vower; voter.

votar, *va.* and *vn.* to vow; to vote.

votivo, va, *adj.* votive.

voto, *m.* vow; vote; opinion, advice; wish; supplication to God; execration.

voz, *f.* voice; outcry; word, term.

V.P. Vicepresidente, Vice Pres. Vice-President.

V.R. Vuestra Reverencia, Your Reverence.

vra., vro. vuestra, vuestro, your, yours (*sing.*).

vras., vros. vuestras, vuestros, your, yours (*pl.*).

vs. or **v.**[s] **varas,** variable unit of length, (*pl.*) about 2.8 feet.

vta. or **v.**[ta]**: vuelta,** turn, over, change; **vista,** sight.

v. tr. verbo transitivo, v.t. transitive verb.

Vuecelencia, *f.* contraction of **Vuestra Excelencia,** Your Excellency.

vuelco, *m.* overturning, spill.

vuelo, *m.* flight; wing; part of a building which projects beyond the wall; width of clothes; ruffle, frill; space flown through at once; loftiness of thought or speech; **a —, al —,** flying, expeditiously.

vuelta, *f.* turn; circuit; detour; return; petition; ruffle; excursion; **a — de correo,** by return mail; **viaje de —,** return trip.

Vuesamerced, *f.* Your Worship, Your Honor (contraction of **Vuestra Merced**).

Vueseñoría, *f.* My Lady (contraction of **Vuestra Señoría**).

vuestro, tra, *pron.* your, yours.

vulcanización, *f.* vulcanization.

vulcanizado, *m.* and *adj.* vulcanizing, vulcanized.

vulcanizar, *va.* to vulcanize.

vulgacho, *m.* mob, populace.

vulgar, *adj.* vulgar, common, ordinary.

vulgaridad, *f.* vulgarity; vulgarism.
vulgata, *f.* Vulgate (applied to the Bible).
vulgo, *m.* populace, mob.
vulneración, *f.* act of wounding.
vulnerar, *va.* to injure the character or reputation.
vulva, *f.* (anat.) vulva.
VV or V.V. ustedes, you (*pl.*).

W

whiskey, *m.* whiskey.

X

xenofobia, *f.* hatred of foreigners.
xenon, *m.* (chem.) xenon.
xilófono, *m.* (mus.) xylophone.
X.^{mo} **diezmo,** tenth.

Y

y, *conj.* and.
ya, *adv.* already; presently; immediately; finally; **— no,** no longer; **— que,** since, seeing that; **¡—!** *interj.* oh, yes, I see!
yacer, *vn.* (YAGO, YAZGO or YAZCO, YACÍ) to lie, to lie down.
yacimiento, *m.* (geol.) bed; ore deposit.
yanqui, *adj.* and *n.* Yankee.
yarda, *f.* yard (measure).
yate, *m.* yacht.
yámbico, ca, *adj.* iambic.
yambo, *m.* iambic foot (in poetry).
ye, *f.* name of letter *y*.
yedra, *f.* ivy; **— terrestre,** ground ivy.
yegua, *f.* mare.
yeguada, *f.* stud (horses).
yeguar, *adj.* belonging to a mare.
yegüero, *m.* keeper of breeding mares.
yelmo, *m.* helmet.
yema, *f.* bud, gem; yolk; **— del dedo,** tip of the finger; **— mejida,** eggnog.
yerba, *f.* herb; grass; **— buena,** mint; **— mate,** Paraguay tea; **—s,** *pl.* greens, vegetables.
yermar, *va.* to depopulate, to lay waste.
yermo, *m.* desert, wilderness; **—, ma,** *adj.* waste, desert.
yerno, *m.* son-in-law.
yerro, *m.* error, mistake, fault.
yerto, ta, *adj.* stiff, inflexible; rigid; cold.
yesar, *m.* gypsum pit.
yesca, *f.* spunk, tinder.
yesera, *f.* kiln where gypsum is calcined.
yesería, *f.* building constructed with gypsum.
yesero, *m.* preparer or seller of gypsum; plasterer.
yeso, *m.* gypsum; plaster, plaster cast; **— mate,** plaster of Paris.
yesón, *m.* fragment of gypsum already used in building.
yesquero, *m.* tinder maker or seller, tinder box.

yo, *pron.* I; **— mismo,** I myself.
yodo, *m.* iodine.
yoquey, *m.* jockey.
yubarta, *f.* finback.
yuca, *f.* (bot.) yucca.
yugada, *f.* yoke of land.
yugo, *m.* yoke.
yugular, *adj.* jugular; **vena —,** jugular vein.
yunque, *m.* anvil; person that is patient in adversity.
yunta, *f.* couple, pair, yoke.
yusera, *f.* bedder, under millstone in oil mills.
yute, *m.* jute (fiber).
yuxtalineal, *adj.* arranged in parallel columns or lines.
yuxtaponer, *va.* (YUXTAPONGO, YUXTAPUSE) to juxtapose.
yuxtaposición, *f.* juxtaposition.

Z

zabordar, *vn.* (naut.) to get ashore, to be stranded.
zabullirse, *vr.* = **zambullirse.**
Zacarías, Zachary, Zachariah.
zacate, *m.* (Mex.) hay, grass.
zacatín, *m.* clothes market.
zafar, *va.* to adorn, to embellish; to lighten a ship; **—se,** to escape; to avoid; to free oneself from trouble.
zafarrancho, *m.* (naut.) clearing for action; (coll.) wrangle, scuffle; **hacer —,** (naut.) to clear.
zafiedad, *f.* boorishness, rusticity, awkwardness.
zafones, *m. pl.* overalls.
zafio, fia, *adj.* boorish, coarse.
zafir or zafiro, *m.* sapphire (jewel).
zafra, *f.* sugar crop, sugar making.
zaga, *f.* load packed at the back of a carriage; rear part; **—,** *m.* last player in a game of cards; **no quedarse en —,** not to be left behind.
zagal, *m.* outrider; swain, boy; shepherd.
zagala, *f.* shepherdess; lass, girl.
zagalejo, *m.* young shepherd; underskirt.
zaguán, *m.* porch; hall, vestibule.
zaheridor, ra, *n.* censurer.
zaherimiento, *m.* censure, blame.
zaherir, *va.* (IE) to reproach; to upbraid.
zahones, *m. pl.* overalls.
zahorí, *m.* cheap impostor pretending to see hidden things.
zahurda, *f.* hogsty; dirty hole.
zaino, na, *adj.* chestnut (color); vicious (applied to animals); treacherous, wicked; **mirar de or a lo —no,** to look sideways.
zalagarda, *f.* ambuscade, ambush; trap, snare; surprise; vulgar noise.
zalamería, *f.* flattery.
zalamero, ra, *n.* wheedler, flatterer.
zalea, *f.* undressed sheepskin.

zamarra, *f.* dress made of undressed sheepskins.

zamarro, *m.* shepherd's coat made of sheepskins; sheep or lambskin; stupid person.

zambo, ba, *adj.* bowlegged; **—,** *n.* sambo or zambo, in Spanish America a person of mixed Indian and Negro blood.

zambomba, *f.* rural drum.

zambombo, *m.* clown, lubber.

zambucar, *va.* to hide (a thing).

zambullida, *f.* dipping, submersion.

zambullirse, *vr.* (ZAMBULLÓ, ZAMBULLENDO) to plunge into water, to dive.

zampar, *va.* to conceal, to hide; to devour eagerly; **—se,** to thrust oneself suddenly into any place.

zampear, *va.* to stake, to prop.

zampoña, *f.* rustic flute.

zampuzar, *va.* to plunge, to dive; to conceal or hide (a thing).

zampuzo, *m.* submersion.

zanahoria, *f.* carrot.

zanca, *f.* shank of a fowl; long shank.

zancada, *f.* stride, long step, long stride.

zancadilla, *f.* trick, deceit.

zancajo, *m.* heel bone.

zancajoso, sa, *adj.* bowlegged; wearing stockings torn at the heels.

zancarrón, *m.* heel bone; thin, old, dirty man.

zanco, *m.* stilt.

zancudo, da, *adj.* long-shanked; wading (bird); **—,** *m.* (Sp. Am.) mosquito.

zanfonía, *f.* hurdy-gurdy.

zanganear, *vn.* to live in idleness.

zángano, *m.* drone; idler, sponger.

zanja, *f.* ditch, trench.

zanjar, *va.* to dig ditches in; to lay a foundation.

zanquear, *vn.* to waddle, to walk much and fast.

zapa, *f.* spade; **caminar a la —,** (mil.) to advance by sap or mine.

zapador, *m.* (mil.) sapper.

zapallo, *m.* (Sp. Am.) calabash; squash.

zapapico, *m.* pickax.

zapar, *vn.* to sap, to mine.

zaparrastrar, *vn.* to trail, to drag along on the ground.

zaparrastroso, sa, *adj.* dirty from trailing along on the ground.

zaparrazo, *m.* violent fall, attended with great noise; sudden calamity.

zapata, *f.* piece of sole leather put on the hinge of a door to prevent its creaking.

zapatazo, *m.* blow with a shoe.

zapatear, *va.* and *vn.* to strike with the shoe; to beat time with the sole of the shoe; **—se,** to resist in debating.

zapatería, *f.* trade of a shoemaker; shoemaker's shop; shoe store.

zapatero, *m.* shoemaker; **— de viejo,** cobbler.

zapatilla, *f.* pump (shoe), slipper; piece of chamois put behind the lock of a gun or pistol.

zapatillero, *m.* shoemaker who makes pumps and children's shoes.

zapato, *m.* shoe; **—s de goma,** rubbers.

¡zape! *interj.* scat!

zapote, *m.* (bot.) sapota (tropical fruit).

zaque, *m.* wine bag; tippler.

zar, *m.* czar.

zarabanda, *f.* saraband (dance); bustle, noise.

zaragalla, *f.* charcoal; boy's gang.

zaragata, *f.* (coll.) turmoil, mixup; quarrel.

zaragüelles, *m. pl.* wide breeches; overalls.

zaramullo, *m.* crafty swindler; upstart.

zaranda, *f.* frame for sifting sand.

zarandajas, *f. pl.* trifles.

zarandar or **zarandear,** *va.* to winnow (grain); **—se,** to move to and fro, to strut.

zarandillo, *m.* frisker; small sieve.

zaratán, *m.* cancer in the breast.

zaraza, *f.* chintz; printed cotton, gingham.

zarcillo, *m.* earring; tendril.

zarigüeya, *f.* opossum.

zarja, *f.* reel (for winding raw silk).

zarpa, *f.* claw.

zarpar, *vn.* to weigh anchor; to sail (away).

zarpazo, *m.* sound or thud of a body falling on the ground; stroke with a paw.

zarza, *f.* bramble.

zarzal, *m.* brambles; brambly place.

zarzamora, *f.* brambleberry; blackberry bush.

zarzaparrilla, *f.* (bot.) sarsaparilla.

zarzo, *m.* hurdle.

zarzoso, sa, *adj.* brambly.

zarzuela, *f.* variety of operetta, musical comedy, musical drama; **— cómica,** comic operetta.

¡zas, zas! *interj.* slap, slap! (sound of a slap, tick).

zascandil, *m.* crafty swindler; upstart.

zatara, *f.* raft.

zepelín, *m.* (aer.) Zeppelin, dirigible.

zeta, *f.* name of letter z.

zigzag, *m.* zigzag.

zinia, *f.* (bot.) zinnia.

¡zis, zas! *interj.* slap, slap! (sound of a slap, tick).

zócalo, *m.* (arch.) socle.

zoclo, *m.* wooden shoe; galosh.

zodíaco, *m.* zodiac.

zona, *f.* zone, district; **— de marcha lenta,** slow-driving zone; **— de peligro,** danger zone; **— de tránsito,** traffic lane.

zonzo, za, *adj.* insipid, tasteless; dull, stupid; **—,** *n.* simpleton; stupid person.

zoología, *f.* zoology.

zoológico, ca, *adj.* zoological.

zopenco, ca, *adj.* doltish, very stupid.

zopo, pa, *adj.* lame, maimed; **—,** *n.* cripple.

zoquete, *m.* block; morsel of bread; (coll.) blockhead, numbskull.

zorra, *f.* fox; (coll.) prostitute, strumpet.

W
X
Y
Z

zorrera, *f.* fox hole.

zorrería, *f.* cunning of a fox; cunning, craft.

zorrillo, *m.* skunk.

zorro, *m.* male fox; cunning fellow.

zorruno, na, *adj.* foxy.

zorzal, *m.* (orn.) thrush.

zote, *m.* stupid, lazy person.

zozobra, *f.* uneasiness, anxiety, anguish.

zozobrar, *vn.* to be weather-beaten; to be in great danger; to be afflicted; (naut.) to founder.

zozobroso, sa, *adj.* anxious, restless.

zuavo, *m.* (mil.) zouave.

zueco, *m.* wooden shoe; galosh.

zumacar, *va.* to tan with sumach.

zumaque, *m.* sumach tree.

zumba, *f.* large bell worn by head mule of a drove; joke, jest; (Sp. Am.) flogging.

zumbador, *m.* buzzer.

zumbar, *vn.* to resound, to hum; to buzz; to ring (the ears); to jest, to joke.

zumbido, *m.* humming, buzzing sound; — **telefónico,** telephone buzzer.

zumbón, ona, *adj.* waggish.

zumo, *m.* sap, juice; — **de cepas** or **parras,** juice of the grape, wine.

zumoso, sa, *adj.* juicy, succulent.

zupia, *f.* wine which is turned; liquor with a bad taste; refuse.

zurcidura, *f.* finedrawing; darning.

zurcir, *va.* to darn, to finedraw; to join, to unite; to hatch lies.

zurdo, da, *adj.* left; left-handed.

zurra, *f.* currying leathers; flogging, drubbing; drudgery.

zurrador, *m.* leather dresser, currier.

zurrapa, *f.* lees, dregs; anything vile or despicable.

zurraposo, sa, *adj.* full of lees and dregs.

zurrar, *va.* to curry, to dress leather; to chastise with a whip; —**se,** to have a sudden and involuntary evacuation of the bowels; to dirty oneself.

zurriaga, *f.* thong; string for tops.

zurriagar, *va.* to flog, to whip.

zurriagazo, *m.* severe lash with a whip; unfortunate calamity.

zurriago, *m.* whip for inflicting punishment.

zurrido, *m.* humming, buzzing; confused noise.

zurrir, *vn.* to hum, to buzz, to tinkle.

zurrón, *m.* shepherd's pouch; husks of grain.

zurrusco, *m.* (coll.) burnt toast; cold, penetrating wind.

zurumbático, ca, *adj.* stunned.

zutano, na, *n.* such a one; — **y fulano,** such and such a one, so and so.

EL FOLLETT
SPANISH DICTIONARY

INGLÉS-ESPAÑOL
y
ESPAÑOL-INGLÉS

por

JOSEPH G. FUCILLA

Profesor de Idiomas Neolatinos de la
Universidad Northwestern, Evanston, Illinois
E.U.A.

FOURTH PRINTING

FOLLETT PUBLISHING COMPANY

CHICAGO · 1948 · ILLINOIS

PART II

INGLÉS - ESPAÑOL

❧

ENGLISH - SPANISH

PREFACIO

Se ha preparado este libro para responder a la creciente demanda de un diccionario completamente moderno de español e inglés de precio popular. Por varios años se ha advertido un constante aumento de las relaciones de buena vecindad entre los pueblos de hablas española e inglesa de Norte y Sud América. Esto ha determinado en los Estados Unidos un desarrollo tremendo del interés por el idioma de la América Hispana. Y también ha estimulado entre los hispanoamericanos similar interés por la lengua de los Estados Unidos.

Este progreso merece por muchas razones que se lo fomente, y el poner a disposición del nuevo interés en estos dos idiomas las herramientas adecuadas para dominarlos es una forma de conseguirlo. Entre las herramientas para dominar un idioma, pocas son más útiles que un buen diccionario bilingüe. Al decir un "buen" diccionario, nos referimos al que suministre traducciones exactas de todas las palabras y expresiones de ambos idiomas que la gente necesite conocer para leer y hablar dichos idiomas eficazmente.

Tal es el tipo de herramienta práctica que se ha querido que este libro sea. Un diccionario manual no puede, naturalmente, comprender un vocabulario completo en ninguno de los dos idiomas, y no se ofrece al estudiante avanzado como equivalente, en la extensión de su lista de palabras, de obras más extensas y más costosas de su índole, tales como el *Diccionario Español de Velázquez* de Follett. Sin embargo, creemos que en este diccionario se hallarán, dentro de los fines comunes, prácticamente cuanta palabra y cuanta expresión puedan necesitarse para un eficaz dominio de ambos idiomas. Se ha preparado con la aspiración de que sea tan útil para el estudiante de habla española que aprende inglés, como para el de habla inglesa que aprende español.

En ambas secciones del libro se ha dado atención máxima a las necesidades de quien lo consulte. Entre las necesidades que constantemente hemos tenido presentes se cuentan:

1. Todas las palabras y expresiones de uso corriente, inclusive el vocabulario necesario para leer periódicos modernos y sostener correspondencia comercial.

2. Un vocabulario técnico adecuado para uso de personas de actividades más especializadas en campos tales como ciencias, ingeniería, arte, comercio, deportes, etc.

3. Traducciones exactas a términos equivalentes o (en casos en que no existan éstos) definiciones claras en la forma más breve posible.

4. Información suficiente sobre cada vocablo tal como parte de la oración, género, número, inflexión, uso, etc., para que haya seguridad de su correcto empleo.

5. Una sola lista de todas las palabras para cada una de las dos partes del diccionario, con lo que se ahorran tiempo y molestias al tener que consultar listas separadas de nombres propios, abreviaturas, modismos, etc.

6. Un tipo claro y grande que hace del uso continuado del diccionario un placer más que un esfuerzo.

Se ha prestado atención especial a la inclusión de palabras nuevas, muchas de ellas de origen demasiado reciente para encontrarse en diccionarios publicados antes de que estallara la segunda guerra mundial. Entre los centenares de neologismos incluídos en el libro se cuentan **radar, electronics, gremlin, air-raid warden, flak, strafe, blood plasma,** y muchos otros de carácter técnico, científico y militar.

Para dar cabida a gran cantidad de palabras adicionales se obtuvo el necesario espacio prescindiendo de dar la pronunciación. Cuando se trata de palabras españolas la pronunciación no ofrece problema alguno para quien se tome la molestia de consultar — o mejor aún, de aprender — las contadas y sencillas reglas de pronunciación que aparecen al principio de la sección española. En el caso de las inglesas, los profesores de idiomas generalmente convienen en que no es posible dar una pronunciación correcta sin el uso de un tercer idioma en forma de un complicado sistema de símbolos fonéticos. La experiencia derivada de diccionarios de inglés-español que utilizan tales sistemas de pronunciación ha demostrado que no son lo suficientemente útiles en una obra de esta índole para que se justifique su inclusión. El espacio ahorrado ha permitido emplear un tipo mayor de letra y añadir varios centenares de palabras.

Entre otras características peculiares de este diccionario pueden mencionarse: (1) gran número de modismos, catalogados según la palabra principal; (2) indicación del género de los sustantivos españoles en *ambas* secciones, con lo que se evita tener que pasar de la sección inglesa a la española en busca de esta información esencial.

Merecen reconocimiento por su ilustrada ayuda en la preparación de esta obra don GRACIANO SALVADOR, profesor de idiomas de la Universidad de Loyola (Chicago), y doña IDA NAVARRO DE HINOJOSA, ex profesora de la Escuela Normal de Panamá y ex traductora de inglés-español de *Rotary International*. El escrupuloso cuidado de la Sra. de Hinojosa al revisar tres veces cada uno de los vocablos del diccionario ha contribuído en gran parte a la excelencia que la obra tenga.

JOSEPH G. FUCILLA.

v

ABREVIATURAS

Abbreviations used in this dictionary.—Abreviaturas usadas en este diccionario.

adj.	adjective, *adjetivo*	Mex.	Mexico, *Méjico*
adv.	adverb, *adverbio*	mil.	military art, *milicia*
aer.	aeronautics, *aeronáutica*	min.	mining, *minería*
agr.	agriculture, *agricultura*	mus.	music, *música*
anat.	anatomy, *anatomía*	*n.*	noun, *sustantivo*
arch.	architecture, *arquitectura*	naut.	nautical, *náutico* or *marino*
Arg.	Argentina, *Argentina*		
art.	article, *artículo*	orn.	ornithology, *ornitología*
ast.	astronomy, *astronomía*	phot.	photography, *fotografía*
auto.	automobile, *automóvil*	phy.	physics, *física*
biol.	biology, *biología*	*pl.*	plural, *plural*
Bol.	Bolivia, *Bolivia*	poet.	poetry, *poética*
bot.	botany, *botánica*	pol.	politics, *política*
chem.	chemistry, *química*	*p.p.*	past participle, *participio pasado*
Col.	Colombia, *Colombia*		
coll.	colloquial, *familiar*	P. R.	Puerto Rico, *Puerto Rico*
com.	commerce, *comercio*	*prep.*	preposition, *preposición*
conj.	conjunction, *conjunción*	print.	printing, *imprenta*
def.	defective, *defectivo*	*pron.*	pronoun, *pronombre*
dent.	dentistry, *dentistería*	rad.	radio, *radiocomunicación*
eccl.	ecclesiastic, *eclesiástico*	rail.	railway, *ferrocarril*
Ecu.	Ecuador, *Ecuador*	rhet.	rhetoric, *retórica*
elec.	electricity, *electricidad*	*sing.*	singular, *singular*
ent.	entomology, *entomología*	Sp. Am.	Spanish America, *Hispanoamérica*
f.	feminine, *femenino*		
fig.	figurative(ly), *figurado*	theat.	theater, *teatro*
geog.	geography, *geografía*	*v.*	verb, *verbo*
geol.	geology, *geología*	va.	transitive verb, *verbo activo*
gram.	grammar, *gramática*		
imp.	impersonal, *ĭmpersonal*	Ven.	Venezuela, *Venezuela*
interj.	interjection, *interjección*	vet.	veterinary, *veterinaria*
interr.	interrogative, *interrogativo*	*vi., vn.*	intransitive verb, *verbo neutro*
m.	masculine, *masculino*	vr.	reflexive verb, *verbo reflexivo*
math.	mathematics, *matemáticas*		
		vt.	transitive verb, *verbo activo*
mech.	mechanics, *mecánica*		
med.	medicine, *medicina*	zool.	zoology, *zoología*

INGLÉS — ESPAÑOL

A

a, *art.*, un, uno, una; —, *prep.* a, al, en.
a. acre, acre.
A.B. Bachelor of Arts, Br. en A. Bachiller en Artes.
aback, *adv.* detrás, atrás; (naut.) en facha; **to be taken —,** quedar desconcertado.
abacus, *n.* ábaco, *m.*; (arch.) tablero de un capitel.
abaft, *adv.* (naut.) a popa, en popa.
abandon, *vt.* abandonar, dejar.
abandoned, *adj.* abandonado.
abandonment, *n.* abandonamiento, abandono, *m.*; desamparo, *m.*
abase, *vt.* rebajar (en rango, puesto, estimación, etc.); degradar.
abasement, *n.* rebajamiento, *m.*; degradación, *f.*
abash, *vt.* avergonzar, causar confusión, sonrojar.
abashment, *n.* confusión, vergüenza, *f.*; rubor, *m.*, consternación, *f.*
abate, *vt.* minorar, disminuir, rebajar; —, *vi.* disminuirse.
abatement, *n.* rebaja, *f.*; diminución, *f.*; reducción, *f.*, descuento, *m.*
abattoir, *n.* desolladero, matadero, *m.*
abbacy, *n.* abadía, *f.*
abbess, *n.* abadesa, *f.*
abbey, *n.* abadía, *f.*; monasterio, *m.*
abbot, *n.* abad, *m.*
abbr. abbreviation, abr. abreviatura.
abbreviate, *vt.* abreviar, acortar, compendiar.
abbreviation, *n.* abreviación, abreviatura, *f.*
abdicate, *vt.* abdicar, renunciar.
abdication, *n.* abdicación, renuncia, *f.*; dimisión, *f.*
abdomen, *n.* abdomen, *m.*, vientre, *m*; barriga, *f.*
abdominal, *adj.* abdominal.
abduct, *vt.* secuestrar, robarse (a alguien); apartar, separar una cosa de otra.
abduction, *n.* abducción, *f.*

abductor, *n.* músculo abductor; secuestrador, *m.*
Abe, Abraham, Abrahán.
abed, *adv.* en (la) cama.
aberrance, aberrancy, *n.* desvío, extravío, *m.*, aberración, *f.*
aberrant, *adj.* errante, extraviado.
aberration, *n.* desvío, extravío, *m.*, aberración, *f.*
abet, *vt.* favorecer, patrocinar, sostener; excitar, animar.
abetment, *n.* apoyo, *m.*, instigación, *f.*
abettor, *n.* fautor, ra; instigador, ra; (law) cómplice, *m.* y *f.*
abeyance, *n.* (law) expectativa, *f.*; supresión temporal; **in —,** (law) en suspenso.
abhor, *vt.* aborrecer, detestar.
abhorrence, *n.* aborrecimiento, odio, *m.*
abhorrent, *adj.* aborrecible, odioso, repugnante; **—ly,** *adv.* aborreciblemente, odiosamente.
abide, *vi.* habitar, morar; permanecer; —, *vt.* soportar, sufrir; defender, sostener; **to — by,** cumplir con, sostenerse en.
ability, *n.* potencia, habilidad, capacidad, aptitud, *f.*; facultad, *f.*; **—ties,** talento, *m.*; bienes, medios, *m. pl.*
abject, *adj.* vil, despreciable, bajo; desanimado; **—ly,** *adv.* abyectamente.
abjection, *n.* abyección, *f.*, servilismo, *m.*
abjectness, *n.* bajeza, vileza, *f.*
abjuration, *n.* abjuración, *f.*
abjure, *vt.* abjurar; renunciar; —, *vi.* retractarse.
ablative, *n.* (gram.) ablativo, *m.*
ablaze, *adj.* en llamas.
able, *adj.* fuerte, capaz, hábil; **to be —,** poder; **to be — to,** saber.
able-bodied, *adj.* robusto, vigoroso.
abloom, *adj.* floreciente, en flor.
ablution, *n.* ablución, *f.*
ably, *adv.* con habilidad.
abnegate, *vt.* negar, renunciar.

abnegation, n. abnegación, f.; resignación, f.; renuncia, f.

abnormal, adj. anormal; deforme; —ly, adv. anormalmente.

abnormality, n. anormalidad, f.; deformidad, f.

aboard, adv. abordo; **to go — a ship,** embarcarse; **all —,** pasajeros al tren listos.

abode, n. domicilio, m., habitación, f.

abolish, vt. abolir, anular, suprimir; destruir o dar fin a alguna cosa; revocar.

abolition, n. abolición, f.

abolitionist, n. abolicionista, m.

abominable, adj. abominable, detestable; —bly, adv. abominablemente.

abominate, vt. abominar, detestar.

abomination, n. abominación, detestación, f.

aboriginal, adj. aborigen, primitivo, originario.

aborigine, n. aborigen, m.

abort, vi. abortar, malparir.

abortion, n. aborto, malparto, m.

abortive, adj. abortivo; infructuoso; intempestivo; —ly, adv. intempestivamente; abortivamente.

abound, vi. abundar; **to — with,** abundar en.

about, prep. cerca de, por ahí, hacia; sobre; acerca; tocante a; —, adv. en contorno, aquí y allá; — **(approximately),** cerca de; **to be — to,** estar para, estar a punto de; **to go —,** andar acá y acullá; **all —,** en todo lugar.

about-face, n. media vuelta; —, vi. dar media vuelta.

above, prep. encima, sobre, superior, más alto (en cuanto a situación, dignidad, etc.); —, adv. arriba; — **all,** sobre todo, principalmente; — **mentioned,** ya mencionado, susodicho; — **par,** sobre la par; — **zero,** sobre cero.

aboveboard, adj. and adv. sincero, al descubierto.

Abp. Archbishop, arz. o arzbpo. arzobispo.

abrade, vt. and vi. raer.

Abraham, Abrahán.

abrasion, n. raspadura, f.; rozamiento, m.; fricción, f.; desgaste por rozamiento o fricción.

abrasive, adj. raspante, abrasivo; —s, n. pl. abrasivos, m. pl.

abreast, adv. de costado; **to be — of the times,** estar al corriente de las cosas.

abridge, vt. abreviar, compendiar; acortar.

abridgment, n. compendio, m.; breviario, m.

abroad, adv. fuera de casa o del país; en todas partes o dirección; **to go —,** salir, ir al extranjero; **to set —,** divulgar, publicar.

abrogate, vt. abrogar, anular.

abrogation, n. abrogación, anulación, f.

abrupt, adj. quebrado, desigual; precipitado, repentino; bronco, rudo; —ly, adv. precipitadamente; bruscamente.

abruptness, n. precipitación, inconsideración, f.; descortesía, f.

abscess, n. absceso, m., apostema, f.

abscond, vi. esconderse; huirse.

absence, n. ausencia, f.; falta, f.; distracción, f.; negligencia, f.; **leave of —,** licencia, f.

absent, adj. ausente; fuera de sí; distraído; —, vt. ausentarse.

absentee, n. el que está ausente de su empleo, etc.

absenteeism, n. ausentismo, m.

absent-minded, adj. distraído; **to be —** estar en Belén, estar absorto.

absinthe, n. ajenjo, m.

absolute, adj. absoluto; categórico; positivo; arbitrario; completo; puro; —ly, adv. absolutamente, terminantemente; por completo.

absolution, n. absolución, f.

absolutism, n. absolutismo, m.

absolutist, n. absolutista, m.

absolve, vt. absolver, dispensar, exentar.

absorb, vt. absorber.

absorbent, adj. (med.) absorbente; —, n. absorbente, m.

absorption, n. absorción, f.

abstain, vi. abstenerse, privarse.

abstemious, adj. abstemio, sobrio, moderado; —ly, adv. moderadamente.

abstention, n. abstención, f.

abstinence, n. abstinencia, f.; templanza, f.

abstinent, adj. abstinente, sobrio; —ly, adv. abstinentemente.

abstract, vt. abstraer; compendiar; —, adj. abstracto; —, n. extracto, m.; sumario, m.; **in the —,** de un modo abstracto; —ly, adv. en abstracto.

abstraction, n. abstracción, f.; distracción, f.

abstruse, adj. abstruso, recóndito, obscuro; —ly, adv. obscuramente.

abstruseness, n. obscuridad, dificultad, f.; misterio, m.

absurd, adj. absurdo; — **speech,** — **act,** majadería, f.; —ly, adv. absurdamente.

absurdity, n. absurdidad, ridiculez, f.

abundance, n. abundancia, copia, plenitud, f.; raudal, m.; **in —,** a rodo.

abundant, adj. abundante; sobrado; —ly, adv. abundantemente, en copia; a manos llenas.

abuse, vt. abusar; engañar; ultrajar, violar; —, n. abuso, engaño, m.; corruptela, seducción, f.; injuria, afrenta, f.; **coarse —,** ribaldería, f.

abusive, adj. abusivo, injurioso; —ly, adv. abusivamente.

abusiveness, n. palabras injuriosas; propensión a injuriar a otro.

abut, vi. terminar, confinar, comarcar.

abutment, n. confín, límite, m.; estribo (de un puente), m.; contrafuerte, m.

abysmal, adj. abismal; insondable.

abyss, n. abismo, m.; golfo, m.; sima, f.

Abyssinia, Abisinia, f.

A.C. Air Corps, Fuerza Aérea.
A.C., a.c. alternating current, C. A.
corriente alterna.
a/c account, c., cta. cuenta.
acacia, *n.* (bot.) acacia, *f.*
academic, academical, *adj.* académico.
academician, academist, *n.* académico,
m., miembro de alguna academia.
academy, *n.* academia, *f.*; universidad, *f.*
acc., acct. account, c., cta. cuenta.
accede, *vi.* acceder, convenir en alguna
cosa, asentir.
accelerate, *vt.* acelerar.
acceleration, *n.* aceleración, prisa, *f.,*
apremio, *m.*
accelerator, *n.* acelerador, *m.*
accent, *n.* acento, *m.,* modulación, *f.,* tono,
m.; (poet.) vocablo, *m.*; —, *vt.* acentuar,
colocar los acentos; (poet.) articular.
accentuate, *vt.* acentuar; intensificar.
accentuation, *n.* acentuación, *f.*
accept, *vt.* aceptar; admitir; recibir favorablemente.
acceptable, *adj.* aceptable, grato, digno de
aceptación.
acceptableness, acceptability, *n.* aceptabilidad, *f.*
acceptance, acceptation, *n.* aceptación,
recepción, *f.*; recibimiento, *m.*; acepción, *f.*
acceptor, *n.* aceptor, aceptante, *m.*; — **of
a draft,** librado, *m.,* librada, *f.*
access, *n.* acceso, *m.*; entrada, *f.*; aumento,
acceso periódico (de alguna enfermedad).
accessibility, *n.* accesibilidad, *f.*
accessible, *adj.* accesible.
accession, *n.* aumento, acrecentamiento, *m.*;
advenimiento, *m.*; acceso, *m.*
accessory, *adj.* accesorio; concomitante;
casual; —, *n.* cómplice, *m.* y *f.*
accidence, *n.* inflexión de las palabras,
rudimentos de la gramática.
accident, *n.* accidente, paso, *m.*; casualidad,
f., suceso imprevisto, lance (funesto), *m.*;
— **insurance,** seguro contra accidentes.
accidental, *adj.* accidental, casual, contingente; —**ly,** *adv.* accidentalmente, casualmente.
acclaim, *vt.* aclamar, aplaudir, vitorear.
acclamation, *n.* aclamación, *f.,* aplauso, *m.*
acclimate, *vt.* aclimatar.
acclimatization, *n.* aclimatación, *f.*
acclimatize, *vt.* aclimatar.
acclivity, *n.* cuesta, rampa, subida, ladera, *f.*
accolade, *n.* acolada, *f.*
accommodate, *vt.* acomodar, ajustar; —,
vi. adaptarse, conformarse.
accommodating, *adj.* servicial, complaciente; obsequioso.
accommodation, *n.* comodidad, *f.*; localidad, *f.*; habitación; cabida, *f.*; cuarto,
m.; —**s,** localidades, *f. pl.*; conciliación, *f.*;
— **bill,** pagaré (endosado, girado o acep-
tado) de una persona por otra.
accompaniment, *n.* (mus.) acompañamiento, *m.*

accompanist, *n.* (mus.) acompañador, ra,
acompañante, *m.* y *f.*
accompany, *vt.* acompañar.
accomplice, *n.* cómplice, *m.* y *f.*
accomplish, *vt.* efectuar, llevar a cabo,
realizar, completar; cumplir.
accomplished, *adj.* perfecto, completo,
elegante, consumado.
accomplishment, *n.* cumplimiento entero
de alguna cosa; —**s,** *n.* habilidades, *f. pl.*;
conocimientos, *m. pl.*; prendas, *f. pl.*
accord, *n.* acuerdo, convenio, *m.*; armonía,
f.; simetría, *f.*; **of one's own** —, espontáneamente; **with one** —, unánimemente;
—, *vt.* ajustar; —, *vi.* acordar; convenir
una cosa con otra.
accordance, *n.* conformidad, *f.*; acuerdo, *m.*
accordant, *adj.* acorde, conforme, conveniente.
according, *adj.* conforme; — **to,** según;
—**ly,** *adv.* en conformidad, de consiguiente,
en efecto.
accordingly, *adv.* en conformidad.
accordion, *n.* acordeón, *m.*
accost, *vt.* saludar a uno yendo hacia él;
trabar conversación.
accoucheur, *n.* comadrón, partero, *m.*
account, *n.* cuenta, *f.,* cálculo, *m.*; caso, *m.*;
estimación, *f.*; aprecio, *m.*; narración, *f.*;
relación, *f.*; motivo, *m.*; **for my** —, **on
my** —, a mi cuenta; **on** — **of,** a causa de,
a cargo de, por motivo de; **on no** —, de
ninguna manera; **pro forma** —, factura o
cuenta simulada; **statement of** —, estado
de cuenta; **to balance an** —, cubrir una
cuenta; **to be of no** —, ser un cero a la
izquierda; **to bring (a person) to** —,
pedir cuentas (a una persona); **to charge
to one's** —, adeudar en cuenta; **to enter
to the** — **of,** sentar en cuenta de; **to keep
an** —, llevar cuenta; **unsettled** —,
cuenta pendiente.
accountability, *n.* responsabilidad, *f.*
accountable, *adj.* responsable.
accountancy, *n.* profesión de contador.
accountant, *n.* contador, *m.,* tenedor de libros.
accounting, *n.* contabilidad, *f.*
accouter, *vt.* equipar, vestir, aviar.
accredit, *vt.* acreditar, patrocinar.
accredited, *adj.* autorizado.
accretion, *n.* aumento, *m.*
accrual, *n.* aumento, *m.*
accrue, *vi.* resultar, provenir.
accumulate, *vt.* acumular; amontonar; —,
vi. crecer, aumentarse.
accumulation, *n.* acumulación, *f.*; amon-
tonamiento, *m.*
accumulator, *n.* acumulador, amortiguador, *m.*
accuracy, *n.* exactitud, precisión, *f.*;
esmero, cuidado, *m.*
accurate, *adj.* exacto, puntual; certero
(de un tiro o un tirador); atinado (en un
cálculo, etc.); —**ly,** *adv.* exactamente.

accursed, *adj.* maldito, maldecido; execrable; excomulgado; — **be!** ¡mal haya!
accusation, *n.* acusación, *f.*; cargo, *m.*
accusative, *n.* (gram.) acusativo, *m.*
accusatory, *adj.* acusatorio.
accuse, *vt.* acusar; culpar; formar causa.
accuser, *n.* acusador, ra; denunciador, ra.
accustom, *vt.* acostumbrar, avezar; — **oneself,** familiarizarse con el uso.
accustomed, *adj.* acostumbrado, habitual; **to be** —, *vi.* soler.
ace, *n.* as (de naipe), *m.*; aviador sobresaliente; migaja, partícula, *f.*; **within an** — **of,** casi casi.
acerbity, *n.* amargura, severidad, aspereza, dureza, acerbidad, *f.*
acetaldehyde, *n.* acetaldehido, *m.*
acetate, *n.* (chem.) acetato, *m.*
acetic, *adj.* acético.
acetone, *n.* (chem.) acetona, *f.*
acetylene, *n.* acetileno, *m.*; — **burner,** torcha de acetileno; — **gas,** gas acetileno.
ache, *n.* dolor continuo, mal, *m.*; —, *vi.* doler.
achievable, *adj.* factible, ganable.
achieve, *vt.* ejecutar, perfeccionar; ganar, obtener; acabar.
achievement, *n.* ejecución, *f.*; acción heroica; hazaña, *f.*; —**s,** sergas, *f. pl.*
Achilles' tendon, tendón de Aquiles.
aching, *adj.* doliente.
achromatic, *adj.* acromático.
acid, *adj.* ácido, agrio, acedo; — **forming,** acidógeno; — **free,** exento de ácido; **acid-proof,** *adj.* resistente a los ácidos; — **test,** ensayo por ácido; —, *n.* ácido, *m.*; **carbolic** —, fenol, *m.*; **sulphuric** —, ácido sulfúrico.
acidify, *vt.* (chem.) acidular.
acidity, *n.* agrura, acedía, acidez, acritud, *f.*
acidosis, *n.* (med.) acidismo, *m.*
acknowledge, *vt.* reconocer; confesar; **to** — **receipt,** acusar recibo.
acknowledgment, *n.* reconocimiento, *m.*; gratitud, *f.*; concesión, *f.*; — **of receipt,** acuse de recibo.
acme, *n.* crisis, *f.*; cima, *f.*; cenit, apogeo, *m.*
acne, *n.* (med.) acne, *m.*
acolyte, *n.* acólito, *m.*
aconite, *n.* (bot.) acónito, *m.*
acorn, *n.* bellota, *f.*; — **harvest,** bellotera, *f.*
acoustics, *n.* acústica, *f.*
acquaint, *vt.* advertir, avisar, enterar, familiarizar, informar; **to be** —**ed,** conocer; **to be** —**ed with,** tener relación con; **to make** —**ed,** relacionar.
acquaintance, *n.* conocimiento, *m.*; familiaridad, *f.*; conocido, *m.*; conocida, *f.*
acquiesce, *vi.* someterse, consentir, asentir.
acquiescence, *n.* asenso, consentimiento, *m.*, sumisión, *f.*
acquiescent, *adj.* deferente; sumiso; condescendiente.
acquire, *vt.* adquirir, ganar, aprender.
acquirement, *n.* adquisición, *f.*, cosa adquirida.

acquisition, *n.* adquisición, obtención, *f.*
acquisitive, *adj.* dispuesto a adquirir.
acquisitiveness, *n.* tendencia a adquirir.
acquit, *vt.* libertar, absolver; pagar; **to** — **oneself well,** comportarse, conducirse bien.
acquitment, acquittal, *n.* absolución, *f.*; pago, pagamento, cumplimiento, *m.*
acquittance, *n.* carta de pago, recibo, finiquito, descargo, *m.*
acre, *n.* acre (medida de tierra que equivale a 40 áreas), *m.*
acreage, *n.* número de acres.
acrid, *adj.* acre, mordaz.
acridity, *n.* acidez, acritud, *f.*
acrimonious, *adj.* acre; corrosivo; sarcástico.
acrimony, *n.* acrimonia, acritud, *f.*
acrobat, *n.* acróbata, *m.* y *f.*, volteador, volatín, volatinero, era.
acrobatic, *adj.* acrobático.
acrobatics, *n.* acrobacia, *f.*
acropolis, *n.* acrópolis, *f.*
across, *adv.* de través, de una parte a otra; —, *prep.* a través de, por; — **the way,** enfrente.
acrostic, *n.* poema acróstico; acróstico, *m.*
act, *vt.* representar; obrar; —, *vi.* hacer; —, *n.* acto, hecho, *m.*; acción, *f.*; efecto, *m.*; jornada (de una comedia), *f.*; —**s,** actas, *f. pl.*; **Acts of the Apostles,** Actos, *m. pl.*
acting, *n.* acción, *f.*; representación, *f.*; —, *adj.* interino, suplente.
actinic, *adj.* actínico.
actinium, *n.* actinio, *m.*
action, *n.* acción, operación, *f.*; batalla, *f.*; gesticulación, *f.*; proceso, *m.*; actividad, *f.*; funcionamiento, *m.*; hecho, *m.*; gestión, *f.*; —**s,** conducta, *f.*, comportamiento, *m.*
actionable, *adj.* acusable; punible.
activate, *vt.* hacer radioactivo; airear aguas sucias; empezar experimentando el desarrollo de un huevo no fecundado.
active, *adj.* activo; eficaz, ocupado; ágil; —**ly,** *adv.* activamente, ágilmente, eficazmente.
activity, *n.* agilidad, actividad, *f.*; prontitud, *f.*; vivacidad, *f.*; expedición, *f.*
actor, *n.* actor, ejecutante, *m.*; agente, *m.*; cómico, actor (en los teatros), *m.*
actress, *n.* comedianta, actriz, cómica, *f.*
actual, *adj.* actual; cierto, real; efectivo; —**ly,** *adv.* en efecto, realmente.
actuality, *n.* actualidad, *f.*
actualize, *vt.* realizar.
actuarial, *adj.* actuarial; relativo al actuario y su trabajo.
actuary, *n.* actuario, *f.*; secretario, *m.*; registrador, *m.*
actuate, *vt.* excitar; mover, impulsar; poner en acción.
acuity, *n.* agudeza, *f.*
acumen, *n.* agudeza, perspicacia, penetración, *f.*; cacumen, *m.*
acuminate, *vt.* aguzar, afilar; —, *adj.* (bot.) acuminado.

acute, *adj.* agudo; ingenioso; **— accent,** acento agudo; **— angle,** ángulo agudo; **—ly,** *adv.* con agudeza.

acuteness, *n.* agudeza, perspicacia, penetración, *f.*

A.D. in the year of our Lord, A.C. Año de Cristo.

adage, *n.* proverbio, *m.*, refrán, *m.*

adagio, *n.* (mus.) adagio, *m.*

Adam, Adán.

adamant, *n.* adamante, diamante, *m.*; **—,** *adj.* firme.

adamantine, *adj.* diamantino; (poet.) impenetrable.

adapt, *vt.* adaptar, acomodar una cosa a otra; ajustar.

adaptability, *n.* adaptabilidad, *f.*: facilidad de adaptarse.

adaptable, *adj.* adaptable.

adaptation, *n.* adaptación, *f.*

add, *vt.* aumentar; juntar; **to — up,** sumar.

addendum, *n.* suplemento, *m.*

adder, *n.* culebra, *f.*; víbora, *f.*

addict, *vt.* dedicar; **to — oneself,** adaptarse; entregarse a.

addicted, *adj.* adicto; **— to,** apasionado por.

addictedness, addiction, *n.* inclinación, propensión, *f.*; dedicación, *f.*; devoción, afición, *f.*

adding machine, *n.* máquina de sumar, máquina de calcular, sumadora mecánica, sumadora, *f.*

addition, *n.* adición, *f.*

additional, *adj.* adicional; **—ly,** *adv.* en o por adición.

addle, *adj.* vacío, vano, infecundo, estéril; **—,** *vt.* hacer estéril; confundir, enredar.

addlebrained, *adj.* estúpido.

address, *vt.* hablar, dirigir la palabra; **—,** *vi.* dirigirse; **— a letter,** dirigir una carta, poner el sobrescrito; **—,** *n.* oración, *f.*, discurso, *m.*; señas, *f. pl.*, dirección, *f.*; trato, *m.*; manera de hablar; **cable —,** dirección cablegráfica; **to deliver an —,** pronunciar un discurso.

addressee, *n.* destinatario, ria.

addressing machine, *n.* máquina para dirigir sobres, tarjetas, etc.

addressograph, *n.* máquina para imprimir sobrescritos (marca comercial registrada).

adduce, *vt.* aducir.

Adelaide, Adelaida.

Adeline, Adelina.

adenoid, *n.* (med.) tumor adenoideo.

adept, *adj.* adepto, sabio, experto; **—,** *n.* sabio, bia, experto, ta.

adequacy, *n.* suficiencia, *f.*; proporcionalidad, *f.*

adequate, *adj.* adecuado, proporcionado; suficiente; a propósito; **—ly,** *adv.* adecuadamente.

adhere, *vi.* adherir; aficionarse; pegarse.

adherence, *n.* adherencia, adhesión, *f.*

adherent, *adj.* pegajoso; tenaz; adherente; **—,** *n.* adherente, partidario, *m.*

adhesion, *n.* adhesión, *f.*; adherencia, *f.*

adhesive, *adj.* pegajoso, tenaz; **— plaster,** **— tape,** esparadrapo, *m.*, tafetán inglés.

adiabatic, *adj.* adiabático.

adieu, *interj.* ¡adiós! **—,** *n.* despedida, *f.*

adipose, *adj.* adiposo; seboso.

adit, *n.* socavón, *m.*; conducto subterráneo; entrada de una mina.

Adj., Adjt. Adjutant, Ayte. Ayudante.

adj. adjective, adj. adjetivo.

adjacency, adjacence, *n.* contigüidad, vecindad, *f.*

adjacent, *adj.* adyacente, contiguo; colindante.

adjectival, *adj.* adjetival; **—ly,** *adv.* adjetivamente.

adjective, *n.* adjetivo, *m.*; **—ly,** *adv.* como adjetivo, adjetivamente.

adjoin, *vt.* juntar; unir; **—,** *vi.* estar contiguo.

adjoining, *adj.* contiguo, siguiente.

adjourn, *vt.* and *vi.* diferir, aplazar; suspender, clausurar (una reunión, etc.).

adjournment, *n.* prórroga, *f.*; aplazamiento, *m.*; clausura (de una reunión, etc.), *f.*

adjudge, adjudicate, *vt.* adjudicar; condenar; decretar.

adjudicate, *vt.* adjudicar.

adjudication, *n.* adjudicación, *f.*

adjudicator, *n.* adjudicador, *m.*

adjunct, *n.* adjunto, *m.*

adjuration, *n.* conjuro, *m.*; juramento, *m.*

adjure, *vt.* juramentar; conjurar.

adjust, *vt.* ajustar, acomodar.

adjustable *adj.* ajustable, graduable, adaptable.

adjuster, *n.* aforador, *m.*; mediador, ajustador, *m.*

adjustment, *n.* ajustamiento, ajuste, *m.*; arreglo, *m.*

adjutancy, *n.* (mil.) ayudantía, *f.*

adjutant, *n.* (mil.) ayudante, *m.*

ad. lib. at pleasure, ad. lib. a voluntad.

Adm. Admiral, Almte. almirante.

admeasurement, *n.* reparto judicial.

administer, *vt.* administrar, gobernar; desempeñar; dar, surtir, proveer; **to — an oath,** tomar juramento.

administration, *n.* administración, *f.*; gobierno, *m.*; dirección, *f.*; (com.) gerencia, *f.*

administrative, *adj.* administrativo.

administrator, *n.* administrador, *m.*

admirable, *adj.* admirable; **—bly,** *adv.* admirablemente, a maravilla.

admiral, *n.* almirante, *m.*; almiranta (nave), *f.*

admiralty, *n.* almirantazgo, *m.*

admiration, *n.* admiración, *f.*; maravilla, *f.*

admire, *vt.* admirar; estimar; contemplar.

admirer, *n.* admirador, *m.*; amante, pretendiente, *m.*

admiring, *adj.* admirativo.

admiringly, *adv.* con admiración.

admissibility, *n.* admisibilidad.

admissible, *adj.* admisible.

admission, *n.* admisión, recepción, entrada, *f.*; concesión, *f.*; ingreso, *m.*; **— fee,** precio de ingreso; **— price,** precio de entrada; **— ticket,** billete de entrada, boleto de entrada, póliza, *f.*

admit, *vt.* admitir, dar entrada; recibir, conceder, permitir; confesar; reconocer.

admittance, *n.* entrada, admisión, *f.*

admittedly, *adv.* según general consenso.

admixture, *n.* mixtura, mezcla, *f.*; agregado en polvo o líquido; ingrediente, *m.*

admonish, *vt.* amonestar, reprender.

admonition, *n.* admonición, amonestación, *f.*

ado, *n.* dificultad, *f.*; bullicio, tumulto, *m.*; fatiga, *f.*; **without further —,** sin más ni menos.

adobe, *n.* adobe, *m.*

adolescence, adolescency, *n.* adolescencia, *f.*

adolescent, *adj.* adolescente.

Adolph, Adolphus, Adolfo.

adopt, *vt.* adoptar, prohijar.

adoption, *n.* adopción, *f.*

adoptive, *adj.* adoptivo.

adorable, *adj.* adorable; **—bly,** *adv.* adorablemente.

adoration, *n.* adoración, *f.*

adore, *vt.* adorar.

adorn, *vt.* hermosear con adornos, adornar; ornar; **to — oneself,** prenderse, adornarse.

adornment, *n.* adorno, atavío, *m.*

adrenal, *adj.* (anat.) suprarrenal.

adrenalin, *n.* adrenalina, *f.*

Adriatic, Adriático, *m.*

adrift, *adj.* and *adv.* flotante, a merced de las olas; al garete.

adroit, *adj.* diestro, hábil, mañoso.

adroitness, *n.* destreza, *f.*

adsorb, *vt.* adsorber.

adsorption, *n.* adsorción, *f.*

adulation, *n.* adulación, lisonja, zalamería, *f.*

adulatory, *adj.* lisonjero.

adult, *adj.* and *n.* adulto, ta.

adulterate, *vt.* adulterar, corromper, falsificar; **—,** *adj.* adúltero; adulterado, falsificado.

adulteration, *n.* adulteración, corrupción, *f.*

adulterer, *n.* adúltero, *m.*

adulteress, *n.* adúltera, *f.*

adulterous, *adj.* adulterino; espurio.

adultery, *n.* adulterio, *m.*

adv. adverb, *adv.* adverbio.

ad val. ad valorem (in proportion to the value), ad val. ad valórem, en proporción al valor.

advance, *vt.* avanzar; promover; pagar adelantado; **—,** *vi.* hacer progresos; **—,** *n.* avance, *m.*; adelanto, *m.*; **— payment,** anticipo, *m.*; **in —,** con anticipación, por adelantado.

advanced, *adj.* adelantado, avanzado.

advancement, *n.* adelantamiento, *m.*; progreso, *m.*; promoción, *f.*

advantage, *n.* ventaja, superioridad, *f.*; provecho, beneficio, *m.*; delantera, *f.*; **to take — of,** aprovecharse de, sacarle partido a; **to have the —,** llevar la ventaja.

advantageous, *adj.* ventajoso, útil; **—ly,** *adv.* ventajosamente. .

advent, *n.* venida, *f.*, advenimiento, *m.*; **Advent,** Adviento, *m.*

adventitious, *adj.* adventicio.

adventure, *n.* aventura, *f.*; riesgo, *m.*; **—,** *vi.* osar, emprender; **—,** *vt.* aventurar.

adventurer, *n.* aventurero, *m.*

adventuresome, adventurous, *adj.* intrépido; atrevido; aventurero; valeroso; **—ly,** *adv.* arriesgadamente.

adventuress, *n.* aventurera, *f.*

adverb, *n.* adverbio, *m.*

adverbial, *adj.* adverbial; **—ly,** *adv.* adverbialmente.

adversary, *n.* adversario, ria, enemigo, ga.

adversative, *adj.* adversativo, contrario.

adverse, *adj.* adverso, contrario; **—ly,** *adv.* adversamente.

adversity, *n.* adversidad, calamidad, *f.*; infortunio, *m.*

advert, *vi.* advertir, hacer notar.

advertise, *vt.* avisar, anunciar.

advertisement, *n.* aviso, *m.*; anuncio, *m.*

advertiser, *n.* anunciante, *m.*

advertising, *n.* anuncio, *m.*; propaganda, *f.*

advice, *n.* consejo, *m.*; aviso, *m.*; parecer, *m.*; **as per —,** según aviso.

advisability, *n.* prudencia, conveniencia, propiedad, *f.*

advisable, *adj.* prudente, conveniente.

advise, *vt.* aconsejar; avisar; **—,** *vi.* consultar, aconsejarse; poner en conocimiento; **to keep —d,** tener al corriente.

advisedly, *adv.* prudentemente, avisadamente.

advisement, *n.* consideración, *f.*

adviser, advisor, *n.* consejero, aconsejador, consultor, *m.*

advisory, *adj.* aconsejador; **— board,** consejo consultivo.

advocacy, *n.* vindicación, defensa, apología, *f.*

advocate, *n.* abogado, *m.*; protector, *m.*; partidario, *m.*; **—,** *vt.* defender; apoyar.

advocateship, *n.* abogacía, *f.*

adze, *n.* azuela, *f.*

A. E. F. American Expeditionary Force, A. E. F. Ejército Expedicionario Americano.

aegis, *n.* égida, *f.*, escudo, *m.*

aeon, *n.* era, *f.*; eternidad, *f.*

aerate, *vt.* airear.

aeration, *n.* aeración, *f.*

aerator, *n.* (mech.) aerador-fumigador, gasógeno, *m.*

aerial, *adj.* aéreo; **—,** *n.* (radio) antena, *f.*

aerie, *n.* nido de águila.

aerobatics, *n.* acrobacia aérea, vuelo acrobático.

aerodynamics, *n.* aerodinámica, *f.*
aerolite, *n.* aerolito, *m.*
aeromechanics, *n.* aeromecánica, *f.*
aerometer, *n.* aerómetro, *m.*
aeronaut, *n.* aeronauta, *m.*
aeronautical, *adj.* aeronáutico.
aeronautics, *n.* aeronáutica, *f.*
aerophotography, *n.* aerofotografía, *f.*
aeroplane, *n.* aeroplano, avión, *m.*
aerostat, *n.* globo aerostático.
aerostatics, *n.* aerostática, *f.*
aerotherapy, *n.* aeroterapia, *f.*
aesthete, *n.* esteta, *m.* y *f.*
aesthetic, *adj.* estético.
aesthetics, *n.* estética, *f.*
aether, *n.* éter, *m.*
afar, *adv.* lejos, distante; **from —,** de algún lugar distante.
affability, *n.* afabilidad, urbanidad, dulzura, *f.*
affable, *adj.* afable, complaciente; **—bly,** *adv.* afablemente.
affair, *n.* asunto, *m.*; negocio, *m.*; lance, duelo, *m.*; **love —,** amorío, *m.*
affect, *vt.* conmover; afectar; hacer mella.
affectation, *n.* afectación, *f.*; culteranismo, *m.*; melindre, *m.*
affected, *adj.* afectado, lleno de afectación; inclinado; **—ly,** *adv.* con afectación.
affecting, *adj.* conmovedor.
affection, *n.* afección, *f.*; amor, afecto, *m.*; afición, *f.*; bienquerencia, *f.*
affectionate, *adv.* afectuoso, benévolo; **to be —,** hacerse unas gachas; **—ly,** *adv.* cariñosamente.
affiance, *n.* compromiso matrimonial; confianza, fe, *f.*; **—,** *vt.* comprometerse, contraer esponsales.
affidavit, *n.* declaración jurada; atestación, *f.*
affiliate, *vt.* ahijar; afiliar.
affiliation, *n.* adopción, *f.*; afiliación, *f.*
affinity, *n.* afinidad, atracción, *f.*
affirm, *vt.* afirmar, declarar, confirmar, ratificar, aprobar.
affirmation, *n.* afirmación, *f.*
affirmative, *adj.* afirmativo; **—ly,** *adv.* afirmativamente.
affix, *vt.* anexar, añadir, fijar; **—,** *n.* (gram.) afijo, *m.*
afflict, *vt.* afligir; atormentar.
affliction, *n.* aflicción, *f.*; dolor, *m.*; pena, *f.*
afflictive, *adj.* aflictivo, penoso.
affluence, *n.* copia, abundancia, *f.*
affluent, *adj.* afluente, opulento.
afflux, *n.* confluencia, afluencia, *f.*
afford, *vt.* dar; proveer; producir; proporcionar; facilitar; tener los medios.
affray, *n.* asalto, *m.*; riña, *f.*
affront, *n.* afrenta, injuria, *f.*; **—,** *vt.* afrentar, insultar, ultrajar.
afghan, *n.* manta tejida de lana.
Afghanistan, Afganistán, *m.*
afield, *adv.* en el campo, afuera.
afire, *adj.* en llamas.
A.F.L., A.F. of L. American Federation

of **Labor,** F.A.T. Federación Americana del Trabajo.
aflame, *adj.* en llamas.
afloat, *adj.* flotante, a flote.
afoot, *adj.* and *adv.* a pie.
afore, *prep.* antes.
afoul, *adv.* en colisión.
afraid, *adj.* temeroso, espantado, tímido, miedoso; **to be —,** temer, tener miedo; **to become —,** sobrecogerse.
afresh, *adv.* de nuevo, otra vez.
African, *n.* and *adj.* africano, na.
aft, *adv.* (naut.) a popa.
after, *prep.* después de, detrás; según; tras de; **— all,** en fin, en suma; **day — day,** día tras día; **day — tomorrow,** pasado mañana; **—,** *adv.* después.
afterbirth, *n.* secundinas, *f. pl.*
aftercost, *n.* gastos extraordinarios.
aftercrop, *n.* segunda cosecha.
afterdays, *n.* tiempo venidero.
aftereffect, *n.* efecto resultante.
afterglow, *n.* reflejo del sol poniente en el cielo.
afterhours, *n.* deshora, tarde, *f.*
afterlife, *n.* vida venidera.
aftermath, *n.* retoño, *m.*, segunda cosecha; consecuencias (generalmente desastrosas), *f. pl.*
afternoon, *n.* tarde, *f.*; pasado meridiano.
afterpains, *n.* dolores de sobreparto.
afterreckoning, *n.* nueva cuenta.
aftertaste, *n.* resabio, *m.*
afterthought, *n.* reflexión tardía.
afterward, afterwards, *adv.* después, en seguida, luego.
A.G. Adjutant General, Ayte. Gral. Ayudante General.
again, *adv.* otra vez; **— and —,** muchas veces, repetidas veces; **as much —,** otro tanto más.
against, *prep.* contra; enfrente; **— the grain,** a contrapelo; de mala gana.
agape, *adj.* con la boca abierta.
agar-agar, *n.* agar-agar.
agate, *n.* ágata, *f.*
agave, *n.* piñuela, *f.*
age, *n.* edad, *f.*; siglo, *m.*; vejez, *f.*; época, *f.*; **under —,** menor de edad; **of —,** mayor de edad; **—,** *vi.* envejecer.
aged, *adj.* envejecido, anciano.
agency, *n.* agencia, *f.*, medio, *m.*
agent, *n.* agente, *m.*; asistente, *m.*; casero, *m.*; (law) poderhabiente, *m.*; mandatario, *m.*; **commission —,** agente comisionista; **insurance —,** agente de seguros.
ageratum, *n.* (bot.) agérato, *m.*
agglomerate, *vt.* aglomerar; **—,** *vi.* ovillarse.
agglomeration, *n.* aglomeración, *f.*
agglutinate, *vt.* conglutinar, unir.
agglutination, *n.* aglutinación, *f.*
aggrandize, *vt.* engrandecer; elevar.
aggrandizement, *n.* engrandecimiento, *m.*
aggravate, *vt.* agravar; empeorar; intensificar.

aggravating, adj. agravante; irritante.
aggravation, n. agravación, f., agravamiento, m.
aggregate, n. agregado, m.; unión, f.; —, vt. juntar, reunir.
aggregation, n. agregación, f.
aggress, vi. acometer; agredir; invadir.
aggression, n. agresión, f.; ataque, asalto, m.
aggressive, adj. agresivo, ofensivo.
aggressiveness, n. calidad de ser agresivo.
aggressor, n. agresor, m.
aggrieve, vt. injuriar; afligir, apesadumbrar; —, vi. lamentar.
aghast, adj. horrorizado.
agile, adj. ágil; vivo, diestro.
agility, n. agilidad, f.; destreza, f.
agitate, vt. agitar; discutir con ahinco; —, vi. excitar los ánimos, alborotar opiniones.
agitation, n. agitación, f.; perturbación, f.
agitator, n. agitador, incitador, m.
aglow, adj. fulgurante.
agnate, n. agnado, da.
agnostic, adj. and n. agnóstico, ca.
agnosticism, n. agnosticismo, m.
ago, adv. pasado, tiempo ha; **a few days** —, hace algunos días; **how long** —? ¿cuánto ha? **long** —, hace mucho.
agog, adj. ansioso, anhelante.
agonizing, adj. agonizante.
agony, n. agonía, f.; angustia extrema.
agrarian, adj. agrario.
agree, vi. concordar, convenir; consentir; **to** — **with,** dar la razón; **to** — **with each other,** estar de cuerdo.
agreeability, n. afabilidad, f.
agreeable, adj. conveniente, agradable; amable; — **with,** según, conforme a; —**bly,** adv. agradablemente.
agreed, adj. establecido, convenido; —! interj. ¡de acuerdo!
agreement, n. acuerdo, m.; concordia, f.; conformidad, f.; unión, f.; ajustamiento, m.; pacto, m.; **by** —, de acuerdo; **general** —, consenso, m.; **to be in** —, estar conforme; **to reach an** —, ponerse de acuerdo.
agric. agriculture, agr. agricultura.
agricultural, adj. agrario, agrícola.
agriculture, n. agricultura, f.
agriculturist, n. agricultor, m.
agrimony, n. (bot.) agrimonía, f.
agronomist, n. agrónomo, m.
agronomy, n. agronomía, f.
aground, adj. and adv. (naut.) varado, encallado.
agt. agent, agte. agente.
ague, n. fiebre, f., calentura intermitente.
aguish, adj. febril.
ah! interj. ¡ah! ¡ay!
aha! interj. ¡ajá!
ahead, adv. más allá, delante de otro; (naut.) por la proa; **to be** — **of,** campar, ir a la cabeza.
ahoy! interj. expresión de saludo entre marineros.

aid, vt. ayudar, socorrer; conllevar; subvenir; —, n. ayuda, f.; auxilio, socorro, m.; concurso, m.
aide, n. ayudante, m.
aide-de-camp, n. (mil.) ayudante de campo, edecán, m.
aigrette, egret, n. garzota, garza, f.
ail, vt. afligir, molestar; **what** —s **you?** ¿qué le duele a Vd.?
ailanthus, n. (bot.) ailanto, m.
aileron, n. (aer.) alerón, m.
ailing, adj. doliente, enfermizo, achacoso.
ailment, n. dolencia, indisposición, f.
aim, vt. apuntar, dirigir el tiro con el ojo; aspirar a; intentar; —, n. designio, intento, punto, m.; mira, f.; puntería, f.; blanco, m.
aimless, adj. sin designio, sin objeto.
ain't, contracción familiar de **am not, is not, are not,** no estar, no ser.
air, n. aire, m.; (mus.) tonada, f.; semblante, m.; **in the open** —, al raso, al aire libre; **to take the** —, tomar el aire; —, adj. aéreo; — **base,** base aérea; — **blast,** chorro de aire; — **brake,** freno neumático, freno de aire; — **chamber,** cámara de aire; — **cock,** llave o válvula o espita de escape de aire; — **conditioning,** purificación del aire; — **cooling,** enfriamiento o refrigeración por aire; — **corps,** cuerpo de aviación; — **cushion,** cojinete rellenado de aire, colchón de viento; — **express,** expreso aéreo; — **letter,** carta aérea; — **line,** línea aérea; — **liner,** avión de línea; — **mail,** correo aéreo, correspondencia aérea, vía aérea; — **pocket,** (aer.) depresión, f.; — **pump,** máquina neumática; — **raid,** bombardeo aéreo; — **shaft,** respiradero de mina; — **sleeve,** — **sock,** (aer.) indicador de dirección del viento; — **valve,** válvula de aire; —, vt. airear; secar; ventilar.
airbrush, n. pulverizador neumático, brocha de aire.
air-condition, vt. acondicionar el clima interior.
air-cooled, adj. enfriado por aire.
aircraft, n. aeronave, f., avión, m.; — **carrier,** portaaviones, m.
airdrome, n. aeródromo, aeropuerto, m.
airfoil, n. (aer.) plano aerodinámico; ala, f.
airiness, n. ventilación, f.
airing, n. caminata, f., paseo para tomar aire; ventilación, f.
airless, adj. falto de ventilación; sin aire.
airman, n. aviador, m.
air-minded, adj. interesado en la aviación o bien dispuesto para ella.
airplane, n. aeroplano, avión, m.; — **carrier,** portaaviones, m.
airport, n. aeropuerto, aeródromo, m.; paradero de aeroplanos o aeronaves.
airproof, adj. hermético.
air-raid shelter, n. refugio contra aeroplanos.

air-raid warden, *n.* jefe de manzana.
air-raid warning, *n.* aviso de ataque aéreo.
airship, *n.* aeronave, *f.*; dirigible, *m.*; aeroplano, *m.*
airsick, *adj.* mareado en naves aéreas.
airsickness, *n.* mal de altura; mareo en viaje aéreo.
airtight, *adj.* herméticamente cerrado, hermético, a prueba de aire.
airway, *n.* vía aérea.
airy, *adj.* aéreo; etéreo; alegre; lleno de aire.
aisle, *n.* nave de una iglesia, pasillo, *m.*; pasadizo, *m.*
ajar, *adj.* entreabierto.
akimbo, *adj.* and *adv.* en jarras.
akin, *adj.* consanguíneo, emparentado; análogo, semejante.
Al: Albert, Alberto; Alexander, Alejandro; Alfred, Alfredo; Alphonso, Alfonso, Alonso o Ildefonso.
Ala. Alabama, Alabama.
alabaster, *n.* alabastro, *m.*; —, *adj.* alabastrino.
à la carte, según lista (de comidas).
alack! alack-a-day! *interj.* ¡ay! (exclamación de dolor o lástima).
alacrity, *n.* alacridad, presteza, *f.*
à la king, en salsa blanca con hongos, pimientos, etc.
à la mode, a la moda; pie —, cake —, pastel o bizcocho servido con helados.
alarm, *n.* alarma, *f.*; rebato, *m.*; — bell, rebato, *m.*; — clock, despertador, *m.*, reloj despertador; — post, puesto de aviso; burglar —, alarma para ladrones; fire —, alarma para incendios; to sound the —, dar la alarma; —, *vt.* alarmar, inquietar.
alarming, *adj.* alarmante; sorprendente.
alarmist, *n.* alarmista, *m.* y *f.*
alas, *interj.* ¡ay!
Alaska seal, *n.* piel de foca de Alaska.
alb, *n.* (eccl.) alba, *f.*
Albanian, *n.* and *adj.* albanés, esa.
albatross, *n.* albatros, *m.*
albeit, *conj.* aunque.
albino, *n.* albino, *m.*
album, *n.* álbum, *m.*
albumen, *n.* albumen, *m.*
albumin, *n.* albúmina, *f.*
alchemist, *n.* alquimista, *m.*
alchemy, *n.* alquimia, *f.*
alcohol, *n.* alcohol, *m.*; denatured —, alcohol desnaturalizado; grain —, alcohol de granos; rubbing —, alcohol para fricciones; wood —, alcohol metílico.
alcoholic, *adj.* alcohólico.
alcove, *n.* alcoba, *f.*
aldehyde, *n.* aldehido, *m.*; methylic —, aldehido metílico.
alder, *n.* (bot.) aliso, *m.*
alderman, *n.* regidor, concejal, *m.*
ale, *n.* variedad de cerveza.
Aleck, Alexander, Alejandro.
alee, *adv.* (naut.) a sotavento.
alehouse, *n.* cervecería, taberna, *f.*

alembic, *n.* alambique, *m.*
alert, *adj.* alerto, vivo.
alertness, *n.* cuidado, *m.*; vigilancia, *f.*; viveza, actividad, *f.*
Alexander, Alejandro.
alfalfa, *n.* alfalfa, *f.*
alg. algebra, álg. álgebra.
alga, *n.* alga (planta que se cría en el mar), *f.*
algebra, *n.* álgebra, *f.*
algebraic, algebraical, *adj.* algebraico.
algebraist, *n.* algebrista, *m.* y *f.*
Algiers, Argel, *m.*
alias, *adv.* alias, de otra manera.
alibi, *n.* (law) coartada, *f.*
alien, *adj.* extraño; —, *n.* forastero, ra; extranjero, ra.
alienable, *adj.* enajenable.
alienate, *vt.* enajenar; malquistar, indisponer.
alienation, *n.* enajenación, *f.*
alienist, *n.* alienista, frenópata, *m.*
alight, *vi.* descender; apearse; —, *adj.* encendido; ardiente.
align, *vt.* alinear.
alignment, *n.* alineación, *f.*
alike, *adj.* semejante, igual; —, *adv.* igualmente.
aliment, *n.* alimento, *m.*
alimentary, *adj.* alimenticio.
alimentation, *n.* alimentación, *f.*
alimony, *n.* alimentos, *m.* *pl.*, cantidad que un cónyuge pasa a otro en caso de divorcio.
aliquot, *adj.* alícuota; — part, parte alícuota.
alive, *adj.* vivo, viviente; activo.
alkali, *n.* álcali, *m.*
alkaline, *adj.* alcalino.
alkalinity, *n.* alcalinidad, *f.*
alkalize, *vt.* alcalizar.
alkaloid, *n.* alcaloide, *m.*
alkanet, *n.* (bot.) alcana, *f.*, raíz de alcana; buglosa, *f.*
all, *adj.* todo; —, *adv.* enteramente; — at once, — of a sudden, de repente, de un tirón; — the same, absolutamente lo mismo; — the better, tanto mejor; not at —, no por cierto, de ninguna manera; no hay de qué; once for —, una vez por todas, una que valga mil; — out, a ultranza; — right, bueno; satisfactorio; — hands on deck, todo el mundo arriba; — year round, todo el año; —, *n.* todo, *m.*
all-American, *adj.* de todos los Estados Unidos (aplícase a los deportistas).
allay, *vt.* aliviar, apaciguar.
allegation, *n.* alegación, *f.*; disculpa, *f.*; cita, *f.*
allege, *vt.* alegar; declarar; to — in pleading, (law) deducir.
allegiance, *n.* lealtad, fidelidad, *f.*; pledging —, jura, *f.*; pledging — to the flag, jura a la bandera.
allegorical, *adj.* alegórico; —ly, *adv.* alegóricamente.

allegorize, *vt.* alegorizar.
allegory, *n.* alegoría, *f.*
allegretto, *adj.* (mus.) alegreto.
allegro, *n.* (mus.) alegro, *m.*
allergic, *adj.* alérgico.
allergy, *n.* alergia, *f.*
alleviate, *vt.* aliviar, aligerar.
alleviation, *n.* alivio, *m.*; mitigación, *f.*
alley, *n.* paseo arbolado, callejuela, *f.*, pasadizo, *m.*, calleja, *f.*, callejón, *m.*
alliance, *n.* alianza, *f.*; parentela, *f.*
allied, *adj.* aliado, confederado.
alligation, *n.* (math.) regla de aligación; (chem.) unión, ligazón, *f.*
alligator, *n.* lagarto, *m.*; — **pear,** aguacate, *m.*
alliteration, *n.* aliteración, *f.*
allocate, *vt.* colocar.
allocation, *n.* distribución, colocación, asignación, fijación, *f.*
allocution, *n.* alocución, *f.*
allodium, *n.* alodio, *m.*
allopathy, *n.* alopatía, *f.*
allot, *vt.* distribuir por suerte; asignar, repartir; adjudicarse.
allotment, *n.* asignación, *f.*; repartimiento, *m.*; lote, *m.*, parte, porción, *f.*
allover, *adj.* de diseño repetido.
allow, *vt.* conceder, aprobar; permitir; dar, pagar; —**ing that,** supuesto que.
allowable, *adj.* admisible, permitido, justo.
allowance, *n.* concesión, *f.*; licencia, *f.*; bonificación, *f.*; (naut.) ración, *f.*, alimentos, *m. pl.*; mesada, *f.*; **month's** —, mensualidad, *f.*
alloy, *vt.* ligar, mezclar un metal con otro; aquilatar oro; —, *n.* liga aleación, mezcla, *f.*
all-round, *adj.* completo; por todas partes, en todas formas.
allspice, *n.* especerías, especias (pimienta, clavos, etc.), *f. pl.*
allude, *vt.* aludir.
allure, *vt.* alucinar; cebar; fascinar; —, *n.* seducción, *f.*
allurement, *n.* seducción, *f.*
alluring, *adj.* halagüeño, seductivo; —**ly,** *adv.* seductoramente.
allusion, *n.* alusión, *f.*
allusive, *adj.* alusivo; —**ly,** *adv.* de un modo alusivo.
alluvial, *adj.* aluvial.
alluvion, *n.* aluvión, *m.*; terrero, *m.*
alluvium, *n.* aluvión, *f.*
ally, *n.* aliado, *m.*; asociado, *m.*; —, *vt.* hacer alianza; vincular.
almanac, *n.* almanaque, *m.*
almighty, *adj.* omnipotente, todopoderoso.
almond, *n.* almendra, *f.*; — **brittle,** crocante, *m.*; — **tree,** almendro, *m.*; **sugared** —, almendra garapiñada.
almoner, *n.* limosnero, *m.*; capellán, *m.*; dispensador de limosnas.
almonry, *n.* lugar donde se reparten limosnas.

almost, *adv.* casi, cerca de.
alms, *n.* limosna, *f.*
almshouse, *n.* hospicio para pobres.
aloe, *n.* áloe, lináloe, *m.*
aloft, *prep.* arriba, sobre.
alone, *adj.* solo; —, *adv.* solamente, sólo; **to let** —, dejar en paz.
along, *adv.* a lo largo; adelante; junto con; **to get** — **with,** entenderse con.
alongside, *adv.* and *prep.* al lado; (naut.) al costado.
aloof, *adv.* lejos, de lejos, en voz alta, a lo largo; —, *adj.* reservado, apartado.
aloud, *adv.* con voz fuerte, recio.
alpaca, *n.* alpaca, *f.*
alpha, *n.* alfa, *f.*; — **and omega,** el primero y el último; — **rays,** rayos alfa.
alphabet, *n.* alfabeto, *m.*
alphabetical, *adj.* alfabético; —**ly,** *adv.* alfabéticamente.
Alphonso, Alfonso, Alonso o Ildefonso.
Alpine, *adj.* alpino.
Alps, Alpes, *m. pl.*
already, *adv.* ya, a la hora de esta, antes de ahora.
Alsace, Alsacia, *f.*
Alsatian, *n.* and *adj.* alsaciano, na.
also, *adv.* también, igualmente, además.
alt. altitude, alt. altitud.
altar, *n.* altar, *m.*
altarpiece, *n.* retablo, *m.*
alter, *vt.* alterar, mudar, modificar.
alteration, *n.* alteración, *f.*; cambio, *m.*
altercate, *vi.* altercar, disputar acaloradamente.
altercation, *n.* altercación, *f.*
alternate, *adj.* alternativo, recíproco; —, *vt.* alternar, variar; —**ly,** *adv.* alternativamente; —, *n.* suplente, *m.* y *f.*
alternating, *adj.* alterno, alternativo; — **current,** corriente alterna o alternativa.
alternation, *n.* alternación, *f.*
alternative, *n.* alternativa, *f.*; —, *adj.* alternativo; —**ly,** *adv.* alternativamente.
alternator, *n.* alternador, *m.*
althea, *n.* (bot.) malvavisco, *m.*, altea, *f.*
although, *conj.* aunque, no obstante, bien que; si.
altimeter, *n.* altímetro, *m.*
altitude, *n.* altitud, altura, *f.*; (aer.) elevación, *f.*
altogether, *adv.* del todo, juntamente.
altruism, *n.* altruismo, *m.*
alum, *n.* alumbre, *m.*
aluminous, *adj.* aluminoso.
aluminum, *n.* (chem.) aluminio, *m.*
alumnus, *n.* persona graduada de una escuela.
always, *adv.* siempre, constantemente, en todo tiempo, sin cesar.
alyssum, *n.* (bot.) alhelí, *m.*
Am., Amer., America, American, América, americano.
A. M., Master of Arts, Maestro o Licenciado en Artes.

A.M., a.m.: before noon, A.M. ante-meridiano; **amplitude modulation,** modulación de amplitud.

A. M. A. American Medical Association, Asociación Americana de Medicina.

am, 1ª persona del singular de indicativo del verbo **be.**

amain, adv. con vehemencia, vigorosamente; a velocidad máxima.

amalgam, n. mezcla de mercurio con un metal o metales.

amalgamate, vt. and vi. amalgamar.

amalgamation, n. amalgamación, f.

amanuensis, n. amanuense, m. y f., secretario, ria.

amaranth, n. (bot.) amaranto, m.

amaryllis, n. (bot.) planta perteneciente a las amarilídeas.

amass, vt. acumular, amontonar.

amateur, n. aficionado, da.

amateurish, adj. novicio.

amatory, adj. amatorio; erótico.

amaze, vt. sorprender, asombrar.

amazedly, adv. pasmadamente.

amazement, n. espanto, pasmo, m.

amazing, adj. extraño, pasmoso; —ly, adv. pasmosamente.

Amazon, Amazonas, m.

amazon, n. amazona, f.

ambassador, n. embajador, m.

ambassador at large, n. embajador acreditado ante varios países.

ambassadress, n. embajadora, f.

amber, n. ámbar, m.; —, adj. ambarino.

ambergris, n. ámbar gris.

ambidextrous, adj. ambidextro.

ambient, adj. ambiente; —, n. ambiente, m.

ambiguity, n. ambigüedad, duda, f.; equívoco, m.

ambiguous, adj. ambiguo; —ly, adv. ambiguamente.

ambit, n. ámbito, circuito, m.

ambition, n. ambición, f.

ambitious, adj. ambicioso; —ly, adv. ambiciosamente.

amble, n. paso de andadura del caballo; —, vi. amblar.

ambler, n. persona o caballo que anda a paso de andadura.

ambrosia, n. ambrosía, f.

ambrosial, adj. digno de los dioses; delicioso.

ambulance, n. ambulancia, f.; (mil.) hospital de campaña.

ambuscade, n. emboscada, celada, f.; sorpresa, f.; —, vi. preparar una emboscada.

ambush, n. emboscada, celada, f.; sorpresa, f.; —, vt. emboscar; **to lie in —,** estar emboscado.

ameliorate, vt. mejorar.

amelioration, n. mejoramiento, m.

amen, interj. amén.

amenable, adj. responsable; sujeto a.

amend, vt. enmendar; —, vi. enmendarse, reformarse, restablecerse.

amendable, adj. emendable, reparable.

amendment, n. enmienda, reforma, f.; remedio, m.

amends, n. recompensa, compensación, f.; satisfacción, f.; **to make —,** reparar.

amenity, n. amenidad, f.

amenorrhea, n. (med.) amenorrea, menostasia, f.; **to contract —,** opilarse.

American, n. and adj. americano, na.

Americana, n. pl. colección de documentos, escritos o objetos americanos.

amethyst, n. amatista, f.

amiability, n. amabilidad, f.

amiable, adj. amable, amigable.

amiably, adv. amablemente.

amicable, adj. amigable, amistoso; **—bly,** adv. amigablemente.

amice, n. (eccl.) amito, m.

amid, amidst, prep. entre, en medio de.

amiss, adj. importuno, impropio; —, adv. fuera de lugar; **to take —,** llevar a mal.

amity, n. amistad, f.

ammeter, n. amperímetro, m.

ammonia, n. amoníaco, m.

ammonium, n. (chem.) amonio, m.

ammunition, n. munición, f.; pertrechos, m. pl.

amnesia, n. amnesia, f.

amnesty, n. amnistía, f., indulto, m.

amoeba, n. amiba, ameba, f.

among, amongst, prep. entre, mezclado con, en medio de.

amoral, adj. amoral.

amorous, adj. amoroso; **—ly,** adv. amorosamente.

amorphous, adj. amorfo.

amortization, n. amortización, f.

amortize, vt. amortizar.

amount, n. importe, m.; cantidad, f.; suma, f.; monto, m.; producto, m.; (com.) montante, m.; **gross —,** importe bruto o total; **net —,** importe líquido o neto; —, vi. montar, importar, subir, ascender; **to — to,** sumar.

amour, n. intriga de amor.

amperage, n. amperaje, m.

ampere, n. (elec.) amperio, m.

amphibian, n. and adj. anfibio, m.

amphibious, adj. anfibio.

amphitheater, n. anfiteatro, m.

ample, adj. amplio, vasto.

amplification, n. amplificación, f.; extensión, f.

amplifier, n. amplificador, m.

amplify, vt. ampliar, extender; —, vi. extenderse.

amplitude, n. amplitud, extensión, f.; abundancia, f.; **— modulation,** modulación de amplitud.

amply, adv. ampliamente, copiosamente.

ampoule, ampule, n. ampolleta, ampolla, f.

amputate, vt. amputar.

amputation, n. amputación, f.; corte, m.

amt. amount, v/ valor.

amuck, adv. furiosamente, frenéticamente;

to run —, atacar a ciegas.
amulet, *n.* amuleto, *m.*
amuse, *vt.* entretener, divertir; hacer gracia.
amusement, *n.* diversión, *f.*, pasatiempo, entretenimiento, *m.*; deporte, *m.*; juego, *m.*; **— park,** parque de diversiones; **— parlor,** sala de recreo.
amusing, *adj.* divertido; **to be —,** tener gracia; **—ly,** *adv.* entretenidamente.
Amy, Amata.
an, *art.* un, uno, una.
anachronism, *n.* anacronismo, *m.*
anaconda, *n.* anaconda, *f.*
anaemia, *n.* anemia, *f.*
anaemic, *adj.* anémico.
anaesthesia, *n.* anestesia, *f.*
anaesthetic, *adj.* anestésico.
anaesthetize, *vt.* anestesiar.
anagram, *n.* anagrama, *m.*; **—s,** *n. pl.* (game) anagramas, *m. pl.*
analgesia, *n.* analgesia, *f.*
analgesic, *adj.* (med.) analgésico.
analogical, *adj.* analógico; **—ly,** *adv.* analógicamente.
analogous, *adj.* análogo.
analogy, *n.* analogía, conformidad, *f.*
analysis, *n.* análisis, *m.* y *f.*
analyst, *n.* analizador, *m.*
analytical, *adj.* analítico; **—ly,** *adv.* analíticamente.
analyze, *vt.* analizar.
anapest, *n.* anapesto, *m.*
anarchic, anarchical, *adj.* anárquico, confuso.
anarchism, *n.* anarquismo, *m.*
anarchist, *n.* anarquista, *m.* y *f.*
anarchy, *n.* anarquía, *f.*
anat. anatomy, anat. anatomía.
anathema, *n.* anatema, *m.* y *f.*, excomunión, *f.*
anathematize, *vt.* anatematizar.
anatomical, *adj.* anatómico; **—ly,** *adv.* anatómicamente.
anatomist, *n.* anatomista, *m.* y *f.*
anatomize, *vt.* anatomizar.
anatomy, *n.* anatomía, *f.*
ancestor, *n.* abuelo, *m.*; **—s,** antepasados, pasados, *m. pl.*
ancestral, *adj.* hereditario.
ancestry, *n.* linaje de antepasados, raza, alcurnia, prosapia, *f.*
anchor, *n.* ancla, áncora, *f.*; **—,** *vi.* ancorar echar las anclas; surgir; **to cast —,** dar fondo; **—,** *vt.* (naut.) sujetar con el ancla; **to swing the — around,** bornear.
anchorage, *n.* anclaje, *m.*; rada, *f.*; surgidero, *m.*
anchorite, *n.* anacoreta, *m.*
anchovy, *n.* anchoa, *f.*
ancient, *adj.* antiguo; **very —,** vetusto; **—ly,** *adv.* antiguamente.
ancillary, *adj.* ancilario.
and, *conj.* y; e (antes de palabras que empiezan con *i* o *hi*, con excepción de *hie*);

— so on, y así sucesivamente.
Andalusia, Andalucía, *f.*
andalusian, *n.* and *adj.* andaluzza.
andante, *adv.* and *adj.* (mus.) andante.
andiron, *n.* morillo, *m.*, caballete de hierro.
Andrew, Andrés.
Andy, Andrew, Andrés.
anecdotal, *adj.* anecdótico.
anecdote, *n.* anécdota, *f.*
anemia, *n.* anemia, *f.*
anemic, *adj.* anémico.
anemometer, *n.* anemómetro, *m.*
anemone, *n.* (bot.) anemone, *f.*
anent, *prep.* contra, respecto a.
anesthesia, *n.* anestesia, *f.*
anesthetic, *adj.* anestésico.
anesthetize, *vt.* anestesiar.
anew, *adv.* de nuevo, nuevamente, otra vez.
angel, *n.* ángel, *m.*
angelic, angelical, *adj.* angélico, angelical.
Angelus, *n.* ángelus, *m.*
anger, *n.* ira, cólera, *f.*; **—,** *vt.* enojar, irritar, encolerizar.
angina pectoris, *n.* angina de pecho; esternalgia, *f.*
angle, *n.* ángulo, *m.*; caña de pescar; **— iron,** cantonera, *f.*; **—,** *vt.* pescar con caña; halagar.
angler, *n.* pescador de caña; cañero, *m.*
angleworm, *n.* lombriz de tierra.
Anglicism, *n.* anglicismo, *m.*
Anglicize, *vt.* inglesar.
angling, *n.* pesca, *f.*
Anglo-Saxon, *n.* and *adj.* anglosajón.
angrily, *adv.* coléricamente, con ira.
angry, *adj.* colérico, irritado, enojado, indignado, resentido.
anguish, *n.* ansia, pena, angustia, *f.*; suplicio, *m.*; tósigo, *m.*; zozobra, *f.*
angular, *adj.* angular.
angularity, *n.* calidad de angular; **—ties,** *pl.* formas angulares.
anil, *n.* añil, *m.*
aniline, *n.* (chem.) anilina, *f.*; **— dye,** tinte de anilina.
animadversion, *n.* animadversión, *f.*; advertencia, *f.*; reprensión, *f.*
animadvert, *vi.* considerar, observar; censurar; reprochar.
animal, *n.* and *adj.* animal, *m.*, alimaña, *f.*
animalcule, *n.* animalejo, *m.*
animality, *n.* animalidad, *f.*
animate, *vt.* animar; alentar; **—,** *adj.* viviente, animado.
animation, *n.* animación, *f.*
animism, *n.* animismo, *m.*
animosity, *n.* animosidad, *f.*
animus, *n.* voluntad, *f.*; intención, *f.*
anise, *n.* anís, *m.*
aniseed, *n.* simiente de anís.
ankle, *n.* maléolo, tobillo, *m.*; **— bone,** hueso del tobillo.
anklet, *n.* tobillera, *f.*, tobillera elástica; calcetín corto.
Ann, Ana.

annals, *n. pl.* anales, *m. pl.*
anneal, *vt.* templar el vidrio.
annealed, *adj.* destemplado.
annealing, *n.* recocción, *f.*
annex, *vt.* anexar, unir, juntar; **—,** *n.* anejo, *m.*; anexo, *m.*; sucursal, *f.*
annexation, *n.* anexión, *f.*
annexed, *adj.* anexo.
annihilable, *adj.* aniquilable.
annihilate, *vt.* aniquilar.
annihilation, *n.* aniquilación, *f.*
anniversary, *n.* aniversario, *m.*; **—,** *adj.* ánual.
annotate, *vt.* anotar.
annotation, *n.* anotación, *f.*
announce, *vt.* anunciar, publicar; notificar, avisar.
announcement, *n.* advertencia, *f.*; aviso, anuncio, *m.*, notificación, *f.*
announcer, *n.* anunciador, ra; avisador, ra; locutor, ra; notificador, ra.
announcing, *adj.* pregonero; anunciante.
annoy, *vt.* molestar; fastidiar.
annoyance, *n.* molestia, *f.*; fastidio, *m.*; (coll.) lata, *f.*
annoying, *adj.* enfadoso, molestoso, fastidioso, importuno.
annual, *adj.* anual; **—ly,** *adv.* anualmente, de año en año.
annuitant, *n.* pensionista, *m.* y *f.*, persona que recibe una pensión.
annuity, *n.* renta anual; pensión, anualidad, *f.*; **life —,** pensión vitalicia, pensión, *f.*; anualidad, *f.*; **life —,** censo de por vida.
annul, *vt.* anular, aniquilar.
annular, *adj.* anular.
annulet, *n.* anillejo, *m.*; (arch.) armilla, *f.*, listel, filete, *m.*
annulment, *n.* anulación, *f.*
annum, *n.* año, *m.*
annunciate, *vt.* anunciar.
annunciation, *n.* anunciación, *f.*
anode, *n.* (elec.) ánodo, *m.*
anodyne, *adj.* (med.) anodino.
anoint, *vt.* untar, ungir.
anomalous, *adj.* anómalo, irregular; **—ly,** *adv.* irregularmente.
anomaly, *n.* anomalía, irregularidad, *f.*
anon, *adv.* presto, al instante, inmediatamente; **ever and —,** a menudo.
anon. anonymous, anón. anónimo.
anonymous, *adj.* anónimo; **—ly,** *adv.* anónimamente.
another, *adj.* otro, diferente; **one —,** uno a otro.
ans. answer, respta. respuesta.
answer, *vi.* responder, contestar, replicar; corresponder; **—,** *vt.* refutar; contestar; satisfacer; surtir efecto; **—,** *n.* respuesta, contestación, réplica, *f.*
answerable, *adj.* responsable; conforme; discutible.
ant, *n.* hormiga, *f.*; **— bear,** oso hormiguero; **white —,** comején, *m.*

antagonism, *n.* antagonismo, *m.*; rivalidad, *f.*
antagonist, *n.* antagonista, *m.* y *f.*; contrario, ria.
antagonistic, *adj.* antagónico.
antagonize, *vt.* contrariar, oponerse a.
antarctic, *adj.* antártico.
anteater, *n.* oso hormiguero.
antecedence, *n.* precedencia, *f.*; ascendencia, *f.*
antecedent, *adj.* antecedente; **—s,** *n. pl.* antecedentes, *m. pl.*
antechamber, *n.* antecámara, *f.*
antedate, *vt.* antedatar.
antediluvian, *adj.* antediluviano.
antelope, *n.* antílope, *m.*
antemeridian, *adj.* antemeridiano.
antenna, *n.* (zool. and rad.) antena, *f.*
anterior, *adj.* anterior, precedente.
anthem, *n.* antífona, *f.*; himno, *m.*
anther, *n.* (bot.) antera, *f.*
anthill, *n.* hormiguero, *m.*
anthology, *n.* antología, *f.*
Anthony, Antonio.
anthracite, *n.* antracita, *f.*, carbón de piedra.
anthrax, *n.* ántrax, *m.*
anthropoid, *n.* and *adj.* antropoide, *m.*
anthropology, *n.* antropología, *f.*
anthropomorphism, *n.* antropomorfismo, *m.*
anthropomorphous, *adj.* antropomorfo.
antiaircraft, *adj.* antiaéreo; **—,** *n.* antiaéreos, *m. pl.*
antibody, *n.* anticuerpo, *m.*
antic, *adj.* raro; grotesco; **—,** *n.* bufón, *m.*; **—s,** *n. pl.* travesuras, gracias, *f. pl.*
Antichrist, *n.* Antecristo, *m.*
anticipate, *vt.* anticipar, prevenir.
anticipation, *n.* anticipación, *f.*
anticipative, *adj.* anticipativo.
anticlerical, *adj.* anticlerical.
anticlericalism, *n.* anticlericalismo, *m.*
anticlimax, *n.* anticlímax, *m.* o *f.*
antidote, *n.* antídoto, contraveneno, *m.*, triaca, *f.*
antifederalist, *n.* antifederalista, *m.*
antifreeze, *n.* solución incongelable.
antifriction, *n.* antifricción, *f.*
antiknock, *adj.* antidetonante; **—,** *n.* antidetonante, *m.*
antimacassar, *n.* funda del reclinatorio de un sofá.
antimony, *n.* antimonio, *m.*
antipathetic, *adj.* antipático.
antipathy, *n.* antipatía, *f.*
antipodal, *adj.* antípoda; diametralmente opuesto.
antipodes, *n. pl.* antípodas, *m. pl.*
antiquarian, antiquary, *n.* anticuario, ria.
antiquated, *adj.* anticuado.
antique, *adj.* antiguo; **—,** *n.* antigualla, *f.*
antiquity, *n.* antigüedad, *f.*; ancianidad, *f.*
antirachitic, *adj.* antirraquítico.
anti-Semitic, *adj.* antisemítico.

antisepsis, *n.* antisepsia, *f.*
antiseptic, *adj.* antiséptico, antipútrido.
antislavery, *n.* antiesclavismo, *m.*
antisocial, *adj.* antisocial.
antispasmodic, *adj.* antiespasmódico.
antitank, *adj.* antitanque.
antithesis, *n.* antítesis, contrariedad, *f.*
antitoxic, *adj.* antitóxico.
antitoxin, *n.* antitoxina, *f.*
antitrust, *adj.* contra monopolios.
antler, *n.* mogote del ciervo.
antonym, *n.* antónimo, *m.*
Antwerp, Amberes, *f.*
anus, *n.* ano, culo, *m.*
anvil, *n.* yunque, *m.*; bigornia, *f.*
anxiety, *n.* ansiedad, ansia, *f.*; afán, *m.*;
cuidado, *m.*
anxious, *adj.* ansioso; inquieto; —ly, *adv.*
ansiosamente.
any, *adj.* and *pron.* cualquier, cualquiera,
alguno, alguna, todo; — **more,** más.
anybody, *pron.* alguno, alguien; cualquiera.
anyhow, *adv.* de cualquier modo; de todos
modos.
anyone, *pron.* alguno, cualquiera.
anything, *pron.* algo.
anyway, *adv.* como quiera; de todos modos.
anywhere, *adv.* en cualquier lugar, dondequiera.
aorta, *n.* aorta, *f.*
Ap., Apr. April, abl. abril.
A. P. Associated Press, P. A. Prensa
Asociada.
apace, *adv.* aprisa, con presteza o prontitud.
apart, *adv.* aparte; separadamente; —, *adj.*
separado.
apartment, *n.* apartamento, apartamiento,
m.; piso, *m.*; — **house,** casa de aparta-
mentos, apartamento.
apathetic, *adj.* apático.
apathy, *n.* apatía, *f.*
ape, *n.* mono, *m.*; simio, *m.*; —, *vt.* contrahacer, imitar.
Apennines, Apeninos, *m. pl.*
aperient, *adj.* (med.) laxante.
aperture, *n.* abertura, *f.*
apex, *n.* ápice, *m.*, cúspide, *f.*; colmo, *m.*;
cima, *f.*
aphid, *n.* afidio, *m.*
aphorism, *n.* aforismo, *m.*; máxima, *f.*
aphoristic, *adj.* aforístico.
apiary, *n.* colmena, *f.*; colmenar, *m.*
apiculture, *n.* apicultura, *f.*
apiece, *adv.* por cabeza, por persona.
apish, *adj.* gestero, mímico; monesco; —ly,
adv. afectadamente.
Apocalypse, *n.* Apocalipsis, *m.*
Apocrypha, *n. pl.* literatura apócrifa.
apocryphal, *adj.* apócrifo, no canónico;
fabuloso, fingido.
apogee, *n.* apogeo, *m.*
apologetic, apologetical, *adj.* apologético;
que se disculpa.
apologetics, *n.* apologética, *f.*
apologist, *n.* apologista, *m.* y *f.*

apologize, *vt.* defender; disculpar, pedir
excusas.
apology, *n.* apología, defensa, *f.*; satisfacción,
disculpa, *f.*
apoplectic or **apoplectical,** *adj.* apoplético.
apoplexy, *n.* apoplejía, *f.*
apostasy, *n.* apostasía, *f.*
apostate, *n.* apóstata, *m.* y *f.*
apostatize, *vi.* apostatar.
a posteriori, *adv.* a posteriori.
apostle, *n.* apóstol, *m.*
apostolic or **apostolical,** *adj.* apostólico.
Apostolic See, sede apostólica.
apostrophe, *n.* apóstrofe, *f.*; (gram.)
apóstrofo, *m.*
apostrophize, *vt.* apostrofar.
apothecary, *n.* boticario, *m.*; —'s **shop,**
n. botica, *f.*
apothegm, *n.* apotegma, *m.*
apotheosis, *n.* apoteosis, deificación, *f.*
appall or **appal,** *vt.* espantar, aterrar;
deprimir, abatir.
appalling, *adj.* aterrador, espantos.
appanage, *m.* dependencia, *f.*; infantado, *m.*
apparatus, *n.* aparato, aparejo, *m.*
apparel, *n.* traje, vestido, *m.*; ropa, *f.*;
wearing —, ropaje, *m.*; —, *vt.* vestir,
trajear; adornar.
apparent, *adj.* evidente, aparente; —ly,
adv. claramente, al parecer, por lo visto.
apparition, *n.* aparición, visión, *f.*
appeal, *vi.* apelar; recurrir; interesar; atraer;
suplicar; **to — from a judgment,** apelar
de un fallo; —, *n.* súplica, *f.*; exhortación,
f.; (law) apelación, *f.*; incentivo, estímulo,
m.; simpatía, atracción, *f.*
appear, *vi.* aparecer, manifestar; ser evidente; salir, parecer; **to — above the
water (as rocks),** velar.
appearance, *n.* apariencia, *f.*, aspecto, *m.*;
vista, *f.*; aparición, *f.*
appeasable, *adj.* aplacable, reconciliable.
appease, *vt.* aplacar, reconciliar; asosegar.
appellant, *n.* (law) apelante, *m.* y *f.*
appellate court, *n.* corte de apelación.
appellation, *n.* (law) apelación, *f.*; nombre,
m.
appellative, *n.* apelativo, *m.*; —, *adj.*
(gram.) apelativo.
appellee, *n.* (law) apelado, da.
append, *vt.* añadir, anexar.
appendage, *n.* cosa accesoria; apéndice,
m.; dependencia, *f.*
appendectomy, *n.* apendicectomía, *f.*
appendicitis, *n.* apendicitis, *f.*
appendix, *n.* apéndice, *m.*
apperception, *n.* apercepción, *f.*, percepción
del conocimiento interior.
appertain, *vi.* pertenecer, relacionarse.
appetite, *n.* apetito, *m.*; **keenness of** —,
gazuza, *f.*, apetito intenso.
appetizer, *n.* aperitivo, *m.*
appetizing, *adj.* apetitivo, apetitoso.
applaud, *vt.* aplaudir; alabar, palmear;
aclamar, palmotear.

applause, *n.* aplauso, *m.*; **thunderous —**, salva de aplausos.

apple, *n.* manzana, *f.*; **— of discord**, manzana de la discordia; **— of one's eye**, niña de los ojos; **— orchard**, manzanal, manzanar, *m.*; **— pie**, **— tart**, pastel o pastelillo de manzanas; **— tree**, manzano; *m.*; **— jack**, especie de chacolí.

applesauce, *n.* compota de manzana, puré de manzana.

appliance, *n.* aplicación, *f.*; utensilio, instrumento, aparato, *m.*, herramienta, *f.*

applicability, *n.* aptitud, aplicabilidad, *f.*

applicable, *adj.* aplicable, apto; conforme; **—bly**, *adv.* de un modo aplicable.

applicant, *n.* aspirante, solicitante, *m.* y *f.*, candidato, ta.

application, *n.* aplicación, *f.*; solicitud, *f.*

applied, *adj.* aplicado, adaptado.

apply, *vt.* aplicar, acomodar; **to — for**, solicitar; **—**, *vi.* dirigirse a, recurrir a; **to — oneself to**, dedicarse.

appoint, *vt.* señalar, determinar, decretar; nombrar, designar.

appointee, *n.* persona nombrada (para algún puesto).

appointment, *n.* estipulación, *f.*; decreto, mandato, *m.*, orden, *f.*; nombramiento, *m.*; cita, *f.*, compromiso, *m.*; designación, *f.*

apportion, *vt.* repartir, prorratear.

apportionment, *n.* repartición, *f.*, prorrateo, *m.*

appose, *vt.* colocar en lugar opuesto; aplicar (a alguna cosa).

apposite, *adj.* adaptado; propio; **—ly**, *adv.* convenientemente, a propósito.

apposition, *n.* aposición, *f.*

appraisal, *n.* avalúo, *m.*; tasación, *f.*; valuación, *f.*

appraise, *vt.* apreciar; tasar; valuar; estimar.

appraisement, *n.* aprecio, *m.*, estimación, *f.*; valuación, tasación, *f.*

appraiser, *n.* apreciador, ra, tasador, ra.

appreciable, *adj.* apreciable; sensible, perceptible.

appreciate, *vt.* apreciar; estimar; valuar.

appreciation, *n.* aprecio, *m.*; tasa, *f.*

appreciative, *adj.* apreciativo; agradecido.

apprehend, *vt.* aprehender, prender; concebir, comprender; temer.

apprehension, *n.* aprehensión, *f.*; recelo, *m.*; presa, captura, *f.*

apprehensive, *adj.* aprehensivo, tímido; perspicaz; **to become —**, sobrecogerse; **—ly**, *adv.* aprehensivamente.

apprentice, *n.* aprendiz, za; **—**, *vt.* poner a alguno de aprendiz.

apprenticeship, *n.* aprendizaje, tirocinio, *m.*

apprise, *vt.* informar, instruir.

approach, *vt.* and *vi.* abordar, aproximar, aproximarse; **—**, *n.* acceso, *m.*; acercamiento, *m.*; proximidad, *f.*

approachable, *adj.* accesible.

approbation, *n.* aprobación, *f.*

appropriate, *vt.* apropiar, adaptar; (com.) asignar (una partida); **—**, *adj.* apropiado; particular, peculiar.

appropriation, *n.* apropiación, *f.*; partida asignada para algún propósito.

approvable, *adj.* digno de aprobación.

approval, *n.* aprobación, *f.*

approve, *vt.* aprobar; dar la razón.

approximate, *vt.* and *vi.* acercar, acercarse; **—**, *adj.* aproximativo, aproximado; **—ly**, *adv.* aproximadamente.

approximation, *n.* aproximación, *f.*

appurtenance, *n.* (law) dependencia, pertenencia, *f.*

apricot, *n.* albaricoque, *m.*; (Mex.) chabacano, *m.*

April, *n.* abril, *m.*

a priori, *adv.* a priori.

apron, *n.* delantal, *m.*; plomada de cañón.

apropos, *adj.* and *adv.* oportuno; a propósito; **— of**, a propósito de.

apse, *n.* ápside, ábside, bóveda, *f.*

apt, *adj.* apto, idóneo; **—ly**, *adv.* aptamente.

aptitude, aptness, *n.* aptitud, *f.*; disposición natural.

aquacade, *n.* espectáculo acuático, natación y saltos ornamentales con acompañamiento musical.

aquaplane, *n.* acuaplano, *m.*; balsa de madera tirada por una lancha automóvil.

aquarium, *n.* acuario, *m.*; pecera, *f.*

Aquarius, *n.* Acuario (signo del zodíaco), *m.*

aquatic, *adj.* acuático, acuátil.

aquatint, *n.* acuatinta, *f.*; grabado al agua tinta.

aqueduct, *n.* acueducto, *m.*

aqueous, *adj.* acuoso.

aquiline, *adj.* aguileño.

Arab, Arabian, *n.* and *adj.* árabe, *m.* y *f.*, arábigo, ga.

arabesque, *n.* arabesco, *m.*

Arabic, *adj.* árabe, arábico; **—**, *n.* árabe, *m.* y *f.*

arable, *adj.* labrantío, cultivable.

Aragonese, *n.* and *adj.* aragonés, esa.

arbiter, *n.* arbitrador, árbitro, *m.*

arbitrament, *n.* arbitrio, *m.*

arbitrarily, *adv.* arbitrariamente.

arbitrariness, *n.* arbitrariedad, *f.*

arbitrary, *adj.* arbitrario, despótico.

arbitrate, *vt.* and *vi.* arbitrar, juzgar como árbitro.

arbitration, *n.* arbitramento, arbitrio, arbitraje, *m.*

arbitrator, *n.* arbitrador, árbitro, *m.*

arbor, *n.* emparrado, *m.*, enramada, *f.*

arboreal, *adj.* arbóreo.

arborescent, *adj.* arborescente.

arboretum, *n.* plantel, criadero, *m.*

arborvitae, *n.* (bot.) tuya, *f.*

arbutus, *n.* (bot.) madroño, *m.*, gayuba, *f.*

arc, *n.* arco, *m.*; **— lamp**, **— light**, lámpara de arco; **— weld**, **— welding**, soldadura de arco.

arcade, *n.* arcada, bóveda, *f.*

arcanum, *n.* arcano, *m.*, secreto muy importante.

arch, *n.* arco (de círculo, de puente, etc.), *m.*; —, *vt.* cubrir con arcos; —, *adj.* principal, insigne; grande; infame; artero, bellaco; (se usa en composición como aumentativo).

arch. architect, arq. arquitecto.

archaeological, *adj.* arqueológico.

archaeology, *n.* arqueología, *f.*

archaic, *adj.* arcaico.

archaism, *n.* arcaísmo, *m.*

archangel, *n.* arcángel, *m.*

archbishop, *n.* arzobispo, *m.*

archbishopric, *n.* arzobispado, *m.*

archdiocese, *n.* arzobispado, *m.*

archduchess, *n.* archiduquesa, *f.*

archduchy, *n.* archiducado, *m.*

archduke, *n.* archiduque, *m.*

arched, *adj.* arqueado, abovedado.

archer, *n.* arquero, *m.*

archery, *n.* arte de tirar con arco y flecha; ballestería, *f.*

archipelago, *n.* archipiélago, *m.*

architect, *n.* arquitecto, *m.*

architectural, *adj.* arquitectural.

architecture, *n.* arquitectura, *f.*

archives, *n. pl.* archivos, *m. pl.*

archivist, *n.* archivero, *m.*

archway, *n.* arcada, bóveda, *f.*

arctic, *adj.* ártico.

Arctic Circle, *n.* círculo ártico.

Arctic zone, *n.* zona ártica.

ardency, *n.* ardor, *m.*; vehemencia, *f.*; pasión, *f.*

ardent, *adj.* ardiente; apasionado; —ly, *adv.* con pasión, ardientemente.

ardor, *n.* ardor, *m.*; vehemencia, *f.*; pasión, *f.*

arduous, *adj.* arduo; laborioso; difícil.

are, plural y 2ª persona del singular de indicativo del verbo **be.**

area, *n.* área, *f.*; espacio, *m.*; superficie, *f.*

arena, *n.* palenque, *m.*; pista, *f.*

argil, *n.* arcilla, *f.*

argol, *n.* tártaro, *m.*

argon, *n.* (chem.) argón, *m.*

argot, *n.* jerigonza, *f.*

argue, *vi.* disputar, argüir; replicar; discurrir; —, *vt.* probar con argumentos; acusar.

argument, *n.* argumento, *m.*, controversia, *f.*

argumentation, *n.* argumentación, *f.*

Argus-eyed, *adj.* que tiene vista de lince.

argyrol, *n.* argirol, *m.*

aria, *n.* (mus.) aria, *f.*

arid, *adj.* árido, seco, estéril.

aridity, *n.* sequedad, *f.*

Aries, *n.* Aries (signo del zodíaco), *m.*

aright, *adv.* rectamente, justamente, bien; **to set** —, rectificar.

arise, *vi.* levantarse; nacer, provenir.

aristocracy, *n.* aristocracia, *f.*

aristocrat, *n.* aristócrata, *m.* y *f.*

aristocratic, *adj.* aristocrático; —ally, *adv.* aristocráticamente.

Aristotelian, *adj.* aristotélico.

arith. arithmetic, arit. aritmética.

arithmetic, *n.* aritmética, *f.*

arithmetical, *adj.* aritmético; —ly, *adv.* aritméticamente; — **progression,** progresión aritmética.

arithmetician, *n.* aritmético, *m.*

Ariz. Arizona, Arizona.

ark, *f.* arca, *f.*; **Ark of the Covenant,** arca del testamento.

Ark. Arkansas, Arkansas.

arm, *n.* brazo, *m.*; rama de árbol, poder, *m.*; arma, *f.*; — **in** —, de bracete; **at** —'s **length,** a una brazada; **to** — (oneself), armar(se); **to ground** —s, clavar las armas; **to walk** — **in** —, ir de bracero.

armadillo, *n.* armadillo, *m.*, mamífero desdentado.

Armageddon, *n.* cualquier grande y terrible conflicto o guerra.

armament, *n.* (naut.) armamento de navíos; (mil.) armamento, *m.*

armature, *n.* armadura, *f.*

armchair, *n.* silla de brazos, poltrona, butaca, *f.*

Armenian, *n.* and *adj.* armenio, nia.

armful, *n.* brazada, *f.*

armhole, *n.* sobaco, *m.*; hueco de la manga.

armistice, *n.* armisticio, *m.*

armlet, *n.* brazuelo, *m.*; brazalete, *m.*; guardabrazo de la armadura.

armor, *n.* armadura, *f.*; — **bearer,** escudero, *m.*; — **plate,** coraza, *f.*; **horse** —, barda, *f.*

armorial, *adj.* heráldico.

armory, *n.* armería, *f.*, arsenal, *m.*

armpit, *n.* sobaco, *m.*, axila, *f.*

army, *n.* ejército, *m.*; tropas, *f. pl.*; — **chaplain,** capellán castrense; — **corps,** cuerpo de ejército; — **engineer,** (mil.) gastador, *m.*; — **register,** escalafón, *m.*; **regular** —, tropa de línea; — **of occupation,** ejército de ocupación; — **worm,** noctua, *f.*, gusano del género de los nóctuidos.

arnica, *n.* árnica, *f.*

aroma, *n.* aroma, *m.*

aromatic, *adj.* aromático, oloroso.

around, *prep.* en, cerca; —, *adv.* al rededor; en o al derredor; en torno de.

arouse, *vt.* despertar; excitar; sublevar.

A R P, A. R. P. air-raid precautions, precauciones contra ataques aéreos.

arpeggio, *n.* (mus.) arpegio, *m.*

arquebus, *n.* arcabuz, *m.*

arraign, *vt.* citar, delatar en justicia; acusar.

arraignment, *n.* acusación, *f.*; proceso criminal.

arrange, *vt.* colocar, poner en orden, arreglar.

arrangement, *n.* colocación, *f.*; orden, arreglo, *m.*

arrant, *adj.* malo, perverso; infame; —ly, *adv.* corruptamente, vergonzosamente.

arras, *n.* tapicerías tejidas.

array, *n.* adorno, vestido, atavío, *m.*; orden de batalla; colocación de los jurados; —, *vt.* colocar; vestir, adornar; colocar los jurados.

arrear, *n.* resto de una deuda; atraso, *m.*

arrest, *n.* arresto, *m.*; detención, *f.*; —, *vt.* arrestar, prender; atraer (la atención).

arrival, *n.* arribo, *m.*; llegada, venida, *f.*

arrive, *vi.* arribar; conseguir; llegar; venir.

arrogance, *n.* arrogancia, presunción, *f.*

arrogant, *adj.* arrogante, presuntuoso; —ly, *adv.* arrogantemente.

arrogate, *vt.* arrogarse, atribuirse, apropiarse.

arrogation, *n.* arrogación, *f.*

arrow, *n.* flecha, saeta, *f.*, dardo, *m.*

arrowhead, *n.* casquillo, *m.*; punta de flecha.

arrowroot, *n.* (bot.) arrurruz, *m.*

arsenal, *n.* (mil.) arsenal, *m.*; (naut.) atarazana, armería, *f.*

arsenic, *n.* arsénico, *m.*

arson, *n.* incendio provocado intencionalmente.

art, *n.* arte, *m.* y *f.*; industria, *f.*; ciencia, *f.*; **the fine** —s, las bellas artes.

art.: article, art. artículo; **artillery,** artill. artillería.

arterial, *adj.* arterial, arterioso.

arteriosclerosis, *n.* arterioesclerosis, *f.*

artery, *n.* arteria, *f.*

artesian well, *n.* pozo artesiano.

artful, *adj.* artificioso; diestro; —ly, *adv.* artificiosamente, diestramente.

artfulness, *n.* astucia, habilidad, *f.*

arthritis, *n.* (med.) artritis, *f.*

arthropod, *n.* artrópodo, *m.*

Arthur, Arturo.

artichoke, *n.* alcachofa, *f.*

article, *n.* artículo, *m.*; **editorial** —, artículo de fondo, editorial, *m.*; —, *vi.* capitular, contratar mutuamente; —, *vt.* formular en artículos; acusar por escrito.

articulate, *adj.* articulado; claro, distinto; —ly, *adv.* distintamente; —, *vt.* articular, pronunciar distintamente.

articulation, *n.* articulación, *f.*; pronunciación, *f.*; (bot.) nudo en las plantas.

artifact, *n.* artefacto, especialmente el producido mediante procedimientos primitivos.

artifice, *n.* artificio, fraude, *m.*

artificer, *n.* artesano, *m.*

artificial, *adj.* artificial; artificioso; sintético; —ly, *adv.* artificialmente; artificiosamente.

artificiality, *n.* arte, astucia, *f.*; afectación, *f.*

artillery, *n.* artillería, *f.*

artilleryman, *n.* artillero, *m.*

artisan, *n.* mecánico, artesano, *m.*

artist, *n.* artista, *m.* y *f.*, pintor, ra.

artistic, *adj.* artístico; —ally, artísticamente.

artistry, *n.* habilidad artística.

artless, *adj.* sencillo, simple; —ly, *adv.* sencillamente, naturalmente.

Aryan, *n.* and *adj.* ario, aria.

as, *conj.* and *adv.* como; mientras; también; pues; en son de; visto que, pues que;

— **much,** tanto; — **a,** a fuer de; — **far** —, hasta; — **it were,** por decirlo; — **for,** — **to,** en cuanto a.

asbestos, *n.* asbesto, amianto, *m.*

ascend, *vi.* ascender, subir.

ascendancy, *n.* ascendiente, influjo, poder, *m.*

ascendant, *n.* ascendiente, *m.*, preeminencia, *f.*; horóscopo, *m.*; —, *adj.* superior, predominante.

ascension, *n.* ascensión, *f.*

ascent, *n.* subida, *f.*; eminencia, *f.*; altura, *f.*

ascertain, *vt.* asegurar, fijar; averiguar; establecer.

ascetic, *adj.* ascético; —, *n.* asceta, *m.*

asceticism, *n.* asceticismo, *m.*

ascribe, *vt.* adscribir; atribuir; adjudicar.

asepsis, *n.* asepsia, *f.*

aseptic, *adj.* aséptico.

asexual, *adj.* asexual, que carece de sexo.

ash, *n.* (bot.) fresno, *m.*; —es, *pl.* ceniza, *f.*; reliquias de un cadáver; — **heap,** — **tray,** — **pit,** cenicero, *m.*

ashamed, *adj.* avergonzado; **to be** —, tener vergüenza.

ashen, *adj.* hecho de fresno; ceniciento, pálido.

ashore, *adv.* en tierra, a tierra; **to get** —, desembarcar.

Ash Wednesday, *n.* miércoles de ceniza.

ashy, *adj.* cenizoso, ceniciento.

Asia Minor, Asia Menor, *f.*

Asiatic, *n.* and *adj.* asiático, ca.

aside, *adv.* al lado, aparte.

asinine, *adj.* asnal; estúpido.

asininity, *n.* asnería, necedad, tontería, *f.*; estupidez, *f.*

ask, *vt.* and *vi.* pedir, rogar, interrogar; demandar; **to** — **out,** convidar.

askance, *adv.* al sesgo, oblicuamente; de refilón; sospechosamente.

askew, *adv.* al lado; de lado; de través; con desdén.

aslant, *adv.* oblicuamente.

asleep, *adj.* dormido; **to fall** —, dormirse.

asp, *n.* áspid, *m.*

asparagus, *n.* espárrago, *m.*

aspect, *n.* aspecto, *m.*; vista, *f.*; aire, *m.*; semblante, *m.*

aspen, *n.* (bot.) tiemblo, *m.*, álamo temblón; —, *adj.* relativo al álamo temblón; tembloroso.

asperity, *n.* aspereza, rudeza, *f.*

asperse, *vt.* calumniar, infamar.

aspersion, *n.* aspersión, *f.*; difamación, calumnia, *f.*

asphalt, *n.* asfalto, *m.*

asphodel, *n.* asfódelo, *m.*

asphyxia, *n.* (med.) asfixia, *f.*

asphyxiate, *vt.* asfixiar.

asphyxiation, *n.* asfixia, sofocación, *f.*

aspirant, *n.* aspirante, *m.* y *f.*; candidato, ta.

aspirate, *vt.* aspirar, pronunciar con aspiración; —, *n.* sonido aspirado.

aspiration, n. aspiración, f.
aspire, vi. aspirar, desear.
aspirin, n. aspirina, f.
ass, n. borrico, asno, m.; **she —,** borrica, f.
assail, vt. asaltar, atacar, acometer.
assailant, assailer, n. asaltador, agresor, m.
assassin, n. asesino, matador, m.
assassinate, vt. asesinar, matar.
assassination, n. asesinato, m.
assault, n. asalto, m.; insulto, m.; **— and battery,** asalto a mano armada; **—,** vt. acometer, asaltar.
assay, n. ensayo, análisis, contraste (de monedas, etc.), m.; **—,** vt. ensayar, copelar.
assemblage, n. multitud, f.; ensambladura, f., empalme, m.
assemble, vt. congregar, convocar; afluir; ensamblar, armar; **—,** vi. juntarse.
assembly, n. asamblea, junta, f.; congreso, m.; montaje, m.; concurso, m.; concurrencia, f.; **gear —,** conjunto de engranaje; **— line,** línea de montaje.
assent, n. asenso, m.; aprobación, f., consentimiento, m.; **—,** vi. asentir, aprobar.
assert, vt. sostener, mantener; afirmar.
assertion, n. aserción, f.
assertive, adj. perentorio.
assess, vt. amillarar, imponer (contribución).
assessable, adj. que puede ser amillarado.
assessment, n. amillaramiento, impuesto, m.; catastro, m.
assessor, n. asesor, m.; **— of taxes,** tasador de impuestos.
assets, n. (com.) haber, activo, m., capital en caja; créditos activos, fondos, valores, activos, m. pl.; **real —,** bienes raíces; **personal —,** bienes muebles.
asseveration, n. aseveración, afirmación, f.
assiduity, n. asiduidad, aplicación, f.; constancia, f.
assiduous, adj. asiduo, aplicado, constante; **—ly,** adv. constantemente; diligentemente.
assign, vt. asignar, destinar, fijar; transferir algún derecho a otro.
assignable, adj. asignable.
assignation, n. asignación, f.; cesión, f.; cita (generalmente clandestina), f.
assignee, n. síndico, apoderado, m.; cesionario, m.; destinatario, m.
assignment, n. asignación, f.; cesión, f.; señalamiento, m.; tarea escolar.
assimilate, vt. asimilar; asemejar.
assimilation, n. asimilación, f.
assimilative, adj. asimilativo.
assist, vt. asistir, ayudar, socorrer, conllevar.
assistance, n. asistencia, f.; socorro, m.; colaboración, f.; **to go to the — of,** acudir en auxilio de.
assistant, n. asistente, ayudante, m.
assize, n. sesión de un tribunal; edicto, m.; tasa, f.
assn. association, asn. asociación.
associate, vt. asociar; acompañar; frecuentar; **—,** adj. asociado; **—,** n. socio, compañero, m.

association, n. asociación, unión, sociedad, agrupación, f.; club, m.
assonance, n. asonancia, f.
assort, vt. clasificar, ordenar.
assortment, n. surtido, m.; variedad, f.
asst. assistant, asistente, ayte. ayudante.
assuage, vt. mitigar, suavizar; **—,** vi. disminuir; apaciguarse.
assuagement, n. mitigación, calma, f.
assume, vt. arrogar, apropiar, presumir; **—,** vi. arrogarse; **—d,** adj. supuesto.
assumption, n. presunción, suposición, f.; **A—,** n. Asunción de la Virgen María.
assurance, n. seguridad, certeza, convicción, f.; fianza, f.; confianza, f.; seguro, m.
assure, vt. asegurar, afirmar; prometer.
assuredly, adv. ciertamente, sin duda, de seguro.
asterisk, n. asterisco, m.
astern, adv. (naut.) por la popa.
asteroid, adj. asteroide; **—,** n. asteroide, m.
asthma, n. asma, f.
asthmatic, adj. asmático.
astigmatism, n. (med.) astigmatismo, m.
astir, adj. agitado; activo; levantado de la cama.
astonish, vt. pasmar, sorprender.
astonishing, adj. asombroso; **—ly,** adv. asombrosamente.
astonishment, n. espanto, pasmo, asombro, m.; sorpresa, f.
astound, vt. consternar, aterrar, pasmar, conturbar.
astounding, adj. asombroso.
astraddle, adj. sentado a horcajadas.
astrakhan, n. astracán, m.
astral, adj. astral, de los astros.
astray, adj. and adv. extraviado, descaminado; en forma descaminada; **to lead —,** desviar, seducir; **to go —,** ir por mal camino.
astride, adj. sentado a horcajadas.
astringent, adj. astringente, estíptico.
astrolabe, n. astrolabio, m.
astrologer, n. astrólogo, m.
astrological, adj. astrológico.
astrology, n. astrología, f.
astronomer, n. astrónomo, m.
astronomical, adj. astronómico.
astronomy, n. astronomía, f.
astrophysics, n. astrofísica, f.
astute, adj. astuto; aleve.
asunder, adv. separadamente, en pedazos.
asylum, n. asilo, refugio, m.; seno, m.; **insane —,** casa de locos, manicomio, m.
asymmetry, n. asimetría, f.
at, prep. a, en; **— once,** al instante, de un golpe; **— all,** generalmente; **— all events,** a todo trance; **— first,** en el principio; **— large,** en libertad; **— last,** al fin, por último; **— your service,** su servidor o servidora; **his honor is — stake,** le va en ello su honor.
atavism, n. atavismo, m.
ataxia, n. ataxia, f.

ate, *p.p.* del verbo **eat.**
atelier, *m.* taller, *m.*
atheism, *n.* ateísmo, *m.*
atheist, *n.* ateísta, ateo, *m.*
atheistic, *adj.* impío.
Athenian, *n.* and *adj.* ateniense, *m.* y *f.*
Athens, Atenas, *f.*
athirst, *adj.* sediento; deseoso.
athlete, *n.* atleta, *m.* y *f.*; —'s foot, (med.) infección entre los dedos de los pies (generalmente contraída por los atletas en los gimnasios).
athletic, *adj.* atlético, vigoroso.
athlétics, *n.pl.* deportes, *m.pl.*
at-home, *n.* recepción en casa de carácter sencillo.
athwart, *prep.* al través; —, *adv.* con perversidad.
atilt, *adj.* inclinado; en ristre.
Atlantic, Atlántico, *m.*; — Charter, Declaración del Atlántico.
atlas, *n.* atlas, *m.*; atlante, *m.*
atmosphere, *n.* atmósfera, *f.*, ambiente, *m.*
atmospherical, *adj.* atmosférico.
atoll, *n.* atol, *m.*, isla de coral.
atom, *n.* átomo, *m.*
atomic, *adj.* atómico; — theory, teoría atómica; — weight, peso atómico.
atomization, *n.* pulverización, *f.*
atomize, *vt.* pulverizar; reducir a átomos.
atomizer, *n.* pulverizador, aromatizador, *m.*
atone, *vt.* expiar, aplacar, pagar.
atonement, *n.* expiación, propiciación, *f.*
atonic, *adj.* átono.
atop, *adv.* encima, en la punta o parte superior de alguna cosa.
atrocious, *adj.* atroz; enorme; odioso; —ly, *adv.* atrozmente.
atrocity, *n.* atrocidad, enormidad, *f.*
atrophy, *n.* (med.) atrofia, *f.*
atropine, *n.* (chem.) atropina, *f.*
att. attention, atención.
attach, *vt.* prender, pillar, asir, coger; ganar, adquirir, atraer a sí; embargar.
attaché, *n.* adjunto o agregado (a alguna legación).
attachment, *n.* adherencia, *f.*; afecto, *m.*; (law) embargo, secuestro, *m.*; aditamento, anexo, *m.*
attack, *vt.* atacar; acometer; to — the enemy, cargar; —, *n.* ataque, *m.*
attain, *vt.* ganar, conseguir, obtener, alcanzar.
attainable, *adj.* asequible.
attainder, *n.* proscripción de derechos civiles.
attainment, *n.* logro, *m.*; consecución de lo que se pretende; —s, *pl.* conocimientos, *m. pl.*
attaint, *vt.* (law) condenar, proscribir; infectar; corromper; deshonrar; —, *n.* baldón, *m.*, deshonra, *f.*; (law) muerte civil.
attar, *n.* aceite rosado o de rosas.
attempt, *vt.* tentar; probar, experimentar;

procurar; —, *n.* empresa, *f.*; experimento (peligroso), *m.*; tentativa, *f.*; prueba, *f.*
attend, *vt.* servir, asistir; acompañar; —, *vi.* prestar atención.
attendance, *n.* corte, *f.*; tren, séquito, *m.*; servicio, *m.*; cuidado, *m.*
attendant, *n.* sirviente, *m.*; cortejo, *m.*; —, *adj.* concomitante.
attending, *adj.* circunstante; — physician, médico de cabecera.
attention, *n.* atención, *f.*; cuidado, *m.*; to attract —, llamar la atención; to call —, hacer presente; to give — to, ocuparse en o de; to pay —, hacer caso, poner atención; to pay no —, no hacer caso.
attentive, *adj.* atento; cuidadoso; to be —, velar; —ly, *adv.* con atención.
attenuate, *vt.* atenuar, disminuir.
attenuation, *n.* atenuación, *f.*
attest, *vt.* atestiguar; dar fe.
attestation, *n.* atestación, *f.*; testimonio, *m.*
attic, *n.* desván, *m.*; guardilla, *f.*; A—, *adj.* ático, ateniense; clásico, refinado (aplícase al estilo literario).
attire, *n.* atavío, *m.*; —, *vt.* adornar, ataviar.
attitude, *n.* actitud, *f.*; postura, *f.*
attitudinize, *vi.* asumir cierta actitud.
attorney, *n.* procurador, abogado, *m.*; (law) mandatario, *m.*; — at law, procurador público; — general, fiscal, *m.*; — in fact, poderhabiente, *m.*
attract, *vt.* atraer; persuadir, seducir; to — attention, llamar la atención.
attraction, *n.* atracción, *f.*; atractivo, *m.*
attractive, *adj.* atractivo, halagüeño; seductor; tentador; —ly, *adv.* por atracción.
attributable, *adj.* imputable.
attribute, *vt.* atribuir, imputar; —, *n.* atributo, *m.*
attribution, *n.* atributo, *m.*; atribución, *f.*; reputación, *f.*
attrition, *n.* trituración, *f.*; fricción, *f.*
attune, *vt.* acordar; armonizar.
atty. attorney, abogado, pror. procurador.
auburn, *adj.* castaño rojizo; —, *n.* color castaño rojizo.
auction, *n.* venta pública, subasta, *f.*, remate, *m.*; to sell at public —, sacar a pública subasta.
auctioneer, *n.* corredor de almoneda, vendutero, *m.*
audacious, *adj.* audaz, temerario; —ly, *adv.* atrevidamente.
audacity, *n.* audacia, osadía, *f.*
audible, *adj.* perceptible al oído; —bly, *adv.* alto, de modo que se pueda oír.
audience, *n.* audiencia, *f.*; auditorio, *m.*; concurrencia, *f.*; oyentes, *m. pl.*; circunstantes, *m. pl.*
audiofrequency, *n.* audiofrecuencia, *f.*
audiometer, *n.* audiómetro, *m.*
audion, *n.* (radio) audión (marca de fábrica), *m.*
audit, *n.* remate de una cuenta; —, *vt.* rematar una cuenta, examinar; peletear.

audition, n. audición, f.

auditor, n. contador, m.; oidor, m.; **to be an —,** asistir de oyente.

auditorium, n. anfiteatro, m.; teatro, m.; sala de conferencias o diversiones, salón de actos.

auditory, n. auditorio, m.; **—,** adj. auditivo.

Aug. August, ag.^{to}, agt. agosto.

auger, n. barrena, f.

aught, n. alguna cosa; cero, m.; **—,** adv. en lo absoluto.

augment, vt. aumentar, acrecentar; **—,** vi. crecer.

augmentation, n. aumento, m.

augur, vi. augurar, adivinar por conjeturas; **to — ill,** no ser de buen augurio; **to — well,** ser de buen augurio.

augury, n. agüero, presagio, m.

August, n. agosto (mes), m.

August, Augustus, Augusto.

august, adj. augusto; majestuoso.

auk, n. pinguino, m., pájaro bobo.

aunt, n. tía, f.

aura, n. aura, f., viento suave y apacible; aureola, f.; (med.) aura, f.

aureole, n. aureola, auréola, f.

auricle, n. oreja, f.; aurícula, f.

auricular, aural, adj. dicho al oído; que se sabe por tradición; **—ly,** adv. al oído; secretamente.

auriferous, adj. aurífero.

aurora, n. aurora, f.; **— borealis,** aurora boreal.

auscultation, n. auscultación, f.

auspices, n. auspicio, m.; protección, f.; **under the — of,** bajo los auspicios de.

auspicious, adj. próspero, favorable; propicio; **—ly,** adv. prósperamente.

austere, adj. austero, severo, rígido; **—ly,** adv. austeramente.

austerity, n. austeridad, f.; mortificación, f.; severidad, f.

Austin, Agustín.

austral, adj. austral, austrino.

Australian, n. and adj. australiano, na.

Austrian, n. and adj. austríaco, ca.

autarchy, n. autarquía, f.

autarky, n. autarquía, f.

authentic, adj. auténtico; (law) fehaciente; **—ally,** adv. auténticamente.

authenticate, vt. autenticar.

authenticity, n. autenticidad, f.

author, n. autor, escritor, m.

authoress, n. autora, escritora, f.

authoritarian, n. and adj. autoritario, m., autoritaria, f.

authoritative, adj. autoritativo; **—ly,** adv. autoritativamente, con autoridad.

authoritativeness, n. presunción, f.; apariencia autoritativa.

authority, n. autoridad, f.; férula, f.

authorization, n. autorización, f.

authorize, vt. autorizar; **—d,** adj. autorizado, facultado.

authorship, n. calidad de autor.

autobiography, n. autobiografía, f.

autobus, n. ómnibus automóvil, autobús, m.

autocade, n. desfile de automóviles.

autocar, n. coche automóvil.

autocracy, n. autocracia, f.

autocrat, n. autócrata, m.

autocratic, autocratical, adj. autocrático.

autogiro, autogyro, n. autogiro, m.

autograph, n. autógrafo, m.

automat, n. restaurante de servicio mecánico.

automatic, adj. automático.

automatism, n. automatismo, m.

automaton, n. autómata, m.

automobile, n. automóvil, m.; **— horn,** bocina, f., (Cuba) fotuto, m.

automotive, adj. automotriz.

autonomous, adj. autónomo.

autonomy, n. autonomía, f.

autopsy, n. autopsia, necroscopía, f.

autosuggestion, n. autosugestión, f.

autotruck, n. autocamión, m.

autumn, n. otoño, m.

autumnal, adj. otoñal; **— equinox,** equinoccio de otoño.

auxiliaries, n. pl. tropas auxiliares.

auxiliary, adj. auxiliar, asistente.

A. V. Authorized Version, V. A. Versión Autorizada.

Av. Average, promedio.

avail, vt. aprovechar; **—,** vi. servir, ser ventajoso; **—,** n. provecho, m.; ventaja, f.; **— oneself of,** aprovecharse de.

available, adj. útil, ventajoso; disponible.

avalanche, n. alud, lurte, m.; torrente, m.

avarice, n. avaricia, f.

avaricious, adj. avaro; **—ly,** adv. avaramente.

avaunt, interj. ¡fuera! ¡quita!

avdp. avoirdupois, sistema de pesos vigente en E.U.A. e Inglaterra.

ave. avenue, av. avenida.

avenge, vt. and vi. vengarse, castigar; vindicar.

avenger, n. vengador, ra.

aventurine, n. venturina, f.

avenue, n. avenida, f.

aver, vt. afirmar, verificar, declarar.

average, vt. tomar un término medio; promediar; **—,** n. promedio, m.; (naut.) avería, f.; **—,** adj. medio.

averse, adj. contrario, repugnante; **—ly,** adv. con repugnancia.

aversion, n. aversión, f., disgusto, m.

avert, vt. desviar, apartar.

aviary, n. pajarera, f.

aviation, n. aviación, f.; **— grounds,** campo de aviación.

aviator, n. aviador, m.

aviatrix, n. aviadora, f.

avid, adj. ávido, codicioso, voraz.

avidity, n. codicia, avidez, f.

avocado, n. aguacate, m.

avocation, n. ocupación accesoria; diversión, chifladura, f.; pasatiempo, m., afición, f.

avoid, *vt.* evitar, escapar, huir; (law) anular.

avoidable, *adj.* evitable.

avoidance, *n.* evitación, fuga, *f.*

avoirdupois, *n.* sistema de pesos vigente en E. U. A. e Inglaterra.

avouch, *vt.* afirmar, justificar, sostener.

avow, *vt.* confesar, declarar.

avowal, *n.* declaración justificativa, confesión, *f.*

avowedly, *adv.* declaradamente, abiertamente.

await, *vt.* aguardar; **—ing your reply,** en espera de sus noticias.

awake, *vt.* and *vi.* despertar; **—,** *adj.* despierto.

awaken, *vi.* despertar.

awakening, *n.* despertamiento, *m.*

award, *vt.* juzgar; otorgar, adjudicar; **—,** *n.* sentencia, decisión, *f.*; premio, *m.*, adjudicación,*f.*

aware, *adj.* cauto, vigilante; sabedor; enterado; consciente; **with —ness,** a sabiendas.

away, *adv.* ausente, fuera; **—!** *interj.* ¡fuera, quita de ahí, marcha! **far and —,** de mucho, con mucho.

awe, *n.* miedo, *m.*, temor reverencial; **—,** *vt.* infundir miedo o temor reverencial.

awe-inspiring, *adj.* imponente.

awesome, *adj.* espantoso. aterrador.

awe-stricken, *adj.* aterrado, espantado.

awe-struck, *adj.* aterrado, espantado; embargado por el respeto.

awful, *adj.* tremendo; funesto; horroroso; **—ly,** *adv.* con respeto y veneración.

awhile, *adv.* por un rato, por algún tiempo.

awkward, *adj.* tosco, inculto, rudo, desmañado; chabacano; torpe, poco diestro; **—ly,** *adv.* groseramente, toscamente.

awkwardness, *n.* tosquedad, grosería, *f.*; poca habilidad.

awl, *n.* lesna, *f.*

awning, *n.* (naut.) toldo (para resguardarse del sol), *m.*; **small —,** toldillo, *m.*

awry, *adj.* and *adv.* oblicuo, oblicuamente, torcidamente, al través.

ax, axe, *n.* segur, *f.*; hacha, *f.*

axiom, *n.* axioma, *m.*

axiomatic, *adj.* axiomático.

axis, *n.* eje, *m.*; alianza, *f.*; **the A—,** el Eje; **the A— nations,** las naciones del Eje (alianza entre Alemania, Italia y el Japón).

axle, *n.* eje de una rueda; **— box,** buje, *m.*; **front —,** eje delantero; **rear —,** eje trasero: **vertical —,** (aer.) eje vertical.

aye, *adv.* sí.

azalea, *n.* (bot.) azalea, *f.*

azure, *adj.* azulado; **—,** *n.* color cerúleo.

B

b.: book, l. libro; **born,** n. nacido.

B.A. Bachelor of Arts, Br. en A. Bachiller en Artes.

baa, *n.* balido, *m.*; **—,** *vi.* balar.

babbitt, *n.* metal blanco, metal antifricción.

babble, *vi.* charlar, parlotear; **—, babbling,** *n.* charla, cháchara, *f.*, murmullo (de un arroyo), *m.*

babbler, *n.* trápala, *m.* **y** *f.*; charlatán, ana.

babe, *n.* niño pequeño, nene, infante, *m.*

babel, *n.* babel, *m.* o *f.*, confusión,*f.*

baboon, *n.* cinocéfalo, *m.*, mono grande; mandril, *m.*

baby, *n.* niño pequeño, nene, infante, *m.*; **— boy,** (coll.) chiquirritín, *m.*; **— girl,** (coll.) chiquirritina, *f.*; **— carriage,** cochecillo para pasear al niño; **—'s diaper,** braga, *f.*, pañal, *m.*; **— grand,** piano de media cola.

babyhood, *n.* niñez, infancia, *f.*

babyish, *adj.* pueril.

baccalaureate, *n.* bachillerato, *m.*

bacchanal, *adj.* bacanal; **—,** *n.*, bacanal, *m.*

bachelor, *n.* soltero, *m.*; bachiller, *m.*

bacillus, *n.* bacilo, microbio, *m.*

back, *n.* dorso, *m.*; espalda, *f.*; lomo, *m.*; revés de la mano; recazo, *m.*; **— of a book,** lomo, *m.*; **flat —,** lomo plano; **loose —,** lomo hueco; **to carry on the —,** llevar o traer a lomo; **to turn one's —,** dar la espalda; **—,** *adj.* posterior; **— number,** número atrasado de algún periódico; (coll.) persona anticuada; **— payment,** paga atrasada; **— seat,** asiento trasero; **—,** *vt.* sostener, apoyar, favorecer: **to — up,** recular; **—,** *adv.* atrás, detrás; **to come —,** regresar; **to come — again,** regresar por segunda vez; **a few years —,** algunos años ha; **to fall —,** hacerse atrás; **to go — to,** remontar a; **— of,** detrás, tras de.

backache, *n.* dolor de espalda.

backbite, *vt.* difamar; **—,** *vi.* difamar a una persona que está ausente.

backbone, *n.* hueso dorsal, espinazo, *m.*, espina, *f.*

backbreaking, *adj.* apurador, agotador.

backdoor, *n.* puerta trasera.

backer, *n.* partidario, sostenedor, *m.*

backfield, *n.* los jugadores detrás de la línea en el juego de fútbol.

backfill, *n.* relleno, *m.*

backfire, *vt.* (mech.) abrir claros mediante fuego para contener un incendio; producirse explosiones prematuras en cilindros o tubos de escape.

backfiring, *n.* encendido prematuro; fogonazo del encendido.

backgammon, *n.* juego de chaquete o tablas.

background, *n.* fondo, *m.*; ambiente, *m.*; antecedentes, *m. pl.*, educación, *f.*

backlog, *n.* tronco trasero en una hoguera: (com.) reserva de pedidos pendientes.

backslide, *vi.* tergiversar; reincidir.

backspin, *n.* retruque, *m.*; **to put a — on a ball,** retrucar.

backstage, *n.* (theat.) parte detrás del

telón o detrás de bastidores.
backstairs, *adj.* clandestino.
back stairs, *n.* escalera trasera; escalera secreta.
backstitch, *n.* pespunte, *m.*
backstop, *n.* reja para detener la pelota en el juego de baseball; la persona que coge la pelota.
backstroke, *n.* reculada, *f.*;' revés, *m.*; movimiento propulsor nadando de espalda.
backtrack, *vi.* retirarse.
backward, *adj.* opuesto; retrógrado; retrospectivo; tardo, lento; **to be —,** ser tímido; **—s, —ly,** *adv.* preposteramente; con repugnancia; de la cola.
backwardness, *n.* torpeza, *f.*; tardanza, *f.*; atraso, *m.*
backwash, *n.* agua de rechazo.
backwater, *n.* contracorriente, *f.*; agua de rechazo, remolino, *m.*; región o condición estacionaria.
bacon, *n.* tocino, *m.*
bacteria, *n. pl.* bacterias, *f. pl.*
bacteriological, *adj.* bacteriológico.
bacteriologist, *n.* bacteriólogo, microbiólogo, *m.*
bacteriology, *n.* bacteriología, *f.*
bacterium, *n.* bacteria, *f.*
bad, *adj.* mal, malo; perverso; infeliz; dañoso; indispuesto; vicioso; **to look —,** tener mala cara; **— debt,** trampa, *f.*; **— humor,** berrinche, *m.*; **—ly,** *adv.* malamente.
badge, *n.* señal, *f.*; símbolo, *m.*; divisa, *f.*; **—,** *vt.* divisar.
badger, *n.* tejón, *m.*; **—,** *vt.* fatigar; cansar, atormentar.
badminton, *n.* badminton, *m.*, juego que se parece al tenis y en que se usan volantes en vez de pelotas.
bad-tempered, *adj.* de mal humor, de mal carácter.
baffle, *vt.* eludir; confundir, hundir; acosar.
bag, *n.* saco, *m.*; talega, *f.*; bolsa, *f.*; talego, *m.*; **coal —,** paniego, *m.*; **sleeping —,** talego de noche; **wine —,** bota, *f.*; **—,** *vt.* entalegar.
bagasse, *n.* bagazo, *m.*
baggage, *n.* bagaje, equipaje, *m.*; **— car,** furgón, *m.*, coche o carro de equipajes, vagón, *m.*; **— check,** talón, *m.*; **— master,** jefe de equipajes; **— office,** equipajes, *m. pl.*; **— room,** sala de equipajes; **— train,** tren de equipaje; **excess —,** exceso de equipaje; **hand —,** equipaje de mano.
baggy, *adj.* flojo, holgado.
bagnio, *n.* casa de baños (italiana o turca); burdel, *m.*
bagpipe, *n.* gaita, *f.*
bail, *n.* fianza, caución (juratoria), *f.*; fiador, *m.*; recuado, *m.*; **to go — for,** salir fiador; **—,** *vt.* caucionar, fiar; salir fiador; dar fianza; **to give —,** sanear; **on —,** bajo fianza; **to — out,** vaciar.
bailee, *n.* (law) depositario, *m.*

bailiff, *n.* alguacil, *m.*; mayordomo, baile, *m.*
bait, *vt.* cebar; azuzar; atraer; **—,** *vt.* tomar un refrigerio; **—,** *n.* cebo, *m.*; anzuelo, *m.*; refrigerio, *m.*; carnada, *f.*
baize, *n.* bayeta, *f.*
bake, *vt.* cocer en horno.
bakelite, *n.* bakelita, *f.*
baker, *n.* hornero, panadero, *m.*; **—'s dozen,** trece piezas; **—'s mop,** barredero, *m.*
bakery, *n.* panadería, *f.*; tahona, *f.*; cocedero, *m.*; **owner of a —,** tahonero, *m.*
baking, *n.* hornada, *f.*; **— soda,** bicarbonato de sosa.
bal. balance, saldo.
balance, *n.* balanza, *f.*; equilibrio, *m.*; resto, *m.*; balance, *m.*; volante de reloj; saldo de una cuenta; **— scale,** peso, *m.*; **— sheet,** balance, *m.*; **credit —,** saldo acreedor; **debit —,** saldo deudor; **net —,** saldo líquido; **to lose one's —,** caerse, dar en tierra; perder el equilibrio; **—,** *vt.* pesar en balanza; contrapesar; saldar; considerar; examinar; **—,** *vi.* dudar, fluctuar; **to — an account,** cubrir una cuenta; **— of power,** equilibrio político; **— of trade,** balanza comercial.
balbriggan, *n.* tejido de algodón para medias y ropa interior.
balcony, *n.* balcón, *m.*; antepecho, *m.*; galería, *f.*; anfiteatro, *m.*
bald, *adj.* calvo; simple, desabrido.
baldness, *n.* calvicie, *f.*; desnudez, *f.*
bale, *n.* bala, *f.*; fardo de mercaderías, *m.*; paca, *f.*; **—,** *vt.* embalar; tirar el agua del bote.
baleful, *adj.* pernicioso, nocivo; **—ly,** *adv.* perniciosamente, en forma nociva.
baling, *n.* embalaje, *m.*; **—,** *adj.* relativo al embalaje; **— machine,** empaquetadora, *f.*
balk, *vt.* viga, *f.*; faja de tierra sin surcar; desliz, *m.*; impedimento, obstáculo, *m.*; yerro, fracaso (en los deportes), *m.*; **—,** *vi.* rebelarse (un caballo, etc.); resistirse.
ball, *n.* bola, *f.*; pelota, *f.*; bala, *f.*; baile, *m.*; **small bowling —,** boliche, bolillo, *m.*; **— (of yarn, etc.),** ovillo (de estambre, etc.), *m.*; **— bearing,** cojinete de bolas; **— player,** pelotari, *m.*; **— and chain,** grillos, *m. pl.*; **— -and-socket joint,** articulación de nuez, articulación esférica o de bola y encastre.
ballad, *n.* balada, *f.*; chanzoneta, *f.*; romance, *m.*
ballast, *n.* lastre, *m.*; (rail.) balasto, *m.*; **—,** *vt.* lastrar.
ballerina, *n.* bailarina, *f.*
ballet, *n.* bailete, ballet, *m.*
ballistics, *n.* balística, *f.*
balloon, *n.* globo, *m.*; máquina aerostática, *f.*; **— tire,** neumático o llanta balón.
ballot, *n.* cédula para votar; escrutinio, *m.*; papeleta, balota, *f.*; **—,** *vi.* votar con balotas; **— box,** urna electoral.
ballplayer, *n.* jugador de pelota.
ballroom, *n.* salón de baile.

ballyhoo, *n.* alharaca, *f.*
balm, balsam, *n.* bálsamo, *m.*; —, *vt.* untar con bálsamo; suavizar.
balmy, *adj.* balsámico; fragante; mitigante.
Baltic, Báltico, *m.*
baluster, *n.* balaústre, *m.*
balustrade, *n.* balaustrada, *f.*
bamboo, *n.* bambú, *m.*
bamboozle, *vt.* (coll.) engañar, embaucar; confundir, aturdir.
ban, *n.* bando, anuncio, *m.*; excomunión, *f.*; proclama, *f.*; prohibición, *f.*; —, *vt.* prohibir, vedar; excomulgar; maldecir.
banal, *adj.* trivial; —**ity,** *n.* trivialidad.
banana, *n.* plátano, *m.*, banana, *f.*, banano, guineo, cambur, *m.*
band, *n.* venda, faja, *f.*; unión, *f.*; cuadrilla, *f.*; banda (de soldados), *f.*; orquesta, capilla, *f.*; —**master,** maestro de capilla, músico mayor; —(on edge of cloth), cenefa, *f.*; —, *vt.* unir, juntar; vendar.
bandage, *n.* venda, faja, *f.*; vendaje, *m.*; — for a rupture, braguero, *m.*; wrist —, pulsera, *f.*; —, *vt.* vendar, fajar.
bandanna, *n.* pañuelo de seda de las Indias Orientales.
bandbox, *n.* caja de cartón; sombrerera, *f.*
bandit, *n.* bandido, da.
bandstand, *n.* quiosco, *m.*, plataforma de banda, quiosco de música.
bandwagon, *n.* carro de banda de música.
bandy, *vt.* pelotear; discutir.
bandy-legged, *adj.* patizambo.
bane, *n.* veneno, *m.*; causa de ruina; —, *vt.* envenenar; perjudicar.
baneful, *adj.* venenoso, destructivo.
bang, *n.* puñada, *f.*; puñetazo, *m.*; ruido de un golpe; —**s,** flequillo (del cabello), *m.*; —, *vt.* dar puñadas, sacudir; cerrar con violencia; —! *interj.* ¡pum!
bangle, *n.* brazalete, *m.*, ajorca, *f.*
banish, *vt.* desterrar, echar fuera, proscribir, expatriar.
banishment, *n.* destierro, *m.*
banister, *n.* balaústre, pasamano, *m.*, baranda, *f.*
banjo, *n.* banjo (especie de guitarrilla), *m.*
bank, *n.* orilla (de río), ribera, *f.*; montón de tierra; banco, cambio, *m.*; dique, *m.*; escollo, *m.*; — **book,** libreta de banco o de depósitos; — **indicator,** (aer.) indicador de viraje; — **note,** billete, *m.*, billete de banco; **blood** —, banco de sangre; **savings** —, banco de ahorros; **state** —, banco del estado; **trust** —, banco de depósito; —, *vt.* poner dinero en un banco; detener el agua con diques; (aer.) banquear; **to** — (an airplane), escorar.
banker, *n.* banquero, cambista, *m.*
banking, *n.* banca, *f.*; —, *adj.* bancario; — **house,** casa de banca.
bankrupt, *adj.* insolvente; quebrado, en bancarrota; —, *n.* fallido, quebrado, *m.*, persona en bancarrota.
bankruptcy, *n.* bancarrota, quiebra, *f.*

banner, *n.* bandera, *f.*; estandarte, *m.*
banneret, *n.* ricohombre de pendón y caldera; bandereta, *f.*
banquet, *n.* banquete, *m.*, comida suntuosa; —, *vt.* banquetear.
bantam, *n.* gallina u otra ave típica de Bantam.
banter, *vt.* zumbar; divertirse a costa de alguno; —, *n.* zumba, burla, *f.*
baptism, *n.* bautismo, bautizo, *m.*
baptismal, *adj.* bautismal.
baptistery, *n.* bautisterio, *m.*
baptize, *vt.* bautizar.
bar, *n.* barra, *f.*; tranca, *f.*; obstáculo, *m.*; (law) estrados, *m. pl.*; aparador, *m.*; cantina, *f.*; barrera, *f.*; palanca, *f.*; —, *vt.* barrear; cerrar con barras; impedir; prohibir; excluir; —**s,** rejas, *f. pl.*; — **room,** taberna, cantina, *f.*; **in** —, **in** —**s,** en barra o barras; — **gold, bullion gold,** oro en barra.
bar.: barometer, barómetro; **barrel,** brl. barril.
barb, *n.* púa, *f.*; lengüeta (de anzuelo, etc.), *f.*; caballo típico de Berbería; especie de barba en algunos animales; —, *vt.* proveer con lengüetas.
Barbados, Barbadas, *f. pl.*
barbarian, *n.* hombre bárbaro; —, *adj.* bárbaro, cruel.
barbarism, *n.* (gram.) barbarismo, *m.*; crueldad, *f.*; barbaridad, *f.*
barbarity, *n.* barbaridad, inhumanidad, *f.*
barbarous, *adj.* bárbaro, cruel; —**ly,** *adv.* bárbaramente, cruelmente.
Barbary, Berbería, *f.*
barbecue, *n.* barbacoa, *f.*
barbed, *adj.* barbado; — **spearhead,** roquete, *m.*; — **wire,** alambre de púas.
barber, *n.* barbero, *m.*; peluquero, *m.*
barberry, *n.* bérbero, agracejo, *m.*; — **confection,** bérbero, *m.*
barbershop, *n.* peluquería, barbería, *f.*
barbette, *n.* (mil.) barbeta, *f.*
barcarole, barcarolle, *n.* barcarola, *f.*
bard, *n.* bardo, poeta, vate, *m.*
bare, *adj.* desnudo, descubierto; simple; público; pobre; puro; —, *vt.* desnudar, descubrir, privar.
bareback (horseback riding), *adj.* en cerro o en pelo (al montar a caballo).
barefaced, *adj.* con la cara descubierta; desvergonzado, imprudente.
barefoot, barefooted, *adj.* descalzo, sin zapatos.
barehanded, *adj.* sin guantes.
bareheaded, *adj.* descubierto, con la cabeza al aire.
barelegged, *adj.* con las piernas desnudas.
barely, *adv.* apenas, solamente; pobremente.
bareness, *n.* desnudez, *f.*; pobreza, *f.*
bargain, *n.* contrato, pacto, *m.*; ganga, *f.*; trato de compra o venta; — **counter,** barato, *m.*; —, *vi.* pactar, negociar; regatear.

barge, _n._ falúa, chalupa, _f._; barcaza, _f._
bargeman, _n._ barquero, _m._
barilla, _n._ barrilla, _f._
baritone, _n._ (mus.) barítono, _m._
barium, _n._ (chem.) bario, _m._
bark, _n._ corteza, _f._; ladrido, _m._, ladra (del perro), _f._; **Peruvian —,** cascarilla, _f._; **—,** _vt._ descortezar; **—,** _vi._ ladrar.
barkeeper, _n._ tabernero, cantinero, _m._
barley, _n._ cebada, _f._
barmaid, _n._ moza de taberna.
barn, _n._ granero, henil, pajar, _m._; establo, _m._
barnacle, _n._ barnacla, _m._; acial, _m._
barnyard, _n._ patio de granja, corral, _m._
barometer, _n._ barómetro, _m._; **— reading,** indicación del barómetro.
barometric, _adj._ barométrico; **— reading,** indicación de barómetro.
baron, _n._ barón, _m._; (coll.) poderoso industrial.
baronage, _n._ baronía, _f._
baroness, _n._ baronesa, _f._
baronet, _n._ título de honor inferior al de barón y superior al de caballero.
baroque, _adj._ barroco.
barouche, _n._ birlocho, _m._
barrack, _n._ cuartel, _m._; caserna, barraca, _f._
barrage, _n._ cortina de fuego; presa de contención; **— balloon,** globo de barrera.
barrel, _n._ barril, _m._; cañón de escopeta; cilindro, _m._; **— organ,** gaita, _f._; organillo de cilindro; **—,** _vt._ embarrilar.
barrelmaker, _n._ pipero, barrilero, tonelero, _m._
barrelmaking, _n._ tonelería, _f._
barren, _adj._ estéril, infructuoso; seco; **—ly,** _adv._ infructuosamente, sin fruto.
barrette, _n._ broche para el cabello.
barretter, _n._ indicador de oscilaciones eléctricas.
barricade, _n._ barricada, _f._; estacada, _f._; barrera, _f._; **—,** _vt._ cerrar con barreras, empalizar; atrincherar.
barrier, _n._ barrera, _f._; obstáculo, _m._
barring, _prep._ excepto, fuera de.
barrister, _n._ abogado, _m._
barrow, _n._ angarillas, _f. pl._; cerdo castrado.
bartender, _n._ tabernero, cantinero, _m._
barter, _vi._ baratar, traficar; **—,** _vt._ cambiar, trocar; **—,** _n._ cambio, trueque, _m._
Bartholomew, Bartolomé, Bartolomeo o Bártolo.
basal, _adj._ basal, fundamental; **— metabolism,** metabolismo basal.
basalt, _n._ basalto, _m._
base, _n._ fondo, _m._; basa, base, _f._; pedestal, _m._; contrabajo, _m._; pie, _m._; **— hit,** golpe de pelota con que se gana un puesto, logro del primer puesto (en baseball); **—,** _vt._ apoyar; basar; **—,** _adj._ bajo, vil; **—d,** basado; **—ly,** _adv._ bajamente, vilmente.
baseball, _n._ baseball, beisbol, _m._; pelota de baseball; juego de baseball.
baseboard, _n._ tabla que sirve de base; zócalo, _m._

baseless, _adj._ sin fondo o base.
baseman, _n._ (baseball) jugador de pelota colocado en uno de los tres primeros puestos o bases en el rombal del campo de baseball; hombre estacionado en uno de los puestos del rombal de baseball.
basement, _n._ basamento, sótano, _m._
baseness, _n._ bajeza, vileza, _f._; ilegitimidad de nacimiento, mezquindad, _f._
bashful, _adj._ vergonzoso, modesto, tímido; **—ly,** _adv._ vergonzosamente tímidamente.
bashfulness, _n._ vergüenza, modestia, timidez, cortedad, esquivez, _f._
basic, _adj._ fundamental; **—ally,** _adv._ fundamentalmente.
Basil, Basilio.
basilica, _n._ basílica, _f._
basilisk, _n._ (zool.) basilisco, _m._
basin, _n._ jofaina, bacía, _f._; **— (for blood),** sangradera, _f._
basis, _n._ base, _f._; fundamento, _m._, suposición, _f._; pie, _m._
bask, _vi._ ponerse a tomar el sol.
basket, _n._ cesta, canasta, _f._; **— maker,** cestero, _m._; **— porter,** capachero, _m._; **— shop, — factory,** cestería, _f._
basketball, _n._ baloncesto, _m._; juego de balón.
basketwork, _n._ fabricación de cestas, cestería, _f._
Basle, Basilea, _f._
Basque, _n. and adj._ vasco; **— cap,** boina, _f._; **— language,** vascuence, _m._
bas-relief, _n._ bajo relieve.
bass, _n._ estera, _f._; esparto, _m._; (mus.) contrabajo, bajo, _m._; (zool.) lobina, _f._, róbalo, _m._; **—,** _adj._ bajo; **— drum,** (mus.) bombo, _m._; **— horn,** tuba, _f._; **— viol,** violoncelo, _m._
bassinet, _n._ cesta-cuna, cuna, _f._
basso, _n._ (mus.) bajo, _m._
bassoon, _n._ (mus.) bajón, _m._
bastard, _n. and adj._ bastardo, da.
bastardy, _n._ bastardía, _f._
baste, _vt._ dar golpes con un bastón; pringar la carne en el asador; hilvanar; bastear.
bastinado, _n._ bastonada, _f._; **—,** _vt._ dar golpes con un bastón.
basting, _n._ hilván, _m._, basta, _f._; apaleamiento, _m._, paliza, _f._
bastion, _n._ (mil.) bastión, _m._
bat, _n._ (baseball) bate, garrote, palo, _m._; (orn.) murciélago, _m._; **—,** _vt._ batear.
bat.: battalion, bat. batallón; **battery,** bat. batería.
batch, _n._ cochura, hornada, _f._; cantidad de cosas producidas a un tiempo; pilada, _f._; carga, _f._; colada, _f._; (Arg.) pastón, _m._; (Cuba) templa, _f._; (Mex.) turno de colada; (Sp. Am.) tongada, _f._
bath, _n._ baño, _m._; **— tub,** bañera, bañadera, _f._, tina de baño.
bathe, _vt. and vi._ bañar, bañarse.
bathhouse, _n._ casa de baños; balneario, _m._
bathing, _n._ baño, _m._; **— beach,** playa de

baños; — **resort,** balneario, m.
bathrobe, n. peinador, m.; bata de baño.
bathroom, n. cuarto de baño.
batik, n. batik, m., método de ejecutar diseños de color sobre paño; tela con este diseño.
baton, n. batuta, f.
battalion, n. (mil.) batallón, m.
batten, n. astilla, f.; — **work,** enlistonado, m.; —, vt. cebar; —, vi. engordar; enlistonar.
batter, n. batido, m.; talud, m.; pasta culinaria; (baseball) voleador (de la pelota), m.; — **post,** tornapunta, f.; —, vt. apalear; batir; cañonear; demoler.
battering-ram, n. (mil.) ariete, m., brigola, f.
battery, n. acumulador, m.; batería, f.; pila, f.; — **box,** caja de batería; — **cell,** elemento de batería; **charged** —, batería cargada; **discharged** —, batería descargada; **dry** —, batería o pila seca; **storage** —, batería de acumuladores; **wet** —, batería líquida.
battle, n. batalla, f.; combate, m.; — **array,** orden de batalla; — **front,** frente de combate; **pitched** —, batalla campal; **sham** —, simulacro, m.; —, vi. batallar, combatir; — **cry,** grito de batalla; — **ground,** campo de batalla; — **royal,** pelotera, f.
battledore, n. raqueta, f.
battlefield, n. campo de batalla.
battlement, n. muralla almenada.
battle-scarred, adj. cicatrizado en batalla; que ha sufrido mucho, que ha tenido mucha experiencia.
battleship, n. acorazado, m.
battling, adj. batallador.
bauble, n. chuchería, f., cosa pequeña de poca importancia.
bauxite, n. bauxita, f.
Bavaria, Baviera, f.
Bavarian, n. and adj. bávaro, ra.
bawl, vi. gritar, vocear; ladrar.
bawler, n. chillón, ona.
bay, n. puerto donde se abrigan las embarcaciones; bahía, f.; laurel, lauro, m.; — **rum,** agua olorosa que sirve de cosmético; — **window,** mirador, m.; ventana saledizа; —, vi. ladrar; balar; —, adj. bayo; **to keep at** —, tener a raya.
bayberry, n. (bot.) arrayán, m.
bayonet, n. bayoneta, f.; —, vt. traspasar con la bayoneta.
bayou, n. canalizo, m.; pasaje entre dos cuerpos de agua; brazo afluente de un río.
bazaar, n. bazar, m.
bazooka, n. (mil.) (coll.) cañón antitanques portátil que dispara cohetes.
bbl. barrel, brl. barril.
B.C. Before Christ, a. de J.C. antes de Jesucristo.
B.C.L. Bachelor of Civil Law, Br. D.C. Bachiller en Derecho Civil.

bdl. bundle, bto. bulto o f/ fardo.
be, vi. ser; estar; quedar; **to** — **ill,** estar malo, estar enfermo; **to** — **in a hurry,** estar de prisa; **to** — **right,** tener razón; **to** — **standing,** estar de pie; **to** — **well,** estar bien o bueno.
beach, n. costa, ribera, orilla, playa, f.; nadadero, m.; — **comber,** vagabundo de las playas; —, vt. and vi. (naut.) encallar.
beachhead, n. desembarque costero adelantado para facilitar la llegada de tropas de refuerzo.
beach wagon, n. automóvil con carrocería parecida a la de carruajes ligeros antiguos, con asientos transversales y toldo plano.
beacon, n. almenara, f., fanal, faro, m.
bead, n. cuenta, chaquira, f.; —s, n. pl. rosario, m.
beadwork, n. abalorio, m.
beagle, n. sabueso, m.
beak, n. pico, m.; espolón de navío.
beaker, n. taza con pico.
beam, n. lanza de coche; rayo de luz; volante, m.; brazos de balanza; **to fly on the** —, volar siguiendo la línea de radiación; — **of timber,** madero, m.; —, vi. emitir rayos, brillar.
beaming, adj. radiante.
bean, n. (bot.) haba, habichuela, f.; frijol, m.; **kidney** —s, frijoles rojos o colorados; **navy** —s, frijoles blancos.
beano, n. variedad de lotería de cartones.
bear, n. oso, m.; (in stocks) bajista (en la bolsa), m.; **grizzly** —, oso grizzli; **she** —, osa, f.; —, vt. llevar alguna cosa como carga; sostener; apoyar; soportar; producir; parir; conllevar, portar; —, vi. sufrir (algún dolor); pasar a algún paraje; tolerar; —, vt. and vi. resistir; **to** — **a grudge,** guardar rencor; **to** — **in mind,** tener presente.
beard, n. barba, f.; arista de espiga; — (**of barley or wheat**), raspa, f.; —, vt. insultar a uno.
bearded, adj. barbado; barbudo; (bot.) aristado.
beardless, adj. desbarbado, joven, imberbe.
bearer, n. portador, ra; arbol fructífero.
bearing, n. situación, f.; comportamiento, m.; relación, f.; sufrimiento, m., paciencia, f.; (mech.) cojinete, m.; chumacera, f.
beast, n. bestia, f.; bruto, m.; res, f.; hombre brutal; — **of burden,** acémila, f.
beastly, adj. bestial, brutal; —, adv. brutalmente.
beat, vt. golpear; batir; **to** — (**with a cane or stick**), bastonear; tocar (un tambor); pisar; abatir; (in a game) ganar (en un juego); —, vi. pulsar, palpitar; —, n. golpe, m.; pulsación, f., ronda, f.
beater, n. maza, f.; batidera, f.; agitador, m.; mezclador, m.; persona que gana un juego.
beatific, adj. beatífico.
beatification, n. beatificación, f.
beatify, vt. beatificar, santificar.

beating, *n.* paliza, zurra, *f.*; soba, *f.*; pulsación, *f.*; **to give one a —,** cimbrar o cimbrear a alguno, dar a alguno una paliza.

beatitude, *n.* beatitud, felicidad, *f.*

Beatrice, Beatriz.

beau, *n.* petimetre, currutaco, *m.*; novio, pretendiente, *m.*

beauteous, *adj.* bello, hermoso.

beautification, *n.* embellecimiento, *m.*

beautiful, *adj.* hermoso, bello; precioso; **—ly,** *adv.* con belleza o perfección.

beautify, *vt.* hermosear, embellecer; adornar; **—,** *vi.* hermosearse.

beauty, *n.* hermosura, belleza, *f.*; preciosidad, *f.*; **— contest,** concurso de pulcritud o belleza; **— parlor,** salón de belleza o peinados; **— spot,** lunar postizo.

beaver, *n.* castor, *m.*; sombrero de pelo de castor; **— board,** cartón de fibras para techos interiores y tabiques.

becalm, *vt.* serenar, calmar alguna tempestad; sosegar.

because, *conj.* porque; pues; que; **— of,** a causa de.

beck, *n.* seña, *f.*, indicación muda; **at one's — and call,** a la mano, a la disposición.

beckon, *vi.* hacer seña con la cabeza, o la mano, llamar con señas.

becloud, *vt.* oscurecer, anublar.

become, *vt.* sentar, quedar bien; **—,** *vi.* hacerse, convertirse; ponerse; llegar a ser; **to — like flesh,** carnificarse; **to — soft,** suavizarse.

becoming, *adj.* sentador, conveniente; **—ly,** *adv.* correctamente; en forma sentadora.

bed, *n.* cama; (geol.) yacimiento, *m.*; **— mat,** traspuntín, *m.*; **— sheet,** sábana, *f.*; **folding —,** cama plegadiza; **head of a —,** cabecera, *f.*; **river —,** cauce, *m.*; **—,** *vt.* acostar, meter en la cama; **to make the —,** hacer la cama; **to stay in —,** guardar cama.

bedaub, *vt.* salpicar; ensuciar.

bedbug, *n.* chinche, *f.*

bedchamber, *n.* dormitorio, *m.*

bedclothes, *n. pl.* cobertores, *m. pl.*, mantas, colchas, *f. pl.*

bedding, *n.* ropa de cama.

bedeck, *vt.* adornar, asear.

bedecked, *adj.* adornado.

bedew, *vt.* rociar; regar.

bedizen, *vt.* ataviar; perifollar.

bedlam, *n.* manicomio, *m.*; bullicio, *m.*; ginebra, confusión, *f.*

Bedouin, *adj.* beduino.

bedpan, *n.* chata, *f.*, silleta para enfermos.

bedplate, *n.* solera, placa, *f.*; plancha de cimiento; (print.) platina, *f.*

bedpost, *n.* pilar de cama.

bedquilt, *n.* cobertor de cama acolchado.

bedraggle, *vt.* ensuciar arrastrando por el suelo.

bedridden, *adj.* postrado en cama (sea por vejez o enfermedad).

bedrock, *n.* lecho de roca, peña sólida, base, *f.*, fondo, *m.*

bedroom, *n.* alcoba, *f.*, cuarto de dormir, dormitorio, *m.*, recámara, *f.*

bedspread, *n.* colcha, cubrecama, sobrecama, *f.*

bedspring, *n.* colchón de muelles.

bedstead, *n.* armazón de cama, cuja, *f.*

bedtime, *n.* hora de acostarse.

bee, *n.* abeja, *f.*; **— glue,** tanque, *m.*, cera aleda.

beech, *n.* (bot.) haya, *f.*

beechen, *adj.* (bot.) de haya.

beechnut, *n.* hayuco, *m.*

beef, *n.* buey, toro, *m.*; vaca, *f.*; carne de res o de vaca; **— tea,** caldo, *m.*; **jerked —,** tasajo, *m.*

beefsteak, *n.* lonja de carne de vaca, biftec, bistec, *m.*

beehive, *n.* colmena, *f.*

beekeeper, *n.* colmenero, *m.*

beeline, *n.* línea recta.

been, *p. p.* del verbo **be.**

beer, *n.* cerveza, *f.*; **small —,** cerveza floja.

beeswax, *n.* cera de abejas.

beet, *n.* remolacha, betarraga, *f.*; (Mex.) betabel, *m.*; **— root,** betarraga, *f.*; **— sugar,** azúcar de remolacha.

beetle, *n.* escarabajo, *m.*; pisón, *m.*

beetle-browed, *adj.* cejudo.

beeves, *n. pl.* de **beef,** carnes de vaca.

befall, *vi.* suceder, acontecer, sobrevenir.

befit, *vt.* convenir, acomodarse a, cuadrar.

befog, *vt.* envolver en niebla; confundir, desconcertar.

befool, *vt.* infatuar; engañar.

before, *adv.* más adelante; delante, enfrente; ante, antes de; **—,** *prep.* antes de, ante; delante de, enfrente de; **—,** *conj.* antes que.

beforehand, *adv.* de antemano, con anterioridad, anticipadamente.

beforetime, *adv.* en tiempo pasado, tiempo atrás.

befoul, *vt.* ensuciar, emporcar.

befriend, *vt.* favorecer, proteger, amparar.

beg, *vt.* mendigar, rogar; suplicar; pedir; **—,** *vi.* vivir de limosna.

began, pretérito del verbo **begin.**

beget, *vt.* engendrar.

beggar, *n.* mendigo, ga; (Sp. Am.) limosnero, ra; **—,** *vt.* empobrecer.

beggarly, *adj.* pobre, miserable; despreciable.

beggary, *n.* mendicidad, mendiguez, *f.*

begin, *vt.* and *vi.* comenzar, principiar.

beginner, *n.* principiante, *m.* y *f.*, novicio, cia.

beginning, *n.* principio, comienzo, *m.*; origen, *m.*; cabecera, *f.*; **—s,** *pl.* rudimentos, *m. pl.*; **at the —,** al principio; **— with,** a partir de.

begone, *interj.* ¡fuera, apártate de ahí!

begonia, *n.* begonia, *f.*

begrime, *vt.* encenagar, ennegrecer, embarrar, manchar.

begrudge, *vt.* envidiar.
beguile, *vt.* engañar.
begun, *p. p.* del verbo **begin.**
behalf, *n.* favor, patrocinio, *m.*; consideración, *f.*; **in — of,** en pro de.
behave, *vi.* comportarse, portarse (bien o mal) manejarse.
behavior, *n.* conducta, *f.*; comportamiento, *m.*; **honorable —,** caballerosidad, *f.*
behaviorism, *n.* behaviorismo, *m.*
behead, *vt.* decapitar, cortar la cabeza; **act of —ing,** degüello, *m.*
behest, *n.* mandato, precepto, *m.*
behind, *prep.* detrás; atrás; de la cola; inferior a; **from —,** por detrás; **—,** *adv.* atrasadamente; fuera de la vista.
behindhand, *adv.* con atraso.
behold, *vt.* ver, contemplar, observar; **—!** *interj.* ¡he aquí! ¡vele ahí!
beholden, *adj.* obligado (por gratitud).
behoof, *n.* provecho, *m.*; utilidad, ventaja, *f.*
behoove, *vi.* importar, ser útil o necesario, incumbir, corresponder, recaer, tocar.
beige, *n.* color entre rojo y amarillo o entre gris y pardo, color arena.
being, *n.* existencia, *f.*; estado, *m.*; ente, *m.*; persona (que existe), *f.*
bejewel, *vt.* enjoyar.
belabor, *vt.* apalear, dar puñadas; atacar verbalmente.
belated, *adj.* demorado, atrasado.
belch, *vi.* eructar, vomitar; **—,** *n.* eructo, *m.*, eructación, *f.*
beldam, beldame, *n.* vejezuela, *f.*; bruja, *f.*
beleaguer, *vt.* sitiar, bloquear.
belfry, *n.* campanario, *m.*
Belgian, *adj.* bélgico, belga; **—,** *n.* belga, *m.* y *f.*
Belgium, Bélgica, *f.*
belie, *vt.* contrahacer; desmentir, calumniar.
belief, *n.* fe, creencia, *f.*; opinión, *f.*; credo, *m.*
believable, *adj.* creíble.
believe, *vt.* creer; **—,** *vi.* pensar, imaginar.
believer, *n.* creyente, fiel, cristano, *m.*
belittle, *vt.* dar poca importancia, achicar.
bell, *n.* campana, *f.*; bronce, *m.*; **— ringer,** campanero, *m.*; **call —,** timbre, *m.*; **sleigh —,** cascabel, *m.*; **—,** *vi.* crecer una planta en figura de campana; gritar (como los ciervos).
belladonna, *n.* (med.) belladona, *f.*
bellboy, *n.* botones, lacayuelo, *m.*, mozo de hotel.
belle, *n.* beldad, *f.*
belles-lettres, *n. pl.* bellas letras, *f. pl.*
bellhop, *n.* mozo de hotel.
bellicose, *adj.* belicoso.
belligerent, *adj.* beligerante.
bellman, *n.* pregonero, *m.*
bellow, *vi.* bramar; rugir; vociferar; **—,** *n.* bramido, *m.*
bellowing, *adj.* rugiente.
bellows, *n.* fuelle, *m.*
belly, *n.* vientre, *m.*; panza, barriga, *f.*
belong, *vi.* pertenecer, tocar a, concernir.

belongings, *n. pl.* propiedad, *f.*; efectos, anexos, *m. pl.*
beloved, *adj.* querido, amado.
below, *adv.* and *prep.* debajo, inferior; abajo.
belt, *n.* cinturón, cinto, *m.*; correa, *f.*; cintura, *f.*; **transmission —,** correa de transmisión; **sword —s,** tiros, *m. pl.*; **below the —,** debajo de la cintura; **to tighten one's —,** tomar aliento, soportar.
bemoan, *vt.* deplorar, lamentar.
bench, *n.* banco, *m.*; tribunal, *m.*
bend, *vt.* encorvar, inclinar, plegar; combar; hacer una reverencia; **—,** *vi.* encorvarse; cimbrarse; inclinarse; **—,** *n.* comba, encorvadura, *f.*; codo, *m.*; giro, *m.*; **sharp —,** curva cerrada.
beneath, *adv.* and *prep.* debajo, abajo; de lo más hondo.
Benedict, Benito.
benediction, *n.* bendición, *f.*
benefactor, *n.* bienhechor, ra.
benefice, *n.* beneficio, *m.*; beneficio eclesiástico.
beneficence, *n.* beneficencia, liberalidad, *f.*
beneficent, *adj.* benéfico; **—ly,** *adv.* benéficamente.
beneficial, *adj.* beneficioso, provechoso, útil; **—ly,** *adv.* provechosamente, ventajosamente.
beneficiary, *n.* beneficiario, ria.
benefit, *n.* beneficio, *m.*; utilidad, *f.*; provecho, *m.*; bien, *m.*; **for the — of,** a beneficio de; **—,** *vt.* beneficiar; **—,** *vi.* beneficiarse; prevalerse; **— of clergy,** inmunidades del clero; sanción de la iglesia.
benevolence, *n.* benevolencia, gracia, *f.*; donativo gratuito.
benevolent, *adj.* benévolo; **— society,** sociedad benéfica.
Bengal, Bengala, *f.*
Bengalese, *n.* and *adj.* bengalí.
benighted, *adj.* anochecido; ignorante, indocto.
benign, *adj.* benigno; afable; liberal; **—ly,** *adv.* benignamente.
benignant, *adj.* bondadoso.
benignity, *n.* benignidad, bondad, dulzura, *f.*
bent, *n.* encorvadura, *f.*; inclinación, *f.*
benumb, *vt.* entorpecer.
benzene, *n.* (chem.) bencina, *f.*
benzoin, *n.* benjuí, *m.*
benzol, *n.* benzol, *m.*
bequeath, *vt.* legar en testamento.
bequest, *n.* legado, *m.*
berate, *vt.* reñir, reprender duramente.
bereave, *vt.* despojar, privar.
bereavement, *n.* despojo, *m.*; luto, duelo, *m.*
bereft, *adj.* despojado, privado.
beret, *n.* boina, *f.*
berlin, *n.* berlina (coche), *f.*
Berlinian, *n.* and *adj.* berlinés, esa.
Bernard, Bernardo.
berry, *n.* baya, *f.*

Bert, Bertie, Albert, Alberto; **Bertram,** Beltrán; **Herbert,** Heriberto.

berth, n. (naut.) alojamiento de un navío, litera, f.; camarote, m.

Bertha, Berta.

Bertram, Beltrán.

beseech, vt. suplicar, implorar, conjurar, rogar.

beseem, vi. convenir, parecer bien.

beset, vt. sitiar; cercar; perseguir; acosar; aturdir, confundir.

besetting, adj. habitual (aplícase al peligro o al pecado).

beside, besides, prep. al lado de; excepto; sobre; fuera de; tras de; —, adv. por otra parte, aun.

besiege, vt. sitiar, bloquear; acosar.

besmear, vt. salpicar, ensuciar.

besmirch, vt. manchar, ensuciar.

besot, vt. infatuar; embrutecer.

bespatter, vt. manchar o salpicar con algo sucio; difamar.

bespeak, vt. ordenar, apalabrar alguna cosa.

besprinkle, vt. rociar, esparcir.

best, adj. mejor; — **man,** padrino de boda; —, adv. mejor; —, n. lo mejor; **to do one's —,** hacer lo posible.

bestial, adj. bestial, brutal; —**ly,** adv. bestialmente.

bestiality, n. bestialidad, brutalidad, f.

bestir, vt. and vi. moverse, excitar a acción.

bestow, vt. dar, conferir; otorgar; dar en matrimonio; regalar; — **upon,** deparar.

bestowal, n. donativo, m., dádiva, f.

bet, n. apuesta, f.; —, vt. apostar.

bethink, vt. recordar algo; —, vi. considerar, pensar.

Bethlehem, Belén, m.

betide, vi. acaecer, suceder.

betoken, vt. anunciar; denotar.

betray, vt. hacer traición, traicionar; divulgar algún secreto.

betrayal, n. traición, f.

betroth, vt. contraer esponsales; desposarse; **to become —ed,** prometerse.

betrothal, n. esponsales, m. pl.

betrothed, adj. comprometido, prometido; —, n. prometido, da.

better, adj. and adv. mejor; más bien; — **half,** cara mitad; **so much the —,** tanto mejor; —**s,** n. pl. superiores, m. pl.; —, vt. mejorar, reformar.

bettor, better, n. apostador, ra.

between, betwixt, prep. entre, en medio de.

bevel, n. cartabón, m.; sesgadura, f.; bisel, m.; — **square,** — **rule,** falsarregla, f.; —, vt. cortar un ángulo al sesgo, biselar.

beverage, n. bebida, f.; trago, m.; **cold —,** refresco, m.

bevy, n. bandada (de aves), f., grupo (de mujeres), m.

bewail, vt. and vi. lamentar, deplorar.

beware, vi. tener cuidado, guardarse; —! interj. ¡cuidado! ¡mira!

bewilder, vt. descaminar; pasmar; —, vi.

extraviarse; confundirse.

bewilderment, n. extravío, m.; confusión, f.

bewitch, vt. encantar, hechizar.

bewitchingly, adv. halagüeñamente; de manera encantadora.

beyond, prep. más allá, más adelante, fuera de.

bezel, n. chatón, m.

b.f., bf. bold-faced (type), letra negra (de imprenta).

biannual, adj. semestral, semianual.

bias, n. propensión, inclinación, parcialidad, f.; preocupación, f.; sesgo, m.; objeto, fin, m.; **on the —,** al sesgo; **to cut on the —,** sesgar; —, vt. inclinar; preocupar; ganar.

biased, adj. predispuesto.

bib, n. babador, babero, m.

Bible, n. Biblia (la sagrada escritura), f.

Biblical, adj. bíblico.

bibliography, n. bibliografía, f.

bibliophile, n. bibliófilo, m.

bicameral, adj. con dos cámaras legislativas.

bicarbonate, n. bicarbonato, m.

bicentenary, n. segundo centenario.

biceps, n. bíceps, m.

bichloride, n. (chem.) bicloruro, m.

bicker, vi. escaramucear, reñir, disputar.

bicuspid, adj. bicúspide; —, n. bicúspide, m.

bicycle, n. bicicleta, f.; **to ride a —,** montar en bicicleta.

bicycling, n. ciclismo, m.

bicyclist, n. biciclista, m. y f.

bid, vt. convidar; mandar, ordenar; ofrecer; — **adieu to,** despedirse; —, n. licitación, proposición, oferta, f.

bidding, n. orden, f., mandato, m.; ofrecimiento, m.

bide, vi. esperar, aguardar; permanecer; —, vt. sufrir, aguantar.

biennial, adj. bienal.

bier, n. féretro, ataúd, m.

bifocal, adj. bifocal.

bifurcated, adj. bifurcado.

bifurcation, n. bifurcación, f.

big, adj. grande, lleno; inflado; **B— Dipper,** (ast.) Osa Mayor; — **game,** casa mayor.

bigamist, n. bígamo, ma.

bigamy, n. bigamia, f.

big-headed, adj. cabezón, cabezudo.

bighearted, adj. generoso, liberal, espléndido, magnánimo.

bight, n. cala, ensenada, bahía, f.

bigness, n. grandeza, f.; tamaño, bulto, m.

bigot, n. persona fanática; hipócrita, m. y f.

bigoted, adj. santurrón, intolerante; —**ly,** adv. como un santurrón.

bilateral, adj. bilateral.

bilberry, n. arándano, m.

bile, n. bilis, f.; cólera, f.; **black —,** atrabilis, f.

bilge, n. pantoque, m.; —, vt. (naut.) hacer agua; — **pump,** bomba de sentina, bomba de carena.

bilingual, adj. bilingüe.

bilious, *adj.* bilioso.

bilk, *vt.* engañar, defraudar; —, *n.* persona indigna; petardista, *m.* y *f.*

bill, *n.* pico de ave; cédula, *f.*; cuenta, *f.*; factura, *f.*; — **of exchange,** cédula o letra de cambio; — **of expenses,** nota de gastos; — **of fare,** menú, *m.*, lista de platos; — **of health,** patente de sanidad; — **of lading,** carta de porte, declaración, *f.*; conocimiento, *m.*; — **of sale,** acta o contrato o escritura de venta; —**s payable,** documentos o efectos por pagar; —**s payable book,** registro de efectos por pagar; —**s receivable,** documentos por cobrar, letras o efectos por cobrar; —**s receivable book,** registro de efectos por cobrar; **accommodation** —, billete de deferencia; **post no** —**s,** no fijar carteles; **show** —, cartelón, *m.*; —, *vt.* enviar una cuenta, facturar; —, *vi.* arrullar.

billboard, *n.* cartelera, *f.*

billet, *n.* billete, *m.*, esquela, *f.*; zoquete de leña; (mil.) orden de alojamiento; —, *vt.* alojar soldados.

billfold, *n.* billetera, *f.*, cartera de bolsillo.

billhead, *n.* encabezamiento de factura.

billiards, *n.* billar, *m.*

billion, *n.* billón, *m.*, millón de millones (en España, Inglaterra, y Alemania); mil millones (en Francia y los Estados Unidos).

billionaire, *n.* billonario, ria.

billow, *n.* ola grande.

billowy, *adj.* hinchado como las olas, ondulado.

billposter, billsticker, *n.* fijacarteles, *m.*

billposting, *n.* fijación de carteles.

bimetalism, *n.* bimetalismo, *m.*

bimonthly, *adj.* bimestral, cada dos meses; —, *adv.* bimestralmente.

bin, *n.* artesón, *m.*; armario, *m.*, despensa, *f.*

binary, *adj.* binario, doble.

bind, *vt.* atar; unir; encuadernar; obligar, constreñir; impedir; poner a uno a servir; —, *vi.* ser obligatorio.

binder, *n.* encuadernador, *m.*

binding, *n.* venda, faja, *f.*; encuadernación, *f.*; pasta (para libros), *f.*; **cardboard** —, encuadernación de cartón; **cloth** —, encuadernación en tela.

bingo, *n.* variedad de lotería de cartones.

binnacle, *n.* (naut.) bitácora, *f.*

binocular, *adj.* binocular; —**s,** *n. pl.* gemelos, lentes, binóculos, *m. pl.*

binomial, *adj.* binomio; — **theorem,** binomio de Newton; —, *n.* binomio, *m.*

biochemistry, *n.* bioquímica, *f.*

biodynamics, *n.* biodinámica, *f.*

biog. biography, biog. biografía.

biogenesis, *n.* biogénesis, *f.*

biographer, *n.* biógrafo, *m.*

biographical, *adj.* biográfico.

biography, *n.* biografía, *f.*

biol. biology, biol. biología.

biology, *n.* biología, *f.*

biometry, *n.* biometría, *f.*, aplicación de los métodos estadísticos a las investigaciones biológicas.

biophysics, *n.* biofísica, *f.*

bipartisan, *adj.* compuesto de o representante de dos partidos políticos.

bipartite, *adj.* bipartido.

biped, *adj.* bípedo; —, *n.* bípedo, *m.*

biplane, *n.* biplano, *m.*

birch, *n.* abedul, *m.*; —, *vt.* varear.

birchen, *adj.* de abedul.

bird, *n.* ave, *f.*, pájaro, *m.*; — **of prey,** ave de rapiña; — **shot,** perdigones, *m. pl.*; **diving** —, mergo, *m.*; —, *vi.* cazar o coger pájaros.

birdie, *n.* (golf) tanto de un golpe menos de par en un agujero (en el juego de golf).

bird lime, *n.* liga, liria, *f.*

bird's-eye view, *n.* vista a ojo de pájaro.

birth, *n.* nacimiento, *m.*; origen, *m.*; parto, *m.*; linaje, *m.*; —**certificate,** certificado o fe de nacimiento; — **control,** prevención voluntaria de la concepción; — **rate,** natalidad, *f.*; **to give** —, dar a luz, parir.

birthday, *n.* cumpleaños, natalicio, *m.*; **to have a** —, cumplir años.

birthmark, *n.* marca de nacimiento.

birthplace, *n.* suelo nativo, lugar de nacimiento.

birthright, *n.* derechos de nacimiento; primogenitura, *f.*

Biscay, Vizcaya, *f.*

Biscayan, *n.* and *adj.* vizcaíno, ina.

biscuit, *n.* bizcocho, bollo, *m.*; galleta, *f.*; **ring-shaped** —, rosca, *f.*

bisect, *vt.* bisecar, dividir en dos partes; —, *vi.* bifurcarse.

bisexual, *adj.* hermafrodita.

bisector, *n.* bisector, *m.*, bisectriz, *f.*

bishop, *n.* obispo, *m.*; (chess) alfil (en el ajedrez), *m.*

bishopric, *n.* obispado, *m.*

bismuth, *n.* bismuto, *m.*

bison, *n.* bisonte, búfalo, *m.*

bisulphate, *n.* (chem.) bisulfato, *m.*

bisulphide, *n.* (chem.) bisulfito, *m.*

bit, *n.* bocado, *m.*; pedacito, *m.*; pizca, *f.*; triza, *f.*; brote, *m.*; trozo, *m.*; — **of a bridle,** bocado del freno; **two** —**s,** (coll. E. U. A.) 25¢ (moneda de E.U.A.); —, *vt.* enfrenar; —, pretérito del verbo **bite.**

bitch, *n.* perra, *f.*; (coll.) zorra, ramera, *f.*

bite, *vt.* morder; punzar, picar; satirizar; engañar; — **the dust,** caer muerto; (fig.) quedar totalmente derrotado; —, *n.* tenteempié, *m.*

biting, *adj.* mordaz, acre, picante.

bitten, *p. p.* del verbo **bite.**

bitter, *adj.* amargo, áspero; mordaz, satírico, penoso; poncil (limón o cidro); —**ly,** *adv.* amargamente; con pena; severamente.

bittern, *n.* alcaraván, bitor, *m.*

bitterness, *n.* amargor, *m.*; amargura, *f.*; rencor, *m.*; pena, *f.*; dolor, *m.*

bittersweet, *n.* (bot.) dulcamara, *f.*

bitumen, n. betún, m.
bituminous, adj. bituminoso; — **coal,** carbón bituminoso.
bivalence, n. (chem.) bivalencia, f.
bivalve, adj. bivalvo; — n. animal bivalvo.
bivouac, n. (mil.) vivac, vivaque, m.; —, vi. vivaquear.
biweekly, adj. quincenal, que sucede cada dos semanas; —, adv. quincenalmente.
bizarre, adj. raro, extravagante.
bk: bank, Bco. banco; **block,** manzana (de una ciudad); bloque; **book,** l. libro.
bkg. banking, banca.
bkt. basket, cesta.
B.L. Bachelor of Law, Br. en L. Bachiller en Leyes.
B/L, b.l. bill of lading, conto. conocimiento de embarque.
bl.: bale, B/ bala, f/ fardo; **barrel,** brl. barril.
blab, vt. parlar, charlar, divulgar; —, vi chismear; —, n. chismoso, sa, soplón, ona.
black, adj. negro, obscuro; tétrico, malvado; funesto; — **art,** nigromancia, f.; — **lead,** lápiz de plomo; — **letter,** letra gótica; — **list,** lista de personas que merecen censura; — **magic,** magia que aspira a producir muerte o daño; — **mark,** fracaso, m.; — **market,** mercado negro, venta clandestina, especialmente de comestibles; — **sheep,** hijo malo; — **widow,** araña americana; —, n. color negro; —, vt. teñir de negro, negrecer; limpiar (las botas).
blackamoor, n. negro, gra.
blackball, vt. excluir a uno votando con una bolita negra; jugar la suerte con una bola negra; votar en contra.
blackberry, n. zarzamora, mora, f.
blackbird, n. mirlo, m.
blackboard, n. pizarra, f., encerado, pizarrón, tablero, m.
blacken, vt. teñir de negro; ennegrecer.
Black Forest, Selva Negra, f.
blackguard, n. hombre soez, galopín, m., tunante, m.; pillo, m.
blackhead, n. espinilla, f.
blackjack, n. cachiporra, f.; especie de vasija grande para cerveza; bandera de pirata.
blackleg, n. bribón, m.; (vet.) morriña, comalía, f.
blackmail, n. chantaje, m.; —, vt. amenazar con chantaje.
blackness, n. negrura, f.
blackout, n. oscurecimiento, m.
blacksmith, n. herrero, chispero, m.
blackthorn, n. (bot.) endrino, m.
bladder, n. vejiga, f.
blade, n. brizna, hoja, f.; pala (de remo), f.; jaquetón, valentón, m.; — **of a propeller,** aleta, f.
blamable, adj. culpable; vituperable; —**bly,** adv. culpablemente.
blame, vt. vituperar; culpar; —, n. culpa, vituperación, imputación, f.

blameless, adj. inocente, irreprensible, intachable, puro; —**ly,** adv. inocentemente.
blanch, vt. blanquear; mondar, pelar; hacer pálido.
Blanche, Blanca.
bland, adj. blando, suave, dulce, apacible, gentil, agradable, sutil.
blandishment, n. halago, m.; zalamería, f.; caricia, f.
blank, adj. blanco; pálido: confuso; vacío, sin interés; — **cartridge,** cartucho en blanco; — **check,** cheque en blanco — **credit,** carta en blanco; — **form,** bianco, esqueleto, m.; — **verse,** verso sin rima; —, n. blanco, m., espacio en blanco.
blanket, n. cubierta de cama, frazada, manta, f.; —, adj. general; — **instructions,** instrucciones generales.
blare, vt. proclamar ruidosamente.
blasé, adj. insensible al placer; hastiado, aburrido.
blaspheme, vt. blasfemar, jurar, decir blasfemias.
blasphemous, adj. blasfematorio; —**ly,** adv. blasfemamente.
blasphemy, n. blasfemia, f., reniego, m.
blast, n. soplo de aire, ráfaga, f.; — **engine,** ventilador, m., máquina soplante — **furnace,** horno alto; —, vt. marchitar, secar; arruinar; volar con pólvora.
blasting, n. voladura, f.
blatant, adj. vocinglero.
blaze, n. llama, f.; hoguera, f.; mancha blanca en la frente de los animales; señal de guía hecha en los troncos de los árboles —, vi. encenderse en llama; brillar, resplandecer; —, vt. inflamar; flamear; llamear· —**s!** interj. ¡chispas! ¡caracoles!
blazon, vt. blasonar; decorar; publicar.
blazonry, n. blasón, m.
bldg. building, ed. edificio.
bleach, vt. blanquear al sol; —, vi. blanquear.
bleachers, n. pl. asientos al aire libre para espectadores de un deporte.
bleaching, n. blanqueo. m.
bleak, adj. pálido, descolorido: frío, helado; sombrío.
bleakness, n. frialdad, f.; palidez, f.
blear, bleared, blear-eyed, adj. lagañoso.
bleat, n. balido, m.; —, vi. balar.
bled, p. p. del verbo **bleed.**
bleed, vt. sacar sangre; (print.) sangrar; —, n. página en que se sangran grabados o texto.
bleeding, n. sangría, f.; —, adj. sangrante; — **heart,** (bot.) dicentra, f.
blemish, vt. manchar, ensuciar; infamar; —, n. tacha, f.; deshonra, infamia, f.; lunar, m.
blench, vi. retroceder, acobardarse; titubear; palidecer.
blend, vt. mezclar, combinar; —, vi. armonizar; —, n. mezcla, f.; armonía, f.
bless, vt. bendecir, alabar; (coll.) santiguar; — **me!** ¡buen Dios! — **their hearts!** ¡benditos sean!

blessed, *adj.* bendito; afortunado.
blessedness, *n.* felicidad, *f.*; santidad, beatitud, *f.*
blessing, *n.* bendición, *f.*; favores del cielo.
blew, pretérito del verbo **blow.**
blight, *n.* tizón, *m.*; pulgón, *m.*; plaga, *f.*; daño, *m.*; —, *vi.* agostarse, perjudicarse.
blimp, *n.* blimp, *m.*, globo dirigible, flexible, semejante al globo cautivo o de observación.
blind, *adj.* ciego; oculto; obscuro; — **alley,** vuelo sin visibilidad, callejón sin salida; — **flying,** (aer.) vuelo con instrumentos; vuelo ciego; — **person,** ciego, ga.; —, *vt.* cegar; deslumbrar; —, *n.* velo, *m.*; subterfugio, *m* ; emboscada, *f.*; **Venetian** —s, persianas, *f. pl.*
blindfold, *vt.* vendar los ojos; —, *adj.* con los ojos vendados.
blindly, *adv.* ciegamente, a ciegas.
blindness, *n.* ceguedad, ceguera, *f.*; alucinación, *f.*
blink, *vi.* guiñar, parpadear; cerrar los ojos; echar llama; —, *n.* guiñada, *f.*, pestañeo, *m.*; destello, *m.*
blinker, *n.* anteojera, *f.*
bliss, *n.* felicidad, *f.*, embeleso, *m.*
blissful, *adj.* feliz en sumo grado; beato, bienaventurado; —**ly,** *adv.* felizmente; embelesadamente.
blister, *n.* vejiga, ampolla, *f.*; vejigatorio, *m.*; —, *vi.* ampollarse; —, *vt.* aplicar un vejigatorio.
blithe, *adj.* alegre, contento, gozoso.
blitzkrieg, *n.* blitzkrieg, *m.*, guerra en la cual la ofensiva es rápida, violenta y difícil de resistir.
blizzard, *n.* chubasco de nieve.
bloat, *vt.* hinchar; —, *vi.* entumecerse; abotagarse.
bloater, *n.* arenque ahumado.
bloc, *n.* bloc, *m.*, grupo político.
block, *n.* zoquete, *m.*; horma (de sombrero), *f.*; bloque, *m.*; cuadernal, *m.*; témpano, *m.*; obstáculo, *m.*; (naut.) motón, *m.*; manzana (de una calle), *f.*; — **of houses,** manzana, cuadra, *f.*; — **system,** (rail.) sistema de cobertura de una vía; —, *vt.* bloquear; **to** — **a wheel,** calzar; — **and tackle,** polea con aparejo.
blockade, *n.* bloqueo, *m.*; cerco, *m.*; **to run a** —, romper el bloqueo; —, *vt.* bloquear.
blockhead, *n.* bruto, necio, zopenco, *m.*
blond, blonde, *n.* and *adj.* rubio, blondo; **peroxide** —, rubia oxigenada.
blood, *n.* sangre, *f.*; linaje, parentesco, *m.*; ira, cólera, *f.*; apetito animal; — **bank,** banco de sangre; — **donor,** donante o donador de sangre; — **poisoning,** envenenamiento de sangre; septicemia, *f.*; — **pressure,** tensión arterial; — **vessel,** vena, *f.*, canal de la sangre; — **plasm,** plasma, *m.*; — **count,** cuenta de los glóbulos de la sangre; **in cold blood,** en sangre fría; — **test,** análisis de la sangre.

bloodhound, *n.* sabueso, *m.*
bloodless, *adj.* exangüe; sin efusión de sangre; muerto.
bloodletter, *n.* sangrador, *m.*
bloodletting, *n.* sangría, *f.*; (med.) flebotomía, *f.*
bloodshed, *n.* efusión de sangre; matanza, *f.*
bloodshot, *adj.* ensangrentado.
bloodstone, *n.* piedra semipreciosa, verde, jaspeada de rojo; sanguinaria, *f.*
bloodsucker, *n.* sanguijuela, *f.*; (fig.) desollador, *m.*
bloody, *adj.* sangriento, ensangrentado; cruel; —**minded,** *adj.* sanguinario.
bloom, *n.* flor, *f.*; florecimiento, *m.*; —, *vi.* florecer.
bloomers, *n.* calzones o pantalones de mujer.
blossom, *n.* flor, *f.*; capullo, botón, *m.*; —, *vi.* florecer.
blot, *vt.* manchar (lo escrito); cancelar; denigrar; **to** — **a writing,** borrar; —, *n.* canceladura, *f.*; mancha, *f.*
blotch, *n.* roncha, *f.*; mancha, *f.*
blotter, *n.* borrador, *m.*; papel secante.
blotting, *adj.* secante; — **paper,** teleta, *f.*, papel secante.
blouse, *n.* blusa, camisa, *f.*
blow, *n.* golpe, *m.*; pedrada, *f.*; —, *vi.* soplar; sonar; florecer; **to** — **(one's nose),** sonarse (las narices); **to** — **up,** volar o volarse por medio de pólvora; ventear; (print.) ampliar mediante proyección; —, *vt.* soplar; inflar; calentar algo con el aliento.
blower, *n.* fuelle, soplador, *m.*
blowgun, *n.* bodoquera, *f.*
blown, *adj.* soplado.
blowout, *n.* reventazón, *f.*; ruptura de neumático, reventón de neumático.
blowpipe, *n.* soplete, *m.*; cerbatana, *f.*
blowtorch, *n.* soplete para soldar.
blubber, *n.* grasa de ballena; —, *vi.* llorar hasta hincharse los carrillos, gimotear.
bludgeon, *n.* cachiporra, *f.*; garrote, *m.*
blue, *adj.* azul, cerúleo; **deep** — **dye,** ultramarino, *m.*; **ultramarine** —, azul ultramarino; —, *vt.* teñir de azul; **to** — **steel,** pavonar.
blueberry, *n.* variedad de mora azul.
bluebird, *n.* (orn.) azulejo, *m.*
blue-blooded, *adj.* de sangre azul, de sangre noble.
bluebottle, *n.* (bot.) campanilla, *f.*; moscarda (mosca), *f.*
bluegrass, *n.* especie de hierba con tallos azulados.
bluejay, *n.* especie de pájaro azul con copete.
blueprint, *n.* heliografía, *f.*, heliógrafo, *m.*; copia al ferroprusiato.
blues, *n. pl.* (coll.) melancolía, *f.*; hipocondría, *f.*
bluff, *n.* risco escarpado, morro, *m.*; fanfarronada, *f.*; —, *adj.* rústico, rudo, francote;

—, *vt.* impedir con pretextos de valentía o de recursos. —, *vi.* baladronear; engañar, hacer alarde.

bluing, blueing, *n.* añil, *m.*

bluish, *adj.* azulado.

blunder, *n.* desatino, *m.*; error craso; atolondramiento, *m.*; patochada, *f.*; pifia, *f.*; —, *vt.* and *vi.* confundir; desatinar.

blunderbuss, *n.* trabuco, *m.*

blunt, *adj.* obtuso; romo, boto; lerdo; bronco; grosero; —, *vt.* embotar; enervar; calmar (un dolor).

blur, *n.* mancha, *f.*; —, *vt.* manchar; infamar.

blurb, *n.* epígrafe, *m.*

blurt (out), *vt.* hablar a tontas y a locas.

blush, *n.* rubor, *m.*; sonrojo, *m.*; —, *vi.* ponerse colorado (de vergüenza), ruborizarse; sonrojarse.

bluster, *n.* ruido, tumulto, *m.*; jactancia, *f.*; —, *vi.* hacer ruido tempestuoso.

blvd. boulevard, bulevar.

boa, *n.* boa (serpiente), *f.*; boa (cuello de pieles), *f.*

boar, *n.* verraco, *m.*; **wild** —, jabalí, *m.*; puerco montés.

board, *n.* tabla, *f.*; mesa, *f.*; tribunal, consejo, *m.*; junta, *f.*; (naut.) bordo, *m.*; — **of directors,** consejo directivo, directorio, *m.*, junta directiva; — **of health,** junta de sanidad; — **of trade,** junta de comercio; — **of trustees,** junta directiva; Bristol —, cartulina, *f.*; **free on** —, franco a bordo (f.o.b.); **on** —, (naut.) a bordo; **planed** —, tablero, *m.*; —, *vt.* abordar; entablar; —, *vi.* estar a pupilaje, residir en casa de huéspedes; tomar pupilos, recibir huéspedes.

boarder, *n.* pensionista, *m.* y *f.*, pupilo, *m.*

boarding, *n.* tablazón, *f.*; — **pike,** botavante, *m.*; — **pupil,** interno, na, pensionista, *m.* y *f.*; — **school,** colegio, *m.*, pensión, *f.*, escuela para internos.

boardinghouse, *n.* casa de pupilos; casa de huéspedes; posada, pensión, *f.*

boardwalk, *n.* paseo entablado a la orilla del mar.

boast, *n.* jactancia, ostentación, *f.*; —, *vi.* presumir; jactarse, hacer alarde, hacer gala; preciarse de; —, *vt.* blasonar; **to** — **about,** jactarse de.

boastful, *adj.* jactancioso, papelón.

boat, *n.* bote, *m.*; barca, chalupa, *f.*; buque, barco, *m.*; **towing** —, remolcador, *m.*; **in the same** —, en una misma situación, en un mismo caso.

boathook, *n.* (naut.) cloque, bichero, *m.*

boating, *n.* barcaje, *m.*; paseo en barco.

boatload, *n.* barcada, *f.*

boatman, *n.* barquero, *m.*

boatswain, *n.* contramaestre, *m.*

bob, *n.* pingajo, *m.*; zarcillo, pendiente, *m.*; pulla, chufleta, *f.*; melena, (corte de pelo corto de las mujeres), *f.*; —, *vt.* and *vi.* menear o mover la cabeza, bambolear; engañar; cortar corto el cabello.

bobbin, *n.* canilla, broca, bobina, *f.*; carrete, *m.*

bobby pin, *n.* horquilla corrugada para el pelo.

bobcat, *n.* especie de lince.

bobolink, *n.* pájaro americano, negro y amarillo, que vive en las praderas y los campos.

bobsled, *n.* rastra corta; trineo de dos rastras.

bobtail, *n.* animal rabón; cola cortada.

bode, *vt.* and *vi.* presagiar, pronosticar; **to** — **ill,** prometer mal; **to** — **well,** prometer bien.

bodice, *n.* corsé, *m.*; cotilla, *f.*

bodied, *adj.* corpóreo.

bodiless, *adj.* incorpóreo.

bodily, *adj.* and *adv.* corpóreo; corporalmente; en peso.

bodkin, *n.* punzón de sastre; aguja de jareta.

body, *n.* cuerpo, *m.*; caja, carro o carrocería de un coche; individuo, *m.*; gremio, *m.*; — **type,** tipo usual, *m.*; **any**—, cualquiera; **every**—, cada uno, todos.

bodyguard, *n.* (mil.) guardia de corps.

bog, *n.* pantano, *m.*; —, *vt.* and *vi.* (a veces con **down**), hundir, hundirse.

bogey, *n.* duende, *m.*; coco, fantasma, *m.*

bogeyman, *n.* espantajo, *m.*

boggy, *adj.* pantanoso, palustre.

bogus, *adj.* fingido, falso.

bogy, *n.* duende, *m.*; coco, fantasma, *m.*

Bohemian, *adj.* bohemio, bohemiano, bohémico; —, *n.* bohemio, mia, bohemiano, na.

boil, *vi.* hervir, bullir, hervirle a uno la sangre; —, *vt.* cocer; —, *n.* (med.) furúnculo, divieso, nacido, *m.*

boiler, *n.* marmita, *f.*; caldera, *f.*, hervidor, *m.*

boilermaker, *n.* calderero, *m.*

boiling, *adj.* hirviendo, hirviente; — **dye,** bullón, *m.*; — **point,** punto de ebullición.

boisterous, *adj.* borrascoso, tempestuoso; violento; ruidoso; —**ly,** *adv.* tumultuosamente, furiosamente, ruidosamente.

bold, *adj.* ardiente, valiente; audaz; temerario; imprudente; majo; —**face,** (print.) letra negra; —**ly,** *adv.* descaradamente.

boldness, *n.* intrepidez, *f.*; valentía, *f.*; osadía, *f.*; confianza, *f.*

bolero, *n.* bolero (baile andaluz), *m.*; especie de chaqueta corta.

bolivar, *n.* bolívar (moneda), *m.*

Bolivian, *n.* and *adj.* boliviano, na.

boliviano, *n.* boliviano (moneda), *m.*

boll, *n.* (bot.) cápsula, *f.*; tallo, *m.*; — **weevil,** especie de gorgojo que ataca la planta de algodón.

bolo (knife), *n.* bolo (especie de machete filipino), *m.*

Bolshevik, *n.* and *adj.* bolchevista, bolchevique, *m.* y *f.*

bolshevism, *n.* bolchevismo, *m.*

bolster, *n.* travesero, *m.*; cabezal, cojín, *m.*;

cabecera, *f.*; **—**, *vt.* recostar la cabeza en el travesero; apoyar, auxiliar; **— up,** sostener, apoyar.

bolt, *n.* dardo, *m.*; flecha, *f.*; cerrojo, *m.*; chaveta, *f.*; tornillo, *m.*; **catch —,** picaporte, *m.*; **door —,** pasador, *m.*; **—,** *vt.* cerrar con cerrojo, amarrar con grillos; cribar; **— from the blue,** sorpresa grande.

bolter, *n.* cedazo, *m.*

bomb, *n.* (mil.) bomba, *f.*; **— release,** lanzabombas, *m.*; **— thrower,** lanzabombas, *m.*; **incendiary —,** bomba incendiaria; **— shelter,** abrigo contra bombas.

bombard, *vt.* bombardear.

bombardier, *n.* bombardero, *m.*

bombardment, *n.* bombardeo, *m.*

bombast, *n.* ampulosidad, *f.*, lenguaje redundante.

bombastic, *adj.* pomposo, redundante, ampuloso.

bomber, *n.* avión de bombardeo.

bombproof, *adj.* a prueba de bombas.

bombshell, *n.* bomba, granada, *f.*

bombsight, *n.* mira de bombardero aéreo.

bona fide, *adj.* de buena fe.

bonanza, *n.* bonanza, *f.*

bonbon, *n.* confite, bombón, *m.*

bond, *n.* ligadura, *f.*; vínculo, lazo, *m.*; vale, *m.*; obligación, *f.*; (com.) bono, *m.*; **government —s,** bonos de gobierno; **—,** *vt.* poner en depósito.

bondage, *n.* esclavitud, servidumbre, *f.*

bondholder, *n.* tenedor de bonos; obligacionista, *m.*

bondsman, bondman, *n.* esclavo, siervo, *m.*; (law) fiador, *m.*

bone, *n.* hueso, *m.*; **—s,** osambre, *m.*, osamenta, *f.*; **—,** *vt.* desosar.

boneless, *adj.* sin huesos, desosado.

bonfire, *n.* hoguera, fogata, *f.*

bonnet, *n.* gorra, *f.*; bonete, *m.*; sombrero, *m.*

bonny, *adj.* bonito, galán, gentil.

bonus, *n.* prima, *f.*; bonificación, gratificación, *f.*

bony, *adj.* huesudo.

boo! *interj.* ¡bu!

booby, *n.* zote, *m.*, persona boba.

book, *n.* libro, *m.*; **— seller,** librero, *m.*; **letter —,** libro copiador; **memorandum —,** carnet, *m.*; **minute —,** libro de actas; **small —,** librillo, *m.*; **—,** *vt.* asentar en un libro; **to bring to —,** pedir cuenta.

bookbinder, *n.* encuadernador de libros.

bookcase, *n.* armario para libros, estante, *m.*

bookie, *n.* (coll.) persona cuyo negocio es apostar a las carreras de caballos.

booking, *n.* registro, *m.*; **— office,** taquilla o despacho de billetes.

bookkeeper, *n.* tenedor de libros.

bookkeeping, *n.* teneduría de libros; contabilidad, *f.*; **double-entry —,** contabilidad por partida doble; **single-entry —,** contabilidad por partida simple o sencilla.

booklet, *n.* folleto, *m.*

bookmaker, *n.* persona cuyo negocio es apostar a las carreras de caballos.

bookmark, *n.* marcador de libro.

bookstand, *n.* puesto de libros.

bookstore, *n.* librería, *f.*

bookworm, *n.* polilla que roe los libros; persona aficionada a los libros.

boom, *n.* (naut.) botalón, *m.*; repentina prosperidad de alguna industria; cadena para cerrar un puerto; rugido seco, estampido, *m.*; **—,** *vi.* zumbar; **— town,** pueblo que goza de prosperidad repentina.

boomerang, *n.* bumerang, *m.*

boon, *n.* presente, regalo, *m.*; favor, *m.*, gracia, *f.*; **—,** *adj.* alegre, festivo; generoso.

boor, *n.* patán, villano, *m.*

boorish, *adj.* rústico, agreste; villano, zafio, palurdo, pardal; **—ly,** *adv.* rústicamente.

boorishness, *n.* zafiedad, rusticidad, grosería, *f.*

boost, *vt.* levantar o empujar hacia arriba; assistir; **—,** *vi.* abogar con entusiasmo; **—,** *n.* ayuda, *f.*, aumento, *m.*

booster, *n.* fomentador, secuaz, *m.*

boot, *n.* bota, *f.*; **double soled —,** bota de dos suelas; **riding —,** bota de montar; **to —,** además, por añadidura.

bootblack, *n.* limpiabotas, *m.*

booted, *adj.* calzado con botas.

bootee, *n.* calzado plástico para niños; bota corta.

booth, *n.* barraca, cabaña, *f.*; puesto, *m.*; reservado en una heladería, etc.; casilla, *f.*

bootjack, *n.* sacabotas, *m.*

bootleg, *vt.* and *vi.* contrabandear (usualmente en licores).

bootlegger, *n.* contrabandista (usualmente de licores), *m.*

bootlegging, *n.* tráfico ilegal de licores.

bootless, *adj.* inútil, sin provecho, vano.

booty, *n.* botín, *m.*; presa, *f.*; saqueo, *m.*

booze, *vi.* emborracharse; **—,** *n.* bebida alcohólica.

bopeep, *n.* escondite, *m.*

bor. borough, villa, burgo.

borate, *n.* borato, *m.*

borax, *n.* bórax, *m.*

Bordeaux, Burdeos, *m.*

border, *n.* orilla, *f.*; borde, *m.*; repulgo, *m.*; vera, *f.*, margen, *m.*; frontera, *f.*; reborde, *m.*; cenefa, *f.*; **—,** *vi.* confinar; bordear; **—,** *vt.* ribetear, limitar; **to — on,** rayar en.

bordering, *n.* orladura, *f.*; **—,** *adj.* contiguo, colindante; **— on,** rayano en.

borderland, *n.* frontera, *f.*, confín, *m.*

borderline, *n.* límite, *m.*, orilla, *f.*; **—,** *adj.* incierto.

bore, *vt.* taladrar, perforar, barrenar; fastidiar; **—,** pretérito del verbo **bear; —,** *n.* taladro, *m.*; calibre, *m.*; perforación, *f.*; (Sp. Am.) cargoso, *m.*; hombre enfadoso; majadero, *m.*; **— of a gun,** alma. *f.*

boreal, *adj.* septentrional, boreal.

Boreas, *n.* viento del septentrión.
boredom, *n.* tedio, fastidio, aburrimiento, *m.*
boresome, *adj.* aburrido, fastidioso.
boric, *adj.* bórico; — **acid,** ácido bórico.
boring, *adj.* fastidioso, chinchoso; — **machine,** taladro, *m.*
born, *adj.* nacido; destinado; **to be** —, nacer.
borne, *p. p.* del verbo **bear.**
borough, *n.* villa, *f.*; burgo, *m.*, distrito administrativo de una ciudad.
borrow, *vt.* tomar fiado; pedir prestado.
borrower, *n.* prestamista, *m.* y *f.*
bosh, *n.* galimatías, *m.*, tontería, *f.*
bosom, *n.* seno, pecho, *m.*; amor, *m.*; cariño, *m.*; — **of a shirt,** guirindola, *f.*; —, *vt.* guardar en el pecho.
Bosphorus, Bósforo, *m.*
boss, *n.* clavo, *m.*; jiba, joroba, *f.*; (coll.) cacique, jefe, *m.*
bot. botany, bot. botánica.
botanical, *adj.* botánico.
botanist, *n.* botánico, *m.*
botanize, *vt.* herborizar.
botany, *n.* botánica, *f.*
botch, *n.* remiendo chapucero; roncha, *f.*; —, *vt.* remendar, chapucear.
both, *pron.* and *adj.* ambos, entrambos; ambas, entrambas; —, *conj.* tanto como.
bother, *vt.* aturrullar; confundir, molestar; incomodar; —, *n.* estorbo, *m.*; mortificación, *f.*
bothersome, *adj.* cargoso, molestoso.
bottle, *n.* botella, *f.*; **earthen** —, caneca, *f.*; **small** —, frasco, *m.*; **vitreous** — **cap,** cápsula, *f.*; —, *vt.* embotellar; — **up,** embotellar; reducir a impotencia.
bottleneck, *n.* cuello de botella; (fig.) obstáculo, impedimento, *m.*
bottling, *n.* embotellamiento, *m.*
bottom, *n.* fondo, *m.*; fundamento, *m.*; valle, *m.*; buque, *m.*; — **of skirts,** ruedo, *m.*; **false** —, *adj.* doble; —, *adj.* bajo; fundamental; —, *vt.* poner fondo (a alguna cosa); cimentar, basar; —, *vi.* apoyarse; **at** —, en el fondo, realmente; — **land,** tierra aluvial.
bottomless, *adj.* insondable; sin fondo.
bottomry, *n.* (naut.) hipoteca de un barco.
boudoir, *n.* tocador, *m.*, recámara, *f.*
bough, *n.* rama (de un árbol), *f.*
bought, pretérito y *p. p.* del verbo **buy.**
bouillon, *n.* caldo, *m.*
boulder, *n.* canto rodado, china, peña, *f.*; guijarro *m.*; peña desprendida de una masa de roca.
boulevard, *n.* avenida, *f.*, paseo, bulevar, *m.*
bounce, *vi.* arremeter, brincar; jactarse; —, *n.* golpazo, brinco, *m.*; bravata, *f.*
bouncer, *n.* (coll.) guardián fornido que echa a los alborotadores de un café.
bouncing, *adj.* fuerte, bien formado, robusto.
bound, *n.* límite, *m.*; salto, *m.*; repercusión, *f.*; **within** —**s,** a raya; —, *vt.* confinar, limitar; destinar; obligar; reprimir; —,

vi. resaltar, brincar; —, pretérito y *p. p.* del verbo **bind;** —, *adj.* destinado; — **for,** con rumbo a, con destino.
boundary, *n.* límite, *m.*; frontera, *f.*; meta, línea, *f.*, aledaño, *m.*
boundless, *adj.* ilimitado, infinito.
bounteous, bountiful, *adj.* liberal, generoso, bienhechor; —**ly,** *adv.* generosamente, liberalmente.
bounty, *n.* liberalidad, bondad, *f.*
bouquet, *n.* ramillete de flores, ramo, *m.*
bourgeois, *adj.* burgués.
bourgeosie, *n.* burguesía, *f.*
bourse, *n.* (com.) bolsa, *f.*; —, *adj.* bursátil.
bout, *n.* turno, *m.*; encuentro, combate, *m.*
bovine, *adj.* bovino, vacuno.
bow, *vt.* encorvar, doblar, oprimir; saludar; —, *vi.* encorvarse; hacer reverencia; —, *n.* reverencia, inclinación, *f.*; (naut.) proa, *f.*
bow, *n.* arco, *m.*; arco de violín; lazo (de cinta, etc.), *m.*
bowels, *n. pl.* intestinos, *m. pl.*; entrañas, *f. pl.*
bower, *n.* enramada de jardín; bóveda, *f.*; aposento retirado.
bowie knife, *n.* puñal largo y ancho.
bowl, *n.* taza, *f.*; bola (juego), *f.*; **wash** —, jofaina, *f.*, lavamanos, *m.*; —, *vi.* jugar boliche o bolos, jugar a las bochas; **to** — **over,** derribar, abatir.
bowlegged, *adj.* patizambo, zancajoso, patiestevado.
bowline, *n.* (naut.) bolina, *f.*
bowling, *n.* bola, *f.*, juego de bolos; juego de boliche; — **alley,** bolera, *f.*; — **pin,** birla, *f.*, bolo, *m.*
bowsprit, *n.* (naut.) bauprés, *m.*; — **shrouds,** mostachos de bauprés.
bowstring, *n.* cuerda de arco.
box, *n.* boj (árbol), *m.*; caja, cajita, *f.*; cofre, *m.*; **axle** —, buje, *m.*; — **elder,** especie de aliso semejante al arce; — **office,** taquilla, *f.*; — **on the ear,** bofetada, *f.*; — **seat,** palco de teatro; —, *vt.* meter alguna cosa en una caja; apuñetear; —, *vi.* combatir a puñadas, boxear.
boxcar, *n.* vagón cubierto, furgón cerrado.
boxer, *n.* púgil, boxeador, pugilista, *m.*
boxing, *n.* boxeo, pugilismo, pugilato, *m.*
boxthorn, *n.* (bot.) tamujo, *m.*
boxwood, *n.* (bot.) boj, *m.*
boy, *n.* muchacho, *m.*; niño, *m.*; criado, lacayo, *m.*; zagal, *m.*; — **scout,** muchacho explorador; **kitchen** —, pinche, *m.*
boycott, *vt.* desacreditar, echar fuera; boicotear; —, *n.* boicoteo, *m.*; exclusión, *f.*; boicot, *m.*
boyhood, *n.* puericia, *f.*
boyish, *adj.* pueril; frívolo; —**ly,** *adv.* puerilmente.
bp. bishop, obo., obpo. obispo.
Br., Brit. British, brit. británico.
brace, *n.* abrazadera, *f.*; sopanda de coche; manija, *f.*; riostra, *f.*; —**s,** *pl.* tirantes para sostener los pantalones; —, *vt.*

ligar, amarrar; (naut.) bracear.
bracelet, *n.* brazalete, *m.*, pulsera, *f.*
brachiopod, *n.* (zool.) braquiópodo, *m.*
brachycephalous, *adj.* braquicéfalo.
bracing, *n.* arriostrado, entibado, *m.*; refuerzo, *m.*; —, *adj.* fortificante, tónico.
bracken, *n.* (bot.) helecho, *m.*
bracket, *n.* puntal, *m.*; listón, *m.*; rinconera, *f.*; consola, *f.*; ménsula, *f.*; — **shelf,** consola, *f.*; **to** — **with,** *vt.* unir, ligar.
brackish, *adj.* salobre.
bradawl, *n.* lesna, *f.*
brag, *n.* jactancia, *f.*; —, *vi.* jactarse, fanfarronear.
braggadocio, *n.* fanfarrón, ona.
braggart, *adj.* and *n.* jactancioso, sa, fanfarrón, ona; valentón, ona.
braid, *n.* trenza, *f.*; pasamano, *m.*, trencilla, *f.*; —, *vt.* trenzar.
braille, *n.* escritura en relieve para uso de los ciegos.
brain, *n.* cerebro, *m.*; seso, juicio, *m.*; — **fever,** meningitis, *f.*, fiebre cerebral; — **storm,** agitación transitoria, confusión, *f.*; —**s,** (coll.) testa, *f.*; —, *vt.* descerebrar, matar a uno.
brainless, *adj.* tonto, insensato.
brake, *n.* (bot.) helecho, *m.*; agramadera, *f.*; amasadera, *f.*; palanca, *f.*; (rail.) freno, *m.*; **to apply the** —**s,** frenar; **to release the** —**s,** quitar el freno; — **band,** cinta o guarnición de freno.
brakeman, *n.* (rail.) guardafrenos, *m.*
bramble, *n.* zarza, espina, *f.*
brambly, *adj.* zarzoso; — **place,** zarzal, *m.*
bran, *n.* salvado, afrecho, *m.*
branch, *n.* rama (de árbol), *f.*; brazo, *m.*; ramal, *m.*; sucursal, *f.*; — **of a compass,** pierna (de un compás), *f.*; — **(of trade, science, art, etc.),** ramo, *m.*; —, *vt.* and *vi.* ramificar, ramificarse; — **out,** ramificarse.
brand, *n.* tizón, *m.*; hierro, *m.*; marca, *f.*; nota de infamia, *f.*; marca de fábrica; —, *vt.* herrar (ganado), infamar.
brandish, *vt.* blandir, ondear; — **a rod,** cimbrar o cimbrear.
brand-new, *adj.* flamante, enteramente nuevo.
brandy, *n.* aguardiente, *m.*; coñac, *m.*
brash, *adj.* frágil, quebradizo (aplícase a la madera); arrebatado, impetuoso, vivo.
brass, *n.* bronce, *m.*; desvergüenza, *f.*; — **band,** charanga, *f.*; **red** —, tumbaga, *f.*
brassart, *n.* brazal, *m.*
brassie, *n.* maza usada en el juego de golf.
brassière, *n.* corpiño para sostener los senos.
brat, *n.* rapaz, *m.*
bravado, *n.* baladronada, *f.*
brave, *adj.* bravo, valiente, atrevido; —, *vt.* bravear; —, *n.* bravo, *m.*; —**ly,** *adv.* bravamente.
bravery, *n.* valor, *m.*; magnificencia, *f.*; braveza, *f.*
bravo, *interj.* ¡bravo!

brawl, *n.* quimera, disputa, camorra, pelotera, *f.*; —, *vi.* alborotar; vocinglear.
brawn, *n.* pulpa, *f.*; carne de verraco.
brawny, *adj.* carnoso, musculoso.
bray, *vt.* triturar; —, *vi.* rebuznar; —, *n.* rebuzno (del asno), *m.*; ruido bronco.
braze, *vt.* soldar con latón; broncear.
brazen, *adj.* de bronce; desvergonzado; imprudente; —, *vi.* encararse con desfachatez.
brazier, *n.* latonero, *m.*; brasero, *m.*;
Brazil, Brasil, *m.*
Brazilian, *n.* and *adj.* brasileño, ña; —, *adj.* (Sp. Am.) brasilero, ra.
brazilwood, *n.* (bot.) brasil, *m.*
breach, *n.* rotura, *f.*; brecha, *f.*; violación, *f.*; — **of trust,** abuso de confianza; — **of faith,** abuso de confianza; — **of promise,** falta de palabra; — **of peace,** violación de la paz.
bread, *n.* pan, *m.*; (fig.) sustento, *m.*; — **basket,** panera, *f.*; — **line,** fila de los que esperan la gratuita distribución de pan; **brown** —, pan moreno; **toasted** —, pan tostado; **whole-wheat** —, pan moreno.
breadboard, *n.* tablero para amasar el pan.
breadstuff, *n.* granos, *m. pl.*
breadth, *n.* anchura, *f.*
breadthwise, *adv.* a lo ancho.
breadwinner, *n.* persona que trabaja para el sustento de su familia.
break, *vt.* and *vi.* quebrar; vencer; quebrantar; violar; domar; arruinar; partir; interrumpir; romperse; reventarse algún tumor; separarse; (com.) quebrar; **to** — **again,** requebrar; **to** — **out,** abrirse salida; derramarse; **to** — **to pieces,** hacer pedazos; **to** — **wind,** peerse; —, *n.* rotura *f.*; rompimiento, *m.*; ruptura, *f.*; interrupción, *f.*; — **of day,** aurora, *f.*
breakage, *n.* rotura, *f.*, destrozo, *m.*
breakdown, *n.* descalabro, *m.*; avería repentina; decadencia, *f.*, decaimiento (de salud, de ánimo), *m.*; desarreglo, *m.*; interrupción, *f.*; postración, *f.*
breaker, *n.* rompedor, *m.*; infractor, *m.*
breakers, *n.* escollo, *m.*
breakfast, *n.* almuerzo, desayuno, *m.*; —, *vi.* almorzar, desayunarse.
breaking, *n.* rompimiento, *m.*; fractura, *f.*; confracción, *f.*; — **up of new ground,** roturación, *f.*
breakneck, *n.* derrumbadero, precipicio, *m.*
breakwater, *n.* muelle, *m.*; dique, *m.* escollera, *f.*
bream, *n.* sargo, *m.*
breast, *n.* pecho, seno, *m.*; tetas, *f. pl.*; corazón, *m.*; —, *vt.* acometer; resistir; arrostrar valerosamente; **to make a clean** — **of,** decir o confesarlo todo; — **stroke,** (natación) braza, *f.*
breastbone, *n.* esternón, *m.*
breasthooks, *n.* buzardas, *f. pl.*
breastplate, *n.* peto, *m.*; pectoral, *m.*; coraza, *f.*

breastwork, *n.* parapeto, *m.*; defensa, *f.*
breath, *n.* aliento, *m.*, respiración, *f.*; soplo de aire; momento, *m.*; **out of —,** jadeante.
breathe, *vt.* and *vi.* respirar; exhalar; resollar; **to — audibly,** resoplar.
breathing, *n.* aspiración, *f.*; respiración, *f.*; respiro, *m.*; **— spell,** desahogo, descanso, reposo, *m.*; aliento, *m.*; **audible —,** resoplido, *m.*
breathless, *adj.* falto de aliento; desalentado.
breath-taking, *adj.* conmovedor, excitante.
bred, pretérito y *p. p.* del verbo **breed.**
breech, *n.* trasero, *m.*; **— of a gun,** culata, *f.*
breeches, *n. pl.* calzones, *m. pl.*; **little —,** braguillas, *f. pl.*; **riding —,** pantalones de equitación o de montar a caballo.
breech-loading, *n.* cargar un arma por la recámara; **—,** *adj.* (mil.) de retrocarga.
breed, *n.* casta, raza, *f.*; **—,** *vt* procrear, engendrar; producir; educar; **—,** *vi.* parir; multiplicarse.
breeder, *n.* criador, *m.*; yegua de cría o vientre.
breeding, *n.* crianza, *f.*; buena educación; modales, *m. pl.*
breeze, *n.* brisa, *f.*, céfiro, *m.*
breezy, *adj.* refrescado con brisas.
brethren, *n. pl.* de **brother,** hermanos (aplícase a los fieles en una iglesia, etc.), *m. pl.*
Breton, *n.* and *adj.* bretón, ona.
breve, *n.* señal para una sílaba o vocal breve; (mus.) breve, *f.*
brevet, *n.* (mil.) grado, *m.*, título honorario.
breviary, *n.* epítome, compendio, *m.*; breviario, *m.*
brevity, *n.* brevedad, concisión, *f.*
brew, *vt.* tramar, maquinar, mezclar; **—,** *vi.* hacer cerveza; **—,** *n.* calderada de cerveza.
brewer, *n.* cervecero, *m.*
brewery, *n.* cervecería, *f.*
briar, brier, *n.* zarza, *f.*, espino, *m.*; **—s,** *pl.* maleza, *f.*
bribe, *n.* cohecho, soborno, *m.*; **—,** *vt.* cohechar, corromper, sobornar.
bribery, *n.* cohecho, soborno, *m.*
bric-a-brac, *n.* bric-à-brac, *m.*; curiosidades, *f. pl.*
brick, *n.* ladrillo, *m.*; ladrillo de pan; hombre alegre y popular; **— kiln,** horno de ladrillo, ladrillera, *f.*, ladrillal, *m.*; **—,** *vt.* enladrillar.
brickbat, *n.* pedazo de ladrillo.
bricklayer, *n.* albañil, *m.*
brickwork, *n.* albañilería, mampostería, *f.*
brickyard, *n.* adobería, *f.*, ladrillar, *m.*
bridal, *adj.* nupcial; **—,** *n.* boda, *f.*
bride, *n.* novia, desposada, *f.*
bridegroom, *n.* novio, desposado, *m.*
bridesmaid, *n.* madrina de boda.
bridge, *n.* puente, *m.*; caballete de la nariz; puente de violín; **suspension —,** puente colgante; **to — (over),** *vt.* construir un puente; salvar un obstáculo; **draw —,** puente levadizo; **pontoon —,** puente de barcas, puente de pontones.
bridgehead, *n.* posición fortificada en el lado enemigo de una corriente para proteger un puente o vado.
Bridget, Brígida.
bridgework, *n.* puente dental; construcción de puentes.
bridging, *n.* crucetas, *f. pl.*; entarimado, *m.*
bridle, *n.* brida, *f.*, freno, *m.*; **—,** *vt.* embridar; reprimir, refrenar; **— path,** camino de herradura.
brief, *adj.* breve, conciso, sucinto; **—,** *n.* compendio, *m.*; breve, *m.*; (law) escrito, *m.*; **— case,** cartera grande, portadocumentos, portapapeles, *m.*; **—ly,** *adv.* brevemente, en pocas palabras; **hold a — for,** defender; **in —,** en pocas palabras, en breve.
brig, *n.* (naut.) bergantín, *m.*
brig. brigadier, brig. brigadier.
brigade, *n.* (mil.) brigada, *f.*
brigadier, *n.* (mil.) general de brigada.
brigand, *n.* bandido, *m.*
brigantine, *n.* bergantín, *m.*
bright, *adj.* claro, luciente, brillante; luminoso; vivo; **—ly,** *adv.* brillantemente; espléndidamente.
brighten, *vt.* pulir, dar lustre; ilustrar; **—,** *vi.* aclarar.
brightness, *n.* esplendor, *m.*, brillantez, *f.*; agudeza, *f.*; claridad, *f.*; lucimiento, *m.*
Bright's disease, *n.* (med.) albuminuria, nefritis, *f.*; inflamación de los riñones.
brilliancy, *n.* brillantez, *f.*, fulgor, *m.*
brilliant, *adj.* brillante; luminoso; resplandeciente; **—ly,** *adv.* espléndidamente; **—,** *n.* brillante (diamante abrillantado), *m.*
brilliantine, *n.* brillantina (grasa para el cabello), *f.*
brim, *n.* borde, extremo, *m.*; orilla, *f.*; ala (de sombrero), *f.*; **—,** *vt.* llenar hasta el borde; **—,** *vi.* estar lleno.
brimful, *adj.* lleno hasta el borde.
brimstone, *n.* azufre, *m.*
brindled, *adj.* abigarrado.
brine, *n.* salmuera, *f.*; (fig.) lágrimas, *f. pl.*
bring, *vt.* llevar, traer; conducir; inducir; persuadir; **to — about,** efectuar; **to — forth,** producir; parir; **to — up,** educar; **— to pass,** efectuar, realizar.
brink, *n.* orilla, *f.*; margen, *m.* y *f.*, borde, *m.*
briny, *adj.* salado.
briquette, *n.* briqueta, *f.*
brisk, *adj.* vivo, alegre, jovial; fresco; **—ly,** *adv.* vigorosamente; alegremente; vivamente.
brisket, *n.* pecho (de un animal), *m.*
bristle, *n.* cerda, seta, *f.*; **—,** *vi.* erizarse.
bristly, *adj.* cerdoso, lleno de cerdas.
Bristol board, *n.* papel de marquilla; cartulina, *f.*
Britain (Great —), Gran Bretaña, *f.*
British, *adj.* bretón, británico; **— Channel,** Canal de la Mancha.
British Columbia, Columbia Británica, *f.*

British East Africa, Africa Oriental Inglesa.
British Guiana, Guayana Inglesa.
British Honduras, Belice, *f.*, Honduras Británica.
Briton, *m.* and *adj.* bretón, ona.
Brittany, Bretaña, *f.*
brittle, *adj.* quebradizo, frágil.
brittleness, *n.* fragilidad, *f.*
bro. brother, hno. hermano.
broach, *n.* asador, *m.*; —, *vt.* espetar; divulgar; barrenar.
broad, *adj.* ancho; abierto; grosero; **at —noon,** en pleno medio día; **— jump,** salto de longitud; **—ly,** *adv.* ampliamente.
broadcast, *n.* radiodifusión, *f.*; —, *vt.* radiodifundir, perifonear.
broadcaster, *n.* radiodifusor, *m.*
broadcasting, *n.* radiodifusión, *f.*; audición, *f.*; perifonía, *f.*; **— station,** emisora, radiodifusora, *f.*; —, *adj.* radioemisor.
broadcloth, *n.* paño fino.
broaden, *vi.* ensancharse.
broad-gauge, *adj.* (rail.) de vía ancha.
broadloom, *adj.* tejido como una alfombra en color sólido.
broad-mindedness, *n.* amplitud de miras.
broadside, *n.* costado de navío; andanada, *f.*; **— gun,** pieza de través, *f.*
broadsword, *n.* espada ancha; alfanje, *m.*
brocade, *n.* brocado, *m.*
broccoli, *n.* bróculi, brécol, *m.*
brochure, *n.* folleto, *m.*
brogue, *n.* abarca, *f.*; idioma corrompido.
broil, *n.* tumulto, *m.*; riña, *f.*; —, *vt.* asar (carne); —, *vi.* padecer calor.
broiler, *n.* parrilla, *f.*
broke, pretérito del verbo **break.**
broken, *adj.* roto, quebrado; interrumpido; **— English,** inglés mal articulado; **— meat,** carne cortada; —, *p. p.* del verbo **break.**
broken-down, *adj.* afligido, abatido; descompuesto.
broken-hearted, *adj.* triste, abatido, transido de dolor.
broker, *n.* corredor, *m.*; chamarillero, chalán, *m.*; agente de bolsa; **exchange —,** corredor de cambio; **insurance —,** corredor de seguros; **money —,** cambista, *m.*
brokerage, *n.* corretaje, *m.*
bromate, *n.* (chem.) bromato, *m.*
bromide, *n.* bromuro, *m.*
bronchial, *adj.* bronquial; **— tube,** bronquio, *m.*
bronchitis, *n.* bronquitis, *f.*
broncho, *n.* caballito cerrero o sin domar.
bronchopneumonia, *n.* bronconeumonía, *f.*
bronchorrhea, *n.* broncorrea, *f.*
bronco, *n.* caballito cerrero o sin domar.
bronze, *n.* bronce, *m.*; —, *vt.* broncear.
brooch, *n.* broche, *m.*; —, *vt.* adornar con joyas.
brood, *vi.* cobijar; pensar alguna cosa con cuidado; madurar; —, *n.* raza, *f.*; nidada, *f.*
brooder, *n.* incubadora, *f.*; clueca, *f.*

brook, *n.* arroyo, *m.*; (Sp. Am.) quebrada, *f.*; —, *vt.* sufrir, tolerar.
broom, *n.* hiniesta, retama, *f.*; escoba, *f.*, escoba de hiniesta; **— seller,** brucero, *m.*
broomcorn, *n.* (bot.) millo de escoba.
broommaker, *n.* brucero, *m.*
broomstick, *n.* palo de escoba.
broth, *n.* caldo, *m.*
brothel, *n.* burdel, *m.*
brother, *n.* hermano, *m.*; **—ly,** *adj.* fraternal; **—ly,** *adv.* fraternalmente.
brotherhood, *n.* hermandad; fraternidad, *f.*
brother-in-law, *n.* cuñado, *m.*, hermano político.
brought, pretérito y *p. p.* del verbo **bring.**
brow, *n.* ceja, *f.*; frente, *f.*; cima, *f.*
browbeat, *vt.* mirar con ceño; intimidar.
brown, *adj.* bruno, moreno; castaño; pardo; **dark —,** bruno, castaño oscuro; **— paper,** papel de estraza; **— sugar,** azúcar terciado, azucar moreno; —, *n.* color moreno; —, *vt.* volver moreno o bruno, dorar, tostar.
brownie, *n.* duende benévolo.
browse, *vt.* and *vi.* ramonear; **to — over a book,** hojear, leer un libro; —, *n.* (bot.) pimpollos, renuevos, vástagos, *m. pl.*
bruin, *n.* oso, *m.*
bruise, *vt.* magullar, machacar, abollar, majar; pulverizar; —, *n.* magulladura, contusión, *f.*
bruit, *vt.* echar voz, dar fama.
brunette, *n.* trigueño, ña; moreno, na; **very dark —,** prieto, ta; —, *adj.* moreno, trigueño.
brunt, *n.* choque, *m.*; esfuerzo, *m.*; desastre, *m.*
brush, *n.* bruza, *f.*; escobilla, *f.*; brocha, *f.*; cepillo, *m.*; asalto, *m.*; combate, *m.*; **artist's —,** pincel, *m.*; **— seller,** brucero, *m.*; **floor —,** escobeta, *f.*; —, *vt.* acepillar; **to — off,** huir; —, *vi.* mover apresuradamente; pasar ligeramente.
brushmaker, *n.* brucero, *m.*
brushwood, *n.* breñal, zarzal, *m.*
brushy, *adj.* cerdoso; velludo.
brusque, *adj.* brusco, rudo, descortés.
Brussels, Bruselas, *f. pl.*; **— sprouts,** (bot.) bretones, *m. pl.*, colecitas de Bruselas.
brutal, *adj.* brutal, bruto; **—ly,** *adv.* brutalmente.
brutality, *n.* brutalidad, *f.*
brutalize, *vt.* and *vi.* embrutecer, embrutecerse.
brute, *n.* bruto, *m.*; —, *adj.* feroz, bestial; irracional.
brutish, *adj.* brutal, bestial; feroz; **—ly,** *adv.* brutalmente.
B.S. Bachelor of Science, Br. en C. Bachiller en Ciencias.
b.s.: bill of sale, C/Vta, C/V.; Cuenta de Ventas; **balance sheet,** balance.
bu. bushel, medida de áridos (Ingl. 36.37 litros; E. U. 35.28 litros).

bubble, n. burbuja, f.; bagatela, f.; engañifa, f.; —, vi. burbujear, bullir; —, vt. engañar; — **over,** estar en efervescencia; borbotar; hervir.
bubbling, n. borbollón, borbotón, m.
bubo, n. buba, f.; —es, pl. (med.) bubas, f. pl.
bubonic, adj. bubónico.
buccaneer, n. corsario (americano), m.; bucanero, m.
Bucephalus, n. Bucéfalo, m.
Bucharest, Bucarest.
buck, n. gamo, m.; macho (de algunos animales), m.; — **private,** (coll.) soldado raso.
bucket, n. cubo, pozal, m.; cangilón, m.; cucharón, m.; — **shop,** juego o apuesta en la bolsa.
buckeye, n. (bot.) castaño de Indias.
buckle, n. hebilla, f.; —, vt. abrochar con hebilla; afianzar; — **down to,** dedicarse (a algo) con empeño; —, vi. encorvarse.
buckler, n. escudo, m.; adarga, f.
buckram, n. bocací, bucarán, m., tela de lino engomada.
bucksaw, n. sierra de bastidor.
buckshot, n. perdigón grande.
buckskin, n. cuero de gamo curtido.
buckthorn, n. (bot.) cambrón, tamujo, m.
bucktooth, n. diente saliente.
buckwheat, n. trigo sarraceno.
bucolic, adj. bucólico.
bud, n. pimpollo, botón, m.; capullo, m.; —, vi. florecer, brotar; —, vt. injertar; pulular.
Buddha, Buda.
budge, vi. moverse, menearse.
budget, n. presupuesto, m.; mochila, f.
budgetary, adj. de presupuesto.
buff, n. ante, m.; búfalo, m.; color amarillo rojizo; —, adj. de ante; de color amarillo rojizo; —, vt. amortiguar (un golpe, etc.).
Buffalo, Búfalo, m.
buffalo, n. búfalo, m.
buffers, n. pl. (rail.) parachoques, topes, m. pl.
buffet, n. puñada, f.; —, vi. combatir a puñadas.
buffet, n. aparador, m.; ambigú, m.
buffoon, n. bufón, chocarrero, matachín, gracioso, m.
buffoonery, n. bufonada, bufonería, f.
bug, n. chinche, f.; insecto, m.
bugaboo, n. coco, espantajo, m.
bugbear, n. espantajo, coco, m.
buggy, n. calesa, f.; **baby —,** cochecito de niño; —, adj. lleno de chinches, etc.
bugle horn, n. trompa de caza, clarín, m.; corneta, f.
bugler, n. corneta, f., trompetero, m.
bugloss, n. (bot.) buglosa, f.
buhl, n. taracea, f.
build, vt. edificar; construir.
builder, n. arquitecto, m.; maestro de obras; constructor, m.

building, n. fábrica, f.; edificio, m.; construcción, f.; — **lot,** solar, m.; — **timber,** madera de construcción.
bulb, n. bulbo, m.; cebolla, f.; **electric light —,** foco o bombilla de luz eléctrica.
bulbous, adj. bulboso.
Bulgarian, n. and adj. búlgaro, ra.
bulge, vi. combarse.
bulk, n. masa, f.; volumen, m.; grosura, f.; mayor parte, f.; capacidad de un buque; buque, m.; **in —,** a granel.
bulkhead, n. (naut.) mamparo, m.
bulkiness, n. bulto, m.; masa, magnitud, f.
bulky, adj. macizo, grueso, grande.
bull, n. toro, m.; disparate, m., bula, f., breve pontificio; dicho absurdo; —'s **eye,** centro de blanco, claraboya, f.
bulldog, n. perro de presa.
bulldoze, vt. (coll.) coercer o reprimir por intimidación.
bulldozer, n. bulldozer, m., máquina para apisonar movida por un tractor (se emplea en la construcción de caminos); (coll.) persona que intimida.
bullet, n. bala, f.
bulletin, n. boletín, m.; — **board,** tablilla, f., tablilla para noticias.
bulletproof, adj. a prueba de bala.
bullfight, n. corrida de toros.
bullfighter, n. torero, toreador, m.
bullfinch, n. (orn.) pinzón real.
bullfrog, n. rana grande.
bullhead, n. gobio (pez), m.
bullion, n. oro o plata en barras.
bullock, n. novillo capado.
bully, n. espadachín, m.; valentón, m.; rufián, m.; (coll.) gallito, m.; —, vi. fanfarronear.
bulrush, n. junco, m.
bulwark, n. baluarte, m.; —, vt. fortificar con baluartes.
bum, n. polizón, bigardo, bribón, m.
bumblebee, n. abejarrón, abejón, abejorro, zángano, m.
bumboat, n. bote vivandero.
bump, n. hinchazón, f.; giba, f.; bollo, m.; golpe, m.; —, vt. and vi. chocar contra.
bumper, n. copa, f.; vaso lleno; amortiguador de golpes; parachoques o paragolpes de un auto; —, adj. (coll.) excelente; abundante.
bumpkin, n. patán, villano, m.
bumptious, adj. presuntuoso.
bun, n. bollo (de pan, etc.), m.
buna, n. variedad de caucho sintético.
bunch, n. tumor, m.; giba, f.; nudo, m.; ramo, racimo, m.; —, vi. formar corcova.
bunchy, adj. racimoso; giboso.
bunco, n. especie de juego con naipes o dados; estafa, f.
bundle, n. atado, haz (de leña, etc.), m.; paquete, m.; rollo, m.; bulto, m.; lío, m.; **small —,** hatillo, m.; —, vt. atar, hacer un lío o un bulto; — **up,** envolver; abrigarse.

bung, *n.* tapón, *m.*; —, *vt.* atarugar.

bungalow, *n.* casa de un piso.

bunghole, *n.* boca (para envasar licores), *f.*

bungle, *vt.* chapucear, chafallar; —, *vi.* hacer algo chabacanamente; —, *n.* yerro, *m.*; obra mal hecha; chabacanería, *f.*

bunion, *n.* juanete, *m.*, callosidad que se forma en los pies.

bunk, *n.* patraña, *f.*, mentira fabulosa.

bunker, *n.* (mil.) fortín, *m.*; (naut.) carbonera, *f.*

bunny, *n.* conejito, *m.*

Bunsen burner, *n.* lámpara Bunsen.

bunt, *n.* (naut.) seno de una vela o red; (baseball) golpe sin fuerza a la pelota; — *vt.* and *vi.* topetar; (baseball) golpear la pelota sin fuerza.

bunting, *n.* lanilla para banderas; (orn.) calandria, *f.*

buntline, *n.* (naut.) briol, *m.*

buoy, *n.* (naut.) boya, *f.*; baliza, *f.*; —, *vt.* boyar; — **up,** apoyar, sostener.

buoyancy, *n.* flotación, *f.*; alegría, *f.*

buoyant, *adj.* boyante.

bur, *n.* carda, *f.*; bardana, *f.*; (mech.) arandela, *f.*; — **oak,** especie de roble; — **parsley,** cadillo, *m.*

burden, *n.* carga, *f.*, cargo, *m.*; estrambote, *m.*; —, *vt.* cargar; gravar.

burdensome, *adj.* gravoso, molesto, incómodo.

burdock, *n.* bardana (planta), *f.*; cadillo, *m.*

bureau, *n.* armario, *m.*; tocador, *m.*, cómoda, *f.*, escritorio, *m.*; negociado, *m.*; oficina, *f.*; departamento, *m.*, división, *f.*

bureaucracy, *n.* burocracia, *f.*

bureaucrat, *n.* burócrata, *m.*

bureaucratic, *adj.* burocrático.

burgess, *n.* ciudadano, *m.*

burgher, *n.* ciudadano, vecino, *m.*

burglar, *n.* salteador, ladrón, *m.*; — **alarm,** alarma para ladrones; — **insurance,** seguro contra robo.

burglary, *n.* asalto y robo nocturno de una casa.

burgomaster, *n.* burgomaestre, *m.*

Burgundian, *n.* and *adj.* borgoñón, ona.

Burgundy, Borgoña, *f.*

burial, *n.* entierro, enterramiento, *m.*; exequias, *f. pl.*; — **place,** cementerio, *m.*

burl, *vt.* desmotar; —, *n.* nudo, nudillo, *m.*

burlesque, *adj.* burlesco; —, *n.* especie de función teatral de género festivo y picaresco; —, *vt.* and *vi.* burlarse; parodiar.

burly, *adj.* voluminoso; vigoroso; turbulento.

Burma, Birmania, *f.*

burn, *vt.* quemar, abrasar o herir, incendiar; —, *vi.* arder; —, *n.* quemadura, *f.*

burner, *n.* quemador, *m.*; mechero, *m.*; **gas —,** mechero de gas.

burning, *n.* quemadura, *f.*; incendio, *m.*; — **glass,** espejo o vidrio ustorio; — **sensation,** (coll.) quemazón, *f.*

burnish, *vt.* bruñir, dar lustre; —, *vi.* tomar lustre.

burnt, *adj.* quemado.

burr, *n.* lóbulo de la oreja; bardana, *f.*; carda, *f.*; (mech.) arandela, *f.*

burrow, *n.* conejera, *f.*; —, *vi.* esconderse en la conejera; excavar un hoyo en la tierra.

bursar, *n.* tesorero, *m.*

burst, *vi.* reventar; abrirse; **to—into tears,** prorrumpir en lágrimas; **to — out laughing,** soltar una carcajada; **to — with laughing,** descoyuntarse de risa; —, *n.* reventón, *m.*; rebosadura, *f.*

bury, *vt.* enterrar, sepultar; esconder.

burying, *n.* soterramiento, entierro, *m.*; — **ground,** cementerio, *m.*

bus, *n.* ómnibus, camión, *m.*

bus. business, negocio.

busby, *n.* gorra de húsar.

bush, *n.* arbusto, espinal, *m.*; cola de zorra; **to beat around the —,** acercarse indirectamente a una cosa, andar con rodeos.

bushel, *n.* medida de áridos (Ingl. 36.37 litros; E. U. 35.28 litros).

bushing, *n.* buje, cojinete, *m.*; (mech.) encastre, encaje, *m.*; casquillo, *m.*; collera (en maquinaria), *f.*; **center pin —,** buje del pivote central.

bushy, *adj.* espeso, lleno de arbustos; lanudo.

busily, *adv.* solícitamente, diligentemente, apresuradamente.

business, *n.* empleo, *m.*, ocupación, *f.*; negocio, *m.*; quehacer, *m.*; — **cycle,** ciclo comercial; — **house,** casa de comercio; — **transaction,** negociación, operación, *f.*; **to do — with,** tratar con.

businessman, *n.* comerciante, *m.*

buskin, *n.* borceguí, coturno, *m.*; drama trágico.

bust, *n.* busto, *m.*

bustard, *n.* avutarda, *f.*

bustle, *n.* baraúnda, *f.*; confusión, *f.*, ruido, *m.*; tontillo, *m.*, caderillas, *f. pl.*; —, *vi.* apurarse con estrépito; menearse; **to — about one's work,** trajinar.

busy, *adj.* ocupado; atareado; entremetido; —, *vt.* ocupar.

busybody, *n.* entremetido, da; veedor, ra; camasquince, *m.* y *f.*

but, *prep.* excepto; —, *conj.* and *adv.* menos; pero; solamente.

butadiene, *n.* butadieno (gas que se emplea en la fabricación de caucho sintético), *m.*

butcher, *n.* carnicero, *m.*; —**'s shop,** carnicería, *f.* —, *vt.* matar atrozmente.

butchery, *n.* matadero, *m.*; matanza, *f.*

butler, *n.* despensero, ra, mayordomo, *m.*; —**'s pantry,** repostería, *f.*

butt, *n.* terrero, *m.*; blanco, hito, *m.*; bota, *f.*, cuba para guardar vino, etc.; persona a quien se ridiculiza; cabezada (golpe de la cabeza), *f.*; —, *vt.* topar.

butter, *n.* manteca, mantequilla, *f.*; — **dish,** mantequillera, *f.*; — **knife,** cuchillo mantequillero; — **seller,** mantequero, *m.*;

—, *vt.* batir la leche; untar con manteca.
buttercup, *n.* (bot.) ranúnculo, *m.*
butterfat, *n.* manteca no batida.
butterfly, *n.* mariposa, *f.*
buttermilk, *n.* nata agria de leche; (Mex.) jocoqui, *m.*
butternut, *n.* nogal americano grueso y oleoso; nuez del nogal americano.
butterscotch, *n.* especie de dulce hecho de azúcar y mantequilla.
buttery, *n.* despensa, *f.*; **—,** *adj.* mantecoso.
buttock, *n.* nalga, *f.*; anca, *f.*; (Sp. Am.) canco, *m.*; (naut.) cucharros, *m. pl.*
button, *n.* botón, *m.*; **call —,** botón de llamada; **push —,** botón de contacto; **—,** *vt.* abotonar.
buttonhole, *n.* ojal, *m.*
buttonhook, *n.* abotonador, *m.*, corchete de botón.
buttress, *n.* contrafuerte, *m.*; sostén, apoyo, *m.*; **—,** *vt.* suministrar un sostén; afianzar.
butyl, *n.* butilo, *m.*
buxom, *adj.* alegre, jovial; robusto y rollizo; **—ly,** *adv.* jovialmente.
buy, *vt.* comprar; **to — at retail,** comprar al por menor; **to — at wholesale,** comprar al por mayor; **to — for cash,** comprar al contado; **to — on credit,** comprar al crédito o fiado; **to — secondhand,** comprar de ocasión; **to — up,** acaparar.
buzz, *n.* susurro, soplo, *m.*; **—,** *vi.* zumbar; cuchuchear.
buzzard, *n.* (orn.) buharro, *m.*; gallinazo, *m.*
buzzer, *n.* zumbador, *m.*
bx. box, c/ caja.
by, *prep.* por; a, en; de, con; al lado de, cerca de; **—,** *adv.* cerca, al lado de; **— all means,** de todos modos, cueste lo que cueste; **— and —,** dentro de poco, luego; **— and large,** por todos conceptos; **— much,** con mucho; **— the way,** de paso, a propósito.
bye-bye, *interj.* ¡adiosito!
by-election, *n.* elección que se celebra entre las elecciones regulares para llenar alguna vacante.
bygone, *adj.* pasado.
bylaws, *n. pl.* estatutos, *m. pl.*, reglamento, *m.*
byname, *n.* apodo, *m.*
by-pass, *n.* desvío, *m.*; **—,** *vt.* desviar.
bypath, *n.* atajo, *m.*, trocha, *f.*
byplay, *n.* acción aparte en el teatro.
by-product, *n.* residuo, *m.*; derivado, *m.*
byroad, *n.* camino descarriado.
bystander, *n.* persona que está presente; **—s,** *pl.* circunstantes, *m. pl.*
bystreet, *n.* callejuela, *f.*
by-way, *n.* camino desviado.
byword, *n.* proverbio, refrán, *m.*
Byzantium, Bizancio, *m.*

C

C.: centigrade, C. centígrado; **current,** corrte. cte. corriente.
c.: about, relativo a; **current,** corrte., etc. corriente.
C.A. Central America, C.A. Centro América.
ca. about, relativo a.
cab, *n.* coche de plaza, coche de alquiler.
cabalistic, *adj.* cabalístico.
cabaret, *n.* cabaret, *m.*
cabbage, *n.* repollo, *m.*, berza, col, *f.*; **—,** *vt.* hurtar, ratear.
cabin, *n.* cabaña, cabina, barraca, *f.*; choza, *f.*; camarote, *m.*; **— boy,** paje de escoba, camarero, *m.*; **— mate,** compañero de camarote; **— steward,** mayordomo, *m.*; **—,** *vt.* and *vi.* hospedar en una cabaña.
cabinet, *n.* gabinete, *m.*; escritorio, *m.*; ministerio, *m.*; **— council,** consejo de ministros.
cabinetmaker, *n.* ebanista, *m.*
cable, *n.* cable, cablegrama, *m.*; (naut.) cable, *m.*; **— address,** dirección cablegráfica; **— control,** cabo, *m.*; **—'s length,** medida de 120 brazas; **electric —,** cabo conductor; **—,** *adj.* cablegráfico.
cablegram, *n.* cablegrama, *m.*
cabman, *n.* cochero de plaza, calesero, *m.*; simón, *m.*
caboose, *n.* (naut.) cocina, *f.*, fogón, *m.*; vagón de cola.
cabstand, *n.* punto de los coches de plaza.
cacao, *n.* cacao, *m.*
cachalot, *n.* cachalote, *m.*
cache, *n.* silo, escondite, *m.*
cackle, *vi.* cacarear, graznar; **—,** *n.* cacareo, *m.*; charla, *f.*
cacophonous, *adj.* cacofónico.
cactus, *n.* (bot.) cacto, *m.*
cad, *n.* persona vil o despreciable.
cadaver, *n.* cadáver, cuerpo, *m.*
cadaverous, *adj.* cadavérico.
caddie, *n.* mensajero, *m.*; ayudante, *m.*; muchacho que lleva los bastones en el juego de golf.
caddy, *n.* caja para el té; muchacho que asiste en el juego de golf; **—,** *vi.* ser o servir de muchacho de golf.
cadence, *n.* (mus.) cadencia, *f.*
cadenza, *n.* (mus.) cadencia, *f.*
cadet, *adj.* cadete, *m.*; hermano menor.
Caesar, César.
Caesarean, *adj.* cesáreo; **— operation,** operación cesárea.
café, *n.* café, restaurante, *m.*, cantina, *f.*; **— keeper,** cantinero, *m.*, dueño de un café o de una cantina.
cafeteria, *n.* restaurante en donde se sirve uno mismo.
caffeine, *n.* cafeína, *f.*
cage, *n.* jaula, *f.*; alambrera, *f.*; prisión, *f.*; **—,** *vt.* enjaular.

cairn, n. montón de piedras para señalar un punto dado.

caisson, n. cajón de dique; (mil.) arcón, m.; carro de municiones; mina portátil; (arch.) casetón, artesón, m.; — **dam,** ataguía, f., dique flotante.

cajole, vt. lisonjear, adular.

cajolery, n. adulación, lisonja, f.; zalamería, f.

cake, n. bollo, m.; torta, tortita, f.; bizcocho, pastel, m.; — **of soap,** pastilla de jabón; —, vi. endurecerse (como el pan en el horno); coagularse.

Cal., Calif. California, California.

calamine, n. calamina, f.

calamitous, adj. calamitoso.

calamity, n. calamidad, miseria, f.

calcareous, adj. calcáreo.

calcify, vt. petrificar.

calcimine, n. lechada, f.

calcine, vt. calcinar.

calcium, n. calcio, m.; — **carbonate,** caliza, f.

calculable, adj. calculable.

calculate, vt. calcular, contar.

calculating, adj. calculador, de calcular; — **machine,** máquina de calcular.

calculation, n. calculación, cuenta, f.; cálculo, m.

calculator, n. calculador, ra.

calculus, n. cálculo, m.

Calcutta, Calcuta, f.

caldron, n. caldera, f.

calendar, n. calendario, almanaque, m.

calender, n. calandria, f.; —, vt. prensar con calandria.

calendula, n. (bot.) caléndula, maravilla, f.

calf, n. ternero, ra; cuero de ternero.

calfskin, n. becerro, becerrillo, m.

caliber, n. calibre, m.

calibrate, vt. calibrar, medir o comprobar el calibre de las armas de fuego o el de otros tubos.

calibration, n. calibración, f.

calibrator, n. calibrador, m.

calico, n. percal, m., zaraza, f.

caliper, n. calibrador, m., compás esférico.

caliph, n. califa, m.

calisthenics, n. pl. ejercicios gimnásticos, calisténica, gimnasia, f.

calk, vt. (naut.) calafatear un navío.

call, vt. llamar, nombrar; convocar, citar; apelar; denominar; **to — attention,** llamar la atención; **to — for,** ir por (algo o alguien); **to — names,** injuriar; **to — the roll,** pasar lista; **to — to order,** llamar al orden, abrir la sesión; **to — upon,** visitar; —, n. llamada, f.; instancia, f.; invitación, f.; urgencia, f.; vocación, profesión, f.; empleo, m.; grito, m.; (naut.) pito, m.; (mil.) toque, m.; — **bell,** timbre, m.; **long-distance —,** llamada de larga distancia.

caller, n. visitador, m., visitadora, f., visitante, m. y f.; persona que llama.

calligraphy, n. caligrafía, f.

calling, n. profesión, vocación, f.

calliope, n. instrumento musical compuesto de una serie de silbatos que tocan mediante un teclado.

callosity, n. callosidad, f., cuerno, m., dureza de la especie del callo.

callous, adj. calloso, endurecido; insensible.

callousness, n. callosidad, f.

callow, adj. pelado, desplumado; joven, inmaturo.

callus, n. callo, m.

calm, n. calma, tranquilidad, f.; —, adj. quieto, tranquilo; —, vt. calmar; aplacar, aquietar; **to — down,** serenarse; —**ly,** adv. tranquilamente, quieta y sosegadamente.

calmness, n. tranquilidad, calma, f.

calomel, n. calomel, m.

caloric, n. calórico, m.

calorie, n. caloría, f.

calorimeter, n. calorímetro, m., medidor del calor específico de los cuerpos.

calumet, n. cañutillo de una pipa de fumar.

calumniate, vt. calumniar.

calumniation, n. calumnia, f.

calumnious, adj. calumnioso.

calumny, n. calumnia, f.

Calvary, n. calvario, m.

calve, vi. parir, producir la vaca.

calves, n. pl. de **calf,** terneros, ras.

Calvinist, n. calvinista, m.

calyx, n. (bot.) cáliz, m.

cam, n. (mech.) leva, f.

camaraderie, n. compañerismo, m., confraternidad, f.

cambric, n. cambray, m., batista, f.

Cambridge, n. Cambrige o Cambrigia, f.

came, pretérito del verbo **come.**

camel, n. camello, m.; **driver of —s,** camellero, m.

camellia, n. (bot.) camelia, f.

camelopard, n. camello pardal; **C —,** (ast.) Camaleopardo, m.

cameo, n. camafeo, m.

camera, n. cámara, f., aparato para fotografiar; **candid —,** fotografías tomadas sin advertirlo el sujeto; **motion picture —,** cámara fotográfica para cine.

camion, n. camión, m.

camlet, n. camelote (especie de tela), m.

camomile, n. manzanilla, camamila, f.

camouflage, n. (mil.) camuflaje, m., simulación, f., fingimiento, engaño, m.; disfraz, m.

camp, n. (mil.) campo, m.; —, vi. acampar; **army —,** campamento del ejército; **break —,** levantar el campo; **concentration —,** campo de concentración; —, adj. campal.

campaign, n. campaña, f.; —, vi. servir en campaña.

campaigner, n. persona que hace campaña; propagandista, m. y f.

campanula, n. (bot.) campánula, f.

campfire, n. hoguera en el campo, reunión militar o de muchachos exploradores alrededor de una hoguera.

camphor, n. alcanfor, m.

campstool, n. silla de tijera, catrecillo, m.

campus, n. patio o terrenos de una universidad, un colegio, un instituto, etc.

can, vi. poder, saber; —, vt. envasar en latas; —, n. lata, f., bote de lata; — **opener,** abrelatas, m., abridor de latas.

Can. Canada, Canadá.

Canada, Canadá, m.

Canadian, n. and adj. canadiense.

canal, n. estanque, m.; canal, m.; **irrigating** —, cacera, f.

canalize, vt. canalizar.

Canal Zone, Zona del Canal, f.

Canaries, Canary Islands, Las Canarias, Islas Canarias, f. pl.

canary, n. canario, m.

cancel, vt. cancelar, borrar; anular, invalidar; barrear.

cancellation, n. cancelación, f.

Cancer, n. Cáncer (signo del zodíaco), m.

cancer, n. (med.) cáncer, m.

cancerous, adj. canceroso.

candelabrum, n. candelabro, m.

candid, adj. cándido, sencillo, ingenuo, sincero; — **camera,** cámara para tomar fotografías sin que lo advierta el sujeto; —**ly,** adv. cándidamente, francamente.

candidacy, n. candidatura, f.

candidate, n. candidato, ta, aspirante (a un puesto, cargo, etc.), m. y f.

candied, adj. garapiñado, en almíbar.

candle, n. candela, vela, bujía, f.; — **grease,** sebo, m.; — **power,** (elec.) potencia luminosa (en bujías); — **store,** cerería, f.; **wax** —, candela de cera, bujía de cera.

candlelight, n. luz artificial; luz de vela; crepúsculo, anochecer, m.

candlemaker, n. cerero, m.

Candlemas, n. Candelaria, f.

candlestick, n. candelero, m.; bujía, f.; **branched** —, araña, f.; **low** —, palmatoria, f.

candor, n. candor, m.; sinceridad, ingenuidad, f.

candy, vt. confitar; garapiñar; —, n. confite, bombón, dulce, m.; — **box,** caja de dulces, confitera, f.

cane, n. caña, f.; bastón, m.; — **plantation,** cañal, cañaveral, m.; — **seller,** bastonero, m.; **small** —, bastoncillo, m.; **to beat with a** —, bastonear; —, vt. bastonear; —, vi. apalear con un bastón o caña.

canemaker, n. bastonero, m.

canine, adj. canino, perruno.

canister, n. canastillo, m., vasija (para guardar té, tabaco, etc.), f.

canker, n. gangrena, f.; cáncer, m.; —, vt. roer, corromper; —, vi. corromperse, roerse.

canned goods, n. pl. productos en lata o en conserva.

cannery, n. fábrica de conservas alimenticias.

cannibal, n. caníbal, m., antropófago, ga.

cannibalism, n. canibalismo, m.

cannon, n. cañón, m.; — **ball,** bala de artillería, f.

cannonade, n. cañoneo, m.; —, vt. cañonear.

cannonier, n. cañonero, artillero, m.

canny, adj. cuerdo, discreto, sagaz.

canoe, n. canoa, f.; bote, m.; (Mex.) chalupa, f.; piragua, f.

canoeist, n. canoero, ra.

canon, n. canon, m., regla, f.; (eccl.) canónigo, m.; — **law,** derecho canónico; — **type** (print.), canon, m.

canonical, adj. canónico; —**s,** n. pl. vestimenta para los eclesiásticos.

canonization, n. canonización, f.

canonize, vt. canonizar.

canonry, n. canonjía, f.

canopy, n. dosel, pabellón, m.

cant, n. jerigonza, f.; canto o esquina de un edificio; —, vi. hablar en jerigonza.

cantaloupe, cantaloup, n. melón de verano.

cantankerous, adj. pendenciero, malicioso.

canteen, n. (mil.) cantina, f., especie de tienda de provisiones para soldados; vasija en que los soldados, viajeros, etc., llevan agua.

canter, n. persona que habla en jerigonza; medio galope.

Canterbury, Canterbury o Cantorberi, f.

canticle, n. cántico, salmo, m.

cantilever, n. ménsula, f.; viga voladiza, viga sostenida por un extremo; (Arg.) consola, f.

canton, n. cantón, m.; —, vt. acantonar.

cantonment, n. acantonamiento, acuartelamiento, m.

canvas, n. cañamazo, m.; lona, f.; tela gruesa de cáñamo usada en velámenes, toldos, etc.

canvass, vt. escudriñar, examinar, controvertir; —, vi. solicitar votos, etc.

canvasser, n. solicitador, ra, persona que solicita votos, etc.

canyon, n. desfiladero, m.

caoutchouc, n. goma elástica, caucho, m.

cap, n. gorra, f., birrete, m.; cachucha, f.; — **and gown,** traje académico o toga y birrete; **Basque** —, boina, f.; **military** —, chaco, m.; —, vt. cubrir la cabeza; **to** — **the climax,** llegar al colmo; **percussion** —, cápsula fulminante, f.

cap. capital letter, may. letra mayúscula.

capability, n. capacidad, aptitud, habilidad, f.

capable, adj. capaz, idóneo.

capacious, adj. capaz; espacioso, vasto.

capacity, n. capacidad, f.; inteligencia, habilidad, f.; calidad, f.; — **of a ship,** capacidad de un barco; **seating** —, cabida, f.

caparison, *n.* caparazón, *m.*; **—,** *vt.* enjaezar un caballo.
cape, *n.* cabo, promontorio, *m.*; capa, *f.*; capota, *f.*; capote, *m.*
Cape Colony, Colonia del Cabo, *f.*
Cape Horn, Cabo de Hornos, *m.*
Cape of Good Hope, Cabo de Buena Esperanza, *m.*
caper, *n.* cabriola, *f.*; travesura, *f.*; alcaparra, *f.*; corsario, *m.*; **to cut a —,** cabriolar; **—,** *vi.* hacer cabriolas, hacer travesuras.
capillary, *adj.* capilar.
capital, *adj.* capital, excelente; principal; **— punishment,** pena de muerte; **—,** *n.* (arch.) capitel, *m.*; capital (la ciudad principal), *f.*; capital, fondo, *m.*; mayúscula, *f.*; **floating —,** capital fluctuante; **rolling —,** capital circulante; **to invest —,** colocar un capital; **—ly,** *adv.* superiormente; admirablemente, capitalmente; con pena de muerte.
capitalist, *n.* capitalista, *m.* y *f.*
capitalization, *n.* capitalización, *f.*
capitalize, *vt.* capitalizar.
capitation, *n.* capitación, *f.*
Capitol, *n.* Capitolio, *m.*
capitular, *n.* capitular, *m.*
capitulary, *adj.* capitular.
capitulate, *vi.* (mil.) capitular.
capitulation, *n.* capitulación, *f.*
capon, *n.* capón (pollo castrado), *m.*
capote, *n.* capote, levitón, *m.*; capota (de coche), *f.*
caprice, *n.* capricho, *m.*; extravagancia, *f.*
capricious, *adj.* caprichoso; **—ly,** *adv.* caprichosamente.
Capricorn, *n.* Capricornio (signo del zodíaco), *m.*
capsicum, *n.* (bot.) pimiento, *m.*
capsize, *vt.* (naut.) trabucar, zozobrar.
capstan, *n.* (naut.) cabrestante, *m.*
capsule, *n.* cápsula, *f.*
Capt. Captain, cap. capitán.
captain, *n.* capitán, *m.*; **ship —,** patrón, *m.*, capitán de un barco.
captaincy, captainship, *n.* capitanía, *f.*
caption, *n.* presa, captura, *f.*; (print.) título, subtítulo, *m.*
captious, *adj.* sofístico, insidioso, engañoso, caviloso; **—ly,** *adv.* cavilosamente.
captivate, *vt.* cautivar; esclavizar.
captivation, *n.* atractivo, *m.*, fascinación, *f.*
captive, *n.* cautivo, va, esclavo, va.
captivity, *n.* cautividad, esclavitud, *f.*, cautiverio, *m.*
captor, *n.* apresador, pirata, *m.*
capture, *n.* captura, *f.*; presa, *f.*; toma, *f.*; **—,** *vt.* apresar; capturar.
capuchin, *n.* capucha, *f.*; **—,** *adj.* capuchino; **— monk,** capuchino, *m.*; **— nun,** capuchina, *f.*
car, *n.* carreta, *f.*; carro, *m.*; **baggage, freight or express —,** furgón, vagón, coche, *m.*; **— body,** carrocería, *f.*, bastidor, *m.*; **— top,** capota, *f.*, capacete,

m.; **dining —,** (rail.) coche comedor; **freight —,** carro, *m.*; **funeral —,** carroza, *f.*; **side — (of a motorcycle),** carro lateral; **sleeping —,** (rail.) coche dormitorio; **smoking —,** coche fumador; **armored —,** automóvil acorazado.
carabine, *n.* carabina, *f.*
carabinier, *n.* carabinero, *m.*
carafe, *n.* garrafa, *f.*
caramel, *n.* caramelo, *m.*
carat, *n.* quilate, *m.*
caravan, *n.* caravana, *f.*
caraway, *n.* (bot.) alcaravea, *f.*
carbide, *n.* (chem.) carburo, *m.*
carbohydrate, *n.* hidrato de carbono, carbohidrato, *m.*
carbolic, *adj.* fénico; **— acid,** ácido carbólico, ácido fénico, fenol, *m.*
carbon, *n.* carbón, *m.*; **— copy,** copia al carbón, copia en papel carbón; **— dioxide,** ácido carbónico, dióxido de carbono; **— paper,** papel carbón.
carbonaceous, *adj.* carbonoso.
carbonate, *n.* carbonato, *m.*
carbonic, *adj.* carbónico.
carboniferous, *adj.* carbonífero.
carbonize, *vt.* carbonizar.
carborundum, *n.* carborundo, *m.*
carboy, *n.* garrafón, *m.*, damajuana para envasar ácidos.
carbuncle, *n.* carbúnculo, rubí, *m.*; (med.) carbunco, *m.*
carburetor, *n.* carburador, *m.*
carcass, *n.* animal muerto; casco, *m.*; armazón, *m.*
card, *n.* naipe, *m.*, carta, *f.*; tarjeta, *f.*; cardencha, *f.*; carda (para cardar lana), *f.*; **— catalogue,** catálogo de fichas; **— index,** fichero, *m.*; **— trick,** baza, *f.*; **cross-reference —,** ficha de referencia; **pack of —s,** conjunto de naipes para jugar baraja; **—,** *vt.* cardar (lana).
cardboard, *n.* cartón, *m.*; **— binding,** encuadernación de cartón; **— fine —,** cartulina, *f.*
cardiac, *adj.* cardíaco.
cardigan, *n.* especie de chaqueta tejida.
cardinal, *adj.* cardinal, principal; rojo, purpurado; **— (point),** cardinal; **—,** *n.* cardenal, *m.*; (orn.) cardenal, *m.*
cardiograph, *n.* (med.) cardiógrafo, *m.*
carditis, *n.* (med.) carditis, *f.*
care, *n.* cuidado, *m.*; solicitud, *f.*; recato, *m.*; miramiento, *m.*; cargo, *m.*; vigilancia, *f.*; **take — of,** cuidar de; **have a —,** estar alerta; **—,** *vi.* cuidar, tener cuidado o pena; inquietarse, estimar, apreciar; **to — about,** preocuparse; **what do I —?** ¿á mí qué me importa? **I don't —,** no me importa un bledo; **not to — a fig,** no dársele a uno un higo; **— for,** guardar; vigilar; cuidar.
careen, *vt.* (naut.) carenar.
career, *n.* carrera, profesión, *f.*; curso, *m.*; **—,** *vi.* correr a carrera tendida.

carefree, *adj.* sin cuidados.
careful, *adj.* cuidadoso, ansioso, diligente, prudente, solícito; **to be —,** tener cuidado; **—ly,** *adv.* cuidadosamente, detenidamente.
carefulness, *n.* cuidado, *m.,* cautela, atención, diligencia, *f.*
careless, *adj.* descuidado, negligente; indolente; **—ly,** *adv.* descuidadamente.
carelessness, *n.* negligencia, indiferencia, *f.*
caress, *n.* caricia, *f.;* **—es,** *n. pl.* gachas, *f. pl.;* **—,** *vt.* acariciar, halagar.
caretaker, *n.* velador, *m.*
careworn, *adj.* cansado, fatigado.
carfare, *n.* pasaje (de tranvía), *m.;* pequeña cantidad de dinero.
cargo, *n.* cargamento de navío; carga, *f.,* consignación, *f.;* **return —,** carga de vuelta.
caribou, *n.* caribú, *m.*
caricature, *n.* caricatura, *f.;* **—,** *vt.* hacer caricaturas; ridiculizar.
caricaturist, *n.* caricaturista, *m.* y *f.*
caries, *n.* caries, *f.*
Carinthia, Carintia, *f.*
carious, *adj.* cariado; **to grow —,** cariarse.
carload, *n.* furgón entero, carro entero, la carga de un carro; galerada, *f.;* (rail.) vagonada, *f.*
carman, *n.* carretero, *m.;* furgonero, *m.*
Carmelite, *n.* carmelita, *m.* y *f.*
carmine, *n.* carmín, *m.*
carnage, *n.* colección de cadáveres; carnicería, matanza, *f.*
carnal, *adj.* carnal; sensual; **—ly,** *adv.* carnalmente.
carnation, *n.* encarnación,*f.;* (bot.) clavel,*m.*
carnelian, *n.* (min.) cornalina, cornerina, *f.*
carnival, *n.* carnaval, *m.*
carnivore, *n.* carnívoro, *m.*
carnivorous, *adj.* carnívoro.
carol, *n.* villancico, *m.,* canción de alegría o piedad; **—,** *vt.* celebrar con villancicos.
Caroline, Carolina.
carom, *n.* carambola, *f.;* **—,** *vi.* hacer carambola.
carotid, *adj.* carotídeo; **— artery,** carótida, *f.*
carousal, *n.* festín, *m.;* parranda, *f.;* (coll.) juerga, *f.*
carouse, *vt.* beber excesivamente; tomar parte en una juerga.
carp, *n.* carpa, *f.;* **—,** *vi.* censurar, criticar, reprobar.
Carpathians, Montes Cárpatos.
carpenter, *n.* carpintero, *m.;* **—'s bench,** banco de carpintero.
carpentry, *n.* carpintería, *f.*
carpet, *n.* tapete de mesa; tapiz, *m.;* **— knight,** caballerete, *m.;* **— sweeper,** barredor de alfombra; **—,** *vt.* cubrir con alfombras.
carpetbag, *n.* baulillo de viandante, *m.*
carpeting, *n.* material para tapices; tapicería, *f.*

carping, *adj.* capcioso, caviloso; **—ly,** *adv.* malignamente.
carriage, *n.* porte, talante, *m.;* coche, *m.,* carroza, *f.;* carruaje, *m.;* vehículo, *m.;* carga,*f.;* cureña de cañón.
carrier, *n.* portador, carretero, *m.;* transportador, *m.;* **aircraft —,** (naut.) portaaviones, *m.;* **— pigeon,** paloma correo o mensajera o viajera.
carrion, *n.* carroña, *f.*
carronade, *n.* carronada, *f.*
carrot, *n.* zanahoria, *f.;* **wild —,** dauco, *m.*
carry, *vt.* llevar, conducir; portar; lograr; cargar; **to — on,** continuar; **to — out,** cumplir, llevar a cabo, realizar; **to — it high,** afectar grandeza; **to — the day,** quedar victorioso; ganar la palma; **to — the prize,** ganar el premio; **to — through,** llevar a cabo.
carryall, *n.* automóvil de carrocería cerrada con dos asientos laterales fronteros.
carrying, *n.* porteo, *m.;* **—,** *adj.* porteador.
cart, *n.* carro, *m.;* carreta, *f.;* carretón, *m.;* **—,** *vt. and vi.* carretear; usar carretas o carros.
cartage, *n.* carretaje, *m.*
carte blanche, *n.* carta blanca.
cartel, *n.* cartel, *m.;* (com., política) cartel (acuerdo entre comerciantes o entre países), *m.;* desafío, *m.*
carter, *n.* carretero, *m.;* furgonero, *m.*
cartilage, *n.* cartílago, *m.,* ternilla, *f.*
carting, *n.* carretaje, *m.*
cartload, *n.* carretada, *f.*
cartographer, *n.* cartógrafo, *m.*
cartography, *n.* cartografía, *f.*
carton, *n.* caja de cartón fino.
cartoon, *n.* caricatura, *f.;* boceto, *m.;* **—,** *vt. and vi.* caricaturizar; bosquejar.
cartoonist, *n.* caricaturista, *m.*
cartouch, *n.* (mil.) cartucho, *m.;* (arch.) cartela, *f.*
cartridge, *n.* cartucho, *m.;* **blank —,** cartucho en blanco; **— shell,** cápsula, *f.*
cartwright, *n.* carretero, *m.*
carve, *vt.* cincelar; trinchar, tajar; grabar; **—,** *vi.* esculpir.
carver, *n.* escultor, *m.;* persona que taja; trinchante, *m.*
carving, *n.* escultura, entalladura, *f.;* **— knife,** cuchillo grande para tajar la carne.
cascade, *n.* cascada, *f.;* salto de agua.
cascara, *n.* cáscara, *f.;* **— sagrada,** cáscara sagrada.
case, *n.* estado, *m.;* situación, *f.;* causa, *f.;* bolsa, *f.;* caso, *m.;* estuche, *m.,* vaina, *f.;* caja, *f.;* (gram.) caso, *m.;* **in —,** si acaso, caso que; **in — of emergency,** en caso de fuerza; **in the — of,** en caso de; **in — that,** dado que, si.
caseharden, *vt.* endurecer superficialmente; hacer insensible.
casein, *n.* caseína, *f.*
casemate, *n.* (mil.) casamata, *f.*
casement, *n.* puerta ventana.

cash, *n.* dinero contante o efectivo; caja, *f.*; **— on delivery,** cóbrese al entregar, contra reembolso; **— on hand,** efectivo en caja; **— payment,** pago al contado; **— register,** registrador, *m.*, caja registradora; **to buy for —,** comprar al contado; **—,** *vt.* cobrar o hacer efectivo (un cheque, etc.)

cashbook, *n.* libro de caja.

cashbox, *n.* caja de hierro.

cashew, *n.* anacardo, *m.*

cashier, *n.* cajero, ra; **—'s check,** cheque de caja; **—,** *vt.* rechazar; privar a uno de su empleo.

cashmere, *n.* casimir (tela), *m.*

Casimir, Casimiro.

casing, *n.* forro, *m.*, cubierta, envoltura, *f.*; caja (de engranaje, etc.), *f.*

casino, *n.* casino, *m.*, casa de juego.

cask, *n.* barril, tonel, *m.*; cuba, *f.*; **water —,** bota, *f.*; **—,** *vt.* entonelar.

casket, *n.* cajita para joyas; ataúd, *m.*; **—,** *vt.* poner en cajita.

Caspian Sea, (Mar) Caspio, *m.*

cassation, *n.* (law) casación, *f.*; **court of —,** tribunal que anula o confirma las sentencias de los tribunales inferiores.

cassava, *n.* (bot.) casabe, cazabe, *m.*

casserole, *n.* cacerola, *f.*

cassia, *n.* casia, *f.*

cassimere, *n.* casimir (tela), *m.*

cassock, *n.* sotana, *f.*

cassowary, *n.* casuario, *m.*

cast, *vt.* tirar, lanzar; ganar; echar; modelar; imponer una pena; **to — lots,** echar suertes; **—,** *vi.* maquinar alguna cosa; **—,** *n.* tiro, golpe, *m.*; forma, *f.*; aire, *m.*, echamiento, *m.*; apariencia exterior; (theat.) reparto de los papeles; **— of characters,** (theat.) reparto, *m.*; **— (of a play),** (theat.) elenco artístico; **— (of the eyes),** ojeada, *f.*; defecto en la mirada; **—,** *adj.* fundido; **— iron,** hierro colado; **— steel,** acero fundido.

castanets, *n. pl.* castañuelas, castañetas, *f. pl.*

castaway, *n.* réprobo, *m.*; náufrago, ga.

cast-down, *adj.* humillado.

caste, *n.* casta, *f.*; clase social; **to lose —,** perder la posición social.

castellan, *n.* castellán, *m.*

caster, *n.* calculador, *m.*; pimentero, *m.*; tirador, *m.*; adivino, *m.*; ruedecita, *f.*

castigate, *vt.* castigar.

castigation, *n.* castigo, *m.*; pena, *f.*

Castile, Castilla, *f.*

Castilian, *n.* and *adj.* castellano, na.

casting, *n.* tiro, *m.*; vaciado, *m.*; (theat.) distribución de papeles a los actores.

castings, *n. pl.* obras de fundición.

castle, *n.* castillo, *m.*; fortaleza, *f.*; **small —,** castillejo, *m.*; **—,** *vt.* encastillar; **to — one's king,** enrocar (en el juego de ajedrez).

castoff, *adj.* descartado; **— clothes,** ropa de desecho; **— iron,** hierro de desecho.

Castor, *n.* (ast.) Cástor, *m.* (estrella en la constelación de Géminis).

castor, *n.* castor, *m.*; sombrero castor; **— oil,** aceite de ricino, de castor o de palmacristi.

castrate, *vt.* castrar, capar.

castration, *n.* capadura, castración, *f.*

casual, *adj.* casual, fortuito; **—ly,** *adv.* casualmente, fortuitamente.

casualty, *n.* casualidad, *f.*; acaso, accidente, *m.*; caso, *m.*; **—ties,** *n. pl.* víctimas de accidentes o de guerra, etc.

casuist, *n.* casuísta; **—ry,** casuística, *f.*

casuistry, *n.* casuística, *f.*

cat, *n.* gato, *m.*, gata, *f.*; **to let the — out of the bag,** revelar un secreto.

cat.: catalog, catálogo; **catechism,** catecismo.

catabolism, *n.* catabolismo, *m.*

cataclysm, *n.* cataclismo, diluvio, *m.*

catacombs, *n. pl.* catacumbas, *f. pl.*

catafalque, *n.* catafalco, *m.*

catalepsis, *n.* (med.) catalepsia, *f.*

catalogue, *n.* catálogo, *m.*; rol, elenco, *m.*, lista, *f.*

Catalonia, Cataluña, *f.*

Catalonian, *n.* and *adj.* catalán, ana.

catalpa, *n.* (bot.) catalpa, *f.*

catalysis, *n.* (chem.) catálisis, *f.*

catalyzer, *n.* (chem.) catalizador, *m.*

catapult, *n.* catapulta, *f.*

cataract, *n.* cascada, catarata, *f.*; (med.) catarata, *f.*

catarrh, *n.* catarro, *m.*; reuma, *f.*

catastrophe, *n.* catástrofe, *f.*

catbird, *n.* tordo mimo.

catcall, *n.* silbido, *m.*; reclamo, *m.*

catch, *vt.* coger, agarrar, asir; atrapar; pillar; sorprender; **—,** *vi.* pegarse, ser contagioso; prender; **to — cold,** resfriarse; **to — fire,** encenderse; **to — up,** alcanzar; **to — at,** coger, descubrir; **—,** *n.* botín, *m.*, presa, *f.*; captura, *f.*; idea, *f.*; buen partido; trampa, *f.*; acto de parar la pelota; **— bolt,** picaporte, *m.*

catchall, *n.* receptáculo para artículos o cosas diversas.

catch-as-catch-can, *n.* lucha libre.

catcher, *n.* cogedor, ra; engañador, ra; (baseball) parador de la pelota.

catching, *adj.* contagioso.

catchword, *n.* (print.) reclamo, *m.*; contraseña, *f.*

catchy, *adj.* atrayente, agradable; engañoso; **— tune,** tonada pegajosa, que se retiene fácilmente.

catechism, *n.* catecismo, *m.*

catechist, *n.* catequista, *m.*

categorical, *adj.* categórico; **—ly,** *adv.* categóricamente.

category, *n.* categoría, *f.*

cater, *vi.* abastecer, proveer; halagar, complacer.

cater-cornered, *adj.* diagonal; **—,** *adv.* diagonalmente.

caterer, n. proveedor, ra, abastecedor, ra.
caterpillar, n. oruga, f.; — **tractor,** tractor de orugas.
caterwaul, vi. maullar; cencerrear; —, n. maullido, maúllo, m.
catfish, n. (pez) barbo, m.
catgut, n. cuerda de violín o guitarra.
catharsis, n. purgación, f.
Cath. Catholic, católico.
cathartic, adj. (med.) catártico; —, n. purgante, laxante, m.
cathedral, n. catedral, f.
Catherine, Catalina.
catheter, n. catéter, m.
cathode, n. cátodo, m.; — **rays,** rayos catódicos.
cathodic, adj. (elec.) catódico.
catholic, n. and adj. católico, ca.
catholicism, n. catolicismo, m.
catkin, n. (bot.) amento, m.
catnip, n. (bot.) calamento, m.
cat-o'-nine-tails, n. cilicio, m.
cat's-paw, n. persona que sirve de instrumento a otra; (naut.) soplo, m.
catsup, n. salsa de tomate.
cattle, n. ganado, m., ganado vacuno; — **car,** vagón de ganado; — **ranch,** rancho, m.
Caucasus, Cáucaso, m.
caucus, n. junta electoral.
caught, pretérito y p. p. del verbo **catch.**
caul, n. membrana, f.; cofia, redecilla, f.
cauliflower, n. colifor, f.
causal, adj. causal.
causality, n. causalidad, f.
causation, n. causalidad, f.
cause, n. causa, f.; razón, f.; motivo, lugar, m.; proceso, m.; —, vt. motivar, causar.
causeless, adj. infundado, sin razón.
causeway, n. arrecife, m.
caustic, adj. cáustico; —, n. cáustico, m.
cauterization, n. cauterización, f., cauterio, m.
cauterize, vt. cauterizar.
caution, n. prudencia, precaución, f.; aviso, m.; —, vt. avisar, amonestar, advertir.
cautionary, adj. de índole preventiva; dado a tomar precauciones.
cautious, adj. prudente, circunspecto, cauto; **to be —,** estar sobre sí.
Cav. Cavalry, caballería.
cavalcade, n. cabalgata, cabalgada, f.
cavalier, n. jinete, m.; caballero, m.
cavalry, n. caballería, f.; **to remount —,** remontar.
cavalryman, n. soldado de a caballo; soldado de caballería.
cave, n. caverna, f.; bodega, f.; hornachuela, f.; — **man,** habitante de las cavernas; troglodita, m.
caveat, n. aviso, m.; advertencia, f.; (law) notificación, f.
cavern, n. caverna, f.; antro, m.
cavernous, adj. cavernoso.
caviar, n. caviar, cavial, m.

cavil, n. cavilación, sofistería, f.; —, vi. cavilar; criticar.
cavity, n. hueco, m., cavidad, f.; seno, m.
caw, vi. graznar, crascitar.
Cayenne, Cayena, f.
cc., c.c. cubic centimeter, centímetro cúbico.
CCC, C.C.C. Civilian Conservation Corps, Cuerpo Civil de Conservación.
cd. cord, cuerda.
C.E. Civil Engineer, Ing. Civil, Ingeniero Civil.
cease, vt. parar, suspender, cesar, dejar de; —, vi. desistir.
ceaseless, adj. incesante, continuo; **—ly,** adv. perpetuamente.
Cebu, Cebú, f.
Cecil, Cecilio.
cedar, n. cedro, m.
cede, vt. ceder, transferir.
ceil, vt. techar.
ceiling, n. techo o cielo raso de una habitación; (aer.) cielo máximo; — **price,** precio tope.
celanese, n. nombre comercial de una seda artificial hecha de acetilcelulosa.
celebrant, n. celebrante, m. y f.
celebrate, vt. celebrar; elogiar.
celebration, n. celebración, f.; alabanza, f.
celebrity, n. celebridad, fama, f.; persona célebre.
celerity, n. celeridad, velocidad, prisa, f.
celery, n. apio, m.
celestial, adj. celeste, divino, celestial; —, n. celícola, m.
celibacy, n. celibato, m., soltería, f.
celibate, n. and adj. soltero, ra, célibe, m. y f.
cell, n. celda, f.; cueva, f.; célula, f.
cellar, n. sótano, m., bodega, f.
cellist, n. violoncelista, m.
cello, n. violoncelo, m.
cellophane, n. celofán, m.; papel transparente y brillante.
cellular, adj. celular.
cellule, n. celdita, f.
celluloid, n. celuloide, m.
cellulose, n. (chem.) celulosa, f.
Celt, n. celta, m. y f.
Celtic, adj. celta; céltico.
cement, n. argamasa, f.; cimento, cemento, m.; (fig.) vínculo, m.; **rubber —,** cemento de caucho; —, vt. pegar con cemento, conglutinar; —, vi. unirse.
cemetery, n. cementerio, m., campo santo.
cen., cent. central, cent. central.
cenobite, n. cenobita, m. y f.
cenotaph, n. cenotafio, m.
censer, n. incensario, m.
censor, n. censor, m.; crítico, m.
censorious, adj. severo, crítico; **—ly,** adv. severamente.
censorship, n. censura, f.
censure, n. censura, reprensión, f.; —, vt. censurar, reprender; criticar.

census, *n.* censo, encabezamiento, *m.*

cent, *n.* ciento, *m.*; **per —,** por ciento; centavo, *m.*; céntimo, *m.*

cent.: centigrade, C. centígrado; **century,** siglo.

centaur, *n.* centauro, *m.*

centenarian, *n.* centenario, ria.

centenary, *n.* centena, *f.*; **—,** *adj.* centenario.

centennial, *n.* and *adj.* centenario, *m.*

center, *n.* centro, *m.*; (football) centro, *m.*; **—,** *vt.* colocar en un centro; reconcentrar; **—,** *vi.* colocarse en el centro, reconcentrarse; **— of gravity,** centro de gravedad.

centigrade, *adj.* centígrado.

centigram, *n.* centigramo, *m.*

centiliter, *n.* centilitro, *m.*

centime, *n.* céntimo, *m.*

centimeter, *n.* centímetro, *m.*

centipede, *n.* escolopendra, *f.*, ciempiés, *m.*

central, *adj.* central; céntrico; **— heating,** calefacción central; **— station,** central *f.*; **—ly,** *adv.* centralmente, en el centro.

Central America, América Central, *f.*

centralization, *n.* centralización, *f.*

centralize, *vt.* centralizar.

centric, *adj.* central, céntrico.

centrifugal, *adj.* centrífugo; **— force,** fuerza centrífuga.

centripetal, *adj.* centrípeto.

centuple, *adj.* céntuplo; **—,** *vt.* centuplicar.

century, *n.* centuria, *f.*; siglo, *m.*

cephalic, *adj.* cefálico.

cephalitis, *n.* (med.) cefalitis, *f.*

ceramics, *n.* cerámica, *f.*

cereal, *n.* cereal, *m.*

cerebellum, *n.* (anat.) cerebelo, *m.*

cerebral, *adj.* cerebral.

cerebrate, *vi.* exhibir actividad mental, pensar.

cerebration, *n.* actividad mental.

cerebrum, *n.* cerebro, *m.*

ceremonial, *adj.* ceremonial; **—,** *n.* ceremonial, *m.*, rito externo.

ceremonious, *adj.* ceremonioso; **—ly,** *adv.* ceremoniosamente.

ceremony, *n.* ceremonia, *f.*, fórmulas exteriores; **without —,** sin empacho.

cerise, *adj.* de color cereza.

cert. certificate, certificado.

certain, *adj.* cierto, evidente; seguro, certero, indudable; efectivo; **— sum, — quantity,** un tanto; **—ly,** *adv.* ciertamente, sin duda; a bien seguro, seguramente.

certainty, certitude, *n.* certeza, *f.*; seguridad, *f.*; certidumbre, *f.*; **with —,** a ciencia cierta.

certificate, *n.* certificado, testimonio, *m.*; (com.) bono, *m.*; certificación, *f.*; **— of registry,** patente de registro.

certification, *n.* certificación, *f.*; certificado, *m.*

certified, *adj.* certificado; **— check,** cheque certificado; **— public accountant,** contador público titulado.

certify, *vt.* certificar, afirmar; dar fe.

certitude, *n.* certidumbre, certeza, *f.*

cerulean, *adj.* cerúleo, azulado.

cerumen, *n.* cerumen, *m.*, cera de los oídos

cervix, *n.* nuca, cerviz, *f.*

Cesarean, *adj.* **Caesarean.**

cessation, *n.* cesación, *f.*

cession, *n.* cesión, *f.*

cesspool, *n.* cloaca, *f.*; sumidero, *m.*

cetacean, *n.* and *adj.* cetáceo, cea.

cf. confer, compare, compárese.

C. G. Consul General, C. G. Cónsul General.

cg. centigram, cg. centigramo.

ch.: chapter, c., cap. capítulo; **church,** igl.ª iglesia.

chafe, *vt.* frotar, enojar, irritar; **—,** *vi.* acalorarse; **—,** *n.* cólera, *f.*; ardor, *m.*

chafer, *n.* escarabajo, *m.*

chaff, *n.* burla, fisga, *f.*; paja menuda; cosa frívola e inútil; **—,** *vt.* and *vi.* dar bromas, chotear.

chaffer, *vi.* regatear, baratear.

chaffinch, *n.* (orn.) pinzón, *m.*

chagrin, *n.* mortificación, *f.*, disgusto, *m.*

chain, *n.* cadena, *f.*; serie, sucesión, *f.*; **— gang,** gavilla de malhechores encadenados juntos, collera, *f.*; **— store,** serie de tiendas al por menor pertenecientes a una misma empresa; **—s,** *n.pl.* esclavitud, *f.*; **—,** *vt.* encadenar, atar con cadena.

chainless, *adj.* desencadenado.

chair, *n.* silla, *f.*; **deck —,** silla de cubierta; **easy —,** silla poltrona; **folding —,** silla plegadiza; **invalid's —,** silla para inválidos; **rocking —,** mecedora, *f.*; **small —,** silleta, *f.*; **swivel —,** silla giratoria; **wheel —,** silla de ruedas; **—,** *vt.* entronizar; colocar en un cargo público.

chairmaker, *n.* sillero, *m.*

chairman, *n.* presidente (de una reunión o junta), *m.*; silletero, *m.*

chairmanship, *n.* presidencia (de una reunión, junta, etc.), *f.*

chaise, *n.* silla volante; calesín, coche, *m.*; **post —,** solitaria, *f.*, silla de posta; **— longue,** canapé, especie de sofá.

chalcedony, *n.* (min.) calcedonia, *f.*

chalet, *n.* chalet, *m.*

chalice, *n.* cáliz, *m.*

chalk, *n.* greda, *f.*; marga, *f.*; tiza, *f.*; yeso, *m.*; **French —,** espuma de mar; **—,** *vt.* dibujar con yeso; bosquejar, lapizar; **to — up,** aumentar un precio; ganar puntos.

chalk talk, *n.* conferencia ilustrada por medio de una pizarra y tiza.

chalky, *adj.* gredoso; yesoso; calcáreo.

challenge, *n.* desafío, cartel, *m.*; pretensión, *f.*; recusación, *f.*; **—,** *vt.* desafiar; retar; provocar, reclamar; (mil.) llamar ¿quién vive?

challenger, *n.* desafiador, ra, retador, ra.

chamber, *n.* cámara, *f.*; aposento, *m.*; (mil.) cámara de mina; **air —,** cámara de aire; **— of commerce,** cámara de comercio; **—(of**

a firearm), **cámara** (de un fusil), *f.*; — **stool, silleta,** *f.*; — **music,** música de cámara.

chamberlain, *n.* camarero, *m.*; chambelán, *m.*

chamber maid, *n.* moza de cámara, camarera, *f.*

chameleon, *n.* camaleón, *m.*

chamois, *n.* gamuza, *f.*

champ, *vt.* morder, mascar.

Champagne, Champaña, *f.*

champagne, *n.* vino de Champaña, champaña, *m.*

champaign, *n.* campiña, llanura, *f.*

champion, *n.* campeón, ona; paladín, *m.*; —, *vt.* desafiar, retar; defender.

championship, *n.* campeonato, *m.*

chance, *n.* ventura, suerte, ocasión, oportunidad, casualidad, *f.*, acaso, *m.*; riesgo, *m.*; **by** —, si acaso, por si acaso, por carambola; **by mere** —, de chiripa; **fortunate** —, (coll.) chiripa, *f.*; —, *vi.* acaecer, acontecer; —, *adj.* fortuito, casual.

chancel, *n.* presbiterio, *m.*

chancellor, *n.* canciller, *m.*; rector, *m.*; **lord high** —, ministro de justicia, gran canciller.

chancellorship, *n.* cancillería, *f.*

chancery, *n.* chancillería, *f.*

chancre, *n.* chancro, *m.*, úlcera venérea.

chandelier, *n.* araña de luces.

chandelle, *n.* (aer.) chandel, *f.*

chandler, *n.* cerero, *m.*; lonjista, *m.*; regatón, *m.*

change, *vt.* cambiar; trasmutar; variar; **to** — **cars,** trasbordar; **to** — **one's clothes,** mudar de ropa; —, *vi.* variar, alterarse; revolverse (el tiempo); —, *n.* mudanza, variedad, *f.*; vicisitud, *f.*; cambio, *m.*; variación, *f.*; suelto (moneda), *m.*; **to make** —, cambiar (moneda); **small** — **(money),** menudo, *m.*; — **of tire,** repuesto de neumático, cambio de gomas o de llantas; — **of heart,** arrepentimiento, *m.*, retractación, *f.*

changeable, changeful, *adj.* variable, inconstante; mudable, cambiante.

changeless, *adj.* inmutable.

change-over, *n.* cambio de ocupación o posición.

channel, *n.* canal, álveo, *m.*; conducto, *m.*; —, *vt.* acanalar, estriar.

chant, *n.* canto llano; sonsonete, *m.*; —, *vt.* cantar; repetir algo monótonamente.

chanticleer, *n.* gallo, *m.*; cantor sonoro.

chantry, *n.* chantría, *f.*

chaos, *n.* caos, *m.*; confusión, *f.*

chaotic, *adj.* confuso; caótico.

chap, *vi.* rajarse, henderse; —, *n.* rendija, *f.*; mandíbula (de animal, etc.), *f.*; (coll.) mozo, chico, *m.*; tipo, *m.*

chap. chapter, c., cap. capítulo.

chape, *n.* chapa de cinturón; charnela de hebilla.

chapel, *n.* capilla, *f.*

chaperon, *n.* persona de respeto, especialmente mujer, que acompaña a jóvenes solteras en público.

chapfallen, *adj.* boquihundido.

chaplain, *n.* capellán, *m.*; **army** —, capellán castrense; **navy** —, capellán de navío.

chaplet, *n.* guirnalda, *f.*; rosario, *m.*

chaps, chaparajos, *n. pl.* chaparreras, *f. pl.*

chapter, *n.* capítulo, *m.*; cabildo, *m.*; sucursal de una confraternidad.

char, *vt.* hacer carbón de leña; carbonizar; —, *vi.* trabajar a jornal; —, *n.* obra de trabajo a jornal; tarea, *f.*; carbón de leña.

character, *n.* carácter, *m.*; señal, *f.*, distintivo, *m.*; letra, *f.*; calidad, *f.*; (theat.) parte, *f.*; papel, *m.*; personaje, *m.*; modalidad, *f.*; **in** —, apropiado a la naturaleza de una personalidad o cosa; **out of** —, no apropiado, etc.; —, *vt.* esculpir, grabar.

characteristic, *adj.* característico; típico; —, *n.* rasgo, *m.*, peculiaridad, *f.*; —**ally,** *adv.* característicamente.

characterization, *n.* caracterización, *f.*

characterize, *vt.* caracterizar, imprimir, calificar.

charade, *n.* charada, *f.*

charcoal, *n.* carbón, *m.*; carbón vegetal; carbón de leña; — **burner,** carbonero, *m.*

charge, *vt.* encargar, comisionar; cobrar; cargar; acusar, imputar; **to** — **to account,** adeudar en cuenta, cargar en cuenta; —, *n.* cargo, cuidado, *m.*; mandato, *m.*; acusación, *f.*; tarifa, *f.*; (mil.) ataque, *m.*; depósito, *m.*; carga, *f.*; — **collect,** porte debido, porte por cobrar; — **prepaid,** porte pagado o cobrado; **extra** —, gasto suplementario; — **account,** cuenta abierta; **in** — **of,** a cargo de.

chargeable, *adj.* que puede atribuirse; imputable.

charger, *n.* caballo de guerra; (elec.) cargador, alimentador, *m.*

chariness, *n.* circunspección, cordura, *f.*; integridad, *f.*

chariot, *n.* faetón, carruaje, *m.*; carro militar.

charioteer, *n.* cochero, *m.*

charitable, *adj.* caritativo, limosnero, benévolo; benigno, clemente; —**bly,** *adv.* caritativamente.

charity, *n.* caridad, benevolencia, *f.*; limosna, *f.*; beneficencia, *f.*; — **society,** sociedad de beneficencia.

charlatan, *n.* charlatán, ana; saltabancos, *m.*

charlatanry, *n.* charlatanería, *f.*

Charles, Carlos.

charlock, *n.* mostaza silvestre.

Charlotte, Carlota.

charm, *n.* encanto, *m.*; atractivo, *m.*; simpatía, *f.*; —, *vt.* encantar, embelesar, atraer; seducir.

charming, *adj.* seductor; simpático; encantador; —**ly,** *adv.* encantadoramente, agradablemente, deleitosamente; seductoramente.

charnel house, *n* carnero, osario, *m.*

chart, *n.* carta de navegar; (aer.) carta, *f.*; hoja de información gráfica, cuadro, *m.*

charter, *n,* carta constitucional; letra patente fletamento, *m.*, privilegio, *m.*; carta, *f.* cédula, *f.*; (com.) contrata de fletamento; **— party,** carta o póliza de fletamento; **—,** *vt.* fletar (un barco, etc.); estatuir; **— member,** miembro o socio fundador.

charterer, *n.* fletador, ra.

chartering, *n.* fletamento, *m.*

charwoman, *n.* jornalera, *f.*, mujer contratada por día para trabajos domésticos.

chary, *adj.* circunspecto; frugal.

chase, *vt.* cazar; perseguir; cincelar; **—,** *n.* caza, *f.*; **to give —,** corretear, perseguir.

chaser, *n.* bebida alcohólica tomada después de café, tabaco, etc.; porción pequeña de agua, cerveza u otra bebida suave que se toma después de algún licor; (aer.) avión de caza.

chasm, *n.* hendidura, *f.*; vacío, *m.*; abismo, *m.*

chassis, *n.* bastidor, armazón, *m.*; (auto.) chasis, *m.*

chaste, *adj.* casto; puro; honesto; púdico.

chasten, *vt.* corregir, castigar.

chastise, *vt.* castigar, reformar, corregir.

chastisement, *n.* castigo, *m.*

chastity, *n.* castidad, pureza, *f.*

chasuble, *n.* casulla, *f.*

chat, *vi.* charlar, platicar; **—,** *n.* plática, charla, conversación, *f*

chattel, *n.* bienes muebles; **—s,** *n.pl.* mobiliario, *m.*

chatter, *vi.* cotorrear; rechinar; charlar; castañetear; **—,** *n.* chirrido, *m.*; charla, *f.*

chatterbox, chatterer, *n.* parlanchín, ina, charlatán, ana.

chattering, *adj.* parlanchín, locuaz; **—,** *n.* charla, *f.*; rechinamiento, *m.*

chatty, *adj.* locuaz, parlanchín.

chauffeur, *n.* chófer, chofer, *m.*

chauvinism, *n.* patriotismo exagerado.

chauvinist, *n.* patriota exagerado; **—ic,** *adj.* de patriotismo exagerado.

cheap, *adj.* barato; **—ly,** *adv.* barato, a poco precio.

cheapen, *vt.* regatear; abaratar; denigrar.

cheapness, *n.* baratura, *f.*

cheat, *vt.* engañar, defraudar; hacer trampa; **—,** *n.* trampa, *f.*; fraude, engaño, *m.*; trampista, trápala, *m.* y *f.*

check, *vt.* reprimir, refrenar; verificar, comprobar; examinar; mitigar; regañar; registrar, facturar; **to —,** tener a raya; **to — (baggage),** facturar (el equipaje); **—,** *n.* restricción, *f.*; freno, *m.*; represión, *f.*; jaque, *m.*; libranza, *f.*; póliza, *f.*; cheque, *m* **— to bearer,** cheque al portador; **cashier's —,** cheque de caja; **traveler's —,** cheque de viajero; **— in,** llegar a un hotel; llegar; **— out,** irse de un hotel, irse; **— off,** eliminar.

checkbook, *n.* libro de cheques.

checker, *vt.* taracear; diversificar; **—,** *n.* verificador, ra.

checkerboard, *n.* tablero de damas.

checkers, *n.* juego de damas.

checking account, *n.* cuenta corriente.

checklist, *n.* lista o catálogo de comprobación.

checkmate, *n.* mate (en ajedrez), *m.*

checkroom, *n.* guardarropía, *f.*

cheek, *n.* cachete, carrillo, *m.*, mejilla, *f.*; (coll.) desvergüenza, *f.*, atrevimiento, *m.*; **— by jowl,** cara a cara.

cheekbone, *n.* hueso del carrillo, pómulo, *m.*

cheer, *n.* viandas, *f. pl.*; alegría, *f.*; aplauso, *m.*; buen humor; vigor, *m.*; **—ing,** *adj.* consolador; **—,** *vt.* animar, alentar; victorear, vitorear; **—,** *vi.* alegrarse, regocijarse; **to — up,** tomar ánimo; **— up!** ¡valor! **—less,** melancólico, triste.

cheerful, *adj.* alegre, vivo, jovial; campechano, genial; **— mien,** buena cara; **—ly,** *adv.* alegremente.

cheerfulness, *n.* alegría, *f.*; buen humor. júbilo, *m.*

cheese, *n.* queso, *m.*; **— dish,** quesera, *f.*; **— rennet,** (bot.) cuajaleche, *f.*; **cottage —,** requesón, *m*

cheesecloth, *n.* estopilla, *f.*, tela de algodón de tejido ralo

cheesemaker, cheeseseller, *n.* quesero, ra.

chem. chemistry, quím. química.

chemical, *adj.* químico; **—,** *n.* substancia química; **— engineering,** ingeniería química.

chemise, *n.* camisa, camisola, *f.*, camisón, *m.*

chemisette, *n.* camiseta, *f.*

chemist, *n.* químico, ca.

chemistry, *n.* química, *f.*

chemurgy, *n.* rama de la química aplicada que tiene que ver con el aprovechamiento industrial de primeras materias orgánicas.

chenille, *n.* felpilla, *f.*

cherish, *vt.* mantener, fomentar, proteger; acariciar; estimar; **to — the hope,** abrigar la esperanza.

cherry, *n.* cereza, *f.*; **— stone,** cuesco de cereza; **—,** *adj.* bermejo.

cherub, *n.* querubín, *m.*

chervil, *n.* (bot.) perifollo, *m.*

chess, *n.* juego de ajedrez; **— player,** ajedrista, *m.* y *f.*

chessboard, *n.* tablero de ajedrez.

chessman, *n.* pieza de ajedrez.

chest, *n.* pecho, *m.*; arca, *f.*; baúl, *m.*; cofre, *m.*; **— of drawers,** cómoda, *f.*

chestnut, *n.* castaña, *f.*; color de castaña; **— tree,** castaño, *m.*; **—,** *adj.* zaino, castaño.

chevron, *n.* cheurón, *m.*

chew, *vt.* and *vi.* mascar, masticar; rumiar; meditar, reflexionar.

chewing gum, n. chicle, m., goma de mascar.

chg. charge, c/ cargo.

chiaroscuro, n. (art) claroscuro, m.

chic, n. chic, m., gracia, elegancia, f.; — adj. elegante, muy de moda.

chicane, n. cavilación, trampa, f.; —, vi. cavilar, sofisticar.

chicanery, n. sofistería, f.; trampa, f., embrollo, m.

chicken, n. polluelo, m.; (fig.) joven, m. y f.; — **pox,** viruelas locas, varicela, f.; **prairie** —, guaco, m., (Mex.) chachalaca, f.; **young** —, pollo, lla.

chicken-hearted, adj. cobarde, tímido; — **person,** (coll.) gallina, m. y f.

chick-pea, n. garbanzo, m.

chickweed, n. (bot.) pamplina, f.

chicle, n. (bot.) chicle, m.

chicory, n. achicoria, chicoria, f.

chide, vt. reprobar, regañar; —, vi. reñir, alborotar.

chief, adj. principal, capital; — **clerk,** oficial mayor; — **part,** cabecera, f.; — **petty officer,** oficial jefe; caudillo, m.; comandante, m.; —**ly,** adv. principalmente, **commander in** —, generalísimo, m., comandante en jefe; — **justice,** presidente de la corte suprema; — **of staff,** jefe de estado mayor.

chieftain, n. jefe, comandante, m.

chiffon, n. chilón, m., gasa, f

chiffonier, n. cómoda, cajonería, f.

chigoe, n. nigua, f.

chilblain, n. sabañón, m.

child, n. infante, m.; hijo, ja; niño, ña; párvulo, m.; **from a** —, desde niño; **with** —, preñada, embarazada.

childbed, n. sobreparto, m.

childhood, n. infancia, niñez, f.

childish, adj. frívolo, pueril; — **action,** niñada, f.; —**ly,** adv. puerilmente.

childless, adj. sin hijos.

childlike, adj. pueril.

children, n.pl. niños, m.pl.; gente menuda; hijos, m.pl.

Chilean, n. and adj. chileno, na.

chili, n. chile, m.; — **sauce,** salsa de chile o de ají.

chill, adj. frío; —, n. frío, m.; (med.) escalofrío, m.; —, vt. enfriar; helar; resfriar.

chilliness, n. escalofrío, m.; tiritona, f.; frialdad, f.

chilly, adj. friolento; frío.

chime, n. armonía, f.; clave, m.; juego de campanas; repique, m.; —, vi. sonar con armonía; concordar; —, vt. repicar.

chimera, n. quimera, f.

chimerical, adj. quimérico; —**ly,** adv. quiméricamente.

chimney, n. chimenea, f.; — **corner,** rincón de chimenea; — **sweep,** limpiador de chimeneas.

chimpanzee, n. chimpancé, m.

chin, n. barba, f., mentón, m.

china, chinaware, n. porcelana, china, loza, f.

chinchilla, n. chinchilla, f.; piel de chinchilla.

chine, n. espinazo, m.; solomo, m.

Chinese n. and adj. chino, na; — **language,** chino, m.; — **lantern,** linterna china.

chink, n. grieta, hendidura, f.; —, vi. henderse; resonar.

chintz, n. zaraza, f.

chip, vt. desmenuzar, picar; —, vi. astillarse; —, n. brizna, astilla, f.; raspaduras de la corteza del pan; — **off the old block,** tal palo tal astilla.

chipmunk, n. especie de ardilla.

chirographer, n. quirógrafo, m.

chirography, n. quirografía, f.

chiropodist, n. pedicuro, m., callista, m. y f.

chiropractor, n. quiropráctico, m.

chirp, vi. chirriar, gorjear; —, n. gorjeo, chirrido, m.

chirping, n. canto de las aves, chirrido, m.

chisel, n. escoplo, cincel, m.; —, vt. escoplear, cincelar, grabar; (coll.) estafar, engañar.

chiseler, n. oportunista, m. y f., estafador, ra.

chit, n. niño, ña; chiquilla, f.; carta breve; comprobante de una deuda pequeña.

chitchat, n. charla, parlería, f.

chitterlings, n. embuchado de tripas.

chivalrous, chivalric, adj. caballeroso.

chivalry, n. caballería, f.; hazaña, f.; caballerosidad, f.

chives, n. cebolleta, f.

chloral, n. (chem.) cloral, m.

chloride, n. cloruro, m.

chlorination, n. tratamiento al cloruro.

chlorine, n. cloro, m.

chloroform, n. cloroformo, m.; **to administer** —, cloroformizar.

chlorophyll, n. clorofila, f.

chlorosis, n. (med.) clorosis, f.

chm. chairman, presidente de una junta o reunión.

chock-full, adj. de bote en bote, completamente lleno.

chocolate, n. chocolate, m.

choice, n. elección, selección, f.; preferencia, f.; opción, f.; —, adj. selecto, exquisito, excelente; escogido; —**ly,** adv. escogidamente, primorosamente.

choir, n. coro, m.

choke, vt. sofocar; oprimir; tapar; —, vi. estrangularse; (auto.) regulador de aire.

choker, n. corbatín, m.; collar apretado, persona que estrangula.

choler, n. cólera, f.; bilis, f.; ira, f.

cholera, n. cólera, m.

choleric, adj. colérico.

choose, vt. escoger, elegir.

chop, vt. tajar, cortar; picar; —, n. chuleta, f., tajada de carne; **lamb** —, chuleta de cordero; **pork** —, chuleta de puerco; **veal** —, chuleta de ternera, **breaded** —s, chuletas empanizadas; — **suey,** olla china; —s, *n. pl.* quijadas, *f. pl.*

chopper, *n.* cuchillo de carnicero.

chopstick, *n.* palillo de madera o marfil con que comen los chinos.

choral, *adj.* coral.

chord, *n.* (mus.) acorde, *m.*; cuerda, *f.*; —, *vt.* encordar.

chore, *n.* quehacer, *m.*; —s, *n. pl.* quehaceres de la casa.

choreography, *n.* coreografía, *f.*

chorister, *n.* corista, *m.* y *f.*

chorus, *n.* coro, *m.*

chose, pretérito del verbo **choose.**

chosen, *p. p.* del verbo **choose.**

chowder, *n.* sancocho de pescado o almejas; sancocho, *m.*

chow mein, *n.* tallarines chinos.

chrestomathy, *n.* crestomatía, *f.*

chrism, *n.* crisma, *m.* y *f.*

Christ, *n.* Jesucristo, Cristo, *m.*

christen, *vt.* cristianar, bautizar.

christendom, *n.* cristianismo, *m.*; cristiandad, *f.*

christening, *n.* bautismo, bautizo, *m.*

Christian, *n.* and *adj.* cristiano, na; —**name,** nombre de pila.

Christianity, *n.* cristianismo, *m.*, cristiandad, *f.*

Christianize, *vt.* cristianizar.

Christmas, *n.* Navidad, Pascua, *f.*; — **box,** aguinaldo, *m.*; — **carol,** villancico de Navidad; — **Eve,** víspera de Navidad, Nochebuena, *f.*; **to wish a Merry —,** dar las Pascuas, desear felices Pascuas; — **tree,** árbol de Navidad; — **Day,** pascua de Navidad.

Christopher, Cristóbal.

chromate, *n.* (chem.) cromato, *m.*

chromatic, *adj.* cromático.

chromatin, *n.* substancia protoplasmática celular.

chrome, *n.* cromo, *m.*

chromium, *n.* cromo, *m.*

chromolithography, *n.* cromolitografía, *f.*

chromosome, *n.* partícula protoplasmática celular.

chromosphere, *n.* cromosfera, *f.*

chronic, *adj.* crónico.

chronicle, *n.* crónica, *f.*, informe, *m.*; —, *vt.* hacer una crónica.

chronicler, *n.* cronista, *m.* y *f.*

chronological, *adj.* cronológico; —**ly,** *adv.* cronológicamente.

chronology, *n.* cronología, *f.*

chronometer, *n.* cronómetro, *m.*, reloj marino.

chrysalis, *n.* crisálida, *f.*

chrysanthemum, *n.* crisantemo, *m.*, santimonia, *f.*

chrysolite, *n.* crisolito, *m.*

chub, *n.* (pez) gobio, *m.*

chubby, *adj.* gordo, cariancho, rechoncho.

chuck, *vi.* cloquear; —, *vt.* hacer la mamola; —, *n.* cloqueo, *m.*; mamola, *f.*

chuckle, *vi.* cloquear; reírse entre dientes.

chum, *n.* camarada, *m.* y *f.*, compañero, ra, amigo íntimo, amiga íntima.

chump, *n.* tajo, tronco, *m.*; (coll.) mastuerzo, *m.*, persona tonta.

chunk, *n.* (coll.) tajo, tronco, *m.*; (fig.) cantidad suficiente; (coll.) persona rechoncha.

church, *n.* iglesia, *f.*; templo, *m.*; — **law,** derecho canónico; — **music,** música sagrada; —, *vt.* llevar a la iglesia (a recibir un sacramento, etc.); ejecutar las ceremonias de la purificación con alguna mujer recién parida.

churchgoer, *n.* persona que asiste fielmente a la iglesia.

churchman, *n.* sacerdote, eclesiástico, *m.*

churchwarden, *n.* mayordomo de la iglesia.

churchyard, *n.* cementerio, *m.*; patio de la iglesia.

churl, *n.* patán, rústico, *m.*

churlish, *adj.* rústico, grosero; tacaño; —**ly,** *adv.* rudamente, brutalmente.

churn, *n.* mantequera, mantequillera, *f.*; —, *vt.* mazar, batir la leche para hacer manteca o mantequilla.

churnstaff, *n.* batidera, *f.*

chute, *n.* vertedor, *m.*

ciborium, *n.* sagrario, *m.*

cicada, *n.* cigarra, *f.*

cicatrice, *n.* cicatriz, *f.*

Cicero, Cicerón.

cider, *n.* sidra, *f.*

C.I.F., c.i.f., cost, insurance and freight, c.s.f. costo, seguro y flete.

cigar, *n.* cigarro, puro, *m.*; — **butt,** colilla, *f.*; — **box,** cigarrera, *f.*; — **case,** petaca para cigarros; — **holder,** boquilla, *f.*; — **store,** — **factory,** estanco, *m.*, tabaquería, *f.*; **Havana —,** habano, *m.*

cigarette, *n.* cigarrillo, cigarro, *m.*; pitillo, *m.*; — **butt,** colilla, *f.*; — **case,** portacigarros, *m.*, pitillera, cigarrera, *f.*; — **holder,** boquilla, *f.*; — **lighter,** encendedor de cigarros; — **paper,** librillo, *m.*

cinch, *n.* cincha, *f.*; (coll.) algo muy fácil.

cinchona, *n.* (bot.) chinchona, *f.*; (Sp. Am.) quinina, *f.*

cincture, *n.* cinto, ceñidor, *m.*; cercado, *m.*; pretinilla, *f.*

cinder, *n.* ceniza gruesa y caliente.

cinema, *n.* cinematógrafo, cine, cinema, *m.*

cinnabar, *n.* cinabrio, *m.*

cinnamate, *n.* (chem.) cinamato, *m.*

cinnamon, *n.* canela, *f.*; — **candy,** canelón, *m.*

C I O, C.I.O. Congress of Industrial Organizations, C.I.O. Congreso de Organizaciones Industriales (de E.U.A.).

cipher, *n.* cifra, *f.*, número, *m.*; cero, *m.*; —, *vi.* numerar, calcular.

circle, *n.* círculo, *m.*; corrillo, *m.*; asamblea, *f.*; rueda, *f.*; —, *vt.* circundar, cercar, ceñir; —, *vi.* circular.

circlet, *n.* círculo pequeño.

circuit, *n.* ámbito, circuito, *m.*; vuelta, *f.*; **— breaker,** (elec.) disyuntor, *m.*; corta-circuitos, *m.*

circuitous, *adj.* circular.

circular, *adj.* circular, redondo; **—,** *n.* carta circular.

circularize, *vt.* hacer circular, anunciar una cosa con circulares.

circulate, *vi.* circular; moverse al rededor.

circulating, *adj.* circulante; **— library,** biblioteca o librería circulante, biblioteca por subscripción; **— pump,** (naut.) bomba de circulación.

circulation, *n.* circulación, *f.*

circulatory, *adj.* circulatorio.

circumcise, *vt.* circuncidar.

circumcision, *n.* circuncisión, *f.*

circumference, *n.* circunferencia, *f.*; circuito, *m.*

circumflex, *n.* acento circunflejo.

circumlocution, *n.* circunlocución, *f.*; requilorios, *m.pl.*; **to use —,** perifrasear.

circumnavigate, *vt.* circunnavegar.

circumnavigation, *n.* circunnavegación, *f.*

circumscribe, *vt.* circunscribir.

circumscription, *n.* circunscripción, *f.*

circumspect, *adj.* circunspecto, prudente, reservado.

circumspection, *n.* circunspección, prudencia, *f.*

circumstance, *n.* circunstancia, condición, *f.*; incidente, *m.*; **—s,** situación económica.

circumstantial, *adj.* accidental; indirecto; circunstancial; accesorio; **— evidence,** evidencia circunstancial; **—ly,** *adv.* circunstanciadamente, exactamente.

circumstantiate, *vt.* detallar, relatar minuciosamente.

circumvent, *vt.* embaucar, engañar.

circumvention, *n.* engaño, *m.*; trampa, *f.*; embrollo, *m.*

circus, *n.* circo, *m.*; arena, *f.*; hipódromo, *m.*

cirrhosis, *n.* (med.) cirrosis, *f.*

cirrus, *n.* cirro, *m.*

cistern, *n.* cisterna, *f.*

citadel, *n.* ciudadela, fortaleza, *f.*

citation, *n.* citación, cita, *f.*

cite, *vt.* citar (a juicio); alegar; citar, referirse a.

cithara, *n.* cítara, *f.*; **— player,** citarista, *m.* y *f.*

citified, *adj.* que tiene las maneras o costumbres de la ciudad.

citizen, *n.* ciudadano, na; **fellow —,** conciudadano, *m.*

citizenry, *n.* masa de ciudadanos.

citizenship, *n.* ciudadanía, *f.*; nacionalidad, *f.*; **— papers,** carta de ciudadanía.

citrate, *n.* (chem.) citrato, *m.*

citric, *adj.* (chem.) cítrico.

citron, *n.* cidra, *f.*

citrus, *adj.* (bot.) auranciáceo.

cittern, cithern, *n.* cítara, *f.*

city, *n.* ciudad, *f.*; **— hall,** ayuntamiento, *m.*; casa del pueblo, palacio municipal;

— of birth, ciudad natal; **— manager,** administrador municipal; **— planning,** planeamiento urbano.

civet, *n.* civeto, *m.*, algalia, *f.*; civeta, *f.*, gato de algalia.

civic, *adj.* cívico; **—s,** *n.* ciencia de gobierno; instrucción cívica.

civil, *adj.* civil, cortés; **— engineer,** ingeniero civil; **— service,** servicio civil; **—ly,** *adv.* civilmente.

civilian, *n.* paisano, na (persona no militar), particular, *m.*; jurisconsulto, *m.*

civility, *n.* civilidad, urbanidad, cortesía, *f.*

civilization, *n.* civilización, *f.*

civilize, *vt.* civilizar.

C.J. Chief Justice, Juez Superior.

c.l. carload, (rail.) vagonada, *f.*, carro entero.

clabber, *n.* cuajo, *m.*; **—,** *vi.* cuajarse; **—,** *vt.* cuajar.

clack, *n.* ruido continuo, golpeo, *m.*; **— valve,** (mech.) chapaleta, *f.*, válvula de charnela; **—,** *vi.* cencerrear.

clad, *adj.* vestido, cubierto.

claim, *vt.* pedir en juicio, reclamar, pretender como cosa debida; **—,** *n.* pretensión, *f.*; derecho, *m.*; reclamo, *m.*; reclamación, *f.*; **to enter a —,** demandar.

claimant, *n.* reclamante, *m.* y *f.*; demandador, ra.

clairvoyance, *n.* clarividencia, *f.*

clam, *n.* almeja, *f.*; **—,** *vi.* pescar almejas.

clambake, *n.* paseo en que se asan almejas.

clamber, *vi.* gatear, trepar.

clamminess, *n.* viscosidad, *f.*

clammy, *adj.* viscoso, tenaz.

clamor, *n.* clamor, grito, *m.*; vocería, *f.*; **prolonged —,** clamoreo, *m.*; **—,** *vi.* vociferar, gritar.

clamorous, *adj.* clamoroso, tumultuoso, estrepitoso; **—ly,** *adv.* clamorosamente.

clamp, *n.* barrilete, *m.*; collar, *m.*; abrazadera, *f.*; manija, *f.*; collera, *f.*; tenazas, pinzas, *f.pl.*; grapa, laña, *f.*; sujetador, *m.*; **—,** *vt.* sujetar, afianzar; empalmar.

clan, *n.* familia, tribu, raza, *f.*

clandestine, *adj.* clandestino, oculto; **—ly,** *adv.* clandestinamente.

clang, *n.* rechino, sonido desapacible; **—,** *vi.* rechinar; sonar.

clangor, *n.* rechinamiento, *m.*; estruendo, *m.*

clangorous, *adj.* ruidoso.

clank, *vi.* rechinar; chillar; **—,** *n.* sonido estridente; retintín, *m.*

clannish, *adj.* estrechamente unido, gregario.

clansman, *n.* miembro de un clan.

clap, *vt.* batir; aplicar; palmear; **—,** *vi.* palmear, palmotear, aplaudir; **to — hands,** batir palmas; **—,** *n.* estrépito, *m.*; golpe, *m.*; trueno, *m.*; palmoteo, *m.*

clapboard, *n.* tejamanil, *m.*; chilla, *f.*

clapper, *n.* palmoteador, ra; badajo de campana; llamador (de una puerta), *m.*

clapping, *n.* palmada, *f.*; aplauso, palmoteo, *m.*

claptrap, *n.* lance de teatro; engañabobos, *m.*

claque, *n.* (theat.) claque, *f.*, aplaudidores de oficio.

claret, *n.* clarete (vino), *m.*

clarification, *n.* clarificación, aclaración, *f.*

clarify, *vt.* clarificar, aclarar; —, *vi.* aclararse.

clarinet, *n.* clarinete, *m.*; **small —,** requinto, *m.*; **— player,** clarinete, *m.*

clarion, *n.* (mus.) clarín, *m.*

clarity, *n.* claridad, *f.*

clash, *vi.* encontrarse; chocar; contradecir; —, *vt.* batir, golpear; —, *n.* rechino, crujido, *m.*; estrépito, *m.*; disputa, *f.*; choque, *m.*; **— of troops,** reencuentro, *m.*

clasp, *n.* broche, *m.*; hebilla, *f.*; sujetador, *m.*; manija, *f.*; abrazo, *m.*; **— knife,** navaja, *f.*; **small —,** trabilla, *f.*; —, *vt.* abrochar; abrazar.

class, *n.* clase, *f.*; género, *m.*; categoría, *f.*; —, *vt.* clasificar.

classic, classical, *adj.* clásico; —, *n.* autor clásico; obra clásica.

classicism, *n.* clasicismo, *m.*

classicist, *n.* clásico, ca, humanista, *m.* y *f.*

classification, *n.* clasificación, *f.*

classify, *vt.* clasificar, graduar.

classmate, *n.* condiscípulo, la.

classroom, *n.* sala de clase.

clatter, *vi.* resonar; hacer ruido; —, *n.* ruido, alboroto, *m.*

clause, *n.* cláusula, *f.*; artículo, *m.*; estipulación, *f.*; condición, *f.*

claustral, *adj.* claustral.

claustrophobia, *n.* claustrofobia, *f.*

clavichord, *n.* clavicordio, clave, *m.*

clavicle, *n.* clavícula, *f.*

clavier, *n.* (mus.) teclado, *m.*

claw, *n.* garra, *f.*; garfa, *f.*; —, *vt.* desgarrar, arañar.

clawed, *adj.* armado de garras.

clay, *n.* barro, *m.*; arcilla, *f.*; **— pit,** barrizal, *m.*, barrera, *f.*, barrero, *m.*

clean, *adj.* limpio; casto; —, *adv.* enteramente; —, *vt.* limpiar.

clean-cut, *adj.* bien portado; claro, bien definido.

cleaner, *n.* limpiador, ra; sacamanchas, quitamanchas, *m.*

cleaning, *n.* limpieza, limpiadura, *f.*; **— rag,** trapo de limpiar; **— rod,** baqueta (para limpiar armas de fuego), *f.*

cleanliness, *n.* limpieza, *f.*; aseo, *m.*

cleanly, *adj.* limpio; puro, delicado; —, *adv.* primorosamente, aseadamente.

cleanness, *n.* limpieza, *f.*; pureza, *f.*

cleanse, *vt.* limpiar, purificar; purgar.

clear, *adj.* claro, lúcido; diáfano; neto; límpido; sereno; evidente; inocente; —, *vt.* clarificar, aclarar; justificar; absolver; **to — accounts,** liquidar cuentas; **to — away (trees, dirt, etc.),** desmontar; **to — the table,** quitar la mesa; **to — up,**

aclararse; —, *vi.* aclararse; **—ly,** *adv.* claramente; enteramente; evidentemente.

clearance, *n.* despejo, *m.*; (com.) despacho de aduana; utilidad líquida; (aer.) espacio, *m.*; (mech.) juego limpio (de una pieza, etc.); **— sale,** liquidación, *f.*

clear-cut, *adj.* claro, bien definido.

clear-headed, *adj.* listo, inteligente.

clearing, *n.* espacio libre; aclaración, *f.*; **— house,** casa de compensación; **— in a forest,** espacio desarbolado.

clearness, *n.* claridad, transparencia, *f.*; esplendor, *m.*

clear-sighted, *adj.* perspicaz, juicioso; clarividente.

clearstarch, *vt.* almidonar con almidón claro.

cleat, *n.* listón de refuerzo; abrazadera, manija, *f.*; (naut.) cornamusa, *f.*

cleavage, *n.* hendimiento, *m.*

cleave, *vt.* and *vi.* hender; partir; dividir; pegarse.

cleaver, *n.* cuchilla de carnicero.

cleek, *n.* maza o mazo para jugar al golf.

clef, *n.* (mus.) clave, *f.*

cleft, *n.* hendedura, abertura, *f.*

clematis, *n.* (bot.) clemátide, *f.*

clemency, *n.* clemencia, *f.*

clement, *adj.* clemente, benigno.

clench, *vt.* cerrar, agarrar, asegurar.

clergy, *n.* clero, *m.*

clergyman, *n.* eclesiástico, *m.*

cleric, *n.* clérigo, *m.*

clerical, *adj.* clerical, eclesiástico; **— work,** trabajo de oficina.

clericalism, *n.* clericalismo, *m.*

clerk, *n.* eclesiástico, clérigo, *m.*; estudiante, *m.*; amanuense, escribiente, *m.*; dependiente, *m.* **chief —,** oficial mayor; **— of a parish,** sacristán, *m.*

clerkship, *n.* empleo de escribiente; secretaría, *f.*

clever, *adj.* diestro, hábil; mañoso; inteligente; **—ly,** *adv.* diestramente, hábilmente; inteligentemente.

cleverness, *n.* destreza, habilidad, *f.*; inteligencia, *f.*; tienta, *f.*

clevis, *n.* abrazadera, *f.*

clew, *n.* ovillo de hilo; pista, *f.*, indicio, *m.*; —, *vt.* (naut.) cargar las velas.

cliché, *n.* clisé, cliché, *m.*

click, *vi.* retiñir.

client, *n.* cliente, *m.* y *f.*

clientele, *n.* clientela, *f.*; (Sp. Am.) casería, *f.*

cliff, *n.* peñasco, risco, *m.*; precipicio, *m.*, barranca, *f.*

climate, *n.* clima, *m.*; temperatura, *f.*

climatic, *adj.* climático.

climax, *n.* colmo, *m.*, culminación, *f.*; clímax, *m.*, gradación, *f.*

climb, *vt.* escalar, trepar; —, *vi.* subir.

clinch, *vt.* empuñar, cerrar el puño; remachar un clavo; —, *vi.* agarrarse; —, *n.* lucha cuerpo a cuerpo.

clincher, *n.* barrilete, remachador, *m.*

cling, *vi.* colgar, adherirse, pegarse.

clinic, *adj.* clínico; —, *n.* clínica, *f.*; consultorio, *m.*; clínica médica.

clinical, *adj.* clínico.

clink, *vt.* hacer resonar; —, *vi.* retiñir, resonar; —, *n.* retintín, *m.*

clinker, *n.* cagafierro, *m.*; ladrillo refractario.

clip, *vt.* abrazar; cortar a raíz; escatimar; —, *n.* tijeretada, *f.*; grapa, *f.*, gancho, *m.*

clipper, *n.* tallador de monedas; (naut.) navío velero; (aer.) clíper, *m.*; trasquilador, *m.*; hidroavión, *m.*; —s, *n. pl.* tijeras podadoras.

clipping, *n.* recorte, *m.*; —s, *n. pl.* tundizno, desbroce, *m.*

clique, *n.* camarilla, pandilla, *f.*

cliquish, *adj.* exclusivista.

clk. clerk, oficial de secretaría; dependiente.

cloak, *n.* capa, *f.*; capote, *m.*; pretexto, *m.*; **short** —, capotillo, *m.*; —, *vt.* encapotar, paliar, encubrir.

cloakroom, *n.* guardarropía, *f.*, vestuario, *m.*

clock, *n.* reloj, *m.*; — **dial,** esfera de reloj; **alarm** —, despertador, *m.*

clockmaker, *n.* relojero, *m.*

clockwork, *n.* mecanismo de un reloj; **like** —, sumamente exacto y puntual.

clod, *n.* terrón, *m.*; tierra, *f.*, suelo, *m.*; césped, *m.*; zoquete, *m.*; hombre estúpido.

clog, *n.* obstáculo, *m.*; galocha, *f.*; —, *vt.* cargar, embarazar; —, *vi.* coagularse; unirse.

cloister, *n.* claustro, monasterio, *m.*

close, *vt.* cerrar, tapar; concluir, terminar; —, *vi.* cerrarse, unirse, convenirse; **to** — **(an account),** finiquitar (una cuenta); **to** — **a transaction,** cerrar una operación; —, *n.* cercado, *m.*; fin, *m.*; conclusión, *f.*; cierre, *m.*; —, *adj.* cerrado; preso; estrecho, angosto; ajustado; secreto; avaro; retirado; obscuro; denso; reservado; — **fight,** combate reñido; — **quarters,** lugar estrecho, espacio limitado; —, *adv.* de cerca; junto; estrechamente; secretamente; — **by,** muy cerca.

closed, *adj.* cerrado; — **shop,** contrato colectivo.

close-fitting, *adj.* entallado, ajustado, estrecho; ceñido al cuerpo.

close-mouthed, *adj.* callado, discreto, reservado.

closeness, *n.* estrechez, espesura, reclusión, *f.*

closet, *n.* retrete, *m.*; gabinete, *m.*; ropero, *m.*; —, *vt.* encerrar en un gabinete o en un ropero.

close-up, *n.* fotografía de cerca.

closing, *n.* cierre, *m.*; conclusión, *f.*; clausura, *f.*; — **the books,** cierre de los libros.

closure, *n.* cerradura, *f.*; conclusión, *f.*

clot, *n.* grumo, *m.*, coagulación, *f.*; —, *vi.* cuajarse, coagularse.

cloth, *n.* paño, *m.*; mantel, *m.*; lienzo, *m.*; material, *m.*; **checked** —, paño a cuadros; — **binding,** encuadernación en tela; **striped** —, paño rayado o listado.

clothe, *vt.* vestir, cubrir.

clothes, *n. pl.* vestidura, *f.*; ropaje, *m.*; — **closet,** ropero, *m.*; — **hanger,** colgador de ropas, percha, *f.*; — **peg,** percha, *f.*; **suit of** —, vestido completo; **bed** —, ropa de cama.

clothesbasket, *n.* cesta para ropa.

clothesbrush, *n.* cepillo para ropa.

clotheshorse, *n.* enjugador, *m.*

clothesline, *n.* cuerda para tender la ropa, tendedero, *m.*

clothespin, *n.* gancho de tendedero; pinza para tender la ropa.

clothespress, *n.* guardarropa, *m.*

clothier, *n.* pañero, *m.*; persona que vende ropa.

clothing, *n.* vestidos, *m. pl.*; ropa, *f.*; **article of** —, prenda de vestir.

cloth-shearing machine, *n.* tundidora, *f.*

cloud, *n.* nube, *f.*; nublado, *m.*; (fig.) adversidad, *f.*; —, *vt.* anublar; obscurecer; —, *vi.* anublarse, nublarse; obscurecerse.

cloudburst, *n.* chaparrón, *m.*, tormenta de lluvia.

cloudiness, *n.* nebulosidad, *f.*; oscuridad, *f.*

cloudy, *adj.* nublado, nubloso; oscuro; sombrío, melancólico; pardo.

clout, *n.* persona estúpida; (coll.) golpe con la mano; —, *vt.* remendar; chapucear.

clove, *n.* (bot.) clavo, *m.*

cloven, *adj.* partido, hendido.

clover, *n.* trébol, *m.*; **to live in** —, vivir lujosamente.

clown, *n.* patán, rústico, *m.*; payaso, sa; gracioso, sa, chulo, la; truhán, ana; **stage** —, bobo, *m.*

clownish, *adj.* rústico; grosero; —**ly,** *adv.* toscamente, groseramente.

cloy, *vt.* empalagar; saciar, hartar.

club, *n.* clava, cachiporra, *f.*; círculo, club, *m.*; garrote, *m.*; —, *vi.* unirse, formar un club; —, *vt.* golpear con un garrote; congregar; contribuir.

clubhouse, *n.* casino, club, *m.*

cluck, clucking, *n.* cloqueo, *m.*

cluck, *vi.* cacarear.

clue, *n.* ovillo de hilo; seña, *f.*; idea, *f.*, vestigio, indicio, *m.*

clump, *n.* trozo sin forma; bosquecillo, *m.*

clumsiness, *n.* zafiedad, rusticidad, *f.*; grosería, *f.*

clumsy, *adj.* tosco, pesado; sin arte; desmañado; — **performance,** chapucería, *f.*

clung, pretérito y *p. p.* del verbo **cling.**

cluster, *n.* racimo, *m.*; manada, *f.*; pelotón, *m.*; —, *vt.* agrupar; —, *vi.* arracimarse; agruparse.

clutch, *n.* (auto.) embrague, *m.*, garra, *f.*; acoplamiento, *m.*; — **lever,** palanca, *f.*; — **pedal,** palanca del embrague; **to step on the** —, **to release the** —, pisar, empujar o soltar el embrague; **to throw in the** —, embragar; **to throw out the** —, desembragar; —, *vt.* embragar, empuñar, agarrar.

clutter, *vt.* poner en desorden; **—**, *vi.* atroparse; **to — up**, poner en desorden; **—**, *n.* confusión, bulla.
clyster, *n.* (med.) clister, *m.*
cm. centimeter, cm. centímetro.
cml. commercial, com. comercial.
Co., co.: company, Cía. Comp. Compañía; **county**, condado.
C.O. Commanding Officer, Comandante en jefe.
c/o, c.o.: carried over, sigue; **in care of**, C/o. a cargo de.
coach, *n.* coche, *m.*; carroza, *f.*; vagón, *m.*; entrenador (en un deporte), *m.*; **through —**, coche directo; **—**, *vt.* entrenar, preparar; llevar en coche.
coachman, *n.* cochero, *m.*
coadjutor, *n.* coadyutor, ayudante, *m.*
coagulate, *vt.* coagular, cuajar; **—**, *vi.* coagularse, cuajarse, espesarse.
coagulation, *n.* coagulación, *f.*
coal, *n.* carbón, *m.*; **bituminous —**, carbón bituminoso; **— dealer, — miner**, carbonero, *m.*; **— heaver**, cargador de carbón; **— mine, — pit**, mina de carbón, carbonería, *f.*; **— oil**, petróleo, *m.*; **— tar**, alquitrán de hulla, brea, *f.*; **anthracite** or **hard —**, antracita; **screened —**, carbón cribado; **soft —**, hulla, *f.*; **—**, *adj.* carbonero.
coalesce, *vi.* juntarse, incorporarse.
coalescence, *n.* coalición, *f.*
coaling station, *n.* (naut.) carbonera, *f.*
coalition, *n.* coalición, confederación, *f.*
coarse, *adj.* basto; ordinario; rústico, grosero; bruto; **— language**, lenguaje grosero; **—ly**, *adv.* groseramente.
coarse-grained, *adj.* de granulación gruesa.
coarsen, *vt.* hacer basto, burdo o vulgar; **—**, *vi.* hacerse basto.
coarseness, *n.* tosquedad, grosería, *f.*
coast, *n.* costa, *f.*; litoral, *m.*; **—**, *adj.* litoral; **— guard**, guardacostas, *m.*; **— line**, litoral, *m.*, costa, *f.*, línea costanera; **— pilot**, piloto, práctico, *m.*; **—**, *vi.* costear; dejar muerto el motor.
coastal, *adj.* costero, costanero.
coast-defense ship, *n.* guardacostas, *m.*
coaster, *n.* piloto, *m.*; buque costanero; **— brake**, freno de bicicleta.
coasting, *n.* cabotaje, *m.*; acción de rodar cuesta abajo.
coastwise, *adj.* costanero, a lo largo de la costa.
coat, *n.* casaca, *f.*, frac, *m.*; gabán, *m.*; hábito, *m.*; chaqueta, *f.*; americana, *f.*; capote, *m.*; **— of arms, — of mail**, cota de malla; escudo de armas; **— of paint**, mano de pintura; **frock —**, casaca, *f.*, levitón, *m.*; **lightweight —**, gabán de entretiempo; **loose —**, sayo, *m.*; **man's —**, saco, *m.*; **—**, *vt.* cubrir, vestir; **to — with**, revestir.
coati, *n.* coatí, *m.*
coating, *n.* revestimiento, *m.*; capa, *f.*;

mano (de pintura, etc.), *f.*
coatroom, *n.* guardarropa, *m.*
coauthor, *n.* coautor, *m.*
coax, *vt.* instar, rogar con lisonja.
cob, *n.* gaviota, *f.*; mazorca de maíz; jaca, *f.*
cobalt, *n.* cobalto, *m.*
cobble, *vt.* chafallar; remendar (zapatos).
cobbler, *n.* chapucero, remendón, *m.*
cobblestone, *n.* guijarro, *m.*
cobra, *n.* (zool.) cobra, *f.*
cobweb, *n.* telaraña, *f.*; (fig.) trama, *f.*
coca, *n.* (bot.) coca, *f.*; **— leaves, — tea**, coca, *f.*
cocaine, *n.* cocaína, *f.*
cochineal, *n.* cochinilla, *f.*
cock, *n.* gallo, *m.*; macho, *m.*; veleta, giraldilla, *f.*; grifo, *m.*, llave, *f.*; montoncillo de heno; aguja de romana; **at half —**, desamartillada (escopeta); **at full —**, amartillada, montada (escopeta); **—**, *vt.* armar el sombrero; amartillar, montar (una escopeta); amontonar heno; **to — the head**, erguir la cabeza.
cockade, *n.* cucarda, *f.*
cock-a-doodle-doo, *n.* canto del gallo.
cockatrice, *n.* basilisco, *m.*
cockchafer, *n.* saltón, *m.*
cockcrow, *n.* canto del gallo.
cocker, *vt.* acariciar, mimar; **—**, *n.* sabueso, *m.*
cockerel, *n.* gallo joven.
cockfight, cockfighting, *n.* pelea de gallos.
cockle, *n.* caracol de mar; (bot.) cizaña, *f.*; **—**, *vt.* arrugar; doblar; **—**, *vi.* plegarse, doblarse.
cockloft, *n.* desván, zaquizamí, *m.*
cockpit, *n.* reñidero de gallos; (naut.) entarimado del sollado; cámara, *f.*; (aer.) casilla o cámara de piloto; cabina, *f.*; (naut.) casilla, *f.*
cockroach, *n.* cucaracha, *f.*
cockscomb, *n.* cresta de gallo; (fig.) currutaco, *m.*
cocksure, *adj.* confiado, seguro, cierto.
cockswain, coxwain, *n.* patrón de bote.
cocktail, *n.* cocktail, coctel, *m.*
coco, cocoa, *n.* coco, *m.*
cocoa, *n.* cacao, *m.*; chocolate, *m.*
coconut, *n.* coco, *m.*; **— tree**, coco, *m.*; **— milk**, agua de coco.
cocoon, *n.* capullo del gusano de seda.
cod, *n.* bacalao, *m.*; merluza, *f.*; (bot.) vaina, *f.*
C.O.D., c.o.d. cash on delivery, collect on delivery, C.A.E. cóbrese al entregar.
coddle, *vt.* sancochar (huevos, etc.); acariciar; consentir, mimar.
code, *n.* código, *m.*; clave, *f.*
codein, *n.* codeína, *f.*
codex, *n.* códice, *m.*
codfish, *n.* bacalao, *m.*
codicil, *n.* (law) codicilo, *m.*
codification, *n.* codificación, *f.*
codify, *vt.* hacer un código, codificar.
cod-liver oil, *n.* aceite de hígado de bacalao.

coeducational, *adj.* coeducativo.
coefficient, *n.* coeficiente, *m.*
cocqual, *adj.* igual (en rango, edad, etc.).
cocrce, *vt.* obligar, forzar.
coercion, *n.* coerción, *f.*
coercive, *adj.* coercitivo.
coeval, *adj.* coevo; —, *n.* contemporáneo, nea.
coexist, *vi.* coexistir.
coexistence, *n.* coexistencia, *f.*
coffee, *n.* café, *m.*; — **plantation,** cafetal, *m.*; — **planter,** — **seller,** cafetero, *m.*; — **store,** cafetería, *f.*; — **table,** mesita para el servicio de café en las salas; — **tree,** cafeto, café, *m.*; — **bean,** grano de café.
coffeepot, *n.* cafetera, *f.*
coffer, *n.* cofre, *m.*, caja, *f.*
coffin, *n.* féretro, ataúd, *m.*; caja, *f.*; —, *vt.* meter en un ataúd.
cog, *n.* diente (de rueda), *m.*; —, *vt.* adular, lisonjear; **to** — **a die,** cargar un dado (con plomo).
cogency, *n.* fuerza, urgencia, *f.*
cogent, *adj.* convincente, urgente; —**ly,** *adv.* de un modo convincente.
cogitate, *vi.* pensar, meditar.
cogitation, *n.* meditación, *f.*
cognac, *n.* coñac, *m.*
cognate, *adj.* consanguíneo; aliado; similar; —, *n.* cognado, da.
cognition, *n.* conocimiento, *m.*; convicción, *f.*
cognizance, *n.* conocimiento, *m.*; divisa, *f.*; competencia, jurisdicción, *f.*
cognizant, *adj.* informado, sabedor; (law) competente.
cogwheel, *n.* rueda dentada, rodezno, *m.*
cohabit, *vi.* cohabitar.
cohabitation, *n.* cohabitación, *f.*
coheir, *n.* coheredero, *m.*
coheiress, *n.* coheredera, *f.*
cohere, *vi.* pegarse; unirse; convenir, conformarse.
coherence, *n.* coherencia, conexión, *f.*
coherent, *adj.* coherente, consistente, lógico.
cohesion, *n.* coherencia, cohesión, *f.*
cohesive, *adj.* cohesivo.
cohort, *n.* cohorte, *f.*
coif, *n.* cofia, redecilla, *f.*
coiffure, *n.* peinado, tocado, *m.*
coil, *vt.* recoger; enrollar; **to** — **a cable,** (naut.) adujar un cable; —, *n.* (elec.) carrete, *m.*; bobina, *f.*; (naut.) adujada, *f.*; espiral, *f.*; rollo, *m.*
coiling, *n.* arrollamiento, *m.*
coin, *n.* cuña, *f.*; moneda acuñada; dinero, *m.*; — **collection,** colección de monedas; —, *vt.* acuñar moneda; falsificar; inventar.
coinage, *n.* acuñación, *f.*, braceaje, *m.*; falsificación, *f.*; invención, *f.*; moneda, *f.*
coincide, *vi.* coincidir, concurrir, convenir.
coincidence, *n.* coincidencia, *f.*; casualidad, *f.*
coincident, *adj.* coincidente.

coiner, *n.* acuñador de moneda; monedero falso; inventor, *m.*
coinsurance, *n.* seguro sobre propiedad por menos de su valor.
coitus, *n.* concúbito, ayuntamiento, *m.*
coke, *n.* cok, coque, *m.*; —, *vt.* convertir en coque.
Col. Colonel, Cnel. Coronel.
col.: colony, col. colonia; **colored,** negro, col. **column,** col. columna.
colander, *n.* coladera, *f.*; colador, pasador, *m.*
cold, *adj.* frío; indiferente, insensible; reservado; yerto; — **cream,** crema para la cara; — **storage,** cámara frigorífica; enfriador, refrigerador, *m.*; **in** — **blood,** en sangre fría; **to be** —, hacer frío; tener frío; —**ly,** *adv.* fríamente; indiferentemente; —, *n.* frío, *m.*; frialdad, *f.*; (med.) resfriado, *m.*; **subject to** —**s,** catarroso; **to take** —, resfriarse.
cold-blooded, *adj.* impasible; cruel; en sangre fría.
coldness, *n.* frialdad, *f.*; indiferencia, insensibilidad, apatía, *f.*
coleslaw, *n.* ensalada de col cruda y picada.
colewort, *n.* berza verde, especie de col.
colic, *n.* cólico, *m.*
coliseum, *n.* coliseo, anfiteatro, *m.*
colitis, *n.* (med.) colitis, *f.*
coll.: collection, colección; **collector,** colector o cobrador; **college,** colegio; **colloquial,** fam. familiar.
collaborate, *vt.* cooperar; colaborar.
collaboration, *n.* colaboración, *f.*; cooperación, *f.*
collapse, *vi.* desplomarse; —, *n.* hundimiento, *m.*; (med.) colapso, *m.*; derrumbe, desplome, *m.*
collapsible, *adj.* plegadizo, que se puede desarmar.
collar, *n.* collar, *m.*; collera, *f.*; —, *vt.* agarrar a uno por el cuello, apercollar.
collarbone, *n.* clavícula, *f.*
collate, *vt.* comparar, confrontar.
collateral, *adj.* colateral; indirecto; —**ly,** *adv.* colateralmente; indirectamente.
collation, *n.* colación, *f.*; colección, *f.*; cotejo, *m.*
collator, *n.* cotejador, ra, confrontador, ra.
colleague, *n.* colega, *m.* y *f.*, compañero, ra.
collect, *vt.* recoger, colegir; cobrar; **to** — (taxes, etc.) recaudar (impuestos, etc.).
collection, *n.* colección, *f.*; compilación, *f.*; cobro, *m.*; **rent** —, **tax** —, recaudo, *m.*
collective, *adj.* colectivo, congregado; — **bargaining,** trato colectivo; —**ly,** *adv.* colectivamente.
collectivism, *n.* colectivismo, *m.*
collectivity, *n.* colectividad, *f.*
collector, *n.* colector, *m.*; agente de cobros; — **of customs,** administrador de aduana.
college, *n.* colegio, *m.*; escuela superior, universidad, *f.*
collegian, *n.* miembro de un colegio.
collegiate, *adj.* colegiado, colegial.

collide, *vi.* chocar, estrellarse.
collie, *n.* perro de pastor, perro de ganado.
collier, *n.* carbonero, *m.*; barco carbonero.
colliery, *n.* carbonera, *f.*
collision, *n.* colisión, *f.*, choque, *m.*; reencuentro, *m.*
colloid, *n.* (chem.) coloide, *m.*
collop, *n.* tajada pequeña de carne.
colloquial, *adj.* dialogal; íntimo; familiar; **—ly,** *adv.* familiarmente.
colloquialism, *n.* expresión familiar.
colloquy, *n.* coloquio, *m.*; conversación, plática, *f.*
collotype, *n.* fototipia, *f.*
collusion, *n.* colusión, *f.*
collusive, *adj.* colusorio; **—ly,** *adv.* colusoriamente.
Cologne, Colonia, *f.*
colon, *n.* colon (parte del intestino grueso), *m.*; dos puntos (signo de puntuación).
colonel, *n.* (mil.) coronel, *m.*
colonelcy, *n.* coronelía, *f.*
colonial, *adj.* colonial.
colonist, *n.* colono, *m.*; colonizador, ra.
colonization, *n.* colonización, *f.*
colonize, *vt.* colonizar.
colonnade, *n.* columnata, *f.*
colony, *n.* colonia, *f.*
colophony, *n.* colofonia, *f.*
color, *n.* color, *m.*; pretexto, *m.*; **— blindness,** daltonismo, *m.*; **—s,** *n. pl.* bandera, *f.*; tafetanes, *m. pl*; **—,** *vt.* colorar; paliar; **—,** *vi.* enrojecerse, ponerse colorado.
coloration, *n.* coloración, *f.*
color-blind, *adj.* daltoniano.
colored, *adj.* colorado, pintado, teñido; de raza negra; con prejuicio.
coloring, *n.* colorido, *m.*; colorante, *m.*; **—,** *adj.* colorativo.
colorist, *n.* colorista, *m. y f.*
colorless, *adj.* descolorido, sin color.
colossal, *adj.* colosal.
colossus, *n.* coloso, *m.*
colt, *n.* potro, *m.*; mozuelo sin juicio.
colter, *n.* reja de arado.
columbine, *n.* (bot.) aguileña, *f.*; **—,** *adj.* columbino, semejante a una paloma.
Columbine, Colombina.
Columbus, Colón.
column, *n.* columna, *f.*
columnar, *adj.* relativo a una columna.
columned, *adj.* con columnas.
columnist, *n.* diarista, *m. y f.*, periodista encargado de una sección especial.
Com.: Commander, jefe; **Commission,** Com. comisión; **Committee,** Com. comité, comisión; **Commodore,** Com. comodoro.
com.: commerce, com. comercio; **commercial,** com. comercial; **common,** común.
coma, *n.* (med.) coma, letargo, *m.*
comatose, *adj.* (med.) comatoso.
comb, *n.* peine, *m.*; almohaza, *f.*; **—,** *vt.* peinar; almohazar; cardar (la lana); **to**

— one's hair, peinarse.
combat, *n.* combate, *m.*; batalla, *f.*; **single —,** duelo, *m.*; **—,** *vt.* and *vi.* combatir; resistir.
combatant, *n.* combatiente, *m. y f.*, batallador, ra.
combative, *adj.* quisquilloso; belicoso.
comber, *n.* cardador, ra.
combination, *n.* combinación, coordinación, *f.*
combine, *vt.* combinar; concretar; **—,** *vi.* unirse; **—,** *n.* (agr.) segadora, trilladora, *f.*; (coll.) combinación de personas u organizaciones para provecho comercial o político.
combustible, *adj.* combustible; **—,** *n.* combustible, *m.*
combustion, *n.* combustión, *f.*; incendio, *m.*; agitación violenta.
Comdr. Commander, jefe.
Comdt. Commandant, Com. comandante.
come, *vi.* venir, acontecer; originar; **to — back,** volver; **to — forward,** avanzar; **to — to pass,** suceder; **to — unexpectedly,** sobrevenir; **to — upon,** encontrarse con; **to — to,** volver en sí; **—!** *interj.* ¡ánimo! **— now!** ¡quia! **to — to pass,** realizarse.
comeback, *n.* vuelta, *f.*; recobro, *m.*; réplica mordaz.
comedian, *n.* comediante, *m. y f.*, cómico, ca.
comedown, *n.* cambio desfavorable de circunstancias; descenso en posición social.
comedy, *n.* comedia, *f.*; sainete, *m.*
comeliness, *n.* gracia, *f.*; garbo, *m.*
comely, *adj.* garboso, gracioso.
comestible, *adj.* comestible; **—s,** *n. pl.* comestibles, *m. pl.*
comet, *n.* cometa, *m.*
comfit, *n.* confite, *m.*
comfort, *n.* confortación, *f.*; ayuda, *f.*; consuelo, *m.*; comodidad, *f.*; bienestar, *m.*; **—,** *vt.* confortar; alentar, consolar.
comfortable, *adj.* cómodo; consolatorio; **—ly,** *adv.* agradablemente, cómodamente.
comforter, *n.* consolador, ra; colcha, *f.*
comforting, *adj.* confortante, confortativo, consolador.
comic, *adj.* cómico, burlesco; chistoso; **— opera,** ópera bufa; **—s,** *n. pl.* historietas cómicas.
comically, *adv.* cómicamente.
coming, *n.* venida, llegada, *f.*; **—,** *adj.* venidero, entrante; **— from,** procedente de.
comity, *n.* cortesía, urbanidad, *f.*
comma, *n.* (gram.) coma, *f.*
command, *vt.* ordenar; mandar; **—,** *vi.* gobernar; imperar; mandar; **—,** *n.* orden, *f.*, comando, *m.*; señorío, *m.*; **by your —,** por su mandato.
commandant, *n.* comandante, *m.*; **—'s office,** comandancia, *f.*
commandeer, *vt.* (mil.) decomisar, confiscar; obligar el reclutamiento.

commander, n. jefe, m., comandante, m.; capitán, m.; capitán de fragata; — **in chief,** capitán general, generalísimo, m.; **lieutenant —,** capitán de corbeta.

commandment, n. mandato, precepto, m.; mandamiento, m.

commando, n. comando, m., incursión o expedición militar.

commemorate, vt. conmemorar; celebrar.

commemoration, n. conmemoración, f.

commemorative, adj. conmemorativo.

commence, vt. and vi. comenzar.

commencement, n. principio, m.; ejercicios de graduación.

commend, vt. encomendar, encargar; alabar.

commendable, adj. recomendable; digno de encomio.

commendation, n. recomendación, f.; encomio, m.

commendatory, adj. recomendatorio.

commensurable, adj. conmensurable.

commensurate, vt. conmensurar; —, adj. conmensurativo, proporcionado.

comment, n. comento, m., glosa, f.; comentario, m.; —, vt. comentar, glosar.

commentary, n. comentario, m.; interpretación, f.; glosa, f.

commentator, n. comentador, ra.

commerce, n. comercio, tráfico, trato, negocio, m.; **chamber of —,** cámara de comercio.

commercial, adj. comercial; — **flying,** navegación aérea comercial; — **house,** casa de comercio.

commercialize, vt. comerciar, explotar un negocio, poner un producto en el mercado.

comminatory, adj. conminatorio.

commingle, vt. mezclar; —, vi. mezclarse.

commisar, n. comisario, m.

commiserate, vt. compadecer, tener compasión; —, vi. compadecerse.

commiseration, n. conmiseración, piedad, f.

commissariat, n. comisaría, f.; comisariato, m.

commissary, n. comisario, m.; comisariato, m.

commission, n. comisión, f.; patente, f.; corretaje, m.; — **agent,** agente comisionista; — **house,** casa de comisión; **in —,** en servicio activo; **out of —,** inutilizado, gastado; — **merchant,** comisionista, m.; —, vt. comisionar; encargar; apoderar.

commissioned officer, n. (mil.) oficial nombrado por el presidente.

commissioner, n. comisionado, delegado, m.

commit, vt. cometer; depositar; encargar; **to — to memory,** aprender de memoria.

commitment, n. compromiso, m.; comisión, f. (law); auto de prisión.

committee, n. comité, m., comisión, junta, f.

commodious, adj. cómodo, conveniente; —ly, adv. cómodamente.

commodity, n. utilidad, f.; provecho, m.; comodidad, f.; mercaderías, f. pl.

commodore, n. (naut.) jefe de escuadra, comodoro, m.

common, adj. común, público, general; ordinario; — **carrier,** empresa de transporte; portador, m.; — **council,** concejo municipal; — **law,** ley a fuerza de costumbre; — **law marriage,** matrimonio por contrato consensual; — **people,** comunal, m.; — **pleas,** (law) causas ajenas; — **sense,** sentido prático; — **stock,** acciones en común u ordinarias; —, n. lo usual; **in —,** en común; —**ly,** adv. comúnmente, frecuentemente.

commoner, n. plebeyo, ya; miembro de la cámara baja (en Inglaterra).

commonplace, n. lugares comunes; —, adj. trivial, banal.

commons, n. pl. pueblo bajo; cámara baja (en Inglaterra).

commonwealth, n. república, f.; estado, m.; nación, f.

commotion, n. tumulto, m.; perturbación del ánimo.

communal, adj. comunal.

commune, vi. conversar; tener confidencias; comulgar; —, n. comuna, f., menor división política de Francia, Italia, etc.; distrito municipal.

communicable, adj. comunicable.

communicant, n. comunicante, m. y f.; comulgante, m. y f.

communicate, vt. comunicar, participar; —, vi. comunicarse.

communication, n. comunicación, f.; participación, f.; escrito, m.

communicative, adj. comunicativo.

communion, n. comunidad, f.; comunión, f.; **to take —,** comulgar.

communique, n. comunicación oficial.

communism, n. comunismo, m.

communist, n. comunista, m. y f.

community, n. comunidad, f.; república, f.; común, m.; colectividad, f.; —, adj. comunal; — **chest,** caja de la comunidad, fondos benéficos de la comunidad; — **center,** lugar que sirve de centro para actividades filantrópicas y educativas.

commutation, n. mudanza, f.; conmutación, f.; — **(of a vow),** relajación, f.: — **ticket,** billete o boleto de abono.

commutator, n. (elec.) conmutador, colector, m.

commute, vt. conmutar; —, vi. viajar diariamente de una ciudad a otra.

commuter, n. persona que viaja diariamente de una localidad a otra.

comp.: comparative, comp. comparativo; **composer,** comp. compositor; **composition,** comp. composición; **compound,** comp. compuesto.

compact, adj. compacto, sólido, denso; —, n. pacto, convenio, m.; neceser, m.; polvera, f.; —**ly,** adv. estrechamente; en pocas palabras.

companion, n. compañero, ra; acompa-

ñante, *m.* y *f.*; (coll.) compinche, *m.* y *f.*
companionable, *adj.* sociable.
companionate, *adj.* en calidad de compañeros, compartido entre compañeros.
companionship, *n.* camaradería, *f.*, compañerismo, *m.*; sociedad, compañía, *f.*
company, *n.* compañía, sociedad, *f.*; compañía comercial; **to keep —,** hacer compañía a; tener relaciones con; **to part —** **(with),** separarse; **— union,** unión de los obreros de una empresa sin otras conexiones.
comparable, *adj.* comparable.
comparative, *adj.* comparativo; **— degree,** (gram.) comparativo, *m.*; **—ly,** *adv.* comparativamente.
compare, *vt.* comparar, colacionar; confrontar; **—,** *n.* comparación, *f.*; **beyond —,** sin igual, sin comparación.
comparison, *n.* comparación, *f.*; símil, *m.*; **in — with,** comparado con; **beyond —,** sin comparación, sin igual.
compartment, *n.* compartimiento, compartimiento, *m.*
compass, *n.* alcance, *m.*; circunferencia, *f.*; compás de la voz; compás, *m.*; **— card,** (naut.) rosa náutica, *f.*; **marine —,** aguja de marear; **—,** *vt.* circundar; lograr; tramar.
compasses, *n. pl.* compás, *m.*
compassion, *n.* compasión, piedad, *f.*
compassionate, *vt.* compadecer (a alguno); **—,** *adj.* compasivo.
compatibility, *n.* compatibilidad, *f.*
compatible, *adj.* compatible.
compatriot, *n.* compatriota, *m.* y *f.*
compeer, *n.* compañero, colega, *m.*
compel, *vt.* compeler, obligar, constreñir.
compend, *n.* compendio, epítome, *m.*
compendious, *adj.* compendioso, sucinto; **—ly,** *adv.* compendiosamente.
compendium, *n.* compendio, *m.*; sinopsis, *f.*
compensate, *vt.* and *vi.* compensar.
compensation, *n.* compensación, *f.*; resarcimiento, *m.*
compensatory, *adj.* compensatorio, compensativo.
compete, *vi.* competir.
competence, *n.* competencia, *f.*; suficiencia, *f.*
competent, *adj.* competente, capaz; adecuado; caracterizado; **—ly,** *adv.* competentemente.
competition, *n.* competencia, *f.*; concurso, *m.*
competitive, *adj.* competidor.
competitor, *n.* competidor, ra; rival, *m* y *f.*
compilation, *n.* compilación, *f.*
compile, *vt.* compilar.
complacence, *n.* complacencia, satisfacción, *f.*
complacent, *adj.* complaciente, deseoso de servir.
complain, *vi.* quejarse, lamentarse; dolerse.

complainant, *n.* (law) querellante, demandante, *m.*
complaining, *adj.* quejoso.
complaint, *n.* queja, pena, *f.*; lamento, llanto, quejido, *m.*; reclamación, *f.*; **to file a —,** (law) querellarse, quejarse.
complaisance, *n.* complacencia, afabilidad, *f.*
complaisant, *adj.* complaciente, cortés.
complement, *n.* complemento, *m.*
complementary, *adj.* complementario.
complete, *adj.* completo, cumplido, perfecto; **—,** *vt.* completar, acabar; llevar a cabo; rematar; **—ly,** *adv.* completamente, a fondo.
completion, *n.* complemento, colmo, *m.*, terminación, *f.*; perfeccionamiento, *m.*
complex, *adj.* complejo, compuesto; **—,** *n.* complejo, *m.*
complexion, *n.* cutis, *m.*, tez, *f.*; aspecto general.
complexioned, *adj.* complexionado.
complexity, *n.* complejidad, *f.*
compliance, *n.* sumisión, condescendencia, *f.*; consentimiento, *m.*; **in — with,** de acuerdo con, accediendo (a sus deseos, etc.).
compliant, *adj.* complaciente, dócil, obediente.
complicate, *vt.* complicar.
complicated, *adj.* complicado, embrollado.
complication, *n.* complicación, *f.*
complicity, *n.* complicidad, *f.*
compliment, *n.* cumplido, *m.*; lisonja, *f.*; (coll.) piropo, requiebro, *m.*; **—,** *vt.* cumplimentar, echar flores; ensalzar, alabar.
complimentary, *adj.* cumplimentero, ceremonioso; piropero.
comply, *vi.* cumplir; condescender, conformarse.
component, *adj.* componente.
comport, *vt.* and *vi.* comportarse, portarse.
comportment, *n.* comportamiento, *m.*, conducta, *f.*
compose, *vt.* componer; sosegar; concertar, reglar, ordenar; **to — oneself,** serenarse.
composed, *adj.* sosegado, moderado; **to be — of,** componerse de; **—ly,** *adv.* tranquilamente, serenamente.
composer, *n.* autor, ra; compositor, ra; cajista, *m.* y *f.*
composition, *n.* composición, *f.*; compuesto, *m.*
compositor, *n.* cajista, *m.* y *f.*; (mus.) compositor, ra.
compost, *n.* abono, estiércol, *m.*
composure, *n.* calma, *f.*; tranquilidad, *f.*; sangre fría; **to lose one's —,** salirse de sus casillas; perder la calma.
compound, *vt.* componer, combinar; confeccionar; **—,** *vi.* concertarse; ajustar; **—,** *adj.* compuesto; **—,** *n.* compuesto, *m.*; (med.) confección, *f.*
comprehend, *vt.* comprender, contener; entender, penetrar.

comprehensible, *adj.* comprensible; **—ly,** *adv.* comprensiblemente.

comprehension, *n.* comprensión, *f.*; inteligencia, *f.*

comprehensive, *adj.* comprensivo; **—ly,** *adv.* comprensivamente.

comprehensiveness, *n.* extensión, *f.*; alcance, *m.*

compress, *vt.* comprimir, estrechar; **—,** *n.* cabezal, *m.*

compression, *n.* compresión, *f.*; **— rate,** índice de compresión.

compressor, *n.* compresor, *m.*

comprisal, *n.* comprensión, inclusión, *f.*

comprise, *vt.* comprender, incluir.

compromise, *n.* compromiso, convenio, *m.*; **—,** *vt.* comprometer; transigir.

comptometer, *n.* contómetro, *m.*

comptroller, *n.* sobrestante, interventor, *m.*

compulsion, *n.* compulsión, *f.*; apremio, *m.*

compulsive, *adj.* coactivo; obligatorio, compulsivo; **—ly,** *adv.* por fuerza.

compulsory, *adj.* obligatorio, compulsivo.

compunction, *n.* compunción, contrición, *f.*

computation, *n.* computación, cuenta, *f.*; cómputo, cálculo, *m.*

compute, *vt.* computar, calcular.

comrade, *n.* camarada, *m.* y *f.*; compañero, ra.

comradeship, *n.* camaradería, *f.*, compañerismo íntimo.

con, *adv.* en contra; **—,** *n.* contra, *m.*, argumento en contra; **—,** *vt.* meditar, estudiar; aprender de memoria.

con: against, contra; **conclusion,** conclusión.

concatenation, *n.* encadenamiento, *m.*; serie, *f.*

concave, *adj.* cóncavo.

concavity, *n.* concavidad, *f.*

conceal, *vt.* ocultar, esconder; zampuzar (una cosa); zampar; **—ed,** *adj.* escondido, oculto; disimulado; secreto.

concealment, *n.* ocultación, *f.*; encubrimiento, *m.*

concede, *vt.* conceder, admitir; **—,** *vi.* asentir, acceder.

conceit, *n.* capricho, *m.*; pensamiento, *m.*; presunción, *f.*; vanagloria, *f.*; amor propio.

conceited, *adj.* afectado, vano, presumido; **—ly,** *adv.* engreídamente.

conceivable, *adj.* concebible, inteligible.

conceive, *vt.* concebir, comprender.

concenter, *vt.* reconcentrar.

concentrate, *vt.* and *vi.* concentrar, concentrarse.

concentration, *n.* concentración, *f.*; **— camp,** campo de concentración.

concentric, concentrical, *adj.* concéntrico.

concept, *n.* concepto, *m.*

conception, *n.* concepción, *f.*; concepto, *m.*

conceptual, *adj.* conceptual, referente a una concepción o idea general.

concern, *vt.* concernir, importar; pertenecer;

—, *n.* negocio, *m.*; interés, *m.*; importancia, consecuencia, *f.*

concerned, *adj.* interesado; inquieto, apesarado, mortificado.

concerning, *prep.* tocante a, respecto a.

concert, *n.* concierto, *m.*; convenio, *m.*; **— performer, — manager,** concertista, *m.* y *f.*; **—,** *vt.* and *vi.* concertar, concertarse.

concertina, *n.* (mus.) concertina, *f.*

concession, *n.* concesión, cesión, *f.*; privilegio, *m.*

concessionaire, *n.* concesionario, *m.*

conch, *n.* concha, *f.*

concierge, *n.* conserje, *m.*; portero, ra.

conciliar, *adj.* conciliar.

conciliate, *vt.* conciliar; atraer.

conciliation, *n.* conciliación, *f.*

conciliator, *n.* conciliador, ra.

conciliatory, *adj.* conciliativo.

concise, *adj.* conciso, sucinto; **—ly,** *adv.* concisamente.

conciseness, *n.* concisión, *f.*; laconismo, *m.*

conclave, *n.* conclave, *m.*

conclude, *vt.* concluir; decidir; finalizar, terminar; epilogar.

conclusion, *n.* conclusión, terminación, *f.*; fin, *m.*; clausura, *f.*; consecuencia, *f.*

conclusive, *adj.* decisivo, conclusivo; **—ly,** *adv.* concluyentemente.

concoct, *vt.* confeccionar; maquinar; mezclar; urdir.

concoction, *n.* maquinación, *f.*; mezcla, *f.*; trama, *f.*

concomitant, *adj.* concomitante; **—,** *n.* concomitante, *m.* y *f.*

concord, *n.* concordia, armonía, *f.*

concordance, *n.* concordancia, *f.*

concordant, *adj.* concordante, conforme.

concordat, *n.* concordato, *m.*; convenio, *m.*

concourse, *n.* concurso, *m.*; reunión, *f.*; multitud, *f.*, gentío, *m.*

concrete, *n.* concreto, *m.*; hormigón, cemento, *m.*; **— mixer,** mezcladora, *f.*; **re-inforced —,** hormigón armado; **—,** *adj.* concreto; **—,** *vt.* and *vi.* concretar.

concretion, *n.* concreción, *f.*; agregado, *m.*; (med.) cálculo, *m.*

concubinage, *n.* concubinato, *m.*

concubine, *n.* concubina, *f.*

concupiscence, *n.* concupiscencia, *f.*; codicia, *f.*

concupiscent, *adj.* lascivo.

concur, *vi.* convenir, coincidir; acceder.

concurrence, *n.* coincidencia, *f.*; acuerdo, convenio, *m.*

concussion, *n.* concusión, *f.*

condemn, *vt.* condenar; desaprobar; vituperar.

condemnation, *n.* condenación, *f.*

condemnatory, *adj.* condenatorio.

condensation, *n.* condensación, *f.*

condense, *vt.* condensar; comprimir.

condenser, *n.* condensador, *m.*; **— pipe,** tubo de condensador; caño de evacuación.

condescend, *vi.* condescender; consentir.

condescending, *adj.* complaciente, afable.
condescension, *n.* condescendencia, *f.*
condiment, *n.* condimento, *m.*; salsa, *f.*
condition, *n.* situación, condición, *f.*; calidad, *f.*; requisito, *m.*; estado, *m.*; circunstancia, *f.*; **on — that,** con tal que.
conditional, *adj.* condicional, hipotético; **—ly,** *adv.* condicionalmente.
conditioned, *adj.* condicionado, acondicionado.
condole, *vi.* condolerse.
condolence, *n.* pésame, *m.*, condolencia, *f.*
condonation, *n.* condonación, *f.*
condone, *vt.* condonar.
condoning, *n.* condonación, *f.*
condor, *n.* (orn.) cóndor, *m.*
conduce, *vt.* conducir.
conducive, *adj.* conducente; útil.
conduct, *n.* conducta, *f.*; manejo, proceder, *m.*; conducción (de tropas), *f.*; porte, *m.*; **safe —,** salvoconducto, *m.*
conduct, *vt.* conducir, guiar.
conduction, *n.* conducción, *f.*
conductive, *adj.* conductivo.
conductivity, *n.* conductibilidad, *f.*
conductor, *n.* conductor, *m.*; guía, director, *m.*; conductor de electricidad.
conduit, *n.* conducto, *m.*; caño, *m.*, cañería, *f.*; **— maker,** cañero, *m.*
cone, *n.* cono, *m.*; **paper —,** cucurucho, *m.*; **ice-cream —,** barquillo de mantecado, de nieve o de helados.
coney, *n.* = **cony.**
confabulate, *vi.* platicar, conversar, charlar.
confection, *n.* confitura, *f.*; confección, *f.*; confite, *m.*
confectioner, *n.* confitero, ra.
confectionery, *n.* dulcería, confitería, *f.*; confitura, *f.*, confite, dulce, *m.*
confederacy, *n.* confederación, *f.*
confederate, *vi.* confederarse; **—,** *adj.* confederado; **—,** *n.* confederado, *m.*
confederation, *n.* federación, confederación, *f.*
confer, *vi.* conferenciar; consultarse; **—,** *vt.* otorgar, dar.
conferee, *n.* persona consultada.
conference, *n.* conferencia, *f.*; sesión, junta, *f.*
confess, *vt.* and *vi.* confesar, confesarse.
confessedly, *adv.* por confesión, admitidamente, sin lugar a duda.
confession, *n.* confesión, *f.*
confessional, *n.* confesionario, *m.*
confessor, *n.* confesor, *m.*
confetti, *n.* confetti, *m.*
confidant, *n.* confidente, *m.* y *f.*, amigo íntimo, amiga íntima.
confide, *vt.* and *vi.* confiar; fiarse.
confidence, *n.* confianza, seguridad, *f.*; confidencia, *f.*; **in strictest —,** con o bajo la mayor reserva.
confident, *adj.* cierto; fiado; seguro; confiado; atrevido; **—,** *n.* confidente, *m.* y *f.*; **—ly,** *adv.* con seguridad.

confidential, *adj.* confidencial; **—ly,** *adv.* en confianza, confidencialmente.
confiding, *adj.* fiel, seguro, confiado.
configuration, *n.* configuración, *f.*
confine, *n.* confín, límite, *m.*; **—,** *vt.* limitar; aprisionar; **—,** *vi.* confinar.
confinement, *n.* prisión, *f.*; encierro, *m.*; parto, *m.*; sobreparto, *m.*
confirm, *vt.* confirmar; ratificar.
confirmation, *n.* confirmación, *f.*; ratificación, *f.*; prueba, *f.*
confirmative, confirmatory, *adj.* confirmativo.
confiscate, *vt.* confiscar, decomisar.
confiscation, *n.* confiscación, *f.*; decomiso, *m.*
conflagration, *n.* conflagración, *f.*, incendio general; quemazón, *f.*
conflict, *n.* conflicto, *m.*; combate, *m.*, pelea, *f.*; **—,** *vt.* contender; combatir; chocar; estar en conflicto.
confluence, *n.* confluencia, *f.*; concurso, *m.*
confluent, *adj.* confluente.
conform, *vt.* and *vi.* conformar, conformarse.
conformation, *n.* conformación, *f.*, arreglo, *m.*
conformable, *adj.* conforme, de acuerdo; **—bly,** *adv.* conformemente.
conformity, *n.* conformidad, *f.*; concordia, *f.*
confound, *vt.* turbar, confundir; destruir; **— it!** *interj.* ¡caracoles! ¡cáspita!
confront, *vt.* afrontar; confrontar, comparar.
Confucius, Confucio.
confuse, *vt.* confundir; desordenar.
confused, *adj.* confuso, desorientado; embrollado; **to become —,** hacerse un lío; trabucarse, trabarse; **—ly,** *adv.* confusamente.
confusion, *n.* confusión, baraúnda, *f.*; desorden, *m.*; perturbación, *f.*; trápala, *f.*; trastorno, *m.*
confute, *vt.* confutar, refutar.
Cong.: Congregational, perteneciente a una Congregación; **Congress,** Cong. Congreso; **Congressional,** relativo al Congreso.
congeal, *vt.* and *vi.* helar, congelar, congelarse.
congelation, *n.* congelación, *f.*
congenial, *adj.* congenial, compatible; **to be —,** simpatizar.
congeniality, *n.* acción de congeniar.
congenital, *adj.* congénito.
conger, *n.* (pez) congrio, *m.*
congestion, *n.* congestión, *f.*
conglomerate, *vt.* conglomerar, aglomerar; **—,** *adj.* aglomerado; **—,** *n.* conglomerado, *m.*
conglomeration, *n.* aglomeración, *f.*
congratulate, *vt.* congratular, felicitar.
congratulation, *n.* congratulación, felicitación, *f.*
congratulatory, *adj.* congratulatorio.
congregate, *vt.* congregar, afluir, reunir.
congregation, *n.* congregación, reunión, *f.*

congregational, *adj.* congregacional.
congress, *n.* congreso, *m.*; conferencia, *f.*
congressional, *adj.* perteneciente o relativo al congreso.
congressman, *n.* diputado al congreso, congresista, *m.* y *f.*
congruent, *adj.* congruente, conforme.
congruity, *n.* congruencia, *f.*
congruous, *adj.* idóneo, congruente, congruo, apto; —ly, *adv.* oportunamente; congruentemente.
conic, conical, *adj.* cónico.
conically, *adv.* en forma cónica.
conifer, *n.* (bot.) conífera, *f.*
coniferous, *adj.* (bot.) conífero.
conj.: conjugation, conj. conjugación; conjunction, conj. conjunción.
conjectural, *adj.* conjetural; —ly, *adv.* conjeturalmente.
conjecture, *n.* conjetura, suposición, *f.*; —, *vt.* conjeturar; pronosticar.
conjoin, *vt.* juntar; asociar; —, *vi.* unirse, ligarse.
conjoint, *adj.* asociado, confederado.
conjugal, *adj.* conyugal, matrimonial; —ly, *adv.* conyugalmente.
conjugate, *vt.* (gram.) conjugar.
conjugation, *n.* (gram.) conjugación, *f.*
conjunct, *adj.* conjunto.
conjunction, *n.* (gram.) conjunción, *f.*; unión, *f.*
conjunctive, *adj.* conjunto; conjuntivo.
conjunctivitis, *n.* (med.) conjuntivitis, *f.*
conjuncture, *n.* coyuntura, *f.*; combinación de acontecimientos; situación crítica.
conjuration, *n.* conjuro, *m.*; conspiración, *f.*
conjure, *vt.* rogar, pedir con instancia; —, *vi.* conjurar, exorcizar; encantar; hechizar.
conjurer, *n.* conjurador, encantador, *m.*; nigromante, *m.*
connate, *adj.* innato, congénito.
connect, *vt.* juntar, unir, enlazar; relacionar.
connecting rod, *n.* biela, *f.*
connection, *n.* conexión, *f.*; —s, *n. pl.* relaciones, *f. pl.*
conning tower, *n.* (naut.) torre de mando.
conniption, conniption fit, *n.* pataleta, *f.*, ataque de histerismo.
connivance, *n.* connivencia, *f.*
connive, *vi.* confabularse; fingir ignorancia; disimular.
connoisseur, *n.* perito, ta, conocedor, ra.
connoisseurship, *n.* conocimiento, *m.*, pericia, *f.*
connotation, *n.* connotación, *f.*
connote, *vt.* connotar.
connubial, *adj.* conyugal, matrimonial.
conquer, *vt.* conquistar; vencer.
conqueror, *n.* vencedor, conquistador, *m.*
conquest, *n.* conquista, *f.*
consanguineous, *adj.* consanguíneo.
consanguinity, *n.* consanguinidad, *f.*
conscience, *n.* conciencia, *f.*; escrúpulo, *m.*; innermost —, fuero interno.
conscience-stricken, *adj.* con remordi-

mientos, hostigado por el remordimiento.
conscientious, *adj.* concienzudo, escrupuloso; meticuloso; —ly, *adv.* según conciencia.
conscientiousness, *n.* rectitud, *f.*; escrupulosidad, *f.*
conscionable, *adj.* justo, razonable.
conscious, *adj.* sabedor, convencido; consciente; —ly, *adv.* a sabiendas.
conscript, *adj.* reclutado, seleccionado; — father, padre conscripto; —, *n.* recluta de servicio forzoso.
conscription, *n.* reclutamiento obligatorio.
consecrate, *vt.* consagrar; dedicar.
consecration, *n.* consagración, *f.*
consecutive, *adj.* consecutivo, consiguiente; —ly, *adv.* consecutivamente, sucesivamente.
consensus, *n.* consenso, asenso, consentimiento, *m.*; — of opinion, opinión colectiva, consentimiento general.
consent, *n.* consentimiento, asenso, *m.*; aprobación, *f.*; —, *vi.* consentir; aprobar.
consequence, *n.* consecuencia, *f.*; importancia, *f.*; efecto, *m.*; resulta, *f.*; as a —, de resultas; in —, como consecuencia; in — of, en vista de.
consequent, *adj.* consecutivo; concluyente; consiguiente; —ly, *adv.* consiguientemente; como consecuencia, por consiguiente.
consequential, *adj.* consiguiente, lógico; importante.
conservation, *n.* conservación, *f.*
conservatism, *n.* calidad de conservador.
conservative, *adj.* conservativo, conservador; —, *n.* conservador, ra.
conservator, *n.* conservador, ra; defensor, *m.*
conservatory, *adj.* conservatorio; —, *n.* conservatorio, *m.*
conserve, *vt.* conservar, cuidar; hacer conservas; —, *n.* conserva, *f.*
consider, *vt.* considerar, examinar; —, *vi.* pensar, deliberar; ponderar; reflexionar; reparar.
considerable, *adj.* considerable; importante; bastante; —bly, *adv.* considerablemente.
considerate, *adj.* considerado, prudente, discreto; deferente; —ly, *adv.* juiciosamente; prudentemente.
consideration, *n.* consideración, *f.*; deliberación, *f.*; importancia, *f.*; valor, mérito, *m.*; to take into —, hacerse cargo de, tomar en cuenta.
considering, *prep.* en atención a; en vista de; — that, a causa de; visto que; en razón a.
consign, *vt.* consignar.
consignation, *n.* consignación, *f.*
consignee, *n.* consignatario, ria; depositario, ria.
consigner, consignor, *n.* consignador, ra.
consignment, *n.* consignación, partida, *f.*
consist, *vi.* consistir.
consistence, consistency, *n.* consistencia, *f.*
consistent, *adj.* consistente; congruente

conveniente, conforme; sólido, estable; **—ly,** *adv.* conformemente; consistente-mente.

consistory, *n.* consistorio, *m.*

consolation, *n.* consolación, *f.*; consuelo, *m.*

consolatory, *adj.* consolatorio.

console, *vt.* consolar; **—,** *n.* (arch.) cartela, *f.*; consola, *f.*

consoler, *n.* consolador, ra.

consolidate, *vt.* and *vi.* consolidar, consolidarse.

consolidation, *n.* consolidación, *f.*

consolidative, *adj.* consolidativo.

consomme, *n.* caldo de carne.

consonance, *n.* consonancia, *f.*; armonía, *f.*

consonant, *adj.* consonante, conforme; **—,** *n.* (gram.) consonante, *f.*

consort, *n.* consorte, socio, *m.*; esposo, sa; **—,** *vi.* asociarse.

conspicuous, *adj.* conspicuo, aparente; notable; llamativo, sobresaliente; **to be —,** destacarse; **—ly,** *adv.* claramente, insignemente.

conspiracy, *n.* conspiración, *f.*; trama, *f.*; complot, *m.*; lío, *m.*

conspirator, *n.* conspirador, ra.

conspire, *vi.* conspirar, maquinar.

Const. Constitution, Const. Constitución.

constable, *n.* condestable, *m.*

constabulary, *n.* policía, *f.*

Constance, Constancia.

constancy, *n.* constancia, perseverancia, persistencia, *f.*

constant, *adj.* constante; seguro, firme; fiel; perseverante; **—ly,** *adv.* constantemente.

Constantine, Constantino.

Constantinople, Constantinopla, *f.*

constellation, *n.* constelación, *f.*

consternation, *n.* consternación, *f.*; terror, *m.*

constipate, *vt.* constipar; obstruir.

constipation, *n.* estreñimiento, *m.*, constipación, obstrucción, *f.*

constituency, *n.* junta electoral.

constituent, *n.* constitutivo, *m.*; elector, votante, *m.*; **—,** *adj.* constituyente.

constitute, *vt.* constituir; establecer, diputar.

constitution, *n.* constitución, *f.*; estado, *m.*; temperamento, *m.*; complexión, *f.*; **weak in —,** delicado.

constitutional, *adj.* constitucional, legal.

constitutionality, *n.* constitucionalidad, *f.*

constrain, *vt.* constreñir; forzar; restringir.

constraint, *n.* constreñimiento, *m.*; fuerza, violencia, *f.*

constrict, *vt.* constreñir, estrechar.

constriction, *n.* constricción, contracción, *f.*

constringent, *adj.* constrictivo.

construct, *vt.* construir, edificar.

construction, *n.* construcción, *f.*; interpretación, *f.*; **— work,** mano de obra.

constructive, *adj.* constructivo, constructor.

construe, *vt.* construir; interpretar.

consul, *n.* cónsul, *m.*

consular, *adj.* consular; **— fees,** derechos consulares.

consulate, consulship, *n.* consulado, *m.*

consult, *vt.* and *vi.* consultar, consultarse; aconsejar, aconsejarse; **— together,** conferenciar.

consultant, *n.* consultante, *m.*

consultation, *n.* consulta, deliberación, *f.*

consume, *vt.* consumir; disipar; destruir; desperdiciar; devorar (alimento); **—,** *vi.* consumirse.

consumer, *n.* consumidor, ra.

consuming, *adj.* consumidor.

consummate, *vt.* consumar, acabar; **—,** *adj.* cumplido, consumado.

consummation, *n.* consumación, perfección, *f.*

consumption, *n.* consunción, *f.*; disipación, *f.*; (med.) tisis, *f.*

consumptive, *adj.* consuntivo; (med.) tísico, ético.

cont.: contents, contenido; **continent,** cont. continente; **continued,** cont. continúa.

contact, *n.* contacto, tocamiento, *m.*; **—,** *vt.* and *vi.* tocar; poner en contacto; ponerse en contacto.

contagion, *n.* contagio, *m.*; infección, *f.*

contagious, *adj.* contagioso.

contain, *vt.* contener, comprender; caber; reprimir, refrenar; refundir.

container, *n.* envase, *m.*; recipiente, *m.*

contaminate, *vt.* contaminar; corromper.

contamination, *n.* contaminación, *f.*

contemn, *vt.* despreciar, menospreciar, desestimar; desdeñar.

contemplate, *vt.* contemplar; **—,** *vi.* meditar, pensar.

contemplation, *n.* contemplación, *f.*

contemplative, *adj.* contemplativo; **—ly,** *adv.* con atención y estudio.

contemporaneous, contemporary, *adj.* contemporáneo.

contempt, *n.* desprecio, desdén, *m.*

contemptible, *adj.* despreciable, vil; **—bly,** *adv.* vilmente.

contemptuous, *adj.* desdeñoso, insolente; **—ly,** *adv.* con desdén, con desprecio; **to look —,** mirar de reojo.

contend, *vi.* contender, disputar, afirmar; lidiar; competir.

content, *adj.* contento, satisfecho; **—,** *vt.* contentar, satisfacer; **—,** *n.* contento, *m.*; satisfacción, *f.*; **to one's heart's —,** a pedir de boca; **—s,** *n. pl.* contenido, *m.*

contention, *n.* contención, altercación, *f.*; tema, *m.*

contentious, *adj.* contencioso, litigioso; **—ly,** *adv.* contenciosamente.

contentment, *n.* contentamiento, placer, *m.*

contest, *vt.* contestar, disputar, litigar; **—,** *n.* concurso, *m.*; competencia, *f.*; disputa, altercación, *f.*; **literary —,** certamen o concurso literario.

contestant, *adj.* contendiente, litigante; **—,**

n. contendiente, litigante, *m.* y *f.*; concursante, *m.* y *f.*
context, *n.* contexto, *m.*; contextura, *f.*
contiguity, *n.* contigüidad, *f.*
contiguous, *adj.* contiguo, vecino; **to be —,** colindar.
continence, continency, *n.* continencia, *f.*; castidad, *f.*
continent, *adj.* continente; **—ly,** *adv.* castamente; **—,** *n.* continente, *m.*
continental, *adj.* continental.
contingency, *n.* contingencia, *f.*; acontecimiento, *m.*; eventualidad, *f.*
contingent, *n.* contingente, *m.*; cuota, *f.*; **—,** *adj.* contingente, casual; **—ly,** *adv.* casualmente.
continual, *adj.* continuo; **—ly,** *adv.* continuamente; de continuo.
continuance, *n.* continuación, permanencia, *f.*; duración, *f.*; prolongación, *f.*
continuation, *n.* continuación, *f.*; serie, *f.*
continue, *vt.* continuar; **—,** *vi.* durar, perseverar, persistir.
continued, *adj.* continuo, continuado, extendido, seguido.
continuity, *n.* continuidad, *f.*
continuous, *adj.* continuo; **—ly,** *adv.* continuamente.
contort, *vt.* torcer.
contortion, *n.* contorsión, *f.*
contour, *n.* contorno, *m.*
contr.: contract, contrato; **contraction,** contracción.
contraband, *n.* contrabando, *m.*; **—,** *adj.* prohibido, ilegal.
contraceptive, *n.* medios contra la procreación.
contract, *vt.* contraer; abreviar; contratar; **—,** *vi.* contraerse; **—,** *n.* contrato, pacto, *m.*
contracting, *adj.* contratante; **— parties,** partes contratantes.
contraction, *n.* contracción, *f.*; abreviatura, *f.*
contractor, *n.* contratante, contratista, *m.*; provisor, ra.
contradict, *vt.* contradecir.
contradiction, *n.* contradicción, oposición, *f.*
contradictory, *adj.* contradictorio.
contralto, *n.* contralto (voz), *m.*; contralto (persona), *m.* y *f.*
contrariety, contrariness, *n.* contrariedad, oposición, *f.*
contrary, *adj.* contrario, opuesto; **—,** *n.* contrario, ria; **on the —,** al contrario, antes bien; **—rily,** *adv.* contrariamente.
contrast, *n.* contraste, *m.*; oposición, *f.*; **—,** *vt.* contrastar, oponer.
contravene, *vt.* contravenir, infringir, violar.
contravention, *n.* contravención, *f.*
contribute, *vt.* contribuir, ayudar.
contribution, *n.* contribución, *f.*; tributo, *m.*; **small —,** óbolo, *m.*
contributor, *n.* contribuidor, ra, contribuyente, *m.* y *f.*

contributory, contributive, *adj.* contribuyente; tributario.
contrite, *adj.* contrito, arrepentido.
contrition, *n.* penitencia, contrición, *f.*
contrivance, *n.* designio, *m.*; invención, *f.*
contrive, *vt.* inventar, trazar, maquinar; manejar; combinar.
control, *n.* contrarregistro, *m.*; inspección, f.; conducción, *f.*; sujeción, *f.*; control, *m.*; dirección, *f.*, mando, *m.*; gobierno, *m.*; **— stick,** palanca de gobierno de un aeroplano; **finger tip —,** control con la punta del dedo; **hydraulic —,** control hidráulico; **— tower,** torre de mando; **—,** *vt.* restringir; gobernar; refutar; registrar; criticar; **to — oneself,** contenerse, comprimirse, vencer.
controllability, *n.* (aer.) controlabilidad, manejabilidad, *f.*
controller, *n.* contralor, registrador, interventor, *m.*
controversial, *adj.* controvertible, discutible.
controversy, *n.* controversia, *f.*
controvert, *vt.* controvertir, disputar.
contumacious, *adj.* contumaz; **—ly,** *adv.* contumazmente.
contumacy, *n.* contumacia, resistencia, *f.*
contumelious, *adj.* contumelioso, injurioso; **—ly,** *adv.* contumeliosamente.
contumely, *n.* contumelia, injuria, *f.*
contusion, *n.* contusión, *f.*, magullamiento, *m.*
conundrum, *n.* adivinanza, *f.*, acertijo, *m.*
convalesce, *vi.* convalecer.
convalescence, *n.* convalecencia, *f.*
convalescent, *adj.* convaleciente.
convection, *n.* convección, *f.*
convene, *vt.* convocar; juntar, unir; **—,** *vi.* convenir, juntarse.
convenience, *n.* conveniencia, comodidad, *f.*; conformidad, *f.*; **at one's —,** cuando le convenga a uno; **does that suit your —?** ¿le conviene a Vd.?
convenient, *adj.* conveniente, apto, cómodo, propio; **—ly,** *adv.* cómodamente, oportunamente.
convent, *n.* convento, claustro, monasterio, *m.*
conventicle, *n.* conventículo, *m.*
convention, *n.* convención, *f.*; contrato, tratado, *m.*
conventional, *adj.* convencional; estipulado; tradicional.
conventionalism, *n.* convencionalismo, *m.*
conventual, *adj.* conventual.
converge, *vi.* convergir.
convergence, *n.* convergencia, *f.*
convergent, *adj.* convergente.
conversant, *adj.* versado, familiarizado; **— with,** versado en.
conversation, *n.* conversación, plática, *f.*; tertulia, *f.*
conversational, *adj.* de conversación.
conversationalist, *n.* persona que conversa

brillantemente o que conversa mucho.

converse, vi. conversar, platicar; —, n.; conversación, plática, f.; familiaridad, f.; comercio, m.; —, adj. inverso; **—ly,** adv. a la inversa, recíprocamente.

conversion, n. conversión, trasmutación, f.

convert, vt. convertir, trasmutar,; reducir; —, vi. convertirse; —, n. converso, convertido, m.; catecúmeno, na.

converter, n. convertidor, m.; depurador, m.

convertibility, n. convertibilidad, f.

convertible, adj. convertible, trasmutable.

convex, adj. convexo; **—ly,** adv. convexamente.

convexity, n. convexidad, f.

convey, vt. trasportar; trasmitir, trasferir; conducir.

conveyance, n. trasporte, m.; conducción, f.; escritura de traspaso.

conveyancer, n. notario para escrituras de traspaso.

conveyer, conveyor, n. conductor, transportador, m.

convict, vt. convencer, probar un delito; condenar.

convict, n. reo, convicto, presidiario, m.

conviction, n. convicción, f.; refutación, f.; certidumbre, f.; condenación, f.

convince, vt. convencer, poner en evidencia; persuadir.

convincing, adj. convincente, con convicción; **—ly,** adv. de una manera convincente.

convivial, adj. sociable; hospitalario.

conviviality, n. sociabilidad, f.

convocation, n. convocación, f.; sínodo, m.

convoke, vt. convocar, reunir.

convolution, n. circunvolución, enroscadura, f.

convolvulus, n. (bot.) enredadera de la familia de las convolvuláceas.

convoy, vt. convoyar; —, n. convoy, m., escolta, f.

convulse, vt. conmover, trastornar.

convulsion, n. convulsión, f.; conmoción, f.

convulsive, adj. convulsivo; **—ly,** adv. convulsivamente.

cony, coney, n. conejo, m.; piel de conejo.

coo, vi. arrullar.

cooing, n. arrullo de palomas; conversación amorosa.

cook, n. cocinero, ra; **pastry —,** repostero, ra; —, vt. cocinar, aderezar las viandas; —, vi. cocer, cocinar; guisar.

cookbook, n. libro culinario, libro de cocina.

cookery, n. arte culinaria, cocina, f.; cocedero, m.

cookhouse, n. fogón de un bajel, cocina de navío.

cooking, n. cocina, f., arte de cocinar; —, adj. relativo a la cocina; **— range,** cocina económica; **— stove,** fogón, m.; estufa, f., cocina económica; cocinilla, f.; **— utensils,** batería de cocina.

cooky, n. bollo, m.; galleta, f.; galletita inglesa.

cool, adj. fresco; indiferente; —, n. frescura, f.; —, vt. enfriar, refrescar, atemperar; resfriar; **to — off,** aplacarse.

cooler, n. enfriadera, f., enfriador, m.; (med.) refrigerante, m.; (coll.) prisión, cárcel, f.

cool-headed, adj. sereno, calmado.

coolie, n. peón oriental.

cooling, adj. refrescante.

coolly, adv. frescamente; indiferentemente.

coolness, n. fresco, m.; frialdad, frescura, f.; estolidez, f.

coop, n. caponera, f.; gallinero, m.; —, vt. enjaular, encarcelar.

coop. cooperative, cooperativo.

cooper, n. cubero, tonelero, m.

cooperage, n. tonelería, f.

co-operate, vi. cooperar.

co-operation, n. cooperación, f.

co-operative, adj. cooperativo, cooperador.

co-ordinate, vt. coordinar.

co-ordination, n. coordinación, f.

co-ordinator, n. coordinador, ra.

copal, n. copal, m.

copartner, n. compañero, ra; socio, cia; socio colectivo.

copartnership, n. sociedad regular colectiva.

cope, n. (eccl.) capa pluvial; arco, m., bóveda, f.; albardilla, f.; —, vi. competir, lidiar con.

Copenhagen, Copenhague, f.

copier, n. copista, m. y f.

coping, n. cumbre de edificio; albardilla, f.

coping saw, n. tipo pequeño de sierra de marquetería.

copious, adj. copioso, abundante; **—ly,** adv. en abundancia.

copiousness, n. abundancia, copia, f.

copper, n. cobre, m.; calderón, m.; cobre (color), m.; moneda de cobre; **— sulphate,** piedra lipis; cobre quemado.

copperas, n. caparrosa, f.

copperplate, n. lámina o plancha de cobre.

coppersmith, n. calderero, m.

coppery, adj. cobrizo.

coppice, copse, n. monte bajo.

copra, n. copra, f.

copula, n. cópula, f.

copulate, vi. copular, juntar una cosa con otra.

copulation, n. cópula, f., coito; m.; conjunción, f.

copy, n. copia, f.; original, m.; ejemplar de algún libro; —, vt. copiar; imitar.

copybook, n. cuaderno para escribir; copiador de cartas (libro).

copyholder, n. persona que lee pruebas en voz alta a otra persona; instrumento en que el impresor coloca el manuscrito que va a imprimir.

copying machine, n. pantógrafo, m.

copyist, n. copista, m. y f.; plagiario, ria.

copyright, *n.* propiedad de una obra literaria; derechos de autor; patente, *f.*

coquet, *vi.* cocar, cortejar, coquetear.

coquetry, *n.* coquetería, *f.*

coquette, *n.* coqueta, *f.*

coquettish, *adj.* coquetón, coqueta.

cor.: corner, esq. esquina; **corrected,** corregido; **corresponding,** correspondiente.

coral, *n.* coral, *m.*; —, *adj.* coralino, de coral; — **reef,** banco de coral.

coralline, *n.* (bot.) coralina, *f.*

cord, *n.* cuerda, *f.*; cordel, *m.*; cuerda (medida para leña), *f.*; cordón, pasamano, *m.*; —, *vt.* encordelar.

cordage, *n.* cordaje, *m.*

cordial, *adj.* cordial, de corazón, amistoso; —**ly,** *adv.* cordialmente; —, *n.* cordial (licor), *m.*

cordiality, *n.* cordialidad, *f.*

cordite, *n.* (chem.) cordita, *f.*

cordon, *n.* cordón, *m.*

corduroy, *n.* pana, *f.*

core, *n.* cuesco, *m.*; interior, centro, corazón, *m.*; núcleo, *m.*

Corfu, Corfú, *f.*

Corinth, Corinto, *m.*

cork, *n.* corcho, *m.*; —, *vt.* tapar con corchos.

corkscrew, *n.* tirabuzón, *m.*

corky, *adj.* de corcho.

cormorant, *n.* corvejón, *m.*; mergo, *m.*; glotón, ona; —, *adj.* glotón, voraz.

corn, *n.* grano, *m.*; callo, *m.*; maíz, *m.*; — **meal,** harina de maíz; — **plaster,** emplasto para los callos; **ear of** —, mazorca, *f.*; —, *vt.* salpresar, salar; granular.

corncob, *n.* mazorca, *f.*

corncrib, *n.* granero de maíz.

corned beef, *n.* cecina, *f.*, carne de vaca preparada en salmuera; carne plateada malaya.

corner, *n.* ángulo, *m.*; rincón, *m.*; esquina, *f.*; extremidad, *f.*; remate, *m.*; — **shelf,** rinconera, *f.*; **to turn the** —, doblar la calle o la esquina; —, *vt.* acaparar.

cornered, *adj.* anguloso; en aprieto.

cornerstone, *n.* piedra angular; mocheta, *f.*

cornet, *n.* corneta, *f.*; portaestandarte, *m.*

cornfield, *n.* maizal, *m.*

cornflower, *n.* aciano, *m.*; trigo azulejo.

cornice, *n.* cornisa, *f.*

cornpopper, *n.* tostador de maíz.

cornstalk, *n.* tallo de maíz.

cornstarch, *n.* almidón de maíz.

Cornwall, Cornwall o Cornualles, *f.*

corolla, *n.* (bot.) corola, *f.*

corollary, *n.* corolario, *m.*

coronation, *n.* coronación, *f.*

coroner, *n.* oficial que hace la inspección jurídica de los cadáveres.

coronet, *n.* corona pequeña.

Corp., corp.: corporal, cabo; **corporation,** S.A. sociedad anónima.

corporal, *n.* (mil.) cabo, *m.*; —, *adj.* corpóreo, corporal; material, físico; —**ly,** *adv.* corporalmente.

corporate, *adj.* formado en cuerpo o en comunidad; colectivo.

corporation, *n.* corporación, *f.*; gremio, *m.*; sociedad anónima.

corporeal, *adj.* corpóreo.

corps, *n.* cuerpo de ejército; regimiento, *m.*; cuerpo, *m.*; **air** —, cuerpo de aviación.

corpse, *n.* cadáver, *m.*

corpulence, corpulency, *n.* corpulencia, *f.*

corpulent, *adj.* corpulento, gordo.

Corpus Christi Day, *n.* día de Corpus.

corpuscle, *n.* corpúsculo, *m.*

corr. correspondent, corresponsal.

corral, *n.* corral, *m.*; —, *vt.* acorralar.

correct, *vt.* corregir, reprender, castigar; enmendar, amonestar; rectificar; —, *adj.* correcto, cierto; —**ly,** *adv.* correctamente.

correction, *n.* corrección, *f.*; castigo, *m.*; enmienda, *f.*; censura, *f.*; remedio, *m.*

corrective, *adj.* correctivo; —, *n.* correctivo, *m.*

correctness, *n.* corrección, *f.*; exactitud, *f.*

corrector, *n.* corrector, ra; revisor, ra.

correlate, *vt.* correlacionar.

correlation, *n.* correlación, *f.*

correlative, *adj.* correlativo.

correspond, *vi.* corresponder; corresponderse.

correspondence, *n.* correspondencia, *f.*; reciprocidad, *f.*; **to carry on the** —, llevar la correspondencia.

correspondent, *adj.* correspondiente; conforme; —, *n.* corresponsal, *m.*

corridor, *n.* crujía, *f.*, pasillo, corredor, *m.*

corrigible, *adj.* corregible.

corroborate, *vt.* corroborar.

corroboration, *n.* corroboración, *f.*

corroborative, *adj.* corroborativo.

corrode, *vt.* corroer.

corrosion, *n.* corrosión, *f.*

corrosive, *adj.* corrosivo; — **sublimate,** sublimado corrosivo.

corrugate, *vt.* corrugar, arrugar.

corrugated, *adj.* corrugado, acanalado, ondulado.

corrugation, *n.* corrugación, ondulación, *f.*

corrupt, *vt.* corromper; sobornar; infectar; —, *vi.* corromperse, pudrirse; —, *adj.* corrompido; depravado.

corruptible, *adj.* corruptible.

corruption, *n.* corrupción, perversión, *f.*; depravación, *f.*; impureza, *f.*

corruptive, *adj.* corruptivo.

corruptness, *n.* corruptela, corrupción, *f.*

corsage, *n.* corpiño, *m.*; ramillete para la cintura.

corsair, *n.* corsario, pirata, *m.*

corset, *n.* corsé, *m.*

Corsica, Córcega, *f.*

Corsican, *n.* and *adj.* corso, sa.

corundum, *n.* corindón, *m.*

coruscation, *n.* resplandor, *m.*; fulgor, *m.*

cortege, *n.* comitiva, *f.*

cortex, *n.* corteza, *f.*

corvette, *n.* (naut.) corbeta, *f.*

cosine, *n.* (math.) coseno, *m.*

cosmetic, *adj.* cosmético;—, *n.* cosmético, *m.*

cosmic, *adj.* cósmico; — **ray,** rayo cósmico.

cosmology, *n.* cosmología, *f.*

cosmopolitan, cosmopolite, *n.* and *adj.* cosmopolita, *m.* y *f.*

cosmos, *n.* cosmos, universo, *m.*

Cossack, *n.* and *adj.* cosaco, ca.

cosset, *vt.* mimar.

cost, *n.* coste, costo, precio, *m.*; expensas, *f. pl.*; **net —,** coste neto; **at all —s,** a todo trance; **production —s,** costo de fabricación; —, *vi.* costar.

costal, *adj.* costal.

costive, *adj.* restringente.

costly, *adj.* costoso, suntuoso, caro; espléndido.

costume, *n.* traje, *m.*; ropa, *f.*; disfraz, *m.*

costumer, *n.* sastre, *m.*

cosy, *adj.* = **cozy.**

cot, *n.* cabaña, *f.*; catre, *m.*

cotangent, *n.* (math.) cotangente, *f.*

cote, *n.* corral, *m.*

coterie, *n.* grupo o círculo de amigos, corrillo, *m.*, tertulia, *f.*

cotillion, *n.* cotillón, *m.*

cottage, *n.* cabaña, casucha, *f.*; borda, *f.*; choza, *f.*; — **cheese,** requesón, *m.*

cotton, *n.* algodón, *m.*; — **flannel,** franela de algodón; — **goods,** cotonía, *f.*; — **lint,** hilaza de algodón desmotado; — **mill,** hilandería de algodón; **printed —,** quimón, *m.*; zaraza, *f.*; **select —,** algodón flor; **skein —,** algodón en madeja; **spun —,** algodón hilado.

cottonseed, *n.* semilla de algodón; — **oil,** aceite de semilla de algodón.

cottontail, *n.* conejo americano común.

cottonwood, *n.* especie de álamo americano.

couch, *vi.* echarse; agobiarse; —, *vt.* acostar; extender; esconder; bajar (los ojos); —, *n.* cama, *f.*, lecho, *m.*; canapé, sofá, *m.*

cougar, *n.* (zool.) cuguar, *m.*, puma, *f.*

cough, *n.* tos, *f.*; —, *vi.* toser; — **drop,** pastilla para la tos.

could, pretérito del verbo **can.**

council, *n.* concilio, concejo, *m.*; junta, *f.*; sínodo, *m.*; — **board,** reunión del consejo; — **house,** consejo, *m.*; **town —,** cabildo, ayuntamiento, *m.*

councilman, *n.* concejal, *m.*

councilor, councillor, *n.* concejal, *m.*, miembro del concejo.

counsel, *n.* consejo, aviso, *m.*; abogado, *m.*

counselor, counsellor, *n.* consejero, abogado, *m.*

count, *vt.* contar, numerar; calcular; **to — on,** confiar, depender de; —, *n.* cuenta, *f.*; cálculo, *m.*; conde (título), *m.*

countenance, *n.* rostro, *m.*; fisonomía, *f.*, aspecto, *m.*; semblante, *m.*; apoyo, *m.*; talante, *m.*; —, *vt.* proteger, ayudar, favorecer.

counter, *n.* contador, *m.*; ficha, *f.*; mostrador, tablero, *m.*; **bargain —,** baratillo,

m.; —, *adv.* contrariamente, al revés; —, *adj.* contrario, adverso.

counteract, *vt.* contrariar, impedir, estorbar; frustrar.

counteraction, *n.* oposición, *f.*

counterattack, *n.* contraataque, *m.*

counterbalance, *vt.* contrapesar; igualar, compensar; —, *n.* contrapeso, *m.*

counterblow, *n.* contragolpe, *m.*

counterclaim, *n.* contrarreclamación, *f.*

counterclockwise, *adj.* and *adv.* que gira a la izquierda.

countercurrent, *n.* contracorriente, *f.*

counterfeit, *vt.* contrahacer, imitar, falsear; —, *n.* contrahacedor, impostor, *m.*; falsificación, *f.*; —, *adj.* falsificado; fingido; — **note,** billete de banco falsificado.

counterfeiter, *n.* contrahacedor, falsario, *m.*; — **of money,** monedero falso.

counterfoil, *n.* contramarca, *f.*

counterjumper, *n.* hortera, *m.*; tendero, dependiente, *m.*

countermand, *vt.* contramandar; revocar.

counteroffensive, *n.* contraofensiva, *f.*

counterpane, *n.* colcha de cama, cobertor, *m.*

counterpart, *n.* parte correspondiente; complemento, *m.*; persona que semeja mucho a otra.

counterplot, *n.* contratreta, *f.*

counterpoint, *n.* contrapunto, *m.*

counterpoise, *vt.* contrapesar; —, *n.* contrapeso, *m.*

counterreformation, *n.* contrarreforma, *f.*

counterrevolution, *n.* contrarevolución, *f.*

counterscarp, *n.* contraescarpa, *f.*

countersign, *vt.* refrendar; firmar (un decreto); visar; —, *n.* (mil.) consigna, *f.*

countervail, *vt.* suministrar un equivalente; compensar.

counterweight, *n.* contrapeso, *m.*

countess, *n.* condesa, *f.*

counting house, *n.* despacho, escritorio, *m.*

countless, *adj.* innumerable.

countrified, *adj.* rústico, campesino.

country, *n.* país, *m.*; campo, *m.*; campiña, *f.*; región, *f.*; patria, *f.*; —, *adj.* rústico; campestre, rural; — **club,** club campestre; — **dance,** baile campestre; — **farm,** hospicio de beneficencia; — **house,** casa de campo, granja, *f.*; — **seat,** pueblo principal de un condado.

countryman, *n.* paisano, *m.*; compatriota, *m.*

countryside, *n.* campo, *m.*, región rural.

countrywoman, *n.* paisana, *f.*; compatriota, *f.*; campesina, *f.*

county, *n.* condado, *m.*

coup d'état, *n.* golpe de estado.

coupé, *n.* cupé, *m.*

couple, *n.* par, *m.*; vínculo, *m.*; —, *vt.* unir, parear, casar; —, *vi.* juntarse carnalmente; juntarse, unirse formando un par.

couplet, *n.* copla, *f.*

coupling, *n.* acoplamiento, *m.*, unión, junta,

f.; empalme, *m.*; **—s,** *n. pl.* (rail.) locomotoras acopladas.

coupón, *n.* cupón, talón, *m.*

courage, *n.* coraje, valor, *m.*; **to lose —,** intimidarse; **to take —,** cobrar ánimo.

courageous, *adj.* corajudo, valeroso, valiente; **to become —,** envalentonarse; **—ly,** *adv.* valerosamente.

courier, *n.* correo, mensajero, *m.*; expreso, *m.*

Courland, Curlandia, *f.*

course, *n.* curso, *m.*; carrera, *f.*; camino, *m.*; ruta, *f.*; rumbo, *m.*; plato, *m.*; capa (de caminos), *f.*; método, *m.*; entrada, *f.*; servicio, *m.*; asignatura, *f.*; **— (of time),** transcurso (del tiempo), *m.*; **of —,** naturalmente, por supuesto, desde luego.

courser, *n.* corcel, corredor, *m.*; cazador, *m.*

court, *n.* corte; palacio, *m.*; patio, *m.*; cortejo, *m.*; frontón, *m.*; **— of justice,** juzgado, *m.*; tribunal de justicia; **— plaster,** tafetán inglés, esparadrapo, *m.*; **—,** *vt.* cortejar; solicitar; adular; requerir, requebrar (una mujer).

courteous, *adj.* cortés; benévolo; caballeresco; **—ly,** *adv.* cortésmente.

courtesan, *n.* cortesana, *f.*

courtesy, *n.* cortesía, *f.*; benignidad, *f.*; **—,** *vi.* hacer la reverencia.

courthouse, *n.* foro, tribunal, *m.*

courtier, *n.* cortesano, palaciego, *m.*; cortejo, *m.*

courtly, *adj.* cortesano, elegante.

court-martial, *n.* (mil.) corte marcial; consejo militar, consejo de guerra.

courtroom, *n.* sala de justicia, tribunal, *m.*

courtship, *n.* cortejo, *m.*; galantería, *f.*

courtyard, *n.* patio, *m.*

cousin, *n.* primo, ma; **first —,** primo hermano, prima hermana.

cove, *n.* (naut.) ensenada, cala, caleta, *f.*

covenant, *n.* contrato, pacto, convenio, *m.*; **—,** *vi.* pactar, estipular.

cover, *n.* cubierta, *f.*; abrigo, *m.*; pretexto, *m.*; tapadillo, *m.*; **table —,** carpeta, cubremesa, *f.*; **under separate —,** bajo sobre separado; **—,** *vt.* cubrir; tapar; ocultar; proteger; paliar.

covering, *n.* ropa, *f.*; vestido, *m.*; cubierta, *f.*

coverlet, coverlid, *n.* colcha, *f.*

covert, *n.* cubierta, *f.*; refugio, *m.*; **—,** *adj.* cubierto; oculto, secreto; **—ly,** *adv.* secretamente.

coverture, *n.* abrigo, refugio, *m.*

covet, *vt.* codiciar, desear con ansia.

covetous, *adj.* avariento, sórdido; **—ly,** *adv.* codiciosamente.

covey, *n.* nidada, pollada, *f.*

cow, *n.* vaca, *f.*; **—,** *vt.* acobardar, intimidar.

coward, *n.* cobarde, *m.* y *f.*

cowardice, *n.* cobardía, timidez, *f.*

cowardly, *adj.* cobarde; pusilánime; **—,** *adv.* cobardemente.

cowboy, *n.* vaquero, gaucho, *m.*

cower, *vi.* agacharse.

cowherd, *n.* vaquero, *m.*

cowhide, *n.* cuero, *m.*; látigo, *m.*

cowl, *n.* capuz, capucho, *m.*

cowlick, *n.* remolino, *m.*, mechón de cabellos.

co-worker, *n.* colaborador, ra, compañero o compañera de trabajo.

cowpea, *n.* (bot.) garbanzo, *m.*

cowpuncher, *n.* vaquero, gaucho, *m.*

coxcomb, *n.* petimetre, *m.*; pedante, *m.*

coy, *adj.* recatado, modesto; tímido; **—ly,** *adv.* con timidez.

coyote, *n.* coyote, *m.*

cozy, *adj.* cómodo y agradable.

cp. compare, compárese.

c.p. candle power, potencia lumínica en bujías.

C.P.A. Certified Public Accountant, C.P.T. Contador Público Titulado.

cr.: credit, crédito, haber; **creditor,** acreedor.

crab, *n.* cangrejo, *m.*; manzana silvestre; persona querellosa y de mal carácter; **— apple,** manzana silvestre.

crabbed, crabby, *adj.* áspero, austero, bronco, tosco.

crack, *n.* crujido, *m.*; hendedura, raja, *f.*; quebraja, *f.*; **—,** *vt.* hender, rajar; romper; **to — a joke,** decir un chiste; **to — down,** compeler; **—,** *vi.* reventar; jactarse; agrietarse; **—,** *adj.* raro, fino, de superior calidad.

crackbrained, *adj.* alocado, loco; estúpido.

cracker, *n.* galletica, galleta, *f.*; cohete, *m.*

crackle, *vi.* crujir, chillar.

crackling, *n.* estallido, crujido, *m.*

cracknel, *n.* hojuela, *f.*

crack-up (of a plane), *n.* acto de estrellarse un aeroplano.

cradle, *n.* cuna, *f.*; **—,** *vt.* mecer la cuna.

cradlesong, *n.* canción de cuna.

craft, *n.* arte, *m.*; artificio, *m.*; astucia, *f.*

craftiness, *n.* astucia, estratagema, *f.*

craftsman, *n.* artífice, artesano, *m.*

crafty, *adj.* astuto, artificioso; **— person,** perillán, ana.

crag, *n.* despeñadero, *m.*

cragged, *adj.* escabroso, áspero.

craggy, *adj.* escabroso, áspero.

cram, *vt.* embutir; engordar; empujar; engullir; recargar; **—,** *vi.* atracarse de comida.

cramp, *n.* calambre, *m.*, retortijón de tripas; laña, *f.*; **—,** *vt.* lañar; constreñir, apretar.

cranberry, *n.* arándano, *m.*

crane, *n.* (orn.) grulla, *f.*; (mech.) grúa, *f.*; pescante, *m.*; **—,** *vt.* levantar con grúa; **to — the neck,** estirar el cuello a manera de grulla.

cranial, *adj.* craneal, del cráneo.

cranium, *n.* cráneo, *m.*

crank, *n.* manivela, *f.*; manija, *f.*; (coll.) maniático, ca; **—,** *vt.* poner en marcha un motor.

crankcase, *n.* (auto.) cárter, *m.*, caja del cigüeñal.

crankpin, *n.* pasador de manivela.
crankshaft, *n.* cigüeñal, *m.*; manivela, *f.*
cranky, *adj.* caprichoso; testarudo.
crannied, *adj.* hendido.
cranny, *n.* grieta, hendedura, *f.*
crape, *n.* crespón, *m.*
craps, crapshooting (dice game), *n.* variedad de juego de dados.
crash, *vi.* estallar, rechinar; estrellar; —, *n.* estallido, fracaso, *m.*; choque, *m.*
crash-dive, *vt.* sumergirse repentinamente como un submarino.
crass, *adj.* craso, grueso, basto, tosco, grosero.
crate, *n.* cesta grande para embalar loza, etc.
crater, *n.* cráter, *m.*
cravat, *n.* corbata, *f.*
crave, *vt.* and *vi.* rogar, suplicar; apetecer; pedir; anhelar.
craven, *adj.* cobarde; —, *n.* cobarde, *m.*
cravenette, *n.* tejido semiimpermeable.
craving, *adj.* insaciable, pedigüeño; —, *n.* deseo ardiente.
craw, *n.* buche de ave.
crawfish, *n.* cangrejo de agua dulce; —, *vi.* (coll.) retroceder; no cumplir con lo prometido.
crawl, *vi.* arrastrar; caminar a rastras; **to — with,** hormiguear; —, *n.* sistema para nadar con gran velocidad.
crayfish, *n.* cangrejo de río.
crayon, *n.* lápiz, pastel, *m.*
craze, *n.* locura, demencia, *f.*; antojo, capricho, *m.*; —, *vt.* enloquecer; —, *vi.* enloquecerse.
craziness, *n.* debilidad, *f.*; locura, *f.*; delirio, *m.*
crazy, *adj.* fatuo, simple; trastornado, loco; **— bone,** cóndilo interno del húmero; **— quilt,** centón, *m.*; **to drive —,** sacar de sus casillas.
creak, *vi.* crujir, chirriar; **—y,** *adj.* crujiente, crujidero.
cream, *n.* crema, nata, *f.*; **— of tartar,** crémor tártaro; **— puff,** bollo de crema; **— separator,** desnatadora, *f.*; **whipped —,** crema batida.
creamery, *n.* lechería, *f.*
creamy, *adj.* lleno de nata o crema; parecido a la crema o a la nata.
crease, *n.* pliegue, *m.*; —, *vt.* plegar.
create, *vt.* crear; causar.
creation, *n.* creación, *f.*; obra creada.
creative, *adj.* creador, con habilidad o facultad para crear.
creator, *n.* criador, ra; **the C—,** el Criador.
creature, *n.* criatura, *f.*
credence, *n.* creencia, *f.*; fe, *f.*; crédito, *m.*
credentials, *n. pl.* credenciales, *f. pl.*
credibility, *n.* credibilidad, *f.*
credible, *adj.* creíble, verisímil, verosímil; **—bly,** *adv.* creíblemente; según se cree.
credit, *n.* crédito, *m.*; creencia, *f.*; reputación, *f.*; autoridad, *f.*; **— balance,** saldo acreedor; **blank —,** carta en blanco; **letter**

of —, carta credencial o de crédito; **on —,** a crédito, al fiado, a plazo; **—,** *vt.* creer; fiar, acreditar; **to buy on —,** comprar al crédito o al fiado; **to — with,** abonar en cuenta.
creditable, *adj.* estimable, digno de encomio; **—bly,** *adv.* honorablemente; de manera encomiable.
creditor, *n.* acreedor, ra, persona que debe dinero.
credo, *n.* credo, *m.*, profesión de fe.
credulity, *n.* credulidad, *f.*
credulous, *adj.* crédulo; **—ly,** *adv.* con credulidad.
creed, *n.* credo, *m.*
creek, *n.* riachuelo, arroyo, *m.*
creep, *vi.* arrastrar, serpear; gatear; **—y,** *adj.* pavoroso.
creeper, *n.* reptil, *m.*; (bot.) enredadera, *f.*; pájaro trepador; vestido de una sola pieza para niños muy pequeños.
creephole, *n.* huronera, *f.*; subterfugio, *m.*; escapatoria, *f.*
cremate, *vt.* incinerar cadáveres.
cremation, *n.* cremación, *f.*
crematory, *n.* crematorio, quemadero, *m.*
Creole, *n.* criollo, *m.*, blanco descendiente de los colonos franceses y españoles de Luisiana; negro nacido en América.
creosote, *n.* creosota, *f.*; **—d wood,** madera creosotada.
crepe, *n.* crepé, crespón, *m.*
crepe de Chine, *n.* crespón de China o de seda.
crept, pretérito y *p. p.* del verbo **creep.**
cres., cresc. abreviatura, cresc. crescendo.
crescent, *adj.* creciente; —, *n.* creciente (fase de la luna), *f.*
cress, *n.* (bot.) mastuerzo, berro, *m.*
crest, *n.* cresta, *f.*; copete, *m.*; orgullo, *m.*; cimera, *f.*
crested, *adj.* crestado.
crestfallen, *adj.* acobardado, abatido de espíritu, decaído; con las orejas caídas.
cretaceous, *adj.* cretáceo.
Cretan, *n.* and *adj.* cretense, *m.* y *f.*
cretinism, *n.* cretinismo, *m.*
cretonne, *n.* cretona, *f.*
crevice, *n.* raja, hendidura, *f.*
crew, *n.* (naut.) tripulación, *f.*; cuadrilla, *f.*
crewel, *n.* ovillo de estambre.
crib, *n.* pesebre, *m.*; casucha, *f.*; cuna, *f.*
cribbage, *n.* especie de juego de naipes.
crick, *n.* (med.) torticolis, *m.*; chirrido, *m.*
cricket, *n.* (zool.) grillo, *m.*; vilorta (juego), *f.*; **field —,** saltamontes, *m.*; caballeta, *f.*
crier, *n.* pregonero, *m.*
crime, *n.* crimen, delito, *m.*
criminal, *adj.* criminal, reo; —, *n.* reo convicto, criminal, *m.* y *f.*; **—ly,** *adv.* criminalmente.
criminality, *n.* criminalidad, *f.*
criminate, *vt.* acriminar; incriminar.
criminology, *n.* criminología, *f.*
crimp, *n.* rizado (de cabello), *m.*; (mil.)

enganchador, _m._; —, _vt._ rizar, encrespar.
crimpy, _adj._ encrespado.
crimson, _n._ carmesí, _m._; —, _adj._ carmesí, bermejo.
cringe, _n._ bajeza, _f._, servilismo, _m._; —, _vi._ incensar, adular servilmente; respingar.
crinkle, _n._ sinuosidad, _f._; arruga, _f._; —, _vt._ serpentear.
crinoline, _n._ crinolina, _f._
cripple, _n._ zopo, pa; lisiado, da; —, _vt._ estropear, derrengar, tullir.
crisis, _n._ crisis, _f._
crisp, _adj._ crespo; frágil, quebradizo; fresco, terso, lozano (aplícase a la lechuga, el apio, etc.); claro, definido; —, _vt._ and _vi._ encrespar; ponerse crespo, rizarse.
crispness, _n._ encrespadura, _f._; lozanía, _f._, verdor (de las legumbres tales como la lechuga, etc.), _m._; fragilidad, _f._
crisscross, _adj._ entrelazado; —, _n._ firma del que no sabe escribir; —, _vt._ entrelazar, cruzar.
criterion, _n._ criterio, _m._
critic, _n._ crítico, _m._
critical, _adj._ crítico; exacto; delicado; —ly, _adv._ exactamente, rigurosamente; en forma crítica.
criticism, _n._ crítica, _f._; censura, _f._
criticize, _vt._ criticar, censurar; **to give cause to** —, dar que decir.
critique, _n._ crítica, _f._, juicio crítico.
croak, _vi._ graznar, crascitar; refunfuñar.
Croatia, Croacia, _f._
Croatian, _n._ and _adj._ croata, _m._ y _f._
crochet, _n._ labor con aguja de gancho; —, _vt._ tejer con aguja de gancho.
crock, _n._ cazuela, olla, _f._
crockery, _n._ loza, _f._; vasijas de barro; vidriado, _m._
crocodile, _n._ cocodrilo, _m._; — **tears,** lágrimas de cocodrilo.
crone, _n._ anciana, vieja, _f._
crony, _n._ amigo (o conocido) antiguo.
crook, _n._ gancho, _m._; curva, _f._; (coll.) fullero, _m._; petardista, _m._ y _f._; ladrón, ona; —, _vt._ encorvar; torcer; pervertir; —, _vi._ desviarse; pervertirse.
crooked, _adj._ torcido, corvo; perverso; deshonesto, avieso; tortuoso; **to go** —, torcerse, desviarse del camino recto de la virtud; **—ly,** _adv._ torcidamente; de mala gana.
croon, _vi._ canturrear, cantar con melancolía exagerada.
crop, _n._ cosecha, _f._, mieses, _f. pl._; producción, _f._; buche de ave; cabello cortado corto; —, _vt._ segar, cosechar.
croquet, _n._ croquet (juego), _m._
croquette, _n._ croqueta, _f._
crosier, _n._ cayado pastoral de obispo.
cross, _n._ cruz, _f._; carga, _f._; trabajo, _m._; pena, aflicción, _f._; tormento, _m._; —, _adj._ contrario, opuesto, atravesado; enojado; travesero; mal humorado; — **reference,** contrarreferencia, comprobación, verifica-

ción, _f._; — **section,** sección transversal; — **wind,** viento de través; —, _prep._ al través; —, _vt._ atravesar, cruzar; **to** — **off,** barrear; **to** — **over,** traspasar; **—ly,** _adv._ enojadamente, malhumoradamente.
crossbar, crossbeam, _n._ tranca, _f._, travesaño, _m._
crossbeam, _n._ viga transversal.
crossbow, _n._ ballesta, _f._
crossbreed, _n._ raza cruzada.
cross-country, _adj._ a campo traviesa.
crosscut, _adj._ de corte transversal; —, _n._ atajo, _m._; corte transversal; — **saw,** sierra de trozar.
crossed, _adj._ cruzado.
cross-examination, _n._ contrainterrogatorio, _m._, comprobación de interrogatorio.
cross-examine, _vt._ hacer preguntas (a un testigo, etc.)
cross-eye, _n._ estrabismo, _m._, torcedura de la vista.
cross-eyed, _adj._ bizco, bisojo.
cross-fertilize, _vt._ and _vi._ fecundar una planta con otra por polinización.
cross-grained, _adj._ de fibra transversal; perverso, intratable.
crossing, crossline, _n._ (rail.) cruzamiento de dos vías; cruce, _m._; travesía, _f._; **street** —, cruce de calle.
cross-legged, _adj._ con las piernas cruzadas.
cross-pollinate, _vt._ polinizar una planta con otra.
cross-pollination, _n._ polinización cruzada, hibridización.
cross-purpose, _n._ propósitos cruzados; **at** —**s,** involuntariamente en desacuerdo.
cross-question, _vt._ interrogar.
cross-reference card, _n._ tarjeta de contrarreferencia o verificación.
crossroad, _n._ paso, _m._, encrucijada, _f._
cross-stitch, _n._ punto cruzado; —, _vt._ and _vi._ hacer puntos cruzados.
crossways, crosswise, _adv._ terciadamente; atravesadamente; en forma de cruz; perversamente; al través.
crossword puzzle, _n._ crucigrama, rompecabezas, _m._
crotch, _n._ gancho, corchete, _m._; bragadura, _f._; bifurcación, _f._
crotchet, _n._ (mus.) semínima, _f._; capricho, _m._; corchete, _m._
crotchety, _adj._ caprichoso.
crouch, _vi._ agacharse, bajarse.
croup, _n._ grupa (de caballo), _f._; (med.) garrotillo, _m._
crouton, _n._ pedacito de pan tostado para sopas, etc.
crow, _n._ (orn.) cuervo, _m._; barra, _f._; canto del gallo; —, _vi._ cantar el gallo; alardearse.
crowbar, _n._ palanca de hierro; (min.) barreta, _f._; pie de cabra.
crowd, _n._ tropel, _m._; turba, muchedumbre, _f._; multitud, _f._; pelotón, _m._; — **of people,** bocanada de gente, gentío, _m._; **noisy** —, bullaje, _m._; —, _vt._ amontonar; **to** — **sail,**

(naut.) hacer fuerza de vela; —, *vi.* amontonarse.

crowded, *adj.* concurrido, lleno de gente.

crown, *n.* corona, *f.*; diadema, guirnalda, *f.*; rueda, *f.*; moneda de plata que vale cinco chelines; complemento, colmo, *m.*; —, *vt.* coronar; recompensar; dar cima; cubrir el peón que ha llegado a ser dama (en ajedrez).

crown prince, *n.* príncipe heredero.

crow's foot, *n.* pata de gallo, arruga que se forma en el ángulo externo del ojo.

crucial, *adj.* en forma de cruz; decisivo, crítico.

crucible, *n.* crisol, *m.*; — **steel,** acero al crisol.

crucifix, *n.* crucifijo, *m.*

crucify, *vt.* crucificar; atormentar.

crude, *adj.* crudo, indigesto, imperfecto; tosco; — (**ore, oil, etc.**), (mineral, petróleo, etc.) bruto; —**ly,** *adv.* crudamente; toscamente.

crudity, *n.* crudeza, *f.*; tosquedad, *f.*

cruel, *adj.* cruel, inhumano; —**ly,** *adv.* cruelmente.

cruelty, *n.* crueldad, *f.*; barbarie, *f.*

cruet, *n.* vinagrera, aceitera, *f.*

cruise, *n.* travesía o viaje por mar y a veces por tierra; —, *vi.* navegar; cruzar (el mar o el país).

cruiser, *n.* crucero, *m.*; navegante, *m.*

cruller, *n.* buñuelo enroscado.

crumb, *n.* miga, *f.*; brote, *m.*; migaja (de pan, etc.), *f.*

crumble, *vt.* desmigajar, desmenuzar; — **away,** derrumbarse; —, *vi.* desmigajarse; desmoronarse.

crumpet, *n.* mollete, *m.*, bollo blando.

crumple, *vt.* arrugar, ajar; rabosear.

crunch, *vi.* crujir; —, *vt.* cascar con los dientes, mascar haciendo ruido.

crusade, *n.* cruzada, *f.*

crusader, *n.* cruzado, *m.*, miembro de una cruzada.

crush, *vt.* apretar, oprimir; aplastar, machacar; —, *n.* choque, *m.*; estrujamiento, *m.*

crusher, *n.* triturador, ra; máquina trituradora.

crushing, *n.* trituración, *f.*; —, *adj.* triturador; — **machine,** triturador, ra.

crust, *n.* costra, *f.*; corteza, *f.*; —, *vt.* encostrar; —, *vi.* encostrarse.

crustaceous, *adj.* crustáceo; conchado.

crusty, *adj.* costroso; bronco, áspero.

crutch, *n.* muleta, *f.*

crux, *n.* problema difícil; momento crítico.

cry, *vt.* and *vi.* gritar; pregonar; exclamar; llorar; —, *n.* grito, *m.*; lloro, *m.*; clamor, *m.*; **to — out,** dar gritos.

crybaby, *n.* niño llorón.

crying, *adj.* lloroso; —, *n.* lloro, grito, *m.*

crypt, *n.* cripta, *f.*, bóveda subterránea.

cryptic, *adj.* escondido, da, secreto, ta.

crystal, *n.* cristal, *m.*

crystalline, *adj.* cristalino: transparente.

crystallization, *n.* cristalización, *f.*

crystallize, *vt.* cristalizar; —, *vi.* cristalizarse;

C.S. Civil Service, Servicio Civil.

CSC Civil Service Commission, Comisión de Servicio Civil.

C.S.T. Central Standard Time, hora normal del centro (de E.U.A.).

ct. cent, cént. céntimo.

cu. cubic, cúbico.

cub, *n.* cachorro, *m.*; — **reporter,** aprendiz de reportero.

Cuban, *n.* and *adj.* cubano, na.

cubbyhole, *n.* casilla, *f.*, cualquier lugar pequeño y encerrado en forma de caverna.

cube, *n.* cubo, *m.*; **in —s,** cubicado.

cubic, cubical, *adj.* cúbico.

cubism, *n.* cubismo, *m.*

cubit, *n.* codo (medida), *m.*

cuckoo, *n.* cuclillo, cuco, *m.*

cucumber, *n.* cohombro, pepino, *m.*

cud, *n.* panza, *f.*; primer estómago de los rumiantes; pasto contenido en la panza; **to chew the —,** rumiar; (fig.) reflexionar.

cuddle, *vt.* and *vi.* abrazar; acariciarse.

cuddy, *n.* (naut.) camarote de proa; cuarto pequeño.

cudgel, *n.* garrote, palo, *m.*; —, *vt.* apalear; — **one's brains,** atormentarse los sesos; **take up the —s for,** salir en defensa de.

cue, *n.* cola, *f.*; apunte de comedia; indirecta, *f.*; taco (de billar), *m.*

cuff, *n.* puño de camisa o de vestido; — **links,** gemelos, *m. pl.*, yugos para los puños de la camisa.

cuirass, *n.* coraza, *f.*

cuirassier, *n.* coracero, *m.*

cuisine, *n.* cocina, *f.*; estilo o clase de cocina; manera de guisar o cocinar.

cuisse, *n.* quijote, *m.*, pieza del arnés que cubre el muslo; parte superior de las ancas de las caballerías.

culinary, *adj.* culinario, de la cocina.

cull, *vt.* escoger, elegir; entresacar.

culm, *n.* carbón fino.

culminate, *vi.* culminar.

culmination, *n.* culminación, *f.*

culottes, *n. pl.* falda pantalón; traje femenino, con falda pantalón.

culpability, *n.* culpabilidad, *f.*

culpable, *adj.* culpable, criminal; —**bly,** *adv.* culpablemente, criminalmente; por la vía criminal.

culpableness, *n.* culpa, culpabilidad, *f.*

culprit, *n.* reo, delincuente, *m.*; criminal, *m.*

cult, *n.* culto, *m.*, devoción, *f.*

cultivate, *vi.* cultivar, mejorar; perfeccionar.

cultivated, *adj.* cultivado, labrado; culto.

cultivation, *n.* cultivación, *f.*; cultivo, *m.*

cultivator, *n.* (agr.) cultivador, ra, agricultor, ra; arado de cultivo.

culture, *n.* cultura, *f.*; luces, *f. pl.*; civilización, *f.*

culverin, *n.* (mil.) culebrina, *f.*

culvert, *n.* alcantarilla, *f.*; conducto subterráneo.

cumber, *vt.* molestar, embrollar.

cumbersome, cumbrous, *adj.* engorroso, pesado, confuso.

cumulate, *vt.* and *vi.* cumular, acumular.

cumulative, *adj.* cumulativo.

cumulus, *m.* cúmulo, *m.*

cunning, *adj.* experto; artificioso, astuto; intrigante; tuno; —**ly,** *adv.* astutamente; expertamente; —, *n.* astucia, sutileza, *f.*; zorrería, *f.*; candonga, *f.*

cup, *n.* taza, jícara, *f.*; (bot.) cáliz, *m.*; oil —, capa aceitadora; —, *vt.* aplicar ventosas; ahuecar en forma de taza.

cupbearer, *n.* copero, escanciador, *m.*

cupboard, *n.* armario, aparador, *m.*, alacena, *f.*; rinconera, *f.*

cupcake, *n.* pastelito, *m.*, bizcocho pequeño.

cupful, *n.* taza (medida), *f.*

cupidity, *n.* concupiscencia, *f.*

cupola, *n.* cúpula, *f.*

cupping, *n.* aplicación de ventosas.

cupric, *adj.* (chem.) cúprico.

cur, *n.* perro de mala ralea; villano, *m.*

cur. currency, m/cte., m/c moneda corriente.

curable, *adj.* curable.

Curaçao, Curazao, *m.*

curacy, *n.* vicariato, *m.*

curare, *n.* curare, *m.*

curate, *n.* ayudante de un párroco.

curative, *adj.* curativo; terapéutico.

curator, *n.* curador, *m.*; guardián, *m.*; conservador, *m.*

curb, *n.* barbada, *f.*; freno, *m.*; restricción, *f.*; orilla de la acera; —, *vt.* refrenar, contener, moderar.

curbstone, *n.* brocal, *m.*; contrafuerte de una acera.

curd, *n.* cuajada, *f.*; requesón, *m.*; —, *vt.* cuajar, coagular.

curdle, *vt.* cuajar, coagular; —, *vi.* cuajarse, coagularse.

cure, *n.* remedio, *m.*; curato, *m.*; —, *vt.* curar, sanar; **to — skins,** curar las pieles.

cure-all, *n.* panacea, *f.*

curfew, *n.* toque de queda.

curing, *n.* curación, *f.*

curio, *n.* chuchería, *f.*, objeto curioso.

curiosity, *n.* curiosidad, *f.*; rareza, *f.*

curious, *adj.* curioso, delicado; —**ly,** *adv.* curiosamente.

curl, *n.* rizo de cabello; tortuosidad, *f.*; —, *vt.* rizar el cabello, ondear; —, *vi,* rizarse, encresparse.

curlicue, *n.* enroscadura, plumada, *f.*

curling, *n.* ensortijamiento, *m.*; — **iron,** — **tongs,** encrespador, *m.*; — **paper,** papel a propósito para rizar el cabello.

curly, *adj.* rizado.

currant, *n.* grosella, *f.*; — **bush,** grosellero, *m.*

currency, *n.* circulación, *f.*; moneda corriente; dinero, *m.*; **national** —, moneda nacional.

current, *adj.* corriente, del día —, *n.* tendencia, *f.*, curso, *m.*; corriente, *f.*; corriente (eléctrica), *f.*; — **exchange,** cambió corriente; —**ly,** *adv.* corrientemente, al día.

curricular, *adj.* perteneciente al curso de estudios en una escuela.

curriculum, *n.* programa de estudios.

currier, *n.* curtidor (de cueros, etc.), *m.*

currish, *adj.* perruno, brutal, regañón; —**ly,** *adv.* brutalmente.

curry, *n.* variedad de condimento de la India; —, *vt.* azotar; condimentar con curry, almohazar; — **favor,** insinuarse, ganar la voluntad de alguno.

currycomb, *n.* almohaza, *f.*

curse, *vt.* maldecir; —, *vi.* imprecar; blasfemar; —, *n.* maldición, *f.*; imprecación, *f.*; reniego, *m.*

cursed, *adj.* maldito; enfadoso.

cursive, *adj.* cursivo.

cursorily, *adv.* precipitadamente.

cursory, *adj.* precipitado, inconsiderado.

curt, *adj.* sucinto; brusco; —**ly,** *adv.* brevemente; bruscamente.

curtail, *vt.* cortar; mutilar; rebajar, reducir.

curtailment, *n.* reducción, *f.*; rebajamiento, *m.*

curtain, *n.* cortina, *f.*, telón en los teatros; — **call,** (theat.) llamada a la escena para recibir los aplausos; — **raiser,** pieza breve con que empieza una función de teatro; —, *vt.* proveer con cortinas.

curtsy, *n.* saludo de una mujer, reverencia, *f.*

curvated, *adj.* corvo, encorvado.

curvature, *n.* curvatura, *f.*

curve, *vt.* encorvar; —, *adj.* corvo, adunco, torcido; —, *n.* curva, combadura, *f.*

curvet, *n.* corveta, *f.*; —, *vi.* corcovear; saltar de alegría.

curvilinear, *adj.* curvilíneo.

cushion, *n.* cojín, *m.*, almohada, *f.*

cusp, *n.* cuerno de la luna; cúspide, *f.*

cuspidor, *n.* escupidera, *f.*

custard, *n.* natillas, *f. pl.*; flan, *m.*, crema, *f.*

custodian, *n.* custodio, *m.*

custody, *n.* custodia, *f.*; prisión, *f.*; cuidado, *m.*

custom, *n.* costumbre, *f.*; uso, *m.*; —**s collector,** aduanero, *m.*, administrador de aduana; — **duties,** derechos de aduana o arancelarios.

customarily, *adv.* comúnmente, ordinariamente.

customary, *adj.* usual, acostumbrado, ordinario.

custom-built, custom-made, *adj.* hecho a la orden o a la medida.

customer, *n.* parroquiano, *m.*; cliente, *m.* y *f.*; comprador, ra.

custom-free, *adj.* exento de derechos.

customhouse, *n.* aduana, *f.*; — **declaration,** manifiesto, *m.*

cut, *vt.* cortar; separar; herir; dividir; alzar (los naipes); **to — capers,** cabriolar; **to — on the bias,** sesgar; **to — short,** interrumpir; **to — teeth,** nacerle los dientes (a un niño); **—,** *adj.* cortado; **— glass,** cristal tallado; **— tobacco,** picadura, *f.*; **—,** *n.* cortadura, *f.*; herida, *f.*; (print.) grabado, *m.*

cutaneous, *adj.* cutáneo.

cutaway, *n.* frac, *m.*

cuticle, *n.* epidermis, *f.*; tapa, *f.*; cutícula, *f.*

cutlass, *n.* espada ancha; alfanje, *m.*; terciado, *m.*

cutler, *n.* cuchillero, *m.*

cutlery, *n.* cuchillería, *f.*

cutlet, *n.* costilla o chuleta asada.

cutout, *n.* (elec.) desconectador, interruptor, *m.*; (auto.) silenciador, *m.*

cutter, *n.* cortador, ra; (naut.) cúter, *m.*

cutthroat, *n.* asesino, *m.*

cutting, *adj.* cortante; sarcástico; **—,** *n.* cortadura, *f.*; incisión, *f.*; alce (de naipes), *m.*; trinchado, *m.*; **wood —s, metal —s,** viruta, *f.*

cuttlebone, *n.* jibión, *m.*

cuttlefish, *n.* pulpo, *m.*, sepia, *f.*

cutwater, *n.* (naut.) tajamar, *m.*

cutworm, *n.* larva destructora.

cwt. hundredweight, ql. quintal.

cyanamide, *n.* cianamida, *f.*

cyanide, *n.* (chem.) cianuro, *m.*

cyclamen, *n.* (bot.) pamporcino, *m.*

cycle, *n.* ciclo, *m.*; **— race track,** velódromo, *m.*

cyclic, cyclical, *adj.* cíclico.

cyclist, *n.* ciclista, *m.* y *f.*

cycloid, *n.* cicloide, *f.*

cyclometer, *n.* odómetro, ciclómetro, *m.*

cyclone, *n.* ciclón, huracán, *m.*

cyclonic, *adj.* ciclónico.

cyclopedia, *n.* enciclopedia, *f.*

cyclorama, *n.* ciclorama, *m.*

cyclotron, *n.* ciclotrón, *m.*

cylinder, *n.* cilindro, *m.*; rollo, *m.*; rodillo, *m.*; **— head,** culata de cilindro.

cylindric, cylindrical, *adj.* cilíndrico.

cymbal, *n.* címbalo, *m.*; platillo, *m.*

cynic, cynical, *adj.* cínico; obsceno.

cynic, *n.* cínico, *m.*

cynicism, *n.* cinismo, *m.*

cynosure, *n.* centro de atracción.

cypher, cipher, *n.* cifra, *f.*, cero, *m.*; persona insignificante.

cypress, *n.* ciprés, *m.*; **— nut,** piñuela, *f.*

Cyprus, *f.* Chipre, *f.*

cyst, *n.* quiste, *m.*; lobanillo, *m.*

cystitis, *n.* (med.) cistitis, *f.*

cytology, *n.* citología, *f.*

cytoplasm, *n.* citoplasma, *m.*

C. Z. Canal Zone, Z. del C. Zona del Canal.

czar, *n.* zar, *m.*

czarina, *n.* zarina, *f.*

Czechoslovak, Czechoslovakian, *n.* and *adj.* checoeslovaco, ca.

Czechoslovakia, Checoeslovaquia, *f.*

D

D. Dutch, hol. holandés.

d.: date, fha. fecha; **daughter,** hija; **day,** día; **diameter,** diámetro; **died,** murió.

D.A. District Attorney, fiscal.

d/a days after acceptance, d/v días vista.

dab, *vt.* frotar suavemente con algo blando o mojado; golpear suavemente; **—,** *n.* pedazo pequeño; salpicadura, *f.*; golpe blando; (pez) barbada, *f.*

dabble, *vt.* rociar, salpicar; **—,** *vi.* chapotear; **to — in politics,** meterse en política.

dace, *n.* (pez) albur, *m.*

dachshund, *n.* perro de origen alemán, de cuerpo largo y patas muy cortas.

dactylology, *n.* dactilología, *f.*

dad, daddy, *n.* papá, *m.*

dadaism, *n.* dadaísmo, *m.*

daffodil, *n.* (bot.) narciso, *m.*

dagger, *n.* puñal, *m.*; **stab with a —,** puñalada, *f.*

daguerreotype, *n.* daguerrotipo, *m.*

dahlia, *n.* (bot.) dalia, *f.*

daily, *adj.* diario, cotidiano; **— routine,** quehacer, *m.*; **—,** *adv.* diariamente, cada día.

daintiness, *n.* elegancia, *f.*; delicadeza, *f.*

dainty, *adj.* delicado; meticuloso, refinado; **—,** *n.* bocado exquisito.

dairy, *n.* lechería, quesera, quesería, *f.*; **— cattle,** vacas lecheras, vacas de leche.

dairymaid, *n.* lechera, mantequera, *f.*

dairyman, *n.* lechero, mantequero, *m.*; comerciante o traficante en productos lácteos.

daisy, *n.* margarita, maya, *f.*

dale, *n.* (poet.) valle, *m.*

dally, *vi.* juguetear, divertirse; tardar, dilatar; pasar el tiempo con gusto.

Dalmatia, Dalmacia, *f.*

Dalmatian, *n.* and *adj.* dálmata, *m.* y *f.*

dam, *n.* madre, *f.* (aplícase especialmente a los animales cuadrúpedos); dique, *m.*; azud, *m.*, presa, *f.*; represa, *f.*; **—,** *vt.* represar; tapar.

damage, *n.* daño, detrimento, *m.*; resarcimiento de daño; perjuicio, *m.*; **—s,** *n. pl.* daños y perjuicios; **—,** *vt.* dañar.

Damascus, Damasco, *m.*

damask, *n.* damasco, *m.*; **—,** *adj.* de damasco; **—,** *vt.* adornar a manera de damasco.

dame, *n.* dama, señora, *f.*

damn, *vt.* condenar; maldecir; **—!** *interj.* ¡caramba! **— it,** ¡maldito sea!

damnable, *adj.* condenable; **—bly,** *adv.* de un modo condenable; horriblemente, detestablemente.

damnation, *n.* condenación, maldición, *f.*

damned, *adj.* condenado.

damp, *adj.* húmedo; **—,** *n.* humedad, *f.*; decaimiento, *m.*; aflicción, *f.*; **—,** *vt.* humedecer; desanimar, abatir.

dampen, *vt.* humedecer; desanimar, abatir.

dampening, *adj.* humectativo.

damper, *n.* sordina, *f.*; apagador, *m.*; registro (de una chimenea), *m.*

dampness, *n.* humedad, *f.*

damsel, *n.* damisela, señorita, *f.*

dance, *n.* danza, *f.*; baile, *m.*; — **hall,** salón de baile; —, *vi.* bailar.

dancer, *n.* danzarín, ina, bailarín, ina.

dandelion, *n.* diente de león, amargón, *m.*

dandle, *vt.* mecer; halagar, acariciar.

dandruff, *n.* caspa, *f.*

dandy, *n.* petimetre, currutaco, *m.*; (coll.) persona o cosa excelente.

Dane, *n.* and *adj.* dinamarqués, esa.

danger, *n.* peligro, riesgo, escollo, *m.*; — **zone,** zona de peligro.

dangerous, *adj.* peligroso; —**ly,** *adv.* peligrosamente.

dangle, *vi.* fluctuar; estar colgado en el aire; colgar, columpiarse.

Danish, *n.* and *adj.* danés, esa, dinamarqués, esa.

dank, *adj.* húmedo.

danseuse, *n.* bailarina, *f.*

Danube, Danubio, *m.*

dapper, *adj.* activo, vivaz, despierto, apuesto.

dapple, *vt.* abigarrar; —, *adj.* vareteado; rayado; —**gray horse,** caballo tordo.

D.A.R. Daughters of the American Revolution, Organización "Hijas de la Revolución Norteamericana."

dare, *vi.* osar, atreverse, arriesgarse; —, *vt.* desafiar, provocar; —, *n.* reto, *m.*

daredevil, *n.* temerario, ria; calavera, *m.*; atrevido, da, valeroso, sa, valiente, *m.* y *f.*; persona que no teme a la muerte, que arriesga su vida.

daring, *n.* osadía, *f.*; —, *adj.* osado, temerario; emprendedor; —**ly,** *adv.* atrevidamente, osadamente.

dark, *adj.* oscuro, obscuro, opaco; ciego; ignorante, hosco, tétrico; moreno, trigueño; — **horse,** candidato incógnito que se postula en el momento más propicio; — **lantern,** linterna sorda; **to become** —, oscurecerse; —, *n.* oscuridad, *f.*; ignorancia, *f.*; **in the** —, a oscuras; —**ly,** *adv.* oscuramente; secretamente.

darken, *vt.* oscurecer; —, *vi.* oscurecerse.

darkness, *n.* oscuridad, *f.*; tinieblas, *f. pl.*

darkroom, *n.* (phot.) cámara oscura; cuarto oscuro.

darksome, *adj.* (poet.) sombrío, oscuro.

darling, *n.* predilecto, ta, favorito, ta; —, *adj.* querido, amado.

darn, *vt.* zurcir.

darnel, *n.* (bot.) cizaña, borrachuela, *f.*

darner, *n.* zurcidor, ra.

darning needle, aguja grande de zurcir.

dart, *n.* dardo, *m.*; —, *vt.* lanzar, tirar; echar; —, *vi.* volar como dardo.

dash, *n.* arranque, *m.*; acometida, *f.*; (gram.) raya, *f.*; — **rule,** (print.) bigote, *m.*; —, *vt.* arrojar, tirar; chocar, estrellar, batir;

— **off,** bosquejar, escribir apresuradamente.

dashboard, *n.* guardafango, paralodo, *m.*

dashing, *adj.* vistoso, brillante.

dastard, *n.* and *adj.* collón, ona, cobarde, *m.* y *f.*

dastardly, *adj.* cobarde, tímido.

data, *n. pl.* datos, *m. pl.*

date, *n.* data, fecha, *f.*; duración, *f.*; cita, *f.*; (bot.) dátil, *m.*; — **line,** límite fijado en el mapa para el cambio de fecha; **newspaper** — **line,** fecha en que se publica un periódico, una revista, etc.; **to** —, hasta la fecha; **out of** —, anticuado; fuera de moda; **under** —, con fecha; **what is the** —? ¿a cómo estamos? —, *vt.* datar; **to** — **from,** remontar a; **up to** —, hasta hoy, de ultima moda.

dated, *adj.* fechado.

dater, *n.* fechador, *m.*

dating machine, *n.* fechadora, *f.*

dative, *adj.* dativo; —, *n.* dativo, *m.*

datum, *n.* dato, *m.*; — **plane,** plano de antecedentes, de comparación o de referencia.

daub, *vt.* pintorrear; untar; manchar; ensuciar.

daughter, *n.* hija, *f.*; —**in-law,** nuera, *f.*

daunt, *vt.* intimidar, espantar.

dauntless, *adj.* intrépido, arrojado.

davit, *n.* (naut.) pescante de ancla.

Dauphin, *n.* delfín, *m.*

davenport, *n.* sofá tapizado generalmente convertible en cama; especie de escritorio pequeño.

daw, *n.* corneja, *f.*

dawdle, *vi.* desperdiciar (el tiempo).

dawn, *n.* alba, *f.*; albor, *m.*; madrugada, *f.*; —, *vi.* amanecer.

day, *n.* día, *m.*; período, *m.*; **by** —, de día; — **after tomorrow,** pasado mañana; — **before,** víspera, *f.*; — **blindness,** hemeralopia, *f.*; — **by** —, día por día; — **laborer,** jornalero, bracero, mercenario, *m.*; — **letter,** telegrama extenso a un precio especial para ser entregado sin urgencia, aunque sí en el curso del mismo día; — **lily,** asfódelo, *m.*; — **nursery,** aposento para los niños cuyos padres trabajan; — **school,** escuela diurna; — **service,** servicio diurno; — **shift,** turno diurno; — **work,** trabajo diurno; **every** —, todos los días; **from** — **to** —, de día en día; **on the following** —, al otro día; **to carry the** —, ganar la palma; —**s,** *n. pl.* tiempo, *m.*; vida, *f.*; **thirty days' sight,** treinta días vista o fecha.

daybook, *n.* libro diario.

daybreak, *n.* alba, *f.*

daydream, *n.* ilusión, fantasía, *f.*; ensueño, *m.*; quimera, *f.*; castillos en el aire; —, *vi.* soñar despierto, hacerse ilusiones.

daylight, *n.* día, *m.*, luz del día, luz natural; — **saving time,** hora adelantada para utilizar la luz del día y ahorrar fuerza eléctrica.

dayspring, *n.* alba, *f.*

daystar, *n.* lucero del alba; (poet.) el sol.

daytime, *n.* tiempo del día.

daze, *vt.* deslumbrar, ofuscar con luz demasiado viva.

dazed, *adj.* aturdido, ofuscado.

dazzle, daze, *vt.* deslumbrar, ofuscar.

D.C. District of Columbia, D.C. Distrito de Columbia, E.U.A.

d.c. direct current, C.D. corriente directa; C.C. corriente continua.

D.C.L. Doctor of Civil Law, Doctor en Derecho Civil.

D.D. Doctor of Divinity, Doctor en Teología.

D.D.S. Doctor of Dental Surgery, Doctor en Cirugía Dental.

deacon, *n.* diácono, *m.*

deaconess, *n.* diaconisa, *f.*

dead, *adj.* muerto, flojo, entorpecido; vacío; inútil; triste; apagado, sin espíritu; despoblado; evaporado; marchito; finado; devuelta (hablando de cartas) ; **— bargain,** precio muy bajo; **— center,** punto muerto; **— end,** extremo de calle que no tiene salida; **— heat,** corrida indecisa; **— letter,** carta no reclamada; **— load,** carga fija o permanente; **— silence,** silencio profundo; **— water,** agua tranquila; **— weight,** carga onerosa; peso propio de una máquina o vehículo; **the —,** los finados, los muertos; **— certainty,** seguridad completa; **— reckoning,** estima, *f.*, derrotero estimado.

deaden, *vt.* amortecer.

dead-end, *adj.* tapado, sin salida.

deadhead, *n.* persona que asiste a teatros con entrada gratis o que viaja con pase; gorrón, ona.

deadline, *n.* fecha fijada para la realización de una cosa, como la fecha de tirada de una revista, periódico, etc.

deadlock, *n.* estancamiento, *m.*, estancación, *f.*; paro, *m.*; interrupción, *f.*; desacuerdo, *m.*

deadly, *adj.* mortal; terrible, implacable; **—,** *adv.* mortalmente.

deadwood, *n.* leña seca; material inútil.

deaf, *adj.* sordo; **— ears,** orejas de mercader; **to fall on — ears,** caer en saco roto.

deafen, *vt.* ensordecer.

deaf-mute, *n.* sordomudo, da.

deafness, *n.* sordera, *f.*; desinclinación a oír.

deal, *n.* negocio, convenio, *m.*; partida, porción, parte, *f.*; (com.) trato, *m.*; negociación, *f.*; (cards) mano (en el juego de naipes), *f.*; **to arrange a —,** cerrar una operación, **—,** *vt.* distribuir; traficar; **to — in,** comerciar en; **to — with,** tratar de.

dealer, *n.* mercader, traficante, *m.*; el que da las cartas en el juego de naipes.

dealing, *n.* conducta, *f.*; trato, *m.*; tráfico,

comercio, *m.*; **—s,** *n.pl.* transacciones, *f.pl.*; relaciones, *f.pl.*

dean, *n.* deán, decano, *m.*

dear, *adj.* predilecto, amado; caro, costoso; querido; **—ly,** *adv.* caramente, tiernamente.

dearth, *n.* carestía, *f.*; hambre, *f.*; **— of news,** escasez de noticias.

death, *n.* muerte, *f.*; (poet.) parca, *f.*; óbito, *m.*; **— penalty,** pena de muerte, pena capital; **— rate,** mortalidad, *f.*; **— warrant,** sentencia de muerte.

deathbed, *n.* lecho de muerte.

deathblow, *n.* golpe mortal.

deathless, *adj.* inmortal, imperecedero.

deathlike, *adj.* cadavérico, inmóvil.

deathly, *adj.* cadavérico; mortal.

deathtrap, *n.* lugar inseguro y peligroso.

deathwatch, *n.* guardia de un reo en capilla.

debacle, *n.* caída, ruina, *f.*

debar, *vt.* excluir, no admitir.

debark, *vt.* and *vi.* desembarcar.

debarkation, *n.* desembarco, *m.*

debase, *vt.* humillar, envilecer; rebajar, deteriorar.

debasement, *n.* rebajamiento, *m.*; envilecimiento, *m.*

debatable, *adj.* disputable, discutible.

debate, *n.* debate, *m.*; riña, disputa, *f.*; **—,** *vt.* discutir; ponderar; **—,** *vi.* deliberar; disputar.

debater, *n.* controversista, polemista, *m.* y *f.*

debauch, *n.* vida disoluta; exceso, libertinaje, *m.*; **—,** *vt.* depravar; corromper; **—,** *vi.* depravarse.

debauchee, *n.* hombre libertino y licencioso.

debauchery, *n.* orgía, *f.*; libertinaje, *m.*

debenture, *n.* vale, *m.*; (com.) obligación, *f.*

debilitate, *vt.* debilitar, enervar.

debility, *n.* debilidad, languidez, *f.*; (med.) adinamia, *f.*

debit, *n.* debe, cargo, *m.*; **— balance,** saldo deudor; **—,** *vt.* (com.) adeudar, cargar en una cuenta, debitar.

debonair, *adj.* afable y cortés; alegre y agraciado.

debouch, *vi.* (mil.) desfilar; surgir, brotar.

debris, *n.* despojos, escombros, *m. pl.*; derribo, *m.*

debt, *n.* deuda, *f.*; débito, *m.*; obligación, *f.*; **bad —,** trampa, *f.*, deuda cuyo pago se demora; **external —,** deuda exterior; **floating —,** deuda flotante; **funded —,** deuda consolidada; **public —,** deuda pública; **to run into —,** adeudar, adeudarse.

debtor, *n.* deudor, ra.

debut, *n.* estreno, debut, *m.*; **to make one's —,** debutar.

debutante, *n.* debutante, *f.*, señorita presentada por primera vez en sociedad.

Dec. December, dic.e, dic. diciembre.

dec.: deceased, M., m. murió o muerto; **decimeter,** dm. decímetro.

decade, *n.* década, *f.*

decadence, n. decadencia, f.
decadent, adj. decadente.
decagon, n. decágono, m.
decagram, m. decagramo, m.
decahedron, n. decaedro, m.
Decalogue, n. Decálogo, m.
decameter, n. decámetro, m.
decamp, vi. (mil.) decampar, levantar el campo; escaparse.
decampment, n. (mil.) levantamiento de un campamento.
decant, vt. decantar, trasegar.
decanter, n. garrafa, ampolla, f., frasco, m., vasija de cristal.
decapitate, vt. decapitar, degollar.
decapitation, n. decapitación, f.
decarbonize, vt. descarbonizar; descarburar.
decay, vi. decaer, descaecer, declinar; degenerar; venir a menos; **to become —ed,** (dent.) cariarse; **—,** n. descaecimiento, m.; decadencia, declinación, diminución, f.; (dent.) caries, f.
decease, n. muerte, f.; **—,** vi. morir.
deceased, adj. muerto, difunto; **—,** n. finado, da, fallecido, da, muerto, ta, difunto, ta.
deceit, n. engaño, fraude, m.; impostura, f.; zancadilla, f.; (coll.) trápala, f.
deceitful, adj. fraudulento, engañoso; falaz; **—ly,** adv. fraudulentamente, falsamente.
deceive, vt. engañar, defraudar, embaucar.
deceiving, adj. delusorio, engañoso.
December, n. diciembre, m.
decency, n. decencia, f.; modestia, f.
decennial, adj. decenal.
decent, adj. decente, razonable; propio, conveniente; **—ly,** adv. decentemente.
decentralization, n. descentralización, f.
deception, n. decepción, impostura, f.; engaño, m.; trapisonda, f.
deceptive, adj. falso, engañoso.
decide, vt. and vi. decidir, determinar, resolver, juzgar; decretar.
decidedly, adv. determinadamente; decididamente, terminantemente.
deciduous, adj. caedizo; temporáneo.
decigram, n. decigramo, m.
deciliter, n. decilitro, m.
decimal, adj. decimal; **— point,** punto decimal, m.; **— fraction,** fracción decimal.
decimate, vt. diezmar.
decimation, n. diezmo, m.; gran mortandad.
decimeter, n. decímetro, m.
decipher, vt. descifrar.
decision, n. decisión, determinación, resolución, f.
decisive, adj. decisivo, terminante; **—ly,** adv. decisivamente.
deck, n. (naut.) bordo, m., cubierta, f.; baraja de naipes; **— bridge,** puente de tablero; **— chair,** silla de cubierta; **— hand,** marinero, estibador, m.; **partial —,** (naut.) tilla, f.; **—,** vt. adornar.
declaim, vi. declamar, perorar.
declamation, n. declamación, arenga, f.

declamatory, adj. declamatorio.
declaration, n. declaración, manifestación, f.; explicación, f.
declaratory, adj. testificativo.
declare, vt. declarar, manifestar.
declension, n. (gram.) declinación, f.; declive, m.; inclinación, f.
declination, n. declinación, f.; decremento, m.; desviación, f.
decline, vt. (gram.) declinar; rehusar; **—,** vi. decaer, desmejorar, venir a menos; inclinarse; **—,** n. declinación, f.; decadencia, f.; declive, m.; consunción, f.; ocaso, m.
declivity, n. declividad, f., declive, m.; pendiente (de algún terreno), f.
decoction, n. decocción, f.; (med.) cocimiento, m.
decode, vt. descifrar (un cable, un escrito, etc.).
décolleté, adj. escotado.
decompose, vt. descomponer; **—,** vi. pudrirse, descomponerse.
decomposition, n. descomposición, f.
decontaminate, vt. desintoxicar, especialmente tratándose de gases venenosos.
decontamination, n. desintoxicación, f.
decorate, vt. decorar, adornar; condecorar.
decoration, n. decoración, f.; decorado, m.
decorative, adj. decorativo.
decorator, n. adornista, m. y f., decorador, ra.
decorous, adj. decente, decoroso; **—ly,** adv. decorosamente.
decorum, n. decoro, garbo, m.; decencia, f.; conveniencia, f.; pudor, m.
decoy, vt. atraer (algún pájaro); embaucar, engañar; **—,** n. seducción, f.; cazadero con señuelo; reclamo, m.; lazo, ardid, m.
decrease, vt. disminuir, reducir, minorar; **—,** vi. menguar; **—,** n. decremento, m., diminución, f.
decree, n. decreto, edicto, m.; **—,** vt. decretar, ordenar.
decrement, n. decremento, m., diminución, f.
decrepit, adj. decrépito.
decrepitude, n. decrepitud, f.
decry, vt. desacreditar, censurar públicamente, difamar.
dedicate, vt. dedicar; consagrar.
dedication, n. dedicación, f.; dedicatoria, f.
dedicatory, adj. dedicatorio.
deduce, vt. deducir; derivar; inferir.
deducible, adj. deducible.
deduct, vt. deducir, sustraer.
deduction, n. deducción, rebaja, f.; descuento, m.
deed, n. acción, f.; hecho, m.; hazaña, f.; instrumento auténtico; (com.) escritura, f.
deem, vt. juzgar, pensar, estimar.
deep, adj. profundo; sagaz; grave; oscuro; taciturno; subido (aplícase al color); intenso; **the —,** n. el piélago, la mar; **—ly,** adv. profundamente; astutamente; intensamente, vivamente; oscuramente.

deepen, *vt.* profundizar; oscurecer; intensificar.

deep-rooted, *adj.* bien arraigado.

deep-sea fishing, *n.* pesca en mar adentro.

deep-seated, *adj.* arraigado, afirmado, profundo.

deep-set, *adj.* hundido, arraigado.

deer, *n. sing.* and *pl.* ciervo(s), venado(s), *m.*

deerhound, *n.* galgo que caza venados.

deerskin, *n.* gamuza, *f.*

def.: definite, defin. definitivo; **definition,** def. definición.

deface, *vt.* borrar, destruir; desfigurar, afear.

defacement, *n.* desfiguración, mutilación, *f.*

de facto, de hecho, actual.

defalcate, *vi.* desfalcar.

defalcation, *n.* desfalco, *m.*

defamation, *n.* difamación, calumnia, *f.*

defamatory, *adj.* calumnioso, difamatorio.

defame, *vt.* difamar; calumniar.

default, *n.* delito de omisión; morosidad en el pago de cuentas; defecto, *m.*, falta, *f.*; **to lose by —,** (deportes) perder por no presentación del participante; **—,** *vt.* and *vi.* faltar, delinquir.

defaulter, *n.* (law) contumaz, *m.*, desfalcador, ra; delincuente, *m.* y *f.*

defeat, *n.* derrota, *f.*; vencimiento, *m.*; **—,** *vt.* derrotar; frustrar.

defeatism, *n.* admisión de derrota de su país, causa o partido, de antemano.

defeatist, *n.* persona que admite la derrota de antemano.

defecate, *vt.* and *vi.* defecar, hacer del cuerpo, obrar.

defecation, *n.* depuración, defecación, *f.*

defect, *n.* defecto, *m.*; falta, *f.*

defection, *n.* defección, *f.*; fracaso, malogro, *m.*

defective, *adj.* defectivo, imperfecto.

defend, *vt.* defender; proteger.

defendant, *adj.* defensivo; **—,** *n.* (law) demandado, da, acusado, da.

defender, *n.* defensor, abogado, *m.*

defense, *n.* defensa, *f.*; protección, *f.*; amparo, apoyo, sostén, *m.*

defenseless, *adj.* indefenso; impotente.

defensible, *adj.* defensible.

defensive, *adj.* defensivo; **—ly,** *adv.* de un modo defensivo; **—,** *n.* defensiva, *f.*

defer, *vt.* diferir, retardar; posponer; postergar; **—,** *vi.* deferir.

deference, *n.* deferencia, *f.*; respeto, *m.*; consideración, *f.*; **in — to,** por consideración a.

deferential, *adj.* respetuoso.

defiance, *n.* desafío, *m.*; **in — of,** a despecho de.

defiant, *adj.* atrevido; porfiado.

deficiency, *n.* defecto, *m.*; imperfección, *f.*; falta, *f.*; insolvencia, *f.*; deficiencia, *f.*

deficient, *adj.* deficiente, pobre.

deficit, *n.* déficit, descubierto, *m.*

defile, *n.* desfiladero, *m.*; **—,** *vt.* corromper;

deshonrar; ensuciar; **—,** *vi.* desfilar.

defilement, *n.* contaminación, corrupción, *f.*

definable, *adj.* definible; determinable.

define, *vt.* definir; limitar; determinar.

definite, *adj.* definido, exacto, preciso, limitado; cierto; concreto.

definition, *n.* definición, *f.*

definitive, *adj.* definitivo; **—ly,** *adv.* definitivamente.

deflate, *vt.* desinflar; **—ed tire,** neumático desinflado, llanta desinflada.

deflation, *n.* desinflación, *f.*

deflect, *vi.* desviarse; ladearse.

deflection, *n.* desvío, rodeo, *m.*

deflector, *n.* deflector, *m.*

deflower, *vt.* desflorar, estuprar.

defoliation, *n.* caída de las hojas.

deforest, *vt.* desboscar.

deforestation, *n.* desboscamiento, *m.*

deform, *vt.* deformar, desfigurar.

deformation, *n.* deformación, desfiguración, *f.*

deformed, *adj.* deformado, desfigurado.

deformity, *n.* deformidad, *f.*

defraud, *vt.* defraudar; frustrar.

defray, *vt.* costear; sufragar; subvenir.

defrayment, *n.* dispendio, gasto, *m.*

defrost, *vt.* descongelar, deshelar.

defroster, *n.* aparato para evitar que se forme hielo, o para destruirlo, especialmente destinado a parabrisas de automóvil.

deft, *adj.* despierto, despejado, diestro; **—ly,** *adv.* con ingenio y viveza.

defunct, *adj.* difunto, muerto; **—,** *n.* difunto, ta.

defy, *vt.* desafiar, retar; despreciar; desdeñar.

deg. degree, gr. grado.

degeneracy, *n.* degeneración, bajeza, depravación, *f.*

degenerate, *vi.* degenerar; **—,** *adj.* degenerado.

degeneration, *n.* degeneración, *f.*

degenerative, *adj.* capaz de degeneración.

degradation, *n.* degradación, *f.*; degeneración, *f.*

degrade, *vt.* degradar; deshonrar, envilecer.

degree, *n.* grado, *m.*; rango, *m.*; condición, *f.*; **by —s,** gradualmente.

dehydrate, *vt.* deshidratar.

dehydrator, *n.* deshidratar, *m.*

de-ice, *vt.* descongelar.

deification, *n.* deificación, *f.*; apoteosis, *f.*

deify, *vt.* deificar; divinizar.

deign, *vi.* dignarse; condescender.

deism, *n.* deísmo, *m.*

deist, *n.* deísta, *m.* y *f.*

deity, *n.* deidad, divinidad, *f.*

deject, *vt.* abatir, desanimar.

dejected, *adj.* abatido; **—ly,** *adv.* abatidamente.

dejection, *n.* decaimiento, *m.*; tristeza, aflicción, *f.*; (med.) evacuación, *f.*

del.: delegate, delegado; **delete,** suprímase.

delay, *vt.* diferir; retardar; postergar; —, *vi.* demorar; —, *n.* dilación, *f.*; retardo, *m.*; retraso, *m.*; **cause of** —, rémora, *f.*

delectable, *adj.* deleitoso, deleitable; —**bly,** *adv.* deleitosamente; con gusto.

delectation, *n.* deleite, encanto, *m.*

delegate, *vt.* delegar, diputar; —, *n.* delegado, da, diputado, da.

delegation, *n.* delegación, diputación, comisión, *f.*

delete, *vt.* suprimir.

deleterious, *adj.* deletéreo.

deletion, *n.* cancelación, supresión, *f.*

delf, delft, *n.* loza vidriada.

deliberate, *vt.* deliberar, considerar; —, *adj.* cauto; avisado, pensado, premeditado; —**ly,** *adv.* deliberadamente, con premeditación.

deliberation, *n.* deliberación, circunspección, *f.*; reflexión, *f.*; consulta, *f.*

deliberative, *adj.* deliberativo.

delicacy, *n.* delicadeza, *f.*; fragilidad, *f.*; escrupulosidad, *f.*; manjar, *m.*

delicate, *adj.* delicado; exquisito; tierno; escrupuloso; —**ly,** *adv.* delicadamente.

delicatessen, *n.* tienda donde se venden fiambres, pescado ahumado, queso, etc.

delicious, *adj.* delicioso; sabroso, exquisito; —**ly,** *adv.* deliciosamente.

delight, *n.* delicia, *f.*; deleite, *m.*; placer, gozo, encanto, *m.*; —, *vt.* deleitar; regocijar; —, *vi.* deleitarse; **to take — in,** tener gusto en, estar encantado de.

delighted, *adj.* complacido, gozoso.

delightful, *adj.* delicioso; deleitable; —**ly,** *adv.* deliciosamente.

delightfulness, *n.* delicia, *f.*, encanto, *m.*

delimitation, *n.* amojonamiento, *m.*

delineament, *n.* delineamiento, *m.*

delineate, *vt.* delinear, diseñar.

delineation, *n.* delineación, *f.*; delineamiento, *m.*

delineator, *n.* delineador, descriptor, *m.*

delinquency, *n.* delito, *m.*; culpa, *f.*; delincuencia, *f.*

delinquent, *n.* delincuente, *m.* y *f.*

delirious, *adj.* delirante, desvariado; **to be** —, delirar.

delirium, *n.* delirio, *m.*; **— tremens,** delírium tremens.

deliver, *vt.* entregar; dar; rendir; libertar; recitar, relatar; partear.

deliverance, *n.* libramiento, *m.*; liberación, *f.*; salvación, *f.*

delivery, *n.* entrega, *f.*; liberación, *f.*; parto, *m.*; **— order,** nota de entrega; **general** —, lista de correos, entrega general.

dell, *n.* valle hondo; hondonada, cañada, *f.*

delouse, *vt.* despiojar.

delphinium, *n.* (bot.) espuela de caballero.

delta, *n.* delta, *f.*; pequeña isla triangular; cuarta letra del alfabeto griego.

deltoid, *adj.* deltoide.

delude, *vt.* engañar, alucinar.

deluge, *n.* inundación, *f.*; diluvio, *m.*; —, *vt.* inundar.

delusion, *n.* engaño, *m.*; ilusión, *f.*

delusive, *adj.* engañoso, falaz.

de luxe, *adj.* lujoso, ostentoso.

delve, *vt.* cavar; penetrar; sondear en busca de información.

Dem. Democrat, demócrata.

demagnetize, *vt.* desimanar, desimantar.

demagogue, *n.* demagogo, *m.*

demagogy, *n.* demagogia, *f.*

demand, *n.* demanda, *f.*; petición jurídica (de una deuda), *f.*; venta continuada, *f.*; **(for merchandise),** consumo (de mercancías), *m.*; —, *vt.* demandar, reclamar, pedir, requerir, exigir.

demarcate, *vt.* amojonar, demarcar.

demarcation, *n.* demarcación, *f.*; límite, *m.*

demean, *vt.* degradar, envilecer; —, *vi.* comportarse.

demeanor, *n.* porte, *m.*; conducta, *f.*; comportamiento, *m.*; **proper** —, corrección, *f.*

demented, *adj.* demente, loco.

dementia praecox, *n.* demencia precoz.

demerit, *vt.* desmerecer.

demesne, *n.* heredad, *f.*; tierra solariega, dominio, *m.*

demigod, *n.* semidiós, *m.*

demijohn, *n.* garrafón, *m.*

demilitarize, *vt.* desmilitarizar.

demimonde, *n.* clase de personas de reputación equívoca.

demise, *vt.* legar, dejar en testamento; ceder, arrendar; —, *n.* muerte, *f.*; óbito, *m.*; trasmisión de la corona por abdicación o muerte.

demisemiquaver, *n.* (mus.) fusa, *f.*

demitasse, *n.* taza pequeña (de café).

demobilize, *vt.* desmovilizar.

democracy, *n.* democracia, *f.*

democrat, *n.* demócrata, *m.* y *f.*

democratic, democratical, *adj.* democrático, demócrata.

democratize, *vt.* democratizar.

demolish, *vt.* demoler, arruinar; arrasar; batir.

demolition, *n.* demolición, *f.*; derribo, *m.*; **— squad,** cuadrilla de demolición; **— bomb,** bomba de demolición.

demon, *n.* demonio, diablo, *m.*

demonetize, *vt.* desmonetizar.

demoniac, *adj.* demoníaco; endemoniado; —, *n.* energúmeno, na.

demoniacal, *adj.* demoníaco.

demonology, *n.* demonología, *f.*

demonstrable, *adj.* demostrable; —**bly,** *adv.* demostrablemente, ostensiblemente.

demonstrate, *vt.* demostrar, probar.

demonstration, *n.* demostración, *f.*; manifestación, *f.*

demonstrative, *adj.* demostrativo; expresivo; —**ly,** *adv.* demostrativamente.

demonstrator, *n.* desmostrador, ra.

demoralization, *n.* desmoralización, *f.*

demoralize, *vt.* desmoralizar.

demote, *vt.* rebajar en clase o en grado.

demotion, *n.* (mil.) degradación, *f.*; descenso de rango, categoría o empleo.

demount, *vt.* desmontar.

demountable, *adj.* desmontable; desarmable.

demur, *vi.* objetar; demorar; vacilar, fluctuar; —, *n.* demora, *f.*; objeción, *f.*

demure, *adj.* reservado; decoroso; grave, serio; **—ly,** *adv.* modestamente.

demurrage, *n.* sobrestadía, *f.*; demora, *f.*

demurrer, *n.* (law) demora, prórroga, *f.*

den, *n.* caverna, *f.*; antro, *m.*; cuarto de lectura o de estudio.

Den. Denmark, Dinamarca.

denationalize, *vt.* privar de carácter o derecho nacional.

denaturalize, *vt.* desnaturalizar.

denature, *vt.* desnaturalizar; **—d alcohol,** alcohol desnaturalizado.

deniable, *adj.* negable.

denial, *n.* denegación, repulsa, *f.*

denim, *n.* mezclilla, *f.*, tela de algodón basta y fuerte.

denizen, *n.* ciudadano, habitante, *m.*; extranjero naturalizado; extranjero residente en un país; —, *vt.* naturalizar.

Denmark, Dinamarca, *f.*

denominate, *vt.* denominar, nombrar.

denomination, *n.* denominación, *f.*; título, nombre, apelativo, *m.*

denominational, *adj.* sectario.

denominator, *n.* (math.) denominador, *m.*

denotation, *n.* denotación, *f.*

denote, *vt.* denotar, indicar.

denouement, *n.* solución, *f.*

denounce, *vt.* denunciar; promulgar; declarar.

dense, *adj.* denso, espeso; cerrado, estúpido; impenetrable.

densimeter, *n.* densímetro, *m.*

density, *n.* densidad, solidez, *f.*

dent, *n.* abolladura, *f.*; mella, *f.*; —, *vt.* abollar.

dental, *adj.* dental; **— clinic,** clínica dental; —, *n.* letra dental.

dentifrice, *adj.* dentífrico; —, *n.* dentífrico, *m.*

dentine, *n.* marfil de los dientes.

dentist, *n.* dentista, *m.*; (coll.) sacamuelas, *m.*

dentistry, *n.* dentistería, *f.*; cirugía dental.

dentition, *n.* dentición, *f.*; dentadura, *f.*

denture, *n.* dentadura, *f.*, dentadura postiza.

denudation, *n.* despojo de ropa, denudación, *f.*

denude, *vt.* desnudar, despojar.

denunciation, *n.* denunciación, *f.*; publicación, *f.*

denunciatory, *adj.* denunciatorio.

deny, *vt.* negar, rehusar; renunciar; abjurar.

deodorant, *adj.* desodorante; —, *n.* desodorante, *m.*, preparación que destruye los olores.

deodorize, *vt.* desinficionar; sahumar.

deodorizer, *n.* substancia para evitar los malos olores.

deoxidize, *vt.* desoxidar.

dep. deputy, diputado; agte. agente.

depart, *vi.* partir; irse, salir; morir; desistir.

department, *n.* departamento, *m.*; distrito, *m.*; **— store,** bazar, *m.*; almacén o tienda grande dividida en secciones o departamentos.

departmental, *adj.* departamental.

departure, *n.* partida, salida, *f.*; desviación, *f.*

depend, *vi.* depender; **it —s,** según y como; **to — on, to — upon,** confiar en, contar con.

dependable, *adj.* digno de confianza.

dependence, *n.* dependencia, confianza, *f.*

dependency, *n.* dependencia, *f.*; **foreign —,** colonia, *f.*

dependent, *n.* dependiente, *m.*; persona que depende de otra persona para su manutención; —, *adj.* dependiente, cifrado; **— upon,** cifrado en.

depict, *vt.* pintar, retratar; describir.

depiction, *n.* descripción, pintura, *f.*

depilatory, *adj.* depilatorio; —, *n.* depilatorio, *m.*

deplete, *vt.* agotar, vaciar.

depletion, *n.* (med.) depleción, *f.*; agotamiento, *m.*

deplorable, *adj.* deplorable, lamentable; **—bly,** *adv.* deplorablemente.

deplore, *vt.* deplorar, lamentar.

deploy, *vt.* (mil.) desplegar.

deployment, *n.* (mil.) despliegue, *m.*

depolarize, *vt.* despolarizar.

deponent, *n.* (gram.) verbo deponente; (law) testigo, *m.*

depopulate, *vt.* despoblar, devastar.

depopulation, *n.* despoblación, *f.*; devastación, *f.*

deport, *vt.* deportar.

deportation, *n.* deportación, *f.*; destierro, *m.*

deportment, *n.* conducta, *f.*; porte, manejo, *m.*

depose, *vt.* deponer; destronar; testificar; **to — upon oath,** declarar.

deposit, *vt.* depositar; —, *n.* depósito, *m.*

deposition, *n.* deposición, *f.*, testimonio, *m.*; destitución, *f.*

depositor, *n.* depositante, *m.* y *f.*

depository, *n.* depositario, ria; almacén, *m.*

depot, *n.* depósito, almacén, *m.*; (rail.) estación, *f.*, paradero, *m.*

deprave, *vt.* depravar, corromper.

depraved, *adj.* depravado.

depravity, *n.* depravación, *f.*

deprecate, *vt.* suplicar con instancia, deprecar.

deprecation, *n.* deprecación, *f.*, súplica para conjurar los males.

deprecatory, *adj.* deprecativo, suplicante.

depreciate, *vt.* rebajar el precio; despreciar, deprimir.

depreciation, *n.* descrédito, *m.*; desestimación, *f.*; depreciación, *f.*

depredation, *n.* depredación, *f.*; pillaje, *m.*

depress, *vt.* deprimir, humillar.

depressed, *adj.* desgraciado, deprimido; — **(in spirit),** descorazonado.

depression, *n.* depresión, *f.*; abatimiento, *m.*

deprivation, *n.* privación, pérdida, *f.*

deprive, *vt.* privar, despojar.

dept. department, dep., depto. departamento.

depth, *n.* hondura, profundidad, *f.*; abismo, *m.*; (fig.) seriedad, *f.*; oscuridad, *f.*; — **bomb,** bomba de profundidad; — **charge,** carga de profundidad; — **of water,** (naut.) braceaje, *m.*; — **charge,** bomba explosiva de profundidad.

deputation, *n.* diputación, *f.*; delegación, *f.*

depute, *vt.* diputar, delegar.

deputy, *n.* diputado, delegado; lugarteniente, *m.*; comisario, *m.*

der.: derivation, deriv. derivación; **derived,** deriv. derivado.

derail, *vt.* descarrilar.

derailment, *n.* descarrilamiento, *m.*

derange, *vt.* desarreglar, desordenar; trastornar, volver loco.

deranged, *adj.* descompuesto, trastornado, enloquecido.

derangement, *n.* desarreglo, desorden, *m.*

derby, *n.* sombrero hongo; (coll.) bombín, *m.*

derelict, *adj.* abandonado; infiel; descuidado; —, *n.* (naut.) derrelicto, *m.*; buque abandonado en alta mar; paria, *m.* y *f.*

dereliction, *n.* desamparo, abandono, *m.*; (law) dejación de bienes.

deride, *vt.* burlar, mofar.

derision, *n.* irrisión, mofa, *f.*; escarnio, *m.*; burla, chulada, *f.*

derisive, *adj.* irrisorio.

derivation, *n.* derivación, *f.*

derivative, *n.* (gram.) derivado, *m.*

derive, *vt.* derivar; proceder; —, *vi.* derivarse.

dermatologist, *n.* dermatólogo, *m.*

dermatology, *n.* dermatología, *f.*

dermis, *n.* (anat.) dermis, *f.*, cutis, *m.*

derogate, *vi.* detraer, sustraer.

derogation, *n.* detracción, *f.*

derogatory, *adj.* derogatorio.

derrick, *n.* grúa, *f.*; pescante, *m.*

dervish, *n.* derviche, *m.*; santón, *m.*

descant, *vi.* discantar; discurrir; —, *n.* (mus.) discante, *m.*

descend, *vi.* descender.

descendant, *n.* vástago, *m.*, descendiente, *m.* y *f.*

descendent, *adj.* descendiente.

descent, *n.* descenso, *m.*; pendiente, *f.*; invasión, *f.*; descendencia, posteridad, *f.*

describable, *adj.* descriptible.

describe, *vt.* describir, delinear; calificar; explicar.

description, *n.* descripción, *f.*; **brief** —, reseña, *f.*

descriptive, *adj.* descriptivo.

descry, *vt.* espiar; observar; descubrir.

desecrate, *vt.* profanar.

desecration, *n.* profanación, *f.*

desensitize, *vt.* insensibilizar; hacer insensible a la luz.

desert, *n.* desierto, *m.*; región desierta; mérito, *m.*; merecimiento, *m.*; —, *vt.* abandonar; —, *vi.* (mil.) desertar.

deserter, *n.* desertor, trásfuga, *m.*

desertion, *n.* deserción, *f.*

deserve, *vt.* merecer; ser digno.

deservedly, *adv.* merecidamente, dignamente.

deserving, *adj.* meritorio; **to be** —, valer, merecer.

deshabille, *n.* desabillé, *m.*; paños menores.

desiccate, *vt.* desecar.

desiccation, *n.* desecación, *f.*

desideratum, *n.* desiderátum, *m.*, cualquier cosa que se desee por ser necesaria.

design, *vt.* designar, proyectar; tramar; diseñar; —, *n.* designio, intento, *m.*; empresa, *f.*; diseño, plan, *m.*

designate, *vt.* apuntar, señalar; distinguir.

designation, *n.* designación, *f.*

designedly, *adv.* de propósito, de intento.

designer, *n.* dibujante, proyectista, *m.* y *f.*; intrigante, *m.* y *f.*

designing, *adj.* insidioso, astuto.

desirability, *n.* ansia, *f.*; conveniencia, *f.*

desirable, *adj.* deseable.

desire, *n.* deseo, *m.*; apetencia, *f.*; —, *vt.* desear, apetecer, querer, pedir.

desirous, *adj.* deseoso, ansioso; —**ly,** *adv.* ansiosamente.

desist, *vi.* desistir.

desk, *n.* escritorio, *m.*; papelera, *f.*; pupitre, *m.*; bufete, *m.*

desolate, *vt.* desolar; devastar; —, *adj.* desolado; solitario.

desolation, *n.* desolación, ruina, destrucción, *f.*

despair, *n.* desesperación, *f.*; —, *vi.* desesperar.

despairing, *adj.* desesperado, sin esperanza.

desperado, *n.* criminal atrevido, malhechor, *m.*

desperate, *adj.* desesperado; furioso; —**ly,** *adv.* desesperadamente, furiosamente.

desperation, *n.* desesperación, *f.*

despicable, *adj.* despreciable, bajo; — **act,** canallada, *f.*; —**bly,** *adv.* despreciablemente.

despise, *vt.* despreciar; desdeñar.

despite, *n.* despecho, *m.*; despique, *m.*; malicia, *f.*; —, *prep.* a despecho de.

despoil, *vt.* despojar; privar.

despoiler, *n.* saqueador, robador, *m.*

despond, *vi.* desanimarse, abatirse; desesperar.

despondency, *n.* desesperación, *f.*; abatimiento, *m.*

despondent, *adj.* abatido, desalentado, desesperado, desanimado.

despot, *n.* déspota, *m.* y *f.*

despotic, despotical, *adj.* despótico. abso luto, arbitrario; **despotically,** *adv.* despóticamente.

despotism, *n.* despotismo, *m.*

dessert, *n.* postre, *m.*

destination, *n.* destinación, *f.*; destino, *m.*; paradero, *m.*

destine, *vt.* destinar, dedicar.

destined, *adj.* destinado, dedicado.

destiny, *n.* destino, hado, sino, *m.*; suerte, *f*

destitute, *adj.* carente; en extrema necesidad.

destitution, *n.* destitución, privación, *f.*; abandono, *m.*

destroy, *vt.* destruir, arruinar; hacer pedazos.

destroyer, *n.* cazatorpedero, *m.*

destructible, *adj.* destructible.

destruction, *n.* destrucción, ruina, *f.*

destructive, *adj.* destructivo, ruinoso; **—ly,** *adv.* destructivamente.

desuetude, *n.* desuso, *m.*

desultory, *adj.* irregular, inconstante, sin método.

detach, *vt.* separar, desprender; (mil.) destacar.

detachment, *n.* (mil.) destacamento, *m.*

detail, *n.* detalle, *m.*; particularidad, *f.*; circunstancia, *f.*; (mil.) destacamento, *m.*; **in —,** al por menor; detalladamente; **to go into —,** menudear; **—,** *vt.* detallar; referir con pormenores.

detain, *vt.* retener, detener; impedir.

detect, *vt.* descubrir; discernir.

detectible, *adj.* que puede averiguarse o descubrirse.

detection, *n.* descubrimiento, *m.*; revelación, *f.*

detective, *n.* oficial de policía secreta, detective, *m.*

detector, *n.* descubridor, ra; detector, ra; indicador, *m.*

detention, *n.* detención, retención, *f.*; cautividad, *f.*; cautiverio, *m.*

deter, *vt.* desanimar; disuadir.

detergent, *adj.* detergente; **—,** *n.* (med.) detersorio, *m.*

deteriorate, *vt.* deteriorar.

deterioration, *n.* deterioración, *f.*, deterioro, *m.*

determent, *n.* disuasión, detención, *f.*

determinable, *adj.* determinable.

determinant, *n.* factor determinante.

determinate, *adj.* determinado, decidido; definido; **—ly,** *adv.* determinadamente.

determination, *n.* determinación, *f.*; decisión, resolución, *f.*

determine, *vt.* determinar, decidir; **—,** *vi.* decidir, resolver; **to be —d,** proponerse.

determinism, *n.* determinismo, *m.*

deterrent, *adj.* disuasivo, desanimador; **—,** *n.* lo que desanima o disuade.

detest, *vt.* detestar, aborrecer.

detestable, *adj.* detestable, abominable; **—bly,** *adv.* detestablemente.

detestation, *n.* detestación, *f.*; aborrecimiento, *m.*

dethrone, *vt.* destronar.

dethronement, *n.* destronamiento, *m.*

detonate, *vi.* detonar.

detonation, *n.* detonación, *f.*

detonator, *n.* detonador, *m.*; cápsula fulminante.

detour, *n.* rodeo, *m.*; desvío, *m.*; desviación, *f.*; vuelta, *f.*

detract, *vt.* detractar, retirar; disminuir; **—,** *vi.* denigrar.

detraction, *n.* detracción, *f.*; denigración, *f.*

detractor, *n.* infamador, ra.

detrain, *vi.* salir del tren; **—,** *vt.* mandar salir del tren.

detriment, *n.* detrimento, daño, perjuicio, *m.*

detrimental, *adj.* perjudicial.

detritus, *n.* (geol.) detrito, *m.*

deuce, *n.* dos (en los juegos de naipes), *m.*; diantre, *m.*; **the —!** *interj.* ¡demonio!

devaluate, *vt.* depreciar, rebajar el valor.

devaluation, *n.* desvaloración, *f.*

devastate, *vt.* devastar; robar.

devastation, *n.* devastación, ruina, *f.*

develop, *vt.* desenvolver; desarrollar; revelar (una fotografía).

developer, *n.* revelador fotográfico.

development, *n.* desarrollo, *m.*

deviate, *vi.* desviarse.

deviation, *n.* desvío, *m.*; desviación, *f.*; (naut.) deriva, *f.*

device, *n.* invento, *m.*; aparato, mecanismo, artefacto, *m.*; plan, ardid, *m.*; lema, *m.*; proyecto, *m.*; artificio, *m.*

devil, *n.* diablo, demonio, *m.*

deviled eggs, *n. pl.* huevos rellenos o con picante.

devilfish, *n.* pulpo, *m.*

devilish, *adj.* diabólico, satánico; **—ly,** *adv.* diabólicamente.

devilment, *n.* diablura, *f.*; travesura, *f.*

devilry, deviltry, *n.* diablura, *f.*; maleficio, *m.*; maldad, *f.*

devious, *adj.* desviado; tortuoso.

devise, *vt.* trazar; inventar; idear; legar; **—,** *n.* legado, *m.*, donación testamentaria.

deviser, *n.* inventor, ra.

devisor, *n.* testador, ra.

devitalize, *vt.* restar vitalidad.

devitalization, *n.* pérdida de vitalidad.

devoid, *adj.* vacío; carente.

devolve, *vt.* rodar abajo; trasmitir.

devote, *vt.* dedicar; consagrar; **— oneself,** consagrarse.

devotee, *n.* aficionado, fanático pío.

devotion, *n.* devoción, *f.*; oración, *f.*, rezo, *m.*; afición, *f.*; dedicación, *f.*

devotional, *adj.* devoto, religioso.

devour, *vt.* devorar.

devout, *adj.* devoto, piadoso; **—ly,** *adv.* devotamente.

dew, *n.* rocío, *m.*; **— point,** punto de rocío; **—,** *vt.* rociar.

dewberry, n. (bot.) zarzamora, f.
dewdrop, n. gota de rocío.
dewlap, n. papada, f.
dewy, adj. rociado.
dexterity, n. destreza, f.
dexterous, adj. diestro, **hábil;** —**ly,** adv. diestramente.
dextrin, n. dextrina, f.
dextrose, n. glucosa, dextrosa, f.
dextrous, adj. diestro, experto; —**ly,** adv. diestramente.
dg. decigram, dg. decigramo.
diabetes, n. diabetes, f.
diabetic, adj. diabético.
diabolic, diabolical, adj. diabólico; —**ally,** adv. diabólicamente.
diacritical, adj. diacrítico; — **mark,** señal diacrítica.
diadem, n. diadema, f.
diaeresis, n. diéresis, crema, f., puntos diacríticos.
diagnose, vt. diagnosticar.
diagnosis, n. (med.) diagnosis, f.
diagnostic, adj. diagnóstico; —, n. diagnóstico, m.
diagonal, n. diagonal, f.; —**ly,** adv. diagonalmente.
diagram, n. esquema, m.; diagrama, m.; gráfico, m.
dial, n. esfera de reloj; reloj de sol; cuadrante, m.; — **telephone,** teléfono automático.
dialing, n. acción de llamar por teléfono automático, sintonización, f.
dialect, n. dialecto, m.
dialectics, n. dialéctica, f.
dialogue, n. diálogo, m.
diam. diameter, diámetro.
diameter, n. diámetro, m.; **inside** — (**of firearms, pipes, etc.**), calibre (de las armas de fuego, de tubos, etc.), m.
diametrical, adj. diametral; —**ly,** adv. diametralmente.
diamond, n. diamante, m.; brillante, m.; oros (de baraja), m. pl.; rombo, rombal (en el juego de baseball), m.; — **cutter,** diamantista, m.; **very small** —, chispa, f.
diapason, n. (mus.) diapasón, m.
diaper, n. lienzo adamascado; **baby's** —, pañal, culero, m.; —, vt. matizar; adamascar; proveer con pañales.
diaphragm, n. diafragma, m.
diarrhea, n. diarrea, f.
diary, n. diario, m.
diastole, n. diástole, f.
diastolic, adj. diastólico.
diathermic, adj. diatérmico.
diathermy, n. (med.) diatermia, f.
diatom, n. (bot.) diatoma, f.
diatribe, n. diatriba, f., denunciación violenta.
dibble, vt. plantar con plantador; —, n. plantador, m.
dice, n. pl. dados, m. pl.
dichotomy, n. dicotomía, f.
dickens, n. (coll.) diablo, m.; **the** —! interj. ¡qué diablos!

dicker, vi. regatear; —, n. regateo, m.
dicky, n. camisolín, peto, m.
dicotyledonous, adj. dicotiledóneo.
dict. dictionary, dicc. diccionario.
dictaphone, n. dictáfono, m., aparato para dictar cartas.
dictate, vt. dictar; —, n. dictamen, m.
dictation, n. dictado, m.
dictator, n. caudillo, m.; dictador, m.
dictatorial, adj. autoritativo, dictatorial, dictatorio, imperioso.
dictatorship, n. dictadura, f.
diction, n. dicción, f.; estilo, m.
dictionary, n. diccionario, léxico, m.
dictograph, n. dictógrafo, m.
dictum, n. fallo, m.; sentencia, f.
did, pretérito del verbo **do.**
didactic, didactical, adj. didáctico.
diddle, vt. and vi. engañar; vacilar.
die, vi. morir, expirar; evaporarse; desvanecerse; marchitarse; caer; —, n. dado, m.; cuño, moide, troquel, m., matriz, f.
dielectric, adj. dieléctrico.
Diesel, adj. Diesel; — **engine,** motor Diesel.
diet, n. dieta, f.; régimen, m.; —, vt. alimentar; —, vi. estar a dieta.
dietary, adj. dietético; —, n. dieta medicinal; tratado sobre dietética.
dietetics, n. dietética, f.
dietician, n. dietista, m. y f.
differ, vi. diferenciarse; contradecir.
difference, n. diferencia, disparidad, f.; variante, f.
different, adj. diferente; desemejante; —**ly,** adv. diferentemente.
differential, n. diferencial, f.; — **calculus,** (math.) cálculo diferencial; — **gear,** (auto.) engranaje diferencial.
differentiate, vt. diferenciar.
differentiation, n. diferenciación, f.
difficult, adj. difícil; áspero; enrevesado; —**ly,** adv. difícilmente.
difficulty, n. dificultad, f.; obstáculo, escollo, m.; trabajo, m.; **to get out of a** —, salir de un apuro; **with** —, a duras penas, trabajosamente.
diffidence, n. timidez, modestia, f.
diffident, adj. tímido, modesto; falto de confianza en sí mismo; —**ly,** adv. tímidamente, modestamente.
diffract, vt. difractar.
diffraction, n. difracción de los rayos luminosos.
diffuse, vt. difundir, esparcir; —, adj. difundido, esparcido; prolijo; —**ly,** adv. copiosamente.
diffusion, n. difusión, prolijidad, f.; esparcimiento, m.
diffusive, adj. difusivo; prolijo.
dig, vt. cavar, ahondar, azadonar; —, n. empuje, m.; — **up,** desenterrar, desarraigar.
digest, vt. clasificar; asimilar mentalmente; digerir; —, vi. digerir; —, n. extracto, compendio, m.

digestible, *adj.* digerible.
digestion, *n.* digestión, *f.*
digestive, *adj.* digestivo.
digger, *n.* cavador, ra.
digging, *n.* excavación, *f.*; **—s,** *n. pl.* lo excavado; lavaderos de arenas auríferas; (coll.) posada, hospedería, *f.*
digit, *n.* dígito, *m.*
digitalis, *n.* (bot.) digital, dedalera, *f.*; (med.) digitalina, *f.*
dignified, *adj.* altivo; serio, grave.
dignify, *vt.* exaltar, elevar.
dignitary, *n.* dignatario, *m.*
dignity, *n.* dignidad, *f.*; rango, *m.*; mesura, *f.*
digress, *vi.* divagar.
digression, *n.* digresión, *f.*; divagación, *f.*; desvío, *m.*
digressive, *adj.* digresivo, prolijo.
dike, *n.* dique, canal, *m.*
dilapidate, *vt.* dilapidar.
dilapidated, *adj.* arruinado; desvencijado.
dilapidation, *n.* dilapidación, *f.*; ruina, *f.*
dilate, *vt.* dilatar, extender; **—,** *vi.* dilatarse, extenderse.
dilated, *adj.* dilatado, extendido; explayado, prolijo, difuso.
dilation, *n.* dilatación, *f.*
dilatory, *adj.* tardo, dilatorio.
dilemma, *n.* dilema, *m.*
dilettante, *n.* aficionado, da (de las bellas artes).
diligence, *n.* diligencia, *f.*; asiduidad, *f.*
diligent, *adj.* diligente, asiduo; aplicado, hacendoso; **—ly,** *adv.* diligentemente.
dill, *n.* (bot.) eneldo, *m.*; **— pickle,** encurtido agrio.
dillydally, *vi.* (coll.) perder el tiempo, vacilar.
dilute, *vt.* diluir.
dilution, *n.* dilución, *f.*
diluvial, *adj.* diluviano.
dim, *adj.* turbio de vista, lerdo; oscuro; **—,** *vt.* ofuscar, oscurecer; eclipsar.
dimension, *n.* dimensión, medida, extensión, *f.*
diminish, *vt.* decrecer, disminuir; **—,** *vi.* ceder; menguar, disminuirse.
diminishing, *adj.* menguante.
diminution, *n.* disminución, *f.*
diminutive, *adj.* diminutivo; **—,** *n.* diminutivo, *m.*; **—ly,** *adv.* diminutivamente.
dimity, *n.* cotonía, *f.*
dimmer (on a light), *n.* (auto.) amortiguador o reductor de intensidad de luz.
dimness, *n.* oscuridad, *f.*; opacidad, *f.*
dim-out, *n.* reducción de la intensidad de luces para protección en tiempo de guerra.
dimple, *n.* hoyuelo, *m.*
din, *n.* ruido violento, alboroto, *m.*; **—,** *vt.* atolondrar.
dine, *vt.* dar de comer o de cenar; **—,** *vi.* comer, cenar.
diner, *n.* coche comedor.
dinginess, *n.* obscuridad, suciedad, *f.*
dingle, *n.* cañada, *f.*

dingy, *adj.* sucio; empañado.
dining, *adj.* comedor; **— car,** coche comedor; **— room,** comedor, *m.*; refectorio, *m.*
dinner, *n.* comida, cena, *f.*
dinosaur, *n.* dinosauro, *m.*
dint, *n.* golpe, *m.*; **by — of,** a fuerza de, a puro.
diocese, *n.* diócesis, *f.*
diorama, *n.* diorama, *m.*
dioxide, *n.* (chem.) deutóxido, bióxido, *m.*
dip, *vt.* remojar, sumergir; **—,** *vi.* sumergirse; penetrar; **—,** *n.* (of the horizon) depresión, *f.*; (of the needle) inclinación, *f.*; plumada de tinta; inmersión, *f.*
diphtheria, *n.* difteria, *f.*
diphthong, *n.* diptongo, *m.*
diploma, *n.* diploma, *m.*
diplomacy, *n.* diplomacia, *f.*; tacto, *m.*
diplomat, diplomatist, *n.* diplomático, *m.*
diplomatic, *adj.* diplomático; **—s,** *n.* diplomacia, *f.*
dipper, *n.* cucharón, cangilón, tanque, *m.*; **D—,** Osa Mayor.
dipsomania, *n.* dipsomanía, *f.*
dipsomaniac, *n.* dipsómano, *m.*
dire, *adj.* horrendo, cruel; deplorable.
direct, *adj.* directo, derecho, recto; claro; **— current,** (elec.) corriente continua; **— hit,** blanco directo; **—,** *vt.* dirigir, enderezar; ordenar; **—ly,** *adv.* directamente, inmediatamente.
direction, *n.* dirección, *f.*; instrucción, *f.*; manejo, *m.*; rumbo, curso, *m.*
directive, *adj.* directivo, que dirige.
director, *n.* director, *m.*; guía, *m.*; superintendente, *m.*; **board of —s,** directorio, *m.*; junta directiva; **managing —,** director gerente.
directorate, *n.* cargo de director; directorio, *m.*, junta directiva.
directory, *n.* directorio, *m.*; guía, *f.*
dirge, *n.* canción lúgubre.
dirigible, *n.* (aer.) dirigible, zepelín, *m.*
dirk, *n.* especie de puñal.
dirndl, *n.* variedad de traje femenino.
dirt, *n.* suciedad, porquería, mugre, *f.*
dirt-cheap, *adj.* extremadamente barato.
dirty, *adj.* puerco, sucio; vil, bajo; **—,** *vt.* ensuciar, emporcar; **— trick,** mala partida.
disability, *n.* impotencia, *f.*; inhabilidad, incapacidad, *f.*
disable, *vt.* hacer incapaz, incapacitar; (naut.) desaparejar (un navío).
disablement, *n.* (law) impedimento, *m.*; (naut.) desaparejo de una nave como resultado de algún combate.
disabuse, *vt.* desengañar.
disaccord, *n.* desacuerdo, *m.*
disadvantage, *n.* desventaja, *f.*; daño, *m.*; **—,** *vt.* dañar, perjudicar.
disadvantageous, *adj.* desventajoso; **—ly,** *adv.* desventajosamente.
disaffect, *vt.* llenar de descontento; indisponer.
disaffection, *n.* desafecto, *m.*; desamor, *m.*

disagree, *vi.* desconvenir, discordar.
disagreeable, *adj.* desagradable; contrario;
—**bly,** *adv.* desagradablemente.
disagreement, *n.* desacuerdo, *m.*, discordia,
desavenencia, *f.*; diferencia, *f.*; desconformidad, *f.*
disallow, *vt.* desaprobar; —, *vi.* negar.
disallowance, *n.* denegación, *f.*
disappear, *vi.* desaparecer; salir; esfumarse;
ausentarse.
disappearance, *n.* desaparecimiento, *m.*,
desaparición, *f.*
disappoint, *vt.* frustrar, faltar a la palabra;
engañar; **to be —ed,** llevarse un disgusto,
llevarse chasco.
disappointment, *n.* chasco, *m.*; contratiempo, *m.*; decepción, *f.*
disapproval, *n.* desaprobación, censura, *f.*
disapprove, *vt.* desaprobar.
disarm, *vt.* desarmar, privar de armas.
disarmament, *n.* desarme, *m.*
disarrange, *vt.* descomponer, desarreglar.
disarrangement, *n.* confusión, *f.*, desorden,
m.
disarray, *n.* desarreglo, *m.*; —, *vt.* desnudar;
desarreglar.
disassociate, *vt.* desunir.
disaster, *n.* desastre, *m.*; infortunio, *m.*;
catástrofe, *f.*
disastrous, *adj.* desastroso, infeliz; funesto;
—**ly,** *adv.* desastradamente.
disavow, *vt.* negar; desconocer; repudiar.
disavowal, *n.* repudiación, *f.*
disband, *vt.* dividir, desunir; —, *vi.*
dispersarse.
disbandment, *n.* disolución, separación, *f.*
disbar, *vt.* excluir del foro; excluir.
disbelief, *n.* incredulidad, desconfianza, *f.*
disbelieve, *vt.* descreer, desconfiar.
disburden, *vt.* descargar; —, *vi.* descargarse,
aliviarse.
disburse, *vt.* desembolsar, pagar.
disbursement, *n.* desembolso, *m.*
disc, *n.* disco, tejo, *m.*
disc. discount, descto. descuento.
discard, *vt.* descartar; —, *n.* descarte (en el
juego de naipes), *m.*
discern, *vt.* and *vi.* discernir, percibir,
distinguir.
discernible, *adj.* perceptible.
discerning, *adj.* juicioso, perspicaz; —**ly,**
adv. juiciosamente.
discernment, *n.* discernimiento, *m.*
discharge, *vt.* descargar, pagar (una deuda,
etc.); dispensar; (mil.) licenciar; ejecutar,
cumplir; descartar; despedir; —, *vi.*
descargarse; cumplir con su obligación;
—, *n.* descarga, *f.*; descargo, *m.*; finiquito,
m.; dimisión, *f.*; absolución, *f.*; —**d
battery,** batería descargada.
disciple, *n.* discípulo, secuaz, *m.*
disciplinarian, *adj.* disciplinario.
disciplinary, *adj.* disciplinario.
discipline, *n.* disciplina, *f.*; enseñanza, *f.*;
rigor, *m.*; —, *vt.* disciplinar, instruir.

disclaim, *vt.* negar, renunciar; repudiar,
rechazar.
disclaimer, *n.* denegación, *f.*
disclose, *vt.* descubrir, revelar.
disclosure, *n.* descubrimiento, *m.*; revelación, *f.*
discolor, *vt.* descolorar.
discoloration, *n.* descoloramiento, *m.*;
mancha, *f.*
discomfit, *vt.* derrotar, desconcertar; vencer, deshacer.
discomfiture, *n.* derrota, *f.*; vencimiento,
m.; desconcierto, *m.*
discomfort, *n.* incomodidad, *f.*; aflicción,
f.; molestia, *f.*
discommode, *vt.* incomodar, molestar.
discompose, *vt.* descomponer, desordenar;
turbar.
discomposure, *n.* descomposición, *f.*; confusión, *f.*
disconcert, *vt.* desconcertar, confundir,
turbar.
disconnect, *vt.* desunir, desembragar; separar.
disconnection, *n.* desunión, *f.*
disconsolate, *adj.* inconsolable; desconsolador; —**ly,** *adv.* desconsoladamente.
discontent, *n.* descontento, *m.*; —, *adj.*
malcontento; —, *vt.* descontentar.
discontented, *adj.* descontento.
discontentment, *n.* descontento, disgusto,
m.
discontinuation, *n.* descontinuación, cesación, interrupción, *f.*
discontinue, *vi.* descontinuar, interrumpir;
cesar.
discontinuity, *n.* incoherencia, *f.*, falta de
continuidad.
discord, discordance, *n.* discordia, *f.*; discordancia, disensión, *f.*
discordant, *adj.* discorde; incongruo; —**ly,**
adv. con discordancia.
discount, *n.* descuento, *m.*; rebaja, *f.*; **rate
of —,** tipo de descuento; —, *vt.* descontar.
discountable, *adj.* descontable.
discountenance, *vt.* aturdir, inmutar; desconcertar.
discourage, *vt.* desalentar, desanimar.
discouragement, *n.* desaliento, *m.*
discourse, *n.* discurso, *m.*; tratado, *m.*; —,
vi. conversar, discurrir, tratar (de).
discourteous, *adj.* descortés, grosero; —**ly,**
adv. descortésmente.
discourtesy, *n.* descortesía, grosería, *f.*
discover, *vt.* descubrir; revelar; manifestar.
discovery, *n.* descubrimiento, *m.*; revelación, *f.*
discredit, *n.* descrédito, deshonor, *m.*; —,
vt. desacreditar, deshonrar.
discreditable, *adj.* ignominioso.
discreet, *adj.* discreto; circunspecto; callado;
—**ly,** *adv.* discretamente.
discrepancy, *n.* discrepancia, diferencia, *f.*;
variante, *f.*

discrete, *adj.* separado; (math.) discreto.
discretion, *n.* discreción, *f.*
discretionary, *adj* discrecional, a voluntad.
discriminable, *adj.* discernible.
discriminate, *vt.* distinguir; señalar; **—ly,** *adv.* con discernimiento.
discriminating, *adj.* parcial, discerniente.
discrimination, *n* distinción, *f.*; discriminación, *f.*
discriminatory, *adj.* discernidor, parcial.
discursive, *adj.* inconstante; discursivo; **—ly,** *adv.* digresivamente.
discus, *n.* disco, *m.*; **— thrower,** discóbolo, *m.*
discuss, *vt.* discutir.
discussion, *n.* discusión, *f.*
disdain, *vt.* desdeñar, despreciar; **—,** *n.* desdén, desprecio, *m.*
disdainful, *adj.* desdeñoso; **—ly,** *adv.* desdeñosamente.
disease, *n.* mal, *m.*; enfermedad, *f.*; **contagious —,** peste, *f.*, enfermedad contagiosa.
diseased, *adj.* enfermo.
disembark, *vt.* and *vi.* desembarcar.
disembarkation, *n.* (mil.) desembarco de tropas.
disembarrass, *vt.* desembarazar.
disembellish, *vt.* desadornar.
disembody, *vt.* separar del cuerpo.
disembowel, *vt.* desentrañar.
disenchant, *vt.* desencantar.
disenchantment, *n.* desencanto, *m.*
disencumber, *vt.* desembarazar.
disengage, *vt.* desenredar, librar; **—,** *vi.* libertarse de, desembarazarse.
disentangle, *vt.* desenredar, separar.
disentanglement, *n.* desenredo, *m.*
disestablish, *vt.* separar (la iglesia del estado, etc.).
disfavor, *vt.* desfavorecer; **—,** *n.* disfavor, *m.*; desaprobación, *f.*
disfiguration, *n.* desfiguración, *f.*
disfigure, *vt.* desfigurar, afear.
disfigurement, *n.* deformidad, *f.*; desfiguración, *f.*
disfranchise, *vt.* quitar franquicias.
disfranchisement, *n.* destitución de los derechos civiles.
disgorge, *vt.* vomitar.
disgrace, *n.* deshonra, *f.*; desgracia, *f.*; disfavor, *m.*; **—,** *vt.* deshonrar; hacer caer en desgracia.
disgraceful, *adj.* deshonroso, ignominioso; **—ly,** *adv.* vergonzosamente.
disguise, *vt.* disfrazar, enmascarar; simular; **—,** *n.* disfraz, *m.*; máscara, *f.*
disgust, *n.* disgusto, *m.*; aversión, *f.*; fastidio, *m.*; **to cause —,** repugnar; **—,** *vt.* disgustar, inspirar aversión.
dish, *n.* fuente, *f.*, plato, *m.*; taza, *f.*; **set of —es,** vajilla, *f.*; **—,** *vt.* servir en un plato.
dishabille, *n.* paños menores, *m. pl.*
disharmony, *n.* discordancia, disonancia, *f.*
dishcloth, dishrag, *n.* paño para lavar platos.

dishearten, *vt.* desalentar, descorazonar.
dishevel, *vt.* desgreñar.
dishonest, *adj.* deshonesto; ignominioso; **—ly,** *adv* deshonestamente.
dishonesty, *n.* deshonestidad, impureza, *f.*
dishonor, *n.* deshonra, ignominia, *f.*; **—,** *vt.* deshonrar, infamar.
dishonorable, *adj.* deshonroso, afrentoso, indecoroso; **—bly,** *adv.* ignominiosamente.
dishpan, *n.* vasija para fregar platos.
dishwasher, *n.* máquina de lavar platos.
dishwater, *n.* agua para lavar platos.
disillusion, *n.* desengaño, *m.*, desilusión, *f.*; **—,** *vt.* desengañar.
disinclination, *n.* desafecto, *m.*, aversión, *f.*
disincline, *vt.* desinclinar.
disinfect, *vt.* desinfectar.
disinfectant, *n.* desinfectante, *m.*
disinfection, *n.* desinfección, *f.*
disinherit, *vt.* desheredar.
disinheritance, *n.* desheredación, *f.*
disintegrate, *vt.* disgregar, despedazar.
disintegration, *n* disgregación, *f.*
disinter, *vt.* desenterrar.
disinterested, *adj.* desinteresado; **—ly,** *adv.* desinteresadamente.
disinterestedness, *n.* desinterés, *m.*
disinterment, *n.* desenterramiento, *m.*
disjoint, *vt.* dislocar, desmembrar; **—,** *vi.* desmembrarse.
disjointed, *adj.* dislocado; **—ly,** *adv.* separadamente.
disk, *n.* disco, tejo, *m.*
dislike, *n.* aversión, repugnancia, *f.*; disgusto, *m.*; **—,** *vt.* disgustar; desagradar.
dislocate, *vt.* dislocar, descoyuntar.
dislocation, *n.* dislocación, *f.*; descoyuntamiento, *m.*
dislodge, *vt.* and *vi.* desalojar.
dislodgement, *n.* desalojamiento, *m.*
disloyal, *adj.* desleal; infiel; **—ly,** *adv.* deslealmente.
disloyalty, *n.* deslealtad, infidelidad, perfidia, *f.*
dismal, *adj.* triste, funesto; horrendo; **—s,** *n. pl.* (coll.) hipocondría, *f.*
dismantle, *vt.* (mil.) desmantelar (una plaza); desamueblar; (naut.) desaparejar.
dismast, *vt.* desarbolar (un navío).
dismay, *n.* desmayo, *m.*; terror, *m.*; **—,** *vt.* and *vi.* desmayar, desmayarse.
dismember, *vt.* desmembrar, despedazar.
dismiss, *vt.* despedir; echar; descartar.
dismissal, dismission, *n.* despedida, *f.*; dimisión, *f.*; destitución, *f.*
dismount, *vt.* desmontar, apearse del caballo; **—,** *vi.* desmontar, descender.
disobedience, *n.* desobediencia, *f.*
disobedient, *adj.* desobediente.
disobey, *vt.* desobedecer.
disoblige, *vt.* desobligar.
disorder, *n.* desorden, *m.*; confusión, *f.*; indisposición, *f.*; desequilibrio, *m.*; **—,** *vt.* desordenar, confundir, perturbar.
disorderly, *adj.* desarreglado, confuso; **—,**

adv. desordenadamente; ilegalmente.
disorganization, *n.* desorganización, *f.*
disorganize, *vt.* desorganizar.
disown, *vt.* negar, desconocer; repudiar.
disparage, *vt.* envilecer; mofar, menospreciar.
disparagement, *n.* menosprecio, desprecio, *m.*; insulto, *m.*
disparate, *adj.* desigual, diferente.
disparity, *n.* disparidad, *f.*
dispassionate, *adj.* sereno, desapasionado; templado.
dispatch, *n.* despacho, *m.*; embarque, *m.*; (com.) envío, *m.*; remisión, *f.*; —, *vt.* despachar; embarcar; remitir, enviar.
dispel, *vt.* disipar, dispersar.
dispensable, *adj.* dispensable.
dispensary, *n.* dispensario, *m.*
dispensation, *n.* dispensación, *f.*; dispensa, *f.*
dispensatory, *n.* farmacopea, *f.*
dispense, *vt.* dispensar; distribuir.
dispenser, *n.* dispensador.
dispersal, *n.* dispersión, *f.*, esparcimiento, *m.*
disperse, *vt.* esparcir, disipar; distribuir.
dispersion, *n.* dispersión, *f.*; separación, *f.*
displace, *vt.* dislocar, desordenar.
displacement, *n.* cambio de situación, mudanza, *f.*; desalojamiento, *m.*; (chem.) coladura, *f.*; (naut.) desplazamiento, *m.*
display, *vt.* desplegar; explicar; exponer; ostentar; —, *n.* ostentación, *f.*; despliegue, *m.*
displease, *vt.* disgustar; ofender; desagradar; chocar.
displeasure, *n.* disgusto, desagrado, *m.*; indignación, *f.*
disport, *vt.* divertir; —, *vi.* divertirse.
disposal, *n.* disposición, *f.*
dispose, *vt.* disponer; dar; arreglar; —, *vi.* vender; trasferir.
disposed, *adj.* dispuesto, inclinado; **well** —, bien dispuesto; **ill** —, mal dispuesto.
disposition, *n.* disposición, *f.*; índole, *f.*; inclinación, *f.*; carácter, *m.*; humor, *m.*; **good** —, buen humor, buen carácter.
dispossess, *vt.* desposeer; desalojar.
dispossession, *n.* desposeimiento, *m.*
dispraise, *vt.* vituperar; menospreciar.
disproof, *n.* confutación, refutación, *f.*
disproportion, *n.* desproporción, *f.*
disproportionate, *adj.* desproporcionado.
disprove, *vt.* confutar; desaprobar.
disputable, *adj.* disputable, contestable.
disputant, *n.* disputador, ra.
disputation, *n.* disputa, controversia, *f.*
dispute, *n.* disputa, controversia, *f.*; —, *vt.* and *vi.* disputar, controvertir, argüir.
disqualification, *n.* incapacidad, *f.*
disqualify, *vi.* inhabilitar.
disquiet, *n.* inquietud, perturbación, *f.*; — *vt.* inquietar, turbar.
disquietude, *n.* inquietud, *f.*
disquisition, *n.* disquisición, *f.*
disregard, *vt.* desatender, desdeñar; —, *n.* desatención, *f.*; desdén, *m.*

disregardful, *adj.* desatento, negligente; **—ly,** *adv.* desatentamente.
disrelish, *n.* disgusto, tedio, hastío, *m.*; —, *vt.* desaprobar; sentir repugnancia (por alguna cosa).
disrepair, *n.* deterioro, *m.*
disreputable, *adj.* deshonroso; despreciable **—bly,** *adv.* deshonrosamente.
disrepute, *n.* descrédito, *m.*; mala fama; **to bring into** —, desacreditar, difamar, desprestigiar.
disrespect, *n.* irreverencia, *f.*, falta de respeto.
disrespectful, *adj.* irreverente, descortés; **—ly,** *adv.* irreverentemente.
disrobe, *vt.* desnudar, despojar.
disrupt, *vt.* and *vi.* desbaratar, hacer pedazos; desorganizar, enredar.
disruption, *n.* rompimiento, *m.*; fractura, *f.*
dissatisfaction, *n.* descontento, disgusto, *m.*
dissatisfied, *adj.* descontento, no satisfecho.
dissatisfy, *vt.* descontentar, desagradar.
dissect, *vt.* disecar.
dissection, *n.* disección, anatomía, *f.*; examen minucioso.
dissemble, *vt.* disimular; —, *vi.* hacer el papel de hipócrita.
dissembler, *n.* disimulador, *m.*
disseminate, *vt.* diseminar, sembrar, esparcir, propagar.
dissemination, *n.* diseminación, *f.*
dissension, *n.* disensión, discordia, *f.*
dissent, *vi.* disentir, estar en desacuerdo. —, *n.* disensión, contrariedad de opinión;
dissenter, *n.* disidente, *m.* y *f.*
dissentient, *adj.* discrepante.
dissertation, *n.* disertación, tesis, *f.*
disservice, *n.* deservicio, *m.*
dissever, *vt.* partir, dividir, separar.
dissident, *adj.* disidente.
dissimilar, *adj.* desemejante, heterogéneo.
dissimilarity, *n.* heterogeneidad, *f.*
dissimulate, *vt.* disimular.
dissimulation, *n.* disimulo, *m.*, disimulación, *f.*; fingimiento, *m.*
dissipate, *vt.* disipar.
dissipated, *adj.* disipado.
dissipation, *n.* disipación, *f.*; libertinaje, *m.*
dissociate, *vt.* disociar.
dissociation, *n.* disociación, separación, *f.*
dissolubility, *n.* disolubilidad, *f.*
dissoluble, *adj.* disoluble.
dissolute, *adj.* disoluto, libertino.
dissolution, *n.* disolución, *f.*; muerte, *f.*
dissolve, *vt.* disolver; —, *vi.* disolverse, derretirse.
dissolvent, *adj.* disolvente; —, *n.* disolvente, *m.*
dissonance, *n.* disonancia, *f.*; desconcierto, *m.*
dissonant, *adj.* disonante; discordante; diferente.
dissuade, *vt.* disuadir.
dissuasion, *n.* disuasión, *f.*
dissuasive, *adj.* disuasivo; que induce.

dissyllable, *adj.* disílabo.
dist.: distance, dist. distancia; **district,** dist. distrito.
distaff, *n.* rueca (para hilar), *f.*
distance, *n.* distancia, *f.*; lejanía, *f.*; lontananza, *f.*; respeto, *m.*; esquivez, *f.*; travesía, *f.*; **at a —,** de lejos; **out of —,** fuera de vista; **—,** *vt.* apartar; sobrepasar; espaciar.
distant, *adj.* distante, lejano; esquivo; **very —,** a leguas.
distaste, *n.* hastío, disgusto, tedio, *m.*
distasteful, *adj.* desabrido, desagradable; chocante; maligno.
Dist. Atty. District Attorney, fiscal.
distemper, *n.* indisposición, enfermedad, *f.*; desasosiego, *m.*; desorden tumultuoso; morbo, *m.*; **—,** *vt.* perturbar; causar una enfermedad.
distend, *vt.* extender, ensanchar; distender.
distension, *n.* distensión, *f.*; dilatación, anchura, *f.*
distich, *n.* dístico, *m.*
distill, *vt.* and *vi.* destilar; gotear.
distillate, *n.* producto de destilación.
distillation, *n.* destilación, *f.*
distiller, *n.* destilador, *m.*
distillery, *n.* destilería, *f.*, destilatorio, *m.*
distinct, *adj.* distinto, diferente; claro, sin confusión; **—ly,** *adv.* con claridad.
distinction, *n.* distinción, diferencia, *f.*
distinctive, *adj.* característico; **—ly,** *adv.* claramente.
distinctness, *n.* claridad, *f.*
distinguish, *vt.* distinguir; discernir; **—ed,** *adj.* distinguido, caracterizado, señalado; eminente; notable, famoso, ilustre, considerado; **to be —ed by,** particularizarse por medio de.
distinguishable, *adj.* distinguible, notable.
distort, *vt.* tergiversar, pervertir, torcer; disfrazar, falsear.
distortion, *n.* contorsión, *f.*; torcimiento, *m.*; perversión, *f.*
distract, *vt.* distraer; perturbar; **—ed,** *adj.* distraído; aturdido; perturbado; **—edly,** *adv.* aturdidamente.
distraction, *n.* distracción, *f.*; confusión, *f.*; frenesí, *m.*, locura, *f.*
distrain, *vt.* embargar, secuestrar.
distraint, *n.* (law) secuestro, *m.*
distraught, *adj.* desconcertado; desesperado; enloquecido.
distress, *n.* aflicción, *f.*; calamidad, miseria, *f.*; secuestro, *m.*; **—,** *vt.* angustiar, acongojar; secuestrar.
distribute, *vt.* distribuir, dividir, repartir; encasillar.
distribution, *n.* distribución, *f.*; reparto, *m.*
distributive, *adj.* distributivo.
distributor, *n.* distribuidor, ra.
district, *n.* distrito, *m.*; región, *f.*; jurisdicción, *f.*; zona, *f.*; vecindario, *m.*; **— (of a town),** barrio (de una ciudad), *m.*
distrust, *vt.* desconfiar; **—,** *n.* desconfianza,

sospecha, *f.*; suspicacia, *f.*
distrustful, *adj.* desconfiado; sospechoso; suspicaz; **—ly,** *adv.* desconfiadamente.
disturb, *vt.* perturbar, estorbar.
disturbance, *n.* disturbio, *m.*; confusión, *f.*; tumulto, *m.*; perturbación, *f.*
disturber, *n.* perturbador, ra, estorbador, ra.
disulphide, *n.* (chem.) bisulfuro, *m.*
disunion, *n.* desunión, discordia, *f.*
disunite, *vt.* desunir, separar; **—,** *vi.* desunirse, separarse.
disuse, *n.* desuso, *m.*; **—,** *vt.* desusar, desacostumbrar, cesar.
ditch, *n.* zanja, *f.*; foso, *m.*; cauce, *m.*; cuneta, *f.*; gavia, *f.*; **intercepting —,** cuneta de coronación; **—,** *vt.* abrir zanjas o fosos; (coll.) desembarazarse, dar calabazas.
dither, *n.* agitación, *f.*
ditto, *n.* ídem, marca('') o abreviatura (id.) que se usa en lugar de **ídem;** copia, *f.*, duplicado, *m.*; **—,** *vt.* copiar, duplicar; **—,** *adv.* también, asimismo.
ditty, *n.* cancioncita, jácara, *f.*
diuresis, *n.* diuresis, *f.*
diuretic, *adj.* (med.) diurético; **—,** *n.* diurético, *m.*
diurnal, *adj.* diurno, cotidiano; **—,** *n.* diario, jornal, *m.*
div.: dividend, div. dividendo; **division,** div. división; **divorced,** divorciado.
diva, *n.* diva, cantante, *f.*
divan, *m.* diván, *m.*, otomana, *f.*
dive, *vi.* sumergirse, zambullirse; bucear; (Mex.) echarse un clavado; **—,** *n.* zambullidura, *f.*; (Mex.) clavado, *m.*; (coll.) garito, *m.*, leonera, *f.*; **— bomber,** avión bombardero en picada.
diver, *n.* buzo, *m.*; (orn.) somorgujo, *m.*
diverge, *vi.* divergir; divergirse; discrepar.
divergence, *n.* divergencia, *f.*
divergent, *adj.* divergente.
divers, *adj.* varios, diversos, muchos.
diverse, *adj.* diverso, diferente, variado; **—ly,** *adv.* diversamente.
diversify, *vt.* diversificar.
diversion, *n.* diversión, *f.*; pasatiempo, *m.*
diversity, *n.* diversidad, *f.*; variedad, *f.*
divert, *vt.* desviar; divertir; recrear.
divertissement, *n.* divertimiento, *m.*
divest, *vt.* desnudar; privar, despojar.
divide, *vt.* dividir, distribuir; repartir; partir; desunir; **—,** *vi.* desunirse, dividirse.
dividend, *n.* dividendo, *m.*; **periodical —,** dividendo ordinario.
divider, *n.* (math.) divisor, *m.*; distribuidor, *m.*; compás de puntas.
divination, *n.* divinación, *f.*
divine, *adj.* divino, sublime, excelente; **—,** *n.* teólogo, *m.*; **—,** *vt.* conjeturar; **—,** *vi.* presentir; profetizar; adivinar; **—ly,** *adv.* divinamente.
diviner, *n.* adivinador, ra, agorero, ra.
diving, *n.* buceo, *m.*; **—,** *adj.* buceador; relativo al buceo; **— bell,** campana de

bucear; — **bird,** (orn.) mergo, *m.*; — **suit,** escafandra, *f.*

divining rod, *n.* vara divinatoria.

divinity, *n.* divinidad, *f.*; deidad, *f.*; teología, *f.*

divisibility, *n.* divisibilidad, *f.*

divisible, *adj.* divisible.

division, *n.* (math.) división, *f.*; desunión, *f.*; separación, *f.*

divisional, *adj.* divisional.

divisor, *n.* (math.) divisor, *m.*

divorce, *n.* divorcio, *m.*; —, *vt.* divorciar; —, *vi.* divorciarse.

divorcé, *n.* divorciado, *m.*

divorcee, *n.* divorciado, da.

divorcée, *n.* divorciada, *f.*

divorcement, *n.* divorcio, *m.*

divulge, *vt.* divulgar, publicar.

dizziness, *n.* vértigo, *m.*; ligereza, *f.*; vahido, *m.*; vaivén, *m.*; mareo, *m.*

dizzy, *adj.* vertiginoso; mareado; (coll.) tonto, estúpido.

dkl. dekaliter, decaliter, Dl. decalitro.

dkm. dekameter, decameter, Dm. decámetro.

dl. deciliter, dl. decilitro.

D. Litt. Doctor of Literature, D. en L. Doctor en Letras.

D.L.O. Dead letter office, Oficina de Cartas No Reclamadas.

dm. decimeter, dm. decímetro.

do, *vt.* hacer, ejecutar, finalizar; despachar; —, *vi.* obrar; comportarse; prosperar; **to — away with,** suprimir, quitar; **how you —?** ¿cómo está usted? **to —without,** pasarse sin, prescindir de.

do. ditto, id. ídem.

doc. document, docum.^{to} documento.

docile, *adj.* dócil, apacible.

docility, *n.* docilidad, *f.*

dock, *n.* (naut.) muelle, *m.*; espigón de descarga; desembarcadero, *m.*; (bot.) bardana, *f.*; **dry —,** astillero, *m.*; —, *vt.* descolar; entrar en muelle; cortar; (law) rescindir; **to — one's wages,** descontarle del salario o jornal.

dockage, *n.* muellaje, *m.*

docket, *n.* extracto, sumario, *m.*; minuta, *f.*; rótulo, marbete, *m.*; **to strike a —,** (com.) declarar a un comerciante en bancarrota; **trial —,** (law) inscripción de los pleitos pendientes; —, *vt.* rotular; inscribir en el orden del día.

dockyard, *n.* (naut.) astillero, *m.*; maestranza, *f.*; arsenal, *m.*

doctor, *n.* doctor, médico, *m.*; **—'s office,** consultorio de médico, gabinete, *m.*; —, *vt.* medicinar.

doctoral, *adj.* doctoral.

doctorate, *n.* doctorado, *m.*

doctoress, *n.* doctora, *f.*

doctrinaire, *n.* doctrinario, teorista, *m.*; —, *adj.* doctrinario, ria.

doctrinal, *adj.* doctrinal, dogmático.

doctrine, *n.* doctrina, *f.*; erudición, *f.*; ciencia, *f.*

document, *n.* documento, *m.*; precepto, *m.*

documentary, *adj.* documental.

documentation, *n.* documentación, *f.*; (com.) juego de documentos de embarque.

dodecasyllable, *n.* dodecasílabo, *m.*

dodge, *vt.* evadir, esquivar.

dodger, *n.* trampista, *m.*

doe, *n.* (zool.) gama, *f.*; — **rabbit,** coneja, *f.*

doer, *n.* hacedor, actor, ejecutante, agente, *m.*

does, tercera persona del singular del verbo **do.**

doff, *vt.* quitar, desnudar; desposeerse de.

dog, *n.* perro, *m.*; — **days,** caniculares, *m. pl.*; — **fancier,** perrero, *m.*; — **fight,** pelea de perros, refriega, *f.*; — **kennel,** perrera, *f.*; — **sledge,** rastra tirada por perros; **—'s mercury,** (bot.) mercurial, *m.*; **D— Star,** Sirio, Canícula; —, *vt.* cazar con perros; espiar.

dogcart, *n.* variedad de coche de dos ruedas; carruaje tirado por perros.

doge, *n.* dux (de Venecia y Génova), *m.*

dogfish, *n.* especie de tiburón pequeño.

dogged, *adj.* tenaz, persistente; ceñudo, intratable, áspero, brutal; **—ly,** *adv.* adustamente; con persistencia, tenazmente.

doggerel, *adj.* vil, bajo (hablando de versos); —, *n.* versos pareados.

doghouse, *n.* perrera, *f.*, casa de perro.

dogma, *n.* dogma, *m.*

dogmatic, dogmatical, *adj.* dogmático; **—ly,** *adv.* dogmáticamente.

dogmatism, *n.* dogmatismo, *m.*

dogmatize, *vi.* dogmatizar.

dog's-ear, *n.* pliegue en los ángulos de la hoja de un libro.

dog-tired, *adj.* rendido de cansancio.

dogtrot, *n.* trote lento.

dogwood, *n.* (bot.) cornejo, *m.*

doily, *n.* pañito de adorno.

doings, *n. pl.* hechos, *m. pl.*; acciones, *f. pl.*; eventos, *m. pl.*

dol. dollar, dl. dólar.

doldrums, *n. pl.* mal humor, fastidio, *m.*; (naut.) vientos bonancibles ecuatoriales.

dole, *n.* distribución, *f.*; porción, *f.*; limosna, *f.*; —, *vt.* repartir, distribuir.

doleful, *adj.* doloroso, lúgubre, triste.

doll, *n.* muñeca, *f.*; **boy —,** muñeco, *m.*

dollar, *n.* dólar, peso (moneda de E.U.A.), *m.*; **silver —,** peso fuerte.

dolly, *n.* muñequita, *f.*; remachador, *m.*; (rail.) plataforma de tracción.

dolman, *n.* dolmán, *m.*; — **sleeves,** tipo especial de mangas anchas en la bocamanga.

dolomite, *n.* dolomía, *f.*

dolor, *n.* (poet.) dolor, pesar, *m.*; dolencia, *f.*

dolorous, *adj.* doloroso, lastimoso.

dolphin, *n.* delfín, *m.*

dolt, *n.* hombre bobo.

dom.: domestic, doméstico; **dominion,** dominio.
domain, n. dominio, m.
dome, n. cúpula, f.; domo, m.
domestic, adj. doméstico; interno; casero; **— exchange,** cambio interior.
domesticate, vt. domesticar.
domestication, n. domesticación, f.
domesticity, n. domesticidad, f.
domicile, n. domicilio, m.
domiciliary, adj. domiciliario.
dominance, n. predominio, m., ascendencia, autoridad, f.
dominant, adj. dominante.
dominate, vt. and vi. dominar, predominar.
domination, n. dominación, f.; imperio, m.
domineer, vi. dominar, señorear.
domineering, adj. tiránico, arrogante.
Dominican Republic, República Dominicana, f.
dominion, n. dominio, territorio, m.; señorío, m.; soberanía, f.
domino, n. dominó, m.: traje de máscara; **—es,** n. pl. dominó (juego), m.
don, vt. vestirse, ponerse.
donate, vt. donar, contribuir; obsequiar.
donation, n. donación, dádiva, contribución, f.
done, adj. hecho; cocido, asado; **well —,** bien hecho; bien cocido, bien asado; **—,** p. p. del verbo **do.**
donkey, n. asno, borrico, m.; **— engine,** máquina auxiliar (generalmente portátil).
donor, n. donador, ra.
doom, n. sentencia, f.; condena, f.; suerte, f.; **—,** vt. sentenciar, juzgar, condenar.
doomsday, n. día del juicio final.
door, n. puerta, f.; **— bolt,** pasador, m.; **— knocker,** picaporte, llamador, m., aldaba, f.; **front —,** puerta de entrada; **within —s,** en casa, bajo techo.
doorbell, n. timbre de llamada.
doorframe, n. dintel, marco, m.
doorhandle, n. picaporte, m.
doorkeeper, n. portero, ujier, m.
doorknob, n. perilla, f.
doorman, n. portero, m.
doornail, n. clavo grande para puertas; **to be as dead as a —,** estar completamente muerto o inmóvil.
doorplate, n. placa en la puerta con el nombre del dueño.
doorstep, n. umbral, m.
doorway, n. portada, f.; portal, m.; puerta de entrada.
dope, n. narcótico, m., droga heroica; (coll.) información, f.; (coll.) persona muy estúpida; **— fiend,** morfinómano, na, persona adicta a las drogas heroicas.
dormancy, n. latencia, letargo, sopor, m.
dormant, adj. durmiente; secreto; latente.
dormer, n. viga maestra; buhardilla, f.; **— window,** lumbrera, f., ventana en un techo.
dormitory, n. dormitorio, m.

dormouse, n. lirón, m.
Dorothy, Dorotea.
dorsal, adj. dorsal.
dose, n. dosis, porción, f.; **—,** vt. disponer la dosis de un remedio.
dossier, n. legajo de papeles documentales.
dot, n. punto, m.; (mus.) puntillo, m.; **—,** vt. poner punto (a una letra).
dotage, n. chochera, chochez, f., cariño excesivo.
dotard, n. viejo que chochea.
dotation, n. dotación, f.
dote, vi. chochear.
doting, adj. senil, chocho, excesivamente aficionado o enamorado.
double, adj. doble, duplicado, duplo; falso, insincero; **— boiler,** caldera de dos piezas o doble; **— chin,** papada, f.; **— entry,** (com.) partida doble; **— play,** (baseball) maniobra que pone fuera de juego a dos de los jugadores rivales; **— time,** paso doble o rápido; **— cross,** engañar; **—,** n. duplo, m.; engaño, m.; artificio, m.; **—,** vt. doblar; duplicar; plegar; disimular; **to — up,** envolver; **—ly,** adv. doblemente.
double-barreled, adj. de dos cañones; (fig.) de dos propósitos.
double-breasted, adj. con dos filas de botones (chaqueta o abrigo).
double-dealing, n. duplicidad, f.
double-edged, adj. de doble filo.
double-faced, adj. de dos caras, pérfido.
double-jointed, adj. con articulaciones dobles.
double-quick, adj. a paso muy rápido.
doubles, n. pl. (tennis) juego de dobles.
doublet, n. justillo, jubón, m.
doubloon, n. doblón (moneda), m.
doubt, n. duda, sospecha, f.; **there is no —,** no cabe duda; **without —,** sin duda; **—,** vt. and vi. dudar; sospechar.
doubter, n. incrédulo, la.
doubtful, adj. dudoso, dudable; incierto; **—ly,** adv. dudosamente.
doubtless, adj. indubitable, indudable; **—ly,** adv. sin duda.
douche, n. ducha, f.
dough, n. masa, pasta, f.
doughboy, n. (coll.) soldado de infantería.
doughnut, n. rosquilla, f.; especie de buñuelo.
doughty, adj. bravo, valeroso; fanfarrón (úsase hoy día en tono festivo).
dour, adj. torvo, austero.
douse, vt. zambullir; empapar; **—,** vi. zambullirse; empaparse.
dove, n. paloma, f.; **ring —,** paloma torcaz.
dovecot, dovecote, dovehouse, n. palomar, m.
dovetail, n. cola de milano; **—,** vi. corresponder, estar de acuerdo.
dowager, n. viuda respetable con viudedad; (coll.) matrona respetable.

dowdy, *adj.* desaliñado; —, *n.* mujer desaliñada.

dowel, *n.* tarugo, zoquete, *m.*

dower, *n.* viudedad, *f.*

down, *n.* plumón, flojel, *m.*; bozo, vello, *m.*; revés de fortuna; **ups and —s,** vaivenes, *m. pl.*; —, *adj.* pendiente; **— payment,** primer plazo; —, *adv.* abajo; **so much —,** tanto al contado; —, *vt.* derribar; — ! *interj.* ¡abajo!

downcast, *adj.* apesadumbrado, cabizbajo.

downfall, *n.* ruina, decadencia, *f.*; desplome, *m.*

downfallen, *adj.* caído, arruinado.

downgrade, *n.* cuesta abajo; bajada, *f.*

downhearted, *adj.* abatido, desanimado.

downhill, *adj.* pendiente, hacia abajo; —, *adv.* colina abajo.

downpour, *n.* aguacero, *m.*; chubasco, chaparrón, *m.*

downright, *adv.* sin ceremonias; de manera patente; por completo.

downstairs, *adv.* abajo de las escaleras; abajo; —, *n.* piso inferior.

downstream, *adv.* aguas abajo.

downtown, *n.* centro, *m.*, parte céntrica de una ciudad.

downtrodden, *adj.* oprimido.

downward, *adj.* inclinado; cabizbajo, triste; —s, *adv.* hacia abajo.

downy, *adj.* velloso; suave.

dowry, *n.* dote, *m.*

doxology, *n.* doxología, *f.*, himno de alabanza a Dios.

doz. dozen, dna., doc. docena.

doze, *n.* sueño ligero; —, *vi.* dormitar.

dozen, *n.* docena, *f.*

dozy, *adj.* soñoliento.

Dr. Doctor, Dr. Doctor.

dr.: debtor, dor. deudor; **dram,** dracma, **drawer,** girador.

drab, *n.* paño castaño; mujer desaliñada; prostituta, *f.*; color entre gris y café; —, *adj.* opaco; murrio; monótono.

drachm, *n.* dracma, *f.*

draft, draught, *n.* dibujo, *m.*; (com.) giro, *m.*, letra de cambio, libranza, *f.*; corriente de aire; (mil.) leva, conscripción, *f.*; (naut.) calado, *m.*; **— board,** junta de conscripción; tabla para dibujar; **—ing board,** tablero de dibujar; **— horse,** caballo de tiro; **rough —,** borrador, *m.*; **sight —,** letra a la vista, giro a la vista; **time —,** letra a plazo; **to honor a —,** dar acogida a una letra o un giro; —, *vt.* dibujar; redactar.

draftee, *n.* quinto, recluta, *m.*

draftsman, *n.* dibujante, *m.*; diseñador, *m.*

drag, *vt.* arrastrar; tirar con fuerza; —, *vi.* arrastrarse por el suelo; —, *n.* rastro, *m.*; rémora, *f.*; (coll.) influencia, *f.*

draggle, *vt.* emporcar (alguna cosa) arrastrándola por el suelo; —, *vi.* ensuciarse (alguna cosa) por llevarla arrastrando.

dragline, *n.* draga de arrastre, cangilón de arrastre.

dragnet, *n.* red barredera.

dragon, *n.* dragón, *m.*

dragonfly, *n.* libélula, *f.*

dragoon, *n.* (mil.) dragón, *m.*

drain, *vt.* desaguar; secar; sanear; —, *n.* desaguadero, *m.*; (naut.) colador, *m.*; cauce, *m.*; cuneta, *f.*; sangradera, *f.*

drainage, *n.* desagüe, *m.*; saneamiento, *m.*

drainpipe, *n.* tubo de desagüe.

drake, *n.* ánade macho.

dram, *n.* dracma, *f.*; porción de licor que se bebe de una vez; —, *vi.* beber licor.

drama, *n.* drama, *m.*

dramatic, dramatical, *adj.* dramático; **—ally,** *adv.* dramáticamente.

dramatist, *n.* dramaturgo, *m.*

dramatization, *n.* versión dramatizada; representación o descripción dramática.

dramatize, *vt.* dramatizar.

dramaturgy, *n.* dramaturgia, *f.*

drank, pretérito del verbo **drink.**

drape, *n.* cortina, colgadura, *f.*; —, *vt.* vestir, colgar decorativamente.

draper, *n.* pañero, *m.*

drapery, *n.* manufactura de paños; colgadura, *f.*; ropaje, *m.*

drastic, *adj.* drástico.

draught, *n.* trago, *m.*, poción, *f.*; corriente de aire; = **draft.**

draw, *vt.* tirar, traer; atraer; arrastrar; dibujar; librar una letra de cambio; **to — lines,** rayar; **to — lots,** echar suertes; **to — nigh,** acercarse; **to — on,** librar a cargo de una persona; **to — on us (me),** girar a nuestro (mi) cargo; **to — out,** sacar; **to — up,** redactar, formular; —, *vi.* tirar, encogerse; moverse.

drawback, *n.* restitución de los derechos al tiempo de exportar los géneros; desventaja, *f.*

drawbridge, *n.* puente levadizo.

drawee, *n.* girado, da, librado, da.

drawer, *n.* gaveta, *f.*; girador de una letra; aguador, *m.*; mozo de taberna; **—s,** *n. pl.* calzones, *m. pl.*; calzoncillos, *m. pl.*

drawing, *n.* dibujo, *m.*; rifa, *f.*; **— room,** sala de recibo.

drawknife, *n.* cuchilla de dos mangos.

drawl, *vi.* hablar con pesadez; —, *n.* enunciación penosa y lenta.

drawn, *adj.* movido; halado; dibujado; desenvainado; estirado; —, *p. p.* del verbo **draw.**

dray (cart), *n.* carro, carretón, *m.*

drayage, *n.* acarreo, arrastre, *m.*

drayman, *n.* carretero, *m.*

dread, *n.* miedo, terror, espanto, *m.*; —, *adj.* terrible; —, *vt.* and *vi.* temer.

dreadful, *adj.* terrible, espantoso; **—ly,** *adv.* terriblemente.

dreadnaught, *n.* gran acorazado.

dream, *n.* sueño, *m.*; fantasía, *f.*; ensueño, *m.*; —, *vi.* soñar; imaginarse.

dreamer, *n.* soñador, ra; visionario, ria.

dreamland, *n.* reino de los sueños.

dreamy, *adj.* quimérico, soñador; soñoliento.

dreariness, *n.* lobreguez, tristeza, *f.*

dreary, *adj.* espantoso, triste.

dredge, *vt.* (naut.) rastrear con el rezón; excavar.

dredger, *n.* draga, *f.*; pescador de ostras.

dredging, *n.* dragado, *m.*; — **machine,** máquina para limpiar un río, estanque, etc.; draga, *f.*

dregs, *n. pl.* heces, *f. pl.*; escoria, *f.*; morralla, *f.*

drench, *vt.* empapar, mojar, humedecer; abrevar; —, *n.* bebida purgante (para ciertos animales); empapada, *f.*

Dresden, Dresde, *f.*

dress, *n.* vestido, *m.*; atavío, tocado, *m.*; traje, *m.*; — **ball,** baile de etiqueta; — **coat,** frac, *m.*; — **suit,** traje de etiqueta; **ready-made** —, traje hecho; —, *vt.* vestir, ataviar; revestir; curar las heridas; almohazar; ajustar; cocinar; —, *vi.* vestirse.

dresser, *n.* el que viste o adereza; aparador, tocador, *m.*; mueble para el tocado; mesa para aderezar carnes.

dressing, *n.* curación, *f.*; adorno, *m.*; salsa, *f.*; — **case,** neceser, *m.*; — **gown,** peinador, *m.*; bata, *f.*, ropa de levantarse o de cámara; — **room,** vestuario, *m.*; gabinete para vestirse; — **table,** tocador, *m.*; **French** —, salsa francesa (para ensaladas).

dressmaker, *n.* modista, *f.*, persona que hace vestidos para señoras y niños.

dressmaking, *n.* modistería, *f.*, confección de vestidos.

dressy, *adj.* aficionado a ataviarse; (coll.) vistoso; elegante.

drew, pretérito del verbo **draw.**

dribble, *vt.* hacer caer gota a gota; —, *vi.* gotear.

dribbling, *n.* (Rugby, basketball), regate, *m.*

driblet, *n.* cantidad pequeña; gota, *f.*; pedacito, *m.*

drift, *n.* impulso, *m.*; tempestad, *f.*; montón, *m.*; tendencia, *f.*, propósito, designio, *m.*; significado, *m.*; (naut.) deriva, *f.*; — **indicator,** indicador de deriva; — **of ice,** hielo flotante; — **of sand,** arena movediza; — **of snow,** nevada con ventisca; —, *vt.* impeler; amontonar; —, *vi.* formar en montones.

driftage, *n.* (naut.) acción de ir a la deriva.

driftwood, *n.* leña acarreada por el agua.

drill, *n.* taladro, *m.*, barrena, *f.*; terraja, *f.*; (mil.) instrucción de reclutas; — **sergeant,** sargento que enseña el ejercicio; —, *vt.* taladrar; (mil.) disciplinar reclutas; —, *vi.* hacer el ejercicio.

driller, *n.* taladrador, *m.*, persona que taladra.

drilling, *n.* perforación, *f.*

drillmaster, *n.* maestro de ejercicios.

drink, *vt.* and *vi.* beber, embeber; absorber; embriagarse; —, *n.* bebida, *f.*

drinkable, *adj.* potable, bebible.

drinker, *n.* bebedor, ra, borracho, cha.

drinking fountain, *n.* fuente pública para beber agua.

drip, *vt.* despedir algún líquido a gotas; —, *vi.* gotear, destilar; —, *n.* gotilla, *f.*; gotera, *f.*

dripping, *n.* pringue, *m.* y *f.*; chorreo, *m.*; —s, *n. pl.* pringue, *m.*; — **pan,** grasera, *f.*

drive, *n.* accionamiento, *m.*; paseo, *m.*; — **lever,** palanca de impulsión; **front wheel** —, accionamiento del eje delantero; **hydraulic** —, accionamiento hidráulico; **motor** —, accionamiento por motor; **to go out for a** —, ir de paseo, dar un paseo; —, *vt.* and *vi.* impeler; guiar, manejar, conducir; llevar; (mech.) impulsar; andar en coche; — **into,** hincar, forzar a; reducir a.

drive-in, *adj.* construído para permitir estacionar automóviles en forma que los automovilistas puedan comprar o ver sin abandonarlos; — **theatre,** teatro que reúna tales condiciones.

drivel, *n.* baba, *f.*; —, *vi.* babear.

driveling, *adj.* baboso.

driven, *p. p.* del verbo **drive.**

driver, *n.* empujador, *m.*; cochero, *m.*; carretero, *m.*; conductor, *m.*; chofer, *m.*; maquinista, *m.*

driveway, *n.* calzada o entrada para coches.

driving, *adj.* motriz; conductor; impulsor; — **lever,** palanca de impulsión; — **license,** matrícula para conducir vehículos; licencia de conductor o de chofer; — **permit,** tarjeta de circulación; licencia de conductor de vehículos; — **wheel,** rueda motriz; **to go out** —, ir de paseo, dar un paseo.

drizzle, *vi.* lloviznar; —, *n.* llovizna, *f.*

droll, *adj.* jocoso, gracioso; —, *n.* bufón, *m.*; —y, *adv.* jocosamente.

drollery, *n.* bufonería, bufonada, *f.*

dromedary, *n.* (zool.) dromedario, *m.*

drone, *n.* zángano de colmena; haragán, *m.*; —, *vi.* zanganear; dar un sonido sordo.

drool, *vi.* babear.

droop, *vi.* inclinarse, colgar; desanimarse, desfallecer; —, *vt.* dejar caer.

drop, *n.* gota, *f.*; pastilla, *f.*; pendiente, arete, *m.*; — **curtain,** telón de boca; — **forge,** forja a troquel; — **hammer,** martinete, *m.*; — **measurer,** bureta, *f.*; — **scene,** telón de foro; **by** —s, gota a gota; **lemon** —, pastilla de limón; **letter** —, buzón, *m.*; —, *vt.* destilar; soltar; cesar; dejar; dejar caer; —, *vi.* gotear; desvanecerse; sobrevenir; languidecer; salirse; **to** — **dead,** morir de repente.

droplet, *n.* gotita, *f.*

dropper, *n.* (med.) cuentagotas, *m.*

droppings, *n.* moquita, *f.*; excrementos de los animales domésticos.

dropsical, *adj.* hidrópico.

dropsy, *n.* hidropesía, *f.*

dross, *n.* escoria de metales; hez, *f.*

drought, *n.* seca, sequía, *f.*; sequedad, *f.*; sed, *f.*

drouth, *n.* sequía, *f.*

drove, *n.* manada, *f.*; hato, *m.*; muchedumbre, *f.*; rebaño, *m.*; **—,** pretérito del verbo **drive.**

drover, *n.* ganadero, *m.*

drown, *vt.* sumergir; anegar; **—,** *vi.* anegarse; ahogarse.

drowse, *vt.* and *vi.* adormercer, adormecerse.

drowsily, *adv.* soñolientamente; lentamente.

drowsiness, *n.* somnolencia, pereza, indolencia, *f.*

drowsy, *adj.* soñoliento; estúpido; **to grow —,** amodorrarse.

drub, *n.* golpe, *m.*, puñada, *f.*; **—,** *vt.* apalear, sacudir.

drubbing, *n.* paliza, zurra, bastonada, *f.*

drudge, *vi.* trabajar ardua y monótonamente; **—,** *n.* ganapán, *m.*; yunque, esclavo, *m.*

drudgery, *n.* trabajo arduo y monótono.

drug, *n.* droga, *f.*, medicamento, *m.*; fruslería de poca venta; **—,** *vt.* narcotizar.

druggist, *n.* droguero, farmacéutico, boticario, *m.*

drugstore, *n.* botica, *f.*

druid, *n.* druida, *m.*

drum, *n.* tambor, *m.*; tímpano (del oído), *m.*; **— barrel,** cilindro del tambor; **— brake band,** banda del freno del tambor; **— major,** tambor mayor.

drumbeat, *n.* toque de tambor.

drumhead, *n.* parche del tambor; tímpano del oído.

drummer, *n.* tambor, tamborilero, tamboritero, *m.*; (com.) viajante, *m.*

drumstick, *n.* palillo de tambor; pata de ave cocida), *f.*

drunk, *adj.* borracho, ebrio, embriagado; **—,** *p. p.* del verbo **drink.**

drunkard, *n.* borrachón, cuero, *m.*, persona que bebe mucho.

drunken, *adj.* ebrio; **— revel,** orgía, *f.*

drunkenness, *n.* embriaguez, borrachera, *f.*

dry, *adj.* árido, seco; sediento; insípido; severo; **— battery,** pila seca, batería seca; **— cell,** pila seca; **— cleaner,** tintorero, *m.*; **—cleaning establishment,** tienda de limpieza al seco **— dock,** dique de carena; **— farming,** labranza sin riego; **— goods,** mercancías generales (como ropas, telas, menudencias, etc.); **—goods store,** mercería, *f.*; **— ice,** hielo seco, anhídrido carbónico solidificado; **— rot,** podredumbre en legumbres y frutas causada por honguillos; (fig.) deterioro o desintegración por falta de sangre nueva o de ideas progresistas; **— wash,** lavado que se entrega seco pero no planchado; **—,** *vt.* secar; enjugar; **— clean,** limpiar en seco; **to make too —,** resecar; **—,** *vi.* secarse, enjugarse; **—ly,** *adv.* secamente, fríamente, estérilmente.

dry-dock, *vt.* poner en un dique de carena.

dryness, *n.* sequedad, *f.*; aridez de estilo.

dry-shod, *adj.* a pie enjuto, con los pies secos.

D.S.: Dental Surgeon, cirujano dentista; **Doctor of Science,** doctor en ciencias.

d.s. daylight saving, aprovechamiento de luz del día.

D.S.C. Distinguished Service Cross, Cruz de Servicios Distinguidos.

D.S.M. Distinguished Service Medal, Medalla de Servicios Distinguidos.

D.S.O. Distinguished Service Order, Orden de Servicios Distinguidos.

D.S.T. Daylight Saving Time, hora oficial (aprovechamiento de luz del día).

dual, *adj.* binario; **— control,** mando doble; mandos gemelos.

dualism, *n.* dualismo, *m.*

dualistic, *adj.* dualista.

dub, *vt.* armar a alguno caballero; apellidar, poner apodo.

dubious, *adj.* dudoso; **—ly,** *adv.* dudosamente.

ducal, *adj.* ducal.

ducat, *n.* ducado (moneda), *m.*

duchess, *n.* duquesa, *f.*

duchy, *n.* ducado, *m.*

duck, *n.* ánade, *m.* y *f.*, pato, ta; tela fuerte más delgada que la lona; sumergida, *f.*; agachada, *f.*; (coll.) apodo cariñoso (querida, linda, etc.); (mil.) camión anfibio para descargar buques de carga; **—,** *vt.* zambullir, somorgujar; **—,** *vi.* zambullirse, somorgujarse; agacharse.

duckbill, *n.* ornitorrinco, *m.*

duckling, *n.* anadeja, *f.*; apodo cariñoso (queridita, linda, etc.).

duct, *n.* canal, tubo, *m.*; conducto, *m.*

ductile, *adj.* dúctil, flexible; tratable.

ductility, *n.* ductilidad, *f.*; docilidad, *f.*

ductless, *adj.* sin canales o tubos.

dud, *n.* bomba que no estalla; (coll.) persona o cosa que resulta un fracaso; (coll.) ropa vieja.

dude, *n.* petimetre, *m.*

dudgeon, *n.* ojeriza, *f.*; resentimiento, *m.*

dudish, *adj.* afectado, peripuesto.

due, *adj.* debido, adecuado; **— bill,** abonaré, pagaré, *m.*; **— in time,** oportunamente; **—,** *adv.* directamente; **—,** *n.* derecho, *m.*; tributo, impuesto, *m.*; **to become —,** (com.) vencerse (una deuda, un plazo, etc.); **— to,** debido a.

duel, *n.* duelo, desafío, *m.*; **—,** *vi.* combatir en un duelo.

duelist, *n.* duelista, *m.*

duenna, *n.* dueña, institutriz, *f.*

duet, *n.* (mus.) dúo, *m.*

dug, *n.* teta, *f.*; **—,** pretérito y *p. p.* del verbo **dig.**

dugout, *n.* refugio subterráneo usado en casos de bombardeo; piragua, *f.*

duke, *n.* duque, *m.*

dukedom, *n.* ducado, *m.*

dulcet, *adj.* dulce, melodioso, armonioso.

dulcimer, *n.* (mus.) dulcémele, *m.*

dull, adj. lerdo, estúpido; insípido; obtuso; tosco; triste, murrio; opaco; romo; **— of hearing,** algo sordo; **—,** vt. entontecer; obstruir; ofuscar; **—y,** adv. estúpidamente; insípidamente.

dullard, n. estólido, da.

dullness, n. estupidez, torpeza, f.; somnolencia, f.; pereza, f.; pesadez, f.

duly, adv. debidamente; puntualmente.

dumb, adj. mudo; (coll.) estúpido; **—ly,** adv. sin chistar, silenciosamente; estúpidamente.

dumbbell, n. palanqueta de gimnasia; (coll.) persona estúpida.

dumbness, n. mudez, f.; silencio, m.; estupidez, f.

dumb-waiter, n. ascensor para comidas, basura, etc.

dumdum bullet, n. bala dumdum de dilatación.

dumfound, vt. and vi. confundir; enmudecer.

dummy, n. mudo, da; estúpido, da; espantajo, m.; maniquí, m.; alzapuertas, m.; modelo que usa un impresor.

dump, n. murria, tristeza, f.; vaciadero, depósito, m.; **— body,** caja de volteo de un camión; volteo, m.; **—s,** n. pl. abatimiento, m., murria, f.; **— truck,** carro de volteo; **to be in the —s,** tener melancolía.

dumper, n. vaciador, m.

dumping, n. vertimiento, m.; acto de arrojar, verter, descargar o volcar (basura, escombros, materiales de construcción, etc.); **— place, — ground,** lugar de descarga, vertedero, m.; **no — allowed,** se prohibe arrojar basura.

dumpling, n. bola de pasta rellena con fruta o carne.

dumpy, adj. gordo, rollizo.

dun, adj. bruno; sombrío; **—,** n. acreedor inoportuno; **—,** vt. and vi. pedir un acreedor a su deudor con importunidad; importunar.

dunce, n. zote, zopenco, m.; tonto, ta, bobo, ba.

dunderhead, n. badulaque, m.

dune, n. mégano, m., duna, f.

dung, n. estiércol, m.; **—,** vt. estercolar.

dungeon, n. calabozo, m.

dunghill, n. estercolero, m.

dunk, vt. and vi. meter, surmergir (pan torta, etc.) en café, té, leche, etc.

Dunkirk, Dunquerque, f.

duodecimal, adj. duodecimal.

duodécimo, n. libro en dozavo.

duodenal, adj. duodenal.

duodenum, n. duodeno, m.

duotone, adj. de dos tonos o colores.

duotype, n. dos fotograbados a media tinta obtenidos del mismo negativo.

dup. duplicate, dupdo., dup.do duplicado.

dupe, n. bobo, ba; víctima, f.; tonto,ta ; **—,** vt. engañar, embaucar.

duplex, adj. duplo, gemelo, doble; **—**

(apartment), apartamento para dos familias.

duplicate, n. duplicado, m.; copia, f.; **—,** vt. duplicar.

duplication, n. duplicación, f.

duplicity, n. duplicidad, f.; doblez, m. y f.

durability, n. duración, f.; estabilidad, f.

durable, adj. durable, duradero; **—bly,** adv. en forma duradera.

duralumin, n. duraluminio (marca de fábrica), m., aleación de cobre y aluminio.

durance, n. cautividad, f.; coacción, f.

duration, n. duración, f.

duress, n. compulsión, f.; prisión, f.

during, prep. durante.

dusk, n. color oscuro; crepúsculo, m.; **—,** vt. oscurecer; **—,** vi. hacerse noche.

dusky, adj. oscuro.

dust, n. polvo, m.; **— of grain,** tamo, m.; **— storm,** vendaval de polvo, tolvanera, f.; **house —,** tamo, m.; **—,** vt. despolvorear; llenar de polvo.

dustbin, n. receptáculo para polvo, ceniza, etc.

duster, n. plumero, m.; persona o cosa que quita el polvo.

dustiness, n. empolvoramiento, m.

dustman, n. barrendero, basurero, m.

dustpan, n. recogedor de basura, basurero, m.

dustwoman, n. barrendera, f.

dusty, adj. polvoriento; empolvado.

Dutch, adj. holandés, esa.

dutiable, adj. sujeto a derechos de aduana; **— goods,** mercancías sujetas a derechos.

dutiful, adj. obediente, sumiso; respetuoso; **—ly,** adv. obedientemente, respetuosamente.

duty, n. deber, m.; obligación, f.; quehacer, m.; respeto, homenaje, m.; (mil.) facción, f.; derechos de aduana; **off —,** libre; **on —,** de servicio, de guardia.

dwarf, n. enano, na; **—,** vt. impedir que alguna cosa llegue a su tamaño natural; **—,** vi. empequeñecerse.

dwarfish, adj. enano, pigmeo.

dwell, vi. habitar, morar; dilatarse; **— upon,** explayarse.

dweller, n. habitante, m. y f., morador, ra.

dwelling, n. habitación, residencia, f.; domicilio, m.; posada, f.; (coll.) cuartel, m.

dwindle, vi. mermar, disminuirse; degenerar; consumirse.

dye, vt. teñir, colorar; **—,** n. tinte, colorante, m.; **boiling —,** bullón, m.; **deep-blue —,** azul ultramarino.

dyed-in-the-wool, adj. convencido, ferviente; fanático, intransigente.

dyeing, n. tintorería, f.; arte o proceso de teñir.

dyer, n. tintorero, ra.

dyestuff, n. artículo de tinte.

dying, adj. agonizante, moribundo.

dyke, n. dique, canal, m., represa, f.

dynamic, adj. dinámico, enérgico; **—s,** n. pl. dinámica, f.; **—ally,** adv. con energía.

dynamite, *n.* dinamita, *f.*
dynamo, *n.* dínamo, *m.* y *f.*
dynamometer, *n.* dinamómetro, *m.*
dynast, *n.* dinasta, *m.*
dynastic, *adj.* dinástico.
dynasty, *n.* dinastía, *f.*
dyne, *n.* (phy.) dina, *f.*
dysentery, *n.* disentería, *f.*
dyspepsia, *n.* (med.) dispepsia, *f.*
dyspeptic, *adj.* dispéptico.
dz. dozen, dna. docena.

E

E. east, E. este, oriente.
ea. each, c/u. cada uno.
E. & O. E. errors and omissions excepted,
S.E. u O. salvo error u omisión.
each, *adj.* cada; **—,** *pron.* cada uno, cada
una, cada cual; **— other,** unos a otros,
mutuamente.
eager, *adj.* deseoso; fogoso; ardiente,
vehemente; celoso, fervoroso; **—ly,** *adv.*
vehementemente, ardientemente.
eagerness, *n.* ansia, *f.*; anhelo, *m.*; vehemencia, *f.*; ardor, *m.*
eagle, *n.* águila, *f.*, moneda de oro equivalente a diez dólares.
eagle-eyed, *adj.* de vista de lince, perspicaz.
eaglet, *n.* aguilucho, *m.*
ear, *n.* oreja, *f.*; oído, *m.*; asa, *f.*; (bot.)
espiga, *f.*; **by —,** de oído; **— muff,**
orejera, *f.*; **— of corn,** mazorca, *f.*; **—
specialist,** otólogo, *m.*; **— trumpet,**
trompetilla, *f.*; **pull by the —,** orejón, *m.*,
tirón de orejas; **—,** *vi.* formar orejas;
echar orejas.
earache, *n.* dolor de oído.
eardrop, *n.* pendiente, arete, *m.*
eardrum, *n.* tímpano, *m.*
earflap, *n.* orejera, *f.*
earl, *n.* conde, *m.*
earlap, *n.* punta de la oreja.
earldom, *n.* condado, *m.*
earlock, *n.* tufo, aladar, *m.*
early, *adj.* temprano, presto; **—,** *adv.* temprano; **— bird,** madrugador, ra.
earmark, *n.* marca de identificación.
earmuff, *n.* orejera, *f.*
earn, *vt.* ganar, obtener, conseguir.
earnest, *adj.* ardiente, fervoroso, serio,
importante; **—,** *n.* seriedad, *f.*; señal, *f.*;
prueba, *f.*; **— money,** caparra, *f.*; **in good
—,** de buena fe; **—ly,** *adv.* seriamente;
ansiosamente; con ahínco.
earnestness, *n.* ansia, *f.*; ardor, celo, *m.*;
seriedad, vehemencia, *f.*; **with —,** con
ahínco.
earnings, *n. pl.* (com.) ingresos, *m. pl.*, ganancias, *f. pl.*
earphone, *n.* audífono, auricular, *m.*
earring, *n.* zarcillo, pendiente, arete, *m.*
earshot, *n.* alcance del oído.

earth, *n.* tierra, *f.*, globo terráqueo; suelo, *m.*
earthborn, *adj.* nacido de la tierra, mortal,
humano.
earthen, *adj.* terreno; hecho de tierra;
de barro.
earthenware, *n.* loza de barro; vajilla
de barro.
earthly, *adj.* terrestre, mundano.
earthquake, *n.* terremoto, *m.*; temblor
de tierra.
earthward, *adv.* and *adj.* hacia la tierra.
earthwork, *n.* terraplén, *m.*; excavaciones
para obras de construcción.
earthworm, *n.* lombriz de tierra; persona
sórdida y despreciable.
earthy, *adj.* mundano, terrestre, terreno.
earwax, *n.* cerumen, *m.*
earwig, *n.* tijereta, *f.*, cortapicos, *m.*
ease, *n.* quietud, *f.*; reposo, ocio, *m.*; comodidad, *f.*; facilidad, *f.*; **at —,** con desahogo;
con soltura; **—,** *vt.* aliviar; mitigar.
easel, *n.* caballete (de los pintores), bastidor, *m.*
easement, *n.* alivio, apoyo, *m.*; ventaja, *f.*;
(law) servidumbre, *f.*
easily, *adv.* fácilmente.
easiness, *n.* facilidad, *f.*
east, *n.* oriente, este, *m.*
Easter, *n.* Pascua de Resurrección; **to wish
one a happy —,** dar las Pascuas, desear
felices Pascuas; **— egg,** huevo real o de
imitación dado como regalo para la
Pascua florida.
easterly, eastern, *adj.* oriental, del este.
East Indies, Indias orientales, *f. pl.*
eastward, *adv.* hacia el oriente, hacia el este.
easy, *adj.* fácil; cortés, sociable; cómodo,
pronto; libre; tranquilo; aliviado; **— chair,**
silla poltrona; **on — street,** próspero;
— mark, víctima, *f.*
easygoing, *adj.* lento, tranquilo, bonazo;
sereno; inalterable.
eat, *vt.* comer; roer; **—,** *vi.* alimentarse;
to — a light meal, merendar; **— up,**
comerse.
eatable, *adj.* comestible; **—s,** *n. pl.* víveres,
m. pl.
eaves, *n. pl.* socarrén, *m.*; alero, *m.*
eavesdrop, *vt.* escuchar escondido.
eavesdropper, *n.* espía, *m.* y *f.*, persona que
escucha a escondidas lo que no debe oír.
ebb, *n.* menguante, *m.*; disminución, *f.*;
decadencia, *f.*; **— tide,** marea menguante;
—, *vi.* menguar; decaer, disminuir; **—
and flow,** flujo y reflujo.
ebon, *adj.* de ébano; negro; **—,** *n.* (poet.)
ébano, *m.*
ebonite, *n.* ebonita, *f.*
ebony, *n.* ébano, *m.*; **to deal in —,** comerciar en negros.
ebullient, *adj.* efervescente, hirviente.
ebullition, *n.* ebullición, fermentación, *f.*;
agitación, emoción, *f.*
eccentric, eccentrical, *adj.* excéntrico.
eccentricity, *n.* excentricidad, *f.*

ecclesiastic, *adj.* eclesiástico; —, *n.* eclesiástico, *m.*

echelon, *n.* (mil.) escalón, *m.*, tropas o barcos de guerra en formación; **to form in** —, escalonar.

echinoderm, *n.* equinodermo, *m.*

echo, *n.* eco, *m.*; —, *vi.* resonar, repercutir (la voz) ; —, *vt.* hacer eco.

éclair, *n.* torta garapiñada llena de nata.

eclectic, *n.* and *adj.* ecléctico, ca.

eclipse, *n.* eclipse, *m.*; —, *vt.* eclipsar.

ecliptic, *n.* eclíptica, *f.*; —, *adj.* eclíptico.

eclogue, *n.* égloga, *f.*

econ. economics, econ. economía.

economic, economical, *adj.* económico, frugal, parco, moderado.

economics, *n.* economía, *f.*

economist, *n.* economista, *m.*

economize, *vt.* and *vi.* economizar; reducirse.

economy, *n.* economía, *f.*; frugalidad, *f.*

ecru, *n.* tejido no blanqueado como seda, lino, etc.; —, *adj.* del color del tejido arriba descrito.

ecstasy, *n.* éxtasi, éxtasis, *m.*

ecstatic, *adj.* extático; —**ally,** *adv.* en éxtasis.

ecumenical, *adj.* ecuménico.

eczema, *n.* eczema, *f.*

ed.: edition, ed. edición; **editor,** director, redactor (de una publicación).

eddy, *n.* reflujo de agua; remolino, *m.*; —, *vi.* remolinar.

edelweiss, *n.* (bot.) flor de los Alpes.

edema, *n.* edema, *m.*

edge, *n.* filo, borde, *m.*; orilla, *f.*; vera, *f.*; punta, *f.*; esquina, *f.*; margen, *m.* y *f.*; acrimonia, *f.*; —, *vt.* afilar, ribetear; introducir; —, *vi.* avanzar poco a poco escurriéndose; — **in,** hacer entrar; **on** —, impaciente, ansioso; — **away,** alejarse; (naut.) inclinarse a sotavento.

edgeways, *adv.* de filo, de lado.

edgewise, *adv.* de canto, de lado.

edging, *n.* orla, orilla, *f.*

edibility, *n.* calidad de comible.

edible, *adj.* comedero, comestible.

edict, *n.* edicto, mandato, *m.*

edification, *n.* edificación, *f.*

edifice, *n.* edificio, *m.*; fábrica, *f.*

edify, *vt.* instruir por medio del ejemplo; aprovechar moral o espiritualmente.

Edinburgh, Edimburgo, *m.*

edit, *vt.* redactar; dirigir (una publicación); revisar o corregir (un artículo, etc.).

edition, *n.* edición, *f.*; publicación, *f.*; impresión, *f.*; tirada, *f.*

editor, *n.* director, redactor (de una publicación), *m.*; persona que corrige o revisa (un artículo, etc.).

editorial, *n.* editorial, *m.*, artículo de fondo; — **staff,** redacción, *f.*, cuerpo de redacción.

editorship, *n.* cargo de redactor o director, dirección (de una publicación).

Edmund, Edmundo.

educate, *vt.* educar; enseñar.

educated, *adj.* educado, instruído.

education, *n.* educación, *f.*; crianza, *f.*

educational, *adj.* educativo.

educator, *n.* pedagogo, educador, maestro, *m.*

educe, *vt.* educir, sacar a luz, poner de manifiesto.

Edward, Eduardo.

eel, *n.* anguila, *f.*

eelpout, *n.* (pez) mustela, *f.*

eerie, *adj.* que infunde terror, como un fantasma; asustado; horripilante.

efface, *vt.* borrar, destruir.

effacement, *n.* cancelación, *f.*

effect, *n.* efecto, *m.*; realidad, *f.*; —**s,** *n. pl.* efectos, bienes, *m. pl.*; —, *vt.* efectuar, ejecutar.

effective, *adj.* eficaz; efectivo; real; —**ly,** *adv.* efectivamente, en efecto; —, *n.* soldado disponible para la guerra.

effectiveness, *n.* efectividad, *f.*

effectual, *adj.* efectivo, adecuado; eficaz; —**ly,** *adv.* eficazmente.

effectuate, *vt.* efectuar.

effeminacy, *n.* afeminación, *f.*

effeminate, *vt.* afeminar, debilitar; —, *vi.* afeminarse, enervarse; —, *adj.* afeminado; — **man,** marica, *m.*; —**ly,** *adv.* con afeminación.

efferent, *adj.* eferente.

effervesce, *vi.* hervir, fermentar.

effervescence, *n.* efervescencia, *f.*; hervor, *m.*

effervescent, *adj.* efervescente.

effete, *adj.* estéril; gastado.

efficacious, *adj.* eficaz; —**ly,** *adv.* eficazmente.

efficacy, *n.* eficacia, *f.*

efficiency, *n.* eficiencia, virtud, *f.*, rendimiento (de una máquina), *m.*

efficient, *adj.* eficaz; eficiente.

Effie, Euphemia, Eufemia.

effigy, *n.* efigie, imagen, *f.*, retrato, *m.*

effloresce, *vi.* eflorescerse.

efflorescence, *n.* eflorescencia, *f.*; excrecencia, *f.*

efflorescent, *adj.* eflorescente.

effluvium, *n.* efluvio, *m.*; emanación, *f.*

effort, *n.* esfuerzo, empeño, *m.*, gestión, *f.*

effortless, *adj.* sin esfuerzo alguno.

effrontery, *n.* descaro, atrevimiento, *m.*; desvergüenza, *f.*

effulgence, *n.* esplendor, fulgor, *m.*

effulgent, *adj.* resplandeciente.

effuse, *vi.* esparcir, verter.

effusion, *n.* efusión, *f.*; flujo de palabras.

effusive, *adj.* expansivo; —**ly,** *adv.* con expansión, expansivamente.

eft, *n.* lagartija, *f.*

e.g. for example, p.ej. por ejemplo, vg. verbigracia.

egg, *n.* huevo, *m.*; — **beater,** batidor de huevos; — **cell,** célula embrionaria; — **white,** clara de huevo; **candied** —, huevo de faltriquera; **deviled** —, huevo relleno;

fried —, huevo frito o estrellado; **hard-boiled** —, huevo cocido; **poached** —, huevo escalfado; **scrambled** —, huevo revuelto; **soft-boiled** —, huevo pasado por agua; —, *vt.* mezclar con huevos; **to** — **on,** airar, incitar.

eggnog, *n.* yema mejida.

eggplant, *n.* (bot.) berenjena, *f.*

eggshell, *n.* cáscara o cascarón de huevo.

egg-yolk, *n.* yema de huevo.

egis, aegis, *n.* égida, protección, defensa, *f.*

eglantine, *n.* agavanzo, *m.*

ego, *n.* ego, yo, *m.*

egocentric, *adj.* egoísta, concentrado en sí mismo.

egoism, egotism, *n.* egoísmo, *m.*

egoist, egotist, *n.* egoísta, *m.* y *f.*

egoistical, egotistical, *adj.* egoísta.

egregious, *adj.* egregio, famoso, excelente; —**ly,** *adv.* egregiamente.

egress, egression, *n.* salida, *f.*

egret, aigrette, *n.* garzota, garza, *f.*: penacho, *m.*

Egypt, Egipto, *m.*

Egyptian, *n.* and *adj.* egipcíaco, ca, egipciano, na, egipcio, cia.

eh! *interj.* ¡eh! ¿qué?

eider, *n.* ganso marino.

eiderdown, *n.* edredón, plumazón, plumón, *m.*

eight, *adj.* ocho; —, *n.* ocho, *m.*

eighteen, *adj.* dieciocho; —, *n.* dieciocho, *m.*

eighteenth, *adj.* décimoctavo, dieciocheno; —, *n.* décimoctavo, dieciocheno, *m.*

eighth, *adj.* octavo; —, *n.* octavo, *m.*; —**ly,** *adv.* en el octavo lugar.

eightieth, *adj.* octogésimo; —, *n.* octogésimo, *m.*

eighty, *adj.* ochenta; —, *n.* ochenta, *m.*

Eire, Erin, *f.*

either, *pron.* and *adj.* cualquiera, uno de dos; —, *conj.* o, sea, ya, ora.

ejaculate, *vt.* arrojar, despedir; exclamar.

ejaculation, *n.* jaculatoria, *f.*

ejaculatory, *adj.* disparado de pronto, repentino; jaculatorio.

eject, *vt.* expeler, desechar.

ejection, *n.* expulsión, *f.*; (med.) evacuación, *f.*

eke, *vt.* adicionar, prolongar.

elaborate, *vt.* elaborar; —, *adj.* trabajado, primoroso; —**ly,** *adv.* cuidadosamente.

elaboration, *n.* elaboración, *f.*

elapse, *vi.* pasar, correr, transcurrir (el tiempo).

elastic, *adj.* elástico; repercusivo.

elasticity, *n.* elasticidad, *f.*

elate, *vt.* ensoberbecer; exaltar, elevar; —**d,** exaltado, animoso.

elation, *n.* júbilo, *m.*

elbow, *n.* codo, *m.*; — **rest,** ménsula, *f.*; —, *vt.* and *vi.* dar codazos, empujar con el codo; codearse.

elbowroom, *n.* anchura, *f.*; espacio suficiente; (fig.) libertad, latitud, *f.*

elder, *adj.* que tiene más edad, mayor; —, *n.* anciano, antepasado, *m.*; eclesiástico, *m.*; jefe de una tribu; (bot.) saúco, *m.*

elderberry, *n.* (bot.) baya del saúco.

elderly, *adj.* de edad madura.

eldest, *adj.* mayor, más anciano.

Eleanor, Leonor.

elec. electricity, elect. electricidad.

elect, *vt.* elegir; —, *adj.* elegido, electo, escogido.

election, *n.* elección, *f.*; —**s,** comicios, *m. pl.*

electioneer, *n.* persona que trabaja por el éxito de un candidato o partido en una elección.

electioneering, *n.* propaganda electoral.

elective, *adj.* electivo; — **attraction,** afinidad química; —**ly,** *adv.* electivamente.

elector, *n.* elector, ra.

electoral, *adj.* electoral; — **college,** colegio electoral.

electorate, *n.* electorado, *m.*

electric, *adj.* eléctrico; — **cable,** cable conductor; — **chair,** silla eléctrica; — **eel,** pez con forma de anguila, del Orinoco y Amazonas, con órganos especiales que trasmiten choques eléctricos; — **eye,** célula fotoeléctrica; — **fixtures,** instalación eléctrica; — **lamp,** bujía eléctrica; — **meter,** contador electrómetro; — **motor,** electromotor, *m.*; — **plant,** planta eléctrica; — **railroad,** ferrocarril eléctrico; — **switch,** conmutador, *m.*; — **wire,** hilo o alambre conductor; — **welding,** soldadura eléctrica.

electrical, *adj.* eléctrico; — **engineering,** electrotecnia, *f.*, ingeniería eléctrica; — **transcription,** radiodifusión por fonógrafo.

electrician, *n.* electricista, *m.*

electricity, *n.* electricidad, *f.*

electrification, *n.* electrificación, electrización, *f.*

electrify, *vt.* electrizar.

electroanalysis, *n.* electroanálisis, *m.*

electrochemistry, *n.* electroquímica, *f.*

electrocute, *vt.* electrocutar, matar por medio de choque eléctrico.

electrocution, *n.* electrocución, *f.*

electrode, *n.* electrodo, *m.*

electrodynamic, *adj.* electrodinámico.

electrodynamics, *n.* electrodinámica, *f.*

electrolysis, *n.* electrólisis, *f.*

electrolyte, *n.* electrólito, *m.*

electrolytic, *adj.* electrolítico.

electrolyzation, *n.* electrolización, *f.*

electrolyze, *vt.* electrolizar; descomponer por electricidad.

electromagnet, *n.* electroimán, *m.*

electromagnetic, *adj.* electromagnético; — **field,** campo electromagnético.

electromagnetism, *n.* electromagnetismo, *m.*

electrometallurgy, *n.* electrometalurgia, *j.*

electrometer, *n.* electrómetro, *m.*

electrometry, *n.* electrometría, *f.*

electromotive, *adj.* electromotriz; **— force,** fuerza electromotriz.

electron, *n.* electrón, *m.*

electronegative, *adj.* electronegativo; **—,** *n.* electronegativo, *m.*

electronic, *adj.* electrónico.

electronics, *n.* electrónica, *f.*, parte de la física que estudia los electrones.

electrophysiology, *n.* electrofisiología, *f.*

electroplate, *vt.* electroplatear, platear; **—,** *n.* artículo electroplateado.

electroplating, *n.* enchapado al galvanismo.

electropositive, *adj.* electropositivo; **—,** *n.* electropositivo, *m.*

electropuncture, *n.* electropuntura, *f.*

electroscope, *n.* electroscopio, *m.*

electrostatic, *adj.* electrostático.

electrostatics, *n. pl.* electrostática, *f.*

electrotechnics, *n.* electrotecnia, *f.*

electrotherapy, *n.* electroterapia, *f.*

electrotype, *n.* electrotipo, *m.*

electrum, *n.* electro, *m.*

eleemosynary, *adj.* caritativo.

elegance, *n.* elegancia, *f.*

elegant, *adj.* elegante, delicado; lujoso; galano; guapo; **—ly,** *adv.* elegantemente.

elegiac, *adj.* elegíaco.

elegy, *n.* elegía, *f.*

element, *n.* elemento, *m.*; fundamento, *m.*; **—s,** *n. pl.* elementos; principios, *m. pl.*; bases, *f. pl.*; elementos atmosféricos; **be in one's —,** estar uno en su elemento.

elemental, *adj.* elemental, simple, inicial.

elementary, *adj.* elemental, simple, inicial; **— school,** escuela primaria.

elephant, *n.* elefante, *m.*

elephantiasis, *n.* (med.) elefantíasis, elefancía, *f.*

elephantine, *adj.* elefantino; grande y chabacano.

elevate, *vt.* elevar, alzar, exaltar.

elevated, *adj.* elevado; **— railroad,** ferrocarril elevado; **— train,** tren elevado.

elevation, *n.* elevación, *f.*; altura, *f.*; alteza (de pensamientos), *f.*

elevator, *n.* ascensor, elevador, *m.*; **— hoist,** montacargas, *m.*

eleven, *n.* and *adj.* once, *m.*, oncena, *f.*

eleventh, *n.* and *adj.* onceno, undécimo, *m.*; **— hour,** la última hora, lo más tarde posible.

elf, *n.* duende, *m.*; persona traviesa.

elfin, *adj.* parecido o relativo a los duendes; **—,** *n.* duende, *m.*; persona traviesa.

elfish, *adj.* como duende; travieso.

elicit, *vt.* incitar; educir; sacar; atraer.

elide, *vt.* elidir.

eligibility, *n.* elegibilidad, *f.*

eligible, *adj.* elegible; deseable.

eliminate, *vt.* eliminar, descartar.

elimination, *n.* eliminación, *f.*

Elinor, Leonor.

Elisha, Eliseo.

elision, *n.* elisión, *f.*

élite, *n.* la flor y nata, la alta sociedad; lo más escogido.

elixir, *n.* elixir, *m.*

Eliza, Elisa.

Elizabeth, Isabel.

elk, *n.* alce, *m.*, anta, *f.*

ell, *n.* ana (medida), *f.*

Ella, Eleanor, Leonor.

Ellen, Elena.

ellipse, *n.* (math.) elipse, *f.*

ellipsis, *n.* (gram.) elipsis, *f.*

elliptic, elliptical, *adj.* elíptico.

Ellis, Eliseo.

elm, *n.* olmo, *m.*

elocution, *n.* elocución, *f.*; declamación, *f.*

elocutionist, *n.* profesor de declamación; declamador, ra.

elongate, *vt.* and *vi.* alargar, extender.

elongation, *n.* alargamiento, *m.*, extensión, *f.*

elope, *vi.* escapar, huir; fugarse con un amante.

elopement, *n.* fuga con un amante; huída, *f.*

eloquence, *n.* elocuencia, *f.*; facundia, *f.*

eloquent, *adj.* elocuente; **—ly,** *adv.* elocuentemente.

Elsa, Alicia.

else, *adj.* otro; **—,** *adv.* en lugar distinto; en forma distinta; **nothing —,** nada más; **somewhere —,** en alguna otra parte; **—,** *conj.* de otro modo; si no.

elsewhere, *adv.* en otra parte.

elucidate, *vt.* dilucidar, explicar.

elucidation, *n.* elucidación, explicación, *f.*

elude, *vt.* eludir, evadir.

elusion, *n.* escapatoria, *f.*; fraude, artificio, *m.*

elusive, elusory, *adj.* artificioso, falaz; evasivo.

elves, *n. pl.* de **elf,** duendes, *m. pl.*

emaciate, *vt.* extenuar, adelgazar.

emaciated, *adj.* demacrado; chupado; **to become —,** demacrarse.

emaciation, *n.* extenuación, *f.*; enflaquecimiento, *m.*

emanate, *vi.* emanar.

emanation, *n.* emanación, *f.*; origen, *m.*

emancipate, *vt.* emancipar; dar libertad.

emancipation, *n.* emancipación, *f.*

emancipator, *n.* libertador, *m.*

Emanuel, Manuel.

emasculate, *vt.* castrar, enflaquecer; debilitar.

emasculation, *n.* castración, *f.*; debilitación, *f.*

embalm, *vt.* embalsamar.

embalmer, *n.* embalsamador, *m.*

embalmment, *n.* embalsamamiento, *m.*

embank, *vt.* terraplenar; represar.

embankment, *n.* encajonamiento, *m.*; malecón, dique, *m.*, presa, *f.*; terraplén, *m.*

embargo, *n.* embargo, *m.*, detención, *f.*; comiso, *m.*; **—,** *vt.* (law) embargar.

embark, *vt.* and *vi.* embarcar; embarcarse.

embarkation, *n.* embarcación, *f.*

embarrass, vt. avergonzar, desconcertar, turbar.

embarrassed, adj. avergonzado, cortado.

embarrassing, adj. penoso.

embarrassment, n. turbación, f.; bochorno, m.; vergüenza, pena, f.

embassy, n. embajada, f.

embattle, vt. formar en orden de batalla; fortificar.

embed, vt. encajar; incrustar.

embellish, vt. hermosear, adornar.

embellishment, n. adorno, m.

embers, n. pl. ascua, pavesa, chispa, f.

embezzle, vt. apropiarse alguna cosa ilícitamente; malgastar, desfalcar.

embezzlement, n. hurto, m.; desfalco, m.

embezzler, n. desfalcador, ra.

embitter, vt. amargar, agriar.

emblazon, vt. blasonar.

emblazonment, n. adorno con blasón; glorificación, f.

emblem, n. emblema, m.

emblematic, emblematical, adj. emblemático, simbólico.

embodiment, n. incorporación, f.

embody, vt. encarnar, incluir.

embolden, vt. animar, envalentonar.

embolism, n. embolismo, m.; (med.) embolia, f.

embolus, n. émbolo, m.

embosom, vt. encerrar, ocultar; acoger con cariño.

emboss, vt. formar alguna cosa en relieve.

embower, vt. and vi. enramar, emparrar.

embrace, vt. abrazar; contener; —, n. abrazo, m.

embrasure, n. tronera, buhedera, f.

embrocation, n. (med.) embrocación, f.

embroider, vt. bordar.

embroiderer, n. bordador, ra, recamador, ra.

embroidery, n. bordado, m.; bordadura, f.; — frame, bastidor, m.; — silk, seda de bordar.

embroil, vt. embrollar; confundir.

embroilment, n. confusión, f., enredo, m.

embryo, n. embrión, m.

embryology, n. embriología, f.

embryonal, adj. embrionario.

embryonic, adj. embrionario.

emend, vt. enmendar, corregir, mejorar.

emendation, n. enmienda, corrección, f.

emerald, n. esmeralda, f.

emerge, vi. salir, proceder; surgir.

emergence, n. emergencia, aparición, f.

emergency, n. aprieto, m.; emergencia, f.; necesidad urgente; — landing field, (aer.) campo de aterrizaje de emergencia; — outlet, aliviadero, m.; in case of —, en caso de fuerza.

emergent, adj. emergente; urgente.

emeritus, adj. emérito, retirado.

emersion, n. emersión, f.

emery, n. esmeril, m.

emetic, n. and adj. emético, vomitivo, m.

E.M.F., e.m.f., electromotive force, F.E.M. fuerza electromotriz.

emigrant, n. and adj. emigrante, m y f.

emigrate, vi. emigrar.

emigration, n. emigración, f.

Emily, Emilia.

eminence, n. altura, sumidad, f.: eminencia, excelencia, f.

eminent, adj. eminente, elevado; distingui-do; relevante; — domain, dominio superior de un poder soberano; —ly, adv. eminentemente.

emissary, n. emisario, m.; espía, m. y f.

emission, n. emisión, f.

emit, vt. emitir, echar de sí; arrojar, despedir.

Emma, Ema, Manuela.

Emmanuel, Manuel.

emollient, n. and adj. emoliente, m.

emolument, n. emolumento, provecho, m.

emotion, n. emoción, f.; conmoción, f.

emotional, adj. sensible, impresionable.

emotionalism, n. emocionalismo, m.

emotive, adj. emotivo, emocional.

empanel, vt. citar a los jurados.

emperor, n. emperador, m.

emphasis, n. énfasis, m. y f.

emphasize, vt. hablar con énfasis; acentuar; hacer hincapié; recalcar.

emphatic, adj. enfático; —ally, adv. enfáticamente; rotundamente.

empire, n. imperio, m.

empiric, n. empírico, medicastro, m.; —, adj. empírico.

empirical, adj. empírico; —ly, adv. como un empírico.

empiricism, n. empirismo, m.

emplacement, n. emplazamiento, m.

employ, vt. emplear, ocupar; —, n. empleo, m.; ocupación, f.; oficio público.

employee, n. empleado, da.

employer, n. amo, ama; dueño, ña; patrón, ona.

employment, n. empleo, m.; ocupación, f.; cargo, m.; to give — to, colocar, dar empleo a.

emporium, n. emporio, m.

empower, vt. autorizar, dar poder.

empress, n. emperatriz, f.

emptiness, n. vaciedad, f.; vacuidad, f.; futilidad, f.

empty, adj. vacío; vano; ignorante; —, vt. vaciar, evacuar, verter.

empty-handed, adj. manivacío.

empty-headed, adj. vano, hueco, frívolo, tonto.

empyrean, adj. empíreo, celestial.

emulate, vt. emular, competir con; imitar.

emulation, n. emulación, f.; rivalidad, f.

emulative, adj. emulativo.

emulous, adj. émulo; —ly, adv. a competencia.

emulsify, vt. emulsionar.

emulsion, n. emulsión, f.

enable, vt. habilitar; poner en estado de; facilitar, proporcionar.

enact, *vt.* establecer, decretar; efectuar; estatuir.

enactment, *n.* decreto, dictamen, *m.*

enamel, *n.* esmalte, charol, *m.*; —, *vt.* esmaltar, charolar.

enameler, *n.* charolista, *m.*

enamelware, *n.* ollas charoladas o esmaltadas.

enamor, *vt.* enamorar.

enamored, *adj.* enamorado.

encamp, *vi.* acamparse.

encampment, *n.* campamento, *m.*

encase, *vt.* encajar, encajonar, incluir.

encaustic, *adj.* encáustico; — **painting,** pintura encáustica.

encephalic, *adj.* encefálico.

encephalitis, *n.* (med.) encefalitis, *f.*, inflamación del cerebro.

enchain, *vt.* encadenar.

enchant, *vt.* encantar.

enchanter, *n.* encantador, nigromante.

enchanting, *adj.* encantador.

enchantment, *n.* encanto, *m.*

enchantress, *n.* encantadora, *f.*; mujer seductora.

enchase, *vt.* engastar, adornar, grabar.

encircle, *vt.* cercar, circundar, circunvalar.

encirclement, *n.* circuición, *f.*; circunvalación, *f.*

enclose, *vt.* cercar, circunvalar, circundar; incluir; encerrar.

enclosure, *n.* cercamiento, *m.*; cercado, *m.*; caja (de engranaje, etc.), *f.*; anexo (en una carta), *m.*

encomium, *n.* encomio, elogio, *m.*

encompass, *vt.* circundar; cercar; circuir.

encore, *n.* (theat.) repetición, *f.*; —! *interj.* ¡otra vez! ¡que se repita! —, *vt.* pedir que un actor repita lo que ha ejecutado.

encounter, *n.* encuentro, *m.*; duelo, *m.*; pelea, *f.*; —, *vt.* encontrar; —, *vi.* encontrarse; combatir.

encourage, *vt.* animar, alentar; envalentonar; dar aliento.

encouragement, *n.* estímulo, aliento, *m.*, animación, *f.*

encouraging, *adj.* alentador.

encroach, *vt.* usurpar, avanzar gradualmente.

encroachment, *n.* usurpación, intrusión, *f.*

encrust, *vt.* encostrar.

encumber, *vt.* embarazar, cargar; estorbar.

encumbrance, *n.* embarazo, impedimento, *m.*; estorbo, *m.*

ency. encyclopedia, Enc. enciclopedia.

encyclical, *adj.* encíclico; —, *n.* encíclica, *f.*

encyclopedia, *n.* enciclopedia, *f.*

encyclopedic, *adj.* enciclopédico.

end, *n.* fin, *m.*; extremidad, *f.*; cabo, *m.*; término, *m.*; propósito, intento, *m.*; punto, *m.*; **at the — of,** al cabo de; **the — of the world,** la consumación de los siglos; **no —,** sinnúmero, *m.*; **on —,** en pie, de pie; **to accomplish one's —,** salirse con la suya; **to no —,** en vano; **to the — that,** para

que; **upper —,** cabecera, *f.*; —, *vt.* matar, concluir, fenecer; terminar; —, *vi.* acabarse, terminarse.

endanger, *vt.* poner en peligro, arriesgar.

endear, *vt.* hacer querer.

endearment, *n.* terneza, *f.*; encarecimiento, afecto, *m.*

endeavor, *vi.* esforzarse; intentar; —, *vt.* tentar; —, *n.* esfuerzo, *m.*

endemic, endemical, *adj.* endémico.

ending, *n.* conclusión, cesación, *f.*; muerte, *f.*

endive, *n.* (bot.) endibia, escarola, *f.*

endless, *adj.* infinito, perpetuo; **—ly,** *adv.* sin fin, perpetuamente.

endocarditis, *n.* (med.) endocarditis, *f.*

endocrine, *adj.* endocrino, de secreción interna; —, *n.* secreción interna.

endometritis, *n.* (med.) endometritis, *f.*

endorse, *vt.* endosar (una letra de cambio); apoyar, sancionar.

endorsee, *n.* endosatario, ria; cesionario, ria.

endorsement, *n.* endorso, endoso, endose, *m.*

endorser (of a draft), *n.* cedente (de un giro o letra), *m.*

endothermic, *adj.* endotérmico.

endow, *vt.* dotar.

endowment, *n.* dote, dotación, *f.*

endue, *vt.* dotar, investir.

endurable, *adj.* soportable.

endurance, *n.* duración, *f.*; paciencia, *f.*; sufrimiento, *m.*

endure, *vt.* sufrir, soportar; —, *vi.* durar; conllevar; sufrir.

endways, endwise, *adv.* de punta, derecho; a lo largo.

ENE, E.N.E. east-northeast, ENE estenordeste.

enema, *n.* lavativa, enema, *f.*

enemy, *n.* enemigo, ga; antagonista, *m.* y *f.*

energetic, *adj.* enérgico, vigoroso.

energize, *vt.* vigorizar, robustecer; —, *vi.* emitir energía.

energy, *n.* energía, fuerza, *f.*

enervate, *vt.* enervar, debilitar, quitar las fuerzas.

enervation, *n.* enervación, *f.*, enflaquecimiento, *m.*

enfeeble, *vt.* debilitar, enervar.

enfilade, *n.* hila, hilera, *f.*; —, *vt.* (mil.) enfilar.

enfold, *vt.* envolver, arrollar; rodear.

enforce, *vt.* compeler; hacer cumplir (una ley), poner en vigor.

enforceable, *adj.* capaz de hacerse cumplir.

enforcement, *n.* compulsión, coacción, *f.*; fuerza, *f.*; cumplimiento (de una ley), *m.*

enfranchise, *vt.* franquear, conceder franquicia; naturalizar.

enfranchisement, *n.* emancipación, *f.*; ciudadanía, *f.*

Eng. England, Ingl. Inglaterra.

eng.: engineering, ingen. ingeniería; **engraving,** grab. grabado.

engage, *vt.* empeñar, obligar; ocupar; —, *vi.* comprometerse.

engaged, *adj.* comprometido.

engagement, *n.* empeño, *m.*; combate, *m.*; pelea, *f.*; obligación, *f.*; noviazgo, compromiso, *m.*; contrato, *m.*; cita, *f.*

engaging, *adj.* simpático, atractivo; **—ly,** de un modo atractivo.

engender, *vt.* engendrar; producir; —, *vi.* producirse.

engine, *n.* máquina, *f.*; locomotora, *f.*; instrumento, *m.*; **— house,** casa de máquinas; **— room,** casa de máquinas; **internal-combustion —,** motor de explosión, motor de combustión interna.

engineer, *n.* ingeniero, *m.*; maquinista, *m.*.

engineering, *n.* ingeniería, *f.*

England, Inglaterra, *f.*

English, *n.* and *adj.* inglés, *m.*; **— Channel,** Canal de la Mancha; **— saddle,** galápago, *m.*, silla de montar a la inglesa.

Englishman, inglés, *m.*

Englishwoman, *n.* inglesa, *f.*

engorge, *vt.* and *vi.* engullir, devorar.

engraft, *vt.* injertar.

engrave, *vt.* grabar; esculpir; tallar.

engraver, *n.* grabador, *m.*

engraving, *n.* grabado, *m.*; estampa, *f.*

engross, *vt.* poner en limpio, copiar en forma legible; concentrar; monopolizar.

engulf, *vt.* engolfar, tragar, sumir.

enhance, *vt.* realzar, elevar, intensificar.

enhancement, *n.* mejoramiento, realce, *m.*

enigma, *n.* enigma, *m.*

enigmatic, *adj.* enigmático.

enigmatical, *adj.* enigmático; **—ly,** *adv.* enigmáticamente.

enjoin, *vt.* ordenar, mandar; advertir; prohibir.

enjoy, *vt.* gozar; poseer; saborear; disfrutar de.

enjoyable, *adj.* agradable.

enjoyment, *n.* goce, disfrute, *m.* placer, *m.*; fruición, *f.*; usufructo, *m.*

enkindle, *vt.* encender, excitar.

enlarge, *vt.* engrandecer, dilatar, extender; ampliar; —, *vi.* extenderse, dilatarse; **— upon,** explayarse.

enlargement, *n.* aumento, *m.*; ampliación (de una fotografía, etc.), *f.*

enlighten, *vt.* aclarar; iluminar; instruir.

enlightenment, *n.* luces, *f. pl.*, ilustración, *f.*; aclaración, *f.*

enlist, *vt.* alistar, reclutar; —, *vi.* inscribirse como recluta, engancharse.

enlistment, *n.* alistamiento, *m.*; **— record,** libreta de la dotación.

enliven, *vt.* animar; avivar; alegrar.

en masse, *adj.* en masa.

enmesh, *vt.* enmarañar; coger con arte o de improviso.

enmity, *n.* enemistad, *f.*; odio, *m.*

ennoble, *vt.* ennoblecer.

ennoblement, *n.* ennoblecimiento, *m.*

ennui, *n.* fastidio, aburrimiento, *m.*

enormity, *n.* enormidad, *f.*; atrocidad, *f.*

enormous, *adj.* enorme; **—ly,** *adv.* enormemente.

enough, *adj.* bastante, suficiente; —, *adv.* suficientemente; —, *n.* suficiencia, *f.*; **—!** *interj.* ¡basta! ¡suficiente! ¡ya!

enquire, *vt.* = **inquire.**

enquiry, *n.* = **inquiry.**

enrage, *vt.* enfurecer, irritar.

enraged, *adj.* colérico, sañoso.

enrapture, *vt.* arrebatar, entusiasmar; encantar.

enrich, *vt.* enriquecer; adornar.

enrichment, *n.* enriquecimiento, *m.*

enrobe, *vt.* vestir.

enroll, *vt.* registrar, inscribir; arrollar.

enrolling office, *n.* oficina de registro.

enrollment, *n.* matriculación, *f.*

en route, en ruta, en el camino.

ensconce, *vt.* esconder, ocultar; acomodar; poner en lugar seguro.

ensemble, *n.* conjunto, *m.*; traje de mujer compuesto de más de una pieza.

enshrine, *vt.* guardar como reliquia; estimar como cosa sagrada.

enshroud, *vt.* amortajar.

ensign, *n.* bandera, *f.*; enseña, *f.*; (naval) alférez, *m.*; subteniente, *m.*

enslave, *vt.* esclavizar, cautivar.

enslavement, *n.* servidumbre, esclavitud, *f.*

ensnare, *vt.* entrampar; engañar.

ensue, *vi.* seguirse; suceder.

ensure, *vt.* asegurar.

entail, *n.* (law) vínculo, mayorazgo, *m.*; —, *vt.* vincular; ocasionar.

entangle, *vt.* enmarañar, embrollar, embarazar.

entangled, *adj.* grifo, enmarañado.

entanglement, *n.* enredo, *m.*; dédalo, laberinto, *m.*; maraña, complicación, *f.*, nudo, *m.*

enter, *vt.* entrar, meter; admitir; registrar; penetrar; —, *vi.* entrar, empeñarse en algo; emprender; aventurar; **to — a contest,** matricularse o tomar parte en un concurso; **to — to the account of,** sentar en cuenta de.

enteric, *adj.* entérico.

enteritis, *n.* enteritis, *f.*

enterprise, *n.* empresa, *f.*

enterprising, *adj.* emprendedor.

entertain, *vt.* entretener; obsequiar, agasajar; divertir; **to — the hope,** abrigar la esperanza.

entertainer, *n.* festejador, ra; persona que divierte a otra; cantante, bailarín, etc., que entretiene en una fiesta.

entertaining, *adj.* divertido, chistoso.

entertainment, *n.* festejo, *m.*; diversión, *f.*, entretenimiento, pasatiempo, *m.*

enthrall, *vt.* esclavizar; encantar, cautivar.

enthrone, *vt.* entronizar.

enthronement, *n.* entronización, *f.*

enthusiasm, *n.* entusiasmo, *m.*

enthusiast, *n.* entusiasta, *m.* y *f.*

enthusiastic, *adj.* entusiasmado, entusiasta.

entice, *vt.* halagar, acariciar, excitar, inducir.

enticement, *n.* instigación, seducción, *f.*

entire, *adj.* entero, cumplido, completo, perfecto, todo; **—ly,** *adv.* enteramente.

entirety, *n.* entereza, integridad, totalidad, *f.*; todo, *m.*

entitle, *vt.* intitular; conferir algún derecho; autorizar.

entity, *n.* entidad, existencia, *f.*

entomb, *vt.* sepultar.

entomology, *n.* entomología, *f.*

entourage, *n.* séquito, cortejo, *m.*

entrails, *n. pl.* entrañas, *f. pl.*; tripa, *f.*; — (of an animal), mondongo, menudo, *m.*

entrance, *n.* entrada, *f.*; admisión, *f.*; principio, *m.*; boca, *f.*; ingreso, *m.*

entrance, *vt.* extasiar.

entrancement, *n.* arrobamiento, *m.*

entrant, *n.* entrante, *m. y f.*; participante, *m. y f.*

entrap, *vt.* entrampar; enredar; engañar.

entreat, *vt.* rogar, suplicar.

entreaty *n.* petición, súplica, instancia, *f.*

entrench, *vt.* = **intrench.**

entrenchment, *n.* trinchera, *f.*; atrincheramiento, *m.*

entrepreneur, *n.* empresario, director, *m.*

entropy, *n.* entropía, *f.*

entrust, intrust, *vt.* confiar.

entry, *n.* entrada, *f.*; (com.) partida, *f.*

entwine, *vt.* entrelazar, enroscar, torcer.

enumerate, *vt.* enumerar, numerar.

enumeration, *n.* enumeración, *f.*

enumerator, *n.* enumerador, *m.*

enunciate, *vt.* enunciar, declarar.

enunciation, *n.* enunciación, *f.*

envelop, *vt.* envolver, cubrir.

envelope, *n.* sobre, *m.*, cubierta, *f.*

envelopment, *n.* envolvimiento, *m.*, envoltura, *f.*

envenom, *vt.* envenenar; amargar.

enviable, *adj.* envidiable.

envious, *adj.* envidioso; **—ly,** *adv.* envidiosamente.

environment, *n.* medio ambiente.

environs, *n. pl.* vecindad, *f.*; alrededores, contornos, *m. pl.*

envisage, *vt.* contemplar.

envoy, *n.* enviado, *m.*; mensajero, *m.*

envy, *n.* envidia, *f.*; malicia, *f.*; **—,** *vt.* envidiar.

enwrap, *vt.* = **wrap.**

enwreathe, *vt.* enguirnaldar.

enzyme, *n.* (chem.) fermento, *m.*

Eocene, *n.* eoceno, *m.*; **—,** *adj.* eoceno.

eon, *n.* eón, *m.*

epaulet, *n.* (mil.) charretera, *f.*

ephemeral, *adj.* efímero.

epic, *adj.* épico; **—,** *n.* epopeya, *f.*

epical, *adj.* épico.

epicure, *n.* gastrónomo, ma.

epicurean, *adj.* epicúreo.

epicycle, *n.* epiciclo, *m.*

epidemic, *adj.* epidémico; **—,** *n.* epidemia, *f.*

epidermal, *adj.* epidérmico.

epidermis, *n.* epidermis, *f.*

epiglottis, *n.* epiglotis, *f.*

epigram, *n.* epigrama, *m.*

epigrammatic, *adj.* epigramático; **—ally,** *adv.* epigramáticamente.

epigraph, *n.* epígrafe, *m.*

epilepsy, *n.* epilepsia, *f.*

epileptic, *adj.* epiléptico; **—,** *n.* epiléptico, ca.

epilogue, *n.* epílogo, *m.*

Epiphany, *n.* Epifanía, *f.*

epiphysis, *n.* epífisis, *f.*

Epis. Episcopal, Episcopal.

episcopacy, *n.* episcopado, *m.*

episcopal, *adj.* episcopal.

episcopalian, *n.* episcopal, *m. y f.*

episcopate, *n.* obispado, *m.*

episode, *n.* episodio, *m.*

episodic, *adj.* episódico.

epistle, *n.* epístola, *f.*

epistolary, *adj.* epistolar.

epitaph, *n.* epitafio, *m.*

epithelium, *n.* epitelio, *m.*

epithet, *n.* epíteto, *m.*

epitome, *n.* epítome, compendio, *m.*; sinopsis, *f.*

epitomize, *vt.* epitomar, abreviar.

epoch, *n.* época, edad, era, *f.*

epochal, *adj.* trascendental.

epoch-making, *adj.* trascendental, que hace época.

Epsom salts, *n.* sal de la Higuera; epsomita, *f.*

equal, *adj.* igual; justo; semejante; imparcial; **—,** *n.* par, *m.*, cantidad igual, persona igual; **—,** *vt* igualar; compensar; **—ly,** *adv.* igualmente.

equality, *n.* igualdad, uniformidad, *f.*

equalization, *n.* igualamiento, *m.*, igualación, *f.*

equalize, *vt.* igualar.

equanimity, *n.* ecuanimidad, *f.*

equation, *n.* equilibrio, *m.*; (math.) ecuación, *f.*

equator, *n.* ecuador, *m.*

equatorial, *adj.* ecuatorial.

equerry, *n.* caballerizo mayor del rey.

equestrian, *adj.* ecuestre; **—,** *n.* jinete, *m.*; **— club,** maestranza, *f.*

equiangular, *adj.* equiángulo.

equidistant, *adj.* equidistante.

equilateral, *n. and adj.* equilátero, *m.*

equilibrate, *vt.* equilibrar.

equilibrium, *n.* equilibrio, *m.*

equine, *adj.* caballar, hípico.

equinoctial, *adj.* equinoccial.

equinox, *n.* equinoccio, *m.*

equip, *vt.* equipar, pertrechar; aprestar (un navío).

equipage, *n.* equipaje, tren, *m.*; carroza, *f.*

equipment, *n.* equipaje, *m.*; equipo, *m.*; **standard —,** equipo corriente.

equipoise, *n.* equilibrio, balance, *m.*

equitable, *adj.* equitativo, imparcial; **—bly,** *adv.* equitativamente.

equity, *n.* equidad, justicia, imparcialidad, *f.*

equivalence, *n.* equivalencia, *f.*

equivalent, *n.* and *adj.* equivalente, *m.*

equivocal, *adj.* equívoco, ambiguo; **—ly,** *adv.* equivocadamente, ambiguamente.

equivocate, *vt.* equivocar, usar equívocos.

equivocation, *n.* equívoco, *m.*; anfibología, *f.*

equivocator, *n.* equivoquista, *m.* y *f.*

era, *n.* edad, época, era, *f.*

eradiate, *vt.* and *vi.* irradiar.

eradicable, *adj.* erradicable, extirpable.

eradicate, *vt.* desarraigar, extirpar.

eradication, *n.* extirpación, *f.*

eradicator, *n.* erradicador, *m.*

erase, *vt.* borrar; cancelar, rayar, tachar.

eraser, *n.* goma de borrar, borrador, *m.*; persona que borra o tacha.

erasure, *n.* borradura, *f.*; cancelación, canceladura, *f.*

ere, *prep.* antes, antes que.

erect, *vt.* erigir; establecer; **—,** *adj.* derecho, erguido.

erection, *n.* erección, *f.*; estructura, construcción, *f.*

erector, *n.* montador, armador, *m.*; erector, *m.*

erelong, *adv.* dentro de poco tiempo.

erg, *n.* ergio, *m.*

ergosterol, *n.* ergosterol, *m.*

ermine, *n.* armiño, *m.*

Ernest, Ernesto.

erode, *vt.* roer, corroer, comer, gastar.

erosion, *n.* erosión, *f.*

erosive, *adj.* erosivo, roedor.

erotic, *adj.* erótico.

eroticism, *n.* erotismo, *m.*

err, *vi.* errar; desviarse.

errand, *n.* recado, mensaje, *m.*; encargo, *m.*; **— boy,** mandadero, *m.*

errant, *adj.* errante, vagabundo.

errantry, *n.* vida errante; caballería andante.

errata, *n. pl.* fe de erratas.

erratic, *adj.* errático, errante; irregular, excéntrico.

erroneous, *adj.* erróneo; falso; **—ly,** *adv.* erróneamente.

error, *n.* error, yerro, *m.*; **— in accounts,** trabacuenta, *f.*; **—s and omissions excepted,** salvo error u omisión.

ersatz, *adj.* sintético, artificial; **—,** *n.* substituto, reemplazo, *m.*

erstwhile, *adv.* antiguamente, en tiempos pasados.

eruct, eructate, *vt.* eructar, erutar.

eructation, *n.* eructación, *f.*; eructo, eruto, *m.*

erudite, *adj.* erudito.

erudition, *n.* erudición, *f.*

erupt, *vi.* hacer erupción.

eruption, *n.* erupción, *f.*; sarpullido, *m.*

erysipelas, *n.* erisipela, *f.*

escadrille, *n.* (mil.) escuadrilla aérea.

escalade, *n.* escalada, *f.*; **—,** *vt.* escalar.

escalator, *n.* escalera móvil o movediza.

escallop, *vt.* asar en salsa con pan molido.

escapade, *n.* fuga, escapada, *f.*; travesura, *f.*; calaverada, *f.*; **youthful —s,** correrías, *f. pl.*

escape, *vt.* evitar; escapar; **—,** *vi.* evadirse, salvarse; **to — from danger,** salvarse; **—,** *n.* escapada, huída, fuga, *f.*; inadvertencia, *f.*; salvamento, salvamiento, *m.*; **to make one's —,** poner pies en polvorosa.

escapement, *n.* escape, *m.*

escapist, *n.* soñador, ra, fantaseador, ra.

escarpment, *n.* escarpa, *f.*, escarpe, *m.*; (mil.) escarpa, *f.*

escheat, *n.* (law) reversión de bienes al estado por desherencia; propiedad confiscada por el estado; confiscación de bienes por el estado; **—,** *vi.* revertir al estado (bienes abintestatos); **—,** *vt.* confiscar.

eschew, *vt.* rehuir, evadir.

escort, *n.* escolta, *f.*; acompañante, *m.*; **—,** *vt.* escoltar, convoyar; acompañar.

escrow, *n.* (law) plica, *f.*

escutcheon, *n.* escudo, *m.*

ESE, E.S.E. east-southeast, ESE estesudeste.

Eskimo, *n.* and *adj.* esquimal, *m.* y *f.*

esophagus, *n.* esófago, tragadero, *m.*

esoteric, *adj.* esotérico.

esp. especially, especialmente.

especial, *adj.* especial, excepcional; **—ly,** *adv.* especialmente; particularmente; sobre todo.

espial, espionage, *n.* espionaje, *m.*

esplanade, *n.* (mil.) explanada, *f.*

espousals, *n. pl.* esponsales, *m. pl.*

espouse, *vt.* desposar.

esprit de corps, espíritu de solidaridad.

espy, *vt.* divisar, percibir; descubrir.

Esq. Esquire, título correspondiente a Don. Se usa después del apellido.

esquire, *n.* señor (título que sigue al apellido), *m.*

essay, *vt.* ensayar, intentar, probar; **—,** *n.* ensayo literario; tentativa, *f.*

essayist, *n.* tratadista, ensayista, *m.* y *f.*

essence, *n.* esencia, *f.*; perfume, *m.*; quid, *m.*; médula, *f.*

essential, *adj.* esencial, sustancial, principal; imprescindible; vital; **—,** *n.* lo esencial; **—ly,** *adv.* esencialmente.

Essie, Esther, Ester.

E.S.T. Eastern Standard Time, hora normal de la región oriental de E.U.A.

est.: established, est. establecido; **estate,** bienes; patrimonio.

establish, *vt.* establecer, estatuir, fundar, fijar; confirmar; **to — oneself,** radicarse.

establishment, *n.* establecimiento, *m.*; estatuto, *m.*; fundación, *f.*; institución, *f.*

estate, *n.* estado, *m.*; patrimonio, *m.*; hacienda, *f.*; bienes, *m. pl.*

esteem, *vt.* estimar, apreciar; **—,** *n.* estima, *f.*; consideración, *f.*

esteemed, *adj.* estimado, considerado.

ester, *n.* (chem.) éster, *m.*

Esther, Ester.

esthetic, *adj.* estético; **—ally,** *adv.* estéticamente; **—s,** *n. pl.* estética, *f.*

Esthonia, Estonia, *f.*

estimable, *adj.* estimable.

estimate, *vt.* estimar, apreciar, tasar; **—,** *n.* presupuesto, *m.*; cálculo, *m.*

estimation, *n.* estimación, *f.*; cálculo, *m.*; opinión, *f.*; juicio, *m.*

estimator, *n.* calculador, *m*

estop, *vt.* tapar, atarugar; impedir; prohibir; (law) prohibir que se hagan afirmaciones contrarias a las que ya se han hecho.

estrange, *vt.* apartar, enajenar, malquistar.

estrangement, *n.* enajenamiento, *m.*

estuary, *n.* estuario, estero, *m.*, brazo de mar; desembocadura de lago o río.

et al. and others, y otros.

etc. and so forth, etc. etcétera.

etch, *vt.* grabar al agua fuerte.

etcher, *n.* acuafortista, *m.* y *f.*

etching, *n.* aguafuerte, *f.*, grabado al agua fuerte.

eternal, *adj.* eterno, perpetuo, inmortal, sempiterno; **—ly,** *adv.* eternamente.

eternity, *n.* eternidad, *f.*

ether, *n.* éter, *m.*

ethereal, *adj.* etéreo; vaporoso.

etherealize, *vt.* espiritualizar.

ethic, *adj.* ético.

ethical, *adj.* ético; **—ly,** *adv.* moralmente.

ethics, *n. pl.* ética, moralidad, *f.*

Ethiopia, Etiopía, *f.*

ethnic, *adj.* étnico.

ethnographer, *n.* etnógrafo, *m.*

ethnography, *n.* etnografía, *f.*

ethnological, *adj.* etnológico.

ethnologist, *n.* etnólogo, *m.*

ethnology, *n.* etnología, *f.*

ethyl, *n.* etilo, *m.*; **— gas,** etilgasolina, *f.*

ethylene, *n.* (chem.) etileno, *m.*

ethylic, *adj.* etílico; **— alcohol,** alcohol etílico.

etiology, *n.* etiología, *f.*

etiquette, *n.* etiqueta, *f.*

Etna, Etna, Aetna.

et seq. and the following, y lo siguiente.

Etta, Enriqueta.

étude, *n.* (mus.) estudio, ensayo, *m.*

etymological, *adj.* etimológico.

etymologist, *n.* etimologista, *m.* y *f.*

etymology, *n.* etimología, *f.*

eucalyptus, *n.* eucalipto, *m.*

Eucharist, *n.* Eucaristía, *f.*; Señor, *m.*

eucharistic, *adj.* eucarístico.

euchre, *n.* variedad de juego de naipes; **—,** *vt.* vencer.

Eugene, Eugenio.

eugenics, *n.* eugenesia, *f.*

eulogistic, *adj.* laudatorio.

eulogize, *vt.* elogiar.

eulogy, *n.* elogio, encomio, *m.*, alabanza, *f.*

eunuch, *n.* eunuco, *m.*

Euphemia, Eufemia.

euphemism, *n.* eufemismo, *m.*

euphonious, *adj.* eufónico.

euphony, *n.* eufonía, *f.*

euphuism, *n.* culteranismo, gongorismo, *m.*

Europe, Europa, *f.*

European, *n.* and *adj.* europeo, pea.

Eustace, Eustaquio.

Eustachian tube, *n.* trompa de Eustaquio.

euthanasia, *n.* eutanasia, *f.*

evacuate, *vt.* evacuar.

evacuation, *n.* evacuación, *f.*

evacuee, *n.* refugiado, da.

evade, *vt.* evadir, escapar, evitar.

evaluate, *vt.* avaluar.

evaluation, *n.* evaluación, valuación, *f.*

evanesce, *vi.* desaparecer gradualmente, disiparse.

evanescence, *n.* desvanecimiento, desaparecimiento, *m.*

evanescent, *adj.* fugitivo; imperceptible.

evangelic, *adj.* evangélico.

evangelical, *adj.* evangélico; **—ly,** *adv.* evangélicamente.

evangelism, *n.* evangelismo, *m.*

evangelist, *n.* evangelista, *m.* y *f.*

evangelize, *vt.* evangelizar.

evaporate, *vt.* convertir en vapor; **—,** *vi.* evaporarse; disiparse; **—d milk,** leche evaporada.

evaporation, *n.* evaporación, *f.*

evasion, *n.* evasión, *f.*; escape, efugio, *m.*, tergiversación, *f.*

evasive, *adj.* evasivo; sofístico; **—ly,** *adv.* sofísticamente.

eve, *n.* tardecita, *f.*; vigilia, víspera, *f.*

even, *adj.* llano, igual; par, semejante; **—,** *adv.* aun, aun cuando, supuesto que; no obstante; **— as,** como; **— now,** ahora mismo; **— so,** lo mismo, de veras; **— or odd,** pares o nones; **not —,** ni siquiera; **—,** *vt.* igualar, allanar; **—ly,** *adv.* igualmente; con suavidad.

even-handed, *adj.* imparcial, equitativo.

evening, *adj.* vespertino; **— clothes,** traje de etiqueta; **—,** *n.* tarde, noche, *f.*

evenness, *n.* llanura, uniformidad, *f.*

evensong, *n.* canción nocturna; vísperas, *f. pl.*

event, *n.* evento, acontecimiento, *m.*; circunstancia, *f.*; caso, *m.*; ocurrencia, *f.*, suceso, *m.*; **at all —s,** en todo caso; **current —s,** sucesos de actualidad.

eventful, *adj.* lleno de acontecimientos; memorable.

eventide, *n.* (poet.) tarde, *f.*, primeras horas de la noche.

eventual, *adj.* eventual, fortuito; **—ly,** *adv.* finalmente, con el tiempo.

eventuality, *n.* eventualidad, *f.*

ever, *adj.* siempre; **for — and —,** por siempre jamás, eternamente; **— since,** desde que; **— and anon,** de cuando en cuando.

everglade, *n.* tierra baja pantanosa o inundable.

evergreen, *adj.* siempre verde; —, *n.* (bot.) siempreviva, *f.*
everlasting, *adj.* eterno; —, *n.* eternidad, *f.*; — **flower,** siempreviva, *f.*
evermore, *adv.* eternamente, para siempre jamás.
every, *adj.* todo, cada; — **day,** todos los días; — **time,** cada vez.
everybody, *pron.* cada uno, cada una; todo el mundo.
everyday, *adj.* ordinario, rutinario, de todos los días.
everyone, *pron.* cada cual, cada uno.
everything, *n.* todo, *m.*
everywhere, *adv.* en todas partes, por todas partes, por doquier.
evict, *vt.* despojar jurídicamente; desalojar, expulsar.
eviction, *n.* evicción, expulsión, *f.*, despojo jurídico.
evidence, *n.* evidencia, *f.*; testimonio, *m.*, prueba, *f.*; **insufficient** —, (law) semiplena, *f.*; —, *vt.* evidenciar.
evident, *adj.* evidente; patente, manifiesto; indudable; —**ly,** *adv.* evidentemente.
evil, *adj.* malo, depravado, pernicioso; dañoso; —, *n.* maldad, *f.*; daño, *m.*; calamidad, *f.*; mal, *m.*
evildoer, *n.* malhechor, ra.
evildoing, *n.* malignidad, *f.*
evil-minded, *adj.* malicioso, mal intencionado.
evince, *vt.* probar, justificar, demostrar.
eviscerate, *vt.* desentrañar.
evisceration, *n.* desentrañamiento, *m.*
evocation, *n.* evocación, *f.*
evoke, *vt.* evocar.
evolution, *n.* evolución, *f.*; desarrollo, *m.*
evolutionary, *adj.* evolucionario.
evolutionist, *n.* evolucionista, *m.*
evolve, *vt.* and *vi.* desenvolver; desplegarse; emitir.
evolvement, *n.* evolución, *f.*, desarrollo, *m.*
ewe, *n.* oveja, (hembra del carnero), *f.*
ewer, *n.* palancana, palangana, *f.*
ex. example, ej. ejemplo.
exacerbate, *vt.* exacerbar; exasperar.
exacerbation, *n.* exacerbación, *f.*
exact, *adj.* exacto, puntual; riguroso; cuidadoso; —, *vt.* exigir; —**ly,** *adv.* exactamente, puntualmente.
exacting, *adj.* severo, exigente.
exaction, *n.* exacción, extorsión, *f.*
exactitude, *n.* exactitud, *f.*
exactness, exactitude, *n.* exactitud, *f.*
exaggerate, *vt.* exagerar; extremar.
exaggeration, *n.* exageración, *f.*
exalt, *vt.* exaltar, elevar; alabar; realzar; enaltecer.
exaltation, *n.* exaltación, elevación, *f.*
exalted, *adj.* sublime.
examination, *n.* examen, *m.*; **medical** —, reconocimiento médico.
examine, *vt.* examinar; escudriñar; ver, revisar.

examinee, *n.* persona examinada.
examiner, *n.* comprobador, ra; persona que examina.
examining, *adj.* revisor; examinador; — **office,** registro, *m.*
example, *n.* ejemplo, *m.*; **to say for** —, poner por caso; **to set an** —, dar el ejemplo.
exasperate, *vt.* exasperar, irritar, enojar, provocar; agravar, amargar.
exasperation, *n.* exasperación, irritación, *f.*
excavate, *vt.* excavar, cavar, ahondar.
excavation, *n.* excavación, *f.*; cavidad, *f.*
excavator, *n.* excavador, ra.
exceed, *vt.* exceder; sobrepujar; rebasar; —, *vi.* excederse; **to** — **in height,** sobresalir.
exceeding, *adj.* excesivo; —**ly,** *adv.* extremadamente, en sumo grado; sobremanera.
excel, *vt.* sobresalir, exceder; descollar; superar.
excellence, *n.* excelencia, *f.*
Excellency, *n.* Excelencia (título), *f.*
excellent, *adj.* excelente; sobresaliente; —**ly,** *adv.* excelentemente.
excelsior, *n.* trizas rizadas de madera para entapizar, empacar, etc.
except, *vt.* exceptuar, excluir; sacar; —, *vi.* recusar; —**ing,** *prep.* salvo, excepto a excepción de.
exception, *n.* excepción, exclusión, *f.*
exceptional, *adj.* excepcional.
excerpt, *vt.* extraer; extractar; —, *n.* extracto, *m.*
excess, *n.* exceso, *m.*, intemperancia, *f.*; desmesura, *f.*; sobra, *f.*; — **baggage,** exceso de equipaje.
excessive, *adj.* excesivo; —**ly,** *adv.* excesivamente, demasiado.
exchange, *vt.* cambiar; trocar, permutar; —, *n.* cambio, *m.*; bolsa, lonja, *f.*; — **at par,** cambio a la par; — **broker,** corredor de cambio, corredor de bolsa; — **office,** casa de cambio; — **on London,** cambio sobre Londres; — **under par,** cambio con quebrado; **at what rate of** — ? ¿a qué cambio? **bill of** —, letra de cambio, cédula de cambio; **current** —, cambio corriente; **domestic** —, cambio interior; **foreign** —, cambio exterior o cambio extranjero; **in** — **for,** a cambio de; **money** —, cambio de moneda, bolsa, *f.*; **rate of** —, tipo de cambio; **stock** —, bolsa, *f.*; bolsa de comercio o financiera; **telephone** —, central telefónica.
exchangeable, *adj.* cambiable.
exchequer, *n.* fisco, *m.*; tesorería, *f.*
excise, *n.* sisa (impuesto), *f.*
excision, *n.* excisión, *f.*
excitability, *n.* excitabilidad, *f.*
excitable, *adj.* excitable; nervioso.
excitant, *n.* and *adj.* excitante, estimulante, *m.*
excitation, *n.* excitación, *f.*
excite, *vt.* excitar; estimular; agitar; conmover.

excitement, *n.* estímulo, *m.*; agitación, *f.*; excitación, *f.*, conmoción, *f.*

exciting, *adj.* excitante, conmovedor.

exclaim, *vi.* exclamar; —, *vt.* proferir.

exclamation, *n.* exclamación, *f.*; clamor, *m.*; — **mark,** — **point,** punto de admiración.

exclamatory, *adj.* exclamatorio.

exclosure, *n.* recinto cercado a prueba de ganado, roedores, insectos, etc.

exclude, *vt.* excluir; exceptuar.

exclusion, *n.* exclusión, exclusiva, *f.*; excepción, *f.*

exclusive, *adj.* exclusivo; —ly, *adv.* exclusivamente.

exclusiveness, *n.* exclusividad, *f.*

excommunicate, *vt.* excomulgar, descomulgar.

excommunication, *n.* excomunión, *f.*

excoriate, *vt.* excoriar.

excoriation, *n.* excoriación, *f.*

excrement, *n.* excremento, *m.*, materias fecales.

excrescence, *n.* excrescencia, *f.*

excreta, *n. pl.* excrementos, *m. pl.*

excrete, *vt.* excretar.

excretion, *n.* excremento, *m.*; excreción, *f.*

excretory, *adj.* excretorio.

excruciating, *adj.* atroz, enorme, grave, muy agudo.

exculpate, *vt.* disculpar; justificar.

exculpation, *n.* disculpa, *f.*

excursion, *n.* excursión, expedición, *f.*; digresión, *f.*; vuelta, *f.*; romería, *f.*; correría, *f.*; jira, *f.*; — **ticket,** billete o boleto de excursión.

excursionist, *n.* excursionista, *m.* y *f.*

excursive, *adj.* errante, viajante.

excusable, *adj.* excusable.

excuse, *vt.* excusar; perdonar; —, *n.* excusa, *f.*

execrable, *adj.* execrable, detestable.

execrate, *vt.* execrar, maldecir.

execration, *n.* execración, maldición, *f.*; reniego, *m.*

execute, *vt.* ejecutar; ajusticiar; llevar a cabo, cumplir.

execution, *n.* ejecución, *f.*

executioner, *n.* ejecutor, *m.*; verdugo, *m.*

executive, *adj.* and *n.* ejecutivo, *m.*

executor, *n.* testamentario, *m.*; (law) albacea, *m.*

executrix, *n.* (law) albacea, *f.*, ejecutora testamentaria.

exegesis, *m.* exégesis, *f.*

exemplar, *n.* ejemplar, original, modelo, *m.*; tipo, *m.*; muestra, *f.*

exemplary, *adj.* ejemplar.

exemplification, *n.* ejemplificación, *f.*

exemplify, *vt.* ejemplificar.

exempt, *adj.* exento, libre por privilegio; —, *vt.* eximir, exentar.

exemption, *n.* exención, franquicia, *f.*

exercise, *n.* ejercicio, *m.*; ensayo, *m.*; tarea, *f.*; práctica, *f.*; —, *vi.* hacer ejercicio; —, *vt.* ejercitar; atarear; practicar; profesar.

exert, *vt.* ejercer; **to** — **oneself,** esforzarse.

exertion, *n.* esfuerzo, *m.*

exhalation, *n.* exhalación, *f.*; vapor, *m.*

exhale, *vt.* exhalar.

exhaust, *n.* cámara de escape; (auto., aer.) escape, *m.*; — **chamber,** cámara de escape; — **collector ring,** colector de escape; — **fan,** expulsor de aire; — **manifold,** múltiple de escape; — **pipe,** tubo de salida de gases; —, *vt.* agotar, consumir.

exhaustible, *adj.* agotable.

exhausting, *adj.* enervante, agotador.

exhaustion, *n.* agotamiento, *m.*, extenuación, *f.*

exhaustive, *adj.* agotable; completo, minucioso.

exhibit, *vt.* exhibir; mostrar; —, *n.* (law) memorial, *m.*; exhibición, *f.*

exhibition, *n.* exhibición, presentación, *f.*; espectáculo, *m.*

exhibitionism, *n.* exhibicionismo, *m.*

exhibitionist, *n.* exhibicionista, *m.* y *f.*

exhibitor, *n.* expositor, ra.

exhilarate, *vt.* alegrar, causar alegría.

exhilaration, *n.* alegría, *f.*; buen humor, regocijo, *m.*

exhort, *vt.* exhortar, excitar.

exhortation, *n.* exhortación, *f.*

exhumation, *n.* exhumación, *f.*

exhume, *vt.* exhumar, desenterrar.

exigent, *adj.* exigente.

exigency, *n.* exigencia, necesidad, urgencia, *f.*

exile, *n.* destierro, *m.*; desterrado, da; proscripto, *m.*; —, *vt.* desterrar, deportar.

exist, *vi.* existir.

existence, *n.* existencia, *f.*

existent, *adj.* existente.

existing, *adj.* actual, presente.

exit, *n.* partida, salida, *f.*

exodus, *n.* éxodo, *m.*, salida, *f.*

ex officio, de oficio.

exonerate, *vt.* exonerar, disculpar.

exoneration, *n.* exoneración, *f.*

exorbitance, *n.* exorbitancia, enormidad, *f.*

exorbitant, *adj.* exorbitante, excesivo.

exorcise, *vt.* exorcizar, conjurar.

exorcism, *n.* exorcismo, *m.*

exordium, *n.* exordio, *m.*

exoteric, *adj.* exotérico.

exotic, *adj.* exótico, extranjero; —, *n.* cosa exótica (como una planta o una palabra).

exp.: expense, gastos; **export,** exportación; **express,** expreso.

expand, *vt.* extender, dilatar.

expanse, *n.* extensión de lugar.

expansion, *n.* expansión, *f.*; desarrollo, *m.*

expansive, *adj.* expansivo.

expatiate, *vi.* espaciarse, explayarse.

expatiation, *n.* digresión, difusión, *f.*

expatriate, *vt.* expatriar.

expatriation, *n.* expatriación, extrañación, *f.*

expect, *vt.* esperar, aguardar; **when least** —**ed,** a lo mejor, cuando menos se espera.

expectance, expectancy, *n.* expectación, esperanza, *f.*

expectant, *adj.* expectante, que espera; preñada, encinta, embarazada.

expectation, *n.* expectativa, *f.*; esperanza, *f.*

expectorate, *vt.* expectorar.

expectoration, *n.* expectoración, *f.*

expediency, *n.* propiedad, *f.*; conveniencia, oportunidad, *f.*

expedient, *adj.* oportuno, conveniente; —, *n.* expediente, medio, *m.*; —**ly,** *adv.* convenientemente.

expedite, *vt.* acelerar; expedir.

expedition, *n.* expedición, excursión, *f.*; cruzada, *f.*; campaña, *f.*

expeditionary, *adj.* expedicionario.

expeditious, *adj.* pronto, expedito; —**ly,** *adv.* prontamente.

expel, *vt.* expeler, expulsar; desterrar.

expend, *vt.* expender; desembolsar.

expenditure, *n.* gasto, desembolso, *m.*

expense, *n.* expensas, *f. pl.*; coste, gasto, *m.*; **bill of** —**s,** nota de gastos.

expensive, *adj.* caro, costoso; —**ly,** *adv.* costosamente.

experience, *n.* experiencia, *f.*; práctica, *f.*; —, *vt.* experimentar; saber.

experienced, *adj.* experimentado; versado, perito.

experiment, *n.* experimento, *m.*; prueba, *f.*; —, *vt.* experimentar, hacer la prueba.

experimental, *adj.* experimental; —**ly,** *adv.* experimentalmente.

expert, *adj.* experto, práctico, diestro; perito; —, *n.* maestro, tra; conocedor, ra; perito, ta; —**in,** conocedor de; —**ly,** *adv.* diestramente.

expertness, *n.* maña, destreza, habilidad, *f.*

expiable, *adj.* expiable.

expiate, *vt.* expiar; reparar un daño.

expiation, *n.* expiación, *f.*

expiatory, *adj.* expiatorio.

expiration, *n.* expiración, *f.*; muerte, *f.*; vapor, vaho, *m.*; vencimiento (plazo de una letra o un pagaré, etc.), *m.*; — **(of credit),** cumplimiento, *m.*

expire, *vi.* expirar, morir.

explain, *vt.* explicar.

explainable, *adj.* explicable.

explanation, *n.* explicación, aclaración, *f.*

explanatory, *adj.* explicativo.

expletive, *adj.* expletivo; —, *n.* interjección, *f.*

explicable, *adj.* explicable.

explication, *n.* explicación, *f.*

explicit, *adj.* explícito; —**ly,** *adv.* explícitamente.

explode, *vt.* and *vi.* disparar con estallido; volar, estallar; refutar.

exploit, *n.* hazaña, proeza, *f.*; hecho heroico; —**s,** *n. pl.* sergas, *f. pl.*; —, *vt.* explotar.

exploitation, *n.* explotación, *f.*

exploiting, *n.* explotación, *f.*

exploration, *n.* exploración, *f.*; examen, *m.*

exploratory, *adj.* exploratorio.

explore, *vt.* explorar, examinar; sondear.

explorer, *n.* explorador, *m.*

explosion, *n.* explosión, *f.*

explosive, *adj.* explosivo, fulminante; — **cotton,** piroxilina, *f.*; **high** —, alto explosivo.

exponent, *n.* (math.) exponente, *m.*

export, *vt.* exportar; — **house,** casa exportadora.

export, exportation, *n.* exportación, *f.*

exporter, *n.* exportador, ra.

exporting, *adj.* exportador.

expose, *vt.* exponer; mostrar; descubrir; poner en peligro.

exposé, *n.* desenmascaramiento, *m.*

exposition, *n.* exposición, exhibición, *f.*

expositor, *m.* expositor, *m.*

expository, *adj.* explicativo.

ex post facto, ex post facto, retroactivo.

expostulate, *vi.* contender; **to — with,** reconvenir á.

expostulation, *n.* debate, *m.*; disputa, *f.*; protesta, *f.*; reconvención, *f.*

exposure, *n.* exposición, *f.*, acción de exponerse (al aire, sol, agua, etc.); (phot.) exposición, *f.*

expound, *vt.* exponer, explicar; interpretar.

expounder, *n.* expositor, ra.

ex-president, *n.* expresidente, *m.*

express, *vt.* expresar, exteriorizar; representar; —, *adj.* expreso, claro, a propósito; — **car,** furgón, *m.*, furgón del expreso, vagón expreso; — **company,** compañía de porteo; — **train,** tren rápido o expreso; —, *n.* expreso, correo expreso; **air** —, expreso aéreo.

expressible, *adj.* decible; que se puede expresar.

expression, *n.* expresión, *f.*; locución, *f.*; animación del rostro.

expressive, *adj.* expresivo; —**ly,** *adv.* expresivamente.

expressly, *adv.* expresamente.

expressman, *n.* cargador, *m.*, empleado de empresa de transporte rápido.

expropriate, *vt.* expropiar, confiscar.

expropriation, *n.* (law) expropiación, *f.*

expulsion, *n.* expulsión, *f.*

expulsive, *adj.* expulsivo.

expunge, *vt.* borrar, cancelar, rayar.

expurgate, *vt.* expurgar.

expurgation, *n.* expurgación, purificación, *f.*

exquisite, *adj.* exquisito, perfecto, excelente; —**ly,** *adv.* exquisitamente.

ex-service, *adj.* ex-militar.

extant, *adj.* estante, existente.

extemporaneous, extemporary, *adj.* extemporáneo, improviso.

extempore, *adv.* de improviso, in promptu; —, *adj.* extemporáneo.

extemporize, *vi.* improvisar.

extend, *vt.* extender; amplificar; **to — (time),** prorrogar (un plazo); —, *vi.* extenderse; cundir.

extended, *adj.* prolongado; — **(in time),** prorrogable.

extensible, *adj.* extensivo, extensible.

extension, *n.* extensión, *f.*; prórroga, *f.*; (com.) respiro, *m.*

extensive, *adj.* extenso; amplio; general; —**ly,** *adv.* extensamente; generalmente; extensivamente.

extent, *n.* extensión, *f.*; grado, *m.*; **to such an** —, a tal grado.

extenuate, *vt.* extenuar, disminuir, atenuar.

extenuation, *n.* extenuación, *f.*; mitigación, *f.*

exterior, *n.* and *adj.* exterior, *m.*

exterminate, *vt.* exterminar; extirpar.

extermination, *n.* exterminación, extirpación, *f.*

exterminator, *n.* exterminador, *m.*

external, *adj.* externo, exterior; —**ly,** *adv.* exteriormente; —**s,** *n. pl.* exterior, *m.*

extinct, *adj.* extinto; abolido.

extinction, *n.* extinción, *f.*; abolición, *f.*

extinguish, *vt.* extinguir; suprimir.

extinguisher, *n.* apagador, *m.*; matacandelas, *m.*; **fire** —, apagador de incendios.

extirpate, *vt.* extirpar.

extirpation, *n.* extirpación, *f.*; exterminio, *m.*

extol, *vt.* alabar, magnificar, exaltar.

extort, *vt.* sacar por fuerza; adquirir por violencia; arrebatar.

extortion, *n.* extorsión, *f.*

extortionate, *adj.* violento; excesivo, exorbitante.

extortioner, *n.* persona que exige dinero sin derecho; opresor, ra.

extortionist, *n.* concusionario, *m.*

extra, *adj.* extraordinario, adicional; de repuesto; —, *n.* suplemento extraordinario de un periódico; algo de calidad extraordinaria; (coll.) actor de cine que desempeña papeles insignificantes.

extract, *vt.* extraer; extractar; —, *n.* extracto, *m.*; compendio, *m.*; **meat** —, carne concentrada.

extractable, *adj.* susceptible de ser extraído.

extraction, *n.* extracción, *f.*; descendencia, *f.*

extractive, *adj.* extractivo.

extractor, *n.* extractor, ra.

extracurricular, *adj.* que no forma parte de un plan de estudios.

extradite, *vt.* entregar por extradición.

extradition, *n.* (law) extradición, *f.*

extralegal, *adj.* extralegal.

extraneous, *adj.* extraño, exótico.

extraordinarily, *adv.* extraordinariamente.

extraordinary, *adj.* extraordinario.

extraterritorial, *adj.* extraterritorial.

extravagance, *n.* extravagancia, *f.*; derroche, *m.*, profusión de lujo.

extravagant, *adj.* extravagante, singular, exorbitante; excesivo; pródigo; gastador, derrochador; —**ly,** *adv.* extravagante-

mente, en forma derrochadora.

extravaganza, *n.* composición musical o dramática que es extravagante.

extreme, *adj.* extremo, supremo; último; —, *n.* extremo, *m.*; **to go to** —**s,** tomar medidas extremas; —**ly,** *adv.* extremadamente; sumamente; sobre todo.

extremist, *n.* extremista, radical, *m.*

extremity, *n.* extremidad, *f.*

extricable, *adj.* que puede desenredarse.

extricate, *vt.* sacar (de un apuro, etc.); desenredar.

extrication, *n.* desembarazo, desenredo, *m.*

extrinsic, extrinsical, *adj.* extrínseco, exterior.

extrovert, *n.* persona que concentra su interés hacia objetos externos.

extrude, *vt.* arrojar, echar; —, *vi.* sobresalir.

extrusion, *n.* expulsión, *f.*

extrusive, *adj.* expulsivo.

exuberance, *n.* exuberancia, *f.*, suma abundancia.

exuberant, *adj.* exuberante, abundantísimo; —**ly,** *adv.* abundantemente.

exudation, *n.* exudación, *f.*

exude, *vi.* traspirar.

exult, *vi.* regocijarse, alegrarse de un triunfo.

exultant, *adj.* regocijado; triunfante, victorioso.

exultation, *n.* exultación, *f.*; regocijo, *m.*

eye, *n.* ojo, *m.*, vista, *f.*; (bot.) yema, *f.*, botón, *m.*; — **of a hook,** hembra, corcheta, *f.*; **in the twinkling of an** —, en un abrir y cerrar de ojos; —, *vt.* ojear, contemplar, observar.

eyeball, *n.* niña del ojo.

eyebolt, *n.* perno de anilla; (naut.) cáncamo de ojo.

eyebrow, *n.* ceja, *f.*

eyecup, *n.* ojera, *f.*, copita para lavar los ojos.

eyeful, *n.* completa visión de algo.

eyeglass, *n.* anteojo, *m.*, luneta, *f.*, ocular, *m.*

eyehole, *n.* atisbadero, *m.*

eyelash, *n.* pestaña, *f.*

eyeless, *adj.* sin ojos, ciego.

eyelet, *n.* resquicio, *m.*; ojete, *m.*

eyelid, *n.* párpado, *m.*, pálpebra, *f.*

eyepiece, *n.* ocular, objetivo, *m.*

eyeshade, *n.* visera, *f.*, guardavista, *m.*

eyesight, *n.* potencia visiva.

eyesore, *n.* cosa ofensiva a la vista.

eyespot, *n.* ojo rudimentario de algunos invertebrados.

eyestrain, *n.* cansancio o tensión de los ojos.

eyetooth, *n.* colmillo, *m.*

eyewash, *n.* colirio, *m.*, loción para los ojos; (coll.) lisonja disparatada.

eyewitness, *n.* testigo ocular.

eyrie, eyry, *n.* nido de ave de rapiña; (fig.) habitación colocada en alto.

F.

F. Fellow, miembro de una sociedad científica o académica; **Fahrenheit,** Fahrenheit; **Friday,** Vier. viernes.

f., fol. folio, f.°, fol. folio.

f. following, sig.te siguiente; **feminine,** f. femenino; **folio,** fol. folio.

fable, n. fábula, f.; ficción, f.

fabled, adj. celebrado o puesto en fábulas.

fabric, n. tejido, m., tela. f.; edificio, m.; construcción, f.

fabricate, vt. fabricar, edificar; inventar (una leyenda, un cuento, una mentira, etc.).

fabrication, n. fabricación, f.

fabrikoid, n. nombre comercial para una imitación de cuero.

fabulous, adj. fabuloso; —ly, adv. fabulosamente.

façade, n. fachada, f., frontispicio de un edificio.

face, n. cara, faz, haz, f.; superficie, f.; fachada, f.; frente, f.; aspecto, m.; apariencia, f.; atrevimiento, m.; **in my —,** en mi presencia; **to lose —,** sufrir pérdida de prestigio; **sallow —,** cara de acelga; **to make —s,** hacer muecas; **— down,** boca abajo; **— to —,** de silla a silla, cara a cara; **— value,** valor nominal o aparente; —, vt. encararse; hacer frente; volver un naipe; **to — about,** volver la cara; **to — the street,** dar a la calle.

facet, n. faceta, f.

facetious, adj. chistoso, jocoso; gracioso; —ly, adv. chistosamente, jocosamente.

facetiousness, n. jocosidad, f.

facial, adj. facial.

facile, adj. fácil; afable, complaciente.

facilitate, vt. facilitar.

facility, n. facilidad, ligereza, f.; afabilidad, f.; destreza, f.

facing, n. paramento, m.; cara, f.; guarnición, f.; forro, m.

facsimile, n. facsímile, m.

fact, n. hecho, m.; realidad, f.; **in —,** en efecto, verdaderamente; **matter of —,** hecho positivo o cierto.

faction, n. facción, f.; disensión, f.

factional, adj. faccionario.

factious, adj. faccioso; —ly, adv. sediciosamente.

factitious, adj. facticio, artificial.

factor, n. factor, m.; agente, m.; (math.) factor, m.; **safety —,** factor o coeficiente de seguridad.

factory, n. fábrica, f., taller, m.; factoría, f.

factotum, n. factótum, m.

factual, adj. actual, relacionado a hechos.

faculty, n. facultad, f.; poder, privilegio, m.; profesorado, m.

fad, n. fruslería, niñería, f.; boga, f.; novedad, f.

faddish, adj. de moda.

faddist, n. aficionado a las novedades.

fade, vi. decaer, marchitarse, fallecer.

fade-out (motion picture), n. desaparecimiento gradual (cinematógrafo).

fag, vt. cansar, fatigar; hacer trabajar como a un esclavo; —, vi. trabajar hasta agotarse; fatigarse; trabajar como un esclavo; —, n. trabajador esclavizado; **— end,** cadillos, m. pl., retazo, m.

fagged out, adj. cansado.

fagot, n. haz, m., gavilla de leña.

Fahr. Fahrenheit, F. Fahrenheit.

fail, vt. abandonar; descuidar; faltar; decepcionar; —, vi. fallar, fracasar; menguar; debilitarse; perecer; **to — in a school subject,** fracasar un curso; —, n. omisión, falta, f.; **without —,** sin falta.

failing, n. falta, f.; defecto, m.

failure, n. falta, f.; culpa, f.; quiebra, bancarrota, f.; fiasco, m.; **to be a —,** quedar o salir deslucido; ser un fracaso.

fain, adj. resignado, conforme; —, adv. de buena gana.

faint, vi. desmayarse; (poet.) debilitarse; —, adj. tímido, lánguido; fatigoso, desfallecido; borroso, sin claridad; —, n. desmayo, deliquio, soponcio, m.; —ly, adv. borrosamente; desmayadamente.

faint-hearted, adj. cobarde, medroso, pusilánime; —ly, adv. medrosamente.

faintness, n. languidez, flaqueza, f.; timidez, f.

fair, adj. hermoso, bello; blanco; rubio; claro, sereno; favorable; recto, justo, franco; **— ball,** (baseball) pelota que cae dentro de los límites permitidos en el juego de baseball; **— catch,** (football) parada de boleo; **— weather,** (naut.) bonanza, f.; buen tiempo; —, n. feria, exposición, f.

fair-dealing, n. proceder justo o equitativo; —, adj. recto, honrado.

fairground, n. cercado al aire libre para feria, exposición o circo.

fair-haired, adj. de cabellos rubios.

fair-lead, n. guía del cable de arrastre.

fairly, adv. positivamente; favorablemente; justamente, honradamente; claramente; bastante, tolerablemente; **— well,** bastante bien.

fair-minded, adj. razonable, imparcial.

fairness, n. hermosura, f.; honradez, f.; justicia, f.

fair-spoken, adj. bien hablado; cortés.

fairway, n. parte de un campo de golf.

fairy, n. hada, f., duende, m.; —, adj. de hadas, relativo a las hadas; **— tale,** cuento de hadas.

fairyland, n. habitación de las hadas.

faith, n. fe, f.; fidelidad, sinceridad, f.; fervor, m.

faithful, adj. fiel, leal; —ly, adv. fielmente.

faithless, adj. infiel, pérfido, desleal.

fake, n. (naut.) aduja, f.; (coll.) imitación fraudulenta; —, adj. (coll.) falso, fraudulento; **— news,** paparrucha, patraña, f.; —, (coll.) engañar; imitar; **to — a piece**

of music, (coll.) tocar una pieza de música en forma superficial y engañosa por no saberse.

faker, *n.* farsante, *m.* y *f.*

fakir, *n.* faquir, *m.*

falchion, *n.* cimitarra, *f.*

falcon, *n.* halcón, *m.*

falconer, *n.* halconero, *m.*

falconry, *n.* halconería, *f.*

fall, *vi.* caer, caerse; perder el poder; disminuir, decrecer en precio; **to —asleep,** dormirse; **to — back,** recular; **to — back again,** recaer; **to — due,** cumplir, vencer; **to — headlong,** caer; **to — short,** faltar, chasquear; **to — sick,** enfermar; **to — in love,** enamorarse; **to — off,** desaparecer, disolverse; caerse; **to — out,** reñir, disputar; **to — upon,** atacar, asaltar; **—,** *n.* caída, *f.;* declive, *m.;* catarata, *f.;* otoño, *m.;* **— in prices,** baja, *f.*

fallacious, *adj.* falaz, fraudulento; delusorio; **—ly,** *adv.* falazmente.

fallacy, *n.* falacia, sofistería, *f.*, engaño, *m.*

fallen, *adj.* caído; arruinado; **—,** *p. p.* del verbo **fall.**

fallibility, *n.* falibilidad, *f.*

fallible, *adj.* falible.

falling sickness, *n.* epilepsia, *f.*

falling star, *n.* exhalación, *f.*

fallow, *adj.* flavo; sin cultivar (aplícase a la tierra); **— deer,** corzo, za; **—,** *n.* barbecho, *m.,* tierra que se deja sin cultivar por un tiempo; **—,** *vt* barbechar.

false, *adj.* falso, pérfido; postizo; supuesto; **— bottom,** fondo doble; **— colors,** bandera falsa; **to sail under — colors,** engañar con pretensiones infundadas; **— teeth,** dientes postizos; **—ly,** *adv.* falsamente; pérfidamente.

falsehood, *n.* falsedad, *f.;* perfidia, *f.;* mentira, *f.*

falsetto, *n.* falsete, *m.;* **— voice,** falsete, *m.*

falsework, *n.* apuntalamiento, *m.;* construcción provisional.

falsification, *n.* falsificación, *f.*

falsify, *vt.* falsificar.

falsity, *n.* falsedad, mentira, *f.*

falter, *vi.* tartamudear; vacilar, titubear.

faltering, *adj.* balbuciente, titubeante.

fame, *n.* fama, *f.;* renombre, *m.*

famed, *adj.* celebrado, famoso.

familiar, *adj.* familiar, casero; conocido; **— with,** acostumbrado a, versado a, conocedor de; **—,** *n.* amigo íntimo; **—ly,** *adv.* familiarmente.

familiarity, *n.* familiaridad, *f.*

familiarize, *vt.* familiarizar.

family, *n.* familia, *f.;* linaje, *m.;* clase, especie, *f.;* **— tree,** árbol genealógico.

famine, *n.* hambre, *f.;* carestía, *f.*

famish, *vt.* hambrear; **—,** *vi.* padecer de hambre intensa; morirse de hambre.

famous, *adj.* famoso, afamado; **most —,** celebérrimo; **—ly,** *adv.* famosamente.

Fan, Fanny, Frasquita, Paquita o Panchita.

fan, *n.* abanico, *m.;* aventador, ventilador, *m.;* aficionado, da; **—,** *vt.* abanicar; aventar; soplar.

fanatic, *n.* and *adj.* fanático, ca; mojigato, ta.

fanatical, *adj.* fanático; **—ly,** *adv.* fanáticamente.

fanaticism, *n.* fanatismo, *m.*

fancied, *adj.* imaginario.

fancier, *n.* aficionado, da.

fanciful, *adj.* imaginativo, caprichoso; fantástico; **—ly,** *adv.* caprichosamente.

fancy, *n.* fantasía, imaginación, imaginativa, *f.;* capricho, *m.;* **— goods,** novedades, modas, *f. pl.;* **foolish —,** quimera, *f.;* **—,** *vt.* imaginar; gustar de; suponer.

fancy-free, *adj.* libre de amor.

fancywork, *n.* labores manuales, trabajo de costura.

fandango, *n.* fandango (baile y tañido), *m.*

fanfare, *n.* (mus.) charanga, *f.;* ostentación, *f.*

fang, *n.* colmillo, *m.;* garra, uña, *f.;* raíz de un diente.

fantasia, *n.* (mus.) fantasía, *f.*

fantastic, *adj.* fantástico; caprichoso; **—ally,** *adv.* fantásticamente.

fantasy, *n.* fantasía, *f.*

far, *adv.* lejos, a una gran distancia; **— be it from me,** ¡abrenuncio! ¡ni lo permita Dios! **—,** *adj.* lejano, distante, remoto; **— off,** lejano, en lontananza.

faraway, *adj.* lejano.

farce, *n.* farsa, *f.*

farcical, *adj.* burlesco; ridículo; que no es natural.

farcy, *n.* (vet.) muermo, *m.*

fare, *n.* alimento, *m.,* comida, *f.;* viajero, ra; pasaje, *m.;* tarifa, *f.;* **—,** *vi.* viajar; **to — well (or ill),** irle a uno bien (o mal.).

farewell, *n.* despedida, *f.;* **—!** *interj.* ¡adiós! ¡que le vaya bien!

farfetched, *adj.* forzado, traído de los cabellos.

far-flung, *adj.* de mucho alcance; muy extendido.

farina, *n.* harina, *f.;* almidón, *m.,* polvo harinoso.

farinaceous, *adj.* harinoso, farináceo.

farm, *n.* tierra arrendada; alquería, *f.;* hacienda, granja, *f* **—,** *vt.* arrendar tomar en arriendo; cultivar; **— hand,** peón de granja.

farmer, *n.* labrador, ra; hacendado, da; agricultor, ra; **small —,** estanciero, ra ranchero, ra.

farmhouse, *n.* hacienda, *f.;* cortijo, *m.*

farming, *n.* agricultura, *f.;* cultivo, *m.*

farmstead, *n.* alquería, hacienda, *f.*

farmyard, *n.* corral, *m.*

far-off, *adj.* remoto, distante.

farrago, *n.* fárrago, *m.;* broza, *f.*

far-reaching, *adj.* de gran alcance, trascendental.

farrier, *n.* herrador, *m.*

farriery, *n.* herrería, *f.*

farrow, *n.* lechigada de puercos; —, *vt.* and *vi.* parir la puerca.

farseeing, *adj.* perspicaz, previsor, precavido.

farsighted, *adj.* présbita, présbite; (fig.) precavido; astuto, sagaz, agudo.

farther, *adv.* más lejos; más adelante; —, *adj.* más lejos, ulterior.

farthermost, *adj.* que está a mayor distancia.

farthest, *adj.* más distante, más remoto; más largo; más extendido; —, *adv.* a la mayor distancia.

farthing, *n.* cuarto de penique.

farthingale, *n.* verdugado, *m.*

fascinate, *vt.* fascinar, encantar.

fascinating, *adj.* fascinador, seductor.

fascination, *n.* fascinación, *f.*; encanto, *m.*

fascine, *n.* fajina, *f.*, haz de leña.

fascism, *n.* fascismo, *m.*

fascist, *n.* fascista, *m.* y *f.*

fashion, *n.* forma, figura, *f.*; moda, *f.*; uso, *m.*, costumbre, *f.*; condición, *f.*; guisa, *f.*; — **plate,** figurín, *m.*; **latest —,** última moda; **people of —,** gente de tono; —, *vt.* formar, amoldar.

fashionable, *adj.* hecho a la moda; en boga, de moda; elegante; **the — world,** el gran mundo; **—bly,** *adv.* según la moda, de acuerdo con la última moda.

fashionableness, *n.* moda, elegancia, *f.*

fast, *vi.* ayunar; —, *n.* ayuno, *m.*; —, *adj.* firme, estable, veloz, pronto; — **day,** día de ayuno; —, *adv.* firmemente; estrechamente; de prisa; a menudo.

fasten, *vt.* afirmar, asegurar, atar; fijar; —, *vi.* fijarse, establecerse.

fastener, *n.* asegurador, sujetador, *m.*; **set of —s,** brochadura, *f.*

fastening, *n.* atadura, ligazón, *f.*; nudo, *m.*

fastidious, *adj.* fastidioso; desdeñoso; delicado, melindroso; **—ly,** *adv.* fastidiosamente.

fastidiousness, *n.* fastidio, *m.*; escrupulosidad, *f.*; delicadeza en extremo; fastidiosa exigencia; melindre, *m.*

fasting, *n.* ayuno, *m.*

fastness, *n.* prontitud, *f.*; ligereza, *f.*; firmeza, *f.*; fortaleza, *f.*

fat, *adj.* gordo, pingüe; **to get —,** echar carnes, engordar; —, *n.* gordo, *m.*, gordura, *f.*; grasa, manteca, *f.*; sebo, *m.*

fatal, *adj.* fatal; funesto; **—ly,** *adv.* fatalmente.

fatalism, *n.* fatalismo, *m.*

fatalist, *n.* fatalista, *m.* y *f.*

fatalistic, *adj.* fatalista.

fatality, *n.* fatalidad, predestinación, *f.*

fat-cheeked, *adj.* molletudo.

fate, *n.* hado, destino, *m.*; fatalidad, *f.*, sino, *m.*; suerte, *f.*; **—s,** *n. pl.* (poet.) Parcas, *f. pl.*

fated, *adj.* decretado por los hados, fatal.

fateful, *adj.* fatídico, ominoso, funesto.

father, *n.* padre, *m.*

fatherhood, *n.* paternidad, *f.*

father-in-law, *n.* suegro, *m.*

fatherland, *n.* patria, *f.*

fatherless, *adj.* huérfano de padre.

fatherly, *adj.* paternal; —, *adv.* paternalmente.

fathom, *n.* braza (medida), *f.*; —, *vt.* sondar; penetrar; **to — a mystery,** desentrañar un misterio.

fathomable, *adj.* sondeable.

fathomless, *adj.* insondable.

fatigue, *n.* fatiga, *f.*, cansancio, *m.*; —, *vt.* and *vi.* fatigar, cansar, rendirse.

fatling, *n.* cebón, *m.*

fatness, *n.* gordura, *f.*

fatten, *vt.* cebar, engordar; —, *vi.* engrosarse, engordarse.

fatty, *adj.* grasoso, untoso, craso, pingüe.

fatuity, *n.* fatuidad, simpleza, *f.*

fatuous, *adj.* fatuo, tonto, imbécil.

faucet, *n.* grifo, *m.*; **water —,** toma, llave, *f.*, caño de agua.

fault, *n.* falta, culpa, *f.*; delito, *m.*; defecto, *m.*; **to find —,** tachar, criticar, poner faltas.

faultfinder, *n.* criticón, ona, censurador, ra.

faultfinding, *adj.* caviloso; criticón.

faultless, *adj.* perfecto, cumplido, sin tacha.

faulty, *adj.* culpable, defectuoso.

faun, *n.* fauno, *m.*

fauna, *n.* (zool.) fauna, *f.*

favor, *n.* favor, beneficio, *m.*; gracia, *f.*; patrocinio, *m.*; **in — of,** a favor de; **in his —,** en su provecho; **with your —,** con licencia o permiso de usted; **your —,** su apreciable, su grata (carta); —, *vt.* favorecer, proteger, apoyar.

favorable, *adj.* favorable, propicio; provechoso; **—bly,** *adv.* favorablemente.

favored, *adj.* favorecido.

favorite, *n.* and *adj.* favorito, ta, favorecido, da.

favoritism, *n.* favoritismo, *m.*

fawn, *n.* cervato, *m.*; —, *vi.* parir la cierva; adular servilmente.

fay, *vi.* cuadrar, venir bien una cosa con otra, empalmar.

FBI, Federal Bureau of Investigation, Comisión Federal de Investigación.

FCC, Federal Communications Commission, Agencia Federal de Comunicaciones.

fealty, *n.* homenaje, *m.*; fidelidad, lealtad, *f.*

fear, *vt.* and *vi.* temer, tener miedo; —, *n.* miedo, terror, pavor, *m.*

fearful, *adj.* medroso, temeroso; tímido; **—ly,** *adv.* medrosamente, temerosamente.

fearless, *adj.* intrépido, atrevido; **—ly,** *adv.* sin miedo.

fearlessness, *n.* intrepidez, *f.*

fearsome, *adj.* espantoso, horroroso.

feasibility, *n.* posibilidad, *f.*

feasible, *adj.* factible, práctico.

feast, *n.* banquete, festín, *m.*; fiesta, *f.*; —,

vt. festejar, regalar; —, *vi.* comer opíparamente.

feat, *n.* hecho, *m.*; acción, hazaña, *f.*

feather, *n.* pluma, *f.*; — **bed,** plumón, *m.*, colchón de plumas; — **duster,** plumero, *m.*; —, *vt.* emplumar; enriquecer.

featherbrained, *adj.* casquivano, tonto, frívolo.

feathered, *adj.* plumado, alado; veloz.

featheredge, *n.* borde o canto muy tenue.

featherweight, *n.* peso pluma.

feathery, *adj.* cubierto de plumas; ligero como una pluma.

feature, *n.* facción del rostro; forma, *f.*; rasgo, *m.*; atracción principal; —s, *n. pl.* facciones, *f. pl.*, fisonomía, *f.*

featured, *adj.* formado; presentado como atracción especial.

featureless, *adj.* sin rasgos distintivos.

Feb. February, Febo., Feb.º febrero.

febrile, *adj.* febril.

February, febrero, *m.*

fecal, *adj.* fecal.

feces, *n. pl.* excrementos, *m. pl.*

fecund, *adj.* fecundo, fértil.

fecundity, *n.* fecundidad, fertilidad, *f.*; abundancia, *f.*

federal, *adj.* federal.

federalism, *n.* federalismo, *m.*

federalist, *n.* federalista, *m.* y *f.*

federalize, *vt.* confederar.

federate, *adj.* confederado; —, *vt.* and *vi.* confederar, confederarse.

federation, *n.* confederación, federación, *f.*

fedora, *n.* fieltro, *m.*; sombrero de fieltro.

fee, *n.* feudo, *m.*; paga, gratificación, *f.*; honorarios, *m. pl.*; derecho, *m.*; cuota, *f.*; —, *vt.* dar propina, gratificar.

feeble, *adj.* flaco, débil.

feeble-minded, *adj.* imbécil, escaso de entendimiento.

feebleness, *n.* debilidad, *f.*

feebly, *adv.* débilmente.

feed, *vt.* pacer; nutrir; alimentar, dar de comer; —, *vi.* alimentarse, nutrirse; —, *n.* alimento, *m.*; pasto, *m.*; — **pump,** (naut.) bomba de alimentación.

feeder, *n.* persona que da de comer; alimentador, *m.*

feeding, *n.* nutrición, *f.*, alimento, *m.*; — **of domestic animals,** cebadura, *f.*

feel, *vt.* sentir; palpar; —, *vi.* tener sensibilidad; —, *n.* tacto, sentido, *m.*

feeler, *n.* antenas, *f. pl.*; (fig.) tentativa, *f.*

feeling, *n.* tacto, *m.*; sensibilidad, *f.*; sentimiento, *m.*

feet, *n. pl.* de **foot,** pies, *m. pl.*; (mil.) infantería, *f.*

feign, *vt.* inventar, fingir; simular; —, *vi.* fingirse, disimular.

feignedly, *adv.* fingidamente.

feint, *n.* ficción, *f.*; finta, treta, *f.*

feldspar, *n.* feldespato, *m.*

Felicia, Felisa.

felicitate, *vt.* felicitar, congratular.

felicitation, *n.* felicitación, congratulación, *f.*

felicitous, *adj.* feliz, dichoso.

felicity, *n.* felicidad, dicha, *f.*

feline, *adj.* gatuno.

fell, *adj.* cruel, bárbaro; —, *n.* cuero, *m.*; piel, *f.*; pellejo, *m.*; —, *vt.* matar las reses; cortar árboles; **to** — **(in sewing),** sobrecargar (en la costura); —, pretérito del verbo **fall.**

felloe, *n.* pina, *f.*, pina de rueda, *f.*

fellow, *n.* compañero, camarada, *m.*; sujeto, *m.*; socio de algún colegio; — **citizen,** conciudadano, na; — **creature,** semejante, *m.*; — **member,** consocio, *m.*; — **student,** condiscípulo, la; — **traveler,** compañero de viaje; correligionario (principalmente comunista) que no pertenece al partido correspondiente.

fellowship, *n.* compañía, sociedad, *f.*; beca (en una universidad), *f.*; camaradería, *f.*

felly, *n.* pina de una rueda.

felon, *n.* reo de un delito capital; —, *adj.* cruel, malvado.

felonious, *adj.* traidor, pérfido; —**ly,** *adv.* traidoramente.

felony, *n.* felonía, *f.*

felt, *n.* fieltro, *m.*

felucca, *n.* faluca, *f.*

fem. feminine, *f.* femenino.

female, *n.* hembra, *f.*; —, *adj.* femenino; afeminado, amujerado.

feminine, *adj.* femenino; femenil, tierno; afeminado, amujerado.

femininity, *n.* femeninidad, *f.*

feminism, *n.* feminismo, *m.*

feminist, *n.* feminista, *m.* y *f.*

femur, *n.* fémur, *m.*

fen, *n.* marjal, pantano, *m.*

fence, *n.* cerca, palizada, valla, *f.*; **wall** —, tapia, *f.*; —, *vt.* cercar; preservar; —, *vi.* esgrimir.

fencer, *n.* esgrimidor, *m.*

fencing, *n.* esgrima, *f.*

fend, *vt.* parar; rechazar; —, *vi.* defenderse.

fender, *n.* guardabarros, guardalodo, guardafango, *m.*: guardafuegos, *m.*

fennel, *n.* (bot.) hinojo, *m.*

Fer., Ferd. Ferdinand, Fern.do Fernando.

Ferdinand, Fernando.

ferment, *n.* fermento, *m.*, levadura, *f.*; —, *vt.* and *vi.* hacer fermentar, fermentarse; revenirse.

fermentation, *n.* fermentación, *f.*

fern, *n.* (bot.) helecho, *m.*

fernery, *n.* helechal, *m.*

ferocious, *adj.* feroz; fiero; —**ly,** *adv.* ferozmente.

ferocity, *n.* ferocidad, fiereza, *f.*

ferret, *n.* (zool.) hurón, *m.*; —, *vt.* huronear; investigar; **to** — **out,** descubrir, echar fuera.

ferreter, *n.* (fig.) espía, *m.* y *f.*

ferriage, *n.* barcaje, *m.*

ferric, *adj.* (chem.) férrico.

Ferris wheel, *n.* rueda de grandes dimensiones movida por fuerza motriz, con vagonetas para pasajeros, que se instala en las ferias y lugares de diversión; (Mex.) rueda de la fortuna.

ferrochrome, *n.* ferrocromo, *m.*

ferroconcrete, *n.* hormigón armado.

ferrotype, *n.* (phot.) ferrotipo, *m.*

ferrous, *adj.* férreo.

ferruginous, *adj.* ferruginoso.

ferrule, *n.* virola, *f.*; garrucha de tornillos.

ferry, *n.* barca de trasporte, barca de trasbordo; —, *vt.* llevar en barca.

ferryboat, *n.* barco para cruzar ríos, etc.

ferryman, *n.* barquero, *m.*

fertile, *adj.* fértil, fecundo, productivo.

fertility, *n.* fertilidad, fecundidad, *f.*

fertilization, *n.* fertilización, *f.*

fertilize, *vt.* fertilizar.

fertilizer, *n.* abono, *m.*

ferulaceous, *adj.* feruláceo.

ferule, *n.* férula, palmeta, *f.*

fervency, *n.* fervor, celo, *m.*

fervent, *adj.* ferviente; fervoroso; —ly, *adv.* con fervor.

fervid, *adj.* ardiente, vehemente, férvido.

fervor, *n.* fervor, ardor, *m.*

fescue, *n.* puntero, *m.*

festal, *adj.* festivo.

fester, *vi.* enconarse, inflamarse.

festival, *adj.* festivo; —, *n.* fiesta, *f.*; día festivo.

festive, *adj.* festivo, alegre.

festivity, *n.* festividad, *f.*

festoon, *n.* festón, *m.*; —, *vt.* festonear.

fetal, *adj.* fetal.

fetch, *vt.* buscar; producir; llevar; arrebatar; —, *n.* estratagema, *f.*; artificio, ardid, *m.*

fete, *n.* fiesta; —, *vt.* festejar, honrar, agasajar con una fiesta.

fetid, *adj.* fétido, hediondo.

fetish, *n.* fetiche, *m.*, adoración ciega de algo.

fetishism, *n.* fetichismo, *m.*

fetlock, *n.* cerneja, *f.*

fetter, *vt.* atar con cadenas.

fetters, *n. pl.* manija, *f.*, grillos, hierros, *m. pl.*, esposas, *f. pl.*

fetus, *n.* feto, *m.*

feud, *n.* riña, contienda, *f.*; feudo, *m.*

feudal, *adj.* feudal.

feudalism, *n.* feudalismo, *m.*

feudatory, *n.* feudatario, *m.*

feuilleton, *n.* folletín, *m.*

fever, *n.* fiebre, *f.*; **yellow** —, fiebre amarilla; **typhoid** —, tifoidea, *f.*, fiebre tifoidea.

feverish, *adj.* febril.

fever therapy, *n.* tratamiento de enfermedades mediante la provocación de altas temperaturas en el paciente.

few, *adj.* pocos; **a** —, algunos; **— and far between,** que ocurre rara vez.

fewer, *adj.* menor; —, *adv.* menos.

ff.: following (after numerals), sig.tes siguientes (después de números); **folios,** fols. folios.

FHA, Federal Housing Administration, Administración Federal (E.U.A.) de la Vivienda.

fiancé, *n.* novio, *m.*

fiancée, *n.* novia, *f.*

fiasco, *n.* fiasco, *m.*

fiat, *n.* fíat, *m.*

fib, *n.* mentira, *f.*; —, *vi.* mentir.

fiber, *n.* fibra, hebra, *f.*

fibrin, *n.* fibrina, *f.*

fibroid, *adj.* fibroso.

fibrous, *adj.* fibroso.

fibula, *n.* peroné, *m.*

fickle, *adj.* voluble, inconstante, mudable, frívolo; caprichoso.

fickleness, *n.* volubilidad, inconstancia, veleidad, *f.*

fiction, *n.* ficción, *f.*; invención, *f.*

fictitious, *adj.* ficticio; fingido; —ly, *adv.* fingidamente.

fiddle, *n.* violín, *m.*; —, *vi.* tocar el violín; jugar nerviosamente con los dedos.

fiddler, *n.* violinista, *m.* y *f.*

fiddlesticks, *interj.* ¡disparates!

fidelity, *n.* fidelidad, lealtad, *f.*

fidget, *vi.* (coll.) contonearse; —, *n.* agitación nerviosa; persona nerviosa e inquieta.

fidgety, *adj.* (coll.) inquieto, impaciente.

fiduciary, *n. and adj.* fiduciario, ria.

fie, *interj.* ¡vaya!

fief, *n.* feudo, *m.*

field, *n.* campo, *m.*; campaña, *f.*; espacio, *m.*; **sown** —, sembrado, *m.*; **to take the** —, salir a campaña; —, *adj.* campal; — **cricket,** caballeta, *f.*, saltamontes, *m.*; — **artillery,** artillería de campaña, *f.*; — **day,** día de la revista, día cuando las tropas hacen ejercicios en sus evoluciones campales; día de concursos gimnásticos al aire libre; — **glass,** gemelo de campaña; — **gun,** cañón de campaña; — **hospital,** hospital de sangre, hospital de campaña; — **marshal,** mariscal de campo; — **mouse,** turón, *m.*; — **officer,** (mil.) oficial del estado mayor.

fielder, *n.* (baseball) jugador que intercepta la pelota en el campo de baseball.

fieldfare, *n.* (orn.) zorzal, *m.*

fieldpiece, *n.* artillería de campaña, cañón de campaña.

fieldwork, *n.* (mil.) fortín, *m.*, fortificación de campaña.

fiend, *n.* demonio, *m.*; persona malvada; enemigo, ga.

fiendish, *adj.* demoníaco.

fierce, *adj.* fiero, feroz; cruel, furioso, torvo; —ly, *adv.* furiosamente.

fierceness, *n.* fiereza, ferocidad, *f.*

fiery, *adj.* ígneo; fogoso, colérico; brioso.

fiesta, *n.* fiesta, *f.*

fife, *n.* pífano, flautín, pito, *m.*

fifteen, *n. and adj.* quince, *m.*

fifteenth, *n. and adj.* décimoquinto, *m.*

fifth, *n. and adj.* quinto, *m.*; quinto de galón (medida de vinos y licores); —

column, quinta columna, partidarios ocultos del enemigo que tratan de facilitar su predominio en un país; **— columnist,** quintacolumnista, *m.* y *f.;* **—ly,** *adv.* en quinto lugar, rodete, *m.;* **—ly,** *adv.* en quinto lugar.
fiftieth, *n.* and *adj.* quincuagésimo, *m.*
fifty, *n.* and *adj.* cincuenta, *m.*
fig, *n.* higo, *m.;* (coll.) bagatela, *f.;* **— tree,** higuera, *f.;* **not to care a —,** no dársele un higo.
fig.: figure, fig. figura, cifra; **figuratively,** figuradamente.
fight, *vt.* and *vi.* reñir; batallar; combatir; **—,** *vt.* luchar; **—,** *vi.* lidiar; **to — one another,** pelearse; **to — to the death,** batirse; **—,** *n.* batalla, *f.;* combate, *m.,* pelea, *f.;* conflicto, *m.*
fighter, *n.* batallador, ra; peleador, ra; **— plane,** aeroplano de combate.
fighting, *n.* combate, *m.;* riña, *f.;* **— top,** cofa militar; **—,** *adj.* pugnante; combatiente.
figment, *n.* invención, *f.,* algo imaginado.
figpecker, *n.* (orn.) becafigo, *m.*
figurative, *adj.* figurativo, figurado; **—ly,** *adv.* figuradamente.
figure, *n.* figura, forma, hechura, *f.;* imagen, *f.;* cifra, *f.;* **— of speech,** tropo, *m.,* frase en sentido figurado; **—,** *vt.* figurar.
figured, *adj.* figurado.
figurehead, *n.* (naut.) roda, *f.;* figurón de proa; jefe nominal.
filament, *n.* filamento, *m.;* fibra, *f.*
filaria, *n.* (zool., med.) filaria, *f.*
filariasis, *n.* (zool., med.) filariosis, *f.*
filbert, *n.* avellana, *f.*
filch, *vt.* ratear.
file, *n.* archivo, *m.;* lista, *f.;* (mil.) fila, hilera, *f.;* lima, *f.;* **— case,** fichero, *m.;* **— clerk,** archivero, ra; **—,** *vt.* archivar; limar; pulir; **to — off,** (mil.) desfilar.
filet, *n.* **= fillet.**
filial, *adj.* filial.
filibuster, *n.* pirata, filibustero, *m.*
filigree, *n.* filigrana, *f.*
filigreed, *adj.* afiligranado.
filing, *n.* clasificación, *f.;* archivo, *m.;* **—s,** *pl.* limaduras, *f. pl.*
fill, *vt.* llenar, henchir; hartar; **to — out,** llenar (un formulario, cuestionario, etc.); **to — up,** colmar; **—,** *vi.* hartarse; **—,** *n.* hartura, abundancia, *f.*
filler, *n.* llenador, *m.*
fillet, *n.* faja, tira, banda, *f.;* filete, solomillo, *m.;* (arch.) filete, *m.*
filling, *n.* tapadura, *f.,* relleno, *m.;* (tooth) orificación, empastadura, *f.;* (of cigars) tripa, *f.;* **— station,** poste o surtidor de gasolina, estación de gasolina.
fillip, *n.* papirote, capirotazo, *m.;* estímulo, *m.;* estimulante, *m.*
filly, *n.* potranca, *f.*
film, *n.* película, *f.;* membrana, *f.;* **— pack,** paquete de planchas fotográficas; **— play,**

drama cinematográfico; **— roll,** rollo de películas.
filmy, *adj.* membranoso.
filter, *n.* filtro, *m.;* **—,** *vt.* filtrar.
filterable, *adj.* capaz de filtración.
filth, filthiness, *n.* inmundicia, porquería, *f.;* fango, lodo, *m.*
filthy, *adj.* sucio, puerco.
filtrate, *vt.* filtrar.
filtration, *n.* filtración, *f.*
fin, *n.* aleta (de un pez), *f.*
final, *adj.* final, último; definitivo; terminal; **—ly,** *adv.* finalmente, por último, al cabo; **—s,** último examen, juego, etc.
finale, *n.* final, *m.;* (mus.) coda, *f.*
finalist, *n.* finalista, *m.,* deportista que llega a disputarse el campeonato con otro en el partido final.
finality, *n.* finalidad, *f.;* finalización, *f.*
finance, *n.* renta, *f.;* hacienda pública; finanzas, *f. pl.*
financial, *adj.* financiero, pecuniario, económico.
financier, *n.* rentista, hacendista, *m.;* financista, *m.*
financing, *n.* financiamiento, *m.*
finback, *n.* yubarta, *f.*
finch, *n.* (orn.) pinzón, *m.*
find, *vt.* hallar, descubrir; proveer; dar con; **to — one's bearings,** orientarse; **to — oneself,** hallarse, estar; verse; **to — out,** descubrir, enterarse (de); **—,** *n.* hallazgo, descubrimiento, *m.*
finder, *n.* descubridor, *m.;* aparato reductor de una cámara.
finding, *n.* (law) resultando, *m.;* resultado, *m.*
fine, *adj.* fino; agudo, cortante; claro; transparente; delicado; astuto; diestro; lindo; elegante; bello; bien criado; bueno; **the — arts,** las bellas artes; **—,** *n.* multa, *f.;* **—,** *vt.* afinar, refinar; multar; **—!** *interj.* ¡bien!
fine-drawn, *adj.* muy tenue.
fine-grained, *adj.* de grano fino.
fineness, *n.* fineza, sutileza, perfección, *f.*
finery, *n.* perifollos, *m. pl.*
finespun, *adj.* sutil, atenuado; insustancial; ilusorio.
finesse, *n.* sutileza, astucia, pericia, *f.*
finger, *n.* dedo, *m.;* **— board,** teclado, *m.,* teclas, *f. pl.;* **— bowl,** enjuague, *m.;* **— glass,** enjuague, *m.;* **— post,** poste indicador; **— wave,** peinado al agua; **little —,** dedillo, *m.;* **—,** *vt.* tocar, manosear; manejar; **to — a keyboard,** teclear.
fingering, *n.* tecleo, *m.;* manoseo, *m.;* modo de tocar un instrumento de música.
fingernail, *n.* uña, *f.;* **— polish,** esmalte para uñas.
fingerprinting, *n.* dactiloscopia, *f.*
fingerprints, *n. pl.* señas dactiloscópicas, impresiones o huellas digitales.
fingerstall, *n.* dedal de pasamanero.
finical, *adj.* afectado, melindroso.

finicky, adj. mimoso, melindroso.
finis, n. fin, m., conclusión, f.
finish, vt. acabar, terminar, concluir, llevar a cabo; —, n. conclusión, f., final, m.; pulimento, m.
finished, adj. concluído; perfeccionado, refinado; retocado.
finishing, n. última mano; — **school,** colegio de señoritas especializado en educación social; —, adj. de retoque.
finite, adj. finito.
Finland, Finlandia, f.
Finlander, n. and adj. finlandés, esa.
finny, adj. armado de aletas; relativo a los peces; abundante en peces.
fiord, n. bahía, f., golfo, m.
fir, n. (bot.) abeto, m.; **Mexican** —, (bot.) oyamel, m.
fire, n. fuego, m.; candela, f.; incendio, m.; quemazón f.; — **alarm,** alarma o llamada de incendios; — **brigade,** bomberos, m. pl.; — **department,** cuerpo de bomberos; — **engine,** bomba de apagar los incendios; — **escape,** aparato de salvamento para incendios, escalera para salvamento; — **extinguisher,** apagador de incendios, matafuegos, m.; — **insurance,** seguro contra incendio; — **power,** potencia de fuego, f.; — **screen,** guardafuegos, m., pantalla, mampara, f.; — **ship,** brulote, m.; — **shovel,** paleta, f.; badil, m.; — **truck,** autobomba, f.; **to catch** —, inflamarse, encenderse; **to open** —, (mil.) hacer una descarga; —, vt. quemar, inflamar; —, vi. encenderse; (mil.) tirar, hacer fuego.
firearms, n. pl. armas de fuego.
fireball, n. granada real o de mano; meteoro, m.
fireboat, n. buque con mangueras para incendios.
firebox, n. caja del fogón.
firebrand, n. tizón, m.; incendiario, ria; persona sediciosa.
firebrick, n. ladrillo refractario.
firebug, n. incendiario, m.
fireclay, n. arcilla refractaria.
firecracker, n. petardo, m.; buscapiés, cohete, m.
firedamp, n. (min.) grisú, m., mofeta, f.
fire-eater, n. juglar que finge comer fuego; fierabrás, m.; jaque, charlatán, m.
firefly, n. luciérnaga, f., cocuyo, cucuyo, m.
fireless, adj. sin fuego; — **cooker,** cocinilla sin fuego.
fireman, n. bombero, m.; (rail.) fogonero, m.
fireplace, n. hogar, fogón, m., chimenea, cocinilla, f.
fireplug, n. boca de incendios, toma de agua.
fireproof, adj. a prueba de fuego, incombustible; refractario.
fireside, n. sitio cerca a la chimenea u hogar; vida de hogar.
firetrap, n. lugar peligroso de incendio.

firewarden, n. guardia encargado de prevenir incendios.
firewater, n. aguardiente, m.
firewood, n. leña para la lumbre.
fireworks, n. pl. fuegos artificiales.
firing, n. encendimiento, m.; leña, f.; (mil.) descarga, f.; — **lever,** (naut.) palanca de descarga, f.; — **line,** línea de fuego; — **party,** (mil.) piquete de salvas.
firkin, n. cuarterola (medida), f.; cuñete, m.
firm, adj. firme, estable, constante; seguro; —, n. (com.) razón social, casa de comercio; — **name,** razón social, f.; —**ly,** adv. firmemente.
firmament, n. firmamento, m.
firmness, n. firmeza, f.; constancia, f.; fijeza, f.
first, adj. primero; primario; delantero; — **aid,** primeros auxilios; — **mate,** piloto, m.; —, adv. primeramente; — **of all,** ante todo; —**ly,** adv. en primer lugar.
first-aid, adj. de primer auxilio; — **kit,** botiquín, m.
first-born, n. primogénito, ta; —, adj. primogénito, ta.
first-class, adj. de primera clase; — **private,** (mil.) soldado de primera.
firsthand, adj. directo, de primera mano.
first-rate, adj. primordial; admirable; de primera clase.
firth, n. estrecho, m.
fisc, n. fisco, m., la hacienda pública.
fiscal, adj. fiscal; —, n. district attorney.
fish, n. pez, m.; pescado, m.; — **cured** —, pescado salado; — **globe,** pecera, f.; — **market,** pescadería, f.; — **pole,** caña de pescar; — **pond,** piscina, pecina, f.; — **story,** (coll.) cuento increíble, relato fabuloso; — **trap,** garlito, m.; —, vt. and vi. pescar.
fishbone, n. espina de pescado.
fisher, n. pescador, ra.
fisherman, n. pescador, m.; —**'s basket,** nasa, f.
fisherwoman, n. pescadora, f.
fishery, n. pesca, f.; pesquera, pesquería, f.
fishhook, n. anzuelo, m.
fishing, n. pesca, f.; — **apparatus,** volantín, m.; — **bait,** cebo para pescar; — **line,** sedal, m.; — **reel,** carretel, m.; — **rod,** caña de pescar; — **smack,** lancha de pescar; — **tackle,** avíos de pescar.
fishplate, n. barra de empalme; (rail.) mordaza, f.; brida, f.
fishwife, n. pescadora, f.; mujer camorrista y pendenciera.
fishworm, n. gusano que sirve de carnada.
fishy, adj. abundante en pescado; que sabe a pescado; (coll.) increíble, fantástico, fabuloso.
fissure, n. grieta, hendedura, f.; —, vt. and vi. agrietar, agrietarse.
fist, n. puño, m.; —, vt. empuñar; dar puñetazos.
fistic, adj. pugilístico.

fístula, n. fístula, f.

fit, adj. apto, idóneo, capaz; cómodo; justo; —, n. paroxismc, m.; convulsión, f.; capricho, m.; ataque repentino de algún mal; —, vt. ajustar, acomodar, adaptar; sentar, quedar bien; **to — out,** proveer; —, vi. convenir, venir; caber; **—ly,** adv. aptamente, justamente.

fitful, adj. alternado con paroxismos; caprichoso; inquieto.

fitness, n. aptitud, conveniencia, f.; proporción, f.; oportunidad, f.

fitter, n. ajustador, m.; arreglador, ra; (naut.) armador, equipador, m.; instalador, m.

fitting, adj. conveniente, idóneo, justo; a propósito; adecuado; —, n. instalación, f.; ajuste, m.; **—s,** n. pl. guarniciones, f. pl.; accesorios, avíos, m. pl.

five, n. and adj. cinco, m.

fix, vt. fijar, establecer; componer; **to — up,** concertar; arreglarse; —, vi. fijarse, determinarse.

fixation, n. fijación, firmeza, estabilidad, f.; (chem.) fijación, f.

fixed, adj. firme, fijo; **—ly,** adv. firmemente, fijamente.

fixedly, adv. fijamente, ciertamente.

fixedness, fixity, n. firmeza, f.; constancia, f.

fixing, n. fijación, f.; ensambladura, f.; **—s,** n. pl. útiles, accesorios, m. pl.

fixings, n. pl. equipajes, m. pl.; pertrechos, m. pl.; ajuar, m.

fixity, n. fijeza, estabilidad, f.

fixture, n. mueble fijo de una casa; **—s,** pl. instalación, f.; enseres, m. pl.

fizz, vi. sisear; —, n. siseo, m.

fizzle, n. fiasco, fracaso, m.; —, vi. sisear; (coll.) fallar.

fl. fluid, flúido.

Fla. Florida, Florida.

flabby, adj. blando, flojo, lacio; fofo, débil.

flaccid, adj. flojo, flaco; fláccido.

flaccidity, n. flojedad, flaqueza.

flag, n. bandera, f.; (naut.) pabellón, m.; (bot.) gladíolo, m.; **— officer,** (naut.) jefe de una escuadra; **— of truce,** bandera de parlamento; —, vt. hacer señales con una bandera; **to — (with stones),** enlosar, embaldosar; **to — (a train),** hacer parar (a un tren); —, vi. pender; flaquear, debilitarse.

flagellant, n. flagelante, m.

flagellate, vt. azotar.

flagellation, n. flagelación, f.

flageolet, n. (mus.) caramillo, m., chirimía, f.

flagging, adj. lánguido, flojo; —, n. enlosado, m.

flagitious, adj. facineroso, malvado.

flagman, n. (rail.) guardavía, vigilante, m.

flagon, n. frasco, m.

flagpole, n. asta de bandera.

flagrancy, n. escándalo, m.; enormidad, f.

flagrant, adj. flagrante; notorio.

flagship, n. navío almirante, capitana, f.

flagstaff, n. asta de pabellón o de bandera.

flagstone, n. losa, f.

flail, n. (agr.) mayal, m.; —, vt. and vi. batir, sacudir.

flair, n. afición, inclinación, f.

flak, n. barrera antiaérea.

flake, n. copo, m.; lámina, f.; **— of fire,** chispa, centella, f.; **— of ice,** carámbano, m., —, vi. romperse en láminas.

flaky, adj. vedijoso; roto en pequeñas laminillas.

flamboyant, adj. flamante, suntuoso; (arch.) de líneas ondulantes.

flame, n. llama, f.; fuego (del amor), m.; **— thrower,** arrojallamas, m.; —, vi. arder; brillar; flamear, llamear.

flaming, adj. llameante; flamante, llamativo.

flamingo, n. (orn.) flamenco, m.

Flanders, Flandes, f.

flange, n. ribete, dobladillo, m.; (arch.) repisa, f.; (mech.) pestaña, f., reborde, m.; herramienta para hacer rebordes; —, vt. hacer un reborde.

flank, n. ijada, f.; (mil.) flanco, m.; —, vt. atacar el flanco; flanquear.

flannel, n. franela, f.; **thick —,** bayeta, f.

flannelette, n. moletón, m.

flap, n. ala (de sombrero), f.; bragueta, f.; solapa, f.; aleta, f.; **— of a pocket,** cartera, f., adorno de bolsillo; —, vt. and vi. aletear; sacudir.

flapjack, n. especie de torta frita.

flare, vi. lucir, brillar; —, n. llama, f.; (aer.) cohete de señales.

flare-up, n. fulguración, f.

flash, n. relámpago, m.; llamarada, f.; borbollón, m.; destello, m.; **— of lightning,** rayo, relámpago, m.; **— of wit,** agudeza, f., rasgo, m.; **— point,** punto de inflamación; —, vt. despedir agua a borbollones; —, vi. relampaguear, brillar; —, adj. rápido; chillón; ladronesco.

flasher, n. (elec.) destellador, m.; generador instantáneo; **— sign,** anuncio intermitente.

flashing, n. centelleo, m.; hoja curva de cobre o hierro galvanizado.

flash lamp, n. (phot.) lámpara especial para tomar fotografías en lugares oscuros.

flashlight, n. linterna, f.; linterna de destellos; lámpara de intermitencia; **— photography,** fotografía instantánea de relámpago.

flashy, adj. resplandeciente; chillón, charro; superficial; vistoso, alegre.

flask, n. frasco, m.; botella, f.

flat, adj. llano, plano; insípido; **— back,** lomo plano; **— tire,** llanta reventada o desinflada, neumático desinflado; —, n. llanura, f.; plano, m.; (naut.) bajío, m.; (mus.) bemol, m.; apartamiento, aparta-mento, m.; **—ly,** adv. horizontalmente; llanamente; enteramente; de plano, de nivel; francamente.

flatboat, n. buque de fondo plano para flete•

flat-bottomed, *adj.* de fondo plano.
flatcar, *n.* vagón de plataforma.
flatfoot, *n.* pie achatado.
flat-footed, *adj.* de pies achatados; (coll.) resuelto, firme.
flatiron, *n.* plancha (para planchar ropa), *f.*
flatness, *n.* llanura, *f.*; insipidez, *f.*
flatten, *vt.* allanar; abatir; chafar; —, *vi.* aplanarse; atontarse.
flatter, *vt.* adular, lisonjear, echar flores; —, *n.* allanador, *m.*
flatterer, *n.* galanteador, ra; zalamero, ra.
flattery, *n.* adulación, lisonja, *f.*; requiebro, *m.*; (coll.) piropo, *m.*
flatulence, *n.* flatulencia, *f.*
flatulent, *adj.* flatulento; hinchado; vano, fútil, frívolo; caduco.
flatware, *n.* vajilla de plata y porcelana.
flatwise, *adv.* con el lado plano hacia abajo.
flaunt, *vi.* pavonearse; —, *n.* alarde, *m.*
flaunting, *n.* ostentación, *f.*, alarde, *m.*
flavor, *n.* sabor, gusto, *m.*; —, *vt.* sazonar, condimentar.
flavoring, *n.* condimento, *m.*
flaw, *n.* resquebradura, hendedura, *f.*; falta, tacha, *f.*; ráfaga, *f.*; —, *vt.* rajar, hender.
flawless, *adj.* sin defecto, sin tacha.
flax, *n.* lino, *m.*; **to dress** —, rastrillar lino.
flaxen, *adj.* de lino, de hilo; blondo, rubio.
flaxseed, *n.* linaza, *f.*
flay, *vt.* desollar, descortezar; censurar severamente.
flea, *n.* pulga, *f.*
fleabane, *n.* pulguera, *f.*
flea-bitten, *adj.* picado de pulgas.
fleck, *n.* mancha, raya, *f.*; —, *vt.* manchar, rayar.
flecked, *adj.* abigarrado, vareteado.
fledge, *vi.* emplumecer; —, *vt.* emplumar.
fledgling, *n.* volantón, *m.*, avecilla, *f.*; inexperto, ta.
flee, *vi.* escapar; huir; tramontarse.
fleece, *n.* vellón, vellocino, *m.*, lana, *f.*; —, *vt.* esquilar; tonsurar; desnudar; despojar.
fleecy, *adj.* lanudo.
fleet, *n.* flota, *f.*; —, *adj.* veloz, acelerado, ligero.
fleeting, *adj.* pasajero, fugitivo.
Fleming, *n.* flamenco, ca.
Flemish, *n.* and *adj.* flamenco.
flesh, *n.* carne, *f.*; **— of fowl,** carne de pluma; **— color,** color de carne; **— wound,** herida superficial o ligera; —, *vt.* hartar, saciar.
flesh-colored, *adj.* encarnado, de color de carne.
fleshpot, *n.* olla, *f.*
fleshy, *adj.* carnoso, pulposo.
fleuron, *n.* (arch.) florón, *m.*
flew, pretérito del verbo **fly.**
flex, *vt.* encorvar, doblar.
flexibility, *n.* flexibilidad, *f.*
flexible, flexile, *adj.* flexible, adaptable, movible.
flexion, *n.* flexión, corvadura, *f.*

flexor, *n.* músculo flexor.
flexure, *n.* flexión, *f.*
flick, *vt.* dar ligeramente con un látigo; —, *n.* golpe como de un látigo; movimiento rápido.
flicker, *vi.* aletear, fluctuar; —, *n.* aleteo, *m.*; **— of an eyelash,** pestañeo, *m.*
flier, *n.* fugitivo, *m.*; volante, *m.*; aviador, ra; tren muy rápido.
flight, *n.* huída, fuga, *f.*; vuelo, *m.*; bandada (de pájaros), *f.*; (fig.) elevación, *f.*; **— strip,** (aer.) pista al borde de una carretera para el aterrizaje de emergencia; **— of stairs,** tramo de una escalera.
flighty, *adj.* veloz; inconstante, voluble, frívolo; casquivano; travieso.
flimflam, *vt.* engañar, estafar; —, *n.* soflama, *f.*; desatino, *m.*; patraña, *f.*; —, *adj.* tonto, absurdo; tramposo.
flimsy, *adj.* débil; fútil.
flinch, *vi.* respingar; desistir, faltar; retirarse; vacilar.
fling, *vt.* lanzar, echar; —, *vi.* lanzarse con violencia; —, *n.* tiro, *m.*; burla, chufleta, *f.*; tentativa, *f.*; **to have one's —,** echar una cana al aire.
flint, *n.* pedernal, *m.*; **— glass,** cristal de piedra.
flintlock, *n.* fusil de chispa.
flinty, *adj.* roqueño; pedregoso; inexorable.
flip, *vt.* arrojar, lanzar.
flippancy, *n.* volubilidad, *f.*; petulancia, *f.*; impertinencia, *f.*
flippant, *adj.* ligero, veloz; petulante, locuaz.
flipper, *n.* aleta de foca.
flirt, *vt.* arrojar, lanzar; —, *vi.* coquetear; mofar; (coll.) pelar la pava; (coll.) hacer cocos; —, *n.* coqueta, *f.*, persona coqueta.
flirtation, *n.* coquetería, *f.*
flirtatious, *adj.* coquetón.
flit, *vi.* volar, huir; aletear.
flitch, *n.* hoja de tocino.
float, *vt.* inundar; —, *vi.* flotar; fluctuar; —, *n.* cosa que flota; carro alegórico.
floater, *n.* flotador, *m.*
floating, *adj.* flotante; **— capital,** capital fluctuante; **— debt,** deuda flotante; **— dock,** (naut.) dique flotante; **— policy,** póliza flotante.
flock, *n.* manada, *f.*; rebaño, *m.*; gentío, *m.*; vedija de lana; —, *vi.* congregarse.
floe, *n.* carámbano, *m.*
flog, *vt.* azotar.
flogging, *n.* tunda, zurra, *f.*
flood, *n.* diluvio, *m.*; inundación, *f.*; llena, *f.*; flujo, *m.*; —, *vt.* inundar; **— tide,** pleamar, *f.*
floodgate, *n.* compuerta, *f.*
flooding, *n.* inundación, *f.*
floodlight, *n.* reflector o lámpara que despide un rayo concentrado de luz.
floodlighting, *n.* alumbrado sin sombras; iluminación intensiva.
floor, *n.* pavimento, suelo, piso, *m.*; piso de una casa; **— brush,** escobeta, *f.*; **ground**

—, piso bajo; **to ask for the** —, pedir la palabra; **to have the** —, tener la palabra; —, *vt.* solar; echar al suelo; (fig.) vencer, derrotar.

flooring, *n.* suelo, pavimento, *m.*; ensamblaje de madera para suelos.

floorwalker, *n.* superintendente de cada departamento de una tienda.

flop, *vi.* caerse, malograrse, fracasar.

flora, *n.* flora, *f.*

floral, *adj.* floral.

Florence, Florencia, *f.*

Florence, Florencio, Florencia.

Florentine, *n.* and *adj.* florentín, florentino, na.

florescence, *n.* florescencia, *f.*

floriculture, *n.* floricultura, *f.*

floriculturist, *n.* floricultor, ra.

florid, *adj.* florido.

Florida Keys, Cayos de la Florida.

florin, *n.* florín, *m.*

florist, *n.* florista, *m.* y *f.*

floss, floss silk, *n.* seda floja.

flossy, *adj.* blando como la seda.

flotation, *n.* flote, *m.*, flotación, *f.*

flotilla, *n.* (naut.) flotilla, *f.*

flotsam and jetsam, pecios, *m. pl.*

flounce, *n.* farfalá, faralá, *m.*; —, *vt.* guarnecer con faralás; —, *vi.* revolcarse en agua o cieno; pernear; voltearse repentinamente con ira o enojo.

flounder, *n.* (pez) rodaballo, *m.*; tropiezo, *m.*; —, *vi.* enlodarse, tropezarse en el cieno.

flour, *n.* harina, *f.*; — **mill,** molino de horina.

flourish, *vt.* exornar, adornar; **to** — (**a sword, etc.**), blandir (una espada, etc.); —, *vi.* gozar de prosperidad; crecer lozanamente; jactarse; rasguear; (mus.) preludiar, florear; —, *n.* floreo de palabras; (mus.) floreo, preludio, *m.*; charanga, *f.*; rasgo (de una pluma), *m.*; lozanía, *f.*

flout, *vt.* and *vi.* mofar, burlarse; —, *n.* mofa, burla, *f.*

flow, *vi.* fluir, manar; crecer (la marea); ondear, verter; correr; —, *n.* creciente de la marea; abundancia, *f.*; flujo, *m.*, corriente, *f.*; caudal, *m.*; — **line,** contorno de inundación.

flower, *n.* flor, *f.*; (fig.) lo mejor; — **girl,** florera, *f.*; — **garden,** vergel, *m.*; —, *vt.* adornar con flores; —, *vi.* florear; florecer.

flowered, *adj.* floreado; abierto en forma de flor; adornado con dibujos florales.

floweret, *n.* florecilla, florecita, *f.*

flowerpot, *n.* tiesto de flores, tiesto, *m.*, maceta, *f.*

flowery, *adj.* florido.

flown, *p. p.* del verbo **fly.**

flu, *n.* (coll.) influenza, gripe, *f.*, trancazo, *m.*

fluctuate, *vi.* fluctuar.

fluctuation, *n.* fluctuación, *f.*

flue, *n.* humero, *m.*; pelusa, *f.*

fluency, *n.* fluidez, facundia, *f.*

fluent, *adj.* flúido; fluente. fácil. corriente;

—**ly,** *adv.* con fluidez.

fluff, *vt.* mullir; — (**from cloth**), tamo, *m.*

fluffy, *adj.* blando y velloso.

fluid, *n.* and *adj.* flúido, *m.*

fluidity, *n.* fluidez, *f.*

fluke, *n.* lengüeta de áncora; (pez) platija, *f.*; ventaja fortuita o inesperada; — (**in billiards**), chiripa (en el billar), *f.*

flume, *n.* canal de esclusa, saetín, *m.*; caz de una rueda hidráulica.

flummery, *n.* especie de manjar blanco; alimento muy suave; patraña, *f.*

flunk, *vt.* dar calabazas; —, *vt.* and *vi.* (coll.) reprobar; —, *n.* persona fracasada.

flunkey, *n.* lacayo, *m.*; estafero, *m.*; persona adulona.

fluorescence, *n.* fluorescencia, *f.*

fluorescent, *adj.* fluorescente.

fluorine, *n.* (chem.) flúor, *m.*

fluorite, *n.* (chem.) fluorita, *f.*

fluoroscope, *n.* fluoroscopio, *m.*

fiuor spar, *n.* espato flúor.

flurry, *n.* ráfaga, *f.*; agitación nerviosa, conmoción, *f.*; —, *vt.* confundir; alarmar.

flush, *vt.* sacar agua de algún lugar; limpiar con un chorro de agua (por ej., un inodoro); animar, alentar; —, *vi.* sonrojarse, ruborizarse; fluir repentinamente; —, *n.* rubor, *m.*; conmoción, *f.*; calor intenso (como de fiebre); chorro de agua que limpia; flux (de naipes), *m.*, una mano de naipes todos del mismo palo; — **on cheek,** chapa, *f.*; (print.) composición pareja en el margen izquierdo; (print.) composición sin sangrías; —, *adj.* bien provisto, vigoroso, lozano; pródigo; parejo.

Flushing, Flesinga, *f.*

fluster, *vt.* confundir, atropellar; —, *vi.* confundirse; —, *n.* agitación y confusión.

flute, *n.* flauta, *f.*; (arch.) estría, *f.*; **rustic** —, zampoña, *f.*; —, *vt.* estriar.

fluted, *adj.* acanalado.

fluting, *n.* estriadura, acanaladura, *f.*

flutist, *n.* flautista, *m.* y *f.*

flutter, *vt.* turbar, desordenar; —, *vi.* revolotear; flamear; estar en agitación; —, *n.* confusión, *f.*; agitación, *f.*

fluvial, *adj.* fluvial.

flux, *n.* flujo, *m.*; disentería, *f.*

fly, *vt.* and *vi.* volar; pasar ligeramente; huir; escapar; — **on the beam,** (rad.) volar por la banda radiofónica; —, *n.* mosca, *f.*; volante, *m.*; (baseball) voleo, *m.*; **Spanish** —, cantárida, *f.*

flyblow, *n.* cresa, *f.*

flyblown, *adj.* contaminado, infestado.

flycatcher, *n.* (orn.) papamoscas, *m.*

fly-fish, *vi.* pescar con moscas.

flying, *n.* vuelo, *m.*; aviación, *f.*; —, *adj.* volante, volador; temporal, de pasada; repentino; — **boat,** hidroavión, *m.*; — **colors,** bandera desplegada; — **column,** (mil.) cuerpo volante; — **field,** campo de aviación, *m.*; — **fish,** volador, *m.*; pez volante; — **fortress,** (aer.) fortaleza aérea, fortaleza volante; — **squirrel,** ardilla voladora.

flypaper, *n.* papel pegajoso para coger moscas.

flyspeck, *n.* mancha de mosca.

flytrap, *n.* mosquero, *m.*

flyweight, *n.* peso mosca.

flywheel, *n.* (mech.) volante, *m.*

F.M., f.m. frequency modulation, (rad.) modulación de frecuencia.

foal, *n.* potro, *m.*, potra, *f.*, buche, *m.·* —, *vt.* and *vi.* parir una yegua.

foam, *n.* espuma, *f.*; —, *vi.* espumar.

foamy, *adj.* espumoso.

fob, *n.* faltriquera pequeña; leopoldina, *f.*; —, *vt.* engañar.

f.o.b., F.O.B. free on board, L.A.B. libre a bordo o f.a.b. franco a bordo.

focal, *adj.* focal.

focalize, *vt.* enfocar.

focus, *n.* foco, *m.*, punto céntrico; enfoque, *m.*; —, *vt.* enfocar.

fodder, *n.* forraje, *m.*, pastura, *f.*

foe, *n.* adversario, ria, enemigo, ga.

fog, *n.* niebla, *f.*; — **bank,** masa de niebla apoyada en la mar.

fogbound, *adj.* rodeado o cubierto de niebla.

fogy, fogey, *n.* persona de ideas o costumbres muy atrasadas.

foggy, *adj.* nebuloso, brumoso.

foghorn, *n.* (naut.) sirena, *f.*; pito de los buques.

foible, *n.* debilidad, *f.*, lado flaco.

foil, *vt.* vencer; frustrar; —, *n.* fracaso, *m.*; hoja (de estaño), *f.*; florete, *m.*

foist, *vt.* insertar (subrepticiamente); engañar.

fol.: folio, f.°, fol., folio, pág. página; **following,** sig.^{te} siguiente.

fold, *n.* redil, aprisco, *m.*; plegadura, *f.*, doblez, *m.*; hoja de una puerta; —, *vt.* apriscar el ganado; plegar, doblar.

folder, *n.* plegador, *m.*, plegadera, *f.*

folderol, *n.* tontería, necedad, *f.*

folding, *n.* plegadura, *f.*; — **bed,** catre de tijera o de campaña; cama plegadiza, catricofre, *m.*; — **chair,** silla de tijera, silla plegadiza; — **door,** puerta plegadiza, puerta de hojas.

foliage, *n.* follaje, ramaje, *m.*

foliation, *n.* (bot.) foliación, *f.*; azogamiento de los espejos.

folio, *n.* folio, infolio, *m.*, libro en folio.

folk, *n.* grupo de personas que forman una nación; gente, *f.*; **common —,** gente común y corriente; — **music,** música tradicional; — **song,** romance, *m.*, copla, *f.*; — **tale,** cuento tradicional.

folklore, *n.* folklóre, *m.*, tradiciones populares.

folkway, *n.* patrón de costumbres o cultura social; manera popular de pensar.

follicle, *n.* folículo, *m.*

follow, *vt.* seguir; acompañar; imitar; —, *vi.* seguirse, resultar, provenir; venir.

follower, *n.* seguidor, ra; imitador, ra; secuaz, *m.* y *f.*, partidario, ria; adherente, *m.* y *f.*; discípulo, la; compañero, ra.

following, *n.* séquito, cortejo, *m.*; profesión, *f.*; —, *adj.* próximo, siguiente.

follow-up, *adj.* que sigue; — **system,** sistema de continuidad (para correspondencia, anuncios, etc.).

folly, *n.* extravagancia, *f.*; bobería, *f.*; temeridad, *f.*; vicio, *m.*

foment, *vt.* fomentar; proteger.

fomentation, *n.* fomentación, *f.*; fomento, *m.*

fond, *adj.* afectuoso; aficionado; demasiado indulgente; **to be — of,** aficionarse, tener simpatía por; —**ly,** *adv.* locamente; cariñosamente.

fondant, *n.* pasta de azúcar que sirve de base a muchos confites.

fondle, *vt.* mimar, hacer caricias.

fondling, *n.* favorito, *m.*, niño mimado.

fondness, *n.* debilidad, terneza, *f.*; afición, *f.*; indulgencia, *f.*; bienquerencia, *f.*

font, *n.* pila bautismal; fundición, *f.*

food, *n.* alimento, *m.*; comida, *f.*; —**s,** comestibles, *m. pl.*; viandas, *f. pl.*

foodstuffs, *n. pl.* productos alimenticios.

fool, *n.* loco, ca, tonto, ta, bobo, ba; bufón, ona; mentecato, ta; —, *vt.* engañar; infatuar; —, *vi.* tontear.

foolery, *n.* tontería, bobería, *f.*

foolhardy, *adj.* temerario, atrevido.

foolish, *adj.* bobo, tonto, majadero; —**ly,** *adv.* bobamente, sin juicio.

foolishness, *n.* tontería, *f.*

foolproof, *adj.* muy evidente, seguro, fácil hasta para un tonto.

foolscap, *n.* papel de oficio (de 43 x 35 cms.).

foot, *n.* pie, *m.*; pezuña (de vacas, cabras, etc.), *f.*; base, *f.*; extremo, final, *m.*; pie (medida), *m.*; paso, *m.*; (poet.) pie, *m.*; — **by —,** paso a paso ; — **soldier,** soldado de infantería; **on —, by —,** a pie; **square —,** pie cuadrado; —, *vi.* bailar, saltar, brincar; ir a pie; —, *vt.* pasar, caminar por encima; **to — the bill,** (coll.) pagar la cuenta.

footage, *n.* largura o cantidad expresada en pies.

football, *n.* fútbol, *m.*; balompié, *m.*, balón de fútbol; balón para jugar con los pies.

footboard, *n.* estribo, *m.*

footbridge, *n.* puente para peatones únicamente.

foot-candle, *n.* patrón de bujía, medida de luz.

footfall, *n.* pisada, *f.*; ruido de pasos.

footgear, *n.* calzado, *m.*

foothill, *n.* cerro al pie de una sierra.

foothold, *n.* espacio en que cabe el pie, apoyo, *m.*; afianzamiento, *m.*

footing, *n.* base, *f.*; pisada, *f.*; paso, *m.*; estado, *m.*; condición, *f.*; fundamento, *m.*

footlights, *n. pl.* luces del proscenio; (fig.) el teatro, las tablas.

foot-loose, adj. libre, sin obligaciones.
footman, n. lacayo, m.; volante, m.; criado de librea.
footmark, n. huella, f.
footnote, n. anotación, f.; glosa, f.; nota, f.
footpace, n. paso de andar.
footpad, n. salteador a pie.
footpath, n. senda para peatones.
foot-pound, n. pie-libra, f.
footprint, n. huella, pisada, f.; vestigio, m.
footrace, n. corrida, carrera, f.
footrail, n. rodapié, m.
footrest, n. apoyo para los pies, escabel, m.
footsore, adj. despeado, con los pies lastimados.
footstep, n. vestigio, m.; huella, f.; paso, m.; pisada, f.
footstool, n. escabel, m., banquillo para los pies.
footway, n. acera de una calle; sendero, m., vereda, f.
footwear, n. calzado, m.
footwork, n. manejo de los pies en boxeo, en el fútbol, etc.; trabajo de periodista recogiendo noticias.
footworn, adj. despeado, cansado de caminar.
fop, n. petimetre, pisaverde, m.
foppery, n. tontería, f.; afectación (en el vestirse), f.
foppish, adj. vanidoso; afectado, currutaco.
for, prep. para; por; —, conj. porque, pues; **as — me,** en cuanto a mí; **what —?** ¿para qué?
for. foreign, extranjero.
forage, n. forraje, m.; —, vt. forrajear; saquear.
forasmuch as, conj. puesto que.
foray, n. correría, f.; saqueo, m.; —, vt. saquear.
forbear, vt. and vi. cesar, detenerse; abstenerse; reprimirse.
forbearance, n. paciencia, f.; indulgencia, f.; longanimidad, f.
forbid, vt. prohibir, vedar; impedir; **God —!** ¡Dios no quiera!
forbidden, adj. prohibido.
forbidding, adj. que prohibe; repugnante, chocante.
force, n. fuerza, f.; poder, vigor, m.; valor, m.; **—s,** tropas, f. pl.; **— pump,** bomba de compresión, bomba impelente; **to be in —,** regir; **with full —,** de plano, en pleno vigor; —, vt. forzar, violentar; esforzar; obligar; constreñir; **to — one's way,** abrirse el paso; —, vi. esforzarse.
forced, adj. forzado, estirado; **—ly,** adv. forzosamente, por fuerza.
forceful, adj. fuerte, poderoso; dominante.
forceps, n. fórceps, m.; pinzas, f. pl.
forcible, adj. fuerte, eficaz, poderoso, enérgico; **—bly,** adv. fuertemente, con energía.
ford, n. vado, m.; —, vt. vadear.
fore, adj. anterior; (naut.) de proa; —, adv.

delante, antes, anteriormente.
forearm, n. antebrazo, m.; —, vt. armar con anticipación.
forebear, n. antepasado, da.
forebode, vt. and vi. pronosticar, presagiar.
foreboding, n. corazonada, f.; pronóstico, m.
forecast, vt. and vi. proyectar, prever; conjeturar de antemano; —, n. previsión, f.; profecía, f.; **weather —,** pronóstico del tiempo.
forecastle, n. (naut.) castillo de proa.
foreclose, vt. (law) entablar, decidir un juicio hipotecario.
foreclosure, n. exclusión, f.; juicio hipotecario.
foredoom, vt. predestinar.
forefather, n. abuelo, antecesor, antepasado, m.
forefinger, n. índice, m.
forefoot, n. pata delantera de un animal.
forefront, n. primera fila; parte delantera
forego, vt. ceder, abandonar, renunciar a; preceder.
foregoing, adj. anterior, precedente.
foregone, adj. pasado; anticipado, predeterminado; previo.
foreground, n. delantera, f.; primer plano.
forehanded, adj. temprano; oportuno; prudente, frugal.
forehand stroke, n. (tennis) golpe con la parte anterior de la mano, golpe derecho.
forehead, n. frente, f.
foreign, adj. extranjero; extraño; **— exchange,** cambio extranjero.
foreign-born, adj. nacido en el extranjero.
foreigner, n. extranjero, ra, forastero, ra.
forejudge, vt. juzgar con anticipación.
foreknow, vt. prever, conocer de antemano.
foreknowledge, n. presciencia, f.
foreland, n. cabo, promontorio, m.
foreleg, n. pata o pierna delantera.
forelock, n. mechón de cabello que cae sobre la frente.
foreman, n. presidente del jurado; capataz, m.
foremast, n. (naut.) palo de trinquete.
foremost, adj. delantero, primero; —, adv. en primer lugar.
forenoon, n. la mañana, las horas antes del mediodía.
forensic, adj. forense, causídico.
foreordain, vt. predestinar, preordinar.
foreordination, n. preordinación, f.
forepart, n. delantera, f.; parte anterior.
forequarter, n. cuarto delantero (de un animal).
forerunner, n. precursor, ra; predecesor, ra.
foresaid, adj. susodicho, antedicho.
foresail, n. (naut.) trinquete, m.
foresee, vt. prever.
foreseer, n. previsor, ra.
foreshadow, vt. pronosticar, anunciar.
foreshorten, vt. recortar.
foreshortening, n. escorzo, m.
foreshow, vt. predecir, pronosticar.

foresight, *n.* previsión, presciencia, *f.*
foresighted, *adj.* perspicaz, previsor.
foreskin, *n.* prepucio, *m.*
forest, *n.* bosque, *m.*; selva, *f.*
forestall, *vt.* anticipar; obstruir, impedir; monopolizar.
forestation, *n.* silvicultura, *f.*, establecimiento de una floresta.
forester, *n.* guardabosque, *m.*
forestry, *n.* silvicultura, *f.*
foretaste, *vt.* probar con anticipación; —, *n.* prueba de antemano; goce anticipado.
foretell, *vt.* predecir, profetizar.
forethought, *n.* providencia, *f.*; premeditación, *f.*
foretop, *n.* copete, *m.*
forever, *adv.* por siempre.
forevermore, *adv.* por siempre jamás.
forewarn, *vt.* prevenir de antemano.
forewoman, *n.* oficiala, *f.*
foreword, *n.* advertencia, *f.*; prefacio, prólogo, preámbulo, *m.*
forfeit, *n.* multa *f.*; confiscación, *f.*; prenda, *f.*; —, *vt.* confiscar, decomisar; perder; pagar una multa.
forfeiture, *n.* confiscación, *f.*, decomiso, *m.*; multa, *f.*
forgather, *vi.* reunirse.
forge, *n.* fragua, *f.*; fábrica de metales; —, *vt.* forjar; contrahacer; inventar; falsear.
forger, *n.* forjador, *m.*; falsario, ria; falsificador, ra.
forgery, *n.* falsificación, *f.*; forjadura, *f.*
forget, *vt.* olvidar; descuidar.
forgetful, *adj.* olvidadizo; descuidado.
forgetfulness, *n.* olvido, *m.*; negligencia, *f.*
forget-me-not, *n.* (bot.) nomeolvides, *f.*, miosota, *f.*
forging, *n.* forjadura, *f.*
forgivable, *adj.* perdonable.
forgive, *vt.* perdonar.
forgiveness, *n.* perdón, *m.*
forgiving, *adj.* misericordioso, clemente, que perdona.
forgot, pretérito del verbo **forget.**
forgotten, *p. p.* del verbo **forget.**
fork, *n.* tenedor, *m.*; horca, *f.*; **tuning —,** diapasón, *m.*; —, *vi.* bifurcarse; —, *vt.* ahorquillar.
forked, forky, *adj.* bifurcado.
forking, *n.* bifurcación, *f.*
forlorn, *adj.* abandonado, perdido; desdichado, triste; **— hope,** (mil.) centinela perdida; empresa casi sin esperanza.
form, *n.* forma, *f.*; esqueleto, modelo, *m.*; modo, *m.*; formalidad, *f.*; método, *m.*; molde, *m.*; patrón, *m.*; **— letter,** carta circular, carta general; **in proper —,** en forma debida; —, *vt.* formar, configurar; idear, concebir; —, *vi.* formarse.
formal, *adj.* formal, metódico; ceremonioso; **—ly,** *adv.* formalmente.
formaldehyde, *n.* (chem.) formaldehido, *m.*
formalin, *n.* (chem.) formalina, *f.*
formalism, *n.* formalismo, *m.*

formality, *n.* formalidad, *f.*; ceremonia, *f.*
formalize, *vt.* formalizar, revestir una cosa de los requisitos legales.
format, *n.* formato, *m.*
formation, *n.* formación, *f.*
formative, *adj.* formativo.
former, *adj.* precedente; anterior, pasado; previo; **the —,** aquél; **—ly,** *adv.* antiguamente, en tiempos pasados, en otro tiempo.
formic, *adj.* hormigoso; **— acid,** ácido fórmico.
formidable, *adj.* formidable, terrible.
formless, *adj.* informe, disforme.
formula, *n.* fórmula, *f.*
formulary, *n.* formulario, *m.*; —, *adj.* relativo a las fórmulas.
formulate, *vt.* formular, articular.
formulation, *n.* formulación, *f.*
fornicate, *vi.* fornicar.
fornication, *n.* fornicación, *f.*
forsake, *vt.* dejar, abandonar.
forsaken, *adj.* desamparado, abandonado.
forsooth, *adv.* en verdad, ciertamente (hoy día se emplea irónicamente).
forswear, *vt.* renunciar con juramento; —, *vi.* perjurar.
fort, *n.* castillo, *m.*; fortaleza, *f.*, fuerte, *m.*; **small —,** fortín, *m.*
forte, *n.* fuerte, *m.*, aquello en que sobresale una persona; (mus.) fuerte, *m.*; —, *adj.* and *adv.* fuerte.
forth, *adv.* en adelante; afuera; **and so —,** y así sucesivamente, et cétera.
forthcoming, *adj.* próximo, pronto a comparecer.
forthright, *adj.* directo; franco; —, *adv.* directamente adelante; con franqueza; inmediatamente.
forthwith, *adv.* inmediatamente, sin tardanza.
fortieth, *n.* and *adj.* cuadragésimo, *m.*
fortification, *n.* fortificación, *f.*
fortify, *vt.* fortificar; corroborar.
fortissimo, *adj.* (mus.) fortísimo; —, *adv.* fortísimo.
fortitude, *n.* fortaleza, *f.*; valor, *m.*, fortitud, *f.*
fortnight, *n.* quincena, *f.*, quince días; dos semanas; **—ly,** *adj.* quincenal; —, *adv.* cada quince días.
fortress, *n.* (mil.) fortaleza, *f.*; castillo, *m.*
fortuitous, *adj.* impensado, casual; **—ly,** *adv.* fortuitamente, casualmente.
fortunate, *adj.* afortunado, dichoso; **—ly,** *adv.* felizmente, por fortuna.
fortune, *n.* fortuna, *f.*; suerte, *f.*; estado, *m.*; condición, *f.*; bienes de fortuna; hacienda, dote, *f.*; **— hunter,** aventurero, ra; persona que busca riquezas al casarse.
fortuneteller, *n.* sortílego, ga, adivino, na.
forty, *n.* and *adj.* cuarenta, *m.*
forum, *n.* foro, tribunal, *m.*
forward, *adj.* anterior, delantero; precoz; atrevido; pronto, activo, dispuesto; —

pass, (fútbol) lance del fútbol en dirección del equipo contrario; **—,** *n.* delantero (en Rugby, basketball), *m.*; **—,** *adv.* adelante, más allá; hacia adelante; **—,** *vt.* expedir, trasmitir, enviar más adelante.

forwards, *adv.* adelante.

fossa, *n.* (anat.) fosa, *f.*

fosse, foss, *n.* foso, *m.*, zanca, *f.*

fossil, *adj.* and *n.* fósil, *m.*

fossilize, *vt.* fosilizar.

foster, *vt.* criar, nutrir; alentar; **— brother,** hermano de leche; **— child,** hijo de leche, hijo adoptivo; **— father,** padre adoptivo, el que cría y enseña a un hijo ajeno; **— mother,** madre adoptiva.

foul, *adj.* sucio, puerco; impuro, detestable; **— ball,** pelota que cae fuera del primer o tercer ángulo del rombal de baseball; **— play,** conducta falsa y pérfida; **—,** *n.* acción de ensuciar; acción de violar las reglas.

foul-mouthed, *adj.* obsceno, abusivo.

found, *vt.* fundar, establecer; edificar; fundir; basar.

foundation, *n.* fundación, *f.*; fundamento, *m.*, pie, *m.*; fondo, *m.*; **— stone,** piedra fundamental, piedra angular.

founder, *n.* fundador, ra; fundidor, *m.*; **—,** *vi.* (naut.) irse a pique; caerse; tropezar.

founding, *n.* establecimiento, *m.*

foundling, *n.* niño expósito.

foundry, *n.* fundición, *f.*

fount, *n.* = **fountain.**

fountain, *n.* fuente, *f.*; manantial, *m.*; **— pen,** plumafuente, estilográfica, *f.*, pluma estilográfica.

fountainhead, *n.* origen, *m.*; fuente, *f.*

four, *n.* and *adj.* cuatro, *m.*; **— o'clock,** las cuatro; **on all —s,** a gatas.

fourflusher, *n.* (poker) lance con un flux de cuatro naipes; embustero, *m.*; persona que miente con respecto a su habilidad, riqueza, etc.

fourfold, *adj.* cuádruplo.

four-footed, *adj.* cuadrúpedo.

four-in-hand, *n.* corbata con nudo corredizo; coche tirado por cuatro caballos.

fourscore, *adj.* ochenta.

four-seater, *n.* vehículo de cuatro pasajeros.

foursquare, *adj.* cuadrangular.

fourteen, *n.* and *adj.* catorce, *m.*

fourteenth, *n.* and *adj.* décimocuarto, *m.*

fourth, *n.* and *adj.* cuarto, *m.*; **— dimension,** cuarta dimensión; **—ly,** *adv.* en cuarto lugar.

fowl, *n.* ave, *f.*; **—s,** volatería, *f.*; **flesh of —,** carne de pluma.

fowler, *n.* pajarero, *m.*

fowling piece, *n.* variedad de escopeta.

fox, *n.* zorra, *f.*; zorro, *m.*; **— terrier,** (perro) fox térrier; **— trot,** variedad de baile.

foxglove, *n.* (bot.) dedalera, *f.*, digital, *f.*

foxhole, *n.* agujero que ofrece protección a las tropas.

foxhound, *n.* perro zorrero.

foxtail, *n.* (bot.) carricera, *f.*

foxy, *adj.* zorruno; astuto.

foyer, *n.* salón de descanso o espera (en un teatro, hotel, etc.).

Fr.: France, Francia; **French,** francés; **Father,** Padre; **Friday,** Vier. viernes.

fr.: from, de; **franc,** fr. franco.

fracas, *n.* riña, arrebatiña, contienda, *f.*

fraction, *n.* fracción, *f.*

fractional, *adj.* fraccionario.

fractious, *adj.* regañón, enojadizo.

fracture, *n.* fractura, confracción, rotura, *f.*; **—,** *vt.* fracturar, romper.

fragile, *adj.* frágil; débil, deleznable.

fragility, *n.* fragilidad, *f.*; debilidad, flaqueza, *f.*

fragment, *n.* fragmento, trozo, *m.*, brizna, *f.*

fragmentary, *adj.* fragmentario.

fragmentation, *n.* fragmentación, *f.*

fragrance, *n.* fragancia, *f.*

fragrant, *adj.* fragante, oloroso; **—ly,** *adv.* con fragancia.

frail, *adj.* frágil, débil.

frailty, *n.* fragilidad, *f.*; debilidad, *f.*

frame, *n.* marco, cerco, *m.*; bastidor, *m.*; armazón, *f.*; telar, *m.*; cuadro de vidriera; estructura, *f.*; sistema, *m.*; figura, forma, *f.*, cuerpo, *m.*; forjadura, *f.*; **embroidery —,** bastidor, *m.*; **structural —,** armazón, *f.*; **—,** *vt.* fabricar, componer; construir, formar; ajustar; idear; poner en bastidor; encuadrar; forjar.

framework, *n.* labor hecha en el bastidor o telar; armazón, *f.*

Fran. Francis, F.co o Fran.co Francisco.

franc, *n.* franco (moneda francesa), *m.*

France, Francia, *f.*

Frances, Francisca.

franchise, *n.* franquicia, inmunidad, *f.*; privilegio, *m.*

Francis, Frank, Francisco.

frank, *adj.* franco, liberal, campechano; **—,** *n.* carta franca; **—,** *vt.* franquear una carta; **—ly,** *adv.* francamente, sin rebozo.

frankfurter, *n.* salchicha, *f.*

frankincense, *n.* variedad de incienso.

frankness, *n.* franqueza, ingenuidad, *f.*, candor, *m.*

frantic, *adj.* frenético, furioso; **—ally,** *adv.* desesperadamente.

frappé, *n.* bebida a base de hielo triturado.

fraternal, *adj.* fraternal; **—ly,** *adv.* fraternalmente.

fraternity, *n.* fraternidad, *f.*

fraternize, *vt.* and *vi.* fraternizar, confraternar.

fratricide, *n.* fratricidio, *m.*; fratricida, *m.* y *f.*

fraud, *n.* fraude, engaño, *m.*

fraudulence, *n.* fraudulencia, *f.*, fraude, *m.*

fraudulent, *adj.* fraudulento; **—ly,** *adv.* fraudulentamente.

fraught, *adj.* cargado, lleno.

fray, *n.* riña, disputa, querella, *f.*; **—,** *vt.* and *vi*, estregar; romper, romperse; desgastar, desgastarse.

freak, *n.* fantasía, *f.*; capricho, *m.*; monstruosidad, *f.*

freakish, *adj.* extravagante, estrambótico.

freckle, *n.* peca, *f.*

freckled, *adj.* pecoso.

Fred. Frederick, Fed. Federico.

Frederic, Frederick, Federico.

free, *adj.* libre; liberal; franco, ingenuo; exento, dispensado, privilegiado; gratuito, gratis; — **lance**, aventurero, ra; persona que escribe para alguna publicación o trabaja para alguna empresa sin contrato u obligación especial; — **on rail**, franco sobre vagón; — **port**, puerto franco; puerto de entrada; — **school**, escuela gratuita; — **thought**, libre pensamiento (esp. en religión); — **trade**, libre cambio; — **trader**, librecambista; — **verse**, verso suelto o libre; — **will**, libre albedrío; voluntariedad, *f.*; —**ly**, *adv.* libremente; espontáneamente; liberalmente; —, *vt.* libertar; librar; eximir.

freebooter, *n.* filibustero, pirata, *m.*

freeborn, *adj.* nacido libre; adecuado para el que ha nacido libre.

freedman, *n.* esclavo manumiso.

freedom, *n.* libertad, *f.*; soltura, *f.*; inmunidad, *f.*; — **of speech**, libertad de palabra.

free-for-all, *n.* (coll.) contienda general; pelotera, *f.*; certamen en que todos pueden participar.

freehand, *adj.* hecho a pulso, sin instrumentos.

freehanded, *adj.* liberal, generoso.

freehold, *n.* feudo franco.

freeholder, *n.* propietario absoluto de una cosa, heredad, etc.

freeman, *n.* hombre libre; ciudadano, *m.*

freemason, *n.* francmasón, *m.*

freemasonry, *n.* francmasonería, masonería, *f.*

freesia, *n.* variedad de hierba sudafricana.

free-spoken, *adj.* dicho sin reserva.

freethinker, *n.* librepensador, ra; libertino, na.

freewill, *adj.* espontáneo.

freewheeling, *n.* rueda libre.

freeze, *vi.* helar, helarse; —, *vt.* helar, congelar, garapiñar.

freezer, *n.* congelador, *m.*; **ice-cream** —, garapiñera, *f.*, aparato para hacer helados o mantecado.

freezing, *n.* congelación, *f.*; — **point**, punto de congelación.

freight, *n.* carga, *f.*; flete, *m.*; conducción, *f.*; porte, *m.*; — **car**, furgón, *m.*, vagón de mercancías o de carga; —, *vt.* (naut.) fletar; cargar.

freighter, *n.* fletador, cargador, *m.*

French, *adj.* francés, esa; — **doors**, puertas vidrieras dobles; — **language**, francés *m.*; — **leave**, despedida a la francesa, despedida precipitada o secreta; — **dressing**, salsa francesa (para ensaladas); — **horn**, (mus.) corno francés; — **windows**, puertas vidrieras dobles; **the** —, *n.* *pl.* los franceses.

French Guiana, Guayana Francesa.

Frenchman, *n.* francés, *m.*

French West Africa, Africa Occidental Francesa.

Frenchwoman, *n.* francesa, *f.*

frenetic, *adj.* frenético.

frenzied, *adj.* loco, delirante, borracho.

frenzy, *n.* frenesí, *m.*; locura, *f.*

frequency, *n.* frecuencia, *f.*; — **modulation**, modulación de frecuencia; **high** —, alta frecuencia.

frequent, *adj.* frecuente; —**ly**, *adv.* frecuentemente, con frecuencia; —, *vt.* frecuentar.

frequenter, *n.* frecuentador, ra.

fresco, *n.* pintura al fresco.

fresh, *adj.* fresco; nuevo, reciente; — **water**, agua dulce.

freshen, *vt.* refrescar.

freshet, *n.* crecida, *f.*

freshman, *n.* estudiante de primer año en la escuela superior o universidad; novicio, cia.

freshness, *n.* frescura, *f.*, frescor, *m.*; (fig.) descaro, *m.*

fresh-water, *adj.* de agua dulce.

fret, *n.* enojo, *m.*; irritación, *f.*; — **(of a guitar)**, traste, *m.*; — **saw**, sierra de calados; —, *vt.* frotar; corroer; cincelar; irritar; enojar; —, *vi.* quejarse; enojarse.

fretful, *adj.* enojadizo, colérico; —**ly**, *adv.* de mala gana.

fretfulness, *n.* mal genio, mal humor.

fretting, *n.* mortificación, *f.*; irritación, *f.*

fretwork, *n.* calado, *m.*

Fri. Friday, Vier. viernes.

friable, *adj.* friable, fácilmente desmenuzado.

friar, *n.* fraile, fray, *m.*

friary, *n.* convento de frailes.

fricassee, *n.* fricasé, *m.*

friction, *n.* fricción, *f.*; rozadura, *f.*; — **block**, bloque de fricción.

Friday, *n.* viernes, *m.*; **Good F**—, Viernes Santo.

fried, *adj.* frito; — **potato**, patata o papa frita; — **toast**, picatoste, *m.*

friedcake, *n.* buñuelo, *m.*

friend, *n.* amigo, ga; **to be close** —**s**, ser uña y carne; **to make** —**s**, trabar amistad.

friendless, *adj.* sin amigos.

friendliness, *n.* amistad, benevolencia, bondad, *f.*

friendly, *adj.* amigable, amistoso; —, *adv.* amigablemente.

friendship, *n.* amistad, *f.*

frieze, *n.* friso, *m.*

frigate, *n.* (naut.) fragata, *f.*

fright, *n.* susto, espanto, pánico, terror, *m.*

frighten, *vt.* espantar; **to** — **away**, remontar, ahuyentar; espantar.

frightful, *adj.* espantoso, horrible; **—ly,** *adv.* espantosamente, terriblemente.
frigid, *adj.* frío, frígido; **— zone,** zona glacial; **—ly,** *adv.* fríamente.
frigidity, *n.* frialdad, *f.*; impotencia, *f.*
frill, *n.* faralá, vuelo, *m.*; (coll.) adorno excesivo; ostentación en el vestir, en los modales, etc.
fringe, *n.* fleco, *m.*; franja, *f.*; **—s,** cenefas, *f.pl.*; borde, *m.*; **—,** *vt.* guarnecer con franjas; adornar con flecos.
frippery, *n.* fruslería, *f.*; cursilería, *f.*
frisk, *vi.* saltar, cabriolar; **—,** *n.* gambeta, *f.*; brinco, *m.*
friskiness, *n.* retozo, *m.*
frisky, *adj.* retozón; alegre.
fritter, *n.* melindre, *m.*, fritura, *f.*; trozo, fragmento, *m.*; **—,** *vt.* desmenuzar; desperdiciar.
frivolity, *n.* frivolidad, *f.*; pamplinada, *f.*
frivolous, *adj.* frívolo, vano; **—ly,** *adv.* frívolamente, sin sustancia.
frizzle, *vt.* rizar, encrespar.
frizzly, *adj.* rizado, frizado.
fro, *adv.* atrás; **to go to and —,** ir y venir.
frock, *n.* blusa, *f.*; bata de niño; sayo, *m.*, túnica, *f.*; **— coat,** casaca, *f.*, levitón, *m.*
frog, *n.* rana, *f.*
frolic, *n.* alegría, *f.*; travesura, *f.*; fiesta, *f.*; **—,** *vi.* retozar, juguetear.
frolicsome, *adj.* jugetón, travieso.
from, *prep.* de; después; desde; **— now on,** en lo sucesivo.
frond, *n.* rama verde.
front, *n.* frente, *f.*; frontispicio, *m.*; portada, *f.*; faz, *f.*; cara, *f.*; **— door,** puerta de entrada; **— seat,** asiento delantero; **in —,** enfrente; **in — of,** delante de; **—,** *vt.* hacer frente; **—,** *vi.* dar cara.
frontage, *n.* extensión frontera; prolongación lineal de frente.
frontal, *n.* venda, *f.*; (Sp.Am.) vincha, *f.*; **—,** *adj.* frontal.
frontier, *n.* frontera, *f.*
frontispiece, *n.* frontispicio, *m.*; portada, *f.*
frontlet, *n.* venda para la frente; frente (de un animal), *f.*
frost, *n.* helada, *f.*; hielo, *m.*; frialdad de temperamento, austeridad, *f.*; (coll.) indiferencia, *f.*; **—,** *vt.* congelar; garapiñar (un pastel, etc.).
frostbitten, *adj.* helado, quemado del hielo.
frosted, *adj.* garapiñado.
frosting, *n.* clara de huevo batida con azúcar; imitación de escarcha.
frosty, *adj.* helado, frío como el hielo.
froth, *n.* espuma (de algún líquido), *f.*; **—,** *vt.* and *vi.* espumar.
frothy, *adj.* espumoso; frívolo, vano.
froward, *adj.* incorregible; impertinente; refractario; **—ly,** *adv.* insolentemente.
frown, *vt.* mirar con ceño; **—,** *vi.* fruncir el entrecejo; **—,** *n.* ceño, *m.*; enojo, *m.*; mala cara.
froze, pretérito del verbo **freeze.**
frozen, *adj.* helado; congelado.
frt. freight, flete.
fructify, *vi.* fructificar.
fructose, *n.* fructosa, *f.*, azúcar de fruta.
frugal, *adj.* frugal; económico; sobrio; **—ly,** *adv.* frugalmente.
frugality, *n.* frugalidad, moderación, *f.*
fruit, *n.* fruto, ta; producto, *m.*; **candied —,** fruta azucarada; **— jar,** vaso para frutas; **— knife,** cuchillo de postres; **— stand,** puesto de frutas; **— store,** frutería, *f.*; **— sugar,** fructosa, *f.*; **— tree,** frutal, *m.*
fruit-bearing, *adj.* frutal.
fruitcake, *n.* torta o pastel de frutas.
fruitful, *adj.* fructífero; fértil; provechoso; útil; **—ly,** *adv.* con fertilidad.
fruitfulness, *n.* fertilidad, *f.*
fruition, *n.* fruición, *f.*, goce, *m.*
fruitless, *adj.* estéril; inútil; **—ly,** *adv.* vanamente, inútilmente.
frustrate, *vt.* frustrar; anular.
frustration, *n.* contratiempo, chasco, malogro, *m.*
fry, *n.* freza, *f.*; fritura, *f.*; enjambre, *m.*; montón, *m.*; asadura, *f.*; **fish —,** fritura de pescado; **—,** *vt.* freír.
frying pan, *n.* sartén, *f.*
ft.: foot, P. pie; **fort,** fuerte, fortaleza, fortificación.
fuchsia, *n.* (bot.) fucsia, *f.*
fuddle, *vt.* and *vi.* emborrachar, emborracharse; confundir.
fuddled, *adj.* (coll.) embriagado.
fudge, *n.* variedad de dulce de chocolate; cuento, embuste, *m.*; **—!** *interj.* ¡que va! (exclamación que indica desdén o menosprecio).
fuel, *n.* combustible, *m.*; **— gauge,** indicador de combustible; **— tank,** depósito de combustible; **— oil,** aceite combustible.
fueling, *n.* aprovisionamiento de combustible.
fugitive, *n.* and *adj.* fugitivo, va.
fugue, *n.* (mus.) fuga, *f.*
fulcrum, *n.* fulcro, *m.*
fulfill, *vt.* colmar; cumplir, realizar.
fulfillment, *n.* cumplimiento, *m.*, realización, *f.*
full, *adj.* lleno, repleto, completo; cumplido; pleno; todo; perfecto; cargado; **— dress,** traje de etiqueta; **— house,** full, fuljan (en el juego de póker), *m.*; **— moon,** luna llena, plenilunio, *m.*; **in — swing,** en plena actividad; **—,** *n.* total, *m.*; **— scale,** tamaño natural; **—,** *adv.* enteramente, del todo; **—,** *vt.* batanar el paño.
fullback, *n.* (fútbol) defensa, *f.*
fuller, *n.* batanero, *m.*
fuller's earth, *n.* arcilla grasa.
full-fashioned, *adj.* entallado con ampli-

tud; — **hose,** medias de costura francesa.
full-fledged, *adj.* maduro, con todos los derechos.
fullness, *n.* plenitud, llenura, abundancia, *f.*
fully, *adv.* llenamente, enteramente ampliamente; a fondo.
fulminate, *vt.* and *vi.* fulminar.
fulminating, *adj.* fulminante.
fulmination, *n.* fulminación, *f.*
fulsome, *adj.* ofensivo, repugnante; insincero.
fumble, *vt.* and *vi.* tartamudear; chapucear; andar a tientas.
fumblingly, *adv.* de manera incierta, a tientas.
fume, *n.* humo, vapor, *m.*; cólera, *f.*; —, *vt.* ahumar; —, *vi.* humear, exhalar; encolerizarse.
fumigate, *vt.* fumigar, sahumar; perfumar.
fumigation, *n.* sahumerio, *m.*; fumigación, *f.*
fumigator, *n.* fumigador, *m.*
fuming, *adj.* humeante.
fun, *n.* chanza, burla, *f.*; chasco, *m.*; diversión, *f.*; **to make — of,** burlarse de; **to have —,** divertirse.
function, *n.* función, *f.*; empleo, *m.*; —, *vi.* funcionar.
functional, *adj.* funcional.
functionary, *n.* empleado, *m.*; oficial, funcionario, *m.*
functioning, *n.* funcionamiento, *m.*
fund, *n.* fondo, *m.*; cantidad de dinero; —, *vt.* colocar en un fondo.
fundamental, *adj.* fundamental, básico, cardinal; **—ly,** *adv.* fundamentalmente.
fundamentalism, *n.* fundamentalismo, *m.*; ortodoxia, *f.*
funeral, *n.* and *adj.* funeral, *m.*; **— car,** carroza, *f.*; **— director,** director de pompas fúnebres; **— parlor,** casa mortuoria, agencia de inhumaciones o funeral.
funereal, *adj.* funeral, fúnebre.
fungous, *adj.* fungoso, esponjoso.
fungus, *n.* hongo, *m.*; seta, *f.*; fungosidad, *f.*
funicular, *adj.* funicular.
funk, *n.* (coll.) estremecimiento causado por temor; pánico, *m.*; persona que se estremece de miedo; **—money,** capital que se ausenta temporalmente por temor de la situación nacional; —, *vi.* estremecerse de miedo.
funnel, *n.* embudo, *m.*; cañón (de chimenea), *m.*; (naut.) chimenea, *f.*
funny, *adj.* burlesco, bufón; cómico; **— bone,** parte del codo donde el nervio cubital se apoya contra el cóndilo medial del húmero; **to strike as —,** hacer gracia.
fur, *n.* piel (para abrigos), *f.*; —, *adj.* hecho de pieles; —, *vt.* aforrar con pieles.
furbelow, *n.* volante, faralá, *m.*; adorno excesivo y de mal gusto.
furbish, *vt.* acicalar, pulir.
furious, *adj.* furioso, frenético, sañoso; **—ly,** *adv.* con furia.

furl, *vt.* enrollar (una bandera, etc.); (naut.) aferrar (las velas).
furlong, *n.* estadio (octava parte de una milla), *m.*
furlough, *n.* (mil.) licencia, *f.*; permiso, *m.*; —, *vt.* conceder un permiso o licencia (a un soldado, etc.).
furnace, *n.* horno, *m.*; hornaza, *f.*; **blast —,** horno alto o de cuba; **open-hearth —,** horno Siemens Martin.
furnish, *vt.* suplir, proporcionar, surtir, proveer; deparar; equipar; **to — a house,** amueblar una casa.
furnished, *adj.* amueblado.
furniture, *n.* ajuar, mueblaje, mobiliario, *m.*, muebles, *m. pl.*; **— set,** juego de muebles; **piece of —,** trasto, mueble, *m.*
furor, *n.* rabia, *f.*; entusiasmo, *m.*
furred, *adj.* forrado o cubierto de piel.
furrier, *n.* peletero, *m.*; pellejero, *m.*; **—'s store,** peletería, *f.*
furriery, *n.* peletería, *f.*
furrow, *n.* surco, *m.*; —, *vt.* and *vi.* surcar; estriar.
furry, *adj.* parecido a la piel; hecho o guarnecido de pieles.
further, *adj.* ulterior, más distante; —, *adv.* más lejos, más allá; aún; además de eso; —, *vt.* adelantar, promover, ayudar, impulsar, fomentar.
furtherance, *n.* adelantamiento, *m.*; progreso, *m.*; ayuda, asistencia, *f.*; fomento, *m.*
furthermore, *adv.* además.
furthest, *adj.* and *adv.* más lejos, más remoto.
furtive, *adj.* furtivo; secreto; **—ly,** *adv.* furtivamente; **to look at —ly,** mirar de reojo.
fury, *n.* furor, *m.*; furia, *f.*; ira, *f.*; **blind —,** saña, *f.*
furze, *n.* (bot.) tojo, *m.*
fuse, *n.* cohete, *m.*; (elec.) fusible, *m.*; detonador, *m.*; mecha, *f.*; espoleta, *f.*; **— box,** caja de fusibles; **large —,** mechón, *m.*; —, *vt.* and *vi.* fundir; derretirse.
fuselage, *n.* fuselaje, *m.*
fusel oil, fusel, *n.* (chem.) alcohol amílico.
fusible, *adj.* fusible, fundible.
fusillade, *n.* descarga cerrada.
fusion, *n.* fusión, licuación, *f.*
fuss, *n.* (coll.) alboroto, tumulto, *m.*; persona molestosa y exigente; —, *vi.* preocuparse por pequeñeces; —, *vt.* molestar con pequeñeces.
fussy, *adj.* melindroso; exigente.
fustian, *n.* fustán, *m.*; pana, *f.*; terciopelo, *m.*; lenguaje altisonante.
fusty, *adj.* mohoso; rancio; atrasado en ideas.
fut. future, futuro.
futile, *adj.* fútil, vano; frívolo.
futility, *n.* futilidad, vanidad, *f.*
future, *adj.* futuro, venidero; —, *n.* lo futuro, el tiempo venidero, porvenir, *m.*;

in the —, en adelante, en lo sucesivo.
futurism, *n.* futurismo, *m.*
futurity, *n.* futuro, *m.*; sucesos venideros.
fuzz, *n.* tamo, *m.*, pelusa, *f.*
fuzzy, *adj.* velloso.

G

G. Gulf, golfo.
g. gram, g. gramo.
G. A. General Agent, Agte. Gral. Agente General.
Ga. Georgia, Georgia.
gab, *n.* (coll.) locuacidad, *f.*
gabardine, *n.* gabardina, *f.*; **— cloak, — coat,** gabán, *m.*, gabardina, *f.*
gabble, *vi.* charlar, parlotear; **—,** *n.* algarabía, *f.*
gable, *n.* socarrén, alero, *m.*, extremidad triangular de un edificio.
gaby, *n.* (coll.) papanatas, *m.*, mentecato, ta.
gad, *vi.* tunar, corretear, callejear; **—,** *n.* aguijón, *m.*; cuña, *f.*
gadabout, *adj.* callejero, tunante; **—,** *n.* persona callejera.
gadfly, *n.* tábano, *m.*
gadget, *n.* baratija, chuchería, *f.*; utensilio, aparato, *m.*; pieza (de máquina), *f.*
Gaelic, *n.* and *adj.* galés, esa.
gaff, *n.* (naut.) cangreja, *f.*; anzuelo grande arponado; (coll.) algo difícil de tolerar.
gag, *n.* mordaza, *f.*; (coll.) expresión aguda y jocosa; **—,** *vt.* tapar la boca con mordaza.
gage, *n.* prenda, fianza, *f.*
gaiety, *n.* alegría, *f.*
gaily, *adv.* alegremente.
gain, *n.* ganancia, *f.*; interés, provecho, beneficio, *m.*; **—,** *vt.* ganar; conseguir; **—,** *vi.* enriquecerse; avanzar.
gainer, *n.* ganador, ra.
gainful, *adj.* ventajoso, lucrativo.
gaining, *adj.* ganador.
gainsay, *vt.* contradecir; prohibir.
gait, *n.* marcha, *f.*; porte, *m.*
gaiter, *n.* polaina, *f.*, borceguí, *m.*
gal. gallon, gal. galón.
gala, *adj.* de gala, de fiesta.
galaxy, *n.* galaxia, *f.*, vía láctea; **— of stars,** congregación de artistas prominentes.
gale, *n.* (naut.) ventarrón, *m.*
Galilee, Galilea, *f.*
gall, *n.* hiel, *f.*; rencor, odio, *m.*; **— bladder,** vesícula biliar; **—,** *vt.* rozar, ludir; irritar, atosigar.
gallant, *adj.* galante, elegante; gallardo; valeroso; **—ly,** *adv.* galantemente; bravamente; **—,** *n.* galán, *m.*; cortejo, *m.*
gallantry, *n.* galantería, gallardía, *f.*; bravura, *f.*
galleon, *n.* (naut.) galeón, *m.*
gallery, *n.* galería, *f.*; corredor, *m.*; **— of**

a cloister, panda, *f.*; **picture —,** pinacoteca, *f.*
galley, *n.* (naut.) galera, *f.*; **— proof,** (print.) galerada, *f.*, primera prueba; **— slave,** galeote, *m.*
gallinaceous, *adj.* gallináceo.
gallipot, *n.* orza, *f.*, pote, *m.*; (coll.) boticario, *m.*; variedad de resina.
gallnut, *n.* agalla, *f.*
gallon, *n.* galón (medida), *m.*
gallop, *n.* galope, *m.*; **—,** *vi.* galopar, galopear.
gallows, *n.* horca, *f.*
gallstone, *n.* cálculo biliario.
galore, *adv.* a montones, abundantemente.
galosh, *n.* galocha (generalmente de goma o caucho), *f.*
galvanism, *n.* galvanismo, *m.*
galvanize, *vt.* galvanizar.
galvanometer, *n.* galvanómetro, *m.*
gambit, *n.* gambito (jugada de ajedrez), *m.*
gamble, *vi.* jugar por dinero; aventurar.
gambler, *n.* tahur, ra, jugador, ra.
gambling, *n.* juego por dinero; **—,** *adj.* de juego; **— house,** garito, *m.*, casa de juego, tahurería, *f.*; casino, *m.*
gamboge, *n.* goma guta, gutagamba, *f.*
gambol, *n.* cabriola, *f.*; **—,** *vi.* brincar, saltar.
game, *n.* juego, *m.*; pasatiempo, *m.*; partida de juego; burla, *f.*; caza, *f.*; **— warden,** guardabosque, *m.*; **—,** *vi.* jugar.
gamebag, *n.* mochila de un cazador.
gamecock, *n.* gallo de pelea.
gamekeeper, *n.* guardabosque, *m.*
gamesome, *adj.* juguetón, retozón; **—ly,** *adv.* alegremente.
gamester, *n.* tahur, jugador, *m.*
gamin, *n.* granuja, *f.*, pilluelo, *m.*
gaming, *n.* juego, *m.*
gammon, *n.* jamón, *m.*; habladuría, *f.*; engaño, *m.*
gamut, *n.* escala, gama, *f.*
gander, *n.* ánsar, ganso, *m.*; simplón, papanatas, *m.*
gang, *n.* cuadrilla, banda, pandilla, patrulla, *f.*; **— plow,** arado de reja múltiple.
gangling, *adj.* delgaducho, larguirucho.
ganglion, *n.* ganglio, *m.*
gangplank, *n.* (naut.) portalón, *m.*, pasamano de un navío, plancha, *f.*; andamio, *m.*
gangrene, *n.* gangrena, *f.*; **—,** *vt.* and *vi.* gangrenar.
gangster, *n.* rufián, *m.*
gangway, *n.* portalón, *m.*; pasamano de un navío, plancha, *f.*; andamio, *m.*
gantry, gauntry, *n.* caballete, *m.*; (rail.) puente trasversal de señales; **— crane,** grúa de pórtico.
gap, *n.* boquete, *m.*; brecha, *f.*; laguna, *f.*
gape, *vi.* bostezar, boquear; ansiar, hendirse; estar con la boca abierta.
G.A.R. Grand Army of the Republic, Gran Ejército de la República (E.U.A.).
garage, *n.* garaje, garage, *m.*, cochera, *f.*

garb, n. vestidura, f.; traje, m.; apariencia exterior.

garbage, n. basura, f., desperdicios, m. pl.

garble, vt. entresacar, mutilar engañosamente (una cuenta, etc.).

garden, n. huerto, m.; jardín, m.; — **bed,** era, f., plantío, cuadro, m.; **vegetable —,** era de hortalizas, huerto de legumbres; —, vi. cultivar un jardín o un huerto.

gardener, n. jardinero, ra.

gardenia, n. (bot.) gardenia, f.

gardening, n. jardinería, f.

gargle, vt. and vi. gargarizar, hacer gárgaras; —, n. gárgara, f., gargarismo, m.

gargoyle, n. gárgola, f., caño de agua adornado en varias formas.

garish, adj. ostentoso y de mal gusto.

garland, n. guirnalda, f.

garlic, n. (bot.) ajo, m.

garment, n. vestidura, f.

garner, n. granero, m.; —, vt. almacenar (grano, etc.).

garnet, n. granate, piropo, m.; (naut.) trinquete, m., cargadera, f.

garnish, vt. guarnecer, adornar, aderezar; —, n. guarnición, f.; adorno, m.

garnishee, n. (law) persona a quien se le embarga el crédito o el sueldo; —, vt. ordenar la retención o embargo de crédito o sueldo.

garnishment, n. adorno, m.; (law) entredicho, m.

garret, n. guardilla, f.; desván, m.; **small —,** buhardilla, f.

garrison, n. (mil.) guarnición, f.; fortaleza, f.; —, vt. (mil.) guarnecer.

garrote, vt. estrangular.

garrulity, n. garrulidad, locuacidad, charladuría, f.

garrulous, adj. gárrulo, locuaz, charlador.

garter, n. liga, f., cenojil, m.; jarretera, f.; —**s,** n. pl. ataderas, f. pl.; — **snake,** culebrilla no venenosa.

gas, n. gas, m.; **carbonic acid —,** gas carbónico; **chlorine —,** cloro, m.; — **burner,** — **jet,** mechero de gas; — **fitter,** gasista, m.; — **main,** cañería, f., alimentadora de gas; — **mask,** mascarilla o careta contra gases asfixiantes; — **meter,** contador de gas; **illuminating —,** gas de alumbrado.

gaseous, adj. gaseoso.

gash, n. cuchillada, f.; —, vt. dar una cuchillada.

gasket, n. relleno, m., empaquetadura, f.

gaslight, n. luz de gas.

gaslighting, n. alumbrado de gas.

gasoline, n. gasolina, f., nafta, f.; — **tank,** depósito o tanque de gasolina.

gasp, vi. boquear; anhelar; —, n. respiración difícil.

gaspipe, n. tubería de gas.

gastric, adj. gástrico.

gastronomic, adj. gastronómico.

gastronomy, n. gastronomía, f.

gastropod, n. gastrópodo, m.

gate, n. puerta, f.; puerta de cercado.

gatekeeper, n. portero, ra.

gateway, n. puerta cochera.

gather, vt. recoger, amontonar, reunir; fruncir; inferir; arrugar, plegar; —, vi. aumentarse, juntarse; supurar.

gathering, n. acumulación, f.; colecta, f.

gauche, adj. tarpo, zurdo.

gaudily, adv. fastuosamente.

gaudy, adj. brillante, fastuoso.

gauge, gage, n. aforo, m.; graduador, m.; indicador, m.; calibrador, m.; manómetro, m.; calibre, m.; **tire —,** medidor, m.; —, vt. aforar; calar; calibrar; graduar, medir.

gauger, n. aforador, m.

Gaul, Galia, f.; —, adj. gálico.

gaunt, adj. flaco, delgado.

gauntlet, n. guantelete, m., variedad de guante; manopla, f.

gauntry, n. = **gantry.**

gauze, n. gasa, f.

gave, pretérito del verbo **give.**

gavel, n. mazo, m., gavilla, f.

gawk, n. majadero, ra; chabacano, na, tonto, ta; —, vi. obrar como un majadero; mirar fijamente como un tonto.

gawky, adj. bobo, tonto, rudo, desgarbado, deslucido.

gay, adj. alegre, festivo; pajarero; **to be —,** estar de buen humor; ser alegre.

gaze, vi. contemplar, considerar; —, n. mirada, f.

gazelle, n. gacela, f.

gazette, n. gaceta, f.

gazetteer, n. gacetero, m.; diccionario geográfico.

G. C. D. Greatest Common Divisor, M. C. D. Máximo Común Divisor.

gear, n. atavío, m.; aparato, m.; engranaje, encaje, m., trasmisión, f.; — **box,** — **case,** caja de velocidades o engranajes; — **changing,** cambio de velocidad, cambio de marcha; — **wheel,** rueda dentada; **in —,** en juego; **out of —,** fuera de juego; **to throw out of —,** desencajar, desmontar, desembragar.

gearing, n. engranaje, m.

gearshift, n. cambio de velocidad, cambio de marcha; — **lever,** palanca de cambios.

gee! interj. ¡caramba! ¡canastos!

geese, n. pl. de **goose,** gansos, m. pl.

gelatin, gelatine, n. gelatina, jaletina, f.; jalea, f.

gelatinous, adj. gelatinoso.

geld, vt. castrar, capar.

gelding, n. caballo capón.

gem, n. joya, f.; piedra preciosa, presea, f.; piedra, f.; —, vt. adornar con piedras preciosas.

Gemini, n. Géminis (signo del zodíaco), m.

Gen. General, Gen.¹, Gral. General.

gen.: gender, gen. género; **genitive,** genit. genitivo.

gen. del. general delivery, entrega general.
gender, *n.* género, *m.*
genealogical, *adj.* genealógico.
genealogist, *n.* genealogista, *m.*
genealogy, *n.* genealogía, *f.*
general, *adj.* general, común, usual; — delivery, lista de correos; — **delivery letter,** carta en lista; — **partnership,** sociedad colectiva; —**ly,** *adv.* generalmente, por lo común; —, *n.* general, *m.*; **in —,** por lo común.
generalissimo, *n.* generalísimo, *m.*
generality, *n.* generalidad, *f.*
generalization, *n.* generalización, *f.*
generalize, *vt.* generalizar.
generalship, *n.* generalato, *m.*
generate, *vt.* engendrar; producir; causar.
generation, *n.* generación, *f.*
generator, *n.* engendrador, dinamo, generador, *m.*
generic, *adj.* genérico.
generosity, *n.* generosidad, liberalidad, *f.*
generous, *adj.* generoso; —**ly,** *adv.* magnánimamente.
genesis, *n.* génesis, *f.*, origen, *m.*
genetics, *n.* genética, eugenesia, *f.*
Geneva, Ginebra, *f.*
genial, *adj.* genial, natural; cordial; alegre; —**ly,** *adv.* genialmente.
geniality, *n.* ingenuidad, *f.*; alegría, *f.*
genital, *adj.* genital.
genitals, *n. pl.* órganos genitales, *m. pl.*
genitive, *n.* genitivo, *m.*
genius, *n.* genio, *m.*
Genoa, Génova, *f.*
Genoese, *n.* and *adj.* genovés, esa.
Gent., gent. gentleman, caballero.
genteel, *adj.* gentil, lindo, elegante; —**ly,** *adv.* gentilmente.
gentian, *n.* (bot.) genciana, *f.*
gentile, *n.* gentil, *m.* y *f.*, pagano, na.
gentility, *n.* gentileza, *f.*, nobleza de sangre.
gentle, *adj.* suave, dócil, manso, moderado; benigno.
gentleman, *n.* caballero, gentilhombre, *m.*; —**'s agreement,** obligación moral.
gentlemanly, *adj.* caballeroso.
gentleness, *n.* gentileza, *f.*; dulzura, *f.*, suavidad de carácter; nobleza, *f.*
gently, *adv.* gentilmente; suavemente, con dulzura.
gentry, *n.* gente educada y de buenos modales; la clase media.
genuflection, *n.* genuflexión, *f.*
genuine, *adj.* genuino, puro; —**ly,** *adv.* puramente, naturalmente, genuinamente.
genuineness, *n.* pureza, *f.*; sinceridad, *f.*
genus, *n.* género, *m.*, clase, especie, *f.*
Geo. George, Jorge.
geocentric, *adj.* geocéntrico.
geodesy, *n.* geodesia, *f.*
geodetic, *adj.* geodésico.
Geoffrey, Geofredo.
geog. geography, geog. geografía.
geographer, *n.* geógrafo, *m.*

geographic, geographical, *adj.* geográfico.
geography, *n.* geografía, *f.*
geol. geology, geol. geología.
geological, *adj.* geológico.
geologist, *n.* geólogo, *m.*
geology, *n.* geología, *f.*
geom. geometry, geom. geometría.
geometric, geometrical, *adj.* geométrico; — **progression,** progresión geométrica.
geometrician, *n.* geómetra, *m.*
geometry, *n.* geometría, *f.*; **solid —,** geometría del espacio; **plane —,** geometría plana.
geophysics, *n.* geofísica, *f.*
geopolitical, *adj.* geopolítico.
geopolitics, *n.* geopolítica, *f.*
George, Jorge.
georgette, *n.* crespón de seda de tejido fino.
geotropism, *n.* geotropismo, *m.*
Ger.: German, al. alemán; **Germany,** Alem. Alemania.
geranium, *n.* (bot.) geranio, *m.*
geriatrics, *n.* (med.) geriatria, *f.*
germ, *n.* germen, *m.*; microbio, *m.*; — **cell,** célula embrional; — **plasm,** germen plasma.
German, *n.* and *adj.* alemán, ana; — **measles,** rubéola, *f.*, especie de sarampión benigno.
germane, *adj.* afín, relacionado.
Germanic, *adj.* alemanisco, germánico.
Germany, Alemania, Germania, *f.*
germicidal, *adj.* germicida.
germicide, *n.* bactericida, germicida, *m.*
germinal, *adj.* germinal.
germinate, *vi.* brotar, germinar.
germination, *n.* germinación, *f.*
gerrymander, *n.* división arbitraria de distritos electorales; argucia, *f.*; —, *vt.* dividir arbitrariamente los distritos electorales.
Gertrude, Gertrudis.
gerund, *n.* gerundio, *m.*
gerundive, *n.* gerundio adjetivado.
gestation, *n.* gestación, preñez, *f.*
gesticulate, *vi.* gesticular; **to — with the hands,** manotear.
gesticulation, *n.* gesticulación, *f.*
gesture, *n.* gesto, movimiento, *m.*
get, *vt.* obtener, conseguir, alcanzar; coger; agarrar, robar; persuadir; **to go and —,** ir a buscar; —, *vi.* alcanzar; llegar; venir; hacerse, ponerse; prevalecer; introducirse; **to — by heart,** aprender de memoria; **to — along,** ir pasando; **to — around,** entrampar, enredar; **to — away,** irse, fugarse, escaparse; **to — the better of,** salir vencedor, sobrepujar; **to — together,** reunirse.
getaway, *n.* escapada, huída, *f.*
getup, *n.* atavío, *m.*, estructura, *f.*
gewgaw, *n.* chuchería, *f.*; miriñaque, *m.*
geyser, *n.* geiser, *m.*, surtidor de agua termal.

ghastliness, *n.* palidez, *f.*; aspecto cadavérico.

ghastly, *adj.* pálido, cadavérico; espantoso.

Ghent, Gante, *m.*

gherkin, *n.* pepinillo, cohombrillo, *m.*

ghetto, *n.* ghetto, *m.*, barrio judío.

ghost, *n.* espectro, *m.*; espíritu, *m.*; fantasma, *m.*; — **writer,** escritor cuyos artículos aparecen bajo el nombre de otra persona.

ghostly, *adj.* espectral, como un espectro.

ghoul, *n.* vampiro, *m.*

G.H.Q. General Headquarters, Cuartel General; Oficinas Generales.

giant, *n.* gigante, *m.*; — **panda,** panda gigante.

giantess, *n.* giganta, *f.*

gibberish, *n.* jerigonza, *f.*

gibbet, *n.* horca, *f.*; —, *vt.* ahorcar.

gibbous, *adj.* giboso, jorobado.

gibe, *vi.* escarnecer, burlarse, mofar; —, *n.* mofa, burla, *f.*

giblets, *n. pl.* despojos y menudillos (de ave).

giddily, *adv.* con vértigos; con volubilidad.

giddiness, *n.* vértigo, *m.*; inconstancia, *f.*

giddy, *adj.* vertiginoso; inconstante.

giddy-headed, *adj.* frívolo; — **person,** tarambana, *m.* y *f.*

gift, *n.* don, *m.*; dádiva, *f.*; talento, *m.*; habilidad, *f.*; presente, obsequio, *m.*; **to make a — of,** obsequiar.

gifted, *adj.* hábil, talentoso.

gig, *n.* tílburi, quitrín, *m.*; trompo, *m.*, perinola, *f.*; (naut.) canoa, *f.*, esquife, *m.*

gigantic, *adj.* gigantesco.

giggle, *vi.* reírse disimuladamente; reírse nerviosamente y sin motivo; —, *n.* risilla disimulada o nerviosa.

gigolo, *n.* hombre que se gana la vida bailando con las mujeres o acompañándolas a fiestas, teatros, etc.

gild, *vt.* dorar.

gilding, *n.* doradura, *f.*; dorado, *m.*

gill, *n.* cuarta parte de una pinta; papada, *f.*; —s, *pl.* barbas del gallo; agallas de los peces.

gillyflower, *n.* (bot.) alelí, *m.*

gilt, *n.* and *adj.* dorado, *m.*

gilt-edged, *adj.* con el borde dorado; (coll.) de la mejor calidad.

gimcrack, *n.* chuchería, *f.*, ornamento de poco valor; —, *adj.* vistoso pero de poco valor.

gimlet, *n.* barrena pequeña.

gimp, *n.* especie de encaje para vestidos y para tapicería.

gin, *n.* trampa, *f.*; cabria, *f.*; ginebra (bebida alcohólica), *f.*; —, *vt.* despepitar (algodón, etc.).

ginger, *n.* jengibre, *m.*; — **ale,** cerveza de jengibre.

gingerbread, *n.* pan de jengibre.

gingerly, *adv.* tímidamente, cautelosamente; —, *adj.* cauteloso, cuidadoso.

gingersnap, *n.* galletica de jengibre.

gingham, *n.* zaraza, guinga, *f.*

gipsy, *n.* = **gypsy.**

giraffe, *n.* jirafa, *f.*

gird, *vt.* ceñir; cercar; —, *vi.* mofarse.

girder, *n.* cuartón, *m.*; viga, *f.*

girdle, *n.* faja, *f.*; cinturón, *m.*; —, *vt.* ceñir.

girl, *n.* muchacha, doncella, niña, *f.*; — **scout,** muchacha exploradora; **young —,** joven, jovencita, *f.*; (coll.) polla, *f.*

girlhood, *n.* niñez, doncellez, *f.*, juventud femenina.

girlish, *adj.* juvenil, propio de una joven o de una niña.

girth, *n.* cincha, *f.*; circunferencia, *f.*

gist, *n.* punto principal de una acusación; quid, *m.*

give, *vt.* and *vi.* dar, donar, conceder; abandonar; aplicarse; dedicarse; **to — account,** dar razón; **to — back,** retornar, devolver; **to — birth,** dar a luz; **to — in,** rendirse, darse; **to — up,** renunciar; rendirse; ceder; transigir; darse por vencido; **to — leave,** permitir; **to — off,** emitir; **to — out,** anunciar públicamente, agotarse, consumirse; **to — security,** dar fianza.

give-and-take, *n.* acción de dar y tomar.

given, *p. p.* del verbo **give.**

giver, *n.* dador, ra, donador, ra.

gizzard, *n.* molleja, *f.*, papo (de ave), *m.*

glacé, *adj.* garapiñado.

glacial, *adj.* glacial.

glacier, *n.* ventisquero, *m.*; glaciar, *m.*

glad, *adj.* alegre, contento; **I am — to see,** me alegro de ver; **to be — of,** celebrar, alegrarse de; **—ly,** *adv.* alegremente, con gusto.

gladden, *vt.* alegrar, recrear; regocijar.

glade, *n.* cañada, *f.*

gladiator, *n.* gladiator, gladiador, *m.*

gladiolus, *n.* gladio, gladíolo, *m.*

gladness, *n.* alegría, *f.*, regocijo, placer, *m.*

gladsome, *adj.* alegre, contento.

glair, *n.* clara de huevo; sustancia viscosa hecha de clara de huevo.

glamor, glamour, *n.* encanto, hechizo, *m.*; elegancia, *f.*

glance, *n.* vislumbre, *f.*; vistazo, *m.*; ojeada, *f.*; vista, *f.*; **at first —,** a primera vista; —, *vt.* lanzar miradas; pasar ligeramente; —, *vi.* ojear.

gland, *n.* glándula, *f.*

glanders, *n.* muermo, *m.*

glandular, *adj.* glanduloso.

glare, *n.* deslumbramiento, *m.*; reflejo, *m.*; mirada feroz y penetrante; —, *vi.* relumbrar, brillar; echar miradas de indignación.

glaring, *adj.* deslumbrante; manifiesto; penetrante.

glass, *n.* vidrio, *m.*; vaso para beber; espejo, *m.*; reloj de arena; — **blower,** soplador de vidrio; — **case,** vidriera, *f.*; **plate —,** vidrio cilindrado; **water —,** vidrio soluble; **—es,** *n. pl.* anteojos, *m. pl.*; —, *adj.* vítreo, de vidrio.

glassful, _n._ vaso, _m._, vaso lleno.
glassware, _n._ cristalería, _f._
glassy, _adj._ vítreo, cristalino, vidrioso.
glaucoma, _n._ (med.) glaucoma, _m._
glaze, _vt._ vidriar, embarnizar.
glazed, _adj._ vidriado, satinado; — **paper,** papel satinado.
glazier, _n._ vidriero, _m._
glazing, _n._ vidriado, _m._
gleam, _n._ claridad, _f._; brillo, destello, centelleo, _m._
glean, _vt._ espigar; recoger.
gleaner, _n._ espigador, ra, rebuscador, ra.
glebe, _n._ gleba, _f._, terrón, _m._
glee, _n._ alegría, _f._; gozo, _m._; jovialidad, _f._; canción sin acompañamiento para más de dos voces; — **club,** coro, _m._
gleeful, _adj._ alegre, gozoso.
glen, _n._ valle, _m._; llanura, _f._
glib, _adj._ de lengua fácil, flúido; —**ly,** _adv._ corrientemente, volublemente; fácilmente.
glide, _vi._ resbalar; pasar ligeramente.
glider, _n._ (aer.) deslizador, planeador, _m._; hidroplano, hidrodeslizador, _m._
gliding, _n._ deslizamiento, _m._; (aer.) planeo, planeamiento, _m._
glim, _n._ farol de ronda; linterna, _f._
glimmer, _n._ vislumbre, _f._; —, _vi._ vislumbrarse.
glimpse, _n._ vislumbre, _f._; ojeada, _f._; —, _vt._ descubrir, percibir.
glint, _n._ reflejo, brillo, _m._
glisten, _vi._ relucir, brillar; —, _n._ brillo, _m._
glitter, _vi._ resplandecer, brillar; —, _n._ brillantez, _f._, brillo, _m._; ostentación, _f._
glittering, _adj._ reluciente.
gloaming, _n._ crepúsculo, _m._
gloat, _vi._ ojear con admiración; deleitarse.
global, _adj._ global.
globe, _n._ globo, _m._; esfera, _f._; orbe, _m._; **fish** —, pecera, _f._
globe-trotter, _n._ persona que viaja extensamente.
globular, _adj._ globoso.
globule, _n._ glóbulo, _m._
gloom, _n._ oscuridad, _f._; melancolía, tristeza, _f._; —**ily,** _adv._ oscuramente; tristemente.
gloomy, _adj._ sombrío, oscuro; nublado; triste, melancólico; hosco, tenebroso.
glorification, _n._ glorificación, alabanza, _f._
glorify, _vt._ glorificar, celebrar.
glorious, _adj._ glorioso, ilustre; —**ly,** _adv._ gloriosamente.
glory, _n._ gloria, fama, celebridad, _f._; lauro, _m._; aureola, _f._; —, _vi._ gloriarse, jactarse.
gloss, _n._ glosa, _f._, escolio, _m._; lustre, _m._; —, _vt._ glosar, interpretar; notar; barnizar.
glossary, _n._ glosario, _m._
glossy, _adj._ lustroso, brillante.
glove, _n._ guante, _m._
glover, _n._ guantero, _m._
glow, _vi._ arder; inflamarse; relucir; —, _n._ fulgor, _m._; color vivo; viveza de color; vehemencia de una pasión.

glower, _vi._ mirar con ceño o con ira.
glowworm, _n._ luciérnaga, _f._
gloze, _vi._ brillar, relucir; comentar, glosar.
glucose, _n._ glucosa, _f._
glue, _n._ cola, _f._, sustancia glutinosa; —, _vt._ encolar, pegar.
gluey, _adj._ viscoso, pegajoso.
glum, _adj._ tétrico; de mal humor.
glut, _vt._ engullir, tragar, devorar; saciar; —, _n._ hartura, abundancia, _f._
gluten, _n._ gluten, _m._
glutenous _adj._ glutenoso.
glutinous, _adj._ glutinoso, viscoso.
glutton, _n._ glotón, ona, tragón, ona.
gluttonous, _adj._ goloso, glotón.
gluttony, _n._ glotonería, _f._
glycerine, _n._ glicerina, _f._
glycogen, _n._ glicógeno, _m._
gm. gram, _g._ gramo.
G-man, _n._ (coll.) agente de la policía federal de E.U.A.
gnarl, _n._ nudo, _m._
gnarled, _adj._ nudoso; enredado.
gnash, _vt._ and _vi._ chocar; **to** — **the teeth,** crujir los dientes, rechinar.
gnat, _n._ jején, _m._
gnaw, _vt._ roer, mordicar.
gnome, _n._ gnomo, _m._
Gnosticism, _n._ gnosticismo, _m._
gnu, _n._ (zool.) bucéfalo, _m._
go, _vi._ ir, irse, andar, caminar; partir; huir; pasar; **to** — **away,** marcharse, salir; **to** — **astray,** extraviarse; **to** — **forward,** ser despachado; **to** — **back,** regresar; remontar a; **to** — **beyond,** rebasar; trascender, ir más allá; **to** — **insane,** perder la razón; **to** — **out,** salir; **to** — **without,** pasarse sin; **to** — **without saying,** sobreentenderse; — **to it!** ¡vamos! ¡a ello! —, _n._ (coll.) energía, _f._; actividad, _f._; espíritu, _m._; **on the** —, en plena actividad, siempre moviéndose; (coll.) moda, _f._, última novedad; **it is all the** — **now,** está ahora muy en boga.
goad, _n._ aguijada, aijada, puya, garrocha, _f._; —, _vt._ aguijar; estimular, incitar.
goal, _n._ meta, _f._; fin, _m._; — **line,** raya de la meta; — **post,** poste de la meta.
goalkeeper, _n._ portero (en los juegos de Rugby, hockey, etc.), _m._
goat, _n._ cabra, chiva, _f._; **he** —, cabrón, _m._
goatee, _n._ perilla, _f._
goatherd, _n._ cabrero, _m._
goatskin, _n._ piel de cabra.
gobble, _vt._ engullir, tragar; —, _vi._ gorgorear como los gallipavos.
gobbler, _n._ pavo, _m._; glotón, ona.
go-between, _n._ mediador, ra; entremetido, da.
goblet, _n._ copa, _f._; cáliz, _m._
goblin, _n._ duende, _m._
gocart, _n._ andaderas, _f. pl._, carretilla, _f._; cochecito para niños.
God, _n._; Dios, _m._; **act of G**—, fuerza mayor; **G**— **willing,** Dios mediante.

god, n. dios, m.
godchild, n. ahijado, da.
goddaughter, n. ahijada, f.
goddess, n. diosa, f.
godfather, n. padrino, m.
God-fearing, adj. timorato.
Godfrey, Gofredo, Godofredo.
Godhead, n. deidad, divinidad, f.
godless, adj. infiel, impío, ateo.
godlike, adj. divino.
godliness, n. piedad, devoción, santidad, f.
godly, adj. piadoso, devoto, religioso;
recto, justificado; —, adv. piadosamente,
justamente.
godmother, n. madrina, f.
godsend, n. cosa llovida del cielo.
godson, n. ahijado, m.
Godspeed, n. bienandanza, f.
goes, 3ª persona del singular del verbo **go.**
goggle, vi. volver los ojos, mirar fijamente.
goggle-eyed, adj. de ojos saltones.
goggles, n. pl. gafas, f. pl.
going, n. paso, m., andadura, f.; partida f.;
progreso, m.; — **concern,** empresa flores-
ciente; — **s on,** (coll.) sucesos, acontecimientos, m. pl.
goiter, goitre, n. papera, f., coto, bocio, m.
gold, n. oro, m.; — **brick,** (coll.) embuste,
m., estafa, f., acción de vender algo sin
valor bajo pretexto de que es un "ladrillo
de oro"; — **foil,** pan de oro; — **leaf,**
hoja de oro batido; — **mine,** mina de
oro; fuente abundante de riqueza; —
standard, patrón de oro.
goldbeater, n. batidor de oro, batihoja, m.
Gold Coast, Costa de Oro.
golden, adj. áureo, de oro; excelente; —
mean, moderación, f., justo medio; —
rule, regla áurea; — **wedding,** bodas
de oro.
gold-filled, adj. enchapado de oro.
goldfinch, n. (orn.) cardelina, f., jilguero, m.
goldfish, n. carpa pequeña dorada.
goldsmith, n. orífice, orfebre, m.
goldstone, n. venturina, f.
golf, n. golf, m., juego de pelota escocés;
— **club,** palo o bastón o mazo de golf;
— **knickers,** pantalones de media pierna
para jugar al golf; — **links,** campo de
golf.
golfer, n. jugador o jugadora de golf.
golosh, n. = **galosh.**
gonad, n. (anat.) gónada (glandula sexual), f.
gondola, n. góndola, f.
gondolier, n. gondolero, m.
gone, adj. ido; perdido; pasado; gastado;
muerto.
gonfalon, n. gonfalon, m.
gong, n. campana chinesca.
gonorrhea, n. (med.) gonorrea, f.
good, adj. bueno, buen, benévolo, bondadoso, cariñoso; conveniente, apto; — **cheer,**
jovialidad, f., regocijo, m.; — **day,**
buenos días; — **evening,** buenas tardes,

buenas noches; — **humor,** buen humor;
— **luck,** suerte, f.; — **morning,** buenos
días; — **nature,** temperamento agradable,
buen carácter; **G— Neighbor Policy,**
política de buena vecindad, política del
buen vecino; — **night,** buenas noches; —
sense, sensatez, f.; — **speed,** buena
suerte, fortuna, f.; — **turn,** favor, m.; —
will, buena voluntad, benevolencia, bondad, f.; bienquerencia, f.; (com.) buena
reputación; crédito mercantil; **to say** —
day, dar los buenos días; —, adv. bien;
—, n. bien, m., prosperidad, ventaja,
f.; —, interj. ¡bien! ¡está bien! — **news!**
¡albricias!
good-by, good-bye, n. adiós; —, interj.
¡adiós! ¡hasta luego! ¡hasta después! ¡hasta
la vista! ¡vaya usted con Dios!
good-for-nothing, adj. despreciable, sin
valor; —, n. haragán, ana.
goodhearted, adj. bondadoso, de buen
corazón.
goodish, adj. bastante bueno, regular.
good-looking, adj. bien parecido, guapo.
goodliness, n. belleza, gracia, f.
goodly, adj. considerable, algo numeroso;
agradable.
good-natured, adj. bondadoso; de buen
carácter.
goodness, n. bondad, f.
goods, n. pl. bienes muebles, m. pl.; mercaderías f. pl.; efectos, m. pl.; **household**
—, enseres, m. pl.
good-sized, adj. de buen tamaño.
goon, n. criminal al servicio de organizaciones de facinerosos o de terroristas
para causar daños a la industria o trabajadores.
goose, n. ganso, m.; oca, f.; plancha de
sastre; tonto, ta; — **flesh,** — **pimples,**
(fig.) carne de gallina; — **step,** (mil.)
paso con las piernas tiesas, estilo alemán.
gooseberry, n. uva espina, grosella, f.
gooseneck, n. cuello de cisne.
**G.O.P. Grand Old Party (Republican
Party),** Partido Republicano (E.U.A.).
gopher, n. variedad de mamífero roedor.
gore, n. sangre cuajada; sesga, f.; —, vt. punzar; herir con puñal; herir un animal con
sus cuernos a otro; acornear.
gorge, n. gorja, gola, garganta, f.; barranco, m.; desfiladero, cañón, m.; —,
vt. engullir, tragar.
gorgeous, adj. primoroso, brillante, vistoso;
—ly, adv. con esplendor y magnificencia.
gorget, n. gola, gorguera, f.
gorilla, n. (zool.) gorila, f.
gormandize, vi. glotonear.
gory, adj. cubierto de sangre grumosa;
sangriento.
gosh, interj. ¡cáscaras! ¡caramba!
goshawk, n. azor, m., halcón palumbario.
gosling, n. gansarón, m.
gospel, n. evangelio, m.

gossamer, *n.* telaraña, *f.*; tejido muy fino como gasa.

gossip, *n.* charla, *f.*; caramillo, *m.*; chisme, *m.*; murmuración, comadrería, *f.*; —, *vi.* charlar, murmurar, decir chismes.

got, pretérito y *p. p.* del verbo **get.**

Gothic, *adj.* gótico; — **type,** letra gótica.

gouge, *n.* gubia, gurbia, *f.*; (coll.) ranura o estría hecha con gubia; (coll.) imposición, *f.*; impostor, ra; —, *vt.* escoplear; (coll.) defraudar, engañar.

goulash, *n.* variedad de plato o guiso húngaro.

gourd, *n.* (bot.) calabaza, *f.*; calabacera, *f.*

gourmand, gormand, *n.* goloso, sa, glotón, ona.

gourmet, *n.* gastrónomo, ma.

gout, *n.* (med.) gota, *f.*; podagra, *f.*

gouty, *adj.* gotoso.

Gov. governor, gob.ʳ gobernador.

govern, *vt.* and *vi.* gobernar, dirigir, regir; mandar.

governess, *n.* aya, institutriz, *f.*

government, *n.* gobierno, *m.*; administración pública; — **bonds,** bonos de gobierno; **municipal** —, ayuntamiento, *m.*

governmental, *adj.* gubernativo, gubernamental.

governor, *n.* gobernador, *m.*; gobernante, *m.*; (mech.) regulador, *m.*; —**'s office,** —**'s mansion,** gobernación, *f.*

governorship, *n.* gobernación, *f.*, oficio de gobernador; espacio de tiempo que dura una gobernación.

govt. government, gob.º gobierno.

gown, *n.* toga, *f.*; vestido de mujer; bata, *f.*; túnica, *f.*; hopalandas, *f. pl.*; **large, loose** —, batón, *m.*

Gr.: Greece, Grecia; **Greek,** gr. griego.

gr.: grain, grano; **gram,** g. gramo; **gross,** gruesa.

grab, *vt.* agarrar, arrebatar; —, *n.* arrebato, *m.*; cosa arrebatada; gancho de arrancar.

grabble, *vi.* tentar, palpar; ir a tientas; arrancar.

Grace, *n.* Engracia; (título) Alteza, *f.*

grace, *n.* gracia, *f.*; favor, *m.*; gentileza, *f.*; sal, *f.*; merced, *f.*; perdón, *m.*; **to say** —, bendecir la mesa; —**s,** *n. pl.* gracias, *f. pl.*; **to get into one's good** —**s,** congraciarse con; —, *vt.* adornar; agraciar.

graceful, *adj.* gracioso, primoroso; gentil; —**ly,** *adv.* elegantemente, con gracia.

graceless, *adj.* sin gracia, desagraciado; réprobo, malvado.

gracious, *adj.* gracioso; atractivo; afable, cortés; —**!** *interj.* ¡cáspita!; —**ly,** *adv.* graciosamente; con gentileza.

graciousness, *n.* gracia, *f.*; bondad, afabilidad, *f.*

grackle, *n.* (orn.) variedad de grajo.

grad. graduate, graduado.

gradation, *n.* gradación, *f.*

grade, *n.* grado, *m.*; pendiente, *f.*; nivel,
m.; categoría, *f.*; calidad, *f.*; rasante, *f.*; — **crossing,** paso a nivel; — **school,** escuela primaria; — **separation,** separación de niveles; **maximum** —, rasante máxima; **passing** —, aprobado, *m.*; **ruling** —, rasante predominante; —, *vt.* graduar.

grader, *n.* nivelador, ra, explanadora, *f.*; **elevating** —, niveladora cargadora.

gradient, *n.* (rail.) pendiente, contrapendiente, *f.*; **falling** —, (rail.) declive, *m.*

grading, *n.* nivelación, *f.*

gradual, *adj.* gradual; —**ly,** *adv.* gradualmente.

graduate, *vt.* graduar; **to be** —**d,** diplomarse; —, *n.* diplomado, da, graduado, da; (chem.) probeta, *f.*

graduation, *n.* graduación, *f.*

graduator, *n.* graduador, *m.*

graft, *n.* injerto, *m.*; soborno público; —, *vt.* injertar, ingerir.

grafter, *n.* concusionario, extorsionista, *m.*

grafting, *n.* concusión, extorsión, *f.*

graham bread, *n.* acemita, *f.*

grain, *n.* grano, *m.*; semilla, *f.*; grana, *f.*; disposición, índole, *f.*; cereal, *m.*; **against the** —, a contrapelo; con repugnancia; —**alcohol,** alcohol de granos; —**elevator,** edificio para guardar cereales; —**merchant,** triguero, *m.*; —**s,** orujo, burujo, *m.*; **mixed** —**s,** comuña, *f.*; —, *vt.* granear.

grained, *adj.* granado; áspero; teñido en crudo.

gram, *n.* gramo (peso), *m.*

gram. grammar, gram. gramática.

grammar, *n.* gramática, *f.*; — **school,** escuela de enseñanza primera, escuela primaria o elemental.

grammarian, *n.* gramático, ca.

grammatical, *adj.* gramatical; —**ly,** *adv.* gramaticalmente.

gramophone, *n.* gramófono, *m.*

granary, *n.* granero, *m.*; lóndiga, alhóndiga, *f.*

grand, *adj.* grande, ilustre; magnífico, esplendido; — **larceny,** robo que pasa cierto valor; — **piano,** piano de cola; — **slam,** (bridge) ganancia de todas las bazas posibles.

grandchild, *n.* nieto, ta.

granddaughter, *n.* nieta, *f.*

grandee, *n.* grande (título de nobleza de España), *m.*

grandeur, *n.* grandeza, *f.*; pompa, *f.*

grandfather, *n.* abuelo, *m.*

grandiloquence, *n.* grandilocuencia, *f.*

grandiloquent, *adj.* grandílocuo.

grandiose, *adj.* grandioso.

grandmother, *n.* abuela, *f.*

grandparent, *n.* abuelo, *m.*

grandson, *n.* nieto, *m.*

grandstand, *n.* andanada, tribuna, *f.*

grange, *n.* granja, *f.*, cortijo, *m.*, casa de labranza.

granger, *n.* granjero, ra, labriego, ga.

granite, *n.* granito, *m.*

grant, *vt.* conceder; conferir; dar; otorgar; **—ing that,** supuesto que; **to take for —ed,** presuponer, dar por sentado; **—,** *n.* concesión, *f.*, subvención, *f.*

grantee, *n.* cesionario, ria.

grantor, *n.* otorgante, *m.* y *f.*

granular, *adj.* granular, granoso.

granulate, *vt.* granular.

granulated, *adj.* granulado.

granulation, *n.* granulación, *f.*

granule, *n.* gránulo, *m.*

grape, *n.* uva, *f.*; **bunch of —s,** racimo de uvas; **white —,** albillo, *m.*

grapefruit, *n.* toronja, *f.*

grapeshot, *n.* (mil.) metralla, *f.*

grapevine, *n.* parra, vid, viña, *f.*; **through the —,** por vía secreta (aplícase a rumores, etc.).

graph, *n.* diagrama, *m.*, gráfico, *m.*

graphic, *adj.* gráfico; pintoresco; **— arts,** artes gráficas; **—ally,** *adv.* gráficamente.

graphite, *n.* grafito, *m.*, plombagina, *f.*, lápiz plomo.

graphology, *n.* grafología, *f.*

grapnel, *n.* (naut.) arpeo, *m.*

grapple, *vt. and vi.* agarrar, agarrarse.

grappling iron, *n.* ancla de una caldera de vapor; arpeo de abordaje; cloque, *m.*

grasp, *vt.* empuñar, asir, agarrar; comprender; **—,** *vi.* esforzarse a agarrar; **—,** *n.* puño, puñado, *m.*; poder, *m.*

grasping, *adj.* codicioso.

grass, *n.* hierba, *f.*; herbaje, *m.*; yerba, *f.*, césped, *m.*; **— seed,** semilla de césped; **— widow,** (coll.) mujer cuyo marido está ausente; mujer divorciada.

grasshopper, *n.* cigarrón, saltamontes, *m.*

grassy, *adj.* herboso.

grate, *n.* reja, verja, rejilla, *f.*; **—,** *vt.* rallar; rechinar (los dientes); enrejar; ofender; irritar.

grateful, *adj.* grato, agradecido; **—ly,** *adv.* agradecidamente.

grater, *n.* rallo, raspador, *m.*

gratification, *n.* gratificación, *f.*

gratify, *vt.* contentar; gratificar; satisfacer.

grating, *n.* rejado, *m.*; reja, *f.*; rejilla, *f.*; **—,** *adj.* áspero; ofensivo.

gratis, *adj.* gratuito, gratis; **—,** *adv.* gratis, de balde.

gratitude, *n.* gratitud, *f.*, agradecimiento, *m.*

gratuitous, *adj.* gratuito, voluntario; **—ly,** *adv.* gratuitamente.

gratuity, *n.* gratificación, propina, *f.*; recompensa, *f.*

grave, *n.* sepultura, *f.*; tumba, fosa, *f.*; **—,** *vt.* grabar, esculpir; **—,** *adj.* grave, serio; **—ly,** *adv.* con gravedad, seriamente.

gravedigger, *n.* sepulturero, *m.*

gravel, *n.* cascajo, *m.*; (med.) piedra, *f.*; mal de piedra; **—,** *vt.* cubrir con cascajo; desconcertar.

graven, *adj.* grabado, esculpido.

graver, *n.* grabador, *m.*; buril, *m.*

gravestone, *n.* piedra sepulcral.

graveyard, *n.* cementerio, *m.*

gravitate, *vi.* gravitar.

gravitation, *n.* gravitación, *f.*

gravity, *n.* gravedad, *f.*; seriedad, *f.*; **— feed,** (aer.) alimentación de gravedad.

gravy, *n.* jugo de la carne, salsa, *f.*; caldillo, *m.*; pringue, *m.*; **— dish,** salsera, salserilla, *f.*

gray, *adj.* gris; cano; **—,** *n.* gris, *m.*

graybeard, *n.* barbicano, *m.*

grayhound, *n.* = **greyhound.**

grayish, *adj.* pardusco; entrecano.

grayling, *n.* (pez) tímalo, *m.*

graze, *vt.* pastorear; tocar ligeramente; **to lead (cattle) to —,** pastar; **—,** *vi.* rozar; pacer.

grazier, *n.* ganadero, *m.*

Gr. Brit. Great Britain, G. B. Gran Bretaña.

grease, *n.* grasa, *f.*; saín, *m.*; pringue, *m.*; **— cup,** vaso de untar; **to remove —,** desgrasar; **—,** *vt.* untar, engrasar, lubricar.

greasy, *adj.* grasiento, craso, gordo, mantecoso.

great, *adj.* gran, grande; principal; ilustre; noble, magnánimo; colosal; revelante; **G— Bear,** (ast.) Osa Mayor; **—ly,** *adv.* muy, mucho; grandemente.

Great Britain, Gran Bretaña, *f.*

greatcoat, *n.* gabán, levitón, *m.*

great-grandchild, *n.* biznieto, ta.

great-granddaughter, *n.* biznieta, *f.*

great-grandfather, *n.* bisabuelo, *m.*

great-grandmother, *n.* bisabuela, *f.*

great-grandparent, *n.* bisabuelo, *m.*

great-grandson, *n.* biznieto, *m.*

great-great-granddaughter, *n.* tataranieta, *f.*

great-great-grandfather *n.* tatarabuelo, *m.*

great-great-grandmother, *n.* tatarabuela, *f.*

great-great-grandson, *n.* tataranieto, *m.*

greatness, *n.* grandeza, *f.*; dignidad, *f.*; poder, *m.*; magnanimidad, *f.*

Grecian, *n. and adj.* griego, ga.

Greece, Grecia, *f.*

greed, greediness, *n.* voracidad, *f.*; gula, *f.*; codicia, *f.*

greedily, *adv.* golosamente, vorazmente; ansiosamente.

greedy, *adj.* voraz, goloso; hambriento; ansioso, deseoso; insaciable.

Greek, *n. and adj.* griego, ga.

green, *adj.* verde, fresco, reciente; no maduro; **—,** *n.* verde, *m.*; verdor, *m.*; llanura verde; **—s,** *n. pl.* verduras, legumbres, *f. pl.*

greenback, *n.* papel moneda.

greenery, *n.* invernáculo, invernadero, *m.*; verdor, *m.*

green-eyed, *adj.* ojiverde.

greengage, *n.* ciruela, verde y amarilla.

greengrocer, *n.* verdulero, *m.*

greenhorn, *n.* joven sin experiencia; neófito, ta; novato, ta.

greenhouse, *n.* invernáculo, invernadero, *m.*

greenish, *adj.* verdoso.

Greenland, Groenlandia, *f.*

Greenlander, *n.* and *adj.* groenlandés, esa.

greens, *n. pl.* verduras, hortalizas, *f. pl.*

greensward, *n.* césped, *m.*

greenwood, *n.* bosque verde.

greet, *vt.* saludar, congratular; —, *vi.* encontrarse y saludarse.

greeting, *n.* salutación, *f.*, saludo, *m.*

Greg. Gregory, Greg.º Gregorio.

gregarious, *adj.* gregario.

Gregory, Gregorio.

gremlin, *n.* diablillo que impone impedimentos a los aviadores.

grenade, *n.* (mil.) granada, *f.*

grenadier, *n.* granadero, *m.*

grew, pretérito del verbo **grow.**

grey, *adj.* = **gray.**

greyhound, *n.* galgo, lebrel, *m.*

grid, *n.* parrilla, rejilla, *f.*; (elec.) soporte de plomo de las placas de acumuladores.

griddle, *n.* plancha, tartera, *f.*

griddlecake, *n.* tortilla de harina cocida en una tartera, torta frita.

gridiron, *n.* parrilla, *f.*; campo marcado para el juego de fútbol.

grief, *n.* dolor, *m.*, aflicción, pena, *f.*; quebranto, *m.*; congoja, *f.*; tósigo, *m.*; suplicio, *m.*

grievance, *n.* pesar, *m.*; molestia, *f.*; agravio, *m.*; injusticia, *f.*; perjuicio, *m.*

grieve, *vt.* agraviar, afligir; —, *vi.* afligirse, llorar.

grievous, *adj.* doloroso; enorme; cargoso; —ly, *adv.* penosamente; cruelmente.

griffin, *n.* grifo, *m.*

grill, *vt.* asar en parrillas; —, *n.* parrilla, *f.*

grillroom, *n.* restaurante, *m.*

grim, *adj.* feo; horrendo; ceñudo; austero.

grimace, *n.* visaje, *m.*; mueca, *f.*, mohín, *m.*

grimalkin, *n.* gataza, *f.*; mujer vieja.

grime, *n.* porquería, *f.*; —, *vt.* ensuciar.

grimness, *n.* grima, *f.*, horror, *m.*, austeridad, *f.*

grimy, *adj.* sucio, manchado.

grin, *n.* visaje, *m.*, mueca, *f.*; especie de risa disimulada; —, *vi.* hacer muecas o gestos; reírse disimuladamente.

grind, *vt.* moler; pulverizar; afilar; estregar; mascar; prepararse para un examen; **to — the teeth,** crujir o rechinar los dientes.

grinder, *n.* molinero, ra; molinillo, *m.*; amolador, *m.*; preparador, *m.*; muela, *f.*; piedra molar, piedra de afilar.

grindstone, *n.* piedra amoladera.

grip, *vt.* agarrar, empuñar, asir; —, *n.* maleta, *f.*

gripe, *vt.* asir, empuñar; —, *vi.* padecer cólico; lamentarse; —, *n.* toma, *f.*; presa, *f.*; opresión, *f.*; —s, *n. pl.* cólico, *m.*

grippe, *n.* (med.) gripe, *f.*, influenza, *f.*

gripping, *n.* agarro, *m.*; —, *adj.* emocionante.

grisly, *adj.* espantoso, horroroso.

grist, *n.* molienda, *f.*; provisión, *f.*

gristle, *n.* tendón, nervio, cartílago, *m.*

gristly, *adj.* tendinoso, nervioso.

gristmill, *n.* molino harinero.

grit, *n.* moyuelo, *m.*; —s, *n. pl.* maíz, avena o trigo descascarado y molido; arena, *f.*; cascajo, *m.*; valor, ánimo, *m.*

gritty, *adj.* arenoso.

grizzled, grizzly, *adj.* mezclado con gris, pardusco; **grizzly bear,** oso pardo.

gro. gross, gsa. gruesa.

groan, *vi.* gemir, suspirar; dar gemidos; —, *n.* gemido, suspiro, *m.*; quejido, *m.*

groat, *n.* moneda del valor de cuatro peniques; —s, *n. pl.* avena mondada y medio molida.

grocer, *n.* especiero, abacero, bodeguero, abarrotero, *m.*

grocery, *n.* especiería, abacería, *f.*; bodega, *f.*; — **store,** tienda de comestibles, tienda de abarrotes; —ries, comestibles, *m. pl.*

grog, *n.* especie de bebida alcohólica.

groggy, *adj.* medio borracho.

groin, *n.* ingle, *f.*

groom, *n.* establero, *m.*; criado, *m.*; mozo de caballos; novio, *m.*; —, *vt.* cuidar los caballos.

groomsman, *n.* padrino de boda.

groove, *n.* cavidad profunda; muesca, *f.*; —, *vt.* acanalar.

grooved, *adj.* acanalado, estriado.

grope, *vt.* and *vi.* tentar, buscar a oscuras; andar a tientas.

grosbeak, *n.* (orn.) cardenal, picogordo, *m.*

grosgrain, *n.* gro, *m.*, especie de tejido de seda.

gross, *adj.* grueso, corpulento, espeso; grosero; estúpido; — **amount,** importe bruto o total, producto bruto o total; — **profits,** beneficio bruto; — **weight,** peso bruto; —ly, *adv.* groseramente; en bruto; —, *n.* gruesa, *f.*; todo, *m.*

grotesque, *adj.* grotesco.

grotto, *n.* gruta, *f.*

grouch, *n.* descontento, mal humor, *m.*; persona malhumorada; —, *vi.* gruñir, refunfuñar.

grouchy, *adj.* mal humorado, de mal humor.

ground, *n.* tierra, *f.*, país, *m.*; terreno, suelo, pavimento, *m.*; fundamento, *m.*; razón fundamental, *f.*; campo (de batalla), *m.*; fondo, *m.*; — **breaking,** roturación, *f.*; — **floor,** piso bajo, planta baja; — **hog,** marmota, *f.*; — **rent,** renta de un bien raiz; — **squirrel,** ardilla, *f.*; — **swell,** undulaciones del océano causadas por ventarrón o terremoto; — **wire,** alambre de tierra; —s, heces, *f. pl.*; poso, sedimento, *m.*; —, *vt.* establecer; —, *vi.* varar.

grounder, *n.* (baseball) pelota que rueda por el suelo.

grounding, *n.* (naut.) varadura, *f.*

groundless, *adj.* infundado; **—ly,** *adv.* sin fundamento, sin razón o motivo.

groundplot, *n.* solar, terreno, *m.*; (fig.) fundamento, *m.*

groundwork, *n.* plan, fundamento, *m.*

group, *n.* grupo, *m.*; **—,** *vt.* agrupar.

grouse, *n.* gallina silvestre, *f.*

grout, *n.* harina basta; hez, *f.*; borras, *f. pl.*

grove, *n.* arboleda, *f.*; boscaje, *m.*; umbría, *f.*

grovel, *vi.* serpear; arrastrarse; envilecerse.

grow, *vt.* cultivar; **—,** *vi.* crecer, aumentarse; nacer, brotar; vegetar; adelantar; hacerse, ponerse, volverse; **to — mild,** suavizarse; **to — soft or tender,** relentecer, lentecer; **to — up,** crecer; **to — young again,** rejuvenecer.

grower, *n.* arrendador, *m.*; cultivador, *m.*

growing, *n.* crecimiento, *m.*; cultivo, *m.*; **—,** *adj.* creciente.

growl, *vi.* regañar, gruñir, rezongar; **—,** *n.* gruñido, *m.*

growling, *n.* refunfuño, *m.*

grown, *p.p.* del verbo **grow.**

growth, *n.* vegetación, *f.*; crecimiento, *m.*; producto, *m.*; aumento, *m.*; progreso, adelanto, *m.*; nacencia, *f.*, tumor, *m.*

grub, *n.* gorgojo, *m.*; (coll.) alimento, *m.*; (coll.) persona desaliñada que trabaja muy fuerte; **—,** *vt.* desarraigar; desmontar, rozar; (coll.) comer; trabajar muy fuerte en la tierra.

grubber, *n.* desyerbador, *m.*

grubby, *adj.* gusarapiento; sucio; desaliñado.

grudge, *n.* rencor, odio, *m.*; envidia, *f.*; **to bear a —,** guardar rencor; **—,** *vt. and vi.* envidiar; repugnar; malquerer.

grudgingly, *adv.* con repugnancia, de mala gana.

gruel, *n.* harina de avena mondada.

grueling, *adj.* muy severo, agotador.

gruesome, *adj.* horrible, espantoso.

gruff, *adj.* ceñudo, grosero, brusco; **—ly,** *adv.* ásperamente.

grumble, *vi.* gruñir; murmurar.

grumpy, *adj.* regañón, quejoso, ceñudo.

grunt, *vi.* gruñir; gemir.

guanaco, *n.* guanaco (especie de llama), *m.*

guano, *n.* guano, *m.*, especie de abono.

guarantee, *n.* garante, *m.* y *f.*, fiador, ra; garantía, fianza, *f.*; **—,** *vt.* garantir, garantizar.

guarantor, *n.* garante, *m.* y f., fiador, ra; **to be a —,** salir fiador, salir garante.

guaranty, *n.* garante, *m.*; garantía, *f.*

guard, *n.* guarda, guardia, *f.*, centinela, *m.* y *f.*; rondador, *m.*; vigilante, *m.*; (rail.) conductor, *m.*; (football) guarda o defensor al lado del atajador en la primera línea o línea de embestida de un equipo de fútbol; **— ship,** navío de guardia o de ronda; **to be on —,** estar de centinela, hacer centinela; estar alerta; **under —,** a buen recaudo; **—,** *vt.* guardar; defender; custodiar; **—,** *vi.* guardarse; prevenirse; velar; **to — against,** cautelar.

guarded, *adj.* mesurado, circunspecto.

guardhouse, *n.* (mil.) cuerpo o cuarto de guardia.

guardian, *n.* tutor, *m.*; curador, *m.*; guardián (prelado), *m.*; **— saint,** patrón, *m.*; **—,** *adj.* tutelar.

guardianship, *n.* tutela, *f.*; guardianía, *f.*

guardrail, *n.* barandilla, *f.*

guardroom, *n.* (mil.) cuerpo o cuarto de guardia.

guardsman, *n.* centinela, *m.*, soldado de guardia.

guava, *n.* (bot.) guayaba, *f.*; guayabo, *m.*

guayule, *n.* (bot.) guayule, *m.*

gudgeon, *n.* (pez) gobio, *m.*; bobo, ba.

guerdon, *n.* galardón, *m.*, recompensa, *f.*

guerrilla, *n.* guerrillero, *m.*

guess, *vt. and vi.* conjeturar; adivinar; **—,** *n.* conjetura, *f.*

guesswork, *n.* conjetura, *f.*

guest, *n.* huésped, invitado, da, convidado, da.

guffaw, *n.* carcajada, risotada, *f.*

guidance, *n.* gobierno, *m.*; dirección, *f.*

guide, *vt.* guiar, dirigir; **—,** *n.* guía, *m.* y *f.*; conductor, *m.*

guidebook, *n.* itinerario, *m.*, guía, *f.*

guidepost, *n.* poste indicador, hito, *m.*

guidon, *n.* guión, *m.*, gallardete llevado por la caballería.

guild, *n.* gremio, *m.*; comunidad, corporación, *f.*

guildhall, *n.* casa consistorial, *f.*

guile, *n.* engaño, fraude, *m.*

guileful, *adj.* engañoso, impostor.

guileless, *adj.* cándido, sincero.

guillotine, *n.* guillotina, *f.*; **—,** *vt.* guillotinar.

guilt, *n.* delito, *m.*; culpa, delincuencia, *f.*

guiltless, *adj.* inocente, libre de culpa.

guilty, *adj.* reo, culpable, culpado.

guimpe, *n.* canesú, *m.*

guinea, *n.* guinea (moneda), *f.*; **— hen,** gallina de Guinea; (Mex.) coquena, *f.*; **— pig,** conejillo de Indias.

guise, *n.* modo, *m.*; manera, *f.*; práctica, *f.*

guitar, *n.* guitarra, *f.*; **small —,** requinto, *m.*

gulch, *n.* barranca, quebrada, cañada, *f.*

gulf, *n.* golfo, *m.*; abismo, *m.*, sima, *f.*; tragadero, *m.*

Gulf Stream, *n.* corriente del Golfo de México.

gull, *n.* (orn.) gaviota, *f.*; persona fácil de engañar o defraudar; **—,** *vi.* engañar, defraudar.

gullet, *n.* gaznate, *m.*; gola, *f.*

gullibility, *n.* credulidad, *f.*

gullible, *adj.* crédulo.

gully, *n.* barranca, *f.*; **—,** *vi.* formar canal.

gulp, *n.* trago, *m.*; **—,** *vi.* engullir, tragar.

gum, *n.* goma, *f.*; encía, *f.*; **chewing —,** chicle, *m.*, goma de mascar; **— arabic,** goma arábiga; **— tree,** árbol gomífero; **—,** *vt.* engomar.

gumbo, *n.* (bot.) quimbombó, *m.*; sopa de quimbombó.

gumdrop, *n.* pastilla de goma.

gummy, *adj.* gomoso.

gumption, *n.* (coll.) inteligencia, *f.*; juicio, *m.*; astucia, *f.*; iniciativa, *f.*

gumwood, *n.* madera del árbol de goma.

gun, *n.* arma de fuego; cañón, *m.*; fusil, *m.*; escopeta, *f.*; pistola, *f.*, revólver, *m.*; — **barrel,** cañón de fusil; — **carriage,** cureña de cañón; — **metal,** bronce de cañones; imitación de cobre; aleación parda; bronce, *m.*; — **room,** (naut.) Santabárbara, *f.*, sala de armas; — **turret,** (naut.) torrecilla de ametralladora.

gunboat, *n.* cañonero, ra.

guncotton, *n.* piroxilina, *f.*, algodón pólvora.

gunfire, *n.* cañoneo, *m.*

gunlock, *n.* llave de arma de fuego.

gunner, *n.* artillero, *m.*

gunnery, *n.* artillería, *f.*

gunny, *n.* tejido basto para sacos; — **sack,** saco de yute.

gunpowder, *n.* pólvora, *f.*

gunshot, *n.* tiro de escopeta; alcance de unas armas.

gunsmith, *n.* arcabucero, armero, *m.*

gunstock, *n.* caja de escopeta.

gunwale, *n.* (naut.) borda, *f.*

gurgle, *vi.* gorgotear, burbujear; —, *n.* gorgoteo, *m.*

gush, *vi.* brotar; chorrear; —, *n.* chorro, *m.*; efusión, *f.*

gusher, *n.* pozo surgente (de petróleo).

gushing, *adj.* superabundante; —, *n.* chorro, *m.*; — **of water,** borbotón, *m.*

gusset, *n.* cuadrado, escudete, cuchillo, *m.*

gust, *n.* soplo de aire; ráfaga, *f.*

gustatory, *adj.* gustativo.

Gustavus, Gustavo.

gusto, *n.* gusto, placer, *m.*

gusty, *adj.* tempestuoso.

gut, *n.* intestino, *m.*, cuerda de tripa; glotonería, *f.*; —**s,** *n. pl.* (coll.) valor, *m.*, valentía, fuerza, *f.*; —, *vt.* desventrar, destripar.

gutta-percha, *n.* gutapercha, *f.*

gutter, *n.* gotera, canal, *f.*; zanja, *f.*; cuneta, *f.*; caño, *m.*; arroyo de la calle; **large —,** canalón, *m.*; —, *vt.* and *vi.* acanalar; caer en gotas.

guttural, *adj.* gutural.

guy, *n.* (naut.) retenida, *f.*; tipo, sujeto, *m.*

guzzle, *vt.* and *vi.* beber o comer con glotonería.

gymnasium, *n.* gimnasio, *m.*

gymnast, *n.* gimnasta, *m.* y *f.*

gymnastic, *adj.* gimnástico; —**s,** *n. pl.* gimnástica, gimnasia, *f.*

gymnosperm, *n.* gimnospermia, *f.*

gynecologist, *n.* ginecólogo, ga.

gynecology, *n.* (med.) ginecología, *f.*

gypsum, *n.* yeso, *m.*

gypsy, *n.* and *adj.* gitano, na; bohemio, mia.

gypsylike, *adj.* gitanesco.

gyrate, *vi.* girar.

gyration, *n.* giro, *m.*, movimiento rotatorio.

gyrocompass, *n.* brújula giroscópica.

gyroscope, *n.* giroscopio, *m.*

gyve, *vt.* encadenar.

H

h.: hardness, dureza; **hour,** hora; **hundred,** cien; **height,** alt. altura.

haberdasher, *n.* tendero, camisero, *m.*

haberdashery, *n.* mercería, camisería, *f.*

habiliment, *n.* vestido, *m.*; indumentaria, *f.*

habilitate, *vt.* habilitar.

habit, *n.* hábito, vestido, *m.*; uso, *m.*; costumbre, *f.*; complexión, *f.*; **to be in the — of,** soler, estar acostumbrado a.

habitable, *adj.* habitable.

habitant, *n.* habitante, morador, *m.*

habitat, *n.* habitación, morada, *f.*

habitation, *n.* habitación, *f.*; domicilio, *m.*

habitual, *adj.* habitual; —**ly,** *adv.* habitualmente.

habituate, *vt.* habituar, acostumbrarse, avezar; frecuentar.

habitude, *n.* costumbre, *f.*

habitué, *n.* parroquiano, na; tertuliano, na.

hack, *n.* caballo de alquiler, rocín, cuártago, *m.*; — **saw,** sierra oscilante, sierra para cortar metal; —, *vt.* tajar, cortar; usar (algo) demasiado hasta vulgarizarlo.

hackle, *n.* rastrillo, *m.*; mosca hecha de plumas para pescar; plumas del cuello de las aves domésticas; —, *vt.* rastrillar.

hackman, *n.* cochero de un coche de alquiler.

hackney, *n.* caballo de alquiler; —, *adj.* alquilado; —**ed,** *adj.* trillado, trivial, manoseado.

hacksaw, *n.* sierra oscilante.

had, pretérito y *p.p.* del verbo **have.**

haddock, *n.* (pez) merluza, *f.*

Hades, *n. pl.* los infiernos, *m. pl.*

haft, *n.* mango, *m.*, asa, manigueta, manija, *f.*; —, *vt.* poner mango a alguna cosa.

hag, *n.* bruja, hechicera, *f.*

haggard, *adj.* feroz, huraño; ojeroso, trasnochado.

haggle, *vt.* cortar en tajadas; —, *vi.* regatear.

Hague, Haya, *f.*

hah! *interj.* ¡ah!

ha-ha, *n.* cerca hundida; —, *interj.* ¡ja! ¡ja!

hail, *n.* granizo, *m.*; saludo, *m.*; —, *vt.* saludar; (naut.) venir a la voz; —, *vi.* granizar; —! *interj.* ¡viva! ¡salve! ¡salud!

hailstone, *n.* piedra de granizo.

hailstorm, *n.* granizada, *f.*

hair, *n.* pelo, *m.*; cabello, pelo, *m.*; **bobbed —,** melena, *f.*; — **net,** redecilla, *f.*, redecilla para el cabello, albanega; *f.*; — **ribbon,** cintillo, *m.*; cinta para el cabello; — **sieve,** tamiz de cerda; — **trigger,** pelo de una pistola; **matted —**, (med.) plica, *f.*; **to comb one's —**, peinarse; **to cut the —of**, tonsurar.

hairbreadth, *n.* ancho de una hebra de cabello; casi nada.

hairbrush, *n.* cepillo para el cabello.

haircloth, *n.* tela de crin.

haircutter, *n.* peluquero, ra.

haircutting, *n.* tonsura, *f.*

hair-do, *n.* (coll.) peinado, *m.*

hairdresser, *n.* peluquero, *m.*; peinador, ra; **—'s shop**, peluquería, *f.*

hairdressing, *n.* peinado, *m.*

hairiness, *n.* pelaje, *m.*

hairless, *adj.* calvo, sin pelo.

hairline, *n.* línea de la cabeza donde comienza el cuero cabelludo; sedal de crin.

hairpin, *n.* horquilla, *f.*, gancho para el cabello.

hair-raising, *adj.* espantoso, aterrador.

hairsplitting, *adj.* sutil; quisquilloso; **—**, *n.* quisquilla,*f.*

hairspring, *n.* pelo o muelle (de reloj), *m.*

hairy, *adj.* peludo, velludo, cabelludo.

Haitian, *n.* haitiano, na; **—**, *adj.* haitiano.

hake, *n.* merluza, *f.*

Hal, Enriquito.

halberd, *n.* alabarda, *f.*

halberdier, *n.* alabardero, *m.*

halcyon, *n.* (orn.) alción, *m.*; **—**, *adj.* quieto, tranquilo.

hale, *adj.* sano, vigoroso; ileso.

half, *n.* mitad, *f.*; **—**, *adj.* medio; **— blood**, parentesco que existe entre hermanos de padre o de madre; medio hermano, media hermana; **— brother**, hermanastro, *m.*; **— holiday**, día quebrado; **— pay**, media paga, medio sueldo; **— sister**, hermanastra, *f.*; **— sole**, media suela; **— story**, entresuelo, *m.*; **— tone**, (mus.) semitono, *m.*; fotograbado a media tinta.

half-and-half, *n.* and *adj.* mitad y mitad; **—**, *adv.* en partes iguales.

halfback, *n.* (fútbol) medio, *m.*, jugador detrás de la línea defensiva o de embestida del equipo.

half-baked, *adj.* asado a medias; (coll.) imperfecto, inmaturo.

half-blooded, *adj.* mestizo; encastado (animales); de padre o de madre (hermanos).

half-breed, *n.* and *adj.* mestizo, za.

half-calf, *adj.* (encuadernación) en media pasta; **— binding**, encuadernación en media pasta vitela.

half-caste, *n.* casta cruzada; (coll.) cholo, la; mestizo, za.

half-cocked, *adj.* desmontado (aplícase a una escopeta).

halfhearted, *adj.* indiferente, sin entusiasmo.

half-hour, *n.* media hora.

half-mast, *n.* media asta; **—**, *adj.* a media asta.

half-moon, *n.* semilunio, *m.*

halfpenny, *n.* medio penique.

half-tone, *n.* fotograbado a media tinta; **—**, *adj.* a media tinta.

halfway, *adv.* a medio camino; **—**, *adj.* medio.

half-witted, *adj.* imbécil.

halibut, *n.* (pez) hipogloso, *m.*

halitosis, *n.* halitosis,*f.*, aliento de mal olor.

hall, *n.* vestíbulo, *m.*, sala, *f.*; salón, colegio, *m.*; sala, *f.*; cámara, *f.*; **recreation —**, salón de recreo.

halliard, *n.* = **halyard.**

hallmark, *n.* marca de pureza, marca de buena calidad.

halloo, *interj.* ¡hola! ¡ea! **—**, *vi.* azuzar (a los perros en la caza); **—**, *vt.* llamar a uno gritando.

hallow, *vt.* consagrar, santificar.

Hallowe'en, *n.* víspera de Todos los Santos.

hallucination, *n.* alucinación, *f.*

hallway, *n.* vestíbulo, atrio, *m.*

halo, *n.* halo, nimbo, *m.*, corona, *f.*

halogen, *n.* halógeno, *m.*

halt, *vi.* cojear; parar, hacer alto; dudar; **—**, *n.* cojera, *f.*; parada, *f.*; alto, *m.*; **—!** *interj.*¡alto!

halter, *n.* soga, *f.*; cuerda, *f.*; cabestro, ronzal, ramal, *m.*; corpiño que se sostiene con cintas al rededor del cuello y espalda, que dejan a la vista brazos y espalda; **to lead by a —**, cabestrar.

halve, *vt.* partir en dos mitades; **by —s**, a medias.

halves, *n. pl.* de **half**, mitades, *f. pl.*

halyard, *n.* (naut.) driza, *f.*

ham, *n.* corva, *f.*; jamón, *m.*

hamburger, *n.* carne picada de res; emparedado de carne molida.

hamlet, *n.* villorrio, *m.*, aldea, *f.*

hammer, *n.* martillo, *m.*; **— of a gun**, serpentín (de fusil); **—**, *vt.* martillar; forjar; **—**, *vi.* trabajar; reiterar esfuerzos.

hammock, *n.* hamaca, *f.*

hamper, *n.* cuévano, *m.*; cesto grande (para ropa, etc.); **—**, *vt.* restringir; estorbar, impedir; entrampar.

hamstring, *n.* tendón de la corva; **—**, *vt.* desjarretar.

hand, *n.* mano, *f.*; palmo (medida), *m.*; carácter de escritura; (coll.) salva de aplausos; poder, *m.*; habilidad, destreza, *f.*; (naut.) marinero, *m.*; obrero, *m.*; mano o manecilla (de un reloj), *f.*; **at —**, a la mano, al lado; **— baggage**, equipaje o bulto de mano; **— bell**, campanilla, *f.*; **— grenade**, granada de mano; **— lever**, manija, *f.*; **— organ**, *n.* organillo, *m.*; **— to —**, cuerpo a cuerpo; **in the —s of**, en poder de; **on the other —**, en cambio, por otra parte; **with bare —s**, a brazo partido; **with one's own —**, de propia mano; **to clap —s**, batir palmas, aplaudir; **—**, *vt.* alargar; guiar por la mano; echar la mano; **to — down**, transmitir, bajar.

handbag, *n.* bolsa, *f.*, saquillo de mano, maletilla, *f.*
handball, *n.* pelota, *f.*; juego de pelota.
handbarrow, *n.* angarillas, *f. pl.*
handbill, *n.* cartel, *m.*
handbook, *n.* manual, prontuario, *m.*
handbreadth, *n.* palmo menor.
handcart, *n.* carretilla de mano.
handcuff, *n.* manilla, *f.*, esposas, *f. pl.*
handed, *adj.* trasmitido, pasado de uno a otro.
handful, *n.* manojo, puñado, *m.*
handicap, *n.* carrera ciega con caballos de peso igualado; obstáculo, *m.*; ventaja, *f.*
handicraft, *n.* arte mecánica; destreza manual; mano de obra.
handicraftsman, *n.* artesano, *m.*
handily, *adv.* con destreza, con habilidad.
handiwork, *n.* obra manual.
handkerchief, *n.* pañuelo, *m.*
handle, *n.* mango, puño, tomadero, *m.*, asa, manija, manigueta, *f.*; palanca, *f.*; — **bar,** manubrio, *m.*; —, *vt.* manejar; tratar.
handling, *n.* manejo, *m.*; toque, *m.*
handmade, *adj.* hecho a mano.
handout, *n.* (coll.) alimento ó ropa que se regala a un limosnero.
hand-picked, *adj.* escogido, selecto, favorecido.
handrail, *n.* barandilla, *f.*, pasamano, *m.*
handsaw, *n.* serrucho, *m.*
handsel, *n.* estreno, *m.*; aguinaldo, *m.*; —, *vt.* estrenar alguna cosa.
handset, *n.* transmisor y receptor telefónico.
handshake, *n.* apretón de manos.
handsome, *adj.* hermoso, bello, gentil, guapo; —**ly,** *adv.* hermosamente, primorosamente.
handspike, *n.* palanca, *f.*
handspring, *n.* voltereta, *f.*
hand-to-mouth, *adj.* impróvido, escaso.
handwork, *n.* obra hecha a mano, trabajo a mano.
handwriting, *n.* escritura, *f.*; caligrafía, *f.*; letra, *f.*
handy, *adj.* manual; diestro, mañoso; — **man,** factótum, *m.*
hang, *vt.* colgar, suspender; ahorcar; entapizar; guindar; —, *vi.* colgar; ser ahorcado; pegarse; quedarse suspenso; depender.
hangar, *n.* (aer.) hangar, *m.*; cobertizo, *m.*
hangdog, *adj.* avergonzado, corrido, degradante; —, *n.* persona vil y despreciable.
hanger, *n.* alfanje, *m.*; espada ancha; colgador, *m.*; **clothes** —, colgador de ropas.
hanger-on, *n.* gorrista, *m.* y *f.*, gorrón, ona, parásito, *m.*
hanging, *adj.* pendiente.
hangings, *n. pl.* tapicería, *f.*; cortinaje, *m.*
hangman, *n.* verdugo, *m.*
hangnail, *n.* respigón, uñero, padrastro, *m.*
hank, *n.* madeja de hilo.

hanker, *vi.* ansiar, apetecer.
hankering, *n.* anhelo, *m.*
Hannah, Ana.
hansom, *n.* cabriolé, *m.*
hap, *n.* acaso, *m.*, casualidad, *f.*
haphazard, *n.* accidente, lance, *m.*; —, *adj.* casual, descuidado.
hapless, *adj.* desgraciado, desventurado.
haply, *adv.* por casualidad.
happen, *vi.* acontecer, acaecer, suceder, sobrevenir, caer.
happening, *n.* suceso, acontecimiento, *m.*
happily, *adv.* felizmente.
happiness, *n.* felicidad, dicha, *f.*
happy, *adj.* feliz, bienaventurado; jubiloso.
happy-go-lucky, *adj.* calmado, sereno, filosófico, sin preocupaciones.
harangue, *n.* arenga, *f.*; —, *vi.* arengar.
harass, *vt.* cansar, fatigar, sofocar, acosar.
harassment, *n.* persecución, *f.*, acción de acosar o importunar.
harbinger, *n.* precursor, ra.
harbor, *n.* albergue, *m.*; puerto, *m.*; bahía, *f.*; asilo, *m.*; — **master,** capitán del puerto; —, *vt.* albergar; hospedar; —, *vi.* tomar albergue.
hard, *adj.* duro, firme; difícil; penoso; cruel, severo, rígido; — **and fast,** rígido; sin excepción; — **cash,** numerario efectivo; — **cider,** sidra fermentada; — **coal,** antracita, *f.*; — **of hearing,** medio sordo, duro de oído; — **sledding,** apuros, *m. pl.*, dificultades, *f. pl.*; —, *adv.* cerca, a la mano, difícilmente; — **by,** muy cerca.
hard-bitten, *adj.* mordaz; terco, tenaz.
hard-earned, *adj.* ganado con mucho trabajo.
harden, *vt.* and *vi.* endurecer, endurecerse.
hardening, *n.* endurecimiento, *m.*
hard-featured, *adj.* de facciones bastas.
hard-handed, *adj.* tacaño; tiránico.
hardheaded, *adj.* testarudo; sagaz, astuto; **to be** —, ser duro de mollera.
hardhearted, *adj.* duro de corazón, insensible.
hardihood, *n.* atrevimiento, valor, *m.*
hardiness, *n.* fatiga, *f.*; intrepidez, *f.*; atrevimiento, *m.*; valor, *f.*; robustez, *f.*
hardly, *adv.* apenas; severamente.
hardness, *n.* dureza, *f.*; dificultad, *f.*; inhumanidad, *f.*; severidad, *f.*
hardpan, *n.* suelo duro subyacente.
hard-pressed, *adj.* apurado.
hardship, *n.* injuria, opresión, *f.*; injusticia, *f.*; penalidad, *f.*; trabajo, *m.*; molestia, fatiga, *f.*
hardtack, *n.* especie de galleta dura.
hardware, *n.* ferretería, quincallería, *f.*; — **store,** quincallería, *f.*
hardwood, *n.* madera dura.
hard-working, *adj.* trabajador.
hardy, *adj.* atrevido, bravo, intrépido; fuerte, robusto, vigoroso.
hare, *n.* liebre, *f.*
harebell, *n.* (bot.) campanilla, *f.*

harebrained, *adj.* aturdido, atolondrado.
hare-lipped, *adj.* labihendido.
harem, *n.* serrallo, harén, *m.*
hark, *vi.* escuchar; —! *interj.* ¡oye! ¡mira!
harlequin, *n.* arlequín, bufón, *m.*
harlot, *n.* puta, meretriz, prostituta, *f.*
harm, *n.* mal, daño, *m.*; desgracia, *f.*; perjuicio, *m.*; —, *vt.* dañar, injuriar, ofender.
harmful, *adj.* dañoso, dañino; perjudicial; — **doctrine,** ponzoña, *f.*, doctrina perjudicial; —**ly,** *adv.* dañosamente.
harmless, *adj.* inocente, inofensivo; —**ly,** *adv.* inocentemente; sin daño.
harmonic, *adj.* armónico; —**s,** *n. pl.* armonía, *f.*
harmonica, *n.* armónica, *f.*
harmonical, *adj.* = **harmonic.**
harmonious, *adj.* armonioso; —**ly,** *adv.* armoniosamente.
harmonize, *vt.* armonizar, concertar, ajustar; concretar; —, *vi.* convenir, corresponder.
harmony, *n.* armonía, *f.*
harness, *n.* arreos de un caballo; —, *vt.* enjaezar.
Harold, Haroldo.
harp, *n.* arpa, *f.*; —, *vt. and vi.* tocar el arpa; **to — upon,** macear, machacar, porfiar.
harpist, *n.* arpista, *m.* y *f.*
harpoon, *n.* arpón, *m.*
harpsichord, *n.* clavicordio, clave, *m.*
harpy, *n.* arpía, *f.*
harridan, *n.* prostituta depravada; mujer perversa.
harrier, *n.* galgo, *m.*
Harriet, Enriqueta.
harrow, *n.* grada, *f.*; rastro, *m.*; —, *vt.* gradar.
harrowing, *adj.* conmovedor; horripilante.
harry, *vt.* atormentar, acosar, molestar.
harsh, *adj.* áspero, agrio, rígido, duro, austero; —**ly,** *adv.* ásperamente, severamente.
harshness, *n.* aspereza, dureza, rudeza, austeridad, severidad, *f.*
hart, *n.* ciervo, *m.*
harum-scarum, *adj.* atolondrado, descuidado; irresponsable; —, *n.* persona atolondrada o irresponsable.
harvest, *n.* cosecha, *f.*; agosto, *m.*; —, *vt.* recoger las mieses.
harvester, *n.* agostero, *m.*, segador, ra; (máquina) segadora, *f.*
has, 3ª persona del singular del verbo **have.**
hasenpfeffer, *n.* guisado muy condimentado de carne de conejo encurtido.
hash, *n.* jigote, picadillo, *m.*; —, *vt.* picar (carne, etc.).
hasp, *n.* aldaba de candado; broche, *m.*; —, *vt.* abrochar; cerrar con aldaba.
hassock, *n.* cojín para los pies.
haste, *n.* prisa, *f.*; presteza, *f.*; **to be in —,** estar de prisa.

hasten, *vt.* acelerar, apresurar; **to — one's steps,** apretar el paso; —, *vi.* estar de prisa, apresurarse.
hastily, *adv.* precipitadamente, airadamente.
hasty, *adj.* pronto, apresurado; colérico.
hat, *n.* sombrero, *m.*; —**s off!** ¡quítense el sombrero! **straw —,** sombrero de paja; **top —,** sombrero de copa alta.
hatband, *n.* cintillo de sombrero.
hatch, *vt.* criar pollos; empollar; tramar; —, *n.* pollada, nidada, *f.*; media puerta; (naut.) cuartel, *m.*; compuerta de esclusa; trampa, *f.*
hatchet, *n.* destral, *m.*, hacha pequeña.
hatching, *n.* incubación, cloquera, *f.*
hatchway, *n.* (naut.) escotilla, *f.*
hate, *n.* odio, aborrecimiento, *m.*; —, *vt.* odiar, detestar.
hateful, *adj.* odioso, detestable; —**ly,** *adv.* detestablemente, con tirria.
hatpin, *n.* aguja o alfiler de sombrero.
hatrack, *n.* cuelgasombreros, *m.*
hatred, *n.* odio, aborrecimiento, *m.*
hatter, *n.* sombrerero, ra.
haughtily, *adv.* fieramente, orgullosamente.
haughtiness, *n.* orgullo, *m.*, altivez, *f.*
haughty, *adj.* altanero, altivo, orgulloso; ceñudo.
haul, *vt.* tirar, halar; —, *n.* estirón, tirón, *m.*
haulage, *n.* acarreo, trasporte, *m.*, tracción, *f.*
haunch, *n.* anca, *f.*
haunt, *vt.* frecuentar, rondar; —, *n.* guarida, *f.*; lugar frecuentado.
haunted, *adj.* encantado, frecuentado por espantos.
have, *vt.* haber, tener; poseer; **to — a relapse,** recaer.
haven, *n.* puerto, *m.*; abrigo, asilo, *m.*
haversack, *n.* mochila, *f.*
havoc, *n.* estrago, *m.*; ruina, *f.*
haw, *n.* (bot.) acerola, *f.*; balbucencia, *f.*; —! *interj.* ¡a la izquierda! —, *vt. and vi.* volver o hacer volver a un lado; —, *vi.* tartamudear.
Hawaii, Hawaí, *f.*
Hawaiian Islands, Islas Hawaianas, *f. pl.*
hawk, *n.* (orn.) halcón, milano, gavilán, *m.*; —, *vi.* cazar con halcón; llevar y vender mercaderías por las calles.
hawker, *n.* vendedor ambulante, buhonero, chalán, *m.*
hawk-eyed, *adj.* lince, agudo.
hawser, *m.* (naut.) guindaleza, amarra, *f.*
hawthorn, *n.* (bot.) espino blanco, acerolo, *m.*
hay, *n.* heno, *m.*; — **fever,** romadizo, *m.*, especie de catarro.
haycock, *n.* almiar, *m.*, pila de heno.
hayfield, *n.* henar, *m.*
hayfork, *n.* horca, laya (para el heno), *f.*
hayloft, *n.* henil, *m.*
haymaker, *n.* guadañil, *m.*; máquina de henear; golpe al aire en pugilato.

haymow, *n.* bálago, *m.*

hayrick, *n.* niara, *f.*

haystack, *n.* niara, *f.*

haywire, *adj.* (coll.) torcido, revesado; loco.

hazard, *n.* acaso, accidente, *m.*; riesgo, *m.*; juego de azar a los dados; —, *vt.* arriesgar; aventurar.

hazardous, *adj.* arriesgado, peligroso; —ly, *adv.* peligrosamente.

haze, *n.* niebla, bruma, *f.*; aturdimiento, *m.*

hazel, *n.* avellano, *m.*; —, *adj.* castaño.

hazelnut, *n.* avellana, *f.*

hazy, *adj.* anieblado, oscuro; aturdido.

H. C. F., h. c. f. highest common factor, máximo factor común.

hd. head, cabeza, jefe.

hdkf. handkerchief, pañuelo.

hdqrs. headquarters, cuartel general; oficinas generales.

he, *pron.* él.

head, *n.* cabeza, *f.*; jefe, *m.*; juicio, *m.*; talento, *m.*; título (de un libro), *m.*; puño (de bastón), *m.*; fuente, *f.*; nacimiento (de un río), *m.*; **bald** —, calva, *f.*; **from** — **to foot,** de arriba abajo; — **of a bed,** cabecera, *f.*; — **of hair,** cabellera, *f.*; —s **or tails,** cara o cruz, cara o sello; — **wind,** viento de frente, viento en contra, viento que sopla en dirección opuesta a la marcha de la embarcación; **top of the** —, testa, *f.*; —, *vt.* gobernar, dirigir, degollar; podar los árboles; — **off,** alcanzar, prevenir.

headache, *n.* dolor de cabeza; (med.) hemicránea, jaqueca, *f.*

headcheese, *n.* queso de cerdo.

headdress, *n.* cofia, *f.*; tocado, *m.*

header, *n.* descabezador de las mieses; salto de cabeza.

headfirst, *adv.* de cabeza.

headgear, *n.* tocado, *m.*

head-hunter, *n.* cazador de cabezas.

headiness, *n.* precipitación, obstinación, *f.*

heading, *n.* título, membrete, *m.*

headland, *n.* promontorio, cabo, *m.*

headless, *adj.* descabezado; estúpido.

headlight, *n.* linterna delantera, farol delantero.

headline, *n.* encabezamiento, título (de un periódico, página, artículo, etc.), *m.*

headlong, *adj.* temerario, precipitoso, inconsiderado; —, *adv.* temerariamente; precipitadamente.

headmaster, *n.* el director de una escuela.

headmost, *adj.* primero, más adelantado.

head-on, *adj.* de cabeza.

headphone, *n.* teléfono para la cabeza.

headpiece, *n.* casco, yelmo, *m.*; cabeza, *f.*, intelecto, *m.*; entendimiento, *m.*; (print.) viñeta, *f.*; auricular telefónico con soporte para la cabeza.

headquarters, *n.* (mil.) cuartel general; jefatura, administración, *f.*; **police** —, jefatura de policía.

headship, *n.* primado, *m.*; autoridad, *f.*

headsman, *n.* verdugo, *m.*

headstall, *n.* cabezada del freno, testera, *f.*

headstock, *n.* cabezal, *m.*

headstone, *n.* lápida, *f.*

headstrong, *adj.* testarudo, cabezudo, obstinado; **to be** —, ser duro de mollera.

headwaiter, *n.* primer mozo, jefe de los mozos de un restaurante.

headwaters, *n.* fuente, cabecera, *f.*

headway, *n.* (naut.) salida, marcha, *f.*; avance, progreso, *m.*; intervalo entre dos trenes en una misma ruta.

headwork, *n.* trabajo mental.

heady, *adj.* temerario; obstinado; violento

heal, *vt. and vi.* curar, sanar, cicatrizar; — *vi.* recobrar la salud.

healer, *n.* curador, ra.

health, *n.* salud, sanidad, *f.*; **bill of** —, patente de sanidad; — **officer,** oficial de sanidad o de cuarentena, sanitario, *m.*; — **resort,** centro de salud; **to be in good** —, estar bien de salud; **to be in poor** —, estar mal de salud.

healthful, *adj.* saludable.

healthy, *adj.* sano; salubre, saludable, lozano.

heap, *n.* montón, *m.*; mojón, *m.*; rima, *f.*, rimero, *m.*; **ash** —, cenicero, *m.*; —, *vt.* amontonar, acumular.

hear, *vt.* oír; entender; acceder; —, *vi.* oír; escuchar.

hearer, *n.* oyente, *m.* y *f.*, oidor, ra.

hearing, *n.* oído, *m.*, oreja, *f.*; audiencia, *f.*

hearken, *vi.* escuchar, atender.

hearsay, *n.* rumor, *m.*, fama, *f.*; voz pública, *f.*; **by** —, de oídas, por oídas.

hearse, *n.* carroza fúnebre.

heart, *n.* corazón, *m.*; alma, *f.*; interior, centro, *m.*; ánimo, valor, *m.*; amor, *m.*; **after one's** —, según los más íntimos deseos de uno; **by** —, de memoria; — **trouble,** enfermedad del corazón; **to one's** —'s **content,** a pedir de boca; **with all my** —, con toda mi alma.

heartache, *n.* angustia, congoja, *f.*

heartbeat, *n.* latido del corazón.

heartbreaking, *adj.* congojoso; conmovedor.

heartbroken, *adj.* transido de dolor.

heartburn, *n.* acedía, *f.*

heartfelt, *adj.* expresivo, muy sentido, muy sincero.

heart-free, *adj.* libre de afectos.

hearth, *n.* hogar, fogón, *m.*, chimenea *f.*, hogar doméstico.

hearthstone, *n.* hogar, *m.*, casa, *f.*

heartily, *adv.* sinceramente, cordialmente.

heartiness, *n.* cordialidad, *f.*

heartless, *adj.* inhumano, cruel; pusilánime; —ly, *adv.* tímidamente; inhumanamente.

heart-rending, *adj.* agudo, penetrante, desgarrador.

heartsease, *n.* (bot.) pensamiento, *m.*, trinitaria, *f.*

heartsick, *adj.* dolorido, afligido.
heart-stricken, *adj.* angustiado, afligido.
heartstrings, *n. pl.* fibras del corazón.
heart-to-heart, *adj.* sincero, abierto; confidencial.
heartwood, *n.* duramen, *m.*; madera de corazón.
hearty, *adj.* sincero; sano; vigoroso; campechano.
heat, *n.* calor, *m.*; ardor, *m.*; vehemencia, *f.*; animosidad, *f.*; — **lightning,** relámpago sin trueno; — **wave,** ola de calor; **in** —, cachondo (aplícase a los animales); **prickly** —, salpullido, *m.*; —, *vt.* calentar, encender.
heater, *n.* escalfador, *m.*; calentador, *m.*, estufa, *f.*; calorífero, *m.*; **water** —, calentador de agua.
heath, *n.* (bot.) brezo, *m.*; brezal, matorral, *m.*
heathen, *n.* gentil, *m.* y *f.*, pagano, na.
heathenish, *adj.* gentílico, pagano; salvaje; —**ly,** *adv.* a manera de los paganos.
heather, *n.* (bot.) brezo, *m.*
heating, *n.* calefacción, *f.*; **central** —, calefacción central; — **apparatus,** calentador, *m.*
heatstroke, *n.* insolación, *f.*
heave, *vt.* alzar; elevar; hincharse; (naut.) virar para proa; —, *vi.* palpitar; respirar trabajosamente; —, *n.* esfuerzo para levantarse; suspiro de congoja.
heaven, *n.* cielo, *m.*; firmamento, *m.*; —**s!** *interj.* ¡caramba!
heavenly, *adj.* celeste, divino; —, *adv.* divinamente.
heaves, *n.* huérfago, *m.*, asma que ataca a los caballos.
heavily, *adv.* pesadamente.
heaviness, *n.* pesadez, *f.*; peso, *m.*; (fig.) carga, *f.*; aflicción, *f.*; opresión, *f.*
heavy, *adj.* grave, pesado; opresivo, penoso, molesto; triste; tardo, soñoliento; oneroso; **to be** —, pesar.
heavy-hearted, *adj.* triste, abatido.
heavy-laden, *adj.* agobiado, recargado.
heavyweight, *n.* boxeador de peso mayor; persona de peso mayor.
Hebrew, *n.* hebreo, ea, judío, ía.
hecatomb, *n.* hecatombe, *f.*
heckle, *vt.* importunar con preguntas.
hectic, *adj.* hético; inquieto, agitado.
hectogram, *n.* hectogramo, *m.*
hectograph, *n.* hectógrafo, *m.*
hectoliter, *n.* hectolitro, *m.*
hectometer, *n.* hectómetro, *m.*
hector, *n.* matasiete, fanfarrón, *m.*; —, *vi.* baladronear, bravear.
hedge, *n.* seto, *m.*; barrera, *f.*; —, *vt.* cercar con un seto.
hedgehog, *n.* erizo, *m.*
hedgerow, *n.* serie de árboles en los cercados.
hedonism, *n.* hedonismo, *m.*
heed, *vt.* atender, observar; —, *n.* cuidado,

m.; atención, precaución, *f.*; **to give** —, reparar, atender.
heedful, *adj.* vigilante, atento; circunspecto; —**ly,** *adv.* cautelosamente.
heedless, *adj.* descuidado, negligente, impróvido; —**ly,** *adv.* negligentemente.
heel, *n.* talón, carcañal, calcañar, *m.*; (coll.) bribón, bellaco, *m.*, pérfido villano; — **bone,** carcañal, calcañar, carcaño, *m.*; **rubber** —, tacón de goma o de caucho; **to take to one's** —**s,** apretar los talones, huir; —, *vt.* taconear.
hegemony, *n.* hegemonía, *f.*
hegira, *n.* égira, *f.*, era de los mahometanos.
heifer, *n.* becerra, vaquilla, ternera, *f.*
height, *n.* altura, elevación, sumidad, *f.*; sublimidad, *f.*
heighten, *vt.* realzar; adelantar, mejorar; exaltar.
heinous, *adj.* atroz, odioso; —**ly,** *adv.* atrozmente, horriblemente.
heir, *n.* heredero, *m.*; — **apparent,** heredero forzoso, presunto heredero.
heirdom, *n.* herencia, heredad, *f.*
heiress, *n.* heredera, *f.*
heirloom, *n.* mueble heredado; reliquia de familia.
heirship, *n.* herencia, *f.*, estado, carácter o privilegio de heredero.
Helen, Helena, Elena.
helical, *adj.* helicoidal, espiral.
helicopter, *n.* helicóptero, *m.*
heliocentric, *adj.* heliocéntrico.
heliochrome, *n.* heliocromía, *f.*
heliograph, *n.* heliografía, *f.*, helióstato, heliógrafo, *m.*
helioscope, *n.* helioscopio, *m.*
heliotherapy, *n.* helioterapia, *f.*
heliotrope, *n.* (bot.) heliotropo, *m.*
heliotropism, *n.* heliotropismo, *m.*
heliotype, *n.* heliotipo, *m.*, fotocolografía, *f.*
helium, *n.* (chem.) helio, *m.*
helix, *n.* hélice, *f.*
hell, *n.* infierno, tártaro, *m.*
hellcat, *n.* bruja, *f.*; persona vil.
hellebore, *n.* (bot.) eléboro, *m.*
Hellenism, *n.* helenismo, *m.*
Hellenist, *n.* helenista, *m.* y *f.*
hellish, *adj.* infernal, malvado; —**ly,** *adv.* diabólicamente.
hello, *interj.* ¡qué hay! ¡qué hubo! (expresión de saludo).
helm, *n.* (naut.) timón, gobernalle, gobierno, *m.*
helmet, *n.* yelmo, casco, *m.*; **diver's** —, casco de buzo.
helmsman, *n.* timonero, *m.*
help, *vt. and vi.* ayudar, asistir, socorrer; aliviar, remediar, reparar; evitar; **to** — **oneself to,** servirse (algún alimento); **I cannot** — **it,** no puedo remediarlo; no puedo dejar de hacerlo; —, *n.* ayuda, *f.*; socorro, remedio, *m.*
helper, *n.* auxiliador, ra, socorredor, ra.
helpful, *adj.* útil, provechoso; saludable.

helpless, *adj.* abandonado; irremediable; **—ly,** *adv.* irremediablemente, sin recurso.

helpmate, *n.* compañero, ra; ayudante, *m.* y *f.*; esposa, *f.*

helpmeet, *n.* = **helpmate.**

helter-skelter, *adv.* (coll.) a trochemoche, en desorden.

helve, *n.* mango, *m.*; astil de hacha; **—,** *vt.* poner mango (a alguna cosa).

hem, *n.* ribete, *m.*; bastilla, *f.*; **—!** *interj.* ¡ejem! **—,** *vt.* bastillar; repulgar; ribetear; **—,** *vi.* vacilar; fingir tos; **— in,** circundar, rodear, ceñir; **to — and haw,** (coll.) tartamudear, vacilar, demostrar indecisión.

hematite, *n.* hematites, *f.*

hemisphere, *n.* hemisferio, *m.*

hemispherical, *adj.* hemisférico.

hemlock, *n.* (bot.) abeto, *m.*; (bot.) cicuta, *f.*

hemoglobin, *n.* (med.) hemoglobina, *f.*

hemophilia, *n.* (med.) hemofilia, *f.*

hemoptysis, *n.* (med.) hemoptisis, *f.*, hemorragia de sangre por la boca.

hemorrhage, *n.* hemorragia, *f.*

hemorrhoids, *n.* *pl.* hemorroides, almorranas, *f.* *pl.*

hemostasis, *n.* (med.) hemóstasis, *f.*, detención de una hemorragia.

hemp, *n.* cáñamo, *m.*

hempen, *adj.* cañameño.

hemstitch, *n.* (costura) vainica, *f.*; **—,** *vt.* (costura) hacer una vainica.

hen, *n.* gallina, *f.*

henbane, *n.* beleño.

hence, *adv.* de aquí; por esto.

henceforth, *adv.* de aquí en adelante; en lo sucesivo.

henceforward, *adv.* = **henceforth.**

henchman, *n.* secuaz servil.

hencoop, *n.* gallinero, *m.*

henhouse, *n.* gallinero, *m.*

henna, *n.* (bot.) alheña, *f.*

hennery, *n.* gallinero, *m.*

henpeck, *vt.* encocorar una mujer a su marido tratando de mandarlo.

Henry, Enrique.

hepatica, *n.* (bot.) hepática, *f.*

heptagon, *n.* heptágono, *m.*

her, *pron.* su, ella, de ella, a ella.

herald, *n.* heraldo, *m.*

heraldry, *n.* heráldica, *f.*

herb, *n.* yerba, hierba, *f.*; **—s,** *pl.* hierbas medicinales.

herbaceous, *adj.* herbáceo.

herbage, *n.* herbaje, *m.*, hierba, *f.*

herbal, *adj.* herbario.

herbalist, *n.* herbolario, *m.*

herbarium, *n.* herbario seco.

Herbert, Heberto.

herbivorous, *adj.* herbívoro.

herculean, *adj.* hercúleo.

herd, *n.* hato, rebaño, *m.*; manada, *f.*; grey, *f.*; **—,** *vi.* ir en hatos; asociarse; **—,** *vt.* guiar (el ganado) en rebaño.

herdsman, *n.* pastor, *m.*, guarda de ganado.

here, *adv.* aquí, acá.

hereabout, hereabouts, *adv.* aquí, al rededor.

hereafter, *adv.* en el tiempo venidero, en lo futuro; **—,** *n.* estado venidero, el futuro.

hereat, *adv.* en esto, por esto.

hereby, *adv.* por esto.

hereditary, *adj.* hereditario.

heredity, *n.* derecho de sucesión.

herefrom, *adv.* de aquí.

herein, *adv.* en esto, aquí dentro.

hereinafter, *adv.* después, más adelante.

hereof, *adv.* de esto, de aquí.

hereon, *adv.* sobre esto.

heresy, *n.* herejía, *f.*

heretic, *n.* hereje, *m.* y *f.*; **—,** *adj.* herético.

heretical, *adj.* herético.

hereto, *adv.* a esto, para esto.

heretofore, *adv.* antes, en tiempos pasados; hasta ahora.

hereunto, *adv.* a esto; hasta ahora.

hereupon, *adv.* sobre esto.

herewith, *adv.* con esto.

heritable, *adj.* que puede heredarse.

heritage, *n.* herencia, *f.*

heritance, *n.* herencia, *f.*

hermaphrodite, *n.* hermafrodito, ta.

hermetic, *adj.* hermético; **—ally,** *adv.* herméticamente.

hermit, *n.* ermitaño, eremita, *m.*; **— crab,** ermitaño, *m.*

hermitage, *n.* ermita, *f.*

hernia, *n.* hernia, rotura, ruptura, *f.*

hero, *n.* héroe, *m.*

heroic, *adj.* heroico; **—s,** *n.* *pl.* expresión o acto extravagantes; **—ally,** *adv.* heroicamente.

heroical, *adj.* = **heroic.**

heroin, *n.* (med.) heroína, *f.*

heroine, *n.* heroína, *f.*

heroism, *n.* heroísmo, *m.*

heron, *n.* garza, *f.*

herring, *n.* arenque, *m.*

herringbone, *n.* punto espigado, punto de ojal.

hers, *pron.* suyo, de ella.

herself, *pron.* sí, ella misma.

hesitancy, *n.* vacilación, *f.*

hesitant, *adj.* indeciso, vacilant.

hesitate, *vi.* vacilar, titubear.

hesitation, *n.* duda, irresolución, vacilación, *f.*, titubeo, *m.*

heterodox, *adj.* heterodoxo.

heterodoxy, *n.* heterodoxia, *f.*

heterodyne, *adj.* heterodino.

heterogeneity, *n.* heterogeneidad, *f.*

heterogeneous, *adj.* heterogéneo.

hew, *vt.* leñar; tajar; cortar, picar.

hexagon, *n.* hexágono, *m.*

hexagonal, *adj.* hexagonal.

hexahedron, *n.* hexaedro, *m.*

hexameter, *n.* hexámetro, *m.*

hexangular, *adj.* hexángulo.

hey, *interj.* ¡he! ¡oye!

heyday, n. apogeo, m., sumo vigor, suma vitalidad; alegría, f., gozo, m.; —, interj. ¡ole!

hf. half, mitad.

hg. hectogram, Hg. hectogramo.

hhd. hogshead, tonel.

H. I. Hawaiian Islands, Islas Hawaianas, Islas Hawaí, f. pl.

hiatus, n. abertura, hendedura, f.; laguna, f.; (gram.) hiato, m.

hibernate, vi. invernar.

hibernation, n. invernada, f.

hibiscus, n. hibisco, m.

hiccough, n. hipo, m.; —, vi. tener hipo.

hiccup, n. hipo, m.; —, vi. hipar, tener hipo.

hickory, n. nogal americano.

hid, pretérito del verbo **hide.**

hide, vt. esconder; —, vi. esconderse; (coll.) apalear; —, n. cuero, m.; piel, f.

hidden, adj. escondido; secreto.

hide-and-seek, n. juego de escondite, escondite.

hidebound, adj. fanático, obstinado.

hideous, adj. horrible, macabro; —ly, adv. horriblemente.

hiding, n. encubrimiento, m.; — **place,** escondite, escondrijo, m., madriguera, f.

hie, vi. apresurarse.

hierarchy, n. jerarquía, f.

hieratic, adj. hierático.

hieroglyphic, adj. and n. jeroglífico, m.

higgle, vi. regatear; vender como buhonero.

higgler, n. revendedor, ra; regateador, ra.

high, adj. alto, elevado; arduo; altivo; noble, ilustre; sublime; violento; solemne; caro; — **altar,** altar mayor; — **frequency,** frecuencia elevada; — **jump,** salto de altura; — **light,** parte subida de una fotografía o pintura; acontecimiento de primordial interés; — **school,** escuela secundaria; — **seas,** alta mar; — **spirits,** alegría, jovialidad, f.; — **tide,** pleamar, f.; — **time,** buena hora, jarana, f.; — **treason,** alta traición, delito de lesa majestad; — **voltage,** alta tensión; — **water,** marea alta, mar llena.

highball, n. highball, m., bebida compuesta de algún aguardiente con soda.

highborn, adj. noble, ilustre por nacimiento.

high-colored, adj. subido de color, encendido, llamativo.

high-flown, adj. altivo, orgulloso.

high-frequency, adj. de alta frecuencia, de frecuencia elevada.

high-grade, adj. de alta calidad, excelente.

highhanded, adj. tiránico, arbitrario.

highland, n. tierra montañosa.

Highlander, n. montañés, esa.

highlight, vt. alumbrar con reflectores eléctricos; subrayar o hacer sobresalir algo en cualquier forma.

highly, adv. altamente; en sumo grado; arrogantemente; ambiciosamente; sumamente;

— seasoned, muy condimentado, picante; (Mex. coll.) picoso.

high-minded, adj. orgulloso, arrogante; magnánimo.

Highness, n. Alteza, f.

highness, n. altura, f.

high-octane, adj. de elevado índice de octano.

high-pitched, adj. agudo; sensitivo.

high-powered, adj. de alta potencia.

high-pressure, adj. de alta presión; intenso, urgente.

high-priced, adj. caro, de precio elevado.

highroad, n. camino, m.

high-sounding, adj. pomposo, retumbante.

high-speed, adj. de gran velocidad.

high-spirited, adj. bizarro, gallardo, valiente.

high-strung, adj. nervioso, excitable.

high-tension, adj. de alta tensión.

high-test, adj. que pasa cierta prueba (aplícase a la gasolina).

high-water mark, n. colmo, pináculo, m.

highway, n. camino real, camino carretero, carretera, f.; **Pan American —,** carretera panamericana.

highwayman, n. salteador de caminos.

hike, n. paseo a pie (generalmente en el campo).

hilarious, adj. alegre y bullicioso.

hilarity, n. alegría bulliciosa.

Hilary, Hilario.

hill, n. collado, cerro, otero, m.

hillock, n. colina, f., otero, m.

hilly, adj. montañoso.

hilt, n. puño de espada.

him, pron. le, a él.

himself, pron. sí, él mismo.

hind, adj. trasero, posterior; — **part,** parte trasera o posterior; —, n. cierva (hembra del ciervo), f.; peón en una hacienda.

hinder, vt. impedir, embarazar, estorbar.

hinder, adj. trasero, posterior.

hindmost, adj. postrero; último.

hindquarter, n. cuarto trasero de algunos animales.

hindrance, n. impedimento, obstáculo, m.; rémora, f.

hindsight, n. mira posterior de una arma de fuego; percepción de la naturaleza y exigencias de un suceso pasado.

hinge, n. charnela, bisagra, f., gozne, m.; punto principal, centro, m.; —, vt. engoznar.

hint, n. seña, f.; sugestión, insinuación, f. luz, f.; aviso, m.; buscapié, m.; **at the least —,** a media palabra; —, vt. apuntar, insinuar; sugerir; hacer señas.

hinterland, n. interior de un país.

hip, n. cadera, f.; (Sp. Am.) canco, m.; (bot.) fruto del rosal silvestre o escaramujo; — **roof,** techo de cuatro aguas.

hipbone, n. hueso de la cadera.

hippodrome, n. hipódromo, m.

hippopotamus, *n.* hipopótamo, *m.*
hire, *vt.* alquilar; arrendar; —, *n.* alquiler, *m.*; salario, *m.*
hireling, *n.* jornalero, *m.*; hombre mercenario; —, *adj.* mercenario, venal.
hirsute, *adj.* hirsuto, velludo, áspero.
his, *pron.* su, suyo, de él.
Hispaniola, Isla Española, *f.*
hiss, *vt.* and *vi.* silbar.
hissing, *n.* chifla, *f.*; siseo, *m.*
hist! *interj.* ¡chito! ¡chitón!
hist.: history, hist. historia; **historical,** hist. histórico.
histology, *n.* histología, *f.*
historian, *n.* historiador, *m.*
historic, *adj.* histórico; **—ally,** *adv.* históricamente.
historical, *adj.* = **historic.**
history, *n.* historia, narración, *f.*
histrionic, *adj.* teatral, histriónico.
hit, *vt.* golpear, dar, atinar; —, *vi.* salir bien; encontrar, encontrarse; **to — against,** estrellar, dar contra; **to — the target,** dar en el blanco; —, *n.* golpe, *m.*; suerte feliz; alcance, *m.*; (coll.) éxito, *m.*; (baseball) golpe, *m.*
hitch, *vt.* enganchar, atar, amarrar; —, *n.* impedimento, *m.*; (naut.) nudo o lazo fácil de soltar.
hitchhike, *vi.* viajar consiguiendo ser llevado gratuitamente el que lo hace por automovilistas que van en la dirección que se propone seguir.
hither, *adv.* acá; hacia acá; —, *adj.* citerior.
hitherto, *adv.* hasta ahora, hasta aquí.
hive, *n.* colmena, *f.*; —, *vt.* enjambrar; —, *vi.* vivir muchos en un mismo lugar.
hives, *n.* (med.) urticaria, *f.*; ronchas, *f. pl.*
H. M. S. His (Her) Majesty's Ship, Barco de la Marina Británica de Guerra.
ho, *interj.* ¡eh! ¡basta!
hoar, *adj.* blanco, cano.
hoard, *n.* montón, *m.*; tesoro escondido; —, *vt.* atesorar, acumular.
hoarding, *n.* acaparamiento, *m.*
hoarfrost, *n.* escarcha, *f.*
hoarhound, *n.* = **horehound.**
hoarse, *adj.* ronco; **—ly,** *adv.* roncamente.
hoarseness, *n.* ronquera, carraspera, *f.*
hoary, *adj.* blanquecino, cano.
hoax, *n.* burla, *f.*; petardo, *m.*; trufa, *f.*; —, *vt.* engañar, burlar.
hob, *n.* repisa interior del hogar; patán, *m.*
hobble, *vi.* cojear; —, *vt.* enredar; —, *n.* dificultad, *f.*; cojera, *f.*; maniota, *f.*; — **skirt,** falda estrecha.
hobby, *n.* caballico, *m.*; manía, afición, *f.*
hobbyhorse, *n.* caballito de madera en que corren los niños.
hobgoblin, *n.* duende, *m.*
hobnail, *n.* clavo de herradura.
hob-nailed, *adj.* con clavos de herradura.
hobnob, *vi.* codearse, rozarse.
hobo, *n.* vagabundo, *m.*

Hobson's choice, *n.* alternativa entre una cosa o ninguna.
hock, *n.* vino añejo del Rin; jarrete, *m.*; —, *vt.* desjarretar; (coll.) dar en prenda, empeñar.
hockey, *n.* variedad de juego de pelota con patines de hielo.
hocus, *vt.* engañar.
hocus-pocus, *n.* pasapasa, *f.*, engaño, *m.*
hod, *n.* cuezo, *m.*; — **carrier,** peón de albañil.
hodgepodge, *n.* almodrote, baturrillo, *m.*; morralla, *f.*
hodman, *n.* peón de albañil.
hoe, *n.* azada, *f.*, azadón, *m.*; —, *vt.* cavar la tierra con azada, azadonar.
hog, *n.* cerdo, puerco, *m.*
hoggish, *adj.* porcuno; egoísta; **—ly,** *adv.* egoístamente; puercamente; vorazmente.
hogshead, *n.* tonel, *m.*; barrica, *f.*; bocoy, *m.*
hoi polloi, *n.* multitud, chusma, *f.*
hoist, *vt.* alzar; (naut.) izar; —, *n.* montacargas, *m.*; cric, *m.*; elevador, *m.*; grúa, *f.*
hoisting, *n.* izamiento, *m.*; — **crane,** montacargas, *m.*; — **engine,** malacate, *m.*
hoity-toity, *adj.* voluble; presuntuoso.
hold, *vt.* tener, asir; detener; sostener; mantener; juzgar, reputar; poseer; continuar, proseguir; contener; celebrar; sujetar; —, *vi.* valer; mantenerse; durar; abstenerse; adherirse; posponer; **to lay —,** echar mano; —! *interj.* ¡tente! ¡para! ¡estate quieto! —, *n.* presa, *f.*; mango, *m.*; asa, *f.*; prisión, *f.*; custodia, *f.*; (naut.) bodega, *f.*; apoyo, *m.*; poder, *m.*
holdback, *n.* freno, *m.*, restricción, *f.*
holder, *n.* tenedor, posesor; mango, *m.*, asa, *f.*; **cigar —, cigarette —,** boquilla, *f.*
holdfast, *n.* grapa, laña, *f.*; prensa, mordaza, *f.*
holding, *n.* tenencia, posesión, *f.*; — **company,** compañía tenedora.
holdup, *n.* salteamiento, *m.*
hole, *n.* agujero, *m.*; cueva, *f.*; hoyo, *m.*; seno, *m.*; hueco, *m.*
holiday, *n.* día de fiesta, día festivo; **half —,** día quebrado; **—s,** *n. pl.* vacaciones, *f. pl.*; días de fiesta.
holiness, *n.* santidad, *f.*
Holland, Holanda, *f.*
Hollander, *n.* and *adj.* holandés, esa.
hollow, *adj.* hueco; falso, engañoso, insincero; —, *n.* cavidad, caverna, *f.*; —, *vt.* excavar, ahuecar.
hollow-eyed, *adj.* con los ojos hundidos.
hollowness, *n.* cavidad, *f.*; falsedad, insinceridad, *f.*; simulación, *f.*
holly, *n.* (bot.) acebo, agrifolio, *m.*
hollyhock, *n.* (bot.) malva hortense.
holocaust, *n.* holocausto, *m.*
holograph, *n.* ológrafo, hológrafo, *m.*
holographic, *adj.* ológrafo.
holster, *n.* funda de pistola.
holy, *adj.* santo, pío; consagrado; — **water,** agua bendita; **Holy Week,** semana santa;

most —, santísimo.
homage, n. homenaje, culto, m.; **to pay —,** rendir homenaje.
home, n. casa, casa propia, morada, f.; patria, f.; domicilio, m.; (coll.) cuartel, m.; **at —,** en casa; **—,** adj. doméstico; **— defense,** defensa patria, defensa del territorio nacional; **— plate,** (baseball) puesto meta en el rombal de baseball; puesto de salida y llegada en baseball; **— rule,** autonomía, f.; **— run** (baseball) golpe dado por el *batter* a la pelota que le permite correr todas las bases sin ayuda de error del equipo contrario.
homebred, adj. nativo; casero.
home-brew, n. cerveza y otros licores hechos en casa.
homeland, n. patria, f., tierra natal.
homeless, adj. sin casa, sin hogar.
homelike, adj. como de casa, cómodo.
homeliness, n. simpleza, f.; fealdad, f.
homely, adj. feo; casero.
homemade, adj. hecho en casa; casero.
homemaker, n. ama de casa.
homeopath, n. homeópata, m. y f.
homeopathy, n. homeopatía, f.
homesick, adj. nostálgico.
homesickness, n. nostalgia, f., mal de la tierra.
homespun, adj. casero; tosco, basto.
homestead, n. heredad, f.; casa solariega; hogar, solar, m.
homestretch, n. último trecho de una carrera.
homeward, homewards, adv. hacia casa, hacia su país.
homeward-bound, adj. con rumbo al hogar, de regreso.
homework, n. tarea, f., trabajo hecho en casa, estudio fuera de la clase.
homicidal, adj. homicida.
homicide, n. homicidio, m.; homicida, m. y f.
homily, n. homilía, f.
homing pigeon, n. paloma mensajera.
hominy, n. maíz machacado o molido.
homogeneity, n. homogeneidad, f.
homogeneous, adj. homogéneo.
homogenize, vt. homogenizar.
homograph, n. homógrafo, m.
homologous, adj. homólogo.
homologue, n. cosa homóloga.
homology, n. homología, f.
homonym, n. homónimo, m.
homophone, n. letra o palabra homófona.
Hon., hon. honorable, honorary, honorable, honorario.
Honduran, n. and adj. hondureño, ña.
hone, n. piedra amoladera, piedra de afilar, f.
honest, adj. honesto, probo; honrado; justo; **—ly,** adv. honestamente; honradamente.
honesty, n. honestidad, justicia, probidad, f., hombría de bien; honradez, f.

honey, n. miel, f.; dulzura, f.; **— locust,** variedad de árbol ornamental de Norte América; **like —,** meloso.
honeybee, n. abeja obrera.
honeycomb, n. panal, m., bresca, f., ceras, f. pl.
honeycombed, adj. horadado por gusanos.
honeydew, n. rocío dulce; **— melon,** variedad de melón.
honeyed, adj. dulce, meloso, enmelado.
honeymoon, n. luna de miel.
honeysuckle, n. (bot.) madreselva, f.
honied, adj. = honeyed.
honor, n. honra, f., honor, lauro, m.; **on my —,** a fe mía; **point of —,** pundonor, m.; **—,** vt. honrar; **to — (a draft),** (com.) aceptar (un giro o letra de cambio).
honorable, adj. honorable; ilustre; respetable; **— behavior,** caballerosidad, f.
honorableness, n. honradez, f.
honorably, adv. honorablemente.
honorarium, n. honorarios, m. pl.
honorary, adj. honorario.
honorific, adj. honorario, honorífico.
honors, n. pl. (bridge) honores, m. pl.
hood, n. caperuza, f.; capirote (de graduados), m.; capucha (de religioso), f.; gorro, m.; (auto.) cubierta del motor; **—,** vt. proveer de caperuza; cubrir con caperuza.
hoodlum, n. (coll.) pillo, tunante, m.
hoodoo, n. (coll.) mal de ojo; persona o cosa que trae mala suerte; **—,** vt. causar mala suerte.
hoodwink, vt. vendar a uno los ojos; engañar.
hoof, n. casco de las bestias caballares, pezuña.
hoofbeat, n. ruido de los cascos.
hoofed, adj. ungulado.
hook, n. gancho, m.; anzuelo, m.; **by — or crook,** de un modo u otro; **eye of a —,** hembra de un broche; **— and eye,** corchete macho y hembra; **—s and eyes,** corchetes, m. pl.; **set of —s and eyes,** brochadura, f.; **—,** vt. enganchar.
hooked, adj. enganchado, encorvado; **— rug,** tapete tejido a mano.
hookup, n. (rad.) circuito, m.; trasmisión en circuito por emisoras conectadas; establecimiento de relaciones o conexiones, como entre dos gobiernos.
hookworm, n. lombriz intestinal.
hooligan, n. cantonero, rufián, m.
hoop, n. cerco, m.; cerco de barril; **— skirt,** miriñaque, m.; **—,** vt. cercar.
hooper, n. tonelero, m.
hoot, vi. gritar; **—,** n. grito, m.
hop, n. salto, m.; **—s,** (bot.) lúpulo, m.; **—,** vi. saltar, brincar; **— (beer),** vt. echar lúpulo (en la cerveza).
hope, n. esperanza, f.; **— chest,** caja en que una mujer guarda trajes, ropa blanca, etc., en anticipación de casamiento; **—,** vi. esperar.
hopeful, adj. lleno de esperanzas, esperan-

zado; optimista; **—ly,** adv. con esperanza; **—,** n. joven prometedor por sus buenas cualidades.

hopeless, adj. desesperado; sin remedio; **—ly,** adv. sin esperanza, desesperadamente.

hopper, n. saltador, m.; tolva (en los molinos), f.

hopscotch, n. coxcojilla, f.

Horace, Horatius, Horacio.

horde, n. horda, f.; enjambre, m.; manada, f.

horehound, n. marrubio, m.

horizon, n. horizonte, m.

horizontal, adj. horizontal; **—ly,** adv. horizontalmente.

hormone, n. hormón, m.

horn, n. cuerno, m.; corneta, f.; trompeta, f.; cacho, m.; bocina, f.; klaxon, m.; clarín, m.; **— of plenty,** cuerno de la abundancia.

hornbill, n. (orn.) cálao, m.

horned, adj. cornudo.

hornet, n. abejón, m.

hornpipe, n. gaita, f.

horny, adj. hecho de cuerno; calloso.

horoscope, n. horóscopo, m.

horrible, adj. horrible, terrible; **—ly,** adv. horriblemente; enormemente.

horrid, adj. horroroso, horrible.

horror, n. horror, terror, m.

horror-stricken, adj. horrorizado.

hors d'oeuvre, n. pl. entremés, m.

horse, n. caballo, m.; caballería, f.; caballete, m.; **— armor,** barda, f.; **— chestnut,** castaño de Indias; **Horse Guards,** guardias de a caballo; **— race,** carrera o corrida de caballos; **—,** vi. cabalgar; **—,** vt. suministrar caballos.

horseback, n. espinazo del caballo; **on —,** a caballo.

horsefly, n. moscarda, f., moscardón, tábano, m.

horsehair, n. crin de caballo; tela de crin.

horsehide, n. corambre de caballo.

horselaugh, n. carcajada; risotada, f.

horseless, adj. sin caballo.

horseman, n. jinete, m.

horsemanship, n. equitación, f.

horseplay, n. chanza pesada, broma de mal gusto.

horsepower, n. caballo de fuerza o potencia.

horse-radish, n. rábano silvestre, rábano picante.

horseshoe, n. herradura de caballo.

horsetail, n. cola de caballo.

horsewhip, n. látigo, m.; fusta, f., (Sp. Am.) fuete, m.; **—,** vt. azotar.

hortioultural, adj. hortícola.

horticulture, n. horticultura, jardinería, f.

horticulturist, n. hortelano, jardinero, m.

hosanna! interj. ¡hosanna!

hose, n. medias, calcetas, f. pl.; calzones, m. pl.; manguera, f.; tubo flexible; **— pipe,** manguera, f.

hosier, n. calcetero, m.

hosiery, n. calcetería, f.; medias, f. pl.; calcetines, m. pl.

hospice, n. hospicio, m.

hospitable, adj. hospitalario; **—bly,** adv. con hospitalidad.

hospital, n. hospital, m.; **— ward,** sala o crujía de hospital; **maternity —,** casa de maternidad.

hospitality, n. hospitalidad, f.

hospitalization, n. hospitalización, f.

host, n. anfitrión, m.; huésped, m.; mesonero, m.; ejército, m.; hostia, f.

hostage, n. rehén, m.

hostel, n. posada, f., hotel, m.; posada para jóvenes (movimiento educativo de excursiones de jóvenes).

hostelry, n. fonda, f., mesón, m.

hostess, n. anfitriona, f.; posadera, mesonera, patrona, f.

hostile, adj. hostil; contrario.

hostility, n. hostilidad, f.

hostler, n. mesonero, posadero, m.

hot, adj. cálido; ardiente; fervoroso; violento; picante; (Mex. coll.) picoso; **— baths,** caldas, termas, f. pl.; **— springs,** termas, f. pl., burga, f.; **while —,** en caliente.

hot-air, adj. de aire caliente.

hotbed, n. era, f.; invernadero (con estufas), m.; semillero, m.; (fig.) foco, m.

hot-blooded, adj. excitable, de sangre ardiente.

hotbox, n. cojinete calentado excesivamente por fricción.

hotel, n. posada, fonda, f., hotel, m.

hotheaded, adj. sañoso, fogoso, exaltado; **— fellow,** calavera, m.

hothouse, n. estufa, f.; invernadero, m.

hotspur, n. hombre colérico y atrevido.

hot-tempered, adj. fogoso.

hot-water tank, n. depósito del agua caliente.

hound, n. sabueso, podenco, m.; hombre vil y despreciable.

hour, n. hora, f.; **— hand,** mano de reloj que señala las horas, horario.

hourglass, n. reloj de arena; (naut.) ampolleta, f.

hourly, adv. a cada hora; frecuentemente; **—,** adj. que sucede a cada hora, frecuente.

house, n. casa, f.; familia, f.; linaje, m.; cámara (del parlamento), f.; **banking —,** casa de banco; **business —,** casa de comercio; **clearing —,** casa de compensación; **commission —,** casa de comisiones; **country —,** casa de campo; **gambling —,** casino, m.; **— of correction,** casa de corrección, reformatorio, m.; **— party,** fiesta en que los invitados permanecen más de un día; tertulia generalmente en una casa de campo; **H— of Representatives,** Cámara de Representantes; **lodging —,** casa de posada o de huéspedes; **publishing —,** casa editora; **to keep —,** poner casa; ser ama de casa;

wholesale —, casa al por mayor; **—,** vt. and vi. albergar; residir; **— of correction,** casa de corrección; **— physician,** médico residente.

houseboat, n. embarcación, especialmente de recreo, con casa habitación construída en ella.

housebreaker, n. ladrón que fuerza las puertas de una casa para robarla.

housefly, n. mosca, f.

houseful, n. casa llena.

household, n. familia, f ; casa, f.; establecimiento, m.; **— duties,** quehaceres de la casa; **— goods,** enseres, bártulos, m. pl.; **— management,** manejo doméstico.

householder, n. amo de casa, padre de familia.

housekeeper, n. ama de casa, jefe de familia; ama de llaves.

housekeeping, n. gobierno doméstico; manejo casero.

housemaid, n. criada de casa.

housetop, n. tejado, m.

housewarming, n. tertulia para el estreno de una casa.

housewife, n. ama de casa; estuche de costura.

housework, n. quehaceres domésticos, trabajo de casa.

housing, n. alojamiento, m.; almacenaje, m.; (mech.) cárter, m.; cubierta, f.; **—s,** gualdrapa, f.

hovel, n. choza, cabaña, f.

hover, vi. colgar; dudar; rondar.

how, adv. cómo, cuán; cuánto; **— do you do?** ¿cómo le va a usted? **— goes it?** ¿qué tal? **— are you getting along?** ¿qué tal? **— so?** ¿por qué? ¿cómo así?

however, adv. como quiera, como quiera que sea; sin embargo, no obstante.

howitzer, n. (mil.) obús, bombero, m.

howl, vi. aullar; **—,** n. aúllo, aullido, m.

howsoever, adv. como quiera, como quiera que sea.

hoyden, n. muchacha ruda y estrepitosa; **—,** adj. estrepitoso, grosero.

H.P., h.p. horse power, H.P. caballo de fuerza, caballo de vapor.

H.R. House of Representatives, Cámara de Representantes.

hr. hour, h. hora.

H.R.H. His (Her) Royal Highness, S.A.R. Su Alteza Real.

H.T. Hawaiian Territory, Territorio de Hawaí.

ht. height, alt. altura.

hub, n. cubo, m.; centro, m.; maza de una rueda.

hubbub, n. grito, ruido, m.; alboroto, tumulto, m.; (coll.) cisco, m.

hubcap, n. tapacubo, m.

huckleberry, n. variedad de gayuba.

huckster, n. revendedor, m., vendedor ambulante.

huddle, vt. amontonar en desorden; **—,** vi. amontonarse en confusión; agruparse para recibir señas (en el juego de fútbol); **—,** n. confusión, f.; (coll.) conferencia secreta.

hue, n. color, m.; tez del rostro; matiz, m., tinta, f.; **— and cry,** alarma que se da contra un criminal.

huff, n. arrebato, m.; cólera, f.; **—,** vt. ofender; tratar con arrogancia; **—,** vi. enojarse, patear dé enfado.

huffy, adj. malhumorado, irascible; arrogante.

hug, vt. abrazar, acariciar; **—,** n. abrazo apretado.

huge, adj. vasto, enorme; gigantesco; **—ly,** adv. inmensamente.

Hugh, Hugo.

hula-hula, n. baile típico de Hawaí.

hulk, n. (naut.) casco de una embarcación; armatoste, m.

hulking, adj. pesado, tosco.

hull, n. cáscara, f.; (naut.) casco (de un buque), m.; **—,** vt. descortezar.

hullabaloo, n. tumulto, alboroto, m.

huller, n. descascarador, m.

hum, vi. zumbar, susurrar, murmurar; **—,** vt. tararear (una canción, etc.); **—,** n. zumbido, m.

human, n. and adj. humano, na; **—ly,** adv. humanamente.

humane, adj. humano; benigno; **—ly,** adv. humanamente.

humanist, n. humanista, m. y f.

humanitarian, n. filántropo, pa; **—,** adj. humanitario.

humanitarianism, n. humanitarianismo, m.

humanity, n. humanidad, f.

humanize, vt. hacer humano; civilizar; **—,** vi. humanizarse.

humankind, n. el género o linaje humano.

humble, adj. humilde, modesto; **—,** vt. humillar, postrar; **to — oneself,** humillarse; doblar o bajar la cerviz.

humblebee, n. = **bumblebee.**

humbleness, n. humildad, f.

humbly, adv. humildemente.

humbug, n. engaño, m.; trampa, f.; **—,** vt. engañar, chasquear.

humdrum, adj. lerdo, estúpido; monótono.

humerus, n. (anat.) húmero, m.

humid, adj. húmedo, algo mojado.

humidifier, n. humedecedor, m.

humidify, vt. humedecer.

humidity, n. humedad, f.

humidor, n. caja humedecida para puros, bote para tabaco de fumar.

humiliate, vt. humillar.

humiliation, n. humillación, mortificación, f., bochorno, m.

humility, n. humildad, f.

hummingbird, n. (orn.) colibrí, m.

hummock, n. colina, f., montecillo, m.

humor, n. humor, m.; humorada, fantasía,

f.; capricho, *m.*; **bad —**, berrinche, *m.*, mal humor; **—**, *vt.* complacer, dar gusto; ejecutar lo que a uno se le manda.

humorist, *n.* humorista, *m.* y *f.*

humorous, *adj.* humorista, chistoso, jocoso; **—ly,** *adv.* de buen humor; en forma jocosa.

hump, *n.* giba, joroba, *f.*

humpbacked, *adj.* jorobado, giboso.

humph! *interj.* exclamación de duda.

Humphrey, Hunfredo.

humus, *n.* humus, mantillo, *m.*, tierra vegetal.

hunch, *n.* giba, *f.*; (coll.) idea, *f.*; pedazo, *m.*

hunchback, *n.* joroba, *f.*; jorobado, da.

hunchbacked, *adj.* = **humpbacked.**

hundred, *adj.* cien, ciento; **—,** *n.* centenar, *m.*; un ciento.

hundredfold, *n.* and *adj.* céntuplo, *m.*

hundredth, *n.* and *adj.* centésimo, *m.*

hundredweight, *n.* quintal, *m.*

hung, pretérito y *p.p.* del verbo **hang.**

Hungarian, *n.* and *adj.* húngaro, ra.

Hungary, Hungría, *f.*

hunger, *n.* hambre, *f.*; **— strike,** abstención de alimento hasta la concesión de ciertas demandas; **—,** *vi.* hambrear.

hungry, *adj.* hambriento; voraz; **to be —,** tener hambre.

hunk, *n.* pedazo grande.

hunt, *vt.* montear, cazar; perseguir; buscar; **—,** *vi.* andar a caza; **—,** *n.* caza, *f.*

hunter, *n.* cazador, *m.*; caballo de caza; perro de monte, perro braco.

hunting, *n.* montería, caza, *f.*; **— horn,** corneta de caza.

huntress, *n.* cazadora, *f.*

huntsman, *n.* cazador, montero, *m.*

hurdle, *n.* zarzo, *m.*; valla, *f.*; **—s,** carrera de obstáculos.

hurdy-gurdy, *n.* (mus.) gaita, zanfonía, *f.*

hurl, *vt.* tirar con violencia; arrojar.

hurly-burly, *n.* alboroto, *m.*; confusión, babilonia, *f.*

hurrah! *interj.* ¡viva!

hurricane, *n.* huracán, *m.*

hurried, *adj.* apresurado, hecho de prisa.

hurry, *vt.* acelerar, apresurar, precipitar; **—,** *vi.* atropellarse, apresurarse; **—,** *n.* precipitación, *f.*; confusión, *f.*; urgencia, *f.*; **to be in a —,** tener prisa, estar de prisa, darse prisa.

hurry-scurry, *n.* tropel, *m.*, confusión, *f.*; **—,** *vt.* and *vi.* andar atropelladamente o de prisa; **—,** *adj.* lleno de confusión y atropello.

hurt, *vt.* dañar, hacer daño, herir; ofender; **—,** *n.* mal, daño, perjuicio, *m.*; golpe, *m.*; herida, *f.*; **—,** *adj.* sentido; lastimado; perjudicado.

hurtful, *adj.* nocivo.

hurtle, *vi.* lanzar, lanzarse con violencia.

husband, *n.* marido, esposo, *m.*; labrador, *m.*; **ship's —,** armador de navío; **—,** *vt.* gobernar con economía; labrar la tierra.

husbandman, *n.* labrador, viñador, *m.*

husbandry, *n.* agricultura, *f.*; economía, *f.*

hush, *n.* silencio, *m.*; **— money,** cohecho que se da a alguno para que calle; **—!** *interj.* ¡chitón! ¡silencio! ¡paz! ¡calla! **—,** *vt.* aquietar; acallar; **—,** *vi.* hacer silencio.

husk, *n.* cáscara, *f.*; pellejo, *m.*; **—,** *vt.* descascarar, mondar.

husker, *n.* descascarador, *m.*

huskiness, *n.* ronquedad, ronquera, *f.*

husky, *adj.* fuerte; lleno de cáscaras; ronco; robusto.

hussar, *n.* (mil.) húsar, *m.*

hussy, *n.* picarona, tunanta, *f.*

hustle, *vt.* and *vi.* bullir; apurar (un trabajo); apurarse, andar de prisa.

hut, *n.* cabaña, barraca, choza, *f.*

hutch, *n.* arca, *f.*; cofre, *m.*; madriguera, *f.*; choza, *f.*

hyacinth, *n.* (bot.) jacinto, *m.*

hybrid, *n.* and *adj.* híbrido, *m.*

hydra, *n.* hidra, *f.*

hydrangea, *n.* (bot.) hortensia, *f.*

hydrant, *n.* llave de un encañado, boca de agua.

hydrate, *n.* (chem.) hidrato, *m.*; **—,** *vt.* hidratar.

hydration, *n.* hidratación, *f.*

hydraulic, *adj.* hidráulico; **— engineering,** hidrotecnia, *f.*

hydraulics, *n.* hidráulica, *f.*

hydrocarbon, *n.* (chem.) hidrocarburo, *m.*

hydrochlorate, *n.* (chem.) hidroclorato, *m.*

hydrochloric, *adj.* hidroclórico, clorhídrico.

hydrocyanic, *adj.* (chem.) prúsico.

hydrodynamics, *n.* hidrodinámica, *f.*

hydroelectric, *adj.* hidroeléctrico.

hydrogen, *n.* (chem.) hidrógeno, *m.*; **carbureted —,** hidrocarburo, *m.*; **— peroxide,** agua oxigenada, peróxido hidrogenado; **— sulphide,** sulfhídrico, *m.*

hydrography, *n.* hidrografía, *f.*

hydrolysis, *n.* hidrólisis, *f.*

hydrometer, *n.* areómetro, *m.*

hydropathy, *n.* hidropatía, *f.*

hydrophobia, *n.* hidrofobia, *f.*

hydrophobic, *adj.* hidrofóbico.

hydroplane, *n.* hidroplano, hidroavión, *m.*

hydroponics, *n.* hidroponía, *f.*, cultivo de vegetales, especialmente legumbres, en mezclas químicas líquidas.

hydrosphere, *n.* hidrósfera, *f.*

hydrostatic, *adj.* hidrostático; **—s,** *n. pl.* hidrostática.

hydrosulphide, *n.* (chem.) hidrosulfuro, sulfhidrato, *m.*

hydrosulphuric, *adj.* (chem.) sulfhídrico.

hydrotherapy, *n.* hidroterapia, *f.*

hydroxide, hydroxid, *n.* hidróxido, *m.*

hyena, *n.* hiena, *f.*

hygiene, *n.* higiene, *f.*

hygienic, *adj.* higiénico.

hygrometer, *n.* higrómetro, *m.*

hygroscope, n. higroscopio, m.
hymen, n. himeneo, m.
hymeneal, adj. nupcial.
hymn, n. himno, m.
hymnal, n. himnario, m.
hyperbole, n. hipérbole, f.; exageración, f.
hyperbolic, adj. hiperbólico; **—ally,** adv. hiperbólicamente.
hypercritic, n. rigorista, m. y f.; crítico austero.
hypercritical, adj. hipercrítico.
hypersensitive, adj. excesivamente impresionable.
hypertrophic, adj. hipertrófico.
hypertrophy, n. hipertrofia, f.
hyphen, n. (gram.) guión, m.
hyphenate, vt. separar con guión.
hypnosis, n. hipnosis, f.
hypnotic, adj. hipnótico.
hypnotism, n. hipnotismo, m.
hypnotize, vt. hipnotizar.
hypochondria, n. hipocondría, f.
hypochondriac, adj. and n. hipocondríaco, ca.
hypocrisy, n. hipocresía, f.
hypocrite, n. hipócrita, m. y f.; mojigato, ta, camandulero, ra; beata, f.
hypocritical, adj. hipócrita, disimulado.
hypodermic, adj. hipodérmico; **— syringe,** jeringa hipodérmica; **—,** n. inyección hipodérmica.
hypotenuse, n. hipotenusa, f.
hypothecate, vt. hipotecar.
hypothesis, n. hipótesis, f.
hypothetic, adj. = **hypothetical.**
hypothetical, adj. hipotético; **—ly,** adv. condicionalmente, hipotéticamente.
hysteria, n. histeria, f., histerismo, m.
hysteric, hysterical, adj. histérico.
hysterics, n. pl. paroxismo histérico.

I

I, pron. yo.
I.: Idaho, Idaho; **Island, Islands,** Isla, Islas.
Ia. Iowa, Iowa.
iambic, adj. yámbico.
ibex, n. íbice, m.
ib., ibid. in the same place, ib. ibídem, en el mismo lugar.
I beam, n. eje en doble T.
Iberian, n. ibero, ra; **—,** adj. ibérico.
ibid. in the same place, ib. ibídem, en el mismo lugar.
ibidem, adv. en el mismo lugar.
ibis, n. (orn.) ibis, m.
I.C.C. Interstate Commerce Commission, Comisión de Comercio entre Estados (E.U.A.).
ice, n. hielo, m.; granizado, m.; **— age,** época glacial; **— cream,** = **ice cream; — field,** témpano de hielo flotante, bancos de hielo; **— hockey,** juego de pelota con

patines; **— pack,** hielo empaquetado para aplicaciones frías; **— pick,** pico para el hielo; **— scraper,** rallo para hielo; **— sheet,** masa de hielo glacial; **— skate,** patín de hielo o de cuchilla; **— spur,** patín, m.; **— water,** agua helada, agua enfriada con hielo; **—,** vt. helar; **to — a cake,** garapiñar un pastel.
iceberg, n. témpano de hielo.
iceboat, n. embarcación con patines para deslizarse sobre el hielo; barco rompehielos.
icebound, adj. rodeado de hielo.
icebox, n. refrigerador, m., nevera, f.
icebreaker, n. rompehielos, m.
ice cream, n. helado, mantecado, m., nieve, f.
ice-cream, adj. de helado o de mantecado; **— cone,** cucurucho o barquillo de helado o de mantecado; **— parlor,** heladería, botillería, f., salón de refrescos.
icehouse, n. nevería, nevera, f., refrigeradora, f.
Iceland, Islandia, f.
Icelander, n. islandés, esa; **—,** adj. islandés, islándico.
iceman, n. repartidor de hielo.
ichthyology, n. ictiología, f.
icicle, n. cerrión, carámbano, m.
iciness, n. congelación, f.; congelamiento, m.; (fig.) frialdad extremada.
icing, n. capa dulce para pasteles.
iconoclast, n. iconoclasta, m. y f.
iconoclastic, adj. iconoclasta.
icy, adj. helado; frío; (fig.) indiferente.
Id., Ida. Idaho, Idaho.
id. the same as previously given, id. ídem, lo mismo que lo anterior.
idea, n. idea, f.; imagen mental; concepto, m.; **clever —,** feliz idea.
ideal, adj. ideal; mental; **—ly,** adv. idealmente.
idealism, n. idealismo, m.
idealist, n. idealista, m. y f.
idealistic, adj. idealista.
idealization, n. idealización, f.
idealize, vt. and vi. idealizar.
idem, pron. and adj. el mismo o lo mismo.
identical, adj. idéntico.
identification, n. identificación, f.; **— card, — papers,** cédula personal o de vecindad.
identify, vt. identificar; **to — oneself,** identificarse.
identity, n. identidad, f.
ideogram, n. ideograma, m.
ideograph, n. ideograma, m.
ideological, adj. ideológico.
ideologist, n. ideólogo, m.
ideology, n. ideología, f.
idiocy, n. idiotismo, m.
idiom, n. idioma, m.; modismo, m.
idiomatic, idiomatical, adj. peculiar a alguna lengua.
idiosyncrasy, n. idiosincrasia, f.
idiot, n. idiota, m. y f., necio, cia.
idiotic, adj. tonto, ta, bobo, ba.
idle, adj. ocioso, perezoso, desocupado

holgazán; inútil, vano, frívolo; **—,** vi.
holgazanear, estar ocioso.
idleness, n. ociosidad, pereza, f.; negligencia, f.; frivolidad, f.
idler, n. holgazán, ana; (coll.) gandul, gandula; (mech.) rueda intermedia.
idly, adv. ociosamente; vanamente.
idol, n. ídolo, m.; imagen, f.
idolater, n. idólatra, m. y f.
idolatrous, adj. idolátrico, idólatra.
idolatry, n. idolatría, f.
idolize, vt. idolatrar.
idyl, n. idilio, m.
idyllic, adj. idílico, como un idilio.
i.e. that is, i.e. es decir, esto es.
if, conj. si; aunque, supuesto que; **— not,** si no.
igloo, n. choza semiesférica de los esquimales que suelen fabricar con bloques de nieve endurecida.
Ignatius, Ignacio.
igneous, adj. ígneo, de fuego.
ignis fatuus, n. fuego fatuo.
ignite, vt. encender, abrasar.
ignition, n. (chem.) ignición, f.; (auto.) ignición, f.; **— switch,** contacto del magneto; **— trouble,** trastorno del encendido.
ignoble, adj. innoble; bajo; **—bly,** adv. vilmente, bajamente.
ignominious, adj. ignominioso; **—ly,** adv. ignominiosamente.
ignominy, n. ignominia, infamia, f.
ignoramus, n. ignorante, m. y f.; tonto, ta.
ignorance, n. ignorancia, f.
ignorant, adj. ignorante, inculto; **—ly,** adv. ignorantemente.
ignore, vt. pasar por alto, desconocer.
iguana, n. (zool.) iguana, f.
ilk, n. especie, f.
ill, adj. malo, enfermo, doliente; **—,** n. mal, infortunio, m.; **— will,** malquerencia, f.; **—,** adv. mal, malamente.
Ill. Illinois, Illinois.
ill., illust. illustration, ilustración, ej. ejemplo.
ill-bred, adj. malcriado, descortés.
ill-deserved, adj. mal merecido, inmerecido.
ill-disposed, adj. malintencionado, contrario.
illegal, adj. ilegal; **—ly,** adv. ilegalmente.
illegality, n. ilegalidad, f.
illegible, adj. ilegible; **—bly,** adv. de un modo ilegible.
illegibility, n. ilegibilidad, f.
illegitimacy, n. ilegitimidad, f.
illegitimate, adj. ilegítimo; **—ly,** adv. ilegítimamente.
ill-fated, adj. desgraciado, desdichado.
ill-favored, adj. repulsivo, desagradable.
ill-gotten, adj. mal habido.
ill-humored, adj. malhumorado.
illiberal, adj. mezquino, iliberal; **—ly,** adv. sin libertad; mezquinamente.
illiberality, n. prejuicio, m.; falta de

cultura; tacañería, f.
illicit, adj. ilícito; **—ly,** adv. ilícitamente.
illimitable, adj. ilimitado.
illiteracy, n. analfabetismo, m.
illiterate, adj. indocto, iliterato, analfabeto.
ill-mannered, adj. malcriado, descortés.
ill-natured, adj. avieso, irascible.
illness, n. enfermedad, f.; maldad, f.; mal, m.
illogical, adj. ilógico.
ill-starred, adj. desdichado.
ill-tempered, adj. malhumorado, de mal carácter.
ill-timed, adj. intempestivo, a deshora.
ill-treat, vt. maltratar.
illuminate, vt. iluminar.
illuminating gas, n. gas de alumbrado.
illumination, n. iluminación, f.; alumbrado, m.
illumine, vt. iluminar.
ill-use, vt. maltratar.
illusion, n. ilusión, f.; ensueño, m.
illusive, adj. ilusivo, ilusorio.
illusory, adj. ilusorio.
illustrate, vt. ilustrar; explicar.
illustrated, adj. ilustrado, de grabados.
illustration, n. ilustración, f.; elucidación, f.; ejemplo, m.; grabado, m.
illustrative, adj. explicativo.
illustrator, n. ilustrador, ra.
illustrious, adj. ilustre, insigne, célebre; **—ly,** adv. ilustremente.
ill-will, n. malevolencia, f., mala voluntad.
image, n. imagen, estatua, f.; **—,** vt. imaginar.
imagery, n. imagen, pintura, f.; vuelos de la fantasía.
imaginable, adj. imaginable, concebible.
imaginary, adj. imaginario.
imagination, n. imaginación, imaginativa, f.; idea fantástica.
imaginative, adj. imaginativo.
imagine, vt. imaginar; idear, inventar.
imbecile, n. and adj. imbécil, m. y f.
imbecility, n. imbecilidad, mentecatez, f.; idiotismo, m.
imbibe, vt. embeber; chupar.
imbreeding, n. cría sin mezclar razas.
imbroglio, n. embrollo, m.; maraña, f.
imbrue, vt. mojar, empapar (aplícase a la sangre).
imbue, vt. imbuir, infundir.
imitable, adj. imitable.
imitate, vt. imitar; copiar.
imitation, n. imitación, copia, f.
imitative, adj. imitativo, imitado.
imitator, n. imitador, ra.
immaculate, adj. inmaculado, puro.
immanence, n. condición o calidad de inmanente.
immanent, adj. inmanente.
immaterial, adj. inmaterial; poco importante.
immature, adj. inmaturo.
immeasurable, adj. inmensurable, inmenso;

—bly, *adv.* inmensamente, inmensurablemente.

immediacy, *n.* inmediación, *f.*

immediate, *adj.* inmediato; **—ly,** *adv.* inmediatamente, luego, en seguida, en el acto, acto continuo.

immemorial, *adj.* inmemorial.

immense, *adj.* inmenso; vasto; **—ly,** *adv.* inmensamente.

immensity, *n.* inmensidad,*f.*; muchedumbre, *f.*

immerge, *vt.* sumergir, zambullir.

immerse, *vt.* sumir, sumergir.

immersion, *n.* inmersión, *f.*

immigrant, *n.* inmigrante, *m.* y *f.*

immigrate, *vi.* inmigrar.

immigration, *n.* inmigración, *f.*

imminence, *m.* inminencia, *f.*

imminent, *adj.* inminente.

immobile, *adj.* inmóvil.

immobility, *n.* inmovilidad, *f.*

immoderate, *adj.* inmoderado, excesivo; **—ly,** *adv.* inmoderadamente.

immodest, *adj.* inmodesto; **—ly,** *adv.* inmodestamente.

immodesty, *n.* inmodestia, *f.*

immolate, *vt.* inmolar, sacrificar.

immolation, *n.* inmolación, *f.*

immoral, *adj.* inmoral, depravado.

immorality, *n.* inmoralidad, *f.*, corrupción de costumbres.

immortal, *adj.* inmortal; **—ly,** *adv.* inmortalmente.

immortality, *n.* inmortalidad, *f.*

immortalize, *vt.* inmortalizar, eternizar.

immovability, *n.* inmutabilidad, *f.*

immovable, *adj.* inmoble; inmovible; **—bly,** *adv.* inmoblemente; **—s,** *n. pl.* bienes raíces.

immunity, *n.* inmunidad, franquicia, *f.*, privilegio, *m.*

immunization, *n.* inmunización, *f.*

immunize, *vt.* inmunizar.

immure, *vt.* emparedar.

immutability, *n.* inmutabilidad, *f.*

immutable, *adj.* inmutable; **—bly,** *adv.* inmutablemente.

imp, *n.* niño travieso; diablillo, *m.*; duende, *m.*

imp.: imperative, imper. imperativo; **imperial,** imperial; **imperfect tense,** imperf. tiempo imperfecto; **import,** importación.

impact, *n.* impulso, *m.*; choque, *m.*

impair, *vt.* empeorar, deteriorar; disminuir.

impairment, *n.* menoscabo, deterioro, *m.*

impale, *vt.* empalar (a un reo).

impalpable, *adj.* impalpable.

impanel, *vt.* (law) formar la lista de personas que han de integrar un jurado, etc.

impart, *vt.* comunicar, dar parte.

impartial, *adj.* imparcial; **—ly,** *adv.* imparcialmente.

impartiality, *n.* imparcialidad, *f.*

impassable, *adj.* intransitable.

impasse, *n.* callejón sin salida; situación embarazosa de la cual no puede uno escaparse.

impassible, *adj.* impasible.

impassion, *vt.* mover las pasiones; conmover.

impassioned, *adj.* apasionado, ardiente.

impassive, *adj.* impasible.

impatience, *n.* impaciencia, *f.*

impatient, *adj.* impaciente; **—ly,** *adv.* impacientemente.

impeach, *vt.* (law) acusar, denunciar, delatar (aplícase especialmente a funcionarios públicos).

impeachable, *adj.* delatable.

impeachment, *n.* acusación pública, delación (aplícase especialmente a funcionarios públicos), *f.*

impeccable, *adj.* impecable.

impecunious, *adj.* indigente, pobre.

impedance, *n.* impedancia, *f.*

impede, *vt.* impedir; paralizar.

impediment, *n.* impedimento, obstáculo, *m.*

impel, *vt.* impeler, impulsar.

impend, *vi.* amenazar, aproximar.

impenetrability, *n.* impenetrabilidad, *f.*

impenetrable, *adj.* impenetrable; **—ly,** *adv.* impenetrablemente.

impenitence, *n.* impenitencia, *f.*

impenitent, *adj.* impenitente; **—ly,** *adv.* sin penitencia.

imperative, *adj.* imperativo, imprescindible; **—ly,** *adv.* imperativamente.

imperceptible, *adj.* imperceptible; **—bly,** *adv.* imperceptiblemente.

imperfect, *adj.* imperfecto, defectuoso; **—ly,** *adv.* imperfectamente; **—,** *n.* (gram.) pretérito imperfecto.

imperfection, *n.* imperfección, *f.*, defecto, *m.*

imperial, *adj.* imperial, supremo, soberano; **—,** *n.* perilla, pera, *f.*

imperialism, *n.* imperialismo, *m.*

imperialist, *n.* and *adj.* imperialista, *m.* y *f.*

imperialistic, *adj.* imperialista.

imperil, *vt.* arriesgar.

imperious, *adj.* imperioso; arrogante; **—ly,** *adv.* imperiosamente, arrogantemente.

imperishable, *adj.* indestructible; eterno; imperecedero.

impermeable, *adj.* impermeable.

impersonal, *adj.* impersonal; **—ly,** *adv.* impersonalmente.

impersonate, *vt.* personificar; representar.

impersonation, *n.* personificación, *f.*; (theat.) representación, *f.*

impersonator, *n.* personificador, ra, imitador, ra.

impertinence, *n.* impertinencia, *f.*; descaro, *m.*; (coll.) chinchorrería, *f.*

impertinent, *adj.* impertinente; inadecuado, inaplicable; **—ly,** *adv.* impertinentemente; fuera de propósito.

imperturbable, *adj.* imperturbable; **—bly,**

adv. sin perturbación.

impervious, *adj.* impenetrable.

impetuosity, *n.* impetuosidad, *f.*, ímpetu, *m.*

impetuous, *adj.* impetuoso; —**ly,** *adv.* impetuosamente, a borbollones.

impetus, *n.* ímpetu, *m.*

impiety, *n.* impiedad, irreligión, *f.*

impinge, *vi.* chocar, tropezar; — **upon,** violar, infringir.

impious, *adj.* impío, irreligioso; desapiadado; —**ly,** *adv.* impíamente.

impish, *adj.* travieso.

implacable, *adj.* implacable, irreconciliable; —**bly,** *adv.* implacablemente, irreconciliablemente.

implant, *vt.* plantar; injertar; imprimir.

implement, *n.* herramienta, *f.*; utensilio, *m.*; mueble, *m.*; —**s,** *n. pl.* aperos, *m. pl.*; enseres, *m. pl.*; —, *vt.* poner en ejecución, ejecutar, completar, cumplir.

implicate, *vt.* implicar, envolver.

implication, *n.* implicación, *f.*

implicit, *adj.* implícito; —**ly,** *adv.* implícitamente.

implied, *adj.* implícito.

implore, *vt.* implorar, suplicar.

imply, *vt.* implicar.

impolite, *adj.* descortés, impolítico.

impolitely, *adv.* descortésmente, incivilmente.

impolitic, impolitical, *adj.* imprudente; impolítico.

imponderable, *adj.* imponderable.

import, *vt.* importar; significar; —, *n.* importancia, *f.*; importe, *m.*; sentido, *m.*; significación, *f.*; — **duties,** derechos de importación.

importance, *n.* importancia, *f.*; trascendencia, *f.*

important, *adj.* importante.

importation, *n.* importación, *f.*

importer, *n.* importador, ra.

importing, *adj.* importador; —, *n.* importación, *f.*

importunate, *adj.* importuno; —**ly,** *adv.* importunamente.

importune, *vt.* importunar.

importunity, *n.* importunidad, *f.*

impose, *vt.* imponer; engañar; **to** — **taxes,** imponer contribuciones.

imposer, *n.* imponedor, ra; vividor, ra.

imposing, *adj.* imponente, que infunde respeto; tremendo.

imposition, *n.* imposición, carga, *f.*; impostura, *f.*

impossibility, *n.* imposibilidad, *f.*

impossible, *adj.* imposible; **to seem** —, parecer mentira.

impost, *n.* impuesto, tributo, *m.*, carga, *f.*

impostor, *n.* impostor, ra; prestigiador, ra.

imposture, *n.* impostura, *f.*; engaño, *m.*

impotence, *n.* impotencia, *f.*; incapacidad, *f.*

impotent, *adj.* impotente; incapaz; —**ly,** *adv.* sin poder, impotentemente.

impound, *vt.* encerrar, acorralar; (law) depositar.

impoverish, *vt.* empobrecer.

impoverishment, *n.* empobrecimiento, *m.*

impracticability, *n.* impracticabilidad, *f.*

impracticable, *adj.* impracticable, imposible.

imprecate, *vt.* maldecir.

imprecation, *n.* imprecación, maldición, *f.*

impregnable, *adj.* inexpugnable.

impregnate, *vt.* impregnar; empreñar.

impregnation, *n.* fecundación, *f.*; impregnación, *f.*

impresario, *n.* (theat.) empresario, *m.*

impress, *vt.* imprimir, estampar; —, *n.* impresión, *f.*; empresa, divisa, *f.*

impression, *n.* impresión, *f.*; edición, *f.*

impressionable, *adj.* impresionable, susceptible de recibir impresiones.

impressionism, *n.* impresionismo, *m.*

impressive, *adj.* penetrante; impresionable; imponente; —**ly,** *adv.* de un modo impresionante.

imprint, *vt.* imprimir; estampar; —, *n.* florón, *m.*, impresión, *f.*; huella, *f.*; pie de imprenta.

imprison, *vt.* aprisionar; prender.

imprisonment, *n.* prisión, *f.*, encierro, *m.*

improbability, *n.* improbabilidad, *f.*

improbable, *adj.* improbable; inverosímil, inverisímil.

impromptu, *adj.* extemporáneo; —, *adv.* extemporáneamente.

improper, *adj.* impropio, indecente; —**ly,** *adv.* impropiamente.

impropriety, *n.* impropiedad, incongruencia, *f.*

improve, *vt. and vi.* mejorar, perfeccionar; —, *vi.* progresar.

improved, *adj.* mejorado, perfeccionado.

improvement, *n.* progreso, mejoramiento, perfeccionamiento, *m.*

improvidence, *n.* imprudencia, *f.*, falta de previsión.

improvident, *adj.* impróvido; —**ly,** *adv.* impróvidamente.

improvisation, *n.* improvisación, *f.*

improvise, *vt.* improvisar.

imprudence, *n.* imprudencia, *f.*

imprudent, *adj.* imprudente; —**ly,** *adv.* imprudentemente.

impudence, *n.* impudencia, *f.*, cinismo, *m.*

impudent, *adj.* impudente; —**ly,** *adv.* desvergonzadamente; impúdicamente.

impugn, *vt.* impugnar.

impulse, *n.* impulsión, *f.*, impulso, *m.*; ímpetu, *m.*

impulsion, *n.* impulsión, *f.*, impulso, *m.*

impulsive, *adj.* impulsivo.

impunity, *n.* impunidad, *f.*

impure, *adj.* impuro; impúdico, sucio; —**ly,** *adv.* impuramente.

impurity, *n.* impuridad, impureza, *f.*

imputation, *n.* imputación, *f.*

impute, *vt.* imputar.

in, *prep.* en; por; a; de; mientras; bajo; dentro de; **—,** *adv.* dentro.

in.: inch, *pl.* pulgada; **inches,** plgs. pulgadas.

inability, *n.* inhabilidad, incapacidad, *f.*

inaccessibility, *n.* inaccesibilidad, *f.*

inaccessible, *adj.* inaccesible.

inaccuracy, *n.* inexactitud, incorrección, *f.*

inaccurate, *adj.* inexacto.

inaction, *n.* inacción, holgazanería, *f.*

inactive, *adj.* inactivo; flojo, perezoso, negligente; pasivo.

inactivity, *n.* ociosidad, desidia, inactividad, *f.*

inadequacy, *n.* insuficiencia, *f.*

inadequate, *adj.* inadecuado, defectuoso; imperfecto, insuficiente.

inadmissible, *adj.* inadmisible.

inadvertence, inadvertency, *n.* inadvertencia, imprevisión, *f.*

inadvertent, *adj.* inadvertido; **—ly,** *adv.* inadvertidamente.

inalienable, *adj.* inajenable, inalienable.

inane, *adj.* sandio, tonto.

inanimate, *adj.* inanimado; exánime.

inanition, *n.* inanición, *f.*; impotencia, *f.*

inanity, *n.* vacuidad, *f.*; nulidad, *f.*

inapplicable, *adj.* inaplicable.

inappreciable, *adj.* inapreciable, inestimable.

inappropriate, *adj.* impropio, inadecuado.

inapt, *adj.* inepto, incapaz.

inaptitude, *n.* ineptitud, *f.*

inarticulate, *adj.* inarticulado; **—ly,** *adv.* indistintamente.

inartistic, *adj.* sin arte, falto de gusto artístico.

inasmuch as, visto o puesto que.

inattention, *n.* desatención, *f.*; descuido, *m.*

inattentive, *adj.* desatento, descuidado.

inaudible, *adj.* que no se puede oír; imperceptible.

inaugural, *adj.* inaugural.

inaugurate, *vt.* inaugurar.

inauguration, *n.* inauguración, *f.*

inauspicious, *adj.* malaventurado; desfavorable; **—ly,** *adv.* desgraciadamente.

inboard, *adv.* (naut.) en el buque.

inborn, *adj.* innato, ínsito, ingénito.

inbred, *adj.* innato.

Inc. Incorporated, Inc. Incorporado.

inc.: inclosure, incluso; **including,** incluyendo; **inclusive,** inclusivo; **incorporated,** (com.) constituído en sociedad por acciones; **increase,** aumento.

Inca, *n.* inca, *m.*

incalculable, *adj.* incalculable.

incandescence, *n.* incandescencia, *f.*

incandescent, *adj.* incandescente; **— light,** luz eléctrica incandescente.

incantation, *n.* encantamiento, *m.*

incapability, *n.* incapacidad, *f.*

incapable, *adj.* incapaz, inhábil.

incapacitate, *vt.* incapacitar; inhabilitar, imposibilitar.

incapacitation, *n.* inhabilitación, *f.*

incapacity, *n.* incapacidad, insuficiencia, *f.*; estolidez, *f.*

incarcerate, *vt.* encarcelar, aprisionar.

incarceration, *n.* encarcelación, prisión, *f.*

incarnate, *adj.* encarnado; **—,** *vt.* encarnar, tomar carne.

incarnation, *n.* encarnación, encarnadura, *f.*

incase, *vt.* encajar, incluir.

incautious, *adj.* incauto; **—ly,** *adv.* incautamente.

incendiarism, *n.* incendiarismo, *m.*

incendiary, *n.* and *adj.* incendiario, ria.

incense, *n.* incienso, *m.*; **— stick,** pebete, *m.*; **—,** *vt.* exasperar, irritar, provocar; incensar.

incentive, *n.* incentivo, estímulo, *m.*

inception, *n.* principio, *m.*

inceptive, *adj.* incipiente; (gram.) relativo al comienzo de una acción, estado, etc. (aplícase a un verbo); **—,** *n.* palabra o frase incipiente.

incertitude, *n.* incertidumbre, *f.*

incessant, *adj.* incesante, constante; **—ly,** *adv.* continuamente.

incest, *n.* incesto, *m.*

incestuous, *adj.* incestuoso.

inch, *n.* pulgada, *f.*; **— by —,** palmo a palmo; **—,** *vi.* avanzar o moverse por pulgadas o a pasos muy pequeños.

inchoate, *adj.* incoado.

incidence, *n.* incidencia, *f.*; **— wires,** (aer.) tirantes o alambres de incidencia.

incident, *adj.* incidente; dependiente; **—,** *n.* incidente, *m.*; circunstancia, ocurrencia, *f.*

incidental, *adj.* accidental, casual; contingente; **—ly,** *adv.* incidentemente, por incidencia.

incinerate, *vt.* incinerar.

incineration, *n.* incineración, *f.*

incinerator, *n.* incinerador, *m.*

incipient, *adj.* incipiente.

incise, *vt.* tajar, cortar, grabar.

incision, *n.* incisión, *f.*

incisive, *adj.* incisivo, incisorio.

incisor, *n.* diente incisivo.

incite, *vt.* incitar, estimular.

incitement, *n.* incitación, instigación, *f.*

incivility, *n.* incivilidad, descortesía, *f.*

inclemency, *n.* inclemencia, severidad, *f.*

inclement, *adj.* inclemente.

inclination, *n.* inclinación, propensión, *f.*; declive, *m.*

incline, *vt.* inclinar; **—,** *vi.* inclinarse; **—,** *n.* pendiente, *f.*

inclined, *adj.* inclinado.

inclinometer, *n.* inclinómetro, *m.*

inclose, *vt.* encerrar, incluir.

inclosure, *n.* cercamiento, *m.*; cercado, *m.*

include, *vt.* incluir, comprender.

inclusion, *n.* inclusión, *f.*

inclusive, *adj.* inclusivo; **—ly,** *adv.* inclusivamente.

incog. incognito, incógnito.

incognito, *adj.* and *adv.* de incógnito.
incoherence, *n.* incoherencia, *f.*
incoherency, *n.* incoherencia, *f.*
incoherent, *adj.* incoherente, inconsecuente; **—ly,** *adv.* incongruamente, incoherentemente.
incombustible, *adj.* incombustible.
income, *n.* renta, *f.*, entradas, *f. pl.*; rendimiento, *m.*; **—** tax, impuesto sobre rentas.
incommensurable, *adj.* inconmensurable.
incommensurate, *adj.* desproporcionado.
incommode, *vt.* incomodar; molestar.
incommodious, *adj.* incómodo; molesto.
incommunicable, *adj.* incomunicable.
incommunicado, *adj.* incomunicado.
incomparable, *adj.* incomparable, excelente; **—bly,** *adv.* incomparablemente.
incompatibility, *n.* incompatibilidad, *f.*
incompatible, *adj.* incompatible; opuesto.
incompetence, *n.* incompetencia, *f.*
incompetency, *n.* incompetencia, *f.*
incompetent, *adj.* incompetente; **—ly,** *adv.* incompetentemente.
incomplete, *adj.* incompleto, falto, imperfecto.
incompletely, *adv.* incompletamente.
incomprehensibility, *n.* incomprensibilidad, *f.*
incomprehensible, *adj.* incomprensible.
incompressible, *adj.* incompresible.
inconceivable, *adj.* incomprensible, inconcebible.
inconclusive, *adj.* no concluyente; sin conclusión; **—ly,** *adv.* en forma no convincente.
incongruity, *n.* incongruencia, incongruidad, *f.*
incongruous, *adj.* incongruo; **—ly,** *adv.* incongruamente.
inconsequential, *adj.* inconsecuente.
inconsiderable, *adj.* frívolo, poco considerable.
inconsiderate, *adj.* inconsiderado; **—ly,** *adv.* inconsideradamente.
inconsistency, *n.* inconsistencia, *f.*; incompatibilidad, incongruencia, *f.*
inconsistent, *adj.* inconsistente; **—ly,** *adv.* incongruamente.
inconsolable, *adj.* inconsolable.
inconspicuous, *adj.* no conspicuo, que pasa desapercibido.
inconstancy, *n.* inconstancia, *f.*
inconstant, *adj.* inconstante, voluble.
incontestable, *adj.* incontestable, incontrastable; **—bly,** *adv.* incontestablemente.
incontinence, *n.* incontinencia, *f.*
incontinent, *adj.* incontinente; **—ly,** *adv.* incontinentemente.
incontrovertible, *adj.* incontrovertible.
inconvenience, *n.* inconveniencia, incomodidad, *f.*; **—,** *vt.* incomodar.
inconvenient, *adj.* incómodo, inconveniente; **—ly,** *adv.* incómodamente.
inconvertible, *adj.* inconvertible.

incorporate, *vt.* incorporar; **—,** *vi.* incorporarse; **—,** *adj.* incorporado.
incorporation, *n.* incorporación, *f.*
incorporeal, *adj.* incorpóreo, incorporal.
incorrect,· *adj.* incorrecto; **—ly,** *adv.* de un modo incorrecto.
incorrigible, *adj.* incorregible.
incorruptibility, *n.* incorruptibilidad, *f.*
incorruptible, *adj.* incorruptible.
increase, *vt.* acrecentar, aumentar; **—,** *vi.* crecer, aumentarse; **—,** *n.* aumento, acrecentamiento, *m.*
increasing, *adj.* creciente.
incredibility, *n.* incredibilidad, *f.*
incredible, *adj.* increíble; **—bly,** *adv.* increíblemente.
incredulity, *n.* incredulidad, *f.*
incredulous, *adj.* incrédulo.
increment, *n.* incremento, *m.*
incriminate, *vt.* acriminar, acusar de algún crimen.
incriminatory, *adj.* incriminatorio.
incrust, *vt.* incrustar.
incrustation, *n.* incrustación, *f.*
incubate, *vi.* empollar, incubar.
incubation, *n.* incubación, empolladura, *f.*
incubator, *n.* horno para empollar, incubadora, *f.*, empollador, *m.*
incubus, *n.* íncubo, *m.*; (med.) pesadilla, *f.*
inculcate, *vt.* inculcar.
inculcation, *n.* inculcación, *f.*
inculpate, *vt.* inculpar.
incumbency, *n.* incumbencia, *f.*; posesión de un beneficio eclesiástico.
incumbent, *adj.* echado; obligatorio; **to be — on,** competer, incumbir; **—,** *n.* beneficiado, da.
incur, *vt.* incurrir; ocurrir.
incurability, *n.* incurabilidad, *f.*, estado incurable.
incurable, *adj.* incurable; **—bly,** *adv.* de un modo incurable.
incursion, *n.* incursión, invasión, *f.*; correría, *f.*
Ind.: **Indiana,** Indiana; **Indian,** indio.
ind.: **independent,** independiente; **indicative,** ind. indicativo; **industrial,** industrial.
indebted, *adj.* endeudado, empeñado, obligado.
indebtedness, *n.*· deuda, obligación, *f.*; pasivo, *m.*
indecency, *n.* indecencia, *f.*
indecent, *adj.* indecente; **—ly,** *adv.* indecentemente.
indecision, *n.* irresolución, indecisión, *f.*
indecisive, *adj.* indeciso.
indeclinable, *adj.* indeclinable.
indecorous, *adj.* indecoroso, indecente.
indecorum, *n.* indecoro, *m.*
indeed, *adv.* verdaderamente, de veras; sí; **no —!** de ninguna manera, ¡quia!
indef. **indefinite,** indef. indefinido.
indefatigable, *adj.* infatigable.
indefensible, *adj.* indefendible.

indefinable, *adj.* indefinible.
indefinite, *adj.* indefinido, indeterminado; **—ly,** *adv.* indefinidamente.
indelible, *adj.* indeleble; **—bly,** *adv.* indeleblemente.
indelicacy, *n.* falta de delicadeza, grosería, indecencia, *f.*
indelicate, *adj.* poco delicado, grosero.
indemnification, *n.* indemnización, *f.*; resarcimiento de daño.
indemnify, *vt.* indemnizar; (law) sanear.
indemnity, *n.* indemnidad, *f.*; **— bond,** contrafianza, *f.*
indent, *vt.* dentar; dar mayor margen.
indentation, *n.* mella, muesca, *f.*; mayor margen.
indented, *adj.* dentado.
indention, *n.* mella, sangría, *f.*
indenture, *n.* escritura, *f.*; contrato de un aprendiz.
independence, *n.* independencia, *f.*
independent, *adj.* independiente; **—ly,** *adv.* independientemente.
indescribable, *adj.* indescriptible.
indestructible, *adj.* indestructible.
indeterminate, *adj.* indeterminado; **—ly,** *adv.* indeterminadamente.
index, *n.* indicador, *m.*; índice, elenco, *m.*; (math.) exponente, *m.*; tabla de un libro, tabla de materias; **— finger,** dedo índice; **—,** *vt.* arreglar por orden alfabético.
India, *n.* India, *f.*; **— ink,** tinta china; **— paper,** papel de China; **— rubber,** goma elástica.
Indiaman, *n.* nave índica.
Indian, *n.* and *adj.* indiano, na; indio, dia; **— summer,** verano tardío; **— file,** en desfilada, en hilera, uno por uno.
indicate, *vt.* indicar.
indication, *n.* indicación, *f.*; indicio, *m.*; señal, *f.*
indicative, *n.* (gram.) indicativo, *m.*; **—,** *adj.* indicativo.
indicator, *n.* indicador, apuntador, *m.*; **bank —,** (aer.) indicador de viraje.
indict, *vt.* procesar.
indictment, *n.* acusación ante el jurado, denuncia, *f.*
Indies, las Indias, *f. pl.*
indifference, *n.* indiferencia, apatía, *f.*
indifferent, *adj.* indiferente; **—ly,** *adv.* indiferentemente.
indigence, *n.* indigencia, pobreza, *f.*
indigenous, *adj.* indígena.
indigent, *adj.* indigente, pobre.
indigestible, *adj.* indigestible.
indigestion, *n.* indigestión, *f.*
indignant, *adj.* airado, indignado.
indignation, *n.* indignación, *f.*; despecho, *m.*
indignity, *n.* indignidad, *f.*
indigo, *n.* añil, *m.*
indirect, *adj.* indirecto; **—ly,** *adv.* indirectamente, de rebote.
indirection, *n.* rodeo, *m.*; indirecta, *f.*
indiscreet, *adj.* indiscreto, inconsiderado;

—ly, *adv.* indiscretamente.
indiscretion, *n.* indiscreción, imprudencia, inconsideración, *f.*
indiscriminate, *adj.* indistinto; **—ly,** *adv.* sin distinción, sin discriminación.
indispensability, *n.* indispensabilidad, *f.*
indispensable, *adj.* indispensable, imprescindible; **—bly,** *adv.* indispensablemente.
indispose, *vt.* indisponer.
indisposed, *adj.* indispuesto, achacoso.
indisposition, *n.* indisposición, *f.*, malestar, *m.*; mala gana.
indisputable, *adj.* indisputable; **—bly,** *adv.* indisputablemente.
indissoluble, *adj.* indisoluble.
indistinct, *adj.* indistinto, confuso; borroso; **—ly,** *adv.* indistintamente.
indistinguishable, *adj.* indistinguible.
indite, *vt.* redactar.
individual, *adj.* individual, individuo; **—,** *n.* individuo, *m.*; **—ly,** *adv.* individualmente.
individuality, *n.* individualidad, *f.*
individualize, *vt.* individualizar.
indivisible, *adj.* indivisible; **—bly,** *adv.* indivisiblemente.
indoctrinate, *vt.* doctrinar.
indolence, *n.* indolencia, pereza, *f.*
indolent, *adj.* indolente; desidioso; **—ly,** *adv.* indolentemente, con negligencia.
indomitable, *adj.* indomable.
indoor, *adj.* interior, de puertas adentro; **—s,** *adv.* bajo techo.
indorse, *vt.* endosar una letra, un vale u otro documento.
indorsee, *n.* endosatario, ria, cesionario, ria.
indorsement, *n.* endorso, endoso, *m.*
indorser, *n.* (com.) endosante (de un giro), *m. y f.*
indrawn, *adj.* aspirado, inhalado.
indubitable, *adj.* indubitable, indudable; **—bly,** *adv.* indubitablemente.
induce, *vt.* inducir, persuadir; causar.
inducement, *n.* motivo, móvil, aliciente, *m.*
induct, *vt.* instalar, iniciar.
inductance, *n.* inductancia, *f.*, coeficiente de autoinducción.
induction, *n.* inducción, deducción, *f.*; ilación, *f.*; **— coil,** carrete de inducción, bobina de inducción.
inductive, *adj.* inductivo; ilativo.
inductor, *n.* inductor, instalador, *m.*
indulge, *vt.* and *vi.* favorecer; conceder; ser indulgente; **to — in,** entregarse a.
indulgence, *n.* indulgencia, *f.*, mimo, *m.*
indulgent, *adj.* indulgente; **—ly,** *adv.* de un modo indulgente.
induration, *n.* endurecimiento, *m.*; dureza de corazón.
industrial, *adj.* industrial.
industrialist, *n.* industrialista, *m.*
industrialism, *n.* industrialismo, *m.*
industrious, *adj.* industrioso, hacendoso; trabajador, laborioso; **—ly,** *adv.* industriosamente.

industry, *n.* industria, *f.*
inebriate, *vt.* embriagar.
inebriation, *n.* embriaguez, *f.*
ineffable, *adj.* inefable.
ineffective, *adj.* ineficaz; —**ly,** *adv.* ineficazmente.
ineffectual, *adj.* ineficaz.
ineffcacious, *adj.* ineficaz.
inefficacy, *n.* ineficacia, *f.*
inefficiency, *n.* ineficacia, *f.*
inefficient, *adj.* ineficaz.
inelegant, *adj.* inelegante; sin pulimento.
ineligibility, *n.* ineligibilidad, *f.*, calidad que excluye elección.
ineligible, *adj.* no eligible, que no llena los requisitos para algún puesto.
inept, *adj.* inepto.
ineptitude, *n.* ineptitud, *f.*
inequality, *n.* desigualdad, disparidad, diferencia, *f.*
inequitable, *adj.* injusto.
inert, *adj.* inerte, perezoso; —**ly,** *adv.* indolentemente.
inertia, *n.* inercia, *f.*
inescapable, *adj.* ineludible.
inestimable, *adj.* inestimable, inapreciable.
inevitability, *n.* calidad de inevitable.
inevitable, *adj.* inevitable, fatal, sin remedio; —**bly,** *adv.* inevitablemente.
inexcusable, *adj.* inexcusable; —**bly,** *adv.* inexcusablemente.
inexhaustible, *adj.* inexhausto, inagotable.
inexorable, *adj.* inexorable, inflexible, duro; inconmovible; —**bly,** *adv.* inexorablemente.
inexpediency, *n.* inconveniencia, *f.*, falta de oportunidad.
inexpedient, *adj.* impropio.
inexpensive, *adj.* de poco costo, barato.
inexperience, *n.* inexperiencia, impericia, *f.*
inexperienced, *adj.* inexperto, bisoño, sin experiencia, novel.
inexplicable, *adj.* inexplicable.
inexplosive, *adj.* inexplosible.
inexpressible, *adj.* indecible.
inextricable, *adj.* intrincado; enmarañado.
Inf. Infantry, inf. infantería.
inf.: infinitive, inf. infinitivo; **infantry,** inf. infantería.
infallibility, *n.* infalibilidad, *f.*
infallible, *adj.* infalible; —**bly,** *adv.* infaliblemente.
infamous, *adj.* vil, infame; —**ly,** *adv.* infamemente.
infamy, *n.* infamia, *f.*, oprobio, *m.*
infancy, *n.* infancia, *f.*
infant, *n.* infante, *m.*; niño, ña.
infanticide, *n.* infanticidio, *m.*; infanticida, *m.* y *f.*
infantile, *adj.* pueril, infantil; — **paralysis,** (med.) parálisis infantil.
infantine, *adj.* = **infantile.**
infantry, *n.* infantería, *f.*
infatuate, *vt.* infatuar, embobar; fascinar.
infatuation, *n.* infatuación, *f.*

infect, *vt.* infectar.
infection, *n.* infección, *f.*
infectious, *adj.* infeccioso: contagioso; —**ly,** *adv.* por infección.
infelicity, *n.* infelicidad, *f.*
infer, *vt.* inferir, deducir, colegir.
inferable, *adj.* = **inferrible.**
inference, *n.* inferencia, ilación, *f.*; conclusión lógica, deducción, *f.*
inferential, *adj.* ilativo.
inferior, *adj.* inferior; **of — quality,** (coll.) de pacotilla, de calidad inferior; —, *n.* oficial subordinado; persona inferior a otra.
inferiority, *n.* inferioridad, *f.*; — **complex,** complejo de inferioridad.
infernal, *adj.* infernal.
inferrible, *adj.* deducible; **to be —,** traslucirse.
infest, *vt.* infestar.
infestation, *n.* infestación, *f.*
infidel, *n.* infiel, *m.* y *f.*; pagano, na.
infidelity, *n.* infidelidad, *f.*; perfidia, *f.*
infield, *n.* (baseball) parte del rombal de baseball en frente del *batter* controlada por los *infielders.*
infielder, *n.* (baseball) jugador colocado dentro o muy cerca del rombal en frente del *batter.*
infighting, *n.* (boxeo) lucha de cuerpo a cuerpo.
infiltrate, *vi.* infiltrarse, penetrar.
infiltration, *n.* infiltración, *f.*
infinite, *adj.* infinito, innumerable; —**ly,** *adv.* infinitamente.
infinitesimal, *adj.* infinitesimal.
infinitive, *n.* infinitivo, *m.*
infinitude, infinity, *n.* infinidad, *f.*
infirm, *adj.* enfermo, débil.
infirmary, *n.* enfermería, *f.*
infirmity, *n.* fragilidad, enfermedad, *f.*
inflame, *vt.* inflamar; —, *vi.* inflamarse.
inflamed, *adj.* encendido.
inflammable, *adj.* inflamable.
inflammation, *n.* inflamación, *f.*, encendimiento, *m.*
inflammatory, *adj.* inflamatorio.
inflate, *vt.* inflar, hinchar.
inflation, *n.* inflación, *f.*; hinchazón, *f.*
inflection, *n.* inflexión, *f.*, modulación de la voz.
inflectional, *adj.* con inflexiones.
inflexibility, *n.* inflexibilidad, *f.*
inflexible, *adj.* inmoble, inflexible; —**bly,** *adv.* inflexiblemente.
inflict, *vt.* castigar; infligir (penas corporales, etc.).
infliction, *n.* imposición de una pena.
inflow, *n.* flujo, *m.*, afluencia, *f.*; entrada, *f.*
influence, *n.* influencia, *f.*; —, *vt.* influir; **to — by suggestion,** sugestionar.
influential, *adj.* influyente.
influenza, *n.* (med.) influenza, gripe, *f.*, trancazo, *m.*
influx, *n.* influjo, *m.*; afluencia, *f.*; desembocadura, *f.*

infold, *vt.* envolver, abrazar.

inform, *vt.* informar, poner en conocimiento; hacer saber, enseñar, poner al corriente, dar razón de; **to — oneself,** enterarse.

informal, *adj.* íntimo, sin formulismos, de confianza; irregular.

informality, *n.* sencillez, intimidad, *f.,* ausencia de formulismos.

informant, *n.* denunciador, ra; informante, *m.* y *f.,* informador, ra.

information, *n.* información, instrucción, *f.;* informe, *m.;* aviso, *m.;* luz, *f.;* — **bureau,** oficina de información.

informed, *adj.* sabedor, bien informado.

informer, *n.* informante, delator, *m.*

infraction, *n.* infracción, violación, *f.*

infrared, *adj.* infrarrojo.

infrequent, *adj.* raro, insólito; **—ly,** *adv.* raramente.

infringe, *vt.* violar (una ley o pacto); contravenir, infringir.

infringement, *n.* violación, infracción, *f.*

infuriate, *vt.* irritar, provocar, enfurecer; sacar de sus casillas.

infuse, *vt.* infundir; vaciar, verter.

infusion, *n.* infusión, *f.*

ingathering, *n.* cosecha, *f.*

ingenious, *adj.* ingenioso; vivo; **—ly,** *adv.* ingeniosamente.

ingenuity, *n.* ingeniosidad, inventiva, *f.;* ingenuidad, *f.;* destreza, *f.*

ingenuous, *adj.* ingenuo, sincero; noble, honorable; **—ly,** *adv.* ingenuamente.

ingle, *n.* llama, llamarada, *f.;* hogar, *m.,* chimenea, *f.*

inglorious, *adj.* ignominioso, vergonzoso; **—ly,** *adv.* ignominiosamente.

ingoing, *adj.* entrante.

ingot, *n.* lingote, *m.,* barra de metal (sin labrar).

ingraft, *vt.* injertar.

ingrained, *adj.* teñido en rama; impregnado.

ingrate, *n.* ingrato, ta.

ingratiate, *vi.* insinuarse; congraciarse.

ingratitude, *n.* ingratitud, *f.*

ingredient, *n.* ingrediente, *m.*

ingress, *n.* entrada, *f.,* ingreso, *m.*

ingrowing, *adj.* que crece hacia dentro.

ingrown, *adj.* crecido hacia dentro; — **nail,** uñero, *m.*

ingulf, *vt.* engolfar, tragar, sumir.

inhabit, *vt.* habitar, ocupar.

inhabitable, *adj.* habitable.

inhabitant, *n.* habitador, ra, habitante, residente, *m.* y *f.*

inhalation, *n.* inhalación, *f.*

inhale, *vt.* aspirar, inhalar.

inhaler, *n.* inhalador, *m.*

inharmonious, *adj.* disonante, discordante.

inhere, *vi.* ser inherente.

inherent, *adj.* inherente; **—ly,** *adv.* inherentemente.

inherit, *vt.* heredar.

inheritable, *adj.* heredable.

inheritance, *n.* herencia, *f.;* patrimonio, *m.;*

— **tax,** contribución o impuesto sobre herencia.

inheritor, *n.* heredero, *m.*

inhibit, *vt.* inhibir, prohibir.

inhibition, *n.* inhibición, prohibición, *f.*

inhospitable, *adj.* inhospitalario, inhospitable.

inhospitality, *n.* inhospitalidad, *f.*

inhuman, *adj.* inhumano, cruel; **—ly,** *adv.* inhumanamente.

inhumanity, *n.* inhumanidad, crueldad, *f.*

inimical, *adj.* enemigo, hostil; adverso, opuesto.

inimitable, *adj.* inimitable.

iniquitous, *adj.* inicuo, injusto.

iniquity, *n.* iniquidad, injusticia, *f.*

initial, *adj.* inicial; **—,** *n.* letra inicial.

initiate, *vt.* principiar, iniciar.

initiation, *n.* principio, *m.;* iniciación, *f.*

initiative, *adj.* iniciativo; **—,** *n.* iniciativa, *f.*

initiatory, *adj.* iniciativo.

inject, *vt.* inyectar.

injection, *n.* inyección, *f.;* (med.) clister, *m.*

injudicious, *adj.* poco juicioso, indiscreto, imprudente; **—ly,** *adv.* sin juicio.

injunction, *n.* mandato, entredicho, *m.*

injure, *vt.* injuriar, ofender; hacer daño; lastimar.

injured, *adj.* lesionado.

injurious, *adj.* injurioso, injusto; perjudicial, nocivo; **—ly,** *adv.* injuriosamente.

injury, *n.* injuria, afrenta, sinrazón, ofensa, *f.;* mal, *m.,* perjuicio, *m.;* daño, *m.*

injustice, *n.* injusticia, *f.;* agravio, *m.*

ink, *n.* tinta, *f.;* **India** —, tinta china; **invisible** —, tinta simpática; **printer's** —, tinta de imprenta; —, *vt.* linear con tinta.

inkhorn, *n.* tintero pequeño; —, *adj.* pedante.

inkling, *n.* insinuación, *f.,* noción vaga.

inkpad, *n.* cojín entintado.

inkstand, *n.* tintero, *m.*

inkwell, *n.* = **inkstand.**

inky, *adj.* de tinta; semejante a la tinta.

inlaid, *adj.* ataraceado; **— work,** embutido, encaje, *m.,* taracea, *f.*

inland, *n.* parte interior de un país; —, *adj.* interior; —, *adv.* dentro de un país.

inlay, *vt.* ataracear; —, *n.* ataracea, *f.;* relleno (en un diente), *m.;* **gold** —, orificación (en un diente), *f.*

inlet, *n.* entrada, *f.;* cala, ensenada, *f.*

inmate, *n.* inquilino, na; ocupante; preso, *m.*

inmost, *adj.* íntimo, muy interior.

inn, *n.* posada, *f.;* mesón, *m.*

innate, *adj.* innato, natural, ínsito.

inner, *adj.* interior; **— tube,** cámara de aire, cámara aérea.

innermost, *adj.* íntimo, muy interior.

inning, *n.* (en juegos) mano, *f.;* mano del partido en mando en un gobierno; mano en mando; **—s,** *pl.* tierras aluviales cerradas en diques.

innkeeper, *n.* posadero, mesonero, *m.*

innocence, *n.* inocencia, *f.*

innocent, *adj.* inocente; **—ly,** *adv.* inocentemente.

innocuous, *adj.* innocuo, inocente; **—ly,** *adv.* inocentemente.

innovate, *vt.* innovar.

innovation, *n.* innovación, *f.*

innovator, *n.* innovador.

innuendo, *n.* indirecta, insinuación, *f.*

innumerable, *adj.* innumerable.

inoculate, *vt.* inocular; injertar.

inoculation, *n.* inoculación, *f.*

inoffensive, *adj.* pacífico; inofensivo.

inopportune, *adj.* inconveniente, inoportuno.

inordinate, *adj.* desordenado; excesivo; **—ly,** *adv.* desordenadamente.

inorganic, *adj.* inorgánico.

input, *n.* (mech.) fuerza necesaria para una máquina; dinero contribuído.

inquest, *n.* pesquisa, indagación, *f.*

inquire, *vt.* preguntar (alguna cosa); **—,** *vi.* inquirir, examinar.

inquirer, *n.* averiguador, ra, investigador, ra, preguntador, ra.

inquiry, *n.* interrogación, pregunta, *f.*; investigación, *f.*; pesquisa, *f.*

inquisition, *n.* inquisición, *f.*; escudriñamiento, *m.*

inquisitive, *adj.* curioso, preguntón; **—ly,** *adv.* en forma inquiridora.

inquisitiveness, *n.* curiosidad, *f.*

inquisitor, *n.* juez pesquisidor; inquisidor, *m.*

inroad, *n.* incursión, invasión, *f.*

ins. insurance, seguro.

insane, *adj.* insano, loco, demente; **— asylum,** casa de locos, manicomio, *m.*; **to go —,** perder la razón.

insanity, *n.* insania, locura, *f.*

insatiable, *adj.* insaciable.

inscribe, *vt.* inscribir; dedicar; grabar.

inscription, *n.* inscripción, letra, leyenda, *f.*; letrero, *m.*; dedicatoria, *f.*

inscrutable, *adj.* inescrutable.

insect, *n.* insecto, bicho, *m.*; **— killer, — poison,** insecticida, *m.*; **— powder,** polvos insecticidas.

insecticide, *n.* insecticida, *m.*

insecure, *adj.* inseguro.

insecurity, *n.* inseguridad, *f.*; incertidumbre, *f.*

insensate, *adj.* insensato.

insensibility, *n.* insensibilidad, *f.*; estupidez, *f.*

insensible, *adj.* insensible; imperceptible; **—bly,** *adv.* insensiblemente.

inseparability, *n.* inseparabilidad, *f.*

inseparable, *adj.* inseparable; **—bly,** *adv.* inseparablemente.

insert, *vt.* insertar, ingerir una cosa en otra, meter.

insertion, *n.* inserción, *f.*

inset, *vt.* injertar, plantar, fijar; grabar; **—,** *n.* hoja intercalada en un libro; carta geográfica o lámina dentro de una más grande; intercalación, *f.*

inshore, *adj.* cerca de la orilla; **—,** *adv.* hacia la orilla.

inside, *n.* and *adj.* interior, *m.*; **—s,** (coll.) entrañas, *f. pl.*; **on the —,** por dentro; **toward the —,** hacia dentro; **—,** *adv.* adentro, dentro; **— of,** dentro de; **— out,** al revés.

insider, *n.* persona que posee información de primera mano.

insidious, *adj.* insidioso; **—ly,** *adv.* insidiosamente.

insight, *n.* conocimiento profundo; perspicacia, *f.*

insignia, *n. pl.* insignias, *f. pl.*; estandartes, *m. pl.*

insignificance, *n.* insignificancia, *f.*; nulidad, *f.*

insignificant, *adj.* insignificante; trivial; **to be —,** ser un cero a la izquierda; **—ly,** *adv.* insignificantemente.

insincere, *adj.* poco sincero, hipócrita.

insincerity, *n.* falta de sinceridad.

insinuate, *vt.* insinuar; **—,** *vi.* congraciarse.

insinuation, *n.* insinuación, *f.*

insipid, *adj.* insípido; insulso; **—ly,** *adv.* insulsamente.

insipidity, *n.* insipidez, insulsez, *f.*

insist, *vi.* insistir, persistir, hacer hincapié.

insistence, *n.* insistencia, *f.*

insistent, *adj.* insistente, persistente.

insolation, *n.* insolación, *f.,* irradiación solar.

insole, *n.* plantilla, *f.*

insolence, *n.* insolencia, *f.*

insolent, *adj.* insolente; **—ly,** *adv.* insolentemente.

insoluble, *adj.* insoluble, indisoluble.

insolvency, *n.* insolvencia, *f.*

insolvent, *adj.* insolvente.

insomnia, *n.* insomnio, *m.*

insomuch, *adv.* de manera que.

inspect, *vt.* reconocer, examinar, inspeccionar.

inspection, *n.* inspección, *f.,* registro, *m.*; (com.) acto de reconocimiento; **tour of —,** requisa, *f.,* jira de inspección.

inspector, *n.* inspector, superintendente, *m.,* registrador, ra; **— of weights and measures,** potador; ra.

inspiration, *n.* inspiración, *f.*; numen, *m.*

inspire, *vt.* inspirar (el aire); inspirar, sugerir.

inspirit, *vt.* alentar, animar; dar vigor.

Inst.: Institute, Inst. instituto; **Institution,** institución.

inst. instant, corr.^te corriente (mes).

instability, *n.* instabilidad, inconstancia, *f.*

install, *vt.* instalar.

installation, *n.* instalación, *f.*

installment, instalment, *n.* instalación, *f.*; pago parcial, plazo, *m.*; entrega, *f.*; **monthly —,** mensualidad, *f.*

instance, n. instancia, f.; ejemplo, caso, m.; instigación, f.; sugestión, f.; **for —,** por ejemplo; **—,** vt. citar ejemplos.

instant, adj. instante, urgente; presente; **the 20th —,** el 20 del presente; **—ly,** adv. en un instante; al punto; **—,** n. instante, momento, m.

instantaneous, adj. instantáneo; **—ly,** adv. instantáneamente.

instead, adv. en lugar de, en vez de.

instep, n. empeine del pie.

instigate, vt. instigar, mover.

instigation, n. instigación, sugestión, f.; provocación a hacer daño.

instigator, n. instigador, ra.

instill, instil, vt. inculcar, infundir, insinuar.

instinct, n. instinto, m.; **—,** adj. animado, impulsado; lleno, cargado.

instinctive, adj. instintivo; **—ly,** adv. por instinto.

institute, vt. instituir, establecer; **—,** n. instituto, m.; principio, m.

institution, n. institución, f.

institutional, adj. institucional.

instruct, vt. instruir, enseñar.

instruction, n. instrucción, enseñanza, f.

instructive, adj. instructivo.

instructor, n. instructor, m.

instrument, n. instrumento, m.; contrato, m., escritura, f.; **— board,** tablero de instrumentos; **—s and supplies of war,** pertrechos, m.pl.

instrumental, adj. instrumental.

instrumentation, n. instrumentación, f.

insubordinate, adj. insubordinado.

insubordination, n. insubordinación, f.

insufferable, adj. insufrible, insoportable; **—ly,** adv. inaguantablemente, de un modo insoportable.

insufficient, adj. insuficiente; **— evidence,** semiplena, f.; **—ly,** adv. insuficientemente.

insular, adj. insular, isleño.

insularity, n. insularidad, f., estrechez de miras.

insulate, vt. aislar (las corrientes eléctricas).

insulating, adj. (elec.) aislante.

insulation, n. (elec.) aislamiento, m.

insulator, n. (elec.) aislador, m.

insulin, n. insulina, f.

insult, vt. insultar; **—,** n. insulto, m.

insulting, adj. insultante; **—ly,** adv. con insultos, con insolencia.

insuperable, adj. insuperable; **—bly,** adv. invenciblemente.

insupportable, adj. insoportable, inaguantable; **—bly,** adv. intolerablemente, insoportablemente.

insurable, adj. asegurable.

insurance, n. (com.) seguro, m., seguridad, f.; **accident —,** seguro contra accidente; **burglary —,** seguro contra robo; **fire —,** seguro contra fuego o incendio; **— agent,** agente de seguros; **— broker,** corredor de seguros; **— policy,** póliza de seguro; **—**

premium, prima de seguro; **life —,** seguro de vida; **life — company,** compañía de seguros.

insure, vt. asegurar.

insurer, n. asegurador, m.

insurgence, n. insurgencia, f.

insurgent, n. and adj. insurgente, insurrecto, rebelde, m.

insurmountable, adj. insuperable.

insurrection, n. insurrección, sedición, f.

insusceptible, adj. no susceptible.

int.: interest, int. interés; **interior,** interior; **international,** int. internacional; **intransitive,** intrans. intransitivo.

intact, adj. intacto, entero.

intake, n. acceso de aire; orificio de entrada o acceso de agua; rigola, f., canal de alimentación; (min.) aereación, f.; válvula de aspiración; cosa tomada o cantidad de ella (como energía eléctrica); **— manifold,** válvula múltiple de admisión.

intangible, adj. intangible; **—bly,** adv. intangiblemente.

integer, n. número entero.

integral, adj. íntegro; (chem.) integrante; **—ly,** adv. integralmente; **—,** n. todo, m.

integrate, vt. integrar.

integration, n. integración, f.

integrity, n. integridad, f.; pureza, f.

integument, n. integumento, m.

intellect, n. entendimiento, intelecto, m.

intellectual, n. intelectual, m. y f.; **—,** adj. intelectual, mental; **—ly,** adv. intelectualmente.

intelligence, n. inteligencia, f.; conocimiento, m.; correspondencia, f.; concierto, m.; **— test,** examen de inteligencia.

intelligent, adj. inteligente; **—ly,** adv. inteligentemente.

intelligentsia, n. círculo de los intelectuales.

intelligibility, n. comprensibilidad, f.

intelligible, adj. inteligible; **—ly,** adv. inteligiblemente.

intemperance, n. intemperancia, f.

intemperate, adj. destemplado; inmoderado; **—ly,** adv. destempladamente; inmoderadamente.

intend, vt. intentar; **—,** vi. proponerse; **to — (to go, to do, etc.)** pensar (ir, hacer, etc.).

intendant, n. intendente, m.

intense, adj. intenso; vehemente; **—ly,** adv. intensamente.

intensification, n. intensificación, f.

intensify, vt. intensificar, hacer más intenso.

intensity, n. intensidad, f.

intensive, adj. completo, concentrado; **— study,** estudio completo; **— bombing,** bombardeo concentrado.

intent, adj. atento, cuidadoso; **—ly,** adv. con aplicación; **—,** n. intento, designio, m.

intention, n. intención, f.; designio, m.; (fig.) mira, f.

intentional, *adj.* intencional; **—ly,** *adv.* de intento.

inter, *vt.* enterrar, soterrar.

interact, *vi.* obrar recíprocamente.

interbreed, *vt.* and *vi.* producir híbridos.

intercede, *vi.* interceder, mediar.

intercept, *vt.* interceptar; impedir.

interception, *n.* intercepción, *f.*

interceptor, *n.* interceptor, *m.*

intercession, *n.* intercesión, mediación, *f.*

intercessor, *n.* intercesor, mediador, *m.*

interchange, *vt.* alternar, trocar; **—,** *n.* comercio, *m.*; canje, intercambio, *m.*

interchangeable, *adj.* intercambiable.

intercollegiate, *adj.* interescolar, interuniversitario.

intercommunicate, *vi.* comunicarse mutuamente.

intercommunication, *n.* comunicación mutua.

intercostal, *adj.* intercostal.

intercourse, *n.* comercio, *m.*; comunicación, *f.*; coito, *m.*, contacto carnal.

interdenominational, *adj.* intersectario.

interdepartmental, *adj.* entre departamentos.

interdependence, *n.* dependencia mutua.

interdict, *n.* entredicho, *m.*; **—,** *vt.* interdecir, prohibir.

interest, *vt.* interesar; empeñar; **—,** *n.* interés, provecho, *m.*; influjo, empeño, *m.*; **compound —,** interés compuesto; **rate of —,** tipo de interés; **simple —,** interés simple.

interested, *adj.* interesado.

interesting, *adj.* interesante, atractivo.

interfere, *vi.* entremeterse, ingerirse, mezclarse; intervenir.

interference, *n.* interposición, mediación, ingerencia, *f.*; (rad.) interferencias estáticas.

interfuse, *vt.* mezclar, fundir.

interim, *n.* intermedio, *m.*; **ad —,** entre tanto; en el ínterim.

interior, *adj.* interior, interno.

interj. interjection, interj. interjección.

interject, *vt.* interponer.

interjection, *n.* (gram.) interjección, *f.*

interlace, *vt.* entretejer, entrelazar.

interlard, *vt.* mechar; interpolar, insertar.

interleave, *vt.* interpolar hojas blancas entre las impresas de un libro.

interline, *vt.* interlinear, entrerrenglonar; entretelar.

interlinear, *adj.* interlineal.

interlineation, *n.* interlineación, *f.*

interlining, *n.* entretela, *f.*

interlink, *vt.* eslabonar.

interlock, *vt.* and *vi.* trabar, trabarse, engranar.

interlocutor, *n.* interlocutor, ra.

interlocutory, *adj.* interlocutorio.

interloper, *n.* entremetido, da, intruso, sa; contrabandista, *m.* y *f.*

interlude, *n.* intermedio, *m.*

intermarriage, *n.* casamiento entre los miembros de dos familias, razas, etc.

intermarry, *vi.* unirse por casamiento distintas familias o razas; mezclarse.

intermeddle, *vi.* meterse, ingerirse, injerirse.

intermediary, *adj.* intermediario; **—,** *n.* intermediario, ria.

intermediate, *adj.* intermedio; **—,** *n.* intermediario, ria.

interment, *n.* entierro, *m.*; sepultura, *f.*

intermezzo, *n.* intermezzo, intermedio, *m.*

interminable, *adj.* interminable, ilimitado.

intermingle, *vt.* and *vi.* entremezclar; mezclarse.

intermission, *n.* intermedio, *m.*, intermisión, *f.*

intermit, *vt.* intermitir; **—,** *vi.* descontinuar, cesar.

intermittent, *adj.* intermitente.

intern, *vt.* internar; encerrar; **—,** *n.* (med.) practicante, *m.*

internal, *adj.* interno; **—ly,** *adv.* internamente.

internal-combustion engine, *n.* motor de combustión interna.

international, *adj.* internacional.

internationalism, *n.* internacionalismo, *m.*

internecine, *adj.* intestino, interno.

internment, *n.* encerramiento, *m.*, concentración, *f.*

internship, *n.* práctica que como médicos residentes hacen los postgraduados en un hospital.

interpellate, *vt.* interpelar.

interpellation, *n.* interpelación, *f.*

interplanetary, *adj.* interplanetario.

interplay, *n.* acción o efecto recíproco o de contraste.

interpolate, *vt.* interpolar.

interpolation, *n.* interpolación, *f.*

interpose, *vt.* interponer, entreponer; **—,** *vi.* interponerse.

interposition, *n.* interposición, *f.*

interpret, *vt.* interpretar.

interpretation, *n.* interpretación, *f.*; versión, *f.*

interpretative, *adj.* interpretativo.

interpreter, *n.* intérprete, *m.* y *f.*

interracial, *adj.* entre razas.

interregnum, *n.* interregno, *m.*

interrelated, *adj.* con relación recíproca.

interrogate, *vt.* interrogar, examinar.

interrogation, *n.* interrogación, pregunta, *f.*

interrogative, *adj.* interrogativo.

interrogator, *n.* interrogante, *m.* y *f.*

interrogatory, *adj.* interrogativo.

interrupt, *vt.* interrumpir, romper.

interruption, *n.* interrupción, *f.*

interruptor, *n.* interruptor, disyuntor, *m.*

interscholastic, *adj.* interescolar.

intersect, *vt.* entrecortar; cortar; cruzar; **—,** *vi.* intersecarse.

intersection, *n.* intersección, *f.*; bocacalle, *f.*

intersperse, *vt.* intercalar, esparcir una cosa entre otras.
interstate, *adj.* entre estados.
interstellar, *adj.* intersideral.
interstice, *n.* intersticio, intervalo, *m.*
intertwine, *vt.* entretejer.
interurban, *n.* and *adj.* interurbano, *m.*
interval, *n.* intervalo, *m.*; **at —s,** a ratos.
intervene, *vi.* intervenir; ocurrir.
intervention, *n.* intervención, interposición, *f.*
interview, *n.* entrevista, *f.*; **—,** *vt.* entrevistar.
interviewer, *n.* persona que celebra entrevistas.
interweave, *vt.* entretejer, enlazar.
interwoven, *adj.* entretejido, entrelazado.
intestate, *adj.* intestado, abintestato.
intestinal, *adj.* intestinal.
intestine, *adj.* intestino, doméstico; **—s,** *n. pl.* intestinos, *m. pl.*
intimacy, *n.* intimidad, confianza, *f.*; familiaridad, *f.*
intimate, *n.* amigo íntimo; **—,** *adj.* íntimo, familiar; **— friend,** muy amigo, amigo íntimo; **—,** *vt.* insinuar, dar a entender; **—ly,** *adv.* íntimamente.
intimation, *n.* insinuación, indirecta, *f.*
intimidate, *vt.* intimidar.
intimidation, *n.* intimidación, *f.*
into, *prep.* en, dentro.
intolerable, *adj.* intolerable; **—bly,** *adv.* intolerablemente.
intolerance, *n.* intolerancia, *f.*
intolerant, *adj.* intolerante; **—ly,** *adv.* intolerablemente.
intonation, *n.* entonación, *f.*
intone, *vt.* entonar, salmodiar.
intoxicant, *n.* bebida alcohólica.
intoxicate, *vt.* embriagar.
intoxicated, *adj.* bebido, ebrio, borracho; (Sp. Am.) caneco; **somewhat —,** algo embriagado; (coll.) calamocano.
intoxicating, *adj.* embriagante.
intoxication, *n.* embriaguez, *f.*; intoxicación, *f.*
intr., intrans. intransitive, intrans. intransitivo.
intractable, *adj.* intratable, huraño.
intramural, *adj.* situado intramuros, que tiene lugar dentro de un pueblo o un colegio.
intransitive, *adj.* (gram.) intransitivo.
intrastate, *adj.* interno, dentro del estado.
intravenous, *adj.* entrevenado.
intrench, *vt.* atrincherar; usurpar, invadir.
intrepid, *adj.* arrojado, intrépido; **—ly,** *adv.* intrépidamente.
intrepidity, *n.* intrepidez, *f.*
intricacy, *n.* embrollo, embarazo, *m.*; dificultad, *f.*
intricate, *adj.* intrincado, complicado; complejo, complexo; **—ly,** *adv.* intrincadamente.

intrigue, *n.* intriga, *f.*; trama, *f.*; **—,** *vi.* intrigar.
intrinsic, *adj.* intrínseco, inherente.
intrinsical, *adj.* intrínseco, interno; **—ly,** *adv.* intrínsecamente.
introd. introduction, introducción.
introduce, *vt.* introducir, meter; **to —** (**a person**), presentar (a una persona).
introduction, *n.* introducción, *f.*; presentación, *f.*; prólogo, preámbulo, *m.*; **letter of —,** carta de presentación.
introductory, *adj.* previo, preliminar, introductorio.
introspection, *n.* examen interior, introversión, *f.*
introversion, *n.* introversión, *f.*
introvert, *n.* introverso, *m.*
intrude, *vi.* entremeterse, introducirse, ingerirse.
intruder, *n.* intruso, sa, entremetido, da.
intrusion, *n.* intrusión, *f.*; entremetimiento, *m.*
intrusive, *adj.* intruso.
intrust, *vt.* confiar.
intuition, *n.* intuición, *f.*
intuitive, *adj.* intuitivo.
inundate, *vt.* inundar.
inundation, *n.* inundación, *f.*
inure, *vt.* acostumbrar, habituar.
inured, *adj.* endurecido; **to become —,** connaturalizarse.
inv.: invoice, fact. factura; **inventor,** inventor.
invade, *vt.* invadir, asaltar.
invader, *n.* usurpador, ra, invasor, ra.
invalid, *adj.* inválido; nulo; **— diet,** dieta para inválidos; **—,** *n.* inválido, da.
invalidate, *vt.* invalidar, anular.
invalidity, *n.* invalidez, *f.*; invalidación, nulidad, *f.*; debilidad, *f.*
invaluable, *adj.* inapreciable.
invariable, *adj.* invariable; **—bly,** *adv.* invariablemente.
invasion, *n.* invasión, *f.*
invective, *n.* invectiva, *f.*
inveigh, *vi.* escribir o decir invectivas, atacar severamente.
inveigle, *vt.* seducir, persuadir.
invent, *vt.* inventar.
invention, *n.* invención, *f.*
inventive, *adj.* inventivo.
inventiveness, *n.* inventiva, *f.*
inventor, *n.* inventor, *m.*; forjador, *m.*
inventory, *n.* inventario, *m.*
inverse, *adj.* inverso, trastornado.
inversion, *n.* inversión, *f.*
invert, *vt.* invertir, trastrocar.
invertebrate, *n.* invertebrado, *m.*; **—,** *adj.* invertebrado.
inverted, *adj.* invertido, permutado.
invest, *vt.* investir; emplear dinero en; (com.) invertir; **to be —ed,** revestirse; **to — capital,** colocar un capital; **to — money,** colocar o invertir dinero.
investigate, *vt.* investigar.

investigation, *n.* investigación, pesquisa, *f.*
investigator, *n.* pesquisador, ra, investigador, ra.
investiture, *n.* investidura, *f.*
investment, *n.* vestido, *m.*, vestidura, *f.*; (com.) inversión, *f.*
investor, *n.* inversionista, *m.* y *f.*
inveterate, *adj.* inveterado.
invidious, *adj.* odioso, difamatorio; **—ly,** *adv.* odiosamente.
invigorate, *vt.* vigorizar, dar vigor, fortificar, confortar, robustecer.
invigoration, *n.* vigorización, *f.*, robustecimiento, *m.*
invincibility, *n.* calidad de invencible.
invincible, *adj.* invencible; **—bly,** *adv.* invenciblemente.
inviolability, *n.* inviolabilidad, *f.*
inviolable, *adj.* inviolable; invulnerable.
inviolate, *adj.* ileso, inviolado.
invisibility, *n.* invisibilidad, *f.*
invisible, *adj.* invisible; **— ink,** tinta simpática; **—bly,** *adv.* invisiblemente.
invitation, *n.* convite, *m.*, invitación, *f.*
invite, *vt.* convidar, invitar.
inviting, *adj.* incitante, atractivo, seductor.
invocation, *n.* invocación, *f.*
invoice, *n.* factura, *f.*; **— book,** libro de facturas; **pro forma —,** factura o cuenta simulada; **shipping —,** factura de remesa o expedición; **—,** *vt.* facturar.
invoke, *vt.* invocar.
involuntarily, *adv.* involuntariamente.
involuntary, *adj.* involuntario.
involve, *vt.* envolver, implicar.
involved, *adj.* intrincado, complejo, complexo.
involvement, *n.* envolvimiento, *m.*, complicación, *f.*
invulnerable, *adj.* invulnerable.
inward, *adj.* interior; interno; **—s, —ly,** *adv.* interiormente; internamente, hacia adentro.
inwrought, *adj.* labrado, incrustado.
iodine, *n.* (chem.) yodo, *m.*
ion, *n.* ion, *m.*
ionization, *n.* ionización, *f.*
ionize, *vt.* and *vi.* ionizar.
iota, *n.* jota, *f.*, punto, *m.*
I.O.U., IOU, I owe you, pagaré, vale.
ipecac, *n.* ipecacuana, *f.*
I.Q., IQ. intelligence quotient, cuociente intelectual.
Ir. Ire. Ireland, Irlanda.
Iran, Irán, *m.*
Iraq, Irak, *m.*
irascibility, *n.* iracundia, irascibilidad, *f.*
irascible, *adj.* irascible.
irate, *adj.* iracundo, colérico
ire, *n.* ira, iracundia, *f.*
ireful, *adj.* = **irate.**
Ireland, Irlanda, *f.*
iridescence, *n.* cambiante, *m.*
iridescent, *adj.* iridiscente, tornasolado.

iris, *n.* arco iris; (anat.) iris, *m.*; (bot.) flor de lis, *f.*
Irish, *n.* and *adj.* irlandés, esa; **— potato,** patata blanca ordinaria.
Irishman, *n.* irlandés, *m.*
Irishwoman, *n.* irlandesa, *f.*
irk, *vt.* fastidiar, cansar.
irksome, *adj.* tedioso, fastidioso.
iron, *n.* hierro, *m.*; **angle —,** hierro en ángulo; **cast —,** hierro fundido o de fundición; **galvanized —,** hierro galvanizado; **— dust,** limadura de hierro; **— rust,** herrumbre, *f.*; **pig —,** fundición, *f.*; **sheet —,** hierro laminado; **wrought —,** hierro forjado o de fragua; **—,** *adj.* férreo; **—,** *vt.* aplanchar, planchar; poner en grillos.
ironbound, *adj.* aherrojado.
ironcased, *adj.* blindado de hierro, con coraza de hierro.
ironclad, *adj.* blindado, acorazado, o armado de hierro.
ironer, *n.* planchador, ra.
ironic, *adj.* irónico.
ironical, *adj.* irónico; **—ly,** *adv.* con ironía, irónicamente.
ironing, *n.* planchado, *m.*; **— board,** tabla de planchar.
ironmonger, *n.* traficante en hierro.
ironware, *n.* ferretería, *f.*; quincallería, *f.*
ironwood, *n.* palo hacha.
ironwork, *n.* herraje, *m.*; **—s,** *n.pl.* herrería, *f.*
irony, *n.* ironía, *f.*
irradiate, *vt.* and *vi.* irradiar, brillar.
irradiated, *adj.* irradiado.
irradiation, *n.* irradiación, iluminación, *f.*
irrational, *adj.* irracional.
irreconcilable, *adj.* irreconciliable, implacable.
irrecoverable, *adj.* irrecuperable; irremediable.
irredeemable, *adj.* no amortizable (deuda); irredimible.
irreducible, *adj.* irreducible.
irrefragable, *adj.* irrefragable.
irrefutable, *adj.* irrefutable.
irregular, *adj.* irregular; **—ly,** *adv.* irregularmente.
irregularity, *n.* irregularidad, *f.*
irrelevance, *n.* inaplicabilidad, *f.*, calidad de no pertinente.
irrelevant, *adj.* no aplicable; que no prueba nada; no concluyente; desatinado.
irreligion, *n.* irreligión, impiedad, *f.*
irreligious, *adj.* irreligioso; **—ly,** *adv.* irreligiosamente.
irremediable, *adj.* irremediable.
irremovable, *adj.* inamovible.
irreparable, *adj.* irreparable.
irrepressible, *adj.* irrefrenable.
irreproachable, *adj.* irreprochable; intachable.
irresistible, *adj.* irresistible.

irresolute, *adj.* irresoluto, vacilante; **—ly,** *adv.* irresolutamente.

irresolution, *n.* irresolución, *f.*

irrespective, *adj.* **— of,** sin consideración a, sin tomar en cuenta.

irresponsibility, *n.* irresponsabilidad, *f.*

irresponsible, *adj.* no responsable, irresponsable.

irretrievable, *adj.* irrecuperable, irreparable; **—bly,** *adv.* irreparablemente.

irreverence, *n.* irreverencia, *f.*

irreverent, *adj.* irreverente; **—ly,** *adv.* irreverentemente.

irreversible, *adj.* irreversible, ininvertible.

irrevocable, *adj.* irrevocable.

irrigate, *vt.* regar, mojar.

irrigating, *n.* irrigación, *f.*, riego, *m.*; **— ditch,** cacera, *f.*; **main — ditch,** madrona, *f.*, cloaca maestra.

irrigation, *n.* riego, *m.*; irrigación, *f.*

irritability, *n.* irritabilidad, *f.*

irritable, *adj.* irritable; colérico.

irritant, *n.* (med.) estimulante, *m.*

irritate, *vt.* irritar, exasperar.

irritation, *n.* irritación, *f.*

irruption, *n.* irrupción, *f.*; entrada forzada.

is., isl. island, isla.

is, 3ª persona del singular del verbo **be.**

Isadore, Isidor, Isidoro, Isidro.

isinglass, *n.* mica, *f.*, cola de pescado.

Islamism, *n.* islamismo, *m.*

island, *n.* isla, *f.*

islander, *n.* isleño, ña; insular, *m. y f.*

isle, *n.* islote, *m.*, isleta, *f.*

islet, *n.* isleta, *f.*

isolate, *vt.* aislar, apartar.

isolation, *n.* aislamiento, *m.*

isolationist, *n.* partidario de una política nacional de aislamiento.

isometric, *adj.* isométrico.

isomorphic, *adj.* isomorfo.

isosceles, *adj.* isósceles.

isotherm, *n.* línea isoterma.

isotope, *n.* isotopos, *m.*

isotropic, *adj.* isotrópico.

issuance, *n.* emisión.

issue, *n.* salida, *f.*; evento, *m.*; resulta, *f.*; fin, término, *m.*; flujo, *m.*; sucesión, *f.*; producto, *m.*; consecuencia, *f.*; punto en debate; (med.) exutorio, *m.*; prole, progenie, *f.*; tirada, edición, *f.*; número (de una publicación), *m.*; **—,** *vi.* salir, nacer, prorrumpir, brotar; venir, proceder; provenir; terminarse; **—,** *vt.* echar, brotar; expedir, despachar; publicar; emitir.

isthmus, *n.* istmo, *m.*

it, *pron.* él, ella, ello, lo, la le.

It., Ital. Italy, Italia.

ital. italic, bastardilla.

Italian, *n.* and *adj.* italiano, na.

italic, *n.* letra cursiva, bastardilla, *f.*

italicize, *vt.* poner en letra bastardilla; subrayar.

Italy, Italia, *f.*

itch, *n.* sarna, picazón, *f.*; prurito, *m.*; **—,** *vi.* picar.

itchy, *adj.* sarnoso; que pica, que produce comezón.

item, *adv.* ítem, otrosí, aun más; **—,** *n.* artículo, suelto, *m.*; (com.) renglón, *m.*; **— in an account,** partida, *f.*

itemize, *vt.* particularizar, detallar estipular.

itinerant, *adj.* ambulante, errante.

itinerary, *n.* itinerario, *m.*

its, *pron.* su, suyo.

itself, *pron.* el mismo, la misma, lo mismo; sí; **by —,** de por sí.

ivory, *n.* marfil, *m.*; **— nut,** marfil vegetal.

ivy, *n.* hiedra, *f.*

I.W.W. Industrial Workers of the World, Trabajadores Industriales del Mundo.

J

J.: Jesus, Jesús; **Judge,** Juez; **Justice,** Justicia.

Ja., Jan. January, En.º enero.

jab, *n.* pinchazo, *m.*; (boxeo) golpe inverso; **—,** *vt.* pinchar.

jabber, *vi.* charlar, farfullar.

Jack, Juanillo, Juanito.

jack, *n.* sacabotas, *m.*; martinete, *m.*; gato, cric, *m.*, clavija, *f.*; torno de asador; jarro de cuero encerado; cota de malla; boliche, *m.*; macho, *m.*; burro, *m.*; sota (de la baraja), *f.*; **— boots,** botas grandes y fuertes; **— pot,** (poker) jugada que no puede abrirse mientras un jugador no tenga un par de sotas o algo mejor; **— tar,** (coll.) marinero, *m.*

jackal, *n.* adiva, *f.*, adive, chacal, *m.*

jackanapes, *n.* pisaverde, mequetrefe *m.*

jackass, *n.* garañón, burro, asno, *m.*

jackdaw, *n.* (orn.) grajo, *m.*

jacket, *n.* chaqueta, *f.*, saco, *m.*; envoltura, *f.*; **— (of a book)** forro de papel (de un libro).

jack-in-the-box, *n.* caja de resorte con muñeco.

jack-in-the-pulpit, *n.* variedad de flor americana.

jackknife, *n.* navaja de bolsillo.

Jack-of-all-trades, *n.* sábelotodo, factótum, *m.*; **to be a —,** meterse en todo.

jack-o'-lantern, *n.* linterna hecha de una calabaza; fuego fatuo.

jackrabbit, *n.* liebre, *f.*

jackscrew, *n.* cric, *m.*, gato de tornillo.

jacksnipe, *n.* becardón, *m.*

jackstone, *n.* taba, *f.*

jackstraw, *n.* títere de paja; **—s,** *pl.* especie de juego con pajitas.

jade, *n.* rocín, *m.*; (min.) nefrita, *f.*, jade, *m.*; **—,** *vt.* cansar.

jag, *n.* diente de sierra; mella, *f.*; diente, *m.*; **—,** *vt.* dentar.

jagged, *adj.* desigual, dentado.

jaguar, n. jaguar, m.

jail, n. cárcel, f.

jailbird, n. preso, m.; criminal, m.

jailer, n. carcelero, bastonero, m.

jam, n. compota, conserva, f.; mermelada de frutas; apretadura, f.; aprieto, m.; —, vt. apiñar, apretar, estrechar.

Jam. Jamaica, Jamaica.

jamb, n. quicial, m.

jamboree, n. borrachera, f., jolgorio, m.; reunión nacional o internacional de muchachos exploradores.

James, Diego, Jaime, Santiago.

Jane, Juana.

jangle, vi. reñir, altercar; sonar en discordancia; —, vt. hacer sonar; —, n. sonido discordante; altercado, m.

janitor, n. ujier, portero, conserje, m.

January, n. enero, m.

Jap. Japan, Japón.

Japan, Japón, m.

japan, n. charol, m.; —, vt. charolar.

Japanese, n. and adj. japonés, esa, nipón, na.

japonica, n. camelia japonesa.

jar, vi. chocar; (mus.) discordar; reñir; —, n. jarro, m.; tinaja, f.; riña, f.; sonido desapacible; tarro, m.; tina, f.; vaso, m., orza, f.

jardiniere, n. jardinera, f., florero, m.

jargon, n. jerga, jerigonza, f.

Jas. James, Santiago, Diego, Jaime.

jasmine, n. (bot.) jazmín, m.

Jasper, Gaspar.

jasper, n. (min.) jaspe, m.

jaundice, n. ictericia, f.

jaunt, n. excursión, f.

jauntiness, n. viveza, f., garbo, m.

jaunty, adj. alegre, festivo.

Java, Java, f.

javelin, n. venablo, m., jabalina, f.

jaw, n. quijada, f.; boca, f.

jawbone, n. quijada, mandíbula, f.

jay, n. picaza, urraca, marica, f.

jazz, n. jazz, m., música popular sincopada.

J. C. Jesus Christ, J.C. Jesucristo.

jct. junction, emp. empalme; confluencia.

J.D. Doctor of Laws, Doctor en Leyes.

Je. Ju. June, jun. junio.

jealous, adj. celoso; envidioso; **to be — of,** tener celos de.

jealousy, n. celos, m. pl.

jeep, n. (mil.) pequeño automóvil de trasporte.

jeer, vi. befar, mofar, escarnecer; —, n. befa, mofa, burla, f.

Jeffrey, Geofredo.

jelly, n. jalea, gelatina, f.

jellyfish, n. aguamar, m.; medusa, f.

Jenny, Jennie, Juanita.

jenny, n. jumenta, f.; torno, m., máquina de hilar.

jeopard, jeopardize, vt. arriesgar, poner en riesgo.

jeopardy, n. peligro, riesgo, m.

Jeremy, Jeremías.

jerk, n. sacudida, sobarbada, f., respingo, m.; —, vt. and vi. sacudir; **—ed beef,** tasajo, m., cecina, f.

jerkin, n. chaquetón, justillo, m.

jerky, adj. espasmódico.

Jerome, Jerónimo.

jerry-builder, n. constructor de fábricas de inferior calidad.

jerry-built, adj. mal construido, de construcción débil.

jersey, n. jersey, m.; jubón, m.; ganado vacuno de la isla de Jersey.

Jerusalem, Jerusalén, m.

jessamine, n. jazmín, m.

Jessie, Jesusita.

jest, n. chanza, burla, f.; zumba, f.; chasco, m.; —, vi. chancear; —, vt. ridiculizar.

jester, n. mofador, ra, bufón, ona.

jestingly, adv. de burla, de broma.

Jesuit, n. jesuíta, m.; **—'s bark,** quina, cascarilla, f.

jesuitic, jesuitical, adj. jesuítico.

Jesus, Jesús.

Jesus Christ, Jesucristo.

jet, n. azabache, m.; surtidor, m.; **gas —,** mechero de gas.

jetsam, n. echazón, f.

jettison, n. (naut.) echazón, f.; —, vt. echar mercancías al mar.

jetty, adj. hecho de azabache; —, n. muelle, m.

Jew, n. judío, m.

jewel, n. joya, alhaja, f.; **small —,** joyel, m.; **—s,** n. pl. rubíes (de un reloj), m. pl.

jewel case, n. joyero, escriño, m., cofre para joyas.

jeweler, n. joyero, m.

jewelry, n. joyería, pedrería, f.; **cheap —, imitation —,** perendengues, m.pl., bisutería, f.; **piece of —,** prenda, f.

Jewess, n. judía, f.

Jewish, adj. judaico, ca, judío, día.

Jewry, n. judería, f.

jew's-harp, n. birimbao, m.

jib, n. (naut.) maraguto, foque, m.

jibe, vt. (naut.) mudar un botavante; —, vi. (coll.) concordar, convenir, estar de acuerdo.

jiffy, n. (coll.) periquete, momentito, m.

jig, n. baile alegre; **— saw,** sierra, f., sierra de vaivén.

jigger flea, n. nigua, f.

jiggle, vt. mover a tirones; —, vi. moverse a tirones.

jigsaw, n. sierra de vaivén.

jigsaw puzzle, n. especie de rompecabezas, enigma, m.

jilt, n. coqueta, f.; —, vi. coquetear; —, vt. dar calabazas, despedir a un galán; (coll.) plantar.

Jim, Jimmy, Santiago, Jaime, Diego.

jimmy, n. pie de cabra, palanca de hierro (que usan los ladrones para abrir cerraduras, etc.).

jingle, *vi.* retiñir, resonar; **—,** *n.* retintín, resonido, *m.*; sonaja, *f.*

jingo, *n.* jingoísta, *m.*; **by —!** (coll.) ¡caramba!

jingoism, *n.* jingoísmo, *m.*

jingoist, *n.* jingoísta, *m.*; **—,** *adj.* jingoísta.

jingoistic, *adj.* jingoísta.

jinriksha, jinricksha, *n.* vehículo japonés de dos ruedas tirado por uno o más hombres.

Jno. John, Juan.

Joan, Juana.

job, *n.* empleo, *m.*; (Mex. coll.) chamba, *f.*; destajo, *m.*; engañifa, *f.*; cucaña, *f.*; **— lot,** colección miscelánea de géneros; **— seeker,** postulante, *m.* y *f.*, persona que busca empleo u ocupación; **—,** *vt.* comprar en calidad de corredor.

jobber, *n.* agiotista, *m.*; destajero, *m.*; usurero, *m.*

jobbery, *n.* engañifa, *f.*

jobbing, *n.* oficio de comprar y revender.

jobless, *adj.* cesante, sin trabajo.

jockey, *n.* jinete, chalán, *m.*; persona apasionada por los caballos; **—,** *vt. and vi.* engañar, estafar.

jocose, *adj.* jocoso, burlesco; **—ly,** *adv.* jocosamente.

jocosity, *n.* jocosidad, chanza, *f.*

jocular, *adj.* jocoso, alegre.

jocund, *adj.* jovial, alegre.

Joe, Pepe, Pepillo, Pepín.

jog, *vt.* empujar; dar un golpe suave; **—,** *vi.* bambolearse; andar a saltos; **—,** *n.* empellón, *m.*; traqueo, *m.*; **— trot,** trote de perro; rutina, *f.*

joggle, *vt.* mover a sacudidas.

John, Juan.

John Bull, apodo para los ingleses.

Johnny, Juanito.

johnnycake, *n.* especie de pan de maíz.

join, *vt.* juntar, unir; **—,** *vi.* unirse, juntarse, asociarse; confluir.

joiner, *n.* carpintero de taller; ensamblador, *m.*

joinery, *n.* ensambladura, *f.*, ensamblaje, *m.*

joint, *n.* coyuntura, articulación, *f.*; charnela, *f.*; (coll.) lugar de reunión; (bot.) nudo, *m.*; **out of —,** desunido; **—,** *adj.* unido; participante; **— account,** cuenta en participación; **— heir,** coheredero, *m.*; **—ly,** *adv.* juntamente, conjuntamente, en común; **—ly liable,** solidario; **—,** *vt.* juntar, ensamblar; descuartizar.

jointure, *n.* bienes parafernales.

joist, *n.* viga de bovedilla o suelo; vigueta, *f.*; abitaque, *m.*

joke, *n.* chanza, burla, zumba, *f.*; chasco, *m.*; **to play a —,** hacer una burla; **to play a — on,** dar broma a; **—,** *vi.* chancear, bromear.

joker, *n.* bromista, *m.* y *f.*; naipe adicional en ciertos juegos.

jollification, *n.* francachela, festividad, *f.*

jollity, *n.* alegría, *f.*, regocijo, *m.*

jolly, *adj.* alegre, jovial; **— boat,** (naut.) serení, *m.*

jolt, *vt. and vi.* traquear, sacudir; **—,** *n.* traqueo, *m.*, sacudida, *f.*

jonquil, *n.* (bot.) junquillo, *m.*

Jos. Joseph, Jph. José.

Joseph, José, Pepe.

jostle, *vt.* rempujar, empellar.

jot, *n.* jota, *f.*, cosa mínima, ápice, *m.*; **— (down),** *vt.* apuntar, tomar apuntes, anotar.

joule, *n.* julio (medida electrica), *m.*

jounce, *vt.* sacudir.

Jour. Journal, diario, revista (publicación).

journal, *n.* diario, periódico, *m.*; libro diario.

journalism, *n.* periodismo, *m.*

journalist, *n.* periodista, *m.* y *f.*

journalistic, *adj.* periodístico.

journey, *n.* jornada, *f.*; viaje, *m.*; **—,** *vi.* viajar.

journeyman, *n.* jornalero, *m.*

joust, *n.* torneo, *m.*; justa, *f.*; **—,** *vi.* justar.

Jove, *n.* Júpiter, *m.*; **by —!** ¡pardiez!

jovial, *adj.* jovial, alegre; **—ly,** *adv.* con jovialidad.

joviality, *n.* jovialidad, *f.*

jowl, *n.* quijada, *f.*

joy, *n.* alegría, *f.*; júbilo, *m.*; **to give —,** alegrar, causar regocijo; **to wish —,** congratular.

joyful, joyous, *adj.* alegre, gozoso; **—ly,** *adv.* alegremente.

joyless, *adj.* triste, sin alegría.

J. P. Justice of the Peace, Juez de Paz.

Jr. Junior, Hijo.

jubilance, *n.* júbilo, regocijo, *m.*

jubilant, *adj.* lleno de júbilo.

jubilation, *n.* júbilo, regocijo, *m.*

jubilee, *n.* jubileo, *m.*

judaism, *n.* judaísmo, *m.*

judge, *n.* juez, *m.*; **—,** *vi.* juzgar; inferir.

judgment, judgement, *n.* juicio, *m.*; sentir, *m.*; meollo, concepto, *m.*; opinión, *f.*; decisión, *f.*; **to pass —,** pronunciar la sentencia; juzgar.

judicial, *adj.* judicial; **—ly,** *adv.* judicialmente.

judiciary, *n.* magistratura, *f.*, administración de justicia.

judicious, *adj.* juicioso, prudente; **—ly,** *adv.* juiciosamente.

jug, *n.* jarro, *m.*

juggle, *n.* juego de manos; **—,** *vi.* hacer juegos de manos, escamotar, escamotear.

juggler, *n.* prestidigitador, *m.*; impostor, estafador, *m.*

Jugoslavia, Yugoeslavia, *f.*

jugular, *adj.* yugular; **— vein,** vena yugular.

juice, *n.* zumo, jugo, *m.*

juicy, *adj.* jugoso.

jujitsu, *n.* arte japonés de defensa propia sin armas.

juke box, n. (coll.) fonógrafo automático que funciona por monedas.

julep, n. julepe (bebida), m.

Juliet, Julieta.

Julius Caesar, Julio César.

Jul., Jy. July, Jul. julio.

July, n. (mes) julio, m.

jumble, vt. mezclar confusamente; —, n. mezcla, confusión, f.

jumbled, adj. destartalado.

jumbo, n. persona o cosa excesivamente voluminosa; —, adj. colosal, excesivamente voluminoso.

jump, vi. saltar, brincar; convenir, concordar; dar saltos; —, n. salto, m.

jumper, n. brincador, ra; blusa de obrero; vestido de mujer o de niña de una sola pieza y sin mangas.

jumping, n. salto, brinco, m.; —, adj. saltante.

jumping jack, n. títere, m.

Jun.: Junior, Hijo; **June,** Jun. junio.

junc. junction, (rail.) emp. empalme; confluencia.

junction, n. junta, unión, f., empalme, contacto, m.; bifurcación, f.; — **box,** caja de conexiones.

juncture, n. juntura, coyuntura, f.; crisis, f., trance, m.

June, n. (mes.) junio, m.; —**bug,** escarabajo americano.

jungle, n. matorral, m.

junior, adj. más joven; —, n. estudiante de tercer año; — **college,** los dos primeros años universitarios; — **high school,** los dos primeros años de escuela secundaria.

juniper, n. (bot.) junípero, enebro, m., sabina, f.

junk, n. hierro viejo; cosa despreciable; (naut.) junco, m.

junket, n. dulce seco; convite familiar; —, vi. dar un convite; asistir a un convite costeado con fondos públicos.

junkman, n. comprador de hierro viejo, de papeles, trapos, etc.

junta, n. junta, asamblea, f.; tribunal, m.

junto, n. facción política; junta, f.

juridical, adj. jurídico, judicial; —**ly,** adv. jurídicamente.

jurisdiction, n. jurisdicción, f.

jurisprudence, n. jurisprudencia, J.

jurist, n. jurista, m. y f., jurisconsulto, m.

juror, n. jurado, m.

jury, n. junta de jurados; jurado, m.

juryman, n. jurado, m.

just, adj. justo, honrado, virtuoso, derecho; —**ly,** adv. justamente, exactamente; — **as,** como, así como; — **now,** ahora mismo.

justice, n. justicia, f., derecho, m.; juez, m.

justifiable, adj. justificable, conforme a razón, según justicia; —**bly,** adv. con justicia y rectitud.

justification, n. justificación, f.; defensa, f.

justify, vt. justificar.

justly, adv. justamente; exactamente.

jut, vi. sobresalir.

jute, n. yute, m.

Jutland, Jutlandia, f.

juvenile, adj. juvenil.

juxtapose, vt. yuxtaponer.

juxtaposition, n. yuxtaposición, f.

K

K. King, Rey.

k.: karat, carat, quilate; **kilogram,** kg. kilogramo.

kaffir corn, n. sorgo, m.

kaiser, n. káiser, m.

kale, n. col, berza, f.

kaleidoscope, n. calidoscopio, m.

Kalmuck, Kalmuk, Kalmuco, Calmuco, m.

Kan. Kans. Kansas, Kansas.

kangaroo, n. canguro, m.

Kantian, n. and adj. kantiano, na, kantista, m. y f.; —, discípulo de Kant; —, adj. relativo al kantismo.

kaolin, n. caolín, m., tierra o arcilla para porcelana.

karakul, n. karacul, m.

katydid, n. cigarra, f.

K.C. Knights of Columbus, Caballeros de Colón.

kc. kilocycle, kc. kilociclo.

keel, n. (naut.) quilla, f.

keen, adj. afilado, agudo; penetrante, sutil, vivo; vehemente; satírico, picante; —**ly,** adv. agudamente; sutilmente; con viveza.

keenness, n. agudeza, sutileza, perspicacia, f.; aspereza, f.

keep, vt. tener, mantener, retener; preservar, guardar; proteger; detener; conservar; reservar; sostener; observar; solemnizar; **to — accounts,** llevar cuentas; **to — aloof,** apartarse; **to — books,** llevar los libros; **to — house,** poner casa; ser ama de casa; —, vi. perseverar; soler; mantenerse; quedar; vivir, residir; tener cuidado; —, n. sustentación, manutención, f.

keeper, n. guardián, tenedor, m.; — **of an insane asylum,** loquero, m.; — **of a prison,** carcelero, m.

keeping, n. custodia, f.; guarda, f.

keepsake, n. dádiva, f., recuerdo, regalo, m.

keg, n. barrilito, m.

kelp, n. sosa, f., alga marina y sus cenizas.

ken, n. vista, f.; percepción, f.

Ken. Kentucky, Kentucky.

kennel, n. perrera, f.; jauría, f.; zorrera, f.

kerchief, n. pañuelo, m.

kernel, n. almendra, pepita, f.; meollo, grano, m.

kerosene, n. kerosene, kerosén, m., kerosina, f.; petróleo de alumbrado.

ketch, n. (naut.) queche, m.

ketchup, n. = catsup.

kettle, n. caldera, marmita, olla, f.

kettledrum, *n.* timbal, atabal, *m.*
key, *n.* llave, *f.*; (mus.) clave, *f.*; clavija, *f.*; chaveta, *f.*; tecla, *f.*; — **ring,** colgajo de llaves; — **word,** palabra clave; **master** —, llave maestra; **tuning** —, templador, *m.*; **keeper of the** —**s,** llavero, ra, clavero, ra.
keyboard, *n.* teclado de órgano o piano, teclado, *m.*
keyed, *adj.* templado.
keyhole, *n.* agujero de la llave.
keynote, *n.* (mus.) tónica, *f.*; idea básica o fundamental.
keystone, *n.* llave de un arco o bóveda.
Key West, Cayohueso, Cayo Hueso, *m.*
K.G. Knight of the Garter, Caballero de la Orden de la Jarretera.
kg. kilogram, kg. kilogramo.
khaki, *adj.* kaki, caqui; —, *n.* kaki, caqui, *m.*
khan, *n.* kan, *m.*, jefe entre los tártaros.
khedive, *n.* jedive, *m.*
kibitzer, *n.* (coll.) espectador en un juego de naipes; camasquince, *m.* y *f.*, mirón, ona, entremetido, da.
kick, *vt.* acocear; —, *vi.* patear; (coll.) reclamar, objetar; —, *n.* puntapié, *m.*; patada, *f.*; culatada de armas de fuego; (coll.) efecto estimulador; placer, *m.*
kickback, *n.* contragolpe, *m.*; parte de una cantidad recibida que se devuelve como consecuencia de un convenio confidencial o de coerción.
kicker, *n.* animal coceador; coceador, *m.*; persona quejumbrosa.
kickoff, *n.* saque (en fútbol), *m.*
kickshaw, *n.* fruslería, bagatela, *f.*
kid, *n.* cabrito, *m.*
kidnap, *vt.* robar niños, secuestrar.
kidnaper, *n.* secuestrador, ra.
kidnaping, *n.* secuestro, *m.*
kidney, *n.* riñón, *m.*; (fig.) clase, índole, especie, *f.*; temperamento, *m.*; — **bean,** variedad de frijol.
kidskin, *n.* cuero de cabritilla.
kill, *vt.* matar, asesinar.
killing, *n.* matanza, *f.*
kill-joy, *n.* aguafiestas, *m.* y *f.*
kiln, *n.* horno, *m.*; **brick** —, horno de ladrillo.
kilo, *n.* kilo, *m.*
kilocycle, *n.* kilociclo, *m.*
kilogram, *n.* kilogramo, *m.*
kilojoule, *n.* (elec.) kilojulio, *m.*
kiloliter, *n.* kilolitro, *m.*
kilometer, *n.* kilómetro, *m.*
kilometric, *adj.* kilométrico.
kilovolt, *n.* kilovoltio, *m.*
kilovolt-ampere, *n.* kilovoltamperio, *m.*
kilowatt, *n.* kilovatio, *m.*; — **hour,** kilovatio-hora, *m.*
kilt, *n.* saya de los escoceses serranos.
kimono, *n.* kimono, quimón, *m.*
kin, *n.* parentesco, *m.*; afinidad, *f.*; **next of** —, pariente próximo.
kind, *adj.* benévolo, benigno, bondadoso,

afable, cariñoso; —, *n.* género, *m.*; clase, *f.*; especie, naturaleza, *f.*; manera, *f.*; tenor, *m.*; calidad, *f.*
kindergarten, *n.* escuela de párvulos, jardín de la infancia.
kindhearted, *adj.* bondadoso.
kindle, *vt.* and *vi.* encender; arder.
kindling wood, *n.* leña, *f.*
kindliness, *n.* benevolencia, benignidad, *f.*
kindly, *adj.* blando, suave, tratable; —, *adv.* benignamente.
kindness, *n.* benevolencia, *f.*; favor, beneficio, *m.*; **have the** — **to,** tenga la bondad de.
kindred, *n.* parentesco, *m.*; parentela, casta, *f.*; —, *adj.* emparentado; parecido.
kinematics, *n.* cinemática, *f.*
kinesthetic, *adj.* cinestésico.
kinetics, *n.* cinética, *f.*
king, *n.* rey, *m.*; rey o doble dama (en el juego de damas); —**ly,** *adv.* regiamente; —**ly,** *adj.* real.
kingdom, *n.* reino, *m.*
kingfisher, *n.* (orn.) martín pescador.
kingpin, *n.* bolo central en un juego de bolos; pasador de charnela o pivote; persona principal en un grupo o empresa.
kinky, *adj.* grifo; ensortijado.
kinsfolk, *n.* parientes, *m.pl.*
kinship, *n.* parentela, *f.*
kinsman, *n.* pariente, *m.*
kinswoman, *n.* parienta, *f.*
kiosk, *n.* quiosco, kiosco, *m.*
kipper, *n.* salmón o arenque ahumado; — *vt.* ahumar (pescado), etc.
kirtle, *n.* vestido de mujer.
kiss, *n.* beso, ósculo, *m.*; —, *vt.* besar.
kissing, *n.* beso, *m.*; acción de besar.
kit, *n.* botellón, *m.*; violín pequeño; vasija, *f.*; colodra, *f.*; **first-aid** —, botiquín, *m.*
kitchen, *n.* cocina, *f.*; cocedero, *m.*; — **boy,** pinche, *m.*; — **maid,** cocinera, *f.*; — **police,** soldado que asiste en el trabajo de cocina; trabajo de cocina en un campamento militar; — **range,** cocina inglesa, cocina económica, fogón inglés; — **utensils,** trastos, *m.pl.*, batería de cocina.
kitchenette, *n.* cocinilla, *f.*, pequeña habitación que combina cocina y despensa.
kitchen midden, *n.* basura que señala el sitio de una habitación primitiva.
kite, *n.* (orn.) milano, *m.*; cometa, birlocha, pandorga, *f.*; (Mex.) papalote, *m.*
kith, *n.* conocidos, *m.pl.*; — **and kin,** parientes y amigos.
kitten, *n.* gatito, ta; —, *vi.* parir (la gata).
kitty, *n.* gatito, *m.*; polla, puesta (en los juegos de naipes), *f.*
K.K.K. Ku Klux Klan, sociedad secreta de E.U.A.
kl. kiloliter, Kl., kl. kilolitro.
kleptomania, *n.* cleptomanía, *f.*
kleptomaniac, *n.* cleptómano, na.
km. kilometer, km. kilómetro.
knack, *n.* chuchería, *f.*; maña, destreza, *f.*

knapsack, *n.* mochila, *f.*
knave, *n.* bribón; pícaro, bellaco, *m.*; (en naipes) sota, *f.*
knavery, *n.* picardía, bribonada, *f.*
knavish, *adj.* fraudulento; pícaro; truhán; **—ly,** *adv.* pícaramente; bellacamente.
knead, *vt.* amasar.
knee, *n.* rodilla, *f.*; ángulo, *m.*; **— bone,** rótula, *f.*
kneecap, *n.* rótula, *f.*
knee-deep, *adj.* metido o subido hasta las rodillas.
knee-high, *adj.* a la altura de la rodilla.
kneel, *vi.* arrodillarse, hincar la rodilla, postrarse.
kneepad, *n.* cojincillo para las rodillas.
kneepan, *n.* rótula, *f.*
knell, *n.* clamoreo, *m.*; tañido fúnebre.
knew, pretérito del verbo **know.**
knickerbockers, knickers, *n. pl.* calzones cortos, pantalones, *m. pl.*; bragas, *f. pl.*
knickknack, *n.* bujería, *f.*; juguete, *m.*
knife, *n.* cuchillo, *m.*
knight, *n.* caballero, paladín, *m.*; **— (in chess),** caballo, *m.*; **—,** *vt.* crear a uno caballero.
knight-errant, *n.* caballero andante.
knight-errantry, *n.* caballería andante.
knighthood, *n.* caballería, *f.*, dignidad de caballero.
knightly, *adj.* propio o digno de caballero; **—,** *adv.* caballerosamente.
knit, *vt.* and *vi.* enlazar; atar, unir; trabajar a punto de aguja, tejer; **to — the brows,** fruncir las cejas, fruncir el ceño.
knitted goods, *n. pl.* géneros de punto.
knitting, *n.* trabajo de punto, tejido con agujas; **— needle,** aguja de hacer medias.
knives, *n. pl.* de **knife,** cuchillos, *m. pl.*
knob, *n.* bulto, *m.*; nudo en la madera.
knobbed, *adj.* nudoso, lleno de nudos.
knobby, *adj.* lleno de nudos.
knock, *vt.* and *vi.* chocar; golpear, tocar; pegar; **to — down,** derribar, tumbar; **—,** *n.* golpe, *m.*; llamada, *f.*
knocker, *n.* llamador, picaporte, *m.*, aldaba, *f.*
knock-kneed, *adj.* patituerto, befo, patizambo.
knockout, *n.* puñetazo que pone fuera de combate, golpe decisivo.
knoll, *n.* otero, *m.*; cima de una colina.
knot, *n.* nudo, *m.*; lazo, *m.*; maraña, *f.*; atadura, *f.*; dificultad, *f.*; confederación, *f.*; **—,** *vt.* enredar, juntar; anudar.
knothole, *n.* agujero que deja un nudo en la madera.
knotted, *adj.* nudoso.
knotty, *adj.* nudoso; dificultoso.
knout, *n.* especie de azote para criminales.
know, *vt.* and *vi.* conocer, saber; tener noticia de; **I — positively,** me consta; **to — a thing perfectly,** saber una cosa al dedillo.
knowing, *adj.* instruído, inteligente, en-

tendido, sabedor; **—ly,** *adv.* hábilmente; a sabiendas.
knowledge, *n.* conocimiento, saber, *m.*; ciencia, *f.*; inteligencia, habilidad, *f.*; luces, *f. pl.*
known, *adj.* conocido.
knuckle, *n.* coyuntura, *f.*, nudillo, *m.*; jarrete de ternero.
k.o. **knockout,** golpe que pone fuera de combate.
kodak, *n.* kodak, *m.*
K. of C. Knights of Columbus, Caballeros de Colón.
K. of P. Knights of Pythias, Sociedad Norteamericana, Caballeros de Pitias.
kohlrabi, *n.* colirrábano, *m.*
Koran, *n.* Corán, *m.*
kosher, *n.* alimento judío; **—,** *adj.* autorizado por la ley judía; (fig.) regular, natural.
K.P.: Kitchen Police, servicio de cocina; **Knights of Pythias,** Sociedad Norteamericana Caballeros de Pitias.
kraft, kraft paper, *n.* papel de estraza.
Kt. Knight, Caballero.
K.T. Knight Templar, Caballero Templario.
kumquat, *n.* auranciáceo chino.
kw. kilowatt, kv. kilovatio.
K.W.H. kilowatt-hour, Kv-H. kilovatio hora.
Ky. Kentucky, Kentucky.

L

L.: Latin, lat. latín; **law,** ley.
l.: law, l. ley; **league,** liga (sociedad); l. legua; **left,** izda. izq.ª izquierda; **length,** long. longitud; **line,** lín. línea; **liter,** l. litro.
£ pound, £ libra esterlina (moneda).
la, *n.* (mus.) la.
La. Louisiana, Luisiana.
L.A. Liberal Arts, Artes Liberales.
label, *n.* esquela, *f.*; marbete, billete, *m.*, etiqueta, *f.*; rótulo, *m.*; **—,** *vt.* rotular o señalar alguna cosa con un rótulo.
labor, *n.* trabajo, *m.*; labor, *f.*; fatiga, *f.*; mano de obra; **hard —,** trabajos forzados; **L — Day,** Día del Trabajo; **— union,** gremio o sindicato obrero; **to be in —,** estar de parto; **—,** *vt.* and *vi.* trabajar; afanarse; estar con dolores de parto.
laboratory, *n.* laboratorio, *m.*; gabinete, *m.*
laborer, *n.* labrador, trabajador, obrero, *m.*; **day —,** mercenario, *m.*
laborious, *adj.* laborioso; difícil; **—ly,** *adv.* laboriosamente, trabajosamente.
laborsaving, *adj.* ahorrador o economizador de trabajo.
labor turnover, *n.* cambio en el personal de obreros o empleados en un plazo dado.
labyrinth, *n.* laberinto, dédalo, *m.*
lac, *n.* laca, *f.*, goma laca.

lace, *n.* lazo, cordón, *m.*; encaje, *m.*; randa, *f.*; galón, pasamano, *m.*; — **trimming,** adorno de encaje, randa, *f.*; **point —,** encaje de aguja; **trimmed with —,** randado; —, *vt.* abrochar, encordonar, galonear; amarrar (los cordones de los zapatos, etc.).

lacerate, *vt.* lacerar, rasgar.

laceration, *n.* laceración, *f.*

lacework, *n.* obra de encaje o parecida al encaje.

lachrymal, *adj.* lacrimal.

lachrymose, *adj.* lacrimoso.

lacing, *n.* cordón, *m.*: acción de atar o amarrar (con un cordón, etc.).

lack, *vt.* and *vi.* carecer, necesitar; faltar algo; —, *n.* falta, *f.*; necesidad, *f.*

lackadaisical, *adj.* lánguido con afectación; indiferente, falto de ánimo.

lackey, *n.* lacayo, *m.*

lacking, *adj.* falto; **to be —,** hacer falta.

laconic, *adj.* lacónico; **—ally,** *adv.* lacónicamente.

lacquer, *n.* laca, *f.*; charol, barniz, *m.*; —, *vt.* charolar.

lacrosse, *n.* variedad de juego de pelota.

lactation, *n.* lactancia, crianza, *f.*

lactic, *adj.* lácteo; **— acid,** ácido láctico.

lactose, *n.* lactina, lactosa, *f.*

lacuna, *n.* laguna, *f.*; espacio en blanco.

lad, *n.* mozo, muchacho, mozalbete, *m.*

ladder, *n.* escala o escalera portátil.

lade, *vt.* cargar; —, *vi.* sacar agua.

laden, *adj.* cargado; oprimido.

lading, *n.* carga, *f.*; cargamento, *m.*; **bill of —,** conocimiento de embarque; (rail.) carta de porte.

ladle, *n.* cucharón, cazo, *m.*; achicador, *m.*

lady, *n.* señora, señorita, dama, *f.*

ladybird, ladybug, *n.* mariquita, *f.*

Lady Day, día de la Anunciación de la Virgen María.

ladyfinger, *n.* melindre, *m.*, especie de bizcocho.

lady-killer, *n.* (coll.) Don Juan, Tenorio, favorito de las mujeres.

ladylike, *adj.* afeminado; elegante.

ladylove, *n.* dama, querida, *f.*

ladyship, *n.* señoría, *f.*

lady's-slipper, *n.* variedad de orquídea.

lag, *vi.* moverse lentamente; quedarse atrás, rezagarse.

lager, *n.* cerveza, *f.*

laggard, lagger, *n.* haragán, ana, holgazán, ana.

lagoon, *n.* laguna, *f.*

laid, pretérito y *p.p.* del verbo **lay.**

lain, *p.p.* del verbo **lie.**

lair, *n.* cubil, *m.*

laity, *n.* estado seglar.

lake, *n.* lago, *m.*; laguna, *f.*

lamb, *n.* cordero, *m.*; —, *vi.* parir corderos.

lambent, *adj.* centelleante.

lambkin, *n.* corderito, *m.*

lambskin, *n.* corderina, *f.*

lame, *adj.* lisiado, estropeado; cojo; imperfecto; **—ly,** *adv.* con cojera; imperfectamente; —, *vt.* lisiar, estropear.

lameness, *n.* cojera, *f.*; imperfección, *f.*

lament, *vt.* lamentar; —, *vi.* lamentarse; —, *n.* lamento, *m.*

lamentable, *adj.* lamentable, deplorable, desconsolador.

lamentation, *n.* lamentación, *f.*, lamento, *m.*

laminate, *vt.* laminar.

lamination, *n.* laminación, *f.*

lamp, *n.* lámpara, *f.*; **electric —,** bujía, *f.*; **— shade,** pantalla, *f.*; **— stand,** velador, *m.*

lampblack, *n.* negro de humo.

lamplight, *n.* luz de lámpara, luz artificial.

lampoon, *n.* sátira, *f.*; libelo, *m.*; —, *vt.* escribir sátiras.

lamppost, *n.* candelabro, *m.*; poste eléctrico, pie de farol de la calle.

lamprey, *n.* lamprea, *f.*

lance, *n.* lanza, *f.*; lanceta, *f.*; —, *vt.* dar un lancetazo; abrir, cortar, perforar; hacer una operación quirúrgica con lanceta.

lancer, *n.* (mil.) lancero, *m.*

lancet, *n.* lanceta, *f.*

land, *n.* país, *m.*; región, *f.*; territorio, *m.*; tierra, *f.*; **— forces,** tropas de tierra; —, *vt.* and *vi.* desembarcar; saltar en tierra.

landau, *n.* (coche) landó, *m.*

landed, *adj.* hacendado.

landholder, *n.* hacendado, *m.*

landing, *n.* desembarco, *m.*; **emergency — field,** (aer.) campo de emergencia; **— field,** campo de aterrizaje; **— (of a staircase),** meseta (de una escalera), *f.*; **— net,** red para pescado; **— place,** desembarcadero, *m.*

landlady, *n.* propietaria, arrendadora, *f.*; mesonera, *f.*; posadera, *f.*; casera, *f.*; **— (of an inn),** patrona, *f.*

landlocked, *adj.* cercado de tierra.

landlord, *n.* propietario, *m.*; huésped, posadero, *m.*; casero, *m.*; **— (of an inn),** patrón, *m.*

landlubber, *n.* marinero bisoño.

landmark, *n.* mojón, linde, *m.*, señal, marca, *f.*; hecho o acontecimiento importante.

landowner, *n.* hacendado, *m.*

landscape, *n.* paisaje, *m.*; **— gardner,** jardinero que proyecta y construye jardines o parques; **— gardening,** jardinería, *f.*

landslide, *n.* derrumbe, *m.*, desprendimiento de tierra; (pol.) mayoría de votos abrumadora.

landsman, *n.* persona que vive en la tierra; marinero de poca experiencia.

landward, *adv.* hacia la tierra.

lane, *n.* callejuela, calle, *f.*; vereda, *f.*; **traffic —,** zona de tránsito.

language, *n.* lengua, *f.*; lenguaje, idioma, *m.*; **Spanish —,** castellano, *m.*

languid, *adj.* lánguido, débil; **—ly,** *adv.*

lánguidamente, débilmente.
languish, *vi.* entristecerse, afligirse, languidecer.
languishing, *adj.* lánguido.
languor, *n.* languidez, *f.*
languorous, *adj.* débil, lánguido.
lank, *adj.* alto y delgado; seco.
lanky, *adj.* alto y delgado.
lanolin, lanoline, *n.* lanolina, *f.*
lantern, *n.* linterna, *f.*; farol, *m.*; **dark —,** linterna sorda; **— slide,** diapositiva, *f.*, fotografía positiva.
lanyard, *n.* (naut.) acollador, *m.*
lap, *n.* falda, *f.*; seno, *m.*; regazo, *m.*; traslapo, *m.*; **— dog,** perro de faldas; **—,** *vt.* arrollar, envolver; traslapar, sobreponer; lamer.
lapel, *n.* solapa, *f.*
lapful, *n.* lo que puede caber en el regazo.
lapidary, *n.* and *adj.* lapidario, *m.*
Lapland, Laponia, *f.*
Laplander, *n.* lapón, ona.
lappet, *n.* doblez o pliegue grande de un vestido; moco de pavo; lóbulo de la oreja.
lapse, *n.* caída, *f.*; falta ligera; traslación de derecho o dominio; lapso, *m.*; **—,** *vi.* escurrir, manar; deslizarse; caer; caducar.
lapwing, *n.* (orn.) avefría, *f.*
larboard, *n.* (naut.) babor, *m.*, lado izquierdo del navío.
larceny, *n.* ratería, *f.*, hurto, *m.*
larch, *n.* (bot.) alerce, lárice, *m.*
lard, *n.* manteca, *f.*, lardo, *m.*, tocino gordo; **—,** *vt.* mechar.
larder, *n.* despensa, *f.*
large, *adj.* grande, amplio, vasto; liberal; **at —,** en libertad, suelto; **— type,** tipo de cartel; **—ly,** *adv.* largamente, copiosamente, liberalmente.
large-scale, *adj.* en gran escala.
largess, *n.* liberalidad, *f.*; dádiva generosa.
lariat, *n.* lazo, *m.*, reata, *f.*
lark, *n.* (orn.) alondra, *f.*
larkspur, *n.* (bot.) espuela de caballero.
larva, *n.* larva, oruga, *f.*
laryngeal, *adj.* laríngeo.
laryngitis, *n.* laringitis, *f.*
larynx, *n.* laringe, *f.*
lascivious, *adj.* lascivo; **—ly,** *adv.* lascivamente.
lash, *n.* latigazo, *m.*; punta del látigo; pihuela, *f.*; sarcasmo, *m.*; **—,** *vt.* dar latigazos, azotar; atar; satirizar.
lass, *n.* doncella, moza, *f.*
lassitude, *n.* lasitud, fatiga, *f.*
lasso, *n.* lazo, *m.*
last, *adj.* último, postrero, pasado; **— straw,** acción que hace perder la paciencia o la fuerza; límite de toleración; el colmo; **— word,** decisión final; última moda; la última palabra; lo mejor; algo que no se puede mejorar; **—ly,** *adv.* a la última vez; al fin; finalmente; **—,** *n.* horma de zapatero; (naut.) carga de un navío; **at —,** últimamente; al fin, al cabo, por último;

—, *vi.* durar; subsistir.
lastex, *n.* hilo elástico hecho de látex y algodón, seda, lana o seda artificial.
lasting, *adj.* duradero, permanente; **—ly,** *adv.* perpetuamente; **—,** *n.* (tela) sempiterna, *f.*
Lat. Latin, lat. latín.
lat. latitude, lat. latitud.
latch, *n.* aldaba (de puerta), *f.*, cerrojo, *m.*; **—,** *vt.* cerrar con aldaba.
latchkey, *n.* llavín, picaporte, *m.*; llave de la puerta principal.
late, *adj.* tardío; tardo, lento; difunto; último; **the train is ten minutes —,** el tren ha sufrido retraso de diez minutos; **—,** *adv.* tarde; **of —,** de poco tiempo acá; **—ly,** *adv.* poco ha, recientemente últimamente.
lateness, *n.* retraso, *m.*, tardanza, *f.*
latent, *adj.* escondido, oculto, latente.
later, *adj.* más tarde; posterior; **—,** *adv.* posteriormente.
lateral, *adj.* lateral; **—ly,** *adv.* lateralmente.
latest, *adj.* último; **— fashion,** última moda; **—,** *adv.* más reciente; **at the —,** a más tardar.
latex, *n.* (bot.) látex, *m.*
lath, *n.* lata, *f.*, listón, *m.*; **—,** *vt.* poner latas en las techumbres, enlistonar.
lathe, *n.* torno, *m.*
lather, *n.* espuma de jabón, jabonaduras, *f. pl.*; **—,** *vt.* and *vi.* bañar con espuma de jabón; espumar.
lathwork, *n.* enlistonado, *m.*
Latin, *n.* latín (lenguaje), *m.*; **—,** *n.* and *adj.* latino, na.
Latin American, *n.* latinoamericano, na.
Latin-American, *adj.* latinoamericano.
latitude, *n.* latitud, *f.*
latrine, *n.* letrina, *f.*
latter, *adj.* posterior, último; **the —,** éste; **—ly,** *adv.* últimamente, recientemente.
lattice, *n.* celosía, *f.*; reja, *f.*; **—,** *vt.* enrejar.
laud, *n.* alabanza, *f.*; (eccl.) laudes, *f. pl.*; **—,** *vt.* alabar, ensalzar.
laudable, *adj.* laudable, loable; meritorio.
laudanum, *n.* láudano, *m.*
laudatory, *adj.* laudatorio.
laugh, *vi.* reír; **— at,** reírse de, burlarse de; **—,** *n.* risa, risotada, *f.*
laughable, *adj.* risible.
laughing, *adj.* risueño; **— gas,** óxido nitroso; **—,** *n.* risa, *f.*; **to burst out —,** soltar una carcajada; **—ly,** *adv.* alegremente, con risa.
laughingstock, *n.* hazmerreír, *m.* y *f.*
laughter, *n.* risa, risotada, *f.*; **hearty —,** carcajada, *f.*; **outburst of —,** risotada, *f.*
launch, *vt.* lanzar; **—,** *vi.* lanzarse; **—,** *n.* (naut.) lancha, *f.*
launder, *vt.* lavar (la ropa).
laundress, *n.* lavandera, *f.*
laundry, *n.* lavadero, *m.*, lavandería, *f.*; ropa lavada o para lavar.
laundryman, *n.* lavandero, *m.*

laureate, *adj.* laureado.
laurel, *n.* (bot.) lauro, laurel, *m.*; honor, *m.*, fama, *f.*
laureled, *adj.* laureado.
Laurence, Lawrence, Lorenzo.
lava, *n.* lava, *f.*
lavaliere, *n.* medallón, *m.*
lavatory, *n.* lavabo, lavatorio, *m.*
lave, *vt.* (poet.) lavar, bañar.
lavender, *n.* (bot.) espliego, *m.*, lavándula, *f.*, cantueso, *m.*
lavish, *adj.* pródigo; gastador; —, *vt.* disipar, prodigar; **—ly,** *adv.* pródigamente.
law, *n.* ley, *f.*; derecho, *m.*; litigio judicial; jurisprudencia, *f.*; regla, *f.*; **according to —,** procedente, de acuerdo con la ley.
law-abiding, *adj.* obediente de las leyes.
lawful, *adj.* legal; legítimo; **—ly,** *adv.* legalmente.
lawgiver, *n.* legislador, *m.*
lawless, *adj.* ilegal; anárquico, sin ley.
lawmaker, *n.* legislador, *m.*
lawn, *n.* prado, *m.*; linón, *m.*; césped, *m.*; **— mower,** segadora de césped, cortacésped, dallador, *m.*; **— tennis,** juego de pelota con raqueta.
lawsuit, *n.* proceso, pleito, lite, *m.*, demanda, *f.*
lawyer, *n.* abogado, jurisconsulto, *m.*; **—'s office,** bufete de abogado.
lax, *adj.* laxo, flojo.
laxative, *n. and adj.* laxativo, purgante, laxante, *m.*
laxity, *n.* laxitud, flojedad, *f.*; relajación, *f.*
lay, *vt.* poner, colocar, extender; calmar, sosegar; imputar; apostar; exhibir; poner (un huevo); **to — claim,** reclamar; pretender; —, *vi.* aovar, poner huevos las aves.
lay, *adj.* laico, secular, seglar; **— brother,** lego, *m.*; —, *n.* canción, melodía, *f.*; **— of the land,** forma del tendido de terreno o suelo; consideración de la disposición o circunstancia; estado de asuntos; —, pretérito del verbo **lie.**
layer, *n.* gallina que pone; estrato, *m.*; **— (of cement, eggs, etc.),** camada, *f.*; **— of ice,** capa de hielo.
layette, canastilla, *f.*
layman, *n.* lego, seglar, *m.*
layoff, *n.* despedida del trabajo; —, *vt.* despedir del trabajo.
layout, *n.* plan, trazado, esquema, arreglo, *m.*, disposición, distribución, *f.*
layover, *n.* parada temporal en un lugar.
lazily, *adv.* perezosamente; lentamente.
laziness, *n.* pereza, *f.*
lazy, *adj.* perezoso, tardo, pesado.
lb. pound, lb. libra.
l.c.: in the place cited, l.c. loco citato (en el lugar citado); **letter of credit,** carta de crédito; **lower case,** min. minúsculas.
l.c.l. less than carload, (rail.) menos de carro entero, menos de vagonada.

l.c.m., L.C.M. least common multiple, M.C.M. mínimo común múltiplo.
lea, *n.* prado, *m.*, pradera, *f.*
leach, *n.* vasija perforada para filtrar; —, *vt.* filtrar.
lead, *vt.* conducir, guiar; gobernar; emplomar; llevar la batuta; **to — by a halter,** cabestrar; —, *vi.* mandar, tener el mando; ser mano (en el juego de naipes); sobresalir, ser el primero; —, *n.* delantera, *f.*; mano (en los naipes), *f.*; **to take the —,** tomar la delantera.
lead, *n.* plomo, *m.*; **— pencil,** lápiz, *m.*; **molten —,** plomo derretido.
leaden, *adj.* hecho de plomo; pesado, estúpido.
leader, *n.* líder, guía, conductor, *m.*; jefe general, *m.*; caudillo, *m.*; **political —,** cacique, *m.*
leading, *adj.* principal; capital; **— article,** artículo de fondo de una publicación; **— hand,** persona que juega primero en las partidas de naipes; **— horse,** caballo de silla; **— strings,** andadores, *m. pl.*; traílla, *f.*
leaf, *n.* folio, *m.*; hoja (de una planta), *f.*; hoja (de un libro), *f.*; hoja (de puerta), *f.*; (bot.) fronda, *f.*; **— tobacco,** tabaco en rama.
leafless, *adj.* deshojado, sin hojas.
leaflet, *n.* hojilla, *f.*
leafstalk, *n.* pecíolo, *m.*
leafy, *adj.* frondoso, hojudo.
league, *n.* liga, alianza, *f.*; legua, *f.*; —, *vi.* confederarse.
leak, *n.* fuga, *f.*, salida o escape (de gas, líquido, etc.); goteo, *m.*, gotera, *f.*; (naut.) vía de agua; —, *vi.* (naut.) hacer agua, gotear, salirse o escaparse (el agua, gas, etc.).
leakage, *n.* derrame, escape, goteo, *m.*; merma, *f.*; filtración, *f.*; gotera, fuga, *f.*
leakproof, *adj.* libre de goteo; a prueba de escape.
leaky, *adj.* roto, agujereado.
lean, *vt. and vi.* ladear, inclinar, apoyarse; **to — back,** retreparse, recostarse; —, *adj.* magro, seco, momio, chupado.
leaning, *n.* ladeo, *m.*; inclinación, tendencia, *f.*
lean-to, *n.* colgadizo, *m.*
leap, *vi.* saltar, brincar; salir con ímpetu; palpitar; dar brincos; —, *n.* salto, *m.*; **— year,** año bisiesto o intercalar.
leaper, *n.* brincador, ra.
leapfrog, *n.* a la una la mula, juego del burro.
learn, *vt. and vi.* aprender, conocer.
learned, *adj.* docto, instruído; **the —,** literatos, *m.pl.*; **—ly,** *adv.* doctamente.
learner, *n.* escolar, *m.*; aprendiz, *m.*
learning, *n.* literatura, ciencia, erudición, *f.*; saber, *m.*; letras, *f.pl.*
lease, *n.* arriendo, arrendamiento, *m.*; contrato de arrendamiento; —, *vt.* arrendar.

leasehold, *n.* arriendo, *m.*
leaseholder, *n.* arrendatario, ria, concesionario, ria.
leash, *n.* pihuela, correa, traílla, *f.*; —, *vt.* atar con correa.
least, *adj.* mínimo; —, *adv.* en el grado mínimo; **at** —, a lo menos; **not in the** —, ni en lo más mínimo; **the — possible,** lo menos posible.
leastwise, *adv.* (coll.) al menos, a lo menos.
leather, *n.* cuero, pellejo, *m.*; **to dress** —, zurrar, curtir pieles.
leatherette, *n.* cuero artificial, imitación de piel.
leathern, *adj.* (hecho) de cuero.
leatheroid, *n.* cuero artificial, imitación de piel o de cuero.
leathery, *adj.* correoso.
leave, *n.* licencia, *f.*; permiso, *m.*; despedida, *f.*; **to give** —, permitir; **to take** —, despedirse; —, *vt. and vi.* dejar, abandonar; ceder; cesar; salir.
leaven, *n.* levadura, *f.*; fermento, *m.*; —, *vt.* fermentar.
leaves, *n. pl.* de **leaf,** hojas, *f. pl.*
leave-taking, *n.* despedida, *f.*
lecherous, *adj.* lascivo.
lechery, *n.* lascivia, lujuria, *f.*
lectern, *n.* atril, facistol, *m.*
lecture, *n.* lectura, conferencia, *f.*; leyenda, *f.*; corrección, *f.*; reprensión, *f.*; —, *vt.* enseñar; censurar, reprender.
lecturer, *n.* conferenciante, *m.* y *f.*; lector, instructor, *m.*
ledge, *n.* capa, tonga, *f.*; borde, *m.*; reborde, *m.*; anaquel, *m.*
ledger, *n.* (com.) libro mayor.
lee, *n.* (naut.) sotavento, *m.*; —, *adj.* sotaventado.
leech, n. sanguijuela, *f.*
leek, *n.* (bot.) puerro, *m.*
leer, *n.* ojeada, *f.*; —, *vi.* ojear al través.
lees, *n.pl.* heces, *f.pl.*; sedimento, foso, *m.*
leeside, *n.* (naut.) banda de sotavento.
leeward, *adv.* (naut.) hacia el sotavento; —, *adj.* relativo al sotavento; —, *n.* sotavento, *m.*
leeway, *n.* desviación, *f.*; libertad, *f.*; margen, *m.*; (naut.) deriva, *f.*
left, *adj.* siniestro, izquierdo; **— behind,** rezagado; **on the** —, a la izquierda; **to be** —; quedarse.
left-handed, *adj.* zurdo; desmañado; insincero, malicioso.
leftist, *n.* and *adj.* (pol.) izquierdista, *m.* y *f.*
leftover, *n.* sobrante, *m.*, lo que queda por hacer; sobras, *f. pl.*, restos, *m. pl.*
leg, *n.* pierna, *f.*; pie, *m.*; (math.) cateto, *m.*; **— of a compass,** pierna, *f.*
leg.: legal, legal; **legislature,** leg. legislatura.
legacy, *n.* legado, *m.*, manda, *f.*
legal, *adj.* legal, legítimo; **— tender,**

moneda legal, curso legal; **—ly,** *adv.* legalmente.
legality, *n.* legalidad, legitimidad, *f.*
legalization, *n.* legalización, *f.*
legalize, *vt.* legalizar, autorizar.
legate, *n.* legado, diputado, *m.*
legatee, *n.* legatario, ria.
legation, *n.* legación, embajada, *f.*
legend, *n.* leyenda, *f.*
legendary, *adj.* fabuloso, quijotesco, legendario.
legerdemain, *n.* prestidigitación, *f.*, juego de manos.
legging, *n.* polaina, *f.*, botín, *m.*
leghorn, *n.* sombrero de paja italiano.
legibility, *n.* legibilidad, *f.*
legible, *adj.* legible, que puede leerse; **—bly,** *adv.* legiblemente.
legion, *n.* legión, *f.*
legionary, *adj.* legionario.
legislate, *vt.* legislar.
legislation, *n.* legislación, *f.*
legislative, *adj.* legislativo.
legislator, *n.* legislador, *m.*
legislature, *n.* legislatura, *f.*, cuerpo legislativo.
legitimacy, *n.* legitimidad, *f.*
legitimate, *adj.* legítimo; **—ly,** *adv.* legítimamente; —, *vt.* legitimar.
legitimize, *vt.* legitimar.
legume, *n.* legumbre, *f.*; **dried —s,** menestra, *f.*
leguminous, leguminose, *adj.* leguminoso.
leisure, *n.* desocupación, *f.*, ocio, *m.*; comodidad, *f.*; **at** —, cómodamente, con sosiego; **—ly,** *adv.* cómodamente, sosegadamente; **— hours,** horas o ratos libres.
lemon, *n.* limón, *m.*; **— drop,** pastilla de limón; **— squeezer,** exprimidera de limones.
lemonade, *n.* limonada, *f.*
lend, *vt.* prestar, dar prestado.
length, *n.* longitud, *f.*; largo, *m.*; duración, *f.*; distancia, *f.*; **at** —, finalmente.
lengthen, *vt.* alargar; —, *vi.* alargarse, dilatarse.
lengthways, lengthwise, *adv.* longitudinalmente, a lo largo; —, *adj.* colocado a lo largo.
lengthy, *adj.* largo; fastidioso.
leniency, *n.* benignidad, lenidad, *f.*
lenient, *adj.* lenitivo, indulgente.
Leningrad, Leningrado, *m.*
lenitive, *adj.* and *n.* lenitivo, *m.*
lenity, *n.* lenidad, benignidad, *f.*
lens, *n.* lente (vidrio convexo), *m.* y *f.*
Lent, *n.* cuaresma, *f.*
lentil, *n.* (bot.) lenteja, *f.*
leonine, *adj.* leonino.
leopard, *n.* (zool.) leopardo, pardal, *m.*
leper, *n.* leproso, sa.
leprosy, *n.* lepra, *f.*
leprous, *adj.* leproso.
lesion, *n.* lesión, *f.*
less, *adj.* inferior, menos; —, *adv.* menos.

lessee, *n.* arrendatario, ria.
lessen, *vt.* minorar, disminuir; —, *vi.* disminuirse.
lesser, *adj.* más pequeño; inferior.
lesson, *n.* lección, *f.*
lessor, *n.* arrendador, casero, *m.*
lest, *conj.* para que no, por temor de que.
let, *vt.* dejar, permitir; arrendar.
letdown, *n.* aflojamiento, *m.*, relajación, *f.*
lethal, *adj.* letal.
lethargic, lethargical, *adj.* letárgico.
lethargy, *n.* letargo, estupor, *m.*
letter, *n.* letra, *f.*; carta, *f.*; **air mail** —, carta aérea; **black** —, **Old English** —, letra gótica; **capital** —, mayúscula, *f.*; **circular** —, carta circular; **form** —, carta general, carta circular; **general delivery** —, carta en lista; — **box,** buzón para las cartas; — **case,** cartera, *f.*; — **drop,** buzón, *m.*; — **file,** archivo para cartas; — **of credit,** carta credencial o de crédito; — **of introduction,** carta de presentación; — **opener,** plegadera, *f.*; **love** —, billete amoroso; **order** —, carta de pedido; **registered** —, carta certificada; **round** —, letra redondilla; **short** —, billete, *m.*; **lower case** —, letra minúscula; **unclaimed** —**s,** cartas rezagadas, cartas no reclamadas.
letterhead, *n.* membrete, *m.*
lettering, *n.* inscripción, leyenda, *f.*; rótulo, *m.*
letter-perfect, *adj.* preciso, exacto; sabido a perfección.
letters patent, *n.* título de privilegio.
lettuce, *n.* lechuga, *f.*
leucocyte, *n.* leucocito, *m.*, glóbulo blanco en la sangre.
leucorrhea, *n.* (med.) leucorrea, *f.*
Levant, *n.* levante, oriente, *m.*
levee, *n.* dique, *m.*; recepción, *f.*, besamanos, *m.*
level, *adj.* llano, igual; nivelado, plano, allanado; —, *n.* llanura, *f.*; plano, *m.*; nivel, *m.*; —, *vt.* allanar; nivelar.
levelheaded, *adj.* discreto, sensato.
leveling, *n.* igualación, nivelación, *f.*; —, *adj.* nivelador.
lever, *n.* palanca, *f.*; **clutch** —, palanca, *f.*; **firing** —, palanca de desenganche; **operating** —, **driving** —, palanca de impulsión; **reverse** —, palanca de cambio de marcha.
leverage, *n.* acción de palanca.
leviathan, *n.* leviatán, *m.*
Levite, *n.* levita, *m.*
levity, *n.* levedad, ligereza, *f.*; inconstancia, veleidad, *f.*
levulose, *n.* (chem.) levulosa, *f.*
levy, *n.* leva (de tropas), *f.*; —, *vt.* embargar una propiedad; imponer (una multa, tributos, etc.).
lewd, *adj.* lascivo, disoluto, libidinoso.
lewdness, *n.* lascivia, disolución, libídine, *f.*, libertinaje, *m.*
lewisite, *n.* especie de vesicante incoloro.

lexicographer, *n.* lexicógrafo, *m.*
lexicography, *n.* lexicografía, *f.*
lexicon, *n.* léxico, diccionario, *m.*
l.h. left hand, izda., izq.ª izquierda.
L.I. Long Island, Long Island.
liability, *n.* responsabilidad, *f.*; —**ies,** (com.) pasivo, *m.*, créditos pasivos.
liable, *adj.* sujeto, expuesto a; responsable; capaz; **jointly** —, solidario, ria.
liaison, *n.* vinculación, *f.*; coordinación, *f.*; — **officer,** (mil.) oficial de intercomunicación y coordinación.
liana, *n.* (bot.) bejuco, jagüey, *m.*
liar, *n.* embustero, ra, mentiroso, sa.
lib. library, biblioteca.
libation, *n.* libación, *f.*
libel, *n.* libelo, *m.*; —, *vt.* difamar.
libeler, libeller, *n.* libelista, *m.* y *f.*
libelous, libellous, *adj.* difamatorio.
liberal, *adj.* liberal, generoso; franco; —, *n.* persona de ideas liberales; miembro del Partido Liberal; — **arts,** artes liberales, *f. pl.*; —**ly,** *adv.* liberalmente; a manos llenas.
liberality, *n.* liberalidad, generosidad, *f.*
liberalize, *vt.* liberalizar.
liberal-minded, *adj.* tolerante, de ideas liberales.
liberate, *vt.* libertar.
liberation, *n.* liberación, *f.*
liberator, *n.* libertador, *m.*
libertine, *n.* libertino, na; —, *adj.* libertino, disoluto.
liberty, *n.* libertad, *f.*; privilegio, *m.*; **to take the** — **to,** permitirse.
libidinous, *adj.* libidinoso.
libido, *n.* libido, *m.*
Libra, *n.* Libra (signo del zodíaco), *f.*
librarian, *n.* bibliotecario, ria.
library, *n.* librería, *f.*; biblioteca, *f.*; gabinete *m.*; **circulating** —, biblioteca por suscripción.
libretto, *n.* (mus.) libreto, *m.*
Libya, Libia, *f.*
lice, *n. pl.* **de louse,** piojos, *m. pl.*
license, licence, *n.* licencia, *f.*; permiso, *m.*; **chauffeur's** —, carnet de chofer; **driver's** —, matrícula para conducir vehículos; — **number,** matrícula, *f.*
licensee, licencee, *n.* concesionario, ria.
licentious, *adj.* licencioso, disoluto; —**ly,** *adv.* licenciosamente.
lichen, *n.* (bot.) liquen, *m.*; (med.) especie de salpullido.
licit, *adj.* lícito.
lick, *vt.* lamer, chupar; (coll.) golpear, tundir; derrotar (en una pelea, etc.).
licking, *n.* paliza, *f.*
licorice, *n.* (bot.) regaliz, orozuz, *m.*
lid, *n.* tapa, *f.*, tapadera, *f.*; — **(of the eye),** párpado, *m.*
lie, *n.* mentira, *f.*; (coll.) trápala, *f.*; **little** —, mentirilla, *f.*; **to give the** — **to,** dar un mentís a; —, *vi.* mentir; echarse; reposar; acostarse; yacer.

lief, *adv.* de buena gana.
liege, *adj.* ligio, feudatario; —, *n.* súbdito, *m.*; señor feudal.
lien, *n.* derecho de retención.
lieu, *n.* lugar, *m.*; **in — of,** en vez de.
Lieut. Lieutenant, ten.te teniente.
lieutenancy, *n.* lugartenencia, *f.*
lieutenant, *n.* lugarteniente, teniente, *m.*; alférez, *m.*; **— commander,** capitán de corbeta; **— colonel,** teniente coronel; **— general,** teniente general; **second —,** subteniente, *m.*
life, *n.* vida, *f.*, ser, *m.*; conducta, *f.*; vivacidad, *f.*; **for —,** por toda la vida; **from —,** del natural; **high —,** el gran mundo; **— annuity,** censo o pensión de por vida; **— belt,** ceñidor para nadar, cinturón salvavidas; **— buoy,** guindola, boya, *f.*; **— guard,** guardia de corps; **— insurance,** seguro de vida; **— preserver,** salvavidas, *m.*; **— raft,** balsa salvavidas.
lifeboat, *n.* bote salvavidas, lancha salvavidas.
lifeguard, *n.* salvavidas (nadador), *m.*
lifeless, *adj.* muerto, inanimado; sin vivacidad.
lifesaver, *n.* salvavidas, *m.*, miembro del servicio de salvavidas.
life-size, *adj.* de tamaño natural.
lifetime, *n.* duración de la vida; —, *adj.* de por vida, que dura toda la vida.
lifework, *n.* obra total o principal de la vida de uno.
lift, *vt.* alzar, elevar, levantar; hurtar, robar; —, *n.* acción de levantar; alza, *f.*; ayuda, *f.*; ascensor (hidráulico), *m.*; **to give one a —,** ayudar a uno; llevar a uno gratuitamente en un vehículo.
lifting, *n.* izamiento, *m.*, acción de levantar.
lift pump, *n.* bomba aspirante.
ligament, ligature, *n.* ligamento, *m.*; ligadura, f.
ligatures, *n.* ligadura, *f.*; letras ligadas.
light, *n.* luz, *f.*; claridad, *f.*; conocimiento, *m.*; día, *m.*; reflejo, *m.*; candela, *f.*; resplandor, *m.*; **— beam,** columna de luz; **— bulb,** bombilla, *f.*; —, *adj.* ligero, leve, fácil; frívolo; superficial; ágil; inconstante; claro; blondo; **— in weight,** ligero, de poco peso; —, *vt.* encender; alumbrar; —, *vi.* hallar, encontrar; desmontarse; desembarcar.
lighten, *vi.* centellear como relámpago, brillar; aclarar; —, *vt.* iluminar; aligerar; aclarar.
lighter, *n.* (naut.) alijador, *m.*; (naut.) chalana, barcaza, gabarra, *f.*; encendedor, *m.*; **cigarette —,** encendedor de cigarrillos.
lighterage, *n.* alijo, *m.*; lanchaje, gabarraje, *m.*
lighterman, *n.* (naut.) gabarrero, *m.*
lightface, *n.* letra delgada de imprenta.
light-faced type, *n.* (print.) tipo delgado.
lighthearted, *adj.* despreocupado; alegre.

lighthouse, *n.* (naut.) faro, fanal, *m.*
lighting, *n.* iluminación, *f.*; **flood —,** iluminación intensiva.
lightly, *adv.* ligeramente; fácilmente; alegremente.
lightness, *n.* ligereza, *f.*; agilidad, velocidad, *f.*
lightning, *n.* relámpago, *m.*; **heat —,** relámpago sin trueno; **— bug,** luciérnaga, *f.*; **— rod,** pararrayos, *m.*
lights, *n.pl.* bofes, *m.pl.*
lightship, *n.* buque fanal, *m.*
lightweight, *adj.* de peso ligero.
light-year, *n.* recorrido de la luz en un año.
ligneous, *adj.* leñoso.
lignin, *n.* lignina, *f.*
lignite, *n.* lignito, *m.*
likable, *adj.* simpático, agradable.
like, *adj.* semejante; igual; verosímil; —, *n.* semejante, *m.*; semejanza, *f.*; —, *adv.* como, del mismo modo que; en son de; —, *vt.* and *vi.* querer, amar; gustar, agradar alguna cosa; **as you — it,** como quisiera usted; **to be —d,** caer en gracia; **to — some one,** tener simpatía por.
likelihood, *n.* probabilidad, *f.*; indicación, *f.*
likely, *adj.* probable, verosímil; —, *adv.* probablemente.
liken, *vt.* asemejar; comparar.
likeness, *n.* semejanza, *f.*; igualdad, *f.*; retrato fiel.
likewise, *adv.* igualmente, asimismo.
liking, *n.* gusto, agrado, *m.*
lilac, *n.* (bot.) lila, *f.*; —, *adj.* de color lila.
lily, *n.* lirio, *m.*; **— of the valley,** lirio de los valles, muguete, *m.*
limb, *n.* miembro (del cuerpo), *m.*; pierna, *f.*; rama (de un árbol), *f.*
limber, *adj.* manejable, flexible; —, *vt.* and *vi.* poner manejable, hacer flexible; —, *vt.* (mil.) poner el avantrén a una cureña; —, *n.* (mil.) avantrén, *m.*
lime, *n.* cal, *f.*; liga, *f.*; variedad de limón; **— tree,** lima, *f.*; tilo, *m.*, tila, *f.*; —, *vt.* untar con liga.
limelight, *n.* centro de atención pública.
limerick, *n.* versos jocosos.
limestone, *n.* piedra de cal, caliza, *f.*
limewater, *n.* agua de cal.
limit, *n.* límite, término, *m.*; línea, *f.*; **to the —,** hasta no más; —, *vt.* restringir; concretar, confinar.
limitation, *n.* limitación, *f.*; restricción, *f.*; coartación, *f.*
limited, *adj.* tasado, limitado.
limitless, *adj.* inmenso, ilimitado, sin límite.
limn, *vt.* pintar; dibujar; retratar.
limousine, *n.* especie de vehículo cerrado.
limp, *vi.* cojear; —, *n.* cojera, *f.*; —, *adj.* fláccido, flojo, blando.
limpid, *adj.* limpio, claro, transparente; límpido.
linchpin, *n.* pezonera, *f.*, perno, sotrozo, *m.*
Lincoln, Lincoln.

linden, linden tree, linden tea, *n.* tila, *f.*, tilo, *m.*

line, *n.* línea, *f.*; (mil.) línea de batalla; raya, *f.*; contorno, *m.*; cola, *f.*; ecuador, *m.*; ferrocarril, *m.*, vía, *f.*; renglón, *m.*; verso, *m.*; linaje, *m.*; cordón (muy delgado), *m.*; **bunt** —, briol, *m.*; **end of** —, (rail.) final del recorrido; **pipe** —, cañería, *f.*; —, *vt.* forrar; revestir; rayar, trazar líneas; —, *vi.* alinearse.

lineage, *n.* linaje, *m.*; descendencia, *f.*; prosapia, *f.*; generación, *f.*

lineal, *adj.* lineal; **—ly,** *adv.* en línea recta.

lineament, *n.* lineamento, *m.*

linear, *adj.* lineal.

lineman, *n.* (rail.) guardavía, guardabarreras, *m.*; reparador de líneas telefónicas; (football) atajador o guarda en la línea de embestida.

linen, *n.* lienzo, lino, *m.*; tela de hilo; ropa blanca; —, *adj.* de lino, de tela de hilo.

liner, *n.* avión o vapor de travesía.

linesman, *n.* (football) juez de línea en el futbol.

line-up, *n.* formación, *f.*; (football) formación de los jugadores antes de principiar el juego.

linger, *vi.* demorarse, tardar, permanecer por un tiempo.

lingering, *n.* tardanza, dilación, *f.*; —, *adj.* moroso, lento; **—ly,** *adv.* lentamente; lánguidamente.

linguist, *n.* lingüista, *m.* y *f.*

liniment, *n.* linimento, *m.*

lining, *n.* forro, *m.*

link, *n.* eslabón, *m.*; vínculo, *m.*; anillo de cadena; hacha de viento; (mech.) articulación, *f.*, gozne, *m.*; —, *vt.* and *vi.* unir, vincular.

linnet, *n.* (orn.) pardillo, pardal, *m.*

linoleum, *n.* linóleo, *m.*

linotype, *n.* linotipo, *m.*, máquina linotipista.

linseed, *n.* linaza, *f.*

lint, *n.* hilas, *f. pl.*; hilaza, *f.*

lintel, *n.* dintel, tranquero, *m.*

linter, *n.* desfibradora de algodón.

lion, *n.* león, *m.*

lioness, *n.* leona, *f.*

lip, *n.* labio, borde, *m.*; **— reading,** acción de interpretar los movimientos de los labios.

lipstick, *n.* lápiz para los labios, lápiz labial.

liq. liquid, liq.º líquido.

liquefy, *vt.* and *vi.* licuar, liquidar; derretir.

liqueur, *n.* licor, aguardiente, *m.*

liquid, *adj.* líquido; **— air,** aire flúido o líquido; **— fire,** fuego líquido; **— measure,** cántara, *f.*, medida para líquidos; —, *n.* licor, líquido, *m.*

liquidate, *vt.* liquidar, saldar (cuentas).

liquidation, *n.* (com.) liquidación, *f.*

liquor, *n.* licor, *m.*; **— case,** licorera, *f.*; **— maker, — dealer,** licorista, *m.*

Lisbon, Lisboa, *f.*

lisle, *n.* tejido de algodón o lino usado en calcetería.

lisp, *vi.* tartamudear, cecear; —, *n.* ceceo, tartamudeo, *m.*

lissome, *adj.* flexible, ágil.

list, *n.* lista, *f.*, elenco, *m.*; cenefa, *f.*; catálogo, *m.*; **— price,** precio de catálogo; **—s,** *n. pl.* liza, *f.*; —, *vt.* poner en lista; registrar; —, *vi.* (mil.) alistarse.

listen, *vi.* escuchar, atender.

lister, *n.* arado doble.

listerine, *n.* listerina, *f.*

listless, *adj.* indiferente, descuidado; **—ly,** *adv.* negligentemente.

lit.: literally, lit. literalmente; **literature,** Lit. Literatura.

litany, *n.* letanía, *f.*

liter, *n.* litro, *m.*

literacy, *n.* capacidad para leer y escribir.

literal, *adj.* literal, al pie de la letra, a la letra; **—ly,** *adv.* literalmente.

literary, *adj.* literario; **— contest,** certamen, *m.*, concurso literario; **— forum,** palestra, *f.*

literature, *n.* literatura, *f.*

lithe, *adj.* flexible, manejable.

lithium, *n.* (chem.) litio, *m.*

lithograph, *n.* litografía, *f.*; —, *vt.* litografiar.

lithographer, *n.* litógrafo, *m.*

lithography, *n.* litografía, *f.*

lithoscope, *n.* litoscopio, *m.*

lithosphere, *n.* litoesfera, *f.*, corteza de la tierra.

litigant, *n.* litigante, *m.* y *f.*

litigate, *vt.* and *vi.* litigar, pleitear.

litigation, *n.* litigio, pleito, *m.*, litigación, *f.*

litigious, *adj.* litigioso.

litmus, *n.* tornasol en pasta; **— paper,** papel reactivo.

Litt. D. Doctor of Letters, D. en L. Doctor en Letras.

litter, *n.* litera, cama, *f.*, cama portátil; lechigada, ventregada, *f.*; —, *vt.* and *vi.* parir los animales; —, *vt.* desordenar; **to — a room,** poner un cuarto en desorden.

little, *adj.* pequeño; poco; chico; **a —,** poquito; **— boy,** chico, chiquito, *m.*; **— by —,** poco a poco; **— girl,** chica, chiquita, *f.*; **very —,** muy poquito; —, *n.* poco, *m.*; parte pequeña.

Little Dipper, *n.* (ast.) Carro Menor.

liturgy, *n.* liturgia, *f.*

live, *vi.* vivir; mantenerse; habitar.

live, *adj.* vivo; **— oak,** roble de Florida; **— wire,** persona lista o muy activa; alambre cargado.

livelihood, *n.* vida, *f.*; subsistencia, *f.*

liveliness, *n.* vivacidad, *f.*

livelong, *adj.* todo.

lively, *adj.* vivo, brioso; gallardo; animado, alegre.

liver, *n.* hígado, *m.*

livery, *n.* librea, *f.*

liverwurst, *n.* salchicha de hígado.
lives, *n. pl.* de **life,** vidas, *f. pl.*
livestock, *n.* ganadería, *f.*; ganado en pie.
livid, *adj.* lívido, cárdeno, amoratado.
living, *n.* modo de vivir; subsistencia, *f.*; —, *adj.* vivo; viviente; — **room,** sala de recibo, salón, *m.*; — **wage,** salario adecuado para vivir.
lizard, *n.* lagarto, *m.*, lagartija, *f.*
ll. lines, lín. líneas.
llama, *n.* (zool.) llama, *f.*
llano, *n.* llano, *m.*
LL.D. Doctor of Laws, Doctor en Derecho.
lo, *interj.* ¡he aquí! ¡ved aquí!
load, *vt.* cargar; **to — a firearm,** cargar; —, *n.* carga, *f.*; cargamento, *m.*; peso, *m.*; — **of a firearm,** carga (de una arma de fuego), *f.*
loader, *n.* cargador, embarcador, *m.*
loading, *n.* cargo, *m.*, acción de cargar.
loaf, *n.* pan, *m.*; — **of sugar,** pilón, *m.*; **small —,** bollo, *m.*; —, *vi.* haraganear, holgazanear.
loafer, *n.* holgazán, ana, gandul, la, cantonero, ra.
loam, *n.* marga, *f.*
loan, *n.* préstamo, empréstito, *m.*; — **office,** casa de préstamos; —, *vt.* prestar.
loath, loth, *adj.* con aversión, poco dispuesto (a hacer algo).
loathe, *vt.* aborrecer, detestar.
loathing, *n.* repugnancia, aversión, *f.*
loathsome, loathly, *adj.* detestable, repugnante.
loaves, *n. pl.* de **loaf,** panes, *m. pl.*
lob, *n.* (tennis) pelota alta.
lobby, *n.* vestíbulo, *m.*; —, *vi.* cabildear.
lobbying, *n.* cabildeo, *m.*
lobe, *n.* lóbulo, *m.*
lobelia, *n.* (bot.) lobelia, *f.*
lobster, *n.* langosta, *f.*
local, *adj.* local; —, *n.* (rail.) tren que para en todas las estaciones.
locale, *n.* local, *m.*
localism, *n.* provincialismo, *m.*
locality, *n.* localidad, *f.*
localize, *vt.* localizar.
locally, *adv.* localmente.
local option, *n.* derecho de una ciudad, distrito, etc., a permitir o no la venta de bebidas alcohólicas.
locate, *vt.* ubicar, colocar, situar.
located, *adj.* situado, ubicado.
location, *n.* ubicación, *f.*; localización, colocación, *f.*
loc. cit. in the place cited, l.c. loco citato (en el lugar citado).
lock, *n.* cerradura, cerraja, *f.*; llave (de arma de fuego), *f.*; vedija (de lana), *f.*; mechón (de cabello), *m.*; compuerta, *f.*; — **nut,** contratuerca, *f.*; — **stitch,** punto de cadeneta; **spring —,** cerradura de golpe o de muelle; —, *vt.* cerrar, cerrar con llave; **to — out,** cerrar la puerta a

uno para que no entre; —, *vi.* cerrarse con llave.
locked, *adj.* cerrado (bajo llave); enganchado; trabado, entrelazado.
locker, *n.* armario, *m.*; cofre, *m.*; gaveta, *f.*; —**s,** *n. pl.* (naut.) cajonada, *f.*
locket, *n.* medallón, guardapelo, *m.*
lockjaw, *n.* trismo, tétano, *m.*
lockout, *n.* cesación del trabajo, paro forzoso, *m.*
locksmith, *n.* cerrajero, *m.*
locomotion, *n.* locomoción, *f.*
locomotive, *n.* locomotora, *f.*
locomotor, *adj.* locomotriz; — **ataxia,** (med.) ataxia locomotriz.
locoweed, *n.* variedad de hierba venenosa.
locus, *n.* (math.) lugar, *m.*, situación, *f.*
locust, *n.* langosta, *f.*
lode, *n.* filón, *m.*, vena, veta, *f.*
lodge, *n.* casa de guarda en el bosque; casita pequeña; surcursal o casa de una sociedad; —, *vt.* alojar; fijar en la memoria; —, *vi.* residir, habitar.
lodger, *n.* huésped, *m.* y *f.*, inquilino, na.
lodging, *n.* posada, casa, habitación, *f.*; hospedaje, *m.*
loess, *n.* especie de tierra muy calcárea depositada al final del período diluvial.
loft, *n.* piso, *m.*; desván, *m.*
loftiness, *n.* altura, *f.*; sublimidad, *f.*; soberbia, *f.*
lofty, *adj.* alto; sublime; altivo; elevado.
log, *n.* leño, *m.*, trozo de árbol; (naut.) barquilla, *f.*; cuaderno de bitácora; — **cabin,** cabaña rústica.
log. logarithm, log. logaritmo.
loganberry, *n.* (bot.) especie de zarzamora.
logarithm, *n.* logaritmo, *m.*
logbook, *n.* (naut.) diario de navegación.
logger, *n.* persona que corta árboles; máquina para el corte y transporte de trozas.
loggerhead, *n.* zote, *m.*; barra de hierro para calentar alquitrán; tortuga marina; **at —s,** en disputa.
logging, *n.* acción de cortar y transportar trozas.
logic, *n.* lógica, *f.*
logical, *adj.* lógico, consecuente.
logician, *n.* lógico, ca.
logistics, *n.* (mil.) logística, *f.*
logrolling, *n.* acuerdo entre los políticos para ayudarse recíprocamente.
logwood, *n.* palo de Campeche, campeche, *m.*
loin, *n.* ijada, *f.*, ijar, *m.*; —**s,** *n. pl.* lomos, *m. pl.*
loiter, *vi.* haraganear, holgazanear.
loiterer, *n.* haragán, ana, holgazán, ana.
loll, *vt.* dejar colgar; —, *vi.* apoyarse, recostarse; dejar colgar la lengua (aplícase a los animales).
lon., long. longitude, long. longitud.
London, Londres, *m.*
lone, *adj.* solitario, soltero.
loneliness, *n.* soledad, *f.*
lonely, *adj.* = **lonesome.**

lonesome, *adj.* solitario, solo; triste, abatido por la soledad.

long, *adj.* largo, prolongado; **a — time,** mucho tiempo, un largo rato; **—,** *adv.* durante mucho tiempo; **so — as you desire it,** todo el tiempo que lo desee; **—,** *vi.* anhelar, desear con vehemencia.

long-distance, *adj.* de larga distancia; **— call,** llamada de larga distancia.

longer, *adj.* más largo; **—,** *adv.* más tiempo; **no —,** ya no.

longevity, *n.* longevidad, *f.*

long-faced, *adj.* carilargo.

longhand, *n.* escritura a mano.

longhorn, *n.* especie de buey español con cuernos muy largos; vaca.

longing, *n.* deseo vehemente, anhelo, *m.*

longitude, *n.* longitud, *f.*

longitudinal. *adj.* longitudinal.

long-lived, *adj.* longevo.

longshoreman, *n.* estibador, *m.*

long-standing, *adj.* de larga duración.

long suit, *n.* especialidad, *f.*; punto fuerte.

look, *vt.* and *vi.* mirar; ver; considerar, pensar, contemplar, esperar; parecer; tener traza de; buscar; **as it —s to me,** a mi ver; **— out!** ¡cuidado! ¡tate! **to — after,** echar una vista, cuidar de; **to — at contemptuously, to—at furtively,** mirar de reojo; **to — bad,** tener mala cara; **to — over,** repasar; **—,** *n.* aspecto, *m.*; mirada, *f.*; ojeada, *f.*

looking, *n.* miramiento, *m.*; **— glass,** espejo, *m.*

lookout, *n.* (mil.) centinela, *m.* y *f.*; (naut.) vigía, *m.*

loom, *n.* telar, *m.*; **— vi.** asomar, aparecer.

loon, *n.* tonto, *m.*

loop, *n.* ojal, *m.*; presilla, *f.*; aro, anillo, *m.*; lazo, *m.*; vuelta, *f.*

loophole, *n.* tronera, buhedera, *f.*; escapatoria, *f.*

loop-the-loop, *n.* (aer.) rizo, *m.*, salto mortal en el aire.

loose, *adj.* suelto, desatado; flojo; suelto de vientre; vago, relajado; disoluto; desenredado; descuidado; **—ly,** *adv.* sueltamente.

loose-jointed, *adj.* con las coyunturas al parecer flojas; capaz de mover las coyunturas con gran facilidad.

loose-leaf, *adj.* de hojas sueltas (insertables en forma de libro).

loosen, *vt.* aflojar, laxar; desliar, desatar.

looseness, *n.* flojedad, *f.*; relajación, *f.*; flujo de vientre.

loot, *n.* pillaje, botín, *m.*; **—,** *vt.* pillar, saquear.

lop, *vt.* desmochar.

lope, *n.* galope tendido.

lop-eared, *adj.* con las orejas caídas.

lopsided, *adj.* desproporcionado, desequilibrado, maniático, ladeado, sesgado.

loquacious, *adj.* locuaz, charlador, palabrero.

loquacity, *n.* locuacidad, charla, garrulidad, *f.*

Lord, *n.* Dios, *m.*; **Almighty —,** el Todopoderoso; **good —!** ¡Dios mío!

lord, *n.* señor, *m.*; amo, dueño, *m.*; lord (título de nobleza inglés), *m.*; **—,** *vi.* señorear, dominar.

lordliness, *n.* señorío, *m.*; altivez, *f.*; orgullo, *m.*

lordling, *n.* lord pequeño.

lordly, *adj.* señoril, orgulloso, imperioso; **—,** *adv.* imperiosamente, altivamente.

lordship, *n.* excelencia, señoría, *f.*; dominio, *m.*, autoridad, *f.*

lore, *n.* saber, *m.*, erudición, *f.*, conocimiento de hechos y costumbres tradicionales.

lorgnette, *n.* impertinentes, *m. pl.*

Lorraine, Lorena.

lorry, *n.* carro de plataforma, autocamión, *m.*

lose, *vt.* perder; disipar, malgastar; **—,** *vi.* perderse, decaer; **to — one's senses,** perder la chaveta; **to — one's temper, to — one's composure,** salirse de sus casillas; **to — out,** ser derrotado.

loss, *n.* pérdida, *f.*; daño, *m.*; **to be at a —,** estar perplejo, estar en duda.

losses, *n. pl.* pérdidas, *f. pl.*

lost sheep, *n.* cordero perdido, oveja descarriada.

lot, *n.* suerte, *f.*; lote, *m.*; cuota, *f.*; porción, *f.*; **building —,** solar, *m.*; **drawing —s,** sorteo, *m.*; **to draw —s,** decidir por suerte, echarlo a suerte.

lotion, *n.* loción, *f.*

lottery, *n.* lotería, rifa, *f.*

lotto, *n.* (juego) lotería, *f.*

lotus, *n.* (bot.) loto, *m.*

loud, *adj.* ruidoso, alto; clamoroso; (coll.) charro, vulgar; **—ly,** *adv.* ruidosamente; en voz alta.

loudness, *n.* ruido, *m.*; (coll.) vulgaridad, *f.*, falta de delicadeza; mal gusto; afición a los colores chillones, etc.

loudspeaker, *n.* altoparlante, *m.*, amplificador de voz.

Louis, Lewis, Luis.

lounge, *n.* sofá, canapé, *m.*; **— room,** sala de esparcimiento social, salón social; **—,** *vi.* haraganear.

louse, *n.* (*pl.* **lice**), piojo, *m.*; **plant —,** pulgón, *m.*; **sheep —,** caparra, *f.*

lousiness, *n.* piojería, *f.*

lousy, *adj.* piojoso; miserable; vil; (coll.) horrible, detestable.

lout, *n.* patán, rústico, zafio, *m.*

loutish, *adj.* rústico, tosco.

louver, *n.* (arch.) lucerna, lumbrera, *f.*

lovable, *adj.* amable, digno de ser querido.

love, *n.* amor, cariño, *m.*; galanteo, *m.*; **— game,** (tennis) juego a cero; **to fall in —,** enamorarse; **to make —,** cortejar, galantear, enamorar; **—,** *vt.* amar; gustar de; querer.

lovebird, *n.* (orn.) periquito, papagayo, *m.*

loveliness, *n.* amabilidad, *f.,* agrado, *m.;* belleza, *f.*

lovely, *adj.* amable, hermoso, bello.

love-making, *n.* enamoramiento, *m.*

lover, *n.* amante, galán, *m.;* (coll.) cortejo, *m.*

lovesick, *adj.* enamorado; herido de amor.

loving, *adj.* amoroso, afectuoso; —ly, *adv.* afectuosamente.

loving-kindness, *n.* terneza, *f.;* afecto, *m.*

low, *adj.* bajo, pequeño; hondo; abatido; vil; —, *vi.* mugir; —, *adv.* a precio bajo; en posición baja; vilmente.

lower, *adj.* más bajo; — **berth,** litera o cama baja; — **case,** (print.) caja baja, caja de minúsculas; —, *vt.* bajar, humillar; disminuir; **to** — **(price),** rebajar (el precio); —, *vi.* disminuirse; encapotarse.

lowering, *adj.* nebuloso; ceñudo.

lowermost, lowest, *adj.* más bajo, ínfimo.

lowing, *n.* mugido, *m.*

lowland, *n.* tierra baja.

lowliness, *n.* bajeza, *f.;* humildad, *f.*

lowly, *adj.* humilde; vil; —, *adv.* humildemente; vilmente.

low-minded, *adj.* bajo, ruin.

low-necked, *adj.* escotado, de cuello bajo.

low-pitched, *adj.* de tono bajo, de calidad baja.

low-pressure, *adj.* de baja presión.

low-priced, *adj.* barato.

low water, *n.* baja mar; **low-water mark,** nivel de agua mínimo o bajo.

loyal, *adj.* leal, fiel; —ly, *adv.* lealmente.

loyalist, *n.* (pol.) realista, *m.* y *f.*

loyalty, *n.* lealtad, fidelidad, *f.*

lozenge, *n.* rombo, *m.;* pastilla en forma de rombo.

L.S. place for stamp, L.S. lugar del sello.

L.S.D., l.s.d., pounds, shillings and pence, libras, chelines y peniques.

Lt. Lieutenant, Ten.te Teniente.

Ltd., ltd. Limited (com.) Ltda. Limitada, S. en C. Sociedad en Comandita.

lubber, *n.* marinero inexperto; patán, *m.;* bobo, *m.*

lubricant, *n.* and *adj.* lubricante, *m.*

lubricate, *vt.* untar con materias crasas, lubricar, engrasar.

lubricating, *adj.* lubricante, lubricador.

lubrication, *n.* lubricación, *f.*

lubricator, *n.* lubricador, *m.;* engrasador, *m.*

lucent, *adj.* brillante, claro.

lucid, *adj.* luciente, luminoso; claro.

lucidity, *n.* esplendor, resplandor, *m.*

Lucifer, *n.* Lucifer, *m.;* **l— (match),** fósforo de fricción.

luck, *n.* acaso, *m.;* fortuna, *f.;* **good** —, suerte, *f.*

luckily, *adv.* por fortuna, afortunadamente.

luckless, *adj.* infeliz, desventurado.

lucky, *adj.* afortunado, feliz, venturoso, dichoso; **to be** —, tener suerte.

lucrative, *adj.* lucrativo.

lucre, *n.* lucro, *m.;* ganancia, *f.*

lucubration, *n.* lucubración, *f.*

Lucy, Lucía.

ludicrous, *adj.* burlesco; ridículo; —ly, *adv.* burlescamente.

luff, *vt.* (naut.) orzar; —, *n.* (naut.) orza, *f.*

lug, *vt.* tirar; arrastrar; (naut.) tirar de un cabo; —, *n.* pértiga, *f.;* agarradera, asa, *f.*

luggage, *n.* equipaje, *m.;* — **rack,** portaequipajes, *m.;* **small** —, (rail.) bultos a la mano.

lugger, *n.* (naut.) lugre, *m.*

lugubrious, *adj.* lúgubre, triste.

lukewarm, *adj.* tibio; templado; —ly, *adv.* tibiamente.

lull, *vt.* arrullar; adormecer; aquietar.

lullaby, *n.* arrullo, *m.;* canción de cuna, *f.*

lumbago, *n.* lumbago, *m.*

lumber, *n.* madera de construcción; — **dealer,** maderero, *m.,* comerciante en maderas.

lumberjack, *n.* leñador, hachero, *m.,* cortador de árboles.

lumberman, *n.* maderero, *m.,* comerciante en maderas.

lumberyard, *n.* depósito de maderas de construcción.

luminary, *n.* luminar, *m.,* lumbrera, *f.*

luminescence, *n.* luminiscencia, *f.*

luminous, *adj.* luminoso, resplandeciente.

lump, *n.* protuberancia, *f.,* masa informe; **by the** — , en grueso, por junto; — **of sugar,** terrón de azúcar; —, *vt.* amontonar; —, *vi.* agrumarse.

lunacy, *n.* locura, *f.;* frenesí, *m.*

Luna moth, *n.* variedad de polilla americana (grande y con largas colas en las alas traseras).

lunar, *adj.* lunar; — **caustic,** nitrato de plata.

lunatic, *adj.* lunático, loco, frenético; fantástico; —, *n.* loco, ca.

lunch, *n.* merienda, colación, *f.,* almuerzo, *m.;* —, *vi.* almorzar, merendar.

luncheon, *n.* almuerzo, *m.,* merienda, colación, *f.*

lunette, *n.* (arch.) luneta, *f.;* (mil.) luneta, *f.,* media luna.

lung, *n.* pulmón, *m.*

lupine, *n.* (bot.) altramuz, lupino, *m.;* —, *adj.* lupino, relativo al lobo; voraz.

lurch, *n.* abandono, *m.;* vaivén, *m.;* (naut.) bandazo, *m.;* sacudida, *f.;* —, *vi.* dar bandazos; caminar con vaivén.

lure, *n.* señuelo, *m.,* añagaza, *f.;* cebo, *m.;* —, *vt.* atraer, inducir.

lurid, *adj.* fantástico, lívido, descolorido.

lurk, *vi.* espiar, ponerse en acecho.

luscious, *adj.* delicioso, sabroso; atractivo, apetitoso.

lush, *adj.* jugoso; suculento.

lust, *n.* lujuria, sensualidad, *f.;* libídine, codicia, *f.;* concupiscencia, *f.;* —, *vi.* lujuriar.

luster, lustre, *n.* lustre, *m.,* brillantez, *f.;* lucimiento, *m.;* realce, *m.;* viso, *m.*

lustful, *adj.* lujurioso, voluptuoso; cachondo, libidinoso; **—ly,** *adv.* lujuriosamente.

lusty, *adj.* fuerte, vigoroso.

lute, *n.* laúd, *m.*

Lutheran, *n.* and *adj.* luterano, na.

luxuriance, *n.* exuberancia, superabundancia, *f.*

luxuriant, *adj.* exuberante, superabundante.

luxuriate, *vi.* crecer con exuberancia.

luxurious, *adj.* lujoso; exuberante; **—ly,** *adv.* lujosamente; voluptuosamente.

luxury, *n.* voluptuosidad, *f.*; exuberancia, *f.*; lujo, *m.*

lycée, *ŋ.* liceo, *m.*

lyceum, *n.* liceo, *m.*

lye, *n.* lejía, *f.*

lying, *n.* acto de mentir, mentira, *f.*; **—,** *adj.* mentiroso.

lying-in, *n.* parto, *m.*

lymph, *n.* linfa, *f.*

lymphatic, *adj.* linfático.

lynch, *vt.* linchar.

lynx, *n.* lince, *m.*

lyre, *n.* lira, *f.*

lyric, lyrical, *adj.* lírico.

lysol, *n.* lisol, *m.*

M

M.: Majesty, M. Majestad; **Master,** M. Maestro; **Monday,** lun. lunes; **Monsieur,** Mr. Monsieur, señor.

m.: married, casado; **masculine,** m. masculino; **meter,** m. metro; **midnight,** medianoche; **mile,** milla; **minute,** m. minuto; **month,** m/ mes; **morning,** m. mañana; **noon,** m. meridiano.

M.A. Master of Arts, M. en A. Maestro en Artes.

macabre, *adj.* macabro.

macadam, *n.* macadán, macádam, *m.*

macadamize, *vt.* macadamizar, macadanizar.

macaroni, *n.* macarrones, *m.pl.*

macaroon, *n.* almendrado, macarrón, *m.*, macarrón de almendras.

mace, *n.* maza, *f.*; macis, *f.*

macerate, *vt.* macerar; mortificar el cuerpo.

machete, *n.* machete, *m.*

Machiavelian, *adj.* maquiavélico.

machinate, *vt.* and *vi.* maquinar.

machination, *n.* maquinación, trama, *f.*

machine, *n.* máquina, *f.*; **— gun,** ametralladora, *f.*; **— shop,** taller de reparación de maquinaria; **— tool,** máquina herramienta; **—** *vt.* fresar.

machinery, *n.* maquinaria, mecánica, *f.*

machinist, *n.* maquinista, mecánico, *m.*

mackerel, *n.* escombro, *m.*, caballa, *f.*

mackinaw, *n.* chamarra, *f.*

mackintosh, *n.* sobretodo impermeable.

macrocosm, *n.* macrocosmo, *m.*

mad, *adj.* loco, furioso, rabioso, insensato; **stark —,** loco rematado; **to go —,**

volverse loco; **—ly,** *adv.* locamente, rabiosamente.

Mad. Madam, Sra. Señora.

madam, *n.* madama, señora, *f.*

madcap, *n.* calavera, *m.*, botarate, *m.* y *f.*

madden, *vt.* enloquecer, trastornar; enfurecer.

madder, *n.* (bot.) rubia, *f.*

made, *adj.* hecho, fabricado, producido.

Madeira, Madera, *f.*

Madeline, Magdalen, Magdalena.

mademoiselle, *n.* señorita, *f.*

made-to-measure, *adj.* hecho a la medida.

made-to-order, *adj.* hecho a la medida o a la orden.

made-up, *adj.* ficticio; artificial; pintado.

madhouse, *n.* casa de locos.

madman, *n.* loco, maniático, *m.*

madness, *n.* locura, manía, *f.*; furor, *m.*

madras, *n.* variedad de tela de algodón para camisas de hombre, vestidos, etc.

maelstrom, *n.* vórtice, remolino, *m.*

maestro, *n.* (mus.) maestro, *m.*, director de orquesta.

mag. magazine, revista (publicación), *f.*

magazine, *n.* almacén, depósito, *m.*; (print.) revista, *f.*; (naut.) Santabárbara, *f.*

Magdalene, Magdalena.

magdalene, *n.* magdalena, *f.*, prostituta penitente.

magenta, *n.* fucsina, *f.*; color rojo azulado que produce la fucsina.

maggot, *n.* gusano, *m.*; noción fantástica.

magic, *n.* magia, nigromancia, *f.*; **—,** *adj.* mágico; **—ally,** *adv.* mágicamente.

magician, *n.* mago, nigromante, *m.*

magic lantern, *n.* linterna mágica.

magisterial, *adj.* dictatorial, magisterial; autoritativo; **—ly,** *adv.* magistralmente.

magistracy, *n.* magistratura, *f.*

magistrate, *n.* magistrado, *m.*

Magna Charta, *n.* Carta Magna.

magnanimity, *n.* magnanimidad, *f.*

magnanimous, *adj.* magnánimo; **—ly,** *adv.* magnánimamente.

magnate, *n.* magnate, *m.*

magnesia, *n.* magnesia, *f.*

magnesium, *n.* magnesio, *m.*

magnet, *n.* imán, *m.*, piedra imán.

magnetic, *adj.* magnético; **— needle,** calamita, brújula, *f.*

magnetism, *n.* magnetismo, *m.*

magnetize, *vt.* magnetizar, imantar.

magneto, *n.* magneto, *m.*

magnificence, *n.* magnificencia, *f.*

magnificent, *adj.* magnífico; pomposo, rumboso; **—ly,** *adv.* pomposamente.

magnify, *vt.* amplificar, magnificar; exaltar, exagerar.

magnifying glass, *n.* vidrio de aumento.

magnitude, *n.* magnitud, grandeza, *f.*

magnolia, *n.* magnolia, *f.*

magpie, *n.* urraca, picaza, *f.*

maguey, *n.* (bot.) maguey, *m.*, pita, *f.*

mahogany, *n.* caoba, caobana, *f.*

maid, maiden, n. doncella, joven, f.; moza, criada, f.

maiden, adj. virgen, virgíneo, virginal; nuevo, intacto.

maidenhood, n. doncellez, virginidad, f.

maidenly, adj. virginal, púdico.

maidservant, n. criada, sirvienta, f.

mail, n. correo, m.; mala, valija, f.; correspondencia, f.; cota de malla; **by registered —,** bajo sobre certificado, por correo certificado; **by return —,** a vuelta de correo; **— coach,** diligencia, f.; **— train,** tren correo.

mailbag, n. portacartas, m., valija de correo.

mailbox, n. buzón, m.

mailman, n. cartero, m.

mail order, m. pedido postal; compra de artículos por correo.

mail-order house, n. casa de ventas por correo.

mailplane, n. avión postal.

maim, vt. mutilar; estropear; tullir.

main, adj. principal; esencial; **— line,** (rail.) línea principal, tronco, m.; **— office,** casa matriz; **—,** n. océano, m., alta mar; fuerza, f.; **in the —,** en general; **—ly,** adv. principalmente, sobre todo.

mainland, n. continente, m.

mainmast, n. palo mayor de un navío.

mainspring, n. muelle (de reloj, etc.), m.

mainstay, n. (naut.) apoyo principal del mastelero; sostén principal.

maintain, vt. and vi. mantener, sostener; conservar.

maintenance, n. mantenimiento, m.; protección, f.; sustento, m.; conservación (de carreteras, caminos, etc.), f.

maintopsail, n. (naut.) gavia, f.

maize, n. maíz, m.

Maj. Major, Mayor, Comte. Comandante.

majestic, majestical, adj. majestuoso; grande; **—ally,** adv. majestuosamente.

majesty, n. majestad, f.

majolica, majolica ware, n. mayólica, f.

major, adj. mayor; **—,** n. (mil.) sargento mayor; (mil.) comandante, m.; primera proposición de un silogismo; **— general,** mariscal de campo.

majordomo, n. mayordomo, m.

majority, n. mayoría, f.; pluralidad, f.; (mil.) sargentía mayor; **— (of votes in an election),** mayoría absoluta.

make, vt. hacer, crear, producir, fabricar; ejecutar; obligar, forzar; confeccionar; vi. hacerse, ir, encaminarse; **to — a fool of,** engañar; **to — a point of,** dar importancia a; **to — over,** hacer de nuevo; **to — ready,** preparar; **to — room,** hacer lugar; **to — use of,** servirse de, utilizar; **to — a show of,** ostentar; **to — fun of,** burlarse de; **to — known,** dar a conocer; **to — no difference,** no importar; **to — out,** divisar, columbrar; **—,** n. hechura, f.; forma, figura, f.

make-believe, n. disimulo, m.; pretexto, m.

makepeace, n. pacificador, ra, conciliador, ra.

maker, n. artífice, m. y f.; fabricante, m. y f.; **— (of a deed),** otorgante, m. y f.; **— of portraits,** retratista, m. y f.

makeshift, n. expediente, medio, m.; **—,** adj. temporal; mal confeccionado, mal hecho.

make-up, n. maquillaje, tocado, m.

makeweight, n. complemento de peso; contrapeso, m.

making, n. composición, f.; estructura, hechura, f.

maladjustment, n. mal ajuste, discordancia, f.

maladroit, adj. chabacano, desmañado.

malady, n. enfermedad, f.

malaria, n. paludismo, m.

malcontent, adj. malcontento; **—,** n. malcontento, ta.

male, adj. masculino; **—,** n. macho, m.

malediction, n. maldición, f.

malefactor, n. malhechor, m.

maleficent, adj. maléfico, maligno.

malevolence, n. malevolencia, f.

malevolent, adj. malévolo; **—ly,** adv. malignamente.

malformation, n. formación o estructura anormal.

malformed, adj. malhecho, contrahecho.

malice, n. malicia, f.

malicious, adj. malicioso; **—ly,** adv. maliciosamente.

malign, adj. maligno; malandrín; **—,** vt. difamar.

malignant, adj. maligno; **—ly,** adv. malignamente.

malignity, n. malignidad, f.

mallard, n. anadón, m.

malleable, adj. maleable.

mallet, n. mazo, m.

mallow, n. (bot.) malva, f.

malnutrition, n. desnutrición, f.

malodorant, n. sustancia mal oliente.

malodorous, adj. hediondo, de mal olor.

malpractice, n. malversación, f.; maltrato, m.

malt, n. cebada fermentada.

maltose, n. (chem.) maltosa, f., azúcar de almidón y malta.

maltreat, vt. maltratar.

maltster, n. obrero que prepara la cebada para hacer cerveza.

mamma, mama, n. mamá, f.

mammal, n. mamífero, m.

mammalian, n. and adj. mamífero, m.

man, n. hombre, m.; marido, m.; criado, peón, m.; **— of the world,** hombre mundano o de mundo; **— overboard,** hombre al agua; **mechanical —,** robota, f.; **young —,** joven, m., (coll.) pollo, m.; **—,** vt. (naut.) tripular, armar.

manacle, n. manilla, maniota, f.; **—s,**

n. pl. esposas, manillas, *f. pl.*; —, *vt.* maniatar.

manage, *vt.* and *vi.* manejar, manipular, gobernar, administrar; dirigir; gestionar.

manageable, *adj.* manejable, dócil, tratable; dirigible.

management, *n.* manejo, *m.*, administración, dirección, *f.*; conducta, *f.*; gestión, *f.*; (com.) gerencia, *f.*

manager, *n.* administrador, director, *m.*; gestor, *m.*; gerente, *m.*; hombre económico; **assistant —,** subgerente, *m.*; **—'s office,** dirección, gerencia, administración, *f.*

managerial, *adj.* administrativo.

managing, *adj.* dirigente; gestor; **— partner,** socio gerente o gestor.

mandamus, *n.* mandamiento, *m.*

mandate, *n.* mandato, *m.*, comisión, *f.*

mandatory, *adj.* obligatorio; —, *n.* mandatario, *m.*

mandolin, *n.* mandolín, bandolín, *m.*, mandolina, bandolina, *f.*

mandrake, *n.* (bot.) mandrágora, *f.*

mane, *n.* melena, *f.*; crines del caballo.

man-eater, *n.* caníbal, antropófago, *m.*

maneuver, *n.* maniobra, *f.*; —, *vt.* and *vi.* maniobrar.

manful, *adj.* bravo, valiente; **—ly,** *adv.* valerosamente.

manganate, *n.* manganato, *m.*

manganese, *n.* manganeso, *m.*

mange, *n.* roña, *f.*, sarna perruna.

manger, *n.* pesebre, *m.*

mangle, *n.* planchadora, *f.*, planchadora mecánica; —, *vt.* mutilar; planchar con una planchadora mecánica.

mango, *n.* (bot.) mango, *m.*

mangy, *adj.* sarnoso.

manhandle, *vt.* maltratar.

manhole, *n.* abertura para la inspección de alcantarillas, calderas, etc.

manhood, *n.* virilidad, *f.*; edad viril; hombría, *f.*; valentía, *f.*; valor, *m.*

mania, *n.* manía, *f.*; tema, *m.*

maniac, maniacal, *adj.* maniático, maníaco; —, *n.* maniático, *m.*

manicure, *n.* manicuro, ra; arte de arreglar las uñas; —, *vt.* arreglar las uñas.

manicurist, *n.* manicuro, ra.

manifest, *adj.* manifiesto, patente; —, *n.* manifiesto, *m.*; —, *vt.* manifestar.

manifestation, *n.* manifestación, *f.*

manifold, *adj.* muchos, varios; múltiple.

manikin, *n.* maniquí, *m.*

Manila hemp, *n.* fibra de Manila.

manioc, *n.* (bot.) casabe o cazabe, *m.*

manipulate, *vt.* manejar, manipular.

manipulation, *n.* manipulación, *f.*

mankind, *n.* género o linaje humano, humanidad, *f.*

manlike, *adj.* varonil.

manliness, *n.* valentía, *f.*; valor, *m.*

manly, *adj.* varonil, valeroso.

man midwife, *n.* comadrón, partero, *m.*

mannequin, *n.* maniquí, *m.*

manner, *n.* manera, *f.*, modo, *m.*; forma, *f.*; método, *m.*; maña, *f.*; hábito, *m.*; moda, *f.*; especie, *f.*; guisa, *f.*; vía, *f.*; **—s,** *m. pl.*, modales, *m. pl.*, urbanidad, crianza, *f.*; **in such a —,** de tal modo; **in the — of,** a fuer de, en son de, a guisa de.

mannerly, *adj.* cortés, atento.

manoeuvre, *n.* maniobra, *f.*; —, *vi.* maniobrar.

man-of-war, *n.* buque de guerra.

manometer, *n.* manómetro, *m.*

manor, *n.* señorío, *m.*; feudo, *m.*

manorial, *adj.* señorial.

manpower, *n.* caudal humano; fuerza colectiva de todos los hombres de una comunidad, país, etc.; (mil.) fuerza de una nación computada por el número de sus hombres.

mansion, *n.* mansión, morada, residencia, *f.*

manslaughter, *n.* homicidio (sin premeditación), *m.*

mantel, *n.* campana de chimenea.

mantelpiece, *n.* repisa de chimenea.

mantilla, *n.* mantilla, *f.*

mantle, *n.* manto, *m.*; capa, *f.*

manual, *n.* manual, *m.*; —, *adj.* manual; **— training,** instrucción en artes y oficios.

manufactory, *n.* fábrica, manufactura, *f.*

manufacture, *n.* manufactura, fabricación, *f.*; artefacto, *m.*; —, *vt.* fabricar, manufacturar, hacer.

manufacturer, *n.* fabricante, manufacturero, *m.*

manufacturing, *n.* fabricación, manufactura, *f.*

manumission, *n.* manumisión, *f.*

manure, *n.* abono, fimo, fiemo, estiércol, *m.*; —, *vt.* abonar, estercolar, cultivar.

manuscript, *n.* manuscrito, escrito, *m.*; original, *m.*

many, *adj.* muchos, muchas; **— a time,** muchas veces; **how —?** ¿cuántos? **as — as,** tantos como.

map, *n.* mapa, *m.*; carta geográfica; **— maker,** cartógrafo, *m.*; —, *vt.* delinear mapas; trazar, hacer planes.

maple, *n.* arce, *m.*; **— syrup,** jarabe de arce.

mapping, *n.* cartografía, *f.*

mar, *vt.* dañar, corromper; desfigurar.

Mar. March, Mzo. marzo.

maraschino, *n.* marrasquino, *m.*

marauder, *n.* merodeador, ra.

marauding, *adj.* merodeador.

marble, *n.* mármol, *m.*; canica, *f.*; bolilla de mármol, bola, *f.*; —, *adj.* marmóreo; —, *vt.* jaspear.

marcasite, *n.* marcasita, marquesita, pirita, *f.*

marcel, marcel wave, *n.* ondulado marcel, peinado con ondulaciones, rizado, *m.*

March, *n.* marzo, *m.*

march, *n.* marcha, *f.*; pasodoble, *m.*; —, *vi.* marchar, caminar.

marchioness, *n.* marquesa, *f.*

marchpane, *n.* mazapán, *m.*

mare, *n.* yegua, *f.*

Marg. Margaret, Marg.ᵗᵃ Margarita.

Margaret, Margarita.

margarine, *n.* margarina, *f.*

margin, *n.* margen, *m.* y *f.*; borde, *m.*; orilla, *f.*; —, *vt.* marginar.

marginal, *adj.* marginal.

marigold, *n.* (bot.) caléndula, *f.*

marijuana, marihuana, *n.* marijuana, marihuana, *f.*

marimba, *n.* marimba, *f.*

marine, *n.* marina, *f.*; soldado de marina; —, *adj.* marino; — **compass,** (naut.) brújula, *f.*, compás de navegación.

mariner, *n.* marinero, *m.*

marionette, *n.* (theat.) títere, muñeco, *m.*

marital, *adj.* marital.

maritime, *adj.* marítimo, naval.

marjoram, sweet marjoram, *n.* (bot.) mejorana, *f.*

Mark, Marcos.

mark, *n.* marca, *f.*; señal, nota, *f.*; seña, *f.*; blanco, *m.*; calificación (en escuela o examen), *f.*; — **down,** reducción (de precio); **printer's** —, pie de imprenta; —, *vt.* marcar; advertir; — **down,** bajar (el precio); — **time,** marcar el paso, llevar el compás; quedar inactivo u ocioso.

marked man, *n.* hombre sospechoso; víctima futura.

marker, *n.* marca, ficha, *f.*; marcador, *m.*

market, *n.* mercado, *m.*; plaza, *f.*; **meat** —, carnicería, *f.*; — **report,** revista del mercado; **open** —, mercado libre; **to be in the** — **for,** estar dispuesto a comprar.

marketable, *adj.* vendible, comercial.

marking, *adj.* marcador.

marksman, *n.* tirador, ra.

marksmanship, *n.* puntería, *f.*

mark up, *vt.* aumentar (el precio).

marl, *n.* marga, *f.*; —, *vt.* margar.

marmalade, *n.* mermelada, *f.*

marmoset, *n.* mono tití.

marmot, *n.* marmota, *f.*

maroon, *n.* esclavo fugitivo; negro descendiente de esclavo fugitivo; color rojo oscuro; —, *vt.* abandonar a uno en una costa desierta.

marplot, *n.* persona cuya acción oficiosa malogra planes, etc.

marquee, *n.* marquesina, *f.*

marquess, *n.* marqués, *m.*

marquetry, *n.* marquetería, ataracea, *f.*

marquis, *n.* marqués, *m.*

marquisette, *n.* tejido fino de malla.

marriage, *n.* matrimonio, casamiento, *m.*

marriageable, *adj.* casadero, núbil.

married, *adj.* casado, conyugal; **to get** —, casarse.

marrow, *n.* tuétano, meollo, *m.*; médula, *f.*; **full of** —, carnoso, carnudo.

marry, *vt.* casar; —, *vi.* casarse.

marsh, *n.* pantano, *m.*, laguna, *f.*

marshal, *n.* mariscal, *m.*; **field** —, capitán general.

marshy, *adj.* pantanoso.

marsupial, *n.* and *adj.* marsupial, *m.*

mart, *n.* emporio, *m.*; comercio, *m.*; feria, *f.*

marten, *n.* (zool.) garduña, marta, *f.*

Martha, Marta.

martial, *adj.* marcial, guerrero; — **law,** derecho militar, estado de guerra o de sitio.

martin, *n.* (orn.) vencejo, *m.*

Martinmas, *n.* día de San Martín.

martyr, *n.* mártir, *m.* y *f.*

martyrdom, *n.* martirio, *m.*

marvel, *n.* maravilla, *f.*, prodigio, *m.*; —, *vi.* maravillarse.

marvelous, *adj.* maravilloso; —**ly,** *adv.* maravillosamente.

marxist, *n.* marxista, *m.* y *f.*

Mary, María.

marzipan, *n.* mazapán, *m.*

masc. masculine, *m.* masculino.

mascara, *n.* preparación para teñir las pestañas.

mascot, *n.* mascota, *f.*

masculine, *adj.* masculino; varonil.

mash, *n.* especie de mezcla; fárrago, *m.*; —, *vt.* amasar; mezclar; majar; —**ed potatoes,** puré de papas.

mashie, *n.* mazo de golf para los golpes de acceso o aproximación.

mask, *n.* máscara, *f.*; pretexto, *m.*; —, *vt.* enmascarar; disimular, ocultar; —, *vi.* andar enmascarado.

masochism, *n.* masoquismo, *m.*

mason, *n.* albañil, *m.*; masón, *m.*

masonite, *n.* cartón hecho de fibras de madera.

masonry, *n.* albañilería, mampostería, *f.*; masonería, *f.*; **stone** —, calicanto, *m.*

masque, *n.* máscara, careta, *f.*

masquerade, *n.* mascarada, *f.*; — **ball,** — **dance,** baile de máscaras o de disfraz.

masquerader, *n.* máscara, *m.* y *f.*

mass, *n.* misa, *f.*; **midnight** —, misa de gallo; **to say** —, cantar o celebrar misa.

mass, *n.* masa, *f.*; montón, *m.*; bulto, *m.*; —**es,** *n. pl.* vulgo, *m.*, las masas, el pueblo en general; — **meeting,** mitin popular, reunión del pueblo en masa; — **production,** fabricación en serie o en gran escala.

Mass. Massachusetts, Massachusetts.

massacre, *n.* carnicería, matanza, *f.*; —, *vt.* matar atrozmente, hacer una carnicería.

massage, *n.* masaje, *m.*, soba, *f.*; —, *vt.* sobar.

masseur, masseuse, *n.* masajista, *m.* y *f.*

massive, *adj.* macizo, sólido.

massiveness, *n.* mole, *f.*, bulto, *m.*; solidez, *f.*

mast, *n.* árbol de navío, palo, *m.*; fabuco, *m.*; **mooring** —, poste de amarre; **topsail** —, verga de garra; —, *vt.* (naut.) arbolar un palo.

master, *n.* amo, dueño, *m.*; maestro, *m.*; señor, *m.*; señorito, *m.*; (naut.) maestre, *m.*; patrón, *m.*; **harbor —,** capitán del puerto; **— hand,** mano maestra, maestría, *f.*; **— stroke, — touch,** golpe de maestro o diestro, golpe magistral; **—,** *vt.* domar, domeñar; gobernar, dominar; sobreponerse.

masterly, *adj.* imperioso, despótico; magistral; **—,** *adv.* con maestría, magistralmente.

masterpiece, *n.* obra o pieza maestra.

mastery, *n.* superioridad, maestría, *f.*

masthead, *n.* (periodismo) cabeza fija.

mastic, *n.* almáciga, *f.*; masilla, resina, *f.*; cemento, *m.*

masticate, *vt.* mascar, masticar.

mastiff, *n.* mastín, *m.*

mastoid, *n.* mastoides, *f.*

mat, *n.* estera, esterilla, *f.*; empalletado, *m.*; **—,** *vt.* esterar; **— down,** chafar.

matador, *n.* matador, *m.*, primer espada; **— and his assistants,** cuadrilla, *f.*

match, *n.* mecha, pajuela, *f.*; fósforo, *m.*; cerilla, *f.*, cerillo, *m.*; partido, *m.*; contrincante, *m.*; pareja, *f.*; casamiento, *m.*; combate, *m.*; **—,** *vt.* igualar; aparear; casar; **—,** *vi.* hermanarse.

matchbox, *n.* cajita de fósforos o cerillos.

matching, *n.* igualación, *f.*, aparejamiento, *m.*

matchless, *adj.* incomparable, sin par.

matchmaker, *n.* casamentero, ra; organizador de juegos o certámenes.

mate, *n.* consorte, *m.* o *f.*; compañero, ra; (naut.) piloto, *m.*; **first —,** (naut.) piloto, *m.*; **—,** *vt.* desposar; igualar.

maté, *n.* mate, *m.*, yerba mate (té del Paraguay).

material, *adj.* material, físico; **—,** *n.* material, *m.*, tela, *f.*; **raw —s,** primeras materias; **—ly,** *adv.* materialmente.

materialism, *n.* materialismo, *m.*

materialistic, *adj.* materialista.

maternal, *adj.* maternal, materno.

maternity, *n.* maternidad, *f.*; **— hospital,** casa de maternidad.

math. mathematics, mat. matemática.

mathematical, *adj.* matemático; **—ly,** *adv.* matemáticamente.

mathematician, *n.* matemático, ca.

mathematics, *n. pl.* matemáticas, *f.pl.*

matinee, *n.* matiné, *f.*, función de tarde.

mating, *n.* apareamiento, *m.*; **— time (of animals),** brama, *f.*

matins, *n. pl.* maitines, *m. pl.*

matriarch, *n.* matriarca, *f.*, mujer que encabeza una familia, grupo, o estado.

matricide, *n.* matricidio, *m.*; matricida, *m.* y *f.*

matriculate, *vt.* matricular.

matriculation, *n.* matrícula, matriculación, *f.*

matrimonial, *adj.* matrimonial, marital.

matrimony, *n.* matrimonio, casamiento, *m.*

matrix, *n.* matriz, *f.*; molde, *m.*

matron, *n.* matrona, *f.*

Matt. Matthew, Mateo.

matted, *adj.* enredado; desgreñado.

matter, *n.* materia, sustancia, *f.*; asunto, objeto, *m.*; cuestión, importancia, *f.*; **it is no —,** no importa; **what is the —?** ¿de qué se trata? **a — of fact,** hecho positivo o cierto; **— of form,** cuestión de fórmula; **—,** *vi.* importar.

matter-of-fact, *adj.* positivo.

mattings, *n. pl.* esteras, *f. pl.*

mattock, *n.* azadón de peto, zapapico, *m.*

mattress, *n.* colchón, *m.*; **air —,** colchón de viento; **— tufting,** basta en los colchones; **spring —,** colchón de muelle.

mature, *adj.* maduro; juicioso; **—,** *vt.* madurar.

maturity, *n.* madurez, *f.*

maudlin, *adj.* lloroso, sentimental en extremo.

maul, *vt.* apalear, maltratar a golpes.

Maurice, Morris, Mauricio.

mausoleum, *n.* mausoleo, *m.*

mauve, *n.* color purpúreo delicado.

maverick, *n.* animal sin marca de hierro.

maw, *n.* cuajar, *m.*, molleja de las aves.

mawkish, *adj.* fastidioso, nauseabundo.

max. maximum, máximo.

maxim, *n.* máxima, *f.*, axioma, *m.*

Maximilian, Maximiliano.

maximum, *adj.* máximo.

May, *n.* mayo, *m.*

may, *vi.* poder; ser posible.

Maya, *n.* Maya, *m.*

maybe, *adv.* quizás, tal vez.

May Day, *n.* día primero de mayo.

mayonnaise, *n.* mayonesa, *f.*, salsa mayonesa.

mayor, *n.* corregidor, alcalde, *m.*

mayoralty, *n.* corregimiento, *m.*, alcaldía, *f.*

mayoress, *n.* corregidora, *f.*

Maypole, *n.* mayo (árbol), *m.*

Mazda lamp, *n.* lámpara de tungsteno.

maze, *n.* laberinto, *m.*; perplejidad, *f.*

mazurka, *n.* mazurca, *f.*

mazy, *adj.* confuso, embrollado.

M. C. Master of Ceremonies, Maestro de Ceremonias.

Mch. March, Mzo., mzo. marzo.

Md. Maryland, Maryland.

M. D. Doctor of Medicine, Doctor en Medicina.

mdse. merchandise, mer. merc.ª mercancías o mercaderías.

me, *pron.* mí; me.

Me. Maine, Maine.

M. E.: Methodist Episcopal, Episcopal Metodista; **Mechanical Engineer,** Ing. Mecán. Ingeniero Mecánico.

mead, *n.* aguamiel, *f.*; (poet.) prado, *m.*

meadow, *n.* pradería, *f.*, prado, *m.*, vega, *f.*

meager, meagre, *adj.* magro; flaco; momio; seco; **—ly,** *adv.* pobremente, estérilmente.

meagerness, meagreness, *n.* flaqueza, *f.*; escasez, *f.*

meal, *n.* comida, *f.*; harina, *f.*

mealy, *adj.* harinoso.

mean, *adj.* bajo, vil, despreciable; abatido; mediocre; mezquino; **in the —time,** **—while,** en el ínterin, mientras tanto; —, *n.* medio, *m.*; expediente, *m.*; **—s,** *pl.* medios, recursos, *m. pl.*; by all **—s,** sin falta; **by no —s,** de ningún modo; —, *vt.* and *vi.* significar; querer decir; **you don't — it!** ¡calla!

meander, *n.* laberinto, *m.*, camino tortuoso; —, *vt.* and *vi.* serpear, seguir un camino tortuoso; caminar sin rumbo.

meaning, *n.* intención, *f.*; inteligencia, *f.*; sentido, significado, *m.*; significación, *f.*

meanly, *adv.* mediocremente; pobremente; vilmente.

meanness, *n.* bajeza, *f.*; pobreza, *f.*; mezquindad, *f.*; mediocridad, *f.*; pequeñez, *f.*

means, *n. pl.* medios, *m. pl.*

meanwhile, *adv.* entretanto, mientras tanto; —, *n.* ínterin, *m.*

meas. measure, medida.

measles, *n. pl.* sarampión, *m.*; rubéola, *f.*

measurable, *adj.* mensurable.

measure, *n.* medida, *f.*; regla, *f.*; (mus.) compás, *m.*; **in some —,** hasta cierto punto; **liquid —,** medida para líquidos; —, *vt.* medir; ajustar; calibrar; calar.

measurement, *n.* medición, *f.*; medida, *f.*

measurer, *n.* medidor, ra.

meat, *n.* carne, vianda, *f.*; **baked —,** carne asada en horno; **broiled —,** carne asada en parrilla; **— ball,** albóndiga, *f.*, pelota de carne molida; **— extract,** carne concentrada, jugo de carne; **— market,** carnicería, *f.*

mechanic, *n.* mecánico, *m.*

mechanical, *adj.* mecánico; rutinario; **— man,** robota, *f.*; **—ly,** *adv.* mecánicamente.

mechanician, *n.* mecánico, maquinista, *m.*

mechanics, *n. pl.* mecánica, *f.*

mechanism, *n.* mecanismo, *m.*

mechanize, *vt.* mecanizar.

Med. Medicine, Med. Medicina; **medieval,** medieval; **medium,** m. mediano.

medal, *n.* medalla, *f.*

medallion, *n.* medallón, *m.*

meddle, *vi.* entremeterse.

meddler, *n.* entremetido, da, camasquince, *m.*

meddlesome, *adj.* entremetido.

median, *adj.* del medio; —, *n.* mediana, *f.*

mediate, *vi.* mediar, promediar.

mediation, *n.* mediación, interposición, *f.*

medical, *adj.* médico; **— examination,** reconocimiento o examen médico.

medicament, *n.* medicamento, *m.*

medicate, *vt.* medicinar.

medicinal, *adj.* medicinal.

medicine, *n.* medicina, *f.*; medicamento, *m.*; **— ball,** pelota grande para gimnasia;

— dropper, cuentagotas, *m.*; **to give —,** medicinar.

medieval, *adj.* medieval.

mediocrity, *n.* mediocridad, *f.*

meditate, *vt.* and *vi.* meditar, idear.

meditation, *n.* meditación, *f.*

meditative, *adj.* meditativo, contemplativo.

Mediterranean, Mediterráneo, *m.*

medium, *n.* medio, *m.*; expediente, *m.*; moderación, *f.*; —, *adj.* mediano.

medium-sized, *adj.* de tamaño regular o mediano.

medlar, *n.* níspero, *m.*; níspola, *f.*

medley, *n.* mezcla, *f.*; baturrillo, *m.*; (mus.) potpourri, *m.*

meek, *adj.* manso, apacible; dulce; **—ly,** *adv.* suavemente; humildemente.

meekness, *n.* suavidad, *f.*; modestia, *f.*; dulzura, *f.*; humildad, *f.*

meerschaum, *n.* piedra loca; espuma de mar; pipa o boquilla de este mineral.

meet, *vt.* encontrar, convocar, reunir, dar con; —, *vi.* encontrarse, juntarse; **till we — again,** hasta la vista; **to go to —,** ir al encuentro; **to — the bill,** hacer frente a una factura; —, *adj.* idóneo, propio.

meeting, *n.* asamblea, *f.*; congreso, *m.*; entrevista, *f.*; sesión, reunión, *f.*, mitin, *m.*; **to call a —,** llamar a junta, convocar a una junta.

megacycle, *n.* megaciclo, *m.*

megalomania, *n.* megalomanía, *f.*

megaphone, *n.* megáfono, portavoz, *m.*

melancholy, *n.* melancolía, *f.*; —, *adj.* melancólico.

mélange, *n.* mezcla, *f.*

meld, *n.* mezcla en que se confunden los elementos; —, *vt.* confundir por mezcla.

melee, *n.* refriega, pelotera, *f.*

mellifluous, *adj.* melifluo.

mellow, *adj.* maduro, meloso; tierno, suave; blando; —, *vt.* and *vi.* madurar, madurarse.

mellowness, *n.* madurez, *f.*

melodious, *adj.* melodioso; **—ly,** *adv.* melodiosamente.

melodrama, *n.* melodrama, *m.*

melody, *n.* melodía, *f.*

melon, *n.* melón, *m.*

melt, *vt.* derretir, fundir; liquidar; enternecer; —, *vi.* derretirse, liquidarse.

melting, *n.* fusión, *f.*; **— point,** punto o temperatura de fusión; **— pot,** crisol, *m.*

member, *n.* miembro, *m.*; parte, *f.*; individuo, socio, *m.*

membership, *n.* número de socios, personal de socios; **— list,** nómina o lista de socios.

membrane, *n.* membrana, *f.*

memento, *n.* memento, *m.*

memo. memorandum, memorándum.

memoir, *n.* memoria, relación, narrativa, *f.*

memorable, *adj.* memorable; **—ly,** *adv.* memorablemente.

memorandum, *n.* memorándum, volante,

m.; — **book**, libreta, *f.*, carnet, *m.*, libro de apuntes.

memorial, *n.* memoria, *f.*; memorial, *m.*; —, *adj.* conmemorativo.

Memorial Day, *n.* Día de los Difuntos.

memory, *n.* memoria, *f.*; recuerdo, *m.*; retentiva, *f.*

men, *n. pl.* de **man,** hombres, *m. pl.*

menace, *n.* amenaza, *f.*; —, *vt.* amenazar.

menagerie, *n.* casa de fieras o animales raros.

mend, *vt.* reparar, remendar, retocar; mejorar, corregir; repasar, recoser (ropa).

mendacious, *adj.* mendaz, embustero, mentiroso.

mendacity, *n.* falsedad, mentira, *f.*

mendicancy, mendicity, *n.* mendiguez, mendicidad, *f.*

mendicant, *adj.* mendicante; —, *n.* mendicante, *m.* y *f.*, mendigo, ga.

menial, *adj.* servil, doméstico.

meningitis, *n.* meningitis, *f.*

menopause, *n.* (med.) menopausia, *f.*

menstruation, *n.* menstruación, *f.*, menstruo, *m.*

mensuration, *n.* medición, *f.*

mental, *adj.* mental, intelectual; —**ly,** *adv.* mentalmente, intelectualmente; **to become —ly unbalanced,** (coll.) chiflarse.

mentality, *n.* mentalidad, *f.*

mentally, *adv.* mentalmente.

menthol, *n.* mentol, *m.*

mentholated, *adj.* mentolado.

mention, *n.* mención, *f.*; —, *vt.* mencionar; **don't — it,** no hay de qué.

mentor, *n.* mentor, ayo, guía, *m.*

menu, *n.* menú, *m.*, lista de platos, comida, *f.*

mercantile, *adj.* mercantil.

mercenary, *adj.* mercenario, venal; —, *n.* mercenario, ria.

mercer, *n.* mercero, sedero, *m.*

mercerize, *vt.* mercerizar, abrillantar, dar lustre.

merchandise, *n.* mercancía, *f.*; efectos comerciales.

merchant, *n.* comerciante, *m.*; mercader, *m.*; negociante, *m.* y *f.*; **wool —,** pañero, *m.*; —, *adj.* mercante; — **ship,** buque mercante.

merchantman, *n.* navío mercantil.

merciful, *adj.* misericordioso, compasivo, piadoso; —**ly,** *adv.* misericordiosamente.

merciless, *adj.* duro de corazón, inhumano; —**ly,** *adv.* cruelmente, sin misericordia.

mercurial, *adj.* vivo, activo; mercurial.

mercurochrome, *n.* mercurocromo, *m.*

mercury, *n.* mercurio, *m.*; **bichloride of —,** solimán, *m.*; — **ointment,** ungüento de soldado.

mercy, *n.* misericordia, piedad, clemencia, *f.*; perdón, *m.*

mere, *adj.* mero, puro; —**ly,** *adv.* simplemente; puramente.

meretricious, *adj.* meretricio

merge, *vt.* unir, juntar, combinar; —, *vi.* absorberse, fundirse.

merger, *n.* consolidación, combinación, *f.*; fusión, *f.*

meridian, *n.* mediodía, *m.*; meridiano, *m.*

meringue, *n.* merengue, *m.*

merino (sheep, wool, cloth), *n.* merino, *m.*

merit, *n.* mérito, *m.*; merecimiento, *m.*; —, *vt.* merecer.

merited, *adj.* meritorio, digno, merecido.

meritorious, *adj.* meritorio; **to be —,** merecer; —**ly,** *adv.* meritoriamente.

mermaid, *n.* sirena, *f.*

merrily, *adv.* alegremente.

merriment, *n.* diversión, *f.*; regocijo, *m.*

merry, *adj.* alegre, jovial, festivo, pajarero.

merry-andrew, *n.* bufón, payaso, *m.*

merry-go-round, *n.* caballitos, *m. pl.*, tíovivo, *m.*

merrymaking, *n.* retozo, bullicio, jolgorio holgorio, *m.*

mesa, *n.* mesa, meseta, altiplanicie, *f.*

mescal, *n.* mezcal, *m.*

mesh, *n.* malla, *f.*

mesmerism, *n.* mesmerismo, *m.*

mesoderm, *n.* mesodermo, *m.*

Mesozoic, *adj.* mesozoico; — **era,** edad mesozoica.

mess, *n.* plato de comida, vianda, *f.*; ración o porción (de comida); grupo de personas que comen juntas; comida para un grupo; (coll.) confusión, *f.*, lío, *m.*; — **hall,** sala de rancho; (mil.) salón comedor.

message, *n.* mensaje, *m.*

messenger, *n.* mensajero, ra.

messmate, *n.* comensal, *m.*, compañero de mesa.

messroom, *n.* comedor para grupos de soldados, trabajadores, etc.

Messrs. Messieurs, Sres. Señores.

met. metropolitan, metropolitano.

metabolism, *n.* metabolismo, *m.*

metacarpus, *n.* metacarpo, *m.*

metal, *n.* metal, *m.*; (fig.) coraje, espíritu, *m.*

metal. metallurgy, metal. metalurgia.

metallic, *adj.* metálico.

metallurgy, *n.* metalurgia, *f.*

metalwork, *n.* metalistería, *f.*

metamorphism, *n.* metamorfismo, *m.*

metamorphose, *vt.* trasformar.

metamorphosis, *n.* metamorfosis, *f.*

metaphor, *n.* metáfora, *f.*

metaphoric, methaphorical, *adj.* metafórico.

metaphysical, *adj.* metafísico; —**ly,** *adv.* metafísicamente.

metaphysics, *n. pl.* metafísica, *f.*

metatarsal, *adj.* metatarsiano.

metazoa, *n. pl.* (zool.) metazoos, *m. pl.*

mete, *vt.* medir.

meteor, *n.* metéoro, meteoro, *m.*

meteorological, *adj.* meteorológico.

meteorology, *n.* meteorología, *f.*

meter, *n.* medidor, contador, *m.*; metro, *m.*

methinks, *v. imp.* (poet.) me parece, creo, pienso.
method, *n.* método, *m.*; vía, *f.*; medio, *m.*
methodic, methodical, *adj.* metódico; **—ly,** *adv.* metódicamente.
methodist, *n.* metodista, *m.* y *f.*
methodology, *n.* metodología, *f.*
methyl, *n.* metilo, *m.*
meticulous, *adj.* meticuloso.
metric, *adj.* métrico; **— system,** sistema métrico.
metrical, *adj.* métrico.
metronome, *n.* metrónomo, *m.*
metropolis, *n.* metrópoli, capital, *f.*
metropolitan, *n.* (eccl.) metropolitano, *m.*; ciudadano de una metrópoli; **—,** *adj.* metropolitano.
mettle, *n.* brío, valor, coraje, *m.*; ardor, *m.*
mettled, mettlesome, *adj.* brioso, vivo, ardiente.
Meuse, Mosa, *m.*
mew, *n.* jaula, *f.*; gaviota, *f.*; caballeriza, *f.*; **—,** *vt.* enjaular; **—,** *vi.* maullar (como el gato).
Mex. Mexico, Mex., Mej. Méjico.
Mexican, *n.* and *adj.* mejicano, na, mexicano, na.
Mexico, Méjico o México, *m.*
mezzanine, *n.* (theat.) entresuelo, *m.*, mezanina, *f.*
mfg. manufacturing, manuf. manufactura.
mfr. manufacturer, fab. fabricante.
mg. milligram, mg. miligramo.
Mgr.: manager, gnte. gerente; **Monsignor,** Mons. Monseñor.
mi, *n.* (mus.) mi, *m.*
mi. mile, milla.
mica, *n.* (min.) mica, *f.*
mice, *n. pl.* de **mouse,** ratones, *m. pl.*
Mich.: Michigan, Míchigan; **Michaelmas,** fiesta de San Miguel.
Michael, Miguel.
Michaelmas, *n.* fiesta de San Miguel.
microbe, *n.* microbio, bacilo, *m.*
microbiologist, *n.* microbiólogo, *m.*
microbiology, *n.* microbiología, *f.*
microcephalism, *n.* microcefalia, *f.*
microcephaly, *n.* microcefalia, *f.*
micrococcus, *n.* micrococo, *m.*
microcosm, *n.* microcosmo, *m.*
microfilm, *n.* película para guardar registro fotográfico de impresos, manuscritos, etc., en corto espacio.
micrometer, *n.* micrómetro, *m.*
micrometric, *adj.* micrométrico.
micron, *n.* micra, *f.*
micro-organism, *m.* microorganismo, *m.*
microphone, *n.* micrófono, *m.*
microphotography, *n.* microfotografía, *f.*
microscope, *n.* microscopio, *m.*; **— slide,** platina, *f.*
microscopic, microscopical, *adj.* microscópico.
mid, *adj.* medio.
mid. middle, mtd. mitad.

midday, *n.* mediodía, *m.*
midden, *n.* acumulación de basura que señala las viviendas primitivas.
middle, *adj.* medio, intermedio; mediocre; **—,** *n.* medio, centro, *m.*; mitad, *f.*; **about the — of,** a mediados de; **— ear,** tímpano del oído.
middle-aged, *adj.* entrado en años, de edad madura.
middle class, *n.* clase media.
middleman, *n.* revendedor, intermediario, *m.*
middleweight, *n.* peso medio; **—,** *adj.* de peso medio.
middling, *adj.* mediano, mediocre.
middy (blouse), *n.* blusa holgada para mujeres y niñas; chaqueta semejante a la que usan los marinos.
midget, *n.* enano, na.
midiron, *n.* especie de palo de golf.
midland, *adj.* mediterráneo.
midnight, *n.* media noche.
midshipman, *n.* guardia marina, aspirante a oficial de marina.
midst, *n.* medio, centro, *m.*
midsummer, *n.* solsticio estival; pleno verano.
midway, *n.* avenida central de una exposición en que suelen instalarse diversiones; **—,** *adj.* medio; **—,** *adv.* a medio camino.
midwife, *n.* comadre, partera, comadrona, *f.*
midwifery, *n.* obstetricia, *f.*
mien, *n.* semblante, parecer, *m.*; talante, *m.*; **cheerful —,** buena cara, semblante agradable.
might, *n.* poder, *m.*, fuerza, *f.*; pretérito del verbo **may;** **— and main,** fuerza máxima.
mightily, *adv.* poderosamente, sumamente.
mightiness, *n.* poder, *m.*; potencia, *f.*
mighty, *adj.* fuerte, potente.
mignonette, *n.* (bot.) reseda, *f.*
migraine, *n.* hemicránea, jaqueca, *f.*
migrant, *adj.* migratorio, de paso, nómade, nómada; **—,** *n.* planta o ave migratoria.
migrate, *vi.* emigrar.
migration, *n.* emigración, *f.*
migratory, *adj.* migratorio.
mil.: military, mil. militar; **militia,** mil. milicia.
milch, *adj.* lactífero, lechero.
mild, *adj.* indulgente, blando, dulce, apacible, suave, moderado; **—ly,** *adv.* suavemente, con blandura.
mildew, *n.* tizón, tizoncillo, *m.*, roya, *f.*
mildness, *n.* clemencia, dulzura, *f.*; suavidad, *f.*
mile, *n.* milla, *f.*
mileage, *n.* longitud en millas; kilometraje, *m.*; **— ticket,** billete kilométrico.
milestone, *n.* piedra miliaria.
milfoil, *n.* (bot.) milenrama, *f.*
militant, *adj.* militante.
militarism, *n.* militarismo, *m.*
military, *adj.* militar; **compulsory — service,** servicio militar obligatorio; **—**

police, policía militar; **— staff,** estado mayor; **— watchword,** santo y seña; **—,** n. ejército, m., tropas, f. pl.

militate, vi. militar, combatir.

militia, n. milicia, f.

milk, n. leche, f.; **— of magnesia,** leche de magnesia; **—,** vt. ordeñar.

milker, n. ordeñador, ra.

milking machine, n. máquina ordeñadora.

milkmaid, n. lechera, f.

milkman, n. lechero, m.

milksop, n. marica, m.

milkweed, n. titímalo, m., cardo lechero.

milky, adj. lácteo, lactífero; lechal, lechoso; lechero.

Milky Way, n. Vía Láctea, Galaxía, f.

mill, n. molino, m.; **—,** vt. moler, batir con el molinillo; estampar; **— wheel,** rueda de molino.

milldam, n. esclusa de molino.

millenary, adj. milenario.

millennium, n. espacio de mil años, milenario, m.

miller, n. molinero, m.

millet, n. (bot.) mijo, m.

milligram, n. miligramo, m.

milliliter, n. mililitro, m.

millimeter, n. milímetro, m.

milliner, n. persona que vende o confecciona sombreros de mujer.

millinery, n. artículos para sombreros de señora; confección de sombreros para señora; **— shop, — store,** sombrerería, f.

million, n. millón, m.

millionaire, n. and adj. millonario, ria.

millionth, adj. millonésimo.

millpond, n. depósito o estanque de agua para mover un molino.

millrace, n. saetín, m.

millstone, n. muela, f., piedra de moler.

millwork, n. fresado, m.; trabajo producido en un molino.

millwright, n. constructor de molinos.

mime, n. mimo, bufón, m.

mimeograph, n. mimeógrafo, m.

mimic, vt. imitar, contrahacer; **—,** adj. burlesco, mímico; **—,** n. mimo, m.

mimicry, n. mímica, f.; bufonería, f.

mimosa, n. (bot.) mimosa, f.

min.: minister, min.º ministro; **minimum,** mínimo; **minute,** m. minuto.

mince, vt. picar (carne); **—,** vi. hablar o pasearse con afectación; andar con pasos muy cortos o muy afectadamente.

mincemeat, n. picadillo de carne.

mincingly, adv. a pedacitos; con afectación.

mind, n. mente, f.; entendimiento, m.; gusto, afecto, m.; voluntad, intención, f.; pensamiento, m.; opinión, f.; ánimo, m.; **of sound —,** consciente; **to make up one's —,** resolverse; **—,** vt. notar, observar, considerar; pensar; obedecer; tener cuidado; importar; **not to —,** no importar; **—,** vi. tener cuidado o cautela; preocu-

parse; obedecer; **never —,** no importa, no se moleste, etc.

minded, adj. inclinado, dispuesto.

mindful, adj. atento, diligente; **—ly,** adv. atentamente.

mindless, adj. descuidado, negligente.

mindreader, n. adivinador del pensamiento.

mine, pron. mío, mía, míos, mías; **—,** n. mina, f.; **— field,** (mil., naut.) campo de minas; cuenca minera; zona donde se han colocado minas explosivas; **— layer,** (naut.) plantaminas o lanzaminas, m.; **— sweeper,** (naut.) dragaminas o recogedor de minas explosivas; **—,** vt. and vi. minar, cavar.

miner, n. minero, minador, m.

mineral, adj. mineral; **— oil,** aceite mineral, petróleo, m.; **— water,** agua mineral; **— wool,** lana de escoria; **—,** n. mineral, m.

mineralogy, n. mineralogía, f.

mingle, vt. and vi. mezclar, mezclarse.

mingled, adj. revuelto, mezclado.

miniature, n. miniatura, f.

minim, n. (mus.) mínima, f.

minimize, vt. reducir a un mínimum; menospreciar.

minimum, n. mínimum, mínimo, m.; **—,** adj. mínimo; **— wage,** jornal mínimo.

mining, n. minería, f., explotación de minas; **—,** adj. minero.

minion, n. favorito, m. (úsase en forma despectiva).

minister, n. ministro, pastor, capellán, m.; **—,** vt. ministrar; servir; suministrar; proveer; socorrer.

ministerial, adj. ministerial.

ministration, n. ministración, f.; ministerio, m.

ministry, n. ministerio, m.

miniver, n. (zool.) gris, m., variedad de ardilla.

mink, n. visón, m.

Minn. Minnesota, Minesota.

minnow, n. variedad de pez pequeño.

minor, adj. menor, pequeño; inferior; (mus.) menor; **—,** n. menor (de edad), m. y f.; asignatura secundaria en las escuelas.

minority, n. minoridad, f.; minoría, f.; (law) menoría, f.

minster, n. iglesia, catedral, f.

minstrel, n. juglar, trovador, m.; actor cómico que imita a los negros del sur de E.U.A.

mint, n. (bot.) menta, f.; ceca, f., casa de moneda; **—,** vt. acuñar.

mintage, n. derechos de cuño; monedería, f.

minuend, n. minuendo, m.

minuet, n. minué, minuete, m.

minus, prep. menos; **seven — four,** siete menos cuatro; **—,** adj. negativo; **— quantity,** cantidad negativa; (coll.) despojado; **— his clothes,** despojado de su ropa; **—,** n. (math.) el signo menos.

minute, adj. menudo, pequeño, nimio;

minucioso; **—ly**, *adv.* exactamente, nimia- | de naipes); **—**, *n.* distribución equivocada.
mente; **set forth —ly**, circunstanciado; | **misdeed**, *n.* delito, *m.*
—, *n.* minuto, *m.*; momento, instante, | **misdemeanor**, *n.* mala conducta; culpa,
m.; minuta, *f.*; **— book**, libro de minutas. | falta, *f.*
minuteness, *n.* minucia, pequeñez, minu- | **misdirect**, *vt.* dirigir erradamente.
ciosidad, *f.* | **misdoing**, *n.* falta, *f.*, mala acción.
minutiae, *n. pl.* minucias, *f. pl.* | **misdoubt**, *vt.* recelar, sospechar.
minx, *n.* moza atrevida y libre. | **miser**, *n.* avaro, ra.
miocene, *adj.* and *n.* mioceno, *m.* | **miserable**, *adj.* miserable, infeliz; pobre;
miracle, *n.* milagro, *m.*; **maravilla**, *f.*; | mísero; mezquino; **—bly**, *adv.* miserable-
— worker, taumaturgo, *m.* | mente, avaramente.
miraculous, *adj.* milagroso; **—ly**, *adv.* | **miserly**, *adj.* mezquino, tacaño.
maravillosamente. | **misery**, *n.* miseria, *f.*; infortunio, *m.*
mirage, *n.* espejismo, *m.* | **misfire**, *vi.* no dar fuego.
mire, *n.* fango, limo, *m.* | **misfit**, *vt.* and *vi.* quedar mal (un vestido,
mirror, *n.* espejo, *m.* | etc.); **—**, *n.* mal ajuste; acción de quedar
mirth, *n.* alegría, *f.*, regocijo, *m.* | o ajustar mal (un vestido, etc.); vestimenta
mirthful, *adj.* alegre, jovial. | que no ajusta o cae bien; persona que no
miry, *adj.* cenagoso, lodoso. | se adapta al ambiente.
misadventure, *n.* desventura, *f.*; infortu- | **misfortune**, *n.* infortunio, revés, *m.*; per-
nio, *m.* | cance, *m.*; calamidad, *f.*, contratiempo, *m.*
misalliance, *n.* boda con persona de posición | **misgive**, *vt.* llenar de dudas; hacer temer.
social inferior. | **misgiving**, *n.* recelo, *m.*; duda, *f.*; pre-
misanthrope, *n.* misántropo, *m.* | sentimiento, *m.*; rescoldo, *m.*
misanthropy, *n.* misantropía, *f.* | **misgovern**, *vt.* gobernar mal.
misapplication, *n.* mala aplicación. | **misguide**, *vt.* guiar mal.
misapply, *vt.* usar de alguna cosa impropia- | **mishandle**, *vt.* maltratar.
mente. | **mishap**, *n.* desventura, *f.*; desastre, con-
misapprehend, *vt.* entender mal. | tratiempo, *m.*
misapprehension, *n.* error, yerro, *m.*; | **misinform**, *vt.* informar mal.
interpretación errónea. | **misinterpret**, *vt.* interpretar mal.
misappropriate, *vt.* malversar. | **misinterpretation**, *n.* mala interpretación.
misbehave, *vi.* portarse mal. | **misjudge**, *vt.* and *vi.* juzgar mal.
misbehavior, *n.* mala conducta, mal | **mislay**, *vt.* colocar mal, extraviar.
comportamiento. | **mislead**, *vt.* extraviar, descaminar; seducir.
misbelief, *n.* incredulidad, *f.*; heterodoxia, *f.* | **mismanage**, *vt.* manejar mal.
misbeliever, *n.* incrédulo, la. | **mismanagement**, *n.* mala administración;
misc. miscellaneous, misceláneo. | desarreglo, *m.*
miscalculate, *vt.* calcular mal. | **misname**, *vt.* dar un nombre falso.
miscall, *vt.* nombrar impropiamente. | **misnomer**, *n.* nombre o título falso.
miscarriage, *n.* aborto, malparto, *m.*; | **misogynist**, *n.* misógino, *m.*
fracaso, malogro, *m.* | **misplace**, *vt.* colocar mal, traspapelar; sacar
miscarry, *vi.* frustrarse, malograrse; abor- | algo de su quicio; extraviar.
tar, malparir. | **misplacement**, *n.* extravío, *m.*
miscegenation, *n.* mezcla de razas. | **misprint**, *vt.* imprimir mal; **—**, *n.* errata de
miscellaneous, *adj.* misceláneo, mezclado. | un libro, errata de imprenta.
miscellany, *n.* miscelánea, *f.* | **mispronounce**, *vt.* pronunciar mal.
mischance, *n.* desventura, *f.*; infortunio, | **mispronunciation**, *n.* pronunciación mala
m., mal suceso. | o incorrecta.
mischief, *n.* travesura, *f.*; daño, infortu- | **misquote**, *vt.* citar falsa o erróneamente.
nio, *m.* | **misrepresent**, *vt.* representar mal; ter-
mischievous, *adj.* travieso; dañoso, mali- | giversar.
cioso, malévolo; **—ly**, *adv.* malignamente. | **misrepresentation**, *n.* representación falsa;
misconceive, *vt.* concebir una idea falsa. | tergiversación, *f.*
misconception, *n.* equivocación, *f.*; falso | **misrule**, *n.* tumulto, *m.*; confusión, *f.*; **—**,
concepto. | *vt.* gobernar mal.
misconduct, *n.* mala conducta; **—**, *vt.* | **miss**, *n.* señorita, *f.*; pérdida, falta, *f.*; **—**,
conducir o manejar mal. | *vt.* errar, perder; omitir; echar de menos;
misconstruction, *n.* mala construcción, | **to — one's mark**, errar el blanco; **to —**
interpretación siniestra. | **(in shooting)**, errar el tiro; **—**, *vi.*
misconstrue, *vt.* interpretar mal. | frustrarse; faltar.
miscreant, *n.* malvado, da, malhechor, ra; | **Miss. Mississippi**, Misisipí.
—, *adj.* sin conciencia, sin escrúpulo. | **missal**, *n.* misal, *m.*
miscue (in billiards), *n.* pifia (en el billar), *f.* | **misshape**, *vt.* deformar, desfigurar.
misdeal, *vt.* dar mal las cartas (en el juego | **misshapen**, *adj.* deformado, desfigurado.

missile, n. proyectil, m.
missing, adj. que falta, perdido.
mission, n. misión, comisión, f.; cometido, m.
missionary, n. misionero, m.
Mississippi, Misisipí, m.
missive, n. carta, misiva, f.; —, adj. misivo.
Missouri, Misuri, m.
misspell, vt. deletrear mal, escribir con mala ortografía.
misstatement, n. aserción equivocada o falsa.
misstep, n. paso en falso.
mist, n. niebla, bruma, f.
mistakable, adj. engañoso, equivocable.
mistake, n. equivocación, f.; yerro, error, m.; —, vt. equivocar; —, vi. equivocarse, engañarse; **to be —n,** haberse equivocado, estar errado.
Mister, n. Señor (título), m.
mistiness, n. nebulosidad, f.
mistletoe, n. (bot.) muérdago, m., liga, f.
mistreat, vt. maltratar, injuriar.
mistreatment, n. mal trato.
mistress, n. ama, f.; señora, f.; concubina, f.
mistrial, n. anulación de un juicio.
mistrust, vt. desconfiar; sospechar; —, n. desconfianza, sospecha, f.
mistrustful, adj. desconfiado, sospechoso.
misty, adj. nebuloso, brumoso.
misunderstand, vt. entender mal una cosa.
misunderstanding, n. mal entendimiento; disensión, f., error, m.
misusage, n. abuso, m.
misuse, vt. maltratar; abusar de algo.
mite, n. pizca, mota, f., ápice, m.
miter, n. (eccl.) mitra, f.
mitigate, vt. mitigar, calmar.
mitigation, n. mitigación, f.
mitosis, n. mitosis, f.
mitt, n. mitón, m.
mitten, n. mitón, m.; **to get the —,** recibir calabazas; **to give the —,** dar calabazas.
mix, vt. mezclar.
mixed, adj. mezclado; **— up,** revuelto.
mixer, n. mezclador, ra; **concrete —,** mezcladora, hormigonera, f., mezcladora de hormigón.
mixture, n. mistura, mixtura, mezcla, f.
mizzen, n. (naut.) mesana, f.
mizzenmast, n. palo de mesana.
mm. millimeter, mm. milímetro.
Mme. Madame, Sra. Señora.
Mo. Missouri, Misuri.
M. O., m. o. money order, giro o libranza postal.
mo. month, mes.
moan, n. lamento, gemido, m.; —, vt. lamentar, gemir; —, vi. afligirse, quejarse.
moanful, adj. lamentable; **—ly,** adv. lamentablemente.
moat, n. foso, m.; —, vt. rodear con fosos.
mob, n. populacho, m., canalla, f.; gentuza, f., gente baja; —, vt. atropellar desordena-

damente, formar un tropel.
mobile, adj. movedizo, móvil; **— kitchen,** cocina ambulante.
mobility, n. movilidad, f.
mobilization, n. movilización, f.
mobilize, vt. (mil.) movilizar.
moccasin, n. mocasín, m., abarca, f.
mock, vt. mofar, burlar, chiflar; —, n. mofa, burla, f.; —, adj. ficticio, falso; **— orange,** (bot.) cambrón, m.
mockery, n. mofa, burla, zumba, f.
mockingbird, n. (orn.) arrendajo, m.
mockingly, adv. burlonamente, en son de burla.
modal, adj. modal.
mode, n. modo, m.; forma, f.; manera, f.; costumbre, f.; vía, f.; (mus.) modalidad, f.
model, n. modelo, m.; pauta, f.; muestra, f.; patrón, m.; tipo, m.; —, vt. modelar.
modeling, n. modelado, m.
moderate, adj. moderado; mediocre; módico; **—ly,** adv. moderadamente; bastante; —, vt. moderar.
moderation, n. moderación, f.; sobriedad, f.
moderator, n. moderador, apaciguador, m.
modern, adj. moderno, reciente.
modernism, n. modernismo, m.
modernistic, adj. modernista.
modernization, n. modernización, f.
modernize, vt. modernizar.
modest, adj. modesto; pudoroso; **—ly,** adv. modestamente.
modesty, n. modestia, decencia, f., pudor, m.
modicum, n. cantidad pequeña, pitanza, f.; poco, m.
modification, n. modificación, f.
modifier, n. modificador, modificante.
modify, vt. modificar.
modulate, vt. modular.
modulating, adj. modulante.
modulation, n. modulación, f.
modulator, n. modulador, ra.
module, n. módulo, m.
modulus, n. módulo, m.
mogul, n. mogol, m.; locomotora grande.
mohair, n. tela hecha de pelo de camello.
Mohammed, Mahoma.
moil, vi. fatigarse.
moist, adj. húmedo, mojado.
moisten, vt. humedecer.
moistened, adj. humedecido.
moisture, n. humedad, f.; jugosidad, f.
molar, adj. molar; **— tooth,** muela, f., diente molar; **— teeth,** muelas, f. pl.
molasses, n. melaza, f.
mold, n. moho, m.; tierra, f.; suelo, m.; molde, m.; matriz, f.; —, vt. enmohecer, moldar; formar; —, vi. enmohecerse.
molder, n. moldeador, m.; —, vt. and vi. convertir o convertirse en polvo.
moldiness, n. moho, m.
molding, n. molduras, f. pl., cornisamiento, m.
moldy, adj. mohoso, lleno de moho.
mole, n. mola, f.; muelle, dique, m.; topo, m.

molecular, *adj.* molecular.
molecule, *n.* molécula, *f.*
molehill, *n.* topinera, *f.*
moleskin, *n.* piel de topo.
molest, *vt.* molestar, atormentar, estorbar.
molestation, *n.* molestia, *f.*; enfado, *m.*
mollify, *vt.* ablandar.
mollusk, *n.* molusco, *m.*
molt, *vi.* mudar, estar de muda las aves.
molten, *adj.* derretido; **the — calf,** el becerro de fundición.
moment, *n.* momento, rato, *m.*; importancia, *f.*
momentarily, *adv.* a cada momento, momentáneamente.
momentary, *adj.* momentáneo.
momentous, *adj.* importante.
momentum, *n.* momento, *m.*, fuerza de impulsión de un cuerpo.
Mon. Monday, lun. lunes.
mon. monastery, monast.º monasterio.
monarch, *n.* monarca, *m.*
monarchic, monarchical, *adj.* monárquico.
monarchy, *n.* monarquía, *f.*
monastery, *n.* monasterio, *m.*
monastic, monastical, *adj.* monástico.
monasticism, *n.* monasticismo, *m.*
Monday, *n.* lunes, *m.*
monetary, *adj.* monetario.
money, *n.* moneda, *f.*; dinero, *m.*; plata, *f.*; oro, *m.*; **— changer,** cambista, *m.*; **— chest,** caja, *f.*; **— exchange,** bolsa, *f.*, cambio de moneda; **— order,** libranza o giro postal; **paper —,** papel moneda; **ready —, — in hand,** dinero contante; **with a limited amount of —,** con el dinero tasado.
moneyed, monied, *adj.* adinerado, rico.
monger, *n.* tratante, traficante, *m.*
mongrel, *adj.* mixto, mestizo; —, *n.* mestizo, za.
monism, *n.* monismo, *m.*
monition, *n.* amonestación, *f.*
monitor, *n.* admonitor, *m.*; (naut.) monitor, *m.*
monitory, *adj.* monitorio.
monk, *n.* monje, *m.*; cenobita, *m.* y *f.*
monkey, *n.* mono, na; simio, mia; **— wrench,** llave inglesa, llave de tuercas.
monkish, *adj.* monástico.
monochrome, *n.* monocromo, *m.*
monocle, *n.* monóculo, *m.*
monogamist, *n.* monógamo, *m.*
monogamy, *n.* monogamia, *f.*
monogram, *n.* monograma, *m.*
monograph, *n.* monografía, *f.*
monolith, *n.* monolito, *m.*
monologue, *n.* monólogo, *m.*
monomania, *n.* monomanía, *f.*
monomaniac, *adj.* monomaníaco.
monomial, *n.* monomio, *m.*
monoplane, *n.* monoplano, *m.*
monopolist, *n.* monopolista, *m.* y *f.*
monopolize, *vt.* monopolizar, acaparar.
monopoly, *n.* monopolio, *m.*

monorail, *adj.* de carril único; —, *n.* monocarril, monorriel, *m.*
monosyllabic, *adj.* monosilábico; —, *n.* monosílabo, *m.*
monotheism, *n.* monoteísmo, *m.*
monotheist, *n.* monoteísta, *m.*
monotonous, *adj.* monótono.
monotony, *n.* monotonía, *f.*
monotype, monotyping, *n.* monotipia, *f.*
monoxide, *n.* (chem.) monóxido, *m.*
Monseigneur, *n.* monseñor, *m.*
monsoon, *n.* (naut.) monzón, *m.*
monster, *n.* monstruo, *m.*
monstrance, *n.* (eccl.) custodia, *f.*
monstrosity, *n.* monstruosidad, *f.*
monstrous, *adj.* monstruoso; **—ly,** *adv.* monstruosamente.
Mont. Montana, Montana.
month, *n.* mes, *m.*; **—'s pay, —'s allowance,** mensualidad, *f.*; **next —,** el mes entrante, el mes que viene; **this —,** el mes corriente.
monthly, *adj.* mensual; **— pay, — salary, — allowance,** mesada, *f.*; **— installment,** mensualidad, *f.*; —, *adv.* mensualmente.
monument, *n.* monumento, *m.*
monumental, *adj.* monumental.
mood, *n.* (gram.), modo, *m.*; humor, talante, *m.*
moodiness, *n.* capricho, *m.*, extravagancia, *f.*
moody, *adj.* caprichoso.
moon, *n.* luna, *f.*
moonbeam, *n.* rayo lunar.
moonlight, *n.* luz de la luna.
moonshine, *n.* claridad de la luna; (fig.) ilusión, *f.*
moon-struck, *adj.* lunático, loco.
Moor, *n.* moro, ra, sarraceno, na.
moor, *n.* pantano, marjal, *m.*; —, *vt.* (naut.) amarrar.
moorage, *n.* ancladero, anclaje, *m.*
mooring, *n.* (naut.) amarra, *f.*; **— mast,** poste de amarre.
Moorish, *adj.* morisco, moro.
moose, *n.* (zool.) alce, *m.*
moot, *vt.* debatir en pro y en contra; —, *adj.* sujeto a discusión; ficticio.
mop, *n.* aljofifa, *f.*, estropajo, *m.*; —, *vt.* aljofifar.
mope, *vi.* dormitar, entontecerse, estar triste.
moraine, *n.* (geol.) morena, *f.*
moral, *adj.* moral, ético; **— support,** apoyo moral; —, *n.* moraleja, *f.*; **—s,** *n. pl.* moralidad, conducta, *f.*, conducta moral; costumbres, *f. pl.*; **—ly,** *adv.* moralmente.
morale, *n.* moralidad, *f.*; animación, *f.*; buen espíritu, entusiasmo entre tropas.
moralist, *n.* moralista, *m.* y *f.*; moralizador, ra.
morality, *n.* ética, moralidad, *f.*
moralize, *vt. and vi.* moralizar.

morass, *n.* lavajo, pantano, *m.*

moratorium, *n.* moratoria, *f.*

morbid, *adj.* enfermo, morboso, mórbido.

mordant, *adj.* mordaz.

more, *adj.* más, adicional; —, *adv.* más, en mayor grado; — **or less,** más o menos; —, *n.* mayor cantidad; **once —,** una vez más; **there's — than enough,** hay de sobra.

moreover, *adv.* además.

mores, *n. pl.* costumbres tradicionales.

morganatic, *adj.* morganático.

morgue, *n.* necrocomio, *m.*

Morisco, *n.* and *adj.* morisco, ca.

morn, *n.* (poet.) mañana, *f.*

morning, *n.* mañana, *f.*; **good —,** buenos días; —, *adj.* matutino; — **gown,** bata, *f.*; — **star,** lucero de la mañana.

morning-glory, *n.* (bot.) dondiego de día.

Moroccan, *n.* and *adj.* marroquín, ina; —, *adj.* marroquí.

Morocco, Marruecos, *m.*

morocco, morocco leather, *n.* marroquí, *m.*

moron, *n.* idiota, *m.* y *f.*, individuo que padece deficiencia mental.

morose, *adj.* hosco, sombrío, adusto; —**ly,** *adv.* adustamente.

morphine, *n.* morfina, *f.*

morphological, *adj.* morfológico.

morphology, *n.* morfología, *f.*

morris chair, *n.* butaca, poltrona, *f.*

morrow, *n.* mañana, *f.*

Morse code, *n.* telegráfico de Morse, clave telegráfica de Morse.

morsel, *n.* bocado, *m.*

mortal, *adj.* mortal; humano; —**ly,** *adv.* mortalmente; —, *n.* mortal, *m.*

mortality, *n.* mortalidad, *f.*

mortar, *n.* mortero, almirez, *m.*; (mil.) obús, *m.*; argamasa, *f.*; — **and pestle,** almirez y mano, mortero y majador.

mortarboard, *n.* gorro académico; esparavel o tabla que usan los albañiles.

mortgage, *n.* hipoteca, *f.*; — **title,** título de propiedad hipotecado; —, *vt.* hipotecar.

mortgagee, *n.* acreedor hipotecario.

mortgagor, mortgager, *n.* deudor hipotecario.

mortician, *n.* sepulturero, enterrador, *m.*; agente funerario; (Sp. Am.) muñidor, zacateca, *m.*

mortification, *n.* mortificación, *f.*; (med.) gangrena, *f.*

mortify, *vt.* and *vi.* mortificar, mortificarse.

mortise, *n.* mortaja, *f.*

mortmain, *n.* (law) manos muertas.

mortuary, *adj.* funeral.

mosaic, *n.* and *adj.* mosaico, *m.*

Moscow, Moscú, *f.*

mosque, *n.* mezquita, *f.*

mosquito, *n.* mosquito, cénzalo, *m.*; (Sp. Am.) zancudo, *m.*; — **boat,** barco mosquito, lancha rápida torpedera dotada de

armamento antiaéreo; — **net,** mosquitero, *m.*

moss, *n.* (bot.) musgo, *m.*; moho, *m.*

mossy, *adj.* mohoso.

most, *adj.* más; —, *adv.* sumamente, en sumo grado; —, *n.* los más; mayor número; mayor valor; **at —,** a lo más, a lo sumo; —**ly,** *adv.* por lo común; principalmente.

mote, *n.* mota, *f.*, átomo, *m.*

moth, *n.* polilla, *f.*; — **ball,** bola de naftalina para la polilla.

mother, *n.* madre, *f.*; — **tongue,** lengua materna.

motherhood, *n.* maternidad, *f.*

mother-in-law, *n.* suegra, *f.*

motherland, *n.* madre patria.

motherless, *adj.* sin madre, huérfana de madre.

motherly, *adj.* maternal, materno.

mother-of-pearl, *n.* madreperla, *f.*

mothy, *adj.* apolillado.

motif, *n.* motivo, tema, *m.*

motile, *adj.* movible.

motion, *n.* movimiento, *m.*, moción, *f.*; vaivén, *m.*; proposición, *f.*; — **picture,** cine, cinema, cinematógrafo, *m.*; —, *vt.* proponer.

motionless, *adj.* inmoble, inmóvil.

motivate, *vi.* motivar, proveer con un motivo; incitar, inducir, estimular interés activo por medio de intereses relacionados o recursos especiales.

motive, *adj.* motriz; móvil; — **power,** fuerza motriz; —, *n.* motivo, móvil, *m.*; razón, *f.*

motley, mottled, *adj.* abigarrado, gayado, barajado.

motor, *n.* motor, *m.*; — **launch,** gasolinera, *f.*; — **truck,** autocamión, *m.*

motorboat, *n.* autobote, *m.*, bote automóvil o de gasolina.

motorbus, *n.* autobús, *m.*

motorcade, *n.* procesión o desfile de automóviles.

motorcar, *n.* automóvil, *m.*

motorcycle, *n.* motocicleta, *f.*

motorist, *n.* automovilista, motorista, *m.* y *f.*

motorization, *n.* motorización, *f.*

motorize, *vt.* motorizar.

motorman, *n.* motorista de un tranvía o tren.

motorship, *n.* motonave, *f.*

motto, *n.* lema, *m.*; mote, *m.*; divisa, *f.*

moulage, *n.* mascarilla empleada en cirugía.

mould, moulder, etc. = mold, molder, etc.

mound, *n.* terraplén, baluarte, dique, terrón, *m.*

mount, *n.* monte, *m.*; montaña, *f.*; montaje, *m.*; —, *vt.* and *vi.* ascender, subir; montar.

mountain, *n.* montaña, sierra, *f.*, monte, *m.*; **range of —s,** cadena de montañas.

mountain ash, *n.* (bot.) serbal, moste-
llar, *m.*
mountaineer, *n.* montañés, esa.
mountainous, *adj.* montañoso.
mountebank, *n.* saltabanco, saltimbanco,
saltimbanqui, charlatán, *m.*
mounted, *adj.* pegado.
mounting, *n.* montaje, *m.*
mourn, *vt.* deplorar; —, *vi.* lamentar; llevar
luto.
mourner, *n.* lamentador, ra; llorón, ona;
doliente, *m.* y *f.*
mourner's bench, *n.* asiento reservado
para los dolientes en algunas reuniones
religiosas.
mournful, *adj.* triste; fúnebre; **—ly,** *adv.*
tristemente.
mourning, *n.* lamento, *m.*; luto, *m.*; **in —,**
de luto.
mourning dove, *n.* tórtola gemidora.
mourningly, *adv.* tristemente.
mouse, *n.* (*pl.* **mice**) ratón, *m.*; **— trap,**
ratonera, *f.*
moustache, *n.* = **mustache.**
mouth, *n.* boca, *f.*; entrada, *f.*; embocadura,
f.; **by word of —,** boca a boca, de palabra;
— organ, armónica, *f.*; **to make the —
water,** hacerse agua la boca; —, *vi.* hablar
a gritos; —, *vt.* poner en la boca; pronunciar.
mouthful, *n.* bocado, *m.*
mouthpiece, *n.* boquilla de un instrumento
de música; vocero, *m.*
movable, moveable, *adj.* movible, movedizo; **—s,** *n. pl.* muebles, *m. pl.*
move, *vt.* mover; proponer; excitar; persuadir; emocionar; bullir; mover a piedad;
—, *vi.* moverse, menearse; andar; marchar
un ejército; **to — to and fro,** zarandarse,
revolverse; **—,** *n.* movimiento, *m.*; movimiento (en el juego de ajedrez), *m.*
movement, *n.* movimiento, *m.*; moción, *f.*
mover, *n.* motor, *m.*; movedor, ra.
movie, *n.* **—s,** *n. pl.* (coll.) cine, cinema,
cinematógrafo, *m.*; **— camera,** cámara
fotográfica para cine.
moving, *n.* movimiento, *m.*; **—,** *adj.* patético, persuasivo; motor; conmovedor;
— picture, cine, cinema, cinematógrafo,
m.; **—ly,** *adv.* patéticamente.
mow, *vt.* guadañar, segar.
mower, *n.* guadañero, *m.*, cortadora, *f.*;
segador, ra.
mowing, *n.* siega, *f.*; **— machine,** guadañadora, *f.*
M. P.: Member of Parliament, Miembro
del Parlamento; **military police,** policía
militar; **mounted police,** policía montada.
mph, m.p.h. miles per hour, m.p.h. millas
por hora.
Mr. Mister, Sr. Señor.
Mrs. Mistress, Sra. Señora.
Ms. MS., ms. manuscript, M.S. manuscrito, original.
M. S. Master of Science, Maestro en Cien-

cias, Licenciado en Ciencias.
Msgr. Monsignor, Mons. Monseñor.
Mss., MSS., mss. manuscripts, (print.)
originales.
Mt. Mount, monte, montaña.
mt. mtn. mountain, montaña.
much, *adj.* mucho; **—,** *adv.* mucho, con
mucho; **so —, as —,** tanto; **too —,**
demasiado.
mucilage, *n.* mucílago *m.*, goma para pegar.
mucilaginous, *adj.* mucilaginoso.
muck, *n.* abono, estiércol, *m.*; basura, *f.*
mucous, *adj.* mocoso, viscoso.
mucus, *n.* moco, *m.*, mucosidad, *f.*
mud, *n.* fango, limo, légamo, lodo, *m.*;
— wall, tapia, *f.*
muddle, *vt.* enturbiar; embriagar; enredar;
confundir.
muddy, *adj.* cenagoso; turbio; lodoso.
mudguard, *n.* guardabarro, guardafango, *m.*
mud hen, *n.* especie de pato marino
americano.
mud turtle, *n.* tortuga americana de agua
dulce.
muff, *n.* manguito, *m.*
muffle, *vt.* embozar; envolver.
muffler, *n.* (auto.) silenciador, *m.*, sordina,
f.; desconectador, *m.*
mufti, *n.* mufti, *m.*
mug, *n.* cubilete, *m.*; (coll.) cara, *f.*
muggy, *adj.* húmedo y caluroso.
mulberry, *n.* mora, *f.*; **— tree,** morera, *f.*
mulch, *n.* cubrir con paja y estiércol.
mulct, *vt.* multar; **—,** *n.* multa, *f.*
mule, *n.* mulo, *m.*, mula, *f.*; **— driver,**
mulero, *m.*
muleteer, *n.* mulero, *m.*
mulish, *adj.* mular; terco.
mull, *vt.* entibiar, calentar cualquier licor;
—, *vt. and vi.* (coll.) cavilar.
mullet, *n.* (pez) múgil, mújol, sargo, capitón, *m.*
multicellular, *adj.* multicelular.
multicolored, *adj.* policromo.
multifarious, *adj.* vario, diferente.
multifold, *adj.* múltiple, numeroso.
multiform, *adj.* multiforme.
multigraph, *n.* multígrafo, *m.*
multigraphing, *n.* policopia, multigrafía, *f.*
multilateral, *adj.* multilateral.
multimillionaire, *n.* multimillonario, ria.
multiple, *adj.* multíplice; múltiple; **—,** *n.*
múltiplo, *m.*
multiplex, *adj.* múltiple; (elec., rad.)
múltiplex.
multiplicand, *n.* (math.) multiplicando, *m.*
multiplication, *n.* multiplicación, *f.*; **—
table,** tabla de multiplicar.
multiplicity, *n.* multiplicidad, *f.*
multiplier, *n.* multiplicador, *m.*
multiply, *vt.* multiplicar; **—,** *vi.* propagarse,
multiplicarse.
multitude, *n.* multitud, *f.*; vulgo, *m.*
multitudinous, *adj.* numeroso.
mum, *interj.* ¡chito! ¡silencio! **—,** *adj.*

silencioso, callado; **to keep —,** callarse.

mumble, vt. barbotar, mascullar; **—,** vi. hablar o decir entre dientes; gruñir; murmurar.

mummer, n. máscara, m. y f.

mummery, n. momería, f.

mummify, vt. momificar.

mummy, n. momia, f.

mumps, n. pl. (med.) papera, parótida, f.

munch, vt. masticar a bocados grandes.

mundane, adj. mundano.

municipal, adj. municipal; **— government,** ayuntamiento, m., gobierno municipal.

municipality, n. municipalidad, f.; comuna, f.

munificence, n. munificencia, liberalidad, f.

munificent, adj. munífico, liberal.

muniment, n. (law) título, documento, m.

munition, n. municiones, f. pl.

mural, adj. mural; **— crown,** corona mural.

murder, n. asesinato, homicidio, m.; **—,** vt. asesinar, cometer homicidio.

murderer, n. asesino, na.

murderess, n. asesina, matadora, f.

murderous, adj. sanguinario, cruel.

murk, n. obscuridad, f.

murky, adj. oscuro, lóbrego; sombrío; turbio; empañado.

murmur, n. murmullo, murmurio, m.; cuchicheo, m.; **—,** vi. murmurar.

murrain, n. morriña, f.

mus.: museum, museo; **music,** mús. música.

muscat, n. (bot.) moscatel, m.

muscle, n. músculo, m.

muscle-bound, adj. con los músculos rígidos por el trabajo muscular excesivo.

muscular, adj. muscular.

muse, n. musa, f.; meditación profunda; **—,** vi. meditar, pensar profundamente.

museum, n. museo, m.

mush, n. gachas, papas.

mushroom, n. (bot.) seta, f., hongo, m.

music, n. música, f.; **— hall,** sala de concierto; **— staff,** pentagrama, m.

musical, adj. musical; melodioso; **— comedy,** zarzuela, f., comedia musical; **—ly,** adv. con armonía.

musicale, n. concierto privado.

musician, n. músico, m.

musing, n. meditación, f.

musk, n. almizcle, m.

musket, n. mosquete, fusil, m.; (coll.) chopo, m.

musketeer, n. mosquetero, m.

musketry, n. mosquetería, f.

muskrat, n. rata almizclera.

musky, adj. almizcleño.

muslin, n. muselina, f.; percal, m.

muss, vt. manosear.

mussel, n. marisco, m.

mussing, n. manoseo, m.

must, vi. estar obligado; ser menester, ser necesario; convenir.

mustache, n. bigotes, m. pl., mostacho, m.

mustang, n. potro mesteño.

mustard, n. mostaza, f.; **— gas,** líquido venenoso e irritante empleado para la guerra; **— seed,** simiente de jenabe o mostaza.

muster, vt. pasar revista de tropa; agregar; **—,** n. (mil.) revista, f.; **— roll,** rol, m., lista de la dotación, rol de la tripulación.

musty, adj. mohoso, añejo.

mutability, n. mutabilidad, inconstancia, f.

mutable, adj. mudable, variable.

mutant, adj. variable, que sufre mutación; **—,** n. el que sufre mutación.

mutate, vt. transformar, alterar.

mutation, n. mudanza, f.; mutación, f.

mute, adj. mudo, silencioso; **—,** n. sordina, f.; **—ly,** adv. mudamente, sin chistar.

mutilate, vt. mutilar.

mutilation, n. mutilación, f.

mutilator, n. mutilador, m.

mutineer, n. amotinador, sedicioso, m.

mutinous, adj. sedicioso; **—ly,** adv. amotinadamente.

mutiny, n. motín, tumulto, m.; **—,** vi. amotinarse, rebelarse.

mutter, vt. and vi. murmurar, musitar, hablar entre dientes; **—,** n. murmuración, f.

mutton, n. carnero, m.

mutual, adj. mutuo, recíproco; **by — consent,** de común acuerdo; **— aid association,** asociación de apoyo mutuo; sociedad de beneficencia; **—ly,** adv. mutuamente, recíprocamente.

mutuality, n. reciprocidad, mutualidad, f.

muzzle, n. bozal, frenillo, m.; hocico, m.; jeta, f.; **—,** vt. embozar.

my, pron. mi, mis.

myocarditis, n. miocarditis, f.

myriad, n. miríada, f.; gran número.

myrrh, n. mirra, f.

myrtle, n. mirto, arrayán, m.

myself, pron. yo mismo.

mysterious, adj. misterioso.

mystery, n. misterio, m.

mystic, mystical, adj. místico; **mystically,** adv. místicamente.

mysticism, n. misticismo, m.

mystification, n. confusión, f., desconcierto m.

mystify, vt. desconcertar, ofuscar.

myth, n. fábula mitológica; mito, m.

mythical, adj. mítico, fabuloso.

mythological, adj. mitológico.

mythology, n. mitología, f.

N

N.: navy, marina; **new,** nuevo; **north,** N. norte; **November,** Nov.ᵉ noviembre.

n.: name, nombre; **neuter,** neutro; **north,** N. norte; **noun,** s. sustantivo; **number,** núm. número.

N. A. North America, N. A. Norte América.

nab, *vt.* atrapar, prender.
nacelle, *n.* (aer.) casilla, barquilla, *f.*
nacre, *n.* nácar, *m.*, madreperla, *f.*
nag, *n.* haca, jaca, *f.*, cuartago, caballejo, *m.*; —, *vt.* and *vi.* regañar, molestar, sermonear.
nail, *n.* uña, *f.*; garra, *f.*; clavo, chillón, *m.*; — **cleaner,** limpiauñas, *m.*; — **file,** lima para las uñas; — **puller,** desclavador, arrancaclavos, sacaclavos, *m.*; —, *vt.* clavar, hincar.
nail set, *n.* punzón, *m.*
nainsook, *n.* nansú, *m.*
naive, *adj.* ingenuo.
naiveté, *n.* ingenuidad, *f.*
naked, *adj.* desnudo; evidente; puro, simple; **entirely** —, en pelota; —**ly,** *adv.* desnudamente; claramente, patentemente.
nakedness, *n.* desnudez, *f.*; claridad, *f.*
name, *n.* nombre, *m.*; fama, reputación, *f.*; **firm** —, razón social; — **plate,** placa de fábrica, plancha con el nombre de una persona; **to give a** — **to,** denominar; —, *vt.* nombrar, mencionar.
nameless, *adj.* anónimo; sin nombre.
namely, *adv.* particularmente; a saber.
namesake, *n.* tocayo, ya.
Nancy, Anita.
nankeen, *n.* mahón, *m.*
nap, *n.* sueño ligero; lanilla, *f.*
nape, *n.* nuca, cerviz, *f.*; testuz, *m.*
naphtha, *n.* nafta, *f.*
naphthalene, *n.* naftalina, *f.*
napkin, *n.* servilleta, *f.*
narcissus, *n.* (bot.) narciso, *m.*
narcosis, *n.* narcosis, *f.*
narcotic, *adj.* narcótico.
narrate, *vt.* narrar, relatar.
narration, *n.* narración, *f.*, relación de alguna cosa.
narrative, *n.* cuento, relato, *m.*; —, *adj.* narrativo.
narrator, *n.* narrador, *m.*
narrow, *adj.* angosto, estrecho; avariento; próximo; escrupuloso; —**ly,** *adv.* estrechamente; —, *vt.* estrechar; limitar.
narrow-gauge, *adj.* (rail.) de trocha o vía angosta; — **railway,** ferrocarril de trocha o vía angosta.
narrowminded, *adj.* mezquino, fanático, intolerante.
narrowness, *n.* angostura, estrechez, *f.*; pobreza, *f.*
nasal, *adj.* nasal.
nascent, *adj.* naciente.
nastily, *adv.* suciamente.
nastiness, *n.* porquería, obscenidad, *f.*
nasturtium, *n.* (bot.) nasturcia, capuchina, *f.*
nasty, *adj.* sucio, puerco; obsceno; sórdido; desagradable.
nat.: national, nac. nacional; **native,** nativo; **natural,** natural.
natal, *adj.* nativo; natal.
natatorium, *n.* piscina de natación.

nation, *n.* nación, *f.*
national, *adj.* nacional; —**ly,** *adv.* nacionalmente.
nationalism, *n.* nacionalismo, *m.*
nationalist, *n.* nacionalista, *m.* y *f.*
nationality, *n.* nacionalidad, *f.*
nationalization, *n.* nacionalización, *f.*
nationalize, *vt.* nacionalizar.
native, *adj.* nativo; — **land,** terruño, *m.*; — **of,** oriundo de; —, *n.* natural, *m.* y *f.*
nativity, *n.* nacimiento, *m.*; natividad, *f.*; horóscopo, *m.*
natl. national, nac. nacional.
natural, *adj.* natural; sencillo; ilegítimo; ingénito; — **gas,** gas natural; — **science,** ciencias naturales; —**ly,** *adv.* naturalmente; —, *n.* (mus.) becuadro, *m.*
naturalist, *n.* naturalista, *m.*
naturalistic, *adj.* a lo natural, al vivo.
naturalize, *vt.* naturalizar.
naturalness, *n.* sencillez, naturalidad, *f.*
natural resources, *n. pl.* riquezas naturales, *f. pl.*
natural selection, *n.* selección natural.
nature, *n.* naturaleza, *f.*; índole, *f.*; modalidad, *f.*; carácter, *m.*; tenor, *m.*; humor, *m.*; genio, *m.*; temperamento, *m.*; **good** —, buen humor.
nature study, *n.* estudio objetivo de la naturaleza especialmente en las escuelas elementales.
naught, *n.* nada, *f.*; cero, *m.*; —, *adj.* nulo.
naughtily, *adv.* pícaramente.
naughtiness, *n.* picardía, travesura, *f.*
naughty, *adj.* travieso, pícaro; desobediente.
nausea, *n.* náusea, basca, *f.*, deseo de vomitar.
nauseate, *vt.* dar disgusto; nausear.
nauseous, *adj.* fastidioso; —**ly,** *adv.* con náusea.
naut. nautical, náut. náutico.
nautical, *adj.* náutico, naval.
nav.: naval, naval; **navigation,** nav. navegación.
naval, *adj.* náutico, naval; — **stores,** artículos navales, *m. pl.*; alquitrán, trementina y otros productos resinosos.
nave, *n.* cubo (de rueda), *m.*; nave (de la iglesia), *f.*
navel, *n.* ombligo, *m.*
navicert, *n.* certificado expedido por autoridad británica para que un embarque pueda cruzar el bloqueo británico.
navigable, *adj.* navegable.
navigate, *vt.* and *vi.* navegar.
navigation, *n.* navegación, *f.*
navigator, *n.* navegante, *m.*
navy, *n.* marina, *f.*; armada, *f.*; — **bean,** frijol blanco; — **blue,** azul oscuro; — **chaplain,** capellán de navío; — **yard,** arsenal de la marina de guerra.
nay, *adv.* no; y aun, más aun.
Nazi, *adj.* and *n.* nazi, nazista, *m.* y *f.*
N. B., n. b. note well, take notice, N. B. Nota Bene.

N. C. North Carolina, Carolina del Norte.
N. C. O. noncommissioned officer, (mil.) oficial nombrado por el jefe de un cuerpo.
N. D., N. Dak., North Dakota, Dakota del Norte.
NE, N. E., n. e., northeast, N. E. nordeste.
N. E. New England, Nueva Inglaterra.
N. E. A. National Education Association, Asociación Nacional de Educación.
neap tide, *n.* marea muerta.
near, *prep.* cerca de, junto a; —, *adv.* casi; cerca, cerca de; —, *adj.* cercano, próximo, inmediato; allegado.
nearby, *adj.* cercano, próximo; —, *adv.* cerca, a la mano.
nearer, *adj.* citerior, más cerca (comparativo de **near**).
nearest, *adj.* próximo, más cerca (superlativo de **near**).
nearly, *adv.* casi, cerca de.
nearness, *n.* proximidad, *f.*; mezquindad, *f.*
near-sighted, *adj.* miope; — **person,** miope, *m.* y *f.*
neat, *adj.* hermoso, pulido; puro; neto; pulcro; ordenado; —**ly,** *adv.* elegantemente; con nitidez; —, *n.* ganado vacuno.
neatness, *n.* pulidez, elegancia, *f.*; pulcritud, nitidez, *f.*
Neb. Nebr. Nebraska, Nebraska.
nebula, *n.* (ast.) nebulosa, *f.*
nebular, *adj.* nebuloso.
nebulous, *adj.* nebuloso.
necessaries, *n. pl.* cosas necesarias, *f. pl.*
necessarily, *adv.* necesariamente.
necessary, *adj.* necesario; **to be** —, hacer falta, ser menester.
necessitate, *vt.* necesitar.
necessitous, *adj.* indigente, pobre.
necessity, *n.* necesidad, *f.*; **of** —, forzosamente.
neck, *n.* cuello, *m.*; — **of land,** lengua de tierra entre dos mares.
neckband, *n.* cabezón de camisa.
neckerchief, *n.* corbata, *f.*; pañuelo de cuello.
necklace, *n.* collar, *m.*
necktie, *n.* corbata, *f.*
neckwear, *n.* cuellos, *m. pl.*, corbatas, *f. pl.*
necromancer, *n.* nigromante, *m.*
necromancy, *n.* necromancía, *f.*
necropolis, *n.* necrópolis, *f.*
nectar, *n.* néctar, *m.*
need, *n.* necesidad, *f.*; pobreza, *f.*; —, *vt.* and *vi.* necesitar; requerir.
needful, *adj.* necesario, indispensable; —**ly,** *adv.* necesariamente.
neediness, *n.* indigencia, pobreza, necesidad, *f.*
needle, *n.* aguja, *f.*; **darning** —, aguja de zurcir; **hypodermic** —, aguja hipodérmica; **magnetic** —, calamita, brújula, *f.*; — **point,** obra de punto; **phonographic** —, aguja fonográfica; **to be on** —**s and pins,** estar en espinas.
needlecase, *n.* alfiletero, *m.*

needless, *adj.* superfluo, inútil.
needlework, *n.* costura, *f.*; bordado de aguja; obra de punto.
needs, *adv.* necesariamente.
needy, *adj.* indigente, necesitado, pobre.
nefarious, *adj.* nefario.
neg. negative, negat. negativo.
negation, *n.* negación, *f.*
negative, *adj.* negativo; —**ly,** *adv.* negativamente; —, *n.* negativa, *f.*
neglect, *vt.* descuidar, desatender; —, *n.* negligencia, *f.*
negligee, *n.* bata de casa.
negligence, *n.* negligencia, *f.*; descuido, *m.*
negligent, *adj.* negligente, descuidado; —**ly,** *adv.* negligentemente.
negligible, *adj.* insignificante.
negotiable, *adj.* negociable.
negotiate, *vt.* gestionar; —, *vi.* negociar; comerciar.
negotiation, *n.* negociación, *f.*; negocio, *m.*
negress, *n.* negra, *f.*
negro, *n.* negro, etíope, *m.*
neigh, *vi.* relinchar; —, *n.* relincho, *m.*
neighbor, *n.* vecino, na; —, *vt.* estar contiguo; acercar; —, *vi.* confinar.
neighborhood, *n.* vecindad, *f.*; vecindario, *m.*; inmediación, cercanía, *f.*
neighboring, *adj.* cercano.
neighborly, *adj.* sociable, amigable.
neither, *conj.* ni; —, *adj.* ninguno; —, *pron.* ninguno, ni uno ni otro.
Nell, Nelly, Nellie, Eleanor, Leonor.
neolithic, *adj.* neolítico.
neologism, *n.* neologismo, *m.*
neon, *n.* neón, *m.*; — **light,** lámpara neón.
neophyte, *n.* neófito, ta, novicio, cia.
Neozoic, *adj.* (geol.) neozoico.
nephew, *n.* sobrino, *m.*
nepotism, *n.* nepotismo, *m.*
nerve, *n.* nervio, *m.*; vigor, *m.*; (coll.) audacia, *f.*, descaro, *m.*
nerveless, *adj.* enervado, débil.
nervous, *adj.* nervioso; excitable; nervudo.
nervous system, *n.* sistema nervioso.
nest, *n.* nido, *m.*; nidada, *f.*; — **egg,** nidal, *m.*; (fig.) ahorros, *m. pl.*
nestle, *vi.* acurrucarse; —, *vt.* abrigar; acomodar (como en un nido).
nestling, *n.* pollo, *m.*
net, *n.* red, *f.*; malla, *f.*; —, *adj.* neto, líquido; — **balance,** saldo líquido; — **cost,** costo neto; — **proceeds,** producto líquido; — **weight,** peso neto.
nether, *adj.* inferior, más bajo.
Netherlands, Países Bajos, *m. pl.*
Netherlands East Indies, Indias Neerlandesas, *f. pl.*
Netherlands Guiana, Guayana holandesa, *f.*
netting, *n.* elaboración de redes; pesca con redes; pedazo de red.
nettle, *n.* ortiga, *f.*; —, *vt.* picar como ortiga; irritar.

network, *n.* (rad.) red de estaciones radio-difusoras; red radiodifusora.
neural, *adj.* neural.
neuralgia, *n.* neuralgia, *f.*
neurasthenia, *n.* neurastenia, *f.*
neurasthenic, *adj.* neurasténico.
neuritis, *n.* neuritis, *f.*, inflamación de los nervios.
neurology, *n.* neurología, *f.*
neurone, *n.* (anat.), neurona, *f.*
neuropathic, *adj.* neuropático.
neuropathy, *n.* neuropatía, *f.*
neurosis, *n.* (med.) neurosis, *f.*
neurotic, *adj.* neurótico.
neut. neuter, neutro.
neuter, *n.* and *adj.* (gram.) neutro, *m.*
neutral, *adj.* neutral; **—ly,** *adv.* neutralmente.
neutrality, *n.* neutralidad, *f.*
neutralization, *n.* neutralización, *f.*
neutralize, *vt.* neutralizar.
neutron, *n.* neutrón, *m.*
Nev. Nevada, Nevada.
never, *adv.* nunca, jamás; **— mind,** no importa; **— a whit,** ni una pizca.
nevermore, *adv.* jamás, nunca.
nevertheless, *adv.* no obstante que, no obstante, así y todo, con todo, sin embargo.
new, *adj.* nuevo, fresco, reciente; original; **—ly,** *adv.* nuevamente.
New Castle, Castilla la Nueva, *f.*
newcomer, *n.* recién llegado, da.
New Deal, *n.* (pol.) nuevo régimen (por antonomasia, los procedimientos económico sociales aplicados por el Presidente de E. U. A., Franklin D. Roosevelt).
newfangled, *adj.* novedoso, de última novedad.
newlywed, *n.* recién casado, da.
newness, *n.* novedad, *f.*, calidad de nuevo.
news, *n. pl.* novedad, *f.*, nuevas, noticias, *f. pl.*
newsboy, *n.* vendedor de periódicos.
newscaster, *n.* perifoneador de noticias que redacta él mismo.
newsdealer, *n.* vendedor de periódicos.
newsmonger, *n.* novelero, ra; chismoso, sa.
newspaper, *n.* gaceta, *f.*; periódico, *m.*; diario, *m.*; **— clipping,** recorte de periódico; **— seller,** gacetero, *m.*; **— serial,** folletín, *m.*
newsprint, *n.* papel para periódicos.
newsreel, *n.* película que ilustra las noticias del día.
newsstand, *n.* puesto de periódicos.
newsy, *adj.* noticioso.
newt, *n.* lagartija acuática.
New York, Nueva York, *f.*
New Yorker, *n.* and *adj.* neoyorquino, na.
next, *adj.* próximo; entrante, venidero; **the — day,** el día siguiente; **—,** *adv.* luego, inmediatamente después.
nexus, *n.* nexo, vínculo, *m.*
N. F. Newfoundland, Terranova.

N. G.: National Guard, Guardia Nacional; **no good,** no sirve.
n. g. no good, no sirve.
N. H. New Hampshire, Nueva Hampshire.
nib, *n.* pico, *m.*, punta, *f.*
nibble, *vt.* and *vi.* mordiscar, picar.
niblick, *n.* uno de los palos de golf (morder).
Nicaraguan, *n.* and *adj.* nicaragüense, *m* y *f.*
nice, *adj.* delicado, exacto, solícito; circunspecto; tierno; fino; elegante; escrupuloso; **—ly,** *adv.* primorosamente.
nicety, *n.* exactitud, *f.*; esmero, *m.*; delicadeza, *f.*; **niceties,** *n. pl.* delicadezas, *f. pl.*; sutilezas, *f. pl.*
niche, *n.* nicho, *m.*
Nicholas, Nicolás.
nick, *n.* muesca, *f.*; punto crítico; ocasión oportuna; **Old N—,** el diablo; **in the — of time,** exactamente a tiempo; **—,** *vt.* dar en el hito; mellar; astillar; (coll.) coger desprevenido.
nickel, *n.* níquel, *m.*
nickel-chrome steel, *n.* acero al cromoníquel.
nickel-plate, *vt.* niquelar.
nickel-plated, *adj.* niquelado.
nickname, *n.* mote, apodo, *m.*; **—,** *vt.* poner apodos.
nicotine, *n.* nicotina, *f*
nicotinic acid, *n.* acído nicotínico.
niece, *n.* sobrina, *f.*
niggard, *n.* hombre avaro y mezquino.
niggardliness, *n.* tacañería, *f.*; miseria, *f.*
niggardly, *adj.* avaro, sórdido; **—,** *adv.* tacañamente, miserablemente.
nigh, *adv.* casi; **—,** *adj.* directo, corto.
night, *n.* noche, *f.*; **by —,** de noche; **good —,** buenas noches; **— blindness,** nictalopia, *f.*; **— club,** cabaret, *m.*; **— letter,** telegrama trasmitido durante la noche sujeto a una tarifa reducida; **— light,** vela de noche, lamparilla de noche; **— owl,** trasnochador, ra; **— school,** escuela de noche o nocturna; **— service,** servicio nocturno; **— watch,** sereno, *m.*, vela, *f.*
nightfall, *n.* anochecer, *m.*; caída de la tarde.
nightgown, *n.* camisón, *m.*, camisa de dormir.
nighthawk, *n.* pájaro nocturno; trasnochador, ra.
nightingale, *n.* ruiseñor, *m.*
nightly, *adv.* por las noches, todas las noches; **—,** *adj.* nocturno.
nightmare, *n.* pesadilla, *f.*
nightshade, *n.* (bot.) hierbamora, dulcamara, *f.*
nightshirt, *n.* camisa de dormir.
nihilist, *n.* nihilista, *m.* y *f.*
nimble, *adj.* ligero, activo, listo, ágil.
nimbly, *adv.* ágilmente.
nimbus, *n.* auréola, *f.*
nincompoop, *n.* tonto, simplón, *m.*
nine, *n.* and *adj.* nueve, *m.*

ninepin, *n*. bolo, *m*.; **game of —s,** juego de bolos.

nineteen, *n*. and *adj*. diez y nueve, dieci-nueve, *m*.

nineteenth, *n*. and *adj*. décimonono, *m*.

ninetieth, *n*. and *adj*. nonagésimo, *m*.

ninety, *n*. and *adj*. noventa, *m*.

ninny, *n*. badulaque, *m*., bobo, ba, tonto, ta.

ninth, *n*. and *adj*. nono, noveno, *m*.; **—ly,** *adv*. en nono lugar.

nip, *vt*. arañar, rasguñar; morder.

nippers, *n. pl*. alicates, *m. pl*.; pinzas, *f. pl*.

nipping, *adj*. mordaz, picante; sensible (frío).

nipple, *n*. pezón, *m*.

Nipponese, *n*. and *adj*. nipón, ona.

nit, *n*. liendre, *f*.

niter, *n*. nitro, *m*., salitre, *m*., nitrato de potasa.

nitrate, *n*. nitrato, *m*.

nitration, *n*. nitración, *f*.

nitric, *adj*. (chem.) nítrico, azótico.

nitrification, *n*. nitrificación, *f*.

nitrify, *vt*. nitrificar.

nitrobenzene, *n*. nitrobenzol, nitroben-ceno, *m*.

nitrocellulose, *n*. nitrocelulosa, *f*.

nitrogen, *n*. nitrógeno, *m*.; **— peroxide,** peróxido de nitrógeno.

nitroglycerine, *n*. nitroglicerina, *f*.

nitrous, *adj*. nitroso.

nitrous oxide, *n*. óxido nitroso.

N. J. New Jersey, Nueva Jersey.

N. M., N. Mex. New Mexico, Nuevo Méjico.

NNE, N.N.E. north-northeast, NNE nornordeste.

NNW, N.N.W. north-northwest, NNO nornoroeste.

no, *adv*. no; **—,** *adj*. ningún, ninguno; **by — means, in — way,** de ningún modo; **— end,** sinnúmero; **— longer,** no más; **there is — such thing,** no hay tal cosa.

No. north, N. norte.

no. number, núm. número.

nobility, *n*. nobleza, *f*.

noble, *adj*. noble; insigne; generoso; so-lariego; **—,** *n*. noble, *m*.

nobleman, *n*. noble, *m*.

nobleness, *n*. nobleza, caballerosidad, *f*.

nobly, *adv*. noblemente.

nobody, *pron*. nadie, ninguno, na; **—,** *n*. persona insignificante.

nocturnal, *adj*. nocturnal, nocturno.

nocturne, *n*. nocturno, *m*.

nod, *n*. cabeceo, *m*.; señal, *f*.; **—,** *vt*. inclinar (la cabeza) en señal de asentimiento; **—,** *vi*. cabecear.

node, *n*. nudo, *m*.; nodo, tumor, *m*.

nodular, *adj*. con nódulos.

nodule, *n*. nódulo, nudillo, *m*.

noise, *n*. ruido, estruendo, *m*.; baraúnda, *f*.; bulla, *f*.; rumor, *m*.; **to make —,** hacer ruido, meter bulla; **—,** *vt*. divulgar alguna noticia; **—,** *vi*. hablar mucho o en voz muy alta.

noiseless, *adj*. silencioso, sin ruido.

noisily, *adv*. con ruido, estrepitosamente.

noisome, *adj*. nocivo, malsano; asqueroso.

noisy, *adj*. ruidoso, turbulento, fragoso, vocinglero.

nom. nominative, nominat. nominativo.

nom de plume, *n*. seudónimo, *m*.

nomad, *n*. and *adj*. nómada, *m*. y *f*.

nomadic, *adj*. nómada.

no man's land, *n*. tierra de nadie; faja de terreno no reclamada o en disputa; terreno que separa dos ejércitos enemigos.

nomenclature, *n*. nomenclatura, *f*.

nominal, *adj*. nominal; **—ly,** *adv*. nominal-mente.

nominate, *vt*. nombrar; proponer (a alguna persona para un puesto, cargo, etc.).

nomination, *n*. nominación, *f*.; propuesta, *f*.

nominative, *n*. (gram.) nominativo, *m*.

nominator, *n*. nominador, ra.

nonacceptance, *n*. falta de aceptación.

nonage, *n*. minoridad, *f*., minoría de edad.

nonagenarian, *n*. nonagenario, ria; **—,** *adj*. nonagenario.

nonaggression, *n*. no agresión, *f*.

nonattendance, *n*. inasistencia, *f*., falta de asistencia.

nonbreakable, *adj*. irrompible.

nonchalance, *n*. indiferencia, *f*.

nonchalant, *adj*. indiferente, calmado.

noncom. noncommissioned officer, (mil.) oficial nombrado por el jefe de un cuerpo.

noncombatant, *n*. no combatiente, *m*.

noncommissioned, *adj*. (mil.) subordinado, sin comisión; **— officer,** sargento, cabo, *m*., oficial nombrado por el jefe de un cuerpo.

noncommittal, *adj*. evasivo, esquivo, reser-vado.

nonconformist, *n*. and *adj*. disidente, *m*. y *f*.

nondescript, *adj*. de difícil descripción o clasificación; **—,** *n*. persona o cosa que no pertenece a determinada clase o categoría; persona o cosa indescriptible.

none, *pron*. nadie, ninguno.

nonentity, *n*. nada, nulidad, *f*.

nones, *n*. (eccl.) nona, *f*.

nonesuch, *n*. cosa o persona sin par.

nonexplosive, *adj*. inexplosivo.

nonferrous, *adj*. no férreo.

nonfluid, *adj*. consistente, sólido.

nonintervention, *n*. no intervención.

nonpareil, *adj*. sin par, sin rival; **—,** *n*. algo de excelencia sin par.

nonpartisan, *adj*. sin afiliación política; **—,** *n*. miembro o grupo sin afiliación política.

nonpayment, *n*. falta de pago.

nonperformance, *n*. falta de ejecución.

nonplus, *n*. incertidumbre, perplejidad, *f*.; **—,** *vt*. confundir.

nonproductive, *adj*. no productivo.

nonresistance, *n*. obediencia pasiva.

nonsectarian, *adj.* no sectario, que no pertenece a denominación alguna.

nonsense, *n.* tontería, *f.*; disparate, absurdo, *m.*; (coll.) pamplinada, *f.*

nonsensical, *adj.* absurdo; tonto.

nonshattering, *adj.* inastillable, irrompible.

nonskid, *adj.* antirresbaladizo, antideslizante.

nonstop, *adj.* directo, sin parar o sin etapas.

nonsuit, *n.* desistimiento de un proceso; —, *vt.* absolver de la instancia.

nonsupport, *n.* falta de mantenimiento.

nontechnical, *adj.* no técnico.

nontransferable, *adj.* no transferible.

nonunion, *adj.* que no forma parte de gremios obreros, que no reconoce ningún sindicato obrero.

noodle, *n.* simplón, mentecato, *m.*; tallarín, fideo, *m.*; — **soup,** sopa de tallarines o de fideos.

nook, *n.* rincón, ángulo, *m.*

noon, *n.* mediodía, *m.*

noontide, *n.* mediodía, *m.*; medianoche, *f.*

noose, *n.* lazo corredizo; —, *vt.* enlazar.

nor, *conj.* ni.

Nordic, *adj.* and *n.* nórdico, ca.

norm, *n.* norma, *f.*, tipo, *m.*

normal, *adj.* normal; — **school,** escuela normal.

normality, *n.* normalidad, *f.*

north, *n.* norte, *m.*; —, *adj.* septentrional.

North America, América del Norte, Norte América.

North American, *n.* and *adj.* norteamericano, na.

northerly, northern, *adj.* septentrional.

northern, *adj.* septentrional, del norte.

northern lights, *n. pl.* aurora boreal.

north-northeast, *n.* nornordeste, *m.*

north-northwest, *n.* nornoroeste, *m.*

North Pole, *n.* Polo Artico, Polo Norte, *m.*

northward, northwards, *adv.* hacia el norte.

northwest, *n.* noroeste, *m.*

Norway, Noruega, *f.*

nose, *n.* nariz, *f.*; olfato, *m.*; sagacidad, *f.*; **large** —, narigón, *m.*

nosebag, *n.* morral, *m.*

noseband, *n.* muserola, sobarba, *f.*

nosebleed, *n.* epistaxis, *f.*, hemorragia nasal.

nose dive, *n.* clavado de proa; descenso repentino de un aeroplano.

nosegay, *n.* ramillete, *m.*

nostalgia, *n.* nostalgia, *f.*

nostril, *n.* ventana de la nariz.

nostrum, *n.* medicina de patente; cúralotodo, *m.*; remedio favorito para algún mal social.

not, *adj.* no; **if** —, si no; — **any,** ningún, ninguno; — **at all,** de ninguna manera; — **even,** ni siquiera.

notable, *adj.* notable; memorable; —**bly,** *adv.* notablemente.

notarize, *vt.* autorizar ante notario.

notary, *n.* notario, *m.*

notation, *n.* notación, *f.*

notch, *n.* muesca, *f.*; —, *vt.* hacer muescas.

notchboard (of a winding staircase), *n.* (arch.) bolo, nabo, *m.*

note, *n.* nota, marca, *f.*; señal, *f.*; aprecio, *m.*; billete, *m.*; consecuencia, *f.*; noticia, *f.*; explicación, *f.*; comentario, *m.*; (mus.) nota, *f.*; **bank** —, billete de banco; **counterfeit** —, billete de banco falso; **treasury** —, billete del tesoro; —, *vt.* notar, marcar; observar.

notebook, *n.* librito de apuntes, carnet, *m.*

noted, *adj.* afamado, célebre.

noteworthy, *adj.* notable, digno de encomio, digno de atención.

nothing, *n.* nada, *f.*, ninguna cosa; **good for** —, que no sirve para nada.

nothingness, *n.* nada, insignificancia, *f.*

notice, *n.* noticia, *f.*; aviso, *m.*; nota, *f.*; —, *vt.* observar, reparar, echar de ver.

noticeable, *adj.* notable, reparable.

notification, *n.* notificación, *f.*

notify, *vt.* notificar; requerir.

notion, *n.* noción, *f.*; opinión, *f.*; idea, *f.*; —**s,** *n. pl.* novedades, *f. pl.*, mercería, *f.*

notoriety, *n.* notoriedad, *f.*

notorious, *adj.* notorio; —**ly,** *adv.* notoriamente.

notwithstanding, *conj.* no obstante, aunque; a pesar de, sin embargo, con todo.

nougat, *n.* dulce de almendras u otras nueces.

nought, *n.* nada, *f.*

noun, *n.* (gram.) sustantivo, nombre, *m.*

nourish, *vt.* nutrir, alimentar.

nourishing, *adj.* sustancioso, nutritivo.

nourishment, *n.* nutrición, *f.*, nutrimento, alimento, *m.*; alimentación, *f.*

Nov. November, Nov.º noviembre.

novel, *n.* novela, *f.*; —, *adj.* novedoso, original.

novelist, *n.* novelista, *m.* y *f.*

novelty, *n.* novedad, *f.*; —**ties,** *n. pl.* artículos de fantasía.

November, *n.* noviembre, *m.*

novena, *n.* novena, *f.*

novice, *n.* novicio, cia; novato, ta; catecúmeno, na; bisoño, ña.

novitiate, *n.* noviciado, *m.*

novocaine, *n.* novocaína, *f.*

now, *adv.* ahora, en el tiempo presente; — **and then,** de cuando en cuando; **till** —, hasta ahora, hasta aquí; —! *interj.* ¡vaya!

nowadays, *adv.* hoy día.

nowhere, *adv.* en ninguna parte.

nowise, *adv.* de ningún modo.

noxious, *adj.* nocivo, dañoso; —**ly,** *adv.* perniciosamente.

nozzle, *n.* boquilla (de una manguera, etc.), *f.*; gollete, *m.*; nariz de un animal; (coll.) hocico, *m.*

N. S.: Nova Scotia, N. E. Nueva Escocia; **New Style,** nuevo estilo.

N. T. New Testament, Nuevo Testamento.

nt. net, nto. neto.

nt. wt. net weight, peso neto.

nuance, *n.* ligera diferencia; cambio de voz o de matiz.

nubbin, *n.* maíz que tiene la mazorca imperfecta; pedacito saliente de alguna cosa.

nucleus, *n.* núcleo, *m.*

nude, *adj.* desnudo, en carnes, en cuero, sin vestido; (law) nulo.

nudge, *vt.* dar del codo a uno para avisarle secretamente, dar a uno un codazo disimuladamente.

nudism, *n.* nudismo, *m.*, costumbre de vivir en un estado de desnudez.

nudist, *n.* desnudista, *m.* y *f.*

nudity, *m.* desnudez, *f.*

nugatory, *adj.* nugatorio, frívolo.

nugget, *n.* pepita, *f.*

nuisance, *n.* daño, perjuicio, *m.*; incomodidad, *f.*, estorbo, *m.*; (coll.) lata, chinchorrería, *f.*

null, *adj.* nulo, inválido.

nullification, *n.* anulación, *f.*

nullify, *vt.* anular, invalidar.

nullity, *n.* nulidad, *f.*

numb, *adj.* entumecido, entorpecido; **—,** *vt.* entorpecer, entumecer; **—ly,** *adv.* entorpecidamente.

number, *n.* número, *m.*; cantidad, *f.*; cifra, *f.*; **back —,** número atrasado; **round —,** número redondo; **—,** *vt.* numerar.

numbering, *n.* numeración, *f.*

numberless, *adj.* innumerable, sin número.

numbness, *n.* torpor, entumecimiento, *m.*

numeral, *adj.* numeral; **—,** *n.* número, *m.*, cifra, *f.*

numeration, *n.* numeración, *f.*

numerator, *n.* (math.) numerador, *m.*

numerical, *adj.* numérico.

numerous, *adj.* numeroso.

numismatics, *n. pl.* numismática, *f.*

numismatist, *n.* numismático, *m.*

numskull, *n.* zote, *m.*, estúpido, da.

nun, *n.* monja, religiosa, *f.*

nunnery, *n.* convento de monjas.

nuptial, *adj.* nupcial; **—s,** *n. pl.* nupcias, *f. pl.*, boda, *f.*

nurse, *n.* ama de cría; enfermera, *f.*; **wet —,** nodriza, nutriz, *f.*; **—,** *vt.* criar, alimentar, amamantar; cuidar (un enfermo).

nursery, *n.* cuarto dedicado a los niños; lugar donde se amamantan los niños; plantel, criadero, *m.*; almáciga, *f.*

nursemaid, *n.* niñera, aya, *f.*; (Mex.) nana, *f.*

nursing, *n.* crianza, *f.*; **— bottle,** mamadera, *f.*, biberón, *m.*

nursling, *n.* niño de teta.

nurture, *vt.* criar, educar.

nut, *n.* nuez, *f.*; (mech.) tuerca, *f.*; **lock —,** contratuerca, *f.*; **cypress —,** piñuela, *f.*

nutcracker, *n.* cascanueces, *m.*

nutgall, *n.* agalla de monte.

nutmeg, *n.* nuez moscada.

nutriment, *n.* nutrimento, alimento, *m.*

nutrition, *n.* nutrición, *f.*, nutrimento, *m.*

nutritious, nutritive, *adj.* nutritivo, alimenticio; sustancioso.

nutshell, *n.* cáscara de nuez.

NW, N.W., n.w. northwest, NO noroeste.

N. Y. New York (State), Nueva York.

NYA, N.Y.A. National Youth Administration, Administración Nacional de la Juventud (E. U. A.).

N. Y. C. New York City, Ciudad de Nueva York.

nylon, *n.* nilón, *m.*

nymph, *n.* ninfa, *f.*

N. Z. New Zealand, Nueva Zelandia.

O

O. Ohio, Ohio.

O/a, o/a on account of, a causa de.

oaf, *n.* idiota, zote, zoquete, *m.*

oafish, *adj.* estúpido, tonto, torpe.

oak, *n.* roble, *m.*, encina, *f.*; **— apple,** agalla, *f.*

oaken, *adj.* de roble.

oakum, *n.* estopa, *f.*

oar, *n.* remo, *m.*

oarsman, *n.* remero, *m.*

oasis, *n.* oasis, *m.*

oat, *n.* avena, *f.*

oatcake, *n.* torta de avena.

oath, *n.* juramento, *m.*; jura, *f.*; blasfemia, *f.*

oatmeal, *n.* harina de avena, avena, *f.*

obbligato, *n.* (mus.) obligado, *m.*

obduracy, *n.* endurecimiento, *m.*; dureza de corazón.

obdurate, *adj.* endurecido, duro; **—ly,** *adv.* tercamente; ásperamente.

obedience, *n.* obediencia, *f.*

obedient, *adj.* obediente; **—ly,** *adv.* obedientemente.

obeisance, *n.* cortesía, reverencia, *f.*; deferencia, *f.*; homenaje, *m.*

obelisk, *n.* obelisco, *m.*

obese, *adj.* obeso, gordo.

obesity, *n.* obesidad, crasitud, gordura, *f.*

obey, *vt.* obedecer.

obfuscate, *vt.* ofuscar.

obfuscation, *n.* ofuscación, *f.*

obituary, *n.* necrología, *f.*; obituario, *m.*

obj.: object, (gram.) comp. complemento; **objection,** objeción, **objective,** (gram.) acus. acusativo.

object, *n.* objeto, *m.*; punto, *m.*; (gram.) complemento, *m.*; **— lesson,** lección objetiva o práctica, enseñanza objetiva; **—,** *vt.* objetar, poner reparo; oponer.

objection, *n.* oposición, objeción, réplica, *f.*; **to raise an —,** poner objeción.

objectionable, *adj.* censurable, reprensible.

objective, *adj.* objetivo; **—,** *n.* meta, *f.*; objetivo, *m.*

objectivity, *n.* objetividad, *f.*

objector, *n.* objetante, *m.* y *f.*

oblation, *n.* oblación, ofrenda, *f.*

obligation, *n.* obligación, *f.*; compromiso, *m.*; cargo, *m.*; **to be under —,** verse obligado.

obligatory, *adj.* obligatorio.

oblige, *vt.* obligar; complacer, favorecer.

obliging, *adj.* servicial; condescendiente; **—ly,** *adv.* cortésmente; gustosamente.

oblique, *adj.* oblicuo; indirecto, de refilón; **—ly,** *adv.* oblicuamente.

obliquity, *n.* oblicuidad, *f.*

obliterate, *vt.* borrar; destruir; (med.) obliterar.

obliteration, *n.* obliteración, cancelación, *f.*

oblivion, *n.* olvido, *m.*

oblivious, *adj.* olvidadizo.

oblong, *adj.* oblongo.

obloquy, *n.* maledicencia, difamación, *f.*; deshonra, *f.*

obnoxious, *adj.* odioso, aborrecible.

oboe, *n.* (mus.) oboe, obué, *m.*

oboist, *n.* oboe, *m.*

obs. obsolete, ant. anticuado.

obscene, *adj.* obsceno, impúdico.

obscenity, *n.* obscenidad, *f.*

obscurantism, *n.* oscurantismo, *m.*

obscure, *adj.* oscuro; **—ly,** *adv.* oscuramente; **—,** *vt.* oscurecer.

obscurity, *n.* oscuridad, *f.*

obsequies, *n. pl.* exequias, honras funerales.

obsequious, *adj.* obsequioso; servicial; **—ly,** *adv.* obsequiosamente.

observable, *adj.* observable; conspicuo.

observance, *n.* observancia, *f.*; costumbre, *f.*; rito, *m.*, ceremonia, *f.*

observant, *adj.* observante, respetuoso, atento, considerado.

observation, *n.* observación, *f.*

observatory, *n.* observatorio, *m.*

observe, *vt.* observar, mirar; reparar; ver; notar; guardar (una fiesta, etc.); **—,** *vi.* comentar.

observer, *n.* observador, ra.

observing, *adj.* observador.

obsess, *vt.* obsesionar, causar obsesión.

obsession, *n.* obsesión, *f.*

obsolescence, *n.* estado de desuso.

obsolete, *adj.* anticuado.

obstacle, *n.* obstáculo, *m.*; valla, *f.*

obstetrician, *n.* partero, *m.*

obstetrics, *n.* obstetricia, *f.*

obstinacy, *n.* obstinación, terquedad, *f.*

obstinate, *adj.* terco, porfiado; **—ly,** *adv.* obstinadamente.

obstreperous, *adj.* estrepitoso, turbulento.

obstruct, *vt.* obstruir; impedir; entullecer; estorbar.

obstruction, *n.* obstrucción, *f.*; impedimento, *m.*; obstruccionismo, *m.*

obstructionist, *n.* obstruccionista, *m.* y *f.*

obstructive, *adj.* obstructivo.

obtain, *vt.* obtener, adquirir, lograr; **—,** *vi.* estar establecido.

obtainable, *adj.* asequible.

obtrude, *vt.* introducir con violencia; **—,** *vi.* entrometerse.

obtrusive, *adj.* intruso, importuno.

obtuse, *adj.* obtuso, romo, sin punta; sordo, apagado.

obviate, *vt.* obviar, evitar.

obvious, *adj.* obvio, evidente, visto; **—ly,** *adv.* patentemente.

ocarina, *n.* ocarina (instrumento músico), *f.*

occasion, *n.* ocasión, ocurrencia, *f.*; caso, *m.*; tiempo oportuno; acontecimiento, *m.*; **to give —,** dar pie; **—,** *vt.* ocasionar, causar.

occasional, *adj.* ocasional, casual; **—ly,** *adv.* ocasionalmente, a veces, a ratos.

occidental, *adj.* occidental.

occiput, *n.* occipucio, cogote, *m.*

occlude, *vt.* tapar, cerrar, obstruir.

occlusion, *n.* oclusión, *f.*

occult, *adj.* oculto, escondido.

occultism, *n.* ocultismo, *m.*

occupancy, *n.* toma de posesión.

occupant, occupier, *n.* ocupador, ra; poseedor, ra; inquilino, na.

occupation, *n.* ocupación, *f.*; empleo, *m.*; quehacer, *m.*

occupied, *adj.* ocupado.

occupy, *vt.* ocupar, emplear.

occur, *vi.* ocurrir; suceder; **to — frequently,** menudear, acontecer a menudo.

occurrence, *n.* ocurrencia, *f.*; incidente, *m.*; caso, *m.*

ocean, *n.* océano, *m.*, alta mar.

oceanic, *adj.* oceánico.

oceanography, *n.* oceanografía, *f.*

ocelot, *n.* (zool.) ocelote, *m.*, especie de gato montés.

ocher, *n.* ocre, *m.*

Oct. October, oct. oct.° octubre.

octagon, *n.* octágono, *m.*

octane, *n.* (chem.) octano, *m.*; **— rating,** número empleado para medir las propiedades antidetonantes de combustibles líquidos.

octave, *n.* octava, *f.*

Octavius, Octavio.

octavo, *n.* libro en octavo; **—,** *adj.* en octavo.

octet, *n.* (mus.) octeto, *m.*

October, *n.* octubre, *m.*

octogenarian, *n.* octogenario, ria.

octopus, *n.* (zool.) pulpo, pólipo, *m.*

ocular, *adj.* ocular.

oculist, *n.* oculista, oftalmólogo, *m.*

O.D.: officer of the day, oficial de guardia; **olive drab,** verde aceituna mate.

odd, *adj.* impar; raro; particular; extravagante; extraño; **one hundred and — dollars,** cien dólares y pico; **—ly,** *adv.* extrañamente, raramente.

oddity, *n.* singularidad, particularidad, rareza, *f.*

oddness, *n.* disparidad, desigualdad, *f.*; singularidad, *f.*

odds, *n. pl.* diferencia, disparidad, *f.*; ventaja, *f.*; **— and ends,** trozos o fragmentos sobrantes.

ode, *n.* oda, *f.*

odious, *adj.* odioso; **—ly,** *adv.* odiosamente.

odium, *n.* odiosidad, *f.*; odio, *m.*

odometer, *n.* odómetro, *m.*

odontologist, *n.* odontólogo, *m.*

odontology, *n.* odontología, *f.*

odontorrhagia, *n.* odontorragia, *f.*

odor, odour, *n.* olor, *m.*; fragancia, *f.*

odorous, *adj.* odorífero.

of, *prep.* de; tocante; según.

off, *adj.* and *adv.* lejos, a distancia; **hands —,** no tocar; **— and on,** de quitaipón; **— flavor,** desabrido, que no tiene el verdadero sabor; **— stage,** entre bastidores, lejos de la parte o región del escenario que puede ver el auditorio; **— hand,** de repente; **—!** *interj.* ¡fuera! ¡abajo!

offal, *n.* sobras, *f. pl.*; desecho, *m.*

off-color, *adj.* descolorido; impropio, inapropiado.

offend, *vt.* ofender, irritar; injuriar; **—,** *vi.* pecar.

offender, *n.* delincuente, *m.* y *f.*, ofensor, ra, transgresor, ra.

offending, *adj.* ofensor.

offense, *n.* ofensa, *f.*; injuria, *f.*; delincuencia, *f.*, crimen, delito, *m.*

offensive, *adj.* ofensivo; injurioso; **—,** *n.* (mil.) ofensiva, *f.*; **—ly,** *adv.* ofensivamente.

offer, *vt.* ofrecer; inmolar; atentar; brindar; **to — one's services,** brindarse; **—,** *vi.* ofrecerse; **—,** *n.* oferta, proposición, propuesta, *f.*

offering, *n.* sacrificio, *m.*; oferta, *f.*; propuesta, *f.*

offertory, *n.* ofertorio, *m.*

office, *n.* oficina, *f.*; oficio, empleo, *m.*; servicio, *m.*; cargo, *m.*; lugar, *m.*; **doctor's —,** consultorio, *m.*; **exchange —,** casa de cambio; **enrolling —, examining —,** registro, *m.*; **main —,** casa matriz; **— seeker,** pretendiente a un puesto, aspirante, *m.* y *f.*; **— supplies,** artículos para escritorio; **secretary's —,** secretaría, *f.*

officeholder, *n.* empleado público, funcionario, *m.*

officer, *n.* oficial, *m.*; funcionario, *m.*; agente de policía.

official, *adj.* oficial; **—,** *n.* oficial, *m.*; funcionario, *m.*; **public —,** funcionario público; **—ly,** *adv.* oficialmente.

officialdom, *n.* funcionarios públicos como entidad.

officiate, *vi.* oficiar; ejercer un cargo.

officious, *adj.* oficioso; **—ly,** *adv.* oficiosamente.

offing, *n.* pleamar, *f.*

offscouring, *n.* basura, *f.*; lavaduras, *f. pl.*

offset, *n.* pimpollo, *m.*; **—,** *vt.* balancear, compensar; neutralizar.

offshoot, *n.* retoño, vástago, *m.*; ramal, *m.*

offshore, *adv.* en la cercanía de la costa.

off side, *adv.* en el lado contrario (en ciertos juegos de pelota); (football) en posición fuera de juego.

offspring, *n.* prole, *f.*; linaje, *m.*; descendencia, *f.*; vástago, *m.*

off-stage, *adj.* (theat.) fuera del escenario.

oft, often, oftentimes, *adv.* muchas veces, frecuentemente, a menudo.

ogive, *n.* ojiva, *f.*

ogle, *vt.* mirar al soslayo; guiñar.

ogre, *n.* ogro, *m.*

ohm, *n.* ohmio, *m.*

ohmmeter, *n.* ohmímetro, *m.*

oil, *n.* aceite, *m.*; óleo, *m.*; petróleo, *m.*; **crude —,** aceite crudo; **drying —,** aceite secante; **heavy —,** aceite pesado; **mineral —,** aceite mineral; **— color,** color preparado con aceite; **— cup,** copa aceitadora o lubricadora; **— field,** campo de petróleo, cuenca petrolífera; **— painting,** pintura al óleo; **— pipe line,** oleoducto, *m.*; **— silk,** encerado, hule, *m.*; **vegetable —,** aceite vegetal; **—,** *vt.* aceitar, engrasar.

oilcan, *n.* aceitera, alcuza, *f.*, lata de aceite.

oilcloth, *n.* encerado, hule, *m.*

oiler, *n.* lubricador, engrasador, *m.*

oilman, *n.* aceitero, *m.*

oilpaper, *n.* papel encerado.

oilskin, *n.* encerado, hule, *m.*

oilstone, *n.* piedra de amolar con aceite.

oily, *adj.* aceitoso, oleaginoso.

ointment, *n.* ungüento, *m.*

O. K.: all correct, correcto, V.º B.º visto bueno; **approval,** aprobación.

okay, *adj.* and *adv.* bueno, está bien; **—,** *vt.* aprobar; dar el visto bueno; **—,** *n.* aprobación, *f.*, visto bueno.

Okla. Oklahoma, Oklahoma.

okra, *n.* (bot.) quimbombó, *m.*

old, *adj.* viejo; antiguo; rancio; **of —,** antiguamente; **— bachelor,** soltero, solterón, *m.*; **— hand,** experto, ta, persona experimentada; **— line,** conservador, de ideas antiguas; **— maid,** soltera, solterona, *f.*; persona remilgada; **— school,** grupo conservador de ideas antiguas; **to become —,** envejecerse, gastarse.

Old Castile, Castilla la Vieja.

old-fashioned, *adj.* anticuado, fuera de moda.

oldster, *n.* persona de edad madura.

old-time, *adj.* antiguo, anciano.

oleaginous, *adj.* oleaginoso.

oleander, *n.* (bot.) adelfa, *f.*, baladre, *m.*

oleomargarine, *n.* oleomargarina, *f.*

olfactory, *adj.* olfatorio.

oligarchy, *n.* oligarquía, *f.*

olive, *n.* olivo, *m.*; oliva, aceituna, *f.*; **— branch,** ramo de olivo, emblema de paz; **— drab,** color verde amarillo oscuro (de los uniformes del ejército de los Estados Unidos); **— grove,** olivar, *m.*; **— oil,** aceite de oliva; **— press,** trapiche, *m.*; **— tree,** olivo, *m.*; **pickled —s,** aceitunas en salmuera.

omber, ombre, *n.* tresillo, calzón (juego de naipes), *m.*

omelet, omelette, *n.* tortilla de huevos.

omen, *n.* agüero, presagio, *m.*

omened, *adj.* fatídico, augural.

ominous, *adj.* ominoso, de mal agüero; **—ly,** *adv.* ominosamente.

omission, *n.* omisión, *f.*; descuido, *m.*; salto, *m.*; olvido, *m.*

omit, *vt.* omitir.

omnibus, *n.* ómnibus, *m.*; libro que comprende diversos trabajos, bien de un mismo autor, bien del mismo tipo.

omnipotence, *n.* omnipotencia, *f.*

omnipotent, *adj.* omnipotente, todopoderoso.

omnipresence, *n.* omnipresencia, *f.*

omniscience, *n.* omnisciencia, *f.*

omniscient, *adj.* omnisciente, omniscio.

omnivorous, *adj.* omnívoro.

on, *prep.* sobre, encima, en; de; a; **—,** *adv.* adelante, sin cesar; **—!** *interj.* ¡vamos! ¡adelante!

once, *adv.* una vez; **— for all,** una vez por todas; **at —,** de un golpe, cuanto antes, a un tiempo; **all at —,** de una vez, de seguida, de un tirón; **— more,** más todavía, otra vez.

oncoming, *adj.* próximo, cercano, venidero.

one, *adj.* un, uno; **at — stroke,** de un tirón; **— by —,** uno a uno, uno por uno.

one-horse, *adj.* tirado por un caballo; inferior, de poca importancia; **— town,** pueblo insignificante.

oneness, *n.* unidad, *f.*

onerous, *adj.* oneroso, molesto, cargoso.

oneself, *pron.* sí mismo; **with —,** consigo.

one-sided, *adj.* unilateral, parcial.

one-step, *n.* especie de baile de salón; determinado ritmo musical para dicho baile.

onetime, *adj.* antiguo, primero.

one-track, *adj.* (rail.) de una sola vía; estrecho; que entiende o hace una sola cosa a la vez.

one-way, *adj.* en una sola dirección; **— trip,** viaje sencillo o de una sola vía; **— ticket,** billete sencillo, boleto de una sola vía.

onion, *n.* cebolla, *f.*

onionskin, *n.* papel trasparente o de seda.

onlooker, *n.* espectador, ra.

only, *adj.* único, solo; mero; **—,** *adv.* solamente, únicamente.

onrush, *n.* arranque, *m.*, embestida, *f.*

onset, onslaught, *n.* primer ímpetu; ataque, *m.*

onshore, *adj.* que se mueve o se dirige hacia las orillas.

Ont. Ontario, Ontario.

ontogeny, *n.* ontogenia, *f.*

ontology, *n.* ontología, *f.*

onward, onwards, *adv.* adelante.

onyx, *n.* ónice, ónique, ónix, *m.*

ooze, *n.* fango, *m.*; **—,** *vi.* escurrir o fluir (algún líquido), manar o correr (algún líquido) suavemente; trazumarse, exudar.

op.: opposite, opuesto, al otro lado; **opus,** op. opus, obra; **opera,** op. ópera, obras.

opacity, *n.* opacidad, *f.*

opal, *n.* ópalo, *m.*

opalescence, *n.* opalescencia, *f.*

opaque, *adj.* opaco.

op. cit. in the work cited, en la obra citada.

open, *adj.* abierto; patente, evidente; sincero, franco; cándido; rasgado; **— air,** aire libre; **— house,** casa abierta para todo mundo; **— letter,** carta abierta (de protesta o súplica); **— question,** cuestión dudosa o sujeta a duda; **— secret,** secreto que todo el mundo sabe; **— shop,** taller que emplea obreros que pertenezcan o no a un gremio; **— sesame,** sésamo ábrete (frase mágica de contraseña); **—ly,** *adv.* con franqueza, francamente, claramente, sin rebozo; **—,** *vt.* abrir; descubrir; **—,** *vi.* abrirse, descubrirse.

open-eyed, *adj.* vigilante, alerta; pasmado, asombrado.

openhanded, *adj.* dadivoso, liberal.

openhearted, *adj.* franco, sincero, sencillo.

open hearth, *n.* horno de reverbero.

open-hearth furnace, *n.* horno Siemens-Martin.

opening, *n.* abertura, grieta, *f.*; (com.) salida, *f.*; principio, *m.*; boca, *f.*; orificio, *m.*; apertura, *f.*

open-minded, *adj.* liberal; imparcial; receptivo.

openmouthed, *adj.* boquiabierto, ávido, voraz, rapaz, bocón, bocudo.

openness, *n.* claridad, *f.*; franqueza, *f.*; sinceridad, *f.*; llaneza, *f.*

openwork, *n.* obra a claros, calado, *m.*

opera, *n.* ópera, *f.*

opera glasses, *n. pl.* anteojos de ópera, gemelos, *m.pl.*

opera hat, *n.* clac, *m.*, sombrero de copa alta.

operate, *vi.* obrar; operar; **—,** *vt.* explotar.

operatic, *adj.* de ópera, relativo a la ópera.

operating table, *n.* mesa de operaciones.

operation, *n.* operación, *f.*; funcionamiento, *m.*; **to have an —,** (med.) operarse.

operative, *adj.* operativo.

operator, *n.* operario, ria; (med.) operador, *m.*

operetta, *n.* opereta, *f.*

ophthalmologist, *n.* oftalmólogo, *m.*

ophthalmology, *n.* oftalmología, *f.*

opiate, *n.* opiato, *m.*, opiata, *f.*; **—,** *adj.* opiato.

opine, *vi.* opinar, juzgar.

opinion, *n.* opinión, *f.*; juicio, *m.*; parecer, *m.*; sentencia, *f.*; concepto, *m.*; **in my —,** a mi ver; **to give an —,** opinar; **to have a high — of oneself,** presumir, vanagloriarse.

opinionated, *adj.* obstinado, pertinaz; doctrinal.

opium, *n.* opio, *m.*

opponent, *n.* antagonista, *m.* y *f.*; contrario, ria; contendiente, *m.* y *f.*

opportune, *adj.* oportuno, tempestivo, favorable; apropiado; **—ly,** *adv.* oportunamente.

opportunism, *n.* oportunismo, *m.*

opportunity, *n.* oportunidad, sazón, *f.*

oppose, *vi.* oponer, oponerse.

opposite, *adj.* fronterizo, opuesto; contrario; frente; de cara; **to take the —side,** llevar la contraria; **—ly,** *adv.* enfrente; **—,** *n.* antagonista, *m.* y *f.*, adversario, ria.

opposition, *n.* oposición, *f.*; resistencia, *f.*; impedimento, *m.*

oppress, *vt.* oprimir.

oppression, *n.* opresión, vejación, *f.*

oppressive, *adj.* opresivo, cruel.

oppressor, *n.* opresor, ra.

opprobrious, *adj.* oprobioso, ignominioso.

opprobrium, *n.* ignominia, *f.*; oprobio, *m.*

oppugn, *vt.* opugnar, resistir, oponer.

optative, *adj.* optativo.

optic, optical, *adj.* óptico; **—s,** *n.pl.* óptica, *f.*

optician, *n.* óptico, *m.*

optimism, *n.* optimismo, *m.*

optimist, *n.* optimista, *m.* y *f.*

optimistic, *adj.* optimista.

optimum, *n.* lo óptimo en grado, cantidad, calidad, etc.; la condición más favorable para la reproducción de organismos; **—** *adj.* óptimo.

option, *n.* opción, *f.*; deseo, *m.*

optional, *adj.* facultativo, opcional.

optometrist, *n.* optómetra, *m.*

optometry, *n.* optometría, *f.*

opulence, *n.* opulencia, riqueza, *f.*

opulent, *adj.* opulento; **—ly,** *adv.* opulentamente.

opus, *n.* obra literaria o musical.

or, *conj.* o; ó (entre números) u (antes de o y ho).

oracle, *n.* oráculo, *m.*

oracular, *adj.* oscuro, ambiguo.

oral, *adj.* oral, vocal; **—ly,** *adv.* verbalmente, de palabra.

orange, *n.* naranja, *f.*; **— juice,** jugo de naranja; **— tree,** naranjo, *m.*

orangeade, *n.* naranjada, *f.*

oration, *n.* oración, arenga, *f.*; **to make an —,** perorar.

orator, *n.* orador, ra, tribuno, *m.*

oratorical, *adj.* retórico, oratorio.

oratorio, *n.* (mus.) oratorio, *m.*

oratory, *n.* oratoria, *f.*; oratorio, *m.*; elocuencia, *f.*, arte oratoria.

orb, *n.* orbe, *m.*, esfera, *f.*; (poet.) ojo, *m.*

orbicular, *adj.* orbicular, circular, round.

orbit, *n.* órbita, *f.*

orbital, *adj.* orbital.

orchard, *n.* pomar, verjel, huerto, *m.*, huerta, *f.*

orchestra, *n.* orquesta, *f.*; **— seat,** luneta, platea, *f.*

orchestration, *n.* orquestación, *f.*

orchid, *n.* orquídea, *f.*

ordain, *vt.* (eccl.) ordenar; establecer.

ordeal, *n.* ordalías, *f.pl.*; prueba severa.

order, *n.* orden, *m.* y *f.*; regla, *f.*; mandato, *m.*; serie, clase, *f.*; encargo, *m.*; (com.) pedido, *m.*; **delivery —,** nota de entrega; **in — that,** para que; **— of the day,** orden del día; **out of —,** descompuesto; **rush —,** pedido de precisión; **trial —,** pedido de ensayo; **unfilled —,** pedido pendiente; **—,** *vt.* ordenar, arreglar; mandar; pedir, hacer un pedido.

orderly, *adj.* ordenado, regular; **—,** *n.* asistente o criado de hospital.

ordinal, *adj.* ordinal.

ordinance, *n.* ordenanza, *f.*

ordinarily, *adv.* ordinariamente.

ordinary, *adj.* ordinario; burdo, vulgar; **—,** *n.* ordinario, *m.*; hostería, *f.*

ordination, *n.* ordenación, *f.*

ordnance, *n.* artillería, *f.*; cañones, *m.pl.*, pertrechos de guerra.

ore, *n.* mineral, *m.*, mena, *f.*; **— deposit,** yacimiento, *m.*

Ore., Oreg. Oregon, Oregón.

organ, *n.* órgano, *m.*; **internal —s,** víscera, *f.*; **— pipe,** cañón de órgano; **— stop,** registro de un órgano.

organdy, *n.* organdí, *m.*

organ-grinder, *n.* organillero, *m.*

organic, *adj.* orgánico.

organism, *n.* organismo, *m.*

organist, *n.* organista, *m.* y *f.*

organization, *n.* organización, *f.*; organismo, *m.*

organize, *vt.* organizar.

organizer, *n.* organizador, ra.

orgy, *n.* orgía, *f.*

orient, *n.* oriente, *m.*; **—,** *vt.* orientar.

oriental, *adj.* oriental.

orientate, *vt.* orientar.

orientation, *n.* orientación, posición, *f.*

orifice, *n.* orificio, *m.*

origin, *n.* origen, principio, *m.*; procedencia, *f.*; tronco, *m.*

original, *adj.* original, primitivo; ingenioso; **—ly,** *adv.* originalmente.

originality, *n.* originalidad, *f.*

originate, *vt.* originar; **—,** *vi.* originar, provenir, originarse.

originator, *n.* inventor, *m.*, iniciador, *m.*

oriole, *n.* (orn.) oriol, *m.*, oropéndola, *f.*; (Sp. Am.) turpial, *m.*

orison, *n.* oración, *f.*, rezo, *m.*

ormolu, *n.* similor, *m.*, oro molido.

ornament, *n.* ornamento, *m.*, decoración, *f.*; **—,** *vt.* ornamentar, adornar.

ornamental, *adj.* que sirve de adorno.

ornamentation, *n.* ornamentación, *f.*

ornate, *adj.* muy adornado, historiado.

ornery, *adj.* de mal carácter, difícil de manejar.

ornithologist, *n.* ornitólogo, *m.*
ornithology, *n.* ornitología, *f.*
orotund, *adj.* sonoro, musical; retumbante, ostentoso.
orphan, *n.* and *adj.* huérfano, na.
orphanage, *n.* orfandad, *f.*; orfanato, *m.*, asilo de huérfanos.
orthodontia, *n.* ortopedia dental.
orthodox, *adj.* ortodoxo.
orthodoxy, *n.* ortodoxia, *f.*
orthographical, *adj.* ortográfico; **—ly,** *adv.* ortográficamente.
orthography, *n.* ortografía, *f.*
orthopedic, *adj.* ortopédico.
orthopedist, *n.* ortopedista, *m.*
O.S. Old Style, estilo antiguo.
oscillate, *vi.* oscilar, vibrar.
oscillation, *n.* oscilación, vibración, *f.*
oscillator, *n.* oscilador, *m.*
osculation, *n.* osculación, *f.*, beso, *m.*
osier, *n.* (bot.) mimbrera, *f.*; **—** *adj.* de mimbre.
osmosis, *n.* ósmosis, *f.*
osprey, *n.* águila marina.
osseous, *adj.* óseo, huesoso.
ossification, *n.* osificación, *f.*
ossify, *vt.* convertir en hueso; **—,** *vi.* osificarse.
ostensible, *adj.* ostensible, aparente; **—bly,** *adv.* ostensiblemente.
ostentation, *n.* ostentación, *f.*
ostentatious, *adj.* ostentoso, fastuoso; **—ly,** *adv.* pomposamente, con ostentación.
osteology, *n.* osteología, *f.*
osteomyelitis, *n.* (med.) osteomielitis, *f*
osteopath, *n.* osteópata, *m.*
osteopathy, *n.* osteopatía, *f.*
ostracism, *n.* ostracismo, *m.*
ostracize, *vt.* desterrar por medio del ostracismo.
ostrich, *n.* avestruz, *m.*
O.T. Old Testament, Antiguo Testamento.
other, *pron.* and *adj.* otro.
otherwise, *adv.* de otra manera, por otra parte.
Otho, Otón.
otology, *n.* (med.) otología, *f.*
otoscopy, *n.* otoscopia, *f.*
otter, *n.* nutra, nutria, *f.*
ottoman, *n.* otomana, *f.*; sofá, *m.*
ought, *vi.* deber, ser menester.
ouija, *n.* nombre comercial de una especie de tabla de escritura espiritista.
ounce, *n.* onza, *f.*
our, ours, *pron.* nuestro, tra, nuestros, tras.
Our Lady, Nuestra Señora.
ourselves, *pron. pl.* nosotros mismos.
oust, *vt.* quitar; desposeer, desalojar.
ouster, *n.* despojo, desposeimiento, *m.*
out, *adv.* fuera, afuera; **—,** *adj.* de fuera; **—!** *interj.* ¡fuera! **—,** *n.* acción de sacar o dejar fuera a un jugador (en el juego de baseball); **—,** *vt.* expeler, desposeer.
out-and-out, *adj.* sin reserva, completo.

outbid, *vt.* pujar, ofrecer más dinero (en subasta, etc.).
outboard, *adj.* and *adv.* (naut.) fuera del buque.
outbreak, *n.* erupción, *f.*; estallido, *m.*; principio, *m.*
outbuilding, *n.* edificio accesorio
outburst, *n.* explosión, *f.*
outcast, *adj.* desechado; desterrado, expulso; **—,** *n.* desterrado, da.
outclass, *vt.* aventajar, ser superior a.
outcome, *n.* conclusión, *f.*; consecuencia, *f.*, resultado, *m.*
outcry, *n.* clamor, *m.*; gritería, *f.*; venta pública.
outdated, *adj.* anticuado, atrasado.
outdistance, *vt.* dejar detrás, sobrepasar.
outdo, *vt.* exceder a otro, sobrepujar.
outdoor, *adj.* al aire libre, fuera de casa, al raso; **— exercise,** ejercicio al aire libre.
outdoors, *adv.* al aire libre, a la intemperie, fuera de la casa; **—,** *adj.* relativo al aire libre o a la intemperie.
outer, *adj.* exterior.
outermost, *adj.* extremo; lo más exterior.
outface, *vt.* humillar; desafiar.
outfield, *n.* la parte fuera del cuadro (en baseball).
outfielder, *n.* (baseball) uno de los tres jugadores colocados fuera del cuadro.
outfit, *n.* vestido, *m.*, vestimenta, *f.*; ropa, *f*; **—,** *vt.* equipar, ataviar.
outgeneral, *vt.* mostrarse superior en táctica militar.
outgoing, *n.* salida, *f.*; **—,** *adj.* saliente; **— mail,** correspondencia de salida; **—s,** *n. pl.* gasto, *m.*
outgrow, *vt.* sobrecrecer; exceder en vegetación; quedar chico, no servirle a uno por quedar ya chico (vestido, calzado, etc.).
outgrowth, *n.* resultado, *m.*; consecuencia, *f.*; producto accesorio.
outguess, *vt.* acertar más o más pronto que otro.
outhouse, *n.* dependencia de una casa; retrete situado fuera de la casa.
outing, *n.* excursión o salida al campo, jira campestre.
outlandish, *adj.* de apariencia exótica; ridículo, grotesco.
outlast, *vt.* exceder en duración.
outlaw, *n.* proscripto, *m.*; bandido, *m.*; **—,** *vt.* proscribir.
outlawry, *n.* proscripción, *f.*
outlay, *n.* gastos, *m. pl.*
outlet, *n.* salida, *f.*; sangrador, tomadero, *m.*
outline, *n.* contorno, *m.*; bosquejo, *m.*; esbozo, *m.*; silueta, *f.*; **—,** *vt.* esbozar.
outlined, *adj.* perfilado; delineado.
outlive, *vt.* sobrevivir.
outlook, *n.* perspectiva, *f.*
outlying, *adj.* lejos de la parte central; remoto.
outmaneuver, outmanoeuvre, *vt.* pre-

valecer en táctica militar, mostrarse superior, distinguirse.

outmatch, vt. prevalecer, mostrarse superior, distinguirse, sobresalir.

outmoded, adj. anticuado, pasado de moda.

outnumber, vt. exceder en número.

out-of-date, adj. anticuado, pasado o fuera de moda.

out-of-door, out-of-doors, adj. fuera de casa, al aire libre.

out-of-print, adj. (print.) agotado; — **edition,** agotada la edición.

out-of-stock, adj. (com.) agotada (la existencia), sin existencia (de cierta mercancía).

outpatient, n. enfermo o paciente externo de un hospital.

outpoint, vt. exceder en puntos al adversario.

outpost, n. puesto avanzado.

outpouring, n. efusión, f.

output, n. capacidad, f., rendimiento, m., producción total; cantidad producida.

outrage, n. ultraje, m., infamia, f.; —, vt. ultrajar.

outrageous, adj. ultrajoso; atroz; —ly, adv. injuriosamente; enormemente; infamemente.

outrank, vt. sobresalir, exceder, exceder en rango, grado o posición.

outreach, vt. alcanzar, sobrepasar.

outrider, n. batidor, palafrenero, m., criado que va a caballo delante o al lado de un carruaje.

outrigger, n. (naut.) escora, f.

outright, adv. cumplidamente, luego, al momento.

outrun, vt. correr más que otro.

outset, n. principio, m.

outshine, vt. exceder en brillantez, eclipsar.

outside, n. superficie, f.; exterior, m.; apariencia, f.; —s, n. pl. delanteros exteriores en Rugby; —, adv. afuera.

outsider, n. forastero, ra, extranjero, ra; persona no perteneciente a determinada institución, partido, etc.

outskirts, n. pl. suburbio, m., parte exterior (de una población, etc.).

outspoken, adj. franco; que habla en forma atrevida.

outspread, adj. esparcido; —, vt. and vi. extender, extenderse.

outstanding, adj. sobresaliente, notable, extraordinario.

outstay, vt. durar más tiempo, resistir más.

outstretch, vt. extender, alargar.

outstrip, vt. dejar atrás; sobrepujar.

outtalk, vt. hablar más que (el otro).

outward, adj. exterior, externo; —ly, adv. fuera; exteriormente.

outwear, vt. durar más que; gastar por uso excesivo.

outweigh, vt. preponderar, exceder en peso o en valor.

outwit, vt. engañar a uno a fuerza de tretas.

outworks, n. pl. (mil.) obras avanzadas.

outworn, adj. usado, gastado, anticuado, ajado.

ouzel, n. (orn.) mirlo, m.

oval, n. óvalo, m.; —, adj. oval, ovalado.

ovary, n. ovario, m.

ovation, n. ovación, f.

oven, n. horno, m.

over, prep. sobre, encima; all —, por todos lados; —, adv. más, demás; — again, otra vez; — against, enfrente; — and above, de sobra; — and —, repetidas veces.

overabundance, n. plétora, superabundancia, f., exceso, m.

overabundant, adj. sobreabundante.

overage, adj. demasiado viejo desde el punto de vista de la eficacia de su servicio.

over-all, adj. que incluye todo.

overalls, n. pl. zahones, m. pl., pantalones amplios para librarse del polvo, basura, etc.

overawe, vt. tener a freno; imponer respeto.

overbalance, vt. preponderar; —, n. preponderancia, f.

overbear, vt. sujetar, oprimir, agobiar.

overbearing, adj. ultrajoso, despótico.

overboard, adv. (naut.) al agua, al mar.

overburden, vt. sobrecargar.

overcapitalization, n. capitalización excesiva, cálculo de capital exagerado.

overcast, vt. anublar, oscurecer; repulgar; valuar demasiado; **to be —,** nublarse.

overcharge, vt. sobrecargar; poner alguna cosa a precio muy subido; (coll.) cargar la mano.

overcloud, vt. cubrir de nubes.

overcoat, n. gabán, abrigo, sobretodo, m.

overcome, vt. vencer; superar; salvar (obstáculos).

overconfident, adj. demasiado confiado, demasiado atrevido.

overcooked, adj. recocido.

overcrowd, vt. atestar, llenar demasiado.

overdevelop, vt. desarrollar demasiado.

overdo, vt. cocer demasiado (la carne, etc.); —, vi. hacer más de lo necesario.

overdose, n. dosis excesiva.

overdraft, n. giro o libranza en descubierto.

overdraw, vt. girar en descubierto.

overdress, vt. engalanar con exceso.

overdue, adj. (com.) atrasado, vencido; — **draft,** letra vencida.

overeat, vi. hartarse, comer demasiado.

overestimate, vt. estimar o avaluar en exceso.

overexposure, n. exceso de exposición.

overfeed, vt. sobrealimentar.

overfill, vt. llenar con exceso.

overflow, vt. inundar; —, vi. salir de madre; rebosar; desbordar; redundar; —, n. inundación, f.; superabundancia, f.

overflowing, n. desbordamiento, m.

overgrow, vi. crecer demasiado.

overgrowth, *n.* vegetación exuberante.

overhang, *vt.* estar colgando sobre alguna cosa; salir algo fuera del nivel (de un edificio, etc.).

overhaul, *vt.* remendar por completo, componer; alcanzar.

overhead, *adv.* sobre la cabeza, en lo alto; **—,** *n.* (com.) gastos de administración.

overhear, *vt.* oír algo por casualidad.

overheat, *vt.* acalorar, calentar demasiado.

overhung, *adj.* colgante, que cuelga.

overindulge, *vt.* consentir o mimar demasiado; darse uno gusto en exceso.

overjoyed, *adj.* muy gozoso.

overland, *adv.* por tierra.

overlap, *vt.* sobreponer; sobrepasar; montar; traslapar.

overlapping, *n.* acción de traslapar; **—,** *adj.* traslapado.

overlay, *vt.* cubrir, extender sobre; abrumar.

overlie, *vt.* tenderse sobre, echarse encima; sofocar echándose encima.

overload, *vt.* sobrecargar; **—,** *n.* sobrecarga, *f.*, recargo, *m.*

overlook, *vt.* mirar desde lo alto; examinar; rever; repasar; pasar por alto; tolerar; descuidar; desdeñar.

overlord, *n.* señor, jefe, *m.*

overmuch, *adj.* demasiado.

overnight, *adv.* de noche, durante o toda la noche; **—,** *adj.* de una noche; **— guests,** visitantes que se quedan a pasar la noche.

overpass, *vt.* and *vi.* atravesar, cruzar; vencer; transgredir; exceder, sobrepasar; pasar por alto; **—,** *n.* puente o camino por encima de un ferrocarril, canal u otra vía.

overplay, *vt.* jugar con habilidad excesiva; (golf) lanzar la pelota más allá del *green.*

overplus, *n.* sobrante, *m.*, sobra, *f.*

overpower, *vt.* predominar, oprimir.

overproduction, *n.* exceso de producción, sobreproducción, *f.*

overrate, *vt.* apreciar o valuar alguna cosa en más de lo que vale.

overreach, *vt.* sobresalir, exceder en altura; engañar.

override, *vt.* fatigar un caballo con exceso; prevalecer.

overrule, *vt.* predominar, dominar.

overrun, *vt.* hacer correrías; cubrir enteramente; inundar; infestar; repasar; **—,** *vi.* rebosar.

overscore, *vt.* señalar por arriba, con una línea u otra marca, una palabra, una frase, etc.

oversea, overseas, *adv.* ultramar; **—,** *adj.* de ultramar.

oversee, *vt.* inspeccionar; examinar.

overseer, *n.* superintendente, *m.*; capataz, *m.*

oversell, *vt.* vender a un precio más alto que otro.

overset, *vt.* volcar; trastornar; **—,** *vi.* volcarse, caerse.

overshadow, *vt.* asombrar, oscurecer; predominar.

overshoe, *n.* galocha, *f.*

overshoot, *vt.* tirar más allá del blanco; **—,** *vi.* pasar de raya.

oversight, *n.* yerro, *m.*; equivocación, *f.*; olvido, *m.*

oversize, *adj.* grande en exceso.

overskirt, *n.* sobre falda.

oversleep, *vi.* dormir demasiado.

overspread, *vt.* desparramar.

overstate, *vi.* exagerar.

overstatement, *n.* exageración, *f.*

overstay, *vt.* permanecer demasiado tiempo.

overstep, *vt.* pasar más allá; extralimitarse, excederse.

overstuff, *vt.* rellenar (un cojín, una almohada, etc.).

overstuffed, *adj.* relleno o rellenado (aplícase a muebles).

oversubscribe, *vt.* and *vi.* contribuir más de lo pedido; comprar más bonos de los que se han emitido.

oversupply, *n.* provisión, cantidad excesiva.

overt, *adj.* abierto, público; **—ly,** *adv.* abiertamente.

overtake, *vt.* alcanzar; coger en el hecho.

overtax, *vt.* oprimir con tributos.

overthrow, *vt.* trastornar; demoler; destruir; derribar, derrocar; **—,** *n.* trastorno, *m.*; ruina, derrota, *f.*

overtime, *n.* trabajo en exceso de las horas regulares.

overtrain, *vt.* entrenar con exceso.

overture, *n.* abertura, *f.*; (mus.) obertura, *f.*; proposición formal (de paz, etc.).

overturn, *vt.* subvertir, trastornar.

overturning, *n.* volteo, *m.*

overweening, *adj.* presuntuoso, arrogante, exagerado, pretencioso.

overweight, *n.* preponderancia, *f.*; exceso de peso.

overwhelm, *vt.* abrumar; oprimir; sumergir.

overwhelming, *adj.* abrumador, arrollador, dominante.

overwork, *vt.* hacer trabajar demasiado; **—,** *vi.* trabajar demasiado.

overwrought, *adj.* sobreexcitado.

Ovid, Ovidio.

oviparous, *adj.* ovíparo.

ovule, *n.* óvulo, *m.*

ovum, *n.* (biol.) huevo, *m.*

owe, *vt.* deber, tener deudas; estar obligado.

owing, *adj.* que es debido; **— to,** a causa de.

owl, owlet, *n.* lechuza, *f.*

own, *adj.* propio; **my —,** mío, mía; **—,** *vt.* reconocer; poseer; **to — up,** confesar.

owner, *n.* dueño, ña, propietario, ria; poseedor, ra; **— of a ship,** naviero, *m.*

ownership, *n.* dominio, *m.*; propiedad, *f.*

ox, *n.* buey, *m.*; **— driver,** boyero, *m.*

oxbow, *n.* horcate de yugo.

oxen, *n. pl.* de **ox,** bueyes, *m. pl.*

oxidation, *n.* oxidación, *f.*

oxidize, *vt.* oxidar.

oxyacetylene, *adj.* oxiacetilénico.
oxyacetylene torch, *n.* antorcha de oxiacetileno.
oxygen, *n.* oxígeno, *m.*; **— tent,** tienda de oxígeno.
oxygenated, *adj.* oxigenado.
oxygenation, *n.* oxigenación, *f.*
oxyhydrogen, *n.* gas oxhídrico; **— torch,** soplete oxhídrico.
oyster, *n.* ostra, *f.*, ostión, *m.*
oyster cracker, *n.* galletica salada.
oz. ounce, ounces, onz. onza, onzas.
ozone, *n.* (chem.) ozona, *f.*, ozono, *m.*

P

p.: page, pág, página; **past,** pasado; **participle,** p. participio.
Pa. Pennsylvania, Pensilvania.
Pac. Pacific, Pacífico.
paca, *n.* (zool.) paca, *f.*
pace, *n.* paso, *m.*, marcha, *f.*; **—,** *vt.* medir a pasos; **—,** *vi.* pasear; **to — one's beat,** hacer la ronda.
pacemaker, *n.* establecedor de marcha, de paso, andadura, etc.
pacer, *n.* caballo de paso, de andadura.
pachyderm, *n.* paquidermo, *m.*
Pacific, *n.* Pacífico, *m.*
pacific, *adj.* pacífico.
pacification, *n.* pacificación, *f.*
pacifist, *n.* pacifista, *m.* y *f.*
pacify, *vt.* pacificar, asosegar.
pack, *n.* lío, fardo, *m.*; baraja de naipes; muta, perrada, *f.*; cuadrilla, *f.*; carga, *f.*; **— animal,** acémila, *f.*, animal de carga; **— horse,** caballo de carga; **— of cigarettes,** cajetilla de cigarros; **— saddle,** albarda, *f.*; **— train,** reata, recua, *f.*; **—,** *vt.* empaquetar; empacar; enfardelar, embalar; empandillar el naipe.
package, *n.* fardo, bulto, *m.*; embalaje, *m.*; paquete, *m.*
packer, *n.* empaquetador, embalador, *m.*
packet, *n.* paquete, *m.*; **— boat,** paquebote, *m.*
packing, *n.* embalaje, *m.*; envase, *m.*; empaque, *m.*; relleno, *m.*; empaquetadura, *f.*; **— house,** empresa empacadora, frigorífico, *m.*
pack rat, *n.* mozo de hotel de veraneo; ratero, *m.*
packthread, *n.* bramante, *m.*, hilo de acarreto.
pact, *n.* pacto, convenio, acuerdo, arreglo, contrato, *m.*
pad, *n.* cojincillo, *m.*, almohadilla, *f.*, relleno, *m.*; **— (of paper),** bloc (de papel), *m.*; **—,** *vt.* rellenar, proveer con cojincillo.
padded, *adj.* acojinado, relleno, rellenado (de algodón, paja, papel, etc.).
padding, *n.* relleno, *m.*
paddle, *vi.* remar; chapotear; **—,** *n.* canalete (especie de remo), *m.*; **— wheel,** rueda de paletas.

paddock, *n.* dehesa, *f.*
padlock, *n.* candado, *m.*
pagan, *n.* and *adj.* pagano, na.
paganism, *n.* paganismo, *m.*
page, *n.* página, *f.*; paje, *m.*; **—,** *vt.* foliar.
pageant, *n.* espectáculo público, procesión, *f.*
pageantry, *n.* fausto, *m.*, pompa, *f.*
pagination, *n.* paginación, *f.*
pail, *n.* colodra, *f.*; cubo, pozal, *m.*; **small —,** cubeto, *m.*
pain, *n.* pena, *f.*; castigo, *m.*; dolor, *m.*; **—,** *vt.* afligir; doler.
painful, *adj.* dolorido; penoso; **—ly,** *adv.* dolorosamente, con pena.
painless, *adj.* sin pena; sin dolor.
painstaker, *n.* trabajador asiduo, persona afanosa.
painstaking, *adj.* laborioso, afanoso; esmerado; **—ly,** *adv.* detenidamente.
paint, *vt.* and *vi.* pintar; **—,** *n.* pintura, *f.*
paintbrush, *n.* brocha, *f.*, pincel, *m.*
painter, *n.* pintor, ra.
painting, *n.* pintura, *f.*
pair, *n.* par, *m.*; **—,** *vt.* parear; **—,** *vi.* aparearse.
paisley, *adj.* que se parece a un chal de Paisley.
pajamas, *n.pl.* pijamas, *m. pl.*
palace, *n.* palacio, *m.*
palatable, *adj.* sabroso.
palate, *n.* paladar, *m.*; gusto, *m.*
palatial, *adj.* propio de palacios, palaciego.
palatinate, *n.* palatinado, *m.*
palatine, *adj.* palatino, palaciego.
palaver, *n.* charla, *f.*; fruslería, *f.*; zalamería, *f.*; **—,** *vi.* congraciarse con zalamerías; charlar.
pale, *adj.* pálido; claro; **to turn —,** palidecer; **—,** *n.* palizada, *f.*; estaca, *f.*; límite, *m.*; **—,** *vt.* empalizar, cercar, rodear.
paleface, *n.* caripálido, da.
paleness, *n.* palidez, *f.*
paleographer, *n.* paleógrafo, *m.*
paleography, *n.* paleografía, *f.*
paleolithic, *adj.* paleolítico.
paleontologist, *n.* paleontólogo, *m.*
paleontology, *n.* paleontología, *f.*; estudio de restos fósiles.
Paleozoic, *adj.* paleozoico.
palette, *n.* paleta (de pintor), *f.*
palfrey, *n.* palafrén, *m.*
paling, *n.* estacada, palizada, *f.*
palisade, *n.* palizada, *f.*, palenque, *m.*
pall, *n.* paño de tumba; palio de arzobispo; palia, *f.*; **—,** *vi.* desvanecerse; **—,** *vt.* evaporar; condecorar con palio.
pallbearer, *n.* el que acompaña a un cadáver.
pallet, *n.* camilla, *f.*, cama pequeña y pobre.
palliate, *vt.* paliar.
palliation, *n.* paliación, *f.*
palliative, *adj.* paliativo; **—,** *n.* paliativo, *m.*
pallid, *adj.* pálido.
pallor, *n.* palidez, *f.*
palm, *n.* (bot.) palma, *f.*; victoria, *f.*; palma (de la mano), *f.*; **— oil,** aceite de palma o

palmera; **—**, *vt.* escamotar; tocar con la palma de la mano.

palmated, *adj.* palmeado.

Palm Beach suit, *n.* traje de Palm Beach, traje de tela fresca para el verano.

palmetto, *n.* (bot.) palmito, *m.*

palmistry, *n.* quiromancia, *f.*

Palm Sunday, *n.* domingo de Ramos.

palpability, *n.* palpabilidad, *f.*

palpable, *adj.* palpable; evidente; **—bly,** *adv.* palpablemente; claramente.

palpitate, *vi.* palpitar.

palpitation, *n.* palpitación, *f.*

palsied, *adj.* paralítico.

palsy, *n.* parálisis, perlesía, *f.*

paltry, *adj.* vil; mezquino.

pampas, *n. pl.* pampas, *f. pl.*; **— man, — woman,** pampero, ra.

pamper, *vt.* mimar.

pamphlet, *n.* folleto, libreto, *m.*; **small —,** folletín, *m.*

pamphleteer, *n.* folletista, *m.*

pan, *n.* cazuela, cacerola, *f.*; **earthen —,** barreña, *f.*, barreño, *m.*

panacea, *n.* panacea, *f.*

Panama, Panamá, *f.*; **from —,** panameño; **— hat,** sombrero de jipijapa, sombrero panamá.

Panamanian, *n.* and *adj.* panameño, ña.

pancake, *n.* especie de tortilla de masa que se cuece en una plancha metálica.

panchromatic, *adj.* pancromático.

pancreas, *n.* (anat.) páncreas, *m.*

panda, *n.* pequeño mamífero de las Himalayas parecido al coatí; **giant —,** mamífero habitante del Tibet parecido al oso.

pander, *n.* alcahuete, ta; **—,** *vt.* alcahuetear.

pane, *n.* cuadro de vidrio.

panegyric, *n.* panegírico, *m.*

panel, *n.* entrepaño, *m.*; bastidor, *m.*; (law) lista de jurados; **— discussion,** discusión de asuntos de interés general, como problemas públicos, a cargo de oradores previamente seleccionados.

pang, *n.* angustia, congoja, *f.*

panhandle, *n.* proyección de un territorio en otro; **—,** *vi.* mendigar en público.

panhandler, *n.* pordiosero, ra, mendigo, ga; callejero, ra.

panic, *n.* pánico, *m.*, terror pánico; **—,** *adj.* pánico; **— grass,** adaza, *f.*, panizo, *m.*

panicky, *adj.* consternado, aterrorizado.

panic-stricken, *adj.* aterrorizado, pasmado, espantado.

pannier, *n.* cuévano, cesto, *m.*

panoplied, *adj.* con armadura de caballero.

panoply, *n.* panoplia, *f.*

panorama, *n.* panorama, *m.*

pansy, *n.* (bot.) pensamiento, *m.*; trinitaria, *f.*

pant, *vi.* palpitar; jadear; **to — for, to — after,** suspirar por; **—,** *n.* jadeo, *m.*; **—s,** *n.pl.* bragas, *f.pl.*, pantalones, *m.pl.*

pantaloon, *n.* bufón, *m.*; **—s,** *n.pl.* pantalones, *m.pl.*

panther, *n.* pantera, *f.*; **American —,** puma, *f.*

panties, *n.pl.* pantalones, *m.pl.*, pantalones de mujer.

panting, *adj.* jadeante, anhelante, sin respiración, sin aliento.

pantograph, *n.* pantógrafo, *m.*

pantomime, *n.* pantomimo, *m.*; pantomima, *f.*

pantomimist, *n.* pantomimo, *m.*

pantry, *n.* despensa, *f.*

pants, *n. pl.* pantalones, *m. pl.*

panzer, *n.* ejército motorizado.

pap, *n.* cosa parecida a un pezón; papa, papilla, *f.*, gachas, *f. pl.*; carne (de la fruta), *f.*

papacy, *n.* papado, *m.*

papal, *adj.* papal.

papaw, *n.* papaya, *f.*

paper, *n.* papel, *m.*; periódico, *m.*; **—s,** *n. pl.* escrituras, *f. pl.*; documento, *m.*; **blotting —,** papel secante; **brown —,** papel de estraza; **carbon —,** papel carbón; **heap of disordered —s,** papelería, *f.*; **glazed —,** papel satinado; **granulated —,** papel imitación chagrín; **in a — cover,** a la rústica (encuadernación); **litmus —,** (chem.) papel reactivo; **tissue —,** papel de seda; **toilet —,** papel de excusado; **vellum —,** papel avitelado; **wrapping —,** papel de envolver; **writing —,** papel de escribir; **marbled —,** papel jaspeado; **— clip,** presilla, *f.*; **— cone,** cucurucho, *m.*; **— cutter, — knife,** cortapapel *m.*; **— money,** papel moneda; **stamped —,** papel sellado; **—,** *adj.* de papel; **—,** *vt.* entapizar con papel.

paper profits, *n. pl.* ganancias no realizadas sobre transacciones no concluídas.

paperweight, *n.* sujetapapeles, pisapapeles, prensapapeles, *m.*

papillary, *adj.* papilar.

papist, *n.* papista, *m.*

papoose, *n.* niñito de los indios norteamericanos.

pappy, *adj.* mollar, jugoso.

paprika, *n.* pimentón, *m.*

papyrus, *n.* papiro, *m.*

par, *n.* equivalencia, *f.*; igualdad, *f.*; (golf) número de jugadas para un agujero; **at —,** (com.) a la par; **exchange at —,** cambio a la par; **exchange under —,** cambio con quebrado; **— excellence,** por excelencia; **— value,** valor a la par.

par. paragraph, párrafo.

parable, *n.* parábola, *f.*

parabola, *n.* (math.) parábola, *f.*

parabolic, *adj.* parabólico.

parachute, *n.* paracaídas, *m.*; **— troops,** cuerpo de paracaidistas.

parachutist, *n.* paracaidista, *m.* y *f.*

parade, *n.* ostentación, pompa, *f.*; desfile, *m.*; (mil.) parada, *f.*; **—,** *vt.* and *vi.* formar parada; tomar parte en un desfile; pasear; hacer gala.

paradigm, *n.* paradigma, *m.*

paradise, *n.* paraíso, *m.*

paradox, *n.* paradoja, *f.*

paradoxical, *adj.* paradójico, paradojo.

paraffin, *n.* parafina, *f.*

paragon, *n.* modelo perfecto; (print.) parangona, *f.*; —, *vt.* comparar, comparar con.

paragraph, *n.* párrafo, *m.*

Paraguayan, *n.* and *adj.* paraguayo, ya.

Paraguay tea, *n.* yerba mate.

parakeet, *n.* periquito, *m.*

parallel, *n.* línea paralela; —, *adj.* paralelo; —, *vt.* parangonar.

parallelism, *n.* paralelismo, *m.*

parallelogram, *n.* paralelogramo, *m.*

paralysis, *n.* parálisis, *f.*

paralytic, paralytical, *adj.* paralítico.

paralyze, *vt.* paralizar.

paramecium, *n.* (zool.) paramecio, *m.*

paramount, *adj.* supremo, superior; —, *n.* jefe, superior, *m.*

paramour, *n.* amante (generalmente ilícito), *m.*

paranoia, *n.* (psych.) paranoia, *f.*

paranoiac, *n.* paranoico, *m.*

parapet, *n.* pretil, *m.*

paraphrase, *n.* paráfrasis, *f.*; —, *vt.* parafrasear.

parasite, *n.* parásito, *m.*

parasitic, *adj.* parásito.

parasol, *n.* parasol, quitasol, *m.*

parathyroid, *adj.* (anat.) paratiroideo.

paratroops, *n. pl.* tropas de paracaídas; paracaidistas, *m. pl.*

paratyphoid, *n.* paratifus, *m.*

parboil, *vt.* medio cocer; sancochar.

parcel, *n.* paquete, *m.*; porción, cantidad, *f.*; bulto, *m.*; lío, *m.*; — **post,** paquete postal; —, *vt.* partir, dividir.

parch, *vt.* tostar.

parcheesi, parchesi, *n.* especie de juego de chaquete.

parchment, *n.* pergamino, *m.*

pardon, *n.* perdón, *m.*, gracia, *f.*; —, *vt.* perdonar.

pardonable, *adj.* perdonable.

pare, *vt.* recortar; pelar, quitar la corteza.

paregoric, *adj.* and *n.* calmante, paregórico, *m.*

paren. parenthesis, paréntesis.

parent, *n.* padre, *m.*; madre, *f.*; —s, *n. pl.* padres, *m. pl.*

parentage, *n.* ascendencia, extracción, *f.*, origen; *m.*

parental, *adj.* paternal; maternal.

parenthesis, *n.* paréntesis, *m.*

parenthetic, *adj.* entre paréntesis.

parenthood, paternidad o maternidad, *f.*

paresis, *n.* (med.) paresia, *f.*

parfait, *n.* variedad de postre congelado.

pariah, *n.* paria, *m.* y *f.*

parietal, *adj.* parietal; —, *n.* parietal, *m.*, hueso parietal.

pari-mutuel, *n.* sistema de apuestas en las carreras de caballos; máquina para registro de apuestas.

paring knife, *n.* cuchillo para pelar legumbres, etc.

parings, *n. pl.* peladuras, mondaduras, *f. pl.*

Paris green, *n.* cardenillo, *m.*

parish, *n.* parroquia, *f.*; —, *adj.* parroquial.

parishioner, *n.* parroquiano, na.

Parisian, *adj.* parisiense; —, *n.* parisiense, *m.* y *f.*

parity, *n.* paridad, igualdad, *f.*

park, *n.* parque, *m.*; —, *vt.* cerrar o cercar un coto; estacionar (vehículos).

parka, *n.* camisa de lana con capucha.

parking, *n.* estacionamiento (de automóviles), *m.*; — **place,** plaza de estacionamiento; — **station,** estación de vehículos.

parkway, *n.* bulevar, *m.*; borde de tierra entre la acera y la calle; faja de césped entre la acera y el pavimento de la calle.

parlance, *n.* conversación, *f.*; dicción, *f.*

parley, *n.* conferencia, plática, *f.*

parliament, *n.* parlamento, *m.*; **member of** —, parlamentario, *m.*

parliamentary, *adj.* parlamentario.

parlor, *n.* sala, *f.*, sala de recibo, parlatorio, *m.*; **funeral** —, casa mortuoria; — **car,** coche salón.

parlous, *adj.* (coll.) perspicaz, demasiado agudo; travieso en exceso.

parochial, *adj.* parroquial.

parody, *n.* parodia, *f.*; —, *vt.* parodiar.

parole, *n.* libertad que se da a un prisionero, libertad bajo palabra.

paroquet, *n.* periquito, *m.*, papagayo pequeño.

paroxysm, *n.* paroxismo, *m.*

parquet, *n.* (theat.) platea, *f.*; piso de mosaico de madera.

parquetry, *n.* mosaico de madera.

parricidal, *adj.* parricida.

parricide, *n.* parricidio, *m.*; parricida, *m.* y *f.*

parrot, *n.* papagayo, loro, *m.*; (Sp. Am.) cata, *f.*

parry, *vi.* evadir; rechazar; —, *n.* rechazo, *m.*

parse, *vt.* (gram.) construir.

parsimonious, *adj.* económico, moderado en sus gastos; —**ly,** *adv.* con parsimonia, con economía.

parsimony, *n.* parsimonia, *f.*

parsley, *n.* (bot.) perejil, *m.*

parsnip, *n.* (bot.) chirivía, *f.*

parson, *n.* párroco, *m.*

parsonage, *n.* beneficio, curado, *m.*; rectoría, *f.*, casa cural.

part, *n.* parte, *f.*; oficio, *m.*; papel (de un actor), *m.*; obligación, *f.*; **in** —, parcialmente; — **of speech,** parte de la oración; — **time,** trabajo de unas cuantas horas por día, trabajo temporal por semana; **rear** —, zaga, *f.*; —**s,** *n. pl.* partes, *f. pl.*, paraje, distrito, *m.*; —, *vt.* partir, separar, desunir; —, *vi.* partirse, separarse; — **from,** despedirse; — **with,** deshacerse de; —**ly,** *adv.* en parte.

part.: participle, p. participio; **partner,** socio.

partake, vt. and vi. participar, tomar parte.

partaker, n. participante, m. y f.

parthenogenesis, n. partenogénesis, f.

partial, adj. parcial; **—ly,** adv. parcialmente.

partiality, n. parcialidad, f.

participant, adj. participante; **—,** n. partícipe, participante, m. y f.

participate, vt. participar.

participation, n. participación, f.

participator, n. partícipe, m. y f.

participial, adj. participial.

participle, n. (gram.) participio, m.

particle, n. partícula, f.

parti-colored, adj. abigarrado, de diversos colores.

particular, adj. particular, singular; **—ly,** adv. particularmente; **—,** n. particular, m.; particularidad, f.

particularity, n. particularidad, f.

particularization, n. particularización, f.

particularize, vt. particularizar.

parting, n. separación, partida, f.; raya (en el cabello), f.

partisan, n. partidario, ria; **—,** adj. partidario.

partisanship, n. partidarismo, m.

partition, n. partición, separación, f.; tabique, m.; **—,** vt. partir, dividir en varias partes.

partly, adv. en parte.

partner, n. socio, cia, compañero, ra; **active —, managing —,** socio gerente o gestor; **silent —,** socio comanditario; **working —,** socio industrial.

partnership, n. compañía, sociedad, f., sociedad de comercio, sociedad mercantil, asociación comercial, consorcio, m.; **general —,** sociedad regular colectiva; **limited —,** sociedad limitada; **silent —,** sociedad en comandita o comanditaria.

partridge, n. perdiz, f.

part-time, adj. parcial; **— work,** trabajo de unas cuantas horas al día.

parturition, n. parto, m.

party, n. partido, m.; parte, f.; función, f.; tertulia, f.; (mil.) partida, f.; **— line,** línea telefónica usada por dos o más abonados; posición oficial de un partido político; **— wall,** pared medianera.

parvenu, n. advenedizo, za; **—,** adj. advenedizo.

paschal, adj. pascual.

pasha, n. bajá, m.

pass, vt. pasar; traspasar; trasferir; **—,** vi. pasar, ocurrir; trascurrir; **—,** n. pasillo, m.; paso, camino, m.; pase, m.; estado, m.; condición, f.; estocada, f.; (football) pase, m.; **narrow —,** callejón, m.

pass. passive, p. pasivo.

passable, adj. pasadero, transitable.

passage, n. pasaje, m.; travesía, f.; pasadizo, m.

passageway, n. pasadizo, pasaje, callejón, m.; paso, m.

passbook, n. libreta de banco.

passé, adj. pasado, anticuado.

passenger, n. pasajero, ra.

passer-by, n. transeúnte, m. y f.

passing, adj. pasajero, transitorio, momentáneo; casual; que pasa; **— grade,** calificación que permite pasar (el examen, etc.); **— bell,** toque de difuntos; **—,** adv. excesivamente; eminentemente; **—,** n. paso, m.; **in —,** al paso, al pasar.

passion, n. pasión, f.; amor, m.; celo, ardor, m.; **to fly into a —,** montar en cólera.

passionate, adj. apasionado; colérico; **—ly,** adv. apasionadamente; ardientemente.

passionflower, n. pasionaria, f.

passive, adj. pasivo; **—ly,** adv. pasivamente.

passivity, n. pasividad, f.

passkey, n. llave maestra.

Passover, n. Pascua, f.

passport, n. pasaporte, salvoconducto, m.

password, n. (mil.) seña, contraseña, f., palabra de pase.

past, adj. pasado; gastado; **— tense,** (gram.) pretérito, m.; **— master,** experto, m.; autoridad, f.; exfuncionario de una logia o sociedad; **— participle,** participio pasado; **— perfect,** n. and adj. pretérito perfecto; **—,** n. pasado, m.; (gram.) pretérito, m.; **—,** prep. más allá de, fuera de.

paste, n. pasta, f.; engrudo, m.; **—,** vt. engrudar, pegar.

pasteboard, n. cartón fuerte.

pastel, n. (bot.) hierba pastel, glasto, m.; pastel, m.; pintura al pastel.

pastern, n. cuartilla del caballo.

pasteurization, n. pasteurización, f.

pasteurize, vt. pasteurizar.

pastime, n. pasatiempo, m.; diversión, f.; recreo, m.; distracción, f.

past master, n. ex maestro (de una logia masónica); experto, ta, conocedor, ra.

pastor, n. pastor, m.

pastoral, adj. pastoril; pastoral, bucólico; **— poetry,** bucólica, f.

pastorate, n. curato, m.

pastry, n. pastelería, f.; **— cook,** repostero, m.; **— shop,** repostería, f.

pasturage, n. pasturaje, m.

pasture, n. pastura, dehesa, f.; **—,** vt. pastar, apacentar; **—,** vi. pastar, pacer.

pasty, adj. pastoso.

pat, adj. apto, conveniente, propio; **—,** adj. and adv. (coll.) firme, fijo; imposible de olvidar; **to have a lesson —,** saberse una lección al dedillo; **to stand —,** mantenerse firme; **—,** n. golpecillo, m.; **—,** vt. dar golpecillos; **stand —,** no cambiar de posición o de ideas.

patch, n. remiendo, m.; lunar, m.; pegado, m.; parche, m.; **rubber —,** cauchal, m.; **—,** vt. remendar; **— up,** remendar.

patcher, n. remendón, m.
patchwork, n. obra de retacitos; chapucería, f.
pate, n. (coll.) cabeza, f.
patella, n. (anat.) rótula, f.
paten, n. patena de cáliz, patena, f.
patent, adj. patente, manifiesto; — **agent,** agente de patentes o privilegios de invención; — **leather,** charol, m., cuero embarnizado; — **medicine,** remedio de patente, medicina patentada; —, n. patente, f., privilegio de invención; cédula, f.; —, vt. patentar.
patentee, n. persona que posee una patente.
paternal, adj. paternal.
paternalism, n. paternalismo, m.
paternalistic, adj. paternalista.
paternity, n. paternidad, f.
path, n. senda, f., sendero, m.; trocha, f.
pathetic, adj. patético; —**ally,** adv. patéticamente.
pathfinder, n. explorador, m.; descubridor de senderos.
pathless, adj. sin senda, intransitable.
pathogenic, adj. patógeno, patogénico.
pathological, adj. patológico.
pathologist, n. patólogo, m.
pathology, n. patología, f.
pathos, n. sentimiento, m.
pathway, n. vereda, senda, f.
patience, n. paciencia, f.
patient, adj. paciente, sufrido; —**ly,** adv. con paciencia; —, n. enfermo, ma; paciente, doliente, m. y f.
patina, n. pátina, f.
patio, n. patio, m.
patriarch, n. patriarca, m.
patriarchal, adj. partriarcal.
patrician, n. patricio, m.; —, adj. patricio.
patricide, n. parricidio, m.; parricida, m. y f.
Patrick, Patricio.
patrimonial, adj. patrimonial.
patrimony, n. patrimonio, m.
patriot, n. patriota, m.
patriotic, adj. patriótico.
patriotism, n. patriotismo, m.
patrol, n. patrulla, f.; —, vi. and vt. patrullar; — **wagon,** camión de policía.
patrolman, n. rondador, m., guardia municipal, vigilante de policía.
patron, n. patrón, protector, m.; — **saint,** santo patrón, santo titular de una iglesia.
patronage, n. patrocinio, m.; patronato, patronazgo, m.; clientela, f.
patroness, n. patrona, f.
patronize, vt. patrocinar, proteger.
patronymic, n. and adj. patronímico, ca.
patten, n. galocha, f.
patter, vi. patalear, patear; charlar; —, n. charlatanería, f.; serie de golpecitos; pataleo, m.
pattern, n. modelo, m.; ejemplar, m.; patrón, m.; muestra, f.; molde, m.; tipo, m.
patternmaker, n. modelista, m. y f.
patty, n. pastelillo, m.

paucity, n. poquedad, f., pequeña cantidad; insuficiencia, f.
Paul, Pablo.
Pauline, Paula, Paulina.
paunch, n. panza, f.; vientre, m.
paunchy, adj. panzado, barrigudo.
pauper, n. pobre, m. y f., limosnero, ra.
pauperism, n. pauperismo, m.
pause, n. pausa, f.; —, vi. pausar; deliberar.
pave, vt. empedrar; enlosar, embaldosar; pavimentar.
pavement, n. pavimento, piso, suelo, m., empedrado de calle.
pavilion, n. (naut.) pabellón, m.; quiosco, m.; (anat.) pabellón (de la oreja), m.
paving, n. pavimento, piso, m.; pavimentación, f.
paw, n. garra, f.; —, vt. herir con el pie delantero; manosear alguna cosa con poca maña.
pawl, n. seguro, fiador, linguete, m., gatillo de trinquete; diente de encaje.
pawn, n. prenda, f.; peón (de ajedrez), m.; —, vt. empeñar.
pawnbroker, n. prendero, m.; prestamista, m. y f.
pawnshop, n. casa de préstamos o empeños.
pawpaw, n. = **papaw.**
pay, vt. pagar; saldar; sufrir (por); **to — back,** devolver; pagar (una deuda); vengarse de; **to — no attention,** no hacer caso; **to — off,** despedir; castigar; recompensar; **to — up,** pagar por completo; —, n. paga, f., pago, m.; sueldo, salario, m.; **monthly —,** mensualidad, mesada, f.; — **roll,** nómina, f., nómina de sueldos.
payable, adj. pagadero.
payday, n. día de paga.
pay dirt, n. tierra, peña, mineral etc., que produce ganancias al minero.
payee, n. portador de una libranza o giro.
paying teller, n. pagador, ra.
paymaster, n. pagador, m.
payment, n. pago, m.; paga, f.; recompensa, f.; premio, m.; pagamento, m.; **cash —,** pago al contado; **on — of,** mediante el pago de; **order of —,** libramiento, m.; — **in advance,** pago adelantado, anticipo, m.; — **in full,** saldo de cuenta; **terms of —,** condiciones de pago; **to delay —,** to **defer —,** diferir o aplazar el pago; **to make —,** efectuar un pago; **to present for —,** presentar al cobro; **to stop —,** suspender el pago.
payt. payment, pago.
pc. piece, pieza, pedazo.
p. c.: per cent, % por ciento; **post card,** tarjeta postal.
pd. paid, pagd.º, pagd.ª, pagado, pagada.
p.d. for each day, para cada día; **potential difference,** diferencia potencial.
P. E. Protestant Episcopal, Episcopal Protestante.

pea, *n.* guisante, chícharo, *m.*; — **green,** verde claro.

peace, *n.* paz, *f.*; — **pipe,** pipa de paz (de los indios de Norte América); —! *interj.* ¡paz! ¡silencio!

peaceable, peaceful, *adj.* tranquilo, pacífico.

peaceful, *adj.* pacífico, apacible, tranquilo; silencioso.

peacemaker, *n.* pacificador, ra.

peace offering, *n.* sacrificio propiciatorio.

peace pipe, *n.* pipa de los indios de Norte América.

peach, *n.* melocotón, durazno, *m.*; — **tree,** melocotonero, duraznero, *m.*

peacock, *n.* pavón, *m.*, pavo real.

peafowl, *n.* pavo real.

peahen, *n.* pava real, *f.*

peajacket, *n.* chaquetón de marinero.

peak, *n.* cima, *f.*; cúspide, *f.*

peaked, *adj.* puntiagudo; endeble.

peal, *n.* campaneo, *m.*; estruendo, *m.*; repique, *m.*; —, *vt.* and *vi.* hacer resonar; devolver el eco los sonidos.

peanut, *n.* cacahuate, cacahuete, maní, *m.*; — **brittle,** crocante, *m.*, especie de turrón; — **butter,** pasta o mantequilla de cacahuate o maní; — **vendor,** manicero, *m.*

pear, *n.* pera, *f.*; — **orchard,** peral, *m.*; — **preserves,** perada, *f.*; — **tree,** peral, *m.*

pearl, *n.* perla, *f.*

pearled, *adj.* perlado.

pearly, *adj.* perlino, que tiene perlas o se parece a ellas.

peasant, *n.* labriego, ga, campesino, na.

peashooter, *n.* cerbatana, *f.*

peat, *n.* turba, *f.*

peaty, *adj.* turboso.

peavey, *n.* palanca con gancho.

pebble, *n.* guija, *f.*, guijarro, *m.*, piedrecilla, *f.*

pebbly, *adj.* guijarroso.

pecan, *n.* pacana, *f.*; — **tree,** pacana, *f.*

peccadillo, *n.* pecadillo, *m.*

peck, *n.* picotazo, *m.*; celemín (medida de granos), *m.*; —, *vt.* picotear; picar.

pectin, *n.* pectina, *f.*

pectoral, *adj.* pectoral; —, *n.* medicamento pectoral.

peculate, *vi.* robar al público.

peculation, *n.* peculado, *m.*

peculiar, *adj.* peculiar, particular, singular; —**ly,** *adv.* peculiarmente.

peculiarity, *n.* particularidad, singularidad, *f.*

pecuniary, *adj.* pecuniario.

pedagogic, *adj.* pedagógico; —**ally,** *adv.* pedagógicamente.

pedagogue, *n.* pedagogo, *m.*; pedante, *m.* y *f.*

pedagogy, *n.* pedagogía, *f.*

pedal, *n.* pedal, *m.*; —, *adj.* relativo a los pies.

pedant, *n.* pedante, *m.*; —, *adj.* pedante.

pedantic, *adj.* pedantesco.

pedantry, *n.* pedantería, *f.*

peddle, *vt.* and *vi.* vender menudencias de casa en casa.

peddler, *n.* buhonero, *m.*

pedestal, *n.* pedestal, *m.*, basa, *f.*; **large** —, podio, *m.*

pedestrian, *n.* andador, ra, peatón, ona; —, *adj.* pedestre.

pediatrician, *n.* (med.) pediatra, *m.* y *f.*

pediatrics, *n.* (med.) pediatría, *f.*

pedicular, *adj.* pedicular.

pedigree, *n.* genealogía, *f.*

pedigreed, *adj.* de casta escogida.

pediment, *n.* (arch.) frontón, *m.*

pedometer, *n.* pedómetro, *m.*

peduncle, *n.* (bot.) pedúnculo, *m.*

peek, *vi.* atisbar; —, *n.* atisbo, *m.*, atisbadura, *f.*

peel, *vt.* descortezar, pelar; —, *n.* corteza, *f.*, pellejo (de frutas), *m.*; pala de horno.

peeling, *n.* peladura, mondadura, *f.*

peep, *vi.* asomar; atisbar; piar, pipiar; clavar la mirada; —, *n.* asomo, *m.*; alba, *f.*; ojeada, *f.*

peephole, *n.* atisbadero, *m.*

peer, *n.* compañero, *m.*; par (grande de Inglaterra), *m.*; —, *vi.* mirar fijamente; fisgar.

peerage, *n.* dignidad de par, nobleza, *f.*

peeress, *n.* mujer de un par; señora noble.

peerless, *adj.* incomparable, sin par.

peevish, *adj.* regañón, bronco; enojadizo; —**ly,** *adv.* con impertinencia.

peevishness, *n.* mal humor.

peg, *n.* clavija, espita, estaquilla, *f.*, gancho, *m.*; —, *vt.* clavar.

pegged, *adj.* enclavijado, con clavijas.

pelagic, *adj.* pelágico.

pelf, *n.* riquezas mal ganadas; despojos, *m. pl.*; dinero, *m.*; ganancias, *f. pl.*

pelican, *n.* pelícano, *m.*

pelisse, *n.* pelliza, *f.*

pellagra, *n.* (med.) pelagra, *f.*

pellet, *n.* pelotilla, *f.*; píldora, *f.*; bodoque, *m.*

pellicle, *n.* película, telilla, *f.*

pell-mell, *adv.* a trochemoche.

pellucid, *adj.* diáfano, trasluciente.

pelota, *n.* pelota vasca; — **player,** pelotari, *m.*

pelt, *n.* pellejo, cuero, *m.*; pelta, *f.*

pelvic, *adj.* pélvico.

pelvis, *n.* pelvis, *f.*

pemmican, *n.* tasajo de los indios norteamericanos.

pen, *n.* pluma, *f.*; corral, *m.*; caponera, *f.*; — **name,** seudónimo, *m.*; **stroke of the** —, plumazo, *m.*; —, *vt.* enjaular, encerrar; escribir.

pen. peninsula, península.

penal, *adj.* penal.

penalize, *vt.* penar, imponer pena a.

penalty, *n.* pena, *f.*, castigo, *m.*; multa, *f.*

penance, *n.* penitencia, *f.*; **to do** —, penar.

penatin, *n.* (med.) droga para evitar heridas infectadas.

pence, *n. pl.* de **penny,** centavos, *m. pl.*

penchant, *n.* tendencia, inclinación, *f.*

pencil, *n.* pincel, *m.*; lápiz, *m.*; **mechanical** —, lapicero, *m.*; — **case,** estuche para lápices; — **holder,** lapicero, *m.*; — **sharpener,** tajalápices, *m.*; —, *vt.* pintar; escribir con lápiz.

pendant, *n.* pendiente, *m.*; (naut.) gallardete, *m.*

pendent, *adj.* pendiente.

pending, *adj.* pendiente; indeciso; — **payment,** pendiente de pago; **to be** —, pender.

pendulous, *adj.* colgante.

pendulum, *n.* péndulo, *m.*

peneplain, *n.* superficie desgastada por rozamiento.

penetrability, *n.* penetrabilidad, *f.*

penetrate, *vt.* and *vi.* penetrar.

penetrating, *adj.* penetrante.

penetration, *n.* penetración, *f.*; sagacidad, *f.*

penguin, *n.* alca, *f.*

penholder, *n.* portapluma, *m.*

penicillin, *n.* (med.) penicilina, droga usada en infecciones, heridas, etc.

peninsula, *n.* península, *f.*

peninsular, *adj.* peninsular.

penis, *n.* pene, *m.*, verga, *f.*, miembro genital masculino de los mamíferos.

penitence, *n.* penitencia, *f.*

penitent, *adj.* and *n.* penitente, *m.* y *f.*; —**ly,** *adv.* con arrepentimiento.

penitential, *adj.* penitencial.

penitentiary, *n.* penitenciaría, *f.*, penitenciario, *m.*

penknife, *n.* cortaplumas, *m.*

penman, *n.* pendolista, *m.* y *f.*; escritor, ra.

penmanship, *n.* caligrafía, *f.*

Penn. Pennsylvania, Pensilvania.

pennant, pennon, *n.* (naut.) flámula, banderola, *f.*; jirón, gallardete, *m.*

penniless, *adj.* falto de dinero, indigente.

pennon, *n.* pendón, *m.*

Pennsylvania, Pensilvania, *f.*

penny, *n.* centavo, *m.*; penique, *m.*; dinero, *m.*

pennyweight, *n.* peso de 24 granos.

penny-wise, *adj.* económico sólo en cosas pequeñas; — **and pound-foolish,** tacaño en los gastos menores, gastador en los mayores.

pennyworth, *n.* valor de un penique.

penology, *n.* penología, *f.*

pension, *n.* pensión, *f.*; **widow's** —, viudedad, *f.*; —, *vt.* dar alguna pensión.

pensioner, *n.* pensionista, *m.* y *f.*, pensionado, da.

pensive, *adj.* pensativo; reflexivo; —**ly,** *adv.* melancólicamente; pensativamente.

pentagon, *n.* pentágono, *m.*

pentameter, *n.* pentámetro, *m.*, verso de cinco pies.

pentathlon, *n.* péntalo, pentatlo, *m.*

Pentecost, *n.* Pentecostés, *m.*

penthouse, *n.* cobertizo, tejadillo, *m.*; habitación construida en un techo.

pent-up, *adj.* acorralado, encerrado, reprimido.

penult, *n.* penúltima sílaba.

penultimate, *adj.* penúltimo.

penumbra, *n.* penumbra, *f.*

penurious, *adj.* tacaño, avaro.

penury, *n.* penuria, carestía, *f.*

peon, *n.* peón, criado, *m.*

peonage, *n.* peonaje, *m.*

peony, *n.* peonía, *f.*

people, *n.* gente, *f.*; pueblo, *m.*; nación, *f.*; vulgo, *m.*; —, *vt.* poblar.

peplum, *n.* peplo, *m.*

pepper, *n.* pimienta, *f.*; — **pot,** sopa de carne y legumbres condimentada con pimientos, ají, etc.; **red** —, pimiento, chile, *m.*; **red** — **(the vegetable),** pimiento (la legumbre), *m.*; —, *vt.* sazonar con pimienta; golpear, azotar.

pepper-and-salt, *adj.* mezclado de negro y blanco.

pepperbox, *n.* pimentero, *m.*

peppercorn, *n.* semilla de pimienta.

peppermint, *n.* menta, hierbabuena, *f.*; — **drop,** pastilla de menta.

peppery, *adj.* picante; de mal humor; mordaz.

pepsin, *n.* pepsina, *f.*

peptic, *adj.* péptico, digestivo.

peptone, *n.* peptona, *f.*

per, *prep.* por; — **annum,** al año; — **capita,** por persona, por cabeza; — **cent,** por ciento (%, p %); — **diem,** por día.

peradventure, *adv.* por si acaso.

perambulate, *vt.* transitar, recorrer algún territorio.

perambulator, *n.* cochecito para niños.

percale, *n.* percal, *m.*

percaline, *n.* percalina, *f.*

perceive, *vt.* percibir, comprender.

percentage, *n.* porcentaje, *m.*, tanto por ciento.

perceptibility, *n.* perceptibilidad, *f.*

perceptible, *adj.* perceptible; —**bly,** *adv.* perceptiblemente.

perception, *n.* percepción, idea, noción, *f.*

perch, *n.* (pez) perca, *f.*; (medida) pértica, *f.*; percha, *f.*; —, *vt.* emperchar; —, *vi.* posarse, encaramarse.

perchance, *adv.* acaso, quizá.

percolate, *vt.* colar; filtrar; trascolar.

percolator, *n.* cafetera filtradora, percolador, *m.*, colador de café.

percussion, *n.* percusión, *f.*; golpe, *m.*; — **cap,** *n.* pistón, fulminante, *m.*; — **instrument,** instrumento de percusión.

perdition, *n.* perdición, ruina, *f.*

peregrinate, *vi.* peregrinar.

peregrination, *n.* peregrinación, *f.*

Peregrine, Peregrino.

peremptorily, *adv.* perentoriamente, definitivamente, rotundamente.

peremptory, *adj.* perentorio; decisivo, rotundo.

perennial, adj. perenne, perpetuo.
perf. perfect, perf. perfecto.
perfect, adj. perfecto, acabado; puro; derecho; —**ly,** adv. perfectamente, a fondo; —, vt. perfeccionar, acabar.
perfecting, n. perfeccionamiento, m.
perfection, n. perfección, f.
perfidious, adj. pérfido, desleal; —**ly,** adv. pérfidamente.
perfidy, n. perfidia, f.
perforate, vt. horadar, perforar.
perforation, n. perforación, f.
perforce, adv. forzosamente.
perform, vt. ejecutar; efectuar; ejercer; hacer; realizar; —, vi. representar, hacer papel.
performance, n. ejecución, f.; cumplimiento, m.; obra, f.; representación teatral, función, f.; funcionamiento, m.; **first** —, estreno, m.
performer, n. ejecutor, ra, ejecutante, m. y f., actor, m., actriz, f.
perfume, n. perfume, m.; fragancia, f.; — **bottle,** frasco de perfume; —, vt. perfumar.
perfumer, n. perfumero, perfumista, m.
perfumery, n. perfumería, f.
perfunctory, adj. descuidado, superficial, negligente.
pergola, n. emparrado, cenador, m.; galería exterior.
perhaps, adv. quizá, quizás, tal vez.
perianth, n. (bot.) periantio, m.
pericarditis, n. (med.) pericarditis, f.
pericardium, n. (anat.) pericardio, m.
perihelion, n. perihelio, m.
peril, n. peligro, riesgo, m.
perilous, adj. peligroso; —**ly,** adv. peligrosamente.
perimeter, n. perímetro, m.
period, n. período, m.; época, f.; **for a fixed** —, a plazo fijo.
periodic, adj. periódico; —**ally,** adv. periódicamente.
periodical, n. periódico, m.; —, adj. periódico.
peripatetic, adj. peripatético.
peripheral, adj. periférico, ca.
periphery, n. periferia, f.
periphrase, n. perífrasis, circunlocución, f.
periphrastic, adj. perifrástico.
periscope, n. periscopio, m.
perish, vi. perecer; sucumbir.
perishable, adj. perecedero.
peristyle, n. peristilo, m.
peritoneum, n. (anat.) peritoneo, m.
peritonitis, n. (med.) peritonitis, f.
periwig, n. peluca, f.
periwinkle, n. caracol marino; (bot.) vincapervinca, f.
perjure, vt. and vi. perjurar.
perjured, adj. perjurado, jurado en falso.
perjurer, n. perjuro, ra.
perjury, n. perjurio, m.
perk, vi. pavonearse.

perky, adj. garboso, gallardo.
permanence, n. permanencia, f.
permanent, adj. permanente, perenne; — **wave,** ondulado permanente, ondulación permanente; —**ly,** adv. permanentemente.
permanganate, n. permanganato, m.
permeability, n. permeabilidad, f.
permeable, adj. permeable.
permeate, vt. penetrar, atravesar.
permeation, n. penetración, f.
permissible, adj. lícito, permitido.
permission, n. permiso, m., licencia, f.
permissive, adj. admisible.
permit, vt. permitir; —, n. permiso, m., cédula, f.
permutation, n. permutación, f.
pernicious, adj. pernicioso; perjudicial; — **anemia,** (med.) anemia perniciosa; —**ly,** adv. perniciosamente.
peroration, n. peroración, f.
peroxide, n. peróxido, m.; **hydrogen** —, peróxido hidrogenado; — **blonde,** rubia oxigenada.
perpendicular, adj. perpendicular; —**ly,** adv. perpendicularmente; —, n. línea perpendicular.
perpetrate, vt. perpetrar, cometer (algún delito).
perpetration, n. perpetración, f.
perpetual, adj. perpetuo; —**ly,** adv. perpetuamente.
perpetuate, vt. perpetuar, eternizar.
perpetuation, n. perpetuación, f.
perpetuity, n. perpetuidad, f.
perplex, vt. confundir, embrollar.
perplexity, n. perplejidad, f.
perquisite, n. emolumento, gaje, m.; obvención, f.; propina, gratificación, f.
pers. personal, pers. personal.
persecute, vt. perseguir; importunar.
persecution, n. persecución, f.
persecutor, n. perseguidor, m.
perseverance, n. perseverancia, f.
persevere, vi. perseverar; obstinarse.
persiflage, n. zumba, fisga, f.
persimmon, n. níspero (árbol), m.; níspola (fruto), f.
persist, vi. persistir.
persistency, n. persistencia, f.
persistent, adj. persistente.
person, n. persona, f.
personable, adj. bien parecido, donoso.
personage, n. personaje, m.
personal, adj. personal; — **estate,** — **goods,** bienes muebles, m. pl.; — **equation,** ecuación personal; — **property,** bienes muebles, m. pl.; —**ly,** adv. personalmente.
personality, n. personalidad, f.
personalty, n. (law) bienes muebles.
personate, vt. representar.
personation, n. personificación, f.
personification, n. prosopopeya, f.; personificación, f.

personify, vt. personificar.
personnel, n. personal, m., cuerpo de empleados; tripulación, f.
perspective, n. perspectiva, f.; —, adj. en perspectiva.
perspicacious, adj. perspicaz, penetrante.
perspicacity, n. perspicacia, viveza, f.
perspicuity, n. perspicuidad, f.
perspicuous, adj. perspicuo, transparente.
perspiration, n. traspiración, f., sudor, m.
perspire, vi. traspirar, sudar.
perspiring, adj. sudorífico.
persuade, vt. persuadir.
persuasion, n. persuasión, f.
persuasive, adj. persuasivo; —ly, adv. de un modo persuasivo.
pert, adj. listo, vivo; petulante.
pertain, vi. pertenecer; relacionar, tocar.
pertaining, adj. perteneciente; — to, relativo a.
pertinacious, adj. pertinaz, obstinado; —ly, adv. pertinazmente.
pertinacity, n. pertinacia, f.
pertinence, n. conexión, f., relación de una cosa con otra.
pertinent, adj. pertinente; perteneciente; —ly, adv. oportunamente.
perturb, vt. perturbar.
perturbation, n. perturbación, f., agitación de ánimo.
Peru, Perú, m.
peruke, n. peluca, f.
perusal, n. lectura o estudio cuidadoso (de algo).
peruse, vt. leer; examinar o estudiar (algo) atentamente.
Peruvian, adj. and n. peruano, na; — bark, cascarilla, quina, f.
pervade, vt. penetrar.
pervasive, adj. penetrante.
perverse, adj. perverso, depravado; malandrín; protervo; —ly, adv. perversamente.
perversion, n. perversión, f.
perversity, n. perversidad, f.; protervia, f.
pervert, vt. pervertir, corromper.
pervious, adj. penetrable; penetrante.
pessimism, n. pesimismo, m.
pessimist, n. pesimista, m. y f.
pessimistic, adj. pesimista.
pest, n. peste, pestilencia, f.
pester, vt. molestar, cansar, fastidiar, importunar.
pesthouse, n. lazareto, m.; hospital de contagiosos.
pestilence, n. pestilencia, f.
pestilent, pestilential adj. pestilente, pestífero.
pestle, n. majador, majadero, m., mano de almirez, majadero de mortero; **mortar and** —, mortero y majador.
pet, n. enojo, enfado, m.; favorito, ta; —, vt. mimar.
petal, n. (bot.) pétalo, m.
petard, n. petardo, m.

petcock, n. llave de desagüe.
Peter, Pedro.
petiole, n. pecíolo, m.
petition, n. memorial, m.; solicitud, f.; petición, súplica, f.; **to make a** —, elevar una instancia o solicitud; —, vt. suplicar, demandar, pedir; requerir en justicia.
petitioner, n. peticionario, ria.
petrel, n. (orn.) petrel, m.
petrification, n. petrificación, f.
petrify, vt. and vi. petrificar.
petrography, n. petrografía, f.
petrol, n. gasolina, f., petróleo, m.
petrolatum, n. ungüento de petróleo.
petroleum, n. petróleo, m.; — jelly, ungüento de petróleo, vaselina, f.
petrology, n. petrología, f.
petticoat, n. enagua, f., zagalejo, m., basquiña, f.
pettifogger, n. abogado de guardilla, picapleitos, m.
pettifogging, n. mangoneo, m.
pettiness, n. pequeñez, f.; mezquindad, f.
petting, n. mimo, m.; acción de acariciar.
pettish, adj. caprichudo, regañón.
petty, adj. pequeño, corto; mezquino; — cash, efectivo para el pago de gastos menores; — larceny, hurto, m., ratería, f.; — officer, oficial de marina entre alférez y teniente; — thief, pillo, m.
petulance, n. petulancia, f.
petulant, adj. petulante; —ly, adv. con petulancia.
petunia, n. petunia, f.
pew, n. banco de iglesia.
pewter, n. peltre, m.
pfd. preferred, preferido.
phaeton, n. faetón, m.
phagocyte, n. (biol.) fagocito, m.
phalanx, n. falange, f.
phantasm, phantom, n. fantasma, m.
phantasmagoria, n. fantasmagoría, f.
phantasy, n. fantasía, f.
phantom, n. espectro, fantasma, m.; —, adj. espectral.
phantomlike, adj. semejante a un espectro o fantasma.
phar.: pharmacopoeia, farmacopea; **pharmacy,** Farm. farmacia.
Pharisaic, Pharisaical, adj. farisaico.
Pharisee, n. fariseo, m.
pharmaceutic, pharmaceutical, adj. farmacéutico.
pharmaceutics, n. pl. farmacéutica, f.
pharmacist, n. boticario, farmacéutico, m.
pharmacologist, n. farmacólogo, m.
pharmacology, n. farmacología, f.
pharmacopoeia, n. farmacopea, f.
pharmacy, n. farmacia, botica, f.
pharyngitis, n. faringitis, f.
pharynx, n. faringe, f.
phase, phasis, n. fase, f., aspecto, m.
Ph.B. Bachelor of Philosophy, Bachiller en Filosofía.

Ph.D. Doctor of Philosophy, Doctor en Filosofía.
pheasant, *n.* faisán, *m.*
phenacetin, *n.* fenacetina, *f.*
phenol, *n.* fenol, *m.*
phenolphthalein, *n.* fenol rojo.
phenomena, *n. pl.* fenómenos, *m. pl.*
phenomenal, *adj.* prominente, fenomenal.
phenomenon, *n.* fenómeno, *m.*
phew! *interj.* ¡fo!
phial, *n.* redomilla, *f.*, frasco, *m.*
Philadelphia, Filadelfia, *f.*
philander, *vi.* galantear.
philanthropic, philanthropical, *adj.* filantrópico.
philanthropist, *n.* filántropo, pa.
philanthropy, *n.* filantropía, *f.*
philatelic, *adj.* filatélico.
philatelist, *n.* filatelista, *m.* y *f.*
philately, *n.* filatelia, *f.*
philharmonic, *adj.* filarmónico.
philippic, *n.* filípica, *f.*
Philippine Islands, Islas Filipinas, *f. pl.*
philological, *adj.* filológico.
philologist, *n.* filólogo, *m.*
philology, *n.* filología, *f.*
philosopher, *n.* filósofo, *m.*
philosophic, philosophical, *adj.* filosófico; **philosophically,** *adv.* filosóficamente.
philosophize, *vi.* filosofar.
philosophy, *n.* filosofía, *f.*
philter, *n.* filtro (bebida) *m.*
phlebotomy, *n.* flebotomía, *f.*
phlegm, *n.* flema, *f.*
phlegmasia, *n.* (med.) flegmasía, *f.*
phlegmatic, phlegmatical, *adj.* flemático.
phlox, *n.* flox, *m.*
phobia, *n.* fobia, obsesión, *f.*
phoenix, *n.* fénix, *m.*
phone, *n.* (coll.) teléfono, *m.*; —, *vt.* (coll.) telefonear.
phonetic, *adj.* fonético.
phonetics, *n. pl.* fonética, *f.*
phonic, *adj.* fónico; —s, *n.* fonología, *f.*
phonograph, *n.* fonógrafo, gramófono, *m.*; — **record,** disco de fonógrafo.
phonography, *n.* fonografía, *f.*; taquigrafía, *f.*
phonology, *n.* fonología, *f.*
phosgene, *n.* fosgeno, *m.*
phosphate, *n.* fosfato, *m.*
phosphoresce, *vi.* fosforescer.
phosphorescence, *n.* fosforescencia, *f.*
phosphorescent, *adj.* fosforescente.
phosphoric, *adj.* fosfórico; — **acid,** ácido fosfórico.
phosphorus, *n.* fósforo, *m.*
photo, *n.* (coll.) = **photograph.**
photochemical, *adj.* fotoquímico.
photoelectric, *adj.* fotoeléctrico.
photoengraved, *adj.* fotograbado.
photoengraving, *n.* fotograbado, *m.*
photo finish, *n.* llegada de corredores a la meta con tan poca diferencia que el triunfador se determina al examinar la fotografía tomada al concluir la carrera.
photogenic, *adj.* fotogénico.
photograph, *n.* fotografía, *f.*; retrato, *m.*; — **developer,** revelador, *m.*; —, *vt.* fotografiar, retratar; **to be** —ed, retratarse.
photographer, *n.* fotógrafo, *m.*
photographic, *adj.* fotográfico.
photography, *n.* fotografía, *f.*
photogravure, *n.* fotograbado, *m.*
photolithography, *n.* fotolitografía, *f.*
photometer, *n.* fotómetro, *m.*
photometry, *n.* fotometría, *f.*
photomicrography, *n.* fotomicrografía, *f.*
photon, *m.* (phy.) fotón, *m.*
photoplay, *n.* representación cinematográfica.
photostat, *n.* fotostato, *m.*
photostatic, *adj.* fotostático.
photosynthesis, *n.* fotosíntesis, *f.*
phototype, *n.* clisé fototipográfico.
phrase, *n.* frase, *f.*; estilo, *m.*; (mus.) frase musical; —, *vt.* expresar; (mus.) dividir en frases musicales.
phraseology, *n.* fraseología, dicción, *f.*
phrenology, *n.* frenología, *f.*
phthisis, *n.* tisis, *f.*
phylogeny, *n.* (biol.) filogenia, *f.*
phylum, *n.* una de las divisiones primarias del reino animal o vegetal.
phys. physician, médico.
physic, *n.* medicina, *f.*, medicamento, *m.*; purgante, *m.*, purga, *f.*; —s, *n. pl.* física, *f.*; —, *vt.* purgar, dar un purgante; aliviar, sanar.
physical, *adj.* físico; — **education,** educación física; — **geography,** geografía física; — **sciences,** ciencias físicas; —ly, *adv.* físicamente.
physician, *n.* médico, *m.*; **attending** —, médico de cabecera.
physicist, *n.* físico, *m.*
physics, *n.* física, *f.*
physiochemical, *adj.* fisicoquímico.
physiognomist, *n.* fisonomista, fisónomo, *m.*
physiognomy, *n.* fisonomía, *f.*; facciones, *f. pl.*
physiographer, *n.* fisiógrafo, *m.*
physiography, *n.* fisiografía, *f.*
physiological, *adj.* fisiológico.
physiologist, *n.* fisiólogo, *m.*
physiology, *n.* fisiología, *f.*
physiotherapy, *n.* fisioterapia, *f.*
physique, *n.* físico, *m.*
pi, pie, *n.* (print.) pastel, *m.*, letras de imprenta en confusión o desorden; —, *vt.* (print.) empastelar, mezclar desordenadamente las letras de imprenta.
P. I. Philippine Islands, Islas Filipinas.
pianissimo, *n.* pianísimo, *m.*
pianist, *n.* pianista, *m.* y *f.*
piano, *n.* piano, pianoforte, *m.*; **grand** —, piano de cola; **player** —, piano mecánico.
pianoforte, *n.* pianoforte, piano, *m.*
piaster, *n.* piastra, *f.*; peso, *m.*

piazza, n. corredor cubierto, m., galería, f., pórtico, m.

pica, n. cícero, m.; — **type,** tipo cícero.

picador, n. picador, m.

picaresque, adj. picaresco.

picaroon, n. picarón, m.; ladrón, pirata, m.

picayune, n. bagatela, chuchería, pequeñez, f.; —, adj. de poco valor, mezquino.

piccalilli, n. legumbres escabechadas, f. pl.

piccolo, n. flautín, m.

pick, vt. escoger, elegir; recoger, mondar, limpiar; **to — a pocket,** ratear la faltriquera; —, vi. mascullar, roer; **to — out,** escoger, señalar; **to — over,** escoger, examinar; —, n. pico (herramienta), m.; lo escogido, lo mejor.

pickaback, adv. sobre los hombros, a modo de fardo; — **plane,** aeroplano para travesías largas que, con fuerte carga de combustible, se eleva sobre un avión mayor, del que se desprende a cierta altura.

pickaninny, n. negrito, ta.

pickax, n. pico, zapapico, m.

pickerel, n. (pez) sollo, m.

picket, n. estaca, f.; piquete, m.; (mil.) piquete, m.; guardia de huelguistas; —, vt. cercar con estacas o piquetes; hacer guardia o colocar guardias de huelguistas; — **fence,** adj. cerca hecha de estacas puntiagudas.

pickings, n. pl. desperdicios, residuos, m. pl.; beneficios pequeños o de poco valor.

pickle, n. salmuera, f.; encurtido, m.; (coll.) dificultad, f.; —, vt. escabechar.

picklock, n. ganzúa, f.

pickpocket, n. ratero, ra, ladrón, ona, cortabolsas, m.

pickup, n. (auto.) aceleración, f.

picnic, n. comida, merienda, f.; romería, f.; partida de campo, jira o paseo campestre, día de campo.

picnicker, n. persona que va a un día de campo, participante en una fiesta campestre.

picric, adj. (chem.) pícrico; — **acid,** ácido carbazótico, ácido pícrico.

pictograph, n. pictografía, f.

pictography, n. pictografía, f.

pictorial, adj. pictórico.

picture, n. pintura, f.; retrato, m.; fotografía, f.; cuadro, m.; **motion —,** película, f.; — **gallery,** pinacoteca, f., salón de pinturas, museo de cuadros; — **writing,** pictografía, f.; —, vt. pintar; figurar; fotografiar; describir gráficamente.

picturesque, adj. pintoresco.

piddle, vi. ocuparse en pequeñeces; (coll.) orinar.

piddling, adj. trivial, insignificante.

pie, n. pastel, m.; empanada, f.; (orn.) urraca, f.

piebald, adj. pío, pintado; manchado de varios colores; — n. animal pío (caballo, asno, etc.).

piece, n. pedazo, m.; pieza, obra, f.; cañón o fusil, m.; **to tear to —s,** hacer pedazos; —, vt. remendar; unir los pedazos.

piecemeal, adv. en pedazos; a remiendos.

piecework, n. obra que se paga por pieza.

pieceworker, n. persona que hace obra pagada por pieza.

pied, adj. manchado de varios colores.

pieplant, n. ruibarbo, m.

pier, n. estribo de puente; muelle, m.; — **glass,** espejo alto que generalmente se coloca en un entrepaño.

pierce, vt. penetrar, agujerear, taladrar; excitar; internar; traspasar.

piercing, adj. penetrante, conmovedor; —**ly,** adv. agudamente.

pietism, n. pietismo, m.

piety, n. piedad, devoción, f.; **affected —,** beatería, f.

pig, n. cochinillo, lechón, m.; lingote, m.; cerdo, m., puerco, ca; —, vi. parir la puerca; — **iron,** hierro en lingotes.

pigeon, n. palomo, m., paloma, f.; **homing —,** paloma viajera o mensajera; **wood —,** paloma zorita.

pigeonhole, n. mechinal, m.; casilla, f.; cajita para guardar cartas.

pigeon-toed, adj. patituerto.

pigeonwing, n. ala de paloma.

piggish, adj. voraz; puerco; cochino.

pigheaded, adj. terco.

pigment, n. pigmento, m.; especie de solución para pinturas.

pigmentation, n. pigmentación, f.

pigmy, n. and adj. pigmeo, mea.

pigpen, n. zahurda, f.

pigskin, n. piel de cerdo; fútbol, m.

pigsty, n. zahurda, pocilga, f.

pigtail, n. cola de cochino; tabaco torcido; chino, m.

pike, n. (pez.) lucio, m.; pica, f.

pilaster, n. pilastra, f.

pile, n. estaca, f.; pila, f.; montón, m.; pira, f.; edificio grande y macizo; pelo, m.; pelillo (en las telas de lana), m.; rimero, m.; — **driver,** martinete, m.; —**s,** n. pl. (med.) hemorroides, almorranas, f. pl.; —, vt. amontonar, apilar.

pilfer, vt. ratear, hurtar.

pilgrim, n. peregrino, na, romero, ra.

pilgrimage, n. peregrinación, romería, f.

pill, n. píldora, f.

pillage, n. pillaje, botín, saqueo, m.; —, vt. pillar, hurtar.

pillar, n. pilar, poste, m., columna, f.; (fig.) sostén, m.

Pillars of Hercules, Columnas de Hércules.

pillbox, n. (mil.) fortín con ametralladoras.

pillion, n. jalma, enjalma, f.

pillory, n. argolla, picota, f.; cepo, m.; —, vt. empicotar, poner a un malhechor en alguna picota o argolla, poner públicamente en ridículo.

pillow, n. almohada, f., cojín, m.; cabezal, m.

pillowcase, pillowslip, *n.* funda, *f.*
pilot, *n.* piloto, *m.*; **harbor —, coast —,** (naut.) piloto práctico; **— house,** timonera, *f.*, sitio del timonel; **— light,** lámpara de comprobación o piloto; luz pequeña y permanente que se usa para encender el mechero de gas; **—,** *vt.* pilotear, pilotar.
pilotage, *n.* pilotaje, *m.*
pimento, pimiento, *n.* pimiento, *m.*, pimienta de Jamaica.
pimp, *n.* alcahuete, ta.
pimpernel, *n.* pimpinela, *f.*
pimple, *n.* postilla, pupa, buba, bubilla, *f.*; grano, barro, *m.*
pimpled, *adj.* engranujado; barroso.
pin, *n.* alfiler, *m.*; prendedor, *m.*; clavija, *f.*; chaveta, *f.*; **— money,** alfileres, *m. pl.*; dinero para alfileres; **safety —,** alfiler de seguridad; **—,** *vt.* asegurar con alfileres; fijar con clavija.
pinafore, *n.* delantal, *m.*
pince-nez, *m.* quevedos, *m. pl.*
pincers, pinchers, *n. pl.* pinzas, tenazuelas, *f. pl.*; **pincer movement,** (mil.) movimiento de pinzas.
pinch, *vt.* pellizcar, apretar con pinzas; **—,** *vi.* ser frugal, escatimar gastos; **—,** *n.* pellizco, *m.*; pulgarada, *f.*; aprieto, *m.*
pinchbeck, *n.* similor, *m.*, tumbaga, *f.*
pinchers, *n.* pinzas, tenacillas, *f. pl.*
pinch-hit, *vi.* (baseball) batear en lugar de otro; tomar el lugar de otro en un aprieto.
pincushion, *n.* alfiletero, acerico, *m.*
pine, *n.* (bot.) pino, *m.*; **— needle,** pinocha, *f.*; **—,** *vi.* languidecer; **to — for,** anhelar, ansiar (alguna cosa).
pineal, *adj.* pineal.
pineapple, *n.* piña, *f.*; ananas, *m.*
pinfeather, *n.* cañón, pluma de las aves cuando empieza a nacer.
pingpong, *n.* pingpong, *m.*, juego parecido al tenis jugado con pelota de celuloide.
pinhead, *n.* cabeza de alfiler; algo muy pequeño o sin valor.
pinhole, *n.* agujero que hace un alfiler; agujero muy pequeño.
pinion, *n.* piñón, *m.*; ala, *f.*; **—,** *vt.* atar las alas; maniatar.
pink, *n.* (bot.) clavel, *m.*; (naut.) pingüe, *m.*; **—,** *adj.* rojizo; rosado, sonrosado.
pinkeye, *n.* conjuntivitis, *f.*
pinnace, *n.* (naut.) pinaza, *f.*
pinnacle, *n.* pináculo, chapitel, *m.*; cima, cumbre, *f.*
pinochle, *n.* pinocle (juego de naipes), *m.*
pint, *n.* pinta (medida de líquidos), *f.*
pintail, *n.* ánade de cola larga.
pinwheel, *n.* rueda de engranaje clavijada; rueda de encuentro; (mech.) linterna, *f.*; girándula, *f.*; molino de viento hecho de papel para jugar los niños.
pioneer, *n.* (mil.) zapador, *m.*; descubridor, explorador, precursor.

pious, *adj.* pío, devoto, piadoso; **—ly,** *adv.* piadosamente.
pip, *n.* pepita, *f.*; **—,** *vi.* piar ciertas aves.
pipe, *n.* tubo, cañón, conducto, caño, *m.*; pipa para fumar; (Sp. Am.) cachimbo, ba (de fumar); (mus.) churumbela, *f.*; **condenser —,** caño de evacuación; **oil — line,** oleoducto, *m.*; **organ —,** cañón de órgano; **— clay,** arcilla refractaria; **— line,** cañería, tubería, *f.*; **— maker,** pipero, *m.*; **— organ,** órgano de cañones; **small —,** cañutillo, *m.*; **—,** *vt. and vi.* tocar (la flauta, churumbela, etc.); cantar con voz aguda; **—,** *vt.* proveer de cañerías; conducir por medio de cañerías; (costura) adornar con vivos.
piper, *n.* flautista, *m.* y *f.*
piping, *adj.* hirviente; **—,** *n.* tubería, *f.*
pipkin, *n.* olla pequeña de barro.
pippin, *n.* (bot.) camuesa, *f.*
piquancy, *n.* picante, *m.*; acrimonia, *f.*; picardía, *f.*
piquant, *adj.* punzante, picante; mordaz; **—ly,** *adv.* con picardía.
pique, *n.* pique, *m.*; desazón, *f.*; ojeriza, *f.*; pundonor, *m.*; **—,** *vt.* picar; irritar.
piqué, *n.* piqué, *m.*
piquet, *n.* juego de los cientos.
piracy, *n.* piratería, *f.*
piragua, *n.* piragua, *f.*
pirate, *n.* pirata, *m.*; **—,** *vt. and vi.* piratear; robar; plagiar.
piratical, *adj.* pirático.
pirouette, *n.* pirueta, cabriola, *f.*; **—,** *vi.* hacer piruetas o cabriolas.
Pisces, *n.* Piscis (signo del zodíaco), *m.*
pish! *interj.* ¡quita allá! ¡bah!
pistachio, *n.* (bot.) alfóncigo, pistacho, *m.*
pistil, *n.* pistilo, *m.*
pistillate, *adj.* con pistilos.
pistol, *n.* pistola, *f.*; revólver, *m.*; pistolete, *m.*; **— shot,** pistoletazo, *m.*
piston, *n.* pistón, émbolo, *m.*; **— ring,** anillo de empaquetadura del émbolo o pistón; **— rod,** vástago del émbolo.
pit, *n.* hoyo, *m.*; sepultura, *f.*; patio, *m.*; (min.) pozo, *m.*; **— ash,** cenicero, *m.*; **engine —,** (rail.) cenicero, *m.*; **—,** *vi.* azuzar a uno para que riña.
pitapat, *adv.* con una serie rápida de palpitaciones; agitadamente; **—,** *vi.* moverse o palpitar agitadamente.
pitch, *n.* pez, brea, *f.*; alquitrán, *m.*; cima, *f.*; grado de elevación; (mus.) tono, *m.*; (en baseball, etc.) lanzamiento, *m.*; **— pine,** pino de tea, pino rizado; **— pipe,** diapasón vocal; **—,** *vt.* fijar, plantar; colocar; ordenar; tirar; arrojar; embrear; oscurecer; **—,** *vi.* caerse alguna cosa hacia abajo; caer de cabeza; escoger.
pitchblende, *n.* pecblenda, *f.*
pitch-dark, *adj.* negro como la pez, perfectamente negro.
pitched battle, *n.* batalla campal.
pitcher, *n.* cántaro, *m.*; (baseball) lanzador

de pelota; — **plant,** planta con hojas en forma de odres, como la sarracenia.

pitchfork, *n.* horca, horquilla, *f.*

pitching, *n.* (aer., naut.) cabeceo, *m.*

piteous, *adj.* lastimoso; compasivo, tierno; —**ly,** *adv.* lastimosamente.

pitfall, *n.* trampa, *f.*, armadijo, *m.*

pith, *n.* meollo, *m.*; médula, *f.*; energía, *f.*

pithily, *adv.* vigorosamente.

pithy, *adj.* enérgico; meduloso.

pitiable, *adj.* lastimoso.

pitiful, *adj.* lastimoso, compasivo; —**ly,** *adv.* lastimosamente.

pitiless, *adj.* desapiadado, cruel; —**ly,** *adv.* cruelmente.

pittance, *n.* pitanza, ración, porcioncilla, *f.*

pitted, *adj.* cavado, picado.

pitter-patter, *n.* repiqueteo, *m.*; parloteo, *m.*

Pittsburgh, Pittsburgo, *m.*

pituitary, *adj.* pituitario; — **gland,** glándula pituitaria.

pity, *n.* piedad, compasión, *f.*; misericordia, *f.*; —, *vt.* compadecer; —, *vi.* tener piedad.

pivot, *n.* espigón, *m.*; quicio, *m.*; chaveta, *f.*; eje de rotación.

pix, *n.* píxide, *f.*

pixy, *n.* duende, *m.*; diablillo, *m.*

pk.: park, parque; **peck,** medida de áridos; **peak,** pico, cima.

pkg. package, bto. bulto, paquete.

pl.: place, lug. lugar; **plural,** pl. plural.

placable, *adj.* aplacable.

placard, *n.* placarte, *m.*; cartel, letrero, anuncio, *m.*

placate, *vt.* aplacar, sosegar.

place, *n.* lugar, sitio, *m.*; local, *m.*; colocación, *f.*; posición, *f.*; recinto, *m.*; rango, empleo, *m.*; (mil.) plaza, fortaleza, *f.*; — **kick,** (football) acción de patear la pelota después de colocarla en tierra; **stopping —,** paradero, *m.*; **to take —,** verificarse; —, *vt.* colocar; poner; poner (dinero a ganancias).

placement, *n.* empleo, *m.*; colocación, *f.*

placer, *n.* (min.) placer, lavadero, *m.*; — **mining,** minería de placer.

placid, *adj.* plácido, quieto; —**ly,** *adv.* apaciblemente.

placidity, *n.* apacibilidad, dulzura, *f.*

placing, *n.* localización, *f.*; colocación, *f.*

placket, *n.* abertura (de un traje, un vestido, etc.).

plagiarism, *n.* plagio, *m.*

plagiarist, *n.* plagiario, ria.

plagiarize, *vt.* plagiar.

plagiary, *n.* plagio, *m.*; plagiario, ria.

plague, *n.* peste, plaga, *f.*; —, *vt.* atormentar; infestar, apestar.

plaice, *n.* (pez) platija, *f.*

plaid, *n.* capa suelta de sarga listada que usan los montañeses de Escocia; tela listada a cuadros.

plain, *adj.* liso, llano, abierto, sencillo;

sincero; puro, simple; común; claro, evidente; — **sailing,** (fig.) camino fácil; — **spoken,** sencillo, sincero en el hablar; — **dealing,** buena fe; llaneza, *f.*; —**ly,** *adv.* llanamente; claramente; —, *n.* llano, *m.*, llanada, vega, *f.*

plain-clothes man, *n.* detective, *m.*

plainness, *n.* llaneza, igualdad, *f.*; sinceridad, *f.*; claridad, *f.*

plainsman, *n.* llanero, *m.*

plainswoman, *n.* llanera, *f.*

plaint, *n.* queja, *f.*; lamento, *m.*

plaintiff, *n.* (law) demandador, ra, demandante, *m.* y *f.*

plaintive, *adj.* lamentoso, lastimoso; —**ly,** *adv.* de manera lastimosa.

plait, *n.* pliegue, *m.*; trenza, *f.*; —, *vt.* plegar; trenzar; rizar; tejer.

plan, *n.* plano, *m.*; sistema, *m.*; proyecto, plan, *m.*; delineación (de un edificio, etc.), *f.*; —, *vt.* proyectar, planear; plantear; —, *vi.* proponerse; pensar.

plane, *n.* plano, *m.*; cepillo de carpintería; **grooving —,** acanalador, *m.*; — **geometry,** geometría plana; — **tree,** plátano, *m.*; **reconnaisance —,** aeroplano de reconocimiento; —, *vt.* allanar; acepillar.

planer, *n.* cepillo mecánico, acepilladora mecánica, aplanador, *m.*

planet, *n.* planeta, *m.*

planetarium, *n.* planetario, *m.*

planetary, *adj.* planetario.

planetesimal, *n.* pequeño cuerpo sólido probablemente similar a un meteoro; —, *adj.* perteneciente a pequeñísimos cuerpos del firmamento.

planetoid, *n.* asteroide, *m.*

planimeter, *n.* planímetro, *m.*

plank, *n.* tablón, *m.*; (naut.) tablaje, *m.*; —, *vt.* entablar, asegurar con tablas.

plankton, *n.* flotante vegetación marítima.

planned, *adj.* planeado; — **economy,** economía dirigida.

plant, *n.* mata, planta; *f.*; planta (del pie), *f.*; — **louse,** pulgón, *m.*; —, *vt.* plantar, sembrar.

plantain, *n.* (bot.) llantén, *m.*; plátano, *m.*

plantation, *n.* plantación, planta, *f.*, plantío, *m.*; **coffee —,** cafetal, *m.*; **rubber —,** cauchal, *m.*

planter, *n.* plantador, *m.*; colono, *m.*; hacendado, *m.*; sembrador, ra.

planting, *n.* plantación, *f.*

plaque, *n.* (art) placa, *f.*

plash, *n.* charquillo, lagunajo, *m.*

plasma, plasm, *n.* (biol., min.) plasma, *m.*

plaster, *n.* yeso, *m.*; emplasto, *m.*; enlucido, estuco, revoque, *m.*; repello, *m.*; **corn —,** emplasto para los callos; — **cast,** vendaje enyesado, yeso, *m.*; — **coating,** enlucido, enyesado, *m.*; — **of Paris,** yeso, *m.*, yeso mate; **sticking —,** pegado, *m.*; —, *vt.* enyesar; emplastar.

plasterboard, *n.* plancha de yeso y fieltro usada para tabiques.

plasterer, *n.* albañil que enyesa, yesero, *m.*

plastering, *n.* revoque, *m.*, revocadura, *f.*

plastic, *adj.* plástico, formativo; — **surgery,** anaplastia, *f.*; —**s,** *n.* plástica, *f.*; arte de modelar en barro, yeso, etc.

plat, *n.* parcela, *f.*, solar, *m.*; plano o mapa de una ciudad; —, *vt.* entretejer, trenzar; trazar el plano (de una ciudad).

plate, *n.* plancha o lámina de metal; placa, *f.*; clisé, *m.*; plata labrada; vajilla, *f.*; plato, *m.*; **name** —, placa de fábrica; — **glass,** vidrio cilindrado o en planchas; —, *vt.* planchear; batir hoja.

plateau, *n.* mesa, meseta, *f.*

platen, *n.* (print.) platina, *f.*

platform, *n.* plataforma, tarima, *f.*; tribunal, *m.*; — **scale,** báscula, *f.*; — **ticket,** billete de andén.

plating, *n.* electrogalvanización, *f.*

platinum, *n.* platino, *m.*; — **ore,** platina, *f.*

platitude, *n.* perogrullada, *f.*, la verdad de Perogrullo, trivialidad, *f.*

platitudinous, *adj.* trivial.

platonic, *adj.* platónico.

platoon, *n.* (mil.) pelotón, *m.*

platter, *n.* fuente, *f.*, plato grande.

plaudit, *n.* aplauso, *m.*

plausibility, *n.* plausibilidad, *f.*

plausible, *adj.* plausible, verisímil, verosímil; —**bly,** *adv.* plausiblemente.

play, *n.* juego, *m.*; recreo, *m.*; representación dramática, comedia, *f.*; — **on words,** juego de palabras, *m.*; —, *vt.* and *vi.* jugar; juguetear; burlarse; representar (un papel); (mus.) tocar, tañer, hacer sonar; **to** — **a joke,** hacer una burla; —**ed out,** exhausto, agotado, postrado; **to** — **up to,** adular.

playable, *adj.* capaz de ser jugado o tocado.

playbill, *n.* programa de espectáculo.

playboy, *n.* hombre disoluto amante de los placeres.

player, *n.* jugador, ra; comediante, ta, actor, *m.*, actriz, *f.*; (mus.) tocador, ra; ejecutante, *m.* y *f.*; **pelota** —, pelotari, *m.*; **ball** —, jugador o jugadora de pelota; — **piano,** pianola, *f.*, piano mecánico o automático.

playfellow, playmate, *n.* camarada, *m.* y *f.*, compañero o compañera de juego.

playful, *adj.* juguetón, travieso; —**ly,** *adv.* juguetonamente, en forma retozona.

playfulness, *n.* jovialidad, *f.*

playgoer, *n.* persona que frecuenta los teatros.

playground, *n.* campo de deportes o de juegos; campo o patio de recreo.

playhouse, *n.* teatro, *m.*

playing card, *n.* naipe *m.*, carta (de baraja), *f.*

playlet, *n.* comedia corta, especie de entremés teatral.

playmate, *n.* compañero o compañera de juego.

plaything, *n.* juguete, *m.*

playtime, *n.* hora de recreo.

playwright, *n.* dramaturgo, *m.*

plea, *n.* defensa, *f.*; excusa, *f.*; pretexto, socolor, efugio, *m.*; ruego, *m.*; argumento, *m.*; súplica, *f.*; petición, *f.*

plead, *vt.* defender en juicio; alegar; suplicar.

pleader, *n.* abogado, da, defensor, ra.

pleading, *n.* acto de abogar; alegación, *f.*; (law) informe, *m.*; —**s,** *n. pl.* debates, litigios, *m. pl.*

pleasant, *adj.* agradable; placentero, alegre; risueño, genial; —**ly,** *adv.* alegremente, placenteramente.

pleasantry, *n.* chocarrería, chanza, *f.*

please, *vt.* agradar, complacer, tener la bondad de; **do as you** —, haga usted lo que guste; **if you** —, con permiso de usted; — **be seated,** sírvase tomar asiento; —**d to meet you,** me alegro de conocer a usted.

pleasing, *adj.* agradable, placentero, grato; **to be** —, caer bien.

pleasurable, *adj.* deleitante, agradable.

pleasure, *n.* gusto, placer, *m.*; arbitrio, *m.*; recreo, *m.*

pleat, *vt.* plegar; rizar; —, *n.* pliegue, *m.*

pleated, *adj.* plegado.

pleater, *n.* plegador, *m.*

pleating, *n.* plegado, *m.*, plegadura, *f.*

plebeian, *adj.* plebeyo, vulgar, bajo; —, *n.* plebeyo, ya.

plebiscite, *n.* plebiscito, *m.*; resolución de un pueblo.

plectrum, *n.* plectro, *m.*

pledge, *n.* prenda, *f.*; fianza, *f.*; compromiso, *m.*; garantía, *f.*; empeño, *m.*, pignoración, *f.*; —, *vt.* empeñar, pignorar; dar fianza.

Pleiades *n.* (ast.) Pléyades, *f. pl.*

plenary, *adj.* plenario, entero.

plenipotentiary, *n.* and *adj.* plenipotenciario, *m.*

plenitude, *n.* plenitud, abundancia, *f.*

plenteous, plentiful, *adj.* copioso, abundante; —**ly,** *adv.* con abundancia, copiosamente.

plenty, *n.* copia, abundancia, *f.*; plenitud, *f.*; —, *adj.* abundante.

pleonasm, *n.* pleonasmo, *m.*

plethora, *n.* plétora, *f.*; repleción, *f.*

plethoric, *adj.* pletórico, repleto.

pleura, *n.* (anat.) pleura, *f.*

pleurisy, *n.* pleuresía, *f.*

plexus, *n.* plexo, *m.*

plf. plaintiff, demandante, *m.* y *f.*

pliable, pliant, *adj.* flexible, dócil, blando; tratable.

pliancy, *n.* flexibilidad, *f.*

pliers, *n. pl.* tenacillas, *f. pl.*

plight, *n.* estado, *m.*; condición, *f.*; apuro, aprieto, *m.*; —, *vt.* empeñar; prometer.

plinth, *n.* zócalo, *m.*

pliocene, *adj.* (geol.) plioceno.

plod, *vi.* afanarse mucho, ajetrearse.

plodder, *n.* persona laboriosa y asidua.

plop, *n.* voz onomatopéyica que describe la caída o movimiento rápido de un objeto, como en el agua; —, *vi.* caer o moverse un objeto en la forma descrita.

plot, *n.* pedazo pequeño de terreno; plano, *m.*; conspiración, trama, *f.*; complot, *m.*; estratagema, *f.*; —, *vt.* and *vi.* trazar; conspirar, tramar.

plotter, *n.* conspirador, ra.

plough, ploughboy, etc. = **plow, plow-boy, etc.**

plover, *n.* (orn.) ave fría, frailecillo, *m.*

plow, *n.* arado, *m.*; **disc** —, arado de discos; **gang** —, arado múltiple; **hoe** —, arado de azada; **hook** —, arado de gancho; **rotary** —, arado giratorio; **stubble** —, arado desterronador; —, *vt.* arar, labrar la tierra; **to — (a ship through waves),** (fig.) surcar (el mar); **to — a second time,** binar.

plowboy, *n.* arador, *m.*

plowing, *n.* rompimiento, *m.*; aradura, *f.*

plowland, *n.* tierra labrantía.

plowman, *n.* surcador, *m.*

plowshare, *n.* reja de arado.

pluck, *vt.* tirar con fuerza; arrancar; desplumar; —, *n.* asadura, *f.*, hígado y bofes; arranque, tirón, *m.*

plucky, *adj.* valiente, gallardo.

plug, *n.* tapón, tarugo, *m.*; obturador, *m.*; clavija, *f.*; (elec.) tapón, *m.*, clavija eléctrica o de contacto; **to pull the —,** desenchufar; —, *vt.* atarugar, tapar; (elec.) poner en contacto con los fusibles.

plum, *n.* ciruela, *f.*; — **pudding,** especie de pudín; — **tree,** ciruelo, *m.*

plumage, *n.* plumaje, *m.*

plumb, *n.* plomada, *f.*; — **line,** cuerda de plomada; nivel, *m.*; —, *adj.* a plomo, vertical; —, *adv.* verticalmente, a plomo; —, *vt.* aplomar.

plumbago, *n.* lápiz plomo, grafito, *m.*

plumber, *n.* plomero, emplomador, *m.*; fontanero, *m.*

plumbing, *n.* plomería, *f.*, instalación de cañerías; arte del plomero.

plume, *n.* pluma, *f.*; plumaje, penacho, *m.*; —, *vt.* desplumar; adornar con plumas.

plummet, *n.* plomada, *f.*; (naut.) sonda, *f.*; criterio, *m.*

plump, *adj.* gordo, rollizo; —, *adv.* de repente; —, *vt.* and *vi.* engordar; caer a plomo.

plumpness, *n.* gordura, corpulencia, obesidad, *f.*

plumule, *n.* (bot.) plúmula, *f.*

plunder, *vt.* saquear, pillar, robar; —, *n.* pillaje, botín, *m.*, despojos, *m. pl.*

plunge, *vt.* and *vi.* sumergir, sumergirse, precipitarse.

plunger, *n.* buzo, somorgujador, *m.*; — **of a pump,** émbolo, *m.*

pluperfect, *adj.* (gram.) pluscuamperfecto;

—, *n.* pluscuamperfecto, *m.*

plur. plural, pl. plural.

plural, *adj.* and *n.* plural, *m.*

plurality, *n.* pluralidad, *f.*; mayoría relativa.

pluralize, *vt.* pluralizar.

plus, *prep.* más.

plush, *n.* tripe (tela felpada), *m.*

plutocracy, *n.* plutocracia, *f.*

plutocrat, *n.* plutócrata, *m.* y *f.*

plutocratic, *adj.* plutocrático.

plutonic, *adj.* plutónico.

pluvial, *adj.* pluvial.

ply, *vt.* trabajar con ahinco; importunar, solicitar; —, *vi.* afanarse; aplicarse; (naut.) barloventear.

plywood, *n.* madera enchapada.

P.M.: afternoon, p.m. tarde; **Postmaster,** Agente de Correos; Admor. de Correos, Administrador de Correos.

p.m. afternoon, p.m. tarde, pasado meridiano.

pneumatic, pneumatical, *adj.* neumático.

pneumococcus, *n.* (med.) neumococo, *m.*

pneumonia, *n.* neumonía, pulmonía, *f.*

P.O. postoffice, oficina de correos.

poach, *vt.* medio cocer (huevos); —, *vi.* cazar en vedado.

poacher, *n.* cazador furtivo.

pock, *n.* viruela, pústula, *f.*

pocket, *n.* bolsillo, *m.*, faltriquera, *f.*; — **battleship,** acorazado de bolsillo; — **money,** dinero para los gastos menudos; — **veto,** retención de parte del presidente de los Estados Unidos de un proyecto de ley; —, *vt.* embolsar.

pocketbook, *n.* portamonedas, *m.*, cartera, *f.*; (fig.) dinero, *m.*, recursos económicos.

pocketful, *n.* bolsillo lleno, bolsillado, *m.*

pocketknife, *n.* cortaplumas, *m.*

pock-marked, *adj.* picado de viruelas.

pod, *n.* vaina, *f.*

podium, *n.* (arch.) podio, *m.*

poem, *n.* poema, *m.*

poesy, *n.* poesía, *f.*

poet, *n.* poeta, *m.*; vate, *m.*; bardo, *m.*

poetaster, *n.* poetastro, *m.*

poetess, *n.* poetisa, *f.*

poetic, poetical, *adj.* poético; — **justice,** justicia poética; — **license,** licencia poética.

poetically, *adv.* poéticamente.

poetics, *n.* poética, *f.*

poetry, *n.* poesía, *f.*; **pastoral —,** bucólica, *f.*; **to write —,** poetizar; trovar.

pogrom, *n.* pogrom, *m.*, ataque organizado en contra de los judíos.

poignancy, *n.* picante, *m.*; acrimonia, *f.*

poignant, *adj.* picante; punzante; satírico; conmovedor; —**ly,** *adv.* conmovedoramente.

poinsettia, *n.* (bot.) nochebuena, catalina, flor de la Pascua.

point, *n.* punta, *f.*; punto, *m.*; promontorio, *m.*: puntillo, *m.*; estado, *m.*; pico, *m.*;

—**s,** *n. pl.* tantos, *m. pl.*; **main** —, quid, *m.*; **make a** — **of,** tener presente; **stretch a** —, exagerar; — **lace,** encaje de aguja o de punto; — **of honor,** pundonor, *m.*; — **of order,** cuestión de orden o reglamento; — **of view,** punto de vista; — **rationing,** racionamiento por puntos; **to get to the** —, ir al grano; **to the** —, en plata; —, *vt.* apuntar; aguzar; **to** — **out,** señalar.

point-blank, *adv.* directamente; —, *adj.* directo, sin rodeos.

pointed, *adj.* puntiagudo; epigramático; conspicuo; satírico; —**ly,** *adv.* sutilmente.

pointer, *n.* apuntador, *m.*; ventor, *m.*, perro ventor.

pointless, *adj.* obtuso, sin punta; insustancial, insípido, tonto.

poise, *n.* peso, *m.*; equilibrio, *m.*; reposo, *m.*; —, *vt.* pesar, equilibrar.

poison, *n.* veneno, *m.*; — **ivy,** especie de hiedra venenosa; — **sumac,** variedad de zumaque venenoso que causa erupción cutánea; —, *vt.* envenenar; pervertir.

poisoner, *n.* envenenador, ra; corruptor, ra.

poisoning, *n.* envenenamiento, *m.*

poisonous, *adj.* venenoso.

poke, *n.* sombrero de mujer con ala abovedada al frente; empujón, *m.*; hurgonazo, *m.*; — **bonnet,** sombrero de mujer con ala abovedada al frente; —, *vt.* aguijonear, hurgar; asomar; **to** — **fun at,** burlarse de; —, *vi.* andar asomándose.

poker, *n.* hurgón, *m.*; póker (juego de naipes), *m.*

poky, *adj.* despacioso, lento, flojo.

Poland, Polonia, *f.*

polar, *adj.* polar; — **bear,** oso blanco o polar.

polariscope, *n.* polariscopio, *m.*

polarity, *n.* polaridad, *f.*

polarization, *n.* polarización, *f.*

polarize, *vt.* polarizar.

Pole, *n.* polaco, ca.

pole, *n.* polo, *m.*; (naut.) palo, *m.*; pértiga, *f.*; lanza de coche; percha, *f.*; — **vault,** salto de garrocha.

poleax, poleaxe, *n.* hachuela de mano.

polecat, *n.* gato montés.

polemic, *adj.* polémico; —, *n.* polémica, *f.*; polemista, *m.* y *f.*; —, controversista, *m.* y *f.*; —**s,** *n. pl.* polémica, *f.*

polestar, *n.* estrella polar.

police, *n.* policía, *f.*; — **court,** tribunal de policía; — **dog,** perro de policía; — **headquarters,** jefatura de policía.

policeman, *n.* policía, *m.*, agente de policía, gendarme, *m.*

policewoman, *n.* agente femenino de policía.

policy, *n.* política de estado; póliza, *f.*; astucia, *f.*; sistema, *m.*; **insurance** —, póliza de seguro.

policyholder, *n.* asegurado, da, persona que tiene póliza de seguro.

poliomyelitis, *n.* (med.) poliomielitis, *f.*, parálisis infantil.

Polish, *n.* and *adj.* polaco, ca; — (language), polaco, *m.*

polish, *vt.* pulir, alisar; limar; charolar; —, *vi.* recibir pulimento; —, *n.* pulimento, *m.*; barniz, lustre, *m.*

polished, *adj.* elegante, pulido; bruñido.

polite, *adj.* pulido, cortés; —**ly,** *adv.* urbanamente, cortésmente.

politeness, *n.* cortesía, *f.*

politic, *adj.* político, astuto.

political, *adj.* político; — **economy,** economía política; — **group,** bloc, *m.*; — **leader,** cacique, *m.*; — **science,** ciencia política; —**ly,** *adv.* según reglas de política.

politician, *n.* político, *m.*

politics, *n. pl.* política, *f.*

polka, *n.* polca, *f.*; — **dot,** diseño de puntos regularmente distribuídos en una tela.

Poll, Polly, Maruja.

poll, *n.* cabeza, *f.*; lista de los que votan en una elección; voto, *m.*; —**s,** *n. pl.* comicios, *m. pl.*; — **tax,** capitación, *f.*; —, *vt.* descabezar; desmochar; —, *vi.* dar voto en las elecciones.

pollen, *n.* (bot.) polen, *m.*

pollinate, *vt.* polinizar.

pollination, *n.* polinización, *f.*

polling, *n.* votación, *f.*; — **booth,** puesto de votación; — **place,** lugar donde se vota.

pollute, *vt.* ensuciar; corromper.

pollution, *n.* corrupción, contaminación, *f.*

polo, *n.* juego de polo.

polonaise, *n.* (mus.) polonesa, *f.*

poltroon, *n.* collón, cobarde, *m.*

polyandry, *n.* poliandria, *f.*

polychrome, *adj.* polícromo, de muchos colores.

polygamist, *n.* polígamo, ma.

polygamy, *n.* poligamia, *f.*

polyglot, *adj.* poligloto; —, *n.* poligloto, ta.

polygon, *n.* polígono, *m.*

polyhedron, *n.* poliedro, *m.*

polymorphism, *n.* (chem.) polimorfismo, *m.*

polynomial, *n.* polinomio, *m.*; —, *adj.* de varios términos.

polyp, *n.* (zool.) pólipo, pulpo, *m.*; (med.) pólipo, *m.*

polyphonic, *adj.* polifónico.

polypus, *n.* pólipo, *m.*

polysyllabic, *adj.* polisílabo.

polysyllable, *n.* polisílabo, *m.*

polytechnic, *adj.* politécnico.

polytheism, *n.* politeísmo, *m.*

pomade, pomatum, *n.* pomada, *f.*

pomegranate, *n.* (bot.) granado, *m.*; granada, *f.*

Pomeranian, *adj.* and *n.* pomerano, na.

pomology, *n.* pomología, *f.*

pomp, *n.* pompa, *f.*; esplendor, *m.*; solemnidad, *f.*

pompadour, *n.* copete, *m.*

pompano, n. (pez) pámpano, m.
pompon, n. pompón, m.
pomposity, n. ostentación, f.
pompous, adj. pomposo; **—ly,** adv. pomposamente.
poncho, n. poncho, m.
pond, n. charca, f., estanque de agua.
ponder, vt. and vi. ponderar, considerar, deliberar, meditar.
ponderous, adj. ponderoso, pesado; **—ly,** adv. pesadamente.
pongee, n. variedad de tela de seda.
poniard, n. puñal, m.; **—,** vt. herir con puñal.
pontiff, n. pontífice, papa, m.
pontifical, adj. pontifical; **—,** n. pontifical (libro), m.
pontificate, n. pontificado, papado, m.
pontoon, n. pontón, m.; **— bridge,** puente de pontones.
pony, n. haca, f., jaco, m.; caballito, m.
poodle, n. perro de aguas.
pooh! interj. ¡puf!
pooh-pooh, vt. tratar o hablar con burla; **—!** interj. ¡bah!
pool, n. charco, m.; lago, m.; tanque, m.; dinero o cosas reunidas por varias personas; **—,** vt. reunir.
poolroom, n. salón de billares.
poop, n. (naut.) popa, f.; toldilla, f.
poor, adj. pobre; humilde; de poco valor; deficiente; estéril; mísero; **— box,** caja de limosnas para los pobres; **— farm,** casa de caridad, casa del pobre; **— law,** ley de asistencia pública; **the —,** los pobres, m. pl.; **to become —,** venir a menos, empobrecer; **—ly,** adv. pobremente.
poorhouse, n. casa de caridad.
pop, n. chasquido, m.; bebida gaseosa; **—,** vt. and vi. entrar o salir de sopetón; meter alguna cosa repentinamente.
pop.: popular, popular; population, h., hab. número de habitantes.
popcorn, n. palomitas de maíz, maíz tostado y reventado.
Pope, n. papa, m.
popery, n. papismo, m.
popgun, n. escopetilla con que juegan los muchachos.
popinjay, n. pisaverde, m.
popish, adj. papal, romano; **—ly,** adv. a manera de los papistas.
poplar, n. álamo temblón.
poplin, n. (tela) papelina, popelina, f., poplín, m.
popover, n. panecillo ligero y hueco.
popper, n. vasija para tostar maíz.
poppet, n. válvula que se mueve verticalmente.
poppy, n. (bot.) adormidera, amapola, f.
populace, n. populacho, m.; pueblo, m.
popular, adj. popular; **—ly,** adv. popularmente.
popularity, n. popularidad, boga, f.
popularize, vt. popularizar.

populate, vi. poblar.
population, n. población, f., número de habitantes (en una ciudad, país, etc.).
populous, adj. populoso.
porcelain, n. porcelana, china, f., loza fina.
porch, n. pórtico, vestíbulo, m.
porcine, adj. porcino, porcuno.
porcupine, n. puerco espín.
pore, n. poro, m.
pork, n. carne de puerco; **— sausage,** longaniza, f.
porker, n. porcino, cochino, m.
pornographic, adj. pornográfico.
pornography, n. pornografía, f.
porosity, n. porosidad, f.
porous, adj. poroso.
porphyry, n. pórfido, m.
porpoise, n. puerco marino.
porridge, n. potaje, m.; sopa, f.
porringer, n. escudilla, f.
port, n. puerto, m.; (naut.) babor, m., escala, f.; vino de Oporto; **to stop at a —,** hacer escala en un puerto.
portable, adj. portátil; **— typewriter,** máquina de escribir portátil.
portage, n. porte, acarreo, m.; portaje, m.
portal, n. portal, m., portada, f.
portend, vt. pronosticar, augurar.
portent, n. portento, prodigio, m.; presagio, m.
portentous, adj. portentoso.
porter, n. portero, m.; mozo, m.
porterage, n. oficio de ganapán; portaje, m.
porterhouse steak, n. biftec de solomillo, filete, m.
portfolio, n. cartera, f., cartera portapapeles; **— (of a minister of state, etc.),** cartera (de un ministro de estado, etc.).
portico, n. pórtico, portal, m.
portion, n. porción, parte, f.; ración, f.; dote, m. y f.; **—,** vt. partir, dividir; dotar.
portliness, n. porte majestuoso; corpulencia, f.
portly, adj. majestuoso; rollizo, corpulento.
portmanteau, n. portamanteo, m., maleta, f.
portrait, n. retrato, m.; **maker of —s,** retratista, m. y f.; **to make a — of,** retratar; **to sit for a —,** retratarse.
portray, vt. retratar.
portrayal, n. descripción, f.; representación gráfica.
Portuguese, n. and adj. portugués, esa; **— language,** portugués, m.
portulaca, n. (bot.) verdolaga, f.
pose, vt. colocar en determinada posición (para retratar, etc.); confundir, turbar; **—,** vi. asumir cierta actitud o postura; **—,** n. postura, actitud, f.
poser, n. examinador, ra; pregunta que confunde; persona que asume cierta actitud o postura.
poseur, n. persona afectada, fingidor, ra.
position, n. posición, situación, f.; estación, f.; orientación, f.

positive, *adj.* positivo, real, verdadero; definitivo; —**ly,** *adv.* positivamente; ciertamente; perentoriamente.

positiveness, *n.* carácter positivo; realidad, *f.*; determinación, *f.*; obstinación, *f.*

positivism, *n.* positivismo, *m.*; certeza, *f.*

posse, *n.* fuerza armada; fuerza con autoridad legal.

possess, *vt.* poseer.

possession, *n.* posesión, *f.*; **to take — of,** hacerse dueño de.

possessive, *adj.* posesivo.

possessor, *n.* poseedor, ra.

posset, *n.* suero, *m.*, agua de leche.

possibility, *n.* posibilidad, *f.*

possible, *adj.* posible; **as soon as —,** cuanto antes; —**bly,** *adv.* quizá, quizás, posiblemente.

post, *n.* correo, *m.*; puesto, *m.*; empleo, *m.*; poste, *m.*; palo, *m.*; — **card,** tarjeta postal; — **chaise,** silla de posta; — **office,** oficina de correos, administración de correos; **post-office box,** apartado de correos, casilla de correos; —, *vt.* apostar; fijar; — **no bills,** se prohibe fijar carteles; —, *vi.* ir en posta, correr la posta.

postage, *n.* porte de carta, franqueo, *m.*; — **stamp,** sello, *m.*, estampilla, *f.*, sello de correo o de franqueo.

postal, *adj.* postal; — **card,** tarjeta postal.

postboy, *n.* postillón, *m.*

postdate, *vt.* posfechar.

poster, *n.* cartel, cartelón, letrero, *m.*

posterior, *adj.* posterior, trasero.

posterity, *n.* posteridad, *f.*; venideros, *m. pl.*

postern, *n.* postigo, *m.*; poterna, *f.*; —, *adj.* trasero o lateral.

postgraduate, *adj.* relativo a estudios para graduados; —, *n.* estudiante graduado que hace estudios avanzados.

posthaste, *adv.* a rienda suelta, con gran celeridad.

posthumous, *adj.* póstumo.

postilion, *n.* postillón, *m.*

postlude, *n.* (mus.) postludio, *m.*, pieza final.

postman, *n.* cartero, *m.*; correo, *m.*; **rural —,** peatón, *m.*

postmark, *n.* timbre de posta, sello o marca de la oficina de correos.

postmaster, *n.* administrador de correos.

postmeridian, *adj.* postmeridiano.

post-mortem, *adj.* que sucede después de la muerte; —, *n.* autopsia, *f.*, examen de un cadáver.

postnatal, *adj.* postnatal.

post-office, *n.* correo, *m.*, oficina postal.

postpaid, *adj.* franco; porte pagado; franco de porte.

postpone, *vt.* diferir, suspender; posponer; trasladar.

postponement, *n.* aplazamiento, *m.*

postscript, *n.* posdata, *f.*

postulant, *n.* postulante, *m.* y *f.*

posture, *n.* postura, *f.*

posy, *n.* mote, *m.*; flor, *f.*; ramillete de flores.

pot, *n.* marmita, *f.*; olla, *f.*; tarro, *m.*; — **roast,** carne asada en marmita; — **shot,** tiro corto y fácil, tiro o ataque en contra de las reglas del juego limpio y que no requiere esfuerzo ni habilidad; —, *vt.* preservar en marmitas.

potable, *adj.* potable.

potash, *n.* potasa, *f.*

potassium, *n.* potasio, *m.*

potation, *n.* bebida, *f.*, trago, *m.*

potato, *n.* patata, papa, *f.*; **fried —es,** patatas o papas fritas; **mashed —es,** puré de patata o de papa; — **beetle,** — **bug,** leptinotarsa, *f.*, coleóptero de la patata; **sweet —,** camote, *m.*, batata, *f.*; — **blight,** plaga de los patatas.

potbellied, *adj.* panzudo.

potboiler, *n.* obra hecha de prisa para ganar dinero.

potboy, *n.* mozo de taberna.

potency, *n.* potencia, energía, fuerza, *f.*; influjo, *m.*

potent, *adj.* potente, poderoso, eficaz.

potentate, *n.* potentado, *m.*

potential, *adj.* potencial, poderoso.

potentiality, *n.* potencialidad, *f.*

pothanger, *n.* llares, *f. pl.*

pother, *n.* baraúnda, *f.*; alboroto, bullicio, *m.*; nube de polvo o de vapor que asfixia; —, *vt.* and *vi.* atormentar, mortificar; confundir.

potherb, *n.* hierba (tal como hierbabuena) que se emplea para sazonar.

potholder, *n.* portaollas, *m.*

pothole, *n.* agujero grande.

pothook, *n.* asa de cadera.

pothouse, *n.* ventorrillo, bodegón, *m.*

potion, *n.* poción, *f.*, bebida medicinal.

potluck, *n.* comida ordinaria; **to take —,** comer varias personas juntas sin formalidad.

potpie, *n.* torta o fricasé de carne.

potpourri, *n.* revoltillo, *m.*, mezcolanza, *f.*

potsherd, *n.* fragmento de una vasija de barro; cacharro, casco, *m.*

pottage, *n.* potaje, *m.* menestra, *f.*

potted, *adj.* en marmita u olla.

potter, *n.* alfarero, *m.*; —**'s ware,** alfarería, *f.*, cacharros, *m.pl.*

pottery, *n.* alfarería, *f.*; **broken —,** cachivaches, *m.pl.*

pouch, *n.* buche, *m.*; bolsillo, *m.*, faltriquera, *f.*; bolsa, *f.*

poulterer, *n.* pollero, ra, gallinero, ra.

poultice, *n.* cataplasma, *f.*, pegado, *m.*

poultry, *n.* aves caseras, aves de corral; — **yard,** corral de aves caseras.

pounce, *n.* garra, *f.*; grasilla, *f.*; cisquero, *m.*; —, *vt.* apomazar; —, *vi.* entrar repentinamente.

pound, *n.* libra, *f.*; libra esterlina; corral público; — **sterling,** libra esterlina; —, *vt.* machacar.

poundal, *n.* unidad de fuerza capaz de impeler una masa con peso de una libra a razón de un pie por segundo.

poundcake, *n.* pastel hecho con una libra de cada ingrediente principal (azúcar, mantequilla, etc.)

pounder, *n.* cosa que pesa una libra (úsase en combinación con números, por ej., **twelve-pounder,** cañón de doce libras).

pour, *vt.* echar o vaciar líquidos de una parte a otra; arrojar alguna cosa continuadamente; verter; —, *vi.* fluir con rapidez; llover a cántaros.

pourer, *n.* vaciador, trasegador, *m.*

pout, *vi.* hacer pucheros, ponerse ceñudo; —, *n.* puchero, *m.*, mueca fingida.

pouter pigeon, *n.* paloma de cuello grueso.

poverty, *n.* pobreza, *f.*

poverty-stricken, *adj.* muy pobre, desamparado.

powder, *n.* polvo, *m.*; pólvora, *f.*; — **case,** polvera, *f.*; — **horn,** frasco para pólvora; — **magazine,** polvorín, *m.*, santabárbara, *f.*, pañol de pólvora; — **puff,** borla o mota de empolvarse; —, *vt.* pulverizar; empolvar.

powdered, *adj.* en polvo, pulverizado.

powdery, *adj.* polvoriento.

power, *n.* poder, *m.*; potestad, *f.*; imperio, *m.*; potencia, *f.*; autoridad, *f.*; valor, *m.*; fuerzas militares; — **dive,** (aer.) picada a todo motor; — **drill,** taladradora de fuerza; **in** —, en el poder; — **of attorney,** carta poder, poder, *m.*; — **plant,** casa de máquinas, de calderas, de fuerza motriz; motor, *m.*; (auto.) motor y sus accesorios; **the** —**s that be,** los superiores, los que dominan; **to grant** — **of attorney,** dar poder.

powerboat, *n.* bote impulsado por un motor, bote automóvil.

powerful, *adj.* poderoso; —**ly,** *adv.* poderosamente, con mucha fuerza.

powerhouse, *n.* central, *f.*; casa de máquinas, de calderas o de fuerza motriz.

powerless, *adj.* impotente.

powwow, *n.* conjuración; reunión de jefes de partidos; —, *vi.* conjurar; reunirse.

pox, *n.* viruelas, *f. pl.*; **chicken** —, viruelas locas; **cow** —, vacuna, *f.*

pp.: pages, págs. páginas; **past participle,** p. pdo. participio pasado.

p. p.: parcel post, paquete postal; **past participle,** p. pdo. participio pasado; **postpaid,** p. p. porte pagado.

ppr., p. pr. present participle, p. pr. participio presente.

pr.: pair, par; **present,** pr. presente; **price,** precio.

P. R. Puerto Rico, Puerto Rico.

practicability, *n.* factibilidad, *f.*

practicable, *adj.* practicable, factible; hacedero; —**bly,** *adv.* posiblemente, factiblemente.

practical, *adj.* práctico; — **joke,** chasco, *m.*, burla, *f.*, broma pesada; — **nurse,** enfermera práctica (sin graduar); —**ly,** *adv.* prácticamente.

practice, *n.* práctica, *f.*; uso, *m.*, costumbre, *f.*; —**s,** *n. pl.* intrigas, *f. pl.*; costumbres, *f. pl.*; —, *vt. and vi.* practicar, ejercer; ensayar.

practitioner, *n.* persona que ejerce una profesión; en "Ciencia Cristiana," persona autorizada para curar.

pragmatic, pragmatical, *adj.* pragmático; entremetido; —**ally,** *adv.* impertinentemente.

pragmatism, *n.* pragmatismo, *m.*

prairie, *n.* prado, *m.*, pampa, *f.*; — **chicken,** chocha, *f.*; — **dog,** especie de roedor americano, aranata, *f.*

praise, *n.* fama, *f.*; renombre, *m.*; alabanza, loa, *f.*; —, *vt.* celebrar, alabar, enaltecer, ensalzar.

praiseworthy, *adj.* digno de alabanza.

praline, *n.* especie de dulce de azúcar y nueces o almendras, almendra confitada.

prance, *vi.* cabriolar.

prank, *n.* travesura, extravagancia, *f.*

prase, *n.* (min.) prasio, *m.*

prate, *vt. and vi.* charlar, parlotear; —, *n.* parlería, charla.

prattle, *vi.* charlar, parlotear; —, *n.* parlería, charla, *f.*

pray, *vt. and vi.* suplicar, rogar, orar.

prayer, *n.* oración, súplica, *f.*; the **Lord's P**—, el Padre Nuestro; — **book,** libro de devociones; capitulario, *m.*; — **meeting,** reunión para orar en común.

preach, *vt. and vi.* predicar.

preacher, *n.* predicador, *m.*

preaching, *n.* predicación, *f.*

preamble, *n.* preámbulo, *m.*

prearrange, *vt.* preparar de antemano.

prebend, *n.* prebenda, *f.*

prebendary, *n.* prebendado, *m.*

precarious, *adj.* precario, incierto; —**ly,** *adv.* precariamente.

precariousness, *n.* incertidumbre, *f.*

precaution, *n.* precaución, *f.*

precautionary, *adj.* preventivo.

precede, *vt.* anteceder, preceder.

precedence, *n.* precedencia, *f.*

precedent, *adj.* precedente; —, *n.* precedente, *m.*

preceding, *adj.* precursor.

precept, *n.* precepto, *m.*

preceptor, *n.* preceptor, *m.*

precession, *n.* precesión, *f.*

precinct, *n.* límite, lindero, *m.*; barriada, *f.*; distrito electoral.

preciosity, *n.* refinamiento en el lenguaje.

precious, *adj.* precioso; — **stone,** piedra preciosa; —**ly,** *adv.* preciosamente.

precipice, *n.* precipicio, *m.*

precipitant, *adj.* precipitado; —, *n.* (chem.) precipitante, *m.*

precipitate, *vt.* precipitar; —, *vi.* precipitarse; —, *adj.* precipitado; —**ly,** *adv.*

precipitadamente; —, n. (chem.) precipitado, m.
precipitation, n. precipitación, inconsideración, f.
precipitous, adj. precipitoso.
précis, n. resumen, m.
precise, adj. preciso, exacto; **—ly,** adv. precisamente, exactamente.
precision, n. precisión, limitación exacta.
preclude, vt. prevenir, impedir, excluir.
preclusion, n. exclusión, f.
precocious, adj. precoz, temprano, prematuro.
precocity, n. precocidad, f.
preconceive, vt. opinar o imaginar con antelación, preconcebir.
preconception, n. idea preconcebida; prejuicio, m.
preconcert, vt. concertar, convenir o estipular de antemano.
precursive, adj. precursor.
precursor, n. precursor, ra.
pred. predicate, pred. predicado.
predatory, adj. rapaz, voraz.
predecessor, n. predecesor, ra, antecesor, ra.
predestination, n. predestinación, f.
predestine, vt. predestinar.
predetermination, n. predeterminación, f.
predetermine, vt. predeterminar.
predicament, n. predicamento, m., situación desagradable.
predicate, vt. predicar; afirmar; —, n. (gram.) atributo, predicado, m.
predication, n. predicación, f.; afirmación, f.
predicative, adj. profético.
predict, vt. predecir.
prediction, n. predicción, f.
predigest, vt. predigerir.
predilection, n. predilección, f.
predispose, vt. predisponer.
predisposed, adj. predispuesto.
predisposition, n. predisposición, f.
predominance, n. predominio, m.
predominant, adj. predominante.
predominate, vt. predominar.
predomination, n. predominio, m., superioridad, f.
pre-eminence, n. preeminencia, f.
pre-eminent, adj. preeminente.
pre-emption, n. compra de antemano.
preen, vt. limpiar, concertar y componer sus plumas las aves; componerse.
pre-establish, vt. preestablecer, establecer anticipadamente.
pre-exist, vi. preexistir.
pre-existence, n. preexistencia, f.
pref.: preface, prefacio; **preferred,** preferido; **prefix,** pref. prefijo.
prefabricate, vt. fabricar piezas intercambiables (de una casa, por ejemplo) de tal modo que la construcción consista sólo en armarlas.
preface, n. prefacio, preámbulo, prólogo, m.; —, vt. hacer un prólogo (a un libro, etc.)

prefatory, adj. preliminar.
prefect, n. prefecto, m.
prefecture, n. prefectura, f.
prefer, vt. preferir, proponer, presentar.
preferable, adj. preferible, preferente; **—bly,** adv. preferiblemente, de preferencia.
preference, n. preferencia, f.
preferential, adj. privilegiado; de preferencia.
preferment, n. promoción, f.; preferencia, f.
preferred, adj. preferente; predilecto; — **stock,** acciones preferidas o preferentes.
prefix, vt. prefijar; —, n. (gram.) prefijo, m.
pregnancy, n. preñez, gravidez, f.
pregnant, adj. preñada, encinta; fértil.
preheat, vt. calentar previamente.
prehensile, adj. prehensil.
prehistoric, adj. prehistórico.
prejudge, vt. juzgar provisionalmente, prejuzgar.
prejudice, n. prejuicio, daño, m.; preocupación, f.; —, vt. perjudicar, hacer daño; preocupar.
prejudicial, adj. perjudicial, dañoso.
prelacy, n. prelacía, f.
prelate, n. prelado, m.
prelim. preliminary, preliminar.
preliminary, adj. preliminar.
prelude, n. preludio, m.; —, vt. preludiar.
premature, adj. prematuro; **—ly,** adv. anticipadamente, prematuramente.
premedical, adj. preparatorio para el estudio de medicina.
premeditate, vi. premeditar.
premeditation, n. premeditación, f.
premier, n. primer ministro.
premiere, n. estreno, m.
premiership, n. dignidad y funciones de primer ministro.
premise, n. premisa, f.; predio rústico, predio urbano; **—s,** n. pl. premisas, f. pl.; —, vt. exponer premisas.
premium, n. premio, m.; remuneración, f.; prima, f.; **at a —,** a premio; muy valioso debido a su escasez.
premolar, n. colmillo, m.
premonition, n. presentimiento, m
premonitory, adj. preventivo.
prenatal, adj. antenatal.
preoccupation, n. anticipación de la adquisición; preocupación (del ánimo), f.
preoccupy, vt. preocupar.
preordain, vt. preordinar.
preordination, n. preordinación, f., determinación anterior.
prep.: preparatory, preparatorio; **preposition,** prep. preposición.
prepaid, adj. franco de porte, porte pagado.
preparation, n. preparación, f.; preparativo, m.
preparatory, adj. preparatorio.
prepare, vt. preparar; —, vi. prepararse; —, vt. and vi. disponer.
prepay, vt. franquear (una carta), pagar anticipadamente.

prepayment, *n.* franqueo o pago adelantado.

prepense, *adj.* (law) premeditado.

preponderance, *n.* preponderancia, *f.*

preponderant, *adj.* preponderante.

preponderate, *vt.* and *vi.* preponderar.

preposition, *n.* preposición, *f.*

prepositional, *adj.* prepositivo.

prepossessing, *adj.* atractivo.

prepossession, *n.* preocupación, *f.*; prevención, *f.*

preposterous, *adj.* prepóstero; absurdo; **—ly,** *adv.* al revés, sin razón.

prepuce, *n.* prepucio, *m.*

prerequisite, *n.* condición o requisito necesario; **—,** *adj.* exigido anticipadamente; necesario para el fin que uno se propone.

prerogative, *n.* prerrogativa, *f.*

Pres.: Presbyterian, Presbiteriano; **President,** Presidente.

pres. present, pte. presente.

presage, *n.* presagio, pronóstico, *m.*; **—,** *vt.* presagiar.

presbytery, *n.* presbiterio, *m.*, ábside, *m.* o *f.*

preschool, *adj.* preescolar.

prescience, *n.* presciencia, *f.*

prescient, *adj.* profético.

prescribe, *vt.* and *vi.* prescribir, ordenar; (med.) recetar.

prescription, *n.* prescripción, *f.*, receta medicinal.

presence, *n.* presencia, *f.*; porte, aspecto, *m.*; **— chamber,** sala de recibimiento; **— of mind,** serenidad de ánimo.

present, *n.* presente, regalo, *m.*; **given as a —,** regalado; **to make a — of,** regalar; **—,** *adj.* presente; **—ly,** *adv.* al presente, luego; **—,** *vt.* ofrecer, presentar; regalar; (law) acusar, denunciar; **to — oneself,** presentarse; **to — itself,** surgir; **to — oneself to view,** aparecerse.

presentable, *adj.* presentable, decente, decoroso.

presentation, *n.* presentación, *f.*

present-day, *adj.* corriente, de hoy, del presente.

presentiment, *n.* presentimiento, *m.*

presentment, *n.* presentación, *f.*

preservation, *n.* preservación, *f.*

preservative, *n.* and *adj.* preservativo, *m.*

preserve, *vt.* preservar, conservar; hacer conservas (de frutas, etc.); **to — with salt,** salpresar; **—,** *n.* conserva, confitura, *f.*; **—s,** *n. pl.* compota, *f.*

preserver, *n.* conservador, ra.

preside, *vi.* presidir; dirigir; llevar la batuta.

presidency, *n.* presidencia, *f.*

president, *n.* presidente, *m.*; rector, *m.*; rector de una escuela.

presidential, *adj.* presidencial.

press, *vt.* planchar; aprensar, apretar; oprimir, angustiar; compeler; importunar; estrechar; **—,** *vi.* apresurarse; agolparse la gente al rededor de una persona o cosa; **—,** *n.* prensa, *f.*; imprenta, *f.*; turba, muchedumbre, *f.*; armario, *m.*; **Associated P—,** Prensa Asociada; **— agent,** agente de publicidad, agente encargado de los anuncios teatrales; **— gang,** (naut.) ronda de matrícula.

pressed ham, *n.* jamón planchado.

pressing, *adj.* urgente; **—ly,** *adv.* urgentemente.

pressure, *n.* prensadura, *f.*; presión, *f.*; opresión, *f.*; **— cooker,** autoclave, *m.*, cocina de presión; **— gauge,** manómetro, *m.*; **— group,** minoría que en cuerpos legisladores ejerce presión por medios extraoficiales o inconfesables.

presswork, *n.* impresión, tirada, *f.*

prestidigitator, *n.* prestidigitador, ra.

prestige, *n.* prestigio, *m.*, reputación, fama, *f.*

presumable, *adj.* presumible.

presume, *vi.* presumir, suponer.

presumed, *adj.* presunto.

presumption, *n.* presunción, *f.*

presumptive, *adj.* presunto.

presumptuous, *adj.* presuntuoso; **—ly,** *adv.* presuntuosamente.

presuppose, *vt.* presuponer.

presupposition, *n.* presuposición, *f.*

pretend, *vt.* and *vi.* presumir; **—,** *vt.* pretender, simular.

pretender, *n.* pretendiente, *m.*

pretendingly, *adv.* presuntuosamente.

pretense, pretence, pretexto, *m.*; pretensión, *f.*

pretension, *n.* pretensión, *f.*

pretentious, *adj.* presumido, pretencioso, presuntuoso, vanidoso.

preterite, *n.* pretérito, *m.*

preternatural, *adj.* sobrenatural, inexplicable.

pretext, *n.* pretexto, socolor, viso, *m.*; **on —,** a título.

prettily, *adv.* bonitamente; agradablemente.

prettiness, *n.* belleza, *f.*

pretty, *adj.* hermoso, lindo, bien parecido, bonito; **—,** *adv.* algo, un poco, bastante.

pretzel, *n.* bizcocho duro y salado generalmente en forma de nudo.

prevail, *vi.* prevalecer, predominar, imperar.

prevailing, *adj.* dominante, prevaleciente (uso, costumbre, etc.).

prevalence, *n.* predominio, *m.*; superioridad, *f.*

prevalent, *adj.* prevaleciente, que existe extensamente; que sucede con frecuencia en determinado lugar.

prevaricate, *vi.* prevaricar; transgredir; mentir.

prevarication, *n.* prevaricación, transgresión, *f.*; mentira, *f.*

prevaricator, *n.* prevaricador, ra.

prevent, *vt.* prevenir; impedir; remediar.

prevention, *n.* prevención, *f.*

preventive, adj. preventivo; **—,** n. preventivo, preservativo, m.

preview, n. vista o examen de antemano.

previous, adj. previo; antecedente; **—ly,** adv. de antemano.

prevision, n. previsión, f.

prewar, adj. antebélico.

prey, n. botín, m.; rapiña, f.; presa, f.; **—,** vt. rapiñar, pillar, robar.

price, n. precio, premio, valor, m.; **best —,** **lowest —,** último precio; **cost —,** precio de costo; **fall in —s,** baja, f.; **fixed —,** precio fijo; **high —s,** carestía, f.; **ceiling,** límite máximo de precios; **— control,** control de precios; **— fixing,** fijación de precios; **— list,** lista de precios, tarifa, f.; **sale —,** precio de venta; **to set a —,** poner precio; **trade —,** precio de costo; **—,** vt. apreciar, valuar.

priceless, adj. inapreciable.

prick, vt. punzar, picar; apuntar; hincar; clavar; **—,** n. puntura, f.; picadura, f.; punzada, f.; pista, f.; pinchazo, m.

pricker, n. picador, m.

pricking, n. picadura, f.; punzada, f.; picada, f.; **—,** adj. picante.

prickle, n. pincho, m.; espina, f.

prickly, adj. espinoso; **— heat,** salpullido causado por el calor; **— pear,** higo chumbo o de pala.

pride, n. orgullo, m.; vanidad, f.; jactancia, f.; **—,** vi. jactarse; **to — oneself on,** enorgullecerse de; **to take — in,** preciarse de.

prier, n. atisbador, ra, acechador, ra.

priest, n. sacerdote, presbítero, cura, m.

priestess, n. sacerdotisa, f.

priesthood, n. sacerdocio, m.

priestly, adj. sacerdotal.

prig, n. persona pedante y remilgada; **—,** vt. and vi. suplicar, rogar.

priggish, adj. afectado.

prim, adj. peripuesto, afectado.

primacy, n. primacía, f.

prima donna, n. prima donna.

primarily, adv. primariamente, sobre todo.

primary, adj. primario, principal, primero; **— accent,** acento tónico; **— colors,** colores primitivos; **— education,** primera enseñanza; **— election,** elección primaria; **— school,** escuela primaria.

primate, n. primado, m.

prime, n. madrugada, alba, f.; (fig.) flor, nata, f.; primavera, f.; principio, m.; **—,** adj. primero; primoroso, excelente; **—,** vt. cebar; imprimir.

primer, n. cartilla para los niños; cebador, m.; (mil.) fulminante, m.

primeval, adj. primitivo.

priming, n. cebo, m.; imprimación, f.; cebadura (de una bomba), f.; **— coat,** primera mano; capa de imprimación.

primitive, adj. primitivo; **—ly,** adv. primitivamente.

primness, n. afectación, f.

primogeniture, n. primogenitura, f.

primordial, adj. primordial.

primrose, n. (bot.) primavera, f.; color amarillo rojizo.

prin. principal, pral. principal.

prince, n. príncipe, soberano, m.

princely, adj. principesco; **—,** adv. como un príncipe.

princess, n. princesa, f.

principal, adj. principal; **—ly,** adv. principalmente; **—,** n. principal, jefe, m.; rector, director (de un colegio), m.; capital (dinero empleado), m.

principality, n. principado, m.

principally, adv. principalmente, máxime.

principalship, n. oficio de director de escuelas primarias, dirección de escuelas.

principle, n. principio, m.; causa primitiva; fundamento, motivo, m.

print, vt. estampar, imprimir; **—,** n. impresión, estampa, edición, f.; impreso, m.; **out of —,** vendido, agotado (libros, etc.).

print. printing, imp. imprenta.

printed, adj. impreso; **— cotton,** zaraza, f.; **— goods,** estampados, m. pl.; **— matter,** impresos, m. pl.

printer, n. impresor, m.; **—'s devil,** aprendiz de impresor; **—'s ink,** tinta de imprenta; **—'s mark,** pie de imprenta; **—'s proof,** prueba de imprenta.

printing, n. tipografía, imprenta, f.; impresión, f.; **— office,** imprenta, f.; **— press,** prensa tipográfica.

printshop, n. imprenta, f.

prior, adj. anterior, precedente; **—,** n. prior (prelado), m.

prioress, n. priora, f.

priority, n. prioridad, prelación, antelación, f.

priory, n. priorato, m.

prism, n. prisma, m.

prismatic, adj. prismático.

prison, n. prisión, cárcel, f., presidio, m.

prisoner, n. prisionero, ra, cautivo, va.

pristine, adj. prístino, antiguo.

privacy, n. secreto, m.; retiro, m.

private, adj. secreto, privado; particular; **—,** n. (mil.) soldado raso; **in —,** secreto; **—ly,** adv. en secreto, en particular, privadamente.

privateer, n. corsario, m.

privation, n. privación, f.

privet, n. (bot.) ligustro, m., alheña, f.

privilege, n. privilegio, m.; **—,** vt. privilegiar.

privily, adv. secretamente, privadamente.

privy, adj. privado, secreto; confidente; **—,** n. secreta, letrina, f., retrete, m.

prize, n. premio, m.; precio, m.; presa, f.; **— fight,** pugilato, m.; **— ring,** plataforma, tribuna o cuadrángulo para un pugilato; **—,** vt. apreciar, valuar.

prizefighter, n. pugilista, boxeador, m.

pro, prep. para, pro; **—,** adj. en el lado afirmativo (de un debate, etc.); **—,** n. persona que toma el afirmativo (en algún debate, votación, etc.); **the —s and cons,** el pro y el contra.

probability, n. probabilidad, f.

probable, adj. probable, verisímil, verosímil; **—bly,** adv. probablemente.

probate, n. verificación de los testamentos; **—,** adj. testamentario.

probation, n. prueba, f.; examen, m.; libertad condicional; noviciado, m.

probationary, adj. probatorio.

probationer, n. novicio, m.; delincuente que disfruta de libertad condicional.

probe, n. (med.) tienta, f.; **—,** vt. tentar (alguna herida); sondar.

probity, n. probidad, sinceridad, f.; hombría de bien.

problem, n. problema, m.

problematic, adj. problemático.

problematical, adj. problemático; **—ly,** adv. problemáticamente.

proboscis, n. probóscide, trompa (del elefante), f.

procedure, n. procedimiento, m.; progreso, proceso, m.

proceed, vi. proceder; provenir; portarse; originarse; ponerse en marcha; **—s,** n. pl. producto, rédito, m.; resultado, m.; **gross —s,** producto íntegro; **net —s,** producto neto o líquido.

proceeding, n. procedimiento, m.; proceso, m.; conducta, f.; **—s,** n. pl. actas, f. pl.; expediente, m.; memoria o informe (de una conferencia, etc.).

process, n. proceso, m.; procedimiento, m.; progreso, m.; **—,** vt. fabricar, tratar o preparar con un método especial.

procession, n. procesión, f.

processional, adj. procesional; **—,** n. procesionario, m.

processor, n. el que beneficia productos agrícolas para darles la forma que requieren los mercados.

proclaim, vt. proclamar; publicar.

proclamation, n. proclamación, f.; decreto, bando, m.; pregón, m.; cedulón, m.

proclivity, n. propensión, inclinación, f.

proconsul, n. procónsul, m.

procrastinate, vt. diferir, retardar.

procrastination, n. dilación, tardanza, f.

procrastinator, n. persona morosa; persona que todo lo deja para otra ocasión.

proctor, n. procurador, m.; juez escolástico.

proctorship, n. procuraduría, f.

procurable, adj. asequible.

procurator, n. procurador, m.

procure, vt. procurar.

procurement, n. procuración, f.

prodigal, adj. pródigo; derramador; **—ly,** adv. pródigamente; **—,** n. disipador, ra, derramador, ra.

prodigality, n. prodigalidad, f.

prodigious, adj. prodigioso; **—ly,** adv. prodigiosamente.

prodigy, n. prodigio, m.

produce, vt. producir, criar; rendir; causar; **—,** n. producto, m.

producer, n. productor, ra.

product, n. producto, m.; obra, f.; efecto, m.

production, n. producción, f.; producto, m.; **— cost,** costo de fabricación o de producción.

productive, adj. productivo.

productiveness, n. producibilidad, fertilidad, fecundidad, f.

Prof., prof. professor, Prof. profesor.

profanation, n. profanación, f.

profane, adj. profano; **—ly,** adv. profanamente; **—,** vt. profanar.

profanity, n. blasfemia, impiedad, f., lenguaje profano.

profess, vt. profesar; ejercer; declarar.

professedly, adv. declaradamente; públicamente.

profession, n. profesión, f.

professional, adj. profesional.

professor, n. profesor, ra, catedrático, m.

professorate, n. profesorado, m.

professorship, n. profesorado, m.; cátedra, f.

proffer, vt. proponer, ofrecer; **—,** n. oferta, f.

proficiency, n. aprovechamiento, m.; habilidad, f.

proficient, adj. proficiente, adelantado.

profile, n. perfil, m.

profit, n. ganancia, f.; provecho, m.; ventaja, f.; utilidad, f.; **net —,** ganancia líquida; **— and loss,** ganancias y pérdidas, lucros y daños; **— sharing,** distribución de la ganancia entre los empleados; **—,** vt. and vi. aprovechar, servir, ser útil; adelantar; **—,** vi. aprovecharse; **—,** vt. beneficiar; **to — by,** beneficiarse con.

profitable, adj. provechoso, ventajoso; productivo; **—bly,** adv. provechosamente.

profiteer, vi. usurar, usurear, explotar; **—,** n. usurero, ra, explotador, ra.

profligacy, n. perversidad, disolución, f., relajación de costumbres; desarreglo, m.

profligate, adj. licencioso, perdido; **—ly,** adv. disolutamente.

pro forma invoice, n. factura o cuenta simulada.

profound, adj. profundo; **—ly,** adv. profundamente.

profundity, n. profundidad, f.

profuse, adj. profuso, pródigo; **—ly,** adv. profusamente.

profusion, n. prodigalidad, f.; abundancia, profusión, f.

progenitor, n. progenitor, ra.

progeny, n. progenie, casta, f.

prognosis, n. (med.) pronóstico, m.; predicción, f.

prognostic, n. pronóstico, m.

prognosticate, vt. pronosticar.

prognostication, n. pronosticación, f.; pronóstico, m.

program, programme, n. programa, m.

progress, n. progreso, m.; adelanto, m.; viaje, curso, m.; **—,** vi. progresar.

progression, *n.* progresión, *f.*; adelantamiento, *m.*

progressive, *adj.* progresivo; **—ly,** *adv.* progresivamente.

prohibit, *vt.* prohibir, vedar; impedir.

prohibition, *n.* prohibición, *f.*; auto prohibitorio.

prohibitionist, *n.* prohibicionista, *m.* y *f.*

prohibitive, prohibitory, *adj.* prohibitivo.

project, *vt.* proyectar, trazar; **—,** *n.* proyecto, *m.*

projectile, *n.* proyectil, *m.*

projecting, *adj.* saliente.

projection, *n.* proyección, *f.*; proyectura, *f.*

projector, *n.* proyectista, proyector, *m.*, aparato de proyección.

proletarian, *n.* and *adj.* proletario, ria.

proletariat, *n.* proletariado, *m.*

prolific, *adj.* prolífico, fecundo.

prolix, *adj.* prolijo, difuso, nimio.

prolixity, *n.* prolijidad, *f.*

prologue, *n.* prólogo, *m.*

prolong, *vt.* prolongar; diferir; prorrogar.

prolongation, *n.* prolongación, dilatación, *f.*

promenade, *vi.* pasearse; **—,** *n.* paseo, *m.*

promenader, *n.* paseante, *m.* y *f.*

prominence, *n.* prominencia, eminencia, *f.*

prominent, *adj.* prominente; saledizo; conspicuo; **to be —,** sobresalir.

promiscuous, *adj.* promiscuo; **—ly,** *adv.* promiscuamente.

promise, *n.* promesa, *f.*; prometido, *m.*; **—,** *vt.* prometer.

promising, *adj.* prometedor.

promissory, *adj.* promisorio; **— note,** pagaré, *m.*

promontory, *n.* promontorio, *m.*

promote, *vt.* promover.

promoter, *n.* promotor, promovedor, *m.*

promotion, *n.* promoción, *f.*

prompt, *adj.* pronto; constante; **—ly,** *adv.* prontamente, con toda precisión; pronto; **—,** *vt.* sugerir, insinuar; apuntar (en el teatro).

prompter, *n.* apuntador de teatro.

promptitude, promptness, *n.* prontitud, presteza, prisa, *f.*

promulgate, *vt.* promulgar, publicar.

promulgation, *n.* promulgación, *f.*

pron.: pronoun, pron. pronombre; **pronounced,** se pronuncia.

prone, *adj.* prono, inclinado.

proneness, *n.* inclinación, propensión, *f.*

prong, *n.* púa, *f.*; dientes de una horca de labrador.

pronominal, *adj.* pronominal.

pronoun, *n.* pronombre, *m.*

pronounce, *vt.* pronunciar; recitar.

pronouncement, *n.* declaración formal, anuncio oficial.

pronto, *adv.* pronto.

pronunciation, *n.* pronunciación, *f.*

proof, *n.* prueba, *f.*; **—,** *adj.* impenetrable; de prueba.

proofread, *vt.* corregir pruebas.

proofreader, *n.* corrector o correctora de pruebas.

prop, *vt.* sostener; apuntalar; **—,** *n.* apoyo, puntal, *m.*; sostén, *m.*

propaganda, *n.* propaganda, *f.*

propagate, *vt.* propagar; **—,** *vi.* propagarse.

propagation, *n.* propagación, *f.*

propel, *vt.* impeler.

propeller, *n.* propulsor, *m.*; hélice, *f.*; **— blade,** segmento o paleta de hélice.

propensity, *n.* propensión, tendencia, *f.*

proper, *adj.* propio; conveniente; exacto; decente; debido; **in — form,** en forma debida; **—ly,** *adv.* propiamente, justamente.

property, *n.* propiedad, *f.*, bien, *m.*; peculiaridad, cualidad, *f.*

prophecy, *n.* profecía, *f.*

prophesy, *vt.* profetizar; predicar.

prophet, *n.* profeta, *m.*

prophetess, *n.* profetisa, *f.*

prophetic, *adj.* profético; **—ally,** *adv.* proféticamente.

prophylactic, *n.* profiláctico, *m.*

prophylaxis, *n.* (med.) profilaxis, *f.*

propinquity, *n.* propincuidad, proximidad, *f.*; parentesco, *m.*

propitiate, *vi.* propiciar.

propitiation, *n.* propiciación, *f.*

propitiatory, *adj.* propiciatorio.

propitious, *adj.* propicio, favorable; **—ly,** *adv.* propiciamente.

proponent, *n.* proponente, *m.* y *f.*

proportion, *n.* proporción, *f.*; simetría, *f.*; **in —,** a prorrata; **—,** *vt.* proporcionar.

proportionable, proportional, *adj.* proporcional, proporcionable.

proposal, *n.* propuesta, proposición, *f.*; oferta, *f.*

propose, *vt.* proponer.

proposition, *n.* proposición, propuesta, *f.*

propound, *vt.* proponer; sentar una proposición.

proprietary, *adj.* propietario; **—,** *n.* dueño, ña, propietario, ria.

proprietor, *n.* propietario, ria, dueño, ña.

proprietress, *n.* propietaria, *f.*

propriety, *n.* propiedad, *f.*

propulsion, *n.* propulsión, *f.*

prorata, *adv.* en proporción.

prorate, *vt.* prorratear.

prorogation, *n.* prorrogación, *f.*

prorogue, *vt.* aplazar o suspender la sesión (de una asamblea legislativa).

prosaic, *adj.* prosaico, en prosa.

proscenium, *n.* proscenio, *m.*

proscribe, *vt.* proscribir.

proscription, *n.* proscripción, *f.*

prose, *n.* prosa, *f.*; **— writer,** prosador, *m.*

prosecute, *vt.* proseguir.

prosecution, *n.* prosecución, *f.*

prosecutor, *n.* acusador, *m.*

proselyte, *n.* prosélito, *m.*

prosody, *n.* prosodia, *f.*

prospect, *n.* perspectiva, *f.*; esperanza, *f.*

prospective, *adj.* prevenido; en perspectiva; próvido.

prospectus, *n.* prospecto, *m.*

prosper, *vt.* and *vi.* prosperar.

prosperity, *n.* prosperidad, bonanza, *f.*

prosperous, *adj.* próspero, feliz; —**ly,** *adv.* prósperamente.

prostitute, *vt.* prostituir; —, *n.* prostituta, *f.*

prostitution, *n.* prostitución, *f.*

prostrate, *adj.* postrado, prosternado; —, *vt.* postrar; —, *vi.* prosternarse, postrarse.

prostrated, *adj.* decaído, postrado.

prostration, *n.* postración, adinamia, *f.*; colapso, *m.*

Prot. Protestant, Protestante.

protagonist, *n.* protagonista, *m.* y *f.*

protean, *adj.* proteiforme, proteico.

protect, *vt.* proteger, amparar.

protection, *n.* protección, *f.*

protectionism, *n.* proteccionismo, *m.*

protective, *adj.* protector; protectorio; — **coloring,** coloración protectora.

protector, *n.* protector, ra, patrono, na, defensor, ra.

protectorate, *n.* protectorado, *m.*

protégé, protégée, *n.* protegido, da; paniaguado, da.

protein, *n.* proteína, *f.*

Proterozoic, *adj.* (geol.) proterozoico.

protest, *vt.* and *vi.* protestar; —, *n.* protesta, *f.*; (com.) protesto (de una libranza), *m.*

Protestant, *n.* and *adj.* protestante, *m.* y *f.*

Protestantism, *n.* protestantismo, *m.*

protestation, *n.* protestación, *f.*; protesta, *f.*

protochloride, *n.* (chem.) protocloruro, *m.*

protocol, *n.* protocolo, *m.*

proton, *n.* (elec.) proton, *m.*

protoplasm, *n.* protoplasma, *m.*

prototype, *n.* prototipo, *m.*

protozoan, *n.* protozoario, *m.*

protract, *vt.* prolongar, dilatar, diferir.

protraction, *n.* prolongación, dilatación, *f.*

protractor, *n.* transportador, *m.*

protrude, *vt.* empujar; impeler; —, *vi.* sobresalir.

protuberance, *n.* protuberancia, *f.*

protuberant, *adj.* prominente, saliente.

proud, *adj.* soberbio, orgulloso; —**ly,** *adv.* soberbiamente.

prov. province, prov.ᵃ provincia.

prove, *vt.* probar, justificar; experimentar; —, *vi.* resultar; salir (bien o mal).

provender, *n.* forraje, *m.*

proverb, *n.* proverbio, *m.*

proverbial, *adj.* proverbial; —**ly,** *adv.* proverbialmente.

provide, *vt.* proveer, surtir; proporcionar; **to — oneself with,** proveerse de.

provided, *adj.* provisto; — **that,** con tal que, a condición de que, dado que, si.

providence, *n.* providencia, *f.*; economía, *f.*

provident, *adj.* próvido; providente; —**ly,** *adv.* próvidamente.

providential, *adj.* providencial; —**ly,** *adv.* providencialmente.

provider, *n.* proveedor, ra.

province, *n.* provincia, *f.*; obligación particular; jurisdicción, *f.*

provincial, *adj.* provincial; —, *n.* provinciano, na.

provision, *n.* provisión, *f.*; precaución, *f.*; —**s,** *n.* *pl.* comestibles, *m.* *pl.*

provisional, *adj.* provisional; —**ly,** *adv* provisionalmente.

proviso, *n.* estipulación, *f.*

provisory, *adj.* provisional, condicional.

provocation, *n.* provocación, *f.*; apelación, *f.*

provocative, *adj.* provocativo; estimulante; —, *n.* excitante, *m.*

provoke, *vt.* provocar; apelar.

provoking, *adj.* provocativo; —**ly,** *adv.* de un modo provocativo.

provost, *n.* preboste, *m.*

prow, *n.* (naut.) proa, *f.*

prowess, *n.* proeza, valentía, *f.*

prowl, *vi.* andar en busca de pillaje; rondar, vagar; rastrear.

prowler, *n.* ladrón, vago, *m.*

prox. of the next month, pmo. (mes) próximo.

proximate, *adj.* próximo; —**ly,** *adv.* próximamente.

proximity, *n.* proximidad, cercanía, *f.*

proxy, *n.* procuración, *f.*; procurador, *m.*; apoderado, da; **by —,** por poder.

prude, *n.* mojigato, ta.

prudence, *n.* prudencia, *f.*; precaución, *f.*

prudent, *adj.* prudente, circunspecto, cauteloso, cauto; —**ly,** *adv.* con juicio.

prudential, *adj.* juicioso.

prudery, *n.* gazmoñería, mojigatez, *f.*

prudish, *adj.* gazmoño, mojigato.

prune, *vt.* podar; escamondar los árboles; —, *n.* ciruela seca, ciruela pasa.

pruning, *n.* poda, *f.*; — **hook,** — **knife,** podadera, *f.*

pruriency, *n.* comezón, *f.*; prurito, *m.*; lascividad, *f.*

prurient, *adj.* lascivo; anheloso.

prussiate, *n.* (chem.) prusiato, *m.*

prussic, *adj.* prúsico; — **acid,** ácido prúsico.

pry, *vi.* espiar, acechar; curiosear; alzaprimar.

P.S. postscript, P.D. posdata.

psalm, *n.* salmo, *m.*

psalter, *n.* salterio, libro de salmos.

psaltery, *n.* (mus.) salterio, *m.*

pseudonym, *n.* seudónimo, *m.*

pseudonymous, *adj.* seudónimo.

pshaw! *interj.* ¡vaya! ¡fuera! ¡quita! ¡bah!

P. S. T. Pacific Standard Time, hora normal de la región del Pacífico (E. U. A.)

psychiatric, *adj.* psiquiátrico.

psychiatrist, *n.* psicópata, *m.* y *f.*, psiquiatra, *m.* y *f.*

psychiatry, *n.* psiquiatría, *f.*

psychic, *adj.* psíquico.

psychoanalysis, *n.* psicoanálisis, *m.*

psychoanalyst, *n.* psicoanalista, *m.* y *f.*

psychoanalyze, *vt.* psicoanalizar.
psychologic, psychological, *adj.* psicológico.
psychologist, *n.* psicólogo, ga.
psychology, *n.* psicología, *f.*
psychopathic, *adj.* psicopático.
psychosis, *n.* (med.) psicosis, *f.*
psychotherapy, *n.* psicoterapia, *f.*
pt.: part, p.ᵗᵉ parte; **payment,** pago; **pint,** pinta; **point,** pto. punto; **port,** pto. puerto.
P. T. A. Parent-Teacher Association, Asociación de Padres y Maestros.
ptomaine, ptomain, *n.* tomaína, *f.;* — **poison,** envenenamiento por tomaínas.
pub.: public, público; **publisher,** Ed. editor.
puberty, *n.* pubertad, *f.*
public, *adj.* público; común; notorio; — **official,** funcionario público; — **relations,** relaciones con el público; — **utility,** empresa pública, empresa de servicios públicos; — **works,** obras públicas; —**ly,** *adv.* públicamente; —, *n.* público, *m.*
publican, *n.* publicano, *m.*; tabernero, *m.*
publication, *n.* publicación, *f.*
publicist, *n.* publicista, *m.* y *f.*
publicity, *n.* publicidad, *f.*
publicize, *vt.* publicar.
public opinion, *n.* opinión pública.
public school, *n.* escuela pública.
publish, *vt.* publicar, dar a la prensa.
publisher, *n.* publicador, editor, *m.*
publishing, *n.* publicación, *f.;* —, *adj.* editor, editorial; — **house,** casa editorial, casa editora.
pucker, *vt.* arrugar, hacer pliegues.
pudding, *n.* pudín, *m.*; morcilla, *f.*
puddle, *n.* lodazal, cenagal, *m.*; —, *vt.* enlodar; enturbiar el agua con lodo.
pudgy, *adj.* regordete.
puerile, *adj.* pueril.
puff, *n.* bufido, soplo, *m.*; bocanada, *f.*; **powder** —, mota para polvos, mota para empolvarse; —, *vt.* hinchar; soplar; ensoberbecer; —, *vi.* inflarse; bufar; resoplar.
puffiness, *n.* hinchazón, *f.*
puffy, *adj.* hinchado, entumecido.
pug, *n.* variedad de perro muy pequeño de pelo corto; — **nose,** nariz respingona.
pugilism, *n.* pugilato, boxeo, *m.*
pugilist, *n.* púgil, boxeador, *m.*
pugnacious, *adj.* belicoso, pugnaz; —**ly,** *adv.* belicosamente.
pulchritude, *n.* belleza, *f.*
pull, *vt.* tirar, halar; coger; rasgar, desgarrar; **to** — **off,** arrancar; **to** — **out,** sacar; —, *n.* tirón, *m.*; sacudida, *f.*; influencia, *f.*
puller, *n.* el que saca; **nail** —, sacaclavos, *m.*
pullet, *n.* polla, *f.*
pulley, *n.* polea, garrucha, *f.,* cuadernal, *m.*; (naut.) motón, *m.*
pulmonary, pulmonic, *adj.* pulmonar, pulmoníaco.

pulmotor, *n.* espirómetro, *m.,* pulmotor para respiración artificial.
pulp, *n.* pulpa, *f.*; carne (de fruta), *f.*
pulpit, *n.* púlpito, *m.*
pulpy, *adj.* pulposo, mollar.
pulpwood, *n.* madera de pulpa.
pulque, *n.* pulque, *m.*
pulsate, *vi.* pulsar, latir.
pulsation, *n.* pulsación, *f.*
pulse, *n.* pulso, *m.*; legumbres, *f. pl.*
pulverization, *n.* pulverización, *f.*
pulverize, *vt.* pulverizar.
pulverizer, *n.* pulverizador, *m.*
puma, *n.* (zool.) puma, *f.*
pumice, *n.* piedra pómez, *f.*
pump, *n.* bomba, *f.*; escarpín, *m.,* zapatilla, *f.*; **air** —, máquina neumática; **bilge** —, bomba de carena; **circulating** —, bomba de circulación; **feed** —, bomba de alimentación; **tire** —, bomba para neumáticos; **vacuum** —, bomba de vacío; —, *vt.* dar a la bomba; sondear; sonsacar.
pumper, *n.* bombero, *m.*; sonsacador, ra.
pumping, *n.* bombeo, *m.*
pumpkin, *n.* calabaza, *f.*
pun, *n.* equívoco, chiste, *m.*; juego de palabras; —, *vi.* jugar del vocablo, hacer juego de palabras.
punch, *n.* punzón, *m.*; puñetazo, *m.*; sacabocados, *m.*; ponche, *m.*; —, *vt.* punzar, horadar, taladrar; dar puñetazos.
puncheon, *n.* punzón, *m.*; cuño, *m.*; pipa, *f.*, tonel, *m.*; pipa (medida), *f.*
punchinello, *n.* polichinela, bufón, *m.*
punctilio, *n.* puntillo, *m.*
punctilious, *adj.* puntilloso.
punctual, *adj.* puntual, exacto; —**ly,** *adv.* puntualmente.
punctuality, *n.* exactitud, puntualidad, *f.*
punctuate, *vi.* puntuar.
punctuation, *n.* puntuación, *f.*
puncture, *n.* puntura, *f.*; pinchazo, *m.,* pinchadura, *f.*; perforación, *f.*; —, *vt.* perforar.
pundit, *n.* erudito, sabio, *m.*
pungency, *n.* acrimonia, *f.*; picante, *m.*
pungent, *adj.* picante, acre, mordaz.
Punic, *adj.* púnico, pérfido.
punish, *vt.* castigar, penar.
punishable, *adj.* punible.
punishment, *n.* castigo, *m.*; pena, *f.*
punitive, *adj.* punitivo, penal.
punk, *n.* yesca, *f.*; —, *adj.* (coll.) muy malo.
punster, *n.* dichero, ra; persona adicta a a hacer juego de palabras.
punt, *n.* barco llano; (football) puntapié que se da al balón; —, *vt.* apuntar, parar (poner el dinero a las cartas); (football) dar puntapié al balón.
punter, *n.* apuntador (en juegos de azar), *m.*
puny, *adj.* insignificante, pequeño; débil.
pup, *n.* cachorrillo, *m.*; —, *vi.* parir la perra.
pupa, *n.* crisálida, *f.*
pupil, *n.* (anat.) pupila, *f.*; pupilo, *m.*; discípulo, la; — **of the eye,** niña del ojo.

pupillary, *adj.* pupilar.
puppet, *n.* títere, muñeco, *m.*; — **show,** representación de títeres.
puppy, *n.* perrillo, cachorro, *m.*
purblind, *adj.* miope, cegato.
purchase, *vt.* comprar; mercar; **to — in bulk,** comprar en bulto; —, *n.* compra, *f.*; adquisición, *f.*
purchaser, *n.* comprador, ra.
pure, *adj.* puro, mero; —**ly,** *adv.* puramente.
purée, *n.* puré, *m.*
purgation, purging, *n.* purgación, *f.*
purgative, *adj.* purgativo.
purgatory, *n.* purgatorio, *m.*
purge, *vt.* purgar; —, *n.* purga, purgación, *f.*; catártico, *m.*
purification, *n.* purificación, *f.*
purifier, *n.* purificador, depurador, *m.*
purify, *vt.* purificar; —, *vi.* purificarse.
purifying, *adj.* purificativo, depurativo.
purist, *n.* purista, *m.* y *f.*
puritan, *n.* puritano, na.
puritanism, *n.* puritanismo, *m.*
purity, *n.* pureza, *f.*
purl, *n.* murmullo, *m.*; variedad de punto de tejido con agujas; —, *vi.* murmurar; orlar, adornar con flecos; hacer cierto punto en el tejido con agujas.
purlieu, *n.* comarca, *f.*
purloin, *vt.* hurtar, robar.
purple, *adj.* purpúreo, morado; cárdeno; —, *n.* púrpura, *f.*; —, *vi.* ponerse morado; —, *vt.* teñir de color morado.
purplish, *adj.* purpurino.
purport, *n.* designio, *m.*; contenido, *m.*; —, *vt.* significar, designar, implicar, dar a entender.
purpose, *n.* intención, *f.*; designio, proyecto, *m.*; objetivo, *m.*; vista, *f.*; mira, *f.*; efecto, *m.*; **on — ,** de propósito; **to no —,** inútilmente; **to the —,** al propósito, de perilla; **to what — is that?** ¿a qué viene eso? —, *vt.* and *vi.* proponerse, resolver, intentar.
purr, *vi.* ronronear (aplícase a los gatos).
purse, *n.* bolsa, *f.*, portamonedas, *m.*; —, *vt.* embolsar.
purser, *n.* sobrecargo de un navío, sobrecargo, *m.*
purslane, *n.* (bot.) verdolaga, *f.*
pursuance, *n.* prosecución, *f.*
pursuant, *adj.* hecho en consecuencia de, de acuerdo con.
pursue, *vt.* and *vi.* perseguir; seguir; acosar; continuar.
pursuer, *n.* perseguidor, ra.
pursuit, *n.* perseguimiento, *m.*; ocupación, *f.*; persecución, *f.*; — **plane,** avión de combate; caza, *f.*
pursy, *adj.* asmático; regordete.
purulence, *n.* purulencia, *f.*
purulent, *adj.* purulento.
purvey, *vt.* and *vi.* proveer; procurar.
purveyance, *n.* abasto, *m.*; provisión, *f.*
purveyor, *n.* provisor, ra, abastecedor, ra,

surtidor, ra.
push, *vt.* empujar; empellar; apretar; —, *vi.* hacer esfuerzos; **to — ahead, to — through,** pujar; —, *n.* impulso, *m.*; empujón, *m.*; momento crítico; esfuerzo, *m.*; asalto, *m.*; — **button,** botón de contacto, botón interruptor.
pushball, *n.* pelota grande y pesada; juego en el cual se emplea esta especie de pelota.
pushing, *adj.* emprendedor, agresivo.
pusillanimity, *n.* pusilanimidad, *f.*
pusillanimous, *adj.* pusilánime.
puss, *n.* miz (voz de cariño para el gato), *m.*
pussy willow, *n.* pequeño sauce americano.
pustule, *n.* pústula, bubilla, pupa, *f.*
put, *vt.* poner, colocar; proponer; imponer, obligar; **to — forth shoots,** brotar; **to — in order,** orillar, poner en orden; **to — in writing,** poner por escrito; **to — on shoes,** calzar; **to — over,** sobreponer; **to — together,** confeccionar, armar.
putative, *adj.* putativo, reputado.
put-off, *n.* retardo, *m.*; dilatación, *f.*
put-on, *n.* engaño, *m.*
putrefaction, *n.* putrefacción, *f.*
putrefy, *vi.* pudrirse.
putrescence, *n.* pudrición, *f.*
putrescent, putrid, *adj.* podrido, pútrido.
putridity, putridness, *n.* podredumbre, pudrición, *f.*
putt (golf), *vt.* tirada que hace rodar la pelota al agujero o cerca de él.
puttee, *n.* polaina, *f.*
putting green, *n.* (golf) terreno nivelado y cubierto de hierba que circunda cada agujero.
putty, *n.* almáciga, masilla, *f.*; cemento, *m.*; —, *vt.* enmasillar.
puzzle, *n.* acertijo, enigma, rompecabezas, *m.*; perplejidad, *f.*; **jigsaw —,** rompecabezas, *m.*; —, *vt.* embrollar, confundir; —, *vi.* confundirse.
Pvt. Private, privado; soldado raso.
PWA Public Works Administration, Administración de Obras Públicas.
pyemia, *n.* envenenamiento de la sangre.
pygmy, *n.* = **pigmy.**
pyjamas, *n. pl.* pijamas, *m. pl.*
pylon, *n.* mástil, pilón, *m.*; (aer.) poste de anclaje; torre de señal; estructura que sostiene la hélice.
pylorus, *n.* píloro, *m.*
pyorrhea, *n.* (med.) piorrea, *f.*
pyramid, *n.* pirámide, *f.*
pyramidal, *adj.* piramidal.
pyre, *n.* pira, hoguera, *f.*
pyrex, *n.* vidrio resistente al calor.
pyrite, *n.* pirita, *f.*
pyromania, *n.* piromanía, *f.*, monomanía incendiaria.
pyrotechnics, *n. pl.* pirotécnica, *f.*
pyroxyline, *n.* piroxilina, *f.*
python, *n.* pitón atigrado.
pythoness, *n.* pitonisa, *f.*
pyx, *n.* píxide, *f.*, copón, *m.*

Q

Q.: quarto, en 4.º en cuarto; **queen,** reina; **question,** P. pregunta; **quire,** mano de papel.

Q.E.D. which was to be proved, Q.E.D. lo que se trataba de demostrar.

Q.M. quartermaster, (mil.) comisario.

Q.M.G. Quartermaster General, (mil.) intendente de ejército.

qr.: quarter, cuarta parte; **quire,** mano de papel.

qt.: quantity, cantidad; **quart,** cuarto de galón.

qtr. quarter, trimestre, cuarta parte.

quack, *vi.* graznar (como un pato); —, *n.* charlatán, *m.*

quackery, *n.* charlatanería, *f.*

Quadragesima, *n.* cuadragésima, cuaresma, *f.*

quadrangle, *n.* cuadrángulo, *m.*

quadrant, *n.* cuadrante, *m.*; (naut.) octante, *m.*

quadratic, *adj.* (math.) de segundo grado.

quadrennial, *adj.* cuadrienal.

quadrilateral, *adj.* cuadrilátero.

quadrille, *n.* contradanza, *f.*

quadroon, *n.* cuarterón, *m.*

quadruped, *n.* cuadrúpedo, *m.*

quadruple, *adj.* cuádruplo.

quaff, *vt.* beber a grandes tragos; —, *vi.* beber demasiado.

quagmire, *n.* tremedal, *m.*

quail, *n.* codorniz, *f.*

quaint, *adj.* extraño pero agradable por su sabor de antaño; **—ly,** *adv.* en forma extraña pero agradable.

quaintness, *n.* elegancia, *f.*; delicadeza, *f.*

quake, *vi.* temblar, tiritar; —, *n.* temblor, *m.*

Quaker, *n.* cuáquero, ra.

qualification, *n.* calificación, *f.*; requisito, *m.*

qualify, *vt.* calificar; modificar; templar; —, *vi.* habilitarse, llenar los requisitos.

qualitative, *adj.* cualitativo.

quality, *n.* calidad, *f.*; don, *m.*; condición, *f.*; prenda, *f.*; **average** —, calidad media.

qualm, *n.* deliquio, desmayo, *m.*; escrúpulo, *m.*

qualmish, *adj.* desfallecido, lánguido; escrupuloso.

quandary, *n.* incertidumbre, duda, *f.*

quantitative, *adj.* cuantitativo.

quantity, *n.* cantidad, *f.*

quantum, *n.* tanto, *m.*, cantidad, *f.*

quarantine, *n.* cuarentena, *f.*

quarrel, *n.* quimera, riña, pelea, contienda, *f.*; —, *vi.* reñir, disputar.

quarrelsome, *adj.* pendenciero, quimerista, peleador.

quarry, *n.* cantera, *f.*

quarrying, *n.* explotación de canteras.

quart, *n.* un cuarto de galón; cuarta (en el juego de los cientos), *f.*

quart. quarterly, trimestral, trimestralmente.

quartan, *n.* (med.) cuartana,· *f.*; —, *adj.* relativo al cuarto día; que sucede cada cuatro días.

quarter, *n.* cuarto, *m.*; cuarta parte; cuartel, *m.*; barriada, *f.*; barrio, *m.*; moneda de E.U.A. que equivale a 25 centavos de dólar; — **of an hour,** cuarto de hora; —, *vt.* cuartear; acuartelar; dividir en cuatro.

quarterback, *n.* (football) uno de los cuatro jugadores colocados detrás de la línea.

quarter-deck, *n.* (naut.) alcázar, *m.*

quarterly, *adj.* trimestral; —, *adv.* trimestralmente.

quartern, *n.* cuarta parte de un cuartillo.

quartet, *n.* (mus.) cuarteto, *m.*

quarto, *adj.* (print.) en cuarto; —, *n.* libro en cuarto.

quartz, *n.* (min.) cuarzo, *m.*

quash, *vt.* fracasar; cascar; anular, abrogar.

quasi, *adj.* and *adv.* casi, poco más o menos.

quaver, *n.* (mus.) corchea, *f.*; —, *vi.* gorgoritear, trinar; temblar.

quay, *n.* muelle, *m.*

Que. Quebec, Quebec.

quean, *n.* mujercilla, *f.*

queasiness, *n.* hastío, fastidio, *m.*; incomodidad, *f.*

queasy, *adj.* nauseabundo; fastidioso.

quebracho, *n.* (bot.) quebracho.

queen, *n.* reina, *f.*; dama (en el juego de ajedrez), *f.*

queenly, *adj.* majestuoso, como una reina.

queer, *adj.* ridículo; enrevesado; raro; **—ly,** *adv.* ridículamente; raramente.

queerness, *n.* rareza, *f.*; ridiculez, *f.*

quell, *vt.* subyugar, postrar, avasallar; mitigar.

quench, *vt.* apagar; extinguir, saciar.

querulous, *adj.* quejoso; **—ly,** *adv.* quejosamente.

querulousness, *n.* tendencia a quejarse.

query, *n.* cuestión, pregunta, *f.*; —, *vt.* preguntar.

quest, *n.* pesquisa, inquisición, *f.*; busca, *f.*

question, *n.* cuestión, *f.*; asunto, *m.*; duda, *f.*; pregunta, *f.*; **to ask a —,** hacer una pregunta; **to be a — of,** tratarse de; —, *vi.* cuestionar, preguntar; —, *vt.* dudar, desconfiar, poner en duda.

questionable, *adj.* cuestionable, dudoso.

questioner, *n.* inquiridor, ra, preguntador, ra.

questionnaire, *n.* cuestionario, *m.*

quetzal, *n.* (orn.) quetzal, *m.*; quetzal (unidad monetaria de Guatemala), *m.*

quibble, *n.* subterfugio, *m.*; evasiva, *f.*; —, *vi.* sutilizar; hacer uso de subterfugios.

quick, *adj.* vivo, viviente; veloz; ligero, pronto; ágil, ardiente, penetrante; **—ly,** *adv.* con presteza; —, *n.* carne viva; cosa viviente; parte vital.

quicken, *vt.* vivificar; acelerar; animar.

quicklime, *n.* cal viva.
quickness, *n.* ligereza, presteza, *f.*; actividad, *f.*; viveza, penetración, *f.*
quicksand, *n.* arena movediza.
quickset, *n.* plantón, *m.*; — **hedge,** seto vivo.
quicksilver, *n.* azogue, mercurio, *m.*
quick-tempered, *adj.* irascible, irritable, colérico.
quick-witted, *adj.* agudo, perspicaz.
quid, *n.* pedazo de tabaco para mascar.
quiddity, *n.* esencia de algo, quid, *m.*; sutileza, *f.*
quidnunc, *n.* persona chismosa, persona que quiere averiguarlo todo.
quiescence, *n.* quietud, *f.*, reposo, *m.*
quiescent, *adj.* quieto, descansado.
quiet, *adj.* quedo, quieto, tranquilo, callado; —, *n.* calma, serenidad, *f.*; —, *vt.* tranquilizar; —**ly,** *adv.* quietamente, tranquilamente.
quietness, quietude, *n.* quietud, tranquilidad, *f.*
quietus, *n.* finiquito, *m.*; muerte, *f.*
quill, *n.* pluma de ave; pluma (para escribir), *f.*; canilla, *f.*; — **driver,** escritor, *m.*; oficinista, *m.*
quilt, *n.* colcha, *f.*; **crazy** —, centón, *m.*
quince, *n.* (bot.) membrillo, *m.*; **preserved** —, carne de membrillo; — **tree,** membrillero, *m.*
quinine, *n.* chinchona, cincona, quinina, *f.*
quinquennial, *adj.* quinquenal.
quinsy, *n.* (med.) angina, esquinancia, *f.*
quint, *n.* quinta (en algunos juegos de naipes), *f.*
quintal, *n.* quintal, *m.*
quintessence, *n.* quinta esencia.
quintet, *n.* (mus.) quinteto, *m.*
quintuple, *adj.* quíntuplo.
quintuplet, *n.* quintupleto, *m.*
quip, *n.* indirecta, *f.*; —, *vt.* echar pullas.
quire, *n.* mano de papel.
quirk, *n.* desviación, *f.*; pulla, *f.*; sutileza, *f.*; rasgo (como en la escritura), *f.*
quisling, *n.* quisling, político de importancia que ayuda al enemigo a establecerse en su país, o que lo favorece de alguna manera.
quit, *vt.* descargar; desempeñar; absolver; **to** — **work,** dejar de trabajar; —, *vi.* desistir, dejar (de hacer algo); —, *adj.* libre, descargado.
quite, *adv.* totalmente, enteramente, absolutamente, bastante.
quittance, *n.* finiquito, *m.*; recompensa, *f.*
quitter, *n.* el que abandona una obra, un trabajo, etc.
quiver, *n.* aljaba, *f.*; temblor, tiritón, *m.*; —, *vi.* temblar, retemblar, blandir.
Quixote, Quijote.
quixotic, *adj.* quijotesco; — **person,** quijote, *m.*
quiz, *vt.* burlar, chulear; examinar; —, *n.* examen por medio de preguntas.
quoit, *n.* tejo, *m.*

quondam, *adj.* antiguo.
quorum, *n.* quórum, *m.*
quot. quotation, cita.
quota, *n.* cuota, *f.*; prorrata, *f.*
quotation, *n.* citación, cotización, cita, *f.*; **list of** —**s,** boletín de cotizaciones; — **marks,** comillas, *f. pl.*
quote, *vt.* citar; **to** — **(a price),** cotizar (precio).
quoth, *v. imp.* — **I,** dije yo; — **he,** dijo él.
quotidian, *adj.* cotidiano; —, *n.* calentura cotidiana.
quotient, *n.* cociente, *m.*; **intelligence** —, cociente de edad, cociente intelectual.
q.v. which see, q.v. véase.

R

R.: railroad, F.C. ferrocarril; **Republican,** Republicano; **right,** (theat.) Der. derecha; **river,** río; **royal,** R.[1] real (del rey).
r.: railroad, f.c. ferrocarril; **road,** camino; **rod,** pértica.
R.A.: Rear Admiral, contralmirante; **Royal Academy,** Real Academia.
rabbet, *n.* ranura, *f.*
rabbi, *n.* rabí, rabino, *m.*
rabbit, *n.* conejo, *m.*
rabble, *n.* gentuza, *f.*, gente baja.
rabid, *adj.* rabioso, furioso.
rabies, *n.* hidrofobia, *f.*
raccoon, *n.* (zool.) mapache, *m.*; — **skin,** mapache, *m.*
race, *n.* raza, casta, *f.*; carrera, corrida, *f.*; sabor rancio del vino; — **suicide,** suicidio de la raza; — **track,** corredera, pista, carrera, *f.*; —, *vi.* correr con mucha ligereza; (auto.) acelerar una máquina o un motor con carga disminuida.
racer, *n.* caballo de carrera; corredor, ra.
rachitis, *n.* (med.) raquitis, *f.*, raquitismo, *m.*
racial, *adj.* racial, de raza.
racism, *n.* racismo, *m.*
rack, *n.* tormento, *m.*; rueca, *f.*; morillos de asador; pesebre, *m.*; cremallera, *f.*; —, *vi.* atormentar; trasegar.
racket, *n.* baraúnda, confusión, *f.*; raqueta, *f.*; cualquier ardid fraudulento.
racketeer, *n.* individuo que recurre a amenazas o a la violencia para robar dinero; —, *vi.* robar dinero recurriendo a amenazas o violencia.
raconteur, *n.* cuentista, anecdotista, *m.* y *f.*
racquet, *n.* raqueta, *f.*
racy, *adj.* fresco, con su aroma natural (vino); picante, espiritoso.
radar, *n.* aparato radiofónico para determinar la presencia de aviones, barcos u obstáculos elevados y calcular la distancia a que se encuentran.
radial, *adj.* radial; — **engine,** motor de cilindros radiales, motor o máquina radial, motor en estrella.
radiance, *n.* brillo, esplendor, *m.*

radiant, *adj.* radiante, brillante; —, *n.* energía radiante.
radiate, *vi.* echar rayos, centellear.
radiation, *n.* irradiación, *f.*
radiator, *n.* calorífero, calentador, *m.*, estufa, *f.*; (auto.) radiador, *m.*; **steam** —, calorífero de vapor.
radical, *adj.* radical; —, *n.* (math.) radical, *m.*; —**ly,** *adv.* radicalmente.
radicalism, *n.* radicalismo, *m.*
radio, *n.* radio, *m.*, radiocomunicación, *f.*; **electrical** — **transcription,** radiodifusión por fonógrafo; — **amateur,** radioaficionado, da; — **amplifier,** radioamplificador, *m.*; — **announcer,** prologuista o anunciador de radio; — **beacon,** fanal de radio; — **beam,** radiación rectilínea para orientar aeroplanos; — **broadcasting station,** estación radiodifusora; — **earphones,** audífonos, *m. pl.*; — **hookup,** circuito, *m.*; — **listener,** radioescucha, *m. y f.*, radioyente, *m. y f.*; — **message,** comunicación radioeléctrica; — **receiver,** radiorreceptor, *m.*; — **signature,** tonada especial usada en la radiodifusión para anunciar una orquesta, un programa, etc.; — **tube,** válvula de radio, tubo de radio; — **wave meter,** ondómetro, *m.*
radioactive, *adj.* radioactivo.
radioactivity, *n.* radioactividad, *f.*
radiobroadcast, *vt.* and *vi.* perifonear, difundir por radiotrasmisión.
radiobroadcaster, *n.* perífono, *m.*, radiodifusora, *f.*
radiobroadcasting, *n.* radiodifusión, perifonía, *f.*
radiofrequency, *n.* radiofrecuencia, *f.*
radiogram, *n.* radiograma, *m.*
radiograph, *n.* radiógrafo, *m.*
radiographer, *n.* radiógrafo, *m.*
radiography, *n.* radiografía, *f.*
radiometer, *n.* radiómetro, *m.*
radiophone, *n.* radiófono, *m.*
radiotelegram, *n.* radiotelegrama, *m.*
radiotelegraph, *n.* radiotelégrafo, *m.*
radiotelephone, *n.* radioteléfono, *m.*
radiotherapy, *n.* radioterapia, *f.*
radiothermy, *n.* radiotermia, *f.*
radish, *n.* rábano, *m.*
radium, *n.* (chem.) radio, *m.*
radius, *n.* (math., anat.) radio, *m.*; (math.) semidiámetro, *m.*
R.A.F. Royal Air Force, F.R.A. Fuerza Real Aérea (de Inglaterra).
raffia, *n.* rafia, *f.*
raffle, *n.* rifa, *f.*, sorteo, *m.*; —, *vi.* rifar.
raft, *n.* balsa, jangada, *f.*; almadía, *f.*
rafter, *n.* cabrio, *m.*, viga, *f.*
rag, *n.* trapo, andrajo, jirón, *m.*; —**s,** *n. pl.* trapería, *f.*
ragamuffin, *n.* mendigo, ga, pordiosero, ra; bribón, ona.
rage, *n.* rabia, *f.*; furor, *m.*, cólera, *f.*; **to fly into a** —, montar en cólera; —, *vi.* rabiar, encolerizarse.

ragged, *adj.* andrajoso.
raging, *n.* furia, rabia, *f.*; —**ly,** *adv.* rabiosamente.
raglan, *n.* raglán, abrigo, *m.*; — **sleeves,** mangas típicas de esta clase de abrigo.
ragtime, *n.* música sincopada.
ragweed, *n.* ambrosía, *f.*; **European** —, zuzón, *m.*
ragwort, *n.* zuzón, *m.*
raid, *n.* invasión, *f.*; —, *vt.* invadir, hacer una incursión.
raider, *n.* corsario, *m.*
rail, *n.* baranda, barrera, *f.*; balaustrada, *f.*; (rail.) carril, riel, *m.*; **by** —, por ferrocarril; —, *vt.* cercar con balaustradas; —, *vi.* injuriar de palabra.
railing, *n.* baranda, *f.*, barandal, pretil, *m.*; carril, *m.*
raillery, *n.* chocarrería, burla, *f.*
railroad, *n.* ferrocarril, *m.*; vía férrea; camino de hierro; **belt** —, ferrocarril de circunvalación; **electric** —, ferrocarril eléctrico; **elevated** —, ferrocarril aéreo; **narrow-gauge** —, camino de hierro económico; — **crossing,** paso a nivel; — **stock,** acciones ferrocarrileras; — **track,** vía férrea; **standard-gauge** —, gran camino de hierro.
railway, *n.* ferrocarril, *m.*; **cable** —, funicular —, ferrocarril de cable; — **express,** servicio rápido de carga por ferrocarril; **street** —, ferrocarril urbano o metropolitano.
raiment, *n.* ropa, *f.*; vestido, *m.*
rain, *n.* lluvia, *f.*; — **water,** agua lluvia, agua llovediza; —, *vi.* llover; **to** — **heavily,** llover a chuzos; **to stop** —**ing,** escampar.
rainbow, *n.* arco iris.
raincheck, *n.* contraseña en espectáculos al aire libre para casos de suspensión de función por mal tiempo.
raincoat, *n.* impermeable, *m.*; capote, *m.*
rainfall, *n.* precipitación, *f.*
rainproof, *adj.* impermeable, a prueba de lluvia.
rainy, *adj.* lluvioso.
raise, *vt.* levantar, alzar; fabricar, edificar; engrandecer, elevar; excitar, causar; **to** — **an objection,** poner objeción; **to** — **up,** suspender.
raisin, *n.* pasa (uva seca), *f.*
raising, *n.* izamiento, *m.*
rajah, *n.* rajá, *m.*
rake, *n.* rastro, rastrillo, *m.*; tunante, *m.*; —, *vt.* rastrillar; raer; rebuscar.
rakish, *adj.* libertino, disoluto.
rally, *vt.* (mil.) reunir; ridiculizar; —, *vi.* reunirse; burlarse de alguno.
Ralph, Rafael, Rodolfo, Rodulfo.
ram, *n.* morueco, *m.*; ariete, *m.*; **battering** —, brígola, *f.*; —, *vt.* impeler con violencia; atestar, henchir.
ramble, *vi.* vagar; callejear; —, *n.* correría, *f.*
rambler, *n.* vagabundo, da, callejero, ra.

ramification, *n.* ramificación, *f.*, ramal, *m.*
ramify, *vi.* ramificarse.
rammer, *n.* maza, *f.*; baqueta de escopeta; (mil.) roquete, *m.*
ramp, *n.* rampa, *f.*
rampage, *n.* conducta violenta o desenfrenada.
rampant, *adj.* exuberante.
rampart, *n.* baluarte, *m.*; terraplén, *m.*; (mil.) muralla, *f.*
ramrod, *n.* banqueta, *f.*; atacador, *m.*; (mil.) roquete, *m.*
ramshackle, *adj.* en ruina, ruinoso.
ran, pretérito del verbo **run.**
ranch, *n.* granja, *f.*; hacienda de ganado.
rancher, *n.* hacendado, da, ranchero, ra.
rancid, *adj.* rancio; **to become —,** ponerse rancio, enaceitarse.
rancidity, *n.* rancidez, *f.*
rancor, *n.* rencor, *m.*
rancorous, *adj.* rencoroso.
random, *n.* ventura, casualidad, *f.*; **at —,** a trochemoche, al azar, de volatería.
rang, pretérito del verbo **ring.**
range, *vt.* colocar, ordenar; clasificar; —, *vi.* fluctuar; vagar; —, *n.* clase, *f.*; orden, *m.*; hilera, *f.*; correría, *f.*; línea de un tiro de artillería; cocina económica, estufa, *f.*; **— finder,** telémetro, *m.*; **— of mountains,** sierra, *f.*; cadena de montañas.
ranger, *n.* batidor, *m.*; vigilante, *m.*; guardabosque, *m.*, (mil.) comando (de E.U.A.).
rank, *adj.* exuberante; rancio; fétido; vulgar; indecente; —, *n.* fila, hilera, *f.*; clase, *f.*; grado, *m.*; **— and file,** (mil.) individuos de tropa; las masas; miembros de algún cuerpo o institución excluídos los funcionarios o jefes.
rankle, *vi.* enconarse, inflamarse.
ransack, *vt.* saquear, pillar.
ransom, *vt.* rescatar; —, *n.* rescate, *m.*
rant, *vi.* decir disparates; regañar con vehemencia.
ranter, *n.* declamador, ra.
rap, *vt.* and *vi.* dar un golpe vivo y repentino; arrebatar; —, *n.* golpe ligero y vivo; **I don't give a —,** no me importa un bledo.
rapacious, *adj.* rapaz; **—ly,** *adv.* con rapacidad.
rapacity, *n.* rapacidad, *f.*
rape, *n.* fuerza, *f.*; estupro, *m.*; (bot.) nabo silvestre; —, *vt.* estuprar.
rapid, *adj.* rápido; **— fire,** de tiro rápido; **—ly,** *adv.* rápidamente.
rapidity, *n.* rapidez, *f.*
rapier, *n.* espadín, *m.*
rapine, *n.* rapiña, *f.*
rapscallion, *n.* villano, *m.*; vagabundo, *m.*
rapt, *adj.* encantado, enajenado.
rapture, *n.* rapto, éxtasis, *m.*
rapturous, *adj.* embelesado.
rare, *adj.* raro, extraordinario; **—ly,** *adv.* raramente.

rarebit, *n.* tostada hecha con queso y cerveza.
rarefaction, *n.* rarefacción, *f.*
rarefied, *adj.* enrarecido.
rarefy, *vt.* rarificar.
rarity, *n.* raridad, rareza, *f.*
rascal, *n.* pícaro, ra, bribón, ona, pillo, lla, perillán, ana, truhán, ana.
rascality, *n.* pillada, bribonería, *f.*
rascally, *adj.* truhán, truhanesco, tuno; —, *adv.* en forma truhanesca.
rash, *adj.* precipitado, temerario; **—ly,** *adv.* temerariamente; —, *n.* roncha, *f.*; urticaria, *f.*; erupción, *f.*, sarpullido, *m.*
rasher, *n.* torrezno, *m.*
rashness, *n.* temeridad, *f.*, arrojo, *m.*
rasp, *n.* escofina, *f.*, raspador, *m.*; —, *vt.* raspar; escofinar.
raspberry, *n.* frambuesa, sangüesa, *f.*; **— bush,** frambueso, sangüeso, *m.*
rat, *n.* rata, *f.*
ratchet, *n.* rueda o diente de engrane; trinquete, *m.*
rate, *n.* tipo, *m.*, tasa, *f.*, precio, valor, *m.*; grado, *m.*; manera, *f.*; tarifa, *f.*; razón, *f.*; tipo, *m.*; **at the — of,** a razón de; **at the — of exchange,** al cambio de; **at what — of exchange?** ¿a qué cambio? **— of discount,** tipo de descuento; **— of exchange,** tipo de cambio, curso de la bolsa; **— of interest,** tipo de interés; —, *vt.* tasar, apreciar; calcular, calificar; reñir a uno.
rate-of-climb indicator, *n.* (aer.) indicador de subida y bajada.
rather, *adv.* de mejor gana; más bien; antes; antes bien; bastante; mejor dicho.
ratification, *n.* ratificación, *f.*
ratify, *vt.* ratificar.
rating, *n.* valuación, *f.*
ratio, *n.* proporción, *f.*; razón, *f.*; **direct —,** razón directa; **inverse —,** razón inversa.
ration, *n.* (mil.) ración, *f.*; **— board,** junta de racionamiento; **— card,** tarjeta de racionamiento; —, *vt.* racionar.
rational, *adj.* racional; razonable; **—ly,** *adv.* racionalmente.
rationalism, *n.* racionalismo, *m.*
rationality, *n.* razón, racionalidad, *f.*
rationalization, *n.* racionalización, *f.*
rationing, *n.* racionamiento, *m.*
ratsbane, *n.* arsénico, *m.*
rattan, *n.* (bot.) rota, *f.*, roten, *m.*
rattle, *vt.* and *vi.* hacer ruido; regañar; zumbar, zurrir; rechinar; **to become —d,** perder la chaveta; confundirse; —, *n.* ruido (como el de matracas), *m.*; sonajero, *m.*; matraca, *f.*
rattlesnake, *n.* culebra de cascabel.
raucous, *adj.* rauco, ronco.
ravage, *vi.* saquear, pillar; asolar; —, *n.* saqueo, *m.*
rave, *vi.* delirar; enfurecerse; echar chispas.
ravel, *vt.* embrollar; enredar; deshebrar;

—, *vi.* deshilarse, destorcerse.
raven, *n.* cuervo, *m.*
ravenous, *adj.* voraz, famélico; —**ly,** *adv.* vorazmente.
ravine, *n.* barranca, cañada, *f.*
raving, *adj.* furioso, frenético; —**ly,** *adv.* como un loco furioso.
ravish, *vt.* estuprar; arrebatar.
ravishing, *adj.* encantador.
ravishingly, *adv.* arrobadoramente.
ravishment, *n.* rapto, *m.*; éxtasis, *m.*
raw, *adj.* crudo; puro; nuevo; **in a —
(unmanufactured) state,** en bruto; — **materials,** primeras materias.
rawboned, *adj.* huesudo; magro.
rawness, *n.* crudeza, *f.*; falta de experiencia.
ray, *n.* rayo de luz; (pez) raya, *f.*
Raymond, Raimundo, Ramón.
rayon, *n.* rayón, *m.*
raze, *vt.* arrasar; extirpar; borrar.
razor, *n.* navaja de afeitar; — **blade,** hoja de afeitar; — **strop,** asentador, *m.*; **safety** —, navaja de seguridad.
R.C.: Red Cross, C.R. Cruz Roja; **reserve corps,** cuerpo de reserva; **Roman Catholic,** católico romano.
Rd. road, camino.
rd.: road, camino; **rod,** pértica.
R.D. Rural Delivery, entrega en zonas rurales.
reach, *vt.* alcanzar; llegar hasta; —, *vi.* extenderse, llegar; alcanzar, penetrar; esforzarse; —, *n.* alcance, poder, *m.*; capacidad, *f.*; astucia, *f.*
react, *vt.* reaccionar; rechazar; obrar recíprocamente.
reactance, *n.* (elec.) reactancia, *f.*
reaction, *n.* reacción, *f.*
reactionary, *n.* reaccionario, ria; (pol.) derechista, *m.* y *f.*; —, *adj.* reaccionario.
read, *vt.* leer; interpretar; adivinar, predecir; —, *vi.* leer; estudiar; —, *adj.* literato, erudito.
readable, *adj.* legible.
reader, *n.* lector, ra.
readily, *adv.* prontamente; de buena gana.
readiness, *n.* facilidad, *f.*; vivacidad del ingenio; voluntad, gana, *f.*; prontitud, *f.*
reading, *n.* lectura, *f.*; — **room,** gabinete de lectura.
readjust, *vt.* recomponer; reajustar.
ready, *adj.* listo, pronto; inclinado; fácil; ligero.
ready-made, *adj.* hecho, confeccionado, ya hecho; — **clothes,** ropa hecha.
reagent, *n.* (chem.) reactivo, *m.*
real, *adj.* real, verdadero, efectivo; inmoble; — **estate,** bienes raíces o inmuebles; — **wages,** salario real; —**ly,** *adv.* realmente, en verdad.
realism, *n.* realismo, *m.*
realist, *n.* realista, *m.* y *f.*
realistic, *adj.* realista; natural.
reality, *n.* realidad, *f.*; efectividad, *f.*

realization, *n.* comprensión, *f.*; realización, *f.*
realize, *vt.* realizar; hacerse cargo de, darse cuenta de.
really, *adv.* realmente, verdaderamente.
realm, *n.* reino, *m.*; dominio, *m.*
ream, *n.* resma, *f.*
reamer, *n.* escariador, *m.*
reanimate, *vt.* reanimar.
reap, *vt.* segar.
reaper, *n.* segador, ra.
reappear, *vi.* reaparecer.
rear, *n.* retaguardia, *f.*; parte posterior; —, *adj.* posterior; — **admiral,** contraalmirante; — **part,** zaga, *f.*; **rear-vision, rearview mirror,** espejo de retrovisión, —, *vi.* encabritarse el caballo; —, *vt.* criar, educar; levantar; construir.
rearguard, *n.* retaguardín, *f.*
rearmament, *n.* rearme, rearmamento, *m.*
rearrange, *vt.* refundir, dar nueva forma (a una comedia, discurso, etc.); volver a arreglar.
rearview, *n.* vista posterior.
rearward, *adj.* de atrás; —, *adv.* hacia atrás.
reascend, *vt.* and *vi.* subir otra vez.
reason, *n.* razón, *f.*; causa, *f.*; motivo, *m.*; juicio, *m.*; quid, *m.*; **by** — **of,** con motivo de, a causa de; **for this** —, por esto; **without** —, sin qué ni para qué, sin razón; —, *vt.* razonar, raciocinar.
reasonable, *adj.* razonable, módico, lógico.
reasonableness, *n.* razón, *f.*; racionalidad, *f.*; sensatez, *f.*
reasonably, *adv.* razonablemente.
reasoning, *n.* raciocinio, *m.*
reassure, *vt.* volver a asegurar; (com.) dar un nuevo seguro.
rebate, *n.* rebaja, *f.*
rebel, *n.* rebelde, *m.* y *f.*, insurrecto, ta; —, *adj.* insurrecto; —, *vi.* rebelarse; insubordinarse.
rebellion, *n.* rebelión, insubordinación, *f.*
rebellious, *adj.* rebelde.
rebirth, *n.* renacimiento, *m.*
rebound, *vt.* and *vi.* repercutir; —, *n.* bote (de una pelota), *m.*
rebroadcast, *n.* retrasmisión radiofónica, *f.*
rebuff, *vt.* rechazar; —, *n.* desaire, *m.*
rebuild, *vt.* reedificar.
rebuke, *vt.* reprender, regañar; —, *n.* reprensión, *f.*, regaño, *m.*
rebus, *n.* rompecabezas, *m.*; jeroglífico, *m.*
rebut, *vt.* refutar, contradecir.
rec.: receipt, Rbí. recibí; **recipe,** receta; **record,** R.ᵉ registro; **recorder,** registrador.
recalcitrant, *adj.* recalcitrante.
recall, *vt.* llamar, hacer volver; revocar; — **to mind,** recapacitar; —, *n.* revocación, *f.*
recant, *vt.* retractarse, desdecirse.
recantation, *n.* retractación, *f.*
recapitulate, *vt.* recapitular.
recapitulation, *n.* recapitulación, *f.*

recapping, (of tires), n. revestimiento (de neumáticos), m.

recapture, n. represa (de un navío, etc.), f.; —, vt. volver a tomar; represar.

recast, n. refundición, f.; —, vt. fundir de nuevo; calcular de nuevo.

recd. received, recib.° recibido.

recede, vi. retroceder; desistir.

receipt, n. recibo, m.; receta, f., ingreso, m.; (com.) recibí, m.; **to acknowledge** —, acusar recibo.

receivable, adj. recibidero, admisible; **bills** —, cuentas por cobrar.

receive, vt. recibir; aceptar, admitir; cobrar.

receiver, n. receptor, m.; recipiente, m.; audífono, m.; depositario, m.; — **in bankruptcy,** síndico, m.

receivership, n. sindicatura, f.

receiving set, n. (rad.) radiorreceptor, m.

recent, adj. reciente, nuevo; fresco; **—ly,** adv. recientemente.

receptacle, n. receptáculo, m.

reception, n. acogida, f.; recepción, f.

receptionist, n. recibidor, ra.

receptive, adj. receptivo.

receptor, n. receptor, m.

recess, n. retiro, m.; nicho, m.; lugar apartado; grieta, f.; tregua, f.; (Mex.) receso, m.; recreo, m.; — **hour,** hora de recreo.

recession, n. retirada, f.; receso, m.

recessive, adj. de receso.

recharge, vt. recargar.

recipe, n. receta de cocina; receta de médico.

recipient, n. receptor, ra.

reciprocal, adj. recíproco; **—ly,** adv. recíprocamente.

reciprocate, vi. corresponder; —, vt. reciprocar, compensar.

reciprocity, n. reciprocidad, f.

recital, n. recitación, f.; (mus.) especie de concierto musical.

recitation, n. recitación, f.

recitative, n. (mus.) recitativo, m.

recite, vt. recitar; referir; relatar; declamar; **to — a lesson,** dar una lección.

reciter, n. declamador, ra.

reck, vt. cuidar, atender; —, vi. interesar, importar.

reckless, adj. descuidado; audaz; **—ly,** adv. con descuido; audazmente.

reckon, vt. contar, numerar; —, vi. computar, calcular.

reckoning, n. cuenta, f.; calculación, f.

reclaim, vt. reformar, corregir; (law) reclamar.

reclaimable, adj. reclamable.

reclamation, n. aprovechamiento, m., utilización, f.; reclamación, f.

recline, vt. and vi. reclinar; reposar; recostar.

recluse, adj. recluso, retirado; —, n. recluso, sa.

reclusion, n. reclusión, f.

recognizable, adj. que puede reconocerse.

recognizance, n. reconocimiento, m.; obligación, f.

recognize, vt. reconocer.

recognition, n. reconocimiento, m.; agradecimiento, m.

recoil, vi. recular, retirarse; —, n. rechazo, m.; reculada, f.; — **of a firearm,** culatada, f.

recollect, vt. acordarse; recobrarse.

recollection, n. recuerdo, m.; reminiscencia, f.

recommend, vt. recomendar.

recommendation, n. recomendación, f.

recommendatory, adj. recomendatorio.

recommit, vt. confiar de nuevo, someter a nuevo examen.

recompense, n. recompensa, f.; —, vt. recompensar.

recompose, vt. volver a componer; tranquilizar de nuevo.

reconcilable, adj reconciliable.

reconcile, vt. reconciliar.

reconciliation, n. reconciliación, f.

recondite, adj. recóndito, reservado.

recondition, vt. reacondicionar.

reconnaissance, n. reconocimiento, m., exploración, f.; — **plane,** aeroplano de reconocimiento.

reconnoiter, vt. (mil.) reconocer.

reconnoitering, n. (mil.) reconocimiento, m.

reconsider, vt. considerar de nuevo.

reconstitute, vt. reconstituir.

reconstruct, vt. reedificar, reconstruir.

record, vt. registrar; protocolar; —, n. registro, archivo, m.; **—s,** m. pl. anales. m. pl.; **off the** —, confidencialmente (tratándose de una declaración que no debe publicarse); —, adj. sin precedente; **off-the-record,** confidencial, extraoficial.

record-breaking, adj. que supera precedentes.

recorder, n. registrador, archivero, medidor, m.

recount, vt. referir, recontar, contar de nuevo; —, n. recuento, m.

recoup, vt. resarcir, desquitarse de.

recouple, vt. (mech.) reenganchar, reacoplar.

recourse, n. recurso, retorno, m.

recover, vt. recobrar; cobrar; reparar; restablecer; —, vi. convalecer, restablecerse; **to — (health),** sanar, reponerse; **to — (property),** recobrar (propiedad); **to — one's senses,** volver en sí.

recoverable, adj. recuperable.

recovery, n. convalecencia, f.; recobro, m.; recuperación, f., restablecimiento, m.

recpt. receipt, Rbí. Recibí.

recreant, adj. cobarde; —, n. cobarde, m. y f.; apóstata, m. y f.

recreate, vt. recrear, deleitar, divertir.

recreation, n. recreación, f.; recreo, m.

recreative, adj. recreativo.

recriminate, vt. and vi. recriminar; acusar al acusador.

recrimination, *n.* recriminación, *f.*
recrudescence, *n.* recrudescencia, *f.*, encrudecimiento, *m.*
recrudescent, *adj.* recrudescente.
recruit, *vt.* reclutar; —, *n.* (mil.) recluta, *m.*
recruiting, *n.* recluta, *f.*, reclutamiento, *m.*; — **office (army, navy, etc.),** caja de reclutamiento.
rectangle, *n.* rectángulo, *m.*
rectangular, *adj.* rectangular.
rectification, *n.* rectificación, *f.*
rectifier, *n.* rectificador, ra.
rectify, *vt.* rectificar.
rectilinear, *adj.* rectilíneo.
rectitude, *n.* rectitud, derechura, *f.*
rector, *n.* rector, *m.*; párroco, *m.*; jefe, *m.*
rectory, *n.* rectoría, *f.*
recumbent, *adj.* recostado, reclinado.
recuperate, *vi.* restablecerse, recuperarse; —, *vt.* recobrar, recuperar.
recuperative, *adj.* recuperativo.
recur, *vi.* recurrir.
recurrence, *n.* retorno, *m.*; vuelta, *f.*; repetición, *f.*
recurrent, *adj.* periódico.
recusant, *n.* and *adj.* recusante, *m.* y *f.*
red, *adj.* rojo; rubio; colorado; — **herring,** arenque ahumado; acción para distraer la atención del asunto principal; — **lead,** minio, bermellón, *m.*; — **man,** piel roja, indio norteamericano; — **pepper,** pimiento, pimentón, *m.*; — **tape,** balduque, *m.*; expedienteo, *m.*; (Mex.) papeleo, *m.*; —, *n.* rojez, *f.*
redbird, *n.* (orn.) cardenal, *m.*
red-blooded, *adj.* valiente, denodado.
redbreast, *n.* petirrojo, pechirrojo, *m.*
redcap, *n.* (orn.) cardelina, *f.*; mozo de cordel, cargador, *m.*
redcoat, *n.* soldado inglés.
redden, *vt.* teñir de color rojo; —, *vi.* ponerse colorado.
reddish, *adj.* rojizo, bermejizo.
redeem, *vt.* redimir, rescatar.
redeeming, *adj.* redentor.
redeemable, *adj.* redimible.
redeemer, *n.* redentor, ra, salvador, ra; **the R—,** el Redentor.
redemption, *n.* redención, *f.*
red-haired, *adj.* pelirrojo.
redhanded, *adj.* en fragante, en el acto.
redhead, *n.* persona de cabello rojo.
red-hot, *adj.* candente, ardiente.
red-letter, *adj.* notable, extraordinario, fuera de lo común; — **day,** día de fiesta, día especial, día extraordinario.
redness, *n.* rojez, bermejura, *f.*
redolence, *n.* fragancia, *f.*
redolent, *adj.* fragante, oloroso.
redouble, *vt.* redoblar; —, *vi.* redoblarse.
redoubt, *n.* (mil.) reducto, *m.*
redoubtable, *adj.* formidable, terrible.
redound, *vi.* resaltar, rebotar; redundar.
redress, *vt.* enderezar; corregir; reformar; rectificar; —, *n.* reforma, corrección, *f.*

Red Sea, Mar Rojo.
redskin, *n.* piel roja, indio nortemericano.
redtop, *n.* especie de hierba forrajera.
reduce, *vt.* reducir; disminuir; sujetar.
reducible, *adj.* reducible.
reducing agent, *n.* agente reductor.
reduction, *n.* reducción, rebaja, *f.*
redundancy, *n.* redundancia, *f.*
redundant, *adj.* redundante, superfluo; **to be —,** redundar.
reduplicate, *vt.* reduplicar.
reduplication, *n.* reduplicación, *f.*
redwing, *n.* malvís, *m.*
redwood, *n.* (bot.) pino de California.
re-echo, *vi.* resonar el eco, repercutir.
reed, *n.* caña, *f.*; flecha, *f.*; — **plantation,** cañal, *m.*
reedy, *adj.* lleno de cañas.
reef, *vt.* (naut.) tomar rizos a las velas; —, *n.* arrecife, escollo, *m.*
reek, *n.* humo, vapor, *m.*; —, *vi.* humear; vahar, vahar.
reel, *n.* aspa, devanadera, *f.*; variedad de baile; carrete, *m.*; película de cine; **fishing —,** carretel, *m.*; —, *vt.* aspar; —, *vi.* vacilar al andar, tambalearse.
re-election, *n.* reelección, *f.*
re-embark, *vt.* reembarcar.
reencounter, *n.* encuentro, *m.*; (mil.) refriega, *f.*
re-enforce, *vt.* reforzar.
re-engage, *vt.* empeñar de nuevo.
re-engagement, *n.* empeño renovado.
re-enter, *vt.* volver a entrar.
re-establish, *vt.* restablecer, volver a establecer una cosa.
re-establishment, *n.* restablecimiento, *m.*; restauración, *f.*
ref.: referee, juez (en los deportes); **reference,** ref. referencia; **referred,** referido; **reformation,** reforma; **reformed,** reformado.
refection, *n.* refección, *f.*; merienda, *f.*
refectory, *n.* refectorio, *m.*
refer, *vt.* and *vi.* referir, remitir; dirigir; referirse; — **to,** véase (imperativo).
referee, *n.* arbitrador, árbitro, *m.*; componedor, *m.*; —, *vt.* and *vi.* servir de árbitro o de juez.
reference, *n.* referencia, relación, *f.*
referendum, *n.* plebiscito, *m.*
refill, *vt.* rellenar; —, *n.* relleno, *m.*; producto comercial destinado a rellenar envases originales.
refine, *vt.* refinar, purificar; —, *vi.* purificarse.
refinement, *n.* refinación, *f.*; refinamiento, *m.*; refinadura, *f.*; elegancia afectada.
refinery, *n.* refinería, *f.*
refit, *vt.* reparar; (naut.) embonar.
reflect, *vt.* and *vi.* reflejar, repercutir; reflexionar; recaer, refluir en.
reflection, *n.* reflexión, meditación, *f.*; reflejo, *m.*
reflective, *adj.* reflexivo; reflejo; pensativo.

reflector, *n.* telescopio de reflexión; reflector, *m.*

reflex, *adj.* reflejo.

reforest, *vt.* restablecer bosques.

reforestation, *n.* restablecimiento de bosques.

reform, *vt.* reformar; —, *vi.* reformarse; —, *n.* reforma, *f.*

reformation, *n.* reformación, *f.*; reforma, *f.*

reformatory, *n.* reformatorio, *m.*

reformer, *n.* reformador, ra.

refract, *vt.* refractar, refringir.

refraction, *n.* refracción, *f.*

refractor, *n.* refractor, *m.*, telescopio de refracción.

refractory, *adj.* refractario, obstinado, reacio.

refrain, *vi.* reprimirse, abstenerse; mesurarse; —, *n.* estribillo, *m.*

refresh, *vt.* refrigerar, refrescar.

refresher, *adj.* recordativo.

refreshing, *adj.* refrescante.

refreshment, *n.* refresco, refrigerio, *m.*

refrigerator, *n.* enfriadera, *f.*, enfriador, refrigerador, frigorífero, *m.*

refuel, *vt.* poner nuevo combustible.

refuge, *n.* refugio, asilo, *m.*; seno, *m.*; recurso, *m.*

refugee, *n.* refugiado, da.

refund, *vt.* restituir; devolver, reembolsar.

refurbish, *vt.* renovar, retocar.

refusal, *n.* repulsa, denegación, *f.*; negativa, *f.*

refuse, *vt.* rehusar, repulsar; —, *n.* desecho, *m.*, sobra, *f.*; limpiaduras, *f. pl.*; basura, *f.*

refutation, *n.* refutación, *f.*

refute, *vt.* refutar; confutar.

reg.: register, registrar, inscribir; **registrar,** registrador; **registry,** registro; **regularly,** regularmente.

regain, *vt.* recobrar, recuperar.

regal, *adj.* real.

regale, *vt.* and *vi.* agasajar, festejarse.

regalia, *n.* insignias, *f. pl.*

regard, *vt.* estimar; considerar; —, *n.* consideración, *f.*; respeto, *m.*; —s, *n. pl.* recuerdos, *m. pl.*, memorias, *f. pl.*; **in —to,** en cuanto a, respecto a, con respecto a; **in this —,** a este respecto; **to give —s,** dar memorias; **with — to,** a propósito de, relativo a.

regardful, *adj.* atento; **—ly,** *adv.* atentamente.

regarding, *prep.* concerniente a.

regardless, *adj.* descuidado, negligente; indiferente; **— of,** a pesar de.

regatta, *n.* regata, *f.*

regency, *n.* regencia, *f.*; gobierno, *m.*

regenerate, *vt.* regenerar; —, *adj.* regenerado.

regeneration, *n.* regeneración, *f.*; renacimiento, *m.*

regent, *n.* regente, *m.*

regicide, *n.* regicida, *m.*; regicidio, *m.*

regime, *n.* régimen, *m.*; administración, *f.*

regimen, *n.* régimen, *m.*; dieta, *f.*

regiment, *n.* regimiento, *m.*; —, *vt.* regimentar; asignar a un regimiento o grupo; regimentar (en el sentido del estado totalitario).

regimentals, *n. pl.* uniforme, *m.*, traje militar.

regimentation, *n.* regimentación, *f.*

Reginald, Reginaldo.

region, *n.* región, *f.*; distrito, *m.*; país, *m.*

regionalism, *n.* regionalismo, *m.*

register, *n.* registro, *m.*; **cash —,** caja registradora; —, *vt.* inscribir; registrar; certificar (una carta); —, *vi.* matricularse, registrarse.

registered, *adj.* registrado, matriculado; **— letter,** carta certificada.

registrar, *n.* registrador, ra.

registration, *n.* registro, *m.*; inscripción, *f.*; empadronamiento, *m.*

registry, *n.* asiento, registro, *m.*

regress, *n.* retroceso, *m.*; —, *vi.* retrogadar.

regressive, *adj.* regresivo.

regret, *n.* arrepentimiento, *m.*; pesar, *m.*; —, *vt.* sentir (pena o dolor), lamentar, deplorar.

regretful, *adj.* pesaroso.

regrettable, *adj.* sensible, lamentable, deplorable.

Regt.: regiment, regimiento; **regent,** regente.

regular, *adj.* regular; ordinario; **— army,** tropas de línea; **—ly,** *adv.* regularmente; **—,** *n.* regular, *m.*

regularity, *n.* regularidad, *f.*

regulate, *vt.* regular, ordenar.

regulation, *n.* regulación, *f.*; regla, *f.*, reglamentación, *f.*; arreglo, *m.*

regulator, *n.* regulador, *m.*; registro de reloj.

regurgitate, *vt.* and *vi.* regurgitar; rebosar.

rehabilitate, *vt.* rehabilitar.

rehabilitation, *n.* rehabilitación, *f.*

rehash, *vt.* refundir, recomponer; —, *n.* refundición, *f.*

rehearsal, *n.* repetición, *f.*; (theat.) ensayo, *m.*

rehearse, *vt.* repetir, recitar; (theat.) ensayar.

reheating, *n.* recalentamiento, *m.*

reign, *n.* reinado, reino, *m.*; —, *vi.* reinar, prevalecer, imperar.

reimburse, *vt.* reembolsar.

reimbursement, *n.* reembolso, reintegro, *m.*

rein, *n.* rienda, *f.*; —, *vt.* refrenar.

reincarnation, *n.* reencarnación, *f.*

reindeer, *n. sing.* y *pl.* reno(s), rangífero(s), *m.*

reinforced, *adj.* reforzado, armado; **— concrete,** hormigón armado.

reinforcement, *n.* refuerzo, *m.*

reinstate, *vt.* instalar de nuevo; restablecer.

reinsure, *vt.* (com.) reasegurar, volver a asegurar.

reinvigorate, *vt.* revigorizar; robustecer.

reinvigoration, *n.* revigorización, *f.*; robustecimiento, *m.*

reissue, *n.* reimpresión, *f.*; nueva edición; —, *vt.* reimprimir.

reiterate, *vt.* reiterar.

reiteration, *n.* reiteración, repetición, *f.*

reject, *vt.* rechazar, rebatir; despreciar.

rejectable, *adj.* rechazable.

rejection, *n.* desecho, rechazamiento, rechazo, *m.*, repudiación, *f.*

rejoice, *vt.* regocijar; —, *vi.* regocijarse.

rejoicing, *n.* regocijo, *m.*

rejoin, *vi.* volver a juntarse; —, *vt.* replicar.

rejoinder, *n.* contrarréplica, *f.*

rejuvenate, *vt.* and *vi.* rejuvenecer, rejuvenecerse.

rel.: relating, con relación a; **relative,** relativo; **religion,** Rel. religión.

relapse, *vi.* recaer; —, *n.* reincidencia, recidiva, *f.*; recaída, *f.*

relapsed, *adj.* relapso.

relate, *vt.* and *vi.* relatar, contar; referirse.

related, *adj.* emparentado, relacionado.

relater, *n.* relator, ra.

relation, *n.* relación, *f.*; parentesco, *m.*; pariente, *m.* y *f.*

relationship, *n.* parentesco, *m.*; relación, *f.*

relative, *adj.* relativo; **—ly,** *adv.* relativamente; —, *n.* pariente, *m.* y *f.*

relativity, *n.* relatividad, *f.*

relator, *n.* relator, ra.

relax, *vt.* relajar, aflojar; —, *vi.* descansar, reposar.

relaxation, *n.* reposo, descanso, *m.*; relajación, *f.*

relay, *n.* parada, posta, *f.*; **— race,** corrida entre un grupo de competidores cada uno de los cuales cubre una parte de la carrera; remuda, *f.*

release, *vt.* soltar, libertar; relevar; dar al público; —, *n.* soltura, *f.*; descargo, *m.*; permiso para publicar o exhibir (una noticia, película, etc.).

relegate, *vt.* desterrar, relegar.

relegation, *n.* relegación, *f.*; destierro, *m.*

relent, *vi.* relentecer, ablandarse.

relentless, *adj.* empedernido, inflexible.

relevance, relevancy, *n.* pertinencia, *f.*

relevant, *adj.* pertinente; concerniente.

reliable, *adj.* digno de confianza, responsable.

reliance, *n.* confianza, *f.*

reliant, *adj.* de confianza.

relic, *n.* reliquia, *f.*

relict, *n.* viuda, *f.*

relief, *n.* relieve (escultura), *m.*; alivio, consuelo, *m.*; **— map,** mapa de relieve.

relieve, *vt.* aliviar, consolar; socorrer.

religion, *n.* religión, *f.*; culto, *m.*; **to instruct in** —, catequizar.

religious, *adj.* religioso; **— instruction,** catequismo, *m.*; **—ly,** *adv.* religiosamente.

relinquish, *vt.* abandonar, dejar.

relinquishment, *n.* abandono, *m.*

reliquary, *n.* relicario, *m.*

relish, *n.* sabor, *m.*; gusto, deleite, *m.*; condimento, *m.*; —, *vt.* agradar; saborear; —, *vi.* tener sabor apetecible.

relocation, *n.* relocalización, *f.*

reluctance, *n.* repugnancia, *f.*, disgusto, *m.*

reluctant, *adj.* renuente, con disgusto.

rely, *vi.* confiar en; contar con.

remain, *vi.* quedar, restar, permanecer, durar.

remainder, *n.* resto, residuo, *m.*; restante, *m.*; sobra, *f.*

remains, *n. pl.* restos, residuos, *m. pl.*, sobras, *f. pl.*

remand, *vt.* devolver al lugar de procedencia; reencarcelar.

remark, *n.* observación, nota, *f.*, comentario, *m.*; —, *vt.* notar, observar, comentar.

remarkable, *adj.* notable, interesante; **—bly,** *adv.* notablemente.

remediable, *adj.* remediable.

remedial, *adj.* curativo, terapéutico.

remediless, *adj.* sin remedio, irreparable.

remedy, *n.* remedio, medicamento, *m.*; cura, *f.*; —, *vt.* remediar.

remember, *vt.* recordar, tener presente; dar memorias; —, *vi.* acordarse.

remembrance, *n.* memoria, *f.*; recuerdo, *m.*

remind, *vt.* acordar, recordar.

reminder, *n.* recuerdo, recordatorio, *m.*

reminisce, *vi.* recordar, contar recuerdos.

reminiscent, *adj.* recordativo, que recuerda acontecimientos pasados.

reminiscence, *n.* reminiscencia, *f.*

remiss, *adj.* remiso, flojo, perezoso, negligente, tibio; **—ly,** *adv.* negligentemente.

remissable, *adj.* remisible, perdonable.

remission, *n.* remisión, *f.*; perdón, *m.*

remissness, *n.* incurria, indolencia, *f.*

remit, *vt.* and *vi.* remitir, perdonar; disminuir; debilitarse.

remittance, *n.* remesa, *f.*; remisión, *f.*

remittent, *adj.* remitente.

remitter, *n.* remitente, *m.* y *f.*

remnant, *n.* resto, residuo, *m.*; retazo, *m.*

remodel, *vt.* reformar.

remonstrance, *n.* súplica motivada, protesta, reconvención, *f.*

remonstrant, *adj.* que censura o echa en cara alguna cosa.

remonstrate, *vi.* protestar, reconvenir.

remorse, *n.* remordimiento, *m.*; compunción, *f.*; cargo de conciencia.

remorseful, *adj.* con remordimiento.

remorseless, *adj.* insensible a los remordimientos.

remote, *adj.* remoto, lejano; **—ly,** *adv.* remotamente, lejos.

remotely, *adv.* lejanamente.

remoteness, *n.* alejamiento, *m.*; distancia, *f.*; lejanía, *f.*

remount, *vt.* and *vi.* remontar; volver a subir.

removable, *adj.* amovible.

removal, *n.* remoción, deposición, *f.*; alejamiento, *m.*; acción de quitar.

remove, *vt.* remover, alejar; deponer (del empleo); quitar; —, *vi.* mudarse.
remover, *n.* quitador, ra; **spot** —, sacamanchas, *m.*
remunerate, *vt.* remunerar.
remuneration, *n.* remuneración, *f.*
remunerative, *adj.* remuneratorio.
Renaissance, *n.* Renacimiento, *m.*
rename, *vt.* nombrar de nuevo.
renascence, *n.* renacimiento, *m.*
renascent, *adj.* que renace, que revive.
rend, *vt.* lacerar, hacer pedazos, rasgar.
render, *vt.* volver, restituir; traducir; rendir.
rendezvous, *n.* cita (particularmente amorosa), *f.*; lugar señalado para encontrarse.
rendition, *n.* rendimiento, *m*; ejecución, *f.*
renegade, *n.* renegado, da, apóstata, *m.* y *f.*
renew, *vt.* renovar, restablecer, reanudar, instaurar.
renewal, *n.* renovación, *f.*; renuevo, *m.*; prórroga, *f.*
rennet, *n.* cuajo, *m.*; — **bag (of ruminants),** cuajar, *m.*
rennin, *n.* fermento del cuajo.
renomination, *n.* nuevo nombramiento.
renounce, *vt.* renunciar.
renouncement, *n.* renuncia, *f.*, renunciamiento, *m.*
renovate, *vt.* renovar, instaurar.
renovation, *n.* renovación, *f.*
renovator, *n.* renovador, *m.*
renown, *n.* renombre, *m.*; celebridad, *f.*
renowned, *adj.* célebre.
rent, *n.* renta, *f.*; arrendamiento, *m.*; rendimiento, *m.*; alquiler, *m.*; rasgón, *m.*; cisma, *m.* y *f.*; —, *vt.* arrendar, alquilar.
rental, *n.* renta, *f.*, arriendo, alquiler, *m.*; —, *adj.* relativo a renta o alquiler.
renter, *n.* rentero, ra, arrendador, ra.
renunciation, *n.* renuncia, renunciación, *f.*
reopen, *vt.* abrir de nuevo.
reorganization, *n.* reorganización, *f.*
reorganize, *vt.* reorganizar.
reorder, *vt.* volver a pedir, ordenar, arreglar.
Rep.: Republic, Rep. República; **Republican,** Republicano.
rep.: report, inf. informe; **reported,** informado; **reporter,** reportero; **representative,** rpte. representante.
repair, *vt.* reparar, resarcir, restaurar; —, *vi.* ir; regresar; —, *n.* reparo, remiendo, *m.*, reparación, compostura, *f.*; — **ship,** buque taller; — **shop,** maestranza, *f.*, taller de reparaciones.
repaired, *adj.* compuesto, remendado.
repairer, *n.* componedor, ra.
reparable, *adj.* reparable.
reparation, *n.* reparación, *f.*, remedio, *m.*
repartee, *n.* réplica aguda o picante.
repass, *vt.* and *vi.* repasar.
repast, *n.* comida, colación, *f.*
repatriate, *vt.* repatriar.
repatriation, *n.* repatriación, *f.*
repay, *vt.* volver a pagar, restituir, devolver.
repayment, *n.* pago, *m.*

repeal, *vt.* abrogar, revocar; —, *n.* revocación, anulación, casación, *f.*
repeat, *vt.* repetir.
repeated, *adj.* repetido, reiterado.
repeatedly, *adv.* repetidamente.
repeater, *n.* reloj de repetición; arma de repetición.
repel, *vt.* repeler, rechazar.
repellent, *adj.* repelente, repulsivo.
repent, *vi.* arrepentirse.
repentance, *n.* arrepentimiento, *m.*
repentant, *adj.* arrepentido.
repercussion, *n.* repercusión, *f.*
repertoire, *n.* repertorio, *m.*
repertory, *n.* repositorio, *m.*; repertorio, *m.*
repetition, *n.* repetición, reiteración, *f.*
repetitious, *adj.* redundante, que contiene repeticiones.
rephrase, *vt.* volver a expresar, volver a formular.
repine, *vi.* afligirse, arrepentirse.
repining, *n.* pesar, *m.*
replace, *vt.* reemplazar; reponer; sustituir.
replacement, *n.* reemplazo, *m.*, sustitución, *f.*; pieza de repuesto.
replant, *vt.* trasplantar.
replenish, *vt.* llenar, surtir.
replete, *adj.* repleto, lleno.
repletion, *n.* repleción, plenitud, *f.*
replica, *n.* réplica, *f.*
reply, *vt.* replicar, contestar, responder; —, *n.* réplica, respuesta, contestación, *f.*; **awaiting your** —, en espera de su respuesta, en espera de sus noticias.
report, *vt.* referir, contar; informar; dar cuenta; —, *n.* voz, *f.*; rumor, *m.*; fama, *f.*; relación, *f.*; informe, *m.*; memoria, *f.*
reporter, *n.* relator, ra; reportero, *m.*; periodista, *m.* y *f*, cronista, *m.* y *f.*; **society** —, cronista de salones.
repose, *vt.* fiar, confiar; —, *vi.* reposar; fiarse de; —, *n.* reposo, *m.*
repository, *n.* depósito, *m.*
repossess, *vt.* recuperar (lo perdido); restaurar (un auto, etc.).
reprehend, *vt.* reprender.
reprehensible, *adj.* reprensible.
reprehension, *n.* reprensión, fraterna, *f.*
represent, *vt.* representar.
representation, *n.* representación, *f.*
representative, *adj.* representativo; —, *n.* representante, *m.* y *f.*; **House of R—s,** Cámara de Representantes.
repress, *vt.* reprimir, domar.
repressible, *adj.* que puede ser reprimido.
repression, *n.* represión, *f.*
repressive, *adj.* represivo.
reprieve, *vt.* suspender una ejecución; demorar un castigo; —, *n.* dilación (de algún castigo), *f.*; suspensión, *f.*
reprimand, *vt.* reprender, corregir; regañar; —, *n.* reprensión, *f.*; reprimenda, *f.*
reprint, *n.* tirada aparte; reimpresión, *f.*; —, *vt.* reimprimir.
reprisal, *n.* represalia, *f.*

reproach, *n.* improperio, oprobio, *m.*; reproche, *m.*; censura, *f.*; —, *vt.* culpar, reprochar; vituperar; improperar.
reproachful, *adj.* represor, increpante; —ly, *adv.* contumeliosamente.
reprobate, *vt.* reprobar; —, *n.* réprobo, malvado, *m.*
reprobation, *n.* reprobación, *f.*
reproduce, *vt.* reproducir .
reproduction, *n.* reproducción, *f.*
reproof, *n.* reprensión, censura, *f.*
reprove, *vt.* censurar; improperar; regañar.
reptile, *n.* reptil, *m.*
republic, *n.* república, *f.*
republican, *n.* and *adj.* republicano, na.
republicanism, *n.* republicanismo, *m.*
repudiate, *vt.* repudiar.
repudiation, *n.* repudio, *m.*, repudiación, *f.*
repugnance, *n.* repugnancia, desgana, *f.*
repugnant, *adj.* repugnante; —ly, *adv.* de muy mala gana, con repugnancia.
repulse, *vt.* repulsar, desechar; —, *n.* repulsa, *f.*; rechazo, *m.*
repulsion, *n.* repulsión, repulsa, *f.*
repulsive, *adj.* repulsivo.
repurchase, *vt.* recomprar.
reputable, *adj.* honroso, estimable.
reputation, *n.* reputación, *f.*
repute, *vt.* reputar.
request, *n.* solicitud, petición, súplica, *f.*; pedido, *m.*; encargo, *m*; on —, (com.) a solicitud; —, *vt.* rogar, suplicar; pedir, solicitar.
require, *vt.* requerir, demandar.
required, *adj.* obligatorio.
requirement, *n.* requisito, *m.*; exigencia, *f.*
requisite, *adj.* necesario, indispensable; —, *n.* requisito, *m.*
requisition, *n.* pedimento, *m.*, requisición, *f.*; petición, demanda, *f.*
requital, *n.* retorno, *m.*; recompensa, *f.*
requite, *vt.* recompensar.
reroute, *vt.* dirigir por otra vía.
resale, *n.* reventa, *f.*, venta de segunda mano.
rescind, *vt.* rescindir, abrogar.
rescript, *n.* rescripto, edicto, *m.*
rescue, *n.* rescate, libramiento, recobro, *m.*; —, *vt.* librar, rescatar; socorrer; salvar.
rescuer, *n.* salvador, ra.
research, *n.* escudriñamiento, *m.*; investigación, *f.*
reseat, *vt.* sentar de nuevo.
resell, *vt.* revender.
resemblance, *n.* semejanza, *f.*
resemble, *vi.* asemejarse a, parecerse a.
resent, *vt.* resentir.
resentful, *adj.* resentido; vengativo; —ly, *adv.* con resentimiento.
resentment, *n.* resentimiento, *m.*; (fig.) escama, *f.*
reservation, *n.* reservación, *f.*; reserva, *f.*; restricción mental.
reserve, *vt.* reservar; —, *n.* reserva, *f.*; sigilo, *m.*

reserved, *adj.* reservado; callado; —ly, *adv.* con reserva.
reservist, *n.* soldado o marinero de reserva.
reservoir, *n.* depósito, *m.*; cambija, *f.*, tanque, *m.*
reset, *vt.* reengastar; montar de nuevo.
reshape, *vt.* reformar, formar de nuevo.
reshipment, *n.* reembarque, *m.*
reside, *vi.* residir, morar.
residence, *n.* residencia, morada, *f.*
resident, *n.* and *adj.* residente, *m.* y *f.*
residential, *adj.* residencial.
residual, *adj.* residual.
residuary, *adj.* sobrado; — legatee, (law) legatario universal.
residue, *n.* residuo, resto, *m.*
residuum, *n.* (chem.) residuo, *m.*
resign, *vt.* and *vi.* resignar, renunciar, ceder; resignarse, rendirse, conformarse.
resignation, *n.* resignación, *f.*; renuncia, *f.*
resigned, *adj.* resignado.
resilience, *n.* elasticidad, *f.*
resilient, *adj.* elástico, flexible.
resin, *n.* resina, colofonia, *f.*, pez griega; —, *vt.* dar con resina.
resinous, *adj.* resinoso.
resist, *vt.* and *vi.* resistir; oponerse.
resistance, *n.* resistencia, *f.*; — coil, bobina de resistencia.
resistant, *adj.* resistente.
resistibility, *n.* resistibilidad *f.*
resistible, *adj.* resistible.
resistless, *adj.* irresistible.
resole, *vt.* remontar, poner media suela (a los zapatos).
resoling, *n.* (zapatos) remonta, *f.*
resolute, *adj.* resuelto; —ly, *adv.* resueltamente.
resolution, *n.* resolución, *f.*
resolve, *vt.* resolver; decretar; —, *vi.* resolverse.
resolved, *adj.* resuelto.
resonance, *n.* resonancia, *f.*
resonant, *adj.* resonante.
resonator, *n.* resonador, *m.*
resort, *vi.* recurrir, frecuentar; —, *n.* concurso, *m.*; resorte, *m.*; bathing —, balneario, *m.*
resound, *vi.* resonar.
resource, *n.* recurso, *m.*; expediente, *m.*
respect, *n.* respecto, *m.*; respeto, *m.*; motivo, *m.*; —s, *n. pl.* enhorabuena, *f.*; —, *vt.* apreciar; respetar; venerar.
respectability, *n.* respetabilidad, *f.*
respectable, *adj.* respetable; decente; considerable; —bly, *adv.* notablemente; respetablemente.
respected, *adj.* considerado, apreciado.
respectful, *adj.* respetuoso; —ly, *adv.* respetuosamente.
respecting, *prep.* con respecto a.
respective, *adj.* respectivo, relativo; —ly, *adv.* respectivamente.
respiration, *n.* respiración, *f.*
respirator, *n.* respirador, *m.*

respiratory, *adj.* respiratorio.
respire, *vi.* respirar, resollar; recobrar el ánimo.
respite, *n.* suspensión, *f.*; respiro, *m.*; tregua, *f.*; —, *vt.* suspender, diferir.
resplendence, *n.* resplandor, brillo, *m.*
resplendent, *adj.* resplandeciente, fulgurante, reluciente.
respond, *vt.* responder; corresponder.
respondent, *n.* (law) defensor, *m.*
response, *n.* respuesta, réplica, *f.*
responsibility, *n.* responsabilidad, *f.*; encargo, *m.*; **to assume —,** tomar por su cuenta.
responsible, *adj.* responsable.
responsive, *adj.* conforme; sensible.
rest, *n.* reposo, *m.*; sueño, *m.*; quietud, *f.*; (mus.) pausa, *f.*; resto, residuo, restante, *m.*, sobra, *f.*; **— room,** sala de descanso; retrete, *m.*; —, *vt.* poner a descansar; apoyar; —, *vi.* dormir, reposar, recostar; **to — upon,** basar, apoyar.
restate, *vt.* repetir.
restaurant, *n.* restaurante, *m.*, fonda, *f.*
restful, *adj.* sosegado, tranquilo.
restitution, *n.* restitución, *f.*
restive, *adj.* repropio; inquieto.
restless, *adj.* inquieto, intranquilo, revuelto.
restlessness, *n.* impaciencia, inquietud, *f.*
restock, *vt.* renovar, volver a surtir.
restoration, *n.* restauración, *f.*
restorative, *adj.* restaurativo; —, *n.* medicamento restaurativo.
restore, *vt.* restaurar, restituir, restablecer, devolver, instaurar.
restrain, *vt.* restringir, refrenar; **to — oneself,** comprimirse.
restraint, *n.* refrenamiento, *m.*, coerción, *f.*; **without —,** a rienda suelta.
restrict, *vt.* restringir, limitar.
restriction, *n.* restricción, coartación, *f.*
restrictive, *adj.* restrictivo.
result, *n.* resultado, *m.*; resulta, consecuencia, *f.*; éxito, *m.*; —, *vi.* resultar; redundar en.
resume, *vt.* resumir, reanudar; empezar de nuevo.
resumption, *n.* reasunción, *f.*
resurface, *vt.* revestir, renovar; recargar (un camino).
resurrect, *vt.* resucitar.
resurrection, *n.* resurrección, *f.*
resuscitate, *vt.* resucitar.
resuscitation, *n.* resurrección, *f.*; renovación, *f.*
retail, *vt.* revender, vender al por menor; —, *n.* venta al por menor, menudeo, *m.*; **at —,** al menudeo, al por menor.
retailer, *n.* comerciante al por menor, revendedor, *m.*
retain, *vt.* retener, guardar.
retainer, *n.* retenedor, ra; adherente, partidario, *m.*; (law) honorario, *m.*
retake, *vt.* volver a tomar.
retaliate, *vi.* talionar, vengarse,

retaliation, *n.* talión, *m.*
retaliatory, *adj.* que usa represalias.
retard, *vt.* retardar.
retardation, *n.* retardación, *f.*
retch, *vi.* esforzarse a vomitar.
retention, *n.* retención, *f.*
retentive, *adj.* retentivo.
reticence, *n.* reticencia, *f.*
reticent, *adj.* reticente.
reticle, *n.* retículo, *m.*
reticule, *n.* ridículo, *m.*, bolsa manual.
retina, *n.* retina (del ojo), *f.*
retire, *vt.* retirar; —, *vi.* retirarse, sustraerse.
retired, *adj.* apartado, retirado.
retirement, *n.* retiro, retiramiento, *m.*; receso, *m.*
retiring, *adj.* recatado, callado.
retort, *vt.* redargüir, retorcer (un argumento); —, *n.* redargución, *f.*; (chem.) retorta, *f.*
retouch, *vt.* retocar.
retrace, *vt.* volver a trazar.
retract, *vt.* retractar, retirar; retraer.
retraction, *n.* retracción, revocación, *f.*
retractor, *n.* retractor, *m.*
retread, *vt.* reponer la superficie rodante de un neumático; reandar (un camino, etc.).
retreat, *n.* retirada, *f.*; (mil.) retreta, *f.*; (eccl.) retiro, *m.*; —, *vi.* retirarse.
retrench, *vt.* cercenar; (mil.) atrincherar; —, *vi.* economizar.
retrenchment, *n.* cercenadura, economía, *f.*; atrincheramiento, *m.*; trinchera, *f.*
retribution, *n.* retribución, recompensa, *f.*; refacción, *f.*
retributive, *adj.* retribuyente.
retrievable, *adj.* recuperable; reparable.
retrieve, *vt.* recuperar, recobrar.
retriever, *n.* sabueso, *m.*
retroactive, *adj.* retroactivo.
retrograde, *adj.* retrógrado; —, *vi.* retrogradar, retroceder.
retrogress, *vi.* retrogradar, retroceder.
retrogression, *n.* retrogradación, *f.*
retrospect, retrospection, *n.* reflexión de las cosas pasadas.
retrospective, *adj.* retrospectivo.
return, *vt.* retribuir; restituir; volver; devolver; —, *n.* retorno, *m.*; vuelta, *f.*; recompensa, retribución, *f.*; recaída, *f.*; **by — mail,** a vuelta de correo; **— trip,** viaje de vuelta.
returnable, *adj.* susceptible de devolverse; **— goods,** efectos susceptibles de devolverse.
reunion, *n.* reunión, *f.*
reunite, *vt.* reunir, volver a unir; —, *vi.* reunirse, reconciliarse.
Rev. Reverend, R. Reverendo.
rev.: revenue, ingresos; **reverse,** reverso; **review,** revista; **revised,** revisado; **revision,** revisión, *f.*; **revolution,** revolución.
revaluation, *n.* revaluación, *f.*
revalue, *vt.* valorizar de nuevo.

revamp, *vt.* meter capellada nueva; remendar.

reveal, *vt.* revelar; publicar.

revealment, *n.* revelamiento, *m.*, revelación, *f.*

revel, *vi.* andar en borracheras; —, *n.* borrachera; **drunken** —, orgía, *f.*

revelation, *n.* revelación, *f.*

reveler, reveller, *n.* borrasquero, ra; fiestero, ra.

revelry, *n.* borrachera, *f.*; jarana, *f.*

revenge, *vt.* vengar; —, *n.* venganza, *f.*

revengeful, *adj.* vengativo; —**ly,** *adv.* con venganza.

revenue, *n.* renta, *f.*; rédito, *m*; ingreso, *m.*; — **cutter,** guardacostas, *m.*; — **stamp,** sello de impuesto.

reverberant, *adj.* reverberante.

reverberate, *vt.* and *vi.* reverberar; resonar, retumbar.

reverberation, *n.* repercusión, *f.*; reverberación, *f.*

reverberator, *n.* reverberador, *m.*

reverberatory, *adj.* reverberatorio.

revere, *vt.* reverenciar, venerar.

reverence, *n.* reverencia, *f.*; —, *vt.* reverenciar.

reverend, *adj.* reverendo; venerable; —, *n.* abad, *m.*; pastor, *m.*

reverent, reverential, *adj.* reverencial, respetuoso; —**ly,** *adv.* reverencialmente.

reverential, *adj.* reverencial.

reverie, revery, *n.* ensueño, *m.*; embelesamiento, *m.*; ilusión, *f*

reversal, *n.* revocación (de una sentencia), *f.*; reversión, *f.*

reverse, *n.* vicisitud, *f*; contrario, *m*; reverso (de una moneda), *m.*; revés, *m.* a través *m.*; contramarcha, *f.*; — **lever,** palanca de cambio de marcha; —, *adj.* inverso; contrario; —, *vt.* trastrocar; abolir.

reversibility, *n.* reversibilidad. *f*

reversible, *adj.* revocable, reversible.

reversing, *adj.* de inversión; — **switch,** inversor, *m.*

reversion, *n.* futura, *f.*; reversión, *f.*

revert, *vt.* and *vi.* revertir, trastrocar; volverse atrás.

revery, *n.* ensueño, *m.*

revet, *vt.* revestir.

revetment, *n.* revestimiento, *m.*

review, *n.* revista, *f*; reseña, *f.*; repaso, *m.*; **to make a** —, reseñar; —, *vt.* rever; (mil.) revistar; repasar.

reviewer, *n.* revisor, ra; crítico profesional de libros.

revile, *vt.* ultrajar; difamar.

revilement, *n.* difamación, injuria, *f.*

revise, *vt.* revisar, rever; —, *n.* revista, revisión, *f.*; (print.) segunda prueba.

reviser, *n.* revisor, ra.

revising, *adj.* revisor.

revision, *n.* revisión, *f.*

revival, *n.* restauración, *f.*; renacimiento,

m.; (theat.) nueva representación de una obra antigua.

revive, *vt.* avivar; restablecer; (theat.) volver a presentar (una comedia antigua, etc.); —, *vi.* revivir.

revocable, *adj.* revocable.

revocation, *n.* revocación, *f.*

revoke, *vt.* revocar, anular.

revolt, *vi.* rebelarse; alzarse en armas; —, *n.* rebelión, *f.*

revolting, *adj.* repugnante.

revolution, *n.* revolución, *f.*

revolutionary, *n.* and *adj.* revolucionario, ria.

revolutionist, *n.* revolucionario, ria

revolutionize, *vt.* revolucionar.

revolve, *vt.* revolver; meditar; —, *vi.* girar.

revolver, *n.* revólver, *m.*, pistola, *f.*

revolving, *adj.* giratorio.

revue, *n.* revista teatral.

revulsion, *n.* (med) revulsión, *f.*

Rev. Ver. Revised Version, Versión Revisada.

reward, *n.* recompensa, *f.*; fruto, *m.*; pago, *m.*; —, *vt.* recompensar.

rewire, *vt.* and *vi.* volver a proveer de alambre; volver a telegrafiar.

rewrite, *vt.* volver a escribir, escribir de nuevo.

R. F., r. f. radio frequency, radiofrecuencia.

RFC Reconstruction Finance Corporation, Institución Financiera de Reconstrucciones.

RFD, r.f.d. rural free delivery, distribución gratuita del correo en regiones rurales.

R.H. Royal Highness, A.R. Alteza Real.

rhapsody, *n.* rapsodia, *f.*

rheostat, *n.* (elec.) reóstato, *m.*

rhetoric, *n.* retórica, *f.*

rhetorical, *adj.* retórico.

rhetorician, *n.* retórico, ca.

rheum, *n.* reuma, *m.* y *f.*

rheumatic, *adj.* reumático.

rheumatism, *n.* reumatismo, *m.*

rhinoceros, *n.* rinoceronte, *m.*

rhizome, *n.* (bot.) rizoma, *f.*

rhododendron, *n.* (bot.) rododendro, *m.*

rhomb, *n.* rombo, *m.*

rhomboid, *n.* romboide, *m.*

rhubarb, *n.* ruibarbo, *m.*

rhyme, *n.* rima, *f.*; poema, *m.*; —, *vi.* rimar.

rhymer, *n.* versista, *m.* y *f.*, versificador, ra.

rhymester, *n.* coplero, ra; versista de rimas malas.

rhythm, *n.* ritmo, *m.*

rhythmic, rhythmical, *adj.* rítmico.

rhythmically, *adv.* rítmicamente.

R.I. Rhode Island, Rhode Island.

rib, *n.* costilla, *f.*; nervio, *m.*, nervadura, (de un puente, barco, etc.), *f*; varilla (de un paraguas), *f.*

ribald, *adj.* obsceno, ribaldo; —, *n.* persona lasciva.

ribaldry, *n.* lenguaje ruin u obsceno.

ribbon, *n.* listón, *m.*, cinta, *f.*; —**s**, *n. pl.* perifollos, *m. pl.*

rice, *n.* arroz, *m.*; — **field**, arrozal, *m.*; — **paper**, papel de paja de arroz.

rich, *adj.* rico; opulento; abundante; —**ly**, *adv.* ricamente.

Richard, Ricardo.

riches, *n. pl.* riqueza, *f.*; bienes, *m. pl.*

richness, *n.* riqueza, *f.*; suntuosidad, *f.*

rick, *n.* niara, *f.*, pajar en el campo.

rickets, *n.* raquitis, *f.*, raquitismo, *m.*

rickety, *adj.* raquítico, desvencijado.

ricksha, rickshaw, *n.* vehículo japonés de dos ruedas tirado por uno o más hombres.

rid, *vt.* librar, desembarazar.

riddance, *n.* libramiento, *m.*; zafada, *f.*

ridden, *p. p.* del verbo **ride**.

riddle, *n.* enigma, rompecabezas, *m.*; criba, *f.*; (min.) garbillo, *m.*; —, *vt.* cribar.

ride, *vi.* cabalgar; andar en coche; **to — a bicycle**, montar en bicicleta; —, *n.* paseo a caballo o en coche.

rider, *n.* caballero, cabalgador, *m.*

ridge, *n.* espinazo, lomo, *m.*; cordillera, *f.*; arruga, *f.*; — **of a roof**, caballete, *m.*; —, *vt.* formar lomos o surcos.

ridicule, *n.* ridiculez, *f.*; ridículo, *m.*; —, *vt.* ridiculizar.

ridiculous, *adj.* ridículo; —**ly**, *adv.* ridículamente.

riding, *n.* acción de andar a caballo o en coche; paseo a caballo o en coche; —, *adj.* relativo a la equitación; — **boot**, bota de montar; — **breeches**, pantalones de equitación o de montar a caballo; — **habit**, — **outfit**, traje de montar, traje de amazona; — **master**, proiesor de equitación.

rife, *adj.* común, frecuente; — **with**, lleno de; abundante en.

riffle, *vt.* barajar dejando caer alternativamente, para que se mezclen, los naipes de una y otra mano.

riffraff, *n.* desecho, desperdicio, *m.*; gentuza, *f.*

rifle, *vt.* robar, pillar; estriar, rayar; —, *n.* fusil, *m.*, carabina rayada; — **case**, carcaj. *m* ; — **corps**, fusilería, *f.*; — **range**, alcance de proyectil de rifle; lugar para tirar al blanco.

rifleman, *n.* escopetero, fusilero, *m.*

rift, *n.* hendidura, *f.*; división, *f.*; disensión, *f.*

rig, *vt.* ataviar; (naut.) aparejar; —, *n.* aparejo, *m.*; traje ridículo o de mal gusto.

rigging, *n.* (naut.) aparejo, *m.*

right, *adj.* derecho, recto; justo; honesto; — **wing**, (pol.) derecha, *f.*; —! *interj.* ¡bueno! ¡bien! **all** —, ¡bien! —, *adv.* derechamente, rectamente; justamente; bien; — **away**, en seguida, luego, inmediatamente; — **off**, en seguida, inmediatamente; **to be** —, tener razón; **to set** —,

poner en claro; —**ly**, *adv.* rectamente, justamente; —, *n.* justicia, *f.*; razón *f.*; derecho, *m.*; mano derecha; **all** —**s reserved**, derechos reservados; — **of way**, derecho de vía; —, *vt.* hacer justicia.

rightabout, *n.* vuelta a la derecha, vuelta atrás, media vuelta.

right angle, *n.* ángulo recto.

right away, *adv.* en seguida.

righteous, *adj.* justo, honrado; —**ly**, *adv.* justamente.

righteousness, *n.* equidad, *f.*; honradez, *f.*

right-hand, *adj.* a la derecha; **to the — side**, a la derecha.

rightist, *n.* (pol.) derechista, *m.* y *f.*

right of way, *n.* derecho a la vía.

rigid, *adj.* rígido; austero, severo; —**ly**, *adv.* con rigidez.

rigidity, *n.* rigidez, austeridad, *f.*

rigmarole, *n.* (coll.) galimatías, *m.*

rigor, *n.* rigor, *m.*; severidad, *f.*

rigorous, *adj.* riguroso; —**ly**, *adv.* rigurosamente.

rill, *n.* riachuelo, *m.*

rim, *n.* margen, *m.* y *f.*, orilla, *f.*, borde, *m.*; llanta, *f.*

rime, *n.* escarcha, *f.*, rima, *f.*

rimy, *adj.* nebuloso, húmedo.

rind, *n.* corteza, *f.*; hollejo, *m.*

ring, *n.* círculo, cerco, *m.*; anillo, *m.*; campaneo, *m* ; (mech.) manija, *f.*; — **finger**, dedo anular; —, *vt.* sonar; **to — the bell**, tirar la campanilla, tocar el timbre; —, *vi.* retiñir, retumbar; resonar; **to — (the ears)**, zumbar (los oídos).

ringbolt, *n.* cáncamo, *m.*, perno de armella o argolla.

ringdove, *n.* paloma torcaz.

ringer, *n.* campanero, *m.*; tejo o herradura colocado al rededor de la estaca de los juegos respectivos.

ringing, *adj.* sonoro, resonante; —, *n.* repique, *m.*

ringleader, *n.* cabecilla, *m.*, cabeza de partido o bando.

ringlet, *n.* anillejo, *m.*; rizo, *m.*

ringworm, *n.* (med.) empeine, *m.*, tiña, *f.*

rink, *n.* patinadero, *m.*

rinse, *vt.* lavar, limpiar, enjuagar.

riot, *n.* tumulto, bullicio, *m.*, pelotera, *f.*; orgía, *f* ; borrachera, *f.*; motín, *m.*; —, *vi.* andar en orgías; causar alborotos; armar motines.

rioter, *n.* amotinador, ra; revoltoso, sa; (coll.) bullanguero, ra, alborotador, ra.

riotous, *adj.* bullicioso, sedicioso; disoluto; —**ly**, *adv.* disolutamente.

rip, *vt.* rasgar, lacerar; descoser; —, *n.* rasgadura, *f.*; — **cord**, (aer.) cuerda que al tirar de ella abre el paracaídas.

riparian, *adj.* ribereño.

ripe, *adj.* maduro, sazonado; —**ly**, *adv.* maduramente.

ripen, *vt. and vi.* madurar.

ripple, *vi.* manar el agua a borbotones;

susurrar; ondular; rizar, ondear; —, *n.* susurro, *m.*

ripsaw, *n.* sierra para cortar madera longitudinalmente.

rise, *vi.* levantarse; nacer, salir (los astros); rebelarse; ascender; hincharse; elevarse; resucitar; surgir; **to — above,** trascender; —, *n.* levantamiento, *m.*; elevación, *f.*; subida, *f.*; salida (del sol), *f.*; causa, *f.*

risen, *p. p.* del verbo **rise.**

riser, *n.* persona o cosa que se levanta; (arch.) contrahuella, *f.*; **early —,** madrugador, ra, buen madrugador.

risible, *adj.* risible.

risk, *n.* riesgo, peligro, *m.*; **without —,** sobre seguro; —, *vt.* arriesgar.

risky, *adj.* peligroso.

rite, *n.* rito, *m.*

ritual, *adj.* and *n.* ritual, *m.*

riv. river, río.

rival, *adj.* émulo; —, *n.* rival, *m.* y *f.*; —, *vt.* competir, emular.

rivalry, *n.* rivalidad, *f.*

rive, *vt.* rajar, hender; —, *vi.* henderse, rajarse.

river, *n.* río, *m.*; **— basin,** cuenca de un río; **— bed,** cauce, *m.*; **— waterways,** vías fluviales.

riverside, *n.* ribera, *f.*; —, *adj.* situado a la orilla de un río.

rivet, *n.* remache, roblón, *m.*; **— plate,** roseta, *f.*, plancha de contrarremache; —, *vt.* remachar, roblar.

riveter, *n.* remachador, *m.*

riveting, *n.* remache, remachado, *m.*, robladura, *f.*

rivulet, *n.* riachuelo, *m.*

rm.: ream, resma; **room,** cto. cuarto.

R.N.: registered nurse, enfermera titulada; **Royal Navy,** Marina Real (de Inglaterra).

roach, *n.* escarcho, rubio, *m.*; cucaracha, *f.*

road, *n.* camino, *m.*; çamino real; vía, *f.*; ruta, *f.*; carretera, *f.*; **main —,** carretera, *f.*; **paved —,** carretera empedrada; **— scraper,** traílla, *f.*

roadbed, *n.* cimiento de un camino; base de balasto de vía férrea o carretera.

roadhouse, *n.* posada o venta a la vera de un camino.

roadside, *adj.* al lado de un camino; **— inn,** venta, posada, *f.*

roadstead, *n.* (naut.) rada, *f.*

roadster, *n.* coche, *m.*, automóvil pequeño de turismo.

roadway, *n.* camino afirmado; firme del camino; calzada, *f.*

roam, *vt.* and *vi.* corretear; tunar, vagar.

roan, *adj.* roano, ruano; **— horse,** caballo roano.

roar, *vi.* rugir; aullar; bramar; —, *n.* rugido, *m.*; bramido, estruendo, *m.*; mugido, *m.*

roaring, *n.* bramido, *m.*; —, *adj.* rugiente.

roast, *vt.* asar; tostar; **— beef,** asado de vaca, rosbif, *m.*

roaster, *n.* asador, *m.*

rob, *vt.* robar, hurtar.

robber, *n.* ladrón, ona.

robbery, *n.* robo, *m.*

robe, *n.* manto, *m.*; toga, *f.*; **—s,** *n. pl.* ropa, vestimenta, *f.*; —, *vt.* vestir de gala.

Robert, Roberto.

robin, *n.* (orn.) petirrojo, pechirrojo, pechicolorado, *m.*

robot, *n.* hombre mecánico; (aer.) piloto mecánico.

robust, *adj.* robusto.

rock, *n.* roca, *f.*; escollo, *m.*; (naut.) vigía, *m.*; **— bottom,** el fondo, lo más profundo; **— crystal,** cuarzo, *m.*; **— garden,** jardín entre rocas; **— salt,** sal gema; **— wool,** material fibroso con aspecto de lana que se forma al arrojar un chorro de vapor a través de roca fundida. Se emplea como aislador del calor y del sonido; —, *vt.* mecer; arrullar; apedrear; —, *vi.* bambolear, balancearse, oscilar.

rock-bound, *adj.* rodeado de rocas.

rocker, *n.* mecedora, *f.*; cunera, *f.*; silla de columpio.

rocket, *n.* cohete, volador, *m.*

rocking, *n.* balanceo, *m.*; —, *adj.* mecedor; **— chair,** mecedora, *f.*, silla de columpio.

rock-ribbed, *adj.* fuerte, firme, sólido.

rocky, *adj.* peñascoso, pedregoso, rocoso, roqueño; **R— Mountains,** Montañas Roqueñas o Rocosas.

rod, *n.* varilla, caña, *f.*; **connecting —,** (mech.) biela, *f.*

rode, pretérito del verbo **ride.**

rodent, *n.* roedor, *m.*

rodeo, *n.* rodeo, *m.*

Roderick, Rodrigo.

rodomontade, *n.* fanfarria, jactancia, *f.*

roe, *n.* corzo, *m.*; hueva, *f.*

roebuck, *n.* corzo, *m.*

rogation, *n.* rogaciones, *f. pl.*

Roger, Rogerio, Rogelio.

rogue, *n.* bribón, pícaro, pillo, villano, *m.*; (coll.) granuja, *m.*; **rogues' gallery,** colección de retratos de malhechores para uso de la policía.

roguery, *n.* picardía, *f.*

roguish, *adj.* pícaro, pillo.

roister, *vi.* bravear, fanfarronear.

role, rôle, *n.* papel, *m.*, parte, *f.*

roll, *vt.* rodar; volver; arrollar, enrollar; —, *vi.* rodar; girar; —, *n.* rodadura, *f.*; rollo, *m.*; lista, *f.*; catálogo, *m.*; rasero, *m.*; voluta, *f.*; panecillo, *m.*; **film —,** rollo de películas; **muster —,** rol, *m.*; **— call,** acto de pasar lista; **to call the —,** pasar lista.

roller, *n.* rodillo, cilindro, aplanador, *m.*; rodo, *m.*; aplanadora, *f.*; rueda, *f.*; **— bearing,** cojinete de rodillos; **— coaster,** montaña rusa; **— skate,** patín de ruedas, patín, *m.*; **— towel,** toalla sin fin.

rollicking, *adj.* jovial, retozón.

rolling, *adj.* rodante; undulado; **— capital,**

capital circulante; **— mill,** taller de laminar; **— pin,** rodillo de pastelero; **— stock,** (rail.) material rodante; **—,** *n.* rodadura, *f.*; (aer.) balanceo, *m.*; (naut.) balance, *m.*

roll-top, *adj.* de cubierta plegadiza o corrediza.

roly-poly, *adj.* rechoncho; **—,** *n.* persona rechoncha; variedad de pudín.

Rom.: Roman, romano, **Romance,** romance, neolatino.

romaine, *n.* especie de lechuga.

Roman, *adj.* romano; romanesco; **—,** *n.* romano, na; **— type,** letra redonda,

romance, *n.* romance, *m.*; ficción, *f.*; cuento, *m.*; fábula, *f.*; **R—,** adj. romance.

romancist, *n.* romancista, *m.* y *f.*

romantic, *adj.* romántico; sentimental.

romanticism, *n.* romanticismo, *m.*

romanticist, *n.* romántico, ca.

Rom. Cath. Roman Catholic, católico romano.

Rome, Roma, *f.*

romp, *n.* muchacha retozona; **—,** *vi.* retozar.

rompers, *n. pl.* traje de niño de una sola pieza y en forma de pantalón.

rondo, *n.* (mus.) rondó, *m.*

rood, *n.* pértiga para medir; (eccl.) cruz *f.*, crucifijo, *m.*

roof, *n.* tejado, techo, *m.*; azotea, *f.*; paladar, *m.*; imperial de un coche; **— garden,** azotea, *f.*; **—,** *vt.* techar.

roofing, *n.* techado, *m.*; material para techos.

rook, *n.* (orn.) corneja, *f.*; roque (en el juego de ajedrez), *m.*; trampista, *m.* y *f.*; **—,** *vt.* and *vi.* trampear, engañar.

rookery, *n.* árboles donde hacen sus nidos muchas cornejas; habitación escuálida.

rookie, *n.* bisoño, *m.*

room, *n.* cuarto, *m.*, habitación, cámara, *f.*; aposento, *m.*; lugar, espacio, *m.*

roomer, *n.* inquilino, na, persona que ocupa un cuarto en una casa de huéspedes.

roommate, *n.* compañero o compañera de cuarto.

roomy, *adj.* espacioso.

roorback, *n.* pasquín, panfleto, libelo, *m.*

roost, *n.* pértiga del gallinero; **—,** *vi.* dormir las aves en una pértiga.

rooster, *n.* gallo, *m.*

root, *n.* raíz *f.*; origen, *m.*; **— beer,** bebida de extractos de varias raíces; **to take —,** echar raíces, prender; radicarse **—,** *vt.* and *vi.* arraigar; echar raíces; (coll.) gritar o aplaudir ruidosamente a los jugadores para animarlos; **to — out,** desarraigar.

rooted, *adj.* inveterado; arraigado.

rooter, *n.* arrancatocones, *m.*; (coll.) persona que grita y aplaude ruidosamente a los jugadores para animarlos.

rope, *n.* cuerda, *f.*; cordel, *m.*; cable, *m.*; **wheel —, tiller —,** guardín, *m.*; **—,** *vt.* atar con un cordel.

ropedancer, *n.* volatín, volatinero, *m.*

ropewalk, *n.* cordelería, *f.*

ropewalker, *n.* volatinero, ra.

roque, *n.* variación del juego de croquet.

Rosalie, Rosalía.

rosary, *n.* rosario, *m.*

Rose, Rosa.

rose, *n.* (bot.) rosa, *f.*; color de rosa; **—,** pretérito del verbo **rise.**

roseate, *adj.* róseo.

rosebud, *n.* capullo de rosa.

rosebush, *n.* (bot.) rosal, *m.*

rosemary, *n.* (bot.) romero, *m.*

rosette, *n.* roseta, *f.*; (arch.) florón, *m.*

rosewood, *n.* palo de rosa, palisandro, *m.*

rosin, *n.* resina, *f.*, pez griega; **—,** *vt.* dar con resina.

roster, *n.* lista, *f.*; matrícula, *f.*; registro, *m.*

rostrum, *n.* tribuna, *f.*; rostro, *m.*

rosy, *adj.* róseo.

rot, *vi.* pudrirse; **—,** *n.* morriña, *f.*; putrefacción, *f.*

rotary, *adj.* giratorio; **— press,** máquina rotativa.

rotate, *vt.* girar; alternar; dar vueltas; **—,** *vi.* alternarse; girar.

rotating, *adj.* giratorio, rotativo.

rotation, *n.* rotación, *f.*

rotatory, *adj.* que rueda, rotatorio, giratorio.

R.O.T.C. Reserve Officers' Training Corps, Cuerpo de Instrucción para Oficiales de la Reserva.

rote, *n.* uso, *m.*; práctica, *f.*

rotogravure, *n.* rotograbado, *m.*

rotor, *n.* (mech.) rotor, *m.*

rotten, *adj.* podrido, corrompido.

rottenness, *n.* podredumbre, putrefacción, *f.*

rotund, *adj.* rotundo, redondo, circular, esférico.

rotunda, *n.* rotonda, *f.*

rotundity, *n.* rotundidad, redondez, *f.*

rouble, *n.* = **ruble.**

roué, *n.* libertino, *m.*

rouge, *n.* arrebol, colorete, afeite, *m.*

rough, *adj.* áspero; bronco, brusco; bruto, tosco; tempestuoso; **in the —,** en bruto; **— draft,** borrador, *m.*; **— sea,** mar borrascoso; **—ly,** *adv.* rudamente, toscamente.

roughage, *n.* alimento o forraje difícil de digerir.

rough-and-ready, *adj.* tosco pero eficaz en acción.

rough-and-tumble, *adj.* desordenado; fuerte, resistente.

roughcast, *vt.* bosquejar una figura o cuadro; **—,** *n.* modelo en bruto.

roughdry, *adj.* seco y sin planchar.

roughen, *vt.* poner áspero; **—,** *vi.* ponerse o hacerse áspero.

roughhew, *vt.* modelar toscamente alguna cosa; desbastar.

roughness, *n.* aspereza, *f.*; rudeza, tosquedad, *f.*; tempestad, *f.*

roughrider, *n.* domador, *m.*; soldado irregular a caballo.

roulette, *n.* ruleta, *f.*; rueda de la fortuna.

Roumania, = **Rumania.**

Roumanian, *n.* and *adj.* = **Rumanian.**

round, *adj.* redondo; circular; cabal; rotundo, franco, sincero; — **number,** número redondo; — **steak,** corte especial de carne de vaca; — **trip,** viaje redondo, viaje de ida y vuelta; **to make** —, redondear; —, *n.* círculo, *m.*; redondez *f.*; vuelta, *f.*; giro, *m.*; escalón, *m.*; (mil.) ronda, *f.*; andanada de cañones; descarga, *f.*; —, *adv.* redondamente; por todos lados; —, *vt.* cercar, rodear; redondear; **to** — **up,** rodear, recoger el ganado; —**ly,** *adv.* redondamente; francamente.

roundabout, *adj.* amplio; indirecto, a la redonda.

round-cheeked, *adj.* carrilludo, cachetudo.

roundelay, *n.* coplas que se cantan en rueda.

roundhouse, *n.* casa de máquinas; (rail.) rotunda, *f.*; (naut.) toldilla, *f.*

roundness, *n.* redondez, *f.*

round-shouldered, *adj.* cargado de espaldas.

round table, *n.* mesa redonda, reunión de un grupo para discutir problemas de interés mutuo.

roundup, *n.* rodeo de ganado.

roundworm, *n.* gusano del género de los nematodes.

roup, *n.* catarro de las aves domésticas; ronquera, *f.*

rouse, *vt.* despertar; excitar.

roustabout, *n.* peón de embarcadero, gañán, *m.*

rout, *n.* rota, derrota, *f.*; —, *vt.* derrotar.

route, *n.* ruta, vía, *f.*, camino, *m.*

routine, *n.* rutina, *f.*; hábito, *m.*; —, *adj.* rutinario.

rove, *vi.* vagar, vaguear.

rover, *n.* vagamundo, *m.*; pirata, *m.*

row, *n.* riña, camorra, *f.*, zipizape, *m.*

row, *n.* hilera, fila, *f.*; — **of seats,** tendido, *m.*; —, *vt.* and *vi.* (naut.) remar, bogar.

rowboat, *n.* (naut.) bote de remos.

rowdy, *n.* alborotador, ra, bullanguero, ra; —, *adj.* alborotoso, bullanguero.

rowel, *n.* estrella de espuela.

rower, *n.* (naut.) remero, ra, bogador, ra, boga, *m.* y *f.*

rowing, *n.* (naut.) boga, *f.*

rowlock, *n.* (naut.) chumacera, *f.*

royal, *adj.* real; regio; —**ly,** *adv.* regiamente.

royalist, *n.* realista, *m.* y *f.*

royalty, *n.* realeza, dignidad real; —**ties,** *n. pl.* regalías, *f. pl.*, derechos de autor.

r.p.m. revolutions per minute, r.p.m. revoluciones por minuto.

r.p.s. revolutions per second, r.p.s. revoluciones por segundo.

R.R.: railroad, f.c. ferrocarril; **Right Reverend,** Reverendísimo.

R.S.V.P. please answer, sírvase enviar respuesta.

rt. right, der. derecha.

Rt. Hon. Right Honorable, Muy Honorable.

rub, *vt.* estregar, fregar, frotar, raspar, restregar; friccionar; **to** — **against,** rozar; **to** — **down,** almohazar, limpiar; —, *n.* frotamiento, *m.*; roce, *m.*; (fig.) tropiezo, obstáculo, *m.*; dificultad, *f.*

rubber, *n.* goma, *f.*, goma elástica, caucho, *m.*; **hard** —, caucho endurecido; — **band,** faja de goma o de caucho; — **cement,** cemento de caucho; — **heel,** tacón de goma; — **plant,** cauchera, *f.*; — **plantation,** cauchal, *m.*; — **stamp,** sello de goma; (coll.) imitador, ra, satélite, *m.* y *f.*; (coll.) persona que obra de una manera rutinaria; **synthetic** —, caucho artificial; **vulcanized** —, caucho vulcanizado; —**s,** *n. pl.* chanclos, *m. pl.*, zapatos de goma; —, *adj.* de goma, de caucho.

rubberize, *vt.* engomar.

rubberizing, *n.* impregnación de caucho.

rubber-sheathed, *adj.* encauchado.

rubber-stamp, *vt.* aprobar servilmente; estampar con un sello de goma.

rubbish, *n.* escombro, *m.*; ruinas, *f. pl.*; andrajos, *m. pl.*; cacharro, ripio, *m.*

rubble, *n.* ripio, *m.*, cascotes, *m. pl.*

rubdown, *n.* frotación, *f.*; — *vt.* frotar.

rubicund, *adj.* rubicundo.

ruble, *n.* rublo, *m.*

rubric, *n.* rúbrica, *f.*

ruby, *n.* rubí, *m.*

ruche, *n.* lechuguilla, *f.*

ruching, *n.* material para hacer lechuguillas.

rudder, *n.* timón, gobernalle, *m.*, timón de dirección.

ruddy, *adj.* colorado, rubio; lozano.

rude, *adj.* rudo, brutal, rústico, grosero, tosco; —**ly,** *adv.* rudamente, groseramente.

rudeness, *n.* descortesía, *f.*; rudeza, insolencia, *f.*; barbaridad, *f.*; brusquedad, *f.*

rudiment, *n.* rudimento, *m.*

Rudolph, Rodolfo.

rue, *vi.* compadecerse; —, *n.* (bot.) ruda, *f.*; pesar, *m.*; decepción, *f.*

rueful, *adj.* lamentable, triste.

ruff, *n.* lechuguilla, *f.*

ruffian, *n.* malhechor, bandolero, rufián, *m.*; —, *adj.* brutal; —**ly,** *adj.* malvado, perverso.

ruffle, *vt.* desordenar, desazonar; rizar; fruncir (un volante, una vuelta, etc.); irritar, enojar; —, *n.* volante fruncido, vuelta, *f.*; conmoción, *f.*; enojo, enfado, *m.*

Rufus, Rufo.

rug, *n.* paño burdo; alfombra, *f.*; **steamer** —, manta de viaje.

rugged, *adj.* áspero, tosco; brutal; peludo; robusto, vigoroso.

ruin, *n.* ruina, *f.*; perdición, *f.*; escom-

bros, *m. pl.*; —, *vt.* arruinar; destruir, echar a perder, dar al traste con.
ruinous, *adj.* ruinoso; —ly, *adv.* ruinosamente.
rule, *n.* mando, *m.*; regla, *f.*; máxima, *f.*; norma, *f.*; férula, *f.*; ordenanza, *f.*; **as a —,** por lo general; **bevel —,** falsarregla, *f.*; **by —,** a regla, por regla; **standard —,** regla fija; **to make it a —,** tener por costumbre; —, *vt.* and *vi.* gobernar; reglar; dirigir; imperar, mandar; —, *vt.* rayar.
ruler, *n.* gobernador, gobernante, *m.*; mandatario, *m.*; regla, *f.*
ruling, *n.* rayadura, *f.*; (law) decisión, *f.*; —, *adj.* gobernante, dirigente.
rum, *n.* ron, *m.*; —, *adj.* (coll.) extraño, singular; peligroso.
Rumania, Rumania, *f.*
Rumanian, *n.* and *adj.* rumano, na.
rumba, *n.* rumba, *f.*
rumble, *vi.* crujir, rugir; — **seat,** (auto.) asiento trasero descubierto.
rumen, *n.* panza, *f.*, primer estómago de los rumiantes.
ruminant, *n.* rumiante, *m.*
ruminate, *vt.* and *vi.* rumiar.
rumination, *n.* meditación, *f.*
rummage, *vt.* trastornar, revolver, escudriñar; —, *n.* confusión, *f.*; — **sale,** venta de artículos usados; venta de remates.
rummy, *n.* variedad de juego de naipes.
rumor, *n.* rumor, *m.*; —, *vt.* divulgar alguna noticia.
rump, *n.* obispillo de ave; nalga (de animal), *f.*
rumple, *n.* arruga, *f.*; —, *vt.* ajar, arrugar.
rumrunner, *n.* contrabandista de aguardiente.
run, *vt.* arrojar con violencia; traspasar; —, *vi.* correr; fluir, manar; pasar rápidamente; proceder; **to — across,** tropezar con; **to — aground,** encallar; **to — down,** averiguar; alcanzar; pararse (un reloj); descargarse, agotarse; **to — into,** topar, chocar con; **to — off,** escaparse, escurrir; **to — out of,** no tener más (de algo); **to — the risk of,** arriesgar, aventurar; —, *n.* corrida, carrera, *f.*; curso, *m.*; recorrido, *m.*; serie, *f.*; moda, *f.*; excursión, *f.*; libertad en el uso de cosas; (mus.) escala, *f.*; tanto (en baseball); **in the long —,** a la larga.
runabout, *n.* automóvil pequeño de dos asientos; vagabundo, da.
runaway, *n.* fugitivo, va, desertor, ra.
rundlet, runlet, *n.* barrilejo, *m.*
run-down, *adj.* cansado, rendido, agotado, fatigado; parado por falta de cuerda (un reloj).
rung, *n.* escalón, peldaño (de escalera de mano), *m.*; —, *p.p.* del verbo **ring.**
runner, *n.* corredor, ra; mensajero, ra; alfombra larga y angosta.
runner-up, *n.* competidor que queda en segundo lugar.

running, *n.* carrera, corrida, *f.*; curso, *m.*; — **board,** estribo, *m.*; — **gear,** juego de ruedas y ejes de un vehículo; tren de ruedas; — **water,** agua corriente; —, *adj.* corriente, que corre o fluye.
runoff, *n.* agua de drenaje; carrera final de caballos para decidir el vencedor.
runway, *n.* cauce, *m.*; corredera, *f.*; vía, *f.*; pasadizo para ganado; (aer.) pista de aterrizaje en un aeropuerto.
Rupert, Ruperto.
rupture, *n.* rotura, *f.*; hernia, quebradura, *f.*; —, *vt.* reventar, romper.
rural, *adj.* rural, campestre, rústico.
ruse, *n.* astucia, maña, *f.*
rush, *n.* (bot.) junco, *m.*; ímpetu, *m.*; prisa, *f.*; — **hour,** hora de tránsito intenso; — **order,** pedido urgente, pedido de precisión; —, *vi.* alabanzarse, tirarse; ir de prisa, apresurarse.
rushlight, *n.* vela o lamparilla de noche.
rusk, *n.* galleta, *f.*
russet, *adj.* bermejizo.
Russia, Rusia, *f.*; — **leather,** cuero de Moscovia.
Russian, *n.* and *adj.* ruso, sa; — **language,** ruso, *m.*
rust, *n.* herrumbre, *f.*, moho, *m.*; (bot.) roya, *f.*; color bermejo o rojizo; —, *vi.* enmohecerse.
rustic, *adj.* rústico, pardal; —, *n.* patán, rústico, *m.*
rustical, *adj.* rústico, pardal.
rusticate, *vi.* vivir en el campo; —, *vt.* desterrar al campo.
rusticity, *n.* rusticidad, *f.*
rustiness, *n.* herrumbre, *f.*
rustle, *n.* susurro, *m.*; —, *vi.* crujir, susurrar.
rustling, *n.* crujido, *m.*
rustproof, *adj.* a prueba de herrumbre, inoxidable.
rusty, *adj.* mohoso, enmohecido, oriniento, ruginoso; rancio.
rut, *vi.* bramar los venados y ciervos cuando están en celo; —, *n.* costumbre, rutina, *f.*; brama, *f.*
rutabaga, *n.* (bot.) naba, *f.*
ruthless, *adj.* cruel, insensible; —ly, *adv.* inhumanamente.
R.V. Revised Version, Versión Revisada.
Ry. Railway, f.c. ferrocarril.
rye, *n.* (bot.) centeno, *m.*; — **field,** centenal, *m.*

S

S.: Saint, Sto. Sta. Santo, Santa; **Saturday,** sáb. sábado; **September,** septiembre; **South,** S. sur; **Sunday,** dom.º domingo.
s.: school, escuela, **shilling,** chelín; **second,** S. segundo; **singular,** sing. singular; **son,** h. hijo; **south,** S. sur.
S.A.: Salvation Army, Ejército de Salvación; **South America,** S.A. Sud América; **South Africa,** Sud África.

sabbath, *n.* día de descanso (sábado para los judíos, domingo para los cristianos).

saber, sabre, *n.* sable, *m.*; —, *vt.* herir o matar con sable.

sable, *m.* cebellina, marta, *f.*

sabotage, *n.* sabotaje, *m.*

saboteur, *n.* persona que comete sabotaje.

saccharine, *n.* sacarina, *f.*; —, *adj.* sacarino, azucarado.

sacerdotal, *adj.* sacerdotal.

sachet, *n.* sachet, *m.*, bolsita con polvo perfumado.

sack, *n.* saco, talego, *m.*; especie de vino blanco; — **coat,** americana, *f.*, saco de hombre; —, *vt.* meter en sacos; saquear.

sacrament, *n.* sacramento, *m.*; Eucaristía, *f.*

sacramental, *adj.* sacramental; **—ly,** *adv.* sacramentalmente.

sacred, *adj.* sagrado, sacro; inviolable; **—ly,** *adv.* sagradamente, inviolablemente.

sacredness, *n.* santidad, *f.*

sacrifice, *n.* sacrificio, *m.*; —, *vt.* sacrificar; **to — oneself,** sacrificarse.

sacrificial, *adj.* relativo a los sacrificios.

sacrilege, *n.* sacrilegio, *m.*

sacrilegious, *adj.* sacrílego.

sacrum, *n.* (anat.) sacro, *m.*

sad, *adj.* triste, melancólico; infausto; **—ly,** *adv.* tristemente.

sadden, *vt.* entristecer.

saddle, *n.* silla, *f.*, silla de montar; — **horse,** caballo de montar; —, *vt.* ensillar.

saddlebag, *n.* alforja, *f.*

saddlecloth, *n.* mantilla de silla.

saddler, *n.* sillero, *m.*

saddlery, *n.* guarnicionería, talabartería, *f.*

sadism, *n.* sadismo, *m.*

sadist, *n.* hombre lúbrico y cruel.

sadness, *n.* tristeza, *f.*; aspecto tétrico.

safari, *n.* expedición, especialmente de caza, y tambien su caravana.

safe, *adj.* seguro; incólume; salvo; — **and sound,** sano y salvo; —, *n.* caja fuerte; **—ly,** *adv.* a salvo.

safe-conduct, *n.* salvoconducto, seguro, *m.*, carta de amparo.

safe-deposit, *adj.* de seguridad; — **box,** caja de seguridad.

safeguard, *n.* salvaguardia, *f.*; —, *vt.* proteger.

safety, *n.* seguridad, *f.*; salvamento, *m.*; — **belt,** cinto salvavidas; — **island,** plataforma de seguridad, refugio, *m.*; — **match,** fósforo de seguridad; — **pin,** alfiler de seguridad, imperdible, *m.*; — **razor,** navaja de seguridad; — **valve,** válvula de seguridad.

saffron, *n.* azafrán, *m.*; —, *adj.* de color amarillo como el del azafrán.

S. Afr. South Africa, Sud África.

sag, *n.* desviación, *f.*, pandeo, seno, *m.*; —, *vi.* empandarse, combarse; doblegarse.

saga, *n.* saga, *f.*, leyenda de los Eddas.

sagacious, *adj.* sagaz, sutil; **—ly,** *adv.* sagazmente.

sagacity, *n.* sagacidad, astucia, tienta, *f.*

sage, *n.* sabio, *m.*; (bot.) salvia, *f.*; —, *adj.* sabio; **—ly,** *adv.* sabiamente.

sagebrush, *n.* (bot.) artemisa, *f.*

Sagittarius, *n.* (ast.) Sagitario, *m.*

sago, *n.* (bot.) sagú, *m.*

sail, *n.* vela, *f.*; —, *vi.* dar a la vela, navegar.

sailboat, *n.* velero, *m.*, buque de vela.

sailcloth, *n.* lona, *f.*

sailer, *n.* navío, buque, *m.*

sailfish, *n.* especie de pez espada.

sailing, *n.* navegación, *f.*; partida, salida, *f.*; —, *adj.* de vela.

sailor, *n.* marinero, *m.*

sailplane, *n.* hidroplano, hidroavión, *m.*

saint, *n.* santo, ta; ángel, *m.*; **guardian —,** santo patrón; **to —,** *vt.* canonizar.

sainted, *adj.* santo; bendito.

saintlike, *adj.* como santo; **a — person,** santo, ta.

saintly, *adj.* santo.

sake, *n.* causa, razón, *f.*; amor, *m.*, consideración, *f.*; **for God's —,** por amor de Dios.

salable, saleable, *adj.* vendible.

salad, *n.* ensalada, *f.*; — **bowl,** ensaladera, *f.*; — **dressing,** salsa para ensalada.

salamander, *n.* salamandra, *f.*

salary, *n.* salario, sueldo, *m.*, paga, *f.*

sale, *n.* venta, *f.*; (com.) realización, *f.*; **auction —,** remate, *m.*; **clearance —,** liquidación, *f.*; — **price,** precio de venta; **—s tax,** impuesto sobre ventas.

saleratus, *n.* salerato, *m.*, bicarbonato de sosa o de potasa.

salesclerk, *n.* vendedor, ra, dependiente, *m.* y *f.*

salesgirl, *n.* vendedora, dependiente, *f.*

salesman, *n.* ropero, vendedor, tendero, *m.*; **traveling —,** comisionista, viajante, *m.*, agente viajero.

salesmanship, *n.* arte de vender.

salesperson, *n.* vendedor, ra.

salesroom, *n.* salón de ventas.

saleswoman, saleslady, *n.* vendedora, *f.*

salicylate, *n.* salicilato, *m.*

salicylic, *adj.* salicílico.

salient, *adj.* saliente, saledizo.

saline, *adj.* salino.

saliva, *n.* saliva, *f.*

sallet, *n.* celada (pieza de armadura), *f.*

sallow, *adj.* cetrino, pálido; — **face,** cara de acelga.

sally, *n.* (mil.) salida, surtida, *f.*; excursión, *f.*, paseo, *m.*; agudeza, *f.*; —, *vi.* salir.

salmon, *n.* salmón, *m.*; —, *adj.* salmón, de color salmón; — **trout,** trucha salmonada.

saloon, *n.* cantina, taberna, *f.*; cámara de un vapor.

salsify, *n.* salsifí, *m.*

sal soda, salsoda, *n.* sal de sosa.

salt, *n.* sal, *f.*; (fig.) sabor, *m.*; gracia, *f.*; agudeza, *f.*; —, *adj.* salado; —, *vt.* salar; salpresar.

saltcellar, *n.* salero, *m.*, receptáculo para sal.

salted, *adj.* salado; **— fish,** pescado salado; **— meat,** carne salpresa.

salter, *n.* salinero, *m.*

saltine, *n.* galletica, *f.*

salting, *n.* saladura, *f.*

saltpeter, saltpetre, *n.* nitro, salitre, nitrato, *m.*; **— works,** salitral, *m.*

saltshaker, *n.* salero, *m.*, receptáculo para sal.

salty, *adj.* salado, salobre; **very —,** resalado.

salubrious, *adj.* salubre, saludable.

salubrity, *n.* salubridad, *f.*

salutary, *adj.* saludable, salubre, salutífero.

salutation, *n.* salutación, *f.*, saludo, *m.*

salute, *vt.* saludar; **—,** *n.* salutación, *f.*

Salvadorean, *n.* and *adj.* salvadoreño, ña.

salvage, *n.* salvamento, *m.*; (naut.) derecho de salvamento; **—,** *vt.* salvar.

salvarsan, *n.* (med.) salvarsán, *m.*

salvation, *n.* salvación, *f.*

salve, *n.* emplasto, ungüento, *m.*, pomada, *f.*

salver, *n.* salvilla, bandeja, salva, *f.*

salvia, *n.* (bot.) salvia, *f.*, cierta planta medicinal.

salvo, *n.* salva, *f.*

Sam. Saml. Samuel, Samuel.

S. Am., S. Amer. South America. S. A. Sud América.

sambo, *n.* zambo, ba.

same, *adj.* mismo; idéntico; propio.

sameness, *n.* identidad, *f.*

sample, *n.* muestra, *f.*; ejemplo, *m.*; **— book,** muestrario, *m.*; **—s,** muestrario, *m.*; **—,** *vt.* catar, probar una muestra.

sampler, *n.* muestra, *f.*; dechado, modelo, *m.*

sanatorium, *n.* sanatorio, *m.*

sanctification, *n.* santificación, *f.*; consagración, *f.*

sanctify, *vt.* santificar.

sanctimonious, *adj.* hipócritamente piadoso.

sanctimony, *n.* santimonia, santidad, *f.*

sanction, *n.* sanción, *f.*; **—,** *vt.* sancionar.

sanctity, *n.* santidad, santimonia, *f.*

sanctuary, *n.* santuario, *m.*; asilo, *m.*

sand, *n.* arena, *f.*; **— pit,** arenal, *m.*; **—,** *vt.* enarenar.

sandal, *n.* sandalia, *f.*

sandalwood, *n.* sándalo, *m.*

sandbag, *n.* saco de arena; **—,** *vt.* resguardar con sacos de arena; golpear con sacos de arena.

sandbank, *n.* banco de arena.

sandblast, *n.* máquina sopladora de arena; chorro de arena lanzado por aire o vapor para grabar o cortar vidrio, piedra, etc.; soplete de arena; **—,** *vt.* lanzar por aire o vapor un chorro de arena para grabar o cortar vidrio, piedra, etc.

sandbox, *n.* caja de arena; banco de arena; salvadera, *f.*

sandpaper, *n.* papel de lija, lija, *f.*; **—,** *vt.* lijar.

sandstone, *n.* piedra arenisca.

sandstorm, *n.* tormenta de arena.

sandwich, *n.* sandwich, emparedado, *m.*; **—,** *vt.* emparedar; intercalar.

sandy, *adj.* arenoso, arenisco.

sane, *adj.* sano.

Sanforize, *vt.* and *vi.* tratar telas de algodón o lino por un procedimiento mecánico patentado para que encojan permanentemente.

sang, pretérito del verbo **sing.**

sanguinary, *adj.* sanguinario.

sanguine, *adj.* sanguíneo.

sanguineous, *adj.* sanguino; sanguíneo.

sanitarium, *n.* sanatorio, *m.*

sanitary, *adj.* sanitario; **— napkin,** almohadilla higiénica.

sanitation, *n.* saneamiento, *m.*

sanity, *n.* cordura, *f.*; juicio sano, sentido común.

sank, pretérito del verbo **sink.**

sap, *n.* savia, *f.*; (mil.) zapa, *f.*; **—,** *vt.* zapar.

sapient, *adj.* sabio, cuerdo.

sapling, *n.* renuevo, vástago, *m.*; mozalbete, *m.*

saponin, saponine, *n.* (chem.) saponina, *f.*

sapota, *n.* (bot.) zapote, *m.*

sapper, *n.* (mil.) zapador, *m.*

sapphire, *n.* zafir, zafiro, *m.*

saprophyte, *n.* (biol.) saprofito, *m.*

sapwood, *n.* albura, *f.*; sámago, *m.*

sarcasm, *n.* sarcasmo, *m.*

sarcastic, *adj.* sarcástico, mordaz, cáustico; **—ally,** *adv.* sarcásticamente, mordazmente.

sarcenet, *n.* tafetán de Florencia.

sarcophagus, *n.* sarcófago, sepulcro, *m.*

sard, *n.* sardio, sardo, *m.*, sardónice, *f.*

sardine, *n.* sardina, *f.*

sarsaparilla, *n.* zarzaparrilla, *f.*

sash, *n.* faja, *f.*, cinturón, *m.*; cíngulo, *m.*; cinta, *f.*; bastidor de ventana o de puerta.

sassafras, *n.* sasafrás, *m.*

sat, pretérito y *p.p.* del verbo **sit.**

Sat. Saturday, sáb. sábado.

Satan, *n.* Satanás, *m.*

satanic, *adj.* diabólico, satánico.

satanical, *adj.* satánico, diabólico; **—ly,** *adv.* satánicamente.

satchel, *n.* saquillo de mano, maletín, *m.*, maleta, *f.*

sate, *vt.* = **satiate.**

sateen, *n.* rasete, *m.*, tela similar al raso pero de inferior calidad.

satellite, *n.* satélite, *m.*

satiate, *vt.* saciar, hartar; **—,** *vi.* saciarse, hartarse.

satiety, *n.* saciedad, hartura, *f.*

satin, *n.* raso, *m.*

satinet, satinette, *n.* rasete, *m.*

satire, *n.* sátira, *f.*

satirical, *adj.* satírico; **—ly,** *adv.* satíricamente.

satirist, *n.* autor satírico, persona que usa sátira.

satirize, *vt.* satirizar.
satisfaction, *n.* satisfacción, *f.*
satisfactorily, *adv.* satisfactoriamente.
satisfactory, *adj.* satisfactorio; **to be — to you,** ser de su agrado.
satisfy, *vt.* satisfacer.
satrap, *n.* sátrapa, *m.*
saturate, *vt.* saturar.
saturation, *n.* saturación, *f.*
Saturday, *n.* sábado, *m.*
saturnine, *adj.* saturnino, melancólico.
satyr, *n.* sátiro, *m.*
sauce, *n.* salsa, *f.*, caldo, *m.*; **—,** *vt.* condimentar.
saucedish, *n.* salsera, *f.*
saucepan, *n.* cacerola, *f.*
saucer, *n.* plato pequeño.
saucy, *adj.* atrevido, malcriado, respondón.
sauerkraut, *n.* col fermentada.
saunter, *vi.* callejear, vagar, andar sin rumbo.
sausage, *n.* salchicha, *f.*; **pork —,** longaniza, *f.*
savage, *adj.* salvaje, bárbaro; **—ly,** *adv.* bárbaramente; **—,** *n.* salvaje, *m.*
savagery, *n.* salvajismo, *m.*, salvajez, *f.*
savanna, savannah, *n.* sabana, llanura, *f.*
savant, *n.* sabio, bia, erudito, ta.
save, *vt.* salvar; economizar; conservar; **—,** *prep.* excepto.
saveloy, *n.* variedad de chorizo.
saver, *n.* libertador, ra; ahorrador, ra.
saving, *adj.* frugal, económico; salvador; **—,** *prep.* fuera de, excepto; **—ly,** *adv.* económicamente; parcamente; **—,** *n.* salvamento, *m.*; **—s,** *n. pl.* ahorros, *m. pl.*, economías, *f. pl.*; **—s bank,** caja de ahorros, banco de ahorros.
savior, saviour, *n.* salvador, ra.
Saviour, *n.* Redentor, *m.*
savoire-faire, *n.* don de gentes.
savor, savour, *n.* olor, *m.*; sabor, *m.*; **—,** *vt. and vi.* gustar, saborear; **to — of,** oler a, saber a; tener la característica de.
savory, savoury, *adj.* sabroso.
saw, *n.* sierra, *f.*; **—,** *vt.* serrar; **—,** pretérito del verbo **see.**
sawdust, *n.* aserraduras, *f. pl.*, aserrín, *m.*
sawfish, *n.* priste, *m.*
sawhorse, *n.* caballete de aserrar.
sawmill, *n.* molino de aserrar.
sawyer, *n.* aserrador, *m.*
saxhorn, *n.* (mus.) bombardino, *m.*
saxophone, *n.* (mus.) saxófono, *m.*
say, *vt.* decir, hablar; proferir; **that is to —,** es decir; **to — mass,** cantar misa; **to — to oneself,** decir para su capote; **—,** *n.* habla, *f.*
saying, *n.* dicho, proverbio, refrán, *m.*
sb. substantive, s. sustantivo.
S. B. Bachelor of Science, Bachiller en Ciencias.
sc.: namely, es decir; **science,** cienc. ciencia; **scene,** esc. escena.
S. C.: Signal Corps, cuerpo de señales;

South Carolina, C. del S. Carolina del Sur; **Supreme Court,** Corte Suprema;
s.c. small capitals, pequeñas mayúsculas.
scab, *n.* costra, *f.*; roña, *f.*; (coll.) hombre roñoso; bribón, *m.*
scabbard, *n.* vaina de espada; cobertura, *f.*; carcaj, *m.*
scabby, scabious, *adj.* sarnoso; costroso; roñoso.
scabies, *n.* sarna, *f.*
scaffold, *n.* tablado, *m.*; cadalso, *m.*
scaffolding, *n.* andamiaje, *m.*; construcción de tablados o andamios.
scald, *vt.* escaldar; **—,** *n.* tiña, *f.*; escaldadura, *f.*; quemadura, *f.*
scale, *n.* balanza, *f.*; escama, *f.*; escala, *f.*; **game,** *f.*; lámina delgada; **balance —,** peso, *m.*, balanza, *f.*; **platform —,** báscula, *f.*; **—,** *vt. and vi.* escalar; descostrarse; desconchar (una pared, un techo, etc.).
Scales, *n.* = **Libra.**
scaling, *n.* desconchamiento (de una pared o un techo, etc.), *m.*; (mil.) escalamiento, *m.*; escamadura, *f.*; **— ladder,** escala de sitio.
scallion, *n.* ascalonia, cebolleta, *f.*
scallop, *n.* venera, pechina, *f.*; festón, *m.*; **—,** *vt.* festonear.
scalp, *n.* cráneo, *m.*; cuero cabelludo; **—,** *vt.* arrancar el cuero cabelludo; comprar y revender billetes de teatro, etc., por una ganancia.
scalper, *n.* revendedor, *m.*, persona que revende billetes de teatro, etc., por una ganancia; **ticket —,** revendedor, *m.*
scamp, *n.* bribón, ona; ladrón, ona.
scamper, *vi.* escapar, huir.
scan, *vt.* escudriñar; medir las sílabas de un verso.
scandal, *n.* escándalo, *m.*; infamia, *f.*
scandalize, *vt.* escandalizar.
scandalous, *adj.* escandaloso; **—ly,** *adv.* escandalosamente.
Scandinavia, Escandinavia, *f.*
Scandinavian, *n. and adj.* escandinavo, va.
scant, scanty, *adj.* escaso, parco; sórdido.
scantling, *n.* listón, *m.*; alfarda, *f.*
scapegoat, *n.* víctima inocente; (Mex.) chivo expiatorio.
scapegrace, *n.* pícaro incorregible, bribón, ona.
scapula, *n.* (anat.) omóplato, *m.*, escápula, *f.*
scar, *n.* cicatriz, *f.*; **—,** *vt.* hacer alguna cicatriz.
scarce, *adj.* raro; **—ly,** *adv.* apenas, escasamente; solamente; pobremente.
scarcity, *n.* escasez, *f.*; raridad, *f.*
scare, *n.* susto, *m.*; **to get a —,** llevarse un susto; **—,** *vt.* espantar.
scarecrow, *n.* espantajo, mamarracho, *m.*
scaremonger, *n.* terrorista, *m.*
scarf, *n.* bufanda, *f.*; trena, *f.*; corbata, *f.*; faja, chalina, *f.*
scarfpin, *n.* alfiler de corbata.

scarify, vt. sajar; lastimar (los sentimientos, etc.)

scarlatina, n. escarlatina, f.

scarlet, n. escarlata, f.; —, adj. de color escarlata o grana; — **fever,** (med.) escarlatina, f.

scarp, n. escarpa, f.; declive, m.; —, vt. (mil.) escarpar.

scat! interj. ¡zape!

scatter, vt. esparcir, dispersar; disipar; —, vi. derramarse, disiparse.

scatterbrained, adj. atolondrado.

scavenger, n. basurero, m., barrendero, ra; animal que se alimenta de carroña.

scenario, n. escenario, m., argumento de una película cinematográfica.

scenarist, n. escritor de argumentos cinematográficos.

scene, n. escena, perspectiva, vista, f.; celaje, m.; (theat.) escena, f.; lugar de un suceso.

scenery, n. vista, f.; (theat.) decoración, f.

sceneshifter, n. tramoyista, m.

scenic, scenical, adj. escénico.

scent, n. olfato, m.; olor, m.; rastro, m.; —, vt. oler, olfatear; —, vi. olfatear.

scentless, adj. sin olfato; inodoro.

scepter, sceptre, n. cetro, m.

sceptic, n. = skeptic.

sceptic, sceptical, etc., adj. = skeptic, skeptical.

scepticism, n. = skepticism.

schedule, n. plan, programa, m.; catálogo, m.; horario, m.; cédula, f.; —, vt. fijar en un plan o en un programa.

schematic, adj. esquemático.

scheme, n. proyecto, designio, m.; esquema, plan, modelo, m.; —, vt. proyectar.

schemer, n. proyectista, m. y f.; intrigante, m. y f.

schism, n. cisma, m.

schismatic, n. and adj. cismático, ca.

schist, (geol.) n. esquisto, m.

scholar, n. escolar, estudiante, m. y f.; literato, ta; erudito, ta.

scholarly, adj. de estudiante; —, adv. muy instruído.

scholarship, n. educación literaria; beca, f.; erudición, f.

scholastic, adj. escolástico; estudiantil.

school, n. escuela, f.; **high** —, escuela secundaria, escuela superior; — **of fish,** banco de peces; **training** —, plantel, m.; —, vt. instruir, enseñar; disciplinar.

schooling, n. instrucción, enseñanza, f.

schooner, n. (naut.) goleta, f.

schottische, n. schottis (baile), m.

sciatica, n. (med.) ciática, f.

science, n. ciencia, f.

scientific, adj. científico; —**ally,** adv. científicamente.

scientist, n. hombre de ciencia.

scil. namely, es decir.

scimitar, scimiter, n. cimitarra, f.

scintillate, vi. chispear, centellear.

scintillation, n. centelleo, m.; chispazo, m.

sciolist, n. persona con conocimientos superficiales.

scion, n. vástago, m.; renuevo, verduguillo, m.

scission, n. separación, partición, f.

scissors, n. pl. tijeras, f. pl.; **small** —, tijeretas, f. pl.

scleroma, n. escleroma, m.

sclerosis, n. (med.) esclerosis, f.

scoff, vi. mofarse, burlarse; —, n. mofa, burla, f.

scoffer, n. burlón, ona.

scoffingly, adv. con mofa y escarnio.

scold, vt. and vi. regañar, reñir, refunfuñar; —, n. persona regañona.

scolding, n. regaño, m.; —, adj. regañón.

scoliosis, n. (med.) escoliosis, f.

sconce, n. cornucopia, f.; cobertizo, m.; baluarte, m.; (coll.) cabeza, f.; juicio, sentido, m.; —, vt. proveer de baluarte o fortificación; proteger.

scoop, n. cucharón, m.; (naut.) achicador, m.; cesta (en el juego de pelota), f.; (coll. periodismo) acción de ganar una noticia; —, vt. cavar, socavar.

scooter, n. velero especial de fondo plano; especie de arado; juguete que consiste en una tablilla con dos ruedas pequeñas en que corren los niños.

scope, n. alcance, m.; blanco, espacio, m.; libertad, f.

scorbutic, adj. escorbútico.

scorch, vt. quemar por encima; tostar; socarrar; calcinar; —, vi. quemarse, secarse.

scorched, adj. chamuscado; abrasado, agostado; — **earth,** tierra chamuscada, tierra abrasada.

score, n. muesca, f.; consideración, f.; cuenta, f.; razón, f.; motivo, m.; veintena, f.; (deportes) tantos, m. pl.; tanteo, m.; (mus.) partitura, f.; —, vt. sentar alguna deuda; imputar; señalar con una línea; —, vi. hacer tantos (en un juego).

scoria, n. escoria, hez, f.

scorn, vt. and vi. despreciar; mofar; —, n. desdén, menosprecio, m.

scornful, adj. desdeñoso; —**ly,** adv. con desdén.

Scorpio, n. Escorpión (signo del zodíaco), m.

scorpion, n. escorpión, m.

Scot, n. escocés, esa; **scot,** escote, m., cuota, contribución, f.; impuesto, m.

Scotch, Scottish, adj. escoces.

scotch, n. cortadura, incisión, f.; —, vt. escoplear; herir levemente.

Scotchman, n. escocés, m.

Scotchwoman, n. escocesa, f.

Scotland, Escocia, f.

scoundrel, n. belitre, m. y f., pícaro, ra, bribón, ona, infame, m. y f.; canalla, m.

scour, vt. fregar, estregar; limpiar; —, vi. correr velozmente en busca de algo.

scourge, n. azote, m.; castigo, m.; —, vt. azotar, castigar.

scout, *n.* (mil.) batidor, corredor, *m.*, escucha, *f.*; centinela avanzada; **boy —,** niño explorador, niño de la Asociación de Niños Exploradores; **girl —,** niña exploradora, niña de la Asociación de Niñas Exploradoras; **—,** *vi.* reconocer secretamente los movimientos del enemigo; (mil.) explorar; **—,** *vt.* and *vi.* rechazar una idea con desdén.

scoutmaster, *n.* jefe de tropa de niños exploradores.

scow, *n.* chalana, gabarra, *f.*

scowl, *n.* ceño, *m.*, semblante ceñudo; **—,** *vi.* mirar con ceño.

scraggy, *adj.* áspero; macilento.

· scramble, *vi.* trepar; arrebatar, disputar; esparcirse en forma irregular; **—,** *vt.* mezclar confusamente; **—d eggs,** huevos revueltos; **—,** *n.* disputa, arrebatiña, *f.*

scrap, *n.* migaja, *f.*; sobras, *f. pl.*; pedacito, *m.*; **— heap,** montón de desechos, pila de desperdicios; **— iron,** hierro viejo; **— metal,** hierro viejo; **—,** *vt.* descartar; **—,** *vi.* (coll.) disputar, reñir.

scrapbook, *n.* álbum de recortes.

scrape, *vt.* and *vi.* raer, raspar; raspear; arañar; tocar mal un instrumento; juntar gradualmente (dinero, etc.); **—,** *n.* dificultad, *f.*, lío, *m.*

scraper, *n.* rascador, raspador, *m.*; aprendiz de violín.

scratch, *vt.* rascar, raspar; borrar; raer, garrapatear; **—,** *n.* rascadura, *f.*

scratcher, *n.* arañador, ra.

scratch-pad, *n.* cuadernillo de apuntes.

scrawl, *vt.* and *vi.* garrapatear; **—,** *n.* garabatos, *m. pl.*

scrawny, *adj.* flaco y huesudo.

scream, *vi.* chillar, dar alaridos; **—,** *n.* chillido, grito, alarido, *m.*

screamer, *n.* chillón, ona.

screech, *vi.* chillar, dar alaridos; **—,** *n.*; chillido, grito, alarido, *m.*; **— owl,** variedad de buho de Norte América.

screechy, *adj.* chillón.

screen, *n.* pantalla, *f.*, biombo, *m.*; mampara, *f.*; volante, *m.*; cine (fotografía cinematográfica), *m.*; pantalla de cine; **fire —,** pantalla de chimenea; **—,** *vt.* abrigar, esconder; cribar, cerner.

screenings, *n. pl.* desperdicios, *m. pl.*

screw, *n.* tornillo, *m.*; **female —,** tuerca, *f.*; **nut of a —,** hembra, *f.*; **— and nut,** rosca, *f.*; **— driver,** destornillador, *m.*; **— propeller,** hélice, *f.*; **—,** *vt.* atornillar; forzar, apretar.

scribble, *vi.* escarabajear, borrajear; **—,** *n.* escrito de poco mérito.

scribe, *n.* escritor, *m.*; escriba, *m.*; escribiente, *m.*

scrim, *n.* tejido de algodón y lino ligero y basto.

scrimmage, *n.* arrebatiña, *f.*

scrimp, *vt.* and *vi.* escatimar, economizar, pasarse sin.

scrip, *n.* cédula, *f.*; esquela, *f.*

script, *n.* (rad.) argumento, libreto, *m.*; (law) documento original; escritura, *f.*; (print.) plumilla inglesa.

scriptural, *adj.* bíblico.

Scripture, *n.* Escritura Sagrada.

scrivener, *n.* escribano, notario público.

scrofula, *n.* escrófula, *f.*

scrofulous, *adj.* escrofuloso.

scroll, *n.* rollo (de papel o pergamino), *m.*; voluta, *f.*; **— saw,** sierra de cinta, sierra de marquetería; **—,** *vt.* decorar con volutas.

scrollwork, *n.* adornos de voluta.

scrub, *vt.* estregar con un estropajo; fregar, restregar; **—,** *n.* estropajo, *m.*; ganapán, *m.*; (Mex.) afanador, *m.*

scrubbing, *n.* fregadura, *f.*; **— brush,** fregador, *m.*, cepillo para fregar.

scruff, *n.* nuca, *f.*

scruple, *n.* escrúpulo, rescoldo, *m.*; **—,** *vi.* escrupulizar, tener duda.

scrupulosity, *n.* escrupulosidad, *f.*

scrupulous, *adj.* escrupuloso; **—ly,** *adv.* escrupulosamente.

scrutinize, *vt.* escudriñar, examinar.

scrutiny, *n.* escrutinio, examen, *m.*

scud, *vi.* huirse, escaparse rápidamente.

scuff, *vt.* arrastrar los pies; dañar una superficie dura; restregar; **—,** *n.* variedad de chinela.

scuffle, *n.* quimera, riña, *f.*; **—,** *vi.* reñir, pelear.

scull, *n.* espadilla de bote; remo, *m.*; **—,** *vt.* and *vi.* bogar con espadilla.

scullery, *n.* espetera, *f.*; fregadero, *m.*

scullion, *n.* marmitón, *m.*; fregona, *f.*, pinche, *m.*

sculptor, *n.* escultor, *m.*

sculptress, *n.* escultora, *f.*

sculpture, *n.* escultura, *f.*; **—,** *vt.* esculpir.

scum, *n.* nata, *f.*; espuma, *f.*; escoria, *f.*; **—,** *vt.* espumar.

scupper, *n.* sentina, *f.*

scurf, *n.* tiña, *f.*; costra de una herida.

scurrility, *n.* bufonería, bufonada, *f.*

scurrilous, *adj.* vil, bajo; injurioso; **—ly,** *adv.* injuriosamente.

S curve, *n.* recodo, *m.*, curva doble.

scurvy, *n.* escorbuto, *m.*; **—,** *adj.* escorbútico; vil, despreciable.

scutcheon, *n.* escudo de armas.

scuttle, *n.* banasta, *f.*; balde para carbón; paso veloz; **—,** *vi.* apretar a correr; **—,** *vt.* (naut.) echar a pique.

scythe, *n.* guadaña, *f.*

s.d. sight draft, giro a la v/, giro a la vista.

S. Dak., S.D. South Dakota, Dakota del Sur.

SE, S.E., s.e. southeast, SE. sureste.

sea, *n.* mar, *m.* y *f.*; **heavy —,** oleada, *f.*, golpe de mar; **rough —,** mar alta; **— breeze,** viento de mar; **— food,** mariscos o pescado; **— gull,** gaviota, *f.*; **— horse,** morsa, *f.*; **— wall,** malecón, *m.*; **—,** *adj.* de mar.

seaboard, *n.* costa, playa, *f.*; —, *adj.* al lado del mar, costanero.

seacoast, *n.* costa marítima.

seadrome, *n.* aeródromo marino.

seafarer, *n.* navegante, marino, *m.*

seafaring, *adj.* marino, de mar; —, *n.* viajes por el mar.

seagoing, *adj.* capaz de navegar en el océano, navegante.

seal, *n.* sello, *m.*; (zool.) foca, *f.*; becerro marino; **Alaska —,** piel de foca de Alaska; —, *vt.* sellar ; —, *vi.* cazar focas.

sea level, *n.* nivel del mar.

sealing, *n.* caza de focas; selladura, *f.*; **— wax,** lacre, *m.*

sealskin, *n.* piel de foca.

seam, *n.* costura, *f.*; cicatriz, *f.*; sutura, *f.*; —, *vt.* coser.

seaman, *n.* marinero, marino, *m.*

seamanship, *n.* pericia en la navegación; marinería, *f.*

seamstress, *n.* costurera, *f.*

seamy, *adj.* con costuras.

seaplane, *n.* hidroavión, *m.*

seaport, *n.* puerto de mar.

sear, *vt.* cauterizar; quemar; dorar o freír (la superficie de la carne, etc.); secar.

search, *vt.* examinar, registrar; escudriñar; inquirir, tentar, pesquisar; —, *n.* pesquisa, *f.*; busca, *f.*; buscada, *f.*; búsqueda, *f.*; **in — of,** en busca de.

searchlight, *n.* reflector eléctrico, reflector, *m.*

seascape, *n.* escena marina.

seashore, *n.* ribera, *f.*, litoral, *m.*

seasick, *adj.* mareado.

seasickness, *n.* mareamiento, mareo, *m.*

seaside, *n.* orilla o ribera del mar.

season, *n.* estación, *f.*; tiempo *m.*; tiempo oportuno; sazón, *f.*; temporada, *f.*; **— ticket,** billete de estación; (rail) abono de pasaje; —, *vt.* sazonar; imbuir; curar; **to — food,** condimentar; —, *vi.* sazonarse.

seasonable, *adj.* oportuno, tempestivo, a propósito.

seasonably, *adv.* en sazón.

seasoned, *adj.* curado; sazonado; **highly —,** picante.

seasoning, *n.* condimento, *m.*

sea squirt, *n.* ascidia, *f.*

seat, *n.* silla, *f.*; localidad, *f.*; morada, *f.*; domicilio, *m.*; situación, *f.*; **front —,** silla delantera; **— cover,** cubreasiento, *m.*; —, *vt.* situar; colocar; asentar; sentar.

seating, *n.* acción de sentar; material para entapizar sillas; **— capacity,** cabida, *f.*, número de asientos.

seaward, *adj.* del litoral; —, **—s,** *adv.* hacia el mar.

seaweed, *n.* alga marina.

seaworthy, *adj.* a propósito para navegar, marinero.

sebaceous, *adj.* sebáceo.

Sebastian, Sebastián.

sec.: according to, de acuerdo con; **second,** S. segundo; **secretary,** secretario; **section,** sección.

S. E. C. Securities and Exchange Commission, Comisión de Valores y Cambios.

secant, *n.* (math.) secante, *f.*

secede, *vi.* apartarse, separarse.

secession, *n.* separación, *f.*; secesión, *f.*

seclude, *vt.* apartar, excluir, recluir.

seclusion, *n.* separación, *f.*; reclusión, *f.*; aislamiento, *m.*

second, *adj.* segundo; **— childhood,** chochera, *f.*; **— hand,** segundero (de un reloj), *m.*; **— lieutenant,** alférez, subteniente, *m.*; **— nature,** costumbre arraigada; **—ly,** *adv.* en segundo lugar; —, *n.* padrino (en un duelo), *m.*; defensor, *m.*; segundo, *m.*; (mus.) segunda, *f.*; —, *vt.* apoyar, ayudar; —, *vi.* segundar.

secondary, *adj.* secundario; **— school,** escuela secundaria.

second-class, *adj.* de segunda clase, mediocre.

second-front, *adj.* del segundo frente.

secondhand, *adj.* de ocasión; usado; de segunda mano; **— dealer,** prendero, *m.*; **— shop,** baratillo, *m.*

secrecy, *n.* secreto, *m.*; reserva, *f.*; reticencia, *f.*

secret, *n.* secreto, *m.*; **in —,** en secreto; —, *adj.* privado; secreto; reservado; **— service,** policía secreta; **—ly,** *adv.* secretamente, a escondidas, de rebozo.

secretariat, *n.* secretaría, *f.*

secretary, *n.* secretario, ria; papelera, *f.*; **private —,** secretario (o secretaria) particular; **—'s office,** secretaría, *f.*

secretaryship, *n.* secretaría, *f.*

secrete, *vt.* esconder; (med.) secretar.

secretion, *n.* secreción, *f.*

secretive, *adj.* misterioso; reservado; secretorio.

sect, *n.* secta, *f.*

sect. section, sección.

sectarian, sectary, *n.* and *adj.* sectario, ria; secuaz, *m.* y *f.*

section, *n.* sección, *f.*; departamento, *m.*; **— of a bridge,** tramo, *m.*

sectionalism, *n.* regionalismo, *m.*

sector, *n.* sector, *m.*

secular, *adj.* secular, seglar.

secularity, *n.* secularidad, mundanalidad, *f.*

secularize, *vt.* secularizar.

secure, *adj.* seguro; salvo; **—ly,** *adv.* seguramente, al seguro; —, *vt.* asegurar; conseguir; resguardar.

security, *n.* seguridad, *f.*; defensa, *f.*; confianza, *f.*; fianza, *f.*; **to give —,** dar o prestar fianza.

secy., sec'y, secretary, secret.° secretario.

sedan, *n.* (auto.) sedán, *m.*; **— chair,** silla de manos.

sedate, *adj.* sosegado, tranquilo; **—ly,** *adv.* tranquilamente.

sedative, *n.* and *adj.* sedativo, calmante, confortante, *m.*

sedentary, *adj.* sedentario.
sedge, *n.* (bot.) lirio espadañal.
sediment, *n.* sedimento, *m.*; hez, *f.*; poso, *m.*
sedimentation, *n.* sedimentación, *f.*
sedition, *n.* sedición, *f.*; tumulto, alboroto, motín, *m.*; revuelta, *f.*
seditious, *adj.* sedicioso; —ly, *adv.* sediciosamente.
seduce, *vt.* seducir; engañar.
seducer, *n.* seductor, ra.
seduction, *n.* seducción, *f.*
seductive, *adj.* seductivo, seductor.
sedulous, *adj.* asiduo, perseverante; —ly, *adv.* diligentemente.
sedum, *n.* (bot.) variedad de hierba de la familia de las crasuláceas.
see, *vt.* and *vi.* ver, observar, descubrir; advertir; conocer, juzgar, comprender; presenciar; **let's** —, vamos a ver, a ver; **to — to it that,** encargarse de; —, véase; —! *interj.* ¡mira! —, *n.* silla episcopal; **the Holy See,** la Santa Sede.
seed, *n.* semilla, simiente, *f.*; — **corn,** semilla para maíz; —s, comuñas, *f. pl.*; —, *vi.* granar, sembrar.
seedcase, *n.* cápsula o vaina (de legumbre), *f.*
seeder, *n.* sembradora, *f.*; aparato para despepitar fruta.
seeding, *n.* siembra, *f.*
seedling, *n.* planta de semillero.
seedsman, *n.* tratante en semillas.
seedtime, *n.* sementera, siembra, *f.*
seedy, *adj.* lleno de semillas; (coll.) andrajoso, de aspecto miserable.
seeing, *n.* vista, *f.*; acto de ver, ver, *m.*; — **that,** visto que.
seek, *vt.* and *vi.* buscar; pretender.
seeker, *n.* buscador, ra.
seem, *vi.* parecer, semejarse; —ly, *adj.* decente, decoroso; agradable.
seeming, *n.* apariencia, *f.*; —ly, *adv.* al parecer.
seen, *p. p.* del verbo **see.**
seep, *vi.* colarse, escurrirse.
seepage, *n.* coladura, *f.*, escape, *m.*
seer, *n.* profeta, vidente, *m.*
seersucker, *n.* sirsaca, *f.*, variedad de tela de algodón.
seesaw, *n.* vaivén, *m.*; columpio de tabla; —, *vi.* balancear.
seethe, *vi.* hervir, bullir.
segment, *n.* segmento, *m.*
segmentation, *n.* fraccionamiento, *m.*; segmentación, *f.*
segregate, *adj.* selecto; —, *vt.* segregar.
seismic, *adj.* sísmico.
seismograph, *n.* sismógrafo, *m.*
seismology, *n.* sismología, *f.*
seize, *vt.* asir, agarrar, prender; secuestrar bienes o efectos; decomisar.
seizure, *n.* captura, toma, *f.*; secuestro, *m.*
seldom, *adv.* raramente, rara vez.
select, *vt.* elegir, escoger; —, *adj.* selecto, escogido, granado.
selection, *n.* selección, *f.*; trozo, *m.*

selective, *adj.* selectivo, relativo a la selección; que escoge.
selectivity, *n.* selectividad, *f.*
selectman, *n.* miembro de la administración municipal elegido anualmente.
self, *adj.* propio, mismo.
self-addressed, *adj.* que tiene el nombre y dirección de uno mismo.
self-assurance, *n.* confianza en sí mismo.
self-centered, *adj.* absorbido en sí mismo; independiente; estacionario.
self-command, *n.* imperio sobre sí mismo.
self-complacency, *n.* satisfacción de los propios actos y carácter.
self-conceit, *n.* presunción, *f.*
self-confident, *adj.* que tiene confianza en sí mismo.
self-contained, *adj.* reservado; completo, que contiene todos sus elementos.
self-controlled, *adj.* dueño de sí mismo.
self-denial, *n.* abnegación, *f.*
self-esteem, *n.* amor propio.
self-evident, *adj.* natural, patente; **to be —,** caerse de suyo.
self-explanatory, *adj.* que se explica por sí mismo.
self-expression, *n.* expresión de personalidad; aserción de rasgos individuales.
self-governing, *adj.* autónomo, que tiene dominio sobre sí mismo.
self-help, *n.* ayuda de sí mismo.
self-importance, *n.* presunción, vanagloria, *f.*
self-improvement, *n.* mejoramiento de sí mismo.
self-induction, *n.* (elec.) autoinducción, *f.*
self-indulgence, *n.* entrega a la satisfacción de los propios deseos.
self-interest, *n.* propio interés.
selfish, *adj.* interesado; egoísta; —ly, *adv.* interesadamente; egoístamente.
selfishness, *n.* egoísmo, *m.*
self-liquidating, *adj.* de propia liquidación.
self-made, *adj.* formado o desarrollado por sus propios esfuerzos; — **man,** hombre forjado por sus propios esfuerzos.
self-perfection, *n.* perfeccionamiento de sí mismo.
self-possession, *n.* sangre fría, tranquilidad de ánimo.
self-propelling, *adj.* automotor.
self-reliance, *n.* confianza en sí mismo.
self-respect, *n.* estima de sí mismo.
self-righteous, *adj.* que tiene un concepto justo de sí mismo.
self-righteousness, *n.* confianza en la justicia de su propia causa.
self-sacrifice, *n.* abnegación, *f.*
selfsame, *adj.* idéntico, el mismo, exactamente lo mismo.
self-satisfied, *adj.* satisfacción de sí mismo.
self-seeking, *adj.* egoísta, interesado.
self-starter, *n.* motor de arranque, arranque automático,

self-styled, *adj.* titulado o llamado por sí mismo.

self-sufficient, *adj.* capaz de mantenerse; confiado en sí mismo; altanero.

self-support, *n.* sostenimiento económico propio.

self-taught, *adj.* autodidacto.

self-willed, *adj.* obstinado.

sell, *vt.* and *vi.* vender; traficar; —, *vt.* realizar; —, *n.* (coll.) patraña, *f.*, engaño, *m.*

seller, *n.* vendedor, ra.

seltzer, *n.* agua de seltzer, agua carbónica.

selvage, *n.* orilla del paño.

selves, *n. pl.* de **self,** mismos, mas.

semantics, *n.* semántica, *f.*

semaphore, *n.* semáforo, *m.*

semblance, *n.* semejanza, apariencia, *f.*

semen, *n.* sémen, *m.*; semilla, *f.*

semester, *n.* semestre, *m.*

semiannual, *adj.* semianual, semestral.

semibreve, *n.* (mus.) semibreve, *f.*

semicircle, *n.* semicírculo, *m.*

semicircular, *adj.* semicircular.

semicolon, *n.* punto y coma.

semifinal, *adj.* semifinal; —s, *n. pl.* partida o combate antes de los finales.

semimonthly, *adj.* quincenal; — **pay,** quincena, *f.*, paga quincenal.

seminar, *n.* seminario (en el sentido de un grupo de estudiantes dirigido por un profesor que hace estudios superiores), *m.*

seminary, *n.* seminario, *m.*

semiquaver, *n.* (mus.) semicorchea, *f.*

Semitic, *adj.* semítico; —, *n.* semita, *m.* y. *f.*

semitone, *n.* (mus.) semitono, *m.*

semitropical, *adj.* semitropical.

semiweekly, *adj.* bisemanal; —, *adv.* bisemanalmente.

semiyearly, *adj.* semestral.

sempstress, *n.* = **seamstress.**

Sen., sen.: Senate, senado; **Senator,** senador; **senior,** padre; socio más antiguo o más caracterizado.

senate, *n.* senado, *m.*

senator, *n.* senador, *m.*

senatorial, *adj.* senatorio, senatorial.

send, *vt.* enviar, despachar, mandar; enviar; producir; trasmitir.

sender, *n.* remitente, *m.* y *f.*; (elec.) trasmisor, *m.*

sending, *n.* trasmisión, *f.*

senescence, *n.* envejecimiento, *m.*

seneschal, *n.* senescal, *m.*

senile, *adj.* senil.

senility, *n.* senectud, vejez, *f.*

senior, *adj.* anciano; estudiante de cuarto año; — **high school,** años superiores de una escuela secundaria.

seniority, *n.* antigüedad, ancianidad, *f.*

senna, *n.* (bot.) sen, *m.*, sena, *f.*

sensation, *n.* sensación, *f.*; sentimiento, *m.*

sense, *n.* sentido, *m.*; entendimiento, *m.*; razón, *f.*; juicio, *m.*; sentimiento, *m.*; sensatez, *f.*; **common —,** sentido práctico; — **of guilt,** cargo de conciencia; — **of sight,** ver, *m.*; — **organ,** órgano sensorio; —, *vt.* percibir; sentir.

senseless, *adj.* insensible; insensato; —ly, *adv.* insensatamente.

senselessness, *n.* insensatez, *f.*, absurdo, *m.*

sensibility, *n.* sensibilidad, *f.*

sensible, *adj.* sensible, sensitivo; juicioso; —bly, *adv.* sensiblemente; juiciosamente.

sensitive, *adj.* sensible; sensitivo; —, *n.* (bot.) sensitiva, *f.*; —ly, *adv.* sensiblemente.

sensitization, *n.* (photo.) sensibilización, *f.*

sensitize, *vt.* sensibilizar.

sensory, *adj.* sensorio.

sensual, *adj.* sensual; —ly, *adv.* sensualmente.

sensualist, *n.* persona sensual; sensualista, *m.* y *f.*

sensuality, *n.* sensualidad, *f.*

sensuous, *adj.* sensorio, sensitivo; afectivo.

sentence, *n.* sentencia, *f.*; (gram.) oración, *f.*; —, *vt.* sentenciar, condenar.

sententious, *adj.* sentencioso; —ly, *adv.* sentenciosamente.

sentience, *n.* sensibilidad, conciencia, *f.*

sentient, *adj.* consciente; —, *n.* persona consciente.

sentiment, *n.* sentimiento, *m.*; opinión, *f.*

sentimental, *adj.* sentimental.

sentimentalist, *n.* sentimentalista, *m.* y *f.*

sentinel, *n.* centinela, *m.* y *f.*

sentry, *n.* centinela, *m.* y *f.*; — **box,** garita de centinela.

Sep. Sept. September, sept.ᵉ septiembre.

sep. separate, separado.

sepal, *n.* (bot.) sépalo, *m.*

separable, *adj.* separable.

separate, *vt.* separar; —, *vi.* separarse; —, *adj.* separado; **under — cover,** (com.) por separado; —ly, *adv.* separadamente.

separation, *n.* separación, *f.*

separator, *n.* abaleador, *m.*; **cream —,** desnatadora, *f.*

sepia, *n.* sepia, *f.*

sepoy, *n.* soldado natural de la Indias orientales.

sepsis, *n.* (med.) sepsis, infección, *f.*

Sept. September, Sept. septiembre, setiembre.

September, *n.* septiembre; setiembre, *m.*

septennial, *adj.* sieteñal.

septic, *adj.* séptico; — **matter,** (med.) levadura, *f.*; — **tank,** foso séptico.

septicemia, *n.* (med.) septicemia, *f.*, condición mórbida de la sangre.

septuagenarian, *n.* septuagenario, ria, setentón, ona.

sepulchral, *adj.* sepulcral, fúnebre.

sepulchre, *n.* sepulcro, *m.*

sepulture, *n.* sepultura, *f.*

seq. the following, lo siguiente.

sequel, *n.* secuela, consecuencia, *f.*; continuación, *f.*

sequence, *n.* serie, continuación, *f.*

sequester, *vt.* secuestrar (bienes, etc.); segregar, separar.

sequestration, *n.* secuestro, *m.*

sequin, *n.* cequí (moneda anticuada), *m.*; lentejuela, *f.*

sequoia, *n.* pino gigantesco californiano.

seraglio, *n.* serrallo, *m.*

serape, *n.* sarape, *m.*, capote mejicano.

seraph, *n.* serafín, *m.*

serenade, *n.* serenata, *f.*; **noisy, mocking** —, cantaleta, *f.*; —, *vt.* dar serenatas.

serene, *adj.* sereno; —**ly,** *adv.* serenamente.

serenity, *n.* serenidad, *f.*

serf, *n.* siervo, esclavo, *m.*

serge, *n.* sarga, *f.*

sergeant, serjeant, *n.* sargento, *m.*; alguacil, *m.*

serial, *adj.* que se publica en series; —, *n.* publicación en cuadernos periódicos; película cinematográfica de episodios.

series, *n.* serie, cadena, *f.*

serious, *adj.* serio, grave; —**ly,** *adv.* seriamente.

seriousness, *n.* gravedad, seriedad, *f.*

sermon, *n.* sermón, *m.*

sermonize, *vt.* sermonear.

serology, *n.* suerología, *f.*

serous, *adj.* seroso.

serpent, *n.* serpiente, sierpe, *f.*

serpentine, *adj.* serpentino; —, *n.* (chem.) serpentina, *f.*; —, *vi.* serpentear.

serrate, serrated, *adj.* serrado.

serum, *n.* suero, *m.*

serv. servant, sirviente.

servant, *n.* criado, da; servidor, ra; sirviente, ta; paniaguado, *m.*

serve, *vt. and vi.* servir; asistir (a la mesa); ser a propósito; **to — a warrant,** ejecutar un auto de prisión.

service, *n.* servicio, *m.*; servidumbre, utilidad, *f.*; culto divino; acomodo, empleo, *m.*; **at your —,** servidor, ra, a sus órdenes; **day —,** servicio diurno; **night —,** servicio nocturno; **— station,** estación de servicios; taller de repuestos y reparaciones; **to be of —,** ser útil.

serviceable, *adj.* servible, útil; beneficioso, ventajoso.

servile, *adj.* servil; —**ly,** *adv.* servilmente.

servility, *n.* bajeza, vileza de ánimo.

servitude, *n.* servidumbre, esclavitud, *f.*

sesame, *n.* (bot.) sésamo, *m.*; **open —,** sésamo ábrete (frase mágica de contraseña).

session, *n.* junta, *f.*; sesión, *f.*; **joint —,** sesión plena.

set, *vt.* poner, colocar, fijar; establecer, determinar; parar (en el juego); basar; —, *vi.* ponerse (el sol o los astros); tramontar (el sol o los astros); cuajarse; aplicarse; **to — a diamond,** montar un diamante; **to — aside,** poner a un lado; **to — back,** hacer retroceder; **to — forward,** hacer adelantar; **to — on fire,** pegar fuego a; **to — the table,** poner la mesa; **to — up,** erigir; sentar; —, *n.* juego, *m.*, conjunto (de cartas), *m.*; servicio (de plata), *m.*; conjunto o agregado de muchas cosas, colección, *f.*; cuadrilla, bandada, *f.*; **— of dishes,** vajilla, *f.*; —, *adj.* puesto, fijo.

setback, *n.* revés, *m.*; (arch.) voladizo, *m.*

setscrew, *n.* tornillo de presión o de sujeción; tornillo de retén.

settee, *n.* canapé pequeño.

setter, *n.* perro de muestra.

setting, *n.* establecimiento, *m.*; colocación, *f.*; asentamiento, *m.*; fraguado, *m.*; montadura, *f.*; (theat.) escenario, decorado, *m.*; marco, *m.*; **— of the sun,** puesta del sol.

settle, *vt.* colocar, fijar, afirmar; componer; arreglar; calmar; solventar (deudas); —, *vi.* reposarse; establecerse, radicarse; sosegarse; **to — an account,** finiquitar, saldar, ajustar una cuenta; —, *n.* asiento, *m.*

settlement, *n.* establecimiento, *m.*; domicilio, *m.*; contrato, *m.*; arreglo, *m.*; liquidación, *f.*; sedimento, *m.*; empleo, *m.*; colonia, *f.*

settler, *n.* colono, *m.*

set-to, *n.* combate, *m.*; contienda, *f.*

setup, *n.* disposición, *f.*, arreglo, *m.*

seven, *n. and adj.* siete, *m.*

sevenfold, *adj.* séptuplo.

seventeen, *adj.* diez y siete, diecisiete; —, *n.* diecisiete, *m.*

seventeenth, *adj.* décimoséptimo.

seventh, *adj.* séptimo; **— heaven,** séptimo cielo; (fig.) éxtasis, *m.*; —**ly,** *adv.* en séptimo lugar.

seventieth, *adj.* septuagésimo.

seventy, *n. and adj.* setenta, *m.*

sever, *vt. and vi.* separar, dividir; cortar; desligar.

several, *adj.* diversos, varios; —**ly,** *adv.* separadamente.

severance, *n.* separación, *f.*

severe, *adj.* severo, riguroso; serio; áspero; duro, torvo, cruel; —**ly,** *adv.* severamente.

severity, *n.* severidad, *f.*

sew, *vt. and vi.* coser; —**er,** *n.* costurera, *f.*

sewage, *n.* alcantarillado, *m.*

sewer, *n.* albañal, *m.*, cloaca, *f.*; caño, *m.*

sewerage, *n.* construcción de albañales; agua de sumidero; alcantarillado, *m.*; sistema de alcantarillas.

sewing, *n.* costura, *f.*; **— machine,** máquina de coser.

sex, *n.* sexo, *m.*

sexagenarian, *n.* sesentón, ona, sexagenario, ria.

sextant, *n.* sextante, *m.*

sextet, *n.* sexteto, *m.*

sexton, *n.* sacristán, *m.*; sepulturero, *m.*

sextuple, *adj.* séxtuplo.

sexual, *adj.* sexual.

s.g. specific gravity, peso específico.

Sgt. Sergeant, Sar. Sargento.

shabbily, *adv.* vilmente; ruinmente; pobremente.

shabbiness, *n.* vileza, bajeza, miseria, *f.*

shabby, *adj.* vil, bajo; desharrapado; tacaño; destartalado.

shackle, *vt.* encadenar; **—s,** *n. pl.* grillos *m. pl.*

shad, *n.* (pez) alosa, *f.*, sábalo, *m.*

shadbush, *n.* amelanquier, guillomo, *m.*

shade, *n.* sombra, oscuridad, *f.*; matiz, *m.*; sombrilla, *f.*; umbría, *f.*; **—,** *vt.* asombrar, dar sombra; matizar; esconder.

shadow, *n.* sombra, *f.*; protección, *f.*; **—,** *vt.* sombrear.

shadowboxing, *n.* acto de pelear o boxear con un adversario imaginario.

shadowy, *adj.* umbroso; oscuro; quimérico.

shady, *adj.* opaco, oscuro, sombrío, umbroso; (fig.) sospechoso.

shaft, *n.* flecha, saeta, *f.*; fuste de columna; pozo de una mina; cañón de chimenea.

shag, *n.* pelo áspero y lanudo; felpa, *f.*

shagbark, *n.* nogal americano.

shaggy, *adj.* afelpado.

shagreen, *n.* zapa, lija, *f.*; chagrín, *m.*

shake, *vt.* sacudir; agitar; **—,** *vi.* vacilar; temblar; **to — hands,** darse las manos; **—,** *n.* concusión, sacudida, *f.*; vibración, *f.*

shakedown, *n.* cama improvisada; (coll.) demanda de dinero por compulsión.

shake-up, *n.* reorganización, *f.*

shaking, *n.* sacudimiento, *m.*; temblor, *m.*

shako, *n.* chacó, *m.*

shaky, *adj.* titubeante, tembloroso.

shale, *n.* arcilla esquistosa.

shall, *vi.* verbo auxiliar para indicar el futuro en la primera persona del singular y del plural, o el imperativo en las demás personas, por ej., **I — eat,** comeré; **we — eat,** comeremos; **he — eat,** comerá de todos modos, tendrá que comer, etc.

shallop, *n.* (naut.) chalupa, *f.*

shallow, *adj.* somero, superficial; trivial; **—,** *n.* bajío (banco de arena), *m.*

sham, *vt.* engañar, chasquear; **—,** *n.* socolor, *m.*; fingimiento, *m.*; impostura, *f.*; **—,** *adj.* fingido, disimulado; **— battle,** simulacro de combate.

shambles, *n. pl.* carnicería, *f.*

shame, *n.* vergüenza, *f.*; deshonra, *f.*; **—,** *vt.* avergonzar, deshonrar.

shamefaced, *adj.* vergonzoso, pudoroso.

shameful, *adj.* vergonzoso; deshonroso; **—ly,** *adv.* ignominiosamente.

shameless, *adj.* desvergonzado; **—ly,** *adv.* desvergonzadamente.

shammy, *n.* = **chamois.**

shampoo, *vt.* dar champú, lavar la cabeza; **—,** *n.* champú, *m.*

shamrock, *n.* trébol, trifolio, *m.*

shank, *n.* pierna, *f.*; asta, *f.*; asta de ancla; cañón de pipa.

shantung, *n.* variedad de tela de seda en rama.

shanty, *n.* cabaña, *f.*

shape, *vt. and vi.* formar; concebir; configurar; dar forma; adaptar; **—,** *n.* forma, figura, *f.*; modelo, *m.*

shapeless, *adj.* informe, sin forma.

shapely, *adj.* bien hecho, bien formado.

share, *n.* parte, porción, cuota, *f.*; (com.) acción, *f.*; reja del arado; participación, *f.*; **— of profits, — of lands,** quiñón, *m.*; **—,** *vt. and vi.* repartir, participar; compartir.

sharecropper, *n.* persona que paga el alquiler de la tierra que cultiva con parte de los frutos.

shareholder, *n.* (com.) accionista, *m.* y *f.*

shark, *n.* tiburón, *m.*; petardista, *m.*

sharkskin, *n.* tela ordinaria en su mayor parte de algodón, tejida con hilos de varias hebras finas y que tiene apariencia sedosa.

sharp, *adj.* agudo, aguzado; astuto; perspicaz, sagaz; penetrante; picante, acre, mordaz, severo, rígido; vivo, violento; **— bend,** curva cerrada; **—,** *n.* (mus.) sostenido, *m.*; **two o'clock —,** las dos en punto; **—ly,** *adv.* con filo; severamente, agudamente; ingeniosamente; ásperamente.

sharpen, *vt.* afilar, aguzar.

sharpener, *n.* aguzador, afilador, amolador *m.*; máquina de afilar; **pencil —,** cortalápiz, tajalápices, *m.*

sharper, *n.* petardista, estafador, *m.*

sharpness, *n.* agudeza, *f.*; sutileza, perspicacia, *f.*; acrimonia, *f.*

shatter, *vt.* destrozar, estrellar; **—,** *vi.* hacerse pedazos; **—,** *n.* pedazo, fragmento, *m.*

shatterproof, *adj.* que no puede astillarse.

shave, *vt.* rasurar, afeitar; raspar; rozar; (fig.) escatimar; **—,** *n.* afeitada, *f.*; (coll.) escape, *m.*

shaver, *n.* barbero, *m.*; usurero, *m.*; (coll.) muchacho, chico, *m.*

shaving, *n.* raedura, acepilladura, *f.*; rasura, afeitada, *f.*; **— cream,** crema de afeitar; **—s,** *pl.* virutas, *f. pl.*

shawl, *n.* chal, mantón, *m.*; sarape, *m.*; **woman's —,** manteleta, *f.*, rebozo, *m.*

she, *pron.* ella.

sheaf, *n.* gavilla, *f.*; **—,** *vt.* agavillar.

shear, *vt.* atusar; tundir; tonsurar; **—s,** *n. pl.* tijeras grandes, cizalla, *f.*

shearing, *n.* tonsura, *f.*; trasquiladura, *f.*

sheath, *n.* vaina, *f.*; **—,** *vt.* envainar; (naut.) aforrar el fondo de un navío.

sheave, *n.* rueda de polea, roldana, *f.*; **—s,** *n. pl.* de **sheaf,** haces, *m. pl.*

shed, *vt.* verter, derramar; esparcir; **—,** *n.* sotechado, tejadillo, *m.*; cabaña, barraca, *f.*; cobertizo, *m.*; techo, *m.*; choza, *f.*; **— for cattle,** tenada, *f.*

sheen, *n.* resplandor, *m.*; brillo, *m.*

sheep, *n. sing.* y *pl.* oveja(s), *f.*, carnero, *m.*; (coll.) papanatas, *m.*; **— louse,** caparra, garrapata, *f.*; **— raiser,** ovejero, *m.*

sheepcote, sheepcot, *n.* redil, *m.*

sheepfold, n. = **sheepcote.**

sheepherder, n. ganadero, m.

sheepish, adj. vergonzoso; tímido; cortado.

sheepskin, n. piel de carnero; (fig.) diploma, m.

sheepwalk, n. dehesa, f.; carneril, pasto de ovejas.

sheer, adj. puro, claro, sin mezcla; delgado, trasparente; —, adv. de un solo golpe; completamente; —, vi. desviarse.

sheet, n. pliego de papel; (naut.) escota, f.; **bed —,** sábana, f.; **blank —,** hoja en blanco; **book in —s,** libro no encuadernado; **— anchor,** áncora mayor de un navío; **— glass,** vidrio en lámina; **— iron,** plancha de hierro batido; **— lightning,** relampagueo a manera de fucilazos; **— metal,** hoja metálica, metal en hojas, palastro, m., lámina, f.; **— music,** música publicada en hojas sueltas; **— (of paper),** **— (of metal),** hoja, f.; —, vt. ensabanar; extender en láminas.

sheeting, n. tela para sábanas; encofrado, m.

shelf, n. anaquel, estante, m.; (naut.) arrecife, m.; escollera, f.; **corner —,** rinconera, f.; **on the —,** (coll.) desechado, archivado.

shell, n. cáscara, f.; silicua, f.; concha, f.; corteza, f.; bomba, f.; cartucho, m.; granada, f.; carapacho, m.; **cartridge —,** cápsula, f.; **— room,** (naut.) pañol de granadas; **— shock,** condición psiconeurótica producida por la guerra moderna en algunos de los combatientes; neurosis de guerra, f.; **turtle —,** carey, m.; —, vt. descascarar, descortezar; bombardear; —, vi. descascararse.

shellac, n. goma laca; —, vt. cubrir con laca.

sheller, n. descascarador, m.

shellfire, n. fuego de bomba o metralla.

shellfish, n. marisco, m.

shellproof, adj. a prueba de bombas.

shelter, n. guarida, f.; amparo, abrigo, m.; asilo, refugio, m.; cubierta, f.; —, vt. guarecer, abrigar; acoger.

shelve, vt. echar a un lado, arrinconar; —s, n. pl. de **shelf,** anaqueles, m. pl.

shelving, n. estantería, f.; material para anaqueles.

shepherd, n. pastor, m.; zagal, m.; **young —,** zagalejo, m.

shepherdess, n. pastora, ovejera, f.; zagala, f.

sherbet, n. sorbete, m.

sheriff, n. alguacil, m., funcionario administrativo de un condado.

sherry, n. vino de Jerez.

shield, n. escudo, m.; patrocinio, m.; —, vt. defender; amparar.

shift, vi. cambiarse; mudarse el vestido; ingeniarse; trampear; —, vt. mudar; cambiar; trasportar; —, n. último recurso; (mech.) cambio de marcha, tanda, f.; conmutación, f.; artificio, m.; astucia, f.; efugio, m.

shiftless, adj. perezoso; negligente; descuidado; **—ly,** adv. negligentemente.

shillelagh, shillalah, n. palo, m., cachiporra, f.

shilling, n. chelín, m.

shimmy, n. baile con movimiento de las caderas y los hombros; (auto.) vibración anormal de las ruedas delanteras.

shin, n. espinilla, f.

shinbone, n. tibia, espinilla, f.

shine, vi. lucir, brillar, resplandecer; —, vt. dar lustre (a los zapatos, etc.); embolar; —, n. brillo, m.; resplandor, m.

shingle, n. ripia, f., tejamaní, tejamanil, m.; muestra de oficina; —, vt. cubrir (un techo, etc.) con ripias; trasquilar, cinglar; tejar con lata.

shingles, n. (med.) herpes, m. y f. pl.

shining, adj. resplandeciente, luciente, reluciente; —, n. esplendor, m.

shiny, adj. brillante, luciente.

ship, n. nave, f.; bajel, navío, buque, barco, m.; **capacity of a —, hull of —,** buque, m.; **merchant —,** buque mercante; **repair —,** buque taller; **scouting —,** buque explorador; **—'s captain,** patrón, m.; **—'s papers,** documentación de a bordo; —, vt. embarcar; expedir.

shipboard, n. tablón de navío; **on —,** a bordo.

shipbuilder, n. arquitecto naval.

shipbuilding, n. arquitectura naval, construcción de buques.

shipmate, n. (naut.) ayudante, m.; compañero de camarote.

shipment, n. cargazón, expedición, f.; cargamento, m.; envío, despacho, embarque, m., remesa, f.

shipowner, n. naviero, m.

shipper, n. expedidor, remitente, m.; (com.) embarcador, m.

shipping, n. navegación, f.; marina, flota, f.; expedición, f., embarque, m.; **— clerk,** dependiente encargado de embarques y remisiones; **— company,** compañía naviera; **— expenses,** gastos de expedición; **— room,** departamento de embarques; **— documents,** documentos de embarque; **—, adj. naviero.**

shipwreck, n. naufragio, m.

shipwrecked, adj. náufrago; **— person,** náufrago, ga.

shipyard, n. varadero, m.

shire, n. condado (de Inglaterra), m.

shirk, vt. esquivar, evitar; —, n. persona que elude o se esquiva de hacer algo.

shirr, vt. (costura) fruncir; (cocina) escalfar; **—ed eggs,** huevos escalfados.

shirt, n. camisa de hombre; **— band,** cabezón de camisa; **— bosom,** pechera, f.; **— store,** camisería, f.; **sport —,** camisa de deporte.

shirting, n. tela para camisas.

shiver, n. cacho, pedazo, fragmento, m.; estremecimiento, m.; —, vi. tiritar de miedo o frío; —, vt. romper, estrellar.

shivering, n. horripilación, f.; temblor, m.

shoal, n. multitud, muchedumbre, f.; bajío, m.; (naut.) vigía, f.; — **of fish,** manada de peces; —, adj. bajo, vadoso; —, vi. perder profundidad gradualmente.

shoaly, adj. lleno de bajíos.

shock, n. choque, encuentro, m.; concusión, f.; combate, m.; ofensa, f ; hacina, f.; —**absorber,** amortiguador, m.; — **troops,** tropas escogidas, tropas ofensivas o de asalto; —, vt. sacudir; ofender.

shockproof, adj. a prueba de choques.

shoddy, n. caedura, f.; —, adj. cursi.

shoe, n. zapato, m.; herradura de caballo; **old** —, chancla, f.; **rubber** —, chanclo, m., zapato de goma; — **polish,** grasa para calzado; betún, m.; — **store,** zapatería, f.; — **tree,** horma de zapatos; **to put on one's** —**s,** calzarse; —, vt. calzar; herrar un caballo.

shoeblack, n. limpiabotas, m.

shoehorn, shoeing-horn, n. calzador, m.

shoelace, n. cordón de zapato. agujeta, f.

shoemaker, n. zapatero, m.

shoestring, n. cordón o lazo de zapato, agujeta.

shone, pretérito y p. p. del verbo **shine.**

shoot, vt. tirar, disparar; arrojar, lanzar; fusilar; matar o herir con escopeta; **to** — **at a target,** tirar al blanco; —, vi. brotar, germinar; sobresalir; lanzarse; —, n. tiro, m.; brote, vástago, retoño, tallo, m.

shop, n. tienda, f.; taller, m.; **in the** —**s,** en el comercio, en las tiendas; **pastry** —, **confectionery** —, repostería, f.; **watch** —, relojería, f.; —, vt. hacer compras.

shopkeeper, n. tendero, ra; mercader, m.

shoplifter, n. ladrón de tiendas, ratero, m.

shopman, n. mancebo de tienda.

shopping, n. compras, f. pl.; **to go** —, ir de compras.

shopwindow, n. vidriera, f.

shore, n. costa, ribera, playa, orilla, f.; — **leave,** (naut.) permiso para ir a tierra; — **line,** ribera, costa, f.; línea de barcos costeros.

short, adj. corto; breve, sucinto, conciso; brusco; **a** — **while,** dentro de poco, al poco rato; — **circuit,** (elec.) corto circuito, cortocircuito, m.; **to** — **circuit,** causar un cortocircuito; — **sale,** promesa de venta de valores u otros bienes que no se poseen, pero cuya adquisición se espera pronto; — **wave,** onda corta; **on** — **notice,** con poco tiempo de aviso; —, n. (com.) déficit, m.; **in** —, en concreto, en definitiva; —**ly,** adv. brevemente; presto; en pocas palabras; dentro de poco.

shortage, n. escasez, falta, f.; merma, f.; déficit, m.

shortbread, n. tortita dulce hecha con manteca.

shortcake, n. torta, f.

shortchange, vt. defraudar al devolver el

sobrante de un pago.

shortcoming, n. insuficiencia, f.; déficit, m.

shorten, vt. acortar; abreviar.

shorthand, n. taquigrafía, estenografía, fonografía, f.

shorthorn, n. variedad de ganado vacuno de cuernos cortos.

short-lived, adj. de breve vida o duración.

shorts, n. pl. calzones cortos; calzoncillos, m. pl.

shortsighted, adj. corto de vista, miope.

shortstop, n. (baseball) jugador que se pone entre el segundo y tercer puesto de un rombal de baseball.

short-tempered, adj. de mal genio, irascible.

short-term, adj. de período breve o limitado.

shot, n. tiro, m.; alcance, m.; escote, m., cuota, f.; **bird** —, perdigones m. pl.

shotgun, n. escopeta, f.

shot-put, n. lanzamiento de peso.

shoulder, n. hombro, m.; brazuelo, m.; **round-** —**ed,** cargado de espaldas; — **blade,** omóplato, m.; —, vt. cargar al hombro; soportar.

shout, vi. dar vivas, aclamar; reprobar con gritos; gritar; —, n. aclamación, f., grito, m.

shove, vt. and vi. empujar; impeler; —, n. empujón, m.

shovel, n. pala, f.; **fire** —, paleta, f.; —, vt. traspalar; secar, desaguar.

shoveler, n. palero, m.

shovelful, n. palada, f.

show, vt. mostrar, enseñar, explicar, hacer ver; descubrir, manifestar; probar; —, vi. parecer; **to** — **off,** lucirse; **to** — **oneself superior to,** sobreponerse; —, n. espectáculo, m.; muestra, f.; exposición, f.; (theat.) función, f.; — **bill,** cartelón, cartel, m.; — **boat,** buqueteatro, m.; — **card,** rótulo, cartel, letrero, m.; — **window,** escaparate, m.

showcase, n. escaparate, mostrador, m., vitrina, f.

shower, n. nubada, f., aguacero, chubasco, m.; llovizna, f.; (fig.) abundancia, f.; — **bath,** baño de ducha; —, vi. llover; —, vt. derramar profusamente.

showery, adj. lluvioso.

showmanship, n. habilidad para presentar espectáculos.

shown, p. p. del verbo **show.**

showroom, n. sala de muestras; sala de exhibición de modelos.

showy, adj. ostentoso, suntuoso; vistoso, llamativo, chillón.

shrank, pretérito del verbo **shrink.**

shrapnel, n. granada de metralla.

shred, n. cacho, pedazo pequeño, triza, f.; jirón, m.; —, vt. picar, hacer trizas; rallar; —**ded cocoanut,** coco rallado.

shrew, n. mujer de mal genio; (zool.) musgaño, m.

shrewd, *adj.* astuto, sagaz; mordaz; **—ly,** *adv.* astutamente.

shrewdness, *n.* astucia, *f.*; sagacidad, *f.*

shrewish, *adj.* regañón; **—ly,** *adv.* con mal humor.

shrewmouse, *n.* musgaño, *m.*, musaraña, *f.*

shriek, *vi.* chillar; **—,** *n.* chillido, *m.*

shrill, *adj.* agudo, penetrante, chillón.

shrimp, *n.* camarón, *m.*; hombrecillo, *m.*

shrine, *n.* relicario, *m.*; tumba de santo; (eccl.) trono, *m.*

shrink, *vi.* encogerse; angostarse, acortarse.

shrinkage, *n.* contracción, *f.*, encogimiento, *m.*

shrivel, *vi.* arrugarse, encogerse; **—,** *vt.* arrugar.

shroud, *n.* cubierta, *f.*; mortaja, *f.*, sudario, *m.*; **—s,** *n. pl.* (naut.) obenques, *m. pl.*; **—,** *vt.* cubrir, esconder; amortajar.

Shrovetide, *n.* martes de carnaval.

shrub, *n.* arbusto, *m.*

shrubbery, *n.* arbustos, *m. pl.*

shrug, *vt.* encogerse de hombros; **—,** *n.* encogimiento de hombros.

shrunk, *p. p.* del verbo **shrink.**

shuck, *n.* cáscara, *f.*; **—,** *vt.* descascar, desgranar.

shudder, *vi.* estremecerse, despeluzarse; **—,** *n.* despeluzamiento, temblor, *m.*

shuffle, *vt.* and *vi.* poner en confusión, desordenar; barajar los naipes; trampear; tergiversar; arrastrar (los pies); **—,** *n.* barajadura, *f.*; treta, *f.*

shuffleboard, *n.* juego de tejo.

shuffling, *n.* tramoya, *f.*; acción de arrastrar (los pies).

shun, *vt.* huir, evitar.

shunt, *n.* (rail.) bifurcación, *f.*, cambio de vía.

shut, *vt.* cerrar, encerrar.

shutdown, *n.* cesación de trabajo.

shut-in, *n.* persona encamada en su casa o en un hospital por enfermedad.

shutout, *n.* (deportes) triunfo en que se deja sin tantos al contrario.

shutter, *n.* persiana, celosía, *f.*; obturador de aparato fotográfico.

shuttle, *n.* lanzadera, *f.*

shuttlecock, *n.* volante, rehilete, *m.*

shy, *adj.* tímido; reservado; vergonzoso; contenido; pudoroso; **—ly,** *adv.* tímidamente.

shyness, *n.* timidez, *f.*

sibyl, *n.* sibila, profetisa, *f.*

sick, *adj.* malo, enfermo; disgustado, aburrido.

sicken, *vt.* enfermar; **—,** *vi.* enfermarse.

sickle, *n.* hoz, segadera, *f.*

sickly, *adj.* enfermizo, malsano.

sickness, *n.* enfermedad, *f.*

side, *n.* lado, *m.*; costado, *m.*; facción, *f.*; partido, *m.*; **— arms,** armas llevadas al cinto; **— dish,** platillo, entremés, *m.*; **— light,** luz lateral, información incidental; **— line,** negocio o actividad accesorios;

— show, función o diversión secundaria; **— whiskers,** patillas, *f. pl.*; **—,** *adj.* lateral, oblicuo; **— by —,** juntos; **—,** *vt.* poner a un lado; **—,** *vi.* apoyar la opinión (de alguien), declararse a favor (de alguien o algún partido).

sideboard, *n.* aparador, *m.*; alacena, *f.*

sideburns, *n.* patillas, *f. pl.*

sidecar, *n.* carro lateral.

sidelong, *adj.* lateral; **—,** *adv.* de lado.

sidepiece, *n.* pieza lateral.

siderurgy, *n.* siderurgia, *f.*

sideslip, *vi.* resbalar hacia un lado.

side-step, *vt.* evitar, evadir; **—,** *vi.* hacerse a un lado.

side-stepping, *n.* (boxeo) esquivada lateral.

sideswipe, *vt.* (coll.) dar un golpe oblicuo en el costado.

sidetrack, *vt.* (rail.) desviar a un apartadero; (coll.) apartarse del asunto principal, arrinconar.

sidewalk, *n.* banqueta, acera, vereda, *f.*

sideways, *adv.* de lado, al través.

side-wheel, *adj.* de ruedas laterales (barco).

siding, *n.* cobertura exterior de una casa de madera; (rail.) apartadero, desviadero, *m.*

sidle, *vi.* estar echado de lado, ir de lado.

siege, *n.* (mil.) sitio, *m.*

sienna, *n.* siena, *f.*

sierra, *n.* sierra, *f.*, cadena de montañas.

siesta, *n.* siesta, *f.*

sieve, *n.* tamiz, *m.*; criba, bo; garbillo, *m.*; **small —,** zarandillo, *m.*

sift, *vt.* cerner; cribar; examinar; investigar.

sigh, *vi.* suspirar, gemir; **—,** *n.* suspiro, *m.*

sight, *n.* vista, mira, *f.*; perspectiva, *f.*; mamarracho, espantajo, *m.*; **at first —,** a primera vista; **at —,** a presentación; **gun —,** punto (de escopeta), *m.*; **on —,** a la vista; **sense of —,** ver, *m.*; **— draft,** letra o giro a la vista; **thirty days' —,** treinta días vista.

sighting hood, *n.* mantelete, *m.*

sightless, *adj.* ciego.

sightly, *adj.* vistoso, hermoso.

sight-seeing, *n.* paseo, *m.*; excursión, *f.*; **— car,** ómnibus de excursión, coche de turismo.

sight-seer, *n.* excursionista, *m.* y *f.*

Sigismund, Segismundo.

sign, *n.* señal, *f.*, indicio, *m.*; tablilla, *f.*; signo, *m.*; firma, *f.*; seña, *f.*; letrero, *m.*; marca, *f.*; rótulo, *m.*; **—,** *vt.* and *vi.* señalar, hacer señas; suscribir, firmar.

signal, *n.* señal, seña, *f.*, aviso, *m.*; **—,** *adj.* insigne, señalado; **— light,** (rail.) farol (de mano o de disco), *m.*; (naut.) fanal, faro, *m.*; **— man,** (rail.) guardavía, *m.*; **— mast,** semáforo, *m.*; mástil de señales.

signalize, *vt.* señalar.

signatory, *n.* signatario, ria.

signature, *n.* firma, *f.*; seña, *f.*; signatura, *f.*

signboard, *n.* tablero de anuncios.

signet, *n.* sello, *m.*

significance, *n.* importancia, significación, *f.*

significant, *adj.* significante, importante.
signification, *n.* significación, *f.*; sentido, significado, *m.*
signify, *vt.* significar; —, *vi.* importar.
sign language, *n.* lenguaje de señales.
signpost, *n.* pilar de anuncio.
silage, *n.* ensilaje, *m.*
silence, *n.* silencio, *m.*; —, *vt.* imponer silencio, hacer callar.
silencer, *n.* silenciador, apagador, *m.*; (Mex.) mofle, *m.*
silent, *adj.* silencioso; callado; mudo; — **partner,** socio comanditario; —**ly,** *adv.* silenciosamente.
silex, *n.* sílice, pedernal, *m.*
silhouette, *n.* silueta, *f.*
silica, *n.* (chem.) sílice, *f.*
silicon dioxide, *n.* sílice, *f.*
silicosis, *n.* (med.) silicosis, *f.*
silk, *n.* seda, *f.*; —**s,** sedería, *f.*; — **stocking,** media de seda.
silken, *adj.* hecho de seda; sedeño.
silkiness, *n.* blandura, molicie, *f.*; cualidad de la seda.
silkworm, *n.* gusano de seda.
silky, *adj.* hecho de seda; sedeño.
sill, *n.* umbral de puerta.
silliness, *n.* simpleza, bobería, tontería, necedad, *f.*
silly, *adj.* tonto, mentecato, imbécil, bobo.
silo, *n.* silo, *m.*
silt, *n.* cieno, limo, légamo, *m.*
silver, *n.* plata, *f.*; — **dollar,** peso fuerte; — **fox,** zorro plateado; piel de zorro plateado; — **nitrate,** nitrato de plata; — **screen,** pantalla cinematográfica; — **wedding,** bodas de plata; —, *adj.* de plata; —, *vt.* platear; **to** — **plate,** platear.
silverbeater, *n.* batidor de plata.
silversmith, *n.* platero, *m.*
silverware, *n.* vajilla de plata, plata labrada.
silvery, *adj.* plateado.
simian, *n.* simio, mia; —, *adj.* símico.
similar, *adj.* similar; semejante; —**ly,** *adv.* en forma similar.
similarity, similitude, *n.* semejanza, *f.*
simile, *n.* semejanza, similitud, *f.*; símil, *m.*
similitude, *n.* similitud, semejanza, *f.*
simmer, *vi.* hervir a fuego lento.
simoniacal, *adj.* simoníaco.
simonize, *vt.* simonizar.
simon-pure, *adj.* genuino, puro.
simony, *n.* simonía, *f.*; **person guilty of** —, simoníaco, ca.
simper, *vi.* sonreír tontamente; —, *n.* sonrisilla tonta.
simple, *adj.* simple, puro, sencillo.
simpleton, *n.* simplón, ona, simplonazo, za, mentecato, ta, pazguato, ta, zonzo, za; (coll.) papamoscas, *m.*
simplicity, *n.* simplicidad, *f.*; simpleza, llaneza, *f.*
simplification, *n.* simplificación, *f.*
simplify, *vt.* simplificar.
simply, *adv.* simplemente.

simulate, *vt.* simular, fingir.
simulation, *n.* simulación, *f.*
simultaneous, *adj.* simultáneo, sincrónico.
sin, *n.* pecado, *m.*, culpa, *f.*; — **offering,** sacrificio propiciatorio; —, *vi.* pecar, faltar.
since, *adv.* desde entonces; —, *conj.* ya que, pues que, pues, puesto que; —, *prep.* desde, después.
sincere, *adj.* sencillo; sincero, franco; —**ly,** *adv.* sinceramente; —**ly yours,** (despedida en una carta), su seguro servidor, de usted muy sinceramente, etc.
sincerity, *n.* sinceridad, *f.*; llaneza, *f.*
sine, *n.* (math.) seno, *m.*
sinecure, *n.* sinecura, prebenda, canonjía, *f.*
sinew, *n.* tendón, *m.*; nervio, *m.*
sinewy, *adj.* nervudo, robusto.
sinful, *adj.* pecaminoso, malvado; —**ly,** *adv.* malvadamente.
sinfulness, *n.* corrupción, perversidad, *f.*
sing, *vt.* and *vi.* cantar; gorjear (los pájaros); (poet.) celebrar.
sing. singular, sing. singular.
singe, *vt.* chamuscar, socarrar.
singer, *n.* cantor *m.*, cantora, *f.*, cantante, *m.* y *f.*
singing, *n.* canto, *m.*, acción de cantar.
single, *adj.* sencillo, simple, solo; soltero; soltera; — **file,** hilera, *f.*, uno tras otro; — **man,** soltero, *m.*; — **woman,** soltera, *f.*; —, *vt.* singularizar; separar.
single-breasted, *adj.* de botonadura sencilla (chaqueta u otra prenda similar).
single-handed, *adj.* sin ayuda.
single-minded, *adj.* cándido, sencillo; con un solo propósito.
singleness, *n.* sencillez, sinceridad, *f.*; celibato, *m.*, soltería, *f.*
single-track, *adj.* de una sola vía; (fig.) estrecho.
singletree, *n.* volea, *f.*
singly, *adv.* separadamente.
singsong, *n.* sonsonete, tonillo, *m.*
singular, *adj.* singular, peculiar; —**ly,** *adv.* singularmente.
singularity, *n.* singularidad, *f.*
sinister, *adj.* siniestro, izquierdo; viciado; infeliz, funesto.
sink, *vi.* hundirse; sumergirse; bajarse; penetrar; arruinarse, decaer, sucumbir; —, *vt.* hundir, echar a lo hondo; echar a pique; sumergir; deprimir, destruir; —, *n.* alcantarilla, *f.*; sentina, *f.*; fregadero, *m.*
sinkable, *adj.* sumergible.
sinking fund, *n.* caja de amortización.
sinner, *n.* pecador, ora.
sintonize, *vt.* (rad.) sintonizar.
sinuosity, *n.* sinuosidad, *f.*
sinuous, *adj.* sinuoso.
sinus, *n.* seno, *m.*, cavidad, *f.*; hondanada, *f.*
sip, *vt.* and *vi.* beborrotear, tomar a sorbos, sorber; —, *n.* sorbo, *m.*
siphon, *n.* sifón, *m.*; — **bottle,** sifón, *m.*, botella de sifón.
sippet, *n.* rebanada de pan tostado.

sir, *n.* señor, *m.*; **my dear —,** muy señor mío, muy señor nuestro.

sire, *n.* caballero, *m.*; (poet.) padre, *m.*

siren, *n.* sirena, *f.*

sirloin, *n.* lomo de buey o vaca, solomillo, *m.*

sirup, *n.* jarabe, *m.*

sisal, *n.* sisal, *m.*

sister, *n.* hermana, *f.*; religiosa, *f.*

sisterhood, *n.* hermandad, *f.*

sister-in-law, *n.* cuñada, *f.*

sisterly, *adj.* como hermana.

sit, *vi.* sentarse; estar situado.

sit-down strike, *n.* huelga de brazos caídos.

site, *n.* sitio, *m.*; situación, *f.*; emplazamiento, *m.*; localización, *f.*

sitting, *n.* sesión, junta, *f.*; sentada, *f.*; **— room,** sala de descanso, salón de descanso.

situate, *adj.* situado; **—,** *vt.* colocar.

situated, *adj.* situado.

situation, *n.* situación, *f.*; ubicación, *f.*; estación, *f.*

six, *n.* and *adj.* seis, *m.*

sixpence, *n.* seis peniques (medio chelín).

sixshooter, *n.* revólver de seis cámaras.

sixteen, *n.* and *adj.* dieciseis, diez y seis.

sixteenth, *adj.* décimosexto.

sixth, *adj.* sexto; **— sense,** sexto sentido, sentido intuitivo; **—ly,** *adv.* en sexto lugar.

sixtieth, *adj.* sexagésimo.

sixty, *n.* and *adj.* sesenta, *m.*

size, *n.* tamaño, talle, *m.*; calibre, *m.*; dimensión, *f.*; estatura, *f.*; condición, *f.*; variedad de cola o goma; **—,** *vt.* encolar; ajustar, calibrar.

sized, *adj.* de tamaño especial; preparado con una especie de cola o goma.

sizzle, *vi.* chamuscar, sisear; **—,** *n.* siseo, *m.*

S. J. Society of Jesus, S. de J. Sociedad de Jesús.

skate, *n.* patín, *m.*; **ice —,** patín de hielo; **roller —,** patín de ruedas; **—,** *vi.* patinar.

skater, *n.* patinador, ra.

skating, *n.* acto de patinar; **— rink,** patinadero, *m.*

skein, *n.* madeja, *f.*

skeleton, *n.* esqueleto, *m.*; **— key,** llave maestra.

skeptic, *n.* and *adj.* escéptico, ca.

skeptic, skeptical, *adj.* escéptico.

skepticism, *n.* escepticismo, *m.*

sketch, *n.* esbozo, *m.*; esquicio, *m.*; bosquejo, *m.*; boceto, *m.*; esquema, *m.*; gráfico, *m.*; **—,** *vt.* bosquejar, esbozar.

skew, *adj.* oblicuo.

skewer, *n.* aguja de lardear; espetón, *m.*; **—,** *vt.* espetar.

ski, *n.* ski, *m.*; **— jump,** salto en skis; pista para esquiar; **—,** *vi.* patinar con skis.

skid, *n.* arrastradera de un carruaje; **—,** *vt.* enrayar, deslizar; **—,** *vi.* patinar.

skidding, *n.* patinaje, *m.*

skiff, *n.* esquife, *m.*

skill, *n.* destreza, pericia, *f.*, ingenio, *m.*; maestría, maña, *f.*

skilled, *adj.* práctico, instruído, versado, diestro.

skillet, *n.* cazuela, sartén, *f.*

skillful, skilful, *adj.* práctico, diestro, perito; mañoso; **—ly,** *adv.* diestramente.

skim, *vt.* espumar; tratar superficialmente; **—,** *n.* espuma, *f.*

skimmer, *n.* espumadera, *f.*

skimp, *vt.* and *vi.* (coll.) ser parco; escatimar.

skimpy, *adj.* tacaño, miserable; corto, escaso.

skin, *n.* cutis, *m.*; cuero, *m.*, piel, *f.*; **—,** *vt.* desollar.

skinned, *adj.* desollado.

skinner, *n.* pellejero, *m.*; peletero, *m.*

skinny, *adj.* flaco, macilento.

skin-tight, *adj.* ajustado al cuerpo.

skip, *vi.* saltar, brincar; **—,** *vt.* pasar, omitir; **—,** *n.* salto, brinco, *m.*

skipper, *n.* capitán de una embarcación pequeña.

skirmish, *n.* escaramuza, *f.*; tiroteo, *m.*; **—,** *vi.* escaramuzar.

skirmisher, *n.* escaramuzador, *m.*; **—s,** *n. pl.* tropas ligeras.

skirt, *n.* falda, enagua, pollera, *f.*; **—,** *vt.* orillar.

skit, *n.* burla, zumba, *f.*, pasquín, *m.*; sainete, *m.*, piececita cómica o dramática.

skitter, *vi.* deslizarse, avanzar a pequeños saltos.

skittish, *adj.* espantadizo, retozón; caprichoso; frívolo; **—ly,** *adv.* caprichosamente.

skittle, *n.* especie de bolo; especie de juego de bolos.

skulk, *vi.* escuchar, acechar.

skull, *n.* cráneo, *m.*; casquete, *m.*

skullcap, *n.* gorro, *m.*; casquete, *m.*

skunk, *n.* zorrillo, zorrino, *m.*; persona despreciable.

sky, *n.* cielo, firmamento, *m.*; **— blue,** azul celeste.

skylight, *n.* claraboya, *f.*

skyline, *n.* horizonte, *m.*; perspectiva de una ciudad.

skyrocket, *n.* cohete, *m.*

skyscraper, *n.* rascacielos, *m.*

skywriting, *n.* dibujo de letras o signos en el aire con humo arrojado por aviones.

slab, *n.* losa, *f.*; plancha, *f.*; tablilla, *f.*

slabber, *vi.* babear; ensuciar.

slack, *adj.* flojo, perezoso, negligente, lento; **—s,** *n. pl.* pantalones bombachos.

slack, slacken, *vt.* and *vi.* aflojar; ablandar; entibiarse; decaer; relajar; aliviar.

slacker, *n.* cobarde, *m.* y *f.*; hombre que elude sus deberes militares en tiempo de guerra.

slackness, *n.* flojedad, *f.*; descuido, *m.*

slag, *n.* escoria, *f.*

slake, *vt.* extinguir, apagar.

slam, *n.* capote (en los juegos de naipes), *m.*; portazo, *m.*; **—,** *vt.* dar capote; empujar con violencia; **to — the door,** dar un portazo, cerrar la puerta de golpe.

slander, *vt.* calumniar, infamar; —, *n.* calumnia, *f.*

slanderer, *n.* calumniador, ra, maldiciente, *m.* y *f.*

slanderous, *adj.* calumnioso; —**ly**, *adv.* calumniosamente.

slang, *n. slang*, vulgarismo, *m.*, jerga, *f.*

slant, *vi.* pender oblicuamente; —, *vt.* oblicuar.

slanting, *adj.* sesgado, oblicuo, terciado.

slap, *n.* manotada, *f.*; — **on the face**, bofetada, *f.*; —, *adv.* de sopetón; —, *vt.* golpear, dar una bofetada.

slapstick, *n.* farsa con actividad física rápida y violenta.

slash, *vt.* acuchillar; —, *n.* cuchillada, *f.*

slat, *n.* tablilla, *f.*

slate, *n.* pizarra, *f.*; —, *vt.* empizarrar; golpear; castigar; criticar severamente.

slate pencil, *n.* lápiz de pizarra.

slater, *n.* pizarrero, *m.*; crítico severo.

slating, *n.* techo de pizarras.

slattern, *n.* mujer desaliñada.

slatternly, *adj.* desaliñado; —, *adv.* desaliñadamente.

slaughter, *n.* carnicería, matanza, *f.*; —, *vt.* matar atrozmente; matar en la carnicería.

slaughterer, *n.* matador, asesino, *m.*

slaughterhouse, *n.* rastro, matadero, degolladero, *m.*

slave, *n.* esclavo, va; — **trade**, trata, *f.*; —, *vi.* trabajar como esclavo.

slaver, **slave ship**, *n.* negrero (navío), *m.*

slaver, *n.* baba, *f.*; —, *vt. and vi.* babosear, babear.

slavery, *n.* esclavitud, *f.*; **white** —, trata de blancas.

Slavic, *adj.* eslavo.

slavish, *adj.* servil, humilde; —**ly**, *adv.* servilmente.

slavishness, *n.* bajeza, servidumbre, *f.*

slaw, *n.* ensalada de col.

slay, *vt.* matar, quitar la vida.

slayer, *n.* asesino, *m.*

sled, **sledge**, **sleigh**, *n.* rastra, narria, *f.*; trineo, *m.*

sledge, *n.* rastra, *f.*; — **hammer**, macho, *m.*, mandarria, *f.*

sleek, *adj.* liso, bruñido; —, *vt.* alisar, pulir.

sleep, *vi.* dormir; **to** — **soundly**, dormir profundamente, dormir como un bendito; —, *n.* sueño, *m.*

sleeper, *n.* persona que duerme; zángano, *m.*; durmiente, *m.*; (rail.) coche dormitorio.

sleepily, *adv.* con somnolencia o torpeza, con sueño.

sleepiness, *n.* adormecimiento, *m.*; **to cause** —, adormecer.

sleeping, *n.* sueño, *m.*; — **bag**, especie de talego para dormir a la intemperie; — **car**, coche dormitorio, vagón cama; — **room**, dormitorio, *m.*; — **sickness**, letargo epidémico, encefalitis letárgica.

sleepless, *adj.* desvelado.

sleeplessness, *n.* insomnio, *m.*

sleepwalker, *n.* sonámbulo, la.

sleepwalking, *n.* sonambulismo, *m.*

sleepy, *adj.* soñoliento; **to be** —, tener sueño.

sleepyhead, *n.* dormilón, ona.

sleet, *n.* aguanieve, *f.*; —, *vi.* caer aguanieve.

sleeve, *n.* manga, *f.*

sleigh, *n.* trineo, *m.*; — **bell**, cascabel, *m.*

sleight, *n.* astucia, maña, *f.*

slender, *adj.* delgado, sutil, débil, pequeño; escaso; —**ly**, *adv.* delgadamente.

slenderness, *n.* delgadez, *f.*; tenuidad, *f.*; pequeñez, *f.*

sleuth, *n.* detective, *m.*

slice, *n.* rebanada, lonja, *f.*; espátula, *f.*; —, *vt.* rebanar.

slicer, *n.* rebanador, *m.*

slicing, *adj.* rebanador; — **machine**, máquina cortadora o rebanadora.

slick, *adj.* liso; lustroso; —, *vt.* hacer liso o lustroso.

slicker, *n.* impermeable, *m.*; trampista, petardista, *m.*

slide, *vi.* resbalar, deslizarse; —, *n.* resbalón, *m.*; resbaladero, *m.*; corredera, *f.*; **lantern** —, diapositiva, *f.*; — **rule**, regla de cálculo; — **valve**, válvula corrediza.

sliding, *n.* deslizamiento, *m.*

slight, *adj.* ligero, leve, pequeño; —, *n.* descuido, *m.*; —, *vt.* despreciar; —**ly**, *adv.* ligeramente.

slightingly, *adv.* con desprecio.

slightness, *n.* debilidad, *f.*; negligencia, *f.*

slim, *adj.* delgado, sutil.

slime, *n.* lodo, *m.*; sustancia viscosa; pecina, *f.*

sliminess, *n.* viscosidad, *f.*

slimness, *n.* delgadez, *f.*; sutileza, tenuidad, *f.*

slimy, *adj.* viscoso, pegajoso.

sling, *n.* honda, *f.*; hondazo, *m.*; —, *vt.* tirar con honda; (naut.) embragar.

slingshot, *n.* tirador, *m.*

slink, *vi.* escaparse; esconderse.

slip, *vi.* resbalar; escapar, huirse; —, *vt.* meter o introducir secretamente; dejar; —, *n.* resbalón, *m.*; tropiezo, *m.*; escapada, *f.*; — **cover**, funda de mueble; — **knot**, nudo corredizo.

slip-on, *n.* prenda de vestir que se pone por la cabeza.

slipper, *n.* chinela, zapatilla, *f.*; **house** —, chancleta, *f.*

slipperiness, *n.* calidad de resbaladizo.

slippery, *adj.* resbaladizo, deleznable, resbaloso.

slipshod, *adj.* desaliñado, negligente; descuidado.

slipstream, *n.* (aer.) corriente de aire que produce una hélice de aeroplano.

slit, *vt.* rajar, hender; —, *n.* raja, hendedura, *f.*

sliver, *n.* astilla, tira, *f.*; —, *vt.* rasgar, cortar en tiras.

slobber, *n.* baba, *f.*
sloe, *n.* endrina, *f.*; endrino, *m.*
sloop, *n.* (naut.) balandra, *f.*
slop, *n.* aguachirle, *f.*; lodazal, *m.*; —**s,** *pl.* gregüescos, *m. pl.*; ropa barata.
slope, *n.* sesgo, *m.*; escarpa, *f.*; ladera, vertiente, *f.*; declive, *m.*; cuesta, *f.*; —, *vt.* sesgar; —, *vi.* inclinarse.
sloping, *adj.* oblicuo; inclinado; (poet.) clivoso.
slop pail, *n.* cubeta, *f.*
sloppy, *adj.* lodoso, fangoso; (coll.) desaliñado, descuidado.
slot, *n.* hendedura, *f.*; — **machine,** máquina automática con ranura para monedas.
sloth, *n.* pereza, *f.*; (zool.) perezoso, *m.*
slothful, *adj.* perezoso.
slouch, *vt.* and *vi.* estar cabizbajo (como un patán); bambolearse pesadamente; ponerse gacho; —, *n.* persona incompetente y perezosa; joroba, *f.*
slough, *n.* lodazal, cenagal, *m.*
slough, *n.* pellejo de serpiente; escara (de una herida), *f.*
sloughy, *adj.* lodoso.
sloven, *n.* persona desaliñada.
slovenliness, *n.* desaliño, *m.*; porquería, *f.*; descuido, *m.*
slovenly, *adj.* desaliñado, puerco, sucio.
slow, *adj.* tardío, lento, torpe, perezoso; — **motion,** velocidad reducida; — **speed,** baja velocidad; —, *vt.* and *vi.* retardar, demorar; **to** — **down,** reducir o acortar la marcha; —**ly,** *adv.* lentamente.
slow-driving zone, *n.* zona de marcha lenta.
slowness, *n.* lentitud, tardanza, pesadez, *f.*
slug, *n.* holgazán, zángano, *m.*; (zool.) babosa, *f.*; (print.) lingote, *m.*; —, *vt.* golpear fuertemente.
sluggard, *n.* haragán, holgazán, *m.*
sluggish, *adj.* perezoso; lento; —**ly,** *adv.* perezosamente.
sluggishness, *n.* pereza, lentitud, *f.*
sluice, *n.* compuerta, *f.*; —, *vt.* soltar la compuerta de un canal, etc.
slum, *vi.* visitar viviendas o barrios bajos o escuálidos; —**s,** *n. pl.* barrios bajos; viviendas escuálidas.
slumber, *vi.* dormitar; —, *n.* sueño ligero.
slump, *n.* hundimiento, *m.*; quiebra, *f.*; baja considerable de precios o actividades en los negocios.
slur, *vt.* ensuciar; pasar ligeramente; —, *n.* (mus.) ligado, *m.*; afrenta, estigma, calumnia, *f.*
slush, *n.* lodo, barro, cieno, *m.*
slut, *n.* mujer sucia.
sly, *adj.* astuto; furtivo; —**ly,** *adv.* astutamente.
slyness, *n.* astucia, maña, *f.*
S. M. Master of Science, Maestro o Licenciado en Ciencias.
smack, *n.* sabor, gusto, *m.*; beso fuerte que

se oye; chasquido de látigo, *m.*; —, *vi.* saber, tener sabor de; besar con ruido.
small, *adj.* pequeño, menudo, chico; — **arms,** armas de fuego portátiles; — **beer,** cerveza floja o insípida; algo de poca importancia; — **change,** suelto, *m.*; — **fry,** niños, *m. pl.*, gente menuda; cosa trivial; — **hours,** primeras horas matinales; — **intestine,** intestino delgado; — **potatoes,** (coll.) persona o cosa de poca importancia; — **talk,** charla frívola; —, *n.* parte estrecha de cualquier cosa.
smallish, *adj.* algo pequeño, más bien pequeño.
small-minded, *adj.* mezquino, despreciable.
smallness, *n.* pequeñez, *f.*
small of the back, *n.* parte más estrecha de la espalda.
smallpox, *n.* viruelas, *f. pl.*
smart, *n.* escozor, *m.*; —, *adj.* punzante, agudo, agrio; ingenioso; mordaz; doloroso; inteligente; elegante; —, *vi.* escocer.
smartly, *adv.* agudamente, vivamente; elegantemente.
smartness, *n.* agudeza, viveza, sutileza, *f.*; elegancia, *f.*
smash, *vt.* romper, quebrantar; —, *n.* fracaso, *m.*; (tennis) bolea alta.
smash-up, *n.* choque desastroso.
smatterer, *n.* persona que sabe las cosas superficialmente.
smattering, *n.* conocimiento superficial.
smear, *vt.* untar; emporcar; manchar.
smell, *vt.* and *vi.* oler; percibir; olfatear; —, *n.* olfato, *m.*; olor, *m.*; hediondez, *f.*; **sense of** —, olfato, *m.*
smelling bottle, *n.* frasco de sales.
smelt, *n.* (pez) eperlano, *m.*; —, *vt.* fundir (el metal).
smelter, *n.* fundidor, *m.*
smile, *vi.* sonreír, sonreírse; —, *n.* sonrisa, *f.*
smirk, *vi.* sonreír burlonamente.
smite, *vt.* herir, golpear.
smith, *n.* forjador de metales.
smithery, smithy, *n.* herrería, *f.*
smock, *n.* camisa de mujer; sayo, *m.*; — **frock,** blusa, *f.*
smoke, *n.* humo, *m.*; vapor, *m.*; — **consumer,** locomotora fumívora; — **pipe,** humero, *m.*; — **screen,** cortina de humo; —, *vt.* and *vi.* ahumar; humear; fumar (tabaco).
smoke-dry, *vt.* ahumar, secar al humo.
smokehouse, *n.* lugar para ahumar carnes.
smokeless, *adj.* sin humo; — **powder,** pólvora sin humo.
smoker, *n.* fumador, *m.*; (rail.) coche fumador.
smokestack, *n.* chimenea, *f.*
smoking, *adj.* fumífero; — **car,** (rail.) coche fumador; — **jacket,** batín, *m.*; **no** —, se prohibe fumar.
smoky, *adj.* humeante; humoso.
smolder, *vi.* arder sin llama; existir en forma latente; —, *n.* humo, *m.*

smooth, adj. liso, pulido, llano; suave; afable; **—,** vt. allanar; alisar; lisonjear.

smoothly, adv. llanamente; con blandura.

smoothness, n. lisura, f.; llanura, f.; suavidad, f.

smother, vt. sofocar; apagar; **—,** n. humareda, f.

smothering, n. sofocación, f.

smoulder, vi. arder debajo de la ceniza; existir en forma latente.

smudge, vt. ahogar, asfixiar; ensuciar, tiznar; **—,** n. tiznadura, mugre, f.

smug, adj. atildado; escrupulosamente limpio o compuesto; satisfecho de sí mismo.

smuggle, vt. contrabandear.

smuggler, n. contrabandista, m. y f.

smuggling, n. contrabando, m.

smut, n. tiznón, m.; suciedad, f.; **—,** vt. tiznar; ensuciar.

smutty, adj. tiznado; anieblado; obsceno.

snack, n. parte, porción, f.; tentempié, refrigerio, m.

snaffle, n. brida con muserola.

snag, n. protuberancia, f.; raigón de diente; diente que sobresale; rama de un árbol escondida en el fondo de un lago o río; tocón, m.; obstáculo inesperado.

snail, n. caracol, m.

snake, n. culebra, sierpe, serpiente, f.; **—,** vi. culebrear.

snaky, adj. serpentino; traicionero, pérfido.

snap, vt. and vi. romper; agarrar; morder; insultar; chasquear, estallar; **to — one's fingers,** castañetear; **—,** n. estallido, m.; castañeteo, m.; corchete, m.; **— shooting,** tiroteo, m.

snapdragon, n. (bot.) antirrino, m., hierba becerra.

snapper, n. persona o cosa que castañetea; tortuga voraz; (pez) pargo, m.

snapping, n. acción de romper; acción de agarrar; **— turtle,** tortuga voraz.

snappish, adj. mordaz; regañón; **—ly,** adv. agriamente.

snappy, adj. vivaz, animado; elegante.

snapshot, n. instantánea, fotografía, f.

snare, n. lazo, m.; trampa, f.; garlito, m.; trapisonda, f.; **— drum,** pequeño tambor militar; **to fall into a —,** caer en la ratonera; **—,** vt. cazar animales con lazos; trapisondear.

snarl, vi. regañar, gruñir; enredar; **—,** n. gruñido, m.; complicación, f.

snatch, vt. arrebatar; agarrar; **—,** n. arrebatamiento, m.; arrebatiña, f.; pedazo, m.; ratito, m.

sneak, vi. arrastrar; ratear; **to — out,** tomar las de Villadiego; **—,** n. persona traicionera; **— thief,** ratero, ra.

sneer, vi. hablar con desprecio; fisgarse; **—,** n. fisga, f.

sneeze, vi. estornudar; **—,** n. estornudo, m.

snicker, vi. reír a menudo y socarronamente; **—,** n. risita socarrona.

sniff, vi. resollar con fuerza; **—,** vt. olfatear;

—, n. olfateo, m.

sniffle, vt. aspirar ruidosamente por la nariz; **—,** n. moquita, f.

snigger, vi. and n. = **snicker.**

snip, vt. tijeretear; **—,** n. tijeretada, f.; pedazo pequeño; porción, f.

snipe, n. (orn.) agachadiza, f., becardón, m.; **—,** vt. cazar becardones; tirar de un apostadero.

sniper, n. tirador apostado.

snivel, n. moquita, f.; **—,** vi. moquear; **—ly,** adj. mocoso.

snob, n. snob, m. y f., persona presuntuosa; advenedizo social o intelectual.

snobbish, adj. presuntuoso; jactancioso; propio del snob.

snood, n. especie de gorro tejido que sujeta el cabello de las mujeres.

snooze, n. sueño ligero; **—,** vi. dormir ligeramente, dormitar.

snore, vi. roncar; **—,** n. ronquido, m.

snort, vi. resoplar, bufar como un caballo fogoso.

snorting, n. resoplido, m.

snout, n. hocico, m.; trompa de elefante; (coll.) nariz, f.; boquilla (de manguera, etc.), f.

snow, n. nieve, f.; **— line,** límite de las nieves perpetuas; **—,** vi. nevar.

snowball, n. pelota de nieve.

snowberry, n. baya blanca americana.

snowbird, n. (orn.) variedad de pinzón.

snow-blind, snow-blinded, adj. cegado por el brillo del sol en la nieve.

snowbound, adj. bloqueado por la nieve.

snow-clad, adj. cubierto de nieve.

snowdrop, n. (bot.) campanilla blanca.

snowfall, n. nevada, f.

snowflake, n. copo de nieve.

snowplow, n. quitanieve, m.

snowshed, n. guardaaludes, m.

snowstorm, n. nevada, nevasca, f., tormenta de nieve.

snowy, adj. nevoso; nevado.

snub, vt. desairar, tratar con desprecio; **—,** n. altanería, f.; desaire, m.

snub-nosed, adj. de nariz chata.

snuff, n. moco de candela; pabilo, m.; tabaco en polvo; rapé, m.; **—,** vt. atraer en la nariz con el aliento; despabilar; oler.

snuffbox, n. tabaquera, f.

snuffer, n. despabilador, m.; despabiladeras, f.pl.

snuffle, vi. ganguear; hablar gangoso; **—s,** n.pl. catarro, m.

snug, adj. abrigado; conveniente, cómodo, agradable, grato.

snuggle, vi. acurrucarse; estar como apretado; arrimarse a otro en busca de calor o cariño.

so, adv. así; tal; de modo que; tanto; **and — forth,** y así sucesivamente; **— and —,** Fulana de Tal, m., Fulana de Tal, f.; **— much,** tanto; **— that,** para que, de modo que; **— then,** conque; **that is —,**

eso es, así es.

So. South, S. Sur.

soak, *vt.* and *vi.* remojarse; calarse; empapar, remojar; **to — through,** calarse (un líquido, etc.); **—,** *n.* calada (de un líquido, etc.), *f.*; (coll.) borrachín, *m.*

soap, *n.* jabón, *m.*; **cake of —,** pastilla de jabón; **— bubble,** ampolla o globo de jabón; **—,** *vt.* jabonar, enjabonar.

soapbox, *n.* plataforma improvisada para oradores de las calles.

soapstone, *n.* esteatita, *f.*

soapsuds, *n. pl.* jabonaduras, *f. pl.*, espuma de jabón.

soapy, *adj.* jabonoso.

soar, *vi.* remontarse, sublimarse.

soaring, *n.* vuelo muy alto; acción de remontarse.

sob, *n.* sollozo, *m.*; **—,** *vi.* sollozar.

sober, *adj.* sobrio; serio; **—ly,** *adv.* sobriamente; juiciosamente.

sobriety, *n.* sobriedad, *f.*; seriedad, gravedad, *f.*

sobriquet, *n.* apodo, sobrenombre, *m.*

Soc. soc. Society, S. Sociedad.

so-called, *adj.* así llamado.

soccer, *n.* variedad de juego de fútbol; balompié, *m.*

sociability, *n.* sociabilidad, *f.*

sociable, *adj.* sociable, comunicativo; **—ly,** *adv.* sociablemente.

social, *adj.* social, sociable; **— sciences,** ciencias sociales; **— security,** seguro social; **— service,** **— work,** servicio social, servicio en pro de las clases pobres; **—,** *n.* tertulia, *f.*; **— worker,** empleado encargado del bienestar social público; **—ly,** *adv.* sociablemente.

socialism, *n.* socialismo, *m.*

socialist, *n.* and *adj.* socialista, *m.* y *f.*

socialistic, *adj.* socialista.

socialite, *n.* (coll.) persona prominente en sociedad.

socialization, *n.* socialización, *f.*

socialize, *vt.* socializar.

society, *n.* sociedad, *f.*; compañía, *f.*

sociological, *adj.* sociológico.

sociologist, *n.* sociólogo, *m.*

sociology, *n.* sociología, *f.*

sock, *n.* escarpín, *m.*; zueco, *m.*; calcetín, *m.*

socket, *n.* cañón de candelero; cubo, encaje, casquillo, *m.*; alvéolo de un diente; encastre, *m.*; **eye —,** órbita, *f.*, cuenca del ojo; **lamp —,** portalámpara, *m.*; **— joint,** enchufe, *m.*

sod, *n.* césped, *m.*; turba, tierra, *f.*; **—,** *vt.* enyerbar.

soda, *n.* sosa, soda, *f.*; **baking —,** bicarbonato de sosa o de soda; **— cracker,** galletica de soda; **— fountain,** aparato de aguas gaseosas; **— water,** gaseosa, *f.*

sodality, *n.* hermandad, cofradía, fraternidad, *f.*

sodden, *adj.* empapado; de aspecto pesado por la disipación; ebrio.

sodium, *n.* (chem.) sodio, *m.*; **— chloride,** cloruro de sodio, sal de cocina.

sofa, *n.* sofá, *m.*

soft, *adj.* blando, mole, suave; benigno; tierno, compasivo; jugoso; afeminado; **— coal,** hulla grasa, carbón bituminoso; **— water,** agua dulce, agua no cruda; **—ly,** *adv.* suavemente; paso a paso; quedamente.

softball, *n.* juego parecido al baseball que se juega con pelota blanda.

soft-boiled, *adj.* pasado por agua; **— eggs,** huevos pasados por agua.

soften, *vt.* ablandar, mitigar; enternecer; reblandecer, suavizar.

softhearted, *adj.* compasivo; sensible, de buen corazón.

softness, *n.* suavidad, blandura, *f.*; dulzura, *f.*

soft-pedal, *vt.* suavizar; contener, reprimir.

soft-spoken, *adj.* afable, que habla con dulzura.

softwood, *n.* madera blanda.

soil, *vt.* ensuciar, emporcar; **—,** *n.* mancha, porquería, *f.*; terreno, *m.*; tierra, *f.*; estiércol, *m.*

soiree, soirée, *n.* velada, *f.*

sojourn, *vi.* residir, morar; **—,** *n.* morada, *f.*; residencia, permanencia, *f.*

sol, *n.* (mus.) sol, *m.*; sueldo (moneda antigua francesa), *m.*; moneda del Perú.

sol.: soluble, soluble; **solution,** solución.

solace, *vt.* solazar, consolar; **—,** *n.* consuelo, solaz, *m.*

solar, *adj.* solar; **— plexus,** (anat.) plexo solar; **— system,** sistema solar; **— year,** año solar.

solarium, *n.* solana, *f.*; habitación para tomar el sol con propósitos terapéuticos.

sold, *p.p.* vendido; **— out,** agotado.

solder, *vt.* soldar; **—,** *n.* soldadura, *f.*

soldier, *n.* soldado, *m.*; **—ly,** *adj.* soldadesco; marcial; **—** *vi.* prestar servicio militar.

soldiery, *n.* soldadesca, *f.*

sole, *n.* planta del pie; suela del zapato; **—,** *adj.* único, solo; **—,** *vt.* solar, poner suela al calzado.

solecism, *n.* (gram.) solecismo, *m.*

solemn, *adj.* solemne; **—ly,** *adv.* solemnemente.

solemnity, *n.* solemnidad, *f.*

solemnization, *n.* solemnización, *f.*

solemnize, *vt.* solemnizar.

solenoid, *n.* (elec.) solenoide, *m.*

solicit, *vt.* solicitar; implorar; pedir.

solicitation, *n.* solicitación, *f.*

solicitor, *n.* procurador, solicitador, *m.*

solicitous, *adj.* solícito, diligente; **—ly,** *adv.* solícitamente.

solicitude, *n.* solicitud, *f.*, cuidado, *m.*

solid, *adj.* sólido, compacto; **— color,** color entero; **— geometry,** geometría del espacio; **—,** *n.* sólido, *m.*; **—ly,** *adv.* sólidamente.

solidarity, *n.* solidaridad, *f.*
solidary, *adj.* solidario.
solidification, *n.* congelación, *f.*; solidificación, *f.*
solidify, *vt.* congelar; solidar; solidificar.
solidity, *n.* solidez, *f.*
solidus, *n.* sueldo antiguo (moneda).
soliloquize, *vi.* soliloquiar, hablar a solas.
soliloquy, *n.* soliloquio, *m.*
solitaire, *n.* solitario (diamante grueso), *m.*; solitario (juego de una sola persona, generalmente de naipes), *m.*
solitary, *adj.* solitario, retirado; —, *n.* ermitaño, *m.*
solitude, *n.* soledad, *f.*; vida solitaria.
solmizate, *vi.* solfear.
solo, *n.* and *adj.* solo, *m.*
soloist, *n.* solista *m.* y *f.*
Solomon, Salomón.
solstice, *n.* solsticio, *m.*; **summer —,** solsticio estival; **winter —,** solsticio hiemal.
soluble, *adj.* soluble.
solution, *n.* solución, *f.*
solve, *vt.* solver, disolver; aclarar, resolver.
solvency, *n.* solvencia, *f.*
solvent, *adj.* solvente.
soma, *n.* soma, *f.*
some, *adj.* algo de, un poco, algún, alguno, alguna, unos pocos, ciertos.
somebody, *n.* alguien, *m.*, alguno, na.
somehow, *adv.* de algún modo.
somersault, somerset, *n.* salto mortal; —, *vt.* dar un salto mortal.
something, *n.* alguna cosa, algo, *m.*; — **else,** otra cosa, alguna otra cosa; —, *adv.* (coll.) en cierto grado, algún tanto.
sometime, *adv.* en algún tiempo.
sometimes, *adv.* algunas veces, a veces.
somewhat, *n.* alguna cosa, algo, *m.*; —, *adv.* algún tanto, un poco.
somewhere, *adv.* en alguna parte.
somnambulism, *n.* somnambulismo, sonambulismo, *m.*
somnambulist, *n.* sonámbulo, la, somnámbulo, la.
somnolence, *n.* somnolencia, *f.*
somnolent, *adj.* soñoliento.
son, *n.* hijo, *m.*
sonata, *n.* (mus.) sonata, *f.*
song, *n.* canción, *f.*, canto, *m.*; cántico, *m.*; **Song of Solomon,** Cantar de los Cantares; — **sparrow,** gorrión canoro; — **thrush,** tordo canoro; — **writer,** compositor de canciones.
songbook, *n.* cancionero, *m.*, libro de canciones.
songster, *n.* cantor, *m.*
songstress, *n.* cantatriz, cantante, *f.*
son-in-law, *n.* yerno, *m.*
sonnet, *n.* soneto, *m.*
sonometer, *n.* sonómetro, *m.*
sonorous, *adj.* sonoro; **—ly,** *adv.* sonoramente.
soon, *adv.* presto, pronto, prontamente; **as — as,** luego que, en cuanto; **as — as**

possible, lo más pronto posible.
sooner, *adv.* más pronto, primero que.
soonest, *adv.* cuanto antes.
soot, *n.* hollín, *m.*
sooth, *n.* verdad, *f.*
soothe, *vt.* adular; calmar, tranquilizar.
soothsayer, *n.* adivino, *m.*
sooty, *adj.* holliniento, fuliginoso.
sop, *n.* pan mojado; soborno, *m.*, adulación, *f.*
sop. soprano, soprano.
Sophia, Sofía.
sophism, *n.* sofisma, *m.*
sophist, *n.* sofista, *m.* y *f.*
sophistical, sophistic, *adj.* sofístico.
sophisticate, *vt.* sofisticar; desilusionar; —, *n.* persona de mundo.
sophistication, *n.* mundanalidad, *f.*
sophistry, *n.* sofistería, *f.*
sophomore, *n.* estudiante de segundo año de una escuela superior o universidad.
soporific, *adj.* soporífero.
sopping, *adj.* ensopado; — **wet,** empapado.
soprano, *n.* (mus.) soprano, tiple, *m.*; — **singer,** tiple, soprano, *m.* y *f.*; — **voice,** tiple, soprano, *m.*; —, *adj.* relativo al soprano.
sorcerer, *n.* hechicero, brujo, *m.*
sorceress, *n.* hechicera, bruja, *f.*
sorcery, *n.* hechizo, encanto, *m.*; hechicería, *f.*
sordid, *adj.* sórdido, sucio; avariento; **—ly,** *adv.* codiciosamente.
sordidness, *n.* sordidez, mezquindad, *f.*
sordine, *n.* (mus.) sordina, *f.*
sore, *n.* llaga, úlcera, *f.*; —, *adj.* doloroso, penoso; (coll.) enojado, resentido; — **throat,** carraspera, *f.*, mal de garganta; **—ly,** *adv.* penosamente.
sorghum, *n.* (bot.) sorgo, *m.*, zahina, *f.*; melaza de sorgo.
sorority, *n.* hermandad de mujeres.
sorrel, *n.* (bot.) acedera, *f.*; —, *adj.* alazán.
sorrow, *n.* pesar, *m.*; tristeza, *f.*; —, *vi.* entristecerse.
sorrowful, *adj.* pesaroso, afligido; sentido; triste; **—ly,** *adv.* con aflicción.
sorry, *adj.* triste; afligido; pesaroso; miserable; **to be —,** sentir; **I am very —,** lo siento mucho.
sort, *n.* género, *m.*, especie, *f.*; calidad, clase, *f.*; manera, *f.*; —, *vt.* separar en varias clases; escoger, elegir.
sortie, *n.* (mil.) incursión, *f.*
S O S (signal of distress in Morse code), señal internacional de peligro.
so-so, *adv.* así así.
sot, *n.* zote, *m.*
sottish, *adj.* torpe, rudo; **—ly,** *adv.* torpemente.
soul, *n.* alma, *f.*; esencia, *f.*; persona, *f.*
sound, *adj.* sano; entero; puro; firme; (com.) solvente; — **track,** guía sonora (en películas cinematográficas); — **wave,** onda sonora; — **detector,** fonolocalización de

aviones; **—ly,** *adv.* sanamente, vigorosamente; **—,** *n.* tienta, sonda, *f.*; sonido,
ruido, *m.*; son, *m.*; estrecho, *m.*; **at the
— of,** al son de; **—,** *vt.* (naut.) sondar;
tocar; celebrar; sondar (intenciones) ; **—,**
vi. sonar, resonar.
soundboard, sounding board, *n.* diapasón, *m.*; tornavoz, *m.*, sombrero de púlpito.
sounder, *n.* (naut.) sondeador, *m.*; receptor
acústico, resonador, *m.*
sounding, *n.* (naut.) sondeo, *m.*; (naut.)
surgidero profundo; **—,** *adj.* sonante; **—
line,** sondaleza, *f.*
soundness, *n.* sanidad, *f.*; fuerza, solidez, *f.*
soundproof, *adj.* a prueba de ruido; **—,** *vt.*
hacer a prueba de ruido.
soup, *n.* sopa, *f.*; **— plate,** sopero, *m.*;
thick —, puré, *m.*; **vegetable —,** menestra, *f.*, sopa de legumbres.
sour, *adj.* agrio, ácido; áspero; **— grapes,**
uvas verdes; (fig.) indiferencia hacia algo
que no se puede poseer; **—ly,** *adv.* agriamente; **—,** *vt.* and *vi.* agriar, acedar;
agriarse.
source, *n.* manantial, *m.*, mina, *f.*; principio,
origen, *m.*
souse, *n.* salmuera, *f.*; zambullida, *f.*; **—,** *vt.*
escabechar; **—,** *vt.* and *vi.* empapar,
chapuzar; **—,** *adv.* zas, con violencia.
south, *n.* sur, sud, mediodía, *m.*; **S—,** la
región meridional (en Estados Unidos
generalmente la región al sur del Río
Ohio) ; **—,** *adj.* meridional, del sur.
South America, América del Sur, Sur o
Sud América, Sudamérica, *f.*
South American, *n.* and *adj.* sudamericano, na.
South Carolina, Carolina del Sur.
South Dakota, Dakota del Sur.
southerly, *adj.* = **southern.**
southern, *adj.* meridional; **—most,** lo más
al sur.
southerner, *n.* persona de la región meridional; **S—,** en Estados Unidos generalmente el nacido o que reside al sur del
Río Ohio.
southward, *adv.* hacia el sur, con rumbo
al sur.
southwest, *n.* sudoeste, *m.*; **—,** *adj.*
sudoeste; **—,** *adv.* del sudoeste; hacia el
sudoeste.
southwester, *n.* (naut.) viento de sudoeste;
sombrero grande de los marineros.
souvenir, *n.* recuerdo, *m.*, memoria, *f.*
sovereign, *n.* and *adj.* soberano, na; **—ly,**
adv. soberanamente.
sovereignty, *n.* soberanía, *f.*
soviet, *n.* soviet, *m.*
sow, *n.* puerca, marrana, *f.*
sow, *vt.* sembrar, sementar; esparcir.
sowbread, *n.* (bot.) pamporcino, *m.*
sowing, *n.* siembra, *f.*
soybean, *n.* soya, *f.*
Sp.: Spain, Esp. España; **Spaniard,** esp.

español.
sp.: special, esp. especial; **species,** gro-
género; especie; **specific,** específico; **specimen,** esp. espécimen; **spelling,** deletreo.
spa, *n.* burga, *f.*, balneario de aguas mine-
rales.
space, *n.* espacio, trecho, *m.*; intersticio, *m.*;
lugar, *m.*; **—,** *vt.* espaciar.
spacer, *n.* separador, espaciador, *m.*
spacing, *n.* espacio, *m.*; acción de espaciar.
spacious, *adj.* espacioso, amplio; **—ly,** *adv.*
con bastante espacio, espaciosamente.
spade, *n.* laya, azada, *f.*; (en los naipes)
espada, *f.*; **—,** *vt.* azadonar.
spaghetti, *n.* fideos, macarrones, *m. pl.*
Spain, España, *f.*
span, *n.* palmo, *m.*; espacio, *m.*; **— of a
bridge,** tramo, *m.*; **—,** *vt.* medir a palmos;
extenderse sobre; atravesar.
spangle, *n.* lentejuela, *f.*; **—,** *vt.* adornar
con lentejuelas.
Spaniard, *n.* and *adj.* español, la.
spaniel, *n.* sabueso, *m.*
Spanish, *adj.* español; **— America,** Hispanoamérica, *f.*, América española; **—
American,** hispanoamericano, na; **—
ballad,** romance, *m.*; **— fly,** cantárida,
f.; **— language,** castellano, *m.*; **—
leather,** cordobán, *m.*
spank, *n.* palmada, *f.*; **—,** *vt.* dar palmadas,
dar nalgadas.
spanking, *n.* nalgada, *f.*
spar, *n.* espato, *m.*; **—,** *vi.* reñir a pun-
tapiés o patadas; boxear de acuerdo con
las reglas.
spare, *vt.* and *vi.* ahorrar, economizar, perdonar; vivir con economía; **—,** *adj.* escaso, económico; **— time,** tiempo desocupado; **— tire,** neumático o llanta de
repuesto o de reserva; **— parts,** piezas
de repuesto, piezas de recambio.
sparely, *adv.* escasamente; **— built,** magro.
sparerib, *n.* costilla de puerco.
sparing, *adj.* escaso, raro, económico; **—ly,**
adv. parcamente, frugalmente.
spark, *n.* chispa, *f.*; (poet.) centella, *f.*;
(coll.) pisaverde, *m.*; **— plug,** bujía, *f.*;
—, *vi.* echar chispas, chispear; **—,** *vt.*
and *vi.* (coll.) enamorar, cortejar.
sparkle, *n.* centella, chispa, *f.*; **—,** *vi.*
chispear; espumar.
sparrow, *n.* gorrión, pardal, *m.*; **— hawk,**
gavilán, *m.*
sparse, *adj.* delgado, tenue; **—ly,** *adv.*
tenuemente.
sparse-bearded, *adj.* barbilampiño.
spasm, *n.* espasmo, *m.*
spasmodic, *adj.* espasmódico.
spastic, *adj.* (med.) espástico; espasmódico.
spat, *n.* riña, *f.*; huevas de ostras; pal-
madita, *f.*; polaina corta; **—,** *vi.* reñir;
golpear, dar una palmada.
spats, *n. pl.* polainas, *f. pl.*
spatter, *n.* salpicadura, *f.*; **—,** *vt.* salpicar,

manchar; esparcir.

spattering, *n.* salpicadura, *f.*

spatula, *n.* espátula, *f.*

spavin, *n.* esparaván, *m.*

spawn, *n.* freza, *f.*; hueva, *f.*; **—,** *vt.* and *vi.* desovar; engendrar.

spawning, *n.* freza, *f.*

S.P.C.A. Society for the Prevention of Cruelty to Animals, Sociedad Protectora de Animales.

S.P.C.C. Society for the Prevention of Cruelty to Children, Sociedad Protectora de Niños.

speak, *vt.* and *vi.* hablar; decir; arengar; conversar; pronunciar; **to — plainly,** hablar en romance, hablar con claridad; **to — in torrents,** hablar a borbotones; **to — to,** dirigirse a.

speaker, *n.* el que habla; orador, ra; **impertinent —,** prosador, ra; **S— of the House,** presidente de la Cámara de Representantes (en E.U.A.).

speaking, *n.* habla, *f.*; oratoria, *f.*; **—,** *adj.* hablante; **— of,** a propósito de; **— trumpet,** portavoz, *m.*; **— tube,** tubo acústico.

spear, *n.* lanza, *f.*; pica, *f.*; arpón, *m.*; **—,** *vt.* herir con lanza; alancear.

spearhead, *n.* roquete, *m.*; tropas en el puesto delantero de un ataque.

spearmint, *n.* hierbabuena, *f.*, menta verde.

spec. special, especial.

spec. del. special delivery, entrega inmediata.

special, *adj.* especial, particular; **— delivery,** carta urgente, carta de entrega inmediata; expreso, *m.*; **—ly,** *adv.* especialmente.

special-delivery, *adj.* de urgencia; de entrega inmediata, de bicicleta; **— letter,** carta urgente, carta de entrega inmediata; **— stamp,** sello de bicicleta, sello de entrega inmediata.

specialist, *n.* especialista, *m.* y *f.*

specialize, *vt.* especializar; **—,** *vi.* especializarse.

specialty, speciality, *n.* especialidad, *f.*

specie, *n.* dinero contante; (com.) efectivo, *m.*, dinero en efectivo.

species, *n.* especie, clase, *f.*, género, *m.*

specif. specifically, específicamente.

specific, *adj.* específico; **— gravity,** densidad específica, peso específico **—,** *n.* específico, *m.*; **—ally,** *adv.* en especie.

specification, *n.* especificación, *f.*; **—s,** *pl.* pliego de condiciones.

specify, *vt.* especificar.

specimen, *n.* espécimen, *m.*, muestra, *f.*; prueba, *f.*

specious, *adj.* aparentemente correcto o justo; engañoso; plausible; **—ly,** *adv.* plausiblemente.

speck, speckle, *n.* mancha, mácula, tacha, *f.*; **—,** *vt.* manchar, abigarrar.

spectacle, *n.* espectáculo, *m.*; exhibición,

f.; **—s,** *n. pl.* anteojos, espejuelos, *m. pl.*, gafas, *f. pl.*; **— case,** anteojera, *f.*; **— maker,** anteojero, *m.*

spectator, *n.* espectador, ra.

specter, spectre, *n.* espectro, *m.*

spectral, *adj.* aduendado; espectrométrico; **— analysis,** análisis espectral, análisis del espectro solar.

spectrometer, *n.* espectrómetro, *m.*

spectroscope, *n.* espectroscopio, *m.*

spectroscopy, *n.* espectroscopia, *f.*

spectrum, *n.* espectro, *m.*, imagen, *f.*

speculate, *vi.* especular; reflexionar.

speculation, *n.* especulación, *f.*; especulativa, *f.*; meditación, *f.*

speculative, *adj.* especulativo, teórico.

speech, *n.* habla, *f.*; discurso, *m.*, oración, arenga, *f.*; conversación, *f.*; perorata, *f.*; (theat.) parlamento, *m.*; **to make a —,** perorar, pronunciar un discurso.

speechless, *adj.* mudo, sin habla.

speed, *n.* prisa, *f.*; celeridad, rapidez, *f.*; prontitud, *f.*; velocidad, *f.*; **at full —,** a todo escape, a toda velocidad, a toda prisa, de corrida; **— limit,** límite de velocidad, velocidad máxima; **—,** *vt.* apresurar; despachar; ayudar; **—,** *vi.* darse prisa; salir bien.

speedboat, *n.* lancha de carrera.

speeder, *n* (auto.) persona que excede el límite de velocidad permitida; persona que anda a gran velocidad.

speedily, *adv.* aceleradamente, de prisa.

speedometer, *n.* velocímetro, celerímetro, *m.*

speed-up, *n.* aceleramiento, *m.*, aceleración, *f.*

speedway, *n.* pista pública; autódromo, *m.*

speedy, *adj.* veloz, pronto, diligente.

spell, *n.* hechizo, encanto, *m.*; período de descanso; período corto; **—,** *vt.* and *vi.* deletrear; escribir con buena ortografía; hechizar, encantar.

speller, *n.* libro de deletrear; deletreador, ra.

spelling, *n.* ortografía, *f.*; deletreo, *m.*

spelt, *n.* (bot.) espelta, *f.*

spelter, *n.* zinc, *m.*

spend, *vt.* gastar; disipar; consumir; **to — (time),** pasar (tiempo); **—,** *vi.* hacer gastos; consumirse.

spendthrift, *n.* pródigo, ga, derrochador, ra, botarate, *m.* y *f.*

spent, *adj.* alcanzado de fuerzas; gastado.

sperm, *n.* esperma, *f.*, semen, *m.*

spermaceti, *n.* espermaceti, *m.*

spermatophyte, *n.* (bot.) cualquier planta que produce semillas.

spermatozoon, *n.* espermatozoide, *m.*

spew, *vt.* and *vi.* vomitar.

sp. gr. specific gravity, peso específico.

sphere, *n.* esfera, *f.*

spheric, spherical, *adj.* esférico; **—ly,** *adv.* en forma esférica.

spheroid, *n.* esferoide, *m.*; **—,** *adj.* esferoidal.

sphinx, *n.* esfinge, *f.*, persona de carácter misterioso e indescifrable.

spice, *n.* especia, *f.*; sal, *f.*, picante, *m.*; —s, especiería, *f.*, especias, *f. pl.*; —, *vt.* sazonar con especias.

spick-and-span, *adj.* flamante, muy limpio o muy nuevo; pulcro y ordenado.

spicy, *adj.* aromático; (coll.) picante.

spider, *n.* araña, *f.*

spigot, *n.* llave de fuente; tapón de espita.

spill, *vt.* derramar, verter; —, *n.* clavija, espiga, *f.*; astilla, *f.*; (coll.) vuelco, *m.*

spillway, *n.* vertedero lateral; canal de desagüe.

spin, *vt.* hilar; alargar, prolongar; —, *vi.* hilar; correr hilo a hilo; —, *n.* vuelta, *f.*; paseo, *m.*

spinach, *n.* espinaca, *f.*

spinal, *adj.* espinal; — column, espina dorsal.

spindle, *n.* huso, *m.*; quicio, *m.*; carretel, *m.*; — of a lathe, (mech.) mandril, *m.*

spindle-legged, spindle-shanked, *adj.* zanquivano.

spine, *n.* espinazo, *m.*, espina, *f.*

spinet, *n.* (mus.) espineta, *f.*

spinner, *n.* hilador, *m.*; hilandera, *f.*

spinney, *n.* maleza, *f.*

spinning, *n.* hilandería, *f.*; rotación, *f.*; —, *adj.* de hilar; — jenny, máquina de hilar; — mill, hilandería, *f.*; — top, trompo, *m.*; — wheel, torno de hilar.

spinster, *n.* hilandera, *f.*; doncella, soltera, *f.*

Spiraea, spirea, *n.* (bot.) espirea, *f.*

spiral, *adj.* espiral; —ly, *adv.* en forma espiral.

spire, *n.* espira, *f.*; pirámide, *f.*; aguja (de una torre), *f.*

spirit, *n.* aliento, *m.*; espíritu, *m.*; ánimo, valor, *m.*; brío, *m.*; humor, *m.*; fantasma, *m.*; —, *vt.* incitar, animar; to — away, quitar secretamente; desvanecerse.

spirited, *adj.* vivo, brioso; —ly, *adv.* con espíritu.

spiritless, *adj.* abatido, sin espíritu.

spiritual, *adj.* espiritual; —ly, *adv.* espiritualmente.

spiritualism, spiritism, *n.* espiritismo, *m.*

spiritualist, *n.* espiritualista, *m.* y *f.*

spirituality, *n.* espiritualidad, inmaterialidad, *f.*

spirituous, *adj.* espiritoso; espirituoso.

spirochete, *m.* (biol.) espiroqueta, *f.*

spirometer, *n.* espirómetro, *m.*

spit, *n.* asador, *m.*; —, *vt.* and *vi.* espetar; escupir, salivar.

spite, *n.* rencor, *m.*, malevolencia, *f.*; in — of, a pesar de, a despecho de; —, *vt.* dar pesar, mortificar.

spiteful, *adj.* rencoroso, malicioso; —ly, *adv.* malignamente, con tirria.

spitfire, *n.* fierabrás, *m.*

spittle, *n.* saliva, *f.*; esputo, *m.*

spittoon, *n.* escupidera, *f.*

spitz, *n.* perro pomerano.

splash, *vt.* salpicar, enlodar; —, *n.* salpicadura, rociada, *f.*

splashboard, *n.* guardafango, guardalodo, *m.*

splay, *vt.* despaldar; extender; achaflanar: —, *adj.* extendido; desmañado; —, *n.* chaflán, *m.*

splayfoot, splayfooted, *adj.* de pies aplastados.

spleen, *n.* bazo, *m.*; esplín, *m.*

splendid, *adj.* espléndido, magnífico; —ly, *adv.* espléndidamente.

splendor, splendour, *n.* esplendor, *m.*; pompa, *f.*; brillo, *m.*

splenetic, splenetical, *adj.* esplénico, atrabiliario; melancólico; enojadizo.

splice, *vt.* (naut.) empalmar, unir; (coll.) casar; —, *n.* empalme, *m.*

splint, *n.* astilla, *f.*; —s, *n. pl.* tablillas para entablillar; —, *vt.* entablillar.

splinter, *n.* cacho, *m.*; astilla, *f.*; brizna, *f.*; —, *vt.* hender; —, *vi.* henderse.

split, *vt.* hender, rajar; —, *vi.* henderse; —, *n.* hendida, raja, *f.*

splotch, *vt.* manchar, salpicar; —, *n.* mancha, *f.*, borrón, *m.*

spoil, *vt.* pillar, robar; despojar; contaminar; arruinar; dañar; pudrir; mimar demasiado, echar a perder; —, *vi.* corromperse; dañarse; —s, *n. pl.* despojo, botín, *m.*

spoiler, *n.* corruptor, robador, *m.*

spoilsman, *n.* (política, en E. U. A.) el que sirve a un partido por la parte del botín que le toca en el triunfo.

spoils system, *n.* (política, en E. U. A.) sistema que consiste en considerar los puestos públicos como botín a distribuirse entre los del partido victorioso.

spoke, *n.* rayo de la rueda; —, pretérito del verbo speak.

spoken, *p. p.* del verbo speak.

spokesman, *n.* interlocutor, *m.*; vocero, *m.*

spoliation, *n.* despojo, pillaje, saqueo, *m.*

sponge, *n.* esponja, *f.*; —, *vt.* limpiar con esponja; —, *vi.* meterse de mogollón, ser gorrón.

spongecake, *n.* bizcochuelo, *m.*

sponger, *n.* pegote, mogollón, *m.*, gorrón, ona; vividor, ra.

sponginess, *n.* esponjosidad, *f.*

spongy, *adj.* esponjoso.

sponsor, *n.* fiador, *m.*; padrino, *m.*; madrina, *f.*; garante, *m.* y *f.*, persona responsable.

spontaneity, *n.* espontaneidad, voluntariedad, *f.*

spontaneous, *adj.* espontáneo; — combustion, combustión espontánea; —ly, *adv.* espontáneamente, de sí.

spool, *n.* canilla, broca, bobina, *f.*, carrete, carretel, *m.*

spoon, *n.* cuchara, *f.*; —, *vi.* acariciarse los enamorados.

spoonful, *n.* cucharada, *f.*

sporadic, *adj.* esporádico.

spore, *n.* espora, *f.*

sport, *n.* juego, retozo, *m.*; juguete, divertimiento, recreo, pasatiempo, *m.*; deporte, *m.*; **—,** *adj.* deportivo; **— shirt,** camisa de deporte, camisa de sport; **—,** *vt.* divertirse; **—,** *vi.* chancear, juguetear.

sporting, *adj.* deportivo.

sportive, *adj.* festivo, juguetón.

sportiveness, *n.* festividad, holganza, *f.*; espíritu deportivo.

sportsman, *n.* aficionado a los deportes, deportista, *m.*

sportsmanship, *n.* espíritu de equidad en los deportes y en los negocios.

spot, *n.* mancha, *f.*; borrón, *m.*; sitio, lugar, *m.*; **— cash,** dinero al contado; **— remover,** sacamanchas, *m.*; **—,** *vt.* abigarrar; manchar; (coll.) observar, reconocer.

spotless, *adj.* limpio, inmaculado; puro; sin mancha.

spotlight, *n.* luz concentrada; proyector, *m.*; proyector orientable; proyector de automóvil.

spotted, spotty, *adj.* lleno de manchas, sucio; moteado.

spotter, *n.* persona que descubre la posición de un adversario.

spousal, *adj.* matrimonial, nupcial; **—s,** *n. pl.* nupcias, *f. pl.*

spouse, *n.* esposo, sa.

spout, *vt.* and *vi.* arrojar agua con mucho ímpetu; borbotar; chorrear; **—,** *n.* llave de fuente; gárgola, *f.*, bomba marina; chorro de agua; pico (de una cafetera, etc.), *m.*

sprain, *vt.* dislocar, descoyuntar; **—,** *n.* dislocación, torcedura, *f.*

sprang, pretérito del verbo **spring.**

sprat, *n.* (pez) clupeo, *m.*

sprawl, *vi.* revolcarse; arrastrarse con las piernas extendidas; extenderse irregularmente (como las viñas); **—,** *n.* arrastrada, *f.*

spray, *n.* leña menuda; vástago, *m.*; espuma del mar; rociador, pulverizador, *m.*; vaporizador, *m.*; **— gun,** pistola pulverizadora; **—,** *vt.* rociar, pulverizar.

sprayer, *n.* regador, *m.*; rociador, pulverizador, *m.*; vaporizador, *m.*

spraying, *n.* regadera, *f.*; riego, *m.*; pulverización, *f.*

spread, *vt.* extender, desplegar, tender; esparcir, divulgar; regar; untar; propagar; generalizar; **—,** *vi.* extenderse, desplegarse; **— over,** cubrir; **—,** *n.* extensión, dilatación, *f.*; cubierta de cama; **—,** *adj.* extendido, aumentado.

spree, *n.* fiesta, *f.*, festín, *m.*; (coll.) juerga, *f.*

sprig, *n.* ramito, *m.*

sprightly, *adj.* alegre, despierto, vivaracho.

spring, *vi.* brotar, arrojar; nacer, provenir; dimanar, originarse; saltar, brincar; **—,** *vt.* ojear la caza; hacer volar; **to — back,** saltar hacia atrás; **to — forward,** arrojarse; **to — from,** venir, proceder de; **to — a leak,** (naut.) declararse una vía de

agua; **—,** *n.* primavera, *f.*; elasticidad, *f.*; muelle, resorte, *m.*; salto, *m.*; manantial, *m.*; (Sp. Am.) casimba, *f.*; **hot —s,** burga, *f.*; **— beauty,** (bot.) claitonia, *f.*; **— mattress,** colchón de muelles; **— of water,** fuente, *f.*; **— tide,** marea viva.

springboard, *n.* trampolín, *m.*

springe, *n.* lazo de cazador; trampa, *f.*

springer, *n.* brincador, ra, saltador, ra; pollo tierno mediano propio para freír.

springlike, *adj.* primaveral.

springtide, *n.* primavera, *f.*

springtime, *n.* = **springtide.**

springy, *adj.* elástico.

sprinkle, *vt.* rociar; hisopear; salpimentar; salpicar; (coll.) bautizar; **—,** *vi.* lloviznar; **—,** *n.* rociada, *f.*; lluvia ligera.

sprinkler, *n.* rociador, *m.*, regadera francesa.

sprinkling, *n.* rociada, aspersión, *f.*

sprint, *n.* carrera breve a todo correr; **—** *vi.* correr velozmente.

sprite, *n.* espíritu, *m.*; fantasma, *m.*; duende, *m.*, hada, *f.*

sprocket, *n.* diente de rueda de cadena; **— wheel,** (mech.) erizo, *m.*, rueda dentada para cadena; rueda catalina, rueda de cabillas.

sprout, *n.* vástago, renuevo, tallo, retoño, *m.*; **—s,** *n. pl.* bretones, *m. pl.*; **—,** *vi.* brotar, pulular.

spruce, *adj.* pulido, gentil; **—ly,** *adv.* bellamente, lindamente; **—,** *n.* (bot.) abeto, *m.*; **—,** *vi.* vestirse con afectación.

sprung, *p. p.* del verbo **spring.**

spt. seaport, puerto marítimo.

spume, *n.* espuma, *f.*; **—,** *vi.* espumar.

spun glass, *n.* lana de vidrio.

spur, *n.* espuela, *f.*; espolón (de gallo), *m.*; **ice —,** patín de hielo; **— stone,** guardacantón, *m.*; **on the — of the moment,** en un impulso repentino; **—,** *vt.* espolear; estimular.

spurge, *n.* (bot.) titímalo, *m.*

spurious, *adj.* espurio, falso; contrahecho; supuesto; bastardo.

spurn, *vt.* acocear; despreciar.

spurt, *vt.* and *vi.* arrojar un líquido en un chorro; hacer un gran esfuerzo; **—,** *n.* chorro, *m.*; esfuerzo grande.

sputter, *vi.* escupir con frecuencia; babosear; barbotar.

sputum, *n.* (med.) esputo, *m.*; saliva, *f.*

spy, *n.* espía, *m.*; **—,** *vt.* and *vi.* espiar; columbrar.

spyglass, *n.* anteojo de larga vista.

sq. square, cuadrado.

squab, *adj.* implume; cachigordo, regordete; **—,** *n.* canapé, sofá, *m.*; cojín, *m.*; pichón, *m.*, palomita, *f.*

squabble, *vi.* reñir, disputar; **—,** *n.* riña, disputa, *f.*

squad, *n.* patrulla, *f.*; escuadra, *f.*; **— car,** automóvil de patrulla de policía.

squadron, *n.* (mil.) escuadrón, *m.*

squalid, *adj.* sucio, puerco, escuálido.

squall, *n.* grito desgarrador; chubasco, *m.*; *vi.* chillar.

squally, *adj.* borrascoso.

squalor, *n.* porquería, suciedad, escualidez, *f.*

squander, *vt.* malgastar, disipar, derrochar.

squanderer, *n.* derrochador, ra, disipador, ra.

square, *adj.* cuadrado, cuadrángulo; exacto; cabal; **— dance,** contradanza, *f.*, baile de figuras; **— deal,** trato equitativo; **— foot,** pie cuadrado; **—,** *n.* cuadro, *m.*; plaza, *f.*; **bevel —,** falsarregla, *f.*; **carpenter's —,** escuadra, *f.*; **— of a chessboard,** casilla, *f.*; **— root,** raíz cuadrada; **—,** *vt.* cuadrar; ajustar, arreglar; **—,** *vi.* ajustarse.

squash, *vt.* aplastar; **—,** *n.* calabaza, *f.*; calabacera, *f.*

squat, *vi.* agacharse, sentarse en cuclillas; **—,** *adj.* agachado; rechoncho.

squatter, *n.* colono usurpador.

squaw, *n.* mujer india.

squawk, *vi.* graznar; (coll.) delatar; **—,** *n.* graznido, *m.*

squeak, *vi.* chillar; **—,** *n.* grito, chillido, *m.*

squeal, *vi.* plañir, gritar; delatar.

squeamish, *adj.* fastidioso; demasiado delicado.

squeamishness, *n.* fastidio, *m.*, repugnancia, *f.*

squeegee, *n.* escobilla de goma para secar superficies húmedas.

squeeze, *vt.* apretar, comprimir; estrechar; **—,** *n.* compresión, *f.*, acción de apretar; abrazo, *m.*

squeezer, *n.* exprimidor, estrujador, *m.*

squelch, *vt.* aplastar; hacer callar.

squib, *n.* cohete, *m.*; sátira, *f.*, escrito breve e ingenioso.

squid, *n.* calamar, *m.*

squint, *adj.* ojizaino; bizco; **—,** *vi.* mirar de reojo; mirar con los ojos medio cerrados.

squire, *n.* caballero (título de cortesía), *m.*; (en Inglaterra) hacendado, *m.*; alcalde, *m.*; **—,** *vt.* acompañar (a una señora, etc.).

squirm, *vi.* retorcerse, contorcerse.

squirrel, *n.* ardilla, *f.*

squirt, *vt.* jeringar; **—,** *n.* jeringa, *f.*; chorro, *m.*; (coll.) pisaverde, *m.*

Sr.: Senior, Padre; socio más antiguo o más caracterizado; **Sir,** Sr. señor.

S. R. O. standing room only, lugar sólo para estar de pie.

S. S. steamship, v. vapor; **Sunday School,** escuela dominical.

SSE, S. S. E. south-southeast, SSE, sudsudeste.

SSW, S. S. W. south-southwest, SSO, sudsudoeste.

St.: Saint, Sto., San, Santo; Sta., Santa; **Strait,** Estrecho; **Street,** Calle.

st.: stanza, estrofa; **stet,** (print.) reténgase; **street,** calle.

stab, *vt.* matar a puñaladas; **—,** *n.* puñalada, *f.*

stability, *n.* estabilidad, solidez, fijeza, *f.*

stabilization, *n.* estabilización, *f.*

stabilize, *vt.* estabilizar, hacer firme.

stabilizer, *n.* estabilizador, *m.*

stable, *n.* establo, *m.*; **— boy,** palafrenero, *m.*; **—,** *vt.* poner en el establo; **—,** *adj.* estable.

staccato, *adj.* and *adv.* (mus.) staccato.

stack, *n.* niara, *f.*; **—,** *vt.* hacinar.

stactometer, *n.* cuentagotas, *m.*

stadium, *n.* estadio, *m.*

staff, *n.* báculo, palo, *m.*; apoyo, *m.*; cuerpo, *m.*; personal, *m.*; **editorial —,** redacción, *f.*, cuerpo de redacción; **music —,** pentagrama, *m.*; **ruled —,** (mus.) pauta, *f.*; **— officer,** oficial del estado mayor.

stag, *n.* ciervo, *m.*; (coll.) hombre que va a una fiesta sin una mujer; **— party,** tertulia para hombres.

stage, *n.* tablado, *m.*; teatro, escenario, *m.*; parada, *f.*; escalón, *m.*; **— fright,** nerviosidad al presentarse en público; **— lights,** batería de teatro; **— scenery,** decoración, *f.*, decorado, *m.*; bastidores, *m. pl.*; **— setting,** decoración, *f.*; **—,** *vt.* (theat.) poner en escenario.

stagecraft, *n.* arte teatral.

stager, *n.* hombre experimentado.

stage whisper, *n.* cuchicheo de actores que pueden oír los espectadores.

stagger, *vi.* vacilar, titubear; estar incierto; **—,** *vt.* escalonar, alternar; asustar; hacer vacilar; **to — business hours,** alternar las horas de entrada y de salida de los trabajadores para facilitarles el trasporte.

staging, *n.* andamiada, *f.*; tráfico de diligencias u ómnibus; (theat.) presentación de obras teatrales.

stagnancy, stagnation, *n.* estancamiento, *m.*; (med.) estagnación, *f.*

stagnant, *adj.* estancado.

stagnate, *vi.* estancarse.

staid, *adj.* grave, serio.

staidness, *n.* gravedad, seriedad, *f.*

stain, *vt.* manchar; empañar la reputación; **—,** *n.* mancha, tacha, *f.*, borrón, *m.*; deshonra, *f.*

stainless, *adj.* limpio, inmaculado; impecable; inoxidable; **— steel,** acero inoxidable.

stair, *n.* escalón, *m.*; **—s,** *n. pl.* escalera, *f.*; **back —s,** escalera de servicio.

staircase, *n.* escalera, *f.*

stake, *n.* estaca, *f.*; posta (en el juego), *f.*; **—,** *vt.* estacar; poner en el juego; apostar; arriesgar.

stalactite, *n.* estalactita, *f.*

stalagmite, *n.* estalagmita, *f.*

stale, *adj.* añejo, viejo, rancio; **—,** *vi.* hacerse rancio o viejo; orinar el ganado; **—,** *n.* orina de ganado.

stalemate, *n.* tablas (en el juego de ajedrez), *f. pl.*; empate, *m.*; **—,** *vt.* hacer tablas (en el juego de ajedrez); parar, paralizar.

staleness, *n.* vejez, *f.*; rancidez, *f.*

stalk, *vi.* andar con paso majestuoso; —, *n.* paso majestuoso; tallo, pie, tronco, *m.*; troncho (de ciertas hortalizas), *m.*

stalking-horse, *n.* caballo verdadero o figurado que sirve a los cazadores para ocultarse y cazar; máscara, *f.*; disfraz, *m.*

stall, *n.* pesebre, *m.*; tienda portátil; tabanco, *m.*; barraca, *f.*; (aer.) desplome, *m.*; silla (de coro), *f.*; butaca en el teatro; —, *vt.* meter en el establo.

stallion, *n.* caballo padre.

stalwart, *adj.* robusto, vigoroso.

stamen, *n.* (bot.) estambre, *m.*

stamina, *n.* fuerza vital, vigor, *m.*, resistencia, *f.*

stammer, *vi.* tartamudear, balbucear.

stammerer, *n.* tartamudo, da.

stamp, *vt.* patear (los pies); estampar, imprimir, sellar; acuñar; —, *n.* cuño, *m.*; sello, *m.*; impresión, *f.*; estampa, *f.*; timbre, *m.*; **postage** —, sello de correo; **revenue** —, sello de impuesto; **special-delivery** —, sello de bicicleta o de entrega inmediata.

stampede, *n.* huída atropellada; susto, terror pánico, *m.*, estampida, *f.*; —, *vi.* huir en tropel.

stance, *n.* posición, postura, *f.*

stanch, *vt.* estancar; —, *vi.* estancarse; —, *adj.* sano; leal; firme, seguro.

stanchion, *n.* puntal, *m.*, apoyo que se pone en tierra firme para sostener las paredes, etc.

stand, *vi.* estar en pie o derecho; sostenerse; resistir; permanecer; pararse; hacer alto, estar situado; hallarse; erizarse el pelo; — **by,** estar cerca o listo para ayudar; —, *vt.* sostener, defender; **to** — **aloof,** retraerse de; **to** — **aside,** apartarse; **to** — **in line,** hacer cola; **to** — **out,** resaltar, destacarse; **to** — **still,** estarse parado o quieto; **to** — **up,** ponerse de pie, pararse; —, *n.* puesto, sitio, *m.*; posición, *f.*; parada, *f.*; tarima, *f.*; velador para poner la luz; estante, vasar, *m.*

standard, *n.* estandarte, *m.*; modelo, *m.*; precio ordinario; norma, *f.*; pauta, *f.*; tipo, *m.*; regla fija; patrón, *m.*; **gold** —, patrón de oro; — **equipment,** equipo corriente, equipo regular; — **of living,** nivel o norma de vida; — **time,** hora normal; — **measure,** medida patrón; —, *adj.* normal.

standard-gauge, *adj.* de medida normal; — **railroad,** gran camino de hierro.

standardization, *n.* uniformidad, igualación, *f.*

stand-by, *n.* cosa o persona con que se puede contar en un momento dado.

standing, *adj.* permanente, fijado, establecido; estancado; — **room,** espacio para estar de pie; —, *n.* duración, *f.*; posición, *f.*; puesto, *m.*

standpipe, *n.* tubo vertical de alimentación hacia un depósito de agua.

standpoint, *n.* punto de vista.

standstill, *n.* pausa, *f.*; alto, *m.*

stanza, *n.* verso, *m.*, estrofa, *f.*

staple, *n.* materia prima; almacén de depósito; presilla, grapa, *f.*; —**s,** *n. pl.* artículos de primera necesidad; —, *adj.* ajustado, establecido; principal.

stapler, *n.* engrapador, *m.*; negociante en los artículos principales de consumo.

star, *n.* estrella, *f.*; asterisco, *m.*; placa, *f.*; — (**of stage, screen, radio, etc.**), estrella (del teatro, la pantalla, etc.), *f.*; —, *vt.* decorar con estrellas; marcar con asterisco; presentar en calidad de estrella; —, *vi.* (theat.) ser estrella, tomar el papel principal.

starboard, *n.* (naut.) estribor, *m.*

starch, *n.* almidón, *m.*; —, *vt.* almidonar.

stardust, *n.* cúmulo estelar.

stare, *vt.* clavar la vista; —, *n.* mirada fija.

stark, *adj.* fuerte, áspero; puro; —, *adv.* del todo, completamente; — **mad,** loco rematadamente.

starless, *adj.* sin estrellas.

starling, *n.* (orn.) estornino, *m.*; esquina del estribo de un puente.

starred, starry, *adj.* estrellado.

start, *vi.* sobrecogerse, sobresaltarse, estremecerse; levantarse de repente; salir los caballos en las carreras; —, *vt.* sobrecoger; suscitar; descubrir; **to** — **machinery,** cebar; **to** — **off, to** — **out,** ponerse en marcha; —, *n.* sobresalto, *m.*; ímpetu, *m.*; principio, *m.*; **to get a** —, tomar la delantera.

starter, *n.* iniciador, ra; arrancador, ra; principio, *m.*; (auto.) arranque, *m.*; **to step on the** —, pisar el arranque.

starting, *n.* principio, *m.*; origen, *m.*; comienzo, *m.*; — **point,** punto de partida; poste de salida (en las carreras).

startle, *vi.* sobresaltarse, estremecerse de repente; —, *n.* espanto, susto repentino.

startling, *adj.* espantoso, pasmoso, alarmante.

starvation, *n.* muerte de hambre; (med.) inanición, *f.*

starve, *vi.* perecer de hambre.

starveling, *n.* persona hambrienta.

state, *n.* estado, *m.*; condición, *f.*; (política) Estado, *m.*; pompa, grandeza, *f.*; situación, *f.*; estación, *f.*; circunstancia, *f.*; —**'s evidence,** testimonio en favor del estado, especialmente confesión de un acusado que denuncia a sus cómplices; —, *vt.* ajustar, arreglar; plantear; declarar; precisar.

statecraft, *n.* arte de gobernar.

statehouse, *n.* palacio del estado.

stately, *adj.* augusto, majestuoso.

statement, *n.* relación, cuenta, *f.*; afirmación, *f.*; (com.) estado de cuenta; relato, *m.*; manifestación, *f.*; declaración, *f.*

stateroom, *n.* (naut.) camarote, *m.*; (rail.) compartimiento, *m.*

statesman, *n.* estadista, político, *m.*; hombre de estado.

statesmanship, *n.* política, *f.*; arte de gobernar.

static, *n.* (rad.) estática, *f.*, disturbio eléctrico; —, *adj.* estático; — **ceiling,** (aer.) techo estático; — **weight,** momento estático.

statics, *n.* estática, *f.*

station, *n.* estación, *f.*; empleo, puesto, *m.*; situación, postura, *f.*; grado, *m.*; condición, *f.*; (rail.) estación, *f.*, paradero, *m.*; **central —, main —,** central, *f.*; — **intermediate —,** estación auxiliar de señales; — **agent,** agente de estación; — **wagon,** pequeño ómnibus automóvil; —, *vt.* apostar, situar, alojar.

stationary, *adj.* estacionario, fijo.

stationer, *n.* papelero, *m.*, comerciante en útiles de escritorio.

stationery, *n.* útiles o efectos de escritorio; papel de escribir; — **store,** papelería, *f.*

statist, *n.* estadista, *m.*

statistic, statistical, *adj.* estadístico.

statistician, *n.* estadístico, *m.*

statistics, *n. pl.* estadística, *f.*

statoscope, *n.* estatoscopio, *m.*

statuary, *n.* estatuario, escultor, *m.*; escultura de estatuas; grupo de estatuas; —, *adj.* estatuario.

statue, *n.* estatua, *f.*

stature, *n.* estatura, talla, *f.*

status, *n.* posición, condición, *f.*; — **quo,** statu quo.

statute, *n.* estatuto, *m.*; reglamento, *m.*; regla, *f.*

stave, *vt.* descabezar algún barril; desfondar; —, *n.* duelas de barril; (mus.) pentagrama, *m.*

stay, *n.* estancia, permanencia, *f.*; (law) suspensión, *f.*; cesación, *f.*; apoyo, *m.*; estribo, *m.*; —**s,** corsé, justillo, *m.*; —, *vi.* quedarse, permanecer, estarse; tardar, detenerse, aguardarse, esperarse; **to — in bed,** guardar cama; —, *vt.* detener; contener; apoyar.

stead, *n.* lugar, sitio, paraje, *m.*

steadfast, *adj.* firme, estable, sólido; —**ly,** *adv.* firmemente, con constancia.

steadily, *adv.* firmemente; invariablemente.

steadiness, *n.* firmeza, estabilidad, *f.*

steady, *adj.* firme, fijo; —, *vt.* hacer firme.

steak, *n.* bistec, *m.*

steal, *vt.* and *vi.* hurtar, robar; introducirse clandestinamente; escapar sin ser visto; —, *n.* (coll.) robo, *m.*

stealth, *n.* hurto, *m.*; **by —,** a hurtadillas.

stealthily, *adv.* furtivamente, a hurtadillas.

stealthy, *adj.* furtivo.

steam, *n.* vapor, *m.*; —, *adj.* de vapor; — **bath,** baño de vapor; — **boiler,** caldera de una máquina de vapor; — **engine,** bomba de vapor, máquina de vapor; — **fitter,** montador de tubos y calderas de vapor; — **heat,** calefacción por vapor; — **radiator,** calorífero de vapor; — **roller,** aplanadora de vapor; — **shovel,** pala de vapor; — **vessel,** vapor, *m.*, buque de vapor; — **pressure,** presión del vapor; —, *vi.* vahear; —, *vt.* limpiar con vapor.

steamboat, *n.* vapor, *m.*, buque de vapor.

steamer, *n.* vapor, *m.*, buque de vapor; máquina o carro de vapor; — **rug,** manta de viaje.

steamship, *n.* vapor, *m.*, buque de vapor; — **agency,** agencia de vapores; — **line,** línea de vapores.

steapsin, *n.* esteapsina, *f.*

stearine, *n.* (chem.) estearina, *f.*

steed, *n.* caballo de regalo; caballo brioso.

steel, *n.* acero, *m.*; **alloy —,** acero aleación; **bar —,** acero en barras; **carbon —,** acero al carbón; **chrome —,** acero al cromo; **hard —,** acero fundido; **nickel —,** acero níquel; **raw —,** acero bruto; **silver —,** acero de plata; **stainless —,** acero inoxidable; **wool —,** lana de acero; **tempered —,** acero recocido; **vanadium —,** acero al vanadio; —, *vt.* acerar; fortalecer, endurecer.

steelwork, *n.* obra de acero; fábrica de acero.

steelworker, *n.* obrero en una fábrica de acero.

steelworks, *n.* acería, *f.*, fábrica de acero, talleres de acero.

steelyard, *n.* romana, *f.*

steep, *adj.* escarpado, pino; (coll.) exorbitante; —, *n.* precipicio, *m.*; —, *vt.* empapar, remojar.

steeple, *n.* torre, *f.*; campanario, *m.*; espira, *f.*

steeplechase, *n.* carrera ciega, carrera de obstáculos.

steeplejack, *n.* reparador de espiras, chimeneas, etc.

steer, *n.* novillo, *m.*; (coll.) dirección, *f.*; —, *vt.* gobernar; guiar, dirigir.

steerage, *n.* gobierno, *m.*; (naut.) antecámara de un navío; proa, *f.*

steerageway, *n.* (naut.) estela, *f.*

steering, *n.* dirección, *f.*; —, *adj.* de gobierno (de automóvil, etc.); — **gear,** (naut.) aparato de gobierno; — **wheel,** volante, *m.*

stele, *n.* (arch.) losa que sirve de lápida sepulcral.

stellar, *adj.* estrellado.

stem, *n.* vástago, tallo, *m.*; estirpe, *f.*; (naut.) branque, *m.*; —, *vt.* cortar (la corriente).

stench, *n.* hedor, *m.*

stencil, *n.* patrón, dechado, *m.*; patrón estarcidor, estarcidor, *m.*; estarcido, *m.*; —, *vt.* estarcir.

stenographer, *n.* taquígrafo, fa, estenógrafo, fa; mecanógrafo, fa.

stenographic, stenographical, *adj.* estenográfico.

stenography, *n.* taquigrafía, estenografía, *f.*; fonografía, *f.*

stenotype, *n.* estenotipia, *f.*

stenotyping, *n.* estenomecanografía, *f.*

stenotypist, *n.* estenomecanógrafo, fa, mecanotaquígrafo, fa.

step, *n.* paso, escalón, *m.*; huella, *f.*; trámite, *m.*; gestión, *f.*; **flight of** —s, tramo, *m.*; **in** —, de acuerdo; **to be in** —, guardar el paso; **short** —, pasillo, pasito, *m.*; **to hasten one's** —s, apretar el paso; —, *vi.* dar un paso; andar; —, *vt.* escalonar; pisar; **to** — **in,** entrar, visitar; **to** — **out,** ir fuera de casa; (coll.) vivir vida disoluta; **to** — **up,** acelerar, avivar.

stepbrother, *n.* medio hermano, hermanastro, *m.*

stepdaughter, *n.* hijastra, *f.*

stepfather, *n.* padrastro, *m.*

Stephen, Steven, Esteban.

stepladder, *n.* escalera de mano; gradilla, *f.*

stepmother, *n.* madrastra, *f.*

steppe, *n.* estepa, *f.*

steppingstone, *n.* pasadera, *f.*

stepsister, *n.* media hermana, hermanastra, *f.*

stepson, *n.* hijastro, *m.*

stereograph, *n.* dibujo o fotografía propios para verse con el estereoscopio.

stereopticon, *n.* estereóptico, *m.*

stereoscope, *n.* estereoscopio, *m.*

stereotype, *n.* estereotipia, *f.*; —, *vt.* estereotipar.

stereotyping, *n.* estereotipia, *f.*

sterile, *adj.* estéril.

sterility, *n.* esterilidad, *f.*

sterilization, *n.* esterilización, *f.*

sterilize, *vt.* desinfectar.

sterilizer, *n.* esterilizador, *m.*

sterling, *adj.* genuino, verdadero; —, *n.* moneda esterlina; — **silver,** plata esterlina.

stern, *adj.* austero, rígido, severo; ceñudo; —, *n.* (naut.) popa, *f.*; —**ly,** *adv.* austeramente, severamente.

sternum, (anat.) *n.* esternón, *m.*

stern-wheeler, *n.* vapor de ruedas.

stertorous, *adj.* estertoroso.

stet, (print.) reténgase.

stethoscope, *n.* (med.) estetoscopio, *m.*

stevedore, *n.* (naut.) estibador, *m.*

stew, *vt.* estofar; guisar; —, *n.* estufa, *f.*; guisado, guiso, *m.*; sancocho, *m.*

steward, *n.* mayordomo, *m.*; (naut.) despensero, *m.*; **cabin** —, camarero, *m.*

stewardship, *n.* mayordomía, *f.*

stewpan, *n.* cazuela, *f.*

stick, *n.* palo, bastón, *m.*; vara, *f.*; **goad** —, puya, *f.*; **incense** —, pebete, *m.*; **small** —, palillo, *m.*; —, *vt.* pegar, hincar; picar, punzar; —, *vi.* pegarse; detenerse; perseverar; dudar; **to** — **together,** soldarse.

sticker, *n.* etiqueta con reverso engomado.

sticking, *n.* pegadura, *f.*; — **plaster,** pegado, *m.*

stickle, *vi.* tomar partido; disputar.

stickleback, *n.* (pez) espino.

stickler, *n.* porfiador, ra; persona escrupulosa.

stickpin, *n.* alfiler de corbata; (Mex.) fistol, *m.*

sticky, *adj.* viscoso, pegajoso, pegadizo.

stiff, *adj.* tieso; duro, torpe; rígido; obstinado; — **neck,** torticolis, *m.*; —**ly,** *adv.* obstinadamente.

stiffen, *vt.* atiesar, endurecer; —, *vi.* endurecerse.

stiffness, *n.* tesura, rigidez, *f.*; obstinación, *f.*

stifle, *vt.* sofocar.

stifling, *adj.* sofocante.

stigma, *n.* nota de infamia, estigma, borrón, *m.*

stigmatize, *vt.* infamar, manchar.

stile, *n.* portillo con escalones (para pasar de un cercado a otro).

stiletto, *n.* puñal, *m.*; punzón, *m.*

still, *vt.* aquietar, aplacar; destilar; —, *adj.* silencioso, tranquilo; —, *n.* silencio, *m.*; alambique, *m.*; fotografía para anunciar una película; —, *adv.* todavía; siempre; hasta ahora; no obstante.

stillborn, *adj.* nacido muerto.

stillness, *n.* calma, quietud, *f.*

stilt, *n.* zanco, *m.*

stilted, *adj.* altisonante.

stimulant, *n.* estimulante, *m.*

stimulate, *vt.* estimular, aguijonear.

stimulation, *n.* estímulo, *m.*; estimulación, *f.*

stimulative, *adj.* estimulante; —, *n.* estimulante, *m.*

stimulus, *n.* estímulo, *m.*

sting, *vt.* picar o morder (un insecto); —, *n.* aguijón, *m.*; punzada, picadura, picada, *f.*; remordimiento de conciencia.

stinginess, *n.* tacañería, avaricia, *f.*

stinging, *adj.* picante; —, *n.* resquemo, *m.*; — **nettle,** (bot.) ortiga, *f.*

stingy, *adj.* mezquino, tacaño, avaro.

stink, *vi.* heder; —, *n.* hedor, *m.*

stint, *vt.* limitar; ser económico; —, *n.* límite, *m.*; restricción, *f.*; cuota, *f.*

stipend, *n.* estipendio, *m.*; sueldo, salario, *m.*

stipendiary, *adj.* estipendiario.

stipple, *n.* punteado, *m.*; —, *vt.* puntear.

stiptic, *adj.* estíptico.

stipulate, *vt.* and *vi.* estipular.

stipulation, *n.* estipulación, *f.*; contrato mutuo.

stir, *vt.* remover; agitar; revolver; incitar; —, *vt.* moverse; bullir; —, *n.* tumulto, *m.*; turbulencia, *f.*

stirrup, *n.* estribo, *m.*

stitch, *vt.* coser, bastear; —, *n.* puntada, *f.*; punto, *m.*

stoat, *n.* (zool.) comadreja, *f.*

stock, *n.* tronco, *m.*; injerto, *m.*; zoquete, *m.*; mango, *m.*; corbatín, *m.*; estirpe, *m.*; linaje, *m.*; (com.) capital, principal, *m.*; fondo, *m.*; (com.) acción, *f.*; ganado, *m.*; **in** —, en existencia; **preferred** —, acciones preferentes; — **company,** sociedad anónima; — **exchange,** bolsa, *f.*, bolsa de comercio, bolsa financiera; — **market,** mercadería de valores, mercado de valores; —s, acciones en los fondos públicos; **supply** —, provisión, *f.*; **to speculate in** —s, jugar a la bolsa; —, *vt.* proveer, abastecer.

stockade, *n.* palizada, *f.*; estocada, *f.*

stockbroker, *n.* agente de cambio, corredor de bolsa, bolsista, *m.*

stockfish, *n.* bacalao seco.

stockholder, *n.* accionista, *m.* y *f.*

Stockholm, Estocolmo, *m.*

stocking, *n.* media, *f.*

stock in trade, *n.* artículos vendibles.

stockjobber, *n.* agiotador, *m.*, corredor de bolsa.

stockjobbing, *n.* juego de bolsa, agiotaje, *m.*

stockroom, *n.* depósito, *m.*

stock-still, *adj.* inmoble, inmóvil.

stocky, *adj.* rechoncho.

stockyard, *n.* rastro, *m.*; corral de ganado.

stodgy, *adj.* hinchado; regordete; (coll.) pesado, indigesto.

stoic, *n.* and *adj.* estoico, ca.

stoical, *adj.* estoico; —**ly,** *adv.* estoicamente.

stoicism, *n.* estoicismo, *m.*

stoke, *vt.* and *vi.* atizar el fuego.

stoker, *n.* fuellero, fogonero, *m.*; cargador, *m.*

stole, *n.* estola, *f.*; —, pretérito del verbo **steal.**

stolen, *p. p.* del verbo **steal.**

stolid, *adj.* estólido.

stomach, *n.* estómago, *m.*; apetito, *m.*; **on the** —, boca abajo; —, *vt.* aguantar; soportar.

stomacher, *n.* peto, *m.*

stomatitis, *n.* (med.) estomatitis, *f.*

stone, *n.* piedra, *f.*; canto, *m.*; cálculo, cuesco, *m.*, pepita, *f.*, hueso de fruta; testículo, *m.*; piedra preciosa; **hewn** —, cantería, *f.*; **of** —, pétreo; — **for grinding corn, etc.,** (Mex.) metate, *m.*; — **fruit,** fruta de hueso; **corner** —, piedra angular; **foundation** —, piedra fundamental; —, *vt.* apedrear; quitar los huesos de las frutas; empedrar; trabajar de albañilería.

stone-blind, *adj.* enteramente ciego.

stonecutter, *n.* picapedrero, *m.*

stone-deaf, *adj.* completamente sordo.

stonemasonry, *n.* calicanto, *m.*

stoneware, *n.* loza de piedra.

stony, *adj.* de piedra, pétreo; duro.

stood, pretérito y *p. p.* del verbo **stand.**

stooge, *n.* cómico, *m.*; paniaguado, *m.*; el que hace tareas desagradables para otro.

stool, *n.* banquillo, taburete, *m.*; silleta, *f.*; evacuación, *f.*; **piano** —, banqueta, *f.*; — **pigeon,** cimbel, *m.*; persona empleada para embaucar.

stoop, *n.* inclinación hacia abajo; abatimiento, *m.*; escalinata, *f.*; —, *vi.* encorvarse; inclinarse; bajarse; agacharse.

stop, *vt.* detener, parar, diferir; cesar, suspender, paralizar; tapar; —, *vi.* pararse, hacer alto; **to** — **a clock,** parar un reloj; —, *n.* pausa, *f.*; obstáculo, *m.*; parada, *f.*; detención, *f.*; (mus.) tecla, *f.*; — **light,** farol de parada; — **on an organ,** tapadillo, *m.*; — **signal,** señal de alto o de parada; — **watch,** cronógrafo, *m.*

stopcock, *n.* grifo, *m.*

stopover, *n.* parada en un punto intermediario del camino, escala, *f.*

stoppage, *n.* obstrucción, *f.*; impedimento, *m.*; (rail.) alto, *m.*

stopper, *n.* obturador, *m.*; botana, *f.*; —s, (naut.) bozas, *f. pl.*; —, *vt.* entaponar.

stopping, *n.* obstrucción, *f.*; impedimento, *m.*; (rail.) alto, *m.*; — **place,** paradero, *m.*

stopple, *n.* tapón, *m.*

storage, *n.* almacenamiento, *m.*; almacenaje, *m.*; **cold** —, cámara frigorífica; — **battery,** batería, *f.*, batería de acumuladores, acumulador, *m.*

store, *n.* abundancia, *f.*; provisión, *f.*; almacén, *m.*; **department** —, bazar, *m.*; **dry goods** —, mercería, *f.*; —, *vt.* surtir, proveer, abastecer.

storehouse, *n.* almacén, *m.*

storekeeper, *n.* guardaalmacén, *m.*; (naut.) pañolero, *m.*

storeroom, *n.* almacén, depósito, *m.*; (naut.) pañol, *m.*

storied, *adj.* historiado; con pisos; **two-house,** casa de dos pisos.

stork, *n.* cigüeña, *f.*

storm, *n.* tempestad, borrasca, *f.*; (mil.) asalto, *m.*; tumulto, *m.*; — **center,** centro tempestuoso; — **door,** guardapuerta, *f.*; — **troops,** tropas de asalto; — **window,** contraventana, *f.*; —, *vt.* tomar por asalto; —, *vi.* haber tormenta.

stormy, *adj.* tempestuoso; violento, turbulento.

story, *n.* cuento, *m.*; historia, *f.*; crónica, *f.*; fábula, *f.*; (coll.) mentira, *f.*; piso de una casa; —, *vt.* adornar con un cuento o con algún acontecimiento histórico.

stout, *adj.* robusto, vigoroso; corpulento; fuerte; —**ly,** *adv.* valientemente; obstinadamente; —, *n.* cerveza fuerte; persona corpulenta; vestido propio para personas gruesas.

stove, *n.* estufa, *f.*; fogón, *m.*; hornillo, *m.*

stow, *vt.* ordenar, colocar; aprensar; (naut.) estibar.

stowage, *n.* almacenaje, *m.*; (naut.) arrumaje, *m.*

stowaway, *n.* polizón, ona.

str.: steamer, vapor; **strait,** estrecho.

strabismus, *n.* (med.) estrabismo, *m.*

straddle, *vi.* montar a horcajadas; (coll.) evitar tomar un partido; —, *n.* posición en que se monta a horcajadas.

strafe, *vt.* (coll.) castigar; bombardear furiosamente.

straggle, *vi.* vagar; extenderse.

straggler, *n.* vagamundo, *m.*

straight, *adj.* derecho, recto; justo; **— line,** línea recta; **— razor,** navaja ordinaria de afeitar; **—,** *adv.* directamente; en línea recta.

straight-arm, *vt.* (fútbol) detener (a un contrario) extendiendo el brazo; **—,** *n.* (fútbol) acción de detener (a un contrario) extendiendo el brazo.

straightaway, *n.* curso directo; **—,** *adj.* derecho, en dirección continua.

straightedge, *n.* regla (para trazar línea recta), *f.*

straighten, *vt.* endrezar.

straightforward, *adj.* derecho; franco; leal; **—,** *adv.* derechamente.

straightway, *adv.* inmediatamente, luego.

strain, *vt.* colar, filtrar, cerner, trascolar; apretar (a uno contra sí); forzar, violentar; **—,** *vi.* esforzarse; **—,** *n.* retorcimiento, *m.*; raza, *f.*; linaje, *m.*; estilo, *m.*; sonido, *m.*; armonía, *f.*; tensión, tirantez, *f.*

strainer, *n.* colador, *m.*, coladera, *f.*

strait, *adj.* estrecho, angosto; íntimo; rígido; exacto; escaso; **— jacket,** camisa de fuerza; **—ly,** *adv.* estrechamente; **—,** *n.* (geog.) estrecho, *m.*; aprieto, *m.*, angustia, *f.*; penuria, *f.*

straiten, *vt.* acortar, estrechar, angostar; **—ed circumstances,** circunstancias reducidas, escasos recursos.

strand, *n.* costa, playa, ribera, *f.*; cordón, *m.*; **—,** *vt.* and *vi.* encallar; **to be —ed,** perderse, estar uno solo y abandonado.

strange, *adj.* extraño; curioso; raro; peculiar; **—ly,** *adv.* extrañamente, extraordinariamente.

strangeness, *n.* extrañeza, rareza, *f.*

stranger, *n.* extranjero, ra, desconocido, da; persona extraña.

strangle, *vt.* ahogar, estrangular; **— hold,** entre luchadores presa que ahoga al antagonista.

strangulation, *n.* ahogamiento, *m.*, estrangulación, *f.*

strap, *n.* correa, *f.*, tira de cuero; tirante de bota; **—,** *vt.* atar con correas.

strapping, *adj.* abultado, corpulento.

stratagem, *n.* estratagema, *f.*; astucia, *f.*

strategic, *adj.* estratégico.

strategist, *n.* estratégico, ca.

strategy, *n.* estrategia, *f.*

stratosphere, *n.* estratosfera, *f.*

stratum, *n.* lecho, estrato, *m.*; bancal, *m.*

stratus, *n.* estrato, *m.*

straw, *n.* paja, *f.*; bagatela, *f.*; **—,** *adj.* de paja, falso; **— hat,** sombrero de paja; **— vote,** voto no oficial para determinar la opinión pública.

strawberry, *n.* fresa, *f.*

strawboard, *n.* cartón de paja.

strawflower, *n.* siempreviva, perpetua, *f.*

stray, *vi.* extraviarse; perder el camino; **—,** *n.* persona descarriada; animal extraviado; **—,** *adj.* extraviado, perdido, aislado, sin conexión.

streak, *n.* raya, lista, *f.*; **—,** *vt.* rayar.

stream, *n.* arroyo, río, torrente, raudal, *m.*; corriente, *f.*; **down —,** agua abajo; **—,** *vt.* and *vi.* correr, fluir; **—,** *vi.* echar rayos.

streamer, *n.* (naut.) flámula, *f.*, gallardete, *m.*; cinta colgante.

streamlet, *n.* arroyo, arroyuelo, *m.*

streamline, *n.* línea en que corre una corriente; **—,** *vt.* dar forma aerodinámica (a alguna cosa); **—,** *adj.* relativo a la aerodinámica.

streamlined, *adj.* aerodinámico.

street, *n.* calle, *f.*; **— crossing,** cruce de calle; **— intersection,** bocacalle, *f.*; **— railway,** tranvía, *m.*

streetcar, *n.* tranvía, *m.*; **— conductor,** cobrador, motorista, *m.*

streetwalker, *n.* prostituta de calle; ramera, *f.*

strength, *n.* fuerza, robustez, *f.*, vigor, *m.*; fortitud, *f.*; potencia, *f.*; fortaleza, resistencia, *f.*; **to gain —,** cobrar fuerzas; **tensile —,** resistencia a la tracción.

strengthen, *vt.* corroborar, consolidar; fortificar; reforzar; **—,** *vi.* fortalecerse.

strengthening, *adj.* tónico, vigorizador; **—,** *n.* refuerzo, *m.*

strenuous, *adj.* estrenuo, fuerte; agitado, con mucha actividad; **—ly,** *adv.* acérrimamente; vigorosamente.

streptococcus, *n.* estreptococo, *m.*

stress, *n.* fuerza, *f.*; peso, *m.*; importancia, *f.*; esfuerzo, *m.*; acento, *m.*; tensión, *f.*; **—ed syllable,** sílaba acentuada; **—,** *vt.* acentuar, dar énfasis, hacer hincapié en.

stretch, *vt.* and *vi.* extender, alargar; estirar; extenderse; esforzarse; **—,** *n.* extensión, *f.*; esfuerzo, *m.*; estirón, *m.*; lapso, *m.*

stretcher, *n.* estirador, *m.*; tendedor, *m.*, parihuela, camilla, *f.*

stretching, *n.* tendedura, *f.*, estiramiento, *m.*

strew, *vt.* esparcir; sembrar.

striate, *vt.* estriar.

striated, *adj.* estriado.

strict, *adj.* estricto, estrecho; exacto; riguroso, severo; terminante; **— order,** orden terminante; **—ly,** *adv.* exactamente; con severidad.

strictness, *n.* exactitud, *f.*; severidad, estrictez, *f.*

stricture, *n.* censura, *f.*; (med.) constricción mórbida; contracción, *f.*

stride, *n.* tranco, *m.*; adelanto, avance, *m.*; **—,** *vt.* cruzar, pasar por encima; **—,** *vi.* andar a pasos largos.

strident, *adj.* estridente.

strife, *n.* contienda, disputa, *f.*; rivalidad, *f.*

strike, *vt.* and *vi.* golpear; dar; rayar; herir; castigar; tocar; chocar; cesar de trabajar; **— out,** tachar; (baseball) hacer perder el tanto al *batter* que falla en golpear la pelota en tres *strikes* consecutivos; **to — (the sun),** batir (el sol); **—,** *n.* golpe, *m.*; rasero, *m.*; cesación de trabajadores, huelga, *f.*; (baseball) pelota no tocada por el *batter* que pasa sobre el *home plate* y entre el hombro y la rodilla.

strikebreaker, *n.* rompehuelgas, *m.* y *f.*

striker, *n.* huelguista, *m.* y *f.*; golpeador, ra.

striking, *adj.* que sorprende, sorprendente, llamativo; **—ly,** *adv.* de un modo sorprendente.

string, *n.* cordon, *m.*; cuerda, *f.*; hilo, *m.*; hilera, *f.*; fibra, *f.*; **— bean,** habichuela verde, judía, *f.*, (Mex.) ejote, *m.*; **— (for tops),** zurriaga, *f.*; **— instrument,** instrumento de cuerda.

stringed, *adj.* encordado; **— instrument,** instrumento de cuerda.

stringent, *adj.* severo, riguroso, rígido; convincente.

stringer, *n.* vigueta, *f.*; larguero, *m.*; viga longitudinal; cepo longitudinal; pie que sostiene una escalera.

stringpiece, *n.* larguero, *m.*; maderamen de enrejado; especie de armazón que cubre las estacas de un puente.

stringy, *adj.* fibroso.

strip, *n.* tira, faja, *f.*; **—,** *vt.* desnudar, despojar.

stripe, *n.* raya, lista, *f.*; roncha, *f.*, cardenal, *m.*; azote, *m.*; **—,** *vt.* rayar.

striped, *adj.* rayado.

stripling, *n.* mozuelo, mozalbete, *m.*

stripper, *n.* despojador, ra; despaldillador, *m.*

stripping *n.* despojo, *m.*; desmonte, *m.*; desmoldamiento, *m.*; descimbramiento, *m.*

strive, *vi.* esforzarse; empeñarse; disputar, contender; oponerse.

stroke, *n.* golpe, *m.*; toque (en la pintura), *m.*; sonido (de reloj), *m.*; (golf) tirada, *f.*; golpe de émbolo; caricia con la mano; **— (of a pen),** plumada, *f.*, palote, *m.*; **— (with a paw),** zarpazo, *m.*; **—,** *vt.* acariciar.

stroll, *vi.* tunar, vagar, pasearse, barzonear; **—,** *n.* paseo, barzón, *m.*

stroller, *n.* paseante, *m.* y *f.*

strong, *adj.* fuerte, vigoroso, robusto; concentrado; picante; poderoso; violento; pujante; **— room,** cuarto de depósito para cosas de valor; **—ly,** *adv.* fuertemente, con violencia.

strong-arm, *vt.* (coll.) asaltar; tratar con fuerza; batir, golpear.

strongbox, *n.* cofre fuerte.

stronghold, *n.* plaza fuerte.

strop, *n.* asentador, suavizador (de navajas), *m.*; **—,** *vt.* asentar (navajas).

strophe, *n.* estrofa, *f.*

struck, *adj.* cerrado o afectado por huelga; golpeado.

structural, *adj.* construccional; de construcción; **— iron,** hierro de construcciones.

structure, *n.* estructura, *f.*; edificio, *m.*; fábrica, *f.*

struggle, *n.* lucha, contienda, *f.*, conflicto,

m.; brega, *f.*; **—,** *vi.* esforzarse; luchar; lidiar; agitarse; contender.

strum, *vt.* (mus.) tocar defectuosamente (un instrumento de cuerda); rasguear (una guitarra, etc.).

strumpet, *n.* ramera, puta, *f.*

strut, *vi.* pavonearse, zarandarse; **—,** *n.* pavonada, *f.*; contoneo, *m.*; poste, puntal, *m.*; adema, *f.*

strychnine, *n.* estricnina, *f.*

stub, *n.* tronco, talón, *m.*; **— book,** libro talonario; **—,** *vt.* tropezar con alguna cosa en el suelo.

stubble, *n.* rastrojo, *m.*

stubborn, *adj.* obstinado, terco, testarudo; enrevesado; cabezón; **—ly,** *adv.* obstinadamente; **to be —,** obstinarse, ser porfiado.

stubbornness, *n.* terquedad, obcecación, *f.*; obstinación, pertinacia, *f.*

stubby, *adj.* cachigordete; gordo.

stucco, *n.* estuco, *m.*, escayola, *f.*

stuck-up, *adj.* (coll.) arrogante, presumido, presuntuoso.

stud, *n.* botón de camisa; tachón, *m.*; yeguada, *f.*; **— mare,** yegua para cría; **—,** *vt.* tachonar.

studding, *n.* tachonería, *f.*; **— sail,** (naut.) ala, *f.*

student, *n.* estudiante, *m.*, alumno, na; **—,** *adj.* estudiantil.

studhorse, *n.* caballo entero.

studied, *adj.* docto, leído, versado.

studio, *n.* estudio de un artista.

studious, *adj.* estudioso; diligente; **—ly,** *adv.* estudiosamente, diligentemente.

study, *n.* estudio, *m.*; aplicación, *f.*; meditación profunda; gabinete, *m.*; **—,** *vt.* estudiar, cursar; observar; **—,** *vi.* estudiar, aplicarse.

stuff, *n.* materia, *f.*; material, *m.*; ropa, *f.*; estofa, *f.*; **—!** *interj.* ¡bagatela! ¡niñería! **—,** *vt.* henchir, llenar; cebar; rellenar; **—,** *vi.* atracarse; tragar; **to — oneself,** soplarse.

stuffing, *n.* relleno, *m.*; atestadura, *f.*

stuffy, *adj.* mal ventilado; (coll.) enojado y terco; (coll.) estirado, presuntuoso.

stultify, *vt.* atontar, atolondrar.

stumble, *vt.* tropezar; **—,** *n.* traspié, tropiezo, *m.*

stumbling, *n.* tropezón, *m.*; **— block,** tropezadero, *m.*; obstáculo, impedimento, *m.*

stump, *n.* tronco, *m.*; tocón, *m.*; muñón, *m.*; **— speech,** discurso de la política; **—,** *vt.* tropezar; confundir, dejar estupefacto; retar; **—,** *vi.* (coll.) pronunciar discursos políticos.

stun, *vt.* aturdir, ensordecer.

stung, pretérito y *p. p.* del verbo **sting.**

stunner, *n.* cualquier cosa que sorprende.

stunning, *adj.* elegante, atractivo; sorprendente.

stunt, *vt.* no dejar crecer; reprimir; **—,** *n.* acción que demuestra destreza.

stupefaction, *n.* aturdimiento, estupor, *m.*

stupefy, *vt.* atontar, atolondrar.

stupendous, *adj.* estupendo, maravilloso; **—ly,** *adv.* estupendamente.

stupid, *adj.* estúpido; (Arg.) calzonudo; **to be —,** ser duro de mollera; **—,** *n.* bobo, ba; **—ly,** *adv.* estúpidamente.

stupidity, *n.* estupidez, *f.*

stupor, *n.* estupor, *m.*

sturdily, *adv.* robustamente, vigorosamente.

sturdy, *adj.* fuerte, tieso, robusto, rollizo; determinado, firme.

sturgeon, *n.* esturión, *m.*

stutter, *vi.* tartamudear; (Sp. Am.) gaguear; **—,** *n.* tartamudeo, *m.*

stuttering, *n.* tartamudeo, *m.*; **—,** *adj.* tartamudo.

sty, *n.* zahurda, pocilga, *f.*; (med.) orzuelo, *m.*

style, *n.* estilo, *m.*; título, *m.*; gnomon, *m.*; modo, *m.*; **—,** *vt.* intitular, nombrar.

stylish, *adj.* elegante, de moda.

stylist, *n.* estilista, *m.* y *f.*

stylograph, *n.* estilógrafo, *m.*

stylographic, *adj.* estilográfico; **— pen, (fountain pen),** pluma estilográfica, pluma fuente.

stylus, *n.* estilo, estilete, punzón, *m.*

stymie, *n.* stymie, *m.*, situación en el juego de golf en que la pelota más próxima al agujero está en la línea a recorrer por la otra; **—,** *vt.* obstruir con un stymie; impedir.

styptic, *adj.* estíptico.

Styx, Estigia, *f.*

suasion, *n.* persuasión, *f.*, convencimiento, *m.*

suave, *adj.* pulido y cortés; **—ly,** *adv.* pulida y cortésmente.

suavity, *n.* suavidad, *f.*; dulzura, *f.*; cortesía, *f.*

sub, *n.* (coll.) substituto, ta; submarino, *m.*; subordinado, da.

sub.: substitute, supl.^te suplente; **subscription,** subscripción; **substitute,** substituto; **suburban,** suburbano.

subacetate, *n.* (chem.) subacetato, *m.*

subagency, *n.* subagencia, *f.*

subagent, *n.* subagente, *m.*

subaltern, *n.* and *adj.* subalterno, na.

subcarbonate, *n.* (chem.) subcarbonato, *m.*

subcommittee, *n.* subcomisión, *f.*, subcomité, *m.*

subconscious, *adj.* subconsciente; **—,** *n.* subconsciencia, *f.*

subconsciousness, *n.* subconsciencia, *f.*

subcontract, *n.* subcontrato, *m.*; **—,** *vt.* subcontratar.

subcutaneous, *adj.* subcutáneo.

subdivide, *vt.* subdividir.

subdivision, *n.* subdivisión, *f.*

subdue, *vt.* sojuzgar, rendir, sujetar; conquistar; mortificar.

subhead, *n.* subtítulo, *m.*, título o encabezamiento secundario.

subj.: subject, sujeto, tema; **subjective,**

subjetivo; **subjunctive,** subj. subjuntivo.

subject, *n.* sujeto, tema, tópico, *m.*; asignatura, *f.*; materia, *f.*; **—,** *adj.* sujeto, sometido a; **— matter,** asunto, tema, *m.*; **—,** *vt.* sujetar, someter; supeditar; rendir, exponer.

subjection, *n.* sujeción, *f.*; supeditación, *f.*

subjective, *adj.* subjetivo; **—ly,** *adv.* subjetivamente.

subjoin, *vt.* añadir, anexar.

subjugate, *vt.* sojuzgar, sujetar.

subjugation, *n.* sujeción, subyugación, *f.*

subjunctive, *n.* and *adj.* subjuntivo, *m.*

sublease, *vt.* subarrendar; **—,** *n.* subarriendo, *m.*

sublet, *vt.* subarrendar, dar en alquiler.

sublimate, *n.* sublimado, *m.*; **—,** *vt.* (chem.) sublimar; purificar.

sublime, *adj.* sublime, excelso; **—ly,** *adv.* de un modo sublime; **—,** *n.* sublimidad, *f.*; **—,** *vt.* hacer sublime, exaltar; purificar; (chem.) sublimar.

sublimity, *n.* sublimidad, *f.*

sublunary, sublunar, *adj.* sublunar; terrestre.

sub-machine gun, *n.* ametralladora pequeña.

submarginal, *adj.* submarginal.

submarine, *n.* and *adj.* submarino, *m.*; **—,** *vt.* (coll.) atacar con un submarino.

submerge, submerse, *vt.* sumergir.

submersible, *adj.* sumergible.

submersion, *n.* sumersión, *f.*

submission, *n.* sumisión, *f.*, rendimiento, *m.*; resignación, *f.*; humildad, *f.*

submissive, *adj.* sumiso, obsequioso; **—ly,** *adv.* con sumisión.

submit, *vt.* someter, rendir; **—,** *vi.* someterse.

subnitrate, *n.* (chem.) hiponitrato, *m.*

subnormal, *adj.* subnormal.

subordinate, *n.* and *adj.* subordinado, subalterno, inferior, dependiente, *m.*; **—,** *vt.* subordinar; someter.

subordination, *n.* subordinación, *f.*

suborn, *vt.* sobornar, cohechar.

subpoena, subpena, *n.* comparendo, *m.*; **—,** *vt.* citar con comparendo.

subscribe, *vt.* and *vi.* suscribir, subscribir, certificar con su firma; consentir.

subscriber, *n.* suscriptor, ra, abonado, da.

subscription, *n.* suscripción, *f.*, abono, *m.*

subsequent, *adj.* subsiguiente, subsecuente; **—ly,** *adv.* subsiguientemente, posteriormente.

subserve, *vt.* servir; **—,** *vi.* estar subordinado.

subserviency, *n.* servicio, *m.*; utilidad, *f.*; concurso, *m.*; ayuda, *f.*

subservient, *adj.* subordinado; útil; **—ly,** *adv.* subordinadamente.

subside, *vi.* sumergirse; apaciguarse.

subsidence, *n.* derrumbamiento, *m.*

subsidiary, *adj.* subsidiario, afiliado, auxiliar; **—,** auxiliar, *m.*

subsidize, *vt.* dar subsidios.

subsidy, *n.* subsidio, socorro, *m.*, subvención, *f.*

subsist, *vi.* subsistir; existir.

subsistence, *n.* existencia, *f.*; subsistencia, *f.*

subsistent, *adj.* subsistente.

subsoil, *n.* subsuelo, *m.*

subst.: substantive, *s.* sustantivo; **substitute,** sustituto.

substance, *n.* substancia, sustancia, *f.*; entidad, *f.*; esencia, *f.*

substantial, *adj.* sustancial; real, material; substancioso, sustancioso; fuerte; **—ly,** *adv.* sustancialmente.

substantiality, *n.* substancialidad, sustancialidad, *f.*; solidez, *f.*

substantiate, *vt.* corroborar; verificar; comprobar; substanciar, sustanciar.

substantive, *n.* (gram.) sustantivo, substantivo, *m.*; **—,** *adj.* substantivo; independiente; sustancial.

substation, *n.* estación o central subalternas.

substitute, *vt.* sustituir, substituir; reemplazar; relevar; **—,** *n.* substituto, *m.*; reemplazo, *m.*; suplente, *m.*; lugarteniente, *m.*; sobresaliente, *m.*; **—,** *adj.* de substituto.

substitution, *n.* sustitución, substitución, *f.*

substratum, *n.* substrato, lecho, *m.*; capa, *f.*

substructure, *n.* infraestructura, subestructura, *f.*

subterfuge, *n.* subterfugio, *m.*; evasión, *f.*

subterranean, subterraneous, *adj.* subterráneo; oculto; secreto.

subtitle, *n.* subtítulo, *m.*, título secundario.

subtle, subtile, *adj.* sutil, delicado, tenue; agudo, penetrante; astuto.

subtlety, subtility, *n.* sutilidad, sutileza, *f.*; astucia, *f.*

subtly, *adv.* sutilmente.

subtract, *vt.* sustraer; (math.) restar.

subtraction, *n.* sustracción, *f.*; (math.) resta, *f.*

subtrahend, *n.* sustraendo, *m.*

subtreasurer, *n.* subtesorero, *m.*

subtropical, *adj.* subtropical.

suburb, *n.* suburbio, arrabal, *m.*; **—s,** afueras, *f. pl.*

suburban, *adj.* suburbano.

suburbanite, *n.* suburbano, *m.*, morador de suburbio.

subvention, *n.* subvención, ayuda, *f.*

subversion, *n.* subversión, *f.*; destrucción, *f.*

subversive, *adj.* subversivo.

subvert, *vt.* subvertir, destruir.

subway, *n.* túnel, *m.*; ferrocarril subterráneo; (coll.) metro, *m.*

succeed, *vt.* and *vi.* suceder, seguir; conseguir, lograr, tener éxito.

success, *n.* éxito, *m.*, buen éxito; lucimiento, *m.*

successful, *adj.* próspero, dichoso; **to be —,** tener buen éxito; **—ly,** *adv.* prósperamente.

succession, *n.* sucesión, *f.*; descendencia, *f.*; herencia, *f.*

successive, *adj.* sucesivo, **—ly,** *adv.* sucesivamente.

successor, *n.* sucesor, ra.

succinct, *adj.* sucinto, compendioso; **—ly,** *adv.* sucintamente, de modo compendioso.

succor, *vt.* socorrer, ayudar; subvenir; **—,** *n.* socorro, *m.*; ayuda, asistencia, *f.*

succotash, *n.* combinación de habas y maíz.

succulence, *n.* jugosidad, suculencia, *f.*

succulent, *adj.* suculento, jugoso.

succumb, *vi.* sucumbir.

such, *adj.* and *pron.* tal, semejante; **— as,** tal como; **— as (go there, etc.),** los o las que (van allí etc.); **in — a manner,** de tal modo.

suck, *vt.* and *vi.* chupar, mamar; **—,** *n.* chupada, *f.*

sucker, *n.* chupador, ra; persona fácil de engañar; (coll.) caramelo, *m.*, (Mex.) paleta, *f.*

sucking, *n.* chupadura, *f.*; **—,** *adj.* mamante; chupador.

suckle, *vt.* amamantar.

suckling, *n.* mamantón, ona.

sucre, *n.* sucre, *m.*

suction, *n.* succión, *f.*; chupada, *f.*; **— fan,** aspirador de aire o ventalle de succión.

sudden, *adj.* repentino, no prevenido; **—ly,** *adv.* de repente, súbitamente, de pronto, repentinamente.

suddenness, *n.* precipitación, *f.*

sudorific, *n.* and *adj.* sudorífico, *m.*

suds, *n. pl.* lejía de agua y jabón, espuma de jabón.

sue, *vt.* and *vi.* poner pleito, demandar.

suede, *n.* piel curtida semejante a la de gamuza.

suet, *n.* sebo, *m.*, grasa, *f.*

suffer, *vt.* and *vi.* sufrir; tolerar, padecer.

sufferable, *adj.* sufrible, soportable; **—ly,** *adv.* sufriblemente.

sufferance, *n.* sufrimiento, *m.*; tolerancia, *f.*

suffering, *n.* sufrimiento, *m.*, pena, *f.*; dolor, *m.*; **—,** *adj.* doliente.

suffice, *vt.* and *vi.* bastar, ser suficiente.

sufficiency, *n.* suficiencia, *f.*; capacidad, *f.*

sufficient, *adj.* suficiente, bastante; **—ly,** *adv.* bastante, suficientemente.

suffix, *n.* (gram.) sufijo, *m.*; **—,** *vt.* añadir un sufijo.

suffocate, *vt.* sofocar, ahogar; **—,** *vi.* sofocarse.

suffocating, *adj.* sofocante.

suffocation, *n.* sofocación, *f.*

suffragan, *n.* sufragáneo, *m.*, obispo sufragáneo.

suffrage, *n.* sufragio, voto, *m.*

suffragette, *n.* sufragista, *f.*

suffragist, *n.* sufragista, *m.* y *f.*

suffuse, *vt.* difundir, derramar, extender.

suffusion, *n.* (med.) sufusión, *f.*; difusión, *f.*

sugar, *n.* azúcar, *m.* y *f.* (coll.) lisonja, *f.*; **beet —,** azúcar de remolacha; **brown —,** azúcar terciado, da; **cube —,** azúcar cubicado, da; **fruit —,** fructosa, *f.*; **gran-**

ulated —, azúcar granulado, da; **loaf** —, azúcar de pilón; **raw** —, (Sp. Am.) papelón, *m.*; — **pine**, pino de los estados norteamericanos de California y Oregon; **refined** —, azúcar blanco, ca; — **bowl**, azucarero, *m.*, azucarera, *f.*; — **cane**, caña de azúcar; — **crop**, zafra, *f.*; — **loaf**, pan de azúcar; — **making**, zafra, *f.*; — **of lead**, azúcar de plomo; — **mill**, trapiche, *m.*; (Sp. Am.) central, *f.*; —, *vt.* azucarar; confitar.

sugar-cane, *adj.* de caña de azúcar; —**plantation**, cañaveral, *m.*; — **juice**, guarapo, *m.*

sugar-coat, *vt.* azucarar, garapiñar; hermosear lo feo; ocultar la verdad.

sugared, *adj.* azucarado; — **almond**, almendra garapiñada.

sugarplum, *n.* confite, *m.*

sugary, *adj.* azucarado, dulce.

suggest, *vt.* sugerir; proponer.

suggestion, *n.* sugestión, *f.*

suicidal, *adj.* suicida.

suicide, *n.* suicidio, *m.*; suicida, *m. y f.*; **to commit** —, suicidarse.

suit, *n.* vestido entero; traje, *m.*; galanteo, *m.*; petición, *f.*; pleito, *m.*; surtido, *m.*; **ready-made** —, traje hecho; — **made to order**, traje a la medida; **to bring** —, (law) formar causa, demandar, entablar un juicio; —, *vt. and vi.* adaptar; surtir; ajustarse, acomodarse; convenir; —, *vt.* sentar, caer bien.

suitability, *n.* conveniencia, *f.*; compatibilidad, *f.*

suitable, *adj.* conforme, conveniente, satisfactorio; —**ly**, *adv.* según, conforme, en conformidad; congruamente.

suitcase, *n.* maleta, *f.*; (Mex.) castaña, *f.*

suite, *n.* serie, *f.*; tren, *m.*, comitiva, *f.*; — **of rooms**, crujía de piezas, apartado de habitaciones.

suitor, *n.* suplicante, *m.*; amante, cortejo, *m.*; demandante, *m.*

sulfa drugs, *n. pl.* sulfanilamidos, *m. pl.*, drogas derivadas de la sulfanilamida.

sulfanilamide, *n.* sulfanilamida, *f.*

sulfapyridine, *n.* sulfapiridina, *f.*

sulfathiazole, *n.* sulfatiazol, *m.*

sulk, *n.* mal humor; —, *vi.* ponerse malhumorado, demostrar resentimiento.

sulky, *adj.* regañón, malhumorado, resentido; —, *n.* especie de carruaje para una sola persona.

sullen, *adj.* malcontento; intratable; hosco; —**ly**, *adv.* de mal humor; tercamente.

sullenness, *n.* mal humor; obstinación, pertinacia, terquedad, *f.*

sully, *vt.* manchar, ensuciar; —, *vi.* empañarse.

sulphate, *n.* sulfato, *m.*; **copper** —, piedra lipis.

sulphide, *n.* (chem.) sulfuro, sulfido, *m.*

sulphite, *n.* sulfito, *m.*

sulphur, *n.* azufre, *m.*; — **dioxide**, gas sulfuroso, bióxido sulfuroso.

sulphuric, *adj.* sulfúrico.

sulphurous, *adj.* sulfúreo, azufroso.

sultan, *n.* sultán, *m.*

sultana, *n.* sultana, *f.*

sultry, *adj.* caluroso y húmedo; sofocante.

sum, *n.* suma, *f.*; monto, *m.*; (com.) montante, *m.*; **certain** —, tanto, *m.*; — **total**, total, *m.*, cifra total; —, *vt.* sumar; recopilar; **to** — **up**, epilogar.

sumac, *n.* zumaque, *m.*

summarily, *adv.* sumariamente.

summarize, *vt.* resumir; recopilar.

summary, *n.* epítome, sumario, *m.*; —, *adj.* sumario.

summation, *n.* total, *m.*, suma, *f.*

summer, *n.* verano, estío, *m.*; —, *adj.* estival; — **house**, glorieta de jardín, cenadero, quiosco, *m.*; — **resort**, lugar de veraneo; — **sausage**, variedad de salchicha; —, *vi.* veranear.

summering, *n.* veraneo, *m.*

summersault, *n. and vt.* = **somersault**.

summertime, *n.* verano, *m.*

summit, *n.* ápice, *m.*; cima, cresta, *f.*

summon, *vt.* citar; requerir por auto de juez; convocar, convidar; (mil.) intimar la rendición.

summoner, *n.* convocador, ra; convidador, ra; citador, ra.

summons, *n. pl.* citación, *f.*; requerimiento, *m.*; (law) emplazamiento, *m.*

sumptuary, *adj.* suntuario.

sumptuous, *adj.* suntuoso; —**ly**, *adv.* suntuosamente.

sun, *n.* sol, *m.*; — **bath**, solanera, *f.*, baño de sol; — **parlor**, solana, *f.*; — **porch**, solana, *f.*; — **visor**, visera contra el sol; —, *vt.* asolear.

Sun. Sunday, dom.º domingo.

sunbeam, *n.* rayo de sol.

sunbonnet, *n.* gorra de mujer que protege la cara contra los rayos del sol.

sunburn, *n.* solanera, *f.*; —, *vi.* quemarse por el sol.

sunburnt, *adj.* tostado por el sol, asoleado.

sundae, *n.* helado cubierto con jarabe, fruta o nueces machacadas.

Sunday, *n.* domingo, *m.*; — **School**, escuela donde se estudia la religión los domingos.

sunder, *vt.* separar, apartar.

sundial, *n.* reloj de sol, cuadrante, *m.*

sundown, *n.* = **sunset**.

sundries, *n. pl.* varias cosas.

sundry, *adj.* varios, muchos, diversos.

sunfast, *adj.* que no descolora el sol.

sunfish, *n.* rueda, *f.*

sunflower, *n.* girasol, mirasol, tornasol, *m.*

sung, *p. p. del verbo* **sing**.

sunglass, *n.* espejo ustorio; lentes para el resplandor; —**es**, anteojos contra el sol.

sunk, *p. p. del verbo* **sink**.

sunless, *adj.* sin sol; sin luz.

sunlight, *n.* luz del sol.

sunny, *adj.* semejante al sol; asoleado;

brillante; alegre; **it is —,** hace sol.

sunproof, *adj.* a prueba de sol.

sunrise, *n.* salida del sol.

sunroom, *n.* solana, *f.*

sunset, *n.* puesta del sol; ocaso, *m.*

sunshade, *n.* quitasol, *m.*; pantalla, *f.*; visera contra el sol.

sunshine, *n.* claridad de sol; luz solar, luz del sol.

sunshiny, *adj.* lleno de sol; resplandeciente como el sol.

sunspot, *n.* mancha solar.

sunstroke, *n.* insolación, *f.*

sup, *vt.* sorber, beber a sorbos; dar de cenar; **—,** *vi.* cenar; **—,** *n.* bocado de algo líquido.

sup.: above, encima, arriba; **superior,** sup. superior; **superlative,** superl. superlativo; **supine,** supino; **supplement,** sup. suplemento.

super, *n.* (theat.) comparsa, *m.* y *f.*; (com.) cosa de superior calidad; (com.) tamaño o medida muy grande.

superable, *adj.* superable.

superabound, *vi.* superabundar.

superabundance, *n.* superabundancia, *f.*; lo superfluo.

superabundant, *adj.* superabundante; **—ly,** *adv.* superabundantemente.

superadd, *vt.* sobreañadir.

superaddition, *n.* sobreañadidura, *f.*

superannuated, *adj.* pensionado, retirado; añejado.

superannuation, *n.* pensión, jubilación, *f.*; retiro, *m.*

superb, *adj.* soberbio, espléndido, excelente; **—ly,** *adv.* soberbiamente.

supercargo, *n.* (naut.) sobrecargo, *m.*

supercharge, *vt.* sobrealimentar (un motor).

supercharger, *n.* (aer.) superalimentador, sobrecargador, *m.*

supercilious, *adj.* arrogante, altanero; **—ly,** *adv.* con altivez.

superdreadnought, *n.* (naut.) acorazado, *m.*

supererogation, *n.* supererogación, *f.*

supererogatory, *adj.* supererogatorio.

superficial, *adj.* superficial; **—ly,** *adv.* superficialmente.

superficiary, *n.* superficiario, *m.*

superficies, *n.* superficie, *f.*

superfine, *adj.* superfino.

superfluity, *n.* superfluidad, *f.*

superfluous, *adj.* superfluo; prolijo; redundante; **—ly,** *adv.* superfluamente.

superheterodyne, *n.* and *adj.* (rad.) superheterodino, *m.*

superhuman, *adj.* sobrehumano.

superimpose, *vt.* sobreponer.

superintend, *vt.* inspeccionar, vigilar, dirigir.

superintendence, *n.* superintendencia, *f.*

superintendent, *n.* superintendente, mayordomo, *m.*

superior, *n.* and *adj.* superior, *m.*

superiority, *n.* superioridad, *f.*; mayoría, *f.*

superl. superlative, superl. superlativo.

superlative, *adj.* and *n.* superlativo, *m.*; **—ly,** *adv.* superlativamente, en sumo grado.

superman, *n.* superhombre, *m.*

supernatural, *adj.* sobrenatural; **—,** *n.* cosa sobrenatural; **—ly,** *adv.* sobrenaturalmente.

supernumerary, *adj.* and *n.* supernumerario, *m.*; **—,** *n.* (theat.) comparsa, *m.* y *f.*, actor que toma un papel insignificante.

superphosphate, *n.* (chem.) superfosfato, *m.*; **— of lime,** superfosfato de cal.

superscribe, *vt.* sobrescribir.

superscription, *n.* sobrescrito, *m.*

supersede, *vt.* sobreseer; diferir; invalidar.

superstition, *n.* superstición, *f.*

superstitious, *adj.* supersticioso; **—ly,** *adv.* supersticiosamente.

superstructure, *n.* superestructura, *f.*; edificio levantado sobre otra fábrica.

supertax, *n.* impuesto adicional.

supervene, *vi.* sobrevenir.

supervise, *vt.* inspeccionar, dirigir, vigilar.

supervision, *n.* superintendencia, *f.*; dirección, inspección, *f.*

supervisor, *n.* superintendente, *m.* y *f.*; inspector, ra.

supine, *adj.* supino; negligente; **—ly,** *adv.* descuidadamente.

supp., suppl. supplement, sup. suplemento.

supper, *n.* cena, *f.*; **Lord's Supper,** institución de la Eucaristía; **— room,** cenadero, *m.*; **to have —,** cenar.

supplant, *vt.* suplantar.

supple, *adj.* flexible, manejable; blando; **—,** *vt.* hacer flexible.

supplement, *n.* suplemento, *m.*; **—,** *vt.* suplir; adicionar.

supplemental, supplementary, *adj.* adicional, suplementario.

suppleness, *n.* flexibilidad, *f.*

suppliant, supplicant, *n.* and *adj.* suplicante, *m.* y *f.*

supplicate, *vt.* suplicar.

supplication, *n.* súplica, suplicación, *f.*

supplicatory, *adj.* suplicante.

supply, *vt.* suplir, completar; surtir; proporcionar; dar, proveer; **—,** *n.* surtido, *m.*; provisión, *f.*; **— and demand,** oferta y demanda.

support, *vt.* sostener; soportar, asistir; basar; **—,** *n.* sustento, *m.*; apoyo, *m.*

supportable, *adj.* soportable.

supporter, *n.* sustentáculo, *m.*; apoyo, *m.*; protector, ra, defensor, ra.

suppose, *vt.* suponer.

supposed, *adj.* supuesto.

supposition, *n.* suposición, *f.*, supuesto, *m.*

suppositional, *adj.* supositivo.

supposititious, *adj.* supositicio, fingido, fraudulento.

suppress, *vt.* suprimir; reprimir.

suppression, *n.* supresión, *f.*

suppressor, *n.* supresor, ra.
suppurate, *vi.* supurar.
suppuration, *n.* supuración, *f.*
suprarenal, *adj.* suprarrenal.
supremacy, *n.* supremacía, *f.*
supreme, *adj.* supremo; **—ly,** *adv.* supremamente.
Supt., supt. superintendent, super.ᵗᵉ superintendente.
surcease, *n.* cesación, parada, *f.*; final, *m.*
surcharge, *vt.* sobrecargar; **—,** *n.* sobrecarga, *f.*, recargo, *m.*
surcingle, *n.* sobrecincha, *f.*
surcoat, *n.* sobretodo, gabán, *m.*
sure, *adj.* seguro, cierto, certero; firme; estable; **to be —,** sin duda; seguramente; ya se ve; **—ly,** *adv.* ciertamente, seguramente, sin duda.
sure-footed, *adj.* seguro, de pie firme.
surety, *n.* seguridad, *f.*; fiador, *m.*; **to go —,** salir fiador.
surf, *n.* (naut.) resaca, *f.*; oleaje, *m.*; **— bathing,** baño de oleaje.
surface, *n.* superficie, sobrefaz, cara, *f.*; **— tension,** tensión superficial, *f.*; **—,** *vt.* alisar; emerger, surgir.
surfacing, *n.* recubrimiento (de un camino), *m.*; revestimiento, *m.*; alisamiento, *m.*
surfboard, *n.* tabla para flotar sobre la rompiente.
surfboat, *n.* embarcación para navegar a través de rompientes fuertes.
surfeit, *vt.* and *vi.* hartar, saciar; ahitarse, saciarse; **—,** *n.* ahito, empacho, *m.*; indigestión, *f.*
surg.: surgeon, cirujano; **surgery,** cir. cirugía.
surge, *n.* ola, onda, *f.*; golpe de mar; **—,** *vi.* embravecerse el mar; agitarse; **—,** *vt.* surgir.
surgeon, *n.* cirujano, *m.*
surgery, *n.* cirugía, *f.*
surgical, *adj.* quirúrgico.
surlily, *adv.* ásperamente, con mal humor.
surly, *adj.* áspero de genio; furioso.
surmise, *vt.* sospechar; suponer; **—,** *n.* sospecha, *f.*; suposición, *f.*
surmount, *vt.* sobrepujar; superar.
surmountable, *adj.* superable.
surname, *n.* apellido, sobrenombre, patronímico, *m.*; **—,** *vt.* apellidar.
surpass, *vt.* sobresalir, sobrepujar, exceder, aventajar, sobrepasar.
surplice, *n.* sobrepelliz, *f.*
surplus, surplusage, *n.* sobrante, *m.*, sobra, *f.*
surprise, *vt.* sorprender; **—,** *n.* sorpresa, extrañeza, *f.*
surprising, *adj.* sorprendente; **—ly,** *adv.* sorprendentemente.
surrealism, *n.* surrealismo, *m.*
surrender, *vt.* rendir; ceder, renunciar; **—,** *vi.* rendirse; **—,** *n.* rendición, *f.*; sumisión, *f.*
surreptitious, *adj.* subrepticio; **—ly,** *adv.* subrepticiamente.

surrogate, *vt.* subrogar; **—,** *n.* suplente, sustituto, *m.*
surround, *vt.* circundar, cercar, rodear.
surrounding, *adj.* circunstante; **—,** *n.* acción de circundar; **—s,** cercanías, *f. pl.*; ambiente, *m.*
surtax, *n.* impuesto especial, impuesto adicional.
surveillance, *n.* vigilancia, *f.*
survey, *vt.* inspeccionar, examinar; apear (tierras); **—,** *n.* inspección, *f.*; apeo (de tierras), *m.*
surveyor, *n.* sobrestante, *m.*; agrimensor, topógrafo, *m.*
surveyorship, *n.* empleo de sobrestante.
survival, *n.* supervivencia, *f.*
survive, *vi.* sobrevivir.
surviving, *adj.* sobreviviente.
survivor, *n.* sobreviviente, *m.* y *f.*
Susan, Susanna, Susana.
susceptibility, *n.* susceptibilidad, *f.*
susceptible, *adj.* susceptible.
suspect, *vt.* and *vi.* sospechar, tener malicia; barruntar; **—,** *n.* persona sospechosa.
suspend, *vt.* suspender, colgar; **to — payment,** declarar inhabilidad para hacer pagos.
suspender, *n.* suspendedor, ra; **—s,** tirantes, *m. pl.*, tiradores elásticos.
suspense, *n.* suspensión, *f.*; detención, *f.*; incertidumbre, duda, *f.*
suspension, *n.* suspensión, *f.*; **— bridge,** puente colgante o colgado; **— of work,** paro, *m.*
suspensory, suspenser, *n.* and *adj.* suspensorio, *m.*; **—,** *n.* braguero, *m.*
suspicion, *n.* sospecha, *f.*
suspicious, *adj.* suspicaz; sospechoso, receloso; **to make —,** dar que pensar.
sustain, *vt.* sostener, sustentar, mantener; apoyar; sufrir.
sustainer, *n.* apoyo, sostén, *m.*, sostenedor, ra.
sustaining, *adj.* que sustenta; **— program,** (rad.) programa radiofónico que perifonean por su cuenta las radiodifusoras.
sustenance, *n.* sostenimiento, sustento, *m.*; alimentos, *m. pl.*
sutler, *n.* vivandero, ra.
suture, *n.* sutura, costura, *f.*
suzerain, *n.* soberano, *m.*
s.v. (under the word or heading), bajo el rubro o la palabra.
S W, S.W., s.w. southwest, SO. Sudoeste.
swab, *n.* (naut.) lampazo, *m.*; (med.) esponja, *f.*; **—,** *vt.* fregar, limpiar; (naut.) lampacear.
swabber, *n.* lampacero, *m.*
swaddle, *vt.* fajar; **—,** *n.* pañal, *m.*
swaddling, *n.* empañadura, *f.*; **— clothes,** pañales, *m. pl.*, envolturas, *f. pl.*
swagger, *vi.* baladronear; **—,** *n.* baladronada, *f.*; **— stick,** bastón corto y ligero.
swaggerer, *n.* fanfarrón, baladrón, *m.*
swain, *n.* enamorado, *m.*; zagal, *m.*

swale, *n.* terreno de baja presión.

swallow, *n.* golondrina, *f.*; bocado, *m.*; esófago, *m.*; **—,** *vt.* tragar, engullir.

swallow-tailed, *adj.* de cola bifurcada como una golondrina; **— coat,** frac, *m.*

swam, pretérito del verbo **swim.**

swamp, *n.* pantano, fangal, *m.*; **—,** *vt.* sumergir; **—ed with work,** abrumado de trabajo.

swampy, *adj.* pantanoso.

swan, *n.* cisne, *m.*; **— song,** canto del cisne; última obra de un poeta o un músico; **— dive,** (natación) salto ornamental.

swank, *adj.* (coll.) elegante; **—,** *n.* (coll.) moda, *f.*; **—,** *vi.* (coll.) baladronear.

swanky, *adj.* (coll.) de moda ostentosa; elegante.

swan's-down, *n.* plumón de cisne; paño grueso de lana mezclada con seda, rayón o algodón.

swap, *vt.* and *vi.* (coll.) cambalachear, cambiar; (coll.) hacer permutas; **—,** *n.* (coll.) cambio, trueque, *m.*

sward, *n.* césped, *m.*

swarm, *n.* enjambre, *m.*; gentío, *m.*; hormiguero, *m.*; **—,** *vi.* enjambrar; hormiguear de gente; abundar.

swarthiness, *n.* tez morena.

swarthy, swart, *adj.* atezado, moreno.

swashbuckler, *n.* fanfarrón, valentón, *m.*

swastika, *n.* svástica, *f.*

swatch, *n.* marbete puesto en la ropa antes de enviarla al tintorero; muestra de tejido.

swath, *n.* rastro, *m.*, huella, *f.*; hilera, *f.*; guadañada, *f.*

swathe, *n.* faja, *f.*; rastro, *m.*, huella, *f.*; guadañada, *f.*; **—,** *vt.* fajar, envolver.

sway, *vt.* empuñar; cimbrar; dominar, gobernar; **—,** *vi.* ladearse, inclinarse; tener influjo; **—,** *n.* bamboleo, *m.*; poder, imperio, influjo, *m.*

sway-backed, *adj.* (coll.) pando.

swear, *vt.* and *vi.* jurar; juramentar.

swearing, *n.* jura, *f.*

sweat, *n.* sudor, *m.*; **—,** *vi.* sudar; trabajar con fatiga.

sweater, *n.* chaqueta de punto de lana; persona que suda.

sweating, *n.* exudación, *f.*

sweatshop, *n.* taller donde se trabaja excesivamente por paga escasa.

Swede, *n.* sueco, ca.

Sweden, Suecia, *f.*

Swedish, *adj.* sueco.

sweep, *vt.* and *vi.* barrer; arrebatar, deshollinar; pasar o tocar ligeramente; oscilar; **—,** *n.* barredura, *f.*; vuelta, *f.*; giro, *m.*; alcance, *m.*

sweeper, *n.* barredor, ra; basurero (persona), *m.*; **carpet —,** barredera de alfombra.

sweeping, *adj.* rápido; barredero; vasto; **—,** *n.* barrido, *m.*; **—s,** *pl.* barreduras, *f. pl.*, desperdicios, *m. pl.*

sweepstakes, *n. sing.* and *pl.* carrera en que se ponen apuestas; el premio de una carrera en que se ponen apuestas.

sweet, *adj.* dulce, grato, meloso, gustoso; suave; oloroso; melodioso; hermoso; amable; **— alyssum,** alhelí dulce; **— basil,** alábega, *f.*; **— clover,** trébol, *m.*; **— corn,** maíz tierno; **— flag,** cálamo, *m.*; **— gum,** ocozol, *m.*; **— potato,** batata, *f.*, camote, moniato, buniato, *m.*; (Cuba) boniato, *m.*; **— william,** dianto, *m.*, especie de clavel; **to have a — tooth,** ser amante del dulce, ser goloso; **—,** *n.* dulzura, *f.*; querida, *f.*; **—s,** dulces, *m. pl.*; **—ly,** *adv.* dulcemente, suavemente.

sweetbread, *n.* mollejas de ternera.

sweetbrier, sweetbriar, *n.* (bot.) escaramujo, *m.*

sweeten, *vt.* endulzar; suavizar; aplacar; perfumar.

sweetheart, *n.* querida, *f.*; novio, via; galanteador, *m.*

sweetmeats, *n. pl.* dulces secos; compota, *f.*

sweetness, *n.* dulzura, suavidad, *f.*

swell, *vi.* hincharse; ensoberbecerse; embravecerse; **—,** *vt.* hinchar, inflar, agravar; **— up,** soplar; **—,** *n.* hinchazón, *f.*; bulto, *m.*; petimetre, *m.*; mar de leva; **—,** *adj.* (coll.) elegante, a la moda.

swelling, *n.* hinchazón, *f.*; tumor, *m.*; bulto, *m.*, protuberancia, *f.*

swelter, *vi.* sofocarse, ahogarse de calor; sudar.

swept, *adj.* barrido.

swerve, *vi.* vagar; desviarse; **—,** *vt.* desviar, torcer; **—,** *n.* desviación, *f.*

swift, *adj.* veloz, ligero, rápido; **—,** *n.* (orn.) vencejo, *m.*; **—ly,** *adv.* velozmente.

swiftness, *n.* velocidad, rapidez, *f.*

swig, *vt.* beber vorazmente; **—,** *n.* trago, *m.*

swill, *vt.* and *vi.* beber con exceso, emborrachar; **—,** *n.* bazofia, basura, *f.*; trago, *m.*

swim, *vi.* nadar; abundar en; ser vertiginoso; **—,** *vt.* pasar a nado; **—,** *n.* nadadera de pez; natación, *f.*

swimmer, *n.* nadador, ra.

swimming, *n.* natación, *f.*; vértigo, *m.*; **— pool,** piscina de natación; **—ly,** *adv.* lisamente, sin dificultad.

swindle, *vt.* petardear, estafar; **—,** *n.* estafa, *f.*, petardo, *m.*

swindler, *n.* petardista, trampista, *m.* y *f.*

swine, *n. sing.* y *pl.* puerco(s), cochino(s) *m.*; ganado de cerda.

swineherd, *n.* porquero, *m.*

swing, *vi.* balancear, columpiarse, oscilar; mecerse; vibrar; agitarse; **—,** *vt.* esgrimir; mecer; vibrar; **—,** *n.* vibración, *f.*; balanceo, *m.*; columpio, *m.*; **— bar,** balancín, *m.*; **— music,** variedad de *jazz.*

swinging, *n.* vibración, *f.*; balanceo, *m.*; oscilación, *f.*; **—,** *adj.* oscilante.

swingtree, *n.* = **singletree.**

swinish, *adj.* porcuno, cochino; grosero.

swipe, *n.* báscula, *f.*, flecha de puente

levadizo, mango de bomba; (coll.) golpe fuerte; **—, vt.** dar golpes fuertes; (coll.) hurtar.

swirl, *vt.* and *vi.* hacer remolinos el agua; arremolinar; **—,** *n.* torcimiento, *m.*

swish, *n.* ruido como el que hace el látigo al hendir el aire; ruido como el roce de la ropa de seda.

Swiss, *n.* and *adj.* suizo, za.

switch, *n.* varilla, *f* ; (rail.) aguja, *f.*; (elec.) interruptor, conmutador, *m.*; **ignition —,** contacto del magneto; **reversing —,** inversor, *m.*; **— box,** caja de interruptores; **—,** *vt.* varear; desviar; (elec.) cambiar; **to — off,** desviar.

switchback, *n.* resbaladero, *m.*; arreglo en zigzag de la vía para reducir la pendiente.

switchboard, *n.* cuadro de distribución o conmutador telefónico.

switching, *n.* conmutación, *f.*

switchman, *n.* (rail.) guardagujas, *m.*

switchyard, *n.* (rail.) patio de maniobras.

Switzerland, Suiza, *f.*

swivel, *n.* alacrán, *m.*; **— chair,** silla giratoria; **—,** *vt.* and *vi.* girar.

swollen, *adj.* hinchado, inflado; **—,** *p. p.* del verbo **swell.**

swoon, *vi.* desmayarse; **—,** *n.* desmayo, deliquio, pasmo, soponcio, *m.*

swoop, *vt.* coger, agarrar; **—,** *n.* acto de echarse un ave de rapiña sobre su presa; **at one —,** de un golpe.

sword, *n.* espada, *f.*; **— belt,** talabarte, *m.*; **— belts,** tiros, *m. pl.,* correas de espada.

swordfish, *n.* pez espada.

swordsman, *n.* guerrero, soldado, *m.*

swore, pretérito del verbo **swear.**

sworn, *p. p.* del verbo **swear.**

swum, *p. p.* del verbo **swim.**

swung, pretérito y *p. p.* del verbo **swing.**

sybarite, *n.* sibarita, *m.* y *f.*

sybaritic, *adj.* sibarítico.

sycamore, *n.* sicómoro (árbol), *m.*

sycophant, *n.* gorrista, *m.* y *f.*, lisonjeador, ra, adulador, ra.

Sydney, Sidney, *f.*

syllabic, syllabical, *adj.* silábico.

syllabication, syllabification, *n.* silabeo, *m.*

syllable, *n.* sílaba, *f.*

syllabus, *n.* extracto, resumen, *m.*

syllogism, *n.* silogismo, *m.*

syllogize, *vi.* silogizar.

sylph, *n.* silfo, *m.*; sílfide, *f.*

sylvan, *adj.* silvestre, campestre.

Sylvester, Silvestre.

symbiosis, *n.* (biol.) simbiosis, *f.*

symbol, *n.* símbolo, *m.*

symbolic, *adj.* simbólico.

symbolical, *adj.* simbólico; **—ly,** *adv.* simbólicamente.

symbolism, *n.* simbolismo, *m.*

symbolize, *vt.* simbolizar.

symmetrical, *adj.* simétrico; **—ly,** *adv.* con simetría.

symmetry, *n.* simetría, *f.*

sympathetic, *adj.* que congenia; inclinado a sentir simpatía o compasión; **—ally,** *adv.* simpáticamente.

sympathize, *vi.* compadecerse, simpatizar; **— with,** compadecer.

sympathy, *n.* simpatía, *f.*; pésame, *m.*

symphonious, *adj.* armonioso.

symphony, *n.* sinfonía, armonía, *f.*

symposium, *n.* simposia, *f.,* festín o banquete de los antiguos griegos en donde se cruzaban ideas; conferencia para discutir un tema; colección de opiniones sobre un mismo tema.

symptom, *n.* síntoma, *m.*

syn.: **synonym,** sin. sinónimo; **synonymous,** sin. sinónimo.

synagogue, *n.* sinagoga, *f.*

synapse, *n.* lugar donde el estímulo de los nervios pasa desde una célula a otra.

synchronism, *n.* sincronismo, *m.*

synchronize, *vt.* sincronizar.

synchronous, *adj.* sincrónico.

syncopation, *n.* (gram., mus.) síncopa, *f.*

syndic, *n.* síndico, *m.*

syndicalism, *n.* sindicalismo, *m.*

syndicate, *n.* sindicato, *m.*; **—,** *vt.* and *vi.* sindicar.

synod, *n.* sínodo, *m.*

synonym, *n.* sinónimo, *m.*

synonymous, *adj.* sinónimo; **—ly,** *adv.* con sinonimia.

synopsis, *n.* sinopsis, *f.*; sumario, resumen, *m.*

synoptic, *adj.* sinóptico; **— table,** sinóptica, *f.*

synoptical, *adj.* sinóptico.

syntax, *n.* sintaxis, *f.*

synthesis, *n.* síntesis, *f.*

synthetic, *adj.* sintético; fabricado; **— rubber,** caucho artificial.

syntonize, *vt.* (rad.) sintonizar.

syphilis, *n.* sífilis, *f.,* gálico, *m.*

syringe, *n.* jeringa, lavativa, *f.*; **hypodermic —,** jeringa hipodérmica.

syrup, *n.* jarabe, *m.*

system, *n.* sistema, *m.*; instalación, *f.*; **follow-up —,** sistema de continuidad.

systematic, *adj.* sistemático, metódico; **—ally,** *adv.* sistemáticamente.

systole, *n.* sístole, *f.*

T

T.: Territory, territ. territorio; **Testament,** test.^mto testamento; **Tuesday,** mart. martes.

t.: teaspoon, cucharita; **temperature,** temp. temperatura; **tense,** (gram.) tpo. tiempo; **territory,** territ. territorio; **time,** tpo. tiempo; **ton,** t. tonelada; **town,** pobl. población; **transitive,** transitivo.

tab, *n.* proyección, *f* ; (coll.) cuenta, razón, *f.*

tabasco, *n.* tabasco, *m.,* salsa muy picante.

tabby, *n.* tabí, *m.*; gata, *f.*; chismosa, *f.*;

table 289 tam

—, *adj.* que tiene rayas.

table, *n.* mesa, *f.*; velador, *m.*; tabla, *f.*; elenco, *m.*; **on the —,** sobre la mesa; **round —,** mesa redonda; **side —,** trinchero, *m.*; **synoptic —,** sinóptica, *f.*; **— cover,** carpeta, *f.*; **— d'hote,** mesa redonda, comida a la orden; **— lamp,** lámpara de mesa; **— linen,** mantelería, *f.*; **— service,** vajilla, *f.*; **to set the —,** poner la mesa; **—,** *vt.* apuntar en forma sinóptica; poner sobre la mesa.

tableau, *n.* cuadro, *m.*, representación de una pintura o escena por una persona o un grupo.

tablecloth, *n.* mantel, *m.*

tableland, *n.* meseta, altiplanicie, *f.*; llanura alta.

tablespoon, *n.* cuchara.

tablespoonful, *n.* cucharada, *f.*

tablet, *n.* tableta, *f.*; tablilla, *f.*; pastilla, *f.*; plancha, lámina, *f.*; (med.) oblea, *f.*; **— of paper,** bloc de papel.

tableware, *n.* servicio de mesa.

tabloid, *n.* noticiero ilustrado.

taboo, tabu, *n.* tabú, *m.*; —, *adj.* prohibido; encartado; —, *vt.* interdecir.

tabor, *n.* tamboril, *m.*; **— player,** tamborilero, tamboritero, *m.*

tabular, *adj.* en forma de tabla, tabular.

tabulate, *vt.* presentar cifras o datos en forma de tabla.

tabulation, *n.* presentación de cifras o datos en forma de tabla.

tachometer, *n.* taqueómetro, *m.*; taquímetro, *m.*

tacit, *adj.* tácito; **—ly,** *adv.* tácitamente.

taciturn, *adj.* taciturno, callado.

taciturnity, *n.* taciturnidad, *f.*

tack, *n.* tachuela, *f.*; —, *vt.* clavar; atar; pegar; —, *vi.* (naut.) virar.

tackle, *n.* todo género de instrumentos o aparejos; (naut.) cordaje, cuadernal, *m.*; jarcia, *f.*; (football) atajador, *m.*, jugador en la primera línea de un equipo; —, *vt.* asir, forcejear; atajar; acometer, emprender, intentar.

tact, *n.* tacto, *m.*

tactical, *adj.* táctico.

tactician, *n.* táctico, *m.*

tactics, *n.pl.* táctica, *f.*

tactile, *adj.* táctil.

tactless, *adj.* sin tacto, imprudente.

tactual, *adj.* relativo al sentido del tacto.

tadpole, *n.* ranilla, *f.*; sapillo, renacuajo, *m.*

taffeta, *n.* tafetán, *m.*

taffy, *n.* arropía, *f.*; (coll.) zalamería, *f.*

tag, *n.* herrete, marbete, *m.*, marca, *f.*; **— day,** día de carteles, día de colectas de caridad en que se dan etiquetas al contribuyente.

tail, *n.* cola, *f.*, rabo, *m.*; **— spin,** (aer.) barrena de cola; **— wheel,** (aer.) rueda de cola; **— wind,** viento de cola.

taillight, *n.* farol de cola.

tailor, *n.* sastre, *m.*

tailoring, *n.* sastrería, *f.*

tailor-made, *adj.* a la medida.

tailpiece, *n.* apéndice, *m.*

tailrace, *n.* canal de escape de agua.

taint, *vt.* tinturar, manchar; inficionar; viciar; —, *n.* mácula, mancha, *f.*

take, *vt.* tomar, coger, asir; recibir, aceptar; hurtar, pillar; prender; admitir; —, *vi.* encaminarse, dirigirse; salir bien, efectuarse una cosa; arraigar; prender (el fuego); **to — a breath,** resollar; **to — apart,** desarmar, desmontar; **to — a walk,** pasear; **to — away,** llevar; **to — away with,** llevarse; **to — charge of,** encargarse de; **to — for granted,** dar por sentado; **to — off,** (aer.) despegar; **to — out,** suprimir; **to — place,** verificarse; **to — the liberty,** permitirse; **to — upon oneself,** encargarse de; —, *n.* toma, *f.*; presa, *f.*

take-in, *n.* engaño. *m.*

taken, *p. p.* del verbo **take.**

take-off, *n.* caricatura, *f.*; parodia, *f.*; (aer.) despegue, *m.*

taker, *n.* tomador, ra.

taking, *adj.* agradable, simpático, cautivador; (coll.) contagioso; —, *n.* presa, *f.*; secuestro, *m.*; **—s,** *pl.* colectas, *f. pl.,* dinero recogido.

talc, *n.* talco, *m.*

talcum, *n.* talco, *m.*; **— powder,** polvo de talco.

tale, *n.* cuento, *m.*, fábula, *f.*

talebearer, *n.* soplón, ona, chismero, ra.

talent, *n.* talento, *f.*; ingenio, *m.*; capacidad, *f.*; **—s,** prendas, habilidades, *f. pl.*

talented, *adj.* talentoso.

talion, *n.* talión, *m.*

talisman, *n.* talismán, *m.*

talk, *vi.* hablar, conversar; charlar; —, *n.* plática, habla, *f.*; charla, *f.*; fama, *f.*; conferencia, *f.*, discurso, *m.*

talkative, *adj.* gárrulo, locuaz, palabrero, hablador, parlero, charlatán.

talker, *n.* charlador, ra.

talking, *adj.* hablante; **— machine,** fonógrafo, *m.*; **— picture,** película sonora.

tall, *adj.* alto, elevado; (coll.) raro, increíble.

tallness, *n.* altura, estatura, *f.*

tallow, *n.* sebo, *m.*; —, *vt.* ensebar.

tallowy, *adj.* seboso.

tally, *n.* cuenta, *f.*; **— sheet,** hoja de apuntes; —, *vt.* ajustar; tarjar.

talon, *n.* garra del ave de rapiña.

tamable, *adj.* domable.

tamale, *n.* tamal, *m.*

tamarack, *n.* (bot.) alerce americano.

tamarind, *n.* tamarindo, *f.*

tamarisk, *n.* tamarisco, *m.*

tambourine, *n.* pandero, *m.*, pandereta, *f.*

tame, *adj.* amansado, domado, domesticado; abatido; manso; sumiso; **—ly,** *adv.* mansamente; —, *vt.* domar, domesticar.

taming, *n.* domadura, *f.*

tam o' shanter, *n.* boina escocesa.

tamp, *vt.* apisonar, compactar; —, *n.* herramienta de apisonar.

tamper, *vi.* tramar; sobornar; entremeterse en lo que no se debe.

tampon, *n.* (med.) tapón, *m.*; —, *vt.* taponar.

tan, *vt.* curtir, zurrar (pieles, etc.); —, *n.* casca, *f.*; color café claro, color de arena; —, *vi.* dorarse por el sol.

tan. tang. tangent, tang. tangente.

tanager, *n.* (orn.) tángara, *f.*

tanbark, *n.* casca rica en tanino.

tandem, *adv.* a lo largo; —, *n.* tándem, *m.*, bicicleta usada por dos ciclistas al mismo tiempo; coche con caballos uno tras otro; —, *adj.* tándem.

tang, *n.* sabor, *m.*; retintín, *m.*; —, *vi.* retiñir.

tangency, *n.* tangencia, *f.*

tangent, *n.* and *adj.* tangente, *f.*

tangerine, *n.* naranja tangerina o mandarina.

tangible, *adj.* tangible.

tangle, *vt.* enredar, embrollar; —, *vi.* enredarse; —, *n.* enredo, embrollo, *m.*; confusión, *f.*; maraña, *f.*

tango, *n.* tango, *m.*

tank, *n.* (mil.) tanque, *m.*, tractor blindado; depósito, tanque, *m.*; cisterna, *f.*, aljibe, *m.*; **cleansing** —, depurador, *m.*; — **car,** (rail.) vagón-tanque, *m.*; — **farming** = **hydroponics;** — **trap,** (mil.) trampa u obstáculo para tanques; —, *vt.* almacenar.

tankage, *n.* capacidad de un tanque.

tankard, *n.* cántaro con tapadera.

tanker, *n.* buque petrolero.

tanned, *adj.* curtido; tostado del sol.

tanner, *n.* curtidor, *m.*

tannery, *n.* curtiduría, tenería, *f.*

tannic, *adj.* tánico.

tannin, *n.* tanino, *m.*

tanning, *n.* curtimiento, *m.*

tantalize, *vt.* atormentar a alguno mostrándole placeres que no puede alcanzar.

tantalizing, *adj.* atormentador.

tantamount, *adj.* equivalente.

tantivy, *adj.* veloz, rápido.

tantrum, *n.* berrinche, *m.*

tanyard, *n.* = **tannery.**

tap, *vt.* tocar ligeramente; barrenar; golpear; extraer el jugo de un árbol por incisión; sacar agua del cuerpo humano; —, *n.* palmada suave; toque ligero; espita, *f.*; tomadero, *m.*; — **dance,** baile zapateado (común en los Estados Unidos).

tap-dance, *vt.* bailar una especie de zapateado (común en los Estados Unidos).

tape, *n.* cinta, *f.*; galón, *m.*; —s, tiras de papel del telégrafo que contienen los telegramas; — **measure,** cinta de medir; —, *vt.* arrollar con cinta, vendar.

taper, *n.* candela, *f.*; cirio, *m.*; taladro de reducción; —, *adj.* cónico; —, *vi.* rematar en punta, ahusar; —, *vt.* dar forma ahusada.

tapestry, *n.* tapiz, *m.*; tapicería, *f.*; — **maker,** tapicero, *m.*

tapeworm, *n.* tenia, *f.*, lombriz solitaria, solitaria, *f.*

tapioca, *n.* tapioca, *f.*

tappet, *n.* aleta, *f.*

taproom, *n.* taberna, *f.*

taproot, *n.* raíz que penetra verticalmente.

taps, *n. pl.* (mil.) toque de silencio.

tar, *n.* brea, *f.*; (coll.) marinero, *m.*; alquitrán, *m.*, pez, *f.*; —, *vt.* embrear.

tarantula, *n.* tarántula, *f.*

tardily, *adv.* lentamente.

tardiness, *n.* lentitud, tardanza, *f.*

tardy, *adj.* tardo, lento.

tare, *n.* (bot.) cizaña, *f.*; tara, *f.*

target, *n.* rodela, *f.*; blanco (para tirar), *m.*; — **practice,** tiro al blanco, ejercicios de tiro; **to hit the** —, dar en el blanco.

tariff, *n.* tarifa, *f.*

tarlatan, *n.* tarlatana, *f.*

tarn, *n.* laguna entre montañas.

tarnish, *vt.* deslustrar; manchar; —, *vi.* deslustrarse; —, *n.* borrón, *m.*, mancha, *f.*

tarpaulin, *n.* tela embreada; toldo, *m.*

tarpon, *n.* tarpon, *m.*

tarry, *vi.* tardar, pararse; demorar; —, *adj.* embreado.

tarsal, *adj.* tarsal.

tart, *adj.* acedo, acre; —ly, *adv.* agriamente.

tart, *n.* torta, *f.*, pastelillo, *m.*

tartan, *n.* tartana, *f.*

Tartar, *n.* and *adj.* tártaro, ra.

tartar, *n.* tártaro, *m.*; sarro (de los dientes), *m.*

Tartarus, Tártaro, *m.*

task, *n.* tarea, *f.*; cometido, quehacer, *m.*; — **force,** tropa o contingente naval a los cuales se asignan tareas de combate.

tassel, *n.* borlita, *f.*; —s, capotas, *f. pl.*; —, *vt.* decorar con borlitas; —, *vi.* crecer capotas.

taste, *n.* gusto, *m.*; sabor, *m.*; prueba, *f.*; saboreo, *m.*; ensayo, *m.*; — **bud,** órgano terminal del gusto; —, *vt.* and *vi.* gustar; probar; experimentar; agradar; tener sabor; **to** — **of,** saber a.

tasteful, *adj.* elegante, galano, de buen gusto; —ly, *adv.* con buen gusto, elegantemente.

tasteless, *adj.* insípido, sin sabor.

taster, *n.* catador, *m.*

tastily, *adv.* con gusto.

tasty, *adj.* sabroso, gustoso.

tat, *vt.* and *vi.* hacer encaje de hilo.

tatter, *n.* andrajo, arrapiezo, *m.*

tatterdemalion, *n.* pobre andrajoso; pelafustán, ana.

tattered, *adj.* andrajoso, haraposo.

tatting, *n.* encaje de hilo.

tattle, *vt.* and *vi.* charlar, parlotear; —, *n.* charla, *f.*

tattletale, *n.* chismoso, sa, chismero, ra.

tattoo, *n.* tatuaje, *m.*; (mil.) retreta, *f.*; *vt.* tatuar.

taunt, *vt.* mofar; ridiculizar; dar chanza; —, *n.* mofa, burla, chanza, *f.*; pulla, *f.*

taunting, *adj.* insolente; —**ly,** *adv.* con mofa.

taupe, *n.* and *adj.* gris pardo.

Taurus, *n.* Tauro (signo del zodíaco), *m.*

taut, *adj.* tieso, terco, tirante; nítido, en orden.

tautological, *adj.* tautológico.

tautology, *n.* tautología, *f.*

tavern, *n.* taberna, *f.*; posada, *f.*; **roadside** —, ventorrillo, *m.*

taw, *vt.* ablandar pieles; —, *n.* bolita de mármol.

tawdrily, *adv.* vistosa y chabacanamente.

tawdry, *adj.* chabacano y vistoso.

tawny, *adj.* moreno; de color tostado.

tax, *n.* impuesto, tributo, gravamen, *m.*, contribución, *f.*; carga, *f.*; **additional** —, recargo, *m.*; **income** —, impuesto de entradas, impuesto de rentas; — **collector,** colector de impuestos; — **rate,** tarifa de impuesto, cupo, *m.*; —, *vt.* imponer tributos; acusar; **to** — **one's strength,** abusar de la propia fuerza.

taxable, *adj.* sujeto a impuestos.

taxation, *n.* imposición de impuestos.

tax-exempt, *adj.* exento de impuesto.

taxi, *n.* taxímetro, *m.*, automóvil de plaza; — **dancer,** pareja femenina de baile en establecimientos donde los parroquianos pagan un tanto por cada pieza que bailan; —, *vi.* ir en un taxímetro o automóvil de plaza; (aer.) moverse sobre la superficie.

taxidermal, *adj.* taxidérmico.

taxidermist, *n.* taxidermista, *m.* y *f.*

taxidermy, *n.* taxidermia, *f.*

taximeter, *n.* taxímetro, *m.*; automóvil de plaza.

taxpayer, *n.* contribuyente, *m.* y *f.*

t.b. tuberculosis, tuberculosis.

T bolt, *n.* perno en T.

tbs., tbsp. tablespoon, cuchara para servir.

tea, *n.* té, *m.*; **Paraguay** —, yerba mate; — **ball,** bola metálica perforada para té, bolsita con hojas de té.

teacart, *n.* carretilla para servir el té.

teach, *vt.* enseñar, instruir; —, *vi.* tener por oficio la enseñanza pública o particular.

teachable, *adj.* dócil; educable.

teacher, *n.* maestro, tra, profesor, ra, preceptor, ra, enseñador, ra, pedagogo, ga.

teaching, *n.* enseñanza, *f.*; —, *adj.* docente; — **staff,** personal docente.

teacup, *n.* taza para té.

teak, *n.* (bot.) teca, *f.*

teakettle, *n.* tetera, *f.*

teal, *n.* cerceta, zarceta, *f.*

team, *n.* tiro de caballos; pareja, *f.*; (deportes) equipo, *m.*

teamster, *n.* galerero, *m.*

teamwork, *n.* trabajo de cooperación; auxilio mutuo.

teapot, *n.* tetera, *f.*

tear, *vt.* despedazar, lacerar; rasgar; arrancar; —, *n.* rasgón, *m.*; raja, *f.*; jirón, *m.*

tear, *n.* lágrima, *f.*; gota, *f.*; — **bomb,** bomba lacrimógena; — **gas,** gas lacrimógeno.

teardrop, *n.* lágrima, *f.*

tearful, *adj.* lloroso, lacrimoso; —**ly,** *adv.* con lloro.

tearless, *adj.* sin lágrimas.

tearoom, *n.* salón de té.

tease, *vt.* cardar (lana o lino); molestar, atormentar; dar broma; (coll.) tomar el pelo.

teasel, *n.* (bot.) capota, *f.*; carda, *f.*; —, *vt.* cardar paño.

teaseler, *n.* carmenador, *m.*

teaspoon, *n.* cucharita, *f.*

teat, *n.* ubre, *f.*; teta, *f.*

teazel, *n.* and *vt.* = **teasel.**

technical, *adj.* técnico; — **staff,** personal técnico.

technicality, *n.* asunto técnico; cuestión técnica.

technician, *n.* experto, técnico, *m.*

technicolor, *n.* tecnicolor, *m.*

technique, *n.* técnica, *f.*, método, *m.*

technocracy, *n.* tecnocracia, *f.*, gobierno de personas con conocimientos técnicos referente a los servicios públicos del estado.

technological, *adj.* tecnológico.

technology, *n.* tecnología, *f.*

techy, *adj.* caprichoso, enojadizo.

tedder, *n.* heneador, *m.*

teddy bear, *n.* oso (juguete), *m.*

Te Deum, *n.* tedéum, *m.*

tedious, *adj.* tedioso, fastidioso; —**ly,** *adv.* fastidiosamente.

tedium, tediousness, *n.* tedio, fastidio, aburrimiento, *m.*

tee, *n.* (golf) tee, *m.*; meta, *f.*; —, *vt.* (golf) colocar la pelota de golf en el tee.

teem, *vt.* producir; —, *vi.* abundar; ser fértil.

teens, *n. pl.* números y años desde 13 hasta 20; período de trece a diecinueve años de edad.

teepee, *n.* = **tepee.**

teeter, *vt.* and *vi.* balancearse; —, *n.* balanceo, *m.*; columpio de tabla.

teeth, *n. pl.* de **tooth,** dientes, *m. pl.*; (coll.) herramienta, *f.*; **false** —, dientes postizos; **in the** — **of,** contra todos obstáculos; **set of** —, dentadura, *f.*

teethe, *vi.* endentecer, echar los dientes.

teething, *n.* dentición, *f.*; — **ring,** chupador, *m.*

teetotal, *adj.* (coll.) entero; total; moderado, sobrio.

teetotaler, teetotaller, *n.* abstemio, mia, persona que se abstiene de bebidas alcohólicas.

teetotalism, *n.* sobriedad, abstinencia de bebidas alcohólicas.

teetotally, *adv.* totalmente.

teetotum, *n.* perinola, *f.*

tel.: telegram, teleg. telegrama; **telegraph,** teleg. telégrafo; **telephone,** telef. teléfono; **television,** televisión.

telecast, *vt.* and *vi.* trasmitir imágenes por televisión.

telegram, *n.* telegrama, *m.*

telegraph, *n.* telégrafo, *m.*; — **operator,** telegrafista, *m.* y *f.*; —, *vi.* telegrafiar.

telegrapher, *n.* telegrafista, *m.* y *f.*

telegraphic, *adj.* telegráfico.

telegraphy, *n.* telegrafía, *f.*

teleological, *adj.* teleológico.

teleology, *n.* teleología, *f.*

telepathy, *n.* telepatía, *f.*

telephone, *n.* teléfono, *m.*; **dial —,** teléfono automático; — **booth,** cabina telefónica; — **exchange,** central telefónica; — **operator,** telefonista, *m.* y *f.*; — **receiver,** micrófono, *m.*; — **directory,** directorio de teléfonos, lista de abonados al teléfono; —, *vt.* and *vi.* telefonear.

telephoto, *adj.* = **telephotographic.**

telephotograph, *n.* telefotografía, *f.*; —, *vt.* and *vi.* fotografiar a distancia.

telephotographic, *adj.* telefotográfico; — **lens,** lente telefotográfica.

telephotography, *n.* telefotografía, *f.*

telescope, *n.* telescopio, *m.*; —, *vi.* enchufar.

telescopic, *adj.* telescópico.

telescopical, *adj.* telescópico; **—ly,** *adv.* a manera de telescopio.

teletype, *n.* teletipo, *m.*; —, *vt.* enviar un mensaje por teletipo.

teletypewriter, *n.* máquina de escribir telegráfica.

teleview, *vt.* and *vi.* ver en un receptor de televisión.

television, *n.* televisión, *f.*

tell, *vt.* and *vi.* decir; informar, contar; numerar, revelar; mandar; —, *vi.* hacer efecto.

teller, *n.* relator, ra; computista, *m.* y *f.*; **paying —,** pagador, ra; **receiving —,** recibidor, ra.

telltale, *n.* soplón, ona.

temerarious, *adj.* temerario.

temerity, *n.* temeridad, *f.*

temp. temperature, temp. temperatura.

temper, *vt.* templar, moderar; atemperar; —, *n.* temperamento, *m.*; humor, genio, *m.*; **ill —,** mal humor; **to lose one's —,** enojarse; salirse de sus casillas.

temperament, *n.* temperamento, *m.*; carácter, genio, *m.*

temperamental, *adj.* genial; de carácter caprichoso; **—ly,** *adv.* genialmente.

temperance, *n.* templanza, moderación, *f.*; sobriedad, *f.*

temperate, *adj.* templado, moderado, sobrio; — **zone,** zona templada; **—ly,** *adv.* templadamente.

temperature, *n.* temperatura, *f.*

tempered, *adj.* templado, acondicionado.

temperer, *n.* templador, *m.*

tempest, *n.* tempestad, *f.*

tempestuous, *adj.* tempestuoso, proceloso; **—ly,** *adv.* tempestuosamente.

Templar, *n.* templario, *m.*; **t—,** *n.* estudiante de leyes (en Inglaterra).

temple, *n.* templo, *m.*; sien, *f.*

tempo, *n.* tiempo, compás, *m.*

temporal, *adj.* temporal, provisional; (anat., zool.) temporal; secular, profano.

temporarily, *adv.* temporalmente, provisionalmente; por lo pronto.

temporary, *adj.* provisional, temporario, temporal.

temporize, *vi.* temporizar, contemporizar.

tempt, *vt.* tentar; provocar.

temptation, *n.* tentación, *f.*; prueba, *f.*

tempter, *n.* tentador, ra.

tempting, *adj.* tentador; **—ly,** *adv.* en forma tentadora.

ten, *n.* and *adj.* diez, *m.*; (math.) decena, *f.*

tenable, *adj.* defendible.

tenacious, *adj.* tenaz; adhesivo; **—ly,** *adv.* tenazmente.

tenacity, *n.* tenacidad, *f.*; porfía, *f.*

tenancy, *n.* tenencia, *f.*

tenant, *n.* arrendador, ra, tenedor, ra, inquilino, na; —, *vi.* arrendar.

tench, *n.* (pez) tenca, *f.*

tend, *vt.* guardar, velar; atender; —, *vi.* tirar, dirigirse; atender.

tendency, *n.* tendencia, *f.*; inclinación, *f.*

tender, *adj.* tierno, delicado; sensible; **—ly,** *adv.* tiernamente; —, *n.* oferta, propuesta, *f.*; (naut.) patache, *m.*; (rail.) ténder (de una locomotora), *m.*; (com.) lo que se emplea para pagar; —, *vt.* ofrecer, proponer; estimar; —, *vi.* ofrecerse.

tenderfoot, *n.* recién llegado; novato, principiante, *m.*

tender-hearted, *adj.* compasivo, simpático.

tenderloin, *n.* filete, solomillo, *m.*

tenderness, *n.* terneza, delicadeza, *f.*

tendon, *n.* tendón, *m.*

tendril, *n.* (bot.) zarcillo, *m.*; filamento, *m.*

tenement, *n.* tenencia, habitación, *f.*; — **house,** casa de vecindad.

tenet, *n.* dogma, *m.*; aserción, *f.*; credo, *m.*

tenfold, *adj.* décuplo.

Tenn. Tennessee, Tennessee.

tennis, *n.* tenis, *m.*, raqueta (juego), *f.*; — **court,** campo de tenis; — **player,** tenista, *m.* y *f.*

tenor, *n.* (mus.) tenor, *m.*; tenor, curso, *m.*; contenido, *m.*; substancia, *f.*; —, *adj.* de tenor.

tenpenny, *adj.* de valor de diez peniques; de clavo de tamaño grande.

tenpin, *n.* bolo, *m.*; **game of —s,** juego de bolos.

tense, *adj.* tieso; tenso; —, *n.* (gram.) tiempo, *m.*; **past —,** pasado, *m.*

tenseness, *n.* tirantez, *f.*

tensile, *adj.* extensible; — **strength,** resistencia a la tracción o tensión.

tension, *n.* tensión, tirantez, *f.*; (elec.) voltaje, *m.*

ten-strike, _n._ chuza, _f._, jugada en que se derriban todos los bolos.

tent, _n._ (mil.) tienda de campaña; pabellón, _m._; tienta, _f._; **oxygen —,** tienda oxígena; **— fly,** toldo de tienda; **—,** _vi._ alojarse en tienda de campaña.

tentacle, _n._ tentáculo, _m._

tentative, _adj._ tentativo; de ensayo; de prueba; **—ly,** _adv._ como prueba.

tenter, _n._ rama, _f._, tendedor, _m._; **—,** _vt._ estirar.

tenterhook, _n._ clavija de rama; **on —s,** ansioso, bajo tensión nerviosa.

tenth, _n._ and _adj._ décimo, ma; **—ly,** _adv._ en décimo lugar.

tenuity, _n._ tenuidad, _f._; delgadez, _f._

tenuous, _adj._ tenue, delgado.

tenure, _n._ tenencia, incumbencia, _f._

tepee, _n._ cabaña indígena (E. U. A.).

tepid, _adj._ tibio.

tepidity, _n._ tibieza, _f._

tequila, _n._ tequila, _f._

ter. terr. territory, territ. territorio.

tergiversate, _vi._ tergiversar.

tergiversation, _n._ tergiversación, _f._

term, _n._ término, confín, _m._; plazo, _m._; tiempo, período, _m._; estipulación, _f._; **—s of payment,** condiciones de pago; **—,** _vt._ nombrar, llamar.

termagant, _n._ diabla, _f._; arpía, _f._; mujer bulliciosa, turbulenta y pendenciera; **—,** _adj._ turbulento; regañón; bullicioso, pendenciero.

terminable, _adj._ terminable.

terminal, _adj._ terminal, final; **—,** _n._ terminal, _m._; (rail.) estación terminal.

terminate, _vt._ and _vi._ terminar, limitar.

termination, _n._ terminación, conclusión, _f._

terminative, _adj._ terminativo.

terminology, _n._ terminología, _f._

terminus, _n._ (rail.) última estación; terminal, _m._

termite, _n._ comején, _m._, termita, _f._

terra, _n._ tierra, _f._; **— cotta,** terracota, _f._, barro, _m._; **— firma,** tierra firme.

terrace, _n._ terraza, _f._, terrado, _m._; terraplén, _m._; **—,** _vt._ terraplenar.

terrain, _n._ terreno, campo, _m._

terrapin, _n._ variedad de tortuga.

terrazzo, _n._ piso de pedacitos de mármol y cemento.

terrestrial, _adj._ terrestre, terreno.

terrible, _adj._ terrible, espantoso; **how —!** ¡qué barbaridad! **—ly,** _adv._ terriblemente.

terrier, _n._ zorrero, _m._

terrific, _adj._ terrífico, terrible, espantoso; (coll.) tremendo, maravilloso.

terrify, _vt._ espantar, llenar de terror.

territory, _n._ territorio, _m._

terror, _n._ terror, espanto, _m._

terrorist, _n._ terrorista, _m._

terror-stricken, _adj._ aterrorizado.

terse, _adj._ terso, elegante, sucinto.

terseness, _n._ brevedad, concisión, _f._

tertian, _n._ terciana, _f._; **—,** _adj._ tercianario.

tertiary, _adj._ terciario; **Tertiary,** (geología) terciario.

tessellate, _vt._ taracear.

test, _n._ ensayo, _m._, prueba, _f._; copela, _f._; piedra de toque; examen, _m._; **— flight,** vuelo experimental o de prueba, _m._; **— pilot,** piloto de prueba; **— tube,** probeta, _f._; **—,** _vt._ ensayar, probar; examinar.

Test. Testament, Test.ᵐᵗᵒ Testamento.

testaceous, _adj._ testáceo.

testacy, _n._ (law) testación, _f._

Testament, _n._ Testamento, _m._; **New —,** el Nuevo Testamento; **Old —,** el Viejo Testamento.

testament, _n._ testamento, _m._

testamentary, _adj._ testamentario.

testate, _adj._ testado.

testator, _n._ testador, _m._

testatrix, _n._ testadora, _f._

tester, _n._ probador, ra; cielo de cama.

testicle, _n._ testículo, _m._

testicular, _adj._ testicular.

testify, _vt._ testificar, atestiguar.

testily, _adv._ con displicencia, con mal humor.

testimonial, _n._ atestación, _f._; recomendación, _f._, elogio, _m._; **—,** _adj._ testimonial.

testimony, _n._ testimonio, _m._

testiness, _n._ mal humor.

testing, _n._ ensayo, _m._, prueba, _f._

testis, _n._ = **testicle.**

testy, _adj._ displicente, descontentadizo; quisquilloso.

tetanus, _n._ tétano, _m._

tête-à-tête, _adj._ cara a cara; confidencial; **—,** _n._ conversación confidencial entre dos.

tether, _n._ correa, maniota, _f._; traba, _f._; **—,** _vt._ atar con una correa.

tetrahedral, _adj._ tetraédrico.

tetrahedron, _n._ tetraedro, _m._

tetroxide, _n._ (chem.) tetróxido, _m._, compuesto de un radical y cuatro átomos de oxígeno.

tetter, _n._ herpes, _m._ y _f._ _pl._; serpigo, _m._

Texas, Tejas, _m._

text, _n._ texto, _m._; tema, _m._

textbook, _n._ texto, _m._, libro de texto.

textile, _adj._ hilable; textil; **—,** _n._ tejido, _m._

textual, _adj._ textual.

textural, _adj._ textorio.

texture, _n._ textura, _f._; tejido, _m._

Th., Thurs. Thursday, jueves.

T. H. Territory of Hawaii, Territorio de Hawaí.

thalamus, _n._ (bot.) tálamo, _m._; (anat.) tálamos ópticos.

thallophyte, _n._ talofitas, _f._ _pl._

thallus, _n._ (bot.) talo, _m._

than, _conj._ que o de (en sentido comparativo).

thane, _n._ caballero (Inglaterra), _m._

thank, _vt._ agradecer, dar gracias; **— offering,** ofrecimiento en acción de gracias; **—s,** gracias, _f._ _pl._; **— you,** gracias, _f._ _pl._

thankful, _adj._ grato, agradecido; **—ly,** _adv._ con gratitud.

thankfulness, *n.* gratitud, *f.*

thankless, *adj.* ingrato.

Thanksgiving, Thanksgiving Day, *n.* día de dar gracias, día de acción de gracias (en Estados Unidos).

thanksgiving, *n.* acción de gracias.

that, *dem. pron.* ese, esa, eso; aquel, aquella, aquello; —, *rel. pron.* que, quien, el cual, la cual, lo cual; —, *conj.* que, por que, para que; —, *adv.* (coll.) así, a tal grado; de este tamaño; **not — large,** no tan grande.

thatch, *n.* techo de paja; —, *vt.* techar con paja; —**ed roof,** techo de paja.

thaw, *n.* deshielo, *m.*; —, *vi.* derretirse, disolverse; deshelarse; —, *vt.* derretir.

the, *art.* el, la, lo; los, las.

theater, *n.* teatro, *m.*

theatrical, *adj.* teatral; —**ly,** *adv.* en forma teatral.

thee, *pron.* (acusativo de **thou**) ti, a ti.

theft, *n.* hurto, robo, *m.*

theine, *n.* (chem.) teína, *f.*, especie de cafeína.

their, *pron.* su, suyo, suya; sus, suyos, suyas; —**s,** el suyo, la suya, los suyos, las suyas.

theism, *n.* teísmo, *m.*

theist, *n.* teísta, *m. y f.*

theistic, *adj.* teísta.

them, *pron.* (acusativo y dativo de **they**) los, las, les; ellos, ellas.

thematic, *adj.* temático.

theme, *n.* tema, asunto, *m.*; (mus.) motivo, *m.*

themselves, *pron. pl.* ellos mismos, ellas mismas; sí mismos.

then, *adv.* entonces, después; en tal caso; **now and —,** de cuando en cuando.

thence, *adv.* desde allí, de ahí.

thenceforth, *adv.* desde entonces.

thenceforward, *adv.* = **thenceforth.**

theocracy, *n.* teocracia, *f.*

theocratic, *adj.* teocrático.

theodolite, *n.* (math.) teodolito, *m.*

theologian, *n.* teólogo, *m.*

theological, *adj.* teológico; —**ly,** *adv.* teológicamente.

theology, *n.* teología, *f.*

theorem, *n.* teorema, *m.*; **binomial —,** binomio de Newton.

theoretical, *adj.* teórico; —**ly,** *adv.* teóricamente.

theorist, *n.* teórico, *m.*

theorize, *vt.* teorizar.

theory, *n.* teoría, *f.*

theosofist, *n.* teósofo, *m.*

theosophical, *adj.* teosófico; —**ly,** *adv.* teosóficamente.

theosophy, *n.* teosofía, *f.*

therapeutic, therapeutical, *adj.* terapéutico.

therapeutics, *n.* terapéutica, *f.*

therapeutist, *n.* terapeuta, *m. y f.*

therapy, *n.* terapia, *f.*

there, *adv.* allí, allá; úsase también como voz expletiva; —**!** *interj.* ¡mira! ¡ya lo ves! ¡te lo dije!

thereabouts, *adv.* por allí, cerca de allí; casi.

thereafter, *adv.* después; subsiguientemente; de acuerdo con eso; de acuerdo.

thereat, *adv.* allí, en ese lugar; en ese momento; por eso.

thereby, *adv.* por medio de eso; con eso.

therefore, *adv.* por lo tanto, por esto, por esa razón; a consecuencia de eso.

therefrom, *adv.* de allí, de allá, de eso.

therein, *adv.* en ese lugar; en ese particular; en esto, en eso.

thereinto, *adv.* dentro de eso, dentro de ello.

thereof, *adv.* de eso, de ello; de allí; de ese particular.

thereon, *adv.* en eso, sobre eso.

thereto, thereunto, *adv.* a eso, a ello; además.

theretofore, *adv.* hasta entonces.

thereupon, *adv.* en eso, sobre eso; por lo tanto; inmediatamente después; en seguida.

therewith, *adv.* con eso; inmediatamente.

therewithal, *adv.* con todo; además; inmediatamente.

thermal, *adj.* termal; — **waters,** termas, caldas, *f. pl.*

thermic, *adj.* termal; térmico.

thermite, *n.* (chem.) termita, *f.*

thermochemistry, *n.* termoquímica, *f.*

thermodynamics, *n.* termodinámica, *f.*

thermoelectric, thermoelectrical, *adj.* termoeléctrico.

thermoelectricity, *n.* termoelectricidad, *f.*

thermometer, *n.* termómetro, *m.*

thermos, thermos bottle, *n.* termos, *m.*

thermostat, *n.* termóstato, *m.*

thermostatic, *adj.* relativo al termóstato.

thesaurus, *n.* tesauro, *m.*

these, *pron. pl.* estos, estas.

thesis, *n.* tesis, *f.*

thews, *n.pl.* poder muscular, fuerza, *f.*, vigor, *m.*

they, *pron. pl.* ellos, ellas.

thick, *adj.* espeso, denso; grueso; turbio; frecuente; torpe; ronco; **through — and thin,** por toda situación difícil o penosa (expresión que demuestra la lealtad de alguien); —, *n.* la parte más gruesa; —**ly,** *adv.* espesamente; frecuentemente; continuadamente.

thicken, *vt.* and *vi.* espesar, condensar; condensarse, espesarse.

thickening, *n.* sustancia espesativa; acción de espesarse.

thicket, *n.* espesar, matorral, *m.*, maleza, *f.*

thickhead, *n.* (coll.) persona torpe, estúpido, da.

thick-headed, *adj.* estúpido, torpe; terco.

thickness, *n.* espesura, densidad, *f.*; grosor, grueso, *m.*

thickset, *adj.* muy espeso (aplícase a un

bosque); rechoncho.

thick-skinned, *adj.* paquidermo; indiferente; sin vergüenza; insensible.

thick-witted, *adj.* estúpido, torpe.

thief, *n.* ladrón, ona.

thieve, *vt.* and *vi.* hurtar, robar; —s *n. pl.* de **thief,** ladrones, *m. pl.*

thievery, *n.* robo, hurto, *m.*

thievish, *adj.* propenso a robar o a hurtar; —**ly,** *adv.* como un ladrón.

thievishness, *n.* latrocinio, *m.*

thigh, *n.* muslo, *m.*

thighbone, *n.* fémur, *m.*

thill, *n.* limonera (de un carruaje o carreta), *f.*

thimble, *n.* dedal, *m.*

thimbleful, *n.* cantidad que cabe en un dedal, cantidad muy pequeña.

thin, *adj.* delgado, delicado; sutil; flaco; claro; ralo; —, *vt.* enrarecer; atenuar; adelgazar; aclarar; —**ly,** *adv.* ralamente; sutilmente.

thine, *pron.* tuyo, tuya, tuyos, tuyas.

thing, *n.* cosa, *f.*

think, *vt.* and *vi.* pensar, imaginar, meditar, considerar; creer, juzgar.

thinker, *n.* pensador, ra.

thinking, *n.* pensamiento, *m.*; juicio, *m.*; opinión, *f.*

thinness, *n.* tenuidad, delgadez, *f.*; raleza, *f.*; escasez, *f.*

thin-skinned, *adj.* de piel fina; sensible, demasiado susceptible a la crítica.

third, *n.* and *adj.* tercero, *m.*; — **degree,** (coll.) abuso de autoridad por parte de la policía para obtener información; — **person,** (gram.) tercera persona; tercero, *m.*; —**ly,** *adv.* en tercer lugar.

thirst, *n.* sed, *f.*; anhelo, *m.*; —, *vi.* tener sed, padecer sed.

thirstiness, *n.* sed, *f.*; anhelo, *m.*

thirsty, *adj.* sediento; **to be —,** tener sed.

thirteen, *n.* and *adj.* trece, *m.*

thirteenth, *n.* and *adj.* décimotercio, *m.*

thirtieth, *n.* and *adj.* treintavo, *m.*; —, *adj.* trigésimo.

thirty, *n.* and *adj.* treinta.

this, *adj.* and *pron.* este, esta; esto.

thistle, *n.* cardo silvestre, abrojo, *m.*; espina, *f.*

thither, *adv.* allá, a aquel lugar; —, *adj.* más remoto.

Thomas, Tom, Tomás.

thong, *n.* correa, correhuela, *f.*

thorax, *n.* tórax, *m.*

thorn, *n.* espino, *m.*; espina, *f.*; — **in the side,** (coll.) molestia, *f.*; —, *vt.* pinchar; proveer de espinas.

thorny, *adj.* espinoso; arduo.

thorough, *adj.* entero, cabal, perfecto; —**ly,** *adv.* enteramente, cabalmente, detenidamente.

thoroughbred, *adj.* de sangre, de casta (de caballos); —, *n.* persona bien nacida o de buena crianza, persona de sangre

azul; caballo u otro animal de casta.

thoroughfare, *n.* paso, tránsito, *m.*; vía pública, vía principal; **no —,** se prohibe el paso.

thoroughgoing, *adj.* completo, entero, hasta el final.

thoroughness, *n.* entereza, *f.*

Thos. Thomas, Tomás.

those, *adj.* and *pron.pl.* de **that,** aquellos, aquellas.

thou, *pron.* tú; —, *vt.* tutear.

though, *conj.* aunque, no obstante; como que, como sí; —, *adv.* (coll.) sin embargo, no obstante.

thought, *n.* pensamiento, juicio, *m.*; opinión, *f.*; cuidado, *m.*; concepto, *m.*; **to give —,** pensar en; —, pretérito y *p. p.* del verbo **think.**

thoughtful, *adj.* pensativo, meditabundo; pensado; —**ly,** *adv.* de un modo muy pensativo.

thoughtfulness, *n.* meditación profunda; atención, consideración, *f.*

thoughtless, *adj.* inconsiderado, descuidado; insensato; —**ly,** *adv.* descuidadamente, sin reflexión.

thousand, *n.* mil, *m.*; millar, *m.*; **per —** por mil; —, *adj.* mil.

thousandfold, *adj.* and *adv.* mil veces más.

thousandth, *n.* and *adj.* milésimo, *m.*

thrall, *n.* esclavo, va.

thralldom, thraldom, *n.* esclavitud, *f.*

thrash, *vt.* golpear; batir; sacudir; trillar (grano).

thrasher, *n.* trillador, *m.*

thrashing, *n.* desgranamiento, *m.*

thread, *n.* hilo, *m.*; fibra, *f.*; —, *vt.* enhebrar; atravesar.

threadbare, *adj.* raído, muy usado.

threat, *n.* amenaza, *f.*

threaten, *vt.* amenazar.

threatening, *n.* amenaza, *f.*; —, *adj.* amenazador; —**ly,** *adv.* con amenazas.

three, *n.* and *adj.* tres, *m.*

threefold, *adj.* tríplice, triplo. triple.

three-legged, *adj.* de tres pies; — **stool,** tajuela, *f.*

three-ply, *adj.* triple.

threescore, *n.* and *adj.* tres veintenas.

threnody, *n.* canto fúnebre.

thresh, *vt.* trillar; desgranar; golpear, batir; sacudir.

thresher, *n.* trillador, *m.*

threshing, *adj.* trillador; — **machine,** trilladora, *f.*, máquina trilladora, trillo, *m.*

threshold, *n.* umbral, *m.*; entrada, *f.*

threw, pretérito del verbo **throw.**

thrice, *adv.* tres veces.

thrift, *n.* economía, frugalidad, *f.*; —**ily,** *adv.* frugalmente.

thriftiness, *n.* frugalidad, parsimonia, *f.*

thriftless, *adj.* manirroto, pródigo.

thrifty, *adj.* frugal, económico; próspero; vigoroso.

thrill, *vt.* emocionar; —, *vi.* estremecerse;

—, *n.* estremecimiento, *m.*, emoción, *f.*
thrilling, *adj.* excitante; emocionante; conmovedor.
thrive, *vi.* prosperar, adelantar, aprovechar.
thriving, *adj.* próspero; **—ly,** *adv.* prósperamente.
throat, *n.* garganta, *f.*, cuello, *m.*; **sore —,** carraspera, *f.*
throatband, *n.* ahogadero, *m.*
throb, *vi.* palpitar; vibrar; **—,** *n.* palpitación, *f.*; latido, *m.*
throe, *n.* agonía, *f.*; dolores de parto; **—s,** agonía, *f.*
thrombosis, *n.* (med.) trombosis, *f.*
throne, *n.* trono, *m.*; **—,** *vt.* entronizar.
throng, *n.* muchedumbre, *f.*, tropel de gente; **—,** *vt.* atestar; **—,** *vi.* apiñarse.
throttle, *n.* gaznate, garguero, *m.*; regulador, *m.*; **— of an engine,** estrangulador, *m.*; **—,** *vt.* ahogar; estrangular.
through, *prep.* a través, por medio de; por conducto de; **—,** *adj.* continuo; **—,** *adv.* del principio al fin, de extremo a extremo; completamente; **— and —,** de un lado a otro, por completo.
throughout, *prep.* por todos lados; **—,** *adv.* en todas partes.
throw, *vt.* echar, arrojar, tirar, lanzar; botar; **to — down,** derribar; **to — into gear,** engranar; **to — out of gear,** desengranar; **—,** *n.* tiro, *m.*, tirada, *f.*; golpe, *m.*
throwback, *n.* atavismo, *m.*
thrown, *p. p.* del verbo **throw.**
thrum, *vt.* rascar las cuerdas de un instrumento; teclear; **—,** *n.* hilo basto; orla, *f.*
thrush, *n.* (orn.) tordo, *m.*
thrust, *vt.* empujar, impeler; estrechar; **—,** *vi.* entremeterse, introducirse; **to — aside,** rechazar; **to — in,** hincar; **—,** *n.* estocada, *f.*; puñalada, *f.*; lanzada, *f.*; bote, *m.*; derrumbe, *m.*
thud, *n.* sonido sordo; **—,** *vi.* hacer un sonido sordo.
thug, *n.* fanático asesino; bribón, *m.*
thumb, *n.* pulgar, *m.*; **— notches,** muescas para el dedo pulgar (como índice de libros, etc.); **—,** *vt.* manosear con poca destreza; emporcar con los dedos; **to — a ride,** (coll.) solicitar ser llevado en un automóvil que pasa señalando con el pulgar la deseada dirección.
thumbnail, *n.* uña del pulgar; **—,** *adj.* en miniatura.
thumbscrew, *n.* tornillo de mano; empulgueras, *f. pl.*
thumbstall, *n.* dedal, *m.*
thumbtack, *n.* chinche, *m.* y *f.*, especie de tachuela.
thump, *n.* porrazo, golpe, *m.*; **—,** *vt.* and *vi.* aporrear, apuñear.
thunder, *n.* trueno, *m.*; estrépito, *m.*; **—,** *vt.* and *vi.* tronar; atronar; fulminar.
thunderbolt, *n.* rayo, *m.*, centella, *f.*
thunderclap, *n.* tempestad de truenos, tronada, *f.*

thundercloud, *n.* nube cargada de electricidad.
thunderhead, *n.* conjunto de cúmulos que suelen preceder a la tempestad.
thundering, *adj.* atronador, fulminante.
thundershower, *n.* tormenta, *f.*
thunderstorm, *n.* temporal, *m.*, tormenta, tronada, *f.*
thunderstruck, *adj.* atónito, estupefacto.
Thur. or Thurs. Thursday, juev. jueves.
Thursday, *n.* jueves, *m.*
thus, *adv.* así, de este modo.
thuya, *n.* (bot.) tuya, *f.*
thwack, *vt.* aporrear, apuñear; golpear; **—,** *n.* porrazo, *m.*; golpe, *m.*
thwart, *vt.* frustrar, desbaratar; **—,** *n.* (naut.) banco de remero.
thy, *pron.* tu, tus.
thyme, *n.* (bot.) tomillo, *m.*
thymus, *n.* (anat.) timo, *m.*
thyroid, *n.* (anat.) tiroides, *m.*; **—,** *adj.* tiroideo.
thyroxine, *n.* (med.) remedio para paperas, obesidad y cretinismo.
thyrsus, *n.* tirso, *m.*
thyself, *pron.* ti mismo.
tiara, *n.* tiara, *f.*
tibia, *n.* (anat.) tibia, *f.*
tic, *n.* movimiento espasmódico local y habitual de ciertos músculos; contracción nerviosa de la cara.
tick, *n.* garrapata, *f.*; (coll.) sonido de tictac; (coll.) crédito, *m.*, cuenta abierta; **—,** *vi.* hacer sonido de tictac; **—,** *vt.* marcar en lista.
ticker, *n.* receptor telegráfico de cotizaciones y noticias de bolsa de comercio; lo que produce tictac; (coll.) reloj de bolsillo.
ticket, *n.* boleto, *m.*, boleta, *f.*; cédula, *f.*; (rail.) billete, *m.*, localidad, *f.*; **round-trip —,** billete de ida y vuelta; **season —,** billete de abono; **— collector,** (rail.) expendedor de billetes; **— office,** (rail.) despacho, *m.*, taquilla, *f.*; **— scalper,** revendedor, *m.*; **— seller,** taquillero, ra; **— window,** taquilla, *f.*; **—,** *vt.* marcar.
ticking, *n.* terliz, cotí, cutí *m.*; tictac, *m.*
tickle, *vt.* hacer cosquillas a alguno; cosquillear; **—,** *vi.* tener cosquillas; **—,** *n.* cosquilla, *f.*
tickling, *n.* cosquillas, *f. pl.*
ticklish, *adj.* cosquilloso.
ticklishness, *n.* propiedad de ser cosquilloso.
ticktock, *n.* tictac, *m.*
tidal, *adj.* (naut.) de la marea; **— wave,** marejada, *f.*
tidbit, *n.* = **titbit.**
tiddlywinks, *n. pl.* juego con discos de colores que se echan en una taza.
tide, *n.* tiempo, *m.*; estación, *f.*; marea, *f.*; **high —,** marea alta, pleamar, *f.*; **—,** *vt.* llevar.
tidewater, *n.* agua de marea; litoral, *m.*; **—,** *adj.* a lo largo del litoral.

tideway, *n.* canal en que corre la marea; la corriente en canal de marea.

tidily, *adv.* con orden, con aseo, con pulcritud.

tidiness, *n.* aseo, *m.*

tidings, *n. pl.* noticias, *f. pl.*

tidy, *adj.* airoso, aseado, pulcro; diestro.

tie, *vt.* anudar, atar; enlazar; —, *n.* nudo, *m.*; corbata, *f.*; lazo, *m.*; (mus.) ligadura, *f.*; (rail.) traviesa, *f.*; — **beam,** tirante, *m.*

tier, *n.* fila, hilera, *f.*; (theat.) hilera de palcos.

tie-up, *n.* (coll.) suspensión de tráfico o de trabajo, interrupción de trabajo.

tiff, *n.* pique, disgusto, *m.*; —, *vi.* picarse.

tiger, *n.* tigre, *m.*; lacayo, *m.*; — **lily,** (bot.) tigridia, *f.*; — **moth,** variedad grande de polilla.

tight, *adj.* tirante, tieso, tenso, estrecho; apretado; escaso; (coll.) tacaño; — **squeeze,** apuro, *m.*; —**ly,** *adv.* estrechamente; severamente.

tighten, *vt.* tirar, estirar; apretar.

tight-lipped, *adj.* callado, reservado.

tightness, *n.* tensión, tirantez, *f.*

tightrope, *n.* cuerda tiesa; cuerda de volatinero.

tights, *n. pl.* calzas entalladas; trajes ajustados que usan los acróbatas.

tigress, *n.* tigre hembra.

tilde, *n.* tilde o marca que se pone sobre la letra ñ y algunas abreviaturas; censura, *f.*, pequeña crítica.

tile, *n.* teja, *f.*; losa, *f.*, azulejo, *m.*; —, *vt.* tejar.

tiling, *n.* tejado, *m.*; azulejos, *m. pl.*

till, *prep.* and *conj.* hasta que, hasta; — **now,** hasta ahora; —, *n.* cajón, *m.*; gaveta, *f.*; —, *vt.* cultivar, labrar, laborar.

tillable, *adj.* labrantío.

tillage, *n.* labranza, *f.*

tiller, *n.* agricultor, ra; (naut.) caña del timón; — **rope,** guardín, *m.*

tilt, *n.* declive, *m.*, inclinación, *f.*; cubierta, *f.*; justa, *f.*; —, *vt.* inclinar, empinar; apuntar la lanza; —, *vi.* justar.

tilth, *n.* labranza, *f.*

Tim. Timothy, Timoteo.

timbal, *n.* (mus.) timbal, tímpano, *m.*

timber, *n.* madera, *f.*; **beam of —,** madero, *m.*; **building —,** madera de construcciones; — **line,** límite del bosque maderable; — **wolf,** lobo gris; —, *vt.* enmaderar.

timbered, *adj.* enmaderado.

timberland, *n.* terreno maderable.

timberwork, *n.* maderamen, maderaje, *m.*

timbre, *n.* timbre, tono, *m.*

timbrel, *n.* pandero, *m.*; tamboril, *m.*

time, *n.* tiempo, *m.*; (mus.) compás, *m.*; edad, época, *f.*; hora, *f.*; vez, *f.*; **at any —,** cuando quiera; **a long — ago,** hace mucho tiempo; **at the proper —,** a su tiempo; **at the same —,** a un tiempo, a la vez; **at the same — that,** a medida que; **at this —,** al presente; **at —s,** a tiempos; **behind —,** atrasado; **from — to —,** de cuando en cuando; **in olden —s,** antiguamente; **in —,** a tiempo, de perilla; **on —,** en tiempo, a plazo; — **signature** signo para indicar el compás musical; **some — ago,** tiempo atrás; **spare —,** tiempo desocupado; — **ball,** (naut.) horario eléctrico; — **clock,** reloj que indica las horas de entrada y salida de los obreros; — **exposure,** exposición de tiempo; **to mark —,** marcar el paso; **to take —,** tomarse tiempo; — **bomb,** bomba de explosión demorada; —, *vt.* medir el tiempo de; hacer a tiempos regulares; escoger el tiempo.

timecard, *n.* tarjeta para marcar las horas de entrada y salida del trabajo.

timekeeper, *n.* listero, *m.*; cronómetro, *m.*

timeless, *adj.* eterno.

timeliness, *n.* oportunidad, *f.*

timely, *adv.* con tiempo; a propósito; —, *adj.* oportuno, tempestivo; a buen tiempo.

timepiece, *n.* reloj, *m.*

timer, *n.* persona o instrumento para registrar el tiempo; regulador o marcador de tiempo.

timesaver, *n.* ahorrador de tiempo.

timeserver, *n.* (fig.) veleta, *f.*; oportunista, *m.* y *f.*

timeserving, *n.* servilismo, *m.*

timetable, *n.* (rail.) horario, itinerario, *m.*

timeworn, *adj.* usado, gastado, deslustrado.

timid, *adj.* tímido, temeroso; —**ly,** *adv.* con timidez.

timidity, *adj.* timidez, pusilanimidad, *f.*

timing, *n.* regulación de tiempo.

timorous, *adj.* temeroso, timorato; —**ly,** *adv.* temerosamente.

Timothy, Timoteo.

timothy, *n.* especie de hierba gruesa con espigas largas usada como heno.

timpani, *n.* tímpano, *m.*; (mus.) timbales, *m. pl.*

tin, *n.* estaño, *m.*; hojalata, *f.*; — **can,** lata, *f.*; — **foil,** hoja de estaño; — **plate,** hoja de lata, hojalata, *f.*; —, *vt.* estañar; cubrir con hojalata.

tincture, *n.* tintura, *f.*; tinta, *f.*; —, *vt.* teñir, tinturar.

tinder, *n.* yesca, *f.*; — **maker,** yesquero, *m.*

tinderbox, *n.* yesquero, *m.*

tine, *n.* diente o punta (de un tenedor, una horquilla, etc.).

tinge, *n.* tinte, *m.*; traza, *f.*; —, *vt.* tinturar, teñir.

tingle, *vi.* zumbar los oídos; latir, punzar; —, *n.* retintín, *m.*; picazón, *m.*

tinker, *n.* latonero, *m.*; calderero, remendón, *m.*; —, *vt.* remendar; desabollar.

tinkle, *vt.* and *vi.* cencerrear; zumbar los oídos; —, *vi.* tintinear; retiñir; —, *n.* retintín, *m.*

tinkling, *n.* retintín, *m.*

tinman, *n.* = **tinsmith.**

tinned, *adj.* en lata, estañado.

tinner, *n.* minero de estaño; hojalatero, *m.*

tinsel, *n.* brocadillo, *m.*; oropel, *m.*; —, *vt.* adornar con oropel.

tinsmith, *n.* hojalatero, *m.*

tint, *n.* tinta, *f.*; tinte, *m.*; —, *vt.* teñir, colorar.

tintype, *n.* ferrotipo, *m.*

tinware, *n.* cosas de hojalata.

tiny, *adj.* pequeño, chico.

tip, *n.* punta, extremidad, *f.*; cabo, *m.*; gratificación, propina, *f.*; información oportuna; —, *vt.* herretear; golpear ligeramente; dar propina; inclinar, ladear; volcar.

tippet, *n.* palatina, *f.*

tipple, *vi.* beber con exceso; —, *n.* bebida (alcohólica), *f.*, licor, *m.*

tippler, *n.* borrachón, *m.*

tipsily, *adv.* instablemente; como borracho.

tipsiness, *n.* embriaguez, *f.*

tipsy, *adj.* borrachuelo, algo borracho; instable.

tiptoe, *n.* punta del pie; **on —,** de puntillas.

tiptop, *n.* cumbre, *f.*; —, *adj.* (coll.) excelente, de la más alta calidad.

tirade, *n.* invectiva, diatriba, *f.*

tire, *n.* llanta, goma, *f.*, neumático, *m.*; **balloon —,** neumático balón, llanta balón; **change of —,** repuesto, *m.*; **flat —,** pinchazo, *m.*, llanta desinflada; **spare —,** goma o llanta de repuesto; **— cover,** cubrellanta, *m.*; **— gauge,** medidor de presión en los neumáticos; —, *vt.* cansar, fatigar; proveer con una llanta; —, *vi.* cansarse, fastidiarse; rendirse.

tired, *adj.* fatigado, cansado; rendido.

tiredness, *n.* cansancio, *m.*

tireless, *adj.* incansable.

tiresome, *adj.* tedioso; molesto.

tiresomeness, *n.* tedio, fastidio, *m.*

T iron, *n.* hierro en T.

tissue, *n.* tisú, *m.*; (anat.) tejido, *m.*; **— paper,** papel de seda; —, *vt.* entretejer.

tit, *n.* jaca, haca, *f.*; (orn.) paro, *m.*; **— for tat,** dando y dando.

titanic, *adj.* titánico.

titbit, *n.* bocado delicado.

tithe, *n.* diezmo, *m.*; —, *vi.* diezmar.

titillate, *vt.* and *vi.* titilar.

titillation, *n.* titilación, *f.*

title, *n.* título, *m.*; **— deed,** derecho de propiedad; **— page,** portada, carátula, *f.*; frontispicio (de un libro), *m.*; **— role,** papel principal; **to obtain a —,** titular; —, *vt.* titular, intitular.

titmouse, *n.* (orn.) paro, *m.*

titration, *n.* dosificación, *f.*, método o proceso para determinar la fuerza de una solución.

titter, *vi.* reírse disimuladamente; —, *n.* risilla disimulada.

tittle, *n.* tilde, *m.*; mínima, *f.*

tittle-tattle, *n.* charla, murmuración, *f.*; —, *vi.* charlar, murmurar.

titular, *n.* and *adj.* titular, *m.*

Titus, Tito.

T joint, *n.* (rail.) enchufe de bifurcación.

tn. ton, t. tonelada.

T N T, T.N.T. trinitrotolueno, trinitrotolueno, *m.*, trilita, *f.*

to, *prep.* a, para; por; de; hasta; en; con; que; —, (delante de un verbo indica sólo el infinitivo y no se traduce); —, *adv.* hacia determinado objeto; **he came —,** volvió en sí.

toad, *n.* sapo, escuerzo, *m.*

toadstool, *n.* (bot.) especie de hongo venenoso.

toady, *n.* adulador, ra; **—ish,** *adj.* adulador; —, *vi.* and *vt.* adular; ser aludador.

to-and-fro, *adj.* and *adv.* de acá para allá; de un lado a otro.

toast, *vt.* tostar; brindar; —, *n.* tostada, *f.*, pan tostado; brindis, *m.*; **burnt —,** (coll.) churrusco, *m.*

toasted, *adj.* tostado.

toaster, *n.* parrilla, *f.*, tostador, *m.*

toasting, *n.* tostadura, torrefacción, *f.*

toastmaster, *n.* maestro de ceremonias.

tobacco, *n.* tabaco, *m.*; **cut —,** picadura, *f.*; **— box,** tabaquera, *f.*; **— pouch,** bolsa para tabaco.

tobacconist, *n.* tabaquero, *m.*

toboggan, *n.* tobogán, *m.*, trineo para deslizarse; —, *vi.* deslizarse en tobogán.

tocsin, *n.* campana de rebato, toque de alarma.

today, to-day, *n.* and *adv.* hoy, *m.*; **a week from —,** en ocho días, de hoy en ocho días.

toddle, *vi.* andar con pasillos inciertos; tambalearse.

toddler, *n.* el que da pasillos inciertos; niño de uno a tres años de edad.

toddy, *n.* grog, *m.*, especie de bebida fermentada.

to-do, *n.* (coll.) alboroto, *m.*

toe, *n.* dedo del pie; punta del calzado; —, *vt.* tocar con los dedos del pie; **to — the line,** comportarse bien, hacer lo que se le manda al pie de la letra.

toenail, *n.* uña del dedo del pie.

tog, *n.* (coll.) vestido, *m.*; **—s,** ropa, *f.*; —, *vt.* (coll.) vestir en ropa especial.

toga, *n.* toga, *f.*

together, *adv.* juntamente, en compañía de otro; al mismo tiempo; **to get —,** unirse, juntarse.

toggery, *n.* fruslería, *f.*; ropería. *f.*

toil, *vi.* fatigarse, trabajar mucho; afanarse; —, *n.* trabajo, *m.*; fatiga, *f.*; afán, *m.*

toilet, *n.* tocado, *m.*; tocador, *m.*; excusado, retrete, *m.*; **— articles,** artículos de tocador; **— paper,** papel de excusado; **— water,** agua de tocador.

toilsome, *adj.* trabajoso; fatigoso.

Tokay, *n.* vino de Tokay; uvas de Tokay.

token, *n.* señal, *f.*; memoria, *f.*; recuerdo, *m.*; prueba, *f.*; **— payment,** (com.) pago parcial como reconocimiento de un adeudo.

Tokyo, Tokio, *m.*

told, pretérito del verbo **tell.**

tolerable, *adj.* tolerable; mediocre; **—ly,** *adv.* tolerablemente, así así.

tolerance, *n.* tolerancia, *f.*

tolerant, *adj.* tolerante.

tolerate, *vt.* tolerar.

toleration, *n.* tolerancia, *f.*

toll, *n.* peaje, portazgo, *m.*; tañido lento de las campanas; **— bridge,** puente de peaje; **— call,** llamada telefónica de larga distancia; **—,** *vt.* tocar una campana; colectar peajes; **—,** *vi.* sonar las campanas.

toller, *n.* campanero, *m.*

tollgate, *n.* barrera de portazgo.

tolling, *n.* campaneo, *m.*; **— of bells,** repique o tañido de las campanas.

tollman, *n.* portazguero, *m.*

toluene, *n.* tolueno, *m.*

tomahawk, *n.* hacha de armas de los indios americanos; **—,** *vt.* golpear con una hacha de los indios.

tomato, *n.* tomate, *m.*; **— sauce,** salsa de tomate.

tomb, *n.* tumba, *f.*; sepulcro, *m.*; **—,** *vt.* poner en tumba.

tomboy, *n.* doncella pizpireta y respingona; (coll.) marimacho, *m.*

tombstone, *n.* piedra sepulcral, lápida sepulcral.

tomcat, *n.* gato, *m.*

tome, *n.* tomo, *m.*

tomfoolery, *n.* tontería, payasada, *f.*, frioleras, *f. pl.*

tommy gun, *n.* ametralladora pequeña.

tomorrow, *n.* and *adv.* mañana, *f.*; **day after —,** pasado mañana; **— morning,** mañana por la mañana.

tomtit, *n.* (orn.) paro, *m.*

tom-tom, *n.* tambor de origen oriental; tam-tam, *m.*

ton, *n.* tonelada, *f.*

tonal, *adj.* tonal.

tone, *n.* tono, *m.*; tono de la voz; acento, *m.*; (mus.) modalidad, *f.*; **—,** *vt.* cambiar el tono; armonizar el tono; **to — down,** suavizar; **to — up,** animar.

tonette, *n.* instrumento musical parecido al plautín.

tongs, *n. pl.* tenaza, *f.*

tongue, *n.* (anat.) lengua, *f.*; lengua, *f.*, lenguaje, *m.*; habla, *f.*; lengua de tierra; **to hold one's —,** callarse; **—,** *vi.* hablar.

tongue-tied, *adj.* con frenillo; mudo, sin habla.

tonic, *n.* (med.) tónico, reconstituyente, *m.*; (mus.) tónica, *f.*; tónico, *m.*; **—,** *adj.* tónico.

tonicity, *n.* tonicidad, *f.*

tonight, to-night, *n.* and *adv.* esta noche.

tonite, *n.* tonita, *f.*, explosivo usado en granadas.

tonnage, *n.* tonelaje, *m.*, porte de un buque.

tonneau, *n.* parte posterior de un automóvil

con asientos laterales.

tonsil, *n.* tonsila, amígdala, agalla, *f.*

tonsillectomy, *n.* amigdaltomía, tonsilotomía, *f.*, operación de las amígdalas.

tonsillitis, *n.* tonsilitis, amigdalitis, *f.*

tonsorial, *adj.* de barbería.

tonsure, *n.* tonsura, *f.*

too, *adv.* demasiado; así mismo, aun; también.

took, pretérito del verbo **take.**

tool, *n.* herramienta, *f.*; utensilio, *m.*; persona usada como instrumento; **— bag,** talega de herramientas, cartera de herramientas; **— chest,** caja de herramientas; **—s,** pertrechos, *m. pl.*; útiles, bártulos, *m. pl.*; **— room,** cuarto de herramientas; **—,** *vt.* labrar con herramientas.

toot, *vt.* and *vi.* sonar un cuerno o una bocina; **—,** *n.* sonido de cuerno o de bocina.

tooth, *n.* diente, *m.*; gusto, *m.*; (mach.) diente de rueda; **molar —,** diente molar; **to have a sweet —,** ser muy goloso; **— powder,** dentífrico, *m.*, polvo dentífrico; **—,** *vt.* dentar; encajar.

toothache, *n.* dolor de muelas.

toothbrush, *n.* cepillo de dientes.

toothdrawer, *n.* sacamuelas, *m.*

toothless, *adj.* desdentado.

toothpaste, *n.* pasta dentífrica.

toothpick, *n.* mondadientes, escarbadientes, palillo de dientes.

toothsome, *adj.* sabroso; comedero.

top, *n.* cima, cumbre, cresta, *f.*; último grado; cabeza, *f.*, capota, *f.*; trompo, peón, *m.*; (naut.) cofa, *f.*; **— hat,** sombrero de copa, sombrero de copa alta; **—,** *vt.* and *vi.* elevarse por encima; sobrepujar, exceder; descabezar los árboles.

topaz, *n.* topacio, *m.*; **yellow —,** crisolito oriental.

topcoat, *n.* sobretodo, abrigo, gabán, *m.*

toper, *n.* bebedor, borrachón, *m.*

topgallant, *n.* (naut.) juanete, *m.*; **—,** *adj.* (naut.) de juanete.

topic, *n.* tópico, particular, asunto, *m.*; principio general.

topical, *adj.* tópico.

topknot, *n.* copete, *m.*

topmast, *n.* (naut.) mastelero de gavia.

topmost, *adj.* superior, más alto.

topographer, *n.* topógrafo, *m.*

topographic, *adj.* topográfico.

topographical, *adj.* topográfico; **—ly,** *adv.* topográficamente.

topography, *n.* topografía, *f.*

topple, *vi.* volcarse.

topsail, *n.* (naut.) gavia, *f.*; **— mast,** verga de garra; **— yard,** verga de gavia.

topside, *n.* parte superior.

topsoil, *n.* suelo de superficie.

topsy-turvy, *adv.* patas arriba, desordenadamente; **—,** *adj.* de patas arriba, revuelto.

toque, *n.* cofia, *f.*

torch, *n.* antorcha, hacha, *f.*

torchbearer, *n.* hachero, *m.*

torchlight, *n.* luz de antorcha; **— procession,** procesión con antorchas.

tore, pretérito del verbo **tear.**

toreador, *n.* torero, *m.*

torment, *n.* tormento, *m.*; pena, *f.*; **—,** *vt.* atormentar.

tormentor, tormenter, *n.* atormentador, ra.

torn, *adj.* destrozado, rasgado, descosido.

tornado, *n.* tornado, huracán, *m.*

torpedo, *n.* torpedo, *m.*; (pez) tremielga, *f.*; **to fire a —,** lanzar un torpedo; **— boat,** torpedero, *m.*; **— tube,** lanzatorpedos, *m.*, tubo lanzatorpedos; **—,** *vt.* torpedear.

torpedo-boat, *adj.* de torpedero; **— destroyer,** cazatorpederos, *m.*

torpid, *adj.* entorpecido.

torpor, *n.* entorpecimiento, estupor, *m.*

torque, *n.* (mech.) fuerza de torsión.

torrent, *n.* torrente, *m.*

torrential, *adj.* torrencial.

torrid, *adj.* tórrido, ardiente; **— zone,** zona tórrida.

torsion, *n.* torsión, *f.*

torso, *n.* torso, *m.*

tortilla, *n.* tortilla, *f.*

tortoise, *n.* tortuga, *f.*; carey, *m.*; **— shell,** concha de tortuga, carey, *m.*

tortoise-shell, *adj.* de carey.

tortuous, *adj.* tortuoso, sinuoso.

torture, *n.* tortura, *f.*, suplicio, *m.*; martirio, *m.*; **—,** *vt.* atormentar, torturar, martirizar.

torturer, *n.* atormentador, ra.

Tory, *n.* tory, *m.*, miembro del partido conservador de Inglaterra; partido conservador de Inglaterra; **—,** *adj.* relativo al partido tory.

tory, *n.* conservador, ra; **—,** *adj.* conservador en extremo.

toss, *vt.* tirar, lanzar, arrojar; agitar, sacudir; **to — in a blanket,** mantear; **to — up,** lanzar algo al aire; jugar a cara o cruz; **—,** *vi.* agitarse; mecerse; **—,** *n.* sacudida, *f.*; alboroto, *m.*, conmoción, *f.*

toss-up, *n.* incertidumbre sobre el resultado; cara o cruz.

tot, *n.* niño, ña.

total, *n.* total, *m.*; **—,** *adj.* entero, completo; **— war,** la guerra total; **— loss,** pérdida total; **— weight,** peso total; **—ly,** *adv.* totalmente.

totalitarian, *adj.* totalitario.

totality, *n.* totalidad, *f.*

totalizator, *n.* instrumento para registrar apuestas en las carreras de caballo.

totalize, *vt.* totalizar.

totem, *n.* tótem, *m.*, objeto o animal que representa una tribu de indios de Norte América; **— pole,** palo totémico.

totter, *vi.* bambolear; tambalear, vacilar, titubear.

tottering, *adj.* vacilante, titubeante; **—ly,** *adv.* en forma tambaleante.

touch, *vt.* tocar, palpar; emocionar, conmover; **—,** *vi.* aproximarse a; **— and go,** tratar de un asunto a la ligera; (naut.) tocar el fondo.

touchable, *adj.* tangible.

touch-and-go, *adj.* precario, incierto, arriesgado.

touchback, *n.* (football) posesión de la pelota detrás de la propia meta.

touchdown, *n.* (football) acción del jugador al poner el fútbol detrás del **goal** del contrario.

touchhole, *n.* fogón, *m.*

touching, *adj.* patético, conmovedor; tocante; **—,** *prep.* por lo que toca a; **—ly,** *adv.* patéticamente, conmovedoramente.

touch-me-not, *n.* (bot.) mercurial, *f.*, (coll.) mírame y no me toques.

touchstone, *n.* piedra de toque; ensayo, *m.*, prueba, *f.*

touchwood, *n.* yesca, *f.*

touchy, *adj.* cosquilloso, vidrioso; sensitivo.

tough, *adj.* tosco; correoso; tieso; vicioso; fuerte, vigoroso; **—ly,** *adv.* tiesamente; toscamente; **—,** *n.* (coll.) alborotador.

toughen, *vi.* hacerse correoso; endurecerse; **—,** *vt.* hacer tosco; hacer correoso; endurecer.

toughness, *n.* tenacidad, *f.*; viscosidad, *f.*; tesura, *f.*; endurecimiento, *m.*

toupee, *n.* tupé, *m.*

tour, *n.* viaje, *m.*, peregrinación, *f.*; vuelta, *f.*; **—,** *vt.* viajar.

touring, *n.* turismo, *m.*; **— agency,** agencia de turismo; **— car,** automóvil de turismo, coche de turismo; **— map,** mapa de turismo.

tourism, *n.* turismo, *m.*

tourist, *n.* turista, *m.* y *f.*; viajero, ra.

tourmaline, *n.* turmalina, *f.*

tournament, *n.* torneo, combate, concurso, *m.*

tourniquet, *n.* torniquete, *m.*

tousle, *vt.* desordenar, desgreñar; despeinar.

tout, *n.* espía, acechador, *m.*; **—,** *vt.* (coll.) solicitar clientes; espiar en las carreras de caballos.

tow, *n.* estopa, *f.*; remolque, *m.*; **—,** *vt.* (naut.) remolcar.

towage, *n.* (naut.) remolque, atoaje, *m.*

toward, towards, *prep.* hacia, con dirección a; cerca de, con respecto a.

towboat, *n.* remolcador, *m.*

towel, *n.* toalla, *f.*; **roller —,** toalla sin fin.

tower, *n.* torre, *f.*; ciudadela, *f.*; **fortified —,** torreón, *m.*; **—,** *vi.* remontarse; elevarse a una altura.

towhead, *n.* cabellera suave y blanca; persona con cabello suave y blanco.

towline, *n.* cable, *m.*, soga o cadena de remolque.

town, *n.* ciudad, *f.*; pueblo, *m.*, población, *f.*; villa, *f.*; **home —,** ciudad natal; **— council,** ayuntamiento, cabildo, *m.*;

— **crier,** pregonero, voceador, *m.*; — **hall,** — **house,** casa de ayuntamiento, casa consistorial, comuna, *f.*; — **planning,** urbanismo, *m.*

townsfolk, *n. pl.* gente de la ciudad.

township, *n.* ayuntamiento, *m.*

townsman, *n.* conciudadano, *m.*

towplane, *n.* (aer.) aeroplano de remolque.

toxemia, *n.* toxemia, *f.*

toxic, *adj.* tóxico.

toxin, *n.* toxina, *f.*, veneno, *m.*

toy, *n.* juguete, *m.*; chuchería, *f.*; miriñaque, *m.*; —, *vi.* jugar, divertirse.

tp. township, municipalidad.

tr.: transitive, tr. transitivo; **transpose,** transponer; **treasurer,** tesorero.

trace, *n.* huella, pisada, *f.*; vestigio, *m.*, señal, *f.*; —, *vt.* delinear, trazar; seguir la pista.

traceable, *adj.* que se puede trazar.

tracer, *n.* cédula de investigación; trazador, *m.*

trachea, *n.* (med.) traquearteria, *f.*

trachoma, *n.* (med.) tracoma, *f.*

tracing, *n.* calco, *m.*; trazo, *m.*

track, *n.* vestigio, *m.*; huella, pista, *f.*; rodada, *f.*; **race** —, hipódromo, *m.*; — **of a wheel,** carrilera, *f.*; —, *vt.* rastrear.

trackless, *adj.* sin huella.

tract, *n.* trecho, *m.*; región, comarca, *f.*; serie, *f.*; tratado, *m.*

tractable, *adj.* tratable, manejable.

traction, *n.* acarreamiento, *m.*, tracción, *f.*; — **engine,** máquina de tracción, máquina de arrastre.

tractor, *n.* tractor, *m.*

trade, *n.* comercio, tráfico, *m.*; negocio, trato, *m.*, contratación, *f.*; **board of** —, junta de comercio; — **directory,** anuario comercial; — **name,** nombre de fábrica; — **price,** precio para el comerciante; — **school,** escuela de artes y oficios; — **union,** asociación de los artesanos, gremio, *m.*; — **winds,** vientos alisios; —, *vi.* comerciar, traficar, negociar.

trade-in, *n.* objeto dado como pago o pago parcial en la compra de otro.

trade-last, *n.* elogio que se hace esperando reciprocidad.

trade-mark, *n.* marca de fábrica.

trader, *n.* comerciante, traficante, *m.*; navío mercante.

tradesman, *n.* tendero, mercader, *m.*; artesano, *m.*

tradesmen, *n. pl.* de **tradesman,** comerciantes, *m. pl.*; artesanos, *m. pl.*

tradespeople, *n. pl.* comerciantes, *m.* y *f. pl.*

trade-unionism, *n.* sistema de gremios obreros.

trading, *n.* comercio, *m.*; — **post,** factoría, *f.*; —, *adj.* comercial.

tradition, *n.* tradición, *f.*

traditional, *adj.* tradicional; —**ly,** *adv.* por tradición, tradicionalmente.

traduce, *vt.* vituperar; calumniar; acusar; propagar.

traducer, *n.* calumniador, ra.

traffic, *n.* tráfico, *m.*, circulación, *f.*; mercaderías, *f. pl.*; tránsito, *m.*; transporte, *m.*; **heavy** —, tránsito intenso; **light** —, tránsito ligero; — **lane,** zona de tránsito; — **light,** farol de tránsito; — **sign,** señal de tránsito; —, *vi.* traficar, comerciar.

trafficker, *n.* traficante, comerciante, mercader, *m.*

tragedian, *n.* actor trágico; autor de tragedias.

tragedienne, *n.* actriz trágica.

tragedy, *n.* tragedia, *f.*

tragic, *adj.* trágico.

tragical, *adj.* trágico; —**ly,** *adv.* trágicamente.

tragicomedy, *n.* tragicomedia, *f.*

tragicomical, *adj.* tragicómico.

trail, *vt.* and *vi.* rastrear; arrastrar; —, *n.* rastro, *m.*; pisada, *f.*; vereda, trocha, *f.*; sendero, *m.*; — **blazer,** abrebrechas, *m.* y *f.*

trailer, *n.* remolque, *m.*, carro de remolque; persona que sigue una pista o un rastro; el que sigue.

trailing, *adj.* rastrero; — **arbutus,** (bot.) gayuba, *f.*

train, *vt.* arrastrar, amaestrar, enseñar, criar, adiestrar; disciplinar; entrenar; —, *n.* (rail.) tren, *m.*; séquito, tren, *m.*; serie, *f.*; cola (de vestido), *f.*; **pack** —, recua, *f.*; — **conductor,** motorista, cobrador, *m.*; — **oil,** aceite de ballena.

trainband, *n.* milicia, *f.*

trainer, *n.* enseñador, *m.*; entrenador, *m.*

training, *n.* educación, disciplina, *f.*; entrenamiento, *m.*; —, *adj.* de instrucción.

trainload, *n.* carga de un tren.

trainman, *n.* hombre empleado en un tren.

trait, *n.* rasgo de carácter; toque, *m.*

traitor, *n.* traidor, *m.*

traitorous, *adv.* pérfido, traidor; —**ly,** *adv.* traidoramente.

traitress, *n.* traidora, *f.*

trajectory, *n.* trayectoria, *f.*

tram, tramcar, *n.* (Inglaterra) tranvía, *m.*

trammel, *n.* trasmallo, *m.*; obstáculo, *m.*; garabato, *m.*; —, *vt.* coger, interceptar; impedir.

tramp, *n.* sonido de pasos pesados; paso fuerte; caminata, *f.*; vagabundo, *m.*; bigardo, *m.*; — **steamer,** vapor que toma carga donde y cuando puede; —, *vi.* vagabundear; —, *vt.* patear.

trample, *vi.* pisar muy fuerte, hollar; —, *n.* pisoteo, *m.*; sonido de pisoteo.

tramway, *n.* tranvía, *m.*

trance, *n.* rapto, *m.*; éxtasis, *m.*; estado hipnótico.

tranquil, *adj.* tranquilo; —**ly,** *adv.* tranquilamente.

tranquilize, *vt.* tranquilizar.

tranquillity, *n.* tranquilidad, paz, calma, *f.*

trans.: transitive, tr. transitivo; **translated,** traducido; **transportation,** trasporte.

transact, vt. negociar, transigir.

transaction, n. transacción, f.; negociación, f.; tramitación, f.

transactor, n. negociador, m.

transalpine, adj. transalpino.

transatlantic, adj. transatlántico, trasatlántico; **— airship,** aeronave trasatlántica; **— liner,** vapor trasatlántico.

transcend, vt. trascender, pasar; exceder.

transcendency, n. trascendencia, f.

transcendent, adj. trascendente; sobresaliente; **—ly,** adv. admirablemente.

transcendental, adj. trascendental; sobresaliente.

transcontinental, adj. trascontinental.

transcribe, vt. transcribir, copiar, trasladar; (rad.) perifonear lo grabado en un disco fonográfico.

transcript, n. trasunto, traslado, m.

transcription, n. traslado, m.; copia, f.

transect, vt. cortar transversalmente.

transept, n. nave transversal de una iglesia.

transfer, vt. transferir, trasferir, transportar, transbordar, trasladar, transponer; **—,** n. cesión, transferencia, f., traspaso, m.; traslado, m.

transferable, adj. transferible.

transference, n. transferencia, f.

transfiguration, n. transfiguración, f.

transfigure, vt. trasformar, transfigurar.

transfix, vt. traspasar.

transform, vt. trasformar; **—,** vi. trasformarse.

transformable, adj. transformable.

transformation, n. trasformación, f.

transformer, n. trasformador, m.

transfuse, vt. trasfundir.

transfusion, n. transfusión, f.

transgress, vt. and vi. transgredir, violar.

transgression, n. transgresión, f.

transgressor, n. transgresor, ra.

transient, adj. pasajero, transitorio; **—,** n. transeúnte, m. y f.; **—ly,** adv. de un modo transitorio.

transit, n. tránsito, m.; trámite, m.; **—,** vi. pasar por.

transition, n. transición, f.; tránsito, m.

transitional, adj. que se transfiere de uno a otro.

transitive, adj. transitivo; **—,** n. verbo transitivo.

transitory, adj. transitorio; **—ily,** adv. transitoriamente.

translate, vt. trasladar, traducir, verter; interpretar.

translation, n. traducción, f.; interpretación, f.; acción de traducir

translator, n. traductor, ra.

translucency, n. traslucimiento, m.

translucent, adj. trasluciente, diáfano.

transmarine, adj. trasmarino.

transmigrate, vi. transmigrar

transmigration, n. transmigración, f.

transmission, n. transmisión, f.; **— belt** correa de transmisión; **— gearbox,** caja de velocidades.

transmit, vt. trasmitir.

transmitter, n. trasmisor, m.

transmutable, adj. trasmutable.

transmutation, n. trasmutación, f.

transmute, vt. trasmutar.

transoceanic, adj. transoceánico.

transom, n. travesaño, m.

transpacific, adj. transpacífico.

transparency, n. trasparencia, f.

transparent, adj. trasparente, diáfano.

transpiration, n. traspiración, f.

transpire, vt. traspirar, exhalar; **—,** vi. (coll.) acontecer.

transplant, vt. trasplantar.

transplantation, n. trasplantación, f., trasplante, m.

transport, vt. transportar; deportar; llevar; transponer; **—,** n. transportación, f.; rapto, m.; (naut.) transporte, m.; criminal condenado a la deportación; **— company,** empresa porteadora, compañía de transportes.

transportable, adj. transportable.

transportation, n. transportación, f., transportamiento, transporte, acarreo, m.

transporter, n. transportador, m.

transporting, adj. de transporte, transportador.

transposal, n. = **transposition.**

transpose, vt. transponer; (mus.) transportar.

transposition, n. transposición, traspuesta, f.

transubstantiate, vt. transubstanciar.

transubstantiation, n. transubstanciación, f.

transversal, n. and adj. transversal, m. y f.

transverse, adj. transverso, travesero; **—ly,** adv. transversalmente.

trap, n. trampa, f.; garlito, lazo, m.; especie de carruaje; **— door,** puerta disimulada; escotillón, m.; **—,** vt. hacer caer en la trampa; atrapar.

trapeze, n. trapecio, m.

trapezist, n. acróbata en el trapecio.

trapezoid, n. trapecio, m.

trapper, n. cazador de animales de piel.

trappings, n. pl. jaeces, m. pl.

trappist, n. and adj. trapense, m.

traps, n. pl. címbalos, m. pl.

trapshooter, n. tirador al vuelo o a blancos movibles.

trash, n. heces, f. pl., desecho, m.; zupia, patarata, f.; cachivache, cacharro, m.; basura, f.

trashy, adj. vil, despreciable, de ningún valor.

trauma, n. (med.) traumatismo, m., lesión, f.

traumatic, adj. traumático.

travail, n. trabajo, m.; dolores de parto; **—,** vi. trabajar; estar de parto.

travel, *vt.* and *vi.* viajar; **to — over**, recorrer; **—**, *n.* viaje, *m.*; carrera, *f.*
traveler, **traveller**, *n.* viajante, *m.* y *f.*, viajero, ra.
traveling, *adj.* de viaje; **— companion**, compañero de viaje; **— salesman**, agente viajero, viajante, *m.*; **— expenses**, viáticos, *m. pl.*
travelogue, *n.* conferencia ilustrada sobre viajes.
traversable, *adj.* atravesable.
traverse, *vt.* atravesar, cruzar; recorrer; examinar con cuidado; **—**, *vi.* atravesarse; recorrer; **—**, *adj.* poligonal, transversal; **—**, *n.* traviesa, *f.*; travesaño, *m.*; (law) negación, *f.*
travesty, *n.* parodia, *f.*; **—**, *vt.* disfrazar.
trawl, *vi.* pescar con red rastrera; **—**, *n.* red larga para rastrear.
trawler, *m.* embarcación para pescar o dragar a la rastra; persona que pesca o draga a la rastra.
trawling, *n.* rastreo, *m.*
tray, *n.* salvilla, *f.*; batea, *f.*; artesa, *f.*; bandeja, *f.*
treacherous, *adj.* traidor, pérfido; **—ly**, *adv.* traidoramente.
treachery, *n.* perfidia, deslealtad, traición, *f.*
treacle, *n.* triaca, *f.*
tread, *vt.* and *vi.* pisar, hollar, apretar con el pie; pisotear; patalear; caminar con majestad; **—**, *n.* pisa, *f.*; pisada, *f.*; galladura, *f.*
treadle, *n.* cárcola, *f.*
treadmill, *n.* molino que se mueve mediante persona o animal en una correa movible; trabajo pesado y fatigoso.
treas.: treasurer, tesorero; **treasury**, tesorería.
treason, *n.* traición, *f.*; **high —**, delito de lesa majestad.
treasonable, *adj.* traidor; **—bly**, *adv.* a traición.
treasure, *n.* tesoro, *m.*; riqueza, *f.*; **—**, *vt.* atesorar; guardar riquezas.
treasurer, *n.* tesorero, ra.
treasury, *n.* tesorería (oficina), *f.*; **— note**, billete de tesorero.
treat, *vt.* and *vi.* tratar; regalar; **to — a patient**, medicinar; **to — of**, versar; **—**, *n.* trato, *m.*; banquete, festín, *m.*, convidada, *f.*
treatise, *n.* tratado, *m.*
treatment, *n.* trato, *m.*; (med.) tratamiento, *m.*
treaty, *n.* tratado, pacto, trato, *m.*
treble, *adj.* triple, tríplice; **—**, *vt.* triplicar; **—**, *vi.* triplicarse; **—**, *n.* (mus.) tiple, *m.*; **—bly**, *adv.* triplicadamente.
tree, *n.* árbol, *m.*; cepo, palo, *m.*; **family —**, árbol genealógico; **— frog**, rana arbórea.
treeless, *adj.* sin árboles.
trefoil, *n.* trébol, trifolio, *m.*
trek, *n.* prolongado viaje lento en carromato u otro vehículo; jornada, *f.*; **—**,

vt. viajar en carromatos.
trellis, *n.* enrejado, *m.*; **—**, *vt.* proveer un enrejado.
trelliswork, *n.* enrejado, *m.*
tremble, *vi.* temblar; estremecerse; **—**, *n.* temblor, *m.*
trembling, *adj.* tembloroso; **—**, *n.* estremecimiento, *m.*; temor, *m.*; **—ly**, *adv.* trémulamente, temblorosamente.
tremendous, *adj.* tremendo; inmenso; **—ly**, *adv.* de un modo tremendo.
tremor, *n.* temblor, estremecimiento, tremor, *m.*
tremulous, *adj.* trémulo, tembloroso; **—ly**, *adv.* trémulamente.
trench, *n.* foso, *m.*; (mil.) trinchera, *f.*; cauce, *m.*; **—**, *vt.* cortar; atrincherar; hacer cauces; **— fever**, fiebre de trinchera; **— mouth**, inflamación de las encías, inflamación de la boca.
trenchant, *adj.* afilado, cortante.
trencher, *n.* trinchero, *m.*
trencherman, *n.* comilón, *m.*; gorrista, vividor, *m.*
trend, *n.* tendencia, *f.*, curso, *m.*; **—**, *vi.* tender, inclinarse.
trepan, *n.* trépano, *m.*; petardista, *m.*; trampa, *f.*; **—**, *vt.* trepanar; petardear.
trepidation, *n.* trepidación, *f.*
trespass, *vt.* quebrantar, traspasar, violar; **—**, *n.* transgresión, violación, *f.*
trespasser, *n.* transgresor, ra.
tress, *n.* trenza, *f.*; rizo de pelo.
trestle, *n.* bastidor, *m.*; caballete, *m.*; armazón, *m.*
trestlework, *n.* caballete, *m.*
trey, *n.* tres (en los naipes), *m.*
triad, *n.* (mus.) acorde, *m.*; terno, *m.*
trial, *n.* prueba, *f.*; ensayo, *m.*; (law) examen, juicio, *m.*, vista, *f.*; **— balance**, balance de prueba; **— order**, pedido de ensayo; **— run**, carrera de ensayo.
triangle, *n.* triángulo, *m.*; grupo de tres personas.
triangular, *adj.* triangular; **—ly**, *adv.* triangularmente.
triangulate, *vt.* triangular.
triangulation, *n.* triangulación, *f.*
tribal, *adj.* tribal, perteneciente a una tribu.
tribe, *n.* tribu, *f.*; raza, casta, *f.*
tribesman, *n.* miembro de una tribu.
tribulation, *n.* tribulación, *f.*
tribunal, *n.* tribunal, *m.*; juzgado, *m.*
tribune, *n.* tribuno, *m.*; tribuna, *f.*
tributary, *n.* and *adj.* tributario, *m.*
tribute, *n.* tributo, *m.*; **to render —**, (coll.) rendir pleitesía, tributar homenaje.
trice, *n.* momento, tris, *m.*
trichina, *n.* triquina, *f.*, parásito de los músculos.
trichinosis, *n.* (med.) triquinosis, *f.*
trick, *n.* engaño, fraude, *m.*; superchería, astucia, *f.*; baza, *f.*; maña, *f.*; baza (en el juego de naipes), *f.*; **wrestler's —**, traspié, *m.*; **—**, *vt.* engañar; **ataviar;**

hacer juegos de manos; embaucar.

trickery, *n.* engaño, dolo, fraude, *m.*

trickle, *vi.* gotear; **—,** *n.* chorrito, *m.,* corriente pequeña.

trickster, *n.* engañador, ra.

tricky, *adj.* astuto, artificioso.

tricolor, *n.* bandera tricolor; **—,** *adj.* tricolor.

tricuspid, *adj.* tricúspide.

tricycle, *n.* triciclo, velocípedo, *m.*

trident, *n.* tridente, *m.*

tried, *adj.* ensayado; probado; fiel.

triennial, *adj.* trienal; **—,** *n.* tercer aniversario; acontecimiento trienal.

trifle, *n.* bagatela, niñería, pamplina, pequeñez, bicoca, *f.*; **—,** *vi.* bobear; chancear, juguetear.

trifler, *n.* necio, *m.*; persona coqueta o juguetona.

trifling, *adj.* frívolo, inútil; **—ly,** *adv.* frívolamente, sin consecuencia.

trig. trigonometry, trigon. trigonometría.

trigger, *n.* gatillo, *m.*; pararruedas, *m.*

trigonometric, *adj.* trigonométrico.

trilateral, *adj.* trilátero.

trilingual, *adj.* trilingüe.

trill, *n.* trino, *m.*; **—,** *vt.* trinar, gorgoritear.

trillion, *n.* trillón, *m.,* la tercera potencia de un millón, o 1,000,000,000,000,000,000 (en la América Ibera, España, Inglaterra, y Alemania); un millón de millones, o 1,000,000,000,000 (en Francia y los Estados Unidos).

trillium, *n.* (bot.) planta de la familia de las convalarias con hojas en grupos de tres.

trilogy, *n.* trilogía, *f.*

trim, *adj.* acicalado, compuesto, bien ataviado; **—ly,** *adv.* lindamente; en buen estado; **—,** *n.* atavío, adorno, aderezo, *m.*; **—,** *vt.* aparejar, preparar; acomodar; adornar, ornar; podar, recortar, cortar; recortar el cabello; (naut.) orientar (las velas); equilibrar.

trimming, *n.* guarnición de vestido; galón, *m.*; adorno, *m.*

trimonthly, *adj.* trimestral.

Trinidad, Trinidad, *f.*

trinitrotoluene, *n.* trinitrotolueno, *m.*

Trinity, *n.* Trinidad, *f.*

trinity, *n.* grupo de tres, trinidad, *f.*

trinket, *n.* joya, alhaja, *f.*; adorno, *m.*; fruslería, chuchería, bujería, *f.*; juguete, *m.*

trio, *n.* (mus.) terceto, trío, *m.*; terno, *m.*

trioxide, *n.* trióxido, *m.*

trip, *vt.* saltar, brincar; hacer tropezar; **—,** *vi.* tropezar; resbalar; **—,** *n.* zancadilla, *f.*; traspié, *m.*; resbalón, *m.*; viaje, *m.*; **one-way —,** viaje sencillo; **return —,** viaje de vuelta; **round —,** viaje redondo, viaje de ida y vuelta; **— hammer,** martinete, *m.*

tripartite, *adj.* tripartito.

tripe, *n.* tripas, *f. pl.*, callos, *m. pl.*, menudo, *m.*

triphthong, *n.* triptongo, *m.*

triplane, *n.* triplano, *m.*

triple, *adj.* tríplice, triple, triplo; **—,** *vt.* triplicar.

triplet, *n.* (poet.) terceto, *m.*; **—s,** trigemelos, *m. pl.*

triplex, *adj.* tríplice, triple; **—,** *n.* triplo, *m.*

triplicate, *vt.* triplicar; hacer tres copias; **—,** *adj.* triplicado; **—,** *n.* una de tres copias idénticas.

tripod, *n.* trípode, *m.*

tripping, *adj.* veloz, ágil, ligero; **—,** *n.* baile ligero; tropiezo, tropezón, *m.*; **—ly,** *adv.* velozmente.

trireme, *n.* trirreme, *m.*

trisect, *vt.* tripartir.

trisection, *n.* trisección, *f.*

trisyllable, *n.* trisílabo, *m.*, palabra trisílaba.

trite, *adj.* trivial, usado, banal; **—ly,** *adv.* vulgarmente.

triteness, *n.* trivialidad, vulgaridad, *f.*

triton, *n.* tritón, *m.*

tritone, *n.* tritono, *m.*

triturate, *vt.* triturar; **—,** *n.* trituración, *f.*

triumph, *n.* triunfo, *m.*; **—,** *vi.* triunfar; vencer.

triumphal, *adj.* triunfal.

triumphant, *adj.* triunfante; victorioso; **—ly,** *adv.* triunfalmente.

triumvirate, *n.* triunvirato, *m.*

trivial, *adj.* trivial, vulgar; **—ly,** *adv.* trivialmente.

triviality, *n.* trivialidad, *f.*

triweekly, *adj.* trisemanal.

troll, *n.* canción en tres partes sucesivas; carrete, *m.*; anzuelo para pescar; duende, enano, *m.*; **—,** *vt.* arrastrar el anzuelo al pescar; seducir; tentar; **—,** *vi.* pescar arrastrando el anzuelo; cantar alegremente; hablar rápidamente.

trolley, *n.* tranvía, *m.*; **— bus, — coach,** ómnibus eléctrico; **— car,** coche de tranvía.

trollop, *n.* ramera, gorrona, *f.*

trombone, *n.* (mus.) trombón, *m.*

troop, *n.* tropa, *f.*; cuadrilla, turba, *f.*; **—,** *vi.* atroparse.

trooper, *n.* soldado a caballo; policía a caballo; caballo de caballería.

troopship, *n.* transporte de guerra.

trophy, *n.* trofeo, *m.*

tropic, *n.* and *adj.* trópico, *m.*; **—s,** trópico, *m.*

tropical, *adj.* trópico, tropical; **—ly,** *adv.* tropicalmente; metafóricamente.

trot, *n.* trote, *m.*; **—,** *vi.* trotar.

troth, *n.* fe, fidelidad, *f.*; desposorio, *m.*; **—,** *vt.* desposarse.

trotline, *n.* especie de cordel de pescar.

trotter, *n.* caballo trotón; trotador, *m.*

trotting, *adj.* trotador.

troubadour, *n.* trovador, *m.*

trouble, *vt.* disturbar, perturbar; afligir; incomodar, molestar; **—,** *vi.* incomodarse; **—,** *n.* turbación, *f.*; disturbio, *m.*; inquietud, *f.*; aflicción, pena, *f.*; congoja, *f.*; trabajo, *m.*; **to be in —,** verse en apuros.

troubled, *adj.* afligido; agitado.

troublemaker, *n.* perturbador, ra.

troublesome, *adj.* penoso, fatigoso; importuno; fastidioso, molesto, majadero.

troublous, *adj.* turbulento, confuso.

trough, *n.* artesa, gamella, *f.*, dornajo, *m.*

trounce, *vt.* golpear, batir, apalear.

troupe, *n.* compañía o tropa, especialmente de actores de teatro.

trouper, *n.* miembro de una compañía teatral.

troupial, *n.* (orn.) turpial, *m.*

trousers, *n. pl.* calzones, pantalones, *m. pl.*

trousseau, *n.* avíos de boda, ajuar de novia.

trout, *n.* trucha, *f.*

trowel, *n.* trulla, llana, paleta, *f.*

truancy, *n.* tuna, *f.*, vida holgazana.

truant, *n.* and *adj.* holgazán, ana, haragán, ana, novillero, ra.

truce, *n.* tregua, *f.*, suspensión de armas.

truck, *vt.* and *vi.* trocar, cambiar; acarrear; transportar; **—,** *n.* camión, carretón, *m.*; cambio, trueque, *m.*; rueda de cureña; (rail.) truck, *m.*; legumbres para mercado; **small —,** camioneta, *f.*; **— body,** carrocería, *f.*, caja o bastidor de camión; **— farm,** pequeña labranza en que se producen legumbres para vender en el mercado; **— frame,** bastidor para camión.

truckage, *n.* acarreo, *m.*

trucker, *n.* carretero, *m.*

truckle, *vi.* someterse; **—,** *n.* ruedecita, *f.*; **— bed,** carriola, *f.*

truckman, *n.* carretero, *m.*; traficante, *m.*; verdulero, *m.*

truculence, *n.* fiereza, crueldad, *f.*

truculent, *adj.* truculento, cruel.

trudge, *vi.* andar con afán; afanarse; **—,** *n.* paseo fatigoso.

true, *adj.* verdadero, cierto; sincero, exacto; efectivo; **— bill,** acusación de un gran jurado; **—,** *adv.* realmente; **—,** *vt.* arreglar, corregir; alinear.

truehearted, *adj.* leal, sincero, franco, fiel.

truelove, *n.* amante fiel; **— knot,** nudo difícil de desatar; lazo de amor.

truffle, *n.* (bot.) criadilla de tierra, trufa, *f.*

truism, *n.* verdad indubitable; verdad de Perogrullo.

truly, *adv.* en verdad; sinceramente.

trump, *n.* trompeta, *f.*; triunfo (en el juego de naipes), *m.*; (poet.) trompeta, *f.*; (coll.) excelente persona; **—,** *vt.* ganar con el triunfo; **— card,** triunfo (en los juegos de naipes, *m.*; **to — up,** forjar, inventar.

trumpery, *n.* hojarasca, *f.*; bujería, baratija, *f.*, cachivache, *m.*

trumpet, *n.* trompeta, trompa, *f.*; **— creeper,** jasmín trompeta; **—,** *vt.* trompetear; divulgar.

trumpeter, *n.* trompetero, *m.*

truncate, *vt.* truncar, troncar; **—,** *adj.* troncado.

truncheon, *n.* cachiporra, *f.*: mazo (de policía, etc.), *m.*; **—,** *vt.* golpear con cachiporra o con un palo o mazo.

trundle, *n.* rueda baja; carreta de ruedas bajas; rodillo, *m.*; **— bed,** carriola, *f.*; **—,** *vt.* and *vi.* rodar; girar.

trunk, *n.* tronco, *m.*; baúl, cofre, *m.*; **leather —,** petaca, *f.*; **— line,** (rail.) tronco, *m.*, línea principal; **— of an elephant,** trompa, *f.*; **— (of trees and plants),** pie, tronco, *m.*; **—,** *adj.* de tronco.

trunks, *n. pl.* calzones cortos entallados; calzoncillos cortos.

trunnion, *n.* muñón, *m.*

truss, *n.* braguero, *m.*; haz, *m.*; atado, *m.*; **—,** *vt.* empaquetar; arremangar.

trussing, *n.* armadura, *f.*

trust, *n.* confianza, *f.*; cargo, depósito, fideicomiso, *m.*; crédito, *m.*; cometido, *m.*; cuidado, *m.*; asociación comercial para monopolizar la venta de algún género; consorcio, *m.*; **in —,** en administración, **on —,** al fiado; **—,** *vt.* and *vi.* confiar: encargar y fiar; dar crédito; esperar; **—,** *vi.* confiarse, fiarse.

trustee, *n.* fideicomisario, curador, depositario, síndico, *m.*

trusteeship, *n.* sindicatura, *f.*

trustful, *adj.* fiel; confiado.

trustiness, *n.* probidad, integridad, *f.*

trusting, *adj.* confiado.

trustworthiness, *n.* honradez, *f.*; confianza, *f.*

trustworthy, *adj.* digno de confianza, confiable.

trusty, *adj.* fiel, leal; seguro.

truth, *n.* verdad, *f.*; fidelidad, *f.*; realidad, *f.*; **in —,** en verdad.

truthful, *adj.* verídico, veraz.

truthfulness, *n.* veracidad, *f.*

truthless, *adj.* sin verdad, falso.

try, *vt.* and *vi.* examinar, ensayar, probar; experimentar; tentar; intentar; juzgar; purificar, refinar; **—,** *vt.* procurar; **to — on clothes,** probarse ropa; **—,** *n.* prueba, *f.*, ensayo, *m.*; **— square,** escuadra de reborde.

trying, *adj.* crítico; penoso; cruel; agravante.

tryout, *n.* prueba, ensayo, *m.*

trypsin, *n.* tripsina, *f.*

trysquare, *n.* escuadra de comprobación, escuadra de reborde.

tryst, *n.* cita, *f.*; lugar de cita; **—,** *vt.* and *vi.* convenir en encontrarse; arreglar; nombrar; ponerse de acuerdo.

tsar, *n.* = **czar.**

tsetse fly, *n.* tsetsé, *f.*

tsp. teaspoon, cucharita, *f.*

T. square, *n.* doble escuadra, regla en T.

Tu., Tues. Tuesday, mart. martes.

tub, *n.* tina, *f.*; cuba, *f.*; cubo, barreño, *m.*, barreña, *f.*; **large —,** tinajón, *m.*; **—,** *vt.* encubar; (coll.) bañar.

tuba, *n.* (mus.) bombardino, *m.*

tubbing, n. baño, lavamiento, m.

tubby, adj. de forma de un cubo.

tube, n. tubo, **cañón,** cañuto, caño, m.; (rail.) ferrocarril subterráneo; **amplifying —,** válvula amplificadora; **electronic —,** tubo electrónico; **inner —,** cámara de aire; **test —,** probeta, f.; **vacuum —,** tubo al vacío; **—,** vt. poner en tubo; entubar.

tuber, n. tubérculo, m.; (anat.) protuberancia, prominencia, f.

tubercle, n. (med.) tubérculo, m.

tubercular, adj. tísico, tuberculoso.

tuberculin, n. tuberculina, f.

tuberculosis, n. (med.) tuberculosis, tisis, f.

tuberose, n. (bot.) tuberosa, f., nardo, m.

tubing, n. tubería, f.

tubular, adj. tubular.

tuck, n. alforza, f.; pliegue, m.; estoque, m.; **—,** vt. arremangar, recoger.

tucker, n. camisolín, m.; alforzador, m.; **—,** vt. (coll.) fatigar.

Tuesday, n. martes, m.

tuft, n. borla, f.; penacho, m.; moño, m.; **—,** vt. adornar con borlas; dividir en borlas.

tufted, adj. frondoso, velludo.

tug, vt. tirar con fuerza; arrancar; **—,** vi. esforzarse; **—,** n. tirada, f.; esfuerzo, m.; tirón, m.; (naut.) remolcador, m.; **— of war,** tiro de cuerda entre dos grupos opuestos; (fig.) contienda ferozmente disputada.

tugboat, n. remolcador, m.

tuition, n. instrucción, enseñanza, f.; precio de enseñanza.

tularemia, n. tuleremia, f.

tulip, n. tulipa, f.; tulipán, m.

tulle, n. tul, m.

tumble, vi. caer, hundirse, voltear; revolcarse; **—,** vt. revolver; rodar; volcar; **—,** n. caída, f.; vuelco, m.; confusión, f.

tumblebug, n. escarabajo, m.

tumble-down, adj. destartalado, dilapidado, a punto de caerse.

tumbler, n. volteador, m.; especie de vaso para beber; (orn.) volteador, m.; (mech.) tambor, m.; seguro, fiador (de cerradura), m.

tumbleweed, n. planta americana cuya semilla esparce el viento otoñal.

tumbrel, tumbril, n. chirrión, m., carreta, f., carreta de armas.

tumefaction, n. (med.) tumefacción, f.

tumefy, vt. and vi. entumecer, entumecerse.

tumescence, n. tumescencia, f.

tumescent, n. tumescente.

tumid, adj. túmido; prominente.

tumor, n. tumor, m., hinchazón, nacencia, f.

tumult, n. tumulto, m.; agitación, f.; alboroto, m.

tumultuous, adj. tumultuoso; alborotado; **—ly,** adv. tumultuosamente.

tun, n. tonel, m.; tonelada, f.; **—,** vt. entonelar.

tuna, n. (bot.) tuna, f.; **— fish,** atún, m.

tunable, adj. armonioso, melodioso; que puede entonarse.

tundra, n. tundra, f.

tune, n. tono, m.; armonía, f.; aria, f.; **—,** vt. templar un instrumento músico; armonizar; (rad.) sintonizar.

tuneful, adj. armonioso, acorde, melodioso; sonoro.

tuneless, adj. disonante.

tuner, n. afinador, templador, m.

tungsten, n. tungsteno, volframio, m.

tunic, n. túnica, f.

tunicate, n. and adj. tunicado, m.

tuning, n. afinación, f.; templadura, f.; **— dial,** cuadrante de sintonización; **— fork,** horquilla tónica; **— key,** templador, m.

Tunis, Túnez, f.

Tunisia, Tunisia, f.

Tunisian, n. and adj. tunecino, na.

tunnel, n. túnel, m.; embudo, m.; **—,** vt. hacer una cosa en forma de túnel.

tunny, n. (pez) atún, m.

turban, n. turbante, m.

turbid, adj. turbio, cenagoso; turbulento.

turbidity, n. turbiedad, f.; turbulencia, f.

turbine, n. turbina, f.; **blast —,** turbosopladora, f.

turbot, n. (pez) rodaballo, rombo, m.

turbulence, n. turbulencia, confusión, f.

turbulent, adj. turbulento, tumultuoso; **—ly,** adv. tumultuariamente, turbulentamente.

tureen, n. sopera, f.

turf, n. césped, m.; turba, f.; hipódromo, m.; carrera de caballos; **—,** vt. cubrir con césped.

turfman, n. hombre interesado en las carreras de caballos.

turgescence, n. turgencia, f.

turgescent, adj. turgente.

turgid, adj. túmido, inflado.

Turk, n. turco, ca.

Turkey, Turquía, f.

turkey, n. pavo, m.; **— buzzard,** gallinazo, m.; **— hen,** pava, f.

Turkish, n. and adj. turco, ca; **— bath,** baño turco; **— towel,** toalla de algodón afelpado.

turmoil, n. disturbio, m., baraúnda, confusión, f.

turn, vt. volver, trocar; verter, traducir; cambiar; tornear; **—,** vi. volver, girar, rodar; voltear; dar vueltas; volverse a, mudarse, trasformarse; dirigirse; **to — back,** regresar, volver atrás; (coll.) virar; **to — down,** poner boca abajo, voltear; rehusar, bajar (la llama de gas); **to — off,** cerrar; **to — on,** abrir; **to — over,** revolver; **to — pale,** palidecer; **to — the corner,** doblar la calle; **to — to,** recurrir a; **—,** n. vuelta, f.; giro, m.; rodeo, recodo, m.; turno, m.; vez, f.; procedimiento, m.; habilidad, inclinación, f.; servicio, m.;

forma, figura, hechura, *f.*; **a good —,** un favor; **sharp —,** codo, *m.*

turnbuckle, *n.* picolete, *m.*

turncoat, *n.* apóstata, *m.* y *f.*; renegado, da.

turndown, *adj.* rehusado, volteado, doblado hacia abajo; **—,** *n.* denegación, *f.*

turning, *n.* vuelta, *f.*; rodeo, *m.*; recodo, *m.*; **—,** *adj.* de vuelta; **— point,** punto culminante; cambio de dirección en el terreno.

turnip, *n.* (bot.) nabo, *m.*

turnkey, *n.* demandadero de una cárcel.

turnout, *n.* coche y demás aparejos; (rail.) aguja, *f.*; producto limpio o neto; asamblea grande de personas.

turnover, *n.* vuelco, *m.*; (com.) ventas, *f. pl.*, evolución o movimiento de mercancías; **—,** *adj.* doblado hacia abajo, volteado.

turnpike, *n.* carretera de portazgo; barrera de peatones.

turnscrew, *n.* destornillador, *m.*

turnsole, *n.* (bot.) heliotropo, *m.*

turnspit, *n.* galopín de cocina que da vueltas al asador.

turnstile, *n.* torniquete, *m.*

turntable, *n.* (rail.) plataforma giratoria, tornavía, *f.*

turpentine, *n.* trementina, *f.*; **oil of —,** aguarrás, *m.*

turpitude, *n.* maldad, infamia, *f.*

turquoise, *n.* turquesa, *f.*

turret, *n.* torrecilla, *f.*

turreted, *adj.* armado con torrecillas; de torres.

turtle, *n.* tortuga, *f.*; galápago, *m.*

turtledove, *n.* tórtola, *f.*

tush, *interj.* ¡tararira! ¡bah! **—,** *n.* = **tusk.**

tusk, *n.* colmillo, *m.*; diente, *m.*

tussle, *n.* lucha a brazo partido; pelea, *f.*; rebatiña, *f.*; **—,** *vt.* pelear; luchar a brazo partido.

tut! *interj.* ¡tararira! ¡tate! ¡bah!

tutelage, *n.* tutela, tutoría, *f.*

tutelar, *adj.* = **tutelary.**

tutelary, *adj.* tutelar.

tutor, *n.* tutor, *m.*; preceptor, *m.*; **—,** *vt.* enseñar, instruir.

tutorage, *n.* tutela, tutoría, *f.*

tutti-frutti, *n.* tutifruti, *m.*; **—,** *adj.* de tutifruti.

tuxedo, *n.* smoking, *m.*; **— coat,** smoking, *m.*

TVA, Tennessee Valley Authority, Administración del Valle del Tennessee.

twaddle, *vi.* charlar; **—,** *n.* charla, *f.*

twain, *n.* and *adj.* (poet.) dos, *m.*

twang, *vt.* and *vi.* producir un sonido agudo; restallar; hablar con tono nasal.

tweak, *vt.* agarrar y halar con un tirón retorcido; **—,** *n.* tirón retorcido.

tweed, *n.* género tejido de lana de superficie áspera y de dos colores; **—s,** ropa hecha de paño de lana y de superficie áspera.

tweet, *n.* gorgorito (de pájaro, etc.), *m.*

tweezers, *n. pl.* tenacillas, *f. pl.*

twelfth, *adj.* duodécimo; **—,** *n.* duodécimo, *m.*

Twelfth-day, *n.* día de reyes; Epifanía, *f.*

Twelfth-night, *n.* víspera de reyes; Epifanía, *f.*

twelve, *n.* and *adj.* doce, *m.*

twelvemonth, *n.* año, *m.*; doce meses.

twentieth, *adj.* vigésimo, veintavo; **—,** *n.* vigésimo, veintavo, *m.*

twenty, *n.* and *adj.* veinte, *m.*; **— odd,** veintitantos.

twice, *adv.* dos veces; al doble.

twice-told, *adj.* que se ha dicho dos veces; repetido.

twiddle, *vt.* hacer girar; enroscar (los dedos, etc.); **—,** *n.* vuelta, *f.*; movimiento giratorio (de los dedos, etc.).

twig, *n.* varita, varilla, *f.*; vástago, *m.*

twilight, *n.* crepúsculo, *m.*; **—,** *adj.* crepuscular; **— sleep,** narcosis obstétrica parcial.

twill, *n.* paño tejido en forma cruzada; **—,** *vt.* tejer paño en forma cruzada.

twin, *n.* and *adj.* gemelo, la, mellizo, za; **—,** *vi.* parir gemelos.

twine, *vt.* torcer, enroscar; **—,** *vi.* entrelazarse; caracolear; **—,** *n.* guita, *f.*; amarradura, *f.*; bramante, *m.*

twinge, *vt.* punzar, pellizcar; **—,** *vi.* arder; sufrir dolor (de una punzada, etc.); **—,** *n.* dolor agudo o punzante.

twinkle, *vi.* centellear; parpadear; **—,** *n.* centelleo, *m.*; pestañeo, *m.*; movimiento rápido.

twinkling, *n.* guiñada, *f.*; pestañeo, *m.*; momento, *m.*; **in the — of an eye,** en un abrir y cerrar de ojos.

twin-screw, *adj.* (naut.) de dos hélices.

twirl, *vt.* voltear; hacer girar; **—,** *n.* rotación, *f.*

twist, *vt.* and *vi.* torcer, retorcer; entretejer; retortijar; **to — one's body,** contorcerse; **—,** *n.* trenza, *f.*; hilo de algodón; torcedura, *f.*

twisted, *adj.* torcido; enredado.

twister, *n.* torcedor, ra; remolino de viento; tornado, *m.*

twisting, *adj.* torcedor; **—,** *n.* torcedura, *f.* torcimiento, *m.*

twit, *vt.* vituperar; censurar; regañar; **—,** *n.* dicterio, *m.*; reproche, *m.*

twitch, *vt.* tirar bruscamente, agarrar; arrancar; **—,** *vi.* crisparse, contorcerse, tener una contracción nerviosa; **—,** *n.* tirón, *m.*; crispatura, *f.*, contracción nerviosa.

twitching, *n.* = **twitch.**

twitter, *vi.* gorjear; **—,** *n.* gorjeo, *m.*

two, *n.* and *adj.* dos, *m.*; **—,** *adj.* de dos.

two-base hit, *n.* (baseball) golpe a la pelota que permite al bateador llegar a segunda base.

two-by-four, *n.* pedazo de madera que

mide cuatro pulgadas por dos pulgadas.

two-faced, *adj.* falso; de dos caras; disimulado.

two-fisted, *adj.* belicoso, denodado, viril.

twofold, *adj.* doble, duplicado; **—,** *adv.* al doble.

two-motored, *adj.* bimotor.

twopence, *n.* moneda de valor de dos peniques en Inglaterra.

two-ply, *adj.* de dos chapas o capas; de dos hilos o tramas.

two-seater, *n.* vehículo de dos asientos.

twosome, *n.* juego en que toman parte dos personas.

two-step, *n.* paso doble (música y baile).

tycoon, *n.* título dado antiguamente al jefe del ejército japonés; (coll.) magnate industrial.

tympan, *n.* tímpano, *m.*

tympanitis, *n.* (med.) timpanitis, *f.*, inflamación del tímpano del oído.

tympanum, *n.* tímpano, *m.*

type, *n.* tipo, *m.*; letra, *f.*; carácter, *m.*; clase, *f.*; género, *m.*; **body —,** tipo usual; **bold-faced —,** tipo negro; **canon —,** canon, *m.*; **large —,** tipo de cartel; **light-faced —,** tipo delgado; **lower-case —,** letra minúscula; **Old English —,** letra gótica; **pica —,** tipo cícero; **roman —,** letra redonda; **upper-case —,** letra mayúscula; **— bar,** línea de tipos; **—,** *vt.* and *vi.* escribir en máquina.

typesetter, *n.* cajista, *m.* y *f.*

typesetting, *n.* cajistería, *f.*; composición tipográfica.

typewrite, *vt.* escribir a máquina.

typewriter, *n.* máquina de escribir; dactilógrafo, *m.*, dactilografista, *m.* y *f.*; **portable —,** máquina de escribir portátil.

typewriting, *n.* acción de escribir a máquina; dactilografía, mecanografía, *f.*; escritura a máquina; trabajo hecho en una máquina de escribir.

typhoid, *n.* fiebre tifoidea; **—,** *adj.* tifoideo; **— fever,** fiebre tifoidea.

typhoon, *n.* tifón, huracán, *m.*

typhus, *n.* (med.) tifus, tifo, *m.*

typical, *adj.* típico; **—ly,** *adv.* en forma típica.

typify, *vt.* simbolizar, representar.

typing, *n.* mecanografía, dactilografía, *f.*

typist, *n.* mecanógrafo, fa.

typographer, *n.* tipógrafo, *m.*

typographic, *adj.* tipográfico.

typographical, *adj.* tipográfico; **—ly,** *adv.* tipográficamente.

typography, *n.* tipografía, *f.*

tyrannic, *adj.* tiránico.

tyrannical, *adj.* tiránico; **—ly,** *adv.* tiránicamente.

tyrannize, *vt.* tiranizar.

tyrannous, *adj.* tiránico, tirano, arbitrario; cruel; injusto.

tyrant, *n.* tirano, *m.*

tyro, tiro, *n.* aprendiz, *m.*; bisoño, *m.*

U

U. University, Universidad.

ubiquitous, *adj.* ubicuo.

ubiquity, *n.* ubicuidad, *f.*

U-boat, *n.* submarino alemán.

u. c. upper case, (print.) mayúsculas.

udder, *n.* ubre, *f.*

ugh! *interj.* ¡uf!

uglily, *adv.* feamente; (coll.) rudamente.

ugliness, *n.* fealdad, deformidad, *f.*; (coll.) rudeza, *f.*

ugly, *adj.* feo, disforme; (coll.) rudo, desagradable.

uhlan, *n.* ulano, *m.*

U. K. United Kingdom, Reino Unido.

Ukraine, Ukrania, *f.*

ukulele, *n.* guitarrita de cuatro cuerdas.

ulcer, *n.* úlcera, *f.*

ulcerate, *vt.* ulcerar.

ulceration, *n.* ulceración, *f.*

ulcerous, *adj.* ulceroso.

ulna, *n.* cúbito, *m.*

ulster, *n.* abrigo flojo y pesado.

ult.: in the past month, p. pdo. ppdo. próximo pasado; **last,** ult/o. último.

ulterior, *adj.* ulterior.

ultimate, *adj.* último; **—ly,** *adv.* últimamente; **—,** *n.* lo último.

ultimatum, *n.* ultimátum, *m.*; última condición irrevocable.

ultimo, *adj.* and *adv.* en o del mes próximo pasado.

ultra, *adj.* extremo, más allá; **—,** *n.* extremista, *m.* y *f.*; persona radical.

ultramarine, *n.* azul de ultramar; **—,** *adj.* ultramarino; **— blue,** ultramarino, *m.*

ultraviolet, *adj.* ultraviolado, ultravioleta; **— rays,** rayos ultraviolados.

umber, *n.* tierra de sombra, tierra de Nocera, tierra de Umbría; **—,** *adj.* de tierra de sombra; pardo.

umbilical, *adj.* umbilical; **— cord,** ombligo, *m.*

umbra, *n.* sombra, *f.*

umbrage, *n.* follaje, *m.*; umbría, *f.*; resentimiento, *m.*; **to take —,** tener sospecha.

umbrageous, *adj.* sombrío, umbrío, sombroso.

umbrella, *n.* paraguas, *m.*; parasol, quitasol, *m.*; **— stand,** portaparaguas, paragüero, *m.*

umiak, *n.* buque esquimal.

umlaut, *n.* diéresis, *f.*

umpire, *n.* árbitro, arbitrador, *m.*; **—,** *vt.* arbitrar.

unabashed, *adj.* desenvuelto, descocado.

unabated, *adj.* no disminuído, no agotado; cabal.

unable, *adj.* incapaz; **to be —,** no poder.

unabridged, *adj.* completo.

unaccompanied, *adj.* solo.

unaccomplished, *adj.* incompleto, no acabado.

unaccountable, *adj.* inexplicable, extraño;

—bly, adv. extrañamente.
unaccustomed, adj. desacostumbrado, desusado.
unacquainted, adj. desconocido; ignorado.
unadorned, adj. sin adorno.
unadulterated, adj. genuino, puro; sin mezcla.
unaffected, adj. sin afectación, sincero, natural; **—ly,** adv. en forma natural, sencillamente.
unaided, adj. sin ayuda.
unaltered, adj. invariado; sin ningún cambio.
unambitious, adj. sin ambición.
unanimity, n. unanimidad, f.
unanimous, adj. unánime; **—ly,** adv. unánimemente, por aclamación, por unanimidad.
unanswerable, adj. incontestable, incontrovertible.
unanswered, adj. no contestado, no respondido; **an — letter,** carta sin contestar.
unapproachable, adj. inaccesible.
unarmed, adj. inerme, desarmado.
unassailable, adj. inatacable; inexpugnable.
unassisted, adj. sin ayuda, solo; sin auxilio.
unassuming, adj. modesto, sencillo, sin pretensiones.
unattached, adj. separado, independiente; disponible.
unattainable, adj. inasequible.
unattempted, adj. no intentado.
unattended, adj. solo, sin comitiva.
unavailing, adj. inútil, vano, infructuoso.
unavoidable, adj. inevitable; **to be —,** no tener remedio, no poder evitarse; **—bly,** inevitablemente.
unaware, adj. incauto; de sorpresa, sin saber.
unawares, adv. inadvertidamente; de improviso, inesperadamente.
unbalanced, adj. trastornado.
unbar, vt. desatrancar; abrir.
unbearable, adj. intolerable; **—bly,** adv. intolerablemente.
unbeaten, adj. no derrotado, no batido; **— path,** camino no frecuentado.
unbecoming, adj. indecoroso; que no queda bien, que no sienta (un vestido, etc.); **—ly,** adv. indecorosamente.
unbelief, n. incredulidad, f.
unbeliever, n. incrédulo, la, infiel, m. y f.
unbend, vt. aflojar; **—,** vi. condescender; descansar.
unbending, adj. inflexible.
unbiased, unbiassed, adj. imparcial, exento de prejuicios.
unbidden, adj. no invitado; no ordenado; espontáneo.
unbind, vt. desatar; aflojar.
unbleached, adj. sin blanquear; sin teñir.
unblemished, adj. sin mancha, sin tacha.
unblest, adj. maldito; no consagrado.

unblushing, adj. descarado, sin sonrojarse.
unbolt, vt. desatrancar.
unborn, adj. sin nacer, no nacido todavía.
unbosom, vt. desembuchar, confesar.
unbound, adj. sin encuadernar, a la rústica (aplícase a libros); desatado.
unbounded, adj. infinito; ilimitado; **—ly,** adv. ilimitadamente.
unbreakable, adj. irrompible.
unbridle, vt. desenfrenar; **—d,** adj. desenfrenado, licencioso; violento.
unbroken, adj. indómito; entero; no interrumpido, continuado.
unbuckle, vt. deshebillar.
unburden, vt. descargar, aliviar.
unburied, adj. insepulto; no enterrado; al descubierto.
unbutton, vt. desabotonar.
uncalled-for, adj. que no viene al caso, que está fuera de lugar; impertinente, grosero; inmerecido.
uncared-for, adj. descuidado, desatendido.
unceasing, adj. sin cesar, continuo; **—ly,** adv. sin tregua.
uncertain, adj. inseguro; incierto, dudoso; vacilante.
uncertainty, n. incertidumbre, f.
unchangeable, adj. inmutable, invariable.
unchanged, adj. no alterado.
unchanging, adj. inalterable, inmutable.
uncharitable, adj. cruel, nada caritativo.
unchecked, adj. desenfrenado.
unchristian, adj. indigno de un cristiano; pagano; bárbaro.
uncivil, adj. grosero, descortés, incivil.
uncivilized, adj. tosco, salvaje, no civilizado, bárbaro.
unclad, adj. desnudo, sin vestir.
unclaimed, adj. no reclamado, sin reclamar; **— letters,** cartas rezagadas.
uncle, n. tío, m.; (coll.) prendero, m.
unclean, adj. inmundo, sucio, puerco; obsceno; inmoral.
uncleanliness, n. falta de limpieza, suciedad, f.
uncleanly, adj. sucio; incasto.
unclose, vt. abrir; descubrir, revelar.
unclouded, adj. sereno, despejado; sin nubes.
uncock, vt. desarmar o desmontar (una escopeta).
uncoil, vt. desarrollar, devanar.
uncombed, adj. despeinado, desgreñado.
uncomely, adj. indecente; feo; desagradable.
uncomfortable, adj. incómodo; intranquilo; desagradable; **—bly,** adv. incómodamente, intranquilamente.
uncommon, adj. raro, extraordinario, fuera de lo común; **—ly,** adv. extraordinariamente, raramente.
uncompromising, adj. inflexible; irreconciliable.
unconcern, n. indiferencia, f.; descuido, m.; despreocupación, f.

unconcerned, *adj.* indiferente; **—ly,** *adv.* indiferentemente; sin empacho.

unconditional, *adj.* incondicional, absoluto; **— surrender,** rendición absoluta, rendición incondicional; **—ly,** *adv.* incondicionalmente.

unconfined, *adj.* libre, ilimitado.

unconfirmed, *adj.* no confirmado; incierto, inseguro.

unconnected, *adj.* inconexo.

unconquerable, *adj.* invencible, insuperable; indomable.

unconscionable, *adj.* injusto, sin escrúpulo; **—bly,** *adv.* injustamente.

unconscious, *adj.* inconsciente; desmayado; **—ly, adv.** inconscientemente.

unconsciousness, *n.* inconsciencia, *f.*

unconstrained, *adj.* libre, voluntario.

uncontrolled, *adj.* desenfrenado, irresistible.

unconventional, *adj.* informal, sin ceremonia, sin formulismos.

unconvincing, *adj.* no convincente.

uncork, *vt.* destapar, quitar el corcho (a una botella, etc.)

uncorrected, *adj.* no corregido.

uncorrupted, *adj.* incorrupto, no pervertido.

uncouple, *vt.* desatraillar.

uncouth, *adj.* extraño; incivil, tosco, grosero; **— word,** palabrota, *f.*; **—ly,** *adv.* groseramente.

uncover, *vt.* descubrir.

uncovered, *adj.* descubierto.

uncrown, *vt.* destronar.

unction, *n.* unción, *f.*

unctuous, *adj.* untuoso.

uncultivated, *adj.* inculto.

uncurl, *vt.* desenrizar (el cabello).

uncut, adj. no cortado, entero.

undamaged, *adj.* ileso, libre de daño.

undaunted, adj. intrépido, atrevido.

undeceive, *vt.* desengañar.

undecided, adj. indeciso.

undefiled, *adj.* impoluto, puro.

undeniable, *adj.* innegable; indudable; **—bly, adv.** indubitablemente.

under, *prep.* debajo de, bajo; **— penalty of fine, — penalty of death,** so pena de multa, so pena de muerte; **—,** *adv.* debajo, abajo, más abajo.

underage, *adj.* menor de edad.

underarmed, *adj.* sin armas suficientes.

underbid, *vt.* ofrecer por algo menos de lo que vale.

underbrush, *n.* maleza, *f.*; breñal, breñar, *m.*

undercarriage, *n.* bastidor auxiliar; tren de aterrizaje (de un aeroplano).

undercharge, *vt.* cobrar de menos.

underclothing, *n.* ropa interior.

under cover, *adv.* bajo cuerda, secretamente.

undercurrent, *n.* tendencia oculta; corriente submarina.

undercut, *n.* solomo, *m.*; puñetazo hacia arriba; **—,** *vi.* vender a precios más bajos que el competidor; socavar.

underdevelopment, *n.* revelado insuficiente.

underdog, *n.* persona oprimida; el que lleva la peor parte.

underdone, *adj.* poco cocido.

underestimate, *vt.* menospreciar; calcular de menos; subestimar.

underexposure, *n.* (phot.) insuficiente exposición.

underfeeding, *n.* alimentación insuficiente.

underframe, *n.* infraestructura, *f.*

undergo, *vt.* sufrir; sostener.

undergraduate, *n.* estudiante no graduado.

underground, *adj.* subterráneo; subrepticio; **—,** *adv.* debajo de la tierra; en secreto; subrepticiamente; **—,** *n.* subterráneo, *m.*; ferrocarril subterráneo.

undergrowth, *n.* soto, monte, tallar, *m.*

underhand, *adj.* secreto, clandestino; fraudulento; injusto; **—,** *adv.* secretamente; por debajo de cuerda, clandestinamente; con las manos hacia abajo.

underhanded, *adj.* bajo cuerda, por debajo de cuerda, secreto, clandestino; **—ly,** *adv.* en forma clandestina.

underlie, *vi.* estar debajo.

underline, *vt.* subrayar.

underling, *n.* subordinado, *m.*; suboficial, *m.*

undermine, *vt.* minar; desprestigiar por debajo de cuerda.

undermost, *adj.* ínfimo.

underneath, *adv.* debajo.

undernourishment, *n.* desnutrición, *f.*

underpass, *n.* viaducto, *m.*

underpay, *vt.* and *vi.* remunerar deficientemente.

underpinning, *n.* apuntalamiento (de un edificio), *m.*

underprivileged, *adj.* desvalido, menesteroso, necesitado.

underproduction, *n.* producción insuficiente.

underrate, *vt.* menoscabar; deslustrar; menospreciar.

underscore, *vt.* subrayar.

undersea, *adj.* submarino, que está bajo la superficie del mar.

undersecretary, *n.* subsecretario, ria.

undersell, *vt.* vender por menos (que otro).

undershirt, *n.* camiseta, *f.*

undersigned, *adj.* suscrito; **—,** *n.* suscrito, ta.

undersized, *adj.* achaparrado, de tamaño menor que lo normal.

underskirt, *n.* enagua, *f.*, refajo, fondo, zagalejo, *m.*

undersleeve, *n.* manga interior, manga llevada bajo otra.

underslung, *adj.* con bajo centro de gravedad (aplícase a los vehículos de motor).

understand, *vt.* entender, comprender; **do you —?** ¿entiende Vd.? **we — each other,** nos comprendemos.

understanding, *n.* entendimiento, *m.*, comprensión, *f.*; inteligencia, *f.*; conocimiento, *m.*; correspondencia, *f.*; meollo, *m.*; **slow in —,** boto, torpe; **—,** *adj.* comprensivo; inteligente, perito.

understatement, *n.* declaración o manifestación incompleta donde no se hacen constar todos los hechos.

understudy, *n.* (theat.) sustituto, ta, actor o actriz que se prepara para reemplazar a otro en un momento dado; **—,** *vt.* and *vi.* (theat.) prepararse para tomar el papel de otro en un momento dado.

undertake, *vt.* and *vi.* emprender.

undertaker, *n.* empresario o director de pompas fúnebres.

undertaking, *n.* empresa, obra, *f.*; empeño, *m.*; **— establishment,** funeraria, *f.*

undertone, *n.* tono (de voz) bajo; voz baja; color tenue u opaco.

undertow, *n.* resaca, *f.*

undervalue, *vt.* desapreciar, menoscabar, apreciar en menos.

underwater, *adj.* que está debajo de la superficie del agua; que se usa debajo del agua.

underwear, *n.* ropa interior.

underweight, *adj.* de bajo peso, que pesa menos del término medio.

underwood, *n.* monte bajo.

underwrite, *vt.* suscribir; asegurar contra riesgos.

underwriter, *n.* asegurador, *m.*

undesigning, *adj.* sin propósitos fraudulentos; sincero; sencillo; sin astucia.

undesirable, *adj.* no deseable, nocivo.

undeveloped, *adj.* no desarrollado; **— country,** país no explotado; **— photograph,** fotografía no revelada.

undigested, *adj.* que no se ha digerido.

undiluted, *adj.* puro, sin diluir.

undiminished, *adj.* entero, sin disminuir.

undiscerning, *adj.* falto de discernimiento.

undisciplined, *adj.* indisciplinado, sin instrucción.

undisguised, *adj.* sin disfraz; cándido, sincero; natural.

undismayed, *adj.* intrépido.

undisputed, *adj.* incontestable.

undisturbed, *adj.* quieto, tranquilo, sin haber sido estorbado.

undivided, *adj.* indiviso, entero.

undo, *vt.* deshacer, desatar.

undoubted, *adj.* indubitado, evidente; **—ly,** *adv.* indudablemente, sin duda.

undress, *vt.* desnudar; **—,** *n.* paños menores; ropa de casa.

undue, *adj.* indebido; injusto.

undulant fever, *n.* fiebre mediterránea.

undulate, *vi.* ondear, ondular.

undulation, *n.* undulación, *f.*

unduly, *adv.* excesivamente; indebidamente; ilícitamente.

undying, *adj.* inmortal; imperecedero.

unearned, *adj.* inmerecido; que no se ha ganado.

unearth, *vt.* desenterrar; revelar, divulgar.

unearthly, *adj.* celeste; sobrenatural; espantoso.

uneasiness, *n.* malestar, *m.*; inquietud, intranquilidad, *f.*; desasosiego, *m.*

uneasy, *adj.* inquieto, desasosegado; incómodo; intranquilo.

unemployed, *adj.* desocupado; ocioso.

unemployment, *n.* paro, *m.*

unenlightened, *adj.* no iluminado.

unequal, *adj.* desigual; **—ly,** *adv.* desigualmente.

unequaled, *adj.* incomparable.

unerring, *adj.* infalible; **—ly,** *adv.* infaliblemente.

unessential, *adj.* no esencial; **—,** *m.* cosa no esencial, cosa accesoria.

uneven, *adj.* desigual; barrancoso; disparejo, impar; **—ly,** *adv.* desigualmente.

unexpected, *adj.* inesperado; inopinado; **—ly,** *adv.* de repente; inesperadamente.

unexplored, *adj.* ignorado, no descubierto, sin explorar.

unexposed, *adj.* (photo.) inexpuesto.

unfading, *adj.* inmarcesible.

unfailing, *adj.* infalible, seguro.

unfair, *adj.* injusto; **—ly,** *adv.* injustamente.

unfaithful, *adj.* infiel, pérfido.

unfaithfulness, *n.* infidelidad, perfidia, *f.*

unfaltering, *adj.* firme, asegurado.

unfamiliar, *adj.* desacostumbrado, desconocido.

unfasten, *vt.* desatar, soltar, aflojar.

unfathomable, *adj.* insondable, impenetrable.

unfavorable, *adj.* desfavorable; **—ly,** *adv.* desfavorablemente.

unfed, *adj.* sin haber comido.

unfeeling, *adj.* insensible, duro, cruel.

unfeigned, *adj.* verdadero, genuino; **—ly,** *adv.* sinceramente.

unfelt, *adj.* no sentido.

unfinished, *adj.* imperfecto, no acabado.

unfit, *adj.* inepto, incapaz; inadecuado; indigno; **—,** *vt.* incapacitar; inhabilitar; **—ly,** *adv.* inadecuadamente; impropiamente.

unfix, *vt.* soltar, aflojar; descomponer.

unfledged, *adj.* implume.

unfold, *vt.* desplegar; revelar; desdoblar.

unforeseen, *adj.* imprevisto.

unforgettable, *adj.* inolvidable.

unformed, *adj.* sin forma, amorfo.

unfortunate, *adj.* desafortunado, infeliz; malhadado; **—ly,** *adv.* por desgracia, infelizmente, desgraciadamente.

unfounded, *adj.* sin fundamento.

unfreezable, *adj.* incongelable.

unfrequented, *adj.* poco frecuentado.

unfriendly, *adj.* nada afable; hostil.

unfruitful, *adj.* infructuoso; estéril.

unfurl, *vt.* desplegar, extender.

unfurnished, *adj.* sin muebles, no amueblado; **— apartment,** piso sin amueblar.

ungainly, *adj.* desmañado; desgarbado.

ungear, *vt.* desembragar, desengranar, desconectar.

ungenerous, *adj.* ignoble, bajo; poco generoso.

ungentlemanly, *adj.* indigno de un caballero; incivil, descortés.

unglazed, *adj.* sin vidriar.

ungodliness, *n.* impiedad, *f.*

ungodly, *adj.* impío.

ungovernable, *adj.* indomable, ingobernable.

ungoverned, *adj.* desgobernado, desenfrenado.

ungrammatical, *adj.* contrario a las reglas de la gramática.

ungrateful, *adj.* ingrato, malagradecido; **—ly,** *adv.* ingratamente.

ungratefulness, *n.* ingratitud, *f.*

ungrounded, *adj.* infundado.

ungrudgingly, *adv.* de buena gana, sin refunfuñar.

unguarded, *adj.* sin guardia o defensa; descuidado.

unguent, *n.* ungüento, *m.*

unhallowed, *adj.* profano.

unhand, *vt.* soltar de las manos.

unhandy, *adj.* desmañado; inconveniente.

unhappily, *adv.* infelizmente.

unhappiness, *n.* infelicidad, *f.*; tristeza, *f.*

unhappy, *adj.* infeliz; descontento, triste.

unharmed, *adj.* ileso, sano y salvo, incólume.

unhealthiness, *n.* insalubridad, *f.*, falta de salud.

unhealthy, *adj.* enfermizo; insalubre, malsano.

unheard (of) *adj.* inaudito, extraño; no imaginado.

unheeded, *adj.* despreciado, no atendido.

unheedful, unheeding, *adj.* negligente; distraído.

unhinge, *vt.* desgonzar; desquiciar.

unholy, *adj.* profano, impío.

unhonored, *adj.* despreciado, no venerado.

unhook, *vt.* desganchar; desabrochar.

unhorse, *vt.* botar de la silla al jinete.

unhurt, *adj.* ileso, sin haber sufrido daño.

unicameral, *adj.* unicameral.

unicellular, *adj.* unicelular.

unicorn, *n.* unicornio, *m.*

unification, *n.* unificación, *f.*

uniform, *n.* uniforme, *m.*; **—,** *adj.* uniforme; **—ly,** *adv.* uniformemente.

uniformity, *n.* uniformidad, *f.*

unilateral, *adj.* unilateral.

unimpaired, *adj.* no disminuído, no alterado, intacto.

unimpeachable, *adj.* incontestable; irreprochable.

unimportant, *adj.* nada importante, insignificante.

uninformed, *adj.* ignorante.

uninhabitable, *adj.* inhabitable.

uninhabited, *adj.* inhabitado, desierto.

uninjured, *adj.* ileso, sin haber sufrido daño.

uninstructed, *adj.* ignorante, ignaro, no instruído.

uninstructive, *adj.* no instructivo.

unintelligible, *adj.* ininteligible; **—bly,** *adv.* en forma ininteligible.

unintentional, *adj.* no intencional, sin premeditación.

uninterested, *adj.* desinteresado.

uninteresting, *adj.* poco interesante.

uninterrupted, *adj.* ininterrumpido, sin interrupción, continuo; **—ly,** *adv.* continuamente, ininterrumpidamente.

uninvited, *adj.* no convidado, no invitado.

union, *n.* unión, *f.*; conjunción, *f.*; fusión, *f.*

unionism, *n.* unionismo, *m.*, sindicalismo obrero, agrupación obrera, formación de gremios obreros.

unionist, *n.* unitario, ria.

unionize, *vt.* sindicar; unionizar; incorporar en un gremio.

Union of South Africa, Unión Sudafricana.

Union of Soviet Socialist Republics, Unión de las Repúblicas Soviéticas Socialistas.

unique, *adj.* único, uno; singular, extraordinario.

unison, *n.* unisonancia, *f.*; concordancia, unión, *f.*; **in —,** al unísono.

unit, *n.* unidad, *f.*

Unitarian, *n.* (eccl.) unitario, ria; **u—,** *adj.* unitario.

unitary, *adj.* unitario.

unite, *vt.* and *vi.* unir, unirse, juntarse; concretar.

united, *adj.* unido, junto; **—ly,** *adv.* unidamente, de acuerdo.

United Kingdom, Reino Unido de la Gran Bretaña e Irlanda del Norte.

United States (of North America), Estados Unidos (de Norte América), *m. pl.*

unity, *n.* unidad, concordia, conformidad, *f.*

univ.: universal, universal; **universalist,** universalista; **university,** universidad.

univalence, *n.* univalencia, *f.*

universal, *adj.* universal; **— joint,** junta universal; **—ly,** *adv.* universalmente.

universality, *n.* universalidad, *f.*

universe, *n.* universo, *m.*

university, *n.* universidad, *f.*, escuela superior.

unjust, *adj.* injusto; **—ly,** *adv.* injustamente.

unjustifiable, *adj.* indisculpable; **—bly,** *adv.* inexcusablemente.

unkempt, *adj.* despeinado; descuidado en el traje; tosco.

unkind, *adj.* poco bondadoso; cruel; **—ly,** *adv.* cruelmente; desfavorablemente; ásperamente.

unknowingly, *adv.* sin saberlo; desapercibidamente.

unknown, adj. incógnito, ignoto.
unlace, vt. desenlazar, desamarrar.
unlawful, adj. ilegal; ilegítimo; ilícito; —**ly,** adv. ilegalmente.
unlearn, vt. desaprender, olvidar.
unlearned, adj. indocto, inculto.
unleavened, adj. ácimo, ázimo.
unless, conj. a menos que, si no.
unlettered, adj. iliterato.
unlicensed, adj. sin licencia.
unlike, adj. disímil, desemejante; —, adv. en forma disímil.
unlikelihood, unlikeliness, n. improbabilidad, inverosimilitud, f.
unlikely, adj. improbable; inverosímil, inverisímil.
unlimited, adj. ilimitado; —**ly,** adv. ilimitadamente.
unload, vt. descargar.
unloading, n. descarga, m.; — **permit,** permiso de descarga.
unlock, vt. abrir alguna cerradura.
unloose, vt. desatar.
unluckily, adv. desafortunadamente.
unlucky, adj. desafortunado; siniestro.
unmake, vt. deshacer.
unman, vt. afeminar; castrar, capar; desarmar.
unmanageable, adj. inmanejable, intratable.
unmanly, adj. inhumano; cobarde; afeminado.
unmannerly, adj. malcriado, descortés, incivil.
unmarried, adj. soltero; soltera; — **woman,** soltera, f.; — **man,** soltero, m.
unmask, vt. quitar la máscara; revelar; —, vi. quitarse la máscara.
unmeaning, adj. insignificativo; sin expresión; sin sentido.
unmentionable, adj. que no se puede mencionar, indigno de mencionarse; —**s,** n. pl. cosas que no pueden mencionarse, por ejemplo, (en forma jocosa) ropa interior, etc.
unmerciful, adj. desapiadado, despiadado, cruel, desalmado, inhumano.
unmerited, adj. desmerecido.
unmindful, adj. olvidadizo, negligente.
unmingled, adj. puro, sin mezcla.
unmistakable, adj. evidente; inequívoco; —**bly,** adv. inequívocamente.
unmixed, adj. sin mezcla.
unmounted, adj. desmontado.
unmoved, adj. inmoto, firme; impasible.
unnatural, adj. artificial; contrario a las leyes de la naturaleza; —**ly,** adv. contra la naturaleza.
unnecessarily, adv. innecesariamente, sin necesidad; inútilmente.
unnecessary, adj. innecesario, inútil.
unnerve, vt. enervar.
unnoticed, adj. no observado.
unnumbered, adj. innumerable.
unobserved, adj. no observado.

unobtainable, adj. que no puede obtenerse, inasequible.
unobtrusive, adj. modesto.
unoccupied, adj. desocupado.
unoffending, adj. inofensivo; inocente.
unofficial, adj. extraoficial; particular, privado.
unorthodox, adj. heterodoxo.
unpack, vt. desempacar; desempaquetar; desenvolver.
unpaid, adj. pendiente de pago.
unpalatable, adj. desabrido.
unparalleled, adj. sin paralelo; sin par.
unpardonable, adj. imperdonable; irremisible; —**bly,** adv. imperdonablemente.
unparliamentary, adj. contrario a las reglas del parlamento.
unperceived, adj. no percibido.
unpitying, adj. incompasivo.
unpleasant, adj. desagradable; —**ly,** adv. desagradablemente.
unpleasantness, n. desagrado, m.
unpolished, adj. sin pulir; rudo, grosero; bruto.
unpolluted, adj. impoluto, inmaculado.
unpopular, adj. impopular.
unpracticed, adj. inexperto, no versado.
unprecedented, adj. sin precedente.
unprejudiced, adj. sin prejuicios.
unpremeditated, adj. sin premeditación.
unprepared, adj. no preparado.
unpretending, adj. sin pretensiones, sencillo, modesto.
unprincipled, adj. sin principios morales, sin escrúpulos.
unproductive, adj. estéril, infructuoso.
unprofitable, adj. inútil, vano, que no rinde utilidad o provecho; —**bly,** adv. inútilmente, en forma infructuosa.
unpropitious, adj. infausto, desfavorable.
unprotected, adj. sin protección, sin defensa; desvalido.
unprovided, adj. desprovisto.
unpublished, adj. inédito, no publicado.
unpunctual, adj. inexacto; falto de puntualidad.
unpunished, adj. impune.
unquenchable, adj. inextinguible.
unquestionable, adj. indiscutible, indudable, indubitable, indisputable; —**bly,** adv. sin lugar a duda.
unquestioned, adj. incontestable; no interrogado.
unquiet, adj. inquieto, agitado.
unravel, vt. desenredar; resolver.
unread, adj. no leído, ignorante.
unreal, adj. fantástico, ilusorio, que no tiene realidad.
unreasonable, adj. irrazonable; irracional; inmoderado, exorbitante; —**bly,** adv. en forma irrazonable; irracionalmente.
unrecognizable, adj. irreconocible.
unregarded, adj. despreciado, no considerado.
unrelenting, adj. inflexible; inexorable.

unremitting, adj. perseverante, constante, incansable.

unrepentant, unrepenting, adj. impenitente.

unreserved, adj. franco, abierto; sin restricción; —ly, adv. abiertamente.

unresisting, adj. sin resistencia.

unrest, n. inquietud, impaciencia, f.; movimiento, m.

unrestrained, adj. desenfrenado; ilimitado.

unriddle, vt. desatar un enigma.

unrighteous, adj. injusto; malvado; —ly, adv. inicuamente.

unripe, adj. inmaturo; precoz, prematuro; **unripened fruit,** fruta verde, fruta no madura.

unrivaled, adj. sin rival, sin igual.

unroll, vt. desenrollar, desplegar.

unroof, vt. destechar.

unruffled, adj. plácido, sereno, calmado.

unruliness, n. turbulencia, f.; falta de sumisión; desenfreno, m., indisciplina, f.

unruly, adj. desenfrenado, inmanejable, refractario; desarreglado.

unsaddle, vt. desensillar.

unsafe, adj. inseguro, peligroso; —ly, adv. inseguramente.

unsalable, adj. invendible.

unsanitary, adj. antihigiénico.

unsatisfactory, adj. que no satisface, insatisfactorio.

unsatisfied, adj. descontento; no satisfecho.

unsavory, adj. desabrido, insípido.

unschooled, adj. indocto; sin escuela.

unscrew, vt. destornillar, desentornillar.

unscrupulous, adj. sin escrúpulos, inmoral, desalmado.

unseasonable, adj. intempestivo, fuera de propósito; **at an — hour,** a deshora; —bly, adv. intempestivamente.

unseat, vt. quitar del asiento; privar del derecho de formar parte de una cámara legislativa.

unseemly, adj. indecente, indecoroso.

unseen, adj. no visto; invisible.

unselfish, adj. desinteresado, generoso.

unsettle, vt. perturbar; desarreglar; alterar.

unsettled, adj. voluble, inconstante; incierto, indeciso; no establecido; — **accounts,** cuentas por pagar, cuentas no liquidadas.

unshakable, adj. inmutable, firme, estable; impasible, inconmovible; insacudible.

unshaken, adj. firme, estable, inmoble.

unsheathe, vt. desenvainar.

unsheltered, adj. sin techo; desvalido.

unship, vt. desembarcar; desmontar; **to — the oars,** (naut.) desarmar los remos.

unshod, adj. descalzo; desherrado.

unshorn, adj. sin esquilar.

unshrinking, adj. intrépido.

unsightliness, n. fealdad, deformidad, f.

unsightly, adj. desagradable a la vista, feo.

unskilled, adj. inexperto, inhábil.

unskillful, unskilful, adj. inexperto, inhábil, sin destreza, chambón; —ly, adv. con poca maña, en forma inexperta.

unsociable, adj. insociable, intratable, huraño.

unsold, adj. no vendido.

unsoldierly, adj. indigno de un soldado.

unsought, adj. hallado sin buscarlo, no solicitado.

unsound, adj. falto de salud; falto de sentido; inestable; erróneo, falso.

unsparing, adj. generoso, liberal; incompasivo, cruel; —ly, adv. generosamente; sin compasión.

unspeakable, adj. indecible; —ly, adv. en forma indecible, de modo inexpresable.

unstable, adj. instable, inconstante.

unsteadily, adv. inconstantemente; irresolutamente; inestablemente.

unsteadiness, n. inestabilidad, f.; inconstancia, f.

unsteady, adj. voluble, inconstante; inestable; inseguro; —ily, adv. inconstantemente; irresolutamente; inestablemente.

unstruck, adj. impávido.

unstudied, adj. no estudiado, natural.

unsubdued, adj. indomado.

unsubstantial, adj. impalpable, insustancial.

unsuccessful, adj. infructuoso; infeliz, desafortunado; —ly, adv. infructuosamente.

unsuitable, adj. inadecuado, impropio; —bly, adv. inadecuadamente, impropiamente.

unsullied, adj. inmaculado, puro, limpio.

unsurpassable, adj. inmejorable.

unswerving, adj. indesviable.

untamable, adj. indomable.

untamed, adj. indómito, indomado.

untangle, vt. desenredar.

untaught, adj. ignorante, sin instrucción.

unteachable, adj. incapaz de ser enseñado.

untenable, adj. insostenible.

untenanted, adj. desarrendado.

unthankful, adj. ingrato, malagradecido; —ly, adv. ingratamente.

unthinking, adj. desatento, inconsiderado, indiscreto; irreflexivo.

unthought (of), adj. impensado.

untidily, adj. desaliñadamente, desaseadamente.

untidy, adj. desarreglado, descuidado, desaliñado.

untie, vt. desatar, deshacer, soltar, desamarrar.

until, prep. and conj. hasta, hasta que.

untimely, adj. intempestivo; prematuro.

untiring, adj. incansable.

unto, prep. (poet.) a, en, para, hasta.

untold, adj. no relatado, no dicho.

untouched, adj. intacto, no tocado.

untoward, adj. perverso; siniestro, adverso; refractario, testarudo.

untraveled, adj. no frecuentado por viajeros, aislado.

untried, *adj.* no ensayado o probado.

untrod, untrodden, *adj.* que no ha sido pisado, no recorrido.

untroubled, *adj.* no perturbado, tranquilo, calmado.

untrue, *adj.* falso, incierto; desleal.

untrustworthy, *adj.* indigno de confianza.

untruth, *n.* falsedad, mentira, *f.*

untutored, *adj.* instruído, sin escuela; sencillo.

unused, *adj.* inusitado; desacostumbrado.

unusual, *adj.* inusitado, raro, insólito; poco común; **—ly,** *adv.* inusitadamente, raramente.

unutterable, *adj.* inefable, indecible, inexpresable.

unvaried, *adj.* invariado.

unvarying, *adj.* invariable.

unveil, *vt.* and *vi.* descubrir; revelar; quitar el velo (a alguna cosa).

unveiled, *adj.* descubierto; (de una estatua, etc.) a cara descubierta.

unvoiced, *adj.* no expresado; mudo.

unwarrantable, *adj.* indisculpable, injustificable.

unwarranted, *adj.* injustificable, inexcusable.

unwary, *adj.* incauto, desprevenido.

unwelcome, *adj.* inoportuno; mal acogido, no recibido con gusto.

unwell, *adj.* mal de salud, enfermo.

unwholesome. *adj.* malsano, insalubre; inmoral.

unwieldy, *adj.* pesado, difícil de manejar.

unwilling, *adj.* renuente, sin deseos, sin querer; **—ly,** *adv.* de mala gana.

unwind, *vt.* desenredar, desenrollar; desenmarañar.

unwise, *adj.* imprudente; **—ly,** *adv.* imprudentemente, sin juicio.

unwittingly, *adv.* sin saber, sin darse cuenta.

unwonted, *adj.* insólito.

unworthily, *adv.* indignamente.

unworthiness, *n.* indignidad, bajeza, *f.*

unworthy, *adj.* indigno, vil.

unwound, *adj.* sin cuerda; desenrollado.

unwrap, *vt.* desenvolver; abrir; revelar.

unwritten, *adj.* verbal, no escrito; **— law,** ley de la costumbre, derecho consuetudinario.

unyielding, *adj.* inflexible.

unyoke, *vt.* desuncir.

up, *adv.* arriba, en lo alto; **—,** *prep.* hasta; **— to,** hasta; **—,** *adj.* levantado; hacia arriba; **— and down,** acá y allá, arriba y abajo.

upbraid, *vt.* echar en cara, vituperar.

upbraidingly, *adv.* por vía de reconvención.

upbringing, *n.* educación, crianza, *f.*

upbuild, *vt.* reconstruir; vigorizar.

upcountry, *n.* (coll.) el interior de un país; **—,** *adj.* que reside en el interior de un país.

upgrade, *n.* cuesta arriba, pendiente arriba.

upheaval, *n.* alzamiento, lavantamiento, *m.*; conmoción, *f.*

uphill, *adj.* difícil, penoso; **—,** *adv.* en grado ascendente; **—,** *n.* subida, *f.*

uphold, *vt.* levantar en alto; sostener; apoyar, proteger; defender.

upholster, *vt.* entapizar.

upholsterer, *n.* tapicero, *m.*

upholstery, *n.* tapicería, *f.*, tapizado, *m.*

upkeep, *n.* conservación, *f.*, mantenimiento, *m.*

upland, *n.* tierra montañosa; **—,** *adj.* alto, elevado.

uplift, *vt.* levantar en alto; mejorar.

upon, *prep.* sobre, encima.

upper, *adj.* superior; más elevado; **— berth,** cama o litera alta (en un tren, un vapor, etc.); **— case,** (print.) caja alta, letras mayúsculas; **— end,** cabecera, *f.*; **— deck,** (naut.) sobrecubierta, *f.*; **— hand,** dominio, *m.*, predominancia, *f.*

upper-case, *adj.* (print.) de caja alta.

upper-class, *adj.* aristocrático; relativo a los grados superiores de un colegio.

uppercut, *n.* puñetazo con el brazo encogido dirigido hacia arriba.

Upper House, *n.* Senado, *m.*, Cámara de los Lores.

uppermost, *adj.* superior en posición, rango, poder, etc.; **to be —,** predominar.

uppish, *adj.* (coll.) engreído, altivo, orgulloso, pretencioso.

upright, *adj.* derecho, recto, justo; perpendicular; **—ly,** *adv.* rectamente; perpendicularmente.

uprightness, *n.* elevación perpendicular; rectitud, probidad, *f.*

uprise, *vi.* levantarse.

uprising, *n.* subida, *f.*, acto de levantarse.

uproar, *n.* tumulto, alboroto, *m.*

uproarious, *adj.* tumultuoso, ruidoso.

uproot, *vt.* desarraigar, extirpar.

upset, *vt.* and *vi.* volcar, trastornar; **—,** *adj.* desordenado; volcado; agitado (de ánimo); mortificado; **—,** *n.* trastorno, *m.*; vuelco, *m.*

upshot, *n.* remate, *m.*; fin, *m.*, conclusión, *f.*

upside-down, *adj.* de arriba abajo.

upstairs, *adv.* en el piso de arriba, arriba.

upstanding, *adj.* erguido; superior; probo.

upstart, *n.* zaramullo, zascandil, *m.*; advenedizo, *m.*

upstream, *adv.* aguas arriba, río arriba.

up-to-date, *adj.* moderno, de última moda, reciente.

uptown, *n.* cierta sección de la ciudad fuera del centro; parte alta de la ciudad.

upturn, *vt.* dar vueltas, poner encima lo que está abajo; **—,** *n.* vuelta hacia arriba.

upward, *adv.* hacia arriba.

uranium, *n.* uranio, *m.*

urban, *adj.* urbano.

urbane, *adj.* civil, atento, cortés.

urbanity, *n.* urbanidad, *f.*

urbanization, *n.* urbanización, *f.*

urbanize, vt. urbanizar.
urchin, n. (zool.) erizo, m.; pilluelo, m., (coll.) granuja, m.
uremia, n. uremia, f.
uremic, adj. urémico.
urethra, n. uretra, f.
urethritis, n. (med.) uretritis, f.
urge, vt. and vi. incitar, hurgar; activar; urgir, instar.
urgency, n. urgencia, f.; premura, f.
urgent, adj. urgente; **—ly,** adv. urgentemente.
uric, adj. úrico.
urinal, n. orinal, m.
urinalysis, n. (med.) urinálisis, f.
urinary, adj. urinario.
urinate, vi. orinar, mear.
urine, n. orina, f., orines, m. pl.
urn, n. urna, f.
urticaria, n. (med.) urticaria, f.
Uru. Uruguay, Uruguay.
Uruguayan, n. and adj. uruguayo, ya.
U. S. United States, E. U. Estados Unidos.
us, pron. nos; nosotros.
U.S.A.: United States Army, Ejército de los Estados Unidos; **United States of America,** E.U.A. Estados Unidos de América.
usable, adj. apto, hábil; utilizable.
usage, n. uso, m.; tratamiento, m.
usance, n. uso, m., usanza, f.; costumbre, f.
use, n. uso, m., utilidad, f.; servicio, m. **—,** vt. and vi. usar, emplear, servirse de; acostumbrar; soler; **to make — of,** utilizar.
used, adj. gastado, usado; de ocasión; **— car,** automóvil de ocasión o de segunda mano.
useful, adj. útil; **to be made —,** utilizarse; **—ly,** adv. en forma útil.
usefulness, n. utilidad, f.
useless, adj. inútil; deslucido; **to become —,** gastarse; **—ly,** adv. inútilmente.
uselessness, n. inutilidad, f.
usher, n. acomodador, m.; ujier, m.; **—,** vt. introducir; anunciar; acomodar (en un teatro, iglesia, etc.).
U.S.M.: United States Mail, Correo de los Estados Unidos; **United States Marines,** Marinos de los Estados Unidos.
U.S.M.A. United States Military Academy, Academia Militar de los Estados Unidos.
U.S.M.C. United States Marine Corps, Cuerpo de Marinos de los E. U. A.
U.S.N. United States Navy, Marina de los Estados Unidos.
U.S.N.A. United States Naval Academy, Academia Naval de los E.U.A.
U.S.N.G. United States National Guard, Guardia Nacional de los E.U.A.
U.S.S. United States Ship, United States Steamer, Vapor Norteamericano, Vapor de los E.U.A.
USSR, U.S.S.R. Union of Soviet Socialist Republics, U.R.S.S. Unión de las Repú-

blicas Soviéticas Socialistas.
usual, adj. usual, común, usado; general, ordinario; **—ly,** adv. usualmente, ordinariamente, de costumbre.
usurer, n. usurero, m.
usurious, adj. usurario.
usurp, vt. usurpar.
usurpation, n. usurpación, f.
usury, n. usura, f.; **to practice —,** usurear.
Ut. Utah, Utah.
utensil, n. utensilio, m.; **—s,** n. pl. útiles, m. pl.; **kitchen —s,** trastos, m. pl., batería de cocina.
uterine, adj. uterino.
uterus, n. útero, m., matriz, f.
utilitarian, adj. utilitario.
utility, n. utilidad, f.; **public —ies,** servicios públicos.
utilization, n. utilización, f.
utilize, vt. utilizar; emplear.
utmost, adj. extremo, sumo; último; **to the —,** hasta no más.
Utopia, utopia, n. utopía, f.
Utopian, utopian, adj. utópico; imaginario; **—,** n. persona que cree en una utopía.
utter, adj. exterior; todo; extremo; entero; **—,** vt. proferir; expresar; publicar.
utterance, n. habla, expresión, manifestación, f.
utterly, adv. enteramente, del todo.
uvula, n. úvula, f., galillo, m.
uxoricide, n. uxoricida, m., marido que mata a su esposa.
uxorious, adj. gurrumino; **—ly,** adv. con gurrumina.

V.

V.: Venerable, Venerable; **Vice,** V. Vice.
v.: verb, v. verbo; **verse,** verso; **versus,** contra; **vice-,** vice; **volume,** tomo; **see,** V. Véa. véase.
Va. Virginia, Virginia.
V.A. Vice Admiral, Vicealmirante.
vacancy, n. vacante, f.; vacío, m.; **— in an office,** resulta, vacante, f.
vacant, adj. vacío, desocupado, vacante.
vacate, vt. desocupar; anular, invalidar.
vacation, n. vacación, f., vacaciones, f. pl.
vaccinate, vt. vacunar.
vaccination, n. vacuna, f.; vacunación, f.
vaccine, n. vacuna, f.
vacillate, vi. vacilar.
vacillation, n. vaivén, m.; vacilación, f.; irresolución, f.
vacuity, n. vacuidad, f.
vacuous, adj. vacío.
vacuum, n. vacuo, vacío, m.; **— bottle,** termos, m.; **— cleaner,** aspirador de polvo, barredor al vacío; **— filter,** filtro al vacío; **— pump,** bomba aspirante, bomba de vacío; **— tube,** tubo de vacío; audión, m.
vagabond, n. and adj. vagabundo, vagamundo, m.

vagary, *n.* capricho, *m.*; extravagancia, *f.*
vagina, *n.* (anat.) vagina, *f.*; (bot.) vaina, *f.*
vagrancy, *n.* vagancia, tuna, *f.*
vagrant, *adj.* vagabundo; —, *n.* bribón, *m.*
vague, *adj.* vago; —ly, *adv.* vagamente.
vain, *adj.* vano, inútil; vanidoso, presuntuoso; **in —,** en vano; —ly, *adv.* vanamente.
vainglorious, *adj.* vanaglorioso.
vainglory, *n.* vanagloria, *f.*
val. value, V. valor.
valance, *n.* cenefa, doselera, *f.*
vale, *n.* (poet.) valle, *m.*
valediction, *n.* despedida (especialmente de los graduados de un colegio), *f.*
valedictory, *adj.* de despedida; —, *n.* discurso de despedida.
valence, *n.* (chem.) valencia, *f.*
valency, *n.* valencia, *f.*
valentine, *n.* persona a quien se le tributa amor el día de San Valentín (14 de febrero); tarjeta o regalo que se envía el día de San Valentín en señal de amor.
Valerian, Valeriano.
valerian, *n.* (bot.) valeriana, *f.*
valet, *n.* criado, camarero, *m.*; (Mex.) camarista, *m.*
valetudinarian, *adj.* valetudinario, enfermizo; —, *n.* persona enfermiza o débil.
valiant, *adj.* valiente, valeroso; —ly, *adv.* valientemente.
valid, *adj.* válido.
validate, *vt.* validar, hacer válido.
validation, *n.* validación, *f.*
validity, *n.* validación, validez, *f.*
valise, *n.* maleta, valija, *f.*; (Mex.) castaña, *f.*
valley, *n.* valle, *m.*, cuenca, *f.*
valor, *n.* valor, aliento, brío, *m.*, fortaleza, *f.*
valorous, *adj.* valeroso; —ly, *adv.* con valor.
valuable, *adj.* precioso, valioso; **to be —,** valer; —s, *n. pl.* tesoros, *m. pl.*, joyas preciosas, etc.
valuation, *n.* tasa, valuación, *f.*
value, *n.* valor, precio, importe, *m.*; **real —,** valor efectivo; **— stipulated, — agreed on,** valor entendido; **face —,** valor nominal o aparente; —, *vt.* valuar, apreciar.
valueless, *adj.* sin valor, que no vale nada.
valve, *n.* válvula, *f.*, regulador, *m.*; **safety —,** válvula de seguridad; **slide —,** válvula corrediza; **air —,** válvula de aires.
vamp, *vt.* remendar; (coll.) cautivar con coqueteos; —, *n.* pala (de un zapato), *f.*
van, *n.* vagón, *m.*, vehículo grande y cerrado para trasportar muebles, animales, etc.; **cattle —,** vagón cuadra; **brake —,** vagón freno; **goods —,** vagón de mercancías.
vanadium, *n.* vanadio, *m.*
vandal, *n.* vándalo, *m.*; —, *adj.* vándalo.
vandalism, *n.* vandalismo, *m.*
vane, *n.* veleta, *f.*; (naut.) grímpola, *f.*
vanguard, *n.* vanguardia, *f.*
vanilla, *n.* vainilla, *f.*

vanish, *vi.* desvanecerse, desaparecer.
vanishing point, *n.* punto de fuga.
vanity, *n.* vanidad, *f.*; **— case,** neceser, *m.*, polvera, *f.*, estuche o caja de afeites.
vanman, *n.* conductor de vagones.
vanquish, *vt.* vencer, conquistar.
vantage, vantage ground, *n.* ventaja, *f.*; provecho, *m.*; oportunidad, *f.*; superioridad, *f.*
vapid, *adj.* insípido, sin espíritu; falto de sabor.
vapor, *n.* vapor, *m.*; exhalación, *f.*
vaporizer, *n.* vaporizador, *m.*
vaporous, *adj.* vaporoso.
var. variant, variante.
variable, *adj.* variable; —bly, *adv.* variablemente.
variance, *n.* discordia, desavenencia, *f.*; diferencia, *f.*; desviación, *f.*; discrepancia, *f.*
variation, *n.* variación, mudanza, *f.*
varicose, *adj.* varicoso; **— vein,** várice, *f.*
varied, *adj.* variado; cambiado, alterado.
variegated, *adj.* abigarrado.
variegation, *n.* variedad de colores.
variety, *n.* variedad, *f.*
variometer, *n.* variómetro, *m.*
various, *adj.* vario, diverso, diferentes; —ly, *adv.* variamente.
varnish, *n.* barniz, *m.*; —, *vt.* barnizar; charolar.
varsity, *n.* equipo deportivo principal seleccionado para representar a una universidad, etc.
vary, *vt. and vi.* variar, diferenciar; cambiar, mudarse, discrepar.
varying, *adj.* variante.
vase, *n.* vaso, jarrón, florero, *m.*
vaseline, *n.* vaselina, *f.*, ungüento de petróleo, *m.*
vassal, *n.* vasallo, *m.*
vassalage, *n.* vasallaje, *m.*
vast, *adj.* vasto; inmenso; —ly, *adv.* excesivamente; vastamente.
vat, *n.* tina, paila, *f.*, tacho, *m.*
vaudeville, *n.* (theat.) función de variedades.
vault, *n.* bóveda, *f.*; cueva, caverna, *f.*; salto, *m.*, voltereta, *f.*; —, *vt.* abovedar; —, *vi.* saltar, dar una voltereta.
vaunt, *vi.* jactarse, vanagloriarse.
vb.: verb, v. verbo; **verbal,** verbal.
veal, *n.* ternera, *f.*; ternero, *m.*; **— cutlet,** chuleta de ternera.
vector, *n.* (math., phys.) vector, *m.*
veer, *vi.* (naut.) virar, rondar, cambiar (el viento).
vegetable, *adj.* vegetal; **— man,** verdulero, *m.*; **— soup,** menestra, *f.*, sopa de legumbres; —, *n.* vegetal, *m.*; —s, *n. pl.* legumbres, *f. pl.*
vegetarian, *n.* and *adj.* vegetariano, na.
vegetarianism, *n.* vegetarianismo, *m.*
vegetate, *vi.* vegetar.
vegetation, *n.* vegetación, *f.*
vegetative, *adj.* vegetativo.

vehemence, *n.* vehemencia, violencia, *f.*; viveza, *f.*
vehement, *adj.* vehemente, violento; **—ly,** *adv.* vehementemente.
vehicle, *n.* vehículo, *m.*
veil, *n.* velo, *m.*; disfraz, *m.*; **—,** *vt.* encubrir, ocultar, cubrir con velo.
vein, *n.* vena, *f.*; cavidad, *f.*; inclinación del ingenio; humor, *m.*
veined, veiny, *adj.* venoso; vetado.
vellum, *n.* vitela, *f.*; pergamino, *m.*; cuero curtido; **— paper,** papel avitelado.
velocity, *n.* velocidad, *f.*
velodrome, *n.* velódromo, *m.*
velour, *n.* terciopelo, *m.*
velvet, *n.* terciopelo, *m.*; **—,** *adj.* de terciopelo; terciopelado.
velveteen, *n.* pana, *f.*, velludillo, *m.*
velvetlike, *adj.* aterciopelado, terciopelado.
velvety, *adj.* terciopelado, aterciopelado.
Ven. Venerable, Ven. Venerable.
venal, *adj.* venal, mercenario.
venality, *n.* venalidad, *f.*
vend, *vt.* vender por menor; exclamar públicamente.
vender, *n.* vendedor, ra.
veneer, *vt.* taracear; **—,** *n.* chapa, capa, *f.*; apariencia, ostentación, *f.*, brillo, *m.*
venerable, *adj.* venerable; **—bly,** *adv.* venerablemente.
venerate, *vt.* venerar, honrar.
veneration, *n.* veneración, *f.*; culto, *m.*
venereal, *adj.* venéreo.
Venetian, *n.* and *adj.* veneciano, na.
Venez. Venezuela, Venezuela.
venezuelan, *n.* and *adj.* venezolano, na.
vengeance, *n.* venganza, *f.*
venial, *adj.* venial.
Venice, Venecia, *f.*
venire, *n.* orden de convocación del jurado.
venison, *n.* carne de venado.
venom, *n.* veneno, *m.*
venomous, *adj.* venenoso; **—ly,** *adv.* venenosamente.
vent, *n.* respiradero, *m.*; salida, *f.*; apertura, *f.*; **— of a gun,** fogón, *m.*; **—,** *vt.* dar salida; echar fuera; divulgar (un proyecto, etc.).
ventilate, *vt.* ventilar; discutir, airear.
ventilation, *n.* ventilación, *f.*
ventilator, *n.* ventilador, abanico, *m.*
ventricle, *n.* ventrículo, *m.*
ventriloquist, *n.* ventrílocuo, *m.*
venture, *n.* riesgo, *m.*; ventura, *f.*; **—,** *vi.* osar, aventurarse; **—,** *vt.* arriesgar.
venturesome, venturous, *adj.* osado, atrevido; **—ly,** *adv.* osadamente.
Venus, (goddess or **planet),** *n.* (diosa o planeta) Venus, *f.*
veracious, *adj.* veraz; honrado.
veracity, *n.* veracidad, *f.*
veranda or **verandah,** *n.* veranda, terraza, galería, *f.*, mirador, *m.*
verb, *n.* (gram.) verbo, *m.*
verbal, *adj.* verbal, literal; **—ly,** *adv.*

verbalmente, oralmente, de palabra.
verbalism, *n.* palabrería, *f.*
verbatim, *adv.* palabra por palabra.
verbena, *n.* (bot.) verbena, *f.*
verbiage, *n.* verbosidad, *f.*, ripio, *m.*
verbose, *adj.* verboso.
verbosity, *n.* verbosidad, *f.*
verdant, *adj.* verde.
verdict, *n.* (law) veredicto, *m.*; sentencia, *f.*, dictamen, *m.*; fallo (del jurado), *m.*
verdigris, *n.* cardenillo, verdín, *m.*
verdure, *n.* verdura, *f.*, verdor, *m.*
verge, *n.* vara, *f.*; maza, *f.*; borde, *m.*; margen, *m.* y *f.*; **—,** *vi.* inclinarse; tirar parecerse a (colores, etc.).
verger, *n.* pertiguero, *m.*
verification, *n.* verificación, *f.*
verify, *vt.* verificar; sustanciar.
verily, *adv.* en verdad; ciertamente.
veritable, *adj.* verdadero, cierto.
verity, *n.* verdad, realidad, *f.*
verjuice, *n.* agraz, *m.*
vermicelli, *n. pl.* fideos, *m.pl.*
vermicular, *adj.* vermicular.
vermifuge, *n.* and *adj.* vermífugo, *m.*
vermilion, *n.* bermellón, *m.*; **—,** *vt.* teñir de bermellón, teñir de cinabrio.
vermin, *n.* bichos, *m.pl.*
verminous, *adj.* verminoso.
vernacular, *adj.* nativo.
vernal, *adj.* vernal.
veronal, *n.* veronal (nombre de fábrica de un narcótico), *m.*
versatile, *adj.* hábil para muchas cosas; versátil, voluble.
versatility, *n.* variedad de habilidades; veleidad, *f.*
verse, *n.* verso, *m.*; versículo, *m.*; **blank —,** verso blanco; **free —,** verso suelto o libre.
versed, *adj.* versado.
versify, *vt.* and *vi.* versificar, trovar, hacer versos.
version, *n.* versión, traducción, *f.*
versus, *prep.* contra.
vertebra, *n.* vértebra, *f.*
vertebral, vertebrate, *adj.* vertebral, vertebrado.
vertex, *n.* cenit, vértice, *m.*
vertical, *adj.* vertical; **— fin,** (aer.) estabilizador vertical; **—ly,** *adv.* verticalmente.
vertigo, *n.* vértigo, *m.*
verve, *n.* estro poético; energía, animación, *f.*, entusiasmo, *m.*; numen, *m.*, inspiración, *f.*
very, *adj.* idéntico, mismo; especial; **—,** *adv.* muy, mucho, sumamente.
vesicle, *n.* vesícula, vejiguilla, *f.*
vespers, *n.pl.* vísperas, *f.pl.*
vessel, *n.* vasija, *f.*, vaso, *m.*; buque, bajel, *m.*
vest, *n.* chaleco, *m.*; **—,** *vt.* vestir; investir.
vestal, *adj.* casto, puro; **— virgin,** vestal, *f.*
vested, *adj.* vestido, investido.
vestibule, *n.* zaguán, *m.*, casapuerta, *f.*

vestige, *n.* vestigio, *m.*
vestigial, *adj.* (biol.) atrofiado.
vestment, *n.* vestido, *m.*; vestidura, *f.*
vest-pocket, *adj.* propio para el bolsillo del chaleco; pequeño; — **edition,** edición en miniatura.
vestry, *n.* sacristía, *f.*
vesture, *n.* vestidura, *f.*, atavío, *m.*
vet.: veteran, veterano; **veterinary,** veter. veterinario.
vetch, *n.* (bot.) arveja, alverjana, *f.*
veteran, *n.* and *adj.* veterano, na.
veterinary, *n.* and *adj.* veterinario, *m.*
veto, *n.* veto, *m.*
vex, *vt.* vejar, molestar, contrariar; **—ed,** *adj.* picado, molesto, contrariado.
vexation, *n.* vejamen, *m.*, vejación, molestia, *f.*
vexatious, *adj.* penoso, molesto, enfadoso; **—ly,** *adv.* penosamente.
V.F.W. Veterans of Foreign Wars, Veteranos de Guerras Extranjeras.
V.I. Virgin Islands, Islas Vírgenes.
v.i. intransitive verb, v. intr. verbo intransitivo.
viability, *n.* viabilidad, *f.*
viaduct, *n.* viaducto, *m.*
vial, *n.* redoma, ampolleta, *f.*, frasco, *m.*
viand, *n.* vianda, *f.*
viaticum, *n.* viático, *m.*
vibrant, *adj.* vibrante.
vibrate, *vt.* vibrar.
vibrating, *adj.* vibrante.
vibration, *n.* vibración, *f.*
vibrator, *n.* vibrador, *m.*
vicar, *n.* vicario, *m.*
vicarage, *n.* vicaría, *f.*
vicar-general, *n.* vicario general.
vicarious, *adj.* sustituto.
vice, *n.* vicio, *m.*; maldad, *f.*; deformidad física; mancha, *f.*, defecto, *m.*; — **versa,** viceversa, al contrario. —, *prep.* en lugar de; —, (prefijo) vice.
vice-admiral, *n.* vicealmirante, *m.*
vice-chairman, *n.* vicepresidente (de una reunión, etc.), *m.*
vice-consul, *n.* vicecónsul, *m.*
Vice Pres. Vice-President, V.P. Vice-presidente.
vice-president, *n.* vicepresidente, *m.*
viceroy, *n.* virrey, *m.*
vicinity, *n.* vecindad, proximidad, *f.*
vicious, *adj.* vicioso; — **circle,** círculo vicioso; **—ly,** *adv.* de manera viciosa.
vicissitude, *n.* vicisitud, *f.*
victim, *n.* víctima, *f.*
victimize, *vt.* sacrificar; engañar.
victor, *n.* vencedor, *m.*
victorious, *adj.* victorioso, vencedor; **—ly,** *adv.* victoriosamente.
victory, *n.* victoria, *f.*
victrola (trade name), *n.* victrola (nombre comercial), *f.*
victual, *vt.* proveer, abastecer de comestibles.

victualer, victualler, *n.* abastecedor, proveedor, *m.*; tabernero, *m.*
victuals, *n. pl.* vituallas, viandas, *f. pl.*, comestibles, *m. pl.*
vid. see, V. véase.
videlicet, *adv.* a saber.
vie, *vi.* competir.
Vienna, Viena, *f.*
Viennese, *n.* and *adj.* vienés, esa.
view, *n.* vista, *f.*; perspectiva, *f.*; aspecto, *m.*; examen, *m.*; apariencia, *f.*; ver, *m.*; **bird's-eye** —, vista a vuelo de pájaro; **in** — **of,** en vista de; **point of** —, punto de vista; —, *vt.* mirar, ver; examinar.
vigil, *n.* vela, *f.*; vigilia, *f.*
vigilance, *n.* vigilancia, *f.*
vigilant, *adj.* vigilante, atento; **—ly,** *adv.* con vigilancia.
vigilante, *n.* persona que se autonombra para ejercer funciones policíacas donde no hay policía o donde legal o ilegalmente no alcanza la acción de ésta; equivale a veces a terrorista.
vignette, *n.* viñeta, *f.*
vigor, *n.* vigor, *m.*; robustez, *f.*; energía, *f.*
vigorous, *adj.* vigoroso; valiente; **—ly,** *adv.* vigorosamente.
vile, *adj.* vil, bajo; **—ly,** *adv.* vilmente.
vilify, *vt.* envilecer; degradar.
villa, *n.* quinta, *f.*, casa de campo.
village, *n.* aldea, *f.*; lugar, *m.*
villager, *n.* aldeano, *m.*
villain, *n.* malvado, miserable, *m.*
villainous, *adj.* bellaco, vil, ruin; villano; **—ly,** *adv.* vilmente.
villainy, *n.* villanía, vileza, *f.*
vim, *n.* energía, *f.*, vigor, *m.*
Vincent, Vicente.
vindicate, *vt.* vindicar, defender.
vindication, *n.* vindicación, *f.*; justificación, *f.*
vindictive, *adj.* vengativo; **—ly,** *adv.* por vindicación.
vine, *n.* vid, *f.*
vinegar, *n.* vinagre, *m.*
vineyard, *n.* viña, *f.*, viñedo, *m.*; **keeper of a** —, viñador, viñero, *m.*
vintage, *n.* vendimia, *f.*
vintager, *n.* vendimiador, *m.*
vintner, *n.* vinatero, *m.*
viol, *n.* (mus.) violón, *m.*
viola, *n.* (mus.) viola, *f.*
violate, *vt.* violar.
violation, *n.* violación, *f.*
violator, *n.* violador, *m.*
violence, *n.* violencia, *f.*
violent, *adj.* violento; **—ly,** *adv.* violentamente.
Violet, Violeta.
violet, *n.* (bot.) violeta, viola, *f.*; violeta (color), *f.*
violet-colored, *adj.* violáceo.
violet ray, *n.* rayo violeta o ultravioleta.
violin, *n.* (mus.) violín, *m.*
violinist, *n.* violinista, *m.* y *f.*

violoncello, *n.* (mus.) violoncelo, violon- chelo, *m.*

viosterol, *n.* viosterol, *m.*

viper, *n.* víbora, *f.*

virago, *n.* virago, *f.*, mujer varonil, mujer alborotosa y pendenciera.

virescence, *n.* virescencia, *f.*

virgin, *n.* virgen, *f.*; —, *adj.* virginal; virgen.

virginal, *adj.* virginal.

Virgin Islands, Islas Vírgenes, *f. pl.*

virginity, *n.* virginidad, *f.*

Virgo, *n.* Virgo (signo del zodíaco), *m.*

viridescence, *n.* estado o condición de verdor.

virile, *adj.* viril.

virility, *n.* virilidad, *f.*

virtu, *n.* gusto para las bellas artes; pro- ducciones de arte en forma colectiva.

virtual, *adj.* virtual; —**ly,** *adv.* virtualmente.

virtue, *n.* virtud, *f.*

virtuous, *adj.* virtuoso; —**ly,** *adv.* virtuosa- mente.

virtuosity, *n.* virtuosidad, *f.*, disposición extraordinaria para ejercer las bellas artes.

virulence, *n.* virulencia, *f.*

virulent, *adj.* virulento; —**ly,** *adv.* maligna- mente.

virus, *n.* (med.) virus, *m.*

visa, *n.* visa, *f.*, permiso para entrar en un país; visto bueno; —, *vt.* visar (un pasa- porte).

visage, *n.* rostro, *m.*; cara, *f.*

viscera, *n. pl.* vísceras, entrañas, *f. pl.*

viscid, *adj.* viscoso, pegajoso.

viscose, *n.* material plástico usado en la fabricación de seda artificial, etc.; —, *adj.* viscoso.

viscosity, *n.* viscosidad, *f.*

viscount, *n.* vizconde, *m.*

viscountess, *n.* vizcondesa, *f.*

viscous, *adj.* viscoso, glutinoso.

vise, *n.* tornillo, torno, *m.*

visé, *vt.* visar (un pasaporte).

visibility, *n.* visibilidad, *f.*

visible, *adj.* visible; —**bly,** *adv.* visible- mente.

vision, *n.* visión, *f.*, fantasma, *m.*; vista, *f.*

visionary, *n.* and *adj.* visionario, ria.

visit, *vt.* and *vi.* ver; visitar; —, *n.* visita, *f.*; **farewell** —, visita de despedida; **to pay** —**s,** hacer visitas.

visitant, *n.* visitador, ra, visitante, *m.* y *f.*; ave migratoria.

visitation, *n.* visitación, *f.*; visita, *f.*

visiting card, *n.* tarjeta de visita.

visitor, *n.* visitante, *m.* y *f.*, visitador, ra.

visor, vizor, *n.* visera, *f.*; máscara, *f.*

vista, *n.* vista, perspectiva, *f.*

visual, *adj.* visual.

visualization, *n.* visualización, *f.*

vital, *adj.* vital; — **statistics,** estadística demográfica; —**ly,** *adv.* vitalmente; —**s,** *n. pl.* partes vitales, *f. pl.*

vitalism, *n.* (biol.) vitalismo, *m.*

vitality, *n.* vitalidad, *f.*

vitamin, *n.* vitamina, *f.*

vitiate, *vt.* viciar, corromper.

vitiation, *n.* depravación, *f.*

viticulture, *n.* viticultura, *f.*

viticulturist, *n.* viñero, *m.*

vitreous, *adj.* vítreo, de vidrio.

vitrify, *vt.* and *vi.* vitrificar, vitrificarse.

vitriol, *n.* vitriolo, *m.*

vituperate, *vt.* vituperar.

vivacious, *adj.* vivaz.

vivacity, *n.* vivacidad, *f.*

vivid, *adj.* vivo, vivaz; gráfico; —**ly,** *adv.* vivamente, vivazmente.

vividness, *n.* vivacidad, intensidad, *f.*

vivification, *n.* vivificación, *f.*

vivify, *vt.* vivificar.

viviparous, *adj.* vivíparo.

vivisection, *n.* vivisección, *f.*

vivisectionist, *n.* viviseccionista, *m.*, par- tidario de la vivisección.

vivisector, *n.* vivisector, *m.*

vixen, *n.* zorra, raposa, *f.*; mujer regañona y de mal genio.

vixenish, *adj.* quimerista.

viz. *adv.* a saber, esto es.

vizier, *n.* visir, *m.*

vizor, *n.* = **visor.**

v.n. verb neuter, v.n. verbo neutro.

voc. vocative, vocat. vocativo.

vocab. vocabulary, vocabulario.

vocabulary, *n.* vocabulario, *m.*

vocal, *adj.* vocal; — **cords,** cuerdas vocales, *f. pl.*

vocalist, *n.* cantante, *m.* y *f.*

vocation, *n.* vocación, carrera, profesión, *f.*; oficio, *m.*

vocational, *adj.* práctico, profesional; — **school,** escuela de artes y oficios, escuela práctica; — **training,** instrucción práctica.

vocative, *n.* vocativo, *m.*

vociferate, *vi.* vociferar.

vociferation, *n.* vociferación, vocería, gri- tería, *f.*

vociferous, *adj.* vocinglero, clamoroso; —**ly,** *adv.* clamorosamente.

vogue, *n.* moda, *f.*; boga, *f.*

voice, *n.* voz, *f.*; sufragio, *m.*

void, *adj.* vacío, desocupado; nulo; —, *n.* vacío, *m.*; —, *vt.* hacer nulo, anular; abandonar, salir; incapacitar; vaciar.

voile, *n.* espumilla (tela), *f.*

vol. volume, tom. tomo, volumen.

volatile, *adj.* volátil; voluble.

volatility, *n.* volatilidad, *f.*

volcanic, *adj.* volcánico.

volcano, *n.* volcán, *m.*

volition, *n.* voluntad, *f.*

volley, *n.* descarga de armas de fuego; salva, *f.*; rociada de insultos, etc.; (tennis) bolea, *f.*

volleyball, *n.* pelota de voleo, volibol (variedad de juego de pelota), *m.*

volplane, *vi.* (aer.) planear.

volt, *n.* vuelta (entre jinetes), *f.*; (elec.) voltio, *m.*

voltage, *n.* (elec.) voltaje, *m.*
voltaic, *adj.* voltaico.
voltameter, *n.* voltámetro, *m.*
volt-ampere, *n.* voltamperio, *m.*
voltmeter, *n.* voltímetro, *m.*
volubility, *n.* volubilidad, *f.*
voluble, *adj.* voluble; flúido, corriente; gárrulo.
volume, *n.* volumen, *m.*; libro, tomo, *m.*
voluminous, *adj.* voluminoso; muy grande.
voluntarily, *adv.* voluntariamente.
voluntary, *adj.* voluntario; —, *n.* (mus.) capricho, *m.*
volunteer, *n.* (mil.) voluntario, *m.*; —, *vi.* servir como voluntario; ofrecerse para alguna cosa.
voluptuary, *n.* sensualista, *m.* y *f.*, persona voluptuosa.
voluptuous, *adj.* voluptuoso; —ly, *adv.* voluptuosamente.
volute, *n.* voluta, *f.*
vomit, *vt.* and *vi.* vomitar, (coll.) devolver; —, *n.* vómito, *m.*; vomitivo, *m.*
voracious, *adj.* voraz; —ly, *adv.* vorazmente.
voracity, *n.* voracidad, *f.*
vortex, *n.* vórtice, remolino, torbellino, *m.*, vorágine, *f.*
votary, *n.* persona consagrada a algún ideal, a algún estudio, religión, etc.
vote, *n.* voto, sufragio, *m.*; —, *vt.* votar.
voter, *n.* votante, *m.* y *f.*
votive, *adj.* votivo; — offering, exvoto, *m.*
vouch, *vt.* atestiguar, certificar, afirmar.
voucher, *n.* testigo, *m.*; documento justificativo; comprobante, recibo, *m.*
vouchsafe, *vt.* conceder, adjudicar; —, *vi.* dignarse, condescender.
vow, *n.* voto, *m.*; —, *vt.* and *vi.* dedicar, consagrar; hacer votos.
vowel, *n.* vocal, *f.*
voyage, *n.* viaje por mar; travesía, *f.*, viaje, *m.*; —, *vi.* hacer viaje por mar.
voyager, *n.* navegador, ra, viajero, ra, navegante, *m.* y *f.*
V.P. Vice-President, V.P. Vicepresidente.
vs.: verse, verso, versículo; **versus,** contra.
V.S. Veterinary Surgeon, Cirujano Veterinario.
v.s. see above, véase arriba.
Vt. Vermont, Vermont.
v.t. transitive verb, v.tr. verbo transitivo.
vulcanite, *n.* ebonita, vulcanita, *f.*
vulcanize, *vt.* vulcanizar; —ed rubber, caucho vulcanizado.
vulcanizing, *n.* vulcanización, *f.*; vulcanizado, *m.*
Vulg. Vulgate, Vulgata.
vulgar, *adj.* vulgar, cursi; —ly, *adv.* vulgarmente.
vulgarism, *n.* vulgarismo, *m.*
vulgarity, *n.* vulgaridad, *f.*; bajeza, *f.*
vulgarize, *vt.* vulgarizar.
vulnerable, *adj.* vulnerable.
vulpine, *adj.* vulpino, zorruno.

vulture, *n.* buitre, *m.*
vying, *adj.* que emula; —ly, *adv.* emuladoramente.

W

W.:Wednesday, mierc. miércoles; **west,** O. oeste.
w.:week, semana; **west,** O. oeste; **width,** ancho; **wife,** esposa.
wad, *n.* atado de paja, heno, etc.; borra, *f.*; taco, *m.*; (coll.) rollo de papel moneda; riqueza en general; —, *vt.* acolchar, rellenar; atacar (una arma de fuego).
wadding, *n.* entretela, *f.*; taco, *m.*; recolchado, *m.*
waddle, *vi.* anadear.
wade, *vi.* vadear.
wafer, *n.* hostia, *f.*; oblea, *f.*; sello (en farmacias), *m.*; galletica, *f.*
waffle, *n.* hojuela, *f.*
waft, *vt.* llevar por el aire o por encima del agua; —, *vi.* flotar; —, *n.* banderín, gallardete, *m.*
wag, *vt.* mover ligeramente; **to — the tail,** menear la cola; —, *n.* meneo, *m.*; bromista, *m.* y *f.*
wage, *vt.* apostar, emprender; **to — war,** hacer guerra; —s, *n. pl.* sueldo, salario, *m.*, paga, *f.*; **monthly —s,** mesada, *f.*; **— earner,** jornalero, *m.*; asalariado, *m.*
wager, *n.* apuesta, *f.*; —, *vt.* apostar.
wageworker, *n.* jornalero, *m.*; asalariado, *m.*
waggery, *n.* chocarrería, bufonada, *f.*
waggish, *adj.* chocarrero.
waggle, *vi.* anadear, menearse.
wagon, *n.* carro grande para mercancía; carreta, *f.*; (rail.) vagón, *m.*
wagoner, waggoner, *n.* carretero, *m.*
wagon train, *n.* tren de vagones.
wagtail, *n.* (orn.) motolita, nevatilla, aguzanieve, *f.*
waif, *n.* niño sin hogar, granuja, *m.*; algo perdido o sin dueño; animal extraviado.
wail, *n.* lamento, gemido, *m.*; —, *vi.* lamentarse.
wain, *n.* carruaje, *m.*, carreta, *f.*
wainscot, *n.* enmaderado, entablonado, *m.*; —, *vt.* revestir, entablar.
waist, *n.* cintura, *f.*; chaqueta, *f.*
waistcoat, *n.* chaleco, *m.*
waistline, *n.* cintura, *f.*
wait, *vi.* esperar, aguardar; asechar; quedarse; —, *n.* acción de esperar; demora, *f.*; asechanza, celada, *f.*
waiter, *n.* sirviente, mozo, servidor, mesero, camarero, criado, *m.*
waiting, *n.* espera, *f.*; **— room,** sala de espera; **— maid, — woman,** moza, camarera, criada, *f.*
waitress, *n.* camarera, criada, mesera, *f.*
waive, *vt.* abandonar, renunciar (a un derecho, privilegio, etc.); posponer.
waiver, *n.* renuncia (a un derecho o privilegio, etc.), *f.*

wake, *vi.* velar; despertarse; —, *vt.* despertar; —, *n.* vela, *f.*; vigilia, *f.*; velorio, *m.*; (naut.) estela, *f.*

wakeful, *adj.* vigilante; despierto.

wakefulness, *n.* vigilancia, *f.*; insomnia, *f.*

waken, *vt.* and *vi.* despertar, despertarse.

waking, *n.* vela, *f.*; acto de despertar.

wale, *n.* (naut.) cinta, *f.*; (med.) equimosis, *f.*, cardenal, *m.*; larguero, cepo, *m.*; —, *vt.* golpear, levantar cardenales.

Wales, Gales, *m.*

walk, *vt.* and *vi.* pasear, andar, caminar, ir a pie; **to — arm in arm,** ir de bracero; —, *n.* paseo, *m.*, caminata, *f.*; esfera de acción; **to take a —,** dar un paseo; (baseball) marcha de un jugador a la primera base después de cuatro *balls.*

walker, *n.* paseador, ra; andador, ra; andaniño, *m.*

walking, *n.* acción de pasear, paseo, *m.*; **to go —,** dar un paseo, ir de paseo.

wall, *n.* pared, muralla, *f.*, muro, *m.*; **— board,** tablilla de fibra de madera; **— fence,** tapia, *f.*; —, *vt.* cercar con muros.

wallet, *n.* mochila, *f.*; cartera de bolsillo.

wallflower, *n.* (bot.) alelí doble; (coll.) persona que se queda sin bailar en las fiestas; **to be a —,** (coll.) comer pavo.

wallop, *vt.* azotar, tundir; —, *n.* golpe, *m.*

wallow, *vi.* encenagarse; **to — in luxury,** nadar en riquezas.

wallpaper, *n.* papel de entapizar.

walnut, *n.* nogal, *m.*; nuez, *f.*

walrus, *n.* (zool.) morsa, *f.*

Walter, Gualterio.

waltz, *n.* vals, *m.*

wampum, *n.* ciertas conchas usadas por los indios norteamericanos como dinero o adorno; (coll.) dinero, *m.*

wan, *adj.* pálido.

wand, *n.* vara, varita, *f.*; varita mágica; batuta, *f.*

wander, *vi.* vagar, rodar; desviarse, extraviarse.

wanderer, *n.* vagamundo, *m.*; peregrino, *m.*

wane, *vi.* disminuir; decaer; menguar; —, *n.* decadencia, *f.*; **— (of the moon),** menguante (de la luna), *m.*; bisel, chaflán, *m.*

wangle, *vt.* engatusar, obtener algo bajo pretexto o con dificultad.

want, *vt.* and *vi.* desear, querer, anhelar; faltar; —, *vi.* estar necesitado; sufrir la falta de algo; —, *n.* falta, carencia, *f.*; indigencia, *f.*; deseo, *m.*; necesidad, *f.*

wanting, *adj.* falto, defectuoso, necesitado; menos.

wanton, *adj.* lascivo, licencioso; desenfrenado; —, *n.* persona lasciva; —, *vi.* hacerse lascivo o licencioso; **—ly,** *adv.* desenfrenadamente, lascivamente.

war, *n.* guerra, *f.*; —, *vi.* guerrear; —, *adj.* relativo a la guerra; **man-of-—,** buque de guerra.

warble, *vi.* trinar; gorjear; —, *n.* trino, gorjeo, *m.*

ward, *vt.* repeler; **to — off,** evitar; desviar; —, *n.* guardia, defensa, *f.*; sala de hospital; pupilo, *m.*

warden, *n.* custodio, guardián, *m.*; alcaide de una cárcel; bedel, *m.*; comandante, *m.*

wardenship, *n.* bedelía, *f.*; alcaidía, *f.*

warder, *n.* guardia, *f.*; fortificación, *f.*

wardrobe, *n.* guardarropa, *f.*, ropero, *m.*; ropa, *f.*, vestuario, *m.*

wardroom, *n.* sala-comedor de la oficialidad de un buque de guerra; oficialidad de un buque de guerra.

wardship, *n.* tutela, *f.*; pupilaje, *m.*

ware, *n.* mercadería, *f.*; loza, *f.*; **—s,** *n. pl.* efectos, *m. pl.*, mercancías, *f. pl.*

warehouse, *n.* almacén, depósito, *m.*, bodega, *f.*; **— man,** guardalmacén, almacenero, *m.*

warfare, *n.* guerra, *f.*, conflicto armado.

warily, *adv.* prudentemente, con cautela.

wariness, *n.* cautela, prudencia, *f.*

warlike, *adj.* guerrero, belicoso, marcial.

warlock, *n.* brujo, hechicero, *m.*

warm, *adj.* cálido; caliente; abrigador; cordial, caluroso; **to be —,** hacer calor; tener calor; —, *vt.* calentar; **—ing pan,** calentador, *m.*; **—ly,** *adv.* calurosamente, cordialmente; con calor.

warm-blooded, *adj.* de sangre ardiente; vehemente, entusiasta, fervoroso, apasionado.

warm-hearted, *adj.* afectuoso, generoso, benévolo, de buenos sentimientos.

warming, *n.* calefacción, *f.*

warmonger, *n.* propagador de guerra.

warmth, *n.* calor, *m.*; ardor, fervor, *m.*

warn, *vt.* avisar; advertir; prevenir.

warning, *n.* amonestación, *f.*; advertencia, *f.*, aviso, *m.*

warp, *n.* urdimbre, *f.*; comba, *f.*; —, *vi.* torcerse, alabearse, combarse; —, *vt.* torcer; pervertir.

warplane, *n.* avión de guerra.

warrant, *vt.* autorizar; privilegiar; garantir, garantizar, asegurar; —, *n.* testimonio, *m.*; justificación, *f.*; decreto de prisión; autorización, *f.*

warrantable, *adj.* justificable.

warranter, *n.* garante, *m.* y *f.*, fiador, ra.

warranty, *n.* garantía, seguridad, *f.*

warren, *n.* conejera, *f.*, conejar, *m.*

warrior, *n.* guerrero, soldado, batallador, *m.*

Warsaw, Varsovia, *f.*

warship, *n.* barco de guerra.

wart, *n.* verruga, *f.*

warty, *adj.* verrugoso.

wary, *adj.* cauto, prudente.

was, 1ª y 3ª persona del singular del pretérito del verbo **be.**

wash, *vt.* lavar; bañar; —, *vi.* lavarse; —, *n.* lavadura, *f.*; loción, ablución, *f.*; lavado, *m.*; bazofia, *f.*; especie de pintura para acuarela; **— bowl, — basin,** jofaina, *f.*; **— stand,** lavabo, *m.*

Wash. Washington, Wáshington.

washer, *n.* máquina de lavar ropa; lavadora, *f.*; (mech.) arandela, *f.*
washerwoman, *n.* lavandera, *f.*
washing, *n.* lavadura, *f.*; lavado, *m.*; ropa para lavar; — **machine,** máquina de lavar, lavadora, *f.*
washout, *n.* deslave, *m.*; socavación, *f.*; (coll.) fracasado, da.
washstand, *n.* lavabo, aguamanil, *m.*
washy, *adj.* húmedo; débil, aguado.
wasp, *n.* avispa, *f.*
waspish, *adj.* parecido a una avispa; de talle esbelto (como una avispa); caprichudo, enojadizo.
wassail, *n.* especie de brindis; orgía, *f.*
wastage, *n.* desgaste, desperdicio, *m.*
waste, *vt.* consumir, gastar; malgastar, disipar; destruir, arruinar, asolar; —, *vi.* gastarse; **to — away,** demacrarse; —, *n.* desperdicio, *m.*; estopa, *f.*; destrucción, *f.*; despilfarro, *m.*; merma, *f.*; limpiaduras, *f. pl.*; — **pipe,** tubería de desagüe; desaguadero, *m.*
wastebasket, *n.* cesto o cesta para papeles.
wasteful, *adj.* destructivo, pródigo, despilfarrador; —**ly,** *adv.* pródigamente, en forma despilfarradora.
wastefulness, *n.* prodigalidad, *f.*, despilfarro, *m.*
wastepaper, *n.* papel de desecho.
waster, *n.* disipador, ra, gastador, ra.
watch, *n.* desvelo, *m.*; vigilia, vela, *f.*; vigía, *f.*, centinela, *f.*; reloj de bolsillo; **wrist —,** reloj de pulsera; **stop —,** cronógrafo, *m.*; **night —,** vela, *f.*; — **shop,** rolojería, *f.*; **works of a —,** movimiento de reloj; **to be on the —,** estar alerta; —, *vt.* observar; —, *vi.* velar, guardar, custodiar; espiar; **to — jealously over,** celar; — **out!** *interj.* ¡cuidado!
watchcase, *n.* caja de reloj de bolsillo; relojera, *f.*
watchdog, *n.* perro guardián.
watchful, *adj.* vigilante; cuidadoso; observador; —**ly,** *adv.* cuidadosamente.
watchfulness, *n.* vigilancia, *f.*
watching, *n.* vigía, *f.*; observación, *f.*
watchmaker, *n.* relojero, *f.*
watchman, *n.* sereno, velador, *m.*
watchtower, *n.* atalaya, garita, vigía, *f.*
watchword, *n.* (mil.) santo y seña, contraseña, *f.*
watchwork, *n.* mecanismo de un reloj de bolsillo.
water, *n.* agua, *f.*; **fresh —,** agua dulce; **hard —,** agua cruda; **high —,** mar llena; **lime —,** agua de cal; **low —,** baja mar; **mineral —,** agua mineral; **running —,** agua corriente; **salt —,** agua salada; **soda —,** agua de soda; **toilet —,** agua de tocador; — **cask,** bota, cuba, *f.*; — **closet,** común, excusado, retrete, *m.*, letrina, *f.*; — **color,** acuarela, *f.*; — **cress,** berro, *m.*; — **cure,** (med.) hidropatía, *f.*; — **dog,** perro de aguas; (coll.)

buen nadador, buena nadadora; — **faucet,** grifo, grifón, *m.*, caño de agua; — **front,** litoral con edificios y muelles o sin ellos; — **gap,** quebrador en una montaña por donde pasa una corriente de agua; — **gas,** gas de agua; — **gate,** arbollón, *m.*, compuerta del caz; — **glass,** vidrio soluble, silicato de sosa; clepsidra, *f.*, reloj de agua, *m.*; — **heater,** calentador de agua; — **lily,** ninfea, *f.*, nenúfar, *m.*, lirio acuático; — **main,** cañería maestra de agua; — **meter,** contador del agua; — **moccasin,** mocasín, *f.*, culebra venenosa de agua; — **polo,** polo acuático; — **power,** fuerza hidráulica; — **softener,** purificador de agua; generador de agua dulce; — **tower,** torre para servicio de agua; — **wing,** nadadera, *f.*; —, *vt.* regar, mojar, bañar; —, *vi.* chorrear agua; **to make one's mouth —,** hacerse la boca agua.
water-cooled, *adj.* enfriado por agua.
watercourse, *n.* corriente de agua; lecho de un río; conducto natural de agua; canal para conducir agua.
watercraft, *n.* habilidad en el manejo de buques, natación y buceo.
watered (silk), *adj.* tornasolado (aplícase a la seda).
waterfall, *n.* cascada, catarata, *f.*, salto de agua, caída de agua.
watering, *n.* riego, *m.*; —, *adj.* que riega; — **place,** balneario, *m.*; — **pot,** regadera, *f.*
waterline, *n.* (naut.) flotación, *f.*
waterlogged, *adj.* anegado; saturado de agua.
waterman, *n.* barquero, *m.*
watermark, *n.* filigrana o marca en el papel que indica su procedencia; señal de agua.
watermelon, *n.* sandía, badea, *f.*
waterproof, *adj.* impermeable, a prueba de agua.
watershed, *n.* vertiente, *f.*, cumbre de las vertientes de las aguas.
waterspout, *n.* manga, *f.*, bomba marina.
watertight, *adj.* impermeable.
waterway, *n.* cañería, *f.*; corriente de agua.
waterworks, *n.* establecimiento para la distribución de las aguas.
waterworn, *adj.* gastado por la acción del agua.
watery, *adj.* acuoso, aguado, mojado.
watt, *n.* vatio, *m.*
wattage, *n.* vatiaje, *m.*, energía vatimétrica.
watt-hour, *n.* vatio-hora, *f.*
wattle, *n.* zarzo, *m.*; barbas de gallo; —, *vt.* enzarzar.
wave, *n.* ola, onda, *f.*; **short —,** onda corta; **sound —,** onda sonora; — **length,** longitud de onda; —, *vi.* fluctuar; ondear; flamear.
waved, *adj.* ondulado.
waver, *vi.* vacilar, titubear; estar en suspenso.
wavering, *n.* titubeo, *m.*

waving, *n.* ondulación, *f.*

wavy, *adj.* ondeado, ondulado.

wax, *n.* cera, *f.*; — **candle,** vela de cera; — **paper, —ed paper,** papel encerado; — **match,** cerilla, *f.*, (Mex.) cerillo, fósforo, *m.*; — **taper,** cerilla, *f.*; —, *vt.* encerar; —, *vi.* aumentarse, crecer.

waxen, *adj.* de cera.

waxwork, *n.* figura de cera.

waxy, *adj.* ceroso.

way, *n.* camino, *m.*, senda, ruta, *f.*; modo, *m.*, forma, *f.*; medio, *m.*; **by the —,** a propósito; **in no —,** de ningún modo, de ninguna manera; **on the —,** al paso, en el camino; **this —,** por aquí; así; **to force one's —,** abrirse el paso; **to give —,** ceder; — **of the cross,** vía crucis; —**s and means,** orientación y fines; — **station,** (rail.) estación intermediaria; — **train,** tren local, tren que para en todas las estaciones.

wayfarer, *n.* pasajero, ra, transeúnte, *m.* y *f.*

waylay, *vt.* insidiar.

wayward, *adj.* caprichoso; desobediente; delincuente.

w.c. water closet, inodoro, excusado, retrete.

W.C.T.U. Women's Christian Temperance Union, Unión Femenina Cristiana de Temperancia (E.U.A.).

we, *pron.* nosotros, nosotras.

weak, *adj.* débil; flojo; decaído; deleznable; — **in constitution,** delicado; —**ly,** *adv.* débilmente.

weaken, *vt.* debilitar; —, *vt.* aflojarse; ceder; debilitarse.

weak-kneed, *adj.* débil de rodillas; falto de fuerza moral, cobarde.

weakling, *n.* persona débil ya sea física o mentalmente; cobarde, *m.* y *f.*; persona delicada; (coll.) alfeñique, *m.*

weak-minded, *adj.* de poca mentalidad, sin carácter.

weakness, *n.* debilidad, *f.*

weal, *n.* prosperidad, *f.*; bien, *m.*; **common —,** bien público.

wealth, *n.* riqueza, *f.*; bienes, *m. pl.*; bonanza, *f.*

wealthy, *adj.* rico, opulento, adinerado; — **class,** clase acomodada, clase adinerada.

wean, *vt.* destetar.

weapon, *n.* arma, *f.*; —**s of war,** pertrechos de guerra.

wear, *vt.* gastar, consumir; usar, llevar, llevar puesto, traer; —, *vi.* consumirse, gastarse; **to — out a person,** fastidiar, aburrir o cansar a una persona; —, *n.* uso, *m.*

weariness, *n.* cansancio, rendimiento, *m.*, fatiga, *f.*; enfado, *m.*

wearing apparel, *n.* ropa, *f.*, ropaje, *m.*, vestidos, *m. pl.*

wearisome, *adj.* cansado, tedioso; laborioso; —**ly,** *adv.* tediosamente; laboriosamente.

weary, *vt.* cansar, fatigar; molestar; —, *adj.*

cansado, fatigado, fatigoso.

weasel, *n.* comadreja, *f.*

weather, *n.* tiempo, *m.*, temperatura, *f.*; **bad —,** intemperie, *f.*; **the — is good,** hace buen tiempo; — **conditions,** *n. pl.* condiciones meteorológicas; —, *vt.* sufrir, aguantar (un temporal, adversidad, etc.).

weather-beaten, *adj.* dañado por haber estado expuesto a la intemperie; endurecido a la intemperie.

weatherboarding, *n.* tablas solapadas.

weathercock, *n.* giralda, veleta, *f.*

weatherman, *n.* meteorologista, *m.*

weather report, *n.* boletín meteorológico.

weathershore, *n.* (naut.) costa de barlovento.

weather-strip, *vt.* proteger con burlete; **weather strip,** *n.* burlete, *m.*

weather-wise, *adj.* hábil para vaticinar los cambios del tiempo.

weave, *vt.* tejer; trenzar; —, *n.* tejido, *m.*

weaver, *n.* tejedor, ra.

web, *n.* tela, *f.*; tejido, *m.*; red, *f.*; —, *vt.* unir en forma de red; enmarañar, enredar.

webbed, *adj.* unido como especie de red; enmarañado, enredado.

wed, *vt.* and *vi.* casar, casarse.

Wed. Wednesday, miérc. miércoles.

wedding, *n.* boda, *f.*, casamiento, matrimonio ,*m.*, nupcias, *f. pl.*; **silver —,** bodas de plata; **golden —,** bodas de oro; — **cake,** torta o pastel de boda.

wedge, *n.* cuña, *f.*; —, *vt.* acuñar; apretar.

wedlock, *n.* matrimonio, *m.*

Wednesday, *n.* miércoles, *m.*

wee, *adj.* pequeñito.

weed, *n.* mala hierba; (coll.) cigarro, tabaco, *m.*; —**s,** *pl.* vestido de luto; —, *vt.* escardar.

weedy, *adj.* lleno de malas hierbas.

week, *n.* semana, *f.*; — **end,** fin de semana.

weekday, *n.* día de trabajo, cualquier día de la semana que no sea domingo.

week-end, *adj.* de fin de semana.

weekly, *adj.* semanal, semanario; — **publication,** semanario, *m.*; —, *adv.* semalmente, por semana.

weep, *vi.* llorar, lamentarse.

weevil, *n.* gorgojo, *m.*

weft, *n.* trama, *f.*; tejido, *m.*

weigh, *vt.* and *vi.* pesar; examinar, considerar.

weight, *n.* peso, *m.*; pesadez, *f.*; **gross —,** peso bruto; **net —,** peso neto; **inspector of —s and measures,** potador, *m.*

weighty, *adj.* ponderoso; importante.

weir, *n.* azud, *m.*, pesquera, *f.*

welcome, *adj.* recibido con agrado; —! ¡bienvenido! —, *n.* bienvenida, *f.*; —, *vt.* dar la bienvenida.

weld, *vt.* soldar.

welding, *n.* soldadura autógena.

welfare, *n.* prosperidad, *f.*; bienestar, bien, *m.*; — **society,** sociedad benéfica, sociedad de beneficencia; — **work,** trabajo social, obra de beneficencia.

well, *n.* fuente, *f.*; manantial, *m.*; pozo, *m.*, cisterna, *f.*, (Sp. Am.) casimba, *f.*; — **sweep,** cigoñal, *m.*; —, *adj.* bueno, sano; **to be** —, estar bien; —, *adv.* bien, felizmente; favorablemente; suficientemente; **as** — **as,** así como, lo mismo que, también como; — **then,** conque; **very** —! ¡está bien! —! *interj.* ¡vaya!

well-aimed, *adj.* bien intencionado; certero.

well-attended, *adj.* bien concurrido.

well-balanced, *adj.* bien equilibrado.

well-behaved, *adj.* bien criado, cortés, bien portado.

well-being, *n.* felicidad, prosperidad, *f.*

wellborn, *adj.* bien nacido.

well-bred, *adj.* bien criado, bien educado.

well-defined, *adj.* bien delineado, bien definido.

well-deserved, *adj.* bien merecido.

well-disposed, *adj.* favorable, bien dispuesto.

well-doing, *n.* beneficio, *m.*

well-done, *adj.* bien hecho.

well-favored, *adj.* agradecido.

well-founded, *adj.* bien fundado.

well-groomed, *adj.* vestido elegantemente.

well-grounded, *adj.* bien fundado.

well-known, *adj.* notorio, bien conocido.

well-modulated, *adj.* cadente, cadencioso.

well-off, *adj.* acomodado, rico.

well-shaped, *adj.* bien hecho, bien formado.

well-spoken, *adj.* bien dicho.

wellspring, *n.* fuente, *f.*, origen, manantial, *m.*

well-suited, *adj.* apropiado, adecuado.

well-timed, *adj.* oportuno, hecho a propósito.

well-to-do, *adj.* acomodado, próspero, rico.

well-wisher, *n.* amigo, partidario, *m.*

well-worn, *adj.* bien gastado, raído; común.

Welsh, *n.* and *adj.* galés, esa.

welt, *n.* ribete, *m.*; roncha, *f.*; —, *vt.* ribetear; (coll.) golpear hasta causar ronchas.

welter, *vi.* revolcarse en el lodo; estar en un torbellino.

welterweight, *n.* pugilista o luchador de 60 a 68 kilos de peso.

wen, *n.* lobanillo, callo, *m.*, lupia, *f.*

wench, *n.* mozuela, *f.*; sirvienta, *f.*

wend, *vt.* encaminar, dirigir; —, *vi.* ir, atravesar, pasar, encaminarse.

went, pretérito del verbo **go.**

were, 2ª persona del singular y plural del verbo **be.**

west, *n.* poniente, occidente, oeste, *m.*; —, *adj.* occidental.

westerly, western, *adj.* occidental; — **wind,** favonio, céfiro, poniente, *m.*

West Indies, Indias Occidentales, Las Antillas, *f. pl.*

west-northwest, *n.* oesnorueste, *m.*

west-southwest, *n.* oessudueste, *m.*

West Virginia, Virginia Occidental, *f.*

westward, *adv.* hacia el poniente u occidente.

wet, *adj.* húmedo, mojado; — **nurse,** nodriza, nutriz, *f.*; —, *n.* humedad, *f.*; —, *vt.* mojar, humedecer.

wet battery, *n.* batería líquida.

wet blanket, *n.* aguafiestas, *m.* y *f.*; **wetblanket,** *vt.* desanimar, desalentar.

wether, *n.* carnero llano.

wet-nurse, *vt.* servir de nodriza, amamantar a un hijo ajeno.

w.f. wrong font, (print.) tipo incorrecto.

whack, *vt.* aporrear; —, *n.* golpe, *m.*; intento, *m.*, prueba, *f.*; porción, participación, *f.*

whale, *n.* ballena, *f.*; — **oil,** aceite de ballena.

whaleback, *n.* algo en forma de lomo de ballena, especialmente ciertos vapores de carga.

whaler, *n.* pescador de ballena.

wharf, *n.* muelle, *m.*

wharfage, *n.* muellaje, *m.*

wharfinger, *n.* administrador de un muelle.

wharves, *n. pl.* de **wharf,** muelles, *m. pl.*

what, *pron.* qué; lo que, aquello que; — **is the matter?** ¿qué pasa?

whatever, whatsoever, *pron.* and *adj.* cualquier cosa, lo que sea.

whatnot, *n.* rinconera, *f.*; óbjeto curioso; algo indescriptible.

wheat, *n.* trigo, *m.*; **winter** —, trigo mocho; — **field,** trigal, *m.*

wheaten, *adj.* de trigo, hecho de trigo.

wheedle, *vt.* and *vi.* halagar, engañar con lisonjas, internarse, insinuarse.

wheel, *n.* rueda, *f.*; — **chair,** silla de ruedas; — **base,** distancia entre ejes; — **and axle,** cabria, *f.*; **driving** —, rueda motriz; **gambling** —, rueda de la fortuna; **gear** —, rueda dentada; **paddle** —, rueda de paletas; **small** —, rodaja, *f.*; **water** —, rodezno, *m.*; — **horse,** caballo de tronco; — **rope,** (naut.) guardín, *m.*; — **track,** carril, *m.*; —, *vt.* rodar, hacer rodar, girar; —, *vi.* girar, dar vueltas.

wheelbarrow, *n.* carretilla, *f.*, carretón de una rueda.

wheeler, *n.* girador, ra, rodador, ra; caballo de tronco.

wheelguard, *n.* guardacantón, *m.*

wheelhouse, *n.* (naut.) timonera, *f.*

wheeling, *n.* rodaje, *m.*; **free** —, rueda libre.

wheelwright, *n.* carpintero de carretas.

wheeze, *vi.* resollar con sonido fuerte.

whelm, *vt.* and *vi.* dominar; cubrir; oprimir.

whelp, *n.* cachorro, *m.*; chiquillo (úsase en forma despectiva), *m.*; —, *vi.* parir (la perra, etc.).

when, *adv.* cuando; cuándo; mientras que; entonces; así que.

whence, *adv.* de donde; de quien.

whencesoever, *adv.* de donde quiera.

whenever, whensoever, *adv.* cuando quiera que, siempre que.

where, *adv.* donde; dónde.

whereabouts, *n.* paradero, *m.*; —, *adv.* por donde, hacia donde.

whereas, *conj.* por cuanto, mientras que; pues que, ya que, considerando.

whereat, *adv.* a lo cual; por lo cual.

whereby, *adv.* con lo cual, por donde, por lo cual.

wherefore, *adv.* por lo que, por cuyo motivo.

wherein, *adv.* en donde, en lo cual, en que.

whereinto, *adv.* dentro de lo que.

whereof, *adv.* de lo cual, de que.

whereon, *adv.* sobre lo cual, sobre que.

wheresoever, *adv.* dondequiera, en cualquier parte que.

whereto, *adv.* a lo que, a que.

whereupon, *adv.* sobre que; en consecuencia de lo cual.

wherever, *adv.* dondequiera que.

wherewith, *adv.* con que, con lo cual; por medio de lo cual; —, *pron.* aquello con que.

wherewithal, *adv.* and *pron.* con que, con lo cual, por medio de lo cual; aquello con que; —, *n.* dinero necesario (para comprar algo).

wherry, *n.* esquife, *m.*, barca, *f.*

whet, *vt.* afilar, amolar; excitar.

whether, *conj.* que; si; ora.

whetstone, *n.* aguzadera, *f.*, piedra de afilar.

whey, *n.* suero, *m.*

which, *pron.* que, el cual, la cual, los cuales, las cuales; cuál.

whichever, whichsoever, *pron.* and *adj.* cualquiera que, cualesquiera.

whiff, *n.* vaharada, *f.*; bocanada de humo, fumada, *f.*

whiffletree, *n.* balancín, *m.*

Whig, *n.* partido liberal en Inglaterra.

while, *n.* rato, *m.*; vez, *f.*; momento, *m.*; **to be worth** —, valer la pena; —, *conj.* mientras, a la vez que, durante.

whilst, *conj.* and *adv.* mientras, a la vez que.

whim, *n.* antojo, capricho, *m.*

whimper, *vi.* sollozar, gemir; —, *n.* sollozo, gemido, *m.*

whimsical, *adj.* caprichoso, fantástico.

whimsicalness, *n.* veleidad, *f.*

whimsy, *n.* fantasía, *f.*, capricho, *m.*

whine, *vi.* llorar, lamentarse; (coll.) gimotear; —, *n.* quejido, lamento, *m.*

whining, *n.* (coll.) gimoteo, lloriqueo, *m.*

whinny, *vi.* relinchar los caballos.

whip, *n.* azote, látigo, *m.*; — **hand,** mano que sostiene el látigo; ventaja, *f.*; —, *vt.* azotar; —, *vi.* andar de prisa.

whipped cream, *n.* crema batida.

whippet, *n.* perro lebrero.

whipping, *n.* flagelación, paliza, *f.*

whippletree, *n.* balancín (de coche), *m.*; volea, *f.*

whirl, *vt.* and *vi.* girar; hacer girar; moverse rápidamente; —, *n.* giro muy rápido; vuelta, *f.*

whirligig, *n.* perinola, *f.*; tiovivo, *m.*

whirlpool, *n.* vórtice, remolino, *m.*, vorágine, olla, *f.*

whirlwind, *n.* torbellino, remolino, *m.*

whisk, *n.* movimiento rápido como de una escobilla; escobilla, *f.*, cepillo, *m.*; —, *vi.* moverse ligera y rápidamente; —, *vt.* batir (huevos, etc.).

whisker, *n.* patilla, *f.*, mostacho, *m.*; —**s,** *pl.* barba, *f.*

whiskey, whisky, *n.* whisky, aguardiente, *m.*

whisper, *vi.* cuchichear, susurrar, hablar al oído; —, *n.* cuchicheo, secreto, *m.*

whist, *n.* especie de juego de naipes.

whistle, *vt.* and *vi.* silbar; chiflar; —, *n.* silbido, *m.*; pito, *m.*

whistling, *n.* chiflido, silbido, *m.*

whit, *n.* partícula, pizca, *f.*, algo muy pequeño; **he doesn't care a** —, no le importa un bledo.

white, *adj.* blanco, pálido; cano, canoso; puro; **to become** —, blanquearse; — **clover,** trébol blanco; — **elephant,** elefante blanco; — **feather,** pluma blanca, señal de cobardía; — **gold,** oro blanco, oro aleado con níquel y cinc o platino; — **heat,** incandescencia, *f.*; rojo blanco; estado de intensa conmoción física o mental; — **lead,** cerusa, *f.*, blanco de plomo; — **lie,** mentirilla, *f.*; — **matter,** (anat.) tejido nervioso blanco (especialmente cerebral y medular); — **oak,** roble blanco; — **pine,** pino blanco; — **poplar,** álamo blanco; — **sauce,** salsa blanca; — **slave,** víctima de la trata de blancas; — **slavery,** trata de blancas; —, *n.* color blanco; clara de huevo.

whitebait, *n.* (pez) albur, gobio, *m.*; boquerón, *m.*

white-collar, *adj.* de oficinista; — **worker,** oficinista, *m.* y *f.*

white-hot, *adj.* incandescente.

whiten, *vt.* and *vi.* blanquear; blanquearse, emblanquecerse.

whiteness, *n.*, blancura, *f.*; palidez, *f.*

whitewash, *n.* jalbegue, blanquete, enlucimiento, *m.*; —, *vt.* encalar; jalbegar; encubrir.

whither, *adv.* adonde, a qué lugar.

whithersoever, *adv.* al lugar que fuere, a dondequiera.

whiting, *n.* (pez) albur, gobio, cadoce, *m.*; blanquimiento, *m.*

whitish, *adj.* blanquizco, blanquecino.

whitlow, *n.* panadizo, panarizo, *m.*

Whitsuntide, *n.* Pentecostés, *m.*

whittle, *vt.* cortar con navaja; tallar, tajar, afilar, mondar, sacar punta.

whiz, *vi.* zumbar, silbar; —, *n.* zumbido, *m.*

who, *pron.* quien, que; quién.

whoa, *interj.* ¡so!

whoever, whosoever, *pron.* quienquiera; cualquiera que; quien.

whole, *adj.* todo, total; sano, entero; —, *n.* todo, total, *m.*; **the** —, conjunto, *m.*; — **note** (mus.) redonda, semibreve, *f.*; — **number,** número entero.

wholehearted, *adj.* sincero, cordial.

wholesale, n. venta al por mayor; **— house,** casa al por mayor.

wholesome, adj. sano, saludable; **—ly,** adv. saludablemente, en forma sana.

whole-wheat, adj. de trigo entero.

wholly, adv. enteramente, totalmente.

whom, pron. acusativo de **who** (quien).

whomsoever, pron. acusativo de **whosoever** (quienquiera).

whoop, n. gritería, f.; **—,** vi. gritar, vocear, huchear.

whooping cough, n. tos ferina.

whore, n. puta, f.

why, adv. ¿por qué? **— not?** ¿pues y qué? ¿por qué no?

W.I. West Indies, Las Antillas.

wick, n. torcida, mecha, f., pabilo, m.

wicked, adj. malvado, perverso; **—ly,** adv. perversamente.

wickedness, n. perversidad, maldad, f.

wicker, n. mimbre, m.; **—,** adj. de mimbre.

wicket, n. postigo, m., portezuela, f.

wide, adj. ancho, vasto, extenso; remoto; **far and —,** por todos lados; **—ly,** adv. ampliamente.

wide-awake, adj. despierto, alerta, vivo.

wide-eyed, adj. asombrado, con los ojos muy abiertos.

widen, vt. ensanchar, extender, ampliar.

widespread, adj. extenso, difuso, esparcido, diseminado.

widgeon, n. avucasta, avutarda, f.

widow, n. viuda, f.; **—,** vt. privar a una mujer de su marido.

widower, n. viudo, m.

widowhood, n. viudez, viudedad, f.

width, n. anchura, f.

wield, vt. manejar, empuñar; ejercer.

wienerwurst, n. especie de salchicha.

wife, n. esposa, consorte, mujer, f.

wig, n. peluca, f.

wiggler, n. lo que se mueve como un gusano; persona inquieta.

wigmaker, n. peluquero, m.

wigwag, vi. menear; comunicarse por señales o banderolas; **—,** n. comunicación por señales o banderolas.

wigwam, n. cabaña de los indios.

wild, adj. silvestre, feroz; desierto; salvaje; **—,** n. desierto, yermo, m.; **— boar,** jabalí, m.; **— oats,** indiscreciones de la juventud.

wildcat, n. gato montés; persona alocada, casquivana o traviesa; **—,** adj. (com.) corrompido, quimérico.

wilderness, n. desierto, m., selva, f.

wildfire, n. fuego griego; sarpullido, m.

wile, n. dolo, engaño, m.; astucia, f.

wilful, adj. voluntarioso, obstinado; **—ly,** adv. obstinadamente, voluntariosamente.

will, n. voluntad, f.; capricho, m.; testamento, m.; **at —,** a gusto; **against one's —,** contra la voluntad de uno; **—,** vt. legar, dejar en testamento; **—,** verbo auxiliar que indica futuro.

willing, adj. deseoso, listo, dispuesto a servir; **—ly,** adv. de buen grado, de buena gana, voluntariamente.

willingness, n. buena voluntad, deseo de servir.

will-o'-the-wisp, n. fuego fatuo.

willow, n. (bot.) sauce, m.

willy-nilly, adj. and adv. de buena o mala gana; por fuerza, sin manera de escoger.

wilt, n. enfermedad hongosa que marchita las plantas.

wily, adj. astuto, insidioso.

wimble, n. taladro, berbiquí, m.

wimple, n. especie de velo para mujer.

win, vt. and vi. ganar, obtener, conquistar; alcanzar, lograr; **to — the favor (of),** caer en gracia (de).

wince, vi. cocear; respingar; aguantar dolor con valor y sin quejarse.

winch, n. cabria, f., torno, cabrestante, malacate, montacargas, m.

wind, n. viento, m.; aliento, m.; pedo, m.; **to break —,** peerse; **— instrument,** instrumento de viento; **— tunnel,** (aer.) túnel aerodinámico.

wind, vt. enrollar; dar vuelta, dar cuerda (a un reloj, etc.); torcer; envolver; **—,** vi. caracolear, serpentear; insinuarse; arrollarse; **to — up,** ultimar (un asunto).

windage, n. pérdida de energía por efecto del viento.

windbreak, n. protección contra el viento.

winded, adj. desalentado, sin fuerzas.

windfall, n. fruta caída del árbol; ganancia inesperada; acontecimiento feliz e inesperado.

winding, n. vuelta, revuelta, f.; arrollamiento (de un alambre), m.; cuerda (de un reloj, etc.), f.; **—,** adj. tortuoso, sinuoso; **— road,** camino tortuoso; **— sheet,** mortaja, f., sudario, m.; **— stair,** escalera de caracol; **— tackle,** (naut.) aparejo de estrelleras.

windlass, n. árgano, torno, m., grúa, f.; malacate, m.

windmill, n. molino de viento.

window, n. ventana, f.; **— frame,** marco de la ventana; **small —,** ventanilla, f.; **— blind,** celosía, f., persiana de ventana; **— shade,** visillo, m.; **— shutter,** puertaventana, contraventana, f.; **— sill,** repisa de ventana.

windowpane, n. vidrio de ventana.

windpipe, n. (anat.) traquearteria, traquea, f.

windrow, n. puñado de cereales cortados y depositados en el surco; montón de turba o césped; **—,** vt. recoger el heno o los cereales con un rastro.

windshield, n. guardabrisa, parabrisas, m.

windshield wiper, n. limpiavidrio, m.

windward, n. (naut.) barlovento, m.; **to ply to the —,** (naut.) bordear; **—,** adv. (naut.) a barlovento.

windy, adj. ventoso; **it is —,** hace viento.

wine, *n.* vino, *m.*; **red —,** vino tinto; **— bag,** bota, *f.*; **— cellar,** candiotera, *f.*; bodega, *f.*; **— merchant,** vinatero, *m.*; **— press,** prensa, *f.*, lagar, *m.*

winebibber, *n.* bebedor, borracho, *m.*

winery, *n.* candiotera, *f.*

winesap, *n.* variedad de manzana de invierno.

wing, *n.* ala, *f.*; lado, costado, *m.*; **—s,** *pl.* (theat.) bastidores, *m.pl.*; **— area,** superficie de sustentación, *f.*; **— cannon,** cañón de ala, *m.*; **— case,** élitro (de un insecto), *m.*; **— chair,** especie de sillón con respaldo en forma de alas; **— spread,** extensión del ala de un aeroplano, de un pájaro, etc.; **—,** *vt.* proveer con alas; **—,** *vi.* volar.

wingers, *n.pl.* alas (en Rugby), *f.pl.*

wink, *vt.* and *vi.* guiñar, pestañear; **—,** *n.* pestañeo, guiño, *m.*

winner, *n.* ganador, ra, vencedor, ra.

winning, *n.* ganancia, *f.*, lucro, *m.*; **—,** *adj.* atractivo, encantador; ganador.

winnow, *vt.* aventar, cerner (el grano).

winsome, *adj.* alegre, jovial; simpático.

winter, *n.* invierno, *m.*; **— wheat,** trigo mocho; **—,** *adj.* invernal; **—,** *vi.* invernar, pasar el invierno.

wintry, *adj.* invernal.

wipe, *vt.* secar, limpiar; borrar; **to — out,** obliterar; **—,** *n.* limpión, *m.*, limpiadura, *f.*

wire, *n.* alambre, *m.*; **barbed —,** alambre de púas; **conducting —,** alambre conductor; **live —,** persona lista o activa; alambre cargado de electricidad; **screen —,** alambre para rejas; **sheathed —,** alambre envuelto o forrado; **— fence, — fencing,** alambrado, *m.*, cerca o cercado de alambre; **— gauge,** calibrador de alambre; **— photo,** telefoto, *f.*; **— screen,** tela metálica; **— tapping,** conexión telefónica o telegráfica para interceptar mensajes; **—,** *vt.* alambrar; **—,** *vi.* (coll.) telegrafiar, cablegrafiar.

wiredraw, *vt.* tirar o estirar el hilo de hierro, de plata, etc.; prolongar.

wireless, *n.* telegrafía sin hilos, telegrafía inalámbrica, radiotelefonía, *f.*; **— station,** radioemisora, *f.*, estación radioemisora; **— transmission,** radioemisión, *f.*

wirepuller, *n.* titiritero, *m.*; intrigante político.

wirepulling, *n.* empleo de alambres para los títeres; (coll.) intrigas políticas.

wiring, *n.* instalación de alambres eléctricos.

wiry, *adj.* hecho de alambre; parecido al alambre; flaco pero a la vez fuerte.

Wis. Wisc. Wisconsin, Wisconsin.

wisdom, *n.* sabiduría, prudencia, *f.*; juicio, *m.*

wisdom tooth, *n.* muela del juicio, muela cordal.

wise, *adj.* sabio, docto, juicioso, prudente, sensato; **—,** *n.* modo, *m.*, manera, *f.*; **—ly,** *adv.* sabiamente, con prudencia.

wiseacre, *n.* persona que presume de sabia.

wisecrack, *n.* chiste o dicho agudo y gracioso; **—,** *vi.* decir cosas con agudeza y en forma chistosa.

wish, *vt.* desear, anhelar, ansiar, querer; **to — one a happy Christmas, to — one a happy Easter,** dar las Pascuas; **—,** *n.* anhelo, deseo, *m.*

wishbone, *n.* hueso bifurcado de la pechuga de las aves.

wishful, *adj.* deseoso; ávido; **—ly,** *adv.* anhelosamente.

wishy-washy, *adj.* débil, insípido.

wisp, *n.* manojo de paja, de heno, etc.; fragmento, *m.*, pizca, *f.*

wisteria, *n.* (bot.) vistaria, *f.*

wistful, *adj.* anheloso y sin esperanza de satisfacer sus deseos; **—ly,** *adv.* anhelosamente.

wit, *n.* ingenio, *m.*, agudeza, sal, *f.*; **to —,** a saber.

witch, *n.* bruja, hechicera, *f.*; **— hazel,** carpe, *m.*, loción de carpe.

witchcraft, *n.* brujería, *f.*; sortilegio, *m.*

witchery, *n.* hechicería, *f.*; encanto, *m.*; influencia fascinadora.

with, *prep.* con; por; de; a.

withal, *adv.* inmediatamente, después; por otro lado, a pesar de eso; todavía.

withdraw, *vt.* quitar; privar; retirar; **—,** *vi.* retirarse, apartarse, sustraerse.

withdrawal, *n.* retiro, *m.*, retirada, *f.*; **— bank,** retiro de depósitos del banco.

withe, *n.* mimbre, *m.*

wither, *vi.* marchitarse, secarse; **—,** *vt.* marchitar.

withhold, *vt.* detener, impedir, retener.

within, *prep.* dentro, adentro; **— bounds,** a raya; **—,** *adv.* adentro, en casa, en el lado de adentro.

without, *prep.* sin; fuera, afuera; **—,** *adv.* exteriormente.

withstand, *vt.* oponer, resistir.

withy, *n.* mimbre, *m.*; **—,** *adj.* flexible y tosco; flaco y ágil.

witless, *adj.* necio, tonto, falto de ingenio.

witness, *n.* testimonio, *m.*; testigo, *m.*; **—,** *vt.* atestiguar, testificar; **—,** *vi.* servir de testigo, presenciar.

wittily, *adv.* ingeniosamente.

wittiness, *n.* agudeza, *f.*; chiste ingenioso; viveza de ingenio.

wittingly, *adv.* intencionalmente, de adrede.

witty, *adj.* ingenioso, agudo, chistoso.

wives, *n. pl.* de **wife,** esposas, mujeres, *f. pl.*

wizard, *n.* brujo, hechicero, mago, *m.*

wk. week, semana.

w.l. wave length, longitud de onda.

Wm. William, Guill⁰. Guillermo.

WNW, W.N.W. west-northwest, ONO. oesnorueste.

woad, *n.* hierba pastel, gualda, *f.*

wobble, *vt.* bambolear; **—,** *n.* bamboleo, *m.*

wobbly, *adj.* instable, que se bambolea.

woe, *n.* dolor, *m.*, aflicción, *f.*

woeful, *adj.* triste, funesto; **—ly**, *adv.* tristemente, dolorosamente.

wolf, *n.* lobo, *m.*; **she —**, loba, *f.*; **— pack**, manada de lobos.

wolfish, *adj.* lobero, característico del lobo; feroz.

wolfram, *n.* tungsteno, volframio, *m.*

wolves, *n. pl.* de **wolf**, lobos, *m. pl.*

woman, *n.* mujer, *f.*

womanhood, *n.* la mujer en general.

womanish, *adj.* mujeril.

womankind, *n.* sexo femenino.

womanly, *adj.* mujeril, femenino.

woman suffrage, *n.* sufragio femenino.

womb, *n.* útero, *m.*, matriz, *f.*

women, *n. pl.* de **woman**, mujeres, *f. pl.*

wonder, *n.* milagro, *m.*; portento, *m.*; prodigio, *m.*; maravilla, *f.*; **—**, *vi.* maravillarse (de).

wonderful, *adj.* maravilloso, prodigioso; **—ly**, *adv.* maravillosamente.

wonderment, *n.* extrañeza, *f.*; admiración, *f.*; sorpresa, *f.*; embeleso, *m.*

wondrous, *adj.* maravilloso.

wont, *n.* uso, *m.*, costumbre, *f.*

won't, contracción de **will not**.

wonted, *adj.* acostumbrado, habituado.

woo, *vt.* cortejar, hacer el amor (a alguien).

wood, *n.* madera, *f.*; leña, *f.*; **creosoted —**, madera creosotada; **— alcohol**, alcohol metílico; **— anemone**, anemona de los bosques; **— louse**, milpiés, *m.*, cochinilla, *f.*; **— nymph**, napea, *f.*; **— pigeon**, paloma zorita; **— pulp**, pulpa de madera; **— thrush**, especie de tordo; **— turning**, arte de trabajar la madera con el torno para sacar piezas de distintas formas; **—s**, *pl.* bosque, *m.*

woodbine, *n.* (bot.) madreselva, *f.*   ●

woodchuck, *n.* (zool.) marmota, *f.*

woodcock, *n.* (orn.) chocha, becada, *f.*

woodcraft, *n.* destreza en trabajos de madera; conocimiento de la vida en el bosque.

woodcut, *n.* grabado en madera; estampa de un grabado en madera.

woodcutter, *n.* hachero, *m.*; leñador, *m.*

wooded, *adj.* arbolado.

wooden, *adj.* de madera.

woodland, *n.* bosque, *m.*, selva, *f.*

woodman, *n.* cazador, *m.*; guardabosque, *m.*

woodpecker, *n.* (orn.) picamaderos, picaposte, becafigo, *m.*

woodwork, *n.* obra de madera, obra de carpintería, maderaje, *m.*; molduras, *f. pl.*

woodworker, *n.* persona que trabaja la madera.

woody, *adj.* lleno de árboles; abundante en madera; **— fiber**, celulosa, *f.*

wooer, *n.* galanteador, *m.*

woof, *n.* trama, *f.*; textura, *f.*; tela, *f.*

wool, *n.* lana, *f.*; **— merchant**, pañero, *m.*

woolen, *adj.* de lana, lanoso.

woolgathering, *n.* fantasías, *f. pl.*; distracción, *f.*; **—**, *adj.* con ideas fantásticas.

woolliness, *n.* pelaje, *m.*; lanosidad, *f.*

woolly, *adj.* lanudo, lanoso.

word, *n.* palabra, voz, *f.*; **by — of mouth**, de palabra; **on my —**, a fe mía, bajo mi palabra; **to leave —**, dejar dicho; **in other —s**, en otros terminos; **—**, *vt.* expresar.

wordiness, *n.* verbosidad, *f.*

wording, *n.* dicción, *f.*; fraseología, *f.*

wordy, *adj.* verboso.

wore, pretérito del verbo **wear**.

work, *vi.* trabajar; laborar; funcionar; **—**, *vt.* trabajar, labrar; laborar; formar; **—**, *n.* trabajo, *m.*, obra, *f.*; gestión, *f.*; fatiga, *f.*; quehacer, *m.*; **metal —**, metalistería, *f.*; **— of art**, obra de arte.

workaday, *adj.* laborioso, prosaico, ordinario.

workbag, *n.* saco de labor, *m.*; bolsa de costura, *f.*

workbench, *n.* banco de taller.

workbook, *n.* manual, *m.*; libro con espacios en blanco en que el estudiante ha de escribir las respuestas a los problemas propuestos.

workhouse, *n.* casa de corrección.

working, *n.* funcionamiento, *m.*; trabajo, *m.*; explotación, *f.*; **— day**, día de trabajo; **— partner**, socio industrial.

workingman, *n.* obrero, *m.*

working-plan, *n.* (arch.) montea, *f.*; plan de trabajo.

workingwoman, *n.* obrera, *f.*

workman, *n.* labrador, *m.*; obrero, *m.*; artífice, *m.*

workmanship, *n.* manufactura, *f.*; destreza del artífice; trabajo, *m.*

workout, *n.* ensayo, ejercicio, *m.*

workroom, *n.* taller, *m.*

works, *n.* fábrica, *f.*, taller, *m.*

workshop, *n.* taller, *m.*

workwoman, *n.* obrera, trabajadora, *f.*

world, *n.* mundo, *m.*; universo, *m.*; gente, *f.*; cantidad, *f.*

worldliness, *n.* mundanalidad, *f.*, vanidad mundana.

worldling, *n.* hombre mundano, persona amante de las cosas superficiales del mundo.

worldly, *adj.* mundano, profano, terrenal.

world-wide, *adj.* mundial, del mundo entero.

worm, *n.* gusano, gorgojo, *m.*; **— gear**, (mech.) engranaje de tornillo sin fin, engranaje de rosca; **— of a screw**, rosca de tornillo; **—**, *vi.* moverse insidiosamente; **—**, *vt.* librar de gusanos; efectuar por medios insidiosos.

worm-eaten, *adj.* carcomido, apolillado.

wormwood, *n.* (bot.) ajenjo, *m.*

wormy, *adj.* gusarapiento.

worn, *p. p.* del verbo **wear**.

worn-out, *adj.* rendido, raído, gastado.

worry, *n.* cuidado, *m.*; preocupación, intranquilidad, *f.*; ansia, *f.*, desasosiego, *m.*; **—**, *vt.* molestar, atormentar; **—**, *vi.*

preocuparse; **to be worried,** estar con cuidado, estar preocupado.

worse, *adj.* and *adv.* peor; **to get —,** empeorarse; **so much the —,** tanto peor.

worship, *n.* culto, *m.*; adoración, *f.*; **your —,** vuestra merced; **—,** *vt.* adorar, venerar.

worshipful, *adj.* venerable, respetable, honorable.

worst, *adj.* pésimo, malísimo; **—,** *n.* lo peor, lo más malo; **—,** *vt.* aventajar; derrotar.

worsted, *n.* especie de estambre.

wort, *n.* especie de hierba; cerveza nueva.

worth, *n.* valor, precio, *m.*; mérito, *m.*, valía, *f.*; **—,** *adj.* meritorio, digno; **to be — while,** merecer o valer la pena; **to be —,** valer.

worthily, *adv.* dignamente, en forma meritoria.

worthiness, *n.* dignidad, *f.*; mérito, *m.*

worthless, *adj.* indigno, sin valor; **— person,** cachivache, *m.*; **to be —,** ser inútil, ser como la carabina de Ambrosio.

worth-while, *adj.* que vale la pena, digno de tenerse en cuenta.

worthy, *adj.* digno, benemérito; merecedor; **—,** *n.* varón ilustre.

would-be, *adj.* que aspira o desea ser; llamado, considerado.

wound, *n.* herida, llaga, *f.*; **—,** *vt.* herir.

wove, pretérito del verbo **weave.**

woven, *p. p.* del verbo **weave.**

WPA Works Projects Administration, Administración de Obras Públicas (E.U.A.)

wraith, *n.* fantasma, *m.*

wrangle, *vi.* reñir, discutir; **to — with one another,** repiquetear; **—,** *n.* pelotera, riña, *f.*

wrangler, *n.* pendenciero, ra, disputador, ra.

wrap, *vt.* arrollar; envolver.

wrapper, *n.* envolvedor; ra; envoltura, *f.*; ropa de casa; chal pequeño; forro de un libro.

wrapping, *n.* envoltura, *f.*; cubierta, *f.*, forro exterior.

wrapping paper, *n.* papel de envolver.

wrath, *n.* ira, rabia, cólera, *f.*

wrathful, *adj.* furioso, colérico.

wreak, *vt.* descargar (la cólera), etc.; **to — one's vengeance,** vengarse.

wreath, *n.* corona, guirnalda, *f.*

wreathe, *vt.* and *vi.* torcer; enrollar; arrugarse; coronar.

wreck, *n.* naufragio, *m.*; destrucción, *f.*; **—,** *vt.* arruinar; destruir; **—,** *vi.* arruinarse.

wreckage, *n.* restos, despojos, *m. pl.*; ruinas, *f. pl.*; naufragio, *m.*; choque, accidente (de automóvil, tren, aeroplano, etc.), *m.*

wrecker, *n.* automóvil de auxilio.

wren, *n.* (orn.) reyezuelo, *m.*

wrench, *vt.* arrancar; dislocar; torcer; **—,** *n.* torcedura (del pie, etc.); destornillador, *m.*

wrest, *vt.* arrancar, quitar a fuerza.

wrestle, *vi.* luchar a brazo partido; disputar; **—,** *n.* lucha, *f.*

wrestler, *n.* luchador (a brazo partido), *m.*

wrestling, *n.* lucha, *f.*

wretch, *n.* pobre infeliz; infame, *m.*; **poor —!** ¡pobre diablo!

wretched, *adj.* infeliz, miserable; mezquino; mísero; deplorable, lamentable; **—ly,** *adv.* miserablemente.

wretchedness, *n.* miseria, *f.*; vileza, *f.*; desdicha, *f.*

wriggle, *vi.* menearse, agitarse; culebrear.

wright, *n.* artesano, obrero, *m.*

wring, *vt.* torcer; arrancar; estrujar.

wringer, *n.* torcedor, *m.*, exprimidor o estrujador de ropa acabada de lavar.

wrinkle, *n.* arruga, *f.*; **—,** *vt.* arrugar.

wrist, *n.* muñeca (de la mano), *f.*; **— bandage,** pulsera, *f.*, venda para la mano; **— pin,** eje de émbolo; **— watch,** reloj de pulsera.

wristband, *n.* puño de camisa.

writ, *n.* escrito, *m.*; escritura, *f.*; orden, *f.*

write, *vt.* escribir; componer; **to — poetry,** trovar; **— off,** cancelar; hacer un descuento por depreciación; **— up,** dar cuenta, completar; alabar en la prensa.

writer, *n.* escritor, ra, autor, ra; novelista, *m.* y *f.*; **prose —,** prosador, ra.

write-up, *n.* crónica de prensa.

writhe, *vt.* torcer; **—,** *vi.* contorcerse.

writing, *n.* escritura, *f.*; escrito, *m.*; manuscrito, *m.*; **in —,** por escrito; **to put in —,** poner por escrito; **the present —,** la presente; **— desk,** escritorio, bufete, pupitre, *m.*; **— paper,** papel de escribir.

written, *p. p.* del verbo **write.**

wrong, *n.* injuria, *f.*; injusticia, *f.*; error, *m.*; **—,** *adj.* malo, incorrecto, erróneo; injusto; **— side,** revés, *m.*; **to be —,** no tener razón; **—,** *vt.* hacer un mal, injuriar; **—,** **—ly,** *adv.* mal, injustamente; al revés.

wrongdoer, *n.* pecador, ra, malvado, da.

wrongful, *adj.* injusto, inicuo; **—ly,** *adv.* injustamente.

wrote, pretérito del verbo **write.**

wroth, *adj.* encolerizado.

wrought, *adj.* labrado, hecho; **— iron,** hierro forjado.

wry, *adj.* torcido; tuerto; **— face,** mohín, *m.*, mueca, *f.*

wryneck, *n.* (orn.) torcecuello, *m.*; (coll.) persona con el cuello torcido.

WSW, W.S.W. west-southwest, OSO. oessudueste.

wt. weight, P. peso.

W. Va. West Virginia, Virginia Occidental.

Wy. Wyo. Wyoming, Wyoming.

X

xebec, *n.* (naut.) jabeque, *m.*

xenon, *n.* (chem.) xenón, *m.*

Xmas. Christmas, Navidad, Pascua de Navidad.

X ray, *n.* rayo X o Roentgen; **X-ray picture,** radiografía, *f.*; **X-ray specialist,** radiógrafo, *m.*; **X-ray,** *adj.* de rayos X; —, *vt.* examinar con rayos X, radiografiar.

xylem, *n.* parte leñosa de las plantas.

xylography, *n.* arte de grabar en láminas de madera.

xylophone, *n.* (mus.) xilófono, *m.*, especie de marimba.

Y

y.: yard, yd. yarda; **year,** a. año.

yacht, *n.* (naut.) yate, *m.*

yak, *n.* yack, *m.*

yam, *n.* (bot.) batata, *f.*, camote, *m.*

Yankee, *n.* y *adj.* yanqui, *m.* y *f.*

yard, *n.* corral, *m.*; yarda (medida), *f.*; (naut.) verga, *f.*

yardarm, *n.* penol de la verga.

yardmaster, *n.* mayordomo de un patio de ferrocarril o del batey de un ingenio, etc.

yardstick, *n.* yarda de medir.

yarn, *n.* estambre, *m.*; hilo de lino; (coll.) cuento de aventuras por lo general exageradas o ficticias.

yarrow, *n.* milhojas, *f.*

yaw, *vi.* (naut.) guiñar.

yawing, *n.* (aer., naut.) guiñada, *f.*

yawl, *n.* (naut.) canoa, *f.*, serení, *m.*

yawn, *vi.* bostezar; —, *n.* bostezo, *m.*

yd. yard, yd. yarda.

ye, *pron.* (poet.) vos.

yea, *adv.* sí, verdaderamente; — **or nay,** sí o no.

yean, *vi.* parir (la oveja, etc.)

year, *n.* año, *m.*; **all — round,** todo el año; **many —s ago,** hace muchos años.

yearbook, *n.* anuario, *m.*, anales, *m. pl.*

yearling, *n.* animal de un año de edad.

yearly, *adj.* anual; —, *adv.* anualmente, todos los años.

yearn, *vi.* anhelar.

yearning, *n.* anhelo, *m.*, deseo ferviente.

yeast, *n.* levadura, *f.*; giste, *m.*; — **cake,** pastilla de levadura.

yelk, *m.* = **yolk.**

yell, *vi.* aullar, gritar; —, *n.* grito, aullido, *m.*

yellow, *adj.* amarillo; —, *n.* color amarillo; — **bedstraw,** (bot.) cuajaleche, *m.*, amor de hortelano; — **fever,** fiebre amarilla; — **jacket,** avispa amarilla; — **pine,** pino americano.

yellowish, *adj.* amarillento.

yelp, *vi.* latir, gañir, ladrar; —, *n.* aullido, gañido, latido, *m.*

yeoman, *n.* (naut.) contramaestre, pañolero, *m.*; alabardero, *m.*; guardalmacén en la marina; hacendado, *m.*

yeomanry, *n.* cuerpo de guardias del rey; cuerpo de hacendados de alguna provincia.

yes, *adv.* sí.

yes-man, *n.* (coll.) persona que siempre

está de acuerdo con sus superiores ya sea con razón o sin ella.

yesterday, *adv.* ayer; **day before —,** anteayer.

yet, *adv.* todavía, aún; —, *conj.* sin embargo, con todo.

yew, *n.* (bot.) tejo, *m.*

yield, *vi.* producir, rendir; ceder; sucumbir; darse por vencido; asentir; —, *vt.* producir, rendir; —, *n.* producto, rendimiento, *m.*; (mech.) rendimiento, *m.*

yielding, *adj.* condescendiente, que cede.

Y.M.C.A. Young Men's Christian Association, A.C.J. Asociación Cristiana de Jóvenes.

Y.M.H.A. Young Men's Hebrew Association, Asociación Hebrea de Jóvenes.

yodel, *vt.* cantar con modulación del tono natural al falsete; —, *n.* canto con modulación del tono natural al falsete.

yoga, *n.* yoga, *f.*

yoke, *n.* yugo, *m.*; yunta, *f.*; férula, *f.*; —, *vt.* uncir; ligar; casar; sojuzgar.

yoke elm, *n.* (bot.) carpe, ojaranzo, *m.*

yokel, *n.* paleto, patán, payo, campesino, *m.*

yolk, *n.* yema (de huevo), *f.*

yon, yonder, *adv.* allí, allá; —, *adj.* de allí, de allá; aquel.

yore, *n.* tiempo antiguo, tiempo atrás.

you, *pron.* tú, usted; vosotros, vosotras, ustedes.

young, *adj.* joven, mozo; tierno; — **man,** joven, *m.*; — **woman,** joven, señorita, *f.*

your, yours, *pron.* tu, su, vuestro, de ustedes, de vosotros; **sincerely —,** su seguro servidor, de usted muy sinceramente (despedida en las cartas).

yourself, *pron.* usted mismo; **yourselves,** ustedes mismos.

youth, *n.* juventud, mocedad, adolescencia, *f.*; joven, *m.*

youthful, *adj.* juvenil; **—ly,** *adv.* de un modo juvenil.

youthfulness, *n.* juventud, *f.*

youth hostel, *n.* = **hostel.**

yr.: year, a. año; **your,** su, sus.

yucca, *n.* (bot.) yuca, *f.*

Yugoslavia, Yugoeslavia, *f.*

Yule, *n.* Navidad, *f.*

Yuletide, *n.* Pascua de Navidad, *f.*

Y.W.C.A. Young Women's Christian Association, A.C.M. Asociación Cristiana de Mujeres.

Z

zambo, *n.* zambo.

zany, *n.* and *adj.* tonto, mentecato, bufón, *m.*

zeal, *n.* celo, ardor, ahinco, *m.*

zealot, *n.* fanático, *m.*

zealous, *adj.* celoso, fervoroso; **—ly,** *adv.* celosamente, fervorosamente.

zebra, *n.* zebra, cebra, *f.*

W X Y Z

zenith, *n.* cenit, *m.*
zephyr, *n.* céfiro, favonio, *m.*
zeppelin, *n.* (aer.) zepelín, *m.*
zero, *n.* cero, *m.*; **— hour,** (mil.) hora fijada para un ataque, etc., hora del peligro, hora crítica.
zest, *n.* gusto, *m.*, sabor agudo; gozo, *m.*
Z.G. Zoological Gardens, Jardines Zoológicos.
zigzag, *n.* zigzag, *m.*; **—,** *vt.* and *vi.* hacer un zigzag, ir en forma de zigzag.
zinc, *n.* (chem.) cinc, zinc, *m.*; **— chloride,** cloruro de cinc.
zinnia, *n.* (bot.) zinia, *f.*, planta que pertenece al género de las astéreas.
zipper, *n.* cierre de corredera.
zither, *n.* cítara, *f.*; **— player,** citarista, *m.* y *f.*
zodiac, *n.* zodíaco, *m.*

zone, *n.* zona, *f.*; **danger —,** zona del peligro; **slow driving —,** zona de marcha lenta.
zoo, *n.* jardín zoológico.
zoography, *n.* zoografía.
zool. zoology, zool. zoología.
zoological, *adj.* zoológico.
zoologist, *n.* zoólogo, *m.*
zoology, *n.* zoología, *f.*
zoom, *vi.* (aer.) levantar el vuelo repentinamente; subirse rápidamente o elevarse (como un aeroplano, etc.).
zooming, *n.* subida vertical.
zoophyte, *n.* zoófito, *m.*
zouave, *n.* (mil.) zuavo, *m.*
zounds, *interj.* ¡cáscaras! ¡cáspita!
zwieback, *n.* especie de bizcocho o molleta.
zygote, *n.* (zool.) zigote, *m.*
zymase, *n.* (chem.) zimasa, *f.*